COLLINS

THESAURUS

THE ULTIMATE WORDFINDER

from A *to* Z

COLLINS

THESAURUS

THE ULTIMATE WORDFINDER

from A *to* Z

HarperCollins*Publishers*

First Published 1995
Reprinted 1998 (twice), 1999
Latest reprint 2000

5 6 7 8 9

PO Box, Glasgow G4 0NB

Standard Edition ISBN 0 00 470454-1
With Thumb Tabs ISBN 0 00 470717-6

The HarperCollins website address is
www.**fireandwater**.com

A catalogue record for this book is available
from the British Library

Typeset by Morton Word Processing Ltd.
Scarborough, England

Printed and bound in Spain by
Mateu Cromo, S.A. Pinto (Madrid)

Contents

Editorial Staff

Publishing Manager
Diana Adams

Managing Editor
Lorna Gilmour

Lexicographers

Elspeth Summers
Mike Munro
Alice Grandison
Ian Brookes
Tom Shearer
Sheila Ferguson
Mary O'Neill
Andrew Holmes
Danielle McGinley

Editorial Assistance
Alison Foy

Computer Staff
Jane Creevy
Ray Carrick

FOREWORD

When Collins A-Z Thesaurus was first published in 1984, it revolutionized the whole concept of thesauruses. It represented a new idea, a thesaurus in which the material was arranged in a single A-Z listing of main-entry words, with all the alternatives for any word found at the one place where you would be most likely to look it up. The simplicity and practicality of this approach made the book an instant success and it has been a consistent best-seller ever since.

The **Collins Thesaurus** retains all the virtues of this A-Z arrangement, but the original text has been massively expanded upon to provide a unique new book which once again widens the whole concept of the thesaurus. In addition to generous synonym lists, the **Collins Thesaurus** includes an entirely new dimension of fascinating and useful information connected with the entry words.

A wide range of main-entry words – over 16,500 – is included, the criterion for selection being that the word or term in question is likely to be looked up as an entry in its own right. If the word which you have in mind does not feature as a main entry (for instance, *gallimaufry*) you can still find synonyms for this concept by trying a more familiar word with the same general meaning (for instance, *jumble* or *hotchpotch*). Having looked up the word which you have in mind, you will find at one place in the book alternatives for all the possible meanings of it. These are numbered for ease of reference to enable you to find the particular meaning which fits the context you have in mind. All the synonyms given have been chosen as being fully substitutable for the headword in at least one context. Because of this, and because of the range of alternatives given, you can always find the better or more appropriate word that you are searching for. The handsome large format, spacious layout and exceptionally clear typography make the book even more practical and easy to use than ever before.

The **Collins Thesaurus** also includes antonym lists at many of the main-entry words. These lists give a very generous range of opposites and as well as being interesting in their own right, provide you with another way of expressing yourself. For instance, if you wish to say that something is difficult, it can sometimes be effective to use a negative construction and, taking a word from the antonym list, you may think of a phrase such as "by no means straightforward".

But the **Collins Thesaurus** gives you much more than just a wide choice of synonyms and antonyms.

One helpful feature is that of "related words". If you look up the entry for *morning* you will find that its related adjective is *matutinal*. Look up *lake* to find its related adjective *lacustrine*, and *star* to find the related adjectives *astral*, *sidereal*, and *stellar*. Such information is usually difficult to find unless you already have an idea of what the related word might be, but the A-Z arrangement of the thesaurus enables you to go to it straight away.

Informative and comprehensive vocabulary lists provide a wealth of material connected with or relevant to many of the entry words. For example, look up the entry for *horse* and you will find not only a choice of synonyms for the word *horse* itself, but a fascinating range of lists including Breeds of horse; Legendary, fictional and historical horses; Horse colours; Horse parts; People associated with horses; Tack and equipment; and Horse-drawn vehicles. Or look up the entry *phobia* and you will find a full and fascinating list which includes the object of each phobia. With nearly 500 such lists, the thesaurus is an invaluable crossword aid, but in addition, these lists provide information not normally available in this helpful form in a single reference book, such as Capital cities (at entry *capital*); Currencies of the world (at entry *currency*); lists of British Prime Ministers, U.S. Presidents, and Prime Ministers of Australia, Canada and New Zealand (at entry *politician*); Major political parties of the world (at entry *politics*); as well as Ports, Rivers, Islands, Deserts, Lakes, Mountains, and many other encyclopedic sets. The essential vocabulary of all the arts and sciences is also included, making this the most comprehensive thesaurus available.

In the preface to his Dictionary of the English Language (1755), Dr. Samuel Johnson, probably the most famous lexicographer of all, said, "Every quotation contributes something to the stability or enlargement of the language". With this in mind, the **Collins Thesaurus** has included over 2750 useful and entertaining quotations and proverbs for hundreds of key entries. The wit and wisdom of centuries is here, with memorable and apt quotations from philosophers and actors, classical novelists and rock stars, literary critics and gossip columnists, politicians and comedians - making the thesaurus a delight to browse through as well as a uniquely practical reference book.

The whole range of language from taboo and slang to formal and technical is represented, with helpful labels to identify areas of usage. Vocabulary is also included from all the regions of the world where English is spoken, while the wide coverage of idiomatic English will help you to add colour to your language.

The name *Thesaurus* came to us from Greek, where it meant, "treasure, treasury or store house", and our thesaurus is so named because it is a treasury or store house of words. The **Collins Thesaurus** gives you much more than any other thesaurus, and is the ultimate wordfinder for anyone who wants to increase their command of English, or simply enjoy its enormous variety and scope.

Explanatory Notes

1. Under each main entry word, the synonyms are arranged alphabetically. When a word has distinctly separate meanings, separate numbered lists are given for the different senses.

2. Where it is desirable to distinguish between different parts of speech, labels have been added as follows: *noun, verb, adjective, adverb, pronoun, conjunction, preposition, interjection*. See entries for *living, loaf, loan, local.*

3. Usually the synonyms for a particular part of speech are grouped together. Thus, in the entry *catch* synonyms for all verb senses are given first, followed by synonyms for all the noun senses. Sometimes, however, noun and verb functions are very closely associated in specific meanings, and where this is the case the synonyms are grouped by meanings, as in the entry for *cover.*

4. When a headword has more than one meaning and can function as more than one part of speech, a new part-of-speech function is shown by a swung dash (~), as in the entry for *glance* or *grasp.*

5. Much-used phrases appear as main entries; for instance, *act for* comes after *act.* Expressions such as *a priori* or *en route* are also given as main entries within the alphabetical listing. Short idiomatic phrases are entered under their key word and are to be found either at the end of the entry or immediately following the sense with which they are associated. Thus, the phrase *take a dim view* appears as sense 7 of the entry *dim*, since the synonyms in sense 6 most closely approximate to the meaning of the phrase.

6. Plural forms that have a distinctly separate meaning, such as *provisions*, are entered at their own alphabetical position, while those with a less distinct difference, such as *appurtenances*, are given as a separate sense under the singular form, e.g. *appurtenance*... **2**. *plural*...

7. The antonym lists which follow many entries are arranged alphabetically, and, where appropriate, treated according to the rules given for synonyms.

8. A label in brackets applies only to the synonym or antonym preceding it, while one which is not bracketed relates to the whole of that particular sense.

9. A swung dash symbol (~) is also used to show that a word has been broken merely because it happens to fall at the end of a line, while the conventional sign (-) is used to distinguish a word which is always written with a hyphen.

A

aback take aback astonish, astound, bewilder, disconcert, flabbergast (*informal*), floor (*informal*), nonplus, stagger, startle, stun, surprise

abaft *Nautical* aft, astern, behind

abandon *verb* **1.** desert, forsake, jilt, leave, leave behind, leave in the lurch, let (someone) stew in their own juice, strand **2.** evacuate, quit, vacate, withdraw from **3.** abdicate, cede, give up, relinquish, renounce, resign, surrender, waive, yield **4.** desist, discontinue, drop, forgo, kick (*informal*) *~noun* **5.** careless freedom, dash, recklessness, unrestraint, wantonness, wild impulse, wildness
Antonyms *verb* claim, continue, defend, hold, keep, maintain, take, uphold *~noun* control, moderation, restraint

abandoned 1. cast aside, cast away, cast out, derelict, deserted, discarded, ditched, dropped, forlorn, forsaken, jilted, left, neglected, outcast, out of the window, rejected, relinquished, stranded, unoccupied, vacant **2.** corrupt, debauched, depraved, dissipated, dissolute, profligate, reprobate, sinful, wanton, wicked **3.** uncontrolled, uninhibited, unrestrained, wild
Antonyms (*sense 1*) claimed, kept, maintained, occupied (*sense 2*) good, high-principled, honest, moral, pure, reputable, righteous, upright, virtuous, worthy (*sense 3*) conscious, restrained

abandonment 1. dereliction, desertion, forsaking, jilting, leaving **2.** evacuation, quitting, withdrawal from **3.** abdication, cession, giving up, relinquishment, renunciation, resignation, surrender, waiver **4.** desistance, discontinuation, dropping

abase belittle, bring low, cast down, debase, degrade, demean, demote, denigrate, depress, disgrace, dishonour, downgrade, humble, humiliate, lower, mortify, put in one's place, reduce
Antonyms advance, aggrandize, dignify, elevate, exalt, glorify, honour, prefer, promote, raise, upgrade

abasement belittlement, debasement, degradation, demotion, depression, disgrace, dishonour, downgrading, humbling, humiliation, lowering, mortification, reduction, shame

abasement: decent and customary mental attitude in the presence of wealth and power
Ambrose Bierce *The Devil's Dictionary*

abash affront, astound, bewilder, chagrin, confound, confuse, discomfit, discompose, disconcert, discountenance, embarrass, faze, humble, humiliate, mortify, perturb, shame, take the wind out of someone's sails

abashed affronted, ashamed, astounded, bewildered, chagrined, confounded, confused, discomfited, discomposed, disconcerted, discountenanced, dismayed, embarrassed, humbled, humiliated, mortified, perturbed, shamefaced, taken aback
Antonyms at ease, blatant, bold, brazen, composed, confident, unashamed, undaunted, undismayed, unperturbed

abashment astonishment, bewilderment, chagrin, confusion, consternation, discomfiture, discomposure, disconcertion, dismay, embarrassment, humiliation, mortification, perturbation, shame

abate 1. alleviate, appease, attenuate, decline, decrease, diminish, dull, dwindle, ease, ebb, fade, lessen, let up, mitigate, moderate, quell, reduce, relax, relieve, sink, slacken, slake, slow, subside, taper off, wane, weaken **2.** deduct, discount, subtract
Antonyms add to, amplify, augment, boost, enhance, escalate, increase, intensify, magnify, multiply, strengthen

abatement 1. alleviation, allowance, attenuation, cessation, decline, decrease, diminution, dulling, dwindling, easing, extenuation, fading, lessening, let-up (*informal*), mitigation, moderation, quelling, reduction, relief, remission, slackening, slaking, slowing, tapering off, waning, weakening **2.** deduction, discount, subtraction

abattoir butchery, shambles, slaughterhouse

abbey cloister, convent, friary, monastery, nunnery, priory

abbreviate abridge, abstract, clip, compress, condense, contract, curtail, cut, digest, epitomize, précis, reduce, shorten, summarize, trim, truncate
Antonyms amplify, draw out, elongate, expand, extend, increase, lengthen, prolong, protract, spin out, stretch out

abbreviated abridged, brief, compressed, concise, condensed, cut, pruned, reduced, shortened, shorter, summarized, trimmed
Antonyms amplified, diffuse, drawn out, expanded, increased, prolonged, protracted, unabbreviated, unabridged

abbreviation abridgment, abstract, clipping, compendium, compression, condensation, conspectus, contraction, curtailment, digest, epitome, précis, reduction, résumé, shortening, summary, synopsis, trimming, truncation

abdicate abandon, abjure, abnegate, cede, forgo, give up, quit, relinquish, renounce, resign, retire, step down (*informal*), surrender, vacate, waive, yield

abdication abandonment, abjuration, abnegation, cession, giving up, quitting, relinquishment, renunciation, resignation, retiral (*especially Scot.*), retirement, surrender, waiver, yielding

abdomen belly, breadbasket (*slang*), corporation (*informal*), guts (*slang*), midriff, midsection, paunch, pot, stomach, tummy (*informal*)

abdominal gastric, intestinal, stomachic, stomachical, visceral

abduct carry off, kidnap, make off with, run away with, run off with, seize, snatch (*slang*)

abduction carrying off, kidnapping, seizure

aberrance abnormality, anomaly, deviance, deviation, divergence, eccentricity, irregularity, oddness, peculiarity, variance
Antonyms conformity, consistency, normality, regularity, uniformity

aberrant **1.** abnormal, anomalous, defective, deviant, divergent, eccentric, irregular, odd, oddball (*informal*), off-the-wall (*slang*), outré, peculiar, queer, rambling, straying, untypical, wacko (*slang*), wandering **2.** delusive, delusory, disordered, hallucinatory, illusive, illusory, unstable **3.** corrupt, corrupted, degenerate, depraved, deviant, erroneous, perverse, perverted, wrong

aberration **1.** aberrancy, abnormality, anomaly, defect, deviation, divergence, eccentricity, irregularity, lapse, oddity, peculiarity, quirk, rambling, straying, wandering **2.** delusion, hallucination, illusion, instability, mental disorder, vagary

abet **1.** aid, assist, back, condone, connive at, help, promote, sanction, second, succour, support, sustain, uphold **2.** egg on, encourage, incite, prompt, spur, urge

abetting *noun* abetment, abettal, aid, assistance, encouragement, facilitation, furtherance, help, support

abettor **1.** accessory, accomplice, assistant, associate, backer, confederate, conniver, cooperator, helper, henchman, second **2.** encourager, fomenter, inciter, instigator, prompter

abeyance **1.** adjournment, deferral, discontinuation, inactivity, intermission, postponement, recess, reservation, suspense, suspension, waiting **2. in abeyance** hanging fire, in cold storage (*informal*), on ice (*informal*), pending, shelved, suspended

abeyant adjourned, deferred, discontinued, dormant, inactive, intermitted, latent, postponed, put off, quiescent, reserved, shelved, suspended, waiting

abhor abominate, detest, execrate, hate, loathe, recoil from, regard with repugnance *or* horror, shrink from, shudder at
Antonyms admire, adore, cherish, covet, delight in, desire, enjoy, like, love, relish

abhorrence abomination, animosity, aversion, detestation, disgust, distaste, enmity, execration, hate, hatred, horror, loathing, odium, repugnance, revulsion

abhorrent abominable, detestable, disgusting, distasteful, execrable, hated, hateful, heinous, horrible, horrid, loathsome, obnoxious, obscene, odious, offensive, repellent, repugnant, repulsive, revolting, yucky *or* yukky (*slang*)

abide **1.** accept, bear, brook, endure, hack (*slang*), put up with, stand, stomach, submit to, suffer, tolerate **2.** dwell, linger, live, lodge, reside, rest, sojourn, stay, stop, tarry, wait **3.** continue, endure, last, persist, remain, survive

abide by **1.** acknowledge, agree to, comply with, conform to, follow, obey, observe, submit to, toe the line **2.** adhere to, carry out, discharge, fulfil, hold to, keep to, persist in, stand by

abiding constant, continuing, durable, enduring, eternal, everlasting, fast, firm, immortal, immutable, indissoluble, lasting, permanent, persistent, persisting, steadfast, surviving, tenacious, unchanging, unending
Antonyms brief, ephemeral, evanescent, fleeting, momentary, passing, short, short-lived, temporary, transient, transitory

ability adeptness, aptitude, capability, capacity, competence, competency, craft, dexterity, endowment, energy, expertise, expertness, facility, faculty, flair, force, gift, knack, know-how (*informal*), potentiality, power, proficiency, qualification, skill, talent
Antonyms inability, incapability, incapacity, incompetence, powerlessness, weakness

> *From each according to his abilities, to each according to his needs*
>
> Karl Marx *Critique of the Gotha Programme*

ab initio *ab ovo*, from first principles, from scratch (*informal*), from the beginning (first, start, word go (*informal*)), initially, originally, to begin *or* start with

abject **1.** base, contemptible, cringing, debased, degraded, despicable, dishonourable, fawning, grovelling, humiliating, ignoble, ignominious, low, mean, servile, slavish, sordid, submissive, vile, worthless **2.** deplorable, forlorn, hopeless, miserable, outcast, pitiable, wretched
Antonyms august, dignified, distinguished, elevated, eminent, exalted, grand, great, high, lofty, noble, patrician, worthy

abjectness **1.** abjection, baseness, contemptibleness, debasement, degradation, dishonour, humbleness, humiliation, ignominy, lowness, meanness, servility, slavishness, sordidness, submissiveness, vileness, worthlessness **2.** destitution, forlornness, hopelessness, misery, pitiableness, pitifulness, squalor, wretchedness

abjuration **1.** denial, disavowal, disclaiming, disclamation, forswearing, recantation, renunciation, retraction **2.** abnegation, abstention, eschewal, rejection, relinquishment, self-denial

abjure **1.** deny, disavow, disclaim, forswear, recant, renege on, renounce, retract **2.** abandon, abnegate, abstain from, eschew, forsake, give up, kick (*informal*), refrain from, reject, relinquish

ablaze **1.** afire, aflame, alight, blazing, burning, fiery, flaming, ignited, lighted, on fire **2.** aglow, brilliant, flashing, gleaming, glowing, illuminated, incandescent, luminous, radiant, sparkling **3.** angry, aroused, enthusiastic, excited, fervent, fit to be tied (*slang*), foaming at the mouth, frenzied, fuming, furious, impassioned, incensed, on the warpath, passionate, raging, stimulated

able accomplished, adept, adequate, adroit, capable, clever, competent, effective, efficient, experienced, expert, fit, fitted, gifted, highly endowed, masterful, masterly, powerful, practised, proficient, qualified, skilful, skilled, strong, talented
Antonyms amateurish, inadequate, incapable, incompetent, ineffective, inefficient, inept, mediocre, no great shakes (*informal*), unfit, unskilful, weak

able-bodied firm, fit, hale, hardy, healthy, hearty, lusty, powerful, right as rain (*Brit. informal*), robust, sound, staunch, stout, strapping, strong, sturdy, vigorous
Antonyms ailing, debilitated, feeble, fragile, frail, sickly, tender, weak

ablution bath, bathing, cleansing, lavation, purification, shower, wash, washing

abnegate abandon, abdicate, abjure, abstain from, concede, decline, deny, disallow, eschew, forbear, forgo, forsake, give up, kick (*informal*), refrain from, refuse, reject, relinquish, renounce, sacrifice, surrender, yield

abnegation abandonment, abjuration, abstinence, continence, disallowance, eschewal, forbearance, giving up, refusal, rejection, relinquishment, renunciation, sacrifice, self-denial, surrender, temperance

abnormal aberrant, anomalous, atypical, curious, deviant, eccentric, erratic, exceptional, extraordinary, irregular, monstrous, odd, oddball (*informal*), off-the-wall (*slang*), outré, peculiar, queer, singular, strange, uncommon, unexpected, unnatural, untypical, unusual, wacko (*slang*), weird
Antonyms common, conventional, customary, familiar, natural, normal, ordinary, regular, unexceptional, usual

abnormality aberration, anomaly, atypicalness, bizarreness, deformity, deviation, eccentricity, exception, extraordinariness, flaw, irregularity, monstrosity, oddity, peculiarity, queerness, singularity, strangeness, uncommonness, unexpectedness, unnaturalness, untypicalness, unusualness, weirdness

abnormally atypically, bizarrely, disproportionately, exceptionally, excessively, extraordinarily, extremely, fantastically, freakishly, inordinately, in the extreme, oddly, overly, particularly, peculiarly, prodigiously, singularly, strangely, subnormally, supernormally, uncannily, uncommonly, unnaturally, unusually

abode domicile, dwelling, dwelling-place, habitat, habitation, home, house, lodging, pad (*slang*), quarters, residence

abolish abrogate, annihilate, annul, axe (*informal*), blot out, cancel, destroy, do away with, eliminate, end, eradicate, expunge, exterminate, extinguish, extirpate, invalidate, nullify, obliterate, overthrow, overturn, put an end to, quash, repeal, repudiate, rescind, revoke, stamp out, subvert, suppress, terminate, vitiate, void, wipe out
Antonyms authorize, continue, create, establish, found, institute, introduce, legalize, promote, reinstate, reintroduce, restore, revive, sustain

abolition abrogation, annihilation, annulment, blotting out, cancellation, destruction, elimination, end, ending, eradication, expunction, extermination, extinction, extirpation, invalidation, nullification, obliteration, overthrow, overturning, quashing, repeal, repudiation, rescission, revocation, stamping out, subversion, suppression, termination, vitiation, voiding, wiping out, withdrawal

abominable abhorrent, accursed, atrocious, base, contemptible, despicable, detestable, disgusting, execrable, foul, godawful (*slang*), hateful, heinous, hellish, horrible, horrid, loathsome, nauseous, obnoxious, obscene, odious, repellent, reprehensible, repugnant, re~

pulsive, revolting, terrible, vile, villainous, wretched, yucky *or* yukky (*slang*)
Antonyms admirable, agreeable, charming, commendable, delightful, desirable, good, laudable, likable *or* likeable, lovable, pleasant, pleasing, wonderful

abominably abhorrently, contemptibly, deplor~ ably, despicably, detestably, disgustingly, dreadfully, execrably, foully, heinously, hid~ eously, horribly, horridly, nauseatingly, ob~ noxiously, odiously, offensively, reprehensibly, repugnantly, repulsively, revoltingly, shame~ fully, terribly, unpalatably, vilely
Antonyms admirably, commendably, delight~ fully, excellently, impeccably, perfectly, won~ derfully

abominate abhor, detest, execrate, hate, loathe, recoil from, regard with repugnance, shudder at
Antonyms admire, adore, cherish, dote on, esteem, idolize, love, revere, treasure, worship

abomination **1.** abhorrence, antipathy, aver~ sion, detestation, disgust, distaste, execration, hate, hatred, horror, loathing, odium, repug~ nance, revulsion **2.** anathema, bête noire, bugbear, curse, disgrace, evil, horror, plague, shame, torment

aboriginal ancient, autochthonous, earliest, first, indigenous, native, original, primary, primeval, primitive, primordial, pristine

aborigine aboriginal, autochthon, indigene, native, original inhabitant

abort **1.** miscarry, terminate (*a pregnancy*) **2.** arrest, axe (*informal*), call off, check, end, fail, halt, stop, terminate

abortion **1.** aborticide, deliberate miscarriage, feticide, miscarriage, termination **2.** disap~ pointment, failure, fiasco, misadventure, mon~ strosity, vain effort

abortive *adjective* **1.** bootless, failed, failing, fruitless, futile, idle, ineffectual, miscarried, unavailing, unsuccessful, useless, vain **2.** *Bi~ ology* imperfectly developed, incomplete, rudi~ mentary, stunted *~noun* **3.** *Medical* abortifa~ cient

abound be jammed with, be packed with, be plentiful, crowd, flourish, increase, infest, luxuriate, overflow, proliferate, superabound, swarm, swell, teem, thrive

abounding abundant, bountiful, copious, filled, flourishing, flowing, flush, full, lavish, luxuri~ ant, overflowing, plenteous, plentiful, profuse, prolific, rank, replete, rich, superabundant, teeming, thick on the ground, two a penny

about *preposition* **1.** anent (*Scot.*), as regards, concerned with, concerning, connected with, dealing with, on, re, referring to, regarding, relating to, relative to, respecting, touching, with respect to **2.** adjacent, beside, circa (*used with dates*), close to, near, nearby **3.** around, encircling, on all sides, round, surrounding **4.** all over, over, through, throughout *~adverb* **5.** almost, approaching, approximately, around, close to, more or less, nearing, nearly, roughly **6.** from place to place, here and there, hither and thither, to and fro *~adjective* **7.** active, around, astir, in motion, present, stirring

about to intending to, on the point of, on the verge *or* brink of, ready to

about-turn *or U.S.* **about-face** **1.** *noun* change of direction, reversal, reverse, right about (turn), turnabout, turnaround, U-turn, volte-face **2.** *verb* change direction, do *or* perform a U-turn *or* volte-face, face the opposite direc~ tion, reverse, turn about *or* around, turn through 180 degrees, volte-face

above *preposition* **1.** atop, beyond, exceeding, higher than, on top of, over, upon **2.** before, beyond, exceeding, prior to, superior to, sur~ passing *~adverb* **3.** aloft, atop, in heaven, on high, overhead *~adjective* **4.** aforementioned, aforesaid, earlier, foregoing, preceding, previ~ ous, prior
Antonyms *preposition* (*sense 1*) below, be~ neath, under, underneath (*sense 2*) inferior, lesser, less than, lower than, subordinate

aboveboard **1.** *adverb* candidly, forthrightly, frankly, honestly, honourably, openly, overtly, straightforwardly, truly, truthfully, uprightly, veraciously, without guile **2.** *adjective* candid, fair and square, forthright, frank, guileless, honest, honourable, kosher (*informal*), legiti~ mate, on the up and up, open, overt, square, straight, straightforward, true, trustworthy, truthful, upfront (*informal*), upright, veracious
Antonyms *adjective* clandestine, crooked, de~ ceitful, deceptive, devious, dishonest, fraudu~ lent, furtive, secret, secretive, shady, sly, sneaky, underhand

ab ovo *ab initio*, from first principles, from scratch (*informal*), from the beginning (egg, first, start, word go (*informal*))

abracadabra **1.** chant, charm, conjuration, hocus-pocus, incantation, invocation, magic, mumbo jumbo, sorcery, spell, voodoo, witch~ craft **2.** babble, balderdash, blather, drivel, gibberish, gobbledegook, Greek (*informal*), jabber, jargon, nonsense, pap, twaddle

abrade erase, erode, file, grind, rub off, scour, scrape away, scrape out, wear away, wear down, wear off

abrasion **1.** *Medical* chafe, graze, scrape, scratch, scuff, surface injury, trauma (*Pathol~ ogy*) **2.** abrading, chafing, erosion, friction, grating, rubbing, scouring, scraping, scratch~ ing, scuffing, wearing away, wearing down

abrasive *adjective* **1.** chafing, erosive, frictional, grating, rough, scraping, scratching, scratchy, scuffing **2.** annoying, biting, caustic, cutting, galling, grating, hurtful, irritating, nasty, rough, sharp, unpleasant, vitriolic *~noun* **3.** abradant, burnisher, grinder, scarifier, scourer

abreast 1. alongside, beside, level, neck and neck, shoulder to shoulder, side by side **2.** acquainted, *au courant*, au fait, conversant, familiar, informed, in the picture, in touch, keeping one's finger on the pulse, knowledgeable, up to date

abridge abbreviate, abstract, clip, compress, concentrate, condense, contract, curtail, cut, cut down, decrease, digest, diminish, downsize, epitomize, lessen, précis, reduce, shorten, summarize, synopsize (*U.S.*), trim
Antonyms amplify, augment, enlarge, expand, extend, go into detail, lengthen, prolong, protract, spin out, stretch out

abridged abbreviated, brief, compressed, concise, condensed, curtailed, cut, diminished, pruned, reduced, shortened, shorter, summarized, trimmed
Antonyms amplified, diffuse, drawn out, expanded, increased, prolonged, protracted, unabbreviated, unabridged

abridgment abbreviation, abstract, compendium, condensation, conspectus, contraction, curtailment, cutting, decrease, digest, diminishing, diminution, epitome, lessening, limitation, outline, précis, reduction, restraint, restriction, résumé, shortening, summary, synopsis

abroad 1. beyond the sea, in foreign lands, out of the country, overseas **2.** about, at large, away, circulating, current, elsewhere, extensively, far, far and wide, forth, in circulation, out, out-of-doors, outside, publicly, widely, without

Abroad is unutterably bloody and foreigners are fiends
Nancy Mitford *The Pursuit of Love*

Go abroad and you'll hear news of home

abrogate abolish, annul, cancel, countermand, end, invalidate, nullify, obviate, override, quash, repeal, repudiate, rescind, retract, reverse, revoke, scrap (*informal*), set aside, void, withdraw

abrogation abolition, annulment, cancellation, countermanding, ending, invalidation, nullification, overriding, quashing, repeal, repudiation, rescission, retraction, reversal, revocation, scrapping (*informal*), setting aside, voiding, withdrawal

abrupt 1. blunt, brisk, brusque, clipped, curt, direct, discourteous, gruff, impatient, impolite, monosyllabic, rough, rude, short, snappish, snappy, terse, unceremonious, uncivil, ungracious **2.** precipitous, sharp, sheer, steep, sudden **3.** hasty, headlong, hurried, precipitate, quick, sudden, surprising, swift, unanticipated, unexpected, unforeseen **4.** broken, disconnected, discontinuous, irregular, jerky, uneven
Antonyms (*sense 1*) civil, courteous, gracious, polite (*sense 2*) gradual (*sense 3*) easy, leisurely, slow, thoughtful, unhurried

abruptly 1. bluntly, briskly, brusquely, curtly, gruffly, rudely, sharply, shortly, snappily, tersely **2.** all at once, all of a sudden, hastily, hurriedly, precipitately, quickly, sharply, short, suddenly, unexpectedly
Antonyms (*sense 1*) courteously, politely (*sense 2*) bit by bit, gently, gradually, little by little, progressively, slowly, steadily

abruptness 1. bluntness, briskness, brusqueness, brusquerie, curtness, gruffness, sharpness, shortness, terseness **2.** precipitateness, suddenness, unexpectedness
Antonyms (*sense 1*) courteousness, politeness (*sense 2*) gradualness, steadiness

abscess boil, bubo, carbuncle, felon, furuncle (*Pathology*), gathering, gumboil, infection, inflammation, parulis (*Pathology*), pustule, whitlow

abscond bolt, clear out, decamp, disappear, do a bunk (*Brit. slang*), do a runner (*slang*), escape, flee, flit (*informal*), fly, fly the coop (*U.S. & Canad. informal*), make off, run off, skedaddle (*informal*), slip away, sneak away, steal away, take a powder (*U.S. & Canad. slang*), take it on the lam (*U.S. & Canad. slang*)

abscond: to "move in a mysterious way", commonly with the property of another
Ambrose Bierce *The Devil's Dictionary*

absence 1. absenteeism, nonappearance, nonattendance, truancy **2.** default, defect, deficiency, lack, need, nonexistence, omission, privation, unavailability, want **3.** absent-mindedness, abstraction, distraction, inattention, preoccupation, reverie

Absence makes the heart grow fonder,
Isle of Beauty, Fare thee well!
Thomas Haynes Bayly *Isle of Beauty*

Absence is to love what wind is to fire; it extinguishes the small, it inflames the great
Comte de Bussy-Rabutin *Histoire amoureuse des Gaules*

That out of sight is out of mind
Is true of most we leave behind
Arthur Hugh Clough *That Out of Sight*

absent *adjective* **1.** away, elsewhere, gone, lacking, missing, nonattendant, nonexistent, not present, out, truant, unavailable, wanting **2.** absent-minded, absorbed, abstracted, bemused, blank, daydreaming, distracted, dreamy, empty, faraway, heedless, inattentive, musing, oblivious, preoccupied, unaware, unconscious, unheeding, unthinking, vacant,

vague *~verb* 3. **absent oneself** abscond, bunk off (*slang*), depart, keep away, play truant, remove, slope off (*informal*), stay away, truant, withdraw
Antonyms *adjective* (*sense 1*) attendant, in attendance, present (*sense 2*) alert, attentive, aware, conscious, thoughtful *~verb* attend, show up (*informal*)

Greater things are believed of those who are absent

Tacitus *Histories*

absentee nonattender, no-show, stay-at-home, stayaway, truant

absently absent-mindedly, abstractedly, bemusedly, blankly, distractedly, dreamily, emptily, heedlessly, inattentively, obliviously, on automatic pilot, unconsciously, unheedingly, vacantly, vaguely

absent-minded absent, absorbed, abstracted, bemused, distracted, dreaming, dreamy, engrossed, faraway, forgetful, heedless, in a brown study, inattentive, musing, oblivious, preoccupied, unaware, unconscious, unheeding, unthinking, vague
Antonyms alert, awake, observant, on one's toes, on the ball, perceptive, quick, vigilant, wary, wide-awake

absent-mindedness absence of mind, abstraction, daydreaming, distractedness, forgetfulness, inattention, musing, obliviousness, preoccupation, vagueness, woolgathering

absolute 1. arrant, complete, consummate, deep-dyed (*usually derogatory*), downright, entire, full-on (*informal*), out-and-out, outright, perfect, pure, sheer, thorough, total, unadulterated, unalloyed, unmitigated, unmixed, unqualified, utter 2. actual, categorical, certain, conclusive, decided, decisive, definite, exact, genuine, infallible, positive, precise, sure, unambiguous, unequivocal, unquestionable 3. absolutist, arbitrary, autarchical, autocratic, autonomous, despotic, dictatorial, full, peremptory, sovereign, supreme, tyrannical, unbounded, unconditional, unlimited, unqualified, unquestionable, unrestrained, unrestricted

absolutely 1. completely, consummately, entirely, every inch, fully, lock, stock and barrel, one hundred per cent, perfectly, purely, thoroughly, totally, to the hilt, unmitigatedly, utterly, wholly 2. actually, categorically, certainly, conclusively, decidedly, decisively, definitely, exactly, genuinely, infallibly, positively, precisely, surely, truly, unambiguously, unequivocally, unquestionably 3. arbitrarily, autocratically, autonomously, despotically, dictatorially, fully, peremptorily, sovereignly, supremely, tyrannically, unconditionally, unquestionably, unrestrainedly, without qualification
Antonyms conditionally, fairly, probably, reasonably, somewhat

absoluteness 1. consummateness, entirety, perfection, purity, thoroughness, totality, unmitigatedness, wholeness 2. assuredness, certainty, certitude, conclusiveness, correctness, decidedness, decisiveness, definiteness, exactitude, genuineness, infallibility, positiveness, precision, sureness, surety, truth, unambiguousness, unequivocalness 3. arbitrariness, autonomy, despotism, dictatorialness, fullness, peremptoriness, supremacy, tyranny, unboundedness, unquestionability, unrestrainedness, unrestrictedness

absolution acquittal, amnesty, deliverance, discharge, dispensation, exculpation, exemption, exoneration, forgiveness, freeing, indulgence, liberation, mercy, pardon, release, remission, setting free, shriving, vindication

absolutism absoluteness, arbitrariness, autarchy, authoritarianism, autocracy, despotism, dictatorship, totalitarianism, tyranny

absolutist arbiter, authoritarian, autocrat, despot, dictator, totalitarian, tyrant

absolve acquit, clear, deliver, discharge, exculpate, excuse, exempt, exonerate, forgive, free, let off, liberate, loose, pardon, release, remit, set free, shrive, vindicate
Antonyms blame, censure, charge, condemn, convict, damn, denounce, excoriate, pass sentence on, reprehend, reproach, reprove, sentence, upbraid

absorb 1. assimilate, consume, devour, digest, drink in, exhaust, imbibe, incorporate, ingest, osmose, receive, soak up, suck up, take in 2. captivate, engage, engross, enwrap, fascinate, fill, fill up, fix, hold, immerse, monopolize, occupy, preoccupy, rivet

absorbed 1. captivated, concentrating, engaged, engrossed, fascinated, fixed, held, immersed, involved, lost, occupied, preoccupied, rapt, riveted, up to one's ears, wrapped up 2. assimilated, consumed, devoured, digested, exhausted, imbibed, incorporated, received

absorbency ability to soak up *or* take in, permeability, permeableness, perviousness, porousness, receptiveness, retentiveness, sponginess
Antonyms impermeability, impermeableness, imperviousness

absorbent absorptive, assimilative, blotting, imbibing, penetrable, permeable, pervious, porous, receptive, spongy

absorbing arresting, captivating, engrossing, fascinating, gripping, interesting, intriguing, preoccupying, riveting, spellbinding
Antonyms boring, dreary, dull, humdrum,

mind-numbing, monotonous, tedious, tiresome, unexciting

absorption 1. assimilation, consumption, digestion, exhaustion, incorporation, osmosis, soaking up, sucking up 2. captivation, concentration, engagement, fascination, holding, immersion, intentness, involvement, occupation, preoccupation, raptness

abstain avoid, cease, decline, deny (oneself), desist, fast, forbear, forgo, give up, keep from, kick (*informal*), refrain, refuse, renounce, shun, stop, withhold

Antonyms abandon oneself, give in, indulge, partake, yield

abstainer: a weak person who yields to the temptation of denying himself a pleasure
Ambrose Bierce *The Devil's Dictionary*

abstemious abstinent, ascetic, austere, continent, frugal, moderate, self-denying, sober, sparing, temperate

Antonyms edacious (*chiefly humorous*), gluttonous, greedy, immoderate, incontinent, intemperate, self-indulgent

abstemiousness abstinence, asceticism, austerity, continence, forbearance, frugality, moderation, plain *or* simple living, restraint, self-denial, self-restraint, sobriety, temperance

Antonyms dissipation, drunkenness, excess, gluttony, incontinence, self-indulgence

abstention abstaining, abstinence, avoidance, desistance, eschewal, forbearance, nonindulgence, refraining, refusal, self-control, self-denial, self-restraint

abstinence abstemiousness, asceticism, avoidance, continence, forbearance, moderation, refraining, self-denial, self-restraint, soberness, sobriety, teetotalism, temperance

Antonyms abandon, acquisitiveness, covetousness, excess, gluttony, greediness, indulgence, self-indulgence, wantonness

If God forbade drinking, would he have made wine so good?
Cardinal Richelieu

I am a beer teetotaller, not a champagne teetotaller
George Bernard Shaw

To many, total abstinence is easier than perfect moderation
St. Augustine of Hippo *On the Good of Marriage*

abstinent abstaining, abstemious, continent, forbearing, moderate, self-controlled, self-denying, self-restraining, sober, temperate

abstract *adjective* 1. abstruse, arcane, complex, conceptual, deep, general, generalized, hypothetical, indefinite, intellectual, nonconcrete, notional, occult, philosophical, profound, recondite, separate, subtle, theoretic, theoretical, unpractical, unrealistic ~*noun* 2. abridgment, compendium, condensation, digest, epitome, essence, outline, précis, recapitulation, résumé, summary, synopsis ~*verb* 3. abbreviate, abridge, condense, digest, epitomize, outline, précis, shorten, summarize, synopsize (*U.S.*) 4. detach, dissociate, extract, isolate, remove, separate, steal, take away, take out, withdraw

Antonyms *adjective* actual, concrete, definite, factual, material, real, specific ~*noun* enlargement, expansion ~*verb* (*sense 4*) add, combine, inject

abstracted 1. absent, absent-minded, bemused, daydreaming, dreamy, faraway, inattentive, preoccupied, remote, withdrawn, woolgathering 2. abbreviated, abridged, condensed, digested, epitomized, shortened, summarized, synopsized (*U.S.*)

abstraction 1. absence, absent-mindedness, bemusedness, dreaminess, inattention, pensiveness, preoccupation, remoteness, woolgathering 2. concept, formula, generality, generalization, hypothesis, idea, notion, theorem, theory, thought

abstruse abstract, arcane, complex, dark, deep, Delphic, enigmatic, esoteric, hidden, incomprehensible, mysterious, mystical, obscure, occult, perplexing, profound, puzzling, recondite, subtle, unfathomable, vague

Antonyms apparent, bold, clear, conspicuous, evident, manifest, open, overt, patent, perceptible, plain, self-evident, transparent, unsubtle

abstruseness arcaneness, complexity, deepness, depth, esotericism, incomprehensibility, mysteriousness, obscurity, occultness, perplexity, profundity, reconditeness, subtlety, vagueness

absurd crazy (*informal*), daft (*informal*), farcical, foolish, idiotic, illogical, inane, incongruous, irrational, laughable, ludicrous, meaningless, nonsensical, preposterous, ridiculous, senseless, silly, stupid, unreasonable

Antonyms intelligent, logical, prudent, rational, reasonable, sagacious, sensible, smart, wise

absurdity bêtise (*rare*), craziness (*informal*), daftness (*informal*), farce, farcicality, farcicalness, folly, foolishness, idiocy, illogicality, illogicalness, incongruity, irrationality, joke, ludicrousness, meaninglessness, nonsense, preposterousness, ridiculousness, senselessness, silliness, stupidity, unreasonableness

absurdity: a statement of belief manifestly inconsistent with one's own opinion
Ambrose Bierce *The Devil's Dictionary*

absurdly farcically, foolishly, idiotically, illogically, implausibly, inanely, inconceivably, incongruously, incredibly, irrationally, laughably, ludicrously, preposterously, ridiculously, senselessly, unbelievably, unreasonably

abundance **1.** affluence, ampleness, bounty, copiousness, exuberance, fullness, heap (*informal*), plenitude, plenteousness, plenty, profusion **2.** affluence, big bucks (*informal, chiefly U.S.*), big money, fortune, megabucks (*U.S. & Canad. slang*), opulence, pretty penny (*informal*), riches, tidy sum (*informal*), wad (*U.S. & Canad. slang*), wealth
Antonyms dearth, deficiency, lack, need, paucity, scantiness, scarcity, sparseness

a land flowing with milk and honey
Bible: Exodus

abundant ample, bounteous, bountiful, copious, exuberant, filled, full, lavish, luxuriant, overflowing, plenteous, plentiful, profuse, rank, rich, teeming, thick on the ground, two a penny, well-provided, well-supplied
Antonyms deficient, few, few and far between, inadequate, in short supply, insufficient, lacking, rare, scant, scanty, scarce, short, sparse, thin on the ground

abundantly amply, bounteously, bountifully, copiously, extensively, exuberantly, freely, fully, in abundance, in great *or* large numbers, in plentiful supply, in profusion, lavishly, luxuriantly, plenteously, plentifully, profusely, richly
Antonyms inadequately, in short supply, insufficiently, rarely, scantily, scarcely, sparsely

abuse *verb* **1.** damage, dump on (*slang, chiefly U.S.*), exploit, harm, hurt, ill-treat, impose upon, injure, maltreat, manhandle, mar, misapply, misuse, oppress, shit on (*taboo slang*), spoil, take advantage of, wrong **2.** calumniate, castigate, curse, defame, disparage, insult, inveigh against, libel, malign, revile, scold, slander, slate (*informal, chiefly Brit.*), smear, swear at, traduce, upbraid, vilify, vituperate *~noun* **3.** damage, exploitation, harm, hurt, ill-treatment, imposition, injury, maltreatment, manhandling, misapplication, misuse, oppression, spoiling, wrong **4.** blame, calumniation, castigation, censure, character assassination, contumely, curses, cursing, defamation, derision, disparagement, insults, invective, libel, opprobrium, reproach, revilement, scolding, slander, swearing, tirade, traducement, upbraiding, vilification, vituperation **5.** corruption, crime, delinquency, fault, injustice, misconduct, misdeed, offence, sin, wrong, wrongdoing
Antonyms *verb* (*sense 1*) care for, protect (*sense 2*) acclaim, commend, compliment, extol, flatter, praise, respect

abusive **1.** calumniating, castigating, censorious, contumelious, defamatory, derisive, disparaging, insulting, invective, libellous, maligning, offensive, opprobrious, reproachful, reviling, rude, scathing, scolding, slanderous, traducing, upbraiding, vilifying, vituperative **2.** brutal, cruel, destructive, harmful, hurtful, injurious, rough
Antonyms (*sense 1*) approving, complimentary, eulogistic, flattering, laudatory, panegyrical, praising

abusiveness **1.** calumniation, coarse language, contumely, derisiveness, foul language, insults, invective, offensiveness, philippics, rudeness, traducement, vilification, vitriol, vituperation **2.** abuse, brutality, cruelty, exploitation, ill-treatment, maltreatment

abut adjoin, border, impinge, join, meet, touch, verge

abutment brace, bulwark, buttress, pier, prop, strut, support

abutting adjacent, adjoining, bordering, contiguous, joining, meeting, next to, touching, verging

abysmal bottomless, boundless, complete, deep, endless, extreme, immeasurable, incalculable, infinite, profound, thorough, unending, unfathomable, vast

abyss abysm, bottomless depth, chasm, crevasse, fissure, gorge, gulf, pit, void

academia academe (*literary*), academic life, learning, scholarship, the groves of Academe (*literary*), university life

academic *adjective* **1.** bookish, campus, college, collegiate, erudite, highbrow, learned, lettered, literary, scholarly, scholastic, school, studious, university **2.** abstract, conjectural, hypothetical, impractical, notional, speculative, theoretical *~noun* **3.** academician, don, fellow, lecturer, master, professor, pupil, scholar, scholastic, schoolman, student, tutor

academy centre of learning, college, institute, institution, school

accede **1.** accept, acquiesce, admit, agree, assent, comply, concede, concur, consent, endorse, grant, own, yield **2.** assume, attain, come to, enter upon, inherit, succeed, succeed to (*as heir*)

accelerate advance, expedite, forward, further, hasten, hurry, pick up speed, precipitate, quicken, speed, speed up, spur, step up (*informal*), stimulate
Antonyms decelerate, delay, hinder, impede, obstruct, slow down

acceleration expedition, hastening, hurrying, quickening, speeding up, spurring, stepping up (*informal*), stimulation

accent *noun* **1.** beat, cadence, emphasis, force, ictus, pitch, rhythm, stress, timbre, tonality **2.** articulation, brogue, enunciation, inflection, intonation, modulation, pronunciation, tone *~verb* **3.** accentuate, emphasize, stress, underline, underscore

The accent of one's birthplace lingers in the

mind and in the heart as it does in one's speech
Duc de la Rochefoucauld *Maximes*

accentuate accent, draw attention to, emphasize, highlight, stress, underline, underscore
Antonyms gloss over, make light of, make little of, minimize, play down, soft-pedal (*informal*), underplay

accept **1**. acquire, gain, get, have, obtain, receive, secure, take **2**. accede, acknowledge, acquiesce, admit, adopt, affirm, agree to, approve, believe, buy (*slang*), concur with, consent to, cooperate with, recognize, swallow (*informal*), take on board **3**. bear, bow to, brook, defer to, like it or lump it (*informal*), put up with, stand, submit to, suffer, take, yield to **4**. acknowledge, admit, assume, avow, bear, take on, undertake
Antonyms decline, deny, disown, rebut, refuse, reject, repudiate, spurn

acceptability acceptableness, adequacy, admissibility, appropriateness, fitness, permissibility, propriety, satisfactoriness, suitability
Antonyms impropriety, inadequacy, inadmissibility, inappropriateness, unacceptability, unsatisfactoriness, unsuitability

acceptable **1**. agreeable, delightful, grateful, gratifying, pleasant, pleasing, welcome **2**. adequate, admissible, all right, fair, moderate, passable, satisfactory, so-so (*informal*), standard, tolerable, up to scratch (*informal*)
Antonyms unacceptable, unsatisfactory, unsuitable

acceptably **1**. agreeably, delightfully, gratifyingly, pleasantly, pleasingly **2**. adequately, passably, satisfactorily, tolerably
Antonyms unacceptably, unsatisfactorily, unsuitably

acceptance **1**. accepting, acquiring, gaining, getting, having, obtaining, receipt, securing, taking **2**. accedence, accession, acknowledgment, acquiescence, admission, adoption, affirmation, agreement, approbation, approval, assent, belief, compliance, concession, concurrence, consensus, consent, cooperation, credence, O.K. *or* okay (*informal*), permission, recognition, stamp *or* seal of approval **3**. deference, standing, submission, taking, yielding **4**. acknowledgment, admission, assumption, avowal, taking on, undertaking

accepted acceptable, acknowledged, admitted, agreed, agreed upon, approved, authorized, common, confirmed, conventional, customary, established, normal, received, recognized, regular, sanctioned, standard, time-honoured, traditional, universal, usual
Antonyms abnormal, irregular, unconventional, uncustomary, unorthodox, unusual, unwonted

access **1**. admission, admittance, approach, avenue, course, door, entering, entrance, entrée, entry, gateway, key, passage, passageway, path, road **2**. *Medical* attack, fit, onset, outburst, paroxysm

accessibility **1**. approachability, attainability, availability, handiness, nearness, obtainability, possibility, readiness **2**. affability, approachability, conversableness, cordiality, friendliness, informality **3**. exposedness, openness, susceptibility

accessible **1**. achievable, a hop, skip and a jump away, at hand, at one's fingertips, attainable, available, get-at-able (*informal*), handy, near, nearby, obtainable, on hand, possible, reachable, ready **2**. affable, approachable, available, conversable, cordial, friendly, informal **3**. exposed, liable, open, subject, susceptible, vulnerable, wide-open
Antonyms far-off, hidden, inaccessible, secreted, unapproachable, unavailable, unobtainable, unreachable

accession **1**. addition, augmentation, enlargement, extension, increase **2**. assumption, attaining to, attainment of, entering upon, succession (*to a throne, dignity, or office*), taking on, taking over **3**. accedence, acceptance, acquiescence, agreement, assent, concurrence, consent

accessorize, accessorise add on to, adorn, augment, complement, decorate, embellish, ornament, supplement, trim

accessory *noun* **1**. abettor, accomplice, assistant, associate (*in crime*), colleague, confederate, helper, partner **2**. accent, accompaniment, addition, add-on, adjunct, adornment, aid, appendage, attachment, component, convenience, decoration, extension, extra, frill, help, supplement, trim, trimming *~adjective* **3**. abetting, additional, aiding, ancillary, assisting in, auxiliary, contributory, extra, secondary, subordinate, supplemental, supplementary

accident **1**. blow, calamity, casualty, chance, collision, crash, disaster, misadventure, mischance, misfortune, mishap, pile-up (*informal*) **2**. chance, fate, fluke, fortuity, fortune, hazard, luck

Accidents will occur in the best-regulated families
Charles Dickens *David Copperfield*

accidental adventitious, casual, chance, contingent, fortuitous, haphazard, inadvertent, incidental, inessential, nonessential, random, uncalculated, uncertain, unessential, unexpected, unforeseen, unintended, unintentional, unlooked-for, unplanned, unpremeditated, unwitting
Antonyms calculated, designed, expected, foreseen, intended, intentional, planned, prepared

accidentally adventitiously, by accident, by chance, by mistake, casually, fortuitously, haphazardly, inadvertently, incidentally, randomly, unconsciously, undesignedly, unexpectedly, unintentionally, unwittingly
Antonyms by design, consciously, deliberately, designedly, on purpose, wilfully

acclaim 1. *verb* applaud, approve, celebrate, cheer, clap, commend, crack up (*informal*), eulogize, exalt, extol, hail, honour, laud, praise, salute, welcome 2. *noun* acclamation, applause, approbation, approval, celebration, cheering, clapping, commendation, eulogizing, exaltation, honour, laudation, plaudits, praise, welcome
Antonyms *noun* bad press, brickbats, censure, criticism, denigration, disparagement, fault-finding, flak (*informal*), panning (*informal*), stick (*slang*), vituperation

acclaimed acknowledged, admired, celebrated, distinguished, famed, famous, highly esteemed (rated, thought of), much touted, much vaunted, noted, renowned, well received, well thought of
Antonyms badly *or* poorly received, criticized, unacclaimed, unacknowledged, undistinguished

acclamation acclaim, adulation, approbation, cheer, cheering, cheers, enthusiasm, laudation, loud homage, ovation, plaudit, praise, salutation, shouting, tribute

acclimatization acclimation, accommodation, acculturation, adaptation, adjustment, habituation, inurement, naturalization

acclimatize accommodate, acculturate, acculture, accustom, adapt, adjust, become seasoned to, get used to, habituate, inure, naturalize

acclimatized, acclimatised acclimated, acculturated, accultured, accustomed, adapted, adjusted, familiarized, inured, orientated, oriented, seasoned, used

acclivity ascent, hill, rise, rising ground, steep upward slope

accolade acclaim, acclamation, applause, approval, commendation, compliment, congratulation, eulogy, homage, honour, laud (*literary*), laudation (*formal*), ovation, plaudit, praise, recognition, tribute

accommodate 1. billet, board, cater for, entertain, harbour, house, lodge, put up, quarter, shelter 2. afford, aid, assist, furnish, help, oblige, provide, purvey, serve, supply 3. accustom, adapt, adjust, comply, compose, conform, fit, harmonize, modify, reconcile, settle

accommodating complaisant, considerate, co-operative, friendly, helpful, hospitable, kind, obliging, polite, unselfish, willing
Antonyms disobliging, inconsiderate, rude, uncooperative, unhelpful

accommodation 1. adaptation, adjustment, compliance, composition, compromise, conformity, fitting, harmony, modification, reconciliation, settlement 2. board, digs (*Brit. informal*), harbouring, house, housing, lodging(s), quartering, quarters, shelter, sheltering 3. aid, assistance, help, provision, service, supply

accompaniment 1. accessory, companion, complement, supplement 2. backing, backing music

accompany 1. attend, chaperon, conduct, convoy, escort, go with, hold (someone's) hand, squire, usher 2. belong to, coexist with, coincide with, come with, follow, go cheek by jowl, go together with, join with, occur with, supplement

accompanying accessory, added, additional, appended, associate, associated, attached, attendant, complementary, concomitant, concurrent, connected, fellow, joint, related, supplemental, supplementary

accomplice abettor, accessory, ally, assistant, associate, coadjutor, collaborator, colleague, confederate, helper, henchman, partner

accomplish achieve, attain, bring about, bring off (*informal*), carry out, complete, conclude, consummate, do, effect, effectuate, execute, finish, fulfil, manage, perform, produce, put the tin lid on, realize
Antonyms fail, fall short, forsake, give up

accomplishable achievable, attainable, doable, feasible, makable, manageable, obtainable, on (*informal*), possible, practicable, realizable, viable, within one's grasp *or* reach, workable
Antonyms impossible, impracticable, outside one's grasp *or* reach, unattainable, unfeasible, unobtainable

accomplished 1. achieved, attained, brought about, carried out, completed, concluded, consummated, done, effected, executed, finished, fulfilled, in the can (*informal*), managed, performed, produced, realized 2. adept, consummate, cultivated, expert, gifted, masterly, polished, practised, proficient, skilful, skilled, talented
Antonyms (*sense 2*) amateurish, incapable, incompetent, inexpert, unestablished, unproven, unrealized, unskilled, untalented

accomplishment 1. achievement, attainment, bringing about, carrying out, completion, conclusion, consummation, doing, effecting, execution, finishing, fulfilment, management, performance, production, realization 2. achievement, act, attainment, coup, deed, exploit, feat, stroke, triumph 3. ability, achievement, art, attainment, capability, craft, gift, proficiency, skill, talent

accord *verb* **1**. agree, assent, be in tune (*informal*), concur, conform, correspond, fit, harmonize, match, suit, tally **2**. allow, bestow, concede, confer, endow, give, grant, present, render, tender, vouchsafe *~noun* **3**. accordance, agreement, assent, concert, concurrence, conformity, congruence, correspondence, harmony, rapport, sympathy, unanimity, unison
Antonyms *verb* (*sense 1*) conflict, contrast, differ, disagree, discord (*sense 2*) hold back, refuse, withhold *~noun* conflict, contention, disagreement, discord

accordance **1**. accord, agreement, assent, concert, concurrence, conformity, congruence, correspondence, harmony, rapport, sympathy, unanimity **2**. according, allowance, bestowal, concession, conferment, conferral, endowment, gift, giving, granting, presentation, rendering, tendering

accordingly **1**. appropriately, correspondingly, fitly, properly, suitably **2**. as a result, consequently, ergo, hence, in consequence, so, therefore, thus

according to **1**. commensurate with, in proportion, in relation **2**. as believed by, as maintained by, as stated by, in the light of, on the authority of, on the report of **3**. after, after the manner of, consistent with, in accordance with, in compliance with, in conformity with, in harmony with, in keeping with, in line with, in obedience to, in step with, in the manner of, obedient to

accost address, approach, buttonhole, confront, greet, hail, halt, salute, solicit (*as a prostitute*), stop

account *noun* **1**. chronicle, description, detail, explanation, history, narration, narrative, recital, record, relation, report, statement, story, tale, version **2**. *Commerce* balance, bill, book, books, charge, computation, inventory, invoice, ledger, reckoning, register, score, statement, tally **3**. advantage, benefit, consequence, distinction, esteem, honour, import, importance, merit, note, profit, rank, repute, significance, standing, use, value, worth **4**. basis, cause, consideration, ground, grounds, interest, motive, reason, regard, sake, score *~verb* **5**. appraise, assess, believe, calculate, compute, consider, count, deem, esteem, estimate, explain, gauge, hold, judge, rate, reckon, regard, think, value, weigh

accountability **1**. answerability, chargeability, culpability, liability, responsibility **2**. comprehensibility, explainability, explicability, intelligibility, understandability

accountable **1**. amenable, answerable, charged with, liable, obligated, obliged, responsible **2**. comprehensible, explainable, explicable, intelligible, understandable

account for **1**. answer for, clarify, clear up, elucidate, explain, illuminate, justify, rationalize **2**. destroy, incapacitate, kill, put out of action, put paid to

accounting accountancy, auditing, bookkeeping

accoutre adorn, appoint, array, bedeck, deck, decorate, equip, fit out, furnish, kit out, outfit, provide, supply

accoutrements adornments, appurtenances, array, bells and whistles, clothing, decorations, dress, equipage, equipment, fittings, fixtures, furnishings, garb, gear, kit, ornamentation, outfit, paraphernalia, tackle, trappings, trimmings

accredit **1**. appoint, authorize, certify, commission, depute, empower, endorse, entrust, guarantee, license, recognize, sanction, vouch for **2**. ascribe, assign, attribute, credit

accredited appointed, authorized, certified, commissioned, deputed, deputized, empowered, endorsed, guaranteed, licensed, official, recognized, sanctioned, vouched for

accretion accumulation, addition, augmentation, enlargement, growth, increase, increment, supplement

accrue accumulate, amass, arise, be added, build up, collect, enlarge, ensue, flow, follow, grow, increase, issue, spring up

accumulate accrue, amass, build up, collect, cumulate, gather, grow, hoard, increase, pile up, stockpile, store
Antonyms diffuse, disperse, disseminate, dissipate, distribute, propagate, scatter

accumulation aggregation, augmentation, build-up, collection, conglomeration, gathering, growth, heap, hoard, increase, mass, pile, rick, stack, stock, stockpile, store

accuracy accurateness, authenticity, carefulness, closeness, correctness, exactitude, exactness, faithfulness, faultlessness, fidelity, meticulousness, niceness, nicety, precision, strictness, truth, truthfulness, veracity, verity
Antonyms carelessness, erroneousness, imprecision, inaccuracy, incorrectness, inexactitude, laxity, laxness

accurate authentic, careful, close, correct, exact, faithful, faultless, just, meticulous, nice, on the money (*U.S.*), precise, proper, regular, right, scrupulous, spot-on (*Brit. informal*), strict, true, truthful, unerring, veracious
Antonyms careless, defective, faulty, imperfect, imprecise, inaccurate, incorrect, inexact, slovenly, wrong

accurately authentically, carefully, closely, correctly, exactly, faithfully, faultlessly, justly, meticulously, nicely, precisely, properly, regularly, rightly, scrupulously, strictly, to the letter, truly, truthfully, unerringly, veraciously

accursed **1.** bedevilled, bewitched, condemned, cursed, damned, doomed, hopeless, ill-fated, ill-omened, jinxed, luckless, ruined, undone, unfortunate, unlucky, wretched **2.** abominable, despicable, detestable, execrable, hateful, hellish, horrible
Antonyms (*sense 1*) blessed, charmed, favoured, fortunate, lucky

accusation allegation, arraignment, attribution, charge, citation, complaint, denunciation, impeachment, imputation, incrimination, indictment, recrimination

accusatory accusative, accusatorial, accusing, censorious, condemnatory, critical, denunciatory, imputative, incriminatory, recriminatory, reproachful

accuse allege, arraign, attribute, blame, censure, charge, cite, denounce, impeach, impute, incriminate, indict, point a *or* the finger at, recriminate, tax
Antonyms absolve, answer, defend, deny, exonerate, plea, reply, vindicate

accustom acclimatize, acquaint, adapt, discipline, exercise, familiarize, habituate, inure, season, train

accustomed **1.** acclimatized, acquainted, adapted, disciplined, exercised, familiar, familiarized, given to, habituated, in the habit of, inured, seasoned, trained, used **2.** common, conventional, customary, established, everyday, expected, fixed, general, habitual, normal, ordinary, regular, routine, set, traditional, usual, wonted
Antonyms (*sense 1*) unaccustomed, unfamiliar, unused (*sense 2*) abnormal, infrequent, occasional, odd, peculiar, rare, strange, unaccustomed, uncommon, unfamiliar, unusual

ace *noun* **1.** *Cards, dice, etc.* one, single point **2.** *informal* adept, buff (*informal*), champion, dab hand (*Brit. informal*), expert, genius, hotshot (*informal*), master, maven (*U.S.*), star, virtuoso, whiz (*informal*), winner, wizard (*informal*) ~*adjective* **3.** *informal* awesome (*slang*), brilliant, champion, excellent, expert, fine, great, masterly, outstanding, superb, virtuoso

acerbic **1.** acid, acrid, acrimonious, bitter, brusque, churlish, harsh, nasty, rancorous, rude, severe, sharp, stern, unfriendly, unkind **2.** acerb, acetic, acid, acidulous, acrid, astringent, bitter, harsh, sharp, sour, tart, vinegary

acerbity **1.** acrimony, asperity, bitterness, brusqueness, churlishness, harshness, nastiness, pungency, rancour, rudeness, severity, sharpness, sternness, unfriendliness, unkindness **2.** acidity, acidulousness, acridity, acridness, astringency, bitterness, sourness, tartness

ache *verb* **1.** hurt, pain, pound, smart, suffer, throb, twinge **2.** agonize, eat one's heart out, grieve, mourn, sorrow, suffer **3.** covet, crave, desire, eat one's heart out over, hanker, hope, hunger, long, need, pine, set one's heart on, thirst, yearn ~*noun* **4.** hurt, pain, pang, pounding, smart, smarting, soreness, suffering, throb, throbbing **5.** anguish, grief, mourning, sorrow, suffering **6.** craving, desire, hankering, hope, hunger, longing, need, pining, thirst, yearning

achievable accessible, accomplishable, acquirable, attainable, feasible, obtainable, possible, practicable, reachable, realizable, winnable, within one's grasp

achieve accomplish, acquire, attain, bring about, carry out, complete, consummate, do, earn, effect, execute, finish, fulfil, gain, get, obtain, perform, procure, put the tin lid on, reach, realize, win

achievement **1.** accomplishment, acquirement, attainment, completion, execution, fulfilment, performance, production, realization **2.** accomplishment, act, deed, effort, exploit, feat, feather in one's cap, stroke

> *When I look at the works of the masters, I see what they have done. When I consider my own trifles, I see what I ought to have done*
> Johann Wolfgang von Goethe

achiever doer, go-getter (*informal*), high-flier, man *or* woman of action, overachiever, success, winner

aching *adjective* **1.** hurting, painful, pounding, smarting, sore, suffering, throbbing, tired **2.** craving, desirous, eager, hankering, hungering, longing, pining, thirsting, yearning

acid **1.** acerb, acerbic, acetic, acidulous, acrid, biting, pungent, sharp, sour, tart, vinegarish, vinegary **2.** acerbic, biting, bitter, caustic, cutting, harsh, hurtful, mordacious, mordant, pungent, sharp, stinging, trenchant, vitriolic
Antonyms (*sense 1*) alkaline, bland, mild, pleasant, sweet (*sense 2*) benign, bland, gentle, kindly, mild, pleasant, sweet

acidity **1.** acerbity, acidulousness, acridity, acridness, bitterness, pungency, sharpness, sourness, tartness, vinegariness, vinegarishness **2.** acerbity, acridity, acridness, bitterness, causticity, causticness, harshness, hurtfulness, mordancy, pungency, sharpness, trenchancy

acidly acerbically, acridly, bitingly, bitterly, caustically, cuttingly, harshly, hurtfully, mordantly, pungently, sharply, stingingly, tartly, trenchantly
Antonyms benignly, blandly, gently, kindly, mildly, pleasantly, sweetly

acidulous **1.** acerb, acerbic, acetic, acid, bitter, harsh, sharp, sour, tart, vinegarish, vinegary **2.** acid, biting, bitter, caustic, cutting, harsh, pungent, sharp, sour, vitriolic

acknowledge 1. accede, accept, acquiesce, admit, allow, concede, confess, declare, grant, own, profess, recognize, yield 2. address, greet, hail, notice, recognize, salute 3. answer, notice, react to, recognize, reply to, respond to, return
Antonyms (*sense 1*) contradict, deny, disclaim, discount, reject, renounce, repudiate (*senses 2 & 3*) deny, disavow, disdain, disregard, ignore, rebut, reject, snub, spurn

acknowledged accepted, accredited, admitted, answered, approved, conceded, confessed, declared, professed, recognized, returned

acknowledgment 1. acceptance, accession, acquiescence, admission, allowing, confession, declaration, profession, realization, yielding 2. addressing, greeting, hail, hailing, notice, recognition, salutation, salute 3. answer, appreciation, Brownie points, credit, gratitude, reaction, recognition, reply, response, return, thanks

acme apex, climax, crest, crown, culmination, height, high point, optimum, peak, pinnacle, summit, top, vertex, zenith
Antonyms bottom, depths, low point, minimum, nadir, rock bottom, zero

acolyte adherent, admirer, altar boy, assistant, attendant, follower, helper

acquaint advise, announce, apprise, disclose, divulge, enlighten, familiarize, inform, let (someone) know, notify, reveal, tell

acquaintance 1. associate, colleague, contact 2. association, awareness, cognizance, companionship, conversance, conversancy, experience, familiarity, fellowship, intimacy, knowledge, relationship, social contact, understanding
Antonyms (*sense 1*) buddy, good friend, intimate, stranger (*sense 2*) ignorance, unfamiliarity

Should auld acquaintance be forgot,
And never brought to mind?
Robert Burns *Auld Lang Syne*

I look upon every day to be lost, in which I do not make a new acquaintance
Dr. Johnson

acquaintance: a person whom we know well enough to borrow from, but not well enough to lend to
Ambrose Bierce *The Devil's Dictionary*

acquaintanceship acquaintance, association, companionship, fellowship, knowledge, relationship, social contact

acquainted alive to, apprised of, *au fait*, aware of, cognizant of, conscious of, conversant with, experienced in, familiar with, informed of, in on, knowledgeable about, privy to, versed in

acquiesce accede, accept, agree, allow, approve, assent, bow to, comply, concur, conform, consent, give in, go along with, play ball (*informal*), submit, yield
Antonyms balk at, contest, demur, disagree, dissent, fight, object, protest, refuse, resist, veto

acquiescence acceptance, accession, agreement, approval, assent, compliance, concurrence, conformity, consent, giving in, obedience, submission, yielding

acquiescent acceding, accepting, agreeable, agreeing, approving, assenting, compliant, concurrent, conforming, consenting, obedient, submissive, yielding

acquire achieve, amass, attain, buy, collect, earn, gain, gather, get, land, obtain, pick up, procure, realize, receive, score (*slang*), secure, win
Antonyms be deprived of, forfeit, forgo, give up, lose, relinquish, renounce, surrender, waive

acquirement accomplishment, achievement, acquisition, attainment, gathering, grip, knowledge, learning, mastery, qualification, skill

acquisition 1. buy, gain, possession, prize, property, purchase 2. achievement, acquirement, attainment, gaining, learning, obtainment, procurement, pursuit

acquisitive avaricious, avid, covetous, grabbing, grasping, greedy, predatory, rapacious
Antonyms bounteous, bountiful, generous, lavish, liberal, munificent, open-handed, unselfish, unstinting

acquisitiveness avarice, avidity, avidness, covetousness, graspingness, greed, predatoriness, rapaciousness, rapacity

acquit 1. absolve, clear, deliver, discharge, exculpate, exonerate, free, fulfil, liberate, release, relieve, vindicate 2. discharge, pay, pay off, repay, satisfy, settle 3. bear, behave, comport, conduct, perform
Antonyms (*sense 1*) blame, charge, condemn, convict, damn, find guilty, sentence

acquittal absolution, clearance, deliverance, discharge, exculpation, exoneration, freeing, liberation, release, relief, vindication

acquittance acknowledgment, discharge, payment, receipt, release, settlement, settling

acrid 1. acerb, acid, astringent, biting, bitter, burning, caustic, harsh, irritating, pungent, sharp, stinging, vitriolic 2. acrimonious, biting, bitter, caustic, cutting, harsh, mordacious, mordant, nasty, sarcastic, sharp, trenchant, vitriolic

acridity 1. acerbity, acidity, acridness, astringency, bitterness, pungency, sharpness, sting, tartness 2. acridness, acrimony, asperity, bitterness, harshness, mordancy, nastiness, sarcasm, sharpness, trenchancy, vitriol

acrimonious acerbic, astringent, biting, bitter, caustic, censorious, churlish, crabbed, cutting, irascible, mordacious, mordant, peevish, petulant, pungent, rancorous, sarcastic, severe, sharp, spiteful, splenetic, tart, testy, trenchant, vitriolic
Antonyms affable, benign, forgiving, good-tempered

acrimony acerbity, asperity, astringency, bitterness, churlishness, harshness, ill will, irascibility, mordancy, peevishness, pungency, rancour, sarcasm, spleen, tartness, trenchancy, virulence
Antonyms amity, friendliness, friendship, good feelings, goodwill, liking, warmth

acrobat gymnast, tumbler

across *preposition* **1.** facing, opposite **2.** beyond, on the other *or* far side of, over, past **3.** all through, covering, over, over the length and breadth of, straddling, throughout *~adverb* **4.** athwart, crossways *or* crosswise, from side to side, transversely **5.** beyond, over, past, to the other *or* far side

across-the-board all-embracing, all-encompassing, all-inclusive, blanket, complete, comprehensive, full, general, indiscriminate, sweeping, thorough, thoroughgoing, total, universal, wall-to-wall, wholesale, widespread, without exception *or* omission
Antonyms discriminate, limited, partial, restricted, selective, specific

act *noun* **1.** accomplishment, achievement, action, blow, deed, doing, execution, exertion, exploit, feat, move, operation, performance, step, stroke, undertaking **2.** bill, decree, edict, enactment, law, measure, ordinance, resolution, statute **3.** affectation, attitude, counterfeit, dissimulation, fake, feigning, front, performance, pose, posture, pretence, sham, show, stance **4.** performance, routine, show, sketch, turn *~verb* **5.** acquit, bear, behave, carry, carry out, comport, conduct, do, enact, execute, exert, function, go about, make, move, operate, perform, react, serve, strike, take effect, undertake, work **6.** affect, assume, counterfeit, dissimulate, feign, imitate, perform, pose, posture, pretend, put on, seem, sham **7.** act out, characterize, enact, impersonate, mime, mimic, perform, personate, personify, play, play *or* take the part of, portray, represent

act for cover for, deputize for, fill in for, function in place of, replace, represent, serve, stand in for, substitute for, take the place of

acting *adjective* **1.** interim, *pro tem*, provisional, substitute, surrogate, temporary *~noun* **2.** characterization, dramatics, enacting, impersonation, performance, performing, playing, portrayal, portraying, stagecraft, theatre **3.** assuming, counterfeiting, dissimulation, feigning, imitating, imitation, imposture, play-acting, posing, posturing, pretence, pretending, putting on, seeming, shamming

The art of acting consists in keeping people from coughing

Ralph Richardson

She ran the whole gamut of emotions from A to B

Dorothy Parker (of Katherine Hepburn)

action **1.** accomplishment, achievement, act, blow, deed, exercise, exertion, exploit, feat, move, operation, performance, step, stroke, undertaking **2.** activity, energy, force, liveliness, spirit, vigour, vim, vitality **3.** activity, effect, effort, exertion, force, functioning, influence, motion, movement, operation, power, process, work, working **4.** battle, combat, conflict, fighting, warfare **5.** affray, battle, clash, combat, contest, encounter, engagement, fight, fray, skirmish, sortie **6.** case, cause, lawsuit, litigation, proceeding, prosecution, suit

An ounce of action is worth a ton of theory

Friedrich Engels

Actions speak louder than words

actions bearing, behaviour, comportment, conduct, demeanour, deportment, manners, ways

activate actuate, animate, arouse, energize, galvanize, get going, impel, initiate, kick-start (*informal*), mobilize, motivate, move, prod, prompt, propel, rouse, set going, set in motion, set off, start, stimulate, stir, switch on, trigger (off), turn on
Antonyms arrest, check, deactivate, halt, impede, stall, stop, terminate, turn off

activation actuation, animation, arousal, initiation, mobilization, setting in motion, start, switching on, triggering, turning on

active **1.** acting, astir, at work, doing, effectual, functioning, in action, in business, in force, in operation, live, moving, operative, running, stirring, working **2.** bustling, busy, engaged, full, hard-working, involved, occupied, on the go (*informal*), on the move, strenuous **3.** alert, alive and kicking, animated, diligent, energetic, industrious, lively, nimble, on the go (*informal*), quick, spirited, sprightly, spry, vibrant, vigorous, vital, vivacious **4.** activist, aggressive, ambitious, assertive, committed, devoted, energetic, engaged, enterprising, enthusiastic, forceful, forward, hard-working, industrious, militant, zealous
Antonyms dormant, dull, idle, inactive, inoperative, lazy, sedentary, slow, sluggish, torpid, unimaginative, unoccupied

activity **1.** action, activeness, animation, bustle, enterprise, exercise, exertion, hurly-burly, hustle, labour, life, liveliness, motion, movement, stir, work **2.** act, avocation, deed, endeavour, enterprise, hobby, interest, job, la~

bour, occupation, pastime, project, pursuit, scheme, task, undertaking, venture, work
Antonyms (*sense 1*) dullness, idleness, immobility, inaction, inactivity, indolence, inertia, lethargy, passivity, sluggishness, torpor

A rolling stone gathers no moss

act on, act upon **1.** act in accordance with, carry out, comply with, conform to, follow, heed, obey, yield to **2.** affect, alter, change, impact, influence, modify, sway, transform

actor **1.** actress, dramatic artist, leading man, luvvie (*informal*), performer, play-actor, player, Thespian, tragedian, trouper **2.** agent, doer, executor, factor, functionary, operative, operator, participant, participator, performer, perpetrator, practitioner, worker

Actors

Woody Allen [U.S.]
Fred Astaire [U.S.]
Richard Attenborough [British]
John Barrymore [U.S.]
Alan Bates [British]
Warren Beatty [U.S.]
Jean-Paul Belmondo [French]
Dirk Bogarde [British]
Humphrey Bogart [U.S.]
Charles Boyer [French]
Kenneth Branagh [British]
Marlon Brando [U.S.]
Richard Burbage [English]
Richard Burton [British]
James Cagney [U.S.]
Michael Caine [British]
Simon Callow [British]
Charlie Chaplin [British]
Maurice Chevalier [French]
Sean Connery [British]
Gary Cooper [U.S.]
Kevin Costner [U.S.]
Tom Cruise [U.S.]
James Dean [U.S.]
Robert De Niro [U.S.]
Gerard Depardieu [French]
Kirk Douglas [U.S.]
Michael Douglas [U.S.]
Clint Eastwood [U.S.]
Douglas Fairbanks Jr. [U.S.]
Douglas Fairbanks Snr. [U.S.]
Fernandel [French]
WC Fields [U.S.]
Albert Finney [British]
Errol Flynn [Australian]
Henry Fonda [U.S.]
Harrison Ford [U.S.]
Jean Gabin [France]
Clark Gable [U.S.]
David Garrick [British]
Mel Gibson [Australian]
John Gielgud [British]
Cary Grant [British - U.S.]
Alec Guinness [British]
Gene Hackman [U.S.]
Tom Hanks [U.S.]
Oliver Hardy [U.S.]
Rex Harrison [British]
Dustin Hoffman [U.S.]
Bob Hope [U.S.]
Anthony Hopkins [British]
Michael Hordern [British]
Leslie Howard [British]
Trevor Howard [British]
Rock Hudson [U.S.]
John Hurt [British]
Jeremy Irons [British]
Henry Irving [British]
Derek Jacobi [British]
Al Jolson [U.S.]
Boris Karloff [British]
Edmund Kean [British]
Buster Keaton [U.S.]
Harvey Keitel [U.S.]
Gene Kelly [U.S.]
Ben Kingsley [British]
Burt Lancaster [U.S.]
Charles Laughton [British - U.S.]
Stan Laurel [British - U.S.]
Harold Lloyd [U.S.]
Bela Lugosi [Hungarian]
Ian McKellen [British]
Steve McQueen [U.S.]
James Mason [British]
Marcello Mastroianni [Italian]
John Mills [British]
Robert Mitchum [U.S.]
Paul Newman [U.S.]
Jack Nicholson [U.S.]
Liam Neeson [Irish]
David Niven [British]
Gary Oldman [British]
Laurence Olivier [British]
Peter O'Toole [Irish - British]
Al Pacino [U.S.]
Gregory Peck [U.S.]
Donald Pleasence [British]
Anthony Quayle [British]
Anthony Quinn [U.S.]
Robert Redford [U.S.]
Michael Redgrave [British]
Fernando Rey [Spanish]
Ralph Richardson [British]
Paul Robeson [U.S.]
Edward G Robinson [U.S.]
Tim Roth [British]
Arnold Schwarzenegger [Austrian - U.S.]
Paul Scofield [British]
Peter Sellers [British]
Sylvester Stallone [U.S.]
Konstantin Stanislavsky [Russian]
James Stewart [U.S.]
Donald Sutherland [Canadian]
Jacques Tati [French]
Spencer Tracy [U.S.]
John Travolta [U.S.]
Peter Ustinov [British]
Rudolph Valentino [Italian - U.S.]
Max Von Sydow [Swedish]
John Wayne [U.S.]
Johnny Weissmuller [U.S.]

An actor's a guy who, if you ain't talking about him, ain't listening
Marlon Brando

Actors should be treated like cattle
Alfred Hitchcock

actress actor, dramatic artist, leading lady, performer, play-actor, player, starlet, Thespian, tragedienne, trouper

Actresses

Yvonne Arnaud [French]
Peggy Ashcroft [British]
Tallulah Bankhead [U.S.]
Brigitte Bardot [French]
Ingrid Bergman [Swedish - U.S.]
Sarah Bernhardt [French]
Clara Bow [U.S.]
Fanny Brice [U.S.]
Glenn Close [U.S.]
Claudette Colbert [French - U.S.]
Joan Crawford [U.S.]
Bette Davis [U.S.]
Geena Davis [U.S.]
Judy Davis [Australian]

Judi Dench [British]
Catherine Deneuve [French]
Marlene Dietrich [German]
Faye Dunaway [U.S.]
Edith Evans [British]
Jane Fonda [U.S.]
Jodie Foster [U.S.]
Greta Garbo [Swedish]
Ava Gardner [U.S.]
Judy Garland [U.S.]
Lillian Gish [U.S.]
Joyce Grenfell [British]
Jean Harlow [U.S.]
Audrey Hepburn [Belgian - U.S.]
Katharine Hepburn [U.S.]
Wendy Hiller [British]
Holly Hunter [U.S.]
Isabelle Huppert [French]
Glenda Jackson [British]
Diane Keaton [U.S.]
Grace Kelly [U.S.]
Fanny Kemble [British - U.S.]
Jessica Lange [U.S.]
Gertrude Lawrence [British]
Vivien Leigh [British]
Lotte Lenya [Austrian]
Margaret Lockwood [British]
Sophia Loren [Italian]
Siobhan McKenna [Irish]
Shirley MacLaine [U.S.]
Melina Mercouri [Greek]
Liza Minnelli [U.S.]
Helen Mirren [British]
Marilyn Monroe [U.S.]
Jeanne Moreau [French]
Michelle Pfeiffer [U.S.]
Mary Pickford [U.S.]
Joan Plowright [British]
Vanessa Redgrave [British]
Julia Roberts [U.S.]
Flora Robson [British]
Ginger Rogers [U.S.]
Margaret Rutherford [British]
Susan Sarandon [U.S.]
Delphine Seyrig [French]
Sarah Siddons [British]
Simone Signoret [French]
Maggie Smith [British]
Meryl Streep [U.S.]
Barbra Streisand [U.S.]
Janet Suzman [South African]
Elizabeth Taylor [British - U.S.]
Shirley Temple [U.S.]
Ellen Terry [British]
Emma Thompson [British]
Sybil Thorndike [British]
Sigourney Weaver [U.S.]
Raquel Welch [U.S.]
Mae West [U.S.]
Billie Whitelaw [British]
Peg Woffington [Irish]

I'm an actor. An actress is someone who wears boa feathers

Sigourney Weaver

actual **1.** absolute, categorical, certain, concrete, corporeal, definite, factual, indisputable, indubitable, physical, positive, real, substantial, tangible, undeniable, unquestionable **2.** authentic, confirmed, genuine, real, realistic, true, truthful, verified **3.** current, existent, extant, live, living, present, present-day, prevailing
Antonyms (*senses 1 & 2*) fictitious, hypothetical, made-up, probable, supposed, theoretical, unreal, untrue

actuality **1.** corporeality, factuality, materiality, reality, realness, substance, substantiality, truth, verity **2.** fact, reality, truth, verity

actualize, actualise bring about, bring into being, bring to life, effect, effectuate, give life *or* substance to, incarnate, make concrete, make happen, make real, objectify, put into effect, realize, reify

actually absolutely, as a matter of fact, de facto, essentially, indeed, in fact, in point of fact, in reality, in truth, literally, really, truly, veritably

actuate animate, arouse, cause, dispose, drive, excite, get going, impel, incite, induce, influence, inspire, instigate, motivate, move, prompt, quicken, rouse, set off, spur, stimulate, stir, urge

act up be naughty, carry on, cause trouble, give bother, give trouble, horse around (*informal*), malfunction, mess about, misbehave, piss about (*taboo slang*), piss around (*taboo slang*), play up (*Brit. informal*), raise Cain

act upon *see* ACT ON

acumen acuteness, astuteness, cleverness, discernment, ingenuity, insight, intelligence, judgment, keenness, penetration, perception, perspicacity, perspicuity, sagacity, sharpness, shrewdness, smartness, smarts (*slang, chiefly U.S.*), wisdom, wit

acute **1.** astute, canny, clever, discerning, discriminating, incisive, ingenious, insightful, intuitive, keen, observant, on the ball (*informal*), penetrating, perceptive, perspicacious, piercing, sensitive, sharp, smart, subtle **2.** critical, crucial, dangerous, decisive, essential, grave, important, serious, severe, sudden, urgent, vital **3.** cutting, distressing, excruciating, exquisite, fierce, harrowing, intense, overpowering, overwhelming, piercing, poignant, powerful, racking, severe, sharp, shooting, shrill, stabbing, sudden, violent **4.** cuspate, needle-shaped, peaked, pointed, sharp, sharpened
Antonyms (*sense 1*) dense, dim, dim-witted, dull, obtuse, slow, stupid, unintelligent (*sense 4*) blunt, blunted, dull, obtuse, unsharpened

acuteness **1.** acuity, astuteness, canniness, cleverness, discernment, discrimination, ingenuity, insight, intuition, intuitiveness, keenness, perception, perceptiveness, perspicacity, sensitivity, sharpness, smartness, subtleness, subtlety, wit **2.** criticality, criticalness, cruciality, danger, dangerousness, decisiveness, essentiality, gravity, importance, seriousness, severity, suddenness, urgency, vitalness **3.** distressingness, exquisiteness, fierceness, intenseness, intensity, poignancy, pow~

erfulness, severity, sharpness, shrillness, sud~denness, violence **4.** pointedness, sharpness

adage aphorism, apophthegm, axiom, by-word, dictum, maxim, motto, precept, proverb, saw, saying

adamant 1. determined, firm, fixed, immovable, inexorable, inflexible, insistent, intransigent, obdurate, relentless, resolute, rigid, set, stiff, stubborn, unbending, uncompromising, unre~lenting, unshakable, unyielding **2.** adaman~tine, flinty, hard, impenetrable, indestructible, rock-hard, rocky, steely, stony, tough, un~breakable

Antonyms (*sense 1*) compliant, compromising, easy-going, flexible, lax, pliant, receptive, re~sponsive, susceptible, tensile, tractable, yielding (*sense 2*) bendy, ductile, flexible, pli~able, pliant, yielding

adapt acclimatize, accommodate, adjust, alter, apply, change, comply, conform, convert, cus~tomize, familiarize, fashion, fit, habituate, harmonize, make, match, modify, prepare, qualify, remodel, shape, suit, tailor, tweak (*informal*)

adaptability adaptableness, adjustability, al~terability, changeability, compliancy, convert~ibility, flexibility, malleability, modifiability, plasticity, pliability, pliancy, resilience, vari~ability, versatility

adaptable adjustable, alterable, changeable, compliant, conformable, convertible, easy-going, easy-oasy (*slang*), flexible, malleable, modifiable, plastic, pliant, resilient, variable, versatile

adaptation 1. adjustment, alteration, change, conversion, modification, refitting, remodel~ling, reworking, shift, transformation, vari~ation, version **2.** acclimatization, accus~tomedness, familiarization, habituation, na~turalization

add 1. adjoin, affix, amplify, annex, append, attach, augment, enlarge by, include, increase by, supplement **2.** add up, compute, count up, reckon, sum up, total, tot up

Antonyms deduct, diminish, lessen, reduce, remove, subtract, take away, take from

addendum addition, adjunct, affix, appendage, appendix, attachment, augmentation, codicil, extension, extra, postscript, supplement

addict 1. dope-fiend (*slang*), fiend (*informal*), freak (*informal*), head (*slang*), junkie (*infor~mal*), pill-popper (*informal*), user (*informal*) **2.** adherent, buff (*informal*), devotee, enthusiast, fan, follower, freak (*informal*), nut (*slang*)

addicted absorbed, accustomed, dedicated, de~pendent, devoted, disposed, fond, habituated, hooked (*slang*), inclined, obsessed, prone

addiction craving, dependence, enslavement, habit, obsession

Every form of addiction is bad, no matter whether the narcotic be alcohol or morphine or idealism

Carl Gustav Jung *Memories, Dreams, and Reflections*

addictive causing addiction *or* dependency, compelling, habit-forming, moreish *or* morish (*informal*)

addition 1. accession, adding, adjoining, affix~ing, amplification, annexation, attachment, augmentation, enlargement, extension, inclu~sion, increasing **2.** addendum, additive, ad~junct, affix, appendage, appendix, extension, extra, gain, increase, increment, supplement **3.** adding up, computation, counting up, reck~oning, summation, summing up, totalling, totting up **4. in addition (to)** additionally, also, as well (as), besides, into the bargain, moreover, over and above, to boot, too, withal

Antonyms deduction, detachment, diminution, lessening, reduction, removal, subtraction

additional added, add-on, affixed, appended, extra, fresh, further, increased, more, new, other, over-and-above, spare, supplementary

additive added ingredient, artificial *or* syn~thetic ingredient, E number, extra, sup~plement

addle 1. befuddle, bewilder, confuse, fluster, fuddle, mix up, muddle, perplex, stupefy **2.** go bad, go off (*Brit. informal*), rot, spoil, turn, turn bad

addle-brained *or* **addle-pated** befuddled, be~wildered, confused, daft (*informal*), dead from the neck up (*informal*), dim-witted, dopey (*in~formal*), dozy (*Brit. informal*), flustered, fool~ish, goofy (*informal*), halfwitted, mixed-up, muddled, muddleheaded, nonsensical, per~plexed, silly, simple, simple-minded, stupid, thick, thickheaded, witless, woolly-minded

addled 1. at sea, befuddled, bewildered, con~fused, flustered, foolish, mixed-up, muddled, perplexed, silly **2.** bad, gone bad, off, rancid, rotten, turned

address *noun* **1.** abode, domicile, dwelling, home, house, location, lodging, pad (*slang*), place, residence, situation, whereabouts **2.** di~rection, inscription, superscription **3.** dis~course, disquisition, dissertation, harangue, lecture, oration, sermon, speech, talk **4.** adroitness, art, dexterity, discretion, expert~ness, ingenuity, skilfulness, skill, tact *~verb* **5.** accost, apostrophize, approach, greet, hail, in~voke, salute, speak to, talk to **6.** discourse, give a speech, give a talk, harangue, lecture, orate, sermonize, speak, spout, talk **7. ad~dress (oneself) to** apply (oneself) to, attend to, concentrate on, devote (oneself) to, engage in, focus on, knuckle down to, look to, take care of, take up, turn to, undertake

adduce advance, allege, cite, designate, mention, name, offer, present, quote

add up 1. add, compute, count, count up, reckon, sum up, total, tot up 2. amount, come to, imply, indicate, mean, reveal, signify 3. be plausible, be reasonable, hold water, make sense, ring true, stand to reason

adept 1. *adjective* able, accomplished, adroit, dexterous, expert, masterful, masterly, practised, proficient, skilful, skilled, versed 2. *noun* buff (*informal*), dab hand (*Brit. informal*), expert, genius, hotshot (*informal*), master, maven (*U.S.*), whiz (*informal*)
Antonyms *adjective* amateurish, awkward, clumsy, inept, unskilled

adeptness ability, adroitness, aptitude, deftness, dexterity, expertise, facility, mastery, proficiency, skilfulness, skill
Antonyms amateurishness, awkwardness, clumsiness, ineptitude, inexpertness

adequacy capability, commensurateness, competence, fairness, requisiteness, satisfactoriness, sufficiency, suitability, tolerability

adequate capable, commensurate, competent, enough, fair, passable, requisite, satisfactory, sufficient, suitable, tolerable, up to scratch (*informal*)
Antonyms deficient, inadequate, insufficient, lacking, meagre, scant, short, unsatisfactory, unsuitable

adhere 1. attach, cement, cleave, cling, cohere, fasten, fix, glue, glue on, hold fast, paste, stick, stick fast, unite 2. abide by, be attached, be constant, be devoted, be faithful, be loyal, be true, cleave to, cling, follow, fulfil, heed, keep, keep to, maintain, mind, obey, observe, respect, stand by, support

adherent 1. *noun* admirer, advocate, devotee, disciple, fan, follower, hanger-on, henchman, partisan, protagonist, sectary, supporter, upholder, votary 2. *adjective* adhering, adhesive, clinging, gluey, glutinous, gummy, holding, mucilaginous, sticking, sticky, tacky, tenacious
Antonyms *noun* adversary, antagonist, disputant, dissentient, enemy, foe, opponent, opposer, opposition, rival

adhesion 1. adherence, adhesiveness, attachment, coherence, cohesion, grip, holding fast, sticking, union 2. allegiance, attachment, constancy, devotion, faithfulness, fidelity, fulfilment, heed, loyalty, obedience, observation, respect, support, troth (*archaic*)

adhesive 1. *adjective* adhering, attaching, clinging, cohesive, gluey, glutinous, gummy, holding, mucilaginous, sticking, sticky, tacky, tenacious 2. *noun* cement, glue, gum, mucilage, paste

ad hoc 1. *adjective* expedient, impromptu, improvised, jury-rigged (*chiefly nautical*), makeshift, stopgap 2. *adverb* as the need arises, for present purposes
Antonyms *adjective* fixed, lasting, permanent, regular, standing (*of a committee*)

adieu congé, farewell, goodbye, leave-taking, parting, valediction

ad infinitum always, boundlessly, endlessly, eternally, evermore, for all time, for ever (and ever), infinitely, in perpetuity, *in perpetuum*, interminably, limitlessly, perpetually, to infinity, unceasingly, unendingly, without end *or* limit

adipose fat, fatty, greasy, obese, oily, oleaginous, sebaceous

adjacent abutting, adjoining, alongside, beside, bordering, cheek by jowl, close, contiguous, near, neighbouring, next door, proximate, touching, within sniffing distance (*informal*)
Antonyms distant, far away, remote, separated

adjoin abut, add, affix, annex, append, approximate, attach, border, combine, communicate with, connect, couple, impinge, interconnect, join, link, neighbour, touch, unite, verge

adjoining abutting, adjacent, bordering, connecting, contiguous, impinging, interconnecting, joined, joining, near, neighbouring, next door, touching, verging

adjourn defer, delay, discontinue, interrupt, postpone, prorogue, put off, put on the back burner (*informal*), recess, stay, suspend, take a rain check on (*U.S. & Canad. informal*)
Antonyms assemble, continue, convene, gather, open, remain, reopen, stay

adjournment deferment, deferral, delay, discontinuation, interruption, postponement, prorogation, putting off, recess, stay, suspension

adjudge adjudicate, allot, apportion, assign, award, decide, declare, decree, determine, distribute, judge, order, pronounce

adjudicate adjudge, arbitrate, decide, determine, judge, mediate, referee, settle, umpire

adjudication adjudgment, arbitration, conclusion, decision, determination, finding, judgment, pronouncement, ruling, settlement, verdict

adjudicator arbiter, arbitrator, judge, moderator, referee, umpire

adjunct accessory, addendum, addition, add-on, appendage, appurtenance, auxiliary, complement, supplement

adjure 1. appeal to, beg, beseech, entreat, implore, invoke, pray, supplicate 2. charge, command, direct, enjoin, order

adjust acclimatize, accommodate, accustom, adapt, alter, arrange, compose, convert, customize, dispose, fit, fix, harmonize, make conform, measure, modify, order, reconcile, rectify, redress, regulate, remodel, set, settle, suit, tune (up), tweak (*informal*)

adjustable adaptable, alterable, flexible, malleable, modifiable, mouldable, movable, tractable

adjustment **1.** adaptation, alteration, arrangement, arranging, fitting, fixing, modification, ordering, rectification, redress, regulation, remodelling, setting, tuning **2.** acclimatization, harmonization, orientation, reconciliation, settlement, settling in

ad-lib **1.** *verb* busk, extemporize, improvise, make up, speak extemporaneously, speak impromptu, speak off the cuff, vamp, wing it (*informal*) **2.** *adjective* extemporaneous, extempore, extemporized, impromptu, improvised, made up, off-the-cuff (*informal*), off the top of one's head, unprepared, unrehearsed **3.** *adverb* extemporaneously, extempore, impromptu, off the cuff, off the top of one's head (*informal*), without preparation, without rehearsal

administer **1.** conduct, control, direct, govern, handle, manage, oversee, run, superintend, supervise **2.** apply, contribute, dispense, distribute, execute, give, impose, mete out, perform, provide

administrate administer, conduct, control, direct, govern, handle, manage, oversee, run, superintend, supervise

administration **1.** administering, application, conduct, control, direction, dispensation, distribution, execution, governing, government, management, overseeing, performance, provision, running, superintendence, supervision **2.** executive, governing body, government, management, ministry, term of office

administrative directorial, executive, governmental, gubernatorial (*chiefly U.S.*), management, managerial, organizational, regulatory, supervisory

administrator agent, bureaucrat, executive, functionary, manager, mandarin, minister, officer, official, organizer, supervisor

admirable choice, commendable, estimable, excellent, exquisite, fine, laudable, meritorious, praiseworthy, rare, sterling, superior, valuable, wonderful, worthy
Antonyms bad, commonplace, deplorable, disappointing, displeasing, mediocre, no great shakes (*informal*), worthless

admiration adoration, affection, amazement, appreciation, approbation, approval, astonishment, delight, esteem, pleasure, praise, regard, respect, surprise, veneration, wonder, wonderment

admire **1.** adore, appreciate, approve, esteem, idolize, look up to, praise, prize, respect, take one's hat off to, think highly of, value, venerate, worship **2.** appreciate, delight in, marvel at, take pleasure in, wonder at
Antonyms contemn, deride, despise, look down on, look down one's nose at (*informal*), misprize, scorn, sneer at, spurn, undervalue

admirer **1.** beau, boyfriend, lover, suitor, sweetheart, wooer **2.** adherent, buff (*informal*), devotee, disciple, enthusiast, fan, follower, partisan, protagonist, supporter, votary, worshipper

admissible acceptable, allowable, allowed, passable, permissible, permitted, tolerable, tolerated
Antonyms disallowed, inadmissible, intolerable, unacceptable

admission **1.** acceptance, access, admittance, entrance, entrée, entry, ingress, initiation, introduction **2.** acknowledgment, admitting, affirmation, allowance, avowal, concession, confession, declaration, disclosure, divulgence, profession, revelation

admit **1.** accept, allow, allow to enter, give access, initiate, introduce, let in, receive, take in **2.** acknowledge, affirm, avow, concede, confess, cough (*slang*), declare, disclose, divulge, 'fess up (*U.S. slang*), own, profess, reveal **3.** agree, allow, grant, let, permit, recognize
Antonyms (*sense 1*) exclude, keep out (*senses 2 & 3*) deny, dismiss, forbid, negate, prohibit, reject

admittance acceptance, access, admitting, allowing, entrance, entry, letting in, passage, reception

admittedly allowedly, avowedly, certainly, confessedly, it cannot be denied, it must be admitted (allowed, confessed, said), to be fair *or* honest, undeniably

admix add, alloy, amalgamate, blend, combine, commingle, commix, include, incorporate, intermingle, meld, merge, mingle, mix, put in

admixture **1.** alloy, amalgamation, blend, combination, compound, fusion, intermixture, medley, meld **2.** component, constituent, element, ingredient

admonish advise, bawl out (*informal*), berate, carpet (*informal*), caution, censure, check, chew out (*U.S. & Canad. informal*), chide, counsel, enjoin, exhort, forewarn, give a rocket (*Brit. & N.Z. informal*), rap over the knuckles, read the riot act, rebuke, reprimand, reprove, scold, slap on the wrist, tear into (*informal*), tear (someone) off a strip (*Brit. informal*), tell off (*informal*), upbraid, warn

Antonyms applaud, commend, compliment, congratulate, praise

admonition advice, berating, caution, chiding, counsel, rebuke, remonstrance, reprimand, re~proach, reproof, scolding, telling off (*informal*), upbraiding, warning

admonitory admonishing, advisory, cautionary, rebuking, reprimanding, reproachful, reprov~ing, scolding, warning

ad nauseam ad infinitum, again and again, on and on, over and over (again), time after time, time and (time) again, times without number

ado agitation, bother, bustle, commotion, con~fusion, delay, disturbance, excitement, flurry, fuss, pother, stir, to-do, trouble

adolescence **1.** boyhood, girlhood, juvenes~cence, minority, teens, youth **2.** boyishness, childishness, girlishness, immaturity, juvenil~ity, puerility, youthfulness

adolescent **1.** *adjective* boyish, girlish, growing, immature, juvenile, puerile, teenage, young, youthful **2.** *noun* juvenile, minor, teenager, youngster, youth

adopt **1.** accept, appropriate, approve, assume, choose, embrace, endorse, espouse, follow, maintain, ratify, select, support, take on, take over, take up **2.** foster, take in

Antonyms (*sense 1*) abandon, abnegate, cast aside, cast off, disavow, disclaim, disown, forswear, give up, reject, renounce, repudiate, spurn, wash one's hands of

adoption **1.** acceptance, approbation, appro~priation, approval, assumption, choice, em~bracing, endorsement, espousal, following, maintenance, ratification, selection, support, taking on, taking over, taking up **2.** adopting, fosterage, fostering, taking in

adorable appealing, attractive, captivating, charming, cute, darling, dear, delightful, fetching, lovable, pleasing, precious

Antonyms despicable, displeasing, hateful, unlikable *or* unlikeable, unlovable

adoration admiration, esteem, estimation, ex~altation, glorification, honour, idolatry, idoli~zation, love, reverence, veneration, worship, worshipping

adore admire, bow to, cherish, dote on, esteem, exalt, glorify, honour, idolize, love, revere, reverence, venerate, worship

Antonyms abhor, abominate, despise, detest, execrate, hate, loathe

adoring admiring, adulatory, affectionate, ar~dent, devoted, doting, enamoured, fond, idol~izing, loving, reverent, reverential, venerating, worshipping

Antonyms abhorring, abominating, despising, detesting, hating, loathing

adorn array, beautify, bedeck, deck, decorate, embellish, emblazon, engarland, enhance, en~rich, festoon, garnish, gild the lily, grace, or~nament, trim

adornment **1.** accessory, decoration, embellish~ment, festoon, frill, frippery, ornament, trim~ming **2.** beautification, decorating, decoration, embellishment, ornamentation, trimming

adrift **1.** afloat, drifting, unanchored, unmoored **2.** aimless, directionless, goalless, purposeless **3.** amiss, astray, off course, wrong

adroit able, adept, apt, artful, bright (*infor~mal*), clever, cunning, deft, dexterous, expert, ingenious, masterful, neat, nimble, proficient, quick-witted, skilful, skilled

Antonyms awkward, blundering, bungling, cack-handed (*informal*), clumsy, ham-fisted (*informal*), inept, inexpert, maladroit, unco~ordinated, unhandy, unskilful

adroitness ability, ableness, address, adept~ness, aptness, artfulness, cleverness, craft, cunning, deftness, dexterity, expertise, ingen~iousness, ingenuity, masterfulness, mastery, nimbleness, proficiency, quick-wittedness, skilfulness, skill

adulation blandishment, bootlicking (*informal*), extravagant flattery, fawning, fulsome praise, servile flattery, sycophancy, worship

Antonyms abuse, calumniation, censure, con~demnation, disparagement, revilement, ridi~cule, vilification, vituperation

adulatory blandishing, bootlicking (*informal*), fawning, flattering, obsequious, praising, ser~vile, slavish, sycophantic, worshipping

adult **1.** *adjective* full grown, fully developed, fully grown, grown-up, mature, of age, ripe **2.** *noun* grown *or* grown-up person (man *or* woman), grown-up, person of mature age

adulterate **1.** *verb* attenuate, bastardize, con~taminate, corrupt, debase, depreciate, deterio~rate, devalue, make impure, mix with, thin, vitiate, water down, weaken **2.** *adjective* adul~terated, attenuated, bastardized, contaminat~ed, corrupt, debased, depreciated, deteriorat~ed, devalued, mixed, thinned, vitiated, wa~tered down, weakened

adulterer, adulteress cheat (*informal*), forni~cator, love cheat (*Journalistic slang*), love rat (*Journalistic slang*)

adulterous cheating (*informal*), extramarital, fornicating, unchaste, unfaithful

adultery cheating (*informal*), extracurricular sex (*informal*), extramarital congress (rela~tions, sex), fornication, having an affair *or* a fling, illicit sex, infidelity, playing away from home (*slang*), playing the field (*slang*), unchastity, unfaithfulness

Antonyms chastity, faithfulness, fidelity

What men call gallantry, and gods adultery,
Is much more common where the climate's sultry
Lord Byron *Don Juan*

Do not adultery commit
Advantage rarely comes of it
Arthur Hugh Clough *The Latest Decalogue*

adumbrate **1.** delineate, indicate, outline, silhouette, sketch, suggest **2.** augur, forecast, foreshadow, foretell, portend, predict, prefigure, presage, prognosticate, prophesy **3.** bedim, darken, eclipse, obfuscate, obscure, overshadow

adumbration **1.** delineation, draft, indication, outline, rough, silhouette, sketch, suggestion **2.** augury, forecast, foreshadowing, foretelling, omen, portent, prediction, prefiguration, prefigurement, presage, prognostication, prophecy, sign **3.** bedimming, cloud, darkening, darkness, eclipse, eclipsing, obfuscation, obscuring, overshadowing, shadow

advance *verb* **1.** accelerate, bring forward, bring up, come forward, elevate, go ahead, go forward, go on, hasten, make inroads, move onward, move up, press on, proceed, progress, promote, send forward, send up, speed, upgrade **2.** benefit, further, grow, improve, multiply, prosper, thrive **3.** adduce, allege, cite, offer, present, proffer, put forward, submit, suggest **4.** lend, pay beforehand, supply on credit *~noun* **5.** advancement, development, forward movement, headway, inroad, onward movement, progress **6.** advancement, amelioration, betterment, breakthrough, furtherance, gain, growth, improvement, progress, promotion, step **7.** appreciation, credit, deposit, down payment, increase *(in price)*, loan, prepayment, retainer, rise *(in price)* **8. advances** approach, approaches, moves, overtures, proposals, proposition *~adjective* **9.** beforehand, early, foremost, forward, in front, leading, prior **10. in advance** ahead, beforehand, earlier, in the forefront, in the lead, in the van, on the barrelhead, previously
Antonyms *verb (sense 1)* demote, hold back, impede, move back, regress, retard, retreat, set back, withdraw *(sense 2)* decrease, diminish, lessen, weaken *(sense 3)* hide, hold back, suppress, withhold *(sense 4)* defer payment, withhold payment

advanced ahead, avant-garde, extreme, foremost, forward, higher, late, leading, precocious, progressive
Antonyms backward, behind, retarded, underdeveloped, undeveloped

advancement **1.** advance, forward movement, headway, onward movement, progress **2.** advance, amelioration, betterment, gain, growth, improvement, preferment, progress, promotion, rise

advantage ace in the hole, ace up one's sleeve, aid, ascendancy, asset, assistance, avail, benefit, blessing, boon, boot *(obsolete)*, convenience, dominance, edge, gain, good, help, inside track, interest, lead, mileage *(informal)*, precedence, pre-eminence, profit, service, start, superiority, sway, upper hand, use, utility, welfare
Antonyms curse, difficulty, disadvantage, downside, drawback, handicap, hindrance, inconvenience, snag

advantageous **1.** dominant, dominating, favourable, superior **2.** beneficial, convenient, expedient, helpful, of service, profitable, useful, valuable, worthwhile
Antonyms detrimental, unfavourable, unfortunate, unhelpful, useless

advent appearance, approach, arrival, coming, entrance, occurrence, onset, visitation

adventitious accidental, casual, chance, extraneous, foreign, fortuitous, incidental, nonessential, unexpected

adventure **1.** *noun* chance, contingency, enterprise, escapade, experience, exploit, hazard, incident, occurrence, risk, speculation, undertaking, venture **2.** *verb* dare, endanger, hazard, imperil, jeopardize, risk, venture

An adventure is only an inconvenience rightly considered. An inconvenience is only an adventure wrongly considered
G.K. Chesterton *All Things Considered*

adventurer **1.** daredevil, hero, heroine, knight-errant, soldier of fortune, swashbuckler, traveller, venturer, voyager, wanderer **2.** charlatan, fortune-hunter, gambler, mercenary, opportunist, rogue, speculator

adventurous adventuresome, audacious, bold, dangerous, daredevil, daring, enterprising, foolhardy, have-a-go *(informal)*, hazardous, headstrong, intrepid, rash, reckless, risky, temerarious *(rare)*, venturesome
Antonyms careful, cautious, chary, circumspect, hesitant, prudent, safe, tentative, timid, timorous, unadventurous, wary

adversary antagonist, competitor, contestant, enemy, foe, opponent, opposer, rival
Antonyms accomplice, ally, associate, collaborator, colleague, confederate, co-worker, friend, helper, partner, supporter

adverse antagonistic, conflicting, contrary, detrimental, disadvantageous, hostile, inexpedient, inimical, injurious, inopportune, negative, opposing, opposite, reluctant, repugnant, unfavourable, unfortunate, unfriendly, unlucky, unpropitious, unwilling
Antonyms advantageous, auspicious, beneficial, favourable, fortunate, helpful, lucky, opportune, promising, propitious, suitable

adversity affliction, bad luck, calamity, catastrophe, deep water, disaster, distress, hardship, hard times, ill-fortune, ill-luck, misery, misfortune, mishap, reverse, sorrow, suffering, trial, trouble, woe, wretchedness

advert *verb* allude, draw attention (to), mention, notice, observe, refer, regard, remark

advertise advise, announce, apprise, blazon, crack up (*informal*), declare, display, flaunt, inform, make known, notify, plug (*informal*), praise, proclaim, promote, promulgate, publicize, publish, puff, push (*informal*), tout

advertisement ad (*informal*), advert (*Brit. informal*), announcement, bill, blurb, circular, commercial, display, notice, placard, plug (*informal*), poster, promotion, publicity, puff

advertising

You can fool all the people all the time if the advertising is right and the budget is big enough
Joseph E. Levine

Promise, large promise, is the soul of an advertisement
Dr. Johnson

Advertising is the rattle of a stick inside a swill bucket
attributed to George Orwell

advice **1.** admonition, caution, counsel, guidance, help, injunction, opinion, recommendation, suggestion, view **2.** information, instruction, intelligence, notice, notification, warning, word

There is nothing we receive with so much reluctance as advice
Joseph Addison *The Spectator*

It was, perhaps, one of those cases in which advice is good or bad only as the event decides
Jane Austen *Persuasion*

The best way to give advice to your children is to find out what they want and advise them to do it
Harry S. Truman

advisability appropriateness, aptness, desirability, expediency, fitness, judiciousness, profitability, propriety, prudence, seemliness, soundness, suitability, wisdom

advisable appropriate, apt, desirable, expedient, fit, fitting, judicious, politic, profitable, proper, prudent, recommended, seemly, sensible, sound, suggested, suitable, wise
Antonyms ill-advised, impolitic, improper, imprudent, inappropriate, inexpedient, injudicious, silly, stupid, undesirable, unfitting, unprofitable, unseemly, unsound, unsuitable, unwise

advise **1.** admonish, caution, commend, counsel, enjoin, prescribe, recommend, suggest, urge **2.** acquaint, apprise, inform, make known, notify, report, tell, warn

Advise none to marry or go to war
George Herbert *Outlandish Proverbs*

advisedly after careful consideration, by design, calculatedly, deliberately, designedly, intentionally, judiciously, on purpose, premeditatedly, prudently, with intent

adviser aide, authority, coach, confidant, consultant, counsel, counsellor, guide, helper, lawyer, mentor, right-hand man, solicitor, teacher, tutor

advisory advising, consultative, counselling, helping, recommending

advocacy advancement, argument for, backing, campaigning for, championing, defence, encouragement, espousal, justification, pleading for, promotion, promulgation, propagation, proposal, recommendation, spokesmanship, support, upholding, urging

advocate *verb* **1.** advise, argue for, campaign for, champion, commend, countenance, defend, encourage, espouse, favour, hold a brief for (*informal*), justify, plead for, prescribe, press for, promote, propose, recommend, speak for, support, uphold, urge *~noun* **2.** apologist, apostle, backer, campaigner, champion, counsellor, defender, pleader, promoter, proponent, proposer, speaker, spokesman, supporter, upholder **3.** *Law* attorney, barrister, counsel, lawyer, solicitor
Antonyms *verb* contradict, oppose, resist, speak against, take a stand against, take issue with

aegis advocacy, auspices, backing, favour, guardianship, patronage, protection, shelter, sponsorship, support, wing

aesthetic artistic, in good taste, pleasing, tasteful

affability amiability, amicability, approachability, benevolence, benignity, civility, congeniality, cordiality, courtesy, friendliness, geniality, good humour, good nature, graciousness, kindliness, mildness, obligingness, pleasantness, sociability, urbanity, warmth

affable amiable, amicable, approachable, benevolent, benign, civil, congenial, cordial, courteous, friendly, genial, good-humoured, good-natured, gracious, kindly, mild, obliging, pleasant, sociable, urbane, warm
Antonyms brusque, cold, discourteous, distant, haughty, rude, stand-offish, surly, unapproachable, uncivil, unfriendly, ungracious, unpleasant, unsociable

affair **1.** activity, business, circumstance, concern, episode, event, happening, incident, interest, matter, occurrence, proceeding, project, question, subject, transaction, undertaking **2.** amour, intrigue, liaison, relationship, romance

affect **1.** act on, alter, bear upon, change, concern, impact, impinge upon, influence, inter~

est, involve, modify, prevail over, regard, relate to, sway, transform **2.** disturb, impress, move, overcome, perturb, stir, touch, tug at (someone's) heartstrings (*often facetious*), upset **3.** adopt, aspire to, assume, contrive, counterfeit, feign, imitate, pretend, put on, sham, simulate

affectation act, affectedness, appearance, artificiality, assumed manners, façade, fakery, false display, insincerity, mannerism, pose, pretence, pretension, pretentiousness, sham, show, simulation, unnatural imitation

affected 1. afflicted, altered, changed, concerned, damaged, deeply moved, distressed, hurt, impaired, impressed, influenced, injured, melted, stimulated, stirred, touched, troubled, upset **2.** artificial, assumed, camp (*informal*), conceited, contrived, counterfeit, feigned, insincere, la-di-da (*informal*), mannered, mincing, phoney *or* phony (*informal*), pompous, precious, pretended, pretentious, put-on, sham, simulated, spurious, stiff, studied, unnatural

Antonyms (*sense 1*) cured, unaffected, unconcerned, unharmed, uninjured, unmoved, untouched (*sense 2*) genuine, natural, real, unaffected

affecting moving, pathetic, piteous, pitiable, pitiful, poignant, sad, saddening, touching

affection amity, attachment, care, desire, feeling, fondness, friendliness, goodwill, inclination, kindness, liking, love, passion, propensity, tenderness, warmth

affectionate attached, caring, devoted, doting, fond, friendly, kind, loving, tender, warm, warm-hearted

Antonyms cold, cool, glacial, indifferent, stony, uncaring, undemonstrative, unfeeling, unresponsive

affiance betroth, bind, engage, pledge, promise

affiliate ally, amalgamate, annex, associate, band together, combine, confederate, connect, incorporate, join, unite

affiliated allied, amalgamated, associated, confederated, conjoined, connected, federated, incorporated, joined, linked, united

affiliation alliance, amalgamation, association, banding together, coalition, combination, confederation, connection, incorporation, joining, league, merging, relationship, union

affinity 1. alliance, analogy, closeness, compatibility, connection, correspondence, kinship, likeness, relation, relationship, resemblance, similarity **2.** attraction, fondness, inclination, leaning, liking, partiality, rapport, sympathy

Antonyms (*sense 1*) difference, disparity, dissimilarity (*sense 2*) abhorrence, animosity, antipathy, aversion, dislike, hatred, hostility, loathing, repugnance, revulsion

affirm assert, asseverate, attest, aver, avouch, avow, certify, confirm, declare, maintain, pronounce, ratify, state, swear, testify

Antonyms deny, disallow, rebut, refute, reject, renounce, repudiate, rescind, retract

affirmation assertion, asseveration, attestation, averment, avouchment, avowal, certification, confirmation, declaration, oath, pronouncement, ratification, statement, testimony

affirmative agreeing, approving, assenting, concurring, confirming, consenting, corroborative, favourable, positive

Antonyms denying, disagreeing, disapproving, dissenting, negating, negative

affix add, annex, append, attach, bind, fasten, glue, join, paste, put on, stick, subjoin, tack, tag

Antonyms detach, disconnect, remove, take off, unfasten, unglue

afflict beset, burden, distress, grieve, harass, hurt, oppress, pain, plague, rack, smite, torment, trouble, try, wound

affliction adversity, calamity, cross, curse, depression, disease, distress, grief, hardship, misery, misfortune, ordeal, pain, plague, scourge, sickness, sorrow, suffering, torment, trial, tribulation, trouble, woe, wretchedness

affluence abundance, big bucks (*informal, chiefly U.S.*), big money, exuberance, fortune, megabucks (*U.S. & Canad. slang*), opulence, plenty, pretty penny (*informal*), profusion, prosperity, riches, tidy sum (*informal*), wad (*U.S. & Canad. slang*), wealth

affluent 1. loaded (*slang*), moneyed, opulent, prosperous, rich, rolling in money (*slang*), wealthy, well-heeled (*informal*), well-off, well-to-do **2.** abundant, copious, exuberant, plenteous, plentiful

Antonyms (*sense 1*) broke (*informal*), destitute, down at heel, hard-up (*informal*), impecunious, impoverished, indigent, on the breadline, penniless, penurious, poor, poverty-stricken, skint (*Brit. slang*), stony-broke (*Brit. slang*)

afford 1. bear, spare, stand, sustain **2.** bestow, furnish, give, grant, impart, offer, produce, provide, render, supply, yield

affordable 1. bearable, manageable, sustainable **2.** cheap, economical, fair, inexpensive, low-cost, low-price, moderate, modest, reasonable

Antonyms beyond one's means, costly, dear, exorbitant, expensive, prohibitively expensive, unaffordable, uneconomical

affray *bagarre*, brawl, contest, disturbance, dogfight, encounter, feud, fight, fracas, free-for-all (*informal*), mêlée, outbreak, quarrel, scrap, scrimmage, scuffle, set-to (*informal*), shindig (*informal*), shindy (*informal*), skir~ mish, tumult

affront 1. *verb* abuse, anger, annoy, displease, insult, offend, outrage, pique, provoke, put *or* get one's back up, slight, vex 2. *noun* abuse, indignity, injury, insult, offence, outrage, provocation, slap in the face (*informal*), slight, slur, vexation, wrong

affronted angry, annoyed, cross, displeased, incensed, indignant, insulted, irate, miffed (*informal*), offended, outraged, peeved (*infor~ mal*), piqued, slighted, stung, upset

aficionado addict, adherent, admirer, buff (*in~ formal*), connoisseur, devotee, disciple, enthu~ siast, fan, fanatic, follower, freak (*informal*), lover, nut (*slang*), supporter, votary

afire 1. ablaze, aflame, alight, blazing, burning, fiery, flaming, ignited, lighted, lit, on fire 2. aglow, aroused, excited, fervent, impassioned, passionate, stimulated

aflame 1. ablaze, afire, alight, blazing, burning, fiery, flaming, ignited, lighted, lit, on fire 2. afire, aroused, excited, fervent, impassioned, passionate, stimulated 3. aglow, flushed, in~ flamed, red, ruddy

afloat 1. buoyant, floating, keeping one's head above water, on the surface, unsubmerged 2. aboard, at sea, on board (ship), on shipboard, sailing, under sail 3. awash, flooded, inundat~ ed, submerged, swamped, under water 4. adrift, aweigh, cast off, drifting, unanchored, unmoored 5. afoot, current, going about *or* around, in circulation, in the air 6. above wa~ ter, in business, solvent

Antonyms (*sense 1*) capsized, immersed, sub~ merged, sunken, under water (*sense 4*) an~ chored, held fast, moored (*sense 6*) bankrupt, bust (*informal*), in receivership, insolvent, out of business

afoot about, abroad, afloat, astir, brewing, cir~ culating, current, going on, hatching, in preparation, in progress, in the wind, on the go (*informal*), operating, up (*informal*)

afraid 1. alarmed, anxious, apprehensive, cow~ ardly, faint-hearted, fearful, frightened, in~ timidated, nervous, reluctant, scared, suspi~ cious, timid, timorous 2. regretful, sorry, un~ happy

Antonyms audacious, bold, fearless, happy, inapprehensive, indifferent, pleased, unafraid

afresh again, anew, newly, once again, once more, over again

after afterwards, behind, below, following, lat~ er, subsequently, succeeding, thereafter

Antonyms before, earlier, in advance, in front, previously, prior to, sooner

aftereffect 1. consequence, delayed response, hangover (*informal*), repercussion, spin-off 2. *usually plural* afterglow, aftermath, after~ shock, trail, wake

aftermath after-effects, consequences, effects, end, end result, outcome, results, sequel, upshot, wake

afterwards, afterward after, after that, at a later date *or* time, following that, later, sub~ sequently, then, thereafter

again 1. afresh, anew, another time, once more 2. also, besides, furthermore, in addition, moreover, on the contrary, on the other hand

against 1. anti (*informal*), averse to, contra (*informal*), counter, hostile to, in contrast to, in defiance of, in opposition to, in the face of, opposed to, opposing, resisting, versus 2. abutting, close up to, facing, fronting, in con~ tact with, on, opposite to, touching, upon 3. in anticipation of, in expectation of, in prepara~ tion for, in provision for

agape 1. gaping, wide, wide open, yawning 2. agog, amazed, astonished, astounded, awestricken, dumbfounded, eager, expectant, flabbergasted, gobsmacked (*Brit. slang*), spell~ bound, surprised, thunderstruck

age *noun* 1. date, day(s), duration, epoch, era, generation, lifetime, period, span, time 2. ad~ vancing years, decline (*of life*), majority, ma~ turity, old age, senescence, senility, seniority *~verb* 3. decline, deteriorate, grow old, ma~ ture, mellow, ripen

Antonyms *noun* (*sense 2*) adolescence, boy~ hood, childhood, girlhood, immaturity, ju~ venescence, salad days, young days, youth

Every man desires to live long, but no man would be old

Jonathan Swift *Thoughts on Various Subjects*

The days of our age are threescore years and ten

Bible: Psalm 90

Youth, which is forgiven everything, forgives itself nothing; age, which forgives itself anything, is for~ given nothing

George Bernard Shaw *Maxims for Revolutionists*

If I'd known I was gonna live this long, I'd have taken better care of myself

Eubie Blake (on reaching the age of 100)

Grow old along with me!
The best is yet to be

Robert Browning *Rabbi Ben Ezra*

Growing old is like being increasingly penalized for a crime you haven't committed

Anthony Powell *Temporary Kings*

aged age-old, ancient, antiquated, antique, cobwebby, elderly, getting on, grey, hoary, old, past it (*informal*), senescent, superannuated

Antonyms adolescent, boyish, childish, girlish, immature, juvenile, young, youthful

ageing, aging 1. *noun* decay, decline, degen~ eration, deterioration, growing old, matura~ tion, senescence, senility 2. *adjective* declining, deteriorating, getting on *or* past it (*informal*), growing old *or* older, in decline, long in the tooth, maturing, mellowing, senescent, senile

But at my back I always hear
Time's wingèd chariot hurrying near
Andrew Marvell *To his Coy Mistress*

ageless abiding, deathless, enduring, eternal, immortal, perennial, timeless, unchanging, unfading
Antonyms ephemeral, fleeting, momentary, passing, temporary, transitory

agency 1. action, activity, auspices, efficiency, force, influence, instrumentality, intercession, intervention, means, mechanism, mediation, medium, operation, power, work **2.** bureau, business, department, office, organization

agenda calendar, diary, list, plan, programme, schedule, timetable

agent 1. advocate, deputy, emissary, envoy, factor, go-between, negotiator, rep (*informal*), representative, substitute, surrogate **2.** actor, author, doer, executor, mover, officer, operative, operator, performer, worker **3.** agency, cause, force, instrument, means, power, vehicle

ages aeons, a long time *or* while, a month of Sundays (*informal*), an age *or* eternity, centuries, coon's age (*U.S. slang*), donkey's years (*informal*), for ever (*informal*), years, yonks (*informal*)
Antonyms a flash, a jiffy (*informal*), a little while, a moment, an instant, a second, a short time, a split second, no time at all, the twinkling *or* wink of an eye, two shakes of a lamb's tail (*informal*)

agglomeration accumulation, clump, cluster, collection, heap, lump, mass, pile, rick, stack

agglutinate adhere, attach, bond, cement, fasten, glue, gum, join, solder, stick, unite

aggrandize advance, amplify, augment, dignify, elevate, enlarge, ennoble, enrich, exaggerate, exalt, inflate, intensify, magnify, promote, widen

aggravate 1. add insult to injury, exacerbate, exaggerate, fan the flames of, heighten, increase, inflame, intensify, magnify, make worse, worsen **2.** *informal* annoy, be on one's back (*slang*), bother, exasperate, gall, get in one's hair (*informal*), get on one's nerves (*informal*), get on one's wick (*Brit. slang*), get under one's skin (*informal*), get up one's nose (*informal*), hassle (*informal*), irk, irritate, nark (*Brit., Austral., & N.Z. slang*), needle (*informal*), nettle, pester, piss one off (*taboo slang*), provoke, rub (someone) up the wrong way (*informal*), tease, vex
Antonyms (*sense 1*) alleviate, assuage, calm, diminish, ease, improve, lessen, mitigate, smooth (*sense 2*) assuage, calm, pacify, please

aggravating 1. exacerbating, exaggerating, heightening, increasing, inflaming, intensifying, magnifying, worsening **2.** *informal* annoying, exasperating, galling, irksome, irritating, provoking, teasing, vexing

aggravation 1. exacerbation, exaggeration, heightening, increase, inflaming, intensification, magnification, worsening **2.** *informal* annoyance, exasperation, gall, hassle (*informal*), irksomeness, irritation, provocation, teasing, vexation

aggregate 1. *verb* accumulate, amass, assemble, collect, combine, heap, mix, pile **2.** *noun* accumulation, agglomeration, amount, assemblage, body, bulk, collection, combination, heap, lump, mass, mixture, pile, sum, total, whole **3.** *adjective* accumulated, added, assembled, collected, collective, combined, composite, corporate, cumulative, mixed, total

aggregation accumulation, agglomeration, assemblage, body, bulk, collection, combination, heap, lump, mass, mixture, pile

aggression 1. assault, attack, encroachment, injury, invasion, offence, offensive, onslaught, raid **2.** aggressiveness, antagonism, belligerence, destructiveness, hostility, pugnacity

aggressive 1. belligerent, destructive, hostile, offensive, pugnacious, quarrelsome **2.** assertive, bold, dynamic, energetic, enterprising, forceful, in-your-face (*slang*), militant, pushing, pushy (*informal*), vigorous, zealous
Antonyms friendly, mild, peaceful, quiet, retiring, submissive

aggressor assailant, assaulter, attacker, invader

aggrieved afflicted, distressed, disturbed, harmed, hurt, ill-used, injured, peeved (*informal*), saddened, unhappy, woeful, wronged

aghast afraid, amazed, appalled, astonished, astounded, awestruck, confounded, frightened, horrified, horror-struck, shocked, startled, stunned, thunder-struck

agile active, acute, alert, bright (*informal*), brisk, clever, limber, lissom(e), lithe, lively, nimble, prompt, quick, quick-witted, sharp, sprightly, spry, supple, swift
Antonyms awkward, clumsy, heavy, lumbering, ponderous, slow, slow-moving, stiff, ungainly, unsupple

agility activity, acuteness, alertness, briskness, cleverness, litheness, liveliness, nimbleness, promptitude, promptness, quickness, quick-wittedness, sharpness, sprightliness, spryness, suppleness, swiftness

agitate 1. beat, churn, convulse, disturb, rock, rouse, shake, stir, toss **2.** alarm, arouse, confuse, disconcert, disquiet, distract, disturb, excite, faze, ferment, fluster, incite, inflame, perturb, rouse, ruffle, stimulate, trouble, un~

nerve, upset, work up, worry **3**. argue, debate, discuss, dispute, examine, ventilate

Antonyms (*sense 2*) appease, assuage, calm, calm down, mollify, pacify, placate, quiet, quieten, soothe, still, tranquillize

agitated alarmed, all of a flutter (*informal*), anxious, discomposed, disconcerted, disquiet~ed, distracted, distressed, disturbed, edgy, ex~cited, fazed, flapping (*informal*), flustered, hot and bothered (*informal*), hot under the collar (*informal*), ill at ease, in a flap (*informal*), nervous, on edge, perturbed, rattled (*infor~mal*), ruffled, shaken, troubled, uneasy, un~nerved, unsettled, upset, worked up, worried

Antonyms at ease, calm, collected, composed, cool, relaxed, sedate, unexcited, unfazed (*in~formal*), unperturbed, unruffled, untroubled

agitation **1**. churning, convulsion, disturbance, rocking, shake, shaking, stir, stirring, tossing, turbulence, upheaval **2**. alarm, arousal, clam~our, commotion, confusion, discomposure, dis~quiet, distraction, disturbance, excitement, ferment, flurry, fluster, incitement, lather (*in~formal*), outcry, stimulation, trouble, tumult, turmoil, upheaval, upset, worry **3**. argument, controversy, debate, discussion, disputation, dispute, ventilation

agitator agent provocateur, demagogue, fire~brand, inciter, instigator, rabble-rouser, revo~lutionary, stirrer (*informal*), troublemaker

agog avid, curious, eager, enthralled, enthusi~astic, excited, expectant, impatient, in sus~pense, keen

Antonyms apathetic, incurious, indifferent, unconcerned, uninterested

agonize afflict, be in agony, be in anguish, distress, go through the mill, harrow, labour, pain, rack, strain, strive, struggle, suffer, tor~ment, torture, worry, writhe

agonized, agonised anguished, broken-hearted, distressed, grief-stricken, racked, suffering, tormented, tortured, wounded, wretched

agonizing, agonising bitter, distressing, ex~cruciating, grievous, harrowing, heart~breaking, heart-rending, hellish, painful, tor~turous

agony affliction, anguish, distress, misery, pain, pangs, suffering, throes, torment, tor~ture, woe

agrarian agrestic, agricultural, country, farm~ing, land, rural, rustic

Antonyms industrial, urban

agree **1**. accede, acquiesce, admit, allow, assent, be of the same mind, comply, concede, concur, con~sent, engage, grant, permit, see eye to eye, settle, shake hands **2**. accord, answer, chime, coincide, conform, correspond, fit, get on (together), har~monize, match, square, suit, tally

Antonyms contradict, deny, differ, disagree, dispute, dissent, rebut, refute, retract

agreeable **1**. acceptable, congenial, delightful, enjoyable, gratifying, likable *or* likeable, pleasant, pleasing, pleasurable, satisfying, to one's liking, to one's taste **2**. appropriate, be~fitting, compatible, consistent, fitting, in keeping, proper, suitable **3**. acquiescent, ame~nable, approving, complying, concurring, con~senting, in accord, responsive, sympathetic, well-disposed, willing

Antonyms (*sense 1*) disagreeable, displeasing, horrid, offensive, unlikable *or* unlikeable, unpleasant (*sense 2*) inappropriate, unaccep~table, unfitting, unsuitable

I do not want people to be very agreeable, as it saves me the trouble of liking them a great deal
Jane Austen

My idea of an agreeable person is a person who agrees with me
Benjamin Disraeli *Lothair*

agreed **1**. *adjective* arranged, definite, estab~lished, firm, fixed, given, guaranteed, prede~termined, settled, stipulated **2**. *interjection* all right, done, it's a bargain *or* deal, O.K. *or* okay (*informal*), settled, you're on (*informal*)

Antonyms (*sense 1*) indefinite, negotiable, to be arranged *or* decided, up in the air, vari~able

agreement **1**. accord, accordance, affinity, analogy, assent, compatibility, compliance, concert, concord, concurrence, conformity, congruity, consistency, correspondence, har~mony, similarity, suitableness, union, unison **2**. arrangement, bargain, compact, contract, covenant, deal (*informal*), pact, settlement, treaty, understanding

Antonyms (*sense 1*) altercation, argument, clash, conflict, difference, discord, discrepan~cy, disparity, dispute, dissent, dissimilarity, diversity, division, falling-out, incompatibil~ity, incongruity, quarrel, row, squabble, strife, tiff, wrangle

agricultural agrarian, agrestic, agronomic, ag~ronomical, country, farming, rural, rustic

agriculture agronomics, agronomy, cultivation, culture, farming, husbandry, tillage

aground ashore, beached, foundered, grounded, high and dry, on the rocks, stranded, stuck

ahead along, at an advantage, at the head, before, forwards, in advance, in front, in the foreground, in the lead, in the vanguard, leading, on, onwards, to the fore, winning

aid *verb* **1**. abet, assist, befriend, encourage, fa~vour, give a leg up (*informal*), help, promote, relieve, second, serve, subsidize, succour, sup~port, sustain *~noun* **2**. assistance, benefit, en~couragement, favour, help, promotion, relief, service, succour, support **3**. abettor, adjutant,

aide, aide-de-camp, assistant, helper, second, supporter
Antonyms *verb* detract from, harm, hinder, hurt, impede, obstruct, oppose, thwart ~*noun* hindrance

aide adjutant, assistant, attendant, coadjutor (*rare*), deputy, helper, helpmate, henchman, right-hand man, second, supporter

ail **1.** afflict, annoy, be the matter with, bother, distress, irritate, pain, sicken, trouble, upset, worry **2.** be ill, be indisposed, be *or* feel off colour, be sick, be unwell, feel unwell

ailing debilitated, diseased, feeble, ill, indisposed, infirm, invalid, off colour, poorly, sick, sickly, suffering, under the weather (*informal*), unsound, unwell, weak

ailment affliction, complaint, disease, disorder, illness, infirmity, lurgi (*informal*), malady, sickness

aim **1.** *verb* aspire, attempt, design, direct, draw a bead (on), endeavour, intend, level, mean, plan, point, propose, purpose, resolve, seek, set one's sights on, sight, strive, take aim (at), train, try, want, wish **2.** *noun* ambition, aspiration, course, design, desire, direction, end, goal, Holy Grail (*informal*), intent, intention, mark, object, objective, plan, purpose, scheme, target, wish

aimless chance, directionless, erratic, frivolous, goalless, haphazard, pointless, purposeless, random, stray, undirected, unguided, unpredictable, vagrant, wayward
Antonyms decided, deliberate, determined, firm, fixed, positive, purposeful, resolute, resolved, settled, single-minded

air *noun* **1.** atmosphere, heavens, sky **2.** blast, breath, breeze, draught, puff, waft, whiff, wind, zephyr **3.** ambience, appearance, atmosphere, aura, bearing, character, demeanour, effect, feeling, flavour, impression, look, manner, mood, quality, style, tone, vibes (*slang*) **4.** circulation, display, dissemination, exposure, expression, publicity, utterance, vent, ventilation **5.** aria, lay, melody, song, tune ~*verb* **6.** aerate, expose, freshen, ventilate **7.** circulate, communicate, declare, disclose, display, disseminate, divulge, exhibit, expose, express, give vent to, make known, make public, proclaim, publicize, reveal, take the wraps off, tell, utter, ventilate, voice
Related adjective: aerial

> *air: a nutritious substance supplied by a bountiful Providence for the fattening of the poor*
> Ambrose Bierce *The Devil's Dictionary*

Fresh air keeps the doctor poor

airborne floating, flying, gliding, hovering, in flight, in the air, on the wing, soaring, volitant, wind-borne

aircraft aeroplane, airplane (*U.S. & Canad.*), flying machine, kite (*Brit. slang*), plane

Types of Aircraft

aerodyne
aerostat
airliner
airship
amphibian
autogiro *or* autogyro
balloon
biplane
blimp
bomber
canard
coleopter
convertiplane, convertaplane *or* convertoplane
cyclogiro
delta-wing
dirigible
dive bomber
drone
fighter
fighter-bomber
flying boat
flying wing
freighter
gas-filled balloon
glider
gyrodyne
hang-glider
helicopter
helicopter gunship
hot-air balloon
interceptor *or* intercepter
jet *or* jet plane
jetliner
jumbo jet
jump jet
lifting body
light aircraft
microlight *or* microlite
monoplane
multiplane
night fighter
ornithopter *or* orthopter
rotaplane
sailplane
seaplane
skiplane
Stealth bomber *or* Stealth plane
STOL
swept-wing
swing-wing
tanker
triplane
troop carrier
turbofan
turbojet
turboprop *or* propjet
VTOL
warplane
wing
zeppelin

Aircraft Parts

aerofoil
aerometeorograph
aerostructure
aileron
airframe
air-intake
airlock
air scoop
airscrew
all-flying tail
altimeter
anti-icer
astrodome *or* astrohatch
athodyd
autopilot
auxiliary power unit
basket
black box
body
bomb bay
bombsight
bulkhead
cabin
canopy
cantilever
capsule
chassis
clamshell
cockpit
control column *or* control stick
cowling *or* cowl
dashboard
drop tank
ejection seat
elevator
elevon
empennage
engine
engine pod
fairing
fin
flap
flight deck
flight recorder

fuel tank
fuselage
galley
gondola
heat sink
hold
horn *or* horn balance
hydroplane
inclinometer
instrument panel
jet engine
jet pipe
joystick
keel
landing gear
landing light
launching shoe *or* launch shoe
longeron
main plane
nacelle
nose
nose wheel
Pitot tube
pod
propeller
pulsejet
pusher
pylon
ramjet *or* ramjet engine
rotor
rudder
slat
slinger ring
spinner
spoiler
stabilizer
tab
tail
tailplane
tailskid
tail wheel
trailing edge
trim tab
turret
undercarriage
waist
wing
winglet
wing tip

airfield aerodrome, airdrome (*U.S.*), airport, air station, airstrip, landing strip

airily **1.** animatedly, blithely, breezily, buoyantly, gaily, happily, high-spiritedly, jauntily, light-heartedly **2.** daintily, delicately, ethereally, gracefully, lightly

airiness **1.** breeziness, draughtiness, freshness, gustiness, lightness, openness, windiness **2.** ethereality, immateriality, incorporeality, insubstantiality, lightness, weightlessness **3.** animation, blitheness, breeziness, buoyancy, gaiety, happiness, high spirits, jauntiness, light-heartedness, lightness of heart

airing **1.** aeration, drying, freshening, ventilation **2.** excursion, jaunt, outing, promenade, stroll, walk **3.** circulation, display, dissemination, exposure, expression, publicity, utterance, vent, ventilation

airless breathless, close, heavy, muggy, oppressive, stale, stifling, stuffy, suffocating, sultry, unventilated

Antonyms airy, blowy, breezy, draughty, fresh, gusty, light, open, spacious, well-ventilated

airport aerodrome, airdrome (*U.S.*), airfield

Airport Identification Codes	Airport
ABZ	Aberdeen
ACC	Accra
ACE	Lanzarote
ADB	Izmir
ADD	Addis Ababa
ADL	Adelaide
AGP	Malaga
AKL	Auckland
ALA	Alma-Ata
ALY	Alexandria
AMS	Amsterdam
ANR	Antwerp
ANU	Antigua
ARN	Stockholm
ASM	Asmara
ATH	Athens
ATL	Atlanta
AUH	Abu Dhabi
BAH	Bahrain
BCN	Barcelona
BDA	Bermuda
BEB	Benbecula
BEY	Beirut
BFS	Belfast International
BGI	Bridgetown, Barbados
BGO	Bergen
BHD	Belfast City
BHX	Birmingham
BKK	Bangkok
BIA	Bastia
BIO	Bilbao
BLQ	Bologna
BNE	Brisbane
BOD	Bordeaux
BOG	Bogotá
BOM	Bombay
BOS	Boston
BRE	Bremen
BRR	Barra
BRS	Bristol
BRU	Brussels
BSL	Basle/Mulhouse
BUD	Budapest
BWI	Baltimore
CAG	Cagliari
CAI	Cairo
CAL	Campbeltown
CCS	Caracas
CCU	Calcutta
CDG	Paris (Charles de Gaulle)
CFN	Donegal
CGN	Cologne/Bonn
CGK	Djakarta
CLT	Charlotte
CMN	Casablanca
CPH	Copenhagen
CPT	Cape Town
CTA	Catania
CUN	Cancun (Mexico)
CWL	Cardiff
DAC	Dhaka
DAR	Dar es Salaam
DAM	Damascus
DEL	Delhi
DEN	Denver
DFW	Dallas/Fort Worth

DHA	Dharan
DND	Dundee
DPS	Denpasar (Bali)
DRS	Dresden
DTM	Dortmund
DTW	Detroit
DUB	Dublin
DUR	Durban
DUS	Düsseldorf
DXB	Dubai
EBB	Entebbe
EDI	Edinburgh
EOI	Eday
ERF	Erfurt
ESB	Ankara
EXT	Exeter
EWR	New York (Newark)
EZE	Buenos Aires
FAO	Faro
FBU	Oslo
FCO	Rome
FDH	Friedrichshafen
FIE	Fair Isle
FLR	Florence
FMO	Münster/Osnabrück
FNC	Funchal
FOA	Foula
FRA	Frankfurt
FUE	Fuerteventura
GBE	Gaborone
GCI	Guernsey
GIG	Rio de Janeiro
GLA	Glasgow
GND	Grenada
GOA	Genoa
GOT	Göthenburg
GRU	São Paulo
GRZ	Graz
GVA	Geneva
HAJ	Hanover
HAM	Hamburg
HEL	Helsinki
HER	Heraklion
HKG	Hong Kong
HNL	Honolulu
HRE	Harare
IAD	Washington
IAH	Houston
IBZ	Ibiza
ILY	Islay
INN	Innsbruck
INV	Inverness
IOM	Isle of Man
ISB	Islanabad
IST	Istanbul
JED	Jeddah
JER	Jersey
JFK	New York (John F. Kennedy)
JNB	Johannesburg
JRS	Jerusalem
KAN	Kano
KBP	Kiev
KEL	Kiel
KHI	Karachi
KIN	Kingston
KIX	Osaka
KLU	Klagenfurt
KOI	Kirkwall
KRT	Khartoum
KTM	Kathmandu
KTW	Katowice
KUL	Kuala Lumpur
KWI	Kuwait
LAS	Las Vegas
LAX	Los Angeles
LBA	Leeds (Bradford)
LCA	Larnaca
LCY	London (City)
LDY	Londonderry
LED	Saint Petersburg
LEI	Almeira
LEJ	Leipzig
LGA	London (Gatwick)
LHR	London (Heathrow)
LIM	Lima
LIN	Milan
LIS	Lisbon
LJU	Ljubljana
LLW	Lilongwe
LNZ	Linz
LOS	Lagos
LPA	Las Palmas
LPB	La Paz
LSI	Sumburgh
LTN	Luton
LUN	Lusaka
LUX	Luxembourg
LWK	Lerwick
LYS	Lyon
MAA	Madras
MAD	Madrid
MAN	Manchester
MBJ	Montego Bay
MCO	Orlando
MCT	Muscat
MDW	Chicago (Midway)
MEL	Melbourne
MEX	Mexico City
MIA	Miami
MNL	Manila
MPL	Montpellier
MRS	Marseilles
MRU	Mauritius
MSQ	Minsk
MUC	Munich
NAP	Naples
NBO	Nairobi
NCE	Nice
NCL	Newcastle
NDY	Sanday
NGO	Nagoya

NOC	Connaught
NQY	Newquay
NRL	North Ronaldsay
NRT	Tokyo
NUE	Nuremberg
NWI	Norwich
OPO	Oporto
ORD	Chicago (O'Hare)
ORK	Cork
ORY	Paris (Orly)
OTP	Bucharest
OUK	Outer Skerries
OVB	Novosibirsk
PEK	Beijing
PER	Perth
PGF	Perpignan
PHL	Philadelphia
PHX	Phoenix
PIT	Pittsburgh
PLH	Plymouth
PMI	Palma (Majorca)
PPW	Papa Westray
PRG	Prague
PSA	Pisa/Florence
PSV	Papa Stour
REC	Recife
RIX	Riga
RTM	Rotterdam
RUH	Riyadh
SAH	Sanaa
SCL	Santiago
SCN	Saarbrucken
SDQ	Santo Domingo
SEA	Seattle
SEL	Seoul
SEZ	Seychelles
SFO	San Francisco
SGN	Ho Chi Minh City
SHA	Shanghai
SIN	Singapore
SJO	San Jose (Costa Rica)
SJU	San Juan
SKG	Thessaloniki
SLU	St. Lucia
SNN	Shannon
SOF	Sofia
SOU	Southampton
SOY	Stronsay
SPC	Santa Cruz
SSA	Salvador
STL	St. Louis
STN	London (Stanstead)
STR	Stuttgart
SVG	Stavanger
SVO	Moscow
SVX	Ekaterinburg
SXF	Berlin (Schönefeld)
SXM	St. Maarten
SYD	Sydney
SYY	Stornoway
SZG	Salzburg
TAS	Tashkent
TFS	Tenerife
THF	Berlin (Tempelhof)
THR	Tehran
TKU	Turku
TLL	Tallinn
TLS	Toulouse
TLV	Tel Aviv
TPE	Taipei
TRE	Tiree
TRN	Turin
TRS	Trieste
TUN	Tunis
TXL	Berlin (Texel)
UIO	Quito
UNT	Unst
UVF	St. Lucia
VCE	Venice
VIE	Vienna
VLC	Valencia
VNO	Vilnius
VRN	Verona
WAW	Warsaw
WDH	Windhoek
WIC	Wick
WRY	Westray
YMX	Montreal (Mirabel)
YOW	Ottawa
YUL	Montreal (Dorval)
YVR	Vancouver
YYZ	Toronto
YYC	Calgary
ZAG	Zagreb
ZRH	Zurich

airs affectation, affectedness, arrogance, haughtiness, hauteur, pomposity, pretensions, superciliousness, swank (*informal*)

airy **1**. blowy, breezy, draughty, fresh, gusty, light, lofty, open, spacious, uncluttered, well-ventilated, windy **2**. aerial, delicate, ethereal, fanciful, flimsy, illusory, imaginary, immaterial, incorporeal, insubstantial, light, vaporous, visionary, weightless, wispy **3**. animated, blithe, buoyant, cheerful, cheery, chirpy (*informal*), debonair, frolicsome, gay, genial, graceful, happy, high-spirited, jaunty, light, light-hearted, lively, merry, nonchalant, sprightly, upbeat (*informal*)
Antonyms (*sense 1*) airless, close, heavy, muggy, oppressive, stale, stifling, stuffy, suffocating, unventilated (*sense 2*) concrete, corporeal, material, real, realistic, substantial, tangible (*sense 3*) cheerless, dismal, gloomy, glum, melancholy, miserable, morose, sad

airy-fairy chimerical, fanciful, feeble, flimsy, incorporeal, insubstantial, lightweight, shaky, unconvincing, unsound, without substance
Antonyms concrete, firm, solid, sound, substantial

aisle alley, corridor, gangway, lane, passage, passageway, path

ajar agape, gaping, open, partly open, unclosed

akin affiliated, alike, allied, analogous, cognate, comparable, congenial, connected, consan~guineous, corresponding, kin, kindred, like, of a piece, parallel, related, similar

alacrity alertness, avidity, briskness, cheerful~ness, dispatch, eagerness, enthusiasm, gaiety, hilarity, joyousness, liveliness, promptness, quickness, readiness, speed, sprightliness, willingness, zeal
Antonyms apathy, dullness, inertia, lethargy, reluctance, slowness, sluggishness, unconcern, unwillingness

à la mode all the go (*informal*), all the rage (*informal*), chic, fashionable, in (*informal*), in fashion, in vogue, latest, modish, popular, stylish, the latest rage (*informal*), with it (*in~formal*)

alarm *verb* **1.** daunt, dismay, distress, frighten, give (someone) a turn (*informal*), make (someone's) hair stand on end, panic, put the wind up (someone) (*informal*), scare, startle, terrify, unnerve **2.** alert, arouse, signal, warn *~noun* **3.** anxiety, apprehension, consterna~tion, dismay, distress, fear, fright, nervous~ness, panic, scare, terror, trepidation, unease, uneasiness **4.** alarm-bell, alert, bell, danger signal, distress signal, hooter, siren, tocsin, warning **5.** *archaic* call to arms, summons to arms
Antonyms *verb* (*sense 1*) assure, calm, com~fort, reassure, relieve, soothe *~noun* (*sense 3*) calm, calmness, composure, sang-froid, seren~ity

alarmed anxious, apprehensive, daunted, dis~mayed, distressed, disturbed, fearful, fright~ened, in a panic, nervous, scared, shocked, startled, terrified, troubled, uneasy, unnerved
Antonyms assured, calm, composed, fearless, serene, undaunted, untroubled

alarming daunting, dismaying, distressing, disturbing, dreadful, frightening, scaring, shocking, startling, terrifying, unnerving

albeit although, even if, even though, notwith~standing that, tho' (*U.S. or poetic*), though

album **1.** book, collection, scrapbook **2.** LP, rec~ord **3.** anthology, compilation, miscellany

alchemy magic, sorcery, witchcraft, wizardry

alcohol **1.** ethanol, ethyl alcohol **2.** booze (*in~formal*), drink, Dutch courage (*informal*), falling-down juice (*slang*), firewater, grog (*in~formal, chiefly Austral. & N.Z.*), hooch *or* hootch (*informal, chiefly U.S. & Canad.*), in~toxicant, John Barleycorn, juice (*informal*), liquor, spirits, strong drink, the bottle (*infor~mal*), the hard stuff (*informal*)

alcoholic **1.** *adjective* brewed, distilled, fer~mented, hard, inebriant, inebriating, intoxi~cating, spirituous, strong, vinous **2.** *noun* bib~ber, boozer (*informal*), dipsomaniac, drunk, drunkard, hard drinker, inebriate, soak (*slang*), sot, sponge (*informal*), tippler, toper, tosspot (*informal*), wino (*informal*)

alcove bay, bower, compartment, corner, cubbyhole, cubicle, niche, nook, recess

alert **1.** *adjective* active, agile, attentive, bright-eyed and bushy-tailed (*informal*), brisk, careful, circumspect, heedful, keeping a weather eye on, lively, nimble, observant, on guard, on one's toes, on the ball (*informal*), on the lookout, on the watch, perceptive, quick, ready, spirited, sprightly, vigilant, wary, watchful, wide-awake **2.** *noun* alarm, signal, siren, warning **3.** *verb* alarm, forewarn, in~form, notify, signal, warn
Antonyms *adjective* careless, heedless, inac~tive, languid, lethargic, listless, oblivious, slow, unaware, unconcerned, unwary *~noun* all clear *~verb* lull

alertness activeness, agility, attentiveness, briskness, carefulness, circumspection, heed~fulness, liveliness, nimbleness, perceptiveness, promptitude, quickness, readiness, spirited~ness, sprightliness, vigilance, wariness, watchfulness

alias **1.** *adverb* also called, also known as, otherwise, otherwise known as **2.** *noun* as~sumed name, *nom de guerre*, nom de plume, pen name, pseudonym, stage name

alibi defence, excuse, explanation, justification, plea, pretext, reason

alien **1.** *adjective* adverse, beyond one's ken, conflicting, contrary, estranged, exotic, for~eign, inappropriate, incompatible, incongru~ous, not native, not naturalized, opposed, out~landish, remote, repugnant, separated, strange, unfamiliar **2.** *noun* foreigner, new~comer, outsider, stranger
Antonyms *adjective* affiliated, akin, alike, al~lied, analogous, cognate, connected, corre~sponding, kindred, like, parallel, related, similar *~noun* citizen, countryman, dweller, inhabitant, national, resident

alienate **1.** break off, disaffect, divert, divorce, estrange, make unfriendly, separate, set against, turn away, withdraw **2.** *Law* abalienate, convey, transfer

alienation **1.** breaking off, disaffection, diver~sion, divorce, estrangement, indifference, re~moteness, rupture, separation, setting against, turning away, withdrawal **2.** *Law* abalien~ation, conveyance, transfer

alight[1] *verb* come down, come to rest, descend, disembark, dismount, get down, get off, land, light, perch, settle, touch down

Antonyms ascend, climb, float up, fly up, go up, lift off, mount, move up, rise, scale, soar, take off

alight² *adjective* 1. ablaze, aflame, blazing, burning, fiery, flaming, flaring, ignited, lighted, lit, on fire 2. bright, brilliant, illuminated, lit up, shining

align 1. arrange in line, coordinate, even, even up, line up, make parallel, order, range, regulate, sequence, straighten 2. affiliate, agree, ally, associate, cooperate, join, side, sympathize

alignment 1. adjustment, arrangement, coordination, evening, evening up, line, lining up, order, ranging, regulating, sequence, straightening up 2. affiliation, agreement, alliance, association, cooperation, sympathy, union

alike 1. *adjective* akin, analogous, corresponding, cut from the same cloth, duplicate, equal, equivalent, even, identical, like two peas in a pod, of a piece, parallel, resembling, similar, the same, uniform 2. *adverb* analogously, correspondingly, equally, evenly, identically, similarly, uniformly
Antonyms *adjective* different, dissimilar, diverse, separate, unlike *~adverb* differently, distinctly, unequally

aliment fare, feed, fodder, food, meat, nourishment, nutriment, nutrition, provender, sustenance, tack (*informal*), vittles (*obsolete or dialect*)

alimentary beneficial, nourishing, nutritional, nutritious, nutritive, sustaining, wholesome

alive 1. animate, breathing, having life, in the land of the living (*informal*), living, subsisting 2. active, existent, existing, extant, functioning, in existence, in force, operative, unquenched 3. active, alert, animated, awake, brisk, cheerful, chirpy (*informal*), eager, energetic, full of beans (*informal*), full of life, lively, quick, spirited, sprightly, spry, vigorous, vital, vivacious, zestful
Antonyms (*sense 1*) dead, deceased, departed, expired, extinct, gone, inanimate, lifeless (*sense 2*) extinct, inactive, inoperative, lost (*sense 3*) apathetic, dull, inactive, lifeless, spiritless

alive to alert to, awake to, aware of, cognizant of, eager for, sensible of, sensitive to, susceptible to

alive with abounding in, bristling with, bustling with, buzzing with, crawling with, hopping with, infested with, jumping with, lousy with (*slang*), overrun by, packed with, swarming with, teeming with, thronged with

all *adjective* 1. every bit of, the complete, the entire, the sum of, the totality of, the total of, the whole of 2. each, each and every, every, every one of, every single 3. complete, entire, full, greatest, perfect, total, utter *~noun* 4. aggregate, entirety, everything, sum, sum total, total, total amount, totality, utmost, whole, whole amount *~adverb* 5. altogether, completely, entirely, fully, totally, utterly, wholly

allay alleviate, appease, assuage, blunt, calm, check, compose, diminish, dull, ease, lessen, mitigate, moderate, mollify, pacify, pour oil on troubled waters, quell, quiet, reduce, relax, relieve, smooth, soften, soothe, subdue

allegation accusation, affirmation, assertion, asseveration, averment, avowal, charge, claim, declaration, deposition, plea, profession, statement

allege advance, affirm, assert, asseverate, aver, avow, charge, claim, declare, depose, maintain, plead, profess, put forward, state
Antonyms abjure, contradict, deny, disagree with, disavow, disclaim, gainsay (*archaic or literary*), oppose, refute, renounce, repudiate

alleged 1. affirmed, asserted, averred, declared, described, designated, stated 2. doubtful, dubious, ostensible, professed, purported, so-called, supposed, suspect, suspicious

allegedly apparently, by all accounts, purportedly, reportedly, reputedly, supposedly

allegiance adherence, constancy, devotion, duty, faithfulness, fealty, fidelity, homage, loyalty, obedience, obligation, troth (*archaic*)
Antonyms disloyalty, faithlessness, falseness, inconstancy, infidelity, perfidy, treachery, treason, unfaithfulness

You cannot run with the hare and hunt with the hounds

allegorical emblematic, figurative, parabolic, symbolic, symbolizing

allegory apologue, emblem, fable, myth, parable, story, symbol, symbolism, tale

allergic 1. affected by, hypersensitive, sensitive, sensitized, susceptible 2. *informal* antipathetic, averse, disinclined, hostile, loath, opposed

allergy 1. antipathy, hypersensitivity, sensitivity, susceptibility 2. *informal* antipathy, aversion, disinclination, dislike, hostility, loathing, opposition

alleviate abate, allay, assuage, blunt, check, diminish, dull, ease, lessen, lighten, mitigate, moderate, mollify, palliate, quell, quench, quiet, reduce, relieve, slacken, slake, smooth, soften, soothe, subdue

alleviation diminution, dulling, easing, lessening, lightening, mitigation, moderation, palliation, quelling, quenching, reduction, relief, slackening, slaking

alley alleyway, backstreet, lane, passage, passageway, pathway, walk

alliance affiliation, affinity, agreement, association, coalition, combination, compact, concordat, confederacy, confederation, connection, federation, league, marriage, pact, partnership, treaty, union
Antonyms alienation, breach, break, disaffection, dissociation, disunion, disunity, division, rupture, separation, severance, split, split-up

> *alliance: in international politics, the union of two thieves who have their hands so deeply inserted in each other's pocket that they cannot separately plunder a third*
> Ambrose Bierce *The Devil's Dictionary*

allied affiliated, amalgamated, associated, bound, combined, confederate, connected, hand in glove (*informal*), in cahoots (*U.S. informal*), in league, joined, joint, kindred, leagued, linked, married, related, unified, united, wed

all-important central, consequential, critical, crucial, essential, key, momentous, necessary, pivotal, significant, urgent, vital

allocate allot, apportion, appropriate, assign, budget, designate, earmark, mete, set aside, share out

allocation allotment, allowance, apportionment, appropriation, grant, lot, measure, portion, quota, ration, share, stint, stipend

allot allocate, apportion, appropriate, assign, budget, designate, earmark, mete, set aside, share out

allotment **1.** allocation, allowance, apportionment, appropriation, grant, lot, measure, portion, quota, ration, share, stint, stipend **2.** kitchen garden, patch, plot, tract

allotted allocated, apportioned, assigned, designated, earmarked, given, set aside

all-out complete, determined, exhaustive, full, full-on (*informal*), full-scale, maximum, optimum, outright, resolute, supreme, thorough, thoroughgoing, total, undivided, unlimited, unremitting, unrestrained, unstinted, utmost
Antonyms careless, cursory, half-hearted, negligent, off-hand, perfunctory, unenthusiastic

allow **1.** acknowledge, acquiesce, admit, concede, confess, grant, own **2.** approve, authorize, bear, brook, enable, endure, give leave, let, permit, put up with (*informal*), sanction, stand, suffer, tolerate **3.** allocate, allot, assign, deduct, give, grant, provide, remit, spare
Antonyms (*sense 1*) contradict, deny, disagree with, gainsay (*archaic or literary*), oppose (*sense 2*) ban, disallow, forbid, prohibit, proscribe, refuse (*sense 3*) deny, forbid, refuse

allowable acceptable, admissible, all right, appropriate, approved, permissible, sanctionable, sufferable, suitable, tolerable

allowance **1.** allocation, allotment, amount, annuity, apportionment, grant, lot, measure, pension, portion, quota, ration, remittance, share, stint, stipend, subsidy **2.** admission, concession, sanction, sufferance, toleration **3.** concession, deduction, discount, rebate, reduction

allow for arrange for, consider, foresee, keep in mind, make allowances for, make concessions for, make provision for, plan for, provide for, set (something) aside for, take into account, take into consideration

alloy *noun* **1.** admixture, amalgam, blend, combination, composite, compound, hybrid, meld, mixture *~verb* **2.** admix, amalgamate, blend, combine, compound, fuse, meld, mix **3.** adulterate, debase, devalue, diminish, impair

Alloys

Alnico (*Trademark*)
austenitic stainless steel
Babbit metal
bell bronze
bell metal
billon
brass
brazing solder
Britannia metal
bronze
chromel
constantan
cupronickel
Duralumin (*Trademark*)
electrum
ferrochromium
ferromanganese
ferromolybdenum
ferronickel
ferrosilicon
Invar (*Trademark*)
kamacite
magnolia metal
magnox
Manganin (*Trademark*)
misch metal
Monel *or* Monell metal
Nichrome (*Trademark*)
nickel silver
nimonic alloy
ormolu
oroide
osmiridium
permalloy
pewter
phosphor bronze
pinchbeck
platina
platiniridium
soft solder
speculum metal
steel
Stellite (*Trademark*)
sterling silver
terne
tombac *or* tambac
type metal
white gold
zircalloy

all-powerful almighty, omnipotent, supreme
Antonyms helpless, impotent, powerless

all right *adjective* **1.** acceptable, adequate, average, fair, O.K. *or* okay (*informal*), passable, satisfactory, so-so (*informal*), standard, unobjectionable, up to scratch (*informal*) **2.** hale, healthy, out of the woods, safe, sound, unharmed, unimpaired, uninjured, well, whole *~adverb* **3.** acceptably, adequately, O.K. *or* okay (*informal*), passably, satisfactorily, unobjectionably, well enough
Antonyms *adjective* (*sense 1*) bad, inadequate, not good enough, not up to scratch (*informal*), objectionable, poor, unacceptable, unsatisfactory (*sense 2*) ailing, bad, ill, injured, off col~

our, out of sorts, poorly, sick, sickly, un~ healthy, unwell

allude advert, glance, hint, imply, insinuate, intimate, mention, refer, remark, speak of, suggest, tip the wink, touch upon

allure 1. *verb* attract, beguile, cajole, captivate, charm, coax, decoy, enchant, entice, inveigle, lead on, lure, persuade, seduce, tempt, win over 2. *noun* appeal, attraction, charm, en~ chantment, enticement, glamour, lure, per~ suasion, seductiveness, temptation

alluring attractive, beguiling, bewitching, cap~ tivating, come-hither, enchanting, fascinating, fetching, glamorous, intriguing, seductive, sexy, tempting
Antonyms abhorrent, off-putting (*Brit. infor~ mal*), repellent, repugnant, repulsive, unat~ tractive

allusion casual remark, glance, hint, implica~ tion, indirect reference, innuendo, insinuation, intimation, mention, suggestion

ally 1. *noun* abettor, accessory, accomplice, as~ sociate, coadjutor, collaborator, colleague, con~ federate, co-worker, friend, helper, partner 2. *verb* affiliate, associate, band together, col~ laborate, combine, confederate, connect, join, join battle with, join forces, league, marry, unify, unite
Antonyms *noun* adversary, antagonist, com~ petitor, enemy, foe, opponent, rival *~verb* al~ ienate, disaffect, disunite, divide, drive apart, separate, set at odds

almighty 1. absolute, all-powerful, invincible, omnipotent, supreme, unlimited 2. *informal* awful, desperate, enormous, excessive, great, intense, loud, severe, terrible
Antonyms (*sense 1*) helpless, impotent, pow~ erless, weak (*sense 2*) feeble, insignificant, paltry, poor, slight, tame, weak

almost about, all but, approximately, as good as, close to, just about, nearly, not far from, not quite, on the brink of, practically, so near (and) yet so far, virtually, well-nigh

alms benefaction, bounty, charity, donation, gift, relief

aloft above, heavenward, higher, high up, in the air, in the sky, on high, overhead, sky~ ward, up, up above, upward

alone 1. abandoned, apart, by itself, by oneself, deserted, desolate, detached, forlorn, forsaken, isolated, lonely, lonesome, only, on one's tod (*slang*), out on a limb, separate, single, single-handed, sole, solitary, unaccompanied, unaided, unassisted, unattended, uncombined, unconnected, under one's own steam, un~ escorted 2. incomparable, matchless, peerless, singular, unequalled, unique, unparalleled, unsurpassed
Antonyms (*sense 1*) accompanied, aided, among others, assisted, escorted, helped, jointly, together (*sense 2*) equalled, surpassed

I want to be alone
Greta Garbo *Grand Hotel (film)*

aloof 1. chilly, cold, cool, detached, distant, forbidding, formal, haughty, indifferent, re~ mote, reserved, standoffish, supercilious, un~ approachable, unfriendly, uninterested, unre~ sponsive, unsociable, unsympathetic 2. above, apart, at a distance, at arm's length, away, distanced, distant
Antonyms (*sense 1*) friendly, gregarious, neighbourly, open, sociable, sympathetic, warm

aloud 1. audibly, clearly, distinctly, intelligibly, out loud, plainly 2. clamorously, loudly, noisi~ ly, vociferously

alphabet letters, script, syllabary, writing sys~ tem

Related vocabulary

Cyrillic	lexigraphy
hiragana	Linear A
kana	Linear B
kanji	logogram *or* logograph
katakana	Nagari
Kufic *or* Cufic	Roman
Latin	

Greek letters

alpha	omega
beta	omicron
chi	phi
delta	pi
epsilon	psi
eta	rho
gamma	sigma
iota	tau
kappa	theta
lambda	upsilon
mu	xi
nu	zeta

Hebrew letters

aleph	pe
ayin *or* ain	resh
beth	sadhe, sade *or* tsade
daleth *or* daled	samekh
gimel	shin
he	sin
heth *or* cheth	tav *or* taw
kaph	teth
koph *or* qoph	vav *or* waw
lamed *or* lamedh	yod *or* yodh
mem	zayin
nun	

Communications code words for the alpha~ bet

Alpha	Echo
Bravo	Foxtrot
Charlie	Golf
Delta	Hotel

India
Juliet
Kilo
Lima
Mike
November
Oscar
Papa
Quebec
Romeo
Sierra
Tango
Uniform
Victor
Whiskey
X-Ray
Yankee
Zulu

already as of now, at present, before now, by now, by that time, by then, by this time, even now, heretofore, just now, previously

also additionally, along with, and, as well, as well as, besides, further, furthermore, in addition, including, into the bargain, moreover, on top of that, plus, to boot, too

alter adapt, adjust, amend, change, convert, diversify, metamorphose, modify, recast, reform, remodel, reshape, revise, shift, transform, transmute, turn, tweak (*informal*), vary

alteration adaptation, adjustment, amendment, change, conversion, difference, diversification, metamorphosis, modification, reformation, remodelling, reshaping, revision, shift, transformation, transmutation, variance, variation

altercate argue, be at sixes and sevens, bicker, clash, contend, controvert, cross swords, disagree, dispute, dissent, fall out (*informal*), quarrel, row, squabble, wrangle

altercation argument, bickering, clash, contention, controversy, disagreement, discord, dispute, dissension, quarrel, row, squabble, wrangle

alternate *verb* **1.** act reciprocally, alter, change, fluctuate, follow in turn, follow one another, interchange, intersperse, oscillate, rotate, substitute, take turns, vary ~*adjective* **2.** alternating, every other, every second, interchanging, rotating **3.** alternative, another, different, second, substitute

alternating fluctuating, interchanging, occurring by turns, oscillating, rotating, seesawing, shifting, swinging, vacillating

alternation change, fluctuation, oscillation, rotation, swing, vacillation, variation, vicissitude

alternative **1.** *noun* choice, option, other (*of two*), preference, recourse, selection, substitute **2.** *adjective* alternate, another, different, other, second, substitute

alternatively as an alternative, by way of alternative, if not, instead, on the other hand, or, otherwise

although albeit, despite the fact that, even if, even supposing, even though, notwithstanding, tho' (*U.S. or poetic*), though, while

altitude elevation, height, loftiness, peak, summit

altogether **1.** absolutely, completely, every inch, fully, lock, stock and barrel, perfectly, quite, thoroughly, totally, utterly, wholly **2.** all in all, all things considered, as a whole, collectively, generally, in general, *in toto*, on the whole **3.** all told, everything included, in all, in sum, *in toto*, taken together
Antonyms (*sense 1*) halfway, incompletely, in part, in some measure, not fully, partially, relatively, slightly, somewhat, to a certain degree *or* extent, up to a certain point

altruism beneficence, benevolence, bigheartedness, charitableness, charity, consideration, generosity, goodwill, greatheartedness, magnanimity, philanthropy, selflessness, self-sacrifice, unselfishness
Antonyms egoism, egotism, greed, looking out for number one (*informal*), meanness, mercenariness, narrowness, self-absorption, self-centredness, self-interest, selfishness, self-seeking

altruist humanitarian, philanthropist

altruistic benevolent, charitable, considerate, generous, humanitarian, philanthropic, public-spirited, self-sacrificing, unselfish
Antonyms egoistic, egoistical, egotistic, egotistical, greedy, looking out for number one (*informal*), mean, self-centred, self-interested, selfish, self-seeking, ungenerous

always aye (*Scot.*), consistently, constantly, continually, eternally, ever, everlastingly, evermore, every time, forever, *in perpetuum*, invariably, perpetually, repeatedly, unceasingly, without exception
Antonyms hardly, hardly ever, infrequently, once in a blue moon, once in a while, only now and then, on rare occasions, rarely, scarcely ever, seldom

amalgam admixture, alloy, amalgamation, blend, combination, composite, compound, fusion, meld, mixture, union

amalgamate alloy, ally, blend, coalesce, combine, commingle, compound, fuse, incorporate, integrate, intermix, meld, merge, mingle, unite
Antonyms disunite, divide, part, separate, split, split up

amalgamation admixture, alliance, alloy, amalgam, amalgamating, blend, coalition, combination, commingling, composite, compound, fusion, incorporation, integration, joining, meld, merger, mingling, mixing, mixture, union

amass accumulate, aggregate, assemble, collect, compile, garner, gather, heap up, hoard, pile up, rake up, scrape together

amateur dabbler, dilettante, layman, nonprofessional

amateurish amateur, bungling, clumsy, crude, inexpert, unaccomplished, unprofessional, unskilful
Antonyms experienced, expert, practised, professional, skilled

amatory amorous, aphrodisiac, erotic, lascivious, libidinous, passionate, romantic, sensual, sexual, sexy, steamy (*informal*)

amaze alarm, astonish, astound, bewilder, boggle the mind, bowl over (*informal*), confound, daze, dumbfound, electrify, flabbergast, shock, stagger, startle, stun, stupefy, surprise

amazement admiration, astonishment, bewilderment, confusion, marvel, perplexity, shock, stupefaction, surprise, wonder

amazing astonishing, astounding, breathtaking, eye-opening, mind-boggling, overwhelming, staggering, startling, stunning, surprising

ambassador agent, consul, deputy, diplomat, emissary, envoy, legate, minister, plenipotentiary, representative

An ambassador is an honest man sent to lie abroad for the commonwealth
Henry Wotton

ambience air, atmosphere, aura, character, complexion, feel, flavour, impression, milieu, mood, quality, setting, spirit, surroundings, temper, tenor, tone, vibes (*slang*), vibrations (*slang*)

ambiguity doubt, doubtfulness, dubiety, dubiousness, enigma, equivocacy, equivocality, equivocation, inconclusiveness, indefiniteness, indeterminateness, obscurity, puzzle, tergiversation, uncertainty, unclearness, vagueness

ambiguous clear as mud (*informal*), cryptic, Delphic, doubtful, dubious, enigmatic, enigmatical, equivocal, inconclusive, indefinite, indeterminate, obscure, oracular, puzzling, uncertain, unclear, vague
Antonyms clear, definite, explicit, obvious, plain, simple, specific, unequivocal, unmistakable, unquestionable

ambit 1. extent, radius, range, reach, scope, sweep 2. border, boundary, circumference, circumscription, compass, confine, edge, extremity, frontier, limit, margin, parameter, perimeter, restraint, restriction, verge

ambition 1. aspiration, avidity, desire, drive, eagerness, enterprise, get-up-and-go (*informal*), hankering, longing, striving, yearning, zeal 2. aim, aspiration, desire, dream, end, goal, Holy Grail (*informal*), hope, intent, objective, purpose, wish

Ambition is the growth of every clime
William Blake *King Edward the Third*

Well is it known that ambition can creep as well as soar
Edmund Burke *Letters on a Regicide Peace*

Ambition, in a private man a vice,
Is in a prince the virtue
Philip Massinger *The Bashful Lover*

Ah, but a man's reach should exceed his grasp,
Or what's a Heaven for?
Robert Browning *Andrea del Sarto*

The glorious fault of angels and gods
Alexander Pope *Elegy to the Memory of an Unfortunate Lady*

Every eel hopes to become a whale

ambitious 1. aspiring, avid, desirous, driving, eager, enterprising, hopeful, intent, purposeful, striving, zealous 2. arduous, bold, challenging, demanding, difficult, elaborate, energetic, exacting, formidable, grandiose, hard, impressive, industrious, pretentious, severe, strenuous
Antonyms (*sense 1*) apathetic, good-for-nothing, lazy, unambitious, unaspiring (*sense 2*) easy, modest, simple, unambitious

ambivalence clash, conflict, contradiction, doubt, equivocation, fluctuation, hesitancy, indecision, irresolution, opposition, uncertainty, vacillation, wavering

ambivalent clashing, conflicting, contradictory, debatable, doubtful, equivocal, fluctuating, hesitant, inconclusive, in two minds, irresolute, mixed, opposed, uncertain, undecided, unresolved, unsure, vacillating, warring, wavering
Antonyms certain, clear, conclusive, convinced, decided, definite, free from doubt, positive, sure, unwavering

amble dawdle, meander, mosey (*informal*), ramble, saunter, stroll, walk, wander

ambush 1. *noun* ambuscade, concealment, cover, hiding, hiding place, lying in wait, retreat, shelter, trap, waylaying 2. *verb* ambuscade, bushwhack (*U.S.*), ensnare, surprise, trap, waylay

ameliorate advance, allay, alleviate, amend, assuage, benefit, better, ease, elevate, improve, meliorate, mend, mitigate, promote, raise, reform, relieve

amelioration advance, amendment, betterment, change for the better, correction, enhancement, improvement, melioration, recovery, upswing

amenability 1. accessibility, acquiescence, agreeableness, compliance, cooperativeness *or* co-operativeness, impressionability, malleability, open-mindedness, openness, persuadability, perviousness, pliancy *or* pliantness, readiness, receptiveness, responsiveness, suggestibleness, susceptibility, tractability, willingness 2. accountability, answerability, answerableness, incumbency, liability, responsibility
Antonyms (*sense 1*) doggedness, fixedness, headstrongness, imperviousness, obduracy *or*

obdurateness, obstinacy, self-willedness, single-mindedness, steadfastness, stubbornness

amenable 1. able to be influenced, acquiescent, agreeable, open, persuadable, responsive, susceptible, tractable 2. accountable, answerable, chargeable, liable, responsible
Antonyms (*sense 1*) inflexible, intractable, mulish, obdurate, obstinate, pig-headed, recalcitrant, stiff-necked, stubborn, unbending, unyielding

amend alter, ameliorate, better, change, correct, enhance, fix, improve, mend, modify, rectify, reform, remedy, repair, revise, tweak (*informal*)

amendment 1. alteration, amelioration, betterment, change, correction, emendation, enhancement, improvement, mending, modification, rectification, reform, remedy, repair, revision 2. addendum, addition, adjunct, alteration, attachment, clarification

amends apology, atonement, compensation, expiation, indemnity, recompense, redress, reparation, requital, restitution, restoration, satisfaction

amenity 1. advantage, comfort, convenience, facility, service 2. affability, agreeableness, amiability, complaisance, courtesy, mildness, pleasantness (*of situation*), politeness, refinement, suavity
Antonyms (*sense 2*) bad manners, discourtesy, impoliteness, incivility, rudeness, ungraciousness

America

The business of America is business
Calvin Coolidge

America had often been discovered before, but it had always been hushed up
Oscar Wilde

America is the only nation in history which, miraculously, has gone directly from barbarism to degeneration without the usual interval of civilization
Georges Clemenceau

No one ever went broke underestimating the taste of the American public
H.L. Mencken

America is God's Crucible, the great Melting-Pot where all the races of Europe are melting and reforming!
Israel Zangwill *The Melting Pot*

America, thou half-brother of the world;
With something good and bad of every land
Philip James Bailey *Festus*

Europe is the unfinished negative of which America is the proof
Mary McCarthy *On the Contrary*

American 1. *adjective* stateside, U.S., Yankee *or* Yank 2. *noun* Yankee *or* Yank, Yankee Doodle

I am willing to love all mankind, except an American
Dr. Johnson

Good Americans, when they die, go to Paris
Thomas Gold Appleton

amiability affability, agreeableness, amiableness, attractiveness, benignity, charm, cheerfulness, delightfulness, engagingness, friendliness, friendship, geniality, good humour, good nature, kindliness, kindness, lovableness, pleasantness, pleasingness, sociability, sweetness, sweetness and light (*informal*), sweet temper, winsomeness

amiable affable, agreeable, attractive, benign, charming, cheerful, congenial, delightful, engaging, friendly, genial, good-humoured, good-natured, kind, kindly, likable *or* likeable, lovable, obliging, pleasant, pleasing, sociable, sweet-tempered, winning, winsome
Antonyms disagreeable, displeasing, hostile, ill-natured, loathsome, repellent, sour, unfriendly, unpleasant

amicability amiability, amicableness, amity, brotherliness, civility, cordiality, courtesy, fraternity, friendliness, friendship, goodwill, harmony, kindliness, kindness, neighbourliness, peace, peaceableness, peacefulness, politeness, sociability

amicable amiable, brotherly, civil, cordial, courteous, fraternal, friendly, good-humoured, harmonious, kind, kindly, neighbourly, peaceable, peaceful, polite, sociable
Antonyms antagonistic, bellicose, belligerent, disagreeable, hostile, ill-disposed, impolite, inimical, pugnacious, quarrelsome, uncivil, unfriendly, unkind, unsociable

amid amidst, among, amongst, in the middle of, in the midst of, in the thick of, surrounded by

amidst amid, among, amongst, in the middle of, in the midst of, in the thick of, midst, with

amiss 1. *adjective* awry, confused, defective, erroneous, fallacious, false, faulty, improper, inaccurate, inappropriate, incorrect, mistaken, out of order, unsuitable, untoward, wrong 2. *adverb* as an insult, as offensive, erroneously, faultily, improperly, inappropriately, incorrectly, mistakenly, out of turn, unsuitably, wrongly
Antonyms *adjective* accurate, appropriate, correct, in order, O.K. *or* okay (*informal*), perfect, proper, right, suitable, true ~*adverb* appropriately, correctly, properly, rightly, suitably, well

amity accord, amicability, brotherhood, comity, comradeship, concord, cordiality, fellowship, fraternity, friendliness, friendship, goodwill, harmony, kindliness, peace, peacefulness, tranquillity, understanding

ammunition armaments, cartridges, explosives, materiel, munitions, powder, rounds, shells, shot, shot and shell

amnesty absolution, condonation, dispensation, forgiveness, general pardon, immunity, oblivion, remission (*of penalty*), reprieve

amok *see* AMUCK

among, amongst **1.** amid, amidst, in association with, in the middle of, in the midst of, in the thick of, midst, surrounded by, together with, with **2.** between, to each of **3.** in the class of, in the company of, in the group of, in the number of, out of **4.** by all of, by the joint action of, by the whole of, mutually, with one another

amoral nonmoral, unethical, unvirtuous

amorous affectionate, amatory, ardent, attached, doting, enamoured, erotic, fond, impassioned, in love, lovesick, loving, lustful, passionate, tender
Antonyms aloof, cold, distant, frigid, frosty, indifferent, passionless, stand-offish, undemonstrative, unfeeling, unloving

amorousness affection, ardour, concupiscence, desire, fondness, lovingness, lust, passion, the hots (*slang*)

amorphous characterless, formless, inchoate, indeterminate, irregular, nebulous, nondescript, shapeless, unformed, unshaped, unshapen, unstructured, vague
Antonyms definite, distinct, regular, shaped, structured

amount **1.** bulk, expanse, extent, lot, magnitude, mass, measure, number, quantity, supply, volume **2.** addition, aggregate, entirety, extent, lot, sum, sum total, total, whole **3.** full effect, full value, import, result, significance

Many a mickle makes a muckle

amount to add up to, aggregate, become, come to, develop into, equal, grow, mean, purport, total

amour affair, *affaire de coeur*, intrigue, liaison, love affair, relationship, romance

amour-propre dignity, faith in oneself, morale, pride, self-esteem, self-respect

amphibian

Amphibians

axolotl
bullfrog
caecilian
congo eel *or* snake
eft
frog *or (Caribbean)* crapaud
Goliath frog
hairy frog
hellbender
hyla
midwife toad
mud puppy
natterjack
newt *or (dialect or archaic)* eft
olm
pipa *or* Surinam toad
Queensland cane toad
salamander
siren
toad *or (Caribbean)* crapaud
tree frog

ample abounding, abundant, big, bountiful, broad, capacious, commodious, copious, enough and to spare, expansive, extensive, full, generous, great, large, lavish, liberal, plenteous, plentiful, plenty, profuse, rich, roomy, spacious, substantial, two a penny, unrestricted, voluminous, wide
Antonyms inadequate, insufficient, little, meagre, restricted, scant, skimpy, small, sparse, unsatisfactory

amplification augmentation, boosting, deepening, development, dilation, elaboration, enlargement, expansion, expatiation, extension, fleshing out, heightening, increase, intensification, lengthening, magnification, raising, rounding out, strengthening, stretching, supplementing, widening

amplify augment, boost, deepen, develop, dilate, elaborate, enlarge, expand, expatiate, extend, flesh out, go into detail, heighten, increase, intensify, lengthen, magnify, raise, round out, strengthen, stretch, supplement, widen
Antonyms abbreviate, abridge, boil down, condense, curtail, cut down, decrease, reduce, simplify

amplitude **1.** bigness, breadth, bulk, capaciousness, compass, dimension, expanse, extent, greatness, hugeness, largeness, magnitude, mass, range, reach, scope, size, spaciousness, sweep, vastness, width **2.** abundance, ampleness, completeness, copiousness, fullness, plenitude, plethora, profusion, richness

amply abundantly, bountifully, capaciously, completely, copiously, extensively, fully, generously, greatly, lavishly, liberally, plenteously, plentifully, profusely, richly, substantially, thoroughly, unstintingly, well, with a blank cheque, with a free hand, without stinting
Antonyms inadequately, insufficiently, meagrely, poorly, scantily, skimpily, sparsely, thinly

amputate curtail, cut off, lop, remove, separate, sever, truncate

amuck, amok berserk, destructively, ferociously, frenziedly, in a frenzy, insanely, madly, maniacally, murderously, savagely, uncontrollably, violently, wildly

amulet charm, fetish, juju, periapt (*rare*), talisman

amuse beguile, charm, cheer, delight, divert, enliven, entertain, gladden, gratify, interest, occupy, please, recreate, regale, tickle
Antonyms be tedious, bore, jade, pall on, send to sleep, tire, weary

We are not amused

Queen Victoria

amusement 1. beguilement, cheer, delight, di~version, enjoyment, entertainment, fun, glad~dening, gratification, hilarity, interest, jollies (*slang*), laughter, merriment, mirth, pleasing, pleasure, recreation, regalement, sport 2. dis~traction, diversion, entertainment, game, hob~by, joke, lark, pastime, prank, recreation, sport
Antonyms boredom, displeasure, monotony, sadness, tedium

amusing charming, cheerful, cheering, comical, delightful, diverting, droll, enjoyable, enter~taining, facetious, funny, gladdening, gratify~ing, humorous, interesting, jocular, laughable, lively, merry, pleasant, pleasing, rib-tickling, witty
Antonyms boring, dead, dull, flat, humdrum, monotonous, stale, tedious, tiresome, unamusing, unexciting, unfunny, uninterest~ing, wearisome

anaemic ashen, bloodless, characterless, col~ourless, dull, enervated, feeble, frail, infirm, like death warmed up (*informal*), pale, pallid, sickly, wan, weak
Antonyms blooming, florid, full-blooded, glowing, hearty, radiant, rosy, rosy-cheeked, rubicund, ruddy, sanguine

anaesthetic 1. *noun* analgesic, anodyne, nar~cotic, opiate, painkiller, sedative, soporific, stupefacient, stupefactive 2. *adjective* analge~sic, anodyne, deadening, dulling, narcotic, numbing, opiate, pain-killing, sedative, sleep-inducing, soporific, stupefacient, stu~pefactive

analogous agreeing, akin, alike, comparable, corresponding, equivalent, homologous, like, of a piece, parallel, related, resembling, similar
Antonyms contrasting, different, discrepant, disparate, dissimilar, diverse, unlike

analogy agreement, comparison, correlation, correspondence, equivalence, homology, like~ness, parallel, relation, resemblance, similar~ity, similitude

analyse 1. assay, estimate, evaluate, examine, interpret, investigate, judge, research, test, work over 2. anatomize, break down, consider, dissect, dissolve, divide, resolve, separate, study, think through

analysis 1. anatomization, anatomy, assay, breakdown, dissection, dissolution, division, enquiry, examination, investigation, perusal, resolution, scrutiny, separation, sifting, test 2. estimation, evaluation, finding, interpretation, judgment, opinion, reasoning, study

analytic, analytical detailed, diagnostic, dis~crete, dissecting, explanatory, expository, in~quiring, inquisitive, interpretative, interpre~tive, investigative, logical, organized, problem-solving, questioning, rational, search~ing, studious, systematic, testing

anarchic chaotic, confused, disordered, disor~ganized, lawless, misgoverned, misruled, off the rails, rebellious, revolutionary, rioting, ri~otous, ungoverned
Antonyms controlled, decorous, disciplined, law-abiding, ordered, peaceable, peaceful, qui~et, restrained, well-behaved

anarchist insurgent, nihilist, rebel, revolution~ary, terrorist

anarchy chaos, confusion, disorder, disorgani~zation, lawlessness, misgovernment, misrule, rebellion, revolution, riot
Antonyms control, discipline, government, law, law and order, order, peace, rule

anathema 1. ban, condemnation, curse, dam~nation, denunciation, excommunication, ex~ecration, imprecation, malediction, proscrip~tion, taboo 2. abomination, bane, bête noire, bugbear, enemy, pariah

anathematize abominate, ban, condemn, curse, damn, denounce, excommunicate, execrate, imprecate, proscribe

anatomize analyse, break down, dissect, dis~solve, divide, examine, resolve, scrutinize, separate, study

anatomy 1. analysis, dismemberment, dissec~tion, division, enquiry, examination, investi~gation, study 2. build, composition, frame, framework, make-up, structure

ancestor forebear, forefather, forerunner, pre~cursor, predecessor, progenitor
Antonyms descendant, inheritor, issue, off~spring, progeny, successor

ancestral ancestorial, antecedent, forefatherly, genealogical, hereditary, inherited, lineal, pa~triarchal

ancestry ancestors, antecedents, blood, deriva~tion, descent, extraction, family, forebears, forefathers, genealogy, house, line, lineage, origin, parentage, pedigree, progenitors, race, stock

anchor *noun* 1. bower (*Nautical*), drogue, hook (*Nautical*), kedge, mooring, sheet anchor ~*verb* 2. cast anchor, come to anchor, dock, drop anchor, drop the hook, kedge, kedge off, lay anchor, let go the anchor, moor, tie up 3. *verb* attach, bolt, chain, fix, secure, tie

anchorage berth, dock, dockage, harbour, har~bourage, haven, moorage, port, quay

anchorite eremite, hermit, recluse

ancient aged, age-old, antediluvian, antiquat~ed, antique, archaic, bygone, cobwebby, early, hoary, obsolete, old, old as the hills, olden, old-fashioned, outmoded, out-of-date, pri~meval, primordial, superannuated, timeworn
Antonyms current, fresh, in vogue, late, mod~

ern, modish, new, newfangled, new-fashioned, novel, recent, state-of-the-art, up-to-date, with it (*informal*), young

ancillary accessory, additional, auxiliary, con~ tributory, extra, secondary, subordinate, sub~ sidiary, supplementary
Antonyms cardinal, chief, main, major, prem~ ier, primary, prime, principal

and along with, also, as well as, furthermore, in addition to, including, moreover, plus, to~ gether with

androgynous androgyne, bisexual, epicene, hermaphrodite, hermaphroditic

android *Science fiction* automaton, bionic man *or* woman, cyborg, humanoid, mechanical man, robot

anecdote reminiscence, short story, sketch, story, tale, urban legend, yarn

anew afresh, again, another time, from scratch, from the beginning, once again, once more, over again

angel 1. archangel, cherub, divine messenger, guardian spirit, seraph, spiritual being 2. *in~ formal* beauty, darling, dear, dream, gem, ideal, jewel, paragon, saint, treasure

Angels

Azrael	Raphael
Gabriel	Uriel
Michael	

Angelic orders

angels	principalities *or* princedoms
archangels	seraphim
cherubim	thrones
dominations *or* do~ minions	virtues
powers	

I am on the side of the angels
Benjamin Disraeli

angelic 1. celestial, cherubic, ethereal, heaven~ ly, seraphic 2. adorable, beatific, beautiful, entrancing, innocent, lovely, pure, saintly, virtuous
Antonyms (*sense 1*) demonic, devilish, diabol~ ic, diabolical, fiendish, hellish, infernal, sa~ tanic

anger 1. *noun* annoyance, antagonism, choler, displeasure, exasperation, fury, ill humour, ill temper, indignation, ire, irritability, irritation, outrage, passion, pique, rage, resentment, seeing red, spleen, temper, vexation, wrath 2. *verb* affront, aggravate (*informal*), annoy, an~ tagonize, be on one's back (*slang*), displease, enrage, exasperate, excite, fret, gall, get in one's hair (*informal*), get one's back up, get one's dander up (*informal*), get on one's nerves (*informal*), hassle (*informal*), incense, infuriate, irritate, madden, make one's blood boil, nark (*Brit., Austral., & N.Z. slang*), net~ tle, offend, outrage, pique, piss one off (*taboo slang*), provoke, put one's back up, rile, vex
Antonyms *noun* acceptance, amiability, ap~ proval, calmness, forgiveness, goodwill, grati~ fication, liking, patience, peace, pleasure ~*verb* appease, calm, pacify, placate, please, soothe

Usually when people are sad, they don't do any~ thing. They just cry over their condition. But when they get angry, they bring about a change
Malcolm X *Malcolm X Speaks*

Anger is a short madness
Horace *Epistles*

Anger and jealousy can no more bear to lose sight of their objects than love
George Eliot *The Mill on the Floss*

Never let the sun go down on your anger

angle *noun* 1. bend, corner, crook, crotch, cusp, edge, elbow, intersection, knee, nook, point 2. approach, aspect, outlook, perspective, point of view, position, side, slant, standpoint, view~ point ~*verb* 3. cast, fish

angle for aim for, be after (*informal*), cast about for, contrive, fish for, hunt, invite, look for, scheme, seek, set one's sights on, solicit, try for

angler fisher, fisherman, piscator *or* piscatrix

angling fishing

a worm at one end and a fool at the other
Dr. Johnson

God never did make a more calm, quiet, inno~ cent recreation than angling
Izaak Walton

Fishing is always a form of madness but happily....there is no cure
Alexander Douglas Home

an excellent angler, and now with God
Izaak Walton

angry annoyed, antagonized, as black as thun~ der, at daggers drawn, choked, choleric, cross, displeased, enraged, exasperated, fit to be tied (*slang*), foaming at the mouth, furious, hacked (off) (*U.S. slang*), heated, hot, hot under the collar (*informal*), ill-tempered, incensed, in~ dignant, infuriated, in high dudgeon, irascible, irate, ireful, irritable, irritated, mad (*infor~ mal*), nettled, on the warpath, outraged, pas~ sionate, piqued, pissed off (*taboo slang*), pro~ voked, raging, resentful, riled, splenetic, tu~ multuous, up in arms, uptight (*informal*), wrathful
Antonyms agreeable, amiable, calm, congen~ ial, friendly, gratified, happy, loving, mild, peaceful, pleasant, pleased

When angry, count four; when very angry, swear
Mark Twain *Pudd'nhead Wilson*

angst agitation, anxiety, apprehension, care, disquietude, distress, fretfulness, inquietude,

malaise, perturbation, torment, unease, vexation, worry
Antonyms calmness, collectedness, composure, contentment, ease, fulfilment, nonchalance, peace of mind, satisfaction

anguish agony, distress, grief, heartache, heartbreak, misery, pain, pang, sorrow, suffering, throe, torment, torture, woe

anguished afflicted, agonized, brokenhearted, distressed, grief-stricken, suffering, tormented, tortured, wounded, wretched

angular bony, gaunt, lank, lanky, lean, macilent (*rare*), rangy, rawboned, scrawny, skinny, spare

animadversion blame, censure, comment, condemnation, criticism, knocking (*informal*), rebuke, reprehension, reproach, reproof, stick (*slang*), strictures

animal *noun* **1.** beast, brute, creature **2.** *applied to a person* barbarian, beast, brute, monster, savage, wild man *~adjective* **3.** bestial, bodily, brutish, carnal, fleshly, gross, physical, sensual

Related words

ant	formic
ass	asinine
bear	ursine
bee	apian
bird	avian *or* ornithic
bull	taurine
cat	feline
crab	cancroid
crow	corvine
deer	cervine
dog	canine
dove	columbine
eagle	aquiline
elephant	elephantine
falcon	falconine
fish	piscine *or* icthyoid
fowl	gallinaceous
fox	vulpine
goat	caprine *or* hircine
goose	anserine *or* anserous
gull	larine
hare	leporine
hawk	accipitrine
horse	equine
lion	leonine
lynx	lyncean
mite *or* tick	acaroid
monkey	simian
ox	bovine
parrot	psittacine
peacock	pavonine
pig	porcine
puffin	alcidine
seal	phocine
sheep	ovine
snake	serpentine, anguine, ophidian *or* colubrine
swallow	hirundine
wasp	vespine
wolf	lupine

Collective animals

antelopes	herd
apes	shrewdness
asses	pace *or* herd
badgers	cete
bears	sloth
bees	swarm *or* grist
birds	flock, congregation, flight *or* volery
bitterns	sedge *or* siege
boars	sounder
bucks	brace *or* lease
buffaloes	herd
capercailzies	tok
cats	clowder
cattle	drove *or* herd
choughs	chattering
colts	rag
coots	covert
cranes	herd, sedge *or* siege
crows	murder
cubs	litter
curlews	herd
curs	cowardice
deer	herd
dolphins	school
doves	flight *or* dule
ducks	paddling *or* team
dunlins	flight
elk	gang
fish	shoal, draught, haul, run *or* catch
flies	swarm *or* grist
foxes	skulk
geese	gaggle *or* skein
giraffes	herd
gnats	swarm *or* cloud
goats	herd *or* tribe
goldfinches	charm
grouse	brood, covey *or* pack
gulls	colony
hares	down *or* husk
hawks	cast
hens	brood
herons	sedge *or* siege
herrings	shoal *or* glean
hounds	pack, mute *or* cry
insects	swarm
kangaroos	troop
kittens	kindle
lapwings	desert
larks	exaltation
leopards	leap
lions	pride *or* troop

mallards	sord *or* sute
mares	stud
martens	richesse
moles	labour
monkeys	troop
mules	barren
nightingales	watch
owls	parliament
oxen	yoke, drove, team *or* herd
partridges	covey
peacocks	muster
pheasants	nye *or* nide
pigeons	flock *or* flight
pigs	litter
plovers	stand *or* wing
pochards	flight, rush, bunch *or* knob
ponies	herd
porpoises	school *or* gam
poultry	run
pups	litter
quails	bevy
rabbits	nest
racehorses	field *or* string
ravens	unkindness
roes	bevy
rooks	building *or* clamour
ruffs	hill
seals	herd *or* pod
sheep	flock
sheldrakes	dopping
snipe	walk *or* wisp
sparrows	host
starlings	murmuration
swallows	flight
swans	herd *or* bevy
swifts	flock
swine	herd, sounder *or* dryft
teal	bunch, knob *or* spring
whales	school, gam *or* run
whelps	litter
whiting	pod
wigeon	bunch, company, knob *or* flight
wildfowl	plump, sord *or* sute
wolves	pack, rout *or* herd
woodcocks	fall

Habitations

ant	ant hill *or* formicary
badger	set *or* sett
beaver	lodge
bee	hive *or* apiary
bird	nest
eagle	aerie *or* eyrie
fish	redd
fox	earth
otter	holt
pig	sty
puffin	puffinry
rabbit	warren
rook	rookery
seal	sealery
squirrel	drey *or* dray
termite	termitarium
wasp	vespiary *or* bike

Male

ass	jack
bird	cock
cat	tom
deer	hart *or* stag
donkey	jack
duck	drake
elephant	bull
falcon	tercel *or* tiercel
ferret	hob
fowl	cock
fox	dog
goat	billy *or* buck
goose	gander
hare	buck
horse	stallion
kangaroo	buck *or* old man
lobster	cock
ox	bull
peafowl	peacock
pig	boar
rabbit	buck
reindeer	buck
ruff	ruff
sheep	ram *or* tup
swan	cob
weasel	whittret
whale	bull

Female

ass	jenny
bird	hen
cat	tabby
deer	doe *or* hind
dog	bitch
donkey	jenny
elephant	cow
ferret	gill *or* jill
fowl	hen
fox	vixen
goat	nanny
hare	doe
horse	mare
leopard	leopardess
lion	lioness
lobster	hen
mink	sow
ox	cow
peafowl	peahen
pig	sow
rabbit	doe
ruff	reeve
sheep	ewe

swan	pen
tiger	tigress
whale	cow
wolf	bitch
wren	jenny

Young

bear	cub
bird	chick, fledg(e)ling *or* nestling
butterfly	caterpillar, chrysalis *or* chrysalid
cat	kitten
cod	codling
deer	fawn
dog	pup *or* puppy
duck	duckling
eagle	eaglet
eel	elver *or* grig
elephant	calf
falcon	eyas
ferret	kit
fish	fry *or* fingerling
frog	tadpole
fox	kit *or* cub
goat	kid *or* yeanling
goose	gosling
hare	leveret
herring	alevin, brit *or* sparling
horse	foal, colt *or* filly
kangaroo	joey
lion	cub
moth	caterpillar
owl	owlet
ox	calf
pig	piglet
pigeon	squab
salmon	alevin, grilse, parr *or* smolt
seal	pup
sheep	lamb *or* yeanling
sprat	brit
swan	cygnet
tiger	cub
toad	tadpole
whale	calf
wolf	cub *or* whelp

Mammals
see MAMMAL

Birds
see BIRD

Amphibians
see AMPHIBIAN

Reptiles
see REPTILE

Dinosaurs
see DINOSAUR

Fish
see FISH

Insects
see INSECT

Invertebrates
see INVERTEBRATE

Animals, whom we have made our slaves, we do not like to consider our equal
Charles Darwin

animate *verb* **1.** activate, breathe life into, embolden, encourage, energize, enliven, excite, fire, gladden, impel, incite, inspire, inspirit, instigate, invigorate, kick-start (*informal*), kindle, move, prod, quicken, revive, rouse, spark, spur, stimulate, stir, urge, vitalize, vivify *~adjective* **2.** alive, alive and kicking, breathing, live, living, moving **3.** gay, lively, spirited, vivacious
Antonyms *verb* check, curb, deaden, deter, devitalize, discourage, dull, inhibit, kill, make lifeless, put a damper on, restrain

animated active, airy, alive and kicking, ardent, brisk, buoyant, dynamic, ebullient, elated, energetic, enthusiastic, excited, fervent, full of beans (*informal*), gay, lively, passionate, quick, sparky, spirited, sprightly, vibrant, vigorous, vital, vivacious, vivid, zealous, zestful
Antonyms apathetic, boring, dejected, depressed, dull, inactive, lethargic, lifeless, listless, monotonous, passive

animation action, activity, airiness, ardour, brio, briskness, buoyancy, dynamism, ebullience, elation, energy, enthusiasm, excitement, exhilaration, fervour, gaiety, high spirits, life, liveliness, passion, pep, pizzazz *or* pizazz (*informal*), sparkle, spirit, sprightliness, verve, vibrancy, vigour, vitality, vivacity, zeal, zest, zing (*informal*)

animosity acrimony, animus, antagonism, antipathy, bad blood, bitterness, enmity, hate, hatred, hostility, ill will, malevolence, malice, malignity, rancour, resentment, virulence
Antonyms amity, benevolence, congeniality, friendliness, friendship, goodwill, harmony, kindness, love, rapport, sympathy

animus 1. acrimony, animosity, antagonism, antipathy, bad blood, bitterness, enmity, hate, hatred, hostility, ill will, malevolence, malice, malignity, rancour, resentment, virulence **2.** animating force, intention, motive, purpose, will

annals accounts, archives, chronicles, history, journals, memorials, records, registers

anneal case-harden, harden, indurate, steel, strengthen, temper, toughen

annex 1. add, adjoin, affix, append, attach, connect, fasten, join, subjoin, tack, unite **2.** acquire, appropriate, arrogate, conquer, expropriate, occupy, seize, take over

Antonyms (*sense 1*) detach, disconnect, disengage, disjoin, disunite, remove, separate, unfasten

annexation annexing, appropriation, arrogation, conquest, expropriation, occupation, seizure, takeover

annexe **1.** ell, extension, supplementary building, wing **2.** addendum, addition, adjunct, affix, appendix, attachment, supplement

annihilate abolish, destroy, eradicate, erase, exterminate, extinguish, extirpate, liquidate, nullify, obliterate, root out, wipe from the face of the earth, wipe out

annihilation abolition, destruction, eradication, erasure, extermination, extinction, extinguishing, extirpation, liquidation, nullification, obliteration, rooting out, wiping out

annihilator deracinator, destroyer, eradicator, expunger, exterminator, extinguisher, extirpator, nullifier, obliterator

annotate commentate, comment on, elucidate, explain, footnote, gloss, illustrate, interpret, make observations, note

annotation comment, commentary, elucidation, exegesis, explanation, explication, footnote, gloss, illustration, interpretation, note, observation

announce **1.** advertise, blow wide open (*slang*), broadcast, declare, disclose, divulge, give out, intimate, make known, proclaim, promulgate, propound, publish, report, reveal, shout from the rooftops (*informal*), tell **2.** augur, betoken, foretell, harbinger, herald, portend, presage, signal, signify

Antonyms (*sense 1*) bury, conceal, cover up, hide, hold back, hush, hush up, keep back, keep quiet, keep secret, suppress, withhold

announcement advertisement, broadcast, bulletin, communiqué, declaration, disclosure, divulgence, intimation, proclamation, promulgation, publication, report, revelation, statement

announcer anchor man, broadcaster, commentator, master of ceremonies, newscaster, news reader, reporter

annoy aggravate (*informal*), anger, badger, bedevil, be on one's back (*slang*), bore, bother, bug (*informal*), displease, disturb, exasperate, gall, get (*informal*), get in one's hair (*informal*), get one's back up, get one's dander up (*informal*), get one's goat (*slang*), get on one's nerves (*informal*), get on one's wick (*Brit. slang*), get under one's skin (*informal*), get up one's nose (*informal*), harass, harry, hassle (*informal*), incommode, irk, irritate, madden, make one's blood boil, molest, nark (*Brit., Austral., & N.Z. slang*), needle (*informal*), nettle, peeve, pester, piss one off (*taboo slang*), plague, provoke, put one's back up, rile, rub (someone) up the wrong way (*informal*), ruffle, tease, trouble, vex

Antonyms appease, calm, comfort, console, mollify, solace, soothe

annoyance **1.** aggravation, anger, bedevilment, bother, displeasure, disturbance, exasperation, harassment, hassle (*informal*), irritation, nuisance, provocation, trouble, vexation **2.** bind (*informal*), bore, bother, drag (*informal*), gall, nuisance, pain (*informal*), pain in the arse (*taboo informal*), pain in the neck (*informal*), pest, plague, tease

annoyed aggravated (*informal*), bothered, browned off (*informal*), displeased, exasperated, harassed, harried, hassled (*informal*), irked, irritated, maddened, miffed (*informal*), nettled, peeved (*informal*), piqued, pissed off (*taboo slang*), riled, ruffled, vexed

annoying aggravating, bedevilling, boring, bothersome, displeasing, disturbing, exasperating, galling, harassing, irksome, irritating, maddening, peeving (*informal*), provoking, teasing, troublesome, vexatious

Antonyms agreeable, amusing, charming, delightful, diverting, enjoyable, entertaining, gratifying, pleasant

annual once a year, yearlong, yearly

annually by the year, each year, every year, once a year, per annum, per year, year after year, yearly

annul abolish, abrogate, cancel, countermand, declare *or* render null and void, invalidate, negate, nullify, obviate, recall, repeal, rescind, retract, reverse, revoke, void

Antonyms bring back, re-enforce, re-establish, reimpose, reinstate, reintroduce, restore

annulment abolition, abrogation, cancellation, countermanding, invalidation, negation, nullification, recall, repeal, rescindment, rescission, retraction, reversal, revocation, voiding

anodyne **1.** *noun* analgesic, narcotic, painkiller, painreliever, palliative **2.** *adjective* analgesic, deadening, dulling, narcotic, numbing, pain-killing, pain-relieving, palliative

anoint **1.** daub, embrocate, grease, oil, rub, smear, spread over **2.** anele (*archaic*), bless, consecrate, hallow, sanctify

anomalous aberrant, abnormal, atypical, bizarre, deviating, eccentric, exceptional, incongruous, inconsistent, irregular, odd, oddball (*informal*), off-the-wall (*slang*), outré, peculiar, rare, unusual

Antonyms common, customary, familiar, natural, normal, ordinary, regular, typical, usual

anomaly aberration, abnormality, departure, deviation, eccentricity, exception, incongruity, inconsistency, irregularity, oddity, peculiarity, rarity

anon before long, betimes (*archaic*), erelong (*archaic or poetic*), forthwith, in a couple of shakes (*informal*), presently, promptly, shortly, soon

anonymity 1. innominateness, namelessness 2. characterlessness, unremarkability *or* unremarkableness, unsingularity

anonymous 1. incognito, innominate, nameless, unacknowledged, unattested, unauthenticated, uncredited, unidentified, unknown, unnamed, unsigned 2. characterless, nondescript, unexceptional
Antonyms (*sense 1*) accredited, acknowledged, attested, authenticated, credited, identified, known, named, signed

answer *noun* 1. acknowledgment, comeback, counterattack, defence, explanation, plea, reaction, refutation, rejoinder, reply, report, resolution, response, retort, return, riposte, solution, vindication *~verb* 2. acknowledge, explain, react, refute, rejoin, reply, resolve, respond, retort, return, solve 3. conform, correlate, correspond, do, fill, fit, fulfil, measure up, meet, pass, qualify, satisfy, serve, suffice, suit, work
Antonyms *noun* inquiry, interrogation, query, question *~verb* (*sense 2*) ask, inquire, interrogate, query, question

answerable 1. accountable, amenable, chargeable, liable, responsible, subject, to blame 2. explainable, refutable, resolvable, solvable

answer back argue, be cheeky, be impertinent, cheek (*informal*), contradict, disagree, dispute, rebut, retort, talk back

answer for 1. be accountable for, be answerable for, be chargeable for, be liable for, be responsible for, be to blame for, take the rap for (*slang*) 2. atone for, make amends for, pay for, suffer for

answer to 1. be accountable to, be answerable to, be responsible to, be ruled by, obey 2. agree, confirm, correspond, fit, match, meet

antagonism antipathy, competition, conflict, contention, discord, dissension, friction, hostility, opposition, rivalry
Antonyms accord, agreement, amity, friendship, harmony, love, peacefulness, sympathy

antagonist adversary, competitor, contender, enemy, foe, opponent, opposer, rival

antagonistic adverse, antipathetic, at odds, at variance, averse, conflicting, contentious, hostile, ill-disposed, incompatible, in dispute, inimical, opposed, unfriendly

antagonization, antagonisation 1. aggravation (*informal*), annoyance, exacerbation, hassle (*informal*), infuriation, irritation, offence, provocation 2. adverseness, antipathy, aversion, competition, conflict, contention, counteraction, enmity, friction, hostility, inimicalness *or* inimicality, opposition, oppugnancy (*rare*), rivalry, variance

antagonize 1. aggravate (*informal*), alienate, anger, annoy, be on one's back (*slang*), disaffect, estrange, gall, get in one's hair (*informal*), get on one's nerves (*informal*), get on one's wick (*Brit. slang*), get under one's skin (*informal*), get up one's nose (*informal*), hassle (*informal*), insult, irritate, nark (*Brit., Austral., & N.Z. slang*), offend, piss one off (*taboo slang*), repel, rub (someone) up the wrong way (*informal*) 2. contend with, counteract, neutralize, oppose, struggle with, work against
Antonyms (*sense 1*) appease, calm, conciliate, disarm, mollify, pacify, placate, propitiate, soothe, win over

antecedent anterior, earlier, foregoing, former, preceding, precursory, preliminary, previous, prior
Antonyms after, coming, consequent, ensuing, following, later, posterior, subsequent, succeeding, successive

antecedents 1. ancestors, ancestry, blood, descent, extraction, family, forebears, forefathers, genealogy, line, progenitors, stock 2. background, history, past

antedate anticipate, come first *or* before, forego, go before, precede, predate

antediluvian 1. prehistoric, primeval, primitive, primordial 2. ancient, antiquated, antique, archaic, obsolete, old as the hills, old-fashioned, out-of-date, out of the ark (*informal*), passé

anterior 1. fore, forward, front, frontward 2. antecedent, earlier, foregoing, former, introductory, preceding, previous, prior

anteroom antechamber, foyer, lobby, outer room, reception room, vestibule, waiting room

anthem 1. canticle, carol, chant, chorale, hymn, psalm 2. paean, song of praise

anthology analects, choice, collection, compendium, compilation, digest, garland, miscellany, selection, treasury

anticipate 1. apprehend, await, count upon, expect, forecast, foresee, foretell, hope for, look for, look forward to, predict, prepare for 2. antedate, beat (someone) to it (*informal*), forestall, intercept, prevent

anticipation apprehension, awaiting, expectancy, expectation, foresight, foretaste, forethought, hope, preconception, premonition, prescience, presentiment

anticipatory apprehensive, expectant, forecasting, foreseeing, foretelling, forethoughtful, predicting, provident

anticlimax bathos, comedown (*informal*), disappointment, letdown
Antonyms climax, culmination, height, highlight, high point, peak, summit, top, zenith

This is the way the world ends
Not with a bang but a whimper
T.S. Eliot *The Hollow Men*

antics buffoonery, capers, clowning, escapades, foolishness, frolics, horseplay, larks, mischief, monkey tricks, playfulness, pranks, silliness, skylarking, stunts, tomfoolery, tricks

antidote antitoxin, antivenin, corrective, counteragent, countermeasure, cure, neutral~izer, nostrum, preventive, remedy, specific

antipathetic abhorrent, antagonistic, averse, disgusting, distasteful, hateful, hostile, in~compatible, invidious, loathsome, obnoxious, odious, offensive, repellent, repugnant, repul~sive, revolting, yucky *or* yukky (*slang*)

antipathy abhorrence, animosity, animus, an~tagonism, aversion, bad blood, contrariety, disgust, dislike, distaste, enmity, hatred, hos~tility, ill will, incompatibility, loathing, odium, opposition, rancour, repugnance, repulsion
Antonyms affection, affinity, attraction, bond, empathy, fellow-feeling, goodwill, harmony, partiality, rapport, sympathy, tie

I do not love thee, Dr. Fell.
The reason why I cannot tell;
But this I know, and know full well,
I do not love thee, Dr. Fell
Thomas Brown

antiquated **1.** antediluvian, antique, archaic, dated, obsolete, old-fashioned, old hat, out~moded, out-of-date, outworn, passé **2.** aged, ancient, cobwebby, elderly, hoary, old, old as the hills, past it (*informal*), superannuated
Antonyms all-singing, all-dancing, current, fashionable, fresh, modern, modish, new, state-of-the-art, stylish, up-to-date, young

antique *adjective* **1.** aged, ancient, elderly, old, superannuated **2.** archaic, obsolete, old-fashioned, outdated **3.** antiquarian, classic, olden, vintage *~noun* **4.** bygone, heirloom, ob~ject of virtu, relic

antiquity **1.** age, ancientness, elderliness, old age, oldness **2.** ancient times, distant past, olden days, time immemorial **3.** antique, relic, ruin

When my sonnet was rejected, I exclaimed,
"Damn the age; I will write for Antiquity!"
Charles Lamb

antiseptic **1.** *adjective* aseptic, clean, germ-free, hygienic, pure, sanitary, sterile, uncontami~nated, unpolluted **2.** *noun* bactericide, disin~fectant, germicide, purifier
Antonyms *adjective* contaminated, dirty, im~pure, infected, insanitary, polluted, septic, unhygienic

antisocial **1.** alienated, asocial, misanthropic, reserved, retiring, uncommunicative, un~friendly, unsociable, withdrawn **2.** antagonis~tic, belligerent, disorderly, disruptive, hostile, menacing, rebellious
Antonyms (*sense 1*) companionable, friendly, gregarious, philanthropic, sociable, social

antithesis **1.** antipode, contrary, contrast, con~verse, inverse, opposite, reverse **2.** contradic~tion, contraposition, contrariety, contrast, in~version, opposition, reversal

antithetical, antithetic antipodal, contradic~tory, contrary, contrasted, contrasting, con~verse, counter, inverse, opposed, opposite, poles apart, reverse

anxiety angst, apprehension, care, concern, disquiet, disquietude, distress, foreboding, fretfulness, misgiving, nervousness, restless~ness, solicitude, suspense, tension, trepida~tion, unease, uneasiness, watchfulness, worry
Antonyms assurance, calmness, confidence, contentment, relief, security, serenity

anxious **1.** apprehensive, careful, concerned, disquieted, distressed, disturbed, fearful, fret~ful, hot and bothered, in suspense, nervous, neurotic, on pins and needles, on tenterhooks, overwrought, restless, solicitous, taut, tense, troubled, twitchy (*informal*), uneasy, unquiet (*chiefly literary*), watchful, wired (*slang*), wor~ried **2.** ardent, avid, desirous, eager, expec~tant, impatient, intent, itching, keen, yearn~ing
Antonyms (*sense 1*) assured, calm, certain, collected, composed, confident, cool, noncha~lant, unfazed (*informal*), unperturbed (*sense 2*) disinclined, hesitant, loath, nonchalant, re~luctant

apace at full speed, expeditiously, posthaste, quickly, rapidly, speedily, swiftly, with dis~patch, without delay

apart **1.** afar, alone, aloof, aside, away, by it~self, by oneself, cut off, distant, distinct, di~vorced, excluded, independent, independently, isolated, out on a limb, piecemeal, separate, separated, separately, singly, to itself, to one~self, to one side **2.** asunder, in bits, in pieces, into parts, to bits, to pieces **3.** **apart from** aside from, besides, but, except for, excluding, not counting, other than, save

apartment accommodation, chambers, com~partment, flat, living quarters, penthouse, quarters, room, rooms, suite

apathetic cold, cool, emotionless, impassive, indifferent, insensible, listless, passive, phleg~matic, sluggish, stoic, stoical, torpid, uncon~cerned, unemotional, unfeeling, uninterested, unmoved, unresponsive
Antonyms active, anxious, aroused, bothered, caring, committed, concerned, emotional, en~thusiastic, excited, interested, moved, pas~sionate, responsive, troubled, worried, zealous

apathy coldness, coolness, emotionlessness, impassibility, impassivity, indifference, iner~

tia, insensibility, listlessness, nonchalance, passiveness, passivity, phlegm, sluggishness, stoicism, torpor, unconcern, unfeelingness, uninterestedness, unresponsiveness
Antonyms anxiety, attention, concern, emotion, enthusiasm, feeling, interest, zeal

ape affect, caricature, copy, counterfeit, echo, imitate, mimic, mirror, mock, parody, parrot

aperture breach, chink, cleft, crack, eye, eyelet, fissure, gap, hole, interstice, opening, orifice, passage, perforation, rent, rift, slit, slot, space, vent

apex acme, apogee, climax, crest, crown, culmination, height, high point, peak, pinnacle, point, summit, tip, top, vertex, zenith
Antonyms base, bottom, depths, lowest point, nadir, perigee, rock bottom

aphorism adage, apothegm, axiom, dictum, gnome, maxim, precept, proverb, saw, saying

aphrodisiac 1. *noun* love potion, philter 2. *adjective* arousing, erotic *or* erotical, exciting, stimulating, venereal

apiece each, for each, from each, individually, respectively, separately, severally, to each
Antonyms all together, as a group, collectively, en masse, overall, together

apish 1. affected, foolish, foppish, silly, stupid, trifling 2. imitative, mimicking

aplenty 1. *adjective* à gogo (*informal*), galore, in abundance, in plenty, in profusion, in quantity, to spare 2. *adverb* abundantly, copiously, in abundance, in plenty, in quantity, plenteously, plentifully

aplomb balance, calmness, composure, confidence, coolness, equanimity, level-headedness, poise, sang-froid, self-assurance, self-confidence, self-possession, stability
Antonyms awkwardness, chagrin, confusion, discomfiture, discomposure, embarrassment, self-consciousness

apocalypse 1. disclosure, prefigurement, prophecy, revelation, telling, vaticination (*rare*) 2. carnage, conflagration, destruction, devastation, havoc, holocaust

apocalyptic bodeful, ominous, oracular, portentous, prophetic, revelational, vatic

apocryphal doubtful, dubious, equivocal, fictitious, legendary, mythical, questionable, spurious, unauthenticated, uncanonical, unsubstantiated, unverified
Antonyms attested, authentic, authenticated, authorized, canonical, credible, factual, substantiated, true, undisputed, unquestionable, verified

apogee acme, apex, climax, crest, crown, culmination, height, high point, peak, pinnacle, summit, tip, top, vertex, zenith

apologetic contrite, penitent, regretful, remorseful, rueful, sorry

apologia apology, argument, case, defence, explanation, justification, plea

apologist advocate, arguer, champion, defender, justifier, maintainer, pleader, spokesman, supporter, vindicator

apologize ask forgiveness, beg pardon, express regret, say one is sorry, say sorry

apologue allegory, fable, parable, story, tale

apology 1. acknowledgment, confession, defence, excuse, explanation, extenuation, justification, plea, vindication 2. caricature, excuse, imitation, makeshift, mockery, stopgap, substitute, travesty

apoplectic *informal* beside oneself, boiling, enraged, frantic, frenzied, fuming, furious, incensed, infuriated, livid (*informal*), mad, raging

apoplexy attack, convulsion, fit, paroxysm, seizure

apostasy backsliding, defection, desertion, disloyalty, faithlessness, falseness, heresy, perfidy, recreance *or* recreancy (*archaic*), treachery, unfaithfulness

apostate 1. *noun* backslider, defector, deserter, heretic, recreant (*archaic*), renegade, traitor, turncoat 2. *adjective* backsliding, disloyal, faithless, false, heretical, perfidious, recreant, traitorous, treacherous, unfaithful, untrue

apostatize backslide, defect, desert, renege, turn traitor

apostle 1. evangelist, herald, messenger, missionary, preacher, proselytizer 2. advocate, champion, pioneer, propagandist, propagator, proponent

apothegm adage, aphorism, axiom, dictum, gnome, maxim, precept, proverb, saw, saying

apotheosis deification, elevation, exaltation, glorification, idealization, idolization

apotheosize deify, elevate, exalt, glorify, idealize, idolize

appal alarm, astound, daunt, dishearten, dismay, frighten, harrow, horrify, intimidate, make one's hair stand on end (*informal*), outrage, petrify, scare, shock, terrify, unnerve

appalled alarmed, astounded, daunted, disheartened, dismayed, disquieted, frightened, horrified, outraged, petrified, scared, shocked, stunned, terrified, unnerved

appalling alarming, astounding, awful, daunting, dire, disheartening, dismaying, dreadful, fearful, frightening, frightful, from hell (*informal*), ghastly, godawful (*slang*), grim, harrowing, hellacious (*U.S. slang*), hideous, horrible, horrid, horrific, horrifying, intimidating, petrifying, scaring, shocking, terrible, terrifying, unnerving
Antonyms comforting, consolatory, consoling, encouraging, heartening, reassuring

apparatus 1. appliance, contraption (*informal*), device, equipment, gear, implements, ma~chine, machinery, materials, means, mecha~nism, outfit, tackle, tools, utensils 2. bureau~cracy, chain of command, hierarchy, network, organization, setup (*informal*), structure, sys~tem

apparel accoutrements, array (*poetic*), attire, clothes, clothing, costume, dress, equipment, garb, garments, gear (*informal*), habiliments, habit, outfit, raiment (*archaic or poetic*), robes, schmutter (*slang*), threads (*slang*), trappings, vestments

apparent 1. blatant, bold, clear, conspicuous, discernible, distinct, evident, indubitable, manifest, marked, obvious, open, overt, pa~tent, plain, plain as the nose on your face, salient, understandable, unmistakable, visible 2. ostensible, outward, seeming, specious, superficial
Antonyms (*sense 1*) ambiguous, doubtful, du~bious, hazy, indefinite, indistinct, obscure, uncertain, unclear, vague (*sense 2*) actual, authentic, bona fide, genuine, honest, intrin~sic, real, sincere, true

apparently it appears that, it seems that, on the face of it, ostensibly, outwardly, seeming~ly, speciously, superficially

apparition 1. appearance, manifestation, ma~terialization, presence, vision, visitation 2. chimera, eidolon, ghost, phantom, revenant, shade (*literary*), spectre, spirit, spook (*infor~mal*), visitant, wraith

appeal *noun* 1. adjuration, application, en~treaty, invocation, petition, plea, prayer, re~quest, solicitation, suit, supplication 2. allure, attraction, attractiveness, beauty, charm, en~gagingness, fascination, interestingness, pleasingness *~verb* 3. adjure, apply, ask, beg, beseech, call, call upon, entreat, implore, pe~tition, plead, pray, refer, request, resort to, solicit, sue, supplicate 4. allure, attract, charm, engage, entice, fascinate, interest, in~vite, please, tempt
Antonyms *noun* (*sense 1*) denial, refusal, re~jection, repudiation (*sense 2*) repulsiveness *~verb* (*sense 3*) deny, refuse, reject, repudiate, repulse (*sense 4*) alienate, bore, repulse, revolt

appeal: in law, to put the dice into the box for another throw
Ambrose Bierce *The Devil's Dictionary*

appealing alluring, attractive, charming, de~sirable, endearing, engaging, inviting, prepos~sessing, taking, winning, winsome
Antonyms disgusting, forbidding, loathsome, objectionable, obnoxious, odious, offensive, re~pellent, repugnant, repulsive, revolting, sick~ening, unalluring, unappealing, unattractive, undesirable, uninviting, unprepossessing

appear 1. arise, arrive, attend, be present, come forth, come into sight, come into view, come out, come to light, crop up (*informal*), develop, emerge, issue, loom, materialize, oc~cur, show (*informal*), show one's face, show up (*informal*), surface, turn out, turn up 2. look (like *or* as if), occur, seem, strike one as 3. be apparent, be clear, be evident, be manifest, be obvious, be patent, be plain 4. become avail~able, be created, be developed, be invented, be published, come into being, come into exist~ence, come out 5. act, be exhibited, come on, come onstage, enter, perform, play, play a part, take part
Antonyms be doubtful, be unclear, disappear, vanish

appearance 1. advent, appearing, arrival, com~ing, debut, emergence, introduction, presence, showing up (*informal*), turning up 2. air, as~pect, bearing, demeanour, expression, face, figure, form, image, look, looks, manner, mien (*literary*) 3. front, guise, illusion, image, im~pression, outward show, pretence, semblance

All that glisters is not gold
William Shakespeare *The Merchant of Venice*

Men are valued, not for what they are, but for what they seem to be
E.G. Bulwer-Lytton *Money*

Appearances are deceptive

You can't tell a book by its cover

appease allay, alleviate, assuage, blunt, calm, compose, conciliate, diminish, ease, lessen, lull, mitigate, mollify, pacify, placate, pour oil on troubled waters, quell, quench, quiet, sat~isfy, soften, soothe, subdue, tranquillize
Antonyms aggravate (*informal*), anger, annoy, antagonize, arouse, be on one's back (*slang*), disturb, enrage, get in one's hair (*informal*), get on one's nerves (*informal*), hassle (*infor~mal*), incense, inflame, infuriate, irritate, madden, nark (*Brit., Austral., & N.Z. slang*), piss one off (*taboo slang*), provoke, rile, upset

appeasement 1. acceding, accommodation, compromise, concession, conciliation, placa~tion, propitiation 2. abatement, alleviation, assuagement, blunting, easing, lessening, lulling, mitigation, mollification, pacification, quelling, quenching, quieting, satisfaction, softening, solace, soothing, tranquillization

appellation address, description, designation, epithet, name, sobriquet, style, term, title

append add, adjoin, affix, annex, attach, fas~ten, hang, join, subjoin, tack on, tag on
Antonyms detach, disconnect, disengage, re~move, separate, take off

appendage 1. accessory, addendum, addition, adjunct, affix, ancillary, annexe, appendix, appurtenance, attachment, auxiliary, sup~

plement **2.** *Zoology* extremity, limb, member, projection, protuberance

appendant *adjective* **1.** added, additional, adjoined, affixed, annexed, appended, attached, auxiliary, fastened, joined, subjoined, supplementary, tacked on, tagged on **2.** accompanying, associated, attendant, concomitant, connected, consequential, following, related, resulting *~noun* **3.** addition, adjunct, affix, annexe, appendage, appendix, attachment, supplement

appendix addendum, addition, add-on, adjunct, appendage, codicil, postscript, supplement

appertain *usually with* **to** apply, bear upon, be characteristic of, be connected, belong, be part of, be pertinent, be proper, be relevant, have to do with, inhere in, pertain, refer, relate, touch upon

appetence, appetency **1.** ache, appetite, craving, desire, hankering, hunger, longing, need, yearning **2.** bent, drive, inclination, instinct, leaning, penchant, propensity **3.** affection, affinity, allurement, attraction, fondness, liking, partiality

appetite appetence, appetency, craving, demand, desire, hankering, hunger, inclination, liking, longing, passion, proclivity, propensity, relish, stomach, taste, willingness, yearning, zeal, zest

Antonyms abhorrence, aversion, disgust, disinclination, dislike, distaste, loathing, repugnance, repulsion, revulsion

The appetite grows by eating
François Rabelais *Gargantua*

appetizer **1.** antipasto, canapé, cocktail, hors d'oeuvre, titbit **2.** apéritif, cocktail **3.** foretaste, sample, taste

appetizing appealing, delicious, inviting, mouthwatering, palatable, savoury, scrumptious (*informal*), succulent, tasty, tempting

Antonyms distasteful, nauseating, unappetizing, unpalatable, unsavoury

applaud acclaim, approve, cheer, clap, commend, compliment, crack up (*informal*), encourage, eulogize, extol, give (someone) a big hand, laud, magnify (*archaic*), praise

Antonyms blast, boo, censure, condemn, criticize, decry, deprecate, deride, disparage, excoriate, hiss, lambast(e), pan (*informal*), put down, ridicule, run down, slag (off) (*slang*), tear into (*informal*), vilify

applause acclaim, acclamation, accolade, approbation, approval, big hand, cheering, cheers, commendation, eulogizing, hand, hand-clapping, laudation, ovation, plaudit, praise

appliance apparatus, device, gadget, implement, instrument, machine, mechanism, tool, waldo

applicable apposite, appropriate, apropos, apt, befitting, fit, fitting, germane, pertinent, relevant, suitable, suited, to the point, to the purpose, useful

Antonyms inapplicable, inappropriate, irrelevant, unsuitable, wrong

applicant aspirant, candidate, claimant, inquirer, petitioner, postulant, suitor, suppliant

application **1.** appositeness, exercise, function, germaneness, pertinence, practice, purpose, relevance, use, value **2.** appeal, claim, inquiry, petition, request, requisition, solicitation, suit **3.** assiduity, attention, attentiveness, commitment, dedication, diligence, effort, hard work, industry, perseverance, study **4.** balm, cream, dressing, emollient, lotion, ointment, poultice, salve, unguent

apply **1.** administer, assign, bring into play, bring to bear, carry out, employ, engage, execute, exercise, exert, implement, practise, put to use, use, utilize **2.** appertain, be applicable, be appropriate, bear upon, be fitting, be relevant, fit, pertain, refer, relate, suit **3.** anoint, bring into contact with, cover with, lay on, paint, place, put on, smear, spread on, touch to **4.** appeal, claim, inquire, make application, petition, put in, request, requisition, solicit, sue **5.** address, be assiduous, be diligent, be industrious, buckle down (*informal*), commit, concentrate, dedicate, devote, direct, give, make an effort, pay attention, persevere, study, try, work hard

appoint **1.** allot, arrange, assign, choose, decide, designate, determine, establish, fix, set, settle **2.** assign, choose, commission, delegate, elect, install, name, nominate, select **3.** command, decree, direct, enjoin, ordain **4.** equip, fit out, furnish, provide, supply

Antonyms (*sense 1*) cancel (*sense 2*) discharge, dismiss, fire, give the sack (*informal*), sack (*informal*) (*sense 4*) dismantle, divest, strip

appointed **1.** allotted, arranged, assigned, chosen, decided, designated, determined, established, fixed, set, settled **2.** assigned, chosen, commissioned, delegated, elected, installed, named, nominated, selected **3.** commanded, decreed, directed, enjoined, ordained **4.** equipped, fitted out, furnished, provided, supplied

appointment **1.** arrangement, assignation, consultation, date, engagement, interview, meeting, rendezvous, session, tryst (*archaic*) **2.** allotment, assignment, choice, choosing, commissioning, delegation, designation, election, installation, naming, nomination, selection **3.** assignment, berth (*informal*), job, office, place, position, post, situation, station **4.** appointee, candidate, delegate, nominee, office-holder, representative **5.** *usually plural* accoutrements, appurtenances, equipage, fittings, fixtures, furnishings, gear, outfit, paraphernalia, trappings

apportion allocate, allot, assign, deal, dispense, distribute, divide, dole out, measure out, mete out, parcel out, ration out, share

apportionment allocation, allotment, assignment, dealing out, dispensing, distribution, division, doling out, measuring out, meting out, parcelling out, rationing out, sharing

apposite appertaining, applicable, appropriate, apropos, apt, befitting, fitting, germane, pertinent, proper, relevant, suitable, suited, to the point, to the purpose
Antonyms inapplicable, inappropriate, inapt, irrelevant, unsuitable, unsuited

appraisal **1.** assessment, estimate, estimation, evaluation, judgment, opinion, recce (*slang*), sizing up (*informal*) **2.** assay, pricing, rating, reckoning, survey, valuation

appraise assay, assess, estimate, evaluate, eye up, gauge, inspect, judge, price, rate, recce (*slang*), review, size up (*informal*), survey, value

appreciable ascertainable, clear-cut, considerable, definite, detectable, discernible, distinguishable, evident, marked, material, measurable, noticeable, obvious, perceivable, perceptible, pronounced, recognizable, significant, substantial, visible
Antonyms immaterial, imperceptible, inappreciable, indiscernible, indistinguishable, insignificant, invisible, minor, minute, negligible, small, trivial, undetectable, unnoticeable, unsubstantial

appreciably ascertainably, considerably, definitely, detectably, discernibly, distinguishably, evidently, markedly, measurably, noticeably, obviously, palpably, perceivably, perceptively, recognizably, significantly, substantially, visibly

appreciate **1.** be appreciative, be grateful for, be indebted, be obliged, be thankful for, give thanks for **2.** acknowledge, be alive to, be aware (cognizant, conscious) of, comprehend, estimate, know, perceive, realize, recognize, sympathize with, take account of, understand **3.** admire, cherish, enjoy, esteem, like, prize, rate highly, regard, relish, respect, savour, treasure, value **4.** enhance, gain, grow, improve, increase, inflate, raise the value of, rise
Antonyms (*sense 1*) be ungrateful (*sense 2*) be unaware, misunderstand, underrate (*sense 3*) belittle, denigrate, disdain, disparage, scorn (*sense 4*) deflate, depreciate, devaluate, fall

appreciation **1.** acknowledgment, gratefulness, gratitude, indebtedness, obligation, thankfulness, thanks **2.** admiration, appraisal, assessment, awareness, cognizance, comprehension, enjoyment, esteem, estimation, knowledge, liking, perception, realization, recognition, regard, relish, respect, responsiveness, sensitivity, sympathy, understanding, valuation **3.** enhancement, gain, growth, improvement, increase, inflation, rise **4.** acclamation, criticism, critique, notice, praise, review, tribute
Antonyms (*sense 1*) ingratitude (*sense 2*) antipathy, dislike, ignorance, incomprehension (*sense 3*) decline, depreciation, devaluation, fall

appreciative **1.** beholden, grateful, indebted, obliged, thankful **2.** admiring, aware, cognizant, conscious, enthusiastic, in the know (*informal*), knowledgeable, mindful, perceptive, pleased, regardful, respectful, responsive, sensitive, supportive, sympathetic, understanding

apprehend **1.** arrest, bust (*informal*), capture, catch, collar (*informal*), feel one's collar (*slang*), lift (*slang*), nab (*informal*), nail (*informal*), nick (*slang, chiefly Brit.*), pinch (*informal*), run in (*slang*), seize, take, take prisoner **2.** appreciate, believe, comprehend, conceive, get the message, get the picture, grasp, imagine, know, perceive, realize, recognize, think, understand **3.** be afraid of, dread, fear
Antonyms (*sense 1*) discharge, free, let go, liberate, release (*sense 2*) be at cross-purposes, be unaware of, be unconscious of, get one's lines crossed, misapprehend, misconceive, miss, misunderstand

apprehension **1.** alarm, anxiety, apprehensiveness, concern, disquiet, doubt, dread, fear, foreboding, misgiving, mistrust, on pins and needles, premonition, suspicion, trepidation, unease, uneasiness, worry **2.** arrest, capture, catching, seizure, taking **3.** awareness, comprehension, grasp, intellect, intelligence, ken, knowledge, perception, understanding **4.** belief, concept, conception, conjecture, idea, impression, notion, opinion, sentiment, thought, view
Antonyms (*sense 1*) assurance, composure, confidence, nonchalance, serenity, unconcern (*sense 2*) discharge, liberation, release (*sense 3*) incomprehension

apprehensive afraid, alarmed, anxious, concerned, disquieted, doubtful, fearful, foreboding, mistrustful, nervous, neurotic, suspicious, twitchy (*informal*), uneasy, worried
Antonyms assured, at ease, composed, confident, nonchalant, unafraid

apprehensiveness alarm, anxiety, anxiousness, concern, disquietedness *or* disquietness, disquietude, doubtfulness, fear, fearfulness, foreboding, forebodingness, misgiving, mistrustfulness, nervousness, suspiciousness, trepidation, uneasiness, worry

apprentice beginner, learner, neophyte, novice, probationer, pupil, student, trainee, tyro
Antonyms ace (*informal*), adept, dab hand

(*Brit. informal*), expert, master, past master, pro

apprenticeship novitiate *or* noviciate, probation, studentship, traineeship

apprise acquaint, advise, communicate, enlighten, give notice, inform, make aware, make cognizant, notify, tell, warn

approach *verb* **1.** advance, catch up, come close, come near, come to, draw near, gain on, meet, move towards, near, push forward, reach **2.** appeal to, apply to, broach the matter with, make advances to, make a proposal to, make overtures to, sound out **3.** begin, begin work on, commence, embark on, enter upon, make a start, set about, undertake **4.** approximate, be comparable to, be like, come close to, come near to, compare with, resemble *~noun* **5.** access, advance, advent, arrival, avenue, coming, drawing near, entrance, nearing, passage, road, way **6.** approximation, likeness, semblance **7.** *often plural* advance, appeal, application, invitation, offer, overture, proposal, proposition **8.** attitude, course, manner, means, method, mode, modus operandi, procedure, style, technique, way

approachability **1.** accessibility, attainability, openness **2.** affability, congeniality, conversableness, cordiality, expansiveness, friendliness, sociability

Antonyms (*sense 1*) inaccessibility, remoteness (*sense 2*) aloofness, chilliness, coolness, detachment, distance, frigidity, frostiness, remoteness, reservedness, standoffishness, unaffability, uncongeniality, unexpansiveness, unfriendliness, unsociability, withdrawnness

approachable **1.** accessible, attainable, come-at-able (*informal*), get-at-able (*informal*), reachable **2.** affable, congenial, cordial, friendly, open, sociable

Antonyms (*sense 1*) inaccessible, out of reach, out-of-the-way, remote, un-get-at-able (*informal*), unreachable (*sense 2*) aloof, chilly, cold as ice, cool, distant, frigid, remote, reserved, standoffish, unfriendly, unsociable, withdrawn

approbation acceptance, acclaim, applause, approval, assent, commendation, congratulation, encouragement, endorsement, favour, laudation, praise, ratification, recognition, sanction, support

Antonyms blame, censure, condemnation, disapprobation, disapproval, disfavour, dislike, displeasure, dissatisfaction, reproof, stricture

approbatory accepting, acclamatory, applauding, approving, commendatory, congratulatory, encouraging, favourable, laudatory, supportive

appropriate *adjective* **1.** adapted, applicable, apposite, appurtenant, apropos, apt, becoming, befitting, belonging, congruous, correct, felicitous, fit, fitting, germane, meet (*archaic*), opportune, pertinent, proper, relevant, right, seemly, suitable, to the point, to the purpose, well-suited, well-timed *~verb* **2.** allocate, allot, apportion, assign, devote, earmark, set apart **3.** annex, arrogate, assume, commandeer, confiscate, expropriate, impound, pre-empt, seize, take, take over, take possession of, usurp **4.** embezzle, filch, misappropriate, pilfer, pocket, steal

Antonyms *adjective* improper, inappropriate, incompatible, incorrect, inopportune, irrelevant, unfitting, unsuitable, untimely *~verb* cede, donate, give, relinquish, withhold

appropriateness applicability, appositeness, aptness, becomingness, congruousness, correctness, felicitousness, felicity, fitness, fittingness, germaneness, opportuneness, pertinence, properness, relevance, rightness, seemliness, suitability, timeliness, well-suitedness

appropriation **1.** allocation, allotment, apportionment, assignment, earmarking, setting apart **2.** annexation, arrogation, assumption, commandeering, confiscation, expropriation, impoundment, pre-emption, seizure, takeover, taking, usurpation

approval **1.** acquiescence, agreement, assent, authorization, blessing, compliance, concurrence, confirmation, consent, countenance, endorsement, imprimatur, leave, licence, mandate, O.K. *or* okay (*informal*), permission, ratification, recommendation, sanction, the go-ahead (*informal*), the green light, validation **2.** acclaim, admiration, applause, appreciation, approbation, Brownie points, commendation, esteem, favour, good opinion, liking, praise, regard, respect

Antonyms denigration, disapproval, dislike, disparagement, displeasure, dissatisfaction, objection

approve **1.** acclaim, admire, applaud, appreciate, be pleased with, commend, esteem, favour, have a good opinion of, like, praise, regard highly, respect, think highly of **2.** accede to, accept, advocate, agree to, allow, assent to, authorize, bless, concur in, confirm, consent to, countenance, endorse, give the go-ahead (*informal*), give the green light, go along with, mandate, O.K. *or* okay (*informal*), pass, permit, ratify, recommend, sanction, second, subscribe to, uphold, validate

Antonyms (*sense 1*) blame, censure, condemn, deplore, deprecate, disapprove, dislike, find unacceptable, frown on, look down one's nose at (*informal*), object to, take exception to (*sense 2*) disallow, discountenance, veto

approving acclamatory, admiring, applauding, appreciative, commendatory, favourable, respectful

approximate *adjective* **1.** almost accurate, almost exact, close, near **2.** estimated, inexact, loose, rough **3.** analogous, close, comparable, like, near, relative, similar, verging on **4.** adjacent, bordering, close together, contiguous, near, nearby, neighbouring *~verb* **5.** approach, border on, come close, come near, reach, resemble, touch, verge on

Antonyms *adjective* (*senses 1 & 2*) accurate, correct, definite, exact, precise, specific

approximately about, almost, around, circa (*used with dates*), close to, generally, in the neighbourhood of, in the region of, in the vicinity of, just about, loosely, more or less, nearly, not far off, relatively, roughly

approximation **1.** ballpark estimate (*informal*), ballpark figure (*informal*), conjecture, estimate, estimation, guess, guesswork, rough calculation, rough idea **2.** approach, correspondence, likeness, resemblance, semblance

appurtenance **1.** accessory, accompaniment, adjunct, annexe, appendage, appurtenant, attachment, auxiliary, concomitant, incidental, piece of equipment, subordinate, subsidiary, supplement **2.** *plural* accessories, accompaniments, accoutrements, appendages, equipment, impedimenta, paraphernalia, trappings

appurtenant accessory, appertaining, applicable, appropriate, belonging, concerned, connected, germane, incidental, pertaining, pertinent, proper, related, relating, relevant

a priori **1.** deduced, deductive, from cause to effect, inferential **2.** conjectural, postulated, postulational, presumptive, self-evident, suppositional, theoretical

apron pinafore, pinny (*informal*)

apropos *adjective* **1.** applicable, apposite, appropriate, apt, befitting, belonging, correct, fit, fitting, germane, meet (*archaic*), opportune, pertinent, proper, related, relevant, right, seemly, suitable, to the point, to the purpose *~adverb* **2.** appropriately, aptly, opportunely, pertinently, relevantly, suitably, timely, to the point, to the purpose **3.** by the bye, by the way, incidentally, in passing, parenthetically, while on the subject

apropos of *preposition* in respect of, on the subject of, re, regarding, respecting, with reference to, with regard to, with respect to

apt **1.** applicable, apposite, appropriate, apropos, befitting, correct, fit, fitting, germane, meet (*archaic*), pertinent, proper, relevant, seemly, suitable, timely, to the point, to the purpose **2.** disposed, given, inclined, liable, likely, of a mind, prone, ready **3.** astute, bright, clever, expert, gifted, ingenious, intelligent, prompt, quick, sharp, skilful, smart, talented, teachable

Antonyms (*sense 1*) ill-fitted, ill-suited, ill-timed, improper, inapplicable, inapposite, inappropriate, infelicitous, inopportune, irrelevant, unsuitable, untimely (*sense 3*) awkward, clumsy, dull, gauche, incompetent, inept, inexpert, maladroit, slow, stupid

aptitude **1.** bent, disposition, inclination, leaning, predilection, proclivity, proneness, propensity, tendency **2.** ability, aptness, capability, capacity, cleverness, faculty, flair, gift, giftedness, intelligence, knack, proficiency, quickness, talent **3.** applicability, appositeness, appropriateness, fitness, relevance, suitability, suitableness

aptness **1.** applicability, appositeness, appropriateness, becomingness, congruousness, correctness, felicitousness, felicity, fitness, fittingness, germaneness, opportuneness, pertinence, properness, relevance, rightness, seemliness, suitability, timeliness, well-suitedness **2.** aptitude, bent, disposition, inclination, leaning, liability, likelihood, likeliness, predilection, proclivity, proneness, propensity, readiness, tendency **3.** ability, capability, capacity, cleverness, faculty, fitness, flair, gift, giftedness, intelligence, knack, proficiency, quickness, suitability, talent

If the cap fits, wear it

arable cultivable, farmable, fecund, fertile, fruitful, ploughable, productive, tillable

arbiter **1.** adjudicator, arbitrator, judge, referee, umpire **2.** authority, controller, dictator, expert, governor, lord, master, pundit, ruler

arbitrariness **1.** capriciousness, fancifulness, inconsistency, randomness, subjectivity, unreasonableness, whimsicality, wilfulness **2.** absoluteness, despotism, dictatorialness, dogmatism, domineeringness, high-handedness, imperiousness, magisterialness, overbearingness, peremptoriness, summariness, tyrannicalness, tyrannousness, tyranny, uncontrolledness, unlimitedness, unrestrainedness

arbitrary **1.** capricious, chance, discretionary, erratic, fanciful, inconsistent, optional, personal, random, subjective, unreasonable, whimsical, wilful **2.** absolute, autocratic, despotic, dictatorial, dogmatic, domineering, high-handed, imperious, magisterial, overbearing, peremptory, summary, tyrannical, tyrannous, uncontrolled, unlimited, unrestrained

Antonyms (*sense 1*) consistent, judicious, logical, objective, rational, reasonable, reasoned, sensible, sound

arbitrate adjudge, adjudicate, decide, determine, judge, mediate, pass judgment, referee, settle, sit in judgment, umpire

arbitration adjudication, arbitrament, decision, determination, judgment, settlement

arbitrator adjudicator, arbiter, judge, referee, umpire

arc arch, bend, bow, crescent, curve, half-moon

arcane cabbalistic, esoteric, hidden, mysterious, occult, recondite, secret

arch[1] *noun* 1. archway, curve, dome, span, vault 2. arc, bend, bow, curvature, curve, hump, semicircle *~verb* 3. arc, bend, bow, bridge, curve, embow, span

arch[2] *adjective* 1. accomplished, chief, consummate, expert, finished, first, foremost, greatest, head, highest, lead, leading, main, major, master, pre-eminent, primary, principal, top 2. artful, frolicsome, knowing, mischievous, pert, playful, roguish, saucy, sly, waggish, wily

archaeology prehistory, protohistory

Archaeological periods

Acheulean *or* Acheulian	Levalloisian *or* Levallois
Asturian	Magdalenian
Aurignacian	Mesolithic
Azilian	Minoan
Bronze Age	Mousterian
chalcolithic	Mycenaean
Châtelperronian	Neo-Babylonian
Eneolithic	Neolithic *or* New Stone Age
Gravettian	Old Babylonian
Helladic	Palaeolithic *or* Old Stone Age
Ice age	Solutrean
Iron Age	
La Tène	

Archaeological terms

acropolis	graffito
alignment	henge
arcade	hillfort
archaeomagnetism *or* archeomagnetism	hogback
barrow	hut circle
baulk	larnax
bifacial	ley line
blade	microlith
bogman	megalith
bracteate	mound
burin	neolith
cairn	obelisk
callais	palmette
cartouch *or* cartouche	palstave
caveman	patella
celt	pylon
cirque	radiocarbon dating
cist *or* kist	retouch
clovis point	robber trench
core	sondage
cromlech	souterrain
cross-dating	stela *or* stele
dolmen	stone circle
earthwork	stratigraphy
eolith	tribrach
flake	tumulus
flint	vallum

archaic ancient, antiquated, antique, behind the times, bygone, obsolete, old, olden (*archaic*), old-fashioned, old hat, outmoded, out of date, passé, primitive, superannuated
Antonyms contemporary, current, fresh, latest, modern, modish, new, newfangled, novel, present, recent, state-of-the-art, up-to-date, up-to-the-minute, with it (*informal*)

arched curved, domed, embowed, vaulted

archer bowman (*archaic*), toxophilite (*formal*)

archetypal, archetypical classic, exemplary, ideal, model, normal, original, paradigmatic, prototypal, prototypic *or* prototypical, standard

archetype classic, exemplar, form, ideal, model, norm, original, paradigm, pattern, prime example, prototype, standard

architect 1. designer, master builder, planner 2. author, contriver, creator, deviser, engineer, founder, instigator, inventor, maker, originator, planner, prime mover, shaper

> *architect: one who drafts a plan of your house, and plans a draft of your money*
> Ambrose Bierce *The Devil's Dictionary*

architecture 1. architectonics, building, construction, design, planning 2. construction, design, framework, make-up, structure, style

Architectural styles

Art Deco	Jacobean
Art Nouveau	Louis Quatorze
Baroque	Louis Quinze
Bauhaus	Louis Seize
brutalism	Louis Treize
Byzantine	Mannerist
churrigueresque *or* churrigueresco	moderne
classical	Moorish
colonial	Mudéjar
Composite	neoclassicist
Corinthian	new brutalism
Decorated	Norman
Doric	Palladian
Early Christian	perpendicular
Early English	postmodernist
Edwardian	Queen-Anne
Elizabethan	Regency
Empire	Renaissance
Federation (*Austral.*)	Rococo
Georgian	Roman
Gothic	Romanesque
Gothic Revival	Saxon
Greek Revival	transition *or* transitional
International Style *or* Modernist	Tudor
Ionic	Tuscan
	Victorian

Architectural features

abacus	ancon *or* ancone
accolade	annulet
acroter	anta
ambulatory	antefix
amphiprostyle	anthemion
amphistylar	apophyge *or* hy~

pophyge
apteral
arcature
architrave
archivolt
arcuation
astragal
atlas (*plural* atlantes) *or* telamon
atrium
attic
baguette *or* baguet
ballflower
band
banderole, banderol, *or* bannerol
barrel vault
base
bay window
bead
beak
bezant, bezzant *or* byzant
billet
bolection *or* bilection
bow
bow window
brattishing
calotte
capital, chapiter *or* cap
caryatid
cavetto
cella *or* naos
chaplet
cinquefoil
colonnade
column
columniation
compass window
concha *or* conch
congé
corbeil *or* corbeille
corbel *or* truss
corbie-step, corbel step *or* crow step
cordon, string course, belt course *or* table
cornice
corona
cove *or* coving
crenel *or* crenelle
crocket *or* crochet
cupola
curtail step
cushion
cusp
cuspidation
cyma
cymatium
dado
decastyle
dentil
die
dogtooth
drip
dripstone, label *or* hood mould
echinus
ectype
egg and dart, egg and tongue *or* egg and anchor
entablature
extrados
facet
fan
fanlight
fantail
fascia *or* facia
fascial *or* facial
fenestella
fenestra
festoon
finial
flute
flying buttress *or* arc-boutant
foil
French windows
frieze
frontispiece
frustum
gable
gable end
gable window
gadroon or godroon
gallery
gambrel
gargoyle
garret
gatehouse
gazebo
griffe
groin
gutta
haunch *or* hance
helicline
imperial
impost
intrados
keystone, quoin *or* headstone
lancet arch, Gothic arch *or* ogive
lancet window
lantern
leaded
long-and-short work
louvre
lucarne
meander
medallion
metope
modillion
moulding
mutule
neck
necking *or* gorgerin
newel
Norman arch *or* Ro~man arch
oeil-de-boeuf
ogee, ogee arch *or* talon
ogive
onion dome
oriel *or* oriel window
ovolo, quarter round *or* thumb
pace
pedestal
pediment
peristyle
perron
quad
poppyhead
quadrangle
quatrefoil
quirk
quoin, coign *or* coigne
reed
reeding
reglet
relief
respond
return
reveal
rose window
rotunda
saddle roof
sash window
scotia
scrollwork
semidome
shaft
shafting
skew arch
skylight
spandrel *or* spandril
spire
springer
squinch
squint *or* hagioscope
steeple
stele *or* stela
stoa
strap work
strigil
taenia *or (U.S.)* tenia
tambour
term, terminal *or* ter~minus
torus *or* tore
transept
trefoil
tribune
triforium
triglyph
trumeau
tympanum *or* tympan
underpitch vault
veranda *or* verandah
verge
vignette
volute *or* helix
web
whispering gallery

Architectural terms

abutment *or* abuttal
architectonic
architectonics
architectural
astylar
bolster
bracket
cinquecento
colossal *or* giant
cradling
crenellate *or (U.S.)* crenelate
denticulate
diastyle
diminish
dipteral
discharge
drum
engaged
fenestrated
filler
flamboyant
floriated *or* floreated
florid
foliated
foliation
galilee
galleria
hexastyle
hip
hypostyle
imbricate *or* imbri~cated
intercolumniation
invert
joggle post *or* king post
lanceted
lierne
lintel *or* summer
listed
loggia

module
Moresque
naos
order
polychromy
postiche
pulvinate *or* pulvinated
queen post
rampant
rendering
respond
return
rhythm
rusticate
Saracen
shaft
shafting
soffit
springing, spring, springing line *or* springing point
stilted
storey
stria
stringer, string *or* string course
stylobate
subbase
summer *or* summer tree
supercolumnar
surbase
tailpiece *or* tail beam
trabeate *or* trabeated
tympanic
underpitch vault

Architects
Alvar Aalto [Finnish]
Sir (Leslie) Patrick Abercrombie [English]
James Adam [Scottish]
Robert Adam [Scottish]
Leon Battista Alberti [Italian]
Sir Charles Barry [English]
Frédéric August Bartholdi [French]
Peter Behrens [German]
Gian Lorenzo Bernini [Italian]
Francesco Borromini [Italian]
Donato Bramante [Italian]
Marcel Lajos Breuer [Hungarian-U.S.]
Filippo Brunelleschi [Italian]
William Butterfield [English]
Callicrates [Greek]
Felix Candela [Mexican]
Sir Hugh (Maxwell) Casson [English]
Daedalus [Greek]
Philibert Delorme *or* de l'Orme [French]
Johann Bernhard Fischer von Erlach [Austrian]
Sir Norman Foster [English]
(Richard) Buckminster Fuller [U.S.]
Jacques-Ange Gabriel [French]
Antonio Gaudí [Spanish]
Sir Frederick Gibberd [English]
James Gibbs [English]
Giulio Romano [Italian]
Walter Gropius [German]
Nicholas Hawksmoor [English]
Henry Holland [English]
Victor Horta [Belgian]
Ictinus [Greek]
Imhotep [Egyptian]
Arne Jacobsen [Danish]
Inigo Jones [English]
Louis I(sadore) Kahn [U.S.]
William Kent [English]
Sir Denys Lasdun [English]
Le Corbusier [French]
Leonardo da Vinci [Italian]
Adolf Loos [Austrian]
Sir Edwin Lutyens [English]
Charles Rennie Mackintosh [Scottish]
François Mansart [French]
Jules Hardouin Mansart [French]
Michelangelo [Italian]
Michelozzo [Italian]
Ludwig Mies van der Rohe [German-U.S.]
John Nash [English]
Pier Luigi Nervi [Italian]
Johann Balthasar Neumann [German]
Oscar Niemeyer [Brazilian]
Andrea Orcagna [Italian]
Andrea Palladio [Italian]
Sir Joseph Paxton [English]
I(eoh) M(ing) Pei [Chinese-U.S.]
Baldassare Tommaso Peruzzi [Italian]
Pietro da Cortona [Italian]
Giambattista Piranesi [Italian]
Andrea Pisano [Italian]
Augustus (Welby Northmore) Pugin [English]
Raphael [Italian]
Sir Richard Rogers [English]
Eero Saarinen [Finnish-U.S.]
Michele Sanmicheli [Italian]
Scopas [Greek]
Sir George Gilbert Scott [English]
Sir Giles Gilbert Scott [English]
Sebastiano Serlio [Italian]
Richard Norman Shaw [English]
Sir John Soane [English]
Sir Basil (Unwin) Spence [Scottish]
Louis (Henri) Sullivan [U.S.]
Kenzo Tange [Japanese]
(John) Quinlan Terry [English]
Sir John Vanbrugh [English]
Henry van de Velde [Belgian]
Giorgio Vasari [Italian]
Robert Venturi [U.S.]
Giacomo Barozzi da Vignola [Italian]
Eugène Emmanuel Viollet-le-Duc [French]
Marcus Vitruvius Pollio [Roman]
Charles (Francis Annesley) Voysey [English]
Otto Wagner [Austrian]
Alfred Waterhouse [English]
Sir Aston Webb [English]
John Wood [English]
Sir Christopher Wren [English]
Frank Lloyd Wright [U.S.]
James Wyatt [English]
Minoru Yamasaki [U.S.]

Architecture in general is frozen music
Friedrich von Schelling *Philosophie der Kunst*

Architecture is the art of how to waste space
Philip Johnson *New York Times*

Architecture, of all the arts, is the one which acts the most slowly, but the most surely, on the soul
Ernest Dimnet *What We Live By*

archives 1. annals, chronicles, documents, papers, records, registers, rolls 2. museum, record office, registry, repository

archness 1. superiority 2. artfulness, canniness, cunning, cuteness, frolicsomeness, guile, impishness, knowingness, mischievousness, pert~

ness, playfulness, roguishness, sauciness, sly~ness, waggishness, wiliness

arctic 1. far-northern, hyperborean, polar 2. *in~formal* chilly, cold, cold as ice, freezing, frigid, frost-bound, frosty, frozen, gelid, glacial, icy

ardent ablaze, avid, eager, enthusiastic, fer~vent, fervid, fierce, fiery, flaming, hot, hot-blooded, impassioned, intense, keen, keen as mustard, lusty, passionate, spirited, vehe~ment, warm, warm-blooded, zealous
Antonyms apathetic, cold, cool, frigid, impas~sive, indifferent, lukewarm, unenthusiastic, unloving

ardour avidity, devotion, eagerness, earnest~ness, enthusiasm, feeling, fervour, fierceness, fire, heat, intensity, keenness, passion, spirit, vehemence, warmth, zeal

arduous backbreaking, burdensome, difficult, exhausting, fatiguing, formidable, gruelling, hard, harsh, heavy, laborious, onerous, pain~ful, punishing, rigorous, severe, steep, strenu~ous, taxing, tiring, toilsome, tough, trouble~some, trying
Antonyms child's play (*informal*), easy, easy-peasy (*slang*), effortless, facile, light, no both~er, no trouble, painless, simple, undemanding

area 1. district, domain, locality, neck of the woods (*informal*), neighbourhood, patch, plot, realm, region, sector, sphere, stretch, terri~tory, tract, turf (*U.S. slang*), zone 2. ambit, breadth, compass, expanse, extent, range, scope, size, width 3. arena, department, do~main, field, province, realm, sphere, territory 4. part, portion, section, sector 5. sunken space, yard

arena 1. amphitheatre, bowl, coliseum, field, ground, park (*U.S. & Canad.*), ring, stadium, stage 2. area, battlefield, battleground, do~main, field, field of conflict, lists, province, realm, scene, scope, sector, sphere, territory, theatre

argot cant, dialect, idiom, jargon, lingo (*infor~mal*), parlance, patois, patter, slang, vernacu~lar

arguably 1. contestably, controversially, con~trovertibly, debatably, deniably, disputably, dubitably, questionably, refutably 2. conceiv~ably, feasibly, plausibly, possibly, potentially

argue 1. altercate, bandy words, be at sixes and sevens, bicker, cross swords, disagree, dispute, fall out (*informal*), feud, fight, fight like cat and dog, go at it hammer and tongs, have an argument, quarrel, squabble, wrangle 2. assert, claim, contend, controvert, debate, discuss, dispute, expostulate, hold, maintain, plead, question, reason, remonstrate 3. con~vince, persuade, prevail upon, talk into, talk round 4. demonstrate, denote, display, evince, exhibit, imply, indicate, manifest, point to, show, suggest

argument 1. altercation, barney (*informal*), bickering, clash, controversy, difference of opinion, disagreement, dispute, falling out (*informal*), feud, fight, quarrel, row, squabble, wrangle 2. assertion, claim, contention, de~bate, discussion, dispute, expostulation, plea, pleading, questioning, remonstrance, remon~stration 3. argumentation, case, defence, dia~lectic, ground(s), line of reasoning, logic, po~lemic, reason, reasoning 4. abstract, gist, out~line, plot, story, story line, subject, summary, synopsis, theme
Antonyms (*senses 1 & 2*) accord, agreement, concurrence

Argument seldom convinces anyone contrary to his inclinations
Thomas Fuller *Gnomologia*

The aim of argument, or of discussion, should not be victory, but progress
Joseph Joubert *Pensées*

argumentative 1. belligerent, combative, con~tentious, contrary, disputatious, litigious, opinionated, quarrelsome 2. contentious, con~troversial, disputed, polemic
Antonyms (*sense 1*) accommodating, ame~nable, complaisant, compliant, conciliatory, easy-going, obliging

arid 1. barren, desert, dried up, dry, moisture~less, parched, sterile, torrid, waterless 2. as dry as dust, boring, colourless, dreary, dry, dull, flat, jejune, lifeless, spiritless, tedious, tiresome, uninspired, uninteresting, vapid
Antonyms (*sense 1*) fertile, fruitful, lush, rich, verdant (*sense 2*) exciting, interesting, lively, sexy (*informal*), spirited, stimulating, viva~cious

aridity, aridness 1. barrenness, dryness, moisturelessness, parchedness, sterility, waterlessness 2. boredom, colourlessness, dreariness, dryness, dullness, flatness, jejune~ness, jejunity, lifelessness, spiritlessness, te~diousness, tedium, uninspiredness, uninter~estingness, vapidity, vapidness

aright accurately, appropriately, aptly, correct~ly, duly, exactly, fitly, in due order, justly, properly, rightly, suitably, truly, without error

arise 1. appear, begin, come into being, come to light, commence, crop up (*informal*), emanate, emerge, ensue, follow, happen, issue, occur, originate, proceed, result, set in, spring, start, stem 2. get to one's feet, get up, go up, rise, stand up, wake up 3. ascend, climb, lift, mount, move upward, rise, soar, tower

aristocracy body of nobles, elite, gentry, *haut monde*, nobility, noblesse (*literary*), patricians, patriciate, peerage, ruling class, upper class, upper crust (*informal*)

Antonyms commoners, common people, hoi polloi, lower classes, masses, plebeians, plebs, proles (*derogatory slang, chiefly Brit.*), proletariat, working classes

Democracy means government by the uneducated, while aristocracy means government by the badly educated

G.K. Chesterton *New York Times*

An aristocracy in a republic is like a chicken whose head has been cut off; it may run about in a lively way, but in fact it is dead

Nancy Mitford *Noblesse Oblige*

aristocrat aristo (*informal*), childe (*archaic*), grandee, lady, lord, noble, nobleman, noblewoman, patrician, peer, peeress

aristocratic **1.** blue-blooded, elite, gentle (*archaic*), gentlemanly, highborn, lordly, noble, patrician, titled, upper-class, well-born **2.** courtly, dignified, elegant, fine, haughty, polished, refined, snobbish, stylish, well-bred
Antonyms (*sense 1*) common, lower-class, plebeian, proletarian, working-class (*sense 2*) boorish, coarse, common, crass, crude, ill-bred, uncouth, unrefined, vulgar

arm[1] *noun* **1.** appendage, limb, upper limb **2.** bough, branch, department, detachment, division, extension, offshoot, projection, section, sector **3.** branch, channel, estuary, firth, inlet, sound, strait, tributary **4.** authority, command, force, might, potency, power, strength, sway

arm[2] *verb* **1.** *especially with weapons* accoutre, array, deck out, equip, furnish, issue with, outfit, provide, rig, supply **2.** mobilize, muster forces, prepare for war, take up arms **3.** brace, equip, forearm, fortify, gird one's loins, guard, make ready, outfit, prepare, prime, protect, strengthen

armada fleet, flotilla, navy, squadron

armaments ammunition, arms, guns, materiel, munitions, ordnance, weaponry, weapons

armed accoutred, arrayed, carrying weapons, equipped, fitted out, forearmed, fortified, furnished, girded, guarded, in arms, prepared, primed, protected, provided, ready, rigged out, strengthened, supplied, under arms

armistice ceasefire, peace, suspension of hostilities, truce

armour armour plate, covering, protection, sheathing, shield

Armour

armet
basinet *or* bascinet
breastplate
camail
chamfrain, chamfron *or* chanfron
coat-of-mail
corselet *or* corslet
couter
crinet
cuirass
cuisse *or* cuish
culet
gauntlet
gorget
greave
gusset
helmet
jack
jambeau, jambart *or* jamber
jupon
lance rest
mail
nosepiece
pavloron
poleyn
roundel
sabaton
sword belt
tasset, tasse *or* tace
umbo
vambrace
ventail
visor *or* vizor

armoured armour-plated, bombproof, bulletproof, ironclad, mailed, protected, steel-plated

armoury ammunition dump, arms depot, arsenal, magazine, ordnance depot

arms **1.** armaments, firearms, guns, instruments of war, ordnance, weaponry, weapons **2.** blazonry, crest, escutcheon, heraldry, insignia

army **1.** armed force, host (*archaic*), land forces, legions, military, military force, soldiers, soldiery, troops **2.** *figurative* array, horde, host, multitude, pack, swarm, throng, vast number

I don't know what effect these men will have upon the enemy, but, by God, they terrify me

Duke of Wellington

An army marches on its stomach

aroma bouquet, fragrance, odour, perfume, redolence, savour, scent, smell

aromatic balmy, fragrant, odoriferous, perfumed, pungent, redolent, savoury, spicy, sweet-scented, sweet-smelling
Antonyms acrid, bad-smelling, fetid, foul, foul-smelling, malodorous, niffy (*Brit. slang*), noisome, offensive, olid, rank, reeking, smelly, stinking, whiffy (*Brit. slang*)

around *preposition* **1.** about, encircling, enclosing, encompassing, environing, on all sides of, on every side of, surrounding **2.** about, approximately, circa (*used with dates*), roughly ~*adverb* **3.** about, all over, everywhere, here and there, in all directions, on all sides, throughout, to and fro **4.** at hand, close, close at hand, close by, near, nearby, nigh (*archaic or dialect*)

arousal agitation, animation, awakening, enlivenment, excitement, exhilaration, incitement, inflammation, movement, provocation, reaction, response, rousedness, stimulation

arouse agitate, animate, awaken, call forth, enliven, excite, foment, foster, goad, incite, inflame, instigate, kindle, move, prod, provoke, quicken, rouse, sharpen, spark, spur, stimulate, stir up, summon up, waken, wake up, warm, whet, whip up
Antonyms allay, alleviate, assuage, calm, dampen, dull, end, lull, pacify, quell, quench, still

arraign accuse, call to account, charge, com~

plain about, denounce, impeach, incriminate, indict, prosecute, take to task

arraignment accusation, charge, complaint, denunciation, impeachment, incrimination, indictment, prosecution

arrange 1. align, array, class, classify, dispose, file, form, group, line up, marshal, order, organize, position, put in order, range, rank, sequence, set out, sort, sort out (*informal*), systematize, tidy 2. adjust, agree to, come to terms, compromise, construct, contrive, determine, devise, fix up, organize, plan, prepare, project, schedule, settle 3. adapt, instrument, orchestrate, score

Antonyms (*senses 1 & 2*) disarrange, disorganize, disturb, mess up, scatter

arrangement 1. alignment, array, classification, design, display, disposition, form, grouping, line-up, marshalling, order, ordering, organization, ranging, rank, setup (*informal*), structure, system 2. *often plural* adjustment, agreement, compact, compromise, construction, deal, devising, organization, plan, planning, preparation, provision, schedule, settlement, terms 3. adaptation, instrumentation, interpretation, orchestration, score, version

arrant absolute, atrocious, blatant, complete, deep-dyed (*usually derogatory*), downright, egregious, extreme, flagrant, gross, infamous, monstrous, notorious, out-and-out, outright, rank, thorough, thoroughgoing, undisguised, unmitigated, utter, vile

array *noun* 1. arrangement, collection, display, disposition, exhibition, formation, line-up, marshalling, muster, order, parade, show, supply 2. *poetic* apparel, attire, clothes, dress, finery, garb, garments, raiment (*archaic or poetic*), regalia, schmutter (*slang*), threads (*slang*) *~verb* 3. align, arrange, display, dispose, draw up, exhibit, form up, group, line up, marshal, muster, order, parade, place in order, range, sequence, set in line (*Military*), show 4. accoutre, adorn, apparel (*archaic*), attire, bedeck, caparison, clothe, deck, decorate, dress, equip, festoon, fit out, garb, get ready, outfit, robe, supply, wrap

arrest *verb* 1. apprehend, bust (*informal*), capture, catch, collar (*informal*), detain, feel one's collar (*slang*), lay hold of, lift (*slang*), nab (*informal*), nail (*informal*), nick (*slang, chiefly Brit.*), pinch (*informal*), run in (*slang*), seize, take, take into custody, take prisoner 2. block, check, delay, end, halt, hinder, hold, inhibit, interrupt, obstruct, restrain, retard, slow, stall, stay, stop, suppress 3. absorb, catch, engage, engross, fascinate, grip, hold, intrigue, occupy *~noun* 4. apprehension, bust (*informal*), capture, cop (*slang*), detention, seizure 5. blockage, check, delay, end, halt, hindrance, inhibition, interruption, obstruction, restraint, stalling, stay, stoppage, suppression

Antonyms *verb* (*sense 1*) free, let go, release, set free (*sense 2*) accelerate, encourage, precipitate, promote, quicken, speed up *~noun* (*sense 4*) freeing, release (*sense 5*) acceleration, encouragement, precipitation, promotion, quickening

arresting conspicuous, dramatic, engaging, extraordinary, impressive, noticeable, outstanding, remarkable, salient, striking, stunning, surprising

Antonyms inconspicuous, unimpressive, unnoticeable, unremarkable

arrival 1. advent, appearance, arriving, coming, entrance, happening, occurrence, taking place 2. arriver, caller, comer, entrant, incomer, newcomer, visitant, visitor

arrive 1. appear, attain, befall, come, enter, get to, happen, occur, reach, show up (*informal*), take place, turn up 2. *informal* achieve recognition, become famous, make good, make it (*informal*), make one's mark (*informal*), make the grade (*informal*), reach the top, succeed

Antonyms (*sense 1*) depart, disappear, exit, go, go away, leave, pack one's bags (*informal*), retire, take (one's) leave, vanish, withdraw

arriviste adventurer *or* adventuress, climber, parvenu *or* parvenue, social climber, status seeker, upstart, would-be

arrogance bluster, conceit, conceitedness, contemptuousness, disdainfulness, haughtiness, hauteur, high-handedness, imperiousness, insolence, loftiness, lordliness, overweeningness, pomposity, pompousness, presumption, pretension, pretentiousness, pride, scornfulness, superciliousness, swagger, uppishness (*Brit. informal*)

Antonyms bashfulness, diffidence, humility, meekness, modesty, politeness, shyness

arrogant assuming, blustering, conceited, contemptuous, disdainful, haughty, high and mighty (*informal*), high-handed, imperious, insolent, looking down one's nose at, lordly, overbearing, overweening, pompous, presumptuous, pretentious, proud, scornful, supercilious, swaggering, too big for one's boots *or* breeches, turning up one's nose at, uppish (*Brit. informal*)

Antonyms bashful, deferential, diffident, humble, modest, polite, servile, shy, unassuming

arrogate appropriate, assume, claim unduly, commandeer, demand, expropriate, presume, seize, usurp

arrogation appropriation, assumption, commandeering, demand, expropriation, presumption, seizure, usurpation

arrow 1. bolt, dart, flight, quarrel, reed (*archaic*), shaft (*archaic*) 2. indicator, pointer

arsenal ammunition dump, armoury, arms depot, magazine, ordnance depot, stock, stockpile, store, storehouse, supply

art 1. adroitness, aptitude, artifice (*archaic*), artistry, craft, craftsmanship, dexterity, expertise, facility, ingenuity, knack, knowledge, mastery, method, profession, skill, trade, virtuosity 2. artfulness, artifice, astuteness, craftiness, cunning, deceit, duplicity, guile, trickery, wiliness

Art styles and movements

abstract expressionism	minimal art
abstractionism	modernism
Art Deco	Nabis
Arte Povera	naturalism
Art Nouveau	Nazarene
Barbizon School	neoclassicism
baroque	neoimpressionism
Der Blaue Reiter	neoplasticism
Brücke	op art
classicism	pointillism
conceptual art	pop art
constructivism	postimpressionism
cubism	postmodernism
Dada *or* Dadaism	Pre-Raphaelite
De Stijl	realism
divisionism	rococo
expressionism	Romanesque
Fauvism	romanticism
futurism	Suprematism
Gothic	surrealism
Impressionism	symbolism
Jugendstil	synthetism
mannerism	ukiyo-e
	vorticism

Art equipment

acrylic	linseed oil
airbrush	oil paint
brush	paint
canvas	paintbox
chalk	paintbrush
charcoal	palette
crayon	palette knife
drawing paper	pastel
easel	pencil
fixative	sketchbook
glaze	spatula
ground	spray gun
ink	varnish
lay figure	watercolour

Art is a jealous mistress
Ralph Waldo Emerson *Conduct of Life*

All art constantly aspires towards the condition of music
Walter Pater *Studies in the History of the Renaissance*

Art is a lie that makes us realise the truth
Pablo Picasso

In art the best is good enough
Johann Wolfgang von Goethe *Italienische Reise*

Life is short, the art long
Hippocrates *Aphorisms*

Art does not reproduce the visible; rather, it makes visible
Paul Klee *Inward Vision*

Art is a revolt against fate
André Malraux *Les Voix du silence*

Art is...pattern informed by sensibility
Herbert Read *The Meaning of Art*

art for art's sake
Victor Cousin

It's clever, but is it Art?
Rudyard Kipling *The Conundrum of the Workshops*

Art is meant to disturb. Science reassures
Georges Braque *Pensées sur l'art*

a product of the untalented, sold by the unprincipled to the utterly bewildered
Al Capp (of abstract art)

Formerly, painting and sculpture were combined in the same work; the ancients painted their statues. The only present alliance between the two arts is that the modern painter chisels his patrons
Ambrose Bierce *The Devil's Dictionary*

artful adept, adroit, clever, crafty, cunning, deceitful, designing, dexterous, foxy, ingenious, intriguing, masterly, politic, proficient, resourceful, scheming, sharp, shrewd, skilful, sly, smart, subtle, tricky, wily
Antonyms artless, clumsy, frank, ingenuous, open, simple, straightforward, unadept, unskilled, untalented

article 1. commodity, item, object, piece, substance, thing, unit 2. composition, discourse, essay, feature, item, paper, piece, story, treatise 3. branch, clause, count, detail, division, head, heading, item, matter, paragraph, part, particular, passage, piece, point, portion, section

articulacy clarity, clearness, coherence, comprehensibility, comprehensibleness, eloquence, expressiveness, fluency, intelligibility, lucidity, meaningfulness, vocality
Antonyms dumbness, haltingness, hesitancy, incoherence, incomprehensibility, indistinctness, muteness, silence, speechlessness, stammering, stuttering, unclearness, unintelligibility, voicelessness

articulate *adjective* 1. clear, coherent, comprehensible, eloquent, expressive, fluent, intelligible, lucid, meaningful, understandable, vocal, well-spoken *~verb* 2. enounce, enunciate, express, pronounce, say, speak, state, talk, utter, verbalize, vocalize, voice 3. connect, couple, fit together, hinge, join, joint
Antonyms *adjective* dumb, faltering, halting, hesitant, incoherent, incomprehensible, indistinct, mumbled, mute, poorly-spoken, silent,

speechless, stammering, stuttering, tongue-tied, unclear, unintelligible, voiceless

articulation **1**. delivery, diction, enunciation, expression, pronunciation, saying, speaking, statement, talking, utterance, verbalization, vocalization, voicing **2**. connection, coupling, hinge, joint, jointing, juncture

artifice **1**. contrivance, device, dodge, expedient, hoax, machination, manoeuvre, ruse, stratagem, subterfuge, tactic, trick, wile **2**. artfulness, chicanery, craft, craftiness, cunning, deception, duplicity, guile, scheming, slyness, trickery **3**. adroitness, cleverness, deftness, facility, finesse, ingenuity, invention, inventiveness, skill

artificer **1**. artisan, craftsman, mechanic **2**. architect, builder, contriver, creator, designer, deviser, inventor, maker, originator

artificial **1**. man-made, manufactured, non-natural, plastic, synthetic **2**. bogus, counterfeit, ersatz, fake, imitation, mock, phoney *or* phony (*informal*), pseudo (*informal*), sham, simulated, specious, spurious **3**. affected, assumed, contrived, false, feigned, forced, hollow, insincere, meretricious, phoney *or* phony (*informal*), pretended, spurious, unnatural
Antonyms authentic, frank, genuine, honest, natural, sincere, true, unaffected

artillery battery, big guns, cannon, cannonry, gunnery, ordnance

artisan artificer, craftsman, handicraftsman, journeyman, mechanic, skilled workman, technician

artist artisan (*obsolete*), craftsman, creator, maker, master

Artists

Agostino di Duccio [Italian]
Josef Albers [German-U.S.]
Leon Battista Alberti [Italian]
Washington Allston [U.S.]
Lawrence Alma-Tadema [Dutch-English]
Albrecht Altdorfer [German]
Fra Angelico [Italian]
Pietro Annigoni [Italian]
Antonello da Messina [Italian]
Apelles [Greek]
Karel Appel [Dutch]
Aleksandr Porfiryevich Archipenko [Russian]
Giuseppe Arcimboldo [Italian]
Jean *or* Hans Arp [French]
Frank Auerbach [British-German]
Francis Bacon [Irish]
Leon Nikolayevich Bakst [Russian]
Balthus [Polish-French]
Frédéric August Bartholdi [French]
Fra Bartolommeo [Italian]
Max Beckmann [German]
Vanessa Bell [English]
Giovanni Bellini [Italian]
Thomas Hart Benton [U.S.]
Gian Lorenzo Bernini [Italian]
Peter Blake [British]
William Blake [English]
Umberto Boccioni [Italian]
David Bomberg [British]
Rosa Bonheur [French]
Pierre Bonnard [French]
Richard Parkes Bonnington [British]
Gutzon Borglum [U.S.]
Hieronymus Bosch [Dutch]
Sandro Botticelli [Italian]
Eugène Boudin [French]
Arthur Boyd [Australian]
Constantin Brancusi [Romanian]
Georges Braque [French]
Agnolo Bronzino [Italian]
Ford Madox Brown [British]
Jan Brueghel [Flemish]
Pieter Brueghel the Elder [Flemish]
Pieter Brueghel the Younger [Flemish]
Bernard Buffet [French]
Edward Burne-Jones [English]
Edward Burra [British]
Reg Butler [British]
Alexander Calder [U.S.]
Callimachus [Greek]
Robert Campin [Flemish]
Canaletto [Italian]
Antonio Canova [Italian]
Michelangelo Merisi da Caravaggio [Italian]
Anthony Caro [British]
Vittore Carpaccio [Italian]
Agostino Carracci [Italian]
Annibale Carracci [Italian]
Ludovico Carracci [Italian]
Mary Cassatt [U.S.]
Pietro Cavallini [Italian]
Benvenuto Cellini [Italian]
Lynn Chadwick [British]
Marc Chagall [Russian-French]
Philippe de Champaigne [French]
Jean-Baptiste Siméon Chardin [French]
Giovanni Cimabue [Italian]
Claude Lorrain [French]
François Clouet [French]
Jean Clouet [French]
John Constable [English]
John Copley [U.S.]
Jean Baptiste Camille Corot [French]
Antonio Allegri da Corregio [Italian]
Gustave Courbet [French]
David Cox [English]
Antoine Coypel [French]
Lucas Cranach [German]
Walter Crane [British]
John Crome [English]
Aelbert Cuyp *or* Kuyp [Dutch]
Paul Cézanne [French]
Richard Dadd [English]
Salvador Dali [Spanish]
Francis Danby [Irish]
Charles François Daubigny [French]
Honoré Daumier [French]
Jacques Louis David [French]
Peter de Wint [English]
Hilaire Germain

Edgar Degas [French]
Eugène Delacroix [French]
Paul Delaroche [French]
Robert Delaunay [French]
Paul Delvaux [Belgian]
Maurice Denis [French]
André Derain [French]
William Dobell [Australian]
Domenichino [Italian]
Domenico del Barbiere [Italian]
Donatello [Italian]
Gerrit Dou [Dutch]
George Russell Drysdale [Australian]
Jean Dubuffet [French]
Duccio di Buoninsegna [Italian]
Marcel Duchamp [French-U.S.]
Raoul Dufy [French]
Albrecht Dürer [German]
Thomas Eakins [U.S.]
El Greco [Greek-Spanish]
James Ensor [Belgian]
Jacob Epstein [British]
Max Ernst [German]
Henri Fantin-Latour [French]
John Flaxman [English]
Jean Fouquet [French]
Jean Honoré Fragonard [French]
Lucian Freud [British]
Caspar David Friedrich [German]
Roger Fry [English]
Henry Fuseli [Swiss]
Naum Gabo [Russian-U.S.]
Thomas Gainsborough [English]
Henri Gaudier-Brzeska [French]
Paul Gauguin [French]
Gentile da Fabriano [Italian]
Lorenzo Ghiberti [Italian]
Domenico Ghirlandaio [Italian]
Alberto Giacometti [Swiss]
Giambologna [Italian]
Grinling Gibbons [Dutch]
Gilbert (Proesch) and George (Passmore) [British]
Eric Gill [British]
Giorgione da Castelfranco [Italian]
Giotto di Bondone [Italian]
Giulio Romano [Italian]
Hugo van der Goes [Flemish]
Julio González [Spanish]
Arshile Gorky [U.S.]
Francisco de Goya [Spanish]
Jan van Goyen [Dutch]
Duncan Grant [British]
Jean Baptiste Greuze [French]
Juan Gris [Spanish]
Antoine Jean Gros [French]
George Grosz [German-U.S.]
Grünewald [German]
Francesco Guardi [Italian]
François Gérard [French]
Théodore Géricault [French]
Frans Hals [Dutch]
Richard Hamilton [British]
Ando Hiroshige [Japanese]
Meindert Hobbema [Dutch]
David Hockney [English]
Hans Hofmann [German-U.S.]
William Hogarth [English]
Katsushika Hokusai [Japanese]
Hans Holbein [German]
Winslow Homer [U.S.]
Pieter de Hooch *or* Hoogh [Dutch]
Edward Hopper [U.S.]
Jean Antoine Houdon [French]
William Holman Hunt [English]
Jean Auguste Dominique Ingres [French]
Augustus John [British]
Gwen John [British]
Jasper Johns [U.S.]
Johan Barthold Jongkind [Dutch]
Jacob Jordaens [Flemish]
Wassily Kandinsky [Russian]
Angelica Kauffmann [Swiss]
Ernst Ludwig Kirchner [German]
Ron B. Kitaj [U.S.]
Paul Klee [Swiss]
Gustav Klimt [Austrian]
Franz Kline [U.S.]
Godfrey Kneller [German-English]
Laura Knight [British]
Oscar Kokoschka [Austrian]
Willem de Kooning [Dutch-U.S.]
Leon Kossoff [British]
Georges de La Tour [French]
Edwin Landseer [English]
Thomas Lawrence [English]
Charles Lebrun [French]
Wilhelm Lehmbruck [German]
Frederic Leighton [British]
Peter Lely [Dutch-English]
Leonardo da Vinci [Italian]
Wyndham Lewis [British]
Roy Lichtenstein [U.S.]
Jacques Lipchitz [Lithuanian-U.S.]
Filippino Lippi [Italian]
L(awrence) S(tephen) Lowry [English]
Lysippus [Greek]
Fernand Léger [French]
Jan Mabuse [Flemish]
Charles Rennie Mackintosh [Scottish]
René Magritte [Belgian]
Aristide Maillol [French]
Kasimir Severinovich Malevich [Russian]
Edouard Manet [French]
Andrea Mantegna [Italian]
Franz Marc [German]
John Martin [British]
Simone Martini [Italian]
Masaccio [Italian]
Quentin Massys [Flemish]
Henri Matisse [French]
Hans Memling *or* Memlinc [Flemish]
Franz Xavier Messerschmidt [Austrian]
Ivan Meštrović [Yugoslav-U.S.]
Michelangelo Buonarroti [Italian]
Michelozzi Michelozzo [Italian]
John Everett Millais [English]
Jean François Millet [French]
Joan Miró [Spanish]
Amedeo Modigliani [Italian]
László Moholy-Nagy [Hungarian]
Piet Mondrian [Dutch]
Claude Oscar Monet [French]
Henry Moore [British]
Gustave Moreau [French]
Berthe Morisot

[French]
William Morris [English]
Samuel Finley Breese Morse [U.S.]
Grandma Moses [U.S.]
Edvard Munch [Norwegian]
Alfred Munnings [British]
Bartolomé Esteban Murillo [Spanish]
Myron [Greek]
Paul Nash [English]
Ernst Wilhelm Nay [German]
Barnett Newman [U.S.]
Ben Nicholson [British]
Sidney Nolan [Australian]
Emil Nolde [German]
Joseph Nollekens [Dutch-English]
Georgia O'Keefe [U.S.]
Claes Oldenburg [Swedish-U.S.]
Orcagna [Italian]
José Clemente Orozco [Mexican]
Jean Baptiste Oudry [French]
Palma Vecchio [Italian]
Samuel Palmer [English]
Eduardo Paolozzi [British]
Parmigianino [Italian]
Joachim Patinir *or* Patenier [Flemish]
Perugino [Italian]
Baldassare Peruzzi [Italian]
Antoine Pevsner [Russian-French]
Phidias [Greek]
Francis Picabia [French]
Pablo Picasso [Spanish]
Piero della Francesca [Italian]
Piero di Cosimo [Italian]
Pietro da Cortona [Italian]
Jean Baptiste Pigalle [French]
Germain Pilon [French]
Pinturicchio [Italian]
Pisanello [Italian]
Andrea Pisano [Italian]
Giovanni Pisano [Italian]
Nicola Pisano [Italian]
Camille Pissarro [French]
Antonio del Pollaiuolo [Italian]
Piero del Pollaiuolo [Italian]
Jackson Pollock [U.S.]
Polyclitus [Greek]
Polygnotus [Greek]
Pontormo [Italian]
Paulus Potter [Dutch]
Nicolas Poussin [French]
Praxiteles [Greek]
Pierre Paul Prud'hon [French]
Pierre Puget [French]
Pierre Puvis de Chavannes [French]
Jacopa della Quercia [Italian]
Henry Raeburn [Scottish]
Allan Ramsay [Scottish]
Raphael [Italian]
Man Ray [U.S.]
Odilon Redon [French]
Rembrandt Harmensz van Rijn [Dutch]
Guido Reni [Italian]
Pierre Auguste Renoir [French]
Joshua Reynolds [English]
Bridget Riley [British]
Diego Rivera [Mexican]
Andrea della Robbia [Italian]
Luca della Robbia [Italian]
Alexander Mikhailovich Rodchenko [Russian]
Auguste Rodin [French]
George Romney [English]
Dante Gabriel Rossetti [English]
Mark Rothko [U.S.]
Louis-François Roubiliac *or* Roubillac [French]
Henri Julien Rousseau [French]
Théodore Rousseau [French]
Peter Paul Rubens [Flemish]
Rublyov *or* Rublev Andrei [Russian]
Jacob van Ruisdael [Dutch]
Philipp Otto Runge [German]
Salomen van Ruysdael [Dutch]
John Singer Sargent [U.S.]
Egon Schiele [Austrian]
Martin Schongauer [German]
Kurt Schwitters [German]
Scopas [Greek]
Sesshu [Japanese]
Georges Seurat [French]
Walter Richard Sickert [British]
Paul Signac [French]
Luca Signorelli [Italian]
David Alfaro Siqueiros [Mexican]
Alfred Sisley [French]
John Sloan [U.S.]
Claus Sluter [Dutch]
David Smith [U.S.]
Chaim Soutine [Lithuanian-French]
Stanley Spencer [English]
Jan Steen [Dutch]
Veit Stoss [German]
George Stubbs [British]
Yves Tanguy [French]
Vladimir Tatlin [Russian]
David Teniers the Elder [Flemish]
David Teniers the Younger [Flemish]
Gerard Ter Borch *or* Terborch [Dutch]
Hendrik Terbrugghen [Dutch]
James Thornhill [English]
Bertel Thorvaldsen [Danish]
Giambattista Tiepolo [Italian]
Jacopo Tintoretto [Italian]
James Jacques Joseph Tissot [French]
Titian [Italian]
Henri Marie Raymond de Toulouse-Lautrec [French]
J(oseph) M(allord) W(illiam) Turner [English]
Paolo Uccello [Italian]
Utagawa Kuniyoshi [Japanese]
Maurice Utrillo [French]
Adriaen van de Velde [Dutch]
Willem van de Velde the Elder [Dutch]
Willem van de Velde the Younger [Dutch]
Rogier van der Weyden [Flemish]
Anthony Van Dyck [Flemish]
Jan van Eyck [Flemish]
Vincent van Gogh [Dutch]
Victor Vasarely [Hungarian-French]
Giorgio Vasari [Italian]
Diego Rodríguez de Silva y Velázquez [Spanish]
Jan Vermeer [Dutch]
Paolo Veronese [Italian]
Andrea del Verrocchio [Italian]
Élisabeth Vigée-Lebrun [French]
Jacques Villon [French]
Maurice de Vlaminck [French]
Jean Antoine Watteau [French]
George Frederick Watts [English]
Benjamin West [U.S.]
James Abbott McNeill Whistler [U.S.]
Richard Wilson

[Welsh]
Joseph Wright [English]
Xia Gui *or* Hsia Kuei [Chinese]
Zeuxis [Greek]
Johann Zoffany [German]
Anders Zorn [Swedish]
Gaetano Giulio Zumbo [Italian]
Francisco Zurbarán [Spanish]

The artist must be in his work as God is in creation, invisible and all-powerful; one must sense him everywhere but never see him

Gustave Flaubert

artiste **1.** entertainer, performer **2.** craftsman, expert, master

artistic aesthetic, beautiful, creative, cultivated, cultured, decorative, elegant, exquisite, graceful, imaginative, ornamental, refined, sensitive, sophisticated, stylish, tasteful
Antonyms inartistic, inelegant, tasteless, unattractive, untalented

artistry accomplishment, art, artistic ability, brilliance, craft, craftsmanship, creativity, finesse, flair, genius, mastery, proficiency, sensibility, skill, style, talent, taste, touch, virtuosity, workmanship

artless **1.** candid, direct, fair, frank, genuine, guileless, honest, open, plain, round, sincere, straightforward, true, undesigning, upfront (*informal*) **2.** humble, natural, plain, pure, simple, unadorned, unaffected, uncontrived, unpretentious **3.** awkward, bungling, clumsy, crude, incompetent, inept, maladroit, primitive, rude, unskilled, untalented **4.** childlike, ingenuous, innocent, jejune, naive, trustful, trusting, unsophisticated
Antonyms (*sense 1*) artful, crafty, cunning, designing, dishonest, false, insincere (*sense 2*) affected, artificial, unnatural (*sense 3*) aesthetic, artful, artistic, crafty, cunning, sophisticated (*sense 4*) sophisticated, suspicious

artlessness **1.** bluntness, candidness, candour, directness, fairness, forthrightness, frankness, genuineness, guilelessness, honesty, openheartedness, openness, plainness, sincerity, straightforwardness, trueness **2.** humbleness, naturalness, plainness, purity, simplicity, unaffectedness, unassumingness, unpretentiousness **3.** awkwardness, clumsiness, crudeness, crudity, incompetence, ineptness, inexpertness, maladroitness, primitiveness, rudeness **4.** ingenuousness, innocence, jejuneness, jejunity, naïveté *or* naivety, trustfulness, trustingness, unguardedness, unsophisticatedness, unsophistication, unwariness

arty *informal* artistic, arty-crafty (*informal*), arty-farty (*derogatory slang*)

as *conjunction* **1.** at the time that, during the time that, just as, when, while **2.** in the manner that, in the way that, like **3.** that which, what **4.** because, considering that, seeing that, since **5.** in the same manner with, in the same way that, like **6.** for instance, like, such as *~preposition* **7.** being, in the character of, in the role of, under the name of **8.** **as for** as regards, in reference to, on the subject of, with reference to, with regard to, with respect to **9.** **as it were** in a manner of speaking, in a way, so to say, so to speak

ascend climb, float up, fly up, go up, lift off, mount, move up, rise, scale, slope upwards, soar, take off, tower
Antonyms alight, descend, dip, drop, fall, go down, incline, move down, plummet, plunge, sink, slant, slope, subside, tumble

ascendancy, ascendency authority, command, control, dominance, domination, dominion, hegemony, influence, mastery, power, predominance, pre-eminence, prevalence, reign, rule, sovereignty, superiority, supremacy, sway, upper hand
Antonyms inferiority, servility, subjection, subordination, weakness

ascendant, ascendent *adjective* **1.** ascending, climbing, going upwards, mounting, rising **2.** authoritative, commanding, controlling, dominant, influential, powerful, predominant, pre-eminent, prevailing, ruling, superior, supreme, uppermost *~noun* **3.** **in the ascendant** ascending, climbing, commanding, dominant, dominating, flourishing, growing, increasing, mounting, on the rise, on the way up, prevailing, rising, supreme, up-and-coming, uppermost, winning

ascension ascent, climb, mounting, moving upwards, rise, rising

ascent **1.** ascending, ascension, clambering, climb, climbing, mounting, rise, rising, scaling, upward movement **2.** acclivity, gradient, incline, ramp, rise, rising ground, upward slope

ascertain confirm, determine, discover, establish, ferret out, find out, fix, identify, learn, make certain, settle, suss (out) (*slang*), verify

ascetic **1.** *noun* abstainer, anchorite, hermit, monk, nun, recluse, self-denier **2.** *adjective* abstemious, abstinent, austere, celibate, frugal, harsh, plain, puritanical, rigorous, self-denying, self-disciplined, severe, Spartan, stern
Antonyms *noun* hedonist, sensualist, voluptuary *~adjective* abandoned, comfortable, luxurious, self-indulgent, sensuous, voluptuous

asceticism abstemiousness, abstinence, austerity, celibacy, frugality, harshness, mortification of the flesh, plainness, puritanism, rigorousness, rigour, self-abnegation, self-denial, self-discipline, self-mortification

ascribe assign, attribute, charge, credit, impute, put down, refer, set down

asexual neuter, neutral, sexless

asexuality neutrality, sexlessness

ashamed abashed, bashful, blushing, chagrined, conscience-stricken, crestfallen, discomfited, distressed, embarrassed, guilty, humbled, humiliated, mortified, prudish, reluctant, remorseful, shamefaced, sheepish, shy, sorry
Antonyms gratified, honoured, pleased, proud, satisfied, unashamed, vain

ashen anaemic, ashy, colourless, grey, leaden, like death warmed up (*informal*), livid, pale, pallid, pasty, wan, white
Antonyms blooming, blushing, florid, flushed, glowing, radiant, red, reddish, rosy, rosy-cheeked, rubicund, ruddy

ashore aground, landwards, on dry land, on land, on the beach, on the shore, shorewards, to the shore

aside **1.** *adverb* alone, alongside, apart, away, beside, in isolation, in reserve, on one side, out of mind, out of the way, privately, separately, to one side, to the side **2.** *noun* departure, digression, excursion, excursus, interpolation, interposition, parenthesis, tangent

asinine braindead (*informal*), brainless, daft (*informal*), dead from the neck up (*informal*), dunderheaded, fatuous, foolish, goofy (*informal*), gormless (*Brit. informal*), halfwitted, idiotic, imbecile, imbecilic, inane, moronic, obstinate, senseless, silly, stupid, thickheaded, thick-witted
Antonyms brainy (*informal*), bright, clever, intelligent, quick-witted, sage, sane, sensible, sharp, smart, wise

asininity brainlessness, cloddishness, daftness, doltishness, fatuity, fatuousness, foolishness (*informal*), goofiness, gormlessness (*Brit. informal*), half-wittedness, idiocy, imbecility, inanity, moronism, moronity, oafishness, obstinacy, senselessness, silliness, stupidness, thickheadedness, thick-wittedness
Antonyms braininess (*informal*), brightness, cleverness, intelligence, keenness, quickness, quick-wittedness, sagacity, sageness, saneness, sensibleness, sharpness, sharp-wittedness, smartness, wisdom

ask **1.** inquire, interrogate, query, question, quiz **2.** appeal, apply, beg, beseech, claim, crave, demand, entreat, implore, petition, plead, pray, request, seek, solicit, sue, supplicate **3.** bid, invite, summon
Antonyms (*sense 1*) answer, reply, respond

askance **1.** awry, indirectly, obliquely, out of the corner of one's eye, sideways, with a side glance **2.** disapprovingly, distrustfully, doubtfully, dubiously, mistrustfully, sceptically, suspiciously

askew *adverb / adjective* aslant, awry, cockeyed (*informal*), crooked, crookedly, lopsided, oblique, obliquely, off-centre, skewwhiff (*Brit. informal*), to one side
Antonyms aligned, even, in line, level, right, square, straight, true

aslant **1.** *adverb* aslope, at a slant, atilt, slantingly, slopingly **2.** *preposition* across, athwart

asleep crashed out (*slang*), dead to the world (*informal*), dormant, dozing, fast asleep, napping, out for the count, sleeping, slumbering, snoozing (*informal*), sound asleep

aspect **1.** air, appearance, attitude, bearing, condition, countenance, demeanour, expression, look, manner, mien (*literary*) **2.** bearing, direction, exposure, outlook, point of view, position, prospect, scene, situation, view **3.** angle, facet, feature, side

asperity acerbity, acrimony, bitterness, churlishness, crabbedness, crossness, harshness, irascibility, irritability, moroseness, peevishness, roughness, ruggedness, severity, sharpness, sourness, sullenness

asperse abuse, calumniate, cast aspersions (on), defame, detract, disparage, reproach, slander, slur, smear, traduce, vilify, vituperate

aspersion abuse, calumny, censure, character assassination, defamation, denigration, detraction, disparagement, obloquy, reproach, slander, slur, smear, traducement, vilification, vituperation

asphyxiate choke, smother, stifle, strangle, strangulate, suffocate, throttle

asphyxiation strangulation, suffocation

aspirant **1.** *noun* applicant, aspirer, candidate, hopeful, postulant, seeker, suitor **2.** *adjective* ambitious, aspiring, eager, endeavouring, hopeful, longing, striving, wishful

aspiration aim, ambition, craving, desire, dream, eagerness, endeavour, goal, hankering, Holy Grail (*informal*), hope, longing, object, objective, wish, yearning

> *We are all in the gutter, but some of us are looking at the stars*
>
> Oscar Wilde *Lady Windermere's Fan*

aspire aim, be ambitious, be eager, crave, desire, dream, hanker, hope, long, pursue, seek, set one's heart on, wish, yearn

aspiring *adjective* ambitious, aspirant, eager, endeavouring, hopeful, longing, striving, wishful, would-be

ass **1.** donkey, jennet, moke (*slang*) **2.** airhead (*slang*), berk (*Brit. slang*), blockhead, bonehead (*slang*), charlie (*Brit. informal*), coot, daftie (*informal*), dickhead (*slang*), dickwit (*slang*), dipstick (*Brit. slang*), divvy (*Brit. slang*), dolt, dope (*informal*), dork (*slang*), dunce, dweeb (*U.S. slang*), fathead (*informal*), fool, fuckwit (*taboo slang*), geek (*slang*), gobshite (*Irish taboo slang*), gonzo (*slang*), halfwit, idiot, jackass, jerk (*slang, chiefly U.S. & Canad.*), nerd *or* nurd (*slang*), nincompoop, ninny, nitwit (*informal*), numpty (*Scot. informal*), numskull *or* numbskull, oaf, pillock (*Brit. slang*), plank (*Brit. slang*), plonker (*slang*), prat (*slang*), prick (*slang*), schmuck (*U.S. slang*), simpleton, twerp *or* twirp (*informal*), twit (*informal, chiefly Brit.*), wally (*slang*), weenie (*U.S. informal*)

assail **1.** assault, attack, belabour, beset, charge, encounter, fall upon, invade, lay into (*informal*), maltreat, set about, set upon **2.** abuse, berate, blast, criticize, go for the jugular, impugn, lambast(e), malign, put down, revile, tear into (*informal*), vilify

assailable **1.** attackable, chargeable, invadable **2.** criticizable *or* criticisable, impugnable

assailant aggressor, assailer, assaulter, attacker, invader

assassin eliminator (*slang*), executioner, hatchet man (*slang*), hit man (*slang*), killer, liquidator, murderer, slayer

assassinate blow away (*slang, chiefly U.S.*), eliminate (*slang*), hit (*slang*), kill, liquidate, murder, slay, take out (*slang*)

assassination elimination (*slang*), hit (*slang*), killing, liquidation, murder, purge, removal (*euphemistic*), slaying

Assassination is the quickest way
Molière *Le Sicilien*

assault **1.** *noun* aggression, attack, campaign, charge, incursion, inroad, invasion, offensive, onset, onslaught, storm, storming, strike **2.** *verb* assail, attack, belabour, beset, charge, fall upon, invade, lay into (*informal*), set about, set upon, storm, strike at
Antonyms *noun* defence, protection, resistance ~*verb* defend, protect, resist

assay *verb* **1.** analyse, appraise, assess, evaluate, examine, inspect, investigate, prove, test, try, weigh ~*noun* **2.** *archaic* attempt, endeavour, essay, stab (*informal*), try, venture **3.** analysis, examination, inspection, investigation, test, trial

assemblage accumulation, aggregation, assembly, body, collection, company, conclave, congregation, convocation, crowd, flock, gathering, group, mass, meeting, multitude, rally, throng

assemble **1.** accumulate, amass, bring together, call together, collect, come together, congregate, convene, convoke, flock, forgather, gather, marshal, meet, muster, rally, round up, summon **2.** build up, connect, construct, erect, fabricate, fit together, join, make, manufacture, piece together, put together, set up
Antonyms adjourn, break up (*informal*), disassemble, disband, dismiss, disperse, distribute, divide, scatter, take apart

assembly **1.** accumulation, aggregation, assemblage, body, collection, company, conclave, conference, congregation, congress, convention, convocation, council, crowd, diet, flock, gathering, group, house, mass, meeting, multitude, rally, synod, throng **2.** building up, connecting, construction, erection, fabrication, fitting together, joining, manufacture, piecing together, putting together, setting up

assent **1.** *verb* accede, accept, acquiesce, agree, allow, approve, comply, concur, consent, fall in with, go along with, grant, permit, sanction, subscribe **2.** *noun* acceptance, accession, accord, acquiescence, agreement, approval, compliance, concurrence, consent, permission, sanction
Antonyms *verb* deny, differ, disagree, dissent, object, protest, rebut, reject, retract ~*noun* denial, disagreement, disapproval, dissension, dissent, objection, refusal

assert **1.** affirm, allege, asseverate, attest, aver, avouch (*archaic*), avow, contend, declare, maintain, predicate, profess, pronounce, state, swear **2.** claim, defend, insist upon, press, put forward, stand up for, stress, uphold, vindicate **3.** **assert oneself** exert one's influence, make one's presence felt, put oneself forward, put one's foot down (*informal*)
Antonyms (*senses 1 & 2*) deny, disavow, disclaim, rebut, refute, retract

assertion **1.** affirmation, allegation, asseveration, attestation, avowal, contention, declaration, predication, profession, pronouncement, statement **2.** defence, insistence, maintenance, stressing, vindication

assertive aggressive, can-do (*informal*), confident, decided, decisive, demanding, dogmatic, domineering, emphatic, feisty (*informal, chiefly U.S. & Canad.*), firm, forceful, forward, insistent, overbearing, positive, pushy (*informal*), self-assured, strong-willed
Antonyms backward, bashful, diffident, hesitant, insecure, meek, modest, reserved, retiring, self-conscious, self-effacing, sheepish, shrinking, shy, timid, timorous, unassertive, unobtrusive

assertiveness aggressiveness, confidence, decidedness, decisiveness, dogmatism, domineeringness, firmness, forcefulness, forwardness, insistence, positiveness, pushiness (*informal*), self-assuredness
Antonyms backwardness, bashfulness, diffidence, hesitancy, insecurity, meekness, modesty, reservedness, self-consciousness, self-effacement, sheepishness, shyness, tentativeness, timidity, timidness, timorousness

assess **1.** appraise, compute, determine, estimate, evaluate, eye up, fix, gauge, judge, rate, size up (*informal*), value, weigh **2.** demand, evaluate, fix, impose, levy, rate, tax, value

assessable appraisable, computable, determinable, estimable (*rare*), gaugeable *or* gageable, judgeable, measurable, ratable *or* rateable

assessment **1.** appraisal, computation, determination, estimate, estimation, evaluation, judgment, rating, valuation **2.** charge, demand, duty, evaluation, fee, impost, levy, rate, rating, tariff, tax, taxation, toll, valuation

asset **1.** ace in the hole, ace up one's sleeve, advantage, aid, benefit, blessing, boon, feather in one's cap, help, resource, service **2.** *plural* capital, estate, funds, goods, holdings, means, money, possessions, property, reserves, resources, valuables, wealth
Antonyms (*sense 1*) albatross, burden, disadvantage, drag, drawback, encumbrance, handicap, hindrance, impediment, liability, millstone, minus (*informal*), nuisance

asseverate affirm, assert, attest, aver, avouch (*archaic*), avow, declare, maintain, predicate, profess, pronounce, protest, state, swear

asseveration affirmation, assertion, attestation, averment, avowal, declaration, predication, profession, pronouncement, protestation, statement, vow

assiduity application, assiduousness, attentiveness, constancy, diligence, indefatigability, industriousness, industry, laboriousness, perseverance, persistence, sedulity, sedulousness, steadiness, studiousness, tirelessness

assiduous attentive, constant, diligent, hard-working, indefatigable, industrious, laborious, persevering, persistent, sedulous, steady, studious, unflagging, untiring, unwearied
Antonyms careless, idle, inattentive, indolent, lax, lazy, negligent, slack

assign **1.** appoint, choose, delegate, designate, name, nominate, select **2.** allocate, allot, apportion, consign, distribute, give, give out, grant, make over **3.** appoint, appropriate, determine, fix, set apart, stipulate **4.** accredit, ascribe, attribute, put down

assignation **1.** clandestine meeting, illicit meeting, rendezvous, secret meeting, tryst (*archaic*) **2.** allocation, allotment, appointment, apportionment, appropriation, ascription, assignment, attribution, choice, consignment, delegation, designation, determination, distribution, giving, grant, nomination, selection, specification, stipulation

assignment **1.** appointment, charge, commission, duty, job, mission, position, post, responsibility, task **2.** allocation, allotment, appointment, apportionment, appropriation, ascription, assignation (*Law, chiefly Scot.*), attribution, choice, consignment, delegation, designation, determination, distribution, giving, grant, nomination, selection, specification, stipulation

assimilate **1.** absorb, digest, imbibe (*literary*), incorporate, ingest, learn, take in **2.** acclimatize, accommodate, acculturate, accustom, adapt, adjust, become like, become similar, blend in, conform, fit, homogenize, intermix, mingle

assist abet, aid, back, benefit, boost, collaborate, cooperate, encourage, expedite, facilitate, further, give a leg up (*informal*), help, lend a helping hand, promote, reinforce, relieve, second, serve, succour, support, sustain, work for, work with
Antonyms frustrate, hamper, handicap, hinder, hold back, hold up, impede, obstruct, resist, thwart, work against

assistance abetment, aid, backing, benefit, boost, collaboration, cooperation, encouragement, furtherance, help, helping hand, promotion, reinforcement, relief, service, succour, support, sustenance
Antonyms hindrance, obstruction, opposition, resistance

assistant abettor, accessory, accomplice, aide, aider, ally, associate, auxiliary, backer, coadjutor (*rare*), collaborator, colleague, confederate, cooperator, helper, helpmate, henchman, partner, protagonist, right-hand man, second, supporter

associate *verb* **1.** affiliate, ally, combine, confederate, conjoin, connect, correlate, couple, identify, join, league, link, lump together, mention in the same breath, mix, pair, relate, think of together, unite, yoke **2.** accompany, befriend, be friends, consort, fraternize, hang about, hang out (*informal*), hang with (*informal, chiefly U.S.*), hobnob, mingle, mix, run around (*informal*) *~noun* **3.** ally, collaborator, colleague, companion, compeer, comrade, confederate, confrère, co-worker, follower, friend, mate, partner
Antonyms (*sense 1*) detach, disconnect, dissociate, distance, distinguish, divorce, isolate, segregate, separate, set apart (*sense 2*) avoid, be alienated, be estranged, break off, part company

associated affiliated, allied, bound, combined, confederated, connected, correlated, involved, joined, leagued, linked, related, syndicated, tied, united, yoked

association **1.** affiliation, alliance, band, clique, club, coalition, combine, company, confederacy, confederation, cooperative, corporation, federation, fraternity, group, league, order, organization, partnership, society, syndicate, union **2.** affinity, companionship, comradeship, familiarity, fellowship, fraternization, friendship, intimacy, liaison, partnership, relations, relationship **3.** blend, bond, combination, concomitance, connection, correlation, identification, joining, juxtaposition, linkage, linking, lumping together, mixing, mixture, pairing, relation, tie, union, yoking

assort arrange, array, categorize, classify, dispose, distribute, file, grade, group, range, rank, sort, type

assorted **1.** different, diverse, diversified, heterogeneous, manifold, miscellaneous, mixed, motley, sundry, varied, variegated, various **2.** arranged, arrayed, categorized, classified, disposed, filed, graded, grouped, ranged, ranked, sorted, typed
Antonyms (*sense 1*) alike, homogeneous, identical, like, same, similar, uniform, unvaried

assortment **1.** array, choice, collection, diversity, farrago, hotchpotch, jumble, medley, *mélange*, miscellany, mishmash, mixed bag (*informal*), mixture, pick 'n' mix, potpourri, salmagundi, selection, variety **2.** arrangement, categorizing, classification, disposition, distribution, filing, grading, grouping, ranging, ranking, sorting, typing

assuage **1.** allay, alleviate, calm, ease, lessen, lighten, mitigate, moderate, palliate, quench, relieve, soothe, temper **2.** appease, calm, lull, mollify, pacify, pour oil on troubled waters, quiet, relax, satisfy, soften, soothe, still, tranquillize
Antonyms (*sense 1*) aggravate, exacerbate, heighten, increase, intensify, worsen (*sense 2*) aggravate, embitter, enrage, infuriate, madden, provoke

assume **1.** accept, believe, expect, fancy, guess (*informal, chiefly U.S. & Canad.*), imagine, infer, presume, presuppose, suppose, surmise, suspect, take for granted, think **2.** adopt, affect, counterfeit, feign, imitate, impersonate, mimic, pretend to, put on, sham, simulate **3.** accept, acquire, attend to, begin, don, embark upon, embrace, enter upon, put on, set about, shoulder, take on, take over, take responsibility for, take up, undertake **4.** acquire, appropriate, arrogate, commandeer, expropriate, pre-empt, seize, take, take over, usurp
Antonyms (*sense 1*) know, prove (*senses 3 & 4*) give up, hand over, leave, put aside, relinquish

assumed **1.** affected, bogus, counterfeit, fake, false, feigned, fictitious, imitation, made-up, make-believe, phoney *or* phony (*informal*), pretended, pseudonymous, sham, simulated, spurious **2.** accepted, expected, hypothetical, presumed, presupposed, supposed, surmised, taken for granted **3.** appropriated, arrogated, pre-empted, seized, usurped
Antonyms (*senses 1 & 2*) actual, authentic, known, natural, positive, real, stated, true

assuming *adjective* arrogant, bold, conceited, disdainful, domineering, egotistic, forward, haughty, imperious, overbearing, presumptuous, pushy (*informal*), rude

assumption **1.** acceptance, belief, conjecture, expectation, fancy, guess, hypothesis, inference, postulate, postulation, premise, premiss, presumption, presupposition, supposition, surmise, suspicion, theory **2.** acceptance, acquisition, adoption, embracing, entering upon, putting on, shouldering, takeover, taking on, taking up, undertaking **3.** acquisition, appropriation, arrogation, expropriation, pre-empting, seizure, takeover, taking, usurpation **4.** arrogance, conceit, imperiousness, presumption, pride, self-importance

assurance **1.** affirmation, assertion, declaration, guarantee, oath, pledge, profession, promise, protestation, vow, word, word of honour **2.** assertiveness, assuredness, boldness, certainty, certitude, confidence, conviction, coolness, courage, faith, firmness, nerve, poise, positiveness, security, self-confidence, self-reliance, sureness **3.** arrogance, brass neck (*Brit. informal*), chutzpah (*U.S. & Canad. informal*), effrontery, gall (*informal*), impudence, neck (*informal*), nerve (*informal*), presumption, sassiness (*U.S. informal*)
Antonyms (*sense 1*) falsehood, lie (*sense 2*) apprehension, diffidence, distrust, doubt, self-doubt, self-effacement, shyness, timidity, uncertainty

assure **1.** comfort, convince, embolden, encourage, hearten, persuade, reassure, soothe **2.** affirm, attest, certify, confirm, declare confidently, give one's word to, guarantee, pledge, promise, swear, vow **3.** clinch, complete, confirm, ensure, guarantee, make certain, make sure, seal, secure

assured **1.** beyond doubt, clinched, confirmed, dependable, ensured, fixed, guaranteed, indubitable, in the bag (*slang*), irrefutable, made certain, sealed, secure, settled, sure, unquestionable **2.** assertive, audacious, bold, brazen, certain, complacent, confident, overconfident, poised, positive, pushy (*informal*), resting on one's laurels, self-assured, self-confident, self-possessed, sure of oneself
Antonyms (*sense 1*) ambiguous, doubtful, indefinite, questionable, uncertain, unconfirmed, unsettled, unsure (*sense 2*) bashful, diffident, hesitant, retiring, self-conscious, self-effacing, timid

astir active, afoot, awake, in motion, on the go (*informal*), on the move (*informal*), out of bed, roused, up and about, up and around

astonish amaze, astound, bewilder, boggle the

mind, confound, daze, dumbfound, flabbergast (*informal*), stagger, stun, stupefy, surprise

astonished amazed, astounded, bewildered, confounded, dazed, dumbfounded, flabbergast~ ed (*informal*), gobsmacked (*informal*), per~ plexed, staggered, stunned, stupefied, sur~ prised

astonishing amazing, astounding, bewildering, breathtaking, brilliant, impressive, sensation~ al (*informal*), staggering, striking, stunning, stupefying, surprising, wondrous (*archaic or literary*)
Antonyms anticipated, expected, foreseen

astonishment amazement, awe, bewilderment, confusion, consternation, stupefaction, sur~ prise, wonder, wonderment

astound amaze, astonish, bewilder, boggle the mind, confound, daze, dumbfound, flabbergast (*informal*), overwhelm, stagger, stun, stupefy, surprise, take one's breath away

astounding amazing, astonishing, bewildering, breathtaking, brilliant, impressive, sensation~ al (*informal*), staggering, striking, stunning, stupefying, surprising, wondrous (*archaic or literary*)

astray *adjective/adverb* **1.** adrift, afield, amiss, lost, off, off course, off the mark, off the right track, off the subject **2.** into error, into sin, to the bad, wrong

astringent **1.** acerbic, austere, caustic, exact~ ing, grim, hard, harsh, rigid, rigorous, severe, stern, strict, stringent **2.** contractile, contrac~ tive, styptic

astrology astromancy, horoscopy, stargazing

Related vocabulary

air
Ascendant *or* Ascend~ ent
aspect
birthchart
cardinal
conjunction
cusp
Descendant *or* De~ scendent
earth
element
fire
fixed
horoscope
house
Midheaven *or* MC
mutable
opposition
quintile
ruling planet
satellitium
square
stars
star sign
sun sign
trine
water
zodiac

Signs

Aquarius (the Water Carrier)
Aries (the Ram)
Cancer (the Crab)
Capricorn (the Goat)
Gemini (the Twins)
Leo (the Lion)
Libra (the Scales)
Pisces (the Fishes)
Sagittarius (the Arch~ er)
Scorpio (the Scorpion)
Taurus (the Bull)
Virgo (the Virgin)

astronaut cosmonaut, spaceman, space pilot, space traveller, spacewoman

astronomical, astronomic boundless, colossal, enormous, galactic, Gargantuan, giant, gigan~ tic, great, huge, immeasurable, immense, infi~ nite, massive, monumental, titanic, vast

astronomy

Astronomy terms

achondrite
aerolite
aerospace
aerosphere
albedo
almucantar *or* alma~ cantar
altitude
analemma
annular eclipse
anthelion
aphelion
apocynthion
apolune
appulse
apapsis
apsis *or* apse
asteroid
asteroid belt
astrobleme
atmosphere
aureola *or* aureole
aurora
aurora australis
aurora borealis
azimuth
barycentre
basin
binary star
black drop
black hole
blue straggler
bolide
brown dwarf
burst
cataclysmic variable
Cepheid variable
Chandrasekhar limit
chemosphere
chondrite
chromosphere
circumlunar
circumpolar
circumsolar
circumstellar
cislunar
cluster
collapsar
colour index
colure
coma
comet
companion
conjunction
constellation
cooordinate system
Copernican system
corona
cosmic
cosmogony
cosmology
crater
crescent
crust
culmination
cusp
dwarf
dynamics
eccentric
ecosphere
effective temperature
ejecta
ellipse
elongation
emersion
ephemeris
epoch
equator
escape velocity
equinox
evection
evolved star
exosphere
extinction
facula
farside
filament
fireball
flare
flocculus
galactic centre
galactic equator
galactic rotation
galaxy
giant
gravitation
heliocentric system
heliosphere
immersion *or* ingress
inclination
inequality
inertia
inferior planet
inner planet

insolation
interplanetary
interstellar
ionosphere
jet
light year
limb
lodestar *or* loadstar
luminosity
lunar
lunar eclipse
magnetosphere
magnitude
major planet
maria
mass
mass loss
mass transfer
merger
meridian
meridian passage
mesosphere
metallicity
metal ratio
meteor
meteorite
meteoroid
meteoroid stream
meteor shower
meteor storm
missing mass
molecular cloud
moonquake
moving cluster
multiple star
nadir
naked singularity
nearside
nebula
neutron star
new moon
node
north celestial pole
northern hemisphere
northern lights
northing
north polar distance
nova
nucleosynthesis
nucleus
nutation
oblateness
obliquity
observatory
occultation
octant
open cluster
opposition
orbit
orbital elements
orbital velocity
oscillating universe
outer planet
parallax
partial eclipse
penumbral eclipse
periapsis
periastron
percentre
perigee
perihelion
photosphere
physical libration
plages
planetary
planetary alignment
planetary system
planetesimal
planetoid
plasmasphere
plerion
polar axis
pole
precession
precession of the equinoxes
primary
prominence
proper motion
protogalaxy
protoplanet
protostar
Ptolemaic system
pulsating universe
pulsating variable
quadrature
quarter
quasar
quasi-stellar object
quiet
radiant
radio source
ray
reciprocal mass
red giant
red supergiant
regolith
retardation
revolution
ring
ring plain
rising
rotation
rupes
saros
satellite
Schwarzschild radius
scintillation
secondary
sextile
Seyfert galaxy
shell star
shepherd satellite
sidereal time
singularity
solar
solar constant
solar eclipse
solar spectrum
solar system
solstice
south celestial pole
southern hemisphere
southern lights
southing
south polar distance
space
spacetime
spectral type *or* spectral class
spherule
spicule
spinar
spray
star
star cloud
stellar
stellar evolution
stellar structure
stellar wind
Strömgren sphere
sublunar point
subsolar point
substellar point
sunspot
sunspot cycle
supercluster
supergiant
superior planet
supernova
symbiotic star
synodic period
syzygy
telluric line
terminator
terrestrial planet
tidal capture
tidal force
tidal friction
tide
total eclipse
total magnitude
thermosphere
train
transient lunar phenomena
triple star
tropical year
troposphere
universal time
universe
variable star
variation
velocity dispersion
vertical circle
visual magnitude
white dwarf
white hole
zenith
zenith distance

Planets
see PLANET

Stars
see STAR

Constellations
see STAR

observatory: a place where astronomers conjecture away the guesses of their predecessors
Ambrose Bierce *The Devil's Dictionary*

astute adroit, artful, bright, calculating, canny, clever, crafty, cunning, discerning, foxy, insightful, intelligent, keen, knowing, on the ball (*informal*), penetrating, perceptive, politic, sagacious, sharp, shrewd, sly, subtle, wily **Antonyms** dull, ingenuous, naive, slow, straightforward, stupid, unintelligent, unknowing

astuteness acumen, adroitness, artfulness, brightness, canniness, cleverness, craftiness, cunning, discernment, foxiness, insight, intelligence, keenness, knowledge, penetration, perceptiveness, sagacity, sharpness, shrewdness, slyness, smarts (*slang, chiefly U.S.*), subtlety, suss (*slang*), wiliness

asunder *adverb/adjective* apart, in pieces, into pieces, rent, to bits, to pieces, torn, to shreds

asylum 1. harbour, haven, preserve, refuge, retreat, safety, sanctuary, shelter 2. *old-fashioned* funny farm (*facetious*), hospital, institution, laughing academy (*U.S. slang*), loony bin (*slang*), madhouse (*informal*), mental hospital, nuthouse (*slang*), psychiatric hospital, rubber room (*U.S. slang*)

atheism disbelief, freethinking, godlessness, heathenism, infidelity, irreligion, nonbelief, paganism, scepticism, unbelief

atheist disbeliever, freethinker, heathen, infidel, irreligionist, nonbeliever, pagan, sceptic, unbeliever

An atheist is a man who has no invisible means of support
John Buchan *On Being a Real Person*

By night an atheist half believes a God
Edward Young *The Complaint: Night Thoughts*

No one has ever died an atheist
Plato *Laws*

There are no atheists in the foxholes
William Thomas Cummings *I Saw the Fall of the Phillipines*

atheistic disbelieving, faithless, freethinking, godless, heathen, infidel, irreligious, nonbelieving, nullifidian, paganistic, sceptic, unbelieving

athlete competitor, contender, contestant, games player, gymnast, player, runner, sportsman, sportswoman

athletic 1. *adjective* able-bodied, active, brawny, energetic, fit, herculean, husky (*informal*), lusty, muscular, powerful, robust, sinewy, strapping, strong, sturdy, vigorous, well-proportioned 2. *plural noun* contests, exercises, games of strength, gymnastics, races, sports, track and field events
Antonyms (*sense 1*) delicate, feeble, frail, puny, sickly, weedy (*informal*)

Athletic events
see SPORT

atmosphere 1. aerosphere, air, heavens, sky 2. air, ambience, aura, character, climate, environment, feel, feeling, flavour, mood, quality, spirit, surroundings, tone, vibes (*slang*)

Layers of the atmosphere

ionosphere	stratosphere
mesosphere	thermosphere
ozone layer *or* ozonosphere	troposphere

atom bit, crumb, dot, fragment, grain, iota, jot, mite, molecule, morsel, mote, particle, scintilla (*rare*), scrap, shred, speck, spot, tittle, trace, whit

atone 1. *with* **for** answer for, compensate, do penance for, make amends for, make redress, make reparation for, make up for, pay for, recompense, redress 2. appease, expiate, make expiation for, propitiate, reconcile, redeem

atonement amends, compensation, expiation, payment, penance, propitiation, recompense, redress, reparation, restitution, satisfaction

atrocious 1. barbaric, brutal, cruel, diabolical, fiendish, flagrant, godawful (*slang*), heinous, hellacious (*U.S. slang*), infamous, infernal, inhuman, monstrous, nefarious, ruthless, savage, vicious, villainous, wicked 2. appalling, detestable, execrable, grievous, horrible, horrifying, shocking, terrible
Antonyms admirable, civilized, fine, generous, gentle, good, honourable, humane, kind, merciful, tasteful

atrocity 1. abomination, act of savagery, barbarity, brutality, crime, cruelty, enormity, evil, horror, monstrosity, outrage, villainy 2. atrociousness, barbarity, barbarousness, brutality, cruelty, enormity, fiendishness, grievousness, heinousness, horror, infamy, inhumanity, monstrousness, nefariousness, ruthlessness, savagery, shockingness, viciousness, villainousness, wickedness

atrophy 1. *noun* decay, decaying, decline, degeneration, deterioration, diminution, meltdown (*informal*), shrivelling, wasting, wasting away, withering 2. *verb* decay, decline, degenerate, deteriorate, diminish, dwindle, fade, shrink, shrivel, waste, waste away, wilt, wither

attach 1. add, adhere, affix, annex, append, bind, connect, couple, fasten, fix, join, link, make fast, secure, stick, subjoin, tie, unite 2. accompany, affiliate, associate, become associated with, combine, enlist, join, join forces with, latch on to, sign on with, sign up with, unite with 3. ascribe, assign, associate, attribute, connect, impute, invest with, lay, place, put 4. allocate, allot, appoint, assign, consign, designate, detail, earmark, second, send
Antonyms detach, disconnect, dissociate, loosen, remove, retire, separate, untie, withdraw

attached 1. affectionate towards, devoted, fond of, full of regard for, possessive 2. accompanied, engaged, married, partnered, spoken for

attachment 1. adapter *or* adaptor, bond, clamp, connection, connector, coupling, fastener, fastening, joint, junction, link, tie 2. affection, affinity, attraction, bond, devotion, fidelity, fondness, friendship, liking, love, loyalty, partiality, possessiveness, predilection, regard, tenderness 3. accessory, accoutrement, adapter, addition, add-on, adjunct, appendage, appurtenance, auxiliary, extension, extra, fitting, fixture, supplement, supplementary part
Antonyms (*sense 2*) animosity, antipathy, aversion, disinclination, distaste, hatred, hostility, loathing

attack *noun* 1. aggression, assault, campaign, charge, foray, incursion, inroad, invasion, of~

fensive, onset, onslaught, raid, rush, strike **2.** abuse, blame, calumny, censure, character as~sassination, criticism, denigration, impugn~ment, stick (*slang*), vilification **3.** access, bout, convulsion, fit, paroxysm, seizure, spasm, spell, stroke *~verb* **4.** assail, assault, charge, fall upon, invade, lay into (*informal*), raid, rush, set about, set upon, storm, strike (at) **5.** abuse, berate, bite someone's head off, blame, blast, censure, criticize, excoriate, go for the jugular, have a go (at) (*informal*), impugn, lambast(e), malign, put down, revile, snap someone's head off, tear into (*informal*), vilify
Antonyms *noun* defence, retreat, support, vindication, withdrawal *~verb* defend, guard, protect, retreat, support, sustain, vindicate, withdraw

Attack is the best form of defence

attacker aggressor, assailant, assaulter, in~truder, invader, raider

attain accomplish, achieve, acquire, arrive at, bring off, complete, earn, effect, fulfil, gain, get, grasp, land, obtain, procure, reach, real~ize, reap, score (*slang*), secure, win

attainable accessible, accomplishable, achiev~able, at hand, feasible, gettable, graspable, likely, obtainable, possible, potential, practi~cable, probable, procurable, reachable, realiz~able, within reach
Antonyms impossible, impracticable, improb~able, inaccessible, out of reach, unattainable, unfeasible, unlikely, unobtainable, unprocur~able, unreachable

attainment **1.** accomplishment, achievement, acquirement, acquisition, arrival at, comple~tion, feat, fulfilment, gaining, getting, obtain~ing, procurement, reaching, realization, reap~ing, winning **2.** ability, accomplishment, achievement, art, capability, competence, gift, mastery, proficiency, skill, talent

attempt **1.** *noun* assault, attack, bid, crack (*in~formal*), effort, endeavour, essay, experiment, go (*informal*), shot (*informal*), stab (*informal*), trial, try, undertaking, venture **2.** *verb* en~deavour, essay, experiment, have a crack (go (*informal*), shot (*informal*), stab (*informal*)) (*informal*), jump through hoops (*informal*), seek, strive, tackle, take on, take the bit be~tween one's teeth, try, try one's hand at, undertake, venture

attempted assayed, endeavoured, tried, undertaken, ventured

attend **1.** appear, be at, be here, be present, be there, frequent, go to, haunt, make one (*ar~chaic*), put in an appearance, show oneself, show up (*informal*), turn up, visit **2.** care for, look after, mind, minister to, nurse, take care of, tend **3.** follow, hear, hearken (*archaic*), heed, listen, look on, mark, mind, note, notice, observe, pay attention, pay heed, regard, take to heart, watch **4.** accompany, arise from, be associated with, be connected with, be conse~quent on, follow, go hand in hand with, issue from, occur with, result from **5.** *with* **to** apply oneself to, concentrate on, devote oneself to, get to work on, look after, occupy oneself with, see to, take care of **6.** accompany, chap~eron, companion, convoy, escort, guard, squire, usher **7.** be in the service of, serve, wait upon, work for
Antonyms (*sense 1*) be absent, miss, play tru~ant (*sense 2*) neglect (*senses 3 & 5*) discount, disregard, ignore, neglect (*sense 4*) dissociate

attendance **1.** appearance, attending, being there, presence **2.** audience, crowd, gate, house, number present, turnout

attendant **1.** *noun* aide, assistant, auxiliary, chaperon, companion, custodian, escort, flunky, follower, guard, guide, helper, lackey, menial, servant, steward, underling, usher, waiter **2.** *adjective* accessory, accompanying, associated, concomitant, consequent, related

attention **1.** concentration, consideration, con~templation, deliberation, heed, heedfulness, intentness, mind, scrutiny, thinking, thought, thoughtfulness **2.** awareness, consciousness, consideration, notice, observation, recognition, regard **3.** care, concern, looking after, mini~stration, treatment **4.** *often plural* assiduities, care, civility, compliment, consideration, cour~tesy, deference, gallantry, mindfulness, polite~ness, regard, respect, service
Antonyms carelessness, discourtesy, disre~gard, disrespect, distraction, impoliteness, in~attention, laxity, laxness, negligence, thoughtlessness, unconcern

attentive **1.** alert, awake, careful, concentrat~ing, heedful, intent, listening, mindful, obser~vant, on one's toes, regardful, studious, watchful **2.** accommodating, civil, conscien~tious, considerate, courteous, devoted, gallant, gracious, kind, obliging, polite, respectful, thoughtful
Antonyms absent-minded, careless, distract~ed, dreamy, heedless, inattentive, neglectful, negligent, preoccupied, remiss, thoughtless, unheeding, unmindful

attenuate *verb* **1.** adulterate, contract, de~crease, devaluate, dilute, diminish, enervate, enfeeble, lessen, lower, reduce, sap, water down, weaken **2.** draw out, elongate, extend, lengthen, make fine, make slender, rarefy, re~fine, slim, spin out, stretch out, thin *~adjec~tive Also* **attenuated** **3.** adulterated, contract~ed, decreased, devalued, dilute, diluted, di~minished, enervated, enfeebled, lessened, low~ered, reduced, sapped, watered down, weak~ened **4.** drawn out, elongated, extended, lengthened, rarefied, refined, slender, slimmed, spun out, stretched out, thinned

attest adjure, affirm, assert, authenticate, aver, bear out, bear witness, certify, confirm, corroborate, declare, demonstrate, display, evince, exhibit, give evidence, invoke, mani~fest, prove, ratify, seal, show, substantiate, swear, testify, verify, vouch for, warrant, wit~ness
Antonyms contradict, controvert, deny, dis~prove, gainsay (*archaic or literary*), give the lie to, make a nonsense of, prove false, rebut, refute

attic[1] *adjective* chaste, classical, correct, el~egant, graceful, polished, pure, refined, sim~ple, tasteful

attic[2] *noun* garret, loft

attire **1.** *noun* accoutrements, apparel, array (*poetic*), clothes, clothing, costume, dress, garb, garments, gear (*informal*), habiliments, habit, outfit, raiment (*archaic or poetic*), robes, schmutter (*slang*), threads (*slang*), uni~form, vestment, wear **2.** *verb* accoutre, apparel (*archaic*), array, clothe, costume, deck out, dress, equip, fit out, garb, get ready, rig out, robe, turn out

attitude **1.** approach, disposition, frame of mind, mood, opinion, outlook, perspective, point of view, position, posture, stance, stand~ing, view **2.** air, aspect, bearing, carriage, condition, demeanour, manner, mien (*liter~ary*), pose, position, posture, stance

attorney lawyer

attract allure, appeal to, bewitch, captivate, catch (someone's) eye, charm, decoy, draw, enchant, endear, engage, entice, fascinate, in~cline, induce, interest, invite, lure, pull (*infor~mal*), tempt
Antonyms disgust, give one the creeps (*infor~mal*), put one off, repel, repulse, revolt, turn one off (*informal*)

attraction allure, appeal, attractiveness, bait, captivation, charm, come-on (*informal*), draw, enchantment, endearment, enticement, fasci~nation, incentive, inducement, interest, invi~tation, lure, magnetism, pull (*informal*), temptation, temptingness

attractive agreeable, alluring, appealing, beau~tiful, captivating, charming, comely, cute, en~gaging, enticing, fair, fascinating, fetching, glamorous, good-looking, gorgeous, handsome, interesting, inviting, likable *or* likeable, love~ly, magnetic, pleasant, pleasing, prepossess~ing, pretty, seductive, tempting, winning, winsome
Antonyms disagreeable, displeasing, distaste~ful, offensive, repulsive, ugly, unappealing, unbecoming, uninviting, unlikable *or* unlike~able, unpleasant, unsightly

attractiveness agreeability, agreeableness, al~lure, appeal, beauty, charm, comeliness, de~sirability, engagingness, enticingness, fair~ness, glamorousness *or* glamourousness, good looks, gorgeousness, handsomeness, likable~ness *or* likeableness, loveliness, magnetism, pleasantness, pleasingness, prepossessingness, prettiness, pulchritude (*formal or literary*), seductiveness, takingness, temptingness, win~ningness, winsomeness
Antonyms disagreeability, disagreeableness, distastefulness, offensiveness, repulsiveness, ugliness, unbecomingness, unpleasantness, unsightliness

attributable accountable, applicable, ascrib~able, assignable, blamable *or* blameable, ex~plicable, imputable, placeable, referable *or* re~ferrable, traceable

attribute **1.** *verb* apply, ascribe, assign, blame, charge, credit, impute, lay at the door of, put down to, refer, set down to, trace to **2.** *noun* aspect, character, characteristic, facet, fea~ture, idiosyncrasy, indication, mark, note, pe~culiarity, point, property, quality, quirk, sign, symbol, trait, virtue

attribution ascription, assignation, assignment, attachment, blame, charge, credit, imputation, placement, referral

attrition **1.** abrasion, chafing, erosion, friction, grinding, rubbing, scraping, wear, wearing away, wearing down **2.** attenuation, debilita~tion, harassment, harrying, thinning out, weakening, wearing down

attune acclimatize, accord, accustom, adapt, adjust, coordinate, familiarize, harmonize, modulate, regulate, set, tune

attuned acclimatized, accustomed, adjusted, coordinated, familiarized, harmonized, in ac~cord, in harmony, in tune

atypical deviant, exceptional, nonconforming, out of keeping, out of the ordinary, singular, uncharacteristic, uncommon, unconforming, unconventional, uncustomary, unique, un~orthodox, unrepresentative, unusual
Antonyms archetypal, average, characteristic, classic, conforming, conventional, customary, illustrative, in character, in keeping, model, normal, ordinary, orthodox, representative, standard, stock, true to type, unexceptional, unsingular, usual

auburn chestnut-coloured, copper-coloured, henna, nutbrown, reddish-brown, russet, rust-coloured, tawny, Titian red

au courant abreast of, acquainted, *au fait*, conversant, enlightened, in the know, in the swim, knowledgeable, up-to-date, well-informed, well up

audacious **1.** adventurous, bold, brave, coura~geous, daredevil, daring, dauntless, death-

defying, enterprising, fearless, intrepid, rash, reckless, risky, valiant, venturesome **2.** assuming, brazen, cheeky, defiant, disrespectful, forward, fresh (*informal*), impertinent, impudent, insolent, pert, presumptuous, rude, sassy (*U.S. informal*), shameless
Antonyms (*sense 1*) careful, cautious, cowardly, frightened, guarded, prudent, timid, unadventurous, unenterprising (*sense 2*) deferential, gracious, tactful, unassuming

audacity **1.** adventurousness, audaciousness, boldness, bravery, courage, daring, dauntlessness, enterprise, face (*informal*), fearlessness, front, guts (*informal*), intrepidity, nerve, rashness, recklessness, valour, ventureomeness **2.** audaciousness, brass neck (*Brit. informal*), cheek, chutzpah (*U.S. & Canad. informal*), defiance, disrespectfulness, effrontery, forwardness, gall (*informal*), impertinence, impudence, insolence, neck (*informal*), nerve, pertness, presumption, rudeness, sassiness (*U.S. informal*), shamelessness

Being tactful in audacity is knowing how far one can go too far
Jean Cocteau *Le Rappel à l'ordre*

audible clear, detectable, discernible, distinct, hearable, perceptible
Antonyms faint, imperceptible, inaudible, indistinct, low, out of earshot

audience **1.** assemblage, assembly, congregation, crowd, gallery, gathering, house, listeners, onlookers, spectators, turnout, viewers **2.** devotees, fans, following, market, public **3.** consultation, hearing, interview, meeting, reception

audit *Accounting* **1.** *noun* balancing, check, checking, examination, inspection, investigation, review, scrutiny, verification **2.** *verb* balance, check, examine, go over, go through, inspect, investigate, review, scrutinize, verify

au fait abreast of, *au courant*, clued-up (*informal*), conversant, expert, familiar, fully informed, in the know, in touch, knowledgeable, on the ball (*informal*), well-acquainted, well up

augment add to, amplify, boost, build up, dilate, enhance, enlarge, expand, extend, grow, heighten, increase, inflate, intensify, magnify, multiply, raise, reinforce, strengthen, swell
Antonyms contract, curtail, cut down, decrease, diminish, lessen, lower, reduce, shrink

augmentation accession, addition, amplification, boost, build-up, dilation, enhancement, enlargement, expansion, extension, growth, heightening, increase, inflation, intensification, magnification, multiplication, reinforcement, rise, strengthening, swelling

augur **1.** *noun* auspex, diviner, haruspex, oracle, prophet, seer, soothsayer **2.** *verb* be an omen of, bespeak (*archaic*), betoken, bode, foreshadow, harbinger, herald, portend, predict, prefigure, presage, promise, prophesy, signify

augury **1.** divination, prediction, prophecy, soothsaying, sortilege **2.** auspice, forerunner, forewarning, harbinger, herald, omen, portent, precursor, presage, prognostication, promise, prophecy, sign, token, warning

august dignified, exalted, glorious, grand, high-ranking, imposing, impressive, kingly, lofty, magnificent, majestic, monumental, noble, regal, solemn, stately, superb

aura air, ambience, aroma, atmosphere, emanation, feel, feeling, mood, odour, quality, scent, suggestion, tone, vibes (*slang*), vibrations (*slang*)

auspice *noun* **1.** *usually plural* advocacy, aegis, authority, backing, care, championship, charge, control, countenance, guidance, influence, patronage, protection, sponsorship, supervision, support **2.** augury, indication, omen, portent, prognostication, prophecy, sign, token, warning

auspicious bright, encouraging, favourable, felicitous, fortunate, happy, hopeful, lucky, opportune, promising, propitious, prosperous, rosy, timely
Antonyms bad, black, discouraging, ill-omened, inauspicious, infelicitous, ominous, unfavourable, unfortunate, unlucky, unpromising, unpropitious

austere **1.** cold, exacting, forbidding, formal, grave, grim, hard, harsh, inflexible, rigorous, serious, severe, solemn, stern, stiff, strict, stringent, unfeeling, unrelenting **2.** abstemious, abstinent, ascetic, chaste, continent, economical, exacting, puritanical, rigid, self-denying, self-disciplined, sober, solemn, Spartan, strait-laced, strict, unrelenting **3.** bleak, economical, harsh, plain, severe, simple, spare, Spartan, stark, subdued, unadorned, unornamented
Antonyms abandoned, affable, cheerful, comfortable, convivial, flexible, free-and-easy, genial, immoral, indulgent, jovial, kindly, loose, luxurious, permissive, sweet

austerity **1.** coldness, exactingness, forbiddingness, formality, gravity, grimness, hardness, harshness, inflexibility, rigour, seriousness, severity, solemnity, sternness, stiffness, strictness **2.** abstemiousness, abstinence, asceticism, chasteness, chastity, continence, economy, exactingness, puritanism, rigidity, self-denial, self-discipline, sobriety, solemnity, Spartanism, strictness **3.** economy, plainness, severity, simplicity, spareness, Spartanism, starkness

authentic accurate, actual, authoritative, bona fide, certain, dependable, factual, faithful, genuine, legitimate, on the level (*informal*), original, pure, real, reliable, simon-pure (*rare*), the real McCoy, true, true-to-life, trustworthy, valid, veritable
Antonyms counterfeit, fake, false, fictitious, fraudulent, hypothetical, imitation, misleading, mock, pseudo (*informal*), spurious, supposed, synthetic, unfaithful, unreal, untrue

authenticate attest, authorize, avouch, certify, confirm, endorse, guarantee, validate, verify, vouch for, warrant
Antonyms annul, invalidate, render null and void

authenticity accuracy, actuality, authoritativeness, certainty, dependability, factualness, faithfulness, genuineness, legitimacy, purity, realness, reliability, trustworthiness, truth, truthfulness, validity, veritableness, verity

author architect, composer, creator, designer, doer, fabricator, father, founder, framer, initiator, inventor, maker, mover, originator, parent, planner, prime mover, producer, writer
Related adjective: auctorial

There is probably no hell for authors in the next world - they suffer so much from critics and publishers in this
C.N. Bovee

authoritarian **1.** *adjective* absolute, autocratic, despotic, dictatorial, disciplinarian, doctrinaire, dogmatic, domineering, harsh, imperious, rigid, severe, strict, tyrannical, unyielding **2.** *noun* absolutist, autocrat, despot, dictator, disciplinarian, tyrant
Antonyms *adjective* broad-minded, democratic, flexible, indulgent, lenient, liberal, permissive, tolerant

authoritative **1.** accurate, authentic, definitive, dependable, factual, faithful, learned, reliable, scholarly, sound, true, trustworthy, truthful, valid, veritable **2.** assertive, autocratic, commanding, confident, decisive, dictatorial, dogmatic, dominating, imperative, imperious, imposing, lordly, masterly, peremptory, self-assured **3.** approved, authorized, commanding, legitimate, official, sanctioned, sovereign
Antonyms (*sense 1*) deceptive, undependable, unreliable (*sense 2*) humble, subservient, timid, weak (*sense 3*) unauthorized, unofficial, unsanctioned

authority **1.** ascendancy, charge, command, control, direction, domination, dominion, force, government, influence, jurisdiction, might, power, prerogative, right, rule, say-so, strength, supremacy, sway, weight **2.** **the authorities** administration, government, management, officialdom, police, powers that be, the establishment **3.** a blank cheque, authorization, justification, licence, permission, permit, sanction, say-so, warrant **4.** arbiter, bible, connoisseur, expert, judge, master, professional, scholar, specialist, textbook **5.** attestation, avowal, declaration, evidence, profession, say-so, statement, testimony, word

Authority is never without hate
Euripides *Ion*

I am a man under authority, having soldiers under me; and I say to this man, Go, and he goeth; and to another, Come, and he cometh; and to my servant, Do this, and he doeth it
Bible: St. Matthew

authorization **1.** ability, a blank cheque, authority, power, right, say-so, strength **2.** approval, credentials, leave, licence, permission, permit, sanction, say-so, warrant

authorize **1.** accredit, commission, empower, enable, entitle, give authority **2.** accredit, allow, approve, confirm, countenance, give a blank cheque to, give authority for, give leave, give the green light for, license, permit, ratify, sanction, vouch for, warrant
Antonyms ban, debar, disallow, exclude, forbid, outlaw, preclude, prohibit, proscribe, rule out, veto

authorized, authorised allowed, approved, commissioned, confirmed, countenanced, licensed, official, permitted, ratified, sanctioned, signed and sealed, warranted

autobiography history, life story, memoirs, record, résumé

An autobiography is an obituary in serial form with the last instalment missing
Quentin Crisp *The Naked Civil Servant*

autocracy absolutism, despotism, dictatorship, tyranny

autocrat absolutist, despot, dictator, tyrant

autocratic absolute, all-powerful, despotic, dictatorial, domineering, imperious, tyrannical, tyrannous, unlimited

automatic **1.** automated, mechanical, mechanized, push-button, robot, self-acting, self-activating, self-moving, self-propelling, self-regulating **2.** habitual, kneejerk, mechanical, perfunctory, routine, unconscious **3.** instinctive, instinctual, involuntary, mechanical, natural, reflex, spontaneous, unconscious, unwilled **4.** assured, certain, inescapable, inevitable, necessary, routine, unavoidable
Antonyms (*sense 1*) done by hand, hand-operated, human, manual, physical (*senses 2 & 3*) conscious, deliberate, intentional, voluntary

autonomous free, independent, self-determining, self-governing, self-ruling, sovereign

autonomy freedom, home rule, independence,

self-determination, self-government, self-rule, sovereignty
Antonyms dependency, foreign rule, subjection

autopsy dissection, necropsy, postmortem, postmortem examination

auxiliary **1.** *adjective* accessory, aiding, ancillary, assisting, back-up, emergency, fall-back, helping, reserve, secondary, subsidiary, substitute, supplementary, supporting **2.** *noun* accessory, accomplice, ally, assistant, associate, companion, confederate, helper, henchman, partner, protagonist, reserve, subordinate, supporter
Antonyms *adjective* cardinal, chief, essential, first, leading, main, primary, prime, principal

avail *verb* **1.** aid, assist, be effective, benefit, be of advantage, be of use, be useful, help, profit, serve, work **2. avail oneself of** employ, exploit, have recourse to, make the most of, make use of, profit from, take advantage of, turn to account, use, utilize *~noun* **3.** advantage, aid, assistance, benefit, boot (*obsolete*), effectiveness, efficacy, good, help, mileage (*informal*), profit, purpose, service, use, usefulness, utility

availability accessibility, attainability, handiness, obtainability, readiness

available accessible, applicable, at hand, at one's disposal, at one's fingertips, attainable, convenient, free, handy, obtainable, on hand, on tap, ready, ready for use, to hand, vacant
Antonyms busy, engaged, inaccessible, in use, occupied, spoken for, taken, unattainable, unavailable, unobtainable

avalanche **1.** landslide, landslip, snow-slide, snow-slip **2.** barrage, deluge, flood, inundation, torrent

avant-garde *adjective* experimental, far-out (*slang*), ground-breaking, innovative, innovatory, pioneering, progressive, unconventional, way-out (*informal*)
Antonyms conservative, conventional, hidebound, reactionary, traditional

avarice acquisitiveness, close-fistedness, covetousness, cupidity, graspingness, greed, greediness, meanness, miserliness, niggardliness, parsimony, penny-pinching, penuriousness, rapacity, stinginess
Antonyms benevolence, bountifulness, extravagance, generosity, largess *or* largesse, liberality, unselfishness

The love of money is the root of all evil
Bible: I Timothy

avarice, the spur of industry
David Hume *Essays: Moral and Political*

avaricious acquisitive, close-fisted, covetous, grasping, greedy, mean, miserable, miserly, niggardly, parsimonious, penny-pinching, penurious, rapacious, stingy, tight-arsed (*taboo slang*), tight as a duck's arse (*taboo slang*), tight-assed (*U.S. taboo slang*)

avenge even the score for, get even for (*informal*), get one's own back, hit back, pay (someone) back in his *or* her own coin, punish, repay, requite, retaliate, revenge, take satisfaction for, take vengeance

avenue access, alley, approach, boulevard, channel, course, drive, driveway, entrance, entry, pass, passage, path, pathway, road, route, street, thoroughfare, way

aver affirm, allege, assert, asseverate, avouch, avow, declare, maintain, proclaim, profess, pronounce, protest, say, state, swear

average *noun* **1.** common run, mean, medium, midpoint, norm, normal, par, rule, run, run of the mill, standard **2. on average** as a rule, for the most part, generally, normally, typically, usually *~adjective* **3.** banal, bog-standard (*Brit. & Irish slang*), common, commonplace, fair, general, indifferent, mediocre, middle-of-the-road, middling, moderate, no great shakes (*informal*), normal, not bad, ordinary, passable, regular, run-of-the-mill, so-so (*informal*), standard, tolerable, typical, undistinguished, unexceptional, usual, vanilla (*slang*) **4.** intermediate, mean, median, medium, middle *~verb* **5.** balance out to, be on average, do on average, even out to, make on average
Antonyms *adjective* abnormal, awful, bad, different, exceptional, great, maximum, memorable, minimum, notable, outstanding, remarkable, special, terrible, unusual

averse antipathetic, backward, disinclined, hostile, ill-disposed, indisposed, inimical, loath, opposed, reluctant, unfavourable, unwilling
Antonyms agreeable, amenable, disposed, eager, favourable, inclined, keen, sympathetic, willing

aversion abhorrence, animosity, antipathy, detestation, disgust, disinclination, dislike, distaste, hate, hatred, horror, hostility, indisposition, loathing, odium, opposition, reluctance, repugnance, repulsion, revulsion, unwillingness
Antonyms desire, inclination, liking, love, willingness

avert **1.** turn, turn aside, turn away **2.** avoid, fend off, forestall, frustrate, preclude, prevent, stave off, ward off

aviate fly, pilot

aviation aeronautics, flight, flying, powered flight

Aviation terms

aerobatics	air miss
air corridor	airside

airspeed
air traffic control
anhedral
approach *or* approach path
attitude
automatic pilot *or* autopilot
autorotation
bank
barrel roll
batsman
belly landing
bird strike
boarding pass
bunt
ceiling
chandelle
charter flight
clearway
contact flight
copilot
crab
crash-dive
crash-land
cruise
dihedral
ditch
dive
drogue
feather
flameout
flight management systems
flight path
fly-by-wire
gate
glide
groundspeed
head-up display
holding pattern
hunt
Immelmann turn *or* Immelmann
in-flight
landing
landside
loading
loop
Mach
navigator
nose dive
overfly
overshoot
pancake landing
pilot
pitch
pitch axis
power dive
rake
redeye *or* redeye flight
reheat
roll
roll axis
runway
SBA *or* standard beam approach
scheduled flight
shockstall
sideslip
snap roll
sonic boom
sound barrier
spin
stack
stall
subsonic
supersonic
tailspin
takeoff
taxi
taxiway
trim
undershoot
vapour trail
victory roll
wide-body
wingover
yaw
yaw axis

aviator aeronaut, airman, flier, pilot

avid 1. ardent, devoted, eager, enthusiastic, fanatical, fervent, intense, keen, keen as mustard, passionate, zealous 2. acquisitive, athirst, avaricious, covetous, grasping, greedy, hungry, insatiable, rapacious, ravenous, thirsty, voracious
Antonyms (*sense 1*) apathetic, impassive, indifferent, lukewarm, unenthusiastic

avidity 1. ardour, devotion, eagerness, enthusiasm, fervour, keenness, zeal 2. acquisitiveness, avarice, covetousness, cupidity, desire, graspingness, greediness, hankering, hunger, insatiability, longing, rapacity, ravenousness, thirst, voracity

avocation 1. diversion, hobby, occupation, pastime, recreation 2. business, calling, employment, job, occupation, profession, pursuit, trade, vocation, work

avoid avert, body-swerve (*Scot.*), bypass, circumvent, dodge, duck (out of) (*informal*), elude, escape, eschew, evade, fight shy of, give a wide berth to, keep aloof from, keep away from, prevent, refrain from, shirk, shun, sidestep, slip through the net, steer clear of
Antonyms approach, confront, contact, face, find, invite, pursue, seek out, solicit

avoidable avertible *or* avertable, escapable, evadable, preventable, stoppable
Antonyms inescapable, inevitable, necessary, unavoidable, unpreventable, unstoppable

avoidance body swerve (*Scot.*), circumvention, dodging, eluding, escape, eschewal, evasion, keeping away from, prevention, refraining, shirking, shunning, steering clear of

avouch acknowledge, affirm, allege, assert, asseverate, aver, avow, declare, guarantee, maintain, proclaim, profess, pronounce, state, swear, vouch for

avow acknowledge, admit, affirm, allege, assert, asseverate, aver, confess, declare, maintain, own, proclaim, profess, recognize, state, swear

avowal acknowledgment, admission, affirmation, allegation, assertion, asseveration, averment, confession, declaration, maintenance, oath, owning, proclamation, profession, recognition, statement

avowed acknowledged, admitted, confessed, declared, open, professed, self-proclaimed, sworn

await 1. abide, anticipate, expect, look for, look forward to, stay for, wait for 2. attend, be in readiness for, be in store for, be prepared for, be ready for, wait for

awake *verb* 1. awaken, rouse, wake, wake up 2. activate, alert, animate, arouse, awaken, breathe life into, call forth, enliven, excite, fan, incite, kick-start (*informal*), kindle, provoke, revive, stimulate, stir up, vivify *~adjective* 3. alert, alive, aroused, attentive, awakened, aware, bright-eyed and bushy-tailed, conscious, heedful, not sleeping, observant, on guard, on one's toes, on the alert, on the lookout, vigilant, wakeful, waking, watchful, wide-awake
Antonyms *adjective* asleep, crashed out (*slang*), dead to the world (*informal*), dormant, dozing, inattentive, napping, sleeping, unaware, unconscious

awaken activate, alert, animate, arouse, awake, breathe life into, call forth, enliven, excite, fan, incite, kick-start (*informal*), kindle, provoke, revive, rouse, stimulate, stir up, vivify, wake

awakening *noun* activation, animating, arousal, awaking, birth, enlivening, incitement, kindling, provocation, revival, rousing, stimulation, stirring up, vivification, waking, waking up

award *verb* **1.** accord, adjudge, allot, apportion, assign, bestow, confer, decree, distribute, endow, gift, give, grant, hand out, present, render *~noun* **2.** adjudication, allotment, bestowal, conferment, conferral, decision, decree, endowment, gift, hand-out, order, presentation, stipend **3.** decoration, gift, grant, prize, trophy, verdict

aware acquainted, alive to, appreciative, apprised, attentive, *au courant*, clued-up (*informal*), cognizant, conscious, conversant, enlightened, familiar, hip (*slang*), informed, in the picture, keeping one's finger on the pulse, knowing, knowledgeable, mindful, sensible, sentient, wise (*slang*)

Antonyms ignorant, insensible, oblivious, unaware, unfamiliar with, unknowledgeable

awareness acquaintance, appreciation, attention, cognizance, consciousness, enlightenment, familiarity, knowledge, mindfulness, perception, realization, recognition, sensibility, sentience, understanding

awash afloat, deluged, drowned, engulfed, flooded, immersed, inundated, overburdened, overwhelmed, submerged, submersed, swamped, swept

away *adverb* **1.** abroad, elsewhere, from here, from home, hence, off **2.** apart, at a distance, far, remote **3.** aside, out of the way, to one side **4.** continuously, incessantly, interminably, relentlessly, repeatedly, uninterruptedly, unremittingly *~adjective* **5.** abroad, absent, elsewhere, gone, not at home, not here, not present, not there, out *~interjection* **6.** beat it (*slang*), begone, be off, bugger off (*taboo slang*), fuck off (*offensive taboo slang*), get lost (*informal*), get out, go, go away, on your bike (*slang*), on your way

awe 1. *noun* admiration, amazement, astonishment, dread, fear, horror, respect, reverence, terror, veneration, wonder **2.** *verb* amaze, astonish, cow, daunt, frighten, horrify, impress, intimidate, put the wind up (*informal*), stun, terrify

Antonyms *noun* arrogance, boldness, contempt, disrespect, fearlessness, irreverence, scorn

awed afraid, amazed, astonished, cowed, daunted, dumbfounded, fearful, frightened, horrified, impressed, intimidated, shocked, stunned, terrified, wonder-stricken, wonder-struck

awe-inspiring amazing, astonishing, awesome, breathtaking, daunting, fearsome, impressive, intimidating, magnificent, striking, stunning (*informal*), wonderful, wondrous (*archaic or literary*)

Antonyms bland, boring, dull, flat, humdrum, insipid, prosaic, tame, tedious, unimpressive, uninspiring, vapid

awesome alarming, amazing, astonishing, awe-inspiring, awful, breathtaking, daunting, dreadful, fearful, fearsome, formidable, frightening, horrible, horrifying, imposing, impressive, intimidating, magnificent, majestic, overwhelming, redoubtable, shocking, solemn, striking, stunning, stupefying, terrible, terrifying, wonderful, wondrous (*archaic or literary*)

awe-struck *or* **awe-stricken** afraid, amazed, astonished, awed, awe-inspired, cowed, daunted, dumbfounded, fearful, frightened, horrified, impressed, intimidated, shocked, struck dumb, stunned, terrified, wonder-stricken, wonder-struck

awful 1. abysmal, alarming, appalling, deplorable, dire, distressing, dreadful, fearful, frightful, from hell (*informal*), ghastly, godawful (*slang*), gruesome, harrowing, hellacious (*U.S. slang*), hideous, horrendous, horrible, horrid, horrific, horrifying, nasty, shocking, terrible, tremendous, ugly, unpleasant, unsightly **2.** *archaic* amazing, awe-inspiring, awesome, dread, fearsome, majestic, portentous, solemn

Antonyms (*sense 1*) amazing, brilliant, excellent, fabulous (*informal*), fantastic, great (*informal*), magnificent, marvellous, miraculous, sensational (*informal*), smashing (*informal*), super (*informal*), superb, terrific, tremendous, wonderful

awfully 1. badly, disgracefully, disreputably, dreadfully, inadequately, reprehensibly, shoddily, unforgivably, unpleasantly, wickedly, woefully, wretchedly **2.** *informal* badly, dreadfully, exceedingly, exceptionally, excessively, extremely, greatly, immensely, quite, seriously (*informal*), terribly, very, very much

awhile briefly, for a little while, for a moment, for a short time, for a while

awkward 1. all thumbs, artless, blundering, bungling, clownish, clumsy, coarse, gauche, gawky, graceless, ham-fisted, ham-handed, ill-bred, inelegant, inept, inexpert, lumbering, maladroit, oafish, rude, skill-less, stiff, uncoordinated, uncouth, ungainly, ungraceful, unpolished, unrefined, unskilful, unskilled **2.** clunky (*informal*), cumbersome, difficult, inconvenient, troublesome, unhandy, unmanageable, unwieldy **3.** compromising, cringe-making (*Brit. informal*), delicate, difficult, embarrassed, embarrassing, ill at ease, incon~

venient, inopportune, painful, perplexing, sticky (*informal*), thorny, ticklish, troublesome, trying, uncomfortable, unpleasant, untimely **4**. annoying, bloody-minded (*Brit. informal*), difficult, disobliging, exasperating, hard to handle, intractable, irritable, perverse, prickly, stubborn, touchy, troublesome, trying, uncooperative, unhelpful, unpredictable, vexatious, vexing **5**. chancy (*informal*), dangerous, difficult, hazardous, perilous, risky **Antonyms** (*sense 1*) adept, adroit, dexterous, graceful, skilful (*sense 2*) convenient, easy, handy (*sense 3*) comfortable, pleasant

awkwardness **1**. artlessness, clownishness, clumsiness, coarseness, gaucheness, gaucherie, gawkiness, gracelessness, ill-breeding, inelegance, ineptness, inexpertness, maladroitness, oafishness, rudeness, stiffness, uncoordination, uncouthness, ungainliness, unskilfulness, unskilledness **2**. cumbersomeness, difficulty, inconvenience, troublesomeness, unhandiness, unmanageability, unwieldiness **3**. delicacy, difficulty, discomfort, embarrassment, inconvenience, inopportuneness, painfulness, perplexingness, stickiness (*informal*), thorniness, ticklishness, unpleasantness, untimeliness **4**. bloody-mindedness (*Brit. informal*), difficulty, disobligingness, intractability, irritability, perversity, prickliness, stubbornness, touchiness, uncooperativeness, unhelpfulness, unpredictability **5**. chanciness (*informal*), danger, difficulty, hazardousness, peril, perilousness, risk, riskiness

awry *adverb/adjective* amiss, askew, asymmetrical, cockeyed (*informal*), crooked, crookedly, misaligned, obliquely, off-centre, off course, out of line, out of true, skew-whiff (*informal*), to one side, twisted, uneven, unevenly, wrong

axe *noun* **1**. adze, chopper, hatchet **2**. **an axe to grind** grievance, personal consideration, pet subject, private ends, private purpose, ulterior motive **3**. **the axe** *informal* cancellation, cutback, discharge, dismissal, termination, the boot (*slang*), the chop (*slang*), the (old) heave-ho (*informal*), the order of the boot (*slang*), the sack (*informal*), wind-up ~*verb* **4**. chop, cut down, fell, hew **5**. *informal* cancel, cut back, discharge, dismiss, dispense with, eliminate, fire (*informal*), get rid of, give (someone) their marching orders, give the boot to (*slang*), give the bullet to (*Brit. slang*), give the push, oust, pull, pull the plug on, relegate, remove, sack (*informal*), terminate, throw out, turn off (*informal*), wind up

axiom adage, aphorism, apophthegm, dictum, fundamental, gnome, maxim, postulate, precept, principle, truism

axiomatic **1**. absolute, accepted, apodictic *or* apodeictic, assumed, certain, fundamental, given, granted, indubitable, manifest, presupposed, self-evident, understood, unquestioned **2**. aphoristic, apophthegmatic, epigrammatic, gnomic, pithy, terse

axis **1**. axle, centre line, pivot, shaft, spindle **2**. alliance, bloc, coalition, compact, entente, league, pact

axle arbor, axis, mandrel, pin, pivot, rod, shaft, spindle

azure blue, cerulean, clear blue, sky-blue, sky-coloured, ultramarine

B

babble 1. *verb* blab, burble, cackle, chatter, gabble, gibber, gurgle, jabber, mumble, murmur, mutter, prate, prattle, rabbit (on) (*Brit. informal*), run off at the mouth (*slang*), waffle (*informal, chiefly Brit.*) 2. *noun* burble, clamour, drivel, gabble, gibberish, murmur, waffle (*informal, chiefly Brit.*)

babe 1. ankle-biter (*Austral. slang*), baby, bairn (*Scot.*), child, infant, nursling, rug rat (*slang*), sprog (*slang*), suckling 2. babe in arms, ingénue *or* (*masc.*) ingénu, innocent

babel bedlam, clamour, confusion, din, disorder, hubbub, hullabaloo, hurly-burly, pandemonium, tumult, turmoil, uproar

baby 1. *noun* ankle-biter (*Austral. slang*), babe, babe in arms, bairn (*Scot.*), child, infant, newborn child, rug rat (*slang*), sprog (*slang*) 2. *adjective* diminutive, dwarf, little, midget, mini, miniature, minute, pygmy *or* pigmy, small, teensy-weensy, teeny-weeny, tiny, wee 3. *verb* coddle, cosset, humour, indulge, mollycoddle, overindulge, pamper, pet, spoil, spoon-feed

People who say they sleep like a baby usually don't have one

Leo Burke

baby: a misshapen creature of no particular age, sex or condition, chiefly remarkable for the violence of the sympathies and antipathies it excites in others, itself without sentiment or emotion

Ambrose Bierce *The Devil's Dictionary*

babyish baby, childish, foolish, immature, infantile, juvenile, namby-pamby, puerile, silly, sissy, soft (*informal*), spoiled

Antonyms adult, grown-up, mature, of age

bacchanal 1. carouser, debauchee, drunkard, reveller, roisterer, winebibber 2. debauch, debauchery, orgy, revel, revelry

bachelor

A bachelor never quite gets over the idea that he is a thing of beauty and a boy forever

Helen Rowland

It is a truth universally acknowledged, that a single man in possession of a good fortune, must be in want of a wife

Jane Austen *Pride and Prejudice*

back *verb* 1. abet, advocate, assist, champion, countenance, encourage, endorse, espouse, favour, finance, promote, sanction, second, side with, sponsor, subsidize, support, sustain, underwrite 2. back off, backtrack, go back, move back, regress, retire, retreat, reverse, turn tail, withdraw ~*noun* 3. backside, end, far end, hind part, hindquarters, posterior, rear, reverse, stern, tail end ~*adjective* 4. end, hind, hindmost, posterior, rear, tail 5. *From an earlier time* delayed, earlier, elapsed, former, overdue, past, previous 6. **behind one's back** covertly, deceitfully, secretly, sneakily, surreptitiously

Antonyms *verb* (*sense 1*) attack, combat, hinder, thwart, undermine, weaken (*sense 2*) advance, approach, move forward, progress ~*noun* face, fore, front, head ~*adjective* advance, fore, front, future, late

backbite abuse, bad-mouth (*slang, chiefly U.S. & Canad.*), calumniate, defame, denigrate, detract, knock (*informal*), libel, malign, revile, rubbish (*informal*), slag (off) (*slang*), slander, traduce, vilify, vituperate

backbiting abuse, aspersion, bitchiness (*slang*), calumniation, calumny, cattiness (*informal*), defamation, denigration, detraction, disparagement, gossip, malice, scandalmongering, slander, spite, spitefulness, vilification, vituperation

backbone 1. *Medical* spinal column, spine, vertebrae, vertebral column 2. bottle (*Brit. slang*), character, courage, determination, firmness, fortitude, grit, hardihood, mettle, moral fibre, nerve, pluck, resolution, resolve, stamina, steadfastness, strength of character, tenacity, toughness, will, willpower 3. basis, foundation, mainstay, support

backbreaking arduous, crushing, exhausting, gruelling, hard, killing, laborious, punishing, strenuous, toilsome, wearing, wearying

backchat answering back, cheek, impertinence, impudence, insolence, lip (*slang*), sass (*U.S. & Canad. informal*), talking back, verbals (*Brit. slang*)

back down accede, admit defeat, back-pedal, concede, give in, surrender, withdraw, yield

backer advocate, angel (*informal*), benefactor, patron, promoter, second, sponsor, subscriber, supporter, underwriter, well-wisher

backfire boomerang, disappoint, fail, flop (*informal*), miscarry, rebound, recoil

background breeding, circumstances, credentials, culture, education, environment, experience, grounding, history, milieu, preparation, qualifications, tradition, upbringing

backhanded ambiguous, double-edged, equivocal, indirect, ironic, oblique, sarcastic, sardonic, two-edged, with tongue in cheek

backing abetment, accompaniment, advocacy, aid, assistance, championing, encouragement, endorsement, espousal, funds, grant, moral support, patronage, promotion, sanction, seconding, sponsorship, subsidy, support

backlash backfire, boomerang, counteraction, counterblast, kickback, reaction, recoil, repercussion, resentment, resistance, response, retaliation, retroaction

backlog accumulation, build-up, excess, hoard, reserve, reserves, resources, stock, supply

back out abandon, cancel, chicken out (*informal*), cop out (*slang*), give up, go back on, recant, renege, resign, retreat, withdraw

backside **1.** back, end, far end, hind part, hindquarters, posterior, rear, reverse, stern, tail end **2.** arse (*taboo slang*), ass (*U.S. & Canad. taboo slang*), behind (*informal*), bottom, bum (*Brit. slang*), buns (*U.S. slang*), butt (*U.S. & Canad. informal*), buttocks, cheeks (*informal*), coit (*Austral. slang*), derrière (*euphemistic*), fanny (*slang, chiefly U.S. & Canad.*), fundament, jacksy (*Brit. slang*), keister *or* keester (*slang, chiefly U.S.*), nates (*technical name*), posterior, rear, rear end, rump, seat, tail (*U.S.*)

backslide fall from grace, go astray, go wrong, lapse, regress, relapse, renege, retrogress, revert, sin, slip, stray, weaken

backslider apostate, deserter, recidivist, recreant, renegade, reneger, turncoat

backtrack **1.** back, backpedal, go back, move back, retrace one's steps, retreat, reverse **2.** draw back, eat one's words, recant, retract, retreat, withdraw

back up aid, assist, bolster, confirm, corroborate, reinforce, second, stand by, substantiate, support

backup **1.** aid, assistance, backing, help, reinforcement, reserves, support **2.** locum, relief, replacement, reserve, second string, stand-by, stand-in, substitute, understudy

backward *adjective* **1.** bashful, diffident, hesitating, late, reluctant, shy, sluggish, tardy, unwilling, wavering **2.** behind, behindhand, braindead (*informal*), dead from the neck up (*informal*), dense, dozy (*Brit. informal*), dull, obtuse, retarded, slow, stupid, subnormal, underdeveloped, undeveloped *~adverb* **3.** aback, behind, in reverse, rearward
Antonyms *adjective* advanced, ahead, bold, brash, eager, forward, pushy (*informal*), willing *~adverb* correctly, forward, frontward, properly

backwardness **1.** bashfulness, diffidence, dilatoriness, hesitancy, reluctance, restraint, reticence, shyness, sluggishness, tardiness, unwillingness **2.** arrested development, denseness, doziness (*informal*), dullness, learning difficulties, retardation, slowness, underdevelopment
Antonyms (*sense 1*) assertiveness, boldness, confidence, forwardness, willingness (*sense 2*) brightness, precociousness, precocity, quickness, smartness

backwoods **1.** *adjective* agrestic, hick (*informal, chiefly U.S. & Canad.*), isolated, remote, rustic, uncouth **2.** *noun* back country (*U.S.*), backlands (*U.S.*), back of beyond, middle of nowhere, outback, sticks (*informal*)

bacteria bacilli, bugs (*slang*), germs, microbes, microorganisms, pathogens, viruses

bad **1.** chickenshit (*U.S. slang*), defective, deficient, duff (*Brit. informal*), erroneous, fallacious, faulty, imperfect, inadequate, incorrect, inferior, low-rent (*informal, chiefly U.S.*), of a sort *or* of sorts, pathetic, poor, poxy (*slang*), substandard, unsatisfactory **2.** damaging, dangerous, deleterious, detrimental, harmful, hurtful, injurious, ruinous, unhealthy **3.** base, corrupt, criminal, delinquent, evil, immoral, mean, sinful, vile, villainous, wicked, wrong **4.** disobedient, mischievous, naughty, unruly **5.** decayed, mouldy, off, putrid, rancid, rotten, sour, spoiled **6.** disastrous, distressing, grave, harsh, painful, serious, severe, terrible **7.** ailing, diseased, ill, sick, unwell **8.** apologetic, conscience-stricken, contrite, guilty, regretful, remorseful, sad, sorry, upset **9.** adverse, discouraged, discouraging, distressed, distressing, gloomy, grim, low, melancholy, troubled, troubling, unfortunate, unpleasant **10.** **not bad** all right, average, fair, fair to middling (*informal*), moderate, O.K. *or* okay (*informal*), passable, respectable, so-so (*informal*), tolerable
Antonyms (*sense 1*) adequate, fair, satisfactory (*sense 2*) agreeable, beneficial, good, healthful, safe, sound, wholesome (*sense 3*) ethical, fine, first-rate, good, moral, righteous, virtuous (*sense 4*) biddable, docile, good, obedient, well-behaved

> *When I'm good, I'm very good, but when I'm bad I'm better*
>
> Mae West

bad blood acrimony, anger, animosity, antagonism, dislike, enmity, feud, hatred, ill feeling, ill will, malevolence, malice, rancour, resentment, seeing red

baddie, baddy antihero, bad guy, villain
Antonyms good guy, goody, hero, heroine

badge brand, device, emblem, identification, insignia, mark, sign, stamp, token

badger bend someone's ear (*informal*), bully, chivvy, goad, harass, harry, hound, importune, nag, pester, plague, torment

badinage banter, chaff, drollery, mockery, persiflage, pleasantry, raillery, repartee, teasing, waggery, wordplay

badly **1.** carelessly, defectively, erroneously, faultily, imperfectly, inadequately, incorrectly, ineptly, poorly, shoddily, wrong, wrongly **2.** unfavourably, unfortunately, unsuccessfully **3.** criminally, evilly, immorally, improperly, naughtily, shamefully, unethically, wickedly **4.** acutely, deeply, desperately, exceedingly, extremely, gravely, greatly, intensely, painfully, seriously, severely
Antonyms ably, competently, correctly, ethically, morally, properly, righteously, rightly, satisfactorily, splendidly, well

bad manners boorishness, churlishness, coarseness, discourtesy, disrespect, impoliteness, incivility, inconsideration, indelicacy, rudeness, unmannerliness
Antonyms civility, cordiality, courteousness, courtesy, good manners, graciousness, politeness, urbanity

badness baseness, corruption, delinquency, evil, foulness, immorality, impropriety, meanness, naughtiness, rottenness, shamefulness, sin, sinfulness, vileness, villainy, wickedness, wrong
Antonyms excellence, good, goodness, morality, rectitude, righteousness, uprightness, virtue

bad-tempered angry, cantankerous, choleric, crabbed, cross, crotchety (*informal*), grouchy (*informal*), grumbling, huffy, ill-tempered, irascible, irritable, liverish, peevish, petulant, querulous, ratty (*Brit. & N.Z. informal*), splenetic, sulky, sullen, surly, testy, tetchy
Antonyms affable, amiable, cheerful, genial, good-humoured, good-tempered, happy, pleasant, sanguine

baffle **1.** amaze, astound, bewilder, boggle the mind, confound, confuse, daze, disconcert, dumbfound, elude, flummox, mystify, nonplus, perplex, puzzle, stump, stun **2.** balk, check, defeat, foil, frustrate, hinder, thwart, upset
Antonyms (*sense 1*) clarify, clear up, elucidate, explain, explicate, interpret, make plain, shed *or* throw light upon, spell out

baffling bewildering, confusing, difficult, elusive, enigmatic, inexplicable, misleading, mysterious, mystifying, perplexing, puzzling, strange, unaccountable, unfathomable, weird
Antonyms clear, easy, intelligible, obvious, simple, understandable

bag *verb* **1.** balloon, bulge, droop, sag, swell **2.** acquire, capture, catch, gain, get, kill, land, shoot, take, trap *~noun* **3.** poke (*Scot.*), receptacle, sac, sack

Types of bag

backpack
bergen
briefcase
bum bag
carpetbag
carrier bag
clutch bag
ditty bag
duffel bag
Gladstone bag
handbag
haversack
holdall *or* (*U.S. & Canad.*) carryall
kitbag
knapsack
nunny bag (*Canad.*)
reticule
rucksack
sabretache
saddlebag
satchel
sea bag
shoulder bag
suitcase
tucker bag
valise
vanity bag, vanity case *or* vanity box
water bag
workbag

baggage accoutrements, bags, belongings, equipment, gear, impedimenta, luggage, paraphernalia, suitcases, things

baggy billowing, bulging, droopy, floppy, ill-fitting, loose, oversize, roomy, sagging, seated, slack
Antonyms close, close-fitting, constricted, cramped, narrow, snug, stretched, taut, tight, tight-fitting

bail[1] *noun* bond, guarantee, guaranty, pledge, security, surety, warranty

bail[2], **bale** *verb* dip, drain off, ladle, scoop

bail out, bale out **1.** aid, help, relieve, rescue, save (someone's) bacon (*informal, chiefly Brit.*) **2.** escape, quit, retreat, withdraw

bait *noun* **1.** allurement, attraction, bribe, carrot and stick, decoy, enticement, incentive, inducement, lure, snare, temptation *~verb* **2.** aggravate (*informal*), annoy, be on one's back (*slang*), bother, gall, get *or* take a rise out of, get in one's hair (*informal*), get one's back up, get on one's nerves (*informal*), harass, hassle (*informal*), hound, irk, irritate, nark (*Brit., Austral. & N.Z. slang*), needle (*informal*), persecute, piss one off (*taboo slang*), provoke, put one's back up, tease, torment, wind up (*Brit. slang*) **3.** allure, beguile, entice, lure, seduce, tempt

baked arid, desiccated, dry, parched, scorched, seared, sun-baked, torrid

balance *verb* **1.** level, librate, match, parallel, poise, stabilize, steady **2.** adjust, compensate for, counteract, counterbalance, counterpoise, equalize, equate, make up for, neutralize, offset **3.** assess, compare, consider, deliberate, estimate, evaluate, weigh **4.** calculate, compute, settle, square, tally, total *~noun* **5.** correspondence, equilibrium, equipoise, equity,

equivalence, evenness, parity, symmetry **6.** composure, equanimity, poise, self-control, self-possession, stability, steadiness **7.** differ~ence, remainder, residue, rest, surplus
Antonyms *verb* outweigh, overbalance, upset *~noun* disproportion, instability, shakiness, unbalance, uncertainty

balanced disinterested, equitable, even-handed, fair, impartial, just, unbiased, un~prejudiced
Antonyms biased, distorted, jaundiced, lop~sided, one-sided, partial, predisposed, preju~diced, slanted, unfair, warped, weighted

balance sheet account, budget, credits and debits, ledger, report, statement

balcony **1.** terrace, veranda **2.** gallery, gods, upper circle

bald **1.** baldheaded, baldpated, depilated, gla~brous (*Biology*), hairless **2.** barren, bleak, ex~posed, naked, stark, treeless, uncovered **3.** bare, blunt, direct, downright, forthright, out~right, plain, severe, simple, straight, straight~forward, unadorned, unvarnished, upfront (*informal*)

balderdash balls (*taboo slang*), bilge (*infor~mal*), bosh (*informal*), bull (*slang*), bullshit (*taboo slang*), bunk (*informal*), bunkum *or* buncombe (*chiefly U.S.*), claptrap (*informal*), cobblers (*Brit. taboo slang*), crap (*slang*), driv~el, eyewash (*informal*), garbage (*informal*), gibberish, guff (*slang*), hogwash, hokum (*slang, chiefly U.S. & Canad.*), horsefeathers (*U.S. slang*), hot air (*informal*), moonshine, nonsense, pap, piffle (*informal*), poppycock (*informal*), rot, rubbish, shit (*taboo slang*), tommyrot, tosh (*slang, chiefly Brit.*), trash, tripe (*informal*), twaddle

balding losing one's hair, receding, thin on top

baldness **1.** alopecia (*Pathology*), baldheaded~ness, baldpatedness, glabrousness (*Biology*), hairlessness **2.** barrenness, bleakness, naked~ness, sparseness, starkness, treelessness **3.** austerity, bluntness, plainness, severity, sim~plicity, spareness

bale *see* BAIL[2]

baleful calamitous, deadly, evil, harmful, hurt~ful, injurious, maleficent, malevolent, malig~nant, menacing, mournful, noxious, ominous, pernicious, ruinous, sad, sinister, venomous, woeful
Antonyms beneficial, benevolent, benign, friendly, good, healthy, salubrious

bale out *see* BAIL OUT

balk **1.** demur, dodge, evade, flinch, hesitate, jib, recoil, refuse, resist, shirk, shrink from **2.** baffle, bar, check, counteract, defeat, discon~cert, foil, forestall, frustrate, hinder, obstruct, prevent, thwart
Antonyms (*sense 1*) accede, accept, acquiesce, comply, relent, submit, yield (*sense 2*) abet, advance, aid, assist, further, help, promote, support, sustain

balky intractable, obstinate, stubborn, unco~operative, unmanageable, unpredictable, un~ruly

ball **1.** drop, globe, globule, orb, pellet, sphere, spheroid **2.** ammunition, bullet, grapeshot, pellet, shot, slug

ballast balance, counterbalance, counterweight, equilibrium, sandbag, stability, stabilizer, weight

balloon *verb* belly, billow, bloat, blow up, di~late, distend, enlarge, expand, grow rapidly, inflate, puff out, swell

ballot election, poll, polling, vote, voting

balls *plural noun* **1.** bollocks *or* ballocks (*taboo slang*), cobblers (*Brit. taboo slang*), *cojones* (*U.S. taboo slang*), family jewels (*slang*), gon~ads, goolies (*taboo slang*), nuts (*taboo slang*), rocks (*U.S. taboo slang*), testes, testicles **2.** backbone, bottle (*slang*), *cojones* (*U.S. taboo slang*), courage, face (*informal*), grit, guts (*in~formal*), nerve, spirit, spunk (*informal*), toughness *~plural noun/interjection* **3.** bull (*slang*), bullshit (*taboo slang*), claptrap (*infor~mal*), cobblers (*Brit. taboo slang*), codswallop (*Brit. slang*), crap (*slang*), garbage (*informal*), horsefeathers (*U.S. slang*), nonsense, poppy~cock (*informal*), rubbish, tosh (*slang, chiefly Brit.*)

ballyhoo **1.** babble, commotion, fuss, hubbub, hue and cry, hullabaloo, noise, racket, to-do **2.** advertising, build-up, hype, promotion, propa~ganda, publicity

balm **1.** balsam, cream, embrocation, emollient, lotion, ointment, salve, unguent **2.** anodyne, comfort, consolation, curative, palliative, re~storative, solace

balmy **1.** clement, mild, pleasant, summery, temperate **2.** *Also* **barmy** crackpot (*informal*), crazy, daft (*informal*), doolally (*slang*), foolish, gonzo (*slang*), goofy (*informal*), idiotic, insane, loony (*slang*), loopy (*informal*), nuts (*slang*), nutty (*slang*), odd, off one's rocker (*slang*), off one's trolley (*slang*), out of one's mind, out to lunch (*informal*), round the twist (*Brit. slang*), silly, stupid, up the pole (*informal*), wacko *or* whacko (*informal*)
Antonyms (*sense 1*) annoying, discomforting, harsh, inclement, intense, irksome, rough, stormy

bamboozle **1.** cheat, con (*informal*), deceive, defraud, delude, dupe, fool, hoax, hoodwink, pull a fast one on (*informal*), skin (*slang*), swindle, trick **2.** baffle, befuddle, confound, confuse, mystify, perplex, puzzle, stump

ban **1.** *verb* banish, bar, black, blackball, block, boycott, debar, disallow, disqualify, exclude, forbid, interdict, outlaw, prohibit, proscribe, restrict, suppress **2.** *noun* block, boycott, censorship, disqualification, embargo, interdict, interdiction, prohibition, proscription, restriction, stoppage, suppression, taboo

Antonyms *verb* allow, approve, authorize, enable, let, permit, sanction *~noun* allowance, approval, permission, sanction

banal clichéd, cliché-ridden, commonplace, everyday, hackneyed, humdrum, mundane, old hat, ordinary, pedestrian, platitudinous, stale, stereotyped, stock, threadbare, tired, trite, unimaginative, unoriginal, vanilla (*slang*), vapid

Antonyms challenging, distinctive, fresh, ground-breaking, imaginative, interesting, new, novel, original, stimulating, unique, unusual

banality bromide (*informal*), cliché, commonplace, platitude, triteness, trite phrase, triviality, truism, vapidity

band[1] *noun* bandage, belt, binding, bond, chain, cord, fetter, fillet, ligature, manacle, ribbon, shackle, strap, strip, tie

band[2] *noun* **1.** assembly, association, bevy, body, camp, clique, club, company, coterie, crew (*informal*), gang, horde, party, posse (*informal*), society, troop **2.** combo, ensemble, group, orchestra *~verb* **3.** affiliate, ally, consolidate, federate, gather, group, join, merge, unite

Antonyms *verb* cleave, disperse, disunite, divide, part, segregate, separate, split, sunder

bandage 1. *noun* compress, dressing, gauze, plaster **2.** *verb* bind, cover, dress, swathe

bandit brigand, crook, desperado, footpad, freebooter, gangster, gunman, highwayman, hijacker, marauder, outlaw, pirate, racketeer, robber, thief

bandy 1. *verb* barter, exchange, interchange, pass, shuffle, swap, throw, toss, trade **2.** *adjective* bandy-legged, bent, bowed, bow-legged, crooked, curved

bane affliction, bête noire, blight, burden, calamity, curse, despair, destruction, disaster, downfall, misery, nuisance, pest, plague, ruin, scourge, torment, trial, trouble, woe

Antonyms blessing, comfort, consolation, joy, pleasure, relief, solace, support

baneful baleful, calamitous, deadly, deleterious, destructive, disastrous, fatal, harmful, hurtful, injurious, maleficent, noxious, pernicious, pestilential, ruinous, venomous

bang *noun* **1.** boom, burst, clang, clap, clash, detonation, explosion, peal, pop, report, shot, slam, thud, thump **2.** belt (*informal*), blow, box, bump, cuff, hit, knock, punch, smack, stroke, wallop (*informal*), whack *~verb* **3.** bash (*informal*), beat, belt (*informal*), bump, clatter, crash, hammer, knock, pound, pummel, rap, slam, strike, thump **4.** boom, burst, clang, detonate, drum, echo, explode, peal, resound, thump, thunder *~adverb* **5.** abruptly, hard, headlong, noisily, precisely, slap, smack, straight, suddenly

banish 1. deport, drive away, eject, evict, exclude, excommunicate, exile, expatriate, expel, ostracize, outlaw, shut out, transport **2.** ban, cast out, discard, dislodge, dismiss, dispel, eliminate, eradicate, get rid of, oust, remove, shake off

Antonyms accept, admit, embrace, hail, invite, offer hospitality to, receive, welcome

banishment deportation, exile, expatriation, expulsion, proscription, transportation

banisters balusters, balustrade, handrail, rail, railing

bank[1] 1. *noun* accumulation, depository, fund, hoard, repository, reserve, reservoir, savings, stock, stockpile, store, storehouse **2.** *verb* deal with, deposit, keep, save, transact business with

bank[2] *noun* **1.** banking, embankment, heap, mass, mound, pile, ridge **2.** brink, edge, margin, shore, side *~verb* **3.** amass, heap, mass, mound, pile, stack **4.** camber, cant, heel, incline, pitch, slant, slope, tilt, tip

bank[3] *noun* array, file, group, line, rank, row, sequence, series, succession, tier, train

bank on assume, believe in, count on, depend on, lean on, look to, rely on, trust

bankrupt broke (*informal*), depleted, destitute, exhausted, failed, impoverished, in queer street, insolvent, in the red, lacking, on one's uppers, on the rocks, ruined, spent, wiped out (*informal*)

Antonyms in the money (*informal*), on the up and up, prosperous, solvent, sound, wealthy

bankruptcy disaster, exhaustion, failure, indebtedness, insolvency, lack, liquidation, ruin

banner banderole, burgee, colours, ensign, fanion, flag, gonfalon, pennant, pennon, standard, streamer

banquet dinner, feast, meal, repast, revel, treat

banter 1. *verb* chaff, deride, jeer, jest, joke, josh (*slang, chiefly U.S. & Canad.*), kid (*informal*), make fun of, rib (*informal*), ridicule, take the mickey (*informal*), taunt, tease, twit **2.** *noun* badinage, chaff, chaffing, derision, jeering, jesting, joking, kidding (*informal*), mockery, persiflage, pleasantry, raillery, repartee, ribbing (*informal*), ridicule, wordplay

baptism 1. christening, immersion, purification, sprinkling **2.** beginning, debut, dedication, initiation, introduction, launching, rite of passage

baptize 1. besprinkle, cleanse, immerse, purify 2. admit, enrol, initiate, recruit 3. call, christen, dub, name, title

bar *noun* 1. batten, crosspiece, paling, palisade, pole, rail, rod, shaft, stake, stick 2. barricade, barrier, block, deterrent, hindrance, impediment, interdict, obstacle, obstruction, rail, railing, stop 3. boozer (*Brit., Austral. & N.Z. informal*), canteen, counter, hostelry (*archaic or facetious*), inn, lounge, pub (*informal, chiefly Brit.*), public house, saloon, taproom, tavern, watering hole (*facetious slang*) 4. bench, court, courtroom, dock, law court 5. *Law* barristers, body of lawyers, counsel, court, judgment, tribunal ~*verb* 6. barricade, bolt, fasten, latch, lock, secure 7. ban, black, blackball, exclude, forbid, hinder, keep out, obstruct, prevent, prohibit, restrain
Antonyms *noun* (*sense 2*) aid, benefit, help ~*verb* (*sense 7*) accept, admit, allow, clear, let, open, permit, receive

barb 1. bristle, point, prickle, prong, quill, spike, spur, thorn 2. affront, cut, dig, gibe, insult, rebuff, sarcasm, scoff, sneer

barbarian *noun* 1. brute, hooligan, lout, lowbrow, ned (*slang*), ruffian, savage, vandal, yahoo 2. bigot, boor, ignoramus, illiterate, lowbrow, philistine ~*adjective* 3. boorish, crude, lowbrow, philistine, primitive, rough, uncouth, uncultivated, uncultured, unsophisticated, vulgar, wild
Antonyms *adjective* civil, civilized, cultured, genteel, highbrow, refined, sophisticated, urbane, well-mannered

barbaric 1. primitive, rude, uncivilized, wild 2. barbarous, boorish, brutal, coarse, crude, cruel, fierce, inhuman, savage, uncouth, vulgar
Antonyms civilized, cultivated, cultured, gentlemanly, gracious, humane, refined, sophisticated, urbane

barbarism 1. coarseness, crudity, savagery, uncivilizedness 2. atrocity, barbarity, enormity, outrage 3. corruption, misusage, misuse, solecism, vulgarism

barbarity brutality, cruelty, inhumanity, ruthlessness, savagery, viciousness

barbarous 1. barbarian, brutish, primitive, rough, rude, savage, uncivilized, uncouth, wild 2. barbaric, brutal, cruel, ferocious, heartless, inhuman, monstrous, ruthless, vicious 3. coarse, crude, ignorant, uncultured, unlettered, unrefined, vulgar

barbed 1. hooked, jagged, prickly, pronged, spiked, spiny, thorny, toothed 2. acid, acrid, catty (*informal*), critical, cutting, hostile, hurtful, nasty, pointed, scathing, unkind

bard minstrel, poet, rhymer, singer, troubadour

bare 1. buck naked (*slang*), denuded, exposed, in the bare scud (*slang*), in the raw (*informal*), naked, naked as the day one was born (*informal*), nude, peeled, scuddy (*slang*), shorn, stripped, unclad, unclothed, uncovered, undressed, without a stitch on (*informal*) 2. barren, blank, empty, lacking, mean, open, poor, scanty, scarce, unfurnished, vacant, void, wanting 3. austere, bald, basic, cold, essential, hard, literal, plain, severe, sheer, simple, spare, spartan, stark, unadorned, unembellished, unfussy, unvarnished
Antonyms abundant, adorned, attired, clad, clothed, concealed, covered, dressed, full, hidden, plentiful, profuse, well-stocked

barefaced 1. audacious, bold, brash, brazen, impudent, insolent, shameless 2. bald, blatant, flagrant, glaring, manifest, naked, obvious, open, palpable, patent, transparent, unconcealed
Antonyms concealed, covered, hidden, inconspicuous, masked, obscured, secret, tucked away, unseen

barely almost, at a push, by the skin of one's teeth, hardly, just, only just, scarcely
Antonyms amply, completely, fully, profusely

bargain *noun* 1. agreement, arrangement, business, compact, contract, convention, engagement, negotiation, pact, pledge, promise, stipulation, transaction, treaty, understanding 2. (cheap) purchase, discount, giveaway, good buy, good deal, good value, reduction, snip (*informal*), steal (*informal*) ~*verb* 3. agree, contract, covenant, negotiate, promise, stipulate, transact 4. barter, buy, deal, haggle, sell, trade, traffic

bargain for anticipate, contemplate, expect, foresee, imagine, look for, plan for

bargain on assume, bank on, count on, depend on, plan on, rely on

barge canal boat, flatboat, lighter, narrow boat, scow

barge in break in, burst in, butt in, infringe, interrupt, intrude, muscle in (*informal*)

barge into bump into, cannon into, collide with, hit, push, shove

bark[1] 1. *noun* casing, cortex (*Anatomy, Botany*), covering, crust, husk, rind, skin 2. *verb* abrade, flay, rub, scrape, shave, skin, strip

bark[2] 1. *noun/verb* bay, growl, howl, snarl, woof, yap, yelp 2. *verb, figurative* bawl, bawl at, berate, bluster, growl, shout, snap, snarl, yell

barmy 1. *Also* **balmy** crackpot (*informal*), crazy, daft (*informal*), dippy, doolally (*slang*), foolish, gonzo (*slang*), goofy (*informal*), idiotic, insane, loony (*slang*), loopy (*informal*), nuts (*slang*), nutty (*slang*), odd, off one's rocker (*slang*), off one's trolley (*slang*), out of one's mind, out to lunch (*informal*), round the twist (*Brit. slang*), silly, stupid, up the pole (*infor~*

mal), wacko *or* whacko (*informal*) **2.** fermenting, foamy, frothy, spumy, yeasty
Antonyms (*sense 1*) all there (*informal*), in one's right mind, of sound mind, rational, reasonable, sane, sensible

baroque bizarre, convoluted, elaborate, extravagant, flamboyant, florid, grotesque, ornate, overdecorated, rococo

barrack abuse, boo, criticize, gibe *or* jibe, heckle, jeer, mock, taunt

barracks billet, camp, cantonment, casern, encampment, garrison, quarters

barrage **1.** battery, bombardment, cannonade, curtain of fire, fusillade, gunfire, salvo, shelling, volley **2.** assault, attack, burst, deluge, hail, mass, onslaught, plethora, profusion, rain, storm, stream, torrent

barred **1.** banded, crosshatched, lined, marked, ribbed, ridged, streaked, striped, veined **2.** banned, excluded, forbidden, off limits, outlawed, prohibited, proscribed, taboo

barren **1.** childless, infecund, infertile, sterile, unprolific **2.** arid, desert, desolate, dry, empty, unfruitful, unproductive, waste **3.** boring, dull, flat, fruitless, lacklustre, stale, uninformative, uninspiring, uninstructive, uninteresting, unrewarding, useless, vapid
Antonyms fecund, fertile, fruitful, instructive, interesting, lush, productive, profitable, rich, useful

barricade **1.** *noun* barrier, blockade, bulwark, fence, obstruction, palisade, rampart, stockade **2.** *verb* bar, block, blockade, defend, fortify, obstruct, protect, shut in

barrier **1.** bar, barricade, block, blockade, boundary, ditch, fence, fortification, obstacle, obstruction, pale, railing, rampart, stop, wall **2.** *figurative* check, difficulty, drawback, handicap, hazard, hindrance, hurdle, impediment, limitation, obstacle, restriction, stumbling block

barter bargain, drive a hard bargain, exchange, haggle, sell, swap, trade, traffic

base[1] *noun* **1.** bed, bottom, foot, foundation, groundwork, pedestal, rest, stand, support **2.** basis, core, essence, essential, fundamental, heart, key, origin, principle, root, source **3.** camp, centre, headquarters, home, post, settlement, starting point, station *~verb* **4.** build, construct, depend, derive, establish, found, ground, hinge, locate, station
Antonyms (*sense 1*) apex, crest, crown, peak, summit, top, vertex

base[2] *adjective* **1.** abject, contemptible, corrupt, depraved, despicable, dishonourable, disreputable, evil, ignoble, immoral, infamous, scandalous, shameful, sordid, vile, villainous, vulgar, wicked **2.** downtrodden, grovelling, low, lowly, mean, menial, miserable, paltry, pitiful, poor, servile, slavish, sorry, subservient, worthless, wretched **3.** adulterated, alloyed, counterfeit, debased, fake, forged, fraudulent, impure, inferior, pinchbeck, spurious
Antonyms admirable, good, honest, honourable, just, lofty, moral, noble, pure, rare, righteous, unalloyed, upright, valuable, virtuous

baseless groundless, unconfirmed, uncorroborated, unfounded, ungrounded, unjustifiable, unjustified, unsubstantiated, unsupported
Antonyms authenticated, confirmed, corroborated, proven, substantiated, supported, validated, verified, well-founded

baseness **1.** contemptibility, degradation, depravation, depravity, despicability, disgrace, ignominy, infamy, notoriety, obloquy, turpitude **2.** lowliness, meanness, misery, poverty, servility, slavishness, subservience, vileness, worthlessness, wretchedness **3.** adulteration, debasement, fraudulence, phoneyness *or* phoniness (*informal*), pretence, speciousness, spuriousness

bash **1.** *verb* belt (*informal*), biff (*slang*), break, chin (*slang*), crash, crush, deck (*slang*), hit, lay one on (*slang*), punch, slosh (*Brit. slang*), smash, sock (*slang*), strike, wallop (*informal*) **2.** *noun* attempt, crack (*informal*), go (*informal*), shot (*informal*), stab (*informal*), try

bashful abashed, blushing, confused, constrained, coy, diffident, easily embarrassed, nervous, overmodest, reserved, reticent, retiring, self-conscious, self-effacing, shamefaced, sheepish, shrinking, shy, timid, timorous
Antonyms aggressive, arrogant, bold, brash, conceited, confident, egoistic, fearless, forward, immodest, impudent, intrepid, pushy (*informal*), self-assured

bashfulness constraint, coyness, diffidence, embarrassment, hesitation, modesty, reserve, self-consciousness, sheepishness, shyness, timidity, timorousness

basic bog-standard (*informal*), central, elementary, essential, fundamental, immanent, indispensable, inherent, intrinsic, key, necessary, primary, radical, underlying, vital
Antonyms complementary, minor, peripheral, secondary, supplementary, supporting, trivial, unessential

basically at bottom, at heart, *au fond*, essentially, firstly, fundamentally, inherently, in substance, intrinsically, mostly, primarily, radically

basics brass tacks (*informal*), core, essentials, facts, fundamentals, hard facts, necessaries, nitty-gritty (*informal*), nuts and bolts (*informal*), practicalities, principles, rudiments

basis **1.** base, bottom, footing, foundation, ground, groundwork, support **2.** chief ingredi~

ent, core, essential, fundamental, heart, premise, principal element, principle, theory

bask 1. laze, lie in, loll, lounge, relax, sun~bathe, swim in, toast oneself, warm oneself 2. delight in, enjoy, indulge oneself, luxuriate, relish, revel, savour, take pleasure, wallow

bass deep, deep-toned, grave, low, low-pitched, resonant, sonorous

bastard 1. *noun* by-blow (*archaic*), illegitimate (child), love child, natural child, whoreson (*archaic*) 2. *adjective* adulterated, baseborn, counterfeit, false, illegitimate, imperfect, im~pure, inferior, irregular, misbegotten, sham, spurious

bastardize adulterate, cheapen, corrupt, de~base, defile, degrade, demean, devalue, dis~tort, pervert

bastion bulwark, citadel, defence, fastness, fortress, mainstay, prop, rock, stronghold, support, tower of strength

bat bang, hit, punch, rap, smack, strike, swat, thump, wallop (*informal*), whack

batch accumulation, aggregation, amount, as~semblage, bunch, collection, crowd, group, lot, pack, quantity, set

bath 1. *noun* ablution, cleansing, douche, douse, scrubbing, shower, soak, soaping, sponging, tub, wash, washing 2. *verb* bathe, clean, douse, lave (*archaic*), scrub down, shower, soak, soap, sponge, tub, wash
Related adjective: balneal *or* balneary

bathe 1. *verb* cleanse, cover, dunk, flood, im~merse, moisten, rinse, soak, steep, suffuse, wash, wet 2. *noun* dip, dook (*Scot.*), swim, wash

bathetic anticlimactic, mawkish, sentimental

bathing costume bathing suit, bikini, swim~ming costume, swimsuit, trunks

bathos anticlimax, false pathos, letdown, mawkishness, sentimentality

bathroom comfort station (*U.S.*), convenience (*chiefly Brit.*), lavatory, powder room, rest room, shower, toilet, washroom, water closet, WC

baton club, crook, mace, rod, sceptre, staff, stick, truncheon, wand

battalion army, brigade, company, contingent, division, force, horde, host, legion, multitude, regiment, squadron, throng

batten[1] *verb* board up, clamp down, cover up, fasten, fasten down, fix, nail down, secure, tighten

batten[2] *verb* fatten, flourish, gain, grow, in~crease, prosper, thrive, wax

batter 1. assault, bash (*informal*), beat, beat the living daylights out of, belabour, break, buffet, clobber (*slang*), dash against, lam~bast(e), lash, pelt, pound, pummel, smash, smite, thrash, wallop (*informal*) 2. bruise, crush, deface, demolish, destroy, disfigure, hurt, injure, mangle, mar, maul, ruin, shatter, shiver, total (*slang*), trash (*slang*)

battered beaten, beat-up (*informal*), black-and-blue, broken-down, bruised, crushed, damaged, dilapidated, injured, ramshackle, squashed, weather-beaten

battery 1. chain, ring, sequence, series, set, suite 2. assault, attack, beating, mayhem, on~slaught, physical violence, thumping 3. artil~lery, cannon, cannonry, gun emplacements, guns

battle *noun* 1. action, attack, combat, encoun~ter, engagement, fight, fray, hostilities, skir~mish, war, warfare 2. agitation, campaign, clash, conflict, contest, controversy, crusade, debate, disagreement, dispute, head-to-head, strife, struggle *~verb* 3. agitate, argue, clam~our, combat, contend, contest, dispute, feud, fight, lock horns, strive, struggle, war
Antonyms *noun* accord, agreement, armistice, ceasefire, concord, entente, peace, suspension of hostilities, truce

Battles

Aboukir Bay *or* Abu~kir Bay
Actium
Agincourt
Alamo
Arnhem
Atlantic
Austerlitz
Balaklava *or* Balacla~va
Bannockburn
Barnet
Bautzen
Belleau Wood
Blenheim
Borodino
Bosworth Field
Boyne
Britain
Bulge
Bull Run
Bunker Hill
Cannae
Crécy
Culloden
Dien Bien Phu
Edgehill
El Alamein
Falkirk
Flodden
Guadalcanal
Gettysburg
Hastings
Hohenlinden
Imphal
Inkerman
Issus
Jemappes
Jena
Killiecrankie
Kursk
Ladysmith
Le Cateau
Leipzig
Lepanto
Leyte Gulf
Little Bighorn
Lützen
Manassas
Mantinea *or* Manti~neia
Marathon
Marengo
Marston Moor
Missionary Ridge
Navarino
Omdurman
Passchendaele
Philippi
Plains of Abraham
Plassey
Plataea
Poltava
Prestonpans
Pydna
Quatre Bras
Ramillies
Roncesvalles
Sadowa *or* Sadová
Saint-Mihiel

Salamis
Sedgemoor
Sempach
Shiloh
Shipka Pass
Somme
Stalingrad
Stamford Bridge
Stirling Bridge
Tannenberg
Tewkesbury
Thermopylae
Tobruk
Trafalgar
Trenton
Verdun
Vitoria
Wagram
Waterloo
Ypres
Zama

battle-axe ballbreaker (*slang*), disciplinarian, fury, harridan, scold, shrew, tartar, termagant, virago, vixen

battle cry catchword, motto, slogan, war cry, war whoop, watchword

battlefield battleground, combat zone, field, field of battle, front

battlement barbican, bartizan, bastion, breastwork, bulwark, crenellation, fortification, parapet, rampart

battleship capital ship, gunboat, man-of-war, ship of the line, warship

batty as daft as a brush (*informal, chiefly Brit.*), barking (*slang*), barking mad (*slang*), barmy (*slang*), bats (*slang*), bonkers (*slang, chiefly Brit.*), cracked (*slang*), crackers (*Brit. slang*), crackpot (*informal*), cranky (*informal*), crazy, daft (*informal*), doolally (*slang*), dotty (*slang, chiefly Brit.*), eccentric, gonzo (*slang*), insane, loony (*slang*), loopy (*informal*), lunatic, mad, not the full shilling (*informal*), nuts (*slang*), nutty (*slang*), odd, oddball (*informal*), off one's rocker (*slang*), off one's trolley (*slang*), off the rails, off-the-wall (*slang*), out of one's mind, outré, out to lunch (*informal*), peculiar, potty (*Brit. informal*), queer (*informal*), round the twist (*Brit. slang*), screwy (*informal*), touched, up the pole (*informal*), wacko *or* whacko (*slang*)

bauble bagatelle, gewgaw, gimcrack, kickshaw, knick-knack, plaything, toy, trifle, trinket

baulk *see* BALK

bawd brothel-keeper, madam, pimp, procuress, prostitute, whore, working girl (*facetious slang*)

bawdy blue, coarse, dirty, erotic, gross, indecent, indecorous, indelicate, lascivious, lecherous, lewd, libidinous, licentious, lustful, near the knuckle (*informal*), obscene, prurient, ribald, risqué, rude, salacious, smutty, steamy (*informal*), suggestive, vulgar, X-rated (*informal*)
Antonyms chaste, clean, decent, good, modest, moral, respectable, seemly, undefiled, upright, virtuous

bawl **1.** bellow, call, clamour, halloo, howl, roar, shout, vociferate, yell **2.** blubber, cry, sob, squall, wail, weep

bay¹ *noun* bight, cove, gulf, inlet, natural harbour, sound

bay² *noun* alcove, compartment, embrasure, niche, nook, opening, recess

bay³ **1.** *verb/noun* bark, bell, clamour, cry, growl, howl, yelp **2.** *noun* **at bay** caught, cornered, trapped

bayonet *verb* impale, knife, run through, spear, stab, stick, transfix

bays chaplet, garland, glory, laurel crown, praise, prize, renown, trophy

bazaar **1.** exchange, market, marketplace, mart **2.** bring-and-buy, fair, fête, sale of work

be **1.** be alive, breathe, exist, inhabit, live **2.** befall, come about, come to pass, happen, occur, take place, transpire (*informal*) **3.** abide, continue, endure, last, obtain, persist, prevail, remain, stand, stay, survive

beach coast, lido, littoral, margin, plage, sands, seaboard (*chiefly U.S.*), seashore, seaside, shingle, shore, strand, water's edge

beachcomber forager, loafer, scavenger, scrounger, tramp, vagabond, vagrant, wanderer

beached abandoned, aground, ashore, deserted, grounded, high and dry, marooned, stranded, wrecked

beacon beam, bonfire, flare, lighthouse, pharos, rocket, sign, signal, signal fire, smoke signal, watchtower

bead blob, bubble, dot, drop, droplet, globule, pellet, pill, spherule

beads chaplet, choker, necklace, necklet, pearls, pendant, rosary

beak **1.** bill, mandible, neb (*archaic or dialect*), nib **2.** nose, proboscis, snout **3.** *Nautical* bow, prow, ram, rostrum, stem

beaked curved, hooked, pointed, sharp

beam *noun* **1.** girder, joist, plank, rafter, spar, support, timber **2.** bar, emission, gleam, glimmer, glint, glow, radiation, ray, shaft, streak, stream *~verb* **3.** broadcast, emit, glare, gleam, glitter, glow, radiate, shine, transmit **4.** grin, laugh, smile

beaming **1.** beautiful, bright, brilliant, flashing, gleaming, glistening, glittering, radiant, scintillating, shining, sparkling **2.** cheerful, grinning, happy, joyful, smiling, sunny

bear **1.** bring, carry, convey, hump (*Brit. slang*), move, take, tote (*informal*), transport **2.** cherish, entertain, exhibit, harbour, have, hold, maintain, possess, shoulder, support, sustain, uphold, weigh upon **3.** abide, admit, allow, brook, endure, hack (*slang*), permit, put up with (*informal*), stomach, suffer, tolerate, undergo **4.** beget, breed, bring forth, develop, engender, generate, give birth to, produce, yield

Antonyms abandon, cease, desert, discontinue, drop, give up, leave, put down, quit, relinquish, shed

bearable admissible, endurable, manageable, passable, sufferable, supportable, sustainable, tolerable

Antonyms insufferable, insupportable, intolerable, oppressive, too much (*informal*), unacceptable, unbearable, unendurable

beard 1. *noun* bristles, five-o'clock shadow, stubble, whiskers 2. *verb* brave, confront, dare, defy, face, oppose, tackle

bearded bewhiskered, bristly, bushy, hairy, hirsute, shaggy, stubbly, unshaven, whiskered

beardless 1. barefaced, clean-shaven, hairless, smooth, smooth-faced 2. callow, fresh, green, immature, inexperienced

bear down 1. burden, compress, encumber, press down, push, strain, weigh down 2. advance on, approach, attack, close in, converge on, move in

bearer 1. agent, carrier, conveyor, messenger, porter, runner, servant 2. beneficiary, consignee, payee

bearing 1. air, aspect, attitude, behaviour, carriage, demeanour, deportment, manner, mien, posture 2. *Nautical* course, direction, point of compass 3. application, connection, import, pertinence, reference, relation, relevance, significance

Antonyms (*sense 3*) inappositeness, inappropriateness, inaptness, inconsequence, irrelevance, irrelevancy, non sequitur

bearings aim, course, direction, location, orientation, position, situation, track, way, whereabouts

bearish 1. churlish, clumsy, gruff, rough, sullen, surly 2. *Stock Exchange* declining, falling, slumping

bear on affect, appertain to, belong to, concern, involve, pertain to, refer to, relate to, touch upon

bear out confirm, corroborate, endorse, justify, prove, substantiate, support, uphold, vindicate

bear up bear the brunt, carry on, endure, go through the mill, grin and bear it (*informal*), keep one's chin up, persevere, suffer, take it on the chin (*informal*), withstand

bear with be patient, forbear, make allowances, put up with (*informal*), suffer, tolerate, wait

beast 1. animal, brute, creature 2. barbarian, brute, fiend, ghoul, monster, ogre, sadist, savage, swine

And what rough beast, its hour come round at last,
Slouches towards Bethlehem to be born?
W.B. Yeats *The Second Coming*

beastly 1. animal, barbarous, bestial, brutal, brutish, coarse, cruel, depraved, inhuman, monstrous, repulsive, sadistic, savage 2. awful, disagreeable, foul, horrid, mean, nasty, rotten, shitty (*taboo slang*), terrible, unpleasant

Antonyms agreeable, fine, good, humane, pleasant, sensitive

beat *verb* 1. bang, batter, belt (*informal*), break, bruise, buffet, cane, chin (*slang*), clobber (*slang*), cudgel, deck (*slang*), drub, flog, hit, knock, lambast(e), lash, lay one on (*slang*), lick (*informal*), maul, pelt, pound, punch, strike, thrash, thwack, whip 2. best, blow out of the water (*slang*), bring to their knees, clobber (*slang*), conquer, defeat, excel, knock spots off (*informal*), lick (*informal*), make mincemeat of (*informal*), master, outdo, outrun, outstrip, overcome, overwhelm, pip at the post, put in the shade (*informal*), run rings around (*informal*), stuff (*slang*), subdue, surpass, tank (*slang*), undo, vanquish, wipe the floor with (*informal*) 3. fashion, forge, form, hammer, model, shape, work 4. flap, flutter, palpitate, pound, pulsate, pulse, quake, quiver, shake, throb, thump, tremble, vibrate 5. **beat it** bugger off (*taboo slang*), depart, exit, fuck off (*offensive taboo slang*), get lost (*informal*), get on one's bike (*Brit. slang*), go away, go to hell (*informal*), hook it (*slang*), hop it (*slang*), leave, make tracks, pack one's bags (*informal*), piss off (*taboo slang*), scarper (*Brit. slang*), scram (*informal*), shoo, skedaddle (*informal*), sling one's hook (*Brit. slang*), vamoose (*slang, chiefly U.S.*) ~*noun* 6. belt (*informal*), blow, hit, lash, punch, shake, slap, strike, swing, thump 7. flutter, palpitation, pulsation, pulse, throb 8. accent, cadence, ictus, measure (*Prosody*), metre, rhythm, stress, time 9. circuit, course, path, rounds, route, way ~*adjective* 10. *slang* clapped out (*Austral. & N.Z. informal*), exhausted, fatigued, on one's last legs, shagged out (*Brit. slang*), tired, wearied, wiped out (*informal*), worn out, zonked (*slang*)

beaten 1. baffled, cowed, defeated, disappointed, disheartened, frustrated, overcome, overwhelmed, thwarted, vanquished 2. forged, formed, hammered, shaped, stamped, worked 3. much travelled, trampled, trodden, well-trodden, well-used, worn 4. blended, foamy, frothy, mixed, stirred, whipped, whisked

beatific blessed, blissed out, blissful, divine, ecstatic, enraptured, exalted, glorious, heavenly, joyful, rapt, rapturous, sent, serene, sublime

beating 1. belting (*informal*), caning, chastisement, corporal punishment, flogging, pasting (*slang*), slapping, smacking, thrashing, whip~

ping **2.** conquest, defeat, downfall, overthrow, pasting (*slang*), rout, ruin

beatitude beatification, blessedness, bliss, ecstasy, exaltation, felicity, happiness, holy joy, saintliness

beat up assault, attack, batter, beat the living daylights out of (*informal*), clobber (*slang*), do over (*Brit., Austral. & N.Z. slang*), duff up (*Brit. slang*), fill in (*Brit. slang*), knock about *or* around, lambast(e), put the boot in (*slang*), thrash, work over (*slang*)

beau **1.** admirer, boyfriend, escort, fancy man (*slang*), fiancé, guy (*informal*), leman (*archaic*), lover, suitor, swain, sweetheart **2.** cavalier, coxcomb, dandy, fop, gallant, ladies' man, popinjay, swell (*informal*)

beautiful alluring, appealing, attractive, charming, comely, delightful, drop-dead (*slang*), exquisite, fair, fine, glamorous, good-looking, gorgeous, graceful, handsome, lovely, pleasing, radiant, ravishing, stunning (*informal*)

Antonyms awful, bad, hideous, repulsive, terrible, ugly, unattractive, unpleasant, unsightly

Have nothing in your houses that you do not know to be useful, or believe to be beautiful
William Morris *Hopes and Fears for Art*

Remember that the most beautiful things in the world are the most useless; peacocks and lilies for instance
John Ruskin *Stones of Venice*

beautify adorn, array, bedeck, deck, decorate, embellish, enhance, festoon, garnish, gild, glamorize, grace, ornament

beauty **1.** allure, attractiveness, bloom, charm, comeliness, elegance, exquisiteness, fairness, glamour, grace, handsomeness, loveliness, pulchritude, seemliness, symmetry **2.** belle, charmer, cracker (*slang*), goddess, good-looker, humdinger (*slang*), lovely (*slang*), stunner (*informal*), Venus **3.** advantage, asset, attraction, benefit, blessing, boon, excellence, feature, good thing

Antonyms detraction, disadvantage, flaw, repulsiveness, ugliness, unpleasantness, unseemliness

If you get simple beauty and nought else,
You get about the best thing God invents
Robert Browning *Fra Lippo Lippi*

A thing of beauty is a joy forever;
Its loveliness increases; it will never
Pass into nothingness
John Keats *Endymion*

It is amazing how complete is the delusion that beauty is goodness
Leo Tolstoy *The Kreutzer Sonata*

All changed, changed utterly;
A terrible beauty is born
W.B. Yeats *Easter 1916*

Beauty vanishes; beauty passes
Walter de la Mare *Epitaph*

Beauty is mysterious as well as terrible. God and devil are fighting there, and the battlefield is the heart of man
Fedor Dostoevsky *The Brothers Karamazov*

Beauty is no quality in things themselves. It exists merely in the mind which contemplates them
David Hume *Essays, Moral, Political, and Literary*

I always say beauty is only sin deep
Saki (H.H. Munro) *Reginald*

Beauty is all very well at first sight; but who ever looks at it when it has been in the house three days?
George Bernard Shaw *Man and Superman*

Beauty is truth, truth beauty
John Keats *Ode on a Grecian Urn*

When a woman isn't beautiful, people always say "You have lovely eyes, you have lovely hair"
Anton Chekhov *Uncle Vanya*

Your looks are laughable, unphotographable, yet you're my favourite work of art
Lorenz Hart *My Funny Valentine*

Was this the face that launched a thousand ships
And burnt the topless towers of Ilium?
Christopher Marlowe *Doctor Faustus*

Beauty and Truth, though never found, are worthy to be sought
Robert Williams Buchanan *To David in Heaven*

beauty: the power by which a woman charms a lover and terrifies a husband
Ambrose Bierce *The Devil's Dictionary*

I never saw an ugly thing in my life: for let the form of an object be what it may, - light, shade, and perspective will always make it beautiful
John Constable

Beauty is in the eye of the beholder

Beauty is only skin deep

beaver away exert oneself, graft (*informal*), hammer away, keep one's nose to the grindstone, peg away, persevere, persist, plug away (*informal*), slog, work

becalmed motionless, settled, still, stranded, stuck

because as, by reason of, in that, on account of, owing to, since, thanks to

beck gesture, nod, signal, summons, wave

beckon **1.** bid, gesticulate, gesture, motion, nod, signal, summon, wave at **2.** allure, attract, call, coax, draw, entice, invite, lure, pull, tempt

becloud bedim, befog, complicate, confuse, darken, muddle, muddy the waters, obfuscate, obscure, overcast, screen, veil

become **1.** alter to, be transformed into, change into, develop into, evolve into, grow into, mature into, metamorphose into, ripen into 2. embellish, enhance, fit, flatter, grace, harmonize, ornament, set off, suit

becoming 1. attractive, comely, enhancing, flattering, graceful, neat, pretty, tasteful 2. appropriate, befitting, *comme il faut*, compatible, congruous, decent, decorous, fit, fitting, in keeping, meet (*archaic*), proper, seemly, suitable, worthy
Antonyms improper, ugly, unattractive, unbecoming, unfit, unsuitable, unworthy

bed *noun* 1. bedstead, berth, bunk, cot, couch, divan, pallet 2. area, border, garden, patch, plot, row, strip 3. base, bottom, foundation, groundwork, substratum *~verb* 4. base, embed, establish, fix, found, implant, insert, plant, settle, set up

Types of bed
see FURNITURE

And so to bed
Samuel Pepys *Diary*

As you make your bed, so you must lie in it

bedaub besmear, smear, smirch, soil, spatter, splash, stain

bedazzle amaze, astound, bewilder, blind, captivate, confuse, daze, dazzle, dumbfound, enchant, overwhelm, stagger, stun, sweep off one's feet

bedclothes bedding, bed linen, blankets, coverlets, covers, duvets, eiderdowns, pillowcases, pillows, quilts, sheets

bedding bedclothes, bed linen, linen, sheets

bed down hit the hay (*slang*), lie, retire, settle down, sleep, turn in (*informal*)

bedeck adorn, array, bedight (*archaic*), bedizen (*archaic*), decorate, embellish, engarland, festoon, garnish, ornament, trim

bedevil afflict, aggravate (*informal*), annoy, be on one's back (*slang*), breathe down someone's neck, confound, distress, fret, frustrate, get in one's hair (*informal*), get on one's nerves (*informal*), get on one's wick (*Brit. slang*), get under one's skin (*informal*), get up one's nose (*informal*), harass, hassle (*informal*), irk, irritate, pester, plague, torment, torture, trouble, vex, worry

bedew besprinkle, dampen, drench, moisten, shower, soak, spray, sprinkle, water, wet

bedim becloud, bedarken, cloak, cloud, darken, dim, obscure, overcast, shade, shadow

bedlam chaos, clamour, commotion, confusion, furore, hubbub, hullabaloo, madhouse (*informal*), noise, pandemonium, tumult, turmoil, uproar

bedraggled dirty, dishevelled, disordered, drenched, dripping, messy, muddied, muddy, sodden, soiled, stained, sullied, unkempt, untidy

bedridden confined, confined to bed, flat on one's back, incapacitated, laid up (*informal*)

bedrock 1. bed, bottom, foundation, nadir, rock bottom, substratum, substructure 2. basics, basis, core, essentials, fundamentals, nuts and bolts (*informal*), roots

beef 1. *informal* brawn, flesh, heftiness, muscle, physique, robustness, sinew, strength 2. *slang* complaint, criticism, dispute, grievance, gripe (*informal*), grouch (*informal*), grouse, grumble, objection, protest, protestation

beefy *informal* 1. brawny, bulky, burly, hulking, muscular, stalwart, stocky, strapping, sturdy, thickset 2. chubby, corpulent, fat, fleshy, heavy, obese, overweight, paunchy, plump, podgy, portly, pudgy, rotund
Antonyms feeble, frail, puny, scrawny, skinny, weak

beehive apiary, comb, hive, honeycomb

beer ale, amber fluid *or* nectar (*Austral. informal*), brew, hop juice, swipes (*Brit. slang*), wallop (*Brit. slang*)

Beers

ale	lager
barley wine	lambic
Bière de Garde	light (*Scot.*)
bitter	light ale
black and tan	mild
bock beer *or* bock	milk stout
boilermaker	nog *or* nogg (*dialect*)
bottle-conditioned beer *or* ale	pale ale
brown ale	Pils
cask-conditioned beer *or* ale	Pilsner *or* Pilsener
Christmas beer *or* ale	plain (*Irish*)
draught beer	porter
eighty shilling *or* eighty	Rauchbier
export	real ale
fruit beer	seventy shilling *or* seventy
guest beer	shandy
gueuze	shebeen *or* shebean (*Irish & U.S.*)
half-and-half	sixty shilling *or* sixty
heavy (*Scot.*)	special
home-brew	stingo
ice beer	stout
India Pale Ale *or* IPA	sweet stout
Kaffir beer	Trappist beer
keg beer	weissbier
Kölsch	Weizenbier
	wheat beer

And malt does more than Milton can
To justify God's ways to man
A E Housman *A Shropshire Lad*

When money's tight and is hard to get
And your horse was also ran,
When all you have is a heap of debt
A pint of plain is your only man
Flann O'Brien *At Swim-Two-Birds*

Lo! the poor toper whose untutored sense,
Sees bliss in ale, and can with wine dispense;
Whose head proud fancy never taught to steer,
Beyond the muddy ecstasies of beer
George Crabbe *Inebriety*

then to the spicy nut-brown ale
John Milton *L'Allegro*

beetle, beetling *adjective* hanging over, jutting, leaning over, overhanging, pendent, projecting, prominent, protruding, sticking out, swelling over

beetle-browed frowning, glowering, lowering, pouting, scowling, sullen

befall bechance, betide, chance, come to pass, ensue, fall, follow, happen, materialize, occur, supervene, take place, transpire (*informal*)

befit be appropriate, become, be fitting, behoove (*U.S.*), behove, be seemly, be suitable, suit

befitting apposite, appropriate, becoming, fit, fitting, meet (*archaic*), proper, right, seemly, suitable
Antonyms improper, inappropriate, irrelevant, unbecoming, unfit, unsuitable, wrong

befog becloud, blur, confuse, darken, fuzz, make hazy (indistinct, vague), muddle, muddy the waters, obfuscate, obscure

befool bamboozle (*informal*), beguile, cheat, con, cozen, delude, dupe, fool, hoax, hoodwink, humbug, impose on, mislead, outwit, trick

before 1. *adverb* ahead, earlier, formerly, in advance, in front, previously, sooner 2. *preposition* earlier than, in advance of, in front of, in the presence of, prior to
Antonyms *adverb* after, afterwards, behind, later, subsequently, thereafter ~*preposition* after, behind, following, succeeding

beforehand ahead of time, already, before, before now, earlier, in advance, in anticipation, previously, sooner

befriend advise, aid, assist, back, benefit, encourage, favour, help, patronize, side with, stand by, succour, support, sustain, uphold, welcome

befuddle baffle, bewilder, confuse, daze, disorient, intoxicate, muddle, puzzle, stupefy
Antonyms clarify, clear up, elucidate, explicate, illuminate, interpret, make clear, make plain, resolve, simplify, throw *or* shed light on

befuddled at sea, confused, dazed, fuddled, groggy (*informal*), inebriated, intoxicated, muddled, woozy (*informal*)

beg 1. beseech, crave, desire, entreat, implore, importune, petition, plead, pray, request, solicit, supplicate 2. blag (*slang*), cadge, call for alms, mooch (*slang*), scrounge, seek charity, solicit charity, sponge on, touch (someone) for (*slang*) 3. *As in* **beg the question** avoid, dodge, duck (*informal*), equivocate, eschew, evade, fend off, flannel (*Brit. informal*), hedge, parry, shirk, shun, sidestep
Antonyms (*sense 1*) apportion, award, bestow, commit, confer, contribute, donate, give, grant, impart, present (*sense 2*) claim, demand, exact, extort, insist on

beget 1. breed, father, generate, get, procreate, propagate, sire 2. bring, bring about, cause, create, effect, engender, give rise to, occasion, produce, result in

begetter 1. father, genitor, parent, procreator, sire 2. architect, author, creator, founder, inventor, originator

beggar *noun* 1. bag lady (*chiefly U.S.*), bum (*informal*), cadger, mendicant, scrounger (*informal*), sponger (*informal*), supplicant, tramp, vagrant 2. bankrupt, down-and-out, pauper, starveling ~*verb* 3. *As in* **beggar description** baffle, challenge, defy, surpass

beggarly abject, base, contemptible, despicable, destitute, impoverished, inadequate, indigent, low, meagre, mean, miserly, needy, niggardly, pathetic, pitiful, poor, poverty-stricken, stingy, vile, wretched

beggary bankruptcy, destitution, indigence, need, pauperism, poverty, vagrancy, want, wretchedness

begin 1. commence, embark on, get the show on the road (*informal*), inaugurate, initiate, instigate, institute, prepare, set about, set on foot, start 2. appear, arise, be born, come into being, come into existence, commence, crop up (*informal*), dawn, emerge, happen, originate, spring, start
Antonyms cease, complete, end, finish, stop, terminate

beginner amateur, apprentice, cub, fledgling, freshman, greenhorn (*informal*), initiate, learner, neophyte, novice, recruit, starter, student, tenderfoot, trainee, tyro
Antonyms authority, expert, master, old hand, old stager, old-timer, past master, past mistress, pro (*informal*), professional, trouper, veteran

beginning 1. birth, commencement, inauguration, inception, initiation, onset, opening, opening move, origin, outset, overture, preface, prelude, rise, rudiments, source, start, starting point 2. embryo, fount, fountainhead, germ, root, seed
Antonyms (*sense 1*) closing, completion, conclusion, end, ending, finish, termination

begrime besmirch, blacken, dirty, muddy, smear, smirch, soil, spatter, stain, sully, tarnish

begrudge be jealous, be reluctant, be stingy, envy, grudge, resent

begrudgingly grudgingly, hesitantly, reluctantly, resentfully, stingily, unenthusiastical~

ly, unwillingly, with bad grace, without enthusiasm
Antonyms enthusiastically, freely, generously, gladly, willingly, with good grace

beguile 1. befool, cheat, deceive, delude, dupe, fool, hoodwink, impose on, mislead, take for a ride (*informal*), trick 2. amuse, charm, cheer, delight, distract, divert, engross, entertain, occupy, solace, tickle the fancy of
Antonyms alarm, alert, enlighten, put right

beguiling alluring, attractive, bewitching, captivating, charming, diverting, enchanting, entertaining, enthralling, interesting, intriguing

behalf account, advantage, benefit, defence, good, interest, part, profit, sake, side, support

behave 1. act, function, operate, perform, run, work 2. act correctly, conduct oneself properly, keep one's nose clean, mind one's manners
Antonyms act up (*informal*), be bad, be insubordinate, be naughty, carry on (*informal*), get up to mischief (*informal*), misbehave, muck about (*Brit. slang*)

behaviour 1. actions, bearing, carriage, comportment, conduct, demeanour, deportment, manner, manners, ways 2. action, functioning, operation, performance

behead decapitate, decollate (*archaic*), execute, guillotine, truncate

behemoth Brobdingnagian, colossus, giant, leviathan, mammoth, monster, titan

behest bidding, canon, charge, command, commandment, decree, dictate, direction, expressed desire, injunction, instruction, mandate, order, precept, wish

behind *preposition* 1. after, at the back of, at the heels of, at the rear of, following, later than 2. at the bottom of, causing, initiating, instigating, responsible for 3. backing, for, in agreement, on the side of, supporting *~adverb* 4. after, afterwards, following, in the wake (of), next, subsequently 5. behindhand, in arrears, in debt, overdue *~noun* 6. arse (*taboo slang*), ass (*U.S. & Canad. taboo slang*), bottom, bum (*Brit. slang*), buns (*U.S. slang*), butt (*U.S. & Canad. informal*), buttocks, derrière (*euphemistic*), jacksy (*Brit. slang*), posterior, rump, seat, tail (*informal*)
Antonyms (*sense 1*) earlier than, in advance of, in front of, in the presence of, prior to (*sense 4*) ahead, earlier, formerly, in advance, previously, sooner

behindhand backward, behind time, dilatory, late, remiss, slow, tardy

behind the times antiquated, dated, *démodé*, obsolete, old-fashioned, old hat, outmoded, out of date, out of the ark (*informal*), passé
Antonyms advanced, avant-garde, experimental, far-out (*slang*), ground-breaking, innovative, pioneering, progressive, trendy (*Brit. informal*), unconventional, way-out (*informal*)

behold 1. *verb* check, check out (*informal*), clock (*Brit. slang*), consider, contemplate, discern, eye, eyeball (*U.S. slang*), get a load of (*informal*), look at, observe, perceive, recce (*slang*), regard, scan, survey, take a dekko at (*Brit. slang*), view, watch, witness 2. *interjection* lo, look, mark, observe, see, watch

beholden bound, grateful, indebted, obligated, obliged, owing, under obligation

behove be advisable, befit, be fitting, be incumbent upon, be necessary, benefit, be obligatory, beseem, be wise

beige biscuit, buff, *café au lait*, camel, cinnamon, coffee, cream, ecru, fawn, khaki, mushroom, neutral, oatmeal, sand, tan

being 1. actuality, animation, existence, life, living, reality 2. entity, essence, nature, soul, spirit, substance 3. animal, beast, body, creature, human being, individual, living thing, mortal, thing
Antonyms nihility, nonbeing, nonexistence, nothingness, nullity, oblivion

belabour 1. batter, beat, clobber (*slang*), flog, lambast(e), thrash, whip 2. attack, berate, blast, castigate, censure, criticize, excoriate, flay, go for the jugular, lambast(e), lay into (*informal*), put down, tear into (*informal*)

belated behindhand, behind time, delayed, late, late in the day, overdue, tardy

belch 1. burp (*informal*), eruct, eructate, hiccup 2. discharge, disgorge, emit, erupt, give off, gush, spew forth, vent, vomit

beleaguer 1. assail, beset, besiege, blockade, encompass, environ, hem in, surround 2. aggravate (*informal*), annoy, badger, be on one's back (*slang*), bother, breathe down someone's neck, get in one's hair (*informal*), get on one's nerves (*informal*), get on one's wick (*Brit. slang*), harass, hassle (*informal*), pester, vex

beleaguered badgered, beset, besieged, bothered, harassed, nagged, persecuted, plagued, put upon, set upon, vexed

belie 1. confute, contradict, deny, disprove, gainsay (*archaic or literary*), give the lie to, make a nonsense of, negate, rebut, repudiate 2. conceal, deceive, disguise, falsify, gloss over, mislead, misrepresent

belief 1. admission, assent, assurance, confidence, conviction, credit, feeling, impression, judgment, notion, opinion, persuasion, presumption, reliance, theory, trust, view 2. credence, credo, creed, doctrine, dogma, faith, ideology, principles, tenet
Antonyms disbelief, distrust, doubt, dubiety, incredulity, mistrust, scepticism

It is necessary to the happiness of man that he be mentally faithful to himself. Infidelity does not consist in believing, or in disbelieving, it consists in professing to believe what one does not believe

Thomas Paine *The Age of Reason*

believable acceptable, authentic, credible, creditable, imaginable, likely, plausible, possible, probable, reliable, trustworthy, verisimilar

Antonyms cock-and-bull (*informal*), doubtful, dubious, fabulous, implausible, incredible, questionable, unacceptable, unbelievable

believe 1. accept, be certain of, be convinced of, buy (*slang*), count on, credit, depend on, have faith in, hold, place confidence in, presume true, rely on, swallow (*informal*), swear by, take as gospel, take on board, trust 2. assume, conjecture, consider, gather, guess (*informal, chiefly U.S. & Canad.*), imagine, judge, maintain, postulate, presume, reckon, speculate, suppose, think

Antonyms disbelieve, distrust, doubt, know, question

To believe with certainty we must begin with doubting

Stanislaus I of Poland *Maxims*

Man can believe the impossible, but man can never believe the improbable

Oscar Wilde *The Decay of Lying*

Though you can believe what you choose, you must believe what you ought

Cardinal Newman

I can believe anything, provided that it is incredible

Oscar Wilde *The Picture of Dorian Gray*

Lord, I believe; help thou mine unbelief

Bible: St. Mark

Except ye see signs and wonders, ye will not believe

Bible: St. John

Though ye believe not me, believe the works

Bible: St. John

believer adherent, convert, devotee, disciple, follower, proselyte, protagonist, supporter, upholder, zealot

Antonyms agnostic, atheist, disbeliever, doubting Thomas, infidel, sceptic, unbeliever

belittle decry, denigrate, deprecate, depreciate, deride, derogate, detract, diminish, disparage, downgrade, minimize, scoff at, scorn, sneer at, underestimate, underrate, undervalue

Antonyms boast about, elevate, exalt, magnify, praise, vaunt

belle beauty, cracker (*informal*), good-looker, looker (*informal*), lovely, peach (*informal*), stunner (*informal*), Venus

bellicose aggressive, antagonistic, belligerent, combative, defiant, hawkish, hostile, jingoistic, militaristic, provocative, pugnacious, quarrelsome, sabre-rattling, warlike, warloving, warmongering

bellicosity aggression, aggressiveness, antagonism, belligerence, combativeness, hostility, pugnacity, truculence, warlike nature

belligerence aggressiveness, animosity, antagonism, combativeness, hostility, pugnacity, unfriendliness

belligerent 1. *adjective* aggressive, antagonistic, argumentative, bellicose, combative, contentious, hostile, litigious, pugnacious, quarrelsome, unfriendly, warlike, warring 2. *noun* combatant, fighter, warring nation

Antonyms amicable, benign, conciliatory, friendly, harmonious, nonviolent, without hostility

bellow *noun/verb* bawl, bell, call, clamour, cry, howl, roar, scream, shout, shriek, yell

belly 1. *noun* abdomen, breadbasket (*slang*), corporation (*informal*), gut, insides (*informal*), paunch, potbelly, stomach, tummy, vitals 2. *verb* billow, bulge, fill, spread, swell, swell out

belong 1. *with* **to** be at the disposal of, be held by, be owned by, be the property of 2. *with* **to** be affiliated to, be allied to, be a member of, be associated with, be included in 3. attach to, be connected with, be fitting, be part of, fit, go with, have as a proper place, pertain to, relate to

belonging acceptance, affiliation, affinity, association, attachment, fellowship, inclusion, kinship, loyalty, rapport, relationship

belongings accoutrements, chattels, effects, gear, goods, paraphernalia, personal property, possessions, stuff, things

beloved admired, adored, cherished, darling, dear, dearest, loved, pet, precious, prized, revered, sweet, treasured, worshipped

below *adverb* 1. beneath, down, lower, under, underneath *~preposition* 2. inferior, lesser, lesser than, subject, subordinate, unworthy of 3. **below par** below average, imperfect, inferior, off colour, off form, poor, second-rate, unfit

belt 1. band, cincture, cummerbund, girdle, girth, sash, waistband 2. *Geography* area, district, layer, region, stretch, strip, tract, zone 3. **below the belt** cowardly, foul, not playing the game (*informal*), unfair, unjust, unscrupulous, unsporting, unsportsmanlike

bemoan bewail, cry over spilt milk, deplore, express sorrow, grieve for, lament, moan over, mourn, regret, rue, weep for

bemuse amaze, bewilder, confuse, daze, flummox, muddle, nonplus, overwhelm, perplex, puzzle, stun

bemused absent-minded, at sea, bewildered, confused, dazed, engrossed, flummoxed, fud~

dled, half-drunk, muddled, nonplussed, per~plexed, preoccupied, stunned, stupefied, tipsy

bemusement amazement, befuddlement, be~wilderment, confusion, mystification, perplex~ity, puzzlement, stupefaction

bench **1.** form, pew, seat, settle, stall **2.** board, counter, table, trestle table, workbench, worktable **3.** court, courtroom, judge, judges, judiciary, magistrate, magistrates, tribunal

benchmark criterion, example, gauge, level, measure, model, norm, par, reference, refer~ence point, standard, touchstone, yardstick

bend *verb* **1.** arc, arch, bow, buckle, contort, crouch, curve, deflect, diverge, flex, incline, incurvate, lean, stoop, swerve, turn, twist, veer, warp **2.** compel, direct, influence, mould, persuade, shape, subdue, submit, sway, yield ~*noun* **3.** angle, arc, arch, bow, corner, crook, curve, hook, loop, turn, twist, zigzag

beneath **1.** *adverb* below, in a lower place, underneath **2.** *preposition* below, inferior to, less than, lower than, unbefitting, under~neath, unworthy of

Antonyms (*sense 2*) above, atop, beyond, ex~ceeding, higher than, on top of, over, upon

benediction beatitude, *benedictus*, benison, blessing, consecration, favour, grace, grati~tude, invocation, orison, prayer, thankfulness, thanksgiving

benefaction **1.** beneficence, benevolence, char~ity, generosity, largess *or* largesse, liberality, munificence, philanthropy **2.** alms, bequest, boon, charity, contribution, donation, endow~ment, gift, grant, gratuity, hand-out, largess *or* largesse, legacy, offering, present, stipend

benefactor angel (*informal*), backer, contribu~tor, donor, helper, patron, philanthropist, pro~moter, sponsor, subscriber, subsidizer, sup~porter, well-wisher

benefice Church living, emolument, incum~bency, office, prebend, preferment, sinecure, stipend

beneficence **1.** altruism, benevolence, compas~sion, generosity, goodness, goodwill, helpful~ness, kindness, largess *or* largesse, liberality, love, unselfishness, virtue **2.** aid, benefaction, bestowal, donation, gift, hand-out, largess *or* largesse, present, relief, succour

beneficent benevolent, benign, bounteous, bountiful, charitable, generous, helpful, kind, liberal, munificent, princely

beneficial advantageous, benign, expedient, fa~vourable, gainful, healthful, helpful, profitable, salubrious, salutary, serviceable, useful, valuable, wholesome

Antonyms detrimental, disadvantageous, harmful, pernicious, useless

beneficiary assignee, heir, inheritor, legatee, payee, receiver, recipient, successor

benefit **1.** *noun* advantage, aid, asset, assis~tance, avail, betterment, blessing, boon, boot (*obsolete*), favour, gain, good, help, inside track (*informal*), interest, mileage (*informal*), profit, use, utility **2.** *verb* advance, advantage, aid, ameliorate, assist, avail, better, enhance, further, improve, profit, promote, serve

Antonyms *noun* damage, detriment, disad~vantage, downside, harm, impairment, injury, loss ~*verb* damage, deprive, detract from, harm, impair, injure, worsen

benevolence altruism, charity, compassion, fellow feeling, generosity, goodness, goodwill, humanity, kind-heartedness, kindness, sym~pathy

Antonyms ill will, malevolence, selfishness, stinginess, unkindness

benevolent affable, altruistic, beneficent, be~nign, bounteous, bountiful, caring, charitable, compassionate, considerate, generous, hu~mane, humanitarian, kind, kind-hearted, lib~eral, philanthropic, tender-hearted, warm-hearted, well-disposed

benighted backward, crude, ignorant, illiter~ate, primitive, uncivilized, uncultivated, un~enlightened

benign **1.** affable, amiable, complaisant, friendly, generous, genial, gracious, kind, kindly, liberal, obliging, sympathetic **2.** balmy, gentle, healthful, mild, refreshing, temperate, warm, wholesome **3.** advantageous, auspicious, beneficial, encouraging, favourable, good, lucky, propitious, salutary **4.** *Medical* curable, harmless, limited, remediable, slight, superfi~cial

Antonyms bad, disobliging, harsh, hateful, inhumane, malicious, malign, severe, stern, unfavourable, unkind, unlucky, unpleasant, unsympathetic

bent *adjective* **1.** angled, arched, bowed, crook~ed, curved, hunched, stooped, twisted **2.** *with* **on** determined, disposed, fixed, inclined, in~sistent, predisposed, resolved, set ~*noun* **3.** ability, aptitude, bag (*slang*), cup of tea (*in~formal*), facility, faculty, flair, forte, inclina~tion, knack, leaning, penchant, preference, proclivity, propensity, talent, tendency

Antonyms (*sense 1*) aligned, erect, even, hori~zontal, in line, level, perpendicular, plumb, smooth, square, straight, true, upright, verti~cal

benumb anaesthetize, chill, deaden, freeze, numb, paralyse, shock, stun, stupefy

benumbed anaesthetized, dazed, deadened, frozen, immobilized, insensible, insensitive, numb, paralysed, stunned, stupefied, unfeel~ing, unresponsive

bequeath bestow, commit, endow, entrust,

give, grant, hand down, impart, leave to by will, pass on, transmit, will

bequest bequeathal, bestowal, dower, endowment, estate, gift, heritage, inheritance, legacy, settlement, trust

berate bawl out (*informal*), blast, carpet (*informal*), castigate, censure, chew out (*U.S. & Canad. informal*), chide, criticize, excoriate, give a rocket (*Brit. & N.Z. informal*), lambast(e), put down, rail at, rap over the knuckles, read the riot act, rebuke, reprimand, reproach, reprove, revile, scold, slap on the wrist, slate (*informal, chiefly Brit.*), tear into (*informal*), tear (someone) off a strip (*Brit. informal*), tell off (*informal*), upbraid, vituperate

Antonyms acclaim, admire, applaud, approve, cheer, commend, compliment, congratulate, extol, laud, praise, take one's hat off to

bereave afflict, deprive of kindred, dispossess, divest, make destitute, strip, take away from, widow

bereavement affliction, death, deprivation, loss, misfortune, tribulation

bereft cut off, deprived, destitute, devoid, lacking, minus, parted from, robbed of, shorn, wanting

berserk amok, ape (*slang*), apeshit (*slang*), crazy, enraged, frantic, frenzied, insane, mad, maniacal, manic, rabid, raging, uncontrollable, violent, wild

berth *noun* **1.** bed, billet, bunk, cot (*Nautical*), hammock **2.** anchorage, dock, harbour, haven, pier, port, quay, slip, wharf **3.** appointment, employment, job, living, position, post, situation *~verb* **4.** *Nautical* anchor, dock, drop anchor, land, moor, tie up

beseech adjure, ask, beg, call upon, crave, entreat, implore, importune, petition, plead, pray, solicit, sue, supplicate

beset 1. assail, attack, besiege, encircle, enclose, encompass, environ, hem in, surround **2.** *figurative* badger, bedevil, embarrass, entangle, harass, perplex, pester, plague

besetting habitual, harassing, inveterate, persistent, prevalent, troublesome

beside 1. abreast of, adjacent to, alongside, at the side of, cheek by jowl, close to, near, nearby, neighbouring, next door to, next to, overlooking **2. beside oneself** apoplectic, at the end of one's tether, berserk, crazed, delirious, demented, deranged, desperate, distraught, frantic, frenzied, insane, mad, out of one's mind, unbalanced, uncontrolled, unhinged

besides 1. *adverb* also, as well, further, furthermore, in addition, into the bargain, moreover, otherwise, too, what's more **2.** *preposition* apart from, barring, excepting, excluding, in addition to, other than, over and above, without

beside the point extraneous, immaterial, inapplicable, inapposite, inappropriate, inconsequent, irrelevant, neither here nor there, unconnected

Antonyms admissible, applicable, apposite, appropriate, appurtenant, apt, fitting, germane, pertinent, relevant, significant, to the point

besiege 1. beleaguer, beset, blockade, confine, encircle, encompass, environ, hedge in, hem in, invest (*rare*), lay siege to, shut in, surround **2.** badger, bend someone's ear (*informal*), bother, harass, harry, hassle (*informal*), hound, importune, nag, pester, plague, trouble

besmirch daub, defame, dishonour, slander, smear, smirch, soil, stain, sully, tarnish

besotted 1. befuddled, bevvied (*dialect*), blitzed (*slang*), blotto (*slang*), bombed (*slang*), Brahms and Liszt (*slang*), drunk, intoxicated, legless (*informal*), lit up (*slang*), out of it (*slang*), out to it (*Austral. & N.Z. slang*), paralytic (*informal*), pissed (*taboo slang*), rat-arsed (*taboo slang*), smashed (*slang*), steamboats (*Scot. slang*), steaming (*slang*), stupefied, wasted (*slang*), wrecked (*slang*), zonked (*slang*) **2.** doting, hypnotized, infatuated, smitten, spellbound **3.** confused, foolish, muddled, witless

bespatter bedaub, befoul, begrime, besmirch, besprinkle, muddy, smear, spatter, splatter, sully

bespeak 1. engage, order beforehand, prearrange, solicit **2.** betoken, denote, display, evidence, evince, exhibit, foretell, imply, indicate, predict, proclaim, reveal, show, signify, suggest, testify to

best *adjective* **1.** chief, finest, first, first-class, first-rate, foremost, highest, leading, most excellent, outstanding, perfect, pre-eminent, principal, superlative, supreme, unsurpassed **2.** advantageous, apt, correct, golden, most desirable, most fitting, right **3.** greatest, largest, most *~adverb* **4.** advantageously, attractively, excellently, most fortunately **5.** extremely, greatly, most deeply, most fully, most highly *~noun* **6.** choice, cream, *crème de la crème*, elite, favourite, finest, first, flower, pick, prime, top **7.** hardest, highest endeavour, utmost *~verb* **8.** beat, blow out of the water (*slang*), conquer, defeat, get the better of, lick (*informal*), master, outclass, outdo, put in the shade (*informal*), run rings around (*informal*), stuff (*slang*), surpass, tank (*slang*), thrash, triumph over, trounce, undo, wipe the floor with (*informal*)

bestial animal, barbaric, barbarous, beastlike, beastly, brutal, brutish, carnal, degraded, de~

praved, gross, inhuman, low, savage, sensual, sordid, vile

bestiality 1. barbarity, beastliness, brutality, brutishness, carnality, cruelty, depravity, in~humanity, savagery 2. zooerastia, zoophilia

bestir activate, actuate, animate, awaken, ex~ert, get going, incite, motivate, rouse, set off, stimulate, stir up, trouble

bestow accord, allot, apportion, award, com~mit, confer, donate, entrust, give, grant, hand out, honour with, impart, lavish, present, render to

Antonyms acquire, attain, come by, earn, gain, get, land, make, net, obtain, procure, secure

bestowal allotment, award, bestowment, con~ferment, conferral, donation, endowment, gift, grant, presentation

bestride bestraddle, bridge, dominate, extend, mount, span, step over, straddle, tower over

bestseller blockbuster (*informal*), chart-topper (*informal*), hit (*informal*), number one, run~away success, smash (*informal*), smash hit (*informal*)

Antonyms dud (*informal*), failure, flop (*infor~mal*), turkey (*slang, chiefly U.S. & Canad.*)

best-selling chart-topping (*informal*), highly successful, hit (*informal*), number one, smash (*informal*), smash-hit (*informal*), successful

bet 1. *noun* ante, gamble, hazard, long shot, pledge, risk, speculation, stake, venture, wa~ger 2. *verb* chance, gamble, hazard, pledge, punt (*chiefly Brit.*), put money on, put one's shirt on, risk, speculate, stake, venture, wa~ger

bête noire abomination, anathema, aversion, bane, bogey, bugaboo, bugbear, curse, devil, dread, nemesis, nightmare, pet hate, scourge, thorn in the flesh *or* side

bethink cogitate, consider, ponder, recall, rec~ollect, reconsider, reflect, remember, review, take thought

betide bechance, befall, chance, come to pass, crop up (*informal*), ensue, happen, occur, overtake, supervene, take place, transpire (*informal*)

betimes anon, beforehand, before long, early, erelong (*archaic or poetic*), first thing, in good time, punctually, seasonably, soon

betoken augur, bespeak, bode, declare, denote, evidence, indicate, manifest, mark, portend, presage, prognosticate, promise, represent, signify, suggest, typify

betray 1. be disloyal (treacherous, unfaithful), break one's promise, break with, double-cross (*informal*), grass (*Brit. slang*), inform on *or* against, put the finger on (*informal*), sell down the river (*informal*), sell out (*informal*), sell the pass (*informal*), shop (*slang, chiefly Brit.*), stab in the back 2. blurt out, disclose, divulge, evince, expose, give away, lay bare, let slip, manifest, reveal, show, tell, tell on, uncover, unmask 3. beguile, corrupt, deceive, delude, dupe, ensnare, entrap, lead astray, mislead, take for a ride (*informal*), undo 4. abandon, desert, forsake, jilt, walk out on

To betray, you must first belong

Kim Philby

betrayal 1. deception, disloyalty, double-cross (*informal*), double-dealing, duplicity, falseness, perfidy, sell-out (*informal*), treachery, treason, trickery, unfaithfulness 2. blurting out, disclo~sure, divulgence, giving away, revelation, tell~ing

Antonyms (*sense 1*) allegiance, constancy, de~votion, faithfulness, fealty, fidelity, loyalty, steadfastness, trustiness, trustworthiness (*sense 2*) guarding, keeping, keeping secret, preserving, safeguarding

If I had to choose between betraying my country and betraying my friend, I hope I should have the guts to betray my country

E.M. Forster *Two Cheers for Democracy*

betrayer apostate, conspirator, deceiver, ren~egade, snake in the grass, traitor

betroth affiance, contract, engage to marry, pledge in marriage, plight, plight one's troth (*old-fashioned*), promise, take the plunge (*in~formal*), tie the knot (*informal*)

betrothal affiancing, betrothing, engagement, espousal (*archaic*), marriage compact, plight, promise, troth, vow

betrothed 1. *adjective* affianced, engaged, pledged, plighted, promised 2. *noun* bride- *or* husband-to-be, fiancé *or* fiancée, future wife *or* husband, intended, prospective spouse

better *adjective* 1. bigger, excelling, finer, fitter, greater, higher-quality, larger, more appropri~ate (desirable, expert, fitting, suitable, useful, valuable), preferable, streets ahead, superior, surpassing, worthier 2. cured, fitter, fully re~covered, healthier, improving, less ill, mend~ing, more healthy, on the mend (*informal*), progressing, recovering, stronger, well 3. big~ger, greater, larger, longer ~*adverb* 4. in a more excellent manner, in a superior way, more advantageously (attractively, compe~tently, completely, effectively, thoroughly), to a greater degree ~*verb* 5. advance, ameliorate, amend, correct, enhance, forward, further, improve, meliorate, mend, promote, raise, rectify, reform 6. beat, cap (*informal*), clobber (*slang*), exceed, excel, improve on *or* upon, knock spots off (*informal*), lick (*informal*), outdo, outstrip, put in the shade (*informal*), run rings around (*informal*), surpass, top ~*noun* 7. **get the better of** beat, best, defeat, get the upper hand, outdo, outsmart (*infor~*

mal), outwit, prevail over, score off, surpass, triumph over, worst
Antonyms *adjective* inferior, lesser, smaller, substandard, worse *~adverb* worse *~verb* depress, devaluate, go downhill, impoverish, lessen, lower, weaken, worsen

betterment amelioration, edification, improvement, melioration

between amidst, among, betwixt, halfway, in the middle of, mid

bevel **1.** *noun* angle, bezel, cant, chamfer, diagonal, mitre, oblique, slant, slope **2.** *verb* cant, chamfer, cut at an angle, mitre

beverage bevvy (*dialect*), draught, drink, libation (*facetious*), liquid, liquor, potable, potation, refreshment

bevy **1.** band, bunch (*informal*), collection, company, crowd, gathering, group, pack, troupe **2.** covey, flight, flock

bewail bemoan, cry over, deplore, express sorrow, grieve for, keen, lament, moan, mourn, regret, repent, rue, wail, weep over

beware avoid, be careful (cautious, wary), guard against, heed, look out, mind, refrain from, shun, steer clear of, take heed, watch out

bewilder baffle, befuddle, bemuse, confound, confuse, daze, flummox, mix up, mystify, nonplus, perplex, puzzle, stupefy

bewildered at a loss, at sea, awed, baffled, bamboozled (*informal*), confused, disconcerted, dizzy, flummoxed, giddy, mystified, nonplussed, perplexed, puzzled, speechless, startled, stunned, surprised, taken aback, uncertain

bewildering amazing, astonishing, astounding, baffling, confusing, mystifying, perplexing, puzzling, staggering, stunning, stupefying, surprising

bewitch absorb, allure, attract, beguile, captivate, charm, enchant, enrapture, entrance, fascinate, hypnotize, ravish, spellbind
Antonyms disgust, give one the creeps (*informal*), make one sick, offend, repel, repulse, sicken, turn off (*informal*)

bewitched charmed, enchanted, entranced, mesmerized, possessed, spellbound, transformed, under a spell, unrecognizable

beyond above, apart from, at a distance, away from, before, farther, out of range, out of reach, outwith (*Scot.*), over, past, remote, superior to, yonder

bias *noun* **1.** bent, bigotry, favouritism, inclination, intolerance, leaning, narrow-mindedness, one-sidedness, partiality, penchant, predilection, predisposition, prejudice, proclivity, proneness, propensity, tendency, turn, unfairness **2.** angle, cross, diagonal line, slant *~verb* **3.** distort, influence, predispose, prejudice, slant, sway, twist, warp, weight
Antonyms (*sense 1*) equality, equity, fairness, impartiality, neutrality, objectivity, open-mindedness

biased distorted, embittered, jaundiced, one-sided, partial, predisposed, prejudiced, slanted, swayed, twisted, warped, weighted

Bible

Books of the Bible (Old Testament)

Genesis	Ecclesiastes
Exodus	Song of Solomon
Leviticus	Isaiah
Numbers	Jeremiah
Deuteronomy	Lamentations
Joshua	Ezekiel
Judges	Daniel
Ruth	Hosea
1 Samuel	Joel
2 Samuel	Amos
1 Kings	Obadiah
2 Kings	Jonah
1 Chronicles	Micah
2 Chronicles	Nahum
Ezra	Habakkuk
Nehemiah	Zephaniah
Esther	Haggai
Job	Zechariah
Psalms	Malachi
Proverbs	

Books of the Bible (New Testament)

Matthew	1 Timothy
Mark	2 Timothy
Luke	Titus
John	Philemon
Acts	Hebrews
Romans	James
1 Corinthians	1 Peter
2 Corinthians	2 Peter
Galatians	1 John
Ephesians	2 John
Philippians	3 John
Colossians	Jude
1 Thessalonians	Revelation
2 Thessalonians	

Books of the Bible (Apocrypha)

Tobit	Daniel and Susanna
Judith	Daniel, Bel and the Snake
1 Maccabees	Song of the Three
2 Maccabees	Esdras
Wisdom	Manasseh
Ecclesiasticus	
Baruch	

Characters in the Bible

Aaron	Ahithophel
Abednego	Adam
Abel	Ahab
Abigail	Ahasuerus
Abraham	Ammon
Absalom	Amos
Achitophel *or*	Ananias

Andrew
apostles
Asher
Balaam
Balthazar
Barabbas
Bartholomew
Baruch
Bathsheba
Beelzebub
Belial
Belshazzar
Benjamin
Boanerges
Boaz
Caiaphas
Cain
Caspar
Cush *or* Kush
Dan
Daniel
David
Deborah
Delilah
Dinah
Dives
Dorcas
Elias
Elijah
Elisha
Enoch
Enos
Ephraim
Esau
Esther
Eve
Ezekiel
Ezra
Gabriel
Gad
Gideon
Gilead
Gog and Magog
Goliath
Good Samaritan
Habakkuk
Hagar
Haggai
Ham
Hannah
Herod
Hezekiah
Hiram
Holofernes
Hosea
Isaac
Isaiah
Ishmael
Issachar
Jacob
Jael
James
Japheth
Jehoshaphat
Jehu
Jephthah *or* Jephte
Jeremiah
Jeroboam
Jesse
Jesus
Jethro
Jezebel
Joab
Job
Joel
John
John the Baptist
Jonah *or* Jonas
Jonathan
Joseph
Joshua
Josiah
Jubal
Judah
Judas
Jude
Judith
Laban
Lazarus
Leah
Levi
Lot
Lot's wife
Luke
Magus
Malachi
Manasseh
Mark
Martha
Mary
Mary Magdalene
Matthew
Matthias
Melchior
Melchizedek *or* Melchisedech
Meshach
Methuselah
Micah
Midian
Miriam
Mordecai
Moses
Nabonidus
Naboth
Nahum
Naomi
Naphtali
Nathan
Nathanael
Nebuchadnezzar *or* Nebuchadrezzar
Nehemiah
Nicodemus
Nimrod
Noah
Obadiah
Paul
Peter
Philip
Potiphar
Queen of Sheba
Rachel
Rebecca
Reuben
Ruth
Salome
Samson
Samuel
Sarah
Saul
Seth
Shadrach
Shem
Simeon
Simon
Solomon
Susanna
Tetragrammaton
Thaddeus *or* Thadeus
Thomas
Tobit
Tubal-cain
Uriah
Virgin Mary
Zacharias, Zachariah *or* Zachary
Zebedee
Zebulun
Zechariah
Zedekiah
Zephaniah
Zilpah

Place names in the Bible

Aceldama
Antioch
Aram
Ararat
Arimathaea *or* Arimathea
Babel
Bashan
Bethesda
Bethlehem
Calvary
Cana
Canaan
Capernaum
Eden
Galilee
Garden of Eden
Gath
Gaza
Gehenna
Gethsemane
Golgotha
Gomorrah *or* Gomorrha
Goshen
Horeb
Jericho
Jerusalem
Judaea *or* Judea
Judah
land of milk and honey
land of Nod
Moab
Nazareth
On
Ophir
Rabbath Ammon
Samaria
Shiloh
Shinar
Shittim
Sodom
Tadmor
Tophet *or* Topheth
wilderness

There's a great text in Galatians,
Once you trip on it, entails
Twenty-nine distinct damnations,
One sure, if another fails
Robert Browning *Soliloquy of the Spanish Cloister*

the English Bible, a book which, if everything else in our language should perish, would alone suffice to show the whole extent of its beauty and power
Lord Macaulay *Miscellaneous Writings*

bicker argue, cross swords, disagree, dispute, fight, fight like cat and dog, go at it hammer and tongs, quarrel, row (*informal*), scrap (*informal*), spar, squabble, wrangle

Antonyms accord, acquiesce, agree, assent, concur, cooperate, get on, harmonize

bid *verb* 1. offer, proffer, propose, submit, tender 2. call, greet, say, tell, wish 3. ask, call, charge, command, desire, direct, enjoin, instruct, invite, require, solicit, summon, tell *~noun* 4. advance, amount, offer, price, proposal, proposition, submission, sum, tender 5. attempt, crack (*informal*), effort, endeavour, go (*informal*), stab (*informal*), try, venture

biddable amenable, complaisant, cooperative, docile, obedient, teachable, tractable
Antonyms awkward, difficult, disobedient, intractable, petulant, querulous, refractory, unruly

bidding 1. beck, beck and call, behest, call, canon, charge, command, demand, direction, injunction, instruction, invitation, order, request, summons 2. auction, offer, offers, proposal, tender

big 1. bulky, burly, colossal, considerable, elephantine, enormous, extensive, gigantic, great, huge, hulking, humongous *or* humungous (*U.S. slang*), immense, large, mammoth, massive, ponderous, prodigious, sizable *or* sizeable, spacious, stellar (*informal*), substantial, vast, voluminous 2. big-time (*informal*), eminent, important, influential, leading, main, major league (*informal*), momentous, paramount, powerful, prime, principal, prominent, serious, significant, valuable, weighty 3. adult, elder, grown, grown-up, mature 4. altruistic, benevolent, generous, gracious, heroic, magnanimous, noble, princely, unselfish 5. arrogant, boastful, bragging, conceited, haughty, inflated, pompous, pretentious, proud
Antonyms (*senses 1 & 3*) diminutive, immature, insignificant, little, mini, miniature, petite, pint-sized (*informal*), pocket-sized, pygmy *or* pigmy, small, tiny, wee, young (*sense 2*) humble, ignoble, insignificant, minor, modest, ordinary, unimportant, unknown

The bigger they come, the harder they fall
Robert Fitzsimmons

bighead blowhard (*informal*), boaster, braggadocio, braggart, egotist, know-all (*informal*), swell-head (*informal*)

big-hearted benevolent, big, charitable, generous, gracious, great-hearted, kind-hearted, magnanimous, noble, open-hearted, unselfish, warm
Antonyms hard-hearted, mean, selfish, uncharitable, ungenerous, ungracious

bigot dogmatist, fanatic, persecutor, sectarian, zealot

bigot: one who is obstinately and zealously attached to an opinion that you do not entertain
Ambrose Bierce *The Devil's Dictionary*

bigoted biased, dogmatic, illiberal, intolerant, narrow-minded, obstinate, opinionated, prejudiced, sectarian, twisted, warped
Antonyms broad-minded, equitable, open-minded, tolerant, unbiased, unbigoted, unprejudiced

bigotry bias, discrimination, dogmatism, fanaticism, ignorance, injustice, intolerance, mindlessness, narrow-mindedness, pig-ignorance (*slang*), prejudice, provincialism, racialism, racism, sectarianism, sexism, unfairness
Antonyms broad-mindedness, forbearance, open-mindedness, permissiveness, tolerance

Bigotry may roughly be defined as the anger of men who have no opinions
G.K. Chesterton *Heretics*

Bigotry tries to keep truth safe in its hand
With a grip that kills it
Rabindranath Tagore *Fireflies*

bigwig big cheese (*slang, old-fashioned*), big gun (*informal*), big name, big noise (*informal*), big shot (*informal*), celeb (*informal*), celebrity, dignitary, heavyweight (*informal*), mogul, nob (*slang*), notability, notable, panjandrum, personage, somebody, V.I.P.
Antonyms cipher, lightweight (*informal*), nobody, nonentity, nothing, zero

bile anger, bitterness, churlishness, ill humour, irascibility, irritability, nastiness, peevishness, rancour, spleen

bilious 1. liverish, nauseated, out of sorts, queasy, sick 2. bad-tempered, cantankerous, crabby, cross, crotchety, edgy, grouchy (*informal*), grumpy, ill-humoured, ill-tempered, irritable, like a bear with a sore head, nasty, peevish, ratty (*Brit. & N.Z. informal*), short-tempered, testy, tetchy, touchy

bilk bamboozle (*informal*), cheat, con (*informal*), cozen, deceive, defraud, do (*slang*), fleece, pull a fast one on (*informal*), rook (*slang*), sell a pup, skin (*slang*), stiff (*slang*), swindle, trick

bill[1] *noun* 1. account, charges, invoice, note of charge, reckoning, score, statement, tally 2. advertisement, broadsheet, bulletin, circular, handbill, handout, leaflet, notice, placard, playbill, poster 3. agenda, card, catalogue, inventory, list, listing, programme, roster, schedule, syllabus 4. measure, piece of legislation, projected law, proposal *~verb* 5. charge, debit, figure, invoice, reckon, record 6. advertise, announce, give advance notice of, post

bill[2] *noun* beak, mandible, neb (*archaic or dialect*), nib

billet 1. *noun* accommodation, barracks, lodging, quarters 2. *verb* accommodate, berth, quarter, station

billow *noun* **1.** breaker, crest, roller, surge, swell, tide, wave **2.** cloud, deluge, flood, out~pouring, rush, surge, wave *~verb* **3.** balloon, belly, puff up, rise up, roll, surge, swell

billowy heaving, rippling, rolling, surging, swelling, swirling, undulating, waving, wavy

bind *verb* **1.** attach, fasten, glue, hitch, lash, paste, rope, secure, stick, strap, tie, tie up, truss, wrap **2.** compel, constrain, engage, force, necessitate, obligate, oblige, prescribe, require **3.** confine, detain, hamper, hinder, re~strain, restrict **4.** bandage, cover, dress, en~case, swathe, wrap **5.** border, edge, finish, hem, trim *~noun* **6.** *informal* bore, difficulty, dilemma, drag (*informal*), hot water (*infor~mal*), nuisance, pain in the arse (*taboo infor~mal*), pain in the neck (*informal*), predica~ment, quandary, spot (*informal*), tight spot
Antonyms (*senses 1 & 3*) free, loosen, release, unbind, undo, unfasten, untie

binding *adjective* compulsory, conclusive, im~perative, indissoluble, irrevocable, mandatory, necessary, obligatory, unalterable
Antonyms discretionary, free, noncompulsory, optional, uncompelled, unconstrained, un~forced, voluntary

binge beano (*Brit. slang*), bender (*informal*), blind (*slang*), bout, feast, fling, jag (*slang*), orgy, spree

biography account, curriculum vitae, CV, life, life history, life story, memoir, memoirs, pro~file, record

Read no history: nothing but biography, for that is life without theory
Benjamin Disraeli *Contarini Fleming*

Discretion is not the better part of biography
Lytton Strachey

The Art of Biography
Is different from Geography
Geography is about Maps,
But Biography is about Chaps
Edmund Clerihew Bentley *Biography for Begin~ners*

biology

Branches of biology

actinobiology
aerobiology
agrobiology
astrobiology
bacteriology
biochemistry
biodynamics
biogeography
biometry
biophysics
biostatics
botany
chronobiology
cryobiology
cytogenetics
cytology
ecology
genetics
histology
microbiology
morphology
oceanography
organography
organology
palaeontology
parasitology
photobiology
photodynamics
radiobiology
sociobiology
somatology
stoichiology
taxonomy
teratology
zoology

Biology terms

aerobic
agglutination
albino
allele *or* allelomorph
anaerobic
anterior
asexual reproduction
assimilation
bacteria
binary fission
biomass
blood
blood vessel
bone
cell
chromosome
circulation
circulatory system
class
clone
codominance
cold-blooded
conception
copulation
cytoplasm
diffusion
digestion
diploid
division
DNA *or* deoxyribonu~cleic acid
dominant
dorsal
ecosystem
egg
embryo
environment
enzyme
epidermis
evolution
excretion
family
fermentation
fertilization
flower
foetus
food chain
fossil
fruit
fungus
gamete
gene
genus
germination
gestation
gland
gonad
growth
haploid
heredity
hermaphrodite
hormone
hybrid
inheritance
invertebrate
kingdom
Krebs cycle
life cycle
meiosis
menstruation
metabolism
metamorphosis
mitosis
muscle
mutation
natural selection
nitrogen cycle
nucleus
order
organ
osmosis
ovulation
ovum
parasite
pathogen
pectoral
photosynthesis
phylum
poikilothermic
pollen
pollination
pollution
posterior
predator
pregnancy
progeny
propagation
protein
protoplasm
puberty
recessive
reproduction
respiration
RNA *or* ribose nucleic acid
ribosome
root
seed
sexual reproduction
skeleton

skin
soil
species
spermatozoon *or* sperm
spore
symbiosis
translocation
transpiration
ventral
vertebrate
virus
vitamin
viviparous
warm-blooded
X-chromosome
Y-chromosome
zygote

Famous biologists

John Boyd Orr [Scottish]
Francis Harry Compton Crick [English]
Charles (Robert) Darwin [English]
Alexander Fleming [Scottish]
William Harvey [English]
Thomas Henry Huxley [English]
Robert Koch [German]
Hans Adolf Krebs [British]
Anton van Leeuwenhoek [Dutch]
Linnaeus (Carl von Linné) [Swedish]
Gregor Mendel [Austrian]
Louis Pasteur [French]
James Dewey Watson [U.S.]

bird

Related adjective: avian

Birds

accentor
accipiter
albatross *or (informal)* gooney bird
amazon
American wigeon *or* baldpate
ani
auk
auklet
avadavat *or* amadavat
avocet
babbler
bald eagle
Baltimore oriole
barbet
barnacle goose
barn owl
bateleur eagle
beccafico
bee-eater
bellbird
Bewick's swan
bird of paradise
bishopbird
bittern
black-backed gull
blackbird
blackcap
blackcock
black grouse
black guillemot
blackpoll
black swan
bluebird
blue duck
blue goose
blue grouse
blue jay
bluethroat
bluetit
boatbill *or* boat-billed heron
bobolink
bobwhite
bokmakierie
boobook
bowerbird
brain-fever bird
brambling
broadbill
brolga, Australian crane *or (Austral.)* native companion
brown owl
brush turkey
budgerigar
bufflehead
bulbul
bullfinch
bunting
bush shrike
bushtit
bush wren
bustard
button quail
buzzard
cacique
Canada goose
canary
canvasback
Cape pigeon
capercaillie *or* capercailzie
Cape sparrow
capuchin
caracara
cardinal *or* cardinal grosbeak
carrion crow
cassowary
catbird
chaffinch
chat
chickadee
chicken *or (Austral. inf.)* chook *see* CHICKEN
chiffchaff
chimney swallow *or* chimney swift
chipping sparrow
chough
chuck-will's-widow
chukar
cliff swallow
coal tit *or* coletit
cock
cockatiel *or* cockateel
cockatoo
cockerel
cock-of-the-rock
collared dove
coly *or* mousebird
condor
conure
Cooper's hawk
coot
coppersmith
coquette
corella
cormorant
corn bunting
corncrake
cotinga *or* chatterer
coucal
cowbird
crake
crane
crested tit
crocodile bird
crombec
crossbill
crow *or (Scot.)* corbie
cuckoo
cumulet
curassow
curlew
currawong *or* bell magpie
darter, anhinga *or* snakebird
demoiselle (crane) *or* Numidian crane
diamond bird *or* pardalote
dipper *or* water ouzel
diver
dollarbird
dotterel *or* dottrel
dove *or (archaic or poetic)* culver
dowitcher
drongo
duck
duck hawk
dunlin *or* red-backed sandpiper
eagle
eagle-hawk *or* wedge-tailed eagle
egret
eider *or* eider duck
Emperor penguin
emu
emu-wren
falcon
falconet
fantail
fernbird
fieldfare
fig-bird
finch
finfoot
firebird
firecrest
fish hawk
flamingo
flower-pecker
flycatcher
francolin
friarbird
frogmouth
fulmar
gadwall
galah
gang-gang
gannet
garganey
glaucous gull
gnatcatcher
go-away bird
godwit
goldcrest
goldeneye
golden eagle
golden oriole
goldfinch
goosander
goose

goshawk
grackle *or* crow blackbird
grassfinch
grassquit
great crested grebe
great northern diver
great tit
grebe
greenfinch
green leek
greenlet
greenshank
green woodpecker
greylag *or* greylag goose
grey warbler *or* riro~riro (*N.Z.*)
grosbeak
grouse
guan
guillemot
guinea fowl
gull *or (Archaic or dialect)* cob(b)
gyrfalcon *or* gerfalcon
hadedah
harlequin duck
harrier
hawfinch
hawk
hawk owl
hazelhen
hedge sparrow *or* dunnock
helldiver, pie-billed grebe *or* dabchick
hen
hen harrier *or (U.S. & Canad.)* marsh harrier
heron
herring gull
hill myna
hoatzin *or* hoactzin
hobby
homing pigeon
honey buzzard
honey creeper
honey-eater
honey guide
honeysucker
hooded crow
hoopoe
hoot owl
hornbill
horned owl
house martin
house sparrow
hummingbird *or* trochilus
ibis
ivory gull
jabiru
jacamar
jaçana *or* lily-trotter
jackdaw
jacksnipe
Jacobin
jaeger (*U.S. & Canad.*)
Java sparrow
jay
junco
jungle fowl
kagu
kaka
kakapo
kea
kestrel
killdeer
kingbird
kingfisher
king penguin
kite
kittiwake
kiwi *or* apteryx
knot
koel
kokako
kookaburra *or* laugh~ing jackass
kotuku
Lahore
lammergeier, lam~mergeyer, bearded vulture *or (archaic)* ossifrage
lanner
lapwing *or* green plover
lark
limpkin *or* courlan
linnet
little owl
locust bird
loggerhead shrike
long-eared owl
longspur
long-tailed tit
lorikeet
lory
lourie
lovebird
lyrebird
macaw
magpie
magpie goose
magpie lark
Major Mitchell
mallard
mallee fowl *or (Aus~tral.)* gnow
mandarin duck
man-of-war bird
marabou
marsh hen
marsh tit
martin
meadowlark
meadow pipit
megapode
merganser *or* sawbill
merlin
minivet
mistle thrush *or* mis~sel thrush
mockingbird
monal *or* monaul
Montagu's harrier
moorhen
mopoke *or (N.Z.)* ruru
motmot *or* sawbill
mourning dove
murrelet
Muscovy duck *or* musk duck
mute swan
mutton bird
myna, mynah *or* mina
nene
nighthawk, bullbat *or* mosquito hawk
night heron
nightingale
nightjar *or (U.S. & Canad.)* goatsucker
noddy
noisy miner
nun
nutcracker
nuthatch
oil bird *or* guacharo
old squaw *or* oldwife
oriole
ortolan *or* ortolan bunting
osprey, fish eagle *or (archaic)* ossifrage
ostrich
ouzel *or* ousel
ovenbird
owl
oxpecker *or* tick-bird
oystercatcher
paradise duck
parakeet *or* parrakeet
parrot
partridge
peacock
peafowl
peewit
pelican
penguin
peregrine falcon
petrel
phalarope
pheasant
pied wagtail
pigeon
pintail
pipit
plover
pochard
pratincole
prion
ptarmigan
puffbird
puffin
pukeko
purple gallinule
pyrrhuloxia
quail
quarrian *or* quarrion
quetzal
racket-tail
rail
rainbow bird
raven
razorbill *or* razor-billed auk
red-backed shrike
redbreast
red grouse
redhead
red kite *or (archaic)* gled(e)
red-legged partridge
redpoll
redshank
redstart
redwing
reedbird
reed bunting
reedling *or* bearded tit
reed warbler
regent-bird
rhea *or* American os~trich
ricebird
riflebird
rifleman
ringed plover
ring-necked pheasant
ring ouzel
roadrunner *or* chap~arral cock
robin *or* robin red~breast
rock dove *or* rock pi~geon
rockhopper

roller
rook
rosella
rosy finch
rough-legged buzzard
ruddy duck
ruff
ruffed grouse
runt
saddleback
saddlebill *or* jabiru
sage grouse
saker
sanderling
sandgrouse
sand martin
sandpiper
sapsucker
sawbill
Scandaroon
scarlet tanager
scaup *or* scaup duck
scoter
screamer
screech owl
scrub bird
sea duck
sea eagle, erne *or* ern
seagull
secretary bird
sedge warbler
seriema
serin
shearwater
sheathbill
shelduck
shoebill
shore bird *or* *(Brit.)* wader
shoveler
shrike *or* butcherbird
sicklebill
siskin *or* *(formerly)* aberdevine
sitella *or* tree-runner
skimmer
skua
skylark
smew
snipe
snow bunting
snow goose
snowy egret
snowy owl
solitaire
song sparrow
song thrush *or* mavis
sora
sparrow
sparrowhawk
spoonbill
spotted crake
spotted flycatcher
spotted sandpiper *or* *(U.S.)* peetweet
squacco
starling
stilt
stint
stock dove
stonechat
stone curlew *or* thick-knee
stork
storm petrel, stormy petrel *or* Mother Carey's chicken
sugar bird
sultan
sunbird
sun bittern
surfbird
surf scoter *or* surf duck
swallow
swan
swift
swiftlet
swordbill
tailorbird
takahe
tanager
tattler
tawny owl
tawny pippit
teal
tern
thornbill
thrasher
thrush *or* *(poetic)* throstle
tit
titmouse
tody
torticollis *or* wryneck
toucan
touraco, turaco *or* plantain-eater
towhee
tragopan
tree creeper
tree sparrow
trochilus
trogon
tropicbird
troupial
trumpeter
trumpeter swan
tui
turkey
turkey buzzard *or* vulture
turtledove
twite
umbrella bird
veery
velvet scoter
verdin
vulture
wader *or* wading bird
wagtail
wall creeper
wandering albatross
warbler
water rail
water thrush
wattlebird
waxbill
waxwing
weaverbird *or* weaver
weka, Maori hen *or* wood hen
wheatear
whimbrel
whinchat
whip bird
whippoorwill
whistling swan
white-eye *or* *(N.Z.)* blighty, silvereye *or* waxeye
whitethroat
whooper *or* whooper swan
whooping crane
wigeon *or* widgeon
willet
willow grouse
willow tit
willow warbler
Wilson's petrel
wonga-wonga
woodchat *or* woodchat shrike
woodcock
wood duck
wood ibis
woodlark
woodpecker
wood pigeon, ring-dove, cushat, *(Scot.)* cushie-doo *or* *(English dialect)* quist
woodswallow
wood warbler
wren
wrybill
wryneck
yellowhammer
zebra finch

Extinct birds

archaeopteryx
archaeornis
dodo
great auk
huia
ichthyornis
moa
notornis
passenger pigeon
solitaire

Be ye therefore wise as serpents, and harmless as doves
Bible: St. Matthew

magpie: a bird whose thievish disposition suggested to someone that it might be taught to talk
Ambrose Bierce *The Devil's Dictionary*

Oh, a wondrous bird is the pelican!
His beak can hold more than his belican.
He takes in his beak
Food enough for a week.
But I'll be darned if I know how the helican
Dixon Lanier Merritt

A bird in the hand is worth two in the bush

Birds of a feather flock together

birth **1**. childbirth, delivery, nativity, parturition **2**. beginning, emergence, fountainhead, genesis, origin, rise, source **3**. ancestry, background, blood, breeding, derivation, descent, extraction, forebears, genealogy, line, lineage, nobility, noble extraction, parentage, pedigree, race, stock, strain
Antonyms (*senses 1 & 2*) death, demise, end, extinction, passing, passing away *or* on

Birth, and copulation, and death.
That's all the facts when you come to brass tacks:
Birth, and copulation and death.
I've been born, and once is enough.
T.S. Eliot *Sweeney Agonistes*

It as natural to die as to be born; and to a little infant, perhaps, the one is as painful as the other
Francis Bacon

There is no cure for birth and death save to enjoy the interval
George Santayana *Soliloquies in England*

bisect bifurcate, cross, cut across, cut in half, cut in two, divide in two, halve, intersect, separate, split, split down the middle

bisexual AC/DC (*slang*), ambidextrous (*slang*), androgyne, androgynous, bi (*slang*), epicene, gynandromorphic *or* gynandromorphous (*Entomology*), gynandrous, hermaphrodite, hermaphroditic, monoclinous (*Botany*), swinging both ways (*slang*)

It immediately doubles your chances for a date on Saturday night
Woody Allen (on bisexuality)

bishopric diocese, episcopacy, episcopate, primacy, see

bit[1] *noun* **1.** atom, chip, crumb, fragment, grain, iota, jot, mite, morsel, mouthful, part, piece, remnant, scrap, segment, slice, small piece, speck, tittle, whit **2.** instant, jiffy (*informal*), little while, minute, moment, period, second, spell, tick (*Brit. informal*), time

bit[2] *noun* **1.** brake, check, curb, restraint, snaffle **2. take the bit in** *or* **between one's teeth** defy, disobey, get stuck into (*informal*), get to grips with, rebel, resist, revolt, run amok, rush into, set about

bitchy backbiting, catty (*informal*), cruel, malicious, mean, nasty, rancorous, shrewish, snide, spiteful, venomous, vicious, vindictive, vixenish
Antonyms charitable, generous, gracious, kindly, magnanimous, nice

bite *verb* **1.** champ, chew, clamp, crunch, crush, cut, gnaw, grip, hold, masticate, nibble, nip, pierce, pinch, rend, seize, snap, tear, wound **2.** burn, corrode, eat away, eat into, erode, smart, sting, tingle, wear away ~*noun* **3.** itch, nip, pinch, prick, smarting, sting, tooth marks, wound **4.** food, light meal, morsel, mouthful, piece, refreshment, snack, taste **5.** edge, kick (*informal*), piquancy, punch (*informal*), pungency, spice

biting 1. bitter, blighting, cold, cold as ice, cutting, freezing, harsh, nipping, penetrating, piercing, sharp **2.** caustic, cutting, incisive, mordacious, mordant, sarcastic, scathing, severe, sharp, stinging, trenchant, vitriolic, withering

bitter 1. acerb, acid, acrid, astringent, sharp, sour, tart, unsweetened, vinegary **2.** acrimonious, begrudging, crabbed, embittered, hostile, morose, rancorous, resentful, sore, sour, sullen, with a chip on one's shoulder **3.** calamitous, cruel, dire, distressing, galling, grievous, harsh, heartbreaking, merciless, painful, poignant, ruthless, savage, vexatious **4.** biting, fierce, freezing, intense, severe, stinging
Antonyms appreciative, balmy, bland, fortunate, friendly, gentle, grateful, happy, mellow, mild, pleasant, sugary, sweet, thankful

bitterly 1. acerbically, acidly, acridly, sharply, sourly, tartly **2.** acrimoniously, caustically, grudgingly, irascibly, mordantly, resentfully, sorely, sourly, sullenly, tartly, testily **3.** cruelly, distressingly, grievously, harshly, mercilessly, painfully, poignantly, ruthlessly, sadly, savagely, terribly **4.** bitingly, fiercely, intensely, severely

bitterness 1. acerbity, acidity, sharpness, sourness, tartness, vinegariness **2.** animosity, chip on one's shoulder (*informal*), grudge, hostility, pique, rancour, resentment **3.** acrimoniousness, asperity, pungency, sarcasm, venom, virulence

bitty disconnected, disjointed, fragmentary, fragmented, incoherent, incomplete, jumbled, patchy, scrappy, sketchy
Antonyms all-embracing, coherent, complete, comprehensive, unified

bizarre abnormal, comical, curious, eccentric, extraordinary, fantastic, freakish, grotesque, left-field (*informal*), ludicrous, odd, oddball (*informal*), off-beat, off the rails, off-the-wall (*slang*), outlandish, outré, peculiar, queer, ridiculous, rum (*Brit. slang*), strange, unusual, wacko (*slang*), way-out (*informal*), weird, zany
Antonyms common, customary, normal, ordinary, regular, routine, standard, typical

blab blow the gaff (*Brit. slang*), blow wide open (*slang*), blurt out, disclose, divulge, gossip, let slip, let the cat out of the bag, reveal, shop (*slang, chiefly Brit.*), sing (*slang, chiefly U.S.*), spill one's guts (*slang*), spill the beans (*informal*), tattle, tell, tell all, tell on

blabber 1. *noun* busybody, gossip, informer, rumour-monger, scandalmonger, talebearer, tattler, telltale **2.** *verb* blather, blether (*Scot.*), chatter, gab (*informal*), jabber, prattle, run off at the mouth

blabbermouth bigmouth (*slang*), blatherskite, flibbertigibbet, gossip, loudmouth (*informal*), motormouth (*slang*), windbag (*slang*)

black *adjective* **1.** coal-black, dark, dusky, ebony, inky, jet, murky, pitchy, raven, sable, starless, stygian, swarthy **2.** *figurative* atrocious, depressing, dismal, distressing, doleful, foreboding, funereal, gloomy, hopeless, horri~

ble, lugubrious, mournful, ominous, sad, sombre **3.** dingy, dirty, filthy, grimy, grubby, soiled, sooty, stained **4.** angry, furious, hostile, menacing, resentful, sullen, threatening **5.** bad, evil, iniquitous, nefarious, villainous, wicked *~verb* **6.** ban, bar, blacklist, boycott *~noun* **7. in the black** in credit, in funds, solvent, without debt
Antonyms (*sense 1*) bright, illuminated, light, lighted, lit, moonlit, sunny (*sense 2*) cheerful, happy, warm (*sense 3*) clean, pure, white, whitish (*sense 4*) amicable, cheerful, friendly, happy, pleased, warm (*sense 5*) good, honourable, moral, pure

blackball *verb* ban, bar, blacklist, debar, drum out, exclude, expel, ostracize, oust, repudiate, snub, vote against

blacken 1. befoul, begrime, cloud, darken, grow black, make black, smudge, soil **2.** bad-mouth (*slang, chiefly U.S. & Canad.*), calumniate, decry, defame, defile, denigrate, dishonour, knock (*informal*), malign, rubbish (*informal*), slag (off) (*slang*), slander, smear, smirch, stain, sully, taint, tarnish, traduce, vilify

blackguard bad egg (*old-fashioned informal*), bastard (*offensive*), blighter (*Brit. informal*), bounder (*old-fashioned Brit. slang*), bugger (*taboo slang*), miscreant, rascal, rogue, scoundrel, scumbag (*slang*), shit (*taboo slang*), son-of-a-bitch (*slang, chiefly U.S. & Canad.*), swine, villain, wretch

blacklist *verb* ban, bar, blackball, boycott, debar, exclude, expel, ostracize, preclude, proscribe, reject, repudiate, snub, vote against

black magic black art, diabolism, necromancy, sorcery, voodoo, witchcraft, wizardry

blackmail 1. *noun* bribe, exaction, extortion, hush money (*slang*), intimidation, milking, pay-off (*informal*), protection (*informal*), ransom, shakedown (*U.S. slang*), slush fund **2.** *verb* bleed (*informal*), bribe, coerce, compel, demand, exact, extort, force, hold to ransom, milk, squeeze, threaten

blackness darkness, duskiness, gloom, inkiness, melanism, murkiness, nigrescence, nigritude (*rare*), swarthiness
Antonyms brightness, brilliance, effulgence, incandescence, lambency, light, lightness, luminescence, luminosity, phosphorescence, radiance

blackout *noun* **1.** coma, faint, loss of consciousness, oblivion, swoon, syncope (*Pathology*), unconsciousness **2.** power cut, power failure **3.** censorship, noncommunication, radio silence, secrecy, suppression, withholding news

black out *verb* **1.** conceal, cover, darken, eclipse, obfuscate, shade **2.** collapse, faint, flake out (*informal*), lose consciousness, pass out, swoon

black sheep bad egg (*old-fashioned informal*), disgrace, dropout, ne'er-do-well, outcast, prodigal, renegade, reprobate, wastrel

blamable answerable, blameworthy, culpable, deserving of censure, faulty, guilty, in the wrong, liable, reprehensible, reproachable, reprovable, responsible

blame *noun* **1.** accountability, culpability, fault, guilt, incrimination, liability, onus, rap (*slang*), responsibility **2.** accusation, castigation, censure, charge, complaint, condemnation, criticism, recrimination, reproach, reproof, stick (*slang*) *~verb* **3.** accuse, admonish, blast, censure, charge, chide, condemn, criticize, disapprove, express disapprobation, find fault with, hold responsible, lambast(e), point a *or* the finger at, put down, reprehend, reproach, reprove, tax, tear into (*informal*), upbraid
Antonyms *noun* absolution, acclaim, alibi, Brownie points, commendation, credit, excuse, exoneration, honour, praise, tribute, vindication *~verb* absolve, acclaim, acquit, approve of, clear, commend, compliment, excuse, exonerate, forgive, praise, vindicate

blameless above suspicion, clean, faultless, guiltless, immaculate, impeccable, innocent, in the clear, irreproachable, perfect, squeaky-clean, stainless, unblemished, unimpeachable, unoffending, unspotted, unsullied, untarnished, upright, virtuous
Antonyms at fault, censurable, culpable, guilty, reprovable, responsible, to blame

blameworthy discreditable, disreputable, indefensible, inexcusable, iniquitous, reprehensible, reproachable, shameful

blanch become *or* grow white, become pallid, bleach, blench, drain, fade, pale, turn pale, wan, whiten

bland 1. boring, dull, flat, humdrum, insipid, monotonous, tasteless, tedious, tiresome, undistinctive, unexciting, uninspiring, uninteresting, unstimulating, vanilla (*informal*), vapid, weak **2.** affable, amiable, congenial, courteous, debonair, friendly, gentle, gracious, smooth, suave, unemotional, urbane **3.** balmy, calm, mild, mollifying, nonirritant *or* nonirritating (*Medical*), soft, soothing, temperate
Antonyms (*sense 1*) distinctive, exciting, inspiring, interesting, rousing, stimulating, turbulent, volatile (*sense 3*) annoying, harsh, irritating, rough, severe

blandish beguile, butter up, cajole, coax, entice, fawn, flannel (*Brit. informal*), flatter, ingratiate, inveigle, lick someone's arse (*taboo slang*), lick someone's boots (*slang*), pander to, soft-soap (*informal*), sweet-talk (*informal*), toady, wheedle

blandishments blarney, cajolery, coaxing, compliments, fawning, flattery, ingratiation, inveiglement, soft soap (*informal*), soft words, sweet talk (*informal*), wheedling, winning caresses

blank *adjective* **1.** bare, clean, clear, empty, plain, spotless, uncompleted, unfilled, unmarked, void, white **2.** deadpan, dull, empty, expressionless, hollow, impassive, inane, lifeless, poker-faced (*informal*), vacant, vacuous, vague **3.** at a loss, at sea, bewildered, confounded, confused, disconcerted, dumbfounded, flummoxed, muddled, nonplussed, uncomprehending **4.** absolute, complete, out and out, outright, thorough, unqualified, utter *~noun* **5.** emptiness, empty space, gap, nothingness, space, tabula rasa, vacancy, vacuity, vacuum, void
Antonyms alert, busy, completed, expressive, filled in, full, intelligent, interested, lively, marked, productive, profitable, rewarding, significant, thoughtful, useful, valuable

blanket *noun* **1.** afghan, cover, coverlet, rug **2.** carpet, cloak, coat, coating, covering, envelope, film, layer, mantle, sheet, wrapper, wrapping *~adjective* **3.** across-the-board, all-inclusive, comprehensive, overall, sweeping, wide-ranging *~verb* **4.** cloak, cloud, coat, conceal, cover, eclipse, hide, mask, obscure, suppress, surround

blankness abstraction, fatuity, inanity, indifference, no recollection, obliviousness, vacancy, vacuity

blare blast, boom, clamour, clang, honk, hoot, peal, resound, roar, scream, sound out, toot, trumpet

blarney blandishment, cajolery, coaxing, exaggeration, flattery, honeyed words, overpraise, soft soap (*informal*), spiel, sweet talk (*informal*), wheedling

blasé apathetic, bored, cloyed, glutted, indifferent, jaded, lukewarm, nonchalant, offhand, satiated, surfeited, unconcerned, unexcited, uninterested, unmoved, weary, world-weary
Antonyms affected, caring, enthusiastic, excited, interested, responsive, stimulated

blaspheme abuse, anathematize, curse, damn, desecrate, execrate, profane, revile, swear

blasphemous godless, impious, irreligious, irreverent, profane, sacrilegious, ungodly
Antonyms devout, God-fearing, godly, pious, religious, respectful, reverent, reverential

blasphemy cursing, desecration, execration, impiety, impiousness, indignity (*to God*), irreverence, profanation, profaneness, profanity, sacrilege, swearing

blast *noun/verb* **1.** blare, blow, clang, honk, peal, scream, toot, wail *~noun* **2.** bang, blow-up, burst, crash, detonation, discharge, eruption, explosion, outburst, salvo, volley **3.** gale, gust, squall, storm, strong breeze, tempest *~verb* **4.** blow sky-high, blow up, break up, burst, demolish, destroy, explode, put paid to, ruin, shatter **5.** blight, kill, shrivel, wither **6.** attack, castigate, criticize, flay, lambast(e), put down, rail at, tear into (*informal*)

blasted blighted, desolated, destroyed, devastated, ravaged, ruined, shattered, spoiled, wasted, withered

blastoff *noun* discharge, expulsion, firing, launch, launching, liftoff, projection, shot

blatant **1.** bald, brazen, conspicuous, flagrant, flaunting, glaring, naked, obtrusive, obvious, ostentatious, outright, overt, prominent, pronounced, sheer, unmitigated **2.** clamorous, deafening, ear-splitting, harsh, loud, noisy, piercing, strident
Antonyms agreeable, cultured, dignified, hidden, inconspicuous, quiet, refined, soft, subtle, tasteful, unnoticeable, unobtrusive, well-mannered

blather claptrap (*informal*), drivel, gibberish, gobbledegook, jabber, jabbering, moonshine, pap, twaddle

blaze *noun* **1.** bonfire, conflagration, fire, flame, flames **2.** beam, brilliance, flare, flash, glare, gleam, glitter, glow, light, radiance **3.** blast, burst, eruption, flare-up, fury, outbreak, outburst, rush, storm, torrent *~verb* **4.** beam, burn, fire, flame, flare, flash, glare, gleam, glow, shine **5.** boil, explode, flare up, fume, seethe

blazing **1.** ablaze, afire, aflame, alight, burning, fiery, flaming, on fire **2.** aglow, brilliant, coruscating, flashing, gleaming, glowing, illuminated, incandescent, luminous, radiant, sparkling **3.** angry, excited, fervent, frenzied, fuming, furious, impassioned, incensed, passionate, raging, seething

blazon broadcast, celebrate, flourish, make known, proclaim, renown, trumpet

bleach blanch, etiolate, fade, grow pale, lighten, peroxide, wash out, whiten

bleached achromatic, etiolated, faded, lightened, peroxided, stone-washed, washed-out

bleak **1.** bare, barren, chilly, cold, desolate, exposed, gaunt, open, raw, stark, unsheltered, weather-beaten, windswept, windy **2.** cheerless, comfortless, depressing, discouraging, disheartening, dismal, dreary, gloomy, grim, hopeless, joyless, sombre, unpromising
Antonyms cheerful, cosy, encouraging, promising, protected, sheltered, shielded

bleary blurred, blurry, dim, fogged, foggy,

fuzzy, hazy, indistinct, misty, murky, rheumy, watery

bleed 1. exude, flow, gush, lose blood, ooze, run, seep, shed blood, spurt, trickle, weep 2. deplete, drain, draw *or* take blood, exhaust, extort, extract, fleece, leech, milk, phlebotomize (*Medical*), reduce, sap, squeeze 3. ache, agonize, feel for, grieve, pity, suffer, sympathize

blemish 1. *noun* blot, blotch, blot on one's escutcheon, blur, defect, demerit, disfigurement, disgrace, dishonour, fault, flaw, imperfection, mark, scar, smirch, smudge, speck, spot, stain, taint 2. *verb* blot, blotch, blur, damage, deface, disfigure, flaw, impair, injure, mar, mark, smirch, smudge, spoil, spot, stain, sully, taint, tarnish

Antonyms *noun* enhancement, improvement, ornament, perfection, purity, refinement *~verb* correct, enhance, improve, perfect, purify, refine, restore

blench cower, cringe, falter, flinch, hesitate, quail, quake, quiver, recoil, shrink, shudder, shy, start, wince

blend *verb* 1. amalgamate, coalesce, combine, compound, fuse, intermix, meld, merge, mingle, mix, synthesize, unite 2. complement, fit, go well, go with, harmonize, suit *~noun* 3. alloy, amalgam, amalgamation, combination, composite, compound, concoction, fusion, meld, mix, mixture, synthesis, union

bless 1. anoint, consecrate, dedicate, exalt, extol, give thanks to, glorify, hallow, invoke happiness on, magnify, ordain, praise, sanctify, thank 2. bestow, endow, favour, give, grace, grant, provide

Antonyms (*sense 1*) accuse, anathematize, curse, damn, excommunicate, execrate, fulminate, imprecate (*sense 2*) afflict, blight, burden, curse, destroy, doom, plague, scourge, torment, trouble, vex

blessed 1. adored, beatified, divine, hallowed, holy, revered, sacred, sanctified 2. endowed, favoured, fortunate, granted, jammy (*Brit. slang*), lucky 3. blissful, contented, glad, happy, joyful, joyous

He alone is blessed who ne'er was born
Matthew Prior *Solomon on the Vanity of the World*

blessedness beatitude, bliss, blissfulness, content, felicity, happiness, heavenly joy, pleasure, sanctity, state of grace, *summum bonum*

blessing 1. benediction, benison, commendation, consecration, dedication, grace, invocation, thanksgiving 2. approbation, approval, backing, concurrence, consent, favour, good wishes, leave, permission, regard, sanction, support 3. advantage, benefit, boon, boot (*obsolete*), bounty, favour, gain, gift, godsend, good fortune, help, kindness, manna from heaven, profit, service, windfall

Antonyms condemnation, curse, damage, deprivation, disadvantage, disapproval, disfavour, drawback, harm, malediction, misfortune, objection, reproof

blight *noun* 1. canker, decay, disease, fungus, infestation, mildew, pest, pestilence, rot 2. affliction, bane, contamination, corruption, curse, evil, plague, pollution, scourge, woe *~verb* 3. blast, destroy, injure, nip in the bud, ruin, shrivel, taint with mildew, wither 4. *figurative* annihilate, crush, dash, disappoint, frustrate, mar, nullify, put a damper on, ruin, spoil, undo, wreck

Antonyms *noun* benefaction, blessing, boon, bounty, favour, godsend, help, service

blind *adjective* 1. destitute of vision, eyeless, sightless, stone-blind, unseeing, unsighted, visionless 2. *figurative* careless, heedless, ignorant, inattentive, inconsiderate, indifferent, indiscriminate, injudicious, insensitive, morally darkened, neglectful, oblivious, prejudiced, thoughtless, unaware of, unconscious of, uncritical, undiscerning, unmindful of, unobservant, unreasoning 3. hasty, impetuous, irrational, mindless, rash, reckless, senseless, uncontrollable, uncontrolled, unthinking, violent, wild 4. closed, concealed, dark, dead-end, dim, hidden, leading nowhere, obscured, obstructed, without exit *~noun* 5. camouflage, cloak, cover, façade, feint, front, mask, masquerade, screen, smoke screen

Antonyms *adjective* alive to, attentive, aware, concerned, conscious, discerning, heedful, knowledgeable, noticeable, observant, obvious, open, seeing, sighted

If the blind lead the blind, both shall fall into the ditch
Bible: St. Matthew

In the country of the blind the one-eyed man is king
Desiderius Erasmus *Adagia*

There's none so blind as those who will not see

A nod's as good as a wink to a blind horse

blinding 1. bedazzling, blurring, dazzling 2. bright, brilliant, coruscating, dazzling, flaming, glaring, intense, scintillating, searing, vivid

blindly 1. aimlessly, at random, confusedly, frantically, indiscriminately, instinctively, madly, purposelessly, wildly 2. carelessly, heedlessly, impulsively, inconsiderately, passionately, recklessly, regardlessly, senselessly, thoughtlessly, unreasonably, wilfully

blink 1. bat, flutter, glimpse, nictate, nictitate, peer, squint, wink 2. flash, flicker, gleam, glimmer, scintillate, shine, sparkle, twinkle, wink 3. *figurative* condone, connive at, disre~

gard, ignore, overlook, pass by, turn a blind eye to **4. on the blink** *slang* faulty, malfunctioning, not working (properly), on the fritz (*U.S. slang*), out of action, out of order, playing up

blinkered biased, constricted, discriminatory, hidebound, insular, lopsided, narrow, narrow-minded, one-eyed, one-sided, parochial, partial, prejudiced, restrictive, selective
Antonyms broad-minded, impartial, open-minded, unbiased, unprejudiced

bliss beatitude, blessedness, blissfulness, ecstasy, euphoria, felicity, gladness, happiness, heaven, joy, paradise, rapture
Antonyms affliction, anguish, distress, grief, heartbreak, misery, mourning, regret, sadness, sorrow, unhappiness, woe, wretchedness

blissful cock-a-hoop, delighted, ecstatic, elated, enchanted, enraptured, euphoric, happy, heavenly (*informal*), in ecstasies, joyful, joyous, over the moon (*informal*), rapt, rapturous

blister abscess, blain, bleb, boil, bubble, canker, carbuncle, cyst, furuncle (*Pathology*), pimple, pustule, sore, swelling, ulcer, welt, wen

blistering 1. baking, boiling, flaming, hot, like a furnace *or* an oven, roasting, scalding, scorching, searing, sizzling, sweltering, tropical, very hot **2.** ferocious, fierce, powerful, scathing, vehement, violent, vitriolic
Antonyms (*sense 1*) arctic, freezing, icy (*sense 2*) bland, gentle, mild

blithe 1. animated, buoyant, carefree, cheerful, cheery, chirpy (*informal*), debonair, gay, genial, gladsome (*archaic*), happy, jaunty, light-hearted, merry, mirthful, sprightly, sunny, upbeat (*informal*), vivacious **2.** careless, casual, heedless, indifferent, nonchalant, thoughtless, unconcerned, untroubled
Antonyms concerned, dejected, depressed, gloomy, kind-hearted, melancholy, morose, preoccupied, sad, thoughtful, unhappy

blitz assault, attack, blitzkrieg, bombardment, campaign, offensive, onslaught, raid, strike

blizzard blast, gale, snowstorm, squall, storm, tempest

bloat balloon, blow up, dilate, distend, enlarge, expand, inflate, puff up, swell
Antonyms contract, deflate, shrink, shrivel, wither, wrinkle

bloated blown-up, bulging, dilated, distended, enlarged, expanded, inflated, puffed up, puffy, swollen, tumescent, tumid, turgid
Antonyms contracted, deflated, flaccid, shrivelled, shrunken, withered, wrinkled

blob ball, bead, bubble, dab, dewdrop, drop, droplet, glob, globule, lump, mass, pearl, pellet, pill

bloc alliance, axis, cabal, clique, coalition, combine, entente, faction, group, league, ring, schism, union, wing

block *noun* **1.** bar, brick, cake, chunk, cube, hunk, ingot, lump, mass, nugget, piece, square **2.** bar, barrier, blockage, hindrance, impediment, jam, obstacle, obstruction, occlusion, stoppage *~verb* **3.** bung up (*informal*), choke, clog, close, obstruct, plug, stem the flow, stop up **4.** arrest, bar, check, deter, halt, hinder, impede, obstruct, put a spoke in someone's wheel, stop, throw a spanner in the works, thwart
Antonyms *verb* (*sense 3*) clear, open, unblock, unclog (*sense 4*) advance, aid, expedite, facilitate, foster, further, lend support to, promote, push, support

blockade barricade, barrier, block, closure, encirclement, hindrance, impediment, obstacle, obstruction, restriction, siege, stoppage

blockage block, blocking, impediment, obstruction, occlusion, stoppage, stopping up

blockhead berk (*Brit. slang*), bimbo (*slang*), bonehead (*slang*), charlie (*Brit. informal*), chump (*informal*), coot, dickhead (*slang*), dickwit (*slang*), dipstick (*Brit. slang*), divvy (*Brit. slang*), dolt, dork (*slang*), dullard, dunce, dweeb (*U.S. slang*), fathead (*informal*), fool, fuckwit (*taboo slang*), geek (*slang*), gobshite (*Irish taboo slang*), gonzo (*slang*), idiot, ignoramus, jerk (*slang, chiefly U.S. & Canad.*), nerd *or* nurd (*slang*), noodle, numpty (*Scot. informal*), numskull *or* numbskull, pillock (*Brit. slang*), plank (*Brit. slang*), plonker (*slang*), prat (*slang*), prick (*slang*), schmuck (*U.S. slang*), thickhead, twit (*informal, chiefly Brit.*), wally (*slang*)

block out chart, map out, outline, plan, sketch

bloke bastard (*informal*), bod (*informal*), body, boy, bugger (*slang*), chap, character (*informal*), customer (*informal*), fellow, guy (*informal*), individual, man, person, punter (*informal*)

blond, blonde fair, fair-haired, fair-skinned, flaxen, golden-haired, light, light-coloured, light-complexioned, tow-headed

blood 1. gore, lifeblood, vital fluid **2.** ancestry, birth, consanguinity, descendants, descent, extraction, family, kindred, kinship, lineage, noble extraction, relations **3.** *figurative* anger, disposition, feeling, passion, spirit, temper
Related adjective: haemal
You cannot get blood from a stone
Blood is thicker than water

bloodcurdling appalling, chilling, dreadful, fearful, frightening, hair-raising, horrendous, horrifying, scaring, spine-chilling, terrifying

bloodless 1. cold, languid, lifeless, listless, passionless, spiritless, torpid, unemotional, unfeeling **2.** anaemic, ashen, chalky, colour~less, like death warmed up (*informal*), pale, pallid, pasty, sallow, sickly, wan

bloodshed blood bath, bloodletting, butchery, carnage, gore, killing, massacre, murder, slaughter, slaying

bloodthirsty barbarous, brutal, cruel, cut~throat, ferocious, gory, inhuman, murderous, ruthless, savage, vicious, warlike

bloody **1.** bleeding, blood-soaked, blood-spattered, bloodstained, gaping, raw, unstaunched **2.** cruel, ferocious, fierce, sangui~nary, savage

bloody-minded awkward, contrary, cussed (*informal*), obstructive, perverse, uncoopera~tive, unhelpful, unreasonable
Antonyms accommodating, cooperative, fair-minded, helpful, open-minded, reasonable

bloom *noun* **1.** blossom, blossoming, bud, efflo~rescence, flower, opening (*of flowers*) **2.** *figura~tive* beauty, blush, flourishing, flush, fresh~ness, glow, health, heyday, lustre, perfection, prime, radiance, rosiness, vigour *~verb* **3.** blossom, blow, bud, burgeon, open, sprout **4.** develop, fare well, flourish, grow, prosper, succeed, thrive, wax
Antonyms *noun* (*sense 2*) bloodlessness, pale~ness, pallor, wanness, whiteness *~verb* (*senses 3 & 4*) decay, decline, die, droop, fade, fail, languish, perish, shrink, shrivel, wane, waste, wilt, wither

blossom *noun* **1.** bloom, bud, floret, flower, flowers *~verb* **2.** bloom, burgeon, flower **3.** *fig~urative* bloom, develop, flourish, grow, mature, progress, prosper, thrive

blot *noun* **1.** blotch, mark, patch, smear, smudge, speck, splodge, spot **2.** blemish, blot on one's escutcheon, blur, defect, demerit, disgrace, fault, flaw, scar, smirch, spot, stain, taint *~verb* **3.** bespatter, disfigure, disgrace, mark, smirch, smudge, spoil, spot, stain, sul~ly, tarnish **4.** absorb, dry, soak up, take up **5.** **blot out** cancel, darken, destroy, efface, erase, expunge, obliterate, obscure, shadow

blotch blemish, blot, mark, patch, scar, smirch, smudge, smutch, splash, splodge, spot, stain

blotchy blemished, macular, patchy, reddened, scurvy, spotty, uneven

blow[1] *verb* **1.** blast, breathe, exhale, fan, pant, puff, waft **2.** flow, rush, stream, whirl **3.** bear, buffet, drive, fling, flutter, sweep, waft, whirl, whisk **4.** blare, mouth, pipe, play, sound, toot, trumpet, vibrate *~noun* **5.** blast, draught, flurry, gale, gust, puff, strong breeze, tempest, wind

blow[2] *noun* **1.** bang, bash (*informal*), belt (*in~formal*), buffet, clomp (*slang*), clout (*informal*), clump (*slang*), knock, punch, rap, slosh (*Brit. slang*), smack, sock (*slang*), stroke, thump, wallop (*informal*), whack **2.** *figurative* afflic~tion, bolt from the blue, bombshell, bummer (*slang*), calamity, catastrophe, comedown (*in~formal*), disappointment, disaster, jolt, misfor~tune, reverse, setback, shock, upset, whammy (*informal, chiefly U.S.*)

blowout **1.** blast, detonation, eruption, explo~sion **2.** break, burst, escape, flat, flat tyre, fuse, leak, puncture, rupture, tear **3.** beano (*Brit. slang*), binge (*informal*), carousal, ca~rouse, feast, hooley *or* hoolie (*chiefly Irish & N.Z.*), party, rave (*Brit. slang*), rave-up (*Brit. slang*), spree

blow out **1.** extinguish, put out, snuff **2.** burst, erupt, explode, rupture, shatter

blow over be forgotten, cease, die down, dis~appear, end, finish, pass, pass away, subside, vanish

blow up **1.** bloat, distend, enlarge, expand, fill, inflate, puff up, pump up, swell **2.** blast, blow sky-high, bomb, burst, detonate, dynamite, explode, go off, rupture, shatter **3.** blow out of (all) proportion, enlarge, enlarge on, exagger~ate, heighten, magnify, make a mountain out of a molehill, make a production out of, over~state **4.** *informal* become angry, become en~raged, blow a fuse (*slang, chiefly U.S.*), crack up (*informal*), erupt, flip one's lid (*slang*), fly off the handle (*informal*), go ballistic (*slang, chiefly U.S.*), go off the deep end (*informal*), go up the wall (*slang*), hit the roof (*informal*), lose one's temper, rage, see red (*informal*), wig out (*slang*)

blowy blustery, breezy, draughty, exposed, fresh, stormy, well-ventilated, windy

blowzy, blowsy **1.** bedraggled, dishevelled, frowzy, slatternly, slipshod, sloppy, slovenly, sluttish, tousled, unkempt, untidy **2.** florid, red-faced, ruddy

bludgeon *noun* **1.** club, cosh (*Brit.*), cudgel, shillelagh, truncheon *~verb* **2.** beat, beat up, club, cosh (*Brit.*), cudgel, knock down, strike **3.** browbeat, bulldoze (*informal*), bully, coerce, dragoon, force, hector, put the screws on, railroad (*informal*), steamroller

blue **1.** azure, cerulean, cobalt, cyan, navy, sapphire, sky-coloured, ultramarine **2.** *figura~tive* dejected, depressed, despondent, dismal, downcast, down-hearted, down in the dumps (*informal*), down in the mouth, fed up, gloomy, glum, low, melancholy, sad, unhappy **3.** *informal* bawdy, dirty, indecent, lewd, naughty, near the knuckle (*informal*), ob~scene, risqué, smutty, vulgar, X-rated (*infor~mal*)
Antonyms (*sense 2*) blithe, cheerful, cheery, chirpy (*informal*), elated, genial, happy, jolly, merry, optimistic, sunny (*sense 3*) decent, re~spectable

blueprint design, draft, layout, norm, outline, pattern, pilot scheme, plan, project, prototype, scheme, sketch

blues dejection, depression, despondency, doldrums, dumps (*informal*), gloom, gloominess, glumness, low spirits, melancholy, moodiness, the hump (*Brit. informal*)

bluff[1] **1.** *verb* con, deceive, defraud, delude, fake, feign, humbug, lie, mislead, pretend, pull the wool over someone's eyes, sham **2.** *noun* bluster, boast, braggadocio, bragging, bravado, deceit, deception, fake, feint, fraud, humbug, idle boast, lie, mere show, pretence, sham, show, subterfuge

bluff[2] *noun* **1.** bank, cliff, crag, escarpment, headland, peak, precipice, promontory, ridge, scarp *~adjective* **2.** abrupt, blunt, blustering, downright, frank, genial, good-natured, hearty, open, outspoken, plain-spoken **3.** abrupt, perpendicular, precipitous, sheer, steep, towering

Antonyms (*sense 2*) delicate, diplomatic, discreet, judicious, sensitive, tactful, thoughtful

blunder *noun* **1.** error, fault, inaccuracy, mistake, oversight, slip, slip-up (*informal*) **2.** bloomer (*Brit. informal*), boob (*Brit. slang*), boo-boo (*informal*), clanger (*informal*), faux pas, gaffe, gaucherie, howler (*informal*), impropriety, indiscretion, mistake *~verb* **3.** bodge (*informal*), botch, bungle, drop a brick (*Brit. informal*), drop a clanger (*informal*), err, flub (*U.S. slang*), put one's foot in it (*informal*), slip up (*informal*) **4.** bumble, confuse, flounder, misjudge, stumble

Antonyms *noun* accuracy, achievement, correctness, success *~verb* be correct, be exact, get it right, go alertly

blunt *adjective* **1.** dull, dulled, edgeless, pointless, rounded, unsharpened **2.** *figurative* bluff, brusque, discourteous, downright, explicit, forthright, frank, impolite, outspoken, plain-spoken, rude, straightforward, straight from the shoulder, tactless, trenchant, uncivil, unpolished, upfront (*informal*) *~verb* **3.** dampen, deaden, dull, numb, soften, take the edge off, water down, weaken

Antonyms *adjective* acute, courteous, diplomatic, keen, pointed, sensitive, sharp, subtle, tactful *~verb* animate, put an edge on, sharpen, stimulate, vitalize

bluntness candour, forthrightness, frankness, ingenuousness, openness, outspokenness, plain speaking, truthfulness

A loose, plain, rude writer .... I call a spade a spade

Robert Burton *Anatomy of Melancholy*

blur *verb* **1.** becloud, bedim, befog, blear, cloud, darken, dim, fog, make hazy, make indistinct, make vague, mask, obscure, soften **2.** blot, smear, smudge, spot, stain *~noun* **3.** blear, blurredness, cloudiness, confusion, dimness, fog, haze, indistinctness, obscurity **4.** blot, smear, smudge, spot, stain

blurred bleary, blurry, faint, foggy, fuzzy, hazy, ill-defined, indistinct, lacking definition, misty, nebulous, out of focus, unclear, vague

blurt out babble, blab, blow the gaff (*Brit. slang*), cry, disclose, exclaim, gush, let the cat out of the bag, reveal, run off at the mouth (*slang*), spill, spill one's guts (*slang*), spill the beans (*informal*), spout (*informal*), sputter, tattle, tell all, utter suddenly

blush 1. *verb* colour, crimson, flush, go red as a beetroot, redden, turn red, turn scarlet **2.** *noun* colour, flush, glow, pink tinge, reddening, rosiness, rosy tint, ruddiness

Antonyms *verb* blanch, blench, drain, fade, pale, turn pale, whiten

Man is the Only Animal that Blushes. Or needs to.

Mark Twain *Following the Equator*

bluster 1. *verb* blow one's own horn (*U.S. & Canad.*), blow one's own trumpet, boast, brag, bulldoze, bully, domineer, hector, rant, roar, roister, storm, swagger, swell, vaunt **2.** *noun* bluff, boasting, boisterousness, bombast, bragging, bravado, crowing, hot air (*informal*), swagger, swaggering

blustery blusterous, boisterous, gusty, inclement, squally, stormy, tempestuous, violent, wild

board *noun* **1.** panel, piece of timber, plank, slat, timber **2.** daily meals, food, meals, provisions, victuals **3.** advisers, advisory group, committee, conclave, council, directorate, directors, panel, quango, trustees *~verb* **4.** embark, embus, enplane, enter, entrain, mount **5.** accommodate, feed, house, lodge, put up, quarter, room

Antonyms (*sense 4*) alight, arrive, disembark, dismount, get off, go ashore, land

boast *verb* **1.** blow one's own trumpet, bluster, brag, crow, exaggerate, puff, strut, swagger, talk big (*slang*), vaunt **2.** be proud of, congratulate oneself on, exhibit, flatter oneself, possess, pride oneself on, show off *~noun* **3.** avowal, brag, gasconade (*rare*), rodomontade (*literary*), swank (*informal*), vaunt **4.** gem, joy, pride, pride and joy, source of pride, treasure

Antonyms *verb* cover up, depreciate, disavow, disclaim *~noun* disavowal, disclaimer

A mule always boasts that its ancestors were horses

boastful bragging, cocky, conceited, crowing, egotistical, full of oneself, puffed-up, swaggering, swanky (*informal*), swollen-headed, vainglorious, vaunting

Antonyms deprecating, humble, modest, self-belittling, self-effacing, unassuming

boat **1.** barge (*informal*), barque, craft, ship, vessel **2. in the same boat** alike, equal, even, on a par, on equal *or* even terms, on the same *or* equal footing, together **3. miss the boat** be too late, blow one's chance (*informal*), let slip, lose out, miss one's chance *or* opportunity, miss out **4. push the boat out** celebrate, go the whole hog (*informal*), kill the fatted calf, put the flags out **5. rock the boat** cause trouble, dissent, make waves (*informal*), throw a spanner in the works, upset the apple cart

> *There is nothing - absolutely nothing - half so much worth doing as simply messing about in boats*
>
> Kenneth Grahame *The Wind in the Willows*

bob bounce, duck, hop, jerk, leap, nod, oscillate, quiver, skip, waggle, weave, wobble

bob up appear, arise, emerge, materialize, pop up, rise, spring up, surface, turn up

bode augur, betoken, forebode, foreshadow, foretell, forewarn, impart, omen, portend, predict, presage, prophesy, signify, threaten

bodiless disembodied, ghostly, immaterial, incorporeal, insubstantial, spectral, spiritual, supernatural

bodily **1.** *adjective* actual, carnal, corporal, corporeal, fleshly, material, physical, substantial, tangible **2.** *adverb* altogether, as a body, as a group, collectively, completely, en masse, entirely, fully, totally, wholly

body **1.** build, figure, form, frame, physique, shape, torso, trunk **2.** cadaver, carcass, corpse, dead body, relics, remains, stiff (*slang*) **3.** being, creature, human, human being, individual, mortal, person **4.** bulk, essence, main part, mass, material, matter, substance **5.** association, band, bloc, collection, company, confederation, congress, corporation, society **6.** crowd, horde, majority, mass, mob, multitude, throng **7.** consistency, density, firmness, richness, solidity, substance

Related adjective: corporal

Parts of the body	**Technical names**	**Related adjectives**
abdomen	-	abdominal
adenoids	pharyngeal tonsil	adenoid *or* adenoidal
alimentary canal	-	-
ankle	talus	-
anus	-	anal
appendix	vermiform appendix	appendicular
arm	brachium	brachial
armpit	axilla	axillary
artery	-	arterial
back	-	dorsal
belly	venter	ventral
bladder	urinary bladder	vesical
blood	-	haemal, haemic *or* haematic
bone	os	osseous, osteal *or* osteoid
brain *see* BRAIN	encephalon	cerebral
breast	-	-
buttocks	nates	natal *or* gluteal
caecum	-	caecal
calf	-	-
capillary	-	capillary
cervix	-	cervical
cheek	gena	genal
chest	-	pectoral
chin	-	genial *or* mental
clitoris	-	clitoral
colon	-	colonic
duodenum	-	duodenal
ear *see* EAR	-	aural
elbow	-	-
epiglottis	-	epiglottal
external ear	auricle *or* pinna	-
eye *see* EYE	-	ocular *or* opthalmic
eyebrow	-	superciliary
eyelash	cilium	ciliary
eyelid	-	palpebral
Fallopian tube	oviduct	oviducal *or* oviductal
finger	-	digital
fingernail	-	ungual *or* ungular
fist	-	-
follicle	-	follicular
fontanelle *or (chiefly U.S.)* fontanel	-	-
foot	pes	pedal
forearm	-	cubital
forehead	-	frontal
foreskin	prepuce	preputial
gall bladder	-	-
gland	-	adenoid
glottis	-	glottic
groin	-	inguinal
gullet	oesophagus	oesophageal
gum	gingiva	gingival
hamstring	-	popliteal
hard palate	-	-
hair	-	-
half-moon	lunula *or* lunule	-
hand	manus	manual

head	caput	capital
heart *see* HEART	-	cardiac
heel	-	-
hip	-	-
ileum	-	ileac *or* ileal
inner ear *or* internal ear	labyrinth	-
instep	-	-
intestine	-	alvine
jaw	-	gnathic *or* gnathal
jejunum	-	jejunal
jugular vein	-	-
kidney	-	renal *or* nephritic
knee	genu	genicular
knuckle	-	-
labia majora	-	labial
labia minora	-	labial
large intestine	-	-
leg	crus	crural
lip	-	labial
liver	-	hepatic
loin	lumbus	lumbar
lung	-	pulmonary
lymph cell	lymphocyte	-
lymph node	-	-
midriff	diaphragm	-
mons pubis	-	-
mons veneris	-	-
mouth	-	stomatic
nape	nucha	nuchal
navel *or* omphalos	umbilicus	umbilical
neck	cervix	cervical
nerve	-	neural
nerve cell	neuron *or* neurone	neuronic
nipple *or* teat	mamilla *or* papilla	mamillary
nose	-	nasal
nostril	naris	narial *or* narine
occiput	-	occipital
ovary	-	ovarian
pancreas	-	pancreatic
penis	-	penile
pharynx	-	pharyngeal
pubes	-	pubic
rectum	-	rectal
red blood cell	erythrocyte	erythrocytic
ribcage	-	-
scalp	-	-
scrotum	-	scrotal
shin	-	-
shoulder	-	-
side	-	-
skin	cutis	cutaneous
small intestine	-	-
soft palate	-	-
sole	-	plantar
spleen	-	lienal *or* splenetic
stomach	-	gastric
tear duct	lacrimal duct	-
temple	-	temporal
tendon	-	-
testicle	-	testicular
thigh	-	femoral *or* crural
thorax	-	thoracic
throat	-	guttural, gular *or* jugular
thumb	pollex	pollical
toe	-	-
toenail	-	ungual *or* ungular
tongue	lingua	lingual *or* glottic
tonsil	-	tonsillar *or* tonsillary
torso	-	-
transverse colon	-	-
trunk	-	-
umbilical cord	-	-
ureter	-	ureteral *or* ureteric
urethra	-	urethral
vagina	-	vaginal
vein	vena	venous
vocal cords	glottis	glottal
voice box	larynx	laryngeal
vulva	-	vulval *or* vulvar *or* vulvate
waist	-	-
white blood cell	leucocyte	leucocytic
windpipe	trachea	tracheal *or* tracheate
womb	uterus	uterine
wrist	carpus	-

Bones	**Nontechnical names**
astragalus	anklebone
calcaneus	heel bone
carpal	wrist
carpus	wrist
clavicle	collarbone
coccyx	-
costa	rib

cranium	brainpan
cuboid	-
ethmoid	-
femur	thighbone
fibula	-
frontal bone	-
hallux	-
humerus	-
hyoid	-
ilium	-
incus	anvil
innominate bone	hipbone
ischium	-
malleus	hammer
mandible	lower jawbone
maxilla	upper jawbone
metacarpal	-
metatarsal	-
metatarsus	-
occipital bone	-
parietal bone	-
patella	kneecap
pelvis	-
phalanx	-
pubis	-
radius	-
rib	-
sacrum	-
scapula	shoulder blade
skull	-
sphenoid	-
spinal column *or* spine	backbone
stapes	stirrup
sternum	breastbone
talus	anklebone
tarsal	-
tarsus	-
temporal bone	-
tibia	shinbone
ulna	-
vertebra	-
vertebral column	backbone
zygomatic bone	cheekbone

Muscles

accelerator
accessorius
adductor
agonist
antagonist
arytenoid
biceps
buccinator
compressor
constrictor
contractor
corrugator
deltoid
depressor
digrastic
dilator
elevator
erector
evertor
extensor
flexor
gastrocnemius
gluteus *or* glutaeus
levator
lumbricalis
masseter
opponent
pectoral
peroneal muscle
pronator
psoas
quadriceps
rectus
retractor
rhomboideus
rotator
sartorius
scalenus
soleus
sphincter
supinator
suspensory *or* suspensor
tensor
trapezius
triceps

Glands

adrenal gland
endocrine gland
exocrine gland
hypothalamus
islets of Langerhans *or* islands of Langerhans
lacrimal gland
liver
mammary gland
mucus gland
ovary
pancreas
parathyroid gland
pituitary gland
prostate
salivary gland
sebaceous gland
sweat gland
testicle
thyroid gland

diaphragm: a muscular partition separating disorders of the chest from disorders of the bowels
Ambrose Bierce *The Devil's Dictionary*

mouth: in man, the gateway to the soul; in woman, the outlet of the heart
Ambrose Bierce *The Devil's Dictionary*

boffin authority, bluestocking (*usually disparaging*), brain(s) (*informal*), brainbox, egghead, genius, intellect, intellectual, inventor, mastermind, maven (*U.S.*), planner, thinker, virtuoso, wizard

bog fen, marsh, marshland, mire, morass, moss (*Scot. & Northern English dialect*), peat bog, quagmire, slough, swamp, wetlands

bog down delay, halt, impede, sink, slow down, slow up, stall, stick

bogey **1.** apparition, bogeyman, goblin, hobgoblin, imp, spectre, spirit, spook (*informal*), sprite **2.** bête noire, bugaboo, bugbear, nightmare

boggle **1.** be alarmed (confused, surprised, taken aback), shy, stagger, startle, take fright **2.** demur, dither (*chiefly Brit.*), doubt, equivocate, falter, hang back, hesitate, hover, jib, shillyshally (*informal*), shrink from, vacillate, waver

boggy fenny, marshy, miry, muddy, oozy, quaggy, soft, spongy, swampy, waterlogged, yielding

bogus artificial, counterfeit, dummy, ersatz, fake, false, forged, fraudulent, imitation, phoney *or* phony (*informal*), pseudo (*informal*), sham, spurious
Antonyms actual, authentic, genuine, real, true

bohemian **1.** *adjective* alternative, artistic, arty (*informal*), avant-garde, eccentric, exotic, left bank, nonconformist, oddball (*informal*), offbeat, off-the-wall (*slang*), outré, unconven~

tional, unorthodox, way-out (*informal*) 2. *noun* beatnik, dropout, hippie, iconoclast, nonconformist
Antonyms *adjective* bourgeois, conservative, conventional, Pooterish, square (*informal*), straight (*slang*), straight-laced, stuffy

boil[1] *verb* 1. agitate, bubble, churn, effervesce, fizz, foam, froth, seethe 2. be angry, be indignant, blow a fuse (*slang, chiefly U.S.*), crack up (*informal*), fly off the handle (*informal*), foam at the mouth (*informal*), fulminate, fume, go ballistic (*slang, chiefly U.S.*), go off the deep end (*informal*), go up the wall (*slang*), rage, rave, see red (*informal*), storm, wig out (*slang*)

boil[2] *noun* blain, blister, carbuncle, furuncle (*Pathology*), gathering, pustule, tumour, ulcer

boil down come down, condense, decrease, reduce, summarize

boiling 1. baking, blistering, hot, roasting, scorching, tropical, very hot 2. angry, choked, cross, enraged, fit to be tied (*slang*), foaming at the mouth, fuming, furious, incensed, indignant, infuriated, on the warpath

boisterous 1. bouncy, clamorous, disorderly, impetuous, loud, noisy, obstreperous, riotous, rollicking, rowdy, rumbustious, unrestrained, unruly, uproarious, vociferous, wild 2. blustery, gusty, raging, rough, squally, stormy, tempestuous, tumultuous, turbulent
Antonyms calm, controlled, peaceful, quiet, restrained, self-controlled, subdued

bold 1. adventurous, audacious, brave, courageous, daring, dauntless, enterprising, fearless, gallant, gritty, heroic, intrepid, lion-hearted, valiant, valorous 2. barefaced, brash, brazen, cheeky, confident, feisty (*informal, chiefly U.S. & Canad.*), forward, fresh (*informal*), impudent, insolent, pert, pushy (*informal*), rude, sassy (*U.S. informal*), saucy, shameless 3. bright, colourful, conspicuous, eye-catching, flashy, forceful, lively, loud, prominent, pronounced, salient, showy, spirited, striking, strong, vivid
Antonyms conservative, cool, courteous, cowardly, dull, faint-hearted, fearful, meek, modest, ordinary, pale, polite, retiring, shy, soft, tactful, timid, timorous, unimaginative

Bold knaves thrive without one grain of sense,
But good men starve for want of impudence
John Dryden *Constantine the Great*

The bold are always lucky

bolster aid, assist, augment, boost, brace, buoy up, buttress, cushion, give a leg up (*informal*), help, hold up, maintain, pillow, prop, reinforce, shore up, stay, strengthen, support

bolt *noun* 1. bar, catch, fastener, latch, lock, sliding bar 2. peg, pin, rivet, rod 3. bound, dart, dash, escape, flight, rush, spring, sprint 4. arrow, dart, missile, projectile, shaft, thunderbolt *~verb* 5. bar, fasten, latch, lock, secure 6. cram, devour, gobble, gorge, gulp, guzzle, stuff, swallow whole, wolf 7. abscond, bound, dash, decamp, do a runner (*slang*), escape, flee, fly, fly the coop (*U.S. & Canad. informal*), hurtle, jump, leap, make a break (for it), run, run for it, rush, skedaddle (*informal*), spring, sprint, take a powder (*U.S. & Canad. slang*), take it on the lam (*U.S. & Canad. slang*)

bomb 1. *noun* bombshell, charge, device, explosive, grenade, mine, missile, projectile, rocket, shell, torpedo 2. *verb* attack, blow sky-high, blow up, bombard, destroy, shell, strafe, torpedo

Bombs

atom bomb *or* A-bomb	incendiary (bomb)
bangalore torpedo	Mills bomb
blockbuster	Molotov cocktail
bouncing bomb	nail bomb
cluster bomb	neutron bomb
depth charge	nuclear bomb
fusion bomb	petrol bomb
grenade	plastic bomb
hand grenade	stun grenade
hydrogen bomb	

bombard 1. assault, blast, blitz, bomb, cannonade, fire upon, open fire, pound, shell, strafe 2. assail, attack, barrage, batter, beset, besiege, harass, hound, pester

bombardment assault, attack, barrage, blitz, bombing, cannonade, fire, flak, fusillade, shelling, strafe

bombast bluster, brag, braggadocio, extravagant boasting, fustian, gasconade (*rare*), grandiloquence, grandiosity, hot air (*informal*), magniloquence, pomposity, rant, rodomontade (*literary*)

bombastic declamatory, fustian, grandiloquent, grandiose, high-flown, histrionic, inflated, magniloquent, pompous, ranting, turgid, verbose, windy, wordy

bona fide actual, authentic, genuine, honest, kosher (*informal*), lawful, legal, legitimate, on the level (*informal*), real, the real McCoy, true
Antonyms bogus, counterfeit, ersatz, fake, false, imitation, phoney *or* phony (*informal*), sham

bond *noun* 1. band, binding, chain, cord, fastening, fetter, ligature, link, manacle, shackle, tie 2. affiliation, affinity, attachment, connection, link, relation, tie, union 3. agreement, compact, contract, covenant, guarantee, obligation, pledge, promise, word *~verb* 4. bind, connect, fasten, fix together, fuse, glue, gum, paste

bondage captivity, confinement, duress, enslavement, enthralment, imprisonment, serfdom, servitude, slavery, subjection, subjugation, thraldom, vassalage, yoke

bonhomie affability, cheerfulness, congeniality, conviviality, cordiality, friendliness, geniality, good cheer, good humour, heartiness, hospitality, warmth

bonny **1.** beautiful, comely, fair, handsome, lovely, pretty, sweet **2.** bouncing, buxom, chubby, fine, plump, rounded, shapely **3.** blithe, cheerful, cheery, gay, joyful, merry, sunny, winsome

bonus benefit, bounty, commission, dividend, extra, gift, gratuity, hand-out, honorarium, icing on the cake, perk (*Brit. informal*), plus, premium, prize, reward

bon viveur *bon vivant*, epicure, epicurean, foodie, gastronome, gourmet, hedonist, luxurist, pleasure-seeker, voluptuary
Antonyms abstainer, ascetic, celibate, self-denier

bony angular, emaciated, gangling, gaunt, lanky, lean, macilent (*rare*), rawboned, scrawny, skin and bone, skinny, thin

booby berk (*Brit. slang*), blockhead, charlie (*Brit. informal*), coot, dickhead (*slang*), dickwit (*slang*), dimwit (*informal*), dipstick (*Brit. slang*), divvy (*Brit. slang*), dork (*slang*), duffer (*informal*), dunce, dweeb (*U.S. slang*), fathead (*informal*), fool, fuckwit (*taboo slang*), geek (*slang*), gobshite (*Irish taboo slang*), gonzo (*slang*), goof (*informal*), idiot, jerk (*slang, chiefly U.S. & Canad.*), lamebrain (*informal*), muggins (*Brit. slang*), nerd *or* nurd (*slang*), nitwit, numpty (*Scot. informal*), numskull *or* numbskull, oaf, pillock (*Brit. slang*), plank (*Brit. slang*), plonker (*slang*), prat (*slang*), prick (*slang*), schmuck (*U.S. slang*), simpleton, twit (*informal, chiefly Brit.*), wally (*slang*), weenie (*U.S. informal*)

book *noun* **1.** hardback, manual, paperback, publication, roll, scroll, textbook, title, tome, tract, volume, work **2.** album, diary, exercise book, jotter, notebook, pad *~verb* **3.** arrange for, bill, charter, engage, line up, make reservations, organize, procure, programme, reserve, schedule **4.** enrol, enter, insert, list, log, mark down, note, post, put down, record, register, write down

Types of book

album
almanac
anatomy
annual
anthology
armorial
A to Z
atlas
autobiography
Baedeker
bestiary
bibelot
Bible
biography
breviary
brochure
casebook
catalogue
catechism
coffee-table book
comic book
commonplace book
companion
compendium
concordance
confessional
cookery book
copybook
diary
dictionary
directory
dispensatory
encyclopedia *or* encyclopaedia
exercise book
formulary
gazetteer
gradus
grammar
graphic novel
grimoire
guidebook
handbook
hymn book
jotter
journal
lectionary
ledger
lexicon
log *or* logbook
manual
miscellany
missal
monograph
notebook
novel
novelette
novella
ordinal
peerage
pharmacopoeia
phrase book
prayer book
primer
prospectus
psalter
reader
reference book
register
road book
score
scrapbook
service book
sketchbook
song book
speller
statute book
storybook
telephone directory
textbook
thesaurus
vade mecum
who's who
wordbook
workbook
yearbook

Parts of a book

acknowledgments
addendum
afterword
appendix
back
back matter
bibliography
binding
blurb
chapter
contents
corrigenda
cover
dedication
dust jacket *or* cover
endpaper
epigraph
epilogue
errata
flyleaf
folio
fore-edge
foreword
frontispiece
front matter
glossary
gutter
half-title
illustration
index
interleaf
introduction
leaf
margin
page
plate
postscript
preface
prelims
proem
prolegomenon
prologue
recto
rubric
running head
slipcase
spine
tail

title page wrapper
verso

A good book is the precious life-blood of a master spirit, embalmed and treasured up on purpose to a life beyond life
John Milton *Areopagitica*

Of all the needs a book has the chief need is that it be readable
Anthony Trollope *Autobiography*

There is no such thing as a moral or an immoral book. Books are well written, or badly written
Oscar Wilde *The Picture of Dorian Gray*

I never read a book before reviewing it; it prejudices a man so
Revd Sidney Smith

A room without books is as a body without a soul
John Lubbock

Style and structure are the essence of a book; great ideas are hogwash
Vladimir Nabokov

When I am dead, I hope it may be said:
"His sins were scarlet, but his books were read."
Hilaire Belloc *On His Books*

All books are divisible into two classes, the books of the hour, and the books of all time
John Ruskin *Sesame and Lilies*

No furniture so charming as books
Revd Sidney Smith

Books will speak plain when counsellors blanch
Francis Bacon *Essays*

Some books are to be tasted, others to be swallowed, and some few to be chewed and digested
Francis Bacon *Essays*

Of making many books there is no end; and much study is a weariness of the flesh
Bible: Ecclesiastes

All books are either dreams or swords,
You can cut, or you can drug, with words
Amy Lowell *Sword Blades and Poppy Seeds*

As good almost kill a man as kill a good book: who kills a man kills a reasonable creature, God's image; but he who destroys a good book, kills reason itself, kills the image of God, as it were in the eye
John Milton *Areopagitica*

booking **1.** appointment, date, reservation **2.** commission, engagement, gig (*informal*)

bookish academic, donnish, erudite, intellectual, learned, literary, pedantic, scholarly, studious, well-read

booklet brochure, leaflet, pamphlet

boom *verb* **1.** bang, blast, crash, explode, resound, reverberate, roar, roll, rumble, thunder **2.** develop, expand, flourish, gain, grow, increase, intensify, prosper, spurt, strengthen, succeed, swell, thrive *~noun* **3.** bang, blast, burst, clap, crash, explosion, roar, rumble, thunder **4.** advance, boost, development, expansion, gain, growth, improvement, increase, jump, push, spurt, upsurge, upswing, upturn
Antonyms *verb* (*sense 2*) crash, fail, fall, slump *~noun* (*sense 4*) bust (*informal*), collapse, crash, decline, depression, downturn, failure, hard times, recession, slump

boomerang backfire, come back, come home to roost, rebound, recoil, return, reverse, ricochet

booming **1.** bellowing, deafening, echoing, loud, resonant, resounding, rich, sonorous, stentorian, thundering **2.** expanding, flourishing, on the up and up (*Brit.*), prospering, thriving

boon[1] *noun* advantage, benefaction, benefit, blessing, donation, favour, gift, godsend, grant, gratuity, hand-out, manna from heaven, present, windfall

boon[2] *adjective* close, intimate, special

boor barbarian, brute, bumpkin, churl, clodhopper (*informal*), clodpole, hayseed (*U.S. & Canad. informal*), hick (*informal, chiefly U.S. & Canad.*), lout, oaf, peasant, philistine, redneck (*U.S. slang*), vulgarian

boorish awkward, barbaric, bearish, churlish, clownish, coarse, crude, gross, gruff, hick (*informal, chiefly U.S. & Canad.*), ill-bred, loutish, lubberly, oafish, rude, rustic, uncivilized, uncouth, uneducated, unrefined, vulgar
Antonyms cultured, gallant, genteel, polite, refined, sophisticated, urbane

boost *noun* **1.** encouragement, help, hype, improvement, praise, promotion **2.** heave, hoist, lift, push, raise, shove, thrust **3.** addition, expansion, improvement, increase, increment, jump, rise *~verb* **4.** advance, advertise, assist, crack up (*informal*), encourage, foster, further, hype, improve, inspire, plug (*informal*), praise, promote, support, sustain **5.** elevate, heave, hoist, lift, push, raise, shove, thrust **6.** add to, amplify, develop, enlarge, expand, heighten, hoick, increase, jack up, magnify, raise
Antonyms *noun* condemnation, criticism, cut-back, decline, decrease, deterioration, fall, knock (*informal*), reduction *~verb* condemn, criticize, cut, decrease, diminish, drop, hinder, hold back, knock (*informal*), lessen, let down, lower, moderate, pare, reduce, scale down

boot *verb* **1.** drive, drop-kick, kick, knock, punt, put the boot in(to) (*slang*), shove **2.** *informal* dismiss, eject, expel, give (someone) their marching orders, give the boot (*slang*), give the bullet (*Brit. slang*), give the bum's rush (*slang*), give the heave *or* push (*informal*), kick out, kiss off (*slang, chiefly U.S. & Canad.*), oust, relegate, sack (*informal*), show one the door, throw out, throw out on one's ear (*informal*)

bootleg *adjective* black-market, contraband, hooky (*slang*), illegal, illicit, outlawed, pirate,

unauthorized, under-the-counter, under-the-table, unlicensed, unofficial
Antonyms authorized, legal, licensed, licit, official, on the level (*informal*)

bootless fruitless, futile, ineffective, profitless, unavailing, unsuccessful, useless, vain

bootlicker ass-kisser (*U.S. & Canad. taboo slang*), brown-noser (*taboo slang*), fawner, flatterer, flunky, lackey, spaniel, sycophant, toady, yes man

booty boodle (*slang, chiefly U.S.*), gains, haul, loot, pillage, plunder, prey, spoil, spoils, swag (*slang*), takings, winnings

booze *noun* **1.** alcohol, drink, firewater, grog (*informal, chiefly Austral. & N.Z.*), hooch *or* hootch (*informal, chiefly U.S. & Canad.*), intoxicant, John Barleycorn, juice (*informal*), liquor, spirits, strong drink, the bottle (*informal*), the hard stuff (*informal*) **2.** bevvy (*dialect*), booze-up (*Brit., Austral. & N.Z. slang*), drink, sesh (*slang*), session (*informal*), wet (*informal*) *~verb* **3.** bevvy (*dialect*), carouse, drink, drink like a fish, get drunk, get plastered (soused, tanked up) (*informal*), go on a binge *or* bender (*informal*), hit the booze *or* bottle (*informal*), imbibe, indulge, tipple, tope

boozer **1.** alcoholic, drinker, drunk, drunkard, inebriate, lush (*slang*), soak (*slang*), sot, tippler, toper, wino (*informal*) **2.** alehouse (*archaic*), bar, hostelry, inn, local (*Brit. informal*), pub (*informal, chiefly Brit.*), public house, roadhouse, taproom, tavern, watering hole (*facetious slang*)

border *noun* **1.** bound, boundary, bounds, brim, brink, confine, confines, edge, flange, hem, limit, limits, lip, margin, pale, rim, skirt, verge **2.** borderline, boundary, frontier, line, march *~verb* **3.** bind, decorate, edge, fringe, hem, rim, trim

borderline *adjective* ambivalent, doubtful, equivocal, indecisive, indefinite, indeterminate, inexact, marginal, unclassifiable

border on **1.** abut, adjoin, connect, contact, impinge, join, march, neighbour, touch, verge on **2.** approach, approximate, be like, be similar to, come close to, come near, echo, match, parallel, resemble

bore[1] **1.** *verb* burrow, drill, gouge out, mine, penetrate, perforate, pierce, sink, tunnel **2.** *noun* borehole, calibre, drill hole, hole, shaft, tunnel

bore[2] **1.** *verb* annoy, be tedious, bother, exhaust, fatigue, jade, pall on, pester, send to sleep, tire, trouble, vex, wear out, weary, worry **2.** *noun* anorak (*informal*), bother, drag (*informal*), dullard, dull person, headache (*informal*), nuisance, pain (*informal*), pain in the arse (*taboo informal*), pain in the neck (*informal*), pest, tiresome person, wearisome talker, yawn (*informal*)
Antonyms *verb* amuse, divert, engross, excite, fascinate, hold the attention of, interest, stimulate

Bore: a person who talks when you wish him to listen
Ambose Bierce *The Devil's Dictionary*

The way to be a bore is to say everything
Voltaire *Sept Discours en vers sur l'Homme*

He was not only a bore; he bored for England
Malcolm Muggeridge *Tread Softly (writing of Sir Anthony Eden)*

A bore is a man who, when you ask him how he is, tells you
Bert Leston Taylor

Some people can stay longer in an hour than others can in a week
W.D. Howells

bored ennuied, fed up, listless, stupefied, tired, uninterested, wearied

boredom apathy, doldrums, dullness, ennui, flatness, irksomeness, monotony, sameness, tediousness, tedium, weariness, world-weariness
Antonyms amusement, entertainment, excitement, interest, stimulation

Boredom is a sign of satisfied ignorance, blunted apprehension, crass sympthies, dull understanding, feeble powers of attention and irreclaimable weakness of character
James Bridie *Mr. Bolfry*

One can be bored until boredom becomes the most sublime of all emotions
Logan Pearsall Smith *Afterthoughts*

Boredom is...a vital problem for the moralist, since half the sins of mankind are caused by the fear of it
Bertrand Russell *The Conquest of Happiness*

boring dead, dull, flat, ho-hum (*informal*), humdrum, insipid, mind-numbing, monotonous, old, repetitious, routine, stale, tedious, tiresome, tiring, unexciting, uninteresting, unvaried, wearisome

borrow **1.** blag (*slang*), cadge, mooch (*slang*), scrounge (*informal*), take and return, take on loan, touch (someone) for (*slang*), use temporarily **2.** acquire, adopt, appropriate, copy, filch, imitate, obtain, pilfer, pirate, plagiarize, simulate, steal, take, use, usurp
Antonyms advance, give, lend, loan, provide, return, supply

Neither a borrower nor a lender be
William Shakespeare *Hamlet*

bosom *noun* **1.** breast, bust, chest **2.** affections, emotions, feelings, heart, sentiments, soul, spirit, sympathies **3.** centre, circle, core, midst, protection, shelter *~adjective* **4.** boon, cherished, close, confidential, intimate, very dear

boss[1] **1.** *noun* administrator, big cheese (*slang, old-fashioned*), chief, director, employer, executive, foreman, gaffer (*informal, chiefly Brit.*), governor (*informal*), head, kingpin, leader, manager, master, Mister Big (*slang, chiefly U.S.*), numero uno (*informal*), overseer, owner, superintendent, supervisor, torchbearer **2.** *verb* administrate, call the shots, call the tune, command, control, direct, employ, manage, oversee, run, superintend, supervise, take charge

boss[2] *noun* knob, nub, nubble, point, protuberance, stud, tip

boss around bully, dominate, domineer, oppress, order, overbear, push around (*slang*), put upon, ride roughshod over, tyrannize

bossy arrogant, authoritarian, autocratic, despotic, dictatorial, domineering, hectoring, high-handed, imperious, lordly, overbearing, tyrannical

botany

Branches of botany

agrostology
algology
archaeobotany *or* archeobotany
astrobotany
bryology
carpology
dendrology
ethnobotany
floristics
mycology
palaeobotany
palaeoethnobotany
phytogenesis
phytogeography
phytography
phytopathology
pteridology

Botany terms

abscission
androecium
androgynous
anther
archegonium
auxin
axil
axis
berry
bulb
calyx
cambium
carpel
chlorophyll
chloroplast
corm
corolla
corona
cortex
cotyledon
cross-pollination
cuticle
dicotyledon
epidermis
filament
flower
foliation
fruit
geotropism
germination
guard cell
gynaecium
hilum
hydrotropism
inflorescence
insect pollination
integument
key
lamina
leaf
legume
lenticel
meristem
mesophyll
micropyle
monocotyledon
nastic movement
nut
operculum
ovary
ovule
palisade mesophyll
phloem
photosynthesis
phototropism
pistil
pith
plumule
pollen
pollination
raceme
radicle
receptacle
rhizome
root
root cap
root hair
root nodule
rosette
runner
sap
seed
seed capsule *or* seedcase
seed pod
seed vessel
self-pollination
sepal
shoot
spadix
spongy mesophyll
sporangium
spore
stamen
stem
stigma
stolon
stoma
style
testa
translocation
transpiration
tropism
tuber
vascular bundle
vegetative reproduction
wind pollination
xylem

Famous botanists

Joseph Banks [British]
David (James) Bellamy [British]
Auguste Pyrame de Candolle [Swiss]
August Wilhelm Eichler [German]
Joseph Dalton Hooker [British]
William Jackson Hooker [British]
Linnaeus (Carl von Linné) [Swedish]
Gregor Johann Mendel [Austrian]
John Ray [English]
John Tradescant [English]

botch 1. *verb* balls up (*taboo slang*), blunder, bodge (*informal*), bungle, butcher, cobble, cock up (*Brit. slang*), flub (*U.S. slang*), fuck up (*offensive taboo slang*), fumble, make a nonsense of (*informal*), make a pig's ear of (*informal*), mar, mend, mess, mismanage, muff, patch, screw up (*informal*), spoil **2.** *noun* balls-up (*taboo slang*), blunder, bungle, bungling, cock-up (*Brit. slang*), failure, fuck-up (*offensive taboo slang*), fumble, hash, mess, miscarriage, pig's breakfast (*informal*), pig's ear (*informal*)

bother 1. *verb* alarm, annoy, bend someone's ear (*informal*), breathe down someone's neck, concern, dismay, distress, disturb, gall, get on one's nerves (*informal*), get on one's wick (*Brit. slang*), harass, hassle (*informal*), inconvenience, irritate, molest, nag, nark (*Brit., Austral. & N.Z. slang*), pester, plague, put out, trouble, upset, vex, worry **2.** *noun* aggravation, annoyance, bustle, difficulty, flurry, fuss, gall, hassle (*informal*), inconvenience, irritation, molestation, nuisance, perplexity, pest, problem, strain, trouble, vexation, worry
Antonyms *verb* aid, assist, facilitate, further, help, relieve, succour, support *~noun* advan-

tage, aid, benefit, comfort, convenience, help, service, use

bothersome aggravating, annoying, distressing, exasperating, inconvenient, irritating, tiresome, troublesome, vexatious, vexing
Antonyms appropriate, beneficial, commodious, convenient, handy, helpful, serviceable, useful

bottleneck block, blockage, congestion, hold-up, impediment, jam, obstacle, obstruction, snarl-up (*informal, chiefly Brit.*)

bottle up check, contain, curb, keep back, restrict, shut in, suppress, trap

bottom *noun* **1.** base, basis, bed, deepest part, depths, floor, foot, foundation, groundwork, lowest part, pedestal, support **2.** lower side, sole, underneath, underside **3.** arse (*taboo slang*), ass (*U.S. & Canad. taboo slang*), backside, behind (*informal*), bum (*Brit. slang*), buns (*U.S. slang*), butt (*U.S. & Canad. informal*), buttocks, derrière (*euphemistic*), fundament, jacksy (*Brit. slang*), posterior, rear, rear end, rump, seat, tail (*informal*) **4.** base, basis, cause, core, essence, ground, heart, mainspring, origin, principle, root, source, substance *~adjective* **5.** base, basement, basic, fundamental, ground, last, lowest, undermost
Antonyms *noun* cover, crown, height, lid, peak, summit, surface, top *~adjective* higher, highest, top, upper

bottomless boundless, deep, fathomless, immeasurable, inexhaustible, infinite, unfathomable, unlimited

bounce *verb* **1.** bob, bound, bump, jounce, jump, leap, rebound, recoil, resile, ricochet, spring, thump **2.** *slang* boot out (*informal*), eject, fire (*informal*), kick out (*informal*), oust, relegate, throw out *~noun* **3.** bound, elasticity, give, rebound, recoil, resilience, spring, springiness **4.** animation, brio, dynamism, energy, go (*informal*), life, liveliness, pep, vigour, vitality, vivacity, zip (*informal*)

bouncing alive and kicking, blooming, bonny, fighting fit, fit as a fiddle (*informal*), healthy, robust, thriving, vigorous

bouncy **1.** bubbly, confident, ebullient, effervescent, enthusiastic, exuberant, full of beans (*informal*), irrepressible, lively, vivacious, zestful **2.** elastic, springy
Antonyms (*sense 1*) dull, listless, unenthusiastic (*sense 2*) flat, inelastic

bound[1] *adjective* **1.** cased, fastened, fixed, pinioned, secured, tied, tied up **2.** certain, destined, doomed, fated, sure **3.** beholden, committed, compelled, constrained, duty-bound, forced, obligated, obliged, pledged, required

bound[2] *verb/noun* bob, bounce, caper, frisk, gambol, hurdle, jump, leap, lope, pounce, prance, skip, spring, vault

bound[3] *noun* **1.** *usually plural* border, boundary, confine, edge, extremity, fringe, limit, line, march, margin, pale, periphery, rim, termination, verge **2. out of bounds** banned, barred, forbidden, off-limits (*chiefly U.S. military*), prohibited, taboo *~verb* **3.** circumscribe, confine, define, delimit, demarcate, encircle, enclose, hem in, limit, restrain, restrict, surround, terminate

boundary barrier, border, borderline, bounds, brink, confines, edge, extremity, fringe, frontier, limits, march, margin, pale, precinct, termination, verge

boundless endless, illimitable, immeasurable, immense, incalculable, inexhaustible, infinite, limitless, measureless, the sky's the limit, unbounded, unconfined, unending, unlimited, untold, vast
Antonyms bounded, confined, limited, little, restricted, small

bountiful **1.** abundant, ample, bounteous, copious, exuberant, lavish, luxuriant, plenteous, plentiful, prolific **2.** beneficent, bounteous, generous, liberal, magnanimous, munificent, open-handed, princely, prodigal, unstinting

bounty **1.** almsgiving, assistance, beneficence, benevolence, charity, generosity, kindness, largess *or* largesse, liberality, open-handedness, philanthropy **2.** bonus, donation, gift, grant, gratuity, largess *or* largesse, meed (*archaic*), premium, present, recompense, reward

bouquet **1.** boutonniere, bunch of flowers, buttonhole, corsage, garland, nosegay, posy, spray, wreath **2.** aroma, fragrance, perfume, redolence, savour, scent

bourgeois conventional, hidebound, materialistic, middle-class, Pooterish, traditional

How beastly the bourgeois is
Especially the male of the species
D.H. Lawrence *How beastly the bourgeois is*

bourn[1] *noun, archaic* border, boundary, confine, destination, goal, limit

bourn[2] *noun* **1.** *chiefly southern Brit.* brook, burn, rill, rivulet, stream, torrent **2.** *figurative* death

bout **1.** course, fit, period, round, run, session, spell, spree, stint, stretch, term, time, turn **2.** battle, boxing match, competition, contest, encounter, engagement, fight, head-to-head, match, set-to, struggle

bovine dense, dozy (*Brit. informal*), dull, slow, sluggish, stolid, stupid, thick

bow[1] *verb* **1.** bend, bob, droop, genuflect, incline, make obeisance, nod, stoop **2.** accept, acquiesce, comply, concede, defer, give in, kowtow, relent, submit, succumb, surrender, yield **3.** cast down, conquer, crush, depress, overpower, subdue, subjugate, vanquish, weigh down ~*noun* **4.** bending, bob, genuflexion, inclination, kowtow, nod, obeisance, salaam

bow[2] *noun, Nautical* beak, fore, head, prow, stem

bowdlerize blue-pencil, censor, clean up, expurgate, mutilate, sanitize

bowed bent, crooked, curved, hunched, inclined, lowered, procumbent, stooped
Antonyms erect, straight-backed, upright

bowels **1.** entrails, guts, innards (*informal*), insides (*informal*), intestines, viscera, vitals **2.** belly, core, deep, depths, hold, inside, interior **3.** *archaic* compassion, mercifulness, mercy, pity, sympathy, tenderness

> *A good reliable set of bowels is worth more to a man than any quantity of brains*
>
> Josh Billings

bower alcove, arbour, grotto, leafy shelter, shady recess, summerhouse

bowl[1] *noun* basin, deep dish, vessel

bowl[2] *verb* fling, hurl, pitch, revolve, roll, rotate, spin, throw, trundle, whirl

bowl over **1.** amaze, astonish, astound, dumbfound, stagger, startle, stun, surprise, sweep off one's feet **2.** bring down, deck (*slang*), fell, floor, knock down, overthrow, overturn

bow out abandon, back out, call it a day *or* night, cop out (*slang*), get out, give up, pull out, quit, resign, retire, step down (*informal*), throw in the sponge, throw in the towel, withdraw

box[1] **1.** *noun* ark (*dialect*), carton, case, casket, chest, container, kist (*Scot. & Northern English dialect*), pack, package, portmanteau, receptacle, trunk **2.** *verb* pack, package, wrap

box[2] *verb* **1.** exchange blows, fight, spar **2.** belt (*informal*), buffet, butt, chin (*slang*), clout (*informal*), cuff, deck (*slang*), hit, lay one on (*slang*), punch, slap, sock (*slang*), strike, thwack, wallop (*informal*), whack ~*noun* **3.** belt (*informal*), blow, buffet, clout (*informal*), cuff, punch, slap, stroke, thumping, wallop (*informal*)

boxer fighter, prizefighter, pugilist, sparrer, sparring partner

box in cage, confine, contain, coop up, enclose, hem in, isolate, shut in, surround, trap

boxing fisticuffs, prizefighting, pugilism, sparring, the fight game (*informal*), the ring

Boxing weights
see SPORT

boy fellow, junior, lad, schoolboy, stripling, youngster, youth

Never send a boy to do a man's job

Boys will be boys

boycott ban, bar, black, blackball, blacklist, embargo, exclude, ostracize, outlaw, prohibit, proscribe, refrain from, refuse, reject, spurn
Antonyms accept, advocate, back, champion, defend, espouse, help, patronize, promote, support, welcome

boyfriend admirer, beau, date, follower, leman (*archaic*), lover, man, steady, suitor, swain, sweetheart, toy boy, young man

boyish adolescent, childish, immature, innocent, juvenile, puerile, young, youthful

brace **1.** *noun* bolster, bracer, bracket, buttress, prop, reinforcement, stanchion, stay, strut, support, truss **2.** *verb* bandage, bind, bolster, buttress, fasten, fortify, hold up, prop, reinforce, shove, shove up, steady, strap, strengthen, support, tie, tighten

bracing brisk, chilly, cool, crisp, energizing, exhilarating, fortifying, fresh, invigorating, lively, refreshing, restorative, reviving, rousing, stimulating, tonic, vigorous
Antonyms debilitating, draining, enervating, exhausting, fatiguing, sapping, soporific, taxing, tiring, weakening

brackish bitter, briny, saline, salt, salty, undrinkable
Antonyms clean, clear, fresh, pure, sweet, unpolluted

brag blow one's own horn (*U.S. & Canad.*), blow one's own trumpet, bluster, boast, crow, swagger, talk big (*slang*), vaunt

braggart bigmouth (*slang*), bluffer, blusterer, boaster, brag, braggadocio, bragger, hot dog (*chiefly U.S.*), show-off (*informal*), swaggerer, swashbuckler

braid entwine, interlace, intertwine, interweave, lace, plait, ravel, twine, weave

brain bluestocking (*usually disparaging*), brainbox, egghead (*informal*), genius, highbrow, intellect, intellectual, mastermind, prodigy, pundit, sage, scholar

Parts of the brain

amygdala
brainstem
Broca's area
central sulcus
cerebellum
cerebral aqueduct
cerebral cortex *or* *(nontechnical)* grey matter
cerebrospinal fluid
cerebrum
choroid plexus
corpus callosum
diencephalon
fourth ventricle
frontal lobe
hippocampus
hypothalamus
infundibulum
limbic system
mamillary body
medulla oblongata
meninges
midbrain
myelencephalon *or* *(nontechnical)* afterbrain
occipital lobe
optic chiasma
parietal lobe
pineal body
pituitary gland
pons Varolli
substantia alba *or* *(nontechnical)* white matter
temporal lobe
thalamus

third ventricle
Wernicke's area
vermis

Our brains may be too big - dooming us as Triceratops was doomed by his armour
Arthur C. Clarke

brainless braindead (*informal*), dead from the neck up (*informal*), foolish, idiotic, inane, inept, mindless, senseless, stupid, thoughtless, unintelligent, witless

brainpower aptitude, braininess, brains (*informal*), brilliance, cleverness, intellect, intelligence, IQ, mental acuity, perception, understanding

brains capacity, intellect, intelligence, mind, nous (*Brit. slang*), reason, sagacity, savvy (*slang*), sense, shrewdness, smarts (*slang, chiefly U.S.*), suss (*slang*), understanding, wit

brainwashing alteration, conditioning, indoctrination, persuasion, re-education

brainy bright, brilliant, clever, intelligent, smart

brake **1.** *noun* check, constraint, control, curb, rein, restraint **2.** *verb* check, decelerate, halt, moderate, reduce speed, slacken, slow, stop

branch **1.** arm, bough, limb, offshoot, prong, ramification, shoot, spray, sprig **2.** chapter, department, division, local office, office, part, section, subdivision, subsection, wing

branch out add to, develop, diversify, enlarge, expand, extend, have a finger in every pie, increase, multiply, proliferate, ramify, spread out

brand *noun* **1.** cast, class, grade, kind, make, quality, sort, species, type, variety **2.** emblem, hallmark, label, mark, marker, sign, stamp, symbol, trademark **3.** blot, disgrace, infamy, mark, reproach, slur, smirch, stain, stigma, taint ~*verb* **4.** burn, burn in, label, mark, scar, stamp **5.** censure, denounce, discredit, disgrace, expose, mark, stigmatize

brandish display, exhibit, flaunt, flourish, parade, raise, shake, swing, wield

brash **1.** audacious, foolhardy, hasty, impetuous, impulsive, indiscreet, precipitate, rash, reckless **2.** bold, brazen, cocky, forward, heedless, impertinent, impudent, insolent, pushy (*informal*), rude
Antonyms careful, cautious, polite, prudent, reserved, respectful, thoughtful, timid, uncertain

brass audacity, brass neck (*Brit. informal*), cheek, chutzpah (*U.S. & Canad. informal*), effrontery, face (*informal*), front, gall, impertinence, impudence, insolence, neck (*informal*), nerve (*informal*), presumption, rudeness, sassiness (*U.S. informal*)

brassy **1.** barefaced, bold, brash, brazen, forward, impudent, insolent, loud-mouthed, pert, pushy (*informal*), saucy **2.** blatant, flashy, garish, gaudy, hard, jazzy (*informal*), loud, obtrusive, showy, vulgar **3.** blaring, cacophonous, dissonant, grating, harsh, jangling, jarring, loud, noisy, piercing, raucous, shrill, strident
Antonyms discreet, low-key, modest, played down, quiet, restrained, subdued, toned down, understated

brat cub, guttersnipe, jackanapes, kid (*informal*), puppy (*informal*), rascal, spoilt child, urchin, whippersnapper, youngster

bravado bluster, boast, boastfulness, boasting, bombast, brag, braggadocio, fanfaronade (*rare*), swagger, swaggering, swashbuckling, vaunting

brave **1.** *adjective* ballsy (*taboo slang*), bold, courageous, daring, dauntless, fearless, gallant, gritty, heroic, intrepid, plucky, resolute, undaunted, valiant, valorous **2.** *verb* bear, beard, challenge, confront, dare, defy, endure, face, face the music, go through the mill, stand up to, suffer, tackle, walk into the lion's den, withstand
Antonyms *adjective* afraid, chickenshit (*U.S. slang*), cowardly, craven, faint-hearted, fearful, frightened, scared, shrinking, timid ~*verb* give in to, retreat from, surrender to

None but the brave deserves the fair
John Dryden *Alexander's Feast*

Fortune favours the brave
Terence *Phormio*

bravery balls (*taboo slang*), ballsiness (*taboo slang*), boldness, bravura, courage, daring, dauntlessness, doughtiness, fearlessness, fortitude, gallantry, grit, guts (*informal*), hardihood, hardiness, heroism, indomitability, intrepidity, mettle, pluck, pluckiness, spirit, spunk (*informal*), valour
Antonyms cowardice, faint-heartedness, fearfulness, fright, timidity

bravo assassin, bandit, brigand, cutthroat, desperado, hired killer, murderer, villain

bravura animation, audacity, boldness, brilliance, brio, daring, dash, display, élan, energy, exhibitionism, ostentation, panache, punch (*informal*), spirit, verve, vigour, virtuosity

brawl **1.** *noun* affray (*Law*), altercation, argument, *bagarre*, battle, broil, clash, disorder, dispute, donnybrook, fight, fracas, fray, free-for-all (*informal*), melee *or* mêlée, punch-up (*Brit. informal*), quarrel, row (*informal*), ruckus (*informal*), rumpus, scrap (*informal*), scrimmage, scuffle, shindig (*informal*), shindy (*informal*), skirmish, squabble, tumult, uproar, wrangle **2.** *verb* altercate, argue, battle, dispute, fight, fight like Kilkenny cats, go at it hammer and tongs, quarrel, row (*informal*), scrap (*informal*), scuffle, tussle, wrangle, wrestle

brawn beef (*informal*), beefiness (*informal*), brawniness, flesh, might, muscle, muscles, muscularity, power, robustness, strength, vigour

brawny athletic, beefy (*informal*), bulky, burly, fleshy, hardy, hefty (*informal*), herculean, husky (*informal*), lusty, muscular, powerful, robust, sinewy, stalwart, strapping, strong, sturdy, thewy, thickset, vigorous, well-built, well-knit
Antonyms frail, scrawny, skinny, thin, undeveloped, weak, weakly, weedy (*informal*), wimpish *or* wimpy (*informal*)

bray **1.** *verb* bell, bellow, blare, heehaw, hoot, roar, screech, trumpet **2.** *noun* bawl, bell, bellow, blare, cry, harsh sound, heehaw, hoot, roar, screech, shout

brazen *adjective* **1.** audacious, barefaced, bold, brash, brassy (*informal*), defiant, forward, immodest, impudent, insolent, pert, pushy (*informal*), saucy, shameless, unabashed, unashamed **2.** brass, brassy, bronze, metallic ~*verb* **3.** *with* **out** be impenitent, be unashamed, confront, defy, outface, outstare, persevere, stare out
Antonyms (*sense 1*) cautious, decorous, diffident, mannerly, modest, reserved, respectful, reticent, secret, shy, stealthy, timid

breach **1.** aperture, break, chasm, cleft, crack, fissure, gap, hole, opening, rent, rift, rupture, split **2.** contravention, disobedience, infraction, infringement, noncompliance, nonobservance, offence, transgression, trespass, violation **3.** alienation, difference, disaffection, disagreement, dissension, division, estrangement, falling-out (*informal*), parting of the ways, quarrel, schism, separation, severance, variance
Antonyms (*sense 2*) adherence to, attention, compliance, discharge, fulfilment, heeding, honouring, observation, performance

Once more unto the breach, dear friends, once more

William Shakespeare *Henry V*

bread **1.** aliment, diet, fare, food, necessities, nourishment, nutriment, provisions, subsistence, sustenance, viands, victuals **2.** *slang* ackers (*slang*), brass (*Northern English dialect*), cash, dibs (*slang*), dosh (*Brit. & Austral. slang*), dough (*slang*), finance, funds, money, necessary (*informal*), needful (*informal*), rhino (*Brit. slang*), shekels (*informal*), silver, spondulicks (*slang*), tin (*slang*)

Breads
see FOOD

breadth **1.** beam (*of a ship*), broadness, latitude, span, spread, wideness, width **2.** amplitude, area, compass, comprehensiveness, dimension, expanse, extensiveness, extent, magnitude, measure, range, reach, scale, scope, size, space, spread, sweep, vastness **3.** broad-mindedness, freedom, latitude, liberality, open-mindedness, openness, permissiveness

break *verb* **1.** batter, burst, crack, crash, demolish, destroy, disintegrate, divide, fracture, fragment, part, rend, separate, sever, shatter, shiver, smash, snap, splinter, split, tear, total (*slang*), trash (*slang*) **2.** breach, contravene, disobey, disregard, infract (*Law*), infringe, renege on, transgress, violate **3.** cow, cripple, demoralize, dispirit, enervate, enfeeble, impair, incapacitate, subdue, tame, undermine, weaken **4.** abandon, cut, discontinue, give up, interrupt, pause, rest, stop, suspend **5.** bust (*informal*), degrade, demote, discharge, dismiss, humiliate, impoverish, make bankrupt, reduce, ruin **6.** announce, come out, come out in the wash, disclose, divulge, impart, inform, let out, make public, proclaim, reveal, tell **7.** *of a record, etc.* beat, better, cap (*informal*), exceed, excel, go beyond, outdo, outstrip, surpass, top **8.** appear, burst out, come forth suddenly, emerge, erupt, happen, occur **9.** cut and run (*informal*), dash, escape, flee, fly, get away, hook it (*slang*), run away **10.** cushion, diminish, lessen, lighten, moderate, reduce, soften, weaken ~*noun* **11.** breach, cleft, crack, division, fissure, fracture, gap, gash, hole, opening, rent, rift, rupture, split, tear **12.** breather (*informal*), breathing space, entr'acte, halt, hiatus, interlude, intermission, interruption, interval, let-up (*informal*), lull, pause, recess, respite, rest, suspension **13.** alienation, breach, disaffection, dispute, divergence, estrangement, rift, rupture, schism, separation, split **14.** *informal* advantage, chance, fortune, opening, opportunity, stroke of luck
Antonyms (*sense 1*) attach, bind, connect, fasten, join, repair, unite (*sense 2*) abide by, adhere to, conform, discharge, follow, obey, observe

breakable brittle, crumbly, delicate, flimsy, fragile, frail, frangible, friable
Antonyms durable, indestructible, infrangible, lasting, nonbreakable, resistant, rugged, shatterproof, solid, strong, toughened, unbreakable

breakage breach, break, cleft, crack, cut, fissure, fracture, rent, rift, rupture, tear

breakaway *adjective* dissenting, heretical, rebel, schismatic, seceding, secessionist

break away **1.** decamp, escape, flee, fly, hook it (*slang*), make a break for it, make a run for it (*informal*), make off, run away **2.** break with, detach, part company, secede, separate

breakdown **1.** collapse, crackup (*informal*), disintegration, disruption, failure, mishap, stoppage **2.** analysis, categorization, classification, detailed list, diagnosis, dissection, itemization

break down be overcome, collapse, come unstuck, conk out (*informal*), crack up (*informal*), fail, fall apart at the seams, give way, go kaput (*informal*), go phut, go to pieces, seize up, stop, stop working

breaker billow, comber, roller, wave, whitecap, white horse

break-in breaking and entering, burglary, invasion, robbery

break in **1.** barge in, burst in, butt in, interfere, interject, interpose, interrupt, intervene, intrude, put one's oar in, put one's two cents in (*U.S. slang*) **2.** break and enter, burgle, invade, rob **3.** accustom, condition, get used to, habituate, initiate, prepare, tame, train

break into begin, burst into, burst out, commence, dissolve into, give way to, launch into

breakneck dangerous, excessive, express, headlong, precipitate, rapid, rash, reckless

break off **1.** detach, divide, part, pull off, separate, sever, snap off, splinter **2.** belay (*Nautical*), cease, desist, discontinue, end, finish, halt, pause, pull the plug on, stop, suspend, terminate

break out **1.** appear, arise, begin, commence, emerge, happen, occur, set in, spring up, start **2.** abscond, bolt, break loose, burst out, escape, flee, get free **3.** burst out, erupt

breakthrough advance, development, discovery, find, finding, gain, improvement, invention, leap, progress, quantum leap, step forward

break through achieve, burst through, crack it (*informal*), cut it (*informal*), emerge, get past, pass, penetrate, shine forth, succeed

break-up breakdown, breaking, crackup (*informal*), disintegration, dispersal, dissolution, divorce, ending, parting, rift, separation, split, splitting, termination, wind-up

break up adjourn, disband, dismantle, disperse, disrupt, dissolve, divide, divorce, end, part, scatter, separate, sever, split, stop, suspend, terminate

breakwater groyne, jetty, mole, sea wall, spur

break with break away from, depart from, ditch (*slang*), drop (*informal*), jilt, part company, reject, renounce, repudiate, separate from

breast **1.** boob (*slang*), bosom, bust, chest, front, teat, thorax, tit (*slang*), udder **2.** being, conscience, core, emotions, feelings, heart, seat of the affections, sentiments, soul, thoughts

breath **1.** air, animation, breathing, exhalation, gasp, gulp, inhalation, pant, respiration, wheeze **2.** aroma, niff (*Brit. slang*), odour, smell, vapour, whiff **3.** break, breather, breathing-space, instant, moment, pause, respite, rest, second **4.** faint breeze, flutter, gust, puff, sigh, slight movement, waft, zephyr **5.** hint, murmur, suggestion, suspicion, undertone, whisper **6.** animation, energy, existence, life, lifeblood, life force, vitality

breathe **1.** draw in, gasp, gulp, inhale and exhale, pant, puff, respire, wheeze **2.** imbue, impart, infuse, inject, inspire, instil, transfuse **3.** articulate, express, murmur, say, sigh, utter, voice, whisper

breather break, breathing space, breath of air, halt, pause, recess, respite, rest

breathless **1.** choking, exhausted, gasping, gulping, out of breath, out of whack (*informal*), panting, short-winded, spent, wheezing, winded **2.** agog, anxious, astounded, avid, eager, excited, flabbergasted (*informal*), gobsmacked (*Brit. slang*), on tenterhooks, open-mouthed, thunderstruck, with bated breath

breathtaking amazing, astonishing, awe-inspiring, awesome, brilliant, dramatic, exciting, heart-stirring, impressive, magnificent, moving, overwhelming, sensational, striking, stunning (*informal*), thrilling, wondrous (*archaic or literary*)

breech arse (*taboo slang*), ass (*U.S. & Canad. taboo slang*), backside (*informal*), behind (*informal*), bum (*Brit. slang*), buns (*U.S. slang*), butt (*U.S. & Canad. informal*), buttocks, derrière (*euphemistic*), fundament, jacksy (*Brit. slang*), posterior, rump, seat, tail (*informal*)

breed *verb* **1.** bear, beget, bring forth, engender, generate, hatch, multiply, originate, procreate, produce, propagate, reproduce **2.** bring up, cultivate, develop, discipline, educate, foster, instruct, nourish, nurture, raise, rear **3.** arouse, bring about, cause, create, generate, give rise to, induce, make, occasion, originate, produce, stir up ~*noun* **4.** brand, class, extraction, family, ilk, kind, line, lineage, pedigree, progeny, race, sort, species, stamp, stock, strain, type, variety

breeding **1.** ancestry, cultivation, development, lineage, nurture, raising, rearing, reproduction, training, upbringing **2.** civility, conduct, courtesy, cultivation, culture, gentility, manners, polish, refinement, sophistication, urbanity

You cannot make a silk purse out of a sow's ear

breeze **1.** *noun* air, breath of wind, capful of wind, current of air, draught, flurry, gust, light wind, puff of air, waft, whiff, zephyr **2.** *verb* flit, glide, hurry, move briskly, pass, sail, sally, sweep, trip

breezy **1.** airy, blowing, blowy, blusterous, blustery, fresh, gusty, squally, windy **2.** airy,

animated, blithe, buoyant, carefree, casual, cheerful, chirpy (*informal*), debonair, easy-going, free and easy, full of beans (*informal*), genial, informal, jaunty, light, light-hearted, lively, sparkling, sparky, spirited, sprightly, sunny, upbeat (*informal*), vivacious
Antonyms calm, depressed, dull, heavy, life~less, mournful, oppressive, sad, serious, wind~less

brevity **1.** conciseness, concision, condensation, crispness, curtness, economy, pithiness, suc~cinctness, terseness **2.** briefness, ephemerality, impermanence, shortness, transience, transi~toriness
Antonyms (*sense 1*) circuity, diffuseness, dis~cursiveness, long-windedness, prolixity, ram~bling, redundancy, tautology, tediousness, verbiage, verboseness, verbosity, wordiness

Brevity is the soul of wit
William Shakespeare *Hamlet*

I strive to be brief, and I become obscure
Horace *Ars Poetica*

brew *verb* **1.** boil, ferment, infuse (*tea*), make (*beer*), prepare by fermentation, seethe, soak, steep, stew **2.** breed, concoct, contrive, devel~op, devise, excite, foment, form, gather, hatch, plan, plot, project, scheme, start, stir up *~noun* **3.** beverage, blend, concoction, distilla~tion, drink, fermentation, infusion, liquor, mixture, preparation

bribe **1.** *noun* allurement, backhander (*slang*), boodle (*slang, chiefly U.S.*), corrupting gift, enticement, graft (*informal*), hush money (*slang*), incentive, inducement, kickback (*U.S.*), pay-off (*informal*), payola (*informal*), reward for treachery, sop, sweetener (*slang*) **2.** *verb* buy off, corrupt, get at, grease the palm *or* hand of (*slang*), influence by gifts, lure, oil the palm of (*informal*), pay off (*informal*), re~ward, square, suborn

bribery buying off, corruption, graft (*informal*), inducement, palm-greasing (*slang*), payola (*informal*), protection, subornation

bric-a-brac baubles, bibelots, curios, gewgaws, kickshaws, knick-knacks, objects of virtu, *ob~jets d'art*, ornaments, trinkets

bridal bride's, conjugal, connubial, hymeneal, marital, marriage, matrimonial, nuptial, spousal, wedding

bridge *noun* **1.** arch, flyover, overpass, span, viaduct **2.** band, bond, connection, link, tie *~verb* **3.** arch over, attach, bind, connect, cou~ple, cross, cross over, extend across, go over, join, link, reach across, span, traverse, unite
Antonyms *verb* cleave, come apart, disjoin, divide, keep apart, separate, sever, split, sun~der, widen
Related adjective: pontine

bridle *verb* **1.** check, constrain, control, curb, govern, have in one's pocket, keep a tight rein on, keep in check, keep on a string, master, moderate, rein, repress, restrain, subdue **2.** be indignant, bristle, draw (oneself) up, get an~gry, get one's back up, raise one's hackles, rear up *~noun* **3.** check, control, curb, rein, restraint, trammels

brief *adjective* **1.** clipped, compendious, com~pressed, concise, crisp, curt, laconic, limited, monosyllabic, pithy, short, succinct, terse, thumbnail, to the point **2.** ephemeral, fast, fleeting, hasty, little, momentary, quick, quickie (*informal*), short, short-lived, swift, temporary, transitory **3.** abrupt, blunt, brusque, curt, sharp, short, surly *~noun* **4.** abridgment, abstract, digest, epitome, outline, précis, sketch, summary, synopsis **5.** argu~ment, case, contention, data, defence, demon~stration *~verb* **6.** advise, clue in (*informal*), explain, fill in (*informal*), gen up (*Brit. infor~mal*), give (someone) a rundown, give (some~one) the gen (*Brit. informal*), inform, instruct, keep posted, prepare, prime, put (someone) in the picture (*informal*)
Antonyms *adjective* circuitous, detailed, dif~fuse, extensive, lengthy, long, long-drawn-out, long-winded, protracted

briefing conference, directions, guidance, infor~mation, instruction, instructions, meeting, preamble, preparation, priming, rundown

briefly abruptly, briskly, casually, concisely, cursorily, curtly, fleetingly, hastily, hurriedly, in a few words, in a nutshell, in brief, in out~line, in passing, momentarily, precisely, quickly, shortly, temporarily

brigade band, body, camp, company, contin~gent, corps, crew, force, group, organization, outfit, party, squad, team, troop, unit

brigand bandit, desperado, footpad (*archaic*), freebooter, gangster, highwayman, marauder, outlaw, plunderer, robber, ruffian

bright **1.** beaming, blazing, brilliant, dazzling, effulgent, flashing, gleaming, glistening, glit~tering, glowing, illuminated, intense, lambent, luminous, lustrous, radiant, resplendent, scintillating, shimmering, shining, sparkling, twinkling, vivid **2.** clear, clement, cloudless, fair, limpid, lucid, pellucid, pleasant, sunny, translucent, transparent, unclouded **3.** acute, astute, aware, brainy, brilliant, clear-headed, clever, ingenious, intelligent, inventive, keen, quick, quick-witted, sharp, smart, wide-awake **4.** auspicious, encouraging, excellent, favour~able, golden, good, hopeful, optimistic, palmy, promising, propitious, prosperous, rosy **5.** cheerful, chirpy (*informal*), full of beans (*in~formal*), gay, genial, glad, happy, jolly, joyful, joyous, light-hearted, lively, merry, sparky, upbeat (*informal*), vivacious **6.** distinguished,

famous, glorious, illustrious, magnificent, outstanding, remarkable, splendid
Antonyms (*senses 1 & 2*) cloudy, dark, dim, dusky, gloomy, grey, overcast, poorly lit (*sense 3*) dense, dim, dim-witted (*informal*), dull, dumb (*informal*), foolish, idiotic, ignorant, retarded, simple, slow, stupid, thick, unintelligent, witless

brighten 1. clear up, enliven, gleam, glow, illuminate, lighten, light up, make brighter, shine 2. become cheerful, buck up (*informal*), buoy up, cheer, encourage, enliven, gladden, hearten, make happy, perk up
Antonyms (*sense 1*) becloud, blacken, cloud over *or* up, dim, dull, obscure, overshadow, shade, shadow (*sense 2*) become angry, become gloomy, blacken, cloud, deject, depress, dispirit, look black, sadden

brightness 1. brilliance, effulgence, glare, incandescence, intensity, light, luminosity, radiance, refulgence, resplendence, shine, sparkle, splendour, vividness 2. acuity, alertness, awareness, cleverness, intelligence, quickness, sharpness, smartness, smarts (*slang, chiefly U.S.*)
Antonyms dimness, dullness

brilliance, brilliancy 1. blaze, brightness, dazzle, effulgence, gleam, glitter, intensity, luminosity, lustre, radiance, refulgence, resplendence, sheen, sparkle, vividness 2. acuity, aptitude, braininess, cleverness, distinction, excellence, genius, giftedness, greatness, inventiveness, talent, wisdom 3. éclat, gilt, glamour, gorgeousness, grandeur, illustriousness, magnificence, pizzazz *or* pizazz (*informal*), splendour
Antonyms darkness, dimness, dullness, folly, idiocy, inanity, incompetence, ineptitude, obscurity, paleness, silliness, simple-mindedness, stupidity, thickness

brilliant 1. ablaze, bright, coruscating, dazzling, glittering, glossy, intense, luminous, lustrous, radiant, refulgent, resplendent, scintillating, shining, sparkling, vivid 2. celebrated, eminent, exceptional, famous, glorious, illustrious, magnificent, notable, outstanding, splendid, superb 3. accomplished, acute, astute, brainy, clever, discerning, expert, gifted, intellectual, intelligent, inventive, masterly, penetrating, profound, quick, talented
Antonyms (*sense 1*) dark, dim, dull, gloomy, obscure (*senses 2 & 3*) dim, dull, ordinary, run-of-the-mill, simple, slow, stupid, unaccomplished, unexceptional, untalented

brim 1. *noun* border, brink, circumference, edge, flange, lip, margin, rim, skirt, verge 2. *verb* fill, fill up, hold no more, overflow, run over, spill, well over

brimful brimming, filled, flush, full, level with, overflowing, overfull, packed, running over

brindled mottled, patched, speckled, spotted, streaked, tabby

brine pickling solution, saline solution, salt water, sea water, the sea

bring 1. accompany, bear, carry, conduct, convey, deliver, escort, fetch, gather, guide, import, lead, take, transfer, transport, usher 2. cause, contribute to, create, effect, engender, inflict, occasion, produce, result in, wreak 3. compel, convince, dispose, force, induce, influence, make, move, persuade, prevail on *or* upon, prompt, sway 4. command, earn, fetch, gross, net, produce, return, sell for, yield

bring about accomplish, achieve, bring to pass, cause, compass, create, effect, effectuate, generate, give rise to, make happen, manage, occasion, produce, realize

bring down abase, cut down, drop, fell, floor, lay low, level, lower, overthrow, overturn, pull down, reduce, shoot down, undermine, upset

bring in accrue, bear, be worth, fetch, gross, produce, profit, realize, return, yield

bring off accomplish, achieve, bring home the bacon (*informal*), bring to pass, carry off, carry out, crack it (*informal*), cut it (*informal*), discharge, execute, perform, pull off, succeed

bring up 1. breed, develop, educate, form, nurture, raise, rear, support, teach, train 2. advance, allude to, broach, introduce, mention, move, propose, put forward, submit

brink border, boundary, brim, edge, fringe, frontier, limit, lip, margin, point, rim, skirt, threshold, verge

brio animation, dash, élan, energy, enthusiasm, get-up-and-go (*informal*), gusto, liveliness, panache, pep, spirit, verve, vigour, vivacity, zest, zip (*informal*)

brisk 1. active, agile, alert, animated, bustling, busy, energetic, lively, nimble, no-nonsense, quick, sparky, speedy, sprightly, spry, vigorous, vivacious 2. biting, bracing, crisp, exhilarating, fresh, invigorating, keen, nippy, refreshing, sharp, snappy, stimulating
Antonyms boring, dull, enervating, heavy, lazy, lethargic, slow, sluggish, tiring, unenergetic, wearisome

briskly actively, apace, brusquely, coolly, decisively, efficiently, energetically, firmly, incisively, nimbly, pdq (*slang*), posthaste, promptly, pronto (*informal*), quickly, rapidly, readily, smartly, vigorously

bristle *noun* 1. barb, hair, prickle, spine, stubble, thorn, whisker *~verb* 2. horripilate, prickle, rise, stand on end, stand up 3. be angry, be infuriated, be maddened, bridle, flare up, get one's dander up (*slang*), go ballistic (*slang, chiefly U.S.*), rage, see red, seethe, spit (*informal*), wig out (*slang*) 4. *with* **with**

abound, be alive, be thick, crawl, hum, swarm, teem

bristly bearded, bewhiskered, hairy, prickly, rough, stubbly, unshaven, whiskered

Briton Anglo-Saxon, Brit (*informal*), Britisher, limey (*U.S. & Canad. slang*), pommy *or* pom (*Austral. & N.Z. slang*)

brittle **1.** breakable, crisp, crumbling, crumbly, delicate, fragile, frail, frangible, friable, shatterable, shivery **2.** curt, edgy, irritable, nervous, prim, stiff, stilted, tense, wired (*slang*)
Antonyms durable, elastic, flexible, infrangible, nonbreakable, resistant, rugged, shatterproof, strong, sturdy, toughened

broach **1.** approach, bring up, hint at, introduce, mention, open up, propose, raise the subject, speak of, suggest, talk of, touch on **2.** crack, draw off, open, pierce, puncture, start, tap, uncork

broad **1.** ample, beamy (*of a ship*), capacious, expansive, extensive, generous, large, roomy, spacious, vast, voluminous, wide, widespread **2.** all-embracing, catholic, comprehensive, encyclopedic, far-reaching, general, global, inclusive, nonspecific, sweeping, undetailed, universal, unlimited, wide, wide-ranging **3.** *As in* **broad daylight** clear, full, obvious, open, plain, straightforward, undisguised **4.** broad-minded, liberal, open, permissive, progressive, tolerant, unbiased **5.** blue, coarse, gross, improper, indecent, indelicate, near the knuckle (*informal*), unrefined, vulgar
Antonyms close, confined, constricted, cramped, limited, meagre, narrow, restricted, tight

broadcast *verb* **1.** air, beam, cable, put on the air, radio, relay, show, televise, transmit **2.** advertise, announce, circulate, disseminate, make public, proclaim, promulgate, publish, report, shout from the rooftops (*informal*), spread *~noun* **3.** programme, show, telecast, transmission

broaden augment, develop, enlarge, expand, extend, fatten, increase, open up, spread, stretch, supplement, swell, widen
Antonyms circumscribe, constrain, diminish, narrow, reduce, restrict, simplify, tighten

broadly **1.** expansively, extensively, far and wide, greatly, hugely, vastly, widely **2.** commonly, generally, popularly, universally, widely **3.** for the most part, generally, in general, in the main, largely, mainly, mostly, on the whole, predominantly, widely
Antonyms exclusively, limitedly, narrowly

broad-minded catholic, cosmopolitan, dispassionate, flexible, free-thinking, indulgent, liberal, open-minded, permissive, responsive, tolerant, unbiased, unbigoted, undogmatic, unprejudiced
Antonyms biased, bigoted, closed-minded, dogmatic, inflexible, intolerant, narrow-minded, prejudiced, uncharitable

broadside abuse, assault, attack, battering, bombardment, censure, criticism, denunciation, diatribe, philippic, stick (*slang*)

brochure advertisement, booklet, circular, folder, handbill, hand-out, leaflet, mailshot, pamphlet

broil **1.** *noun* affray, altercation, *bagarre*, brawl, brouhaha, dispute, feud, fracas, fray, quarrel, scrimmage, shindig (*informal*), shindy (*informal*), skirmish, strife, wrangle **2.** *verb* brawl, dispute, quarrel, scrimmage, wrangle

broke bankrupt, bust (*informal*), cleaned out (*slang*), dirt-poor (*informal*), down and out, flat broke (*informal*), impoverished, in queer street, insolvent, in the red, not have a penny to one's name, on one's uppers, penniless, penurious, ruined, short, skint (*Brit. slang*), stony-broke (*Brit. slang*), strapped for cash (*informal*), without two pennies to rub together (*informal*)
Antonyms affluent, comfortable, flush (*informal*), in the money (*informal*), prosperous, rich, solvent, wealthy, well-to-do

broken **1.** burst, demolished, destroyed, fractured, fragmented, rent, ruptured, separated, severed, shattered, shivered **2.** buggered (*slang, chiefly Brit.*), defective, exhausted, feeble, imperfect, kaput (*informal*), not functioning, on one's last legs, on the blink (*slang*), out of order, ruined, run-down, spent, weak **3.** disconnected, discontinuous, disturbed, erratic, fragmentary, incomplete, intermittent, interrupted, spasmodic **4.** beaten, browbeaten, crippled, crushed, defeated, demoralized, humbled, oppressed, overpowered, subdued, tamed, vanquished **5.** dishonoured, disobeyed, disregarded, forgotten, ignored, infringed, isolated, retracted, traduced, transgressed **6.** disjointed, halting, hesitating, imperfect, stammering

broken-down collapsed, dilapidated, in disrepair, inoperative, kaput (*informal*), not functioning, not in working order, old, on the blink (*slang*), on the fritz (*U.S. slang*), out of commission, out of order, worn out

brokenhearted choked, crestfallen, desolate, despairing, devastated, disappointed, disconsolate, down in the dumps (*informal*), grief-stricken, heartbroken, heart-sick, inconsolable, miserable, mournful, prostrated, sorrowful, wretched

broker agent, dealer, factor, go-between, intermediary, middleman, negotiator

bromide banality, cliché, commonplace, hack~

neyed saying, platitude, stereotype, trite remark, truism

bronze brownish, chestnut, copper, copper-coloured, metallic brown, reddish-brown, reddish-tan, rust, tan

bronzed brown, sunburnt, suntanned, tanned

brood *verb* **1.** agonize, dwell upon, eat one's heart out, fret, have a long face, meditate, mope, mull over, muse, ponder, repine, ruminate, think upon **2.** cover, hatch, incubate, set, sit upon *~noun* **3.** breed, chicks, children, clutch, family, hatch, infants, issue, litter, offspring, progeny, young

brook[1] *noun* beck, burn, gill (*dialect*), rill, rivulet, runnel (*literary*), stream, streamlet, watercourse

brook[2] *verb* abide, accept, allow, bear, countenance, endure, hack (*slang*), put up with (*informal*), stand, stomach, suffer, support, swallow, thole (*dialect*), tolerate, withstand

brothel bagnio, bawdy house (*archaic*), bordello, cathouse (*U.S. slang*), house of ill fame, house of ill repute, house of prostitution, knocking shop (*slang*), red-light district, stews (*archaic*), whorehouse

> *Prisons are built with stones of Law, brothels with bricks of Religion*
> William Blake *The Marriage of Heaven and Hell*

brother **1.** blood brother, kin, kinsman, relation, relative, sibling **2.** associate, chum (*informal*), cock (*Brit. informal*), colleague, companion, compeer, comrade, confrère, fellow member, mate, pal (*informal*), partner **3.** cleric, friar, monk, regular, religious
Related adjective: fraternal

brotherhood **1.** brotherliness, camaraderie, companionship, comradeship, fellowship, friendliness, kinship **2.** alliance, association, clan, clique, community, coterie, fraternity, guild, league, order, society, union

brotherly affectionate, altruistic, amicable, benevolent, cordial, fraternal, friendly, kind, neighbourly, philanthropic, sympathetic

brow **1.** air, appearance, aspect, bearing, countenance, eyebrow, face, forehead, front, mien, temple **2.** brim, brink, crest, crown, edge, peak, rim, summit, tip, top, verge

browbeat badger, bulldoze (*informal*), bully, coerce, cow, domineer, dragoon, hector, intimidate, lord it over, oppress, overawe, overbear, ride roughshod over, threaten, tyrannize
Antonyms beguile, cajole, coax, entice, flatter, inveigle, lure, manoeuvre, seduce, sweet-talk (*informal*), tempt, wheedle

brown **1.** *adjective* auburn, bay, brick, bronze, bronzed, browned, brunette, chestnut, chocolate, coffee, dark, donkey brown, dun, dusky, fuscous, ginger, hazel, rust, sunburnt, tan, tanned, tawny, toasted, umber **2.** *verb* cook, fry, grill, sauté, seal, sear

browned off cheesed off (*Brit. slang*), discontented, discouraged, disgruntled, disheartened, fed up, pissed off (*taboo slang*), sick as a parrot (*informal*), weary

brown study absorption, abstractedness, abstraction, contemplation, meditation, musing, preoccupation, reflection, reverie, rumination

browse **1.** dip into, examine cursorily, flip through, glance at, leaf through, look round, look through, peruse, scan, skim, survey **2.** crop, eat, feed, graze, nibble, pasture

bruise *verb* **1.** blacken, blemish, contuse, crush, damage, deface, discolour, injure, mar, mark, pound, pulverize **2.** displease, grieve, hurt, injure, insult, offend, pain, sting, wound *~noun* **3.** black-and-blue mark, black mark, blemish, contusion, discoloration, injury, mark, swelling, trauma (*Pathology*)

bruiser bully, bully boy, gorilla (*informal*), hard man, heavy (*slang*), hoodlum, rough (*informal*), roughneck (*slang*), rowdy, ruffian, thug, tough, tough guy

bruising **1.** *noun* contusion, discoloration, ecchymosis, marking, swelling **2.** *adjective* ferocious, fierce, hard, rough, rumbustious, tough, violent

brunt burden, force, full force, impact, pressure, shock, strain, stress, thrust, violence

brush[1] *noun* **1.** besom, broom, sweeper **2.** clash, conflict, confrontation, encounter, fight, fracas, scrap (*informal*), set-to (*informal*), skirmish, slight engagement, spot of bother (*informal*), tussle *~verb* **3.** buff, clean, paint, polish, sweep, wash **4.** caress, contact, flick, glance, graze, kiss, scrape, stroke, sweep, touch

brush[2] *noun* brushwood, bushes, copse, scrub, shrubs, thicket, undergrowth, underwood

brush aside discount, dismiss, disregard, have no time for, ignore, kiss off (*slang, chiefly U.S. & Canad.*), override, sweep aside

brush-off *noun* bum's rush (*slang*), cold shoulder, cut, dismissal, go-by (*slang*), kick in the teeth (*slang*), kiss-off (*slang, chiefly U.S. & Canad.*), knock-back (*slang*), rebuff, refusal, rejection, repudiation, repulse, slight, snub, the (old) heave-ho (*informal*)

brush off *verb* cold-shoulder, cut, deny, disdain, dismiss, disown, disregard, ignore, kiss off (*slang, chiefly U.S. & Canad.*), put down, rebuff, refuse, reject, repudiate, scorn, send to Coventry, slight, snub, spurn

brush up bone up on (*informal*), cram, go over, polish up, read up, refresh one's memory, relearn, revise, study

brusque abrupt, blunt, curt, discourteous, gruff, hasty, impolite, monosyllabic, sharp, short, surly, tart, terse, unmannerly

Antonyms accommodating, civil, courteous, gentle, patient, polite, well-mannered

brutal 1. barbarous, bloodthirsty, cruel, ferocious, heartless, inhuman, merciless, pitiless, remorseless, ruthless, savage, uncivilized, vicious 2. animal, beastly, bestial, brute, brutish, carnal, coarse, crude, sensual 3. bearish, callous, gruff, harsh, impolite, insensitive, rough, rude, severe, uncivil, unfeeling, unmannerly

Antonyms civilized, gentle, humane, kind, merciful, polite, refined, sensitive, soft-hearted

brutality atrocity, barbarism, barbarity, bloodthirstiness, brutishness, cruelty, ferocity, inhumanity, ruthlessness, savageness, savagery, viciousness

brutalize 1. bestialize, degrade, dehumanize 2. barbarize, terrorize, vandalize

brutally barbarically, barbarously, brutishly, callously, cruelly, ferociously, fiercely, hardheartedly, heartlessly, in cold blood, inhumanly, meanly, mercilessly, murderously, pitilessly, remorselessly, ruthlessly, savagely, unkindly, viciously

brute *noun* 1. animal, beast, creature, wild animal 2. barbarian, beast, devil, fiend, ghoul, monster, ogre, sadist, savage, swine *~adjective* 3. bodily, carnal, fleshly, instinctive, mindless, physical, senseless, unthinking 4. bestial, coarse, depraved, gross, sensual

brutish barbarian, boorish, coarse, crass, crude, cruel, gross, loutish, savage, stupid, subhuman, swinish, uncouth, vulgar

bubble *noun* 1. air ball, bead, blister, blob, drop, droplet, globule, vesicle 2. bagatelle, delusion, fantasy, illusion, toy, trifle, vanity *~verb* 3. boil, effervesce, fizz, foam, froth, percolate, seethe, sparkle 4. babble, burble, gurgle, murmur, purl, ripple, trickle, trill

bubbles effervescence, fizz, foam, froth, head, lather, spume, suds

bubbly 1. carbonated, curly, effervescent, fizzy, foamy, frothy, lathery, sparkling, sudsy 2. alive and kicking, animated, bouncy, elated, excited, full of beans (*informal*), happy, lively, merry, sparky

buccaneer corsair, freebooter, pirate, privateer, sea-rover

buck *noun* 1. *archaic* beau, blade, blood, coxcomb, dandy, fop, gallant, popinjay, spark *~verb* 2. bound, jerk, jump, leap, prance, spring, start, vault 3. dislodge, throw, unseat 4. *informal* cheer, encourage, gladden, gratify, hearten, inspirit, please

buckle *noun* 1. catch, clasp, clip, fastener, hasp 2. bulge, contortion, distortion, kink, warp *~verb* 3. catch, clasp, close, fasten, hook, secure 4. bend, bulge, cave in, collapse, contort, crumple, distort, fold, twist, warp

buckle down apply oneself, exert oneself, launch into, pitch in, put one's shoulder to the wheel, set to

buck up 1. get a move on, hasten, hurry up, shake a leg, speed up 2. brighten, cheer up, encourage, hearten, inspirit, perk up, rally, take heart

bucolic agrarian, agrestic, agricultural, country, pastoral, rural, rustic

bud 1. *noun* embryo, germ, shoot, sprout 2. *verb* burgeon, burst forth, develop, grow, pullulate, shoot, sprout

budding beginning, burgeoning, developing, embryonic, fledgling, flowering, germinal, growing, incipient, nascent, potential, promising

budge 1. dislodge, give way, inch, move, propel, push, remove, roll, shift, slide, stir 2. bend, change, convince, give way, influence, persuade, sway, yield

budget 1. *noun* allocation, allowance, cost, finances, financial statement, fiscal estimate, funds, means, resources 2. *verb* allocate, apportion, cost, cost out, estimate, plan, ration

> *Annual income twenty pounds, annual expenditure nineteen pounds nineteen six, result happiness. Annual income twenty pounds, annual expenditure twenty pound ought and six, result misery*
>
> Charles Dickens *David Copperfield*

buff[1] 1. *adjective* sandy, straw, tan, yellowish, yellowish-brown 2. *noun* **in the buff** bare, buck naked (*slang*), in one's birthday suit (*informal*), in the altogether (*informal*), in the bare scud (*slang*), in the raw (*informal*), naked, nude, scuddy (*slang*), unclad, unclothed, with bare skin, without a stitch on (*informal*) 3. *verb* brush, burnish, polish, rub, shine, smooth

buff[2] *noun, informal* addict, admirer, aficionado, connoisseur, devotee, enthusiast, expert, fan, fiend (*informal*), freak (*informal*), grandmaster, hotshot (*informal*), maven (*U.S.*), whiz (*informal*)

buffer bulwark, bumper, cushion, fender, intermediary, safeguard, screen, shield, shock absorber

buffet[1] *noun* brasserie, café, cafeteria, cold table, counter, cupboard, refreshment-counter, salad bar, sideboard, snack bar

buffet[2] 1. *verb* bang, batter, beat, box, bump, clobber (*slang*), cuff, flail, knock, lambast(e), pound, pummel, punch, push, rap, shove, slap, strike, thump, wallop (*informal*) 2. *noun* bang, blow, box, bump, cuff, jolt, knock, push, rap, shove, slap, smack, thump, wallop (*informal*)

buffoon clown, comedian, comic, droll, fool, harlequin, jester, joculator *or (fem.)* joculatrix, joker, merry-andrew, silly billy (*informal*), wag

buffoonery clowning, drollery, jesting, non~ sense, silliness, tomfoolery, waggishness

bug *noun* **1.** *informal* bacterium, disease, germ, infection, lurgi (*informal*), microorganism, vi~ rus **2.** craze, fad, mania, obsession, rage **3.** blemish, catch, defect, error, failing, fault, flaw, glitch, gremlin, imperfection, snarl-up (*informal, chiefly Brit.*), virus *~verb* **4.** *infor~ mal* aggravate (*informal*), annoy, badger, be on one's back (*slang*), bother, disturb, gall, get in one's hair (*informal*), get on one's nerves (*informal*), get on one's wick (*Brit. slang*), get under one's skin (*informal*), get up one's nose (*informal*), harass, hassle (*informal*), irk, irri~ tate, nark (*Brit., Austral. & N.Z. slang*), nee~ dle (*informal*), nettle, pester, piss one off (*ta~ boo slang*), plague, vex **5.** eavesdrop, listen in, spy, tap, wiretap

bugbear anathema, bane, bête noire, bogey, bogeyman, bugaboo, devil, dread, fiend, hor~ ror, nightmare, pet hate

build *verb* **1.** assemble, construct, erect, fabri~ cate, form, make, put up, raise **2.** base, begin, constitute, establish, formulate, found, in~ augurate, initiate, institute, originate, set up, start **3.** accelerate, amplify, augment, develop, enlarge, escalate, extend, improve, increase, intensify, strengthen *~noun* **4.** body, figure, form, frame, physique, shape, structure
Antonyms *verb* contract, debilitate, decline, decrease, demolish, dilute, dismantle, end, finish, harm, impair, lower, reduce, relin~ quish, sap, suspend, tear down, weaken

building **1.** domicile, dwelling, edifice, fabric, house, pile, structure **2.** architecture, con~ struction, erection, fabricating, raising

build-up **1.** accumulation, development, en~ largement, escalation, expansion, gain, growth, increase **2.** ballyhoo (*informal*), hype, plug (*informal*), promotion, publicity, puff **3.** accretion, accumulation, heap, load, mass, rick, stack, stockpile, store

build up **1.** add to, amplify, augment, develop, enhance, expand, extend, fortify, heighten, improve, increase, intensify, reinforce, strengthen **2.** advertise, boost, plug (*informal*), promote, publicize, spotlight

built-in essential, immanent, implicit, in-built, included, incorporated, inherent, inseparable, integral, part and parcel of

bulbous bloated, bulging, convex, rounded, swelling, swollen

bulge *noun* **1.** bump, hump, lump, projection, protrusion, protuberance, swelling **2.** boost, increase, intensification, rise, surge *~verb* **3.** bag, dilate, distend, enlarge, expand, project, protrude, puff out, sag, stand out, stick out, swell, swell out
Antonyms bowl, cave, cavity, concavity, crat~ er, dent, depression, hole, hollow, indentation, pit, trough

bulk *noun* **1.** amplitude, bigness, dimensions, immensity, largeness, magnitude, massive~ ness, size, substance, volume, weight **2.** better part, body, generality, lion's share, main part, majority, major part, mass, most, nearly all, plurality, preponderance *~verb* **3.** **bulk large** be important, carry weight, dominate, loom, loom large, preponderate, stand out, threaten

bulky big, colossal, cumbersome, elephantine, enormous, ginormous (*informal*), heavy, huge, hulking, humongous *or* humungous (*U.S. slang*), immense, mammoth, massive, massy, mega (*slang*), ponderous, substantial, unman~ ageable, unwieldy, very large, voluminous, weighty
Antonyms convenient, handy, manageable, neat, slim, small, wieldy

bulldoze **1.** demolish, flatten, level, raze **2.** drive, force, propel, push, shove, thrust **3.** browbeat, bully, coerce, cow, dragoon, hector, intimidate, put the screws on, railroad (*infor~ mal*)

bullet ball, missile, pellet, projectile, shot, slug

bulletin account, announcement, communica~ tion, communiqué, dispatch, message, news flash, notification, report, statement

bull-headed headstrong, inflexible, mulish, ob~ stinate, pig-headed, stiff-necked, stubborn, stupid, tenacious, uncompromising, unyield~ ing, wilful

bullish assured, bold, confident, expectant, im~ proving, positive, rising

bully **1.** *noun* big bully, browbeater, bully boy, coercer, intimidator, oppressor, persecutor, ruffian, tormentor, tough **2.** *verb* bluster, browbeat, bulldoze (*informal*), bullyrag, co~ erce, cow, domineer, hector, intimidate, op~ press, overbear, persecute, push around (*slang*), ride roughshod over, swagger, terror~ ize, tyrannize **3.** *adjective* admirable, excellent, fine, nifty (*informal*), radical (*informal*), very good **4.** *interjection* bravo, capital, good, grand, great, well done

bulwark **1.** bastion, buttress, defence, embank~ ment, fortification, outwork, partition, ram~ part, redoubt **2.** buffer, guard, mainstay, safe~ guard, security, support

bumbler blunderer, bungler, duffer (*informal*), fumbler, geek (*slang*), klutz (*U.S. & Canad. slang*), lummox (*informal*), muddler

bumbling awkward, blundering, botching, bungling, clumsy, incompetent, inefficient, in~ ept, lumbering, maladroit, muddled, stum~ bling

Antonyms able, brisk, capable, competent, efficient, equal, fit

bump *verb* **1**. bang, collide (with), crash, hit, knock, slam, smash into, strike **2**. bounce, jar, jerk, jolt, jostle, jounce, rattle, shake **3**. budge, dislodge, displace, move, remove, shift *~noun* **4**. bang, blow, collision, crash, hit, impact, jar, jolt, knock, rap, shock, smash, thud, thump **5**. bulge, contusion, hump, knob, knot, lump, node, nodule, protuberance, swelling

bumper *adjective* abundant, bountiful, excellent, exceptional, jumbo (*informal*), massive, mega (*slang*), prodigal, spanking (*informal*), teeming, unusual, whacking (*informal, chiefly Brit.*), whopping (*informal*)

bump into chance upon, come across, encounter, happen upon, light upon, meet, meet up with, run across, run into

bumpkin boor, clodhopper, clown, country bumpkin, hayseed (*U.S. & Canad. informal*), hick (*informal, chiefly U.S. & Canad.*), hillbilly, lout, lubber, oaf, peasant, rustic, yokel

bump off assassinate, blow away (*slang, chiefly U.S.*), dispatch, do away with, do in (*slang*), eliminate, finish off, kill, knock off (*slang*), liquidate, murder, remove, rub out (*U.S. slang*), take out (*slang*), wipe out (*informal*)

bumptious arrogant, boastful, brash, cocky, conceited, egotistic, forward, full of oneself, impudent, overbearing, overconfident, presumptuous, pushy (*informal*), self-assertive, showy, swaggering, vainglorious, vaunting

bumpy bone-breaking, bouncy, choppy, irregular, jarring, jerky, jolting, jolty, knobby, lumpy, pitted, potholed, rough, rutted, uneven

bunch *noun* **1**. assortment, batch, bouquet, bundle, clump, cluster, collection, heap, lot, mass, number, parcel, pile, quantity, rick, sheaf, spray, stack, tuft **2**. band, bevy, crew (*informal*), crowd, flock, gang, gathering, group, knot, mob, multitude, party, posse (*informal*), swarm, team, troop *~verb* **3**. assemble, bundle, cluster, collect, congregate, cram together, crowd, flock, group, herd, huddle, mass, pack

bundle *noun* **1**. accumulation, assortment, batch, bunch, collection, group, heap, mass, pile, quantity, rick, stack **2**. bag, bale, box, carton, crate, pack, package, packet, pallet, parcel, roll *~verb* **3**. bale, bind, fasten, pack, package, palletize, tie, tie together, tie up, truss, wrap **4**. *with* **out, off, into,** *etc.* hurry, hustle, push, rush, shove, throw, thrust **5**. *with* **up** clothe warmly, muffle up, swathe, wrap up

Related adjective: fascicular

bungle blow (*slang*), blunder, bodge (*informal*), botch, butcher, cock up (*Brit. slang*), drop a brick *or* clanger (*informal*), flub (*U.S. slang*), foul up, fuck up (*offensive taboo slang*), fudge, louse up (*slang*), make a mess of, make a nonsense of (*informal*), make a pig's ear of (*informal*), mar, mess up, miscalculate, mismanage, muff, ruin, screw up (*informal*), spoil

Antonyms accomplish, achieve, carry off, effect, fulfil, succeed, triumph

bungler blunderer, botcher, butcher, butterfingers (*informal*), duffer (*informal*), fumbler, incompetent, lubber, muddler, muff

bungling awkward, blundering, botching, cack-handed (*informal*), clumsy, ham-fisted (*informal*), ham-handed (*informal*), incompetent, inept, maladroit, unskilful

bunk[1] *verb* abscond, beat it (*slang*), bolt, clear out (*informal*), cut and run (*informal*), decamp, do a bunk (*Brit. slang*), do a runner (*slang*), flee, fly the coop (*U.S. & Canad. informal*), run for it (*informal*), scram (*informal*), skedaddle (*informal*), take a powder (*U.S. & Canad. slang*), take it on the lam (*U.S. & Canad. slang*)

bunk[2], **bunkum** *noun* balderdash, balls (*taboo slang*), baloney (*informal*), bilge (*informal*), bosh (*informal*), bullshit (*taboo slang*), cobblers (*Brit. taboo slang*), crap (*slang*), eyewash (*informal*), garbage (*informal*), guff (*slang*), havers (*Scot.*), hogwash, hokum (*slang, chiefly U.S. & Canad.*), hooey (*slang*), horsefeathers (*U.S. slang*), hot air (*informal*), moonshine, nonsense, piffle (*informal*), poppycock (*informal*), rot, rubbish, shit (*taboo slang*), stuff and nonsense, tarradiddle, tomfoolery, tommyrot, tosh (*slang, chiefly Brit.*), trash, tripe (*informal*), truck (*informal*), twaddle

buoy **1**. *noun* beacon, float, guide, marker, signal **2**. *verb with* **up** boost, cheer, cheer up, encourage, hearten, keep afloat, lift, raise, support, sustain

buoyancy **1**. floatability, lightness, weightlessness **2**. animation, bounce (*informal*), cheerfulness, cheeriness, good humour, high spirits, liveliness, pep, spiritedness, sunniness, zing (*informal*)

buoyant **1**. afloat, floatable, floating, light, weightless **2**. animated, blithe, bouncy, breezy, bright, carefree, cheerful, chirpy (*informal*), debonair, full of beans (*informal*), genial, happy, jaunty, joyful, light-hearted, lively, peppy (*informal*), sparky, sunny, upbeat (*informal*), vivacious

Antonyms (*sense 2*) cheerless, depressed, despairing, dull, forlorn, gloomy, glum, hopeless, melancholy, moody, morose, pessimistic, sad, sullen, unhappy

burden *noun* **1**. affliction, albatross, anxiety, care, clog, encumbrance, grievance, load, millstone, obstruction, onus, pigeon (*informal*),

responsibility, sorrow, strain, stress, trial, trouble, weight, worry **2.** *Nautical* cargo, freight, lading, tonnage *~verb* **3.** bother, encumber, handicap, load, oppress, overload, overwhelm, saddle with, strain, tax, weigh down, worry
Related adjective: onerous

burdensome crushing, difficult, exacting, heavy, irksome, onerous, oppressive, taxing, troublesome, trying, weighty

bureau **1.** desk, writing desk **2.** agency, branch, department, division, office, service

bureaucracy **1.** administration, authorities, civil service, corridors of power, directorate, government, ministry, officialdom, officials, the system **2.** bumbledom, officialdom, officialese, red tape, regulations

bureaucrat administrator, apparatchik, civil servant, functionary, mandarin, minister, office-holder, officer, official, public servant

burgeon bloom, blossom, bud, develop, flourish, flower, grow, increase, mature, progress, prosper, sprout, thrive
Antonyms droop, languish, shrivel, wilt, wither

burglar cat burglar, filcher, housebreaker, picklock, pilferer, robber, sneak thief, thief

burglary break-in, breaking and entering, filching, housebreaking, larceny, pilferage, robbery, stealing, theft, thieving

burial burying, entombment, exequies, funeral, inhumation, interment, obsequies, sepulture

burial ground cemetery, churchyard, God's acre, golgotha (*rare*), graveyard, necropolis

buried **1.** coffined, consigned to the grave, entombed, interred, laid to rest **2.** dead and buried, dead and gone, in the grave, long gone, pushing up the daisies, six feet under **3.** covered, forgotten, hidden, repressed, sunk in oblivion, suppressed **4.** cloistered, concealed, hidden, private, sequestered, tucked away **5.** caught up, committed, concentrating, devoted, engrossed, immersed, intent, lost, occupied, preoccupied, rapt

burlesque **1.** *noun* caricature, mock, mockery, parody, satire, send-up (*Brit. informal*), spoof (*informal*), takeoff (*informal*), travesty **2.** *adjective* caricatural, comic, farcical, hudibrastic, ironical, ludicrous, mock, mock-heroic, mocking, parodic, satirical, travestying **3.** *verb* ape, caricature, exaggerate, imitate, lampoon, make a monkey out of, make fun of, mock, parody, ridicule, satirize, send up (*Brit. informal*), spoof (*informal*), take off (*informal*), take the piss out of (*taboo slang*), travesty

burly beefy (*informal*), big, brawny, bulky, hefty, hulking, muscular, powerful, stocky, stout, strapping, strong, sturdy, thickset, well-built

Antonyms lean, puny, scraggy, scrawny, slight, spare, thin, weak, weedy (*informal*), wimpish *or* wimpy (*informal*)

burn **1.** be ablaze, be on fire, blaze, flame, flare, flash, flicker, glow, go up in flames, smoke **2.** brand, calcine, char, ignite, incinerate, kindle, light, parch, reduce to ashes, scorch, set on fire, shrivel, singe, toast, wither **3.** bite, hurt, pain, smart, sting, tingle **4.** be excited (angry, aroused, inflamed, passionate), blaze, desire, fume, seethe, simmer, smoulder, yearn **5.** consume, eat up, expend, use

burning **1.** blazing, fiery, flaming, flashing, gleaming, glowing, hot, illuminated, scorching, smouldering **2.** ablaze, all-consuming, ardent, eager, earnest, fervent, fervid, flaming, frantic, frenzied, impassioned, intense, passionate, vehement, zealous **3.** acrid, biting, caustic, irritating, painful, piercing, prickling, pungent, reeking, smarting, stinging, tingling **4.** acute, compelling, critical, crucial, essential, important, now or never, pressing, significant, urgent, vital
Antonyms apathetic, calm, cool, cooling, faint, indifferent, mild, numbing, passive, soothing

burnish **1.** *verb* brighten, buff, furbish, glaze, polish, rub up, shine, smooth **2.** *noun* gloss, lustre, patina, polish, sheen, shine
Antonyms *verb* abrade, graze, scratch, scuff

burrow **1.** *noun* den, hole, lair, retreat, shelter, tunnel **2.** *verb* delve, dig, excavate, hollow out, scoop out, tunnel

burst *verb* **1.** blow up, break, crack, disintegrate, explode, fly open, fragment, puncture, rend asunder, rupture, shatter, shiver, split, tear apart **2.** barge, break, break out, erupt, gush forth, run, rush, spout *~noun* **3.** bang, blast, blasting, blowout, blow-up, breach, break, crack, discharge, explosion, rupture, split **4.** eruption, fit, gush, gust, outbreak, outburst, outpouring, rush, spate, spurt, surge, torrent *~adjective* **5.** flat, punctured, rent, ruptured, split

bury **1.** consign to the grave, entomb, inearth, inhume, inter, lay to rest, sepulchre **2.** conceal, cover, cover up, draw a veil over, enshroud, hide, secrete, shroud, stash (*informal*), stow away **3.** drive in, embed, engulf, implant, sink, submerge **4.** absorb, engage, engross, immerse, interest, occupy
Antonyms (*senses 1 & 2*) bring to light, dig up, discover, disinter, dredge up, exhume, expose, find, reveal, turn up, uncover, unearth

bush **1.** hedge, plant, shrub, shrubbery, thicket **2.** back country (*U.S.*), backlands (*U.S.*), backwoods, brush, scrub, scrubland, the wild, woodland

bushy bristling, bristly, fluffy, fuzzy, luxuriant,

rough, shaggy, spreading, stiff, thick, unruly, wiry

busily actively, assiduously, briskly, carefully, diligently, earnestly, energetically, industri~ously, intently, purposefully, speedily, strenu~ously

business 1. calling, career, craft, employment, function, job, line, métier, occupation, profes~sion, pursuit, trade, vocation, work 2. compa~ny, concern, corporation, enterprise, estab~lishment, firm, organization, venture 3. bar~gaining, commerce, dealings, industry, manu~facturing, merchandising, selling, trade, trad~ing, transaction 4. affair, assignment, concern, duty, function, issue, matter, pigeon (*infor~mal*), point, problem, question, responsibility, subject, task, topic

The business of America is business
Calvin Coolidge

The trouble with the rat race is that even if you win, you're still a rat
Lily Tomlin

The public be damned! I'm working for my stockholders
William H. Vanderbilt

The superior man understands what is right; the inferior man understands what will sell
Confucius

business before pleasure

businesslike correct, efficient, matter-of-fact, methodical, orderly, organized, practical, pro~fessional, regular, routine, systematic, thor~ough, well-ordered, workaday
Antonyms careless, disorderly, disorganized, frivolous, impractical, inefficient, irregular, sloppy, unprofessional, unsystematic, untidy

businessman, businesswoman capitalist, employer, entrepreneur, executive, financier, *homme d'affaires*, industrialist, merchant, tradesman, tycoon

bust[1] *noun* bosom, breast, chest, torso

bust[2] *verb* 1. break, burst, fracture, rupture 2. bankrupt, break, crash, fail, impoverish, ruin 3. arrest, catch, collar (*informal*), cop (*slang*), feel one's collar (*slang*), lift (*slang*), nab (*in~formal*), nail (*informal*), raid, search ~*adjec~tive* 4. **go bust** become insolvent, be ruined, break, fail, go bankrupt ~*noun* 5. arrest, cap~ture, cop (*slang*), raid, search, seizure

bustle 1. *verb* beetle, bestir, dash, flutter, fuss, hasten, hurry, rush, scamper, scramble, scur~ry, scuttle, stir, tear 2. *noun* activity, ado, agitation, commotion, excitement, flurry, fuss, haste, hurly-burly, hurry, pother, stir, to-do, tumult
Antonyms *verb* be indolent, idle, laze, lie around, loaf, loiter, loll, relax, rest, take it easy ~*noun* inaction, inactivity, quiet, quiet~ness, stillness, tranquillity

bustling active, astir, busy, buzzing, crowded, energetic, eventful, full, humming, hustling, lively, rushing, stirring, swarming, teeming, thronged

busy *adjective* 1. active, assiduous, brisk, dili~gent, employed, engaged, engrossed, hard at work, industrious, in harness, occupied, on active service, on duty, persevering, rushed off one's feet, slaving, working 2. active, ener~getic, exacting, full, hectic, hustling, lively, on the go (*informal*), restless, strenuous, tireless, tiring 3. fussy, inquisitive, interfering, med~dlesome, meddling, nosy, officious, prying, snoopy, stirring, troublesome ~*verb* 4. absorb, employ, engage, engross, immerse, interest, occupy
Antonyms (*senses 1 & 2*) idle, inactive, indo~lent, lackadaisical, lazy, off duty, relaxed, shiftless, slothful, unoccupied

busybody eavesdropper, gossip, intriguer, in~truder, meddler, nosy parker (*informal*), pry, scandalmonger, snoop, snooper, stirrer (*infor~mal*), troublemaker

but *conjunction* 1. further, however, moreover, nevertheless, on the contrary, on the other hand, still, yet 2. bar, barring, except, except~ing, excluding, notwithstanding, save, with the exception of ~*adverb* 3. just, merely, only, simply, singly, solely

butcher *noun* 1. destroyer, killer, murderer, slaughterer, slayer ~*verb* 2. carve, clean, cut, cut up, dress, joint, prepare, slaughter 3. as~sassinate, cut down, destroy, exterminate, kill, liquidate, massacre, put to the sword, slaughter, slay 4. bodge (*informal*), botch, de~stroy, mess up, mutilate, ruin, spoil, wreck

butchery blood bath, blood-letting, bloodshed, carnage, killing, massacre, mass murder, murder, slaughter

butt[1] *noun* 1. haft, handle, hilt, shaft, shank, stock 2. base, end, fag end (*informal*), foot, leftover, stub, tail, tip

butt[2] *noun* Aunt Sally, dupe, laughing stock, mark, object, point, subject, target, victim

butt[3] *verb/noun* 1. *With or of the head or horns* buck, buffet, bump, bunt, jab, knock, poke, prod, punch, push, ram, shove, thrust ~*verb* 2. abut, join, jut, meet, project, protrude 3. *with* **in** *or* **into** chip in (*informal*), cut in, interfere, interrupt, intrude, meddle, put one's oar in, put one's two cents in (*U.S. slang*), stick one's nose in

butt[4] *noun* barrel, cask, pipe

butter up blarney, brown-nose (*taboo slang*), cajole, coax, fawn on *or* upon, flatter, honey up, kiss (someone's) ass (*U.S. slang*), oil one's tongue, pander to, soft-soap, suck up to (*in~formal*), wheedle

buttocks arse (*taboo slang*), ass (*U.S. & Canad. taboo slang*), backside (*informal*), behind (*informal*), bottom, bum (*Brit. slang*), buns (*U.S. slang*), butt (*U.S. & Canad. informal*), derrière (*euphemistic*), fundament, gluteus maximus (*Anatomy*), haunches, hindquarters, jacksy (*Brit. slang*), nates (*technical name*), posterior, rear, rump, seat, tail (*informal*)

buttonhole *verb, figurative* accost, bore, catch, detain in talk, grab, importune, persuade importunately, take aside, waylay

buttress **1.** *noun* abutment, brace, mainstay, pier, prop, reinforcement, shore, stanchion, stay, strut, support **2.** *verb* augment, back up, bolster, brace, prop, prop up, reinforce, shore, shore up, strengthen, support, sustain, uphold

buxom ample, bosomy, busty, comely, curvaceous, debonair, fresh-looking, full-bosomed, healthy, hearty, jocund, jolly, lively, lusty, merry, plump, robust, sprightly, voluptuous, well-rounded, winsome
Antonyms delicate, frail, slender, slight, slim, svelte, sylphlike, thin, trim

buy *verb* **1.** acquire, get, invest in, obtain, pay for, procure, purchase, score (*slang*), shop for **2.** *often with* **off** bribe, corrupt, fix (*informal*), grease someone's palm (*slang*), square, suborn ~*noun* **3.** acquisition, bargain, deal, purchase
Antonyms *verb* auction, barter, retail, sell, vend

buzz *noun* **1.** bombilation *or* bombination (*literary*), buzzing, drone, hiss, hum, murmur, purr, ring, ringing, sibilation, susurration *or* susurrus (*literary*), whir, whisper **2.** dirt (*U.S. slang*), gen (*Brit. informal*), gossip, hearsay, latest (*informal*), news, report, rumour, scandal, scuttlebutt (*U.S. slang*), whisper ~*verb* **3.** bombilate *or* bombinate (*literary*), drone, fizzle, hum, murmur, reverberate, ring, sibilate, susurrate (*literary*), whir, whisper, whizz **4.** chatter, gossip, natter, rumour, tattle

by *preposition* **1.** along, beside, by way of, close to, near, next to, over, past, via **2.** through, through the agency of, under the aegis of ~*adverb* **3.** aside, at hand, away, beyond, close, handy, in reach, near, past, to one side

by and by before long, erelong (*archaic or poetic*), eventually, in a while, in the course of time, one day, presently, soon

bygone ancient, antiquated, departed, erstwhile, extinct, forgotten, former, gone by, lost, of old, of yore, olden, one-time, past, past recall, previous, sunk in oblivion
Antonyms coming, forthcoming, future, prospective, to be, to come

bypass avoid, body-swerve (*Scot.*), circumvent, depart from, detour round, deviate from, get round, give a wide berth to, go round, ignore, neglect, outflank, pass round
Antonyms abut, adjoin, come together, connect, converge, cross, intersect, join, link, meet, touch, unite

bystander eyewitness, looker-on, observer, onlooker, passer-by, spectator, viewer, watcher, witness
Antonyms contributor, partaker, participant, party

byword adage, aphorism, apophthegm, dictum, epithet, gnome, maxim, motto, precept, proverb, saw, saying, slogan

C

cab hackney, hackney carriage, minicab, taxi, taxicab

cabal camp, caucus, clique, coalition, combination, conclave, confederacy, conspiracy, coterie, faction, intrigue, junta, league, machination, party, plot, scheme, schism, set

cabbalistic cryptic, dark, esoteric, fanciful, mysterious, mystic, mystical, obscure, occult, secret

cabin **1.** berth, bothy, chalet, cot, cottage, crib, hovel, hut, lodge, shack, shanty, shed **2.** berth, compartment, deckhouse, quarters, room

cabinet **1.** case, chiffonier, closet, commode, cupboard, dresser, escritoire, locker **2.** administration, assembly, council, counsellors, ministry **3.** *archaic* apartment, boudoir, chamber (*archaic*),

Cabinets and cupboards
see FURNITURE

cache **1.** *noun* accumulation, fund, garner (*archaic*), hiding place, hoard, nest egg, repository, reserve, stash (*informal*), stockpile, store, storehouse, supply, treasury **2.** *verb* bury, conceal, hide, put away, secrete, stash (*informal*), store

cackle babble, blather, chatter, chuckle, cluck, crow, gabble, gibber, giggle, jabber, prattle, snicker, snigger, titter

cacophonous discordant, dissonant, grating, harsh, inharmonious, jarring, raucous, strident

cacophony caterwauling, discord, disharmony, dissonance, stridency

cad bounder (*old-fashioned Brit. slang*), churl, cur, dastard (*archaic*), heel (*slang*), knave, rat (*informal*), rotter (*slang, chiefly Brit.*), scrote (*slang*), scumbag (*slang*)

cadaverous ashen, blanched, bloodless, corpselike, deathlike, deathly, emaciated, exsanguinous, gaunt, ghastly, haggard, hollow-eyed, like death warmed up (*informal*), pale, pallid, wan

caddish despicable, ill-bred, low, ungentlemanly, unmannerly
Antonyms gentlemanly, honourable, laudable, mannerly, pleasant, praiseworthy

cadence **1.** beat, lilt, measure (*Prosody*), metre, pulse, rhythm, swing, tempo, throb **2.** accent, inflection, intonation, modulation

cadge **1.** *verb* beg, freeload (*slang*), scrounge (*informal*), sponge **2.** *noun* beggar, bloodsucker (*informal*), freeloader (*slang*), hanger-on, leech, parasite, scrounger (*informal*), sponger

cadre core, framework, hard core, infrastructure, key group, nucleus

café brasserie, cafeteria, coffee bar, coffee shop, lunchroom, restaurant, snack bar, tearoom

cage **1.** *verb* confine, coop up, fence in, immure, impound, imprison, incarcerate, lock up, mew, pound, restrain, shut up **2.** *noun* corral (*U.S.*), enclosure, pen, pound

cagey, cagy careful, cautious, chary, discreet, guarded, noncommittal, shrewd, wary, wily
Antonyms careless, dull, imprudent, indiscreet, reckless, stolid, unthinking, unwary

caitiff **1.** *noun* coward, knave, miscreant, rascal, rogue, scoundrel, traitor, vagabond, villain, wretch **2.** *adjective* base, cowardly, craven, dastardly, ignoble

cajole beguile, coax, decoy, dupe, entice, entrap, flatter, inveigle, lure, manoeuvre, mislead, seduce, sweet-talk (*informal*), tempt, wheedle

cajolery beguilement, blandishments, blarney, coaxing, enticement, flattery, inducement(s), inveigling, persuasion, soft soap (*informal*), sweet talk (*informal*), wheedling

cake **1.** *verb* bake, cement, coagulate, congeal, consolidate, dry, encrust, harden, inspissate (*archaic*), ossify, solidify, thicken **2.** *noun* bar, block, cube, loaf, lump, mass, slab

Cakes and pastries
see FOOD

calamitous blighting, cataclysmic, catastrophic, deadly, devastating, dire, disastrous, fatal, pernicious, ruinous, tragic, woeful
Antonyms advantageous, beneficial, favourable, fortunate, good, helpful

calamity adversity, affliction, cataclysm, catastrophe, disaster, distress, downfall, hardship, misadventure, mischance, misfortune, mishap, reverse, ruin, scourge, tragedy, trial, tribulation, woe, wretchedness
Antonyms advantage, benefit, blessing, boon, good fortune, good luck, help

Calamities are of two kinds: misfortune to ourselves, and good fortune to others
Ambrose Bierce *The Devil's Dictionary*

calculable appraisable, assessable, computable, determinable, estimable (*rare*), gaugeable *or* gageable, judgeable, measurable, quantifiable, ratable *or* rateable

calculate 1. adjust, compute, consider, count, determine, enumerate, estimate, figure, gauge, judge, rate, reckon, value, weigh, work out 2. aim, design, intend, plan

calculated considered, deliberate, intended, intentional, planned, premeditated, purposeful
Antonyms haphazard, hasty, heedless, hurried, impetuous, impulsive, rash, spontaneous, unintentional, unplanned, unpremeditated

calculating canny, cautious, contriving, crafty, cunning, designing, devious, Machiavellian, manipulative, politic, scheming, sharp, shrewd, sly
Antonyms blunt, direct, downright, frank, guileless, honest, open, outspoken, sincere, undesigning

calculation 1. answer, computation, estimate, estimation, figuring, forecast, judgment, reckoning, result 2. caution, circumspection, contrivance, deliberation, discretion, foresight, forethought, planning, precaution

calibrate gauge, measure

calibre 1. bore, diameter, gauge, measure 2. *figurative* ability, capacity, distinction, endowment, faculty, force, gifts, merit, parts, quality, scope, stature, strength, talent, worth

call *verb* 1. announce, arouse, awaken, cry, cry out, hail, halloo, proclaim, rouse, shout, waken, yell 2. assemble, bid, collect, contact, convene, convoke, gather, invite, muster, rally, summon 3. give (someone) a bell (*Brit. slang*), phone, ring up (*informal, chiefly Brit.*), telephone 4. christen, denominate, describe as, designate, dub, entitle, label, name, style, term 5. announce, appoint, declare, decree, elect, ordain, order, proclaim, set apart 6. consider, estimate, judge, regard, think *~noun* 7. cry, hail, scream, shout, signal, whoop, yell 8. announcement, appeal, command, demand, invitation, notice, order, plea, request, ring (*informal, chiefly Brit.*), summons, supplication, visit 9. cause, claim, excuse, grounds, justification, need, occasion, reason, right, urge
Antonyms *verb* (*sense 1*) be quiet, be silent, murmur, mutter, speak softly, whisper (*senses 2 & 5*) call off, cancel, dismiss, disperse, excuse, release *~noun* (*sense 7*) murmur, mutter, whisper (*sense 8*) dismissal, release

call for 1. demand, entail, involve, necessitate, need, occasion, require, suggest 2. collect, fetch, pick up, uplift (*Scot.*)

calling business, career, employment, life's work, line, métier, mission, occupation, profession, province, pursuit, trade, vocation, walk of life, work
Antonyms affliction, avocation, curse, dislike, hobby

call on 1. drop in on, look in on, look up, see, visit 2. appeal to, ask, bid, call upon, entreat, invite, invoke, request, summon, supplicate

callous apathetic, case-hardened, cold, hard-bitten, hard-boiled (*informal*), hardened, hardhearted, harsh, heartless, indifferent, indurated (*rare*), insensate, insensible, insensitive, inured, obdurate, soulless, thick-skinned, torpid, uncaring, unfeeling, unresponsive, unsusceptible, unsympathetic
Antonyms caring, compassionate, considerate, gentle, sensitive, soft, sympathetic, tender, understanding

callously apathetically, brutally, coldly, hardheartedly, harshly, heartlessly, indifferently, insensately, insensibly, insensitively, obdurately, soullessly, torpidly, unfeelingly

callousness apathy, coldness, hardheartedness, hardness, harshness, heartlessness, indifference, induration (*rare*), insensateness, insensibility, insensibleness, insensitivity, inuredness *or* enuredness, obduracy, obdurateness, soullessness, torpidity, unfeelingness

callow green, guileless, immature, inexperienced, jejune, juvenile, naive, puerile, raw, unfledged, unsophisticated, untried

callowness greenness, guilelessness, immaturity, inexperience, innocence, jejuneness, jejunity, juvenileness, naïveté *or* naivety, puerility, rawness, unsophisticatedness, unsophistication

calm *adjective* 1. balmy, halcyon, mild, pacific, peaceful, placid, quiet, restful, serene, smooth, still, tranquil, windless 2. as cool as a cucumber, collected, composed, cool, dispassionate, equable, impassive, imperturbable, keeping one's cool, relaxed, sedate, self-possessed, undisturbed, unemotional, unexcitable, unexcited, unfazed (*informal*), unflappable (*informal*), unmoved, unruffled *~verb* 3. hush, mollify, placate, quieten, relax, soothe *~noun* 4. calmness, hush, peace, peacefulness, quiet, repose, serenity, stillness
Antonyms *adjective* agitated, aroused, discomposed, disturbed, emotional, excited, fierce, frantic, heated, perturbed, rough, shaken, stormy, troubled, wild, worried *~verb* aggravate, agitate, arouse, disturb, excite, irritate, stir *~noun* agitation, disturbance, wildness

calmly casually, collectedly, composedly, coolly, dispassionately, equably, impassively, imperturbably, nonchalantly, placidly, relaxedly, sedately, self-possessedly, serenely, tranquilly, unflappably, unflinchingly

calmness **1.** calm, composure, equability, hush, motionlessness, peace, peacefulness, placidity, quiet, repose, restfulness, serenity, smoothness, stillness, tranquillity **2.** composure, cool (*slang*), coolness, dispassion, equanimity, impassivity, imperturbability, poise, sang-froid, self-possession

calumniate asperse, backbite, bad-mouth (*slang, chiefly U.S. & Canad.*), blacken, defame, denigrate, detract, knock (*informal*), lampoon, libel, malign, misrepresent, revile, rubbish (*informal*), slag (off) (*slang*), slander, stigmatize, traduce, vilify, vilipend (*rare*)

calumnious abusive, aspersive, backbiting, defamatory, derogatory, detractive, insulting, libellous, lying, slanderous, vituperative

calumny abuse, aspersion, backbiting, calumniation, defamation, denigration, derogation, detraction, evil-speaking, insult, libel, lying, misrepresentation, obloquy, revilement, slander, smear, stigma, vilification, vituperation

camaraderie brotherhood, brotherliness, companionability, companionship, comradeship, esprit de corps, fellowship, fraternization, good-fellowship, togetherness

camouflage **1.** *noun* blind, cloak, concealment, cover, deceptive markings, disguise, false appearance, front, guise, mask, masquerade, mimicry, protective colouring, screen, subterfuge **2.** *verb* cloak, conceal, cover, disguise, hide, mask, obfuscate, obscure, screen, veil
Antonyms *verb* bare, display, exhibit, expose, reveal, show, uncover, unmask, unveil

camp¹ *noun* bivouac, camping ground, camp site, cantonment (*Military*), encampment, tents

camp² *adjective* affected, artificial, camped up (*informal*), campy (*informal*), effeminate, mannered, ostentatious, poncy (*slang*), posturing

campaign attack, crusade, drive, expedition, jihad (*rare*), movement, offensive, operation, push

campaigner activist, crusader, demonstrator

canaille hoi polloi, masses, mob, plebs, populace, proletariat, rabble, ragtag, riffraff, scum, vulgar herd

canal channel, conduit, duct, passage, watercourse, waterway

cancel **1.** abolish, abort, abrogate, annul, blot out, call off, countermand, cross out, delete, do away with, efface, eliminate, erase, expunge, obliterate, obviate, quash, repeal, repudiate, rescind, revoke **2.** balance out, compensate for, counterbalance, make up for, neutralize, nullify, obviate, offset, redeem

cancellation abandoning, abandonment, abolition, annulment, deletion, elimination, quashing, repeal, revocation

cancer blight, canker, carcinoma (*Pathology*), corruption, evil, growth, malignancy, pestilence, rot, sickness, tumour

candid **1.** blunt, downright, fair, forthright, frank, free, guileless, impartial, ingenuous, just, open, outspoken, plain, round, sincere, straightforward, truthful, unbiased, unequivocal, unprejudiced, upfront (*informal*) **2.** impromptu, informal, uncontrived, unposed
Antonyms biased, complimentary, diplomatic, flattering, kind, subtle

candidate applicant, aspirant, claimant, competitor, contender, contestant, entrant, nominee, possibility, runner, solicitant, suitor

candour artlessness, directness, fairness, forthrightness, frankness, guilelessness, honesty, impartiality, ingenuousness, naïveté, openness, outspokenness, simplicity, sincerity, straightforwardness, truthfulness, unequivocalness
Antonyms bias, cunning, deceit, diplomacy, dishonesty, flattery, insincerity, prejudice, subtlety

canker **1.** *verb* blight, consume, corrode, corrupt, embitter, envenom, inflict, poison, pollute, rot, rust, waste away **2.** *noun* bane, blight, blister, cancer, corrosion, corruption, infection, lesion, rot, scourge, sore, ulcer

canniness acuteness, artfulness, astuteness, carefulness, cautiousness, circumspection, judiciousness, knowingness, perspicaciousness, perspicacity, prudence, sagacity, sageness, sharpness, shrewdness, subtlety, wariness, wisdom, worldliness

cannon **1.** artillery piece, big gun, field gun, gun, mortar **2.** *plural* artillery, battery, big guns, cannonry, field guns, guns, ordnance

cannonade barrage, battery, bombardment, broadside, pounding, salvo, shelling, volley

canny acute, artful, astute, careful, cautious, circumspect, clever, judicious, knowing, on the ball (*informal*), perspicacious, prudent, sagacious, sharp, shrewd, subtle, wise, worldly-wise
Antonyms bumbling, inept, lumpen (*informal*), obtuse, unskilled

canon **1.** criterion, dictate, formula, precept, principle, regulation, rule, standard, statute, yardstick **2.** catalogue, list, roll

canonical accepted, approved, authoritative, authorized, orthodox, recognized, sanctioned

canopy awning, baldachin, covering, shade, sunshade, tester

cant *noun* **1.** affected piety, humbug, hypocrisy, insincerity, lip service, pious platitudes, pretence, pretentiousness, sanctimoniousness, sham holiness **2.** argot, jargon, lingo, patter, slang, vernacular *~verb* **3.** angle, bevel, incline, rise, slant, slope, tilt

cantankerous bad-tempered, captious, choleric, contrary, crabby, cranky (*U.S., Canad., & Irish informal*), crotchety (*informal*), crusty, difficult, disagreeable, grouchy (*informal*), grumpy, ill-humoured, irascible, irritable, liverish, peevish, perverse, quarrelsome, ratty (*Brit. & N.Z. informal*), testy, tetchy
Antonyms agreeable, amiable, breezy, cheerful, complaisant, congenial, genial, good-natured, happy, kindly, merry, placid, pleasant, vivacious

canter *noun* amble, dogtrot, easy gait, jog, lope

canting hypocritical, insincere, Janus-faced, sanctimonious, two-faced

canvass *verb* **1.** analyse, campaign, electioneer, examine, fly a kite, inspect, investigate, poll, scan, scrutinize, sift, solicit, solicit votes, study, ventilate **2.** agitate, debate, discuss, dispute *~noun* **3.** examination, investigation, poll, scrutiny, survey, tally

canyon coulee (*U.S.*), gorge, gulch (*U.S.*), gulf, gully, ravine

cap *verb* beat, better, clobber (*slang*), complete, cover, crown, eclipse, exceed, excel, finish, lick (*informal*), outdo, outstrip, overtop, put in the shade, run rings around (*informal*), surpass, top, transcend

capability ability, capacity, competence, facility, faculty, means, potential, potentiality, power, proficiency, qualification(s), wherewithal
Antonyms inability, incompetence, inefficiency, ineptitude, powerlessness

capable able, accomplished, adapted, adept, adequate, apt, clever, competent, efficient, experienced, fitted, gifted, intelligent, masterly, proficient, qualified, skilful, suited, susceptible, talented
Antonyms incapable, incompetent, ineffective, inept, inexpert, unqualified, unskilled

capacious ample, broad, comfortable, commodious, comprehensive, expansive, extended, extensive, generous, liberal, roomy, sizable *or* sizeable, spacious, substantial, vast, voluminous, wide
Antonyms confined, constricted, cramped, enclosed, incommodious, insubstantial, limited, narrow, poky, restricted, small, tight, tiny, uncomfortable, ungenerous

capaciousness ampleness, commodiousness, roominess, sizableness *or* sizeableness, spaciousness

capacity **1.** amplitude, compass, dimensions, extent, magnitude, range, room, scope, size, space, volume **2.** ability, aptitude, aptness, brains, capability, cleverness, competence, competency, efficiency, facility, faculty, forte, genius, gift, intelligence, power, readiness, strength **3.** appointment, function, office, position, post, province, role, service, sphere

cape chersonese (*poetic*), head, headland, ness (*archaic*), peninsula, point, promontory

caper **1.** *verb* bounce, bound, cavort, cut a rug (*informal*), dance, frisk, frolic, gambol, hop, jump, leap, romp, skip, spring, trip **2.** *noun* antic, dido (*informal*), escapade, gambol, high jinks, hop, jape, jest, jump, lark (*informal*), leap, mischief, practical joke, prank, revel, shenanigan (*informal*), sport, stunt

capital *adjective* **1.** cardinal, central, chief, controlling, essential, foremost, important, leading, main, major, overruling, paramount, pre-eminent, primary, prime, principal, prominent, vital **2.** excellent, fine, first, first-rate, prime, splendid, sterling, superb, world-class *~noun* **3.** assets, cash, finance, finances, financing, funds, investment(s), means, money, principal, property, resources, stock, wealth, wherewithal

Capital city	Country
Abu Dhabi	United Arab Emirates
Abuja	Nigeria
Accra	Ghana
Addis Ababa	Ethiopia
Agaña	Guam
Akmola	Kazakhstan
Algiers	Algeria
Amman	Jordan
Amsterdam	Netherlands
Andorra la Vella	Andorra
Ankara	Turkey
Antananarivo	Madagascar
Apia	Western Samoa
Ashkhabad	Turkmenistan
Asmara	Eritrea
Asunción	Paraguay
Athens	Greece
Baghdad	Iraq
Baku	Azerbaijan
Bamako	Mali
Bandar Seri Begawan	Brunei
Bangkok	Thailand
Bangui	Central African Republic
Banjul	Gambia
Basseterre	St. Kitts and Nevis
Basse-Terre	Guadeloupe
Beijing	People's Republic of China
Beirut *or* Beyrouth	Lebanon
Belfast	Northern Ireland
Belgrade	Serbia
Belmopan	Belize
Berlin	Germany
Berne *or* Bern	Switzerland
Bissau *or* Bissão	Guinea-Bissau

Bloemfontein	judicial capital of South Africa
Bogotá	Colombia
Brasília	Brazil
Bratislava	Slovakia
Brazzaville	Congo Republic
Bridgetown	Barbados
Brussels	Belgium
Bucharest	Romania
Budapest	Hungary
Buenos Aires	Argentina
Bujumbura	Burundi
Cairo	Egypt
Canberra	Australia
Cape Town	legislative capital of South Africa
Caracas	Venezuela
Cardiff	Wales
Castries	St. Lucia
Cayenne	French Guiana
Charlotte Amalie	U.S. Virgin Islands
Colombo	Sri Lanka
Conakry *or* Konakry	Guinea
Copenhagen	Denmark
Dakar	Senegal
Damascus	Syria
Dhaka *or* Dacca	Bangladesh
Djibouti *or* Jibouti	Djibouti *or* Jibouti
Dodoma	Tanzania
Doha	Qatar
Douglas	Isle of Man
Dublin	Republic of Ireland
Dushanbe	Tadzhikistan
Edinburgh	Scotland
Fort-de-France	Martinique
Freetown	Sierra Leone
Funafuti	Tuvalu
Gaborone	Botswana
Georgetown	Cayman Islands
Georgetown	Guyana
Grand Turk	Turks and Caicos Islands
Guatemala City	Guatemala
Hamilton	Bermuda
Hanoi	Vietnam
Harare	Zimbabwe
Havana	Cuba
Helsinki	Finland
Honiara	Solomon Islands
Islamabad	Pakistan
Jakarta *or* Djakarta	Indonesia
Jerusalem	Israel
Kabul	Afghanistan
Kampala	Uganda
Katmandu *or* Kathmandu	Nepal
Khartoum *or* Khartum	Sudan
Kiev	Ukraine
Kigali	Rwanda
Kingston	Jamaica
Kingstown	St. Vincent and the Grenadines
Kinshasa	Zaïre
Kishinev	Moldavia
Kolonia	Micronesia
Koror	Belau
Kuala Lumpur	Malaysia
Kuwait City	Kuwait
Laâyoune	Western Sahara
La Paz	administrative capital of Bolivia
Lhasa *or* Lassa	Tibet
Libreville	Gabon
Lilongwe	Malawi
Lima	Peru
Lisbon	Portugal
Ljubljana	Slovenia
Lomé	Togo
London	England and United Kingdom
Luanda *or* Loanda	Angola
Lusaka	Zambia
Luxembourg-Ville	Luxembourg
Macao City	Macao
Madrid	Spain
Majuro	Marshall Islands
Malabo	Equatorial Guinea
Malé	Republic of Maldives
Managua	Nicaragua
Manama	Bahrain
Manila	Philippines
Maputo	Mozambique
Maseru	Lesotho
Mbabane	Swaziland
Mecca *or* Mekka	joint capital with Riyadh of Saudi Arabia
Mexico City	Mexico
Minsk	Byelorussia
Mogadishu *or* Mogadiscio	Somalia
Monaco-Ville	Monaco
Monrovia	Liberia
Montevideo	Uruguay
Moroni	Comoros
Moscow	Russia and Russian Federation
Muscat	Oman
Nairobi	Kenya
Nassau	Bahamas
Ndjamena *or* N'djamena	Chad
New Delhi	India
Niamey	Niger
Nicosia	Cyprus
Nouakchott	Mauritania
Nuku'alofa	Tonga
Nuuk	Greenland
Oslo	Norway
Ottawa	Canada
Ouagadougou	Burkina-Faso

Pago Pago	American Samoa
Panama City	Panama
Paramaribo	Surinam
Paris	France
Phnom Penh *or* Pnom Penh	Cambodia
Pishpek	Kirghizia
Plymouth	Montserrat
Podgorica	Montenegro
Port-au-Prince	Haiti
Port Louis	Mauritius
Port Moresby	Papua New Guinea
Port of Spain	Trinidad and Tobago
Porto Novo	Benin
Prague	Czech Republic
Praia	Cape Verde
Pretoria	administrative capital of South Africa
Pyongyang *or* P'yong-yang	North Korea
Quito	Ecuador
Rabat	Morocco
Reykjavik	Iceland
Riga	Latvia
Riyadh	joint capital with Mecca of Saudi Arabia
Road Town	British Virgin Islands
Rome	Italy
Roseau	Dominica
San'a *or* Sanaa	Yemen
San José	Costa Rica
San Juan	Puerto Rico
San Marino	San Marino
San Salvador	El Slavador
Santiago	Chile
Santo Domingo	Dominican Republic
São Tomé	São Tomé and Principe
Sarajevo *or* Serajevo	Bosnia and Herzegovina
Seoul	South Korea
Singapore	Singapore
Skopje	Macedonia
Sofia	Bulgaria
Stanley	Falkland Islands
St-Denis	Réunion
St. George's	Grenada
St. John's	Antigua and Barbuda
Stockholm	Sweden
Sucre	legislative and judicial capital of Bolivia
Suva	Fiji
Taipei *or* T'ai-pei	Taiwan
Tallin *or* Tallinn	Estonia
Tarawa	Kiribati
Tashkent	Uzbekistan
Tbilisi	Georgia
Tegucigalpa	Honduras
Tehran *or* Teheran	Iran
Thimphu *or* Thimbu	Bhutan
Thorshavn	Faeroe Islands
Tirana *or* Tiranë	Albania
Tokyo	Japan
Tripoli	Libya
Tunis	Tunisia
Ulan Bator	Mongolia
Vaduz	Liechtenstein
Valletta *or* Valetta	Malta
Vatican City	Vatican City
Victoria	Hong Kong
Victoria	Seychelles
Vienna	Austria
Vientiane	Laos
Vila	Vanuatu
Vilnius *or* Vilngus	Lithuania
Warsaw	Poland
Washington DC	USA
Wellington	New Zealand
Willemstad	Netherlands Antilles
Windhoek	Namibia
Yamoussoukro	Côte d'Ivoire
Yangon	Myanmar
Yaoundé *or* Yaunde	Cameroon
Yaren	Nauru
Yerevan	Armenia
Zagreb	Croatia

capitalism free enterprise, *laissez faire or laisser faire*, private enterprise, private ownership

I think that Capitalism, wisely managed, can probably be made more efficient for attaining economic ends than any alternative system yet in sight, but that in itself it is in many ways extremely objectionable
John Maynard Keynes *The End of Laissez-Faire*

capitalize, capitalise *with* **on** benefit from, cash in on (*informal*), exploit, gain from, make the most of, profit from, take advantage of

capitulate come to terms, give in, give up, relent, submit, succumb, surrender, yield
Antonyms beat, conquer, crush, defeat, get the better of, lick (*informal*), overcome, overpower, subdue, subjugate, vanquish

capitulation accedence, submission, surrender, yielding

caprice changeableness, fad, fancy, fickleness, fitfulness, freak, humour, impulse, inconstancy, notion, quirk, vagary, whim, whimsy

capricious changeful, crotchety (*informal*), erratic, fanciful, fickle, fitful, freakish, impulsive, inconsistent, inconstant, mercurial, odd, queer, quirky, unpredictable, variable, wayward, whimsical
Antonyms certain, consistent, constant, decisive, determined, firm, resolute, responsible,

stable, unchangeable, unmoveable, unwavering

capriciousness changefulness, crotchetiness (*informal*), fancifulness, fickleness, fitfulness, freakishness, impulsiveness, inconstancy, mercuriality, mercurialness, oddness, queerness, quirkiness, unpredictability, unpredictableness, variability, variableness, waywardness, whimsicality, whimsicalness
Antonyms constancy, fidelity, firmness, fixedness, invariability, invariableness, loyalty, predictability, predictableness, single-mindedness, steadfastness, steadiness

capsize invert, keel over, overturn, tip over, turn over, turn turtle, upset

capsule 1. bolus, lozenge, pill, tablet, troche (*Medical*) 2. case, pericarp (*Botany*), pod, receptacle, seed vessel, sheath, shell, vessel

captain boss, chief, chieftain, commander, head, leader, master, number one (*informal*), officer, (senior) pilot, skipper, torchbearer

captious 1. carping, cavilling, censorious, critical, deprecating, disparaging, fault-finding, hypercritical, nagging, nit-picking (*informal*) 2. acrimonious, cantankerous, crabbed, cross, irritable, peevish, ratty (*Brit. & N.Z. informal*), testy, tetchy, touchy

captivate absorb, allure, attract, beguile, bewitch, charm, dazzle, enamour, enchant, enrapture, enslave, ensnare, enthral, entrance, fascinate, hypnotize, infatuate, lure, mesmerize, ravish, seduce, sweep off one's feet, win
Antonyms alienate, disenchant, disgust, repel, repulse

captivation absorption, allurement, attraction, beguilement, enchantment, enslavement, ensnarement, enthralment, entrancement, fascination, hypnotization *or* hypnotisation, infatuation, mesmerization *or* mesmerisation, ravishment, seduction, tantalization *or* tantalisation

captive 1. *noun* bondservant, convict, detainee, hostage, internee, prisoner, prisoner of war, slave 2. *adjective* caged, confined, enslaved, ensnared, imprisoned, incarcerated, locked up, penned, restricted, subjugated

captivity bondage, confinement, custody, detention, durance (*archaic*), duress, enthralment, imprisonment, incarceration, internment, restraint, servitude, slavery, thraldom, vassalage

A robin red breast in a cage
Puts all Heaven in a rage
William Blake *Auguries of Innocence*

captor confiner, custodian, detainer, enslaver, ensnarer, imprisoner, incarcerator, jailer *or* gaoler

capture 1. *verb* apprehend, arrest, bag, catch, collar (*informal*), feel one's collar (*slang*), lift (*slang*), nab (*informal*), nail (*informal*), secure, seize, take, take into custody, take prisoner 2. *noun* apprehension, arrest, catch, imprisonment, seizure, taking, taking captive, trapping
Antonyms *verb* free, let go, let out, liberate, release, set free, turn loose

car 1. auto (*U.S.*), automobile, jalopy (*informal*), machine, motor, motorcar, vehicle, wheels (*informal*) 2. buffet car, cable car, coach, dining car, (railway) carriage, sleeping car, van

Car parts

accelerator
air bag
alternator
ammeter
anti-roll bar
ashtray
automatic choke
axle
battery
bearing
big end
body
bonnet
boot
brake
brake light
brake pad
bucket seat
bulb
bumper
camshaft
carburettor
catalytic converter
chassis
childproof lock
choke
clutch
coil
connecting rod
convertible top
cowl
crank
crankcase
crankshaft
cylinder
cylinder head
dashboard
demister
dipstick
disc brakes
distributor
distributor cap
door
door handle
driveshaft
engine
exhaust
fan
fan belt
fascia
fender (*U.S. & Canad.*)
flywheel
fog lamp
fuel gauge
fuse
fuse box
gasket
gear
gearbox
gear lever *or (U.S. & Canad.)* gearshift
generator
glove compartment
grille *or* radiator grille
handbrake
hard top
hazard light
headlight
headrest
heater
hood
horn
hubcap
ignition
indicator
jack
light
little end
lock
luggage rack
manifold
mileometer, milometer *or (U.S. & Canad.)* odometer
mud flap
numberplate
oil filter
oil pump
oil-pressure gauge
parcel shelf
parking light
pedal
petrol cap
petrol gauge

petrol tank
piston
plug
points
radiator
radius arm
rear light *or* *(U.S. & Canad.)* taillight
rear-view mirror
reversing light
roof
seat
seat belt *or* safety belt
shock absorber
silencer
soft top
spare wheel
speedometer
springs
sprocket
starter
steering column
steering wheel
sump
sunroof *or* sunshine roof
suspension
tailgate
tailpipe
tank
top
torsion bar
towbar
transmission
trim
tyre
universal joint
valve
wheel
wheel brace
wheel nut
wheel trim
window
windscreen
windscreen wiper
wing
wing mirror
wing nut

International car registration letters	**Country**
A	Austria
ADN	Yemen
AFG	Afghanistan
AL	Albania
AND	Andorra
AUS	Australia
B	Belgium
BD	Bangladesh
BDS	Barbados
BG	Bulgaria
BH	Belize
BR	Brazil
BRN	Bahrain
BRU	Brunei
BS	Bahamas
BUR	Myanmar
C	Cuba
CDN	Canada
CH	Switzerland
CI	Côte d'Ivoire
CL	Sri Lanka
CO	Colombia
CR	Costa Rica
CY	Cyprus
CZ	Czech Republic
D	Germany
DK	Denmark
DOM	Dominican Republic
DY	Benin
DZ	Algeria
E	Spain
EAK	Kenya
EAT	Tanzania
EAU	Uganda
EC	Ecuador
ES	El Salvador
ET	Egypt
ETH	Ethiopia
EW	Estonia
F	France
FIN	Finland
FJI	Fiji
FL	Liechtenstein
FR	Faeroe Islands
GB	United Kingdom
GBA	Alderney
GBG	Guernsey
GBJ	Jersey
GBM	Isle of Man
GBZ	Gibraltar
GCA	Guatemala
GH	Ghana
GR	Greece
GUY	Guyana
H	Hungary
HK	Hong Kong
HKJ	Jordan
HR	Croatia
I	Italy
IL	Israel
IND	India
IR	Iran
IRL	Republic of Ireland
IRQ	Iraq
IS	Iceland
J	Japan
JA	Jamaica
K	Cambodia
KWT	Kuwait
L	Luxembourg
LAO	Laos
LAR	Libya
LB	Liberia
LS	Lesotho
LT	Lithuania
LV	Latvia
M	Malta
MA	Morocco
MAL	Malaysia
MC	Monaco
MEX	Mexico
MS	Mauritius
MW	Malawi
N	Norway
NA	Netherlands Antilles
NIC	Nicaragua
NL	Netherlands
NZ	New Zealand
OMAN	Oman
P	Portugal
PA	Panama
PE	Peru
PK	Pakistan
PL	Poland

PNG	Papua New Guinea
PY	Paraguay
RA	Argentina
RB	Botswana
RC	Taiwan
RCA	Central African Re~ public
RCB	Congo Republic
RCH	Chile
RH	Haiti
RI	Indonesia
RIM	Mauritania
RL	Lebanon
RM	Madagascar
RMM	Mali
RO	Romania
ROK	South Korea
ROU	Uruguay
RP	Philippines
RSM	San Marino
RU	Burundi
RUS	Russian Federation
RWA	Rwanda
S	Sweden
SD	Swaziland
SGP	Singapore
SK	Slovakia
SME	Surinam
SN	Senegal
SWA	Namibia
SY	Seychelles
SYR	Syria
T	Thailand
TG	Togo
TN	Tunisia
TR	Turkey
TT	Trindad and Tobago
USA	United States of America
V	Vatican City
VN	Vietnam
WAG	Gambia
WAL	Sierra Leone
WAN	Nigeria
WD	Dominica
WG	Grenada
WL	St. Lucia
WS	Western Samoa
WV	St. Vincent and the Grenadines
YU	Yugoslavia
YV	Venezuela
Z	Zambia
ZA	South Africa
ZRE	Zaire
ZW	Zimbabwe

carafe decanter, flagon, flask, jug, pitcher

carcass body, cadaver (*Medical*), corpse, corse (*archaic*), dead body, framework, hulk, re~ mains, shell, skeleton

cardinal capital, central, chief, essential, first, foremost, fundamental, greatest, highest, im~ portant, key, leading, main, paramount, pre-eminent, primary, prime, principal
Antonyms dispensable, inessential, least im~ portant, lowest, secondary, subordinate

care **1**. affliction, anxiety, burden, concern, dis~ quiet, hardship, interest, perplexity, pressure, responsibility, solicitude, stress, tribulation, trouble, vexation, woe, worry **2**. attention, carefulness, caution, circumspection, consid~ eration, direction, forethought, heed, manage~ ment, meticulousness, pains, prudence, re~ gard, vigilance, watchfulness **3**. charge, con~ trol, custody, guardianship, keeping, manage~ ment, ministration, protection, supervision, ward
Antonyms (*sense 1*) pleasure, relaxation (*sense 2*) abandon, carelessness, heedlessness, inattention, indifference, laxity, laxness, ne~ glect, negligence, unconcern

What is this life if, full of care,
We have no time to stand and stare?
W.H. Davies *Leisure*

career *noun* **1**. calling, employment, life's work, livelihood, occupation, pursuit, vocation **2**. course, passage, path, procedure, progress, race, walk *~verb* **3**. barrel (along) (*informal, chiefly U.S. & Canad.*), bolt, burn rubber (*in~ formal*), dash, hurtle, race, rush, speed, tear

care for **1**. attend, foster, look after, mind, minister to, nurse, protect, provide for, tend, watch over **2**. be fond of, desire, enjoy, find congenial, like, love, prize, take to, want

carefree airy, blithe, breezy, buoyant, careless, cheerful, cheery, chirpy (*informal*), easy-going, halcyon, happy, happy-go-lucky, insouciant, jaunty, light-hearted, lightsome (*archaic*), ra~ diant, sunny, untroubled
Antonyms blue, careworn, cheerless, dejected, depressed, desolate, despondent, down, down in the dumps (*informal*), gloomy, low, melan~ choly, miserable, sad, unhappy, worried

careful **1**. accurate, attentive, cautious, chary, circumspect, conscientious, discreet, fastidious, heedful, painstaking, precise, prudent, punc~ tilious, scrupulous, thoughtful, thrifty **2**. alert, concerned, judicious, mindful, particular, pro~ tective, solicitous, vigilant, wary, watchful
Antonyms abandoned, careless, casual, inac~ curate, inattentive, inexact, neglectful, negli~ gent, reckless, remiss, slovenly, thoughtless, unconcerned, untroubled

Softly, softly, catchee monkey

careless **1**. absent-minded, cursory, forgetful, hasty, heedless, incautious, inconsiderate, in~ discreet, negligent, perfunctory, regardless, remiss, thoughtless, unconcerned, unguarded, unmindful, unthinking **2**. inaccurate, irre~

sponsible, lackadaisical, neglectful, offhand, slapdash, slipshod, sloppy (*informal*) **3.** artless, casual, nonchalant, unstudied
Antonyms accurate, alert, anxious, attentive, careful, cautious, concerned, correct, neat, on the ball (*informal*), orderly, painstaking, tidy, wary, watchful

carelessness inaccuracy, inattention, inconsiderateness, indiscretion, irresponsibility, laxity, laxness, neglect, negligence, omission, remissness, slackness, sloppiness (*informal*), thoughtlessness

To lose one parent, Mr. Worthing, may be regarded as a misfortune; to lose both looks like carelessnesss
Oscar Wilde *The Importance of Being Earnest*

Don't throw out the baby with the bathwater

caress 1. *verb* cuddle, embrace, fondle, hug, kiss, neck (*informal*), nuzzle, pet, stroke **2.** *noun* cuddle, embrace, fondling, hug, kiss, pat, stroke

caretaker 1. *noun* concierge, curator, custodian, janitor, keeper, porter, superintendent, warden, watchman **2.** *adjective* holding, interim, short-term, temporary

careworn heavy-laden, overburdened

cargo baggage, consignment, contents, freight, goods, lading, load, merchandise, shipment, tonnage, ware

caricature 1. *noun* burlesque, cartoon, distortion, farce, lampoon, mimicry, parody, pasquinade, satire, send-up (*Brit. informal*), takeoff (*informal*), travesty **2.** *verb* burlesque, distort, lampoon, mimic, mock, parody, ridicule, satirize, send up (*Brit. informal*), take off (*informal*)

caring compassionate, considerate, kindly, loving, receptive, responsive, sensitive, soft, softhearted, sympathetic, tender, tenderhearted, touchy-feely (*informal*), warm, warmhearted

carnage blood bath, bloodshed, butchery, havoc, holocaust, massacre, mass murder, murder, shambles, slaughter

carnal 1. amorous, animal, erotic, fleshly, impure, lascivious, lecherous, lewd, libidinous, licentious, lustful, prurient, randy (*informal, chiefly Brit.*), raunchy (*slang*), salacious, sensual, sensuous, sexual, sexy (*informal*), steamy (*informal*), unchaste, voluptuous, wanton **2.** bodily, corporeal, earthly, human, mundane, natural, physical, profane, secular, sublunary, temporal, unregenerate, unspiritual, worldly

carnality bestiality, corporeality, fleshliness, lechery, lust, lustfulness, prurience, salaciousness, sensuality, voluptuousness, worldliness

carnival celebration, fair, festival, fête, fiesta, gala, holiday, jamboree, jubilee, Mardi Gras, merrymaking, revelry

carol canticle, canzonet, chorus, ditty, hymn, lay, noel, song, strain

carouse bend the elbow (*informal*), bevvy (*dialect*), booze (*informal*), drink, imbibe, make merry, quaff, roister, wassail

carp beef (*slang*), cavil, censure, complain, criticize, find fault, hypercriticize, knock (*informal*), kvetch (*U.S. slang*), nag, pick holes, quibble, reproach
Antonyms admire, applaud, approve, commend, compliment, extol, laud (*literary*), pay tribute to, praise, sing the praises of, speak highly of

carpenter cabinet-maker, joiner, woodworker

carpet

Types of carpet and rug

Aubusson	Kidderminster
Axminster	kilim
broadloom	Kirman
Brussels carpet	numdah
Bukhara rug	Persian carpet *or* Persian rug
chenille	Turkey carpet
durrie	Wilton
flat-woven	
ingrain	

carping captious, cavilling, critical, fault-finding, grouchy (*informal*), hard to please, hypercritical, nagging, nit-picking (*informal*), on someone's back (*informal*), picky (*informal*), reproachful

carriage 1. carrying, conveyance, conveying, delivery, freight, transport, transportation **2.** cab, coach, conveyance, vehicle **3.** *figurative* air, bearing, behaviour, comportment, conduct, demeanour, deportment, gait, manner, mien, posture, presence

carry 1. bear, bring, conduct, convey, fetch, haul, hump (*Brit. slang*), lift, lug, move, relay, take, tote (*informal*), transfer, transmit, transport **2.** accomplish, capture, effect, gain, secure, win **3.** drive, impel, influence, motivate, spur, urge **4.** bear, bolster, hold up, maintain, shoulder, stand, suffer, support, sustain, underpin, uphold **5.** broadcast, communicate, display, disseminate, give, offer, publish, release, stock

carry on 1. continue, endure, keep going, last, maintain, perpetuate, persevere, persist **2.** administer, manage, operate, run **3.** *informal* create (*slang*), make a fuss, misbehave, raise Cain

carry-on commotion, disturbance, fracas, fuss, hubbub, racket, rumpus, shindy (*informal*), tumult

carry out accomplish, achieve, carry through, consummate, discharge, effect, execute, fulfil, implement, perform, realize

carton box, case, container, pack, package, packet

cartoon animated cartoon, animated film, animation, caricature, comic strip, lampoon, parody, satire, sketch, takeoff (*informal*)

cartridge **1.** capsule, case, cassette, container, cylinder, magazine **2.** charge, round, shell

carve chip, chisel, cut, divide, engrave, etch, fashion, form, grave (*archaic*), hack, hew, incise, indent, inscribe, mould, sculpt, sculpture, slash, slice, whittle

carving engraving, etching, inscription, sculpture
Related adjective: glyptic

cascade **1.** *noun* avalanche, cataract, deluge, downpour, falls, flood, fountain, outpouring, shower, torrent, waterfall **2.** *verb* descend, flood, gush, overflow, pitch, plunge, pour, spill, surge, teem, tumble

case **1.** box, cabinet, canister, capsule, carton, cartridge, casket, chest, compact, container, crate, holder, receptacle, suitcase, tray, trunk **2.** capsule, casing, cover, covering, envelope, folder, integument, jacket, sheath, shell, wrapper, wrapping **3.** circumstance(s), condition, context, contingency, dilemma, event, plight, position, predicament, situation, state **4.** example, illustration, instance, occasion, occurrence, specimen **5.** *Law* action, cause, dispute, lawsuit, proceedings, process, suit, trial

cash ackers (*slang*), banknotes, brass (*Northern English dialect*), bread (*slang*), bullion, change, coin, coinage, currency, dibs (*slang*), dosh (*Brit. & Austral. slang*), dough (*slang*), funds, money, necessary (*informal*), needful (*informal*), notes, payment, ready (*informal*), ready money, resources, rhino (*Brit. slang*), shekels (*informal*), silver, specie, spondulicks (*slang*), tin (*slang*), wherewithal

cashier **1.** *noun* accountant, bank clerk, banker, bursar, clerk, purser, teller, treasurer **2.** *verb* break, cast off, discard, discharge, dismiss, drum out, expel, give the boot to (*slang*)

casing cover, covering, integument, shell

cask barrel, cylinder, drum

casket ark (*dialect*), box, case, chest, coffer, jewel box, kist (*Scot. & Northern English dialect*)

cast *verb* **1.** chuck (*informal*), drive, drop, fling, hurl, impel, launch, lob, pitch, project, shed, shy, sling, throw, thrust, toss **2.** bestow, deposit, diffuse, distribute, emit, give, radiate, scatter, shed, spread **3.** allot, appoint, assign, choose, name, pick, select **4.** add, calculate, compute, figure, forecast, reckon, total **5.** form, found, model, mould, set, shape *~noun* **6.** fling, lob, throw, thrust, toss **7.** air, appearance, complexion, demeanour, look, manner, mien, semblance, shade, stamp, style, tinge, tone, turn **8.** actors, characters, company, dramatis personae, players, troupe

cast down deject, depress, desolate, discourage, dishearten, dispirit

caste class, estate, grade, lineage, order, race, rank, social order, species, station, status, stratum

castigate bawl out (*informal*), beat, berate, blast, cane, carpet (*informal*), censure, chasten, chastise, chew out (*U.S. & Canad. informal*), correct, criticize, discipline, dress down (*informal*), excoriate, flail, flay, flog, give a rocket (*Brit. & N.Z. informal*), haul over the coals (*informal*), lambast(e), lash, put down, rap over the knuckles, read the riot act, rebuke, reprimand, scold, scourge, slap on the wrist, slate (*informal, chiefly Brit.*), tear into (*informal*), tear (someone) off a strip (*Brit. informal*), whip

castigation bawling-out (*informal*), beating, blast, caning, censure, chastisement, condemnation, correction, criticism, discipline, dressing down (*informal*), excoriation, flogging, fustigation (*archaic*), put-down, whipping

castle chateau, citadel, donjon, fastness, fortress, keep, mansion, palace, peel, stronghold, tower

castrate emasculate, geld, neuter, unman

casual **1.** accidental, chance, contingent, fortuitous, hit-and-miss *or* hit-or-miss (*informal*), incidental, irregular, occasional, random, serendipitous, uncertain, unexpected, unforeseen, unintentional, unpremeditated **2.** apathetic, blasé, cursory, indifferent, informal, insouciant, lackadaisical, nonchalant, offhand, perfunctory, relaxed, unconcerned **3.** informal, non-dressy, sporty
Antonyms (*sense 1*) arranged, deliberate, expected, fixed, foreseen, intentional, planned, premeditated (*sense 2*) committed, concerned, direct, enthusiastic, passionate, serious, systematic (*sense 3*) ceremonial, dressy, formal

casualties dead, fatalities, losses, missing, wounded

casualty **1.** loss, sufferer, victim **2.** accident, calamity, catastrophe, chance, contingency, disaster, misadventure, misfortune, mishap

casuistry chicanery, equivocation, oversubtleness, sophism, sophistry, speciousness

cat feline, gib, grimalkin, kitty, malkin (*archaic*), moggy (*slang*), mouser, puss (*informal*), pussy (*informal*), tabby
Related adjective: feline

Breeds of cat

Abyssinian	Himalayan
Angora	Havana
Burmese	Maine coon
colourpoint *or (U.S.)*	Manx

Persian
Rex
Russian blue
Siamese
tabby
tortoiseshell
Turkish

cat: a soft, indestructible automaton provided by nature to be kicked when things go wrong in the domestic circle
Ambrose Bierce *The Devil's Dictionary*

When I play with my cat, who knows whether she isn't amusing herself with me more than I am with her?
Montaigne *Essais*

When the cat's away, the mice will play

The cat would eat fish, but would not wet her feet

All cats are grey in the dark

cataclysm calamity, catastrophe, collapse, convulsion, debacle, disaster, upheaval

cataclysmic calamitous, catastrophic, convulsionary, disastrous

catacomb crypt, ossuary, tomb, vault

catalogue 1. *noun* directory, gazetteer, index, inventory, list, record, register, roll, roster, schedule 2. *verb* accession, alphabetize, classify, file, index, inventory, list, register, tabulate

catapult 1. *noun* ballista, sling, slingshot (*U.S.*), trebuchet 2. *verb* heave, hurl, hurtle, pitch, plunge, propel, shoot, toss

cataract 1. cascade, deluge, downpour, falls, Niagara, rapids, torrent, waterfall 2. *Medical* opacity (*of the eye*)

catastrophe 1. adversity, affliction, blow, bummer (*slang*), calamity, cataclysm, deep water, devastation, disaster, failure, fiasco, ill, meltdown (*informal*), mischance, misfortune, mishap, reverse, tragedy, trial, trouble, whammy (*informal, chiefly U.S.*) 2. conclusion, culmination, curtain, debacle, dénouement, end, finale, termination, upshot, winding-up

catastrophic calamitous, cataclysmic, devastating, disastrous, tragic

catcall 1. *verb* boo, deride, gibe, give the bird to (*informal*), hiss, jeer, whistle 2. *noun* boo, gibe, hiss, jeer, raspberry, whistle

catch *verb* 1. apprehend, arrest, capture, clutch, ensnare, entangle, entrap, feel one's collar (*slang*), get, grab, grasp, grip, lay hold of, lift (*slang*), nab (*informal*), nail (*informal*), seize, snare, snatch, take 2. catch in the act, detect, discover, expose, find out, surprise, take unawares, unmask 3. bewitch, captivate, charm, delight, enchant, enrapture, fascinate 4. contract, develop, get, go down with, incur, succumb to, suffer from 5. apprehend, discern, feel, follow, get, grasp, hear, perceive, recognize, sense, take in, twig (*Brit. informal*) ~*noun* 6. bolt, clasp, clip, fastener, hasp, hook, hook and eye, latch, sneck (*dialect, chiefly Scot. & N. English*), snib (*Scot.*) 7. disadvantage, drawback, fly in the ointment, hitch, snag, stumbling block, trap, trick
Antonyms *verb* (*sense 1*) drop, free, give up, liberate, loose, release (*sense 3*) alienate, bore, disenchant, disgust, fail to interest, repel (*sense 4*) avert, avoid, escape, ward off ~*noun* (*sense 7*) advantage, benefit, bonus, boon, reward

catching 1. communicable, contagious, infectious, infective, transferable, transmittable 2. attractive, captivating, charming, enchanting, fascinating, fetching, taking, winning
Antonyms (*sense 1*) incommunicable, non-catching, non-contagious, non-infectious, non-transmittable

catch on comprehend, find out, get the picture, grasp, see, see the light of day, see through, twig (*Brit. informal*), understand

catchword byword, motto, password, refrain, slogan, watchword

catchy captivating, haunting, memorable, popular

catechize cross-examine, drill, examine, grill (*informal*), interrogate, question

catechumen convert, disciple, initiate, learner, neophyte, novice, probationer, tyro

categorical absolute, direct, downright, emphatic, explicit, express, positive, unambiguous, unconditional, unequivocal, unqualified, unreserved
Antonyms conditional, hesitant, indefinite, qualified, questionable, uncertain, vague

category class, classification, department, division, grade, grouping, head, heading, list, order, rank, section, sort, type

cater furnish, outfit, provide, provision, purvey, supply, victual

cater to coddle, fawn on, feed, gratify, humour, indulge, minister to, mollycoddle, pamper, pander to, spoil

caterwaul bawl, howl, scream, screech, shriek, squall, wail, yowl

caterwauling bawling, howling, screaming, screeching, shrieking, squalling, wailing, yowling

catharsis abreaction, cleansing, lustration, purgation, purging, purification, release

catholic all-embracing, all-inclusive, broad-minded, charitable, comprehensive, eclectic, ecumenical, general, global, liberal, tolerant, unbigoted, universal, unsectarian, whole, wide, world-wide
Antonyms bigoted, exclusive, illiberal, limited, narrow-minded, parochial, sectarian

catnap 1. *verb* doze, drowse, kip (*Brit. slang*), nap, snooze, take forty winks (*informal*) 2.

noun doze, forty winks (*informal*), kip (*Brit. slang*), nap, siesta, sleep, snooze

cattiness bitchiness (*informal*), ill-naturedness, malevolence, maliciousness, meanness, rancorousness, shrewishness, snideness, spitefulness, venomousness, virulence

cattle beasts, bovines, cows, kine (*archaic*), livestock, neat (*archaic*), stock
Related adjective: bovine

Breeds of cattle

Aberdeen Angus	Highland
Africander	Holstein
Alderney	Illawarra
Ayrshire	Jersey
Blonde d'Aquitaine	Kerry
Brown Swiss	kyloe
Belted Galloway	Limousin
cattalo *or* catalo	longhorn
Charolais *or* Charollais	Meuse-Rhine-Ijssel
Devon	Normandy
dexter	Norwegian Red
Durham	Red Poll *or* Red Polled
Friesian	Santa Gertrudis
Galloway	shorthorn
Gelbvieh	Simmental
Guernsey	Sussex
Hereford	Texas longhorn

The cow is of the bovine ilk;
One end is moo, the other, milk
Ogden Nash *The Cow*

catty backbiting, bitchy (*informal*), ill-natured, malevolent, malicious, mean, rancorous, shrewish, snide, spiteful, venomous
Antonyms benevolent, charitable, compassionate, considerate, generous, kind, pleasant

caucus assembly, conclave, congress, convention, get-together (*informal*), meeting, parley, session

cause *noun* **1.** agent, beginning, creator, genesis, mainspring, maker, origin, originator, prime mover, producer, root, source, spring **2.** account, agency, aim, basis, consideration, end, grounds, incentive, inducement, motivation, motive, object, purpose, reason, the why and wherefore **3.** attempt, belief, conviction, enterprise, ideal, movement, purpose, undertaking *~verb* **4.** begin, bring about, compel, create, effect, engender, generate, give rise to, incite, induce, lead to, motivate, occasion, precipitate, produce, provoke, result in
Antonyms *noun* consequence, effect, end, outcome, result *~verb* deter, foil, inhibit, prevent, stop

caustic **1.** acrid, astringent, biting, burning, corroding, corrosive, keen, mordant, vitriolic **2.** acrimonious, cutting, mordacious, pungent, sarcastic, scathing, severe, stinging, trenchant, virulent, vitriolic
Antonyms agreeable, bland, gentle, healing, kind, loving, mild, pleasant, pleasing, soft, soothing, sweet, temperate

caution *noun* **1.** alertness, belt and braces, care, carefulness, circumspection, deliberation, discretion, forethought, heed, heedfulness, prudence, vigilance, watchfulness **2.** admonition, advice, counsel, injunction, warning *~verb* **3.** admonish, advise, tip off, urge, warn
Antonyms *noun* carelessness, daring, imprudence, rashness, recklessness *~verb* dare

You should know a man seven years before you stir his fire

Once bitten, twice shy

cautious alert, belt-and-braces, cagey (*informal*), careful, chary, circumspect, discreet, guarded, heedful, judicious, keeping a weather eye on, on one's toes, prudent, tentative, vigilant, wary, watchful
Antonyms adventurous, bold, careless, daring, foolhardy, heedless, impetuous, inattentive, incautious, indiscreet, madcap, rash, reckless, unguarded, unheedful, venturesome, venturous

cautiously alertly, cagily (*informal*), carefully, circumspectly, discreetly, guardedly, heedfully, judiciously, mindfully, prudently, tentatively, vigilantly, warily, watchfully

cavalcade array, march-past, parade, procession, spectacle, train

cavalier *noun* **1.** chevalier, equestrian, horseman, knight, royalist **2.** beau, blade (*archaic*), escort, gallant, gentleman *~adjective* **3.** arrogant, condescending, curt, disdainful, haughty, insolent, lofty, lordly, offhand, scornful, supercilious

cavalry horse, horsemen, mounted troops
Antonyms foot soldiers, infantrymen

cave cavern, cavity, den, grotto, hollow

caveat admonition, caution, warning

cavern cave, hollow, pothole

cavernous **1.** concave, deep-set, hollow, sunken, yawning **2.** echoing, resonant, reverberant, sepulchral

cavil beef (*slang*), carp, censure, complain, find fault, hypercriticize, kvetch (*U.S. slang*), object, quibble

cavilling captious, carping, censorious, critical, fault-finding, hypercritical, nit-picking (*informal*), quibbling

cavity crater, dent, gap, hole, hollow, pit

cavort caper, caracole, frisk, frolic, gambol, prance, romp, sport

cease belay (*Nautical*), break off, bring *or* come to an end, conclude, culminate, desist, die away, discontinue, end, fail, finish, halt, leave off, refrain, stay, stop, terminate

Antonyms begin, commence, continue, initiate, start

ceaseless constant, continual, continuous, endless, eternal, everlasting, incessant, indefatigable, interminable, never-ending, nonstop, perennial, perpetual, unending, unremitting, untiring
Antonyms broken, erratic, intermittent, irregular, occasional, periodic, spasmodic, sporadic

cede abandon, abdicate, allow, concede, convey, grant, hand over, make over, relinquish, renounce, resign, step down (*informal*), surrender, transfer, yield

celebrate bless, commemorate, commend, crack up (*informal*), drink to, eulogize, exalt, extol, glorify, honour, keep, kill the fatted calf, laud, observe, perform, praise, proclaim, publicize, put the flags out, rejoice, reverence, solemnize, toast

celebrated acclaimed, distinguished, eminent, famed, famous, glorious, illustrious, lionized, notable, outstanding, popular, pre-eminent, prominent, renowned, revered, well-known
Antonyms dishonoured, forgotten, insignificant, obscure, trivial, unacclaimed, undistinguished, unknown, unnotable, unpopular

celebration **1.** beano (*Brit. slang*), carousal, -fest (*in combination*), festival, festivity, gala, hooley *or* hoolie (*chiefly Irish & N.Z.*), jollification, jubilee, junketing, merrymaking, party, rave (*Brit. slang*), rave-up (*Brit. slang*), red-letter day, revelry **2.** anniversary, commemoration, honouring, observance, performance, remembrance, solemnization

celebrity **1.** big name, big shot (*informal*), bigwig (*informal*), celeb (*informal*), dignitary, lion, luminary, megastar (*informal*), name, personage, personality, star, superstar, V.I.P. **2.** distinction, éclat, eminence, fame, glory, honour, notability, popularity, pre-eminence, prestige, prominence, renown, reputation, repute, stardom
Antonyms has-been, nobody, obscurity, unknown

The celebrity is a person who is known for his well-knownness
Daniel Boorstin *The Image*

celerity dispatch, expedition, fleetness, haste, promptness, quickness, rapidity, speed, swiftness, velocity, vivacity

celestial angelic, astral, divine, elysian, empyrean (*poetic*), eternal, ethereal, godlike, heavenly, immortal, seraphic, spiritual, sublime, supernatural

celibacy chastity, continence, purity, singleness, virginity

Marriage has many pains, but celibacy has no pleasures
Dr. Johnson *Rasselas*

Marriage may often be a stormy lake, but celibacy is almost always a muddy horsepond
Thomas Love Peacock *Melincourt*

cell **1.** cavity, chamber, compartment, cubicle, dungeon, stall **2.** caucus, coterie, group, nucleus, unit

cement **1.** *verb* attach, bind, bond, cohere, combine, glue, gum, join, plaster, seal, solder, stick together, unite, weld **2.** *noun* adhesive, binder, glue, gum, paste, plaster, sealant

cemetery burial ground, churchyard, God's acre, graveyard, necropolis

censor blue-pencil, bowdlerize, cut, expurgate

censorious captious, carping, cavilling, condemnatory, disapproving, disparaging, fault-finding, hypercritical, scathing, severe

censorship blue pencil, bowdlerization *or* bowdlerisation, expurgation, purgation, sanitization *or* sanitisation

God forbid that any book should be banned. The practice is as indefensible as infanticide
Rebecca West *The Strange Necessity*

Wherever books are burned, in the end people too will be burned
Heinrich Heine *Almansor*

Is it a book you would even wish your wife or your servants to read?
Mervyn Griffith-Jones (of D.H. Lawrence's "Lady Chatterley's Lover")

censurable at fault, blamable, blameworthy, chargeable, contemptible, culpable, faulty, guilty, reprehensible, scandalous

censure **1.** *verb* abuse, bawl out (*informal*), berate, blame, blast, carpet (*informal*), castigate, chew out (*U.S. & Canad. informal*), chide, condemn, criticize, denounce, excoriate, give (someone) a rocket (*Brit. & N.Z. informal*), lambast(e), put down, rap over the knuckles, read the riot act, rebuke, reprehend, reprimand, reproach, reprove, scold, slap on the wrist, slate (*informal, chiefly U.S.*), tear into (*informal*), tear (someone) off a strip (*Brit. informal*), upbraid **2.** *noun* blame, castigation, condemnation, criticism, disapproval, dressing down (*informal*), obloquy, rebuke, remonstrance, reprehension, reprimand, reproach, reproof, stick (*slang*), stricture
Antonyms *verb* applaud, commend, compliment, laud (*literary*) ~*noun* approval, commendation, compliment, encouragement

central chief, essential, focal, fundamental, inner, interior, key, main, mean, median, mid, middle, primary, principal
Antonyms exterior, minor, outer, outermost, secondary, subordinate, subsidiary

centralize amalgamate, compact, concentrate, concentre, condense, converge, incorporate, rationalize, streamline, unify

centre 1. *noun* bull's-eye, core, crux, focus, heart, hub, kernel, mid (*archaic*), middle, midpoint, nucleus, pivot 2. *verb* cluster, con~ centrate, converge, focus, revolve
Antonyms *noun* border, boundary, brim, cir~ cumference, edge, fringe, limit, lip, margin, perimeter, periphery, rim ~*verb* bestrew, dif~ fuse, disseminate, fling, scatter, spread, sprinkle, strew, toss

centrepiece cynosure, epergne, focus, high~ light, hub, star

centrifugal diffusive, divergent, diverging, ef~ ferent, radial, radiating

ceremonial 1. *adjective* formal, liturgical, ritu~ al, ritualistic, solemn, stately 2. *noun* ceremo~ ny, formality, rite, ritual, solemnity
Antonyms casual, informal, relaxed, simple

ceremonious civil, courteous, courtly, deferen~ tial, dignified, exact, formal, precise, punctili~ ous, ritual, solemn, starchy (*informal*), stately, stiff

ceremony 1. commemoration, function, obser~ vance, parade, rite, ritual, service, show, so~ lemnities 2. ceremonial, decorum, etiquette, form, formal courtesy, formality, niceties, pomp, propriety, protocol

certain 1. assured, confident, convinced, posi~ tive, satisfied, sure 2. ascertained, conclusive, incontrovertible, indubitable, irrefutable, known, plain, true, undeniable, undoubted, unequivocal, unmistakable, valid 3. bound, definite, destined, fated, ineluctable, inescap~ able, inevitable, inexorable, sure 4. decided, definite, established, fixed, settled 5. assured, constant, dependable, reliable, stable, staunch, steady, trustworthy, unfailing, un~ questionable 6. express, individual, particular, precise, special, specific
Antonyms disputable, doubtful, dubious, equivocal, fallible, indefinite, questionable, uncertain, unconvinced, undecided, unlikely, unreliable, unsettled, unsure

certainly absolutely, assuredly, come hell or high water, decidedly, definitely, doubtlessly, indisputably, indubitably, irrefutably, posi~ tively, surely, truly, undeniably, undoubtedly, unequivocally, unquestionably, without doubt, without question

certainty 1. assurance, authoritativeness, cer~ titude, confidence, conviction, faith, indubi~ tableness, inevitability, positiveness, sureness, trust, validity 2. fact, reality, sure thing (*in~ formal*), surety, truth
Antonyms disbelief, doubt, indecision, qualm, scepticism, uncertainty, unsureness

In this world nothing is certain but death and taxes
Benjamin Franklin

If a man will begin with certainties, he shall end in doubts; but if he will be content to begin with doubts, he shall end in certainties
Francis Bacon *The Advancement of Learning*

certificate authorization, credential(s), diplo~ ma, document, licence, testimonial, voucher, warrant

certify ascertain, assure, attest, authenticate, aver, avow, confirm, corroborate, declare, en~ dorse, guarantee, notify, show, testify, vali~ date, verify, vouch, witness

certitude assurance, certainty, confidence, con~ viction

cessation abeyance, arrest, break, ceasing, discontinuance, ending, entr'acte, halt, halt~ ing, hiatus, intermission, interruption, inter~ val, let-up (*informal*), pause, recess, remis~ sion, respite, rest, standstill, stay, stoppage, suspension, termination, time off

cession abandonment, abnegation, capitula~ tion, ceding, conceding, concession, convey~ ance, grant, relinquishment, renunciation, surrender, yielding

chafe abrade, anger, annoy, exasperate, fret, fume, gall, get *or* take a rise out of, get on someone's nerves, get on someone's wick (*Brit. slang*), grate, incense, inflame, irritate, nark (*Brit., Austral., & N.Z. slang*), offend, pro~ voke, rage, rasp, rub, rub (someone) up the wrong way (*informal*), ruffle, scrape, scratch, vex, worry
Antonyms allay, alleviate, appease, assuage, calm, conciliate, mollify, pacify, placate, please, soothe

chaff *noun* 1. dregs, glumes, hulls, husks, ref~ use, remains, rubbish, trash, waste 2. badi~ nage, banter, joking, josh (*slang, chiefly U.S. & Canad.*), persiflage, raillery, teasing ~*verb* 3. banter, deride, jeer, josh (*slang, chiefly U.S. & Canad.*), mock, rib (*informal*), ridicule, scoff, take the piss out of (*taboo slang*), taunt, tease

chagrin 1. *noun* annoyance, discomfiture, discom~ posure, displeasure, disquiet, dissatisfaction, embarrassment, fretfulness, humiliation, ill-humour, irritation, mortification, peevishness, spleen, vexation 2. *verb* annoy, discomfit, dis~ compose, displease, disquiet, dissatisfy, embar~ rass, humiliate, irk, irritate, mortify, peeve, vex

chain *verb* 1. bind, confine, enslave, fetter, gyve (*archaic*), handcuff, manacle, restrain, shack~ le, tether, trammel, unite ~*noun* 2. bond, cou~ pling, fetter, link, manacle, shackle, union 3. concatenation, progression, sequence, series, set, string, succession, train

chairman chairperson, chairwoman, director, master of ceremonies, president, presider, speaker, spokesman, toastmaster

chalk up accumulate, achieve, attain, credit, enter, gain, log, mark, record, register, score, tally, win

challenge **1.** *verb* accost, arouse, beard, brave, call out, call (someone's) bluff, claim, confront, dare, defy, demand, dispute, face off (*slang*), impugn, investigate, object to, provoke, question, require, stimulate, summon, tackle, tax, test, throw down the gauntlet, try **2.** *noun* confrontation, dare, defiance, face-off (*slang*), interrogation, provocation, question, summons to contest, test, trial, ultimatum

chamber **1.** apartment, bedroom, cavity, compartment, cubicle, enclosure, hall, hollow, room **2.** assembly, council, legislative body, legislature

champion **1.** *noun* backer, challenger, conqueror, defender, guardian, hero, nonpareil, patron, protector, title holder, upholder, victor, vindicator, warrior, winner **2.** *verb* advocate, back, commend, defend, encourage, espouse, fight for, promote, stick up for (*informal*), support, uphold

chance *noun* **1.** liability, likelihood, occasion, odds, opening, opportunity, possibility, probability, prospect, scope, time, window **2.** accident, casualty, coincidence, contingency, destiny, fate, fortuity, fortune, luck, misfortune, peril, providence **3.** gamble, hazard, jeopardy, risk, speculation, uncertainty *~verb* **4.** befall, betide, come about, come to pass, fall out, happen, occur **5.** endanger, gamble, go out on a limb, hazard, jeopardize, risk, skate on thin ice, stake, try, venture, wager *~adjective* **6.** accidental, casual, contingent, fortuitous, inadvertent, incidental, random, serendipitous, unforeseeable, unforeseen, unintentional, unlooked-for

Antonyms *noun* certainty, design, impossibility, improbability, intention, surety, unlikelihood *~adjective* arranged, deliberate, designed, expected, foreseen, intentional, planned

chancy dangerous, dicey (*informal, chiefly Brit.*), dodgy (*Brit., Austral., & N.Z. slang*), hazardous, perilous, problematical, risky, speculative, uncertain

Antonyms certain, reliable, safe, secure, sound, stable, sure

change *verb* **1.** alter, convert, diversify, fluctuate, metamorphose, moderate, modify, mutate, reform, remodel, reorganize, restyle, shift, transform, transmute, vacillate, vary, veer **2.** alternate, barter, convert, displace, exchange, interchange, remove, replace, substitute, swap (*informal*), trade, transmit *~noun* **3.** alteration, difference, innovation, metamorphosis, modification, mutation, permutation, revolution, transformation, transition, transmutation, vicissitude **4.** conversion, exchange, interchange, substitution, trade **5.** break (*informal*), departure, diversion, novelty, variation, variety, whole new ball game (*informal*)

Antonyms *verb* hold, keep, remain, stay *~noun* constancy, invariability, monotony, permanence, stability, uniformity

A state without the means of some change is without the means of its conservation
Edmund Burke *Reflections on the Revolution in France*

Can the Ethiopian change his skin, or the leopard his spots?
Bible: Jeremiah

The more things change, the more they are the same
Alphonse Karr *Les Guêpes*

Change is not made without inconvenience, even from worse to better
Dr. Johnson *Dictionary of the English Language*

The old order changeth, yielding place to new
Alfred, Lord Tennyson *The Passing of Arthur*

Philosophers have only interpreted the world in various ways; the point, however, is to change it
Karl Marx *Theses on Feuerbach*

When it is not necessary to change, it is necessary not to change
Lucius Cary *Discourses of Infallibility*

Don't change horses in midstream

A change is as good as a rest

A new broom sweeps clean

changeable capricious, changeful, chequered, erratic, fickle, fitful, fluid, inconstant, irregular, kaleidoscopic, labile (*Chemistry*), mercurial, mobile, mutable, protean, shifting, temperamental, uncertain, uneven, unpredictable, unreliable, unsettled, unstable, unsteady, vacillating, variable, versatile, volatile, wavering

Antonyms constant, invariable, irreversible, regular, reliable, stable, steady, unchangeable

changeless abiding, consistent, constant, eternal, everlasting, fixed, immovable, immutable, permanent, perpetual, regular, reliable, resolute, settled, stationary, steadfast, steady, unalterable, unchanging, uniform, unvarying

channel *noun* **1.** canal, chamber, conduit, duct, fluting, furrow, groove, gutter, main, passage, route, strait **2.** *figurative* approach, artery, avenue, course, means, medium, path, route, way *~verb* **3.** conduct, convey, direct, guide, transmit

chant **1.** *noun* carol, chorus, melody, psalm, song **2.** *verb* carol, chorus, croon, descant, intone, recite, sing, warble

chaos anarchy, bedlam, confusion, disorder, disorganization, entropy, lawlessness, pandemonium, tumult
Antonyms neatness, orderliness, organization, tidiness

The whole worl's in a state o' chassis!
Sean O'Casey *Juno and the Paycock*

chaotic anarchic, confused, deranged, disordered, disorganized, lawless, purposeless, rampageous, riotous, topsy-turvy, tumultuous, uncontrolled

chap bloke (*Brit. informal*), character, cove (*slang*), customer (*informal*), dude (*U.S. & Canad. informal*), fellow, guy (*informal*), individual, person, sort, type

chaperon 1. *noun* companion, duenna, escort, governess **2.** *verb* accompany, attend, escort, protect, safeguard, shepherd, watch over

chaplet bouquet, coronal, garland, wreath

chapter clause, division, episode, part, period, phase, section, stage, topic

char carbonize, cauterize, scorch, sear, singe

character 1. attributes, bent, calibre, cast, complexion, constitution, disposition, individuality, kidney, make-up, marked traits, nature, personality, quality, reputation, temper, temperament, type **2.** honour, integrity, rectitude, strength, uprightness **3.** card (*informal*), eccentric, nut (*slang*), oddball (*informal*), odd bod (*informal*), oddity, original, queer fish (*Brit. informal*), wacko *or* whacko (*informal*) **4.** cipher, device, emblem, figure, hieroglyph, letter, logo, mark, rune, sign, symbol, type **5.** part, persona, portrayal, role **6.** fellow, guy (*informal*), individual, person, sort, type

Genius is formed in quiet, character in the stream of human life
Goethe *Torquato Tasso*

Character is much easier kept than recovered
Thomas Paine *The American Crisis*

A man's character is his fate
Heraclitus *On the Universe*

You can tell a lot about a fellow's character by the way he eats jelly beans
Ronald Reagan

Fate and character are the same concept
Novalis *Heinrich von Ofterdingen*

characteristic 1. *adjective* distinctive, distinguishing, idiosyncratic, individual, peculiar, representative, singular, special, specific, symbolic, symptomatic, typical **2.** *noun* attribute, faculty, feature, idiosyncrasy, mark, peculiarity, property, quality, quirk, trait
Antonyms *adjective* rare, uncharacteristic, unrepresentative, unusual

characterize brand, distinguish, identify, indicate, inform, mark, represent, stamp, typify

charade fake, farce, pantomime, parody, pretence, travesty

charge *verb* **1.** accuse, arraign, blame, impeach, incriminate, indict, involve *~noun* **2.** accusation, allegation, imputation, indictment *~verb* **3.** assail, assault, attack, rush, stampede, storm *~noun* **4.** assault, attack, onset, onslaught, rush, sortie, stampede *~verb* **5.** afflict, burden, commit, entrust, tax *~noun* **6.** burden, care, concern, custody, duty, office, responsibility, safekeeping, trust, ward **7.** amount, cost, damage (*informal*), expenditure, expense, outlay, payment, price, rate *~verb* **8.** fill, instil, lade, load, suffuse **9.** bid, command, demand, enjoin, exhort, instruct, order, require *~noun* **10.** canon, command, demand, dictate, direction, exhortation, injunction, instruction, mandate, order, precept
Antonyms *verb* (*sense 1*) absolve, acquit, clear, exonerate, pardon *~noun* (*sense 2*) absolution, acquittal, clearance, exoneration, pardon, reprieve *~verb* (*sense 3*) back off, retreat, withdraw *~noun* (*sense 4*) retreat, withdrawal

charisma allure, attraction, charm, lure, magnetism, personality

charismatic alluring, attractive, charming, enticing, influential, magnetic

charitable 1. beneficent, benevolent, bountiful, eleemosynary, generous, kind, lavish, liberal, philanthropic **2.** broad-minded, considerate, favourable, forgiving, gracious, humane, indulgent, kindly, lenient, magnanimous, sympathetic, tolerant, understanding
Antonyms inconsiderate, mean, stingy, strict, uncharitable, unforgiving, ungenerous, unkind, unsympathetic

charity 1. alms-giving, assistance, benefaction, contributions, donations, endowment, fund, gift, hand-out, largess *or* largesse, philanthropy, relief **2.** affection, Agape, altruism, benevolence, benignity, bountifulness, bounty, compassion, fellow feeling, generosity, goodness, goodwill, humanity, indulgence, love, pity, tenderheartedness
Antonyms (*sense 1*) miserliness, selfishness, stinginess, uncharitableness (*sense 2*) hatred, ill will, intolerance, malice

The living need more charity than the dead
George Arnold *The Jolly Old Pedagogue*

Knowledge puffeth up, but charity edifieth
Bible: 1 Corinthians

Though I speak with the tongues of men and of angels, and have not charity, I am become as sounding brass, or a tinkling cymbal. And though I have the gift of prophecy, and understand all mysteries, and all knowledge; and though I have all faith; so that I could remove mountains; and have

not charity, I am nothing
Bible: 1 Corinthians

Charity sufferreth long, and is kind; charity envieth not; charity vaunteth not itself, is not puffed up... Beareth all things, believeth all things, hopeth all things, endureth all things. Charity never faileth
Bible: 1 Corinthians

Charity shall cover the multitude of sins
Bible: 1 Peter

He gives the poor man twice as much good who gives quickly
Publilius Syrus

Charity begins at home

charlatan cheat, con man (*informal*), fake, fraud, fraudster, grifter (*slang, chiefly U.S. & Canad.*), impostor, mountebank, phoney *or* phony (*informal*), pretender, quack, sham, swindler

charm *verb* **1.** absorb, allure, attract, beguile, bewitch, cajole, captivate, delight, enamour, enchant, enrapture, entrance, fascinate, mesmerize, please, ravish, win, win over ~*noun* **2.** allure, allurement, appeal, attraction, desirability, enchantment, fascination, magic, magnetism, sorcery, spell **3.** amulet, fetish, good-luck piece, lucky piece, periapt (*rare*), talisman, trinket
Antonyms *verb* alienate, repel, repulse ~*noun* (*sense 2*) repulsiveness, unattractiveness

You know what charm is: a way of getting the answer yes without having asked any clear question
Albert Camus *The Fall*

Charm... it's a sort of bloom on a woman. If you have it, you don't need to have anything else; and if you don't have it, it doesn't much matter what else you have
J.M. Barrie *What Every Woman Knows*

charming appealing, attractive, bewitching, captivating, cute, delectable, delightful, engaging, eye-catching, fetching, irresistible, likable *or* likeable, lovely, pleasant, pleasing, seductive, winning, winsome
Antonyms disgusting, horrid, repulsive, unappealing, unattractive, unlikable *or* unlikeable, unpleasant, unpleasing

chart 1. *noun* blueprint, diagram, graph, map, plan, table, tabulation **2.** *verb* delineate, draft, graph, map out, outline, plot, shape, sketch

charter 1. *noun* bond, concession, contract, deed, document, franchise, indenture, licence, permit, prerogative, privilege, right **2.** *verb* authorize, commission, employ, hire, lease, rent, sanction

chary 1. careful, cautious, circumspect, guarded, heedful, leery (*slang*), prudent, reluctant, scrupulous, slow, suspicious, uneasy, wary **2.** careful (*Brit.*), frugal, niggardly, parsimonious, thrifty

chase 1. *verb* course, drive, drive away, expel, follow, hound, hunt, pursue, put to flight, run after, track **2.** *noun* hunt, hunting, pursuit, race, venery (*archaic*)

chasm abyss, alienation, breach, cavity, cleft, crater, crevasse, fissure, gap, gorge, gulf, hiatus, hollow, opening, ravine, rent, rift, split, void

chassis anatomy, bodywork, frame, framework, fuselage, skeleton, substructure

chaste austere, decent, decorous, elegant, immaculate, incorrupt, innocent, modest, moral, neat, pure, quiet, refined, restrained, simple, unaffected, uncontaminated, undefiled, unsullied, vestal, virginal, virtuous, wholesome
Antonyms blemished, corrupt, dirty, dishonourable, gaudy, immoral, impure, married, ornate, promiscuous, self-indulgent, tainted, unchaste, unclean, unrestrained, wanton

chasten afflict, castigate, chastise, correct, cow, curb, discipline, humble, humiliate, put in one's place, repress, soften, subdue, tame

chastise beat, berate, castigate, censure, correct, discipline, flog, lash, lick (*informal*), punish, scold, scourge, upbraid, whip
Antonyms caress, commend, compliment, congratulate, cuddle, embrace, fondle, hug, praise, reward

chastity celibacy, continence, innocence, maidenhood, modesty, purity, virginity, virtue
Antonyms debauchery, immorality, lewdness, licentiousness, profligacy, promiscuity, wantonness

Give me chastity and continence, but not just now
St. Augustine of Hippo *Confessions*

chastity - the most unnatural of all the sexual perversions
Aldous Huxley *Eyeless in Gaza*

I'd the upbringing a nun would envy...Until I was fifteen I was more familiar with Africa than my own body
Joe Orton *Entertaining Mr. Sloane*

'Tis chastity, my brother, chastity;
She that has that, is clad in complete steel
John Milton *Comus*

chat 1. *noun* chatter, chinwag (*Brit. informal*), confab (*informal*), gossip, heart-to-heart, natter, talk, tête-à-tête **2.** *verb* chatter, chew the rag *or* fat (*slang*), gossip, jaw (*slang*), natter, rabbit (on) (*Brit. informal*), run off at the mouth (*U.S. slang*), shoot the breeze (*U.S. slang*), talk

chatter *noun/verb* babble, blather, chat, gab (*informal*), gossip, jabber, natter, prate, prattle, rabbit (on) (*Brit. informal*), run off at the mouth (*U.S. slang*), tattle, twaddle

chatterbox *informal* babbler, blather *or* blether (*Scot.*), gossip, jabberer, natterer, prater, prattler, tattler, tattletale (*chiefly U.S. & Canad.*), twaddler

chatty colloquial, familiar, friendly, gossipy, informal, newsy (*informal*), talkative
Antonyms aloof, cold, distant, formal, hostile, quiet, reserved, shy, silent, standoffish, taciturn, timid, unfriendly, unsociable

cheap **1.** bargain, cheapo (*informal*), cut-price, economical, economy, inexpensive, keen, low-cost, low-priced, reasonable, reduced, sale **2.** bush-league (*Austral. & N.Z. informal*), chickenshit (*U.S. slang*), common, crappy (*slang*), dime-a-dozen (*informal*), inferior, low-rent (*informal, chiefly U.S.*), paltry, piss-poor (*U.S. taboo slang*), poor, poxy (*slang*), second-rate, shoddy, tatty, tawdry, tinhorn (*U.S. slang*), two a penny, two-bit (*U.S. & Canad. slang*), worthless **3.** base, contemptible, despicable, low, mean, scurvy, sordid, vulgar
Antonyms (*sense 1*) costly, dear, expensive, pricey (*informal*), steep (*senses 2 & 3*) admirable, charitable, decent, elegant, generous, good, high-class, honourable, superior, tasteful, valuable

cheapen belittle, debase, degrade, demean, denigrate, depreciate, derogate, devalue, discredit, disparage, lower

cheapness **1.** affordability, inexpensiveness, reasonableness **2.** commonness, crappiness (*slang*), inferiority, paltriness, poorness, shoddiness, tattiness, tawdriness, valuelessness, worthlessness

cheat *verb* **1.** bamboozle (*informal*), beguile, bilk, con (*informal*), cozen, deceive, defraud, diddle (*informal*), do (*informal*), do the dirty on (*Brit. informal*), double-cross (*informal*), dupe, finagle (*informal*), fleece, fool, gull (*archaic*), hoax, hoodwink, kid (*informal*), mislead, pull a fast one on (*informal*), rip off (*slang*), skin (*slang*), stiff (*slang*), sting (*informal*), stitch up (*slang*), swindle, take for a ride (*informal*), take in (*informal*), thwart, trick, victimize **2.** baffle, check, defeat, deprive, foil, frustrate, prevent, thwart *~noun* **3.** artifice, deceit, deception, fraud, imposture, rip-off (*slang*), scam (*slang*), sting (*informal*), swindle, trickery **4.** charlatan, cheater, chiseller (*informal*), con man (*informal*), deceiver, dodger, double-crosser (*informal*), fraudster, grifter (*slang, chiefly U.S. & Canad.*), impostor, knave (*archaic*), rogue, shark, sharper, swindler, trickster
Cheats never prosper

check *verb* **1.** check out (*informal*), compare, confirm, enquire into, examine, inspect, investigate, look at, look over, make sure, monitor, note, probe, research, scrutinize, study, take a dekko at (*Brit. slang*), test, tick, verify, vet, work over **2.** arrest, bar, bridle, control, curb, delay, halt, hinder, impede, inhibit, limit, nip in the bud, obstruct, pause, put a spoke in someone's wheel, rein, repress, restrain, retard, stem the flow, stop, thwart **3.** admonish, bawl out (*informal*), blame, carpet (*informal*), chew out (*U.S. & Canad. informal*), chide, give (someone) a rocket (*Brit. & N.Z. informal*), give (someone) a row (*informal*), rap over the knuckles, rate, read the riot act, rebuff, rebuke, reprimand, reprove, scold, slap on the wrist, tear into (*informal*), tear (someone) off a strip (*Brit. informal*), tell off (*informal*) *~noun* **4.** examination, inspection, investigation, once-over (*informal*), research, scrutiny, test **5.** constraint, control, curb, damper, hindrance, impediment, inhibition, limitation, obstacle, obstruction, rein, restraint, stoppage **6.** blow, disappointment, frustration, rejection, reverse, setback, whammy (*informal, chiefly U.S.*)
Antonyms *verb* (*sense 1*) disregard, ignore, neglect, overlook, pass over, pay no attention to (*sense 2*) accelerate, advance, begin, encourage, further, give free rein, help, release, start

cheek audacity, brass neck (*Brit. informal*), brazenness, chutzpah (*U.S. & Canad. informal*), disrespect, effrontery, face (*informal*), front, gall (*informal*), impertinence, impudence, insolence, lip (*slang*), neck (*informal*), nerve, sassiness (*U.S. informal*), sauce (*informal*), temerity

cheeky audacious, disrespectful, forward, fresh (*informal*), impertinent, impudent, insolent, insulting, lippy (*U.S. & Canad. slang*), pert, sassy (*U.S. informal*), saucy
Antonyms civil, complaisant, courteous, decorous, deferential, mannerly, polite, respectful, well-behaved, well-mannered

cheer *verb* **1.** animate, brighten, buoy up, cheer up, comfort, console, elate, elevate, encourage, enliven, exhilarate, gladden, hearten, incite, inspirit, solace, uplift, warm **2.** acclaim, applaud, clap, hail, hurrah *~noun* **3.** animation, buoyancy, cheerfulness, comfort, gaiety, gladness, glee, hopefulness, joy, liveliness, merriment, merry-making, mirth, optimism, solace **4.** acclamation, applause, ovation, plaudits
Antonyms *verb* (*sense 1*) darken, depress, discourage, dishearten, sadden (*sense 2*) blow a raspberry, boo, hiss, jeer, ridicule

cheerful animated, blithe, bright, bucked (*informal*), buoyant, cheery, chirpy (*informal*), contented, enlivening, enthusiastic, gay, genial, glad, gladsome (*archaic*), happy, hearty, jaunty, jolly, joyful, light-hearted, lightsome (*archaic*), merry, optimistic, pleasant, sparkling, sprightly, sunny, upbeat (*informal*)

Antonyms cheerless, dejected, depressed, depressing, despondent, dismal, down, downcast, down in the dumps (*informal*), dull, gloomy, lifeless, low, melancholy, miserable, morose, pensive, sad, unhappy, unpleasant

cheerfulness buoyancy, exuberance, gaiety, geniality, gladness, good cheer, good humour, high spirits, jauntiness, joyousness, light-heartedness

cheering auspicious, bright, comforting, encouraging, heartening, promising, propitious

cheerless austere, bleak, comfortless, dark, dejected, depressed, desolate, despondent, disconsolate, dismal, dolorous, drab, dreary, dull, forlorn, funereal, gloomy, grim, joyless, melancholy, miserable, mournful, sad, sombre, sorrowful, sullen, unhappy, woebegone, woeful
Antonyms cheerful, cheery, elated, happy, jolly, joyful, light-hearted, merry

cheer up brighten, buck up (*informal*), comfort, encourage, enliven, gladden, hearten, jolly along (*informal*), perk up, rally, take heart

cheery breezy, carefree, cheerful, chirpy (*informal*), full of beans (*informal*), genial, good-humoured, happy, jovial, lively, pleasant, sunny, upbeat (*informal*)

chef d'oeuvre brainchild, crowning achievement, *magnum opus*, masterpiece, masterwork

chemical compound, drug, potion, synthetic

Chemical elements	Symbols	Atomic numbers
hydrogen	H	1
helium	He	2
lithium	Li	3
beryllium	Be	4
boron	B	5
carbon	C	6
nitrogen	N	7
oxygen	O	8
fluorine	F	9
neon	Ne	10
sodium	Na	11
magnesium	Mg	12
aluminium *or (U.S.)* aluminum	Al	13
silicon	Si	14
phosphorus	P	15
sulphur *or (U.S.)* sulfur	S	16
chlorine	Cl	17
argon	Ar	18
potassium	K	19
calcium	Ca	20
scandium	Sc	21
titanium	Ti	22
vanadium	V	23
chromium	Cr	24
manganese	Mn	25
iron	Fe	26
cobalt	Co	27
nickel	Ni	28
copper	Cu	29
zinc	Zn	30
gallium	Ga	31
germanium	Ge	32
arsenic	As	33
selenium	Se	34
bromine	Br	35
krypton	Kr	36
rubidium	Rb	37
strontium	Sr	38
yttrium	Y	39
zirconium	Zr	40
niobium	Nb	41
molybdenum	Mo	42
technetium	Tc	43
ruthenium	Ru	44
rhodium	Rh	45
palladium	Pd	46
silver	Ag	47
cadmium	Cd	48
indium	In	49
tin	Sn	50
antimony	Sb	51
tellurium	Te	52
iodine	I	53
xenon	Xe	54
caesium *or (U.S.)* cesium	Cs	55
barium	Ba	56
lanthanum	La	57
cerium	Ce	58
praseodymium	Pr	59
neodymium	Nd	60
promethium	Pm	61
samarium	Sm	62
europium	Eu	63
gadolinium	Gd	64
terbium	Tb	65
dysprosium	Dy	66
holmium	Ho	67
erbium	Er	68
thulium	Tm	69
ytterbium	Yb	70
lutetium *or* lutecium	Lu	71
hafnium	Hf	72
tantalum	Ta	73
tungsten *or* wolfram	W	74
rhenium	Re	75
osmium	Os	76
iridium	Ir	77
platinum	Pt	78
gold	Au	79
mercury	Hg	80

thallium	Tl	81
lead	Pb	82
bismuth	Bi	83
polonium	Po	84
astatine	At	85
radon	Rn	86
francium	Fr	87
radium	Ra	88
actinium	Ac	89
thorium	Th	90
protactin~ium	Pa	91
uranium	U	92
neptunium	Np	93
plutonium	Pu	94
americium	Am	95
curium	Cm	96
berkelium	Bk	97
californium	Cf	98
einsteinium	Es	99
fermium	Fm	100
mende~levium	Md	101
nobelium	No	102
lawrencium	Lr	103
rutherfordium	Rf	104
dubnium	Db	105
seaborgium	Sg	106
bohrium	Bh	107
hassium	Hs	108
meitnerium	Mt	109

chemistry

Branches of chemistry

analytical chemistry
astrochemistry
biochemistry
chemurgy
cytochemistry
electrochemistry
geochemistry
histochemistry
immunochemistry
inorganic chemistry
kinetics
magnetochemistry
neurochemistry
nuclear chemistry
organic chemistry
petrochemistry
phonochemistry
photochemistry
physical chemistry
phytochemistry
radiochemistry
stereochemistry
stoichiometry
thermochemistry
zoochemistry
zymurgy

Chemistry terms

acid
alcohol
alkali
alkali metal
alkaline earth metal
alkane
allotrope
alloy
amino acid
analysis
anion
anode
atom
atomic mass
atomic number
base
boiling point
bond
Brownian motion
carbohydrate
catalyst
cathode
cation
chain
chain reaction
chromatography
combustion
compound
concentrated
condensation
corrosion
covalent bond
crystal
crystallization
diffusion
dilute
distillation
electrode
electrolysis
electron
electrovalency
element
emulsion
equation
ester
ether
evaporation
fat
fatty acid
fermentation
fission
foam
formula
fuel
fusion
gas
halogen
hydrocarbon
hydrolysis
inert
inorganic
insoluble
ion
ionic bond
ionization
isomer
isotope
lanthanide *or* rare-earth element
liquid
litmus test
melting point
metal
metalloid
mineral
mixture
molarity
mole
molecule
monomer
neutral
neutron
noble gas *or* inert gas
nonmetal
nucleus
oil
ore
organic
oxidation
periodic table
pH
plastic
polymer
precipitate
proton
radioactivity
reaction
reagent
redox reaction
reduction
salt
saponification
saturated
soap
solid
soluble
solution
solvent
sublimation
substitution reaction
sugar
suspension
synthesis
transition metal
unsaturated
valency
van der Waals forces

Famous Chemists

Robert Boyle [Irish]
Robert Wilhelm Bun~sen [German]
Marie Curie [French]
Pierre Curie [French]
John Dalton [English]
Humphrey Davy [English]
Antoine Laurent Lavoisier [French]
Dmitri Ivanovich Mendeleyev [Rus~sian]
Alfred Bernhard Nobel [Swedish]
Louis Pasteur [French]
Linus Carl Pauling [U.S.]
Joseph Priestley [English]

cherish care for, cleave to, cling to, comfort, cosset, encourage, entertain, foster, harbour,

hold dear, nourish, nurse, nurture, prize, shelter, support, sustain, treasure
Antonyms abandon, desert, despise, disdain, dislike, forsake, hate, neglect

cherubic adorable, angelic, heavenly, innocent, lovable, seraphic, sweet

chest ark (*dialect*), box, case, casket, coffer, crate, kist (*Scot. & Northern English dialect*), strongbox, trunk

chew 1. bite, champ, crunch, gnaw, grind, masticate, munch 2. *figurative usually with* **over** consider, deliberate upon, meditate, mull (over), muse on, ponder, reflect upon, ruminate, weigh

chic elegant, fashionable, modish, sexy (*informal*), smart, stylish, trendy (*Brit. informal*), up-to-date, urbane
Antonyms dinosaur, inelegant, naff (*Brit. slang*), old-fashioned, outmoded, out-of-date, passé, shabby, unfashionable

chicanery artifice, cheating, chicane, deception, deviousness, dodge, double-dealing, duplicity, intrigue, sharp practice, skulduggery (*informal*), sophistry, stratagems, subterfuge, trickery, underhandedness, wiles, wire-pulling (*chiefly U.S.*)

chicken

Breeds of chicken

Ancona	Houdan
Andalusian	Leghorn
Australorp	Minorca
bantam	New Hampshire
Brahma	Orpington
Campine	Plymouth Rock
Cochin	Rhode Island Red
Dorking	Sumatra
Faverolle	Sussex
Hamburg	Wyandotte

chide admonish, bawl out (*informal*), berate, blame, blast, carpet (*informal*), censure, check, chew out (*U.S. & Canad. informal*), criticize, find fault, give (someone) a rocket (*Brit. & N.Z. informal*), give (someone) a row (*informal*), lambast(e), lecture, put down, rap over the knuckles, read the riot act, rebuke, reprehend, reprimand, reproach, reprove, scold, slap on the wrist, slate (*informal, chiefly Brit.*), tear into (*informal*), tear (someone) off a strip (*Brit. informal*), tell off (*informal*), upbraid

chief 1. *adjective* big-time (*informal*), capital, cardinal, central, especial, essential, foremost, grand, highest, key, leading, main, major league (*informal*), most important, outstanding, paramount, predominant, pre-eminent, premier, prevailing, primary, prime, principal, superior, supreme, uppermost, vital 2. *noun* boss (*informal*), captain, chieftain, commander, director, governor, head, leader, lord, manager, master, principal, ringleader, ruler, superintendent, suzerain, torchbearer
Antonyms *adjective* least, minor, subordinate, subsidiary *~noun* follower, subject, subordinate

chiefly above all, especially, essentially, in general, in the main, largely, mainly, mostly, on the whole, predominantly, primarily, principally, usually

child ankle-biter (*Austral. slang*), babe, babe in arms (*informal*), baby, bairn (*Scot.*), brat, chit, descendant, infant, issue, juvenile, kid (*informal*), little one, minor, nipper (*informal*), nursling, offspring, progeny, rug rat (*slang*), sprog (*slang*), suckling, toddler, tot, wean (*Scot.*), youngster
Related adjective: filial

The child is father of the man
William Wordsworth *My Heart Leaps Up*

I love children. Especially when they cry - for then someone takes them away
Nancy Mitford

The first half of our life is ruined by our parents and the second half by our children
Clarence Darrow

Your children are not your children.
They are the sons and daughters of life's longing for itself.
They came through you but not from you
And though they are with you yet they belong not to you
Kahlil Gibran *The Prophet*

Children should be seen and not heard

little children, little sorrows; big children, great sorrows

childbirth accouchement, child-bearing, confinement, delivery, labour, lying-in, parturition, travail
Related adjectives: natal, parturient

In sorrow thou shalt bring forth children
Bible: Genesis

Death and taxes and childbirth! There's never any convenient time for any of them
Margaret Mitchell *Gone with the Wind*

childhood boyhood, girlhood, immaturity, infancy, minority, schooldays, youth

Childhood is the kingdom where nobody dies.
Nobody that matters, that is
Edna St. Vincent Millay *Childhood is the Kingdom where Nobody dies*

childish boyish, foolish, frivolous, girlish, immature, infantile, juvenile, puerile, silly, simple, trifling, weak, young
Antonyms adult, grown-up, manly, mature, sensible, sophisticated, womanly

childlike artless, credulous, guileless, ingenuous, innocent, naive, simple, trustful, trusting, unfeigned

chill *adjective* **1.** biting, bleak, chilly, cold, freezing, frigid, parky (*Brit. informal*), raw, sharp, wintry **2.** *figurative* aloof, cool, depressing, distant, frigid, hostile, stony, unfriendly, ungenial, unresponsive, unwelcoming *~verb* **3.** congeal, cool, freeze, refrigerate **4.** *figurative* dampen, deject, depress, discourage, dishearten, dismay *~noun* **5.** bite, cold, coldness, coolness, crispness, frigidity, nip, rawness, sharpness

chilly **1.** blowy, breezy, brisk, cool, crisp, draughty, fresh, nippy, parky (*Brit. informal*), penetrating, sharp **2.** cold as ice, frigid, hostile, unfriendly, unresponsive, unsympathetic, unwelcoming
Antonyms (*sense 1*) balmy, hot, mild, scorching, sunny, sweltering, warm (*sense 2*) affable, chummy (*informal*), congenial, cordial, friendly, responsive, sociable, sympathetic, warm, welcoming

chime boom, clang, dong, jingle, peal, ring, sound, strike, tinkle, tintinnabulate, toll

chimera bogy, delusion, dream, fantasy, figment, hallucination, ignis fatuus, illusion, monster, monstrosity, snare, spectre, will-o'-the-wisp

chimerical delusive, fabulous, fanciful, fantastic, hallucinatory, illusive, illusory, imaginary, quixotic, unfounded, unreal, vain, visionary, wild

china ceramics, crockery, porcelain, pottery, service, tableware, ware

chink aperture, cleft, crack, cranny, crevice, cut, fissure, flaw, gap, opening, rift

chip **1.** *noun* dent, flake, flaw, fragment, nick, notch, paring, scrap, scratch, shard, shaving, sliver, wafer **2.** *verb* chisel, damage, gash, nick, whittle

chip in contribute, donate, go Dutch (*informal*), interpose, interrupt, pay, subscribe

chirp cheep, chirrup, peep, pipe, tweet, twitter, warble

chirpy *informal* animated, blithe, bright, buoyant, cheerful, enlivening, enthusiastic, full of beans (*informal*), happy, in high spirits, jaunty, jolly, light-hearted, lively, radiant, sparkling, sprightly, sunny

chivalrous bold, brave, courageous, courteous, courtly, gallant, gentlemanly, heroic, high-minded, honourable, intrepid, knightly, magnanimous, true, valiant
Antonyms boorish, cowardly, cruel, dishonourable, disloyal, rude, uncourtly, ungallant, unmannerly

chivalry courage, courtesy, courtliness, gallantry, gentlemanliness, knight-errantry, knighthood, politeness

chivvy annoy, badger, bend someone's ear (*informal*), breathe down someone's neck (*informal*), bug (*informal*), harass, hassle (*informal*), hound, nag, pester, plague, pressure (*informal*), prod, torment

choice **1.** *noun* alternative, discrimination, election, option, pick, preference, say, selection, variety **2.** *adjective* bad (*slang*), best, crucial (*slang*), dainty, def (*slang*), elect, elite, excellent, exclusive, exquisite, hand-picked, nice, precious, prime, prize, rare, select, special, superior, uncommon, unusual, valuable

You pays your money and you takes your choice
Punch

choke asphyxiate, bar, block, bung, clog, close, congest, constrict, dam, gag, obstruct, occlude, overpower, smother, stifle, stop, strangle, suffocate, suppress, throttle

choleric angry, bad-tempered, cross, fiery, hasty, hot, hot-tempered, ill-tempered, irascible, irritable, passionate, petulant, quick-tempered, ratty (*Brit. & N.Z. informal*), testy, tetchy, touchy

choose adopt, cull, designate, desire, elect, espouse, fix on, opt for, pick, predestine, prefer, see fit, select, settle upon, single out, take, wish
Antonyms decline, dismiss, exclude, forgo, leave, refuse, reject, throw aside

If you run after two hares you will catch neither

choosy discriminating, exacting, faddy, fastidious, finicky, fussy, particular, picky (*informal*), selective
Antonyms easy (*informal*), easy to please, indiscriminate, undemanding, unselective

chop **1.** *verb* axe, cleave, cut, fell, hack, hew, lop, sever, shear, slash, truncate **2.** *noun* **the chop** *slang* dismissal, one's cards, sacking (*informal*), termination, the axe (*informal*), the boot (*slang*), the (old) heave-ho (*informal*), the order of the boot (*slang*), the sack (*informal*)

choppy blustery, broken, rough, ruffled, squally, tempestuous
Antonyms calm, smooth, windless

chop up cube, dice, divide, fragment, mince

chore burden, duty, errand, fag (*informal*), job, no picnic, task

chortle cackle, chuckle, crow, guffaw

chorus **1.** choir, choristers, ensemble, singers, vocalists **2.** burden, refrain, response, strain **3.** accord, concert, harmony, unison

Christ the Galilean, the Good Shepherd, Jesus Christ, Our Lord, the Nazarene

christen baptize, call, designate, dub, name, style, term, title

chronic **1.** confirmed, deep-rooted, deep-seated, habitual, incessant, incurable, ineradicable, ingrained, inveterate, persistent **2.** *informal*

abysmal, appalling, atrocious, awful, dreadful
Antonyms infrequent, occasional, temporary

chronicle 1. *noun* account, annals, diary, history, journal, narrative, record, register, story 2. *verb* enter, narrate, put on record, record, recount, register, relate, report, set down, tell

chronicler annalist, diarist, historian, historiographer, narrator, recorder, reporter, scribe

chronological consecutive, historical, in sequence, ordered, progressive, sequential
Antonyms haphazard, intermittent, irregular, out-of-order, random

chubby buxom, flabby, fleshy, plump, podgy, portly, rotund, round, stout, tubby
Antonyms lean, skinny, slender, slight, slim, sylphlike, thin

chuck cast, discard, fling, heave, hurl, pitch, shy, sling, throw, toss

chuckle chortle, crow, exult, giggle, laugh, snigger, titter

chum cock (*Brit. informal*), companion, comrade, crony, friend, mate (*informal*), pal (*informal*)

chummy affectionate, buddy-buddy (*slang, chiefly U.S. & Canad.*), close, friendly, intimate, matey *or* maty (*Brit. informal*), pally (*informal*), palsy-walsy (*informal*), thick (*informal*)

chunk block, dollop (*informal*), hunk, lump, mass, nugget, piece, portion, slab, wad, wodge (*Brit. informal*)

chunky beefy (*informal*), dumpy, stocky, stubby, thickset

churl 1. boor, lout, oaf 2. bumpkin, clodhopper (*informal*), clown, hayseed (*U.S. & Canad. informal*), hick (*informal, chiefly U.S. & Canad.*), hillbilly, peasant, rustic, yokel 3. curmudgeon, miser, niggard, skinflint

churlish 1. boorish, brusque, crabbed, harsh, ill-tempered, impolite, loutish, morose, oafish, rude, sullen, surly, uncivil, uncouth, unmannerly, vulgar 2. close-fisted, illiberal, inhospitable, mean, miserly, niggardly, unneighbourly, unsociable
Antonyms admirable, agreeable, amiable, civil, courteous, cultivated, generous, good-tempered, mannerly, noble, pleasant, polite, well-bred

churlishness boorishness, crassness, crudeness, loutishness, oafishness, rudeness, surliness, uncouthness

churn agitate, beat, boil, convulse, foam, froth, seethe, stir up, swirl, toss

chute channel, gutter, incline, ramp, runway, slide, slope, trough

cicerone courier, dragoman, escort, guide, mentor, pilot

cigarette cancer stick (*slang*), ciggy (*informal*), coffin nail (*slang*), fag (*Brit. slang*), gasper (*slang*), smoke
see TOBACCO

cinema big screen (*informal*), films, flicks (*slang*), motion pictures, movies, pictures

Photography is truth. The cinema is truth 24 times per second
Jean-Luc Godard *Le Petit Soldat*

A film must have a beginning, a middle and an end. But not necessarily in that order
Jean-Luc Godard

To wish the movies to be articulate is about as sensible as wishing the drama to be silent
George Jean Nathan

Pictures are for entertainment, messages should be delivered by Western Union
Sam Goldwyn

cipher 1. nil, nothing, nought, zero 2. nobody, nonentity 3. character, digit, figure, number, numeral, symbol 4. code, cryptograph 5. device, logo, mark, monogram

circa about, approximately, around, in the region of, roughly

circle *noun* 1. band, circumference, coil, cordon, cycle, disc, globe, lap, loop, orb, perimeter, periphery, revolution, ring, round, sphere, turn 2. area, bounds, circuit, compass, domain, enclosure, field, orbit, province, range, realm, region, scene, sphere 3. assembly, class, clique, club, company, coterie, crowd, fellowship, fraternity, group, order, school, set, society *~verb* 4. belt, circumnavigate, circumscribe, coil, compass, curve, encircle, enclose, encompass, envelop, gird, hem in, pivot, revolve, ring, rotate, surround, tour, whirl

circuit 1. area, compass, course, journey, lap, orbit, perambulation, revolution, round, route, tour, track 2. boundary, bounding line, bounds, circumference, compass, district, limit, pale, range, region, tract

circuitous ambagious (*archaic*), devious, indirect, labyrinthine, meandering, oblique, rambling, roundabout, tortuous, winding
Antonyms as the crow flies, direct, straight, undeviating, unswerving

circuitousness deviousness, indirectness, obliqueness, rambling, roundaboutness, tortuousness

circular *adjective* 1. annular, discoid, globelike, orbicular, ring-shaped, rotund, round, spherical 2. circuitous, cyclical, orbital *~noun* 3. advertisement, notice

circulate 1. broadcast, diffuse, disseminate, distribute, issue, make known, promulgate, propagate, publicize, publish, spread 2. flow, gyrate, radiate, revolve, rotate

circulation 1. currency, dissemination, distribution, spread, transmission, vogue **2**. circling, flow, motion, rotation **3**. bloodstream

circumference border, boundary, bounds, cir~cuit, edge, extremity, fringe, limits, outline, pale, perimeter, periphery, rim, verge

circumlocution beating about the bush (*infor~mal*), diffuseness, discursiveness, euphemism, indirectness, periphrasis, prolixity, redundan~cy, wordiness

circumscribe bound, confine, define, delimit, delineate, demarcate, encircle, enclose, en~compass, environ, hem in, limit, mark off, re~strain, restrict, straiten, surround

circumspect attentive, canny, careful, cau~tious, deliberate, discreet, discriminating, guarded, heedful, judicious, observant, politic, prudent, sagacious, sage, vigilant, wary, watchful

Antonyms bold, careless, daring, foolhardy, heedless, imprudent, rash, venturous

circumspection canniness, care, caution, chariness, deliberation, discretion, keeping one's head down, prudence, wariness

Don't put all your eggs in one basket

circumstance accident, condition, contingency, detail, element, event, fact, factor, happening, incident, item, occurrence, particular, position, respect, situation

circumstances lie of the land, lifestyle, means, position, resources, situation, state, state of affairs, station, status, times

circumstantial conjectural, contingent, de~tailed, founded on circumstances, hearsay, in~cidental, indirect, inferential, particular, pre~sumptive, provisional, specific

circumvent beguile, bypass, deceive, dupe, elude, ensnare, entrap, evade, hoodwink, mis~lead, outflank, outgeneral, outwit, overreach, sidestep, steer clear of, thwart, trick

circumvention chicanery, deceit, deception, dodge, duplicity, evasion, fraud, guile, imposi~tion, imposture, trickery, wiles

cistern basin, reservoir, sink, tank, vat

citadel bastion, fastness, fortification, fortress, keep, stronghold, tower

citation **1**. commendation, excerpt, illustration, passage, quotation, quote, reference, source **2**. award, commendation, mention

cite **1**. adduce, advance, allude to, enumerate, evidence, extract, mention, name, quote, specify **2**. *Law* call, subpoena, summon

citizen burgess, burgher, denizen, dweller, freeman, inhabitant, ratepayer, resident, sub~ject, townsman

city **1**. *noun* conurbation, megalopolis, me~tropolis, municipality **2**. *adjective* civic, metro~politan, municipal, urban

The city is not a concrete jungle, it is a human zoo

Desmond Morris *The Human Zoo*

civic borough, communal, community, local, municipal, public

civil **1**. civic, domestic, home, interior, munici~pal, political **2**. accommodating, affable, civi~lized, complaisant, courteous, courtly, oblig~ing, polished, polite, refined, urbane, well-bred, well-mannered

Antonyms (*sense 1*) military, religious, state (*sense 2*) discourteous, ill-mannered, impolite, rude, uncivil, unfriendly, ungracious, unpleas~ant

civility affability, amiability, breeding, com~plaisance, cordiality, courteousness, courtesy, good manners, graciousness, politeness, poli~tesse, tact, urbanity

Civility costs nothing and buys everything

Mary Wortley Montagu

A civil question deserves a civil answer

civilization **1**. advancement, cultivation, cul~ture, development, education, enlightenment, progress, refinement, sophistication **2**. com~munity, nation, people, polity, society **3**. cus~toms, mores, way of life

civilize cultivate, educate, enlighten, humanize, improve, polish, refine, sophisticate, tame

civilized cultured, educated, enlightened, hu~mane, polite, sophisticated, tolerant, urbane

Antonyms barbarous, green, ignorant, naive, primitive, simple, uncivilized, uncultivated, uncultured, undeveloped, uneducated, unen~lightened, unsophisticated, untutored, wild

clad accoutred, apparelled, arrayed, attired, clothed, covered, decked out, draped, dressed, fitted out, invested, rigged out (*informal*)

claim **1**. *verb* allege, ask, assert, call for, chal~lenge, collect, demand, exact, hold, insist, maintain, need, pick up, profess, require, take, uphold **2**. *noun* affirmation, allegation, application, assertion, call, demand, petition, pretension, privilege, protestation, request, requirement, right, title

claimant applicant, petitioner, pretender, sup~pliant, supplicant

clairvoyant **1**. *adjective* extrasensory, fey, oracular, prescient, prophetic, psychic, second-sighted, sibylline, telepathic, vatic, vi~sionary **2**. *noun* augur, diviner, fortune-teller, haruspex, oracle, prophet, prophetess, seer, sibyl, soothsayer, telepath, telepathist, vision~ary

clairvoyant: a person, commonly a woman, who has the power of seeing that which is invisible to her patron - namely, that he is a blockhead

Ambrose Bierce *The Devil's Dictionary*

clamber claw, climb, scale, scrabble, scramble, shin

clamminess airlessness, closeness, dampness, dankness, drizzliness, heaviness, humidity, humidness, moistness, mugginess, oppressiveness, pastiness, sliminess, stickiness, stuffiness, sultriness, sweatiness, thickness

clammy close, damp, dank, drizzly, moist, pasty, slimy, sticky, sweating, sweaty

clamorous blaring, deafening, insistent, lusty, noisy, riotous, strident, tumultuous, uproarious, vehement, vociferous

clamour agitation, babel, blare, brouhaha, commotion, din, exclamation, hubbub, hullabaloo, noise, outcry, racket, shout, shouting, uproar, vociferation

clamp 1. *noun* bracket, fastener, grip, press, vice **2.** *verb* brace, clinch, fasten, fix, impose, make fast, secure

clan band, brotherhood, clique, coterie, faction, family, fraternity, gens, group, house, order, race, schism, sect, sept, set, society, sodality, tribe

clandestine cloak-and-dagger, closet, concealed, covert, fraudulent, furtive, hidden, private, secret, sly, stealthy, surreptitious, underground, underhand, under-the-counter

clang 1. *verb* bong, chime, clank, clash, jangle, resound, reverberate, ring, toll **2.** *noun* clangour, ding-dong, knell, reverberation

clannish cliquish, exclusive, insular, narrow, sectarian, select, unfriendly

clannishness cliquishness, exclusiveness, exclusivity, insularity, narrowness, sectarianism, selectness, unfriendliness

clap 1. acclaim, applaud, cheer, give (someone) a big hand **2.** bang, pat, punch, slap, strike gently, thrust, thwack, wallop (*informal*), whack

Antonyms (*sense 1*) blow a raspberry, boo, catcall, hiss, jeer

claptrap affectation, balls (*taboo slang*), bilge (*informal*), blarney, bombast, bosh (*informal*), bull (*slang*), bullshit (*taboo slang*), bunk (*informal*), bunkum *or* buncombe (*chiefly U.S.*), cobblers (*Brit. taboo slang*), crap (*slang*), drivel, eyewash (*informal*), flannel (*Brit. informal*), garbage (*informal*), guff (*slang*), hogwash, hokum (*slang, chiefly U.S. & Canad.*), horsefeathers (*U.S. slang*), hot air (*informal*), humbug, insincerity, moonshine, nonsense, pap, piffle (*informal*), poppycock (*informal*), rodomontade (*literary*), rot, rubbish, shit (*taboo slang*), tommyrot, tosh (*slang, chiefly Brit.*), trash, tripe (*informal*)

clarification elucidation, explanation, exposition, illumination, interpretation, simplification

clarify 1. clear the air, clear up, elucidate, explain, explicate, illuminate, interpret, make plain, resolve, simplify, throw *or* shed light on **2.** cleanse, purify, refine

clarion *adjective* blaring, clear, inspiring, loud, ringing, stirring, strident

clarity clearness, comprehensibility, definition, explicitness, intelligibility, limpidity, lucidity, obviousness, precision, simplicity, transparency

Antonyms cloudiness, complexity, complication, dullness, haziness, imprecision, intricacy, murkiness, obscurity

Everything that can be said can be said clearly
Ludwig Wittgenstein *Tractatus Logico-Philosophicus*

clash *verb* **1.** bang, clang, clank, clatter, crash, jangle, jar, rattle **2.** conflict, cross swords, feud, grapple, lock horns, quarrel, war, wrangle *~noun* **3.** brush, collision, conflict, confrontation, difference of opinion, disagreement, fight, showdown (*informal*)

clasp *verb* **1.** concatenate, connect, fasten **2.** attack, clutch, embrace, enfold, grapple, grasp, grip, hold, hug, press, seize, squeeze *~noun* **3.** brooch, buckle, catch, clip, fastener, fastening, grip, hasp, hook, pin, press stud, snap **4.** embrace, grasp, grip, hold, hug

class 1. *noun* caste, category, classification, collection, denomination, department, division, genre, genus, grade, group, grouping, kind, league, order, rank, set, sort, species, sphere, stamp, status, type, value **2.** *verb* brand, categorize, classify, codify, designate, grade, group, label, rank, rate

The history of all hitherto existing society is the history of class struggles
Karl Marx and Friedrich Engels *The Communist Manifesto*

There are but two families in the world as my grandmother used to say, the Haves and the Have-nots
Miguel de Cervantes *Don Quixote*

The rich man in his castle,
The poor man at his gate,
God made them, high or lowly,
And ordered their estate
Cecil Frances Alexander *All Things Bright and Beautiful*

classic *adjective* **1.** best, consummate, finest, first-rate, masterly, world-class **2.** archetypal, definitive, exemplary, ideal, master, model, paradigmatic, quintessential, standard **3.** characteristic, regular, standard, time-honoured, typical, usual **4.** abiding, ageless, deathless, enduring, immortal, lasting, undying *~noun* **5.** exemplar, masterpiece, masterwork, model, paradigm, prototype, standard

Antonyms *adjective* inferior, modern, poor, second-rate, terrible, unrefined, unrepresentative *~noun* trash

A classic is something that everybody wants to have read and nobody wants to read
Mark Twain

classical 1. chaste, elegant, harmonious, pure, refined, restrained, symmetrical, understated, well-proportioned 2. Attic, Augustan, Grecian, Greek, Hellenic, Latin, Roman

The great tragedy of the classical languages is to have been born twins
Geoffrey Madan

Every man with a bellyful of the classics is an enemy to the human race
Henry Miller *Tropic of Cancer*

That's the classical mind at work, runs fine inside but looks dingy on the surface
Robert M. Pirsig *Zen and the Art of Motorcycle Maintenance*

classification analysis, arrangement, cataloguing, categorization, codification, grading, sorting, taxonomy

classify arrange, catalogue, categorize, codify, dispose, distribute, file, grade, pigeonhole, rank, sort, systematize, tabulate

classy elegant, exclusive, high-class, high-toned, posh (*informal, chiefly Brit.*), ritzy (*slang*), select, stylish, superior, swanky (*informal*), swish (*informal, chiefly Brit.*), top-drawer, up-market, urbane

clause 1. article, chapter, condition, paragraph, part, passage, section 2. heading, item, point, provision, proviso, rider, specification, stipulation

claw 1. *noun* nail, nipper, pincer, talon, tentacle, unguis 2. *verb* dig, graze, lacerate, mangle, maul, rip, scrabble, scrape, scratch, tear

clean *adjective* 1. faultless, flawless, fresh, hygienic, immaculate, impeccable, laundered, pure, sanitary, spotless, squeaky-clean, unblemished, unsoiled, unspotted, unstained, unsullied, washed 2. antiseptic, clarified, decontaminated, natural, purified, sterile, sterilized, unadulterated, uncontaminated, unpolluted 3. chaste, decent, exemplary, good, honourable, impeccable, innocent, moral, pure, respectable, undefiled, upright, virtuous 4. delicate, elegant, graceful, neat, simple, tidy, trim, uncluttered 5. complete, conclusive, decisive, entire, final, perfect, thorough, total, unimpaired, whole *~verb* 6. bath, cleanse, deodorize, disinfect, do up, dust, launder, lave, mop, purge, purify, rinse, sanitize, scour, scrub, sponge, swab, sweep, vacuum, wash, wipe
Antonyms *adjective* (*sense 1*) dirty, filthy, mucky, scuzzy (*slang, chiefly U.S.*), soiled, sullied, unwashed (*sense 2*) adulterated, contaminated, infected, polluted (*sense 3*) dishonourable, immoral, impure, indecent, unchaste (*sense 4*) chaotic, disorderly, disorganized, higgledy-piggledy (*informal*), shambolic (*informal*), untidy *~verb* adulterate, defile, dirty, disorder, disorganize, infect, mess up, pollute, soil, stain

clean-cut chiselled, clear, definite, etched, neat, outlined, sharp, trim, well-defined

cleanliness asepsis, cleanness, freshness, immaculacy, immaculateness, neatness, purity, sanitariness, spotlessness, stainlessness, sterility, tidiness, unspottedness, whiteness

Cleanliness is next to godliness

cleanse absolve, clean, clear, lustrate, purge, purify, rinse, scour, scrub, wash

cleanser detergent, disinfectant, purifier, scourer, soap, soap powder, solvent

clear[1] *adjective* 1. bright, cloudless, fair, fine, halcyon, light, luminous, shining, sunny, unclouded, undimmed 2. apparent, articulate, audible, blatant, bold, coherent, comprehensible, conspicuous, cut-and-dried (*informal*), definite, distinct, evident, explicit, express, incontrovertible, intelligible, lucid, manifest, obvious, palpable, patent, perceptible, plain, pronounced, recognizable, unambiguous, unequivocal, unmistakable, unquestionable 3. empty, free, open, smooth, unhampered, unhindered, unimpeded, unlimited, unobstructed 4. crystalline, glassy, limpid, pellucid, see-through, translucent, transparent 5. certain, convinced, decided, definite, positive, resolved, satisfied, sure 6. clean, guiltless, immaculate, innocent, pure, sinless, stainless, unblemished, undefiled, untarnished, untroubled
Antonyms (*sense 1*) cloudy, dark, dull, foggy, hazy, misty, murky, overcast, stormy (*sense 2*) ambiguous, confused, doubtful, equivocal, hidden, inarticulate, inaudible, incoherent, indistinct, inexplicit, obscured, unrecognizable (*sense 3*) barricaded, blocked, closed, engaged, hampered, impeded, obstructed (*sense 4*) cloudy, muddy, non-translucent, non-transparent, opaque, turbid

clear[2] *verb* 1. clean, cleanse, erase, purify, refine, sweep away, tidy (up), wipe 2. break up, brighten, clarify, lighten 3. absolve, acquit, excuse, exonerate, justify, vindicate 4. emancipate, free, liberate, set free 5. disengage, disentangle, extricate, free, loosen, open, rid, unblock, unclog, unload, unpack 6. jump, leap, miss, pass over, vault 7. acquire, earn, gain, make, reap, secure
Antonyms (*sense 3*) accuse, blame, charge, condemn, convict, find guilty

clearance 1. authorization, blank cheque, consent, endorsement, go-ahead (*informal*), green light, leave, O.K. *or* okay (*informal*), permission, sanction 2. allowance, gap, headroom, margin 3. depopulation, emptying, evacuation, eviction, removal, unpeopling, withdrawal

clear-cut black-and-white, cut-and-dried (*informal*), definite, explicit, plain, precise, specific, straightforward, unambiguous, unequivocal

clearing dell, glade

clearly beyond doubt, distinctly, evidently, incontestably, incontrovertibly, markedly, obviously, openly, overtly, undeniably, undoubtedly

clearness audibility, brightness, clarity, coherence, distinctness, glassiness, intelligibility, lucidity, luminosity, transparency

clear out 1. empty, exhaust, get rid of, sort, tidy up 2. beat it (*slang*), decamp, depart, hook it (*slang*), leave, make oneself scarce, make tracks, pack one's bags (*informal*), retire, slope off, take oneself off, withdraw

clear up 1. answer, clarify, elucidate, explain, resolve, solve, straighten out, unravel 2. order, rearrange, tidy (up)

cleave[1] *verb* abide by, adhere, agree, attach, be devoted to, be true, cling, cohere, hold, remain, stand by, stick

cleave[2] *verb* crack, dissever, disunite, divide, hew, open, part, rend, rive, sever, slice, split, sunder, tear asunder

cleft 1. *noun* breach, break, chasm, chink, crack, cranny, crevice, fissure, fracture, gap, opening, rent, rift 2. *adjective* cloven, parted, rent, riven, ruptured, separated, split, sundered, torn

clemency compassion, forbearance, forgiveness, humanity, indulgence, kindness, leniency, mercifulness, mercy, mildness, moderation, pity, quarter, soft-heartedness, tenderness

clement 1. compassionate, forbearing, forgiving, gentle, humane, indulgent, kind, kind-hearted, lenient, merciful, mild, soft-hearted, tender 2. balmy, calm, fair, fine, mild, temperate

clergy churchmen, clergymen, clerics, ecclesiastics, first estate, holy orders, ministry, priesthood, the cloth

I remember the average curate at home as something between a eunuch and a snigger
Ronald Firbank *The Flower Beneath the Foot*

clergyman chaplain, cleric, curate, divine, father, man of God, man of the cloth, minister, padre, parson, pastor, priest, rabbi, rector, reverend (*informal*), vicar

clerical 1. ecclesiastical, pastoral, priestly, sacerdotal 2. book-keeping, clerkish, clerkly, office, secretarial, stenographic

clever able, adroit, apt, astute, brainy (*informal*), bright, canny, capable, cunning, deep, dexterous, discerning, expert, gifted, ingenious, intelligent, inventive, keen, knowing, knowledgeable, quick, quick-witted, rational, resourceful, sagacious, sensible, shrewd, skilful, smart, talented, witty

Antonyms awkward, boring, clumsy, dense, dull, ham-fisted (*informal*), inept, inexpert, maladroit, slow, stupid, thick, unaccomplished, unimaginative, witless

cleverness ability, adroitness, astuteness, brains, brightness, canniness, dexterity, flair, gift, gumption (*Brit. informal*), ingenuity, intelligence, nous (*Brit. slang*), quickness, quick wits, resourcefulness, sagacity, sense, sharpness, shrewdness, smartness, smarts (*slang, chiefly U.S.*), suss (*slang*), talent, wit

cliché banality, bromide, chestnut (*informal*), commonplace, hackneyed phrase, old saw, platitude, stereotype, truism

click *noun/verb* 1. beat, clack, snap, tick ~*verb* 2. *informal* become clear, come home (to), fall into place, make sense 3. *slang* be compatible, be on the same wavelength, feel a rapport, get on, get on like a house on fire (*informal*), go over, hit it off (*informal*), make a hit, succeed, take to each other

client applicant, buyer, consumer, customer, dependant, habitué, patient, patron, protégé, shopper

clientele business, clients, customers, following, market, patronage, regulars, trade

cliff bluff, crag, escarpment, face, overhang, precipice, rock face, scar, scarp

climactic climactical, critical, crucial, decisive, paramount, peak

climate 1. clime, country, region, temperature, weather 2. ambience, disposition, feeling, mood, temper, tendency, trend

You don't need a weatherman to know which way the wind blows
Bob Dylan *Subterranean Homesick Blues*

climax 1. *noun* acme, apogee, crest, culmination, head, height, highlight, high spot (*informal*), *ne plus ultra*, pay-off (*informal*), peak, summit, top, zenith 2. *verb* come to a head, culminate, peak

climb ascend, clamber, mount, rise, scale, shin up, soar, top

climb down 1. descend, dismount 2. back down, eat crow (*U.S. informal*), eat one's words, retract, retreat

clinch 1. assure, cap, conclude, confirm, decide, determine, seal, secure, set the seal on, settle, sew up (*informal*), tip the balance, verify 2. bolt, clamp, fasten, fix, make fast, nail, rivet, secure 3. clutch, cuddle, embrace, grasp, hug, squeeze

cling adhere, attach to, be true to, clasp, cleave to, clutch, embrace, fasten, grasp, grip, hug, stick, twine round

clinical analytic, antiseptic, cold, detached, disinterested, dispassionate, emotionless, impersonal, objective, scientific, unemotional

clip[1] 1. *verb* crop, curtail, cut, cut short, dock, pare, prune, shear, shorten, snip, trim 2. *noun/verb, informal* belt (*informal*), blow, box, clout (*informal*), cuff, knock, punch, skelp (*dialect*), smack, thump, wallop (*informal*), whack 3. *noun, informal* gallop, lick (*informal*), rate, speed, velocity

clip[2] *verb* attach, fasten, fix, hold, pin, staple

clipping cutting, excerpt, extract, piece

clique cabal, circle, clan, coterie, crew (*informal*), crowd, faction, gang, group, mob, pack, posse (*informal*), schism, set

cloak 1. *verb* camouflage, conceal, cover, disguise, hide, mask, obscure, screen, veil 2. *noun* blind, cape, coat, cover, front, mantle, mask, pretext, shield, wrap

clobber *slang* 1. *verb* assault, bash (*informal*), batter, beat, beat up (*informal*), belabour, duff up (*informal*), lambast(e), lash, pound, pummel, rough up (*informal*), smash, thrash, wallop (*informal*) 2. *noun* accoutrements, belongings, effects, gear, possessions

clod block, chunk, clump, hunk, lump, mass, piece

clodhopper booby, boor, bumpkin, clown, galoot (*slang, chiefly U.S.*), loon (*informal*), lout, oaf, yokel

clog 1. *verb* block, bung, burden, congest, dam up, hamper, hinder, impede, jam, obstruct, occlude, shackle, stop up 2. *noun* burden, dead weight, drag, encumbrance, hindrance, impediment, obstruction

cloistered cloistral, confined, hermitic, insulated, reclusive, restricted, secluded, sequestered, sheltered, shielded, shut off, withdrawn

Antonyms extrovert, genial, gregarious, outgoing, public, sociable, social

close[1] *verb* 1. bar, block, bung, choke, clog, confine, cork, fill, lock, obstruct, plug, seal, secure, shut, shut up, stop up 2. axe (*informal*), cease, complete, conclude, culminate, discontinue, end, finish, mothball, shut down, terminate, wind up 3. come together, connect, couple, fuse, grapple, join, unite

Antonyms (*sense 1*) clear, free, open, release, unblock, unclog, uncork, unstop, widen (*sense 2*) begin, commence, initiate, open, start (*sense 3*) disconnect, disjoin, disunite, divide, part, separate, split, uncouple

close[2] *adjective* 1. adjacent, adjoining, a hop, skip and a jump away, approaching, at hand, cheek by jowl, handy, hard by, imminent, impending, just round the corner, near, nearby, neighbouring, nigh, proximate, upcoming, within sniffing (spitting (*informal*), striking (*informal*)) distance (*informal*) 2. compact, congested, cramped, cropped, crowded, dense, impenetrable, jam-packed, packed, short, solid, thick, tight 3. accurate, conscientious, exact, faithful, literal, precise, strict 4. alert, assiduous, attentive, careful, concentrated, detailed, dogged, earnest, fixed, intense, intent, keen, minute, painstaking, rigorous, searching, thorough 5. attached, confidential, dear, devoted, familiar, inseparable, intimate, loving 6. airless, confined, frowsty, fuggy, heavy, humid, muggy, oppressive, stale, stifling, stuffy, suffocating, sweltering, thick, unventilated 7. hidden, private, reticent, retired, secluded, secret, secretive, taciturn, uncommunicative, unforthcoming 8. illiberal, mean, mingy (*Brit. informal*), miserly, near, niggardly, parsimonious, penurious, stingy, tight as a duck's arse (*taboo slang*), tight-fisted, ungenerous

Antonyms (*sense 1*) distant, far, far away, far off, future, outlying, remote (*sense 2*) dispersed, empty, free, loose, penetrable, porous, uncongested, uncrowded (*sense 5*) alienated, aloof, chilly, cold, cool, distant, indifferent, standoffish, unfriendly (*sense 6*) airy, fresh, refreshing, roomy, spacious (*sense 8*) charitable, extravagant, generous, lavish, liberal, magnanimous, unstinting

close[3] *noun* cessation, completion, conclusion, culmination, denouement, end, ending, finale, finish, run-in, termination

closed 1. fastened, locked, out of business, out of service, sealed, shut 2. concluded, decided, ended, finished, over, resolved, settled, terminated 3. exclusive, restricted

Antonyms (*sense 1*) ajar, open, unclosed, unfastened, unlocked, unsealed

closeness 1. adjacency, handiness, imminence, imminentness, impendence, impendency, nearness, proximity 2. compactness, crowdedness, denseness, impenetrability, impenetrableness, snugness, solidness, thickness, tightness 3. accuracy, exactness, faithfulness, literality, literalness, preciseness, strictness 4. alertness, assiduousness, attentiveness, carefulness, doggedness, earnestness, fixedness, intensiveness, intentness, keenness, minuteness, painstakingness, rigorousness, searchingness, thoroughness 5. confidentiality, confidentialness, dearness, devotedness, familiarness, inseparability, intimacy, intimateness, lovingness 6. airlessness, confinedness, frowstiness, heaviness, humidity, humidness, mugginess, oppressiveness, staleness, stuffiness, sultriness, thickness 7. reticence, secludedness, secretiveness, taciturnity, uncommunicativeness 8. illiberality, illiberalness, meanness, minginess (*Brit. informal*), miserliness, niggardliness, parsimony, penuriousness, stinginess

closet *noun* 1. cabinet, cubbyhole, cubicle, cupboard, recess 2. den, retreat *~adjective* 3. concealed, covert, hidden, private, secret

closure 1. cessation, closing, conclusion, end, finish, stoppage 2. bung, cap, lid, plug, seal, stopper 3. *in a deliberative assembly* cloture, guillotine

clot *noun* 1. clotting, coagulation, curdling, embolism, embolus, gob, lump, mass, occlu~ sion, thrombus 2. ass, berk (*Brit. slang*), buf~ foon, charlie (*Brit. informal*), coot, dickhead (*slang*), dickwit (*slang*), dipstick (*Brit. slang*), divvy (*Brit. slang*), dolt, dope (*informal*), dork (*slang*), dunderhead, dweeb (*U.S. slang*), fat~ head (*informal*), fool, fuckwit (*taboo slang*), geek (*slang*), gobshite (*Irish taboo slang*), gonzo (*slang*), idiot, jerk (*slang, chiefly U.S. & Canad.*), nerd *or* nurd (*slang*), nincompoop, nit (*informal*), nitwit (*informal*), numpty (*Scot. informal*), numskull *or* numbskull, pil~ lock (*Brit. slang*), plank (*Brit. slang*), plonker (*slang*), prat (*slang*), prick (*slang*), schmuck (*U.S. slang*), twerp *or* twirp (*informal*), twit (*informal, chiefly Brit.*), wally (*slang*) ~*verb* 3. coagulate, coalesce, congeal, curdle, jell, thicken

cloth dry goods, fabric, material, stuff, textiles

clothe accoutre, apparel, array, attire, bedizen (*archaic*), caparison, cover, deck, doll up (*slang*), drape, dress, endow, enwrap, equip, fit out, garb, get ready, habit, invest, outfit, rig, robe, swathe

Antonyms disrobe, divest, expose, strip, strip off, unclothe, uncover, undress

clothes, clothing apparel, attire, clobber (*Brit. slang*), costume, dress, duds (*informal*), en~ semble, garb, garments, gear (*informal*), get-up (*informal*), glad rags (*informal*), habits, outfit, raiment (*archaic or poetic*), rigout (*in~ formal*), schmutter (*slang*), threads (*slang*), togs (*informal*), vestments, vesture, wardrobe, wear

Types of clothing

academic dress
armour
baby clothes
beachwear
black tie
canonicals
civvies *or* civies
clericals
coordinates
coveralls
evening dress
fancy dress
fatigues
froufrou
Highland dress
hose
hosiery
knitwear
lingerie
livery
long-coats *or (archa~ ic)* long clothes
millinery
morning dress
mufti
neckwear
nightclothes
nightwear
overgarments
sackcloth
samfoo
separates
skivvy (*slang, chiefly U.S.*)
slops
sportswear
swaddling clothes
swimwear
undergarments
underthings
underwear
uniform
weepers
white tie
widow's weeds

Articles of clothing

apron
baldric
basque
bathrobe
bikini
blouse
body
body stocking
bodysuit
braces *or (U.S.)* sus~ penders
bustier
cardigan *or (infor~ mal)* cardie *or* cardy
chapeau
chaps, chaparajos *or* chaparejos
chuddah, chuddar, chudder *or* chador
cilice
coat
coatee
codpiece
cummerbund *or* kum~ merbund
dress
dressing gown
dungarees
frock
galluses (*dialect*)
garter
gown
glove
halter
housecoat
jacket
jerkin
jersey
jumper
jump suit
kaftan *or* caftan
kimono
kilt
leotard
loincloth *or* breech~ cloth
maillot
manteau
mantle (*archaic*)
mitten
muff
negligee *or* negligée
nightdress, nightgown *or (Brit. informal)* nightie
nightshirt
overall
overcoat
overskirt
oversleeve
peignoir
plaid
pullover
pyjamas *or (U.S.)* pa~ jamas
rompers
sash
sari *or* saree
sarong
serape
shawl
shift
shirt
shoe
shorts
slop
smock
sock
sporran
sweater
swimming costume, bathing costume, costume *or (Austral. informal)* cossie
swimming trunks *or* trunks
swimsuit
tanga
tank top
thong
tie *or (U.S.)* necktie
tights
T-shirt *or* tee shirt
undergarment
waistcoat *or (U.S. & Canad.)* vest
wrap
wrapper
yashmak *or* yashmac

Parts of clothing

arm
armhole
bodice
buttonhole
collar
cuff
epaulette
gusset
hem
hemline

hood
lapel
leg
lining
neckline
pocket
seam
shoulder
sleeve
tail
train
waist
waistline
yoke

Religious clothing
alb
almuce
amice
biretta *or* berretta
calotte
canonicals
capuche *or* capouche
cassock
chasuble
chimere, chimer *or* chimar
clerical collar
clericals
coif
cope
cornet
cotta
cowl
dalmatic
dog collar (*informal*)
gremial
guimpe
habit
infulae
maniple
mantelletta
mitre
mozzetta *or* mozetta
pallium
peplos *or* peplus
pontificals
rochet
scapular
shovel hat
soutane
superhumeral
surcingle
surplice
tippet
wimple
zucchetto

Suits
boiler suit
catsuit
double-breasted suit
dress suit
G-suit *or* anti-G suit
judogi
jump suit
lounge suit
Mao suit
penguin suit
playsuit
pyjamas *or* (*U.S.*) pa~jamas
romper suit
safari suit
sailor suit
shell suit
single-breasted suit
ski suit
sunsuit
spacesuit
sweat suit
swimsuit
three-piece suit
tracksuit
trouser suit *or* (*U.S. & Canad.*) pant suit
wet suit
zoot suit

Coats and cloaks
afghan
balmacaan
bathrobe
box coat
Burberry (*Trade~mark*)
burnous, burnouse *or* burnoose
cape
capote
capuchin
cardinal
chesterfield
coat dress
coatee
cope
covert coat
cutaway
dolman
domino
dreadnought *or* dreadnaught
dress coat
dressing gown
duffel coat
duster coat
fearnought *or* fear~naught
frock coat
fur coat
greatcoat
hacking coat
housecoat
Inverness
jellaba *or* jellabah
Jodhpuri coat
joseph
loden coat
mac *or* mack
mackintosh *or* macin~tosh
manta
mantelet
mantilla
morning coat
newmarket
opera cloak *or* opera hood
overcoat
paletot
pea jacket *or* peacoat
parka
peignoir
pelisse
peplum
poncho
Prince Albert
raglan
raincoat
redingote
roquelaure
sheepskin coat
sherwani
slicker (*U.S. & Canad.*)
snorkel
sou'wester
spencer
surcoat
surtout
swallow-tailed coat *or* swallowtail
tailcoat *or* tails
tippet
trench coat
ulster
undercoat
waterproof

Jackets
acton
anorak
bed jacket
biker jacket
blazer
blouson
body warmer
bomber jacket
bolero
boxy jacket
bumfreezer
cagoule *or* cag
cymar
denim jacket
dinner jacket *or* (*U.S. & Canad.*) tuxedo *or* tux
donkey jacket
doublet
duvet *or* duvet jacket
Eton jacket
gambeson
gilet
hacking jacket
jerkin
leather jacket
lumberjacket
Mackinaw coat *or* mackinaw (*chiefly U.S. & Canad.*)
matinée jacket
mess jacket
monkey jacket
Norfolk jacket
pourpoint
reefing jacket
sack *or* sacque
shell jacket
shrug
smoking jacket
spencer
sports jacket
tabard
windcheater *or* wind~jammer

Sweaters
Aran sweater
Cowichan sweater, Indian sweater, si~wash *or* siwash sweater (*Canad.*)
cowl-necked sweater
crew-neck *or* crew-necked sweater
Guernsey (*Austral.*)
Icelandic
jumper
polo *or* polo neck
pullover
rollneck
skivvy (*Austral. & N.Z.*)
slipover
sloppy joe

sweatshirt
turtleneck
V-neck *or* V-necked sweater

Shirts

blouse
boiled shirt
bush shirt
camise
chemise
cover-shoulder
dashiki
dress shirt
garibaldi
guimpe
Jacky Howe (*Austral. informal*)
hair shirt
kerbaya
kurta *or* khurta
lava-lava
middy blouse
overblouse
polo shirt
sark (*Scot.*)
sports shirt
T-shirt *or* tee shirt

Gowns and dresses

ballgown
burka
busuuti
button-through dress
chemise
cheongsam
chiton
coat dress
cocktail dress
dirndl
gymslip
kaftan *or* caftan
kimono
mantua
maxidress
microdress
midi
minidress
Mother Hubbard
muu-muu
negligee *or* negligée
nightdress *or* (*U.S. & Canad.*) nightrobe
nightgown *or* (*infor~mal*) nightie *or* nighty
nightshirt
overdress
peignoir
pinafore dress, pina~fore, pinny (informal) *or* (*U.S. & Canad.*) jumper
riding habit
sack
sari *or* saree
sheath
shift
shirtdress
shirtwaister *or* (*U.S. and Canad.*) shirt~waist
sundress
sweater dress
tea gown
tunic
wedding dress

Skirts

A-line
button-through
crinoline
dirndl
divided skirt
drop-waisted
filibeg, fillibeg *or* philibeg
full skirt
fustanella *or* fusta~nelle
gaberdine *or* gabar~dine
grass skirt
half-slip *or* waist-slip
hobble skirt
hoop skirt
kilt
maxiskirt
microskirt
midiskirt
miniskirt
overskirt
pencil skirt
petticoat
puffball skirt
ra-ra skirt
riding skirt
sarong
tutu
underskirt
wrapover *or* wrap~round

Trousers and shorts

bell-bottoms
Bermuda shorts
bloomers
breeches
Capri pants *or* Capris
chinos
churidars
cords
corduroys
culottes
cycling shorts
denims
drainpipes
flares
galligaskins *or* gally~gaskins
hot pants
jeans
jodhpurs
knickerbockers *or* (*U.S.*) knickers
lederhosen
leggings
Levis (*Trademark*)
loon pants *or* loons
overalls
Oxford bags
palazzo pants
pedal pushers
plus fours
pyjamas
riding breeches
salopettes
ski pants
slacks
slops
smallclothes
spatterdashes
stovepipes
toreador pants
trews
trouse (*Brit.*)
trunk hose

Hosiery

ankle sock *or* (*U.S.*) anklet
argyle
bed sock
bobby sock
half-hose
hose (*history*)
knee-high sock
legwarmer
lisle stocking
maillot
nylons
pop sock
puttee *or* putty
tights *or* (*esp. U.S. & Austral.*) pantihose
sock
stay-up
stock (*archaic*)
stocking

Underwear

Balmoral
basque
bloomers
body
body stocking
boxer shorts *or* boxers
brassiere *or* bra
briefs
camiknickers
camisole
chemisette
combinations *or* (*U.S. & Canad.*) union suit
corset
crinoline
drawers *or* underdrawers
foundation garment
French knickers
garter
girdle
G-string
half-slip *or* waist-slip
jockstrap *or* athletic support
knickers
liberty bodice
lingerie
long johns
pannier
panties
pants
petticoat
shift
shorts *or* undershorts (*chiefly U.S. & Canad.*)
singlet (*chiefly Brit.*)
step-ins
string vest
suspender *or* (*U.S.*) garter
suspender belt *or* (*U.S.*) garter belt
teddy
thermals
trunks
underpants
underskirt
vest, undervest, undershirt, T-shirt (*U.S. & Canad.*), *or* (*Austral.*) singlet
Y-fronts

Headgear

Akubra (*Austral. Trademark*)
anadem (*poetic*)
babushka
Balaclava helmet *or* Balaclava
Balmoral
bandanna *or* bandana
bandeau
barret
baseball cap
basinet *or* bascinet
beanie *or* beany
bearskin
beaver
beret
billycock (*rare, chiefly Brit.*)
biretta *or* berretta
blackcap
bluebonnet *or* bluecap
boater
bonnet
bowler *or (U.S. & Canad.)* derby
broadbrim
busby
calash *or* caleche
calotte
calpac, calpack *or* kalpak
capuche *or* capouch
castor
chaplet
cheese cutter
circlet
cloche
cloth cap
cocked hat
coif
commode
coonskin
cornet
coronet
cossack hat
crash helmet
crown
curch *or* curchef
deerstalker
diadem
Dolly Varden
dunce cap
earmuff
fascinator (*rare*)
fedora
fez
flat cap
fool's cap
forage cap
frontlet *or* frontal
Gandhi cap
glengarry
hard hat
havelock
headband
headdress
heaume
helmet
homburg
hood
Juliet cap
keffiyeh, kaffiyeh *or* kufiyah
kepi
laurels
leghorn
liberty cap
lum-hat (*Scot.*)
mitre
mobcap *or* mob
montero
morion
mortarboard, trencher *or* trencher cap
mutch
nightcap
opera hat *or* gibus
Panama hat
paper hat
peaked cap
petasus
Phrygian cap
picture hat
pillbox
pinner
pith helmet, topee *or* topi
poke *or* poke bonnet
porkpie hat
sailor hat
sallet, salet *or* salade
shako *or* shacko
shovel hat
shower cap
silk hat
skullcap
slouch hat
snood
sombrero
songkok
sou'wester *or* nor'wester
stetson
stocking cap
stovepipe
straw hat
sunbonnet
sunhat
taj
tam-o'-shanter *or* tammy (*Scot.*)
tarboosh, tarbouche *or* tarbush
tarpaulin
ten-gallon hat
tiara
tin hat (*informal*)
tricorn *or* tricorne
toorie *or* tourie (*Scot.*)
top hat
topper (*informal*)
toque
tricorn
trilby
tuque
turban
veil
visor *or* vizor
watch cap
wimple
yarmulke

Neckwear

ascot
bertha
black tie
boa
bow tie
carcanet (*archaic*)
comforter (*chiefly Brit.*)
cravat
dicky *or* dicky bow
falling band
fichu
foulard
kerchief
madras
muffler
neckcloth
neckerchief
rebozo
scarf
school tie
stock
stole
tie *or (U.S.)* necktie
white tie
Windsor tie

Footwear

ankle boot
arctic (*U.S.*)
Balmoral
blucher (*obsolete*)
bootee
bottine
bovver boot (*Brit. slang*)
brogan
brogue
brothel creeper (*informal*)
buskin
chopine *or* chopin
chukka boot
clog
co-respondent
cothurnus *or* cothurn
court shoe
creeper (*informal*)
crowboot
deck shoe
Doc Marten (*Trademark*)
espadrille
field boot
flats *or* flatties
flip-flop
gaiter *or* spat
galosh
ghillie (*Scot.*)
gumboot
gumshoe
gym shoe
half boot
Hessian boot
high heel
hobnail boot
jackboot
Jandal (*N.Z., Trademark*)
lace-up
larrigan
loafer
moccasin
moonboot
mukluk
mule
overshoe
Oxford
pantofle, pantoffle *or* pantoufle (*archaic*)
platform
plimsoll *or* plimsole
pump
racket *or* racquet
running shoe
rock boot
sabot
sandal
sandshoe
scuff
slingback
slip-on
slipper
sneaker
snowshoe
spike

stiletto
surgical boot
tennis shoe
top boot
track shoe
training shoe *or* trainer
veldskoen
wader
wedge *or* wedge heel
welly
Wellington boot
winkle-picker

Thou shalt not wear a garment of divers sort, as of woollen and linen together
Bible: Deuteronomy

kilt: a costume sometimes worn by Scotchmen in America and Americans in Scotland
Ambrose Bierce *The Devil's Dictionary*

Sure, deck your lower limbs in pants;
Yours are the limbs, my sweeting.
You look divine as you advance -
Have you seen yourself retreating?
Ogden Nash *What's the Use?*

cloud *noun* **1.** billow, darkness, fog, gloom, haze, mist, murk, nebula, nebulosity, obscurity, vapour **2.** crowd, dense mass, flock, horde, host, multitude, shower, swarm, throng ~*verb* **3.** becloud, darken, dim, eclipse, obfuscate, obscure, overcast, overshadow, shade, shadow, veil **4.** confuse, disorient, distort, impair, muddle, muddy the waters

Cloud types
see WEATHER

I wander'd lonely as a cloud
William Wordsworth *I Wandered Lonely as a Cloud*

cloudy blurred, confused, dark, dim, dismal, dull, dusky, emulsified, gloomy, hazy, indistinct, leaden, louring *or* lowering, muddy, murky, nebulous, obscure, opaque, overcast, sombre, sullen, sunless
Antonyms bright, clear, distinct, fair, obvious, plain, sunny, uncloudy

clout **1.** *verb* box, chin (*slang*), clobber (*slang*), cuff, deck (*slang*), hit, lay one on (*slang*), punch, skelp (*dialect*), sock (*slang*), strike, thump, wallop (*informal*), wham **2.** *noun* authority, bottom, influence, power, prestige, pull, standing, weight

cloven bisected, cleft, divided, split

clown *noun* **1.** buffoon, comedian, dolt, fool, harlequin, jester, joculator *or (fem.)* joculatrix, joker, merry-andrew, mountebank, pierrot, prankster, punchinello **2.** boor, clodhopper (*informal*), hind (*obsolete*), peasant, swain (*archaic*), yahoo, yokel ~*verb* **3.** act the fool, act the goat, jest, mess about, piss about *or* around (*taboo slang*), play the fool, play the goat

clownish **1.** comic, foolish, galumphing (*informal*), nonsensical, slapstick, zany **2.** awkward, boorish, churlish, clumsy, ill-bred, rough, rude, rustic, uncivil, ungainly, vulgar

cloy disgust, glut, gorge, nauseate, sate, satiate, sicken, surfeit, weary

cloying excessive, icky (*informal*), nauseating, oversweet, sickly, treacly

club **1.** *noun* bat, bludgeon, cosh (*Brit.*), cudgel, stick, truncheon **2.** *verb* bash, baste, batter, beat, bludgeon, clobber (*slang*), clout (*informal*), cosh (*Brit.*), hammer, pommel (*rare*), pummel, strike **3.** *noun* association, circle, clique, company, fraternity, group, guild, lodge, order, set, society, sodality, union

Clubs
blackjack
bludgeon
cudgel
knobkerrie *or* knobstick
lathi
life preserver
nightstick
nulla-nulla
quarterstaff
shillelagh *or* shillala
truncheon
waddy

I wouldn't want to belong to any club that would have me as a member
Groucho Marx

clue evidence, hint, indication, inkling, intimation, lead, pointer, sign, suggestion, suspicion, tip, tip-off, trace

clump **1.** *noun* bunch, bundle, cluster, mass, shock **2.** *verb* bumble, clomp, lumber, plod, stamp, stomp, stump, thud, thump, tramp

clumsiness accident-proneness, awkwardness, gaucheness, gawkiness, gracelessness, heaviness, heavy-handedness, inelegance, inelegancy, ineptitude, ineptness, inexpertness, lumberingness, maladroitness, ponderosity, ponderousness, uncouthness, ungainliness, unskilfulness, unwieldiness
Antonyms adeptness, adroitness, agility, deftness, dexterity, dexterousness *or* dextrousness, expertise, finesse, grace, gracefulness, handiness, nimbleness, proficiency, skill

clumsy accident-prone, awkward, blundering, bumbling, bungling, butterfingered (*informal*), cack-handed (*informal*), gauche, gawky, ham-fisted (*informal*), ham-handed (*informal*), heavy, ill-shaped, inept, inexpert, klutzy (*U.S. & Canad. slang*), like a bull in a china shop, lumbering, maladroit, ponderous, uncoordinated, uncouth, ungainly, unhandy, unskilful, unwieldy
Antonyms adept, adroit, competent, deft, dexterous, expert, graceful, handy, proficient, skilful

cluster **1.** *noun* assemblage, batch, bunch, clump, collection, gathering, group, knot **2.** *verb* assemble, bunch, collect, flock, gather, group

clutch catch (up), clasp, cling to, embrace, fasten, grab, grapple, grasp, grip, seize, snatch

clutches claws, control, custody, grasp, grip, hands, keeping, possession, power, sway

clutter 1. *noun* confusion, disarray, disorder, hotchpotch, jumble, litter, mess, muddle, un~tidiness 2. *verb* litter, scatter, strew
Antonyms *noun* neatness, order, organization, tidiness *~verb* arrange, order, organize, straighten, tidy

cluttered confused, disarrayed, disordered, jumbled, littered, messy, muddled, untidy

coach *noun* 1. bus, car, carriage, charabanc, vehicle 2. handler, instructor, teacher, trainer, tutor *~verb* 3. cram, drill, exercise, instruct, prepare, train, tutor

coagulate clot, congeal, curdle, jell, thicken

coalesce amalgamate, blend, cohere, combine, come together, commingle, commix, consoli~date, fraternize, fuse, incorporate, integrate, meld, merge, mix, unite

coalition affiliation, alliance, amalgam, amal~gamation, association, bloc, combination, com~pact, confederacy, confederation, conjunction, fusion, integration, league, merger, union

coarse 1. boorish, brutish, coarse-grained, foul-mouthed, gruff, loutish, rough, rude, un~civil 2. bawdy, earthy, immodest, impolite, improper, impure, indelicate, inelegant, mean, offensive, raunchy (*slang*), ribald, rude, smut~ty, vulgar 3. coarse-grained, crude, homespun, impure, rough-hewn, unfinished, unpolished, unprocessed, unpurified, unrefined
Antonyms (*senses 1 & 2*) civilized, cultured, elegant, fine, genteel, inoffensive, pleasant, polished, polite, proper, refined, sophisticated, urbane, well-bred, well-mannered (*sense 3*) fine-grained, polished, purified, refined, smooth, soft

coarsen anaesthetize, blunt, callous, deaden, desensitize, dull, harden, indurate, roughen

coarseness bawdiness, boorishness, crudity, earthiness, indelicacy, offensiveness, poor taste, ribaldry, roughness, smut, smuttiness, uncouthness, unevenness

coast 1. *noun* beach, border, coastline, littoral, seaboard, seaside, shore, strand 2. *verb* cruise, drift, freewheel, get by, glide, sail, taxi
Related adjective: littoral

coat *noun* 1. fleece, fur, hair, hide, pelt, skin, wool 2. coating, covering, layer, overlay *~verb* 3. apply, Artex (*Trademark*), cover, plaster, smear, spread

Coats and cloaks
see CLOTHES

coating blanket, coat, covering, dusting, film, finish, glaze, lamination, layer, membrane, patina, sheet, skin, varnish, veneer

coax allure, beguile, cajole, decoy, entice, flat~ter, inveigle, persuade, prevail upon, soft-soap (*informal*), soothe, sweet-talk (*informal*), talk into, twist (someone's) arm, wheedle
Antonyms browbeat, bully, coerce, force, har~ass, intimidate, pressurize, threaten

cobble botch, bungle, clout, mend, patch, tink~er

cock 1. *noun* chanticleer, cockerel, rooster 2. *verb* perk up, prick, raise, stand up

cockeyed absurd, askew, asymmetrical, awry, crazy, crooked, lopsided, ludicrous, nonsensi~cal, preposterous, skewwhiff (*Brit. informal*), squint (*informal*)

cockiness arrogance, big-headedness, brash~ness, bumptiousness, cocksureness, conceit, conceitedness, confidence, egotism, lordliness, overconfidence, presumptuousness, self-assurance, vanity

cocksure arrogant, brash, bumptious, cocky, full of oneself, hubristic, overconfident, pre~sumptuous

cocky arrogant, brash, cocksure, conceited, egotistical, full of oneself, lordly, swaggering, swollen-headed, vain
Antonyms hesitant, lacking confidence, mod~est, self-effacing, uncertain, unsure

cocoon cushion, envelop, insulate, pad, pro~tect, swaddle, swathe, wrap

coddle baby, cosset, humour, indulge, molly~coddle, nurse, pamper, pet, spoil, wet-nurse (*informal*)

code 1. cipher, cryptograph 2. canon, conven~tion, custom, ethics, etiquette, manners, max~im, regulations, rules, system

codify catalogue, classify, collect, condense, di~gest, organize, summarize, systematize, tabu~late

coerce browbeat, bulldoze (*informal*), bully, compel, constrain, dragoon, drive, force, in~timidate, press-gang, pressurize, railroad (*in~formal*), twist (someone's) arm (*informal*)

coercion browbeating, bullying, compulsion, constraint, duress, force, intimidation, pres~sure, strong-arm tactics (*informal*), threats

coeval coetaneous (*rare*), coexistent, contempo~raneous, contemporary, synchronous

coffee

Coffees

arabica	decaffinated *or* decaf
black coffee	espresso
Blue mountain	French roast
Brazilian	instant coffee
brown coffee	Java
café au lait	Kenyan
café noir	mocha
cappuccino	Turkish coffee
Colombian	robusta
Continental	white coffee
Costa Rican	

Look here, Steward, if this is coffee, I want tea; but

if this is tea, then I wish for coffee
Punch

coffer ark (*dialect*), case, casket, chest, kist (*Scot. & Northern English dialect*), repository, strongbox, treasure chest, treasury

coffers assets, capital, finances, funds, means, reserves, treasury, vaults

cogency conviction, force, potency, power, strength

cogent compelling, compulsive, conclusive, convincing, effective, forceful, forcible, influ~ential, irresistible, potent, powerful, strong, urgent, weighty

cogitate consider, contemplate, deliberate, meditate, mull over, muse, ponder, reflect, ruminate, think

cogitation consideration, contemplation, delib~eration, meditation, reflection, rumination, thought

cognate affiliated, akin, alike, allied, analo~gous, associated, connected, kindred, related, similar

cognition apprehension, awareness, compre~hension, discernment, insight, intelligence, perception, reasoning, understanding

cognizance acknowledgment, apprehension, cognition, knowledge, notice, perception, per~cipience, recognition, regard

cognizant acquainted, aware, clued-up (*infor~mal*), conscious, conversant, familiar, in~formed, knowledgeable, versed

cohere **1.** adhere, bind, cling, coalesce, com~bine, consolidate, fuse, glue, hold, stick, unite **2.** agree, be connected, be consistent, corre~spond, hang together, harmonize, hold good, hold water, square

coherence agreement, comprehensibility, con~cordance, congruity, connection, consistency, consonance, correspondence, intelligibility, ra~tionality, union, unity

coherent articulate, comprehensible, consist~ent, intelligible, logical, lucid, meaningful, or~derly, organized, rational, reasoned, system~atic
Antonyms confusing, disjointed, illogical, in~comprehensible, inconsistent, meaningless, rambling, unintelligible, vague

cohort **1.** band, company, contingent, legion, regiment, squadron, troop **2.** *chiefly U.S.* ac~complice, assistant, comrade, follower, hench~man, mate, myrmidon, partner, protagonist, sidekick (*slang*), supporter

coil convolute, curl, entwine, loop, snake, spi~ral, twine, twist, wind, wreathe, writhe

coin **1.** *verb* conceive, create, fabricate, forge, formulate, frame, invent, make up, mint, mould, originate, think up **2.** *noun* cash, change, copper, dosh (*Brit. & Austral. slang*), money, silver, specie
Related adjective: nummary

coincide **1.** be concurrent, coexist, occur simul~taneously, synchronize **2.** accord, harmonize, match, quadrate, square, tally **3.** acquiesce, agree, concur, correspond
Antonyms be inconsistent, be unlike, contra~dict, differ, disagree, diverge, divide, part, separate

coincidence **1.** accident, chance, eventuality, fluke, fortuity, happy accident, luck, stroke of luck **2.** concomitance, concurrence, conjunc~tion, correlation, correspondence, synchronism

coincident coinciding, concomitant, concurring, consonant, contemporaneous, coordinate, cor~respondent, synchronous

coincidental **1.** accidental, casual, chance, fluky (*informal*), fortuitous, unintentional, un~planned **2.** coincident, concomitant, concur~rent, simultaneous, synchronous
Antonyms (*sense 1*) calculated, deliberate, done on purpose, intentional, planned, prear~ranged

coitus coition, congress, copulation, coupling, mating, nookie (*slang*), rumpy-pumpy (*slang*), sexual intercourse, the other (*informal*), union

cold *adjective* **1.** arctic, biting, bitter, bleak, brumal, chill, chilly, cool, freezing, frigid, frosty, frozen, gelid, harsh, icy, inclement, parky (*Brit. informal*), raw, wintry **2.** be~numbed, chilled, chilly, freezing, frozen to the marrow, numbed, shivery **3.** aloof, apathetic, cold-blooded, dead, distant, frigid, glacial, in~different, inhospitable, lukewarm, passionless, phlegmatic, reserved, spiritless, standoffish, stony, undemonstrative, unfeeling, unmoved, unresponsive, unsympathetic *~noun* **4.** chill, chilliness, coldness, frigidity, frostiness, ici~ness, inclemency
Antonyms (*sense 1*) balmy, heated, hot, mild, sunny, warm (*sense 3*) alive, animated, caring, compassionate, conscious, demonstrative, emotional, friendly, loving, open, passionate, responsive, spirited, sympathetic, warm

cold-blooded barbarous, brutal, callous, cruel, dispassionate, heartless, inhuman, merciless, pitiless, ruthless, savage, steely, stony-hearted, unemotional, unfeeling, unmoved
Antonyms caring, charitable, civilized, con~cerned, emotional, feeling, friendly, humane, involved, kind, kind-hearted, merciful, open, passionate, sensitive, warm

cold-hearted callous, detached, frigid, hard~hearted, harsh, heartless, indifferent, inhu~man, insensitive, stony-hearted, uncaring, un~feeling, unkind, unsympathetic

cold-heartedness callousness, chilliness, cold~ness, detachment, flintiness, frigidity, frigid~ness, hardheartedness, harshness, heartless~

ness, indifference, inhumanity, insensitiveness, insensitivity, mercilessness, pitilessness, steeliness, stony-heartedness, unfeelingness, unkindness, unresponsiveness

collaborate 1. cooperate, coproduce, join forces, participate, play ball (*informal*), team up, work together 2. collude, conspire, cooperate, fraternize

collaboration alliance, association, concert, cooperation, partnership, teamwork

collaborator 1. associate, colleague, confederate, co-worker, partner, team-mate 2. collaborationist, fraternizer, quisling, traitor, turncoat

collapse 1. *verb* break down, cave in, come to nothing, crack up (*informal*), crumple, fail, faint, fall, fall apart at the seams, fold, founder, give way, go belly-up (*informal*), subside 2. *noun* breakdown, cave-in, disintegration, downfall, exhaustion, failure, faint, flop, prostration, subsidence

collar *verb* apprehend, appropriate, capture, catch, catch in the act, grab, lay hands on, nab (*informal*), nail (*informal*), seize

collate adduce, analogize, collect, compare, compose, gather (*Printing*)

collateral *noun* 1. assurance, deposit, guarantee, pledge, security, surety *~adjective* 2. concurrent, confirmatory, corroborative, indirect, not lineal, parallel, related, supporting 3. ancillary, auxiliary, secondary, subordinate

colleague aider, ally, assistant, associate, auxiliary, coadjutor (*rare*), collaborator, companion, comrade, confederate, confrère, fellow worker, helper, partner, team-mate, workmate

collect 1. accumulate, aggregate, amass, assemble, gather, heap, hoard, save, stockpile 2. assemble, cluster, congregate, convene, converge, flock together, rally 3. acquire, muster, obtain, raise, secure, solicit

Antonyms disperse, distribute, scatter, spread, strew

Collectors and enthusiasts

ailurophile	cats
arctophile	teddy bears
audiophile	high-fidelity sound reproduction
automobilist	cars
bibliophile	books
brolliologist	umbrellas
campanologist	bell-ringing
cartophilist	cigarette cards
cruciverbalist	crosswords
deltiologist	picture postcards
discophile	gramophone records
fusilatelist	phonecards
herbalist	herbs
lepidopterist	moths and butterflies
medallist	medals
numismatist	coins
oenophile	wine
paranumismatist	coin-like objects
philatelist	stamps
phillumenist	matchbox labels
phraseologist	phrases
scripophile	share certificates
vexillologist	flags
zoophile	animals

collected as cool as a cucumber, calm, composed, confident, cool, keeping one's cool, placid, poised, sedate, self-possessed, serene, together (*slang*), unfazed (*informal*), unperturbable, unperturbed, unruffled

Antonyms agitated, distressed, emotional, excitable, irritable, nervous, perturbed, ruffled, shaky, troubled, twitchy (*informal*), unpoised, unsteady

collection 1. accumulation, anthology, compilation, congeries, heap, hoard, mass, pile, set, stockpile, store 2. assemblage, assembly, assortment, cluster, company, congregation, convocation, crowd, gathering, group 3. alms, contribution, offering, offertory

collective aggregate, combined, common, composite, concerted, cooperative, corporate, cumulative, joint, shared, unified, united

Antonyms divided, individual, piecemeal, split, uncombined, uncooperative

collector acquirer, amasser, gatherer, hoarder, saver, stockpiler

collide clash, come into collision, conflict, crash, meet head-on

collision 1. accident, bump, crash, impact, pile-up (*informal*), prang (*informal*), smash 2. clash, clashing, conflict, confrontation, encounter, opposition, skirmish

colloquial conversational, demotic, everyday, familiar, idiomatic, informal, vernacular

colloquy confabulation, conference, conversation, debate, dialogue, discourse, discussion, talk

collude abet, be in cahoots (*informal*), collaborate, complot, connive, conspire, contrive, intrigue, machinate, plot, scheme

collusion cahoots (*informal*), complicity, connivance, conspiracy, craft, deceit, fraudulent artifice, intrigue, secret understanding

colonist colonial, colonizer, frontiersman, homesteader (*U.S.*), immigrant, pioneer, planter, settler

colonize open up, people, pioneer, populate, put down roots, settle

colonnade arcade, cloisters, covered walk, peristyle, portico

colony community, dependency, dominion, outpost, possession, province, satellite state, settlement, territory

colossal Brobdingnagian, elephantine, enormous, gargantuan, gigantic, ginormous (*informal*), herculean, huge, humongous *or* humungous (*U.S. slang*), immense, mammoth, massive, monstrous, monumental, mountainous, prodigious, stellar (*informal*), titanic, vast **Antonyms** average, diminutive, little, miniature, minute, ordinary, pygmy *or* pigmy, slight, small, tiny, weak, wee

colour *noun* **1.** colorant, coloration, complexion, dye, hue, paint, pigment, pigmentation, shade, tincture, tinge, tint **2.** animation, bloom, blush, brilliance, flush, glow, liveliness, rosiness, ruddiness, vividness **3.** *figurative* appearance, disguise, excuse, façade, false show, guise, plea, pretence, pretext, semblance ~*verb* **4.** colourwash, dye, paint, stain, tinge, tint **5.** *figurative* disguise, distort, embroider, exaggerate, falsify, garble, gloss over, misrepresent, pervert, prejudice, slant, taint **6.** blush, burn, crimson, flush, go as red as a beetroot, go crimson, redden

Colours

almond
almond green
amber
amethyst
apple green
aqua
aquamarine
ash
aubergine
auburn
avocado
azure
baby pink
bay
beige
bisque
bistre
black
blue
bronze
brown
buff
burgundy
burnt sienna
burnt umber
butternut
café au lait
Cambridge blue
camel
canary yellow
cardinal
cardinal red
carmine
carnation
celadon
cerise
cerulean
champagne
charcoal
chartreuse
cherry
chestnut
chocolate
cinnabar
cinnamon
citron
claret
cobalt blue
cocoa
coffee
Copenhagen blue
copper
coral
cream
crimson
cyanic (*rare*)
cyclamen
daffodil
damask
drab
dubonnet
duck-egg blue
dun
eau de nil
ebony
ecru
eggshell
electric blue
emerald green
fawn
flame
flesh
fuchsia
gamboge
gentian
ginger
gold
green
grenadine
grey
gunmetal
hazel
heather
heliotrope
henna
indigo
iron
ivory
jade
jasmine
jet
khaki
lapis lazuli
lavender
lemon
lilac
lime green
Lincoln green
liver
magenta
magnolia
mahogany
maize
maroon
mauve
midnight blue
mocha
mulberry
mustard
nankeen
navy
navy blue
Nile blue
Nile green
nutbrown
nutmeg
oatmeal
ochre
off-white
old gold
old rose
olive
orange
oxblood
Oxford blue
oyster pink
oyster white
pansy
peach
peach-blow
peacock blue
pea green
pearl
periwinkle
perse
petrol blue
pewter
pine green
pink
pistachio
platinum
plum
poppy
primrose
primrose yellow
puce
purple
putty
raspberry
raven
red
rose
royal blue
royal purple
ruby
russet
rust
sable
saffron
salmon pink
sand
sapphire
saxe blue
scarlet
sea green
seal brown
sepia
shell pink
sienna
silver
sky blue
slate
sorrel
steel blue
steel grey
stone
straw
strawberry
tan
tangerine
taupe
tawny
teak
teal
tea rose
terracotta
Titian
topaz
tortoiseshell
Turkey red
turquoise
Tyrian purple
ultramarine
umber
vermilion
violet

walnut
Wedgwood blue
white
wine
yellow

colourful 1. bright, brilliant, Day-glo (*Trademark*), intense, jazzy (*informal*), kaleidoscopic, motley, multicoloured, psychedelic, rich, variegated, vibrant, vivid 2. characterful, distinctive, graphic, interesting, lively, picturesque, rich, stimulating, unusual, vivid
Antonyms (*sense 1*) colourless, dark, drab, dreary, dull, faded, pale, washed out (*sense 2*) boring, characterless, dull, flat, lifeless, monotonous, unexciting, uninteresting, unvaried

colourless 1. achromatic, achromic, anaemic, ashen, bleached, drab, faded, neutral, sickly, wan, washed out 2. characterless, dreary, insipid, lacklustre, tame, uninteresting, unmemorable, vacuous, vapid
Antonyms (*sense 1*) blooming, flushed, glowing, healthy, radiant, robust, ruddy (*sense 2*) animated, bright, colourful, compelling, distinctive, exciting, interesting, unusual

colours 1. banner, emblem, ensign, flag, standard 2. *figurative* aspect, breed, character, identity, nature, stamp, strain

coltish frisky, frolicsome, lively, ludic (*literary*), playful, romping, skittish, sportive, unruly

column 1. cavalcade, file, line, list, procession, queue, rank, row, string, train 2. caryatid, obelisk, pilaster, pillar, post, shaft, support, upright

columnist correspondent, critic, editor, gossip columnist, journalist, journo (*slang*), reporter, reviewer

coma insensibility, lethargy, oblivion, somnolence, stupor, torpor, trance, unconsciousness

comatose drugged, insensible, lethargic, somnolent, soporose (*Medical*), stupefied, torpid, unconscious

comb *verb* 1. arrange, curry, dress, groom, untangle 2. *of flax, wool, etc.* card, hackle, hatchel, heckle, tease, teasel, teazle 3. *figurative* forage, go through with a fine-tooth comb, hunt, rake, ransack, rummage, scour, screen, search, sift, sweep

combat 1. *noun* action, battle, conflict, contest, encounter, engagement, fight, skirmish, struggle, war, warfare 2. *verb* battle, contend, contest, cope, defy, do battle with, engage, fight, oppose, resist, strive, struggle, withstand
Antonyms *noun* agreement, armistice, peace, surrender, truce *~verb* accept, acquiesce, declare a truce, give up, make peace, support, surrender

combatant 1. *noun* adversary, antagonist, belligerent, contender, enemy, fighter, fighting man, gladiator, opponent, serviceman, soldier, warrior 2. *adjective* battling, belligerent, combative, conflicting, contending, fighting, opposing, warring

combative aggressive, antagonistic, bellicose, belligerent, contentious, militant, pugnacious, quarrelsome, truculent, warlike
Antonyms nonaggressive, nonbelligerent, nonviolent, pacific, pacifist, peaceable, peaceful, peace-loving

combination 1. amalgam, amalgamation, blend, coalescence, composite, connection, meld, mix, mixture 2. alliance, association, cabal, cartel, coalition, combine, compound, confederacy, confederation, consortium, conspiracy, federation, merger, syndicate, unification, union

combine amalgamate, associate, bind, blend, bond, compound, connect, cooperate, fuse, incorporate, integrate, join (together), link, marry, meld, merge, mix, pool, put together, synthesize, unify, unite
Antonyms detach, dissociate, dissolve, disunite, divide, part, separate, sever

combustible explosive, flammable, incendiary, inflammable

come 1. advance, appear, approach, arrive, become, draw near, enter, happen, materialize, move, move towards, near, occur, originate, show up (*informal*), turn out, turn up (*informal*) 2. appear, arrive, attain, enter, materialize, reach, show up (*informal*), turn up (*informal*) 3. fall, happen, occur, take place 4. arise, emanate, emerge, end up, flow, issue, originate, result, turn out 5. extend, reach 6. be available (made, offered, on offer, produced)

come about arise, befall, come to pass, happen, occur, result, take place, transpire (*informal*)

come across bump into (*informal*), chance upon, discover, encounter, find, happen upon, hit upon, light upon, meet, notice, stumble upon, unearth

come along develop, improve, mend, perk up, pick up, progress, rally, recover, recuperate

come apart break, come unstuck, crumble, disintegrate, fall to pieces, give way, separate, split, tear

come at 1. attain, discover, find, grasp, reach 2. assail, assault, attack, charge, fall upon, fly at, go for, light into, rush, rush at

comeback 1. rally, rebound, recovery, resurgence, return, revival, triumph 2. rejoinder, reply, response, retaliation, retort, riposte

come back reappear, recur, re-enter, return

come between alienate, divide, estrange, interfere, meddle, part, separate, set at odds

come by acquire, get, land, lay hold of, obtain, procure, score (*slang*), secure, take possession of, win

come clean acknowledge, admit, come out of the closet, confess, cough up (*slang*), 'fess up (*U.S.*), get (something) off one's chest (*informal*), make a clean breast of, own up, reveal, sing (*slang, chiefly U.S.*), spill one's guts (*slang*)

comedian card (*informal*), clown, comic, funny man, humorist, jester, joculator *or (fem.)* joculatrix, joker, laugh (*informal*), wag, wit

comedown anticlimax, blow, decline, deflation, demotion, disappointment, humiliation, letdown, reverse, whammy (*informal, chiefly U.S.*)

come down **1.** decline, degenerate, descend, deteriorate, fall, go downhill, go to pot (*informal*), reduce, worsen **2.** choose, decide, favour, recommend

come down on bawl out (*informal*), blast, carpet (*informal*), chew out (*U.S. & Canad. informal*), criticize, dress down (*informal*), give (someone) a rocket (*Brit. & N.Z. informal*), jump on (*informal*), lambast(e), put down, rap over the knuckles, read the riot act, rebuke, reprimand, tear into (*informal*), tear (someone) off a strip (*Brit. informal*)

come down to amount to, boil down to, end up as, result in

come down with ail, be stricken with, catch, contract, fall ill, fall victim to, get, sicken, take, take sick

comedy chaffing, drollery, facetiousness, farce, fun, hilarity, humour, jesting, joking, light entertainment, sitcom (*informal*), slapstick, wisecracking, witticisms
Antonyms high drama, melancholy, melodrama, opera, sadness, seriousness, serious play, soap opera, solemnity, tragedy

Comedy is an imitation of the common errors of our life
Sir Philip Sidney *The Defence of Poetry*

The world is a comedy to those that think, a tragedy to those that feel
Horace Walpole *Letters*

All tragedies are finish'd by a death,
All comedies are ended by a marriage
Lord Byron *Don Juan*

come forward offer one's services, present *or* proffer oneself, volunteer

come in appear, arrive, cross the threshold, enter, finish, reach, show up (*informal*)

come in for acquire, bear the brunt of, endure, get, receive, suffer

comely **1.** attractive, beautiful, becoming, blooming, bonny, buxom, cute, fair, good-looking, graceful, handsome, lovely, pleasing, pretty, wholesome, winsome **2.** *archaic* decent, decorous, fit, fitting, proper, seemly, suitable
Antonyms affected, disagreeable, distasteful, faded, homely, improper, indecorous, mumsy, plain, repulsive, ugly, unattractive, unbecoming, unfitting, unnatural, unpleasant, unseemly

come off go off, happen, occur, succeed, take place, transpire (*informal*)

come on **1.** advance, develop, improve, make headway, proceed, progress **2.** appear, begin, take place

come out **1.** appear, be published (announced, divulged, issued, released, reported, revealed) **2.** conclude, end, result, terminate

come out with acknowledge, come clean, declare, disclose, divulge, lay open, own, own up, say

come round **1.** accede, acquiesce, allow, concede, grant, mellow, relent, yield **2.** come to, rally, recover, regain consciousness, revive **3.** call, drop in, pop in, stop by, visit

come through **1.** accomplish, achieve, make the grade (*informal*), prevail, succeed, triumph **2.** endure, survive, weather the storm, withstand

come up arise, crop up, happen, occur, rise, spring up, turn up

comeuppance chastening, deserts, due reward, dues, merit, punishment, recompense, requital, retribution

come up to admit of comparison with, approach, compare with, equal, match, measure up to, meet, resemble, rival, stand *or* bear comparison with

come up with advance, create, discover, furnish, offer, present, produce, propose, provide, submit, suggest

comfort *verb* **1.** alleviate, assuage, cheer, commiserate with, compassionate (*archaic*), console, ease, encourage, enliven, gladden, hearten, inspirit, invigorate, reassure, refresh, relieve, solace, soothe, strengthen *~noun* **2.** aid, alleviation, cheer, compensation, consolation, ease, encouragement, enjoyment, help, relief, satisfaction, succour, support **3.** cosiness, creature comforts, ease, luxury, opulence, snugness, wellbeing
Antonyms *verb* aggravate (*informal*), agitate, annoy, bother, depress, discomfort, distress, excite, hassle (*informal*), irk, irritate, rile, ruffle, sadden, trouble *~noun* aggravation, annoyance, discouragement, displeasure, hassle (*informal*), inconvenience, irritation

comfortable **1.** adequate, agreeable, ample, commodious, convenient, cosy, delightful, easy, enjoyable, homely, loose, loose-fitting, pleasant, relaxing, restful, roomy, snug **2.** at ease, at home, contented, gratified, happy, relaxed, serene **3.** affluent, in clover (*informal*), prosperous, well-off, well-to-do
Antonyms (*sense 1*) disagreeable, inadequate, skin-tight, tight, tight-fitting, uncomfortable,

unpleasant (*sense 2*) distressed, disturbed, ill at ease, like a fish out of water, miserable, nervous, on tenterhooks, tense, troubled, un~ comfortable, uneasy

comforting cheering, consolatory, consoling, encouraging, heart-warming, inspiriting, re~ assuring, soothing
Antonyms alarming, dismaying, disturbing, perplexing, upsetting, worrying

comfortless **1.** bleak, cheerless, cold, desolate, dismal, dreary **2.** disconsolate, forlorn, incon~ solable, miserable, sick at heart, woebegone, wretched

comic **1.** *adjective* amusing, comical, droll, fa~ cetious, farcical, funny, humorous, jocular, joking, light, rich, waggish, witty **2.** *noun* buf~ foon, clown, comedian, funny man, humorist, jester, joculator *or (fem.)* joculatrix, wag, wit
Antonyms depressing, melancholy, pathetic, sad, serious, solemn, touching, tragic

comical absurd, amusing, comic, diverting, droll, entertaining, farcical, funny, hilarious, humorous, laughable, ludicrous, priceless, ri~ diculous, risible, side-splitting, silly, whimsi~ cal, zany

coming *adjective* **1.** approaching, at hand, due, en route, forthcoming, future, imminent, im~ pending, in store, in the wind, just round the corner, near, next, nigh, on the cards, upcom~ ing **2.** aspiring, future, promising, up-and-coming *~noun* **3.** accession, advent, approach, arrival

command *verb* **1.** bid, charge, compel, demand, direct, enjoin, order, require **2.** administer, call the shots, call the tune, control, domi~ nate, govern, handle, head, lead, manage, reign over, rule, supervise, sway *~noun* **3.** be~ hest, bidding, canon, commandment, decree, demand, direction, directive, edict, fiat, in~ junction, instruction, mandate, order, precept, requirement, ultimatum **4.** authority, charge, control, direction, domination, dominion, gov~ ernment, grasp, management, mastery, power, rule, supervision, sway, upper hand
Antonyms (*sense 1*) appeal (to), ask, beg, be~ seech, plead, request, supplicate (*sense 2*) be inferior, be subordinate, follow

commandeer appropriate, confiscate, expro~ priate, hijack, requisition, seize, sequester, sequestrate, usurp

commander boss, captain, chief, C in C, C.O., commander-in-chief, commanding officer, di~ rector, head, leader, officer, ruler

commanding **1.** advantageous, controlling, de~ cisive, dominant, dominating, superior **2.** as~ sertive, authoritative, autocratic, compelling, forceful, imposing, impressive, peremptory
Antonyms retiring, shrinking, shy, submis~ sive, timid, unassertive, unimposing, weak

commemorate celebrate, honour, immortalize, keep, memorialize, observe, pay tribute to, remember, salute, solemnize
Antonyms disregard, forget, ignore, omit, overlook, pass over, take no notice of

commemoration ceremony, honouring, memo~ rial service, observance, remembrance, tribute

commemorative celebratory, dedicatory, in honour, in memory, in remembrance, memo~ rial

commence begin, embark on, enter upon, get the show on the road (*informal*), inaugurate, initiate, open, originate, start
Antonyms bring *or* come to an end, cease, complete, conclude, desist, end, finish, halt, stop, terminate, wind up

commencement beginning, birth, dawn, em~ barkation, inauguration, inception, initiation, launch, onset, opening, origin, outset, square one (*informal*), start

commend **1.** acclaim, applaud, approve, com~ pliment, crack up (*informal*), eulogize, extol, praise, recommend, speak highly of **2.** commit, confide, consign, deliver, entrust, hand over, yield
Antonyms (*sense 1*) attack, blast, censure, condemn, criticize, denounce, disapprove, knock (*informal*), lambast(e), put down, slam, tear into (*informal*), (*sense 2*) hold back, keep, keep back, retain, withdraw, withhold

commendable admirable, creditable, deserv~ ing, estimable, exemplary, laudable, meritori~ ous, praiseworthy, worthy

commendation acclaim, acclamation, appro~ bation, approval, Brownie points, credit, enco~ mium, encouragement, good opinion, panegyr~ ic, praise, recommendation

> *commendation: the tribute that we pay to achievements that resemble, but do not equal, our own*
>
> Ambrose Bierce *The Devil's Dictionary*

commensurate adequate, appropriate, coex~ tensive, comparable, compatible, consistent, corresponding, due, equivalent, fit, fitting, in accord, proportionate, sufficient

comment *verb* **1.** animadvert, interpose, men~ tion, note, observe, opine, point out, remark, say, utter **2.** annotate, criticize, elucidate, ex~ plain, interpret *~noun* **3.** animadversion, ob~ servation, remark, statement **4.** annotation, commentary, criticism, elucidation, explana~ tion, exposition, illustration, note

commentary analysis, critique, description, exegesis, explanation, narration, notes, re~ view, treatise, voice-over

commentator **1.** commenter, reporter, special correspondent, sportscaster **2.** annotator, crit~ ic, expositor, interpreter, scholiast

commerce 1. business, dealing, exchange, merchandising, trade, traffic 2. communication, dealings, intercourse, relations, socializing

commercial 1. business, mercantile, profit-making, sales, trade, trading 2. in demand, marketable, popular, profitable, saleable 3. exploited, materialistic, mercenary, monetary, pecuniary, profit-making, venal

commingle amalgamate, blend, combine, commix, intermingle, intermix, join, meld, mingle, unite

commiserate compassionate (*archaic*), condole, console, feel for, pity, sympathize

commiseration compassion, condolence, consolation, fellow feeling, pity, sympathy

commission *noun* 1. appointment, authority, charge, duty, employment, errand, function, mandate, mission, task, trust, warrant 2. allowance, brokerage, compensation, cut, fee, percentage, rake-off (*slang*), royalties 3. board, body of commissioners, commissioners, committee, delegation, deputation, representative ~*verb* 4. appoint, authorize, contract, delegate, depute, empower, engage, nominate, order, select, send

commit 1. carry out, do, enact, execute, perform, perpetrate 2. commend, confide, consign, deliver, deposit, engage, entrust, give, hand over 3. align, bind, compromise, endanger, make liable, obligate, pledge, rank 4. confine, imprison, put in custody
Antonyms (*sense 1*) omit (*sense 2*) receive, withhold (*sense 3*) disavow, vacillate, waver (*sense 4*) free, let out, release, set free

commitment 1. duty, engagement, liability, obligation, responsibility, tie 2. adherence, dedication, devotion, involvement, loyalty 3. assurance, guarantee, pledge, promise, undertaking, vow, word
Antonyms disavowal, indecisiveness, negation, vacillation, wavering

In for a penny, in for a pound

One might as well be hanged for a sheep as a lamb

committed 1. adherent, dedicated, devoted, devout, dutiful, faithful, intent, loyal, resolute 2. aligned, avowed, duty-bound, engaged, entrusted, involved, obliged, pledged, promised, tied

committee commission, delegation, deputation, group, panel, subcommittee

a group of men who individually can do nothing but as a group decide that nothing can be done
attributed to Fred Allen

a group of the unwilling, chosen from the unfit, to do the unnecessary
Anon.

A committee is a group of men who keep minutes and waste hours

commodious ample, capacious, comfortable, convenient, expansive, extensive, large, loose, roomy, spacious

commodities goods, merchandise, produce, products, stock, wares

common 1. a dime a dozen, average, bog-standard (*Brit. & Irish slang*), commonplace, conventional, customary, daily, everyday, familiar, frequent, general, habitual, humdrum, obscure, ordinary, plain, regular, routine, run-of-the-mill, simple, standard, stock, usual, vanilla (*slang*), workaday 2. accepted, general, popular, prevailing, prevalent, universal, widespread 3. collective, communal, community, popular, public, social 4. coarse, hackneyed, inferior, low, pedestrian, plebeian, stale, trite, undistinguished, vulgar
Antonyms (*sense 1*) abnormal, distinguished, famous, formal, important, infrequent, noble, outstanding, rare, scarce, sophisticated, strange, superior, uncommon, unknown, unpopular, unusual (*sense 3*) personal, private (*sense 4*) cultured, gentle, refined, sensitive

commonness 1. commonplaceness, conventionality, customariness, familiarness, generalness, habitualness, humdrumness, ordinariness, plainness, regularity, simpleness, usualness 2. baseness, coarseness, inferiority, lowness, vulgarity
Antonyms abnormality, extraordinariness, rarity, strangeness, uncommonness, unfamiliarness, uniqueness

commonplace 1. *adjective* banal, common, customary, dime-a-dozen (*informal*), everyday, humdrum, mundane, obvious, ordinary, pedestrian, run-of-the-mill, stale, threadbare, trite, uninteresting, vanilla (*slang*), widespread, worn out 2. *noun* banality, cliché, platitude, truism
Antonyms *adjective* exciting, extraordinary, ground-breaking, infrequent, interesting, left-field (*informal*), new, novel, original, rare, strange, uncommon, unfamiliar, unique, unusual

common-sense, common-sensical *adjective* astute, down-to-earth, hard-headed, judicious, level-headed, matter-of-fact, practical, realistic, reasonable, sane, sensible, shrewd, sound
Antonyms airy-fairy (*informal*), daft (*informal*), foolish, impractical, irrational, unrealistic, unreasonable, unthinking, unwise

common sense good sense, gumption (*Brit. informal*), horse sense, level-headedness, mother wit, native intelligence, nous (*Brit. slang*), practicality, prudence, reasonableness, smarts (*slang, chiefly U.S.*), sound judgment, soundness, wit

commotion ado, agitation, brouhaha, bustle, disorder, disturbance, excitement, ferment, furore, fuss, hubbub, hue and cry, hullabaloo, hurly-burly, perturbation, racket, riot, rum~ pus, to-do, tumult, turmoil, upheaval, uproar

communal collective, communistic, community, general, joint, neighbourhood, public, shared
Antonyms exclusive, individual, personal, private, single, unshared

commune[1] *verb* **1.** communicate, confer, con~ fide in, converse, discourse, discuss, parley **2.** contemplate, meditate, muse, ponder, reflect

commune[2] *noun* collective, community, co~ operative, kibbutz

communicable catching, contagious, infectious, taking, transferable, transmittable

communicate acquaint, announce, be in con~ tact, be in touch, connect, convey, correspond, declare, disclose, disseminate, divulge, impart, inform, make known, pass on, phone, pro~ claim, publish, report, reveal, ring up (*infor~ mal, chiefly Brit.*), signify, spread, transmit, unfold
Antonyms conceal, cover up, hold back, hush up, keep back, keep secret, keep under wraps, repress, sit on (*informal*), suppress, white~ wash (*informal*), withhold

communication **1.** connection, contact, conver~ sation, correspondence, dissemination, inter~ course, link, transmission **2.** announcement, disclosure, dispatch, information, intelligence, message, news, report, statement, word

communications **1.** routes, transport, travel **2.** information technology, media, publicity, pub~ lic relations, telecommunications

communicative candid, chatty, conversable, expansive, forthcoming, frank, informative, loquacious, open, outgoing, talkative, unre~ served, voluble
Antonyms quiet, reserved, reticent, secretive, taciturn, uncommunicative, uninformative, untalkative

communion **1.** accord, affinity, agreement, closeness, communing, concord, consensus, converse, fellowship, harmony, intercourse, participation, rapport, sympathy, together~ ness, unity **2.** *Church* Eucharist, Lord's Sup~ per, Mass, Sacrament

communiqué announcement, bulletin, dis~ patch, news flash, official communication, re~ port

communism Bolshevism, collectivism, Marx~ ism, socialism, state socialism

A spectre is haunting Europe - the spectre of Communism
Karl Marx *The Communist Manifesto*

[Russian Communism is] the illegitimate child of Karl Marx and Catherine the Great
Clement Attlee

Communism is Soviet power plus the electrifica~ tion of the whole country
Lenin

communist Bolshevik, collectivist, Marxist, Red (*informal*), socialist

community **1.** association, body politic, brotherhood, commonwealth, company, dis~ trict, general public, locality, people, populace, population, public, residents, society, state **2.** affinity, agreement, identity, likeness, same~ ness, similarity

commute **1.** barter, exchange, interchange, substitute, switch, trade **2.** *Law: of penalties, etc.* alleviate, curtail, mitigate, modify, reduce, remit, shorten, soften

commuter **1.** *noun* daily traveller, straphanger (*informal*), suburbanite **2.** *adjective* suburban

compact[1] *adjective* **1.** close, compressed, con~ densed, dense, firm, impenetrable, imper~ meable, pressed together, solid, thick **2.** brief, compendious, concise, epigrammatic, laconic, pithy, pointed, succinct, terse, to the point *~verb* **3.** compress, condense, cram, pack down, stuff, tamp
Antonyms *adjective* (*sense 1*) dispersed, large, loose, roomy, scattered, spacious, sprawling (*sense 2*) circumlocutory, garrulous, lengthy, long-winded, prolix, rambling, verbose, wordy *~verb* disperse, loosen, separate

compact[2] *noun* agreement, alliance, arrange~ ment, bargain, bond, concordat, contract, cov~ enant, deal, entente, pact, stipulation, treaty, understanding

companion **1.** accomplice, ally, associate, bud~ dy (*informal*), colleague, comrade, confederate, consort, crony, friend, gossip (*archaic*), home~ boy (*slang, chiefly U.S.*), mate (*informal*), partner **2.** aide, assistant, attendant, chaper~ on, duenna, escort, squire **3.** complement, counterpart, fellow, match, mate, twin

companionable affable, congenial, conversable, convivial, cordial, familiar, friendly, genial, gregarious, neighbourly, outgoing, sociable

companionship amity, camaraderie, company, comradeship, conviviality, esprit de corps, fel~ lowship, fraternity, friendship, rapport, to~ getherness

company **1.** assemblage, assembly, band, bevy, body, camp, circle, collection, community, con~ course, convention, coterie, crew, crowd, en~ semble, gathering, group, league, party, set, throng, troop, troupe, turnout **2.** association, business, concern, corporation, establishment, firm, house, partnership, syndicate **3.** callers, companionship, fellowship, guests, party, presence, society, visitors

Every man is like the company he is wont to keep
Euripides *Phoenix*

A wise man may look ridiculous in the company of fools
Thomas Fuller *Gnomologia*

Tell me thy company, and I'll tell thee what thou art
Miguel de Cervantes *Don Quixote*
A man is known by the company he keeps
Two is company, three's a crowd

comparable **1.** a match for, as good as, commensurate, equal, equivalent, in a class with, on a par, proportionate, tantamount **2.** akin, alike, analogous, cognate, corresponding, cut from the same cloth, of a piece, related, similar
Antonyms different, dissimilar, incommensurable, incomparable, unequal

comparative approximate, by comparison, qualified, relative

compare **1.** *with* **with** balance, collate, contrast, juxtapose, set against, weigh **2.** *with* **to** correlate, equate, identify with, liken, mention in the same breath, parallel, resemble **3.** *be the equal of* approach, approximate to, bear comparison, be in the same class as, be on a par with, come up to, compete with, equal, hold a candle to, match, vie

comparison **1.** collation, contrast, distinction, juxtaposition **2.** analogy, comparability, correlation, likeness, resemblance, similarity
Comparisons are odious
John Fortescue *De laudibus legum Angliae*

compartment **1.** alcove, bay, berth, booth, carrel, carriage, cell, chamber, cubbyhole, cubicle, locker, niche, pigeonhole, section **2.** area, category, department, division, section, subdivision

compartmentalize, compartmentalise categorize *or* categorise, classify, pigeonhole, sectionalize *or* sectionalise

compass *noun* **1.** area, bound, boundary, circle, circuit, circumference, enclosure, extent, field, limit, range, reach, realm, round, scope, sphere, stretch, zone *~verb* **2.** beset, besiege, blockade, circumscribe, encircle, enclose, encompass, environ, hem in, invest (*rare*), surround **3.** accomplish, achieve, attain, bring about, effect, execute, fulfil, perform, procure, realize

compassion charity, clemency, commiseration, compunction, condolence, fellow feeling, heart, humanity, kindness, mercy, pity, quarter, ruth (*archaic*), soft-heartedness, sorrow, sympathy, tender-heartedness, tenderness
Antonyms apathy, cold-heartedness, indifference, mercilessness, unconcern

compassionate benevolent, charitable, humane, humanitarian, indulgent, kind-hearted, kindly, lenient, merciful, pitying, sympathetic, tender, tender-hearted, understanding
Antonyms callous, harsh, heartless, inhumane, pitiless, uncaring, unfeeling, unmerciful, unsympathetic

compatibility affinity, agreement, amity, concord, congeniality, empathy, harmony, like-mindedness, rapport, single-mindedness, sympathy

compatible accordant, adaptable, agreeable, congenial, congruent, congruous, consistent, consonant, harmonious, in harmony, in keeping, like-minded, reconcilable, suitable
Antonyms contradictory, inappropriate, inapt, incompatible, unfitting, unharmonious, unsuitable

compatriot countryman, fellow citizen, fellow countryman

compel bulldoze (*informal*), coerce, constrain, dragoon, drive, enforce, exact, force, hustle (*slang*), impel, make, necessitate, oblige, railroad (*informal*), restrain, squeeze, urge

compelling **1.** cogent, conclusive, convincing, forceful, irrefutable, powerful, telling, weighty **2.** enchanting, enthralling, gripping, hypnotic, irresistible, mesmeric, spellbinding **3.** binding, coercive, imperative, overriding, peremptory, pressing, unavoidable, urgent
Antonyms (*sense 1*) boring, dull, humdrum, monotonous, ordinary, repetitious, tiresome, uneventful, uninteresting, wearisome

compendious abbreviated, abridged, brief, comprehensive, concise, condensed, contracted, short, succinct, summarized, summary, synoptic

compendium **1.** collection, compilation, digest **2.** abbreviation, abridgment, abstract, capsule, epitome, outline, précis, summary, synopsis

compensate **1.** atone, indemnify, make good, make restitution, recompense, refund, reimburse, remunerate, repay, requite, reward, satisfy **2.** balance, cancel (out), counteract, counterbalance, countervail, make amends, make up for, offset, redress
What you lose on the swings you gain on the roundabouts

compensation amends, atonement, damages, indemnification, indemnity, meed (*archaic*), payment, recompense, reimbursement, remuneration, reparation, requital, restitution, reward, satisfaction

compete be in the running, challenge, contend, contest, emulate, fight, pit oneself against, rival, strive, struggle, vie

competence ability, adequacy, appropriateness, capability, capacity, competency, craft, expertise, fitness, proficiency, skill, suitability
Antonyms inability, inadequacy, incompetence
He has, indeed, done it very well; but it is a foolish thing well done
Dr. Johnson

competent able, adapted, adequate, appropriate, capable, clever, endowed, equal, fit, pertinent, proficient, qualified, sufficient, suitable

Antonyms cowboy (*informal*), inadequate, in~capable, incompetent, inexperienced, inexpert, undependable, unqualified, unskilled

competition 1. contention, contest, emulation, one-upmanship (*informal*), opposition, rivalry, strife, struggle 2. championship, contest, event, head-to-head, puzzle, quiz, tournament 3. challengers, field, opposition, rivals

competitive aggressive, ambitious, antagonis~tic, at odds, combative, cutthroat, dog-eat-dog, emulous, opposing, rival, vying

competitor adversary, antagonist, challenger, competition, contestant, emulator, opponent, opposition, rival

compilation accumulation, anthology, assem~blage, assortment, collection, treasury

compile accumulate, amass, anthologize, col~lect, cull, garner, gather, marshal, organize, put together

complacency contentment, gratification, pleasure, satisfaction, self-satisfaction, smug~ness

complacent contented, gratified, pleased, pleased with oneself, resting on one's laurels, satisfied, self-assured, self-contented, self-righteous, self-satisfied, serene, smug, uncon~cerned

Antonyms discontent, dissatisfied, insecure, rude, troubled, uneasy, unsatisfied

complain beef (*slang*), bellyache (*slang*), be~moan, bewail, bitch (*slang*), bleat, carp, de~plore, find fault, fuss, grieve, gripe (*informal*), groan, grouch (*informal*), grouse, growl, grumble, kick up a fuss (*informal*), kvetch (*U.S. slang*), lament, moan, put the boot in (*slang*), whine, whinge (*informal*)

complaint 1. accusation, annoyance, beef (*slang*), bitch (*slang*), charge, criticism, dis~satisfaction, fault-finding, grievance, gripe (*informal*), grouch (*informal*), grouse, grumble, lament, moan, plaint, protest, remonstrance, trouble, wail 2. affliction, ailment, disease, disorder, illness, indisposition, malady, sick~ness, upset

complaisance accommodativeness, acquies~cence, agreeableness, compliance, deference, obligingness

complaisant accommodating, amiable, compli~ant, conciliatory, deferential, obliging, polite, solicitous

complement *noun* 1. companion, completion, consummation, correlative, counterpart, fin~ishing touch, rounding-off, supplement 2. ag~gregate, capacity, entirety, quota, total, total~ity, wholeness *~verb* 3. cap (*informal*), com~plete, crown, round off, set off

complementary companion, completing, cor~relative, corresponding, fellow, interdepend~ent, interrelating, matched, reciprocal

Antonyms contradictory, different, incompat~ible, incongruous, uncomplementary

complete *adjective* 1. all, entire, faultless, full, intact, integral, plenary, unabridged, unbro~ken, undivided, unimpaired, whole 2. accom~plished, achieved, concluded, ended, finished 3. absolute, consummate, deep-dyed (*usually derogatory*), dyed-in-the-wool, outright, per~fect, thorough, thoroughgoing, total, utter *~verb* 4. accomplish, achieve, cap, close, con~clude, crown, discharge, do, end, execute, fill in, finalize, finish, fulfil, perfect, perform, put the tin lid on, realize, round off, settle, termi~nate, wrap up (*informal*)

Antonyms *adjective* deficient, imperfect, in~complete, inconclusive, partial, spoilt, unac~complished, unfinished, unsettled *~verb* begin, commence, initiate, mar, spoil, start

completely absolutely, a hundred per cent, al~together, down to the ground, en masse, en~tirely, every inch, from A to Z, from beginning to end, fully, heart and soul, hook, line and sinker, in full, *in toto*, lock, stock and barrel, one hundred per cent, perfectly, quite, root and branch, solidly, thoroughly, totally, utterly, wholly

completion accomplishment, attainment, bitter end, close, conclusion, consummation, culmi~nation, end, expiration, finalization, fruition, fulfilment, realization

complex *adjective* 1. circuitous, complicated, convoluted, Daedalian (*literary*), intricate, in~volved, knotty, labyrinthine, mingled, mixed, tangled, tortuous 2. composite, compound, compounded, heterogeneous, manifold, multi~farious, multiple *~noun* 3. aggregate, compo~site, network, organization, scheme, structure, synthesis, system 4. fixation, fixed idea, *idée fixe*, obsession, phobia, preoccupation

Antonyms (*sense 1*) clear, easy, easy-peasy (*slang*), elementary, obvious, simple, straight~forward, uncomplicated

complexion 1. colour, colouring, hue, pigmen~tation, skin, skin tone 2. appearance, aspect, cast, character, countenance, disposition, guise, light, look, make-up, nature, stamp

complexity complication, convolution, elabora~tion, entanglement, intricacy, involvement, multiplicity, ramification

compliance acquiescence, agreement, assent, complaisance, concession, concurrence, con~formity, consent, deference, obedience, obser~vance, passivity, submission, submissiveness, yielding

Antonyms defiance, disobedience, non-compliance, nonconformity, opposition, refusal, resistance, revolt

compliant accepting, accommodating, accord~ant, acquiescent, agreeable, assentient, com~

plaisant, concessive, concurrent, conformable, conformist, consentient, co-operative, deferen~tial, obedient, obliging, passive, submissive, willing, yielding

complicate confuse, entangle, interweave, in~volve, make intricate, muddle, ravel, snarl up
Antonyms clarify, clear up, disentangle, elu~cidate, explain, facilitate, simplify, spell out, unsnarl

complicated **1.** Byzantine (*of attitudes, etc.*), complex, convoluted, elaborate, interlaced, in~tricate, involved, labyrinthine **2.** difficult, in~volved, perplexing, problematic, puzzling, troublesome
Antonyms clear, easy, easy-peasy (*slang*), simple, straightforward, uncomplicated, unde~manding, understandable, uninvolved, user-friendly

complication **1.** combination, complexity, con~fusion, entanglement, intricacy, mixture, web **2.** aggravation, difficulty, drawback, embar~rassment, factor, obstacle, problem, snag

complicity abetment, collaboration, collusion, concurrence, connivance

compliment **1.** *noun* admiration, bouquet, commendation, congratulations, courtesy, eulogy, favour, flattery, honour, praise, tribute **2.** *verb* commend, congratulate, crack up (*in~formal*), extol, felicitate, flatter, laud, pat on the back, pay tribute to, praise, salute, sing the praises of, speak highly of, wish joy to
Antonyms *noun* complaint, condemnation, criticism, disparagement, insult, reproach *~verb* blast, condemn, criticize, decry, dispar~age, insult, lambast(e), put down, reprehend, reproach, tear into (*informal*)

complimentary **1.** appreciative, approving, commendatory, congratulatory, eulogistic, flattering, laudatory, panegyrical **2.** courtesy, donated, free, free of charge, gratis, gratui~tous, honorary, on the house
Antonyms (*sense 1*) abusive, critical, dispar~aging, fault-finding, insulting, scathing, un~complimentary, unflattering

compliments good wishes, greetings, regards, remembrances, respects, salutation

comply abide by, accede, accord, acquiesce, adhere to, agree to, conform to, consent to, defer, discharge, follow, fulfil, obey, observe, perform, play ball (*informal*), respect, satisfy, submit, toe the line, yield
Antonyms break, defy, disobey, disregard, fight, ignore, oppose, refuse to obey, reject, repudiate, resist, spurn, violate

component **1.** *noun* constituent, element, in~gredient, item, part, piece, unit **2.** *adjective* composing, constituent, inherent, intrinsic

comport **1.** accord, agree, coincide, correspond, fit, harmonize, square, suit, tally **2.** acquit, act, bear, behave, carry, conduct, demean

compose **1.** build, compound, comprise, consti~tute, construct, fashion, form, make, make up, put together **2.** contrive, create, devise, frame, imagine, indite, invent, produce, write **3.** ad~just, arrange, reconcile, regulate, resolve, set~tle **4.** appease, assuage, calm, collect, control, pacify, placate, quell, quiet, soothe, still, tranquillize
Antonyms (*sense 1*) bulldoze, demolish, de~stroy, dismantle, obliterate, raze (*sense 4*) agitate, disturb, excite, perturb, trouble, un~settle, upset

composed as cool as a cucumber, at ease, calm, collected, confident, cool, imperturbable, keeping one's cool, laid-back (*informal*), level-headed, poised, relaxed, sedate, self-possessed, serene, together (*slang*), tranquil, unfazed (*informal*), unflappable, unruffled, unworried
Antonyms agitated, anxious, disturbed, excit~ed, hot and bothered (*informal*), nervous, ruf~fled, twitchy (*informal*), uncontrolled, uneasy, unpoised, upset

composite **1.** *adjective* blended, combined, complex, compound, conglomerate, mixed, synthesized **2.** *noun* amalgam, blend, com~pound, conglomerate, fusion, meld, synthesis

composition **1.** arrangement, configuration, constitution, design, form, formation, layout, make-up, organization, structure **2.** compila~tion, creation, fashioning, formation, formula~tion, invention, making, mixture, production **3.** creation, essay, exercise, literary work, opus, piece, study, treatise, work, writing **4.** ar~rangement, balance, concord, consonance, harmony, placing, proportion, symmetry

compost humus, mulch, organic fertilizer

composure aplomb, calm, calmness, collected~ness, cool (*slang*), coolness, dignity, ease, equanimity, imperturbability, placidity, poise, sang-froid, sedateness, self-assurance, self-possession, serenity, tranquillity
Antonyms agitation, discomposure, excitabil~ity, impatience, nervousness, perturbation, uneasiness

compound *verb* **1.** amalgamate, blend, coa~lesce, combine, concoct, fuse, intermingle, meld, mingle, mix, synthesize, unite **2.** add insult to injury, add to, aggravate, augment, complicate, exacerbate, heighten, intensify, magnify, worsen **3.** *used of a dispute, differ~ence, etc.* adjust, arrange, compose, settle *~noun* **4.** alloy, amalgam, blend, combination, composite, composition, conglomerate, fusion, medley, meld, mixture, synthesis *~adjective* **5.** complex, composite, conglomerate, intricate, multiple, not simple
Antonyms *verb* decrease, divide, lessen, mini~

mize, moderate, modify, part, segregate *~noun* element *~adjective* pure, simple, single, unmixed

comprehend 1. apprehend, assimilate, conceive, discern, fathom, get the hang of (*informal*), get the picture, grasp, know, make out, perceive, see, see the light of day, take in, understand 2. comprise, contain, embody, embrace, enclose, encompass, include, involve, take in
Antonyms (*sense 1*) be at cross-purposes, get (it) wrong, get one's lines crossed, get the wrong end of the stick, misapprehend, misconceive, misconstrue, misinterpret, miss the point of, mistake, misunderstand, pervert

comprehensibility apprehensibility, clarity, clearness, conceivability, conceivableness, explicitness, intelligibility, intelligibleness, plainness, user-friendliness

comprehensible clear, coherent, conceivable, explicit, graspable, intelligible, plain, understandable, user-friendly

comprehension 1. conception, discernment, grasp, intelligence, judgment, knowledge, perception, realization, sense, understanding 2. compass, domain, field, limits, province, range, reach, scope
Antonyms (*sense 1*) incomprehension, misapprehension, misunderstanding, unawareness

comprehensive all-embracing, all-inclusive, blanket, broad, catholic, complete, encyclopedic, exhaustive, extensive, full, inclusive, sweeping, thorough, umbrella, wide
Antonyms incomplete, limited, narrow, restricted, specialized, specific

compress abbreviate, compact, concentrate, condense, constrict, contract, cram, crowd, crush, knit, press, pucker, shorten, squash, squeeze, summarize, wedge

compressed abridged, compact, compacted, concentrated, concise, consolidated, constricted, flattened, reduced, shortened, squashed, squeezed

compression condensation, consolidation, constriction, crushing, pressure, squeezing, wedging

comprise 1. be composed of, comprehend, consist of, contain, embrace, encompass, include, take in 2. compose, constitute, form, make up

compromise 1. *verb* adjust, agree, arbitrate, compose, compound, concede, give and take, go fifty-fifty (*informal*), meet halfway, settle, strike a balance 2. *noun* accommodation, accord, adjustment, agreement, concession, give-and-take, half measures, middle ground, settlement, trade-off 3. *verb* discredit, dishonour, embarrass, endanger, expose, hazard, imperil, implicate, jeopardize, prejudice, weaken
Antonyms *verb* argue, assure, boost, contest, differ, disagree, enhance, support *~noun* contention, controversy, difference, disagreement, dispute, quarrel

If the mountain will not come to Mahomet,
Mahomet must go to the mountain

compulsion 1. coercion, constraint, demand, duress, force, obligation, pressure, urgency 2. drive, necessity, need, obsession, preoccupation, urge

compulsive besetting, compelling, driving, irresistible, neurotic, obsessive, overwhelming, uncontrollable, urgent

compulsory binding, *de rigueur*, forced, imperative, mandatory, obligatory, required, requisite
Antonyms discretionary, non-obligatory, non-requisite, optional, unimperative, unnecessary, voluntary

compunction contrition, misgiving, penitence, qualm, regret, reluctance, remorse, repentance, sorrow, stab *or* sting of conscience

compute add up, calculate, cast up, cipher, count, enumerate, estimate, figure, figure out, measure, rate, reckon, sum, tally, total

computer

Computer parts

adder
analogue-digital converter
arithmetic logic unit *or* ALU
central processing unit *or* CPU
chip
coaxial cable
console
counter
daisywheel
digitizer
disk
disk unit
emulator
encoder
floppy disk
hard disk
hard disk drive
integrated circuit
interface
joystick
keyboard
light pen
microfloppy
microprocessor
modem
monitor
mouse
multiplexor
optical disk
port
printed circuit board
printer
scanner
screen
silicon disk
transistor
visual display unit *or* VDU
Winchester disk
Winchester disk drive

Computer terms

absolute address
access
access time
accumulator
address
address bus
algorithm
analogue computer
AND gate
architecture
array
artificial intelligence *or* AI
assembler
assembly language
backup
base address
batch processing

binary digit
binary notation
bit
bomb
boot *or* bootstrap
buffer
bug
bulletin board
bus
byte
cache memory
CD-Rom
character
code
command
command language
communications
compiler
complex instruction set computer *or* CISC
computer-aided design *or* CAD
computer-aided management *or* CAM
constant
core memory
crash
cursor
cut and paste
data
database
databus
data processing
data structure
debugging
default
desktop
digit
digital computer
direct-access storage
directory
disassembler
DOS (*Trademark*)
dot matrix
downloading
down time
dumb terminal
dump
editor
electronic mail *or* E-mail
emulator
encryption
error
exit
fail-safe
field
file
firmware
flowchart
function
gate
gigabyte
graphical user interface
graphics
hacker
handshake
hard copy
hardware
high-level language
icon
idle time
information technology
input
instruction
Internet
interpreter
job
keyword
kilobyte
language
laptop
linked list
load
location
local area network
logic circuit
loop
low-level language
machine code
macro
main frame
megabyte
memory
menu
minicomputer
NAND gate
network
NOR gate
notebook
NOT gate
operating system
OR gate
output
overflow
package
packet
palmtop
parallel processing
parameter
password
personal computer *or* PC
pixel
pointer
printout
procedure
program
programmable read only memory *or* PROM
programming language
prompt
protocol
query language
queue
random access memory *or* RAM
Random Instruction Set Computer *or* RISC
read only memory *or* ROM
real-time processing
reboot
record
routine
run
scroll
serial access memory *or* SAM
serial processing
shareware
software
software engineering
sort
sprite
stack
store
string
subroutine
syntax
system
systems analysis
terminal
tetrabyte
toggle
transputer
underflow
UNIX (*Trademark*)
user group
variable
virtual address
virtual memory
virtual reality
virus
volatile memory
wild card
window
windows icons menus pointers *or* WIMP
word processor
work station
WYSIWIG

Programming languages

Ada
Algol
Awk
BASIC *or* Basic
C
C++
COBOL *or* Cobol
FORTH *or* Forth
FORTRAN *or* Fortran
Haskell
LISP
LOGO
OCCAM *or* Occam
Pascal
Perl
PL/1
PROLOG *or* Prolog
Simula
Smalltalk
SML
SNOBOL

Computer scientists

Ada, Countess of Lovelace [British]
Howard Aiken [U.S.]
Charles Babbage [British]
Seymour Cray [U.S.]
Bill Gates [U.S.]
Herman Hollerith [U.S.]
Clive Sinclair [British]
Alan Mathison Turing [British]

To err is human but to really foul things up requires a computer

Farmers' Almanac for 1978

comrade ally, associate, buddy (*informal*), cock (*Brit. informal*), colleague, companion, compatriot, compeer, confederate, co-worker, crony, fellow, friend, homeboy (*slang, chiefly U.S.*), mate (*informal*), pal (*informal*), partner

comradely associatory, fraternal

comradeship alliance, association, camaraderie, companionship, fellowship, fraternity, membership, partnership, sodality

con 1. *verb* bamboozle (*informal*), bilk, cheat, cozen, deceive, defraud, diddle (*informal*), do the dirty on (*Brit. informal*), double-cross (*in~ formal*), dupe, gull (*archaic*), hoax, hoodwink, humbug, inveigle, kid (*informal*), mislead, pull a fast one on (*informal*), rip off (*slang*), rook (*slang*), sell a pup, skin (*slang*), stiff (*slang*), sting (*informal*), swindle, take for a ride (*in~ formal*), trick 2. *noun* bluff, canard, deception, fraud, scam (*slang*), sting (*informal*), swindle, trick

concatenation chain, connection, interlocking, linking, nexus, sequence, series, succession

concave cupped, depressed, excavated, hollow, hollowed, incurved, indented, scooped, sunken
Antonyms bulging, convex, curving, protuber~ ant, rounded

conceal bury, camouflage, cover, disguise, dis~ semble, draw a veil over, hide, keep dark, keep secret, keep under one's hat, mask, ob~ scure, screen, secrete, shelter, stash (*informal*)
Antonyms disclose, display, divulge, expose, lay bare, reveal, show, uncover, unmask, un~ veil

concealed covered, hidden, inconspicuous, masked, obscured, screened, secret, secreted, tucked away, under wraps, unseen

concealment camouflage, cover, disguise, hideaway, hide-out, hiding, secrecy
Antonyms disclosure, display, exposure, give-away, leak, revelation, showing, uncover~ ing

concede 1. accept, acknowledge, admit, allow, confess, grant, own 2. cede, give up, hand over, relinquish, surrender, yield
Antonyms (*sense 1*) contest, deny, disclaim, dispute, protest, refute, reject (*sense 2*) beat, conquer, defeat, fight to the bitter end, make a stand

conceit 1. amour-propre, arrogance, compla~ cency, egotism, narcissism, pride, self-importance, self-love, swagger, vainglory, vanity 2. *archaic* belief, fancy, fantasy, idea, image, imagination, judgment, notion, opinion, quip, thought, vagary, whim, whimsy

As for conceit, what man will do any good who is not conceited? Nobody holds a good opinion of a man who has a low opinion of himself
Anthony Trollope *Orley Farm*

conceited arrogant, bigheaded (*informal*), cocky, egotistical, full of oneself, immodest, narcissistic, overweening, puffed up, self-important, stuck up (*informal*), swollen-headed, too big for one's boots *or* breeches, vain, vainglorious
Antonyms humble, modest, self-effacing, un~ assuming

conceivable believable, credible, imaginable, possible, thinkable
Antonyms inconceivable, incredible, unbeliev~ able, unimaginable, unthinkable

conceive 1. appreciate, apprehend, believe, comprehend, envisage, fancy, get the picture, grasp, imagine, realize, suppose, understand 2. contrive, create, design, develop, devise, form, formulate, produce, project, purpose, think up 3. become impregnated, become pregnant

concentrate 1. be engrossed in, consider close~ ly, focus attention on, give all one's attention to, put one's mind to, rack one's brains 2. bring to bear, centre, cluster, converge, focus 3. accumulate, cluster, collect, congregate, gather, huddle
Antonyms (*sense 1*) disregard, let one's mind wander, lose concentration, pay no attention to, pay no heed to (*senses 2 & 3*) deploy, dif~ fuse, disperse, dissipate, scatter, spread out

concentrated 1. all-out (*informal*), deep, hard, intense, intensive 2. boiled down, condensed, evaporated, reduced, rich, thickened, undilut~ ed

concentration 1. absorption, application, heed, single-mindedness 2. bringing to bear, cen~ tralization, centring, combination, compres~ sion, consolidation, convergence, focusing, in~ tensification 3. accumulation, aggregation, cluster, collection, convergence, horde, mass
Antonyms (*sense 1*) absent-mindedness, dis~ regard, distraction, inattention (*senses 2 & 3*) diffusion, dispersion, scattering, spreading-out

concept abstraction, conception, conceptualiza~ tion, hypothesis, idea, image, impression, no~ tion, theory, view

conception 1. concept, design, idea, image, no~ tion, plan 2. beginning, birth, formation, in~ ception, initiation, invention, launching, ori~ gin, outset 3. appreciation, clue, comprehen~ sion, impression, inkling, perception, picture, understanding 4. fertilization, germination, impregnation, insemination

concern *verb* 1. affect, apply to, bear on, be relevant to, interest, involve, pertain to, re~ gard, touch *~noun* 2. affair, business, charge, department, field, interest, involvement, job, matter, mission, occupation, pigeon (*informal*), responsibility, task, transaction 3. bearing, importance, interest, reference, relation, rel~ evance *~verb* 4. bother, disquiet, distress, dis~ turb, make anxious, make uneasy, perturb, trouble, worry *~noun* 5. anxiety, apprehen~ sion, attention, burden, care, consideration, disquiet, disquietude, distress, heed, respon~ sibility, solicitude, worry 6. business, compa~ ny, corporation, enterprise, establishment, firm, house, organization

concerned 1. active, implicated, interested, in~ volved, mixed up, privy to 2. anxious, both~

ered, distressed, disturbed, exercised, trou~bled, uneasy, upset, worried **3.** attentive, car~ing, interested, solicitous
Antonyms aloof, carefree, detached, indiffer~ent, neglectful, unconcerned, uninterested, untroubled, without a care

concerning about, anent (*Scot.*), apropos of, as regards, as to, in the matter of, on the subject of, re, regarding, relating to, respecting, touching, with reference to

concert *noun* **1.** accord, agreement, concord, concordance, harmony, unanimity, union, uni~son **2.** **in concert** concertedly, in collabora~tion, in league, in unison, jointly, shoulder to shoulder, together, unanimously

concerted agreed upon, collaborative, com~bined, coordinated, joint, planned, prear~ranged, united
Antonyms disunited, separate, uncontrived, uncooperative, unplanned

concession **1.** acknowledgment, admission, as~sent, confession, surrender, yielding **2.** adjust~ment, allowance, boon, compromise, grant, in~dulgence, permit, privilege, sop

conciliate appease, clear the air, disarm, me~diate, mollify, pacify, placate, pour oil on troubled waters, propitiate, reconcile, restore harmony, soothe, win over

conciliation appeasement, disarming, mollifi~cation, pacification, placation, propitiation, reconciliation, soothing

conciliatory appeasing, disarming, irenic, mol~lifying, pacific, peaceable, placatory, propitia~tive

concise brief, compact, compendious, com~pressed, condensed, epigrammatic, in a nut~shell, laconic, pithy, short, succinct, summary, synoptic, terse, to the point
Antonyms diffuse, discursive, garrulous, lengthy, long-winded, prolix, rambling, ver~bose, wordy

conciseness brevity, briefness, compactness, compendiousness, compression, laconicism, pithiness, shortness, succinctness, summariness, synoptic, terseness
Antonyms diffuseness, discursiveness, garru~lity, garrulousness, lengthiness, long-windedness, prolixity, verboseness, verbosity, wordiness

conclave assembly, cabinet, conference, con~gress, council, parley, secret *or* private meet~ing, session

conclude **1.** bring down the curtain, cease, close, come to an end, complete, draw to a close, end, finish, round off, terminate, wind up **2.** assume, decide, deduce, gather, infer, judge, reckon (*informal*), sum up, suppose, surmise **3.** accomplish, bring about, carry out, clinch, decide, determine, effect, establish, fix, pull off, resolve, settle, work out
Antonyms (*sense 1*) begin, commence, extend, initiate, open, protract, start

conclusion **1.** bitter end, close, completion, end, finale, finish, result, termination **2.** con~sequence, culmination, end result, issue, out~come, result, sequel, upshot **3.** agreement, conviction, decision, deduction, inference, judgment, opinion, resolution, settlement, verdict **4.** **in conclusion** finally, in closing, lastly, to sum up

conclusive clinching, convincing, decisive, defi~nite, definitive, final, irrefutable, ultimate, unanswerable, unarguable
Antonyms contestable, disputable, doubtful, dubious, impeachable, inconclusive, indecisive, indefinite, questionable, refutable, unconvinc~ing, vague

concoct brew, contrive, cook up (*informal*), de~sign, devise, fabricate, formulate, hatch, in~vent, make up, manufacture, mature, plot, prepare, project, think up, trump up

concoction blend, brew, combination, com~pound, contrivance, creation, mixture, prepa~ration

concomitant accompanying, associative, atten~dant, coexistent, coincidental, collateral, com~plementary, concurrent, contemporaneous, contributing, coterminous, synchronous

concord **1.** accord, agreement, amity, concert, consensus, consonance, friendship, good understanding, goodwill, harmony, peace, rapport, unanimity, unison **2.** agreement, compact, concordat, convention, entente, protocol, treaty

concourse **1.** assemblage, assembly, collection, confluence, convergence, crowd, crush, gather~ing, meeting, multitude, rout (*archaic*), throng **2.** entrance, foyer, gathering *or* meeting place, hall, lounge, rallying point

concrete *adjective* **1.** actual, definite, explicit, factual, material, real, sensible, specific, sub~stantial, tangible **2.** calcified, compact, com~pressed, conglomerated, consolidated, firm, petrified, solid, solidified *~noun* **3.** cement (*not in technical usage*), concretion
Antonyms (*sense 1*) abstract, immaterial, in~definite, insubstantial, intangible, notional, theoretical, unspecified, vague

concubine courtesan, kept woman, leman (*ar~chaic*), mistress, odalisque, paramour

concupiscence appetite, desire, horniness (*slang*), lasciviousness, lechery, libidinousness, libido, lickerishness (*archaic*), lust, lustful~ness, randiness (*informal, chiefly Brit.*)

concupiscent horny (*slang*), lascivious, lecher~ous, lewd, libidinous, lickerish (*archaic*), lust~ful, randy (*informal, chiefly Brit.*)

concur accede, accord, acquiesce, agree, approve, assent, coincide, combine, consent, cooperate, harmonize, join

concurrent 1. coexisting, coincident, concerted, concomitant, contemporaneous, simultaneous, synchronous 2. confluent, convergent, converging, uniting 3. agreeing, at one, compatible, consentient, consistent, cooperating, harmonious, in agreement, in rapport, like-minded, of the same mind

concussion clash, collision, crash, impact, jarring, jolt, jolting, shaking, shock

condemn 1. blame, censure, damn, denounce, disapprove, excoriate, reprehend, reproach, reprobate, reprove, upbraid 2. convict, damn, doom, pass sentence on, proscribe, sentence
Antonyms (*sense 1*) acclaim, applaud, approve, commend, compliment, condone, praise (*sense 2*) acquit, free, liberate

Society needs to condemn a little more and understand a little less
John Major

condemnation 1. blame, censure, denouncement, denunciation, disapproval, reproach, reprobation, reproof, stricture 2. conviction, damnation, doom, judgment, proscription, sentence

condemnatory accusatory, accusing, censorious, critical, damnatory, denunciatory, disapproving, proscriptive, reprobative, scathing

condensation 1. abridgment, contraction, digest, précis, synopsis 2. condensate, deliquescence, distillation, liquefaction, precipitate, precipitation 3. compression, concentration, consolidation, crystallization, curtailment, reduction

condense 1. abbreviate, abridge, compact, compress, concentrate, contract, curtail, encapsulate, epitomize, précis, shorten, summarize 2. boil down, coagulate, concentrate, decoct, precipitate (*Chemistry*), reduce, solidify, thicken
Antonyms (*sense 1*) elaborate, enlarge, expand, expatiate, increase, lengthen, pad out, spin out (*sense 2*) dilute, make thinner, thin (out), water down, weaken

condensed 1. abridged, compressed, concentrated, curtailed, shortened, shrunken, slimmed down, summarized 2. boiled down, clotted, coagulated, concentrated, precipitated (*Chemistry*), reduced, thickened

condescend 1. be courteous, bend, come down off one's high horse (*informal*), deign, humble *or* demean oneself, lower oneself, see fit, stoop, submit, unbend (*informal*), vouchsafe 2. patronize, talk down to

condescending disdainful, lofty, lordly, on one's high horse (*informal*), patronizing, snobbish, snooty (*informal*), supercilious, superior, toffee-nosed (*slang, chiefly Brit.*)

condescension 1. airs, disdain, haughtiness, loftiness, lordliness, patronizing attitude, superciliousness, superiority 2. affability, civility, courtesy, deference, favour, graciousness, humiliation, obeisance

condign *used especially of a punishment* adequate, appropriate, deserved, fitting, just, meet (*archaic*), merited, richly-deserved, suitable

condition *noun* 1. case, circumstances, lie of the land, plight, position, predicament, shape, situation, state, state of affairs, *status quo* 2. arrangement, article, demand, limitation, modification, prerequisite, provision, proviso, qualification, requirement, requisite, restriction, rider, rule, stipulation, terms 3. fettle, fitness, health, kilter, order, shape, state of health, trim 4. ailment, complaint, infirmity, malady, problem, weakness 5. caste, class, estate, grade, order, position, rank, status, stratum *~verb* 6. accustom, adapt, educate, equip, habituate, inure, make ready, prepare, ready, tone up, train, work out

conditional contingent, dependent, limited, provisional, qualified, subject to, with reservations
Antonyms absolute, categorical, unconditional, unrestricted

conditioned acclimatized, accustomed, adapted, adjusted, familiarized, habituated, inured, made ready, prepared, seasoned, trained, used

conditioning *noun* 1. grooming, preparation, readying, training 2. accustoming, familiarization, hardening, inurement, reorientation, seasoning *~adjective* 3. astringent, toning

conditions circumstances, environment, milieu, situation, surroundings, way of life

condole commiserate, compassionate (*archaic*), console, feel for, sympathize

condolence commiseration, compassion, consolation, fellow feeling, pity, sympathy

condom flunky (*slang*), Frenchie (*slang*), French letter (*slang*), French tickler (*slang*), rubber (*U.S. slang*), rubber johnny (*Brit. slang*), safe (*U.S. & Canad. slang*), scumbag (*U.S. slang*), sheath

condone disregard, excuse, forgive, let pass, look the other way, make allowance for, overlook, pardon, turn a blind eye to, wink at
Antonyms censure, condemn, denounce, disapprove, punish

conduce advance, aid, avail, contribute, lead, promote, tend

conducive calculated to produce, contributive, contributory, favourable, helpful, leading, productive of, promotive, tending

conduct *noun* 1. administration, control, direction, guidance, leadership, management, organization, running, supervision *~verb* 2. administer, carry on, control, direct, govern, handle, lead, manage, organize, preside over, regulate, run, supervise 3. accompany, attend, chair, convey, escort, guide, pilot, preside over, steer, usher *~noun* 4. attitude, bearing, behaviour, carriage, comportment, demeanour, deportment, manners, mien (*literary*), ways *~verb* 5. acquit, act, behave, carry, comport, deport

conduit canal, channel, duct, main, passage, pipe, tube

confab, confabulation chat, chinwag (*Brit. informal*), conversation, discussion, gossip, natter, powwow, session, talk

confabulate chat, chew the rag *or* fat (*slang*), converse, discuss, gossip, natter, shoot the breeze (*slang, chiefly U.S.*), talk

confederacy alliance, bund, coalition, compact, confederation, conspiracy, covenant, federation, league, union

confederate 1. *adjective* allied, associated, combined, federal, federated, in alliance 2. *noun* abettor, accessory, accomplice, ally, associate, colleague, partner 3. *verb* ally, amalgamate, associate, band together, combine, federate, merge, unite

confer 1. accord, award, bestow, give, grant, hand out, present, vouchsafe 2. consult, converse, deliberate, discourse, parley, talk

conference colloquium, congress, consultation, convention, convocation, discussion, forum, meeting, seminar, symposium, teach-in

confess 1. acknowledge, admit, allow, blurt out, come clean (*informal*), come out of the closet, concede, confide, disclose, divulge, 'fess up (*U.S.*), get (something) off one's chest (*informal*), grant, make a clean breast of, own, own up, recognize, sing (*slang, chiefly U.S.*), spill one's guts (*slang*) 2. affirm, assert, attest, aver, confirm, declare, evince, manifest, profess, prove, reveal

Antonyms button one's lips, conceal, cover, deny, hide, hush up, keep mum, keep secret, keep under wraps, repudiate, suppress, withhold

confession acknowledgment, admission, avowal, disclosure, divulgence, exposure, revelation, unbosoming

Confession is good for the soul

confidant, confidante alter ego, bosom friend, close friend, crony, familiar, intimate

confide 1. admit, breathe, confess, disclose, divulge, impart, reveal, whisper 2. commend, commit, consign, entrust

confidence 1. belief, credence, dependence, faith, reliance, trust 2. aplomb, assurance, boldness, courage, firmness, nerve, self-possession, self-reliance 3. **in confidence** between you and me (and the gatepost), confidentially, in secrecy, privately

Antonyms (*sense 1*) disbelief, distrust, doubt, misgiving, mistrust (*sense 2*) apprehension, fear, self-doubt, shyness, uncertainty

confident 1. certain, convinced, counting on, positive, satisfied, secure, sure 2. assured, bold, can-do (*informal*), dauntless, fearless, self-assured, self-reliant

Antonyms (*sense 1*) doubtful, dubious, not sure, tentative, uncertain, unconvinced, unsure (*sense 2*) afraid, hesitant, insecure, jittery, lacking confidence, mousy, nervous, scared, self-doubting, unsure

confidential 1. classified, hush-hush (*informal*), intimate, off the record, private, privy, secret 2. faithful, familiar, trusted, trustworthy, trusty

confidentially behind closed doors, between ourselves, in camera, in confidence, in secret, personally, privately, sub rosa

configuration arrangement, cast, conformation, contour, figure, form, outline, shape

confine 1. *verb* bind, bound, cage, circumscribe, clip someone's wings, enclose, hem in, hold back, immure, imprison, incarcerate, intern, keep, limit, repress, restrain, restrict, shut up, straiten 2. *noun* border, boundary, frontier, limit, precinct

confined 1. enclosed, limited, restricted 2. in childbed, in childbirth, lying-in

confinement 1. custody, detention, imprisonment, incarceration, internment, porridge (*slang*) 2. *accouchement*, childbed, childbirth, labour, lying-in, parturition, time, travail

confines boundaries, bounds, circumference, edge, limits, pale, precincts

confirm 1. assure, buttress, clinch, establish, fix, fortify, reinforce, settle, strengthen 2. approve, authenticate, bear out, corroborate, endorse, ratify, sanction, substantiate, validate, verify

confirmation 1. authentication, corroboration, evidence, proof, substantiation, testimony, validation, verification 2. acceptance, agreement, approval, assent, endorsement, ratification, sanction

Antonyms (*sense 1*) contradiction, denial, disavowal, repudiation (*sense 2*) annulment, cancellation, disapproval, refusal, rejection

confirmed chronic, dyed-in-the-wool, habitual, hardened, ingrained, inured, inveterate, long-established, rooted, seasoned

confiscate appropriate, commandeer, expropriate, impound, seize, sequester, sequestrate

Antonyms free, give, give back, hand back, release, restore, return

confiscation appropriation, expropriation, forfeiture, impounding, seizure, sequestration, takeover

conflagration blaze, fire, holocaust, inferno, wildfire

conflict *noun* **1.** battle, clash, collision, combat, contention, contest, encounter, engagement, fight, fracas, head-to-head, set-to (*informal*), strife, war, warfare **2.** antagonism, bad blood, difference, disagreement, discord, dissension, divided loyalties, friction, hostility, interference, opposition, strife, variance *~verb* **3.** be at variance, clash, collide, combat, contend, contest, differ, disagree, fight, interfere, strive, struggle
Antonyms *noun* accord, agreement, harmony, peace, treaty, truce *~verb* agree, coincide, harmonize, reconcile

conflicting antagonistic, clashing, contradictory, contrary, discordant, inconsistent, opposed, opposing, paradoxical
Antonyms accordant, agreeing, compatible, congruous, consistent, harmonious, similar, unopposing

confluence **1.** concurrence, conflux, convergence, junction **2.** assemblage, assembly, concourse, concurrence, crowd, host, meeting, multitude, union

conform **1.** adapt, adjust, comply, fall in with, follow, follow the crowd, obey, run with the pack, toe the line, yield **2.** accord, agree, assimilate, correspond, harmonize, match, square, suit, tally

conformation anatomy, arrangement, build, configuration, form, framework, outline, shape, structure

conformist *noun* Babbitt (*U.S.*), conventionalist, stick-in-the-mud (*informal*), traditionalist, yes man

conformity **1.** allegiance, Babbittry (*U.S.*), compliance, conventionality, observance, orthodoxy **2.** affinity, agreement, conformance, congruity, consonance, correspondence, harmony, likeness, resemblance, similarity

confound **1.** amaze, astonish, astound, baffle, be all Greek to (*informal*), bewilder, boggle the mind, confuse, dumbfound, flabbergast (*informal*), flummox, mix up, mystify, nonplus, perplex, startle, surprise **2.** annihilate, contradict, demolish, destroy, explode, make a nonsense of, overthrow, overwhelm, refute, ruin

confront accost, beard, brave, bring face to face with, call out, challenge, defy, encounter, face, face off (*slang*), face the music, face up to, oppose, stand up to, tackle, walk into the lion's den
Antonyms avoid, body-swerve (*Scot.*), circumvent, dodge, evade, flee, give a wide berth to, keep clear of, sidestep, steer clear of

confrontation conflict, contest, crisis, encounter, face-off (*slang*), head-to-head, set-to (*informal*), showdown (*informal*)

confuse **1.** baffle, be all Greek to (*informal*), bemuse, bewilder, darken, faze, flummox, muddy the waters, mystify, nonplus, obscure, perplex, puzzle **2.** blend, confound, disarrange, disorder, intermingle, involve, jumble, mingle, mistake, mix up, muddle, ravel, snarl up (*informal*), tangle **3.** abash, addle, demoralize, discomfit, discompose, disconcert, discountenance, disorient, embarrass, fluster, mortify, nonplus, rattle (*informal*), shame, throw off balance, unnerve, upset

confused **1.** at a loss, at sea, at sixes and sevens, baffled, bewildered, dazed, discombobulated (*informal, chiefly U.S. & Canad.*), disorganized, disorientated, flummoxed, muddled, muzzy (*U.S. informal*), nonplussed, not knowing if one is coming or going, not with it (*informal*), perplexed, puzzled, taken aback, thrown off balance, upset **2.** at sixes and sevens, chaotic, disarranged, disarrayed, disordered, disorderly, disorganized, higgledy-piggledy (*informal*), hugger-mugger (*archaic*), in disarray, jumbled, mistaken, misunderstood, mixed up, out of order, topsy-turvy, untidy
Antonyms arranged, aware, enlightened, informed, in order, on the ball (*informal*), ordered, orderly, organized, tidy, with it (*informal*)

If you are sure you understand everything that is going on, you are hopelessly confused
Walter Mondale

Anyone who isn't confused doesn't really understand the situation
Ed Murrow (on the Vietnam War)

confusing ambiguous, baffling, clear as mud (*informal*), complicated, contradictory, disconcerting, inconsistent, misleading, muddling, perplexing, puzzling, unclear
Antonyms clear, definite, explicit, plain, simple, straightforward, uncomplicated, understandable

confusion **1.** befuddlement, bemusement, bewilderment, disorientation, mystification, perplexity, puzzlement **2.** bustle, chaos, clutter, commotion, disarrangement, disarray, disorder, disorganization, hodgepodge (*U.S.*), hotchpotch, jumble, mess, muddle, pig's breakfast (*informal*), shambles, state, tangle, turmoil, untidiness, upheaval **3.** abashment, chagrin, demoralization, discomfiture, distraction, embarrassment, fluster, mind-fuck (*taboo slang*), perturbation
Antonyms (*sense 1*) clarification, composure, enlightenment, explanation, solution (*sense 2*)

arrangement, neatness, order, organization, tidiness

Confusion is a word we have invented for an order which is not understood
Henry Miller *Tropic of Capricorn*

with ruin upon ruin, rout on rout,
Confusion worse confounded
John Milton *Paradise Lost*

confute blow out of the water (*slang*), controvert, disprove, invalidate, oppugn, overthrow, prove false, rebut, refute, set aside

congeal benumb, clot, coagulate, condense, curdle, freeze, gelatinize, harden, jell, set, solidify, stiffen, thicken

congenial adapted, affable, agreeable, companionable, compatible, complaisant, favourable, fit, friendly, genial, kindly, kindred, like-minded, pleasant, pleasing, suitable, sympathetic, well-suited

congenital **1.** constitutional, immanent, inborn, inbred, inherent, innate, natural **2.** *informal* complete, deep-dyed (*usually derogatory*), inveterate, thorough, utter

congested blocked-up, clogged, crammed, crowded, jammed, overcrowded, overfilled, overflowing, packed, stuffed, stuffed-up, teeming

Antonyms clear, empty, free, half-full, uncongested, uncrowded, unhampered, unhindered, unimpeded, unobstructed

congestion bottleneck, clogging, crowding, jam, mass, overcrowding, snarl-up (*informal, chiefly Brit.*), surfeit

conglomerate **1.** *adjective* amassed, clustered, composite, heterogeneous, massed **2.** *verb* accumulate, agglomerate, aggregate, cluster, coalesce, snowball **3.** *noun* agglomerate, aggregate, multinational

conglomeration accumulation, aggregation, assortment, combination, composite, hotchpotch, mass, medley, miscellany, mishmash, potpourri

congratulate compliment, felicitate, pat on the back, wish joy to

congratulations best wishes, compliments, felicitations, good wishes, greetings, pat on the back

congratulation: the civility of envy
Ambrose Bierce *The Devil's Dictionary*

congregate assemble, collect, come together, concentrate, convene, converge, convoke, flock, forgather, gather, mass, meet, muster, rally, rendezvous, throng

Antonyms break up, dispel, disperse, dissipate, part, scatter, separate, split up

congregation assembly, brethren, crowd, fellowship, flock, host, laity, multitude, parish, parishioners, throng

congress assembly, chamber of deputies, conclave, conference, convention, convocation, council, delegates, diet, house, legislative assembly, legislature, meeting, parliament, quango, representatives

congruence accord, agreement, coincidence, compatibility, concurrence, conformity, congruity, consistency, correspondence, harmony, identity

congruous appropriate, apt, becoming, compatible, concordant, congruent, consistent, consonant, correspondent, corresponding, fit, meet, seemly, suitable

conic, conical cone-shaped, conoid, funnel-shaped, pointed, pyramidal, tapered, tapering

conjectural academic, hypothetical, speculative, supposed, suppositional, surmised, tentative, theoretical

conjecture **1.** *verb* assume, fancy, guess, hypothesize, imagine, infer, suppose, surmise, suspect, theorize **2.** *noun* assumption, conclusion, fancy, guess, guesstimate (*informal*), guesswork, hypothesis, inference, notion, presumption, shot in the dark, speculation, supposition, surmise, theorizing, theory

conjugal bridal, connubial, hymeneal, marital, married, matrimonial, nuptial, spousal, wedded

conjunction association, coincidence, combination, concurrence, juxtaposition, union

conjuncture combination, concurrence, connection, crisis, crossroads, crucial point, emergency, exigency, juncture, pass, predicament, stage, turning point

conjure **1.** juggle, play tricks **2.** bewitch, call upon, cast a spell, charm, enchant, fascinate, invoke, raise, rouse, summon up **3.** adjure, appeal to, beg, beseech, crave, entreat, implore, importune, pray, supplicate

conjurer, conjuror illusionist, magician, miracle-worker, sorcerer, thaumaturge (*rare*), wizard

conjure up bring to mind, contrive, create, evoke, produce as by magic, recall, recollect

conjuring juggling, magic, sorcery, thaumaturgy (*rare*), wizardry

connect affix, ally, associate, attach, cohere, combine, couple, fasten, join, link, relate, unite

Antonyms detach, disconnect, dissociate, divide, part, separate, sever, unfasten

connected **1.** affiliated, akin, allied, associated, banded together, bracketed, combined, coupled, joined, linked, related, united **2.** *of speech* coherent, comprehensible, consecutive, intelligible

connection **1.** alliance, association, attachment, coupling, fastening, junction, link, tie, union **2.**

affiliation, affinity, association, bond, com~ merce, communication, correlation, corre~ spondence, intercourse, interrelation, liaison, link, marriage, relation, relationship, rel~ evance, tie-in **3**. context, frame of reference, reference **4**. acquaintance, ally, associate, con~ tact, friend, sponsor **5**. kin, kindred, kinsman, kith, relation, relative

connivance abetment, abetting, collusion, complicity, conspiring, tacit consent

connive **1**. cabal, collude, conspire, cook up (*informal*), intrigue, plot, scheme **2**. *with* **at** abet, aid, be an accessory to, be a party to, be in collusion with, blink at, disregard, lend oneself to, let pass, look the other way, over~ look, pass by, shut one's eyes to, turn a blind eye to, wink at

conniving caballing, calculating, collusive, conspiring, contriving, designing, plotting, scheming

connoisseur aficionado, appreciator, arbiter, authority, buff (*informal*), cognoscente, devo~ tee, expert, judge, maven (*U.S.*), savant, spe~ cialist, whiz (*informal*)

connoisseur: a specialist who knows everything about something and nothing about anything else

Ambrose Bierce *The Devil's Dictionary*

connotation association, colouring, implication, nuance, significance, suggestion, undertone

connote betoken, hint at, imply, indicate, inti~ mate, involve, signify, suggest

connubial conjugal, marital, married, matri~ monial, nuptial, wedded

conquer **1**. beat, blow out of the water (*slang*), bring to their knees, checkmate, clobber (*slang*), crush, defeat, discomfit, get the better of, humble, lick (*informal*), make mincemeat of (*informal*), master, overcome, overpower, overthrow, prevail, put in their place, quell, rout, run rings around (*informal*), stuff (*slang*), subdue, subjugate, succeed, surmount, tank (*slang*), triumph, undo, vanquish, wipe the floor with (*informal*) **2**. acquire, annex, obtain, occupy, overrun, seize, win

Antonyms (*sense 1*) be defeated, capitulate, give in, give up, lose, quit, submit, surrender, throw in the towel, yield

I came, I saw, I conquered (veni, vidi, vici)

Julius Caesar

conqueror champion, conquistador, defeater, hero, lord, master, subjugator, vanquisher, victor, winner

conquest **1**. defeat, discomfiture, mastery, overthrow, pasting (*slang*), rout, triumph, vanquishment, victory **2**. acquisition, annexa~ tion, appropriation, coup, invasion, occupation, subjection, subjugation, takeover **3**. captiva~ tion, enchantment, enthralment, enticement, seduction **4**. acquisition, adherent, admirer, catch, fan, feather in one's cap, follower, prize, supporter, worshipper

consanguinity affinity, blood-relationship, family tie, kin, kindred, kinship

conscience **1**. moral sense, principles, scruples, sense of right and wrong, still small voice **2**. **in all conscience** assuredly, certainly, fairly, honestly, in truth, rightly, truly

Conscience: the inner voice which warns us that someone may be looking

H.L. Mencken *A Little Book in C Major*

Thus conscience does make cowards of us all

William Shakespeare *Hamlet*

Conscience is thoroughly well-bred and soon leaves off talking to those who do not wish to hear it

Samuel Butler

A guilty conscience needs no accuser

conscience-stricken ashamed, compunctious, contrite, disturbed, guilty, penitent, remorse~ ful, repentant, sorry, troubled

conscientious **1**. careful, diligent, exact, faith~ ful, having one's nose to the grindstone, me~ ticulous, painstaking, particular, punctilious, thorough **2**. high-minded, high-principled, honest, honourable, incorruptible, just, moral, responsible, scrupulous, straightforward, strict, upright

Antonyms careless, irresponsible, negligent, remiss, slack, thoughtless, unconscientious, unprincipled, unreliable, unscrupulous, un~ trustworthy

conscious **1**. alert, alive to, awake, aware, clued-up (*informal*), cognizant, percipient, re~ sponsive, sensible, sentient, wise to (*slang*) **2**. calculated, deliberate, intentional, knowing, premeditated, rational, reasoning, reflective, responsible, self-conscious, studied, wilful

Antonyms (*sense 1*) ignorant, insensible, oblivious, unaware, unconscious (*sense 2*) ac~ cidental, uncalculated, unintended, uninten~ tional, unplanned, unpremeditated, unwitting

consciousness apprehension, awareness, knowledge, realization, recognition, sensibility

Consciousness... is the phenomenon whereby the universe's very existence is made known

Roger Penrose *The Emperor's New Mind*

consecrate dedicate, devote, exalt, hallow, or~ dain, sanctify, set apart, venerate

consecutive chronological, following, in se~ quence, in turn, running, sequential, seriatim, succeeding, successive, uninterrupted

consensus agreement, assent, common con~ sent, concord, concurrence, general agreement, harmony, unanimity, unity

consent **1**. *verb* accede, acquiesce, agree, allow, approve, assent, comply, concede, concur, per~ mit, play ball (*informal*), yield **2**. *noun* acqui~

escence, agreement, approval, assent, compliance, concession, concurrence, go-ahead (*informal*), green light, O.K. *or* okay (*informal*), permission, sanction
Antonyms *verb* decline, demur, disagree, disapprove, dissent, refuse, resist ~*noun* disagreement, disapproval, dissent, refusal, unwillingness

consequence 1. effect, end, end result, event, issue, outcome, repercussion, result, sequel, upshot 2. account, concern, import, importance, interest, moment, note, portent, significance, value, weight 3. bottom, distinction, eminence, notability, rank, repute, standing, status 4. **in consequence** as a result, because, following

As you sow, so shall you reap

consequent ensuing, following, resultant, resulting, sequential, subsequent, successive

consequential 1. eventful, far-reaching, grave, important, momentous, serious, significant, weighty 2. arrogant, bumptious, conceited, inflated, pompous, pretentious, self-important, supercilious, vainglorious 3. consequent, indirect, resultant

consequently accordingly, ergo, hence, necessarily, subsequently, therefore, thus

conservation custody, economy, guardianship, husbandry, maintenance, preservation, protection, safeguarding, safekeeping, saving, upkeep

conservative 1. *adjective* cautious, conventional, die-hard, guarded, hidebound, middle-of-the-road, moderate, quiet, reactionary, right-wing, sober, tory, traditional 2. *noun* middle-of-the-roader, moderate, reactionary, right-winger, stick-in-the-mud (*informal*), tory, traditionalist
Antonyms *adjective* imaginative, innovative, liberal, progressive, radical ~*noun* changer, innovator, progressive, radical

No amount of cajolery, and no attempts at ethical or social seduction, can eradicate from my heart a deep burning hatred for the Tory Party... So far as I am concerned they are lower than vermin
Aneurin Bevan

conservative: a statesman who is enamoured of existing evils, as distinguished from the Liberal, who wishes to replace them with others
Ambrose Bierce *The Devil's Dictionary*

We know what happens to people who stay in the middle of the road. They get run down
Aneurin Bevan

The most conservative man in this world is the British Trade Unionist when you want to change him
Ernest Bevin

I do not know which makes a man more conservative - to know nothing but the present, or nothing but the past
John Maynard Keynes *The End of Laissez-Faire*

conservatory glasshouse, greenhouse, hothouse

conserve go easy on, hoard, husband, keep, nurse, preserve, protect, save, store up, take care of, use sparingly
Antonyms be extravagant, blow (*slang*), dissipate, fritter away, misspend, misuse, spend, spend like water, squander, use up, waste

consider 1. chew over, cogitate, consult, contemplate, deliberate, discuss, examine, eye up, meditate, mull over, muse, ponder, reflect, revolve, ruminate, study, think about, turn over in one's mind, weigh, work over 2. believe, deem, hold to be, judge, rate, regard as, think 3. bear in mind, care for, keep in view, make allowance for, reckon with, regard, remember, respect, take into account

considerable 1. abundant, ample, appreciable, comfortable, goodly, great, large, lavish, marked, much, noticeable, plentiful, reasonable, sizable *or* sizeable, substantial, tidy, tolerable 2. distinguished, important, influential, noteworthy, renowned, significant, venerable
Antonyms insignificant, insubstantial, meagre, ordinary, paltry, small, unimportant, unremarkable

considerably appreciably, greatly, markedly, noticeably, remarkably, seriously (*informal*), significantly, substantially, very much

considerate attentive, charitable, circumspect, concerned, discreet, forbearing, kind, kindly, mindful, obliging, patient, tactful, thoughtful, unselfish
Antonyms heedless, inconsiderate, selfish, thoughtless

consideration 1. analysis, attention, cogitation, contemplation, deliberation, discussion, examination, perusal, reflection, regard, review, scrutiny, study, thought 2. concern, factor, issue, point 3. concern, considerateness, friendliness, kindliness, kindness, respect, solicitude, tact, thoughtfulness 4. fee, payment, perquisite, recompense, remuneration, reward, tip 5. **take into consideration** bear in mind, make allowance for, take into account, weigh

considering all in all, all things considered, insomuch as, in the light of, in view of

consign commend to, commit, convey, deliver, deposit with, entrust, hand over, relegate, ship (*cargo*), transfer, transmit

consignment 1. *act of consigning* assignment, committal, dispatch, distribution, entrusting, handing over, relegation, sending, shipment, transmittal 2. *something consigned* batch, delivery, goods, shipment

consist 1. *with* **of** amount to, be composed of, be made up of, comprise, contain, embody, include, incorporate, involve 2. *with* **in** be expressed by, be found *or* contained in, inhere, lie, reside

consistency 1. compactness, density, firmness, thickness, viscosity 2. accordance, agreement, coherence, compatibility, congruity, correspondence, harmony 3. constancy, evenness, regularity, steadfastness, steadiness, uniformity

Consistency is the last refuge of the unimaginative
Oscar Wilde

A foolish consistency is the hobgoblin of little minds
Ralph Waldo Emerson *Essays: Self-Reliance*

consistent 1. constant, dependable, persistent, regular, steady, true to type, unchanging, undeviating 2. accordant, agreeing, all of a piece, coherent, compatible, congruous, consonant, harmonious, logical
Antonyms (*sense 1*) changing, deviating, erratic, inconsistent, irregular (*sense 2*) contradictory, contrary, discordant, incompatible, incongruous, inconsistent, inharmonious

consolation alleviation, assuagement, cheer, comfort, ease, easement, encouragement, help, relief, solace, succour, support

console assuage, calm, cheer, comfort, encourage, express sympathy for, relieve, solace, soothe
Antonyms aggravate (*informal*), agitate, annoy, discomfort, distress, hassle (*informal*), hurt, sadden, torment, trouble, upset

Anything that consoles is fake
Iris Murdoch

consolidate 1. amalgamate, cement, combine, compact, condense, conjoin, federate, fuse, harden, join, solidify, thicken, unite 2. fortify, reinforce, secure, stabilize, strengthen

consolidation alliance, amalgamation, association, compression, condensation, federation, fortification, fusion, reinforcement, strengthening

consonance accord, agreement, concord, conformity, congruence, congruity, consistency, correspondence, harmony, suitableness, unison

consonant accordant, according, compatible, concordant, congruous, consistent, correspondent, harmonious, in agreement, suitable

consort *noun* 1. associate, companion, fellow, husband, partner, significant other (*U.S. informal*), spouse, wife ~*verb* 2. associate, fraternize, go around with, hang about, around *or* out with, hang with (*informal, chiefly U.S.*), keep company, mingle, mix 3. accord, agree, correspond, harmonize, square, tally

conspectus abstract, compendium, digest, epitome, outline, précis, résumé, summary, survey, syllabus, synopsis

conspicuous 1. apparent, blatant, clear, discernible, easily seen, evident, manifest, noticeable, obvious, patent, perceptible, salient, visible 2. celebrated, distinguished, eminent, famous, illustrious, notable, outstanding, prominent, remarkable, salient, signal, striking 3. blatant, flagrant, flashy, garish, glaring, showy
Antonyms (*sense 1*) concealed, hidden, imperceptible, inconspicuous, indiscernible, invisible, obscure, unnoticeable (*sense 2*) humble, inconspicuous, insignificant, ordinary, unacclaimed, undistinguished, unmemorable, unnotable

conspiracy cabal, collusion, confederacy, frame-up (*slang*), intrigue, league, machination, plot, scheme, treason

conspirator cabalist, conspirer, intriguer, plotter, schemer, traitor

conspire 1. cabal, confederate, contrive, devise, hatch treason, intrigue, machinate, manoeuvre, plot, scheme 2. combine, concur, conduce, contribute, cooperate, tend, work together

constancy decision, determination, devotion, fidelity, firmness, fixedness, permanence, perseverance, regularity, resolution, stability, steadfastness, steadiness, tenacity, uniformity

I am constant as the northern star
William Shakespeare *Julius Caesar*

constant 1. continual, even, firm, fixed, habitual, immovable, immutable, invariable, permanent, perpetual, regular, stable, steadfast, steady, unalterable, unbroken, uniform, unvarying 2. ceaseless, continual, continuous, endless, eternal, everlasting, incessant, interminable, never-ending, nonstop, perpetual, persistent, relentless, sustained, uninterrupted, unrelenting, unremitting 3. determined, dogged, persevering, resolute, unflagging, unshaken, unwavering 4. attached, dependable, devoted, faithful, loyal, stalwart, staunch, tried-and-true, true, trustworthy, trusty, unfailing
Antonyms (*senses 1 & 2*) changeable, changing, deviating, erratic, inconstant, intermittent, irregular, occasional, random, uneven, unstable, unsustained, variable (*sense 4*) disloyal, fickle, irresolute, undependable

constantly all the time, always, aye (*Scot.*), continually, continuously, endlessly, everlastingly, incessantly, interminably, invariably, morning, noon and night, night and day, nonstop, perpetually, persistently, relentlessly
Antonyms (every) now and then, every so often, from time to time, intermittently, irregu~

larly, now and again, occasionally, off and on, periodically, sometimes

consternation alarm, amazement, anxiety, awe, bewilderment, confusion, dismay, distress, dread, fear, fright, horror, panic, shock, terror, trepidation

constituent *adjective* **1.** basic, component, elemental, essential, integral *~noun* **2.** component, element, essential, factor, ingredient, part, principle, unit **3.** elector, voter

constitute 1. compose, comprise, create, enact, establish, fix, form, found, make, make up, set up **2.** appoint, authorize, commission, delegate, depute, empower, name, nominate, ordain

constitution 1. composition, establishment, formation, organization **2.** build, character, composition, disposition, form, habit, health, make-up, nature, physique, structure, temper, temperament

constitutional *adjective* **1.** congenital, immanent, inborn, inherent, intrinsic, organic **2.** chartered, statutory, vested *~noun* **3.** airing, stroll, turn, walk

constrain 1. bind, coerce, compel, drive, force, impel, necessitate, oblige, pressure, pressurize, urge **2.** chain, check, confine, constrict, curb, hem in, rein, restrain, straiten

constrained embarrassed, forced, guarded, inhibited, reserved, reticent, subdued, unnatural

constraint 1. coercion, compulsion, force, necessity, pressure, restraint **2.** bashfulness, diffidence, embarrassment, inhibition, repression, reservation, restraint, timidity **3.** check, curb, damper, deterrent, hindrance, limitation, rein, restriction

constrict choke, compress, contract, cramp, inhibit, limit, narrow, pinch, restrict, shrink, squeeze, strangle, strangulate, tighten

constriction blockage, compression, constraint, cramp, impediment, limitation, narrowing, pressure, reduction, restriction, squeezing, stenosis (*Pathology*), stricture, tightness

construct assemble, build, compose, create, design, elevate, engineer, erect, establish, fabricate, fashion, form, formulate, found, frame, make, manufacture, organize, put up, raise, set up, shape
Antonyms bulldoze, demolish, destroy, devastate, dismantle, flatten, knock down, level, pull down, raze, tear down

construction 1. assembly, building, composition, creation, edifice, erection, fabric, fabrication, figure, form, formation, shape, structure **2.** explanation, inference, interpretation, reading, rendering, take (*informal, chiefly U.S.*)

constructive helpful, positive, practical, productive, useful, valuable
Antonyms destructive, futile, ineffective, limp-wristed, negative, unhelpful, unproductive, useless, vain, worthless

construe analyse, deduce, explain, expound, interpret, parse, read, read between the lines, render, take, translate

consult 1. ask, ask advice of, commune, compare notes, confer, consider, debate, deliberate, interrogate, pick (someone's) brains, question, refer to, take counsel, turn to **2.** consider, have regard for, regard, respect, take account of, take into consideration

consult: to seek another's approval of a course already decided on
Ambrose Bierce *The Devil's Dictionary*

consultant adviser, authority, specialist

consultation appointment, conference, council, deliberation, dialogue, discussion, examination, hearing, interview, meeting, seminar, session

consume 1. absorb, deplete, dissipate, drain, eat up, employ, exhaust, expend, finish up, fritter away, lavish, lessen, spend, squander, use, use up, utilize, vanish, waste, wear out **2.** devour, eat, eat up, gobble (up), guzzle, polish off (*informal*), put away, swallow **3.** annihilate, decay, demolish, destroy, devastate, lay waste, ravage **4.** *often passive* absorb, devour, dominate, eat up, engross, monopolize, obsess, preoccupy

consumer buyer, customer, purchaser, shopper, user

The consumer isn't a moron; she is your wife
David Ogilvy *Confessions of an Advertising Man*

consuming absorbing, compelling, devouring, engrossing, excruciating, gripping, immoderate, overwhelming, tormenting

consummate 1. *verb* accomplish, achieve, carry out, compass, complete, conclude, crown, effectuate, end, finish, perfect, perform, put the tin lid on **2.** *adjective* absolute, accomplished, complete, conspicuous, deep-dyed (*usually derogatory*), finished, matchless, perfect, polished, practised, skilled, superb, supreme, total, transcendent, ultimate, unqualified, utter
Antonyms *verb* begin, commence, conceive, get under way, inaugurate, initiate, originate, start

consummation achievement, completion, culmination, end, fulfilment, perfection, realization

consumption 1. consuming, decay, decrease, depletion, destruction, diminution, dissipation, drain, exhaustion, expenditure, loss, use, using up, utilization, waste **2.** *Medical* atrophy, emaciation, phthisis, T.B., tuberculosis

contact *noun* **1.** association, communication, connection **2.** approximation, contiguity, junction, juxtaposition, touch, union **3.** acquaintance, connection *~verb* **4.** approach, call, com~

municate with, get hold of, get *or* be in touch with, phone, reach, ring (up) (*informal, chiefly Brit.*), speak to, touch base with (*U.S. & Canad. informal*), write to

contagion 1. contamination, corruption, infec~tion, pestilence, plague, pollution, taint 2. communication, passage, spread, transference, transmittal

contagious catching, communicable, epidemic, epizootic (*Veterinary medicine*), infectious, pestiferous, pestilential, spreading, taking (*informal*), transmissible

contain 1. accommodate, enclose, have capacity for, hold, incorporate, seat 2. comprehend, comprise, embody, embrace, include, involve 3. control, curb, hold back, hold in, keep a tight rein on, repress, restrain, stifle

container holder, receptacle, repository, vessel

Drinking vessels

canteen	mug
champagne flute	porrón
chalice	quaich
copita	schooner
cup	tankard
demitasse	tassie
glass	tumbler
goblet	water bottle

Containers for storing drink

amphore (*historical*)	jeroboam
ampulla (*historical*)	jug
Balthazar	keg
barrel	magnum
bottle	Methuselah
can	miniature
carafe	Nebuchadnezzar
carton	pitcher
cask	polypin
coldie (*Austral. slang*)	rehoboam
	Salmanazar
decanter	screw-top (*informal*)
firkin	stubby (*Austral. informal*)
flagon	
flask	tantalus
gourd	tin
half-bottle	tinny (*Austral. slang*)
hogshead	tube (*Austral. slang*)
jar	

contaminate adulterate, befoul, corrupt, defile, deprave, infect, pollute, radioactivate, smirch, soil, stain, sully, taint, tarnish, vitiate
Antonyms clean, cleanse, decontaminate, de~odorize, disinfect, fumigate, purify, sanitize, sterilize

contaminated adulterated, corrupted, defiled, depraved, dirtied, infected, poisoned, polluted, smirched, soiled, stained, sullied, tainted, tar~nished, vitiated

contamination adulteration, contagion, cor~ruption, decay, defilement, dirtying, filth, foulness, impurity, infection, poisoning, pollu~tion, radioactivation, rottenness, taint

contemn despise, disdain, disregard, hold cheap, neglect, scorn, slight, spurn, treat with contempt

contemplate 1. brood over, consider, deliber~ate, meditate, meditate on, mull over, muse over, observe, ponder, reflect upon, revolve *or* turn over in one's mind, ruminate (upon), study 2. behold, check out (*informal*), exam~ine, eye, eye up, gaze at, inspect, recce (*slang*), regard, scrutinize, stare at, survey, view, weigh 3. aspire to, consider, design, en~visage, expect, foresee, have in view *or* in mind, intend, mean, plan, propose, think of

contemplation 1. cogitation, consideration, de~liberation, meditation, musing, pondering, re~flection, reverie, rumination, thought 2. ex~amination, gazing at, inspection, looking at, observation, recce (*slang*), scrutiny, survey, viewing

contemplative deep *or* lost in thought, in a brown study, intent, introspective, meditative, musing, pensive, rapt, reflective, ruminative, thoughtful

contemporary *adjective* 1. coetaneous (*rare*), coeval, coexistent, coexisting, concurrent, con~temporaneous, synchronous 2. à la mode, cur~rent, happening (*informal*), in fashion, latest, modern, newfangled, present, present-day, re~cent, trendy (*Brit. informal*), ultramodern, up-to-date, up-to-the-minute, with it (*infor~mal*) ~*noun* 3. compeer, fellow, peer
Antonyms *adjective* antecedent, antique, ear~ly, obsolete, old, old-fashioned, out-of-date, passé, succeeding

contempt 1. condescension, contumely, deri~sion, despite (*archaic*), disdain, disregard, dis~respect, mockery, neglect, scorn, slight 2. *a state of contempt* disgrace, dishonour, hu~miliation, shame
Antonyms admiration, esteem, honour, liking, regard, respect

contemptible abject, base, cheap, degenerate, despicable, detestable, ignominious, low, low-down (*informal*), mean, measly, paltry, pitiful, scurvy, shabby, shameful, vile, worthless
Antonyms admirable, attractive, honourable, laudable, pleasant, praiseworthy

contemptuous arrogant, cavalier, condescend~ing, contumelious, derisive, disdainful, haughty, high and mighty, insolent, insulting, on one's high horse (*informal*), scornful, sneering, supercilious, withering
Antonyms civil, courteous, deferential, gra~cious, humble, mannerly, obsequious, polite, respectful

contend 1. clash, compete, contest, cope, emu~late, grapple, jostle, litigate, skirmish, strive, struggle, vie **2.** affirm, allege, argue, assert, aver, avow, debate, dispute, hold, maintain

contender competitor, contestant, rival, vier

content[1] **1.** *verb* appease, delight, gladden, gratify, humour, indulge, mollify, placate, please, reconcile, sate, satisfy, suffice **2.** *noun* comfort, contentment, ease, gratification, peace, peace of mind, pleasure, satisfaction **3.** *adjective* agreeable, at ease, comfortable, contented, fulfilled, satisfied, willing to accept

content[2] *noun* **1.** burden, essence, gist, ideas, matter, meaning, significance, substance, text, thoughts **2.** capacity, load, measure, size, volume

contented at ease, at peace, cheerful, comfortable, complacent, content, glad, gratified, happy, pleased, satisfied, serene, thankful
Antonyms annoyed, discontented, displeased, dissatisfied, pissed off (*taboo slang*), troubled, uncomfortable, uneasy

contention **1.** bone of contention, competition, contest, discord, dispute, dissension, enmity, feuding, hostility, rivalry, row, strife, struggle, wrangling **2.** affirmation, allegation, argument, assertion, asseveration, belief, claim, declaration, ground, idea, maintaining, opinion, position, profession, stand, thesis, view

contentious argumentative, bickering, cantankerous, captious, cavilling, combative, controversial, cross, disputatious, factious, litigious, peevish, perverse, pugnacious, quarrelsome, querulous, wrangling

contentment comfort, complacency, content, contentedness, ease, equanimity, fulfilment, gladness, gratification, happiness, peace, pleasure, repletion, satisfaction, serenity
Antonyms discomfort, discontent, discontentment, displeasure, dissatisfaction, uneasiness, unhappiness

Poor and content is rich and rich enough
William Shakespeare *Othello*

contents **1.** constituents, elements, ingredients, load **2.** chapters, divisions, subject matter, subjects, themes, topics

contest *noun* **1.** competition, game, head-to-head, match, tournament, trial **2.** affray, altercation, battle, combat, conflict, controversy, debate, discord, dispute, encounter, fight, shock, struggle *~verb* **3.** compete, contend, fight, fight over, strive, vie **4.** argue, call in *or* into question, challenge, debate, dispute, doubt, litigate, object to, oppose, question

contestant aspirant, candidate, competitor, contender, entrant, participant, player

context **1.** background, connection, frame of reference, framework, relation **2.** ambience, circumstances, conditions, situation

contiguous abutting, adjacent, adjoining, beside, bordering, conterminous, in contact, juxtaposed, juxtapositional, near, neighbouring, next, next door to, touching

continence abstinence, asceticism, celibacy, chastity, moderation, self-control, self-restraint, temperance

You command continence; give what you command, and command what you will
St. Augustine of Hippo *Confessions*

continent[1] *adjective* abstemious, abstinent, ascetic, austere, celibate, chaste, self-restrained, sober

continent[2]

Continents

Africa	Europe
Antarctica	North America
Asia	South America
Australia	

contingency accident, chance, emergency, event, eventuality, fortuity, happening, incident, juncture, possibility, uncertainty

contingent *adjective* **1.** *with* **on** *or* **upon** conditional, controlled by, dependent, subject to **2.** accidental, casual, fortuitous, haphazard, random, uncertain *~noun* **3.** batch, body, bunch (*informal*), deputation, detachment, group, mission, quota, section, set

continual constant, continuous, endless, eternal, everlasting, frequent, incessant, interminable, oft-repeated, perpetual, recurrent, regular, repeated, repetitive, unceasing, uninterrupted, unremitting
Antonyms broken, ceasing, erratic, fluctuating, fragmentary, infrequent, intermittent, interrupted, irregular, occasional, periodic, spasmodic, sporadic, terminable

continually all the time, always, aye (*Scot.*), constantly, endlessly, eternally, everlastingly, forever, incessantly, interminably, nonstop, persistently, repeatedly

continuance continuation, duration, period, protraction, term

continuation **1.** addition, extension, furtherance, postscript, sequel, supplement **2.** maintenance, perpetuation, prolongation, resumption

continue **1.** abide, carry on, endure, last, live on, persist, remain, rest, stay, stay on, survive **2.** go on, keep at, keep on, keep one's hand in, keep the ball rolling, keep up, maintain, persevere, persist in, prolong, pursue, stick at, stick to, sustain **3.** draw out, extend, lengthen, project, prolong, reach **4.** carry on, pick up where one left off, proceed, recommence, resume, return to, take up
Antonyms (*sense 1*) abdicate, leave, quit, resign, retire, step down (*senses 2 & 4*) break off, call it a day, cease, discontinue, give up, leave off, pack in (*Brit. informal*), quit, stop

continuing enduring, in progress, lasting, ongoing, sustained

continuity cohesion, connection, flow, interrelationship, progression, sequence, succession, whole

continuous connected, constant, continued, extended, prolonged, unbroken, unceasing, undivided, uninterrupted
Antonyms broken, disconnected, ending, inconstant, intermittent, interrupted, occasional, passing, severed, spasmodic

contort convolute, deform, distort, gnarl, knot, misshape, twist, warp, wrench, writhe

contortion bend, convolution, deformity, distortion, gnarl, knot, tortuosity, twist, warp

contour curve, figure, form, lines, outline, profile, relief, shape, silhouette

contraband 1. *noun* black-marketing, bootlegging, moonshine (*U.S.*), rum-running, smuggling, trafficking 2. *adjective* banned, black-market, bootleg, bootlegged, forbidden, hot (*informal*), illegal, illicit, interdicted, prohibited, smuggled, unlawful

contract *verb* 1. abbreviate, abridge, compress, condense, confine, constrict, curtail, diminish, dwindle, epitomize, knit, lessen, narrow, pucker, purse, reduce, shrink, shrivel, tighten, wither, wrinkle 2. agree, arrange, bargain, clinch, close, come to terms, commit oneself, covenant, engage, enter into, negotiate, pledge, shake hands, stipulate 3. acquire, be afflicted with, catch, develop, get, go down with, incur ~*noun* 4. agreement, arrangement, bargain, bond, commission, commitment, compact, concordat, convention, covenant, deal (*informal*), engagement, pact, settlement, stipulation, treaty, understanding
Antonyms (*sense 1*) broaden, develop, distend, enlarge, expand, grow, increase, inflate, multiply, spread, stretch, swell, widen (*sense 2*) decline, disagree, refuse, turn down (*sense 3*) avert, avoid, escape, ward off

A verbal contract isn't worth the paper it is written on

Sam Goldwyn

contraction abbreviation, compression, constriction, diminution, drawing in, elision, narrowing, reduction, shortening, shrinkage, shrivelling, tensing, tightening

contradict be at variance with, belie, challenge, contravene, controvert, counter, counteract, deny, dispute, fly in the face of, gainsay (*archaic or literary*), impugn, make a nonsense of, negate, oppose, rebut
Antonyms affirm, agree, authenticate, confirm, defend, endorse, support, verify

contradiction conflict, confutation, contravention, denial, incongruity, inconsistency, negation, opposite

contradictory antagonistic, antithetical, conflicting, contrary, discrepant, incompatible, inconsistent, irreconcilable, opposed, opposite, paradoxical, repugnant

contraption apparatus, contrivance, device, gadget, instrument, mechanism, rig, waldo

contrary *adjective* 1. adverse, antagonistic, clashing, contradictory, counter, discordant, hostile, inconsistent, inimical, opposed, opposite, paradoxical 2. awkward, balky, cantankerous, cussed (*informal*), difficult, disobliging, froward (*archaic*), intractable, obstinate, perverse, stroppy (*Brit. slang*), thrawn (*Northern English dialect*), unaccommodating, wayward, wilful ~*noun* 3. antithesis, converse, opposite, reverse 4. **on the contrary** conversely, in contrast, not at all, on the other hand, quite the opposite *or* reverse
Antonyms (*sense 1*) accordant, congruous, consistent, harmonious, in agreement, parallel, unopposed (*sense 2*) accommodating, agreeable, amiable, cooperative, eager to please, helpful, obliging, tractable, willing

contrast 1. *noun* comparison, contrariety, difference, differentiation, disparity, dissimilarity, distinction, divergence, foil, opposition 2. *verb* compare, differ, differentiate, distinguish, oppose, set in opposition, set off

contravene 1. break, disobey, go against, infringe, transgress, violate 2. conflict with, contradict, counteract, cross, go against, hinder, interfere, oppose, refute, thwart

contravention 1. breach, disobedience, infraction, infringement, transgression, trespass, violation 2. conflict, contradiction, counteraction, disputation, hindrance, impugnation, interference, rebuttal, refutation

contretemps accident, calamity, difficulty, misfortune, mishap, mistake, predicament

contribute 1. add, afford, bestow, chip in (*informal*), donate, furnish, give, provide, subscribe, supply 2. be conducive, be instrumental, be partly responsible for, conduce, help, lead, tend

contribution addition, bestowal, donation, gift, grant, input, offering, stipend, subscription

contributor 1. backer, bestower, conferrer, donor, giver, patron, subscriber, supporter 2. correspondent, freelance, freelancer, journalist, journo (*slang*), reporter

contrite chastened, conscience-stricken, humble, in sackcloth and ashes, penitent, regretful, remorseful, repentant, sorrowful, sorry

contrition compunction, humiliation, penitence, remorse, repentance, self-reproach, sorrow

contrivance 1. artifice, design, dodge, expedient, fabrication, formation, intrigue, inventiveness, machination, measure, plan, plot, project, ruse, scheme, stratagem, trick 2. ap~

paratus, appliance, contraption, device, equipment, gadget, gear, implement, instrument, invention, machine, mechanism

contrive 1. concoct, construct, create, design, devise, engineer, fabricate, frame, improvise, invent, manufacture, wangle (*informal*) 2. arrange, bring about, effect, hit upon, manage, manoeuvre, plan, plot, scheme, succeed

contrived artificial, elaborate, forced, laboured, overdone, planned, recherché, strained, unnatural
Antonyms genuine, natural, relaxed, spontaneous, unaffected, unconstrained, unfeigned, unforced, unpretentious

control *verb* 1. administer, boss (*informal*), call the shots, call the tune, command, conduct, direct, dominate, govern, handle, have charge of, have (someone) in one's pocket, hold the purse strings, keep a tight rein on, keep on a string, lead, manage, manipulate, oversee, pilot, reign over, rule, steer, superintend, supervise 2. bridle, check, constrain, contain, curb, hold back, limit, master, rein in, repress, restrain, subdue 3. *used of a machine, an experiment, etc.* counteract, determine, monitor, regulate, verify *~noun* 4. authority, charge, command, direction, discipline, government, guidance, jurisdiction, management, mastery, oversight, rule, superintendence, supervision, supremacy 5. brake, check, curb, limitation, regulation, restraint

Who controls the past controls the future: who controls the present controls the past
George Orwell *Nineteen Eighty-Four*

controls console, control panel, dash, dashboard, dials, instruments

controversial at issue, contended, contentious, controvertible, debatable, disputable, disputed, open to question, polemic, under discussion

controversy altercation, argument, contention, debate, discussion, dispute, dissension, polemic, quarrel, row, squabble, strife, wrangle, wrangling

controvert 1. challenge, contradict, counter, deny, fly in the face of, make a nonsense of, oppose, refute 2. argue, contest, debate, discuss, dispute, wrangle

contumacious haughty, headstrong, insubordinate, intractable, intransigent, obdurate, obstinate, perverse, pig-headed, rebellious, recalcitrant, refractory, stiff-necked, stubborn

contumacy contempt, contrariety, delinquency, disobedience, haughtiness, insubordination, intransigence, obstinacy, perverseness, pigheadedness, rebelliousness, recalcitrance, refractoriness, stubbornness

contumelious contemptuous, disdainful, insolent, insulting, scornful, sneering, sniffy (*informal*), supercilious, withering

contumely abuse, affront, arrogance, contempt, derision, disdain, humiliation, indignity, insolence, insult, obloquy, opprobrium, rudeness, scorn, superciliousness

contusion bruise, discoloration, injury, knock, swelling, trauma (*Pathology*)

conundrum brain-teaser (*informal*), enigma, poser, problem, puzzle, riddle, teaser

convalesce improve, rally, recover, recuperate, rehabilitate, rest

convalescence improvement, recovery, recuperation, rehabilitation, return to health

convalescent *adjective* getting better, improving, mending, on the mend, recovering, recuperating

convene assemble, bring together, call, come together, congregate, convoke, gather, meet, muster, rally, summon

convenience 1. accessibility, appropriateness, availability, fitness, handiness, opportuneness, serviceability, suitability, usefulness, utility 2. *a convenient time or situation* chance, leisure, opportunity, spare moment, spare time 3. accommodation, advantage, benefit, comfort, ease, enjoyment, satisfaction, service, use 4. *a useful device* amenity, appliance, comfort, facility, help, labour-saving device
Antonyms discomfort, hardship, inconvenience, uselessness

convenient 1. adapted, appropriate, beneficial, commodious, fit, fitted, handy, helpful, labour-saving, opportune, seasonable, serviceable, suitable, suited, timely, useful, well-timed 2. accessible, at hand, available, close at hand, handy, just round the corner, nearby, within reach
Antonyms awkward, distant, inaccessible, inconvenient, out-of-the-way, unsuitable, useless

convent convent school, nunnery, religious community

I like convents, but I wish they would not admit anyone under the age of fifty
Napoleon Bonaparte

convention 1. assembly, conference, congress, convocation, council, delegates, meeting, representatives 2. code, custom, etiquette, formality, practice, propriety, protocol, tradition, usage 3. agreement, bargain, compact, concordat, contract, pact, protocol, stipulation, treaty

conventional 1. accepted, bog-standard (*Brit. & Irish slang*), common, correct, customary, decorous, expected, formal, habitual, normal, ordinary, orthodox, prevailing, prevalent, proper, regular, ritual, standard, traditional, usual, wonted 2. banal, bourgeois, commonplace, hackneyed, hidebound, pedestrian, Pooterish, prosaic, routine, run-of-the-mill, stereotyped, unoriginal, vanilla (*slang*)
Antonyms abnormal, left-field (*informal*),

off-the-wall (*slang*), uncommon, unconventional, unorthodox

converge coincide, combine, come together, concentrate, focus, gather, join, meet, merge, mingle

convergence approach, blending, coincidence, concentration, concurrence, confluence, conflux, conjunction, junction, meeting, merging, mingling

conversant *usually with* **with** acquainted, *au fait*, experienced, familiar, knowledgeable, practised, proficient, skilled, versed, well-informed, well up in (*informal*)

conversation chat, chinwag (*Brit. informal*), colloquy, communication, communion, confab (*informal*), confabulation, conference, converse, dialogue, discourse, discussion, exchange, gossip, intercourse, powwow, talk, tête-à-tête

Conversation is the enemy of good wine and food

Alfred Hitchcock

conversational chatty, colloquial, communicative, informal

converse[1] *verb* **1.** chat, commune, confer, discourse, exchange views, shoot the breeze (*slang, chiefly U.S. & Canad.*) **2.** *obsolete* associate, consort ~*noun* **3.** chat, communication, conference, conversation, dialogue, talk

converse[2] **1.** *noun* antithesis, contrary, obverse, opposite, other side of the coin, reverse **2.** *adjective* contrary, counter, opposite, reverse, reversed, transposed

conversion **1.** change, metamorphosis, transfiguration, transformation, transmogrification (*jocular*), transmutation **2.** adaptation, alteration, modification, reconstruction, remodelling, reorganization **3.** change of heart, proselytization, rebirth, reformation, regeneration

convert[1] *verb* **1.** alter, change, interchange, metamorphose, transform, transmogrify (*jocular*), transmute, transpose, turn **2.** adapt, apply, appropriate, customize, modify, remodel, reorganize, restyle, revise **3.** baptize, bring to God, convince, proselytize, reform, regenerate, save

convert[2] *noun* catechumen, disciple, neophyte, proselyte

convertible adaptable, adjustable, exchangeable, interchangeable

convex bulging, gibbous, outcurved, protuberant, rounded

Antonyms concave, cupped, depressed, excavated, hollowed, indented, sunken

convey **1.** bear, bring, carry, conduct, fetch, forward, grant, guide, move, send, support, transmit, transport **2.** communicate, disclose, impart, make known, relate, reveal, tell **3.** *Law* bequeath, cede, deliver, demise, devolve, grant, lease, transfer, will

conveyance **1.** carriage, movement, transfer, transference, transmission, transport, transportation **2.** transport, vehicle

convict **1.** *verb* condemn, find guilty, imprison, pronounce guilty, sentence **2.** *noun* con (*slang*), criminal, culprit, felon, jailbird, lag (*slang*), malefactor, prisoner, villain

conviction **1.** assurance, certainty, certitude, confidence, earnestness, fervour, firmness, reliance **2.** belief, creed, faith, opinion, persuasion, principle, tenet, view

convince assure, bring round, gain the confidence of, persuade, prevail upon, prove to, satisfy, sway, win over

convincing cogent, conclusive, credible, impressive, incontrovertible, likely, persuasive, plausible, powerful, probable, telling, verisimilar

Antonyms beyond belief, cock-and-bull (*informal*), dubious, far-fetched, implausible, improbable, inconclusive, incredible, unconvincing, unlikely

convivial back-slapping, cheerful, festive, friendly, fun-loving, gay, genial, hearty, hilarious, jolly, jovial, lively, merry, mirthful, partyish (*informal*), sociable

conviviality bonhomie, cheer, cordiality, festivity, gaiety, geniality, good fellowship, jollification, jollity, joviality, liveliness, merrymaking, mirth, sociability

convocation assemblage, assembly, conclave, concourse, congregation, congress, convention, council, diet, meeting, synod

convoke assemble, call together, collect, convene, gather, muster, summon

convolution coil, coiling, complexity, contortion, curlicue, helix, intricacy, involution, loop, sinuosity, sinuousness, spiral, tortuousness, twist, undulation, winding

convoy **1.** *noun* armed guard, attendance, attendant, escort, guard, protection **2.** *verb* accompany, attend, escort, guard, pilot, protect, shepherd, usher

convulse agitate, churn up, derange, disorder, disturb, shake, shatter, twist, work

convulsion **1.** agitation, commotion, disturbance, furore, shaking, tumult, turbulence, upheaval **2.** contortion, contraction, cramp, fit, paroxysm, seizure, spasm, throe (*rare*), tremor

convulsive churning, fitful, jerky, paroxysmal, spasmodic, sporadic, violent

cook

Cookery has become an art, a noble science; cooks are gentlemen

Robert Burton *Anatomy of Melancholy*

Too many cooks spoil the broth

God sends meat and the Devil sends cooks

cookery

Related adjective: culinary

General cookery terms

à la king
à la mode
antipasto
au gratin
au jus
au lait
au naturel
bake
barbecue *or (Austral. slang)* barbie
bard *or* barde
baste
batter
blackened
blanch
boil
boil-in-the-bag
braise
broth
browning
caramelise
carbanado
casserole
caterer
chafing dish
char-grill
chasseur
chef
cobbler
coddle
colander
commis
confectioner
consommé
cook
cookbook *or* cookery book
cook-chill
corned
creole
cuisine
cuisine minceur
cured
curried
custard
dice
dough
dressing
en brochette
en croute
entrée
entremets
fajita
farci
fillet
flambé
flour
fondue
fricassee
fry
fumet
garnish
gelatine
ghee
giblets
glacé
glaze
goujon
goulash
grate
gravy
grill
hors d'oeuvre
ice
icing
jardinière
jerk
julienne
knead
ladle
lard
lardon *or* lardoon
leaven
liaison
luau
lyonnaise
macedoine
marengo
marinade
marinate
marmite
mask
mash
médaillions *or* medaillions
meunière
meze
mirepoix
mornay
Newburg
nouvelle cuisine
offal
oven-ready
panada
parboil
Parmentier
paste
poach
potage
Provençale
purée
ragout
rijstaffel
rise
rissole
roast
roulade
roux
royal icing
salipicon
sauce
sauté
scramble
season
silver service
sippet
smoked
soup
steam
stew
stock
stroganoff
supreme
sweat
sweet-and-sour
tandoori
tenderize
teriyaki
tikka
timbale
topping
undressed
unleavened
unsmoked
whip
wholemeal *or (chiefly U.S. and Canad.)* wholewheat
wholemeal flour *or (chiefly U.S. and Canad.)* Graham flour
yeast

Cuisines and cooking styles

balti
Cantonese
Caribbean
Californian
Chinese
cordon bleu
cuisine minceur
fast food
French
Greek
gutbürgerlich
halal
haute cuisine
home cooking
Indian
Indonesian
international
ital
Italian
Japanese
kosher
Malaysian
Mediterranean
Mexican
nouvelle cuisine
Provençal
seafood
Sichuan *or* Szechuan
tapas
Tex-Mex
Thai
Turkish
vegan
vegetarian

Cooking utensils and kitchen equipment

Aga (*Trademark*)
bain-marie
baking tray
barbecue *or (Austral. slang)* barbie
batterie de cuisine
blender
bottle opener
bread knife
cafetiere
cake tin
carving knife
casserole
chip pan
chopping board
chopsticks
coffee grinder
coffeepot
colander
cooker
cooling rack
corkscrew
deep fat fryer
dessertspoon
double saucepan *or (U.S. & Canad.)* double boiler
egg beater *or* egg whisk
fan-assisted oven
fish slice
flan tin
food processor
fork
frying pan
grater
gravy boat *or* sauce boat
griddle *or (Scot.)* gir~dle

grill
ice-cream maker
icing bag
jelly bag
juicer *or* juice extractor
kettle
knife
masher
mould
ladle
lemon squeezer
liquidizer
loaf tin
mandoline
measuring jug
mezzaluna
microwave *or* microwave oven
mixing bowl
mortar and pestle
nutcracker
olla
oven
pastry cutter
peeler
pepper mill
percolator
poacher
pot
pot-au-feu
ramekin
ricer (*U.S. and Canad.*)
rolling pin
rotisserie
saucepan
scales
sieve
skillet
spatula
spoon
spurtle
steamer
strainer
tablespoon
tagine
tandoor
teapot
teaspoon
tenderizer
timbale
tin-opener
toaster
toasting fork
whisk
wok
wooden spoon

Cookery has become an art, a noble science; cooks are gentlemen
Robert Burton *Anatomy of Melancholy*

Life is too short to stuff a mushroom
Shirley Conran *Superwoman*

The tragedy of English cooking is that 'plain' cooking cannot be entrusted to 'plain' cooks
Countess Morphy *English Recipes*

cook up concoct, contrive, devise, dream up, fabricate, improvise, invent, manufacture, plot, prepare, scheme, trump up

cool *adjective* **1.** chilled, chilling, chilly, coldish, nippy, refreshing **2.** calm, collected, composed, deliberate, dispassionate, imperturbable, laid-back (*informal*), level-headed, placid, quiet, relaxed, sedate, self-controlled, self-possessed, serene, together (*slang*), unemotional, unexcited, unfazed (*informal*), unruffled **3.** aloof, apathetic, distant, frigid, incurious, indifferent, lukewarm, offhand, reserved, standoffish, uncommunicative, unconcerned, unenthusiastic, unfriendly, uninterested, unresponsive, unwelcoming **4.** audacious, bold, brazen, cheeky, impertinent, impudent, presumptuous, shameless **5.** *informal* cosmopolitan, elegant, sophisticated, urbane *~verb* **6.** chill, cool off, freeze, lose heat, refrigerate **7.** abate, allay, assuage, calm (down), dampen, lessen, moderate, quiet, temper *~noun* **8.** *slang* calmness, composure, control, poise, self-control, self-discipline, self-possession, temper
Antonyms *adjective* (*sense 1*) lukewarm, moderately hot, sunny, tepid, warm (*sense 2*) agitated, delirious, excited, impassioned, nervous, overwrought, perturbed, tense, troubled, twitchy (*informal*) (*sense 3*) amiable, chummy (*informal*), cordial, friendly, outgoing, receptive, responsive, sociable, warm *~verb* (*sense 6*) heat, reheat, take the chill off, thaw, warm, warm up

coolness **1.** chilliness, coldness, freshness, nippiness **2.** calmness, collectedness, composedness, composure, control, deliberateness, dispassionateness, imperturbability, level-headedness, placidity, placidness, quietness, sedateness, self-control, self-discipline, self-possession **3.** aloofness, apathy, distantness, frigidity, frigidness, frostiness, impassiveness, impassivity, incuriosity, incuriousness, indifference, lukewarmness, offhandedness, poise, remoteness, reservedness, standoffishness, uncommunicativeness, unconcernedness, unfriendliness, uninterestedness, unresponsiveness **4.** audaciousness, audacity, boldness, brazenness, cheekiness, impertinence, impudence, insolence, presumptuousness, shamelessness **5.** *informal* elegance, sophistication, urbanity
Antonyms (*sense 1*) sunniness, tepidness, warmness (*sense 2*) agitation, deliriousness, discomposure, disconcertedness, excitedness, impassionedness, nervousness, perturbation, tenseness, twitchiness (*informal*) (*sense 3*) affability, amiability, amiableness, chumminess (*informal*), cordiality, friendliness, geniality, receptiveness, receptivity, responsiveness, sociability, sociableness, warmth

coop **1.** *noun* box, cage, corral (*chiefly U.S. & Canad.*), enclosure, hutch, pen, pound **2.** *verb* cage, confine, immure, impound, imprison, pen, pound, shut up

cooperate abet, aid, assist, collaborate, combine, concur, conduce, conspire, contribute, coordinate, go along with, help, join forces, lend a helping hand, pitch in, play ball (*informal*), pool resources, pull together, work together
Antonyms conflict, contend with, fight, hamper, hamstring, hinder, impede, obstruct, oppose, prevent, put the mockers on (*informal*), resist, struggle against, stymie, thwart

cooperation assistance, collaboration, combined effort, concert, concurrence, esprit de corps, give-and-take, helpfulness, participation, responsiveness, teamwork, unity
Antonyms discord, dissension, hindrance, opposition, rivalry

Two heads are better than one

cooperative **1.** accommodating, helpful, obliging, responsive, supportive **2.** coactive, collec~

tive, combined, concerted, coordinated, joint, shared, unified, united

co-opt, coopt appoint, choose, elect

coordinate 1. *verb* correlate, harmonize, integrate, match, mesh, organize, relate, synchronize, systematize 2. *adjective* coequal, correlative, correspondent, equal, equivalent, parallel, tantamount

cope 1. carry on, get by (*informal*), hold one's own, make out (*informal*), make the grade, manage, rise to the occasion, struggle through, survive 2. **cope with** contend, deal, dispatch, encounter, grapple, handle, struggle, tangle, tussle, weather, wrestle

copious abundant, ample, bounteous, bountiful, extensive, exuberant, full, generous, lavish, liberal, luxuriant, overflowing, plenteous, plentiful, profuse, rich, superabundant

copiousness abundance, amplitude, bountifulness, bounty, cornucopia, exuberance, fullness, horn of plenty, lavishness, luxuriance, plentifulness, plenty, richness, superabundance

cop-out alibi, dodge, fraud, pretence, pretext

cop out abandon, desert, dodge, quit, renege, renounce, revoke, skip, skive (*Brit. slang*), withdraw

copulate ball (*taboo slang, chiefly U.S.*), bonk (*informal*), fuck (*taboo slang*), have intercourse, have sex, hump (*taboo slang*), screw (*taboo slang*), shag (*taboo slang, chiefly Brit.*)

copulation carnal knowledge, coition, coitus, congress, coupling, intimacy, legover (*slang*), love, lovemaking, mating, nookie (*slang*), rumpy-pumpy (*slang*), sex, sex act, sexual intercourse, the other (*informal*), venery (*archaic*)

copy *noun* 1. archetype, carbon copy, counterfeit, duplicate, facsimile, fake, fax, forgery, image, imitation, likeness, model, pattern, photocopy, Photostat (*Trademark*), print, replica, replication, representation, reproduction, transcription, Xerox (*Trademark*) ~*verb* 2. counterfeit, duplicate, photocopy, Photostat (*Trademark*), replicate, reproduce, transcribe, Xerox (*Trademark*) 3. ape, echo, emulate, follow, follow suit, follow the example of, imitate, mimic, mirror, parrot, repeat, simulate
Antonyms *noun* model, original, pattern, prototype, the real thing ~*verb* create, originate

coquet dally, flirt, lead on, make eyes at, philander, tease, toy, trifle, vamp (*informal*)

coquetry dalliance, flirtation, wantonness

coquettish amorous, arch, come-hither (*informal*), coy, dallying, flighty, flirtatious, flirty, inviting, teasing

cord 1. line, rope, string, twine 2. bond, connection, link, tie

cordial affable, affectionate, agreeable, cheerful, congenial, earnest, friendly, genial, heartfelt, hearty, invigorating, sociable, warm, warm-hearted, welcoming, wholehearted
Antonyms aloof, cold, distant, formal, frigid, reserved, unfriendly, ungracious

cordiality affability, amiability, friendliness, geniality, heartiness, sincerity, warmth, wholeheartedness

cordon 1. *noun* barrier, chain, line, ring 2. *verb* **cordon off** close off, encircle, enclose, fence off, isolate, picket, separate, surround

core centre, crux, essence, gist, heart, kernel, nub, nucleus, pith

corner *noun* 1. angle, bend, crook, joint 2. cavity, cranny, hideaway, hide-out, hidey-hole (*informal*), hole, niche, nook, recess, retreat 3. hole (*informal*), hot water (*informal*), pickle (*informal*), predicament, spot (*informal*), tight spot ~*verb* 4. bring to bay, run to earth, trap 5. *As in* **corner the market** dominate, engross, hog (*slang*), monopolize

cornerstone 1. quoin 2. basis, bedrock, key, premise, starting point

corny banal, commonplace, dull, feeble, hackneyed, maudlin, mawkish, old-fashioned, old hat, sentimental, stale, stereotyped, trite

corollary conclusion, consequence, deduction, induction, inference, result, sequel, upshot

corporal anatomical, bodily, carnal, corporeal (*archaic*), fleshly, material, physical, somatic

corporate allied, collaborative, collective, combined, communal, joint, merged, pooled, shared, united

corporation 1. association, corporate body, society 2. civic authorities, council, municipal authorities, town council 3. *informal* beer belly (*informal*), middle-age spread (*informal*), paunch, pod, pot, potbelly, spare tyre (*Brit. slang*), spread (*informal*)

> *corporation: an ingenious device for obtaining individual profit without individual responsibility*
>
> Ambrose Bierce *The Devil's Dictionary*

corporeal bodily, fleshy, human, material, mortal, physical, substantial

corps band, body, company, contingent, crew, detachment, division, regiment, squad, squadron, team, troop, unit

corpse body, cadaver, carcass, remains, stiff (*slang*)

corpulence beef (*informal*), blubber, burliness, *embonpoint*, fatness, fleshiness, obesity, plumpness, portliness, rotundity, stoutness, tubbiness

corpulent beefy (*informal*), bulky, burly, fat, fattish, fleshy, large, lusty, obese, overweight, plump, portly, roly-poly, rotund, stout, tubby,

well-padded
Antonyms anorexic, bony, emaciated, gaunt, scrawny, skin and bones (*informal*), skinny, slim, thin, thin as a rake, underweight

corpus body, collection, compilation, complete works, entirety, *oeuvre*, whole

corral **1.** *noun* confine, coop, enclosure, fold, pen, yard **2.** *verb* cage, confine, coop up, en~close, fence in, impound, mew, pen in

correct *verb* **1.** adjust, amend, cure, emend, improve, rectify, redress, reform, regulate, remedy, right, set the record straight **2.** ad~monish, chasten, chastise, chide, discipline, punish, reprimand, reprove *~adjective* **3.** ac~curate, equitable, exact, faultless, flawless, just, O.K. *or* okay (*informal*), on the right lines, precise, regular, right, strict, true **4.** ac~ceptable, appropriate, diplomatic, fitting, ko~sher (*informal*), O.K. *or* okay (*informal*), proper, seemly, standard
Antonyms *verb* (*sense 1*) damage, harm, im~pair, ruin, spoil (*sense 2*) compliment, excuse, praise *~adjective* (*sense 3*) false, inaccurate, incorrect, untrue, wrong (*sense 4*) improper, inappropriate, unacceptable, unfitting, unsuit~able

For whom the Lord loveth he correcteth
Bible: Proverbs

correction **1.** adjustment, alteration, amend~ment, emendation, improvement, modification, rectification, righting **2.** admonition, castiga~tion, chastisement, discipline, punishment, reformation, reproof

corrective *adjective* **1.** palliative, rehabilitative, remedial, restorative, therapeutic **2.** discipli~nary, penal, punitive, reformatory

correctly accurately, aright, perfectly, precise~ly, properly, right, rightly

correctness **1.** accuracy, exactitude, exactness, faultlessness, fidelity, preciseness, precision, regularity, truth **2.** *bon ton*, civility, decorum, good breeding, propriety, seemliness

correlate associate, compare, connect, coordi~nate, correspond, equate, interact, parallel, tie in

correlation alternation, correspondence, equi~valence, interaction, interchange, interde~pendence, interrelationship, reciprocity

correspond **1.** accord, agree, be consistent, co~incide, complement, conform, correlate, dove~tail, fit, harmonize, match, square, tally **2.** communicate, exchange letters, keep in touch, write
Antonyms be at variance, be dissimilar, be inconsistent, belie, be unlike, differ, disagree, diverge, vary

correspondence **1.** agreement, analogy, coinci~dence, comparability, comparison, concur~rence, conformity, congruity, correlation, fit~ness, harmony, match, relation, similarity **2.** communication, letters, mail, post, writing

correspondent *noun* **1.** letter writer, pen friend *or* pal **2.** contributor, gazetteer (*archa~ic*), journalist, journo (*slang*), reporter, special correspondent *~adjective* **3.** analogous, compa~rable, like, of a piece, parallel, reciprocal, similar

corresponding analogous, answering, comple~mentary, correlative, correspondent, equiva~lent, identical, interrelated, matching, recip~rocal, similar, synonymous

corridor aisle, alley, hallway, passage, passageway

corroborate authenticate, back up, bear out, confirm, document, endorse, establish, ratify, substantiate, support, sustain, validate
Antonyms contradict, disprove, invalidate, negate, rebut, refute

corroboration authentication, certification, circumstantiation, confirmation, documenta~tion, endorsement, establishment, fortification, ratification, substantiation, support, sustain~ment, validation

corrode canker, consume, corrupt, deteriorate, eat away, erode, gnaw, impair, oxidize, rust, waste, wear away

corrosive **1.** acrid, biting, caustic, consuming, corroding, erosive, virulent, vitriolic, wasting, wearing **2.** caustic, cutting, incisive, mordant, sarcastic, trenchant, venomous, vitriolic

corrugated channelled, creased, crinkled, flut~ed, furrowed, grooved, puckered, ridged, rum~pled, wrinkled

corrupt *adjective* **1.** bent (*slang*), bribable, crooked (*informal*), dishonest, fraudulent, rot~ten, shady (*informal*), unethical, unprincipled, unscrupulous, venal **2.** abandoned, debased, defiled, degenerate, demoralized, depraved, dishonoured, dissolute, profligate, vicious *~verb* **3.** bribe, buy off, debauch, demoralize, deprave, entice, fix (*informal*), grease (someone's) palm (*slang*), lure, pervert, square, suborn, subvert *~adjective* **4.** adulter~ated, altered, contaminated, decayed, defiled, distorted, doctored, falsified, infected, pollut~ed, putrescent, putrid, rotten, tainted *~verb* **5.** adulterate, contaminate, debase, defile, doctor, infect, putrefy, spoil, taint, tamper with, viti~ate
Antonyms *adjective* (*senses 1 & 2*) ethical, honest, honourable, moral, noble, principled, righteous, scrupulous, straight, undefiled, upright, virtuous *~verb* (*sense 3*) correct, pu~rify, reform

corrupted **1.** abandoned, debased, debauched, defiled, degenerate, demoralized, depraved, dishonoured, perverted, profligate, reprobate, warped **2.** adulterated, altered, contaminated, decayed, defiled, dirtied, distorted, doctored, falsified, infected, polluted, putrefied, rotten, soiled, spoiled, stained, sullied, tainted, tarnished, vitiated

corruption 1. breach of trust, bribery, bribing, crookedness (*informal*), demoralization, dishonesty, extortion, fiddling (*informal*), fraud, fraudulency, graft (*informal*), jobbery, profiteering, shadiness, shady dealings (*informal*), unscrupulousness, venality 2. baseness, decadence, degeneration, degradation, depravity, evil, immorality, impurity, iniquity, perversion, profligacy, sinfulness, turpitude, vice, viciousness, wickedness 3. adulteration, debasement, decay, defilement, distortion, doctoring, falsification, foulness, infection, pollution, putrefaction, putrescence, rot, rottenness

Something is rotten in the state of Denmark
William Shakespeare *Hamlet*

All rising to great place is by a winding stair
Francis Bacon *Essays*

One rotten apple spoils the barrel

corsair buccaneer, freebooter, picaroon (*archaic*), pirate, rover, sea rover

corset 1. belt, bodice, corselet, foundation garment, girdle, panty girdle, stays (*rare*) 2. *figurative* check, curb, limitation, restriction

cortege cavalcade, entourage, procession, retinue, suite, train

cosmetic *adjective* beautifying, nonessential, superficial, surface, touching-up

cosmic grandiose, huge, immense, infinite, limitless, measureless, stellar (*informal*), universal, vast

cosmonaut astronaut, spaceman, space pilot

cosmopolitan 1. *adjective* broad-minded, catholic, open-minded, sophisticated, universal, urbane, well-travelled, worldly, worldly-wise 2. *noun* cosmopolite, jetsetter, man *or* woman of the world, sophisticate

Antonyms *adjective* hidebound, illiberal, insular, limited, narrow-minded, parochial, provincial, restricted, rustic, unsophisticated

cosmos 1. creation, macrocosm, universe, world 2. harmony, order, structure

cosset baby, coddle, cosher (*Irish*), mollycoddle, pamper, pet, wrap up in cotton wool (*informal*)

cost *noun* 1. amount, charge, damage (*informal*), expenditure, expense, figure, outlay, payment, price, rate, worth 2. damage, deprivation, detriment, expense, harm, hurt, injury, loss, penalty, sacrifice, suffering ~*verb* 3. come to, command a price of, sell at, set (someone) back (*informal*) 4. *figurative* do disservice to, harm, hurt, injure, lose, necessitate

costly 1. dear, excessive, exorbitant, expensive, extortionate, highly-priced, steep (*informal*), stiff, valuable 2. gorgeous, lavish, luxurious, opulent, precious, priceless, rich, splendid, sumptuous 3. *entailing loss or sacrifice* catastrophic, damaging, deleterious, disastrous, harmful, loss-making, ruinous, sacrificial

Antonyms (*sense 1*) cheap, cheapo (*informal*), dirt-cheap, economical, fair, inexpensive, low-priced, reasonable, reduced

costs 1. budget, expenses, outgoings 2. **at all costs** at any price, no matter what, regardless, without fail

costume apparel, attire, clothing, dress, ensemble, garb, get-up (*informal*), livery, national dress, outfit, robes, uniform

cosy comfortable, comfy (*informal*), cuddled up, homely, intimate, secure, sheltered, snug, snuggled down, tucked up, warm

coterie cabal, camp, circle, clique, gang, group, outfit (*informal*), posse (*informal*), set

cottage but-and-ben (*Scot.*), cabin, chalet, cot, hut, lodge, shack

couch 1. *verb* express, frame, phrase, set forth, utter, word 2. *noun* bed, chaise longue, chesterfield, daybed, divan, ottoman, settee, sofa

cough 1. *noun* bark, frog *or* tickle in one's throat, hack 2. *verb* bark, clear one's throat, hack, hawk, hem

cough up ante up (*informal, chiefly U.S.*), come across, deliver, fork out (*slang*), give up, hand over, shell out (*informal*), surrender

council assembly, board, cabinet, chamber, committee, conclave, conference, congress, convention, convocation, diet, governing body, house, ministry, panel, parliament, quango, synod

counsel *noun* 1. admonition, advice, caution, consideration, consultation, deliberation, direction, forethought, guidance, information, recommendation, suggestion, warning 2. advocate, attorney, barrister, lawyer, legal adviser, solicitor ~*verb* 3. admonish, advise, advocate, caution, exhort, instruct, prescribe, recommend, urge, warn

count *verb* 1. add (up), calculate, cast up, check, compute, enumerate, estimate, number, reckon, score, tally, tot up 2. consider, deem, esteem, impute, judge, look upon, rate, regard, think 3. carry weight, cut any ice (*informal*), enter into consideration, matter, rate, signify, tell, weigh 4. include, number among, take into account *or* consideration ~*noun* 5. calculation, computation, enumeration, numbering, poll, reckoning, sum, tally

countenance *noun* 1. appearance, aspect, expression, face, features, look, mien, physiognomy, visage 2. aid, approval, assistance, backing, endorsement, favour, sanction, support ~*verb* 3. abet, aid, approve, back, champion, commend, condone, encourage, endorse, help, sanction, support 4. brook, endure, hack (*slang*), put up with (*informal*), stand for (*informal*), tolerate

counter 1. *adverb* against, at variance with, contrarily, contrariwise, conversely, in defiance of, versus 2. *adjective* adverse, against, conflicting, contradictory, contrary, contrasting, obverse, opposed, opposing, opposite 3. *verb* answer, hit back, meet, obviate, offset, parry, resist, respond, retaliate, return, ward off

Antonyms *adverb/adjective* accordant, in agreement, parallel, similar ~*verb* accept, give in, surrender, take, yield

counteract annul, check, contravene, counterbalance, countervail, cross, defeat, foil, frustrate, hinder, invalidate, negate, neutralize, obviate, offset, oppose, resist, thwart

counterbalance balance, compensate, counterpoise, countervail, make up for, offset, set off

counterfeit 1. *verb* copy, fabricate, fake, feign, forge, imitate, impersonate, pretend, sham, simulate 2. *adjective* bogus, copied, ersatz, faked, false, feigned, forged, fraudulent, imitation, phoney *or* phony (*informal*), pseud *or* pseudo (*informal*), sham, simulated, spurious, suppositious 3. *noun* copy, fake, forgery, fraud, imitation, phoney *or* phony (*informal*), reproduction, sham

Antonyms authentic, genuine, good, original, real, the real thing

countermand annul, cancel, override, repeal, rescind, retract, reverse, revoke

counterpane bedcover, bedspread, cover, coverlet, doona (*Austral.*), quilt

counterpart complement, copy, correlative, duplicate, equal, fellow, match, mate, opposite number, supplement, tally, twin

countless endless, immeasurable, incalculable, infinite, innumerable, legion, limitless, measureless, multitudinous, myriad, numberless, uncounted, untold

Antonyms finite, limited, restricted

count on *or* **upon** bank on, believe (in), depend on, lean on, pin one's faith on, reckon on, rely on, take for granted, take on trust, trust

count out disregard, except, exclude, leave out, leave out of account, pass over

countrified agrestic, Arcadian, bucolic, cracker-barrel (*U.S.*), homespun, idyllic, pastoral, picturesque, provincial, rural, rustic

country *noun* 1. commonwealth, kingdom, nation, people, realm, sovereign state, state 2. fatherland, homeland, motherland, nationality, native land, *patria* 3. land, part, region, terrain, territory 4. citizenry, citizens, community, electors, grass roots, inhabitants, nation, people, populace, public, society, voters 5. back country (*U.S.*), backlands (*U.S.*), backwoods, boondocks (*U.S. slang*), countryside, farmland, green belt, outback (*Austral. & N.Z.*), outdoors, provinces, rural areas, sticks (*informal*), the back of beyond, the middle of nowhere, wide open spaces (*informal*) ~*adjective* 6. agrarian, agrestic, Arcadian, bucolic, georgic (*literary*), landed, pastoral, provincial, rural, rustic

Antonyms *noun* (*sense 5*) city, metropolis, town ~*adjective* city, cosmopolitan, sophisticated, urban, urbane

Related adjective: campestral

Countries

Afghanistan
Albania
Algeria
American Samoa
Andorra
Angola
Antigua and Barbuda
Argentina
Armenia
Australia
Austria
Azerbaijan
Bahamas
Bahrain
Bangladesh
Barbados
Belau
Belgium
Belize
Benin
Bermuda
Bhutan
Bolivia
Bosnia and Herzegovina
Botswana
Brazil
British Virgin Islands
Brunei
Bulgaria
Burkina-Faso
Burundi
Byelorussia
Cambodia
Cameroon
Canada
Cape Verde
Cayman Islands
Central African Republic
Chad
Chile
Colombia
Comoros
Congo Republic
Costa Rica
Côte d'Ivoire
Croatia
Cuba
Cyprus
Czech Republic
Denmark
Djibouti *or* Jibouti
Dominica
Dominican Republic
Ecuador
Egypt
El Salvador
England
Equatorial Guinea
Eritrea
Estonia
Ethiopia
Faeroe Islands
Falkland Islands
Fiji
Finland
France
French Guiana
Gabon
Gambia
Georgia
Germany
Ghana
Greece
Greenland
Grenada
Guadeloupe
Guam
Guatemala
Guinea
Guinea-Bissau
Guyana
Haiti
Honduras
Hong Kong
Hungary
Iceland
India
Indonesia
Iran
Iraq
Isle of Man
Israel

Italy
Jamaica
Japan
Jordan
Kazakhstan
Kenya
Kirghizia
Kiribati
Kuwait
Laos
Latvia
Lebanon
Lesotho
Liberia
Libya
Liechtenstein
Lithuania
Luxembourg
Macao
Macedonia
Madagascar
Malawi
Malaysia
Mali
Malta
Marshall Islands
Martinique
Mauritania
Mauritius
Mexico
Micronesia
Moldavia
Monaco
Mongolia
Montenegro
Montserrat
Morocco
Mozambique
Myanmar
Namibia
Nauru
Nepal
Netherlands
Netherlands Antilles
New Zealand
Nicaragua
Niger
Nigeria
Northern Ireland
North Korea
Norway
Oman
Pakistan
Panama
Papua New Guinea
Paraguay
People's Republic of China
Peru
Philippines
Poland
Portugal
Puerto Rico
Qatar
Republic of Ireland
Republic of Maldives
Réunion
Romania
Russian Federation
Rwanda
Saint Kitts and Nevis
Saint Lucia
Saint Vincent and the Grenadines
San Marino
São Tomé and Principe
Saudi Arabia
Scotland
Senegal
Serbia
Seychelles
Sierra Leone
Singapore
Slovakia
Slovenia
Solomon Islands
Somalia
South Africa
South Korea
Spain
Sri Lanka
Sudan
Surinam
Swaziland
Sweden
Switzerland
Syria
Taiwan
Tadzhikistan
Tanzania
Thailand
Tibet
Togo
Tonga
Trinidad and Tobago
Tunisia
Turkey
Turkmenistan
Turks and Caicos Islands
Tuvalu
Uganda
Ukraine
United Arab Emirates
United Kingdom
Uruguay
U.S. Virgin Islands
USA
Uzbekistan
Vanuatu
Vatican City
Venezuela
Vietnam
Wales
Western Sahara
Western Samoa
Yemen
Zaire
Zambia
Zimbabwe

countryman **1.** bumpkin, cockie (*N.Z.*), country dweller, farmer, hayseed (*U.S. & Canad. informal*), hick (*informal, chiefly U.S. & Canad.*), hind (*obsolete*), husbandman, peasant, provincial, rustic, swain, yokel **2.** compatriot, fellow citizen

countryside country, farmland, green belt, outback (*Austral. & N.Z.*), outdoors, panorama, sticks (*informal*), view, wide open spaces (*informal*)

count up add, reckon up, sum, tally, total

county **1.** *noun* province, shire **2.** *adjective* green-wellie, huntin', shootin', and fishin' (*informal*), plummy (*informal*), tweedy, upper-class, upper-crust (*informal*)

English counties

Avon
Bedfordshire
Berkshire
Buckinghamshire
Cambridgeshire
Cheshire
Cleveland
Cornwall
Cumbria
Derbyshire
Devon *or* Devonshire
Dorset
Durham
East Sussex
Essex
Gloucestershire
Greater London
Greater Manchester
Hampshire
Hereford and Worcester
Hertfordshire
Humberside
Isle of Wight
Kent
Lancashire
Leicestershire
Lincolnshire
Merseyside
Norfolk
Northamptonshire
Northumberland
North Yorkshire
Nottinghamshire
Oxfordshire
Shropshire
Somerset
South Yorkshire
Staffordshire
Suffolk
Surrey
Tyne and Wear
Warwickshire
West Midlands
West Sussex
West Yorkshire
Wiltshire

Former English counties

Bedfordshire
Berkshire
Buckinghamshire
Cambridgeshire and Isle of Ely
Cheshire
Cornwall
Cumberland
Derbyshire
Devon
Dorset
Durham
East Suffolk
East Sussex
East Yorkshire
Essex
Gloucestershire
Greater London
Hampshire
Herefordshire
Hertfordshire
Huntingdon and Peterborough
Kent
Lancashire
Leicestershire
Lincolnshire
Norfolk

Northamptonshire
Northumberland
North Yorkshire
Nottinghamshire
Oxfordshire
Rutland
Shropshire
Somerset
Staffordshire
Surrey
Warwickshire
Westmorland
West Suffolk
West Sussex
West Yorkshire
Wiltshire
Worcestershire

Scottish counties

Aberdeenshire
Angus
Argyll and Bute
Borders
City of Aberdeen
City of Dundee
City of Edinburgh
City of Glasgow
Clackmannan
Dumbarton and Clydebank
Dumfries and Galloway
East Ayrshire
East Dunbartonshire
East Lothian
East Renfrewshire
Falkirk
Fife
Highland
Inverclyde
Midlothian
Moray
North Ayrshire
North Lanarkshire
Orkney Islands
Perthshire and Kinross
Renfrewshire
Shetland Islands
South Ayrshire
South Lanarkshire
Stirling
West Lothian
Western Isles

Former Scottish counties

Aberdeen
Aberdeenshire
Angus
Argyll
Ayrshire
Banff *or* Banffshire
Berwickshire
Bute
Caithness
Clackmannanshire
Dumfriesshire
Dunbartonshire
Dundee
East Lothian
Edinburgh
Fife
Glasgow
Inverness-shire
Kincardine *or* Kincardineshire
Kinross *or* Kinross-shire
Kircudbrightshire
Lanarkshire
Midlothian
Moray
Nairn *or* Nairnshire
Orkney
Peeblesshire
Perthshire
Renfrewshire
Ross and Cromarty
Roxburgh *or* Roxburghshire
Selkirkshire
Shetland
Stirlingshire
Sutherland
West Lothian
Wigtownshire

Welsh counties

Clwyd
Dyfed
Gwent
Gwynedd
Mid Glamorgan
Powys
South Glamorgan
West Glamorgan

Former Welsh counties

Anglesey
Brecknock
Caernarvonshire
Cardiganshire
Carmarthenshire
Denbighshire
Flintshire
Glamorgan
Merioneth
Montgomeryshire
Pembrokeshire
Radnor

Northern Irish counties

Antrim
Armagh
Down
Fermanagh
Londonderry
Tyrone

Republic of Ireland counties

Carlow
Cavan
Clare
Cork
Donegal
Dublin
Galway
Kerry
Kildare
Kilkenny
Laois
Leitrim
Limerick
Longford
Louth
Mayo
Meath
Monaghan
Offaly
Roscommon
Sligo
Tipperary
Waterford
Westmeath
Wexford
Wicklow

coup accomplishment, action, deed, exploit, feat, manoeuvre, masterstroke, stratagem, stroke, stroke of genius, stunt, *tour de force*

coup de grâce clincher (*informal*), comeuppance (*slang*), deathblow, final blow, kill, knockout blow, mercy stroke, mortal blow, quietus

coup d'état coup, overthrow, palace revolution, putsch, rebellion, seizure of power, takeover

couple 1. *noun* brace, duo, item, pair, span (*of horses or oxen*), twain (*archaic*), twosome 2. *verb* buckle, clasp, conjoin, connect, hitch, join, link, marry, pair, unite, wed, yoke

coupon card, certificate, detachable portion, slip, ticket, token, voucher

courage balls (*taboo slang*), ballsiness (*taboo slang*), boldness, bottle (*Brit. slang*), bravery, daring, dauntlessness, fearlessness, firmness, fortitude, gallantry, grit, guts (*informal*), hardihood, heroism, intrepidity, lion-heartedness, mettle, nerve, pluck, resolution, spunk (*informal*), valour

Antonyms cowardice, faint-heartedness, fear, timidity

No one can answer for his courage when he has never been in danger
Duc de la Rochefoucauld *Maxims*

Sometimes even to live is an act of courage
Seneca *Letters to Lucilius*

Courage is not simply one of the virtues but the form of every virtue at the testing point
C.S. Lewis

Screw your courage to the sticking place
William Shakespeare *Macbeth*

As to moral courage, I have very rarely met with two o'clock in the morning courage: I mean instantaneous courage
Napoleon Bonaparte

courageous audacious, ballsy (*taboo slang*), bold, brave, daring, dauntless, fearless, gallant, gritty, hardy, heroic, indomitable, intrepid, lion-hearted, plucky, resolute, stalwart, stouthearted, valiant, valorous
Antonyms chicken (*slang*), chicken-hearted, chickenshit (*U.S. slang*), cowardly, craven, dastardly, faint-hearted, gutless (*informal*), lily-livered, pusillanimous, scared, spineless, timid, timorous, yellow (*informal*)

courier **1.** bearer, carrier, emissary, envoy, herald, messenger, pursuivant (*Historical*), runner **2.** guide, representative

course *noun* **1.** advance, advancement, continuity, development, flow, furtherance, march, movement, order, progress, progression, sequence, succession, tenor, unfolding **2.** channel, direction, line, orbit, passage, path, road, route, tack, track, trail, trajectory, way **3.** duration, lapse, passage, passing, sweep, term, time **4.** behaviour, conduct, manner, method, mode, plan, policy, procedure, programme, regimen **5.** cinder track, circuit, lap, race, racecourse, round **6.** classes, course of study, curriculum, lectures, programme, schedule, studies *~verb* **7.** dash, flow, gush, move apace, race, run, scud, scurry, speed, stream, surge, tumble **8.** chase, follow, hunt, pursue **9. in due course** eventually, finally, in the course of time, in the end, in time, sooner or later **10. of course** certainly, definitely, indubitably, naturally, needless to say, obviously, undoubtedly, without a doubt

court *noun* **1.** cloister, courtyard, piazza, plaza, quad (*informal*), quadrangle, square, yard **2.** hall, manor, palace **3.** attendants, cortege, entourage, retinue, royal household, suite, train **4.** bar, bench, court of justice, lawcourt, seat of judgment, tribunal **5.** addresses, attention, homage, respects, suit *~verb* **6.** chase, date, go (out) with, go steady with (*informal*), keep company with, make love to, pay court to, pay one's addresses to, pursue, run after, serenade, set one's cap at, sue (*archaic*), take out, walk out with, woo **7.** cultivate, curry favour with, fawn upon, flatter, pander to, seek, solicit **8.** attract, bring about, incite, invite, prompt, provoke, seek

courteous affable, attentive, ceremonious, civil, courtly, elegant, gallant, gracious, mannerly, polished, polite, refined, respectful, urbane, well-bred, well-mannered
Antonyms discourteous, disrespectful, ill-mannered, impolite, insolent, rude, uncivil, ungracious, unkind

courtesan call girl, demimondaine, *fille de joie*, harlot, hetaera, kept woman, mistress, paramour, prostitute, scarlet woman, whore, working girl (*facetious slang*)

courtesy **1.** affability, civility, courteousness, courtliness, elegance, gallantness, gallantry, good breeding, good manners, graciousness, polish, politeness, urbanity **2.** benevolence, consent, consideration, favour, generosity, indulgence, kindness

courtier attendant, follower, henchman, liegeman, pursuivant (*Historical*), squire, trainbearer

> *The two maxims of any great man at court are, always to keep his countenance, and never to keep his word*
>
> Jonathan Swift *Thoughts on Various Subjects*

courtliness affability, breeding, ceremony, chivalrousness, correctness, courtesy, decorum, elegance, formality, gallantry, gentility, graciousness, politeness, politesse, propriety, refinement, stateliness, urbanity

courtly affable, aristocratic, ceremonious, chivalrous, civil, decorous, dignified, elegant, flattering, formal, gallant, highbred, lordly, obliging, polished, refined, stately, urbane

courtship courting, engagement, keeping company, pursuit, romance, suit, wooing

courtyard area, enclosure, peristyle, playground, quad, quadrangle, yard

cove[1] *noun* anchorage, bay, bayou, creek, firth *or* frith (*Scot.*), inlet, sound

cove[2] *noun* bloke (*Brit. informal*), chap, character, customer, fellow, type

covenant *noun* **1.** arrangement, bargain, commitment, compact, concordat, contract, convention, pact, promise, stipulation, treaty, trust **2.** bond, deed *~verb* **3.** agree, bargain, contract, engage, pledge, shake hands, stipulate, undertake

cover *verb* **1.** camouflage, cloak, conceal, cover up, curtain, disguise, eclipse, enshroud, hide, hood, house, mask, obscure, screen, secrete, shade, shroud, veil *~noun* **2.** cloak, cover-up, disguise, façade, front, mask, pretence, screen, smoke screen, veil, window-dressing *~verb* **3.** defend, guard, protect, reinforce, shelter, shield, watch over *~noun* **4.** camouflage, concealment, defence, guard, hiding place, protection, refuge, sanctuary, shelter, shield, undergrowth, woods *~verb* **5.** canopy, clothe, coat, daub, dress, encase, envelop, invest, layer, mantle, overlay, overspread, put on, wrap *~noun* **6.** awning, binding, canopy, cap, case, clothing, coating, covering, dress, envelope, jacket, lid, sheath, top, wrapper *~verb* **7.** comprehend, comprise, consider, contain, deal with, embody, embrace, encompass, examine, include, incorporate, involve, provide for, refer to, survey, take account of **8.** double for, fill in for, hold the fort (*informal*), relieve, stand in for, substitute, take over, take the rap for (*slang*) **9.** describe, detail, investigate, narrate, recount, relate, report, tell of, write up **10.** balance, compensate, counterbalance, insure, make good, make up for, offset *~noun* **11.** compensation, indemnity, insurance, payment, protection, reimbursement *~verb* **12.** cross, pass through *or* over, range, travel over, traverse **13.** engulf, flood, overrun, submerge, wash over

Antonyms *verb* exclude, exhibit, expose, omit, reveal, show, unclothe, uncover, unmask, un~wrap *~noun* base, bottom

coverage analysis, description, reportage, re~porting, treatment

covering **1.** *noun* blanket, casing, clothing, coating, cover, housing, layer, overlay, protec~tion, shelter, top, wrap, wrapper, wrapping **2.** *adjective* accompanying, descriptive, explana~tory, introductory

covert **1.** *adjective* clandestine, concealed, dis~guised, dissembled, hidden, private, secret, sly, stealthy, surreptitious, underhand, un~suspected, veiled **2.** *noun* brush (*archaic*), bushes, coppice, shrubbery, thicket, under~growth, underwood

cover-up complicity, concealment, conspiracy, front, smoke screen, whitewash (*informal*)

cover up **1.** conceal, cover one's tracks, draw a veil over, feign ignorance, hide, hush up, keep dark, keep secret, keep silent about, keep un~der one's hat (*informal*), repress, stonewall, suppress, sweep under the carpet, whitewash (*informal*) **2.** Artex (*Trademark*), coat, cover, encrust, envelop, hide, plaster, slather (*U.S. slang*), swathe

covet aspire to, begrudge, crave, desire, envy, fancy (*informal*), hanker after, have one's eye on, long for, lust after, set one's heart on, thirst for, would give one's eyeteeth for, yearn for

covetous acquisitive, avaricious, close-fisted, envious, grasping, greedy, jealous, mercenary, rapacious, yearning

covey bevy, brood, cluster, flight, flock, group, nye *or* nide (*of pheasants*)

cow awe, browbeat, bully, daunt, dishearten, dismay, frighten, intimidate, overawe, psych out (*informal*), scare, subdue, terrorize, un~nerve

coward caitiff (*archaic*), chicken (*slang*), cra~ven, dastard (*archaic*), faint-heart, funk (*in~formal*), poltroon, recreant (*archaic*), renegade, scaredy-cat (*informal*), skulker, sneak, wimp (*informal*), yellow-belly (*slang*)

Cowards die many times before their deaths
William Shakespeare *Julius Caesar*

coward: one who in a perilous emergency thinks with his legs
Ambrose Bierce *The Devil's Dictionary*

May coward shame distain his name,
The wretch that dares not die!
Robert Burns *McPherson's Farewell*

All men would be cowards if they durst
John Wilmot *A Satire against Mankind*

cowardice cravenness, dastardliness, faint-heartedness, fearfulness, pusillanimity, recre~ance *or* recreancy (*archaic*), softness, spine~lessness, timorousness, weakness

To know what is right and not to do it is the worst cowardice
Confucius *Analects*

cowardly abject, base, boneless, caitiff (*archa~ic*), chicken (*slang*), chicken-hearted, chickenshit (*U.S. slang*), craven, dastardly, faint-hearted, fearful, gutless (*informal*), lily-livered, pusillanimous, recreant (*archaic*), scared, shrinking, soft, spineless, timorous, weak, weak-kneed (*informal*), white-livered, yellow (*informal*)

Antonyms audacious, bold, brave, courageous, daring, dauntless, doughty, intrepid, plucky, valiant

cowboy broncobuster (*U.S.*), buckaroo (*U.S.*), cattleman, cowhand, cowpuncher (*U.S. infor~mal*), drover, gaucho (*S. American*), herder, herdsman, rancher, ranchero (*U.S.*), stock~man, wrangler (*U.S.*)

cower cringe, crouch, draw back, fawn, flinch, grovel, quail, shrink, skulk, sneak, tremble, truckle

coxcomb beau, Beau Brummell, dandy, dude (*U.S. & Canad. informal*), exquisite, fop, macaroni (*obsolete*), peacock, popinjay, poser (*informal*), prig, puppy, spark (*rare*), swell (*informal*)

coy arch, backward, bashful, coquettish, de~mure, evasive, flirtatious, kittenish, modest, overmodest, prudish, reserved, retiring, self-effacing, shrinking, shy, skittish, timid

Antonyms bold, brash, brass-necked (*Brit. in~formal*), brassy (*informal*), brazen, flip (*infor~mal*), forward, impertinent, impudent, pert, pushy (*informal*), saucy, shameless

coyness affectation, archness, backwardness, bashfulness, coquettishness, demureness, dif~fidence, evasiveness, modesty, primness, pris~siness (*informal*), prudery, prudishness, re~serve, shrinking, shyness, skittishness, timid~ity

Had we but world enough, and time
This coyness, lady, were no crime
Andrew Marvell *To his Coy Mistress*

cozen bilk, cheat, circumvent, con (*informal*), deceive, diddle (*informal*), double-cross (*infor~mal*), dupe, gull (*archaic*), hoodwink, impose on, inveigle, stiff (*slang*), stitch up (*slang*), swindle, take advantage of, take for a ride (*informal*), victimize

crabbed **1.** acrid, acrimonious, captious, churlish, cross, cynical, difficult, fretful, harsh, ill-tempered, irritable, morose, perverse, petulant, prickly, ratty (*Brit. & N.Z. informal*), sour, splenetic, surly, tart, testy, tetchy, tough, trying **2.** *of handwriting* awkward, cramped, hieroglyphical, illegible, indecipherable, laboured, squeezed, unreadable

crabby acid, awkward, bad-tempered, cross, crotchety (*informal*), grouchy (*informal*), ill-humoured, irritable, mardy (*dialect*), misanthropic, nasty-tempered, prickly, ratty (*Brit. & N.Z. informal*), snappish, snappy, sour, surly, testy, tetchy, unsociable

crack *verb* **1.** break, burst, chip, chop, cleave, crackle, craze, fracture, rive, snap, splinter, split *~noun* **2.** breach, break, chink, chip, cleft, cranny, crevice, fissure, fracture, gap, interstice, rift *~verb* **3.** burst, crash, detonate, explode, pop, ring, snap *~noun* **4.** burst, clap, crash, explosion, pop, report, snap *~verb* **5.** break down, collapse, give way, go to pieces, lose control, succumb, yield *~verb/noun* **6.** *informal* buffet, clip (*informal*), clout (*informal*), cuff, slap, thump, wallop (*informal*), whack *~verb* **7.** decipher, fathom, get the answer to, solve, work out *~noun* **8.** *informal* attempt, go (*informal*), opportunity, shot, stab (*informal*), try **9.** *slang* dig, funny remark, gag (*informal*), insult, jibe, joke, quip, smart-alecky remark, wisecrack, witticism *~adjective* **10.** *slang* ace, choice, elite, excellent, first-class, first-rate, hand-picked, superior, world-class

crackbrained cracked (*slang*), crackers (*Brit. slang*), crackpot (*informal*), crazy (*informal*), gonzo (*slang*), idiotic, insane, loopy (*informal*), lunatic, off one's rocker (*slang*), off one's trolley (*slang*), out of one's mind, out to lunch (*informal*), round the twist (*Brit. slang*), up the pole (*informal*), wacko *or* whacko (*informal*)

crackdown clampdown, crushing, repression, suppression

cracked **1.** broken, chipped, crazed, damaged, defective, faulty, fissured, flawed, imperfect, split **2.** *slang* bats (*slang*), batty (*slang*), crackbrained, crackpot (*informal*), crazy (*informal*), daft (*informal*), doolally (*slang*), eccentric, gonzo (*slang*), insane, loony (*slang*), loopy (*informal*), nuts (*slang*), nutty (*slang*), oddball (*informal*), off one's head *or* nut (*slang*), off one's rocker (*slang*), off one's trolley (*slang*), off-the-wall (*slang*), out of one's mind, outré, out to lunch (*informal*), round the bend (*slang*), round the twist (*Brit. slang*), touched, up the pole (*informal*), wacko *or* whacko (*informal*)

cracked up blown up, exaggerated, hyped (up), overpraised, overrated, puffed up

crack up break down, collapse, come apart at the seams (*informal*), flip one's lid (*slang*), fly off the handle (*informal*), freak out (*informal*), go ape (*slang*), go apeshit (*slang*), go berserk, go crazy (*informal*), go off one's head (*slang*), go off one's rocker (*slang*), go off the deep end (*informal*), go out of one's mind, go to pieces, have a breakdown, throw a wobbly (*slang*)

cradle *noun* **1.** bassinet, cot, crib, Moses basket **2.** *figurative* beginning, birthplace, fount, fountainhead, origin, source, spring, wellspring *~verb* **3.** hold, lull, nestle, nurse, rock, support **4.** nourish, nurture, tend, watch over

craft **1.** ability, aptitude, art, artistry, cleverness, dexterity, expertise, expertness, ingenuity, knack, know-how (*informal*), skill, technique, workmanship **2.** artfulness, artifice, contrivance, craftiness, cunning, deceit, duplicity, guile, ruse, scheme, shrewdness, stratagem, subterfuge, subtlety, trickery, wiles **3.** business, calling, employment, handicraft, handiwork, line, occupation, pursuit, trade, vocation, work **4.** aircraft, barque, boat, plane, ship, spacecraft, vessel

craftiness artfulness, astuteness, canniness, cunning, deviousness, duplicity, foxiness, guile, shrewdness, slyness, subtlety, trickiness, wiliness

craftsman artificer, artisan, maker, master, skilled worker, smith, technician, wright

craftsmanship artistry, expertise, mastery, technique, workmanship

crafty artful, astute, calculating, canny, cunning, deceitful, designing, devious, duplicitous, foxy, fraudulent, guileful, insidious, knowing, scheming, sharp, shrewd, sly, subtle, tricksy, tricky, wily

Antonyms as green as grass, candid, ethical, frank, honest, ingenuous, innocent, naive, open, simple, wet behind the ears

crag aiguille, bluff, peak, pinnacle, rock, tor

craggy broken, cragged, jagged, jaggy (*Scot.*), precipitous, rock-bound, rocky, rough, rugged, stony, uneven

cram **1.** compact, compress, crowd, crush, fill to overflowing, force, jam, overcrowd, overfill, pack, pack in, press, ram, shove, squeeze, stuff **2.** glut, gorge, gormandize, guzzle, overeat, overfeed, pig out (*slang*), put *or* pack away, satiate, stuff **3.** *informal* bone up on (*informal*), con, grind, mug up (*slang*), revise, study, swot, swot up

cramp[1] *verb* check, circumscribe, clip someone's wings, clog, confine, constrain, encumber, hamper, hamstring, handicap, hinder, impede, inhibit, obstruct, restrict, shackle, stymie, thwart

cramp[2] *noun* ache, contraction, convulsion,

crick, pain, pang, shooting pain, spasm, stiff~ness, stitch, twinge

cramped **1**. awkward, circumscribed, closed in, confined, congested, crowded, hemmed in, jammed in, narrow, overcrowded, packed, re~stricted, squeezed, uncomfortable **2**. *especially of handwriting* crabbed, indecipherable, ir~regular, small
Antonyms (*sense 1*) capacious, commodious, large, open, roomy, sizable *or* sizeable, spa~cious, uncongested, uncrowded

crank case (*informal*), character (*informal*), freak (*informal*), kook (*U.S. & Canad. infor~mal*), nut (*slang*), oddball (*informal*), odd fish (*informal*), queer fish (*Brit. informal*), rum customer (*Brit. slang*), screwball (*slang, chiefly U.S. & Canad.*), wacko *or* whacko (*in~formal*), weirdo *or* weirdie (*informal*)

cranky bizarre, capricious, eccentric, erratic, freakish, freaky (*slang*), funny (*informal*), idiosyncratic, odd, oddball (*informal*), off-the-wall (*slang*), outré, peculiar, queer, quirky, rum (*Brit. slang*), strange, wacko *or* whacko (*informal*), wacky (*slang*)

cranny breach, chink, cleft, crack, crevice, fis~sure, gap, hole, interstice, nook, opening, rift

crash *noun* **1**. bang, boom, clang, clash, clatter, clattering, din, racket, smash, smashing, thunder *~verb* **2**. break, break up, dash to pieces, disintegrate, fracture, fragment, shat~ter, shiver, smash, splinter **3**. come a cropper (*informal*), dash, fall, fall headlong, give way, hurtle, lurch, overbalance, pitch, plunge, pre~cipitate oneself, sprawl, topple **4**. bang, bump (into), collide, crash-land (*an aircraft*), drive into, have an accident, hit, hurtle into, plough into, run together, wreck *~noun* **5**. accident, bump, collision, jar, jolt, pile-up (*informal*), prang (*informal*), smash, smash-up, thud, thump, wreck **6**. bankruptcy, collapse, debacle, depression, downfall, failure, ruin, smash *~verb* **7**. be ruined, collapse, fail, fold, fold up, go belly up (*informal*), go broke (*informal*), go bust (*informal*), go to the wall, go under, smash *~adjective* **8**. *of a course of studies, etc.* emergency, immediate, intensive, round-the-clock, speeded-up, telescoped, urgent

crass asinine, blundering, boorish, bovine, coarse, dense, doltish, gross, indelicate, insen~sitive, lumpish, oafish, obtuse, stupid, unre~fined, witless
Antonyms brainy (*informal*), bright, clever, elegant, intelligent, polished, refined, sensi~tive, sharp, smart

crassness asininity, boorishness, coarseness, denseness, doltishness, grossness, indelicacy, insensitivity, oafishness, stupidity, tactless~ness, vulgarity

crate **1**. *noun* box, case, container, packing case, tea chest **2**. *verb* box, case, encase, en~close, pack, pack up

crater depression, dip, hollow, shell hole

crave **1**. be dying for, cry out for (*informal*), desire, eat one's heart out over, fancy (*infor~mal*), hanker after, hope for, hunger after, long for, lust after, need, pant for, pine for, require, set one's heart on, sigh for, thirst for, want, would give one's eyeteeth for, yearn for **2**. ask, beg, beseech, entreat, implore, petition, plead for, pray for, seek, solicit, supplicate

craven **1**. *adjective* abject, caitiff (*archaic*), chicken-hearted, chickenshit (*U.S. slang*), cowardly, dastardly, fearful, lily-livered, mean-spirited, niddering (*archaic*), pusillani~mous, scared, timorous, weak, yellow (*infor~mal*) **2**. *noun* base fellow (*archaic*), caitiff (*ar~chaic*), coward, dastard (*archaic*), niddering (*archaic*), poltroon, recreant (*archaic*), ren~egade, wheyface, yellow-belly (*slang*)

craving ache, appetite, cacoethes, desire, hankering, hope, hunger, longing, lust, thirst, urge, yearning, yen (*informal*)

craw crop, gizzard, gullet, maw, stomach, throat

crawl **1**. advance slowly, creep, drag, go on all fours, inch, move at a snail's pace, move on hands and knees, pull *or* drag oneself along, slither, worm one's way, wriggle, writhe **2**. be overrun (alive, full of, lousy (*slang*)), swarm, teem **3**. abase oneself, brown-nose (*taboo slang*), cringe, fawn, grovel, humble oneself, kiss ass (*U.S. & Canad. taboo slang*), lick someone's arse (*taboo slang*), lick someone's boots (*slang*), pander to, toady, truckle
Antonyms (*sense 1*) dart, dash, fly, hasten, hurry, race, run, rush, sprint, step on it (*in~formal*), walk

craze **1**. *noun* enthusiasm, fad, fashion, infat~uation, mania, mode, novelty, passion, preoc~cupation, rage, the latest (*informal*), thing, trend, vogue **2**. *verb* bewilder, confuse, de~ment, derange, distemper, drive mad, enrage, infatuate, inflame, madden, make insane, send crazy *or* berserk, unbalance, unhinge

crazy **1**. *informal* a bit lacking upstairs (*infor~mal*), as daft as a brush (*informal, chiefly Brit.*), barking (*slang*), barking mad (*slang*), barmy (*slang*), batty (*slang*), berserk, bonkers (*slang, chiefly Brit.*), cracked (*slang*), crackpot (*informal*), crazed, cuckoo (*informal*), daft (*in~formal*), delirious, demented, deranged, dool~ally (*slang*), idiotic, insane, loopy (*informal*), lunatic, mad, mad as a hatter, mad as a March hare, maniacal, mental (*slang*), not all there (*informal*), not right in the head, not the full shilling (*informal*), nuts (*slang*), nutty (*slang*), nutty as a fruitcake (*slang*), off one's

head (*slang*), off one's rocker (*slang*), off one's trolley (*slang*), off-the-wall (*slang*), of unsound mind, out of one's mind, out to lunch (*informal*), potty (*Brit. informal*), round the bend (*slang*), round the twist (*Brit. slang*), touched, unbalanced, unhinged, up the pole (*informal*) **2.** bizarre, eccentric, fantastic, odd, oddball (*informal*), outrageous, peculiar, ridiculous, rum (*Brit. slang*), silly, strange, wacko *or* whacko (*informal*), weird **3.** absurd, bird-brained (*informal*), cockeyed (*informal*), derisory, fatuous, foolhardy, foolish, half-baked (*informal*), idiotic, ill-conceived, impracticable, imprudent, inane, inappropriate, irresponsible, ludicrous, nonsensical, potty (*Brit. informal*), preposterous, puerile, quixotic, senseless, short-sighted, unrealistic, unwise, unworkable, wild **4.** *informal* ablaze, ardent, beside oneself, devoted, eager, enamoured, enthusiastic, fanatical, hysterical, infatuated, into (*informal*), mad, passionate, smitten, very keen, wild (*informal*), zealous
Antonyms (*sense 1*) all there (*informal*), *compos mentis*, down-to-earth, in one's right mind, intelligent, mentally sound, practical, prudent, rational, reasonable, sane, sensible, smart, wise (*sense 2*) common, conventional, normal, ordinary, orthodox, regular, usual (*sense 3*) appropriate, brilliant, feasible, possible, practicable, prudent, realistic, responsible, sensible, wise, workable (*sense 4*) cool, indifferent, uncaring, unenthusiastic, uninterested

creak *verb* grate, grind, groan, rasp, scrape, scratch, screech, squeak, squeal

creaky creaking, grating, rasping, raspy, rusty, squeaking, squeaky, unoiled

cream *noun* **1.** cosmetic, emulsion, essence, liniment, lotion, oil, ointment, paste, salve, unguent **2.** best, *crème de la crème*, elite, flower, pick, prime *~adjective* **3.** off-white, yellowish-white

creamy buttery, creamed, lush, milky, oily, rich, smooth, soft, velvety

crease 1. *verb* corrugate, crimp, crinkle, crumple, double up, fold, pucker, ridge, ruck up, rumple, screw up, wrinkle **2.** *noun* bulge, corrugation, fold, groove, line, overlap, pucker, ridge, ruck, tuck, wrinkle

create 1. beget, bring into being *or* existence, coin, compose, concoct, design, develop, devise, dream up (*informal*), form, formulate, generate, give birth to, give life to, hatch, initiate, invent, make, originate, produce, spawn **2.** appoint, constitute, establish, found, install, invest, make, set up **3.** bring about, cause, lead to, occasion
Antonyms annihilate, close, demolish, destroy

creation 1. conception, formation, generation, genesis, making, procreation, siring **2.** constitution, development, establishment, formation, foundation, inception, institution, laying down, origination, production, setting up **3.** achievement, brainchild (*informal*), *chef-d'oeuvre*, concept, concoction, handiwork, invention, *magnum opus*, *pièce de résistance*, production **4.** all living things, cosmos, life, living world, natural world, nature, universe, world

creative artistic, clever, fertile, gifted, imaginative, ingenious, inspired, inventive, original, productive, stimulating, visionary

creativity cleverness, fecundity, fertility, imagination, imaginativeness, ingenuity, inspiration, inventiveness, originality, productivity, talent

creator architect, author, begetter, designer, father, framer, God, initiator, inventor, maker, originator, prime mover

creature 1. animal, beast, being, brute, critter (*U.S. dialect*), dumb animal, living thing, lower animal, quadruped **2.** body, character, fellow, human being, individual, man, mortal, person, soul, wight (*archaic*), woman **3.** cohort (*chiefly U.S.*), dependant, hanger-on, hireling, instrument (*informal*), lackey, minion, puppet, retainer, tool, wretch

credence acceptance, assurance, belief, certainty, confidence, credit, dependence, faith, reliance, trust

credentials attestation, authorization, card, certificate, deed, diploma, docket, letter of recommendation *or* introduction, letters of credence, licence, missive, passport, recommendation, reference(s), testament, testimonial, title, voucher, warrant

credibility believability, believableness, integrity, plausibility, reliability, tenability, trustworthiness

credible 1. believable, conceivable, imaginable, likely, plausible, possible, probable, reasonable, supposable, tenable, thinkable, verisimilar **2.** dependable, honest, reliable, sincere, trustworthy, trusty
Antonyms (*sense 1*) doubtful, implausible, inconceivable, incredible, questionable, unbelievable, unlikely (*sense 2*) dishonest, insincere, not dependable, unreliable, untrustworthy

credit *noun* **1.** acclaim, acknowledgment, approval, Brownie points, commendation, fame, glory, honour, kudos, merit, praise, recognition, thanks, tribute **2.** character, clout (*informal*), esteem, estimation, good name, influence, position, prestige, regard, reputation, repute, standing, status **3.** belief, confidence, credence, faith, reliance, trust **4.** *As in* **be a credit to** feather in one's cap, honour, source of satisfaction *or* pride **5. on credit** by de~

ferred payment, by instalments, on account, on hire-purchase, on (the) H.P., on the slate (*informal*), on tick (*informal*) ~*verb* **6.** *with* **with** accredit, ascribe to, assign to, attribute to, chalk up to (*informal*), impute to, refer to **7.** accept, bank on, believe, buy (*slang*), depend on, fall for, have faith in, rely on, swallow (*informal*), trust
credit where credit is due

creditable admirable, commendable, deserving, estimable, exemplary, honourable, laudable, meritorious, praiseworthy, reputable, respectable, worthy

credulity blind faith, credulousness, gullibility, naïveté, silliness, simplicity, stupidity

credulous as green as grass, born yesterday (*informal*), dupable, green, gullible, naive, overtrusting, trustful, uncritical, unsuspecting, unsuspicious, wet behind the ears (*informal*)
Antonyms cynical, incredulous, sceptical, suspecting, unbelieving, wary

creed articles of faith, belief, canon, catechism, confession, credo, doctrine, dogma, persuasion, principles, profession (*of faith*), tenet

creek **1.** bay, bight, cove, firth *or* frith (*Scot.*), inlet **2.** *U.S., Canad., & Austral.* bayou, brook, rivulet, runnel, stream, streamlet, tributary, watercourse

creep *verb* **1.** crawl, crawl on all fours, glide, insinuate, slither, squirm, worm, wriggle, writhe **2.** approach unnoticed, skulk, slink, sneak, steal, tiptoe **3.** crawl, dawdle, drag, edge, inch, proceed at a snail's pace **4.** bootlick (*informal*), brown-nose (*taboo slang*), cower, cringe, fawn, grovel, kiss (someone's) ass (*U.S. & Canad. taboo slang*), kowtow, pander to, scrape, suck up to (*informal*), toady, truckle ~*noun* **5.** *slang* ass-kisser (*U.S. & Canad. taboo slang*), bootlicker (*informal*), brown-noser (*taboo slang*), sneak, sycophant, toady **6.** **give one the creeps** *or* **make one's flesh creep** disgust, frighten, horrify, make one flinch (quail, shrink, squirm, wince), make one's hair stand on end (*informal*), repel, repulse, scare, terrify, terrorize

creeper climber, climbing plant, rambler, runner, trailing plant, vine (*chiefly U.S.*)

creepy awful, direful, disgusting, disturbing, eerie, forbidding, frightening, ghoulish, goose-pimply (*informal*), gruesome, hair-raising, horrible, macabre, menacing, nightmarish, ominous, scary (*informal*), sinister, terrifying, threatening, unpleasant, weird

crepitate crack, crackle, rattle, snap

crescent *noun* **1.** half-moon, meniscus, new moon, old moon, sickle, sickle-shape ~*adjective* **2.** arched, bow-shaped, curved, falcate, semicircular, sickle-shaped **3.** *archaic* growing, increasing, waxing

Crescent, the Islam, Mohammedanism, Muslim Empire, Turkey

crest **1.** apex, crown, head, height, highest point, peak, pinnacle, ridge, summit, top **2.** aigrette, caruncle (*Zoology*), cockscomb, comb, crown, mane, panache, plume, tassel, topknot, tuft **3.** *Heraldry* badge, bearings, charge, device, emblem, insignia, symbol

crestfallen chapfallen, choked, dejected, depressed, despondent, disappointed, disconsolate, discouraged, disheartened, downcast, downhearted, sick as a parrot (*informal*)
Antonyms cock-a-hoop, elated, encouraged, exuberant, happy, in seventh heaven, joyful, on cloud nine (*informal*), over the moon (*informal*)

crevasse abyss, bergschrund, chasm, cleft, crack, fissure

crevice chink, cleft, crack, cranny, fissure, fracture, gap, hole, interstice, opening, rent, rift, slit, split

crew **1.** hands, (ship's) company, (ship's) complement **2.** company, corps, gang, party, posse, squad, team, working party **3.** *informal* assemblage, band, bunch (*informal*), camp, company, crowd, gang, herd, horde, lot, mob, pack, posse (*informal*), set, swarm, troop

crib *noun* **1.** bassinet, bed, cot, cradle **2.** bin, box, bunker, manger, rack, stall **3.** *informal* key, translation, trot (*U.S. slang*) ~*verb* **4.** *informal* cheat, pass off as one's own work, pilfer, pirate, plagiarize, purloin, steal **5.** box up, cage, confine, coop, coop up, enclose, fence, imprison, limit, pen, rail, restrict, shut in

crick **1.** *noun* convulsion, cramp, spasm, twinge **2.** *verb* jar, rick, wrench

crime **1.** atrocity, fault, felony, job (*informal*), malfeasance, misdeed, misdemeanour, offence, outrage, transgression, trespass, unlawful act, violation, wrong **2.** corruption, delinquency, guilt, illegality, iniquity, lawbreaking, malefaction, misconduct, sin, unrighteousness, vice, villainy, wickedness, wrong, wrongdoing

criminal *noun* **1.** con (*slang*), con man (*informal*), convict, crook (*informal*), culprit, delinquent, evildoer, felon, jailbird, lag (*slang*), lawbreaker, malefactor, offender, sinner, transgressor, villain ~*adjective* **2.** bent (*slang*), corrupt, crooked (*informal*), culpable, felonious, illegal, illicit, immoral, indictable, iniquitous, lawless, nefarious, peccant (*rare*), under-the-table, unlawful, unrighteous, vicious, villainous, wicked, wrong **3.** *informal* deplorable, foolish, preposterous, ridiculous, scandalous, senseless
Antonyms commendable, honest, honourable, innocent, law-abiding, lawful, legal, right

criminality corruption, culpability, delinquency, depravity, guiltiness, illegality, sinfulness, turpitude, villainy, wickedness

cringe 1. blench, cower, dodge, draw back, duck, flinch, quail, quiver, recoil, shrink, shy, start, tremble, wince 2. bend, bootlick (*informal*), bow, brown-nose (*taboo slang*), crawl, creep, crouch, fawn, grovel, kiss ass (*U.S. & Canad. taboo slang*), kneel, kowtow, pander to, sneak, stoop, toady, truckle

crinkle *noun/verb* 1. cockle, crimp, crimple, crumple, curl, fold, pucker, ruffle, rumple, scallop, twist, wrinkle 2. crackle, hiss, rustle, swish, whisper

crinkly buckled, cockled, curly, fluted, frizzy, furrowed, gathered, kinky, knit, puckered, ruffled, scalloped, wrinkled

cripple *verb* 1. debilitate, disable, enfeeble, hamstring, incapacitate, lame, maim, mutilate, paralyse, weaken 2. bring to a standstill, cramp, damage, destroy, halt, impair, put out of action, put paid to, ruin, spoil, vitiate
Antonyms advance, aid, assist, assist the progress of, ease, expedite, facilitate, further, help, promote

crippled bedridden, deformed, disabled, enfeebled, handicapped, housebound, incapacitated, laid up (*informal*), lame, paralysed

crisis 1. climacteric, climax, confrontation, critical point, crunch (*informal*), crux, culmination, height, moment of truth, point of no return, turning point 2. catastrophe, critical situation, deep water, dilemma, dire straits, disaster, emergency, exigency, extremity, meltdown (*informal*), mess, panic stations (*informal*), pass, plight, predicament, quandary, strait, trouble

crisp 1. brittle, crispy, crumbly, crunchy, firm, fresh, unwilted 2. bracing, brisk, fresh, invigorating, refreshing 3. brief, brusque, clear, incisive, pithy, short, succinct, tart, terse 4. clean-cut, neat, orderly, smart, snappy, spruce, tidy, trig (*archaic or dialect*), well-groomed, well-pressed
Antonyms (*sense 1*) drooping, droopy, flaccid, floppy, limp, soft, wilted, withered (*sense 2*) balmy, clement, mild, pleasant, warm

criterion bench mark, canon, gauge, measure, norm, par, principle, proof, rule, standard, test, touchstone, yardstick

critic 1. analyst, arbiter, authority, commentator, connoisseur, expert, expositor, judge, pundit, reviewer 2. attacker, carper, caviller, censor, censurer, detractor, fault-finder, knocker (*informal*), Momus, reviler, vilifier

The proper function of the critic is to save the tale from the artist who created it
D.H. Lawrence

A critic is a man who knows the way but can't drive the car
Kenneth Tynan

critic: a person who boasts himself hard to please because nobody tries to please him
Ambrose Bierce *The Devil's Dictionary*

A critic is a bundle of biases held loosely together by a sense of taste
Whitney Balliet *Dinosaurs in the Morning*

critical 1. captious, carping, cavilling, censorious, derogatory, disapproving, disparaging, fault-finding, nagging, niggling, nit-picking (*informal*), on someone's back (*informal*), scathing 2. accurate, analytical, diagnostic, discerning, discriminating, fastidious, judicious, penetrating, perceptive, precise 3. all-important, crucial, dangerous, deciding, decisive, grave, hairy (*slang*), high-priority, momentous, now or never, perilous, pivotal, precarious, pressing, psychological, risky, serious, urgent, vital
Antonyms appreciative, approving, complimentary, permissive, safe, secure, settled, uncritical, undiscriminating, unimportant

criticism 1. animadversion, bad press, brickbats (*informal*), censure, character assassination, critical remarks, denigration, disapproval, disparagement, fault-finding, flak (*informal*), knocking (*informal*), panning (*informal*), slam (*slang*), slating (*informal*), stick (*slang*), stricture 2. analysis, appraisal, appreciation, assessment, comment, commentary, critique, elucidation, evaluation, judgment, notice, review

criticize 1. animadvert on *or* upon, blast, carp, censure, condemn, disapprove of, disparage, excoriate, find fault with, give (someone *or* something) a bad press, have a go (at) (*informal*), knock (*informal*), lambast(e), nag at, pan (*informal*), pass strictures upon, pick holes in, pick to pieces, put down, slam (*slang*), slate (*informal*), tear into (*informal*) 2. analyse, appraise, assess, comment upon, evaluate, give an opinion, judge, pass judgment on, review
Antonyms commend, compliment, extol, laud (*literary*), praise

There is so much good in the worst of us
And so much bad in the best of us
That it hardly becomes any of us
To talk about the rest of us
Anon.

People in glass houses shouldn't throw stones

critique analysis, appraisal, assessment, commentary, essay, examination, review, treatise

croak *verb* 1. caw, gasp, grunt, squawk, utter *or* speak harshly (huskily, throatily), wheeze 2. *informal* complain, groan, grouse, grumble, moan, murmur, mutter, repine 3. *slang* buy it

(*U.S. slang*), buy the farm (*U.S. slang*), check out (*U.S. slang*), die, expire, go belly-up (*slang*), hop the twig (*informal*), kick it (*slang*), kick the bucket (*informal*), pass away, peg it (*informal*), peg out (*informal*), perish, pop one's clogs (*informal*)

crone beldam (*archaic*), gammer (*dialect*), hag, old bag (*derogatory slang*), old bat (*slang*), witch

crony accomplice, ally, associate, buddy (*informal*), china (*Brit. slang*), chum (*informal*), cock (*Brit. informal*), colleague, companion, comrade, friend, gossip (*archaic*), homeboy (*slang, chiefly U.S.*), mate (*informal*), pal (*informal*), sidekick (*slang*)

crook **1.** *noun, informal* cheat, chiseller (*informal*), criminal, fraudster, grifter (*slang, chiefly U.S. & Canad.*), knave (*archaic*), lag (*slang*), racketeer, robber, rogue, shark, swindler, thief, villain **2.** *verb* angle, bend, bow, curve, flex, hook

crooked **1.** anfractuous, bent, bowed, crippled, curved, deformed, deviating, disfigured, distorted, hooked, irregular, meandering, misshapen, out of shape, tortuous, twisted, twisting, warped, winding, zigzag **2.** angled, askew, asymmetric, at an angle, awry, lopsided, off-centre, skewwhiff (*Brit. informal*), slanted, slanting, squint, tilted, to one side, uneven, unsymmetrical **3.** *informal* bent (*slang*), corrupt, crafty, criminal, deceitful, dishonest, dishonourable, dubious, fraudulent, illegal, knavish, nefarious, questionable, shady (*informal*), shifty, treacherous, underhand, under-the-table, unlawful, unprincipled, unscrupulous

Antonyms (*sense 1*) flat, straight (*sense 3*) ethical, fair, honest, honourable, lawful, legal, straight, upright

crookedness **1.** anfractuosity, contortedness, curvedness, deformedness, deviance, disfigurement, distortedness, hookedness, irregularity, tortuousness, zigzaggedness **2.** asymmetry, lopsidedness, unevenness **3.** corruptness, craftiness, criminality, deceitfulness, dishonesty, dishonourableness, dubiousness, fraudulence, fraudulency, illegality, improbity, knavishness, nefariousness, questionability, questionableness, shadiness (*informal*), shiftiness, treacherousness, underhandedness, unlawfulness, unprincipledness, unscrupulosity, unscrupulousness

Antonyms (*sense 1*) flatness, levelness, straightness (*sense 3*) ethicality, ethicalness, fairness, honesty, honourableness, lawfulness, legality, straightness, trustworthiness, uprightness

croon breathe, hum, purr, sing, warble

crop *noun* **1.** fruits, gathering, harvest, produce, reaping, season's growth, vintage, yield *~verb* **2.** clip, curtail, cut, dock, lop, mow, pare, prune, reduce, shear, shorten, snip, top, trim **3.** bring home, bring in, collect, garner, gather, harvest, mow, pick, reap **4.** browse, graze, nibble

crop up appear, arise, emerge, happen, occur, spring up, turn up

cross *adjective* **1.** angry, annoyed, cantankerous, captious, choked, churlish, crotchety (*informal*), crusty, disagreeable, fractious, fretful, grouchy (*informal*), grumpy, hacked (off) (*U.S. slang*), ill-humoured, ill-tempered, impatient, in a bad mood, irascible, irritable, liverish, out of humour, peeved (*informal*), peevish, pettish, petulant, pissed off (*taboo slang*), put out, querulous, ratty (*Brit. & N.Z. informal*), shirty (*slang, chiefly Brit.*), short, snappish, snappy, splenetic, sullen, surly, testy, tetchy, vexed, waspish *~verb* **2.** bridge, cut across, extend over, ford, meet, pass over, ply, span, traverse, zigzag **3.** crisscross, intersect, intertwine, lace, lie athwart of **4.** blend, crossbreed, cross-fertilize, cross-pollinate, hybridize, interbreed, intercross, mix, mongrelize **5.** block, deny, foil, frustrate, hinder, impede, interfere, obstruct, oppose, resist, thwart *~noun* **6.** affliction, burden, grief, load, misery, misfortune, trial, tribulation, trouble, woe, worry **7.** crucifix, rood **8.** crossing, crossroads, intersection, junction **9.** amalgam, blend, combination, crossbreed, cur, hybrid, hybridization, mixture, mongrel, mutt (*slang*) *~adjective* **10.** crosswise, intersecting, oblique, transverse **11.** adverse, contrary, opposed, opposing, unfavourable **12.** *involving an interchange* opposite, reciprocal

Antonyms (*sense 1*) affable, agreeable, calm, cheerful, civil, congenial, even-tempered, genial, good-humoured, good-natured, nice, placid, pleasant, sweet

cross-examine catechize, grill (*informal*), interrogate, pump, question, quiz

cross-grained awkward, cantankerous, crabby, difficult, disobliging, ill-natured, morose, peevish, perverse, refractory, shrewish, stubborn, truculent, wayward

cross out *or* **off** blue-pencil, cancel, delete, eliminate, strike off *or* out

crosspatch bear, crank (*U.S., Canad., & Irish informal*), curmudgeon, grump (*informal*), killjoy, scold, shrew, sorehead (*informal, chiefly U.S.*), sourpuss (*informal*)

crosswise, crossways across, aslant, at an angle, athwart, at right angles, awry, crisscross, diagonally, from side to side, on the bias, over, sideways, transversely

crotch crutch, groin

crotchet caprice, fad, fancy, quirk, vagary, whim, whimsy

crotchety awkward, bad-tempered, cantankerous, contrary, crabby, cross, crusty, curmudgeonly, difficult, disagreeable, fractious, grumpy, irritable, liverish, obstreperous, peevish, ratty (*Brit. & N.Z. informal*), surly, testy, tetchy

crouch **1.** bend down, bow, duck, hunch, kneel, squat, stoop **2.** abase oneself, cower, cringe, fawn, grovel, pander to, truckle

crow blow one's own trumpet, bluster, boast, brag, drool, exult, flourish, gloat, glory in, strut, swagger, triumph, vaunt

crowd *noun* **1.** army, assembly, bevy, company, concourse, flock, herd, horde, host, mass, mob, multitude, pack, press, rabble, swarm, throng, troupe **2.** bunch (*informal*), circle, clique, group, lot, set **3.** attendance, audience, gate, house, spectators *~verb* **4.** cluster, congregate, cram, flock, forgather, gather, huddle, mass, muster, press, push, stream, surge, swarm, throng **5.** bundle, congest, cram, pack, pile, squeeze **6.** batter, butt, elbow, jostle, shove **7.** **the crowd** hoi polloi, masses, mob, people, populace, proletariat, public, rabble, rank and file, riffraff, vulgar herd

crowded busy, congested, cramped, crushed, full, huddled, jam-packed, mobbed, overflowing, packed, populous, swarming, teeming, thronged

crown *noun* **1.** chaplet, circlet, coronal (*poetic*), coronet, diadem, tiara **2.** bays, distinction, garland, honour, kudos, laurels, laurel wreath, prize, trophy **3.** emperor, empress, king, monarch, monarchy, queen, *rex*, royalty, ruler, sovereign, sovereignty **4.** acme, apex, crest, head, perfection, pinnacle, summit, tip, top, ultimate, zenith *~verb* **5.** adorn, dignify, festoon, honour, invest, reward **6.** be the climax *or* culmination of, cap, complete, consummate, finish, fulfil, perfect, put the finishing touch to, put the tin lid on, round off, surmount, terminate, top **7.** *slang* belt (*informal*), biff (*slang*), box, cuff, hit over the head, punch

crowning *adjective* climactic, consummate, culminating, final, mother (of all), paramount, sovereign, supreme, ultimate

crucial **1.** central, critical, decisive, pivotal, psychological, searching, testing, trying **2.** *informal* essential, high-priority, important, momentous, now or never, pressing, urgent, vital

crucify **1.** execute, harrow, persecute, rack, torment, torture **2.** *slang* lampoon, pan (*informal*), ridicule, tear to pieces, wipe the floor with (*informal*)

crude **1.** boorish, coarse, crass, dirty, gross, indecent, lewd, obscene, smutty, tactless, tasteless, uncouth, vulgar, X-rated (*informal*) **2.** natural, raw, unmilled, unpolished, unprepared, unprocessed, unrefined **3.** clumsy, makeshift, outline, primitive, rough, rough-and-ready, rough-hewn, rude, rudimentary, sketchy, undeveloped, unfinished, unformed, unpolished

Antonyms (*sense 1*) genteel, polished, refined, subtle, tasteful (*sense 2*) fine, fine-grained, polished, prepared, processed, refined

crudely bluntly, clumsily, coarsely, impolitely, indecently, pulling no punches (*informal*), roughly, rudely, sketchily, tastelessly, vulgarly

crudity **1.** coarseness, crudeness, impropriety, indecency, indelicacy, lewdness, loudness, lowness, obscenity, obtrusiveness, smuttiness, vulgarity **2.** clumsiness, crudeness, primitiveness, roughness, rudeness

cruel **1.** atrocious, barbarous, bitter, bloodthirsty, brutal, brutish, callous, cold-blooded, depraved, excruciating, fell (*archaic*), ferocious, fierce, flinty, grim, hard, hard-hearted, harsh, heartless, hellish, implacable, inclement, inexorable, inhuman, inhumane, malevolent, murderous, painful, poignant, ravening, raw, relentless, remorseless, sadistic, sanguinary, savage, severe, spiteful, stony-hearted, unfeeling, unkind, unnatural, vengeful, vicious **2.** merciless, pitiless, ruthless, unrelenting

Antonyms benevolent, caring, compassionate, gentle, humane, kind, merciful, sympathetic, warm-hearted

I must be cruel, only to be kind
William Shakespeare *Hamlet*

cruelly **1.** barbarously, brutally, brutishly, callously, ferociously, fiercely, heartlessly, in cold blood, mercilessly, pitilessly, sadistically, savagely, spitefully, unmercifully, viciously **2.** bitterly, deeply, fearfully, grievously, monstrously, mortally, severely

cruelty barbarity, bestiality, bloodthirstiness, brutality, brutishness, callousness, depravity, ferocity, fiendishness, hardheartedness, harshness, heartlessness, inhumanity, mercilessness, murderousness, ruthlessness, sadism, savagery, severity, spite, spitefulness, venom, viciousness

cruise *verb* **1.** coast, sail, voyage **2.** coast, drift, keep a steady pace, travel along *~noun* **3.** boat trip, sail, sea trip, voyage

crumb atom, bit, grain, mite, morsel, particle, scrap, shred, sliver, snippet, *soupçon*, speck

crumble **1.** bruise, crumb, crush, fragment, granulate, grind, pound, powder, pulverize, triturate **2.** break down, break up, collapse, come to dust, decay, decompose, degenerate, deteriorate, disintegrate, fall apart, go to pieces, go to wrack and ruin, moulder, perish, tumble down

crumbling collapsing, decaying, decomposing, deteriorating, disintegrating, eroding, mouldering

crumbly brashy, brittle, friable, powdery, rotted, short (*of pastry*)

crummy bush-league (*Austral. & N.Z. informal*), cheap, chickenshit (*U.S. slang*), contemptible, crappy (*slang*), dime-a-dozen (*informal*), duff (*Brit. informal*), for the birds (*informal*), half-baked (*informal*), inferior, lousy (*slang*), low-rent (*informal, chiefly U.S.*), miserable, of a sort *or* of sorts, piss-poor (*taboo slang*), poor, poxy (*slang*), rotten (*informal*), rubbishy, second-rate, shitty (*taboo slang*), shoddy, strictly for the birds (*informal*), third-rate, tinhorn (*U.S. slang*), trashy, two-bit (*U.S. & Canad. slang*), useless, weak, worthless

crumple 1. crease, crush, pucker, rumple, screw up, wrinkle 2. break down, cave in, collapse, fall, give way, go to pieces

crumpled creased, crushed, puckered, ruffled, rumpled, shrivelled, wrinkled

crunch 1. *verb* champ, chew noisily, chomp, grind, masticate, munch 2. *noun, informal* crisis, critical point, crux, emergency, hour of decision, moment of truth, test

crusade campaign, cause, drive, holy war, jihad, movement, push

crusader advocate, campaigner, champion, reformer

crush *verb* 1. bray, break, bruise, comminute, compress, contuse, crease, crumble, crumple, crunch, mash, pound, pulverize, rumple, smash, squeeze, wrinkle 2. conquer, extinguish, overcome, overpower, overwhelm, put down, quell, stamp out, subdue, vanquish 3. abash, browbeat, chagrin, dispose of, humiliate, mortify, put down (*slang*), quash, shame 4. embrace, enfold, hug, press, squeeze ~*noun* 5. crowd, huddle, jam, party

crust caking, coat, coating, concretion, covering, film, incrustation, layer, outside, scab, shell, skin, surface

crusty 1. brittle, crisp, crispy, friable, hard, short, well-baked, well-done 2. brusque, cantankerous, captious, choleric, crabby, cross, curt, gruff, ill-humoured, irritable, peevish, prickly, ratty (*Brit. & N.Z. informal*), short, short-tempered, snappish, snarling, splenetic, surly, testy, tetchy, touchy

crux core, decisive point, essence, heart, nub

cry 1. *verb* bawl, bewail, blubber, boohoo, greet (*Scot. or archaic*), howl one's eyes out, keen, lament, mewl, pule, shed tears, snivel, sob, wail, weep, whimper, whine, whinge (*informal*), yowl 2. *noun* bawling, blubbering, crying, greet (*Scot. or archaic*), howl, keening, lament, lamentation, plaint (*archaic*), snivel, snivelling, sob, sobbing, sorrowing, wailing, weep, weeping 3. *verb* bawl, bell, bellow, call, call out, ejaculate, exclaim, hail, halloo, holler (*informal*), howl, roar, scream, screech, shout, shriek, sing out, vociferate, whoop, yell 4. *noun* bawl, bell, bellow, call, ejaculation, exclamation, holler (*informal*), hoot, howl, outcry, roar, scream, screech, shriek, squawk, whoop, yell, yelp, yoo-hoo 5. *verb* advertise, announce, bark (*informal*), broadcast, bruit, hawk, noise, proclaim, promulgate, publish, shout from the rooftops (*informal*), trumpet 6. *noun* announcement, barking (*informal*), noising, proclamation, publication 7. *verb* beg, beseech, clamour, entreat, implore, plead, pray 8. *noun* appeal, entreaty, petition, plea, prayer, supplication

Antonyms *verb* (*sense 1*) chortle, chuckle, giggle, laugh, snicker, snigger, twitter (*sense 3*) drone, mumble, murmur, mutter, speak in hushed tones, speak softly, utter indistinctly, whisper

It is no use crying over spilt milk

cry down asperse, bad-mouth (*slang, chiefly U.S. & Canad.*), belittle, decry, denigrate, disparage, knock (*informal*), rubbish (*informal*), run down, slag (off) (*slang*)

cry off back out, beg off, cop out (*slang*), excuse oneself, quit, withdraw, withdraw from

crypt catacomb, ossuary, tomb, undercroft, vault

cryptic abstruse, ambiguous, apocryphal, arcane, cabbalistic, coded, dark, Delphic, enigmatic, equivocal, esoteric, hidden, mysterious, obscure, occult, oracular, perplexing, puzzling, recondite, secret, vague, veiled

crystallize appear, coalesce, form, harden, materialize, take shape

cub 1. offspring, whelp, young 2. babe (*informal*), beginner, fledgling, greenhorn (*informal*), lad, learner, puppy, recruit, tenderfoot, trainee, whippersnapper, youngster

cubbyhole 1. den, hideaway, hole, snug 2. compartment, niche, pigeonhole, recess, slot

cuddle bill and coo, canoodle (*slang*), clasp, cosset, embrace, fondle, hug, nestle, pet, snuggle

cuddly buxom, cuddlesome, curvaceous, huggable, lovable, plump, soft, warm

cudgel 1. *noun* bastinado, baton, bludgeon, club, cosh (*Brit.*), shillelagh, stick, truncheon 2. *verb* bang, baste, batter, beat, bludgeon, cane, cosh (*Brit.*), drub, maul, pound, pummel, thrash, thump, thwack

cue catchword, hint, key, nod, prompting, reminder, sign, signal, suggestion

cuff[1] 1. *verb* bat (*informal*), beat, belt (*informal*), biff (*slang*), box, buffet, clap, clobber (*slang*), clout (*informal*), knock, lambast(e), pummel, punch, slap, smack, thump, whack **2.** *noun* belt (*informal*), biff (*slang*), box, buffet, clout (*informal*), knock, punch, rap, slap, smack, thump, whack

cuff[2] *noun* **off the cuff** ad lib, extempore, im~promptu, improvised, offhand, off the top of one's head, on the spur of the moment, spon~taneous, spontaneously, unrehearsed

cul-de-sac blind alley, dead end

cull 1. choose, pick, pluck, select, sift, thin, thin out, winnow **2.** amass, collect, gather, glean, pick up

culminate climax, close, come to a climax, come to a head, conclude, end, end up, finish, rise to a crescendo, terminate, wind up

culmination acme, apex, apogee, climax, com~pletion, conclusion, consummation, crown, crowning touch, finale, height, *ne plus ultra*, peak, perfection, pinnacle, punch line, sum~mit, top, zenith

culpability answerability, blame, blameworthi~ness, fault, guilt, liability, responsibility

culpable answerable, at fault, blamable, blameworthy, censurable, found wanting, guilty, in the wrong, liable, reprehensible, sinful, to blame, wrong

Antonyms blameless, clean (*slang*), guiltless, innocent, in the clear, not guilty, squeaky-clean

culprit criminal, delinquent, evildoer, felon, guilty party, malefactor, miscreant, offender, person responsible, rascal, sinner, transgres~sor, villain, wrongdoer

cult 1. body, church, clique, denomination, fac~tion, faith, following, party, religion, school, sect **2.** admiration, craze, devotion, idolization, reverence, veneration, worship

cultivate 1. bring under cultivation, farm, fer~tilize, harvest, plant, plough, prepare, tend, till, work **2.** ameliorate, better, bring on, cher~ish, civilize, develop, discipline, elevate, en~rich, foster, improve, polish, promote, refine, train **3.** aid, devote oneself to, encourage, for~ward, foster, further, help, patronize, promote, pursue, support **4.** associate with, butter up, consort with, court, dance attendance upon, run after, seek out, seek someone's company *or* friendship, take trouble *or* pains with

cultivated accomplished, advanced, civilized, cultured, developed, discerning, discriminat~ing, educated, enlightened, erudite, genteel, polished, refined, sophisticated, urbane, versed, well-bred, well-educated

cultivation 1. agronomy, farming, gardening, husbandry, planting, ploughing, tillage, tilling, working **2.** breeding, civility, civilization, culture, discernment, discrimination, education, en~lightenment, gentility, good taste, learning, let~ters, manners, polish, refinement, sophistica~tion, taste **3.** advancement, advocacy, develop~ment, encouragement, enhancement, fostering, furtherance, help, nurture, patronage, promo~tion, support **4.** devotion to, pursuit, study

cultural artistic, broadening, civilizing, devel~opmental, edifying, educational, educative, el~evating, enlightening, enriching, humane, hu~manizing, liberal, liberalizing

culture 1. civilization, customs, lifestyle, mores, society, stage of development, the arts, way of life **2.** accomplishment, breeding, education, elevation, enlightenment, erudition, gentility, good taste, improvement, polish, politeness, refinement, sophistication, urbanity **3.** agri~culture, agronomy, cultivation, farming, hus~bandry

cultured accomplished, advanced, educated, enlightened, erudite, genteel, highbrow, knowledgeable, polished, refined, scholarly, sophisticated, urbane, versed, well-bred, well-informed, well-read

Antonyms coarse, common, inelegant, uncul~tivated, uneducated, unpolished, unrefined, vulgar

culvert channel, conduit, drain, gutter, water~course

cumbersome awkward, bulky, burdensome, clumsy, clunky (*informal*), cumbrous, embar~rassing, heavy, hefty (*informal*), incommodi~ous, inconvenient, oppressive, unmanageable, unwieldy, weighty

Antonyms compact, convenient, easy to use, handy, manageable, practical, serviceable, wieldy

cumulative accruing, accumulative, aggregate, amassed, collective, heaped, increasing, snow~balling

cunning 1. *adjective* artful, astute, canny, crafty, devious, foxy, guileful, knowing, Machiavellian, sharp, shifty, shrewd, subtle, tricky, wily **2.** *noun* artfulness, astuteness, craftiness, deceitfulness, deviousness, foxiness, guile, shrewdness, slyness, trickery, wiliness **3.** *adjective* adroit, deft, dexterous, imagina~tive, ingenious, skilful **4.** *noun* ability, adroit~ness, art, artifice, cleverness, craft, deftness, dexterity, finesse, ingenuity, skill, subtlety

Antonyms *adjective* artless, dull, ethical, frank, honest, ingenuous, maladroit *~noun* candour, clumsiness, ingenuousness, sincerity

Cunning is the dark sanctuary of incapacity
Lord Chesterfield *Letters...to his Godson and Successor*

cup 1. beaker, cannikin, chalice, demitasse, goblet, teacup **2.** trophy

cupboard ambry (*obsolete*), cabinet, closet, locker, press

Cabinets and cupboards
see FURNITURE

Cupid amoretto, Eros, god of love, love

cupidity acquisitiveness, avarice, avidity, covetousness, graspingness, greed, greediness, hunger, itching, longing, rapaciousness, rapacity, voracity, yearning

cupola dome, onion dome

cur 1. canine, hound, mongrel, mutt (*slang*), stray 2. bad egg (*old-fashioned informal*), bastard (*offensive*), blackguard, bugger (*taboo slang*), cocksucker (*taboo slang*), coward, good-for-nothing, heel (*slang*), rat (*informal*), rotter (*slang, chiefly Brit.*), scoundrel, scumbag (*slang*), shit (*taboo slang*), son-of-a-bitch (*slang, chiefly U.S. & Canad.*), villain, wretch

curative alleviative, corrective, healing, healthful, health-giving, medicinal, remedial, restorative, salutary, therapeutic, tonic

curb 1. *verb* bite back, bridle, check, constrain, contain, control, hinder, impede, inhibit, keep a tight rein on, moderate, muzzle, repress, restrain, restrict, retard, stem the flow, subdue, suppress 2. *noun* brake, bridle, check, control, deterrent, limitation, rein, restraint

curdle clot, coagulate, condense, congeal, curd, solidify, thicken, turn sour

Antonyms deliquesce, dissolve, liquefy, melt, soften, thaw

cure 1. *verb* alleviate, correct, ease, heal, help, make better, mend, rehabilitate, relieve, remedy, restore, restore to health 2. *noun* alleviation, antidote, corrective, healing, medicine, nostrum, panacea, recovery, remedy, restorative, specific, treatment 3. *verb* dry, kipper, pickle, preserve, salt, smoke

It is part of the cure to wish to be cured
Seneca *Phaedra*

The cure is worse than the disease
Philip Massinger *The Bondman*

cure-all catholicon, elixir, *elixir vitae*, nostrum, panacea

curio antique, bibelot, bygone, collector's item, knick-knack, trinket

curiosity 1. inquisitiveness, interest, nosiness (*informal*), prying, snooping (*informal*) 2. celebrity, freak, marvel, novelty, oddity, phenomenon, rarity, sight, spectacle, wonder 3. bibelot, bygone, collector's item, curio, knickknack, *objet d'art*, trinket

Curiosity killed the cat

curious 1. inquiring, inquisitive, interested, puzzled, questioning, searching 2. inquisitive, meddling, nosy (*informal*), peeping, peering, prying, snoopy (*informal*) 3. bizarre, exotic, extraordinary, marvellous, mysterious, novel, odd, peculiar, puzzling, quaint, queer, rare, rum (*Brit. slang*), singular, strange, unconventional, unexpected, unique, unorthodox, unusual, wonderful

Antonyms (*senses 1 & 2*) incurious, indifferent, uninquisitive, uninterested (*sense 3*) common, everyday, familiar, ordinary

curl 1. *verb* bend, coil, convolute, corkscrew, crimp, crinkle, crisp, curve, entwine, frizz, loop, meander, ripple, spiral, turn, twine, twirl, twist, wind, wreathe, writhe 2. *noun* coil, curlicue, kink, ringlet, spiral, twist, whorl

curly corkscrew, crimped, crimpy, crinkly, crisp, curled, curling, frizzy, fuzzy, kinky, permed, spiralled, waved, wavy, winding

curmudgeon bear, bellyacher (*slang*), churl, crosspatch (*informal*), grouch (*informal*), grouser, grumbler, grump (*informal*), malcontent, sourpuss (*informal*)

currency 1. bills, coinage, coins, dosh (*Brit. & Austral. slang*), medium of exchange, money, notes 2. acceptance, circulation, exposure, popularity, prevalence, publicity, transmission, vogue

Country	**Currency**
Afghanistan	afghani
Albania	lek
Algeria	Algerian dinar
American Samoa	U.S. dollar
Andorra	French franc; Spanish peseta
Angola	new kwanza
Antigua and Barbuda	East Caribbean dollar
Argentina	peso
Armenia	dram
Australia	Australian dollar
Austria	schilling
Azerbaijan	manat
Bahamas	Bahamian dollar
Bahrain	dinar
Bangladesh	taka
Barbados	Barbados dollar
Belau	U.S. dollar
Belgium	Belgian franc
Belize	Belize dollar
Benin	CFA franc
Bermuda	Bermuda dollar
Bhutan	ngultrum
Bolivia	boliviano
Bosnia and Herzegovina	dinar
Botswana	pula
Brazil	cruzeiro
British Virgin Isles	U.S. dollar
Brunei	Brunei dollar
Bulgaria	lev
Burkina-Faso	CFA franc
Burundi	Burundi franc
Byelorussia	duktat
Cambodia	riel
Cameroon	CFA franc
Canada	Canadian dollar

Cape Verde	Cape Verdean escu~do
Cayman Islands	Cayman Islands dol~lar
Central African Re~public	CFA franc
Chad	CFA franc
Chile	peso
Colombia	peso
Comoros	CFA franc
Congo Republic	CFA franc
Costa Rica	Costa Rica cólon
Côte d'Ivoire	CFA franc
Croatia	dinar
Cuba	Cuban peso
Cyprus	pound
Czech Republic	koruna
Denmark	Danish krone
Djibouti	Djibouti franc
Dominica	East Caribbean dol~lar
Dominican Republic	peso
Ecuador	sucre
Egypt	Egyptian pound
El Salvador	El Salvador cólon
Equatorial Guinea	bipkwele
Eritrea	birr
Estonia	kroon
Ethiopia	birr
Faeroe Islands	Danish krone
Fiji	Fiji dollar
Finland	markka
France	franc
French Guiana	French franc
Gabon	CFA franc
Gambia	dalasi
Germany	deutschmark
Ghana	cedi
Greece	drachma
Greenland	Danish krone
Grenada	East Caribbean dol~lar
Guadeloupe	franc
Guam	U.S. dollar
Guatemala	quetzal
Guinea	Guinea franc
Guinea-Bissau	peso
Guyana	Guyana dollar
Haiti	gourde
Honduras	lempira
Hong Kong	Hong Kong dollar
Hungary	forint
Iceland	krona
India	rupee
Indonesia	rupiah
Iran	rial
Iraq	dinar
Israel	shekel
Italy	lira
Jamaica	Jamaican dollar
Japan	yen
Jordan	Jordanian dinar
Kazakhstan	rouble
Kenya	Kenyan shilling
Kirghizia	rouble
Kiribati	Australian dollar
Kuwait	Kuwaiti dinar
Laos	new kip
Latvia	lats
Lebanon	Lebanese pound
Lesotho	maloti
Liberia	Liberian dollar
Libya	Libyan dinar
Liechtenstein	Swiss franc
Lithuania	lita
Luxembourg	Luxembourg franc
Macao	pataca
Macedonia	denar
Madagascar	Malagasy franc
Malawi	kwacha
Malaysia	ringgit
Mali	Mali franc
Malta	Maltese pound
Marshall Islands	U.S. dollar
Martinique	French franc
Mauritania	ouguija
Mauritius	Mauritius rupee
Mexico	Mexican peso
Micronesia	U.S. dollar
Moldavia	rouble
Monaco	Monégasque-franc *or* French franc
Mongolia	tugrik
Montserrat	East Caribbean dol~lar
Morocco	dirham
Mozambique	metical
Myanmar	kyat
Namibia	Namibian dollar
Nauru	Australian dollar
Nepal	Nepalese rupee
Netherlands	guilder
Netherlands Antilles	Netherlands Antilles guilder
New Zealand	New Zealand dollar
Nicaragua	córdoba
Niger	CFA franc
Nigeria	naira
North Korea	North Korean won
Norway	krone
Oman	rial Omani
Pakistan	Pakistani rupee
Panama	balboa
Papua New Guinea	kina
Paraguay	guarani
People's Republic of China	yuan
Peru	new sol
Philippines	Philippine peso
Poland	zloty
Portugal	escudo
Puerto Rico	U.S. dollar

Qatar	riyal
Republic of Ireland	punt
Republic of Maldives	rufiyaa
Réunion	French franc
Romania	leu
Russian Federation	rouble
Rwanda	Rwanda franc
San Marino	Italian lira
São Tomé and Principe	dobra
Saudi Arabia	riyal
Senegal	CFA franc
Serbia	dinar
Seychelles	Seychelles rupee
Sierra Leone	leone
Singapore	Singapore dollar
Slovakia	koruna
Slovenia	tolar
Solomon Islands	Solomon Islands dollar
Somalia	Somali shilling
South Africa	rand
South Korea	South Korean won
Spain	peseta
Sri Lanka	rupee
St. Kitts and Nevis	East Caribbean dollar
St. Lucia	East Caribbean dollar
St. Vincent and the Grenadines	East Caribbean dollar
Sudan	Sudanese pound
Surinam	Surinam guilder
Swaziland	lilangeni
Sweden	krona
Switzerland	Swiss franc
Syria	Syrian pound
Tadzhikistan	rouble
Taiwan	New Taiwan dollar
Tanzania	Tanzanian shilling
Thailand	baht
Togo	CFA franc
Tonga	pa'anga
Trinidad and Tobago	Trinidad and Tobago dollar
Tunisia	Tunisian dollar
Turkey	Turkish lira
Turkmenistan	rouble
Turks and Caicos Islands	U.S. dollar
Tuvalu	Australian dollar
Uganda	Ugandan shilling
Ukraine	hryvnia
United Arab Emirates	dirham
United Kingdom	pound sterling
Uruguay	new peso
U.S. Virgin Islands	U.S. dollar
United States of America	U.S. dollar
Uzbekistan	som
Vanuatu	Australian dollar *or* Vanuatu franc
Vatican City	Italian lira
Venezuela	bolívar
Vietnam	dong
Western Sahara	peseta
Western Samoa	tala
Yemen	Yemeni riyal
Zaire	zaire
Zambia	kwacha
Zimbabwe	Zimbabwe dollar

current *adjective* **1.** accepted, circulating, common, common knowledge, customary, general, going around, in circulation, in progress, in the air, in the news, ongoing, popular, present, prevailing, prevalent, rife, topical, widespread **2.** contemporary, fashionable, happening (*informal*), in, in fashion, in vogue, now (*informal*), present-day, sexy (*informal*), trendy (*Brit. informal*), up-to-date, up-to-the-minute *~noun* **3.** course, draught, flow, jet, progression, river, stream, tide, tideway, undertow **4.** atmosphere, drift, feeling, inclination, mood, tendency, trend, undercurrent, vibes (*slang*)

Antonyms (*sense 2*) archaic, obsolete, old-fashioned, outmoded, out-of-date, passé, past

curse *noun* **1.** blasphemy, expletive, oath, obscenity, swearing, swearword **2.** anathema, ban, denunciation, evil eye, excommunication, execration, hoodoo (*informal*), imprecation, jinx, malediction, malison (*archaic*) **3.** affliction, bane, burden, calamity, cross, disaster, evil, hardship, misfortune, ordeal, plague, scourge, torment, tribulation, trouble, vexation *~verb* **4.** be foul-mouthed, blaspheme, cuss (*informal*), swear, take the Lord's name in vain, turn the air blue (*informal*), use bad language **5.** accurse, anathematize, damn, excommunicate, execrate, fulminate, imprecate **6.** afflict, blight, burden, destroy, doom, plague, scourge, torment, trouble, vex

A plague o' both your houses
William Shakespeare *Romeo and Juliet*

[Cursing] is an operation which in literature, particularly in the drama, is commonly fatal to the victim. Nevertheless, the liability to a cursing is a risk that cuts but a small figure in fixing the rates of life insurance
Ambrose Bierce *The Devil's Dictionary*

Curses, like chickens, come home to roost

cursed **1.** accursed, bedevilled, blighted, cast out, confounded, damned, doomed, excommunicate, execrable, fey (*Scot.*), foredoomed, ill-fated, star-crossed, unholy, unsanctified, villainous **2.** abominable, damnable, detestable, devilish, fell (*archaic*), fiendish, hateful, infamous, infernal, loathsome, odious, pernicious, pestilential, vile

cursory brief, careless, casual, desultory, hasty, hurried, offhand, passing, perfunctory, rapid, slapdash, slight, summary, superficial

curt abrupt, blunt, brief, brusque, concise, gruff, monosyllabic, offhand, pithy, rude, sharp, short, snappish, succinct, summary, tart, terse, unceremonious, uncivil, ungracious

curtail abbreviate, abridge, contract, cut, cut back, cut short, decrease, diminish, dock, lessen, lop, pare down, reduce, retrench, shorten, trim, truncate

curtailment abbreviation, abridgment, contraction, cutback, cutting, cutting short, docking, retrenchment, truncation

curtain **1.** *noun* drape (*chiefly U.S.*), hanging **2.** *verb* conceal, drape, hide, screen, shroud, shut off, shutter, veil

curvaceous bosomy, buxom, comely, curvy, shapely, voluptuous, well-rounded, well-stacked (*Brit. slang*)

curvature arching, bend, curve, curving, curvity, deflection, flexure, incurvation

curve **1.** *verb* arc, arch, bend, bow, coil, hook, inflect, spiral, swerve, turn, twist, wind **2.** *noun* arc, bend, camber, curvature, half-moon, loop, trajectory, turn

curved arced, arched, bent, bowed, crooked, humped, rounded, serpentine, sinuous, sweeping, turned, twisted, twisty

cushion **1.** *noun* beanbag, bolster, hassock, headrest, pad, pillow, scatter cushion, squab **2.** *verb* bolster, buttress, cradle, dampen, deaden, muffle, pillow, protect, soften, stifle, support, suppress

cushy comfortable, easy, jammy (*Brit. slang*), soft, undemanding

custodian caretaker, curator, guardian, keeper, overseer, protector, superintendent, warden, warder, watchdog, watchman

custody **1.** aegis, auspices, care, charge, custodianship, guardianship, keeping, observation, preservation, protection, safekeeping, supervision, trusteeship, tutelage, ward, watch **2.** arrest, confinement, detention, durance (*archaic*), duress, imprisonment, incarceration

custom **1.** habit, habitude (*rare*), manner, mode, procedure, routine, way, wont **2.** convention, etiquette, fashion, form, formality, matter of course, observance, observation, policy, practice, praxis, ritual, rule, style, tradition, unwritten law, usage, use **3.** customers, patronage, trade

a custom
More honoured in the breach than the observance

William Shakespeare *Hamlet*

customarily as a rule, commonly, generally, habitually, in the ordinary way, normally, ordinarily, regularly, traditionally, usually

customary accepted, accustomed, acknowledged, bog-standard (*Brit. & Irish slang*), common, confirmed, conventional, established, everyday, familiar, fashionable, general, habitual, normal, ordinary, popular, regular, routine, traditional, usual, wonted
Antonyms exceptional, infrequent, irregular, occasional, rare, uncommon, unusual

customer buyer, client, consumer, habitué, patron, prospect, purchaser, regular (*informal*), shopper

customs duty, import charges, tariff, taxes, toll

cut *verb* **1.** chop, cleave, divide, gash, incise, lacerate, nick, notch, penetrate, pierce, score, sever, slash, slice, slit, wound **2.** carve, chip, chisel, chop, engrave, fashion, form, inscribe, saw, sculpt, sculpture, shape, whittle **3.** clip, dock, fell, gather, hack, harvest, hew, lop, mow, pare, prune, reap, saw down, shave, trim **4.** contract, cut back, decrease, diminish, downsize, ease up on, lower, rationalize, reduce, slash, slim (down) **5.** abbreviate, abridge, condense, curtail, delete, edit out, excise, precis, shorten **6.** *often with* **through, off,** *or* **across** bisect, carve, cleave, cross, dissect, divide, interrupt, intersect, part, segment, sever, slice, split, sunder **7.** avoid, cold-shoulder, freeze (someone) out (*informal*), grieve, hurt, ignore, insult, look straight through (someone), pain, put down, send to Coventry, slight, snub, spurn, sting, turn one's back on, wound ~*noun* **8.** gash, graze, groove, incision, laceration, nick, rent, rip, slash, slit, stroke, wound **9.** cutback, decrease, decrement, diminution, economy, fall, lowering, reduction, saving **10.** *informal* chop (*slang*), division, kickback (*chiefly U.S.*), percentage, piece, portion, rake-off (*slang*), section, share, slice **11.** configuration, fashion, form, look, mode, shape, style **12. a cut above** *informal* better than, higher than, more efficient (capable, competent, reliable, trustworthy, useful) than, superior to **13. cut and dried** *informal* automatic, fixed, organized, prearranged, predetermined, settled, sorted out (*informal*)
Antonyms (*sense 5*) add to, augment, enlarge, expand, extend, fill out, increase (*sense 7*) accept gladly, embrace, greet, hail, receive, welcome with open arms

cut along dash (off), fly, go, hurry (away), leave, press on

cutback cut, decrease, economy, lessening, reduction, retrenchment

cut back check, curb, decrease, downsize, draw *or* pull in one's horns (*informal*), economize, lessen, lower, prune, reduce, retrench, slash, trim

cut down 1. fell, hew, level, lop, raze 2. *sometimes with* **on** decrease, lessen, lower, reduce 3. blow away (*slang, chiefly U.S.*), dispatch, kill, massacre, mow down, slaughter, slay (*archaic*), take out (*slang*) 4. **cut (someone) down to size** abash, humiliate, make (someone) look small, take the wind out of (someone's) sails

cute appealing, attractive, charming, delightful, engaging, lovable, sweet, winning, winsome

cut in break in, butt in, interpose, interrupt, intervene, intrude, move in (*informal*)

cut off 1. disconnect, intercept, interrupt, intersect 2. bring to an end, discontinue, halt, obstruct, suspend 3. isolate, separate, sever 4. disinherit, disown, renounce

cut out 1. cease, delete, extract, give up, kick (*informal*), refrain from, remove, sever, stop 2. *informal* displace, eliminate, exclude, oust, supersede, supplant

cut out for adapted, adequate, competent, designed, eligible, equipped, fitted, qualified, suitable, suited

cut-price bargain, cheap, cheapo (*informal*), cut-rate (*chiefly U.S.*), reduced, sale

cutpurse footpad (*archaic*), mugger (*informal*), pickpocket, robber, thief

cut short abort, break off, bring to an end, check, halt, interrupt, leave unfinished, postpone, pull the plug on, stop, terminate

cutthroat *noun* 1. assassin, bravo, butcher, executioner, heavy (*slang*), hit man (*slang*), homicide, killer, liquidator, murderer, slayer (*archaic*), thug *~adjective* 2. barbarous, bloodthirsty, bloody, cruel, death-dealing, ferocious, homicidal, murderous, savage, thuggish, violent 3. competitive, dog-eat-dog, fierce, relentless, ruthless, unprincipled

cutting *adjective* 1. biting, bitter, chill, keen, numbing, penetrating, piercing, raw, sharp, stinging 2. acid, acrimonious, barbed, bitter, caustic, hurtful, malicious, mordacious, pointed, sarcastic, sardonic, scathing, severe, trenchant, vitriolic, wounding

Antonyms (*sense 1*) balmy, pleasant, soothing (*sense 2*) consoling, flattering, kind, mild

cut up *verb* 1. carve, chop, dice, divide, mince, slice 2. injure, knife, lacerate, slash, wound 3. *informal* blast, criticize, crucify (*slang*), give (someone *or* something) a rough ride, lambast(e), pan (*informal*), put down, ridicule, slate (*informal*), tear into (*informal*), vilify *~adjective* 4. *informal* agitated, dejected, desolated, distressed, disturbed, heartbroken, stricken, upset, wretched

cycle aeon, age, circle, era, period, phase, revolution, rotation, round (*of years*)

cyclone hurricane, tempest, tornado, twister (*U.S. informal*), typhoon, whirlwind

cynic doubter, misanthrope, misanthropist, pessimist, sceptic, scoffer

> *A cynic is a man who knows the price of everything and the value of nothing*
> Oscar Wilde *Lady Windemere's Fan*

> *The cynic is one who never sees a good quality in a man, and never fails to see a bad one*
> H.W. Beecher *Proverbs from Plymouth Pulpit*

> *cynic: a blackguard whose faulty vision sees things as they are, not as they ought to be*
> Ambrose Bierce *The Devil's Dictionary*

cynical contemptuous, derisive, distrustful, ironic, misanthropic, misanthropical, mocking, mordacious, pessimistic, sarcastic, sardonic, sceptical, scoffing, scornful, sneering, unbelieving

Antonyms credulous, green, gullible, hopeful, optimistic, trustful, trusting, unsceptical, unsuspecting

cynicism disbelief, doubt, misanthropy, pessimism, sarcasm, sardonicism, scepticism

> *Cynicism is intellectual dandyism without the coxcomb's feathers*
> George Meredith *The Egoist*

cynosure attraction, centre, centre of attention, focus, focus of attention, leading light (*informal*), point (of attraction), shining example

cyst bleb, blister, growth, sac, vesicle, wen

D

dab *verb* 1. blot, daub, pat, stipple, swab, tap, touch, wipe *~noun* 2. bit, dollop (*informal*), drop, fleck, pat, smidgen *or* smidgin (*informal, chiefly U.S. & Canad.*), smudge, speck, spot 3. flick, pat, peck, smudge, stroke, tap, touch

dabble 1. dip, guddle (*Scot.*), moisten, paddle, spatter, splash, sprinkle, wet 2. dally, dip into, play at, potter, tinker, trifle (with)

dabbler amateur, dilettante, potterer, tinkerer, trifler

dab hand ace (*informal*), adept, buff (*informal*), dabster (*dialect*), expert, hotshot (*informal*), maven (*U.S.*), past master, whiz (*informal*), wizard

daft 1. absurd, asinine, crackpot (*informal*), crazy, doolally (*slang*), dopey (*informal*), foolish, giddy, gonzo (*slang*), goofy (*informal*), idiotic, inane, loopy (*informal*), off one's head (*informal*), off one's trolley (*slang*), out to lunch (*informal*), scatty (*Brit. informal*), silly, simple, stupid, up the pole (*informal*), wacko *or* whacko (*slang*), witless 2. barking (*slang*), barking mad (*slang*), crackers (*Brit. slang*), crazy, demented, deranged, insane, lunatic, mental (*slang*), not right in the head, not the full shilling (*informal*), nuts (*slang*), nutty (*slang*), round the bend (*Brit. slang*), touched, unhinged 3. *with* **about** besotted by, crazy (*informal*), doting, dotty (*slang, chiefly Brit.*), infatuated by, mad, nuts (*slang*), nutty (*informal*), potty (*Brit. informal*), sweet on

daftness absurdity, asininity, brainlessness, craziness, dottiness (*slang, chiefly Brit.*), fatuity, fatuousness, folly, foolhardiness, foolishness, idiocy, inanity, insanity, lunacy, madness, nonsense, scattiness (*Brit. informal*), senselessness, silliness, stupidity, tomfoolery, witlessness
Antonyms common sense, intelligence, judgment, reason, sanity, sense, wisdom

dagger 1. bayonet, dirk, poniard, skean, stiletto 2. **at daggers drawn** at enmity, at loggerheads, at odds, at war, on bad terms, up in arms 3. **look daggers** frown, glare, glower, look black, lour *or* lower, scowl

> *Is this a dagger which I see before me*
> *The handle toward my hand?*
> William Shakespeare *Macbeth*

daily *adjective* 1. circadian, diurnal, everyday, quotidian 2. common, commonplace, day-to-day, everyday, ordinary, quotidian, regular, routine *~adverb* 3. constantly, day after day, day by day, every day, often, once a day, per diem, regularly

dainty *adjective* 1. charming, delicate, elegant, exquisite, fine, graceful, neat, petite, pretty 2. choice, delectable, delicious, palatable, savoury, tasty, tender, toothsome 3. choosy, fastidious, finical, finicky, fussy, mincing, nice, particular, picky (*informal*), refined, scrupulous *~noun* 4. *bonne bouche*, delicacy, fancy, sweetmeat, titbit
Antonyms awkward, clumsy, coarse, gauche, inelegant, maladroit, uncouth, ungainly

dais estrade, platform, podium, rostrum, stage

dale bottom, coomb, dell, dingle, glen, strath (*Scot.*), vale, valley

dalliance *noun* 1. dabbling, dawdling, delay, dilly-dallying (*informal*), frittering, frivolling (*informal*), idling, loafing, loitering, playing, pottering, procrastination, toying, trifling 2. *archaic* amorous play, coquetry, flirtation

dally 1. dawdle, delay, dilly-dally (*informal*), drag one's feet *or* heels, fool (about *or* around), fritter away, hang about, linger, loiter, procrastinate, tarry, waste time, while away 2. *often with* **with** caress, flirt, fondle, fool (about *or* around), frivol (*informal*), lead on, play, play fast and loose (*informal*), tamper, tease, toy, trifle
Antonyms hasten, hurry (up), make haste, push forward *or* on, run, step on it (*informal*)

dam 1. *noun* barrage, barrier, embankment, hindrance, obstruction, wall 2. *verb* barricade, block, block up, check, choke, confine, hold back, hold in, obstruct, restrict

damage *noun* 1. destruction, detriment, devastation, harm, hurt, impairment, injury, loss, mischief, mutilation, suffering 2. *informal* bill, charge, cost, expense, total 3. *plural* compensation, fine, indemnity, reimbursement, reparation, satisfaction *~verb* 4. deface, harm, hurt, impair, incapacitate, injure, mar, mutilate, play (merry) hell with (*informal*), ruin, spoil, tamper with, undo, weaken, wreck
Antonyms *noun* gain, improvement, reparation *~verb* better, fix, improve, mend, repair

damages compensation, fine, indemnity, reimbursement, reparation, satisfaction

damaging deleterious, detrimental, disadvantageous, harmful, hurtful, injurious, prejudicial, ruinous
Antonyms advantageous, favourable, healthful, helpful, profitable, salutary, useful, valuable, wholesome

dame baroness, dowager, *grande dame*, lady, matron (*archaic*), noblewoman, peeress

damn *verb* **1**. blast, castigate, censure, condemn, criticize, denounce, denunciate, excoriate, inveigh against, lambast(e), pan (*informal*), put down, slam (*slang*), slate (*informal*), tear into (*informal*) **2**. abuse, anathematize, blaspheme, curse, execrate, imprecate, revile, swear **3**. condemn, doom, sentence *~noun* **4**. brass farthing, hoot, iota, jot, tinker's curse *or* damn (*slang*), two hoots, whit **5**. **not give a damn** be indifferent, not care, not mind
Antonyms (*sense 1*) acclaim, admire, applaud, approve, cheer, compliment, congratulate, extol, honour, laud, praise, take one's hat off to (*sense 2*) adore, bless, exalt, glorify, magnify (*archaic*), pay homage to

damnable abominable, accursed, atrocious, culpable, cursed, despicable, detestable, execrable, hateful, horrible, offensive, wicked
Antonyms admirable, commendable, creditable, excellent, exemplary, fine, honourable, laudable, meritorious, praiseworthy, worthy

damnably abominably, accursedly, atrociously, despicably, detestably, disgracefully, execrably, hatefully, horribly, offensively, reprehensibly, wickedly
Antonyms admirably, commendably, creditably, excellently, honourably, laudably, worthily

damnation anathema, ban, condemnation, consigning to perdition, damning, denunciation, doom, excommunication, objurgation, proscription, sending to hell

> *For what shall it profit a man, if he shall gain the whole world, and lose his own soul?*
> Bible: St. Mark

damned **1**. accursed, anathematized, condemned, doomed, infernal, lost, reprobate, unhappy **2**. *slang* confounded, despicable, detestable, hateful, infamous, infernal, loathsome, revolting

damnedest best, hardest, utmost

damning accusatorial, condemnatory, damnatory, dooming, implicating, implicative, incriminating

damp *noun* **1**. clamminess, dampness, dankness, dew, drizzle, fog, humidity, mist, moisture, mugginess, vapour *~adjective* **2**. clammy, dank, dewy, dripping, drizzly, humid, misty, moist, muggy, sodden, soggy, sopping, vaporous, wet *~verb* **3**. dampen, moisten, wet **4**. *figurative* allay, check, chill, cool, curb, dash, deaden, deject, depress, diminish, discourage, dispirit, dull, inhibit, moderate, pour cold water on, restrain, stifle *~noun* **5**. *figurative* check, chill, cold water (*informal*), curb, damper, discouragement, gloom, restraint, wet blanket (*informal*)
Antonyms *noun* (*sense 1*) aridity, dryness *~adjective* arid, dry, watertight *~verb* (*sense 4*) encourage, hearten, inspire

dampen **1**. bedew, besprinkle, make damp, moisten, spray, wet **2**. *figurative* check, dash, deaden, depress, deter, dishearten, dismay, dull, lessen, moderate, muffle, reduce, restrain, smother, stifle

damper chill, cloud, cold water (*informal*), curb, discouragement, gloom, hindrance, killjoy, pall, restraint, wet blanket (*informal*)

dampness clamminess, damp, dankness, humidity, moistness, moisture, mugginess, sogginess, wetness
Antonyms aridity, aridness, dryness

dance **1**. *verb* bob up and down, caper, cut a rug (*informal*), frolic, gambol, hop, jig, prance, rock, skip, spin, sway, swing, trip, whirl **2**. *noun* ball, dancing party, disco, discotheque, hop (*informal*), knees-up (*Brit. informal*), social

Dances

allemande
apache dance
ballroom dance
barn dance
beguine
belly dance
black bottom
body popping
bogle
bolero
boogaloo
boogie
bossa nova
boston
bourrée
branle
brawl
break dance
breakdown
buck and wing
bump
bunny hug
butterfly
cachucha
cakewalk
calypso
cancan
carioca
carmagnole
carol
cha-cha-cha *or* cha-cha
chaconne
charleston
clog dance
conga
contredanse *or* contradance
Cossack dance
cotillion
country dance
courante
czardas
Dashing White Sergeant
ecossaise
eightsome reel
excuse-me
fan dance
fandango
farandole
flamenco
folk dance
formation dance
foxtrot
galliard
galop
gavotte
Gay Gordons
german

ghost dance
gigue
gopak
habanera
hay *or* hey
Highland fling
hoedown
hokey cokey
hora
hornpipe
hula *or* hula-hula
hustle
jig
jitterbug
jive
jota
juba
kazachok
kolo
lambada
Lambeth walk
lancers
ländler
limbo
malagueña
mambo
maxixe
mazurka
merengue
minuet
Morisco *or* Moresco
morris dance
mosh
musette
nautch
old-time dance
one-step
palais glide
paso doble
passacaglia
Paul Jones
pavane
pogo
poi dance
polka
polonaise
pyrrhic
quadrille
quickstep
redowa
reel
rigadoon *or* rigaudon
ring-shout
robot dancing *or* ro~botics
ronggeng
round
round dance
roundelay *or* roundel
rumba
salsa
saltarello
samba
saraband
saunter
schottische
seguidilla
shake
shimmy
shuffle
siciliano
Sir Roger de Coverley
skank
snake dance
snowball
square dance
step dance
stomp
strathspey
strip the willow
sword dance
tambourin
tango
tap dance
tarantella
toe dance
twist
two-step
Tyrolienne
Virginia reel
vogueing
volta
waltz
war dance
Zapata

General dance steps and terms

chassé
choreography
dosido
glide
grand chain
keep step
in step
out of step
pas
pas de basque
pas seul
phrase
pigeonwing
progressive
promenade
rhythm
routine
score
sequence
set
shuffle
slip step
steps
time

Ballet steps and terms

abstract *or* absolute ballet
adagio *or* adage
allegro
allongé
aplomb
arabesque
assemblé
attitude
balancé
ballerina
ballet blanc
ballet d'action
ballet de cour
ballon
ballonné
ballotté *or* pas ballotté
battement
batterie
battu
Benesh notation
brisé *or* pas de brisé
cabriole
Cecchetti method
changement *or* changement de pieds
chassé *or* pas de chassé
ciseaux *or* pas ciseaux
classical ballet
contretemps
cou-de-pied
coupé *or* pas coupé
croisé
croisé derrière
croisé devant
déboulé
decor
défilé de corps de bal~let
dégagé
demi-plié
demi-pointe
détournée
dévelopée *or* temps dévelopée
ecarté
échappé *or* pas échappé
emboîté
elevation
enchaînement
en couronne
en dedans
en dehors
en l'air
en pointe
en tire-bouchon
entrechat
entrée de ballet
failli
figurant
foudroyant
fouetté en tournant
gargouillade
glissade
grand écart
grande plié
jeté
ouvert
pas
pas de bourée
pas de bourée couru
pas de chat
pas de deux
pas de sissonne
passé
pirouette
plié
pointe
ports de bras
premier danseur *or* *(fem.)* première danseuse
prima bellerina
prima ballerina assoluta
raccourci
relevé
romantic ballet
rond de jambe
sickling
soubresaut
soutenu
Stepanov notation
sur place
temps de cuisse
temps de flèche
temps de poisson
temps levé
temps lié
terre à terre
toe-dance
tombé
tour en l'air
turn-out
variation
Von Laban notation

You should make a point of trying everything once,

excepting incest and folk-dancing
Arnold Bax *Farewell My Youth*

There are many kinds of dances, but all those requiring the participation of the two sexes have two characteristics in common; they are conspicuously innocent, and warmly loved by the vicious
Ambrose Bierce *The Devil's Dictionary*

Come, knit hands, and beat the ground,
In a light fantastic round
John Milton *Comus*

dandle amuse, caress, cradle, cuddle, dance, fondle, give a knee ride, pet, rock, toss, toy (with)

dandy **1.** *noun* beau, blade (*archaic*), blood (*rare*), buck (*archaic*), coxcomb, dude (*U.S. & Canad. informal*), exquisite (*obsolete*), fop, macaroni (*obsolete*), man about town, peacock, popinjay, swell (*informal*), toff (*Brit. slang*) **2.** *adjective, informal* capital, excellent, fine, first-rate, great, splendid

danger endangerment, hazard, insecurity, jeopardy, menace, peril, pitfall, precariousness, risk, threat, venture, vulnerability

danger, the spur of all great minds
George Chapman *The Revenge of Bussy D'Ambois*

dangerous alarming, breakneck, chancy (*informal*), exposed, hairy (*slang*), hazardous, insecure, menacing, nasty, parlous (*archaic*), perilous, precarious, risky, threatening, treacherous, ugly, unchancy (*Scot.*), unsafe, vulnerable
Antonyms harmless, innocuous, O.K. *or* okay (*informal*), out of danger, out of harm's way, protected, safe, safe and sound, secure

mad, bad, and dangerous to know
Caroline Lamb (of Byron)

dangerously **1.** alarmingly, carelessly, daringly, desperately, harmfully, hazardously, perilously, precariously, recklessly, riskily, unsafely, unsecurely **2.** critically, gravely, seriously, severely

dangle *verb* **1.** depend, flap, hang, hang down, sway, swing, trail **2.** brandish, entice, flaunt, flourish, lure, tantalize, tempt, wave

dangling disconnected, drooping, hanging, loose, swaying, swinging, trailing, unconnected

dank chilly, clammy, damp, dewy, dripping, moist, slimy, soggy

dapper active, brisk, chic, dainty, natty (*informal*), neat, nice, nimble, smart, soigné *or* soignée, spruce, spry, stylish, trig (*archaic or dialect*), trim, well-groomed, well turned out
Antonyms disarrayed, dishevelled, dowdy, frowzy, ill-groomed, rumpled, slobby (*informal*), sloppy (*informal*), slovenly, unkempt, untidy

dapple *verb* bespeckle, dot, fleck, freckle, mottle, speckle, spot, stipple

dappled brindled, checkered, flecked, freckled, mottled, piebald, pied, speckled, spotted, stippled, variegated

dare *verb* **1.** challenge, defy, goad, provoke, taunt, throw down the gauntlet **2.** adventure, brave, endanger, gamble, hazard, make bold, presume, risk, skate on thin ice, stake, venture *~noun* **3.** challenge, defiance, provocation, taunt

Who dares wins
Motto of the British SAS regiment

daredevil **1.** *noun* adventurer, desperado, exhibitionist, hot dog (*chiefly U.S.*), madcap, show-off (*informal*), stunt man **2.** *adjective* adventurous, audacious, bold, daring, death-defying, madcap, reckless

daredevilry adventure, adventurousness, boldness, daring, derring-do (*archaic*), fearlessness, foolhardiness, intrepidity, rashness, recklessness, temerity

daring **1.** *adjective* adventurous, audacious, ballsy (*taboo slang*), bold, brave, daredevil, fearless, game (*informal*), have-a-go (*informal*), impulsive, intrepid, plucky, rash, reckless, valiant, venturesome **2.** *noun* audacity, balls (*taboo slang*), ballsiness (*taboo slang*), boldness, bottle (*Brit. slang*), bravery, courage, derring-do (*archaic*), face (*informal*), fearlessness, grit, guts (*informal*), intrepidity, nerve (*informal*), pluck, rashness, spirit, spunk (*informal*), temerity
Antonyms *adjective* anxious, careful, cautious, cowardly, faint-hearted, fearful, timid, uncourageous, wary *~noun* anxiety, caution, cowardice, fear, timidity

dark *adjective* **1.** black, brunette, dark-skinned, dusky, ebony, sable, swarthy **2.** cloudy, darksome (*literary*), dim, dingy, indistinct, murky, overcast, pitch-black, pitchy, shadowy, shady, sunless, unlit **3.** abstruse, arcane, concealed, cryptic, deep, Delphic, enigmatic, hidden, mysterious, mystic, obscure, occult, puzzling, recondite, secret **4.** bleak, cheerless, dismal, doleful, drab, gloomy, grim, joyless, morbid, morose, mournful, sombre **5.** benighted, ignorant, uncultivated, unenlightened, unlettered **6.** atrocious, damnable, evil, foul, hellish, horrible, infamous, infernal, nefarious, satanic, sinful, sinister, vile, wicked **7.** angry, dour, forbidding, frowning, glowering, glum, ominous, scowling, sulky, sullen, threatening *~noun* **8.** darkness, dimness, dusk, gloom, murk, murkiness, obscurity, semi-darkness **9.** evening, night, nightfall, night-time, twilight **10.** *figurative* concealment, ignorance, secrecy
Antonyms (*sense 1*) blond, blonde, fair, fair-haired, flaxen-haired, light, light-complexioned, towheaded (*senses 2 & 4*)

bright, cheerful, clear, genial, glad, hopeful, pleasant, sunny

The darkest hour is just before the dawn

darken **1.** becloud, blacken, cloud up *or* over, deepen, dim, eclipse, make dark, make darker, make dim, obscure, overshadow, shade, shadow **2.** become angry, become gloomy, blacken, cast a pall over, cloud, deject, depress, dispirit, grow troubled, look black, sadden
Antonyms (*sense 1*) brighten, clear up, enliven, gleam, glow, illuminate, lighten, light up, make bright, shine (*sense 2*) become cheerful, cheer, encourage, gladden, hearten, make happy, perk up

darkling **1.** *adjective* black, dark, darksome (*literary*), dim, dusky, gloomy, pitchy, shadowy, tenebrous **2.** *adverb* at *or* by night, in the dark, in the dead of night, in the night

darkness **1.** blackness, dark, dimness, dusk, duskiness, gloom, murk, murkiness, nightfall, obscurity, shade, shadiness, shadows **2.** *figurative* blindness, concealment, ignorance, mystery, privacy, secrecy, unawareness

darling *noun* **1.** beloved, dear, dearest, love, sweetheart, truelove **2.** apple of one's eye, blue-eyed boy, fair-haired boy (*U.S.*), favourite, pet, spoilt child *~adjective* **3.** adored, beloved, cherished, dear, precious, treasured **4.** adorable, attractive, captivating, charming, cute, enchanting, lovely, sweet

darn **1.** *verb* cobble up, mend, patch, repair, sew up, stitch **2.** *noun* invisible repair, mend, patch, reinforcement

dart **1.** bound, dash, flash, flit, fly, race, run, rush, scoot, shoot, spring, sprint, start, tear, whistle, whiz **2.** cast, fling, hurl, launch, propel, send, shoot, sling, throw

dash *verb* **1.** break, crash, destroy, shatter, shiver, smash, splinter **2.** cast, fling, hurl, slam, sling, throw **3.** barrel (along) (*informal, chiefly U.S. & Canad.*), bolt, bound, burn rubber (*informal*), dart, fly, haste, hasten, hurry, race, run, rush, speed, spring, sprint, tear **4.** abash, chagrin, confound, dampen, disappoint, discomfort, discourage **5.** blight, foil, frustrate, ruin, spoil, thwart, undo *~noun* **6.** bolt, dart, haste, onset, race, run, rush, sortie, sprint, spurt **7.** brio, élan, flair, flourish, panache, spirit, style, verve, vigour, vivacity **8.** bit, drop, flavour, hint, little, pinch, smack, *soupçon*, sprinkling, suggestion, tinge, touch
Antonyms *verb* (*sense 2*) crawl, dawdle, walk (*sense 5*) enhance, improve *~noun* (*sense 8*) lot, much

dashing **1.** bold, daring, debonair, exuberant, gallant, lively, plucky, spirited, swashbuckling **2.** dapper, dazzling, elegant, flamboyant, jaunty, showy, smart, sporty, stylish, swish (*informal, chiefly Brit.*), urbane
Antonyms boring, dreary, dull, lacklustre, stolid, unexciting, uninteresting

dastard *noun* caitiff (*archaic*), coward, craven, niddering (*archaic*), poltroon, recreant (*archaic*), renegade, sneak, traitor, worm

dastardly *adjective* abject, base, caitiff (*archaic*), contemptible, cowardly, craven, despicable, faint-hearted, low, mean, niddering (*archaic*), recreant (*archaic*), sneaking, sneaky, spiritless, underhand, vile, weak-kneed (*informal*)

data details, documents, dope (*informal*), facts, figures, info (*informal*), information, input, materials, statistics

date *noun* **1.** age, epoch, era, period, stage, time **2.** appointment, assignation, engagement, meeting, rendezvous, tryst **3.** escort, friend, partner, steady (*informal*) **4. out of date** antiquated, archaic, dated, obsolete, old, old-fashioned, passé **5. to date** now, so far, up to now, up to the present, up to this point, yet **6. up-to-date** à la mode, contemporary, current, fashionable, modern, trendy (*Brit. informal*), up-to-the-minute *~verb* **7.** assign a date to, determine the date of, fix the period of, put a date on **8.** bear a date, belong to, come from, exist from, originate in **9.** become obsolete, be dated, obsolesce, show one's age

dated antiquated, archaic, *démodé*, obsolete, old-fashioned, old hat, out, outdated, outmoded, out of date, out of the ark (*informal*), passé, unfashionable, untrendy (*Brit. informal*)
Antonyms à la mode, all the rage, chic, cool (*informal*), current, hip (*slang*), in vogue, latest, modern, modish, popular, stylish, trendy (*Brit. informal*), up-to-date

daub *verb* **1.** coat, cover, paint, plaster, slap on (*informal*), smear **2.** bedaub, begrime, besmear, blur, deface, dirty, grime, smirch, smudge, spatter, splatter, stain, sully *~noun* **3.** blot, blotch, smear, smirch, splodge, splotch, spot, stain

daughter

A daughter is an embarrassing and ticklish possession

Menander *Perinthis*

Marry your son when you will; your daughter when you can

George Herbert *Jacula Prudentum*

daunt **1.** alarm, appal, cow, dismay, frighten, frighten off, intimidate, overawe, scare, subdue, terrify **2.** deter, discourage, dishearten, dispirit, put off, shake
Antonyms cheer, comfort, encourage, hearten, inspire, inspirit, reassure, spur, support

daunted *adjective* alarmed, cowed, demoralized, deterred, discouraged, disillusioned, dis~

mayed, dispirited, downcast, frightened, hesitant, intimidated, overcome, put off, unnerved

daunting alarming, awesome, demoralizing, disconcerting, discouraging, disheartening, frightening, intimidating, off-putting (*Brit. informal*), unnerving

Antonyms cheering, comforting, encouraging, heartening, reassuring

dauntless bold, brave, courageous, daring, doughty, fearless, gallant, gritty, heroic, indomitable, intrepid, lion-hearted, resolute, stouthearted, undaunted, unflinching, valiant, valorous

dawdle dally, delay, dilly-dally (*informal*), drag one's feet *or* heels, fritter away, hang about, idle, lag, loaf, loiter, potter, trail, waste time

Antonyms fly, get a move on (*informal*), hasten, hurry, lose no time, make haste, rush, scoot, step on it (*informal*)

dawdler laggard, lingerer, loiterer, slowcoach (*Brit. informal*), slowpoke (*U.S. & Canad. informal*), snail, tortoise

dawn *noun* **1.** aurora (*poetic*), cockcrow, crack of dawn, dawning, daybreak, daylight, dayspring (*poetic*), morning, sunrise, sunup *~verb* **2.** break, brighten, gleam, glimmer, grow light, lighten *~noun* **3.** advent, beginning, birth, dawning, emergence, genesis, inception, onset, origin, outset, rise, start, unfolding *~verb* **4.** appear, begin, develop, emerge, initiate, open, originate, rise, unfold **5.** come into one's head, come to mind, cross one's mind, flash across one's mind, hit, occur, register (*informal*), strike

Related adjective: auroral

rosy-fingered dawn

Homer *Iliad*

day **1.** daylight, daylight hours, daytime, twenty-four hours, working day **2.** age, ascendancy, cycle, epoch, era, generation, height, heyday, period, prime, time, zenith **3.** date, particular day, point in time, set time, time **4.** **call it a day** *informal* end, finish, knock off (*informal*), leave off, pack it in (*slang*), pack up (*informal*), shut up shop, stop **5.** **day after day** continually, monotonously, persistently, regularly, relentlessly **6.** **day by day** daily, gradually, progressively, steadily

Related adjective: diurnal

daybreak break of day, cockcrow, crack of dawn, dawn, dayspring (*poetic*), first light, morning, sunrise, sunup

daydream *noun* **1.** dream, imagining, musing, reverie, stargazing, vision, woolgathering **2.** castle in the air *or* in Spain, dream, fancy, fantasy, figment of the imagination, fond hope, pipe dream, wish *~verb* **3.** dream, envision, fancy, fantasize, hallucinate, imagine, muse, stargaze

daydreamer castle-builder, dreamer, fantast, pipe dreamer, visionary, Walter Mitty, wishful thinker, woolgatherer

daylight **1.** light of day, sunlight, sunshine **2.** broad day, daylight hours, daytime **3.** full view, light of day, openness, public attention

day-to-day accustomed, customary, everyday, habitual, quotidian, regular, routine, run-of-the-mill, usual, wonted

daze *verb* **1.** benumb, numb, paralyse, shock, stun, stupefy **2.** amaze, astonish, astound, befog, bewilder, blind, confuse, dazzle, dumbfound, flabbergast (*informal*), flummox, nonplus, perplex, stagger, startle, surprise *~noun* **3.** bewilderment, confusion, distraction, mind-fuck (*taboo slang*), shock, stupor, trance, trancelike state

dazed at sea, baffled, bemused, bewildered, confused, disorientated, dizzy, dopey (*slang*), flabbergasted (*informal*), flummoxed, fuddled, groggy (*informal*), light-headed, muddled, nonplussed, numbed, perplexed, punch-drunk, shocked, staggered, stunned, stupefied, woozy (*informal*)

dazzle *verb* **1.** bedazzle, blind, blur, confuse, daze **2.** amaze, astonish, awe, bowl over (*informal*), fascinate, hypnotize, impress, overawe, overpower, overwhelm, strike dumb, stupefy, take one's breath away *~noun* **3.** brilliance, éclat, flash, glitter, magnificence, razzle-dazzle (*slang*), razzmatazz (*slang*), sparkle, splendour

dazzling brilliant, divine, drop-dead (*slang*), glittering, glorious, radiant, ravishing, scintillating, sensational (*informal*), shining, sparkling, splendid, stunning, sublime, superb, virtuoso

Antonyms dull, ordinary, tedious, unexceptional, unexciting, uninspiring, uninteresting, unmemorable, unremarkable, vanilla (*slang*)

dead *adjective* **1.** deceased, defunct, departed, extinct, gone, inanimate, late, lifeless, passed away, perished, pushing up (the) daisies **2.** apathetic, callous, cold, dull, frigid, glassy, glazed, indifferent, inert, lukewarm, numb, paralysed, spiritless, torpid, unresponsive, wooden **3.** barren, inactive, inoperative, not working, obsolete, stagnant, sterile, still, unemployed, unprofitable, useless **4.** boring, dead-and-alive, dull, flat, ho-hum (*informal*), insipid, stale, tasteless, uninteresting, vapid **5.** *figurative* absolute, complete, downright, entire, outright, thorough, total, unqualified, utter **6.** *informal* dead beat (*informal*), exhausted, spent, tired, worn out *~noun* **7.** depth, middle, midst *~adverb* **8.** absolutely, completely, directly, entirely, exactly, totally

Antonyms *adjective* active, alive, alive and kicking, animate, animated, effective, existing, full of beans (*informal*), in use, lively, living, operative, productive, responsive, vivacious, working

Dead men tell no tales

Never speak ill of the dead

deadbeat bum (*informal*), cadger, drone, free~loader (*slang*), good-for-nothing, idler, lay~about, loafer, lounger, parasite, scrounger (*in~formal*), skiver (*Brit. slang*), sponge (*infor~mal*), sponger (*informal*), waster, wastrel

deaden abate, alleviate, anaesthetize, benumb, blunt, check, cushion, damp, dampen, dimin~ish, dull, hush, impair, lessen, muffle, mute, numb, paralyse, quieten, reduce, smother, sti~fle, suppress, weaken

deadline cutoff point, limit, target date, time limit

deadlock cessation, dead heat, draw, full stop, halt, impasse, stalemate, standoff, standstill, tie

deadly **1.** baleful, baneful, dangerous, death-dealing, deathly, destructive, fatal, lethal, malignant, mortal, noxious, pernicious, poi~sonous, venomous **2.** cruel, grim, implacable, mortal, ruthless, savage, unrelenting **3.** ashen, deathlike, deathly, ghastly, ghostly, pallid, wan, white **4.** accurate, effective, exact, on target, precise, sure, true, unerring, unfailing **5.** *informal* as dry as dust, boring, dull, ho-hum (*informal*), mind-numbing, monotonous, tedious, tiresome, uninteresting, wearisome

deadpan *adjective* blank, empty, expression~less, impassive, inexpressive, inscrutable, poker-faced, straight-faced

deaf *adjective* **1.** hard of hearing, stone deaf, without hearing **2.** indifferent, oblivious, un~concerned, unhearing, unmoved

There's none so deaf as those that will not hear

deafen din, drown out, make deaf, split *or* burst the eardrums

deafening booming, dinning, ear-piercing, ear-splitting, intense, overpowering, piercing, resounding, ringing, thunderous

deal *verb* **1.** *with* **with** attend to, come to grips with, cope with, get to grips with, handle, manage, oversee, see to, take care of, treat **2.** *with* **with** concern, consider, treat (of) **3.** *with* **with** act, behave, conduct oneself **4.** bargain, buy and sell, do business, negotiate, sell, stock, trade, traffic, treat (with) *~noun* **5.** *in~formal* agreement, arrangement, bargain, contract, pact, transaction, understanding *~verb* **6.** allot, apportion, assign, bestow, dis~pense, distribute, divide, dole out, give, mete out, reward, share *~noun* **7.** amount, degree, distribution, extent, portion, quantity, share, transaction **8.** cut and shuffle, distribution, hand, round, single game

dealer chandler, marketer, merchandiser, mer~chant, purveyor, supplier, trader, tradesman, wholesaler

dealings business, business relations, com~merce, trade, traffic, transactions, truck

dear *adjective* **1.** beloved, cherished, close, dar~ling, esteemed, familiar, favourite, intimate, precious, prized, respected, treasured **2.** at a premium, costly, expensive, high-priced, over~priced, pricey (*informal*) *~noun* **3.** angel, be~loved, darling, loved one, precious, treasure *~adverb* **4.** at a heavy cost, at a high price, at great cost, dearly

Antonyms cheap, common, disliked, hated, inexpensive, worthless

dearly **1.** extremely, greatly, profoundly, very much **2.** affectionately, devotedly, fondly, lov~ingly, tenderly **3.** at a heavy cost, at a high price, at great cost, dear

dearth absence, deficiency, exiguousness, fam~ine, inadequacy, insufficiency, lack, need, paucity, poverty, scantiness, scarcity, short~age, sparsity, want

death **1.** bereavement, cessation, curtains (*in~formal*), decease, demise, departure, dissolu~tion, dying, end, exit, expiration, loss, passing, quietus, release **2.** annihilation, destruction, downfall, eradication, extermination, extinc~tion, finish, grave, obliteration, ruin, ruina~tion, undoing **3.** *sometimes capital* Dark An~gel, grim reaper

Antonyms beginning, birth, emergence, gen~esis, growth, origin, rise, source

I am not so much afraid of death, as ashamed thereof; 'tis the very disgrace and ignominy of our natures

Sir Thomas Browne *Religio Medici*

Any man's death diminishes me, because I am in~volved in Mankind; And therefore never send to know for whom the bell tolls; it tolls for thee

John Donne *LXXX Sermons*

Death hath so many doors to let out life

John Fletcher *The Custom of the Country*

I could not look on Death, which being known,
Men led me to him, blindfold and alone

Rudyard Kipling *Epitaphs of the War*

One dies only once, and it's for such a long time

Molière *Le Dépit Amoureux*

I want death to find me planting my cabbages, but caring little for it, and even less for the imperfec~tions of my garden

Montaigne *Essais*

Anyone can stop a man's life, but no one his death; a thousand doors open on to it

Seneca *Phoenissae*

After the first death, there is no other

Dylan Thomas *A refusal to mourn the death, by fire, of a child in London*

Revenge triumphs over death; love slights it; hon~

our aspireth to it; grief flieth to it
Francis Bacon *Essays*

Fear death? - to feel the fog in my throat,
The mist in my face
Robert Browning *Prospice*

Death never takes the wise man by surprise; he is always ready to go
Jean de la Fontaine *Fables*

If there wasn't death, I think you couldn't go on
Stevie Smith *The Observer*

My name is Death: the last best friend am I
Robert Southey *The Curse of Kehama*

O death, where is thy sting?
Bible: I Corinthians

It is good to die before one has done anything de~serving death
Anaxandrides *fragment*

Fear of death is worse than death itself
William Shakespeare *King Lear*

I have been half in love with easeful death
John Keats *Ode to a Nightingale*

How wonderful is death,
Death and his brother sleep!
Percy Bysshe Shelley *Queen Mab*

Though I walk through the valley of the shadow of death, I will fear no evil
Bible: Psalm 23

Death be not proud, though some have called thee
Mighty and dreadful, for thou art not so
John Donne *Holy Sonnets*

Death hath ten thousand doors
For men to take their exits
John Webster *The Duchess of Malfi*

We all labour against our own cure, for death is the cure of all diseases
Thomas Browne

Death is nothing at all. I have only slipped away into the next room. I am I and you are you. Whatever we were to each other, that we are still...What is death but a negligible acci~dent? Why should I be out of mind because I am out of sight? I am waiting for you. for an interval, somewhere very near, just around the corner. All is well
Henry Scott Holland

Death is nature's way of telling you to slow down
Anon.

Men fear death as children fear to go in the dark; and as that natural fear in children is in~creased with tales, so is the other
Francis Bacon *Essays*

Death and taxes and childbirth! There's never any convenient time for any of them
Margaret Mitchell *Gone with the Wind*

There is no cure for birth and death save to enjoy the interval
George Santayana *Soliloquies in England*

In this world nothing can be said to be certain, except death and taxes
Benjamin Franklin

Death is the great leveller

deathblow clincher (*informal*), *coup de grâce*, finishing stroke, kill, knockout blow *or* punch, lethal *or* mortal blow, quietus

deathless eternal, everlasting, immortal, im~perishable, incorruptible, timeless, undying
Antonyms corporeal, earthly, ephemeral, hu~man, mortal, passing, temporal, transient, transitory

deathly **1.** cadaverous, deathlike, gaunt, ghast~ly, grim, haggard, like death warmed up (*in~formal*), pale, pallid, wan **2.** deadly, extreme, fatal, intense, mortal, terrible

debacle catastrophe, collapse, defeat, devasta~tion, disaster, downfall, fiasco, havoc, over~throw, reversal, rout, ruin, ruination

debar bar, black, blackball, deny, exclude, hin~der, interdict, keep out, obstruct, preclude, prevent, prohibit, refuse admission to, re~strain, segregate, shut out, stop

debase **1.** abase, cheapen, degrade, demean, devalue, disgrace, dishonour, drag down, humble, humiliate, lower, reduce, shame **2.** adulterate, bastardize, contaminate, corrupt, defile, depreciate, impair, pollute, taint, viti~ate
Antonyms elevate, enhance, exalt, improve, purify, uplift

debased **1.** adulterated, depreciated, devalued, impure, lowered, mixed, polluted, reduced **2.** abandoned, base, corrupt, debauched, degrad~ed, depraved, fallen, low, perverted, sordid, vile
Antonyms chaste, decent, ethical, good, hon~ourable, incorruptible, innocent, moral, pure, upright, virtuous

debasement **1.** adulteration, contamination, depreciation, devaluation, pollution, reduction **2.** abasement, baseness, corruption, degrada~tion, depravation, perversion

debatable arguable, borderline, controversial, disputable, doubtful, dubious, iffy (*informal*), in dispute, moot, open to question, problem~atical, questionable, uncertain, undecided, unsettled

debate **1.** *verb* argue, contend, contest, contro~vert, discuss, dispute, question, wrangle **2.** *noun* altercation, argument, contention, con~troversy, discussion, disputation, dispute, po~lemic, row **3.** *verb* cogitate, consider, deliber~ate, meditate upon, mull over, ponder, reflect, revolve, ruminate, weigh **4.** *noun* cogitation, consideration, deliberation, meditation, reflec~tion

debauch *verb* **1.** corrupt, demoralize, deprave, lead astray, pervert, pollute, seduce, subvert, vitiate **2.** deflower, ravish, ruin, seduce, violate *~noun* **3.** bacchanalia, bender (*informal*), binge (*informal*), bout, carousal, carouse, fling, orgy, saturnalia, spree

debauched *adjective* abandoned, corrupt, debased, degenerate, degraded, depraved, dissipated, dissolute, immoral, licentious, perverted, pervy (*slang*), profligate, sleazy, wanton

debauchee libertine, Lothario, playboy, profligate, rake, roué, sensualist, wanton

debauchery carousal, depravity, dissipation, dissoluteness, excess, gluttony, incontinence, indulgence, intemperance, lewdness, licentiousness, lust, orgy, overindulgence, revel

debilitate devitalize, enervate, enfeeble, exhaust, incapacitate, prostrate, relax, sap, undermine, weaken, wear out
Antonyms animate, brighten, energize, enliven, excite, fire, invigorate, pep up, perk up, rouse, stimulate, vitalize, wake up

debilitating devitalizing, draining, enervating, enfeebling, exhausting, fatiguing, incapacitating, sapping, tiring, weakening, wearing, wearisome
Antonyms animating, energizing, enlivening, exciting, invigorating, rousing, stimulating, vitalizing

debility decrepitude, enervation, enfeeblement, exhaustion, faintness, feebleness, frailty, incapacity, infirmity, languor, malaise, sickliness, weakness

debonair affable, buoyant, charming, cheerful, courteous, dashing, elegant, jaunty, light-hearted, refined, smooth, sprightly, suave, urbane, well-bred

debouch come forth, come out, come out in the open, disembogue, emerge, issue, sally, sortie

debrief **1.** cross-examine, examine, interrogate, probe, question, quiz **2.** describe, detail, report

debris bits, brash, detritus, dross, fragments, litter, pieces, remains, rubbish, rubble, ruins, waste, wreck, wreckage

debt **1.** arrears, bill, claim, commitment, debit, due, duty, liability, obligation, score **2. in debt** accountable, beholden, in arrears, in hock (*informal, chiefly U.S.*), in the red (*informal*), liable, owing, responsible

In the midst of life we are in debt
Ethel Watts Mumford et al. *Altogether New Cynic's Calendar*

debtor borrower, defaulter, insolvent, mortgagor

debunk cut down to size, deflate, disparage, expose, lampoon, mock, puncture, ridicule, show up

debut beginning, bow, coming out, entrance, first appearance, inauguration, initiation, introduction, launching, presentation

decadence corruption, debasement, decay, decline, degeneration, deterioration, dissipation, dissolution, fall, perversion, retrogression

decadent corrupt, debased, debauched, decaying, declining, degenerate, degraded, depraved, dissolute, immoral, self-indulgent
Antonyms decent, ethical, good, high-minded, honourable, incorruptible, moral, principled, proper, upright, upstanding, virtuous

decamp **1.** abscond, bolt, desert, do a bunk (*Brit. slang*), do a runner (*slang*), escape, flee, flit (*informal*), fly, fly the coop (*U.S. & Canad. informal*), hightail (*informal, chiefly U.S.*), hook it (*slang*), make off, run away, scarper (*Brit. slang*), skedaddle (*informal*), sneak off, steal away, take a powder (*U.S. & Canad. slang*), take it on the lam (*U.S. & Canad. slang*) **2.** break up camp, evacuate, march off, move off, strike camp, vacate

decant drain, draw off, pour out, tap

decapitate behead, execute, guillotine

decay *verb* **1.** atrophy, break down, crumble, decline, degenerate, deteriorate, disintegrate, dissolve, dwindle, moulder, shrivel, sink, spoil, wane, waste away, wear away, wither **2.** corrode, decompose, mortify, perish, putrefy, rot *~noun* **3.** atrophy, collapse, decadence, decline, degeneracy, degeneration, deterioration, dying, fading, failing, wasting, withering **4.** caries, cariosity, decomposition, gangrene, mortification, perishing, putrefaction, putrescence, putridity, rot, rotting
Antonyms *verb* expand, flourish, flower, grow, increase *~noun* growth

decayed bad, carious, carrion, corroded, decomposed, perished, putrefied, putrid, rank, rotten, spoiled, wasted, withered

decaying crumbling, deteriorating, disintegrating, gangrenous, perishing, putrefacient, rotting, wasting away, wearing away

decease **1.** *noun* death, demise, departure, dissolution, dying, release **2.** *verb* buy it (*U.S. slang*), cease, check out (*U.S. slang*), croak (*slang*), die, expire, go belly-up (*slang*), kick it (*slang*), kick the bucket (*slang*), pass away *or* on *or* over, peg it (*informal*), peg out (*informal*), perish, pop one's clogs (*informal*)

deceased *adjective* dead, defunct, departed, expired, finished, former, gone, late, lifeless, lost, pushing up daisies

deceit **1.** artifice, cheating, chicanery, craftiness, cunning, deceitfulness, deception, dissimulation, double-dealing, duplicity, fraud, fraudulence, guile, hypocrisy, imposition, pretence, slyness, treachery, trickery, underhandedness **2.** artifice, blind, cheat, chicanery, deception, duplicity, fake, feint, fraud, imposture, misrepresentation, pretence, ruse, scam (*slang*), sham, shift, sting (*informal*), strata-

gem, subterfuge, swindle, trick, wile
Antonyms candour, frankness, honesty, openness, sincerity, truthfulness

deceitful counterfeit, crafty, deceiving, deceptive, designing, dishonest, disingenuous, double-dealing, duplicitous, fallacious, false, fraudulent, guileful, hypocritical, illusory, insincere, knavish (*archaic*), sneaky, treacherous, tricky, two-faced, underhand, untrustworthy

deceive **1.** bamboozle (*informal*), beguile, betray, cheat, con (*informal*), cozen, delude, disappoint, double-cross (*informal*), dupe, ensnare, entrap, fool, hoax, hoodwink, impose upon, kid (*informal*), lead (someone) on (*informal*), mislead, outwit, pull a fast one (*slang*), pull the wool over (someone's) eyes, stiff (*slang*), sting (*informal*), swindle, take for a ride (*informal*), take in (*informal*), trick **2.** **be deceived by** be made a fool of, be taken in (by), be the dupe of, bite, fall for, fall into a trap, swallow (*informal*), swallow hook, line, and sinker (*informal*), take the bait

deceiver betrayer, charlatan, cheat, chiseller (*informal*), con man (*informal*), cozener, crook (*informal*), deluder, dissembler, double-dealer, fake, fraud, fraudster, grifter (*slang, chiefly U.S. & Canad.*), hypocrite, impostor, inveigler, mountebank, pretender, sharper, snake in the grass, swindler, trickster

men were deceivers ever
William Shakespeare *Much Ado About Nothing*

decelerate brake, check, put the brakes on, reduce speed, slow, slow down *or* up
Antonyms accelerate, pick up speed, quicken, speed up

decency appropriateness, civility, correctness, courtesy, decorum, etiquette, fitness, good form, good manners, modesty, propriety, respectability, seemliness

decent **1.** appropriate, becoming, befitting, chaste, comely, *comme il faut*, decorous, delicate, fit, fitting, modest, nice, polite, presentable, proper, pure, respectable, seemly, suitable **2.** acceptable, adequate, ample, average, competent, fair, passable, reasonable, satisfactory, sufficient, tolerable **3.** accommodating, courteous, friendly, generous, gracious, helpful, kind, obliging, thoughtful
Antonyms awkward, clumsy, discourteous, immodest, improper, inadequate, incorrect, indecent, inept, unsatisfactory, unseemly, unsuitable

deception **1.** craftiness, cunning, deceit, deceitfulness, deceptiveness, dissimulation, duplicity, fraud, fraudulence, guile, hypocrisy, imposition, insincerity, legerdemain, treachery, trickery **2.** artifice, bluff, canard, cheat, decoy, feint, fraud, hoax, hokum (*slang, chiefly U.S. & Canad.*), illusion, imposture, leg-pull (*Brit. informal*), lie, pork pie (*Brit. slang*), porky (*Brit. slang*), ruse, sham, snare, snow job (*slang, chiefly U.S. & Canad.*), stratagem, subterfuge, trick, wile
Antonyms artlessness, candour, fidelity, frankness, honesty, openness, scrupulousness, straightforwardness, trustworthiness, truthfulness

Deceive boys with toys, but men with oaths
Lysander

O what a tangled web we weave,
When first we practise to deceive!
Walter Scott *Marmion*

you can fool some of the people all of the time, and all of the people some of the time, but you cannot fool all of the people all of the time
ascribed to Abraham Lincoln

One may smile, and smile, and be a villain
William Shakespeare *Hamlet*

deceptive ambiguous, deceitful, delusive, dishonest, fake, fallacious, false, fraudulent, illusory, misleading, mock, specious, spurious, unreliable

decide adjudge, adjudicate, choose, come to a conclusion, commit oneself, conclude, decree, determine, elect, end, make a decision, make up one's mind, purpose, reach *or* come to a decision, resolve, settle, tip the balance
Antonyms be indecisive, be unable to decide, blow hot and cold (*informal*), dither (*chiefly Brit.*), falter, fluctuate, hesitate, hum and haw, seesaw, shillyshally (*informal*), swither (*Scot.*), vacillate

decided **1.** absolute, categorical, certain, clear-cut, definite, distinct, express, indisputable, positive, pronounced, unambiguous, undeniable, undisputed, unequivocal, unquestionable **2.** assertive, decisive, deliberate, determined, emphatic, firm, resolute, strong-willed, unfaltering, unhesitating
Antonyms doubtful, dubious, hesitant, indecisive, irresolute, questionable, undetermined, weak

decidedly absolutely, certainly, clearly, decisively, distinctly, downright, positively, unequivocally, unmistakably

deciding chief, conclusive, critical, crucial, decisive, determining, influential, prime, principal, significant

decipher construe, crack, decode, deduce, explain, figure out (*informal*), interpret, make out, read, reveal, solve, suss (out) (*slang*), understand, unfold, unravel

decision **1.** arbitration, conclusion, finding, judgment, outcome, resolution, result, ruling, sentence, settlement, verdict **2.** decisiveness, determination, firmness, purpose, purposefulness, resoluteness, resolution, resolve, strength of mind *or* will

decisive 1. absolute, conclusive, critical, crucial, definite, definitive, fateful, final, influential, momentous, positive, significant 2. decided, determined, firm, forceful, incisive, resolute, strong-minded, trenchant
Antonyms doubtful, hesitant, hesitating, indecisive, in two minds (*informal*), irresolute, pussy-footing (*informal*), uncertain, undecided, vacillating

deck *verb* 1. adorn, apparel (*archaic*), array, attire, beautify, bedeck, bedight (*archaic*), bedizen (*archaic*), clothe, decorate, dress, embellish, engarland, festoon, garland, grace, ornament, trim 2. **deck up** *or* **out** doll up (*slang*), get ready, prettify, pretty up, prink, rig out, tog up *or* out, trick out

declaim 1. harangue, hold forth, lecture, orate, perorate, proclaim, rant, recite, speak, spiel (*informal*) 2. **declaim against** attack, decry, denounce, inveigh, rail

declamation address, harangue, lecture, oration, rant, recitation, speech, tirade

declamatory bombastic, discursive, grandiloquent, high-flown, incoherent, inflated, magniloquent, orotund, pompous, rhetorical, stagy, stilted, theatrical, turgid

declaration 1. acknowledgment, affirmation, assertion, attestation, averment, avowal, deposition, disclosure, protestation, revelation, statement, testimony 2. announcement, edict, manifesto, notification, proclamation, profession, promulgation, pronouncement, pronunciamento

declarative, declaratory affirmative, definite, demonstrative, enunciatory, explanatory, expository, expressive, positive

declare 1. affirm, announce, assert, asseverate, attest, aver, avow, certify, claim, confirm, maintain, proclaim, profess, pronounce, state, swear, testify, utter, validate 2. confess, convey, disclose, make known, manifest, reveal, show

declension 1. decadence, decay, decline, degeneracy, descent, deterioration, diminution, fall 2. inflection, variation

declination decline, declivity, descent, deviation, dip, divergence, inclination, obliquity, slope

decline *verb* 1. abstain, avoid, deny, forgo, refuse, reject, say 'no', send one's regrets, turn down 2. decrease, diminish, drop, dwindle, ebb, fade, fail, fall, fall off, flag, lessen, shrink, sink, wane *~noun* 3. abatement, diminution, downturn, drop, dwindling, falling off, lessening, recession, slump *~verb* 4. decay, degenerate, deteriorate, droop, languish, pine, weaken, worsen *~noun* 5. decay, decrepitude, degeneration, deterioration, enfeeblement, failing, senility, weakening, worsening 6. *archaic* consumption, phthisis, tuberculosis *~verb* 7. descend, dip, sink, slant, slope *~noun* 8. declivity, hill, incline, slope
Antonyms *verb* (*sense 1*) accept, agree, consent (*sense 2*) improve, increase, rise *~noun* (*sense 3*) improvement, rise, upswing

declivity brae (*Scot.*), declination, descent, incline, slant, slope

decode crack, decipher, decrypt, descramble, interpret, solve, unscramble, work out
Antonyms encipher, encode, encrypt, scramble

décolleté low-cut, low-necked, revealing

decompose 1. break up, crumble, decay, fall apart, fester, putrefy, rot, spoil 2. analyse, atomize, break down, break up, decompound, disintegrate, dissect, dissolve, distil, separate

decomposition atomization, breakdown, corruption, decay, disintegration, dissolution, division, putrefaction, putrescence, putridity, rot

decontaminate clean, cleanse, deodorize, disinfect, disinfest, fumigate, make safe, purify, sanitize, sterilize
Antonyms contaminate, infect, infest, poison, pollute

décor colour scheme, decoration, furnishing style, ornamentation

decorate 1. adorn, beautify, bedeck, deck, embellish, engarland, enrich, festoon, grace, ornament, trim 2. colour, do up (*informal*), furbish, paint, paper, renovate, wallpaper 3. cite, honour, pin a medal on

decoration 1. adornment, beautification, elaboration, embellishment, enrichment, garnishing, ornamentation, trimming 2. arabesque, bauble, cartouch(e), curlicue, falderal, festoon, flounce, flourish, frill, furbelow, garnish, ornament, scroll, spangle, trimmings, trinket 3. award, badge, colours, emblem, garter, medal, order, ribbon, star

decorative adorning, arty-crafty, beautifying, enhancing, fancy, nonfunctional, ornamental, pretty

decorous appropriate, becoming, befitting, comely, *comme il faut*, correct, decent, dignified, fit, fitting, mannerly, polite, proper, refined, sedate, seemly, staid, suitable, well-behaved
Antonyms inapposite, inappropriate, malapropos, out of keeping, unbefitting, undignified, unseemly

decorum behaviour, breeding, courtliness, decency, deportment, dignity, etiquette, gentility, good grace, good manners, gravity, politeness, politesse, propriety, protocol, punctilio, respectability, seemliness
Antonyms bad manners, churlishness, impoliteness, impropriety, indecorum, rudeness, unseemliness

decoy **1.** *noun* attraction, bait, ensnarement, enticement, inducement, lure, pretence, trap **2.** *verb* allure, bait, deceive, ensnare, entice, entrap, inveigle, lure, seduce, tempt

decrease **1.** *verb* abate, contract, curtail, cut down, decline, diminish, drop, dwindle, ease, fall off, lessen, lower, peter out, reduce, shrink, slacken, subside, wane **2.** *noun* abatement, contraction, cutback, decline, diminution, downturn, dwindling, ebb, falling off, lessening, loss, reduction, shrinkage, subsidence

Antonyms *verb* enlarge, expand, extend, increase *~noun* expansion, extension, growth

decreasingly at a declining rate, diminishingly, ever less, less and less, to a lesser *or* smaller extent

Antonyms ever more, increasingly, more and more, to a greater extent

decree **1.** *noun* act, canon, command, demand, dictum, edict, enactment, law, mandate, order, ordinance, precept, proclamation, regulation, ruling, statute **2.** *verb* command, decide, demand, determine, dictate, enact, establish, lay down, ordain, order, prescribe, proclaim, pronounce, rule

decrepit **1.** aged, crippled, debilitated, doddering, effete, feeble, frail, incapacitated, infirm, past it, superannuated, wasted, weak **2.** antiquated, battered, beat-up (*informal*), broken-down, deteriorated, dilapidated, ramshackle, rickety, run-down, tumble-down, weather-beaten, worn-out

decrepitude **1.** debility, dotage, eld (*archaic*), feebleness, incapacity, infirmity, invalidity, old age, senility, wasting, weakness **2.** decay, degeneration, deterioration, dilapidation

decry abuse, asperse, belittle, blame, blast, censure, condemn, criticize, cry down, denigrate, denounce, depreciate, derogate, detract, devalue, discredit, disparage, excoriate, lambast(e), put down, rail against, run down, tear into (*informal*), traduce, underestimate, underrate, undervalue

dedicate **1.** commit, devote, give over to, pledge, surrender **2.** address, assign, inscribe, offer **3.** bless, consecrate, hallow, sanctify, set apart

dedicated committed, devoted, enthusiastic, given over to, purposeful, single-minded, sworn, wholehearted, zealous

Antonyms indifferent, uncaring, uncommitted, unconcerned, uninterested, unresponsive

dedication **1.** adherence, allegiance, commitment, devotedness, devotion, faithfulness, loyalty, single-mindedness, wholeheartedness **2.** address, inscription, message **3.** consecration, hallowing, sanctification

Antonyms apathy, coolness, indifference, insensibility, torpor, unconcern, uninterestedness

deduce conclude, derive, draw, gather, glean, infer, put two and two together, read between the lines, reason, take to mean, understand

deducible derivable, inferable, to be inferred, traceable

deduct decrease by, knock off (*informal*), reduce by, remove, subtract, take away, take from, take off, take out, withdraw

Antonyms add, add to, enlarge

deduction **1.** assumption, conclusion, consequence, corollary, finding, inference, reasoning, result **2.** abatement, allowance, decrease, diminution, discount, reduction, subtraction, withdrawal

deed **1.** achievement, act, action, exploit, fact, feat, performance, reality, truth **2.** *Law* contract, document, indenture, instrument, title, title deed, transaction

deem account, believe, conceive, consider, esteem, estimate, hold, imagine, judge, reckon, regard, suppose, think

deep *adjective* **1.** abyssal, bottomless, broad, far, profound, unfathomable, wide, yawning **2.** abstract, abstruse, arcane, esoteric, hidden, mysterious, obscure, recondite, secret **3.** acute, discerning, learned, penetrating, sagacious, wise **4.** artful, astute, canny, cunning, designing, devious, insidious, knowing, scheming, shrewd **5.** extreme, grave, great, intense, profound, serious (*informal*), unqualified **6.** absorbed, engrossed, immersed, lost, preoccupied, rapt **7.** *of a colour* dark, intense, rich, strong, vivid **8.** *of a sound* bass, booming, full-toned, low, low-pitched, resonant, sonorous *~noun* **9.** *usually preceded by* **the** briny (*informal*), high seas, main, ocean, sea **10.** culmination, dead, middle, mid point *~adverb* **11.** deeply, far down, far into, late

Antonyms *adjective* (*sense 1*) shallow (*sense 2*) shallow (*sense 3*) simple (*sense 4*) shallow, simple (*sense 5*) shallow, superficial (*sense 7*) light, pale (*sense 8*) high, sharp

Still waters run deep

deepen **1.** dig out, dredge, excavate, hollow, scoop out, scrape out **2.** grow, increase, intensify, magnify, reinforce, strengthen

deeply **1.** completely, gravely, profoundly, seriously, severely, thoroughly, to the core, to the heart, to the quick **2.** acutely, affectingly, distressingly, feelingly, intensely, mournfully, movingly, passionately, sadly

deep-rooted *or* **deep-seated** confirmed, dyed-in-the-wool, entrenched, fixed, ineradicable, ingrained, inveterate, rooted, settled, subconscious, unconscious

Antonyms eradicable, exterior, external, on

the surface, peripheral, shallow, skin-deep, slight, superficial, surface

de-escalate check, contain, curb, damp down, decrease, defuse, diminish, lessen, limit, minimize, reduce, take the heat *or* sting out
Antonyms escalate, heighten, increase, intensify, magnify

deface blemish, deform, destroy, disfigure, impair, injure, mar, mutilate, obliterate, spoil, sully, tarnish, total (*slang*), trash (*slang*), vandalize

defacement blemish, damage, destruction, disfigurement, distortion, impairment, injury, mutilation, vandalism

de facto 1. *adverb* actually, in effect, in fact, in reality, really 2. *adjective* actual, existing, real

defalcation default, deficiency, deficit, embezzlement, fraud, misappropriation, shortage

defamation aspersion, calumny, character assassination, denigration, disparagement, libel, obloquy, opprobrium, scandal, slander, slur, smear, traducement, vilification

defamatory abusive, calumnious, contumelious, denigrating, derogatory, disparaging, injurious, insulting, libellous, slanderous, vilifying, vituperative

defame asperse, bad-mouth (*slang, chiefly U.S. & Canad.*), belie, besmirch, blacken, calumniate, cast a slur on, cast aspersions on, denigrate, detract, discredit, disgrace, dishonour, disparage, knock (*informal*), libel, malign, rubbish (*informal*), slag (off) (*slang*), slander, smear, speak evil of, stigmatize, traduce, vilify, vituperate

default 1. *noun* absence, defect, deficiency, dereliction, failure, fault, lack, lapse, neglect, nonpayment, omission, want 2. *verb* bilk, defraud, dodge, evade, fail, levant (*Brit.*), neglect, rat (*informal*), swindle, welsh (*slang*)

defaulter delinquent, embezzler, levanter (*Brit.*), nonpayer, offender, peculator, welsher (*slang*)

defeat *verb* 1. beat, blow out of the water (*slang*), clobber (*slang*), conquer, crush, lick (*informal*), make mincemeat of (*informal*), master, overpower, overthrow, overwhelm, pip at the post, quell, repulse, rout, run rings around (*informal*), stuff (*slang*), subdue, subjugate, tank (*slang*), undo, vanquish, wipe the floor with (*informal*) 2. baffle, balk, confound, disappoint, discomfit, foil, frustrate, get the better of, ruin, thwart ~*noun* 3. beating, conquest, debacle, overthrow, pasting (*slang*), repulse, rout, trouncing, vanquishment 4. disappointment, discomfiture, failure, frustration, rebuff, repulse, reverse, setback, thwarting
Antonyms *verb* bow, lose, submit, succumb, surrender, yield ~*noun* success, triumph, victory

How are the mighty fallen, and the weapons of war perished!
Bible: II Samuel

defeated balked, beaten, bested, checkmated, conquered, crushed, licked (*informal*), overcome, overpowered, overwhelmed, routed, thrashed, thwarted, trounced, vanquished, worsted
Antonyms conquering, dominant, glorious, successful, triumphal, triumphant, undefeated, victorious, winning

defeatist 1. *noun* pessimist, prophet of doom, quitter, submitter, yielder 2. *adjective* pessimistic

defecate crap (*taboo slang*), egest, empty, evacuate (*Physiology*), excrete, move, open the bowels, pass a motion, shit (*taboo slang*), void excrement

defecation egestion, elimination, emptying *or* opening of the bowels, evacuation (*Physiology*), excrement, excretion, motion, movement, voiding excrement

defect *noun* 1. blemish, blotch, error, failing, fault, flaw, foible, imperfection, mistake, spot, taint, want 2. absence, default, deficiency, frailty, inadequacy, lack, shortcoming, weakness ~*verb* 3. abandon, apostatize, break faith, change sides, desert, go over, rebel, revolt, tergiversate, walk out on (*informal*)

defection abandonment, apostasy, backsliding, dereliction, desertion, rebellion, revolt

defective 1. broken, deficient, faulty, flawed, imperfect, inadequate, incomplete, insufficient, not working, on the blink (*slang*), out of order, scant, short 2. abnormal, mentally deficient, retarded, subnormal
Antonyms adequate, intact, normal, perfect, whole, working

defector apostate, deserter, rat (*informal*), recreant (*archaic*), renegade, runagate (*archaic*), tergiversator, turncoat

defence 1. armament, cover, deterrence, guard, immunity, protection, resistance, safeguard, security, shelter 2. barricade, bastion, buckler, bulwark, buttress, fastness, fortification, rampart, shield 3. apologia, apology, argument, excuse, exoneration, explanation, extenuation, justification, plea, vindication 4. *Law* alibi, case, declaration, denial, plea, pleading, rebuttal, testimony

defenceless endangered, exposed, helpless, naked, powerless, unarmed, unguarded, unprotected, vulnerable, wide open
Antonyms free from harm, guarded, out of harm's way, protected, safe, safe and sound, secure

defend 1. cover, fortify, guard, keep safe, preserve, protect, safeguard, screen, secure, shelter, shield, ward off, watch over 2. assert, champion, endorse, espouse, justify, maintain, plead, speak up for, stand by, stand up for, stick up for (*informal*), support, sustain, uphold, vindicate

defendant appellant, defence, litigant, offender, prisoner at the bar, respondent, the accused

defender **1.** bodyguard, escort, guard, protector **2.** advocate, champion, patron, sponsor, supporter, vindicator

defensible **1.** holdable, impregnable, safe, secure, unassailable **2.** justifiable, pardonable, permissible, plausible, tenable, valid, vindicable
Antonyms faulty, inexcusable, insupportable, unforgivable, unjustifiable, unpardonable, untenable, wrong

defensive averting, defending, on the defensive, opposing, protective, safeguarding, uptight (*informal*), watchful, withstanding

defensively at bay, in defence, in self-defence, on guard, on the defensive, suspiciously

defer[1] *verb* adjourn, delay, hold over, postpone, procrastinate, prorogue, protract, put off, put on ice, put on the back burner (*informal*), set aside, shelve, suspend, table, take a rain check on (*U.S. & Canad. informal*)

defer[2] *verb* accede, bow, capitulate, comply, give in, give way to, respect, submit, yield

deference **1.** acquiescence, capitulation, complaisance, compliance, obedience, obeisance, submission, yielding **2.** attention, civility, consideration, courtesy, esteem, homage, honour, obeisance, politeness, regard, respect, reverence, thoughtfulness, veneration
Antonyms (*sense 1*) disobedience, insubordination, noncompliance, nonobservance, revolt (*sense 2*) contempt, discourtesy, dishonour, disregard, disrespect, impertinence, impoliteness, impudence, incivility, insolence, irreverence, lack of respect, rudeness

deferential civil, complaisant, considerate, courteous, dutiful, ingratiating, obedient, obeisant, obsequious, polite, regardful, respectful, reverential, submissive

deferment, deferral adjournment, delay, moratorium, postponement, putting off, stay, suspension

defiance challenge, confrontation, contempt, contumacy, disobedience, disregard, insolence, insubordination, opposition, provocation, rebelliousness, recalcitrance, spite
Antonyms accordance, acquiescence, compliance, deference, obedience, observance, regard, respect, subservience

defiant aggressive, audacious, bold, challenging, contumacious, daring, disobedient, insolent, insubordinate, mutinous, provocative, rebellious, recalcitrant, refractory, truculent
Antonyms cowardly, meek, obedient, respectful, submissive

deficiency **1.** defect, demerit, failing, fault, flaw, frailty, imperfection, shortcoming, weakness **2.** absence, dearth, deficit, inadequacy, insufficiency, lack, scantiness, scarcity, shortage
Antonyms (*sense 2*) abundance, adequacy, sufficiency, superfluity, surfeit

deficient **1.** defective, faulty, flawed, impaired, imperfect, incomplete, inferior, unsatisfactory, weak **2.** exiguous, inadequate, insufficient, lacking, meagre, pathetic, scant, scanty, scarce, short, skimpy, wanting

deficit arrears, default, deficiency, loss, shortage, shortfall

defile[1] *verb* **1.** befoul, contaminate, corrupt, dirty, make foul, pollute, smear, smirch, soil, taint, tarnish, vitiate **2.** besmirch, debase, degrade, disgrace, dishonour, smirch, stain, sully **3.** desecrate, profane, treat sacrilegiously **4.** abuse, deflower, molest, rape, ravish, seduce, violate

defile[2] *noun* gorge, gully, pass, passage, ravine, way through

defiled besmirched, desecrated, dishonoured, impure, polluted, profaned, ravished, spoilt, tainted, unclean
Antonyms chaste, clean, immaculate, innocent, spotless, uncontaminated, uncorrupted, undefiled, unstained, unsullied, untainted

defilement contamination, corruption, debasement, degradation, depravity, desecration, disgrace, pollution, sullying, violation

definable apparent, definite, describable, determinable, explicable, perceptible, specific

define **1.** characterize, describe, designate, detail, determine, explain, expound, interpret, specify, spell out **2.** bound, circumscribe, delimit, delineate, demarcate, limit, mark out, outline

definite **1.** black-and-white, clear, clear-cut, clearly defined, cut-and-dried (*informal*), determined, exact, explicit, express, fixed, marked, obvious, particular, precise, specific **2.** assured, certain, decided, guaranteed, positive, settled, sure
Antonyms confused, fuzzy, general, hazy, ill-defined, imprecise, indefinite, indeterminate, indistinct, inexact, loose, obscure, uncertain, unclear, undetermined, vague

definitely absolutely, beyond any doubt, categorically, certainly, clearly, come hell or high water (*informal*), decidedly, easily, far and away, finally, indubitably, needless to say, obviously, plainly, positively, surely, undeniably, unequivocally, unmistakably, unquestionably, without doubt, without fail, without question

definition 1. clarification, description, elucidation, explanation, exposition, statement of meaning 2. delimitation, delineation, demarcation, determination, fixing, outlining, settling 3. clarity, contrast, distinctness, focus, precision, sharpness

definitive absolute, authoritative, complete, conclusive, decisive, exhaustive, final, mother (of all) (*informal*), perfect, reliable, ultimate

deflate 1. collapse, contract, empty, exhaust, flatten, puncture, shrink, void 2. chasten, dash, debunk (*informal*), disconcert, dispirit, humble, humiliate, mortify, put down (*slang*), squash, take the wind out of (someone's) sails 3. *Economics* decrease, depreciate, depress, devalue, diminish, reduce
Antonyms aerate, amplify, balloon, bloat, blow up, boost, dilate, distend, enlarge, exaggerate, expand, increase, inflate, puff up *or* out, pump up, swell

deflect bend, deviate, diverge, glance off, ricochet, shy, sidetrack, slew, swerve, turn, turn aside, twist, veer, wind

deflection aberration, bend, declination, deviation, divergence, drift, refraction, swerve, veer

deflower 1. assault, force, molest, rape, ravish, ruin, seduce, violate 2. defile, desecrate, despoil, harm, mar, spoil, violate

deform 1. buckle, contort, distort, gnarl, malform, mangle, misshape, twist, warp 2. cripple, deface, disfigure, injure, maim, mar, mutilate, ruin, spoil

deformation contortion, disfiguration, distortion, malformation, misshapenness, warping

deformed 1. bent, blemished, crippled, crooked, disfigured, distorted, maimed, malformed, mangled, marred, misbegotten, misshapen 2. depraved, gross, offensive, perverted, twisted, warped

deformity 1. abnormality, defect, disfigurement, distortion, irregularity, malformation, misproportion, misshapenness, ugliness 2. corruption, depravity, grossness, hatefulness, vileness

defraud beguile, bilk, cheat, con (*informal*), cozen, delude, diddle (*informal*), do (*slang*), dupe, embezzle, fleece, gull (*archaic*), gyp (*slang*), outwit, pilfer, pull a fast one on (*informal*), rip off (*slang*), rob, rook (*slang*), skin (*slang*), stiff (*slang*), stitch up (*slang*), swindle, trick

defray clear, cover, discharge, foot the bill, liquidate, meet, pay, settle

defrayal, defrayment clearance, discharge, liquidation, payment, settlement

defrost de-ice, thaw, unfreeze
Antonyms freeze (up), frost, ice over *or* up

deft able, adept, adroit, agile, clever, dexterous, expert, handy, neat, nimble, proficient, skilful
Antonyms awkward, bumbling, cack-handed (*informal*), clumsy, gauche, inept, maladroit, unskilful

deftness ability, adeptness, adroitness, agility, cleverness, competence, coordination, dexterity, expertise, facility, finesse, neatness, nimbleness, proficiency, skill, touch
Antonyms awkwardness, cack-handedness (*informal*), clumsiness, ham-fistedness (*informal*), incompetence, ineptitude

defunct 1. dead, deceased, departed, extinct, gone 2. a dead letter, bygone, expired, inoperative, invalid, nonexistent, not functioning, obsolete, out of commission

defuse 1. deactivate, disable, disarm, make safe 2. calm, contain, cool, damp down, settle, smooth, stabilize, take the heat *or* sting out
Antonyms (*sense 1*) activate, arm (*sense 2*) aggravate, escalate, exacerbate, inflame, intensify, magnify, make worse, worsen

defy 1. beard, brave, challenge, confront, contemn, dare, despise, disregard, face, flout, hurl defiance at, provoke, scorn, slight, spurn 2. baffle, call (someone's) bluff, defeat, elude, foil, frustrate, repel, repulse, resist, thwart, withstand

degeneracy 1. corruption, decadence, degradation, depravity, dissoluteness, immorality, inferiority, meanness, poorness, turpitude 2. debasement, decay, decline, decrease, depravation, deterioration

degenerate 1. *adjective* base, corrupt, debased, debauched, decadent, degenerated, degraded, depraved, deteriorated, dissolute, fallen, immoral, low, mean, perverted, pervy (*slang*) 2. *verb* decay, decline, decrease, deteriorate, fall off, go to pot, lapse, regress, retrogress, rot, sink, slip, worsen

degeneration debasement, decline, degeneracy, descent, deterioration, dissipation, dissolution, regression

degradation 1. abasement, debasement, decadence, decline, degeneracy, degeneration, demotion, derogation, deterioration, downgrading, perversion 2. discredit, disgrace, dishonour, humiliation, ignominy, mortification, shame

degrade 1. cheapen, corrupt, debase, demean, deteriorate, discredit, disgrace, dishonour, humble, humiliate, impair, injure, pervert, shame, vitiate 2. break, cashier, demote, depose, downgrade, lower, reduce to inferior rank 3. adulterate, dilute, doctor, mix, thin, water, water down, weaken
Antonyms dignify, elevate, enhance, ennoble, honour, improve, promote, raise

degraded abandoned, base, corrupt, debased, debauched, decadent, depraved, despicable, disgraced, disreputable, dissolute, low, mean, profligate, sordid, vicious, vile

degrading cheapening, contemptible, debasing, demeaning, disgraceful, dishonourable, humiliating, infra dig (*informal*), lowering, shameful, undignified, unworthy

degree **1.** class, grade, level, order, position, rank, standing, station, status **2.** division, extent, gradation, grade, interval, limit, mark, measure, notch, point, rung, scale, stage, step, unit **3.** ambit, calibre, extent, intensity, level, measure, proportion, quality, quantity, range, rate, ratio, scale, scope, severity, standard **4.** **by degrees** bit by bit, gently, gradually, imperceptibly, inch by inch, little by little, slowly, step by step

dehydrate desiccate, drain, dry out, dry up, evaporate, exsiccate, parch

deification apotheosis, elevation, ennoblement, exaltation, glorification, idolization

deify apotheosize, elevate, ennoble, enthrone, exalt, extol, glorify, idealize, idolize, immortalize, venerate, worship

deign condescend, consent, deem worthy, lower oneself, see fit, stoop, think fit

deity celestial being, divine being, divinity, god, goddess, godhead, idol, immortal, supreme being

deject cast down, dampen, daunt, demoralize, depress, discourage, dishearten, dismay, dispirit

dejected blue, cast down, crestfallen, depressed, despondent, disconsolate, disheartened, dismal, doleful, down, downcast, downhearted, down in the dumps (*informal*), gloomy, glum, low, low-spirited, melancholy, miserable, morose, sad, sick as a parrot (*informal*), woebegone, wretched
Antonyms blithe, cheerful, chirpy (*informal*), encouraged, genial, happy, joyous, light-hearted, upbeat (*informal*)

dejection blues, depression, despair, despondency, doldrums, downheartedness, dumps (*informal*), gloom, gloominess, heavy-heartedness, low spirits, melancholy, sadness, sorrow, the hump (*Brit. informal*), unhappiness

de jure according to the law, by right, legally, rightfully

delay **1.** *verb* beat about the bush, defer, hold over, play for time, postpone, procrastinate, prolong, protract, put off, put on the back burner (*informal*), shelve, stall, suspend, table, take a rain check on (*U.S. & Canad. informal*), temporize **2.** *noun* deferment, postponement, procrastination, stay, suspension **3.** *verb* arrest, bog down, check, detain, halt, hinder, hold back, hold up, impede, obstruct, retard, set back, slow up, stop, throw a spanner in the works **4.** *noun* check, detention, hindrance, hold-up, impediment, interruption, interval, obstruction, setback, stoppage, wait **5.** *verb* dawdle, dilly-dally (*informal*), drag, drag one's feet *or* heels (*informal*), lag, linger, loiter, tarry **6.** *noun* dawdling, dilly-dallying (*informal*), lingering, loitering, tarrying
Antonyms *verb* accelerate, advance, dispatch, expedite, facilitate, forward, hasten, hurry, precipitate, press, promote, quicken, rush, speed (up), urge

delaying **1.** procrastinating, temporizing **2.** cunctative, halting, hindering, moratory, obstructive, retardant **3.** dallying, dilatory, lingering, slow, tardy, tarrying
Antonyms expeditious, hasty, precipitate, prompt, urgent

delectable adorable, agreeable, appetizing, charming, dainty, delicious, delightful, enjoyable, enticing, gratifying, inviting, luscious, lush, pleasant, pleasurable, satisfying, scrumptious (*informal*), tasty, toothsome, yummy (*slang*)
Antonyms awful, disagreeable, disgusting, distasteful, dreadful, horrible, horrid, nasty, offensive, terrible, unappetizing, unpleasant, yucky *or* yukky (*slang*)

delectation amusement, delight, diversion, enjoyment, entertainment, gratification, happiness, jollies (*slang*), pleasure, refreshment, relish, satisfaction

delegate *noun* **1.** agent, ambassador, commissioner, deputy, envoy, legate, representative, vicar *~verb* **2.** accredit, appoint, authorize, commission, depute, designate, empower, mandate **3.** assign, consign, devolve, entrust, give, hand over, pass on, relegate, transfer

delegation **1.** commission, contingent, deputation, embassy, envoys, legation, mission **2.** assignment, commissioning, committal, deputizing, devolution, entrustment, relegation

delete blot out, blue-pencil, cancel, cross out, cut out, dele, edit, edit out, efface, erase, excise, expunge, obliterate, remove, rub out, strike out

deleterious bad, damaging, destructive, detrimental, harmful, hurtful, injurious, pernicious, prejudicial, ruinous

deliberate *verb* **1.** cogitate, consider, consult, debate, discuss, meditate, mull over, ponder, reflect, think, weigh *~adjective* **2.** calculated, conscious, considered, designed, intentional, planned, prearranged, premeditated, purposeful, studied, thoughtful, wilful **3.** careful, cautious, circumspect, heedful, measured, methodical, ponderous, prudent, slow, thoughtful, unhurried, wary
Antonyms (*sense 2*) accidental, inadvertent, unconscious, unintended, unpremeditated,

unthinking (*sense 3*) fast, haphazard, hasty, heedless, hurried, impetuous, impulsive, rash

deliberately by design, calculatingly, con~ sciously, determinedly, emphatically, in cold blood, intentionally, knowingly, on purpose, pointedly, resolutely, studiously, wilfully, wit~ tingly

deliberation **1.** calculation, care, carefulness, caution, circumspection, cogitation, considera~ tion, coolness, forethought, meditation, pru~ dence, purpose, reflection, speculation, study, thought, wariness **2.** conference, consultation, debate, discussion

deliberation: the act of examining one's bread to determine which side it is buttered on
Ambrose Bierce *The Devil's Dictionary*

delicacy **1.** accuracy, daintiness, elegance, ex~ quisiteness, fineness, lightness, nicety, preci~ sion, subtlety **2.** debility, flimsiness, fragility, frailness, frailty, infirmity, slenderness, ten~ derness, weakness **3.** discrimination, fastidi~ ousness, finesse, purity, refinement, sensibil~ ity, sensitiveness, sensitivity, tact, taste **4.** *bonne bouche*, dainty, luxury, relish, savoury, titbit, treat

delicate **1.** ailing, debilitated, flimsy, fragile, frail, sickly, slender, slight, tender, weak **2.** choice, dainty, delicious, elegant, exquisite, fine, graceful, savoury, tender **3.** faint, muted, pastel, soft, subdued, subtle **4.** accurate, deft, detailed, minute, precise, skilled **5.** consider~ ate, diplomatic, discreet, sensitive, tactful **6.** built on sand, critical, difficult, precarious, sensitive, sticky (*informal*), ticklish, touchy **7.** careful, critical, discriminating, fastidious, nice, prudish, pure, refined, scrupulous, squeamish
Antonyms bright, careless, coarse, crude, harsh, healthy, inconsiderate, indelicate, in~ sensitive, rough, strong, unrefined

delicately carefully, daintily, deftly, elegantly, exquisitely, fastidiously, finely, gracefully, lightly, precisely, sensitively, skilfully, softly, subtly, tactfully

delicious **1.** ambrosial, appetizing, choice, dainty, delectable, luscious, mouthwatering, nectareous, palatable, savoury, scrumptious (*informal*), tasty, toothsome, yummy (*slang*) **2.** agreeable, charming, delightful, enjoyable, entertaining, exquisite, pleasant, pleasing
Antonyms disagreeable, distasteful, unpleas~ ant

delight *noun* **1.** ecstasy, enjoyment, felicity, gladness, gratification, happiness, jollies (*slang*), joy, pleasure, rapture, transport *~verb* **2.** amuse, charm, cheer, divert, enchant, gratify, please, ravish, rejoice, satisfy, thrill **3.** *with* **in** appreciate, enjoy, feast on, glory in, indulge in, like, love, luxuriate in, relish, rev~ el in, savour
Antonyms *noun* disapprobation, disfavour, dislike, displeasure, dissatisfaction, distaste *~verb* (*sense 2*) disgust, displease, dissatisfy, gall, irk, offend, upset, vex

delighted blissed out, captivated, charmed, cock-a-hoop, ecstatic, elated, enchanted, glad~ dened, happy, in seventh heaven, joyous, ju~ bilant, overjoyed, over the moon (*informal*), pleased, rapt, sent, thrilled

delightful agreeable, amusing, captivating, charming, congenial, delectable, enchanting, engaging, enjoyable, entertaining, fascinating, gratifying, heavenly, pleasant, pleasing, pleasurable, rapturous, ravishing, thrilling
Antonyms disagreeable, displeasing, distaste~ ful, horrid, nasty, unpleasant

delimit bound, define, demarcate, determine, fix, mark (out)

delineate characterize, chart, contour, depict, describe, design, draw, figure, map out, out~ line, paint, picture, portray, render, sketch, trace

delineation account, chart, depiction, descrip~ tion, design, diagram, drawing, outline, pic~ ture, portrait, portrayal, representation, trac~ ing

delinquency crime, fault, misbehaviour, mis~ conduct, misdeed, misdemeanour, offence, wrongdoing

delinquent criminal, culprit, defaulter, juvenile delinquent, lawbreaker, malefactor, miscreant, offender, villain, wrongdoer, young offender

delirious **1.** crazy, demented, deranged, gonzo (*slang*), incoherent, insane, light-headed, mad, raving, unhinged **2.** beside oneself, blissed out, carried away, corybantic, ecstatic, excited, frantic, frenzied, hysterical, sent, wild
Antonyms calm, clear-headed, coherent, *com~ pos mentis*, in one's right mind, lucid, ration~ al, sane, sensible

delirium **1.** aberration, derangement, halluci~ nation, insanity, lunacy, madness, raving **2.** ecstasy, fever, frenzy, fury, hysteria, passion, rage

deliver **1.** bear, bring, carry, cart, convey, dis~ tribute, transport **2.** cede, commit, give up, grant, hand over, make over, relinquish, re~ sign, surrender, transfer, turn over, yield **3.** acquit, discharge, emancipate, free, liberate, loose, ransom, redeem, release, rescue, save **4.** announce, declare, give, give forth, present, proclaim, pronounce, publish, read, utter **5.** administer, aim, deal, direct, give, inflict, launch, strike, throw **6.** discharge, dispense, feed, give forth, provide, purvey, release, sup~ ply

deliverance emancipation, escape, liberation, ransom, redemption, release, rescue, salvation

delivery 1. consignment, conveyance, dispatch, distribution, handing over, surrender, transfer, transmission, transmittal 2. articulation, elocution, enunciation, intonation, speech, utterance 3. *Medical* childbirth, confinement, labour, parturition 4. deliverance, escape, liberation, release, rescue

delude bamboozle (*informal*), beguile, cheat, con (*informal*), cozen, deceive, dupe, fool, gull (*archaic*), hoax, hoodwink, impose on, kid (*informal*), lead up the garden path (*informal*), misguide, mislead, pull the wool over someone's eyes, take for a ride (*informal*), take in (*informal*), trick

deluge *noun* 1. cataclysm, downpour, flood, inundation, overflowing, spate, torrent 2. *figurative* avalanche, barrage, flood, rush, spate, torrent *~verb* 3. douse, drench, drown, flood, inundate, soak, submerge, swamp 4. *figurative* engulf, inundate, overload, overrun, overwhelm, swamp

delusion deception, error, fallacy, false impression, fancy, hallucination, illusion, misapprehension, misbelief, misconception, mistake, phantasm, self-deception

delusive chimerical, deceptive, fallacious, illusive, illusory, misleading, specious, spurious

delusory deceptive, deluded, erroneous, fallacious, false, fictitious, illusory, imaginary, imagined, misguided, mistaken, unfounded
Antonyms actual, authentic, genuine, real, true

de luxe choice, costly, elegant, exclusive, expensive, gorgeous, grand, luxurious, opulent, palatial, plush (*informal*), rich, select, special, splendid, splendiferous (*facetious*), sumptuous, superior

delve burrow, dig into, examine, explore, ferret out, forage, investigate, look into, probe, ransack, research, rummage, search, unearth

demagogue agitator, firebrand, haranguer, rabble-rouser, soapbox orator

demand *verb* 1. ask, challenge, inquire, interrogate, question, request 2. call for, cry out for, entail, involve, necessitate, need, require, take, want 3. claim, exact, expect, insist on, order *~noun* 4. bidding, charge, inquiry, interrogation, order, question, request, requisition 5. call, claim, market, necessity, need, requirement, want 6. **in demand** fashionable, in vogue, like gold dust, needed, popular, requested, sought after
Antonyms *verb* come up with, contribute, furnish, give, grant, produce, provide, supply, yield

demanding 1. challenging, difficult, exacting, exhausting, exigent, hard, taxing, tough, trying, wearing 2. clamorous, imperious, importunate, insistent, nagging, pressing, urgent
Antonyms a piece of cake (*informal*), child's play (*informal*), easy, easy-peasy (*slang*), effortless, facile, no bother, painless, simple, straightforward, uncomplicated, undemanding

demarcate define, delimit, determine, differentiate, distinguish between, fix, mark, separate

demarcation 1. bound, boundary, confine, enclosure, limit, margin, pale 2. delimitation, differentiation, distinction, division, separation

demean abase, debase, degrade, descend, humble, lower, stoop

demeaning beneath one's dignity, cheapening, contemptible, debasing, degrading, disgraceful, dishonourable, humiliating, infra dig (*informal*), shameful, undignified, unworthy

demeanour air, bearing, behaviour, carriage, comportment, conduct, deportment, manner, mien

demented barking (*slang*), barking mad (*slang*), crackbrained, crackpot (*informal*), crazed, crazy, daft (*informal*), deranged, distraught, doolally (*slang*), dotty (*slang, chiefly Brit.*), foolish, frenzied, gonzo (*slang*), idiotic, insane, loopy (*informal*), lunatic, mad, maniacal, manic, *non compos mentis*, not the full shilling (*informal*), off one's trolley (*slang*), out to lunch (*informal*), unbalanced, unhinged, up the pole (*informal*), wacko *or* whacko (*slang*)
Antonyms all there (*informal*), *compos mentis*, in one's right mind, lucid, mentally sound, normal, of sound mind, rational, reasonable, sensible, sound

demise *noun* 1. death, decease, departure, expiration 2. collapse, dissolution, downfall, end, failure, fall, ruin, termination 3. *Law* alienation, conveyance, transfer, transmission *~verb* 4. *Law* bequeath, convey, grant, leave, transfer, will

demobilize deactivate, decommission, demob (*Brit. informal*), disband, discharge, release
Antonyms call up, conscript, draft (*U.S.*), enlist, enrol, mobilize, muster, recruit

democracy commonwealth, government by the people, representative government, republic

The ballot is stronger than the bullet
Abraham Lincoln

Man's capacity for justice makes democracy possible; but man's inclination to injustice makes democracy necessary
Reinhold Niebuhr *The Children of Light and the Children of Darkness*

After each war there is a little less democracy to save
Brooks Atkinson *Once Around the Sun*

Democracy means government by discussion, but it

is only effective if you can stop people talking
Clement Atlee

Democracy is the worst form of Government except all those other forms that have been tried from time to time
Winston Churchill

Democracy is the name we give the people whenever we need them
Robert, Marquis de Flers and Arman de Caillavet *L'habit vert*

Democracy substitutes election by the incompetent many for appointment by the corrupt few
George Bernard Shaw *Man and Superman*

All the ills of democracy can be cured by more democracy
Alfred Emanuel Smith

government of the people, by the people, and for the people
Abraham Lincoln *Gettysburg Address*

Democracy means government by the uneducated, while aristocracy means government by the badly educated
G.K. Chesterton *New York Times*

democratic autonomous, egalitarian, popular, populist, representative, republican, self-governing

demolish 1. bulldoze, destroy, dismantle, flatten, knock down, level, overthrow, pulverize, raze, ruin, tear down, total (*slang*), trash (*slang*) **2.** *figurative* annihilate, blow out of the water (*slang*), defeat, destroy, lick (*informal*), master, overthrow, overturn, stuff (*slang*), tank (*slang*), undo, wipe the floor with (*informal*), wreck **3.** consume, devour, eat, gobble up, put away
Antonyms build, construct, create, repair, restore, strengthen

demolition bulldozing, destruction, explosion, knocking down, levelling, razing, wrecking

demon 1. devil, evil spirit, fiend, ghoul, goblin, malignant spirit **2.** *figurative* devil, fiend, ghoul, monster, rogue, villain **3.** ace (*informal*), addict, fanatic, fiend, go-getter (*informal*), master, wizard **4.** daemon, daimon, genius, guardian spirit, ministering angel, numen

demonic, demoniac demoniacal 1. devilish, diabolic, diabolical, fiendish, hellish, infernal, satanic **2.** crazed, frantic, frenetic, frenzied, furious, hectic, like one possessed, mad, maniacal, manic

demonstrable attestable, axiomatic, certain, evident, evincible, incontrovertible, indubitable, irrefutable, obvious, palpable, positive, provable, self-evident, undeniable, unmistakable, verifiable

demonstrate 1. display, establish, evidence, evince, exhibit, indicate, manifest, prove, show, testify to **2.** describe, explain, illustrate, make clear, show how, teach **3.** march, parade, picket, protest, rally

demonstration 1. affirmation, confirmation, display, evidence, exhibition, expression, illustration, manifestation, proof, substantiation, testimony, validation **2.** description, explanation, exposition, presentation, test, trial **3.** march, mass lobby, parade, picket, protest, rally, sit-in

demonstrative 1. affectionate, effusive, emotional, expansive, expressive, gushing, loving, open, unreserved, unrestrained **2.** evincive, explanatory, expository, illustrative, indicative, symptomatic
Antonyms (*sense 1*) aloof, cold, contained, distant, formal, impassive, reserved, restrained, stiff, unaffectionate, undemonstrative, unemotional, unresponsive

demoralization 1. agitation, crushing, devitalization, discomfiture, enervation, lowering *or* loss of morale, panic, perturbation, trepidation, unmanning, weakening **2.** corruption, debasement, depravation, lowering, perversion, vitiation

demoralize 1. cripple, daunt, deject, depress, disconcert, discourage, dishearten, dispirit, enfeeble, psych out (*informal*), rattle (*informal*), sap, shake, undermine, unnerve, weaken **2.** corrupt, debase, debauch, deprave, lower, pervert, vitiate
Antonyms (*sense 1*) boost, cheer, egg on, encourage, hearten, spur

demoralized 1. broken, crushed, depressed, discouraged, disheartened, dispirited, downcast, sick as a parrot (*informal*), subdued, unmanned, unnerved, weakened **2.** bad, base, corrupt, degenerate, depraved, dissolute, immoral, low, reprobate, sinful, wicked

demoralizing crushing, dampening, daunting, depressing, disappointing, discouraging, disheartening, dispiriting
Antonyms cheering, comforting, encouraging, heartening, reassuring

demote declass, degrade, disrate (*Naval*), downgrade, kick downstairs (*slang*), lower in rank, relegate
Antonyms advance, elevate, kick upstairs (*informal*), prefer, raise, upgrade

demotic common, common or garden, grass-roots, humble, lowborn, lowbrow, lower-class, ordinary, plebeian, popular, proletarian, vulgar, working-class
Antonyms aristocratic, blue-blooded, elite, highborn, noble, patrician, upper-class

demulcent calming, easing, emollient, lenitive, mild, mollifying, relieving, sedative, softening, soothing

demur 1. *verb* balk, cavil, disagree, dispute, doubt, hesitate, object, pause, protest, refuse, take exception, waver 2. *noun* compunction, demurral, demurrer, dissent, hesitation, misgiving, objection, protest, qualm, scruple

demure 1. decorous, diffident, grave, modest, reserved, reticent, retiring, sedate, shy, sober, staid, unassuming 2. affected, bashful, coy, niminy-piminy, priggish, prim, prissy (*informal*), prudish, strait-laced
Antonyms brash, brazen, forward, immodest, impudent, shameless

den 1. cave, cavern, haunt, hide-out, hole, lair, shelter 2. cloister, cubbyhole, hideaway, retreat, sanctuary, sanctum, snuggery, study

denial adjuration, contradiction, disavowal, disclaimer, dismissal, dissent, negation, prohibition, rebuff, refusal, rejection, renunciation, repudiation, repulse, retraction, veto
Antonyms acknowledgment, admission, affirmation, avowal, confession, declaration, disclosure, divulgence, profession, revelation

denigrate asperse, bad-mouth (*slang, chiefly U.S. & Canad.*), belittle, besmirch, blacken, calumniate, decry, defame, disparage, impugn, knock (*informal*), malign, revile, rubbish (*informal*), run down, slag (off) (*slang*), slander, vilify
Antonyms acclaim, admire, approve, cheer, compliment, eulogize, extol, honour, laud, praise, take one's hat off to

denigration aspersion, backbiting, defamation, detraction, disparagement, obloquy, scandal, scurrility, slander, vilification

denizen citizen, dweller, inhabitant, occupant, resident

denominate call, christen, designate, dub, entitle, name, phrase, style, term

denomination 1. belief, communion, creed, persuasion, religious group, school, sect 2. grade, size, unit, value 3. body, category, class, classification, group 4. appellation, designation, label, name, style, term, title

denotation designation, indication, meaning, signification, specification

denote betoken, designate, express, imply, import, indicate, mark, mean, show, signify, typify

dénouement climax, conclusion, culmination, finale, outcome, resolution, solution, termination, upshot

denounce accuse, arraign, attack, brand, castigate, censure, condemn, declaim against, decry, denunciate, excoriate, impugn, point a *or* the finger at, proscribe, revile, stigmatize, vilify

dense 1. close, close-knit, compact, compressed, condensed, heavy, impenetrable, opaque, solid, substantial, thick, thickset 2. blockish, brain-dead (*informal*), crass, dead from the neck up (*informal*), dozy (*Brit. informal*), dull, obtuse, slow, slow-witted, stolid, stupid, thick, thick-witted
Antonyms alert, bright, clever, intelligent, light, quick, scattered, sparse, thin, transparent

density 1. body, bulk, closeness, compactness, consistency, crowdedness, denseness, impenetrability, mass, solidity, thickness, tightness 2. crassness, dullness, obtuseness, slowness, stolidity, stupidity, thickness

dent 1. *noun* chip, concavity, crater, depression, dimple, dip, hollow, impression, indentation, pit 2. *verb* depress, dint, gouge, hollow, imprint, make a dent in, make concave, press in, push in

denude bare, divest, expose, lay bare, strip, uncover

denunciate castigate, condemn, curse, damn, denounce, stigmatize, vituperate

denunciation accusation, castigation, censure, character assassination, condemnation, criticism, denouncement, fulmination, incrimination, invective, obloquy, stick (*slang*), stigmatization

denunciatory accusatory, censorious, comminatory, condemnatory, fulminatory, incriminatory, recriminatory, reproachful

deny 1. contradict, disagree with, disprove, gainsay (*archaic or literary*), oppose, rebuff, rebut, refute 2. abjure, disavow, discard, disclaim, disown, recant, renege, renounce, repudiate, retract, revoke 3. begrudge, decline, disallow, forbid, negative, refuse, reject, turn down, veto, withhold
Antonyms accept, acknowledge, admit, affirm, agree, allow, concede, confirm, grant, let, permit, receive, recognize, take on board

deodorant air freshener, antiperspirant, deodorizer, disinfectant, fumigant

deodorize aerate, disinfect, freshen, fumigate, purify, refresh, ventilate

depart 1. absent (oneself), decamp, disappear, escape, exit, go, go away, hook it (*slang*), leave, make tracks, migrate, pack one's bags (*informal*), quit, remove, retire, retreat, set forth, slope off, start out, take (one's) leave, vanish, withdraw 2. deviate, differ, digress, diverge, stray, swerve, turn aside, vary, veer
Antonyms arrive, remain, show up (*informal*), stay, turn up

departed dead, deceased, expired, late

department 1. district, division, province, region, sector 2. branch, bureau, division, office, section, station, subdivision, unit 3. area, domain, function, line, province, realm, responsibility, speciality, sphere

departure 1. exit, exodus, going, going away, leave-taking, leaving, removal, retirement, withdrawal 2. abandonment, branching off,

deviation, digression, divergence, variation, veering **3.** branching out, change, difference, innovation, novelty, shift, whole new ball game (*informal*)
Antonyms advent, appearance, arrival, coming, entrance, return

depend **1.** bank on, build upon, calculate on, confide in, count on, lean on, reckon on, rely upon, trust in, turn to **2.** be based on, be contingent on, be determined by, be subject to, be subordinate to, hang on, hinge on, rest on, revolve around

dependable faithful, reliable, reputable, responsible, staunch, steady, sure, trustworthy, trusty, unfailing
Antonyms irresponsible, undependable, unreliable, unstable, untrustworthy

dependant *noun* child, client, cohort (*chiefly U.S.*), hanger-on, henchman, minion, minor, protégé, relative, retainer, subordinate, vassal

dependence, dependency **1.** assurance, belief, confidence, expectation, faith, hope, reliance, trust **2.** addiction, attachment, helplessness, need, subordination, subservience, vulnerability, weakness

dependent *adjective* **1.** counting on, defenceless, helpless, immature, reliant, relying on, vulnerable, weak **2.** conditional, contingent, depending, determined by, liable to, relative, subject to **3.** feudal, subject, subordinate, tributary
Antonyms autarkic, autonomous, independent, self-determining, self-governing, self-reliant

depict **1.** delineate, draw, illustrate, limn, outline, paint, picture, portray, render, reproduce, sculpt, sketch **2.** characterize, describe, detail, narrate, outline, sketch

depiction delineation, description, drawing, illustration, image, likeness, outline, picture, portrayal, representation, sketch

deplete bankrupt, consume, decrease, drain, empty, evacuate, exhaust, expend, impoverish, lessen, milk, reduce, use up
Antonyms add to, augment, enhance, expand, increase, raise, step up (*informal*), swell

depleted consumed, decreased, depreciated, devoid of, drained, effete, emptied, exhausted, lessened, out of, reduced, short of, spent, used (up), wasted, weakened, worn out

depletion attenuation, consumption, decrease, deficiency, diminution, drain, dwindling, exhaustion, expenditure, lessening, lowering, reduction, using up

deplorable **1.** calamitous, dire, disastrous, distressing, grievous, heartbreaking, lamentable, melancholy, miserable, pitiable, regrettable, sad, unfortunate, wretched **2.** blameworthy, disgraceful, dishonourable, disreputable, execrable, opprobrious, reprehensible, scandalous, shameful
Antonyms A1 *or* A-one (*informal*), admirable, bad (*slang*), bodacious (*slang, chiefly U.S.*), brilliant, excellent, fantastic, great (*informal*), laudable, marvellous, notable, outstanding, praiseworthy, super (*informal*), superb

deplore **1.** bemoan, bewail, grieve for, lament, mourn, regret, rue, sorrow over **2.** abhor, censure, condemn, denounce, deprecate, disapprove of, excoriate, object to, take a dim view of

deploy arrange, dispose, extend, position, redistribute, set out, set up, spread out, station, use, utilize

deport **1.** banish, exile, expatriate, expel, extradite, oust **2.** *used reflexively* acquit, act, bear, behave, carry, comport, conduct, hold

deportation banishment, eviction, exile, expatriation, expulsion, extradition, transportation

deportment air, appearance, aspect, bearing, behaviour, carriage, cast, comportment, conduct, demeanour, manner, mien, posture, stance

depose **1.** break, cashier, degrade, demote, dethrone, dismiss, displace, downgrade, oust, remove from office **2.** *Law* avouch, declare, make a deposition, testify

deposit *verb* **1.** drop, lay, locate, place, precipitate, put, settle, sit down **2.** amass, bank, consign, entrust, hoard, lodge, save, store ~*noun* **3.** down payment, instalment, money (*in bank*), part payment, pledge, retainer, security, stake, warranty **4.** accumulation, alluvium, deposition, dregs, lees, precipitate, sediment, silt

depositary fiduciary (*Law*), guardian, steward, trustee

deposition **1.** dethronement, dismissal, displacement, ousting, removal **2.** *Law* affidavit, declaration, evidence, sworn statement, testimony

depository depot, repository, safe-deposit box, store, storehouse, warehouse

depot **1.** depository, repository, storehouse, warehouse **2.** *Military* arsenal, dump **3.** bus station, garage, terminus

deprave brutalize, corrupt, debase, debauch, degrade, demoralize, lead astray, pervert, seduce, subvert, vitiate

depraved abandoned, corrupt, debased, debauched, degenerate, degraded, dissolute, evil, immoral, lascivious, lewd, licentious, perverted, pervy (*slang*), profligate, shameless, sinful, sink, vicious, vile, wicked
Antonyms chaste, decent, ethical, good, honourable, innocent, moral, principled, proper, pure, upright, virtuous, wholesome

depravity baseness, contamination, corruption, criminality, debasement, debauchery, degen~eracy, depravation, evil, immorality, iniquity, profligacy, sinfulness, turpitude, vice, vicious~ness, vitiation, wickedness

No one ever suddenly became depraved
Juvenal *Satires*

deprecate **1.** condemn, deplore, disapprove of, frown on, object to, protest against, take ex~ception to **2.** belittle, denigrate, depreciate, detract, disparage

deprecatory **1.** censuring, condemnatory, dis~approving, opprobrious, reproachful **2.** apolo~getic, contrite, penitent, regretful, remorseful, rueful

depreciate **1.** decrease, deflate, devaluate, de~value, lessen, lose value, lower, reduce **2.** be~little, decry, denigrate, deride, detract, dis~parage, look down on, ridicule, run down, scorn, sneer at, traduce, underestimate, underrate, undervalue
Antonyms (*sense 1*) add to, appreciate, aug~ment, enhance, enlarge, expand, grow, in~crease, rise (*sense 2*) admire, appreciate, cherish, esteem, like, prize, rate highly, re~gard, respect, value

depreciation **1.** deflation, depression, devalua~tion, drop, fall, slump **2.** belittlement, deni~gration, deprecation, derogation, detraction, disparagement, pejoration

depredation desolation, despoiling, destruc~tion, devastation, harrying, laying waste, ma~rauding, pillage, plunder, ransacking, rapine, ravaging, robbery, spoliation, theft

depredator despoiler, destroyer, looter, ma~rauder, pillager, plunderer, raider, ransacker, ravager, rifler, sacker

depress **1.** cast down, chill, damp, daunt, de~ject, desolate, discourage, dishearten, dispirit, make despondent, oppress, sadden, weigh down **2.** debilitate, devitalize, drain, enervate, exhaust, lower, sap, slow up, weaken **3.** cheapen, depreciate, devaluate, devalue, di~minish, downgrade, impair, lessen, lower, re~duce **4.** flatten, level, lower, press down, push down
Antonyms cheer, elate, hearten, heighten, in~crease, lift, raise, strengthen, uplift

depressed **1.** blue, crestfallen, dejected, de~spondent, discouraged, dispirited, down, downcast, downhearted, down in the dumps (*informal*), fed up, glum, low, low-spirited, melancholy, moody, morose, pessimistic, sad, unhappy **2.** concave, hollow, indented, re~cessed, set back, sunken **3.** *of an area, cir~cumstances* deprived, destitute, disadvant~aged, distressed, grey, needy, poor, poverty-stricken, run-down **4.** cheapened, depreciated, devalued, impaired, weakened

depressing black, bleak, daunting, dejecting, depressive, discouraging, disheartening, dis~mal, dispiriting, distressing, dreary, funereal, gloomy, harrowing, heartbreaking, hopeless, melancholy, sad, saddening, sombre

depression **1.** dejection, despair, despondency, dolefulness, downheartedness, dumps (*infor~mal*), gloominess, hopelessness, low spirits, melancholia, melancholy, sadness, the blues, the hump (*Brit. informal*) **2.** *Commerce* dull~ness, economic decline, hard *or* bad times, in~activity, lowness, recession, slump, stagnation **3.** bowl, cavity, concavity, dent, dimple, dip, excavation, hollow, impression, indentation, pit, sag, sink, valley

It's a recession when your neighbour loses his job; it's a depression when you lose yours
Harry S. Truman

deprivation **1.** denial, deprival, dispossession, divestment, expropriation, removal, with~drawal, withholding **2.** destitution, detriment, disadvantage, distress, hardship, need, priva~tion, want

deprive bereave, despoil, dispossess, divest, expropriate, rob, strip, wrest

deprived bereft, denuded, destitute, disadvan~taged, down at heel, forlorn, in need, in want, lacking, necessitous, needy, poor
Antonyms born with a silver spoon in one's mouth, favoured, fortunate, golden, happy, having a charmed life, lucky, prosperous, sit~ting pretty (*informal*), successful, well-off

depth **1.** abyss, deepness, drop, extent, meas~ure, profoundness, profundity **2.** *figurative* as~tuteness, discernment, insight, penetration, profoundness, profundity, sagacity, wisdom **3.** abstruseness, complexity, obscurity, recon~diteness **4.** intensity, richness, strength **5.** *of~ten plural* abyss, bowels of the earth, deepest (furthest, innermost, most intense, remotest) part, middle, midst, nadir, slough of despond **6. in depth** comprehensively, extensively, in~tensively, thoroughly
Antonyms (*sense 1*) apex, apogee, crest, crown, height, peak, pinnacle, summit, top, vertex, zenith (*sense 2*) *figurative* emptiness, lack of depth *or* substance, superficiality, triviality

deputation **1.** commission, delegates, delega~tion, deputies, embassy, envoys, legation **2.** appointment, assignment, commission, desig~nation, nomination

depute *verb* accredit, appoint, authorize, char~ge, commission, delegate, empower, entrust, mandate

deputize **1.** commission, delegate, depute **2.** act for, stand in for, take the place of, understudy

deputy **1.** *noun* agent, ambassador, commis~sioner, delegate, legate, lieutenant, nuncio, proxy, representative, second-in-command, substitute, surrogate, vicegerent **2.** *adjective* assistant, depute (*Scot.*), subordinate

derange 1. confound, confuse, disarrange, disarray, discompose, disconcert, disorder, displace, disturb, ruffle, unsettle, upset **2.** craze, dement (*rare*), drive mad, madden, make insane, unbalance, unhinge

deranged barking (*slang*), barking mad (*slang*), berserk, crackpot (*informal*), crazed, crazy, delirious, demented, distracted, doolally (*slang*), frantic, frenzied, gonzo (*slang*), insane, irrational, loopy (*informal*), lunatic, mad, maddened, not the full shilling (*informal*), off one's trolley (*slang*), out to lunch (*informal*), unbalanced, unhinged, up the pole (*informal*), wacko *or* whacko (*slang*)
Antonyms all there (*informal*), calm, *compos mentis*, in one's right mind, lucid, mentally sound, normal, of sound mind

derangement 1. confusion, disarrangement, disarray, disorder, disturbance, irregularity, jumble, muddle **2.** aberration, alienation, delirium, dementia, hallucination, insanity, loss of reason, lunacy, madness, mania

derelict *adjective* **1.** abandoned, deserted, dilapidated, discarded, forsaken, neglected, ruined **2.** careless, irresponsible, lax, negligent, remiss, slack *~noun* **3.** bag lady (*chiefly U.S.*), bum (*informal*), down-and-out, good-for-nothing, ne'er-do-well, outcast, tramp, vagrant, wastrel

dereliction 1. delinquency, evasion, failure, faithlessness, fault, neglect, negligence, nonperformance, remissness **2.** abandonment, abdication, desertion, forsaking, relinquishment, renunciation

deride chaff, contemn, detract, disdain, disparage, flout, gibe, insult, jeer, knock (*informal*), mock, pooh-pooh, ridicule, scoff, scorn, sneer, take the piss out of (*taboo slang*), taunt

de rigueur *comme il faut*, conventional, correct, decent, decorous, done, fitting, necessary, proper, required, right, the done thing

derision contempt, contumely, denigration, disdain, disparagement, disrespect, insult, laughter, mockery, raillery, ridicule, satire, scoffing, scorn, sneering

derisive contemptuous, jeering, mocking, ridiculing, scoffing, scornful, taunting

derisory contemptible, insulting, laughable, ludicrous, outrageous, preposterous, ridiculous

derivable attributable, deducible, determinable, extractable, inferable, obtainable, traceable

derivation 1. acquiring, deriving, extraction, getting, obtaining **2.** ancestry, basis, beginning, descent, etymology, foundation, genealogy, origin, root, source

derivative *adjective* **1.** acquired, borrowed, derived, inferred, obtained, procured, transmitted **2.** copied, imitative, plagiaristic, plagiarized, rehashed, secondary, second-hand, uninventive, unoriginal *~noun* **3.** by-product, derivation, descendant, offshoot, outgrowth, spin-off
Antonyms *adjective* archetypal, authentic, first-hand, genuine, master, original, prototypical, seminal

derive 1. collect, deduce, draw, elicit, extract, follow, gain, gather, get, glean, infer, obtain, procure, receive, trace **2.** *with* **from** arise, descend, emanate, flow, issue, originate, proceed, spring from, stem from

derogate 1. cheapen, compromise, depreciate, detract, devaluate, diminish, disparage, lessen, run down **2.** *of oneself* decline, degenerate, degrade, descend, deteriorate, deviate from, retrogress, stoop

derogatory belittling, damaging, defamatory, depreciative, detracting, discreditable, dishonouring, disparaging, injurious, offensive, slighting, uncomplimentary, unfavourable, unflattering
Antonyms appreciative, complimentary, flattering, fulsome, laudatory

descant *verb* **1.** amplify, animadvert, comment on, dilate, discourse, discuss, enlarge, expatiate *~noun* **2.** animadversion, commentary, criticism, discourse, discussion, dissertation **3.** counterpoint, decoration, melody, song, tune

descend 1. alight, dismount, drop, fall, go down, move down, plummet, plunge, sink, subside, tumble **2.** dip, gravitate, incline, slant, slope **3.** be handed down, be passed down, derive, issue, originate, proceed, spring **4.** abase oneself, condescend, degenerate, deteriorate, lower oneself, stoop **5.** *often with* **on** arrive, assail, assault, attack, come in force, invade, pounce, raid, swoop
Antonyms ascend, climb, go up, mount, rise, scale, soar

descendant child, daughter, heir, inheritor, issue, offspring, progeny, scion, son, successor
Antonyms ancestor, antecedent, forebear, forefather, forerunner, precursor, predecessor, progenitor

descent 1. coming down, drop, fall, plunge, swoop **2.** declination, declivity, dip, drop, incline, slant, slope **3.** ancestry, extraction, family tree, genealogy, heredity, lineage, origin, parentage **4.** debasement, decadence, decline, degradation, deterioration **5.** assault, attack, foray, incursion, invasion, pounce, raid, swoop

describe 1. characterize, define, depict, detail, explain, express, illustrate, narrate, portray, recount, relate, report, specify, tell **2.** delineate, draw, mark out, outline, trace

description **1.** account, characterization, delineation, depiction, detail, explanation, narration, narrative, portrayal, report, representation, sketch **2.** brand, breed, category, class, genre, genus, ilk, kidney, kind, order, sort, species, type, variety

descriptive circumstantial, depictive, detailed, explanatory, expressive, graphic, illustrative, pictorial, picturesque, vivid

descry behold, detect, discern, discover, distinguish, espy, make out, mark, notice, observe, perceive, recognize, see, sight, spy out

desecrate abuse, blaspheme, commit sacrilege, contaminate, defile, despoil, dishonour, pervert, pollute, profane, violate
Antonyms esteem, exalt, glorify, hallow, prize, respect, revere, value, venerate, worship

desecration blasphemy, debasement, defilement, impiety, profanation, sacrilege, violation

desert[1] **1.** *noun* solitude, waste, wasteland, wilderness, wilds **2.** *adjective* arid, bare, barren, desolate, infertile, lonely, solitary, uncultivated, uninhabited, unproductive, untilled, waste, wild

Deserts

Arabian	Kara Kum
Atacama	Kyzyl Kum
Dasht-i-Lut *or* Dasht-e-Lut	Libyan
Death Valley	Mohave *or* Mojave
Gibson	Nubian
Gobi	Rub'al Khali
Great Sandy	Sahara
Great Victoria	Taklimakan Shama
Kalahari	Thar

desert[2] *verb* abandon, abscond, betray, decamp, defect, forsake, give up, go over the hill (*Military slang*), jilt, leave, leave high and dry, leave (someone) in the lurch, leave stranded, maroon, quit, rat (on) (*informal*), relinquish, renounce, resign, run out on (*informal*), strand, throw over, vacate, walk out on (*informal*)
Antonyms be a source of strength to, look after, maintain, provide for, succour, sustain, take care of

desert[3] *noun* **1.** *often plural* comeuppance (*slang*), due, guerdon (*poetic*), meed (*archaic*), payment, recompense, requital, retribution, return, reward, right **2.** excellence, merit (*or* demerit), virtue, worth

deserted abandoned, bereft, cast off, derelict, desolate, empty, forlorn, forsaken, godforsaken, isolated, left in the lurch, left stranded, lonely, neglected, solitary, unfriended, unoccupied, vacant

deserter absconder, apostate, defector, escapee, fugitive, rat (*informal*), renegade, runaway, traitor, truant

desertion abandonment, absconding, apostasy, betrayal, defection, departure, dereliction, escape, evasion, flight, forsaking, relinquishment, truancy

deserve be entitled to, be worthy of, earn, gain, justify, merit, procure, rate, warrant, win

deserved appropriate, condign, due, earned, fair, fitting, just, justifiable, justified, meet (*archaic*), merited, proper, right, rightful, suitable, warranted, well-earned

deservedly according to one's due, appropriately, by rights, condignly, duly, fairly, fittingly, justifiably, justly, properly, rightfully, rightly
Antonyms inappropriately, undeservedly, unduly, unfairly, unfittingly, unjustifiably, unjustly, unwarrantedly, wrongfully, wrongly

deserving commendable, estimable, laudable, meritorious, praiseworthy, righteous, worthy
Antonyms not deserving of, not good enough, not worth, undeserving, unworthy

desiccate dehydrate, drain, dry, evaporate, exsiccate, parch

desiccated **1.** dehydrated, dried, dry, powdered **2.** cold, dead, dry, dry-as-dust, dull, empty, inanimate, inert, lifeless, passionless, spiritless

desideratum aim, aspiration, dream, essential, goal, heart's desire, hope, ideal, lack, need, objective, *sine qua non*, want, wish

design *verb* **1.** delineate, describe, draft, draw, outline, plan, sketch, trace *~noun* **2.** blueprint, delineation, draft, drawing, model, outline, plan, scheme, sketch *~verb* **3.** conceive, create, fabricate, fashion, invent, originate, think up *~noun* **4.** arrangement, configuration, construction, figure, form, motif, organization, pattern, shape, style *~verb* **5.** aim, contrive, destine, devise, intend, make, mean, plan, project, propose, purpose, scheme, tailor *~noun* **6.** enterprise, plan, project, schema, scheme, undertaking **7.** aim, end, goal, intent, intention, meaning, object, objective, point, purport, purpose, target, view **8.** *often plural* conspiracy, evil intentions, intrigue, machination, plot, scheme

designate **1.** call, christen, dub, entitle, label, name, nominate, style, term **2.** allot, appoint, assign, choose, delegate, depute, nominate, select **3.** characterize, define, denote, describe, earmark, indicate, pinpoint, show, specify, stipulate

designation **1.** denomination, description, epithet, label, mark, name, title **2.** appointment, classification, delegation, indication, selection, specification

designedly by design, calculatedly, deliberately, intentionally, knowingly, on purpose, purposely, studiously, wilfully, wittingly

designer 1. architect, artificer, couturier, creator, deviser, inventor, originator, stylist 2. conniver, conspirator, intriguer, plotter, schemer

designing artful, astute, conniving, conspiring, crafty, crooked (*informal*), cunning, deceitful, devious, intriguing, Machiavellian, plotting, scheming, sharp, shrewd, sly, treacherous, tricky, unscrupulous, wily

desirability advantage, benefit, merit, profit, usefulness, value, worth

desirable 1. advantageous, advisable, agreeable, beneficial, covetable, eligible, enviable, good, pleasing, preferable, profitable, to die for (*informal*), worthwhile 2. adorable, alluring, attractive, fascinating, fetching, glamorous, seductive, sexy (*informal*)
Antonyms disagreeable, distasteful, unacceptable, unappealing, unattractive, undesirable, unpleasant, unpopular, unsexy (*informal*)

desire *verb* 1. aspire to, covet, crave, desiderate, fancy, hanker after, hope for, long for, set one's heart on, thirst for, want, wish for, yearn for ~*noun* 2. ache, appetite, aspiration, craving, hankering, hope, longing, need, thirst, want, wish, yearning, yen (*informal*) ~*verb* 3. ask, entreat, importune, petition, request, solicit ~*noun* 4. appeal, entreaty, importunity, petition, request, solicitation, supplication 5. appetite, concupiscence, lasciviousness, lechery, libido, lust, lustfulness, passion
Related adjective: orectic

Sooner murder an infant in his cradle than
nurse unacted desires
William Blake *The Marriage of Heaven and Hell*

There are two tragedies in life. One is not to get
your heart's desire. The other is to get it
George Bernard Shaw *Man and Superman*

Other women cloy
The appetites they feed, but she makes hungry
Where most she satisfies
William Shakespeare *Antony and Cleopatra*

desired accurate, appropriate, correct, exact, expected, express, fitting, necessary, particular, proper, required, right

desirous ambitious, anxious, aspiring, avid, craving, desiring, eager, hopeful, hoping, keen, longing, ready, willing, wishing, yearning
Antonyms averse, disinclined, grudging, indisposed, loath, opposed, reluctant, unenthusiastic, unwilling

desist abstain, belay (*Nautical*), break off, cease, discontinue, end, forbear, give over (*informal*), give up, have done with, kick (*informal*), leave off, pause, refrain from, remit, stop, suspend

desolate *adjective* 1. bare, barren, bleak, desert, dreary, godforsaken, ruined, solitary, unfrequented, uninhabited, waste, wild ~*verb* 2. depopulate, despoil, destroy, devastate, lay low, lay waste, pillage, plunder, ravage, ruin ~*adjective* 3. abandoned, bereft, cheerless, comfortless, companionless, dejected, depressing, despondent, disconsolate, dismal, downcast, down in the dumps (*informal*), forlorn, forsaken, gloomy, lonely, melancholy, miserable, wretched ~*verb* 4. daunt, deject, depress, discourage, dishearten, dismay, distress, grieve
Antonyms *adjective* cheerful, happy, inhabited, joyous, light-hearted, populous ~*verb* cheer, develop, encourage, hearten, nourish

desolation 1. destruction, devastation, havoc, ravages, ruin, ruination 2. barrenness, bleakness, desolateness, forlornness, isolation, loneliness, solitariness, solitude, wildness 3. anguish, dejection, despair, distress, gloom, gloominess, melancholy, misery, sadness, unhappiness, woe, wretchedness

despair *verb* 1. despond, give up, lose heart, lose hope ~*noun* 2. anguish, dejection, depression, desperation, despondency, disheartenment, gloom, hopelessness, melancholy, misery, wretchedness 3. burden, cross, hardship, ordeal, pain, trial, tribulation

despairing anxious, at the end of one's tether, broken-hearted, dejected, depressed, desperate, despondent, disconsolate, dismal, downcast, down in the dumps (*informal*), frantic, grief-stricken, hopeless, inconsolable, melancholy, miserable, suicidal, wretched

despatch *see* DISPATCH

desperado bandit, criminal, cutthroat, gangster, gunman, heavy (*slang*), hoodlum (*chiefly U.S.*), lawbreaker, mugger (*informal*), outlaw, ruffian, thug, villain

desperate 1. audacious, dangerous, daring, death-defying, determined, foolhardy, frantic, furious, hasty, hazardous, headstrong, impetuous, madcap, precipitate, rash, reckless, risky, violent, wild 2. acute, critical, dire, drastic, extreme, great, urgent, very grave 3. at the end of one's tether, despairing, despondent, forlorn, hopeless, inconsolable, irrecoverable, irremediable, irretrievable, wretched

desperately 1. badly, dangerously, gravely, perilously, seriously, severely 2. appallingly, fearfully, frightfully, hopelessly, shockingly

desperation 1. defiance, foolhardiness, frenzy, heedlessness, impetuosity, madness, rashness, recklessness 2. agony, anguish, anxiety, despair, despondency, distraction, heartache, hopelessness, misery, pain, sorrow, torture, trouble, unhappiness, worry

The mass of men lead lives of quiet desperation
Henry David Thoreau *Walden*

Beggars can't be choosers

A drowning man will clutch at a straw

despicable abject, base, beyond contempt, cheap, contemptible, degrading, detestable, disgraceful, disreputable, hateful, ignominious, infamous, low, mean, pitiful, reprehensible, scurvy, shameful, sordid, vile, worthless, wretched
Antonyms admirable, estimable, ethical, exemplary, good, honest, honourable, moral, noble, praiseworthy, righteous, upright, virtuous, worthy

despise abhor, contemn, deride, detest, disdain, disregard, flout, have a down on (*informal*), loathe, look down on, neglect, revile, scorn, slight, spurn, undervalue
Antonyms admire, adore, be fond of, be keen on, cherish, dig (*slang*), esteem, fancy (*informal*), love, relish, revel in, take to

despite against, even with, in contempt of, in defiance of, in spite of, in the face of, in the teeth of, notwithstanding, regardless of, undeterred by

despoil denude, deprive, destroy, devastate, dispossess, divest, loot, pillage, plunder, ravage, rifle, rob, strip, total (*slang*), trash (*slang*), vandalize, wreak havoc upon, wreck

despoliation depredation, despoilment, destruction, devastation, havoc, looting, pillage, plunder, ruin, vandalism, wreckage

despond be cast down, be depressed, despair, give up, lose heart, lose hope, mourn, sorrow

despondency dejection, depression, despair, desperation, disconsolateness, discouragement, dispiritedness, downheartedness, gloom, hopelessness, low spirits, melancholy, misery, sadness, the hump (*Brit. informal*), wretchedness

despondent blue, dejected, depressed, despairing, disconsolate, discouraged, disheartened, dismal, dispirited, doleful, down, downcast, downhearted, down in the dumps (*informal*), gloomy, glum, hopeless, in despair, low, low-spirited, melancholy, miserable, morose, sad, sick as a parrot (*informal*), sorrowful, woebegone, wretched
Antonyms buoyant, cheerful, cheery, chirpy (*informal*), genial, glad, happy, hopeful, joyful, light-hearted, optimistic, upbeat (*informal*)

despot autocrat, dictator, monocrat, oppressor, tyrant

despotic absolute, arbitrary, arrogant, authoritarian, autocratic, dictatorial, domineering, imperious, monocratic, oppressive, tyrannical, unconstitutional

despotism absolutism, autarchy, autocracy, dictatorship, monocracy, oppression, totalitarianism, tyranny

dessert afters (*Brit. informal*), last course, pudding, second course, sweet, sweet course
Desserts and sweet dishes
see FOOD

destabilize damage, disable, impair, sabotage, subvert, undermine, weaken
Antonyms buttress, fortify, reinforce, shore up, stabilize, strengthen, sustain

destination 1. harbour, haven, journey's end, landing-place, resting-place, station, stop, terminus 2. aim, ambition, design, end, goal, intention, object, objective, purpose, target

destine allot, appoint, assign, consecrate, decree, design, devote, doom, earmark, fate, intend, mark out, ordain, predetermine, preordain, purpose, reserve

destined 1. bound, certain, designed, doomed, fated, foreordained, ineluctable, inescapable, inevitable, intended, meant, ordained, predestined, unavoidable 2. assigned, booked, bound for, directed, en route, heading, on the road to, routed, scheduled

destiny cup, divine decree, doom, fate, fortune, karma, kismet, lot, portion

destiny: a tyrant's authority for crime and a fool's excuse for failure
Ambrose Bierce *The Devil's Dictionary*

What must be, must be

destitute 1. dirt-poor (*informal*), distressed, down and out, flat broke (*informal*), impecunious, impoverished, indigent, in queer street (*informal*), insolvent, moneyless, necessitous, needy, on one's uppers, on the breadline (*informal*), on the rocks, penniless, penurious, poor, poverty-stricken, short, without two pennies to rub together (*informal*) 2. bereft of, deficient in, depleted, deprived of, devoid of, drained, empty of, in need of, lacking, wanting, without

destitution beggary, dire straits, distress, impecuniousness, indigence, neediness, pauperism, pennilessness, penury, privation, utter poverty, want
Antonyms affluence, fortune, good fortune, life of luxury, luxury, plenty, prosperity, riches, wealth

destroy annihilate, blow sky-high, blow to bits, break down, crush, demolish, desolate, devastate, dismantle, dispatch, eradicate, extinguish, extirpate, gut, kill, put paid to, ravage, raze, ruin, shatter, slay, smash, torpedo, total (*slang*), trash (*slang*), waste, wipe out, wreck

destruction annihilation, crushing, demolition, devastation, downfall, end, eradication, extermination, extinction, havoc, liquidation, massacre, overthrow, overwhelming, ruin, ruination, shattering, slaughter, undoing, wreckage, wrecking

destructive 1. baleful, baneful, calamitous, cataclysmic, catastrophic, damaging, deadly, deleterious, detrimental, devastating, fatal, harmful, hurtful, injurious, lethal, maleficent, noxious, pernicious, ruinous 2. adverse, antagonistic, contrary, derogatory, discouraging, discrediting, disparaging, hostile, invalidating, negative, opposed, undermining, vicious

desuetude abandonment, abeyance, discontinuation, disuse, neglect

desultory aimless, capricious, cursory, disconnected, discursive, disorderly, erratic, fitful, haphazard, inconsistent, inconstant, inexact, irregular, loose, maundering, off and on, rambling, random, roving, spasmodic, unmethodical, unsettled, unsystematic, vague

detach cut off, disconnect, disengage, disentangle, disjoin, disunite, divide, free, isolate, loosen, remove, segregate, separate, sever, tear off, unbridle, uncouple, unfasten, unhitch

Antonyms attach, bind, connect, fasten

detached 1. disconnected, discrete, disjoined, divided, free, loosened, separate, severed, unconnected 2. aloof, disinterested, dispassionate, impartial, impersonal, neutral, objective, reserved, unbiased, uncommitted, uninvolved, unprejudiced

Antonyms biased, concerned, interested, involved, partisan, prejudiced

detachment 1. aloofness, coolness, indifference, nonchalance, remoteness, unconcern 2. disinterestedness, fairness, impartiality, neutrality, nonpartisanship, objectivity 3. disconnection, disengagement, disjoining, separation, severing 4. *Military* body, detail, force, party, patrol, squad, task force, unit

detail *noun* 1. aspect, component, count, element, fact, factor, feature, item, particular, point, respect, specific, technicality 2. *plural* fine points, ins and outs, minutiae, niceties, particulars, parts, trivia, trivialities 3. **in detail** comprehensively, exhaustively, inside out, item by item, point by point, thoroughly 4. *Military* assignment, body, detachment, duty, fatigue, force, party, squad *~verb* 5. catalogue, delineate, depict, describe, enumerate, individualize, itemize, narrate, particularize, portray, recite, recount, rehearse, relate, specify, tabulate 6. allocate, appoint, assign, charge, commission, delegate, detach, send

detailed blow-by-blow, circumstantial, comprehensive, elaborate, exact, exhaustive, full, intricate, itemized, meticulous, minute, particular, particularized, specific, thorough

Antonyms brief, compact, concise, condensed, limited, pithy, short, slight, succinct, summary, superficial, terse

detain 1. check, delay, hinder, hold up, impede, keep, keep back, retard, slow up (*or* down), stay, stop 2. arrest, confine, hold, intern, restrain

detect 1. ascertain, catch, descry, distinguish, identify, note, notice, observe, recognize, scent, spot 2. catch, disclose, discover, expose, find, reveal, track down, uncover, unmask

detection discovery, exposé, exposure, ferreting out, revelation, tracking down, uncovering, unearthing, unmasking

detective bizzy (*slang*), C.I.D. man, constable, cop (*slang*), copper (*slang*), dick (*slang, chiefly U.S.*), gumshoe (*U.S. slang*), investigator, private eye, private investigator, sleuth (*informal*), tec (*slang*)

detention confinement, custody, delay, hindrance, holding back, imprisonment, incarceration, keeping in, porridge (*slang*), quarantine, restraint, withholding

Antonyms acquittal, discharge, emancipation, freedom, liberation, liberty, release

deter caution, check, damp, daunt, debar, discourage, dissuade, frighten, hinder, inhibit from, intimidate, prevent, prohibit, put off, restrain, stop, talk out of

detergent 1. *noun* cleaner, cleanser 2. *adjective* abstergent, cleaning, cleansing, detersive, purifying

deteriorate 1. corrupt, debase, decline, degenerate, degrade, deprave, depreciate, go downhill (*informal*), go to pot, go to the dogs (*informal*), impair, injure, lower, slump, spoil, worsen 2. be the worse for wear (*informal*), break down, crumble, decay, decline, decompose, disintegrate, ebb, fade, fall apart, lapse, retrogress, weaken, wear away

Antonyms advance, ameliorate, get better, improve, upgrade

deterioration atrophy, corrosion, debasement, decline, degeneration, degradation, *dégringolade*, depreciation, descent, dilapidation, disintegration, downturn, drop, fall, lapse, meltdown (*informal*), retrogression, slump, vitiation, worsening

determinable answerable, ascertainable, assessable, definable, describable, discoverable

determinate absolute, certain, conclusive, decided, decisive, defined, definite, definitive, determined, distinct, established, explicit, express, fixed, limited, positive, precise, quantified, settled, specified

determination 1. backbone, constancy, conviction, dedication, doggedness, drive, firmness, fortitude, indomitability, perseverance, persistence, resoluteness, resolution, resolve, single-mindedness, steadfastness, tenacity, willpower **2.** conclusion, decision, judgment, purpose, resolve, result, settlement, solution, verdict

Antonyms doubt, hesitancy, hesitation, indecision, instability, irresolution, vacillation

Nil carborundum illegitimi (Don't let the bastards grind you down)
cod Latin slogan in circulation during the Second World War

When the going gets tough, the tough get going

determine 1. arbitrate, conclude, decide, end, finish, fix upon, ordain, regulate, settle, terminate **2.** ascertain, certify, check, detect, discover, find out, learn, verify, work out **3.** choose, decide, elect, establish, fix, make up one's mind, purpose, resolve **4.** affect, condition, control, decide, dictate, direct, govern, impel, impose, incline, induce, influence, lead, modify, regulate, rule, shape

determined bent on, constant, dogged, firm, fixed, immovable, intent, persevering, persistent, purposeful, resolute, set on, single-minded, stalwart, steadfast, strong-minded, strong-willed, tenacious, unflinching, unwavering

determining conclusive, critical, crucial, deciding, decisive, definitive, essential, final, important, settling

deterrent *noun* check, curb, defensive measures, determent, discouragement, disincentive, hindrance, impediment, obstacle, restraint

Antonyms bait, carrot (*informal*), enticement, incentive, inducement, lure, motivation, spur, stimulus

detest abhor, abominate, despise, dislike intensely, execrate, feel aversion (disgust, hostility, repugnance) towards, hate, loathe, recoil from

Antonyms adore, cherish, dig (*slang*), dote on, love, relish

detestable abhorred, abominable, accursed, despicable, disgusting, execrable, hateful, heinous, loathsome, obnoxious, obscene, odious, offensive, repugnant, repulsive, revolting, shocking, vile, yucky *or* yukky (*slang*)

detestation 1. abhorrence, abomination, animosity, animus, antipathy, aversion, disgust, dislike, execration, hatred, hostility, loathing, odium, repugnance, revulsion **2.** abomination, anathema, bête noire, hate

dethrone depose, oust, uncrown, unseat

detonate blast, blow up, discharge, explode, fulminate, set off, touch off, trigger

detonation bang, blast, blow-up, boom, discharge, explosion, fulmination, report

detour bypass, byway, circuitous route, deviation, diversion, indirect course, roundabout way

detract 1. devaluate, diminish, lessen, lower, reduce, take away from **2.** deflect, distract, divert, shift

Antonyms add to, augment, boost, complement, enhance, improve, reinforce, strengthen

detraction abuse, aspersion, belittlement, calumny, defamation, denigration, deprecation, disparagement, innuendo, insinuation, misrepresentation, muckraking, running down, scandalmongering, scurrility, slander, traducement, vituperation

detractor backbiter, belittler, defamer, denigrator, derogator (*rare*), disparager, muckraker, scandalmonger, slanderer, traducer

detriment damage, disadvantage, disservice, harm, hurt, impairment, injury, loss, mischief, prejudice

detrimental adverse, baleful, damaging, deleterious, destructive, disadvantageous, harmful, inimical, injurious, mischievous, pernicious, prejudicial, unfavourable

Antonyms advantageous, beneficial, efficacious, favourable, good, helpful, salutary

detritus debris, fragments, litter, remains, rubbish, waste

de trop in the way, redundant, superfluous, surplus, unnecessary, unwanted, unwelcome

devastate 1. demolish, desolate, despoil, destroy, lay waste, level, pillage, plunder, ravage, raze, ruin, sack, spoil, total (*slang*), trash (*slang*), waste, wreck **2.** *informal* chagrin, confound, discomfit, discompose, disconcert, floor (*informal*), nonplus, overpower, overwhelm, take aback

devastating caustic, cutting, deadly, destructive, effective, incisive, keen, mordant, overpowering, overwhelming, ravishing, sardonic, satirical, savage, stunning, trenchant, vitriolic, withering

devastation demolition, depredation, desolation, destruction, havoc, pillage, plunder, ravages, ruin, ruination, spoliation

develop 1. advance, blossom, cultivate, evolve, flourish, foster, grow, mature, progress, promote, prosper, ripen **2.** amplify, augment, broaden, dilate upon, elaborate, enlarge, expand, unfold, work out **3.** acquire, begin, breed, commence, contract, establish, form, generate, invent, originate, pick up, start **4.** be a direct result of, break out, come about, ensue, follow, happen, result

development 1. advance, advancement, evolution, expansion, growth, improvement, increase, maturity, progress, progression, spread, unfolding, unravelling **2.** change, circumstance, event, happening, incident, issue, occurrence, outcome, phenomenon, result, situation, turn of events, upshot

deviant 1. *adjective* aberrant, abnormal, bent (*slang*), deviate, devious, freaky (*slang*), heretical, kinky (*slang*), perverse, perverted, pervy (*slang*), queer (*informal, derogatory*), sick (*informal*), sicko (*informal*), twisted, warped, wayward 2. *noun* deviate, freak, misfit, odd type, pervert, queer (*informal, derogatory*), sicko (*informal*)
Antonyms conventional, normal, orthodox, straight, straightforward

deviate avert, bend, deflect, depart, differ, digress, diverge, drift, err, meander, part, stray, swerve, turn, turn aside, vary, veer, wander

deviation aberration, alteration, change, deflection, departure, digression, discrepancy, disparity, divergence, fluctuation, inconsistency, irregularity, shift, variance, variation

device 1. apparatus, appliance, contraption, contrivance, gadget, gimmick, gismo *or* gizmo (*slang, chiefly U.S. & Canad.*), implement, instrument, invention, tool, utensil, waldo 2. artifice, design, dodge, expedient, gambit, improvisation, manoeuvre, plan, ploy, project, purpose, ruse, scheme, shift, stratagem, strategy, stunt, trick, wile 3. badge, colophon, crest, design, emblem, figure, insignia, logo, motif, motto, symbol, token

devil 1. *sometimes capital* Apollyon, archfiend, Beelzebub, Belial, Clootie (*Scot.*), demon, fiend, Lucifer, Old Harry (*informal*), Old Nick (*informal*), Old Scratch (*informal*), Prince of Darkness, Satan 2. beast, brute, demon, fiend, ghoul, monster, ogre, rogue, savage, terror, villain 3. imp, monkey (*informal*), pickle (*Brit. informal*), rascal, rogue, scamp, scoundrel 4. beggar, creature, thing, unfortunate, wretch 5. demon, enthusiast, fiend, go-getter (*informal*)

If the devil doesn't exist, but man has created him, he has created him in his own image and likeness
Fyodor Dostoevsky *The Brothers Karamazov*

How art thou fallen from heaven, O Lucifer, son of the morning!
Bible: Isaiah

Be sober, be vigilant; because your adversary the devil, as a roaring lion, walketh about, seeking whom he may devour
Bible: I Peter

The devil's most devilish when respectable
Elizabeth Barrett Browning *Aurora Leigh*

An apology for the Devil; It must be remembered that we have only heard one side of the case. God has written all the books
Samuel Butler

Better the devil you know than the devil you don't know

The devil looks after his own

He who sups with the devil should have a long spoon

Talk of the devil, and he shall appear

devilish accursed, atrocious, damnable, detestable, diabolic, diabolical, execrable, fiendish, hellish, infernal, satanic, wicked

devil-may-care careless, casual, easy-going, flippant, happy-go-lucky, heedless, insouciant, nonchalant, reckless, swaggering, swashbuckling, unconcerned

devilment devilry, knavery, mischief, mischievousness, naughtiness, rascality, roguery, roguishness

devilry, deviltry 1. devilment, jiggery-pokery (*informal, chiefly Brit.*), knavery, mischief, mischievousness, monkey-business (*informal*), rascality, roguery 2. cruelty, evil, malevolence, malice, vice, viciousness, villainy, wickedness 3. black magic, diablerie, diabolism, sorcery

devious 1. calculating, crooked (*informal*), deceitful, dishonest, double-dealing, evasive, indirect, insidious, insincere, not straightforward, scheming, sly, surreptitious, treacherous, tricky, underhand, wily 2. circuitous, confusing, crooked, deviating, erratic, excursive, indirect, misleading, rambling, roundabout, tortuous, wandering
Antonyms blunt, candid, direct, downright, forthright, frank, honest, straight, straightforward, undeviating, unswerving

devise arrange, conceive, concoct, construct, contrive, design, dream up, form, formulate, frame, imagine, invent, plan, plot, prepare, project, scheme, think up, work out

devitalize cripple, debilitate, enervate, enfeeble, exhaust, reduce, sap, undermine, weaken

devoid barren, bereft, deficient, denuded, destitute, empty, free from, lacking, sans (*archaic*), vacant, void, wanting, without

devolution decentralization, delegation

devolve 1. be transferred, commission, consign, delegate, depute, entrust, fall upon *or* to, rest with, transfer 2. *Law* alienate, be handed down, convey

devote allot, apply, appropriate, assign, commit, concern oneself, consecrate, dedicate, enshrine, give, occupy oneself, pledge, reserve, set apart

devoted ardent, caring, committed, concerned, constant, dedicated, devout, faithful, fond, loving, loyal, staunch, steadfast, true
Antonyms disloyal, inconstant, indifferent, uncommitted, undedicated, unfaithful

devotee addict, adherent, admirer, aficionado, buff (*informal*), disciple, enthusiast, fan, fanatic, follower, supporter, votary

devotion 1. adherence, allegiance, commitment, consecration, constancy, dedication, faithfulness, fidelity, loyalty 2. adoration, devoutness, godliness, holiness, piety, prayer, religiousness, reverence, sanctity, spirituality,

worship **3.** affection, ardour, attachment, earnestness, fervour, fondness, intensity, love, passion, zeal **4.** *plural* church service, divine office, prayers, religious observance
Antonyms (*sense 1*) carelessness, disregard, inattention, indifference, laxity, laxness, neglect, thoughtlessness (*sense 2*) derision, disrespect, impiety, irreverence

devotional devout, holy, pious, religious, reverential, sacred, solemn, spiritual

devour **1.** bolt, consume, cram, dispatch, eat, gobble, gorge, gulp, guzzle, pig out on (*slang*), polish off (*informal*), stuff, swallow, wolf **2.** annihilate, consume, destroy, ravage, spend, waste, wipe out **3.** absorb, appreciate, be engrossed by, be preoccupied, delight in, drink in, enjoy, feast on, go through, read compulsively *or* voraciously, relish, revel in, take in

devouring consuming, excessive, flaming, insatiable, intense, overwhelming, passionate, powerful

devout **1.** godly, holy, orthodox, pious, prayerful, pure, religious, reverent, saintly **2.** ardent, deep, devoted, earnest, fervent, genuine, heartfelt, intense, passionate, profound, serious, sincere, zealous
Antonyms impious, indifferent, irreligious, irreverent, passive, sacrilegious

devoutly fervently, heart and soul, profoundly, sincerely, with all one's heart

dexterity **1.** adroitness, artistry, craft, deftness, effortlessness, expertise, facility, finesse, handiness, knack, mastery, neatness, nimbleness, proficiency, skill, smoothness, touch **2.** ability, address, adroitness, aptitude, aptness, art, cleverness, expertness, ingenuity, readiness, skilfulness, tact
Antonyms clumsiness, gaucheness, inability, incapacity, incompetence, ineptitude, uselessness

dexterous able, active, acute, adept, adroit, agile, apt, clever, deft, expert, handy, ingenious, masterly, neat, nimble, nimble-fingered, proficient, prompt, quick, skilful

diabolic **1.** demoniac, demonic, devilish, fiendish, hellish, infernal, satanic **2.** atrocious, cruel, evil, fiendish, monstrous, nefarious, vicious, villainous, wicked

diabolical abysmal, appalling, atrocious, damnable, difficult, disastrous, dreadful, excruciating, fiendish, from hell (*informal*), hellacious (*U.S. slang*), hellish, nasty, outrageous, shocking, tricky, unpleasant, vile

diadem circlet, coronet, crown, tiara

diagnose analyse, determine, distinguish, identify, interpret, investigate, pinpoint, pronounce, put one's finger on, recognize

diagnosis **1.** analysis, examination, investigation, scrutiny **2.** conclusion, interpretation, opinion, pronouncement

diagnostic demonstrative, distinctive, distinguishing, idiosyncratic, indicative, particular, peculiar, recognizable, symptomatic

diagonal *adjective* angled, cater-cornered (*U.S. informal*), cornerways, cross, crossways, crosswise, oblique, slanting

diagonally aslant, at an angle, cornerwise, crosswise, obliquely, on the bias, on the cross

diagram chart, drawing, figure, layout, outline, plan, representation, sketch

dialect accent, brogue, idiom, jargon, language, lingo (*informal*), localism, patois, pronunciation, provincialism, speech, tongue, vernacular

> *Dialect words - those terrible marks of the beast to the truly genteel*
> Thomas Hardy *The Mayor of Casterbridge*

dialectal dialect, idiomatic, local, nonstandard, regional, restricted, vernacular

dialectic **1.** *adjective* analytic, argumentative, dialectical, logical, polemical, rational, rationalistic **2.** *noun often plural* argumentation, contention, discussion, disputation, logic, polemics, ratiocination, reasoning

dialogue **1.** colloquy, communication, confabulation, conference, conversation, converse, discourse, discussion, duologue, interlocution **2.** conversation, lines, script, spoken part

diametric, diametrical antipodal, antithetical, conflicting, contrary, contrasting, counter, opposed, opposite, poles apart

diametrically absolutely, completely, entirely, utterly

diaphanous chiffon, clear, cobwebby, delicate, filmy, fine, gauzy, gossamer, light, pellucid, see-through, sheer, thin, translucent, transparent

diarrhoea *noun* dysentery, gippy tummy, holiday tummy, looseness, Montezuma's revenge (*informal*), Spanish tummy, the runs, the skits (*informal*), the skitters (*informal*), the trots (*informal*)

diary appointment book, chronicle, daily record, day-to-day account, engagement book, Filofax (*Trademark*), journal

> *Keep a diary and someday it'll keep you*
> Mae West
>
> *Only good girls keep diaries. Bad girls don't have the time*
> Tallulah Bankhead

diatribe abuse, castigation, criticism, denunciation, disputation, harangue, invective, philippic, reviling, stream of abuse, stricture, tirade, verbal onslaught, vituperation

dicey chancy (*informal*), dangerous, difficult, hairy (*slang*), risky, ticklish, tricky

dichotomy bisection, disjunction, division, divorce, separation, split (in two)

dicky *adjective* fluttery, queer, shaky, unreliable, unsound, unsteady, weak

dictate *verb* **1.** read out, say, speak, transmit, utter **2.** command, decree, demand, direct, enjoin, establish, impose, lay down, lay down the law, ordain, order, prescribe, pronounce ~*noun* **3.** behest, bidding, command, decree, demand, direction, edict, fiat, injunction, mandate, order, ordinance, requirement, statute, ultimatum, word **4.** canon, code, dictum, law, precept, principle, rule

dictator absolute ruler, autocrat, despot, oppressor, tyrant

dictatorial **1.** absolute, arbitrary, autocratic, despotic, totalitarian, tyrannical, unlimited, unrestricted **2.** authoritarian, bossy (*informal*), dogmatical, domineering, imperious, iron-handed, magisterial, oppressive, overbearing
Antonyms constitutional, democratic, egalitarian, humble, restricted, servile, suppliant, tolerant

dictatorship absolute rule, absolutism, authoritarianism, autocracy, despotism, reign of terror, totalitarianism, tyranny

diction **1.** expression, language, phraseology, phrasing, style, usage, vocabulary, wording **2.** articulation, delivery, elocution, enunciation, fluency, inflection, intonation, pronunciation, speech

dictionary concordance, encyclopedia, glossary, lexicon, vocabulary, wordbook

To make dictionaries is dull work
Dr. Johnson *Dictionary*

dictionary: a malevolent literary device for cramping the growth of a language and making it hard and inelastic. This dictionary, however, is a most useful work
Ambrose Bierce *The Devil's Dictionary*

Dictionaries are like watches, the worst is better than none, and the best cannot be expected to go quite true
Dr. Johnson

dictum **1.** canon, command, decree, demand, dictate, edict, fiat, order, pronouncement **2.** adage, axiom, gnome, maxim, precept, proverb, saw, saying

didactic edifying, educational, enlightening, homiletic, instructive, moral, moralizing, pedagogic, pedantic, preceptive

die **1.** breathe one's last, buy it (*U.S. slang*), buy the farm (*U.S. slang*), check out (*U.S. slang*), croak (*slang*), decease, depart, expire, finish, give up the ghost, go belly-up (*slang*), hop the twig (*slang*), kick it (*slang*), kick the bucket (*slang*), pass away, peg it (*informal*), peg out (*informal*), perish, pop one's clogs (*informal*), snuff it (*slang*) **2.** decay, decline, disappear, dwindle, ebb, end, fade, lapse, pass, sink, subside, vanish, wane, wilt, wither **3.** break down, fade out *or* away, fail, fizzle out, halt, lose power, peter out, run down, stop **4.** ache, be eager, desire, hunger, languish, long, pine for, set one's heart on, swoon, yearn **5.** *usually with* **of** be overcome, collapse, succumb to
Antonyms be born, begin, build, come to life, exist, flourish, grow, increase, live, survive

It is better to die on your feet than to live on your knees
Dolores Ibárruri (La Pasionaria)

Only we die in earnest, that's no jest
Walter Raleigh *On the Life of Man*

Die, my dear doctor? That's the last thing I shall do!
Lord Palmerston

It's not that I'm afraid to die. I just don't want to be there when it happens
Woody Allen *Death*

To die will be an awfully big adventure
J.M. Barrie *Peter Pan*

Dying is a very dull, dreary affair. And my advice to you is to have nothing whatever to do with it
Somerset Maugham

We shall die alone
Blaise Pascal *Pensées*

Whom the gods love dies young
Menander *Dis Exapaton*

A man dies still if he has done nothing, as one who has done much
Homer *Iliad*

It as natural to die as to be born; and to a little infant, perhaps, the one is as painful as the other
Francis Bacon

die-hard **1.** *noun* fanatic, intransigent, old fogy, reactionary, stick-in-the-mud (*informal*), ultraconservative, zealot **2.** *adjective* dyed-in-the-wool, immovable, inflexible, intransigent, reactionary, ultraconservative, uncompromising, unreconstructed (*chiefly U.S.*)

diet[1] *noun* **1.** abstinence, dietary, fast, regime, regimen **2.** aliment, comestibles, commons, edibles, fare, food, nourishment, nutriment, provisions, rations, subsistence, sustenance, viands, victuals ~*verb* **3.** abstain, eat sparingly, fast, lose weight, reduce, slim
Antonyms *verb* get fat, glut, gobble, gormandize, guzzle, indulge, overindulge, pig out (*slang*), stuff oneself

with cheesecake you've got a choice:
Either EAT it or BE it
Liz Lochhead *Fat Girl's Confession*

diet[2] *noun* chamber, congress, convention, council, legislative assembly, legislature, meeting, parliament, sitting

dieter calorie counter, faster, reducer, slimmer, weight watcher

differ 1. be dissimilar, be distinct, contradict, contrast, depart from, diverge, run counter to, stand apart, vary **2.** clash, contend, debate, demur, disagree, dispute, dissent, oppose, take issue

Antonyms accord, acquiesce, agree, assent, coincide, concur, cooperate, harmonize

difference 1. alteration, change, contrast, deviation, differentiation, discrepancy, disparity, dissimilarity, distinction, distinctness, divergence, diversity, unlikeness, variation, variety **2.** distinction, exception, idiosyncrasy, particularity, peculiarity, singularity **3.** argument, clash, conflict, contention, contrariety, contretemps, controversy, debate, disagreement, discordance, dispute, quarrel, row, set-to (*informal*), strife, tiff, wrangle **4.** balance, remainder, rest, result

Antonyms (*senses 1, 2 & 3*) affinity, agreement, comparability, concordance, conformity, congruence, likeness, relation, resemblance, sameness, similarity, similitude

different 1. altered, at odds, at variance, changed, clashing, contrasting, deviating, discrepant, disparate, dissimilar, divergent, diverse, inconsistent, opposed, streets apart, unlike **2.** another, discrete, distinct, individual, other, separate **3.** assorted, divers (*archaic*), diverse, manifold, many, miscellaneous, multifarious, numerous, several, some, sundry, varied, various **4.** another story, atypical, bizarre, distinctive, extraordinary, left-field (*informal*), out of the ordinary, peculiar, rare, singular, something else, special, strange, uncommon, unconventional, unique, unusual

And now for something completely different
Monty Python's Flying Circus

differential 1. *adjective* diacritical, discriminative, distinctive, distinguishing **2.** *noun* amount of difference, difference, discrepancy, disparity

differentiate 1. contrast, discern, discriminate, distinguish, make a distinction, mark off, separate, set off *or* apart, tell apart **2.** adapt, alter, change, convert, make different, modify, transform

differently 1. contrastingly, in another way, in contrary fashion, otherwise **2.** contradictorily, dissimilarly, diversely, erratically, idiosyncratically, inconsistently, unevenly, variably

Antonyms (*sense 1*) in like manner, in the same way, likewise, similarly (*sense 2*) comparably, consistently, invariably, similarly

difficult 1. arduous, burdensome, demanding, formidable, hard, laborious, like getting blood out of a stone, no picnic (*informal*), onerous, painful, strenuous, toilsome, uphill, wearisome **2.** abstract, abstruse, baffling, complex, complicated, delicate, enigmatical, intricate, involved, knotty, obscure, perplexing, problematical, thorny, ticklish **3.** demanding, fastidious, fractious, fussy, hard to please, intractable, obstreperous, perverse, refractory, rigid, tiresome, troublesome, trying, unaccommodating, unamenable, unmanageable **4.** dark, full of hardship, grim, hard, straitened, tough, trying

Antonyms accommodating, amenable, cooperative, easy, easy-peasy (*slang*), light, manageable, obvious, plain, pleasant, simple, straightforward, uncomplicated

difficulty 1. arduousness, awkwardness, hardship, laboriousness, labour, pain, painfulness, strain, strenuousness, tribulation **2.** deep water, dilemma, distress, embarrassment, fix (*informal*), hot water (*informal*), jam (*informal*), mess, perplexity, pickle (*informal*), plight, predicament, quandary, spot (*informal*), straits, tight spot, trial, trouble **3.** *often plural* complication, hassle (*informal*), hazard, hindrance, hurdle, impediment, objection, obstacle, opposition, pitfall, problem, protest, snag, stumbling block

Ten thousand difficulties do not make one doubt
Cardinal Newman *Apologia pro Vita Sua*

diffidence backwardness, bashfulness, constraint, doubt, fear, hesitancy, hesitation, humility, insecurity, lack of self-confidence, meekness, modesty, reluctance, reserve, self-consciousness, sheepishness, shyness, timidity, timidness, timorousness, unassertiveness

Antonyms assurance, boldness, confidence, courage, firmness, self-confidence, self-possession

diffident backward, bashful, constrained, distrustful, doubtful, hesitant, insecure, meek, modest, reluctant, reserved, self-conscious, self-effacing, sheepish, shrinking, shy, suspicious, timid, timorous, unassertive, unassuming, unobtrusive, unsure, withdrawn

diffuse *adjective* **1.** circumlocutory, copious, diffusive, digressive, discursive, long-winded, loose, maundering, meandering, prolix, rambling, vague, verbose, waffling (*informal*), wordy **2.** dispersed, scattered, spread out, unconcentrated *~verb* **3.** circulate, dispel, dispense, disperse, disseminate, dissipate, distribute, propagate, scatter, spread

Antonyms *adjective* apposite, brief, compendious, concentrated, concise, succinct, terse, to the point

diffusion 1. circulation, dispersal, dispersion, dissemination, dissipation, distribution, expansion, propaganda, propagation, scattering, spread **2.** circuitousness, diffuseness, digressiveness, discursiveness, long-windedness, prolixity, rambling, verbiage, verbosity, wandering, wordiness

dig *verb* **1.** break up, burrow, delve, excavate, gouge, grub, hoe, hollow out, mine, penetrate, pierce, quarry, scoop, till, tunnel, turn over **2.** drive, jab, poke, prod, punch, thrust **3.** delve, dig down, go into, investigate, probe, research, search **4.** *with* **out** *or* **up** bring to light, come across, come up with, discover, expose, extricate, find, retrieve, root (*informal*), rootle, uncover, unearth **5.** *informal* appreciate, enjoy, follow, groove (*dated slang*), like, understand ~*noun* **6.** jab, poke, prod, punch, thrust **7.** barb, crack (*slang*), cutting remark, gibe, insult, jeer, quip, sneer, taunt, wisecrack (*informal*)

digest *verb* **1.** absorb, assimilate, concoct, dissolve, incorporate, macerate **2.** absorb, assimilate, con, consider, contemplate, grasp, master, meditate, ponder, study, take in, understand **3.** arrange, classify, codify, dispose, methodize, systematize, tabulate **4.** abridge, compress, condense, reduce, shorten, summarize ~*noun* **5.** abridgment, abstract, compendium, condensation, epitome, précis, résumé, summary, synopsis

digestion absorption, assimilation, conversion, incorporation, ingestion, transformation

dig in **1.** defend, entrench, establish, fortify, maintain **2.** *informal* begin, fall to, set about, start eating, tuck in (*informal*)

digit **1.** finger, toe **2.** figure, number, numeral

dignified august, decorous, distinguished, exalted, formal, grave, honourable, imposing, lofty, lordly, noble, reserved, solemn, stately, upright

Antonyms crass, inelegant, unbecoming, undignified, unseemly, vulgar

dignify adorn, advance, aggrandize, distinguish, elevate, ennoble, exalt, glorify, grace, honour, promote, raise

dignitary *noun* bigwig (*informal*), celeb (*informal*), high-up (*informal*), notability, notable, personage, pillar of society (the church, the state), public figure, V.I.P., worthy

dignity **1.** courtliness, decorum, grandeur, gravity, hauteur, loftiness, majesty, nobility, propriety, solemnity, stateliness **2.** elevation, eminence, excellence, glory, greatness, honour, importance, nobleness, rank, respectability, standing, station, status **3.** *amour-propre*, pride, self-esteem, self-importance, self-possession, self-regard, self-respect

> *I left the room with silent dignity, but caught my foot in the mat*
>
> George Grossmith *The Diary of a Nobody*

digress be diffuse, depart, deviate, diverge, drift, expatiate, get off the point *or* subject, go off at a tangent, meander, ramble, stray, turn aside, wander

digression apostrophe, aside, departure, detour, deviation, divergence, diversion, footnote, obiter dictum, parenthesis, straying, wandering

digressive anecdotal, circuitous, circumlocutory, diffuse, discursive, divergent, drifting, episodic, excursive, meandering, rambling

digs accommodation, lodgings, quarters, rooms

dilapidated battered, beat-up (*informal*), broken-down, crumbling, decayed, decaying, decrepit, fallen in, falling apart, gone to rack and ruin, in ruins, neglected, ramshackle, rickety, ruined, ruinous, run-down, shabby, shaky, tumbledown, uncared for, worn-out

dilapidation collapse, decay, demolition, destruction, deterioration, disintegration, disrepair, dissolution, downfall, ruin, waste, wear and tear

dilate **1.** broaden, distend, enlarge, expand, extend, puff out, stretch, swell, widen **2.** amplify, be profuse, be prolix, descant, detail, develop, dwell on, enlarge, expand, expatiate, expound, spin out

Antonyms compress, constrict, contract, narrow, shrink

dilation broadening, dilatation, distension, enlargement, expansion, extension, increase, spread

dilatory backward, behindhand, dallying, delaying, laggard, lingering, loitering, procrastinating, putting off, slack, slow, sluggish, snail-like, tardy, tarrying, time-wasting

Antonyms on-the-ball (*informal*), prompt, punctual, sharp (*informal*)

dilemma **1.** difficulty, embarrassment, fix (*informal*), how-do-you-do (*informal*), jam (*informal*), mess, perplexity, pickle (*informal*), plight, predicament, problem, puzzle, quandary, spot (*informal*), strait, tight corner *or* spot **2.** **on the horns of a dilemma** between a rock and a hard place (*informal*), between Scylla and Charybdis, between the devil and the deep blue sea

dilettante aesthete, amateur, dabbler, nonprofessional, trifler

diligence activity, application, assiduity, assiduousness, attention, attentiveness, care, constancy, earnestness, heedfulness, industry, intentness, laboriousness, perseverance, sedulousness

diligent active, assiduous, attentive, busy, careful, conscientious, constant, earnest, hard-working, indefatigable, industrious, laborious, painstaking, persevering, persistent, sedulous, studious, tireless

Antonyms careless, dilatory, good-for-nothing, inconstant, indifferent, lazy

dilly-dally dally, dawdle, delay, dither (*chiefly Brit.*), falter, fluctuate, hesitate, hover, hum and haw, linger, loiter, potter, procrastinate, shillyshally (*informal*), trifle, vacillate, waver

dilute *verb* **1.** adulterate, cut, make thinner, thin (out), water down, weaken **2.** *figurative* attenuate, decrease, diffuse, diminish, lessen, mitigate, reduce, temper, weaken
Antonyms concentrate, condense, intensify, strengthen, thicken

diluted adulterated, cut, dilute, thinned, watered down, watery, weak, weakened, wishy-washy (*informal*)

dim *adjective* **1.** caliginous (*archaic*), cloudy, dark, darkish, dusky, grey, overcast, poorly lit, shadowy, tenebrous, unilluminated **2.** bleary, blurred, faint, fuzzy, ill-defined, indistinct, obscured, shadowy, unclear **3.** braindead (*informal*), dense, doltish, dozy (*Brit. informal*), dull, dumb (*informal*), obtuse, slow, slow on the uptake (*informal*), stupid, thick **4.** confused, hazy, imperfect, indistinct, intangible, obscure, remote, shadowy, vague **5.** dingy, dull, feeble, lacklustre, muted, opaque, pale, sullied, tarnished, weak **6.** dashing, depressing, discouraging, gloomy, sombre, unfavourable, unpromising **7. take a dim view** be displeased, be sceptical, disapprove, look askance, reject, suspect, take exception, view with disfavour *~verb* **8.** bedim, blur, cloud, darken, dull, fade, lower, obscure, tarnish, turn down
Antonyms (*sense 1*) bright, clear, cloudless, fair, limpid, pleasant, sunny, unclouded (*sense 2*) bright, brilliant, clear, distinct, limpid, palpable (*sense 3*) acute, astute, aware, brainy, bright, clever, intelligent, keen, quick-witted, sharp, smart

dimension *often plural* **1.** amplitude, bulk, capacity, extent, measurement, proportions, size, volume **2.** bigness, extent, greatness, importance, largeness, magnitude, measure, range, scale, scope

diminish **1.** abate, contract, curtail, cut, decrease, downsize, lessen, lower, reduce, retrench, shrink, weaken **2.** decline, die out, dwindle, ebb, fade away, peter out, recede, shrivel, slacken, subside, wane **3.** belittle, cheapen, demean, depreciate, devalue
Antonyms amplify, augment, enhance, enlarge, expand, grow, heighten, increase

diminution abatement, contraction, curtailment, cut, cutback, decay, decline, decrease, deduction, lessening, reduction, retrenchment, weakening

diminutive *adjective* bantam, Lilliputian, little, midget, mini, miniature, minute, petite, pocket(-sized), pygmy *or* pigmy, small, teensy-weensy, teeny-weeny, tiny, undersized, wee
Antonyms big, colossal, enormous, giant, gigantic, great, immense, jumbo (*informal*), king-size, massive (*informal*)

dimwit blockhead, bonehead (*slang*), booby, dullard, dunce, dunderhead, fathead (*informal*), gobshite (*Irish taboo slang*), ignoramus, lamebrain (*informal*), nitwit (*informal*), numpty (*Scot. informal*), numskull *or* numbskull

dim-witted braindead (*informal*), dense, dim, doltish, dopey (*informal*), dozy (*Brit. informal*), dull, dumb (*informal*), obtuse, slow, slow on the uptake, stupid, thick (*informal*), thick-skulled, unperceptive
Antonyms alert, astute, bright, clever, keen, perceptive, quick on the uptake, quick-witted, sharp, shrewd, smart

din **1.** *noun* babel, clamour, clangour, clash, clatter, commotion, crash, hubbub, hullabaloo, noise, outcry, pandemonium, racket, row, shout, uproar **2.** *verb usually with* **into** drum into, go on at, hammer into, inculcate, instil, instruct, teach
Antonyms *noun* calm, calmness, hush, peace, quiet, quietness, silence, tranquillity

dine **1.** banquet, chow down (*slang*), eat, feast, lunch, sup **2.** *often with* **on, off** *or* **upon** consume, eat, feed on

dingle dale, dell, glen, hollow, vale, valley

dingy bedimmed, colourless, dark, dim, dirty, discoloured, drab, dreary, dull, dusky, faded, gloomy, grimy, murky, obscure, seedy, shabby, soiled, sombre, tacky (*informal*)

dinky cute, dainty, mini, miniature, natty (*informal*), neat, petite, small, trim

dinner banquet, beanfeast (*Brit. informal*), blowout (*slang*), collation, feast, main meal, meal, refection, repast, spread (*informal*)

dinosaur

Dinosaurs

allosaur(us)	megalosaur(us)
ankylosaur(us)	mosasaur(us)
apatosaur(us)	oviraptor
atlantosaur(us)	plesiosaur(us)
brachiosaur(us)	pteranodon
brontosaur(us)	pterodactyl *or* pterosaur
ceratosaur(us)	protoceratops
compsognathus	stegodon *or* stegodont
dimetrodon	stegosaur(us)
diplodocus	theropod
dolichosaur(us)	titanosaur(us)
dromiosaurus	trachodon
elasmosaur(us)	triceratops
hadrosaur(us)	tyrannosaur(us)
ichthyosaur(us)	velociraptor
iguanodon *or* iguanodont	

dint **1.** *As in* **by dint of** force, means, power,

use, virtue **2.** blow, dent, depression, indentation, stroke

diocese bishopric, see

dip *verb* **1.** bathe, douse, duck, dunk, immerse, plunge, rinse, souse **2.** decline, descend, disappear, droop, drop (down), fade, fall, lower, sag, set, sink, slope, slump, subside, tilt **3.** ladle, scoop, spoon **4.** *with* **in** *or* **into** browse, dabble, glance at, peruse, play at, run over, sample, skim, try **5.** *with* **in** *or* **into** draw upon, reach into *~noun* **6.** douche, drenching, ducking, immersion, plunge, soaking **7.** bathe, dive, plunge, swim **8.** concoction, dilution, infusion, mixture, preparation, solution, suspension **9.** basin, concavity, depression, hole, hollow, incline, slope **10.** decline, drop, fall, lowering, sag, slip, slump

diplomacy **1.** international negotiation, statecraft, statesmanship **2.** artfulness, craft, delicacy, discretion, finesse, savoir-faire, skill, subtlety, tact

Antonyms awkwardness, clumsiness, ineptness, tactlessness, thoughtlessness

Diplomacy is to do and say
The nastiest thing in the nicest way
Isaac Goldberg *The Reflex*

A soft answer turneth away wrath
Bible: Proverbs

A word spoken in due season, how good is it!
Bible: Proverbs

A word fitly spoken is like apples of gold in pictures of silver
Bible: Proverbs

diplomacy: the patriotic art of lying for one's country
Ambrose Bierce *The Devil's Dictionary*

diplomat conciliator, go-between, mediator, moderator, negotiator, politician, public relations expert, tactician

A diplomat is a man who remembers a woman's birthday but never remembers her age
Robert Frost

diplomatic adept, discreet, polite, politic, prudent, sensitive, subtle, tactful

Antonyms impolitic, insensitive, rude, tactless, thoughtless, undiplomatic, unsubtle

dire **1.** alarming, appalling, awful, calamitous, cataclysmic, catastrophic, cruel, disastrous, godawful (*slang*), horrible, horrid, ruinous, terrible, woeful **2.** bodeful, dismal, dreadful, fearful, gloomy, grim, ominous, portentous **3.** critical, crucial, crying, desperate, drastic, exigent, extreme, now or never, pressing, urgent

direct[1] *verb* **1.** administer, advise, call the shots, call the tune, conduct, control, dispose, govern, guide, handle, lead, manage, mastermind, oversee, preside over, regulate, rule, run, superintend, supervise **2.** bid, charge, command, demand, dictate, enjoin, instruct, order **3.** guide, indicate, lead, point in the direction of, point the way, show **4.** address, aim, cast, fix, focus, intend, level, mean, point, train, turn **5.** address, label, mail, route, send, superscribe

direct[2] *adjective* **1.** candid, downright, frank, honest, man-to-man, matter-of-fact, open, outspoken, plain-spoken, round, sincere, straight, straightforward, upfront (*informal*) **2.** absolute, blunt, categorical, downright, explicit, express, plain, point-blank, unambiguous, unequivocal **3.** nonstop, not crooked, shortest, straight, through, unbroken, undeviating, uninterrupted **4.** face-to-face, first-hand, head-on, immediate, personal

Antonyms ambiguous, circuitous, crooked, devious, indirect, mediated, sly, subtle

direction **1.** administration, charge, command, control, government, guidance, leadership, management, order, oversight, superintendence, supervision **2.** aim, bearing, course, line, path, road, route, track, way **3.** bent, bias, current, drift, end, leaning, orientation, proclivity, tack, tendency, tenor, trend **4.** address, label, mark, superscription

Compass Point	Abbreviation
North	N
North by East	N by E
North North East	NNE
North East by North	NE by N
North East	NE
North East by East	NE by E
East North East	ENE
East by North	E by N
East	E
East by South	E by S
East South East	ESE
South East by East	SE by E
South East	SE
South East by South	SE by S
South South East	SSE
South by East	S by E
South	S
South by West	S by W
South South West	SSW
South West by South	SW by S
South West	SW
South West by West	SW by W
West South West	WSW
West by South	W by S
West	W
West by North	W by N
West North West	WNW
North West by West	NW by W
North West	NW
North West by North	NW by N
North North West	NNW
North by West	N by W

Cardinal point	Related adjective
north	arctic *or* boreal
east	oriental
south	meridional *or* austral
west	occidental *or* hesperidan

directions briefing, guidance, guidelines, indication, instructions, plan, recommendation, regulations

directive *noun* canon, charge, command, decree, dictate, edict, fiat, imperative, injunction, instruction, mandate, notice, order, ordinance, regulation, ruling

directly **1.** by the shortest route, exactly, in a beeline, precisely, straight, unswervingly, without deviation **2.** as soon as possible, at once, dead, due, forthwith, immediately, in a second, instantaneously, instantly, pdq (*slang*), posthaste, presently, promptly, pronto (*informal*), quickly, right away, soon, speedily, straightaway **3.** candidly, face-to-face, honestly, in person, openly, overtly, personally, plainly, point-blank, straightforwardly, truthfully, unequivocally, without prevarication

directness bluntness, candour, forthrightness, frankness, honesty, outspokenness, sincerity, straightforwardness

director administrator, boss (*informal*), chairman, chief, controller, executive, governor, head, leader, manager, organizer, principal, producer, supervisor

direful appalling, awful, calamitous, dire, dreadful, fearful, ghastly, gloomy, godawful (*slang*), horrible, horrid, shocking, terrible

dirge coronach (*Scot. & Irish*), dead march, elegy, funeral song, lament, requiem, threnody

dirt **1.** crap (*slang*), crud (*slang*), dust, excrement, filth, grime, grot (*slang*), impurity, mire, muck, mud, shit (*taboo slang*), slime, slob (*Irish*), smudge, stain, tarnish **2.** clay, earth, loam, soil **3.** indecency, obscenity, pornography, sleaze, smut

We must eat a peck of dirt before we die

dirty *adjective* **1.** begrimed, filthy, foul, grimy, grotty (*slang*), grubby, grungy (*slang, chiefly U.S.*), messy, mucky, muddy, nasty, polluted, scuzzy (*slang, chiefly U.S.*), soiled, sullied, unclean **2.** blue, indecent, obscene, off-colour, pornographic, risqué, salacious, sleazy, smutty, vulgar, X-rated (*informal*) **3.** clouded, dark, dull, miry, muddy, not clear **4.** corrupt, crooked, dishonest, fraudulent, illegal, treacherous, unfair, unscrupulous, unsporting **5.** base, beggarly, contemptible, cowardly, despicable, ignominious, low, low-down (*informal*), mean, nasty, scurvy, shabby, sordid, squalid, vile **6.** angry, annoyed, bitter, choked, indignant, offended, resentful, scorching **7.** *of weather* gusty, louring *or* lowering, rainy, squally, stormy *~verb* **8.** begrime, blacken, defile, foul, mess up, muddy, pollute, smear, smirch, smudge, soil, spoil, stain, sully

Antonyms *adjective* clean, decent, honest, moral, pleasant, pure, reputable, respectable, upright *~verb* clean, tidy up

disability **1.** affliction, ailment, complaint, defect, disablement, disorder, handicap, impairment, infirmity, malady **2.** disqualification, impotency, inability, incapacity, incompetency, unfitness, weakness

disable **1.** cripple, damage, debilitate, enfeeble, hamstring, handicap, immobilize, impair, incapacitate, paralyse, prostrate, put out of action, render *hors de combat*, render inoperative, unfit, unman, weaken **2.** disenable, disqualify, invalidate, render *or* declare incapable

disabled bedridden, crippled, handicapped, incapacitated, infirm, lame, maimed, mangled, mutilated, paralysed, weak, weakened, wrecked

Antonyms able-bodied, fit, hale, healthy, hearty, robust, sound, strong, sturdy

disabuse correct, enlighten, free from error, open the eyes of, set right, set straight, shatter (someone's) illusions, undeceive

disadvantage **1.** damage, detriment, disservice, harm, hurt, injury, loss, prejudice **2.** *often plural* burden, downside, drawback, flaw, fly in the ointment (*informal*), handicap, hardship, hindrance, impediment, inconvenience, liability, minus (*informal*), nuisance, privation, snag, trouble, weakness, weak point **3.** **at a disadvantage** boxed in, cornered, handicapped, in a corner, vulnerable, with one's hands tied behind one's back

Antonyms advantage, aid, benefit, convenience, gain, help, merit, profit

disadvantaged deprived, discriminated against, handicapped, impoverished, struggling, underprivileged

disadvantageous adverse, damaging, deleterious, detrimental, harmful, hurtful, ill-timed, inconvenient, inexpedient, injurious, inopportune, prejudicial, unfavourable

disaffect alienate, antagonize, disunite, divide, estrange, repel

disaffected alienated, antagonistic, discontented, disloyal, dissatisfied, estranged, hostile, mutinous, rebellious, seditious, uncompliant, unsubmissive

disaffection alienation, animosity, antagonism, antipathy, aversion, breach, disagreement, discontent, dislike, disloyalty, dissatisfaction, estrangement, hostility, ill will, repugnance, resentment, unfriendliness

disagree **1.** be discordant, be dissimilar, conflict, contradict, counter, depart, deviate, differ, diverge, run counter to, vary **2.** argue, be

at sixes and sevens, bicker, clash, contend, contest, cross swords, debate, differ (in opinion), dispute, dissent, fall out (*informal*), have words (*informal*), object, oppose, quarrel, take issue with, wrangle **3.** be injurious, bother, discomfort, distress, hurt, make ill, nauseate, sicken, trouble, upset
Antonyms accord, agree, coincide, concur, get on (together), harmonize

disagreeable **1.** bad-tempered, brusque, churlish, contrary, cross, difficult, disobliging, ill-natured, irritable, nasty, peevish, ratty (*Brit. & N.Z. informal*), rude, surly, tetchy, unfriendly, ungracious, unlikable *or* unlikeable, unpleasant **2.** disgusting, displeasing, distasteful, horrid, nasty, objectionable, obnoxious, offensive, repellent, repugnant, repulsive, uninviting, unpalatable, unpleasant, unsavoury, yucky *or* yukky (*slang*)
Antonyms agreeable, congenial, delightful, enjoyable, friendly, good-natured, lovely, nice, pleasant

disagreement **1.** difference, discrepancy, disparity, dissimilarity, dissimilitude, divergence, diversity, incompatibility, incongruity, unlikeness, variance **2.** altercation, argument, clash, conflict, debate, difference, discord, dispute, dissent, division, falling out, misunderstanding, quarrel, row, squabble, strife, wrangle **3.** **in disagreement** at daggers drawn, at loggerheads, at odds, at variance, disunited, in conflict, in disharmony
Antonyms accord, agreement, assent, consensus, correspondence, harmony, similarity, unison, unity

It were not best that we should all think alike; it is difference of opinion that makes horse-races
Mark Twain *Pudd'n-head Wilson*

The only sin which we never forgive in each other is difference of opinion
Ralph Waldo Emerson *Clubs*

disallow **1.** abjure, disavow, disclaim, dismiss, disown, rebuff, refuse, reject, repudiate **2.** ban, boycott, cancel, embargo, forbid, prohibit, proscribe, veto

disappear **1.** abscond, be lost to view, depart, drop out of sight, ebb, escape, evanesce, fade away, flee, fly, go, pass, recede, retire, vanish from sight, vanish off the face of the earth, wane, withdraw **2.** cease, cease to be known, die out, dissolve, end, evaporate, expire, fade, leave no trace, melt away, pass away, perish, vanish
Antonyms appear, arrive, materialize, reappear

disappearance departure, desertion, disappearing, disappearing trick, eclipse, evanescence, evaporation, fading, flight, going, loss, melting, passing, vanishing, vanishing point

disappoint **1.** chagrin, dash, deceive, delude, disenchant, disgruntle, dishearten, disillusion, dismay, dissatisfy, fail, let down, sadden, vex **2.** baffle, balk, defeat, disconcert, foil, frustrate, hamper, hinder, thwart

disappointed balked, cast down, choked, depressed, despondent, discontented, discouraged, disenchanted, disgruntled, disillusioned, dissatisfied, distressed, downhearted, foiled, frustrated, let down, saddened, thwarted, upset
Antonyms content, contented, fulfilled, happy, pleased, satisfied

disappointing depressing, disagreeable, disconcerting, discouraging, failing, inadequate, inferior, insufficient, lame, not much cop (*Brit. slang*), pathetic, sad, second-rate, sorry, unexpected, unhappy, unsatisfactory, unworthy, upsetting

disappointment **1.** chagrin, discontent, discouragement, disenchantment, disillusionment, displeasure, dissatisfaction, distress, failure, frustration, ill-success, mortification, regret, unfulfilment **2.** blow, calamity, disaster, failure, fiasco, letdown, miscarriage, misfortune, setback, washout (*informal*), whammy (*informal, chiefly U.S.*)

disapprobation blame, censure, condemnation, disapproval, disfavour, dislike, displeasure, dissatisfaction, reproof, stricture

disapproval censure, condemnation, criticism, denunciation, deprecation, disapprobation, displeasure, dissatisfaction, objection, reproach, stick (*slang*)

disapprove **1.** *often with* **of** blame, censure, condemn, deplore, deprecate, discountenance, dislike, find unacceptable, frown on, have a down on (*informal*), look down one's nose at (*informal*), object to, raise an *or* one's eyebrow, reject, take a dim view of, take exception to **2.** disallow, set aside, spurn, turn down, veto
Antonyms applaud, approve, commend, compliment, endorse, give the go-ahead (to) (*informal*), like, O.K. *or* okay (*informal*)

disapproving censorious, condemnatory, critical, denunciatory, deprecatory, disapprobatory, discouraging, disparaging, frowning, reproachful
Antonyms approbatory, approving, commendatory, encouraging

disarm **1.** disable, render defenceless, unarm **2.** deactivate, demilitarize, demobilize, disband **3.** persuade, set at ease, win over

disarmament arms limitation, arms reduction, de-escalation, demilitarization, demobilization

disarming charming, irresistible, likable *or* likeable, persuasive, winning

disarrange confuse, derange, discompose, disorder, disorganize, disturb, jumble (up), mess (up), scatter, shake (up), shuffle, unsettle, untidy

disarray 1. confusion, discomposure, disharmony, dismay, disorder, disorderliness, disorganization, disunity, indiscipline, unruliness, upset 2. chaos, clutter, dishevelment, hodgepodge (*U.S.*), hotchpotch, jumble, mess, mix-up, muddle, pig's breakfast (*informal*), shambles, state, tangle, untidiness
Antonyms arrangement, harmony, method, neatness, order, orderliness, organization, pattern, plan, regularity, symmetry, system, tidiness

disassemble deconstruct, dismantle, dismount, knock down, strike, take apart, take down

disaster accident, act of God, adversity, blow, bummer (*slang*), calamity, cataclysm, catastrophe, misadventure, mischance, misfortune, mishap, reverse, ruin, ruination, stroke, tragedy, trouble, whammy (*informal, chiefly U.S.*)

disastrous adverse, calamitous, cataclysmal, cataclysmic, catastrophic, destructive, detrimental, devastating, dire, dreadful, fatal, hapless, harmful, ill-fated, ill-starred, ruinous, terrible, tragic, unfortunate, unlucky, unpropitious, untoward

disavow abjure, contradict, deny, disclaim, disown, forswear, gainsay (*archaic or literary*), rebut, reject, repudiate, retract

disavowal abjuration, contradiction, denial, disclaimer, gainsaying (*archaic or literary*), recantation, rejection, renunciation, repudiation, retraction

disband break up, demobilize, dismiss, disperse, dissolve, go (their) separate ways, let go, part company, scatter, send home, separate

disbelief distrust, doubt, dubiety, incredulity, mistrust, scepticism, unbelief
Antonyms belief, credence, credulity, faith, trust

disbelieve discount, discredit, give no credence to, mistrust, not accept, not buy (*slang*), not credit, not swallow (*informal*), reject, repudiate, scoff at, suspect

disbeliever agnostic, atheist, doubter, doubting Thomas, questioner, sceptic, scoffer
Antonyms adherent, believer, devotee, disciple, follower, proselyte, supporter, upholder, zealot

disbelievingly askance, cynically, doubtingly, incredulously, mistrustfully, quizzically, sceptically, suspiciously, with a pinch of salt

disburden alleviate, diminish, discharge, disencumber, ease, free, lighten, relieve, take a load off one's mind, unburden, unload

disburse expend, fork out (*slang*), lay out, pay out, shell out (*informal*), spend

disbursement disposal, expenditure, outlay, payment, spending

disc, disk 1. circle, discus, plate, saucer 2. gramophone record, phonograph record (*U.S. & Canad.*), platter (*U.S. slang*), record, vinyl

discard abandon, axe (*informal*), cast aside, chuck (*informal*), dispense with, dispose of, ditch (*slang*), drop, dump (*informal*), get rid of, jettison, junk (*informal*), reject, relinquish, remove, repudiate, scrap, shed, throw away *or* out
Antonyms hang *or* hold on to, hold back, keep, reserve, retain, save

discern 1. behold, catch sight of, descry, discover, espy, make out, notice, observe, perceive, recognize, see, suss (out) (*slang*) 2. detect, determine, differentiate, discriminate, distinguish, judge, make a distinction, pick out

discernible apparent, appreciable, clear, detectable, discoverable, distinct, distinguishable, noticeable, observable, obvious, perceptible, plain, recognizable, visible

discerning acute, astute, clear-sighted, critical, discriminating, ingenious, intelligent, judicious, knowing, penetrating, perceptive, percipient, perspicacious, piercing, sagacious, sensitive, sharp, shrewd, subtle, wise

discernment acumen, acuteness, astuteness, awareness, clear-sightedness, cleverness, discrimination, ingenuity, insight, intelligence, judgment, keenness, penetration, perception, perceptiveness, percipience, perspicacity, sagacity, sharpness, shrewdness, understanding

discharge *verb* 1. absolve, acquit, allow to go, clear, exonerate, free, liberate, pardon, release, set free *~noun* 2. acquittal, clearance, exoneration, liberation, pardon, release, remittance *~verb* 3. cashier, discard, dismiss, eject, expel, fire (*informal*), give (someone) the boot (*slang*), give (someone) the sack (*informal*), oust, remove, sack (*informal*) *~noun* 4. congé, demobilization, dismissal, ejection, the boot (*slang*), the (old) heave-ho (*informal*), the order of the boot (*slang*), the sack (*informal*) *~verb* 5. detonate, explode, fire, let off, set off, shoot *~noun* 6. blast, burst, detonation, discharging, explosion, firing, fusillade, report, salvo, shot, volley *~verb* 7. disembogue, dispense, emit, empty, excrete, exude, give off, gush, leak, ooze, pour forth, release, void *~noun* 8. emission, emptying, excretion, flow, ooze, pus, secretion, seepage, suppuration, vent, voiding *~verb* 9. disburden, lighten, offload, remove, unburden, unload *~noun* 10. disburdening, emptying, unburdening, unloading *~verb* 11. accomplish, carry out, do, execute, fulfil, observe, perform *~noun* **12.** accomplishment, achievement, execution, fulfilment, observance, performance *~verb* **13.** clear, honour, meet, pay, relieve, satisfy, settle, square up *~noun* **14.** payment, satisfaction, settlement

disciple adherent, apostle, believer, catechumen, convert, devotee, follower, learner, partisan, proselyte, pupil, student, supporter, votary
Antonyms guru, leader, master, swami, teacher

disciplinarian authoritarian, despot, drill sergeant, hard master, martinet, stickler, strict teacher, taskmaster, tyrant

discipline *noun* **1.** drill, exercise, method, practice, regimen, regulation, training **2.** conduct, control, orderliness, regulation, restraint, self-control, strictness **3.** castigation, chastisement, correction, punishment **4.** area, branch of knowledge, course, curriculum, field of study, speciality, subject *~verb* **5.** break in, bring up, check, control, drill, educate, exercise, form, govern, instruct, inure, prepare, regulate, restrain, train **6.** bring to book, castigate, chasten, chastise, correct, penalize, punish, reprimand, reprove

Spare the rod and spoil the child

disclaim abandon, abjure, abnegate, decline, deny, disaffirm, disallow, disavow, disown, forswear, rebut, reject, renege, renounce, repudiate, retract

disclaimer abjuration, contradiction, denial, disavowal, rejection, renunciation, repudiation, retraction

disclose **1.** blow wide open (*slang*), broadcast, communicate, confess, divulge, get off one's chest (*informal*), impart, leak, let slip, make known, make public, publish, relate, reveal, spill one's guts about (*slang*), spill the beans about (*informal*), tell, unveil, utter **2.** bring to light, discover, exhibit, expose, lay bare, reveal, show, take the wraps off, uncover, unveil
Antonyms conceal, cover, dissemble, hide, keep dark, keep secret, mask, obscure, secrete, veil

disclosure acknowledgment, admission, announcement, broadcast, confession, declaration, discovery, divulgence, exposé, exposure, leak, publication, revelation, uncovering

discoloration blemish, blot, blotch, mark, patch, smirch, splotch, spot, stain

discolour fade, mar, mark, rust, soil, stain, streak, tarnish, tinge

discoloured besmirched, blotched, etiolated, faded, foxed, pale, stained, tainted, tarnished, wan, washed out

discomfit **1.** abash, confound, confuse, demoralize, discompose, disconcert, embarrass, faze, flurry, fluster, perplex, perturb, rattle (*informal*), ruffle, take aback, take the wind out of someone's sails, unnerve, unsettle, worry **2.** baffle, balk, beat, checkmate, defeat, foil, frustrate, outwit, overcome, thwart, trump, worst

discomfiture **1.** abashment, chagrin, confusion, demoralization, discomposure, embarrassment, humiliation, shame, unease **2.** beating, defeat, disappointment, failure, frustration, overthrow, rout, ruin, undoing

discomfort **1.** *noun* ache, annoyance, disquiet, distress, gall, hardship, hurt, inquietude, irritation, malaise, nuisance, pain, soreness, trouble, uneasiness, unpleasantness, vexation **2.** *verb* discomfit, discompose, disquiet, distress, disturb, embarrass, make uncomfortable
Antonyms *noun* comfort, ease, reassurance, solace *~verb* alleviate, assuage, comfort, ease, reassure, solace, soothe

discommode annoy, bother, burden, disquiet, disturb, harass, hassle (*informal*), incommode, inconvenience, molest, put out, trouble

discompose agitate, annoy, bewilder, confuse, discomfit, disconcert, displease, disturb, embarrass, faze, flurry, fluster, fret, hassle (*informal*), irritate, nettle, perplex, perturb, provoke, rattle (*informal*), ruffle, unnerve, unsettle, upset, vex, worry

discomposure agitation, anxiety, confusion, discomfiture, disquiet, disquietude, distraction, disturbance, embarrassment, fluster, inquietude, malaise, nervousness, perturbation, trepidation, uneasiness

disconcert **1.** abash, agitate, bewilder, discompose, disturb, faze, flummox, flurry, fluster, nonplus, perplex, perturb, put out of countenance, rattle (*informal*), ruffle, shake up (*informal*), take aback, throw off balance, trouble, unbalance, unnerve, unsettle, upset, worry **2.** baffle, balk, confuse, defeat, disarrange, frustrate, hinder, put off, thwart, undo

disconcerted annoyed, at sea, bewildered, caught off balance, confused, distracted, disturbed, embarrassed, fazed, flummoxed, flurried, flustered, mixed-up, nonplussed, out of countenance, perturbed, rattled (*informal*), ruffled, shook up (*informal*), taken aback, thrown (*informal*), troubled, unsettled, upset

disconcerting alarming, awkward, baffling, bewildering, bothersome, confusing, dismaying, distracting, disturbing, embarrassing, off-putting (*Brit. informal*), perplexing, upsetting

disconnect cut off, detach, disengage, divide, part, separate, sever, take apart, uncouple

disconnected confused, disjointed, garbled, il~ logical, incoherent, irrational, jumbled, mixed-up, rambling, uncoordinated, unintelli~ gible, wandering

disconnection cessation, cut-off, cutting off, discontinuation, discontinuity, interruption, separation, severance, stoppage, suspension

disconsolate crushed, dejected, desolate, des~ pairing, dismal, down in the dumps (*infor~ mal*), forlorn, gloomy, grief-stricken, heart~ broken, hopeless, inconsolable, low, melan~ choly, miserable, sad, unhappy, woeful, wretched

discontent *noun* discontentment, displeasure, dissatisfaction, envy, fretfulness, regret, rest~ lessness, uneasiness, unhappiness, vexation

discontented brassed off (*Brit. slang*), cheesed off (*Brit. slang*), complaining, disaffected, dis~ gruntled, displeased, dissatisfied, exasperated, fed up, fretful, miserable, pissed off (*taboo slang*), unhappy, vexed, with a chip on one's shoulder (*informal*)
Antonyms cheerful, content, contented, hap~ py, pleased, satisfied

discontinuance adjournment, cessation, dis~ continuation, disjunction, intermission, inter~ ruption, separation, stop, stoppage, stopping, suspension, termination

discontinue abandon, axe (*informal*), belay (*Nautical*), break off, cease, drop, end, finish, give up, halt, interrupt, kick (*informal*), leave off, pause, pull the plug on, put an end to, quit, refrain from, stop, suspend, terminate, throw in the sponge, throw in the towel

discontinued abandoned, ended, finished, giv~ en up *or* over, halted, no longer made, termi~ nated

discontinuity disconnectedness, disconnection, disjointedness, disruption, disunion, incoher~ ence, interruption, lack of coherence, lack of unity

discontinuous broken, disconnected, fitful, intermittent, interrupted, irregular, spasmodic

discord 1. clashing, conflict, contention, differ~ ence, disagreement, discordance, dispute, dis~ sension, disunity, division, friction, incompat~ ibility, lack of concord, opposition, row, rup~ ture, strife, variance, wrangling 2. cacophony, din, disharmony, dissonance, harshness, jan~ gle, jarring, racket, tumult
Antonyms accord, agreement, concord, euphony, friendship, harmony, melody, peace, tunefulness, understanding, unison, unity

discordant 1. at odds, clashing, conflicting, contradictory, contrary, different, disagreeing, divergent, incompatible, incongruous, incon~ sistent, opposite 2. cacophonous, dissonant, grating, harsh, inharmonious, jangling, jar~ ring, shrill, strident, unmelodious

discount *verb* 1. brush off (*slang*), disbelieve, disregard, ignore, leave out of account, over~ look, pass over 2. deduct, lower, mark down, rebate, reduce, take off ~*noun* 3. abatement, allowance, concession, cut, cut price, deduc~ tion, drawback, percentage (*informal*), rebate, reduction

discountenance *verb* 1. abash, chagrin, con~ fuse, discompose, disconcert, embarrass, hu~ miliate, put down (*slang*), shame 2. condemn, disapprove, discourage, disfavour, frown on, object to, oppose, resist, take exception to, veto

discourage 1. abash, awe, cast down, cow, damp, dampen, dash, daunt, deject, demoral~ ize, depress, dishearten, dismay, dispirit, frighten, intimidate, overawe, psych out (*in~ formal*), put a damper on, scare, unman, un~ nerve 2. check, curb, deprecate, deter, dis~ countenance, disfavour, dissuade, divert from, hinder, inhibit, prevent, put off, restrain, talk out of, throw cold water on (*informal*)
Antonyms bid, countenance, embolden, en~ courage, hearten, inspire, urge, welcome

discouraged crestfallen, dashed, daunted, de~ terred, disheartened, dismayed, dispirited, downcast, down in the mouth, glum, pessi~ mistic, put off, sick as a parrot (*informal*)

discouragement 1. cold feet (*informal*), dejec~ tion, depression, despair, despondency, disap~ pointment, discomfiture, dismay, down~ heartedness, hopelessness, loss of confidence, low spirits, pessimism 2. constraint, curb, damper, deterrent, disincentive, hindrance, impediment, obstacle, opposition, rebuff, re~ straint, setback

discouraging dampening, daunting, depress~ ing, disappointing, disheartening, dispiriting, off-putting (*Brit. informal*), unfavourable, un~ propitious

discourse *noun* 1. chat, communication, con~ versation, converse, dialogue, discussion, seminar, speech, talk 2. address, disquisition, dissertation, essay, homily, lecture, oration, sermon, speech, talk, treatise ~*verb* 3. confer, converse, debate, declaim, discuss, expatiate, hold forth, speak, talk

discourteous abrupt, bad-mannered, boorish, brusque, curt, disrespectful, ill-bred, ill-mannered, impolite, insolent, offhand, rude, uncivil, uncourteous, ungentlemanly, ungra~ cious, unmannerly
Antonyms civil, courteous, courtly, gracious, mannerly, polite, respectful, well-mannered

discourtesy 1. bad manners, disrespectfulness, ill-breeding, impertinence, impoliteness, inci~ vility, insolence, rudeness, ungraciousness, unmannerliness 2. affront, cold shoulder, in~

sult, kick in the teeth (*slang*), rebuff, slight, snub

discover 1. bring to light, come across, come upon, dig up, find, light upon, locate, turn up, uncover, unearth 2. ascertain, descry, detect, determine, discern, disclose, espy, find out, get wise to (*informal*), learn, notice, perceive, realize, recognize, reveal, see, spot, suss (out) (*slang*), turn up, uncover 3. conceive, contrive, design, devise, invent, originate, pioneer

discoverer author, explorer, founder, initiator, inventor, originator, pioneer

discovery 1. ascertainment, detection, disclosure, espial, exploration, finding, introduction, locating, location, origination, revelation, uncovering 2. bonanza, breakthrough, coup, find, findings, godsend, innovation, invention, secret

Discovery consists of seeing what everybody has seen and thinking what nobody has thought
Albert von Szent-Györgyi

discredit *verb* 1. blame, bring into disrepute, censure, defame, degrade, detract from, disgrace, dishonour, disparage, reproach, slander, slur, smear, vilify *~noun* 2. aspersion, censure, disgrace, dishonour, disrepute, ignominy, ill-repute, imputation, odium, reproach, scandal, shame, slur, smear, stigma *~verb* 3. challenge, deny, disbelieve, discount, dispute, distrust, doubt, mistrust, question *~noun* 4. distrust, doubt, mistrust, question, scepticism, suspicion
Antonyms *verb* acclaim, applaud, commend, honour, laud, pay tribute to, praise *~noun* acclaim, acknowledgment, approval, commendation, credit, honour, merit, praise

discreditable blameworthy, degrading, disgraceful, dishonourable, humiliating, ignominious, improper, infamous, reprehensible, scandalous, shameful, unprincipled, unworthy

discredited brought into disrepute, debunked, discarded, exploded, exposed, obsolete, outworn, refuted, rejected

discreet careful, cautious, circumspect, considerate, diplomatic, discerning, guarded, judicious, politic, prudent, reserved, sagacious, sensible, tactful, wary
Antonyms incautious, indiscreet, injudicious, rash, tactless, undiplomatic, unthinking, unwise

discrepancy conflict, contrariety, difference, disagreement, discordance, disparity, dissimilarity, dissonance, divergence, incongruity, inconsistency, variance, variation

discrepant at variance, conflicting, contradictory, contrary, differing, disagreeing, discordant, incompatible, incongruous, inconsistent

discrete detached, disconnected, discontinuous, distinct, individual, separate, unattached

discretion 1. acumen, care, carefulness, caution, circumspection, consideration, diplomacy, discernment, good sense, heedfulness, judgment, judiciousness, maturity, prudence, sagacity, tact, wariness 2. choice, disposition, inclination, liking, mind, option, pleasure, predilection, preference, responsibility, volition, will, wish
Antonyms carelessness, indiscretion, insensitivity, rashness, tactlessness, thoughtlessness

Discretion is the better part of valour

discretionary arbitrary (*Law*), elective, nonmandatory, open, open to choice, optional, unrestricted

discriminate 1. disfavour, favour, show bias, show prejudice, single out, treat as inferior, treat differently, victimize 2. assess, differentiate, discern, distinguish, draw a distinction, evaluate, segregate, separate, separate the wheat from the chaff, sift, tell the difference

discriminating acute, astute, critical, cultivated, discerning, fastidious, keen, particular, refined, selective, sensitive, tasteful
Antonyms careless, desultory, general, hit or miss (*informal*), indiscriminate, random, undiscriminating, unselective, unsystematic

discrimination 1. bias, bigotry, favouritism, inequity, intolerance, prejudice, unfairness 2. acumen, acuteness, clearness, discernment, insight, judgment, keenness, penetration, perception, refinement, sagacity, subtlety, taste

discriminatory, discriminative 1. biased, favouring, inequitable, one-sided, partial, partisan, preferential, prejudiced, prejudicial, unjust, weighted 2. analytical, astute, differentiating, discerning, discriminating, perceptive, perspicacious

discursive circuitous, desultory, diffuse, digressive, erratic, long-winded, loose, meandering, prolix, rambling, roundabout, roving

discuss argue, confer, consider, consult with, converse, debate, deliberate, examine, exchange views on, get together, go into, reason about, review, sift, talk about, thrash out, ventilate, weigh up the pros and cons

discussion analysis, argument, colloquy, confabulation, conference, consideration, consultation, conversation, debate, deliberation, dialogue, discourse, examination, exchange, review, scrutiny, seminar, symposium

To jaw-jaw is better than to war-war
Winston Churchill

disdain 1. *verb* belittle, contemn, deride, despise, disregard, look down on, look down one's nose at (*informal*), misprize, pooh-pooh, reject, scorn, slight, sneer at, spurn, undervalue 2. *noun* arrogance, contempt, contumely, derision, dislike, haughtiness, hauteur, indiffer~

ence, scorn, sneering, snobbishness, supercili~ ousness

A little disdain is not amiss; a little scorn is al~ luring

William Congreve *The Way of the World*

disdainful aloof, arrogant, contemptuous, deri~ sive, haughty, high and mighty (*informal*), hoity-toity (*informal*), insolent, looking down one's nose (at), on one's high horse (*informal*), proud, scornful, sneering, supercilious, su~ perior, turning up one's nose (at)

disease **1**. affliction, ailment, complaint, condi~ tion, disorder, ill health, illness, indisposition, infection, infirmity, lurgi (*informal*), malady, sickness, upset **2**. *figurative* blight, cancer, canker, contagion, contamination, disorder, malady, plague

Human diseases

absinthism
acariasis
acne
acromegaly
actinodermatitis
actinomycosis
Addison's disease
adrenoleukodystrophy *or* ALD
aeroneurosis
agranulocytosis
ague
Aids *or* AIDS
alcoholism
Alzheimer's disease
amoebiasis
ancylostomiasis, an~ chylostomiasis *or* ankylostomiasis
angina
anorexia *or* anorexia nervosa
anthracosis
anthrax
aortitis
appendicitis
apraxia
arteriosclerosis
arthritis
asbestosis
ascariasis
asthma
atherosclerosis
athlete's foot
avitaminosis
Bell's palsy
beriberi
bilharzia
bilharziasis *or* bilhar~ ziosis
Black Death
black measles
blackwater fever
Bornholm disease
Bright's disease
bronchiolitis
bronchitis
bronchopneumonia
brucellosis
bubonic plague
bulimia *or* bulimia nervosa
Burkitt lymphoma *or* Burkitt's lymphoma
bursitis
byssinosis
calenture
cancer
cardiomyopathy
carditis
caries
carpal tunnel syn~ drome
cellulitis
cerebellar syndrome
Chagas' disease
chickenpox
chin cough
chloracne
chlorosis
cholera
chorea
Christmas disease
chronic fatigue syn~ drome *or* CFS
cirrhosis
coal miner's lung
coccidioidomycosis
coeliac disease
cold
colitis
common cold
conjunctivitis
constipation
consumption
cor pulmonale
coxalgia
Creutzfeldt-Jakob disease
Crohn's disease
Cushing's disease
cystic fibrosis
cystitis
dead fingers
decompression sick~ ness
dengue
depression
dermatitis
dhobi itch
diabetes
diarrhoea
diphtheria
diverticulitis
double pneumonia
dropsy
dysentery
earache
ebola virus disease
Economo's disease
eczema
elephantiasis
emphysema
encephalitis
encephalomyelitis
encephalopathy
endocarditis
enteritis
enterobiasis
enterocolitis
epilepsy
ergotism
erysipelas
erythroblastosis
exophthalmic goitre
farmer's lung
favus
fibrositis
filariasis
fishskin disease
flu
framboesia
furunculosis
gastritis
gastroenteritis
genital herpes
German measles
gingivitis
glandular fever
glaucoma
glomerulonephritis
glossitis
glue ear
goitre
gonorrhoea
gout
grand mal
green monkey disease
greensickness
haemoglobinopathy
haemophilia
Hansen's disease
hebephrenia
hepatitis
hepatitis A
hepatitis B
herpes
herpes simplex
herpes zoster
hidrosis
histoplasmosis
Hodgkin's disease
Huntington's chorea
hypothermia
hypothyroidism
ichthyosis
icterus
impetigo
infectious hepatitis
infectious mononu~ cleosis
influenza
iritis
irritable bowel syn~ drome
jaundice
jungle fever
kala-azar
Kaposi's sarcoma
Kawasaki's disease
Korsakoff's psychosis
kuru
labyrinthitis
laryngitis
Lassa fever
lathyrism
lead poisoning
legionnaire's disease
leishmaniasis *or* leishmaniosis
leprosy
leptospirosis
leukaemia
listeriosis
lockjaw
lumbago
lupus
lupus erythematosus
lupus vulgaris
Lyme disease
lymphoma
malaria
Marburg disease
mastitis
measles
Ménière's syndrome

meningitis
milk sickness
motor neurone disease
multiple sclerosis
mumps
muscular dystrophy
myalgic encephalomyelitis *or* ME
myasthenia gravis
myiasis
myopathy
myxoedema
narcolepsy
necrotising fasciitis
nephritis
nephrosis
neuropathy
non-A, non-B hepatitis
non-Hodgkin's lymphoma
onchocerciasis
ornithosis
osteitis
osteitis deformans
osteoarthritis
osteomalacia
osteomyelitis
osteoporosis
otitis
Paget's disease
paralysis
paratyphoid fever
Parkinson's disease
pellagra
pelvic inflammatory disease
pemphigus
pericarditis
petit mal
pharyngitis
phlebitis
phthisis
pinta
pityriasis
pleurisy
pleuropneumonia
pneumoconiosis
pneumonia
poliomyelitis *or* polio
polycythaemia
porphyria
Pott's disease
pox
presenile dementia
prurigo
psittacosis
psoriasis
purpura
pyorrhoea
Q fever
quinsy
rabies
radiation sickness
ratbite fever *or* rat-bite disease
Raynaud's disease
relapsing fever
retinitis
Reye's syndrome
rheumatic fever
rheumatoid arthritis
rhinitis
rickets
rickettsial disease
ringworm
Rocky Mountain spotted fever
rubella
Saint Vitus's dance
salmonella *or* salmonellosis
salpingitis
sapraemia
sarcomatosis
scabies
scarlet fever *or* scarlatina
schistosomiasis
schizophrenia
schizothymia
sciatica
scleroderma *or* sclerodermia *or* scleriasis
scrofula
scrub typhus
scurvy
seasonal affective disorder
seborrhoea
senile dementia
septicaemia
serpigo
serum sickness
shell shock
shingles
sickle-cell anaemia
siderosis
silicosis
sinusitis
sleeping sickness
smallpox
spina bifida
spirochaetosis
splenitis
splenomegaly
spondylitis
spotted fever
sprue
stomatitis
strongyloidiasis *or* strongyloidosis
sunstroke
sweating sickness
swinepox
sycosis
Sydenham's chorea
synovitis
syphilis
syringomyelia
tarantism
Tay-Sachs disease
tetanus
thalassaemia
thrush
tick fever
tinea
tonsillitis
Tourette syndrome
toxic shock syndrome
trachoma
trench fever
trench mouth
trichinosis
trypanosomiasis
tsutsugamushi disease
tuberculosis
typhoid fever
typhus
uncinariasis
uraemia
urethritis
urticaria
utriculitis
uveitis
vaginitis
vagotonia
valvulitis
varicosis
variola
varioloid
venereal disease
Vincent's angina *or* Vincent's disease
vulvitis
vulvovaginitis
Weil's disease
whooping cough
worms
yaws
yellow fever
yuppie disease *or* yuppie flu

Animal diseases

actinomycosis *or* *(nontechnical)* lumpy jaw
anbury
anthrax
blackleg
bots
braxy
brucellosis *or* undulant fever
BSE (bovine spongiform encephalopathy) *or* *(informal)* mad cow disease
bull nose
bush sickness (*N.Z.*)
canker
cowpox
distemper
dourine
foot-and-mouth disease *or* hoof-and-mouth disease
fowl pest
furunculosis
gallsickness *or* anaplasmosis
gapes
gid
glanders
grapes
hard pad
heaves *or* broken wind
laminitis *or* founder
lampas *or* lampers
loco disease
Lyme disease
malanders, mallanders, *or* mallenders
Marburg disease *or* green monkey disease
milk fever
moon blindness *or* mooneye
murrain
myxomatosis
nagana
Newcastle disease *or* fowl pest
ornithosis
pinkeye
pip
pityriasis
psittacosis
pullorum disease *or* bacillary white diarrhoea
quarter crack
quittor
red water
rinderpest
ringbone
roaring
rot

roup
sand crack
scab
scrapie
scratches
seedy toe
sheep measles
sitfast
spavin
staggers, blind staggers *or* megrims
strangles *or* equine distemper
stringhalt *or* springhalt
surra
swamp fever *or* equine infectious anaemia
sweating sickness
sweeny
swine fever *or (U.S.)* hog cholera
swinepox *or* variola porcina
swine vesicular disease
Texas fever
thoroughpin
thrush
toe crack
trembles *or* milk sickness
warble
whistling
windgall

diseased ailing, infected, rotten, sick, sickly, tainted, unhealthy, unsound, unwell, unwholesome

disembark alight, arrive, get off, go ashore, land, step out of

disembarrass 1. disembroil, disengage, disentangle, disentwine, extricate, unsnarl, untangle 2. disencumber, lighten, relieve, unburden, unload
Antonyms (*sense 1*) embarrass, embroil, engage, ensnarl, entangle, entwine, involve (*sense 2*) burden, encumber, load, saddle with, weigh down

disembodied bodiless, ghostly, immaterial, incorporeal, intangible, phantom, spectral, spiritual, unbodied

disembowel draw, eviscerate, gut, paunch

disenchant break the spell, bring (someone) down to earth, destroy (someone's) illusions, disabuse, disillusion, open (someone's) eyes, undeceive

disenchanted blasé, cynical, disappointed, disillusioned, indifferent, jaundiced, let down, out of love, sick of, soured, undeceived

disenchantment disappointment, disillusion, disillusionment, revulsion, rude awakening

disencumber disburden, discharge, disembarrass, disembroil, extricate, lighten, unburden, unhamper, unload

disengage 1. disentangle, ease, extricate, free, liberate, loosen, release, set free, unbridle, unloose, untie 2. detach, disconnect, disjoin, disunite, divide, separate, undo, withdraw

disengaged 1. apart, detached, free, loose, out of gear, released, separate, unattached, unconnected, uncoupled 2. at ease, at leisure, free, not busy, uncommitted, unoccupied, vacant

disengagement detachment, disconnection, disentanglement, division, separation, withdrawal

disentangle 1. detach, disconnect, disengage, extricate, free, loose, separate, sever, unfold, unravel, unsnarl, untangle, untwist 2. clarify, clear (up), resolve, simplify, sort out, work out

disfavour 1. disapprobation, disapproval, dislike, displeasure 2. *As in* **fall into disfavour** bad books (*informal*), discredit, disesteem, disgrace, doghouse (*informal*), shame, unpopularity 3. bad turn, discourtesy, disservice

disfigure blemish, damage, deface, deform, disfeature, distort, injure, maim, make ugly, mar, mutilate, scar

disfigurement blemish, defacement, defect, deformity, distortion, impairment, injury, mutilation, scar, spot, stain, trauma (*Pathology*)

disgorge 1. barf (*U.S. slang*), belch, chuck (up) (*slang, chiefly U.S.*), chunder (*slang, chiefly Austral.*), discharge, do a technicolour yawn (*slang*), eject, empty, expel, regurgitate, spew, spit up, spout, throw up, toss one's cookies (*U.S. slang*), upchuck (*U.S. slang*), vomit 2. cede, give up, relinquish, renounce, resign, surrender, yield

disgrace *noun* 1. baseness, degradation, dishonour, disrepute, ignominy, infamy, odium, opprobrium, shame 2. aspersion, blemish, blot, blot on one's escutcheon, defamation, reproach, scandal, slur, stain, stigma 3. contempt, discredit, disesteem, disfavour, obloquy *~verb* 4. abase, bring shame upon, defame, degrade, discredit, disfavour, dishonour, disparage, humiliate, reproach, shame, slur, stain, stigmatize, sully, taint
Antonyms *noun* credit, esteem, favour, grace, honour, repute *~verb* credit, grace, honour

disgraced branded, degraded, discredited, dishonoured, humiliated, in disgrace, in the doghouse (*informal*), mortified, shamed, stigmatized, under a cloud

disgraceful blameworthy, contemptible, degrading, detestable, discreditable, dishonourable, disreputable, ignominious, infamous, low, mean, opprobrious, scandalous, shameful, shocking, unworthy

disgruntled annoyed, cheesed off (*Brit. slang*), discontented, displeased, dissatisfied, grumpy, hacked (off) (*U.S. slang*), huffy, irritated, malcontent, peeved, peevish, petulant, pissed off (*taboo slang*), put out, sulky, sullen, testy, vexed

disguise *verb* 1. camouflage, cloak, conceal, cover, hide, mask, screen, secrete, shroud, veil 2. deceive, dissemble, dissimulate, fake, falsify, fudge, gloss over, misrepresent *~noun* 3. camouflage, cloak, costume, cover, get-up (*informal*), mask, screen, veil 4. deception, dissimulation, façade, front, pretence, semblance, trickery, veneer

disguised camouflaged, cloaked, covert, fake, false, feigned, incognito, in disguise, masked, pretend, undercover, unrecognizable

disgust 1. *verb* cause aversion, displease, fill with loathing, gross out (*U.S. slang*), nauseate, offend, outrage, put off, repel, revolt, sicken, turn one's stomach 2. *noun* abhorrence, abomination, antipathy, aversion, detestation, dislike, distaste, hatefulness, hatred, loathing, nausea, odium, repugnance, repulsion, revulsion
Antonyms *verb* delight, impress, please ~*noun* liking, love, pleasure, satisfaction, taste

disgusted appalled, nauseated, offended, outraged, repelled, repulsed, scandalized, sick and tired of (*informal*), sickened, sick of (*informal*)

disgusting abominable, cringe-making (*Brit. informal*), detestable, distasteful, foul, gross, grotty (*slang*), hateful, loathsome, nasty, nauseating, nauseous, objectionable, obnoxious, odious, offensive, repellent, repugnant, revolting, shameless, sickening, stinking, vile, vulgar, yucky *or* yukky (*slang*)

dish *noun* 1. bowl, plate, platter, salver 2. fare, food, recipe ~*verb* 3. *slang* finish, muck up (*slang*), ruin, spoil, torpedo, wreck

disharmony clash, conflict, disaccord, discord, discordance, dissonance, friction, inharmoniousness

dishearten cast down, crush, damp, dampen, dash, daunt, deject, depress, deter, discourage, dismay, dispirit, put a damper on
Antonyms buck up (*informal*), cheer up, encourage, hearten, lift, perk up, rally

disheartened choked, crestfallen, crushed, daunted, dejected, depressed, disappointed, discouraged, dismayed, dispirited, downcast, downhearted, sick as a parrot (*informal*)

dishevelled bedraggled, blowzy, disarranged, disarrayed, disordered, frowzy, hanging loose, messy, ruffled, rumpled, tousled, uncombed, unkempt, untidy
Antonyms chic, dapper, neat, smart, soigné *or* soignée, spick-and-span, spruce, tidy, trim, well-groomed

dishonest bent (*slang*), cheating, corrupt, crafty, crooked (*informal*), deceitful, deceiving, deceptive, designing, disreputable, double-dealing, false, fraudulent, guileful, knavish (*archaic*), lying, mendacious, perfidious, shady (*informal*), swindling, treacherous, unfair, unprincipled, unscrupulous, untrustworthy, untruthful
Antonyms honest, honourable, law-abiding, lawful, principled, true, trustworthy, upright

dishonesty cheating, chicanery, corruption, craft, criminality, crookedness, deceit, duplicity, falsehood, falsity, fraud, fraudulence, graft (*informal*), improbity, mendacity, perfidy, sharp practice, stealing, treachery, trickery, unscrupulousness, wiliness

Thou shalt not steal; an empty feat
When it's so lucrative to cheat
Arthur Hugh Clough *The Latest Decalogue*

dishonour *verb* 1. abase, blacken, corrupt, debase, debauch, defame, degrade, discredit, disgrace, shame, sully 2. defile, deflower, pollute, rape, ravish, seduce ~*noun* 3. abasement, degradation, discredit, disfavour, disgrace, disrepute, ignominy, infamy, obloquy, odium, opprobrium, reproach, scandal, shame 4. abuse, affront, discourtesy, indignity, insult, offence, outrage, sacrilege, slight
Antonyms *verb* esteem, exalt, respect, revere, worship ~*noun* decency, goodness, honour, integrity, morality, principles, rectitude

dishonourable 1. base, contemptible, despicable, discreditable, disgraceful, ignoble, ignominious, infamous, not cricket (*informal*), scandalous, shameful 2. blackguardly, corrupt, disreputable, shameless, treacherous, unprincipled, unscrupulous, untrustworthy

dish out allocate, distribute, dole out, hand out, inflict, mete out

dish-shaped concave, cupped, cup-shaped, depressed, hollow, hollowed out, incurvate, incurved, pushed in, scooped, scooped out, scyphiform, sunken

dish up hand out, ladle, prepare, present, produce, scoop, serve, spoon

disillusion *verb* break the spell, bring down to earth, disabuse, disenchant, open the eyes of, shatter one's illusions, undeceive

disillusioned disabused, disappointed, disenchanted, enlightened, indifferent, out of love, sadder and wiser, undeceived

disillusionment disappointment, disenchantment, disillusion, enlightenment, lost innocence, rude awakening

disincentive damper, determent, deterrent, discouragement, dissuasion, impediment

disinclination alienation, antipathy, aversion, demur, dislike, hesitance, lack of desire, lack of enthusiasm, loathness, objection, opposition, reluctance, repugnance, resistance, unwillingness

disinclined antipathetic, averse, balking, hesitating, indisposed, loath, not in the mood, opposed, reluctant, resistant, unwilling

disinfect clean, cleanse, decontaminate, deodorize, fumigate, purify, sanitize, sterilize
Antonyms contaminate, defile, infect, poison, pollute, taint, vitiate

disinfectant antiseptic, germicide, sanitizer, sterilizer

disingenuous artful, cunning, deceitful, designing, dishonest, duplicitous, feigned, guileful, insidious, insincere, shifty, sly, two-faced, uncandid, underhanded, unfair, wily

disinherit cut off, cut off without a penny, disown, dispossess, oust, repudiate

disintegrate break apart, break up, crumble, disunite, fall apart, fall to pieces, go to pieces, go to seed, reduce to fragments, separate, shatter, splinter

disinter 1. dig up, disentomb, exhume, unearth 2. bring to light, disclose, discover, expose, uncover, unearth

disinterest candidness, detachment, disinterestedness, dispassionateness, equity, fairness, impartiality, justice, neutrality, unbiasedness

disinterested candid, detached, dispassionate, equitable, even-handed, free from self-interest, impartial, impersonal, neutral, outside, unbiased, uninvolved, unprejudiced, unselfish
Antonyms biased, involved, partial, prejudiced, selfish

disjointed 1. aimless, confused, disconnected, disordered, fitful, incoherent, loose, rambling, spasmodic, unconnected 2. disconnected, dislocated, displaced, disunited, divided, separated, split

dislikable, dislikeable detestable, displeasing, distasteful, hatable, nasty, objectionable, odious, unattractive, unlikable *or* unlikeable, unpleasant

dislike 1. *noun* animosity, animus, antagonism, antipathy, aversion, detestation, disapprobation, disapproval, disgust, disinclination, displeasure, distaste, enmity, hatred, hostility, loathing, odium, repugnance 2. *verb* abhor, abominate, be averse to, despise, detest, disapprove, disfavour, disrelish, hate, have a down on (*informal*), have no taste *or* stomach for, loathe, not be able to bear *or* abide, object to, scorn, shun, take a dim view of
Antonyms *noun* admiration, attraction, delight, esteem, inclination, liking ~*verb* esteem, favour, like

dislocate 1. disorder, displace, disrupt, disturb, misplace, shift 2. disarticulate, disconnect, disengage, disjoint, disunite, luxate (*Medical*), put out of joint, unhinge

dislocation 1. disarray, disorder, disorganization, disruption, disturbance, misplacement 2. disarticulation, disconnection, disengagement, luxation (*Medical*), unhinging

dislodge dig out, disentangle, displace, disturb, eject, extricate, force out, knock loose, oust, remove, uproot

disloyal apostate, disaffected, faithless, false, perfidious, seditious, subversive, traitorous, treacherous, treasonable, two-faced, unfaithful, unpatriotic, untrustworthy
Antonyms constant, dependable, dutiful, faithful, loyal, steadfast, true, trustworthy, trusty

disloyalty betrayal of trust, breach of trust, breaking of faith, deceitfulness, double-dealing, falseness, falsity, inconstancy, infidelity, perfidy, Punic faith, treachery, treason, unfaithfulness

dismal black, bleak, cheerless, dark, depressing, despondent, discouraging, dolorous, dreary, forlorn, funereal, gloomy, gruesome, lonesome, louring *or* lowering, lugubrious, melancholy, sad, sombre, sorrowful
Antonyms bright, cheerful, cheery, glad, happy, joyful, light-hearted, sunny

dismantle demolish, disassemble, dismount, raze, strike, strip, take apart, take to pieces, unrig

dismay *verb* 1. affright, alarm, appal, distress, fill with consternation, frighten, horrify, paralyse, scare, terrify, unnerve 2. daunt, disappoint, discourage, dishearten, disillusion, dispirit, put off ~*noun* 3. agitation, alarm, anxiety, apprehension, consternation, distress, dread, fear, fright, horror, panic, terror, trepidation 4. chagrin, disappointment, discouragement, disillusionment, upset

dismember amputate, anatomize, cut into pieces, disjoint, dislimb, dislocate, dissect, divide, mutilate, rend, sever

dismiss 1. axe (*informal*), cashier, discharge, fire (*informal*), give notice to, give (someone) their marching orders, give the boot to (*slang*), give the bullet to (*Brit. slang*), kiss off (*slang, chiefly U.S. & Canad.*), lay off, oust, remove, sack (*informal*), send packing (*informal*) 2. disband, disperse, dissolve, free, let go, release, send away 3. banish, discard, dispel, disregard, drop, lay aside, pooh-pooh, put out of one's mind, reject, relegate, repudiate, set aside, shelve, spurn

dismissal 1. adjournment, congé, end, freedom to depart, permission to go, release 2. discharge, expulsion, kiss-off (*slang, chiefly U.S. & Canad.*), marching orders (*informal*), notice, one's books *or* cards (*informal*), removal, the boot (*slang*), the bum's rush (*slang*), the (old) heave-ho (*informal*), the order of the boot (*slang*), the push (*slang*), the sack (*informal*)

dismount alight, descend, get down, get off, light

disobedience indiscipline, infraction, insubordination, mutiny, noncompliance, nonobservance, recalcitrance, revolt, unruliness, waywardness

disobedient contrary, contumacious, defiant, disorderly, froward (*archaic*), insubordinate, intractable, mischievous, naughty, noncompliant, nonobservant, obstreperous, re-

fractory, undisciplined, unruly, wayward, wilful
Antonyms biddable, compliant, dutiful, manageable, obedient, submissive, well-behaved

disobey contravene, defy, dig one's heels in (*informal*), disregard, flout, go counter to, ignore, infringe, overstep, rebel, refuse to obey, resist, transgress, violate

disoblige **1.** annoy, bother, discommode, disturb, inconvenience, put out, trouble, upset **2.** affront, displease, insult, offend, slight

disobliging awkward, bloody-minded (*Brit. informal*), cussed (*informal*), disagreeable, discourteous, ill-disposed, rude, unaccommodating, uncivil, uncooperative, unhelpful, unobliging, unpleasant

disorder *noun* **1.** chaos, clutter, confusion, derangement, disarray, disorderliness, disorganization, hodgepodge (*U.S.*), hotchpotch, irregularity, jumble, mess, muddle, pig's breakfast (*informal*), shambles, state, untidiness **2.** *bagarre*, brawl, clamour, commotion, disturbance, fight, fracas, hubbub, hullabaloo, quarrel, riot, rumpus, scrimmage, shindig (*informal*), shindy (*informal*), tumult, turbulence, turmoil, unrest, unruliness, upheaval, uproar **3.** *Medical* affliction, ailment, complaint, disease, illness, indisposition, malady, sickness ~*verb* **4.** clutter, confound, confuse, derange, disarrange, discompose, disorganize, disturb, jumble, make hay of, mess up, mix up, muddle, scatter, unsettle, upset

disordered all over the place, confused, deranged, disarranged, disarrayed, dislocated, disorganized, displaced, higgledy-piggledy (*informal*), in a mess, in confusion, jumbled, misplaced, muddled, out of kilter, out of place, untidy

disorderly **1.** chaotic, confused, disorganized, higgledy-piggledy (*informal*), indiscriminate, irregular, jumbled, messy, shambolic (*informal*), unsystematic, untidy **2.** boisterous, disruptive, indisciplined, lawless, obstreperous, rebellious, refractory, riotous, rowdy, stormy, tumultuous, turbulent, ungovernable, unlawful, unmanageable, unruly
Antonyms arranged, neat, orderly, organized, tidy

disorganization chaos, confusion, derangement, disarray, disjointedness, disorder, disruption, incoherence, unconnectedness

disorganize break up, confuse, convulse, derange, destroy, disarrange, discompose, disorder, disrupt, disturb, jumble, make a shambles of, muddle, turn topsy-turvy, unsettle, upset

disorganized chaotic, confused, disordered, haphazard, jumbled, muddled, off the rails, shuffled, unmethodical, unorganized, unsystematic

disorientate, disorient cause to lose one's bearings, confuse, dislocate, mislead, perplex, upset

disorientated, disoriented adrift, all at sea, astray, bewildered, confused, lost, mixed up, not adjusted, off-beam, off-course, out of joint, perplexed, unbalanced, unhinged, unsettled, unstable

disown abandon, abnegate, cast off, deny, disallow, disavow, disclaim, rebut, refuse to acknowledge *or* recognize, reject, renounce, repudiate, retract

disparage asperse, bad-mouth (*slang, chiefly U.S. & Canad.*), belittle, blast, criticize, decry, defame, degrade, denigrate, deprecate, depreciate, deride, derogate, detract from, discredit, disdain, dismiss, knock (*informal*), lambast(e), malign, minimize, put down, ridicule, rubbish (*informal*), run down, scorn, slag (off) (*slang*), slander, tear into (*informal*), traduce, underestimate, underrate, undervalue, vilify

disparagement aspersion, belittlement, condemnation, contempt, contumely, criticism, debasement, degradation, denigration, denunciation, depreciation, derision, derogation, detraction, discredit, disdain, impairment, lessening, prejudice, reproach, ridicule, scorn, slander, underestimation

disparaging abusive, belittling, contemptuous, contumelious, critical, damaging, defamatory, deprecatory, derisive, derogatory, disdainful, dismissive, fault-finding, insulting, libellous, malign, offensive, scathing, scornful, slanderous, slighting, uncomplimentary, unfavourable, unflattering
Antonyms appreciative, approving, commendatory, complimentary, favourable, flattering, laudatory

disparate at odds, at variance, contrary, contrasting, different, discordant, discrepant, dissimilar, distinct, diverse, unlike

disparity difference, discrepancy, disproportion, dissimilarity, dissimilitude, distinction, gap, imbalance, incongruity, inequality, unevenness, unlikeness

dispassion candidness, detachment, disinterestedness, impartiality, neutrality, objectivity

dispassionate **1.** calm, collected, composed, cool, imperturbable, moderate, quiet, serene, sober, temperate, unemotional, unexcitable, unexcited, unfazed (*informal*), unmoved, unruffled **2.** candid, detached, disinterested, fair, impartial, impersonal, indifferent, neutral, objective, unbiased, uninvolved, unprejudiced
Antonyms (*sense 1*) ablaze, ardent, emotional, excited, fervent, impassioned, intense, pas-

sionate (*sense 2*) biased, concerned, interested, involved, partial, prejudiced

dispatch, despatch *verb* **1.** accelerate, consign, dismiss, express, forward, hasten, hurry, quicken, remit, send, transmit **2.** conclude, discharge, dispose of, expedite, finish, make short work of (*informal*), perform, settle **3.** assassinate, blow away (*slang, chiefly U.S.*), bump off (*slang*), butcher, eliminate (*slang*), execute, finish off, kill, murder, put an end to, slaughter, slay, take out (*slang*) *~noun* **4.** alacrity, celerity, expedition, haste, precipitateness, promptitude, promptness, quickness, rapidity, speed, swiftness **5.** account, bulletin, communication, communiqué, document, instruction, item, letter, message, missive, news, piece, report, story

dispel allay, banish, chase away, dismiss, disperse, dissipate, drive away, eliminate, expel, resolve, rout, scatter

dispensable disposable, expendable, inessential, needless, nonessential, superfluous, unnecessary, unrequired, useless
Antonyms crucial, essential, important, indispensable, necessary, requisite, vital

dispensation **1.** allotment, appointment, apportionment, bestowal, conferment, consignment, dealing out, disbursement, distribution, endowment, supplying **2.** award, dole, part, portion, quota, share **3.** administration, direction, economy, management, plan, regulation, scheme, stewardship, system **4.** exception, exemption, immunity, indulgence, licence, permission, privilege, relaxation, relief, remission, reprieve

dispense **1.** allocate, allot, apportion, assign, deal out, disburse, distribute, dole out, mete out, share **2.** measure, mix, prepare, supply **3.** administer, apply, carry out, direct, discharge, enforce, execute, implement, operate, undertake **4.** except, excuse, exempt, exonerate, let off (*informal*), release, relieve, reprieve **5.** *with* **with** abstain from, do without, forgo, give up, omit, relinquish, waive **6.** *with* **with** abolish, brush aside, cancel, dispose of, disregard, do away with, get rid of, ignore, pass over, render needless, shake off

disperse **1.** broadcast, circulate, diffuse, disseminate, dissipate, distribute, scatter, spread, strew **2.** break up, disappear, disband, dismiss, dispel, dissolve, rout, scatter, send off, separate, vanish
Antonyms amass, assemble, collect, concentrate, congregate, convene, gather, muster, pool

dispersion broadcast, circulation, diffusion, dispersal, dissemination, dissipation, distribution, scattering, spread

dispirit cast down, damp, dampen, dash, deject, depress, deter, discourage, dishearten, disincline, sadden

dispirited crestfallen, dejected, depressed, despondent, discouraged, disheartened, down, downcast, gloomy, glum, in the doldrums, low, morose, sad, sick as a parrot (*informal*)

dispiriting crushing, dampening, daunting, demoralizing, depressing, disappointing, discouraging, disheartening, saddening, sickening
Antonyms cheering, comforting, encouraging, heartening, reassuring

displace **1.** derange, disarrange, disturb, misplace, move, shift, transpose **2.** cashier, depose, discard, discharge, dismiss, fire (*informal*), remove, sack (*informal*) **3.** crowd out, oust, replace, succeed, supersede, supplant, take the place of **4.** dislocate, dislodge, dispossess, eject, evict, force out, unsettle

display *verb* **1.** betray, demonstrate, disclose, evidence, evince, exhibit, expose, manifest, open, open to view, present, reveal, show, take the wraps off, unveil **2.** expand, extend, model, open out, spread out, stretch out, unfold, unfurl **3.** boast, flash (*informal*), flaunt, flourish, parade, show off, vaunt *~noun* **4.** array, demonstration, exhibition, exposition, exposure, manifestation, presentation, revelation, show **5.** flourish, ostentation, pageant, parade, pomp, show, spectacle
Antonyms *verb* conceal, cover, hide, keep dark, keep secret, mask, secrete, veil

displease aggravate (*informal*), anger, annoy, disgust, dissatisfy, exasperate, gall, hassle (*informal*), incense, irk, irritate, nark (*Brit., Austral., & N.Z. slang*), nettle, offend, pique, piss one off (*taboo slang*), provoke, put one's back up, put out, rile, upset, vex

displeasure anger, annoyance, disapprobation, disapproval, disfavour, disgruntlement, dislike, dissatisfaction, distaste, indignation, irritation, offence, pique, resentment, vexation, wrath
Antonyms approval, endorsement, pleasure, satisfaction

disport **1.** amuse, beguile, cheer, delight, divert, entertain, make merry **2.** caper, frisk, frolic, gambol, play, revel, romp, sport

disposable **1.** biodegradable, compostable, decomposable, nonreturnable, paper, throwaway **2.** at one's service, available, consumable, expendable, free for use, spendable

disposal **1.** clearance, discarding, dumping (*informal*), ejection, jettisoning, parting with, relinquishment, removal, riddance, scrapping, throwing away **2.** arrangement, array, dispensation, disposition, distribution, grouping, placing, position **3.** assignment, bequest, bestowal, consignment, conveyance, dispensation, gift, settlement, transfer **4.** *As in* **at one's disposal** authority, conduct, control, determination, direction, discretion, govern~ ment, management, ordering, regulation, re~ sponsibility

dispose 1. adjust, arrange, array, determine, distribute, fix, group, marshal, order, place, put, range, rank, regulate, set, settle, stand **2.** actuate, adapt, bias, condition, incline, induce, influence, lead, motivate, move, predispose, prompt, tempt

disposed apt, given, inclined, liable, likely, of a mind to, predisposed, prone, ready, subject, tending towards

dispose of 1. deal with, decide, determine, end, finish with, settle **2.** bestow, give, make over, part with, sell, transfer **3.** bin (*informal*), chuck (*informal*), destroy, discard, dump (*in~ formal*), get rid of, get shot of, jettison, junk (*informal*), scrap, throw out *or* away, unload

disposition 1. character, constitution, make-up, nature, spirit, temper, temperament **2.** bent, bias, habit, inclination, leaning, predisposi~ tion, proclivity, proneness, propensity, readi~ ness, tendency **3.** adjustment, arrangement, classification, disposal, distribution, grouping, ordering, organization, placement **4.** control, direction, disposal, management, regulation

dispossess deprive, dislodge, divest, drive out, eject, evict, expel, oust, strip, take away, turn out

dispossessed destitute, evicted, exiled, ex~ pelled, homeless, landless

dispraise 1. *verb* animadvert on *or* upon, blame, blast, censure, condemn, criticize, dis~ approve, disparage, lambast(e), put down, re~ proach, reprove, tear into (*informal*) **2.** *noun* blame, censure, depreciation, discredit, dis~ grace, dishonour, disparagement, opprobrium, reproach, shame

disproof confutation, counterargument, denial, disproval, invalidation, negation, rebuttal, refutation

disproportion asymmetry, discrepancy, dis~ parity, imbalance, inadequacy, inequality, in~ sufficiency, lopsidedness, unevenness, unsuitableness
Antonyms balance, congruity, harmony, pro~ portion, symmetry

disproportionate excessive, incommensurate, inordinate, out of proportion, too much, un~ balanced, unequal, uneven, unreasonable

disprove blow out of the water (*slang*), con~ fute, contradict, controvert, discredit, expose, give the lie to, invalidate, make a nonsense of, negate, prove false, rebut, refute
Antonyms ascertain, bear out, confirm, evince, prove, show, substantiate, verify

disputable arguable, controversial, debatable, doubtful, dubious, iffy (*informal*), moot, open to discussion, questionable, uncertain

disputant adversary, antagonist, arguer, con~ tender, contestant, debater, opponent

disputation argumentation, controversy, de~ bate, dispute, dissension, polemics

disputatious argumentative, cantankerous, captious, cavilling, contentious, dissentious, litigious, polemical, pugnacious, quarrelsome

dispute *verb* **1.** altercate, argue, brawl, clash, contend, cross swords, debate, discuss, quar~ rel, row, spar, squabble, wrangle **2.** challenge, contest, contradict, controvert, deny, doubt, impugn, question, rebut *~noun* **3.** altercation, argument, *bagarre*, brawl, conflict, disagree~ ment, discord, disturbance, feud, friction, quarrel, shindig (*informal*), shindy (*informal*), strife, wrangle **4.** argument, contention, con~ troversy, debate, discussion, dissension

disqualification 1. disability, disablement, in~ capacitation, incapacity, unfitness **2.** ban, de~ barment, disenablement, disentitlement, elimination, exclusion, incompetence, ineli~ gibility, rejection

disqualified debarred, eliminated, ineligible, knocked out, out of the running

disqualify 1. disable, incapacitate, invalidate, unfit (*rare*) **2.** ban, debar, declare ineligible, disentitle, preclude, prohibit, rule out

disquiet 1. *noun* alarm, angst, anxiety, con~ cern, disquietude, distress, disturbance, fear, foreboding, fretfulness, nervousness, restless~ ness, trepidation, trouble, uneasiness, unrest, worry **2.** *verb* agitate, annoy, bother, concern, discompose, distress, disturb, fret, harass, hassle (*informal*), incommode, make uneasy, perturb, pester, plague, trouble, unsettle, upset, vex, worry

disquieting annoying, bothersome, disconcert~ ing, distressing, disturbing, harrowing, irri~ tating, perturbing, troubling, unnerving, un~ settling, upsetting, vexing, worrying

disquisition discourse, dissertation, essay, ex~ position, lecture, paper, thesis, treatise

disregard *verb* **1.** brush aside *or* away, dis~ count, disobey, ignore, laugh off, leave out of account, make light of, neglect, overlook, pass over, pay no attention to, pay no heed to, take no notice of, turn a blind eye to **2.** brush off (*slang*), cold-shoulder, contemn, despise, disdain, disparage, send to Coventry, slight, snub *~noun* **3.** brushoff (*slang*), contempt, disdain, disrespect, heedlessness, ignoring, in~ attention, indifference, neglect, negligence, oversight, slight, the cold shoulder
Antonyms *verb* attend, heed, listen to, mind, note, pay attention to, regard, respect, take into consideration, take notice of

disrelish 1. *verb* be averse to, be turned off by (*informal*), disfavour, dislike, loathe, regard with distaste 2. *noun* antipathy, aversion, disfavour, disgust, disinclination, dislike, distaste, loathing, repugnance

disrepair 1. collapse, decay, deterioration, dilapidation, ruination 2. **in disrepair** broken, bust (*informal*), decayed, decrepit, kaput (*informal*), not functioning, on the blink (*slang*), out of commission, out of order, worn-out

disreputable 1. base, contemptible, derogatory, discreditable, disgraceful, dishonourable, disorderly, ignominious, infamous, louche, low, mean, notorious, opprobrious, scandalous, shady (*informal*), shameful, shocking, unprincipled, vicious, vile 2. bedraggled, dilapidated, dingy, dishevelled, down at heel, scruffy, seedy, shabby, threadbare, worn

Antonyms decent, reputable, respectable, respected, upright, worthy

disrepute discredit, disesteem, disfavour, disgrace, dishonour, ignominy, ill favour, ill repute, infamy, obloquy, shame, unpopularity

disrespect contempt, discourtesy, dishonour, disregard, impertinence, impoliteness, impudence, incivility, insolence, irreverence, lack of respect, lese-majesty, rudeness, unmannerliness

Antonyms esteem, regard, respect

disrespectful bad-mannered, cheeky, contemptuous, discourteous, ill-bred, impertinent, impolite, impudent, insolent, insulting, irreverent, misbehaved, rude, uncivil

disrobe bare, denude, divest, doff, remove, shed, strip, take off, unclothe, uncover, undress

disrupt 1. agitate, confuse, convulse, disorder, disorganize, disturb, spoil, throw into disorder, upset 2. break up *or* into, interfere with, interrupt, intrude, obstruct, unsettle, upset

disruption confusion, disarray, disorder, disorderliness, disturbance, interference, interruption, stoppage

disruptive confusing, disorderly, distracting, disturbing, obstreperous, troublemaking, troublesome, unruly, unsettling, upsetting

Antonyms biddable, cooperative, docile, obedient, well-behaved

dissatisfaction annoyance, chagrin, disappointment, discomfort, discontent, dislike, dismay, displeasure, distress, exasperation, frustration, irritation, regret, resentment, unhappiness

The grass is always greener on the other side of the fence

dissatisfied disappointed, discontented, disgruntled, displeased, fed up, frustrated, not satisfied, unfulfilled, ungratified, unhappy, unsatisfied

Antonyms content, contented, pleased, satisfied

dissatisfy annoy, disappoint, discontent, disgruntle, displease, give cause for complaint, irritate, leave dissatisfied, not pass muster, not suffice, put out, vex

dissect 1. anatomize, cut up *or* apart, dismember, lay open 2. analyse, break down, explore, inspect, investigate, research, scrutinize, study

dissection 1. anatomization, anatomy, autopsy, dismemberment, necropsy, postmortem (examination) 2. analysis, breakdown, examination, inspection, investigation, research, scrutiny

dissemble 1. camouflage, cloak, conceal, cover up, disguise, dissimulate, hide, mask 2. affect, counterfeit, falsify, feign, pretend, sham, simulate

dissembler charlatan, con man (*informal*), deceiver, dissimulator, feigner, fraud, hypocrite, impostor, pretender, trickster, whited sepulchre

disseminate broadcast, circulate, diffuse, disperse, dissipate, distribute, proclaim, promulgate, propagate, publicize, publish, scatter, sow, spread

dissemination broadcasting, circulation, diffusion, distribution, promulgation, propagation, publication, publishing, spread

dissension conflict, conflict of opinion, contention, difference, disagreement, discord, discordance, dispute, dissent, friction, quarrel, row, strife, variance

dissent 1. *verb* decline, differ, disagree, object, protest, refuse, withhold assent *or* approval 2. *noun* difference, disagreement, discord, dissension, dissidence, nonconformity, objection, opposition, refusal, resistance

Antonyms *verb* agree, assent, concur *~noun* accord, agreement, assent, concurrence, consensus

dissenter disputant, dissident, nonconformist, objector, protestant

dissenting *adjective* conflicting, differing, disagreeing, dissenting, dissident, opposing, protesting

dissertation critique, discourse, disquisition, essay, exposition, thesis, treatise

disservice bad turn, disfavour, harm, ill turn, injury, injustice, unkindness, wrong

Antonyms courtesy, good turn, indulgence, kindness, obligement (*Scot. or archaic*), service

dissever cleave, disunite, divorce, part, rend, rift, separate, sever, sunder

dissidence difference of opinion, disagreement,

discordance, dispute, dissent, feud, rupture, schism

dissident 1. *adjective* differing, disagreeing, discordant, dissentient, dissenting, heterodox, nonconformist, schismatic 2. *noun* agitator, dissenter, protester, rebel, recusant

dissimilar different, disparate, divergent, diverse, heterogeneous, manifold, mismatched, not alike, not capable of comparison, not similar, unlike, unrelated, various
Antonyms alike, comparable, congruous, corresponding, in agreement, much the same, resembling, uniform

dissimilarity difference, discrepancy, disparity, dissimilitude, distinction, divergence, heterogeneity, incomparability, nonuniformity, unlikeness, unrelatedness

dissimilitude difference, discrepancy, disparity, dissimilarity, diversity, heterogeneity, incomparability, nonuniformity, unlikeness, unrelatedness

dissimulate camouflage, cloak, conceal, disguise, dissemble, feign, hide, mask, pretend

dissimulation concealment, deceit, deception, dissembling, double-dealing, duplicity, feigning, hypocrisy, play-acting, pretence, sham, wile

dissipate 1. burn up, consume, deplete, expend, fritter away, indulge oneself, lavish, misspend, run through, spend, squander, waste 2. disappear, dispel, disperse, dissolve, drive away, evaporate, scatter, vanish

dissipated 1. abandoned, debauched, dissolute, intemperate, profligate, rakish, self-indulgent 2. consumed, destroyed, exhausted, scattered, squandered, wasted

dissipation 1. abandonment, debauchery, dissoluteness, drunkenness, excess, extravagance, indulgence, intemperance, lavishness, prodigality, profligacy, squandering, wantonness, waste 2. amusement, distraction, diversion, entertainment, gratification 3. disappearance, disintegration, dispersion, dissemination, dissolution, scattering, vanishing

dissociate 1. break off, disband, disrupt, part company, quit 2. detach, disconnect, distance, divorce, isolate, segregate, separate, set apart

dissociation break, detachment, disconnection, disengagement, distancing, disunion, division, divorce, isolation, segregation, separation, severance

dissolute abandoned, corrupt, debauched, degenerate, depraved, dissipated, immoral, lax, lewd, libertine, licentious, loose, profligate, rakish, unrestrained, vicious, wanton, wild
Antonyms chaste, clean-living, good, moral, squeaky-clean, upright, virtuous

dissolution 1. breaking up, disintegration, division, divorce, parting, resolution, separation 2. death, decay, decomposition, demise, destruction, dispersal, extinction, overthrow, ruin 3. adjournment, conclusion, disbandment, discontinuation, dismissal, end, ending, finish, suspension, termination 4. corruption, debauchery, dissipation, intemperance, wantonness 5. disappearance, evaporation, liquefaction, melting, solution
Antonyms (*sense 1*) alliance, amalgamation, coalition, combination, unification, union

dissolve 1. deliquesce, flux, fuse, liquefy, melt, soften, thaw 2. break down, crumble, decompose, diffuse, disappear, disintegrate, disperse, dissipate, dwindle, evanesce, evaporate, fade, melt away, perish, vanish, waste away 3. axe (*informal*), break up, destroy, discontinue, dismiss, end, overthrow, ruin, suspend, terminate, wind up 4. break into *or* up, collapse, disorganize, disunite, divorce, loose, resolve into, separate, sever

dissonance 1. cacophony, discord, discordance, harshness, jangle, jarring, unmelodiousness, want of harmony 2. difference, disagreement, discord, discrepancy, disparity, dissension, incongruity, inconsistency, variance

dissonant 1. cacophonous, discordant, grating, harsh, inharmonious, jangling, jarring, out of tune, raucous, strident, tuneless, unmelodious 2. anomalous, at variance, different, differing, disagreeing, discrepant, dissentient, incompatible, incongruous, inconsistent, irreconcilable, irregular

dissuade advise against, deter, discourage, disincline, divert, expostulate, persuade not to, put off, remonstrate, talk out of, urge not to, warn
Antonyms bring round (*informal*), coax, convince, persuade, sway, talk into

dissuasion caution, damper, determent, deterrence, deterrent, discouragement, disincentive, expostulation, hindrance, remonstrance, setback

dissuasive admonitory, cautionary, discouraging, disincentive, dissuading, monitory, off-putting (*Brit. informal*), remonstrative, warning

distance *noun* 1. absence, extent, gap, interval, lapse, length, range, reach, remoteness, remove, separation, space, span, stretch, width 2. aloofness, coldness, coolness, frigidity, reserve, restraint, stiffness 3. **go the distance** bring to an end, complete, finish, see through, stay the course 4. **keep one's distance** avoid, be aloof (indifferent, reserved), keep (someone) at arm's length, shun 5. **in the distance** afar, far away, far off, on the horizon, yonder ~*verb* 6. dissociate oneself, put in proportion, separate oneself 7. leave behind, outdistance, outdo, outrun, outstrip, pass

distance: the only thing that the rich are willing for the poor to call theirs and keep
Ambrose Bierce *The Devil's Dictionary*

Distance lends enchantment to the view

distant **1.** abroad, afar, far, faraway, far-flung, far-off, outlying, out-of-the-way, remote, removed **2.** apart, disparate, dispersed, distinct, scattered, separate **3.** aloof, at arm's length, ceremonious, cold, cool, formal, haughty, reserved, restrained, reticent, standoffish, stiff, unapproachable, unfriendly, withdrawn **4.** faint, indirect, indistinct, obscure, slight, uncertain
Antonyms (*senses 1 & 2*) adjacent, adjoining, at hand, close, handy, imminent, just round the corner, near, nearby, neighbouring, nigh, proximate, within sniffing distance (*informal*), (*sense 3*) close, friendly, intimate, warm

distaste abhorrence, antipathy, aversion, detestation, disfavour, disgust, disinclination, dislike, displeasure, disrelish, dissatisfaction, horror, loathing, odium, repugnance, revulsion

distasteful abhorrent, disagreeable, displeasing, loathsome, nauseous, objectionable, obnoxious, obscene, offensive, repugnant, repulsive, undesirable, uninviting, unpalatable, unpleasant, unsavoury
Antonyms agreeable, charming, enjoyable, pleasing, pleasurable

distend balloon, bloat, bulge, dilate, enlarge, expand, increase, inflate, puff, stretch, swell, widen

distended bloated, dilated, enlarged, expanded, inflated, puffy, stretched, swollen, tumescent

distension dilatation, dilation, enlargement, expansion, extension, inflation, intumescence, spread

distil condense, draw out, evaporate, express, extract, press out, purify, rectify, refine, sublimate, vaporize

distillation elixir, essence, extract, quintessence, spirit

distinct **1.** apparent, black-and-white, blatant, bold, clear, clear-cut, decided, definite, evident, lucid, manifest, marked, noticeable, obvious, palpable, patent, plain, recognizable, sharp, unambiguous, unmistakable, well-defined **2.** detached, different, discrete, dissimilar, individual, separate, unconnected
Antonyms common, connected, fuzzy, identical, indefinite, indistinct, obscure, similar, unclear, vague

distinction **1.** differentiation, discernment, discrimination, penetration, perception, separation **2.** contrast, difference, differential, division, fine line, separation **3.** characteristic, distinctiveness, feature, individuality, mark, particularity, peculiarity, quality **4.** account, celebrity, consequence, credit, eminence, excellence, fame, greatness, honour, importance, merit, name, note, prominence, quality, rank, renown, reputation, repute, superiority, worth

distinctive characteristic, different, distinguishing, extraordinary, idiosyncratic, individual, original, peculiar, singular, special, typical, uncommon, unique
Antonyms common, ordinary, run-of-the-mill, typical

distinctly clearly, decidedly, definitely, evidently, manifestly, markedly, noticeably, obviously, palpably, patently, plainly, precisely, sharply

distinctness **1.** clarity, lucidity, obviousness, plainness, sharpness, vividness **2.** detachment, difference, discreteness, disparateness, dissimilarity, dissociation, distinctiveness, individuality, separation

distinguish **1.** ascertain, decide, determine, differentiate, discriminate, judge, tell apart, tell between, tell the difference **2.** categorize, characterize, classify, individualize, make distinctive, mark, separate, set apart, single out **3.** discern, know, make out, perceive, pick out, recognize, see, tell **4.** celebrate, dignify, honour, immortalize, make famous, signalize

distinguishable bold, clear, conspicuous, discernible, evident, manifest, noticeable, obvious, perceptible, plain, recognizable, well-marked

distinguished **1.** acclaimed, celebrated, conspicuous, eminent, famed, famous, illustrious, notable, noted, renowned, well-known **2.** conspicuous, extraordinary, marked, outstanding, signal, striking
Antonyms common, inelegant, inferior, undistinguished, unknown

distinguishing characteristic, different, differentiating, distinctive, individualistic, marked, peculiar, typical

distort **1.** bend, buckle, contort, deform, disfigure, misshape, twist, warp, wrench, wrest **2.** bias, colour, falsify, garble, misrepresent, pervert, slant, twist

distorted **1.** bent, buckled, contorted, crooked, deformed, disfigured, irregular, misshapen, twisted, warped **2.** biased, coloured, false, garbled, one-sided, partial, perverted, slanted, twisted

distortion **1.** bend, buckle, contortion, crookedness, deformity, malformation, twist, twistedness, warp **2.** bias, colouring, falsification, misrepresentation, perversion, slant

distract **1.** divert, draw away, sidetrack, turn aside **2.** amuse, beguile, engross, entertain, occupy **3.** agitate, bewilder, confound, confuse, derange, discompose, disconcert, disturb, harass, madden, perplex, puzzle, torment, trouble

distracted **1.** agitated, at sea, bemused, bewildered, confounded, confused, flustered, harassed, in a flap (*informal*), perplexed, puzzled, troubled **2.** at the end of one's tether, crazy, deranged, desperate, distraught, frantic, frenzied, gonzo (*slang*), grief-stricken, insane, mad, overwrought, raving, wild

distracting bewildering, bothering, confusing, disconcerting, dismaying, disturbing, off-putting (*Brit. informal*), perturbing

distraction **1.** abstraction, agitation, bewilderment, commotion, confusion, discord, disorder, disturbance **2.** amusement, beguilement, diversion, divertissement, entertainment, pastime, recreation **3.** disturbance, diversion, interference, interruption **4.** aberration, alienation, delirium, derangement, desperation, frenzy, hallucination, incoherence, insanity, mania

distrait absent, absent-minded, abstracted, distracted, forgetful, inattentive, oblivious, preoccupied, unaware

distraught agitated, anxious, at the end of one's tether, beside oneself, crazed, desperate, distracted, distressed, frantic, hysterical, mad, out of one's mind, overwrought, raving, wild, worked-up, wrought-up

distress *noun* **1.** affliction, agony, anguish, anxiety, desolation, discomfort, grief, heartache, misery, pain, sadness, sorrow, suffering, torment, torture, woe, worry, wretchedness **2.** adversity, calamity, destitution, difficulties, hardship, indigence, misfortune, need, poverty, privation, straits, trial, trouble ~*verb* **3.** afflict, agonize, bother, disturb, grieve, harass, harrow, pain, perplex, sadden, torment, trouble, upset, worry, wound

distressed **1.** afflicted, agitated, anxious, distracted, distraught, saddened, tormented, troubled, upset, worried, wretched **2.** destitute, down at heel, indigent, needy, poor, poverty-stricken, straitened

distressing affecting, afflicting, distressful, disturbing, grievous, harrowing, heart-breaking, hurtful, lamentable, nerve-racking, painful, sad, upsetting, worrying

distribute **1.** administer, allocate, allot, apportion, assign, deal, dispense, dispose, divide, dole out, give, measure out, mete, share **2.** circulate, convey, deliver, hand out, pass round **3.** diffuse, disperse, disseminate, scatter, spread, strew **4.** arrange, assort, categorize, class, classify, file, group

distribution **1.** allocation, allotment, apportionment, dispensation, division, dole, partition, sharing **2.** circulation, diffusion, dispersal, dispersion, dissemination, propagation, scattering, spreading **3.** arrangement, assortment, classification, disposition, grouping, location, organization, placement **4.** *Commerce* dealing, delivery, handling, mailing, marketing, trading, transport, transportation

district area, community, locale, locality, neck of the woods (*informal*), neighbourhood, parish, quarter, region, sector, vicinity, ward

distrust **1.** *verb* be sceptical of, be suspicious of, be wary of, disbelieve, discredit, doubt, misbelieve, mistrust, question, smell a rat (*informal*), suspect, wonder about **2.** *noun* disbelief, doubt, dubiety, lack of faith, misgiving, mistrust, qualm, question, scepticism, suspicion, wariness

Antonyms *verb* believe, depend, have confidence, have faith, trust ~*noun* confidence, faith, reliance, trust

Trust him no further than you can throw him
Thomas Fuller *Gnomologia*

distrustful chary, cynical, disbelieving, distrusting, doubtful, doubting, dubious, leery (*slang*), mistrustful, sceptical, suspicious, uneasy, wary

disturb **1.** bother, butt in on, disrupt, interfere with, interrupt, intrude on, pester, rouse, startle **2.** confuse, derange, disarrange, disorder, disorganize, muddle, unsettle **3.** agitate, alarm, annoy, confound, discompose, distract, distress, excite, fluster, harass, hassle (*informal*), perturb, ruffle, shake, trouble, unnerve, unsettle, upset, worry

Antonyms calm, compose, lull, pacify, quiet, quieten, reassure, relax, relieve, settle, soothe

disturbance **1.** agitation, annoyance, bother, confusion, derangement, disorder, distraction, hindrance, interruption, intrusion, molestation, perturbation, upset **2.** bother (*informal*), brawl, commotion, disorder, fracas, fray, hubbub, riot, ruckus (*informal*), ruction (*informal*), shindig (*informal*), shindy (*informal*), tumult, turmoil, upheaval, uproar

disturbed **1.** *Psychiatry* disordered, maladjusted, neurotic, troubled, unbalanced, upset **2.** agitated, anxious, apprehensive, bothered, concerned, disquieted, nervous, troubled, uneasy, upset, worried

Antonyms balanced, calm, collected, self-possessed, unfazed (*informal*), untroubled

disturbing agitating, alarming, disconcerting, discouraging, dismaying, disquieting, distressing, frightening, harrowing, perturbing, startling, threatening, troubling, unsettling, upsetting, worrying

disunion **1.** abstraction, detachment, disconnection, disjunction, division, partition, separation, severance **2.** alienation, breach, disagreement, discord, dissension, dissidence, estrangement, feud, rupture, schism, split

disunite **1.** detach, disband, disconnect, disengage, disjoin, disrupt, divide, part, segregate, separate, sever, split, sunder **2.** alienate, embroil, estrange, set at odds, set at variance

disunity alienation, breach, disagreement, discord, discordance, dissension, dissent, estrangement, rupture, schism, split, variance

disuse abandonment, decay, desuetude, discontinuance, idleness, neglect, non-employment, nonuse
Antonyms application, employment, practice, service, usage, use

ditch *noun* **1.** channel, drain, dyke, furrow, gully, moat, trench, watercourse *~verb* **2.** dig, drain, excavate, gouge, trench **3.** *slang* abandon, axe (*informal*), bin (*informal*), chuck (*informal*), discard, dispose of, drop, dump (*informal*), get rid of, jettison, junk (*informal*), scrap, throw out *or* overboard

dither 1. *verb* faff about (*Brit. informal*), falter, haver, hesitate, hum and haw, oscillate, shillyshally (*informal*), swither (*Scot.*), teeter, vacillate, waver **2.** *noun* bother, flap (*informal*), fluster, flutter, pother, stew (*informal*), tiz-woz (*informal*), tizzy (*informal*), twitter (*informal*)
Antonyms *verb* come to a conclusion, conclude, decide, make a decision, make up one's mind, reach *or* come to a decision, resolve, settle

dithery agitated, all of a dither *or* fluster, bothered, dithering, flustered, hesitant, in a flap *or* tizzy (*informal*), indecisive, irresolute, swithering (*Scot.*), tentative, uncertain, unsure, vacillating, wavering
Antonyms certain, decisive, firm, positive, resolute, sure, unhesitating

diurnal circadian, daily, daytime, everyday, quotidian, regular

diva opera singer, prima donna, singer

dive *verb* **1.** descend, dip, disappear, drop, duck, fall, go underwater, jump, leap, nose-dive, pitch, plummet, plunge, submerge, swoop *~noun* **2.** dash, header (*informal*), jump, leap, lunge, nose dive, plunge, spring **3.** *slang* honky-tonk (*U.S. slang*), joint (*slang*), sleazy bar

diverge 1. bifurcate, branch, divaricate, divide, fork, part, radiate, separate, split, spread **2.** be at odds, be at variance, conflict, differ, disagree, dissent **3.** depart, deviate, digress, meander, stray, turn aside, wander

divergence branching out, deflection, departure, deviation, difference, digression, disparity, divagation, ramification, separation, varying

divergent conflicting, deviating, different, differing, disagreeing, dissimilar, diverging, diverse, separate, variant

divers different, manifold, many, multifarious, numerous, several, some, sundry, varied, various

diverse 1. assorted, diversified, manifold, miscellaneous, of every description, several, sundry, varied, various **2.** different, differing, discrete, disparate, dissimilar, distinct, divergent, separate, unlike, varying

diversify alter, assort, branch out, change, expand, have a finger in every pie, mix, modify, spread out, transform, variegate, vary

diversion 1. alteration, change, deflection, departure, detour, deviation, digression, variation **2.** amusement, beguilement, delight, distraction, divertissement, enjoyment, entertainment, game, gratification, jollies (*slang*), pastime, play, pleasure, recreation, relaxation, sport

diversity assortment, difference, dissimilarity, distinctiveness, divergence, diverseness, diversification, heterogeneity, medley, multiplicity, range, unlikeness, variance, variegation, variety

It takes all sorts to make a world

divert 1. avert, deflect, redirect, switch, turn aside **2.** amuse, beguile, delight, entertain, gratify, recreate, regale **3.** detract, distract, draw *or* lead away from, lead astray, sidetrack

diverted 1. changed, deflected, made use of, rebudgeted, rechannelled, reclassified, redirected, taken over, turned aside **2.** amused, entertained, taken out of oneself, tickled

diverting amusing, beguiling, enjoyable, entertaining, fun, humorous, pleasant

divest 1. denude, disrobe, doff, remove, strip, take off, unclothe, undress **2.** deprive, despoil, dispossess, strip

divide 1. bisect, cleave, cut (up), detach, disconnect, part, partition, segregate, separate, sever, shear, split, subdivide, sunder **2.** allocate, allot, apportion, deal out, dispense, distribute, divvy (up) (*informal*), dole out, measure out, portion, share **3.** alienate, break up, cause to disagree, come between, disunite, estrange, set at variance *or* odds, set *or* pit against one another, sow dissension, split **4.** arrange, categorize, classify, grade, group, put in order, separate, sort
Antonyms (*sense 1*) combine, come together, connect, join, knit, marry, splice, unite

Divide and rule

Philip of Macedon

dividend bonus, cut (*informal*), divvy (*informal*), extra, gain, plus, portion, share, surplus

divination augury, clairvoyance, divining, foretelling, fortune-telling, prediction, presage, prognostication, prophecy, soothsaying, sortilege

Methods of divination

astrology	palmistry
clairvoyance	runes
crystal gazing	scrying
dice	sortilege
dowsing	tarot
I Ching	tea leaves
numerology	

Means of divination

ailuromancy	cats
alphitomancy	wheat or barley cakes
arachnomancy	spiders
astragalomancy	dice
bibliomancy	passages from books
cartomancy	cards
catoptromancy	mirror
ceromancy	melted wax
chiromancy	hands
cleidomancy	suspended key
crithomancy	freshly baked bread
cromniomancy	onions
crystallomancy	crystal ball
dactylomancy	suspended ring
geomancy	earth, sand, or dust
hippomancy	horses
hydromancy	water
lampadomancy	oil lamps
lithomancy	precious stones
lychnomancy	flames of wax candles
molybdomancy	molten lead
necromancy	the dead
oneiromancy	dreams
ornithomancy	birds
pegomancy	sacred pool
pyromancy	fire or flames
radiesthesia	pendulum
rhabdomancy	rod or wand
sciomancy	ghosts
tasseography	tea leaves
theomancy	god
tyromancy	cheese

divination: the art of nosing out the occult. Divination is of as many kinds as there are fruit-bearing varieties of the flowering dunce and the early fool

Ambrose Bierce *The Devil's Dictionary*

divine *adjective* **1.** angelic, celestial, godlike, heavenly, holy, spiritual, superhuman, supernatural **2.** consecrated, holy, religious, sacred, sanctified, spiritual **3.** beatific, blissful, exalted, mystical, rapturous, supreme, transcendent, transcendental, transmundane **4.** *informal* beautiful, excellent, glorious, marvellous, perfect, splendid, superlative, wonderful *~noun* **5.** churchman, clergyman, cleric, ecclesiastic, minister, pastor, priest, reverend *~verb* **6.** apprehend, conjecture, deduce, discern, foretell, guess, infer, intuit, perceive, prognosticate, suppose, surmise, suspect, understand **7.** *of water or minerals* dowse

diviner **1.** astrologer, augur, oracle, prophet, seer, sibyl, soothsayer **2.** *of water or minerals* dowser

divinity **1.** deity, divine nature, godhead, godhood, godliness, holiness, sanctity **2.** daemon, deity, genius, god, goddess, guardian spirit, spirit **3.** religion, religious studies, theology

divisible dividable, fractional, separable, splittable

division **1.** bisection, cutting up, detaching, dividing, partition, separation, splitting up **2.** allotment, apportionment, distribution, sharing **3.** border, boundary, demarcation, divide, divider, dividing line, partition **4.** branch, category, class, compartment, department, group, head, part, portion, section, sector, segment **5.** breach, difference of opinion, disagreement, discord, disunion, estrangement, feud, rupture, split, variance

Antonyms (*sense 5*) accord, agreement, concord, harmony, peace, union, unity

If a house be divided against itself, that house cannot stand

Bible: St. Mark

divisive alienating, damaging, detrimental, discordant, disruptive, estranging, inharmonious, pernicious, troublesome, unsettling

divorce **1.** *noun* annulment, breach, break, decree nisi, dissolution, disunion, rupture, separation, severance, split-up **2.** *verb* annul, disconnect, dissociate, dissolve (*marriage*), disunite, divide, part, separate, sever, split up, sunder

divulge betray, blow wide open (*slang*), communicate, confess, cough (*slang*), declare, disclose, exhibit, expose, get off one's chest (*informal*), impart, leak, let slip, make known, proclaim, promulgate, publish, reveal, spill (*informal*), spill one's guts about (*slang*), tell, uncover

Antonyms conceal, hide, keep secret

divvy **1.** *noun* cut (*informal*), dividend, percentage, portion, quota, share, whack (*informal*) **2.** *verb sometimes with* **up** apportion, cut, distribute, divide, parcel out, share (out), split

dizzy **1.** faint, giddy, light-headed, off balance, reeling, shaky, staggering, swimming, vertiginous, weak at the knees, wobbly, woozy (*informal*) **2.** at sea, befuddled, bemused, bewildered, confused, dazed, dazzled, muddled **3.** lofty, steep, vertiginous **4.** *informal* capricious, fickle, flighty, foolish, frivolous, giddy, light-headed, scatterbrained, silly

do *verb* **1.** accomplish, achieve, act, carry out, complete, conclude, discharge, end, execute, perform, produce, transact, undertake, work **2.**

answer, be adequate, be enough, be of use, be sufficient, cut the mustard, pass muster, satisfy, serve, suffice, suit **3.** arrange, be responsible for, fix, get ready, look after, make, make ready, organize, prepare, see to, take on **4.** decipher, decode, figure out, puzzle out, resolve, solve, work out **5.** adapt, render, translate, transpose **6.** bear oneself, behave, carry oneself, comport oneself, conduct oneself **7.** fare, get along, get on, make out, manage, proceed **8.** bring about, cause, create, effect, produce **9.** *of a play, etc.* act, give, perform, present, produce, put on **10.** *informal* cover, explore, journey through *or* around, look at, stop in, tour, travel, visit **11.** *informal* cheat, con (*informal*), cozen, deceive, defraud, diddle (*informal*), dupe, fleece, hoax, pull a fast one on (*informal*), skin (*slang*), stiff (*slang*), swindle, take (someone) for a ride (*informal*), trick ~*noun* **12.** *informal* affair, event, function, gathering, occasion, party **13. do's and don'ts** *informal* code, customs, etiquette, instructions, regulations, rules, standards

Do unto others what you would they should do unto you

do away with **1.** blow away (*slang, chiefly U.S.*), bump off (*slang*), destroy, do in (*slang*), exterminate, kill, liquidate, murder, slay, take out (*slang*) **2.** abolish, axe (*informal*), chuck (*informal*), discard, discontinue, eliminate, get rid of, junk (*informal*), pull, put an end to, put paid to, remove

docile amenable, biddable, compliant, ductile, manageable, obedient, pliant, submissive, teachable (*rare*), tractable
Antonyms difficult, intractable, obstreperous, troublesome, trying, uncooperative, unmanageable

docility amenability, biddableness, compliance, ductility, manageability, meekness, obedience, pliancy, submissiveness, tractability

dock[1] *noun* **1.** harbour, pier, quay, waterfront, wharf ~*verb* **2.** anchor, berth, drop anchor, land, moor, put in, tie up **3.** *of spacecraft* couple, hook up, join, link up, rendezvous, unite

dock[2] *verb* **1.** clip, crop, curtail, cut off, cut short, diminish, lessen, shorten **2.** decrease, deduct, diminish, lessen, reduce, subtract, withhold
Antonyms (*sense 2*) augment, boost, increase, raise

docket **1.** *noun* bill, certificate, chit, chitty, counterfoil, label, receipt, tab, tag, tally, ticket, voucher **2.** *verb* catalogue, file, index, label, mark, register, tab, tag, ticket

doctor *noun* **1.** general practitioner, G.P., medic (*informal*), medical practitioner, physician ~*verb* **2.** apply medication to, give medical treatment to, treat **3.** botch, cobble, do up (*informal*), fix, mend, patch up, repair **4.** alter, change, disguise, falsify, fudge, misrepresent, pervert, tamper with **5.** add to, adulterate, cut, dilute, mix with, spike, water down

God heals, and the doctor takes the fee
Benjamin Franklin *Poor Richard's Almanac*

I am simply in Hell, where there are no doctors - at least, not in a professional capacity
T.S. Eliot *The Cocktail Party*

One finger in the throat and one in the rectum makes a good diagnostician
William Osler *Aphorisms from his Bedside Teachings*

God and the doctor we alike adore
But only when in danger, not before;
The danger o'er, both are alike requited,
God is forgotten, and the Doctor slighted
John Owen *Epigrams*

doctrinaire *adjective* **1.** biased, dogmatic, fanatical, inflexible, insistent, opinionated, rigid **2.** hypothetical, ideological, impractical, speculative, theoretical, unpragmatic, unrealistic

doctrine article, article of faith, belief, canon, concept, conviction, creed, dogma, opinion, precept, principle, teaching, tenet

document **1.** *noun* certificate, instrument, legal form, paper, record, report **2.** *verb* authenticate, back up, certify, cite, corroborate, detail, give weight to, instance, particularize, substantiate, support, validate, verify

dodder quake, quaver, quiver, shake, shamble, shiver, shuffle, stagger, sway, teeter, totter, tremble

doddering aged, decrepit, doddery, faltering, feeble, floundering, infirm, senile, shaky, shambling, tottery, trembly, unsteady, weak

doddle cakewalk (*informal*), child's play (*informal*), cinch (*slang*), easy-peasy (*slang*), money for (jam and) old rope, no sweat (*slang*), picnic (*informal*), piece of cake (*informal*), pushover (*slang*)

dodge *verb* **1.** body-swerve (*Scot.*), dart, duck, shift, sidestep, swerve, turn aside **2.** avoid, body-swerve (*Scot.*), deceive, elude, equivocate, evade, fend off, flannel (*Brit. informal*), fudge, get out of, hedge, parry, shirk, shuffle, trick ~*noun* **3.** contrivance, device, feint, flannel (*Brit. informal*), machination, ploy, ruse, scheme, stratagem, subterfuge, trick, wheeze (*Brit. slang*), wile

dodger evader, shifty so-and-so, shirker, slacker, slippery one, slyboots, trickster

dodgy chancy (*informal*), dangerous, delicate, dicey (*informal, chiefly Brit.*), dicky (*Brit. informal*), difficult, problematic(al), risky, ticklish, tricky, uncertain, unreliable

doer achiever, active person, activist, bustler, dynamo, go-getter (*informal*), live wire (*slang*), organizer, powerhouse (*slang*), wheeler-dealer (*informal*)

doff 1. *of a hat* lift, raise, remove, take off, tip, touch 2. *of clothing* cast off, discard, remove, shed, slip off, slip out of, take off, throw off, undress

do for defeat, destroy, finish (off), kill, ruin, shatter, slay, undo

dog *noun* 1. bitch, canine, cur, hound, kuri *or* goorie (*N.Z.*), man's best friend, mongrel, mutt (*slang*), pooch (*slang*), pup, puppy, tyke 2. *informal* beast, blackguard, cur, heel (*slang*), knave (*archaic*), scoundrel, villain 3. **dog-eat-dog** cutthroat, ferocious, fierce, ruth~less, vicious, with no holds barred 4. **go to the dogs** *informal* degenerate, deteriorate, go down the drain, go to pot, go to ruin ~*verb* 5. haunt, hound, plague, pursue, shadow, tail (*informal*), track, trail, trouble
Related adjective: canine

Breeds of dog

affenpinscher
Afghan hound
Airedale terrier
Akita
Alaskan malamute
Alpine spaniel
Alsatian *or* German shepherd
Australian terrier
barb (*Austral.*)
basenji
basset hound
beagle
bearded collie
Bedlington terrier
Belvoir hound
Bichon Frise
Blenheim spaniel
bloodhound, sleuth~hound *or* sleuth
blue Gascon hound
Border collie
Border terrier
borzoi *or* Russian wolfhound
Boston terrier *or* bull terrier
bouvier
boxer
briard
Bruxellois
bulldog
bull mastiff
bull terrier
cairn terrier *or* cairn
chihuahua
chow-chow *or* chow
clumber spaniel
cocker spaniel
collie
corgi *or* Welsh corgi
Cuban bloodhound
dachshund
Dalmatian *or (for~merly)* carriage dog *or* coach dog
Dandie Dinmont (ter~rier)
deerhound
Doberman pinscher *or* Doberman
Egyptian basset
elkhound *or* Norwe~gian elkhound
English setter
Eskimo dog
field spaniel
foxhound
fox terrier
French bulldog
golden retriever
Gordon setter
Great Dane
greyhound
griffon
harrier
Highland terrier
husky
Irish setter *or* red setter
Irish terrier
Irish water spaniel
Irish wolfhound
Italian greyhound
Jack Russell (terrier)
Japanese spaniel
Japanese tosa
keeshond
kelpie
Kerry blue terrier
King Charles spaniel
komondor
Labrador retriever, Labrador *or* lab
Lakeland terrier
Lhasa apso
malamute *or* mal~emute
Maltese
Manchester terrier *or* black-and-tan terrier
mastiff
Mexican hairless
Newfoundland
Norfolk springer spaniel
Norfolk terrier
Norwich terrier
Old English sheepdog
otterhound
papillon
Pekingese
pit bull terrier *or* American pit bull terrier
pointer
Pomeranian
poodle
pug
puli
Pyrenean mountain dog
raccoon dog *or* coon~hound
retriever
Rhodesian ridgeback
Rottweiler
rough collie
Saint Bernard *or* St. Bernard
Saluki *or* Persian greyhound
Samoyed
schipperke
schnauzer
Scottish, Scotch, *or (formerly)* Aberdeen terrier *or* Scottie
Sealyham terrier
setter
Shetland sheepdog *or* sheltie
shih-tzu
Skye terrier
spaniel
spitz
springer spaniel
Staffordshire bull ter~rier
staghound
Sussex spaniel
talbot
terrier
vizsla
water spaniel
Weimaraner
Welsh terrier
West Highland white terrier
whippet
wire-haired terrier
wolfhound
Yorkshire terrier

Love me, love my dog

St. Bernard

The more I see of men, the better I like dogs

Mme Roland

Histories are more full of examples of the fidelity of dogs than of friends

Alexander Pope

Every dog has its day

Why keep a dog and bark yourself?

If you lie down with dogs, you will get up with fleas

A live dog is better than a dead lion

Let sleeping dogs lie

dogged determined, firm, immovable, indefati~gable, obstinate, persevering, persistent, per~tinacious, resolute, single-minded, staunch, steadfast, steady, stiff-necked, stubborn, tena~cious, unflagging, unshakable, unyielding
Antonyms doubtful, half-hearted, hesitant, irresolute, undetermined, unsteady

doggedness bulldog tenacity, determination, endurance, obstinacy, perseverance, persistence, pertinacity, relentlessness, resolution, single-mindedness, steadfastness, steadiness, stubbornness, tenaciousness, tenacity

doggo **lie doggo** be in hiding, go to earth, keep a low profile, keep one's head down, keep out of the public eye, stay out of sight

dogma article, article of faith, belief, credo, creed, doctrine, opinion, precept, principle, teachings, tenet

dogmatic 1. arbitrary, arrogant, assertive, categorical, dictatorial, doctrinaire, downright, emphatic, imperious, magisterial, obdurate, opinionated, overbearing, peremptory 2. authoritative, canonical, categorical, doctrinal, ex cathedra, oracular, positive

dogmatism arbitrariness, arrogance, dictatorialness, imperiousness, opinionatedness, peremptoriness, positiveness, presumption

dogsbody drudge, general factotum, maid *or* man of all work, menial, skivvy (*chiefly Brit.*), slave

do in 1. blow away (*slang, chiefly U.S.*), butcher, dispatch, eliminate (*slang*), execute, kill, liquidate, murder, slaughter, slay, take out (*slang*) 2. exhaust, fag (*informal*), fatigue, knacker (*slang*), shatter (*informal*), tire, wear out, weary

doing achievement, act, action, carrying out *or* through, deed, execution, exploit, handiwork, implementation, performance

doings actions, affairs, concerns, dealings, deeds, events, exploits, goings-on (*informal*), handiwork, happenings, proceedings, transactions

doldrums apathy, blues, boredom, depression, dullness, dumps (*informal*), ennui, gloom, inertia, lassitude, listlessness, malaise, stagnation, tedium, the hump (*Brit. informal*), torpor

dole *noun* 1. allowance, alms, benefit, donation, gift, grant, gratuity, modicum, parcel, pittance, portion, quota, share 2. allocation, allotment, apportionment, dispensation, distribution, division *~verb* 3. *usually with* **out** administer, allocate, allot, apportion, assign, deal, dispense, distribute, divide, give, hand out, mete, share

doleful cheerless, depressing, dismal, distressing, dolorous, down in the mouth, dreary, forlorn, funereal, gloomy, low, lugubrious, melancholy, mournful, painful, pitiful, rueful, sad, sombre, sorrowful, woebegone, woeful, wretched

dollop gob, helping, lump, portion, scoop, serving

doll up deck out, dress up (like a dog's dinner), get ready, gussy up (*slang*), preen, primp, prink, tart up (*slang*), titivate, trick out

dolorous anguished, dismal, distressing, doleful, grievous, harrowing, heart-rending, melancholy, miserable, mournful, painful, rueful, sad, sorrowful, woebegone, woeful, wretched

dolour anguish, distress, grief, heartache, heartbreak, heaviness of heart, misery, ruth (*archaic*), sadness, sorrow, suffering

dolt ass, berk (*Brit. slang*), blockhead, booby, charlie (*Brit. informal*), chump (*informal*), clot (*Brit. informal*), coot, dickwit (*slang*), dimwit (*informal*), dipstick (*Brit. slang*), dope (*informal*), dork (*slang*), dullard, dunce, dweeb (*U.S. slang*), fathead (*informal*), fool, fuckwit (*taboo slang*), geek (*slang*), gobshite (*Irish taboo slang*), gonzo (*slang*), idiot, ignoramus, jerk (*slang, chiefly U.S. & Canad.*), lamebrain (*informal*), nerd *or* nurd (*slang*), nitwit (*informal*), numpty (*Scot. informal*), numskull *or* numbskull, oaf, plank (*Brit. slang*), plonker (*slang*), prat (*slang*), prick (*slang*), schmuck (*U.S. slang*), simpleton, thickhead, twit (*informal, chiefly Brit.*), wally (*slang*)

doltish asinine, boneheaded (*slang*), brainless, clottish (*Brit. informal*), dense, dim-witted (*informal*), dopey (*informal*), dumb (*informal*), foolish, goofy (*informal*), halfwitted, idiotic, inane, mindless, silly, stupid

domain 1. demesne, dominion, empire, estate, kingdom, lands, policies (*Scot.*), province, realm, region, territory 2. area, authority, bailiwick, concern, department, discipline, field, jurisdiction, orbit, power, realm, scope, speciality, sphere, sway

domestic *adjective* 1. domiciliary, family, home, household, private 2. domesticated, home-loving, homely, housewifely, stay-at-home 3. domesticated, house, house-trained, pet, tame, trained 4. indigenous, internal, native, not foreign *~noun* 5. char (*informal*), charwoman, daily, daily help, help, maid, servant, woman (*informal*)

domesticate 1. break, gentle, house-train, tame, train 2. acclimatize, accustom, familiarize, habituate, naturalize

domesticated 1. *of plants or animals* broken (in), naturalized, tame, tamed 2. *of people* domestic, home-loving, homely, house-trained (*jocular*), housewifely
Antonyms feral, ferocious, savage, unbroken, undomesticated, untamed, wild

domesticity domestication, home life, home-lovingness, homemaking, housekeeping, housewifery

domicile abode, dwelling, habitation, home, house, legal residence, mansion, pad (*slang*), residence, residency, settlement

dominance ascendancy, authority, command, control, domination, government, mastery, paramountcy, power, rule, supremacy, sway

dominant **1.** ascendant, assertive, authoritative, commanding, controlling, governing, leading, presiding, ruling, superior, supreme **2.** chief, influential, main, outstanding, paramount, predominant, pre-eminent, prevailing, prevalent, primary, principal, prominent
Antonyms ancillary, auxiliary, inferior, junior, lesser, lower, minor, secondary, subservient, subsidiary

dominate **1.** control, direct, domineer, govern, have the upper hand over, have the whip hand over, keep under one's thumb, lead, lead by the nose (*informal*), master, monopolize, overbear, rule, rule the roost, tyrannize **2.** bestride, loom over, overlook, stand head and shoulders above, stand over, survey, tower above **3.** detract from, eclipse, outshine, overrule, overshadow, predominate, prevail over

domination **1.** ascendancy, authority, command, control, influence, mastery, power, rule, superiority, supremacy, sway **2.** despotism, dictatorship, oppression, repression, subjection, subordination, suppression, tyranny

domineer bluster, boss around *or* about (*informal*), browbeat, bully, hector, intimidate, lord (it) over, menace, overbear, ride roughshod over, swagger, threaten, tyrannize

domineering arrogant, authoritarian, autocratic, bossy (*informal*), coercive, despotic, dictatorial, high-handed, imperious, iron-handed, magisterial, masterful, oppressive, overbearing, tyrannical
Antonyms meek, obsequious, servile, shy, submissive, subservient

dominion **1.** ascendancy, authority, command, control, domination, government, jurisdiction, mastery, power, rule, sovereignty, supremacy, sway **2.** country, domain, empire, kingdom, patch, province, realm, region, territory, turf (*U.S. slang*)

don clothe oneself in, dress in, get into, pull on, put on, slip on *or* into

donate bequeath, bestow, chip in (*informal*), contribute, gift, give, hand out, make a gift of, present, subscribe

donation alms, benefaction, boon, contribution, gift, grant, gratuity, hand-out, largess *or* largesse, offering, present, stipend, subscription

done *adjective* **1.** accomplished, completed, concluded, consummated, ended, executed, finished, in the can (*informal*), over, perfected, realized, terminated, through **2.** cooked, cooked enough, cooked sufficiently, cooked to a turn, ready **3.** depleted, exhausted, finished, spent, used up **4.** acceptable, conventional, *de rigueur*, proper **5.** *informal* cheated, conned (*informal*), duped, taken for a ride (*informal*), tricked *~interjection* **6.** agreed, it's a bargain, O.K. *or* okay (*informal*), settled, you're on (*informal*) **7.** **done for** *informal* beaten, broken, dashed, defeated, destroyed, doomed, finished, foiled, lost, ruined, undone, wrecked **8.** **done in** *or* **up** *informal* all in (*slang*), bushed (*informal*), clapped out (*Austral. & N.Z. informal*), dead (*informal*), dead beat (*informal*), dog-tired (*informal*), exhausted, fagged out (*informal*), knackered (*slang*), on one's last legs, ready to drop, tired out, worn out, worn to a frazzle (*informal*), zonked (*slang*) **9.** **have done with** be through with, desist, end relations with, finish with, give up, throw over, wash one's hands of

Don Juan Casanova, gallant, ladies' man, lady-killer (*informal*), libertine, Lothario, philanderer, poodle-faker (*slang*), Prince Charming, rake, Romeo, seducer, wolf (*informal*), womanizer

donnish bookish, erudite, formalistic, pedagogic, pedantic, precise, scholarly, scholastic

donor almsgiver, benefactor, contributor, donator, giver, grantor (*Law*), philanthropist
Antonyms assignee, beneficiary, inheritor, legatee, payee, receiver, recipient

doom *noun* **1.** catastrophe, death, destiny, destruction, downfall, fate, fortune, lot, portion, ruin **2.** condemnation, decision, decree, judgment, sentence, verdict **3.** Armageddon, Doomsday, end of the world, Judgment Day, the Last Day, the Last Judgment, the last trump *~verb* **4.** condemn, consign, damn, decree, destine, foreordain, judge, predestine, preordain, sentence, sound the death knell, threaten

doomed bedevilled, bewitched, condemned, cursed, fated, hopeless, ill-fated, ill-omened, luckless, star-crossed

doomsday

> *This is the way the world ends*
> *Not with a bang but a whimper*
> T.S. Eliot *The Hollow Men*

door **1.** doorway, egress, entrance, entry, exit, ingress, opening **2.** **lay at the door of** blame, censure, charge, hold responsible, impute to **3.** **out of doors** alfresco, in the air, out, outdoors, outside **4.** **show someone the door** ask to leave, boot out (*informal*), bounce (*slang*), eject, oust, show out

do-or-die death-or-glory, desperate, going for broke, hazardous, kill-or-cure, risky, win-or-bust

do out of balk, bilk, cheat, con (*informal*), cozen, deprive, diddle (*informal*), swindle, trick

dope *noun* **1.** drugs, narcotic, opiate **2.** berk (*Brit. slang*), blockhead, charlie (*Brit. informal*), coot, dickhead (*slang*), dickwit (*slang*), dimwit (*informal*), dipstick (*Brit. slang*), divvy (*Brit. slang*), dolt, dork (*slang*), dunce, dweeb (*U.S. slang*), fathead (*informal*), fool, fuckwit (*taboo slang*), geek (*slang*), gobshite (*Irish taboo slang*), gonzo (*slang*), idiot, jerk (*slang, chiefly U.S. & Canad.*), lamebrain (*informal*), nerd *or* nurd (*slang*), nitwit (*informal*), numpty (*Scot. informal*), numskull *or* numbskull, oaf, pillock (*Brit. slang*), plank (*Brit. slang*), plonker (*slang*), prat (*slang*), prick (*slang*), schmuck (*U.S. slang*), simpleton, twit (*informal, chiefly Brit.*), wally (*slang*) **3.** details, facts, gen (*Brit. informal*), info (*informal*), information, inside information, lowdown (*informal*), news, tip *~verb* **4.** anaesthetize, doctor, drug, inject, knock out, narcotize, sedate, stupefy

dopey, dopy **1.** asinine, dense, dozy (*Brit. informal*), dumb (*informal*), foolish, goofy (*informal*), idiotic, senseless, silly, simple, slow, stupid, thick **2.** dazed, drowsy, drugged, groggy (*informal*), muzzy, stupefied, woozy (*informal*)

dormant asleep, comatose, fallow, hibernating, inactive, inert, inoperative, latent, quiescent, sleeping, sluggish, slumbering, suspended, torpid
Antonyms active, alert, alive and kicking, aroused, awake, awakened, conscious, wakeful, wide-awake

dose dosage, draught, drench, measure, portion, potion, prescription, quantity

dot *noun* **1.** atom, circle, dab, fleck, full stop, iota, jot, mark, mite, mote, point, speck, speckle, spot **2. on the dot** exactly, on the button (*informal*), on time, precisely, promptly, punctually, to the minute *~verb* **3.** dab, dabble, fleck, speckle, spot, sprinkle, stipple, stud

dotage **1.** decrepitude, eld (*archaic*), feebleness, imbecility, old age, second childhood, senility, weakness **2.** doting, foolish fondness, infatuation

dote on *or* **upon** admire, adore, hold dear, idolize, lavish affection on, prize, treasure

doting adoring, devoted, fond, foolish, indulgent, lovesick

dotty **1.** batty (*slang*), crackpot (*informal*), crazy, doolally (*slang*), eccentric, feeble-minded, loopy (*informal*), oddball (*informal*), off one's trolley (*slang*), off-the-wall (*slang*), outré, out to lunch (*informal*), peculiar, potty (*Brit. informal*), touched, up the pole (*informal*), wacko *or* whacko (*slang*) **2.** *with* **about** crazy (*informal*), daft (*informal*), fond of, keen on

double *adjective* **1.** binate (*Botany*), coupled, doubled, dual, duplicate, in pairs, paired, twice, twin, twofold **2.** deceitful, dishonest, false, hypocritical, insincere, Janus-faced, knavish (*archaic*), perfidious, treacherous, two-faced, vacillating *~verb* **3.** duplicate, enlarge, fold, grow, increase, magnify, multiply, plait, repeat *~noun* **4.** clone, copy, counterpart, dead ringer (*slang*), Doppelgänger, duplicate, fellow, impersonator, lookalike, mate, replica, ringer (*slang*), spitting image (*informal*), twin **5. at** *or* **on the double** at full speed, briskly, immediately, in double-quick time, pdq (*slang*), posthaste, quickly, without delay

double back backtrack, circle, dodge, loop, retrace one's steps, return, reverse

double-cross betray, cheat, cozen, defraud, hoodwink, mislead, sell down the river (*informal*), swindle, trick, two-time (*informal*)

double-dealer betrayer, cheat, con man (*informal*), cozener, deceiver, dissembler, double-crosser (*informal*), fraud, fraudster, grifter (*slang, chiefly U.S. & Canad.*), hypocrite, rogue, snake in the grass (*informal*), swindler, traitor, two-timer (*informal*)

double-dealing **1.** *noun* bad faith, betrayal, cheating, deceit, deception, dishonesty, duplicity, foul play, hypocrisy, mendacity, perfidy, treachery, trickery, two-timing (*informal*) **2.** *adjective* cheating, crooked (*informal*), deceitful, dishonest, duplicitous, fraudulent, hypocritical, lying, perfidious, sneaky, swindling, treacherous, tricky, two-faced, two-timing (*informal*), underhanded, untrustworthy, wily

double entendre ambiguity, double meaning, innuendo, play on words, pun

doublet **1.** jacket, jerkin, vest, waistcoat **2.** couple, pair, set, two

doubly again, as much again, even more, in double measure, once more, over again, twice, twofold

doubt *verb* **1.** discredit, distrust, fear, lack confidence in, misgive, mistrust, query, question, suspect *~noun* **2.** apprehension, disquiet, distrust, fear, incredulity, lack of faith, misgiving, mistrust, qualm, scepticism, suspicion *~verb* **3.** be dubious, be uncertain, demur, fluctuate, hesitate, scruple, vacillate, waver *~noun* **4.** dubiety, hesitancy, hesitation, indecision, irresolution, lack of conviction, suspense, uncertainty, vacillation **5.** ambiguity, can of worms (*informal*), confusion, difficulty, dilemma, perplexity, problem, quandary **6. no doubt** admittedly, assuredly, certainly, doubtless, doubtlessly, probably, surely
Antonyms *verb* accept, believe, buy (*slang*), have faith in, swallow (*informal*), take on board, trust *~noun* belief, certainty, confidence, conviction, trust

There lives more faith in honest doubt,

Believe me, than in half the creeds
Alfred Tennyson *In Memoriam A.H.H.*

I show you doubt, to prove that faith exists
Robert Browning *Balaustion's Adventure*

If a man will begin with certainties, he shall end in doubts; but if he will be content to begin with doubts, he shall end in certainties
Francis Bacon *The Advancement of Learning*

Ten thousand difficulties do not make one doubt
Cardinal Newman *Apologia pro Vita Sua*

doubter agnostic, disbeliever, doubting Thomas, questioner, sceptic, unbeliever

doubtful 1. ambiguous, debatable, dodgy (*Brit., Austral., & N.Z. informal*), dubious, equivocal, hazardous, iffy (*informal*), inconclusive, indefinite, indeterminate, obscure, precarious, problematic(al), questionable, unclear, unconfirmed, unsettled, vague 2. distrustful, hesitating, in two minds (*informal*), irresolute, leery (*slang*), perplexed, sceptical, suspicious, tentative, uncertain, unconvinced, undecided, unresolved, unsettled, unsure, vacillating, wavering 3. disreputable, dodgy (*Brit., Austral., & N.Z. informal*), dubious, questionable, shady (*informal*), suspect, suspicious
Antonyms certain, decided, definite, indubitable, positive, resolute

doubtless 1. assuredly, certainly, clearly, indisputably, of course, precisely, surely, truly, undoubtedly, unquestionably, without doubt 2. apparently, most likely, ostensibly, presumably, probably, seemingly, supposedly

doughty bold, brave, courageous, daring, dauntless, fearless, gallant, gritty, hardy, heroic, intrepid, redoubtable, resolute, stouthearted, valiant, valorous

dour 1. dismal, dreary, forbidding, gloomy, grim, morose, sour, sullen, unfriendly 2. austere, hard, inflexible, obstinate, rigid, rigorous, severe, strict, uncompromising, unyielding
Antonyms carefree, cheerful, cheery, chirpy (*informal*), genial, good-humoured, happy, jovial, pleasant, sunny

douse, dowse 1. drench, duck, dunk, immerse, plunge into water, saturate, soak, souse, steep, submerge 2. blow out, extinguish, put out, smother, snuff (out)

dovetail *verb* 1. fit, fit together, interlock, join, link, mortise, tenon, unite 2. accord, agree, coincide, conform, correspond, harmonize, match, tally

dowdy dingy, drab, frowzy, frumpish, frumpy, ill-dressed, old-fashioned, scrubby (*Brit. informal*), shabby, slovenly, tacky (*U.S. informal*), unfashionable
Antonyms chic, dressy, fashionable, neat, smart, spruce, trim, well-dressed

dower 1. dowry, inheritance, legacy, portion, provision, share 2. endowment, faculty, gift, talent

do without abstain from, dispense with, forgo, get along without, give up, kick (*informal*), manage without

down *adjective* 1. blue, dejected, depressed, disheartened, dismal, downcast, down in the dumps (*informal*), low, miserable, sad, sick as a parrot (*informal*), unhappy ~*verb* 2. bring down, deck (*slang*), fell, floor, knock down, overthrow, prostrate, subdue, tackle, throw, trip 3. *informal* drain, drink (down), gulp, put away, swallow, toss off ~*noun* 4. decline, descent, drop, dropping, fall, falling, reverse 5. **have a down on** *informal* be antagonistic *or* hostile to, be anti (*informal*), bear a grudge towards, be contra (*informal*), be prejudiced against, be set against, feel ill will towards, have it in for (*slang*) 6. **down with** away with, get rid of, kick out (*informal*), oust, push out

down and out 1. *adjective* derelict, destitute, dirt-poor (*informal*), flat broke (*informal*), impoverished, on one's uppers (*informal*), penniless, ruined, short, without two pennies to rub together (*informal*) 2. **down-and-out** *noun* bag lady (*chiefly U.S.*), beggar, bum (*informal*), derelict, dosser (*Brit. slang*), loser, outcast, pauper, tramp, vagabond, vagrant

downbeat depressed, discouraging, disheartening, flat, gloomy, low-key, muted, negative, pessimistic, sober, sombre, subdued, unfavourable
Antonyms buoyant, cheerful, encouraging, favourable, heartening, optimistic, positive, upbeat

downcast cheerless, choked, crestfallen, daunted, dejected, depressed, despondent, disappointed, disconsolate, discouraged, disheartened, dismal, dismayed, dispirited, down in the dumps (*informal*), miserable, sad, sick as a parrot (*informal*), unhappy
Antonyms cheerful, cheery, chirpy (*informal*), contented, elated, genial, happy, joyful, light-hearted, optimistic

downfall 1. breakdown, collapse, comedown, comeuppance (*slang*), debacle, descent, destruction, disgrace, fall, overthrow, ruin, undoing 2. cloudburst, deluge, downpour, rainstorm

downgrade 1. degrade, demote, humble, lower *or* reduce in rank, take down a peg (*informal*) 2. decry, denigrate, detract from, disparage, run down
Antonyms advance, ameliorate, better, elevate, enhance, improve, promote, raise, upgrade

downhearted blue, chapfallen, crestfallen, dejected, depressed, despondent, discouraged, disheartened, dismayed, dispirited, downcast, low-spirited, sad, sick as a parrot (*informal*), sorrowful, unhappy

down-market bush-league (*Austral. & N.Z. informal*), cheap, cheap and nasty (*informal*), inferior, lowbrow, low-grade, low-quality, second-rate, shoddy, tacky (*informal*), tawdry, two-bit (*U.S. & Canad. slang*)
Antonyms elite, exclusive, first-rate, highbrow, high-class, high-quality, posh (*informal, chiefly Brit.*), superior, top-quality, up-market

downpour cloudburst, deluge, flood, inundation, rainstorm, torrential rain

downright **1.** absolute, arrant, blatant, categorical, clear, complete, deep-dyed (*usually derogatory*), explicit, out-and-out, outright, plain, positive, simple, thoroughgoing, total, undisguised, unequivocal, unqualified, utter **2.** blunt, candid, forthright, frank, honest, open, outspoken, plain, sincere, straightforward, straight-from-the-shoulder, upfront (*informal*)

downside bad *or* weak point, disadvantage, drawback, flipside, minus (*informal*), other side of the coin (*informal*), problem, snag, trouble
Antonyms advantage, benefit, good *or* strong point, plus (*informal*)

down-to-earth common-sense, hard-headed, matter-of-fact, mundane, no-nonsense, plain-spoken, practical, realistic, sane, sensible, unsentimental

downtrodden abused, afflicted, distressed, exploited, helpless, oppressed, subjugated, subservient, tyrannized

downward *adjective* declining, descending, earthward, heading down, sliding, slipping

downy feathery, fleecy, fluffy, plumate (*Zoology, Botany*), silky, soft, velvety, woolly

dowse *see* DOUSE

doze **1.** *verb* catnap, drop off (*informal*), drowse, kip (*Brit. slang*), nap, nod, nod off (*informal*), sleep, sleep lightly, slumber, snooze (*informal*), zizz (*Brit. informal*) **2.** *noun* catnap, forty winks (*informal*), kip (*Brit. slang*), little sleep, nap, shuteye (*slang*), siesta, snooze (*informal*), zizz (*Brit. informal*)

dozy **1.** dozing, drowsy, half asleep, nodding, sleepy **2.** *informal* daft (*informal*), goofy (*informal*), not all there, senseless, silly, simple, slow, slow-witted, stupid, witless

drab cheerless, colourless, dingy, dismal, dreary, dull, flat, gloomy, grey, lacklustre, shabby, sombre, uninspired, vapid
Antonyms bright, cheerful, colourful, jazzy (*informal*), vibrant, vivid

drabness banality, cheerlessness, colourlessness, dinginess, dreariness, dullness, flatness, gloom, gloominess, greyness, insipidity, monotony, sobriety, tediousness, vapidity
Antonyms brightness, brilliance, character, cheerfulness, colour, colourfulness, gaiety, interest, liveliness, vividness

Draconian austere, drastic, hard, harsh, pitiless, punitive, severe, stern, stringent

draft *verb* **1.** compose, delineate, design, draw, draw up, formulate, outline, plan, sketch ~*noun* **2.** abstract, delineation, outline, plan, preliminary form, rough, sketch, version **3.** bill (*of exchange*), cheque, order, postal order

drag *verb* **1.** draw, hale, haul, lug, pull, tow, trail, tug, yank **2.** crawl, creep, go slowly, inch, limp along, shamble, shuffle **3.** dawdle, draggle, lag behind, linger, loiter, straggle, trail behind **4.** *with* **on** *or* **out** draw out, extend, keep going, lengthen, persist, prolong, protract, spin out, stretch out **5.** **drag one's feet** *informal* block, hold back, obstruct, procrastinate, stall ~*noun* **6.** *slang* annoyance, bore, bother, nuisance, pain (*informal*), pain in the arse (*taboo informal*), pest

dragging boring, dull, going slowly, humdrum, mind-numbing, monotonous, tedious, tiresome, wearisome

draggle **1.** befoul, bemire, besmirch, drabble, trail **2.** dally, dawdle, dilly-dally (*informal*), lag, straggle, trail behind

dragoon *verb* browbeat, bully, coerce, compel, constrain, drive, force, impel, intimidate, railroad (*informal*), strong-arm (*informal*)

drain *verb* **1.** bleed, draw off, dry, empty, evacuate, milk, pump off *or* out, remove, tap, withdraw **2.** consume, deplete, dissipate, empty, exhaust, sap, strain, tax, use up, weary **3.** discharge, effuse, exude, flow out, leak, ooze, seep, trickle, well out **4.** drink up, finish, gulp down, quaff, swallow ~*noun* **5.** channel, conduit, culvert, ditch, duct, outlet, pipe, sewer, sink, trench, watercourse **6.** depletion, drag, exhaustion, expenditure, reduction, sap, strain, withdrawal **7.** **down the drain** gone, gone for good, lost, ruined, wasted

drainage bilge (water), seepage, sewage, sewerage, waste

dram drop, glass, measure, shot (*informal*), slug, snifter (*informal*), snort (*slang*), tot

drama **1.** dramatization, play, show, stage play, stage show, theatrical piece **2.** acting, dramatic art, dramaturgy, stagecraft, theatre, Thespian art **3.** crisis, dramatics, excitement, histrionics, scene, spectacle, theatrics, turmoil

Drama types

comedy
comedy of manners
commedia dell'arte
costume piece *or* costume drama
farce
Grand Guignol
Jacobean
kabuki
Kathakali

kitchen sink
melodrama
morality play
mystery play
No *or* Noh
passion play
Restoration Comedy
revenge tragedy
shadow play
situation comedy *or* sitcom
sketch
soap opera
street theatre
theatre of cruelty
theatre of the absurd
tragedy
tragicomedy

Drama/theatre terms

act
backstage
catastrophe
chorus
circle
Comédie Française
coup de théâtre
crush bar
cue
curtain
curtain call
curtain-raiser
curtain speech
downstage
dramatis personae
entr'acte
entrance
exit
first night
first-night nerves
flat
flies
fluff
front of house
gallery
gods
greasepaint
greenroom
ham
house
juvenile
leading lady
leading man
lines
monologue
noises off
off-Broadway
off-off-Broadway
offstage
opera house
orchestra *or* orchestra pit
overact
prompt
prompter
prop
proscenium arch
resting
role
scene
scene dock *or* bay
scenery
script
soliloquy
soubrette
speech
stage
stage direction
stage door
stage fright
stagehand
stage left
stage manager
stage right
stage-struck
stage whisper
stalls
theatre-in-the-round
Thespian
understudy
unities
upstage
wings

Drama is life with the dull bits cut out
Alfred Hitchcock

pantomime: a play in which the story is told without violence to the language. The least disagreeable form of dramatic action
Ambrose Bierce *The Devil's Dictionary*

for what's a play without a woman in it?
Thomas Kyd *The Spanish Tragedy*

dramatic 1. dramaturgic, dramaturgical, theatrical, Thespian **2.** breathtaking, climactic, electrifying, emotional, exciting, melodramatic, sensational, shock-horror (*facetious*), startling, sudden, suspenseful, tense, thrilling **3.** affecting, effective, expressive, impressive, moving, powerful, striking, vivid
Antonyms ordinary, run-of-the-mill, undramatic, unexceptional, unmemorable

dramatist dramaturge, playwright, screenwriter, scriptwriter
Dramatists
see WRITER

dramatize act, exaggerate, lay it on (thick) (*slang*), make a performance of, overdo, overstate, play-act, play to the gallery

drape 1. adorn, array, cloak, cover, fold, swathe, wrap **2.** dangle, droop, drop, hang, lean over, let fall, suspend

drastic desperate, dire, extreme, forceful, harsh, radical, severe, strong

draught 1. *of air* current, flow, influx, movement, puff **2.** dragging, drawing, haulage, pulling, traction **3.** cup, dose, drench, drink, potion, quantity

draw *verb* **1.** drag, haul, pull, tow, tug **2.** delineate, depict, design, map out, mark out, outline, paint, portray, sketch, trace **3.** deduce, derive, get, infer, make, take **4.** allure, attract, bring forth, call forth, elicit, engage, entice, evoke, induce, influence, invite, persuade **5.** extort, extract, pull out, take out **6.** attenuate, elongate, extend, lengthen, stretch **7.** breathe in, drain, inhale, inspire, puff, pull, respire, suck **8.** compose, draft, formulate, frame, prepare, write **9.** choose, pick, select, single out, take *~noun* **10.** *informal* attraction, enticement, lure, pull (*informal*) **11.** dead heat, deadlock, impasse, stalemate, tie

drawback defect, deficiency, detriment, difficulty, disadvantage, downside, fault, flaw, fly in the ointment (*informal*), handicap, hazard, hindrance, hitch, impediment, imperfection, nuisance, obstacle, snag, stumbling block, trouble
Antonyms advantage, asset, benefit, gain, help, service, use

draw back back off, recoil, retract, retreat, shrink, start back, withdraw

drawing cartoon, delineation, depiction, illustration, outline, picture, portrayal, representation, sketch, study

drawl *verb, of speech sounds* drag out, draw out, extend, lengthen, prolong, protract

drawling dragging, drawly, droning, dull, twanging, twangy

drawn fatigued, fraught, haggard, harassed, harrowed, pinched, sapped, strained, stressed, taut, tense, tired, worn

draw on employ, exploit, extract, fall back on, have recourse to, make use of, rely on, take from, use

draw out drag out, extend, lengthen, make longer, prolong, prolongate, protract, spin out, stretch, string out
Antonyms curtail, cut, cut short, dock, pare down, reduce, shorten, trim, truncate

draw up **1.** bring to a stop, halt, pull up, run in, stop, stop short **2.** compose, draft, formulate, frame, prepare, write out

dread **1.** *verb* anticipate with horror, cringe at, fear, have cold feet (*informal*), quail, shrink from, shudder, tremble **2.** *noun* affright, alarm, apprehension, aversion, awe, dismay, fear, fright, funk (*informal*), heebie-jeebies (*slang*), horror, terror, trepidation **3.** *adjective* alarming, awe-inspiring, awful, dire, dreaded, dreadful, frightening, frightful, horrible, terrible, terrifying

dreadful abysmal, alarming, appalling, awful, dire, distressing, fearful, formidable, frightful, from hell (*informal*), ghastly, godawful (*slang*), grievous, hellacious (*U.S. slang*), hideous, horrendous, horrible, monstrous, shocking, terrible, tragic, tremendous

dreadfully **1.** abysmally, alarmingly, appallingly, awfully, badly, disgracefully, disreputably, frightfully, horrendously, horribly, inadequately, monstrously, reprehensibly, shockingly, terribly, unforgivably, wickedly, woefully, wretchedly **2.** awfully (*informal*), badly, deeply, desperately, exceedingly, exceptionally, excessively, extremely, greatly, immensely, terribly, tremendously, very, very much

dream *noun* **1.** daydream, delusion, fantasy, hallucination, illusion, imagination, pipe dream, reverie, speculation, trance, vagary, vision **2.** ambition, aspiration, design, desire, goal, Holy Grail (*informal*), hope, notion, thirst, wish **3.** beauty, delight, gem, joy, marvel, pleasure, treasure *~verb* **4.** build castles in the air *or* in Spain, conjure up, daydream, envisage, fancy, fantasize, hallucinate, have dreams, imagine, stargaze, think, visualize
Related adjective: oneiric

Your old men shall dream dreams, your young men shall see visions
Bible: Joel

We are such stuff
As dreams are made on
William Shakespeare *The Tempest*

I talk of dreams;
Which are the children of an idle brain,
Begot of nothing but vain fantasy
William Shakespeare *Romeo and Juliet*

Judge of your natural character by what you do in your dreams
Ralph Waldo Emerson *Journals*

dreamer daydreamer, Don Quixote, fantasist, fantasizer, fantast, idealist, romancer, theorizer, utopian, visionary, Walter Mitty

dreamland cloud-cuckoo-land, cloudland, dream world, fairyland, fantasy, illusion, land of dreams, land of make-believe, land of Nod, never-never land (*informal*), sleep

dreamlike chimerical, hallucinatory, illusory, phantasmagoric, phantasmagorical, surreal, trancelike, unreal, unsubstantial, visionary

dream up concoct, contrive, cook up (*informal*), create, devise, hatch, imagine, invent, spin, think up

dreamy **1.** airy-fairy, dreamlike, fanciful, imaginary, impractical, quixotic, speculative, surreal, vague, visionary **2.** chimerical, dreamlike, fantastic, intangible, misty, phantasmagoric, phantasmagorical, shadowy, unreal **3.** absent, abstracted, daydreaming, faraway, in a reverie, musing, pensive, preoccupied, vague, with one's head in the clouds **4.** calming, gentle, lulling, relaxing, romantic, soothing
Antonyms common-sense, down-to-earth, feet-on-the-ground, practical, pragmatic, realistic, unromantic

dreary **1.** bleak, cheerless, comfortless, depressing, dismal, doleful, downcast, drear, forlorn, funereal, gloomy, glum, joyless, lonely, lonesome, melancholy, mournful, sad, solitary, sombre, sorrowful, wretched **2.** as dry as dust, boring, colourless, drab, dull, ho-hum (*informal*), humdrum, lifeless, mind-numbing, monotonous, routine, tedious, tiresome, uneventful, uninteresting, wearisome
Antonyms bright, cheerful, happy, interesting, joyful

dredge up dig up, discover, drag up, draw up, fish up, raise, rake up, uncover, unearth

dreg bit, drop, mite, particle, piece, remnant, scrap

dregs **1.** deposit, draff, dross, grounds, lees, residue, residuum, scourings, scum, sediment, trash, waste **2.** *slang canaille*, down-and-outs, good-for-nothings, outcasts, rabble, ragtag and bobtail, riffraff, scum

drench **1.** *verb* drown, duck, flood, imbrue, inundate, saturate, soak, souse, steep, wet **2.** *noun, Veterinary* dose, physic, purge

dress *noun* **1.** costume, ensemble, frock, garment, get-up (*informal*), gown, outfit, rigout (*informal*), robe, suit **2.** apparel, attire, clothes, clothing, costume, garb, garments, gear (*informal*), guise, habiliment, raiment (*archaic or poetic*), schmutter (*slang*), threads (*slang*), togs, vestment *~verb* **3.** attire, change, clothe, don, garb, put on, robe, slip on *or* into **4.** adorn, apparel (*archaic*), array, bedeck, deck, decorate, drape, embellish, festoon, furbish, ornament, rig, trim **5.** adjust, align, arrange, comb (out), dispose, do (up), fit, get ready, groom, prepare, set, straighten **6.**

bandage, bind up, plaster, treat
Antonyms (*sense 3*) disrobe, divest oneself of, peel off (*slang*), shed, strip, take off one's clothes

Gowns and dresses
see CLOTHES

> *Singularity in dress is ridiculous; in fact it is generally looked upon as a proof that the mind is somewhat deranged*
> St. John Baptist de la Salle *The Rules of Christian Manners and Civility*

> *Eat to please thyself, but dress to please others*
> Benjamin Franklin *Poor Richard's Almanac*

dress down bawl out (*informal*), berate, carpet (*informal*), castigate, chew out (*U.S. & Canad. informal*), give a rocket (*Brit. & N.Z. informal*), haul over the coals, rap over the knuckles, read the riot act, rebuke, reprimand, reprove, scold, slap on the wrist, tear into (*informal*), tear (someone) off a strip (*Brit. informal*), tell off (*informal*), upbraid

dressmaker couturier, modiste, seamstress, sewing woman, tailor

dress up **1.** doll up (*slang*), dress for dinner, dress formally, put on one's best bib and tucker (*informal*), put on one's glad rags (*informal*) **2.** disguise, play-act, put on fancy dress, wear a costume **3.** beautify, do oneself up, embellish, gild, improve, titivate, trick out *or* up

> *All dressed up with nowhere to go*
> William Allen White

dressy classy (*slang*), elaborate, elegant, formal, ornate, ritzy (*slang*), smart, stylish, swish (*informal, chiefly Brit.*)

dribble **1.** drip, drop, fall in drops, leak, ooze, run, seep, trickle **2.** drip saliva, drivel, drool, slaver, slobber

driblet bit, dash, drop, droplet, fragment, gobbet, morsel, piece, scrap, speck, sprinkling

drift *verb* **1.** be carried along, coast, float, go (aimlessly), meander, stray, waft, wander **2.** accumulate, amass, bank up, drive, gather, pile up *~noun* **3.** accumulation, bank, heap, mass, mound, pile **4.** course, current, direction, flow, impulse, movement, rush, sweep, trend **5.** *figurative* aim, design, direction, gist, implication, import, intention, meaning, object, purport, scope, significance, tendency, tenor, thrust

drifter bag lady (*chiefly U.S.*), beachcomber, bum (*informal*), hobo (*U.S.*), itinerant, rolling stone, tramp, vagabond, vagrant, wanderer

drill *verb* **1.** coach, discipline, exercise, instruct, practise, rehearse, teach, train *~noun* **2.** discipline, exercise, instruction, practice, preparation, repetition, training *~verb* **3.** bore, penetrate, perforate, pierce, puncture, sink in *~noun* **4.** bit, borer, boring-tool, gimlet, rotary tool

drink *verb* **1.** absorb, drain, gulp, guzzle, imbibe, partake of, quaff, sip, suck, sup, swallow, swig (*informal*), swill, toss off, wash down, wet one's whistle (*informal*) **2.** bend the elbow (*informal*), bevvy (*dialect*), booze (*informal*), carouse, go on a binge *or* bender (*informal*), hit the bottle (*informal*), indulge, pub-crawl (*informal, chiefly Brit.*), revel, tipple, tope, wassail *~noun* **3.** beverage, liquid, potion, refreshment, thirst quencher **4.** alcohol, booze (*informal*), Dutch courage, hooch *or* hootch (*informal, chiefly U.S. & Canad.*), liquor, spirits, the bottle (*informal*) **5.** cup, draught, glass, gulp, noggin, sip, snifter (*informal*), swallow, swig (*informal*), taste, tipple **6.** **the drink** *informal* the briny (*informal*), the deep, the main, the ocean, the sea

Spirits
absinth *or* absinthe
aguardiente
applejack, applejack brandy *or* apple brandy
aquavit *or* akvavit
aqua vitae (*archaic*)
Armagnac
arrack *or* arak
Bacardi (*Trademark*)
brandy
bitters
Calvados
Cognac
dark rum
eau de vie
firewater
framboise
gin
grappa
Hollands
hooch
Kirsch *or* Kirschwasser
korn
marc
mescal
ouzo
palinka
poteen *or* poitín
raki *or* rakee
rum
schnapps *or* schnaps
slivovitz
sloe gin
taffia
tequila
triple sec
vodka
whisky *see* WHISKY
white rum

Liqueurs
advocaat
amaretto
Amendoa Amarga
anisette
Bailey's Irish Cream (*Trademark*)
Benedictine
chartreuse
cherry brandy
Cointreau (*Trademark*)
crème
crème de cacao
crème de menthe
Curaçao
Drambuie (*Trademark*)
Frangelico
Galliano (*Trademark*)
Glayva (*Trademark*)
Grand Marnier (*Trademark*)
Kahlua
kümmel
Malibu (*Trademark*)
maraschino
Midori
noyau
pastis
peach schnapps
Pernod (*Trademark*)
pousse-café
prunelle
ratafia *or* ratafee
sambucca
Southern Comfort (*Trademark*)
Tia Maria (*Trade~

mark)
Van der Hum
Veuve Jacquolot

Miscellaneous alcoholic drinks

apéritif
busera
Campari (*Trademark*)
chaser
cider, cyder *or (U.S. & Canad.)* hard cider
caudle
Cinzano (*Trademark*)
cocktail
cordial
dram
Dubonnet (*Trademark*)
elderberry wine
frappé
French vermouth
ginger wine
glogg
gluhwein
grog
hippocras
Irish coffee *or* Gaelic coffee
Italian vermouth
kvass, kvas *or* quass
liqueur
malt liquor
Martini (*Trademark*)
mead
mulled wine
negus
nor'wester
palm wine
posset
pousse-café
pulque
sake, saké, saki *or* rice wine
samshu
shooter
skokiaan
slammer
snakebite
soma
spruce beer
toddy
Tom and Jerry
Tom Collins
vermouth
waragi

Cocktails

Americano
Bellini
Black Russian
black velvet
Bloody Mary
Brandy Alexander
buck's fizz
bullshot
caudle
claret cup
cobbler
cold duck
collins
cooler
Cuba libre
cup
daiquiri
dry martini
eggnog *or* egg flip
Gibson
gimlet
gin sling
glogg
Harvey Wallbanger
highball
julep
kir
Long Island Tea
manhattan
margarita
martini
milk punch
mint julep
mojito
Moscow Mule
negroni
nog *or* nogg
oenomel
old-fashioned
orgasm
piña colada
pink gin
planter's punch
punch
rickey
Rusty Nail
sangaree
sangria
sazerac
screwdriver
sidecar
Singapore sling
sling
Slow Screw Against the Wall
snowball
spritzer
stinger *or* stengah
swizzle
syllabub *or* sillabub
whiskey sour
whisky mac
white lady
zombie

Soft drinks

alcohol-free *or* non-alcoholic beer
apple juice
barley water
bitter lemon
Bovril (*Trademark*)
buttermilk
cassis
Coca-Cola *or* Coke (*Trademark*)
cocoa
coffee *see* COFFEE
cola
cordial
cream soda
crush
dandelion and burdock
fruit juice
fruit tea
ginger ale
ginger beer
grapefruit juice
herb tea *or* herbal infusion
hot chocolate
ice-cream soda
iron brew
juice
kumiss, koumiss, koumis *or* koumyss
lassi
lemonade
lemon squash
lemon tea *or* Russian tea
limeade
lime cordial
lolly water (*Austral. & N.Z.*)
Lucozade (*Trademark*)
maté *or* mate
milk
milk shake
mineral water
nectar
orangeade
orange juice
orgeat
peppermint cordial
Perrier *or* Perrier water (*Trademark*)
prairie oyster
Ribena (*Trademark*)
root beer
sarsaparilla
Seltzer *or* Seltzer water
sherbet
smoothie
soapolallie
soda
soda water
spremuta
squash
sweet cider (*U.S. & Canad.*)
tea *see* TEA
tisane
Tizer (*Trademark*)
tomato juice
tonic
vichy water
Vimto (*Trademark*)
water

Beers

see BEER

Wines

see WINE

Let us eat and drink; for tomorrow we shall die
Bible: Isaiah

I drink when I have occasion for it, and sometimes when I have not
Miguel de Cervantes *Don Quixote*

Drink to me only with thine eyes
Ben Jonson *To Celia*

It's all right to drink like a fish - if you drink what a fish drinks
Mary Pettibone Poole *A Glass Eye at the Keyhole*

One reason I don't drink is that I want to know when I'm having a good time
Nancy Astor

I wasna fou, but just had plenty
Robert Burns *Death and Dr. Hornbook*

I have taken more out of alcohol than alcohol has taken out of me
Winston Churchill

Man wants little drink below,
But wants that little strong
Oliver Wendell Holmes *A Song of other Days*

Give strong drink unto him that is ready to perish, and wine unto those that be of heavy hearts
Bible: Proverbs

Let schoolmasters puzzle their brain,
With grammar, and nonsense, and learning,
Good liquor, I stoutly maintain,
Gives genius a better discerning
Oliver Goldsmith *She Stoops to Conquer*

Candy
Is dandy
But liquor
Is quicker
Ogden Nash *Reflections on Ice-breaking*

I arrived on the job in what I considered to be a perfect state of equilibrium, half man and half alcohol
Eddie Condon *We Called it Music*

Wine is the drink of the gods, milk the drink of babies, tea the drink of women, and water the drink of beasts
John Stuart Blackie

brandy: a cordial composed of one part thunder-and-lightning, one part remorse, two parts bloody murder, one part death-hell-and-the-grave and four parts clarified Satan
Ambrose Bierce *The Devil's Dictionary*

Claret is the liquor for boys; port, for men; but he who aspires to be a hero must drink brandy
Dr. Johnson

rum: generically, fiery liquors that produce madness in total abstainers
Ambrose Bierce *The Devil's Dictionary*

Cocktails have all the disagreeability without the utility of a disinfectant
Shane Leslie *The Observer*

The proper union of gin and vermouth is a great and sudden glory; it is one of the happiest marriages on earth, and one of the shortest lived
Bernard De Voto

drinkable drinking, fit to drink, potable, quaffable

drinker alcoholic, bibber, boozer (*informal*), dipsomaniac, drunk, drunkard, guzzler, inebriate, lush (*slang*), soak (*slang*), sot, sponge (*informal*), tippler, toper, wino (*informal*)

drink in absorb, assimilate, be all ears (*informal*), be fascinated by, be rapt, hang on (someone's) words, hang on the lips of, pay attention

drinking bout bacchanalia, bender (*informal*), bevvy (*dialect*), binge (*informal*), celebration, debauch, orgy, pub-crawl (*informal, chiefly Brit.*), spree, wassail

drink to pledge, pledge the health of, salute, toast

drip *verb* **1.** dribble, drizzle, drop, exude, filter, plop, splash, sprinkle, trickle *~noun* **2.** dribble, dripping, drop, leak, trickle **3.** *informal* milksop, mummy's boy (*informal*), namby-pamby, ninny, softy (*informal*), weakling, weed (*informal*), wet (*Brit. informal*)

drive *verb* **1.** herd, hurl, impel, propel, push, send, urge **2.** direct, go, guide, handle, manage, motor, operate, ride, steer, travel **3.** actuate, coerce, compel, constrain, dragoon, force, goad, harass, impel, motivate, oblige, overburden, overwork, press, prick, prod, prompt, railroad (*informal*), rush, spur **4.** dash, dig, hammer, plunge, ram, sink, stab, thrust *~noun* **5.** excursion, hurl (*Scot.*), jaunt, journey, outing, ride, run, spin (*informal*), trip, turn **6.** action, advance, appeal, campaign, crusade, effort, push (*informal*), surge **7.** ambition, effort, energy, enterprise, get-up-and-go (*informal*), initiative, motivation, pep, pressure, push (*informal*), vigour, zip (*informal*)

drive at aim, allude to, get at, have in mind, hint at, imply, indicate, insinuate, intend, intimate, mean, refer to, signify, suggest

drivel *verb* **1.** dribble, drool, slaver, slobber **2.** babble, blether, gab (*informal*), gas (*informal*), maunder, prate, ramble, waffle (*informal, chiefly Brit.*) *~noun* **3.** balderdash, balls (*taboo slang*), bilge (*informal*), blah (*slang*), bosh (*informal*), bull (*slang*), bullshit (*taboo slang*), bunk (*informal*), bunkum *or* buncombe (*chiefly U.S.*), cobblers (*Brit. taboo slang*), crap (*slang*), dross, eyewash (*informal*), fatuity, garbage (*informal*), gibberish, guff (*slang*), hogwash, hokum (*slang, chiefly U.S. & Canad.*), horsefeathers (*U.S. slang*), hot air (*informal*), moonshine, nonsense, pap, piffle (*informal*), poppycock (*informal*), prating, rot, rubbish, shit (*taboo slang*), stuff, tommyrot, tosh (*slang, chiefly Brit.*), trash, tripe (*informal*), twaddle, waffle (*informal, chiefly Brit.*) **4.** saliva, slaver, slobber

driveller **1.** drooler, slaverer, slobberer, splutterer, sputterer **2.** babbler, blatherskite, prater, prattler, rambler, twaddler, waffler (*informal, chiefly Brit.*), windbag (*slang*)

driving compelling, dynamic, energetic, forceful, galvanic, sweeping, vigorous, violent

drizzle **1.** *noun* fine rain, Scotch mist, smir (*Scot.*) **2.** *verb* mizzle (*dialect*), rain, shower, spot *or* spit with rain, spray, sprinkle

droll amusing, clownish, comic, comical, diverting, eccentric, entertaining, farcical, funny, humorous, jocular, laughable, ludicrous, odd, oddball (*informal*), off-the-wall (*slang*), quaint, ridiculous, risible, waggish, whimsical

drollery absurdity, archness, buffoonery, comicality, farce, fun, humour, jocularity, pleasantry, waggishness, whimsicality, wit

drone[1] *noun* couch potato (*slang*), idler, leech, loafer, lounger, parasite, scrounger (*informal*), skiver (*Brit. slang*), sluggard, sponger (*informal*)

drone[2] *verb* 1. buzz, hum, purr, thrum, vibrate, whirr 2. *often with* **on** be boring, chant, drawl, intone, prose about, speak monotonously, spout, talk interminably ~*noun* 3. buzz, hum, murmuring, purr, thrum, vibration, whirr, whirring

droning 1. buzzing, humming, murmuring, purring, thrumming, vibrating, whirring 2. boring, drawling, monotonous, soporific, tedious

drool 1. *often with* **over** dote on, fondle, gloat over, gush, make much of, pet, rave (*informal*), slobber over, spoil 2. dribble, drivel, salivate, slaver, slobber, water at the mouth

droop 1. bend, dangle, drop, fall down, hang (down), sag, sink 2. decline, diminish, fade, faint, flag, languish, slump, wilt, wither 3. despond, falter, give in, give up, give way, lose heart *or* hope

droopy 1. drooping, flabby, floppy, languid, languorous, lassitudinous, limp, pendulous, sagging, stooped, wilting 2. blue, dejected, disheartened, dispirited, doleful, downcast, down (in the dumps) (*informal*), sick as a parrot (*informal*)

drop *noun* 1. bead, bubble, driblet, drip, droplet, globule, pearl, tear 2. dab, dash, mouthful, nip, pinch, shot (*informal*), sip, spot, taste, tot, trace, trickle 3. abyss, chasm, declivity, descent, fall, plunge, precipice, slope 4. cut, decline, decrease, deterioration, downturn, fall-off, lowering, reduction, slump ~*verb* 5. dribble, drip, fall in drops, trickle 6. decline, depress, descend, diminish, dive, droop, fall, lower, plummet, plunge, sink, tumble 7. abandon, axe (*informal*), cease, desert, discontinue, forsake, give up, kick (*informal*), leave, quit, relinquish, remit, terminate 8. *informal* disown, ignore, jilt, reject, renounce, repudiate, throw over 9. *sometimes with* **off** deposit, leave, let off, set down, unload

drop in (on) blow in (*informal*), call, call in, go and see, look in (on), look up, pop in (*informal*), roll up (*informal*), stop, turn up, visit

drop off 1. decline, decrease, diminish, dwindle, fall off, lessen, slacken 2. allow to alight, deliver, leave, let off, set down 3. *informal* catnap, doze (off), drowse, fall asleep, have forty winks (*informal*), nod (off), snooze (*informal*)

drop out abandon, back out, cop out (*slang*), fall by the wayside, forsake, give up, leave, quit, renege, stop, withdraw

droppings crap (*taboo slang*), doo-doo (*informal*), dung, excrement, excreta, faeces, guano, manure, ordure, shit (*taboo slang*), stool, turd

dross crust, debris, dregs, impurity, lees, recrement, refuse, remains, scoria, scum, waste

drought 1. aridity, dehydration, drouth (*Scot.*), dryness, dry spell, dry weather, parchedness 2. dearth, deficiency, insufficiency, lack, need, scarcity, shortage, want

Antonyms abundance, deluge, downpour, flood, flow, inundation, outpouring, profusion, rush, stream, torrent

drove collection, company, crowd, flock, gathering, herd, horde, mob, multitude, press, swarm, throng

drown 1. deluge, drench, engulf, flood, go down, go under, immerse, inundate, sink, submerge, swamp 2. *figurative* deaden, engulf, muffle, obliterate, overcome, overpower, overwhelm, stifle, swallow up, wipe out

I was much farther out than you thought
And not waving but drowning
Stevie Smith *Not Waving But Drowning*

drowse 1. *verb* be drowsy, be lethargic, be sleepy, doze, drop off (*informal*), kip (*Brit. slang*), nap, nod, sleep, slumber, snooze (*informal*), zizz (*Brit. informal*) 2. *noun* doze, forty winks (*informal*), kip (*Brit. slang*), nap, sleep, slumber, zizz (*Brit. informal*)

drowsiness doziness, heavy eyelids, languor, lethargy, oscitancy, sleepiness, sluggishness, somnolence, tiredness, torpidity, torpor

Antonyms alertness, brightness, liveliness, perkiness, wakefulness

drowsy 1. comatose, dazed, dopey (*slang*), dozy, drugged, half asleep, heavy, lethargic, nodding, sleepy, somnolent, tired, torpid 2. dreamy, lulling, restful, sleepy, soothing, soporific

Antonyms alert, awake, bright-eyed and bushy-tailed, full of beans (*informal*), lively, perky

drub 1. bang, beat, birch, cane, clobber (*slang*), club, cudgel, flog, hit, knock, lambast(e), pound, pummel, punch, strike, thrash, thump, whack 2. beat, best, blow out of the water (*slang*), defeat, hammer (*informal*), lick (*informal*), master, outclass, overcome, rout, run rings around (*informal*), stuff (*slang*), tank (*slang*), trounce, undo, vanquish, wipe the floor with (*informal*), worst

drubbing beating, clobbering (*slang*), defeat, flogging, hammering (*informal*), licking (*informal*), pasting (*slang*), pounding, pummelling, thrashing, trouncing, walloping (*informal*), whipping

drudge 1. *noun* dogsbody (*informal*), factotum, hack, maid *or* man of all work, menial, plodder, scullion (*archaic*), servant, skivvy (*chiefly Brit.*), slave, toiler, worker 2. *verb* grind (*informal*), keep one's nose to the grindstone, labour, moil (*archaic or dialect*), plod, plug away (*informal*), slave, toil, work

drudgery chore, donkey-work, fag (*informal*), grind (*informal*), hack work, hard work, labour, menial labour, skivvying (*Brit.*), slavery, slog, sweat (*informal*), sweated labour, toil

drug *noun* 1. medicament, medication, medicine, physic, poison, remedy 2. dope (*slang*), narcotic, opiate, stimulant *~verb* 3. administer a drug, dope (*slang*), dose, medicate, treat 4. anaesthetize, deaden, knock out, numb, poison, stupefy

Drugs

acetanilide *or* acetanilid
acriflavine
allopurinol
aloin
alum *or* potash alum
amitriptyline
ampicillin
amyl nitrite *or* *(slang)* popper
amphetamine, *(Trademark)* Benzedrine *or (slang)* speed
Amytal (*Trademark*)
Antabuse (*Trademark*)
antipyrine
apomorphine
araroba *or* Goa powder
Argyrol (*Trademark*)
arsphenamine
aspirin *or* acetylsalicylic acid
atropine *or* atropin
azathioprine
azedarach
bacitracin
barbitone *or (U.S.)* barbital
barbiturate
belladonna
Benadryl (*Trademark*)
benzocaine
benzodiazepine
berberine
bhang *or* bang
bitter aloes
bromal
bupivacaine
caffeine
calomel
cannabis *see* MARIJUANA
cantharides
carbamazepine
carbimazole
cascara sagrada
chlorambucil
chloramphenicol
chlordiazepoxide
chloroquine
chlorothiazide
chlorpromazine
chlorpropamide
chlortetracycline
chlorthalidone
chrysarobin
cinchona
cinchonine
cocaine, cocain *or (slang)* coke *or* Charlie
codeine
contrayerva
cortisone
co-trimoxazole
curare *or* curari
cyclopropane
cyclosporin-A
dapsone
DET *or* diethyltryptamine
dextroamphetamine
digitalis
dimenhydrinate *or (Trademark)* Dramamine
disulfiram
DMT *or* dimethyltryptamine *(slang)*
ephedrin *or* ephedrine
fentanyl
ganja *see* MARIJUANA
gemfibrozil
hashish *or* charas
hemlock
hemp
heroin *or* diamorphine
hydrocortisone *or* cortisol
hyoscyamine
ibuprofen
imipramine
indomethacin
ipecac *or* ipecacuanha
ivermectin
kaolin *or* kaoline
ketamine
laudanum
Librium (*Trademark*)
LSD, lysergic acid diethylamide *or (slang)* acid
marijuana *or* marihuana *see* MARIJUANA
mecamylamine
mepacrine, quinacrine *(U.S.)*, Atebrin *(Trademark)*, *or (U.S. Trademark)* Atabrine
meperidine *or* meperidene hydrochloride
merbromin
mercaptopurine
mescaline *or* mescalin
methadone *or* methadon
methamphetamine
methotrexate
methyldopa
Mogadon (*Trademark*)
morphin *or* morphia
neomycin
nepenthe
nicotine
nitrazepam
nitrous oxide, dinitrogen oxide *or* laughing gas
Novocaine *(Trademark) or* procaine hydrochloride
nux vomica
opium
Paludrine (*Trademark*)
paracetamol
paraldehyde
paregoric
PCP *(Trademark)*, phencyclidine *or (informal)* angel dust
penicillin
pentamidine
pentaquine
pentazocine
pentobarbitone sodium, sodium pentabarbital *(U.S.)*, *or (Trademark)* Nembutal
pentylenetetrazol
phenacaine
phenacetin *or* acetophenetidin
phenformin
phenobarbitone
phenolphthalein
phenothiazine
phenylbutazone
phenytoin
poppy
prednisolene
prednisone
primaquine
promethazine
propranolol
psilocybin
quercetin *or* quercitin
quinidine
quinine
reserpine
rhatany *or* krameria
rifampicin *or (U.S.)* rifampin
safflower *or* false saffron
salicin *or* salicine
saloop
salts
sanguinaria
santonin
scammony
scopolamine *or* hyoscine
scopoline
Seidlitz powder, Seidlitz powders *or* Rochelle powder
senna leaf
senna pods
squill
STP
stramonium

streptomycin
sulphadiazine
sulphadimidine *or (U.S.)* sulfamethazine
sulpha drug
sulphanilamide
sulphathiozole
sulphisoxazole
temazepam
terebene
Terramycin (*Trademark*)
tetracycline
thalidomide
thiopentone sodium, thiopental sodium *or (Trademark)* Sodium Pentothal
thiouracil
tricyclic
turpeth
valerian
Valium *(Trademark) or* diazepam
verapamil
vinblastine
vinca alkaloid
vincristine
witch hazel *or* wych-hazel
wormseed
yohimbine
zidovudine *or (Trademark)* Retrovir

Types of drug

abirritant
abortifacient
adjuvant
agrypnotic
alexipharmic
alkylating agent
alterative
anaesthetic *or (U.S.)* anesthetic
analeptic
analgesic
anaphrodisiac
anodyne
antagonist
antibiotic
anticholinergic
anticonvulsant
antidepressant
antidote
antiemetic
antifebrile
antihistamine
anti-inflammatory
antimalarial
antimetabolite
antimycotic
antiperiodic
antiphlogistic
antipyretic
antispasmodic
antitussive
anxiolytic
aphrodisiac
astringent
ataractic *or* ataraxic
attenuant
beta-blocker
bronchodilator
calcium antagonist *or* blocker
calmative
cardiac
carminative
cathartic
cholagogue
cimetedine
cisplatin
clomiphene
colestipol
contraceptive
convulsant
cytotoxin
decongestant
demulcent
depressant
depressomotor
diaphoretic
diuretic
ecbolic
emetic
emmenagogue
errhine
euphoriant
excitant
expectorant
expellant *or* expellent
febrifuge
general anaesthetic *or (U.S.)* general anesthetic
haemagogue *or (U.S.)* hemagogue *or* hemagog
haemostatic *or (U.S.)* hemostatic
hallucinogen
hepatic
hypnotic
immunosuppressive
inotropic
laxative
lenitive
local anaesthetic *or (U.S.)* local anesthetic
masticatory
miticide
narcotic
nervine
neuroleptic
NSAID *or* nonsteroidal anti-inflammatory drug
opiate
oxytocic
painkiller
palliative
pectoral
preventive
prophylactic
psychedelic *or* psychodelic
psychoactive
psychotomimetic
pulmonic (*rare*)
purgative
radio mimetic
recreational
relaxant
resolvent
restorative
revulsive
roborant
sedative
sialagogue *or* sialogogue
soporific
sorbefacient
spermicide *or (less commonly)* spermatocide
steroid
stimulant
stupefacient
styptic
suppurative
sympatholytic
sympathomimetic
synergist
taeniacide *or (U.S.)* teniacide
taeniafuge *or (U.S.)* teniafuge
tetanic
tonic
tranquillizer, tranquilliser *or (U.S.)* tranquilizer
tumefacient
vasoconstrictor
vasodilator
vasoinhibitor
vermifuge, anthelminthic, anthelmintic *or* helminthic
vesicant *or* vesicatory
vomit
vulnenary

General drug terms

absorption
addiction
addictive
adiaphorus
ana
antimonial
aromatic
arsenical
autacoid
bacterin
bioassay
bioavailability
biological
blockade
botanical
chalybeate
chemoprophylaxis
cohobate
confection
contraindicate
control group
decoction
dependency
designer drug
dosage
dose
electuary
elixir
embrocation
emulsion
endermic
ethical
excipient
exhaust
external
extract
fluidextract
galenical
glycoside
hard
hypersensitive
hypodermic
hypodermic needle
hypodermic syringe
idiosyncracy
incompatible
inhalant
intermediate-acting
intoxicating
lethal dose *or* LD
linctus
liquor

local
long-acting
magistral
mass
median lethal dose *or* mean lethal dose
medication
menstruum
mercurial
mind-expanding
minimum lethal dose *or* MLD
mixture
normal
officinal (*obsolete*)
oleoresin
oral
overdose
over-the-counter
parenteral
pessary
placebo
positive
potentiate
prescription
proprietary
reaction
reactor
remedy
route
sensitivity
sensitize *or* sensitise
short-acting
side effect
signature (*U.S.*)
soft
spansule
specific
spirit
suppository
tincture
succedaneum
synergism *or* synergy
tachyphylaxis
tolerant
topical
trituration
unit
unofficial
vehicle
venipuncture *or* venepuncture
vinegar
wafer
wine
withdrawal

Drug abuse terms
acid
acidhead
angel dust
blow
blow someone's mind
bombed
bong
bring down
bummer
burned
bust
buzz
Charlie
chillum
coke
cold turkey
comedown
connection
cook up
cop
crack
crackhead
crank up
dealer
do
dope
downer
drop
dry out
ecstasy *or* E
fix
freebase
gear
get off
get through (*U.S.*)
glue-sniffing
gone
goof
goofball (*U.S.*)
grass
habit
hash
head
high
hit
hooked
hop (*obsolete*)
hophead (*chiefly U.S.*)
hop up (*dated*)
hype
hyped up
jack up
jag
jellies
joint
joypop
junk
junkie
kick
kif
knockout drops
line
lit up
loaded (*chiefly U.S. & Canad.*)
magic mushroom
mainline
make it
Man (*U.S.*)
Mickey Finn
mind-expanding
monkey (*U.S. & Canad.*)
nail
narc (*U.S.*)
nod out
number
OD *or* overdose
opium den
pep pill
pop
popper
pot
pothead
pusher
reefer
roach
score
shooting gallery
shoot up
skin-pop
skin up
smack
smackhead
smashed
smoke
snort
snowball
solvent abuse
space cadet
spaced out *or* spaced
speed
speedball
speedfreak
spliff
stash
step on
stoned
strung out
stuff
swacked
switch on
tab
toke
toot
trip
turn on
upper
user
wasted
weight
withdrawal
withdrawal symptoms
wrecked
zonked

opiate: an unlocked door in the prison of Identity. It leads into the jail yard
Ambrose Bierce *The Devil's Dictionary*

And though she's not really ill,
There's a little yellow pill;
She goes running for the shelter
Of mother's little helper
Mick Jagger *Mother's Little Helper*

Turn on, tune in and drop out
Timothy Leary *The Politics of Ecstasy*

drug addict *noun* acid head (*informal*), crackhead (*informal*), dope-fiend (*slang*), head (*informal*), hop-head (*informal*), junkie (*informal*), tripper (*informal*)

drugged bombed (*slang*), comatose, doped (*slang*), dopey (*slang*), flying (*slang*), high (*informal*), on a trip (*informal*), out of it (*slang*), out of one's mind (*slang*), out to it (*Austral. & N.Z. slang*), smashed (*slang*), spaced out (*slang*), stoned (*slang*), stupefied, turned on (*slang*), under the influence (*informal*), wasted (*slang*), wrecked (*slang*), zonked (*slang*)

drum *verb* **1.** beat, pulsate, rap, reverberate, tap, tattoo, throb **2.** *with* **into** din into, drive home, hammer away, harp on, instil, reiterate

drum out cashier, discharge, dismiss, disown, drive out, expel, oust, outlaw

drum up attract, bid for, canvass, obtain, peti~ tion, round up, solicit

drunk 1. *adjective* bacchic, bevvied (*dialect*), blitzed (*slang*), blotto (*slang*), bombed (*slang*), Brahms and Liszt (*slang*), canned (*slang*), drunken, flying (*slang*), fu' (*Scot.*), fuddled, half seas over (*informal*), inebriated, intoxi~ cated, legless (*informal*), lit up (*slang*), loaded (*slang, chiefly U.S. & Canad.*), maudlin, mer~ ry (*Brit. informal*), muddled, out of it (*slang*), out to it (*Austral. & N.Z. slang*), paralytic (*informal*), pickled (*informal*), pie-eyed (*slang*), pissed (*taboo slang*), plastered (*slang*), rat-arsed (*taboo slang*), sloshed (*slang*), smashed (*slang*), soaked (*informal*), steamboats (*Scot. slang*), steaming (*slang*), stewed (*slang*), stoned (*slang*), tanked up (*slang*), tiddly (*slang, chiefly Brit.*), tight (*informal*), tipsy, tired and emotional (*euphemistic*), under the influence (*informal*), wasted (*slang*), well-oiled (*slang*), wrecked (*slang*), zonked (*slang*) 2. *noun* boozer (*informal*), drunkard, inebriate, lush (*slang*), soak (*slang*), sot, toper, wino (*in~ formal*)

Man, being reasonable, must get drunk;
The best of Life is but intoxication
Lord Byron *Don Juan*

It's the wise man who stays home when he's drunk
Euripides *The Cyclops*

Two things a man cannot hide: that he is drunk, and that he is in love
Antiphanes

A man who exposes himself when he is intoxi~ cated has not the art of getting drunk
Dr. Johnson

drunkard alcoholic, carouser, dipsomaniac, drinker, drunk, lush (*slang*), soak (*slang*), sot, tippler, toper, wino (*informal*)

drunken 1. bevvied (*dialect*), bibulous, blitzed (*slang*), blotto (*slang*), bombed (*slang*), boozing (*informal*), Brahms and Liszt (*slang*), drunk, flying (*slang*), (gin-)sodden, inebriate, intoxi~ cated, legless (*informal*), lit up (*slang*), out of it (*slang*), out to it (*Austral. & N.Z. slang*), paralytic (*informal*), pissed (*taboo slang*), rat-arsed (*taboo slang*), red-nosed, smashed (*slang*), sottish, steamboats (*Scot. slang*), steaming (*slang*), tippling, toping, under the influence (*informal*), wasted (*slang*), wrecked (*slang*), zonked (*slang*) 2. bacchanalian, bac~ chic, boozy (*informal*), debauched, dionysian, dissipated, orgiastic, riotous, saturnalian

drunkenness alcoholism, bibulousness, dipso~ mania, inebriety, insobriety, intemperance, intoxication, sottishness, tipsiness

Drink moderately, for drunkenness neither keeps a secret, nor observes a promise
Miguel de Cervantes *Don Quixote*

What does drunkenness not accomplish? It unlocks secrets, confirms our hopes, urges the indolent into battle, lifts the burden from anxious minds, teaches new arts
Horace *Epistles*

dry *adjective* 1. arid, barren, dehydrated, desic~ cated, dried up, juiceless, moistureless, parched, sapless, thirsty, torrid, waterless 2. *figurative* boring, dreary, dull, ho-hum (*infor~ mal*), monotonous, plain, tedious, tiresome, uninteresting 3. *figurative* cutting, deadpan, droll, keen, low-key, quietly humorous, sar~ castic, sharp, sly *~verb* 4. dehumidify, dehy~ drate, desiccate, drain, make dry, parch, sear 5. *with* **out** *or* **up** become dry, become unpro~ ductive, harden, mummify, shrivel up, wilt, wither, wizen

Antonyms *adjective* (*sense 1*) damp, humid, moist, wet (*sense 2*) entertaining, interesting, lively *~verb* moisten, wet

dryness aridity, aridness, dehumidification, dehydration, drought, thirst, thirstiness

dual binary, coupled, double, duplex, duplicate, matched, paired, twin, twofold

duality biformity, dichotomy, doubleness, dual~ ism, duplexity, polarity

dub 1. bestow, confer, confer knighthood upon, entitle, knight 2. call, christen, denominate, designate, label, name, nickname, style, term

dubiety doubt, doubtfulness, dubiosity, incerti~ tude, indecision, misgiving, mistrust, qualm, scepticism, uncertainty

dubious 1. doubtful, hesitant, iffy (*informal*), leery (*slang*), sceptical, uncertain, uncon~ vinced, undecided, unsure, wavering 2. am~ biguous, debatable, dodgy (*Brit., Austral., & N.Z. informal*), doubtful, equivocal, indefinite, indeterminate, obscure, problematical, un~ clear, unsettled 3. dodgy (*Brit., Austral., & N.Z. informal*), fishy (*informal*), questionable, shady (*informal*), suspect, suspicious, unde~ pendable, unreliable, untrustworthy

Antonyms certain, definite, dependable, obvi~ ous, positive, reliable, sure, trustworthy

dubitable debatable, doubtable, doubtful, du~ bious, iffy (*informal*), in doubt, more than doubtful, open to doubt, problematic(al), questionable, unconvincing

duck 1. bend, bob, bow, crouch, dodge, drop, lower, stoop 2. dip, dive, douse, dunk, im~ merse, plunge, souse, submerge, wet 3. *infor~ mal* avoid, body-swerve (*Scot.*), dodge, escape, evade, shirk, shun, sidestep

duct blood vessel, canal, channel, conduit, fun~ nel, passage, pipe, tube

ductile 1. extensible, flexible, malleable, plastic, pliable, pliant, tensile 2. amenable, biddable, compliant, docile, manageable, tractable, yielding

dud 1. *noun* clinker (*slang, chiefly U.S.*), failure, flop (*informal*), washout (*informal*) 2. *adjective* broken, bust (*informal*), duff (*Brit. informal*), failed, inoperative, kaput (*informal*), not functioning, valueless, worthless

dudgeon 1. *archaic* indignation, ire, resentment, umbrage, wrath 2. **in high dudgeon** angry, choked, fuming, indignant, offended, resentful, vexed

due *adjective* 1. in arrears, outstanding, owed, owing, payable, unpaid 2. appropriate, becoming, bounden, deserved, fit, fitting, just, justified, merited, obligatory, proper, requisite, right, rightful, suitable, well-earned 3. adequate, ample, enough, plenty of, sufficient 4. expected, expected to arrive, scheduled ~*noun* 5. comeuppance (*slang*), deserts, merits, prerogative, privilege, right(s) ~*adverb* 6. dead, direct, directly, exactly, straight, undeviatingly

duel *noun* 1. affair of honour, single combat 2. clash, competition, contest, encounter, engagement, fight, head-to-head, rivalry ~*verb* 3. clash, compete, contend, contest, fight, lock horns, rival, struggle, vie with

dues charge, charges, contribution, fee, levy, membership fee

duff bad, counterfeit, dud (*informal*), fake, false, not working, useless, worthless

duffer blunderer, booby, bungler, clod, clot (*Brit. informal*), galoot (*slang, chiefly U.S.*), lubber, lummox (*informal*), oaf

dulcet agreeable, charming, delightful, euphonious, harmonious, honeyed, mellifluent, mellifluous, melodious, musical, pleasant, pleasing, soothing, sweet

dull *adjective* 1. braindead (*informal*), dense, dim, dim-witted (*informal*), doltish, dozy (*Brit. informal*), obtuse, slow, stolid, stupid, thick, unintelligent 2. apathetic, blank, callous, dead, empty, heavy, indifferent, insensible, insensitive, lifeless, listless, passionless, slow, sluggish, unresponsive, unsympathetic, vacuous 3. as dry as dust, boring, commonplace, dozy, dreary, dry, flat, ho-hum (*informal*), humdrum, mind-numbing, monotonous, plain, prosaic, run-of-the-mill, tedious, tiresome, unimaginative, uninteresting, vapid 4. blunt, blunted, dulled, edgeless, not keen, not sharp, unsharpened 5. cloudy, dim, dismal, gloomy, leaden, opaque, overcast, turbid 6. depressed, inactive, slack, slow, sluggish, torpid, uneventful 7. drab, faded, feeble, indistinct, lacklustre, muffled, murky, muted, sombre, subdued, subfusc, toned-down ~*verb* 8. dampen, deject, depress, discourage, dishearten, dispirit, sadden 9. allay, alleviate, assuage, blunt, lessen, mitigate, moderate, palliate, paralyse, relieve, soften, stupefy, take the edge off 10. cloud, darken, dim, fade, obscure, stain, sully, tarnish

Antonyms *adjective* active, bright, clever, exciting, full of beans (*informal*), intelligent, interesting, lively, sharp

dullard blockhead, clod, dimwit (*informal*), dolt, dope (*informal*), dunce, fathead (*informal*), gobshite (*Irish taboo slang*), lamebrain (*informal*), nitwit (*informal*), numpty (*Scot. informal*), numskull *or* numbskull, oaf

dullness 1. colourlessness, dimness, dinginess, drabness, gloominess, greyness 2. dimness, dim-wittedness, dopiness (*slang*), doziness (*Brit. informal*), obtuseness, slowness, stupidity, thickness 3. banality, dreariness, flatness, insipidity, monotony, tediousness, vapidity 4. bluntness, hebetude

Antonyms (*sense 1*) brightness, brilliance, effulgence, incandescence, shine, sparkle (*sense 2*) brightness, cleverness, intelligence, quickness, sharpness, smartness (*sense 3*) colour, interest, liveliness (*sense 4*) acuteness, keenness, sharpness

duly 1. accordingly, appropriately, befittingly, correctly, decorously, deservedly, fittingly, properly, rightfully, suitably 2. at the proper time, on time, punctually

dumb 1. at a loss for words, inarticulate, mum, mute, silent, soundless, speechless, tongue-tied, voiceless, wordless 2. *informal* asinine, braindead (*informal*), dense, dim-witted (*informal*), dozy (*Brit. informal*), dull, foolish, obtuse, stupid, thick, unintelligent

Antonyms (*sense 2*) articulate, bright, clever, intelligent, quick-witted, smart

dumbfound, dumfound amaze, astonish, astound, bewilder, bowl over (*informal*), confound, confuse, flabbergast (*informal*), flummox, nonplus, overwhelm, stagger, startle, stun, take aback

dumbfounded, dumfounded amazed, astonished, astounded, at sea, bewildered, bowled over (*informal*), breathless, confounded, confused, dumb, flabbergasted (*informal*), flummoxed, gobsmacked (*Brit. slang*), knocked for six (*informal*), knocked sideways (*informal*), lost for words, nonplussed, overcome, overwhelmed, speechless, staggered, startled, stunned, taken aback, thrown, thunderstruck

dummy *noun* 1. figure, form, lay figure, manikin, mannequin, model 2. copy, counterfeit, duplicate, imitation, sham, substitute 3. *slang* berk (*Brit. slang*), blockhead, charlie (*Brit. informal*), coot, dickhead (*slang*), dickwit (*slang*), dimwit (*informal*), dipstick (*Brit. slang*), divvy (*Brit. slang*), dolt, dork (*slang*), dullard, dunce, dweeb (*U.S. slang*), fathead (*informal*), fool, fuckwit (*taboo slang*), geek (*slang*), gobshite (*Irish taboo slang*), gonzo (*slang*), jerk (*slang, chiefly U.S. & Canad.*), lamebrain (*informal*), nerd *or* nurd (*slang*), nitwit (*informal*), numpty (*Scot. informal*), numskull *or* numbskull, oaf, pillock (*Brit. slang*), plank (*Brit. slang*), plonker (*slang*), prat (*slang*), prick (*slang*), schmuck (*U.S. slang*), simpleton, wally (*slang*), weenie (*U.S. informal*) *~adjective* **4**. artificial, bogus, fake, false, imitation, mock, phoney *or* phony (*informal*), sham, simulated **5**. mock, practice, simulated, trial

dump *verb* **1**. deposit, drop, fling down, let fall, throw down **2**. coup (*Scot.*), discharge, dispose of, ditch (*slang*), empty out, get rid of, jettison, scrap, throw away *or* out, tip, unload *~noun* **3**. junkyard, refuse heap, rubbish heap, rubbish tip, tip **4**. *informal* hole (*informal*), hovel, joint (*slang*), mess, pigsty, shack, shanty, slum

dumps blues, dejection, depression, despondency, dolour, gloom, gloominess, low spirits, melancholy, mopes, sadness, the hump (*Brit. informal*), unhappiness, woe

dumpy chubby, chunky, fubsy (*archaic or dialect*), homely, plump, podgy, pudgy, roly-poly, short, squab, squat, stout, tubby

dun *verb* beset, importune, pester, plague, press, urge

dunce ass, blockhead, bonehead (*slang*), dimwit (*informal*), dolt, donkey, duffer (*informal*), dullard, dunderhead, fathead (*informal*), goose (*informal*), halfwit, ignoramus, lamebrain (*informal*), loon (*informal*), moron, nincompoop, nitwit (*informal*), numskull *or* numbskull, oaf, simpleton, thickhead

dungeon cage, calaboose (*U.S. informal*), cell, donjon, lockup, oubliette, prison, vault

dupe *noun* **1**. fall guy (*informal*), gull, mug (*Brit. slang*), pigeon (*slang*), pushover (*slang*), sap (*slang*), simpleton, sucker (*slang*), victim **2**. cat's-paw, instrument, pawn, puppet, stooge (*slang*), tool *~verb* **3**. bamboozle (*informal*), beguile, cheat, con (*informal*), cozen, deceive, defraud, delude, gull (*archaic*), hoax, hoodwink, humbug, kid (*informal*), outwit, overreach, pull a fast one on (*informal*), rip off (*slang*), swindle, take for a ride (*informal*), trick

duplicate **1**. *adjective* corresponding, identical, matched, matching, twin, twofold **2**. *noun* carbon copy, clone, copy, dead ringer (*slang*), double, facsimile, fax, likeness, lookalike, match, mate, photocopy, Photostat (*Trademark*), replica, reproduction, ringer (*slang*), twin, Xerox (*Trademark*) **3**. *verb* clone, copy, double, echo, fax, photocopy, Photostat (*Trademark*), reinvent the wheel, repeat, replicate, reproduce, Xerox (*Trademark*)

duplicity artifice, chicanery, deceit, deception, dishonesty, dissimulation, double-dealing, falsehood, fraud, guile, hypocrisy, perfidy

Antonyms candour, honesty, straightforwardness

durability constancy, durableness, endurance, imperishability, lastingness, permanence, persistence

durable abiding, constant, dependable, enduring, fast, firm, fixed, hard-wearing, lasting, long-lasting, permanent, persistent, reliable, resistant, sound, stable, strong, sturdy, substantial, tough

Antonyms breakable, brittle, delicate, fragile, impermanent, perishable, weak

duration continuance, continuation, extent, length, period, perpetuation, prolongation, span, spell, stretch, term, time

duress **1**. coercion, compulsion, constraint, pressure, threat **2**. captivity, confinement, constraint, hardship, imprisonment, incarceration, restraint

dusk **1**. dark, evening, eventide, gloaming (*Scot. or poetic*), nightfall, sundown, sunset, twilight **2**. *poetic* darkness, gloom, murk, obscurity, shade, shadowiness

Antonyms aurora (*poetic*), cockcrow, dawn, dawning, daybreak, daylight, morning, sunlight, sunup

dusky **1**. dark, dark-complexioned, dark-hued, sable, swarthy **2**. caliginous (*archaic*), cloudy, crepuscular, darkish, dim, gloomy, murky, obscure, overcast, shadowy, shady, tenebrous, twilight, twilit, veiled

dust *noun* **1**. fine fragments, grime, grit, particles, powder, powdery dirt **2**. dirt, earth, ground, soil **3**. *informal* commotion, disturbance, fuss, racket, row **4**. **bite the dust** *informal* die, drop dead, expire, fall in battle, pass away, perish **5**. **lick the dust** *informal* be servile, bootlick (*informal*), demean oneself, grovel, kowtow, toady **6**. **throw dust in the eyes of** con (*slang*), confuse, deceive, fool, have (someone) on, hoodwink, mislead, take in (*informal*) *~verb* **7**. cover, dredge, powder, scatter, sift, spray, spread, sprinkle

dust-up argument, brush, conflict, encounter, fight, fracas, punch-up (*Brit. informal*), quarrel, scrap (*informal*), set-to (*informal*), shindig (*informal*), skirmish, tussle

dusty **1**. dirty, grubby, sooty, unclean, undusted, unswept **2**. chalky, crumbly, friable, granular, powdery, sandy

dutiful compliant, conscientious, deferential, devoted, docile, duteous (*archaic*), filial, obedient, punctilious, respectful, reverential, submissive

Antonyms disobedient, disrespectful, insubordinate, remiss, uncaring

duty **1**. assignment, business, calling, charge, engagement, function, mission, obligation, office, onus, pigeon (*informal*), province, re~

sponsibility, role, service, task, work **2.** allegiance, deference, loyalty, obedience, respect, reverence **3.** customs, due, excise, impost, levy, tariff, tax, toll **4. do duty for** stand in, substitute, take the place of **5. be the duty of** behove (*archaic*), be incumbent upon, belong to, be (someone's) pigeon (*Brit. informal*), be up to (*informal*), devolve upon, pertain to, rest with **6. off duty** at leisure, free, off, off work, on holiday **7. on duty** at work, busy, engaged, on active service

Our duty is to be useful, not according to our desires but according to our powers
Henri Frédéric Amiel *Journal*

Without duty, life is soft and boneless; it cannot hold itself together
Joseph Joubert *Pensées*

When a stupid man is doing something that he is ashamed of, he always declares that it is his duty
George Bernard Shaw *Caesar and Cleopatra*

Do your duty, and leave the outcome to the Gods
Pierre Corneille *Horace*

England expects that every man will do his duty
Horatio Nelson

Duty, honour! We make these words say whatever we want, the same as we do with parrots
Alfred Capus *Mariage bourgeois*

dwarf *noun* **1.** bantam, homunculus, hop-o'-my-thumb, Lilliputian, manikin, midget, munchkin (*informal, chiefly U.S.*), pygmy *or* pigmy, Tom Thumb **2.** gnome, goblin *~adjective* **3.** baby, bonsai, diminutive, dwarfed, Lilliputian, miniature, petite, pocket, small, teensy-weensy, teeny-weeny, tiny, undersized *~verb* **4.** dim, diminish, dominate, minimize, overshadow, tower above *or* over **5.** check, cultivate by bonsai, lower, retard, stunt

Snow White's seven dwarfs

Bashful
Doc
Dopey
Grumpy
Happy
Sleepy
Sneezy

dwarfish diminutive, dwarfed, knee high to a grasshopper (*informal*), low, miniature, minute, pint-size (*informal*), pygmaean, pygmy *or* pigmy, runtish, runty, short, small, stunted, teensy-weensy, teeny-weeny, tiny, undersized

dwell abide, establish oneself, hang out (*informal*), inhabit, live, lodge, quarter, remain, reside, rest, settle, sojourn, stay, stop

dwelling abode, domicile, dwelling house, establishment, habitation, home, house, lodging, pad (*slang*), quarters, residence

Types of dwelling

adobe
apartment
back-to-back
barrack
bedsitter
black house (*Scot.*)
board-and-shingle (*Caribbean*)
boarding house
booth
bungalow
bunker
but and ben (*Scot.*)
cabin
caboose (*Canad.*)
camboose
Cape Cod cottage
caravan
castle
chalet
chateau *or* château
chattel house
consulate
cot *or* cote (*dialect*)
cottage
cottage flat
crannog
croft
dacha (*Russian*)
deanery
digs
doss house
duplex *or* duplex apartment (*U.S. & Canad.*)
embassy
farmhouse
flat
flatlet
flophouse
flotel
garret
grange
guest house
hacienda
hall
hogan
hostel
hotel
house
houseboat
hovel
hut
igloo *or* iglu
inn
lake dwelling
lodge
log cabin
long house
maisonette
manor
manse
mansion
mattamore
mews (*informal*)
mobile home
motel
motor caravan
mud hut
palace
parsonage
penthouse
pied-à-terre
prefab
priory
ranch
rath (*Irish*)
rectory
rest-home
roadhouse
semi
shack
shanty
shooting box
show house
single-end (*Scot. dialect*)
slum
starter home
stately home
studio flat
tavern
tenement
tent
tepee
town house
trailer (*U.S. & Canad.*)
tree house
tupik *or* tupek (*Canad.*)
vicarage
villa
whare (*N.Z.*)
wigwam

dwell on *or* **upon** be engrossed in, continue, elaborate, emphasize, expatiate, harp on, linger over, tarry over

dwindle abate, contract, decay, decline, decrease, die away (down, out), diminish, ebb, fade, fall, grow less, lessen, peter out, pine, shrink, shrivel, sink, subside, taper off, wane, waste away, weaken, wither
Antonyms advance, amplify, develop, dilate, enlarge, escalate, expand, grow, heighten, increase, magnify, multiply, swell, wax

dye **1.** *noun* colorant, colour, colouring, pigment, stain, tinge, tint **2.** *verb* colour, pigment, stain, tincture, tinge, tint

dyed-in-the-wool complete, confirmed, deep-dyed (*usually derogatory*), deep-rooted, die-hard, entrenched, established, inveterate, through-and-through

dying at death's door, ebbing, expiring, fading, failing, final, going, *in extremis*, moribund, mortal, not long for this world, passing, perishing, sinking

dynamic active, alive and kicking, driving, electric, energetic, forceful, full of beans (*informal*), go-ahead, go-getting (*informal*), high-octane (*informal*), high-powered, lively, magnetic, powerful, vigorous, vital, zippy (*informal*)
Antonyms apathetic, couldn't-care-less (*informal*), impassive, inactive, listless, sluggish, torpid, undynamic, unenergetic

dynamism brio, drive, energy, enterprise, forcefulness, get-up-and-go (*informal*), go (*informal*), initiative, liveliness, pep, push (*informal*), vigour, zap (*slang*), zip (*informal*)

dynasty ascendancy, dominion, empire, government, house, regime, rule, sovereignty, sway

E

each 1. *adjective* every 2. *pronoun* each and every one, each one, every one, one and all 3. *adverb* apiece, for each, from each, individ~ually, per capita, per head, per person, re~spectively, singly, to each

eager agog, anxious, ardent, athirst, avid, bright-eyed and bushy-tailed (*informal*), ear~nest, enthusiastic, fervent, fervid, greedy, hot, hungry, impatient, intent, keen, keen as mustard, longing, raring, vehement, yearning, zealous
Antonyms apathetic, blasé, impassive, indif~ferent, lazy, nonchalant, opposed, unambi~tious, unconcerned, unenthusiastic, unim~pressed, uninterested

eagerness ardour, avidity, earnestness, enthu~siasm, fervour, greediness, heartiness, hunger, impatience, impetuosity, intentness, keenness, longing, thirst, vehemence, yearning, zeal

ear *figurative* 1. attention, consideration, hear~ing, heed, notice, regard 2. appreciation, dis~crimination, musical perception, sensitivity, taste

Parts of the ear

ancus
auditory nerve
cochlea
eardrum, tympanic membrane *or* tym~panum
ear lobe
Eustachian tube
external auditory ca~nal
incus
malleus
meatus *or* auditory canal
organ of Corti
oval window
pinna
round window
saccule
semicircular canals
stapes
tragus
utricle

early *adjective* 1. advanced, forward, prema~ture, untimely 2. primeval, primitive, primor~dial, undeveloped, young ~*adverb* 3. ahead of time, beforehand, betimes (*archaic*), in ad~vance, in good time, prematurely, too soon
Antonyms (*sense 2*) developed, mature, ripe, seasoned (*sense 3*) behind, belated, late, over~due, tardy

The early bird catches the worm

Early to bed and early to rise, makes a man healthy, wealthy, and wise

earmark 1. *verb* allocate, designate, flag, keep back, label, mark out, reserve, set aside, tag 2. *noun* attribute, characteristic, feature, hall~mark, label, quality, signature, stamp, tag, token, trademark, trait

earn 1. bring in, collect, draw, gain, get, gross, make, net, obtain, procure, realize, reap, re~ceive 2. acquire, attain, be entitled to, be wor~thy of, deserve, merit, rate, warrant, win

earnest *adjective* 1. close, constant, deter~mined, firm, fixed, grave, intent, resolute, re~solved, serious, sincere, solemn, stable, staid, steady, thoughtful 2. ablaze, ardent, devoted, eager, enthusiastic, fervent, fervid, heartfelt, impassioned, keen, keen as mustard, passion~ate, purposeful, urgent, vehement, warm, zealous ~*noun* 3. determination, reality, reso~lution, seriousness, sincerity, truth 4. assur~ance, deposit, down payment, earnest money (*Law*), foretaste, guarantee, pledge, promise, security, token
Antonyms *adjective* apathetic, couldn't-care-less, flippant, frivolous, half-hearted, indiffer~ent, insincere, light, slack, trifling, uncon~cerned, unenthusiastic, uninterested, unstable ~*noun* apathy, indifference, unconcern

earnestness ardour, determination, devotion, eagerness, enthusiasm, fervour, gravity, in~tentness, keenness, passion, purposefulness, resolution, seriousness, sincerity, urgency, ve~hemence, warmth, zeal

earnings emolument, gain, income, pay, pro~ceeds, profits, receipts, remuneration, return, reward, salary, stipend, takings, wages

earth 1. globe, orb, planet, sphere, terrestrial sphere, world 2. clay, clod, dirt, ground, land, loam, mould, sod, soil, topsoil, turf
Related adjectives: terrestrial, telluric

earthenware ceramics, crockery, crocks, pots, pottery, terracotta

earthiness bawdiness, coarseness, crudeness, crudity, lustiness, naturalness, ribaldry, ro~bustness, uninhibitedness

earthly 1. mundane, sublunary, tellurian, tel~luric, terrene, terrestrial, worldly 2. human, material, mortal, non-spiritual, profane, secu~lar, temporal, worldly 3. base, carnal, fleshly, gross, low, materialistic, physical, sensual, sordid, vile 4. *informal* conceivable, feasible, imaginable, likely, possible, practical
Antonyms ethereal, heavenly, immaterial,

immortal, otherworldly, spiritual, supernatural, unearthly

earthshaking apocalyptic, crucial, earth-shattering, epoch-making, fateful, historic, landmark, momentous, pivotal, vital

earthy bawdy, coarse, crude, down-to-earth, homely, lusty, natural, raunchy (*slang*), ribald, robust, rough, simple, uninhibited, unrefined, unsophisticated

ease *noun* **1.** affluence, calmness, comfort, content, contentment, enjoyment, happiness, leisure, peace, peace of mind, quiet, quietude, relaxation, repose, rest, restfulness, serenity, tranquillity **2.** easiness, effortlessness, facility, readiness, simplicity **3.** flexibility, freedom, informality, liberty, naturalness, unaffectedness, unconstraint, unreservedness **4.** aplomb, composure, insouciance, nonchalance, poise, relaxedness *~verb* **5.** abate, allay, alleviate, appease, assuage, calm, comfort, disburden, lessen, lighten, mitigate, moderate, mollify, pacify, palliate, quiet, relax, relent, relieve, slacken, soothe, still, tranquillize **6.** aid, assist, expedite, facilitate, forward, further, give a leg up (*informal*), lessen the labour of, make easier, simplify, smooth, speed up **7.** edge, guide, inch, manoeuvre, move carefully, slide, slip, squeeze, steer

Antonyms *noun* agitation, arduousness, awkwardness, clumsiness, concern, constraint, difficulty, discomfort, disturbance, effort, exertion, formality, hardship, irritation, pain, poverty, tension, toil, tribulation *~verb* aggravate, discomfort, exacerbate, hinder, irritate, make nervous, make uneasy, retard, worsen

easeful calm, comfortable, easy, peaceful, quiet, reposeful, restful, soothing, tranquil

easily **1.** comfortably, effortlessly, facilely, like a knife through butter, readily, simply, smoothly, standing on one's head, with ease, with one hand tied behind one's back, with one's eyes closed *or* shut, without difficulty, without trouble **2.** absolutely, beyond question, by far, certainly, clearly, definitely, doubtlessly, far and away, indisputably, indubitably, plainly, surely, undeniably, undoubtedly, unequivocally, unquestionably, without a doubt **3.** almost certainly, probably, well

easy **1.** a bed of roses, a piece of cake (*informal*), a piece of piss (*taboo slang*), a pushover (*slang*), child's play (*informal*), clear, easy-peasy (*slang*), effortless, facile, light, no bother, not difficult, no trouble, painless, plain sailing, simple, smooth, straightforward, uncomplicated, undemanding **2.** calm, carefree, comfortable, contented, cushy (*informal*), easeful, leisurely, peaceful, pleasant, quiet, relaxed, satisfied, serene, tranquil, undisturbed, untroubled, unworried, well-to-do **3.** flexible, indulgent, lenient, liberal, light, mild, permissive, tolerant, unburdensome, unoppressive **4.** affable, casual, easy-going, friendly, gentle, graceful, gracious, informal, laid-back (*informal*), mild, natural, open, pleasant, relaxed, smooth, tolerant, unaffected, unceremonious, unconstrained, undemanding, unforced, unpretentious **5.** accommodating, amenable, biddable, compliant, docile, gullible, manageable, pliant, soft, submissive, suggestible, susceptible, tractable, trusting, yielding **6.** comfortable, gentle, leisurely, light, mild, moderate, temperate, undemanding, unexacting, unhurried

Antonyms affected, anxious, arduous, complex, demanding, dictatorial, difficult, exacting, exhausting, forced, formal, formidable, hard, harsh, impossible, inflexible, insecure, intolerant, onerous, poor, rigid, self-conscious, stern, stiff, stressful, strict, uncomfortable, unnatural, unyielding, worried

Easy come, easy go

easy-going amenable, calm, carefree, casual, complacent, easy, easy-oasy (*slang*), even-tempered, flexible, happy-go-lucky, indulgent, insouciant, laid-back (*informal*), lenient, liberal, mild, moderate, nonchalant, permissive, placid, relaxed, serene, tolerant, unconcerned, uncritical, undemanding, unhurried

Antonyms anxious, edgy, fussy, hung-up (*slang*), intolerant, irritated, nervy (*Brit. informal*), neurotic, on edge, strict, tense, uptight (*informal*)

eat **1.** chew, consume, devour, gobble, ingest, munch, scoff (*slang*), swallow **2.** break bread, chow down (*slang*), dine, feed, have a meal, take food, take nourishment **3.** corrode, crumble, decay, dissolve, erode, rot, waste away, wear away **4. eat one's words** abjure, recant, rescind, retract, take (statement) back

Specific eating habits

anthropophagic *or* anthropophagous	fellow humans
apivorous	bees
cannibalistic	other members of the same species
carnivorous	meat
carpophagous, frugivorous *or* fruitarian	fruit
carrion	dead and rotting flesh
coprophagous	dung
geophagous	earth
herbivorous	plants
hylophagous	wood
insectivorous	insects
limivorous	mud
macrophagous	relatively large pieces of food
monophagous	only one food

mycetophagous	fungi
myrmecophagous	ants
nectarivorous	nectar
nucivorous	nuts
omnivorous	meat and plants
omophagic *or* omophagous	raw food
piscivorous	fish
theophagous	gods
vegan	no animal products
vegetarian	no flesh
zoophagous	animals

One should eat to live, and not live to eat
Molière *L'Avare*

Most vegetarians I ever see looked enough like their food to be classed as cannibals
Finley Peter Donne

eatable comestible (*rare*), digestible, edible, esculent, fit to eat, good, harmless, palatable, wholesome

eavesdrop bug (*informal*), earwig (*informal*), listen in, monitor, overhear, snoop (*informal*), spy, tap

eavesdropper listener, monitor, snooper (*informal*), spy

ebb *verb* **1.** abate, fall away, fall back, flow back, go out, recede, retire, retreat, retrocede, sink, subside, wane, withdraw *~noun* **2.** ebb tide, going out, low tide, low water, reflux, regression, retreat, retrocession, subsidence, wane, waning, withdrawal *~verb* **3.** decay, decline, decrease, degenerate, deteriorate, diminish, drop, dwindle, fade away, fall away, flag, lessen, peter out, shrink, sink, slacken, weaken *~noun* **4.** decay, decline, decrease, degeneration, deterioration, diminution, drop, dwindling, fading away, flagging, lessening, petering out, shrinkage, sinking, slackening, weakening

ebullience 1. brio, buoyancy, effervescence, effusiveness, elation, enthusiasm, excitement, exhilaration, exuberance, high spirits, vivacity, zest **2.** boiling, bubbling, ebullition, effervescence, ferment, fermentation, foam, froth, frothing, seething

ebullient 1. buoyant, effervescent, effusive, elated, enthusiastic, excited, exhilarated, exuberant, frothy, gushing, in high spirits, irrepressible, vivacious, zestful **2.** boiling, bubbling, effervescent, foaming, frothing, seething

ebullition 1. boiling, bubbling, effervescence, fermentation, frothing, outburst, overflow, seething **2.** access, fit, outbreak, outburst, overflow, paroxysm, spasm, storm, throe (*rare*)

eccentric 1. *adjective* aberrant, abnormal, anomalous, bizarre, capricious, erratic, freakish, idiosyncratic, irregular, odd, oddball (*informal*), off the rails, off-the-wall (*slang*), outlandish, outré, peculiar, queer (*informal*), quirky, rum (*Brit. slang*), singular, strange, uncommon, unconventional, wacko (*slang*), weird, whimsical **2.** *noun* card (*informal*), case (*informal*), character (*informal*), crank (*informal*), freak (*informal*), kook (*U.S. & Canad. informal*), nonconformist, nut (*slang*), oddball (*informal*), odd fish (*informal*), oddity, queer fish (*Brit. informal*), rum customer (*Brit. slang*), screwball (*slang, chiefly U.S. & Canad.*), wacko (*slang*), weirdo *or* weirdie (*informal*)

Antonyms *adjective* average, conventional, normal, ordinary, regular, run-of-the-mill, straightforward, typical

eccentricity aberration, abnormality, anomaly, bizarreness, caprice, capriciousness, foible, freakishness, idiosyncrasy, irregularity, nonconformity, oddity, oddness, outlandishness, peculiarity, queerness (*informal*), quirk, singularity, strangeness, unconventionality, waywardness, weirdness, whimsicality, whimsicalness

ecclesiastic 1. *noun* churchman, clergyman, cleric, divine, holy man, man of the cloth, minister, parson, pastor, priest **2.** *adjective Also* **ecclesiastical** church, churchly, clerical, divine, holy, pastoral, priestly, religious, spiritual

echelon degree, grade, level, office, place, position, rank, tier

echo *verb* **1.** repeat, resound, reverberate **2.** ape, copy, imitate, mirror, parallel, parrot, recall, reflect, reiterate, reproduce, resemble, ring, second *~noun* **3.** answer, repetition, reverberation **4.** copy, imitation, mirror image, parallel, reflection, reiteration, reproduction, ringing **5.** allusion, evocation, hint, intimation, memory, reminder, suggestion, trace **6.** *often plural* aftereffect, aftermath, consequence, repercussion

echoic imitative, onomatopoeic

éclat 1. brilliance, effect, success **2.** display, lustre, ostentation, pomp, show, showmanship, splendour **3.** celebrity, distinction, fame, glory, renown **4.** acclaim, acclamation, applause, approval, plaudits

eclectic all-embracing, broad, catholic, comprehensive, dilettantish, diverse, diversified, general, heterogeneous, liberal, manifold, many-sided, multifarious, selective, varied, wide-ranging

eclipse *verb* **1.** blot out, cloud, darken, dim, extinguish, obscure, overshadow, shroud, veil **2.** exceed, excel, outdo, outshine, put in the shade (*informal*), surpass, transcend *~noun* **3.** darkening, dimming, extinction, obscuration, occultation, shading **4.** decline, diminution, failure, fall, loss

eclogue bucolic, georgic, idyll, pastoral

economic 1. business, commercial, financial, industrial, mercantile, trade 2. money-making, productive, profitable, profit-making, remunerative, solvent, viable 3. bread-and-butter (*informal*), budgetary, financial, fiscal, material, monetary, pecuniary 4. *informal Also* **economical** cheap, fair, inexpensive, low, low-priced, modest, reasonable

economical 1. cost-effective, efficient, money-saving, neat, sparing, time-saving, unwasteful, work-saving 2. careful, economizing, frugal, prudent, saving, scrimping, sparing, thrifty 3. *Also* **economic** cheap, fair, inexpensive, low, low-priced, modest, reasonable
Antonyms exorbitant, expensive, extravagant, generous, imprudent, lavish, loss-making, profligate, spendthrift, uneconomical, unprofitable, unthrifty, wasteful

economics

Branches of economics

agronomics
cliometrics
econometrics
economic history
industrial economics
macroeconomics
microeconomics
welfare economics

Economics terms

arbitration
asset
autarky
automation
balanced budget
balance of payments
balance of trade
balance sheet
bank
bankruptcy
barriers to entry
barriers to exit
barter
base rate
bear market
bid
black economy
boom
boycott
bridging loan
budget
budget deficit
building society
bull market
business cycle
buyer's market
capacity
capital
capital good
capitalism
cartel
cash
central bank
Chamber of Commerce
closed shop
collective bargaining
command economy *or* planned economy
commercial bank *or* clearing bank
commission
commodity
common market
comparative advantage
competition
conspicuous consumption
consumer
consumer good
consumption
cooperative
corporation
corporation tax
cost-benefit analysis
cost effectiveness
cost of living
cost-push inflation
credit
credit controls
credit squeeze
currency
current account
customs union
debt
deflation
deindustrialization
demand
demand management *or* stabilization policy
demand-pull inflation
deposit account
depreciation
depression
deregulation
devaluation
diminishing returns
discount
discount house (*Brit.*)
discount rate
disequilibrium
disinflation
disposable income
diversification
divestment
dividend
division of labour
dumping
duopoly
durable good
Dutch disease
duty
earned income
earnings
economic growth
economic policy
economic sanctions
economies of scale
embargo
employee
employer
employment
entrepreneur
environmental audit
exchange
exchange rate
expenditure
export
finance
financial year
fiscal drag
fiscal policy
fiscal year
Five-Year Plan
fixed assets
fixed costs
fixed exchange-rate system
fixed investment
floating exchange-rate system
foreclosure
foreign exchange controls
foreign exchange market
forfaiting
franchise
free-market economy
free rider
free trade
free trade area
free trade zone *or* freeport
freight
friendly society
fringe benefits
full employment
funding
futures market *or* forward exchange market
gains from trade
game theory
gilt-edged security *or* government bond
gold standard
greenfield investment
gross domestic product *or* GDP
gross national product *or* GNP
gross profit
hard currency
hedging
hire
hire purchase *or* HP
hoarding
holding
horizontal integration
hot money
human capital
hyperinflation
imperfect competition
import
import restrictions
income
income support
income tax
index-linked
indirect tax
industrial dispute
industrial estate
industrial policy
industrial relations
industrial sector
inflationary spiral
information agreement
infrastructure
inheritance tax
insolvency
instalment credit
institutional investors
insurance
intangible assets
intangibles
intellectual property right
interest
interest rate

international com~
petitiveness
international debt
international reserves
investment
invisible balance
invisible hand
invoice
joint-stock company
joint venture
junk bond
labour
labour market
labour theory of value
laissez-faire *or*
laisser-faire
lease
legal tender
lender
liability
liquidation
liquid asset
liquidity
listed company
loan
lockout
macroeconomic policy
management buy-out
marginal revenue
marginal utility
market
market failure
mass production
means test
mediation
medium of exchange
medium-term finan~
cial strategy
mercantilism
merchant bank
merger
microeconomic policy
middleman
mint
mixed economy
monetarism
monetary compensa~
tory amounts, MCAs,
or green money
monetary policy
money
money supply
monopoly
moonlighting
mortgage
multinational
national debt
national income
national insurance
contributions
nationalization
national product
natural rate of unem~
ployment
net profit
nondurable good
offshore
oligopoly
overheads
overheating
overmanning
overtime
patent
pawnbroker
pay
pay-as-you-earn *or*
PAYE
payroll
pension
pension fund
per capita income
perfect competition
personal equity plan
or PEP
picket
piecework
polluter pays principle
portfolio
poverty trap
premium
premium bond
price
prices and incomes
policy
primary sector
private enterprise
private property
privatization
producer
production
productivity
profit
profitability
profit-and-loss account
profit margin
profit sharing
progressive taxation
protectionism
public expenditure
public finance
public interest
public-sector borrow~
ing requirement *or*
PSBR
public-sector debt re~
payment
public utility
public works
pump priming
purchasing power
quality control
ratchet effect
rational expectations
rationalization
rationing
recession
recommended retail
price
recovery
recycling
redundancy
reflation
regional policy
rent
rent controls
research and develop~
ment *or* R & D
residual unemploy~
ment
restrictive labour
practice
retail
retail price index
revaluation
revenue
risk analysis
salary
sales
saving
savings bank
seasonal unemploy~
ment
self-employment
self service
self-sufficiency
seller's market
sequestration
service sector
share
shareholder
share issue
share price index
shop
shop steward
simple interest
slump
social costs
socio-economic group
soft currency
specialization
speculation
stagflation
standard of living
stock
stockbroker
stock control
stock exchange *or*
stock market
stop-go cycle
structural unemploy~
ment
subsidiary company
subsidy
supplier
supply
supply-side economics
surplus
synergy
takeover
tangible assets
tariff
tax
taxation
tax avoidance
tax evasion
tax haven
terms of trade
trade
trade barrier
trademark
trade union
trade-weighted index
training
transaction
trust
trustee
underwriter
unearned income
unemployment
unemployment benefit
uniform business rate
or UBR
unit of account
unit trust
utility
value-added tax *or*
VAT
variable costs
venture capital
vertical integration
voluntary unemploy~
ment
wage
wage restraint
wealth
welfare state
wholesaler
worker participation
working capital
yield

Organizations and treaties

ACAS *or* Advisory,
Conciliation, and Ar~
bitration Service
Bretton Woods Sys~
tem
CACM *or* Central
American Common
Market

CAP *or* Common Agricultural Policy
CARICOM *or* Caribbean Community and Common Market
CARIFTA *or* Caribbean Free Trade Area
CBI *or* Confederation of British Industry
COMECON *or* Council for Mutual Economic Assistance
ECO *or* European Coal Organization
ECOSOC *or* Economic and Social Council
ECOWAS *or* Economic Community Of West African States
ECSC *or* European Coal and Steel Community
EEA *or* European Economic Area
EFTA *or* European Free Trade association
EMS *or* European Monetary System
EMU *or* European Monetary Union
EU *or* European Union
European Bank for Reconstruction and Development
European Investment Bank
European Monetary Cooperation Fund
European Regional Development Fund
GATT *or* General Agreement on Tariffs and Trade
Group of 7 *or* G7
IFC *or* International Finance Corporation
ILO *or* International Labour Organization
IMF *or* International Monetary Fund
LAFTA *or* Latin American Free Trade Association
Lomé agreements
Maastricht Treaty
Monopolies and Mergers Commission
NAFTA *or* New Zealand and Australia Free Trade Agreement
NAFTA *or* North American Free Trade Agreement
NEDC *or* National Economic Development Council
OECD *or* Organization for Economic Cooperation and Development
Office of Fair Trading
OPEC *or* Organization of Petroleum Exporting Countries
Single European Market Act
Treaty of Rome
TUC *or* Trades Union Congress
UNCTAD *or* United Nations Conference on Trade and Development
UNIDO *or* United Nations Industrial Development Organization
World Bank *or* International Bank for Reconstruction and Development
WTO *or* World Trade Organization

Schools and theories

Austrian school
Chicago school
Classical school
Keynesianism
Marxism
mercantilism
monetarism
neoclassical school
neoKeynesians
Physiocrats
Reaganomics
Rogernomics (*N.Z.*)
Thatcherism

Famous economists

Walter Bagehot [British]
Augustin Cournot [French]
Milton Friedman [U.S.]
Ragnar Frisch [Norwegian]
J(ohn) K(enneth) Galbraith [U.S.]
Friedrich August von Hayek [Austrian-British]
John Maynard Keynes [British]
Arthur Lewis [West Indian]
Thomas Robert Malthus [British]
Alfred Marshall [British]
Karl Marx [German]
Jean Monnet [French]
David Ricardo [British]
Joseph Schumpeter [Austrian]
Adam Smith [British]
Jan Tinbergen [Dutch]
Thorstein Veblen [U.S.]

If all economists were laid end to end, they would not reach a conclusion
George Bernard Shaw

the dismal science
Thomas Carlyle *The Nigger Question*

economize be economical, be frugal, be on a shoestring, be sparing, cut back, draw in one's horns, husband, pull in one's horns, retrench, save, scrimp, tighten one's belt
Antonyms be extravagant, push the boat out (*informal*), spend, splurge, squander

economy frugality, husbandry, parsimony, providence, prudence, restraint, retrenchment, saving, sparingness, thrift, thriftiness

Economy is going without something you do want in case you should, some day, want something you probably won't want
Anthony Hope *The Dolly Dialogues*

Take care of the pence, and the pounds will take care of themselves
William Lowndes

Cut your coat according to your cloth

ecstasy bliss, delight, elation, enthusiasm, euphoria, exaltation, fervour, frenzy, joy, rapture, ravishment, rhapsody, seventh heaven, trance, transport
Antonyms affliction, agony, anguish, distress, hell, misery, pain, suffering, torment, torture

ecstatic blissed out, blissful, cock-a-hoop, delirious, elated, enraptured, enthusiastic, entranced, euphoric, fervent, floating on air, frenzied, in exaltation, in seventh heaven, in transports of delight, joyful, joyous, on cloud nine (*informal*), overjoyed, over the moon (*informal*), rapturous, rhapsodic, sent, transported, walking on air

ecumenical catholic, general, unifying, universal, worldwide

eddy **1.** *noun* counter-current, counterflow, swirl, tideway, undertow, vortex, whirlpool **2.** *verb* swirl, whirl

edge *noun* **1.** border, bound, boundary, brim, brink, contour, flange, fringe, limit, line, lip, margin, outline, perimeter, periphery, rim, side, threshold, verge **2.** acuteness, animation, bite, effectiveness, force, incisiveness, interest, keenness, point, pungency, sharpness, sting, urgency, zest **3.** advantage, ascendancy, dominance, lead, superiority, upper hand **4. on edge** apprehensive, eager, edgy, excited, ill at ease, impatient, irritable, keyed up, nervous, on tenterhooks, tense, tetchy, twitchy (*informal*), uptight (*informal*), wired (*slang*) ~*verb* **5.** bind, border, fringe, hem, rim, shape, trim **6.** creep, ease, inch, sidle, steal, work, worm **7.** hone, sharpen, strop, whet

edginess anxiety, irascibility, irritability, jitters (*informal*), nerves, nervousness, nervous tension, prickliness, restiveness, tenseness, tetchiness, touchiness, twitchiness

edgy anxious, ill at ease, irascible, irritable, keyed up, nervous, nervy (*Brit. informal*), neurotic, on edge, on pins and needles, on tenterhooks, restive, tense, tetchy, touchy, twitchy (*informal*), uptight (*informal*), wired (*slang*)

edible comestible (*rare*), digestible, eatable, esculent, fit to eat, good, harmless, palatable, wholesome

Antonyms baneful, harmful, indigestible, inedible, noxious, pernicious, poisonous, uneatable

edict act, canon, command, decree, demand, dictate, dictum, enactment, fiat, injunction, law, mandate, manifesto, order, ordinance, proclamation, pronouncement, pronunciamento, regulation, ruling, statute, ukase (*rare*)

edification education, elevation, enlightenment, guidance, improvement, information, instruction, nurture, schooling, teaching, tuition, uplifting

edifice building, construction, erection, fabric (*rare*), habitation, house, pile, structure

edify educate, elevate, enlighten, guide, improve, inform, instruct, nurture, school, teach, uplift

edifying elevating, enlightening, improving, inspiring, instructional, uplifting

edit **1.** adapt, annotate, censor, check, condense, correct, emend, polish, redact, rephrase, revise, rewrite **2.** assemble, compose, put together, rearrange, reorder, select

edition copy, impression, issue, number, printing, programme (*TV, Radio*), version, volume

educate civilize, coach, cultivate, develop, discipline, drill, edify, enlighten, exercise, foster, improve, indoctrinate, inform, instruct, mature, rear, school, teach, train, tutor

educated **1.** coached, informed, instructed, nurtured, schooled, taught, tutored **2.** civilized, cultivated, cultured, enlightened, experienced, informed, knowledgeable, learned, lettered, literary, polished, refined, sophisticated, tasteful

Antonyms (*sense 1*) ignorant, illiterate, uneducated, unlettered, unread, unschooled, untaught (*sense 2*) benighted, lowbrow, philistine, uncultivated, uncultured, uneducated

education breeding, civilization, coaching, cultivation, culture, development, discipline, drilling, edification, enlightenment, erudition, improvement, indoctrination, instruction, knowledge, nurture, scholarship, schooling, teaching, training, tuition, tutoring

Educational institutions

academe (*literary*)
academy
alma mater
approved school (*Brit.*)
boarding school
choir school (*Brit.*)
city technology college *or* CTC (*Brit.*)
civic university (*Brit.*)
classical college (*Canad.*)
co-ed (*Brit.*)
college
college of advanced technology *or* CAT
college of education
collegiate institute (*Canad.*)
community college
community home
community school (*Brit.*)
composite school (*Canad.*)
comprehensive *or* comprehensive school (*chiefly Brit.*)
convent *or* convent school
correspondence school
council school
dame school (*old-fashioned*)
day school
direct-grant school (*Brit. old-fashioned*)
district high school (*N.Z.*)
elementary school (*Brit. old-fashioned*)
finishing school
first school (*Brit.*)
grade school (*U.S.*)
grammar school (*U.S.*)
Great Public Schools *or* GPS (*Austral.*)
hedge-school (*Irish history*)
hostel (*Canad.*)
independent school
infant school
integrated school (*N.Z.*)
intermediate school (*N.Z.*)
Ivy League
junior college (*U.S. & Canad.*)
junior school
kindergarten
kindy *or* kindie (*Austral. & N.Z.*)
land grant university (*U.S.*)
List D school (*Scot.*)
magnet school
maintained school
middle school (*Brit.*)
mixed school
multiversity (*chiefly U.S. & Canad.*)
National School
night school
normal school
nursery *or* nursery school
Open College
Open University
polytechnic
preparatory school, prep school *or* (*chiefly U.S.*) prep
primary school
private school
public school
ragged school (*Brit.*)
reformatory *or* reform school
residential school
Sabbath school (*chiefly U.S.*)
schola cantorum
secondary modern school (*Brit. old-fashioned*)
secondary school

seminary
separate school (*Canad.*)
single-sex school
sixth-form college
special school (*Brit.*)
state school
summer school
Sunday school
technical college *or* (*informal*) tech (*Brit.*)
tertiary college (*Brit.*)
trade school
university *or* (*informal*) uni
varsity (*Brit. & N.Z. informal*)
village college
yeshiva

Academic awards	**Abbreviations**
Bachelor of Agriculture	BAgr
Bachelor of Arts	BA
Bachelor of Commerce	BCom
Bachelor of Dental Surgery	BDS
Bachelor of Divinity	BD
Bachelor of Education	BEd
Bachelor of Engineering	BEng
Bachelor of Law	BL
Bachelor of Laws	LLB
Bachelor of Letters	BLitt
Bachelor of Medicine	BM *or* MB
Bachelor of Music	BMus, MusB *or* MusBac
Bachelor of Pharmacy	BPharm
Bachelor of Philosophy	BPhil
Bachelor of Science	BSc
Bachelor of Surgery	BS
Diploma in Education	DipEd
Doctor of Dental Surgery or Science	DDS *or* DDSc
Doctor of Divinity	DD
Doctor of Laws	LLD
Doctor of Letters or Literature	DLitt *or* LittD
Doctor of Medicine	MD
Doctor of Music	DMus, MusD *or* MusDoc
Doctor of Philosophy	PhD
Higher National Certificate	HNC
Higher National Diploma	HND
Master of Arts	MA
Master of Education	MEd
Master of Laws	LLM
Master of Letters	MLitt
Master of Music	MMus
Master of Philosophy	MPhil
Master of Science	MSc
Master of Surgery	MCh
Master of Technology	MTech
Ordinary National Certificate	ONC
Ordinary National Diploma	OND

Education terms
A bursary (*N.Z.*)
academic
accredit (*N.Z.*)
accumulation
Advanced level *or* A level (*Brit.*)
adviser *or* advisor (*Brit.*)
advisory teacher (*Brit.*)
aegrotat (*Brit.*)
alumnus *or* alumna (*chiefly U.S. & Canad.*)
assignment
assistant (*U.S. & Canad.*)
associate (*U.S. & Canad.*)
baccalaureate
banding (*Brit.*)
battels (*Brit.*)
B bursary (*N.Z.*)
bedder (*Brit.*)
binary
boarder (*Brit.*)
boarding house (*Austral.*)
bubs grade (*Austral. & N.Z. slang*)
bursar
bursarial
bursary *or* bursarship (*Scot. & N.Z.*)
campus
campus university
catalogue (*U.S. & Canad.*)
catchment (*Brit.*)
Certificate of Prevocational Education *or* CPVE (*Brit.*)
Certificate of Proficiency *or* COP (*N.Z.*)
chancellor (*Brit., U.S., & Canad.*)
chapterhouse (*U.S.*)
class
classmate
classroom
co-ed (*U.S.*)
coeducation
collegial
collegian
collegiate
comedown (*Brit.*)
commencement (*U.S. & Canad.*)
commoner (*Brit.*)
Common Entrance (*Brit.*)
conductive education
congregation (*chiefly Brit.*)
continuous assessment
convocation
core subjects (*Brit.*)
coursework
crammer
credit
crib (*Brit.*)
cross-curricular (*Brit.*)
Cuisenaire rod (*Trademark*)
curricular
curriculum
dean
deanery
degree
delegacy
department
detention
dissertation
docent (*U.S.*)
dominie (*Scot.*)
don (*Brit.*)
donnish
dropout
dunce
dunce cap
dux
Easter term
educate
education
educational
eleven-plus (*obsolete*)
emeritus
entry
essay
examination *or* exam
exercise
exhibition (*Brit. & Austral.*)
exhibitioner (*Brit.*)
expel
extension
external
extracurricular
extramural

faculty
fail
family grouping *or* vertical grouping
federal
fellow
fellowship
ferule
flunk (*chiefly U.S., Canad. & N.Z. informal*)
fresher *or* freshman
full professor (*U.S. & Canad.*)
further education (*Brit.*)
gaudy (*Brit.*)
General Certificate of Education *or* GCE (*Brit.*)
General Certificate of Secondary Education *or* GCSE (*Brit.*)
gown
grade (*U.S. & Canad.*)
graded post (*Brit.*)
graduand (*chiefly Brit.*)
graduate (*Brit., U.S. & Canad.*)
graduation
grant
grant-in-aid
grant-maintained
Great Public Schools *or* GPS (*Austral.*)
Greats (*Brit.*)
gymnasium
hall
hall of residence
headmaster
headmastership
headmistress
headmistress-ship
headship (*Brit.*)
higher (*Scot.*)
high school
Hilary term
homework
honours *or* (*U.S.*) honors
hood
hooky *or* hookey (*chiefly U.S., Canad. & N.Z. informal*)
house
housefather
housemaster
housemother
imposition (*Brit.*)
incept (*Brit.*)
infant (*Brit.*)
in residence
instructor (*U.S. & Canad.*)
internal
interscholastic
intramural (*chiefly U.S. & Canad.*)
invigilate (*Brit.*)
invigilator (*Brit.*)
janitor (*Scot.*)
jig (*Austral. slang*)
junior
junior common room
key stage (*Brit.*)
lecture
lecturer
level of attainment (*Brit.*)
liaison officer (*N.Z.*)
lines
literae humaniores (*Brit.*)
LMS *or* local management of schools (*Brit.*)
local examinations
lowerclassman (*U.S.*)
lower school
lycée (*chiefly French*)
manciple
marking
master
matriculate
matriculation *or* matric
mature student
Michaelmas term
middle common room
midterm
mistress
mitch *or* mich (*dialect*)
mocks (*informal*)
moderator (*Brit. & N.Z.*)
muck-up day (*Austral. slang*)
National Curriculum (*Brit.*)
Nuffield teaching project (*Brit.*)
open learning
Ordinary grade *or* O grade (*Scot.*)
Ordinary level *or* O level (*Brit.*)
Ordinary National Certificate *or* ONC (*Brit.*)
pandy (*chiefly Scot. & Irish*)
parent teacher association *or* PTA
parietal (*U.S.*)
pass
pedant (*archaic*)
pipe (*U.S. slang*)
porter
postgraduate
prefect (*Brit.*)
prelims (*Scot.*)
prepositor (*Brit., rare*)
primers (*N.Z. informal*)
principal
Privatdocent
proctor (*U.S.*)
professor
professoriate
prospectus
provost
punishment exercise
reader (*chiefly Brit.*)
readership (*chiefly Brit.*)
reception (*Brit.*)
recess (*U.S. & Canad.*)
record of achievement (*Brit.*)
recreation
rector (*chiefly Brit.*)
redbrick (*Brit.*)
refresher course
regent
registrar
Regius professor (*Brit.*)
remedial
remove (*Brit.*)
report (*Brit.*)
resit
rusticate (*Brit.*)
sabbatical
sandwich course
SCE *or* Scottish Certificate of Education
scholastic
School Certificate (*Brit. old-fashioned & N.Z.*)
schoolleaver
schoolman
schoolmarm
schoolmaster
schoolmistress
schoolteacher
second (*Brit.*)
self-educated
semester (*chiefly U.S. & Canad.*)
seminar
senate
send down
senior
senior common room
session
set
shell (*Brit.*)
sixth form (*Brit.*)
sixth-form college (*Brit.*)
sizar (*Brit.*)
sophomore (*chiefly U.S. & Canad.*)
sorority (*chiefly U.S.*)
speech day (*Brit.*)
sports day (*Brit.*)
stage
Standard Grade (*Scot.*)
standard assessment tasks *or* SATS (*Brit.*)
statement (*Brit.*)
stream (*Brit.*)
student teacher
subject
subprincipal
summa cum laude
summative assessment (*Brit.*)
supervisor
teach-in
term
tertiary bursary (*Brit.*)
test
thesis
transcript (*chiefly U.S. & Canad.*)
transfer
trimester (*chiefly U.S. & Canad.*)
Trinity term
truant
tuition
tutee
tutor
tutorial
tutorial system
union
university entrance (examination) *or* UE (*N.Z.*)
undergraduate
unstreamed (*Brit.*)
upper school
vice chancellor (*Brit.*)
visiting professor

wag (*slang*) wrangler (*Brit.*)
warden (*Brit.*) year

The roots of education are bitter, but the fruit is sweet
Aristophanes

Education makes a people easy to lead, but difficult to drive; easy to govern, but impossible to enslave
Lord Henry Brougham

To live for a time close to great minds is the best education
John Buchan *Memory Hold the Door*

Education made us what we are
C.A. Helvétus *Discours XXX*

'Tis education forms the common mind,
Just as the twig is bent, the tree's inclined
Alexander Pope *Epistles to Several Persons*

Even while they teach, men learn
Seneca *Letters*

Education is what survives when what has been learnt has been forgotten
B.F. Skinner *Education in 1984*

Anyone who has passed through the regular gradations of a classical education, and is not made a fool by it, may consider himself as having had a very narrow escape
William Hazlitt *The Ignorance of the Learned*

When you educate a man you educate an individual; when you educate a woman you educate a whole family
Charles D. McIver

Men must be born free; they cannot be born wise, and it is the duty of any university to make free men wise
Adlai Stevenson

There is no such whetstone, to sharpen a good wit and encourage a will to learning, as is praise
Roger Ascham *The Schoolmaster*

education: that which discloses to the wise and disguises from the foolish their lack of understanding
Ambrose Bierce *The Devil's Dictionary*

Better build schoolrooms for 'the boy' than cells and gibbets for 'the man'
Eliza Cook *A Song for the Ragged Schools*

educational cultural, didactic, edifying, educative, enlightening, heuristic, improving, informative, instructive

educative didactic, edifying, educational, enlightening, heuristic, improving, informative, instructive

educator coach, edifier, educationalist *or* educationist, instructor, pedagogue, schoolmaster, schoolmistress, schoolteacher, teacher, trainer, tutor

educe **1.** come out, develop, evolve **2.** bring forth, bring out, derive, draw out, elicit, evoke, extract **3.** *Logic* conclude, deduce, infer

eerie awesome, creepy (*informal*), eldritch (*poetic*), fearful, frightening, ghostly, mysterious, scary (*informal*), spectral, spooky (*informal*), strange, uncanny, unearthly, uneasy, weird

efface **1.** annihilate, blot out, cancel, cross out, delete, destroy, dim, eradicate, erase, excise, expunge, extirpate, obliterate, raze, rub out, wipe out **2.** *of oneself* be modest (bashful, diffident, retiring, timid, unassertive), humble, lower, make inconspicuous, withdraw

effect *noun* **1.** aftermath, conclusion, consequence, end result, event, fruit, issue, outcome, result, upshot **2.** clout (*informal*), effectiveness, efficacy, efficiency, fact, force, influence, power, reality, strength, use, validity, vigour, weight **3.** drift, essence, impact, import, impression, meaning, purport, purpose, sense, significance, tenor **4.** action, enforcement, execution, force, implementation, operation **5.** **in effect** actually, effectively, essentially, for practical purposes, in actuality, in fact, in reality, in truth, really, to all intents and purposes, virtually **6.** **take effect** become operative, begin, come into force, produce results, work *~verb* **7.** accomplish, achieve, actuate, bring about, carry out, cause, complete, consummate, create, effectuate, execute, fulfil, give rise to, initiate, make, perform, produce

effective **1.** able, active, adequate, capable, competent, effectual, efficacious, efficient, energetic, operative, productive, serviceable, useful **2.** cogent, compelling, convincing, emphatic, forceful, forcible, impressive, moving, persuasive, potent, powerful, striking, telling **3.** active, actual, current, in effect, in execution, in force, in operation, operative, real
Antonyms feeble, futile, inactive, inadequate, incompetent, ineffective, ineffectual, inefficient, inoperative, insufficient, pathetic, powerless, tame, unimpressive, unproductive, useless, vain, weak, worthless

effectiveness bottom, capability, clout (*informal*), cogency, effect, efficacy, efficiency, force, influence, potency, power, strength, success, use, validity, vigour, weight

effects belongings, chattels, furniture, gear, goods, movables, paraphernalia, possessions, property, things, trappings

effectual **1.** capable, effective, efficacious, efficient, forcible, influential, potent, powerful, productive, serviceable, successful, telling, useful **2.** authoritative, binding, in force, lawful, legal, licit (*rare*), sound, valid

effectuate accomplish, achieve, bring about, carry out *or* through, cause, complete, create, do, effect, execute, fulfil, make, perform, procure, produce

effeminacy delicacy, femininity, softness, tenderness, unmanliness, weakness, womanishness, womanliness

effeminate camp (*informal*), delicate, feminine, poofy (*slang*), sissy, soft, tender, unmanly, weak, wimpish *or* wimpy (*informal*), womanish, womanlike, womanly
Antonyms butch (*slang*), he-man (*informal*), macho, manly, virile

effervesce bubble, ferment, fizz, foam, froth, sparkle

effervescence **1.** bubbling, ferment, fermentation, fizz, foam, foaming, froth, frothing, sparkle **2.** animation, brio, buoyancy, ebullience, enthusiasm, excitedness, excitement, exhilaration, exuberance, gaiety, high spirits, liveliness, pizzazz *or* pizazz (*informal*), vim (*slang*), vitality, vivacity, zing (*informal*)

effervescent **1.** bubbling, bubbly, carbonated, fermenting, fizzing, fizzy, foaming, foamy, frothing, frothy, sparkling **2.** animated, bubbly, buoyant, ebullient, enthusiastic, excited, exhilarated, exuberant, gay, in high spirits, irrepressible, lively, merry, vital, vivacious, zingy (*informal*)
Antonyms boring, dull, flat, flavourless, insipid, jejune, lacklustre, lifeless, spiritless, stale, unexciting, vapid, watery, weak

effete **1.** corrupt, debased, decadent, decayed, decrepit, degenerate, dissipated, enervated, enfeebled, feeble, ineffectual, overrefined, spoiled, weak **2.** burnt out, drained, enervated, exhausted, played out, spent, used up, wasted, worn out **3.** barren, fruitless, infecund, infertile, sterile, unfruitful, unproductive, unprolific

efficacious active, adequate, capable, competent, effective, effectual, efficient, energetic, operative, potent, powerful, productive, serviceable, successful, useful
Antonyms abortive, futile, ineffective, ineffectual, inefficacious, unavailing, unproductive, unsuccessful, useless

efficacy ability, capability, competence, effect, effectiveness, efficaciousness, efficiency, energy, force, influence, potency, power, strength, success, use, vigour, virtue, weight

efficiency ability, adeptness, capability, competence, economy, effectiveness, efficacy, power, productivity, proficiency, readiness, skilfulness, skill

efficient able, adept, businesslike, capable, competent, economic, effective, effectual, organized, powerful, productive, proficient, ready, skilful, well-organized, workmanlike
Antonyms cowboy (*informal*), disorganized, incompetent, ineffectual, inefficient, inept, slipshod, sloppy, unbusinesslike, unproductive, wasteful

effigy dummy, figure, guy, icon, idol, image, likeness, picture, portrait, representation, statue

effluence discharge, effluent, effluvium, efflux, emanation, emission, exhalation, flow, issue, outflow, outpouring, secretion

effluent *noun* **1.** effluvium, pollutant, sewage, waste **2.** discharge, effluence, efflux, emanation, emission, exhalation, flow, issue, outflow, outpouring *~adjective* **3.** discharged, emanating, emitted, outflowing

effluvium exhalation, exhaust, fumes, malodour, mephitis, miasma, niff (*Brit. slang*), odour, pong (*Brit. informal*), reek, smell, stench, stink

effort **1.** application, blood, sweat, and tears (*informal*), elbow grease (*facetious*), endeavour, energy, exertion, force, labour, pains, power, strain, stress, stretch, striving, struggle, toil, travail (*literary*), trouble, work **2.** attempt, endeavour, essay, go (*informal*), shot (*informal*), stab (*informal*), try **3.** accomplishment, achievement, act, creation, deed, feat, job, product, production

> *Lovely it is, when the winds are churning up the waves on the great sea, to gaze out from the land on the great efforts of someone else*
> Lucretius *De Rerum Natura*

> *Whatever is worth doing at all is worth doing well*
> Lord Chesterfield *Letter to his son*

> *Whatsoever thy hand findeth to do, do it with thy might*
> Bible: Ecclesiastes

effortless easy, easy-peasy (*slang*), facile, painless, plain sailing, simple, smooth, uncomplicated, undemanding, untroublesome
Antonyms demanding, difficult, formidable, hard, onerous, uphill

effrontery arrogance, assurance, audacity, boldness, brashness, brass (*informal*), brass neck (*Brit. informal*), brazenness, cheek (*informal*), cheekiness, chutzpah (*U.S. & Canad. informal*), disrespect, face (*informal*), front, gall (*informal*), impertinence, impudence, incivility, insolence, neck (*informal*), nerve, presumption, rudeness, shamelessness, temerity

effulgence blaze, brightness, brilliance, dazzle, fire, flame, fluorescence, glow, incandescence, luminosity, lustre, radiance, refulgence (*literary*), resplendence, shine, splendour, vividness

effulgent beaming, blazing, bright, brilliant, Day-Glo, dazzling, flaming, fluorescent, fulgent (*poetic*), glowing, incandescent, lucent, luminous, lustrous, radiant, refulgent (*literary*), resplendent, shining, splendid, vivid

effusion **1.** discharge, effluence, efflux, emission, gush, issue, outflow, outpouring, shedding, stream **2.** address, outpouring, speech, talk, utterance, writing

effusive demonstrative, ebullient, enthusiastic, expansive, extravagant, exuberant, free-flowing, fulsome, gushing, lavish, overflowing, profuse, talkative, unreserved, unrestrained, wordy

egg on encourage, exhort, goad, incite, prod, prompt, push, spur, urge
Antonyms deter, discourage, dissuade, hold back, put off, talk out of

egocentric egoistic, egoistical, egotistic, egotistical, self-centred, selfish

egoism egocentricity, egomania, egotism, narcissism, self-absorption, self-centredness, self-importance, self-interest, selfishness, self-love, self-regard, self-seeking

egoist egomaniac, egotist, narcissist, self-seeker

egoistic, egoistical egocentric, egomaniacal, egotistic, egotistical, full of oneself, narcissistic, self-absorbed, self-centred, self-important, self-seeking

egotism conceitedness, egocentricity, egoism, egomania, narcissism, self-admiration, self-centredness, self-conceit, self-esteem, self-importance, self-love, self-praise, superiority, vainglory, vanity

egotist bighead (*informal*), blowhard (*informal*), boaster, braggadocio, braggart, egoist, egomaniac, self-admirer, swaggerer

egotist: a person of low taste, more interested in himself than in me
Ambrose Bierce *The Devil's Dictionary*

egotistic, egotistical boasting, bragging, conceited, egocentric, egoistic, egoistical, egomaniacal, full of oneself, narcissistic, opinionated, self-admiring, self-centred, self-important, superior, vain, vainglorious

egregious arrant, enormous, flagrant, glaring, grievous, gross, heinous, infamous, insufferable, intolerable, monstrous, notorious, outrageous, rank, scandalous, shocking

egress departure, emergence, escape, exit, exodus, issue, outlet, passage out, vent, way out, withdrawal

ejaculate **1.** discharge, eject, emit, spurt **2.** blurt out, burst out, cry out, exclaim, shout

ejaculation **1.** cry, exclamation, shout **2.** discharge, ejection, emission, spurt

eject **1.** cast out, discharge, disgorge, emit, expel, spew, spout, throw out, vomit **2.** banish, boot out (*informal*), bounce (*slang*), deport, dispossess, drive out, evacuate, evict, exile, expel, give the bum's rush (*slang*), oust, relegate, remove, show one the door, throw out, throw out on one's ear (*informal*), turn out **3.** discharge, dislodge, dismiss, fire (*informal*), get rid of, kick out (*informal*), oust, sack (*informal*), throw out

ejection **1.** casting out, disgorgement, expulsion, spouting, throwing out **2.** banishment, deportation, dispossession, evacuation, eviction, exile, expulsion, ouster (*Law*), removal, the bum's rush (*slang*) **3.** discharge, dislodgement, dismissal, firing (*informal*), sacking (*informal*), the boot (*slang*), the sack (*informal*)

eke out **1.** be economical with, be frugal with, be sparing with, economize on, husband, stretch out **2.** add to, enlarge, increase, make up (with), supplement

elaborate *adjective* **1.** careful, detailed, exact, intricate, laboured, minute, painstaking, perfected, precise, skilful, studied, thorough **2.** complex, complicated, decorated, detailed, extravagant, fancy, fussy, involved, ornamented, ornate, ostentatious, showy *~verb* **3.** add detail, amplify, complicate, decorate, develop, devise, embellish, enhance, enlarge, expand (upon), flesh out, garnish, improve, ornament, polish, produce, refine, work out
Antonyms *adjective* basic, minimal, modest, plain, severe, simple, unadorned, unembellished, unfussy *~verb* abbreviate, condense, put in a nutshell, reduce to essentials, simplify, streamline, summarize, truncate

élan animation, brio, dash, esprit, flair, impetuosity, panache, spirit, style, verve, vigour, vivacity, zest

elapse glide by, go, go by, lapse, pass, pass by, roll by, roll on, slip away, slip by

elastic **1.** ductile, flexible, plastic, pliable, pliant, resilient, rubbery, springy, stretchable, stretchy, supple, tensile, yielding **2.** accommodating, adaptable, adjustable, complaisant, compliant, flexible, supple, tolerant, variable, yielding **3.** bouncy, buoyant, irrepressible, resilient
Antonyms firm, immovable, inflexible, intractable, obdurate, resolute, rigid, set, stiff, strict, stringent, unyielding

elasticity **1.** ductileness, ductility, flexibility, give (*informal*), plasticity, pliability, pliancy, pliantness, resilience, rubberiness, springiness, stretch, stretchiness, suppleness **2.** adaptability, adjustability, complaisance, compliantness, flexibility, suppleness, tolerance, variability **3.** bounce (*informal*), buoyancy, irrepressibility, resilience

elated animated, blissed out, blissful, cheered, cock-a-hoop, delighted, ecstatic, elevated, euphoric, excited, exhilarated, exultant, floating *or* walking on air, gleeful, in high spirits, in seventh heaven, joyful, joyous, jubilant, overjoyed, over the moon (*informal*), proud, puffed up, rapt, roused, sent
Antonyms dejected, depressed, discouraged,

dispirited, downcast, down in the dumps (*informal*), miserable, sad, unhappy, woebegone

elation bliss, delight, ecstasy, euphoria, exaltation, exhilaration, exultation, glee, high spirits, joy, joyfulness, joyousness, jubilation, rapture

elbow *noun* **1.** angle, bend, corner, joint, turn **2. at one's elbow** at hand, close by, handy, near, to hand, within reach **3. out at elbow(s)** beggarly, down at heel, impoverished, in rags, ragged, seedy, shabby, tattered **4. rub elbows with** associate, fraternize, hang out (*informal*), hobnob, mingle, mix, socialize **5. up to the elbows** absorbed, busy, engaged, engrossed, immersed, occupied, tied up, up to the ears, wrapped up *~verb* **6.** bump, crowd, hustle, jostle, knock, nudge, push, shoulder, shove

elbowroom freedom, latitude, leeway, play, room, scope, space

elder *adjective* **1.** ancient, earlier born, first-born, older, senior *~noun* **2.** older person, senior **3.** *Presbyterianism* church official, office bearer, presbyter

elect **1.** *verb* appoint, choose, decide upon, designate, determine, opt for, pick, pick out, prefer, select, settle on, vote **2.** *adjective* choice, chosen, elite, hand-picked, picked, preferred, select, selected

election appointment, choice, choosing, decision, determination, judgment, preference, selection, vote, voting

Elections are won by men and women chiefly because most people vote against somebody rather than for somebody
Franklin P. Adams *Nods and Becks*

elector chooser, constituent, selector, voter

electric *figurative* charged, dynamic, exciting, rousing, stimulating, stirring, tense, thrilling

electrify *figurative* amaze, animate, astonish, astound, excite, fire, galvanize, invigorate, jolt, rouse, shock, startle, stimulate, stir, take one's breath away, thrill
Antonyms be tedious, bore, fatigue, jade, send to sleep, weary

eleemosynary almsgiving, altruistic, benevolent, charitable, philanthropic

elegance, elegancy **1.** beauty, courtliness, dignity, exquisiteness, gentility, grace, gracefulness, grandeur, luxury, polish, politeness, refinement, sumptuousness **2.** discernment, distinction, propriety, style, taste

elegant **1.** à la mode, artistic, beautiful, chic, choice, comely, courtly, cultivated, delicate, exquisite, fashionable, fine, genteel, graceful, handsome, luxurious, modish, nice, polished, refined, stylish, sumptuous, tasteful, urbane **2.** appropriate, apt, clever, effective, ingenious, neat, simple
Antonyms (*sense 1*) awkward, clumsy, coarse, gauche, graceless, inelegant, misshapen, plain, tasteless, tawdry, ugly, uncouth, undignified, ungraceful, unrefined

elegiac dirgeful, funereal, keening, lamenting, melancholy, mournful, nostalgic, plaintive, sad, threnodial, threnodic, valedictory

elegy coronach (*Scot. & Irish*), dirge, keen, lament, plaint (*archaic*), requiem, threnody

element **1.** basis, component, constituent, essential factor, factor, feature, hint, ingredient, member, part, section, subdivision, trace, unit **2.** domain, environment, field, habitat, medium, milieu, sphere

elemental **1.** basic, elementary, essential, fundamental, original, primal, primitive, primordial **2.** atmospheric, meteorological, natural

elementary **1.** clear, easy, facile, plain, rudimentary, simple, straightforward, uncomplicated **2.** basic, bog-standard (*informal*), elemental, fundamental, initial, introductory, original, primary, rudimentary
Antonyms advanced, complex, complicated, higher, highly-developed, progressive, secondary, sophisticated

elements **1.** basics, essentials, foundations, fundamentals, nuts and bolts (*informal*), principles, rudiments **2.** atmospheric conditions, atmospheric forces, powers of nature, weather

elephantine bulky, clumsy, enormous, heavy, huge, hulking, humongous *or* humungous (*U.S. slang*), immense, laborious, lumbering, massive, monstrous, ponderous, weighty

elevate **1.** heighten, hoist, lift, lift up, raise, uplift, upraise **2.** advance, aggrandize, exalt, prefer, promote, upgrade **3.** animate, boost, brighten, buoy up, cheer, elate, excite, exhilarate, hearten, lift up, perk up, raise, rouse, uplift **4.** augment, boost, heighten, increase, intensify, magnify, swell

elevated **1.** dignified, exalted, grand, high, high-flown, high-minded, inflated, lofty, noble, sublime **2.** animated, bright, cheerful, cheery, elated, excited, exhilarated, gleeful, in high spirits, overjoyed
Antonyms (*sense 1*) humble, lowly, modest, simple

elevation **1.** altitude, height **2.** acclivity, eminence, height, hill, hillock, mountain, rise, rising ground **3.** exaltedness, grandeur, loftiness, nobility, nobleness, sublimity **4.** advancement, aggrandizement, exaltation, preferment, promotion, upgrading

elfin arch, charming, elfish, elflike, elvish, frolicsome, impish, ludic (*literary*), mischievous, playful, prankish, puckish, sprightly

elicit bring forth, bring out, bring to light, call forth, cause, derive, draw out, educe, evoke, evolve, exact, extort, extract, give rise to, obtain, wrest

eligible acceptable, appropriate, desirable, fit, preferable, proper, qualified, suitable, suited, worthy
Antonyms inappropriate, ineligible, unacceptable, unqualified, unsuitable, unsuited

eliminate 1. cut out, dispose of, do away with, eradicate, exterminate, get rid of, get shot of, remove, stamp out, take out, wipe from the face of the earth 2. axe (*informal*), dispense with, disregard, drop, eject, exclude, expel, ignore, knock out, leave out, omit, put out, reject, throw out 3. *slang* annihilate, blow away (*slang, chiefly U.S.*), bump off (*slang*), kill, liquidate, murder, rub out (*U.S. slang*), slay, take out (*slang*), terminate, waste (*informal*)

elite 1. *noun* aristocracy, best, cream, *crème de la crème*, elect, flower, gentry, high society, nobility, pick, upper class 2. *adjective* aristocratic, best, choice, crack (*slang*), elect, exclusive, first-class, noble, pick, selected, upper-class
Antonyms *noun* dregs, hoi polloi, rabble, riff-raff

elixir 1. cure-all, nostrum, panacea, sovereign remedy 2. concentrate, essence, extract, pith, principle, quintessence 3. mixture, potion, solution, syrup, tincture

elliptical 1. oval 2. abstruse, ambiguous, concentrated, concise, condensed, cryptic, laconic, obscure, recondite, terse

elocution articulation, declamation, delivery, diction, enunciation, oratory, pronunciation, public speaking, rhetoric, speech, speechmaking, utterance, voice production

elongate draw out, extend, lengthen, make longer, prolong, protract, stretch

elongated drawn out, extended, long, long-drawn-out, prolonged, protracted, stretched

elope abscond, bolt, decamp, disappear, escape, leave, run away, run off, slip away, steal away

eloquence expression, expressiveness, fluency, forcefulness, oratory, persuasiveness, rhetoric, way with words

eloquent 1. articulate, fluent, forceful, graceful, moving, persuasive, silver-tongued, stirring, well-expressed 2. expressive, meaningful, pregnant, revealing, suggestive, telling, vivid
Antonyms faltering, halting, hesitant, inarticulate, speechless, stumbling, tongue-tied, wordless

elsewhere abroad, absent, away, hence (*archaic*), in *or* to another place, not here, not present, somewhere else

elucidate annotate, clarify, clear the air, clear up, explain, explicate, expound, gloss, illuminate, illustrate, interpret, make plain, shed *or* throw light upon, spell out, unfold

elucidation annotation, clarification, comment, commentary, explanation, explication, exposition, gloss, illumination, illustration, interpretation

elude 1. avoid, body-swerve (*Scot.*), circumvent, dodge, duck (*informal*), escape, evade, flee, get away from, outrun, shirk, shun, slip through one's fingers, slip through the net 2. baffle, be beyond (someone), confound, escape, foil, frustrate, puzzle, stump, thwart

elusive 1. difficult to catch, shifty, slippery, tricky 2. baffling, fleeting, indefinable, intangible, puzzling, subtle, transient, transitory 3. ambiguous, deceitful, deceptive, elusory, equivocal, evasive, fallacious, fraudulent, illusory, misleading, oracular, unspecific

Elysian blessed, blissful, celestial, charming, delightful, enchanting, glorious, happy, heavenly, paradisiac, paradisiacal, ravishing, seraphic

emaciated atrophied, attenuate, attenuated, cadaverous, gaunt, haggard, lank, lean, macilent (*rare*), meagre, pinched, scrawny, skeletal, skin and bone, thin, undernourished, wasted

emaciation atrophy, attenuation, gauntness, haggardness, leanness, meagreness, scrawniness, thinness, wasting away

emanate 1. arise, come forth, derive, emerge, flow, issue, originate, proceed, spring, stem 2. discharge, emit, exhale, give off, give out, issue, radiate, send forth

emanation 1. arising, derivation, emergence, flow, origination, proceeding 2. discharge, effluent, efflux, effusion, emission, exhalation, radiation

emancipate deliver, discharge, disencumber, disenthral, enfranchise, free, liberate, manumit, release, set free, unbridle, unchain, unfetter, unshackle
Antonyms bind, capture, enchain, enslave, enthral, fetter, shackle, subjugate, yoke

emancipation deliverance, discharge, enfranchisement, freedom, liberation, liberty, manumission, release
Antonyms bondage, captivity, confinement, detention, enthralment, imprisonment, servitude, slavery, thraldom

emasculate 1. castrate, geld 2. cripple, debilitate, deprive of force, enervate, impoverish, soften, weaken

embalm 1. mummify, preserve 2. *of memories* cherish, consecrate, conserve, enshrine, immortalize, store, treasure 3. *poetic* make fragrant, perfume, scent

embargo 1. *noun* ban, bar, barrier, block, blockage, boycott, check, hindrance, impediment, interdict, interdiction, prohibition, pro~ scription, restraint, restriction, stoppage **2.** *verb* ban, bar, block, boycott, check, impede, interdict, prohibit, proscribe, restrict, stop

embark **1.** board ship, go aboard, put on board, take on board, take ship **2.** *with* **on** *or* **upon** begin, broach, commence, engage, enter, get the show on the road (*informal*), initiate, launch, plunge into, set about, set out, start, take up, undertake
Antonyms (*sense 1*) alight, arrive, get off, go ashore, land, step out of

embarrass abash, chagrin, confuse, discomfit, discompose, disconcert, discountenance, dis~ tress, faze, fluster, mortify, put out of counte~ nance, shame, show up (*informal*)

embarrassed ashamed, awkward, blushing, caught with egg on one's face, chagrined, con~ fused, discomfited, disconcerted, discoun~ tenanced, flustered, humiliated, mortified, not know where to put oneself, put out of counte~ nance, red-faced, self-conscious, sheepish, shown-up, thrown, upset, wishing the earth would swallow one up

embarrassing awkward, blush-making, com~ promising, cringe-making (*Brit. informal*), discomfiting, disconcerting, distressing, hu~ miliating, mortifying, sensitive, shameful, shaming, touchy, tricky, uncomfortable

embarrassment **1.** awkwardness, bashfulness, chagrin, confusion, discomfiture, discompo~ sure, distress, humiliation, mortification, self-consciousness, shame, showing up (*infor~ mal*) **2.** bind (*informal*), difficulty, mess, pickle (*informal*), predicament, scrape (*informal*) **3.** excess, overabundance, superabundance, superfluity, surfeit, surplus

embed dig in, drive in, fix, hammer in, im~ plant, plant, ram in, root, set, sink

embellish adorn, beautify, bedeck, deck, deco~ rate, dress up, elaborate, embroider, enhance, enrich, exaggerate, festoon, garnish, gild, gild the lily, grace, ornament, tart up (*slang*), var~ nish

embellishment adornment, decoration, elabo~ ration, embroidery, enhancement, enrichment, exaggeration, gilding, ornament, ornamenta~ tion, trimming

embers ashes, cinders, live coals

embezzle abstract, appropriate, defalcate (*Law*), filch, have one's hand in the till (*infor~ mal*), misapply, misappropriate, misuse, pecu~ late, pilfer, purloin, rip off (*slang*), steal

embezzlement abstraction, appropriation, de~ falcation (*Law*), filching, fraud, larceny, mis~ application, misappropriation, misuse, pecula~ tion, pilferage, pilfering, purloining, stealing, theft, thieving

embitter **1.** alienate, anger, disaffect, disillu~ sion, envenom, make bitter *or* resentful, poi~ son, sour **2.** aggravate, exacerbate, exasperate, worsen

embittered acid, angry, at daggers drawn (*in~ formal*), bitter, disaffected, disillusioned, nursing a grudge, rancorous, resentful, sour, soured, venomous, with a chip on one's shoul~ der (*informal*)

emblazon **1.** adorn, blazon, colour, decorate, embellish, illuminate, ornament, paint **2.** crack up (*informal*), extol, glorify, laud (*liter~ ary*), praise, proclaim, publicize, publish, trumpet

emblem badge, crest, device, figure, image, in~ signia, mark, representation, sigil (*rare*), sign, symbol, token, type

emblematic, emblematical figurative, repre~ sentative, symbolic

embodiment **1.** bodying forth, epitome, exam~ ple, exemplar, exemplification, expression, in~ carnation, incorporation, manifestation, per~ sonification, realization, reification, represen~ tation, symbol, type **2.** bringing together, codification, collection, combination, compre~ hension, concentration, consolidation, inclu~ sion, incorporation, integration, organization, systematization

embody **1.** body forth, concretize, exemplify, express, incarnate, incorporate, manifest, per~ sonify, realize, reify, represent, stand for, symbolize, typify **2.** bring together, codify, col~ lect, combine, comprehend, comprise, concen~ trate, consolidate, contain, include, incorpo~ rate, integrate, organize, systematize

embolden animate, cheer, encourage, fire, hearten, inflame, inspirit, invigorate, nerve, reassure, rouse, stimulate, stir, strengthen, vitalize

embrace *verb* **1.** clasp, cuddle, encircle, enfold, grasp, hold, hug, neck (*informal*), seize, squeeze, take *or* hold in one's arms **2.** accept, adopt, avail oneself of, espouse, grab, make use of, receive, seize, take on board, take up, welcome **3.** comprehend, comprise, contain, cover, deal with, embody, enclose, encompass, include, involve, provide for, subsume, take in, take into account *~noun* **4.** canoodle (*slang*), clasp, clinch (*slang*), cuddle, hug, squeeze

embroil complicate, compromise, confound, confuse, disorder, disturb, encumber, enmesh, ensnare, entangle, implicate, incriminate, in~ volve, mire, mix up, muddle, perplex, stitch up (*slang*), trouble

embryo beginning, germ, nucleus, root, rudi~ ment

embryonic beginning, early, germinal, imma~ ture, inchoate, incipient, primary, rudimenta~

ry, seminal, undeveloped

Antonyms advanced, developed, progressive

emend amend, correct, edit, improve, rectify, redact, revise

emendation amendment, correction, editing, improvement, rectification, redaction, revision

emerge 1. appear, arise, become visible, come forth, come into view, come out, come up, emanate, issue, proceed, rise, spring up, surface 2. become apparent, become known, come out, come out in the wash, come to light, crop up, develop, materialize, transpire, turn up

Antonyms depart, disappear, enter, fade, fall, recede, retreat, sink, submerge, vanish from sight, wane, withdraw

emergence advent, apparition, appearance, arrival, coming, dawn, development, disclosure, emanation, issue, materialization, rise

emergency crisis, danger, difficulty, exigency, extremity, necessity, panic stations (*informal*), pass, pinch, plight, predicament, quandary, scrape (*informal*), strait

emergent appearing, budding, coming, developing, rising

emetic vomitive, vomitory

emigrate migrate, move, move abroad, remove

emigration departure, exodus, migration, removal

eminence 1. celebrity, dignity, distinction, esteem, fame, greatness, illustriousness, importance, notability, note, pre-eminence, prestige, prominence, rank, renown, reputation, repute, superiority 2. elevation, height, high ground, hill, hillock, knoll, rise, summit

eminent big-time (*informal*), celebrated, conspicuous, distinguished, elevated, esteemed, exalted, famous, grand, great, high, high-ranking, illustrious, important, major league (*informal*), notable, noted, noteworthy, outstanding, paramount, pre-eminent, prestigious, prominent, renowned, signal, superior, well-known

Antonyms anonymous, commonplace, infamous, lowly, ordinary, undistinguished, unheard-of, unimportant, unknown, unremarkable, unsung

eminently conspicuously, exceedingly, exceptionally, extremely, greatly, highly, notably, outstandingly, prominently, remarkably, seriously (*informal*), signally, strikingly, surpassingly, well

emissary agent, ambassador, courier, delegate, deputy, envoy, go-between, herald, legate, messenger, representative, scout, secret agent, spy

emission diffusion, discharge, ejaculation, ejection, emanation, exhalation, exudation, issuance, issue, radiation, shedding, transmission, utterance, venting

emit breathe forth, cast out, diffuse, discharge, eject, emanate, exhale, exude, give off, give out, give vent to, issue, radiate, send forth, send out, shed, throw out, transmit, utter, vent

Antonyms absorb, assimilate, consume, devour, digest, drink in, incorporate, ingest, receive, soak up, suck up, take in

emollient 1. *adjective* assuaging, assuasive, balsamic, demulcent, lenitive, mollifying, softening, soothing 2. *noun* balm, lenitive, liniment, lotion, moisturizer, oil, ointment, salve

emolument benefit, compensation, earnings, fee, gain, hire, pay, payment, profits, recompense, remuneration, return, reward, salary, stipend, wages

emotion agitation, ardour, excitement, feeling, fervour, passion, perturbation, sensation, sentiment, vehemence, warmth

emotional 1. demonstrative, excitable, feeling, hot-blooded, passionate, responsive, sensitive, sentimental, susceptible, temperamental, tender, touchy-feely (*informal*), warm 2. affecting, emotive, exciting, heart-warming, moving, pathetic, poignant, sentimental, stirring, tear-jerking (*informal*), three-hankie (*informal*), thrilling, touching 3. ablaze, ardent, enthusiastic, fervent, fervid, fiery, flaming, heated, impassioned, passionate, roused, stirred, zealous

Antonyms apathetic, cold, detached, dispassionate, insensitive, phlegmatic, undemonstrative, unemotional, unenthusiastic, unexcitable, unfeeling, unmoved, unruffled, unsentimental

emotionless blank, cold, cold-blooded, cool, detached, distant, frigid, glacial, impassive, indifferent, remote, toneless, undemonstrative, unemotional, unfeeling

emotive 1. argumentative, controversial, delicate, sensitive, touchy 2. affecting, emotional, exciting, heart-warming, moving, pathetic, poignant, sentimental, stirring, tear-jerking (*informal*), three-hankie (*informal*), thrilling, touching 3. ardent, emotional, enthusiastic, fervent, fervid, fiery, heated, impassioned, passionate, roused, stirred, zealous

empathize feel for, identify with, put oneself in someone else's shoes (*informal*), relate to

emphasis accent, accentuation, attention, decidedness, force, importance, impressiveness, insistence, intensity, moment, positiveness, power, pre-eminence, priority, prominence, significance, strength, stress, underscoring, weight

emphasize accent, accentuate, dwell on, give priority to, highlight, insist on, lay stress on, play up, press home, put the accent on, stress, underline, underscore, weight

Antonyms gloss over, make light of, make little of, minimize, play down, soft-pedal (*informal*), underplay

emphatic absolute, categorical, certain, decided, definite, direct, distinct, earnest, energetic, forceful, forcible, important, impressive, insistent, in spades, marked, momentous, positive, powerful, pronounced, resounding, significant, striking, strong, telling, unequivocal, unmistakable, vigorous
Antonyms commonplace, equivocal, hesitant, insignificant, tame, tentative, uncertain, undecided, unremarkable, unsure, weak

empire **1.** commonwealth, domain, imperium (*rare*), kingdom, realm **2.** authority, command, control, dominion, government, power, rule, sovereignty, supremacy, sway

All empire is no more than power in trust
John Dryden *Absalom and Achitophel*

empirical, empiric experiential, experimental, first-hand, observed, practical, pragmatic
Antonyms academic, assumed, conjectural, hypothetical, putative, speculative, theoretic, theoretical

emplace insert, place, position, put, put in place, set up, station

emplacement **1.** location, lodgment, platform, position, site, situation, station **2.** placement, placing, positioning, putting in place, setting up, stationing

employ *verb* **1.** commission, engage, enlist, hire, retain, take on **2.** engage, fill, keep busy, make use of, occupy, spend, take up, use up **3.** apply, bring to bear, exercise, exert, make use of, ply, put to use, use, utilize ~*noun* **4.** employment, engagement, hire, service

employed active, busy, engaged, in a job, in employment, in work, occupied, working
Antonyms idle, jobless, laid off, on the dole (*Brit. informal*), out of a job, out of work, redundant, unoccupied

employee hand, job-holder, staff member, wage-earner, worker, workman

employer boss (*informal*), business, company, establishment, firm, gaffer (*informal, chiefly Brit.*), organization, outfit (*informal*), owner, patron, proprietor

employment **1.** engagement, enlistment, hire, retaining, taking on **2.** application, exercise, exertion, use, utilization **3.** avocation (*archaic*), business, calling, craft, employ, job, line, métier, occupation, profession, pursuit, service, trade, vocation, work

emporium bazaar, market, mart, shop, store, warehouse

empower allow, authorize, commission, delegate, enable, entitle, license, permit, qualify, sanction, warrant

emptiness **1.** bareness, blankness, desertedness, desolation, destitution, vacancy, vacuum, void, waste **2.** aimlessness, banality, barrenness, frivolity, futility, hollowness, inanity, ineffectiveness, meaninglessness, purposelessness, senselessness, silliness, unreality, unsatisfactoriness, unsubstantiality, vainness, valuelessness, vanity, worthlessness **3.** cheapness, hollowness, idleness, insincerity, triviality, trivialness **4.** absentness, blankness, expressionlessness, unintelligence, vacancy, vacantness, vacuity, vacuousness **5.** *informal* desire, hunger, ravening

empty *adjective* **1.** bare, blank, clear, deserted, desolate, destitute, hollow, unfurnished, uninhabited, unoccupied, untenanted, vacant, void, waste **2.** aimless, banal, bootless, frivolous, fruitless, futile, hollow, inane, ineffective, meaningless, purposeless, senseless, silly, unreal, unsatisfactory, unsubstantial, vain, valueless, worthless **3.** cheap, hollow, idle, insincere, trivial **4.** absent, blank, expressionless, unintelligent, vacant, vacuous **5.** *informal* esurient, famished, hungry, ravenous, starving (*informal*), unfed, unfilled ~*verb* **6.** clear, consume, deplete, discharge, drain, dump, evacuate, exhaust, gut, pour out, unburden, unload, use up, vacate, void
Antonyms *adjective* busy, fulfilled, full, inhabited, interesting, meaningful, occupied, packed, purposeful, satisfying, serious, significant, stuffed, useful, valuable, worthwhile ~*verb* cram, fill, pack, replenish, stock, stuff

empty-headed brainless, dizzy (*informal*), featherbrained, flighty, frivolous, giddy, goofy (*informal*), harebrained, inane, scatterbrained, silly, skittish, vacuous

empyrean, empyreal aerial, airy, celestial, ethereal, heavenly, refined, skylike, sublime

emulate challenge, compete with, contend with, copy, echo, follow, follow in the footsteps of, follow suit, follow the example of, imitate, mimic, rival, take after, take a leaf out of someone's book, vie with

emulation challenge, competition, contention, contest, copying, envy, following, imitation, jealousy, mimicry, rivalry, strife

emulous aspiring, competitive, contending, imitative, vying

enable allow, authorize, capacitate, commission, empower, entitle, facilitate, fit, license, permit, prepare, qualify, sanction, warrant
Antonyms bar, block, hinder, impede, obstruct, prevent, stop, thwart

enact **1.** authorize, command, decree, establish, legislate, ordain, order, pass, proclaim, ratify, sanction **2.** act, act out, appear as, depict, perform, personate, play, play the part of, portray, represent

enactment 1. authorization, canon, command, commandment, decree, dictate, edict, law, legislation, order, ordinance, proclamation, ratification, regulation, statute 2. acting, depiction, performance, personation, play-acting, playing, portrayal, representation

enamour absorb, bewitch, captivate, charm, enchant, endear, enrapture, entrance, fascinate, infatuate, sweep off one's feet

enamoured bewitched, captivated, charmed, crazy about (*informal*), enchanted, enraptured, entranced, fascinated, fond, infatuated, in love, nuts on *or* about (*slang*), smitten, swept off one's feet, taken, wild about (*informal*)

encampment base, bivouac, camp, camping ground, campsite, cantonment, quarters, tents

encapsulate, incapsulate abridge, compress, condense, digest, epitomize, précis, summarize, sum up

enchain bind, enslave, fetter, hold, hold fast, manacle, pinion, put in irons, shackle

enchant beguile, bewitch, captivate, cast a spell on, charm, delight, enamour, enrapture, enthral, fascinate, hypnotize, mesmerize, ravish, spellbind

enchanter conjurer, magician, magus, necromancer, sorcerer, spellbinder, warlock, witch, wizard

enchanting alluring, appealing, attractive, bewitching, captivating, charming, delightful, endearing, entrancing, fascinating, lovely, Orphean, pleasant, ravishing, winsome

enchantment 1. allure, allurement, beguilement, bliss, charm, delight, fascination, hypnotism, mesmerism, rapture, ravishment, transport 2. charm, conjuration, incantation, magic, necromancy, sorcery, spell, witchcraft, wizardry

enchantress 1. conjurer, lamia, magician, necromancer, sorceress, spellbinder, witch 2. charmer, *femme fatale*, seductress, siren, vamp (*informal*)

encircle begird (*poetic*), circle, circumscribe, compass, enclose, encompass, enfold, envelop, environ, enwreath, gird in, girdle, hem in, ring, surround

enclose, inclose 1. bound, circumscribe, cover, encase, encircle, encompass, environ, fence, hedge, hem in, impound, pen, pound, shut in, wall in, wrap 2. include, insert, put in, send with 3. comprehend, contain, embrace, hold, include, incorporate

encomium acclaim, acclamation, applause, compliment, eulogy, homage, laudation, panegyric, praise, tribute

encompass 1. circle, circumscribe, encircle, enclose, envelop, environ, enwreath, girdle, hem in, ring, surround 2. bring about, cause, contrive, devise, effect, manage 3. admit, comprehend, comprise, contain, cover, embody, embrace, hold, include, incorporate, involve, subsume, take in

encounter *verb* 1. bump into (*informal*), chance upon, come upon, confront, experience, face, happen on *or* upon, meet, run across, run into (*informal*) 2. attack, clash with, combat, come into conflict with, contend, cross swords with, do battle with, engage, face off (*slang*), fight, grapple with, join battle with, strive, struggle ~*noun* 3. brush, confrontation, meeting, rendezvous 4. action, battle, clash, collision, combat, conflict, contest, dispute, engagement, face-off (*slang*), fight, head-to-head, run-in (*informal*), set to (*informal*), skirmish

encourage 1. animate, buoy up, cheer, comfort, console, embolden, hearten, incite, inspire, inspirit, rally, reassure, rouse, stimulate 2. abet, advance, advocate, aid, boost, commend, egg on, favour, forward, foster, further, help, promote, prompt, spur, strengthen, succour, support, urge
Antonyms daunt, depress, deter, discourage, dishearten, dispirit, dissuade, hinder, inhibit, intimidate, prevent, retard, scare, throw cold water on (*informal*)

encouragement advocacy, aid, boost, cheer, clarion call, consolation, favour, help, incitement, inspiration, inspiritment, promotion, reassurance, security blanket (*informal*), stimulation, stimulus, succour, support, urging

It's a good thing to shoot an admiral now and then to encourage the others

Voltaire *Candide*

encouraging bright, cheerful, cheering, comforting, good, heartening, hopeful, promising, reassuring, rosy, satisfactory, stimulating
Antonyms daunting, depressing, disappointing, discouraging, disheartening, dispiriting, offputting (*informal*), unfavourable, unpropitious

encroach appropriate, arrogate, impinge, infringe, intrude, invade, make inroads, overstep, trench, trespass, usurp

encroachment appropriation, arrogation, impingement, incursion, infringement, inroad, intrusion, invasion, trespass, usurpation, violation

encumber burden, clog, cramp, embarrass, hamper, handicap, hinder, impede, incommode, inconvenience, make difficult, obstruct, oppress, overload, retard, saddle, slow down, trammel, weigh down

encumbrance albatross, burden, clog, difficulty, drag, embarrassment, handicap, hindrance, impediment, inconvenience, liability, load, millstone, obstacle, obstruction

encyclopedic all-embracing, all-encompassing, all-inclusive, complete, comprehensive, exhaustive, thorough, universal, vast, wide-ranging

end *noun* **1.** bound, boundary, edge, extent, extreme, extremity, limit, point, terminus, tip **2.** attainment, cessation, close, closure, completion, conclusion, consequence, consummation, culmination, denouement, ending, end result, expiration, expiry, finale, finish, issue, outcome, resolution, result, sequel, stop, termination, upshot, wind-up **3.** aim, aspiration, design, drift, goal, intent, intention, object, objective, point, purpose, reason **4.** part, piece, portion, responsibility, share, side **5.** bit, butt, fragment, leftover, oddment, remainder, remnant, scrap, stub, tag end, tail end **6.** annihilation, death, demise, destruction, dissolution, doom, extermination, extinction, ruin, ruination **7.** **the end** *slang* beyond endurance, insufferable, intolerable, the final blow, the last straw, the limit (*informal*), the worst, too much (*informal*), unbearable, unendurable *~verb* **8.** axe (*informal*), belay (*Nautical*), bring to an end, cease, close, complete, conclude, culminate, dissolve, expire, finish, nip in the bud, pull the plug on, put paid to, resolve, stop, terminate, wind up **9.** abolish, annihilate, destroy, exterminate, extinguish, kill, put to death, ruin

Antonyms *noun* beginning, birth, commencement, inception, launch, opening, origin, outset, prelude, source, start *~verb* begin, come into being, commence, initiate, launch, originate, start

The end must justify the means
Matthew Prior *Hans Carvel*

All good things must come to an end

All's well that ends well

endanger compromise, hazard, imperil, jeopardize, put at risk, put in danger, risk, threaten

Antonyms defend, guard, preserve, protect, safeguard, save, secure

endear attach, attract, bind, captivate, charm, engage, win

endearing adorable, attractive, captivating, charming, cute, engaging, lovable, sweet, winning, winsome

endearment **1.** affectionate utterance, loving word, sweet nothing **2.** affection, attachment, fondness, love

endeavour **1.** *noun* aim, attempt, crack (*informal*), effort, enterprise, essay, go (*informal*), shot (*informal*), stab (*informal*), trial, try, undertaking, venture **2.** *verb* aim, aspire, attempt, bend over backwards (*informal*), break one's neck (*informal*), bust a gut (*informal*), do one's best, do one's damnedest (*informal*), essay, give it one's all (*informal*), give it one's best shot (*informal*), go for broke (*slang*), go for it (*informal*), have a go (crack (*informal*), shot (*informal*), stab (*informal*)) (*informal*), jump through hoops (*informal*), knock oneself out (*informal*), labour, make an all-out effort (*informal*), make an effort, rupture oneself (*informal*), strive, struggle, take pains, try, undertake

ended all over (bar the shouting), at an end, closed, complete, concluded, done, finis, finished, over, settled, through, wrapped-up (*informal*)

ending catastrophe, cessation, close, completion, conclusion, consummation, culmination, denouement, end, finale, finish, resolution, termination, wind-up

Antonyms birth, commencement, inauguration, inception, onset, opening, origin, preface, source, start, starting point

endless **1.** boundless, ceaseless, constant, continual, eternal, everlasting, immortal, incessant, infinite, interminable, limitless, measureless, perpetual, unbounded, unbroken, undying, unending, uninterrupted, unlimited **2.** interminable, monotonous, overlong **3.** continuous, unbroken, undivided, whole

Antonyms bounded, brief, circumscribed, finite, limited, passing, restricted, temporary, terminable, transient, transitory

endorse, indorse **1.** advocate, affirm, approve, authorize, back, champion, confirm, espouse, favour, prescribe, promote, ratify, recommend, sanction, subscribe to, support, sustain, vouch for, warrant **2.** countersign, sign, superscribe, undersign

endorsement, indorsement **1.** comment, countersignature, qualification, signature, superscription **2.** advocacy, affirmation, approbation, approval, authorization, backing, championship, confirmation, espousal, favour, fiat, O.K. *or* okay (*informal*), promotion, ratification, recommendation, sanction, seal of approval, subscription to, support, warrant

endow award, bequeath, bestow, confer, donate, endue, enrich, favour, finance, fund, furnish, give, grant, invest, leave, make over, provide, purvey, settle on, supply, will

endowment **1.** award, benefaction, bequest, bestowal, boon, donation, fund, gift, grant, hand-out, income, largess *or* largesse, legacy, presentation, property, provision, revenue, stipend **2.** *often plural* ability, aptitude, attribute, capability, capacity, faculty, flair, genius, gift, power, qualification, quality, talent

endue, indue endow, fill, furnish, invest, provide, supply

end up **1.** become eventually, finish as, finish up, pan out (*informal*), turn out to be **2.** ar~

rive finally, come to a halt, fetch up (*informal*), finish up, stop, wind up

endurable acceptable, bearable, sufferable, supportable, sustainable, tolerable
Antonyms insufferable, insupportable, intolerable, too much (*informal*), unbearable, unendurable

endurance **1.** bearing, fortitude, patience, perseverance, persistence, pertinacity, resignation, resolution, stamina, staying power, strength, submission, sufferance, tenacity, toleration **2.** continuation, continuity, durability, duration, immutability, lastingness, longevity, permanence, stability

endure **1.** bear, brave, cope with, experience, go through, stand, stick it out (*informal*), suffer, support, sustain, take it (*informal*), thole (*Scot.*), undergo, weather, withstand **2.** abide, allow, bear, brook, countenance, hack (*slang*), permit, put up with, stand, stick (*slang*), stomach, submit to, suffer, swallow, take patiently, tolerate **3.** abide, be durable, continue, have a good innings, hold, last, live, live on, persist, prevail, remain, stand, stay, survive, wear well
What can't be cured must be endured

enduring abiding, continuing, durable, eternal, firm, immortal, immovable, imperishable, lasting, living, long-lasting, perennial, permanent, persistent, persisting, prevailing, remaining, steadfast, steady, surviving, unfaltering, unwavering
Antonyms brief, ephemeral, fleeting, momentary, passing, short, short-lived, temporary, transient, transitory

enemy adversary, antagonist, competitor, foe, opponent, rival, the opposition, the other side
Antonyms ally, confederate, friend, supporter
Related adjective: inimical

> *A man cannot be too careful in the choice of his enemies*
>
> Oscar Wilde *Lady Windermere's Fan*

energetic active, alive and kicking, animated, bright-eyed and bushy-tailed (*informal*), brisk, dynamic, forceful, forcible, full of beans (*informal*), high-octane (*informal*), high-powered, indefatigable, lively, potent, powerful, spirited, strenuous, strong, tireless, vigorous, zippy (*informal*)
Antonyms debilitated, dull, enervated, inactive, lazy, lethargic, lifeless, listless, slow, sluggish, torpid, weak

energize **1.** activate, animate, enliven, inspirit, invigorate, liven up, motivate, pep up, quicken, stimulate, vitalize **2.** activate, electrify, kick-start, start up, switch on, turn on

energy activity, animation, ardour, brio, drive, efficiency, élan, elbow grease (*facetious*), exertion, fire, force, forcefulness, get-up-and-go (*informal*), go (*informal*), intensity, life, liveliness, pep, pluck, power, spirit, stamina, strength, strenuousness, verve, vigour, vim (*slang*), vitality, vivacity, zeal, zest, zip (*informal*)

enervate **1.** *verb* debilitate, devitalize, enfeeble, exhaust, fatigue, incapacitate, paralyse, prostrate, sap, tire, unnerve, wash out, weaken, wear out **2.** *adjective* debilitated, devitalized, done in (*informal*), enervated, enfeebled, exhausted, fatigued, feeble, incapacitated, limp, paralysed, prostrate, prostrated, run-down, sapped, spent, tired, undermined, unnerved, washed out, weak, weakened, worn out

enervation debilitation, debility, enfeeblement, exhaustedness, exhaustion, fatigue, feebleness, impotence, incapacity, infirmity, lassitude, paralysis, powerlessness, prostration, tiredness, weakening, weakness

enfeeble debilitate, deplete, devitalize, diminish, exhaust, fatigue, render feeble, sap, undermine, unhinge, unnerve, weaken, wear out

enfold, infold clasp, embrace, enclose, encompass, envelop, enwrap, fold, hold, hug, shroud, swathe, wrap, wrap up

enforce administer, apply, carry out, coerce, compel, constrain, exact, execute, implement, impose, insist on, oblige, prosecute, put in force, put into effect, reinforce, require, urge

enforced compelled, compulsory, constrained, dictated, imposed, involuntary, necessary, ordained, prescribed, required, unavoidable, unwilling

enforcement **1.** administration, application, carrying out, exaction, execution, implementation, imposition, prosecution, reinforcement **2.** coercion, compulsion, constraint, insistence, obligation, pressure, requirement

enfranchise **1.** give the vote to, grant suffrage to, grant the franchise to, grant voting rights to **2.** emancipate, free, liberate, manumit, release, set free

enfranchisement **1.** giving the vote, granting suffrage *or* the franchise, granting voting rights **2.** emancipation, freedom, freeing, liberating, liberation, manumission, release, setting free

engage **1.** appoint, commission, employ, enlist, enrol, hire, retain, take on **2.** bespeak, book, charter, hire, lease, prearrange, rent, reserve, secure **3.** absorb, busy, engross, grip, involve, occupy, preoccupy, tie up **4.** allure, arrest, attach, attract, captivate, catch, charm, draw, enamour, enchant, fascinate, fix, gain, win **5.** embark on, enter into, join, partake, participate, practise, set about, take part, undertake **6.** affiance, agree, betroth (*archaic*), bind, commit, contract, covenant, guarantee, obli~

gate, oblige, pledge, promise, undertake, vouch, vow **7.** *Military* assail, attack, combat, come to close quarters with, encounter, face off (*slang*), fall on, fight with, give battle to, join battle with, meet, take on **8.** activate, ap~ ply, bring into operation, energize, set going, switch on **9.** dovetail, interact, interconnect, interlock, join, mesh

Antonyms (*sense 1*) axe (*informal*), discharge, dismiss, fire (*informal*), give notice to, lay off, oust, remove, sack (*informal*)

engaged **1.** affianced, betrothed (*archaic*), pledged, promised, spoken for **2.** absorbed, busy, committed, employed, engrossed, in use, involved, occupied, preoccupied, tied up, un~ available

Antonyms available, fancy-free, free, unat~ tached, uncommitted, unengaged

engagement **1.** assurance, betrothal, bond, compact, contract, oath, obligation, pact, pledge, promise, troth (*archaic*), undertaking, vow, word **2.** appointment, arrangement, com~ mitment, date, meeting **3.** commission, em~ ployment, gig (*informal*), job, post, situation, stint, work **4.** action, battle, combat, conflict, confrontation, contest, encounter, face-off (*slang*), fight

engaging agreeable, appealing, attractive, captivating, charming, cute, enchanting, fas~ cinating, fetching (*informal*), likable *or* like~ able, lovable, pleasant, pleasing, winning, winsome

Antonyms disagreeable, objectionable, obnox~ ious, offensive, repulsive, unattractive, unlik~ able *or* unlikeable, unlovely, unpleasant

engender **1.** beget, breed, bring about, cause, create, excite, foment, generate, give rise to, hatch, incite, induce, instigate, lead to, make, occasion, precipitate, produce, provoke **2.** be~ get, breed, bring forth, father, generate, give birth to, procreate, propagate, sire, spawn

engine **1.** machine, mechanism, motor **2.** agen~ cy, agent, apparatus, appliance, contrivance, device, implement, instrument, means, tool, weapon

engineer **1.** *noun* architect, contriver, designer, deviser, director, inventor, manager, manipu~ lator, originator, planner, schemer **2.** *verb* bring about, cause, concoct, contrive, control, create, devise, effect, encompass, finagle (*in~ formal*), manage, manoeuvre, mastermind, originate, plan, plot, scheme, wangle (*infor~ mal*)

English

The English take their pleasures sadly after the fashion of their country

Maximilien de Béthune, Duc de Sully *Memoirs*

An Englishman, even if he is alone, forms an or~ derly queue of one

George Mikes *How to be an Alien*

Mad dogs and Englishmen go out in the mid-day sun

Noel Coward *Mad Dogs and Englishmen*

An Englishman's home is his castle

engorge bolt, cram, devour, eat, fill, glut, gob~ ble, gorge, gulp, guzzle, pig out (*slang*), sati~ ate, stuff, wolf

engraft, ingraft graft, implant, incorporate, inculcate, infix, infuse, ingrain, instil

engrain *see* INGRAIN

engrave **1.** carve, chase, chisel, cut, enchase (*rare*), etch, grave (*archaic*), inscribe **2.** im~ press, imprint, print **3.** embed, fix, impress, imprint, infix, ingrain, lodge

engraving **1.** carving, chasing, chiselling, cut~ ting, dry point, enchasing (*rare*), etching, in~ scribing, inscription **2.** block, carving, etching, inscription, plate, woodcut **3.** etching, impres~ sion, print

engross **1.** absorb, arrest, engage, engulf, hold, immerse, involve, occupy, preoccupy **2.** corner, monopolize, sew up (*U.S.*)

engrossed absorbed, captivated, caught up, deep, enthralled, fascinated, gripped, im~ mersed, intent, intrigued, lost, preoccupied, rapt, riveted

engrossing absorbing, captivating, compelling, enthralling, fascinating, gripping, interesting, intriguing, riveting

engulf, ingulf absorb, bury, consume, deluge, drown, encompass, engross, envelop, flood (out), immerse, inundate, overrun, overwhelm, plunge, submerge, swallow up, swamp

enhance add to, augment, boost, complement, elevate, embellish, exalt, heighten, improve, increase, intensify, lift, magnify, raise, re~ inforce, strengthen, swell

Antonyms debase, decrease, depreciate, de~ value, diminish, lower, minimize, reduce, spoil

enhancement addition, augmentation, boost, embellishment, enrichment, heightening, im~ provement, increase, increment, rise

enigma conundrum, mystery, problem, puzzle, riddle, teaser

enigmatic, enigmatical ambiguous, cryptic, Delphic, doubtful, equivocal, incomprehen~ sible, indecipherable, inexplicable, inscrutable, mysterious, obscure, oracular, perplexing, puzzling, recondite, sphinxlike, uncertain, un~ fathomable, unintelligible

Antonyms clear, comprehensible, simple, straightforward, uncomplicated

enjoin **1.** advise, bid, call upon, charge, com~ mand, counsel, demand, direct, instruct, or~ der, prescribe, require, urge, warn **2.** *Law* ban, bar, disallow, forbid, interdict, place an injunction on, preclude, prohibit, proscribe, restrain

enjoy 1. appreciate, be entertained by, be pleased with, delight in, like, rejoice in, relish, revel in, take joy in, take pleasure in *or* from 2. be blessed *or* favoured with, experience, have, have the benefit of, have the use of, own, possess, reap the benefits of, use 3. **enjoy oneself** have a ball (*informal*), have a field day (*informal*), have a good time, have fun, let one's hair down, make merry
Antonyms (*sense 1*) abhor, despise, detest, dislike, hate, have no taste *or* stomach for, loathe

Make hay while the sun shines

enjoyable agreeable, amusing, delectable, delicious, delightful, entertaining, gratifying, pleasant, pleasing, pleasurable, satisfying, to one's liking
Antonyms despicable, disagreeable, displeasing, hateful, loathsome, obnoxious, offensive, repugnant, unenjoyable, unpleasant, unsatisfying, unsavoury

enjoyment 1. amusement, beer and skittles (*informal*), delectation, delight, diversion, entertainment, fun, gladness, gratification, gusto, happiness, indulgence, joy, pleasure, recreation, relish, satisfaction, zest 2. advantage, benefit, exercise, ownership, possession, use

enkindle 1. fire, ignite, kindle, light, put a match to, put to the torch, set ablaze, set alight, set fire to, set on fire, torch 2. arouse, awake, excite, foment, incite, inflame, inspire, provoke, stir

enlarge 1. add to, amplify, augment, blow up (*informal*), broaden, diffuse, dilate, distend, elongate, expand, extend, grow, heighten, increase, inflate, lengthen, magnify, make *or* grow larger, multiply, stretch, swell, wax, widen 2. amplify, descant, develop, dilate, elaborate, expand, expatiate, give details
Antonyms abbreviate, abridge, compress, condense, curtail, decrease, diminish, lessen, narrow, reduce, shorten, shrink, trim, truncate

enlighten advise, apprise, cause to understand, civilize, counsel, edify, educate, inform, instruct, make aware, teach

enlightened aware, broad-minded, civilized, cultivated, educated, informed, knowledgeable, liberal, literate, open-minded, reasonable, refined, sophisticated
Antonyms ignorant, narrow-minded, short-sighted, small-minded, unaware, uneducated, unenlightened

enlightenment awareness, broad-mindedness, civilization, comprehension, cultivation, edification, education, information, insight, instruction, knowledge, learning, literacy, open-mindedness, refinement, sophistication, teaching, understanding, wisdom

enlist engage, enrol, enter (into), gather, join, join up, muster, obtain, procure, recruit, register, secure, sign up, volunteer

enliven animate, brighten, buoy up, cheer, cheer up, excite, exhilarate, fire, gladden, hearten, inspire, inspirit, invigorate, pep up, perk up, quicken, rouse, spark, stimulate, vitalize, vivify, wake up
Antonyms chill, dampen, deaden, depress, put a damper on, repress, subdue

en masse all at once, all together, as a group, as a whole, as one, ensemble, in a group (body, mass), together

enmesh catch, embroil, ensnare, entangle, implicate, incriminate, involve, net, snare, snarl, tangle, trammel, trap

enmity acrimony, animosity, animus, antagonism, antipathy, aversion, bad blood, bitterness, hate, hatred, hostility, ill will, malevolence, malice, malignity, rancour, spite, venom
Antonyms affection, amity, cordiality, friendliness, friendship, geniality, goodwill, harmony, love, warmth

ennoble aggrandize, dignify, elevate, enhance, exalt, glorify, honour, magnify, raise

ennui boredom, dissatisfaction, lassitude, listlessness, tedium, the doldrums

enormity 1. atrociousness, atrocity, depravity, disgrace, evilness, heinousness, monstrousness, nefariousness, outrageousness, turpitude, viciousness, vileness, villainy, wickedness 2. abomination, atrocity, crime, disgrace, evil, horror, monstrosity, outrage, villainy 3. *informal* enormousness, greatness, hugeness, immensity, magnitude, massiveness, vastness

enormous 1. astronomic, Brobdingnagian, colossal, elephantine, excessive, gargantuan, gigantic, ginormous (*informal*), gross, huge, humongous *or* humungous (*U.S. slang*), immense, jumbo (*informal*), mammoth, massive, monstrous, mountainous, prodigious, stellar (*informal*), titanic, tremendous, vast 2. *archaic* abominable, atrocious, depraved, disgraceful, evil, heinous, monstrous, nefarious, odious, outrageous, vicious, vile, villainous, wicked
Antonyms diminutive, dwarf, infinitesimal, insignificant, Lilliputian, little, meagre, microscopic, midget, minute, petite, pint-sized (*informal*), small, tiny, trivial, wee

enough 1. *adjective* abundant, adequate, ample, plenty, sufficient 2. *noun* abundance, adequacy, ample supply, plenty, right amount, sufficiency 3. *adverb* abundantly, adequately, amply, fairly, moderately, passably, reasonably, satisfactorily, sufficiently, tolerably

Enough is as good as a feast

enquire 1. ask, query, question, request information, seek information 2. *Also* **inquire** conduct an inquiry, examine, explore, inspect, investigate, look into, make inquiry, probe, research, scrutinize, search

enquiry 1. query, question 2. *Also* **inquiry** examination, exploration, inquest, inspection, investigation, probe, research, scrutiny, search, study, survey

enrage aggravate (*informal*), anger, exasperate, gall, get one's back up, incense, incite, inflame, infuriate, irritate, madden, make one's blood boil, make one see red (*informal*), nark (*Brit., Austral., & N.Z. slang*), provoke, put one's back up
Antonyms appease, assuage, calm, conciliate, mollify, pacify, placate, soothe

enraged aggravated (*informal*), angered, angry, boiling mad, choked, cross, exasperated, fit to be tied (*slang*), fuming, furious, incensed, inflamed, infuriated, irate, irritated, livid (*informal*), mad (*informal*), on the warpath, raging, raging mad, wild

enrapture absorb, beguile, bewitch, captivate, charm, delight, enamour, enchant, enthral, entrance, fascinate, ravish, spellbind, transport

enrich 1. make rich, make wealthy 2. aggrandize, ameliorate, augment, cultivate, develop, endow, enhance, improve, refine, supplement 3. adorn, decorate, embellish, grace, ornament

enrol 1. chronicle, inscribe, list, note, record 2. accept, admit, engage, enlist, join up, matriculate, recruit, register, sign up *or* on, take on

enrolment acceptance, admission, engagement, enlistment, matriculation, recruitment, registration

en route in transit, on *or* along the way, on the road

ensconce 1. curl up, establish, install, nestle, settle, snuggle up 2. conceal, cover, hide, protect, screen, shelter, shield

ensemble *noun* 1. aggregate, assemblage, collection, entirety, set, sum, total, totality, whole, whole thing 2. costume, get-up (*informal*), outfit, suit 3. band, cast, chorus, company, group, supporting cast, troupe ~*adverb* 4. all at once, all together, as a group, as a whole, at once, at the same time, en masse, in concert

enshrine apotheosize, cherish, consecrate, dedicate, embalm, exalt, hallow, preserve, revere, sanctify, treasure

enshroud cloak, cloud, conceal, cover, enclose, enfold, envelop, enwrap, hide, obscure, pall, shroud, veil, wrap

ensign badge, banner, colours, flag, jack, pennant, pennon, standard, streamer

enslave bind, dominate, enchain, enthral, reduce to slavery, subjugate, yoke

ensnare catch, embroil, enmesh, entangle, entrap, net, snare, snarl, trap

ensue arise, attend, be consequent on, befall, come after, come next, come to pass (*archaic*), derive, flow, follow, issue, proceed, result, stem, succeed, supervene, turn out *or* up
Antonyms antecede, come first, forerun, go ahead of, go before, introduce, lead, pave the way, precede, usher

ensure, insure 1. certify, confirm, effect, guarantee, make certain, make sure, secure, warrant 2. guard, make safe, protect, safeguard, secure

entail bring about, call for, cause, demand, encompass, give rise to, impose, involve, lead to, necessitate, occasion, require, result in

entangle 1. catch, compromise, embroil, enmesh, ensnare, entrap, foul, implicate, involve, knot, mat, mix up, ravel, snag, snare, tangle, trammel, trap 2. bewilder, complicate, confuse, jumble, mix up, muddle, perplex, puzzle, snarl, twist
Antonyms (*sense 1*) detach, disconnect, disengage, disentangle, extricate, free, loose, separate, sever, unfold, unravel, unsnarl, untangle, untwist (*sense 2*) clarify, clear (up), resolve, simplify, work out

entanglement 1. complication, confusion, ensnarement, entrapment, imbroglio (*obsolete*), involvement, jumble, knot, mesh, mess, mix-up, muddle, snare, snarl-up (*informal, chiefly Brit.*), tangle, toils, trap 2. difficulty, embarrassment, imbroglio, involvement, liaison, predicament, tie

entente *Also* **entente cordiale** agreement, arrangement, compact, deal, friendship, pact, treaty, understanding

enter 1. arrive, come *or* go in *or* into, insert, introduce, make an entrance, pass into, penetrate, pierce 2. become a member of, begin, commence, commit oneself to, embark upon, enlist, enrol, join, participate in, set about, set out on, sign up, start, take part in, take up 3. inscribe, list, log, note, record, register, set down, take down 4. offer, present, proffer, put forward, register, submit, tender
Antonyms depart, drop out, exit, go, issue from, leave, pull out, resign, retire, take one's leave, withdraw

enterprise 1. adventure, effort, endeavour, essay, operation, plan, programme, project, undertaking, venture 2. activity, adventurousness, alertness, audacity, boldness, daring, dash, drive, eagerness, energy, enthusiasm, get-up-and-go (*informal*), gumption (*informal*), initiative, pep, push (*informal*), readiness, resource, resourcefulness, spirit, vigour, zeal **3**. business, company, concern, establishment, firm, operation

enterprising active, adventurous, alert, audacious, bold, daring, dashing, eager, energetic, enthusiastic, go-ahead, intrepid, keen, ready, resourceful, spirited, stirring, up-and-coming, venturesome, vigorous, zealous

entertain **1**. amuse, charm, cheer, delight, divert, occupy, please, recreate (*rare*), regale **2**. accommodate, be host to, harbour, have company, have guests *or* visitors, lodge, put up, show hospitality to, treat **3**. cherish, cogitate on, conceive, consider, contemplate, foster, harbour, hold, imagine, keep in mind, maintain, muse over, ponder, support, think about, think over

entertaining amusing, charming, cheering, delightful, diverting, funny, humorous, interesting, pleasant, pleasing, pleasurable, recreative (*rare*), witty

entertainment amusement, beer and skittles (*informal*), cheer, distraction, diversion, enjoyment, fun, good time, leisure activity, pastime, play, pleasure, recreation, satisfaction, sport, treat

Types of entertainment

acrobatics
aerobatics
agon
airshow
all-dayer
all-nighter
antimasque
après-ski
aquashow
ball
ballet
banquet
bear-baiting
bullfighting
burlesque show
busking
cabaret
carnival
ceilidh
charade
circus
cockfighting
comedy
command performance
concert
conjuring
cotillion *or* cotillon (*U.S. & Canad.*)
dance
escapology
exhibition
fair
farce
fashion show
feast
fête *or* fete
film
fireworks *or* pyrotechnics
floor show
funambulism *or* tightrope-walking
gala
galanty show
garden party
gaudy
gig (*informal*)
ice show
juggling
karaoke
kermis *or* kirmess (*U.S. & Canad.*)
levee
light show
masked ball
masque
melodrama
minstrel show
musical
music hall
opera
operetta
pantomime
party
play
puppet show
raree show
rave
reading
reception
recital
recitation
revue *or* review
ridotto
road show
rodeo
shadow play
show
sideshow
singsong
slide show
slot machine
soiree
son et lumière
street theatre
striptease
tragedy
variety
vaudeville
ventriloquism
video game
wall of death
waltzer
warehouse party
whist drive
zarzuela

Types of entertainer

acrobat
actor *or* (*fem.*) actress
artist
artiste
auguste
bareback rider
busker
chorus girl
circus artist
clown
comedian *or* (*fem.*) comedienne
conjurer
contortionist
dancer
diva
equilibrist
escapologist
exotic dancer
fire eater
fool
funambulist *or* tightrope walker
funnyman
go-go dancer
gracioso
guiser
harlequin
illusionist
impersonator
impressionist
jester
jongleur
juggler
lion tamer
magician
merry-andrew
mimic
minstrel
mummer
musician
organ-grinder
performer
prima ballerina
prima donna
puppeteer
quick-change artist
raconteur
ringmaster
show girl
singer
snake charmer
stripteaser *or* stripper
strolling player
strongman
sword swallower
tightrope walker
tragedian *or* (*fem.*) tragedienne
trapeze artist
trouper
tumbler
unicyclist
vaudevillian
ventriloquist

Places of entertainment

amphitheatre
amusement arcade (*Brit.*)
arena
auditorium
ballroom
bandstand
big top
bingo hall
carnival
cinema
circus
coliseum *or* colosseum
concert hall
dance hall
disco
fairground
funfair
gallery
hall
leisure centre
lido

marquee
museum
music hall
nightclub
nightspot
niterie (*slang*)
opera house
social club
stadium
theatre
vaudeville
waxworks
zoo

This day my wife made it appear to me that my late entertainment this week cost me above £12, an expense which I am almost ashamed of, though it is but once in a great while, and it is the end for which, in the most part, we live, to have such a merry day once or twice in a man's life
Samuel Pepys *Diary*

enthral absorb, beguile, captivate, charm, en~chant, enrapture, entrance, fascinate, grip, hold spellbound, hypnotize, intrigue, mesmer~ize, ravish, rivet, spellbind

enthralling beguiling, captivating, charming, compelling, compulsive, enchanting, entranc~ing, fascinating, gripping, hypnotizing, intri~guing, mesmerizing, riveting, spellbinding

enthusiasm **1.** ardour, avidity, devotion, eagerness, earnestness, excitement, fervour, frenzy, interest, keenness, passion, relish, ve~hemence, warmth, zeal, zest, zing (*informal*) **2.** craze, fad (*informal*), hobby, hobbyhorse, interest, mania, passion, rage

enthusiast admirer, aficionado, buff (*informal*), devotee, fan, fanatic, fiend (*informal*), follow~er, freak (*informal*), lover, supporter, zealot

enthusiastic ablaze, ardent, avid, bright-eyed and bushy-tailed (*informal*), devoted, eager, earnest, ebullient, excited, exuberant, fervent, fervid, forceful, full of beans (*informal*), hearty, keen, keen as mustard, lively, pas~sionate, spirited, unqualified, unstinting, ve~hement, vigorous, warm, wholehearted, zeal~ous
Antonyms apathetic, blasé, bored, cool, dis~passionate, half-hearted, indifferent, noncha~lant, unconcerned, unenthusiastic, uninterest~ed

entice allure, attract, beguile, cajole, coax, dangle a carrot in front of (someone's) nose, decoy, draw, inveigle, lead on, lure, persuade, prevail on, seduce, tempt, wheedle

enticement allurement, attraction, bait, blan~dishments, cajolery, coaxing, come-on (*infor~mal*), decoy, incentive, inducement, inveigle~ment, lure, persuasion, seduction, temptation

enticing alluring, attractive, beguiling, capti~vating, come-hither (*informal*), intriguing, in~viting, irresistible, persuasive, seductive, tempting, yummy (*informal*)
Antonyms distasteful, off-putting (*Brit infor~mal*), repellent, unappealing, unattractive

entire **1.** complete, full, gross, total, whole **2.** absolute, full, outright, thorough, total, undi~minished, unmitigated, unreserved, unre~stricted **3.** intact, perfect, sound, unbroken, undamaged, unmarked, unmarred, whole, without a scratch **4.** continuous, integrated, unbroken, undivided, unified

entirely **1.** absolutely, altogether, completely, every inch, fully, in every respect, lock, stock and barrel, perfectly, thoroughly, totally, un~reservedly, utterly, wholly, without exception, without reservation **2.** exclusively, only, solely
Antonyms incompletely, moderately, partially, partly, piecemeal, slightly, somewhat, to a certain extent *or* degree

entirety **1.** absoluteness, completeness, fullness, totality, undividedness, unity, wholeness **2.** aggregate, sum, total, unity, whole

entitle **1.** accredit, allow, authorize, empower, enable, enfranchise, fit for, license, make eli~gible, permit, qualify for, warrant **2.** call, characterize, christen, denominate, designate, dub, label, name, style, term, title

entity **1.** being, body, creature, existence, indi~vidual, object, organism, presence, quantity, substance, thing **2.** essence, essential nature, quiddity (*Philosophy*), quintessence, real na~ture

entomb bury, inhume, inter, inurn, lay to rest, sepulchre

entombment burial, inhumation, interment, inurnment, sepulture

entourage **1.** associates, attendants, compan~ions, company, cortege, court, escort, follow~ers, following, retainers, retinue, staff, suite, train **2.** ambience, environment, environs, mi~lieu, surroundings

entrails bowels, guts, innards (*informal*), in~sides (*informal*), intestines, offal, viscera

entrance[1] *noun* **1.** access, avenue, door, door~way, entry, gate, ingress, inlet, opening, pas~sage, portal, way in **2.** appearance, arrival, coming in, entry, ingress, introduction **3.** ac~cess, admission, admittance, entrée, entry, in~gress, permission to enter **4.** beginning, com~mencement, debut, initiation, introduction, outset, start
Antonyms departure, egress, exit, exodus, leave-taking, outlet, way out

entrance[2] *verb* **1.** absorb, bewitch, captivate, charm, delight, enchant, enrapture, enthral, fascinate, gladden, ravish, spellbind, transport **2.** hypnotize, mesmerize, put in a trance
Antonyms bore, disenchant, irritate, offend, put off, turn off (*informal*)

entrant **1.** beginner, convert, initiate, neophyte, newcomer, new member, novice, probationer, tyro **2.** candidate, competitor, contestant, en~try, participant, player

entrap **1.** capture, catch, ensnare, net, snare, trap **2.** allure, beguile, decoy, embroil, enmesh, ensnare, entangle, entice, implicate, inveigle, involve, lead on, lure, seduce, trick

entreat appeal to, ask, ask earnestly, beg, beseech, conjure, crave, enjoin, exhort, implore, importune, petition, plead with, pray, request, supplicate

entreaty appeal, earnest request, exhortation, importunity, petition, plea, prayer, request, solicitation, suit, supplication

entrench, intrench 1. construct defences, dig in, dig trenches, fortify 2. anchor, dig in, embed, ensconce, establish, fix, implant, ingrain, install, lodge, plant, root, seat, set, settle 3. encroach, impinge, infringe, interlope, intrude, make inroads, trespass

entrenched, intrenched deep-rooted, deep-seated, firm, fixed, indelible, ineradicable, ingrained, rooted, set, unshakable, well-established

entre nous between ourselves, between the two of us, between you and me, confidentially, in confidence, off the record, privately

entrepreneur businessman, businesswoman, contractor, director, financier, impresario, industrialist, magnate, tycoon

entrust, intrust assign, authorize, charge, commend, commit, confide, consign, delegate, deliver, give custody of, hand over, invest, trust, turn over

entry 1. appearance, coming in, entering, entrance, initiation, introduction 2. access, avenue, door, doorway, entrance, gate, ingress, inlet, opening, passage, passageway, portal, way in 3. access, admission, entrance, entrée, free passage, permission to enter 4. account, item, jotting, listing, memo, memorandum, minute, note, record, registration 5. attempt, candidate, competitor, contestant, effort, entrant, participant, player, submission

Antonyms departure, egress, exit, leave, leave-taking, withdrawal

entwine, intwine braid, embrace, encircle, entwist (*archaic*), interlace, intertwine, interweave, knit, plait, ravel, surround, twine, twist, weave, wind

Antonyms disentangle, extricate, free, separate, straighten out, undo, unravel, untangle, unwind

enumerate 1. cite, detail, itemize, list, mention, name, quote, recapitulate, recite, recount, rehearse, relate, specify, spell out, tell 2. add up, calculate, compute, count, number, reckon, sum up, tally, total

enunciate 1. articulate, enounce, pronounce, say, sound, speak, utter, vocalize, voice 2. declare, proclaim, promulgate, pronounce, propound, publish, state

envelop blanket, cloak, conceal, cover, embrace, encase, encircle, enclose, encompass, enfold, engulf, enwrap, hide, obscure, sheathe, shroud, surround, swaddle, swathe, veil, wrap

envelope case, casing, coating, cover, covering, jacket, sheath, shell, skin, wrapper, wrapping

enveloping all-embracing, concealing, encircling, encompassing, enfolding, enwreathing, shrouding, surrounding

envenom 1. contaminate, infect, poison, taint 2. acerbate, aggravate (*informal*), embitter, enrage, exacerbate, exasperate, incense, inflame, irritate, madden, provoke, sour

enviable advantageous, blessed, covetable, desirable, favoured, fortunate, lucky, much to be desired, privileged, to die for (*informal*)

Antonyms disagreeable, painful, thankless, uncomfortable, undesirable, unenviable, unpleasant

envious begrudging, covetous, green-eyed, green with envy, grudging, jaundiced, jealous, malicious, resentful, spiteful

environ beset, besiege, encircle, enclose, encompass, engird, envelop, gird, hem, invest (*rare*), ring, surround

environment atmosphere, background, conditions, context, domain, element, habitat, locale, medium, milieu, scene, setting, situation, surroundings, territory

environmentalist conservationist, ecologist, friend of the earth, green

environs district, locality, neighbourhood, outskirts, precincts, purlieus, suburbs, surrounding area, vicinity

envisage 1. conceive (of), conceptualize, contemplate, fancy, imagine, picture, think up, visualize 2. anticipate, envision, foresee, predict, see

envision anticipate, conceive of, contemplate, envisage, foresee, predict, see, visualize

envoy agent, ambassador, courier, delegate, deputy, diplomat, emissary, intermediary, legate, messenger, minister, plenipotentiary, representative

envy 1. *noun* covetousness, enviousness, grudge, hatred, ill will, jealousy, malice, malignity, resentfulness, resentment, spite, the green-eyed monster (*informal*) 2. *verb* be envious (of), begrudge, be jealous (of), covet, grudge, resent

Nothing sharpens sight like envy
Thomas Fuller *Gnomologia*

Our envy always lasts much longer than the happiness of those we envy
Duc de la Rochefoucauld *Maxims*

Even success softens not the heart of the envious
Pindar *Odes*

ephemeral brief, evanescent, fleeting, flitting, fugacious, fugitive, impermanent, momentary, passing, short, short-lived, temporary, transient, transitory

Antonyms abiding, durable, enduring, eternal, immortal, lasting, long-lasting, persisting, steadfast

epicene *adjective* **1.** androgyne, androgynous, bisexual, gynandrous, hermaphrodite, hermaphroditic **2.** asexual, neuter, sexless **3.** camp (*informal*), effeminate, unmanly, weak, womanish *~noun* **4.** androgyne, bisexual, gynandromorph, hermaphrodite

epicure 1. *bon vivant*, epicurean, foodie, gastronome, gourmet **2.** glutton, gourmand, hedonist, sensualist, sybarite, voluptuary

epicurean 1. *adjective* bacchanalian, gluttonous, gourmandizing, hedonistic, libertine, luscious, lush, luxurious, pleasure-seeking, self-indulgent, sensual, sybaritic, voluptuous **2.** *noun bon vivant*, epicure, foodie, gastronome, gourmet

epidemic 1. *adjective* general, pandemic, prevailing, prevalent, rampant, rife, sweeping, wide-ranging, widespread **2.** *noun* contagion, growth, outbreak, plague, rash, spread, upsurge, wave

epigram aphorism, *bon mot*, quip, witticism

A thing well said will be wit in all languages
John Dryden *Essay of Dramatic Poesy*

epigrammatic concise, laconic, piquant, pithy, pointed, pungent, sharp, short, succinct, terse, witty

epilogue afterword, coda, concluding speech, conclusion, postscript

Antonyms exordium, foreword, introduction, preamble, preface, prelude, prologue

episode 1. adventure, affair, business, circumstance, escapade, event, experience, happening, incident, matter, occurrence **2.** chapter, instalment, part, passage, scene, section

episodic anecdotal, digressive, disconnected, discursive, disjointed, intermittent, irregular, occasional, picaresque, rambling, sporadic, wandering

epistle communication, letter, message, missive, note

epithet appellation, description, designation, moniker *or* monicker (*slang*), name, nickname, sobriquet, tag, title

epitome 1. archetype, embodiment, essence, exemplar, norm, personification, quintessence, representation, type, typical example **2.** abbreviation, abridgment, abstract, compendium, condensation, conspectus, contraction, digest, précis, résumé, summary, syllabus, synopsis

epitomize 1. embody, exemplify, illustrate, incarnate, personify, represent, symbolize, typify **2.** abbreviate, abridge, abstract, condense, contract, curtail, cut, encapsulate, précis, reduce, shorten, summarize, synopsize

epoch age, date, era, period, time

equable 1. agreeable, calm, composed, easy-going, even-tempered, imperturbable, level-headed, placid, serene, temperate, unexcitable, unfazed (*informal*), unflappable (*informal*), unruffled **2.** consistent, constant, even, on an even keel, regular, smooth, stable, steady, temperate, tranquil, unchanging, uniform, unvarying

Antonyms changeable, excitable, fitful, inconsistent, irregular, nervous, temperamental, uneven, unpredictable, unstable, volatile

equal *adjective* **1.** alike, commensurate, equivalent, identical, like, one and the same, proportionate, tantamount, the same, uniform **2.** balanced, corresponding, egalitarian, even, evenly balanced, evenly matched, evenly proportioned, fifty-fifty (*informal*), level pegging (*Brit. informal*), matched, regular, symmetrical, uniform, unvarying **3.** able, adequate, capable, competent, fit, good enough, ready, strong enough, suitable, up to **4.** egalitarian, equable, even-handed, fair, impartial, just, unbiased *~noun* **5.** brother, compeer, counterpart, equivalent, fellow, match, mate, parallel, peer, rival, twin *~verb* **6.** agree with, amount to, balance, be equal to, be even with, be level with, be tantamount to, come up to, correspond to, equalize, equate, even, level, match, parallel, rival, square with, tally with, tie with

Antonyms *adjective* different, disproportionate, dissimilar, diverse, inadequate, inequitable, irregular, unbalanced, unequal, uneven, unlike, unmatched *~verb* be different, be unequal, disagree

equality balance, coequality, correspondence, egalitarianism, equal opportunity, equatability, equivalence, evenness, fairness, identity, likeness, parity, sameness, similarity, uniformity

Antonyms bias, discrimination, disparity, imparity, inequality, lack of balance, prejudice, unevenness, unfairness

We hold these truths to be self-evident: that all men are created equal; that they are endowed by their Creator with inalienable rights; that among these are life, liberty, and the pursuit of happiness
Thomas Jefferson *The Declaration of Independence*

I have a dream that one day this nation will rise up, live out the true meaning of its creed: we hold these truths to be self-evident, that all men are created equal
Martin Luther King

All animals are equal but some animals are more equal than others
George Orwell *Animal Farm*

The defect of equality is that we only desire it with our superiors
Henry Becque *Querelles littéraires*
Even the president of the United States sometimes must have to stand naked
Bob Dylan *It's Alright, Ma (I'm Only Bleeding)*

equalize balance, equal, equate, even up, level, make equal, match, regularize, smooth, square, standardize

equanimity aplomb, calm, calmness, compo~sure, coolness, imperturbability, level-headedness, peace, phlegm, placidity, poise, presence of mind, sang-froid, self-possession, serenity, steadiness, tranquillity

equate agree, balance, be commensurate, com~pare, correspond with *or* to, equalize, liken, make *or* be equal, match, mention in the same breath, offset, pair, parallel, square, tally, think of together

equation agreement, balancing, comparison, correspondence, equality, equalization, equat~ing, equivalence, likeness, match, pairing, parallel

equestrian **1.** *adjective* in the saddle, mounted, on horseback **2.** *noun* cavalier (*archaic*), horseman, knight, rider

equilibrate balance, ballast, compensate (for), counterbalance, counterpoise, countervail, equipoise, even up, neutralize, offset

equilibrium **1.** balance, counterpoise, equipoise, evenness, rest, stability, steadiness, symmetry **2.** calm, calmness, collectedness, composure, coolness, equanimity, poise, self-possession, serenity, stability, steadiness

equip accoutre, arm, array, attire, deck out, dress, endow, fit out, fit up, furnish, kit out, outfit, prepare, provide, rig, stock, supply

equipage **1.** carriage, coach **2.** accoutrements, apparatus, baggage, equipment, gear, materi~el, munitions, stores

equipment accoutrements, apparatus, appur~tenances, baggage, equipage, furnishings, fur~niture, gear, materiel, outfit, paraphernalia, rig, stuff, supplies, tackle, tools

equipoise *noun* **1.** balance, equilibrium, even balance, evenness, stability, steadiness, sym~metry **2.** ballast, counterbalance, counterpoise, counterweight, offset *~verb* **3.** balance, ballast, compensate (for), counterbalance, counter~poise, countervail, equilibrate, neutralize, off~set

equitable candid, disinterested, dispassionate, due, even-handed, fair, honest, impartial, just, nondiscriminatory, proper, proportionate, rea~sonable, right, rightful, unbiased, unpreju~diced

equity disinterestedness, equitableness, even-handedness, fair-mindedness, fairness, fair play, honesty, impartiality, integrity, justice, reasonableness, rectitude, righteousness, uprightness
Antonyms bias, discrimination, injustice, par~tiality, preference, prejudice, unfairness

equivalence agreement, alikeness, conformity, correspondence, equality, evenness, identity, interchangeableness, likeness, match, parallel, parity, sameness, similarity, synonymy

equivalent **1.** *adjective* alike, commensurate, comparable, correspondent, corresponding, equal, even, homologous, interchangeable, of a kind, of a piece, same, similar, synonymous, tantamount **2.** *noun* correspondent, counter~part, equal, match, opposite number, parallel, peer, twin
Antonyms *adjective* different, dissimilar, in~comparable, unequal, unlike

equivocal ambiguous, ambivalent, doubtful, dubious, evasive, indefinite, indeterminate, misleading, oblique, obscure, oracular, pre~varicating, questionable, suspicious, uncertain, vague
Antonyms absolute, certain, clear, clear-cut, cut-and-dried (*informal*), decisive, definite, evident, explicit, incontrovertible, indubitable, manifest, plain, positive, straight, unambigu~ous, unequivocal

equivocate avoid the issue, beat about the bush (*informal*), dodge, evade, fence, flannel (*Brit. informal*), fudge, hedge, parry, prevari~cate, pussyfoot (*informal*), quibble, shuffle, sidestep, tergiversate, waffle (*informal, chiefly Brit.*)

equivocation ambiguity, double talk, doubtful~ness, evasion, hedging, prevarication, quib~bling, shuffling, tergiversation, waffle (*infor~mal, chiefly Brit.*), weasel words (*informal, chiefly U.S.*)

era aeon, age, cycle, date, day *or* days, epoch, generation, period, stage, time

eradicate abolish, annihilate, deracinate, de~stroy, efface, eliminate, erase, excise, expunge, exterminate, extinguish, extirpate, obliterate, put paid to, remove, root out, stamp out, uproot, weed out, wipe from the face of the earth, wipe out

eradication abolition, annihilation, deracina~tion, destruction, effacement, elimination, erasure, expunction, extermination, extinction, extirpation, obliteration, removal

erase blot, cancel, delete, efface, excise, ex~punge, obliterate, remove, rub out, scratch out, wipe out

erect *adjective* **1.** elevated, firm, perpendicular, pricked-up, raised, rigid, standing, stiff, straight, upright, vertical *~verb* **2.** build, con~struct, elevate, lift, mount, pitch, put up, raise, rear, set up, stand up **3.** create, estab~

lish, form, found, initiate, institute, organize, set up
Antonyms *adjective* bent, flaccid, horizontal, leaning, limp, prone, recumbent, relaxed, su~ pine *~verb* demolish, destroy, dismantle, raze, tear down

erection 1. assembly, building, construction, creation, elevation, establishment, fabrication, manufacture 2. building, construction, edifice, pile, structure

erelong *archaic or poetic* before long, early, quickly, shortly, soon, speedily

eremite anchorite, hermit, recluse, solitary

ergo accordingly, consequently, for that reason, hence, in consequence, so, then, therefore, thus

erode abrade, consume, corrode, destroy, de~ teriorate, disintegrate, eat away, grind down, spoil, wear down *or* away

erosion abrasion, attrition, consumption, cor~ rasion, corrosion, destruction, deterioration, disintegration, eating away, grinding down, spoiling, wear, wearing down *or* away

erotic amatory, aphrodisiac, carnal, erogenous, lustful, rousing, seductive, sensual, sexy (*in~ formal*), steamy (*informal*), stimulating, sug~ gestive, titillating, voluptuous

err 1. be inaccurate, be incorrect, be in error, blot one's copybook (*informal*), blunder, drop a brick *or* clanger (*informal*), go astray, go wrong, make a mistake, misapprehend, mis~ calculate, misjudge, mistake, put one's foot in it (*informal*), slip up (*informal*) 2. be out of order, blot one's copybook (*informal*), deviate, do wrong, fall, go astray, lapse, misbehave, offend, sin, transgress, trespass

errand charge, commission, job, message, mis~ sion, task

errant 1. *archaic* itinerant, journeying, nomad~ ic, peripatetic, rambling, roaming, roving, wandering 2. aberrant, deviant, erring, of~ fending, sinning, straying, wayward, wrong

erratic 1. aberrant, abnormal, capricious, changeable, desultory, eccentric, fitful, incon~ sistent, inconstant, irregular, shifting, uneven, unpredictable, unreliable, unstable, variable, wayward 2. directionless, meandering, plan~ etary, wandering
Antonyms certain, consistent, constant, de~ pendable, invariable, natural, normal, pre~ dictable, regular, reliable, stable, steady, straight, unchanging, undeviating

erratum corrigendum, literal, misprint, omis~ sion, typo (*informal*)

erroneous amiss, fallacious, false, faulty, flawed, inaccurate, incorrect, inexact, invalid, mistaken, spurious, unfounded, unsound, un~ true, wide of the mark, wrong
Antonyms accurate, correct, factual, faultless, flawless, precise, right, true, veracious

erroneously falsely, inaccurately, incorrectly, in error, mistakenly, wrongly

error 1. bloomer (*Brit. informal*), blunder, bon~ er (*slang*), boob (*Brit. slang*), delusion, erra~ tum, fallacy, fault, flaw, howler (*informal*), inaccuracy, misapprehension, miscalculation, misconception, mistake, oversight, slip, sol~ ecism 2. delinquency, deviation, fault, lapse, misdeed, offence, sin, transgression, trespass, wrong, wrongdoing

Truth lies within a little and certain compass, but error is immense
Henry St. John, 1st Viscount Bolingbroke *Re~ flections upon Exile*

Crooked things may be as stiff and unflexible as straight; and men may be as positive in error as in truth
John Locke *Essay Concerning Human Under~ standing*

ersatz artificial, bogus, counterfeit, fake, imi~ tation, phoney *or* phony (*informal*), pretended, sham, simulated, spurious, substitute, syn~ thetic

erstwhile bygone, ex (*informal*), former, late, old, once, one-time, past, previous, quondam, sometime

erudite cultivated, cultured, educated, knowl~ edgeable, learned, lettered, literate, scholarly, well-educated, well-read
Antonyms ignorant, illiterate, shallow, un~ educated, uninformed, unlettered, unschooled, untaught, unthinking

erudition education, knowledge, learning, let~ ters, lore, scholarship

erupt 1. be ejected, belch forth, blow up, break out, burst forth, burst into, burst out, dis~ charge, explode, flare up, gush, pour forth, spew forth *or* out, spit out, spout, throw off, vent, vomit 2. *Medical* appear, break out

eruption 1. discharge, ejection, explosion, flare-up, outbreak, outburst, sally, venting 2. *Medical* inflammation, outbreak, rash

escalate amplify, ascend, be increased, en~ large, expand, extend, grow, heighten, in~ crease, intensify, magnify, mount, raise, rise, step up
Antonyms abate, contract, decrease, descend, diminish, fall, lessen, limit, lower, shrink, wane, wind down

escalation acceleration, amplification, build-up, expansion, heightening, increase, intensifica~ tion, rise, upsurge

escapade adventure, antic, caper, fling, lark (*informal*), mischief, prank, romp, scrape (*in~ formal*), spree, stunt, trick

escape 1. *verb* abscond, bolt, break free *or* out, decamp, do a bunk (*Brit. slang*), do a runner (*slang*), flee, fly, fly the coop (*U.S. & Canad. informal*), get away, hook it (*slang*), make *or* effect one's escape, make one's getaway, run away *or* off, skedaddle (*informal*), skip, slip away, slip through one's fingers, take a powder (*U.S. & Canad. slang*), take it on the lam (*U.S. & Canad. slang*) **2.** *noun* bolt, break, break-out, decampment, flight, getaway **3.** *verb* avoid, body-swerve (*Scot.*), circumvent, dodge, duck, elude, evade, pass, shun, slip **4.** *noun* avoidance, circumvention, elusion, evasion **5.** *verb* discharge, drain, emanate, exude, flow, gush, issue, leak, pour forth, seep, spurt **6.** *noun* discharge, drain, effluence, efflux, emanation, emission, gush, leak, leakage, outflow, outpour, seepage, spurt **7.** *verb* baffle, be beyond (someone), be forgotten by, elude, puzzle, stump **8.** *noun* distraction, diversion, pastime, recreation, relief

eschew abandon, abjure, abstain from, avoid, elude, fight shy of, forgo, forswear, give a wide berth to, give up, have nothing to do with, keep *or* steer clear of, kick (*informal*), refrain from, renounce, shun, swear off

escort *noun* **1.** bodyguard, company, convoy, cortege, entourage, guard, protection, retinue, safeguard, train **2.** attendant, beau, chaperon, companion, guide, partner, protector, squire (*rare*) ~*verb* **3.** accompany, chaperon, conduct, convoy, guard, guide, hold (someone's) hand, lead, partner, protect, shepherd, squire, usher

esculent eatable, edible, fit to eat, palatable, wholesome

esoteric abstruse, arcane, cabbalistic, cryptic, hidden, inner, inscrutable, mysterious, mystic, mystical, obscure, occult, private, recondite, secret

especial **1.** chief, distinguished, exceptional, extraordinary, marked, notable, noteworthy, outstanding, principal, signal, special, uncommon, unusual **2.** exclusive, express, individual, particular, peculiar, personal, private, singular, special, specific, unique

especially **1.** chiefly, conspicuously, exceptionally, extraordinarily, largely, mainly, markedly, notably, outstandingly, principally, remarkably, seriously (*informal*), signally, specially, strikingly, supremely, uncommonly, unusually **2.** exclusively, expressly, particularly, peculiarly, singularly, specifically, uniquely

espionage counter-intelligence, intelligence, spying, surveillance, undercover work

espousal **1.** adoption, advocacy, backing, championing, championship, defence, embracing, maintenance, promotion, support, taking up **2.** *archaic* affiancing, betrothal, betrothing (*archaic*), engagement, espousing (*archaic*), marriage, nuptials, plighting, wedding

espouse **1.** adopt, advocate, back, champion, defend, embrace, maintain, promote, stand up for, support, take up **2.** *archaic* betroth (*archaic*), marry, plight one's troth (*old-fashioned*), take as spouse, take to wife, wed

esprit animation, brio, élan, liveliness, quickness, sparkle, spirit, sprightliness, verve, vitality, vivacity, wit, zest

espy behold, catch a glimpse of, catch sight of, descry, detect, discern, discover, glimpse, make out, notice, observe, perceive, sight, spot, spy

essay[1] *noun* article, composition, discourse, disquisition, dissertation, paper, piece, tract, treatise

essay[2] **1.** *noun* aim, attempt, bid, crack (*informal*), effort, endeavour, exertion, experiment, go (*informal*), shot (*informal*), stab (*informal*), struggle, test, trial, try, undertaking, venture **2.** *verb* aim, attempt, endeavour, have a go (bash (*informal*), crack (*informal*), shot (*informal*)) (*informal*), put to the test, strive, take on, test, try, try out, undertake

essence **1.** being, bottom line, core, crux, entity, heart, kernel, life, lifeblood, meaning, nature, pith, principle, quiddity, quintessence, significance, soul, spirit, substance **2.** concentrate, distillate, elixir, extract, spirits, tincture **3.** *rare* cologne, fragrance, perfume, scent **4. in essence** basically, essentially, fundamentally, in effect, in substance, in the main, materially, substantially, to all intents and purposes, virtually **5. of the essence** crucial, essential, indispensable, of the utmost importance, vital, vitally important

essential *adjective* **1.** crucial, important, indispensable, necessary, needed, requisite, vital **2.** basic, cardinal, constitutional, elemental, elementary, fundamental, immanent, inherent, innate, intrinsic, key, main, principal, radical **3.** absolute, complete, ideal, perfect, quintessential **4.** concentrated, distilled, extracted, rectified, refined, volatile ~*noun* **5.** basic, fundamental, must, necessity, prerequisite, principle, requisite, rudiment, *sine qua non*, vital part

Antonyms accessory, dispensable, expendable, extra, extraneous, incidental, inessential, lesser, minor, nonessential, option, secondary, superfluous, surplus, trivial, unimportant, unnecessary

establish **1.** base, constitute, create, decree, enact, ensconce, entrench, fix, form, found, ground, implant, inaugurate, install, institute, organize, plant, put down roots, root, secure, settle, set up, sow the seeds, start **2.** authenticate, certify, confirm, corroborate, demonstrate, prove, ratify, show, substantiate, validate, verify

establishment 1. creation, enactment, formation, foundation, founding, inauguration, installation, institution, organization, setting up 2. business, company, concern, corporation, enterprise, firm, house, institute, institution, organization, outfit (*informal*), setup (*informal*), structure, system 3. building, factory, house, office, plant, quarters 4. abode, domicile, dwelling, home, house, household, pad (*slang*), residence 5. **the Establishment** established order, institutionalized authority, ruling class, the powers that be, the system

estate 1. area, demesne, domain, holdings, lands, manor, property 2. *Property law* assets, belongings, effects, fortune, goods, possessions, property, wealth 3. caste, class, order, rank 4. condition, lot, period, place, position, quality, rank, situation, standing, state, station, status

esteem *verb* 1. admire, be fond of, cherish, honour, like, love, prize, regard highly, respect, revere, reverence, take off one's hat to, think highly of, treasure, value, venerate 2. *formal* account, believe, calculate, consider, deem, estimate, hold, judge, rate, reckon, regard, think, view *~noun* 3. admiration, Brownie points, consideration, credit, estimation, good opinion, honour, regard, respect, reverence, veneration

estimable admirable, esteemed, excellent, good, honourable, honoured, meritorious, reputable, respectable, respected, valuable, valued, worthy

estimate *verb* 1. appraise, assess, calculate roughly, evaluate, gauge, guess, judge, number, reckon, value 2. assess, believe, conjecture, consider, form an opinion, guess, judge, rank, rate, reckon, surmise, think *~noun* 3. appraisal, appraisement, approximate calculation, assessment, ballpark estimate (*informal*), ballpark figure (*informal*), evaluation, guess, guesstimate (*informal*), judgment, reckoning, valuation 4. appraisal, appraisement, assessment, belief, conjecture, educated guess, estimation, judgment, opinion, surmise, thought(s)

estimation 1. appraisal, appreciation, assessment, belief, consideration, considered opinion, estimate, evaluation, judgment, opinion, view 2. admiration, Brownie points, credit, esteem, good opinion, honour, regard, respect, reverence, veneration

estrange alienate, antagonize, disaffect, disunite, divide, drive apart, lose *or* destroy the affection of, make hostile, part, separate, set at odds, withdraw, withhold

Antonyms ally, associate, coalesce, couple, fuse, join, link, marry, unite

estrangement alienation, antagonization, breach, break-up, disaffection, dissociation, disunity, division, hostility, parting, separation, split, withdrawal, withholding

estuary creek, firth, fjord, inlet, mouth

et cetera and others, and so forth, and so on, and the like, and the rest, et al.

etch carve, corrode, cut, eat into, engrave, furrow, impress, imprint, incise, ingrain, inscribe, stamp

etching carving, engraving, impression, imprint, inscription, print

eternal 1. abiding, ceaseless, constant, deathless, endless, everlasting, immortal, infinite, interminable, never-ending, perennial, perpetual, sempiternal (*literary*), timeless, unceasing, undying, unending, unremitting, without end 2. deathless, enduring, everlasting, immortal, immutable, imperishable, indestructible, lasting, permanent

Antonyms changing, ephemeral, evanescent, finite, fleeting, infrequent, irregular, mortal, occasional, perishable, random, rare, temporal, transient, transitory

eternity 1. age, ages, endlessness, for ever, immortality, infinitude, infinity, perpetuity, timelessness, time without end 2. *Theology* heaven, paradise, the afterlife, the hereafter, the next world

> *Eternity's a terrible thought. I mean, where's it all going to end?*
> Tom Stoppard *Rosencrantz and Guildenstern are Dead*

> *Eternity! thou pleasing, dreadful thought!*
> Joseph Addison *Cato*

> *Every instant of time is a pinprick of eternity*
> Marcus Aurelius *Meditations*

> *Eternity is in love with the productions of time*
> William Blake *The Marriage of Heaven and Hell*

ethereal 1. dainty, delicate, exquisite, fine, insubstantial, light, rarefied, refined, subtle, tenuous 2. aerial, airy, fairy, impalpable, intangible, light, rarefied 3. celestial, empyreal, heavenly, spiritual, sublime, unearthly, unworldly

ethical conscientious, correct, decent, fair, fitting, good, honest, honourable, just, moral, principled, proper, right, righteous, upright, virtuous

Antonyms dishonourable, disreputable, immoral, improper, indecent, low-down (*informal*), not cricket (*informal*), underhand, unethical, unfair, unscrupulous, unseemly

ethics conscience, moral code, morality, moral philosophy, moral values, principles, rules of conduct, standards

ethnic cultural, folk, indigenous, national, native, racial, traditional

ethos attitude, beliefs, character, disposition, ethic, spirit, tenor

etiolated achromatic, blanched, bleached, colourless, faded, pale, wan, washed out, white, whitened

etiquette civility, code, convention, courtesy, customs, decorum, formalities, good *or* proper behaviour, manners, politeness, politesse, propriety, protocol, p's and q's, rules, usage

eulogize acclaim, applaud, commend, compliment, crack up (*informal*), cry up, exalt, extol, glorify, laud, magnify (*archaic*), panegyrize, pay tribute to, praise, sing *or* sound the praises of

eulogy acclaim, acclamation, accolade, applause, commendation, compliment, encomium, exaltation, glorification, laudation, paean, panegyric, plaudit, praise, tribute

euphonic, euphonious canorous (*rare*), clear, consonant, dulcet, harmonious, mellifluous, mellow, melodic, melodious, musical, pleasing to the ear, silvery, sweet-toned, tuneful

euphony consonance, harmony, mellifluousness, mellowness, melodiousness, melody, music, musicality, tunefulness, unison

euphoria bliss, ecstasy, elation, exaltation, exhilaration, exultation, glee, high spirits, intoxication, joy, joyousness, jubilation, rapture, transport
Antonyms depression, despair, despondency, dolefulness, downheartedness, dumps (*informal*), gloominess, hopelessness, low spirits, melancholia, melancholy, sadness, the blues

evacuate 1. abandon, clear, decamp, depart, desert, forsake, leave, move out, pull out, quit, relinquish, remove, vacate, withdraw 2. crap (*taboo slang*), defecate, discharge, eject, eliminate, empty, excrete, expel, shit (*taboo slang*), void

evacuation 1. abandonment, clearance, departure, exodus, flight, leaving, pulling out, removal, vacation, withdrawal 2. crap (*taboo slang*), defecation, discharge, ejection, elimination, excretion, purging, shit (*taboo slang*), voiding

evade 1. avoid, body-swerve (*Scot.*), circumvent, decline, dodge, duck, elude, escape, escape the clutches of, eschew, get away from, shirk, shun, sidestep, slip through one's fingers, slip through the net, steer clear of 2. balk, beat about the bush, circumvent, cop out (*slang*), equivocate, fence, fend off, flannel (*Brit. informal*), fudge, hedge, parry, prevaricate, quibble, waffle (*informal, chiefly Brit.*)
Antonyms brave, confront, encounter, face, meet, meet face to face

evaluate appraise, assay, assess, calculate, estimate, gauge, judge, rank, rate, reckon, size up (*informal*), value, weigh

evaluation appraisal, assessment, calculation, estimate, estimation, judgment, opinion, rating, valuation

evanesce clear, disappear, disperse, dissolve, evaporate, fade, melt, vanish, vanish off the face of the earth

evanescence brevity, briefness, ephemerality, ephemeralness, fleetingness, fugaciousness, fugacity, impermanence, momentariness, transience, transitoriness

evanescent brief, ephemeral, fading, fleeting, fugacious, fugitive, impermanent, momentary, passing, short-lived, transient, transitory, vanishing

evangelical, evangelistic crusading, missionary, propagandizing, proselytizing, zealous

evaporate 1. dehydrate, desiccate, dry, dry up, vaporize 2. dematerialize, disappear, dispel, disperse, dissipate, dissolve, evanesce, fade, fade away, melt, melt away, vanish

evaporation 1. dehydration, desiccation, drying, drying up, vaporization 2. dematerialization, disappearance, dispelling, dispersal, dissipation, dissolution, evanescence, fading, fading away, melting, melting away, vanishing

evasion artifice, avoidance, circumvention, cop-out (*slang*), cunning, dodge, elusion, equivocation, escape, evasiveness, excuse, fudging, obliqueness, pretext, prevarication, ruse, shift, shirking, shuffling, sophism, sophistry, subterfuge, trickery, waffle (*informal, chiefly Brit.*)

evasive cagey (*informal*), casuistic, casuistical, cunning, deceitful, deceptive, devious, dissembling, elusive, elusory, equivocating, indirect, misleading, oblique, prevaricating, shifty, shuffling, slippery, sophistical, tricky
Antonyms candid, direct, frank, guileless, honest, open, straight, straightforward, truthful, unequivocating

eve 1. day before, night before, vigil 2. brink, edge, point, threshold, verge

even *adjective* 1. flat, flush, horizontal, level, parallel, plane, plumb, smooth, steady, straight, true, uniform 2. constant, metrical, regular, smooth, steady, unbroken, uniform, uninterrupted, unvarying, unwavering 3. calm, composed, cool, equable, equanimous, even-tempered, imperturbable, peaceful, placid, serene, stable, steady, tranquil, undisturbed, unexcitable, unruffled, well-balanced 4. coequal, commensurate, comparable, drawn, equal, equalized, equally balanced, fifty-fifty (*informal*), identical, level, level pegging (*Brit. informal*), like, matching, neck and neck, on a par, parallel, similar, square, the same, tied, uniform 5. balanced, disinterested, dispassionate, equitable, fair, fair and square, impartial, just, unbiased, unprejudiced 6. **get even (with)** *informal* be revenged *or* revenge one~

self, even the score, get one's own back, give tit for tat, pay back, pay (someone) back in his *or* her own coin, reciprocate, repay, requite, return like for like, settle the score, take an eye for an eye, take vengeance *~adverb* **7.** all the more, much, still, yet **8.** despite, disregarding, in spite of, notwithstanding **9.** **even as** at the same time as, at the time that, during the time that, exactly as, just as, while, whilst **10.** **even so** all the same, be that as it may, despite (that), however, in spite of (that), nevertheless, nonetheless, notwithstanding (that), still, yet *~verb* **11.** *often followed by* **out** *or* **up** align, balance, become level, equal, equalize, flatten, level, match, regularize, smooth, square, stabilize, steady **12.** **even the score** be revenged *or* revenge oneself, equalize, get even (*informal*), get one's own back, give tit for tat, pay (someone) back, reciprocate, repay, requite, return like for like, settle the score, take an eye for an eye, take vengeance

Antonyms (*senses 1 & 2*) asymmetrical, awry, broken, bumpy, changeable, changing, curving, different, fluctuating, irregular, odd, rough, twisting, undulating, uneven, variable, wavy (*sense 3*) agitated, changeable, emotional, excitable, quick-tempered, unpredictable (*sense 4*) disproportionate, ill-matched, imbalanced, irregular, unequal, uneven (*sense 5*) biased, partial, prejudiced, unbalanced, unequal, unfair

even-handed balanced, disinterested, equitable, fair, fair and square, impartial, just, unbiased, unprejudiced

evening crepuscule, dusk, e'en (*archaic or poetic*), eve, even (*archaic*), eventide (*archaic or poetic*), gloaming (*Scot. or poetic*), twilight, vesper (*archaic*)

It is a beauteous evening, calm and free,
The holy time is quiet as a nun,
Breathless with adoration
William Wordsworth *It is a beauteous evening*

The curfew tolls the knell of passing day
Thomas Gray *Elegy Written in a Country Churchyard*

Let us go then, you and I
When the evening is spread out against the sky
Like a patient etherized upon a table
T.S. Eliot *Love Song of J. Alfred Prufrock*

event **1.** adventure, affair, business, circumstance, episode, escapade, experience, fact, happening, incident, matter, milestone, occasion, occurrence **2.** conclusion, consequence, effect, end, issue, outcome, result, termination, upshot **3.** bout, competition, contest, game, tournament **4.** **at all events** at any rate, come what may, in any case, in any event, regardless, whatever happens

even-tempered calm, composed, cool, cool-headed, equable, imperturbable, level-headed, peaceful, placid, serene, steady, tranquil, unexcitable, unruffled

Antonyms emotional, excitable, hasty, highly-strung, hot-headed, hot-tempered, irascible, quick-tempered, temperamental, touchy, volatile

eventful active, busy, consequential, critical, crucial, decisive, dramatic, exciting, fateful, full, historic, important, lively, memorable, momentous, notable, noteworthy, remarkable, significant

Antonyms commonplace, dull, humdrum, insignificant, ordinary, trivial, uneventful, unexceptional, unexciting, unimportant, uninteresting, unremarkable

eventual concluding, consequent, ensuing, final, future, later, overall, prospective, resulting, ultimate

eventuality case, chance, contingency, event, likelihood, possibility, probability

eventually after all, at the end of the day, finally, in the course of time, in the end, in the fullness of time, in the long run, one day, some day, some time, sooner or later, ultimately, when all is said and done

eventuate be a consequence, be consequent, come about, come to pass (*archaic*), ensue, follow, issue, result

ever **1.** at all, at any time (period, point), by any chance, in any case, on any occasion **2.** always, at all times, aye (*Scot.*), constantly, continually, endlessly, eternally, everlastingly, evermore, for ever, incessantly, perpetually, relentlessly, to the end of time, unceasingly, unendingly

everlasting **1.** abiding, deathless, endless, eternal, immortal, imperishable, indestructible, infinite, interminable, never-ending, perpetual, timeless, undying **2.** ceaseless, constant, continual, continuous, endless, incessant, interminable, never-ending, unceasing, uninterrupted, unremitting

Antonyms brief, ephemeral, fleeting, impermanent, passing, short-lived, temporary, transient, transitory

evermore always, eternally, ever, for ever, *in perpetuum*, to the end of time

every all, each, each one, the whole number

everybody all and sundry, each one, each person, everyone, every person, one and all, the whole world

everyday **1.** daily, quotidian **2.** accustomed, banal, bog-standard (*Brit. & Irish slang*), common, common or garden (*informal*), commonplace, conventional, customary, dime-a-dozen (*informal*), dull, familiar, frequent, habitual, informal, mundane, ordinary, routine, run-of-

the-mill, stock, unexceptional, unimaginative, usual, vanilla (*slang*), wonted, workaday
Antonyms best, exceptional, exciting, extraordinary, incidental, individual, infrequent, interesting, irregular, now and then, occasional, original, outlandish, periodic, special, uncommon, unusual

everyone all and sundry, each one, each person, everybody, every person, one and all, the whole world

everything all, each thing, the aggregate, the entirety, the lot, the sum, the total, the whole caboodle (*informal*), the whole kit and caboodle (*informal*), the whole lot

everywhere all around, all over, far and wide *or* near, high and low, in each place, in every nook and cranny, in every place, omnipresent, the world over, to *or* in all places, ubiquitous, ubiquitously

evict boot out (*informal*), chuck out (*informal*), dislodge, dispossess, eject, expel, kick out (*informal*), oust, put out, remove, show the door (to), throw on to the streets, throw out, turf out (*informal*), turn out

eviction clearance, dislodgement, dispossession, ejection, expulsion, ouster (*Law*), removal

evidence **1.** *noun* affirmation, attestation, averment, confirmation, corroboration, data, declaration, demonstration, deposition, grounds, indication, manifestation, mark, proof, sign, substantiation, testimony, token, witness **2.** *verb* demonstrate, denote, display, evince, exhibit, indicate, manifest, prove, reveal, show, signify, testify to, witness

evident apparent, blatant, bold, clear, conspicuous, incontestable, incontrovertible, indisputable, manifest, noticeable, obvious, palpable, patent, perceptible, plain, plain as the nose on your face, salient, tangible, unmistakable, visible
Antonyms ambiguous, concealed, doubtful, dubious, hidden, imperceptible, obscure, questionable, secret, uncertain, unclear, unknown, vague

evidently **1.** clearly, doubtless, doubtlessly, incontestably, incontrovertibly, indisputably, manifestly, obviously, patently, plainly, undoubtedly, unmistakably, without question **2.** apparently, it seems, it would seem, ostensibly, outwardly, seemingly, to all appearances

evil *adjective* **1.** bad, base, corrupt, depraved, heinous, immoral, iniquitous, maleficent, malevolent, malicious, malignant, nefarious, reprobate, sinful, vicious, vile, villainous, wicked, wrong *~noun* **2.** badness, baseness, corruption, curse, depravity, heinousness, immorality, iniquity, maleficence, malignity, sin, sinfulness, turpitude, vice, viciousness, villainy, wickedness, wrong, wrongdoing *~adjective* **3.** baneful (*archaic*), calamitous, catastrophic, deleterious, destructive, detrimental, dire, disastrous, harmful, hurtful, inauspicious, injurious, mischievous, painful, pernicious, ruinous, sorrowful, unfortunate, unlucky, woeful *~noun* **4.** affliction, calamity, catastrophe, disaster, harm, hurt, ill, injury, mischief, misery, misfortune, pain, ruin, sorrow, suffering, woe *~adjective* **5.** foul, mephitic, noxious, offensive, pestilential, putrid, unpleasant, vile

So farewell hope, and with hope farewell fear,
Farewell remorse: all good to me is lost;
Evil be thou my Good
John Milton *Paradise Lost*

Evil be to him who evil thinks (Honi soit qui mal y pense)
Motto of the Order of the Garter

What we call evil is simply ignorance bumping its head in the dark
Henry Ford *Observer*

The evil that men do lives after them
William Shakespeare *Julius Caesar*

Sufficient unto the day is the evil thereof
Bible: St. Matthew

Choose the lesser of two evils

See no evil, hear no evil, speak no evil

evildoer **1.** bad hat (*informal, chiefly Brit*), criminal, crook (*informal*), culprit, delinquent, malefactor, miscreant, offender, villain, wrongdoer, wrong 'un (*informal*) **2.** beast, blackguard, devil, devil incarnate, fiend, mischief-maker, monster, ogre, reprobate, rogue, sinner

evildoing abomination, badness, crime, devilry, evil, fiendishness, harm, iniquity, injury, mischief-making, sin, vice, viciousness, vileness, villainy, wickedness, wrongdoing

evil-minded bitchy (*informal*), depraved, dirty-minded, filthy, foul-mouthed, gossip-mongering, lewd, malicious, nasty, poisonous, salacious, snide, spiteful, venomous

evince attest, bespeak, betoken, demonstrate, display, establish, evidence, exhibit, express, indicate, make clear, make evident, manifest, reveal, show, signify

evoke **1.** arouse, awaken, call, excite, give rise to, induce, recall, rekindle, stimulate, stir up, summon up **2.** call forth, educe (*rare*), elicit, produce, provoke **3.** arouse, call, call forth, conjure up, invoke, raise, summon
Antonyms contain, hold in check, inhibit, muffle, repress, restrain, smother, stifle, suppress

evolution development, enlargement, evolvement, expansion, growth, increase, maturation, progress, progression, unfolding, unrolling, working out

evolve develop, disclose, educe, elaborate, enlarge, expand, grow, increase, mature, open, progress, unfold, unroll, work out

exacerbate add insult to injury, aggravate (*informal*), embitter, enrage, envenom, exasperate, excite, fan the flames of, inflame, infuriate, intensify, irritate, madden, provoke, vex, worsen

exact *adjective* **1.** accurate, careful, correct, definite, explicit, express, faithful, faultless, identical, literal, methodical, on the money (*U.S.*), orderly, particular, precise, right, specific, true, unequivocal, unerring, veracious, very **2.** careful, exacting, meticulous, painstaking, punctilious, rigorous, scrupulous, severe, strict *~verb* **3.** call for, claim, command, compel, demand, extort, extract, force, impose, insist upon, require, squeeze, wrest, wring

Antonyms *adjective* approximate, careless, imprecise, inaccurate, incorrect, indefinite, inexact, loose, rough, slovenly

exacting demanding, difficult, hard, harsh, imperious, oppressive, painstaking, rigid, rigorous, severe, stern, strict, stringent, taxing, tough, unsparing

Antonyms easy, easy-peasy (*slang*), effortless, no bother, simple, undemanding

exaction compulsion, contribution, demand, extortion, imposition, oppression, rapacity, requirement, requisition, shakedown (*U.S. slang*), squeeze (*informal*), tribute

exactitude accuracy, carefulness, correctness, exactness, faithfulness, faultlessness, nicety, orderliness, painstakingness, preciseness, precision, promptitude, regularity, rigorousness, rigour, scrupulousness, strictness, truth, unequivocalness, veracity

exactly *adverb* **1.** accurately, carefully, correctly, definitely, explicitly, faithfully, faultlessly, literally, methodically, precisely, rigorously, scrupulously, severely, strictly, truly, truthfully, unequivocally, unerringly, veraciously **2.** absolutely, bang, explicitly, expressly, indeed, in every respect, just, on the button (*informal*), particularly, precisely, prompt (*informal*), quite, specifically, to the letter **3. not exactly** *ironical* by no means, certainly not, hardly, in no manner, in no way, not at all, not by any means, not quite, not really *~interjection* **4.** absolutely, assuredly, as you say, certainly, indeed, just so, of course, precisely, quite, quite so, spot-on (*Brit. informal*), truly

exactness accuracy, carefulness, correctness, exactitude, faithfulness, faultlessness, nicety, orderliness, painstakingness, preciseness, precision, promptitude, regularity, rigorousness, rigour, scrupulousness, strictness, truth, unequivocalness, veracity

Antonyms imprecision, inaccuracy, incorrectness, inexactness, unfaithfulness

exaggerate amplify, blow out of all proportion, embellish, embroider, emphasize, enlarge, exalt, hyperbolize, inflate, lay it on thick (*informal*), magnify, make a federal case of (*U.S. informal*), make a mountain out of a molehill (*informal*), make a production (out) of (*informal*), overdo, overemphasize, overestimate, overstate

exaggerated amplified, exalted, excessive, extravagant, highly coloured, hyped, hyperbolic, inflated, overblown, overdone, overestimated, overstated, over the top (*informal*), pretentious, tall (*informal*)

exaggeration amplification, embellishment, emphasis, enlargement, exaltation, excess, extravagance, hyperbole, inflation, magnification, overemphasis, overestimation, overstatement, pretension, pretentiousness

Antonyms litotes, meiosis, restraint, underplaying, understatement

The report of my death was an exaggeration
Mark Twain

An exaggeration is a truth that has lost its temper
Kahlil Gibran *Sand and Foam*

exalt **1.** advance, aggrandize, dignify, elevate, ennoble, honour, promote, raise, upgrade **2.** acclaim, apotheosize, applaud, bless, crack up (*informal*), extol, glorify, idolize, laud, magnify (*archaic*), pay homage to, pay tribute to, praise, reverence, set on a pedestal, worship **3.** animate, arouse, electrify, elevate, excite, fire the imagination (of), heighten, inspire, inspirit, stimulate, uplift **4.** delight, elate, exhilarate, fill with joy, thrill

exaltation **1.** advancement, aggrandizement, dignity, elevation, eminence, ennoblement, grandeur, high rank, honour, loftiness, prestige, promotion, rise, upgrading **2.** acclaim, acclamation, apotheosis, applause, blessing, extolment, glorification, glory, homage, idolization, laudation, lionization, magnification, panegyric, plaudits, praise, reverence, tribute, worship **3.** animation, elevation, excitement, inspiration, stimulation, uplift **4.** bliss, delight, ecstasy, elation, exhilaration, exultation, joy, joyousness, jubilation, rapture, transport

exalted **1.** august, dignified, elevated, eminent, grand, high, high-ranking, honoured, lofty, prestigious **2.** elevated, high-minded, ideal, intellectual, lofty, noble, sublime, superior, uplifting **3.** *informal* elevated, exaggerated, excessive, inflated, overblown, pretentious **4.** animated, blissful, cock-a-hoop, ecstatic, elated, elevated, excited, exhilarated, exultant, in high spirits, in seventh heaven, inspired, inspirited, joyous, jubilant, on cloud nine (*infor~*

mal), over the moon (*informal*), rapturous, stimulated, transported, uplifted

examination analysis, assay, catechism, checkup, exploration, inquiry, inquisition, inspection, interrogation, investigation, observation, once-over (*informal*), perusal, probe, questioning, quiz, recce (*slang*), research, review, scrutiny, search, study, survey, test, trial

In examinations the foolish ask questions that the wise cannot answer
Oscar Wilde *Phrases and Philosophies for the Use of the Young*

examine 1. analyse, appraise, assay, check, check out, consider, explore, go over *or* through, inspect, investigate, look over, peruse, ponder, pore over, probe, recce (*slang*), research, review, scan, scrutinize, sift, study, survey, take stock of, test, vet, weigh, work over 2. catechize, cross-examine, grill (*informal*), inquire, interrogate, question, quiz

example 1. case, case in point, exemplification, illustration, instance, sample, specimen 2. archetype, exemplar, ideal, illustration, model, norm, paradigm, paragon, pattern, precedent, prototype, standard 3. admonition, caution, lesson, warning 4. **for example** as an illustration, by way of illustration, e.g., *exempli gratia*, for instance, to cite an instance, to illustrate

Practise what you preach

exasperate aggravate (*informal*), anger, annoy, bug (*informal*), embitter, enrage, exacerbate, excite, gall, get (*informal*), get in one's hair (*informal*), get on one's nerves (*informal*), get on one's wick (*Brit. slang*), hassle (*informal*), incense, inflame, infuriate, irk, irritate, madden, nark (*Brit., Austral., & N.Z. slang*), needle (*informal*), nettle, peeve (*informal*), pique, piss one off (*taboo slang*), provoke, rankle, rile (*informal*), rouse, try the patience of, vex
Antonyms appease, assuage, calm, conciliate, mollify, pacify, placate, soothe

exasperating aggravating (*informal*), annoying, enough to drive one up the wall (*informal*), enough to try the patience of a saint, galling, infuriating, irksome, irritating, maddening, provoking, vexing

exasperation aggravation (*informal*), anger, annoyance, exacerbation, fury, ire (*literary*), irritation, passion, pique, provocation, rage, vexation, wrath

excavate burrow, cut, delve, dig, dig out, dig up, gouge, hollow, mine, quarry, scoop, trench, tunnel, uncover, unearth

excavation burrow, cavity, cut, cutting, dig, diggings, ditch, dugout, hole, hollow, mine, pit, quarry, shaft, trench, trough

exceed 1. beat, be superior to, better, cap (*informal*), eclipse, excel, go beyond, knock spots off (*informal*), outdistance, outdo, outreach, outrun, outshine, outstrip, overtake, pass, put in the shade (*informal*), run rings around (*informal*), surmount, surpass, top, transcend 2. go beyond the bounds of, go over the limit of, go over the top, overstep

exceeding enormous, exceptional, excessive, extraordinary, great, huge, pre-eminent, streets ahead, superior, superlative, surpassing, vast

exceedingly enormously, especially, exceptionally, excessively, extraordinarily, extremely, greatly, highly, hugely, inordinately, seriously (*informal*), superlatively, surpassingly, to a fault, to the nth degree, unusually, vastly, very

excel 1. beat, be superior, better, cap (*informal*), eclipse, exceed, go beyond, outdo, outrival, outshine, pass, put in the shade (*informal*), run rings around (*informal*), steal the show (*informal*), surmount, surpass, top, transcend 2. be good, be master of, be proficient, be skilful, be talented, have (something) down to a fine art, predominate, shine, show talent, take precedence

excellence distinction, eminence, fineness, goodness, greatness, high quality, merit, perfection, pre-eminence, purity, superiority, supremacy, transcendence, virtue, worth

excellent A1 *or* A-one (*informal*), admirable, bodacious (*slang, chiefly U.S.*), boffo (*slang*), brill (*informal*), brilliant, capital, champion, chillin' (*U.S. slang*), choice, cracking (*Brit. informal*), crucial (*slang*), def (*slang*), distinguished, estimable, exemplary, exquisite, fine, first-class, first-rate, good, great, jim-dandy (*slang*), mean (*slang*), mega (*slang*), meritorious, notable, noted, outstanding, prime, select, sovereign, sterling, superb, superior, superlative, tiptop, top-notch (*informal*), topping (*Brit. slang*), world-class, worthy
Antonyms abysmal, bad, dreadful, faulty, imperfect, incompetent, inexpert, inferior, lousy (*slang*), mediocre, no great shakes (*informal*), piss-poor (*taboo slang*), poor, rotten (*informal*), second-class, second-rate, substandard, terrible, unskilled

except 1. *preposition Also* **except for** apart from, bar, barring, besides, but, excepting, excluding, exclusive of, omitting, other than, save (*archaic*), saving, with the exception of 2. *verb* ban, bar, disallow, exclude, leave out, omit, pass over, reject, rule out

exception 1. debarment, disallowment, excepting, exclusion, leaving out, omission, passing over, rejection 2. anomaly, departure, deviation, freak, inconsistency, irregularity, oddity, peculiarity, quirk, special case 3. **take excep~**

tion be offended, be resentful, demur, disagree, object, quibble, take offence, take umbrage

The exception proves the rule
John Wilson *The Cheats*

exceptionable disagreeable, inappropriate, objectionable, unacceptable, unbearable, undesirable, unsatisfactory, unwelcome

exceptional 1. aberrant, abnormal, anomalous, atypical, deviant, extraordinary, inconsistent, irregular, odd, peculiar, rare, singular, special, strange, uncommon, unusual 2. bodacious (*slang, chiefly U.S.*), excellent, extraordinary, marvellous, notable, one in a million, outstanding, phenomenal, prodigious, remarkable, special, superior
Antonyms average, awful, bad, common, customary, familiar, lousy (*slang*), mediocre, no great shakes (*informal*), normal, ordinary, regular, second-rate, straightforward, typical, unexceptional, unremarkable, usual

excerpt 1. *noun* citation, extract, fragment, part, passage, pericope, piece, portion, quotation, quote (*informal*), section, selection 2. *verb* cite, cull, extract, pick out, quote, select, take

excess *noun* 1. glut, leftover, overabundance, overdose, overflow, overload, plethora, remainder, superabundance, superfluity, surfeit, surplus, too much 2. debauchery, dissipation, dissoluteness, exorbitance, extravagance, immoderation, intemperance, overindulgence, prodigality, unrestraint *~adjective* 3. extra, leftover, redundant, remaining, residual, spare, superfluous, surplus
Antonyms (*sense 1*) dearth, deficiency, insufficiency, lack, shortage, want (*sense 2*) moderation, restraint, self-control, self-discipline, self-restraint, temperance

Nothing succeeds like excess
Oscar Wilde *A Woman of No Importance*

Too much of a good thing can be wonderful
Mae West

The road of excess leads to the palace of wisdom
William Blake *The Marriage of Heaven and Hell*

Too many cooks spoil the broth

You can have too much of a good thing

excessive disproportionate, enormous, exaggerated, exorbitant, extravagant, extreme, immoderate, inordinate, intemperate, needless, O.T.T. (*slang*), overdone, overmuch, over the odds, over the top (*slang*), prodigal, profligate, superfluous, too much, unconscionable, undue, unreasonable

exchange *verb* 1. bandy, barter, change, commute, convert into, interchange, reciprocate, swap (*informal*), switch, trade, truck *~noun* 2. barter, dealing, interchange, quid pro quo, reciprocity, substitution, swap (*informal*), switch, tit for tat, trade, traffic, truck 3. Bourse, market

excise¹ *noun* customs, duty, impost, levy, surcharge, tariff, tax, toll

excise² *verb* 1. cross out, cut, delete, destroy, eradicate, erase, expunge, exterminate, extirpate, strike out, wipe from the face of the earth 2. cut off *or* out, extract, remove

excision deletion, destruction, eradication, extermination, extirpation, removal

excitability high spirits, hot-headedness, nervousness, restiveness, restlessness, volatility

excitable edgy, emotional, hasty, highly strung, hot-headed, hot-tempered, irascible, mercurial, nervous, passionate, quick-tempered, sensitive, susceptible, temperamental, testy, touchy, uptight (*informal*), violent, volatile
Antonyms calm, cool, cool-headed, even-tempered, imperturbable, laid-back (*informal*), placid, unexcitable, unruffled

excite agitate, animate, arouse, awaken, discompose, disturb, electrify, elicit, evoke, fire, foment, galvanize, incite, inflame, inspire, instigate, kindle, move, provoke, quicken, rouse, stimulate, stir up, thrill, titillate, waken, whet

excited aflame, agitated, animated, aroused, awakened, discomposed, disturbed, enthusiastic, feverish, flurried, high (*informal*), hot and bothered (*informal*), moved, nervous, overwrought, roused, stimulated, stirred, thrilled, tumultuous, wild, worked up

excitement 1. action, activity, ado, adventure, agitation, animation, commotion, discomposure, elation, enthusiasm, ferment, fever, flurry, furore, heat, kicks (*informal*), passion, perturbation, thrill, tumult, warmth 2. impulse, incitement, instigation, motivation, motive, provocation, stimulation, stimulus, urge

exciting dramatic, electrifying, exhilarating, inspiring, intoxicating, moving, provocative, rip-roaring (*informal*), rousing, sensational, sexy (*informal*), stimulating, stirring, thrilling, titillating
Antonyms boring, dreary, dull, flat, humdrum, mind-numbing, monotonous, unexciting, uninspiring, uninteresting

exclaim call, call out, cry, cry out, declare, ejaculate, proclaim, shout, utter, vociferate, yell

exclamation call, cry, ejaculation, expletive, interjection, outcry, shout, utterance, vociferation, yell

exclude 1. ban, bar, black, blackball, boycott, debar, disallow, embargo, forbid, interdict, keep out, ostracize, prohibit, proscribe, refuse, shut out, veto 2. count out, eliminate, except, ignore, leave out, omit, pass over, preclude,

reject, repudiate, rule out, set aside **3**. bounce (*slang*), drive out, eject, evict, expel, force out, get rid of, oust, remove, throw out
Antonyms accept, admit, allow, count, include, let in, permit, receive, welcome

exclusion **1**. ban, bar, boycott, debarment, disqualification, embargo, forbiddance, interdict, nonadmission, preclusion, prohibition, proscription, refusal, veto **2**. elimination, exception, omission, rejection, repudiation **3**. eviction, expulsion, removal

exclusive **1**. absolute, complete, entire, full, only, private, single, sole, total, undivided, unique, unshared, whole **2**. aristocratic, chic, choice, clannish, classy (*slang*), cliquish, closed, discriminative, elegant, fashionable, high-toned, limited, narrow, posh (*informal, chiefly Brit.*), private, restricted, restrictive, ritzy (*slang*), select, selfish, snobbish, swish (*informal, chiefly Brit.*), top-drawer, upmarket **3**. confined, limited, peculiar, restricted, unique **4**. debarring, except for, excepting, excluding, leaving aside, not counting, omitting, restricting, ruling out
Antonyms common, communal, inclusive, nonexclusive, open, partial, popular, public, shared, sociable, unrestricted

excogitate conceive, contemplate, contrive, deliberate, devise, evolve, frame, invent, mull over, ponder, ruminate, think out *or* up, weigh, work out

excommunicate anathematize, ban, banish, cast out, denounce, eject, exclude, expel, proscribe, remove, repudiate, unchurch

excoriate **1**. abrade, flay, gall, peel, scarify, scrape, scratch, skin, strip **2**. attack, bawl out (*informal*), berate, blast, carpet (*informal*), castigate, censure, chastise, chew out (*U.S. & Canad. informal*), condemn, criticize, denounce, flay, give a rocket (*Brit. & N.Z. informal*), lambast(e), put down, read the riot act, rebuke, reproach, reprove, revile, scold, slam (*slang*), slate (*informal, chiefly Brit.*), tear into (*informal*), tear (someone) off a strip (*Brit. informal*), upbraid, vilify

excrement crap (*taboo slang*), droppings, dung, excreta, faeces, mess (*especially of a domestic animal*), motion, night soil, ordure, shit (*taboo slang*), stool, turd (*taboo slang*)

excrescence **1**. *Medical* growth, lump, swelling, tumour, wart **2**. knob, lump, outgrowth, process, projection, prominence, protrusion, protuberance

excrete crap (*taboo slang*), defecate, discharge, egest, eject, eliminate, evacuate, expel, exude, shit (*taboo slang*), void

excruciate afflict, agonize, harrow, rack, torment, torture

excruciating acute, agonizing, burning, exquisite, extreme, harrowing, insufferable, intense, piercing, racking, searing, severe, tormenting, torturous, unbearable, unendurable, violent

exculpate absolve, acquit, clear, discharge, dismiss, excuse, exonerate, free, justify, pardon, release, vindicate

excursion **1**. airing, day trip, expedition, jaunt, journey, outing, pleasure trip, ramble, tour, trip **2**. detour, deviation, digression, episode, excursus, wandering

excursive devious, diffusive, digressive, discursive, episodic, errant, rambling, roaming, roving, wandering

excusable allowable, defensible, forgivable, justifiable, minor, pardonable, permissible, slight, understandable, venial, warrantable

excuse *verb* **1**. absolve, acquit, bear with, exculpate, exonerate, extenuate, forgive, indulge, make allowances for, overlook, pardon, pass over, tolerate, turn a blind eye to, wink at **2**. apologize for, condone, defend, explain, justify, mitigate, vindicate **3**. absolve, discharge, exempt, free, let off, liberate, release, relieve, spare *~noun* **4**. apology, defence, explanation, grounds, justification, mitigation, plea, pretext, reason, vindication **5**. cop-out (*slang*), disguise, evasion, expedient, makeshift, pretence, pretext, semblance, shift, subterfuge **6**. *informal* apology, makeshift, mockery, substitute, travesty
Antonyms *verb* accuse, arraign, blame, censure, charge, chasten, chastise, compel, condemn, convict, correct, criticize, hold responsible, indict, oblige, point a *or* the finger at, punish, sentence *~noun* (*sense 4*) accusation, charge, imputation, indictment

> *Two wrongs don't make a right, but they make a good excuse*
>
> Thomas Szasz *The Second Sin*

> *Several excuses are always less convincing than one*
>
> Aldous Huxley *Point Counter Point*

execrable abhorrent, abominable, accursed, atrocious, cringe-making (*Brit. informal*), damnable, deplorable, despicable, detestable, disgusting, foul, hateful, heinous, horrible, loathsome, nauseous, obnoxious, obscene, odious, offensive, repulsive, revolting, sickening, vile, yucky *or* yukky (*slang*)

execrate abhor, abominate, anathematize, condemn, curse, damn, denounce, deplore, despise, detest, excoriate, hate, imprecate, loathe, revile, slam (*slang*), vilify

execration abhorrence, abomination, anathema, condemnation, contempt, curse, damnation, detestation, excoriation, hate, hatred, imprecation, loathing, malediction, odium, vilification

execute 1. behead, electrocute, guillotine, hang, kill, put to death, shoot 2. accomplish, achieve, administer, bring off, carry out, com~ plete, consummate, discharge, do, effect, en~ act, enforce, finish, fulfil, implement, perform, prosecute, put into effect, realize, render 3. *Law* deliver, seal, serve, sign, validate

We must execute not only the guilty. Execution of the innocent will impress the masses even more

Nikolai V. Krylenko

execution 1. accomplishment, achievement, administration, carrying out, completion, con~ summation, discharge, effect, enactment, en~ forcement, implementation, operation, perfor~ mance, prosecution, realization, rendering 2. capital punishment, hanging, killing, necktie party (*informal*) 3. delivery, manner, mode, performance, rendition, style, technique 4. *Law* warrant, writ

executioner 1. hangman, headsman 2. assas~ sin, exterminator, hit man (*slang*), killer, liq~ uidator, murderer, slayer

executive *noun* 1. administrator, director, manager, official 2. administration, directo~ rate, directors, government, hierarchy, leader~ ship, management ~*adjective* 3. administra~ tive, controlling, decision-making, directing, governing, managerial

exemplar 1. criterion, epitome, example, ideal, model, paradigm, paragon, pattern, standard 2. example, exemplification, illustration, in~ stance, prototype, specimen, type

exemplary 1. admirable, commendable, correct, estimable, excellent, fine, good, honourable, ideal, laudable, meritorious, model, praise~ worthy, punctilious, sterling 2. admonitory, cautionary, monitory, warning 3. characteris~ tic, illustrative, representative, typical

exemplification embodiment, epitome, exam~ ple, exemplar, illustration, manifestation, paradigm, personification, prototype, repre~ sentation

exemplify demonstrate, depict, display, em~ body, evidence, exhibit, illustrate, instance, manifest, represent, serve as an example of, show

exempt 1. *verb* absolve, discharge, except, ex~ cuse, exonerate, free, grant immunity, let off, liberate, release, relieve, spare 2. *adjective* absolved, clear, discharged, excepted, excused, favoured, free, immune, liberated, not liable, not subject, privileged, released, spared

Antonyms *adjective* accountable, answerable, chargeable, liable, obligated, responsible, sub~ ject

exemption absolution, discharge, dispensation, exception, exoneration, freedom, immunity, privilege, release

exercise *verb* 1. apply, bring to bear, employ, enjoy, exert, practise, put to use, use, utilize, wield 2. discipline, drill, habituate, inure, practise, train, work out 3. afflict, agitate, an~ noy, burden, distress, disturb, occupy, pain, perturb, preoccupy, trouble, try, vex, worry ~*noun* 4. action, activity, discipline, drill, drilling, effort, labour, toil, training, work, work-out 5. accomplishment, application, dis~ charge, employment, enjoyment, exertion, ful~ filment, implementation, practice, use, utilization 6. drill, lesson, practice, problem, schooling, schoolwork, task, work

exert 1. apply, bring into play, bring to bear, employ, exercise, expend, make use of, put forth, use, utilize, wield 2. **exert oneself** ap~ ply oneself, bend over backwards (*informal*), break one's neck (*informal*), bust a gut (*infor~ mal*), do one's best, do one's damnedest (*in~ formal*), endeavour, get one's finger out (*Brit. informal*), give it one's all (*informal*), give it one's best shot (*informal*), go for broke (*slang*), go for it (*informal*), knock oneself out (*informal*), labour, make an all-out effort (*in~ formal*), make an effort, pull one's finger out (*Brit. informal*), rupture oneself (*informal*), spare no effort, strain, strive, struggle, toil, try hard, work

exertion action, application, attempt, effort, elbow grease (*facetious*), employment, endeav~ our, exercise, industry, labour, pains, strain, stretch, struggle, toil, travail (*literary*), trial, use, utilization

exhalation breath, breathing out, discharge, effluvium, emanation, emission, evaporation, exhaust, expiration, fog, fume, mist, smoke, steam, vapour

exhale breathe, breathe out, discharge, eject, emanate, emit, evaporate, expel, give off, is~ sue, respire, steam

exhaust 1. bankrupt, cripple, debilitate, dis~ able, drain, enervate, enfeeble, fatigue, im~ poverish, prostrate, sap, tire, tire out, weak~ en, wear out 2. consume, deplete, dissipate, expend, finish, run through, spend, squander, use up, waste 3. drain, dry, empty, strain, void 4. be emitted, discharge, emanate, es~ cape, issue

exhausted 1. all in (*slang*), beat (*slang*), bug~ gered (*slang*), clapped out (*Austral. & N.Z. informal*), crippled, dead (*informal*), dead beat (*informal*), dead tired, debilitated, disabled, dog-tired (*informal*), done in (*informal*), drained, effete, enervated, enfeebled, fatigued, jaded, knackered (*slang*), on one's last legs (*informal*), out on one's feet (*informal*), pros~ trated, ready to drop, sapped, shagged out

(*Brit. slang*), spent, tired out, wasted, weak, wiped out (*informal*), worn out, worn to a frazzle (*informal*), zonked (*slang*) **2.** at an end, consumed, depleted, dissipated, done, expended, finished, gone, spent, squandered, used up, wasted **3.** bare, drained, dry, empty, void

Antonyms active, alive and kicking, animated, conserved, enlivened, invigorated, kept, preserved, refreshed, rejuvenated, replenished, restored, revived, stimulated

exhaustible delimited, finite, limited

exhausting arduous, backbreaking, crippling, debilitating, difficult, draining, enervating, fatiguing, gruelling, hard, laborious, punishing, sapping, strenuous, taxing, testing, tiring

exhaustion **1.** debilitation, enervation, fatigue, feebleness, lassitude, prostration, tiredness, weariness **2.** consumption, depletion, emptying

exhaustive all-embracing, all-inclusive, all-out (*informal*), complete, comprehensive, detailed, encyclopedic, extensive, far-reaching, full, full-scale, in-depth, intensive, sweeping, thorough, thoroughgoing, total

Antonyms casual, cursory, desultory, incomplete, perfunctory, sketchy, superficial

exhibit **1.** *verb* air, demonstrate, disclose, display, evidence, evince, expose, express, flaunt, indicate, make clear *or* plain, manifest, offer, parade, present, put on view, reveal, show **2.** *noun* display, exhibition, illustration, model, show

exhibition airing, demonstration, display, exhibit, expo (*informal*), exposition, fair, manifestation, performance, presentation, representation, show, showing, spectacle

exhilarate animate, cheer, delight, elate, enliven, exalt, gladden, inspirit, invigorate, lift, pep *or* perk up, rejoice, stimulate, thrill

exhilarating breathtaking, cheering, enlivening, exalting, exciting, exhilarant, exhilarative, exhilaratory, gladdening, invigorating, stimulating, thrilling, vitalizing

exhilaration animation, cheerfulness, delight, elation, exaltation, excitement, gaiety, gladness, gleefulness, high spirits, hilarity, joy, joyfulness, liveliness, mirth, sprightliness, vivacity

Antonyms dejection, depression, despondency, gloom, low spirits, melancholy, misery, sadness

exhort admonish, advise, beseech, bid, call upon, caution, counsel, encourage, enjoin, entreat, goad, incite, persuade, press, prompt, spur, urge, warn

exhortation admonition, advice, beseeching, bidding, caution, clarion call, counsel, encouragement, enjoinder (*rare*), entreaty, goading, incitement, lecture, persuasion, sermon, urging, warning

exhume dig up, disentomb, disinter, unbury, unearth

Antonyms bury, entomb, inearth, inhume, inter

exigency, exigence **1.** acuteness, constraint, criticalness, demandingness, difficulty, distress, emergency, imperativeness, necessity, needfulness, pressingness, pressure, stress, urgency **2.** constraint, demand, necessity, need, requirement, wont **3.** crisis, difficulty, emergency, extremity, fix (*informal*), hardship, jam (*informal*), juncture, panic stations (*informal*), pass, pickle (*informal*), pinch, plight, predicament, quandary, scrape (*informal*), strait

exigent **1.** acute, constraining, critical, crucial, imperative, importunate, insistent, necessary, needful, pressing, urgent **2.** arduous, demanding, difficult, exacting, hard, harsh, rigorous, severe, stiff, strict, stringent, taxing, tough

exiguous bare, meagre, negligible, paltry, scanty, skimpy, slender, spare, sparse

exile *noun* **1.** banishment, deportation, expatriation, expulsion, ostracism, proscription, separation **2.** deportee, émigré, expatriate, outcast, refugee *~verb* **3.** banish, deport, drive out, eject, expatriate, expel, ostracize, oust, proscribe

exiled banished, deported, expat, expatriate, outcast, refugee

exist **1.** abide, be, be extant, be living, be present, breathe, continue, endure, happen, last, live, obtain, occur, prevail, remain, stand, survive **2.** eke out a living, get along *or* by, keep one's head above water, stay alive, subsist, survive

existence **1.** actuality, animation, being, breath, continuance, continuation, duration, endurance, life, subsistence, survival **2.** being, creature, entity, thing **3.** creation, life, reality, the world

To be, or not to be: that is the question
William Shakespeare *Hamlet*

I think; therefore I am
René Descartes *Discourse on Method*

existent abiding, around, current, enduring, existing, extant, in existence, living, obtaining, present, prevailing, remaining, standing, surviving

existing alive, alive and kicking, extant, in existence, living, remaining, surviving

Antonyms dead, defunct, died out, extinct, gone, lost, vanished

exit *noun* **1.** door, egress, gate, outlet, passage out, vent, way out **2.** adieu, departure, evacuation, exodus, farewell, going, goodbye, leave-taking, retirement, retreat, withdrawal **3.** death, decease, demise, expiry, passing away *~verb* **4.** bid farewell, depart, go away,

go offstage (*Theatre*), go out, issue, leave, make tracks, retire, retreat, say goodbye, take one's leave, withdraw
Antonyms (*sense 1*) entrance, entry, ingress, inlet, opening, way in (*sense 4*) arrive, come *or* go in *or* into, enter, make an entrance

exodus departure, evacuation, exit, flight, go~ing out, leaving, migration, retirement, re~treat, withdrawal

exonerate **1.** absolve, acquit, clear, discharge, dismiss, exculpate, excuse, justify, pardon, vindicate **2.** discharge, dismiss, except, excuse, exempt, free, let off, liberate, release, relieve

exoneration **1.** absolution, acquittal, amnesty, discharge, dismissal, exculpation, justification, pardon, vindication **2.** deliverance, discharge, dismissal, exception, exemption, freeing, lib~eration, release, relief

exorbitance excess, excessiveness, extrava~gance, extremeness, immoderateness, immod~eration, inordinateness, preposterousness, un~reasonableness

exorbitant enormous, excessive, extortionate, extravagant, extreme, immoderate, inordinate, outrageous, preposterous, ridiculous, uncon~scionable, undue, unreasonable, unwarranted
Antonyms cheap, fair, moderate, reasonable

exorcise adjure, cast out, deliver (from), drive out, expel, purify

exorcism adjuration, casting out, deliverance, driving out, expulsion, purification

exordium beginning, foreword, introduction, opening, opening remarks, preamble, preface, prelude, proem, prolegomenon, prologue

exotic **1.** alien, external, extraneous, extrinsic, foreign, imported, introduced, naturalized, not native **2.** beyond one's ken, bizarre, colourful, curious, different, extraordinary, fascinating, glamorous, mysterious, outlandish, peculiar, strange, striking, unfamiliar, unusual
Antonyms (*sense 2*) conventional, familiar, ordinary, pedestrian, plain, run-of-the-mill, unmemorable, unremarkable

expand **1.** amplify, augment, bloat, blow up, broaden, develop, dilate, distend, enlarge, ex~tend, fatten, fill out, grow, heighten, increase, inflate, lengthen, magnify, multiply, prolong, protract, swell, thicken, wax, widen **2.** diffuse, open (out), outspread, spread (out), stretch (out), unfold, unfurl, unravel, unroll **3.** ampli~fy, develop, dilate, elaborate, embellish, en~large, expatiate, expound, flesh out, go into detail
Antonyms abbreviate, close, condense, con~tract, decrease, reduce, shorten, shrink

expanse area, breadth, extent, field, plain, range, space, stretch, sweep, tract

expansion amplification, augmentation, devel~opment, diffusion, dilatation, distension, en~largement, expanse, growth, increase, infla~tion, magnification, multiplication, opening out, spread, swelling, unfolding, unfurling

expansive **1.** dilating, distending, elastic, en~largeable, expanding, extendable, inflatable, stretching, stretchy, swelling **2.** all-embracing, broad, comprehensive, extensive, far-reaching, inclusive, thorough, voluminous, wide, wide-ranging, widespread **3.** affable, communica~tive, easy, effusive, free, friendly, garrulous, genial, loquacious, open, outgoing, sociable, talkative, unreserved, warm

expatiate amplify, descant, develop, dilate, dwell on, elaborate, embellish, enlarge, ex~pound, go into detail

expatriate **1.** *adjective* banished, emigrant, émigré, exiled, refugee **2.** *noun* emigrant, émi~gré, exile **3.** *verb* banish, exile, expel, ostra~cize, proscribe

expect **1.** assume, believe, calculate, conjecture, forecast, foresee, imagine, presume, reckon, suppose, surmise, think, trust **2.** anticipate, await, bargain for, contemplate, envisage, hope for, look ahead to, look for, look forward to, predict, watch for **3.** call for, count on, de~mand, insist on, look for, rely upon, require, want, wish

expectancy **1.** anticipation, assumption, belief, conjecture, expectation, hope, looking forward, prediction, presumption, probability, supposi~tion, surmise, suspense, waiting **2.** likelihood, outlook, prospect

expectant **1.** anticipating, anxious, apprehen~sive, awaiting, eager, expecting, hopeful, in suspense, ready, watchful **2.** enceinte, expect~ing (*informal*), gravid, pregnant

expectation **1.** assumption, assurance, belief, calculation, confidence, conjecture, forecast, likelihood, presumption, probability, supposi~tion, surmise, trust **2.** anticipation, apprehen~sion, chance, expectancy, fear, hope, looking forward, outlook, possibility, prediction, promise, prospect, suspense **3.** demand, insist~ence, reliance, requirement, trust, want, wish

Blessed is the man who expects nothing, for he shall never be disappointed
Alexander Pope

expected anticipated, awaited, counted on, forecast, hoped-for, long-awaited, looked-for, predicted, promised, wanted

expecting enceinte, expectant, gravid, in the club (*Brit. slang*), in the family way (*infor~mal*), pregnant, with child

expediency, expedience **1.** advantageousness, advisability, appropriateness, aptness, benefit, convenience, desirability, effectiveness, fitness, helpfulness, judiciousness, meetness, practi~cality, pragmatism, profitability, properness, propriety, prudence, suitability, usefulness, utilitarianism, utility **2.** contrivance, device, expedient, makeshift, manoeuvre, means, measure, method, resort, resource, scheme, shift, stopgap, stratagem, substitute

expedient **1.** *adjective* advantageous, advisable, appropriate, beneficial, convenient, desirable, effective, fit, helpful, judicious, meet, opportune, politic, practical, pragmatic, profitable, proper, prudent, suitable, useful, utilitarian, worthwhile **2.** *noun* contrivance, device, expediency, makeshift, manoeuvre, means, measure, method, resort, resource, scheme, shift, stopgap, stratagem, substitute
Antonyms *adjective* detrimental, disadvantageous, futile, harmful, ill-advised, impractical, imprudent, inadvisable, inappropriate, ineffective, inexpedient, unwise, wrong

expedite accelerate, advance, assist, dispatch, facilitate, forward, hasten, hurry, precipitate, press, promote, quicken, rush, speed (up), urge
Antonyms block, curb, decelerate, delay, handicap, hold up, obstruct, restrict, slow up *or* down

expedition **1.** enterprise, excursion, exploration, journey, mission, quest, safari, tour, trek, trip, undertaking, voyage **2.** company, crew, explorers, team, travellers, voyagers, wayfarers **3.** alacrity, celerity, dispatch, expeditiousness, haste, hurry, promptness, quickness, rapidity, readiness, speed, swiftness

expeditious active, alert, brisk, diligent, efficient, fast, hasty, immediate, instant, nimble, prompt, quick, rapid, ready, speedy, swift

expel **1.** belch, cast out, discharge, dislodge, drive out, eject, remove, spew, throw out **2.** ban, banish, bar, black, blackball, discharge, dismiss, drum out, evict, exclude, exile, expatriate, give the bum's rush (*slang*), oust, proscribe, relegate, send packing, show one the door, throw out, throw out on one's ear (*informal*), turf out (*informal*)
Antonyms (*sense 2*) admit, allow to enter, give access, let in, receive, take in, welcome

expend consume, disburse, dissipate, employ, exhaust, fork out (*slang*), go through, lay out (*informal*), pay out, shell out (*informal*), spend, use (up)

expendable dispensable, inessential, nonessential, replaceable, unimportant, unnecessary
Antonyms crucial, essential, indispensable, key, necessary, vital

expenditure application, charge, consumption, cost, disbursement, expense, outgoings, outlay, output, payment, spending, use

Expenditure rises to meet income
C. Northcote Parkinson *The Law and the Profits*

expense charge, consumption, cost, disbursement, expenditure, loss, outlay, output, payment, sacrifice, spending, toll, use

expensive costly, dear, excessive, exorbitant, extravagant, high-priced, inordinate, lavish, overpriced, rich, steep (*informal*), stiff
Antonyms bargain, budget, cheap, cut-price, economical, inexpensive, low-cost, low-priced, reasonable

experience *noun* **1.** contact, doing, evidence, exposure, familiarity, involvement, know-how (*informal*), knowledge, observation, participation, practice, proof, training, trial, understanding **2.** adventure, affair, encounter, episode, event, happening, incident, occurrence, ordeal, test, trial *~verb* **3.** apprehend, become familiar with, behold, encounter, endure, face, feel, go through, have, know, live through, meet, observe, participate in, perceive, sample, sense, suffer, sustain, taste, try, undergo

Trust one who has gone through it
Virgil *Aeneid*

All experience is an arch to build upon
Henry Brooks Adams *The Education of Henry Adams*

What poor education I have received has been gained in the University of Life
Horatio Bottomley

If you have lived one day you have seen everything; one day is the same as all the others
Montaigne *Essais*

Experience is the best teacher

experienced **1.** accomplished, adept, capable, competent, expert, familiar, knowledgeable, master, practised, professional, qualified, seasoned, skilful, tested, trained, tried, veteran, well-versed **2.** knowing, mature, sophisticated, wise, worldly, worldly-wise
Antonyms apprentice, green, incompetent, inexperienced, new, unqualified, unskilled, untrained, untried

experiment **1.** *noun* assay, attempt, examination, experimentation, investigation, procedure, proof, research, test, trial, trial and error, trial run, venture **2.** *verb* assay, examine, investigate, put to the test, research, sample, test, try, verify

experimental empirical, exploratory, pilot, preliminary, probationary, provisional, speculative, tentative, test, trial, trial-and-error

expert **1.** *noun* ace (*informal*), adept, authority, buff (*informal*), connoisseur, dab hand (*Brit. informal*), hotshot (*informal*), master, maven (*U.S.*), past master, pro (*informal*), professional, specialist, virtuoso, whiz (*informal*), wizard **2.** *adjective* able, adept, adroit, apt, clever, deft, dexterous, experienced, facile, handy, knowledgeable, master, masterly, practised, professional, proficient, qualified,

skilful, skilled, trained, virtuoso
Antonyms *noun* amateur, dabbler, ham, layman, nonprofessional, novice *~adjective* amateurish, cack-handed (*informal*), clumsy, incompetent, inexperienced, unpractised, unqualified, unskilled, untrained

An expert is a man who has made all the mistakes which can be made in a very narrow field
Niels Henrik David Bohr

An expert is one who knows more and more about less and less
Nicholas Murray Butler

An expert is someone who knows some of the worst mistakes that can be make in his subject and who manages to avoid them
Werner Heisenberg *Der Teil und das Ganze*

expertise ableness, adroitness, aptness, cleverness, command, craft, deftness, dexterity, expertness, facility, grasp, grip, judgment, knack, know-how (*informal*), knowing inside out, knowledge, masterliness, mastery, proficiency, skilfulness, skill

expertness ableness, adroitness, aptness, command, craft, deftness, dexterity, expertise, facility, grasp, grip, judgment, know-how (*informal*), knowing inside out, knowledge, masterliness, mastery, proficiency, skilfulness, skill

expiate atone for, do penance for, make amends for, redeem, redress

expiation amends, atonement, penance, redemption, redress, shrift (*archaic*)

expiration **1.** cessation, close, conclusion, end, expiry, finis, finish, termination **2.** death, decease, demise, departure

expire **1.** cease, close, come to an end, conclude, end, finish, lapse, run out, stop, terminate **2.** breathe out, emit, exhale, expel **3.** buy it (*U.S. slang*), check out (*U.S. slang*), croak (*slang*), decease, depart, die, go belly-up (*slang*), kick it (*slang*), kick the bucket (*informal*), pass away *or* on, peg it (*informal*), peg out (*informal*), perish, pop one's clogs (*informal*), snuff it (*informal*)

expiry cessation, close, conclusion, demise, end, ending, expiration, lapsing, termination

explain **1.** clarify, clear up, define, demonstrate, describe, disclose, elucidate, explicate (*formal*), expound, illustrate, interpret, make clear *or* plain, resolve, solve, teach, unfold **2.** account for, excuse, give an explanation for, give a reason for, justify

Never explain - your friends do not need it and your enemies will not believe you anyway
Elbert Hubbard *The Motto Book*

explanation **1.** clarification, definition, demonstration, description, elucidation, explication, exposition, illustration, interpretation, resolution **2.** account, answer, cause, excuse, justification, meaning, mitigation, motive, reason, sense, significance, the why and wherefore, vindication

explanatory demonstrative, descriptive, elucidatory, explicative, expository, illuminative, illustrative, interpretive, justifying

explicable accountable, definable, explainable, intelligible, interpretable, justifiable, resolvable, understandable

explicate **1.** clarify, clear up, elucidate, explain, expound, interpret, make clear *or* explicit, make plain, unfold, untangle **2.** construct, develop, devise, evolve, formulate, work out

explicit absolute, categorical, certain, clear, definite, direct, distinct, exact, express, frank, open, outspoken, patent, plain, positive, precise, round, specific, stated, straightforward, unambiguous, unequivocal, unqualified, unreserved, upfront (*informal*)
Antonyms ambiguous, cryptic, general, implicit, implied, indefinite, indirect, inexact, obscure, oracular, suggested, uncertain, vague

explode **1.** blow up, burst, detonate, discharge, erupt, go off, set off, shatter, shiver **2.** belie, blow out of the water (*slang*), debunk, discredit, disprove, give the lie to, invalidate, refute, repudiate

exploit *noun* **1.** accomplishment, achievement, adventure, attainment, deed, escapade, feat, stunt *~verb* **2.** abuse, dump on (*slang, chiefly U.S.*), impose upon, manipulate, milk, misuse, play on *or* upon, shit on (*taboo slang*), take advantage of **3.** capitalize on, cash in on (*informal*), live off the backs of, make capital out of, make use of, profit by *or* from, put to use, turn to account, use, use to advantage, utilize

exploitation **1.** abuse, imposition, manipulation, misuse, trading upon **2.** capitalization, utilization

exploration **1.** analysis, examination, inquiry, inspection, investigation, once-over (*informal*), probe, research, scrutiny, search, study **2.** expedition, recce (*slang*), reconnaissance, survey, tour, travel, trip

exploratory analytic, experimental, fact-finding, investigative, probing, searching, trial

explore **1.** analyse, examine, inquire into, inspect, investigate, look into, probe, prospect, research, scrutinize, search, work over **2.** case (*slang*), have *or* take a look around, range over, recce (*slang*), reconnoitre, scout, survey, tour, travel, traverse

explosion **1.** bang, blast, burst, clap, crack, detonation, discharge, outburst, report **2.** eruption, fit, outbreak, outburst, paroxysm

explosive **1.** unstable, volatile **2.** fiery, stormy, touchy, vehement, violent **3.** charged, dangerous, hazardous, overwrought, perilous, tense, ugly

exponent **1.** advocate, backer, champion, defender, promoter, propagandist, proponent, spokesman, spokeswoman, supporter, upholder **2.** commentator, demonstrator, elucidator, expositor, expounder, illustrator, interpreter **3.** example, exemplar, illustration, indication, model, norm, sample, specimen, type **4.** executant, interpreter, performer, player, presenter

expose **1.** display, exhibit, manifest, present, put on view, reveal, show, take the wraps off, uncover, unveil **2.** air, betray, blow wide open (*slang*), bring to light, denounce, detect, disclose, divulge, lay bare, let out, make known, reveal, show up, smoke out, uncover, unearth, unmask **3.** endanger, hazard, imperil, jeopardize, lay open, leave open, make vulnerable, risk, subject **4.** *with* **to** acquaint with, bring into contact with, familiarize with, introduce to, make conversant with
Antonyms conceal, cover, hide, keep secret, mask, protect, screen, shelter, shield

exposé disclosure, divulgence, exposure, revelation, uncovering

exposed **1.** bare, exhibited, laid bare, made manifest, made public, on display, on show, on view, revealed, shown, unconcealed, uncovered, unveiled **2.** open, open to the elements, unprotected, unsheltered **3.** in danger, in peril, laid bare, laid open, left open, liable, open, susceptible, vulnerable, wide open

exposition **1.** account, commentary, critique, description, elucidation, exegesis, explanation, explication, illustration, interpretation, presentation **2.** demonstration, display, exhibition, expo (*informal*), fair, presentation, show

expository descriptive, elucidative, exegetic, explanatory, explicative, explicatory, hermeneutic, illustrative, interpretive

expostulate argue (with), dissuade, protest, reason (with), remonstrate (with)

exposure **1.** baring, display, exhibition, manifestation, presentation, publicity, revelation, showing, uncovering, unveiling **2.** airing, betrayal, denunciation, detection, disclosure, divulgence, divulging, exposé, revelation, unmasking **3.** danger, hazard, jeopardy, risk, vulnerability **4.** acquaintance, contact, conversancy, experience, familiarity, introduction, knowledge **5.** aspect, frontage, location, outlook, position, setting, view

expound describe, elucidate, explain, explicate (*formal*), illustrate, interpret, set forth, spell out, unfold

express *verb* **1.** articulate, assert, asseverate, communicate, couch, declare, enunciate, phrase, pronounce, put, put across, put into words, say, speak, state, tell, utter, verbalize, voice, word **2.** bespeak, convey, denote, depict, designate, disclose, divulge, embody, evince, exhibit, indicate, intimate, make known, manifest, represent, reveal, show, signify, stand for, symbolize, testify **3.** extract, force out, press out, squeeze out *~adjective* **4.** accurate, categorical, certain, clear, definite, direct, distinct, exact, explicit, outright, plain, pointed, precise, unambiguous **5.** clear-cut, especial, particular, singular, special **6.** direct, fast, high-speed, nonstop, quick, quickie (*informal*), rapid, speedy, swift

expression **1.** announcement, assertion, asseveration, communication, declaration, enunciation, mention, pronouncement, speaking, statement, utterance, verbalization, voicing **2.** demonstration, embodiment, exhibition, indication, manifestation, representation, show, sign, symbol, token **3.** air, appearance, aspect, countenance, face, look, mien (*literary*) **4.** choice of words, delivery, diction, emphasis, execution, intonation, language, phraseology, phrasing, speech, style, wording **5.** idiom, locution, phrase, remark, set phrase, term, turn of phrase, word

expressionless blank, deadpan, dull, empty, inscrutable, poker-faced (*informal*), straight-faced, vacuous, wooden

expressive **1.** eloquent, emphatic, energetic, forcible, lively, mobile, moving, poignant, striking, strong, sympathetic, telling, vivid **2.** allusive, demonstrative, indicative, meaningful, pointed, pregnant, revealing, significant, suggestive, thoughtful
Antonyms blank, dead-pan, dull, empty, impassive, inscrutable, poker-faced (*informal*), straight-faced, vacuous, wooden

expressly **1.** especially, exactly, intentionally, on purpose, particularly, precisely, purposely, specially, specifically **2.** absolutely, categorically, clearly, decidedly, definitely, distinctly, explicitly, in no uncertain terms, manifestly, outright, plainly, pointedly, positively, unambiguously, unequivocally, unmistakably

expropriate appropriate, arrogate, assume, commandeer, confiscate, impound, requisition, seize, take, take over

expropriation commandeering, confiscation, disseisin (*Law*), impounding, requisitioning, seizure, sequestration, takeover

expulsion banishment, debarment, discharge, dislodgment, dismissal, ejection, eviction, exclusion, exile, expatriation, extrusion, proscription, removal

expunge abolish, annihilate, annul, blot out, cancel, delete, destroy, efface, eradicate, erase, excise, exterminate, extinguish, extirpate, obliterate, raze, remove, strike out, wipe from the face of the earth, wipe out

expurgate blue-pencil, bowdlerize, censor, clean up (*informal*), cut, purge, purify, sanitize

exquisite 1. beautiful, dainty, delicate, elegant, fine, lovely, precious **2.** attractive, beautiful, charming, comely, lovely, pleasing, striking **3.** admirable, choice, consummate, delicious, divine, excellent, fine, flawless, incomparable, matchless, outstanding, peerless, perfect, rare, select, splendid, superb, superlative **4.** appreciative, consummate, cultivated, discerning, discriminating, fastidious, impeccable, meticulous, polished, refined, selective, sensitive **5.** acute, excruciating, intense, keen, piercing, poignant, sharp

Antonyms flawed, ill-favoured, imperfect, ugly, unattractive, unlovely, unsightly

extant existent, existing, in existence, living, remaining, subsisting, surviving, undestroyed

extemporaneous, extemporary 1. ad-lib, extempore, free, impromptu, improvisatory, improvised, made-up, offhand, off-the-cuff (*informal*), off the top of one's head, spontaneous, unplanned, unpremeditated, unprepared, unrehearsed **2.** expedient, improvised, makeshift, on-the-spot, temporary

extempore *adverb/adjective* ad lib, extemporaneous, extemporary, freely, impromptu, improvised, offhand, off the cuff (*informal*), off the top of one's head, on the spot, spontaneously, unplanned, unpremeditated, unprepared

extemporize ad-lib, busk, improvise, make up, play (it) by ear, vamp, wing it (*informal*)

extend 1. carry on, continue, drag out, draw out, elongate, lengthen, make longer, prolong, protract, spin out, spread out, stretch, unfurl, unroll **2.** carry on, continue, go on, last, take **3.** amount to, attain, go as far as, reach, spread **4.** add to, amplify, augment, broaden, develop, dilate, enhance, enlarge, expand, increase, spread, supplement, widen **5.** advance, bestow, confer, give, grant, hold out, impart, offer, present, proffer, put forth, reach out, stretch out, yield

Antonyms abbreviate, abridge, condense, contract, curtail, cut, decrease, limit, reduce, restrict, shorten, take back, withdraw

extendable elastic, flexible, stretchy

extended 1. continued, drawn-out, elongated, enlarged, lengthened, long, prolonged, protracted, spread (out), stretched out, unfolded, unfurled, unrolled **2.** broad, comprehensive, enlarged, expanded, extensive, far-reaching, large-scale, sweeping, thorough, wide, widespread **3.** conferred, outstretched, proffered, stretched out

extension 1. amplification, augmentation, broadening, continuation, delay, development, dilatation, distension, elongation, enlargement, expansion, extent, increase, lengthening, postponement, prolongation, protraction, spread, stretching, widening **2.** addendum, addition, add-on, adjunct, annexe, appendage, appendix, branch, ell, supplement, wing

extensive all-inclusive, broad, capacious, commodious, comprehensive, expanded, extended, far-flung, far-reaching, general, great, huge, humongous *or* humungous (*U.S. slang*), large, large-scale, lengthy, long, pervasive, prevalent, protracted, spacious, sweeping, thorough, universal, vast, voluminous, wholesale, wide, widespread

Antonyms circumscribed, confined, constricted, limited, narrow, restricted, tight

extent 1. ambit, bounds, compass, play, range, reach, scope, sphere, sweep **2.** amount, amplitude, area, breadth, bulk, degree, duration, expanse, expansion, length, magnitude, measure, quantity, size, stretch, term, time, volume, width

extenuate 1. decrease, diminish, excuse, lessen, make allowances for, minimize, mitigate, moderate, palliate, play down, qualify, reduce, soften, temper, weaken **2.** discount, make light of, underestimate, underrate, undervalue

extenuating justifying, mitigating, moderating, qualifying, serving as an excuse

exterior *noun* **1.** appearance, aspect, coating, covering, façade, face, finish, outside, shell, skin, surface *~adjective* **2.** external, outer, outermost, outside, outward, superficial, surface **3.** alien, exotic, external, extraneous, extrinsic, foreign, outside

Antonyms *noun* inner, inside, interior *~adjective* domestic, immanent, inherent, inside, interior, internal, intrinsic

exterminate abolish, annihilate, destroy, eliminate, eradicate, extirpate

extermination annihilation, destruction, elimination, eradication, extirpation, genocide, massacre, mass murder, murder, slaughter, wiping out

> *We seem to be in the midst of an era of delirious ferocity, with half of mankind hell bent upon exterminating the other half*
>
> H.L. Mencken

external 1. apparent, exterior, outer, outermost, outside, outward, superficial, surface, visible **2.** alien, exotic, exterior, extramural, extraneous, extrinsic, foreign, independent, outside

Antonyms immanent, inherent, inner, inside, interior, internal, intrinsic

extinct 1. dead, defunct, gone, lost, vanished **2.** doused, extinguished, inactive, out, quenched, snuffed out **3.** abolished, defunct, ended, obsolete, terminated, void

Antonyms active, alive and kicking, existing, extant, flourishing, living, surviving, thriving

extinction abolition, annihilation, death, de~struction, dying out, eradication, excision, ex~termination, extirpation, obliteration, oblivion

extinguish 1. blow out, douse, put out, quench, smother, snuff out, stifle 2. abolish, annihi~late, destroy, eliminate, end, eradicate, erase, expunge, exterminate, extirpate, kill, obscure, put paid to, remove, suppress, wipe out

extirpate abolish, annihilate, deracinate, de~stroy, eliminate, eradicate, erase, excise, ex~punge, exterminate, extinguish, pull up by the roots, remove, root out, uproot, wipe from the face of the earth, wipe out

extol acclaim, applaud, celebrate, commend, crack up (*informal*), cry up, eulogize, exalt, glorify, laud, magnify (*archaic*), panegyrize, pay tribute to, praise, sing the praises of

extort blackmail, bleed (*informal*), bully, co~erce, exact, extract, force, squeeze, wrest, wring

extortion 1. blackmail, coercion, compulsion, demand, exaction, force, oppression, rapacity, shakedown (*U.S. slang*) 2. enormity, exorbi~tance, expensiveness, overcharging

extortionate 1. excessive, exorbitant, extrava~gant, immoderate, inflated, inordinate, outra~geous, preposterous, sky-high, unreasonable 2. blood-sucking (*informal*), exacting, grasping, hard, harsh, oppressive, rapacious, rigorous, severe, usurious

Antonyms (*sense 1*) fair, inexpensive, moder~ate, modest, reasonable

extra *adjective* 1. accessory, added, additional, add-on, ancillary, auxiliary, fresh, further, more, new, other, supplemental, supplemen~tary 2. excess, extraneous, inessential, left~over, needless, redundant, reserve, spare, supererogatory, superfluous, supernumerary, surplus, unnecessary, unneeded, unused *~noun* 3. accessory, addendum, addition, add-on, adjunct, affix, appendage, appurte~nance, attachment, bonus, complement, ex~tension, supernumerary, supplement *~adverb* 4. especially, exceptionally, extraordinarily, extremely, particularly, remarkably, uncom~monly, unusually

Antonyms *adjective* (*sense 2*) compulsory, es~sential, mandatory, necessary, needed, obliga~tory, required, requisite, vital *~noun* essen~tial, must, necessity, precondition, prerequi~site, requirement, requisite

extract *verb* 1. draw, extirpate, pluck out, pull, pull out, remove, take out, uproot, withdraw 2. bring out, derive, draw, elicit, evoke, exact, gather, get, glean, obtain, reap, wrest, wring 3. deduce, derive, develop, educe, elicit, evolve 4. distil, draw out, express, obtain, press out, separate out, squeeze, take out 5. abstract, choose, cite, copy out, cull, cut out, quote, se~lect *~noun* 6. concentrate, decoction, distillate, distillation, essence, juice 7. abstract, citation, clipping, cutting, excerpt, passage, quotation, selection

extraction 1. drawing, extirpation, pulling, re~moval, taking out, uprooting, withdrawal 2. derivation, distillation, separation 3. ancestry, birth, blood, derivation, descent, family, line~age, origin, parentage, pedigree, race, stock

extraneous 1. accidental, additional, adventi~tious, extra, incidental, inessential, needless, nonessential, peripheral, redundant, superflu~ous, supplementary, unessential, unnecessary, unneeded 2. beside the point, immaterial, im~pertinent, inadmissible, inapplicable, inappo~site, inappropriate, inapt, irrelevant, off the subject, unconnected, unrelated 3. adventi~tious, alien, exotic, external, extrinsic, foreign, out of place, strange

extraordinary amazing, beyond one's ken, bi~zarre, curious, exceptional, fantastic, marvel~lous, notable, odd, out of this world (*infor~mal*), outstanding, particular, peculiar, phe~nomenal, rare, remarkable, serious (*informal*), singular, special, strange, surprising, uncom~mon, unfamiliar, unheard-of, unique, unprec~edented, unusual, unwonted, weird, wonder~ful, wondrous (*archaic or literary*)

Antonyms banal, common, commonplace, cus~tomary, everyday, ordinary, unexceptional, unremarkable, usual

extravagance 1. improvidence, lavishness, overspending, prodigality, profligacy, profu~sion, squandering, waste, wastefulness 2. ab~surdity, dissipation, exaggeration, excess, ex~orbitance, folly, immoderation, outrageous~ness, preposterousness, recklessness, unrea~sonableness, unrestraint, wildness

extravagant 1. excessive, having money to burn, improvident, imprudent, lavish, prodi~gal, profligate, spendthrift, wasteful 2. absurd, exaggerated, excessive, exorbitant, fanciful, fantastic, foolish, immoderate, inordinate, O.T.T. (*slang*), outrageous, over the top (*slang*), preposterous, reckless, unreasonable, unrestrained, wild 3. fancy, flamboyant, flashy, garish, gaudy, grandiose, ornate, os~tentatious, pretentious, showy 4. costly, exces~sive, exorbitant, expensive, extortionate, inor~dinate, overpriced, steep (*informal*), unrea~sonable

Antonyms careful, close, conservative, down-to-earth, economical, frugal, miserly, moder~ate, prudent, realistic, reasonable, restrained, sensible, sober, sparing, thrifty, tight-fisted (*informal*)

extravaganza display, flight of fancy, pageant, show, spectacle, spectacular

extreme *adjective* **1.** acute, great, greatest, high, highest, intense, maximum, mother (of all) (*informal*), severe, supreme, ultimate, utmost, uttermost, worst **2.** downright, egregious, exaggerated, exceptional, excessive, extraordinary, extravagant, fanatical, immoderate, inordinate, intemperate, O.T.T. (*slang*), out-and-out, outrageous, over the top (*slang*), radical, remarkable, sheer, uncommon, unconventional, unreasonable, unusual, utter, zealous **3.** dire, Draconian, drastic, harsh, radical, rigid, severe, stern, strict, unbending, uncompromising **4.** faraway, far-off, farthest, final, last, most distant, outermost, remotest, terminal, ultimate, utmost, uttermost *~noun* **5.** acme, apex, apogee, boundary, climax, consummation, depth, edge, end, excess, extremity, height, limit, maximum, minimum, nadir, pinnacle, pole, termination, top, ultimate, zenith
Antonyms *adjective* average, common, mild, moderate, modest, nearest, ordinary, reasonable, traditional, unremarkable

extremely acutely, awfully (*informal*), exceedingly, exceptionally, excessively, extraordinarily, greatly, highly, inordinately, intensely, markedly, quite, severely, terribly, to a fault, to *or* in the extreme, to the nth degree, ultra, uncommonly, unusually, utterly, very

extremism

Extremism in the defence of liberty is no vice!
Barry Goldwater

extremist die-hard, fanatic, radical, ultra, zealot

extremity **1.** acme, apex, apogee, border, bound, boundary, brim, brink, edge, end, extreme, frontier, limit, margin, maximum, minimum, nadir, pinnacle, pole, rim, terminal, termination, terminus, tip, top, ultimate, verge, zenith **2.** acuteness, climax, consummation, depth, excess, height **3.** adversity, crisis, dire straits, disaster, emergency, exigency, hardship, pass, pinch, plight, setback, trouble **4.** *plural* fingers and toes, hands and feet, limbs

extricate clear, deliver, disembarrass, disengage, disentangle, free, get out, get (someone) off the hook (*slang*), liberate, release, relieve, remove, rescue, withdraw, wriggle out of

extrinsic alien, exotic, exterior, external, extraneous, foreign, imported, outside, superficial

extrovert amiable, exuberant, gregarious, hearty, out-going, sociable, social
Antonyms introspective, introverted, inward-looking, self-contained, withdrawn

extrude eject, expel, force out, press out, squeeze out, thrust out

exuberance **1.** animation, brio, buoyancy, cheerfulness, eagerness, ebullience, effervescence, energy, enthusiasm, excitement, exhilaration, high spirits, life, liveliness, pep, spirit, sprightliness, vigour, vitality, vivacity, zest **2.** effusiveness, exaggeration, excessiveness, fulsomeness, lavishness, prodigality, superfluity **3.** abundance, copiousness, lavishness, lushness, luxuriance, plenitude, profusion, rankness, richness, superabundance, teemingness

Exuberance is Beauty
William Blake *The Marriage of Heaven and Hell*

Exuberance is better than taste
Flaubert *Sentimental Education*

exuberant **1.** animated, buoyant, cheerful, chirpy (*informal*), eager, ebullient, effervescent, elated, energetic, enthusiastic, excited, exhilarated, full of beans (*informal*), full of life, high-spirited, in high spirits, lively, sparkling, spirited, sprightly, upbeat (*informal*), vigorous, vivacious, zestful **2.** effusive, exaggerated, excessive, fulsome, lavish, overdone, prodigal, superfluous **3.** abundant, copious, lavish, lush, luxuriant, overflowing, plenteous, plentiful, profuse, rank, rich, superabundant, teeming
Antonyms (*sense 1*) apathetic, dull, lifeless, subdued, unenthusiastic

exude **1.** bleed, discharge, emanate, emit, excrete, filter through, issue, leak, ooze, secrete, seep, sweat, trickle, weep, well forth **2.** display, emanate, exhibit, manifest, radiate, show

exult **1.** be delighted, be elated, be in high spirits, be joyful, be jubilant, be overjoyed, celebrate, jubilate, jump for joy, make merry, rejoice **2.** boast, brag, crow, drool, gloat, glory (in), revel, take delight in, taunt, triumph, vaunt

exultant cock-a-hoop, delighted, elated, exulting, flushed, gleeful, joyful, joyous, jubilant, overjoyed, over the moon (*informal*), rapt, rejoicing, revelling, transported, triumphant

exultation **1.** celebration, delight, elation, glee, high spirits, joy, joyousness, jubilation, merriness, rejoicing, transport **2.** boasting, bragging, crowing, gloating, glory, glorying, revelling, triumph

eye *noun* **1.** eyeball, optic (*informal*), orb (*poetic*), peeper (*slang*) **2.** appreciation, discernment, discrimination, judgment, perception, recognition, taste **3.** *often plural* belief, judgment, mind, opinion, point of view, viewpoint **4.** **keep an** *or* **one's eye on** guard, keep in view, keep tabs on (*informal*), keep under surveillance, look after, look out for, monitor, observe, pay attention to, regard, scrutinize, supervise, survey, watch, watch like a hawk, watch over **5.** **an eye for an eye** justice, reprisal, requital, retaliation, retribution, revenge, vengeance **6.** **lay, clap** *or* **set eyes on** behold, come across, encounter, meet, notice, observe, run into, see **7.** **see eye to eye** accord, agree, back, be in unison, coincide, concur, fall in, get on, go along, harmonize, jibe (*informal*), subscribe to **8.** **up to one's eyes** busy, caught up, engaged, flooded out, fully occupied, inundated, overwhelmed, up to here, up to one's elbows, wrapped up in *~verb* **9.** behold (*archaic or literary*), check, check out (*informal*), clock (*Brit. slang*), contemplate, eyeball (*U.S. slang*), gaze at, get a load of (*informal*), glance at, have *or* take a look at, inspect, look at, peruse, recce (*slang*), regard, scan, scrutinize, stare at, study, survey, take a dekko at (*Brit. slang*), view, watch **10.** eye up, give (someone) the (glad) eye, leer at, make eyes at, ogle

Parts of the eye

aqueous humour
blind spot
choroid *or* chorioid
ciliary body
cone
conjunctiva
cornea
eyeball
fovea
iris
lens
ocular muscle
optic nerve
pupil
retina
retinal vessels
rod
sclera
suspensory ligament
vitreous body
vitreous humour

If thy right eye offend thee, pluck it out
Bible: St. Matthew

The sight of you is good for sore eyes
Jonathan Swift *Polite Conversation*

The eyes are the windows of the soul

eye-catching arresting, attractive, captivating, dramatic, showy, spectacular, striking

eyeful **1.** butcher's (*Brit. slang*), gander (*informal*), gaze, glance, look, shufti (*Brit. slang*), sight, view **2.** beauty, dazzler, humdinger (*slang*), knockout (*informal*), show, sight, sight for sore eyes (*informal*), spectacle, stunner (*informal*), vision

eyesight observation, perception, range of vision, sight, vision

eyesore atrocity, blemish, blight, blot, disfigurement, disgrace, horror, mess, monstrosity, sight (*informal*), ugliness

eyewitness bystander, looker-on, observer, onlooker, passer-by, spectator, viewer, watcher, witness

F

Fabian attritional, cautious, circumspect, cunctative *or* cunctatory (*rare*), delaying, procrastinating

fable 1. allegory, apologue, legend, myth, parable, story, tale 2. fabrication, fairy story (*informal*), falsehood, fantasy, fib, fiction, figment, invention, lie, romance, tall story (*informal*), untruth, urban legend, white lie, yarn (*informal*)
Antonyms actuality, certainty, fact, reality, truth, verity

fabled fabulous, famed, famous, fictional, legendary, mythical, storied

fabric 1. cloth, material, stuff, textile, web 2. constitution, construction, foundations, framework, infrastructure, make-up, organization, structure

Fabrics

Acrilan (*Trademark*)
alpaca
armure
baize
balbriggan
barathea
barège
batik *or* battik
batiste
bayadere
beige
bengaline
bird's-eye
bobbinet
bombazine *or* bombasine
bouclé
brilliantine
broadcloth
brocade
buckskin
bunting
burlap
calamanco
calico
cambric
camlet
cavalry twill
challis *or* challie
chambray
Charmeuse (*Trademark*)
cheesecloth
chenille
cheviot
chiffon
chintz
cilice
ciré
cloqué
cord
corduroy
cotton
cottonade
cotton flannel
covert cloth
crepe *or* crape
cretonne
Crimplene (*Trademark*)
crinoline
cypress *or* cyprus
Dacron (*Trademark*)
damask
delaine
denim
diamanté
dimity
Donegal tweed
drab
drabbet
Dralon (*Trademark*)
drugget
duck
dungaree
duvetyn, duvetine *or* duvetyne
etamine *or* etamin
façonné *or* faconne
faille
fearnought *or* fearnaught
felt
fishnet
flannel
fleece
folk weave
foulard
frieze
frisé
fur
fustian
gaberdine
galatea
georgette
gingham
gloria
Gore-Tex (*Trademark*)
gossamer
grogram
gros de Londres
grosgrain
gunny (*chiefly U.S.*)
Harris Tweed (*Trademark*)
hessian
honan
hopsack
huckaback *or* huck
India print
jaconet
Jacquard *or* Jacquard weave
jean
jersey
khaki
kincob
knit
lace
lambskin
lamé
lawn
leather
linen
linsey-woolsey
lisle
Lurex (*Trademark*)
Lycra (*Trademark*)
madras
marabou
marocain
marquisette
marseille *or* marseilles
melton
messaline
mohair
moire *or* moiré
moleskin
monk's cloth
moquette
moreen
mousseline
mull
muslin
nainsook
nankeen *or* nankin
needlecord
net
ninon
nun's cloth *or* veiling
oilskin
organdie
organza
organzine
Orlon (*Trademark*)
ottoman
Oxford
paduasoy
paisley pattern
panne
paramatta *or* parramatta
peau de soie
percale
percaline
petersham
piña cloth
piqué
plush
pongee
poplin
poult *or* poult-de-soie
prunella, prunelle *or* prunello

rayon
russet
sailcloth
samite
sarcenet *or* sarsenet
sateen
satin
satinet *or* satinette
saxony
say (*archaic*)
schappe
scrim
seersucker
sendal
serge
shag
shalloon
shantung
sharkskin
sheeting
shirting
shoddy
silesia
silk
silkaline
slipper satin
spandex
spun silk
stockinet
stroud
stuff
suiting
surah
surat
swan's-down
swanskin
swiss muslin
tabaret
tabby
taffeta
tammy
tarlatan
tarpaulin
tartan
tattersall
terry
Terylene (*Trademark*)
tick
ticking
tiffany
toile
towelling
tricot
tricotine
tulle
tussore, tusser *or* (*chiefly U.S.*) tussah
tweed
twill
velours
velure
velvet
velveteen
Viyella (*Trademark*)
voile
wadmal
webbing
whipcord
wild silk
winceyette
wool
worsted

fabricate 1. assemble, build, construct, erect, fashion, form, frame, make, manufacture, shape 2. coin, concoct, devise, fake, falsify, feign, forge, form, invent, make up, trump up

fabrication 1. assemblage, assembly, building, construction, erection, manufacture, production 2. cock-and-bull story (*informal*), concoction, fable, fairy story (*informal*), fake, falsehood, fiction, figment, forgery, invention, lie, myth, pork pie (*Brit. slang*), porky (*Brit. slang*), untruth

fabulous 1. amazing, astounding, breathtaking, fictitious, immense, inconceivable, incredible, legendary, phenomenal, unbelievable 2. *informal* brilliant, fantastic (*informal*), magic (*informal*), marvellous, out-of-this-world (*informal*), sensational (*informal*), spectacular, superb, wonderful 3. apocryphal, fantastic, fictitious, imaginary, invented, legendary, made-up, mythical, unreal
Antonyms actual, common, commonplace, credible, genuine, natural, ordinary, real

façade appearance, exterior, face, front, frontage, guise, mask, pretence, semblance, show, veneer

face *noun* 1. clock (*Brit. slang*), countenance, dial (*Brit. slang*), features, kisser (*slang*), lineaments, mug (*slang*), phiz *or* phizog (*slang*), physiognomy, visage 2. appearance, aspect, expression, frown, grimace, look, *moue*, pout, scowl, smirk 3. air, appearance, disguise, display, exterior, façade, front, mask, pretence, semblance, show 4. authority, dignity, honour, image, prestige, reputation, self-respect, standing, status 5. *informal* assurance, audacity, boldness, brass neck (*Brit. informal*), cheek (*informal*), chutzpah (*U.S. & Canad. informal*), confidence, effrontery, front, gall (*informal*), impudence, neck (*informal*), nerve, presumption, sauce (*informal*) 6. aspect, cover, exterior, facet, front, outside, right side, side, surface 7. **face to face** *à deux*, confronting, eyeball to eyeball, in confrontation, opposite, tête-à-tête, vis-à-vis 8. **fly in the face of** act in defiance of, defy, disobey, go against, oppose, rebel against, snap one's fingers at (*informal*) 9. **on the face of it** apparently, at first sight, seemingly, to all appearances, to the eye 10. **pull** (*or* **make) a long face** frown, grimace, knit one's brows, look black (disapproving, displeased, put out, stern), lour *or* lower, pout, scowl, sulk 11. **show one's face** approach, be seen, come, put in *or* make an appearance, show up (*informal*), turn up 12. **to one's face** directly, in one's presence, openly, straight *~verb* 13. be confronted by, brave, come up against, confront, cope with, deal with, defy, encounter, experience, face off (*slang*), meet, oppose, tackle 14. be opposite, front onto, give towards *or* onto, look onto, overlook 15. clad, coat, cover, dress, finish, level, line, overlay, sheathe, surface, veneer

The face is the image of the soul
Cicero *De Oratore*

Was this the face that launched a thousand ships
And burnt the topless towers of Ilium?
Christopher Marlowe *Dr. Faustus*

face-lift 1. cosmetic surgery, plastic surgery 2. renovation, restoration

facer difficulty, dilemma, how-do-you-do (*informal*), poser, problem, puzzle, teaser

facet angle, aspect, face, part, phase, plane, side, slant, surface

facetious amusing, comical, droll, flippant, frivolous, funny, humorous, jesting, jocose, jocular, merry, playful, pleasant, tongue in cheek, unserious, waggish, witty
Antonyms earnest, genuine, grave, lugubrious, pensive, sedate, serious, sincere, sober, thoughtful

face up to accept, acknowledge, come to terms with, confront, cope with, deal with, face the music, meet head-on, tackle

facile 1. adept, adroit, dexterous, easy, effortless, fluent, light, proficient, quick, ready, simple, skilful, smooth, uncomplicated 2. cursory, glib, hasty, shallow, slick, superficial
Antonyms awkward, careful, clumsy, difficult, intractable, maladroit, slow, thoughtful, unskilful

facilitate assist the progress of, ease, expedite, forward, further, help, make easy, oil the wheels, pave the way for, promote, smooth the path of, speed up
Antonyms delay, encumber, frustrate, hamper, handicap, hinder, hold up *or* back, impede, obstruct, prevent, restrain, thwart

facility 1. ability, adroitness, craft, dexterity, ease, efficiency, effortlessness, expertness, fluency, gift, knack, proficiency, quickness, readiness, skilfulness, skill, smoothness, talent 2. *often plural* advantage, aid, amenity, appliance, convenience, equipment, means, opportunity, resource
Antonyms awkwardness, clumsiness, difficulty, hardship, ineptness, maladroitness, pains

facing 1. *adjective* fronting, opposite, partnering 2. *noun* cladding, coating, façade, false front, front, overlay, plaster, reinforcement, revetment, stucco, surface, trimming, veneer

facsimile carbon, carbon copy, copy, duplicate, fax (*Trademark*), photocopy, Photostat (*Trademark*), print, replica, reproduction, transcript, Xerox (*Trademark*)

fact 1. act, deed, event, *fait accompli*, happening, incident, occurrence, performance 2. actuality, certainty, gospel (truth), naked truth, reality, truth 3. circumstance, detail, feature, item, particular, point, specific 4. **in fact** actually, indeed, in point of fact, in reality, in truth, really, truly
Antonyms delusion, fable, fabrication, falsehood, fiction, invention, lie, tall story, untruth, yarn (*informal*)

> *In this life we want nothing but facts, sir; nothing but facts*
>
> Charles Dickens *Hard Times*

faction 1. bloc, cabal, camp, caucus, clique, coalition, combination, confederacy, contingent, coterie, division, gang, ginger group, group, junta, lobby, minority, party, pressure group, schism, section, sector, set, splinter group 2. conflict, disagreement, discord, disharmony, dissension, disunity, division, divisiveness, friction, infighting, rebellion, sedition, strife, tumult, turbulence
Antonyms (*sense 2*) accord, agreement, amity, assent, concord, consensus, friendship, goodwill, harmony, peace, rapport, unanimity, unity

factious conflicting, contentious, disputatious, dissident, divisive, insurrectionary, litigious, malcontent, mutinous, partisan, rebellious, refractory, rival, sectarian, seditious, troublemaking, tumultuous, turbulent, warring

factitious affected, artificial, assumed, counterfeited, engineered, fabricated, fake, false, imitation, insincere, made-up, manufactured, mock, phoney *or* phony (*informal*), pinchbeck, pseudo (*informal*), put-on, sham, simulated, spurious, synthetic, unnatural, unreal

factor 1. aspect, cause, circumstance, component, consideration, determinant, element, influence, item, part, point, thing 2. *Scot.* agent, deputy, estate manager, middleman, reeve, steward

factory manufactory (*obsolete*), mill, plant, works

factotum Girl Friday, handyman, jack of all trades, Man Friday, man of all work, odd job man

facts data, details, gen (*Brit. informal*), info (*informal*), information, ins and outs, the lowdown (*informal*), the score (*informal*), the whole story

factual accurate, authentic, circumstantial, close, correct, credible, exact, faithful, genuine, literal, matter-of-fact, objective, precise, real, sure, true, true-to-life, unadorned, unbiased, veritable
Antonyms embellished, fanciful, fictitious, fictive, figurative, imaginary, unreal

faculties capabilities, intelligence, powers, reason, senses, wits

faculty 1. ability, adroitness, aptitude, bent, capability, capacity, cleverness, dexterity, facility, gift, knack, power, propensity, readiness, skill, talent, turn 2. branch of learning, department, discipline, profession, school, teaching staff (*chiefly U.S.*) 3. authorization, licence, prerogative, privilege, right
Antonyms (*sense 1*) failing, inability, shortcoming, unskilfulness, weakness, weak point

fad affectation, craze, fancy, fashion, mania, mode, rage, trend, vogue, whim

fade 1. blanch, bleach, blench, dim, discolour, dull, grow dim, lose colour, lose lustre, pale, wash out 2. decline, die away, die out, dim, disappear, disperse, dissolve, droop, dwindle, ebb, etiolate, evanesce, fail, fall, flag, languish, melt away, perish, shrivel, vanish, vanish into thin air, wane, waste away, wilt, wither

faded bleached, dim, discoloured, dull, etiolated, indistinct, lustreless, pale, washed out

fading declining, decreasing, disappearing, dy~ ing, on the decline, vanishing

faeces bodily waste, droppings, dung, excre~ ment, excreta, ordure, stools

fag[1] *noun* bind (*informal*), bore, bother, chore, drag (*informal*), inconvenience, irritation, nui~ sance, pain in the arse (*taboo informal*)

fag[2] *noun* bender (*slang*), catamite, dyke (*slang*), fairy (*slang*), gay, homo (*informal*), homosexual, lesbian, nancy boy (*slang*), poof (*slang*), poofter (*slang*), queen (*slang*), queer (*informal, derogatory*), woofter (*slang*)

fagged out all in (*slang*), beat (*slang*), clapped out (*Austral. & N.Z. informal*), exhausted, fa~ tigued, jaded, jiggered (*informal*), knackered (*slang*), on one's last legs (*informal*), shagged out (*Brit. slang*), wasted, weary, wiped out (*informal*), worn out, zonked (*slang*)

fail 1. be defeated, be found lacking *or* wanting, be in vain, be unsuccessful, bite the dust, break down, come a cropper (*informal*), come to grief, come to naught, come to nothing, come unstuck, fall, fall by the wayside, fall flat, fall flat on one's face, fall short, fall short of, fall through, fizzle out (*informal*), flop (*in~ formal*), founder, go astray, go belly-up (*slang*), go by the board, go down, go down like a lead balloon (*informal*), go up in smoke, lay an egg (*slang, chiefly U.S. & Canad.*), meet with disaster, miscarry, misfire, miss, not make the grade (*informal*), run aground, turn out badly **2.** abandon, break one's word, desert, disappoint, forget, forsake, let down, neglect, omit, turn one's back on **3.** be on one's last legs (*informal*), cease, conk out (*in~ formal*), cut out, decline, die, disappear, droop, dwindle, fade, fall apart at the seams, give out, give up, go phut, gutter, languish, peter out, sicken, sink, stop working, wane, weaken **4.** become insolvent, close down, crash, fold (*informal*), go bankrupt, go broke (*informal*), go bust (*informal*), go into receiv~ ership, go out of business, go to the wall, go under, smash **5. without fail** conscientiously, constantly, dependably, like clockwork, punc~ tually, regularly, religiously, without excep~ tion

Antonyms bloom, flourish, grow, pass, pros~ per, strengthen, succeed, thrive, triumph

failing 1. *noun* blemish, blind spot, defect, defi~ ciency, drawback, error, failure, fault, flaw, foible, frailty, imperfection, lapse, miscarriage, misfortune, shortcoming, weakness **2.** *preposi~ tion* in default of, in the absence of, lacking

Antonyms (*sense 1*) advantage, asset, forte, metier, speciality, strength, strong suit

failure 1. abortion, breakdown, collapse, defeat, downfall, fiasco, frustration, lack of success, miscarriage, overthrow, wreck **2.** black sheep, clinker (*slang, chiefly U.S.*), dead duck (*slang*), disappointment, dud (*informal*), flop (*informal*), incompetent, loser, ne'er-do-well, no-good, no-hoper (*chiefly Austral.*), nonstart~ er, washout (*informal*) **3.** default, deficiency, dereliction, neglect, negligence, nonobserv~ ance, nonperformance, nonsuccess, omission, remissness, shortcoming, stoppage **4.** break~ down, decay, decline, deterioration, failing, loss **5.** bankruptcy, crash, downfall, folding (*informal*), insolvency, ruin

Antonyms adequacy, care, effectiveness, for~ tune, observance, prosperity, strengthening, success, triumph

There's many a slip 'twixt the cup and the lip
R.B. Barham *The Ingoldsby Legends*

fain *adverb* **1.** as lief (*rare*), as soon, cheerfully, eagerly, gladly, willingly *~adjective* **2.** anxious, eager, glad, well-pleased **3.** compelled, con~ strained, with no alternative but

faint *adjective* **1.** bleached, delicate, dim, dis~ tant, dull, faded, faltering, feeble, hazy, hushed, ill-defined, indistinct, light, low, muf~ fled, muted, soft, subdued, thin, vague, whis~ pered **2.** feeble, remote, slight, unenthusiastic, weak **3.** dizzy, drooping, enervated, exhausted, faltering, fatigued, giddy, languid, lethargic, light-headed, muzzy, vertiginous, weak, woozy (*informal*) **4.** faint-hearted, lily-livered, spirit~ less, timid, timorous *~verb* **5.** black out, col~ lapse, fade, fail, flake out (*informal*), keel over (*informal*), languish, lose consciousness, pass out, swoon (*literary*), weaken *~noun* **6.** black~ out, collapse, swoon (*literary*), syncope (*Pa~ thology*), unconsciousness

Antonyms *adjective* bold, brave, bright, clear, conspicuous, courageous, distinct, energetic, fresh, hearty, loud, powerful, strong, vigorous

faint-hearted boneless, chickenshit (*U.S. slang*), cowardly, diffident, half-arsed (*Brit. slang*), half-assed (*U.S. & Canad. slang*), half-hearted, irresolute, spineless, timid, tim~ orous, weak, yellow

Antonyms audacious, bold, brave, courageous, daring, dauntless, fearless, game (*informal*), intrepid, plucky, stouthearted

faintly 1. feebly, in a whisper, indistinctly, softly, weakly **2.** a little, dimly, slightly, somewhat

faintness dimness, dizziness, feebleness, giddi~ ness, indistinctness, languor, loss of strength, shakiness, weakness

fair[1] *adjective* **1.** above board, according to the rules, clean, disinterested, dispassionate, equal, equitable, even-handed, honest, hon~ ourable, impartial, just, lawful, legitimate, objective, on the level (*informal*), proper, square, trustworthy, unbiased, unprejudiced, upright **2.** blond, blonde, fair-haired, flaxen-haired, light, light-complexioned, tow-haired, towheaded **3.** adequate, all right, average, de~

cent, mediocre, middling, moderate, not bad, O.K. *or* okay (*informal*), passable, reasonable, respectable, satisfactory, so-so (*informal*), tolerable **4**. beauteous, beautiful, bonny, comely, handsome, lovely, pretty, well-favoured **5**. bright, clear, clement, cloudless, dry, favourable, fine, sunny, sunshiny, unclouded
Antonyms (*sense 1*) bad, biased, bigoted, discriminatory, dishonest, inequitable, one-sided, partial, partisan, prejudiced, unfair, unjust (*sense 4*) homely, plain, ugly

fair² *noun* bazaar, carnival, expo (*informal*), exposition, festival, fête, gala, market, show

fair-and-square above board, correct, honest, just, kosher (*informal*), on the level (*informal*), straight

fairly **1**. adequately, moderately, pretty well, quite, rather, reasonably, somewhat, tolerably **2**. deservedly, equitably, honestly, impartially, justly, objectively, properly, without fear or favour **3**. absolutely, in a manner of speaking, positively, really, veritably

fair-minded disinterested, even-handed, impartial, just, open-minded, unbiased, unprejudiced

fairness decency, disinterestedness, equitableness, equity, impartiality, justice, legitimacy, rightfulness, uprightness

One should always play fairly when one has the winning cards
Oscar Wilde *An Ideal Husband*

fairy brownie, elf, hob, leprechaun, peri, pixie, Robin Goodfellow, sprite

fairy tale *or* **fairy story** **1**. folk tale, romance **2**. cock-and-bull story (*informal*), fabrication, fantasy, fiction, invention, lie, pork pie (*Brit. slang*), porky (*Brit. slang*), tall story, untruth

faith **1**. assurance, confidence, conviction, credence, credit, dependence, reliance, trust **2**. belief, church, communion, creed, denomination, dogma, persuasion, religion **3**. allegiance, constancy, faithfulness, fealty, fidelity, loyalty, troth (*archaic*), truth, truthfulness **4**. *As in* **keep faith, in good faith** honour, pledge, promise, sincerity, vow, word, word of honour
Antonyms agnosticism, apprehension, denial, disbelief, distrust, doubt, incredulity, infidelity, misgiving, mistrust, rejection, scepticism, suspicion, uncertainty

Faith may be defined briefly as an illogical belief in the occurrence of the improbable
H.L. Mencken *Prejudices: Third Series*

Faith is the substance of things hoped for, the evidence of things not seen
Bible: Hebrews

I show you doubt, to prove that faith exists
Robert Browning *Balaustion's Adventure*

Faith without works is dead
Bible: James

The faith that stands on authority is not faith
Ralph Waldo Emerson *Essays*

Faith will move mountains

faithful **1**. attached, constant, dependable, devoted, immovable, loyal, reliable, staunch, steadfast, true, true-blue, trusty, truthful, unswerving, unwavering **2**. accurate, close, exact, just, precise, strict, true **3**. **the faithful** adherents, believers, brethren, communicants, congregation, followers, the elect
Antonyms disloyal, doubting, faithless, false, false-hearted, fickle, inconstant, perfidious, recreant (*archaic*), traitorous, treacherous, unbelieving, unfaithful, unreliable, untrue, untrustworthy, untruthful

faithfulness **1**. adherence, constancy, dependability, devotion, fealty, fidelity, loyalty, trustworthiness **2**. accuracy, closeness, exactness, justice, strictness, truth

faithless disloyal, doubting, false, false-hearted, fickle, inconstant, perfidious, recreant (*archaic*), traitorous, treacherous, unbelieving, unfaithful, unreliable, untrue, untrustworthy, untruthful

faithlessness betrayal, disloyalty, fickleness, inconstancy, infidelity, perfidy, treachery, unfaithfulness

fake **1**. *verb* affect, assume, copy, counterfeit, fabricate, feign, forge, pretend, put on, sham, simulate **2**. *noun* charlatan, copy, forgery, fraud, hoax, imitation, impostor, mountebank, phoney *or* phony (*informal*), reproduction, sham **3**. *adjective* affected, artificial, assumed, counterfeit, false, forged, imitation, mock, phoney *or* phony (*informal*), pinchbeck, pseudo (*informal*), reproduction, sham
Antonyms *adjective* actual, authentic, bona fide, faithful, genuine, honest, legitimate, real, true, veritable

faker fake, fraud, humbug, impostor, phoney *or* phony (*informal*), pretender, sham

fall *verb* **1**. be precipitated, cascade, collapse, come a cropper (*informal*), crash, descend, dive, drop, drop down, go head over heels, keel over, nose-dive, pitch, plummet, plunge, settle, sink, stumble, subside, topple, trip, trip over, tumble **2**. abate, become lower, decline, decrease, depreciate, diminish, drop, dwindle, ebb, fall off, flag, go down, lessen, slump, subside **3**. be overthrown, be taken, capitulate, give in *or* up, give way, go out of office, pass into enemy hands, resign, succumb, surrender, yield **4**. be a casualty, be killed, be lost, be slain, die, meet one's end, perish **5**. become, befall, chance, come about, come to pass, fall out, happen, occur, take place **6**. **fall foul of** brush with, come into conflict with, cross swords with, have trouble with, make an enemy of **7**. **fall in love (with)** become

attached to, become enamoured of, become fond of, become infatuated (with), be smitten by, conceive an affection for, fall (for), lose one's heart (to), take a fancy to **8**. fall away, incline, incline downwards, slope **9**. backslide, err, go astray, lapse, offend, sin, transgress, trespass, yield to temptation *~noun* **10**. descent, dive, drop, nose dive, plummet, plunge, slip, spill, tumble **11**. cut, decline, decrease, diminution, dip, drop, dwindling, falling off, lessening, lowering, reduction, slump **12**. capitulation, collapse, death, defeat, destruction, downfall, failure, overthrow, resignation, ruin, surrender **13**. declivity, descent, downgrade, incline, slant, slope **14**. degradation, failure, lapse, sin, slip, transgression
Antonyms (*sense 1*) ascend, climb, go up, increase, mount, rise, scale, soar, wax (*sense 2*) advance, appreciate, climb, escalate, extend, heighten, increase (*senses 3 & 4*) endure, hold out, prevail, survive, triumph

fallacious deceptive, delusive, delusory, erroneous, false, fictitious, illogical, illusory, incorrect, misleading, mistaken, sophistic, sophistical, spurious, untrue, wrong

The conclusion of your syllogism, I said lightly, is fallacious, being based upon licensed premises
Flann O'Brien *At Swim-Two-Birds*

fallacy casuistry, deceit, deception, delusion, error, falsehood, faultiness, flaw, illusion, inconsistency, misapprehension, misconception, mistake, sophism, sophistry, untruth

fall apart break up, come apart at the seams, crumble, disband, disintegrate, disperse, dissolve, fall to bits, go *or* come to pieces, go to seed, lose cohesion, shatter

fall asleep doze off, drop off (*informal*), go out like a light, go to sleep, nod off (*informal*)

fall back back off, draw back, recede, recoil, retire, retreat, withdraw

fall back on call upon, employ, have recourse to, make use of, press into service, resort to

fall behind be in arrears, drop back, get left behind, lag, lose one's place, trail

fall down disappoint, fail, fail to make the grade, fall short, go wrong, prove unsuccessful

fallen *adjective* **1**. collapsed, decayed, flat, on the ground, ruinous, sunken **2**. disgraced, dishonoured, immoral, loose, lost, ruined, shamed, sinful, unchaste **3**. dead, killed, lost, perished, slain, slaughtered

fall for **1**. become infatuated with, desire, fall in love with, lose one's head over, succumb to the charms of **2**. accept, be deceived (duped, fooled, taken in) by, buy (*slang*), give credence to, swallow (*informal*), take on board

fallible erring, frail, ignorant, imperfect, mortal, prone to error, uncertain, weak
Antonyms divine, faultless, impeccable, infallible, omniscient, perfect, superhuman, unerring, unimpeachable

fall in cave in, collapse, come down about one's ears, fall apart at the seams, sink

falling off *noun* deceleration, decline, decrease, deterioration, downward trend, drop, slackening, slowing down, slump, waning, worsening

fall in with accept, agree with, assent, concur with, cooperate with, go along with, support, take on board

fall off **1**. be unseated, come a cropper *or* purler (*informal*), plummet, take a fall *or* tumble, topple, tumble **2**. decline, decrease, diminish, drop, dwindle, ebb away, fade, fall away, go down *or* downhill, lessen, peter out, reduce, shrink, slacken, slump, subside, tail off (*informal*), wane, weaken
Antonyms (*sense 2*) improve, increase, pick up, rally, recover, revive

fall on *or* **fall upon** assail, assault, attack, belabour, descend upon, lay (pitch (*informal*), tear (*informal*)) into (*informal*), set upon *or* about, snatch

fall out **1**. altercate, argue, clash, come to blows, differ, disagree, fight, quarrel, squabble **2**. chance, come to pass, happen, occur, pan out (*informal*), result, take place, turn out

fallow dormant, idle, inactive, inert, resting, uncultivated, undeveloped, unplanted, untilled, unused

falls cascade, cataract, force (*Northern English dialect*), linn (*Scot.*), rapids, waterfall

fall short be deficient (lacking, wanting), fail, miss, prove inadequate

fall through come to nothing, fail, fizzle out (*informal*), go by the board, miscarry

fall to **1**. apply oneself to, begin, commence, set about, start **2**. be up to, come down to, devolve upon

false **1**. concocted, erroneous, faulty, fictitious, improper, inaccurate, incorrect, inexact, invalid, mistaken, unfounded, unreal, wrong **2**. lying, mendacious, truthless, unreliable, unsound, untrue, untrustworthy, untruthful **3**. artificial, bogus, counterfeit, ersatz, fake, feigned, forged, imitation, mock, pretended, pseudo (*informal*), sham, simulated, spurious, synthetic **4**. deceitful, deceiving, deceptive, delusive, fallacious, fraudulent, hypocritical, misleading, trumped up **5**. dishonest, dishonourable, disloyal, double-dealing, duplicitous, faithless, false-hearted, hypocritical, perfidious, treacherous, treasonable, two-faced, unfaithful, untrustworthy **6**. **play (someone) false** betray, cheat, deceive, double-cross, give the Judas kiss to, sell down the river (*informal*), stab in the back
Antonyms authentic, bona fide, correct, exact, faithful, genuine, honest, kosher (*informal*),

loyal, real, right, sincere, sound, true, trustworthy, valid

falsehood **1.** deceit, deception, dishonesty, dissimulation, inveracity (*rare*), mendacity, perjury, prevarication, untruthfulness **2.** fabrication, fib, fiction, lie, misstatement, pork pie (*Brit. slang*), porky (*Brit. slang*), story, untruth

The most dangerous of all falsehoods is a slightly distorted truth

G.C. Lichtenberg

falsification adulteration, deceit, dissimulation, distortion, forgery, misrepresentation, perversion, tampering with

falsify alter, belie, cook (*slang*), counterfeit, distort, doctor, fake, forge, garble, misrepresent, misstate, pervert, tamper with

falsity **1.** deceit, deceptiveness, dishonesty, double-dealing, duplicity, fraudulence, hypocrisy, inaccuracy, mendacity, perfidy, treachery, unreality, untruth **2.** cheating, deception, fraud, lie, pork pie (*Brit. slang*), porky (*Brit. slang*)

falter break, hesitate, shake, speak haltingly, stammer, stumble, stutter, totter, tremble, vacillate, waver
Antonyms continue, endure, keep going, last, persevere, persist, proceed, stand firm, stick at, survive

faltering broken, hesitant, irresolute, stammering, tentative, timid, uncertain, weak

fame celebrity, credit, eminence, glory, honour, illustriousness, name, prominence, public esteem, renown, reputation, repute, stardom
Antonyms disgrace, dishonour, disrepute, ignominy, infamy, oblivion, obscurity, shame

If fame is to come only after death, I am in no hurry for it

Martial *Epigrams*

In the future everyone will be famous for fifteen minutes

Andy Warhol

Fame is the spur

John Milton *Lycidas*

Fame is like a river, that beareth up things light and swollen, and drowns things heavy and solid

Francis Bacon *Essays*

Fame is a food that dead men eat, -
I have no stomach for such meat

Henry Austin Dobson *Fame is a Food*

Famous men have the whole earth as their memorial

Pericles

famed acclaimed, celebrated, recognized, renowned, widely-known

familiar **1.** accustomed, common, common or garden (*informal*), conventional, customary, domestic, everyday, frequent, household, mundane, ordinary, recognizable, repeated, routine, stock, well-known **2. familiar with** abreast of, acquainted with, at home with, *au courant*, *au fait*, aware of, conscious of, conversant with, introduced, knowledgeable, no stranger to, on speaking terms with, versed in, well up in **3.** amicable, buddy-buddy (*slang, chiefly U.S. & Canad.*), chummy (*informal*), close, confidential, cordial, easy, free, free-and-easy, friendly, hail-fellow-well-met, informal, intimate, near, open, palsy-walsy (*informal*), relaxed, unceremonious, unconstrained, unreserved **4.** bold, disrespectful, forward, impudent, intrusive, overfree, presuming, presumptuous
Antonyms aloof, cold, detached, distant, formal, ignorant, infrequent, unaccustomed, unacquainted, uncommon, unfamiliar, unfriendly, uninformed, unknown, unskilled, unusual

familiarity **1.** acquaintance, acquaintanceship, awareness, experience, grasp, understanding **2.** absence of reserve, closeness, ease, fellowship, freedom, friendliness, friendship, informality, intimacy, naturalness, openness, sociability, unceremoniousness **3.** boldness, disrespect, forwardness, liberties, liberty, presumption
Antonyms constraint, decorum, distance, formality, ignorance, inexperience, propriety, reserve, respect, unfamiliarity

familiarity breeds contempt

familiarize accustom, bring into common use, coach, get to know (about), habituate, instruct, inure, make conversant, make used to, prime, school, season, train

family **1.** brood, children, descendants, folk (*informal*), household, issue, kin, kindred, kinsfolk, kinsmen, kith and kin, ménage, offspring, one's nearest and dearest, one's own flesh and blood, people, progeny, relations, relatives **2.** ancestors, ancestry, birth, blood, clan, descent, dynasty, extraction, forebears, forefathers, genealogy, house, line, lineage, parentage, pedigree, race, sept, stemma, stirps, strain, tribe **3.** class, classification, genre, group, kind, network, subdivision, system
Related adjective: familial

The family - that dear octopus from whose tentacles we never quite escape

Dodie Smith *Dear Octupus*

All happy families are alike, but every unhappy one is unhappy in its own way

Leo Tolstoy *Anna Karenina*

Blood is thicker than water

family tree ancestry, extraction, genealogy, line, lineage, line of descent, pedigree, stemma, stirps

famine dearth, destitution, hunger, scarcity, starvation

They that die by famine die by inches
Matthew Henry *Expositions on the Old and New Testament*

famished ravening, ravenous, ready to eat a horse (*informal*), starved, starving, voracious

famous acclaimed, celebrated, conspicuous, distinguished, eminent, excellent, far-famed, glorious, honoured, illustrious, legendary, lionized, much-publicized, notable, noted, prominent, remarkable, renowned, signal, well-known
Antonyms forgotten, mediocre, obscure, uncelebrated, undistinguished, unexceptional, unknown, unremarkable

fan[1] *verb* **1.** *Often fig.* add fuel to the flames, agitate, arouse, enkindle, excite, impassion, increase, provoke, rouse, stimulate, stir up, whip up, work up **2.** air-condition, air-cool, blow, cool, refresh, ventilate, winnow (*rare*) *~noun* **3.** air conditioner, blade, blower, propeller, punkah (*in India*), vane, ventilator

fan[2] *noun* adherent, admirer, aficionado, buff (*informal*), devotee, enthusiast, fiend (*informal*), follower, freak (*informal*), groupie (*slang*), lover, rooter (*U.S.*), supporter, zealot

fanatic *noun* activist, addict, bigot, buff (*informal*), devotee, energumen, enthusiast, extremist, militant, visionary, zealot

A fanatic is one who can't change his mind and won't change the subject
Winston Churchill

fanatical bigoted, burning, enthusiastic, extreme, fervent, frenzied, immoderate, mad, obsessive, overenthusiastic, passionate, rabid, visionary, wild, zealous

fanaticism bigotry, dedication, devotion, enthusiasm, extremism, immoderation, infatuation, madness, monomania, obsessiveness, overenthusiasm, single-mindedness, zeal, zealotry

Fanaticism consists in redoubling your effort when you have forgotten your aim
George Santayana *The Life of Reason*

fancier aficionado, amateur, breeder, connoisseur, expert

fanciful capricious, chimerical, curious, extravagant, fabulous, fairy-tale, fantastic, ideal, imaginary, imaginative, mythical, poetic, romantic, unreal, visionary, whimsical, wild
Antonyms conventional, down-to-earth, dry, dull, literal, matter of fact, ordinary, pedestrian, predictable, routine, sensible, sober, unimaginative, uninspired

fancy *verb* **1.** be inclined to think, believe, conceive, conjecture, guess (*informal, chiefly U.S. & Canad.*), imagine, infer, reckon, suppose, surmise, think, think likely **2.** be attracted to, crave, desire, dream of, hanker after, have a yen for, hope for, long for, relish, thirst for, wish for, would like, yearn for **3.** *informal* be attracted to, be captivated by, desire, favour, go for, have an eye for, like, lust after, prefer, take a liking to, take to *~noun* **4.** caprice, desire, humour, idea, impulse, inclination, notion, thought, urge, whim **5.** fondness, hankering, inclination, liking, partiality, predilection, preference, relish, thirst **6.** conception, image, imagination, impression **7.** chimera, daydream, delusion, dream, fantasy, nightmare, phantasm, vision *~adjective* **8.** baroque, decorated, decorative, elaborate, elegant, embellished, extravagant, fanciful, intricate, ornamental, ornamented, ornate **9.** capricious, chimerical, delusive, fanciful, fantastic, far-fetched, illusory, whimsical
Antonyms (*sense 5*) aversion, disinclination, dislike (*sense 8*) basic, cheap, common, inferior, ordinary, plain, simple, unadorned, undecorated, unfussy

Ever let the fancy roam,
Pleasure never is at home.
John Keats *Fancy*

Tell me where is fancy bred,
Or in the heart or in the head?
William Shakespeare *The Merchant of Venice*

fanfare ballyhoo, fanfaronade, flourish, trump (*archaic*), trumpet call, tucket (*archaic*)

fang tooth, tusk

fan out disperse, lay out, open out, space out, spread, spread out, unfurl

fantasize build castles in the air, daydream, dream, envision, give free rein to the imagination, hallucinate, imagine, invent, live in a dream world, romance, see visions

fantastic **1.** comical, eccentric, exotic, fanciful, freakish, grotesque, imaginative, odd, oddball (*informal*), off-the-wall (*slang*), outlandish, outré, peculiar, phantasmagorical, quaint, queer, rococo, strange, unreal, weird, whimsical, zany **2.** ambitious, chimerical, extravagant, far-fetched, grandiose, illusory, ludicrous, ridiculous, unrealistic, visionary, wild **3.** absurd, capricious, cock-and-bull (*informal*), implausible, incredible, irrational, mad, preposterous, unlikely **4.** *informal* enormous, extreme, great, overwhelming, severe, tremendous **5.** *informal* awesome (*slang*), boffo (*slang*), brill (*informal*), chillin' (*U.S. slang*), cracking (*Brit. informal*), crucial (*slang*), def (*slang*), excellent, first-rate, jim-dandy (*slang*), marvellous, mean (*slang*), mega (*slang*), out of this world (*informal*), sensational (*informal*), sovereign, superb, topping (*Brit. slang*), wonderful, world-class
Antonyms common, credible, everyday, moderate, normal, ordinary, poor, rational, realistic, sensible, typical

fantasy, phantasy **1.** creativity, fancy, imagination, invention, originality **2.** apparition, daydream, delusion, dream, fancy, figment of the imagination, flight of fancy, hallucination, illusion, mirage, nightmare, pipe dream, reverie, vision

far *adverb* **1.** afar, a good way, a great distance, a long way, deep, miles **2.** considerably, decidedly, extremely, greatly, incomparably, much, very much **3. by far** by a long chalk (*informal*), by a long shot, by a long way, easily, far and away, immeasurably, incomparably, to a great degree, very much **4. far and wide** broadly, everywhere, extensively, far and near, here, there and everywhere, in every nook and cranny, widely, worldwide **5. so far** thus far, to date, until now, up to now, up to the present *~adjective* **6.** distant, faraway, far-flung, far-off, far-removed, long, outlying, out-of-the-way, remote, removed
Antonyms adjacent, adjoining, alongside, at close quarters, beside, bordering, close, contiguous, just round the corner, near, nearby, neighbouring, proximate, within sniffing distance (*informal*)

faraway **1.** beyond the horizon, distant, far, far-flung, far-off, far-removed, outlying, remote **2.** absent, abstracted, distant, dreamy, lost, vague

farce **1.** broad comedy, buffoonery, burlesque, comedy, satire, slapstick **2.** absurdity, joke, mockery, nonsense, parody, ridiculousness, sham, travesty

farcical absurd, amusing, comic, custard-pie, derisory, diverting, droll, funny, laughable, ludicrous, nonsensical, preposterous, ridiculous, risible, slapstick

fare *noun* **1.** charge, passage money, price, ticket money, transport cost **2.** passenger, pick-up (*informal*), traveller **3.** commons, diet, eatables, feed, food, meals, menu, nosebag (*slang*), provisions, rations, sustenance, table, tack (*informal*), victuals, vittles (*obsolete or dialect*) *~verb* **4.** do, get along, get on, make out, manage, prosper **5.** *used impersonally* go, happen, pan out (*informal*), proceed, turn out

farewell adieu, adieux *or* adieus, departure, goodbye, leave-taking, parting, sendoff (*informal*), valediction

far-fetched cock-and-bull (*informal*), doubtful, dubious, fantastic, hard to swallow (*informal*), implausible, improbable, incredible, preposterous, strained, unbelievable, unconvincing, unlikely, unnatural, unrealistic
Antonyms acceptable, authentic, believable, credible, feasible, imaginable, likely, plausible, possible, probable, realistic, reasonable

farm **1.** *noun* acreage, acres, croft (*Scot.*), farmstead, grange, holding, homestead, land, plantation, ranch (*chiefly North American*), smallholding, station (*Austral. & N.Z.*) **2.** *verb* bring under cultivation, cultivate, operate, plant, practise husbandry, till the soil, work

farmer agriculturist, agronomist, cockie (*N.Z.*), husbandman, smallholder, yeoman

farming agriculture, agronomy, husbandry

far-out advanced, avant-garde, bizarre, off-the-wall (*slang*), outlandish, outré, unconventional, weird, wild

farrago gallimaufry, hash, hodgepodge, hotchpotch, jumble, medley, *mélange*, miscellany, mishmash, mixed bag, mixture, potpourri, salmagundi

far-reaching broad, extensive, important, momentous, pervasive, significant, sweeping, widespread

far-sighted acute, canny, cautious, discerning, far-seeing, judicious, politic, prescient, provident, prudent, sage, shrewd, wise

fascinate absorb, allure, beguile, bewitch, captivate, charm, delight, enamour, enchant, engross, enrapture, enravish, enthral, entrance, hold spellbound, hypnotize, infatuate, intrigue, mesmerize, ravish, rivet, spellbind, transfix
Antonyms alienate, bore, disenchant, disgust, irritate, jade, put one off, sicken, turn one off (*informal*)

fascinated absorbed, beguiled, bewitched, captivated, charmed, engrossed, enthralled, entranced, hooked on, hypnotized, infatuated, smitten, spellbound, under a spell

fascinating alluring, bewitching, captivating, compelling, enchanting, engaging, engrossing, enticing, gripping, intriguing, irresistible, ravishing, riveting, seductive
Antonyms boring, dull, mind-numbing, unexciting, uninteresting

fascination allure, attraction, charm, enchantment, glamour, lure, magic, magnetism, pull, sorcery, spell

fascism *noun* absolutism, authoritarianism, autocracy, dictatorship, Hitlerism, totalitarianism

fashion *noun* **1.** convention, craze, custom, fad, latest, latest style, look, mode, prevailing taste, rage, style, trend, usage, vogue **2.** attitude, demeanour, manner, method, mode, style, way **3.** appearance, configuration, cut, figure, form, guise (*archaic*), line, make, model, mould, pattern, shape, stamp **4.** description, kind, sort, stamp, type **5.** beau monde, fashionable society, high society, jet set **6. after a fashion** in a manner of speaking, in a way, moderately, somehow, somehow or other, to a degree, to some extent *~verb* **7.** construct, contrive, create, design, forge, form, make, manufacture, mould, shape, work **8.** accommodate, adapt, adjust, fit, suit, tailor

It is only the modern that ever becomes old-fashioned
Oscar Wilde

fashionable à la mode, all the go (*informal*), all the rage, chic, cool (*slang*), current, customary, genteel, happening (*informal*), hip (*slang*), in (*informal*), in vogue, latest, modern, modish, popular, prevailing, smart, stylish, trendsetting, trendy (*Brit. informal*), up-to-date, up-to-the-minute, usual, voguish (*informal*), with it (*informal*)
Antonyms behind the times, dated, frumpy, obsolete, old-fashioned, old-hat, outmoded, out of date, out of the ark (*informal*), uncool (*slang*), unfashionable, unpopular, unstylish, untrendy (*Brit. informal*)

fast[1] *adjective* **1.** accelerated, brisk, fleet, flying, hasty, hurried, mercurial, nippy (*Brit. informal*), quick, quickie (*informal*), rapid, speedy, swift, winged *~adverb* **2.** apace, at a rate of knots, hastily, hell for leather (*informal*), hotfoot, hurriedly, in haste, like a bat out of hell (*slang*), like a flash, like a shot (*informal*), like greased lightning (*informal*), like lightning, like nobody's business (*informal*), like the clappers (*Brit. informal*), pdq (*slang*), posthaste, presto, quickly, rapidly, speedily, swiftly, with all haste *~adjective* **3.** close, constant, fastened, firm, fixed, fortified, immovable, impregnable, lasting, loyal, permanent, secure, sound, stalwart, staunch, steadfast, tight, unwavering *~adverb* **4.** deeply, firmly, fixedly, securely, soundly, tightly *~adjective* **5.** dissipated, dissolute, extravagant, gadabout (*informal*), giddy, immoral, intemperate, licentious, loose, profligate, promiscuous, rakish, reckless, self-indulgent, wanton, wild *~adverb* **6.** extravagantly, intemperately, loosely, promiscuously, rakishly, recklessly, wildly **7. pull a fast one** bamboozle (*informal*), cheat, con (*informal*), deceive, defraud, hoodwink, put one over on (*informal*), swindle, take advantage of, take for a ride (*informal*), trick
Antonyms (*sense 1*) leisurely, plodding, slow, slow moving, unhurried (*sense 2*) at a snail's pace, at one's leisure, gradually, leisurely, slowly, steadily, unhurriedly (*sense 3*) inconstant, irresolute, unfaithful, unreliable, unstable, wavering, weak

fast[2] **1.** *verb* abstain, deny oneself, go hungry, go without food, practise abstention, refrain from food *or* eating **2.** *noun* abstinence, fasting

fasten 1. affix, anchor, attach, bind, bolt, chain, connect, fix, grip, join, lace, link, lock, make fast, make firm, seal, secure, tie, unite **2.** *figurative* aim, bend, concentrate, direct, fix, focus, rivet

fastening affixation, attachment, binding, bond, concatenation, connection, coupling, fusion, joint, junction, ligature, link, linking, tie, union

fastidious choosy, critical, dainty, difficult, discriminating, finicky, fussy, hard to please, hypercritical, meticulous, nice, overdelicate, overnice, particular, pernickety, picky (*informal*), punctilious, squeamish
Antonyms careless, casual, disorderly, easygoing, lenient, slack, slipshod, sloppy, slovenly, unsystematic

fat *adjective* **1.** beefy (*informal*), broad in the beam (*informal*), corpulent, elephantine, fleshy, gross, heavy, obese, overweight, plump, podgy, portly, roly-poly, rotund, solid, stout, tubby **2.** adipose, fatty, greasy, lipid, oily, oleaginous, suety **3.** affluent, cushy (*slang*), fertile, flourishing, fruitful, jammy (*Brit. slang*), lucrative, lush, productive, profitable, prosperous, remunerative, rich, thriving *~noun* **4.** adipose tissue, beef (*informal*), blubber, bulk, cellulite, corpulence, fatness, flab, flesh, obesity, overweight, paunch, weight problem
Antonyms angular, barren, bony, empty, gaunt, lank, lean, poor, scanty, scarce, scrawny, skinny, slender, slight, slim, spare, thin, unproductive, unprofitable, unrewarding

Imprisoned in every fat man a thin one is wildly signalling to be let out
Cyril Connolly *The Unquiet Grave*

Let me have men about me that are fat
William Shakespeare *Julius Caesar*

I'm built for comfort, I ain't built for speed
Willie Dixon *Built for Comfort*

Fat is a feminist issue
Susie Orbach

fatal 1. deadly, destructive, final, incurable, killing, lethal, malignant, mortal, pernicious, terminal **2.** baleful, baneful, calamitous, catastrophic, disastrous, lethal, ruinous **3.** critical, crucial, decisive, destined, determining, doomed, fateful, final, foreordained, inevitable, predestined
Antonyms beneficial, benign, harmless, inconsequential, innocuous, inoffensive, minor, non-lethal, non-toxic, salutary, vitalizing, wholesome

fatalism acceptance, determinism, necessitarianism, passivity, predestinarianism, resignation, stoicism

fatality casualty, deadliness, death, disaster, fatal accident, lethalness, loss, mortality

fate 1. chance, destiny, divine will, fortune, kismet, nemesis, predestination, providence, weird (*archaic*) **2.** cup, fortune, horoscope, lot, portion, stars **3.** end, future, issue, outcome, upshot **4.** death, destruction, doom, downfall, end, ruin

Fate keeps on happening
Anita Loos *Gentlemen prefer Blondes*

Fate is not an eagle, it creeps like a rat
Elizabeth Bowen *The House in Paris*

We may become the makers of our fate when we have ceased to pose as its prophets
Karl Popper *The Open Society and its Enemies*

Fate and character are the same concept
Novalis *Heinrich von Ofterdingen*

Man proposes, God disposes

What must be, must be (Che sera, sera)

fated destined, doomed, foreordained, ineluctable, inescapable, inevitable, marked down, predestined, pre-elected, preordained, sure, written

fateful **1.** critical, crucial, decisive, important, portentous, significant **2.** deadly, destructive, disastrous, fatal, lethal, ominous, ruinous
Antonyms inconsequential, insignificant, nugatory, ordinary, unimportant

Fates, the *Greek myth* Providence, the Moirai, the Norns (*Norse myth*), the Parcae (*Roman Myth*), the Three Sisters, the Weird Sisters

Fates

Atropos	Lachesis
Clotho	

fathead ass, berk (*Brit. slang*), booby, charlie (*Brit. informal*), coot, dickhead (*slang*), dickwit (*slang*), dimwit (*informal*), dipstick (*Brit. slang*), divvy (*Brit. slang*), dope (*informal*), dork (*slang*), dunderhead, dweeb (*U.S. slang*), fool, fuckwit (*taboo slang*), geek (*slang*), gobshite (*Irish taboo slang*), gonzo (*slang*), goose, idiot, imbecile, jackass, jerk (*slang, chiefly U.S. & Canad.*), lamebrain (*informal*), nerd *or* nurd (*slang*), nincompoop, nitwit (*informal*), numpty (*Scot. informal*), numskull *or* numbskull, pillock (*Brit. slang*), plank (*Brit. slang*), plonker (*slang*), prat (*slang*), prick (*slang*), schmuck (*U.S. slang*), twerp *or* twirp (*informal*), twit (*informal, chiefly Brit.*), wally (*slang*)

father *noun* **1.** begetter, dad (*informal*), daddy (*informal*), governor (*informal*), old boy (*informal*), old man (*informal*), pa (*informal*), papa (*old-fashioned informal*), pater, paterfamilias, patriarch, pop (*informal*), sire **2.** ancestor, forebear, forefather, predecessor, progenitor **3.** architect, author, creator, founder, inventor, maker, originator, prime mover **4.** city father, elder, leader, patriarch, patron, senator **5.** abbé, confessor, curé, padre (*informal*), pastor, priest *~verb* **6.** beget, get, procreate, sire **7.** create, engender, establish, found, institute, invent, originate

No man is responsible for his father. That is entirely his mother's affair
Margaret Turnbull

No man can know who was his father
Homer *Odyssey*

It's all any reasonable child can expect if the dad is present at the conception
Joe Orton *Entertaining Mr. Sloane*

It is a wise father that knows his own child
William Shakespeare *The Merchant of Venice*

Like father like son

fatherland homeland, land of one's birth, land of one's fathers, motherland, native land, old country

fatherly affectionate, benevolent, benign, forbearing, indulgent, kind, kindly, paternal, patriarchal, protective, supportive, tender

fathom **1.** divine, estimate, gauge, measure, penetrate, plumb, probe, sound **2.** comprehend, get to the bottom of, grasp, interpret, understand

fathomless abysmal, bottomless, deep, immeasurable, impenetrable, incomprehensible, profound, unfathomable, unplumbed

fatigue **1.** *verb* drain, drain of energy, exhaust, fag (out) (*informal*), jade, knacker (*slang*), overtire, poop (*informal*), take it out of (*informal*), tire, weaken, wear out, weary, whack (*Brit. informal*) **2.** *noun* debility, ennui, heaviness, languor, lethargy, listlessness, overtiredness, tiredness
Antonyms *noun* alertness, animation, energy, freshness, get-up-and-go (*informal*), go, indefatigability, life, vigour, zest *~verb* refresh, rejuvenate, relieve, rest, revive, stimulate

fatigued all in (*slang*), bushed (*informal*), clapped out (*Austral. & N.Z. informal*), dead beat (*informal*), exhausted, fagged (out) (*informal*), jaded, jiggered (*informal*), knackered (*slang*), on one's last legs, overtired, tired, tired out, wasted, weary, whacked (*Brit. informal*), zonked (*slang*)

fatness beef (*informal*), bulkiness, corpulence, *embonpoint*, flab, flesh, fleshiness, girth, grossness, heaviness, obesity, overweight, podginess, rotundity, size, stoutness, weight, weight problem

fatten **1.** broaden, coarsen, expand, gain weight, grow fat, put on weight, spread, swell, thicken, thrive **2.** *often with* **up** bloat, build up, cram, distend, feed, feed up, nourish, overfeed, stuff

fatty adipose, fat, greasy, oily, oleaginous, rich

fatuity absurdity, bêtise (*rare*), brainlessness, daftness (*informal*), denseness, fatuousness, folly, foolishness, idiocy, imbecility, insanity, ludicrousness, lunacy, mindlessness, stupidity

fatuous absurd, asinine, brainless, dense, dull, foolish, idiotic, inane, ludicrous, lunatic, mindless, moronic, puerile, silly, stupid, vacuous, weak-minded, witless

fault *noun* **1.** blemish, defect, deficiency, demerit, drawback, failing, flaw, imperfection, infirmity, lack, shortcoming, snag, weakness, weak point **2.** blunder, boob (*Brit. slang*), error, error of judgment, inaccuracy, indiscretion, lapse, mistake, negligence, offence, omission, oversight, slip, slip-up **3.** accountability, culpability, liability, responsibility **4.** delinquency, frailty, lapse, misconduct, misdeed, misdemeanour, offence, peccadillo, sin, transgression, trespass, wrong **5. at fault** answerable, blamable, culpable, guilty, in the wrong, responsible, to blame **6. find fault with** carp at, complain, criticize, pick holes in, pull to pieces, quibble, take to task **7. to a fault** excessively, immoderately, in the extreme, needlessly, out of all proportion, overly (*U.S.*), overmuch, preposterously, ridiculously, unduly *~verb* **8.** blame, call to account, censure, criticize, find fault with, find lacking, hold (someone) accountable (responsible, to blame), impugn
Antonyms (*sense 1*) asset, attribute, credit, goodness, merit, perfection, strength, virtue

The fault, dear Brutus, is not in our stars,
But in ourselves
William Shakespeare *Julius Caesar*

fault-finding **1.** *noun* carping, hairsplitting, nagging, niggling, nit-picking (*informal*) **2.** *adjective* captious, carping, censorious, critical, hypercritical, on (someone's) back (*informal*), pettifogging
Antonyms complimentary, easily pleased, indiscriminate, uncritical, undiscerning, unexacting, unfussy, unperceptive

faultless **1.** accurate, classic, correct, exemplary, faithful, flawless, foolproof, impeccable, model, perfect, unblemished **2.** above reproach, blameless, guiltless, immaculate, impeccable, innocent, irreproachable, pure, sinless, spotless, stainless, unblemished, unspotted, unsullied

faulty bad, blemished, broken, damaged, defective, erroneous, fallacious, flawed, impaired, imperfect, imprecise, inaccurate, incorrect, invalid, malfunctioning, not working, on the blink, out of order, unsound, weak, wrong

faux pas bloomer (*Brit. informal*), blunder, boob (*Brit. slang*), breach of etiquette, clanger (*informal*), gaffe, gaucherie, impropriety, indiscretion, solecism

favour *noun* **1.** approbation, approval, backing, bias, championship, espousal, esteem, favouritism, friendliness, good opinion, goodwill, grace, kindness, kind regard, partiality, patronage, promotion, support **2.** benefit, boon, courtesy, good turn, indulgence, kindness, obligement (*Scot. or archaic*), service **3. in favour of** all for (*informal*), backing, for, on the side of, pro, supporting, to the benefit of **4.** gift, keepsake, love-token, memento, present, souvenir, token **5.** badge, decoration, knot, ribbons, rosette *~verb* **6.** be partial to, esteem, have in one's good books, indulge, pamper, pull strings for (*informal*), reward, side with, smile upon, spoil, treat with partiality, value **7.** advocate, approve, back, be in favour of, champion, choose, commend, countenance, encourage, espouse, fancy, incline towards, like, opt for, patronize, prefer, single out, support **8.** abet, accommodate, advance, aid, assist, befriend, do a kindness to, facilitate, help, oblige, promote, succour **9.** *informal* be the image *or* picture of, look like, resemble, take after **10.** ease, extenuate, spare
Antonyms *noun* animosity, antipathy, disapproval, disfavour, disservice, harm, ill will, injury, malevolence, wrong *~verb* disapprove, disdain, dislike, inconvenience, object to, oppose, thwart

One good turn deserves another
John Fletcher & Philip Massinger *The Little French Lawyer*

favourable **1.** advantageous, appropriate, auspicious, beneficial, convenient, encouraging, fair, fit, good, helpful, hopeful, opportune, promising, propitious, suitable, timely **2.** affirmative, agreeable, amicable, approving, benign, encouraging, enthusiastic, friendly, kind, positive, reassuring, sympathetic, understanding, welcoming, well-disposed
Antonyms disadvantageous, disapproving, ill-disposed, inauspicious, unfavourable, unfriendly, unhelpful, unpromising, unsympathetic, useless

favourably **1.** advantageously, auspiciously, conveniently, fortunately, opportunely, profitably, to one's advantage, well **2.** agreeably, approvingly, enthusiastically, genially, graciously, helpfully, in a kindly manner, positively, with approval (approbation, cordiality), without prejudice

favoured **1.** best-liked, chosen, favourite, pet, preferred, recommended, selected, singled out **2.** advantaged, blessed, elite, jammy (*Brit. slang*), lucky, privileged

favourite **1.** *adjective* best-loved, choice, dearest, esteemed, favoured, preferred **2.** *noun* beloved, blue-eyed boy (*informal*), choice, darling, dear, idol, pet, pick, preference, teacher's pet, the apple of one's eye

favouritism bias, jobs for the boys (*informal*), nepotism, one-sidedness, partiality, partisanship, preference, preferential treatment
Antonyms equality, equity, evenhandedness, fairness, impartiality, neutrality, objectivity, open-mindedness

fawn[1] *adjective* beige, buff, greyish-brown, neutral

fawn[2] *verb often with* **on** *or* **upon** be obsequious, be servile, bow and scrape, brown-nose (*taboo slang*), court, crawl, creep, cringe, curry favour, dance attendance, flatter, grovel, ingratiate oneself, kiss ass (*U.S. & Canad. taboo slang*), kneel, kowtow, lick (someone's) arse (*taboo slang*), lick (someone's) boots, pander to, pay court, toady, truckle

fawning abject, bootlicking (*informal*), bowing and scraping, crawling, cringing, deferential, flattering, grovelling, obsequious, prostrate, servile, slavish, sycophantic

fealty allegiance, devotion, faith, faithfulness, fidelity, homage, loyalty, obeisance, submission, troth (*archaic*)

fear *noun* **1.** alarm, apprehensiveness, awe, blue funk (*informal*), consternation, cravenness, dismay, dread, fright, horror, panic, qualms, terror, timidity, tremors, trepidation **2.** bête noire, bogey, bugbear, horror, nightmare, phobia, spectre **3.** agitation, anxiety, apprehension, concern, disquietude, distress, doubt, foreboding(s), misgiving(s), solicitude, suspicion, unease, uneasiness, worry **4.** awe, reverence, veneration, wonder *~verb* **5.** apprehend, be apprehensive (afraid, frightened, scared), be in a blue funk (*informal*), dare not, dread, have a horror of, have a phobia about, have butterflies in one's stomach (*informal*), have qualms, live in dread of, shake in one's shoes, shudder at, take fright, tremble at **6.** anticipate, apprehend, be afraid, expect, foresee, suspect **7.** *with* **for** be anxious (concerned, distressed) about, be disquieted over, feel concern for, tremble for, worry about **8.** respect, revere, reverence, stand in awe of, venerate

Let me assert my firm belief that the only thing we have to fear is fear itself
Franklin D. Roosevelt

Let them hate, so long as they fear
Accius

Perfect fear casteth out love
Cyril Connolly

fearful **1.** afraid, alarmed, anxious, apprehensive, diffident, faint-hearted, frightened, hellacious (*U.S. slang*), hesitant, intimidated, jittery (*informal*), jumpy, nervous, nervy (*Brit. informal*), neurotic, panicky, pusillanimous, scared, shrinking, tense, timid, timorous, uneasy, wired (*slang*) **2.** appalling, atrocious, awful, dire, distressing, dreadful, frightful, ghastly, grievous, grim, gruesome, hair-raising, harrowing, hideous, horrendous, horrible, horrific, monstrous, shocking, terrible, unspeakable

Antonyms (*sense 1*) ballsy (*taboo slang*), bold, brave, confident, courageous, daring, dauntless, doughty, gallant, game (*informal*), gutsy (*slang*), heroic, indomitable, intrepid, lion-hearted, plucky, unabashed, unafraid, undaunted, unflinching, valiant, valorous

fearfully **1.** apprehensively, diffidently, in fear and trembling, nervously, timidly, timorously, uneasily, with bated breath, with many misgivings *or* forebodings, with one's heart in one's mouth **2.** awfully, exceedingly, excessively, frightfully, terribly, tremendously, very

fearless ballsy (*taboo slang*), bold, brave, confident, courageous, daring, dauntless, doughty, gallant, game (*informal*), gutsy (*slang*), heroic, indomitable, intrepid, lion-hearted, plucky, unabashed, unafraid, undaunted, unflinching, valiant, valorous

fearlessness balls (*taboo slang*), ballsiness (*taboo slang*), boldness, bravery, confidence, courage, dauntlessness, guts (*informal*), indomitability, intrepidity, lion-heartedness, nerve, pluckiness

fearsome alarming, appalling, awe-inspiring, awesome, awful, baleful, daunting, dismaying, formidable, frightening, hair-raising, hellacious (*U.S. slang*), horrendous, horrifying, menacing, unnerving

feasibility expediency, practicability, usefulness, viability, workability

feasible achievable, attainable, likely, possible, practicable, realizable, reasonable, viable, workable

Antonyms impossible, impracticable, inconceivable, unreasonable, untenable, unviable, unworkable

feast *noun* **1.** banquet, barbecue, beanfeast (*Brit. informal*), beano (*Brit. slang*), blowout (*slang*), carousal, carouse, dinner, entertainment, festive board, jollification, junket, repast, revels, slap-up meal (*Brit. informal*), spread (*informal*), treat **2.** celebration, -fest, festival, fête, gala day, holiday, holy day, red-letter day, saint's day **3.** delight, enjoyment, gratification, pleasure, treat *~verb* **4.** eat one's fill, eat to one's heart's content, fare sumptuously, gorge, gormandize, indulge, overindulge, pig out (*slang*), stuff, stuff one's face (*slang*), wine and dine **5.** entertain, hold a reception for, kill the fatted calf for, regale, treat, wine and dine **6.** delight, gladden, gratify, rejoice, thrill

feat accomplishment, achievement, act, attainment, deed, exploit, feather in one's cap, performance

feathers down, plumage, plumes

feathery downy, feathered, fluffy, plumate *or* plumose (*Botany & Zoology*), plumed, plumy, wispy

feature *noun* **1.** aspect, attribute, characteristic, facet, factor, hallmark, mark, peculiarity, point, property, quality, trait **2.** attraction, crowd puller (*informal*), draw, highlight, in~

novation, main item, special, special attraction, speciality, specialty **3.** article, column, comment, item, piece, report, story *~verb* **4.** accentuate, call attention to, emphasize, give prominence to, give the full works (*slang*), headline, play up, present, promote, set off, spotlight, star

featured given prominence, headlined, highlighted, in the public eye, presented, promoted, recommended, specially presented, starred

features countenance, face, lineaments, physiognomy

featuring calling attention to, displaying, drawing attention to, giving a star role, giving prominence to, giving the full works (*slang*), highlighting, making the main attraction, presenting, promoting, pushing, recommending, showing, showing off, starring, turning the spotlight on

febrile delirious, fevered, feverish, fiery, flushed, hot, inflamed, pyretic (*Medical*)

feckless aimless, feeble, futile, good-for-nothing, hopeless, incompetent, ineffectual, irresponsible, shiftless, useless, weak, worthless

fecund fertile, fructiferous, fruitful, productive, prolific, teeming

fecundity fertility, fructiferousness, fruitfulness, productiveness

federate *verb* amalgamate, associate, combine, confederate, integrate, syndicate, unify, unite

federation alliance, amalgamation, association, *Bund*, coalition, combination, confederacy, copartnership, entente, federacy, league, syndicate, union

fed up (with) annoyed, blue, bored, brassed off (*Brit. slang*), browned-off (*informal*), depressed, discontented, dismal, dissatisfied, down, down in the mouth, gloomy, glum, hacked (off) (*U.S. slang*), pissed off (*taboo slang*), sick and tired of (*informal*), tired of, weary of

fee account, bill, charge, compensation, emolument, hire, honorarium, meed (*archaic*), pay, payment, recompense, remuneration, reward, toll

feeble 1. debilitated, delicate, doddering, effete, enervated, enfeebled, etiolated, exhausted, failing, faint, frail, infirm, languid, powerless, puny, shilpit (*Scot.*), sickly, weak, weakened, weedy (*informal*) **2.** flat, flimsy, inadequate, incompetent, indecisive, ineffective, ineffectual, inefficient, insignificant, insufficient, lame, paltry, pathetic, poor, slight, tame, thin, unconvincing, weak
Antonyms ardent, effective, energetic, forceful, hale, healthy, hearty, lusty, robust, stalwart, strong, sturdy, successful, vigorous

feeble-minded addle-pated, bone-headed (*slang*), braindead (*informal*), deficient, dim-witted (*informal*), dozy (*Brit. informal*), dull, dumb (*informal*), half-witted, idiotic, imbecilic, lacking, moronic, obtuse, retarded, simple, slow on the uptake, slow-witted, soft in the head (*informal*), stupid, vacant, weak-minded
Antonyms astute, aware, bright, clear-headed, clever, intelligent, keen, quick-witted, smart

feebleness 1. debility, delicacy, effeteness, enervation, etiolation, exhaustion, frailness, frailty, incapacity, infirmity, lack of strength, languor, lassitude, sickliness, weakness **2.** flimsiness, inadequacy, incompetence, indecisiveness, ineffectualness, insignificance, insufficiency, lameness, weakness

feed *verb* **1.** cater for, nourish, provide for, provision, supply, sustain, victual, wine and dine **2.** *sometimes with* **on** devour, eat, exist on, fare, graze, live on, nurture, partake of, pasture, subsist, take nourishment **3.** augment, bolster, encourage, foster, fuel, minister to, strengthen, supply *~noun* **4.** fodder, food, forage, pasturage, provender, silage **5.** *informal* feast, meal, nosh (*slang*), nosh-up (*Brit. slang*), repast, spread (*informal*), tuck-in (*informal*)

feel *verb* **1.** caress, finger, fondle, handle, manipulate, maul, paw, run one's hands over, stroke, touch **2.** be aware of, be sensible of, endure, enjoy, experience, go through, have, have a sensation of, know, notice, observe, perceive, suffer, take to heart, undergo **3.** explore, fumble, grope, sound, test, try **4.** be convinced, feel in one's bones, have a hunch, have the impression, intuit, sense **5.** believe, be of the opinion that, consider, deem, hold, judge, think **6.** appear, resemble, seem, strike one as **7.** *with* **for** be moved by, be sorry for, bleed for, commiserate, compassionate, condole with, empathize, feel compassion for, pity, sympathize with **8. feel like** could do with, desire, fancy, feel inclined, feel the need for, feel up to, have the inclination, want *~noun* **9.** finish, surface, texture, touch **10.** air, ambience, atmosphere, feeling, impression, quality, sense, vibes (*slang*)

feeler 1. antenna, tentacle, whisker **2.** advance, approach, probe, trial balloon

feeling 1. feel, perception, sensation, sense, sense of touch, touch **2.** apprehension, consciousness, hunch, idea, impression, inkling, notion, presentiment, sense, suspicion **3.** affection, ardour, emotion, fervour, fondness, heat, intensity, passion, sentiment, sentimentality, warmth **4.** appreciation, compassion, concern, empathy, pity, sensibility, sensitivity, sympathy, understanding **5.** inclination, instinct, opinion, point of view, view **6.** air, ambience, atmosphere, aura, feel, mood, quality, vibes (*slang*) 7. **bad feeling** anger, dislike, distrust, enmity, hostility, upset

feelings ego, emotions, self-esteem, sensitivities, susceptibilities

feign act, affect, assume, counterfeit, devise, dissemble, fabricate, fake, forge, give the appearance of, imitate, make a show of, pretend, put on, sham, simulate

feigned affected, artificial, assumed, counterfeit, ersatz, fabricated, fake, false, imitation, insincere, pretended, pseudo (*informal*), sham, simulated, spurious

feint *noun* artifice, blind, bluff, distraction, dodge, expedient, gambit, manoeuvre, mock attack, play, pretence, ruse, stratagem, subterfuge, wile

felicitate compliment, congratulate, wish joy to

felicitous apposite, appropriate, apropos, apt, fitting, happy, inspired, neat, opportune, pat, propitious, suitable, timely, well-chosen, well-timed

felicity 1. blessedness, bliss, blissfulness, delectation, ecstasy, happiness, joy 2. applicability, appropriateness, aptness, becomingness, effectiveness, grace, propriety, suitability, suitableness

feline 1. catlike, leonine 2. graceful, sinuous, sleek, slinky, smooth, stealthy

fell[1] *verb* cut, cut down, deck (*slang*), demolish, flatten, floor, hew, knock down, level, prostrate, raze, strike down

fell[2] *adjective* 1. barbarous, bloody, cruel, ferocious, fierce, grim, implacable, inhuman, malicious, malignant, merciless, murderous, pitiless, relentless, ruthless, sanguinary, savage, vicious 2. baneful, deadly, destructive, fatal, malign, mortal, noxious, pernicious, pestilential, ruinous

fellow *noun* 1. bloke (*Brit. informal*), boy, chap (*informal*), character, customer (*informal*), guy (*informal*), individual, man, person, punter (*informal*) 2. associate, colleague, companion, compeer, comrade, co-worker, equal, friend, member, partner, peer 3. brother, counterpart, double, duplicate, match, mate, twin *~adjective* 4. affiliated, akin, allied, associate, associated, co-, like, related, similar

fellow feeling compassion, empathy, pity, sympathy, understanding

fellowship 1. amity, brotherhood, camaraderie, communion, companionability, companionship, familiarity, fraternization, intercourse, intimacy, kindliness, sociability 2. association, brotherhood, club, fraternity, guild, league, order, sisterhood, society, sodality

Fellowship is heaven, and lack of fellowship is hell

William Morris *A Dream of John Ball*

female

The female of the species is more deadly than the male

Rudyard Kipling *The Female of the Species*

feminine 1. delicate, gentle, girlish, graceful, ladylike, modest, soft, tender, womanly 2. camp (*informal*), effeminate, effete, unmanly, unmasculine, weak, womanish

Antonyms Amazonian, butch, indelicate, manly, mannish, masculine, rough, unfeminine, unladylike, unwomanly, virile

femininity delicacy, feminineness, gentleness, girlishness, muliebrity, softness, womanhood, womanliness

feminist

People call me a feminist whenever I express sentiments that differentiate me from a doormat or a prostitute

Rebecca West

femme fatale charmer, Circe, enchantress, seductress, siren, vamp (*informal*)

fen bog, holm (*dialect*), marsh, morass, moss (*Scot.*), quagmire, slough, swamp

fence *noun* 1. barbed wire, barricade, barrier, defence, guard, hedge, paling, palisade, railings, rampart, shield, stockade, wall 2. **on the fence** between two stools, irresolute, uncertain, uncommitted, undecided, vacillating *~verb* 3. *often with* **in** *or* **off** bound, circumscribe, confine, coop, defend, encircle, enclose, fortify, guard, hedge, impound, pen, pound, protect, restrict, secure, separate, surround 4. beat about the bush, cavil, dodge, equivocate, evade, flannel (*Brit. informal*), hedge, parry, prevaricate, quibble, shift, stonewall, tergiversate

Good fences make good neighbours

fencing *figurative* beating about the bush, double talk, equivocation, evasiveness, hedging, parrying, prevarication, quibbling, stonewalling, tergiversation, weasel words (*informal, chiefly U.S.*)

fend for look after, make do, make provision for, provide for, shift for, support, sustain, take care of

fend off avert, beat off, deflect, drive back, hold *or* keep at bay, keep off, parry, repel, repulse, resist, stave off, turn aside, ward off

feral 1. unbroken, uncultivated, undomesticated, untamed, wild 2. bestial, brutal, fell, ferocious, fierce, savage, vicious

ferment *verb* 1. boil, brew, bubble, concoct, effervesce, foam, froth, heat, leaven, rise, seethe, work *~noun* 2. bacteria, barm, fermentation agent, leaven, leavening, mother, mother-of-vinegar, yeast *~verb* 3. *figurative* agitate, boil, excite, fester, foment, heat, incite, inflame, provoke, rouse, seethe, smoulder, stir up *~noun* 4. *figurative* agitation, brouhaha, commotion, disruption, excitement,

fever, frenzy, furore, glow, heat, hubbub, imbroglio, state of unrest, stew, stir, tumult, turbulence, turmoil, unrest, uproar
Antonyms *noun* calmness, hush, peacefulness, quiet, restfulness, stillness, tranquillity

ferocious 1. feral, fierce, predatory, rapacious, ravening, savage, violent, wild 2. barbaric, barbarous, bloodthirsty, brutal, brutish, cruel, merciless, pitiless, relentless, ruthless, tigerish, vicious
Antonyms calm, docile, gentle, mild, subdued, submissive, tame

ferocity barbarity, bloodthirstiness, brutality, cruelty, ferociousness, fierceness, inhumanity, rapacity, ruthlessness, savageness, savagery, viciousness, wildness

ferret out bring to light, dig up, disclose, discover, drive out, elicit, get at, nose out, root out, run to earth, search out, smell out, trace, track down, unearth

ferry 1. *noun* ferryboat, packet, packet boat 2. *verb* carry, chauffeur, convey, run, ship, shuttle, transport

fertile abundant, fat, fecund, flowering, flowing with milk and honey, fruit-bearing, fruitful, generative, luxuriant, plenteous, plentiful, productive, prolific, rich, teeming, yielding
Antonyms barren, dry, impotent, infecund, infertile, poor, sterile, unfruitful, unimaginative, uninventive, unproductive

fertility abundance, fecundity, fruitfulness, luxuriance, productiveness, richness

fertilization 1. implantation, impregnation, insemination, pollination, procreation, propagation 2. dressing, manuring, mulching, top dressing

fertilize 1. fecundate, fructify, impregnate, inseminate, make fruitful, make pregnant, pollinate 2. compost, dress, enrich, feed, manure, mulch, top-dress

fertilizer compost, dressing, dung, guano, manure, marl

fervent, fervid animated, ardent, devout, eager, earnest, ecstatic, emotional, enthusiastic, excited, fiery, flaming, heartfelt, impassioned, intense, perfervid (*literary*), vehement, warm, zealous
Antonyms apathetic, cold, cool, detached, dispassionate, frigid, impassive, unfeeling, unimpassioned

fervour animation, ardour, eagerness, earnestness, enthusiasm, excitement, fervency, intensity, passion, vehemence, warmth, zeal

fester 1. become inflamed, decay, gather, maturate, putrefy, suppurate, ulcerate 2. *figurative* aggravate, chafe, gall, intensify, irk, rankle, smoulder

festering 1. gathering, inflamed, maturating, poisonous, purulent, pussy, septic, suppurating, ulcerated 2. black-hearted, smouldering, venomous, vicious, virulent

festival 1. anniversary, commemoration, feast, fête, fiesta, holiday, holy day, red-letter day, saint's day 2. carnival, celebration, entertainment, -fest, festivities, fête, field day, gala, jubilee, treat

festive back-slapping, carnival, celebratory, cheery, Christmassy, convivial, festal, gala, gay, gleeful, happy, hearty, holiday, jolly, jovial, joyful, joyous, jubilant, light-hearted, merry, mirthful, sportive
Antonyms depressing, drab, dreary, funereal, gloomy, lugubrious, mournful, sad

festivity 1. amusement, conviviality, fun, gaiety, jollification, joviality, joyfulness, merriment, merrymaking, mirth, pleasure, revelry, sport 2. *often plural* beano (*Brit. slang*), carousal, celebration, entertainment, festival, festive event, festive proceedings, fun and games, hooley *or* hoolie (*chiefly Irish & N.Z.*), jollification, party, rave (*Brit. slang*), rave-up (*Brit. slang*)

festoon 1. *noun* chaplet, garland, lei, swag, swathe, wreath 2. *verb* array, bedeck, beribbon, deck, decorate, drape, engarland, garland, hang, swathe, wreathe

fetch 1. bring, carry, conduct, convey, deliver, escort, get, go for, lead, obtain, retrieve, transport 2. draw forth, elicit, give rise to, produce 3. bring in, earn, go for, make, realize, sell for, yield

fetching alluring, attractive, captivating, charming, cute, enchanting, enticing, fascinating, intriguing, sweet, taking, winsome

fetch up arrive, come, end up, finish up, halt, land, reach, stop, turn up

fête, fete 1. *noun* bazaar, fair, festival, gala, garden party, sale of work 2. *verb* bring out the red carpet for (someone), entertain regally, hold a reception for (someone), honour, kill the fatted calf for (someone), lionize, make much of, treat, wine and dine

fetid corrupt, foul, malodorous, mephitic, noisome, noxious, offensive, olid, rancid, rank, reeking, stinking

fetish 1. amulet, cult object, talisman 2. fixation, *idée fixe*, mania, obsession, thing (*informal*)

fetter *verb* bind, chain, clip someone's wings, confine, curb, encumber, gyve (*archaic*), hamper, hamstring, hobble, hold captive, manacle, put a straitjacket on, restrain, restrict, shackle, straiten, tie, tie up, trammel

fetters *noun* 1. bilboes, bonds, chains, gyves (*archaic*), irons, leg irons, manacles, shackles 2. bondage, captivity, check, curb, hindrance, obstruction, restraint

feud 1. *noun* argument, bad blood, bickering, broil, conflict, contention, disagreement, discord, dissension, enmity, estrangement, faction, falling out, grudge, hostility, quarrel, rivalry, row, strife, vendetta 2. *verb* be at daggers drawn, be at odds, bicker, brawl, clash, contend, dispute, duel, fall out, quarrel, row, squabble, war

fever 1. *figurative* agitation, delirium, ecstasy, excitement, ferment, fervour, flush, frenzy, heat, intensity, passion, restlessness, turmoil, unrest 2. pyrexia (*Medical*)
Related adjective: febrile

Feed a cold and starve a fever

fevered burning, feverish, flushed, hectic, hot, on fire, pyretic (*Medical*)

feverish 1. burning, febrile, fevered, flaming, flushed, hectic, hot, inflamed, pyretic (*Medical*) 2. agitated, desperate, distracted, excited, frantic, frenetic, frenzied, impatient, obsessive, overwrought, restless
Antonyms calm, collected, composed, cool, dispassionate, nonchalant, offhand, serene, tranquil, unemotional, unexcitable, unfazed (*informal*), unruffled

few *adjective* 1. hardly any, inconsiderable, infrequent, insufficient, meagre, negligible, not many, rare, scant, scanty, scarce, scarcely any, scattered, sparse, sporadic, thin 2. **few and far between** at great intervals, hard to come by, infrequent, in short supply, irregular, rare, scarce, scattered, seldom met with, thin on the ground, uncommon, unusual, widely spaced ~*pronoun* 3. handful, scarcely any, scattering, small number, some
Antonyms *adjective* (*senses 1 & 2*) abundant, bounteous, divers (*archaic*), inexhaustible, manifold, many, multifarious, plentiful, sundry

fiancé, fiancée betrothed, intended, prospective spouse, wife- *or* husband-to-be

fiasco balls-up (*taboo slang*), catastrophe, cock-up (*Brit. slang*), debacle, disaster, failure, flap (*informal*), fuck-up (*offensive taboo slang*), mess, rout, ruin, washout (*informal*)

fiat 1. authorization, permission, sanction, warrant 2. canon, command, decree, demand, dictate, dictum, edict, mandate, order, ordinance, precept, proclamation, ukase

fib *noun* fiction, lie, pork pie (*Brit. slang*), porky (*Brit. slang*), prevarication, story, untruth, white lie, whopper (*informal*)

fib: a lie that has not cut its teeth
Ambrose Bierce *The Devil's Dictionary*

fibre 1. fibril, filament, pile, staple, strand, texture, thread, wisp 2. *figurative* essence, nature, quality, spirit, substance 3. *figurative As in* **moral fibre** resolution, stamina, strength, strength of character, toughness

fickle blowing hot and cold, capricious, changeable, faithless, fitful, flighty, inconstant, irresolute, mercurial, mutable, quicksilver, temperamental, unfaithful, unpredictable, unstable, unsteady, vacillating, variable, volatile
Antonyms changeless, constant, faithful, firm, invariable, loyal, reliable, resolute, settled, stable, staunch, steadfast, true, trustworthy

The fickleness of the women I love is matched only by the infernal constancy of the women who love me
George Bernard Shaw *The Philanderer*

fickleness capriciousness, fitfulness, flightiness, inconstancy, mutability, unfaithfulness, unpredictability, unsteadiness, volatility

fiction 1. fable, fantasy, legend, myth, novel, romance, story, storytelling, tale, urban legend, work of imagination, yarn (*informal*) 2. cock and bull story (*informal*), concoction, fabrication, falsehood, fancy, fantasy, figment of the imagination, imagination, improvisation, invention, lie, pork pie (*Brit. slang*), porky (*Brit. slang*), tall story, untruth

Truth may be stranger than fiction, but fiction is truer
Frederic Raphael *Contemporary Novelists*

Literature is a luxury. Fiction is a necessity
G.K. Chesterton *The Defendant*

fictional imaginary, invented, legendary, made-up, nonexistent, unreal

fictitious apocryphal, artificial, assumed, bogus, counterfeit, fabricated, false, fanciful, feigned, imaginary, imagined, improvised, invented, made-up, make-believe, mythical, spurious, unreal, untrue
Antonyms actual, authentic, genuine, legitimate, real, true, truthful, veracious, veritable

fiddle *verb* 1. *often with* **with** fidget, finger, interfere with, mess about *or* around, play, tamper with, tinker, toy, trifle 2. *informal* cheat, cook the books (*informal*), diddle (*informal*), finagle (*informal*), fix, gerrymander, graft (*informal*), manoeuvre, racketeer, sting (*informal*), swindle, wangle (*informal*) ~*noun* 3. violin 4. **fit as a fiddle** blooming, hale and hearty, healthy, in fine fettle, in good form, in good shape, in rude health, in the pink, sound, strong 5. *informal* fix, fraud, graft (*informal*), piece of sharp practice, racket, scam (*slang*), sting (*informal*), swindle, wangle (*informal*)

fiddling futile, insignificant, nickel-and-dime (*U.S. slang*), pettifogging, petty, trifling, trivial

fidelity 1. allegiance, constancy, dependability, devotedness, devotion, faith, faithfulness, fealty, integrity, lealty (*archaic or Scot.*), loyalty, staunchness, troth (*archaic*), true-

heartedness, trustworthiness **2.** accuracy, ad~herence, closeness, correspondence, exactitude, exactness, faithfulness, preciseness, precision, scrupulousness
Antonyms disloyalty, faithlessness, falseness, inaccuracy, inexactness, infidelity, perfidious~ness, treachery, unfaithfulness, untruthful~ness

Histories are more full of examples of the fidelity of dogs than of friends
Alexander Pope

fidget 1. *verb* be like a cat on hot bricks (*in~formal*), bustle, chafe, fiddle (*informal*), fret, jiggle, jitter (*informal*), move restlessly, squirm, twitch, worry **2.** *noun usually* **the fidgets** fidgetiness, jitters (*informal*), nerv~ousness, restlessness, unease, uneasiness

fidgety impatient, jerky, jittery (*informal*), jumpy, nervous, on edge, restive, restless, twitchy (*informal*), uneasy

field *noun* **1.** grassland, green, greensward (*ar~chaic or literary*), lea (*poetic*), mead (*archaic*), meadow, pasture **2.** applicants, candidates, competition, competitors, contestants, en~trants, possibilities, runners **3.** area, bailiwick, bounds, confines, department, discipline, do~main, environment, limits, line, metier, pale, province, purview, range, scope, speciality, specialty, sphere of influence (activity, inter~est, study), territory *~verb* **4.** catch, pick up, retrieve, return, stop **5.** *figurative* deal with, deflect, handle, turn aside
Related adjective: campestral

fiend 1. demon, devil, evil spirit, hellhound **2.** barbarian, beast, brute, degenerate, ghoul, monster, ogre, savage **3.** *informal* addict, en~ergumen, enthusiast, fanatic, freak (*informal*), maniac

fiendish accursed, atrocious, black-hearted, cruel, demoniac, devilish, diabolical, hellish, implacable, infernal, inhuman, malevolent, malicious, malignant, monstrous, satanic, savage, ungodly, unspeakable, wicked

fierce 1. baleful, barbarous, brutal, cruel, dan~gerous, fell (*archaic*), feral, ferocious, fiery, menacing, murderous, passionate, savage, threatening, tigerish, truculent, uncontrol~lable, untamed, vicious, wild **2.** blustery, bois~terous, furious, howling, inclement, powerful, raging, stormy, strong, tempestuous, tumul~tuous, uncontrollable, violent **3.** cutthroat, in~tense, keen, relentless, strong
Antonyms affectionate, calm, civilized, cool, docile, domesticated, gentle, harmless, kind, mild, peaceful, submissive, tame, temperate, tranquil

fiercely ferociously, frenziedly, furiously, in a frenzy, like cat and dog, menacingly, passion~ately, savagely, tempestuously, tigerishly, tooth and nail, uncontrolledly, viciously, with bared teeth, with no holds barred

fierceness 1. ferocity, fieriness, mercilessness, ruthlessness, savageness, viciousness, wild~ness **2.** bluster, destructiveness, roughness, storminess, tempestuousness, turbulence, vio~lence **3.** avidity, fervidness, fervour, intensity, passion, relentlessness, strength

fiery 1. ablaze, afire, aflame, blazing, burning, flaming, glowing, in flames, on fire, red-hot **2.** choleric, excitable, fierce, hot-headed, impetu~ous, irascible, irritable, passionate, peppery, violent **3.** burning, febrile, fevered, feverish, flushed, heated, hot, inflamed

fiesta bacchanal *or* bacchanalia, carnival, ca~rousal, celebration, fair, feast, festival, festiv~ity, fête, gala, holiday, jamboree, jubilee, Mardi Gras, merrymaking, party, revel, rev~elry, saint's day, Saturnalia

fight *verb* **1.** assault, battle, bear arms against, box, brawl, carry on war, clash, close, combat, come to blows, conflict, contend, cross swords, do battle, engage, engage in hostilities, ex~change blows, feud, fight like Kilkenny cats, go to war, grapple, joust, lock horns, row, scrap (*informal*), spar, struggle, take the field, take up arms against, tilt, tussle, wage war, war, wrestle **2.** contest, defy, dispute, make a stand against, oppose, resist, stand up to, strive, struggle, withstand **3.** argue, bicker, dispute, fall out (*informal*), squabble, wrangle **4.** carry on, conduct, engage in, prosecute, wage **5. fight shy of** avoid, duck out of (*in~formal*), keep aloof from, keep at arm's length, shun, steer clear of *~noun* **6.** action, affray (*Law*), altercation, *bagarre*, battle, bout, brawl, brush, clash, combat, conflict, contest, dispute, dissension, dogfight, duel, encounter, engagement, exchange of blows, fracas, fray, free-for-all (*informal*), head-to-head, hostilities, joust, melee *or* mêlée, pas~sage of arms, riot, row, rumble (*U.S. & N.Z. slang*), scrap (*informal*), scrimmage, scuffle, set-to (*informal*), shindig (*informal*), shindy (*informal*), skirmish, sparring match, struggle, tussle, war **7.** *figurative* belligerence, game~ness, mettle, militancy, pluck, resistance, spirit, will to resist

fight back 1. defend oneself, give tit for tat, hit back, put up a fight, reply, resist, retaliate **2.** bottle up, contain, control, curb, hold back, hold in check, restrain

fightback comeback (*informal*), counterattack, counteroffensive, defiance, improvement, rally, reaction, recovery, recuperation, resistance, resurgence, retaliation, revival
Antonyms accedance, acquiescence, capitula~tion, falling off, folding up, giving in *or* up, submission, surrender, yielding

fight down bottle up, control, curb, hold back, repress, restrain, suppress

fighter 1. fighting man, man-at-arms, soldier, warrior 2. boxer, bruiser (*informal*), prize fighter, pugilist 3. antagonist, battler, belligerent, combatant, contender, contestant, disputant, militant

fighting 1. *adjective* aggressive, argumentative, bellicose, belligerent, combative, contentious, disputatious, hawkish, martial, militant, pugnacious, sabre-rattling, truculent, warlike 2. *noun* battle, bloodshed, blows struck, combat, conflict, hostilities, warfare

fight off beat off, keep *or* hold at bay, repel, repress, repulse, resist, stave off, ward off

figment creation, fable, fabrication, falsehood, fancy, fiction, improvisation, invention, production

figurative 1. allegorical, emblematical, metaphorical, representative, symbolical, typical 2. descriptive, fanciful, florid, flowery, ornate, pictorial, poetical, tropical (*Rhetoric*)
Antonyms accurate, exact, factual, faithful, literal, prosaic, simple, true, unpoetical, unvarnished

figure *noun* 1. character, cipher, digit, number, numeral, symbol 2. amount, cost, price, sum, total, value 3. form, outline, shadow, shape, silhouette 4. body, build, chassis (*slang*), frame, physique, proportions, shape, torso 5. depiction, design, device, diagram, drawing, emblem, illustration, motif, pattern, representation, sketch 6. big name, celebrity, character, dignitary, force, leader, notability, notable, personage, personality, presence, somebody, worthy *~verb* 7. *often with* **up** add, calculate, compute, count, reckon, sum, tally, tot up, work out 8. *usually with* **in** act, appear, be conspicuous, be featured, be included, be mentioned, contribute to, feature, have a place in, play a part 9. **it figures** it follows, it goes without saying, it is to be expected

figured adorned, decorated, embellished, marked, ornamented, patterned, variegated

figurehead cipher, dummy, front man (*informal*), leader in name only, man of straw, mouthpiece, name, nonentity, puppet, straw man (*chiefly U.S.*), titular *or* nominal head, token

figure of speech conceit, image, trope, turn of phrase

Figures of speech
alliteration
allusion
anacoluthia
anadiplosis
analogy
anaphora
anastrophe
antiphrasis
antithesis
antonomasia
apophasis
aporia
aposiopesis
apostrophe
catachresis
chiasmus
circumlocution
climax
emphasis
epanaphora
epanorthosis
exclamation
gemination
hendiadys
hypallage
hyperbaton
hyperbole
hysteron proteron
inversion
irony
kenning
litotes
malapropism
meiosis
metaphor
metonymy
onomatopoeia
oxymoron
paralipsis *or* paraleipsis
parenthesis
periphrasis
personification
pleonasm
polysyndeton
prolepsis
prosopopoeia *or* prosopopeia
repetition
rhetorical question
sarcasm
simile
spoonerism
syllepsis
synechdoche
tmesis
zeugma

figure out 1. calculate, compute, reckon, work out 2. comprehend, decipher, fathom, make head or tail of (*informal*), make out, resolve, see, suss (out) (*slang*), understand

filament cilium (*Biology & Zoology*), fibre, fibril, pile, staple, strand, string, thread, wire, wisp

filch abstract, cabbage (*Brit. slang*), crib (*informal*), embezzle, half-inch (*old-fashioned slang*), lift (*informal*), misappropriate, nick (*slang, chiefly Brit.*), pilfer, pinch (*informal*), purloin, rip off (*slang*), snaffle (*Brit. informal*), steal, swipe (*slang*), take, thieve, walk off with

file[1] *verb* abrade, burnish, furbish, polish, rasp, refine, rub, rub down, scrape, shape, smooth

file[2] *noun* 1. case, data, documents, dossier, folder, information, portfolio *~verb* 2. document, enter, pigeonhole, put in place, record, register, slot in (*informal*) *~noun* 3. column, line, list, queue, row, string *~verb* 4. march, parade, troop

filibuster *noun* 1. *chiefly U.S., with reference to legislation* delay, hindrance, obstruction, postponement, procrastination *~verb* 2. *chiefly U.S., with reference to legislation* delay, hinder, obstruct, play for time, prevent, procrastinate, put off *~noun* 3. adventurer, buccaneer, corsair, freebooter, pirate, sea robber, sea rover, soldier of fortune

filigree lace, lacework, lattice, tracery, wirework

fill 1. brim over, cram, crowd, furnish, glut, gorge, inflate, pack, pervade, replenish, sate, satiate, satisfy, stock, store, stuff, supply, swell 2. charge, imbue, impregnate, overspread, pervade, saturate, suffuse 3. block, bung, close, cork, plug, seal, stop **4.** assign, carry out, discharge, engage, execute, fulfil, hold, occupy, officiate, perform, take up **5.** **one's fill** all one wants, ample, a sufficiency, enough, plenty, sufficient

Antonyms diminish, drain, empty, exhaust, shrink, subside, vacate, void

fill in **1.** answer, complete, fill out (*U.S.*), fill up **2.** *informal* acquaint, apprise, bring up to date, give the facts *or* background, inform, put wise (*slang*) **3.** deputize, replace, represent, stand in, sub, substitute, take the place of

filling **1.** *noun* contents, filler, innards (*informal*), inside, insides, padding, stuffing, wadding **2.** *adjective* ample, heavy, satisfying, square, substantial

fillip *noun* goad, incentive, prod, push, spice, spur, stimulus, zest

film *noun* **1.** coat, coating, covering, dusting, gauze, integument, layer, membrane, pellicle, scum, skin, tissue **2.** blur, cloud, haze, haziness, mist, mistiness, opacity, veil **3.** flick (*slang*), motion picture, movie (*U.S. informal*) ~*verb* **4.** photograph, shoot, take, video, videotape **5.** *often with* **over** blear, blur, cloud, dull, haze, mist, veil

Related adjectives: cinematic, filmic

Film directors

Woody Allen [U.S.]
Pedro Almodovar [Spanish]
Robert Altman [U.S.]
Lindsay Anderson [British]
Michelangelo Antonioni [Italian]
Gillian Armstrong [Australia]
Richard Attenborough [British]
Ingmar Bergman [Swedish]
Bernardo Bertolucci [Italian]
Robert Bresson [French]
Peter Brook [British]
Mel Brooks [U.S.]
Tim Burton [U.S.]
Luis Buñuel [Spanish]
James Cameron [U.S.]
Jane Campion [New Zealand]
Frank Capra [U.S]
Marcel Carné [French]
Claude Chabrol [French]
René Clair [French]
Jean Cocteau [French]
Ethan Coen [U.S.]
Joel Coen [U.S.]
Francis Ford Coppola [U.S.]
David Cronenberg [Canadian]
Brian de Palma [U.S.]
Vittoria De Sicca [Italian]
Johnathan Demme [U.S.]
Aleksandr Petrovitch Dovzhenko [Russian]
Clint Eastwood [U.S.]
Blake Edwards [U.S.]
Sergei Mikhailovich Eisenstein [Russian]
Rainer Werner Fassbinder [German]
Federico Fellini [Italian]
John Ford [U.S.]
Miloš Forman [Czech]
Bill Forsyth [British]
Abel Gance [French]
Terry Gilliam [U.S.]
Jean-Luc Godard [French]
Peter Greenaway [British]
John Grierson [British]
D(avid Lewelyn) W(ark) Griffith [U.S.]
Sacha Guitry [French]
Howard Hawks [U.S.]
Werner Herzog [German]
Alfred Hitchcock [British]
John Huston [U.S]
James Ivory [U.S.]
Derek Jarman [British]
Chen Kaige [China]
Elia Kazan [U.S.]
Krzysztof Kieslowski [Polish]
Stanley Kubrick [U.S.]
Akira Kurosawa [Japanese]
Fritz Lang [Austrian]
David Lean [British]
Spike Lee [U.S.]
Mike Leigh [British]
Richard Lester [U.S.]
Ken Loach [British]
George Lucas [U.S]
Sidney Lumet [U.S.]
David Lynch [U.S.]
Alexander Mackendrick [British]
Louis Malle [French]
Georges Méliès [French]
Ismail Merchant [Indian]
Vincente Minelli [U.S.]
Kenji Mizoguchi [Japanese]
Max Ophüls [German]
G(eorge) W(ilhelm) Pabst [German]
Marcel Pagnol [French]
Alan Parker [British]
Pier Paolo Pasolini [Italian]
Sam Peckinpah [U.S.]
Arthur Penn [U.S]
Roman Polanski [Polish]
Sydney Pollack [U.S]
Michael Powell [British]
Otto Preminger [Austrian-U.S.]
Emeric Pressburger [Hungarian]
Vsevolod Pudovkin [Russian]
David Puttnam [British]
Satyajit Ray [Indian]
Carol Reed [British]
Rob Reiner [U.S.]
Edgar Reitz [German]
Jean Renoir [French]
Alain Resnais [French]
Leni Riefenstahl [German]
Hal Roach [U.S.]
Eric Rohmer [France]
Roberto Rossellini [Italian]
Ken Russell [British]
John Schlesinger [British]
Martin Scorsese [U.S.]
Ridley Scott [British]
Steven Spielberg [U.S.]
Oliver Stone [U.S.]
Preston Sturges [U.S.]
Quentin Tarantino [U.S.]
Andrei Tarkovsky [Russian]
Jacques Tati [French]
Bertrand Tavernier [French]
François Truffaut [French]
Roger Vadim [French]
Luchino Visconti [Italian]
Joseph von Sternberg [Austrian-U.S.]
Erich von Stroheim [Austrian-U.S.]
Andrei Wajda [Polish]
Peter Weir [Australian]
Orson Welles [U.S.]
Wim Wenders [German]
Billy Wilder [Austrian-U.S.]
Michael Winner [British]
Zhang Yimou [Chinese]
Franco Zeffirelli [Italian]
Robert Zemeckis [U.S.]

filmy 1. chiffon, cobwebby, delicate, diaphanous, fine, finespun, flimsy, floaty, fragile, gauzy, gossamer, insubstantial, see-through, sheer, transparent 2. bleared, bleary, blurred, blurry, cloudy, dim, hazy, membranous, milky, misty, opalescent, opaque, pearly

filter *verb* 1. clarify, filtrate, purify, refine, screen, sieve, sift, strain, winnow 2. *often with* **through** *or* **out** dribble, escape, exude, leach, leak, ooze, penetrate, percolate, seep, trickle, well ~*noun* 3. gauze, membrane, mesh, riddle, sieve, strainer

filth 1. carrion, contamination, crap (*slang*), crud (*slang*), defilement, dirt, dung, excrement, excreta, faeces, filthiness, foul matter, foulness, garbage, grime, grot (*slang*), muck, nastiness, ordure, pollution, putrefaction, putrescence, refuse, sewage, shit (*taboo slang*), slime, sludge, squalor, uncleanness 2. corruption, dirty-mindedness, impurity, indecency, obscenity, pornography, smut, vileness, vulgarity

filthy 1. dirty, faecal, feculent, foul, nasty, polluted, putrid, scummy, scuzzy (*slang, chiefly U.S.*), slimy, squalid, unclean, vile 2. begrimed, black, blackened, grimy, grubby, miry, mucky, muddy, mud-encrusted, scuzzy (*slang, chiefly U.S.*), smoky, sooty, unwashed 3. bawdy, coarse, corrupt, depraved, dirty-minded, foul, foul-mouthed, impure, indecent, lewd, licentious, obscene, pornographic, smutty, suggestive, X-rated (*informal*) 4. base, contemptible, despicable, low, mean, offensive, scurvy, vicious, vile

final 1. closing, concluding, end, eventual, last, last-minute, latest, terminal, terminating, ultimate 2. absolute, conclusive, decided, decisive, definite, definitive, determinate, finished, incontrovertible, irrevocable, settled
Antonyms earliest, first, initial, introductory, maiden, opening, original, precursory, prefatory, premier, preparatory

finale climax, close, conclusion, crowning glory, culmination, dénouement, epilogue, finis, last act
Antonyms commencement, exordium, foreword, intro (*informal*), lead-in, opening, overture, preamble, preface, preliminaries, prelude, proem, prolegomenon, prologue

finality certitude, conclusiveness, decidedness, decisiveness, definiteness, inevitableness, irrevocability, resolution, unavoidability

finalize agree, clinch, complete, conclude, decide, settle, sew up (*informal*), shake hands, tie up, work out, wrap up (*informal*)

finally 1. at last, at length, at long last, at the end of the day, at the last, at the last moment, eventually, in the end, in the fullness of time, in the long run, lastly, ultimately, when all is said and done 2. in conclusion, in summary, to conclude 3. beyond the shadow of a doubt, completely, conclusively, convincingly, decisively, for all time, for ever, for good, inescapably, inexorably, irrevocably, once and for all, permanently

finance 1. *noun* accounts, banking, business, commerce, economics, financial affairs, investment, money, money management 2. *verb* back, bankroll (*U.S.*), float, fund, guarantee, pay for, provide security for, set up in business, subsidize, support, underwrite

finances affairs, assets, capital, cash, financial condition, funds, money, resources, wherewithal

financial budgeting, economic, fiscal, monetary, money, pecuniary

financing *noun* costs, expenditure, expense(s), funding, operating expenses, outlay

find *verb* 1. catch sight of, chance upon, come across, come up with, descry, discover, encounter, espy, expose, ferret out, hit upon, lay one's hand on, light upon, locate, meet, recognize, run to earth, run to ground, spot, stumble upon, track down, turn up, uncover, unearth 2. achieve, acquire, attain, earn, gain, get, obtain, procure, win 3. get back, recover, regain, repossess, retrieve 4. arrive at, ascertain, become aware, detect, discover, experience, learn, note, notice, observe, perceive, realise, remark 5. be responsible for, bring, contribute, cough up (*informal*), furnish, provide, purvey, supply ~*noun* 6. acquisition, asset, bargain, catch, discovery, good buy
Antonyms (*sense 1*) lose, mislay, misplace, miss, overlook

finders keepers

finding award, conclusion, decision, decree, judgment, pronouncement, recommendation, verdict

find out 1. detect, discover, learn, note, observe, perceive, realize 2. bring to light, catch, detect, disclose, expose, reveal, rumble (*Brit. informal*), suss (out) (*slang*), uncover, unmask

fine[1] *adjective* 1. accomplished, admirable, beautiful, choice, divine, excellent, exceptional, exquisite, first-class, first-rate, great, magnificent, masterly, ornate, outstanding, rare, select, showy, skilful, splendid, sterling, superior, supreme, world-class 2. balmy, bright, clear, clement, cloudless, dry, fair, pleasant, sunny 3. dainty, delicate, elegant, expensive, exquisite, fragile, quality 4. abstruse, acute, critical, discriminating, fastidious, hair-splitting, intelligent, keen, minute, nice, precise, quick, refined, sensitive, sharp, subtle, tasteful, tenuous 5. delicate, diaphanous, fine-grained, flimsy, gauzy, gossamer, light, lightweight, powdered, powdery, pulverized, sheer, slender, small, thin 6. clear, pure, re~

fined, solid, sterling, unadulterated, unalloyed, unpolluted **7.** attractive, bonny, good-looking, handsome, lovely, smart, striking, stylish, well-favoured **8.** acceptable, agreeable, all right, convenient, good, hunky-dory (*informal*), O.K. *or* okay (*informal*), satisfactory, suitable **9.** brilliant, cutting, honed, keen, polished, razor-sharp, sharp
Antonyms (*sense 1*) indifferent, inferior, poor, second rate, substandard (*sense 2*) cloudy, dull, overcast, unpleasant (*senses 3 & 4*) blunt, coarse, crude, dull, heavy, rough, uncultured, unfinished, unrefined

fine[2] **1.** *verb* amerce (*archaic*), mulct, penalize, punish **2.** *noun* amercement (*obsolete*), damages, forfeit, penalty, punishment

finery best bib and tucker (*informal*), decorations, frippery, gear (*informal*), gewgaws, glad rags (*informal*), ornaments, showiness, splendour, Sunday best, trappings, trinkets

finesse *noun* **1.** adeptness, adroitness, artfulness, cleverness, craft, delicacy, diplomacy, discretion, know-how (*informal*), polish, quickness, savoir-faire, skill, sophistication, subtlety, tact **2.** artifice, bluff, feint, manoeuvre, ruse, stratagem, trick, wile *~verb* **3.** bluff, manipulate, manoeuvre

finger *verb* **1.** feel, fiddle with (*informal*), handle, manipulate, maul, meddle with, paw (*informal*), play about with, touch, toy with **2.** **put one's finger on** bring to mind, discover, find out, hit the nail on the head, hit upon, identify, indicate, locate, pin down, place, recall, remember

finicky choosy (*informal*), critical, dainty, difficult, fastidious, finicking, fussy, hard to please, nit-picking (*informal*), overnice, overparticular, particular, picky (*informal*), scrupulous, squeamish

finish *verb* **1.** accomplish, achieve, bring to a close *or* conclusion, carry through, cease, close, complete, conclude, culminate, deal with, discharge, do, end, execute, finalize, fulfil, get done, get out of the way, make short work of, put the finishing touch(es) to, put the tin lid on, round off, settle, stop, terminate, wind up, wrap up (*informal*) **2.** *sometimes with* **up** *or* **off** consume, deplete, devour, dispatch, dispose of, drain, drink, eat, empty, exhaust, expend, spend, use, use up **3.** *often with* **off** administer *or* give the coup de grâce, annihilate, best, bring down, defeat, destroy, dispose of, drive to the wall, exterminate, get rid of, kill, move in for the kill, overcome, overpower, put an end to, put paid to, rout, ruin, worst *~noun* **4.** cessation, close, closing, completion, conclusion, culmination, dénouement, end, ending, finale, last stage(s), run-in, termination, winding up (*informal*), wind-up **5.** annihilation, bankruptcy, curtains (*informal*), death, defeat, end, end of the road, liquidation, ruin *~verb* **6.** elaborate, perfect, polish, refine *~noun* **7.** cultivation, culture, elaboration, perfection, polish, refinement, sophistication *~verb* **8.** coat, face, gild, lacquer, polish, smooth off, stain, texture, veneer, wax *~noun* **9.** appearance, grain, lustre, patina, polish, shine, smoothness, surface, texture
Antonyms *verb* begin, commence, create, embark on, instigate, start, undertake *~noun* beginning, birth, commencement, conception, genesis, inauguration, inception, instigation, preamble, preface, prologue

finished **1.** accomplished, classic, consummate, cultivated, elegant, expert, flawless, impeccable, masterly, perfected, polished, professional, proficient, refined, skilled, smooth, urbane **2.** accomplished, achieved, closed, complete, completed, concluded, done, ended, entire, final, finalized, full, in the past, over, over and done with, sewed up (*informal*), shut, terminated, through, tied up, wrapped up (*informal*) **3.** done, drained, empty, exhausted, gone, played out (*informal*), spent, used up **4.** bankrupt, defeated, devastated, done for (*informal*), doomed, gone, liquidated, lost, ruined, through, undone, washed up (*informal, chiefly U.S.*), wiped out, wound up, wrecked
Antonyms basic, begun, coarse, crude, imperfect, inartistic, incomplete, inelegant, inexperienced, raw, rough, unfinished, unrefined, unskilled, unsophisticated

finite bounded, circumscribed, conditioned, delimited, demarcated, limited, restricted, subject to limitations, terminable
Antonyms boundless, endless, eternal, everlasting, immeasurable, infinite, interminable, limitless, perpetual, unbounded

fire *noun* **1.** blaze, combustion, conflagration, flames, inferno **2.** barrage, bombardment, cannonade, flak, fusillade, hail, salvo, shelling, sniping, volley **3.** *figurative* animation, ardour, brio, burning passion, dash, eagerness, élan, enthusiasm, excitement, fervency, fervour, force, heat, impetuosity, intensity, life, light, lustre, passion, pizzazz *or* pizazz (*informal*), radiance, scintillation, sparkle, spirit, splendour, verve, vigour, virtuosity, vivacity **4.** **hanging fire** delayed, in abeyance, in cold storage, on ice, pending, postponed, put back, put off, shelved, suspended, undecided **5.** **on fire a.** ablaze, aflame, alight, blazing, burning, fiery, flaming, in flames **b.** ardent, eager, enthusiastic, excited, inspired, passionate *~verb* **6.** enkindle, ignite, kindle, light, put a match to, set ablaze, set aflame, set alight, set fire to, set on fire, torch **7.** detonate, discharge, eject, explode, hurl, launch, let off, loose, pull the trigger, set off, shell, shoot, touch off **8.** *figurative* animate, arouse, electrify, enliven, excite, galvanize, impassion, incite, inflame, inspire, inspirit, irritate, quicken, rouse, stir **9.** *informal* cashier, discharge, dismiss, give marching orders, give the boot (*slang*), give the bullet (*Brit. slang*), give the push, kiss off (*slang, chiefly U.S. & Canad.*), make redundant, sack (*informal*), show the door

Fight fire with fire

Fire is a good servant but a bad master

If you play with fire you get burnt

Out of the frying pan, into the fire

firearm gun, handgun, heater (*U.S. slang*), piece (*slang*), pistol, revolver, rod (*slang*), shooter (*slang*)

firebrand *figurative* agitator, demagogue, fomenter, incendiary, instigator, rabble-rouser, soapbox orator, tub-thumper

fireworks 1. illuminations, pyrotechnics **2.** *figurative* fit of rage, hysterics, paroxysms, rage, rows, storm, temper, trouble, uproar, wax (*informal, chiefly Brit.*)

firm[1] *adjective* **1.** close-grained, compact, compressed, concentrated, congealed, dense, hard, inelastic, inflexible, jelled, jellified, rigid, set, solid, solidified, stiff, unyielding **2.** anchored, braced, cemented, embedded, fast, fastened, fixed, immovable, motionless, riveted, robust, rooted, secure, secured, stable, stationary, steady, strong, sturdy, taut, tight, unfluctuating, unmoving, unshakable **3.** adamant, constant, definite, fixed, immovable, inflexible, obdurate, resolute, resolved, set on, settled, stalwart, staunch, steadfast, strict, true, unalterable, unbending, unfaltering, unflinching, unshakable, unshaken, unswerving, unwavering, unyielding

Antonyms flabby, flaccid, flimsy, inconstant, insecure, irresolute, limp, loose, shaky, soft, unreliable, unstable, unsteady, wavering

firm[2] *noun* association, business, company, concern, conglomerate, corporation, enterprise, house, organization, outfit (*informal*), partnership

firmament empyrean (*poetic*), heaven, heavens, sky, the blue, the skies, vault, vault of heaven, welkin (*archaic*)

firmly 1. enduringly, immovably, like a rock, motionlessly, securely, steadily, tightly, unflinchingly, unshakably **2.** determinedly, resolutely, staunchly, steadfastly, strictly, through thick and thin, unchangeably, unwaveringly, with a rod of iron, with decision

firmness 1. compactness, density, fixedness, hardness, inelasticity, inflexibility, resistance, rigidity, solidity, stiffness **2.** immovability, soundness, stability, steadiness, strength, tautness, tensile strength, tension, tightness **3.** constancy, fixedness, fixity of purpose, inflexibility, obduracy, resolution, resolve, staunchness, steadfastness, strength of will, strictness

first *adjective* **1.** chief, foremost, head, highest, leading, pre-eminent, prime, principal, ruling **2.** earliest, initial, introductory, maiden, opening, original, premier, primeval, primitive, primordial, pristine **3.** basic, cardinal, elementary, fundamental, key, primary, rudimentary *~adverb* **4.** at the beginning, at the outset, before all else, beforehand, firstly, initially, in the first place, to begin with, to start with *~noun* **5.** *As in* **from the first** beginning, commencement, inception, introduction, outset, start, starting point, word "go" (*informal*)

Many that are first shall be last; and the last shall be first

Bible: St. Mark

First come, first served

First things first

first-class A1 *or* A-one (*informal*), ace (*informal*), bad (*slang*), blue-chip, boffo (*slang*), brill (*informal*), brilliant, capital, champion, chillin' (*U.S. slang*), choice, crack (*slang*), cracking (*Brit. informal*), crucial (*slang*), def (*slang*), elite, excellent, exceptional, exemplary, first-rate, five-star, great, jim-dandy (*slang*), marvellous, matchless, mean (*slang*), mega (*slang*), outstanding, premium, prime, second to none, sovereign, superb, superlative, tiptop, top, top-class, top-drawer, top-flight, topnotch (*informal*), topping (*Brit. slang*), tops (*slang*), twenty-four carat, very good, world-class

Antonyms inferior, second-class, second-rate, shocking (*informal*), terrible, third-rate

first-hand direct, straight from the horse's mouth

first-rate admirable, A1 *or* A-one (*informal*), bodacious (*slang, chiefly U.S.*), boffo (*slang*), brill (*informal*), chillin' (*U.S. slang*), crack (*slang*), cracking (*Brit. informal*), crucial (*slang*), def (*slang*), elite, excellent, exceptional, exclusive, first class, jim-dandy (*slang*), mean (*slang*), mega (*slang*), outstanding, prime, second to none, sovereign, superb, superlative, tiptop, top, topnotch (*informal*), topping (*Brit. slang*), tops (*slang*), world-class

fiscal budgetary, economic, financial, monetary, money, pecuniary

fish

Related adjectives: piscine, ichthyoid

Fish

alewife
amberjack
anabantid
anabas
anableps
anchoveta
anchovy
angelfish
angel shark, angelfish *or* monkfish
arapaima
archerfish

argentine
barbel
barracouta *or (Austral.)* hake
barracuda
barramunda
barramundi
basking shark *or* sailfish
bass
batfish
beluga
bib, pout *or* whiting pout
bigeye
billfish
bitterling
black bass
blackfish
bleak
blenny
blindfish
bloodfin
blowfish
blue cod, rock cod *or (N.Z.)* rawaru, pakirikiri *or* patutuki
bluefish *or* snapper
bluegill
blue pointer
boarfish
bonefish
bonito
bowfin *or* dogfish
bream *or (Austral.)* brim
brill
brook trout *or* speckled trout
brown trout
buffalo fish
bullhead
bull trout
bully *or (N.Z.)* pakoko, titarakura *or* toi-toi
burbot, eelpout *or* ling
butterfish
butterfish, greenbone *or (N.Z.)* koaea *or* marari
butterfly fish
cabezon *or* cabezone
cabrilla
callop
candlefish *or* eulachon
capelin *or* caplin
carp
carpet shark
catfish
cavalla *or* cavally
cavefish
cero
characin *or* characid
chimaera
Chinook salmon, quinnat salmon *or* king salmon
chub
chum
cichlid
cisco *or* lake herring
climbing fish *or* climbing perch
clingfish
coalfish *or (Brit.)* saithe *or* coley
cobia
cockabully
cod *or* codfish
coelacanth
coho *or* silver salmon
coley
conger
cow shark *or* six-gilled shark
crappie
croaker
crucian
dab
dace
damselfish
danio
darter
dealfish
dentex
dogfish
dollarfish
dorado
dory
dragonet
eel
eelpout
electric eel
fallfish
father lasher *or* short-spined sea scorpion
fighting fish *or* betta
filefish
flatfish
flathead
flounder
flying fish
flying gurnard
four-eyed fish
frogfish
garpike, garfish *or* gar
geelbek
gemfish
gilthead
goby
goldeye
goldfish
goldsinny *or* goldfinny
gourami
grayling
greenling
grenadier *or* rat-tail
groper *or* grouper
grunion
grunt
gudgeon
guitarfish
gunnel
guppy
gurnard *or* gurnet
gwyniad
haddock
hagfish *or* hag
hairtail *or (U.S.)* cutlass fish
hake
halfbeak
halibut
hammerhead
herring
hogfish
horned pout *or* brown bullhead
horse mackerel
houndfish
houting
ice fish
jacksmelt
jewelfish
jewfish
John Dory
jurel
kahawai *or* Australian salmon
killifish
kingfish
kingklip (*S. Afr.*)
kokanee
labyrinth fish
lampern *or* river lamprey
lamprey *or* lamper eel
lancet fish
lantern fish
largemouth bass
latimeria
leatherjacket
lemon sole
lepidosiren
ling
lingcod
lionfish
loach
louvar
luderick
lumpfish *or* lumpsucker
lungfish
mackerel *or (colloquial)* shiner
mako
manta, manta ray, devilfish *or* devil ray
marlin *or* spearfish
megrim
menhaden
milkfish
miller's thumb
minnow *or (Scot.)* baggie minnow
mirror carp
moki
molly
monkfish *or (U.S.)* goosefish
mooneye
moonfish
Moorish idol
moray
morwong
mudcat
mudfish
mudskipper
mullet
mulloway
muskellunge, maskalonge, maskanonge *or (informal)* musky *or* muskie
nannygai *or* redfish
needlefish
numbfish
nursehound
nurse shark
oarfish *or* king of the herrings
oldwife
opah, moonfish *or* kingfish
orange chromide
orfe
ouananiche
paddlefish
panchax
pandora
paradise fish
parrotfish
perch
pickerel
pigfish *or* hogfish
pike, luce *or* jackfish
pikeperch
pilchard
pilot fish
pinfish *or* sailor's choice

pipefish *or* needlefish
piranha *or* piraña
plaice
platy
pogge *or* armed bull~head
pollack *or* pollock
pollan
pomfret
pompano
porbeagle *or* mackerel shark
porcupine fish *or* globefish
porgy *or* pogy
pout
powan *or* lake herring
puffer *or* globefish
pumpkinseed
Queensland lungfish
rabbitfish
rainbow trout
ray
red cod
redfin
redfish
red mullet *or (U.S.)* goatfish
red salmon
red snapper
remora
requiem shark
ribbonfish
roach
robalo
rock bass
rockfish *or (formerly)* rock salmon
rockling
rosefish
rudd
ruffe, ruff *or* pope
runner
sailfish
salmon
salmon trout
sand dab
sand eel, sand lance *or* launce
sardine
sauger
saury *or* skipper
sawfish
scabbard fish
scad
scaldfish
scat
scorpion fish
sculpin (*U.S. & Canad.*)
scup *or* northern porgy
sea bass
sea bream
sea horse
sea lamprey
sea perch
sea raven
sea robin
sea scorpion
sea snail *or* snailfish
sea trout
Sergeant Baker
sergeant major
shad
shanny
shark *or (Austral.)* noah
sheepshead
shiner
shovelhead
shovelnose
Siamese fighting fish
sild
silver belly (*N.Z.*)
silverfish
silverside *or* silver~sides
skate
skelly
skipjack *or* skipjack tuna
sleeper *or* sleeper goby
smallmouth bass
smelt
smooth hound
snapper
snipefish *or* bellows fish
snoek
snook
sockeye *or* red salmon
sole
solenette
soupfin *or* soupfin shark
spadefish
Spanish mackerel
sprat
squeteague
squirrelfish
steelhead
sterlet
stickleback
stingray
stone bass *or* wreck~fish
stonefish
stone roller
sturgeon
sucker
sunfish
surfperch *or* sea perch
surgeonfish
swordfish
swordtail
tailor
tarakihi *or* terakihi
tarpon
tarwhine
tautog *or* blackfish
tench
teraglin
tetra
thornback
threadfin
tiger shark
tilapia
tilefish
toadfish
tope
topminnow
torsk *or (U.S. & Canadian)* cusk
trevally (*Austral. & N.Z.*)
triggerfish
tripletail
trout
trunkfish, boxfish *or* cowfish
tuna *or* tunny
turbot
vendace
wahoo
walleye, walleyed pike *or* dory
weakfish
weever
whale shark
whitebait
whitefish
whiting
wirrah
witch
wobbegong
wolffish *or* catfish
wrasse
yellow belly (*Austral.*)
yellow jack
yellowtail
zander

Extinct fish

ceratodus
ostracoderm
placoderm

Seafood

see FOOD

fish for angle for, elicit, hint at, hope for, hunt for, invite, look for, search for, seek, solicit

fish out extract, extricate, find, haul out, pro~duce, pull out

fishy 1. *informal* cock-and-bull (*informal*), dodgy (*Brit., Austral., & N.Z. informal*), doubtful, dubious, funny (*informal*), implau~sible, improbable, odd, queer, questionable, rum (*Brit. slang*), suspect, suspicious, unlikely 2. blank, deadpan, dull, expressionless, glassy, glassy-eyed, inexpressive, lacklustre, lifeless, vacant, wooden 3. fishlike, piscatorial, pisca~tory, piscine

fission breaking, cleavage, division, parting, rending, rupture, schism, scission, splitting

fissure breach, break, chink, cleavage, cleft, crack, cranny, crevice, fault, fracture, gap, hole, interstice, opening, rent, rift, rupture, slit, split

fit[1] *adjective* 1. able, adapted, adequate, appo~site, appropriate, apt, becoming, capable, competent, convenient, correct, deserving, equipped, expedient, fitted, fitting, good enough, meet (*archaic*), prepared, proper, qualified, ready, right, seemly, suitable, trained, well-suited, worthy 2. able-bodied, as right as rain, hale, healthy, in good condition, in good shape, in good trim, robust, strapping, toned up, trim, well ~*verb* 3. accord, agree, be consonant, belong, concur, conform, correspond, dovetail, go, interlock, join, match, meet, suit, tally 4. *often with* **out** *or* **up** accommodate, accoutre, arm, equip, fit out, kit out, outfit, prepare, provide, rig out 5. adapt, adjust, alter, arrange, customize, dispose, fashion, modify, place, position, shape, tweak (*informal*)

Antonyms (*sense 1*) amiss, ill-fitted, ill-suited, improper, inadequate, inappropriate, unfit, unprepared, unseemly, unsuitable, untimely (*sense 2*) flabby, in poor condition, out of shape, out of trim, unfit, unhealthy

fit[2] *noun* 1. attack, bout, convulsion, paroxysm, seizure, spasm 2. caprice, fancy, humour, mood, whim 3. bout, burst, outbreak, outburst, spell 4. **by fits and starts** erratically, fitfully, intermittently, irregularly, on and off, spasmodically, sporadically, unsystematically

fitful broken, desultory, disturbed, erratic, flickering, fluctuating, haphazard, impulsive, inconstant, intermittent, irregular, spasmodic, sporadic, uneven, unstable, variable

Antonyms constant, equable, even, orderly, predictable, regular, steady, systematic, unchanging, uniform

fitfully by fits and starts, desultorily, erratically, in fits and starts, in snatches, intermittently, interruptedly, irregularly, off and on, spasmodically, sporadically

fitness 1. adaptation, applicability, appropriateness, aptness, competence, eligibility, pertinence, preparedness, propriety, qualifications, readiness, seemliness, suitability 2. good condition, good health, health, robustness, strength, vigour

fitted 1. adapted, cut out for, equipped, fit, qualified, right, suitable, tailor-made 2. *often with* **with** accoutred, appointed, armed, equipped, furnished, outfitted, provided, rigged out, set up, supplied 3. built-in, permanent

fitting 1. *adjective* apposite, appropriate, becoming, *comme il faut*, correct, decent, decorous, desirable, meet (*archaic*), proper, right, seemly, suitable 2. *noun* accessory, attachment, component, connection, part, piece, unit

Antonyms ill-suited, improper, unfitting, unseemly, unsuitable

fittings accessories, accoutrements, appointments, appurtenances, bells and whistles, conveniences, equipment, extras, furnishings, furniture, trimmings

fix *verb* 1. anchor, embed, establish, implant, install, locate, place, plant, position, root, set, settle 2. attach, bind, cement, connect, couple, fasten, glue, link, make fast, pin, secure, stick, tie 3. agree on, appoint, arrange, arrive at, conclude, decide, define, determine, establish, limit, name, resolve, set, settle, specify 4. adjust, correct, mend, patch up, put to rights, regulate, repair, see to, sort 5. congeal, consolidate, harden, rigidify, set, solidify, stiffen, thicken 6. direct, focus, level at, rivet 7. *informal* bribe, fiddle (*informal*), influence, manipulate, manoeuvre, pull strings (*informal*), rig 8. *slang* cook (someone's) goose (*informal*), get even with (*informal*), get revenge on, pay back, settle (someone's) hash (*informal*), sort (someone) out (*informal*), take retribution on, wreak vengeance on ~*noun* 9. *informal* difficult situation, difficulty, dilemma, embarrassment, hole (*slang*), hot water (*informal*), jam (*informal*), mess, pickle (*informal*), plight, predicament, quandary, spot (*informal*), ticklish situation, tight spot

If it ain't broke, don't fix it

fixated absorbed, attached, besotted, captivated, caught up in, devoted, engrossed, fascinated, hung up on (*slang*), hypnotized, infatuated, mesmerized, monomaniacal, obsessed, preoccupied, prepossessed, single-minded, smitten, spellbound, taken up with, wrapped up in

Antonyms detached, disinterested, dispassionate, indifferent, open-minded, uncommitted, unconcerned, uninvolved, unprepossessed

fixation addiction, complex, hang-up (*informal*), *idée fixe*, infatuation, mania, obsession, preoccupation, thing (*informal*)

fixed 1. anchored, attached, established, immovable, made fast, permanent, rigid, rooted, secure, set 2. intent, level, resolute, steady, unbending, unblinking, undeviating, unflinching, unwavering 3. agreed, arranged, decided, definite, established, planned, resolved, settled 4. going, in working order, mended, put right, repaired, sorted 5. *informal* framed, manipulated, packed, put-up, rigged

Antonyms bending, inconstant, mobile, motile, moving, pliant, unfixed, varying, wavering

fixity doggedness, intentness, perseverance, persistence, stability, steadiness

fix up 1. agree on, arrange, fix, organize, plan, settle, sort out 2. *often with* **with** accommodate, arrange for, bring about, furnish, lay on, provide

fizz bubble, effervesce, fizzle, froth, hiss, sparkle, sputter

fizzle out abort, collapse, come to nothing, die away, end in disappointment, fail, fall through, fold (*informal*), miss the mark, peter out

fizzy bubbling, bubbly, carbonated, effervescent, gassy, sparkling

flab beef (*informal*), fat, flabbiness, flesh,

fleshiness, heaviness, overweight, plumpness, slackness, weight

flabbergasted abashed, amazed, astonished, astounded, bowled over (*informal*), confounded, dazed, disconcerted, dumbfounded, gobsmacked (*Brit. slang*), lost for words, nonplussed, overcome, overwhelmed, rendered speechless, speechless, staggered, struck dumb, stunned

flabbiness bloatedness, flaccidity, limpness, looseness, pendulousness, slackness

flabby 1. baggy, drooping, flaccid, floppy, hanging, lax, limp, loose, pendulous, sagging, slack, sloppy, toneless, unfit, yielding 2. boneless, effete, enervated, feeble, impotent, ineffective, ineffectual, nerveless, spineless, weak, wimpish *or* wimpy (*informal*)

Antonyms firm, hard, solid, strong, taut, tense, tight, tough

flaccid drooping, flabby, lax, limp, loose, nerveless, slack, soft, weak

flaccidity flabbiness, limpness, looseness, nervelessness, slackness, softness

flag[1] *verb* abate, decline, die, droop, ebb, fade, fail, faint, fall, fall off, feel the pace, languish, peter out, pine, sag, sink, slump, succumb, taper off, wane, weaken, weary, wilt

flag[2] *noun* 1. banderole, banner, colours, ensign, gonfalon, jack, pennant, pennon, standard, streamer ~*verb* 2. *sometimes with* **down** hail, salute, signal, warn, wave 3. docket, indicate, label, mark, note, tab

Then raise the scarlet standard high!
Within its folds we'll live or die
Tho' cowards flinch and traitors sneer
We'll keep the red flag flying here
James M. Connell *The Red Flag*

flagellate beat, castigate, chastise, flay, flog, lambast(e), lash, scourge, thrash, whip

flagellation beating, flogging, lashing, thrashing, whipping

flagging declining, decreasing, deteriorating, ebbing, fading, failing, faltering, giving up, sinking, slowing down, tiring, waning, weakening, wilting

flagrancy blatancy, enormity, heinousness, infamy, insolence, ostentation, outrageousness, public display, shamelessness

flagrant arrant, atrocious, awful, barefaced, blatant, bold, brazen, crying, dreadful, egregious, enormous, flagitious, flaunting, glaring, heinous, immodest, infamous, notorious, open, ostentatious, out-and-out, outrageous, scandalous, shameless, undisguised

Antonyms delicate, faint, implied, indirect, insinuated, slight, subtle, understated

flagstone block, flag, paving stone, slab

flail *verb* beat, thrash, thresh, windmill

flair 1. ability, accomplishment, aptitude, faculty, feel, genius, gift, knack, mastery, talent 2. chic, dash, discernment, elegance, panache, style, stylishness, taste

flak *figurative* abuse, bad press, brickbats (*informal*), censure, complaints, condemnation, criticism, denigration, disapprobation, disapproval, disparagement, fault-finding, hostility, opposition, stick (*slang*)

flake 1. *noun* disk, lamina, layer, peeling, scale, shaving, sliver, squama (*Biology*), wafer 2. *verb* blister, chip, desquamate, peel (off), scale (off)

flake out collapse, faint, keel over, lose consciousness, pass out, swoon (*literary*)

flamboyance bravura, brio, chic, dash, élan, exhibitionism, extravagance, flair, flamboyancy, flashiness, floridity, glitz (*informal*), ostentation, panache, pizzazz *or* pizazz (*informal*), pomp, show, showiness, sparkle, style, stylishness, swagger, swank (*informal*), theatricality, verve

Antonyms drabness, dullness, flatness, restraint, simplicity, unobtrusiveness

flamboyant 1. actorly, baroque, camp (*informal*), elaborate, extravagant, florid, ornate, ostentatious, over the top (*informal*), rich, rococo, showy, theatrical 2. brilliant, colourful, dashing, dazzling, exciting, glamorous, glitzy (*slang*), swashbuckling

flame *verb* 1. blaze, burn, flare, flash, glare, glow, shine ~*noun* 2. blaze, brightness, fire, light 3. *figurative* affection, ardour, enthusiasm, fervency, fervour, fire, intensity, keenness, passion, warmth 4. *informal* beau, beloved, boyfriend, girlfriend, heart-throb (*Brit.*), ladylove, lover, sweetheart

flameproof fire-resistant, incombustible, non-flammable, non-inflammable

flaming 1. ablaze, afire, blazing, brilliant, burning, fiery, glowing, ignited, in flames, raging, red, red-hot 2. angry, ardent, aroused, frenzied, hot, impassioned, intense, raging, scintillating, vehement, vivid

flammable combustible, ignitable, incendiary, inflammable

flank *noun* 1. ham, haunch, hip, loin, quarter, side, thigh 2. side, wing ~*verb* 3. bookend, border, bound, edge, fringe, line, screen, skirt, wall

flannel *figurative* 1. *noun* baloney (*informal*), blarney, equivocation, flattery, hedging, prevarication, soft soap (*informal*), sweet talk (*U.S. informal*), waffle (*informal, chiefly Brit.*), weasel words (*informal, chiefly U.S.*) 2. *verb* blarney, butter up, equivocate, flatter, hedge, prevaricate, pull the wool over (someone's) eyes, soft-soap (*informal*), sweet-talk (*informal*), waffle (*informal, chiefly Brit.*)

flap *verb* **1.** agitate, beat, flail, flutter, shake, swing, swish, thrash, thresh, vibrate, wag, wave *~noun* **2.** bang, banging, beating, flutter, shaking, swinging, swish, waving *~verb* **3.** *informal* dither (*chiefly Brit.*), fuss, panic *~noun* **4.** *informal* agitation, commotion, fluster, mind-fuck (*taboo slang*), panic, state (*informal*), stew (*informal*), sweat (*informal*), tizzy (*informal*), twitter (*informal*) **5.** apron, cover, fly, fold, lapel, lappet, overlap, skirt, tab, tail

flare *verb* **1.** blaze, burn up, dazzle, flicker, flutter, glare, waver **2.** *often with* **out** broaden, spread out, widen *~noun* **3.** blaze, burst, dazzle, flame, flash, flicker, glare

flare up blaze, blow one's top (*informal*), boil over, break out, explode, fire up, fly off the handle (*informal*), lose control, lose one's cool (*informal*), lose one's temper, throw a tantrum

flash *verb* **1.** blaze, coruscate, flare, flicker, glare, gleam, glint, glisten, glitter, light, scintillate, shimmer, sparkle, twinkle *~noun* **2.** blaze, burst, coruscation, dazzle, flare, flicker, gleam, ray, scintillation, shaft, shimmer, spark, sparkle, streak, twinkle *~verb* **3.** barrel (along) (*informal, chiefly U.S. & Canad.*), bolt, burn rubber (*informal*), dart, dash, fly, race, shoot, speed, sprint, streak, sweep, whistle, zoom *~noun* **4.** bat of an eye (*informal*), instant, jiffy (*informal*), moment, second, shake, split second, trice, twinkling, twinkling of an eye, two shakes of a lamb's tail (*informal*) *~verb* **5.** display, exhibit, expose, flaunt, flourish, show *~noun* **6.** burst, demonstration, display, manifestation, outburst, show, sign, touch *~adjective* **7.** *informal* cheap, glamorous, naff (*Brit. slang*), ostentatious, tacky (*informal*), tasteless, vulgar

flashy brash, cheap, cheap and nasty, flamboyant, flaunting, garish, gaudy, glittery, glitzy (*slang*), in poor taste, jazzy (*informal*), loud, meretricious, naff (*Brit. slang*), ostentatious, over the top (*informal*), showy, snazzy (*informal*), tacky (*informal*), tasteless, tawdry, tinselly

Antonyms downbeat, low-key, modest, natural, plain, unaffected, understated

flat[1] *adjective* **1.** even, horizontal, level, levelled, low, planar, plane, smooth, unbroken **2.** laid low, lying full length, outstretched, prone, prostrate, reclining, recumbent, supine **3.** boring, dead, dull, flavourless, ho-hum (*informal*), insipid, jejune, lacklustre, lifeless, monotonous, pointless, prosaic, spiritless, stale, tedious, tiresome, uninteresting, vapid, watery, weak **4.** absolute, categorical, direct, downright, explicit, final, fixed, out-and-out, peremptory, plain, positive, straight, unconditional, unequivocal, unmistakable, unqualified **5.** blown out, burst, collapsed, deflated, empty, punctured *~noun* **6.** *often plural* lowland, marsh, mud flat, plain, shallow, shoal, strand, swamp *~adverb* **7.** absolutely, categorically, completely, exactly, point blank, precisely, utterly **8.** **flat out** all out, at full gallop, at full speed, at full tilt, for all one is worth, hell for leather (*informal*), posthaste, under full steam

Antonyms (*sense 1*) broken, hilly, irregular, rolling, rough, rugged, slanting, sloping, uneven, up and down (*sense 2*) on end, perpendicular, straight, upright, vertical (*sense 3*) bubbly, effervescent, exciting, fizzy, palatable, sparkling, tasty, zestful

flat[2] *noun* apartment, rooms

flatly absolutely, categorically, completely, positively, unhesitatingly

flatness **1.** evenness, horizontality, levelness, smoothness, uniformity **2.** dullness, emptiness, insipidity, monotony, staleness, tedium, vapidity

flatten **1.** compress, even out, iron out, level, plaster, raze, roll, smooth off, squash, trample **2.** bowl over, crush, deck (*slang*), fell, floor, knock down, knock off one's feet, prostrate, subdue

flatter **1.** blandish, butter up, cajole, compliment, court, fawn, flannel (*Brit. informal*), humour, inveigle, lay it on (thick) (*slang*), pander to, praise, puff, soft-soap (*informal*), sweet-talk (*informal*), wheedle **2.** become, do something for, enhance, set off, show to advantage, suit

flattering **1.** becoming, effective, enhancing, kind, well-chosen **2.** adulatory, complimentary, fawning, fulsome, gratifying, honeyed, honey-tongued, ingratiating, laudatory, sugary

Antonyms (*sense 1*) not shown in the best light, not shown to advantage, plain, unattractive, unbecoming, unflattering (*sense 2*) blunt, candid, honest, straight, uncomplimentary, warts and all

flattery adulation, blandishment, blarney, cajolery, false praise, fawning, flannel (*Brit. informal*), fulsomeness, honeyed words, obsequiousness, servility, soft-soap (*informal*), sweet-talk (*informal*), sycophancy, toadyism

> *I suppose flattery hurts no one, that is, if he doesn't inhale*
>
> Adlai Stevenson

> *Everyone likes flattery; and when you come to Royalty you should lay it on with a trowel*
>
> Benjamin Disraeli

flatulence **1.** borborygmus (*Medical*), eructation, wind **2.** *figurative* boasting, bombast, claptrap, empty words, fanfaronade (*rare*), fustian, hot air (*informal*), pomposity, prolixity, rodomontade, twaddle

flatulent *figurative* bombastic, inflated, long-winded, pompous, pretentious, prolix, swollen, tedious, tiresome, turgid, wordy

flaunt boast, brandish, display, disport, exhibit, flash about, flourish, make an exhibition of, make a (great) show of, parade, show off, sport (*informal*), vaunt

flaunting brazen, flamboyant, gaudy, ostentatious, pretentious

flavour *noun* **1.** aroma, essence, extract, flavouring, odour, piquancy, relish, savour, seasoning, smack, tang, taste, zest, zing (*informal*) **2.** aspect, character, essence, feel, feeling, property, quality, soupçon, stamp, style, suggestion, tinge, tone, touch *~verb* **3.** ginger up, imbue, infuse, lace, leaven, season, spice

Antonyms (*sense 1*) blandness, flatness, insipidity, odourlessness, tastelessness, vapidity

flavouring essence, extract, spirit, tincture, zest

flaw **1.** blemish, chink in one's armour, defect, disfigurement, failing, fault, imperfection, scar, speck, spot, weakness, weak spot **2.** breach, break, cleft, crack, crevice, fissure, fracture, rent, rift, scission, split, tear

flawed blemished, broken, chipped, cracked, damaged, defective, erroneous, faulty, imperfect, unsound

flawless **1.** faultless, impeccable, perfect, spotless, unblemished, unsullied **2.** intact, sound, unbroken, undamaged, whole

flay **1.** excoriate, skin **2.** *figurative* castigate, excoriate, execrate, give a tongue-lashing, pull to pieces (*informal*), revile, slam (*slang*), tear a strip off, tear into (*informal*), upbraid

fleabite drop in the ocean, nothing, piddling amount, pinprick, trifle

flea-bitten crawling, decrepit, fetid, flea-ridden, frowsty, grotty (*slang*), grubby, infested, insalubrious, lousy, mean, mucky, pediculous (*Medical*), run-down, scabby, scruffy, scurfy, sleazy, slummy, sordid, squalid, tatty, unhygienic

fleck **1.** *verb* bespeckle, besprinkle, dapple, dot, dust, mark, mottle, speckle, spot, stipple, streak, variegate **2.** *noun* dot, mark, pinpoint, speck, speckle, spot, streak

fledgling **1.** chick, nestling **2.** apprentice, beginner, learner, neophyte, newcomer, novice, rookie (*informal*), trainee, tyro

flee abscond, avoid, beat a hasty retreat, bolt, cut and run (*informal*), decamp, depart, do a runner (*slang*), escape, fly, fly the coop (*U.S. & Canad. informal*), get away, hook it (*slang*), leave, make a quick exit, make off, make oneself scarce (*informal*), make one's escape, make one's getaway, run away, scarper (*Brit. slang*), shun, skedaddle (*informal*), slope off, split (*slang*), take a powder (*U.S. & Canad. slang*), take flight, take it on the lam (*U.S. & Canad. slang*), take off (*informal*), take to one's heels, turn tail, vanish

fleece **1.** *figurative* bleed (*informal*), cheat, con (*informal*), cozen, defraud, despoil, diddle (*informal*), mulct, overcharge, plunder, rifle, rip off (*slang*), rob, rook (*slang*), sell a pup, skin (*slang*), soak (*U.S. & Canad. slang*), steal, stiff (*slang*), swindle, take for a ride (*informal*), take to the cleaners (*slang*) **2.** clip, shear

fleecy downy, fluffy, shaggy, soft, woolly

fleet[1] *noun* argosy, armada, flotilla, naval force, navy, sea power, squadron, task force, vessels, warships

fleet[2] *adjective* fast, flying, mercurial, meteoric, nimble, nimble-footed, quick, rapid, speedy, swift, winged

fleeting brief, ephemeral, evanescent, flitting, flying, fugacious, fugitive, here today, gone tomorrow, momentary, passing, short, short-lived, temporary, transient, transitory

Antonyms abiding, continuing, durable, enduring, eternal, imperishable, lasting, long-lasting, long-lived, permanent

fleetness celerity, lightning speed, nimble-footedness, nimbleness, quickness, rapidity, speed, speediness, swiftness, velocity

flesh **1.** beef (*informal*), body, brawn, fat, fatness, food, meat, tissue, weight **2.** animality, body, carnality, flesh and blood, human nature, physicality, physical nature, sensuality **3.** homo sapiens, humankind, human race, living creatures, man, mankind, mortality, people, race, stock, world **4. one's own flesh and blood** blood, family, kin, kindred, kinsfolk, kith and kin, relations, relatives

Related adjective: carnal

I saw him even now going the way of all flesh
John Webster & Thomas Dekker *Westward Ho*

The spirit indeed is willing, but the flesh is weak
Bible: St. Matthew

fleshiness chubbiness, corpulence, flabbiness, heaviness, obesity, plumpness, stoutness

fleshly **1.** animal, bodily, carnal, erotic, lascivious, lecherous, lustful, sensual **2.** corporal, corporeal, earthly, human, material, mundane, of this world, physical, secular, terrestrial, worldly

fleshy ample, beefy (*informal*), brawny, chubby, chunky, corpulent, fat, hefty, meaty, obese, overweight, plump, podgy, stout, tubby, well-padded

flex *verb* angle, bend, contract, crook, curve, tighten

flexibility adaptability, adjustability, complaisance, elasticity, give (*informal*), pliability, pliancy, resilience, springiness, tensility

flexible 1. bendable, ductile, elastic, limber, lissom(e), lithe, mouldable, plastic, pliable, pliant, springy, stretchy, supple, tensile, whippy, willowy, yielding 2. adaptable, adjustable, discretionary, open, variable 3. amenable, biddable, complaisant, compliant, docile, gentle, manageable, responsive, tractable
Antonyms absolute, determined, fixed, immovable, inexorable, inflexible, intractable, obdurate, rigid, staunch, stiff, tough, unyielding

flick *verb* 1. dab, fillip, flip, hit, jab, peck, rap, strike, tap, touch 2. *with* **through** browse, flip, glance, skim, skip, thumb *~noun* 3. fillip, flip, jab, peck, rap, tap, touch

flicker *verb* 1. flare, flash, glimmer, gutter, shimmer, sparkle, twinkle 2. flutter, quiver, vibrate, waver *~noun* 3. flare, flash, gleam, glimmer, spark 4. atom, breath, drop, glimmer, iota, spark, trace, vestige

flickering fitful, guttering, twinkling, unsteady, wavering

flier, flyer 1. goer, racer, runner, scorcher (*informal*), speed demon *or* merchant (*informal*), sprinter 2. advert (*Brit. informal*), bill, booklet, circular, handbill, handout, leaf, leaflet, literature (*informal*), notice, pamphlet, promotional material, publicity material, release, throwaway (*U.S.*) 3. aeronaut, airman *or* airwoman, aviator *or* aviatrix, pilot 4. bound, flying *or* running jump, hurdle, jeté, jump, leap, spring, vault

flight[1] *noun* 1. flying, mounting, soaring, winging 2. *of air travel* journey, trip, voyage 3. aerial navigation, aeronautics, air transport, aviation, flying 4. cloud, flock, formation, squadron, swarm, unit, wing

Aviation terms
see AVIATION

flight[2] *noun* 1. departure, escape, exit, exodus, fleeing, getaway, retreat, running away 2. **put to flight** chase off, disperse, drive off, rout, scare off, scatter, send packing, stampede 3. **take (to) flight** abscond, beat a retreat, bolt, decamp, do a bunk (*Brit. slang*), do a runner (*slang*), flee, fly the coop (*U.S. & Canad. informal*), light out (*informal*), make a hasty retreat, run away *or* off, skedaddle (*informal*), take a powder (*U.S. & Canad. slang*), take it on the lam (*U.S. & Canad. slang*), turn tail, withdraw hastily

flightiness capriciousness, fickleness, flippancy, frivolity, giddiness, irresponsibility, levity, lightness, mercurialness, volatility

flighty capricious, changeable, dizzy, fickle, frivolous, giddy, harebrained, impetuous, impulsive, irresponsible, light-headed, mercurial, scatterbrained, skittish, thoughtless, unbalanced, unstable, unsteady, volatile, wild

flimsy 1. delicate, fragile, frail, gimcrack, insubstantial, makeshift, rickety, shaky, shallow, slight, superficial, unsubstantial 2. chiffon, gauzy, gossamer, light, sheer, thin, transparent 3. feeble, frivolous, implausible, inadequate, pathetic, poor, thin, transparent, trivial, unconvincing, unsatisfactory, weak
Antonyms durable, heavy, robust, serious, solid, sound, stout, strong, sturdy, substantial

flinch back off, baulk, blench, cower, cringe, draw back, duck, flee, quail, recoil, retreat, shirk, shrink, shy away, start, swerve, wince, withdraw

fling *verb* 1. cast, catapult, chuck (*informal*), heave, hurl, jerk, let fly, lob (*informal*), pitch, precipitate, propel, send, shy, sling, throw, toss *~noun* 2. cast, lob, pitch, shot, throw, toss 3. bash, beano (*Brit. slang*), binge (*informal*), bit of fun, good time, hooley *or* hoolie (*chiefly Irish & N.Z.*), indulgence, party, rave (*Brit. slang*), rave-up (*Brit. slang*), spree 4. attempt, bash (*informal*), crack (*informal*), gamble, go (*informal*), shot (*informal*), stab (*informal*), trial, try, venture, whirl (*informal*)

flinty adamant, cruel, hard, hard-hearted, harsh, heartless, inflexible, obdurate, pitiless, steely, stern, stony, unfeeling, unmerciful, unyielding

flip *verb/noun* cast, flick, jerk, pitch, snap, spin, throw, toss, twist

flippancy cheek (*informal*), cheekiness, disrespectfulness, frivolity, impertinence, irreverence, levity, pertness, sauciness

flippant cheeky, disrespectful, flip (*informal*), frivolous, glib, impertinent, impudent, irreverent, offhand, pert, rude, saucy, superficial
Antonyms gracious, mannerly, polite, respectful, serious, sincere, solicitous, well-mannered

flirt *verb* 1. chat up (*informal*), coquet, dally, lead on, make advances, make eyes at, make sheep's eyes at, philander 2. *usually with* **with** consider, dabble in, entertain, expose oneself to, give a thought to, play with, toy with, trifle with *~noun* 3. coquette, heart-breaker, philanderer, tease, trifler, wanton

flirtation coquetry, dalliance, intrigue, philandering, teasing, toying, trifling

Merely innocent flirtation,
Not quite adultery, but adulteration
Lord Byron *Don Juan*

flirtatious amorous, arch, come-hither, come-on (*informal*), coquettish, coy, enticing, flirty, provocative, sportive, teasing

flirting amorous play, chatting up (*informal*), coquetry, dalliance, sport

flit dart, flash, fleet, flutter, fly, pass, skim, speed, whisk, wing

float *verb* **1.** be buoyant, be *or* lie on the surface, displace water, hang, hover, poise, rest on water, stay afloat **2.** bob, drift, glide, move gently, sail, slide, slip along **3.** get going, launch, promote, push off, set up
Antonyms (*senses 1 & 2*) dip, drown, founder, go down, settle, sink, submerge (*sense 3*) abolish, annul, cancel, dissolve, terminate

floating **1.** afloat, buoyant, buoyed up, nonsubmersible, ocean-going, sailing, swimming, unsinkable **2.** fluctuating, free, migratory, movable, unattached, uncommitted, unfixed, variable, wandering

flock *verb* **1.** collect, congregate, converge, crowd, gather, group, herd, huddle, mass, throng, troop *~noun* **2.** colony, drove, flight, gaggle, herd, skein **3.** assembly, bevy, collection, company, congregation, convoy, crowd, gathering, group, herd, host, mass, multitude, throng

flog **1.** beat, castigate, chastise, flagellate, flay, lambast(e), lash, scourge, thrash, trounce, whack, whip **2.** drive, oppress, overexert, overtax, overwork, punish, push, strain, tax

flogging beating, caning, flagellation, hiding (*informal*), horsewhipping, lashing, scourging, thrashing, trouncing, whipping

flood *verb* **1.** brim over, deluge, drown, immerse, inundate, overflow, pour over, submerge, swamp, teem **2.** engulf, flow, gush, overwhelm, rush, surge, swarm, sweep **3.** choke, fill, glut, oversupply, saturate *~noun* **4.** deluge, downpour, flash flood, freshet, inundation, overflow, spate, tide, torrent **5.** abundance, flow, glut, multitude, outpouring, profusion, rush, stream, torrent
Related adjective: fluvial

floor **1.** *noun* level, stage, storey, tier **2.** *verb, figurative* baffle, beat, bewilder, bowl over (*informal*), bring up short, confound, conquer, deck (*slang*), defeat, discomfit, disconcert, dumbfound, faze, knock down, nonplus, overthrow, perplex, prostrate, puzzle, stump, throw (*informal*)

flop *verb* **1.** collapse, dangle, droop, drop, fall, hang limply, sag, slump, topple, tumble **2.** *informal* bomb (*U.S. & Canad. slang*), close, come to nothing, come unstuck, fail, fall flat, fall short, fold (*informal*), founder, go belly-up (*slang*), go down like a lead balloon (*informal*), misfire *~noun* **3.** *informal* cockup (*Brit. slang*), debacle, disaster, failure, fiasco, loser, nonstarter, washout (*informal*)
Antonyms *verb* flourish, make a hit, make it (*informal*), prosper, succeed, triumph, work *~noun* hit, success, triumph

floppy baggy, droopy, flaccid, flapping, flip-flop, hanging, limp, loose, pendulous, sagging, soft

floral flower-patterned, flowery

florescence blooming, blossoming, development, flourishing, flowering, fruition, maturity

florid **1.** blowzy, flushed, high-coloured, high-complexioned, rubicund, ruddy **2.** baroque, busy, embellished, euphuistic, figurative, flamboyant, flowery, fussy, grandiloquent, high-flown, ornate, overelaborate
Antonyms anaemic, bare, bloodless, dull, pale, pallid, pasty, plain, unadorned, wan, washed out

flossy downy, feathery, fluffy, satiny, silky, soft

flotsam debris, detritus, jetsam, junk, odds and ends, sweepings, wreckage

flounce *verb* bounce, fling, jerk, spring, stamp, storm, throw, toss

flounder *verb* be in the dark, blunder, fumble, grope, muddle, plunge, struggle, stumble, thrash, toss, tumble, wallow

flourish *verb* **1.** bear fruit, be in one's prime, be successful, be vigorous, bloom, blossom, boom, burgeon, develop, do well, flower, get ahead, get on, go great guns (*slang*), go up in the world, grow, grow fat, increase, prosper, succeed, thrive **2.** brandish, display, flaunt, flutter, shake, sweep, swing, swish, twirl, vaunt, wag, wave, wield *~noun* **3.** brandishing, dash, display, fanfare, parade, shaking, show, showy gesture, twirling, wave **4.** curlicue, decoration, embellishment, ornamentation, plume, sweep
Antonyms decline, diminish, dwindle, fade, fail, grow less, pine, shrink, wane

flourishing blooming, burgeoning, doing well, going places, going strong, in the pink, in top form, lush, luxuriant, mushrooming, on a roll, on the up and up (*informal*), prospering, rampant, successful, thriving

flout defy, deride, gibe at, insult, jeer at, laugh in the face of, mock, outrage, ridicule, scoff at, scorn, scout (*archaic*), show contempt for, sneer at, spurn, take the piss out of (*taboo slang*), taunt, treat with disdain
Antonyms attend, esteem, heed, honour, mind, note, pay attention to, regard, respect, revere, value

flow *verb* **1.** circulate, course, glide, gush, move, pour, purl, ripple, roll, run, rush, slide, surge, sweep, swirl, whirl **2.** cascade, deluge, flood, inundate, issue, overflow, pour, run, run out, spew, spill, spurt, squirt, stream, teem, well forth **3.** arise, emanate, emerge, issue, pour, proceed, result, spring *~noun* **4.** course, current, drift, flood, flux, gush, issue, outflow, outpouring, spate, stream, tide, tideway, undertow **5.** abundance, deluge, effusion, emanation, outflow, outpouring, plenty, plethora, succession, train

flower *noun* **1.** bloom, blossom, efflorescence **2.** *figurative* best, choicest part, cream, *crème de*

la crème, elite, freshness, greatest *or* finest point, height, pick, vigour *~verb* **3.** bloom, blossom, blow, burgeon, effloresce, flourish, mature, open, unfold
Related adjective: floral

Flowers

acacia
acanthus
African violet
aloe
alyssum
amaranth
amaryllis
anemone
arbutus
asphodel
aspidistra
aster
aubrietia, aubrieta *or* aubretia
azalea
begonia
betony
bignonia
black-eyed Susan
bluebell
bog asphodel
bougainvillea
burdock
Busy Lizzie
buttercup
cactus
calendula
camellia
camomile *or* chamomile
cardinal flower
carnation
celandine
Christmas cactus
chrysanthemum
clematis
columbine
cornflower
cotoneaster
cowslip
crocus
cyclamen
daffodil
dahlia
daisy
dandelion
deadly nightshade
delphinium
digitalis
dog rose
edelweiss
eglantine
forget-me-not
foxglove
freesia
geranium
gilliflower *or* gillyflower
gladiolus
godetia
grape hyacinth
groundsel
guelder-rose
gypsophila
harebell
heartsease *or* heart's-ease
heliotrope
hellebore
hemlock
hibiscus
hollyhock
hyacinth
hydrangea
iris
jasmine
jonquil
larkspur
lavender
lily
lily of the valley
lobelia
London pride
lotus
love-in-idleness
love-lies-bleeding
lupin
magnolia
mallow
mandrake
marguerite
marigold
marjoram
meadowsweet
monkshood
Michaelmas daisy
morning-glory
narcissus
nasturtium
old man's beard
orchid
oxeye daisy
oxlip
oxtongue
pansy
passionflower
peony *or* paeony
petunia
phlox
pimpernel
pink
poppy
primrose
primula
ragged robin
ragweed
rose
saffron
samphire
saxifrage
scarlet pimpernel
snapdragon
snowdrop
speedwell
stock
sunflower
sweetbrier
sweet pea
sweet william
tiger lily
tulip
valerian
verbena
violet
wallflower
water lily
willowherb
wintergreen
wisteria
wood anemone
woodbine
yarrow
zinnia

'Tis the last rose of summer
Left blooming alone;
All her lovely companions
Are faded and gone
Thomas Moore *'Tis the last rose of Summer*

There is no 'Why' about the rose, it blossoms because it blossoms
It pays no heed to itself, and does not care whether it is seen
Angelus Silesius

O my love's like a red, red rose
Robert Burns *A Red, Red Rose*

flowering *adjective* abloom, blooming, blossoming, florescent, in bloom, in blossom, in flower, open, out, ready

flowery baroque, embellished, euphuistic, fancy, figurative, florid, high-flown, ornate, overwrought, rhetorical
Antonyms austere, bare, basic, modest, muted, plain, restrained, simple, spartan, unadorned, unembellished

flowing 1. falling, gushing, rolling, rushing, smooth, streaming, sweeping **2.** continuous, cursive, easy, fluent, smooth, unbroken, uninterrupted **3.** abounding, brimming over, flooded, full, overrun, prolific, rich, teeming

fluctuate alter, alternate, change, ebb and flow, go up and down, hesitate, oscillate, rise and fall, seesaw, shift, swing, undulate, vacillate, vary, veer, waver

fluctuation alternation, change, fickleness, inconstancy, instability, oscillation, shift, swing, unsteadiness, vacillation, variation, wavering

fluency articulateness, assurance, command, control, ease, facility, glibness, readiness, slickness, smoothness, volubility

fluent articulate, easy, effortless, facile, flowing, glib, natural, ready, smooth, smooth-spoken, voluble, well-versed
Antonyms faltering, halting, hesitant, hesi~

tating, inarticulate, stammering, stumbling, terse, tongue-tied

fluff 1. *noun* down, dust, dustball, fuzz, lint, nap, oose (*Scot.*), pile 2. *verb, informal* bungle, cock up (*Brit. slang*), foul up (*informal*), fuck up (*offensive taboo slang*), make a mess off, make a nonsense of, mess up (*informal*), muddle, screw up (*informal*), spoil

fluffy downy, feathery, fleecy, flossy, fuzzy, gossamer, silky, soft

fluid *adjective* 1. aqueous, flowing, in solution, liquefied, liquid, melted, molten, running, runny, watery 2. adaptable, adjustable, changeable, flexible, floating, fluctuating, in~ definite, mercurial, mobile, mutable, protean, shifting 3. easy, elegant, feline, flowing, graceful, sinuous, smooth ~*noun* 4. liquid, liq~ uor, solution

Antonyms *adjective* definite, firm, fixed, hard, immobile, immutable, rigid, set, solid

fluke accident, blessing, break, chance, chance occurrence, coincidence, fortuity, freak, lucky break, quirk, quirk of fate, serendipity, stroke, stroke of luck, windfall

fluky 1. accidental, coincidental, fortuitous, lucky 2. at the mercy of events, chancy, incal~ culable, uncertain, variable

flummox baffle, bamboozle (*informal*), bewil~ der, bring up short, defeat, fox, mystify, non~ plus, perplex, stump, stymie

flummoxed at a loss, at sea, baffled, bewil~ dered, foxed, mystified, nonplussed, stumped, stymied

flunk *informal verb* 1. be found lacking, be un~ successful, bust (*U.S. slang*), fail, fall short, flop (*informal*), founder, miss, not come up to scratch, not come up to the mark (*informal*), not make the grade (*informal*), plough (*Brit. slang*), screw up (*informal*), underachieve, underperform, wash out 2. *Also* **flunk out** be dismissed, be expelled, drop out (*informal*), go down ~*noun* 3. fail, failure, nonsuccess

Antonyms (*sense 1*) be successful, come up to scratch (*informal*), excel, get by *or* through, get pass marks, make it, make the grade, meet *or* satisfy requirements, pass, pass with flying colours, stand the test (*sense 2*) gradu~ ate, qualify

flunky 1. assistant, cohort (*chiefly U.S.*), drudge, hanger-on, menial, minion, slave, toady, tool, underling, yes man 2. footman, lackey, manservant, valet

flurry *noun* 1. *figurative* ado, agitation, bustle, commotion, disturbance, excitement, ferment, flap, fluster, flutter, furore, fuss, hurry, stir, to-do, tumult, whirl 2. flaw, gust, squall 3. burst, outbreak, spell, spurt ~*verb* 4. agitate, bewilder, bother, bustle, confuse, disconcert, disturb, faze, fluster, flutter, fuss, hassle (*in~ formal*), hurry, hustle, rattle (*informal*), ruffle, unnerve, unsettle, upset

flush[1] *verb* 1. blush, burn, colour, colour up, crimson, flame, glow, go as red as a beetroot, go red, redden, suffuse ~*noun* 2. bloom, blush, colour, freshness, glow, redness, rosiness ~*verb* 3. cleanse, douche, drench, eject, expel, flood, hose down, rinse out, swab, syringe, wash out

flush[2] *adjective* 1. even, flat, level, plane, square, true 2. abundant, affluent, full, gener~ ous, lavish, liberal, overflowing, prodigal 3. *informal* in funds, in the money (*informal*), moneyed, rich, rolling (*slang*), wealthy, well-heeled (*informal*), well-off, well-supplied ~*ad~ verb* 4. even with, hard against, in contact with, level with, squarely, touching

flush[3] *verb* discover, disturb, drive out, put to flight, rouse, start, uncover

flushed 1. blushing, burning, crimson, embar~ rassed, feverish, glowing, hot, red, rosy, rubi~ cund, ruddy 2. *often with* **with** ablaze, ani~ mated, aroused, elated, enthused, excited, ex~ hilarated, high (*informal*), inspired, intoxicat~ ed, thrilled

fluster 1. *verb* agitate, bother, bustle, confound, confuse, disturb, excite, flurry, hassle (*infor~ mal*), heat, hurry, make nervous, perturb, rattle (*informal*), ruffle, throw off balance, unnerve, upset 2. *noun* agitation, bustle, com~ motion, disturbance, dither (*chiefly Brit.*), flap (*informal*), flurry, flutter, furore, perturbation, ruffle, state (*informal*), turmoil

fluted channelled, corrugated, furrowed, grooved

flutter *verb* 1. agitate, bat, beat, flap, flicker, flit, flitter, fluctuate, hover, palpitate, quiver, ripple, ruffle, shiver, tremble, vibrate, waver ~*noun* 2. palpitation, quiver, quivering, shiver, shudder, tremble, tremor, twitching, vibration 3. agitation, commotion, confusion, dither (*chiefly Brit.*), excitement, flurry, fluster, per~ turbation, state (*informal*), state of nervous excitement, tremble, tumult

flux alteration, change, flow, fluctuation, fluid~ ity, instability, modification, motion, mutabil~ ity, mutation, transition, unrest

fly[1] *verb* 1. flit, flutter, hover, mount, sail, soar, take to the air, take wing, wing 2. aviate, be at the controls, control, manoeuvre, operate, pilot 3. display, flap, float, flutter, show, wave 4. elapse, flit, glide, pass, pass swiftly, roll on, run its course, slip away 5. barrel (along) (*in~ formal, chiefly U.S. & Canad.*), be off like a shot (*informal*), bolt, burn rubber (*informal*), career, dart, dash, hare (*Brit. informal*), has~ ten, hurry, race, rush, scamper, scoot, shoot, speed, sprint, tear, whiz (*informal*), zoom 6. abscond, avoid, beat a retreat, clear out (*in~

formal), cut and run (*informal*), decamp, disappear, do a runner (*slang*), escape, flee, fly the coop (*U.S. & Canad. informal*), get away, hasten away, hightail (*informal, chiefly U.S.*), light out (*informal*), make a getaway, make a quick exit, make one's escape, run, run for it, run from, show a clean pair of heels, shun, skedaddle (*informal*), take a powder (*U.S. & Canad. slang*), take flight, take it on the lam (*U.S. & Canad. slang*), take off, take to one's heels **7. fly off the handle** blow one's top, explode, flip one's lid (*slang*), fly into a rage, go ballistic (*slang, chiefly U.S.*), have a tantrum, hit *or* go through the roof (*informal*), let fly (*informal*), lose one's cool (*slang*), lose one's temper, wig out (*slang*) **8. let fly a.** burst forth, give free reign, keep nothing back, lash out, let (someone) have it, lose one's temper, tear into (*informal*), vent **b.** cast, chuck (*informal*), fire, fling, heave, hurl, hurtle, launch, let off, lob (*informal*), shoot, sling, throw *~noun* **9. fly in the ointment** difficulty, drawback, flaw, hitch, problem, rub, small problem, snag

fly² *adjective* astute, canny, careful, knowing, nobody's fool, not born yesterday, on the ball (*informal*), sharp, shrewd, smart, wide-awake

fly at assail, assault, attack, belabour, fall upon, get stuck into (*informal*), go for, go for the jugular, have a go at (*informal*), lay about, pitch into (*informal*), rush at

fly-by-night *adjective* **1.** cowboy (*informal*), dubious, questionable, shady, undependable, unreliable, untrustworthy **2.** brief, here today, gone tomorrow, impermanent, short-lived

flying *adjective* **1.** brief, fleeting, fugacious, hasty, hurried, rushed, short-lived, transitory **2.** express, fast, fleet, mercurial, mobile, rapid, speedy, winged **3.** airborne, flapping, floating, fluttering, gliding, hovering, in the air, soaring, streaming, volitant, waving, wind-borne, winging

foam 1. *noun* bubbles, froth, head, lather, spray, spume, suds **2.** *verb* boil, bubble, effervesce, fizz, froth, lather

foamy bubbly, foaming, frothy, lathery, spumescent, sudsy

fob off 1. appease, deceive, equivocate with, flannel (*Brit. informal*), give (someone) the run-around (*informal*), put off, stall **2.** dump, foist, get rid of, inflict, palm off, pass off, unload

focus *noun* **1.** bull's eye, centre, centre of activity, centre of attraction, core, cynosure, focal point, headquarters, heart, hub, meeting place, target **2. in focus** clear, distinct, sharp-edged, sharply defined **3. out of focus** blurred, fuzzy, ill-defined, indistinct, muzzy, unclear *~verb* **4.** aim, bring to bear, centre, concentrate, converge, direct, fix, join, meet, pinpoint, rivet, spotlight, zero in (*informal*), zoom in

fodder feed, food, foodstuff, forage, provender, rations, tack (*informal*), victuals, vittles (*obsolete or dialect*)

foe adversary, antagonist, enemy, foeman (*archaic*), opponent, rival
Antonyms ally, companion, comrade, confederate, friend, partner

fog *noun* **1.** gloom, miasma, mist, murk, murkiness, peasouper (*informal*), smog **2.** *figurative* blindness, confusion, daze, haze, mist, obscurity, perplexity, stupor, trance *~verb* **3.** becloud, bedim, befuddle, bewilder, blear, blind, cloud, confuse, darken, daze, dim, muddle, muddy the waters, obfuscate, obscure, perplex, stupefy **4.** cloud, mist over *or* up, steam up

foggy 1. blurred, brumous (*rare*), cloudy, dim, grey, hazy, indistinct, misty, murky, nebulous, obscure, smoggy, soupy, vaporous **2.** *figurative* befuddled, bewildered, clouded, cloudy, confused, dark, dazed, dim, indistinct, muddled, obscure, stupefied, stupid, unclear, vague
Antonyms accurate, alert, awake, bright, clear, decisive, distinct, lucid, palpable, sharp, shrewd, undimmed

fogy, fogey anachronism, antique (*informal*), back number (*informal*), dinosaur, dodo (*informal*), fossil (*informal*), fuddy-duddy (*informal*), relic, square (*informal*), stick-in-the-mud (*informal*)

foible defect, failing, fault, idiosyncrasy, imperfection, infirmity, peculiarity, quirk, weakness, weak point

foil¹ *verb* baffle, balk, check, checkmate, circumvent, cook (someone's) goose (*informal*), counter, defeat, disappoint, elude, frustrate, nip in the bud, nullify, outwit, put a spoke in (someone's) wheel (*Brit.*), stop, thwart

foil² *noun* antithesis, background, complement, contrast, setting

foist fob off, get rid of, impose, insert, insinuate, interpolate, introduce, palm off, pass off, put over, sneak in, unload

fold *verb* **1.** bend, crease, crumple, dog-ear, double, double over, gather, intertwine, overlap, pleat, tuck, turn under *~noun* **2.** bend, crease, double thickness, folded portion, furrow, knife-edge, layer, overlap, pleat, turn, wrinkle *~verb* **3.** do up, enclose, enfold, entwine, envelop, wrap, wrap up **4.** *informal* be ruined, close, collapse, crash, fail, go bankrupt, go belly-up (*slang*), go bust (*informal*), go by the board, go down like a lead balloon (*informal*), go to the wall, go under, shut down

folder binder, envelope, file, portfolio

folk clan, ethnic group, family, kin, kindred, people, race, tribe
There's nowt so queer as folk

follow **1.** come after, come next, step into the shoes of, succeed, supersede, supplant, take the place of **2.** chase, dog, hound, hunt, pursue, run after, shadow, stalk, tail (*informal*), track, trail **3.** accompany, attend, bring up the rear, come after, come *or* go with, escort, tag along, tread on the heels of **4.** act in accordance with, be guided by, comply, conform, give allegiance to, heed, mind, note, obey, observe, regard, toe the line, watch **5.** appreciate, catch, catch on (*informal*), comprehend, fathom, get, get the hang of (*informal*), get the picture, grasp, keep up with, realize, see, take in, understand **6.** arise, be consequent, develop, emanate, ensue, flow, issue, proceed, result, spring, supervene **7.** adopt, copy, emulate, imitate, live up to, pattern oneself upon, take a leaf out of someone's book, take as example **8.** be a devotee *or* supporter of, be devoted to, be interested in, cultivate, keep abreast of, support
Antonyms abandon, avoid, desert, disobey, elude, escape, flout, forsake, give up, guide, ignore, lead, precede, reject, renounce, shun, steer

follower **1.** adherent, admirer, apostle, backer, believer, cohort (*chiefly U.S.*), convert, devotee, disciple, fan, fancier, habitué, henchman, partisan, protagonist, pupil, representative, supporter, votary, worshipper **2.** attendant, companion, hanger-on, helper, henchman, lackey, minion, retainer (*History*), sidekick (*slang*)
Antonyms (*sense 1*) guru, leader, mentor, svengali, swami, teacher, tutor (*sense 2*) antagonist, contender, enemy, foe, opponent, rival

following **1.** *adjective* coming, consequent, consequential, ensuing, later, next, specified, subsequent, succeeding, successive **2.** *noun* audience, circle, clientele, coterie, entourage, fans, patronage, public, retinue, suite, support, supporters, train

follow through bring to a conclusion, complete, conclude, consummate, pursue, see through

follow up **1.** check out, find out about, investigate, look into, make inquiries, pursue, research **2.** consolidate, continue, make sure, reinforce

folly absurdity, bêtise (*rare*), daftness (*informal*), desipience, fatuity, foolishness, idiocy, imbecility, imprudence, indiscretion, irrationality, lunacy, madness, nonsense, preposterousness, rashness, recklessness, silliness, stupidity
Antonyms judgment, level-headedness, moderation, prudence, rationality, reason, sanity, sense, wisdom
As a dog returneth to his vomit, so a fool returneth to his folly
Bible: Proverbs

foment abet, agitate, arouse, brew, encourage, excite, fan the flames, foster, goad, incite, instigate, promote, provoke, quicken, raise, rouse, sow the seeds of, spur, stimulate, stir up, whip up

fomenter agitator, demagogue, firebrand, incendiary, inciter, instigator, rabble-rouser, stirrer (*informal*), troublemaker

fond **1.** *with* **of** addicted to, attached to, enamoured of, have a liking (fancy, taste, soft spot), for hooked on, into (*informal*), keen on, partial to, predisposed towards **2.** adoring, affectionate, amorous, caring, devoted, doting, indulgent, loving, tender, warm **3.** absurd, credulous, deluded, delusive, delusory, empty, foolish, indiscreet, naive, overoptimistic, vain
Antonyms (*senses 1 & 2*) aloof, austere, averse, disinterested, indifferent, rational, sensible, unaffectionate, unconcerned, undemonstrative

fondle caress, cuddle, dandle, pat, pet, stroke

fondly **1.** affectionately, dearly, indulgently, lovingly, possessively, tenderly, with affection **2.** credulously, foolishly, naively, stupidly, vainly

fondness **1.** attachment, fancy, liking, love, partiality, penchant, predilection, preference, soft spot, susceptibility, taste, weakness **2.** affection, attachment, devotion, kindness, love, tenderness
Antonyms antagonism, antipathy, aversion, coldness, contempt, dislike, enmity, harshness, hatred, hostility, loathing, repugnance, repulsion

food **1.** aliment, board, bread, chow (*informal*), comestibles, commons, cooking, cuisine, diet, eatables (*slang*), eats (*slang*), edibles, fare, feed, foodstuffs, grub (*slang*), larder, meat, menu, nosebag (*slang*), nosh (*slang*), nourishment, nutriment, nutrition, pabulum (*rare*), provender, provisions, rations, refreshment, scoff (*slang*), stores, subsistence, sustenance, table, tack (*informal*), tuck (*informal*), viands, victuals, vittles (*obsolete or dialect*) **2.** *Cattle, etc.* feed, fodder, forage, provender
Related noun: gastronomy

Savoury dishes

angels-on-horseback
baked beans
beef bourguinon *or* boeuf bourguignonne
beef stroganoff
blanquette de veau
brawn
bridie *or* Forfar bridie
bubble and squeak
Caesar salad
casserole
cassoulet
cauliflower cheese
cheeseburger

chicken Kiev
chilli con carne
chips
chow mein
clam chowder
cock-a-leekie *or* cockie-leekie
coddle
consommé
corn chowder
Cornish pasty
cottage pie
coulibiac *or* koulibiac
couscous
crêpe
Cullen skink
curry
dolmades
doner kebab
eggs Benedict
enchilada
fish and chips *or* *(Scot.)* fish supper
fish finger
French toast
fry *or* fry-up
galantine
game chips
gefilte fish *or* gefüllte fish
goulash
guacamole
haggis
hamburger
hominy grits *or* grits
hotpot
hummus, houmus *or* humous
jambalaya
jugged hare
Irish stew
kebab
kedgeree
keftedes
kishke
knish
kofta
kromesky
laksa
Lancashire hotpot
laver bread
lobster Newburg
lobster thermidor
macaroni cheese
madrilène
manicotti
matelote *or* matelotte
meat loaf
minestrone
mixed grill
mock turtle soup
moussaka
mulligatawny
nasi goreng
navarin
olla podrida
omelette *or (esp. U.S.)* omelet
open sandwich
osso bucco
paella
pakora
pastitsio
patty
pease pudding
pie
pilau, pilaf, pilaff, pi~lao *or* pilaw
pizza
ploughman's lunch
polenta
porridge
pot-au-feu
prairie oyster
quiche
quiche lorraine
Quorn (*Trademark*)
raita
ratatouille
red pudding
risotto
salad
salade niçoise
salmagundi *or* salma~gundy
salmi *or* salmis
samosa
sandwich
sashimi
sauerbraten
sauerkraut
sausage roll
scaloppine *or* scalop~pini
scampi
Scotch broth
Scotch egg
Scotch pie *or* mutton pie
scrambled eggs
shepherd's pie
skirlie
souvlakia
spanokopita
spring roll
steak-and-kidney pie
steak-and-kidney pudding
steak pie
steak tartare
sukiyaki
sushi
taco
tagine
tamale
taramasalata
teriyaki
toad-in-the-hole
toast
tofu
tomalley
tyropitta
tzatziki *or* tsatsiki
vichyssoise
Waldorf salad
white pudding
Yorkshire pudding

Types and cuts of meat

bacon
baron of beef
Bath chap
beef
beef-ham
black pudding
bockwurst
bratwurst
breast
brisket
cervelat
charqui
Chateaubriand
chicken
chipolata
chitterlings, chitlings *or* chitlins
chop
chorizo
chuck *or* chuck steak
chump
cold cuts
colonial goose
corned beef
crown roast
Cumberland sausage
cutlet
devon
duck
entrecôte
escalope
escargot
fillet
forehock
game
gammon
gigot
goose
gristle
ham
haslet
hogg *or* hogget
kidney
knackwurst *or* knock~wurst
lamb's fry
leg
lights
liver
liver sausage *or (esp. U.S.)* liverwurst
loin
Lorne sausage, square sausage *or* square slice (*Scot.*)
luncheon meat
mince
minute steak
mortadella
mutton
noisette
numbles (*archaic*)
offal
oxtail
oxtongue
Parma ham
parson's nose
pastrami
pepperoni
pheasant
pigeon
polony
pope's eye
pork
porterhouse steak
prosciutto
rack
rib
rolled lamb
round
rump
saddle
salami
salt pork
sausage
saveloy
schnitzel
scrag
shoulder
silverside
sirloin
skirt
Spam (*Trademark*)
sparerib
steak
stewing steak
sweetbread
T-bone
tenderloin
tongue
topside
tournedos

tripe
turkey
undercut
veal
venison

Seafood

abalone
anchovy
Balmain bug (*Austral.*)
barramundi
bass
blackfish
bloater
blue cod
bonito
bream
brill
butterfish
callop
carp
catfish
clam
coalfish *or* saithe
cockle
cod
codling
crab
crayfish *or* crawfish
dab
dogfish
dorado
Dover sole
Dublin Bay prawn
eel
flounder
gemfish
grayling
Greenland halibut
haddock
hake
halibut
herring
huss
jewfish
John Dory
kahawai *or* Australian salmon
kingfish
king prawn
kipper
langoustine
lemon sole
ling
lobster
lumpfish
mackerel
marron
megrim
monkfish
Moreton Bay bug (*Austral.*)
morwong
mullet
mulloway
mussel
nannygai
octopus
oyster
parrotfish
perch
pike
pilchard
pipi
plaice
pollack
pomfret
pout
prawn
queenie *or* queen scallop
rainbow trout
redfish
red snapper
roach
rockfish
salmon
sardine
scallop
sea cucumber
shad
shark
shrimp
sild
skate
skipjack tuna
snapper
snoek
snook
sockeye *or* red salmon
sole
sprat
squid
swordfish
tarakihi *or* terakihi
teraglin
tiger prawn
tilefish
trevally (*Austral. & N.Z.*)
trout
tuna *or* tunny
turbot
wahoo
whelk
whitebait
whiting
winkle
witch
wolffish
yabby *or* yabbie (*Austral.*)
yellow belly (*Austral.*)
zander

Types of curry

achari
balti
bhoona *or* bhuna
chasni
dhal
dhansak
dopiaza
green
jalfrezi
karahi
korma
madras
masala
mussalman
nentara
pasanda
pathia
phal
red
rogan josh
vindaloo

Desserts and sweet dishes

Atholl Brose *or* Athole Brose
baked Alaska
banana split
bavarois *or* Bavarian cream
Black Forest gateau
blancmange
bombe
bread and butter pudding
cabinet pudding
cassata
charlotte
charlotte russe
cheesecake
Christmas pudding
cobbler
college pudding
compote
coupe
cranachan
crème brûlée
crème caramel
crêpe
crêpe suzette
crumble
custard
death by chocolate
duff
dumpling
Easter-ledge pudding
Eve's pudding
flummery
fondant
fool
fruit salad *or* cocktail
gâteau
hasty pudding
ice cream
Île Flottante
jelly *or (U.S.)* jello
junket
knickerbocker glory
kulfi
marrons glacés
milk pudding
Mississippi mud pie
mousse
Neapolitan ice cream
nesselrode
parfait
pashka
pavlova *or (Austral. & N.Z. informal)* pav
peach melba
plum duff
plum pudding
queen of puddings
rice pudding
roly-poly
sabayon
sago
semolina
shoofly pie (*U.S.*)
shortcake
sorbet
sponge pudding
spotted dick
spumone *or* spumoni
steamed pudding
sundae
syllabub *or* sillabub
tapioca
tiramisu
torte
trifle
tutti-frutti
vacherin
water ice
whip
yogurt
zabaglione

Biscuits

abernethy
Bath Oliver
bourbon
brandy snap
captain's biscuit
caramel wafer
chocolate digestive
cookie (*chiefly U.S. & Canad.*)
cracker
cream cracker
crispbread
digestive
Empire biscuit
fairing
flapjack
Florentine
garibaldi
ginger nut *or* ginger snap
graham cracker (*U.S.*)
hardtack *or* ship's biscuit
Jaffa cake (*Trademark*)
langue de chat
lebkuchen
macaroon
matzo
oatcake
petit four
pretzel
ratafia
rich tea
shortbread
shortcake
soda biscuit
sweetmeal biscuit *or* digestive
Tararua (*N.Z.*)
tea biscuit
wafer
water biscuit

Cakes and pastries

angel cake *or* angel food cake
Bakewell tart
baklava
Banbury cake
Battenburg cake
black bun
Black forest gateau
brownie
carrot cake
cherry cake
chocolate cake
Christmas cake
coffee kiss
cream cake
cruller *or* kruller (*U.S. & Canad.*)
crumpet
cupcake
Danish pastry
devil's food cake
doughnut
Dundee cake
Eccles cake
eclair
fairy cake
flapjack
frangipane
fruitcake
fudge cake
gateau
Genoa cake
Genoese sponge
gingerbread
hot cross bun
johnny cake (*Austral.*)
jumble *or* jumbal
koeksister (*S. Afr.*)
kuchen
kuglehopf
ladyfinger *or* sponge finger
lamington (*Austral. & N.Z.*)
lardy cake
layer cake
Linzer torte
Madeira cake
madeleine
marble cake
millefeuille
muffin
parkin
petit four
pound cake
queencake
rock cake
rum baba
Sally Lunn
seedcake
Selkirk bannock
simnel cake
sponge cake
swiss roll
teabread
teacake
tipsy cake
torte
upside-down cake
Victoria sponge
wedding cake
yumyum (*Scot.*)

Herbs, spices and seasonings

allspice
aniseed
asafoetida *or* asafetida
basil
bayleaf
black pepper
borage
capers
caraway seed
cardamom
cayenne pepper
chervil
chilli
chive
cinnamon
clove
coconut
coconut milk
coriander
cress
cumin
curry powder
dill
fennel
fines herbes
five spice powder
galangal *or* galingale
garam masala
garlic
ginger
Kaffir lime leaf
lemon grass
mace
marjoram
mint
mustard
nam pla *or* fish sauce
nutmeg
oregano
paprika
parsley
peppercorn
poppy seed
red pepper
rosemary
saffron
sage
salt
savory
sesame seed
soy sauce, soya sauce, shoyu *or* tamari
star anise
sunflower seed
Szechuan, Szechwan *or* Sichuan peppercorns
tarragon
thyme
turmeric
white pepper

Sauces

apple
barbecue
Béarnaise
béchamel
black bean
bolognese *or* bolognaise
Bordelaise
brandy butter *or* hard sauce
bread
brown
chasseur
chaudfroid
cheese
chilli
chocolate
coulis
cranberry
cream
creole
cumberland
curry
custard
fudge
hoisin
hollandaise
ketchup
mayonnaise
Melba sauce
mint
mornay
mousseline
nam pla *or* fish sauce
orange
oyster
pesto
red pesto
remoulade
sabayon
salad cream
salsa
salsa verde
soubise
soy sauce, shoyu *or* tamari
suprême
sweet-and-sour
Tabasco (*Trademark*)
tartare
tomato
velouté
vinaigrette
white

wine
Worcester *or* Worcestershire

Breads

bagel *or* beigel
baguette
bannock (*Scot.*)
bap
barm cake (*dialect*)
barn-brack (*Irish*)
batch loaf
billy-bread (*N.Z.*)
black bread
bloomer
bridge roll
brioche
brown bread, loaf *or* roll
buttery (*Scot.*)
challah *or* hallah
chapati *or* chapatti
cob
coburg
corn bread, corn pone *or* Indian bread (*U.S.*)
cottage loaf
croissant
damper (*Austral.*)
farmhouse
focaccia
French bread
French stick
fruit loaf
Granary (*Trademark*)
gluten bread
half-quartern
long tin
matzo, matzoh, matza *or* matzah
muffin
naan *or* nan
pan bread *or* loaf (*Scot.*)
paratha
pitta
plain bread *or* loaf (*Scot.*)
plait
poppadom *or* poppadum
pumpernickel
puri
quartern
roll
roti
rye bread *or* rye
soda bread
sourdough
split tin
square tin
stollen
white bread, loaf *or* roll
wholemeal *or (esp. U.S. & Canad.)* whole-wheat

Types of pastry

choux pastry
filo pastry
flaky pastry
hot water pastry
pâte brisée
pâte feuilletée
pâte sucrée
puff pastry
shortcrust pastry
suet pastry

Types of pasta

agnolotti
bavette
bombolotti
bucatini
cannelloni
cappelletti
cellentani
conchiglie
ditali
farfalle
fettuccine, fettucine *or* fettucini
fusilli
gnocchetti
gnocchi
lasagne
lasagnette
linguini
lumache
macaroni *or* maccheroni
maultaschen
noodles
orecchiette
paglia e fieno
pappardelle
penne
pipe
ravioli
rigatoni
ruote
spaghetti
spätzle *or* spaetzle
taglioni
tagliatelle
tortellini
tortelloni
tortiglioni
vermicelli
zita *or* ziti

Cheeses

Bavarian blue
Bel Paese
Bleu d'Auvergne
Bleu de Bresse
blue cheese
Blue Shropshire
Blue Stilton
Blue Vinney *or* Blue Vinny
Bonchester
Brie
Caboc
caciocavallo
Caerphilly
Cambazolla
Camembert
canestrato
Cantal
Chaumes
Cheddar
Cheshire
chèvre
cottage cheese
cream cheese
crowdie
curd cheese
Danish blue
Derby
Dolcellate
Double Gloucester
Dunlop
Dunsyre Blue
Edam
Emmenthal *or* Emmental
Ermite
Esrom
feta
fontina
fromage frais
Gjetost
goats' cheese
Gorgonzola
Gouda
Gruyère
Havarti
Jarlsberg
Lanark Blue
Lancashire
Limburger
mascarpone
mousetrap
mozzarella
Monterey jack
muenster *or* münster
mycella
Neufchâtel
Oka
Parmesan
pecorino
Port-Salut
provolone
Reblochon
Red Leicester
Red Windsor
Ribblesdale
ricotta
Romano
Roquefort
Sage Derby
Saint Agur
Samsø
Stilton
Swiss cheese
Taleggio
Tornegus
Vacherin
vignotte
wensleydale
yarg

Vegetables

ackee
asparagus
aubergine *or* eggplant
baby corn
bean sprout
beef tomato
beetroot *or* beet
broccoli
Brussels sprout *or* sprout
cabbage
calabrese
calalu *or* calaloo
cardoon
carrot
cauliflower
celeriac
celery
chard
cherry tomato
chicory
Chinese cabbage
chive
choko
collard
corn on the cob
cos, cos lettuce *or (U.S. & Canad.)* romaine
courgette *or (U.S., Canad. & Austral.)* zucchini

cress
cucumber
endive
fennel
frisee
gherkin
globe artichoke
horseradish
iceberg lettuce
Jerusalem artichoke
kale *or* kail
kohlrabi
lamb's lettuce *or* corn salad
leek
lettuce
okra, lady's finger *or* bhindi
onion
pak-choi
parsnip
pea
pepper, capsicum *or* *(U.S.)* bell pepper
pimiento *or* pimento
potato
radicchio
radish
salsify *or* oyster plant
savoy cabbage
shallot
silver beet
sorrel
Spanish onion
spinach
spring greens
spring onion, salad onion, scallion *(chiefly U.S.)* *or* syboe *(Scot.)*
squash
swede
sweet corn *or* *(chiefly U.S.)* corn
sweet potato, batata *or* *(N.Z.)* kumera
turnip *or* *(dialect)* neep
vegetable marrow *or* marrow
yam

Potatoes

Arran Comet
Arran Pilot
Arran Victory
Belle de Fontenay
Cara
Catriona
Charlotte
Desiree
Estima
Golden Wonder
Jersey Royal
Kerr's Pink
King Edward
Marfona
Maris Bard
Maris Piper
Pentland Crown
Pentland Dell
Pentland Javelin
Pentland Squire
Pink Fir Apple
Romano
Roseval
Sharpe's Express
Ulster Specre
Wilja

Mushrooms and other edible fungi

black truffle
blewit
button mushroom
cep *or* porcini
champignon
chanterelle
horn of plenty
morel
oyster mushroom
puffball
shaggy ink cap *or* lawyer's wig
shiitake mushroom
straw mushroom
white truffle
wood ear mushroom

Pulses

adzuki bean *or* adsuki bean
black bean
black-eyed bean *or* *(U.S.)* black-eyed pea
bobby bean
borlotti bean
broad bean
butter bean
cannelini bean
chick pea *or* garbanzo
continental lentil
dhal
field bean
flageolet bean
French bean
ful medames
gram
green bean
green lentil
haricot bean *or* *(U.S.)* navy bean
kidney bean
lentil
lima bean
mangetout *or* snow pea
marrowfat pea
mung bean
petit pois
pigeon pea
pinto bean
puy lentil
red kidney bean *or* *(U.S.)* red bean
red lentil
runner bean
soya bean
split pea
string bean
sugar snap pea

Fruits

amarelle cherry
ananas
apple
apricot
avocado, avocado pear *or* *(U.S.)* alligator pear
babaco
banana
Bartlett pear
beach plum
berry
Beurre Hardy pear
bigarreau cherry
bilberry, blaeberry, huckleberry, whortleberry *or* *(Irish)* fraughan
blackberry *or* *(Scot.)* bramble
black cherry
blackcurrant
blackheart cherry
blood orange
blueberry
Bon Chretien pear
boxberry
boysenberry
breadfruit
calamondin
cantaloup *or* canta~loupe melon
carambola *or* star fruit
casaba *or* cassaba melon
Charentais melon
chayote
chempaduk
cherry
chokecherry
choko
citron
clementine
cloudberry *or* *(Canad.)* bakeapple
Conference pear
cranberry
custard apple
damson
date
dewberry
durian *or* durion
elderberry
fig
Galia melon
gooseberry *or* *(infor~mal)* goosegog
grape
grapefruit
greengage
guava
hackberry
heart cherry
honeydew melon
jackfruit *or* jack
Jaffa orange
kiwano *(Trademark)*
Kiwi fruit *or* Chinese gooseberry
kumquat *or* cumquat
lemon
lime
lychee, litchi, lichee *or* lichi
loganberry
longan
loquat *or* Japan plum
mandarin
mango
mangosteen
May apple
medlar
melon
minneola
morello cherry
mulberry
muskmelon
nashi *or* Asian pear
navel orange
nectarine
Ogen melon
olive
orange
ortanique
papaw *or* pawpaw

papaya
passion fruit *or* granadilla
peach
pear
pepper
physalis, Cape gooseberry *or* strawberry tomato
pineapple
plantain
plum
pomegranate
pomelo *or* shaddock
prickly pear
prune
pumpkin
Queensland blue
quince
raisin
rambutan
raspberry
redcurrant
rockmelon
salmonberry
sapota
sapodilla, sapodilla plum *or* naseberry
saskatoon
satsuma
Seville orange
serviceberry
sharon fruit *or* persimmon
sloe
snowberry
sour cherry
sour gourd
soursop
star-apple
strawberry
sultana
sweet cherry
sweetie
sweetsop
tamarillo *or* tree tomato
tamarind
tangelo
tangerine *or (S. African)* naartje
tayberry
tomato *or (archaic)* love apple
Ugli (*Trademark*)
victoria *or* victoria plum
watermelon
white currant
Williams pear
winter melon
youngberry

Apples
biffin (*Brit.*)
Blenheim Orange
Braeburn
bramley
Charles Ross
codlin *or* codling
costard
Cox's orange pippin
crab apple
Discovery
Egremont Russet
Elstar
Empire
Fuji
Golden Delicious
Granny Smith
Greensleeves
Grenadier
Idared
James Grieve
Jonathon
Jonagold
Laxton Superb
Lobo
Lord Lambourne
pippin
Prince Albert
Red Delicious
Red Ellison
Rosemary Russet
Royal Gala
russet
Spartan
sturmer
sunset
sweeting
Worcester Pearmain

Nuts
almond
beech nut
brazil nut
cashew
chestnut
chinquapin, chincapin *or* chinkapin
earthnut *or* pignut
hazelnut, filbert, cobnut *or* cob
macadamia nut
marron
peanut, monkey nut, groundnut *or* goober
pine nut *or* pine kernel
pecan
pistachio
walnut

Types of meal
see MEAL

Specific eating habits
see EAT

A cucumber should be well sliced, and dressed with pepper and vinegar, and then thrown out, as good for nothing
Dr. Johnson

We lived for days on nothing but food and water
W.C. Fields

Food first, then morals
Bertolt Brecht *The Threepenny Opera*

Tell me what you eat and I will tell you what you are
Anthelme Brillat-Savarin *Physiologie du Gout*

The discovery of a new dish does more for the happiness of man than the discovery of a star
Anthelme Brillat-Savarin

After a good dinner one can forgive anybody, even one's own relatives
Oscar Wilde

There is no love sincerer than the love of food
George Bernard Shaw *Man and Superman*

On the Continent people have good food; in England people have good table manners
George Mikes *How to be an Alien*

Stands the church clock at ten to three?
And is there honey still for tea?
Rupert Brooke *Grantchester*

Dinner at the Huntercombes' possessed only two dramatic features - the wine was a farce and the food a tragedy
Anthony Powell *The Acceptance World*

The healsome porritch, chief of Scotia's food
Robert Burns *The Cotter's Saturday Night*

Fair fa' your honest, sonsie face,
Great chieftain o' the puddin'-race!
Robert Burns *To a Haggis*

Doubtless God could have made a better berry, but doubtless God never did
William Butler (on the strawberry)

mayonnaise: one of the sauces which serve the French in place of a state religion
Ambrose Bierce *The Devil's Dictionary*

milk's leap towards immortality
Clifford Fadiman (of cheese) *Any Number Can Play*

sauce: the one infallible sign of civilization and enlightenment. A people with no sauces has one thousand vices; a people with one sauce has only nine hundred and ninety-nine.For every sauce invented and accepted a vice is renounced and forgiven
Ambrose Bierce *The Devil's Dictionary*

If the people have no bread, let them eat cake
ascribed to Marie-Antoinette

Man shall not live by bread alone, but by every word that proceedeth out of the mouth of God
Bible: St. Matthew

Half a loaf is better than no bread

You cannot have your cake and eat it

What's sauce for the goose is sauce for the gander

An apple a day keeps the doctor away

foodie *bon vivant*, *bon viveur*, connoisseur, epicure, gastronome, gourmet

fool *noun* **1.** ass, berk (*Brit. slang*), bird-brain (*informal*), blockhead, bonehead (*slang*), charlie (*Brit. informal*), chump (*informal*), clodpate (*archaic*), clot (*Brit. informal*), coot, dickhead (*slang*), dickwit (*slang*), dimwit (*informal*), dipstick (*Brit. slang*), divvy (*Brit. slang*), dolt, dope (*informal*), dork (*slang*), dunce, dunderhead, dweeb (*U.S. slang*), fathead (*informal*), fuckwit (*taboo slang*), geek (*slang*), gobshite (*Irish taboo slang*), gonzo (*slang*), goose (*informal*), halfwit, idiot, ignoramus, illiterate, imbecile (*informal*), jackass, jerk (*slang, chiefly U.S. & Canad.*), lamebrain (*informal*), loon, mooncalf, moron, nerd *or* nurd (*slang*), nincompoop, ninny, nit (*informal*), nitwit (*informal*), numpty (*Scot. informal*), numskull *or* numbskull, oaf, pillock (*Brit. slang*), plank (*Brit. slang*), plonker (*slang*), prat (*slang*), prick (*slang*), sap (*slang*), schmuck (*U.S. slang*), silly, simpleton, twerp *or* twirp (*informal*), twit (*informal, chiefly Brit.*), wally (*slang*), weenie (*U.S. informal*) **2.** butt, chump (*informal*), dupe, easy mark (*informal*), fall guy (*informal*), greenhorn (*informal*), gull (*archaic*), laughing stock, mug (*Brit. slang*), stooge (*slang*), sucker (*slang*) **3.** buffoon, clown, comic, harlequin, jester, joculator *or (fem.)* joculatrix, merry-andrew, motley, pierrot, punchinello **4. act** *or* **play the fool** act the goat, act up, be silly, cavort, clown, cut capers, frolic, lark about (*informal*), mess about, piss about (*taboo slang*), piss around (*taboo slang*), play (silly) games, play the goat, show off (*informal*) ~*verb* **5.** bamboozle, beguile, bluff, cheat, con (*informal*), deceive, delude, dupe, gull (*archaic*), have (someone) on, hoax, hoodwink, kid (*informal*), make a fool of, mislead, play a trick on, pull a fast one on (*informal*), put one over on (*informal*), stiff (*slang*), take for a ride (*informal*), take in, trick **6.** act the fool, cut capers, feign, jest, joke, kid (*informal*), make believe, piss about (*taboo slang*), piss around (*taboo slang*), pretend, tease **7.** *with* **with, around with,** *or* **about with** fiddle (*informal*), meddle, mess, monkey, piss about (*taboo slang*), piss around (*taboo slang*), play, tamper, toy, trifle

Antonyms (*senses 1 & 2*) expert, genius, master, sage, savant, scholar, wise man

Who loves not woman, wine and song
Remains a fool his whole life long
attributed to Martin Luther

A sucker is born every minute
Phineas T. Barnum

A fool uttereth all his mind
Bible: Proverbs

Natur never makes enny blunders. When she makes a phool she means it
Josh Billings *Josh Billings' Wit and Humour*

A fool sees not the same tree that a wise man sees
William Blake *The Marriage of Heaven and Hell*

If the fool would persist in his folly he would become wise
William Blake *The Marriage of Heaven and Hell*

A knowledgeable fool is a greater fool than an ignorant fool
Molière *Les Femmes savantes*

Fools rush in where angels fear to tread

A fool and his money are soon parted

A fool at forty is a fool indeed

There's no fool like an old fool

Fools ask questions that wise men cannot answer

Fools build houses and wise men live in them

A fool may give a wise man counsel

fool around *or* **about** act the fool, dawdle, footle (*informal*), hang around, idle, kill time, lark, mess about, play about, play the fool, waste time

foolery antics, capers, carry-on (*informal, chiefly Brit.*), childishness, clowning, desipience, folly, fooling, horseplay, larks, mischief, monkey tricks (*informal*), nonsense, practical jokes, pranks, shenanigans (*informal*), silliness, tomfoolery

foolhardy adventurous, bold, hot-headed, impetuous, imprudent, incautious, irresponsible, madcap, precipitate, rash, reckless, temerarious, venturesome, venturous

Antonyms alert, careful, cautious, chary, circumspect, heedful, judicious, prudent, shrewd, solicitous, thoughtful, wary, watchful

fooling *noun* bluffing, buffoonery, clownishness, farce, joking, kidding (*informal*), mockery, nonsense, pretence, shamming, skylarking (*informal*), teasing, tricks, trifling

foolish 1. absurd, asinine, ill-advised, ill-considered, ill-judged, imprudent, inane, incautious, indiscreet, injudicious, nonsensical, senseless, short-sighted, silly, unintelligent, unreasonable, unwise **2.** as daft as a brush (*informal, chiefly Brit.*), braindead (*informal*), brainless, crackpot (*informal*), crazy, daft (*informal*), doltish, fatuous, goofy (*informal*), half-baked (*informal*), half-witted, harebrained, idiotic, imbecilic, inane, loopy (*informal*), ludicrous, mad, moronic, off one's head (*informal*), potty (*Brit. informal*), ridiculous,

senseless, silly, simple, stupid, weak, witless
Antonyms bright, cautious, clever, commonsensical, intelligent, judicious, prudent, rational, sagacious, sane, sensible, sharp, smart, sound, thoughtful, wise

foolishly absurdly, idiotically, ill-advisedly, imprudently, incautiously, indiscreetly, injudiciously, like a fool, mistakenly, shortsightedly, stupidly, unwisely, without due consideration

foolishness 1. absurdity, bêtise (*rare*), folly, idiocy, imprudence, inanity, indiscretion, irresponsibility, silliness, stupidity, weakness 2. bunk (*informal*), bunkum *or* buncombe (*chiefly U.S.*), carrying-on (*informal, chiefly Brit.*), claptrap (*informal*), foolery, nonsense, rigmarole, rubbish, trash

Mix a little foolishness with your prudence; it's good to be silly at the right moment
Horace *Odes*

foolproof certain, guaranteed, infallible, never-failing, safe, sure-fire (*informal*), unassailable, unbreakable

footing 1. basis, establishment, foot-hold, foundation, ground, groundwork, installation, settlement 2. condition, grade, position, rank, relations, relationship, standing, state, status, terms

footling fiddling, fussy, hairsplitting, immaterial, insignificant, irrelevant, minor, nickel-and-dime (*U.S. slang*), niggly, petty, pointless, silly, time-wasting, trifling, trivial, unimportant

footslog hike, hoof it (*slang*), march, plod, tramp, trudge, yomp (*slang*)

footstep 1. footfall, step, tread 2. footmark, footprint, trace, track

footwear footgear

fop beau, Beau Brummel, clotheshorse, coxcomb (*archaic*), dandy, exquisite (*obsolete*), fashion plate, macaroni (*obsolete*), peacock, popinjay, smoothie *or* smoothy (*slang*), swell

foppish coxcombical, dandified, dandyish, dapper, dressy (*informal*), finical, natty (*informal*), preening, prinking, spruce, vain

forage 1. *noun Cattle, etc.* feed, fodder, food, foodstuffs, provender 2. *verb* cast about, explore, hunt, look round, plunder, raid, ransack, rummage, scavenge, scour, scrounge (*informal*), search, seek

foray depredation, descent, incursion, inroad, invasion, irruption, raid, reconnaissance, sally, sortie, swoop

forbear abstain, avoid, cease, decline, desist, eschew, hold back, keep from, omit, pause, refrain, resist the temptation to, restrain oneself, stop, withhold

forbearance 1. indulgence, leniency, lenity, longanimity (*rare*), long-suffering, mildness, moderation, patience, resignation, restraint, self-control, temperance, tolerance 2. abstinence, avoidance, refraining
Antonyms anger, impatience, impetuosity, intolerance, irritability, shortness

forbearing clement, easy, forgiving, indulgent, lenient, long-suffering, merciful, mild, moderate, patient, tolerant

forbid ban, debar, disallow, exclude, hinder, inhibit, interdict, outlaw, preclude, prohibit, proscribe, rule out, veto
Antonyms allow, approve, authorize, bid, enable, endorse, grant, let, license, O.K. *or* okay (*informal*), order, permit, sanction

It is forbidden to forbid
French student graffiti

forbidden banned, outlawed, out of bounds, prohibited, proscribed, taboo, *verboten*, vetoed

Stolen fruit is sweet

forbidding 1. abhorrent, disagreeable, odious, offensive, off-putting (*Brit. informal*), repellent, repulsive 2. baleful, bodeful, daunting, foreboding, frightening, grim, hostile, menacing, ominous, sinister, threatening, unfriendly
Antonyms alluring, attractive, beguiling, enticing, inviting, magnetic, tempting, welcoming, winning

force *noun* 1. dynamism, energy, impact, impulse, life, might, momentum, muscle, potency, power, pressure, stimulus, strength, stress, vigour 2. arm-twisting (*informal*), coercion, compulsion, constraint, duress, enforcement, pressure, violence 3. bite, cogency, effect, effectiveness, efficacy, influence, persuasiveness, power, punch (*informal*), strength, validity, weight 4. drive, emphasis, fierceness, intensity, persistence, vehemence, vigour 5. army, battalion, body, corps, detachment, division, host, legion, patrol, regiment, squad, squadron, troop, unit 6. **in force** **a.** binding, current, effective, in operation, on the statute book, operative, valid, working **b.** all together, in full strength, in great numbers *~verb* 7. bring pressure to bear upon, coerce, compel, constrain, dragoon, drive, impel, impose, make, necessitate, obligate, oblige, overcome, press, press-gang, pressure, pressurize, put the screws on (*informal*), put the squeeze on (*informal*), railroad (*informal*), strong-arm (*informal*), twist (someone's) arm, urge 8. blast, break open, prise, propel, push, thrust, use violence on, wrench, wrest 9. drag, exact, extort, wring
Antonyms *noun* debility, enervation, feebleness, fragility, frailty, impotence, ineffectiveness, irresolution, powerlessness, weakness *~verb* coax, convince, induce, persuade, prevail, talk into

Force is not a remedy
John Bright
Who overcomes
By force, hath overcome but half his foe
John Milton *Paradise Lost*

forced 1. compulsory, conscripted, enforced, involuntary, mandatory, obligatory, slave, unwilling 2. affected, artificial, contrived, false, insincere, laboured, stiff, strained, unnatural, wooden
Antonyms easy, natural, simple, sincere, spontaneous, unforced, unpretending, voluntary

forceful cogent, compelling, convincing, dynamic, effective, persuasive, pithy, potent, powerful, telling, vigorous, weighty
Antonyms enervated, exhausted, faint, feeble, frail, powerless, spent, weak

forcible 1. active, cogent, compelling, effective, efficient, energetic, forceful, impressive, mighty, potent, powerful, strong, telling, valid, weighty 2. aggressive, armed, coercive, compulsory, drastic, violent

forcibly against one's will, by force, by main force, compulsorily, under compulsion, under protest, willy-nilly

forebear ancestor, father, forefather, forerunner, predecessor, progenitor

forebode augur, betoken, foreshadow, foreshow, foretell, foretoken, forewarn, indicate, portend, predict, presage, prognosticate, promise, vaticinate (*rare*), warn of

foreboding 1. anxiety, apprehension, apprehensiveness, chill, dread, fear, misgiving, premonition, presentiment 2. augury, foreshadowing, foretoken, omen, portent, prediction, presage, prognostication, sign, token, warning

forecast 1. *verb* anticipate, augur, calculate, divine, estimate, foresee, foretell, plan, predict, prognosticate, prophesy, vaticinate (*rare*) 2. *noun* anticipation, conjecture, foresight, forethought, guess, outlook, planning, prediction, prognosis, projection, prophecy

forefather ancestor, father, forebear, forerunner, predecessor, primogenitor, procreator, progenitor

forefront centre, fore, foreground, front, lead, prominence, spearhead, van, vanguard

forego *see* FORGO

foregoing above, antecedent, anterior, former, preceding, previous, prior

foreground centre, forefront, front, limelight, prominence

foreign 1. alien, beyond one's ken, borrowed, distant, exotic, external, imported, outlandish, outside, overseas, remote, strange, unfamiliar, unknown 2. extraneous, extrinsic, incongruous, irrelevant, unassimilable, uncharacteristic, unrelated
Antonyms applicable, characteristic, customary, domestic, familiar, intrinsic, native, pertinent, relevant, suited, well-known

foreigner alien, immigrant, incomer, newcomer, outlander, stranger

foreknowledge clairvoyance, foresight, forewarning, precognition, prescience, prevision, prior knowledge

foremost chief, first, front, headmost, highest, inaugural, initial, leading, paramount, preeminent, primary, prime, principal, supreme

forename Christian name, first name, given name

foreordain doom, fate, foredoom, prearrange, predestine, predetermine, preordain, reserve

forerunner 1. ancestor, announcer, envoy, forebear, foregoer, harbinger, herald, precursor, predecessor, progenitor, prototype 2. augury, foretoken, indication, omen, portent, premonition, prognostic, sign, token

foresee anticipate, divine, envisage, forebode, forecast, foretell, predict, prophesy, vaticinate (*rare*)

foreshadow adumbrate, augur, betoken, bode, forebode, imply, indicate, portend, predict, prefigure, presage, promise, prophesy, signal

foresight anticipation, care, caution, circumspection, far-sightedness, forethought, precaution, premeditation, preparedness, prescience, prevision (*rare*), provision, prudence
Antonyms carelessness, hindsight, imprudence, inconsideration, lack of foresight, neglect, retrospection, thoughtlessness, unpreparedness

forestall anticipate, balk, circumvent, frustrate, head off, hinder, intercept, nip in the bud, obviate, parry, preclude, prevent, provide against, thwart

forestry arboriculture, dendrology (*Botany*), silviculture, woodcraft, woodmanship

foretaste *noun* example, foretoken, indication, prelude, preview, sample, trailer, warning, whiff

foretell adumbrate, augur, bode, forebode, forecast, foreshadow, foreshow, forewarn, portend, predict, presage, prognosticate, prophesy, signify, soothsay, vaticinate (*rare*)

forethought anticipation, far-sightedness, foresight, precaution, providence, provision, prudence
Antonyms carelessness, imprudence, impulsiveness, inconsideration, neglect, unpreparedness

foretoken *verb* augur, forebode, foreshadow, foreshow, give notice of, give warning of, portend, presage, signify, warn of

forever 1. always, evermore, for all time, for good and all (*informal*), for keeps, in perpetuity, till Doomsday, till the cows come home (*informal*), till the end of time, world without end 2. all the time, constantly, continually, endlessly, eternally, everlastingly, incessantly, interminably, perpetually, unremittingly

forewarn admonish, advise, alert, apprise, caution, dissuade, give fair warning, put on guard, put on the qui vive, tip off

Forewarned is forearmed

foreword introduction, preamble, preface, preliminary, prolegomenon, prologue

forfeit 1. *noun* amercement (*obsolete*), damages, fine, forfeiture, loss, mulct, penalty 2. *verb* be deprived of, be stripped of, give up, lose, relinquish, renounce, say goodbye to, surrender

forfeiture confiscation, giving up, loss, relinquishment, sequestration (*Law*), surrender

forge *verb* 1. construct, contrive, create, devise, fabricate, fashion, form, frame, hammer out, invent, make, mould, shape, work 2. coin, copy, counterfeit, fake, falsify, feign, imitate

forged 1. beat out, cast, crafted, fashioned, formed, founded, framed, hammered out, minted, modelled, moulded, shaped, stamped, worked 2. artificial, bogus, copy, copycat (*informal*), counterfeit, duplicate, ersatz, fabricated, fake, false, falsified, fraudulent, imitation, mock, phony *or* phoney (*informal*), pretend, pseudo, quasi, reproduction, sham, simulated, synthetic, ungenuine, unoriginal
Antonyms (*sense 2*) actual, authentic, bona fide, *echt*, genuine, honest, kosher (*informal*), legitimate, original, real, true

forger coiner, counterfeiter, falsifier

forgery 1. coining, counterfeiting, falsification, fraudulence, fraudulent imitation 2. counterfeit, fake, falsification, imitation, phoney *or* phony (*informal*), sham

forget 1. consign to oblivion, dismiss from one's mind, let bygones be bygones, let slip from the memory 2. leave behind, lose sight of, omit, overlook
Antonyms bring to mind, mind, recall, recollect, remember, retain

an elephant never forgets

forgetful absent-minded, apt to forget, careless, dreamy, having a memory like a sieve, heedless, inattentive, lax, neglectful, negligent, oblivious, slapdash, slipshod, unmindful, vague
Antonyms attentive, careful, mindful, retentive, unforgetful, unforgetting

forgetfulness absent-mindedness, abstraction, carelessness, dreaminess, heedlessness, inattention, lapse of memory, laxity, laxness, oblivion, obliviousness, woolgathering

forgive absolve, accept (someone's) apology, acquit, bear no malice, condone, excuse, exonerate, let bygones be bygones, let off (*informal*), pardon, remit
Antonyms blame, censure, charge, condemn, find fault with, reproach, reprove

To err is human, to forgive, divine
Alexander Pope *An Essay on Criticism*

forgiveness absolution, acquittal, amnesty, condonation, exoneration, mercy, overlooking, pardon, remission

We read that we ought to forgive our enemies; but we do not read that we ought to forgive our friends
Cosimo de Medici

Always forgive your enemies; nothing annoys them so much
Oscar Wilde

God will forgive me; that is His business
Heinrich Heine

Father, forgive them; for they know not what they do
Bible: St. Luke

Resist not evil; but whosoever shall smite thee on thy right cheek, turn to him the other also
Bible: St. Matthew

Lord, how oft shall my brother sin against me, and I forgive him? till seven times? Jesus said unto him, I say not unto thee, Until seven times; but Until seventy times seven
Bible: St. Matthew

forgiving clement, compassionate, forbearing, humane, lenient, magnanimous, merciful, mild, soft-hearted, tolerant

forgo, forego abandon, abjure, cede, do without, give up, kick (*informal*), leave alone *or* out, relinquish, renounce, resign, sacrifice, say goodbye to, surrender, waive, yield

forgotten blotted out, buried, bygone, consigned to oblivion, gone (clean) out of one's mind, left behind *or* out, lost, obliterated, omitted, past, past recall, unremembered

fork *verb* bifurcate, branch, branch off, diverge, divide, go separate ways, part, split

forked angled, bifurcate(d), branched, branching, divided, pronged, split, tined, zigzag

forlorn abandoned, bereft, cheerless, comfortless, deserted, desolate, destitute, disconsolate, down in the dumps (*informal*), forgotten, forsaken, friendless, helpless, homeless, hopeless, lonely, lost, miserable, pathetic, pitiable, pitiful, unhappy, woebegone, wretched
Antonyms busy, cheerful, happy, hopeful, optimistic, thriving

form[1] *verb* 1. assemble, bring about, build, concoct, construct, contrive, create, devise, establish, fabricate, fashion, forge, found, invent, make, manufacture, model, mould, pro~

duce, put together, set up, shape, stamp **2**. arrange, combine, design, dispose, draw up, frame, organize, pattern, plan, think up **3**. accumulate, appear, become visible, come into being, crystallize, grow, materialize, rise, settle, show up (*informal*), take shape **4**. acquire, contract, cultivate, develop, get into (*informal*), pick up **5**. compose, comprise, constitute, make, make up, serve as **6**. bring up, discipline, educate, instruct, rear, school, teach, train

form[2] *noun* **1**. appearance, cast, configuration, construction, cut, fashion, formation, model, mould, pattern, shape, stamp, structure **2**. anatomy, being, body, build, figure, frame, outline, person, physique, shape, silhouette **3**. arrangement, character, description, design, guise, kind, manifestation, manner, method, mode, order, practice, semblance, sort, species, stamp, style, system, type, variety, way **4**. format, framework, harmony, order, orderliness, organization, plan, proportion, structure, symmetry **5**. condition, fettle, fitness, good condition, good spirits, health, shape, trim **6**. **off form** below par, not in the pink (*informal*), not up to the mark, out of condition, stale, under the weather (*informal*), unfit **7**. behaviour, ceremony, conduct, convention, custom, done thing, etiquette, formality, manners, procedure, protocol, ritual, rule **8**. application, document, paper, sheet **9**. class, grade, rank

formal **1**. approved, ceremonial, explicit, express, fixed, lawful, legal, methodical, official, prescribed, *pro forma*, regular, rigid, ritualistic, set, solemn, strict **2**. affected, aloof, ceremonious, conventional, correct, exact, precise, prim, punctilious, reserved, starched, stiff, unbending

Antonyms casual, easy-going, informal, laid-back (*informal*), relaxed, unceremonious, unofficial

formality **1**. ceremony, convention, conventionality, custom, form, gesture, matter of form, procedure, red tape, rite, ritual **2**. ceremoniousness, correctness, decorum, etiquette, politesse, protocol, p's and q's, punctilio

format appearance, arrangement, construction, form, layout, look, make-up, plan, style, type

formation **1**. accumulation, compilation, composition, constitution, crystallization, development, establishment, evolution, forming, generation, genesis, manufacture, organization, production **2**. arrangement, configuration, design, disposition, figure, grouping, pattern, rank, structure

formative **1**. impressionable, malleable, mouldable, pliant, sensitive, susceptible **2**. determinative, developmental, influential, moulding, shaping

former **1**. antecedent, anterior, *ci-devant*, earlier, erstwhile, ex-, late, one-time, previous, prior, quondam, whilom (*archaic*) **2**. ancient, bygone, departed, long ago, long gone, of yore, old, old-time, past **3**. above, aforementioned, aforesaid, first mentioned, foregoing, preceding

Antonyms coming, current, ensuing, following, future, latter, modern, present, present-day, subsequent, succeeding

formerly aforetime (*archaic*), already, at one time, before, heretofore, lately, once, previously

formidable **1**. appalling, baleful, dangerous, daunting, dismaying, dreadful, fearful, frightful, horrible, intimidating, menacing, shocking, terrifying, threatening **2**. arduous, challenging, colossal, difficult, mammoth, onerous, overwhelming, staggering, toilsome **3**. awesome, great, impressive, indomitable, mighty, powerful, puissant, redoubtable, terrific, tremendous

Antonyms cheering, comforting, easy, encouraging, genial, heartening, pleasant, reassuring

formless amorphous, disorganized, inchoate, incoherent, indefinite, nebulous, shapeless, unformed, vague

formula **1**. form of words, formulary, rite, ritual, rubric **2**. blueprint, method, modus operandi, precept, prescription, principle, procedure, recipe, rule, way

formulate **1**. codify, define, detail, express, frame, give form to, particularize, set down, specify, systematize **2**. coin, develop, devise, evolve, forge, invent, map out, originate, plan, work out

fornication **1**. adultery, extra-curricular sex (*informal*), extra-marital congress *or* relations *or* sex, infidelity, living in sin, pre-marital congress *or* relations *or* sex, unfaithfulness **2**. debauchery, dissipation, dissoluteness, easy virtue, free love, immodesty, immorality, impurity, incontinence, indecency, indelicacy, lasciviousness, lechery, libertinism, loose morals, looseness, promiscuity, salaciousness, shamelessness, sin, sleeping around, unchastity, uncleanness

forsake **1**. abandon, cast off, desert, disown, jettison, jilt, leave, leave in the lurch, quit, repudiate, strand, throw over **2**. abdicate, forgo, forswear, give up, have done with, kick (*informal*), relinquish, renounce, set aside, surrender, turn one's back on, yield

My God, my God, why hast thou forsaken me?
Bible: Psalm 22

forsaken abandoned, cast off, deserted, destitute, disowned, ditched, forlorn, friendless, ignored, isolated, jilted, left behind, left in the lurch, lonely, marooned, outcast, solitary, stranded

forswear 1. abandon, abjure, drop (*informal*), forgo, forsake, give up, renounce, swear off 2. deny, disavow, disclaim, disown, recant, re~ject, repudiate, retract 3. lie, perjure oneself, renege, swear falsely

fort 1. blockhouse, camp, castle, citadel, fast~ness, fortification, fortress, garrison, redoubt, station, stronghold 2. **hold the fort** carry on, keep things moving, keep things on an even keel, maintain the status quo, stand in, take over the reins

forte gift, long suit (*informal*), métier, special~ity, strength, strong point, talent
Antonyms Achilles heel, chink in one's ar~mour, defect, failing, imperfection, short~coming, weak point

forth ahead, away, forward, into the open, on~ward, out, out of concealment, outward

forthcoming 1. approaching, coming, expected, future, imminent, impending, prospective, up~coming 2. accessible, at hand, available, in evidence, obtainable, on tap (*informal*), ready 3. chatty, communicative, expansive, free, in~formative, open, sociable, talkative, unre~served

forthright above-board, blunt, candid, direct, downright, frank, open, outspoken, plain-spoken, straightforward, straight from the shoulder (*informal*), upfront (*informal*)
Antonyms dishonest, furtive, secret, secretive, sneaky, underhand, untruthful

forthwith at once, directly, immediately, in~stantly, quickly, right away, straightaway, *tout de suite*, without delay

fortification 1. bastion, bulwark, castle, citadel, defence, fastness, fort, fortress, keep, protec~tion, stronghold 2. embattlement, reinforce~ment, strengthening

fortify 1. augment, brace, buttress, embattle, garrison, protect, reinforce, secure, shore up, strengthen, support 2. brace, cheer, confirm, embolden, encourage, hearten, invigorate, re~assure, stiffen, strengthen, sustain
Antonyms debilitate, demoralize, dilute, dis~hearten, impair, reduce, sap the strength of, weaken

fortitude backbone, braveness, courage, daunt~lessness, determination, endurance, fearless~ness, firmness, grit, guts (*informal*), hardi~hood, intrepidity, patience, perseverance, pluck, resolution, staying power, stout~heartedness, strength, strength of mind, val~our

fortress castle, citadel, fastness, fort, redoubt, stronghold

fortuitous 1. accidental, arbitrary, casual, chance, contingent, incidental, random, un~foreseen, unplanned 2. fluky (*informal*), fortu~nate, happy, lucky, providential, serendipitous

fortunate 1. born with a silver spoon in one's mouth, bright, favoured, golden, happy, hav~ing a charmed life, in luck, jammy (*Brit. slang*), lucky, on a roll, prosperous, rosy, sit~ting pretty (*informal*), successful, well-off 2. advantageous, auspicious, convenient, encour~aging, expedient, favourable, felicitous, fortui~tous, helpful, opportune, profitable, promising, propitious, providential, timely
Antonyms disastrous, hapless, ill-fated, ill-starred, miserable, poor, unfortunate, unhap~py, unlucky, unsuccessful, wretched

fortunately by a happy chance, by good luck, happily, luckily, providentially

fortune 1. affluence, an arm and a leg (*infor~mal*), big bucks (*informal, chiefly U.S.*), big money, gold mine, megabucks (*U.S. & Canad. slang*), opulence, possessions, pretty penny (*informal*), property, prosperity, riches, tidy sum (*informal*), treasure, wad (*U.S. & Canad. slang*), wealth 2. accident, chance, contingen~cy, destiny, fate, fortuity, hap (*archaic*), haz~ard, kismet, luck, providence 3. *often plural* adventures, circumstances, destiny, doom, ex~pectation, experience(s), history, life, lot, por~tion, star, success 4. bomb (*Brit. slang*), bun~dle (*slang*), king's ransom, mint, packet (*slang*), pile (*informal*), wealth
Antonyms (*sense 1*) destitution, hardship, in~digence, penury, poverty, privation

Fortune, that favours fools
Ben Jonson *The Alchemist*

No woman can be a beauty without a fortune
George Farquhar *The Beaux' Stratagem*

The slings and arrows of outrageous fortune
William Shakespeare *Hamlet*

Base Fortune, now I see, that in thy wheel
There is a point, to which when men aspire,
They tumble headlong down
Christopher Marlowe *Edward II*

forum 1. agora (*in ancient Greece*), assemblage, assembly, body, caucus (*chiefly U.S. & Canad.*), colloquium, conclave, conference, congregation, congress, consistory (*in various Churches*), convention, convergence, convoca~tion, council, court, diet, ecclesia (*in Church use*), folkmoot (*in medieval England*), gather~ing, get-together (*informal*), meeting, moot, parliament, rally, seminar, senate, sympo~sium, synod, tribunal (*archaic or literary*) 2. agora (*in ancient Greece*), amphitheatre, arena, chamber, court, meeting place, plat~form, pulpit, rostrum, stage

forward *adjective* 1. advanced, advancing, ear~ly, forward-looking, onward, precocious, premature, progressive, well-developed 2. ad~vance, first, fore, foremost, front, head, lead~

ing **3.** assuming, bare-faced, bold, brash, brass-necked (*Brit. informal*), brazen, brazen-faced, cheeky, confident, familiar, fresh (*informal*), impertinent, impudent, overassertive, overweening, pert, presuming, presumptuous, pushy (*informal*), sassy (*U.S. informal*) ~*adverb* **4.** *Also* **forwards** ahead, forth, on, onward **5.** into consideration, into prominence, into the open, into view, out, to light, to the fore, to the surface ~*verb* **6.** advance, aid, assist, back, encourage, expedite, favour, foster, further, hasten, help, hurry, promote, speed, support **7.** *Commerce* dispatch, freight, post, route, send, send on, ship, transmit

Antonyms *adjective* backward, diffident, modest, regressive, retiring, shy ~*adverb* backward(s) ~*verb* bar, block, hinder, hold up, impede, obstruct, retard, thwart

forward-looking dynamic, enlightened, enterprising, go-ahead, go-getting (*informal*), liberal, modern, progressive, reforming

forwardness boldness, brashness, brazenness, cheek (*informal*), cheekiness, chutzpah (*U.S. & Canad. informal*), impertinence, impudence, overconfidence, pertness, presumption

fossilized **1.** dead, dead as a dodo, extinct, inflexible, ossified, petrified, prehistoric **2.** anachronistic, antediluvian, antiquated, archaistic, behind the times, *démodé*, obsolete, out of the ark (*informal*), passé, superannuated

foster **1.** cultivate, encourage, feed, foment, nurture, promote, stimulate, support, uphold **2.** bring up, mother, nurse, raise, rear, take care of **3.** accommodate, cherish, entertain, harbour, nourish, sustain

Antonyms combat, curb, curtail, hold out against, inhibit, oppose, resist, restrain, subdue, suppress, withstand

foul *adjective* **1.** contaminated, dirty, disgusting, fetid, filthy, grotty (*slang*), grungy (*slang, chiefly U.S.*), impure, loathsome, malodorous, mephitic, nasty, nauseating, noisome, offensive, olid, polluted, putrid, rank, repulsive, revolting, rotten, scuzzy (*slang, chiefly U.S.*), squalid, stinking, sullied, tainted, unclean, yucky *or* yukky (*slang*) **2.** abusive, blasphemous, blue, coarse, dirty, filthy, foul-mouthed, gross, indecent, lewd, low, obscene, profane, scatological, scurrilous, smutty, vulgar **3.** abhorrent, abominable, base, despicable, detestable, disgraceful, dishonourable, egregious, hateful, heinous, infamous, iniquitous, nefarious, notorious, offensive, scandalous, shameful, shitty (*taboo slang*), vicious, vile, wicked **4.** crooked, dirty, dishonest, fraudulent, inequitable, shady (*informal*), underhand, unfair, unjust, unscrupulous, unsportsmanlike **5.** bad, blustery, disagreeable, foggy, murky, rainy, rough, stormy, wet, wild ~*verb* **6.** begrime, besmear, besmirch, contaminate, defile, dirty, pollute, smear, smirch, soil, stain, sully, taint **7.** block, catch, choke, clog, ensnare, entangle, jam, snarl, twist

Antonyms *adjective* admirable, attractive, clean, clear, decent, fair, fragrant, fresh, pleasant, pure, respectable, spotless, undefiled ~*verb* clean, cleanse, clear, honour, purge, purify, sanitize

foul-mouthed abusive, blasphemous, coarse, Fescennine (*rare*), obscene, offensive, profane

foul play chicanery, corruption, crime, deception, dirty work, double-dealing, duplicity, fraud, perfidy, roguery, sharp practice, skulduggery, treachery, villainy

foul up bodge (*informal*), botch, bungle, cock up (*Brit. slang*), flub (*U.S. slang*), fuck up (*offensive taboo slang*), make a mess of, make a nonsense of, make a pig's ear of (*informal*), mismanage, muck up (*slang*), put a spanner in the works (*Brit. informal*), spoil

found **1.** bring into being, constitute, construct, create, endow, erect, establish, fix, inaugurate, institute, organize, originate, plant, raise, settle, set up, start **2.** base, bottom, build, ground, rest, root, sustain

foundation **1.** base, basis, bedrock, bottom, footing, groundwork, substructure, underpinning **2.** endowment, establishment, inauguration, institution, organization, setting up, settlement

founder[1] *noun* architect, author, beginner, benefactor, builder, constructor, designer, establisher, father, framer, generator, initiator, institutor, inventor, maker, organizer, originator, patriarch

founder[2] *verb* **1.** be lost, go down, go to the bottom, sink, submerge **2.** *figurative* abort, bite the dust, break down, collapse, come to grief, come to nothing, come unstuck, fail, fall by the wayside, fall through, go belly-up (*slang*), go down like a lead balloon (*informal*), miscarry, misfire **3.** collapse, fall, go lame, lurch, sprawl, stagger, stumble, trip

foundling orphan, outcast, stray, waif

fountain **1.** font, fount, jet, reservoir, spout, spray, spring, well **2.** *figurative* beginning, cause, commencement, derivation, fount, fountainhead, genesis, origin, rise, source, wellhead, wellspring

fountainhead *fons et origo*, fount, inspiration, mainspring, origin, source, spring, well, wellspring

foursquare **1.** *adverb* firmly, resolutely, squarely **2.** *adjective* firm, firmly-based, immovable, resolute, solid, steady, strong, unyielding

foxy artful, astute, canny, crafty, cunning, de~

vious, guileful, knowing, sharp, shrewd, sly, tricky, wily

foyer antechamber, anteroom, entrance hall, lobby, reception area, vestibule

fracas affray (*Law*), aggro (*slang*), *bagarre*, brawl, disturbance, donnybrook, fight, free-for-all (*informal*), melee *or* mêlée, quarrel, riot, row, rumpus, scrimmage, scuffle, shindig (*informal*), shindy (*informal*), skirmish, trouble, uproar

fraction **1.** cut, division, moiety, part, percentage, piece, portion, proportion, quota, ratio, section, sector, segment, share, slice, subdivision **2.** atom, bit, bite, chip, crumb, drop, flake, fragment, grain, granule, iota, jot, morsel, mote, particle, scrap, shard, shred, sliver, smithereen (*informal*), splinter, whit **3.** breaching, breaking, breakup, cleaving, cracking, dissection, division, fission, fracturing, fragmentation, rupture, segregation, separation, splintering, splitting

fractious awkward, captious, crabby, cross, fretful, froward (*archaic*), grouchy (*informal*), irritable, peevish, pettish, petulant, querulous, ratty (*Brit. & N.Z. informal*), recalcitrant, refractory, testy, tetchy, touchy, unruly
Antonyms affable, agreeable, amiable, biddable, complaisant, genial, good-natured, good-tempered, tractable

fracture **1.** *noun* breach, break, cleft, crack, fissure, gap, opening, rent, rift, rupture, schism, split **2.** *verb* break, crack, rupture, splinter, split

fragile breakable, brittle, dainty, delicate, feeble, fine, flimsy, frail, frangible, infirm, slight, weak
Antonyms durable, elastic, flexible, hardy, lasting, reliable, resilient, robust, strong, sturdy, tough

fragility brittleness, delicacy, feebleness, frailty, frangibility, infirmity, weakness

fragment **1.** *noun* bit, chip, fraction, morsel, oddment, part, particle, piece, portion, remnant, scrap, shiver, sliver **2.** *verb* break, break up, come apart, come to pieces, crumble, disintegrate, disunite, divide, shatter, shiver, splinter, split, split up
Antonyms *verb* bond, combine, compound, fuse, join together, link, marry, merge, synthesize, unify

fragmentary bitty, broken, disconnected, discrete, disjointed, incoherent, incomplete, partial, piecemeal, scattered, scrappy, sketchy, unsystematic

fragrance aroma, balm, bouquet, fragrancy, perfume, redolence, scent, smell, sweet odour
Antonyms effluvium, miasma, niff (*Brit. slang*), offensive smell, pong (*Brit. informal*), reek, smell, stink, whiff (*Brit. slang*)

fragrant ambrosial, aromatic, balmy, odoriferous, odorous, perfumed, redolent, sweet-scented, sweet-smelling
Antonyms fetid, foul-smelling, malodorous, niffy (*Brit. slang*), noisome, olid, pongy (*Brit. informal*), reeking, smelling, smelly, stinking

frail breakable, brittle, decrepit, delicate, feeble, flimsy, fragile, frangible, infirm, insubstantial, puny, slight, tender, unsound, vulnerable, weak, wispy
Antonyms hale, healthy, robust, sound, stalwart, strong, sturdy, substantial, tough, vigorous

frailty **1.** fallibility, feebleness, frailness, infirmity, peccability, puniness, susceptibility, weakness **2.** blemish, chink in one's armour, defect, deficiency, failing, fault, flaw, foible, imperfection, peccadillo, shortcoming, vice, weak point
Antonyms asset, fortitude, might, robustness, strength, strong point, virtue

frame *verb* **1.** assemble, build, constitute, construct, fabricate, fashion, forge, form, institute, invent, make, manufacture, model, mould, put together, set up **2.** block out, compose, conceive, concoct, contrive, cook up, devise, draft, draw up, form, formulate, hatch, map out, plan, shape, sketch **3.** case, enclose, mount, surround *~noun* **4.** casing, construction, fabric, form, framework, scheme, shell, structure, system **5.** anatomy, body, build, carcass, morphology, physique, skeleton **6.** mount, mounting, setting **7. frame of mind** attitude, disposition, fettle, humour, mood, outlook, spirit, state, temper

frame-up fabrication, fit-up (*slang*), put-up job, trumped-up charge

framework core, fabric, foundation, frame, frame of reference, groundwork, plan, schema, shell, skeleton, structure, the bare bones

franchise authorization, charter, exemption, freedom, immunity, prerogative, privilege, right, suffrage, vote

frank artless, blunt, candid, direct, downright, forthright, free, honest, ingenuous, open, outright, outspoken, plain, plain-spoken, round, sincere, straightforward, straight from the shoulder (*informal*), transparent, truthful, unconcealed, undisguised, unreserved, unrestricted, upfront (*informal*)
Antonyms artful, crafty, cunning, evasive, indirect, inscrutable, reserved, reticent, secretive, shifty, shy, underhand

frankly **1.** candidly, honestly, in truth, to be honest **2.** bluntly, directly, freely, openly, overtly, plainly, straight, straight from the shoulder, without reserve

frankness absence of reserve, bluntness, candour, forthrightness, ingenuousness, laying it on the line, openness, outspokenness, plain speaking, truthfulness

frantic at one's wits' end, at the end of one's tether, berserk, beside oneself, desperate, distracted, distraught, fraught (*informal*), frenetic, frenzied, furious, hectic, mad, overwrought, raging, raving, uptight (*informal*), wild

Antonyms calm, collected, composed, cool, laid-back, poised, self-possessed, together (*slang*), unfazed (*informal*), unruffled

fraternity association, brotherhood, camaraderie, circle, clan, club, companionship, company, comradeship, fellowship, guild, kinship, league, order, set, sodality, union

fraternize associate, concur, consort, cooperate, go around with, hang out (*informal*), hang with (*informal, chiefly U.S.*), hobnob, keep company, mingle, mix, socialize, sympathize, unite

Antonyms avoid, eschew, keep away from, shun, steer clear of

fraud **1.** artifice, canard, cheat, chicane, chicanery, craft, deceit, deception, double-dealing, duplicity, guile, hoax, humbug, imposture, scam (*slang*), sharp practice, spuriousness, sting (*informal*), stratagems, swindling, treachery, trickery **2.** bluffer, charlatan, cheat, counterfeit, double-dealer, fake, forgery, fraudster, grifter (*slang, chiefly U.S. & Canad.*), hoax, hoaxer, impostor, mountebank, phoney *or* phony (*informal*), pretender, quack, sham, swindler

Antonyms (*sense 1*) fairness, good faith, honesty, integrity, probity, rectitude, trustworthiness, virtue

fraudulent counterfeit, crafty, criminal, crooked (*informal*), deceitful, deceptive, dishonest, double-dealing, duplicitous, false, knavish, phoney *or* phony (*informal*), sham, spurious, swindling, treacherous

Antonyms above board, genuine, honest, honourable, lawful, principled, reputable, true, trustworthy, upright

fraught **1.** *with* **with** abounding, accompanied, attended, bristling, charged, filled, full, heavy, laden, replete, stuffed **2.** *informal* agitated, anxious, difficult, distracted, distressed, distressing, emotionally charged, emotive, hag-ridden, on tenterhooks, strung-up, tense, tricky, trying, uptight (*informal*), wired (*slang*)

fray¹ *noun* affray (*Law*), *bagarre*, battle, battle royal, brawl, broil, clash, combat, conflict, disturbance, donnybrook, fight, melee *or* mêlée, quarrel, riot, row, ruckus (*informal*), rumble (*U.S. & N.Z. slang*), rumpus, scrimmage, scuffle, set-to (*informal*), shindig (*informal*), shindy (*informal*), skirmish

fray² *verb* become threadbare, chafe, fret, rub, wear, wear away, wear thin

frayed frazzled, out at elbows, ragged, tattered, threadbare, worn

freak *noun* **1.** aberration, abnormality, abortion, anomaly, grotesque, malformation, monster, monstrosity, mutant, oddity, queer fish (*Brit. informal*), *rara avis*, sport (*Biology*), teratism, weirdo *or* weirdie (*informal*) **2.** caprice, crotchet, fad, fancy, folly, humour, irregularity, quirk, turn, twist, vagary, whim, whimsy **3.** *slang* addict, aficionado, buff (*informal*), devotee, enthusiast, fan, fanatic, fiend (*informal*), nut (*slang*) *~adjective* **4.** aberrant, abnormal, atypical, bizarre, erratic, exceptional, fluky (*informal*), fortuitous, odd, queer, unaccountable, unexpected, unforeseen, unparalleled, unpredictable, unusual

freakish **1.** arbitrary, capricious, changeable, erratic, fanciful, fitful, humorous, odd, unpredictable, vagarious (*rare*), wayward, whimsical **2.** aberrant, abnormal, fantastic, freaky (*slang*), grotesque, malformed, monstrous, odd, outlandish, *outré*, preternatural, strange, teratoid (*Biology*), unconventional, weird

freaky abnormal, bizarre, crazy, far-out (*slang*), freakish, odd, queer, rum (*Brit. slang*), strange, unconventional, weird, wild

free *adjective* **1.** buckshee (*Brit. slang*), complimentary, for free (*informal*), for nothing, free of charge, gratis, gratuitous, on the house, unpaid, without charge **2.** at large, at liberty, footloose, independent, liberated, loose, off the hook (*slang*), on the loose, uncommitted, unconstrained, unengaged, unfettered, unrestrained **3.** able, allowed, clear, disengaged, loose, open, permitted, unattached, unengaged, unhampered, unimpeded, unobstructed, unregulated, unrestricted, untrammelled **4.** *with* **of** above, beyond, deficient in, devoid of, exempt from, immune to, lacking (in), not liable to, safe from, sans (*archaic*), unaffected by, unencumbered by, untouched by, without **5.** autarchic, autonomous, democratic, emancipated, independent, self-governing, self-ruling, sovereign **6.** at leisure, available, empty, extra, idle, not tied down, spare, unemployed, uninhabited, unoccupied, unused, vacant **7.** casual, easy, familiar, forward, frank, free and easy, informal, laid-back (*informal*), lax, liberal, loose, natural, open, relaxed, spontaneous, unbidden, unceremonious, unconstrained, unforced, uninhibited **8.** big (*informal*), bounteous, bountiful, charitable, eager, generous, hospitable, lavish, liberal, munificent, open-handed, prodigal, unsparing, unstinting, willing **9.** **free and easy** casual, easy-going, informal, laid-back (*informal*), lax, lenient, liberal, relaxed, tolerant, unceremonious *~adverb* **10.** at no cost, for love, gratis, without charge **11.** abundantly, copiously, freely, idly, loosely *~verb* **12.** deliver, dis~

charge, disenthrall, emancipate, let go, let out, liberate, loose, manumit, release, set at liberty, set free, turn loose, unbridle, uncage, unchain, unfetter, unleash, untie **13.** clear, cut loose, deliver, disengage, disentangle, exempt, extricate, ransom, redeem, relieve, rescue, rid, unburden, undo, unshackle

Antonyms (*senses 2 & 3*) bound, captive, con~fined, dependent, fettered, immured, incarcer~ated, occupied, restrained, restricted, secured (*sense 7*) constrained, formal, official, stiff, unnatural (*sense 8*) close, mean, mingy (*infor~mal*), stingy, tight, ungenerous (*senses 12 & 13*) confine, imprison, incarcerate, inhibit, limit, restrain, restrict, straiten

I am condemned to be free
Jean-Paul Sartre *L'Être et le néant*

The thoughts of a prisoner - they're not free either. They keep returning to the same things
Alexander Solzhenitsyn *One Day in the Life of Ivan Denisovich*

The best things in life are free

There's no such thing as a free lunch

freebooter bandit, brigand, buccaneer, cateran (*Scot.*), highwayman, looter, marauder, pillag~er, pirate, plunderer, raider, reiver (*dialect*), robber, rover

freedom **1.** autonomy, deliverance, emancipa~tion, home rule, independence, liberty, manu~mission, release, self-government **2.** exemp~tion, immunity, impunity, privilege **3.** ability, a free hand, blank cheque, carte blanche, dis~cretion, elbowroom, facility, flexibility, free rein, latitude, leeway, licence, opportunity, play, power, range, scope **4.** abandon, candour, directness, ease, familiarity, frankness, infor~mality, ingenuousness, lack of restraint *or* re~serve, openness, unconstraint **5.** boldness, brazenness, disrespect, forwardness, imperti~nence, laxity, licence, overfamiliarity, pre~sumption

Antonyms bondage, captivity, caution, de~pendence, imprisonment, limitation, respect~fulness, restraint, restriction, servitude, slav~ery, thraldom

I disapprove of what you say, but I will defend to the death your right to say it
Voltaire

Freedom is always and exclusively freedom for the one who thinks differently
Rosa Luxemburg *Die Russische Revolution*

Man was born free, and everywhere he is in chains
Jean Jacques Rousseau *The Social Contract*

No human being, however great or powerful, was ever so free as a fish
John Ruskin *The Two Paths*

Man is a free agent; were it otherwise, the priests would not damn him
Voltaire *Philosophical Dictionary*

Perfect freedom is reserved for the man who lives by his own work and in that work does what he wants to do
R.G. Collingwood *Speculum Mentis*

Freedom is the freedom to say that two plus two make four. If that is granted, all else follows
George Orwell *Nineteen Eighty-Four*

free-for-all affray (*Law*), *bagarre*, brawl, donnybrook, dust-up (*informal*), fight, fracas, melee *or* mêlée, riot, row, scrimmage, shindig (*informal*), shindy (*informal*)

free hand *noun* authority, blank cheque, carte blanche, discretion, freedom, latitude, liberty, scope

freely **1.** of one's own accord, of one's own free will, spontaneously, voluntarily, willingly, without prompting **2.** candidly, frankly, open~ly, plainly, unreservedly, without reserve **3.** as you please, unchallenged, without let or hin~drance, without restraint **4.** abundantly, am~ply, bountifully, copiously, extravagantly, lav~ishly, liberally, like water, open-handedly, unstintingly, with a free hand **5.** cleanly, easily, loosely, readily, smoothly

freethinker agnostic, deist, doubter, infidel, sceptic, unbeliever

freewheel coast, drift, float, glide, relax one's efforts, rest on one's oars

freeze **1.** benumb, chill, congeal, glaciate, harden, ice over *or* up, stiffen **2.** fix, hold up, inhibit, peg, stop, suspend

freezing arctic, biting, bitter, chill, chilled, cold as ice, cutting, frost-bound, frosty, glacial, icy, numbing, parky (*Brit. informal*), penetrating, polar, raw, Siberian, wintry

freight *noun* **1.** carriage, conveyance, shipment, transportation **2.** bales, bulk, burden, cargo, consignment, contents, goods, haul, lading, load, merchandise, payload, tonnage

French Gallic

frenetic demented, distraught, excited, fanati~cal, frantic, frenzied, hyped up (*slang*), insane, mad, maniacal, obsessive, overwrought, un~balanced, wild

frenzied agitated, all het up (*informal*), con~vulsive, distracted, distraught, excited, fever~ish, frantic, frenetic, furious, hysterical, mad, maniacal, rabid, uncontrolled, wild

frenzy **1.** aberration, agitation, delirium, de~rangement, distraction, fury, hysteria, insan~ity, lunacy, madness, mania, paroxysm, pas~sion, rage, seizure, transport, turmoil **2.** bout, burst, convulsion, fit, outburst, paroxysm, spasm

Antonyms calm, collectedness, composure, coolness, sanity

frequency constancy, frequentness, periodicity, prevalence, recurrence, repetition

frequent[1] *adjective* common, constant, continual, customary, everyday, familiar, habitual, incessant, numerous, persistent, recurrent, recurring, reiterated, repeated, usual
Antonyms few, few and far between, infrequent, occasional, rare, scanty, sporadic

frequent[2] *verb* attend, be a regular customer of, be found at, hang out at (*informal*), haunt, patronize, resort, visit
Antonyms avoid, keep away, shun, spurn

frequenter client, fan, habitué, haunter, patron, regular, regular customer, regular visitor

frequently commonly, customarily, habitually, many a time, many times, much, not infrequently, oft (*archaic or poetic*), often, oftentimes (*archaic*), over and over again, repeatedly, thick and fast, very often
Antonyms hardly ever, infrequently, occasionally, once in a blue moon (*informal*), rarely, seldom

fresh **1**. different, ground-breaking, latest, left-field (*informal*), modern, modernistic, new, new-fangled, novel, original, recent, this season's, unconventional, unusual, up-to-date **2**. added, additional, auxiliary, extra, further, more, other, renewed, supplementary **3**. bracing, bright, brisk, clean, clear, cool, crisp, invigorating, pure, refreshing, spanking, sparkling, stiff, sweet, unpolluted **4**. alert, bouncing, bright, bright-eyed and bushy-tailed (*informal*), chipper (*informal*), energetic, full of beans (*informal*), full of vim and vigour (*informal*), invigorated, keen, like a new man, lively, refreshed, rested, restored, revived, sprightly, spry, vigorous, vital **5**. blooming, clear, fair, florid, glowing, good, hardy, healthy, rosy, ruddy, wholesome **6**. dewy, undimmed, unfaded, unwearied, unwithered, verdant, vivid, young **7**. artless, callow, green, inexperienced, natural, new, raw, uncultivated, untrained, untried, youthful **8**. crude, green, natural, raw, uncured, undried, unprocessed, unsalted **9**. *informal* bold, brazen, cheeky, disrespectful, familiar, flip (*informal*), forward, impudent, insolent, pert, presumptuous, sassy (*U.S. informal*), saucy, smart-alecky (*informal*)
Antonyms (*sense 1*) dull, old, ordinary, stereotyped, trite (*sense 3*) impure, musty, stale, warm (*sense 4*) exhausted, weary (*sense 5*) pallid, sickly (*sense 6*) old, weary (*sense 7*) experienced, old (*sense 8*) preserved, salted, tinned (*sense 9*) well-mannered

freshen **1**. enliven, freshen up, liven up, refresh, restore, revitalize, rouse, spruce up, titivate **2**. air, purify, ventilate

freshness **1**. innovativeness, inventiveness, newness, novelty, originality **2**. bloom, brightness, cleanness, clearness, dewiness, glow, shine, sparkle, vigour, wholesomeness

fret[1] *verb* **1**. affront, agonize, anguish, annoy, brood, chagrin, goad, grieve, harass, irritate, lose sleep over, provoke, ruffle, torment, upset *or* distress oneself, worry **2**. agitate, bother, distress, disturb, gall, irk, nag, nettle, peeve (*informal*), pique, rankle with, rile, trouble, vex

fret[2] *verb* abrade, chafe, erode, fray, gall, rub, wear, wear away

fretful captious, complaining, cross, crotchety (*informal*), edgy, fractious, irritable, out of sorts, peevish, petulant, querulous, ratty (*Brit. & N.Z. informal*), short-tempered, splenetic, testy, tetchy, touchy, uneasy

friable brittle, crisp, crumbly, powdery, pulverizable

friction **1**. abrasion, attrition, chafing, erosion, fretting, grating, irritation, rasping, resistance, rubbing, scraping, wearing away **2**. animosity, antagonism, bad blood, bad feeling, bickering, conflict, disagreement, discontent, discord, disharmony, dispute, dissension, hostility, incompatibility, opposition, resentment, rivalry, wrangling

friend **1**. Achates, alter ego, boon companion, bosom friend, buddy (*informal*), china (*Brit. slang*), chum (*informal*), cock (*Brit. informal*), companion, comrade, confidant, crony, familiar, homeboy (*slang, chiefly U.S.*), intimate, mate (*informal*), pal, partner, playmate, soul mate **2**. adherent, advocate, ally, associate, backer, benefactor, partisan, patron, protagonist, supporter, well-wisher
Antonyms adversary, antagonist, competitor, enemy, foe, opponent, rival

A friend should bear his friend's infirmities
William Shakespeare *Julius Caesar*

What is a friend? A single soul dwelling in two bodies
Aristotle

The belongings of friends are common
Aristotle

I count myself nothing else so happy
As in a soul remembering my good friends
William Shakespeare *Richard II*

True happiness
Consists not in the multitude of friends,
But in the worth and choice
Ben Jonson *Cynthia's Revels*

Friends are God's apology for relatives
Hugh Kingsmill

Old friends are the best. King James used to call for his old shoes; for they were easiest for his feet
John Seldon *Table Talk*

Old friends are the blessing of one's later years - half a word conveys one's meaning
Horace Walpole

When your friend holds you affectionately by both hands you are safe, for you can watch both his

Ambrose Bierce

Of two close friends, one is always the slave of the other

Mikhail Lermontov *A Hero of Our Time*

A friend in need is a friend indeed

friendless abandoned, alienated, all alone, alone, cut off, deserted, estranged, forlorn, forsaken, isolated, lonely, lonesome, ostracized, shunned, solitary, unattached, with no one to turn to, without a friend in the world, without ties

friendliness affability, amiability, companionability, congeniality, conviviality, geniality, kindliness, mateyness *or* matiness (*Brit. informal*), neighbourliness, open arms, sociability, warmth

friendly affable, affectionate, amiable, amicable, attached, attentive, auspicious, beneficial, benevolent, benign, buddy-buddy (*slang, chiefly U.S. & Canad.*), chummy (*informal*), close, clubby, companionable, comradely, conciliatory, confiding, convivial, cordial, familiar, favourable, fond, fraternal, genial, good, helpful, intimate, kind, kindly, matey *or* maty (*Brit. informal*), neighbourly, on good terms, on visiting terms, outgoing, palsy-walsy (*informal*), peaceable, propitious, receptive, sociable, sympathetic, thick (*informal*), welcoming, well-disposed

Antonyms antagonistic, belligerent, cold, contentious, distant, inauspicious, sinister, uncongenial, unfriendly

friendship affection, affinity, alliance, amity, attachment, benevolence, closeness, concord, familiarity, fondness, friendliness, good-fellowship, goodwill, harmony, intimacy, love, rapport, regard

Antonyms animosity, antagonism, antipathy, aversion, bad blood, conflict, enmity, hatred, hostility, resentment, strife, unfriendliness

The only reward of virtue is virtue; the only way to have a friend is to be one

Ralph Waldo Emerson *Essays*

Men seem to kick friendship around like a football, but it doesn't seem to crack. Women treat it as glass and it goes to pieces

Anne Morrow Lindburgh

friendship: a ship big enough to carry two in fair weather, but only one in foul

Ambrose Bierce *The Devil's Dictionary*

fright 1. alarm, apprehension, (blue) funk (*informal*), cold sweat, consternation, dismay, dread, fear, fear and trembling, horror, panic, quaking, scare, shock, terror, the shivers, trepidation 2. *informal* eyesore, frump, mess (*informal*), scarecrow, sight (*informal*)

Antonyms boldness, bravery, courage, pluck, valor

frighten affright (*archaic*), alarm, appal, cow, daunt, dismay, freeze one's blood, intimidate, make one's blood run cold, make one's hair stand on end (*informal*), make (someone) jump out of his skin (*informal*), petrify, put the wind up (someone) (*informal*), scare, scare (someone) stiff, scare the living daylights out of (someone) (*informal*), shock, startle, terrify, terrorize, throw into a fright, throw into a panic, unman, unnerve

Antonyms allay, assuage, calm, comfort, encourage, hearten, reassure, soothe

frightened abashed, affrighted (*archaic*), afraid, alarmed, cowed, dismayed, frozen, get the wind up, in a cold sweat, in a panic, in fear and trepidation, numb with fear, panicky, petrified, scared, scared shitless (*taboo slang*), scared stiff, shit-scared (*taboo slang*), startled, terrified, terrorized, terror-stricken, unnerved

frightening alarming, appalling, baleful, bloodcurdling, daunting, dismaying, dreadful, fearful, fearsome, hair-raising, horrifying, intimidating, menacing, scary (*informal*), shocking, spooky (*informal*), terrifying, unnerving

frightful 1. alarming, appalling, awful, dire, dread, dreadful, fearful, from hell (*informal*), ghastly, godawful (*slang*), grim, grisly, gruesome, harrowing, hellacious (*U.S. slang*), hideous, horrendous, horrible, horrid, lurid, macabre, petrifying, shocking, terrible, terrifying, traumatic, unnerving, unspeakable 2. annoying, awful, disagreeable, dreadful, extreme, great, insufferable, terrible, terrific, unpleasant

Antonyms attractive, beautiful, calming, lovely, moderate, nice, pleasant, slight, soothing

frigid 1. arctic, chill, cold, cool, frost-bound, frosty, frozen, gelid, glacial, hyperboreal, icy, Siberian, wintry 2. aloof, austere, cold as ice, cold-hearted, forbidding, formal, icy, lifeless, passionless, passive, repellent, rigid, stiff, unapproachable, unbending, unfeeling, unloving, unresponsive

Antonyms ardent, cordial, friendly, hospitable, hot, impassioned, passionate, responsive, sensual, stifling, sweltering, warm

frigidity aloofness, austerity, chill, cold-heartedness, coldness, frostiness, iciness, impassivity, lack of response, lifelessness, passivity, touch-me-not attitude, unapproachability, unresponsiveness, wintriness

frill *noun* flounce, furbelow, gathering, purfle, ruche, ruching, ruff, ruffle, tuck

frills additions, affectation(s), bells and whistles, bits and pieces, decoration(s), dressing up, embellishment(s), extras, fanciness, fandangles, finery, frilliness, frippery, fuss, gewgaws, icing on the cake, jazz (*slang*), mannerisms, nonsense, ornamentation, ostentation, superfluities, tomfoolery, trimmings

frilly fancy, flouncy, frothy, lacy, ruched, ruffled

fringe *noun* **1.** binding, border, edging, hem, tassel, trimming **2.** borderline, edge, limits, march, marches, margin, outskirts, perimeter, periphery *~adjective* **3.** unconventional, unofficial, unorthodox *~verb* **4.** border, edge, enclose, skirt, surround, trim

fringed befringed, bordered, edged, margined, outlined, overhung

frippery 1. fanciness, finery, flashiness, foppery, frilliness, frills, fussiness, gaudiness, glad rags (*informal*), meretriciousness, nonsense, ostentation, pretentiousness, showiness, tawdriness **2.** adornment, bauble, decoration, fandangle, gewgaw, icing on the cake, knick-knack, ornament, toy, trinket

frisk 1. bounce, caper, cavort, curvet, dance, frolic, gambol, hop, jump, play, prance, rollick, romp, skip, sport, trip **2.** *informal* check, inspect, run over, search, shake down (*U.S. slang*)

frisky bouncy, coltish, frolicsome, full of beans (*informal*), full of joie de vivre, high-spirited, in high spirits, kittenish, lively, ludic (*literary*), playful, rollicking, romping, spirited, sportive

Antonyms demure, dull, lacklustre, pensive, sedate, stodgy, stolid, wooden

fritter (away) dally away, dissipate, fool away, idle (away), misspend, run through, spend like water, squander, waste

frivolity childishness, desipience, flightiness, flippancy, flummery, folly, frivolousness, fun, gaiety, giddiness, jest, levity, light-heartedness, lightness, nonsense, puerility, shallowness, silliness, superficiality, trifling, triviality

Antonyms earnestness, gravity, humourlessness, importance, sedateness, seriousness, significance, soberness, sobriety

frivolous 1. childish, dizzy, empty-headed, flighty, flip (*informal*), flippant, foolish, giddy, idle, ill-considered, juvenile, light-minded, nonserious, puerile, silly, superficial **2.** extravagant, footling (*informal*), impractical, light, minor, nickel-and-dime (*U.S. slang*), niggling, paltry, peripheral, petty, pointless, shallow, trifling, trivial, unimportant

Antonyms earnest, important, mature, practical, responsible, sensible, serious, solemn, vital

frizzle crisp, fry, hiss, roast, scorch, sizzle, sputter

frizzy corrugated, crimped, crisp, frizzed, tight-curled, wiry

frolic *verb* **1.** caper, cavort, cut capers, frisk, gambol, lark, make merry, play, rollick, romp, sport *~noun* **2.** antic, blast (*U.S. slang*), escapade, gambado, gambol, game, lark, prank, revel, romp, spree **3.** amusement, drollery, fun, fun and games, gaiety, high jinks, merriment, skylarking (*informal*), sport

frolicsome coltish, frisky, full of beans (*informal*), gay, kittenish, lively, ludic (*literary*), merry, playful, rollicking, sportive, sprightly, wanton (*archaic*)

front *noun* **1.** anterior, exterior, façade, face, facing, foreground, forepart, frontage, obverse **2.** beginning, fore, forefront, front line, head, lead, top, van, vanguard **3.** air, appearance, aspect, bearing, countenance, demeanour, expression, exterior, face, manner, mien, show **4.** blind, cover, cover-up, disguise, façade, mask, pretext, show **5. in front** ahead, before, first, in advance, in the lead, in the van, leading, preceding, to the fore *~adjective* **6.** first, foremost, head, headmost, lead, leading, topmost *~verb* **7.** face (onto), look over *or* onto, overlook

Antonyms (*senses 1 & 2*) aft, back, back end, behind, hindmost, nethermost, rear

frontier borderland, borderline, bound, boundary, confines, edge, limit, marches, perimeter, verge

frost freeze, freeze-up, hoarfrost, Jack Frost, rime

frosty 1. chilly, cold, frozen, hoar (*rare*), ice-capped, icicled, icy, parky (*Brit. informal*), rimy, wintry **2.** cold as ice, discouraging, frigid, off-putting (*Brit. informal*), standoffish, unenthusiastic, unfriendly, unwelcoming

froth 1. *noun* bubbles, effervescence, foam, head, lather, scum, spume, suds **2.** *verb* bubble over, come to a head, effervesce, fizz, foam, lather

frothy 1. foaming, foamy, spumescent, spumous, spumy, sudsy **2.** *figurative* empty, frilly, frivolous, light, petty, slight, trifling, trivial, trumpery, unnecessary, unsubstantial, vain

frown 1. give a dirty look, glare, glower, knit one's brows, look daggers, lour *or* lower, scowl **2.** *with* **on** *or* **upon** disapprove of, discountenance, discourage, dislike, look askance at, not take kindly to, show disapproval *or* displeasure, take a dim view of, view with disfavour

frowsty close, fuggy, fusty, ill-smelling, musty, stale, stuffy

frowzy blowzy, dirty, draggletailed (*archaic*), frumpish, messy, slatternly, sloppy, slovenly, sluttish, ungroomed, unkempt, untidy, unwashed

frozen 1. arctic, chilled, chilled to the marrow, frigid, frosted, icebound, ice-cold, ice-covered, icy, numb 2. fixed, pegged (*of prices*), petrified, rooted, stock-still, stopped, suspended, turned to stone

frugal abstemious, careful, cheeseparing, economical, meagre, niggardly, parsimonious, penny-wise, provident, prudent, saving, sparing, thrifty

Antonyms excessive, extravagant, imprudent, lavish, luxurious, prodigal, profligate, spendthrift, wasteful

frugality carefulness, conservation, economizing, economy, good management, husbandry, moderation, providence, thrift, thriftiness

fruit 1. crop, harvest, produce, product, yield 2. advantage, benefit, consequence, effect, end result, outcome, profit, result, return, reward

Fruits
see FOOD

A good tree cannot bring forth evil fruit, neither can a corrupt tree bring forth good fruit
Bible: St. Matthew

He that would eat the fruit must climb the tree

fruitful 1. fecund, fertile, fructiferous 2. abundant, copious, flush, plenteous, plentiful, productive, profuse, prolific, rich, spawning 3. advantageous, beneficial, effective, gainful, productive, profitable, rewarding, successful, useful, well-spent, worthwhile

Antonyms barren, fruitless, futile, ineffectual, infertile, pointless, scarce, sterile, unfruitful, unproductive, useless, vain

fruition actualization, attainment, completion, consummation, enjoyment, fulfilment, materialization, maturation, maturity, perfection, realization, ripeness

fruitless abortive, barren, bootless, futile, idle, ineffectual, in vain, pointless, profitless, to no avail, to no effect, unavailing, unfruitful, unproductive, unprofitable, unprolific, unsuccessful, useless, vain

Antonyms abundant, effective, fecund, fertile, fruitful, productive, profitable, prolific, useful

fruity 1. full, mellow, resonant, rich 2. *informal* bawdy, blue, hot, indecent, indelicate, juicy, near the knuckle (*informal*), racy, ripe, risqué, salacious, sexy, smutty, spicy (*informal*), suggestive, titillating, vulgar

frumpish, frumpy badly-dressed, dated, dingy, dowdy, drab, dreary, frumpy, mumsy, out of date

frustrate 1. baffle, balk, block, check, circumvent, confront, counter, defeat, disappoint, foil, forestall, inhibit, neutralize, nullify, render null and void, stymie, thwart 2. depress, discourage, dishearten

Antonyms advance, cheer, encourage, endorse, forward, further, hearten, promote, satisfy, stimulate

frustrated carrying a chip on one's shoulder (*informal*), choked, disappointed, discontented, discouraged, disheartened, embittered, foiled, irked, resentful, sick as a parrot (*informal*)

frustration 1. blocking, circumvention, contravention, curbing, failure, foiling, nonfulfilment, nonsuccess, obstruction, thwarting 2. annoyance, disappointment, dissatisfaction, grievance, irritation, resentment, vexation

fuddled bevvied (*dialect*), blitzed (*slang*), blotto (*slang*), bombed (*slang*), Brahms and Liszt (*slang*), confused, drunk, flying (*slang*), inebriated, intoxicated, legless (*informal*), lit up (*slang*), muddled, muzzy, out of it (*slang*), out to it (*Austral. & N.Z. slang*), paralytic (*informal*), pissed (*taboo slang*), rat-arsed (*taboo slang*), smashed (*slang*), sozzled (*informal*), steamboats (*Scot. slang*), steaming (*slang*), stupefied, tipsy, wasted (*slang*), woozy (*informal*), wrecked (*slang*), zonked (*slang*)

fuddy-duddy *noun* back number (*informal*), conservative, dinosaur, dodo (*informal*), fossil, museum piece, (old) fogy, square (*informal*), stick-in-the-mud (*informal*), stuffed shirt (*informal*)

fudge *verb* avoid, cook (*slang*), dodge, equivocate, evade, fake, falsify, flannel (*Brit. informal*), hedge, misrepresent, patch up, shuffle, slant, stall

fuel 1. *noun, figurative* ammunition, encouragement, fodder, food, incitement, material, means, nourishment, provocation 2. *verb* charge, fan, feed, fire, incite, inflame, nourish, stoke up, sustain

fug fetidity, fetor, frowst, frowstiness, fustiness, reek, stale air, staleness, stink

fuggy airless, fetid, foul, frowsty, noisome, noxious, stale, stuffy, suffocating, unventilated

fugitive 1. *noun* deserter, escapee, refugee, runagate (*archaic*), runaway 2. *adjective* brief, ephemeral, evanescent, fleeing, fleeting, flitting, flying, fugacious, momentary, passing, short, short-lived, temporary, transient, transitory, unstable

fulfil accomplish, achieve, answer, bring to completion, carry out, complete, comply with, conclude, conform to, discharge, effect, execute, fill, finish, keep, meet, obey, observe, perfect, perform, realise, satisfy

Antonyms disappoint, dissatisfy, fail in, fail to meet, fall short of, neglect

fulfilment accomplishment, achievement, attainment, carrying out *or* through, completion, consummation, crowning, discharge, discharging, effecting, end, implementation, observance, perfection, realization

full 1. brimful, brimming, bursting at the seams, complete, entire, filled, gorged, intact, loaded, replete, sated, satiated, satisfied, saturated, stocked, sufficient 2. abundant, adequate, all-inclusive, ample, broad, comprehensive, copious, detailed, exhaustive, extensive, generous, maximum, plenary, plenteous, plentiful, thorough, unabridged 3. chock-a-block, chock-full, crammed, crowded, in use, jammed, occupied, packed, taken 4. clear, deep, distinct, loud, resonant, rich, rounded 5. baggy, balloonlike, buxom, capacious, curvaceous, large, loose, plump, puffy, rounded, voluminous, voluptuous 6. **in full** completely, in its entirety, in total, *in toto*, without exception 7. **to the full** completely, entirely, fully, thoroughly, to the utmost, without reservation
Antonyms abridged, blank, devoid, empty, exhausted, faint, incomplete, limited, partial, restricted, thin, tight, vacant, void

full-blooded ballsy (*taboo slang*), gutsy (*slang*), hearty, lusty, mettlesome, red-blooded, vigorous, virile

full-blown 1. advanced, complete, developed, entire, full, full-scale, full-sized, fully developed, fully fledged, fully formed, fully grown, progressed, total, whole 2. blossoming, flowering, full, in full bloom, opened out, unfolded
Antonyms (*sense 1*) dormant, latent, potential, undeveloped

full-bodied fruity, full-flavoured, heady, heavy, mellow, redolent, rich, strong, well-matured

full-grown adult, developed, full-fledged, grown-up, in one's prime, marriageable, mature, nubile, of age, ripe
Antonyms adolescent, green, premature, undeveloped, unfledged, unformed, unripe, untimely, young

fullness 1. abundance, adequateness, ampleness, copiousness, fill, glut, plenty, profusion, repletion, satiety, saturation, sufficiency 2. broadness, completeness, comprehensiveness, entirety, extensiveness, plenitude, totality, vastness, wealth, wholeness 3. clearness, loudness, resonance, richness, strength 4. curvaceousness, dilation, distension, enlargement, roundness, swelling, tumescence, voluptuousness

full-scale all-encompassing, all-out, comprehensive, exhaustive, extensive, full-dress, in-depth, major, proper, sweeping, thorough, thoroughgoing, wide-ranging

fully 1. absolutely, altogether, completely, entirely, every inch, from first to last, heart and soul, in all respects, intimately, lock, stock and barrel, one hundred per cent, perfectly, positively, thoroughly, totally, to the hilt, utterly, wholly 2. abundantly, adequately, amply, comprehensively, enough, plentifully, satisfactorily, sufficiently 3. at least, quite, without (any) exaggeration, without a word of a lie (*informal*)

fully-fledged experienced, mature, professional, proficient, qualified, senior, time-served, trained

fulminate animadvert upon, berate, blast, castigate, censure, criticize, curse, denounce, denunciate, excoriate, execrate, fume, inveigh against, lambast(e), protest against, put down, rage, rail against, reprobate, tear into (*informal*), thunder, upbraid, vilify, vituperate

fulmination condemnation, denunciation, diatribe, excoriation, invective, obloquy, philippic, reprobation, tirade

fulsome adulatory, cloying, excessive, extravagant, fawning, gross, icky (*informal*), immoderate, ingratiating, inordinate, insincere, nauseating, overdone, over the top, saccharine, sickening, smarmy (*Brit. informal*), sycophantic, unctuous

fumble 1. bumble, feel around, flounder, grope, paw (*informal*), scrabble 2. bodge (*informal*), botch, bungle, cock up (*Brit. slang*), fuck up (*offensive taboo slang*), make a hash of (*informal*), make a nonsense of, mess up, misfield, mishandle, mismanage, muff, spoil

fume *figurative* 1. *verb* blow a fuse (*slang, chiefly U.S.*), boil, chafe, champ at the bit (*informal*), crack up (*informal*), fly off the handle (*informal*), get hot under the collar (*informal*), get steamed up about (*slang*), go ballistic (*slang, chiefly U.S.*), go off the deep end (*informal*), go up the wall (*slang*), rage, rant, rave, see red (*informal*), seethe, smoulder, storm, wig out (*slang*) 2. *noun* agitation, dither (*chiefly Brit.*), fit, fret, fury, passion, rage, stew (*informal*), storm

fumes effluvium, exhalation, exhaust, gas, haze, miasma, pollution, reek, smog, smoke, stench, vapour

fumigate clean out *or* up, cleanse, disinfect, purify, sanitize, sterilize

fuming all steamed up (*slang*), angry, at boiling point (*informal*), choked, enraged, fit to be tied (*slang*), foaming at the mouth, in a rage, incensed, on the warpath (*informal*), raging, roused, seething, up in arms

fun *noun* 1. amusement, beer and skittles (*informal*), cheer, distraction, diversion, enjoyment, entertainment, frolic, gaiety, good time, high jinks, jollification, jollity, joy, junketing, living it up, merriment, merrymaking, mirth, pleasure, recreation, romp, sport, treat, whoopee (*informal*) 2. buffoonery, clowning, foolery, game, horseplay, jesting, jocularity, joking, nonsense, play, playfulness, skylarking (*informal*), sport, teasing, tomfoolery 3. **in** *or* **for fun** facetiously, for a joke, for a laugh, in jest, jokingly, light-heartedly, mischievously, play~

fully, roguishly, teasingly, tongue in cheek, with a gleam *or* twinkle in one's eye, with a straight face **4. make fun of** deride, hold up to ridicule, lampoon, laugh at, make a fool of, make a monkey of, make game of, make sport of, make the butt of, mock, parody, poke fun at, rag, rib (*informal*), ridicule, satirize, scoff at, send up (*Brit. informal*), sneer at, take off, take the piss out of (*taboo slang*), taunt *~adjective* **5.** amusing, convivial, diverting, enjoyable, entertaining, lively, witty

Antonyms (*sense 1*) depression, desolation, despair, distress, gloom, grief, melancholy, misery, sadness, sorrow, unhappiness, woe

People must not do things for fun. We are not here for fun. There is no reference to fun in any Act of Parliament

A.P. Herbert *Uncommon Law*

function *noun* **1.** activity, business, capacity, charge, concern, duty, employment, exercise, job, mission, occupation, office, operation, part, post, province, purpose, raison d'être, responsibility, role, situation, task *~verb* **2.** act, act the part of, behave, be in business, be in commission, be in operation *or* action, be in running order, do duty, go, officiate, operate, perform, run, serve, serve one's turn, work *~noun* **3.** affair, do (*informal*), gathering, lig (*Brit. slang*), reception, social occasion

functional hard-wearing, operative, practical, serviceable, useful, utilitarian, utility, working

functionary dignitary, employee, office bearer, office holder, officer, official

fund *noun* **1.** capital, endowment, fall-back, foundation, kitty, pool, reserve, stock, store, supply, tontine **2.** hoard, mine, repository, reserve, reservoir, source, storehouse, treasury, vein *~verb* **3.** capitalize, endow, finance, float, pay for, promote, stake, subsidize, support

fundamental 1. *adjective* basic, cardinal, central, constitutional, crucial, elementary, essential, first, important, indispensable, integral, intrinsic, key, necessary, organic, primary, prime, principal, radical, rudimentary, underlying, vital **2.** *noun* axiom, basic, cornerstone, essential, first principle, law, principle, rudiment, rule, *sine qua non*

Antonyms advanced, back-up, extra, incidental, lesser, secondary, subsidiary, superfluous

fundamentally at bottom, at heart, basically, essentially, intrinsically, primarily, radically

funds 1. ackers (*slang*), brass (*Northern English dialect*), bread (*slang*), capital, cash, dibs (*slang*), dosh (*Brit. & Austral. slang*), dough (*slang*), finance, hard cash, money, necessary (*informal*), needful (*informal*), ready money, resources, rhino (*Brit. slang*), savings, shekels (*informal*), silver, spondulicks (*slang*), the ready (*informal*), the wherewithal, tin (*slang*) **2. in funds** flush (*informal*), in the black, solvent, well-off, well-supplied

funeral burial, inhumation, interment, obsequies

funereal dark, deathlike, depressing, dirgelike, dismal, dreary, gloomy, grave, lamenting, lugubrious, mournful, sad, sepulchral, solemn, sombre, woeful

funk 1. *verb* chicken out of (*informal*), dodge, duck out of (*informal*), flinch from, recoil from, take fright, turn tail **2. be in a (blue) funk** be in a cold sweat, be in a panic, be scared stiff, be sick with fear, cower, dread, fear, quail, quake, quiver, shake at the knees, shrink, tremble, tremble in one's boots

funnel *verb* channel, conduct, convey, direct, filter, move, pass, pour

funny *adjective* **1.** absurd, amusing, a scream (card (*informal*), caution (*informal*)) (*informal*), comic, comical, diverting, droll, entertaining, facetious, farcical, hilarious, humorous, jocose, jocular, jolly, killing (*informal*), laughable, ludicrous, rich, ridiculous, riotous, risible, side-splitting, silly, slapstick, waggish, witty **2.** curious, dubious, mysterious, odd, peculiar, perplexing, puzzling, queer, remarkable, rum (*Brit. slang*), strange, suspicious, unusual, weird *~noun* **3.** *informal* crack (*slang*), jest, joke, play on words, pun, quip, wisecrack, witticism

Antonyms (*sense 1*) grave, humourless, melancholy, serious, sober, solemn, stern, unfunny

furbish brighten, burnish, gussy up (*slang, chiefly U.S.*), polish, renovate, restore, rub, shine, smarten up, spruce up

furious 1. angry, beside oneself, boiling, choked, cross, enraged, fit to be tied (*slang*), foaming at the mouth, frantic, frenzied, fuming, incensed, infuriated, in high dudgeon, livid (*informal*), mad, maddened, on the warpath (*informal*), raging, up in arms, wrathful, wroth (*archaic*) **2.** agitated, boisterous, fierce, impetuous, intense, savage, stormy, tempestuous, tumultuous, turbulent, ungovernable, unrestrained, vehement, violent, wild

Antonyms calm, dispassionate, impassive, imperturbable, mild, placated, pleased, serene, tranquil

furnish 1. appoint, decorate, equip, fit (out, up), outfit, provide, provision, purvey, rig, stock, store, supply **2.** afford, bestow, endow, give, grant, hand out, offer, present, provide, reveal, supply

furniture appliances, appointments, chattels, effects, equipment, fittings, furnishings, goods, household goods, movable property, movables, possessions, things (*informal*)

Types of bed

bassinet
berth
box bed
bunk
bunk bed
camp bed
cot
cradle
crib
day bed
divan bed
double bed
field bed
foldaway bed
folding bed
four-poster bed
hammock
hospital bed
king-size *or* king-sized bed
pallet
put-u-up
queen-size *or* queen-sized bed
single bed
sleigh bed
sofa bed
trestle bed
truckle *or* trundle bed
twin bed
water bed

Types of cabinet and cupboard

armoire
bookcase
buffet
bureau
cabinet
canterbury
cellaret
chest
chest of drawers
chest-on-chest
chiffonier *or* chiffonnier
closet
clothes-press
commode
court cupboard
credence table *or* credenza
drawer
dresser
étagère
garderobe (*archaic*)
highboy (*U.S.*)
locker
lowboy (*U.S.*)
press
shelf
sideboard
stand
tallboy
vitrine
wardrobe
Welsh dresser
whatnot

Types of chair

armchair
banquette
barrel chair
bar stool
basket chair
bench
bucket seat
campaign chair
camp chair
carver
corner chair
deck chair
dining chair
director's chair
dos-à-dos
easy chair
fauteuil
folding chair
form
hassock
high chair
ladder-back chair
milking stool
music stool
opsitbank (*S. Afr.*)
ottoman
pew
piano stool
pouf *or* pouffe
reclining chair *or* recliner
rocking chair *or* rocker
sedan chair
settle
shooting stick
stool
straight chair
swing
swivel chair
throne
tub chair
window seat
Windsor chair
wing chair

Types of sofa

chaise longue *or* chaise
chesterfield
couch
davenport (*U.S.*)
day bed
divan
lounge
love seat
settee
settle
squab
studio couch
tête-à-tête
vis-à-vis

Types of tables and desks

bar
bedside table
breakfast bar
breakfast table
buffet
card table
coffee table
console table
counter
davenport (*Brit.*)
desk
dining table
dressing table
drop-leaf table
drum table
escritoire
folding table
gate-leg *or* gate-legged table
kitchen table
nest of tables
occasional table
Pembroke table
piecrust table
reading desk
refectory table
roll-top desk
secretaire *or* secretary
side table
tea table
tea trolley
trestle table
workbench
worktable
writing desk
writing table

Other pieces of furniture

bedpost
bedstead
canopy
cheval glass
coatstand
dumbwaiter
epergne
footstool
girandole *or* girandola
grandfather clock
grandmother clock
hallstand
hatstand
headboard
litter
longcase clock
tester
trolley
umbrella stand
vanitory
vanity unit
washstand

Furniture styles

Art Deco
Bauhaus
Cape Dutch
Edwardian
Elizabethan
Empire
Georgian
Gothic
Greek Revival
Jacobean
Louis Quatorze
Louis Quinze
Louis Seize
Louis Treize
Medieval
New Georgian
Norman
Puritan
Queen Anne
Regency
Restoration
Saxon
Second Empire
Shaker
Tudor
Victorian
William and Mary

Furniture designers

Robert Adam [Scottish]
Charles Bevan [English]
Marcel Lajos Breuer [Hungarian-U.S.]
William Burges [English]

Thomas Chippendale [English]
Ambrose Heal [English]
George Hepplewhite [English]
Inigo Jones [English]
William Jones [English]
William Kent [English]
Kaara Klint [Danish]
Charles Rennie Mackintosh [Scottish]
Daniel Marot [French]
William Morris [English]
Michael Angelo Pergolesi [Italian]
Duncan Phyfe [Scottish-U.S.]
Augustus Pugin [English]
Thomas Sheraton [English]
George Smith [English]
Charles Voysey [English]

furore 1. commotion, disturbance, excitement, flap (*informal*), frenzy, fury, hullabaloo, outburst, outcry, stir, to-do, uproar 2. craze, enthusiasm, mania, rage

furrow 1. *noun* channel, corrugation, crease, crow's-foot, fluting, groove, hollow, line, rut, seam, trench, wrinkle 2. *verb* corrugate, crease, draw together, flute, knit, seam, wrinkle

further 1. *adjective* additional, extra, fresh, more, new, other, supplementary 2. *adverb* additionally, also, as well as, besides, furthermore, in addition, into the bargain, moreover, on top of, over and above, to boot, what's more, yet 3. *verb* advance, aid, assist, champion, contribute to, encourage, expedite, facilitate, forward, foster, hasten, help, lend support to, patronize, pave the way for, plug (*informal*), promote, push, speed, succour, work for
Antonyms *verb* foil, frustrate, hinder, impede, obstruct, oppose, prevent, retard, stop, thwart

furtherance advancement, advocacy, backing, boosting, carrying-out, championship, promotion, prosecution, pursuit

furthermore additionally, as well, besides, further, in addition, into the bargain, moreover, not to mention, to boot, too, what's more

furthest extreme, farthest, furthermost, most distant, outermost, outmost, remotest, ultimate, uttermost

furtive behind someone's back, clandestine, cloaked, conspiratorial, covert, hidden, secret, secretive, skulking, slinking, sly, sneaking, sneaky, stealthy, surreptitious, underhand, under-the-table
Antonyms above-board, candid, forthright, frank, open, public, straightforward, undisguised, unreserved

fury 1. anger, frenzy, impetuosity, ire, madness, passion, rage, wrath 2. ferocity, fierceness, force, intensity, power, savagery, severity, tempestuousness, turbulence, vehemence, violence 3. bacchante, hag, hellcat, shrew, spitfire, termagant, virago, vixen
Antonyms calm, calmness, composure, equanimity, hush, peace, peacefulness, serenity, stillness, tranquillity

fuse *verb* agglutinate, amalgamate, blend, coalesce, combine, commingle, dissolve, federate, integrate, intermingle, intermix, join, meld, melt, merge, run together, smelt, solder, unite, weld
Antonyms diffuse, dispense, disseminate, dissipate, disunite, scatter, separate, spread, strew

fusillade barrage, broadside, burst, fire, hail, outburst, salvo, volley

fusion alloy, amalgam, amalgamation, blend, blending, coalescence, commingling, commixture, federation, integration, liquefaction, meld, merger, merging, mixture, smelting, synthesis, union, uniting, welding

fuss *noun* 1. ado, agitation, bother, bustle, commotion, confusion, excitement, fidget, flap (*informal*), flurry, fluster, flutter, hue and cry, hurry, palaver, pother, stir, storm in a teacup (*Brit.*), to-do, upset, worry 2. altercation, argument, bother, complaint, difficulty, display, furore, hassle (*informal*), objection, row, squabble, trouble, unrest, upset ~*verb* 3. bustle, chafe, fidget, flap (*informal*), fret, fume, get in a stew (*informal*), get worked up, labour over, make a meal of (*informal*), make a thing of (*informal*), niggle, take pains, worry

fusspot fidget, fussbudget (*U.S.*), nit-picker (*informal*), old woman, perfectionist, worrier

fussy 1. choosy (*informal*), dainty, difficult, discriminating, exacting, faddish, faddy, fastidious, finicky, hard to please, nit-picking (*informal*), old-maidish, old womanish, overparticular, particular, pernickety, picky (*informal*), squeamish 2. busy, cluttered, overdecorated, overelaborate, overembellished, overworked, rococo

fustiness airlessness, dampness, frowstiness, fug, mouldiness, mustiness, smell of decay, staleness, stuffiness

fusty 1. airless, damp, frowsty, ill-smelling, malodorous, mildewed, mildewy, mouldering, mouldy, musty, rank, stale, stuffy 2. antediluvian, antiquated, archaic, old-fashioned, old-fogyish, outdated, out-of-date, out of the ark (*informal*), passé

futile 1. abortive, barren, bootless, empty, forlorn, fruitless, hollow, ineffectual, in vain, nugatory, profitless, sterile, to no avail, unavailing, unproductive, unprofitable, unsuccessful, useless, vain, valueless, without rhyme or reason, worthless 2. idle, pointless, trifling, trivial, unimportant, wanky (*taboo slang*)
Antonyms constructive, effective, fruitful,

profitable, purposeful, significant, successful, useful, valuable, worthwhile

futility 1. bootlessness, emptiness, fruitlessness, hollowness, ineffectiveness, spitting in the wind, uselessness 2. pointlessness, triviality, unimportance, vanity

as futile as a clock in an empty house

James Thurber

future 1. *noun* expectation, hereafter, outlook, prospect, time to come 2. *adjective* approaching, coming, destined, eventual, expected, fated, forthcoming, impending, in the offing, later, prospective, subsequent, to be, to come, ultimate, unborn

Antonyms *adjective* bygone, erstwhile, ex-, former, late, past, preceding, previous, quondam

I never think of the future. It comes soon enough

Albert Einstein

fuzz down, fibre, floss, fluff, hair, lint, nap, pile

fuzzy 1. down-covered, downy, flossy, fluffy, frizzy, linty, napped, woolly 2. bleary, blurred, distorted, faint, ill-defined, indistinct, muffled, out of focus, shadowy, unclear, unfocused, vague

Antonyms clear, defined, detailed, distinct, in focus, precise

G

gab **1.** *verb* babble, blabber, blather, buzz, chatter, chew the fat *or* rag (*slang*), gossip, jabber, jaw (*slang*), prattle, rabbit (*Brit. informal*), run off at the mouth (*slang*), spout, talk, waffle (*informal, chiefly Brit.*), yak (*slang*) **2.** *noun* blab, blarney, blather, chat, chatter, chitchat, conversation, gossip, loquacity, palaver, small talk, talk, tête-à-tête, tittle-tattle, tongue-wagging, waffle (*informal, chiefly Brit.*), yackety-yak (*slang*), yak (*slang*)

gabble **1.** *verb* babble, blab, blabber, cackle, chatter, gaggle, gibber, gush, jabber, prattle, rabbit (*Brit. informal*), rattle, run off at the mouth (*slang*), splutter, spout, sputter, waffle (*informal, chiefly Brit.*) **2.** *noun* babble, blabber, cackling, chatter, drivel, gibberish, jargon, pap, prattle, twaddle, waffle (*informal, chiefly Brit.*)

gabby chatty, effusive, garrulous, glib, gossiping, gushing, long-winded, loquacious, mouthy, prattling, prolix, talkative, verbose, voluble, windy, wordy

gad (about *or* **around)** gallivant, ramble, range, roam, rove, run around, stravaig (*Scot. & northern English dialect*), stray, traipse (*informal*), wander

gadabout gallivanter, pleasure-seeker, rambler, rover, wanderer

gadget appliance, contraption (*informal*), contrivance, device, gimmick, gizmo (*slang, chiefly U.S.*), instrument, invention, novelty, thing, tool, waldo

gaffe bloomer (*informal*), blunder, boob (*Brit. slang*), boo-boo (*informal*), clanger (*informal*), faux pas, gaucherie, howler, indiscretion, lapse, mistake, slip, solecism

gaffer **1.** granddad, greybeard, old boy (*informal*), old fellow, old man, old-timer (*U.S.*) **2.** *informal* boss (*informal*), foreman, ganger, manager, overseer, superintendent, supervisor

gag[1] *verb* **1.** curb, muffle, muzzle, quiet, silence, stifle, still, stop up, suppress, throttle **2.** *slang* barf (*slang*), disgorge, heave, puke (*slang*), retch, spew, throw up (*informal*), vomit **3.** *slang* choke, gasp, pant, struggle for breath

gag[2] *noun* crack (*slang*), funny (*informal*), hoax, jest, joke, wisecrack (*informal*), witticism

gage *noun* **1.** bond, deposit, earnest, guarantee, pawn, pledge, security, surety, token **2.** challenge, dare, defiance, gauntlet, glove

gaiety **1.** animation, blitheness, blithesomeness (*literary*), cheerfulness, effervescence, elation, exhilaration, glee, good humour, high spirits, hilarity, *joie de vivre*, jollity, joviality, joyousness, light-heartedness, liveliness, merriment, mirth, sprightliness, vivacity **2.** celebration, conviviality, festivity, fun, jollification, merrymaking, revelry, revels **3.** brightness, brilliance, colour, colourfulness, gaudiness, glitter, show, showiness, sparkle
Antonyms despondency, gloom, melancholy, misery, sadness

gaily **1.** blithely, cheerfully, gleefully, happily, joyfully, light-heartedly, merrily **2.** brightly, brilliantly, colourfully, flamboyantly, flashily, gaudily, showily

gain *verb* **1.** achieve, acquire, advance, attain, bag, build up, capture, collect, enlist, gather, get, glean, harvest, improve, increase, land, net, obtain, pick up, procure, profit, realize, reap, score (*slang*), secure, win, win over **2.** acquire, bring in, clear, earn, get, make, net, obtain, produce, realize, win, yield **3.** *usually with* **on a.** approach, catch up with, close with, get nearer, narrow the gap, overtake **b.** draw *or* pull away from, get farther away, leave behind, outdistance, recede, widen the gap **4.** arrive at, attain, come to, get to, reach **5. gain time** delay, procrastinate, stall, temporize, use delaying tactics *~noun* **6.** accretion, achievement, acquisition, advance, advancement, advantage, attainment, benefit, dividend, earnings, emolument, growth, headway, improvement, income, increase, increment, lucre, proceeds, produce, profit, progress, return, rise, winnings, yield
Antonyms *verb* fail, forfeit, lose, worsen *~noun* damage, forfeiture, injury, loss, privation

gainful advantageous, beneficial, expedient, fruitful, lucrative, moneymaking, paying, productive, profitable, remunerative, rewarding, useful, worthwhile

gains booty, earnings, gainings, pickings, prize, proceeds, profits, revenue, takings, winnings

gainsay contradict, contravene, controvert,

deny, disaffirm, disagree with, dispute, rebut, retract
Antonyms agree with, back, confirm, support

gait bearing, carriage, pace, step, stride, tread, walk

gala **1.** *noun* beano (*Brit. slang*), carnival, celebration, festival, festivity, fête, hooley *or* hoolie (*chiefly Irish & N.Z.*), jamboree, pageant, party, rave (*Brit. slang*), rave-up (*Brit. slang*) **2.** *adjective* celebratory, convivial, festal, festive, gay, jovial, joyful, merry

gale **1.** blast, cyclone, hurricane, squall, storm, tempest, tornado, typhoon **2.** *informal* burst, eruption, explosion, fit, howl, outbreak, outburst, peal, shout, shriek

gall[1] *noun* **1.** *informal* brass (*informal*), brass neck (*Brit. informal*), brazenness, cheek (*informal*), chutzpah (*U.S. & Canad. informal*), effrontery, face (*informal*), impertinence, impudence, insolence, neck (*informal*), nerve (*informal*), sassiness (*U.S. informal*), sauciness **2.** acrimony, animosity, animus, antipathy, bad blood, bile, bitterness, enmity, hostility, malevolence, malice, malignity, rancour, sourness, spite, spleen, venom

gall[2] *noun* **1.** abrasion, chafe, excoriation, raw spot, scrape, sore, sore spot, wound **2.** aggravation (*informal*), annoyance, bother, botheration (*informal*), exasperation, harassment, irritant, irritation, nuisance, pest, provocation, vexation ~*verb* **3.** abrade, bark, chafe, excoriate, fret, graze, irritate, rub raw, scrape, skin **4.** aggravate (*informal*), annoy, be on one's back (*slang*), bother, exasperate, fret, get in one's hair (*informal*), get on one's nerves (*informal*), harass, hassle (*informal*), irk, irritate, nag, nark (*Brit., Austral., & N.Z. slang*), nettle, peeve (*informal*), pester, piss one off (*taboo slang*), plague, provoke, rankle, rile (*informal*), rub up the wrong way, ruffle, vex

gallant *adjective* **1.** bold, brave, courageous, daring, dashing, dauntless, doughty, fearless, game (*informal*), heroic, high-spirited, honourable, intrepid, lion-hearted, manful, manly, mettlesome, noble, plucky, valiant, valorous **2.** attentive, chivalrous, courteous, courtly, gentlemanly, gracious, magnanimous, noble, polite **3.** august, dignified, elegant, glorious, grand, imposing, lofty, magnificent, noble, splendid, stately ~*noun* **4.** admirer, beau, boyfriend, escort, leman (*archaic*), lover, paramour, suitor, wooer **5.** beau, blade (*archaic*), buck (*informal*), dandy, fop, ladies' man, lady-killer (*informal*), man about town, man of fashion **6.** adventurer, cavalier, champion, daredevil, hero, knight, man of mettle, *preux chevalier*
Antonyms churlish, cowardly, discourteous, fearful, ignoble, ill-mannered, impolite, rude

gallantry **1.** audacity, boldness, bravery, courage, courageousness, daring, dauntlessness, derring-do (*archaic*), fearlessness, heroism, intrepidity, manliness, mettle, nerve, pluck, prowess, spirit, valiance, valour **2.** attentiveness, chivalry, courteousness, courtesy, courtliness, elegance, gentlemanliness, graciousness, nobility, politeness
Antonyms churlishness, cowardice, discourtesy, irresolution, rudeness, ungraciousness

galling aggravating (*informal*), annoying, bitter, bothersome, exasperating, harassing, humiliating, irksome, irritating, nettlesome, plaguing, provoking, rankling, vexatious, vexing

gallivant gad about, ramble, range, roam, rove, run around, stravaig (*Scot. & northern English dialect*), stray, traipse (*informal*), wander

gallop barrel (along) (*informal, chiefly U.S. & Canad.*), bolt, career, dart, dash, fly, hasten, hie (*archaic*), hurry, race, run, rush, scud, shoot, speed, sprint, tear along, zoom

galore à gogo (*informal*), all over the place, aplenty, everywhere, in abundance, in great quantity, in numbers, in profusion, to spare

galvanize arouse, awaken, electrify, excite, fire, inspire, invigorate, jolt, kick-start, move, prod, provoke, put a bomb under (*informal*), quicken, shock, spur, startle, stimulate, stir, thrill, vitalize, wake

gamble *verb* **1.** back, bet, game, have a flutter (*informal*), lay *or* make a bet, play, punt, put one's shirt on, stake, try one's luck, wager **2.** back, chance, hazard, put one's faith *or* trust in, risk, skate on thin ice, speculate, stake, stick one's neck out (*informal*), take a chance, take the plunge, venture ~*noun* **3.** chance, leap in the dark, lottery, risk, speculation, uncertainty, venture **4.** bet, flutter (*informal*), punt, wager
Antonyms (*sense 3*) certainty, foregone conclusion, safe bet, sure thing

gambol **1.** *verb* caper, cavort, curvet, cut a caper, frisk, frolic, hop, jump, prance, rollick, skip **2.** *noun* antic, caper, frolic, gambado, hop, jump, prance, skip, spring

game[1] *noun* **1.** amusement, distraction, diversion, entertainment, frolic, fun, jest, joke, lark, merriment, pastime, play, recreation, romp, sport **2.** competition, contest, event, head-to-head, match, meeting, round, tournament **3.** adventure, business, enterprise, line, occupation, plan, proceeding, scheme, undertaking **4.** chase, prey, quarry, wild animals **5.** *informal* design, device, plan, plot, ploy, scheme, stratagem, strategy, tactic, trick **6.** **make (a) game of** deride, make a fool of, make a laughing stock, make a monkey of, make fun of, make sport of, mock, poke fun

at, ridicule, send up (*Brit. informal*)
Antonyms business, chore, duty, job, labour, toil, work

Board Games

acey-deucy
backgammon
bagatelle
chequers
chess
Chinese chequers
Cluedo (*Trademark*)
draughts
fox and geese
go *or* I-go
halma
kriegspiel
lightning chess
ludo
Monopoly (*Trademark*)
nine men's morris
pachisi
reversi
shove-halfpenny
snakes and ladders
solitaire
speed chess

Chess piece	**Abbreviation**
Bishop	B
King	K
King's bishop	KB
King's knight	KN
King's rook	KR
Knight	N
Pawn	P
Queen	Q
Queen's bishop	QB
Queen's knight	QN
Queen's rook	QR

Card games

auction bridge
baccarat
beggar-my-neighbour
bezique
blackjack
boston
bridge
canasta
canfield
casino
chemin-de-fer *or* chemmy
cinch
contract bridge
cooncan *or* conquian
cribbage
duplicate bridge
écarté
euchre
faro
five hundred
gin rummy
happy families
hearts
loo
monte
nap *or* napoleon
old maid
ombre
patience
pinochle, penuchle, penuckle *or* pinocle
piquet
poker
pontoon
quinze
rouge et noir
rubber bridge
rummy
seven up
skat
slapjack
snap
solo
solo whist
spoilfive
stops
strip poker
stud poker
switch
trente et quarante
whist

Bridge terms

contract
double
dummy
east
finesse
grand slam
little slam *or* small slam
north
no-trump
redouble
rubber
ruff
singleton
slam
south
trick
trump
vulnerable
west
yarborough

Poker terms

ante
flush
full house
pair
raise
royal flush
see
showdown
shy
stand pat
straddle
straight
straight flush

Other card terms

ace
clubs
court card *or* (*U.S. & Canad.*) face card
cut
deal
deck
deuce
diamonds
hand
hearts
jack
joker
king
knave
queen
revoke
spades
suit
trey
wild

Party Games

blind man's buff
charades
Chinese whispers
consequences
follow-my-leader
hide-and-seek
I-spy
musical chairs
postman's knock
Simon says
statues

Word Games

acrostic
anagram
crambo
crossword *or* crossword puzzle
hangman
logogriph
The Minister's Cat (*Scot.*)
rebus
Scrabble (*Trademark*)
twenty questions *or* animal, vegetable or mineral

Other games

bar billiards
battleships
beetle
bingo
British bulldog
caber tossing
conkers
craps
crown and anchor
deck tennis
dominoes
French cricket
hoopla
hopscotch
horseshoes
housey-housey
jacks
jigsaw puzzle
keno, keeno, kino *or* quino
king of the castle
knur and spell
lansquenet
leapfrog
lotto
mahjong *or* mah-jongg
marbles
nim
noughts and crosses
paintball
pall-mall
pegboard
pinball
pitch-and-toss

quoits	spillikins *or* jack~ straws
ring taw	tag *or* tig
roque	tangram
roulette	thimblerig
Russian roulette	tiddlywinks
sack race	tipcat
scavenger hunt	trictrac *or* tricktrack
shuffleboard	trugo
skipping	wall game
Space Invaders (*Trademark*)	war game

die: the singular of "dice". We seldom hear the word, because there is a prohibitory proverb, "Nev~ er say die."

Ambrose Bierce *The Devil's Dictionary*

I am sorry I have not learned to play at cards. It is very useful in life; it generates kindness and con~ solidates society

Dr. Johnson

game² *adjective* **1.** ballsy (*taboo slang*), bold, brave, courageous, dauntless, dogged, fearless, feisty (*informal, chiefly U.S. & Canad.*), gal~ lant, gritty, have-a-go (*informal*), heroic, in~ trepid, persevering, persistent, plucky, reso~ lute, spirited, unflinching, valiant, valorous **2.** desirous, disposed, eager, inclined, interested, keen, prepared, ready, willing
Antonyms cowardly, fearful, irresolute

game³ *adjective* bad, crippled, deformed, dis~ abled, gammy (*Brit. slang*), incapacitated, in~ jured, lame, maimed

gamesome coltish, frisky, frolicsome, gay, lively, ludic (*literary*), merry, playful, rollick~ ing, sportive, vivacious

gamin guttersnipe, mudlark (*slang*), ragamuf~ fin, street Arab (*offensive*), (street) urchin, waif

gammon **1.** *verb* beguile, cheat, con, cozen, de~ ceive, dupe, gull (*archaic*), hoax, hoodwink, humbug, kid (*informal*), take for a ride (*infor~ mal*), trick **2.** *noun* deceit, deception, humbug, imposition, nonsense, trick

gamut area, catalogue, compass, field, range, scale, scope, series, sweep

gang band, bevy, camp, circle, clique, club, company, coterie, crew (*informal*), crowd, group, herd, horde, lot, mob, pack, party, pos~ se (*slang*), ring, set, shift, squad, team, troupe

gangling, gangly angular, awkward, lanky, loose-jointed, rangy, rawboned, skinny, spin~ dly, tall

gangster bandit, brigand, crook (*informal*), desperado, gang member, heavy (*slang*), hood (*U.S. slang*), hoodlum (*chiefly U.S.*), mobster (*U.S. slang*), racketeer, robber, ruffian, thug, tough

gaol *see* JAIL

gap **1.** blank, breach, break, breathing space, chink, cleft, crack, cranny, crevice, disconti~ nuity, divide, entr'acte, hiatus, hole, interlude, intermission, interruption, interstice, interval, lacuna, lull, opening, pause, recess, rent, res~ pite, rift, space, vacuity, void **2.** difference, disagreement, disparity, divergence, incon~ sistency

gape **1.** gawk, gawp (*Brit. slang*), goggle, stare, wonder **2.** crack, open, split, yawn

gaping broad, cavernous, great, open, vast, wide, wide open, yawning

garb *noun* **1.** apparel, array, attire, clothes, clothing, costume, dress, garment, gear (*slang*), habiliment, habit, outfit, raiment (*ar~ chaic*), robes, schmutter (*slang*), threads (*slang*), uniform, vestments, wear **2.** cut, fash~ ion, look, mode, style **3.** appearance, aspect, attire, covering, guise, outward form *~verb* **4.** apparel, attire, clothe, cover, dress, rig out, robe

garbage **1.** bits and pieces, debris, detritus, junk, litter, odds and ends, rubbish, scraps **2.** dreck (*slang, chiefly U.S.*), dross, filth, muck, offal, refuse, rubbish, scourings, slops, sweep~ ings, swill, trash (*chiefly U.S.*), wack (*U.S. slang*), waste **3.** balderdash, balls (*taboo slang*), bilge (*informal*), bosh (*informal*), bull (*slang*), bullshit (*taboo slang*), bunkum *or* buncombe (*chiefly U.S.*), claptrap (*informal*), cobblers (*Brit. taboo slang*), codswallop (*Brit. slang*), crap (*slang*), drivel, eyewash (*infor~ mal*), flapdoodle (*slang*), gibberish, guff (*slang*), havers (*Scot.*), hogwash, hokum (*slang, chiefly U.S. & Canad.*), horsefeathers (*U.S. slang*), hot air (*informal*), moonshine, nonsense, pap, piffle (*informal*), poppycock (*informal*), rot, shit (*taboo slang*), stuff and nonsense, tommyrot, tosh (*informal*), trash, tripe (*informal*), twaddle

garble **1.** confuse, jumble, mix up **2.** corrupt, distort, doctor, falsify, misinterpret, misquote, misreport, misrepresent, misstate, mistrans~ late, mutilate, pervert, slant, tamper with, twist
Antonyms clarify, decipher, make intelligible

garbled confused, distorted, double-Dutch, in~ comprehensible, jumbled, mixed up, unintelli~ gible

garden
Related adjective: horticultural

We must cultivate our gardens

Voltaire *Candide*

A garden is a lovesom thing, God wot!

T.E. Brown *My Garden*

God Almighty first planted a garden, and, indeed, it is the purest of human pleasures

Francis Bacon *Essays*

The kiss of the sun for pardon,
The song of the birds for mirth,

One is nearer God's Heart in a garden
Than anywhere else on earth
Dorothy Frances Gurney *God's Garden*

gardening
What a man needs in gardening is a cast-iron back, with a hinge on it
Charles Dudley Warner

If you would be happy for a week, take a wife; if you would be happy for a month, kill your pig; but if you would be happy all your life, plant a garden
Chinese proverb

gargantuan big, Brobdingnagian, colossal, elephantine, enormous, giant, gigantic, ginormous (*informal*), huge, humongous *or* humungous (*U.S. slang*), immense, mammoth, massive, monstrous, monumental, mountainous, prodigious, stellar (*informal*), titanic, towering, tremendous, vast
Antonyms little, meagre, miniature, minute, paltry, petite, puny, pygmy *or* pigmy, small, tiny

garish brash, brassy, brummagem, cheap, flash (*informal*), flashy, flaunting, gaudy, glaring, glittering, loud, meretricious, naff (*Brit. slang*), raffish, showy, tacky (*informal*), tasteless, tawdry, vulgar
Antonyms conservative, elegant, modest, plain, refined, sedate, sombre, unobtrusive

garland 1. *noun* bays, chaplet, coronal, crown, festoon, honours, laurels, wreath **2.** *verb* adorn, crown, deck, festoon, wreathe

garments apparel, array, articles of clothing, attire, clothes, clothing, costume, dress, duds (*informal*), garb, gear (*slang*), habiliment, habit, outfit, raiment (*archaic*), robes, schmutter (*slang*), threads (*slang*), togs, uniform, vestments, wear

garner 1. *verb* accumulate, amass, assemble, collect, deposit, gather, hoard, husband, lay in *or* up, put by, reserve, save, stockpile, store, stow away, treasure **2.** *noun, literary* depository, granary, store, storehouse, vault

garnish 1. *verb* adorn, beautify, bedeck, deck, decorate, embellish, enhance, festoon, grace, ornament, set off, trim **2.** *noun* adornment, decoration, embellishment, enhancement, festoon, garniture, ornament, ornamentation, trim, trimming
Antonyms denude, spoil, strip

garniture accessories, adornment, appendages, appurtenances, decoration, embellishment, furniture, garnish, ornamentation, ornaments, trimmings

garrison *noun* **1.** armed force, command, detachment, troops, unit **2.** base, camp, encampment, fort, fortification, fortress, post, station, stronghold ~*verb* **3.** assign, mount, position, post, put on duty, station **4.** defend, guard, man, occupy, protect, supply with troops

garrulity 1. babble, babbling, chatter, chattering, chattiness, effusiveness, gabbiness (*informal*), garrulousness, gift of the gab (*informal*), glibness, loquacity, mouthiness, prating, prattle, talkativeness, verbosity, volubility **2.** diffuseness, long-windedness, prolixity, prosiness, verbosity, windiness, wordiness

garrulous 1. babbling, chattering, chatty, effusive, gabby (*informal*), glib, gossiping, gushing, loquacious, mouthy, prating, prattling, talkative, verbose, voluble **2.** diffuse, gassy (*slang*), long-winded, prolix, prosy, verbose, windy, wordy
Antonyms concise, reserved, reticent, succinct, taciturn, terse, tight-lipped, uncommunicative

gash 1. *verb* cleave, cut, gouge, incise, lacerate, rend, slash, slit, split, tear, wound **2.** *noun* cleft, cut, gouge, incision, laceration, rent, slash, slit, split, tear, wound

gasp 1. *verb* blow, catch one's breath, choke, fight for breath, gulp, pant, puff **2.** *noun* blow, ejaculation, exclamation, gulp, intake of breath, pant, puff, sharp intake of breath

gate access, barrier, door, doorway, egress, entrance, exit, gateway, opening, passage, port (*Scot.*), portal

gather 1. accumulate, amass, assemble, bring *or* get together, collect, congregate, convene, flock, forgather, garner, group, heap, hoard, marshal, mass, muster, pile up, round up, stack up, stockpile **2.** assume, be led to believe, conclude, deduce, draw, hear, infer, learn, make, surmise, understand **3.** clasp, draw, embrace, enfold, hold, hug **4.** crop, cull, garner, glean, harvest, pick, pluck, reap, select **5.** build, deepen, enlarge, expand, grow, heighten, increase, intensify, rise, swell, thicken, wax **6.** fold, pleat, pucker, ruffle, shirr, tuck
Antonyms diffuse, disperse, dissipate, scatter, separate

gathering 1. assemblage, assembly, company, conclave, concourse, congregation, congress, convention, convocation, crowd, flock, get-together (*informal*), group, knot, meeting, muster, party, rally, throng, turnout **2.** accumulation, acquisition, aggregate, collecting, collection, concentration, gain, heap, hoard, mass, pile, procuring, roundup, stock, stockpile **3.** *informal* abscess, boil, carbuncle, pimple, pustule, sore, spot, tumour, ulcer

gauche awkward, clumsy, graceless, ignorant, ill-bred, ill-mannered, inelegant, inept, insensitive, lacking in social graces, maladroit, tactless, uncultured, unpolished, unsophisticated

Antonyms elegant, gracious, polished, polite, refined, sophisticated, tasteful, urbane, well-mannered

gaucherie **1.** awkwardness, bad taste, clumsiness, gaucheness, gracelessness, ignorance, ill-breeding, inelegance, ineptness, insensitivity, lack of polish, maladroitness, tactlessness, unsophisticatedness **2.** bloomer (*informal*), blunder, boob (*slang*), breach of etiquette, clanger (*informal*), faux pas, gaffe, indiscretion, lapse, mistake, slip, solecism

gaudiness brashness, flashiness, garishness, loudness, naffness, ostentation, poor taste, tastelessness, tawdriness, vulgarity

gaudy brash, bright, brilliant, brummagem, flash (*informal*), flashy, florid, garish, gay, gimcrack, glaring, loud, meretricious, naff (*Brit. slang*), ostentatious, raffish, showy, tacky (*informal*), tasteless, tawdry, vulgar
Antonyms colourless, conservative, dull, elegant, modest, quiet, refined, sedate, subtle, tasteful

gauge *verb* **1.** ascertain, calculate, check, compute, count, determine, measure, weigh **2.** adjudge, appraise, assess, estimate, evaluate, guess, judge, rate, reckon, value *~noun* **3.** basis, criterion, example, exemplar, guide, guideline, indicator, measure, meter, model, par, pattern, rule, sample, standard, test, touchstone, yardstick **4.** bore, capacity, degree, depth, extent, height, magnitude, measure, scope, size, span, thickness, width

gaunt **1.** angular, attenuated, bony, cadaverous, emaciated, haggard, lank, lean, macilent (*rare*), meagre, pinched, rawboned, scraggy, scrawny, skeletal, skin and bone, skinny, spare, thin, wasted **2.** bare, bleak, desolate, dismal, dreary, forbidding, forlorn, grim, harsh, stark
Antonyms (*sense 1*) chubby, corpulent, fat, lush, obese, plump, stout, well-fed (*sense 2*) inviting, lush, luxurious

gauntness **1.** angularity, boniness, cadaverousness, emaciation, leanness, scragginess, scrawniness, thinness, wasted frame **2.** bleakness, desolation, forlornness, grimness, harshness, starkness

gauzy delicate, diaphanous, filmy, flimsy, gossamer, insubstantial, light, see-through, sheer, thin, translucent, transparent

gawk **1.** *noun* boor, churl, clod, clodhopper (*informal*), dolt, dunderhead, galoot (*slang*), ignoramus, lout, lubber, lummox (*informal*), oaf **2.** *verb* gape, gawp (*slang*), gaze open-mouthed, goggle, stare

gawky awkward, clownish, clumsy, gauche, loutish, lumbering, lumpish, maladroit, oafish, uncouth, ungainly

Antonyms elegant, graceful, self-assured, well-coordinated

gay *adjective* **1.** homosexual, lesbian, pink (*informal*), poofy (*offensive slang*), queer (*informal, derogatory*) **2.** animated, blithe, carefree, cheerful, debonair, full of beans (*informal*), glad, gleeful, happy, hilarious, insouciant, jolly, jovial, joyful, joyous, light-hearted, lively, merry, sparkling, sunny, vivacious **3.** bright, brilliant, colourful, flamboyant, flashy, fresh, garish, gaudy, rich, showy, vivid **4.** convivial, festive, frivolous, frolicsome, fun-loving, gamesome, ludic (*literary*), merry, playful, pleasure-seeking, rakish, rollicking, sportive, waggish *~noun* **5.** dyke (*offensive slang*), faggot (*U.S. offens. slang*), fairy (*offensive slang*), homosexual, invert, lesbian, poof (*offensive slang*), queer (*offensive slang*)
Antonyms (*senses 1 & 5*) heterosexual, straight (*sense 2*) cheerless, colourless, conservative, down in the dumps (*informal*), drab, dull, grave, grim, melancholy, miserable, sad, sedate, serious, sober, solemn, sombre, unhappy

gaze **1.** *verb* contemplate, eyeball (*U.S. slang*), gape, look, look fixedly, regard, stare, view, watch, wonder **2.** *noun* fixed look, look, stare

gazette journal, newspaper, news-sheet, organ, paper, periodical

gear *noun* **1.** cog, cogwheel, gearwheel, toothed wheel **2.** cogs, gearing, machinery, mechanism, works **3.** accessories, accoutrements, apparatus, equipment, harness, instruments, outfit, paraphernalia, rigging, supplies, tackle, tools, trappings **4.** baggage, belongings, effects, kit, luggage, stuff, things **5.** *slang* apparel, array, attire, clothes, clothing, costume, dress, garb, garments, habit, outfit, rigout (*informal*), schmutter (*slang*), threads (*slang*), togs, wear *~verb* **6.** adapt, adjust, equip, fit, rig, suit, tailor

gelatinous gluey, glutinous, gummy, jelly-like, mucilaginous, sticky, viscid, viscous

gelid arctic, chilly, cold, freezing, frigid, frosty, frozen, glacial, ice-cold, icy, polar
Antonyms hot, red-hot, scorching, sweltering, torrid

gem **1.** jewel, precious stone, semiprecious stone, stone **2.** flower, jewel, masterpiece, pearl, pick, prize, treasure
Related adjective: lapidary

Gemstones

adularia	andradite
agate	aquamarine
alexandrite	aventurine, aventurin *or* avanturine
almandine	balas
amazonite	beryl
amethyst	black opal
andalusite	

bloodstone
bone turquoise
cairngorm
carnelian
cat's-eye
chalcedony
chrysoberyl
chrysolite
chrysoprase
citrine
Colorado ruby
Colorado topaz
corundum
cymophane
demantoid
diamond
diopside
emerald
fire opal
garnet
girasol, girosol *or* girasole
grossularite
hawk's-eye
helidor
heliotrope
hessonite
hiddenite
hyacinth
indicolite *or* indigolite
jacinth
jadeite *or* jade
jasper
jet
kunzite
lapis lazuli
liver opal
Madagascar aqua~ marine
melanite
moonstone
morganite
morion
moss agate
New Zealand green~ stone
odontolite
onyx
opal
Oriental almandine
Oriental emerald
peridot
plasma
pyrope
quartz
rhodolite
rose quartz
rubellite
ruby
sapphire
sard *or* sardine
sardonyx
smoky quartz
Spanish topaz
spessartite
sphene
spinel
spodumene
staurolite
sunstone
titanite
topaz
topazolite
tourmaline
turquoise
uvarovite
vesuvianite
water sapphire
white sapphire
zircon

genealogy ancestry, blood line, derivation, de~ scent, extraction, family tree, line, lineage, pedigree, progeniture, stemma, stirps, stock, strain

general **1.** accepted, broad, common, extensive, popular, prevailing, prevalent, public, univer~ sal, widespread **2.** accustomed, conventional, customary, everyday, habitual, normal, ordi~ nary, regular, typical, usual **3.** approximate, ill-defined, imprecise, inaccurate, indefinite, inexact, loose, undetailed, unspecific, vague **4.** across-the-board, all-inclusive, blanket, broad, catholic, collective, comprehensive, encyclo~ pedic, generic, indiscriminate, miscellaneous, panoramic, sweeping, total, universal
Antonyms definite, distinctive, exact, excep~ tional, extraordinary, individual, infrequent, particular, peculiar, precise, rare, special, specific, unusual

generality **1.** abstract principle, generalization, loose statement, sweeping statement, vague notion **2.** acceptedness, commonness, exten~ siveness, popularity, prevalence, universality **3.** approximateness, impreciseness, indefinite~ ness, inexactness, lack of detail, looseness, vagueness **4.** breadth, catholicity, comprehen~ siveness, miscellaneity, sweepingness, univer~ sality

generally **1.** almost always, as a rule, by and large, conventionally, customarily, for the most part, habitually, in most cases, largely, mainly, normally, on average, on the whole, ordinarily, regularly, typically, usually **2.** commonly, extensively, popularly, publicly, universally, widely **3.** approximately, broadly, chiefly, for the most part, in the main, large~ ly, mainly, mostly, on the whole, predomi~ nantly, principally
Antonyms especially, individually, occasional~ ly, particularly, rarely, unusually

generate beget, breed, bring about, cause, cre~ ate, engender, form, give rise to, initiate, make, originate, procreate, produce, propa~ gate, spawn, whip up
Antonyms annihilate, crush, destroy, end, ex~ tinguish, kill, terminate

generation **1.** begetting, breeding, creation, engenderment, formation, genesis, origination, procreation, production, propagation, repro~ duction **2.** age group, breed, crop **3.** age, day, days, epoch, era, period, time, times

generic all-encompassing, blanket, collective, common, comprehensive, general, inclusive, sweeping, universal, wide
Antonyms individual, particular, precise, specific

generosity **1.** beneficence, benevolence, boun~ teousness, bounty, charity, kindness, largess *or* largesse, liberality, munificence, open-handedness **2.** disinterestedness, goodness, high-mindedness, magnanimity, nobleness, unselfishness

God loveth a cheerful giver
Bible: II Corinthians

generous **1.** beneficent, benevolent, bounteous, bountiful, charitable, free, hospitable, kind, lavish, liberal, munificent, open-handed, princely, prodigal, ungrudging, unstinting **2.** big-hearted, disinterested, good, high-minded, lofty, magnanimous, noble, unselfish **3.** abun~ dant, ample, copious, full, lavish, liberal, overflowing, plentiful, rich, unstinting
Antonyms avaricious, cheap, close-fisted, greedy, mean, minimal, miserly, parsimoni~ ous, scanty, selfish, small, stingy, tight, tiny

It is easy to be generous with other people's proper~ ty

genesis beginning, birth, commencement, creation, dawn, engendering, formation, generation, inception, origin, outset, propagation, root, source, start
Antonyms completion, conclusion, end, finish, termination

genial affable, agreeable, amiable, cheerful, cheery, congenial, convivial, cordial, easygoing, enlivening, friendly, glad, good-natured, happy, hearty, jolly, jovial, joyous, kind, kindly, merry, pleasant, sunny, warm, warm-hearted
Antonyms cheerless, cool, discourteous, frigid, morose, rude, sardonic, sullen, unfriendly, ungracious, unpleasant

geniality affability, agreeableness, amiability, cheerfulness, cheeriness, congenialness, conviviality, cordiality, friendliness, gladness, good cheer, good nature, happiness, heartiness, jollity, joviality, joy, joyousness, kindliness, kindness, mirth, pleasantness, sunniness, warm-heartedness, warmth

genitals genitalia, loins, private parts, pudenda, reproductive organs, sex organs

genius 1. adept, brain (*informal*), brainbox, buff (*informal*), expert, hotshot (*informal*), intellect (*informal*), maestro, master, master-hand, mastermind, maven (*U.S.*), virtuoso, whiz (*informal*) 2. ability, aptitude, bent, brilliance, capacity, creative power, endowment, faculty, flair, gift, inclination, knack, propensity, talent, turn
Antonyms dolt, dunce, fool, half-wit, idiot, imbecile, nincompoop, simpleton

Genius is one per cent inspiration and ninety-nine per cent perspiration
Thomas Alva Edison *Life*

When a true genius appears in the world, you may know him by this sign, that the dunces are all in confederacy against him
Jonathan Swift *Thoughts on Various Subjects*

The true genius is a mind of large general powers, accidentally determined to some particular direction
Dr. Johnson *Lives of the English Poets*

Genius is...the child of imitation
Joshua Reynolds *Discourses on Art*

Genius must be born, and never can be taught
John Dryden *To Mr. Congreve*

In every work of genius we recognize our own rejected thoughts
Ralph Waldo Emerson *Self-Reliance*

I have nothing to declare but my genius
Oscar Wilde

Every man of genius is considerably helped by being dead
Robert Lynd

Genius does what it must,
And Talent does what it can
Owen Meredith *Last Words of a Sensitive Second-rate Poet*

Genius is only a greater aptitude for patience
Comte de Buffon

genre brand, category, character, class, fashion, genus, group, kind, school, sort, species, stamp, style, type

genteel aristocratic, civil, courteous, courtly, cultivated, cultured, elegant, fashionable, formal, gentlemanly, ladylike, mannerly, polished, polite, refined, respectable, sophisticated, stylish, urbane, well-bred, well-mannered
Antonyms discourteous, ill-bred, impolite, inelegant, low-bred, natural, plebeian, rude, unaffected, uncultured, unmannerly, unpolished, unrefined

gentility 1. breeding, civility, courtesy, courtliness, cultivation, culture, decorum, elegance, etiquette, formality, good breeding, good manners, mannerliness, polish, politeness, propriety, refinement, respectability, sophistication, urbanity 2. blue blood, gentle birth, good family, high birth, nobility, rank 3. aristocracy, elite, gentlefolk, gentry, nobility, nobles, ruling class, upper class

It is almost a definition of a gentleman to say that he is one who never inflicts pain
Cardinal Newman *The Idea of a University*

gentle 1. amiable, benign, bland, compassionate, dove-like, humane, kind, kindly, lenient, meek, merciful, mild, pacific, peaceful, placid, quiet, soft, sweet-tempered, tender 2. balmy, calm, clement, easy, light, low, mild, moderate, muted, placid, quiet, serene, slight, smooth, soft, soothing, temperate, tranquil, untroubled 3. easy, gradual, imperceptible, light, mild, moderate, slight, slow 4. biddable, broken, docile, manageable, placid, tame, tractable 5. *archaic* aristocratic, civil, courteous, cultured, elegant, genteel, gentlemanlike, gentlemanly, high-born, ladylike, noble, polished, polite, refined, upper-class, well-born, well-bred
Antonyms aggressive, cruel, fierce, hard, harsh, heartless, impolite, powerful, rough, savage, sharp, strong, sudden, unkind, unmanageable, violent, wild

gentlemanly civil, civilized, courteous, cultivated, debonair, gallant, genteel, gentlemanlike, honourable, mannerly, noble, obliging, polished, polite, refined, reputable, suave, urbane, well-bred, well-mannered

gentleness compassion, kindliness, kindness, lightness of touch, mansuetude (*archaic*), mildness, softness, sweetness, tenderness

gentry aristocracy, elite, gentility, gentlefolk, nobility, nobles, ruling class, upper class, upper crust (*informal*)

genuine 1. actual, authentic, bona fide, honest, legitimate, natural, on the level, original, pure, real, sound, sterling, the real McCoy, true, unadulterated, unalloyed, veritable 2. artless, candid, earnest, frank, heartfelt, hon~est, sincere, unaffected, unfeigned
Antonyms affected, artificial, bogus, counter~feit, fake, false, feigned, fraudulent, hypo~critical, imitation, insincere, phoney, pseudo (*informal*), sham, simulated, spurious

genus breed, category, class, genre, group, kind, order, race, set, sort, type

geography

Branches of geography

biogeography
cartography
chorography
chorology
climatology
demography
geology
geomorphology
glaciology
hydrology
human geography
meteorology
oceanography
oceanology
orography *or* orology
pedology
physical geography
political geography *or* geopolitics
seismology
topography
vulcanology

Geography terms and features

afforestation
antipodes
arête
atlas
atmosphere
atoll
basin
bay
beach
canyon
cliff
climate
col
conservation
continent
continental drift
continental shelf
contour
conurbation
coombe
coral reef
core
corrie, cirque *or* cwm
crag
crater
crevasse
crust
culvert
deforestation
delta
desert
desertification
dormitory
dyke
earthquake
eastings
environment
epicentre
equator
erosion
escarpment
estuary
fault
fell
fjord
flood plain
glaciation
glacier
glade
glen
global warming
green belt
greenhouse effect
grid reference
hanging valley
headland
ice cap
infrastructure
International Date Line
irrigation
isobar
isobath
isohyet
isotherm
isthmus
jungle
lagoon
latitude
levée
loch
longitude
longshore drift
mantle
map
meander
Mercator projection
moraine
new town
northern hemisphere
northings
North Pole
occidental
ocean
Ordnance Survey
oriental
ozone layer
permafrost
plate tectonics
pollution
precipitation
rainforest
rain shadow
reef
relief map
ridge
rift valley
rill
river basin
rivulet
salt flat
salt lake
sandbank
sand bar
sand dune
savanna *or* savannah
scree
sierra
snow line
southern hemisphere
South Pole
spit
spring
spur
stack
steppe
subsoil
suburb
tarn
temperate
Third World
topsoil
tor
tropics
tsunami
tundra
urbanization
veld *or* veldt
volcano
wadi
watercourse
water cycle
waterfall
watershed
water table
weathering
wetland
whirlpool

Famous geographers

Sir Halford John Mackinder [British]
Gerardus Mercator (Gerhard Kremer) [Flemish]
Ptolemy [Greek]
Mary Somerville [British]
Strabo [Greek]

geology

Geological eras

Cenozoic
Mesozoic
Palaeozoic
Precambrian

Geological periods

Quaternary
Tertiary
Cretaceous
Jurassic
Triassic
Permian
Carboniferous
Devonian
Silurian
Ordovician
Cambrian

Epochs of the Cenozoic era

Holocene
Pleistocene
Pliocene
Miocene
Oligocene
Eocene
Palaeocene

germ 1. bacterium, bug (*informal*), microbe, microorganism, virus 2. beginning, bud, cause, embryo, origin, root, rudiment, seed, source, spark **3.** bud, egg, embryo, nucleus, ovule, ovum, seed, spore, sprout

germane akin, allied, apposite, appropriate, apropos, apt, cognate, connected, fitting, kindred, material, pertinent, proper, related, relevant, suitable, to the point *or* purpose
Antonyms extraneous, foreign, immaterial, inappropriate, irrelevant, unrelated

germinate bud, develop, generate, grow, originate, pullulate, shoot, sprout, swell, vegetate

gestation development, evolution, incubation, maturation, pregnancy, ripening

gesticulate gesture, indicate, make a sign, motion, sign, signal, wave

gesticulation arm-waving, gestures, signalling, waving

gesture 1. *noun* action, gesticulation, indication, motion, sign, signal **2.** *verb* gesticulate, indicate, motion, sign, signal, wave

get 1. achieve, acquire, attain, bag, bring, come by, come into possession of, earn, fall heir to, fetch, gain, glean, inherit, land, make, net, obtain, pick up, procure, realize, reap, receive, score (*slang*), secure, succeed to, win **2.** be afflicted with, become infected with, be smitten by, catch, come down with, contract, fall victim to, take **3.** arrest, capture, collar (*informal*), grab, lay hold of, nab (*informal*), nail (*informal*), seize, take, trap **4.** become, come to be, grow, turn, wax **5.** catch, comprehend, fathom, follow, get the picture, hear, notice, perceive, see, suss (out) (*slang*), take in, understand, work out **6.** arrive, come, make it (*informal*), reach **7.** arrange, contrive, fix, manage, succeed, wangle (*informal*) **8.** coax, convince, induce, influence, persuade, prevail upon, sway, talk into, wheedle, win over **9.** communicate with, contact, get in touch with, reach **10.** *informal* affect, arouse, excite, have an effect on, impact on, impress, move, stimulate, stir, touch, tug at (someone's) heartstrings (*often facetious*) **11.** *informal* annoy, bother, bug (*informal*), gall, get (someone's) goat (*slang*), irk, irritate, nark (*Brit., Austral., & N.Z. slang*), pique, rub (someone) up the wrong way, upset, vex **12.** baffle, confound, mystify, nonplus, perplex, puzzle, stump

get across 1. cross, ford, negotiate, pass over, traverse **2.** bring home to, communicate, convey, get (something) through to, impart, make clear *or* understood, put over, transmit

get ahead 1. advance, be successful, cut it (*informal*), do well, flourish, get on, make good, make one's mark, progress, prosper, succeed, thrive **2.** excel, leave behind, outdo, outmanoeuvre, overtake, surpass

get along 1. agree, be compatible, be friendly, get on, harmonize, hit it off (*informal*) **2.** cope, develop, fare, get by (*informal*), make out (*informal*), manage, progress, shift **3.** be off, depart, get on one's bike (*Brit. slang*), go, go away, go to hell (*informal*), leave, make tracks, move off, sling one's hook (*Brit. slang*), slope off

get at 1. acquire, attain, come to grips with, gain access to, get, get hold of, reach **2.** hint, imply, intend, lead up to, mean, suggest **3.** annoy, attack, be on one's back (*slang*), blame, carp, criticize, find fault with, hassle (*informal*), irritate, nag, nark (*Brit., Austral., & N.Z. slang*), pick on, put the boot into (*slang*), taunt **4.** bribe, buy off, corrupt, influence, suborn, tamper with

getaway break, break-out, decampment, escape, flight

get away abscond, break free, break out, decamp, depart, disappear, escape, flee, leave, make good one's escape, slope off

get back 1. recoup, recover, regain, repossess, retrieve **2.** arrive home, come back *or* home, return, revert, revisit **3.** *with* **at** be avenged, get even with, get one's own back, give tit for tat, hit back, retaliate, settle the score with, take vengeance on

get by 1. circumvent, get ahead of, go around, go past, overtake, pass, round **2.** *informal* contrive, cope, exist, fare, get along, keep one's head above water, make both ends meet, manage, subsist, survive

get down 1. alight, bring down, climb down, descend, disembark, dismount, get off, lower, step down **2.** bring down, depress, dishearten, dispirit

get in alight, appear, arrive, collect, come, embark, enter, include, infiltrate, insert, interpose, land, make inroads (into), mount, penetrate

get off 1. alight, depart, descend, disembark, dismount, escape, exit, leave **2.** detach, remove, shed, take off

get on 1. ascend, board, climb, embark, mount **2.** advance, cope, cut it (*informal*), fare, get along, make out (*informal*), manage, progress, prosper, succeed **3.** agree, be compatible, be friendly, concur, get along, harmonize, hit it off (*informal*)

get out alight, break out, clear out (*informal*), decamp, escape, evacuate, extricate oneself, free oneself, leave, vacate, withdraw

get out of avoid, body-swerve (*Scot.*), dodge, escape, evade, shirk

get over 1. cross, ford, get across, pass, pass over, surmount, traverse **2.** come round, get better, mend, pull through, rally, recover from, revive, survive **3.** defeat, get the better of, master, overcome, shake off **4.** communi~

cate, convey, get *or* put across, impart, make clear *or* understood

get round 1. bypass, circumvent, edge, evade, outmanoeuvre, skirt 2. *informal* cajole, coax, convert, persuade, prevail upon, talk round, wheedle, win over

get together accumulate, assemble, collect, congregate, convene, converge, gather, join, meet, muster, rally, unite

get-together celebration, conference, do (*informal*), function, gabfest (*informal, chiefly U.S.*), gathering, jolly (*Brit. informal*), knees-up (*Brit. informal*), meeting, party, reception, social

get up arise, ascend, climb, increase, mount, rise, scale, stand

gewgaw bagatelle, bauble, bijou, gaud, gimcrack, kickshaw, knick-knack, novelty, plaything, toy, trifle, trinket

ghastly ashen, cadaverous, deathlike, deathly pale, dreadful, frightful, from hell (*informal*), godawful (*slang*), grim, grisly, gruesome, hideous, horrendous, horrible, horrid, like death warmed up (*informal*), livid, loathsome, pale, pallid, repellent, shocking, spectral, terrible, terrifying, wan
Antonyms appealing, attractive, beautiful, blooming, charming, healthy, lovely, pleasing

ghost 1. apparition, eidolon, manes, phantasm, phantom, revenant, shade (*literary*), soul, spectre, spirit, spook (*informal*), wraith 2. glimmer, hint, possibility, semblance, shadow, suggestion, trace

ghostly eerie, ghostlike, illusory, insubstantial, phantasmal, phantom, spectral, spooky (*informal*), supernatural, uncanny, unearthly, weird, wraithlike

ghoulish disgusting, grisly, gruesome, macabre, morbid, sick (*informal*), unwholesome

giant 1. *noun* behemoth, colossus, Hercules, leviathan, monster, ogre, titan 2. *adjective* Brobdingnagian, colossal, elephantine, enormous, gargantuan, gigantic, ginormous (*informal*), huge, humongous *or* humungous (*U.S. slang*), immense, jumbo (*informal*), large, mammoth, monstrous, prodigious, stellar (*informal*), titanic, vast
Antonyms (*sense 2*) dwarf, Lilliputian, miniature, pygmy *or* pigmy, tiny

gibber babble, blab, blabber, blather, cackle, chatter, gabble, jabber, prattle, rabbit (*Brit. informal*), waffle (*informal, chiefly Brit.*)

gibberish all Greek (*informal*), babble, balderdash, balls (*taboo slang*), bilge (*informal*), blather, bosh (*informal*), bull (*slang*), bullshit (*taboo slang*), bunkum *or* buncombe (*chiefly U.S.*), cobblers (*Brit. taboo slang*), crap (*slang*), double talk, drivel, eyewash (*informal*), gabble, garbage (*informal*), gobbledegook (*informal*), guff (*slang*), hogwash, hokum (*slang, chiefly U.S. & Canad.*), horsefeathers (*U.S. slang*), hot air (*informal*), jabber, jargon, moonshine, mumbo jumbo, nonsense, pap, piffle (*informal*), poppycock (*informal*), prattle, shit (*taboo slang*), tommyrot, tosh (*slang, chiefly Brit.*), tripe (*informal*), twaddle, yammer (*informal*)

gibbous bulging, convex, crookbacked, humpbacked, humped, hunchbacked, hunched, protuberant, rounded

gibe, jibe 1. *verb* deride, flout, jeer, make fun of, mock, poke fun at, ridicule, scoff, scorn, sneer, take the piss out of (*slang*), taunt, twit 2. *noun* barb, crack (*slang*), cutting remark, derision, dig, jeer, mockery, ridicule, sarcasm, scoffing, sneer, taunt

giddiness dizziness, faintness, light-headedness, vertigo

giddy 1. dizzy, dizzying, faint, light-headed, reeling, unsteady, vertiginous 2. capricious, careless, changeable, changeful, erratic, fickle, flighty, frivolous, heedless, impulsive, inconstant, irresolute, irresponsible, reckless, scatterbrained, silly, thoughtless, unbalanced, unstable, unsteady, vacillating, volatile, wild
Antonyms calm, constant, determined, earnest, resolute, serious, steady

gift 1. benefaction, bequest, bonus, boon, bounty, contribution, donation, grant, gratuity, hand-out, largess *or* largesse, legacy, offering, present 2. ability, aptitude, attribute, bent, capability, capacity, endowment, faculty, flair, genius, knack, power, talent, turn

gifted able, accomplished, adroit, brilliant, capable, clever, expert, ingenious, intelligent, masterly, skilled, talented
Antonyms amateur, backward, dull, incapable, inept, retarded, slow, talentless, unskilled

gigantic Brobdingnagian, colossal, Cyclopean, elephantine, enormous, gargantuan, giant, herculean, huge, humongous *or* humungous (*U.S. slang*), immense, mammoth, monstrous, prodigious, stellar (*informal*), stupendous, titanic, tremendous, vast
Antonyms diminutive, insignificant, little, miniature, puny, small, tiny, weak

giggle *verb/noun* cackle, chortle, chuckle, laugh, snigger, tee-hee, titter, twitter

gild adorn, beautify, bedeck, brighten, coat, deck, dress up, embellish, embroider, enhance, enrich, garnish, grace, ornament

gimcrack 1. *adjective* cheap, rubbishy, shoddy, tawdry, trashy 2. *noun* bauble, gewgaw, kickshaw, plaything, toy, trinket

gimmick contrivance, device, dodge, gadget, gambit, gizmo (*slang, chiefly U.S.*), ploy, scheme, stratagem, stunt, trick

gingerly 1. *adverb* carefully, cautiously, charily, circumspectly, daintily, delicately, fastidiously, hesitantly, reluctantly, squeamishly, suspiciously, timidly, warily 2. *adjective* careful, cautious, chary, circumspect, dainty, delicate, fastidious, hesitant, reluctant, squeamish, suspicious, timid, wary
Antonyms boldly, carelessly, confidently, rashly

gird[1] *verb* 1. belt, bind, girdle 2. blockade, encircle, enclose, encompass, enfold, engird, environ, hem in, pen, ring, surround 3. brace, fortify, make ready, prepare, ready, steel

gird[2] *verb* deride, gibe, jeer, make fun of, mock, poke fun at, ridicule, scoff, scorn, sneer, taunt

girdle 1. *noun* band, belt, cincture, cummerbund, fillet, sash, waistband 2. *verb* bind, bound, encircle, enclose, encompass, engird, environ, enwreath, gird, hem, ring, surround

girl bird (*slang*), chick (*slang*), colleen (*Irish*), damsel (*archaic*), daughter, female child, lass, lassie (*informal*), maid (*archaic*), maiden (*archaic*), miss, wench

girth bulk, circumference, measure, size

gist core, drift, essence, force, idea, import, marrow, meaning, nub, pith, point, quintessence, sense, significance, substance

give 1. accord, administer, allow, award, bestow, commit, confer, consign, contribute, deliver, donate, entrust, furnish, grant, hand over *or* out, make over, permit, present, provide, purvey, supply, vouchsafe 2. announce, be a source of, communicate, emit, impart, issue, notify, pronounce, publish, render, transmit, utter 3. demonstrate, display, evidence, indicate, manifest, offer, proffer, provide, set forth, show 4. allow, cede, concede, devote, grant, hand over, lend, relinquish, surrender, yield 5. cause, do, engender, lead, make, occasion, perform, produce 6. bend, break, collapse, fall, recede, retire, sink
Antonyms accept, get, hold, keep, receive, take, withdraw

It is more blessed to give than to receive
Bible: Acts

give away betray, disclose, divulge, expose, grass (*Brit. slang*), inform on, leak, let out, let slip, let the cat out of the bag (*informal*), put the finger on (*informal*), reveal, shop (*slang, chiefly Brit.*), uncover

give in admit defeat, capitulate, collapse, comply, concede, quit, submit, succumb, surrender, yield

given addicted, apt, disposed, inclined, liable, likely, prone

give off discharge, emit, exhale, exude, produce, release, send out, smell of, throw out, vent

give out 1. discharge, emit, exhale, exude, produce, release, send out, smell of, throw out, vent 2. announce, broadcast, communicate, disseminate, impart, make known, notify, publish, shout from the rooftops (*informal*), transmit, utter

give up abandon, call it a day *or* night, capitulate, cease, cede, cut out, desist, despair, fall by the wayside, forswear, hand over, kick (*informal*), kiss (something) goodbye, leave off, quit, relinquish, renounce, resign, say goodbye to, step down (*informal*), stop, surrender, throw in the sponge, throw in the towel, waive

glacial 1. arctic, biting, bitter, chill, chilly, cold, freezing, frigid, frosty, frozen, gelid, icy, piercing, polar, raw, wintry 2. antagonistic, cold, frigid, hostile, icy, inimical, unfriendly

glad 1. blithesome (*literary*), cheerful, chuffed (*slang*), contented, delighted, gay, gleeful, gratified, happy, jocund, jovial, joyful, overjoyed, pleased, willing 2. animated, cheerful, cheering, cheery, delightful, felicitous, gratifying, joyous, merry, pleasant, pleasing
Antonyms depressed, discontented, displeased, melancholy, miserable, sad, sorrowful, unhappy

gladden cheer, delight, elate, enliven, exhilarate, gratify, hearten, please, rejoice

gladly cheerfully, freely, gaily, gleefully, happily, jovially, joyfully, joyously, lief (*rare*), merrily, readily, willingly, with (a) good grace, with pleasure
Antonyms dolefully, grudgingly, reluctantly, sadly, unenthusiastically, unwillingly

gladness animation, blitheness, cheerfulness, delight, felicity, gaiety, glee, happiness, high spirits, hilarity, jollity, joy, joyousness, mirth, pleasure

glamorous alluring, attractive, beautiful, bewitching, captivating, charming, dazzling, elegant, enchanting, entrancing, exciting, fascinating, glittering, glitzy (*slang*), glossy, lovely, prestigious, smart
Antonyms colourless, dull, unattractive, unexciting, unglamorous

glamour allure, appeal, attraction, beauty, bewitchment, charm, enchantment, fascination, magnetism, prestige, ravishment, witchery

glance *verb* 1. check, check out (*informal*), clock (*Brit. informal*), gaze, glimpse, look, peek, peep, scan, take a dekko at (*Brit. slang*), view 2. flash, gleam, glimmer, glint, glisten, glitter, reflect, shimmer, shine, twinkle 3. bounce, brush, graze, rebound, ricochet, skim 4. *with* **over, through,** *etc.* browse, dip into, flip through, leaf through, riffle through, run over *or* through, scan, skim through,

thumb through *~noun* **5.** brief look, butcher's (*Brit. slang*), dekko (*slang*), gander (*informal*), glimpse, look, peek, peep, quick look, shufti (*Brit. slang*), squint, view **6.** flash, gleam, glimmer, glint, reflection, sparkle, twinkle **7.** allusion, passing mention, reference
Antonyms (*sense 1*) peruse, scrutinize, study (*sense 5*) examination, good look, inspection, perusal

glare *verb* **1.** frown, give a dirty look, glower, look daggers, lour *or* lower, scowl, stare angrily **2.** blaze, dazzle, flame, flare *~noun* **3.** angry stare, black look, dirty look, frown, glower, lour *or* lower, scowl **4.** blaze, brilliance, dazzle, flame, flare, glow **5.** flashiness, floridness, gaudiness, loudness, meretriciousness, showiness, tawdriness

glaring **1.** audacious, blatant, conspicuous, egregious, flagrant, gross, manifest, obvious, open, outrageous, outstanding, overt, patent, rank, unconcealed, visible **2.** blazing, bright, dazzling, flashy, florid, garish, glowing, loud
Antonyms concealed, hidden, inconspicuous, obscure, soft, subdued, subtle

glasses

Men seldom make passes
At girls who wear glasses

Dorothy Parker

glassy **1.** clear, glossy, icy, shiny, slick, slippery, smooth, transparent **2.** blank, cold, dazed, dull, empty, expressionless, fixed, glazed, lifeless, vacant

glaze **1.** *verb* burnish, coat, enamel, furbish, gloss, lacquer, polish, varnish **2.** *noun* coat, enamel, finish, gloss, lacquer, lustre, patina, polish, shine, varnish

gleam *noun* **1.** beam, flash, glimmer, glow, ray, sparkle **2.** brightness, brilliance, coruscation, flash, gloss, lustre, sheen, splendour **3.** flicker, glimmer, hint, inkling, ray, suggestion, trace *~verb* **4.** coruscate, flare, flash, glance, glimmer, glint, glisten, glitter, glow, scintillate, shimmer, shine, sparkle

gleaming bright, bright as a button, brilliant, burnished, catching the light, glimmering, glistening, glowing, lustrous, scintillating, shining, sparkling
Antonyms dull, lustreless, unpolished

glean accumulate, amass, collect, cull, garner, gather, harvest, learn, pick, pick up, reap, select

glee cheerfulness, delight, elation, exhilaration, exuberance, exultation, fun, gaiety, gladness, hilarity, jocularity, jollity, joviality, joy, joyfulness, joyousness, liveliness, merriment, mirth, sprightliness, triumph, verve
Antonyms depression, gloom, melancholy, misery, sadness

gleeful cheerful, chirpy (*informal*), cock-a-hoop, delighted, elated, exuberant, exultant, gay, gratified, happy, jocund, jovial, joyful, joyous, jubilant, merry, mirthful, overjoyed, over the moon (*informal*), pleased, rapt, triumphant

glib artful, easy, fast-talking, fluent, garrulous, insincere, plausible, quick, ready, slick, slippery, smooth, smooth-tongued, suave, talkative, voluble
Antonyms halting, hesitant, implausible, sincere, tongue-tied

glibness fluency, gift of the gab, patter, plausibility, readiness, slickness, smoothness

glide coast, drift, float, flow, fly, roll, run, sail, skate, skim, slide, slip, soar

glimmer *verb* **1.** blink, flicker, gleam, glisten, glitter, glow, shimmer, shine, sparkle, twinkle *~noun* **2.** blink, flicker, gleam, glow, ray, shimmer, sparkle, twinkle **3.** flicker, gleam, grain, hint, inkling, ray, suggestion, trace

glimpse **1.** *noun* brief view, butcher's (*Brit. slang*), gander (*informal*), glance, look, peek, peep, quick look, shufti (*Brit. slang*), sight, sighting, squint **2.** *verb* catch sight of, clock (*Brit. informal*), descry, espy, sight, spot, spy, view

glint **1.** *verb* flash, gleam, glimmer, glitter, shine, sparkle, twinkle **2.** *noun* flash, gleam, glimmer, glitter, shine, sparkle, twinkle, twinkling

glisten coruscate, flash, glance, glare, gleam, glimmer, glint, glitter, scintillate, shimmer, shine, sparkle, twinkle

glitter *verb* **1.** coruscate, flare, flash, glare, gleam, glimmer, glint, glisten, scintillate, shimmer, shine, sparkle, twinkle *~noun* **2.** beam, brightness, brilliance, flash, glare, gleam, lustre, radiance, scintillation, sheen, shimmer, shine, sparkle **3.** display, gaudiness, gilt, glamour, pageantry, show, showiness, splendour, tinsel

gloaming dusk, eventide (*archaic*), half-light, nightfall, twilight

gloat crow, drool, exult, glory, relish, revel in, rub it in (*informal*), rub one's hands, rub someone's nose in it, triumph, vaunt

global **1.** international, pandemic, planetary, universal, world, worldwide **2.** all-encompassing, all-inclusive, all-out, comprehensive, encyclopedic, exhaustive, general, thorough, total, unbounded, unlimited
Antonyms (*sense 2*) limited, narrow, parochial, restricted, sectional

globe ball, earth, orb, planet, round, sphere, world

globular globate, globelike, globoid, globose, globous, globulous, orbicular, round, spherical, spheroid

globule bead, bubble, drop, droplet, particle, pearl, pellet

gloom **1.** blackness, cloud, cloudiness, dark, darkness, dimness, dullness, dusk, duskiness, gloominess, murk, murkiness, obscurity, shade, shadow, twilight **2.** blues, dejection, depression, desolation, despair, despondency, downheartedness, low spirits, melancholy, misery, sadness, sorrow, the hump (*Brit. informal*), unhappiness, woe
Antonyms brightness, cheerfulness, daylight, delight, happiness, high spirits, jollity, joy, light, mirth, radiance

gloomy **1.** black, crepuscular, dark, dim, dismal, dreary, dull, dusky, murky, obscure, overcast, shadowy, sombre, Stygian, tenebrous **2.** bad, black, cheerless, comfortless, depressing, disheartening, dismal, dispiriting, dreary, funereal, joyless, sad, saddening, sombre **3.** blue, chapfallen, cheerless, crestfallen, dejected, despondent, dismal, dispirited, down, downcast, downhearted, down in the dumps (*informal*), down in the mouth, glum, in low spirits, low, melancholy, miserable, moody, morose, pessimistic, sad, saturnine, sullen
Antonyms blithe, bright, brilliant, cheerful, chirpy (*informal*), happy, high-spirited, jolly, jovial, light, merry, radiant, sunny, upbeat (*informal*)

glorify **1.** add lustre to, adorn, aggrandize, augment, dignify, elevate, enhance, ennoble, illuminate, immortalize, lift up, magnify, raise **2.** adore, apotheosize, beatify, bless, canonize, deify, enshrine, exalt, honour, idolize, pay homage to, revere, sanctify, venerate, worship **3.** celebrate, crack up (*informal*), cry up (*informal*), eulogize, extol, hymn, laud, lionize, magnify, panegyrize, praise, sing *or* sound the praises of
Antonyms condemn, debase, defile, degrade, desecrate, dishonour, humiliate, mock

glorious **1.** celebrated, distinguished, elevated, eminent, excellent, famed, famous, grand, honoured, illustrious, magnificent, majestic, noble, noted, renowned, sublime, triumphant **2.** beautiful, bright, brilliant, dazzling, divine, effulgent, gorgeous, radiant, resplendent, shining, splendid, splendiferous (*facetious*), superb **3.** *informal* delightful, enjoyable, excellent, fine, gorgeous, great, heavenly (*informal*), marvellous, pleasurable, splendid, splendiferous (*facetious*), wonderful
Antonyms awful, dreary, dull, gloomy, horrible, minor, ordinary, trivial, unimportant, unimpressive, unknown, unpleasant

glory *noun* **1.** celebrity, dignity, distinction, eminence, exaltation, fame, honour, illustriousness, immortality, kudos, praise, prestige, renown **2.** adoration, benediction, blessing, gratitude, homage, laudation, praise, thanksgiving, veneration, worship **3.** éclat, grandeur, greatness, magnificence, majesty, nobility, pageantry, pomp, splendour, sublimity, triumph **4.** beauty, brilliance, effulgence, gorgeousness, lustre, radiance, resplendence *~verb* **5.** boast, crow, drool, exult, gloat, pride oneself; relish, revel, take delight, triumph
Antonyms blasphemy, condemnation, disgrace, dishonour, disrepute, infamy, shame, triviality, ugliness

The paths of glory lead but to the grave
Thomas Gray *Elegy Written in a Country Churchyard*

Not in utter nakedness,
But trailing clouds of glory do we come
William Wordsworth *Intimations of Immortality*

to the greater glory of God (ad majorem Dei gloriam)
Motto of the Society of Jesus

Thus passes the glory of the world (sic transit gloria mundi)
Anon.

gloss[1] *noun* **1.** brightness, brilliance, burnish, gleam, lustre, polish, sheen, shine, varnish, veneer **2.** appearance, façade, front, mask, semblance, show, surface *~verb* **3.** burnish, finish, furbish, glaze, lacquer, polish, shine, varnish, veneer **4.** camouflage, conceal, cover up, disguise, hide, mask, smooth over, sweep under the carpet (*informal*), veil, whitewash (*informal*)

gloss[2] **1.** *noun* annotation, comment, commentary, elucidation, explanation, footnote, interpretation, note, scholium, translation **2.** *verb* annotate, comment, construe, elucidate, explain, interpret, translate

glossy bright, brilliant, burnished, glassy, glazed, lustrous, polished, sheeny, shining, shiny, silken, silky, sleek, smooth
Antonyms drab, dull, mat *or* matt, subfusc

glow *noun* **1.** burning, gleam, glimmer, incandescence, lambency, light, luminosity, phosphorescence **2.** brightness, brilliance, effulgence, radiance, splendour, vividness **3.** ardour, earnestness, enthusiasm, excitement, fervour, gusto, impetuosity, intensity, passion, vehemence, warmth **4.** bloom, blush, flush, reddening, rosiness *~verb* **5.** brighten, burn, gleam, glimmer, redden, shine, smoulder **6.** be suffused, blush, colour, fill, flush, radiate, thrill, tingle
Antonyms chill, coolness, dullness, greyness, half-heartedness, iciness, indifference, paleness, pallor, wanness

glower **1.** *verb* frown, give a dirty look, glare, look daggers, lour *or* lower, scowl **2.** *noun* angry stare, black look, dirty look, frown, glare, lour *or* lower, scowl

glowing 1. aglow, beaming, bright, flaming, florid, flushed, lambent, luminous, radiant, red, rich, ruddy, suffused, vibrant, vivid, warm 2. adulatory, complimentary, ecstatic, enthusiastic, eulogistic, laudatory, panegyrical, rave (*informal*), rhapsodic
Antonyms colourless, cool, cruel, dispassionate, dull, grey, pale, pallid, scathing, unenthusiastic, wan

glue 1. *noun* adhesive, cement, gum, mucilage, paste 2. *verb* affix, agglutinate, cement, fix, gum, paste, seal, stick

glum chapfallen, churlish, crabbed, crestfallen, crusty, dejected, doleful, down, gloomy, gruff, grumpy, huffy, ill-humoured, low, moody, morose, pessimistic, saturnine, sour, sulky, sullen, surly
Antonyms cheerful, cheery, chirpy (*informal*), jolly, joyful, merry, upbeat (*informal*)

glut *noun* 1. excess, overabundance, oversupply, plethora, saturation, superabundance, superfluity, surfeit, surplus ~*verb* 2. cram, fill, gorge, overfeed, satiate, stuff 3. choke, clog, deluge, flood, inundate, overload, oversupply, saturate
Antonyms dearth, lack, paucity, scarcity, shortage, want

glutinous adhesive, cohesive, gluey, gooey, gummy, mucilaginous, sticky, viscid, viscous

glutton gannet (*slang*), gobbler, gorger, gormandizer, gourmand, pig (*informal*)

gluttonous edacious, gormandizing, greedy, hoggish, insatiable, piggish, rapacious, ravenous, voracious

gluttony edacity, gormandizing, gourmandism, greed, greediness, piggishness, rapacity, voraciousness, voracity

gnarled contorted, knotted, knotty, knurled, leathery, rough, rugged, twisted, weather-beaten, wrinkled

gnaw 1. bite, chew, munch, nibble, worry 2. consume, devour, eat away *or* into, erode, fret, wear away *or* down 3. distress, fret, harry, haunt, nag, plague, prey on one's mind, trouble, worry

go *verb* 1. advance, decamp, depart, fare (*archaic*), journey, leave, make for, make tracks, move, move out, pass, proceed, repair, set off, slope off, travel, withdraw 2. function, move, operate, perform, run, work 3. connect, extend, fit, give access, lead, reach, run, span, spread, stretch 4. avail, concur, conduce, contribute, incline, lead to, serve, tend, work towards 5. develop, eventuate, fall out, fare, happen, pan out (*informal*), proceed, result, turn out, work out 6. accord, agree, blend, chime, complement, correspond, fit, harmonize, match, suit 7. buy it (*U.S. slang*), check out (*U.S. slang*), croak (*slang*), die, expire, give up the ghost, go belly-up (*slang*), kick it (*slang*), kick the bucket (*slang*), pass away, peg it (*informal*), peg out (*informal*), perish, pop one's clogs (*informal*), snuff it (*informal*) 8. elapse, expire, flow, lapse, pass, slip away ~*noun* 9. attempt, bid, crack (*informal*), effort, essay, shot (*informal*), stab (*informal*), try, turn, whack (*informal*), whirl (*informal*) 10. *informal* activity, animation, brio, drive, energy, force, get-up-and-go (*informal*), life, oomph (*informal*), pep, spirit, verve, vigour, vitality, vivacity
Antonyms (*sense 1*) arrive, halt, reach, remain, stay, stop (*sense 2*) break (down), fail, malfunction, stop

go about 1. circulate, move around, pass around, wander 2. approach, begin, get the show on the road, set about, tackle, take the bit between one's teeth, undertake 3. busy *or* occupy oneself with, devote oneself to

goad 1. *noun* impetus, incentive, incitement, irritation, motivation, pressure, spur, stimulation, stimulus, urge 2. *verb* annoy, arouse, be on one's back (*slang*), drive, egg on, exhort, harass, hassle (*informal*), hound, impel, incite, instigate, irritate, lash, nark (*Brit., Austral., & N.Z. slang*), prick, prod, prompt, propel, spur, stimulate, sting, urge, worry

go-ahead 1. *noun, informal* assent, authorization, consent, green light, leave, O.K. *or* okay (*informal*), permission 2. *adjective* ambitious, enterprising, go-getting (*informal*), pioneering, progressive, up-and-coming

go ahead advance, begin, continue, go forward, go on, proceed, progress

goal aim, ambition, design, destination, end, Holy Grail (*informal*), intention, limit, mark, object, objective, purpose, target

go along 1. acquiesce, agree, assent, concur, cooperate, follow 2. accompany, carry on, escort, join, keep up, move, pass, travel

go at argue, attack, blame, blast, criticize, go for the jugular, impugn, lambast(e), put down, set about, tear into (*informal*)

go away decamp, depart, exit, get on one's bike (*Brit. slang*), go to hell (*informal*), hook it (*slang*), leave, make tracks, move out, pack one's bags (*informal*), recede, sling one's hook (*Brit. slang*), slope off, withdraw

gob blob, chunk, clod, gobbet, hunk, lump, nugget, piece, wad, wodge (*Brit. informal*)

go back 1. retrocede, return, revert 2. change one's mind, desert, forsake, renege, repudiate, retract

gobble bolt, cram, devour, gorge, gulp, guzzle, pig out on (*U.S. & Canad. slang*), stuff, swallow, wolf

gobbledegook babble, cant, double talk, gabble, gibberish, Greek (*informal*), hocus-pocus, jabber, jargon, mumbo jumbo, nonsense, officialese, rigmarole, twaddle

go-between agent, broker, dealer, factor, intermediary, liaison, mediator, medium, middleman

go by 1. elapse, exceed, flow on, move onward, pass, proceed 2. adopt, be guided by, follow, heed, judge from, observe, take as guide

god

Egyptian gods and goddesses

Anubis	Ra *or* Amen-Ra
Hathor	Re
Horus	Serapis
Isis	Set
Osiris	Thoth
Ptah	

Greek gods and goddesses

Aeolus	winds
Aphrodite	love and beauty
Apollo	light, youth, and music
Ares	war
Artemis	hunting and the moon
Asclepius	healing
Athene *or* Pallas Athene	wisdom
Bacchus	wine
Boreas	north wind
Cronos	fertility of the earth
Demeter	agriculture
Dionysus	wine
Eos	dawn
Eros	love
Fates	destiny
Gaea *or* Gaia	the earth
Graces	charm and beauty
Hades	underworld
Hebe	youth and spring
Hecate	underworld
Helios	sun
Hephaestus	fire and metalworking
Hera	queen of the gods
Hermes	messenger of the gods
Horae *or* the Hours	seasons
Hymen	marriage
Hyperion	sun
Hypnos	sleep
Iris	rainbow
Momus	blame and mockery
Morpheus	sleep and dreams
Nemesis	vengeance
Nike	victory
Pan	woods and shepherds
Poseidon	sea and earthquakes
Rhea	fertility
Selene	moon
Uranus	sky
Zephyrus	west wind
Zeus	king of the gods

Roman gods and goddesses

Aesculapius	medicine
Apollo	light, youth, and music
Aurora	dawn
Bacchus	wine
Bellona	war
Bona Dea	fertility
Ceres	agriculture
Cupid	love
Cybele	nature
Diana	hunting and the moon
Faunus	forests
Flora	flowers
Janus	doors and beginnings
Juno	queen of the gods
Jupiter *or* Jove	king of the gods
Lares	household
Luna	moon
Mars	war
Mercury	messenger of the gods
Minerva	wisdom
Neptune	sea
Penates	storeroom
Phoebus	sun
Pluto	underworld
Quirinus	war
Saturn	agriculture and vegetation
Sol	sun
Somnus	sleep
Trivia	crossroads
Venus	love
Victoria	victory
Vulcan	fire and metalworking

Hindu gods and goddesses

Agni	Krishna
Brahma	Lakshmi
Devi	Maya
Durga	Rama
Ganesa	Siva *or* Shiva
Hanuman	Ushas
Indra	Varuna
Kali	Vishnu
Kama	

Norse gods and goddesses

Aegir	Idun *or* Ithunn
Aesir	Loki
Balder	Njord *or* Njorth
Frey *or* Freyr	Norns
Freya *or* Freyja	Odin *or* Othin
Frigg *or* Frigga	Thor
Hel *or* Hela	Tyr *or* Tyrr
Heimdall, Heimdal *or* Heimdallr	Vanir

Fates
see FATES, THE
Graces
see GRACES, THE
Muses
see MUSES, THE

As flies to wanton boys are we to the gods;
They kill us for their sport
William Shakespeare *King Lear*

Bacchus: a convenient deity invented by the ancients as an excuse for getting drunk
Ambrose Bierce *The Devil's Dictionary*

It is convenient that there be gods, and, as it is convenient, let us believe that there are
Ovid *Ars Amatoria*

God

If God didn't exist, man would have to invent him
Voltaire *Epître à l'auteur du nouveau livre des trois imposteurs*

God moves in a mysterious way
William Cowper *Light Shining Out of Darkness*

The voice of the people is the voice of God
Alcuin *Epistles*

God is love, but get it in writing
Gypsy Rose Lee

The nature of God is a circle of which the centre is everywhere and the circumference is nowhere
attributed to Empedocles

God is no respecter of persons
Bible: Acts

It is a fearful thing to fall into the hands of the living God
Bible: Hebrews

Thou shalt have one God only; who
Would be at the expense of two?
Arthur Hugh Clough *The Latest Decalogue*

God is subtle, but he is not malicious
Albert Einstein

God, to me, it seems,
is a verb
not a noun,
proper or improper
R. Buckminster Fuller *No More Secondhand God*

If the triangles were to make a God they would give him three sides
Montesquieu *Lettres Persones*

God and the doctor we alike adore
But only when in danger, not before;
The danger o'er, both are alike requited,
God is forgotten, and the Doctor slighted
John Owen *Epigrams*

God is really only another artist. He invented the giraffe, the elephant, and the cat. He has no real style. He just goes on trying other things
Pablo Picasso

godforsaken abandoned, backward, bleak, deserted, desolate, dismal, dreary, forlorn, gloomy, lonely, neglected, remote, wretched

godless atheistic, depraved, evil, impious, irreligious, profane, ungodly, unprincipled, unrighteous, wicked

godlike celestial, deific, deiform, divine, heavenly, superhuman, transcendent

godly devout, god-fearing, good, holy, pious, religious, righteous, saintly

go down **1.** be beaten, collapse, decline, decrease, drop, fall, founder, go under, lose, set, sink, submerge, submit, suffer defeat **2.** be commemorated (recalled, recorded, remembered)

godsend blessing, boon, manna, stroke of luck, windfall

go far advance, be successful, cut it (*informal*), do well, get ahead (*informal*), get on (*informal*), make a name for oneself, make one's mark, progress, succeed

go for **1.** clutch at, fetch, obtain, reach, seek, stretch for **2.** admire, be attracted to, be fond of, choose, favour, hold with, like, prefer **3.** assail, assault, attack, launch oneself at, rush upon, set about *or* upon, spring upon

goggle gape, gawk, gawp (*slang*), peer, rubberneck (*slang*), stare

go in (for) adopt, embrace, engage in, enter, espouse, practise, pursue, take up, undertake

going-over **1.** analysis, check, examination, inspection, investigation, perusal, recce (*slang*), review, scrutiny, study, survey **2.** beating, buffeting, doing (*informal*), drubbing, pasting (*slang*), thrashing, thumping, whipping **3.** castigation, chastisement, chiding, dressing-down (*informal*), lecture, rebuke, reprimand, row, scolding, talking-to (*informal*), tongue-lashing

go into **1.** begin, develop, enter, participate in, undertake **2.** analyse, consider, delve into, discuss, examine, inquire into, investigate, look into, probe, pursue, research, review, scrutinize, study, work over

golden **1.** blond *or* blonde, bright, brilliant, flaxen, resplendent, shining, yellow **2.** best, blissful, delightful, flourishing, glorious, halcyon, happy, joyful, joyous, precious, prosperous, rich, successful **3.** advantageous, auspicious, excellent, favourable, opportune, promising, propitious, rosy, valuable
Antonyms (*sense 1*) black, brunette, dark, dull (*sense 2*) poorest, sad, unfavourable, worst (*sense 3*) black, dark, sad, unfavourable, untimely, wretched

gone **1.** elapsed, ended, finished, over, past **2.** absent, astray, away, lacking, lost, missing, vanished **3.** dead, deceased, defunct, departed, extinct, no more **4.** consumed, done, finished, spent, used up

good *adjective* **1**. acceptable, admirable, agreeable, awesome (*slang*), bad (*slang*), capital, choice, commendable, crucial (*slang*), divine, excellent, fine, first-class, first-rate, great, hunky-dory (*informal*), pleasant, pleasing, positive, precious, satisfactory, splendid, super (*informal*), superior, tiptop, valuable, wicked (*slang*), world-class, worthy **2**. admirable, estimable, ethical, exemplary, honest, honourable, moral, praiseworthy, right, righteous, trustworthy, upright, virtuous, worthy **3**. able, accomplished, adept, adroit, capable, clever, competent, dexterous, efficient, expert, first-rate, proficient, reliable, satisfactory, serviceable, skilled, sound, suitable, talented, thorough, useful **4**. adequate, advantageous, auspicious, beneficial, convenient, favourable, fit, fitting, healthy, helpful, opportune, profitable, propitious, salubrious, salutary, suitable, useful, wholesome **5**. eatable, fit to eat, sound, uncorrupted, untainted, whole **6**. altruistic, approving, beneficent, benevolent, charitable, friendly, gracious, humane, kind, kind-hearted, kindly, merciful, obliging, well-disposed **7**. authentic, bona fide, dependable, genuine, honest, legitimate, proper, real, reliable, sound, true, trustworthy, valid **8**. decorous, dutiful, mannerly, obedient, orderly, polite, proper, seemly, well-behaved, well-mannered **9**. agreeable, cheerful, congenial, convivial, enjoyable, gratifying, happy, pleasant, pleasing, pleasurable, satisfying **10**. adequate, ample, complete, considerable, entire, extensive, full, large, long, sizable *or* sizeable, solid, substantial, sufficient, whole **11**. best, fancy, finest, newest, nicest, precious, smartest, special, valuable **12**. *of weather* balmy, bright, calm, clear, clement, cloudless, fair, halcyon, mild, sunny, sunshiny, tranquil ~*noun* **13**. advantage, avail, behalf, benefit, gain, interest, mileage (*informal*), profit, service, use, usefulness, welfare, wellbeing, worth **14**. excellence, goodness, merit, morality, probity, rectitude, right, righteousness, uprightness, virtue, worth **15**. **for good** finally, for ever, irrevocably, never to return, once and for all, permanently, *sine die*

Antonyms *adjective* (*sense 1*) awful, bad, boring, disagreeable, dull, inadequate, rotten, tedious, unpleasant (*sense 2*) bad, base, corrupt, dishonest, dishonourable, evil, immoral, improper, sinful (*sense 3*) bad, incompetent, inefficient, unsatisfactory, unskilled (*sense 4*) inappropriate, pathetic, unbecoming, unbefitting, unfavourable, unfitting, unsuitable, useless (*sense 5*) bad, decayed, mouldy, off, rotten, unsound (*sense 6*) cruel, evil, mean (*informal*), selfish, unkind, vicious, wicked (*sense 7*) counterfeit, false, fraudulent, invalid, phoney (*sense 8*) ill-mannered, mischievous, naughty, rude, unkind (*sense 10*) scant, short ~*noun* (*sense 13*) detriment, disadvantage, failure, ill-fortune, loss (*sense 14*) badness, baseness, corruption, cruelty, dishonesty, evil, immorality, meanness, wickedness

No people do so much harm as those who go about doing good
Bishop Mandell Creighton *Life*

Do good by stealth, and blush to find it fame
Alexander Pope *Epilogue to the Satires*

goodbye adieu, farewell, leave-taking, parting

good-for-nothing **1**. *noun* black sheep, idler, layabout, ne'er-do-well, numb-nut (*U.S. slang*), profligate, rapscallion, scapegrace, skiver (*Brit. slang*), waster, wastrel **2**. *adjective* feckless, idle, irresponsible, useless, worthless

good-humoured affable, amiable, cheerful, congenial, genial, good-tempered, happy, pleasant

good-looking attractive, comely, fair, handsome, personable, pretty, well-favoured

goodly **1**. ample, considerable, large, significant, sizable *or* sizeable, substantial, tidy (*informal*) **2**. agreeable, attractive, comely, desirable, elegant, fine, good-looking, graceful, handsome, personable, pleasant, pleasing, well-favoured

good-natured agreeable, benevolent, friendly, good-hearted, helpful, kind, kindly, tolerant, warm-hearted, well-disposed, willing to please

goodness **1**. excellence, merit, quality, superiority, value, worth **2**. beneficence, benevolence, friendliness, generosity, goodwill, graciousness, humaneness, kind-heartedness, kindliness, kindness, mercy, obligingness **3**. honesty, honour, integrity, merit, morality, probity, rectitude, righteousness, uprightness, virtue **4**. advantage, benefit, nourishment, nutrition, salubriousness, wholesomeness

Antonyms badness, corruption, detriment, disadvantage, dishonesty, evil, immorality, wickedness, worthlessness

Goodness is easier to recognise than to define
W.H. Auden *I Believe*

Nobody deserves to be praised for his goodness if he has not the power to be wicked. All other goodness is often only weakness and impotence of the will
Duc de la Rochefoucauld *Maxims*

Goodness is not achieved in a vacuum, but in the company of other men, attended by love
Saul Bellow *Dangling Man*

goods **1**. appurtenances, belongings, chattels, effects, furnishings, furniture, gear, movables, paraphernalia, possessions, property, things, trappings **2**. commodities, merchandise, stock, stuff, wares

goodwill amity, benevolence, favour, friendliness, friendship, heartiness, kindliness, zeal

gooey 1. glucy, glutinous, mucilaginous, soft, sticky, tacky, viscous 2. maudlin, mawkish, sentimental, slushy (*informal*), syrupy (*informal*), tear-jerking (*informal*)

go off 1. blow up, detonate, explode, fire 2. happen, occur, take place 3. decamp, depart, go away, hook it (*slang*), leave, move out, pack one's bags (*informal*), part, quit, slope off 4. *informal* go bad, go stale, rot

go on 1. continue, endure, happen, last, occur, persist, proceed, stay 2. blether, carry on, chatter, prattle, rabbit (*Brit. informal*), ramble on, waffle (*informal, chiefly Brit.*), witter (on) (*informal*)

go out 1. depart, exit, leave 2. be extinguished, die out, expire, fade out

go over 1. examine, inspect, rehearse, reiterate, review, revise, study, work over 2. peruse, read, scan, skim

gore[1] *noun* blood, bloodshed, butchery, carnage, slaughter

gore[2] *verb* impale, pierce, spit, stab, transfix, wound

gorge[1] *noun* canyon, cleft, clough (*dialect*), defile, fissure, pass, ravine

gorge[2] *verb* bolt, cram, devour, feed, fill, glut, gobble, gormandize, gulp, guzzle, overeat, pig out (*U.S. & Canad. slang*), raven, sate, satiate, stuff, surfeit, swallow, wolf

gorgeous 1. beautiful, brilliant, dazzling, drop-dead (*slang*), elegant, glittering, grand, luxuriant, magnificent, opulent, ravishing, resplendent, showy, splendid, splendiferous (*facetious*), stunning (*informal*), sumptuous, superb 2. *informal* attractive, bright, delightful, enjoyable, exquisite, fine, glorious, good, good-looking, lovely, pleasing

Antonyms cheap, dismal, dreary, dull, gloomy, homely, plain, repulsive, shabby, shoddy, sombre, ugly, unattractive, unsightly

gory blood-soaked, bloodstained, bloodthirsty, bloody, ensanguined (*literary*), murderous, sanguinary

gospel 1. certainty, fact, the last word, truth, verity 2. credo, creed, doctrine, message, news, revelation, tidings

gossamer *adjective* airy, delicate, diaphanous, fine, flimsy, gauzy, light, sheer, silky, thin, transparent

gossip *noun* 1. blether, bush telegraph, buzz, chinwag (*Brit. informal*), chitchat, clishmaclaver (*Scot.*), dirt (*U.S. slang*), gen (*Brit. informal*), hearsay, idle talk, jaw (*slang*), latest (*informal*), newsmongering (*old-fashioned*), prattle, scandal, scuttlebutt (*U.S. slang*), small talk, tittle-tattle 2. babbler, blatherskite, blether, busybody, chatterbox (*informal*), chatterer, flibbertigibbet, gossipmonger, newsmonger (*old-fashioned*), prattler, quidnunc, scandalmonger, tattler, telltale *~verb* 3. blather, blether, chat, chew the fat *or* rag (*slang*), dish the dirt (*informal*), gabble, jaw (*slang*), prate, prattle, shoot the breeze (*slang, chiefly U.S.*), tattle

There is only one thing in the world worse than being talked about, and that is not being talked about

Oscar Wilde *The Picture of Dorian Gray*

Gossip is a sort of smoke that comes from the dirty tobacco-pipes of those that diffuse it; it proves nothing but the bad taste of the smoker

George Eliot *Daniel Deronda*

go through 1. bear, brave, endure, experience, suffer, tolerate, undergo, withstand 2. consume, exhaust, squander, use 3. check, examine, explore, forage, hunt, look, search, work over

go together 1. accord, agree, fit, harmonize, make a pair, match 2. *informal* court, date (*informal, chiefly U.S.*), escort, go out with, go steady with (*informal*)

gouge 1. *verb* chisel, claw, cut, dig (out), gash, hollow (out), incise, scoop, score, scratch 2. *noun* cut, furrow, gash, groove, hollow, incision, notch, scoop, score, scratch, trench

go under default, die, drown, fail, fold (*informal*), founder, go down, sink, submerge, succumb

gourmet *bon vivant*, connoisseur, epicure, foodie (*informal*), gastronome

govern 1. administer, be in power, call the shots, call the tune, command, conduct, control, direct, guide, handle, hold sway, lead, manage, order, oversee, pilot, reign, rule, steer, superintend, supervise 2. bridle, check, contain, control, curb, direct, discipline, get the better of, hold in check, inhibit, keep a tight rein on, master, regulate, restrain, subdue, tame 3. decide, determine, guide, influence, rule, sway, underlie

government 1. administration, authority, dominion, execution, governance, law, polity, rule, sovereignty, state, statecraft 2. administration, executive, ministry, powers-that-be, regime 3. authority, command, control, direction, domination, guidance, management, regulation, restraint, superintendence, supervision, sway

Types of government

absolutism	by an absolute ruler
anarchy	absence of government
aristocracy	by nobility
autarchy *or* autocracy	by an unrestricted individual
bureaucracy	by officials
communalism	by self-governing communities

constitutionalism	according to a constitution
corporatism	by corporate groups
democracy	by the people
despotism	by a despot or absolute ruler
diarchy *or* dyarchy	by two rulers
dictatorship	by dictator
ergatocracy	by the workers
gerontocracy	by old people
gynaecocracy *or* gynarchy	by women
hagiocracy *or* hagiarchy	by holy men
heptarchy	by seven rulers
hexarchy	by six rulers
hierocracy *or* hierarchy	by priests
imperialism	by an emperor or empire
isocracy	by equals
meritocracy	by rulers chosen according to ability
mobocracy	by the mob
monarchy	by monarch
monocracy	by one ruler
nomocracy	by rule of law
ochlocracy	by mob
octarchy	by eight rulers
oligarchy	by the few
pantisocracy	by all equally
pentarchy	by five rulers
plutocracy	by the rich
pornocracy	by whores
ptochocracy	by the poor
quangocracy	by quangos
slavocracy	by slaveholders
squirearchy *or* squirarchy	by squires
stratocracy	by the army
technocracy	by experts
tetrarchy	by four rulers
theocracy *or* thearchy	by a deity
triarchy	by three rulers
tyranny	by a tyrant

Government is a contrivance of human wisdom to provide for human wants. Men have a right that these wants should be provided for by this wisdom
Edmund Burke *Reflections on the Revolution in France*

Every country has the government it deserves
Joseph de Maistre *Lettres et Opuscules Inédits*

All government is evil, and the parent of evil...The best government is that which governs least
John L. O'Sullivan

Governments need to have both shepherds and butchers
Voltaire *The Piccini Notebooks*

The worst thing in this world, next to anarchy, is government
Henry Ward Beecher *Proverbs from Plymouth pulpit*

I would not give half a guinea to live under one form of government rather than another. It is of no moment to the happiness of an individual
Dr. Johnson

There is no art which one government sooner learns of another than that of draining money from the pockets of the people
Adam Smith *The Wealth of Nations*

Government is like a baby: an alimentary canal with a big appetite at one end and no sense of responsibility at the other
Ronald Reagan

Nothing appears more surprising to those who consider human affairs with a philosophical eye, than the ease with which the many are governed by the few
David Hume *First Principles of Government*

If the Government is big enough to give you everything you want, it is big enough to take away everything you have
Gerald Ford

When, in countries that are called civilized, you see age going to the workhouse and youth to the gallows, something must be wrong in the system of government
Thomas Paine *The Rights of Man*

governmental administrative, bureaucratic, executive, ministerial, official, political, sovereign, state

governor administrator, boss (*informal*), chief, commander, comptroller, controller, director, executive, head, leader, manager, overseer, ruler, superintendent, supervisor
Related adjective: gubernatorial

go with accompany, agree, blend, complement, concur, correspond, fit, harmonize, match, suit

go without abstain, be denied, be deprived of, deny oneself, do without, go short, lack, want

gown costume, dress, frock, garb, garment, habit, robe

Gowns and dresses
see CLOTHES

grab bag, capture, catch *or* take hold of, catch (up), clutch, grasp, grip, latch on to, nab (*informal*), nail (*informal*), pluck, seize, snap up, snatch

grace *noun* **1.** attractiveness, beauty, charm, comeliness, ease, elegance, finesse, gracefulness, loveliness, pleasantness, poise, polish, refinement, shapeliness, tastefulness **2.** benefaction, beneficence, benevolence, favour, generosity, goodness, goodwill, kindliness, kindness **3.** breeding, consideration, cultivation, decency, decorum, etiquette, mannerli~

ness, manners, propriety, tact **4**. charity, clemency, compassion, forgiveness, indulgence, leniency, lenity, mercy, pardon, quarter, reprieve **5**. benediction, blessing, prayer, thanks, thanksgiving *~verb* **6**. adorn, beautify, bedeck, deck, decorate, dignify, distinguish, elevate, embellish, enhance, enrich, favour, garnish, glorify, honour, ornament, set off

Antonyms *noun* awkwardness, bad manners, clumsiness, condemnation, disfavour, harshness, ill will, inelegance, stiffness, tactlessness, tastelessness, ugliness, ungainliness *~verb* desecrate, dishonour, insult, ruin, spoil

Some have meat and cannot eat,
Some cannot eat that want it;
But we have meat, and we can eat,
Sae let the Lord be thankit

Robert Burns *Grace Before Meat*

graceful agile, beautiful, becoming, charming, comely, easy, elegant, fine, flowing, gracile (*rare*), natural, pleasing, smooth, symmetrical, tasteful

Antonyms awkward, clumsy, gawky, inelegant, plain, ponderous, stiff, ugly, ungainly, ungraceful

graceless **1**. barbarous, boorish, coarse, crude, ill-mannered, improper, indecorous, loutish, rude, shameless, unmannerly, unsophisticated, vulgar **2**. awkward, clumsy, forced, gauche, gawky, inelegant, rough, uncouth, ungainly, untutored

Graces, the *Greek myth* Charities

Graces

Aglaia	Thalia
Euphrosyne	

gracious accommodating, affable, amiable, beneficent, benevolent, benign, benignant, charitable, chivalrous, civil, compassionate, considerate, cordial, courteous, courtly, friendly, hospitable, indulgent, kind, kindly, lenient, loving, merciful, mild, obliging, pleasing, polite, well-mannered

Antonyms brusque, cold, discourteous, gruff, haughty, impolite, mean, remote, rude, surly, unfriendly, ungracious, unpleasant

gradation **1**. array, progression, sequence, series, succession **2**. degree, grade, level, mark, measurement, notch, place, point, position, rank, stage, step **3**. arrangement, classification, grouping, ordering, sorting

grade *noun* **1**. brand, category, class, condition, degree, echelon, group, level, mark, notch, order, place, position, quality, rank, rung, size, stage, station, step **2**. **make the grade** *informal* come through with flying colours, come up to scratch (*informal*), measure up, measure up to expectations, pass muster, prove acceptable, succeed, win through **3**. acclivity, bank, declivity, gradient, hill, incline, rise, slope *~verb* **4**. arrange, brand, class, classify, evaluate, group, order, range, rank, rate, sequence, sort, value

gradient acclivity, bank, declivity, grade, hill, incline, rise, slope

gradual continuous, even, gentle, graduated, moderate, piecemeal, progressive, regular, slow, steady, successive, unhurried

Antonyms abrupt, broken, instantaneous, overnight, sudden

gradually bit by bit, by degrees, drop by drop, evenly, gently, little by little, moderately, piece by piece, piecemeal, progressively, slowly, steadily, step by step, unhurriedly

graduate *verb* **1**. calibrate, grade, mark off, measure out, proportion, regulate **2**. arrange, classify, grade, group, order, range, rank, sequence, sort

graft **1**. *noun* bud, implant, scion, shoot, splice, sprout **2**. *verb* affix, implant, ingraft, insert, join, splice, transplant

grain **1**. cereals, corn **2**. grist, kernel, seed **3**. atom, bit, crumb, fragment, granule, iota, jot, mite, modicum, molecule, morsel, mote, ounce, particle, piece, scintilla (*rare*), scrap, scruple, spark, speck, suspicion, trace, whit **4**. fibre, nap, pattern, surface, texture, weave **5**. character, disposition, humour, inclination, make-up, temper

grammar rules of language, syntax

Grammatical cases

ablative	instrumental
accusative	locative
agentive	nominative
dative	objective
elative	oblique
ergative	possessive
genitive	subjective
illative	vocative

When I split an infinitive, God damn it, I split it so it will stay split

Raymond Chandler

This is the sort of English up with which I will not put

Winston Churchill

grand **1**. ambitious, august, dignified, elevated, eminent, exalted, fine, glorious, gorgeous, grandiose, great, haughty, illustrious, imposing, impressive, large, lofty, lordly, luxurious, magnificent, majestic, monumental, noble, opulent, ostentatious, palatial, pompous, pretentious, princely, regal, splendid, splendiferous (*facetious*), stately, striking, sublime, sumptuous, superb **2**. admirable, awesome (*slang*), divine, excellent, fine, first-class, first-rate, great (*informal*), hunky-dory (*informal*), marvellous (*informal*), outstanding, smashing (*informal*), splendid, splendiferous (*facetious*), super (*informal*), superb, terrific

(*informal*), very good, wonderful, world-class **3.** big-time (*informal*), chief, head, highest, lead, leading, main, major league (*informal*), pre-eminent, principal, supreme
Antonyms awful, bad, base, chickenshit (*U.S. slang*), common, contemptible, crappy (*slang*), inferior, insignificant, little, mean, petty, poor, poxy (*slang*), secondary, small, terrible, triv~ial, undignified, unimportant, unimposing, worthless

grandeur augustness, dignity, greatness, im~portance, loftiness, magnificence, majesty, no~bility, pomp, splendour, state, stateliness, sublimity
Antonyms commonness, inferiority, insignifi~cance, lowliness, pettiness, smallness, trivial~ity, unimportance

grandiloquent bombastic, flowery, fustian, high-flown, high-sounding, inflated, magnilo~quent, orotund, pompous, pretentious, rhe~torical

grandiose **1.** affected, ambitious, bombastic, extravagant, flamboyant, high-flown, ostenta~tious, pompous, pretentious, showy **2.** ambi~tious, grand, imposing, impressive, lofty, magnificent, majestic, monumental, stately
Antonyms down-to-earth, humble, modest, small-scale, unpretentious

grant *verb* **1.** accede to, accord, acknowledge, admit, agree to, allocate, allot, allow, assign, award, bestow, cede, concede, confer, consent to, donate, give, hand out, impart, permit, present, vouchsafe, yield **2.** *Law* assign, con~vey, transfer, transmit *~noun* **3.** admission, allocation, allotment, allowance, award, ben~efaction, bequest, boon, bounty, concession, donation, endowment, gift, hand-out, present, stipend, subsidy

granular crumbly, grainy, granulated, gravelly, gritty, rough, sandy

granulate crumble, crush, crystallize, grind, levigate (*Chemistry*), pound, powder, pulver~ize, triturate

granule atom, crumb, fragment, grain, iota, jot, molecule, particle, scrap, speck

graphic **1.** clear, descriptive, detailed, explicit, expressive, forcible, illustrative, lively, lucid, picturesque, striking, telling, vivid, well-drawn **2.** delineated, diagrammatic, drawn, il~lustrative, pictorial, representational, seen, visible, visual
Antonyms (*sense 1*) generalized, imprecise, impressionistic, unspecific, vague, woolly

grapple **1.** catch, clasp, clutch, come to grips, fasten, grab, grasp, grip, hold, hug, lay *or* take hold, make fast, seize, wrestle **2.** address oneself to, attack, battle, clash, combat, con~front, contend, cope, deal with, do battle, en~counter, engage, face, fight, get to grips with, struggle, tackle, take on, tussle, wrestle

grasp *verb* **1.** catch (up), clasp, clinch, clutch, grab, grapple, grip, hold, lay *or* take hold of, seize, snatch **2.** catch on, catch *or* get the drift of, comprehend, follow, get, get the hang of (*informal*), get the message, get the picture, realize, see, take in, understand *~noun* **3.** clasp, clutches, embrace, grip, hold, posses~sion, tenure **4.** capacity, compass, control, ex~tent, mastery, power, range, reach, scope, sway, sweep **5.** awareness, comprehension, grip, ken, knowledge, mastery, perception, re~alization, understanding

grasping acquisitive, avaricious, close-fisted, covetous, greedy, mean, miserly, niggardly, penny-pinching (*informal*), rapacious, selfish, stingy, tight-arsed (*taboo slang*), tight as a duck's arse (*taboo slang*), tight-assed (*U.S. taboo slang*), tightfisted, usurious, venal
Antonyms altruistic, generous, unselfish

grate *verb* **1.** mince, pulverize, shred, triturate **2.** creak, grind, rasp, rub, scrape, scratch **3.** aggravate (*informal*), annoy, chafe, exasper~ate, fret, gall, get one down, get on one's nerves (*informal*), get on one's wick (*Brit. slang*), get under someone's skin (*informal*), get up someone's nose (*informal*), irk, irritate, jar, nark (*Brit., Austral., & N.Z. slang*), net~tle, peeve, rankle, rub one up the wrong way, set one's teeth on edge, vex

grateful **1.** appreciative, beholden, indebted, obliged, thankful **2.** acceptable, agreeable, fa~vourable, gratifying, nice, pleasing, refreshing, restful, satisfactory, satisfying, welcome

gratification delight, enjoyment, fruition, ful~filment, glee, indulgence, joy, kick *or* kicks (*informal*), pleasure, recompense, relish, re~ward, satisfaction, thrill
Antonyms control, denial, disappointment, discipline, dissatisfaction, frustration, pain, restraint, sorrow

gratify cater to, delight, favour, fawn on, feed, fulfil, give pleasure, gladden, humour, in~dulge, pander to, please, recompense, requite, satisfy, thrill

grating[1] *adjective* annoying, disagreeable, dis~cordant, displeasing, grinding, harsh, irksome, irritating, jarring, offensive, rasping, raucous, scraping, squeaky, strident, unpleasant, vexa~tious
Antonyms agreeable, calming, mellifluous, musical, pleasing, soft, soothing

grating[2] *noun* grate, grid, gridiron, grille, lat~tice, trellis

gratis buckshee (*Brit. slang*), for nothing, free, freely, free of charge, gratuitously, on the house, unpaid

gratitude appreciation, gratefulness, indebtedness, obligation, recognition, sense of obligation, thankfulness, thanks
Antonyms ingratitude, ungratefulness, unthankfulness

gratuitous 1. buckshee (*Brit. slang*), complimentary, free, spontaneous, unasked-for, unpaid, unrewarded, voluntary 2. assumed, baseless, causeless, groundless, irrelevant, needless, superfluous, uncalled-for, unfounded, unjustified, unmerited, unnecessary, unprovoked, unwarranted, wanton
Antonyms compulsory, involuntary, justifiable, paid, provoked, relevant, well-founded

gratuity baksheesh, benefaction, bonus, boon, bounty, donation, gift, largess *or* largesse, perquisite, *pourboire*, present, recompense, reward, tip

grave[1] *noun* burying place, crypt, last resting place, mausoleum, pit, sepulchre, tomb, vault
Related adjective: sepulchral

The grave's a fine and private place,
But none do there, I think, embrace
Andrew Marvell *To his coy Mistress*

grave[2] *adjective* 1. dignified, dour, dull, earnest, gloomy, grim-faced, heavy, leaden, long-faced, muted, quiet, sage (*obsolete*), sedate, serious, sober, solemn, sombre, staid, subdued, thoughtful, unsmiling 2. acute, critical, crucial, dangerous, exigent, hazardous, important, life-and-death, momentous, of great consequence, perilous, pressing, serious, severe, significant, threatening, urgent, vital, weighty
Antonyms carefree, exciting, flippant, frivolous, happy, insignificant, joyous, merry, mild, trifling, undignified, unimportant

graveyard boneyard (*informal*), burial ground, cemetery, charnel house, churchyard, God's acre (*literary*), necropolis

gravitas gravity, seriousness, solemnity

gravitate 1. *with* **to** *or* **towards** be influenced (attracted, drawn, pulled), incline, lean, move, tend 2. be precipitated, descend, drop, fall, precipitate, settle, sink

gravity 1. acuteness, consequence, exigency, hazardousness, importance, moment, momentousness, perilousness, pressingness, seriousness, severity, significance, urgency, weightiness 2. demureness, dignity, earnestness, gloom, gravitas, grimness, reserve, sedateness, seriousness, sobriety, solemnity, thoughtfulness
Antonyms flippancy, frivolity, gaiety, happiness, inconsequentiality, insignificance, joy, levity, merriment, thoughtlessness, triviality, unimportance

graze[1] *verb* browse, crop, feed, pasture

graze[2] *verb* 1. brush, glance off, kiss, rub, scrape, shave, skim, touch 2. abrade, bark, chafe, scrape, scratch, skin ~*noun* 3. abrasion, scrape, scratch

greasy 1. fatty, oily, oleaginous, slick, slimy, slippery 2. fawning, glib, grovelling, ingratiating, oily, slick, smarmy (*Brit. informal*), smooth, sycophantic, toadying, unctuous

great 1. big, bulky, colossal, elephantine, enormous, extensive, gigantic, ginormous (*informal*), huge, humongous *or* humungous (*U.S. slang*), immense, large, mammoth, prodigious, stellar (*informal*), stupendous, tremendous, vast, voluminous 2. extended, lengthy, long, prolonged, protracted 3. big-time (*informal*), capital, chief, grand, head, lead, leading, main, major, major league (*informal*), paramount, primary, principal, prominent, superior 4. considerable, decided, excessive, extravagant, extreme, grievous, high, inordinate, prodigious, pronounced, serious (*informal*), strong 5. consequential, critical, crucial, grave, heavy, important, momentous, serious, significant, weighty 6. celebrated, distinguished, eminent, exalted, excellent, famed, famous, glorious, illustrious, notable, noteworthy, outstanding, prominent, remarkable, renowned, superb, superlative, talented, world-class 7. august, chivalrous, dignified, distinguished, exalted, fine, glorious, grand, heroic, high-minded, idealistic, impressive, lofty, magnanimous, noble, princely, sublime 8. active, devoted, enthusiastic, keen, zealous 9. able, adept, adroit, crack (*slang*), expert, good, masterly, proficient, skilful, skilled 10. *informal* admirable, awesome (*slang*), boffo (*slang*), brill (*informal*), chillin' (*U.S. slang*), cracking (*Brit. informal*), crucial (*slang*), def (*informal*), excellent, fantastic (*informal*), fine, first-rate, good, hunky-dory (*informal*), jim-dandy (*slang*), marvellous (*informal*), mean (*slang*), mega (*slang*), sovereign, superb, terrific (*informal*), topping (*Brit. slang*), tremendous (*informal*), wonderful 11. absolute, arrant, complete, consummate, downright, egregious, flagrant, out-and-out, perfect, positive, thoroughgoing, thundering (*informal*), total, unmitigated, unqualified, utter
Antonyms average, bad, base, diminutive, hateful, ignoble, inconsequential, inconsiderable, inferior, inhumane, insignificant, little, mean, mild, petty, poor, secondary, second-rate, small, terrible, trivial, undistinguished, unimportant, unkind, unnotable, unskilled, weak

greatly abundantly, by leaps and bounds, by much, considerably, enormously, exceedingly, extremely, highly, hugely, immensely, markedly, mightily, much, notably, powerfully, re~

markably, seriously (*informal*), to the nth de~ gree, tremendously, vastly, very much

greatness **1.** bulk, enormity, hugeness, im~ mensity, largeness, length, magnitude, mass, prodigiousness, size, vastness **2.** amplitude, force, high degree, intensity, potency, power, strength **3.** gravity, heaviness, import, impor~ tance, moment, momentousness, seriousness, significance, urgency, weight **4.** celebrity, dis~ tinction, eminence, fame, glory, grandeur, il~ lustriousness, lustre, note, renown **5.** chivalry, dignity, disinterestedness, generosity, gran~ deur, heroism, high-mindedness, idealism, loftiness, majesty, nobility, nobleness, stateli~ ness, sublimity

No really great man ever thought himself so
William Hazlitt *Whether Genius is Conscious of Its Powers?*

There would be no great ones if there were no little ones
George Herbert *Outlandish Proverbs*

I would sooner fail than not be among the greatest
John Keats *letter*

It is the privilege of greatness to confer intense happiness with insignificant gifts
Friedrich Nietzsche *Human, All Too Human*

Some are born great, some achieve greatness, and some have greatness thrust upon 'em
William Shakespeare *Twelfth Night*

No man who wanted to be a great man ever was a great man
John Hunter

greed, greediness **1.** edacity, esurience, glut~ tony, gormandizing, hunger, insatiableness, ravenousness, voracity **2.** acquisitiveness, ava~ rice, avidity, covetousness, craving, cupidity, desire, eagerness, graspingness, longing, ra~ pacity, selfishness
Antonyms altruism, benevolence, generosity, largess *or* largesse, munificence, self-restraint, unselfishness

There is enough in the world for everyone's need, but not enough for everyone's greed
Frank Buchman *Remaking the World*

The more you get, the more you want

The pitcher will go to the well once too often

greedy **1.** edacious, esurient, gluttonous, gor~ mandizing, hoggish, hungry, insatiable, pig~ gish, ravenous, voracious **2.** acquisitive, avari~ cious, avid, covetous, craving, desirous, eager, grasping, hungry, impatient, rapacious, selfish
Antonyms altruistic, apathetic, benevolent, full, generous, indifferent, munificent, self-restrained, unselfish

Greek **1.** *noun* Hellene **2.** *adjective* Hellenic

I fear the Greeks, even when they are bearing gifts
Virgil *Aeneid*

green *adjective* **1.** blooming, budding, flourish~ ing, fresh, grassy, leafy, new, undecayed, ver~ dant, verdurous **2.** fresh, immature, new, raw, recent, unripe **3.** conservationist, ecological, environment-friendly, non-polluting, ozone-friendly **4.** callow, credulous, gullible, igno~ rant, immature, inexperienced, inexpert, in~ genuous, innocent, naive, new, raw, unpol~ ished, unpractised, unskilful, unsophisticated, untrained, unversed, wet behind the ears (*in~ formal*) **5.** covetous, envious, grudging, jealous, resentful **6.** ill, nauseous, pale, sick, under the weather, unhealthy, wan **7.** immature, pliable, supple, tender, undried, unseasoned, young ~*noun* **8.** common, grassplot, lawn, sward, turf

greenhorn apprentice, beginner, ignoramus, ingénue, learner, naïf, neophyte, newcomer, novice, raw recruit, simpleton, tyro

green light approval, authorization, blessing, clearance, confirmation, go-ahead (*informal*), imprimatur, O.K. *or* okay (*informal*), permis~ sion, sanction

greet accost, address, compliment, hail, meet, nod to, receive, salute, tip one's hat to, wel~ come

greeting **1.** address, hail, reception, salutation, salute, welcome **2.** *plural* best wishes, compli~ ments, devoirs, good wishes, regards, respects, salutations

gregarious affable, companionable, convivial, cordial, friendly, outgoing, sociable, social
Antonyms antisocial, reserved, solitary, standoffish, unsociable, withdrawn

grey **1.** ashen, bloodless, colourless, like death warmed up (*informal*), livid, pale, pallid, wan **2.** cheerless, cloudy, dark, depressing, dim, dismal, drab, dreary, dull, foggy, gloomy, misty, murky, overcast, sunless **3.** anonymous, characterless, colourless, dull, indistinct, neu~ tral, unclear, unidentifiable **4.** aged, ancient, elderly, experienced, hoary, mature, old, ven~ erable

grief **1.** affliction, agony, anguish, bereavement, dejection, distress, grievance, hardship, heart~ ache, heartbreak, misery, mournfulness, mourning, pain, regret, remorse, sadness, sor~ row, suffering, trial, tribulation, trouble, woe **2. come to grief** *informal* come unstuck, fail, fall flat on one's face, meet with disaster, miscarry
Antonyms cheer, comfort, consolation, delight, gladness, happiness, joy, rejoicing, solace

Grief is a species of idleness
Dr. Johnson

grief-stricken afflicted, agonized, broken, brokenhearted, crushed, desolate, despairing, devastated, heartbroken, inconsolable, over~ whelmed, sorrowful, sorrowing, woebegone, wretched

grievance affliction, axe to grind, beef (*slang*), chip on one's shoulder (*informal*), complaint, damage, distress, grief, gripe (*informal*), hardship, injury, injustice, protest, resentment, sorrow, trial, tribulation, trouble, unhappiness, wrong

grieve 1. ache, bemoan, bewail, complain, deplore, lament, mourn, regret, rue, sorrow, suffer, wail, weep 2. afflict, agonize, break the heart of, crush, distress, hurt, injure, make one's heart bleed, pain, sadden, wound
Antonyms cheer, comfort, console, ease, gladden, please, rejoice, solace

grievous 1. afflicting, calamitous, damaging, distressing, dreadful, grave, harmful, heavy, hurtful, injurious, lamentable, oppressive, painful, severe, wounding 2. appalling, atrocious, deplorable, dreadful, egregious, flagrant, glaring, heinous, intolerable, lamentable, monstrous, offensive, outrageous, shameful, shocking, unbearable 3. agonized, grief-stricken, heart-rending, mournful, pitiful, sorrowful, tragic
Antonyms delightful, glad, happy, insignificant, joyous, mild, pleasant, trivial, unimportant

grim cruel, ferocious, fierce, forbidding, formidable, frightful, ghastly, godawful (*slang*), grisly, gruesome, hard, harsh, hideous, horrible, horrid, implacable, merciless, morose, relentless, resolute, ruthless, severe, shocking, sinister, stern, sullen, surly, terrible, unrelenting, unyielding
Antonyms amiable, attractive, benign, cheerful, easy, genial, gentle, happy, kind, pleasant, soft, sympathetic

grimace 1. *noun* face, frown, mouth, scowl, sneer, wry face 2. *verb* frown, lour *or* lower, make a face *or* faces, mouth, scowl, sneer

grime dirt, filth, grot (*slang*), smut, soot

grimy begrimed, besmeared, besmirched, dirty, filthy, foul, grubby, scuzzy (*slang*), smutty, soiled, sooty, unclean

grind *verb* 1. abrade, comminute, crush, granulate, grate, kibble, mill, pound, powder, pulverize, triturate 2. file, polish, sand, sharpen, smooth, whet 3. gnash, grate, grit, scrape 4. *with* **down** afflict, harass, hold down, hound, oppress, persecute, plague, trouble, tyrannize (over) ~*noun* 5. *informal* chore, drudgery, hard work, labour, sweat (*informal*), task, toil

grip *noun* 1. clasp, handclasp (*U.S.*), purchase 2. clutches, comprehension, control, domination, grasp, hold, influence, keeping, mastery, perception, possession, power, tenure, understanding 3. **come** *or* **get to grips (with)** close with, confront, contend with, cope with, deal with, encounter, face up to, grapple with, grasp, handle, meet, tackle, take on, take the bit between one's teeth, undertake ~*verb* 4. clasp, clutch, grasp, hold, latch on to, seize, take hold of 5. absorb, catch up, compel, engross, enthral, entrance, fascinate, hold, involve, mesmerize, rivet, spellbind

gripe *verb* 1. *informal* beef (*slang*), bellyache (*slang*), bitch (*slang*), bleat, carp, complain, groan, grouch (*informal*), grouse, grumble, kvetch (*U.S. slang*), moan, nag, whine 2. ache, compress, cramp, hurt, pain, pinch, press, squeeze ~*noun* 3. *often plural* ache, aching, affliction, colic, cramps, distress, griping, pain, pang, pinching, stomachache, twinge 4. *informal* beef (*slang*), complaint, grievance, groan, grouch (*informal*), grouse, grumble, moan, objection, protest

gripping compelling, compulsive, engrossing, enthralling, entrancing, exciting, fascinating, riveting, spellbinding, thrilling, unputdownable (*informal*)

grisly abominable, appalling, awful, dreadful, frightful, ghastly, grim, gruesome, hellacious (*U.S. slang*), hideous, horrible, horrid, macabre, shocking, sickening, terrible, terrifying
Antonyms agreeable, attractive, charming, innocuous, nice, pleasant

grit *noun* 1. dust, gravel, pebbles, sand 2. backbone, balls (*taboo slang*), courage, determination, doggedness, fortitude, gameness, guts (*informal*), hardihood, mettle, nerve, perseverance, pluck, resolution, spirit, tenacity, toughness ~*verb* 3. clench, gnash, grate, grind

gritty 1. abrasive, dusty, grainy, granular, gravelly, rasping, rough, sandy 2. ballsy (*taboo slang*), brave, courageous, determined, dogged, feisty (*informal, chiefly U.S. & Canad.*), game, hardy, mettlesome, plucky, resolute, spirited, steadfast, tenacious, tough

grizzle fret, girn (*Scot.*), pule, snivel, whimper, whine, whinge (*informal*)

grizzled canescent, grey, grey-haired, grey-headed, greying, griseous, grizzly, hoary

groan *noun* 1. cry, moan, sigh, whine 2. *informal* beef (*slang*), complaint, gripe (*informal*), grouse, grumble, objection, protest ~*verb* 3. cry, moan, sigh, whine 4. *informal* beef (*slang*), bemoan, bitch (*slang*), complain, gripe (*informal*), grouse, grumble, lament, object

groggy befuddled, confused, dazed, dizzy, faint, muzzy, punch-drunk, reeling, shaky, staggering, stunned, stupefied, unsteady, weak, wobbly, woozy (*informal*)

groom *noun* 1. currier (*rare*), hostler *or* ostler (*archaic*), stableboy, stableman ~*verb* 2. clean, dress, get up (*informal*), gussy up (*slang, chiefly U.S.*), preen, primp, smarten up, spruce up, tidy, turn out 3. brush, clean, curry, rub down, tend 4. coach, drill, educate, make ready, nurture, prepare, prime, ready, train

groove channel, cut, cutting, flute, furrow, gutter, hollow, indentation, rebate, rut, score, trench, trough

grope cast about, feel, finger, fish, flounder, forage, fumble, grabble, scrabble, search

gross *adjective* **1.** big, bulky, corpulent, dense, fat, great, heavy, hulking, large, lumpish, massive, obese, overweight, thick **2.** aggregate, before deductions, before tax, entire, total, whole **3.** coarse, crude, improper, impure, in~decent, indelicate, lewd, low, obscene, offen~sive, ribald, rude, sensual, smutty, unseemly, vulgar, X-rated (*informal*) **4.** apparent, arrant, blatant, downright, egregious, flagrant, glar~ing, grievous, heinous, manifest, obvious, out~rageous, plain, rank, serious, shameful, sheer, shocking, unmitigated, unqualified, utter **5.** boorish, callous, coarse, crass, dull, ignorant, imperceptive, insensitive, tasteless, uncul~tured, undiscriminating, unfeeling, unrefined, unsophisticated *~verb* **6.** bring in, earn, make, rake in (*informal*), take

Antonyms *adjective* (*sense 1*) delicate, little, petite, slim, small, svelte, thin (*sense 2*) net (*sense 3*) decent, delicate, proper, pure (*sense 4*) partial, qualified (*sense 5*) cultivated, el~egant *~verb* clear, net

grossness **1.** bigness, bulkiness, corpulence, fatness, greatness, heaviness, lumpishness, obesity, thickness **2.** bestiality, coarseness, crudity, impurity, indecency, indelicacy, licen~tiousness, obscenity, offensiveness, ribaldry, rudeness, sensuality, smut, smuttiness, un~seemliness, vulgarity **3.** blatancy, egregious~ness, flagrancy, grievousness, obviousness, rankness, seriousness, shamefulness **4.** coarseness, crassness, ignorance, insensitivity, lack of taste, pig-ignorance (*slang*), tasteless~ness

grotesque absurd, bizarre, deformed, distorted, extravagant, fanciful, fantastic, freakish, in~congruous, ludicrous, malformed, misshapen, odd, outlandish, preposterous, ridiculous, strange, unnatural, weird, whimsical

Antonyms average, classic, graceful, natural, normal, realistic

grouch *verb* **1.** beef (*slang*), bellyache (*slang*), bitch (*slang*), bleat, carp, complain, find fault, gripe (*informal*), grouse, grumble, kvetch (*U.S. slang*), moan, whine, whinge (*informal*) *~noun* **2.** beef (*slang*), complaint, grievance, gripe (*informal*), grouse, grumble, moan, ob~jection, protest **3.** complainer, crab (*informal*), crosspatch (*informal*), curmudgeon, faultfinder, grouser, grumbler, malcontent, moaner, whiner

grouchy cantankerous, cross, discontented, grumbling, grumpy, huffy, ill-tempered, iras~cible, irritable, liverish, peevish, petulant, querulous, ratty (*Brit. & N.Z. informal*), sulky, surly, testy, tetchy

ground *noun* **1.** clod, dirt, dry land, dust, earth, field, land, loam, mould, sod, soil, terra firma, terrain, turf **2.** *often plural* area, coun~try, district, domain, estate, fields, gardens, habitat, holding, land, property, realm, ter~rain, territory, tract **3.** *usually plural* account, argument, base, basis, call, cause, excuse, factor, foundation, inducement, justification, motive, occasion, premise, pretext, rationale, reason **4.** *usually plural* deposit, dregs, grouts, lees, sediment, settlings **5.** arena, field, park (*informal*), pitch, stadium *~verb* **6.** base, es~tablish, fix, found, set, settle **7.** acquaint with, coach, familiarize with, inform, initiate, in~struct, prepare, teach, train, tutor

groundless baseless, chimerical, empty, false, idle, illusory, imaginary, unauthorized, uncalled-for, unfounded, unjustified, unpro~voked, unsupported, unwarranted

Antonyms justified, logical, proven, real, rea~sonable, substantial, supported, true, well-founded

groundwork base, basis, cornerstone, footing, foundation, fundamentals, preliminaries, preparation, spadework, underpinnings

group *noun* **1.** aggregation, assemblage, asso~ciation, band, batch, bevy, bunch, camp, cat~egory, circle, class, clique, clump, cluster, col~lection, company, congregation, coterie, crowd, faction, formation, gang, gathering, organiza~tion, pack, party, posse (*slang*), set, troop *~verb* **2.** arrange, assemble, associate, assort, bracket, class, classify, dispose, gather, mar~shal, order, organize, put together, range, sort **3.** associate, band together, cluster, congre~gate, consort, fraternize, gather, get together

grouse **1.** *verb* beef (*slang*), bellyache (*slang*), bitch (*slang*), bleat, carp, complain, find fault, gripe (*informal*), grouch (*informal*), grumble, kvetch (*U.S. slang*), moan, whine, whinge (*in~formal*) **2.** *noun* beef (*slang*), complaint, griev~ance, gripe (*informal*), grouch (*informal*), grumble, moan, objection, protest

grove brake, coppice, copse, covert, hurst (*ar~chaic*), plantation, spinney, thicket, wood, woodland

grovel abase oneself, bootlick (*informal*), bow and scrape, brown-nose (*taboo slang*), cower, crawl, creep, cringe, crouch, demean oneself, fawn, flatter, humble oneself, kiss ass (*taboo slang*), kowtow, lick someone's arse (*taboo slang*), lick someone's boots, pander to, sneak, toady

Antonyms be proud, domineer, face, hold one's head high, intimidate

grow 1. develop, enlarge, expand, extend, fill out, get bigger, get taller, heighten, increase, multiply, spread, stretch, swell, thicken, widen 2. develop, flourish, germinate, shoot, spring up, sprout, vegetate 3. arise, issue, originate, spring, stem 4. advance, expand, flourish, improve, progress, prosper, succeed, thrive 5. become, come to be, develop (into), get, turn, wax 6. breed, cultivate, farm, nurture, produce, propagate, raise
Antonyms decline, decrease, die, diminish, dwindle, fail, lessen, shrink, subside, wane

grown-up 1. *adjective* adult, fully-grown, mature, of age 2. *noun* adult, man, woman

growth 1. aggrandizement, augmentation, development, enlargement, evolution, expansion, extension, growing, heightening, increase, multiplication, proliferation, stretching, thickening, widening 2. crop, cultivation, development, germination, produce, production, shooting, sprouting, vegetation 3. advance, advancement, expansion, improvement, progress, prosperity, rise, success 4. *Medicine* excrescence, lump, tumour
Antonyms decline, decrease, dwindling, failure, lessening, retreat, shrinkage, slackening, subsiding
Great oaks from little acorns grow

grub *verb* 1. burrow, dig up, probe, pull up, root (*informal*), rootle (*Brit.*), search for, uproot 2. ferret, forage, hunt, rummage, scour, search, uncover, unearth 3. drudge, grind (*informal*), labour, plod, slave, slog, sweat, toil ~*noun* 4. caterpillar, larva, maggot 5. *slang* eats (*slang*), feed, food, nosebag (*slang*), nosh (*slang*), rations, sustenance, tack (*informal*), victuals, vittles (*obsolete or dialect*)

grubby besmeared, dirty, filthy, frowzy, grimy, grungy (*slang chiefly U.S. & Canad.*), manky (*Scot. dialect*), mean, messy, mucky, scruffy, scuzzy (*slang*), seedy, shabby, slovenly, smutty, soiled, sordid, squalid, unkempt, untidy, unwashed

grudge 1. *noun* animosity, animus, antipathy, aversion, bitterness, chip on one's shoulder (*informal*), dislike, enmity, grievance, hard feelings, hate, ill will, malevolence, malice, pique, rancour, resentment, spite, venom 2. *verb* begrudge, be reluctant, complain, covet, envy, hold back, mind, resent, stint
Antonyms *noun* appreciation, goodwill, liking, thankfulness ~*verb* be glad for, celebrate, welcome

gruelling arduous, backbreaking, brutal, crushing, demanding, difficult, exhausting, fatiguing, fierce, grinding, hard, harsh, laborious, punishing, severe, stiff, strenuous, taxing, tiring, trying
Antonyms cushy (*informal*), easy, enjoyable, light, pleasant, undemanding

gruesome abominable, awful, fearful, from hell (*informal*), ghastly, grim, grisly, hellacious (*U.S. slang*), hideous, horrendous, horrible, horrid, horrific, horrifying, loathsome, macabre, obscene, repugnant, repulsive, shocking, spine-chilling, terrible
Antonyms appealing, benign, cheerful, pleasant, sweet

gruff 1. bad-tempered, bearish, blunt, brusque, churlish, crabbed, crusty, curt, discourteous, grouchy (*informal*), grumpy, ill-humoured, ill-natured, impolite, rough, rude, sour, sullen, surly, uncivil, ungracious, unmannerly 2. croaking, guttural, harsh, hoarse, husky, low, rasping, rough, throaty
Antonyms courteous, good-tempered, gracious, kind, mellifluous, pleasant, polite, smooth, sweet

grumble *verb* 1. beef (*slang*), bellyache (*slang*), bitch (*slang*), bleat, carp, complain, find fault, gripe (*informal*), grouch (*informal*), grouse, kvetch (*U.S. slang*), moan, repine, whine, whinge (*informal*) 2. growl, gurgle, murmur, mutter, roar, rumble ~*noun* 3. beef (*slang*), complaint, grievance, gripe (*informal*), grouch (*informal*), grouse, moan, objection, protest 4. growl, gurgle, murmur, muttering, roar, rumble

grumpy cantankerous, crabbed, cross, crotchety (*informal*), edgy, grouchy (*informal*), grumbling, huffy, ill-tempered, irritable, liverish, peevish, petulant, querulous, ratty (*Brit. & N.Z. informal*), sulky, sullen, surly, testy, tetchy

guarantee 1. *noun* assurance, bond, certainty, collateral, covenant, earnest, guaranty, pledge, promise, security, surety, undertaking, warranty, word, word of honour 2. *verb* answer for, assure, certify, ensure, insure, maintain, make certain, pledge, promise, protect, secure, stand behind, swear, vouch for, warrant

guarantor backer, bailsman (*rare*), bondsman (*Law*), guarantee, sponsor, supporter, surety, underwriter, voucher, warrantor

guaranty 1. agreement, assurance, bond, contract, covenant, guarantee, insurance, oath, pledge, promise, undertaking, warrant, warranty, word 2. bail, bond, collateral, deposit, earnest, gage, pawn, pledge, security, token

guard *verb* 1. cover, defend, escort, keep, mind, oversee, patrol, police, preserve, protect, safeguard, save, screen, secure, shelter, shield, supervise, tend, watch, watch over ~*noun* 2. custodian, defender, lookout, picket, protector, sentinel, sentry, warder, watch, watchman 3. convoy, escort, patrol 4. buffer, bulwark, bumper, defence, pad, protection, rampart, safeguard, screen, security, shield 5. attention, care, caution, heed, vigilance, wariness, watchfulness **6. off (one's) guard** napping, unprepared, unready, unwary, with one's defences down **7. on (one's) guard** alert, cautious, circumspect, on the alert, on the lookout, on the qui vive, prepared, ready, vigilant, wary, watchful

guarded cagey (*informal*), careful, cautious, circumspect, discreet, leery (*slang*), noncommittal, prudent, reserved, restrained, reticent, suspicious, wary

guardian attendant, champion, curator, custodian, defender, escort, guard, keeper, preserver, protector, trustee, warden, warder

guerrilla freedom fighter, irregular, member of the underground *or* resistance, partisan, underground fighter

guess *verb* **1.** conjecture, estimate, fathom, hypothesize, penetrate, predict, solve, speculate, work out **2.** believe, conjecture, dare say, deem, divine, fancy, hazard, imagine, judge, reckon, suppose, surmise, suspect, think *~noun* **3.** ballpark figure (*informal*), conjecture, feeling, hypothesis, judgment, notion, prediction, reckoning, shot in the dark, speculation, supposition, surmise, suspicion, theory

Antonyms *verb* be certain, be sure, know, prove, show *~noun* certainty, fact

No great discovery was ever made without a bold guess

ascribed to Sir Isaac Newton

guesswork conjecture, estimation, presumption, speculation, supposition, surmise, suspicion, theory

guest boarder, caller, company, lodger, visitant, visitor

Mankind is divisible into two great classes: hosts and guests

Max Beerbohm *Hosts and Guests*

guff balderdash, balls (*taboo slang*), bilge (*informal*), bosh (*informal*), bull (*slang*), bullshit (*taboo slang*), bunkum *or* buncombe (*chiefly U.S.*), cobblers (*Brit. taboo slang*), crap (*slang*), drivel, empty talk, eyewash (*informal*), garbage (*informal*), guff (*slang*), hogwash, hokum (*slang, chiefly U.S. & Canad.*), horsefeathers (*U.S. slang*), hot air (*informal*), humbug, moonshine, nonsense, pap, piffle (*informal*), poppycock (*informal*), rot, rubbish, shit (*taboo slang*), tommyrot, tosh (*slang, chiefly Brit.*), trash, tripe (*informal*)

guidance advice, auspices, conduct, control, counsel, counselling, direction, government, help, instruction, intelligence, leadership, management, teaching

guide *verb* **1.** accompany, attend, conduct, convoy, direct, escort, lead, pilot, shepherd, show the way, steer, usher **2.** command, control, direct, handle, manage, manoeuvre, steer **3.** advise, counsel, educate, govern, influence, instruct, oversee, regulate, rule, superintend, supervise, sway, teach, train *~noun* **4.** adviser, attendant, chaperon, cicerone, conductor, controller, counsellor, director, dragoman, escort, leader, mentor, monitor, pilot, steersman, teacher, torchbearer, usher **5.** criterion, example, exemplar, ideal, imago (*Psychoanalysis*), inspiration, lodestar, master, model, par, paradigm, standard **6.** beacon, clue, guiding light, key, landmark, lodestar, mark, marker, pointer, sign, signal, signpost **7.** Baedeker, catalogue, directory, guidebook, handbook, instructions, key, manual, vade mecum

guild association, brotherhood, club, company, corporation, fellowship, fraternity, league, lodge, order, organization, society, union

guile art, artfulness, artifice, cleverness, craft, craftiness, cunning, deceit, deception, duplicity, gamesmanship (*informal*), knavery, ruse, sharp practice, slyness, treachery, trickery, trickiness, wiliness

Antonyms candour, frankness, honesty, sincerity, truthfulness

guileful artful, clever, crafty, cunning, deceitful, duplicitous, foxy, sly, sneaky, treacherous, tricky, underhand, wily

guileless above-board, artless, candid, frank, genuine, honest, ingenuous, innocent, naive, natural, open, simple, simple-minded, sincere, straightforward, truthful, undesigning, unsophisticated, upfront (*informal*)

guilt **1.** blame, blameworthiness, criminality, culpability, delinquency, guiltiness, iniquity, misconduct, responsibility, sinfulness, wickedness, wrong, wrongdoing **2.** bad conscience, contrition, disgrace, dishonour, guiltiness, guilty conscience, infamy, regret, remorse, self-condemnation, self-reproach, shame, stigma

Antonyms blamelessness, honour, innocence, pride, righteousness, self-respect, sinlessness, virtue

Will all great Neptune's ocean wash this blood
Clean from my hand?

William Shakespeare *Macbeth*

guiltless blameless, clean (*slang*), clear, immaculate, impeccable, innocent, irreproachable, pure, sinless, spotless, squeaky-clean, unimpeachable, unsullied, untainted, untarnished

guilty **1.** at fault, blameworthy, convicted, criminal, culpable, delinquent, erring, evil, felonious, iniquitous, offending, reprehensible, responsible, sinful, to blame, wicked, wrong **2.** ashamed, conscience-stricken, contrite, hangdog, regretful, remorseful, rueful, shamefaced, sheepish, sorry

Antonyms blameless, innocent, moral, proud, righteous, virtuous

guise air, appearance, aspect, behaviour, demeanour, disguise, dress, façade, face, fashion, form, front, mask, mode, pretence, semblance, shape, show

gulf **1.** bay, bight, sea inlet **2.** abyss, breach, chasm, cleft, gap, opening, rent, rift, separation, split, void, whirlpool

gull **1.** *noun* babe in arms (*informal*), chump (*informal*), dupe, easy mark (*slang*), fool, gudgeon (*slang*), mug (*slang*), sap (*slang*), simpleton, sucker (*slang*) **2.** *verb* beguile, cheat, con (*slang*), cozen, deceive, defraud, dupe, hoax, pull a fast one on (*informal*), put one over on (*informal*), rook (*slang*), sell a pup to, skin (*slang*), stiff (*slang*), swindle, take for a ride (*informal*), take in (*informal*), trick

gullet craw, crop, maw, oesophagus, throat

gullibility credulity, innocence, naïveté, simplicity, trustingness

gullible as green as grass, born yesterday, credulous, easily taken in, foolish, green, innocent, naive, silly, simple, trusting, unsceptical, unsophisticated, unsuspecting, wet behind the ears (*informal*)
Antonyms cynical, sophisticated, suspicious, untrusting, worldly

gully channel, ditch, gutter, watercourse

gulp *verb* **1.** bolt, devour, gobble, guzzle, knock back (*informal*), quaff, swallow, swig (*informal*), swill, toss off, wolf **2.** choke, gasp, stifle, swallow *~noun* **3.** draught, mouthful, swallow, swig (*informal*)

gum **1.** *noun* adhesive, cement, exudate, glue, mucilage, paste, resin **2.** *verb* affix, cement, clog, glue, paste, stick, stiffen

gummy adhesive, gluey, sticky, tacky, viscid

gumption ability, acumen, astuteness, cleverness, common sense, discernment, enterprise, get-up-and-go (*informal*), horse sense, initiative, mother wit, nous (*Brit. slang*), resourcefulness, sagacity, savvy (*slang*), shrewdness, spirit, wit(s)

gun firearm, handgun, heater (*U.S. slang*), piece (*slang*), rod (*slang*), shooter (*slang*)

Guns

AK-47 *or* Kalashnikov
anti-aircraft gun *or* ack-ack gun
Armalite (*Trademark*)
arquebus
BAR
Big Bertha
blunderbuss
Bofors gun
breech-loader
Bren gun
Browning
burp gun
carbine
carronade
chassepot
chokebore
Colt
culverin
derringer *or* deringer
Enfield rifle
firelock
flintlock
forty-five
fusil
Garand rifle
Gatling
howitzer
Lewis gun
Luger (*Trademark*)
M-1 rifle
M-14
M-16
machine gun
Magnum (*Trademark*)
matchlock
Mauser
Maxim gun
mitrailleuse
musket
muzzle-loader
Owen gun
petronel
pistol
pom-pom
pump gun
Quaker gun
repeater
revolver
rifle
scatter-gun
shotgun
six-shooter
Springfield rifle
Sten gun
stern-chaser
sub-machine-gun
Thompson sub-machine gun (*Trademark*)
trench mortar
Uzi (*Trademark*)
Winchester rifle
zip gun

gunman assassin, bandit, bravo, desperado, gangster, gunslinger (*U.S. slang*), heavy (*slang*), hit man (*slang*), killer, mobster (*U.S. slang*), murderer, terrorist, thug

gurgle **1.** *verb* babble, bubble, burble, crow, lap, murmur, plash, purl, ripple, splash **2.** *noun* babble, murmur, purl, ripple

guru authority, guiding light, leader, maharishi, mahatma, master, mentor, sage, swami, teacher, torchbearer, tutor

gush *verb* **1.** burst, cascade, flood, flow, issue, jet, pour, run, rush, spout, spurt, stream **2.** babble, blather, chatter, effervesce, effuse, enthuse, jabber, overstate, spout *~noun* **3.** burst, cascade, flood, flow, issue, jet, outburst, outflow, rush, spout, spurt, stream, torrent **4.** babble, blather, chatter, effusion, exuberance

gushy cloying, effusive, emotional, excessive, fulsome, gushing, icky (*informal*), mawkish, overdone, overenthusiastic, over the top, sentimental

gust *noun* **1.** blast, blow, breeze, flurry, gale, puff, rush, squall **2.** burst, eruption, explosion, fit, gale, outburst, paroxysm, passion, storm, surge *~verb* **3.** blast, blow, puff, squall

gusto appetite, appreciation, brio, delight, enjoyment, enthusiasm, exhilaration, fervour, liking, pleasure, relish, savour, verve, zeal, zest, zing (*informal*)
Antonyms apathy, coolness, disinterest, distaste, inertia

gusty blowy, blustering, blustery, breezy, inclement, squally, stormy, tempestuous, windy

gut *noun* **1.** *often plural* belly, bowels, entrails, innards (*informal*), insides (*informal*), intestines, inwards, paunch, stomach, viscera **2.** *plural informal* audacity, backbone, boldness, bottle (*slang*), courage, daring, forcefulness, grit, hardihood, mettle, nerve, pluck, spirit, spunk (*informal*), willpower *~verb* **3**. clean, disembowel, draw, dress, eviscerate **4**. clean out, despoil, empty, pillage, plunder, ransack, ravage, rifle, sack, strip *~adjective* **5**. *informal* basic, deep-seated, emotional, heartfelt, innate, instinctive, intuitive, involuntary, natural, spontaneous, unthinking, visceral

gutless abject, boneless, chicken (*slang*), chickenshit (*U.S. slang*), cowardly, craven, faint-hearted, feeble, irresolute, lily-livered, spineless, submissive, timid, weak
Antonyms bold, brave, courageous, determined, resolute

gutsy ballsy (*taboo slang*), bold, brave, courageous, determined, feisty (*informal, chiefly U.S. & Canad.*), gallant, game (*informal*), gritty, have-a-go (*informal*), indomitable, mettlesome, plucky, resolute, spirited, staunch

gutter channel, conduit, ditch, drain, duct, pipe, sluice, trench, trough, tube

guttersnipe gamin, mudlark (*slang*), ragamuffin, street Arab (*offensive*), street urchin, waif

guttural deep, gravelly, gruff, hoarse, husky, low, rasping, rough, thick, throaty

guy **1**. *noun, informal* bloke (*Brit. informal*), cat (*slang*), chap, fellow, lad, man, person, youth **2**. *verb* caricature, make (a) game of, make fun of, mock, poke fun at, rib (*informal*), ridicule, send up (*Brit informal*), take off (*informal*), take the piss out of (*slang*)

guzzle bolt, carouse, cram, devour, drink, gobble, gorge, gormandize, knock back (*informal*), pig out (*U.S. & Canad. slang*), quaff, stuff (oneself), swill, tope, wolf

Gypsy, Gipsy Bohemian, nomad, rambler, roamer, Romany, rover, traveller, vagabond, vagrant, wanderer

gyrate circle, pirouette, revolve, rotate, spin, spiral, twirl, whirl

gyration convolution, pirouette, revolution, rotation, spin, spinning, spiral, whirl, whirling

H

habiliment apparel, array, attire, clothes, clothing, costume, dress, garb, garment, habit, raiment (*archaic or poetic*), robes, uniform, vestments

habit *noun* **1.** bent, custom, disposition, manner, mannerism, practice, proclivity, propensity, quirk, tendency, way **2.** convention, custom, mode, practice, routine, rule, second nature, tradition, usage, wont **3.** constitution, disposition, frame of mind, make-up, nature **4.** addiction, dependence, fixation, obsession, weakness **5.** apparel, dress, garb, garment, habiliment, riding dress *~verb* **6.** array, attire, clothe, dress, equip

Habit is a great deadener
Samuel Beckett *Waiting for Godot*

It is hard to teach an old dog new tricks
William Camden *Remains Concerning Britain*

The second half of a man's life is made up of nothing but the habits he has acquired during the first half
Fyodor Dostoevsky

Habit with him was all the test of truth,
"It must be right; I've done it from my youth."
George Crabbe *The Borough*

Old habits die hard

habitat abode, element, environment, home, home ground, locality, natural home, surroundings, terrain, territory

habitation **1.** abode, domicile, dwelling, dwelling house, home, house, living quarters, lodging, pad (*slang*), quarters, residence **2.** inhabitance, inhabitancy, occupancy, occupation, tenancy

habit-forming addictive, compulsive, moreish (*informal*)

habitual **1.** accustomed, common, customary, familiar, fixed, natural, normal, ordinary, regular, routine, standard, traditional, usual, wonted **2.** chronic, confirmed, constant, established, frequent, hardened, ingrained, inveterate, persistent, recurrent
Antonyms abnormal, exceptional, extraordinary, infrequent, irregular, occasional, rare, strange, uncommon, unusual

habituate acclimatize, accustom, acquaint, break in, condition, discipline, familiarize, harden, inure, make used to, school, season, train

habituated acclimatized, accustomed, adapted, broken in, conditioned, disciplined, familiarized, hardened, inured, schooled, seasoned, trained, used (to)
Antonyms unaccustomed, unfamiliar, unused (to)

habitué constant customer, frequenter, frequent visitor, regular (*informal*), regular patron

hack[1] *verb* **1.** chop, cut, gash, hew, kick, lacerate, mangle, mutilate, notch, slash *~noun* **2.** chop, cut, gash, notch, slash *~verb/noun* **3.** *informal* bark, cough, rasp

hack[2] *adjective* **1.** banal, mediocre, pedestrian, poor, stereotyped, tired, undistinguished, uninspired, unoriginal *~noun* **2.** Grub Street writer, literary hack, penny-a-liner, scribbler **3.** drudge, plodder, slave **4.** crock, hired horse, horse, jade, nag, poor old tired horse

hackles make one's hackles rise anger, annoy, bridle at, cause resentment, get one's dander up (*slang*), infuriate, make one see red (*informal*), rub one up the wrong way

hackneyed banal, clichéd, common, commonplace, overworked, pedestrian, played out (*informal*), run-of-the-mill, stale, stereotyped, stock, threadbare, timeworn, tired, trite, unoriginal, worn-out
Antonyms fresh, imaginative, new, novel, original, striking, unusual

Hades hell, infernal regions, lower world, nether regions, realm of Pluto, (the) inferno, underworld

haft handle, helve, shaft

hag ballbreaker (*slang*), beldam (*archaic*), crone, fury, harridan, Jezebel, shrew, termagant, virago, vixen, witch

haggard careworn, drawn, emaciated, gaunt, ghastly, hollow-eyed, pinched, shrunken, thin, wan, wasted, wrinkled
Antonyms bright-eyed, brisk, energetic, fresh, hale, robust, sleek, vigorous

haggle **1.** bargain, barter, beat down, chaffer, dicker (*chiefly U.S.*), drive a hard bargain, higgle, palter **2.** bicker, dispute, quarrel, squabble, wrangle

hag-ridden angst-ridden, anxiety-ridden, careworn, ground down, harassed, tormented, with all the troubles of the world on one's shoulders, worn down, worried

hail[1] *figurative* 1. *noun* barrage, bombardment, downpour, pelting, rain, shower, storm, volley 2. *verb* barrage, batter, beat down upon, bombard, pelt, rain, rain down on, shower, storm, volley

hail[2] *verb* 1. acclaim, acknowledge, applaud, cheer, exalt, glorify, greet, honour, salute, welcome 2. accost, address, call, flag down, halloo, shout to, signal to, sing out, speak to, wave down 3. *with* **from** be a native of, be born in, come from, originate in

Antonyms (*sense 1*) boo, condemn, criticize, hiss, insult, jeer (*sense 2*) avoid, cut (*informal*), ignore, snub

hail-fellow-well-met back-slapping, familiar, free-and-easy, genial, hearty, overfriendly, unceremonious

hair 1. head of hair, locks, mane, mop, shock, tresses 2. **by a hair** by a fraction of an inch, by a hair's-breadth, by a narrow margin, by a split second, by a whisker, by the skin of one's teeth 3. **get in one's hair** aggravate (*informal*), annoy, be on one's back (*slang*), exasperate, get on one's nerves (*informal*), get on one's wick (*Brit. slang*), get up one's nose (*informal*), harass, hassle (*informal*), irritate, nark (*Brit., Austral., & N.Z. slang*), pester, piss one off (*taboo slang*), plague 4. **let one's hair down** chill out (*slang, chiefly U.S.*), let it all hang out (*informal*), let off steam (*informal*), let oneself go, mellow out (*informal*), relax, veg out (*slang, chiefly U.S.*) 5. **not turn a hair** keep one's cool (*slang*), keep one's hair on (*Brit. informal*), not bat an eyelid, remain calm 6. **split hairs** cavil, find fault, overrefine, pettifog, quibble

Doth not even nature itself teach you, that if a man have long hair, it is a shame unto him? But if a woman have long hair, it is a glory to her

Bible: I Corinthians

hairdresser barber, coiffeur, coiffeuse, friseur, stylist
Related adjective: tonsorial

hairstyle coiffure, cut, haircut, hairdo, style

Hairstyles

Afro	dreadlocks	wave	pouf
beehive	duck's arse *or* DA	pigtail	razor-cut
bob	Eton crop	plait	shingle
bouffant	feather-cut	pompadour	skinhead
bun	flat top	ponytail	wedge
bunches	French pleat *or* roll		
buzz cut	marcel *or* marcel wave		
chignon	mohican		
corn row	pageboy		
crew cut	perm *or* permanent		
crop			

hairless bald, baldheaded, beardless, clean-shaven, depilated, glabrous *or* glabrate (*Biology*), shorn, tonsured

hairpiece postiche, switch, toupee, wig

hair-raising alarming, bloodcurdling, breathtaking, creepy, exciting, frightening, horrifying, petrifying, scary, shocking, spine-chilling, startling, terrifying, thrilling

hair's-breadth 1. *noun* fraction, hair, jot, narrow margin, whisker 2. *adjective* close, hazardous, narrow

hairsplitting *adjective* captious, carping, cavilling, fault-finding, fine, finicky, nice, niggling, nit-picking (*informal*), overrefined, pettifogging, quibbling, subtle

hairy 1. bearded, bewhiskered, bushy, fleecy, furry, hirsute, pileous (*Biology*), pilose (*Biology*), shaggy, stubbly, unshaven, woolly 2. *slang* dangerous, difficult, hazardous, perilous, risky, scaring

halcyon 1. calm, gentle, mild, pacific, peaceful, placid, quiet, serene, still, tranquil, undisturbed, unruffled 2. *figurative* carefree, flourishing, golden, happy, palmy, prosperous

hale able-bodied, blooming, fit, flourishing, healthy, hearty, in fine fettle, in the pink, right as rain (*Brit. informal*), robust, sound, strong, vigorous, well

half 1. *noun* bisection, division, equal part, fifty per cent, fraction, hemisphere, portion, section 2. *adjective* divided, fractional, halved, incomplete, limited, moderate, partial 3. *adverb* after a fashion, all but, barely, inadequately, incompletely, in part, partially, partly, pretty nearly, slightly 4. **by half** considerably, excessively, very much

The half is better than the whole

Half a loaf is better than no bread

half-baked 1. brainless, crackpot (*informal*), crazy, foolish, harebrained, inane, loopy (*informal*), senseless, silly, stupid 2. ill-conceived, ill-judged, impractical, poorly planned, short-sighted, unformed, unthought out *or* through

half-hearted apathetic, cool, half-arsed (*Brit. slang*), half-assed (*U.S. & Canad. slang*), indifferent, lacklustre, listless, lukewarm, neutral, passive, perfunctory, spiritless, tame, unenthusiastic, uninterested

Antonyms ambitious, animated, avid, concerned, determined, eager, emotional, energetic, enthusiastic, excited, spirited, warm, wholehearted, zealous

halfway *adverb* 1. midway, to *or* in the middle, to the midpoint 2. incompletely, moderately, nearly, partially, partly, rather **3. meet halfway** accommodate, come to terms, compromise, concede, give and take, strike a balance, trade off *~adjective* **4.** central, equidistant, intermediate, mid, middle, midway **5.** imperfect, incomplete, moderate, partial, part-way

halfwit airhead (*slang*), berk (*Brit. slang*), charlie (*Brit. informal*), coot, dickhead (*slang*), dickwit (*slang*), dimwit (*informal*), dipstick (*Brit. slang*), divvy (*Brit. slang*), dolt, dork (*slang*), dullard, dunce, dunderhead, dweeb (*U.S. slang*), fathead (*informal*), fool, fuckwit (*taboo slang*), geek (*slang*), gobshite (*Irish taboo slang*), gonzo (*slang*), idiot, imbecile (*informal*), jerk (*slang, chiefly U.S. & Canad.*), lamebrain (*informal*), mental defective, moron, nerd *or* nurd (*slang*), nitwit (*informal*), numpty (*Scot. informal*), numskull *or* numbskull, oaf, pillock (*Brit. slang*), plank (*Brit. slang*), plonker (*slang*), prat (*slang*), prick (*slang*), schmuck (*U.S. slang*), simpleton, twit (*informal, chiefly Brit.*), wally (*slang*)

half-witted addle-brained, barmy (*slang*), batty (*slang*), crazy, doltish, doolally (*slang*), dull, dull-witted, feeble-minded, flaky (*U.S. slang*), foolish, goofy (*informal*), idiotic, moronic, nerdish *or* nurdish (*slang*), obtuse, silly, simple, simple-minded, stupid

hall 1. corridor, entrance hall, entry, foyer, hallway, lobby, passage, passageway, vestibule **2.** assembly room, auditorium, chamber, concert hall, meeting place

hallmark 1. authentication, device, endorsement, mark, seal, sign, signet, stamp, symbol **2.** badge, emblem, indication, sure sign, telltale sign

halloo call, cry, hail, holla, shout

hallow bless, consecrate, dedicate, devote, enshrine, glorify, magnify (*archaic*), respect, revere, reverence, sanctify, venerate

hallowed beatified, blessed, consecrated, dedicated, holy, honoured, inviolable, revered, sacred, sacrosanct, sanctified

hallucinate daydream, envision, fantasize, freak out (*informal*), have hallucinations, imagine, trip (*informal*)

hallucination aberration, apparition, delusion, dream, fantasy, figment of the imagination, illusion, mirage, phantasmagoria, vision

hallucinogenic hallucinatory, mind-blowing (*informal*), mind-expanding, psychedelic, psychoactive, psychotropic

halo aura, aureole *or* aureola, corona, halation (*Photography*), nimbus, radiance, ring of light

halt[1] *verb* **1.** belay (*Nautical*), break off, call it a day, cease, close down, come to an end, desist, draw up, pull up, rest, stand still, stop, wait **2.** arrest, block, bring to an end, check, curb, cut short, end, hold back, impede, nip in the bud, obstruct, staunch, stem, stem the flow, terminate *~noun* **3.** arrest, break, close, end, impasse, interruption, pause, stand, standstill, stop, stoppage, termination
Antonyms *verb* aid, begin, boost, commence, continue, encourage, forward, go ahead, maintain, proceed, resume, start *~noun* beginning, commencement, continuation, resumption, start

halt[2] *verb* **1.** be defective, falter, hobble, limp, stumble **2.** be unsure, boggle, dither (*chiefly Brit.*), haver, hesitate, pause, stammer, swither (*Scot.*), think twice, waver *~adjective* **3.** *archaic* crippled, lame, limping

halting awkward, faltering, hesitant, imperfect, laboured, stammering, stumbling, stuttering

halve 1. *verb* bisect, cut in half, divide equally, reduce by fifty per cent, share equally, split in two **2.** *noun plural* **by halves** imperfectly, incompletely, scrappily, skimpily

ham-fisted all fingers and thumbs (*informal*), awkward, bungling, butterfingered (*informal*), cack-handed (*informal*), clumsy, ham-handed (*informal*), inept, maladroit, unhandy

hammer *verb* **1.** bang, beat, drive, hit, knock, lambast(e), strike, tap **2.** beat out, fashion, forge, form, make, shape **3.** *often with* **into** din into, drive home, drub into, drum into, grind into, impress upon, instruct, repeat **4.** *often with* **away (at)** beaver away (*Brit. informal*), drudge, grind, keep on, peg away (*chiefly Brit.*), persevere, persist, plug away (*informal*), pound away, stick at, work **5.** *informal* beat, blow out of the water (*slang*), clobber (*slang*), defeat, drub, lick (*informal*), master, run rings around (*informal*), slate (*informal*), stuff (*slang*), tank (*slang*), thrash, trounce, undo, wipe the floor with (*informal*), worst

hammer out accomplish, bring about, come to a conclusion, complete, excogitate, finish, form a resolution, make a decision, negotiate, produce, settle, sort out, thrash out, work out

hamper *verb* bind, cramp, curb, embarrass, encumber, entangle, fetter, frustrate, hamstring, handicap, hinder, hold up, impede, interfere with, obstruct, prevent, restrain, restrict, slow down, thwart, trammel
Antonyms aid, assist, boost, encourage, expedite, forward, further, help, promote, speed

hamstring 1. cripple, disable, hock, injure, lame **2.** balk, foil, frustrate, prevent, ruin, stop, thwart

hamstrung at a loss, crippled, disabled, helpless, *hors de combat*, incapacitated, paralysed

hand *noun* **1.** fist, hook, meathook (*slang*), mitt (*slang*), palm, paw (*informal*) **2.** agency, direction, influence, part, participation, share **3.**

aid, assistance, help, support **4.** artificer, artisan, craftsman, employee, hired man, labourer, operative, worker, workman **5.** calligraphy, chirography, handwriting, longhand, penmanship, script **6.** clap, ovation, round of applause **7.** ability, art, artistry, skill **8. at** *or* **on hand** approaching, at one's fingertips, available, close, handy, imminent, just round the corner, near, nearby, on tap (*informal*), ready, within reach **9. from hand to mouth** by necessity, improvidently, in poverty, insecurely, on the breadline (*informal*), precariously, uncertainly **10. hand in glove** allied, in cahoots (*informal*), in league, in partnership **11. hand over fist** by leaps and bounds, easily, steadily, swiftly **12. in hand a.** in order, receiving attention, under control **b.** available for use, in reserve, put by, ready *~verb* **13.** deliver, hand over, pass **14.** aid, assist, conduct, convey, give, guide, help, lead, present, transmit
Related adjective: manual

One hand washes the other

Many hands make light work

A bird in the hand is worth two in the bush

handbook Baedeker, guide, guidebook, instruction book, manual, vade mecum

handcuff 1. *verb* fetter, manacle, shackle **2.** *noun plural* bracelets (*slang*), cuffs (*informal*), fetters, manacles, shackles

hand down *or* **on** bequeath, give, grant, pass on *or* down, transfer, will

handful few, small number, small quantity, smattering, sprinkling
Antonyms a lot, crowd, heaps, horde, large number, large quantity, loads (*informal*), masses (*informal*), mob, plenty, scores, stacks

handgun automatic, derringer, piece (*U.S. slang*), pistol, revolver, rod (*U.S. slang*), shooter (*informal*)

handicap *noun* **1.** albatross, barrier, block, disadvantage, drawback, encumbrance, hazard, hindrance, impediment, limitation, millstone, obstacle, restriction, shortcoming, stumbling block **2.** advantage, edge, head start, odds, penalty, upper hand **3.** defect, disability, impairment *~verb* **4.** burden, encumber, hamper, hamstring, hinder, hold back, impede, limit, place at a disadvantage, restrict, retard
Antonyms *noun* (*sense 1*) advantage, asset, benefit, boost, edge *~verb* aid, assist, benefit, boost, forward, further, help, promote

handicraft art, artisanship, craft, craftsmanship, handiwork, skill, workmanship

Handicrafts

basketry *or* basket making
batik
calligraphy
ceramics
cloisonnage
crewelwork
crochet
decoupage
dress-making
embroidery
flower arranging
knitting
knotwork
macramé
needlepoint
patchwork
pottery
quilling
quilting
raffia work
sewing
spinning
sugarcraft
tapestry
weaving
wickerwork

handily 1. adroitly, capably, cleverly, deftly, dexterously, expertly, proficiently, skilfully **2.** accessibly, advantageously, conveniently, helpfully, readily, suitably

handiness 1. accessibility, availability, closeness, convenience, practicality, proximity, usefulness, workability **2.** adroitness, aptitude, cleverness, deftness, dexterity, efficiency, expertise, knack, proficiency, skill

handiwork 1. craft, handicraft, handwork **2.** achievement, artefact, creation, design, invention, product, production, result

handkerchief hanky (*informal*), mouchoir, nose rag (*slang*), snot rag (*slang*), tissue

handle *noun* **1.** grip, haft, handgrip, helve, hilt, knob, stock *~verb* **2.** feel, finger, fondle, grasp, hold, maul, paw (*informal*), pick up, poke, touch **3.** control, direct, guide, manage, manipulate, manoeuvre, operate, steer, use, wield **4.** administer, conduct, cope with, deal with, manage, supervise, take care of, treat **5.** discourse, discuss, treat **6.** carry, deal in, market, sell, stock, trade, traffic in

handling administration, approach, conduct, direction, management, manipulation, running, treatment

hand-me-down *adjective* cast-off, handed down, inherited, passed on, reach-me-down (*informal*), second-hand, used, worn

hand-out 1. alms, charity, dole **2.** bulletin, circular, free sample, leaflet, literature (*informal*), mailshot, press release

hand out deal out, disburse, dish out (*informal*), dispense, disseminate, distribute, give out, mete

hand over deliver, donate, fork out *or* up (*slang*), present, release, surrender, transfer, turn over, yield

hand-picked choice, chosen, elect, elite, recherché, select, selected
Antonyms haphazard, indiscriminate, random, run-of-the-mill, wholesale

hands 1. authority, care, charge, command, control, custody, disposal, guardianship, keeping, possession, power, supervision **2. hands down** easily, effortlessly, with no contest, with no trouble

handsome 1. admirable, attractive, becoming, comely, dishy (*informal, chiefly Brit.*), elegant, fine, good-looking, gorgeous, graceful, majes~

tic, personable, stately, well-proportioned **2.** abundant, ample, bountiful, considerable, generous, gracious, large, liberal, magnanimous, plentiful, sizable *or* sizeable
Antonyms base, cheap, inelegant, meagre, mean, miserly, selfish, small, stingy, tasteless, ugly, unattractive, ungenerous, unprepossessing, unsightly
Handsome is as handsome does

handsomely abundantly, amply, bountifully, generously, liberally, magnanimously, munificently, plentifully, richly

handwriting calligraphy, chirography, fist, hand, longhand, penmanship, scrawl, script
Related noun: graphology

handy **1.** accessible, at *or* on hand, at one's fingertips, available, close, convenient, just round the corner, near, nearby, within reach **2.** convenient, easy to use, helpful, manageable, neat, practical, serviceable, useful, user-friendly **3.** adept, adroit, clever, deft, dexterous, expert, nimble, proficient, ready, skilful, skilled
Antonyms awkward, clumsy, ham-fisted, inaccessible, incompetent, inconvenient, inept, inexpert, maladroit, out of the way, unaccomplished, unavailable, unskilful, unskilled, unwieldy, useless

handyman DIY expert, handy Andy (*informal*), jack-of-all-trades, odd-jobman

hang *verb* **1.** be pendent, dangle, depend, droop, incline, suspend **2.** execute, gibbet, send to the gallows, string up (*informal*) **3.** adhere, cling, hold, rest, stick **4.** attach, cover, deck, decorate, drape, fasten, fix, furnish **5.** be poised, drift, float, hover, remain, swing **6.** bend downward, bend forward, bow, dangle, drop, incline, lean over, let droop, loll, lower, sag, trail **7.** **hang fire** be slow, be suspended, delay, hang back, procrastinate, stall, stick, vacillate *~noun* **8.** **get the hang of** comprehend, get the knack *or* technique, grasp, understand

hang about *or* **around** **1.** dally, linger, loiter, roam, tarry, waste time **2.** associate with, frequent, hang out (*informal*), hang with (*informal, chiefly U.S.*), haunt, resort

hang back be backward, be reluctant, demur, hesitate, hold back, recoil

hangdog *adjective* abject, browbeaten, cowed, cringing, defeated, downcast, furtive, guilty, shamefaced, sneaking, wretched

hanger-on cohort (*chiefly U.S.*), dependant, follower, freeloader (*slang*), lackey, leech, ligger (*slang*), minion, parasite, sponger (*informal*), sycophant

hanging *adjective* **1.** dangling, drooping, flapping, flopping, floppy, loose, pendent, suspended, swinging, unattached, unsupported **2.** undecided, unresolved, unsettled, up in the air (*informal*) **3.** beetle, beetling, jutting, overhanging, projecting, prominent

hang on **1.** carry on, continue, endure, go on, hold on, hold out, persevere, persist, remain, stay the course **2.** cling, clutch, grasp, grip, hold fast **3.** be conditional upon, be contingent on, be dependent on, be determined by, depend on, hinge, rest, turn on **4.** *Also* **hang onto, hang upon** be rapt, give ear, listen attentively **5.** *informal* hold on, hold the line, remain, stop, wait

hang-out den, dive (*slang*), haunt, home, joint (*slang*), resort

hangover aftereffects, crapulence, head (*informal*), morning after (*informal*)

hang over be imminent, impend, loom, menace, threaten

hang-up block, difficulty, inhibition, obsession, preoccupation, problem, thing (*informal*)

hank coil, length, loop, piece, roll, skein

hanker *with* **for** *or* **after** ache, covet, crave, desire, eat one's heart out over, hope, hunger, itch, long, lust, pine, set one's heart on, thirst, want, wish, yearn, yen (*informal*)

hankering ache, craving, desire, hope, hunger, itch, longing, pining, thirst, urge, wish, yearning, yen (*informal*)

hanky-panky chicanery, deception, devilry, funny business (*informal*), jiggery-pokery (*informal, chiefly Brit.*), knavery, machinations, mischief, monkey business (*informal*), shenanigans (*informal*), subterfuge, trickery

haphazard **1.** accidental, arbitrary, chance, fluky (*informal*), random **2.** aimless, careless, casual, disorderly, disorganized, hit or miss (*informal*), indiscriminate, slapdash, slipshod, unmethodical, unsystematic
Antonyms arranged, careful, considered, deliberate, methodical, orderly, organized, planned, systematic, thoughtful

hapless cursed, ill-fated, ill-starred, jinxed, luckless, miserable, unfortunate, unhappy, unlucky, wretched

happen **1.** appear, arise, come about, come off (*informal*), come to pass, crop up (*informal*), develop, ensue, eventuate, follow, materialize, occur, present itself, result, see the light of day, take place, transpire (*informal*) **2.** become of, befall, betide **3.** chance, fall out, have the fortune to be, pan out (*informal*), supervene, turn out

happening accident, adventure, affair, case, chance, episode, escapade, event, experience, incident, occasion, occurrence, phenomenon, proceeding, scene

happen on *or* **upon** chance upon, come upon, discover unexpectedly, find, hit upon, light upon, stumble on, turn up

happily 1. agreeably, contentedly, delightedly, enthusiastically, freely, gladly, heartily, lief (*rare*), willingly, with pleasure 2. blithely, cheerfully, gaily, gleefully, joyfully, joyously, merrily 3. auspiciously, favourably, fortunately, luckily, opportunely, propitiously, providentially, seasonably 4. appropriately, aptly, felicitously, gracefully, successfully

happiness beatitude, blessedness, bliss, cheer, cheerfulness, cheeriness, contentment, delight, ecstasy, elation, enjoyment, exuberance, felicity, gaiety, gladness, high spirits, joy, jubilation, light-heartedness, merriment, pleasure, prosperity, satisfaction, wellbeing
Antonyms annoyance, bane, depression, despondency, distress, grief, low spirits, misery, misfortune, sadness, sorrow, unhappiness

Perfect happiness, even in memory, is not common
Jane Austen *Emma*

A lifetime of happiness! No man alive could bear it: it would be hell on earth
George Bernard Shaw *Man and Superman*

The world of the happy is quite another than the world of the unhappy
Ludwig Wittgenstein *Tracatus Logico-Philosophicus*

To be happy, we must not be too concerned with others
Albert Camus *The Fall*

Happiness does not lie in happiness, but in the achievement of it
Fyodor Dostoevsky *A Diary of a Writer*

The search for happiness is one of the chief sources of unhappiness
Eric Hoffer *The Passionate State of Mind*

I am happy and content because I think I am
Alain René Lesage *Histoire de Gil Blas de Santillane*

Ask yourself whether you are happy, and you cease to be so
John Stuart Mill *Autobiography*

It is not enough to be happy, it is also necessary that others not be
Jules Renard *Journal*

Happiness is not an ideal of reason but of imagination
Immanuel Kant *Fundamental Principles of the Metaphysics of Ethics*

We have no more right to consume happiness without producing it than to consume wealth without producing it
George Bernard Shaw *Candida*

Happiness is an imaginary condition, formerly often attributed by the living to the dead, now usually attributed by adults to children, and by children to adults
Thomas Szasz *The Second Sin*

No man is happy but by comparison
Thomas Shadwell *The Virtuoso*

Unbroken happiness is a bore: it should have ups and downs
Molière *Les fourberies de Scapin*

Nothing ages like happiness
Oscar Wilde *An Ideal Husband*

Happiness is no laughing matter
Richard Whately *Apophthegms*

happiness: an agreeable sensation arising from contemplating the misery of another
Ambrose Bierce *The Devil's Dictionary*

Happiness makes up in height for what it lacks in length
Robert Frost

happy 1. blessed, blest, blissful, blithe, cheerful, cock-a-hoop, content, contented, delighted, ecstatic, elated, floating on air, glad, gratified, jolly, joyful, joyous, jubilant, merry, on cloud nine (*informal*), overjoyed, over the moon (*informal*), pleased, rapt, sunny, thrilled, walking on air (*informal*) 2. advantageous, appropriate, apt, auspicious, befitting, convenient, enviable, favourable, felicitous, fortunate, lucky, opportune, promising, propitious, satisfactory, seasonable, successful, timely, well-timed
Antonyms depressed, despondent, discontented, displeased, down in the dumps (*informal*), forlorn, gloomy, inapt, joyless, low, melancholy, miserable, mournful, sad, sombre, sorrowful, sorry, unfortunate, unhappy, unlucky

Call no man happy till he dies, he is at best but fortunate
Solon

No one can be perfectly free till all are free; no one can be perfectly moral till all are moral; no one can be perfectly happy till all are happy
Herbert Spencer *Social Statics*

We are never happy: we can only remember that we were so once
Alexander Smith

happy-go-lucky blithe, carefree, casual, devil-may-care, easy-going, heedless, improvident, insouciant, irresponsible, light-hearted, nonchalant, unconcerned, untroubled
Antonyms careworn, cheerless, gloomy, melancholy, morose, sad, serious, unhappy

hara-kiri ritual suicide, seppuku

harangue 1. *noun* address, declamation, diatribe, exhortation, lecture, oration, philippic, screed, speech, spiel (*informal*), tirade 2. *verb* address, declaim, exhort, hold forth, lecture, rant, spout (*informal*)

harass annoy, badger, bait, beleaguer, be on one's back (*slang*), bother, breathe down someone's neck, chivvy (*Brit.*), devil (*informal*), disturb, exasperate, exhaust, fatigue, harry, hassle (*informal*), hound, perplex, persecute, pester, plague, tease, tire, torment, trouble, vex, weary, worry

harassed careworn, distraught, harried, has~ sled (*informal*), plagued, strained, tormented, troubled, under pressure, under stress, vexed, worried

harassment aggravation (*informal*), annoy~ ance, badgering, bedevilment, bother, hassle (*informal*), irritation, molestation, nuisance, persecution, pestering, torment, trouble, vexation

harbinger forerunner, foretoken, herald, indi~ cation, messenger, omen, portent, precursor, sign

harbour *noun* **1.** anchorage, destination, haven, port **2.** asylum, covert, haven, refuge, retreat, sanctuary, sanctum, security, shelter *~verb* **3.** conceal, hide, lodge, protect, provide refuge, relieve, secrete, shelter, shield **4.** believe, brood over, cherish, cling to, entertain, foster, hold, imagine, maintain, nurse, nurture, re~ tain

hard *adjective* **1.** compact, dense, firm, impen~ etrable, inflexible, rigid, rocklike, solid, stiff, stony, strong, tough, unyielding **2.** arduous, backbreaking, burdensome, exacting, exhaust~ ing, fatiguing, formidable, Herculean, labori~ ous, rigorous, strenuous, toilsome, tough, uphill, wearying **3.** baffling, complex, compli~ cated, difficult, intricate, involved, knotty, perplexing, puzzling, tangled, thorny, unfath~ omable **4.** callous, cold, cruel, exacting, grim, hardhearted, harsh, implacable, obdurate, pitiless, ruthless, severe, stern, strict, stub~ born, unfeeling, unjust, unkind, unrelenting, unsparing, unsympathetic **5.** calamitous, dark, disagreeable, disastrous, distressing, grievous, grim, intolerable, painful, unpleasant **6.** driv~ ing, fierce, forceful, heavy, powerful, strong, violent **7.** *of feelings or words* acrimonious, angry, antagonistic, bitter, hostile, rancorous, resentful **8.** *of truth or facts* actual, bare, cold, definite, indisputable, plain, undeniable, un~ varnished, verified *~adverb* **9.** energetically, fiercely, forcefully, forcibly, heavily, intensely, powerfully, severely, sharply, strongly, vigor~ ously, violently, with all one's might, with might and main **10.** assiduously, determinedly, diligently, doggedly, earnestly, industriously, intently, persistently, steadily, strenuously, untiringly **11.** agonizingly, badly, distressingly, harshly, laboriously, painfully, roughly, se~ verely, with difficulty **12.** bitterly, hardly, keenly, rancorously, reluctantly, resentfully, slowly, sorely
Antonyms *adjective* agreeable, amiable, care~ less, clear, direct, easy, easy-peasy (*slang*), flexible, friendly, gentle, good, humane, kind, lazy, lenient, light, malleable, merciful, mild, permissive, pleasant, pliable, simple, soft, straightforward, uncomplicated, weak *~adverb* calmly, easily, gently, lazily, lightly, loosely, mildly, serenely, softly, weakly

hard and fast binding, immutable, incontro~ vertible, inflexible, invariable, rigid, set, strict, stringent, unalterable

hard-bitten *or* **hard-boiled** case-hardened, cynical, down-to-earth, hard-headed, hard-nosed (*informal*), matter-of-fact, practical, re~ alistic, shrewd, tough, unsentimental
Antonyms benign, compassionate, gentle, hu~ mane, idealistic, merciful, mild, romantic, sympathetic

hard-core **1.** dedicated, die-hard, dyed-in-the-wool, extreme, intransigent, obstinate, rigid, staunch, steadfast **2.** explicit, obscene, X-rated (*informal*)

harden **1.** anneal, bake, cake, freeze, set, so~ lidify, stiffen **2.** brace, buttress, fortify, gird, indurate, nerve, reinforce, steel, strengthen, toughen **3.** accustom, brutalize, case-harden, habituate, inure, season, train

hardened **1.** chronic, fixed, habitual, incorri~ gible, inveterate, irredeemable, reprobate, set, shameless **2.** accustomed, habituated, inured, seasoned, toughened
Antonyms infrequent, irregular, occasional, rare, unaccustomed

hard-favoured *or* **hard-featured** austere, coarse-featured, forbidding, grim visaged, ill-favoured, severe, ugly

hard-headed astute, cool, hard-boiled (*infor~ mal*), level-headed, practical, pragmatic, real~ istic, sensible, shrewd, tough, unsentimental
Antonyms idealistic, impractical, sentimental, unrealistic

hardhearted callous, cold, cruel, hard, hard as nails, heartless, indifferent, inhuman, insen~ sitive, intolerant, merciless, pitiless, stony, uncaring, unfeeling, unkind, unsympathetic
Antonyms compassionate, forgiving, gentle, humane, kind, loving, merciful, sensitive, soft-hearted, sympathetic, understanding, warm, warm-hearted

hard-hitting critical, no holds barred, pulling no punches, strongly worded, tough, uncom~ promising, unsparing, vigorous

hardihood **1.** backbone, boldness, bottle (*Brit. slang*), bravery, courage, daring, deter~ mination, firmness, grit, guts (*informal*), in~ trepidity, mettle, nerve, pluck, resolution, spirit, spunk (*informal*), strength **2.** assurance, audacity, effrontery, foolhardiness, imperti~ nence, impetuousness, rashness, recklessness, temerity

hardiness boldness, courage, fortitude, intre~ pidity, resilience, resolution, robustness, rug~ gedness, sturdiness, toughness, valour

hardline definite, inflexible, intransigent, tough, uncompromising, undeviating, unyielding

hardly almost not, at a push, barely, by no means, faintly, infrequently, just, not at all, not quite, no way, only, only just, scarcely, with difficulty
Antonyms abundantly, amply, by all means, certainly, completely, easily, fully, indubitably, more than, really, truly, undoubtedly, well over

hard-nosed businesslike, down-to-earth, hard-headed, hardline, practical, pragmatic, realistic, shrewd, tough, uncompromising, unsentimental

hard-pressed harried, hotly pursued, in difficulties, pushed (*informal*), under attack, under pressure, up against it (*informal*), with one's back to the wall

hardship adversity, affliction, austerity, burden, calamity, destitution, difficulty, fatigue, grievance, labour, misery, misfortune, need, oppression, persecution, privation, suffering, toil, torment, trial, tribulation, trouble, want
Antonyms aid, blessing, boon, comfort, ease, good fortune, happiness, help, prosperity, relief

hard up bankrupt, broke (*informal*), bust (*informal*), cleaned out (*slang*), dirt-poor (*informal*), down and out, flat broke (*informal*), impecunious, impoverished, in queer street, in the red (*informal*), on one's uppers (*informal*), on the breadline, out of pocket, penniless, poor, short, short of cash *or* funds, skint (*Brit. slang*), strapped for cash (*informal*), without two pennies to rub together (*informal*)
Antonyms affluent, comfortable (*informal*), fortunate, loaded (*slang*), rich, wealthy, well-heeled (*informal*), well-off

hard-wearing durable, resilient, rugged, stout, strong, tough, well-made

hard-working assiduous, busy, conscientious, diligent, energetic, indefatigable, industrious, sedulous, zealous
Antonyms careless, dilatory, good-for-nothing, inconstant, indifferent, lazy

hardy 1. firm, fit, hale, healthy, hearty, in fine fettle, lusty, robust, rugged, sound, stalwart, stout, strong, sturdy, tough, vigorous 2. bold, brave, courageous, daring, feisty (*informal, chiefly U.S. & Canad.*), gritty, heroic, intrepid, manly, plucky, resolute, stouthearted, valiant, valorous 3. audacious, brazen, foolhardy, headstrong, impudent, rash, reckless
Antonyms delicate, faint-hearted, feeble, fragile, frail, sickly, soft, weak, weedy (*informal*), wimpish *or* wimpy (*informal*)

harebrained asinine, careless, empty-headed, flighty, foolish, giddy, half-baked (*informal*), harum-scarum, heedless, inane, mindless, rash, reckless, scatterbrained, unstable, unsteady, wild

harem gynaeceum (*in ancient Greece*), seraglio, women's quarters, zenana (*in eastern countries*)

hark attend, give ear, give heed, hear, hearken (*archaic*), listen, mark, notice, pay attention

hark back look back, recall, recollect, regress, remember, revert, think back

harlot call girl, fallen woman, hussy, loose woman, pro (*slang*), prostitute, scrubber (*Brit. & Austral. slang*), slag (*Brit. slang*), streetwalker, strumpet, tart (*informal*), tramp (*slang*), whore, working girl (*facetious slang*)

harm *noun* 1. abuse, damage, detriment, disservice, hurt, ill, impairment, injury, loss, mischief, misfortune 2. evil, immorality, iniquity, sin, sinfulness, vice, wickedness, wrong *~verb* 3. abuse, blemish, damage, hurt, ill-treat, ill-use, impair, injure, lay a finger on, maltreat, mar, molest, ruin, spoil, wound
Antonyms *noun* aid, assistance, benefit, blessing, boon, gain, good, goodness, help, improvement, reparation, righteousness *~verb* aid, alleviate, ameliorate, assist, benefit, better, cure, heal, help, improve, repair

harmful baleful, baneful, damaging, deleterious, destructive, detrimental, disadvantageous, evil, hurtful, injurious, maleficent, noxious, pernicious
Antonyms beneficial, good, harmless, healthy, helpful, innocuous, safe, wholesome

harmless gentle, innocent, innocuous, innoxious, inoffensive, nontoxic, not dangerous, safe, unobjectionable
Antonyms dangerous, destructive, harmful, unhealthy, unsafe, unwholesome

harmonious 1. agreeable, compatible, concordant, congruous, consonant, coordinated, correspondent, dulcet, euphonic, euphonious, harmonic, harmonizing, matching, mellifluous, melodious, musical, sweet-sounding, symphonious (*literary*), tuneful 2. agreeable, amicable, compatible, concordant, congenial, cordial, *en rapport*, fraternal, friendly, in accord, in harmony, in unison, of one mind, sympathetic
Antonyms cacophonous, contrasting, discordant, grating, harsh, incompatible, inconsistent, unfriendly, unlike, unmelodious

harmonize accord, adapt, agree, arrange, attune, be in unison, be of one mind, blend, chime with, cohere, compose, coordinate, correspond, match, reconcile, suit, tally, tone in with

harmony 1. accord, agreement, amicability, amity, assent, compatibility, concord, conformity, consensus, cooperation, friendship, goodwill, like-mindedness, peace, rapport,

sympathy, unanimity, understanding, unity **2.** balance, compatibility, concord, congruity, consistency, consonance, coordination, correspondence, fitness, parallelism, suitability, symmetry **3.** euphony, melodiousness, melody, tune, tunefulness, unison
Antonyms antagonism, cacophony, conflict, contention, disagreement, dissension, hostility, incongruity, inconsistency, opposition, unsuitability

harness *noun* **1.** equipment, gear, tack, tackle, trappings **2. in harness** active, at work, busy, in action, working *~verb* **3.** couple, hitch up, put in harness, saddle, yoke **4.** apply, channel, control, employ, exploit, make productive, mobilize, render useful, turn to account, utilize

harp *with* **on** *or* **upon** dwell on, go on, labour, press, reiterate, renew, repeat, rub it in

harping *noun* nagging, reiteration, repetition

harridan ballbreaker (*slang*), battle-axe (*informal*), nag, scold, shrew, tartar, termagant, virago, witch, Xanthippe

harried agitated, anxious, beset, bothered, distressed, hag-ridden, harassed, hard-pressed, hassled (*informal*), plagued, tormented, troubled, worried

harrow *verb, figurative* agonize, distress, harass, lacerate, perturb, rack, rend, tear, torment, torture, vex, wound, wring

harrowing agonizing, alarming, chilling, distressing, disturbing, excruciating, frightening, heartbreaking, heart-rending, nerve-racking, painful, racking, scaring, terrifying, tormenting, traumatic

harry **1.** annoy, badger, bedevil, be on one's back (*slang*), bother, breathe down someone's neck, chivvy, disturb, fret, get in one's hair (*informal*), harass, hassle (*informal*), molest, persecute, pester, plague, tease, torment, trouble, vex, worry **2.** depredate (*rare*), despoil, devastate, pillage, plunder, raid, ravage, rob, sack

harsh **1.** coarse, croaking, crude, discordant, dissonant, glaring, grating, guttural, jarring, rasping, raucous, rough, strident, unmelodious **2.** abusive, austere, bitter, bleak, brutal, comfortless, cruel, dour, Draconian, drastic, grim, hard, pitiless, punitive, relentless, ruthless, severe, sharp, Spartan, stern, stringent, unfeeling, unkind, unpleasant, unrelenting
Antonyms agreeable, gentle, harmonious, kind, loving, mellifluous, merciful, mild, pleasant, smooth, soft, soothing, sweet

harshly brutally, cruelly, grimly, roughly, severely, sharply, sternly, strictly

harshness acerbity, acrimony, asperity, austerity, bitterness, brutality, churlishness, coarseness, crudity, hardness, ill-temper, rigour, roughness, severity, sourness, sternness

harum-scarum careless, erratic, giddy, haphazard, harebrained, hasty, ill-considered, impetuous, imprudent, inconstant, irresponsible, precipitate, rash, reckless, scatterbrained, scatty (*Brit. informal*), wild

harvest *noun* **1.** harvesting, harvest-time, ingathering, reaping **2.** crop, produce, yield **3.** *figurative* consequence, effect, fruition, product, result, return *~verb* **4.** gather, mow, pick, pluck, reap **5.** accumulate, acquire, amass, collect, garner

hash **1.** balls-up (*taboo slang*), cock-up (*Brit. slang*), confusion, fuck-up (*offensive taboo slang*), hodgepodge (*U.S.*), hotchpotch, jumble, mess, mishmash, mix-up, muddle, pig's breakfast (*informal*), pig's ear (*informal*), shambles, state **2. make a hash of** *informal* bodge (*informal*), botch, bungle, cock up (*Brit. slang*), flub (*U.S. slang*), fuck up (*offensive taboo slang*), jumble, make a nonsense of (*informal*), make a pig's ear of (*informal*), mess up, mishandle, mismanage, mix, muddle

hassle *noun* **1.** altercation, argument, bickering, disagreement, dispute, fight, quarrel, row, squabble, tussle, wrangle **2.** bother, difficulty, inconvenience, problem, struggle, trial, trouble, upset *~verb* **3.** annoy, badger, be on one's back (*slang*), bother, breath down someone's neck, bug (*informal*), get in one's hair (*informal*), get on one's nerves (*informal*), harass, harry, hound, pester

hassled bothered, browbeaten, hot and bothered, hounded, hunted, pressured, stressed, under pressure, uptight, worried

haste **1.** alacrity, briskness, celerity, dispatch, expedition, fleetness, nimbleness, promptitude, quickness, rapidity, rapidness, speed, swiftness, urgency, velocity **2.** bustle, hastiness, helter-skelter, hurry, hustle, impetuosity, precipitateness, rashness, recklessness, rush
Antonyms calmness, care, delay, deliberation, leisureliness, slowness, sluggishness, sureness

More haste, less speed

Make haste slowly (festina lente)

hasten **1.** barrel (along) (*informal, chiefly U.S. & Canad.*), beetle, bolt, burn rubber (*informal*), dash, fly, get one's skates on (*informal*), haste, hurry (up), make haste, race, run, rush, scurry, scuttle, speed, sprint, step on it (*informal*), tear (along) **2.** accelerate, advance, dispatch, expedite, goad, hurry (up), precipitate, press, push forward, quicken, speed (up), step up (*informal*), urge
Antonyms crawl, creep, dawdle, decelerate, delay, hinder, impede, move slowly, retard, slow, slow down

hastily **1.** apace, double-quick, fast, hotfoot, pdq (*slang*), posthaste, promptly, pronto (*informal*), quickly, rapidly, speedily, straightaway **2.** heedlessly, hurriedly, impetuously, impulsively, on the spur of the moment, precipitately, rashly, recklessly, too quickly

hasty **1.** brisk, eager, expeditious, fast, fleet, hurried, prompt, rapid, speedy, swift, urgent **2.** brief, cursory, fleeting, passing, perfunctory, rushed, short, superficial **3.** foolhardy, headlong, heedless, impetuous, impulsive, indiscreet, precipitate, rash, reckless, thoughtless, unduly quick **4.** brusque, excited, fiery, hot-headed, hot-tempered, impatient, irascible, irritable, passionate, quick-tempered, snappy
Antonyms careful, cautious, detailed, dispassionate, leisurely, long, protracted, slow, thorough, thoughtful

hatch **1.** breed, bring forth, brood, incubate **2.** *figurative* conceive, concoct, contrive, cook up (*informal*), design, devise, dream up (*informal*), manufacture, plan, plot, project, scheme, think up, trump up

hatchet axe, cleaver, machete, tomahawk

hatchet man assassin, bravo, calumniator, cutthroat, debunker, defamer, destroyer, detractor, gunman, heavy (*slang*), hired assassin, hit man (*slang*), killer, murderer, smear campaigner, thug, traducer

hate *verb* **1.** abhor, abominate, be hostile to, be repelled by, be sick of, despise, detest, dislike, execrate, have an aversion to, loathe, recoil from **2.** be loath, be reluctant, be sorry, be unwilling, dislike, feel disinclined, have no stomach for, shrink from *~noun* **3.** abhorrence, abomination, animosity, animus, antagonism, antipathy, aversion, detestation, dislike, enmity, execration, hatred, hostility, loathing, odium
Antonyms *verb* be fond of, cherish, dote on, enjoy, esteem, fancy, like, love, relish, treasure, wish *~noun* affection, amity, devotion, fondness, goodwill, liking, love

> *Men love in haste, but they detest at leisure*
> Lord Byron *Don Juan*

> *If you hate a person, you hate something in him that is part of yourself. What isn't part of ourselves doesn't disturb us*
> Hermann Hesse *Demian*

hateful abhorrent, abominable, despicable, detestable, disgusting, execrable, forbidding, foul, heinous, horrible, loathsome, obnoxious, obscene, odious, offensive, repellent, repugnant, repulsive, revolting, vile
Antonyms affectionate, attractive, beautiful, charming, desirable, devoted, friendly, good, kind, likable *or* likeable, lovable, loving, pleasant, wonderful

hatred abomination, animosity, animus, antagonism, antipathy, aversion, detestation, dislike, enmity, execration, hate, ill will, odium, repugnance, revulsion
Antonyms affection, amity, attachment, devotion, fondness, friendliness, goodwill, liking, love

haughtiness airs, aloofness, arrogance, conceit, contempt, contemptuousness, disdain, hauteur, insolence, loftiness, pomposity, pride, snobbishness, superciliousness

haughty arrogant, assuming, conceited, contemptuous, disdainful, high, high and mighty (*informal*), hoity-toity (*informal*), imperious, lofty, on one's high horse (*informal*), overweening, proud, scornful, snobbish, snooty (*informal*), stuck-up (*informal*), supercilious, uppish (*Brit. informal*)
Antonyms humble, meek, mild, modest, self-effacing, subservient, wimpish *or* wimpy (*informal*)

haul *verb* **1.** drag, draw, hale, heave, lug, pull, tow, trail, tug **2.** carry, cart, convey, hump (*Brit. slang*), move, transport *~noun* **3.** drag, heave, pull, tug **4.** booty, catch, find, gain, harvest, loot, spoils, takings, yield

haunt *verb* **1.** visit, walk **2.** beset, come back, obsess, plague, possess, prey on, recur, stay with, torment, trouble, weigh on **3.** frequent, hang around *or* about, repair, resort, visit *~noun* **4.** den, gathering place, hangout (*informal*), meeting place, rendezvous, resort, stamping ground

haunted **1.** cursed, eerie, ghostly, jinxed, possessed, spooky (*informal*) **2.** obsessed, plagued, preoccupied, tormented, troubled, worried

haunting disturbing, eerie, evocative, indelible, nostalgic, persistent, poignant, recurrent, recurring, unforgettable

hauteur affectedness, airs, arrogance, contempt, dignity, disdain, haughtiness, loftiness, pride, snobbishness, stateliness, superciliousness

have **1.** hold, keep, obtain, occupy, own, possess, retain **2.** accept, acquire, gain, get, obtain, procure, receive, secure, take **3.** comprehend, comprise, contain, embody, include, take in **4.** endure, enjoy, experience, feel, meet with, suffer, sustain, undergo **5.** *slang* cheat, deceive, dupe, fool, outwit, stiff (*slang*), swindle, take in (*informal*), trick **6.** *usually* **have to** be bound, be compelled, be forced, be obliged, have got to, must, ought, should **7.** allow, consider, entertain, permit, put up with (*informal*), think about, tolerate **8.** bear, beget, bring forth, bring into the world, deliver, give birth to **9.** **have had it** *informal* be defeated, be exhausted, be finished, be out, be past it (*informal*), be pooped (*U.S. slang*), be stonk~ered (*slang*)

haven 1. anchorage, harbour, port, roads (*Nautical*) 2. *figurative* asylum, refuge, re~treat, sanctuary, sanctum, shelter

have on 1. be clothed in, be dressed in, wear 2. be committed to, be engaged to, have on the agenda, have planned 3. *of a person* deceive, kid (*informal*), play a joke on, pull someone's leg, take the mickey, tease, trick, wind up (*Brit. slang*)

havoc 1. carnage, damage, desolation, despo~liation, destruction, devastation, rack and ruin, ravages, ruin, slaughter, waste, wreck 2. *informal* chaos, confusion, disorder, disrup~tion, mayhem, shambles 3. **play havoc (with)** bring into chaos, confuse, convulse, demolish, destroy, devastate, disorganize, dis~rupt, wreck

hawk *verb* 1. bark (*informal*), cry, market, peddle, sell, tout (*informal*), vend 2. *often with* **about** bandy about (*informal*), bruit about, buzz, noise abroad, put about, retail, rumour

hawker barrow boy (*Brit.*), cheap-jack (*infor~mal*), colporteur, crier, huckster, pedlar, ven~dor

hawk-eyed Argus-eyed, gimlet-eyed, having eyes in the back of one's head (*informal*), keen sighted, lynx-eyed, observant, perceptive, sharp-eyed, vigilant

haywire 1. *of things* chaotic, confused, disar~ranged, disordered, disorganized, mixed up, on the blink (*slang*), out of commission, out of order, shambolic (*informal*), tangled, topsy-turvy 2. *of people* crazy, erratic, gonzo (*slang*), mad, wild

hazard *noun* 1. danger, endangerment, imper~ilment, jeopardy, peril, pitfall, risk, threat 2. accident, chance, coincidence, fluke, luck, misfortune, mishap, stroke of luck *~verb* 3. chance, dare, gamble, risk, skate on thin ice, stake 4. advance, conjecture, offer, presume, proffer, speculate, submit, suppose, throw out, venture, volunteer 5. endanger, expose, im~peril, jeopardize, risk, threaten

hazardous 1. dangerous, dicey (*informal, chiefly Brit.*), difficult, fraught with danger, hairy (*slang*), insecure, perilous, precarious, risky, unsafe 2. chancy (*informal*), haphazard, precarious, uncertain, unpredictable
Antonyms reliable, safe, secure, sound, sta~ble, sure

haze cloud, dimness, film, fog, mist, obscurity, smog, smokiness, steam, vapour

hazy 1. blurry, cloudy, dim, dull, faint, foggy, misty, nebulous, obscure, overcast, smoky, veiled 2. *figurative* fuzzy, ill-defined, indefi~nite, indistinct, loose, muddled, muzzy, nebu~lous, uncertain, unclear, vague
Antonyms bright, certain, clear, detailed, light, sunny, well-defined

head *noun* 1. bean (*U.S. & Canad. slang*), conk (*slang*), cranium, crown, loaf (*slang*), noddle (*informal, chiefly Brit.*), noggin, nut (*slang*), pate, skull 2. boss (*informal*), captain, chief, chieftain, commander, director, headmaster, headmistress, head teacher, leader, manager, master, principal, superintendent, supervisor 3. apex, crest, crown, height, peak, pinnacle, pitch, summit, tip, top, vertex 4. cutting edge, first place, fore, forefront, front, van, van~guard 5. beginning, commencement, origin, rise, source, start 6. ability, aptitude, brain, brains (*informal*), capacity, faculty, flair, in~tellect, intelligence, mentality, mind, talent, thought, understanding 7. branch, category, class, department, division, heading, section, subject, topic 8. climax, conclusion, crisis, cul~mination, end, turning point 9. *Geography* cape, foreland, headland, point, promontory 10. **go to one's head** dizzy, excite, intoxicate, make conceited, puff up 11. **head over heels** completely, intensely, thoroughly, uncontrol~lably, utterly, wholeheartedly 12. **put (our, their,** *etc.*) **heads together** *informal* confab (*informal*), confabulate, confer, consult, delib~erate, discuss, palaver, powwow, talk over *~adjective* 13. arch, chief, first, foremost, front, highest, leading, main, pre-eminent, premier, prime, principal, supreme, topmost *~verb* 14. be *or* go first, cap, crown, lead, lead the way, precede, top 15. be in charge of, command, control, direct, govern, guide, lead, manage, rule, run, supervise 16. *often with* **for** aim, go to, make a beeline for, make for, point, set off for, set out, start towards, steer, turn
Related adjective: cephalic

headache 1. cephalalgia (*Medical*), head (*in~formal*), migraine, neuralgia 2. *informal* bane, bother, inconvenience, nuisance, problem, trouble, vexation, worry

headcase crackpot (*informal*), headbanger (*in~formal*), loony (*slang*), nutcase (*slang*), nutter (*Brit. slang*), oddball (*informal*), screwball (*slang, chiefly U.S. & Canad.*)

headfirst 1. *adjective/adverb* diving, headlong, head-on 2. *adverb* carelessly, hastily, head over heels, precipitately, rashly, recklessly

heading 1. caption, headline, name, rubric, ti~tle 2. category, class, division, section

headland hill, bluff, cape, cliff, foreland, head, mull (*Scot.*), point, promontory

headlong 1. *adjective/adverb* headfirst, headforemost, head-on 2. *adjective* breakneck, dangerous, hasty, impetuous, impulsive, in~considerate, precipitate, reckless, thoughtless 3. *adverb* hastily, heedlessly, helter-skelter, hurriedly, pell-mell, precipitately, rashly, thoughtlessly, wildly

headmaster head, head teacher, principal, rector

head off 1. block off, cut off, deflect, divert, intercept, interpose, intervene 2. avert, fend off, forestall, parry, prevent, stop, ward off

headstrong contrary, foolhardy, froward (*archaic*), heedless, imprudent, impulsive, intractable, mulish, obstinate, perverse, pig-headed, rash, reckless, self-willed, stiff-necked, stubborn, ungovernable, unruly, wilful
Antonyms cautious, impressionable, manageable, pliant, subservient, tractable

headway 1. advance, improvement, progress, progression, way 2. **make headway** advance, come *or* get on, cover ground, develop, gain, gain ground, make inroads (into), make strides, progress

heady 1. inebriating, intoxicating, potent, spirituous, strong 2. exciting, exhilarating, intoxicating, overwhelming, stimulating, thrilling 3. hasty, impetuous, impulsive, inconsiderate, precipitate, rash, reckless, thoughtless

heal 1. cure, make well, mend, regenerate, remedy, restore, treat 2. alleviate, ameliorate, compose, conciliate, harmonize, patch up, reconcile, settle, soothe
Antonyms aggravate, exacerbate, harm, hurt, inflame, injure, make worse, reopen, wound

healing 1. analeptic, curative, medicinal, remedial, restorative, restoring, sanative, therapeutic 2. assuaging, comforting, emollient, gentle, lenitive, mild, mitigative, palliative, soothing

health 1. fitness, good condition, haleness, healthiness, robustness, salubrity, soundness, strength, vigour, wellbeing 2. condition, constitution, fettle, form, shape, state, tone
Antonyms (*sense 1*) debility, disease, frailty, illness, sickness, weakness

An apple a day keeps the doctor away

healthful beneficial, bracing, good for one, health-giving, healthy, invigorating, nourishing, nutritious, salubrious, salutary, wholesome

healthy 1. active, alive and kicking, blooming, fighting fit, fit, fit as a fiddle (*informal*), flourishing, hale, hale and hearty, hardy, hearty, in fine feather, in fine fettle, in fine form, in good condition, in good shape (*informal*), in the pink, physically fit, right as rain (*Brit. informal*), robust, sound, strong, sturdy, vigorous, well 2. beneficial, bracing, good for one, healthful, health-giving, hygienic, invigorating, nourishing, nutritious, salubrious, salutary, wholesome
Antonyms ailing, at death's door, debilitated, delicate, diseased, feeble, fragile, frail, ill, infirm, poorly (*informal*), sick, sickly, unfit, unhealthy, unsound, unwell, unwholesome, weak, weedy (*informal*)

heap *noun* 1. accumulation, aggregation, collection, hoard, lot, mass, mound, mountain, pile, rick, stack, stockpile, store 2. *often plural informal* abundance, a lot, great deal, lashings (*Brit. informal*), load(s) (*informal*), lots (*informal*), mass, mint, ocean(s), oodles (*informal*), plenty, pot(s) (*informal*), quantities, stack(s), tons *~verb* 3. accumulate, amass, augment, bank, collect, gather, hoard, increase, mound, pile, stack, stockpile, store 4. assign, bestow, burden, confer, load, shower upon

hear 1. attend, be all ears (*informal*), catch, eavesdrop, give attention, hark, hearken (*archaic*), heed, listen in, listen to, overhear 2. ascertain, be informed, be told of, discover, find out, gather, get wind of (*informal*), hear tell (*dialect*), learn, pick up, understand 3. *Law* examine, investigate, judge, try

hearing 1. audition, auditory, ear, perception 2. audience, audition, chance to speak, interview 3. auditory range, earshot, hearing distance, range, reach, sound 4. industrial tribunal, inquiry, investigation, review, trial

hearsay buzz, dirt (*U.S. slang*), gossip, grapevine (*informal*), idle talk, mere talk, *on dit*, report, rumour, scuttlebutt (*slang, chiefly U.S.*), talk, talk of the town, tittle-tattle, word of mouth

heart 1. character, disposition, emotion, feeling, inclination, nature, sentiment, soul, sympathy, temperament 2. affection, benevolence, compassion, concern, humanity, love, pity, tenderness, understanding 3. balls (*taboo slang*), boldness, bravery, courage, fortitude, guts (*informal*), mettle, mind, nerve, pluck, purpose, resolution, spirit, spunk (*informal*), will 4. central part, centre, core, crux, essence, hub, kernel, marrow, middle, nucleus, pith, quintessence, root 5. **at heart** *au fond*, basically, essentially, fundamentally, in essence, in reality, really, truly 6. **by heart** by memory, by rote, off pat, parrot-fashion (*informal*), pat, word for word 7. **eat one's heart out** agonize, brood, grieve, mope, mourn, pine, regret, repine, sorrow 8. **from (the bottom of) one's heart** deeply, devoutly, fervently, heart and soul, heartily, sincerely, with all one's heart 9. **heart and soul** absolutely, completely, devotedly, entirely, gladly, to the hilt, wholeheartedly 10. **take heart** be comforted, be encouraged, be heartened, brighten up, buck up (*informal*), cheer up, perk up, revive

Parts of the heart

aorta	pulmonary artery
atrium *or* auricle	pulmonary vein
bicuspid valve	semilunar valve

septum vena cava
tricuspid valve ventricle

heartache affliction, agony, anguish, bitterness, despair, distress, grief, heartbreak, heartsickness, pain, remorse, sorrow, suffering, torment, torture

heartbreak anguish, desolation, despair, grief, misery, pain, sorrow, suffering

heartbreaking agonizing, bitter, desolating, disappointing, distressing, grievous, harrowing, heart-rending, pitiful, poignant, sad, tragic
Antonyms cheerful, cheery, comic, glorious, happy, jolly, joyful, joyous, light-hearted

heartbroken brokenhearted, choked, crestfallen, crushed, dejected, desolate, despondent, disappointed, disconsolate, disheartened, dismal, dispirited, downcast, down in the dumps (*informal*), grieved, heartsick, miserable, sick as a parrot (*informal*)
Antonyms cheerful, cock-a-hoop, elated, exuberant, happy, in seventh heaven, joyful, joyous, on cloud nine, over the moon (*informal*)

hearten animate, assure, buck up (*informal*), buoy up, cheer, comfort, console, embolden, encourage, incite, inspire, inspirit, raise someone's spirits, reassure, revivify, rouse, stimulate

heartfelt ardent, cordial, deep, devout, earnest, fervent, genuine, hearty, honest, profound, sincere, unfeigned, warm, wholehearted
Antonyms false, feigned, flippant, fraudulent, frivolous, half-hearted, hypocritical, insincere, phoney *or* phony (*informal*), pretended, put on, reserved, unenthusiastic, unimpassioned

heartily **1.** cordially, deeply, feelingly, genuinely, profoundly, sincerely, unfeignedly, warmly **2.** eagerly, earnestly, enthusiastically, resolutely, vigorously, zealously **3.** absolutely, completely, thoroughly, totally, very

heartless brutal, callous, cold, cold-blooded, cold-hearted, cruel, hard, hardhearted, harsh, inhuman, merciless, pitiless, uncaring, unfeeling, unkind
Antonyms compassionate, generous, humane, kind, merciful, sensitive, sympathetic, warm-hearted

heart-rending affecting, distressing, harrowing, heartbreaking, moving, pathetic, piteous, pitiful, poignant, sad, tragic

heartsick dejected, despondent, dispirited, downcast, heartsore, heavy-hearted, sick at heart

heart-to-heart **1.** *adjective* candid, intimate, open, personal, sincere, unreserved **2.** *noun* cosy chat, tête-à-tête

heart-warming **1.** gratifying, pleasing, rewarding, satisfying **2.** affecting, cheering, encouraging, heartening, moving, touching, warming

hearty **1.** affable, ardent, back-slapping, cordial, eager, ebullient, effusive, enthusiastic, friendly, generous, genial, jovial, unreserved, warm **2.** earnest, genuine, heartfelt, honest, real, sincere, true, unfeigned, wholehearted **3.** active, alive and kicking, energetic, hale, hardy, healthy, right as rain (*Brit. informal*), robust, sound, strong, vigorous, well **4.** ample, filling, nourishing, sizable *or* sizeable, solid, square, substantial
Antonyms cold, cool, delicate, feeble, frail, half-hearted, insincere, mild, sickly, unhealthy, weak

heat *noun* **1.** calefaction, fever, fieriness, high temperature, hotness, hot spell, sultriness, swelter, torridity, warmness, warmth **2.** *figurative* agitation, ardour, earnestness, excitement, fervour, fever, fury, impetuosity, intensity, passion, vehemence, violence, warmth, zeal *~verb* **3.** become warm, chafe, flush, glow, grow hot, make hot, reheat, warm up **4.** animate, excite, impassion, inflame, inspirit, rouse, stimulate, stir, warm
Antonyms *noun* calmness, cold, coldness, composure, coolness *~verb* chill, cool, cool off, freeze
Related adjectives: thermal, calorific
If you can't stand the heat get out of the kitchen

heated angry, bitter, excited, fierce, fiery, frenzied, furious, impassioned, intense, passionate, raging, stormy, tempestuous, vehement, violent
Antonyms calm, civilized, dispassionate, friendly, half-hearted, mellow, mild, peaceful, quiet, rational, reasoned, serene, subdued, unemotional, unfazed (*informal*), unruffled

heathen *noun* **1.** idolater, idolatress, infidel, pagan, unbeliever **2.** barbarian, philistine, savage *~adjective* **3.** godless, heathenish, idolatrous, infidel, irreligious, pagan **4.** barbaric, philistine, savage, uncivilized, unenlightened

heathen: a benighted creature who has the folly to worship something that he can see and feel
Ambrose Bierce *The Devil's Dictionary*

heave **1.** drag (up), elevate, haul (up), heft (*informal*), hoist, lever, lift, pull (up), raise, tug **2.** cast, fling, hurl, pitch, send, sling, throw, toss **3.** breathe heavily, groan, puff, sigh, sob, suspire (*archaic*), utter wearily **4.** billow, breathe, dilate, exhale, expand, palpitate, pant, rise, surge, swell, throb **5.** barf (*U.S. slang*), be sick, chuck (up) (*slang, chiefly U.S.*), chunder (*slang, chiefly Austral.*), do a technicolour yawn (*slang*), gag, retch, spew, throw up (*informal*), toss one's cookies (*U.S. slang*), upchuck (*U.S. slang*), vomit

heaven **1.** abode of God, bliss, Elysium *or* Elysian fields (*Greek myth*), happy hunting ground (*Amerind legend*), Happy Valley, hereafter, life everlasting, life to come, next world, nirvana (*Buddhism, Hinduism*), paradise, Valhalla (*Norse myth*), Zion (*Christianity*) **2.** *usually plural* empyrean (*poetic*), ether, firmament, sky, welkin (*archaic*) **3.** *figurative* bliss, dreamland, ecstasy, enchantment, felicity, happiness, paradise, rapture, seventh heaven, sheer bliss, transport, utopia

In my father's house are many mansions
Bible: St. John

Work and pray
Live on hay
You'll get pie in the sky when you die
Joe Hill *The Preacher and the Slave*

The kingdom of heaven is like to a grain of mustard seed
Bible: St. Matthew

The kingdom of heaven is like unto a merchant man, seeking goodly pearls; who, when he had found one pearl of great price, went and sold all that he had, and bought it
Bible: St. Matthew

heaven: a place where the wicked cease from troubling you with talk of their personal affairs, and the good listen with attention while you expound your own
Ambrose Bierce *The Devil's Dictionary*

heavenly **1.** *informal* alluring, beautiful, blissful, delightful, divine (*informal*), entrancing, exquisite, glorious, lovely, rapturous, ravishing, sublime, wonderful **2.** angelic, beatific, blessed, blest, celestial, cherubic, divine, empyrean (*poetic*), extraterrestrial, godlike, holy, immortal, paradisaical, seraphic, superhuman, supernal (*literary*), supernatural
Antonyms (*sense 1*) abominable, abysmal, appalling, awful, bad, depressing, dire, disagreeable, dreadful, dreary, dull, frightful, gloomy, grim, hellacious (*U.S. slang*), horrible, horrid, lousy (*slang*), miserable, rotten (*informal*), terrible, unpleasant, vile (*sense 2*) earthly, human, secular, worldly

heaven-sent blessed, felicitous, fortunate, opportune, providential, serendipitous, welcome

heavily **1.** awkwardly, clumsily, ponderously, weightily **2.** laboriously, painfully, with difficulty **3.** completely, decisively, roundly, thoroughly, utterly **4.** dejectedly, dully, gloomily, sluggishly, woodenly **5.** closely, compactly, densely, fast, hard, thick, thickly **6.** deep, deeply, profoundly, sound, soundly **7.** a great deal, considerably, copiously, excessively, frequently, to excess, very much

heaviness **1.** gravity, heftiness, ponderousness, weight **2.** arduousness, burdensomeness, grievousness, onerousness, oppressiveness, severity, weightiness **3.** deadness, dullness, languor, lassitude, numbness, sluggishness, torpor **4.** dejection, depression, despondency, gloom, gloominess, glumness, melancholy, sadness, seriousness

heavy **1.** bulky, hefty, massive, ponderous, portly, weighty **2.** burdensome, difficult, grievous, hard, harsh, intolerable, laborious, onerous, oppressive, severe, tedious, vexatious, wearisome **3.** apathetic, drowsy, dull, inactive, indolent, inert, listless, slow, sluggish, stupid, torpid, wooden **4.** crestfallen, dejected, depressed, despondent, disconsolate, downcast, gloomy, grieving, melancholy, sad, sorrowful **5.** complex, deep, difficult, grave, profound, serious, solemn, weighty **6.** abundant, considerable, copious, excessive, large, profuse **7.** burdened, encumbered, laden, loaded, oppressed, weighted **8.** boisterous, rough, stormy, tempestuous, turbulent, violent, wild **9.** dull, gloomy, leaden, louring *or* lowering, overcast
Antonyms agile, alert, bearable, brisk, calm, cheerful, compact, easy, exciting, gentle, handy, happy, inconsequential, joyful, light, mild, moderate, quick, slight, small, soft, sparse, trivial, unimportant, weak

heavy-handed **1.** awkward, bungling, clumsy, graceless, ham-fisted (*informal*), ham-handed (*informal*), inept, inexpert, like a bull in a china shop (*informal*), maladroit, unhandy **2.** bungling, inconsiderate, insensitive, tactless, thoughtless **3.** autocratic, domineering, harsh, oppressive, overbearing
Antonyms adept, adroit, competent, considerate, considered, dexterous, diplomatic, effectual, efficient, gentle, graceful, intelligent, prudent, sensible, skilful, smart, smooth, submissive, subservient, suitable, tactful, well-advised, well-thought-out, wise

heavy-hearted crushed, depressed, despondent, discouraged, disheartened, dismal, downcast, downhearted, down in the dumps (*informal*), forlorn, heartsick, melancholy, miserable, morose, mournful, sad, sick as a parrot (*informal*), sorrowful

heckle bait, barrack (*informal*), boo, disrupt, interrupt, jeer, pester, shout down, taunt

hectic animated, boisterous, chaotic, excited, fevered, feverish, flurrying, flustering, frantic, frenetic, frenzied, furious, heated, riotous, rumbustious, tumultuous, turbulent, wild
Antonyms calm, peaceful, relaxing, tranquil

hector bluster, boast, browbeat, bully, bullyrag, harass, huff and puff, intimidate, menace, provoke, ride roughshod over, roister, threaten, worry

hedge *noun* **1.** hedgerow, quickset **2.** barrier, boundary, screen, windbreak **3.** compensation, counterbalance, guard, insurance cover, protection *~verb* **4.** border, edge, enclose, fence, surround **5.** block, confine, hem in (about, around), hinder, obstruct, restrict **6.** beg the question, be noncommittal, dodge, duck, equivocate, evade, flannel (*Brit. informal*), prevaricate, pussyfoot (*informal*), quibble, sidestep, temporize, waffle (*informal, chiefly Brit.*) **7.** cover, fortify, guard, insure, protect, safeguard, shield

hedonism 1. epicureanism, epicurism, sybaritism **2.** dolce vita, gratification, luxuriousness, pleasure-seeking, pursuit of pleasure, self-indulgence, sensualism, sensuality

hedonist 1. epicure, epicurean, sybarite **2.** *bon vivant*, pleasure seeker, sensualist, voluptuary

hedonistic 1. bacchanalian, epicurean, sybaritic **2.** luxurious, pleasure-seeking, self-indulgent, voluptuous

heed 1. *noun* attention, care, caution, consideration, ear, heedfulness, mind, note, notice, regard, respect, thought, watchfulness **2.** *verb* attend, bear in mind, be guided by, consider, follow, give ear to, listen to, mark, mind, note, obey, observe, pay attention to, regard, take notice of, take to heart
Antonyms *noun* carelessness, disregard, inattention, laxity, laxness, neglect, thoughtlessness ~*verb* be inattentive to, discount, disobey, disregard, flout, ignore, neglect, overlook, reject, shun, turn a deaf ear to

heedful attentive, careful, cautious, chary, circumspect, mindful, observant, prudent, vigilant, wary, watchful

heedless careless, foolhardy, imprudent, inattentive, incautious, neglectful, negligent, oblivious, precipitate, rash, reckless, thoughtless, unmindful, unobservant, unthinking
Antonyms attentive, aware, careful, cautious, concerned, heedful, mindful, observant, thoughtful, vigilant, wary, watchful

heel[1] *noun* **1.** crust, end, remainder, rump, stub, stump **2.** *slang* blackguard, bounder (*old-fashioned Brit. slang*), cad (*Brit informal*), cocksucker (*taboo slang*), rotter (*slang, chiefly Brit.*), scally (*Northwest English dialect*), scoundrel, scumbag (*slang*), swine **3. down at heel** dowdy, impoverished, out at elbows, run-down, seedy, shabby, slipshod, slovenly, worn **4. take to one's heels** escape, flee, hook it (*slang*), run away *or* off, show a clean pair of heels, skedaddle (*informal*), take flight, turn tail, vamoose (*slang, chiefly U.S.*) **5. well-heeled** affluent, flush (*informal*), moneyed, prosperous, rich, wealthy, well-off, well-to-do

heel[2] *verb* cant, careen, incline, keel over, lean over, list, tilt

hefty 1. beefy (*informal*), big, brawny, burly, hulking, husky (*informal*), massive, muscular, robust, strapping, strong **2.** forceful, heavy, powerful, thumping (*slang*), vigorous **3.** ample, awkward, bulky, colossal, cumbersome, heavy, large, massive, ponderous, substantial, tremendous, unwieldy, weighty
Antonyms agile, diminutive, feeble, frail, inconsequential, ineffectual, infinitesimal, insignificant, light, little, mild, minute, narrow, petty, pocket-sized, scanty, short, slight, slim, small, soft, thin, tiny, trivial, weak, weedy (*informal*), wimpish *or* wimpy (*informal*)

hegemony ascendancy, dominance, domination, leadership, mastery, predominance, pre-eminence, supremacy, sway, upper hand

height 1. altitude, elevation, highness, loftiness, stature, tallness **2.** apex, apogee, crest, crown, elevation, hill, mountain, peak, pinnacle, summit, top, vertex, zenith **3.** acme, dignity, eminence, exaltation, grandeur, loftiness, prominence **4.** climax, culmination, extremity, limit, maximum, *ne plus ultra*, ultimate, utmost degree, uttermost
Antonyms abyss, base, bottom, canyon, chasm, depth, lowland, lowness, low point, minimum, moderation, nadir, ravine, shortness, smallness, tininess, triviality, valley

heighten 1. add to, aggravate, amplify, augment, enhance, improve, increase, intensify, magnify, sharpen, strengthen **2.** elevate, enhance, ennoble, exalt, magnify, raise, uplift

heinous abhorrent, abominable, atrocious, awful, evil, execrable, flagrant, grave, hateful, hideous, infamous, iniquitous, monstrous, nefarious, odious, outrageous, revolting, shocking, unspeakable, vicious, villainous

heir beneficiary, heiress (*fem.*), inheritor, inheritress *or* inheritrix (*fem.*), next in line, scion, successor

hell 1. Abaddon, abode of the damned, abyss, Acheron (*Greek myth*), bottomless pit, fire and brimstone, Gehenna (*New Testament, Judaism*), Hades (*Greek myth*), hellfire, infernal regions, inferno, lower world, nether world, Tartarus (*Greek myth*), underworld **2.** affliction, agony, anguish, martyrdom, misery, nightmare, ordeal, suffering, torment, trial, wretchedness **3. hell for leather** at a rate of knots, at the double, full-tilt, headlong, hotfoot, hurriedly, like a bat out of hell (*slang*), pell-mell, posthaste, quickly, speedily, swiftly

Hell is paved with the skulls of priests
St. John Chrysostom *De Sacerdotio*

Let none admire
The riches that grow in hell; that soil may best
Deserve the precious bane
John Milton *Paradise Lost*

But wherefore thou alone? Wherefore with thee
Came not all hell broke loose?
John Milton *Paradise Lost*

If there is no Hell, a good many preachers are obtaining money under false pretenses
William A. Sunday

Hell is other people
Jean-Paul Sartre *Huis Clos*

A perpetual holiday is a good working definition of hell
George Bernard Shaw *Parents and Children*

Hell hath no limits nor is circumscribed
In one self place, where we are is Hell,
And to be short, when all the world dissolves
And every creature shall be purified
All places shall be Hell that are not Heaven
Christopher Marlowe *Doctor Faustus*

Hell is a city much like London -
A populous and smoky city
Percy Bysshe Shelley *Peter Bell the Third*

What is hell?
Hell is oneself,
Hell is alone, the other figures in it
Merely projections
T.S. Eliot *The Cocktail Party*

hellbent bent, determined, fixed, intent, resolved, set, settled

hellish 1. damnable, damned, demoniacal, devilish, diabolical, fiendish, infernal 2. abominable, accursed, atrocious, barbarous, cruel, detestable, execrable, inhuman, monstrous, nefarious, vicious, wicked
Antonyms admirable, agreeable, benevolent, delightful, fine, gentle, good, harmless, honourable, humane, innocuous, kind, merciful, noble, pleasant, virtuous, wonderful

helm 1. *Nautical* rudder, steering gear, tiller, wheel 2. *figurative* command, control, direction, leadership, rule 3. **at the helm** at the wheel, directing, in charge, in command, in control, in the driving seat, in the saddle

help *verb* 1. abet, aid, assist, back, befriend, cooperate, encourage, give a leg up (*informal*), lend a hand, lend a helping hand, promote, relieve, save, second, serve, stand by, succour, support 2. alleviate, ameliorate, cure, ease, facilitate, heal, improve, mitigate, relieve, remedy, restore 3. abstain, avoid, control, eschew, forbear, hinder, keep from, prevent, refrain from, resist, shun, withstand *~noun* 4. advice, aid, assistance, avail, benefit, cooperation, guidance, helping hand, promotion, service, support, use, utility 5. assistant, employee, hand, helper, worker 6. balm, corrective, cure, relief, remedy, restorative, salve, succour
Antonyms *verb* aggravate, bar, block, discourage, fight, foil, frustrate, harm, hinder, hurt, impede, injure, irritate, make worse, obstruct, oppose *~noun* aggravation, bane, block, discouragement, hindrance, irritant, obstruction, opposition

Help yourself, and heaven will help you
Jean de la Fontaine *Fables*

God helps them that help themselves

Many hands make light work

helper abettor, adjutant, aide, aider, ally, assistant, attendant, auxiliary, coadjutor, collaborator, colleague, deputy, helpmate, henchman, mate, partner, protagonist, right-hand man, second, subsidiary, supporter

helpful 1. advantageous, beneficial, constructive, favourable, fortunate, practical, productive, profitable, serviceable, timely, useful 2. accommodating, beneficent, benevolent, caring, considerate, cooperative, friendly, kind, neighbourly, supportive, sympathetic

helpfulness 1. advantage, assistance, benefit, usefulness 2. cooperation, friendliness, good neighbourliness, kindness, neighbourliness, rallying round, support, sympathy

helping *noun* dollop (*informal*), piece, plateful, portion, ration, serving

helpless 1. abandoned, defenceless, dependent, destitute, exposed, forlorn, stranded, unprotected, vulnerable, wide open 2. debilitated, disabled, feeble, impotent, incapable, incompetent, infirm, paralysed, powerless, unfit, weak
Antonyms able, capable, competent, equipped, fit, hardy, healthy, hearty, invulnerable, mighty, powerful, robust, safe, secure, solid, strong, sturdy, thriving, tough, well-protected

helplessness 1. defencelessness, exposed position, forlornness, vulnerability 2. disability, feebleness, impotence, infirmity, powerlessness, weakness

helpmate assistant, associate, companion, consort, helper, helpmeet, husband, partner, significant other (*U.S. informal*), spouse, support, wife

helter-skelter 1. *adverb* carelessly, hastily, headlong, hurriedly, pell-mell, rashly, recklessly, wildly 2. *adjective* anyhow, confused, disordered, haphazard, higgledy-piggledy (*informal*), hit-or-miss, jumbled, muddled, random, topsy-turvy

hem 1. *noun* border, edge, fringe, margin, trimming 2. *verb usually with* **in** beset, border, circumscribe, confine, edge, enclose, environ, hedge in, restrict, shut in, skirt, surround

he-man Atlas, bit of beefcake, Hercules, hunk (*Slang*), muscle man, Tarzan (*informal*)

hem and haw falter, fumble, hesitate, hum and haw, pause, stammer, stutter

hence ergo, for this reason, on that account, therefore, thus

henceforth from now on, from this day forward, hence, hereafter, hereinafter, in the future

henchman aide, associate, attendant, bodyguard, cohort (*chiefly U.S.*), crony, follower, heavy (*slang*), minder (*slang*), minion, myrmidon, right-hand man, satellite, sidekick (*slang*), subordinate, supporter

henpeck browbeat, bully, carp, cavil, chide, criticize, domineer, find fault, harass, hector, intimidate, nag, niggle, pester, pick at, scold, torment

henpecked browbeaten, bullied, cringing, dominated, led by the nose, meek, subject, subjugated, tied to someone's apron strings, timid, treated like dirt
Antonyms aggressive, assertive, bossy (*informal*), dominating, domineering, forceful, macho, overbearing, self-assertive, spirited, wilful

herald *noun* **1.** bearer of tidings, crier, messenger **2.** forerunner, harbinger, indication, omen, precursor, sign, signal, token *~verb* **3.** advertise, announce, broadcast, proclaim, publicize, publish, trumpet **4.** foretoken, harbinger, indicate, pave the way, portend, precede, presage, promise, show, usher in

heraldry

Heraldry terms

- achievement
- annulet
- argent
- armes parlantes
- armiger
- armory
- bandeau
- bar
- base
- baton
- bearing
- bend
- bend sinister
- bezzant, bezant *or* byzant
- blazon
- blazonry
- bordure
- cadency
- canting arms
- canton
- chaplet
- charge
- checky
- chevron
- chief
- cinquefoil
- Clarenceux
- coat armour
- coat of arms
- cockatrice
- cognizance *or* cognisance
- college of arms
- compony *or* compone
- coronet
- couchant
- crescent
- crest
- cross
- crosslet
- crown
- dexter
- difference
- dimidiate
- dormant
- eagle
- embattled
- emblazon
- ermine
- escutcheon
- falcon
- fesse *or* fess
- field
- fillet
- fleur-de-lis *or* fleur-de-lys
- flory *or* fleury
- fret
- fur
- fusil
- garland
- giron *or* gyron
- gironny *or* gyronny
- griffon
- guardant *or* gardant
- gules
- hatchment
- herald
- heraldic *or* fetial
- impale *or* empale
- inescutcheon
- issuant
- king-of-arms
- label
- leopard
- lion
- lozenge
- lozengy
- Lyon King of Arms
- mantling *or* lambrequin
- mascle *or* voided lozenge
- matriculation
- moline
- naissant
- nombril
- octofoil
- officer of arms
- or
- ordinary
- orle
- pale
- pall
- paly
- parted
- party
- passant
- pean
- pile
- potent
- proper
- purpure
- pursuivant
- quarter
- quartered
- quartering
- quarterly
- rampant
- rebus
- regardant
- roundel
- sable
- saltire
- sejant *or* sejeant
- scutcheon
- semé (of) *or* semée (of)
- shield
- sinister
- spread eagle
- statant
- sun in splendour
- supporter
- torse
- tressure
- urdé *or* urdée
- urinant
- vair
- vert
- voided
- volant
- wreath
- wyvern
- yale

The science of fools with long memories
J.R. Planché *The Pursuivant of Arms*

herculean **1.** arduous, demanding, difficult, exhausting, formidable, gruelling, hard, heavy, laborious, onerous, prodigious, strenuous, toilsome, tough **2.** athletic, brawny, husky (*informal*), mighty, muscular, powerful, rugged, sinewy, stalwart, strapping, strong, sturdy **3.** colossal, elephantine, enormous, gigantic, great, huge, humongous *or* humungous (*U.S. slang*), large, mammoth, massive, titanic

herd *noun* **1.** assemblage, collection, crowd, crush, drove, flock, horde, mass, mob, multitude, press, swarm, throng **2.** mob, populace, rabble, riffraff, the hoi polloi, the masses, the plebs *~verb* **3.** assemble, associate, collect, congregate, flock, gather, huddle, muster, rally **4.** drive, force, goad, guide, lead, shepherd, spur

herdsman cowherd, cowman, drover, grazier, stockman

hereafter **1.** *adverb* after this, from now on, hence, henceforth, henceforward, in future **2.** *noun* afterlife, future life, life after death, next world, the beyond

hereditary **1.** family, genetic, inborn, inbred, inheritable, transmissible **2.** ancestral, bequeathed, handed down, inherited, patrimonial, traditional, transmitted, willed

heredity congenital traits, constitution, genetic make-up, genetics, inheritance

heresy apostasy, dissidence, error, heterodoxy, iconoclasm, impiety, revisionism, schism, unorthodoxy

The heresy of one age becomes the orthodoxy of the next

Helen Keller *Optimism*

They that approve a private opinion, call it opinion; but they that mislike it, heresy; and yet heresy signifies no more than private opinion

Thomas Hobbes *Leviathan*

heretic apostate, dissenter, dissident, nonconformist, renegade, revisionist, schismatic, sectarian, separatist

heretical freethinking, heterodox, iconoclastic, idolatrous, impious, revisionist, schismatic, unorthodox

heritage bequest, birthright, endowment, estate, inheritance, legacy, lot, patrimony, portion, share, tradition

hermaphrodite **1.** *noun* androgyne, bisexual, epicene **2.** *adjective* AC/DC (*informal*), androgenous, bisexual, epicene, gynandrous, hermaphroditic

hermetic, hermetical airtight, sealed, shut

hermit anchoret, anchorite, eremite, monk, recluse, solitary, stylite

hero **1.** celeb (*informal*), celebrity, champion, conqueror, exemplar, great man, heart-throb (*Brit.*), idol, man of the hour, megastar (*informal*), popular figure, star, superstar, victor **2.** lead actor, leading man, male lead, principal male character, protagonist

Unhappy the land that is in need of heroes

Bertolt Brecht *Galileo*

If I was to stumble upon Jesus Christ I'd say "Good Afternoon" and then walk on. But if I met Robert Burns or Shakespeare, well, that would be a different matter. I'd stop and talk for a wee while

Robin Jenkins

See, the conquering hero comes!
Sound the trumpets, beat the drums!

Thomas Morell *Judas Maccabeus*

heroic **1.** bold, brave, courageous, daring, dauntless, doughty, fearless, gallant, intrepid, lion-hearted, stouthearted, undaunted, valiant, valorous **2.** classical, Homeric, legendary, mythological **3.** classic, elevated, epic, exaggerated, extravagant, grand, grandiose, high-flown, inflated

Antonyms (*sense 1*) base, chicken (*slang*), cowardly, craven, faint-hearted, ignoble, irresolute, mean, timid (*sense 3*) lowbrow, simple, unadorned

heroine **1.** celeb (*informal*), celebrity, goddess, ideal, megastar (*informal*), woman of the hour **2.** diva, female lead, lead actress, leading lady, prima donna, principal female character, protagonist

heroism boldness, bravery, courage, courageousness, daring, fearlessness, fortitude, gallantry, intrepidity, prowess, spirit, valour

hero worship admiration, adoration, adulation, idealization, idolization, putting on a pedestal, veneration

hesitant diffident, doubtful, half-arsed, half-assed (*U.S. & Canad. slang*), half-hearted, halting, hanging back, hesitating, irresolute, lacking confidence, reluctant, sceptical, shy, timid, uncertain, unsure, vacillating, wavering

Antonyms arrogant, avid, can-do (*informal*), clear, confident, definite, determined, dogmatic, eager, enthusiastic, firm, forceful, keen, positive, resolute, self-assured, spirited, sure, unhesitating, unwavering

hesitate **1.** be uncertain, delay, dither (*chiefly Brit.*), doubt, haver (*Brit.*), hum and haw, pause, shillyshally (*informal*), swither (*Scot.*), vacillate, wait, waver **2.** balk, be reluctant, be unwilling, boggle, demur, hang back, scruple, shrink from, think twice **3.** falter, fumble, hem and haw, stammer, stumble, stutter

Antonyms (*sense 1*) be confident, be decisive, be firm, continue, decide (*sense 2*) be determined, resolve, welcome

It's all right to hesitate if you then go ahead

Bertolt Brecht *The Good Woman of Setzuan*

He who hesitates is lost

hesitation **1.** delay, doubt, dubiety, hesitancy, indecision, irresolution, uncertainty, vacillation **2.** demurral, misgiving(s), qualm(s), reluctance, scruple(s), unwillingness **3.** faltering, fumbling, hemming and hawing, stammering, stumbling, stuttering

heterodox dissident, heretical, iconoclastic, revisionist, schismatic, unorthodox, unsound

heterogeneous assorted, contrary, contrasted, different, discrepant, disparate, dissimilar, divergent, diverse, diversified, incongruous, manifold, miscellaneous, mixed, motley, opposed, unlike, unrelated, varied

hew **1.** axe, chop, cut, hack, lop, split **2.** carve, fashion, form, make, model, sculpt, sculpture, shape, smooth

heyday bloom, flowering, pink, prime, prime of life, salad days

hiatus aperture, blank, breach, break, chasm, discontinuity, entr'acte, gap, interruption, interval, lacuna, lapse, opening, respite, rift, space

hibernate hole up, lie dormant, overwinter, remain torpid, sleep snug, vegetate, winter

hidden abstruse, clandestine, close, concealed, covered, covert, cryptic, dark, hermetic, hermetical, masked, mysterious, mystic, mystical, obscure, occult, recondite, secret, shrouded, ulterior, under wraps, unrevealed, unseen, veiled

hide[1] *verb* **1.** cache, conceal, go into hiding, go to ground, go underground, hole up, lie low, secrete, stash (*informal*), take cover **2.** blot out, bury, camouflage, cloak, conceal, cover, disguise, eclipse, mask, obscure, screen, shelter, shroud, veil **3.** draw a veil over, hush up, keep dark, keep secret, keep under one's hat, suppress, withhold
Antonyms admit, bare, confess, disclose, display, divulge, exhibit, expose, find, flaunt, reveal, show, uncover, unveil

hide[2] *noun* fell, pelt, skin

hideaway haven, hide-out, hiding place, nest, refuge, retreat, sanctuary, sequestered nook

hidebound brassbound, conventional, narrow, narrow-minded, puritan, rigid, set, set in one's ways, strait-laced, ultraconservative
Antonyms broad-minded, flexible, liberal, open, receptive, tolerant, unconventional, unorthodox

hideous **1.** ghastly, grim, grisly, grotesque, gruesome, monstrous, repulsive, revolting, ugly, unsightly **2.** abominable, appalling, awful, detestable, disgusting, dreadful, godawful (*slang*), horrendous, horrible, horrid, loathsome, macabre, obscene, odious, shocking, sickening, terrible, terrifying
Antonyms appealing, beautiful, captivating, charming, entrancing, lovely, pleasant, pleasing

hide-out den, hideaway, hiding place, lair, secret place, shelter

hiding *noun* beating, caning, drubbing, flogging, larruping (*Brit. dialect*), lathering (*informal*), licking (*informal*), spanking, tanning (*slang*), thrashing, walloping (*informal*), whaling, whipping

hierarchy grading, pecking order, ranking

In a hierarchy every employee tends to rise to his level of incompetence
Laurence Peter *The Peter Principle*

hieroglyphic *adjective* enigmatical, figurative, indecipherable, obscure, runic, symbolical

higgledy-piggledy **1.** *adverb* all over the place, all over the shop (*informal*), anyhow, any old how, confusedly, disorderly, haphazard, helter-skelter, pell-mell, topsy-turvy **2.** *adjective* haphazard, helter-skelter, indiscriminate, jumbled, muddled, pell-mell, topsy-turvy

high *adjective* **1.** elevated, lofty, soaring, steep, tall, towering **2.** excessive, extraordinary, extreme, great, intensified, sharp, strong **3.** arch, big-time (*informal*), chief, consequential, distinguished, eminent, exalted, important, influential, leading, major league (*informal*), notable, powerful, prominent, ruling, significant, superior **4.** arrogant, boastful, bragging, despotic, domineering, haughty, lofty, lordly, ostentatious, overbearing, proud, tyrannical, vainglorious **5.** capital, extreme, grave, important, serious **6.** boisterous, bouncy (*informal*), cheerful, elated, excited, exhilarated, exuberant, joyful, light-hearted, merry, strong, tumultuous, turbulent **7.** *informal* delirious, euphoric, freaked out (*informal*), hyped up (*slang*), inebriated, intoxicated, on a trip (*informal*), spaced out (*slang*), stoned (*slang*), tripping (*informal*), turned on (*slang*), zonked (*slang*) **8.** costly, dear, exorbitant, expensive, high-priced, steep (*informal*), stiff **9.** acute, high-pitched, penetrating, piercing, piping, sharp, shrill, soprano, strident, treble **10.** extravagant, grand, lavish, luxurious, rich **11.** gamy, niffy (*Brit. slang*), pongy (*Brit. informal*), strong-flavoured, tainted, whiffy (*Brit. slang*) **12.** **high and dry** abandoned, bereft, destitute, helpless, stranded **13.** **high and low** all over, everywhere, exhaustively, far and wide, in every nook and cranny **14.** **high and mighty** *informal* arrogant, cavalier, conceited, disdainful, haughty, imperious, overbearing, self-important, snobbish, stuck-up (*informal*), superior *~adverb* **15.** aloft, at great height, far up, way up *~noun* **16.** apex, crest, height, peak, record level, summit, top **17.** *informal* delirium, ecstasy, euphoria, intoxication, trip (*informal*)
Antonyms (*sense 1*) dwarfed, low, short, stunted (*sense 2*) average, low, mild, moderate, reduced, restrained, routine, suppressed (*sense 3*) average, common, degraded, ignoble, inconsequential, insignificant, low, lowly, low-ranking, menial, routine, secondary, undistinguished, unimportant (*sense 6*) angry, dejected, depressed, gloomy, low, melancholy, sad (*sense 9*) alto, bass, deep, gruff, low, low-pitched

highborn aristocratic, blue-blooded, gentle (*archaic*), noble, patrician, pedigreed, thoroughbred, well-born

highbrow **1.** *noun* aesthete, Brahmin (*U.S.*), brain (*informal*), brainbox (*slang*), egghead (*informal*), intellectual, mastermind, savant, scholar **2.** *adjective* bookish, brainy (*informal*), cultivated, cultured, deep, highbrowed, intellectual, sophisticated
Antonyms *noun* idiot, ignoramus, illiterate, imbecile (*informal*), lowbrow, moron, philistine *~adjective* ignorant, lowbrow, philistine, shallow, uncultivated, uninformed, unintellectual, unlearned, unsophisticated

A highbrow is a kind of person who looks at a sausage and thinks of Picasso
A.P. Herbert *The Highbrow*

high-class A1 *or* A-one (*informal*), choice, classy (*slang*), elite, exclusive, first-rate, high-quality, high-toned, posh (*informal,*

chiefly Brit.), ritzy (*slang*), select, superior, swish (*informal, chiefly Brit.*), tip-top, top-drawer, top-flight, tops (*slang*), U (*Brit. informal*), up-market, upper-class
Antonyms cheap, cheapo (*informal*), common, inferior, mediocre, ordinary, run-of-the-mill

higher-up boss, director, executive, gaffer (*informal, chiefly Brit.*), manager, senior, superior

highfalutin, highfaluting big, bombastic, florid, grandiose, high-flown, high-sounding, lofty, magniloquent, pompous, pretentious, supercilious, swanky (*informal*)

high-flown elaborate, exaggerated, extravagant, florid, grandiose, high-falutin (*informal*), inflated, lofty, magniloquent, overblown, pretentious
Antonyms down-to-earth, moderate, modest, practical, pragmatic, realistic, reasonable, restrained, sensible, simple, straightforward, unpretentious

high-handed arbitrary, autocratic, bossy (*informal*), despotic, dictatorial, domineering, imperious, inconsiderate, oppressive, overbearing, peremptory, self-willed, tyrannical, wilful

high jinks fun and games, horseplay, jollity, junketing, merrymaking, revelry, skylarking (*informal*), sport, spree

highlands heights, hill country, hills, mesa, mountainous region, plateau, tableland, uplands

highlight **1.** *noun* best part, climax, feature, focal point, focus, high point, high spot, main feature, memorable part, peak **2.** *verb* accent, accentuate, bring to the fore, emphasize, feature, focus attention on, give prominence to, play up, set off, show up, spotlight, stress, underline
Antonyms *noun* disappointment, low point ~*verb* de-emphasize, gloss over, neglect, overlook, play down

highly **1.** decidedly, eminently, exceptionally, extraordinarily, extremely, greatly, immensely, seriously (*informal*), supremely, tremendously, vastly, very, very much **2.** appreciatively, approvingly, enthusiastically, favourably, warmly, well

highly strung easily upset, edgy, excitable, irascible, irritable, nervous, nervy (*Brit. informal*), neurotic, on pins and needles, on tenterhooks, restless, sensitive, stressed, taut, temperamental, tense, tetchy, twitchy (*informal*), wired (*slang*)
Antonyms calm, collected, easy-going, even-tempered, laid-back (*informal*), placid, relaxed, serene, unfazed (*informal*)

high-minded elevated, ethical, fair, good, honourable, idealistic, magnanimous, moral, noble, principled, pure, righteous, upright, virtuous, worthy
Antonyms dishonest, dishonourable, unethical, unfair

high-mindedness integrity, probity, rectitude, scrupulousness, uprightness

high-powered aggressive, driving, dynamic, effective, energetic, enterprising, fast-track, forceful, go-ahead, go-getting (*informal*), highly capable, high-octane (*informal*), vigorous

high-pressure *of salesmanship* aggressive, bludgeoning, coercive, compelling, forceful, high-powered, importunate, insistent, intensive, in-your-face (*slang*), persistent, persuasive, pushy (*informal*)

high-priced costly, dear, excessive, exorbitant, expensive, extortionate, high, steep (*informal*), stiff, unreasonable

high-sounding affected, artificial, bombastic, extravagant, flamboyant, florid, grandiloquent, grandiose, high-flown, imposing, magniloquent, ostentatious, overblown, pompous, pretentious, stilted, strained

high-speed brisk, express, fast, hotted-up (*informal*), quick, rapid, souped-up (*informal*), streamlined, swift

high-spirited alive and kicking, animated, boisterous, bold, bouncy, daring, dashing, ebullient, effervescent, energetic, exuberant, frolicsome, full of beans (*informal*), full of life, fun-loving, gallant, lively, mettlesome, sparky, spirited, spunky (*informal*), vibrant, vital, vivacious

high spirits abandon, boisterousness, exhilaration, exuberance, good cheer, hilarity, *joie de vivre*, rare good humour

hijack commandeer, expropriate, seize, skyjack, take over

hike *verb* **1.** back-pack, hoof it (*slang*), leg it (*informal*), ramble, tramp, walk **2.** *usually with* **up** hitch up, jack up, lift, pull up, raise ~*noun* **3.** journey on foot, march, ramble, tramp, trek, walk

hiker backpacker, rambler, walker

hilarious amusing, comical, convivial, entertaining, exhilarated, funny, gay, happy, humorous, jolly, jovial, joyful, joyous, merry, mirthful, noisy, rollicking, side-splitting, uproarious
Antonyms dull, gloomy, quiet, sad, sedate, serious

hilarity amusement, boisterousness, cheerfulness, conviviality, exhilaration, exuberance, gaiety, glee, high spirits, jollification, jollity, joviality, joyousness, laughter, levity, merriment, mirth

hill **1.** brae (*Scot.*), down (*archaic*), elevation, eminence, fell, height, hillock, hilltop, knoll, mound, mount, prominence, tor **2.** drift, heap, hummock, mound, pile, rick, stack **3**. acclivity, brae (*Scot.*), climb, gradient, incline, rise, slope

hillock barrow, hummock, knap (*dialect*), knoll, monticule, mound, tump (*Western Brit. dialect*)

hilt **1**. grip, haft, handgrip, handle, helve **2**. **to the hilt** completely, entirely, fully, totally, wholly

hind after, back, caudal (*Anatomy*), hinder, posterior, rear

hinder arrest, block, check, debar, delay, deter, encumber, frustrate, hamper, hamstring, handicap, hold up *or* back, impede, interrupt, obstruct, oppose, prevent, retard, slow down, stop, stymie, throw a spanner in the works, thwart, trammel

Antonyms accelerate, advance, aid, benefit, encourage, expedite, facilitate, further, help, hurry, promote, quicken, speed, support

hindmost concluding, final, furthest, furthest behind, last, most remote, rearmost, terminal, trailing, ultimate

hindrance bar, barrier, block, check, deterrent, difficulty, drag, drawback, encumbrance, handicap, hazard, hitch, impediment, interruption, limitation, obstacle, obstruction, restraint, restriction, snag, stoppage, stumbling block, trammel

Antonyms advancement, advantage, aid, asset, assistance, benefit, boon, boost, encouragement, furtherance, help, support

hinge *verb* be contingent, be subject to, depend, hang, pivot, rest, revolve around, turn

hint *noun* **1**. allusion, clue, implication, indication, inkling, innuendo, insinuation, intimation, mention, reminder, suggestion, tip-off, word to the wise **2**. advice, help, pointer, suggestion, tip, wrinkle (*informal*) **3**. breath, dash, *soupçon*, speck, suggestion, suspicion, taste, tinge, touch, trace, undertone, whiff, whisper *~verb* **4**. allude, cue, imply, indicate, insinuate, intimate, let it be known, mention, prompt, suggest, tip off, tip the wink (*informal*)

hip *adjective* aware, clued-up (*informal*), fashionable, in, informed, in on, knowledgeable, onto, trendy (*Brit. informal*), wise (*slang*), with it (*informal*)

hippie beatnik, bohemian, dropout, flower child

hire *verb* **1**. appoint, commission, employ, engage, sign up, take on **2**. charter, engage, lease, let, rent *~noun* **3**. charge, cost, fee, price, rent, rental

hirsute bearded, bewhiskered, bristly, hairy, hispid (*Biology*), shaggy, unshaven

hiss *noun* **1**. buzz, hissing, sibilance, sibilation **2**. boo, catcall, contempt, derision, jeer, raspberry *~verb* **3**. rasp, shrill, sibilate, wheeze, whirr, whistle, whiz **4**. blow a raspberry, boo, catcall, condemn, damn, decry, deride, hoot, jeer, mock, revile, ridicule

historian annalist, biographer, chronicler, historiographer, recorder

historian: a broad-gauge gossip
Ambrose Bierce *The Devil's Dictionary*

historic celebrated, consequential, epoch-making, extraordinary, famous, ground-breaking, momentous, notable, outstanding, red-letter, remarkable, significant

Antonyms ordinary, uncelebrated, unimportant, unknown

historical actual, archival, attested, authentic, chronicled, documented, factual, real, verifiable

Antonyms contemporary, current, fabulous, fictional, legendary, mythical, present-day

history **1**. account, annals, autobiography, biography, chronicle, memoirs, narration, narrative, recapitulation, recital, record, relation, saga, story **2**. ancient history, antiquity, bygone times, days of old, days of yore, olden days, the good old days, the old days, the past, yesterday, yesteryear

Characters in history

Alexander the Great
Alfred the Great
Mark Antony
Attila the Hun
Augustus
Thomas à Becket
Billy the Kid
The Black Prince
Bonnie Prince Charlie (Charles Edward Stuart)
Lucrezia Borgia
Boudicca *or* Boadicea
Brutus
Buddha
Buffalo Bill (William Frederick Cody)
Julius Caesar
Catherine the Great
Charlemagne
Winston Churchill
El Cid
Cleopatra
Clive of India
Christopher Columbus
Captain James Cook
Hernando Cortés
Crazy Horse
Davy Crockett
Oliver Cromwell
George Armstrong Custer
Francis Drake
Guy Fawkes
Yuri Gagarin
Mahatma Gandhi
Giuseppe Garibaldi
Genghis Khan
Geronimo
Gordon of Khartoum
Che Guevara
Haile Selassie
Hannibal
Henry VIII
Hereward the Wake
Hiawatha
Wild Bill (James Butler) Hickok
Adolf Hitler
Ivan the Terrible
Jesse James
Jesus
Joan of Arc
Martin Luther King
Lawrence of Arabia
Robert E(dward) Lee
Vladimir Ilyich Lenin
Abraham Lincoln
Martin Luther
Mary, Queen of Scots
Mao Ze Dong *or* Mao Tse-tung
Marie Antoinette
Mohammed *or* Muhammad
Montezuma
Benito Mussolini
Napoleon Bonaparte

Horatio Nelson
Florence Nightingale
Captain (Lawrence Edward Grace) Oates
Pericles
Marco Polo
Pompey
Walter Raleigh
Grigori Efimovich Rasputin
Richard the Lionheart
Robert the Bruce
Saladin
Robert Falcon Scott
Sitting Bull
Socrates
Joseph Stalin
Tomás de Torquemada
Leon Trotsky
William Wallace
Warwick the King~maker
George Washington
Duke of Wellington
William the Conquer~or
Orville and Wilbur Wright
Emiliano Zapata

Events in history

Agincourt
Alamo
American Civil War *or (chiefly U.S.)* the War between the States
Armistice
Battle of Hastings
Black Death
Bloody Sunday
Boer War
Boston Tea Party
Boxer Rebellion
Charge of the Light Brigade
Civil War
Cold War
Crimean War
Crusades
Cultural Revolution
D-day
Declaration of Inde~pendence
Depression
Diet of Worms
Easter Rising
French Revolution
General Strike
Gettysburg Address
Glorious Revolution
Gordon Riots
Great Fire of London
Great Schism
Great Trek
Gunpowder Plot
Hiroshima
Holocaust
Hundred Years War
Hungarian Uprising
Indian Mutiny
Industrial Revolution
Jacobite Rebellion
Korean War
Kristallnacht *or* Crystal Night
Long March
Magna Carta
Munich Agreement
Night of the Long Knives
Napoleonic Wars
Norman Conquest
Pearl Harbor
Peasants' Revolt
Peterloo Massacre
Potato Famine
Reformation
Reign of Terror
Renaissance
Restoration
Risorgimento
Russian Revolution
Saint Valentine's Day Massacre
South Sea Bubble
Spanish Armada
Spanish Civil War
Spanish Inquisition
Suez Crisis
Thirty Years' War
Tiananmen Square Massacre
Trafalgar
Treaty of Versailles
Vietnam War
Wall Street Crash
Wars of the Roses
Watergate
Waterloo
World War I
World War II

Battles

see BATTLE

The history of all hitherto existing societies is the history of class struggles
Karl Marx and Friedrich Engels *The Communist Manifesto*

History is philosophy from examples
Dionysius of Halicarnassus *Ars Rhetorica*

There is properly no history; only biography
Ralph Waldo Emerson *Essays*

History is more or less bunk
Henry Ford

History is past politics, and politics is present history
E.A. Freeman *Methods of Historical Study*

What experience and history teach is this - that people and governments never have learned any~thing from history, or acted on principles deduced from it
G.W.F. Hegel *Philosophy of History*

History is a nightmare from which I am trying to awake
James Joyce *Ulysses*

The world's history is the world's judgement
Friedrich von Schiller

Indeed, history is nothing more than a tableau of crimes and misfortunes
Voltaire *L'Ingénu*

That great dust-heap called "history"
Augustine Birrell *Obiter Dicta*

History [is] a distillation of rumour
Thomas Carlyle *History of the French Revolution*

History gets thicker as it approaches recent times
A.J.P. Taylor *English History 1914-45*

History repeats itself, first as tragedy, second as farce
Karl Marx

History is littered with wars that everybody knew would never happen
Enoch Powell

History is the essence of innumerable biographies
Thomas Carlyle *Critical and Miscellaneous Essays*

History repeats itself

histrionic actorly, actressy, affected, artificial, bogus, camp (*informal*), dramatic, forced, in~sincere, melodramatic, sensational, theatrical, unnatural

histrionics dramatics, performance, scene, staginess, tantrums, temperament, theatrical~ity

hit *verb* **1.** bang, bash (*informal*), batter, beat, belt (*informal*), chin (*slang*), clip (*informal*), clobber (*slang*), clout (*informal*), cuff, deck (*slang*), flog, knock, lambast(e), lay one on (*slang*), lob, punch, slap, smack, smite (*archa~ic*), sock (*slang*), strike, swat, thump, wallop (*informal*), whack **2.** bang into, bump, clash with, collide with, crash against, meet head-on, run into, smash into **3.** accomplish, achieve, arrive at, attain, gain, reach, secure, strike, touch **4.** affect, damage, devastate, impact on, impinge on, influence, leave a mark on, make an impact *or* impression on, move, overwhelm, touch *~noun* **5.** belt (*informal*), blow, bump, clash, clout (*informal*), collision, cuff, impact, knock, rap, shot, slap, smack, stroke, swipe (*informal*), wallop (*informal*) **6.** *informal* sellout, sensation, smash (*informal*), smasheroo (*informal*), success, triumph, winner

A hit, a very palpable hit
William Shakespeare *Hamlet*

hitch *verb* **1.** attach, connect, couple, fasten, harness, join, make fast, tether, tie, unite, yoke **2.** *often with* **up** hoick, jerk, pull, tug, yank **3.** *informal* hitchhike, thumb a lift *~noun* **4.** catch, check, delay, difficulty, drawback, hassle (*informal*), hazard, hindrance, hold-up, impediment, mishap, obstacle, problem, snag, stoppage, trouble

hither close, closer, here, near, nearer, nigh (*archaic*), over here, to this place

hitherto heretofore, previously, so far, thus far, till now, until now, up to now

hit off 1. capture, catch, impersonate, mimic, represent, take off (*informal*) **2. hit it off** *informal* be on good terms, click (*slang*), get on like a house on fire (*informal*), get on (well) with, take to, warm to

hit on *or* **upon** arrive at, chance upon, come upon, discover, guess, invent, light upon, realize, strike upon, stumble on, think up

hit or miss aimless, casual, cursory, disorganized, haphazard, indiscriminate, perfunctory, random, undirected, uneven
Antonyms arranged, deliberate, organized, planned, systematic

hit out (at) assail, attack, castigate, condemn, denounce, inveigh against, lash out, rail against, strike out at

hive 1. cluster, colony, swarm **2.** *figurative* centre, heart, hub, powerhouse (*slang*)

hoard 1. *noun* accumulation, cache, fall-back, fund, heap, mass, pile, reserve, stockpile, store, supply, treasure-trove **2.** *verb* accumulate, amass, buy up, cache, collect, deposit, garner, gather, hive, lay up, put away, put by, save, stash away (*informal*), stockpile, store, treasure

hoarder collector, magpie (*Brit.*), miser, niggard, saver, squirrel (*informal*), tight-arse (*taboo slang*), tight-ass (*U.S. taboo slang*)

hoarse croaky, discordant, grating, gravelly, growling, gruff, guttural, harsh, husky, rasping, raucous, rough, throaty
Antonyms harmonious, mellifluous, mellow, melodious, smooth

hoarseness a frog in one's throat, croakiness, gruffness, huskiness, rasping, sore throat, throatiness, wheeziness

hoary 1. frosty, grey, grey-haired, grizzled, hoar, silvery, white, white-haired **2.** aged, ancient, antiquated, antique, old, venerable

hoax 1. *noun* canard, cheat, con (*informal*), deception, fast one (*informal*), fraud, imposture, joke, practical joke, prank, ruse, spoof (*informal*), swindle, trick **2.** *verb* bamboozle (*informal*), befool, bluff, con (*slang*), deceive, delude, dupe, fool, gammon (*Brit. informal*), gull (*archaic*), hoodwink, hornswoggle (*slang*), kid (*informal*), swindle, take in (*informal*), take (someone) for a ride (*informal*), trick, wind up (*Brit. slang*)

hoaxer bamboozler (*informal*), hoodwinker, humbug, joker, practical joker, prankster, spoofer (*informal*), trickster

hobble 1. dodder, falter, halt, limp, shamble, shuffle, stagger, stumble, totter **2.** clog, fasten, fetter, hamstring, restrict, shackle, tie

hobby diversion, favourite occupation, (leisure) activity, leisure pursuit, pastime, relaxation, sideline

hobgoblin apparition, bogey, goblin, hob, imp, spectre, spirit, sprite

hobnob associate, consort, fraternize, hang about, hang out (*informal*), keep company, mingle, mix, socialize

hocus-pocus 1. artifice, cheat, chicanery, deceit, deception, delusion, hoax, humbug, imposture, swindle, trickery **2.** abracadabra, cant, gibberish, gobbledegook (*informal*), Greek (*informal*), hokum (*slang, chiefly U.S. & Canad.*), jargon, mumbo jumbo, nonsense, rigmarole **3.** conjuring, jugglery, legerdemain, prestidigitation, sleight of hand

hog *verb* be a dog in the manger, corner, corner the market in, dominate, monopolize, tie up

hoggish brutish, dirty, edacious, filthy, gluttonous, greedy, gross, mean, piggish, rapacious, ravenous, selfish, sordid, squalid, swinish, unclean

hogwash balderdash, balls (*taboo slang*), bilge (*informal*), bosh (*informal*), bull (*slang*), bullshit (*taboo slang*), bunk (*informal*), bunkum *or* buncombe (*chiefly U.S.*), cobblers (*Brit. taboo slang*), crap (*slang*), drivel, eyewash (*informal*), garbage (*informal*), guff (*slang*), hokum (*slang, chiefly U.S. & Canad.*), hooey (*slang*), horsefeathers (*U.S. slang*), hot air (*informal*), moonshine, nonsense, pap, piffle (*informal*), poppycock (*informal*), rot, rubbish, shit (*taboo slang*), tommyrot, tosh (*slang, chiefly Brit.*), trash, tripe (*informal*), twaddle

hoiden *see* HOYDEN

hoi polloi admass, *canaille*, commonalty, riffraff, the (common) herd, the common people, the great unwashed (*informal & derogatory*), the lower orders, the masses, the plebs, the populace, the proles (*derogatory slang, chiefly Brit.*), the proletariat, the rabble, the third estate, the underclass

hoist 1. *verb* elevate, erect, heave, lift, raise, rear, upraise 2. *noun* crane, elevator, lift, tackle, winch

hoity-toity arrogant, conceited, disdainful, haughty, high and mighty (*informal*), lofty, overweening, proud, scornful, snobbish, snooty (*informal*), stuck-up (*informal*), supercilious, toffee-nosed (*slang, chiefly Brit.*), uppish (*Brit. informal*)

hold *verb* 1. have, keep, maintain, occupy, own, possess, retain 2. adhere, clasp, cleave, clinch, cling, clutch, cradle, embrace, enfold, grasp, grip, stick 3. arrest, bind, check, confine, curb, detain, impound, imprison, pound, restrain, stay, stop, suspend 4. assume, believe, consider, deem, entertain, esteem, judge, maintain, presume, reckon, regard, think, view 5. continue, endure, last, persevere, persist, remain, resist, stay, wear 6. assemble, call, carry on, celebrate, conduct, convene, have, officiate at, preside over, run, solemnize 7. bear, brace, carry, prop, shoulder, support, sustain, take 8. accommodate, comprise, contain, have a capacity for, seat, take 9. apply, be in force, be the case, exist, hold good, operate, remain true, remain valid, stand up 10. **hold one's own** do well, hold fast, hold out, keep one's head above water, keep pace, keep up, maintain one's position, stand firm, stand one's ground, stay put, stick to one's guns (*informal*) ~*noun* 11. clasp, clutch, grasp, grip 12. anchorage, foothold, footing, leverage, prop, purchase, stay, support, vantage 13. ascendancy, authority, clout (*informal*), control, dominance, dominion, influence, mastery, pull (*informal*), sway

Antonyms bestow, break, call off, cancel, come undone, deny, disavow, disclaim, free, give, give up, give way, hand over, let go, let loose, loosen, offer, postpone, put down, refute, reject, release, turn over

hold back 1. check, control, curb, inhibit, rein, repress, restrain, stem the flow, suppress 2. desist, forbear, keep back, refuse, withhold

holder 1. bearer, custodian, incumbent, keeper, occupant, owner, possessor, proprietor, purchaser 2. case, container, cover, housing, receptacle, sheath

hold forth declaim, descant, discourse, go on, harangue, lecture, orate, preach, speak, speechify, spiel (*informal*), spout (*informal*)

holdings assets, estate, investments, land interests, possessions, property, resources, securities, stocks and shares

hold off 1. avoid, defer, delay, keep from, postpone, put off, refrain 2. fend off, keep off, rebuff, repel, repulse, stave off

hold out 1. extend, give, offer, present, proffer 2. carry on, continue, endure, hang on, last, persevere, persist, stand fast, stay the course, withstand

hold over adjourn, defer, delay, postpone, put off, suspend, take a rain check on (*U.S. & Canad. informal*), waive

hold-up 1. bottleneck, delay, difficulty, hitch, obstruction, setback, snag, stoppage, traffic jam, trouble, wait 2. burglary, mugging (*informal*), robbery, steaming (*informal*), stick-up (*slang, chiefly U.S.*), theft

hold up 1. delay, detain, hinder, impede, retard, set back, slow down, stop 2. bolster, brace, buttress, jack up, prop, shore up, support, sustain 3. mug (*informal*), rob, stick up (*slang, chiefly U.S.*), waylay 4. display, exhibit, flaunt, present, show 5. bear up, endure, last, survive, wear

hold with agree to *or* with, approve of, be in favour of, countenance, subscribe to, support, take kindly to

Antonyms be against, disagree with, disapprove of, hold out against, oppose

hole 1. aperture, breach, break, crack, fissure, gap, opening, orifice, outlet, perforation, puncture, rent, split, tear, vent 2. cave, cavern, cavity, chamber, depression, excavation, hollow, pit, pocket, scoop, shaft 3. burrow, covert, den, earth, lair, nest, retreat, shelter 4. *informal* dive (*slang*), dump (*informal*), hovel, joint (*slang*), slum 5. *informal* calaboose (*U.S. informal*), cell, dungeon, oubliette, prison 6. defect, discrepancy, error, fallacy, fault, flaw, inconsistency, loophole 7. *slang* dilemma, fix (*informal*), hot water (*informal*), imbroglio, jam (*informal*), mess, predicament, quandary, scrape (*informal*), spot (*informal*), tangle, tight spot 8. **pick holes in** asperse, badmouth (*slang, chiefly U.S. & Canad.*), cavil, crab (*informal*), criticize, denigrate, disparage, disprove, find fault, knock (*informal*), niggle, pull to pieces, put down, rubbish (*informal*), run down, slag (off) (*slang*), slate (*informal*)

hole-and-corner backstairs, clandestine, furtive, secret, secretive, sneaky (*informal*), stealthy, surreptitious, underhand, under the counter (*informal*)

Antonyms above-board, candid, frank, open, public

hole up go to earth, hibernate, hide, shelter, take cover, take refuge

holiday 1. break, leave, recess, time off, vacation 2. anniversary, bank holiday, celebration, feast, festival, festivity, fête, gala, name day,

public holiday, red-letter day, saint's day
Related adjective: ferial

A perpetual holiday is a good working definition of hell
George Bernard Shaw *Parents and Children*

holier-than-thou goody-goody (*informal*), pietistic, pietistical, priggish, religiose, sanctimonious, self-righteous, self-satisfied, smug, squeaky-clean, unctuous

holiness blessedness, devoutness, divinity, godliness, piety, purity, religiousness, righteousness, sacredness, saintliness, sanctity, spirituality, virtuousness

holler *verb/noun* bawl, bellow, call, cheer, clamour, cry, hail, halloo, hollo, hurrah, huzzah (*archaic*), roar, shout, whoop, yell

hollow *adjective* **1.** empty, not solid, unfilled, vacant, void **2.** cavernous, concave, deep-set, depressed, indented, sunken **3.** deep, dull, expressionless, flat, low, muffled, muted, reverberant, rumbling, sepulchral, toneless **4.** empty, fruitless, futile, meaningless, pointless, Pyrrhic, specious, unavailing, useless, vain, wanky (*taboo slang*), worthless **5.** empty, esurient, famished, hungry, ravenous, starved **6.** artificial, cynical, deceitful, faithless, false, flimsy, hollow-hearted, hypocritical, insincere, treacherous, unsound, weak **7. beat (someone) hollow** *informal* defeat, hammer (*informal*), outdo, overcome, rout, thrash, trounce, worst *~noun* **8.** basin, bowl, cave, cavern, cavity, concavity, crater, cup, den, dent, depression, dimple, excavation, hole, indentation, pit, trough **9.** bottom, dale, dell, dingle, glen, valley *~verb* **10.** channel, dig, dish, excavate, furrow, gouge, groove, pit, scoop
Antonyms *adjective* (*sense 1*) full, occupied, solid (*sense 2*) convex, rounded (*sense 3*) expressive, vibrant (*sense 4*) gratifying, meaningful, pleasing, satisfying, valuable, worthwhile (*sense 6*) genuine *~noun* (*sense 8*) bump, mound, projection (*sense 9*) bluff, height, hill, knoll, mountain, rise

Hollywood

A dreary industrial town controlled by hoodlums of enormous wealth
S.J. Perelman

a trip through a sewer in a glass-bottomed boat
Wilson Mizner

holocaust annihilation, carnage, conflagration, destruction, devastation, fire, genocide, inferno, massacre, mass murder, pogrom

holy **1.** devout, divine, faithful, god-fearing, godly, hallowed, pious, pure, religious, righteous, saintly, sublime, virtuous **2.** blessed, consecrated, dedicated, hallowed, sacred, sacrosanct, sanctified, venerable, venerated
Antonyms blasphemous, corrupt, desecrated, earthly, evil, human, immoral, impious, irreligious, sacrilegious, secular, sinful, unconsecrated, unhallowed, unholy, unsanctified, wicked, worldly

Is that which is holy loved by the gods because it is holy, or is it holy because it is loved by the gods?
Plato *Euthyphro*

homage **1.** admiration, adoration, adulation, awe, deference, devotion, duty, esteem, honour, respect, reverence, worship **2.** allegiance, devotion, faithfulness, fealty, fidelity, loyalty, obeisance, service, tribute, troth (*archaic*)
Antonyms condemnation, contempt, disdain, disregard, disrespect, irreverence, scorn

home *noun* **1.** abode, domicile, dwelling, dwelling place, habitation, house, pad (*slang*), residence **2.** birthplace, family, fireside, hearth, homestead, home town, household **3.** abode, element, environment, habitat, habitation, haunt, home ground, range, stamping ground, territory **4. at home a.** available, in, present **b.** at ease, comfortable, familiar, relaxed **c.** entertaining, giving a party, having guests, receiving **d.** *as a noun* party, reception, soirée **5. at home in, on,** *or* **with** conversant with, familiar with, knowledgeable, proficient, skilled, well-versed **6. bring home to** drive home, emphasize, impress upon, make clear, press home *~adjective* **7.** central, domestic, familiar, family, household, inland, internal, local, national, native

Mid pleasures and palaces though we may roam,
Be it ever so humble, there's no place like home.
Home, home, sweet, sweet home!
There's no place like home! There's no place like home!
J.H. Payne *Clari, the Maid of Milan*

Home is where the heart is
Pliny the Elder

Home is the place where, when you have to go there,
They have to take you in
Robert Frost *The Death of the Hired Man*

East, west, home's best

An Englishman's home is his castle

homeland country of origin, fatherland, mother country, motherland, native land

homeless **1.** *adjective* abandoned, destitute, displaced, dispossessed, down-and-out, exiled, forlorn, forsaken, outcast, unsettled **2.** *noun* **the homeless** dossers (*Brit. slang*), squatters, vagrants

homelike cheerful, comfortable, cosy, easy, familiar, homy, informal, intimate, relaxing, snug

homely comfortable, comfy (*informal*), cosy, domestic, downhome (*slang, chiefly U.S.*), down-to-earth, everyday, familiar, friendly, homelike, homespun, homy, informal, modest, natural, ordinary, plain, simple, unaffected, unassuming, unfussy, unpretentious, welcoming

Antonyms affected, elaborate, elegant, grand, ostentatious, pretentious, refined, regal, sophisticated, splendid

Homeric epic, grand, heroic, imposing, impressive

homespun artless, coarse, homely, home-made, inelegant, plain, rough, rude, rustic, unpolished, unsophisticated

homicidal deadly, death-dealing, lethal, maniacal, mortal, murderous

homicide **1.** bloodshed, killing, manslaughter, murder, slaying **2.** killer, murderer, slayer

homily address, discourse, lecture, preaching, preachment, sermon

homogeneity analogousness, comparability, consistency, correspondence, identicalness, oneness, sameness, similarity, uniformity

homogeneous akin, alike, analogous, cognate, comparable, consistent, identical, kindred, similar, uniform, unvarying

Antonyms different, disparate, dissimilar, divergent, diverse, heterogeneous, manifold, mixed, unlike, unrelated, varied, various, varying

homologous analogous, comparable, correspondent, corresponding, like, parallel, related, similar

homosexual *adjective* bent (*slang*), camp (*informal*), gay, homoerotic, lesbian, pink (*informal*), queer (*informal, derogatory*), sapphic

I am the Love that dare not speak its name
Lord Alfred Douglas *Two Loves*

I have heard some say... [homosexual] practices are allowed in France and in other NATO countries. We are not French, and we are not other nationals. We are British, thank God!
Field Marshal Montgomery

homy comfortable, comfy (*informal*), congenial, cosy, domestic, familiar, friendly, informal, intimate, pleasant, warm

hone *verb* edge, file, grind, point, polish, sharpen, strop, whet

honest **1.** conscientious, decent, ethical, high-minded, honourable, law-abiding, reliable, reputable, scrupulous, trustworthy, trusty, truthful, upright, veracious, virtuous **2.** above board, authentic, bona fide, genuine, honest to goodness, on the level (*informal*), on the up and up, proper, real, straight, true **3.** equitable, fair, fair and square, impartial, just **4.** candid, direct, forthright, frank, ingenuous, open, outright, plain, round, sincere, straightforward, undisguised, unfeigned, upfront (*informal*)

Antonyms bad, corrupt, counterfeit, crooked, deceitful, disguised, dishonest, false, fraudulent, guilty, illegitimate, immoral, insincere, secretive, treacherous, unethical, unfair, unfaithful, unlawful, unprincipled, unreliable, unrighteous, unscrupulous, untrustworthy, untruthful

To be honest, as this world goes, is to be one man picked out of ten thousand
William Shakespeare *Hamlet*

An honest man's the noblest work of God
Alexander Pope *An Essay on Man*

honestly **1.** by fair means, cleanly, ethically, honourably, in good faith, lawfully, legally, legitimately, on the level (*informal*), with clean hands **2.** candidly, frankly, in all sincerity, in plain English, plainly, straight (out), to one's face, truthfully

honesty **1.** faithfulness, fidelity, honour, incorruptibility, integrity, morality, probity, rectitude, reputability, scrupulousness, straightness, trustworthiness, truthfulness, uprightness, veracity, virtue **2.** bluntness, candour, equity, even-handedness, fairness, frankness, genuineness, openness, outspokenness, plainness, sincerity, straightforwardness

The surest way to remain poor is to be an honest man
Napoleon Bonaparte *Maxims*

No legacy is so rich as honesty
William Shakespeare *All's Well That Ends Well*

Honesty's a fool
William Shakespeare *Othello*

Honesty is a fine jewel, but much out of fashion
Thomas Fuller *Gnomologia*

Honesty is praised and left to shiver
Juvenal *Satires*

Honesty is the best policy

honeyed agreeable, alluring, cajoling, dulcet, enticing, flattering, mellow, melodious, seductive, soothing, sweet, sweetened, unctuous

honorary complimentary, ex officio, formal, *honoris causa*, in name *or* title only, nominal, titular, unofficial, unpaid

honour *noun* **1.** credit, dignity, distinction, elevation, eminence, esteem, fame, glory, high standing, prestige, rank, renown, reputation, repute **2.** acclaim, accolade, adoration, Brownie points, commendation, deference, homage, kudos, praise, recognition, regard, respect, reverence, tribute, veneration **3.** decency, fairness, goodness, honesty, integrity, morality, principles, probity, rectitude, righteousness, trustworthiness, uprightness **4.** compliment, credit, favour, pleasure, privilege, source of pride *or* satisfaction **5.** chastity, innocence, modesty, purity, virginity, virtue ~*verb* **6.** admire, adore, appreciate, esteem, exalt, glorify, hallow, prize, respect, revere, reverence, value, venerate, worship **7.** be as good as (*informal*), be faithful to, be true to, carry out, discharge, fulfil, keep, live up to, observe **8.** acclaim, celebrate, commemorate, commend, compliment, crack up (*informal*), decorate, dignify, exalt, glorify, laud, lionize, praise **9.** accept, acknowledge, cash, clear, credit, pass, pay, take

Antonyms *noun* condemnation, contempt, degradation, disfavour, disgrace, dishonesty, dishonour, disrepute, disrespect, infamy, insincerity, insult, lowness, meanness, scorn, shame, slight, unscrupulousness *~verb* condemn, defame, degrade, dishonour, disobey, insult, offend, refuse, scorn, slight

Duty, honour! We make these words say whatever we want, the same as we do with parrots
Alfred Capus *Mariage bourgeois*

If I lose mine honour,
I lose myself
William Shakespeare *Antony and Cleopatra*

Remember, you're fighting for this woman's honour....which is probably more than she ever did
Groucho Marx *Duck Soup (film)*

The louder he talked of his honour, the faster we counted our spoons
Ralph Waldo Emerson *The Conduct of Life*

There is honour among thieves

honourable 1. ethical, fair, high-minded, honest, just, moral, principled, true, trustworthy, trusty, upright, upstanding, virtuous **2.** distinguished, eminent, great, illustrious, noble, notable, noted, prestigious, renowned, venerable **3.** creditable, estimable, proper, reputable, respectable, respected, right, righteous, virtuous

For Brutus is an honourable man
William Shakespeare *Julius Caesar*

honours adornments, awards, decorations, dignities, distinctions, laurels, titles

hoodoo bad luck, curse, evil eye, evil star, hex (*U.S. & Canad. informal*), jinx, nemesis, voodoo

hoodwink bamboozle (*informal*), befool, cheat, con (*informal*), cozen, deceive, delude, dupe, fool, gull (*archaic*), hoax, impose, kid (*informal*), lead up the garden path (*informal*), mislead, pull a fast one on (*informal*), rook (*slang*), sell a pup, swindle, take (someone) for a ride (*informal*), trick

hook *noun* **1.** catch, clasp, fastener, hasp, holder, link, lock, peg **2.** noose, snare, springe, trap **3. by hook or by crook** by any means, by fair means or foul, somehow, somehow or other, someway **4. hook, line, and sinker** *informal* completely, entirely, lock, stock and barrel, thoroughly, through and through, totally, utterly, wholly **5. off the hook** *slang* acquitted, cleared, exonerated, in the clear, let off, under no obligation, vindicated *~verb* **6.** catch, clasp, fasten, fix, hasp, secure **7.** catch, enmesh, ensnare, entrap, snare, trap

hookah hubble-bubble, kalian, narghile, water pipe

hooked 1. aquiline, beaked, beaky, bent, curved, falcate (*Biology*), hamate (*rare*), hook-like, hook-shaped, unciform (*Anatomy, etc.*), uncinate (*Biology*) **2.** addicted to, devoted to, enamoured of, obsessed with, taken with, turned on (*slang*)

hooligan casual, delinquent, hoodlum (*chiefly U.S.*), lager lout, ned (*slang*), rowdy, ruffian, tough, vandal, yob *or* yobbo (*Brit. slang*)

hoop band, circlet, girdle, loop, ring, wheel

hoot *noun* **1.** call, cry, toot **2.** boo, catcall, hiss, jeer, yell **3.** *informal* card (*informal*), caution (*informal*), laugh (*informal*), scream (*informal*) *~verb* **4.** boo, catcall, condemn, decry, denounce, execrate, hiss, howl down, jeer, yell at **5.** cry, scream, shout, shriek, toot, whoop, yell

hop 1. *verb* bound, caper, dance, jump, leap, skip, spring, trip, vault **2.** *noun* bounce, bound, jump, leap, skip, spring, step, vault

hope 1. *noun* ambition, anticipation, assumption, belief, confidence, desire, dream, expectancy, expectation, faith, light at the end of the tunnel, longing **2.** *verb* anticipate, aspire, await, believe, contemplate, count on, cross one's fingers, desire, expect, foresee, keep one's fingers crossed, long, look forward to, rely, set one's heart on, trust

Antonyms despair, distrust, doubt, dread, hopelessness

Hope springs eternal in the human breast;
Man never Is, but always To be blest
Alexander Pope *An Essay on Man*

He that lives upon hope will die fasting
Benjamin Franklin *Poor Richard's Almanac*

He that lives in hope danceth without music
George Herbert *Outlandish Proverbs*

While there's life, there's hope
Cicero *Letters to Atticus*

Hope is the poor man's bread
George Herbert *Jacula Prudentum*

What is hope? Nothing but the paint on the face of existence; the least touch of truth rubs it off, and then we see what a hollow-cheeked harlot we have got hold of
Lord Byron

Abandon hope, all ye who enter here
Dante *Divine Comedy*

Hope is a good breakfast but a bad supper

hopeful 1. anticipating, assured, buoyant, confident, expectant, looking forward to, optimistic, sanguine **2.** auspicious, bright, cheerful, encouraging, heartening, promising, propitious, reassuring, rosy

Antonyms (*sense 1*) cheerless, dejected, despairing, hopeless, pessimistic (*sense 2*) depressing, discouraging, disheartening, unpromising

hopefully 1. confidently, expectantly, optimistically, sanguinely 2. *informal* all being well, conceivably, expectedly, feasibly, probably

hopeless 1. defeatist, dejected, demoralized, despairing, desperate, despondent, disconsolate, downhearted, forlorn, in despair, pessimistic, woebegone 2. basket case, helpless, incurable, irremediable, irreparable, irreversible, lost, past remedy, remediless 3. forlorn, futile, impossible, impracticable, not having a prayer, no-win, pointless, unachievable, unattainable, useless, vain 4. *informal* inadequate, incompetent, ineffectual, inferior, no good, pathetic, poor, useless (*informal*)
Antonyms (*sense 1*) assured, cheerful, confident, expectant, happy, heartened, hopeful, optimistic, uplifted (*sense 2*) curable, encouraging, favourable, heartening, promising, reassuring, remediable

hopelessly 1. beyond all hope, despairingly, in despair, irredeemably, irremediably, without hope 2. completely, impossibly, totally, utterly

horde band, crew, crowd, drove, gang, host, mob, multitude, pack, press, swarm, throng, troop

horizon 1. field of vision, skyline, vista 2. ambit, compass, ken, perspective, prospect, purview, range, realm, scope, sphere, stretch

horizontal flat, level, parallel, plane, supine

horny amorous, aroused, excited, lustful, randy (*informal, chiefly Brit.*), raunchy (*slang*), turned on (*slang*)

horrible 1. abhorrent, abominable, appalling, awful, dreadful, fearful, frightful, from hell (*informal*), ghastly, grim, grisly, gruesome, heinous, hellacious (*U.S. slang*), hideous, horrid, loathsome, obscene, repulsive, revolting, shameful, shocking, terrible, terrifying 2. *informal* awful, beastly (*informal*), cruel, disagreeable, dreadful, ghastly (*informal*), horrid, mean, nasty, terrible, unkind, unpleasant
Antonyms agreeable, appealing, attractive, charming, cute, delightful, enchanting, fetching, lovely, pleasant, wonderful

horrid 1. awful, disagreeable, disgusting, dreadful, horrible, nasty, obscene, offensive, terrible, unpleasant, yucky *or* yukky (*slang*) 2. abominable, alarming, appalling, formidable, frightening, from hell (*informal*), hair-raising, harrowing, hideous, horrific, odious, repulsive, revolting, shocking, terrifying, terrorizing 3. *informal* beastly (*informal*), cruel, mean, nasty, unkind

horrific appalling, awful, dreadful, frightening, frightful, from hell (*informal*), ghastly, grim, grisly, hellacious (*U.S. slang*), horrendous, horrifying, shocking, terrifying

horrify 1. affright, alarm, frighten, intimidate, petrify, put the wind up (*informal*), scare, terrify, terrorize 2. appal, disgust, dismay, gross out (*U.S. slang*), make one's hair stand on end, outrage, shock, sicken
Antonyms comfort, delight, enchant, encourage, gladden, hearten, please, reassure, soothe

horror 1. alarm, apprehension, awe, consternation, dismay, dread, fear, fright, panic, terror 2. abhorrence, abomination, antipathy, aversion, detestation, disgust, hatred, loathing, odium, repugnance, revulsion
Antonyms affinity, approval, attraction, delight, liking, love

Where there is no imagination there is no horror
Sir Arthur Conan Doyle *A Study in Scarlet*

horror-struck *or* **horror-stricken** aghast, appalled, awe-struck, frightened to death, horrified, petrified, scared out of one's wits, shocked

horse colt, cuddy *or* cuddie (*dialect, chiefly Scots.*), dobbin, filly, gee-gee (*slang*), gelding, hobby (*archaic or dialect*), jade, mare, moke (*Austral. slang*), mount, nag, stallion, steed (*archaic or literary*), studhorse *or* stud, yarraman (*Austral.*), yearling
Related adjectives: equestrian, equine, horsy
Related noun: equitation

Breeds of horse

Akhal-Teke
American Quarter horse
American Saddle horse
Andalusian
Anglo-Arab
Anglo-Norman
Appaloosa
Arab
Ardennes
Balearic
Barb
Basuto
Batak *or* Deli
boerperd
Beetewk
Brabançon
Breton
Burmese *or* Shan
Cleveland Bay
Clydesdale
Connemara
Criollo
Dales pony
Danish
Dartmoor pony
Don
Dutch Draught
Esthonian, Smudish *or* Zmudzin
Exmoor
Fell pony
Finnish horse
Fjord pony
Flemish
Friesian
Gelderland
Gidran
Groningen
Gudbrandsdal
Hackney
Hafflinger
Hambletonian
Hanoverian
Highland pony
Holstein
Huçul
Iceland pony
Iomud
Jutland
Kabarda
Karabair
Karabakh
Karadagh
Kathiawari
Kladruber
Klepper

Knabstrup
Konik
Kurdistan pony
Limousin
Lipizzaner *or* Lippizaner
Lokai
Manipur
Marwari
Mecklenburg
Mongolian
Morgan
Mustang *or* bronco
New Forest pony
Nonius
North Swedish horse
Oldenburg
Orlov Trotter
Palomino
Percheron
Persian Arab
Pinto
Pinzgauer
Polish Arab
Polish Half-bred
Polish Thoroughbred
Quarter horse
racehorse
Rhenish
Russian saddle horse *or* Orlov Rostopchin
Schleswig
Shagya
Shetland pony
Shirazi *or* Gulf Arab
Shire horse
Spanish Jennet *or* Genet
Spiti
Standard Bred
Strelet
Suffolk *or* Suffolk Punch
Swedish Ardennes
Tarbenian
Tarpan
Tennessee Walking Horse *or* Walking Horse
Thoroughbred
Timor pony
Trakehner
Turk *or* Turkoman
Viatka
Waler
Welsh Cob
Welsh Mountain pony
Welsh pony
Yamoote
Yorkshire Coach horse
Zeeland horse
Zemaitukas

Types of horse

carthorse
cavalry horse
cayuse (*Western U.S. & Canad.*)
charger
cob
courser (*literary*)
cow pony
crock
destrier (*archaic*)
drayhorse
hack
high-stepper
hunter
liberty horse
nag
night horse (*Austral.*)
packhorse
palfrey (*archaic*)
pacer
packhorse
plug (*chiefly U.S.*)
polo pony
pony
racehorse *or (Austral. informal)* neddy
rip (*informal, archaic*)
running mate
saddle horse *or* saddler
screw (*slang*)
show jumper
stalking-horse
stockhorse
sumpter (*archaic*)
trooper
warhorse
weed
workhorse

Wild horses

brumby (*Austral.*)
buckjumper (*Austral.*)
mustang
Przewalski's horse *or* wild horse
quagga
tarpan
warrigal (*Austral.*)
zebra

Extinct horses

hyracotherium *or* eohippus
merychippus
miohippus
pliohippus
quagga
tarpan

Legendary/fictional/historical horses

Bayard
Black Beauty
Black Bess
Boxer
Bucephalus
Champion
El Fideldo
Flicka
Hercules
Incitatus
Mister Ed
Pegasus
Rosinante
Silver
Sleipnir
Traveler
Trigger

Horse colours

albino
bay
black
blue roan
chestnut
claybank
cream
dapple
dapplegrey
dun
fleabitten
grey
mealy
palomino
piebald
pinto (*U.S. & Canad.*)
roan
skewbald
sorrel
strawberry roan

Horse markings

blaze
coronet
snip
sock
star
stocking
stripe
white face

Horse parts

back
bar
barrel
brisket
buttress
cannon bone
chestnut
chin groove
coffin bone
coronet band
counter
coupling
croup *or* croupe
diagonal
dock
ergot
fetlock joint
flank
forearm
forehand
foreleg
forelock
forequarters
frog
gambrel
gaskin *or* second thigh
hamstring
haunch
haw
heel
hock
hoof
loins
mane
muzzle
near-fore
near-hind
neck
off-fore
off-hind
pastern
poll
quarter
saddle
shannon *or* shank
sheath
sole
splint bone
stifle joint
tail
toe
tusk

wall
white line
withers

Horse gaits

amble
canter
extended trot
gallop
jog trot
lope
pace
prance
rising trot
single-foot *or* rack
sitting trot
trot
walk

People associated with horses

broncobuster
buster (*U.S. & Canad.*)
caballero (*Southwestern U.S.*)
cavalier
cavalry
chevalier (*French history*)
coachman
coper
cowboy
currier
equerry
equestrian *or (fem.)* equestrienne
equites (*Roman history*)
farrier
groom
horseman *or (fem.)* horsewoman
hussar
jockey
Jockey Club
knacker
knight
lad (*Brit.*)
ostler
picador
postilion
postrider
rider
roughrider
rustler (*chiefly U.S. & Canad.*)
saddler
stable lad
trainer
wrangler (*Western U.S. & Canad.*)

Tack and equipment and their parts

anti-sweat rug
bar
bard *or* barde
bearing rein *or (U.S.)* check rein
bit
blinkers
body brush
boot
breastplate
breeching
bridle
bridoon
browband
cantle
cavesson
chamfron
cheek-piece
crownpiece
crupper
curb *or* curb bit
curb chain
curb reins
curry comb
dandy brush
day rug
double bridle
double-jointed snaffle
flap
front arch
fulmer snaffle
gag-bit
gambado
girth *or (U.S. & Canad.)* cinch
girth strap
hackamore plate
halter
harness
headpiece
hockboot
hoof pick
horseshoe
jointed egg-butt snaffle
kimblewick
kneecap
lip strap
mane comb
martingale
New Zealand rug
night rug
nosebag
noseband *or* nosepiece
overcheck
pad saddle *or* numnah
pelham
plain snaffle
plate
pommel
rein
roller
saddle
saddlebag
saddlecloth
saddlery
sidesaddle
skirt
sliphead
snaffle *or* snaffle bit
split-eared bridle
spur
stable rubber
stirrup
stirrup bar
stirrup iron
stirrup leather
summer sheet
surcingle
sweat scraper
swingletree, whippletree *or (U.S.)* whiffletree
tack
tail bandage
tail comb
tailguard
throatlash *or* throatlatch
trace
trammel
trappings
twisted snaffle
twitch
underblanket
water brush
Weymouth curb bit
wisp

Horse-drawn vehicles

barouche
brake
britzka
brougham
buckboard (*U.S. & Canad.*)
buggy
cab
cabriolet
calash *or* calèche
Cape cart (*S. African*)
cariole *or* carriole
carriage
carryall
cart
chaise
chariot
clarence
coach
Conestoga wagon
coupe
covered wagon (*U.S. & Canad.*)
curricle
dogcart
drag
droshky
equipage
fiacre
fly
four-in-hand
gharry
gig
Gladstone
hansom
herdic (*U.S.*)
jaunting car *or* jaunty car
landau
phaeton
post chaise
prairie schooner (*chiefly U.S.*)
pung (*Eastern U.S. & Canad.*)
quadriga (*historical*)
randem
ratha
rig
rockaway (*U.S.*)
sledge
spider phaeton *or* spider
stagecoach
sulky
surrey
tandem
tarantass
tilbury
troika
victoria
vis-à-vis
wagon
wagonette
wain (*chiefly poetic*)

Equestrian events

see SPORT

A horse! a horse! my kingdom for a horse!
William Shakespeare *Richard III*

A horse is dangerous at both ends and uncomfortable in the middle
Ian Fleming

Don't change horses in midstream

You can take a horse to water but you cannot make him drink

A nod's as good as a wink to a blind horse

Nothing is so good for the inside of a man as the outside of a horse

horse around *or* **about** clown, fool about *or* around, misbehave, play the fool, play the goat, roughhouse (*slang*)

horseman cavalier, cavalryman, dragoon, equestrian, horse-soldier, rider

horseplay buffoonery, clowning, fooling around, high jinks, pranks, romping, rough-and-tumble, roughhousing (*slang*), skylarking (*informal*)

horse sense common sense, gumption (*Brit. informal*), judgment, mother wit, nous (*Brit. slang*), practicality

hospitable **1.** amicable, bountiful, cordial, friendly, generous, genial, gracious, kind, liberal, sociable, welcoming **2.** accessible, amenable, open-minded, receptive, responsive, tolerant
Antonyms (*sense 1*) inhospitable, parsimonious (*sense 2*) inhospitable, intolerant, narrow-minded, unapproachable, unreceptive

hospitality cheer, conviviality, cordiality, friendliness, heartiness, hospitableness, neighbourliness, sociability, warmth, welcome

Be not forgetful to entertain strangers; for thereby some have entertained angels unawares
Bible: Hebrews

hospitality: the virtue which induces us to feed and lodge certain persons who are not in need of food and lodging
Ambrose Bierce *The Devil's Dictionary*

Welcome the coming, speed the going guest
Alexander Pope *Imitations of Horace*

host[1] *noun* **1.** entertainer, innkeeper, landlord, master of ceremonies, proprietor **2.** anchor man, compere (*Brit.*), presenter *~verb* **3.** compere (*Brit.*), front (*informal*), introduce, present

A host is like a general; it takes a mishap to reveal his genius
Horace *Satires*

Mankind is divisible into two great classes: hosts and guests
Max Beerbohm *Hosts and Guests*

host[2] *noun* army, array, drove, horde, legion, multitude, myriad, swarm, throng

hostage captive, gage, pawn, pledge, prisoner, security, surety

hostile **1.** antagonistic, anti (*informal*), bellicose, belligerent, contrary, ill-disposed, inimical, malevolent, opposed, opposite, rancorous, unkind, warlike **2.** adverse, alien, inhospitable, unfriendly, unpropitious, unsympathetic, unwelcoming
Antonyms affable, agreeable, amiable, approving, congenial, cordial, friendly, kind, peaceful, sympathetic, warm

hostilities conflict, fighting, state of war, war, warfare
Antonyms alliance, ceasefire, peace, treaty, truce

hostility abhorrence, animosity, animus, antagonism, antipathy, aversion, bad blood, detestation, enmity, hatred, ill will, malevolence, malice, opposition, resentment, unfriendliness
Antonyms agreement, amity, approval, congeniality, cordiality, friendliness, goodwill, sympathy

hot **1.** aboil, blistering, boiling, burning, fiery, flaming, heated, piping hot, roasting, scalding, scorching, searing, steaming, sultry, sweltering, torrid, warm **2.** acrid, biting, peppery, piquant, pungent, sharp, spicy **3.** *figurative* ablaze, animated, ardent, excited, fervent, fervid, fierce, fiery, flaming, impetuous, inflamed, intense, irascible, lustful, passionate, raging, stormy, touchy, vehement, violent **4.** fresh, just out, latest, new, recent, up to the minute **5.** approved, favoured, in demand, in vogue, popular, sought-after **6.** close, following closely, in hot pursuit, near
Antonyms (*sense 1*) chilly, cold, cool, freezing, frigid, frosty, icy, parky (*Brit. informal*), (*sense 2*) mild (*sense 3*) apathetic, calm, dispassionate, half-hearted, indifferent, mild, moderate (*sense 4*) old, stale, trite (*sense 5*) out of favour, unpopular (*sense 6*) cold

hot air blather, blether, bombast, bosh (*informal*), bunkum *or* buncombe (*chiefly U.S.*), claptrap (*informal*), empty talk, gas (*informal*), guff (*slang*), rant, tall talk (*informal*), verbiage, wind

hotbed breeding ground, den, forcing house, nest, nursery, seedbed

hot-blooded ardent, excitable, fervent, fiery, heated, impulsive, passionate, rash, spirited, temperamental, wild
Antonyms apathetic, calm, cold, cool, frigid, impassive, restrained, unenthusiastic

hotchpotch conglomeration, farrago, gallimaufry, hash, hodgepodge (*U.S.*), jumble, medley, *mélange*, mess, miscellany, mishmash, mixture, olio, olla podrida, potpourri

hotfoot hastily, helter-skelter, hurriedly, pell-mell, posthaste, quickly, speedily

hothead daredevil, desperado, hotspur, madcap, tearaway

hot-headed fiery, foolhardy, hasty, hot-tempered, impetuous, precipitate, quick-tempered, rash, reckless, unruly, volatile

hothouse 1. *noun* conservatory, glasshouse, greenhouse 2. *adjective* coddled, dainty, delicate, exotic, fragile, frail, overprotected, pampered, sensitive

hotly 1. angrily, fiercely, heatedly, impetuously, indignantly, passionately, vehemently, with indignation 2. closely, eagerly, enthusiastically, hotfoot, with enthusiasm

hound *verb* 1. chase, drive, give chase, hunt, hunt down, pursue 2. badger, goad, harass, harry, impel, persecute, pester, prod, provoke

house *noun* 1. abode, building, domicile, dwelling, edifice, habitation, home, homestead, pad (*slang*), residence 2. family, household, ménage 3. ancestry, clan, dynasty, family tree, kindred, line, lineage, race, tribe 4. business, company, concern, establishment, firm, organization, outfit (*informal*), partnership 5. assembly, Commons, legislative body, parliament 6. hotel, inn, public house, tavern 7. **on the house** for nothing, free, gratis, without expense *~verb* 8. accommodate, billet, board, domicile, harbour, lodge, put up, quarter, take in 9. contain, cover, keep, protect, sheathe, shelter, store

A house is a machine for living in
Le Corbusier *Vers une architecture*

household 1. *noun* family, home, house, ménage 2. *adjective* domestic, domiciliary, family, ordinary, plain

householder homeowner, occupant, resident, tenant

housekeeping home economy, homemaking (*U.S.*), housecraft, household management, housewifery

housing 1. accommodation, dwellings, homes, houses 2. case, casing, container, cover, covering, enclosure, sheath

hovel cabin, den, hole, hut, shack, shanty, shed

hover 1. be suspended, drift, float, flutter, fly, hang, poise 2. hang about, linger, wait nearby 3. alternate, dither (*chiefly Brit.*), falter, fluctuate, haver (*Brit.*), oscillate, pause, seesaw, swither (*Scot. dialect*), vacillate, waver

however after all, anyhow, be that as it may, but, even though, nevertheless, nonetheless, notwithstanding, on the other hand, still, though, yet

howl 1. *noun* bawl, bay, bell, bellow, clamour, cry, groan, hoot, outcry, roar, scream, shriek, ululation, wail, yelp, yowl 2. *verb* bawl, bell, bellow, cry, cry out, lament, quest (*used of hounds*), roar, scream, shout, shriek, ululate, wail, weep, yell, yelp

howler bloomer (*Brit. informal*), blunder, boner (*slang*), boob (*Brit. slang*), booboo (*informal*), bull (*slang*), clanger (*informal*), error, malapropism, mistake, schoolboy howler

hoyden, hoiden romp (*archaic*), tomboy

hoydenish, hoidenish boisterous, bold, ill-mannered, inelegant, rackety, uncouth, unfeminine, ungenteel, unladylike, unruly

hub centre, core, focal point, focus, heart, middle, nerve centre, pivot

hubbub babel, bedlam, brouhaha, clamour, confusion, din, disorder, disturbance, hue and cry, hullabaloo, hurly-burly, noise, pandemonium, racket, riot, ruckus (*informal*), ruction (*informal*), rumpus, tumult, uproar

hubris arrogance, nemesis, pride

huckster barker (*informal*), hawker, pedlar, pitchman (*U.S.*), salesman, vendor

huddle *noun* 1. confusion, crowd, disorder, heap, jumble, mass, mess, muddle 2. *informal* confab (*informal*), conference, discussion, meeting, powwow *~verb* 3. cluster, converge, crowd, flock, gather, press, throng 4. crouch, cuddle, curl up, hunch up, make oneself small, nestle, snuggle

hue 1. colour, dye, shade, tincture, tinge, tint, tone 2. aspect, cast, complexion, light

hue and cry brouhaha, clamour, furore, hullabaloo, much ado, outcry, ruction (*informal*), rumpus, uproar

huff *noun* 1. anger, bad mood, bate (*Brit. slang*), miff (*informal*), passion, pet, pique, rage, temper, wax (*informal, chiefly Brit.*) 2. **in a huff** angered, annoyed, exasperated, hacked (off) (*U.S. slang*), hurt, in high dudgeon, irked, miffed (*informal*), nettled, peeved, piqued, pissed off (*taboo slang*), provoked, put out (*informal*), riled (*informal*), vexed· *~verb* 3. blow, exhale, puff

huffy, huffish angry, choked, crabbed, cross, crotchety (*informal*), crusty, curt, disgruntled, edgy, grumpy, irritable, moody, moping, offended, peevish, pettish, petulant, querulous, ratty (*Brit. & N.Z. informal*), resentful, shirty (*slang, chiefly Brit.*), short, snappy, sulky, sullen, surly, testy, tetchy, touchy, waspish
Antonyms amiable, calm, cheerful, friendly, gay, good-humoured, happy, pleasant, sunny

hug *verb* 1. clasp, cuddle, embrace, enfold, hold close, squeeze, take in one's arms 2. cling to, follow closely, keep close, stay near 3. cherish, cling, hold onto, nurse, retain *~noun* 4. bear hug, clasp, clinch (*slang*), embrace, squeeze

huge Brobdingnagian, bulky, colossal, elephantine, enormous, extensive, gargantuan, giant, gigantic, ginormous (*informal*), great, humongous *or* humungous (*U.S. slang*), immense, jumbo (*informal*), large, mammoth, massive, mega (*slang*), monumental, mountainous, prodigious, stellar (*informal*), stupendous, titanic, tremendous, vast

Antonyms insignificant, little, microscopic, minute, petty, puny, small, tiny

hugely by leaps and bounds, enormously, immensely, massively, monumentally, on a grand scale, prodigiously, stupendously

huggermugger confusion, disarray, disorder, disorganization, guddle (*Scot.*), hodgepodge (*U.S.*), hotchpotch, huddle, jumble, mess, muddle, pig's breakfast (*informal*), shambles, state

hulk **1.** derelict, frame, hull, shell, shipwreck, wreck **2.** lout, lubber, lump (*informal*), oaf

hulking awkward, bulky, clumsy, clunky (*informal*), cumbersome, gross, lubberly, lumbering, lumpish, massive, oafish, overgrown, ponderous, ungainly, unwieldy

hull *noun* **1.** body, casing, covering, frame, framework, skeleton **2.** husk, peel, pod, rind, shell, shuck, skin *~verb* **3.** husk, peel, shell, shuck, skin, trim

hullabaloo babel, bedlam, brouhaha, clamour, commotion, confusion, din, disturbance, furore, hubbub, hue and cry, hurly-burly, noise, outcry, pandemonium, racket, ruckus (*informal*), ruction (*informal*), rumpus, to-do, tumult, turmoil, upheaval, uproar

hum **1.** bombinate *or* bombilate (*literary*), buzz, croon, drone, mumble, murmur, purr, sing, throb, thrum, vibrate, whir **2.** be active, be busy, bustle, buzz, move, pulsate, pulse, stir, vibrate

human *adjective* **1.** anthropoid, fleshly, manlike, mortal **2.** approachable, compassionate, considerate, fallible, forgivable, humane, kind, kindly, natural, understandable, understanding, vulnerable *~noun* **3.** body, child, creature, human being, individual, man, mortal, person, soul, wight (*archaic*), woman

Antonyms *adjective* (*sense 1*) animal, nonhuman (*sense 2*) beastly, brutish, cruel, inhuman, unsympathetic *~noun* animal, god, nonhuman

Drinking when we are not thirsty and making love all year round, madam; that is all there is to distinguish us from other animals

P-A.C. de Beaumarchais *The Marriage of Figaro*

humane benevolent, benign, charitable, clement, compassionate, forbearing, forgiving, gentle, good, good-natured, kind, kind-hearted, kindly, lenient, merciful, mild, sympathetic, tender, understanding

Antonyms barbarous, brutal, cruel, inhuman, inhumane, ruthless, uncivilized, unkind, unmerciful, unsympathetic

humanitarian **1.** *adjective* altruistic, beneficent, benevolent, charitable, compassionate, humane, philanthropic, public-spirited **2.** *noun* altruist, benefactor, Good Samaritan, philanthropist

humanitarianism beneficence, benevolence, charity, generosity, goodwill, humanism, philanthropy

humanities classical studies, classics, liberal arts, literae humaniores

humanity **1.** flesh, Homo sapiens, humankind, human race, man, mankind, men, mortality, people **2.** human nature, humanness, mortality **3.** benevolence, benignity, brotherly love, charity, compassion, fellow feeling, kind-heartedness, kindness, mercy, philanthropy, sympathy, tenderness, tolerance, understanding

Out of the crooked timber of humanity no straight thing can ever be made

Immanuel Kant *Idee zu einer allgemeinen Geschichte in welt bürgerlicher Absicht*

humanize civilize, cultivate, educate, enlighten, improve, mellow, polish, reclaim, refine, soften, tame

humble *adjective* **1.** meek, modest, self-effacing, submissive, unassuming, unostentatious, unpretentious **2.** common, commonplace, insignificant, low, low-born, lowly, mean, modest, obscure, ordinary, plebeian, poor, simple, undistinguished, unimportant, unpretentious **3.** courteous, deferential, obliging, obsequious, polite, respectful, servile, subservient *~verb* **4.** abase, abash, break, bring down, chagrin, chasten, crush, debase, degrade, demean, disgrace, humiliate, lower, mortify, put down (*slang*), put (someone) in their place, reduce, shame, sink, subdue, take down a peg (*informal*) **5.** **humble oneself** abase oneself, eat crow (*U.S. informal*), eat humble pie, go on bended knee, grovel, swallow one's pride

Antonyms *adjective* (*senses 1 & 3*) arrogant, assuming, conceited, haughty, immodest, lordly, ostentatious, overbearing, pompous, presumptuous, pretentious, proud, snobbish, superior, vain (*sense 2*) aristocratic, distinguished, elegant, famous, glorious, high, important, rich, significant, superior, wealthy *~verb* elevate, exalt, magnify, raise

humbly cap in hand, deferentially, diffidently, meekly, modestly, obsequiously, on bended knee, respectfully, servilely, submissively, subserviently, unassumingly

humbug *noun* **1.** bluff, canard, cheat, deceit, deception, dodge, feint, fraud, hoax, imposition, imposture, ruse, sham, swindle, trick, trickery, wile **2.** charlatan, cheat, con man (*informal*), faker, fraud, fraudster, grifter (*slang, chiefly U.S. & Canad.*), impostor, phoney *or* phony (*informal*), quack, swindler, trickster **3.** baloney (*informal*), cant, charlatanry, claptrap (*informal*), eyewash (*informal*), gammon (*Brit. informal*), hypocrisy, nonsense, quackery, rubbish, trash *~verb* **4.** bamboozle (*informal*), befool, beguile, cheat, con (*infor-*

mal), cozen, deceive, delude, dupe, fool, gull (*archaic*), hoax, hoodwink, impose, mislead, swindle, take in (*informal*), trick

humdrum banal, boring, commonplace, dreary, dull, ho-hum (*informal*), mind-numbing, monotonous, mundane, ordinary, repetitious, routine, tedious, tiresome, uneventful, uninteresting, unvaried, wearisome

Antonyms dramatic, entertaining, exciting, extraordinary, interesting, lively, sexy (*informal*), stimulating

humid clammy, damp, dank, moist, muggy, steamy, sticky, sultry, watery, wet

Antonyms arid, dry, sunny, torrid

humidity clamminess, damp, dampness, dankness, dew, humidness, moistness, moisture, mugginess, sogginess, wetness

humiliate abase, abash, bring low, chagrin, chasten, crush, debase, degrade, discomfit, disgrace, embarrass, humble, make (someone) eat humble pie, mortify, put down, put (someone) in their place, shame, subdue, take down a peg (*informal*), take the wind out of someone's sails

Antonyms elevate, honour, magnify, make proud

humiliating cringe-making (*Brit. informal*), crushing, degrading, disgracing, embarrassing, humbling, ignominious, mortifying, shaming

humiliation abasement, affront, chagrin, condescension, degradation, disgrace, dishonour, embarrassment, humbling, ignominy, indignity, loss of face, mortification, put-down, resignation, self-abasement, shame, submission, submissiveness

humility diffidence, humbleness, lack of pride, lowliness, meekness, modesty, self-abasement, servility, submissiveness, unpretentiousness

Antonyms arrogance, conceit, disdain, haughtiness, pomposity, presumption, pretentiousness, pride, snobbishness, superciliousness, superiority, vanity

Humility is the first of the virtues - for other people
Oliver Wendell Holmes *The Professor at the Breakfast Table*

One may be humble out of pride
Montaigne *Essais*

He that humbleth himself wishes to be exalted
Friedrich Nietzsche *Human, All Too Human*

The first test of a truly great man is his humility
John Ruskin *Modern Painters*

For whosoever exalteth himself shall be abased; and he that humbleth himself shall be exalted
Bible: St. Luke

hummock hillock, hump, knoll, mound

humorist card (*informal*), comedian, comic, eccentric, funny man, jester, joculator *or (fem.)* joculatrix, joker, wag, wit

humorous amusing, comic, comical, droll, entertaining, facetious, farcical, funny, hilarious, jocose, jocular, laughable, ludicrous, merry, playful, pleasant, side-splitting, waggish, whimsical, witty

Antonyms earnest, grave, sad, serious, sober, solemn

humour *noun* **1.** amusement, comedy, drollery, facetiousness, fun, funniness, jocularity, ludicrousness, wit **2.** comedy, farce, gags (*informal*), jesting, jests, jokes, joking, pleasantry, wisecracks (*informal*), wit, witticisms, wittiness **3.** disposition, frame of mind, mood, spirits, temper **4.** bent, bias, fancy, freak, mood, propensity, quirk, vagary, whim ~*verb* **5.** accommodate, cosset, favour, fawn on, feed, flatter, go along with, gratify, indulge, mollify, pamper, pander to, spoil

Antonyms *noun* gravity, grief, melancholy, sadness, seriousness, sobriety, solemnity, sorrow ~*verb* aggravate, excite, oppose, rouse, stand up to

Humour is falling downstairs if you do it while in the act of warning your wife not to
Kenneth Bird

Humour is the first of the gifts to perish in a foreign tongue
Virginia Woolf *On Not Knowing Greek*

Humour is emotional chaos remembered in tranquillity
James Thurber

humourless dour, dry, heavy-going, intense, po-faced, serious, solemn, straight, unamused, unamusing, unfunny, unsmiling

hump *noun* **1.** bulge, bump, hunch, knob, lump, mound, projection, protrusion, protuberance, swelling **2. the hump** *Brit. informal* megrims (*rare*), the blues, the doldrums, the dumps (*informal*), the grumps (*informal*), the mopes, the sulks ~*verb* **3.** arch, curve, form a hump, hunch, lift, tense **4.** *slang* carry, heave, hoist, lug, shoulder

hunch **1.** *noun* feeling, idea, impression, inkling, intuition, premonition, presentiment, suspicion **2.** *verb* arch, bend, crouch, curve, draw in, huddle, hump, squat, stoop, tense

hunchback crookback (*rare*), crouch-back (*archaic*), humpback, kyphosis (*Pathology*), Quasimodo

hunchbacked gibbous, humpbacked, humped, malformed, misshapen, stooped

hunger *noun* **1.** appetite, emptiness, esurience, famine, hungriness, ravenousness, starvation, voracity **2.** ache, appetence, appetite, craving, desire, greediness, itch, lust, thirst, yearning, yen (*informal*) ~*verb* **3.** ache, crave, desire, hanker, hope, itch, long, pine, starve, thirst, want, wish, yearn

There's no sauce in the world like hunger
Miguel de Cervantes *Don Quixote*
Hunger drives the wolf from the wood

hungry 1. empty, esurient, famished, famishing, hollow, peckish (*informal, chiefly Brit.*), ravenous, sharp-set, starved, starving, voracious 2. athirst, avid, covetous, craving, desirous, eager, greedy, keen, yearning

A hungry stomach has no ears
Jean de la Fontaine *The Kite and the Nightingale*

hunk block, chunk, gobbet, lump, mass, nugget, piece, slab, wedge, wodge (*Brit. informal*)

hunt *verb* 1. chase, gun for, hound, pursue, stalk, track, trail 2. ferret about, forage, go in quest of, look, look high and low, rummage through, scour, search, seek, try to find *~noun* 3. chase, hunting, investigation, pursuit, quest, search

hunted careworn, desperate, distraught, gaunt, haggard, harassed, harried, persecuted, stricken, terror-stricken, tormented, worn

hunter Artemis, Diana, huntsman *or (fem.)* huntress, jaeger (*rare*), Nimrod, Orion, pink, sportsman

hunting

The English country gentleman galloping after a fox - the unspeakable in full pursuit of the uneatable
Oscar Wilde

hurdle *noun* 1. barricade, barrier, block, fence, hedge, wall 2. barrier, block, complication, difficulty, handicap, hazard, hindrance, impediment, obstacle, obstruction, snag, stumbling block

hurl cast, chuck (*informal*), fire, fling, heave, launch, let fly, pitch, project, propel, send, shy, sling, throw, toss

hurly-burly bedlam, brouhaha, chaos, commotion, confusion, disorder, furore, hubbub, pandemonium, tumult, turbulence, turmoil, upheaval, uproar
Antonyms composure, order, organization, tidiness

hurricane cyclone, gale, storm, tempest, tornado, twister (*U.S. informal*), typhoon, willy-willy (*Austral.*), windstorm

hurried breakneck, brief, cursory, hasty, hectic, perfunctory, precipitate, quick, quickie (*informal*), rushed, short, slapdash, speedy, superficial, swift

hurriedly hastily, hurry-scurry, in a rush, perfunctorily, quickly

hurry *verb* 1. barrel (along) (*informal, chiefly U.S. & Canad.*), burn rubber (*informal*), dash, fly, get a move on (*informal*), get one's skates on (*informal*), lose no time, make haste, rush, scoot, scurry, step on it (*informal*) 2. accelerate, expedite, goad, hasten, hustle, push on, quicken, speed (up), urge *~noun* 3. bustle, celerity, commotion, dispatch, expedition, flurry, haste, precipitation, promptitude, quickness, rush, speed, urgency
Antonyms *verb* crawl, creep, dawdle, delay, drag one's feet, move slowly, retard, slow, slow down *~noun* calmness, slowness

hurt *verb* 1. bruise, damage, disable, harm, impair, injure, lay a finger on, mar, spoil, wound 2. ache, be sore, be tender, burn, pain, smart, sting, throb 3. afflict, aggrieve, annoy, cut to the quick, distress, grieve, pain, sadden, sting, upset, wound *~noun* 4. discomfort, distress, pain, pang, soreness, suffering 5. bruise, sore, wound 6. damage, detriment, disadvantage, harm, injury, loss, mischief, wrong *~adjective* 7. bruised, cut, damaged, grazed, harmed, injured, scarred, scraped, scratched, wounded 8. aggrieved, crushed, injured, miffed (*informal*), offended, pained, piqued, rueful, sad, wounded
Antonyms *verb* aid, alleviate, benefit, calm, compensate, compliment, console, cure, forward, heal, heighten, help, increase, please, relieve, repair, restore, soothe *~noun* delight, happiness, joy, pleasure, pride, satisfaction *~adjective* alleviated, assuaged, calmed, consoled, healed, placated, relieved, repaired, restored, soothed

hurtful cruel, cutting, damaging, destructive, detrimental, disadvantageous, distressing, harmful, injurious, maleficent, malicious, mean, mischievous, nasty, pernicious, prejudicial, spiteful, unkind, upsetting, wounding

hurtle barrel (along) (*informal, chiefly U.S. & Canad.*), burn rubber (*informal*), charge, crash, fly, go hell for leather (*informal*), plunge, race, rush, rush headlong, scoot, scramble, shoot, speed, spurt, stampede, tear

husband[1] *verb* budget, conserve, economize, hoard, manage thriftily, save, store, use sparingly
Antonyms be extravagant, fritter away, spend, splash out (*informal, chiefly Brit.*), squander

husband[2]

A husband is what is left of the lover after the nerve has been extracted
Helen Rowland

The majority of husbands remind me of an orang-utang trying to play the violin
Honoré de Balzac *The Physiology of Marriage*

A good husband should be deaf and a good wife blind
French proverb

husbandry 1. agriculture, agronomy, cultivation, farming, land management, tillage 2. careful management, economy, frugality, good housekeeping, thrift

hush *verb* 1. mute, muzzle, quieten, shush, silence, still, suppress 2. allay, appease, calm, compose, mollify, soothe *~noun* 3. calm, peace, peacefulness, quiet, silence, still (*poetic*), stillness, tranquillity

hush-hush classified, confidential, restricted, secret, top-secret, under wraps

hush up conceal, cover up, draw a veil over, keep dark, keep secret, sit on (*informal*), smother, squash, suppress, sweep under the carpet (*informal*)

husk bark, chaff, covering, glume, hull, rind, shuck

huskiness dryness, harshness, hoarseness, raspingness, roughness

husky 1. croaking, croaky, gruff, guttural, harsh, hoarse, rasping, raucous, rough, throaty 2. *informal* beefy (*informal*), brawny, burly, hefty, muscular, powerful, rugged, stocky, strapping, thickset

hussy baggage (*informal, old-fashioned*), floozy (*slang*), jade, minx, quean (*archaic*), scrubber (*Brit. & Austral. slang*), slut, strumpet, tart (*informal*), tramp (*slang*), trollop, wanton, wench (*archaic*)

hustle bustle, crowd, elbow, force, haste, hasten, hurry, impel, jog, jostle, push, rush, shove, thrust

hut cabin, den, hovel, lean-to, refuge, shanty, shed, shelter

hybrid *noun* amalgam, composite, compound, cross, crossbreed, half-blood, half-breed, mixture, mongrel, mule

hygiene cleanliness, hygienics, sanitary measures, sanitation

hygienic aseptic, clean, disinfected, germ-free, healthy, pure, salutary, sanitary, sterile
Antonyms dirty, filthy, germ-ridden, harmful, insanitary, polluted, unhealthy, unhygienic, unwholesome

hymn anthem, canticle, carol, chant, doxology, paean, psalm, song of praise

hype ballyhoo (*informal*), brouhaha, build-up, plugging (*informal*), promotion, publicity, puffing, racket, razzmatazz (*slang*)

hyperbole amplification, enlargement, exaggeration, magnification, overstatement

hypercritical captious, carping, cavilling, censorious, fault-finding, finicky, fussy, hair-splitting, niggling, overcritical, overexacting, overscrupulous, pernickety (*informal*), strict

hypnotic mesmeric, mesmerizing, narcotic, opiate, sleep-inducing, somniferous, soothing, soporific, spellbinding

hypnotize 1. mesmerize, put in a trance, put to sleep 2. absorb, entrance, fascinate, magnetize, spellbind

hypochondria hypochondriasis, valetudinarianism

hypochondriac *adjective/noun* valetudinarian

hypocrisy cant, deceit, deceitfulness, deception, dissembling, duplicity, falsity, imposture, insincerity, pharisaism, phariseeism, phoneyness *or* phoniness (*informal*), pretence, sanctimoniousness, speciousness, two-facedness
Antonyms honesty, sincerity, truthfulness

Hypocrisy is a tribute which vice pays to virtue
Duc de la Rochefoucauld *Réflexions ou Sentences et Maximes Morales*

I hope you have not been leading a double life, pretending to be wicked and being really good all the time. That would be hypocrisy
Oscar Wilde *The Importance of Being Earnest*

Why beholdest thou the mote that is in thy brother's eye, but considerest not the beam that is in thine own eye?
Bible: St. Matthew

hypocrisy, the only evil that walks
Invisible, except to God alone
John Milton *Paradise Lost*

hypocrite charlatan, deceiver, dissembler, fraud, Holy Willie, impostor, Pecksniff, pharisee, phoney *or* phony (*informal*), pretender, Tartuffe, whited sepulchre

No man is a hypocrite in his pleasures
Dr. Johnson

Ye are like unto whited sepulchres
Bible: St. Matthew

Their sighan', cantan', grace-proud faces,
Their three-mile prayers, and half-mile graces
Robert Burns *To the Rev. John M'Math*

hypocritical canting, deceitful, deceptive, dissembling, duplicitous, false, fraudulent, hollow, insincere, Janus-faced, pharisaical, phoney *or* phony (*informal*), sanctimonious, specious, spurious, two-faced

hypodermic needle, syringe

hypothesis assumption, postulate, premise, premiss, proposition, supposition, theory, thesis

It is a good morning exercise for a research scientist to discard a pet hypothesis every day before breakfast
Konrad Lorenz *On Aggression*

hypothetical academic, assumed, conjectural, imaginary, putative, speculative, supposed, theoretical
Antonyms actual, confirmed, established, known, proven, real, true

hysteria agitation, delirium, frenzy, hysterics, madness, panic, unreason

hysterical 1. berserk, beside oneself, convulsive, crazed, distracted, distraught, frantic, frenzied, mad, overwrought, raving, uncontrollable 2. *informal* comical, farcical, hilari~

ous, screaming, side-splitting, uproarious, wildly funny
Antonyms calm, composed, grave, melancholy, poised, sad, self-possessed, serious, unfazed (*informal*)

I

ice 1. **break the ice** begin, initiate the proceedings, kick off (*informal*), lead the way, make a start, start *or* set the ball rolling (*informal*), take the plunge (*informal*) 2. **on thin ice** at risk, in jeopardy, open to attack, out on a limb, sticking one's neck out (*informal*), unsafe, vulnerable

ice-cold arctic, biting, bitter, chilled to the bone *or* marrow, freezing, frozen, glacial, icy, raw, refrigerated, shivering

iconoclast critic, dissident, heretic, radical, rebel

iconoclastic denunciatory, dissentient, impious, innovative, irreverent, questioning, radical, rebellious, subversive

icy 1. arctic, biting, bitter, chill, chilling, chilly, cold, freezing, frost-bound, frosty, frozen over, ice-cold, parky (*Brit. informal*), raw 2. glacial, glassy, like a sheet of glass, rimy, slippery, slippy (*informal or dialect*) 3. *figurative* aloof, cold, distant, forbidding, frigid, frosty, glacial, hostile, indifferent, steely, stony, unfriendly, unwelcoming
Antonyms (*sense 1*) blistering, boiling, hot, sizzling, warm (*sense 3*) cordial, friendly, gracious, warm

idea 1. abstraction, concept, conception, conclusion, fancy, impression, judgment, perception, thought, understanding 2. belief, conviction, doctrine, interpretation, notion, opinion, teaching, view, viewpoint 3. approximation, ballpark figure, clue, estimate, guess, hint, impression, inkling, intimation, notion, suspicion 4. aim, end, import, intention, meaning, object, objective, plan, purpose, *raison d'être*, reason, sense, significance 5. design, hypothesis, plan, recommendation, scheme, solution, suggestion, theory 6. archetype, essence, form, pattern

Nothing is more dangerous than an idea, when you have only one idea
Alain *Propos sur la religion*

no army can withstand the strength of an idea whose time has come
Victor Hugo

It is better to entertain an idea than to take it home to live with you for the rest of your life
Randall Jarrell *Pictures from an Institution*

ideal *noun* 1. archetype, criterion, epitome, example, exemplar, last word, model, nonpareil, paradigm, paragon, pattern, perfection, prototype, standard, standard of perfection 2. *often plural* moral value, principle, standard *~adjective* 3. archetypal, classic, complete, consummate, model, optimal, perfect, quintessential, supreme 4. abstract, conceptual, hypothetical, intellectual, mental, notional, theoretical, transcendental 5. fanciful, imagal (*Psychoanalysis*), imaginary, impractical, ivory-tower, unattainable, unreal, Utopian, visionary
Antonyms *adjective* (*sense 3*) deficient, flawed, impaired, imperfect, unsuitable (*sense 5*) actual, factual, literal, mundane, ordinary, real

idealist *noun* dreamer, romantic, Utopian, visionary

idealistic impracticable, optimistic, perfectionist, quixotic, romantic, starry-eyed, Utopian, visionary
Antonyms down-to-earth, practical, pragmatic, realistic, sensible

idealization ennoblement, exaltation, glorification, magnification, worship

idealize apotheosize, deify, ennoble, exalt, glorify, magnify, put on a pedestal, romanticize, worship

ideally all things being equal, if one had one's way, in a perfect world, under the best of circumstances

idée fixe bee in one's bonnet, fixation, fixed idea, hobbyhorse, monomania, obsession, one-track mind (*informal*), preoccupation, thing (*informal*)

identical a dead ringer (*slang*), alike, corresponding, duplicate, equal, equivalent, indistinguishable, interchangeable, like, like two peas in a pod, matching, selfsame, the dead spit (*informal*), the same, twin
Antonyms different, disparate, distinct, diverse, separate, unlike

Two things are identical if one can be substituted for the other without affecting the truth
Gottfried Wilhelm Leibniz *Table de définitions*

identifiable ascertainable, detectable, discernible, distinguishable, known, noticeable, recognizable, unmistakable

identification 1. cataloguing, classifying, establishment of identity, labelling, naming, pinpointing, recognition 2. association, connection, empathy, fellow feeling, involvement, rapport, relationship, sympathy 3. credentials, ID, identity card, letters of introduction, papers

identify 1. catalogue, classify, diagnose, flag, label, make out, name, pick out, pinpoint, place, put one's finger on (*informal*), recognize, single out, spot, tag 2. *often with* **with** ally, associate, empathize, feel for, put in the same category, put oneself in the place *or* shoes of, relate to, respond to, see through another's eyes, think of in connection (with)

identity 1. distinctiveness, existence, individuality, oneness, particularity, personality, self, selfhood, singularity, uniqueness 2. accord, correspondence, empathy, rapport, sameness, unanimity, unity

ideology articles of faith, belief(s), creed, dogma, ideas, philosophy, principles, tenets, *Weltanschauung*, world view

idiocy abject stupidity, asininity, cretinism, fatuity, fatuousness, foolishness, imbecility, inanity, insanity, lunacy, senselessness, tomfoolery
Antonyms acumen, sagacity, sanity, sense, soundness, wisdom

idiom 1. expression, locution, phrase, set phrase, turn of phrase 2. jargon, language, mode of expression, parlance, style, talk, usage, vernacular

idiomatic dialectal, native, vernacular

idiosyncrasy affectation, characteristic, eccentricity, habit, mannerism, oddity, peculiarity, personal trait, quirk, singularity, trick

idiosyncratic distinctive, individual, individualistic, peculiar

idiot airhead (*slang*), ass, berk (*Brit. slang*), blockhead, booby, charlie (*Brit. informal*), coot, cretin, dickhead (*slang*), dickwit (*slang*), dimwit (*informal*), dipstick (*Brit. slang*), divvy (*Brit. slang*), dork (*slang*), dunderhead, dweeb (*U.S. slang*), fool, fuckwit (*taboo slang*), geek (*slang*), gobshite (*Irish taboo slang*), gonzo (*slang*), halfwit, imbecile, jerk (*slang, chiefly U.S. & Canad.*), lamebrain (*informal*), mooncalf, moron, nerd *or* nurd (*slang*), nincompoop, nitwit (*informal*), numpty (*Scot. informal*), numskull *or* numbskull, oaf, pillock (*Brit. slang*), plank (*Brit. slang*), plonker (*slang*), prat (*slang*), prick (*slang*), schmuck (*U.S. slang*), simpleton, twit (*informal, chiefly Brit.*), wally (*slang*)

idiotic asinine, braindead (*informal*), crackpot (*informal*), crazy, daft (*informal*), dumb (*informal*), fatuous, foolhardy, foolish, halfwitted, harebrained, imbecile, imbecilic, inane, insane, loopy (*informal*), lunatic, moronic, senseless, stupid, unintelligent
Antonyms brilliant, commonsensical, intelligent, sensible, thoughtful, wise

idle *adjective* 1. dead, empty, gathering dust, inactive, jobless, mothballed, out of action *or* operation, out of work, redundant, stationary, ticking over, unemployed, unoccupied, unused, vacant 2. good-for-nothing, indolent, lackadaisical, lazy, shiftless, slothful, sluggish 3. frivolous, insignificant, irrelevant, nugatory, superficial, trivial, unhelpful, unnecessary 4. abortive, bootless, fruitless, futile, groundless, ineffective, of no avail, otiose, pointless, unavailing, unproductive, unsuccessful, useless, vain, worthless ~*verb* 5. *often with* **away** dally, dawdle, fool, fritter, hang out (*informal*), kill time, laze, loaf, loiter, lounge, potter, waste, while 6. bob off (*Brit. slang*), coast, drift, mark time, shirk, sit back and do nothing, skive (*Brit. slang*), slack, slow down, take it easy, vegetate, veg out (*slang*)
Antonyms (*senses 1 & 2*) active, busy, employed, energetic, functional, industrious, occupied, operative, working (*sense 3*) important, meaningful (*sense 4*) advantageous, effective, fruitful, profitable, useful, worthwhile

As idle as a painted ship
Upon a painted ocean
Samuel Taylor Coleridge *The Ancient Mariner*

It is impossible to enjoy idling thoroughly unless
one has plenty of work to do
Jerome K. Jerome *Idle Thoughts of an Idle Fellow*

Satan finds some mischief still
For idle hands to do
Isaac Watts *Divine Songs for Children*

We would all be idle if we could
Dr. Johnson

idleness 1. inaction, inactivity, leisure, time on one's hands, unemployment 2. hibernation, inertia, laziness, shiftlessness, sloth, sluggishness, torpor, vegetating 3. dilly-dallying (*informal*), lazing, loafing, pottering, skiving (*Brit. slang*), time-wasting, trifling

Idleness is the only refuge of weak minds
Lord Chesterfield *Letters to his Son*

idler clock-watcher, couch potato (*slang*), dawdler, deadbeat (*informal, chiefly U.S. & Canad.*), dodger, drone, laggard, layabout, lazybones, loafer, lounger, malingerer, shirker, skiver (*Brit. slang*), slacker, sloth, slouch (*informal*), slugabed, sluggard, time-waster, Weary Willie (*informal*)

idling *adjective* dawdling, drifting, loafing, pottering, resting, resting on one's oars, taking it easy, ticking over

idly apathetically, casually, inactively, indolently, inertly, lackadaisically, languidly, languorously, lazily, lethargically, passively,

shiftlessly, slothfully, sluggishly, unthinkingly
Antonyms actively, animatedly, busily, dy~namically, energetically, industriously

idol 1. deity, god, graven image, image, pagan symbol 2. *figurative* beloved, darling, favour~ite, hero, pet, pin-up (*slang*), superstar

idolater 1. heathen, idol-worshipper, pagan 2. admirer, adorer, devotee, idolizer, votary, worshipper

idolatrous adoring, adulatory, reverential, un~critical, worshipful

idolatry adoration, adulation, apotheosis, deifi~cation, exaltation, glorification, hero worship, idolizing

idolize admire, adore, apotheosize, bow down before, deify, dote upon, exalt, glorify, hero-worship, look up to, love, revere, reverence, venerate, worship, worship to excess

idyllic arcadian, charming, halcyon, heavenly, ideal, idealized, out of this world, pastoral, peaceful, picturesque, rustic, unspoiled

if 1. *conjunction* admitting, allowing, assuming, granting, in case, on condition that, on the assumption that, provided, providing, suppos~ing, though, whenever, wherever, whether 2. *noun* condition, doubt, hesitation, stipulation, uncertainty

If ifs and ands were pots and pans there'd be no need for tinkers

iffy chancy (*informal*), conditional, doubtful, in the lap of the gods, problematical, uncertain, undecided, unpredictable, up in the air

ignis fatuus bubble, chimera, delusion, illu~sion, mirage, phantasm, self-deception, will-o'-the-wisp

ignite burn, burst into flames, catch fire, fire, flare up, inflame, kindle, light, put a match to (*informal*), set alight, set fire to, take fire, torch, touch off

ignoble 1. abject, base, contemptible, craven, dastardly, degenerate, degraded, despicable, disgraceful, dishonourable, heinous, infamous, low, mean, petty, shabby, shameless, unwor~thy, vile, wretched 2. baseborn (*archaic*), com~mon, humble, lowborn (*rare*), lowly, mean, of humble birth, peasant, plebeian, vulgar

ignominious abject, despicable, discreditable, disgraceful, dishonourable, disreputable, hu~miliating, indecorous, inglorious, mortifying, scandalous, shameful, sorry, undignified
Antonyms creditable, honourable, reputable, worthy

ignominy bad odour, contempt, discredit, dis~grace, dishonour, disrepute, humiliation, infa~my, mortification, obloquy, odium, oppro~brium, reproach, shame, stigma
Antonyms credit, honour, repute

ignoramus ass, blockhead, bonehead (*slang*), dolt, donkey, duffer (*informal*), dullard, dunce, fathead (*informal*), fool, illiterate, lowbrow, numpty (*Scot. informal*), numskull *or* numb~skull, simpleton

ignorance 1. greenness, inexperience, inno~cence, nescience (*literary*), oblivion, unaware~ness, unconsciousness, unfamiliarity 2. be~nightedness, blindness, illiteracy, lack of edu~cation, mental darkness, unenlightenment, unintelligence
Antonyms (*sense 2*) comprehension, enlight~enment, insight, intelligence, knowledge, understanding, wisdom

No more; where ignorance is bliss,
'Tis folly to be wise
Thomas Gray *Ode on a Distant Prospect of Eton College*

We live and learn, but not the wiser grow
John Pomfret *Reason*

To be conscious that you are ignorant is a great step to knowledge
Benjamin Disraeli *Sybil*

Nothing in all the world is more dangerous than sincere ignorance and conscientious stupidity
Martin Luther King *Strength to Love*

If ignorance is indeed bliss, it is a very low grade of the article
Tehyi Hsieh *Chinese Epigrams Inside Out and Proverbs*

Ignorance is not bliss - it is oblivion
Philip Wylie *Generation of Vipers*

Ignorance is not innocence but sin
Robert Browning *The Inn Album*

I know nothing except the fact of my ignorance
Socrates

If you think education is expensive - try igno~rance
Derek Bok

One half of the world does not know how the other half lives

ignorant 1. benighted, blind to, inexperienced, innocent, in the dark about, oblivious, un~aware, unconscious, unenlightened, unin~formed, uninitiated, unknowing, unschooled, unwitting 2. as green as grass, green, illiter~ate, naive, unaware, uncultivated, uneducat~ed, unknowledgeable, unlearned, unlettered, unread, untaught, untrained, untutored, wet behind the ears (*informal*) 3. crass, crude, gross, half-baked (*informal*), insensitive, rude, shallow, superficial, uncomprehending, un~scholarly
Antonyms astute, aware, brilliant, conscious, cultured, educated, informed, knowledgeable, learned, literate, sagacious, sophisticated, wise

ignore be oblivious to, bury one's head in the sand, cold-shoulder, cut (*informal*), discount, disregard, give the cold shoulder to, neglect, overlook, pass over, pay no attention to, re~

ject, send (someone) to Coventry, shut one's eyes to, take no notice of, turn a blind eye to, turn a deaf ear to, turn one's back on
Antonyms acknowledge, heed, note, pay attention to, recognize, regard

ilk brand, breed, character, class, description, disposition, kidney, kind, sort, stamp, style, type, variety

ill *adjective* **1.** ailing, at death's door, dicky (*Brit. informal*), diseased, funny (*informal*), green about the gills, indisposed, infirm, laid up (*informal*), not up to snuff (*informal*), off-colour, on the sick list (*informal*), out of sorts (*informal*), poorly (*informal*), queasy, queer, seedy (*informal*), sick, under the weather (*informal*), unhealthy, unwell, valetudinarian **2.** bad, damaging, deleterious, detrimental, evil, foul, harmful, iniquitous, injurious, ruinous, unfortunate, unlucky, vile, wicked, wrong **3.** acrimonious, adverse, antagonistic, cantankerous, cross, harsh, hateful, hostile, hurtful, inimical, malevolent, malicious, sullen, surly, unfriendly, unkind **4.** bodeful, disturbing, foreboding, inauspicious, ominous, sinister, threatening, unfavourable, unhealthy, unlucky, unpromising, unpropitious, unwholesome *~noun* **5.** affliction, hardship, harm, hurt, injury, misery, misfortune, pain, trial, tribulation, trouble, unpleasantness, woe **6.** ailment, complaint, disease, disorder, illness, indisposition, infirmity, malady, malaise, sickness **7.** abuse, badness, cruelty, damage, depravity, destruction, evil, ill usage, malice, mischief, suffering, wickedness *~adverb* **8.** badly, hard, inauspiciously, poorly, unfavourably, unfortunately, unluckily **9.** barely, by no means, hardly, insufficiently, scantily **10.** *As in* **ill-gotten** criminally, dishonestly, foully, fraudulently, illegally, illegitimately, illicitly, unlawfully, unscrupulously
Antonyms *adjective* (*sense 1*) hale, healthy, strong, well (*sense 2*) favourable, good (*sense 3*) generous, kind *~noun* good, honour, kindness *~adverb* easily, well

ill-advised foolhardy, foolish, ill-considered, ill-judged, impolitic, imprudent, inappropriate, incautious, indiscreet, injudicious, misguided, overhasty, rash, reckless, short-sighted, thoughtless, unseemly, unwise, wrong-headed
Antonyms appropriate, cautious, discreet, judicious, politic, prudent, seemly, sensible, wise

ill-assorted incompatible, incongruous, inharmonious, mismatched, uncongenial, unsuited

ill at ease anxious, awkward, disquieted, disturbed, edgy, faltering, fidgety, hesitant, like a fish out of water, nervous, neurotic, on edge, on pins and needles (*informal*), on tenterhooks, out of place, restless, self-conscious, strange, tense, twitchy (*informal*), uncomfortable, uneasy, unquiet, unrelaxed, unsettled, unsure, wired (*slang*)
Antonyms at ease, at home, comfortable, easy, quiet, relaxed, settled, sure

ill-bred bad-mannered, boorish, churlish, coarse, crass, discourteous, ill-mannered, impolite, indelicate, rude, uncivil, uncivilized, uncouth, ungallant, ungentlemanly, unladylike, unmannerly, unrefined, vulgar
Antonyms civil, courteous, delicate, mannerly, refined, urbane, well-bred

ill-considered careless, hasty, heedless, improvident, imprudent, injudicious, overhasty, precipitate, rash, unwise

ill-defined blurred, dim, fuzzy, indistinct, nebulous, shadowy, unclear, vague, woolly
Antonyms apparent, bold, clear, conspicuous, cut-and-dried, distinct, evident, manifest, obvious, plain

ill-disposed against, antagonistic, anti (*informal*), antipathetic, averse, disobliging, down on (*informal*), hostile, inimical, opposed, uncooperative, unfriendly, unwelcoming
Antonyms cooperative, friendly, obliging, welcoming, well-disposed

illegal actionable (*Law*), banned, black-market, bootleg, criminal, felonious, forbidden, illicit, lawless, off limits, outlawed, prohibited, proscribed, unauthorized, unconstitutional, under-the-counter, under-the-table, unlawful, unlicensed, unofficial, wrongful
Antonyms lawful, legal, licit, permissible

illegality crime, criminality, felony, illegitimacy, illicitness, lawlessness, unlawfulness, wrong, wrongness

illegible crabbed, faint, hard to make out, hieroglyphic, indecipherable, obscure, scrawled, undecipherable, unreadable
Antonyms clear, decipherable, legible, plain, readable

illegitimacy **1.** illegality, illicitness, irregularity, unconstitutionality, unlawfulness **2.** bastardism, bastardy

illegitimate **1.** illegal, illicit, improper, unauthorized, unconstitutional, under-the-table, unlawful, unsanctioned **2.** baseborn (*archaic*), bastard, born on the wrong side of the blanket, born out of wedlock, fatherless, misbegotten (*literary*), natural, spurious (*rare*) **3.** illogical, incorrect, invalid, spurious, unsound
Antonyms (*sense 1*) authorized, constitutional, lawful, legal, legitimate, proper, sanctioned

there are no illegitimate children - only illegitimate parents

Judge Léon R. Yankwich

ill-fated blighted, doomed, hapless, ill-omened, ill-starred, luckless, star-crossed, unfortunate, unhappy, unlucky

ill-favoured hideous, no oil painting (*informal*),

plain, repulsive, ugly, unattractive, unlovely, unprepossessing, unsightly

ill feeling animosity, animus, antagonism, bad blood, bitterness, chip on one's shoulder, disgruntlement, dissatisfaction, dudgeon (*archaic*), enmity, frustration, hard feelings, hostility, ill will, indignation, offence, rancour, resentment
Antonyms amity, benevolence, favour, friendship, goodwill, satisfaction

ill-founded baseless, empty, groundless, idle, unjustified, unproven, unreliable, unsubstantiated, unsupported

ill humour (bad) mood, (bad) temper, bate (*Brit. slang*), crabbiness, crossness, disagreeableness, grumpiness, irascibility, irritability, moodiness, moroseness, petulance, pique, sharpness, spleen, sulkiness, sulks, tartness, testiness

ill-humoured acrimonious, bad-tempered, crabbed, crabby, cross, disagreeable, grumpy, huffy, impatient, irascible, irritable, like a bear with a sore head (*informal*), liverish, mardy (*dialect*), moody, morose, out of sorts, out of temper, petulant, ratty (*Brit. & N.Z. informal*), sharp, snappish, snappy, sulky, sullen, tart, testy, tetchy, thin-skinned, touchy, waspish
Antonyms affable, agreeable, amiable, charming, congenial, delightful, genial, good-humoured, good-natured, pleasant

illiberal **1.** bigoted, hidebound, intolerant, narrow-minded, prejudiced, reactionary, small-minded, uncharitable, ungenerous **2.** close-fisted, mean, miserly, niggardly, parsimonious, selfish, sordid, stingy, tight, tight-arsed (*taboo slang*), tight as a duck's arse (*taboo slang*), tight-assed (*U.S. taboo slang*), tightfisted, ungenerous
Antonyms (*sense 1*) broad-minded, charitable, generous, liberal, open-minded, politically correct *or* PC, right-on (*informal*), tolerant

illicit **1.** black-market, bootleg, contraband, criminal, felonious, illegal, illegitimate, off limits, prohibited, unauthorized, unlawful, unlicensed **2.** clandestine, forbidden, furtive, guilty, immoral, improper, wrong
Antonyms above-board, lawful, legal, legitimate, licit, permissible, proper

illimitable boundless, eternal, immeasurable, immense, infinite, limitless, unbounded, unending, unlimited, vast, without end

illiteracy benightedness, ignorance, illiterateness, lack of education

illiterate benighted, ignorant, uncultured, uneducated, unlettered, untaught, untutored
Antonyms cultured, educated, lettered, literate, taught, tutored

ill-judged foolish, ill-advised, ill-considered, injudicious, misguided, overhasty, rash, short-sighted, unwise, wrong-headed

ill-mannered badly behaved, boorish, churlish, coarse, discourteous, ill-behaved, ill-bred, impolite, insolent, loutish, rude, uncivil, uncouth, unmannerly
Antonyms civil, courteous, cultivated, mannerly, polished, polite, refined, well-mannered

ill-natured bad-tempered, catty (*informal*), churlish, crabbed, cross, cross-grained, disagreeable, disobliging, malevolent, malicious, mean, nasty, perverse, petulant, shrewish, spiteful, sulky, sullen, surly, unfriendly, unkind, unpleasant
Antonyms agreeable, amiable, cheerful, congenial, friendly, good-natured, kind, obliging, pleasant

illness affliction, ailment, attack, complaint, disability, disease, disorder, ill health, indisposition, infirmity, lurgi (*informal*), malady, malaise, poor health, sickness

illogical absurd, fallacious, faulty, inconclusive, inconsistent, incorrect, invalid, irrational, meaningless, senseless, sophistical, specious, spurious, unreasonable, unscientific, unsound
Antonyms coherent, consistent, correct, logical, rational, reasonable, scientific, sound, valid

ill-starred doomed, ill-fated, ill-omened, inauspicious, star-crossed, unfortunate, unhappy, unlucky

ill temper annoyance, bad temper, crossness, curtness, impatience, irascibility, irritability, petulance, sharpness, spitefulness, tetchiness

ill-tempered annoyed, bad-tempered, choleric, cross, curt, grumpy, ill-humoured, impatient, irascible, irritable, liverish, ratty (*Brit. & N.Z. informal*), sharp, spiteful, testy, tetchy, touchy
Antonyms benign, cheerful, good-natured, mild-mannered, patient, pleasant, sweet-tempered

ill-timed awkward, inappropriate, inconvenient, inept, inopportune, unseasonable, untimely, unwelcome
Antonyms appropriate, convenient, opportune, seasonable, timely, well-timed

ill-treat abuse, damage, dump on (*slang, chiefly U.S.*), handle roughly, harass, harm, harry, ill-use, injure, knock about *or* around, maltreat, mishandle, misuse, oppress, shit on (*taboo slang*), wrong

ill-treatment abuse, damage, harm, ill-use, injury, mistreatment, misuse, rough handling

illuminate **1.** brighten, illumine (*literary*), irradiate, light, light up **2.** clarify, clear up, elucidate, enlighten, explain, explicate, give insight into, instruct, interpret, make clear, shed light on **3.** adorn, decorate, illustrate, ornament

Antonyms (*sense 1*) black out, darken, dim, obscure, overshadow (*sense 2*) befog, cloud, dull, obfuscate, overcast, shade, veil

illuminating enlightening, explanatory, helpful, informative, instructive, revealing
Antonyms confusing, obscuring, puzzling, unhelpful

illumination 1. beam, brightening, brightness, light, lighting, lighting up, lights, radiance, ray 2. awareness, clarification, edification, enlightenment, insight, inspiration, instruction, perception, revelation, understanding

illuminations decorations, fairy lights, lights

illusion 1. chimera, daydream, fantasy, figment of the imagination, hallucination, ignis fatuus, mirage, mockery, phantasm, semblance, will-o'-the-wisp 2. deception, delusion, error, fallacy, false impression, fancy, misapprehension, misconception
Antonyms actuality, reality, truth

illusory *or* **illusive** apparent, Barmecide, beguiling, chimerical, deceitful, deceptive, delusive, fallacious, false, hallucinatory, misleading, mistaken, seeming, sham, unreal, untrue
Antonyms authentic, down-to-earth, factual, genuine, real, reliable, solid, true

illustrate 1. bring home, clarify, demonstrate, elucidate, emphasize, exemplify, exhibit, explain, explicate, instance, interpret, make clear, make plain, point up, show 2. adorn, decorate, depict, draw, ornament, picture, sketch

illustrated decorated, embellished, graphic, illuminated, pictorial, picture, pictured, with illustrations

illustration 1. analogy, case, case in point, clarification, demonstration, elucidation, example, exemplification, explanation, instance, interpretation, specimen 2. adornment, decoration, figure, picture, plate, sketch

illustrative delineative, descriptive, diagrammatic, explanatory, explicatory, expository, graphic, illustrational, interpretive, pictorial, representative, sample, typical

illustrious brilliant, celebrated, distinguished, eminent, exalted, famed, famous, glorious, great, noble, notable, noted, prominent, remarkable, renowned, resplendent, signal, splendid
Antonyms humble, ignoble, infamous, lowly, meek, notorious, obscure, unassuming

ill will acrimony, animosity, animus, antagonism, antipathy, aversion, bad blood, dislike, enmity, envy, grudge, hard feelings, hatred, hostility, malevolence, malice, no love lost, rancour, resentment, spite, unfriendliness, venom
Antonyms amiability, amity, charity, congeniality, cordiality, friendship, goodwill

image 1. appearance, effigy, figure, icon, idol, likeness, picture, portrait, reflection, representation, statue 2. chip off the old block (*informal*), counterpart, (dead) ringer (*slang*), Doppelgänger, double, facsimile, replica, similitude, spit (*informal, chiefly Brit.*), spitting image *or* spit and image (*informal*) 3. conceit, concept, conception, figure, idea, impression, mental picture, perception, trope

imaginable believable, comprehensible, conceivable, credible, likely, plausible, possible, supposable, thinkable, under the sun, within the bounds of possibility
Antonyms impossible, incomprehensible, inconceivable, incredible, unbelievable, unimaginable, unlikely, unthinkable

imaginary assumed, chimerical, dreamlike, fancied, fanciful, fictional, fictitious, hallucinatory, hypothetical, ideal, illusive, illusory, imagal (*Psychoanal.*), imagined, invented, legendary, made-up, mythological, nonexistent, phantasmal, shadowy, supposed, suppositious, supposititious, unreal, unsubstantial, visionary
Antonyms actual, factual, genuine, known, proven, real, substantial, tangible, true

imagination 1. creativity, enterprise, fancy, ingenuity, insight, inspiration, invention, inventiveness, originality, resourcefulness, vision, wit, wittiness 2. chimera, conception, idea, ideality, illusion, image, invention, notion, supposition, unreality

People can die of mere imagination
Geoffrey Chaucer *The Miller's Tale*

I imagine, therefore I belong and am free
Lawrence Durrell *Justine*

I have imagination, and nothing that is real is alien to me
George Santayana *Little Essays*

Imagination, that dost so abstract us
That we are not aware, not even when
A thousand trumpets sound about our ears!
Dante *Divine Comedy*

Where there is no imagination there is no horror
Sir Arthur Conan Doyle *A Study in Scarlet*

His imagination resembled the wings of an ostrich.
It enabled him to run, though not to soar
Lord Macaulay *Miscellaneous Writings*

imaginative clever, creative, dreamy, enterprising, fanciful, fantastic, ingenious, inspired, inventive, original, poetical, visionary, vivid, whimsical
Antonyms literal, mundane, ordinary, uncreative, unimaginative, uninspired, unoriginal, unpoetical, unromantic

imagine 1. conceive, conceptualize, conjure up, create, devise, dream up (*informal*), envisage, fantasize, form a mental picture of, frame, invent, picture, plan, project, scheme, see in the mind's eye, think of, think up, visualize **2.** apprehend, assume, believe, conjecture, deduce, deem, fancy, gather, guess (*informal, chiefly U.S. & Canad.*), infer, realize, suppose, surmise, suspect, take for granted, take it, think

imbalance bias, disproportion, inequality, lack of proportion, lopsidedness, partiality, top-heaviness, unevenness, unfairness

imbecile 1. *noun* berk (*Brit. slang*), bungler, charlie (*Brit. informal*), coot, cretin, dickhead (*slang*), dickwit (*slang*), dipstick (*Brit. slang*), divvy (*Brit. slang*), dolt, dork (*slang*), dotard, dweeb (*U.S. slang*), fool, fuckwit (*taboo slang*), geek (*slang*), gobshite (*Irish taboo slang*), gonzo (*slang*), halfwit, idiot, jerk (*slang, chiefly U.S. & Canad.*), moron, nerd *or* nurd (*slang*), numpty (*Scot. informal*), numskull *or* numbskull, pillock (*Brit. slang*), plank (*Brit. slang*), plonker (*slang*), prat (*slang*), prick (*slang*), schmuck (*U.S. slang*), thickhead, tosser (*Brit. slang*), twit (*informal, chiefly Brit.*), wally (*slang*) **2.** *adjective* asinine, braindead (*informal*), dead from the neck up, fatuous, feeble-minded, foolish, idiotic, imbecilic, inane, ludicrous, moronic, simple, stupid, thick, witless

imbecility asininity, childishness, cretinism, fatuity, foolishness, idiocy, inanity, incompetency, stupidity

Antonyms comprehension, intelligence, perspicacity, reasonableness, sagacity, sense, soundness, wisdom

imbibe 1. consume, drink, knock back (*informal*), quaff, sink (*informal*), suck, swallow, swig (*informal*) **2.** *literary* absorb, acquire, assimilate, gain, gather, ingest, receive, take in

imbroglio complexity, complication, embarrassment, entanglement, involvement, misunderstanding, quandary

imbue 1. *figurative* bathe, impregnate, inculcate, infuse, instil, permeate, pervade, saturate, steep **2.** colour, dye, ingrain, stain, suffuse, tinge, tint

imitate affect, ape, burlesque, caricature, copy, counterfeit, do (*informal*), do an impression of, duplicate, echo, emulate, follow, follow in the footsteps of, follow suit, impersonate, mimic, mirror, mock, parody, personate, repeat, send up (*Brit. informal*), simulate, spoof (*informal*), take a leaf out of (someone's) book, take off (*informal*), travesty

imitation *noun* **1.** aping, copy, counterfeit, counterfeiting, duplication, echoing, likeness, mimicry, resemblance, simulation **2.** carbon copy (*informal*), fake, forgery, impersonation, impression, mockery, parody, reflection, replica, reproduction, sham, substitution, takeoff (*informal*), travesty ~*adjective* **3.** artificial, dummy, ersatz, man-made, mock, phoney *or* phony (*informal*), pseudo (*informal*), repro, reproduction, sham, simulated, synthetic

Antonyms *adjective* authentic, genuine, original, real, true, valid

Almost all absurdity of conduct arises from the imitation of those whom we cannot resemble
Dr. Johnson *The Rambler*

Imitation is the sincerest form of flattery
Charles Colton *Lacon*

imitative copied, copycat (*informal*), copying, derivative, echoic, mimetic, mimicking, mock, onomatopoeic, parrotlike, plagiarized, pseudo (*informal*), put-on, second-hand, simulated, unoriginal

imitator aper, carbon copy (*informal*), copier, copycat (*informal*), echo, epigone (*rare*), follower, impersonator, impressionist, mimic, parrot, shadow

immaculate 1. clean, impeccable, neat, neat as a new pin, spick-and-span, spruce, squeaky-clean, trim, unexceptionable **2.** above reproach, faultless, flawless, guiltless, impeccable, incorrupt, innocent, perfect, pure, sinless, spotless, squeaky-clean, stainless, unblemished, uncontaminated, undefiled, unpolluted, unsullied, untarnished, virtuous

Antonyms contaminated, corrupt, dirty, filthy, impeachable, impure, polluted, stained, tainted, unclean

immanent congenital, inborn, indigenous, indwelling, inherent, innate, internal, intrinsic, mental, natural, subjective

immaterial 1. a matter of indifference, extraneous, impertinent, inapposite, inconsequential, inconsiderable, inessential, insignificant, irrelevant, of little account, of no consequence, of no importance, trifling, trivial, unimportant, unnecessary **2.** airy, disembodied, ethereal, ghostly, incorporeal, metaphysical, spiritual, unembodied, unsubstantial

Antonyms (*sense 1*) crucial, essential, germane, important, material, relevant, significant, substantial (*sense 2*) earthly, physical, real, tangible

immature 1. adolescent, crude, green, imperfect, premature, raw, undeveloped, unfinished, unfledged, unformed, unripe, unseasonable, untimely, young **2.** babyish, callow, childish, inexperienced, infantile, jejune, juvenile, puerile, wet behind the ears (*informal*)

Antonyms adult, developed, fully-fledged, mature, mellow, responsible, ripe

immaturity 1. crudeness, crudity, greenness, imperfection, rawness, unpreparedness, unripeness **2.** babyishness, callowness, childishness, inexperience, juvenility, puerility

immeasurable bottomless, boundless, endless, illimitable, immense, incalculable, inestimable, inexhaustible, infinite, limitless, measureless, unbounded, unfathomable, unlimited, vast
Antonyms bounded, calculable, estimable, exhaustible, fathomable, finite, limited, measurable

immediate 1. instant, instantaneous 2. adjacent, close, contiguous, direct, near, nearest, next, primary, proximate, recent 3. actual, current, existing, extant, on hand, present, pressing, up to date, urgent
Antonyms delayed, distant, far, late, later, leisurely, postponed, remote, slow, tardy

immediately 1. at once, before you could say Jack Robinson (*informal*), directly, forthwith, instantly, now, on the nail, posthaste, promptly, pronto (*informal*), right away, right now, straight away, this instant, this very minute, *tout de suite*, unhesitatingly, without delay, without hesitation 2. at first hand, closely, directly, nearly

immemorial age-old, ancient, archaic, fixed, long-standing, of yore, olden (*archaic*), rooted, time-honoured, traditional

immense Brobdingnagian, colossal, elephantine, enormous, extensive, giant, gigantic, ginormous (*informal*), great, huge, humongous *or* humungous (*U.S. slang*), illimitable, immeasurable, infinite, interminable, jumbo (*informal*), large, mammoth, massive, mega (*slang*), monstrous, monumental, prodigious, stellar (*informal*), stupendous, titanic, tremendous, vast
Antonyms infinitesimal, little, microscopic, minuscule, minute, puny, small, tiny

immensity bulk, enormity, expanse, extent, greatness, hugeness, infinity, magnitude, massiveness, scope, size, sweep, vastness

immerse 1. bathe, dip, douse, duck, dunk, plunge, sink, submerge, submerse 2. *figurative* absorb, busy, engage, engross, involve, occupy, take up

immersed *figurative* absorbed, bound up, buried, busy, consumed, deep, engrossed, in a brown study, involved, mesmerized, occupied, rapt, spellbound, taken up, wrapped up

immersion 1. baptism, bathe, dip, dipping, dousing, ducking, dunking, plunging, submerging 2. *figurative* absorption, concentration, involvement, preoccupation

immigrant incomer, newcomer, settler

imminent at hand, brewing, close, coming, fast-approaching, forthcoming, gathering, impending, in the air, in the offing, in the pipeline, just round the corner, looming, menacing, near, nigh (*archaic*), on the cards, on the horizon, on the way, threatening, upcoming
Antonyms delayed, distant, far-off, remote

immobile at a standstill, at rest, fixed, frozen, immobilized, immotile, immovable, like a statue, motionless, rigid, riveted, rooted, stable, static, stationary, stiff, still, stock-still, stolid, unmoving
Antonyms active, mobile, movable, on the move, pliant, portable, vigorous

immobility absence of movement, firmness, fixity, immovability, inertness, motionlessness, stability, steadiness, stillness

immobilize bring to a standstill, cripple, disable, freeze, halt, lay up (*informal*), paralyse, put out of action, render inoperative, stop, transfix

immoderate egregious, enormous, exaggerated, excessive, exorbitant, extravagant, extreme, inordinate, intemperate, O.T.T. (*slang*), over the odds (*informal*), over the top (*slang*), profligate, steep (*informal*), uncalled-for, unconscionable, uncontrolled, undue, unjustified, unreasonable, unrestrained, unwarranted, wanton
Antonyms controlled, judicious, mild, moderate, reasonable, restrained, temperate

immoderation excess, exorbitance, extravagance, intemperance, lack of restraint *or* balance, overindulgence, prodigality, unrestraint

immodest 1. bawdy, coarse, depraved, flirtatious, gross, immoral, improper, impure, indecent, indecorous, indelicate, lewd, obscene, revealing, titillating, unchaste 2. bold, bold as brass, brass-necked (*Brit. informal*), brazen, forward, fresh (*informal*), impudent, pushy (*informal*), shameless, unblushing

immodesty 1. bawdiness, coarseness, impurity, indecorousness, indelicacy, lewdness, obscenity 2. audacity, balls (*taboo slang*), boldness, brass neck (*Brit. informal*), forwardness, gall (*informal*), impudence, shamelessness, temerity
Antonyms (*sense 1*) decency, decorousness, delicacy, modesty, restraint, sobriety

immolate kill, sacrifice

immolation offering up, sacrifice, slaughter

immoral abandoned, bad, corrupt, debauched, degenerate, depraved, dishonest, dissolute, evil, impure, indecent, iniquitous, lewd, licentious, nefarious, obscene, of easy virtue, pornographic, profligate, reprobate, sinful, sink, unchaste, unethical, unprincipled, vicious, vile, wicked, wrong
Antonyms conscientious, good, honourable, inoffensive, law-abiding, moral, pure, upright, virtuous

immorality badness, corruption, debauchery, depravity, dissoluteness, evil, iniquity, licentiousness, profligacy, sin, turpitude, vice,

wickedness, wrong
Antonyms goodness, honesty, lawfulness, mo~ rality, purity

immorally corruptly, degenerately, dishonestly, dissolutely, evilly, sinfully, unethically, un~ righteously, wickedly

immortal *adjective* **1.** abiding, constant, death-defying, deathless, endless, enduring, eternal, everlasting, imperishable, incorrupt~ ible, indestructible, lasting, perennial, perpet~ ual, sempiternal (*literary*), timeless, undying, unfading *~noun* **2.** god, goddess, Olympian **3.** genius, great (*usually plural*), hero, paragon
Antonyms *adjective* ephemeral, fading, fleet~ ing, mortal, passing, perishable, temporary, transitory

immortality **1.** deathlessness, endlessness, eternity, everlasting life, incorruptibility, in~ destructibility, perpetuity, timelessness **2.** ce~ lebrity, fame, glorification, gloriousness, glory, greatness, renown

No young man believes he shall ever die
William Hazlitt *Uncollected Essays*

I don't want to achieve immortality through my work...I want to achieve it by not dying
Woody Allen

Should this my firm persuasion of the soul's immortality prove to be a mere delusion, it is at least a pleasing delusion, and I will cherish it to my last breath
Cicero *De Senectute*

All the doctrines that have flourished in the world about immortality have hardly affected men's natu~ ral sentiment in the face of death
George Santayana *The Life of Reason: Reason in Religion*

Our Creator would never have made such lovely days, and given us the deep hearts to enjoy them, unless we were meant to be immortal
Nathaniel Hawthorne *The Old Manse*

Do not try to live forever. You will not succeed
George Bernard Shaw *The Doctor's Dilemma*

Millions long for immortality who don't know what to do with themselves on a rainy Saturday afternoon
Susan Ertz *Anger in the Sky*

immortalize apotheosize, celebrate, commemo~ rate, enshrine, eternalize, eternize, exalt, glo~ rify, memorialize, perpetuate, solemnize

immovable **1.** fast, firm, fixed, immutable, jammed, rooted, secure, set, stable, stationary, stuck, unbudgeable **2.** adamant, constant, im~ passive, inflexible, obdurate, resolute, stead~ fast, stony-hearted, unchangeable, unimpres~ sionable, unshakable, unshaken, unwavering, unyielding
Antonyms (*sense 2*) changeable, flexible, im~ pressionable, movable, shakable, wavering, yielding

immune clear, exempt, free, insusceptible, in~ vulnerable, let off (*informal*), not affected, not liable, not subject, proof (against), protected, resistant, safe, unaffected
Antonyms exposed, liable, prone, susceptible, unprotected, vulnerable

immunity **1.** amnesty, charter, exemption, ex~ oneration, franchise, freedom, indemnity, in~ vulnerability, liberty, licence, prerogative, privilege, release, right **2.** immunization, pro~ tection, resistance
Antonyms (*sense 1*) exposure, liability, open~ ness, proneness, susceptibility, vulnerability

immunize inoculate, protect, safeguard, vacci~ nate

immure cage, cloister, confine, enclose, impris~ on, incarcerate, jail, shut in *or* up, wall up *or* in

immutability agelessness, changelessness, con~ stancy, durability, invariability, permanence, stability, unalterableness, unchangeableness

immutable abiding, ageless, changeless, con~ stant, enduring, fixed, fixed as the laws of the Medes and Persians, immovable, inflexible, invariable, permanent, perpetual, sacrosanct, stable, steadfast, unalterable, unchangeable

imp brat, demon, devil, gamin, minx, pickle (*Brit. informal*), rascal, rogue, scamp, sprite, urchin

impact *noun* **1.** bang, blow, bump, collision, concussion, contact, crash, force, jolt, knock, shock, smash, stroke, thump **2.** brunt, burden, consequences, effect, full force, impression, influence, meaning, power, repercussions, sig~ nificance, thrust, weight *~verb* **3.** clash, col~ lide, crash, crush, hit, strike

impair blunt, damage, debilitate, decrease, de~ teriorate, diminish, enervate, enfeeble, harm, hinder, injure, lessen, mar, reduce, spoil, undermine, vitiate, weaken, worsen
Antonyms ameliorate, amend, better, en~ hance, facilitate, improve, strengthen

impaired damaged, defective, faulty, flawed, imperfect, unsound

impale lance, pierce, run through, skewer, spear, spike, spit, stick, transfix

impalpable airy, delicate, disembodied, fine, imperceptible, incorporeal, indistinct, insub~ stantial, intangible, shadowy, tenuous, thin, unsubstantial

impart **1.** communicate, convey, disclose, dis~ cover, divulge, make known, pass on, relate, reveal, tell **2.** accord, afford, bestow, confer, contribute, give, grant, lend, offer, yield

impartial detached, disinterested, equal, equi~ table, even-handed, fair, just, neutral, nondis~ criminating, nonpartisan, objective, open-minded, unbiased, unprejudiced, without fear or favour

Antonyms biased, bigoted, influenced, partial, prejudiced, swayed, unfair, unjust

impartiality detachment, disinterest, disinterestedness, dispassion, equality, equity, even-handedness, fairness, lack of bias, neutrality, nonpartisanship, objectivity, open-mindedness
Antonyms bias, favouritism, partiality, partisanship, subjectivity, unfairness

impassable blocked, closed, impenetrable, obstructed, pathless, trackless, unnavigable

impasse blind alley (*informal*), dead end, deadlock, stalemate, standoff, standstill

impassioned ablaze, animated, ardent, blazing, excited, fervent, fervid, fiery, flaming, furious, glowing, heated, inflamed, inspired, intense, passionate, rousing, stirring, vehement, violent, vivid, warm, worked up
Antonyms apathetic, cool, impassive, indifferent, objective, reasoned

impassive aloof, apathetic, callous, calm, composed, cool, dispassionate, emotionless, impassible (*rare*), imperturbable, indifferent, inscrutable, insensible, insusceptible, phlegmatic, poker-faced (*informal*), reserved, self-contained, serene, stoical, stolid, unconcerned, unemotional, unexcitable, unfazed (*informal*), unfeeling, unimpressible, unmoved, unruffled

impassivity aloofness, calmness, composure, dispassion, impassiveness, imperturbability, indifference, inscrutability, insensibility, nonchalance, phlegm, stoicism, stolidity

impatience 1. haste, hastiness, heat, impetuosity, intolerance, irritability, irritableness, quick temper, rashness, shortness, snappiness, vehemence, violence 2. agitation, anxiety, avidity, disquietude, eagerness, edginess, fretfulness, nervousness, restiveness, restlessness, uneasiness
Antonyms (*sense 2*) calm, composure, control, forbearance, patience, restraint, serenity, tolerance

impatient 1. abrupt, brusque, curt, demanding, edgy, hasty, hot-tempered, indignant, intolerant, irritable, quick-tempered, snappy, sudden, testy, vehement, violent 2. agog, athirst, chafing, eager, fretful, headlong, impetuous, like a cat on hot bricks (*informal*), restless, straining at the leash
Antonyms (*sense 1*) calm, composed, cool, easy-going, imperturbable, patient, quiet, serene, tolerant

impeach 1. accuse, arraign, blame, censure, charge, criminate (*rare*), denounce, indict, tax 2. call into question, cast aspersions on, cast doubt on, challenge, disparage, impugn, question

impeachment accusation, arraignment, indictment

impeccable above suspicion, blameless, exact, exquisite, faultless, flawless, immaculate, incorrupt, innocent, irreproachable, perfect, precise, pure, sinless, stainless, unblemished, unerring, unimpeachable
Antonyms blameworthy, corrupt, cursory, defective, deficient, faulty, flawed, shallow, sinful, superficial

impecunious broke (*informal*), cleaned out (*slang*), destitute, dirt-poor (*informal*), down and out, flat broke (*informal*), indigent, in queer street, insolvent, penniless, poverty-stricken, short, skint (*Brit. slang*), stony (*Brit. slang*), strapped (*slang*), without two pennies to rub together (*informal*)
Antonyms affluent, prosperous, rich, wealthy, well-off, well-to-do

impede bar, block, brake, check, clog, curb, delay, disrupt, hamper, hinder, hold up, obstruct, restrain, retard, slow (down), stop, throw a spanner in the works (*Brit. informal*), thwart
Antonyms advance, aid, assist, further, help, promote

impediment bar, barrier, block, check, clog, curb, defect, difficulty, encumbrance, fly in the ointment, hazard, hindrance, millstone around one's neck, obstacle, obstruction, snag, stumbling block
Antonyms advantage, aid, assistance, benefit, encouragement, relief, support

impedimenta accoutrements, baggage, belongings, effects, equipment, gear, junk (*informal*), luggage, movables, odds and ends, paraphernalia, possessions, stuff, things, trappings, traps

impel actuate, chivy, compel, constrain, drive, force, goad, incite, induce, influence, inspire, instigate, motivate, move, oblige, power, prod, prompt, propel, push, require, spur, stimulate, urge
Antonyms check, discourage, dissuade, rebuff, repulse, restrain

impending approaching, brewing, coming, forthcoming, gathering, hovering, imminent, in the offing, in the pipeline, looming, menacing, near, nearing, on the horizon, threatening, upcoming

impenetrable 1. dense, hermetic, impassable, impermeable, impervious, inviolable, solid, thick, unpierceable 2. arcane, baffling, cabbalistic, dark, enigmatic, enigmatical, hidden, incomprehensible, indiscernible, inexplicable, inscrutable, mysterious, obscure, unfathomable, unintelligible
Antonyms (*sense 1*) accessible, enterable, passable, penetrable, pierceable, vulnerable (*sense 2*) clear, explicable, obvious, soluble, understandable

impenitence hardheartedness, impenitency, incorrigibility, obduracy, stubbornness

impenitent defiant, hardened, hardhearted, incorrigible, obdurate, recidivistic, relentless, remorseless, unabashed, unashamed, uncontrite, unreformed, unrepentant

imperative **1**. compulsory, crucial, essential, exigent, indispensable, insistent, obligatory, pressing, urgent, vital **2**. authoritative, auto~cratic, commanding, dictatorial, domineering, high-handed, imperious, lordly, magisterial, peremptory
Antonyms (*sense 1*) avoidable, discretional, nonessential, optional, unimportant, unneces~sary

imperceptible faint, fine, gradual, impalpable, inappreciable, inaudible, indiscernible, indis~tinguishable, infinitesimal, insensible, invis~ible, microscopic, minute, shadowy, slight, small, subtle, teensy-weensy, teeny-weeny, tiny, undetectable, unnoticeable
Antonyms audible, detectable, discernible, distinguishable, noticeable, perceptible, visible

imperceptibly by a hair's-breadth, inappre~ciably, indiscernibly, invisibly, little by little, slowly, subtly, unnoticeably, unobtrusively, unseen

imperceptive impercipient, insensitive, obtuse, superficial, unappreciative, unaware, undis~cerning, unobservant, unseeing

imperfect broken, damaged, defective, defi~cient, faulty, flawed, immature, impaired, in~complete, inexact, limited, partial, patchy, ru~dimentary, sketchy, undeveloped, unfinished
Antonyms complete, developed, exact, fin~ished, flawless, perfect

imperfection blemish, defect, deficiency, fail~ing, fallibility, fault, flaw, foible, frailty, inad~equacy, incompleteness, infirmity, insufficien~cy, peccadillo, scar, shortcoming, stain, taint, weakness, weak point
Antonyms adequacy, completeness, consum~mation, excellence, faultlessness, flawlessness, perfection, sufficiency

imperial **1**. kingly, majestic, princely, queenly, regal, royal, sovereign **2**. august, exalted, grand, great, high, imperious, lofty, magnifi~cent, noble, superior, supreme

imperil endanger, expose, hazard, jeopardize, risk
Antonyms care for, guard, protect, safeguard, secure

imperious arrogant, authoritative, autocratic, bossy (*informal*), commanding, despotic, dic~tatorial, domineering, exacting, haughty, high-handed, imperative, lordly, magisterial, overbearing, overweening, tyrannical, tyran~nous

imperishable abiding, enduring, eternal, ever~lasting, immortal, indestructible, perennial, permanent, perpetual, undying, unfading, un~forgettable
Antonyms destructible, dying, fading, forget~table, mortal, perishable

impermanent brief, elusive, ephemeral, eva~nescent, fleeting, fly-by-night (*informal*), fly~ing, fugacious, fugitive, here today, gone to~morrow (*informal*), inconstant, momentary, mortal, passing, perishable, short-lived, tem~porary, transient, transitory

impermeable hermetic, impassable, impen~etrable, impervious, nonporous, proof, resist~ant

impersonal aloof, bureaucratic, businesslike, cold, detached, dispassionate, formal, inhu~man, neutral, remote
Antonyms friendly, intimate, outgoing, per~sonal, warm

impersonate act, ape, caricature, do (*infor~mal*), do an impression of, enact, imitate, masquerade as, mimic, parody, pass oneself off as, personate, pose as (*informal*), take off (*informal*)

impersonation caricature, imitation, impres~sion, mimicry, parody, takeoff (*informal*)

impertinence assurance, audacity, backchat (*informal*), boldness, brass neck (*Brit. infor~mal*), brazenness, cheek (*informal*), chutzpah (*U.S. & Canad. informal*), disrespect, effron~tery, face (*informal*), forwardness, front, im~pudence, incivility, insolence, neck (*informal*), nerve (*informal*), pertness, presumption, rudeness, sauce (*informal*)

impertinent **1**. bold, brazen, cheeky (*informal*), discourteous, disrespectful, flip (*informal*), forward, fresh (*informal*), impolite, impudent, insolent, interfering, lippy (*U.S. & Canad. slang*), pert, presumptuous, rude, sassy (*U.S. informal*), saucy (*informal*), uncivil, unman~nerly **2**. inapplicable, inappropriate, incongru~ous, irrelevant
Antonyms (*sense 1*) mannerly, polite, respect~ful (*sense 2*) appropriate, germane, important, pertinent, relevant, vital

imperturbable calm, collected, complacent, composed, cool, equanimous, nerveless, sedate, self-possessed, serene, stoical, tranquil, undis~turbed, unexcitable, unfazed (*informal*), un~flappable (*informal*), unmoved, unruffled
Antonyms agitated, excitable, frantic, jittery (*informal*), nervous, panicky, ruffled, touchy, upset

impervious **1**. hermetic, impassable, impen~etrable, impermeable, imperviable, invulner~able, resistant, sealed **2**. closed to, immune, invulnerable, proof against, unaffected by, unmoved by, unreceptive, unswayable, untouched by

impetuosity haste, hastiness, impulsiveness, precipitancy, precipitateness, rashness, vehemence, violence

For fools rush in where angels fear to tread
Alexander Pope *An Essay on Criticism*

impetuous ardent, eager, fierce, furious, hasty, headlong, impassioned, impulsive, passionate, precipitate, rash, spontaneous, spur-of-the-moment, unbridled, unplanned, unpremeditated, unreflecting, unrestrained, unthinking, vehement, violent
Antonyms cautious, leisurely, mild, slow, wary

impetuously helter-skelter, impulsively, in the heat of the moment, on the spur of the moment, passionately, rashly, recklessly, spontaneously, unthinkingly, vehemently, without thinking

impetus **1.** catalyst, goad, impulse, impulsion, incentive, motivation, push, spur, stimulus **2.** energy, force, momentum, power

impiety godlessness, iniquity, irreligion, irreverence, profaneness, profanity, sacrilege, sinfulness, ungodliness, unholiness, unrighteousness, wickedness
Antonyms devoutness, godliness, holiness, piety, respect, reverence, righteousness

impiety: your irreverence towards my deity
Ambrose Bierce *The Devil's Dictionary*

impinge **1.** encroach, invade, make inroads, obtrude, trespass, violate **2.** affect, bear upon, have a bearing on, impact, influence, infringe, relate to, touch, touch upon **3.** clash, collide, dash, strike

impious blasphemous, godless, iniquitous, irreligious, irreverent, profane, sacrilegious, sinful, ungodly, unholy, unrighteous, wicked
Antonyms devout, godly, holy, pious, religious, reverent, righteous

impish devilish, elfin, mischievous, prankish, puckish, rascally, roguish, sportive, waggish

implacability implacableness, inexorability, inflexibility, intractability, mercilessness, pitilessness, relentlessness, ruthlessness, unforgivingness, vengefulness

implacable cruel, inexorable, inflexible, intractable, merciless, pitiless, rancorous, relentless, remorseless, ruthless, unappeasable, unbending, uncompromising, unforgiving, unrelenting, unyielding
Antonyms appeasable, flexible, lenient, merciful, reconcilable, relenting, tolerant, yielding

implant **1.** inculcate, infix, infuse, inseminate, instil, sow **2.** embed, fix, graft, ingraft, insert, place, plant, root, sow

implausible cock-and-bull (*informal*), dubious, far-fetched, flimsy, improbable, incredible, suspect, unbelievable, unconvincing, unlikely, unreasonable, weak

implement **1.** *noun* agent, apparatus, appliance, device, gadget, instrument, tool, utensil **2.** *verb* bring about, carry out, complete, effect, enforce, execute, fulfil, perform, put into action *or* effect, realize
Antonyms *verb* delay, hamper, hinder, impede, weaken

implementation accomplishment, carrying out, discharge, effecting, enforcement, execution, fulfilment, performance, performing, realization

implicate associate, compromise, concern, embroil, entangle, imply, include, incriminate, inculpate, involve, mire, stitch up (*slang*), tie up with
Antonyms acquit, disentangle, dissociate, eliminate, exclude, exculpate, rule out

implicated incriminated, involved, suspected, under suspicion

implication **1.** association, connection, entanglement, incrimination, involvement **2.** conclusion, inference, innuendo, meaning, overtone, presumption, ramification, significance, signification, suggestion

implicit **1.** contained, implied, inferred, inherent, latent, tacit, taken for granted, undeclared, understood, unspoken **2.** absolute, constant, entire, firm, fixed, full, steadfast, total, unhesitating, unqualified, unreserved, unshakable, unshaken, wholehearted
Antonyms (*sense 1*) declared, explicit, expressed, obvious, patent, spoken, stated

implicitly absolutely, completely, firmly, unconditionally, unhesitatingly, unreservedly, utterly, without reservation

implied hinted at, implicit, indirect, inherent, insinuated, suggested, tacit, undeclared, unexpressed, unspoken, unstated

implore beg, beseech, conjure, crave, entreat, go on bended knee to, importune, plead with, pray, solicit, supplicate

imply **1.** connote, give (someone) to understand, hint, insinuate, intimate, signify, suggest **2.** betoken, denote, entail, evidence, import, include, indicate, involve, mean, point to, presuppose

impolite bad-mannered, boorish, churlish, discourteous, disrespectful, ill-bred, ill-mannered, indecorous, indelicate, insolent, loutish, rough, rude, uncivil, uncouth, ungallant, ungentlemanly, ungracious, unladylike, unmannerly, unrefined
Antonyms courteous, decorous, gallant, gracious, mannerly, polite, refined, respectful, well-bred

impoliteness bad manners, boorishness, churlishness, discourtesy, disrespect, incivil~

ity, indelicacy, insolence, rudeness, unmannerliness

Antonyms civility, courtesy, delicacy, mannerliness, politeness, respect

impolitic ill-advised, ill-judged, imprudent, indiscreet, inexpedient, injudicious, maladroit, misguided, undiplomatic, untimely, unwise

Antonyms diplomatic, discreet, expedient, judicious, politic, prudent, timely, wise

import *noun* **1.** bearing, drift, gist, implication, intention, meaning, message, purport, sense, significance, thrust **2.** bottom, consequence, importance, magnitude, moment, significance, substance, weight *~verb* **3.** bring in, introduce, land

importance **1.** concern, consequence, import, interest, moment, momentousness, significance, substance, value, weight **2.** bottom, distinction, eminence, esteem, influence, mark, pre-eminence, prestige, prominence, standing, status, usefulness, worth

important **1.** far-reaching, grave, large, material, meaningful, momentous, of substance, primary, salient, serious, signal, significant, substantial, urgent, weighty **2.** big-time (*informal*), eminent, foremost, high-level, high-ranking, influential, leading, major league (*informal*), notable, noteworthy, of note, outstanding, powerful, pre-eminent, prominent, seminal **3.** *usually with* **to** basic, essential, of concern *or* interest, relevant, valuable, valued

Antonyms inconsequential, insignificant, minor, needless, negligible, secondary, trivial, undistinctive, unimportant, unnecessary

importunate burning, clamant, clamorous, demanding, dogged, earnest, exigent, insistent, persistent, pertinacious, pressing, solicitous, troublesome, urgent

importune badger, beset, besiege, dun, entreat, harass, hound, lay siege to, pester, plague, press, solicit

importunity cajolery, dunning, entreaties, insistence, persistence, pressing, solicitations, urging

impose **1.** decree, establish, exact, fix, institute, introduce, lay, levy, ordain, place, promulgate, put, set **2.** appoint, charge with, dictate, enforce, enjoin, inflict, prescribe, saddle (someone) with **3.** *with* **on** *or* **upon** butt in, encroach, foist, force oneself, gate-crash (*informal*), horn in (*informal*), intrude, obtrude, presume, take liberties, trespass **4.** *with* **on** *or* **upon a.** abuse, exploit, play on, take advantage of, use **b.** con (*informal*), deceive, dupe, hoodwink, pull the wool over (somebody's) eyes, trick

imposing august, commanding, dignified, effective, grand, impressive, majestic, stately, striking

Antonyms insignificant, mean, modest, ordinary, petty, poor, unimposing

imposition **1.** application, decree, introduction, laying on, levying, promulgation **2.** cheek (*informal*), encroachment, intrusion, liberty, presumption **3.** artifice, cheating, con (*informal*), deception, dissimulation, fraud, hoax, imposture, stratagem, trickery **4.** burden, charge, constraint, duty, levy, tax

impossibility hopelessness, impracticability, inability, inconceivability

Probable impossibilities are to be preferred to improbable possibilities

Aristotle *Poetics*

impossible **1.** beyond one, beyond the bounds of possibility, hopeless, impracticable, inconceivable, not to be thought of, out of the question, unachievable, unattainable, unobtainable, unthinkable **2.** absurd, inadmissible, insoluble, intolerable, ludicrous, outrageous, preposterous, unacceptable, unanswerable, ungovernable, unreasonable, unsuitable, unworkable

Antonyms (*sense 1*) conceivable, imaginable, likely, plausible, possible, reasonable

Why, sometimes I've believed as many as six impossible things before breakfast

Lewis Carroll *Through the Looking-Glass*

impostor charlatan, cheat, deceiver, fake, fraud, hypocrite, impersonator, knave (*archaic*), phoney *or* phony (*informal*), pretender, quack, rogue, sham, trickster

imposture artifice, canard, cheat, con trick (*informal*), counterfeit, deception, fraud, hoax, impersonation, imposition, quackery, swindle, trick

impotence disability, enervation, feebleness, frailty, helplessness, inability, inadequacy, incapacity, incompetence, ineffectiveness, inefficacy, inefficiency, infirmity, paralysis, powerlessness, uselessness, weakness

Antonyms ability, adequacy, competence, effectiveness, efficacy, efficiency, powerfulness, strength, usefulness

impotent disabled, emasculate, enervated, feeble, frail, helpless, incapable, incapacitated, incompetent, ineffective, infirm, nerveless, paralysed, powerless, unable, unmanned, weak

Antonyms able, capable, competent, effective, manned, potent, powerful, strong

impoverish **1.** bankrupt, beggar, break, ruin **2.** deplete, diminish, drain, exhaust, pauperize, reduce, sap, use up, wear out

impoverished **1.** bankrupt, destitute, distressed, impecunious, indigent, in reduced *or* straitened circumstances, necessitous, needy, on one's uppers, penurious, poverty-stricken, ruined, straitened **2.** barren, denuded, deplet~

ed, drained, empty, exhausted, played out, reduced, spent, sterile, worn out
Antonyms (*sense 1*) affluent, rich, wealthy, well-off (*sense 2*) fecund, fertile, productive

impracticability futility, hopelessness, impossibility, impracticality, unsuitableness, unworkability, uselessness

impracticable 1. impossible, out of the question, unachievable, unattainable, unfeasible, unworkable **2.** awkward, impractical, inapplicable, inconvenient, unserviceable, unsuitable, useless
Antonyms feasible, possible, practicable, practical, serviceable, suitable

impractical 1. impossible, impracticable, inoperable, nonviable, unrealistic, unserviceable, unworkable, visionary, wild **2.** idealistic, romantic, starry-eyed, unbusinesslike, unrealistic, visionary
Antonyms (*sense 1*) possible, practical, serviceable, viable, workable (*sense 2*) down-to-earth, realistic, sensible

impracticality hopelessness, impossibility, inapplicability, romanticism, unworkability

imprecation anathema, blasphemy, curse, denunciation, execration, malediction, profanity, vilification

imprecise ambiguous, blurred round the edges, careless, equivocal, estimated, fluctuating, hazy, ill-defined, inaccurate, indefinite, indeterminate, inexact, inexplicit, loose, rough, sloppy (*informal*), vague, wide of the mark, woolly
Antonyms accurate, careful, definite, determinate, exact, explicit, precise

impregnable immovable, impenetrable, indestructible, invincible, invulnerable, secure, strong, unassailable, unbeatable, unconquerable, unshakable
Antonyms destructible, exposed, insecure, movable, open, pregnable, shakable, vulnerable

impregnate 1. fill, imbrue (*rare*), imbue, infuse, percolate, permeate, pervade, saturate, seep, soak, steep, suffuse **2.** fecundate, fertilize, fructify, get with child, inseminate, make pregnant

impress 1. affect, excite, grab (*informal*), influence, inspire, make an impression, move, stir, strike, sway, touch **2.** *often with* **on** *or* **upon** bring home to, emphasize, fix, inculcate, instil into, stress **3.** emboss, engrave, imprint, indent, mark, print, stamp

impression 1. effect, feeling, impact, influence, reaction, sway **2. make an impression** arouse comment, be conspicuous, cause a stir, excite notice, find favour, make a hit (*informal*), make an impact, stand out **3.** belief, concept, conviction, fancy, feeling, funny feeling (*informal*), hunch, idea, memory, notion, opinion, recollection, sense, suspicion **4.** brand, dent, hollow, impress, imprint, indentation, mark, outline, stamp, stamping **5.** edition, imprinting, issue, printing **6.** imitation, impersonation, parody, send-up (*Brit. informal*), takeoff (*informal*)
First impressions are the most lasting

impressionability ingenuousness, receptiveness, receptivity, sensitivity, suggestibility, susceptibility, vulnerability

impressionable feeling, gullible, ingenuous, open, receptive, responsive, sensitive, suggestible, susceptible, vulnerable
Antonyms blasé, hardened, insensitive, jaded, unresponsive

impressive affecting, dramatic, exciting, forcible, moving, powerful, stirring, striking, touching
Antonyms ordinary, unimposing, unimpressive, uninspiring, unmemorable, weak

imprint 1. *noun* impression, indentation, mark, print, sign, stamp **2.** *verb* engrave, establish, etch, fix, impress, print, stamp

imprison confine, constrain, detain, immure, incarcerate, intern, jail, lock up, put away, put under lock and key, send down (*informal*), send to prison
Antonyms discharge, emancipate, free, liberate, release

imprisoned behind bars, captive, confined, immured, incarcerated, in irons, in jail, inside (*slang*), interned, jailed, locked up, put away, under lock and key

imprisonment confinement, custody, detention, durance (*archaic*), duress, incarceration, internment, porridge (*slang*)

improbability doubt, doubtfulness, dubiety, uncertainty, unlikelihood

improbable cock-and-bull (*informal*), doubtful, dubious, fanciful, far-fetched, implausible, questionable, unbelievable, uncertain, unconvincing, unlikely, weak
Antonyms certain, convincing, doubtless, likely, plausible, probable, reasonable

improbity chicanery, crookedness (*informal*), dishonesty, faithlessness, fraud, knavery, unfairness, unscrupulousness, villainy

impromptu 1. *adjective* ad-lib, extemporaneous, extempore, extemporized, improvised, offhand, off the cuff (*informal*), spontaneous, unpremeditated, unprepared, unrehearsed, unscripted, unstudied **2.** *adverb* ad lib, off the cuff (*informal*), off the top of one's head (*informal*), on the spur of the moment, spontaneously, without preparation
Antonyms *adjective* considered, planned, premeditated, prepared, rehearsed

improper 1. impolite, indecent, indecorous, indelicate, off-colour, risqué, smutty, suggestive, unbecoming, unfitting, unseemly, untoward, vulgar 2. ill-timed, inapplicable, inapposite, inappropriate, inapt, incongruous, infelicitous, inopportune, malapropos, out of place, uncalled-for, unfit, unseasonable, unsuitable, unsuited, unwarranted 3. abnormal, erroneous, false, inaccurate, incorrect, irregular, wrong

Antonyms (*sense 1*) becoming, decent, decorous, delicate, fitting, proper, seemly (*sense 2*) apposite, appropriate, apt, felicitous, opportune, seasoned, suitable

impropriety 1. bad taste, immodesty, incongruity, indecency, indecorum, unsuitability, vulgarity 2. bloomer (*Brit. informal*), blunder, faux pas, gaffe, gaucherie, lapse, mistake, slip, solecism

Antonyms (*sense 1*) decency, decorum, delicacy, modesty, propriety, suitability

Impropriety is the soul of wit

W. Somerset Maugham *The Moon and Sixpence*

improve 1. advance, ameliorate, amend, augment, better, correct, face-lift, help, mend, polish, rectify, touch up, upgrade 2. develop, enhance, gain strength, increase, look up (*informal*), make strides, perk up, pick up, progress, rally, reform, rise, take a turn for the better (*informal*), take on a new lease of life (*informal*) 3. be on the mend, convalesce, gain ground, gain strength, grow better, make progress, mend, recover, recuperate, turn the corner 4. clean up one's act (*informal*), get it together (*informal*), get one's act together (*informal*), pull one's socks up (*Brit. informal*), reform, shape up (*informal*), turn over a new leaf

Antonyms damage, harm, impair, injure, mar, worsen

improvement 1. advancement, amelioration, amendment, augmentation, betterment, correction, face-lift, gain, rectification 2. advance, development, enhancement, furtherance, increase, progress, rally, recovery, reformation, rise, upswing

improvidence carelessness, extravagance, heedlessness, imprudence, negligence, prodigality, profligacy, short-sightedness, thriftlessness, wastefulness

improvident careless, heedless, imprudent, inconsiderate, negligent, prodigal, profligate, reckless, shiftless, short-sighted, spendthrift, thoughtless, thriftless, uneconomical, unthrifty, wasteful

Antonyms careful, considerate, economical, heedful, provident, prudent, thrifty

improvisation ad-lib, ad-libbing, expedient, extemporizing, impromptu, invention, makeshift, spontaneity

improvise 1. ad-lib, busk, coin, extemporize, invent, play it by ear (*informal*), speak off the cuff (*informal*), vamp, wing it (*informal*) 2. concoct, contrive, devise, make do, throw together

improvised ad-lib, extemporaneous, extempore, extemporized, makeshift, off the cuff (*informal*), spontaneous, spur-of-the-moment, unprepared, unrehearsed

imprudence carelessness, folly, foolhardiness, foolishness, heedlessness, improvidence, inadvisability, incaution, incautiousness, inconsideration, indiscretion, irresponsibility, rashness, recklessness, temerity

imprudent careless, foolhardy, foolish, heedless, ill-advised, ill-considered, ill-judged, impolitic, improvident, incautious, inconsiderate, indiscreet, injudicious, irresponsible, overhasty, rash, reckless, temerarious, unthinking, unwise

Antonyms careful, cautious, considerate, discreet, judicious, politic, provident, prudent, responsible, wise

impudence assurance, audacity, backchat (*informal*), boldness, brass neck (*Brit. informal*), brazenness, bumptiousness, cheek (*informal*), chutzpah (*U.S. & Canad. informal*), effrontery, face (*informal*), front, impertinence, insolence, lip (*slang*), neck (*informal*), nerve (*informal*), pertness, presumption, rudeness, sassiness (*U.S. informal*), sauciness, shamelessness

impudent audacious, bold, bold-faced, brazen, bumptious, cheeky (*informal*), cocky (*informal*), forward, fresh (*informal*), immodest, impertinent, insolent, lippy (*U.S. & Canad. slang*), pert, presumptuous, rude, sassy (*U.S. informal*), saucy (*informal*), shameless

Antonyms courteous, modest, polite, respectful, retiring, self-effacing, timid, well-behaved

impugn assail, attack, call into question, cast aspersions upon, cast doubt upon, challenge, criticize, dispute, gainsay (*archaic or literary*), oppose, question, resist, traduce

impulse 1. catalyst, force, impetus, momentum, movement, pressure, push, stimulus, surge, thrust 2. *figurative* caprice, drive, feeling, incitement, inclination, influence, instinct, motive, notion, passion, resolve, urge, whim, wish

Have no truck with first impulses for they are always generous ones

Casimir, Comte de Montrond

impulsive devil-may-care, emotional, hasty, headlong, impetuous, instinctive, intuitive, passionate, precipitate, quick, rash, spontaneous, unconsidered, unpredictable, unpremeditated

Antonyms arresting, calculating, cautious,

considered, cool, deliberate, halting, planned, premeditated, rehearsed, restrained

impunity dispensation, exemption, freedom, immunity, liberty, licence, nonliability, permission, security

impure 1. admixed, adulterated, alloyed, debased, mixed, unrefined 2. contaminated, defiled, dirty, filthy, foul, infected, polluted, sullied, tainted, unclean, unwholesome, vitiated 3. carnal, coarse, corrupt, gross, immodest, immoral, indecent, indelicate, lascivious, lewd, licentious, lustful, obscene, prurient, ribald, salacious, smutty, unchaste, unclean, X-rated (*informal*)
Antonyms (*sense 2*) clean, immaculate, spotless, squeaky-clean, undefiled, unsullied (*sense 3*) chaste, decent, delicate, modest, moral, pure, wholesome

impurity 1. admixture, adulteration, mixture 2. befoulment, contamination, defilement, dirtiness, filth, foulness, infection, pollution, taint, uncleanness 3. *often plural* bits, contaminant, dirt, dross, foreign body, foreign matter, grime, marks, pollutant, scum, spots, stains 4. carnality, coarseness, corruption, grossness, immodesty, immorality, indecency, lasciviousness, lewdness, licentiousness, obscenity, prurience, salaciousness, smuttiness, unchastity, vulgarity

imputable accreditable, ascribable, attributable, chargeable, referable, traceable

imputation accusation, ascription, aspersion, attribution, blame, censure, charge, insinuation, reproach, slander, slur

impute accredit, ascribe, assign, attribute, credit, lay at the door of, refer, set down to

inability disability, disqualification, impotence, inadequacy, incapability, incapacity, incompetence, ineptitude, powerlessness
Antonyms ability, adequacy, capability, capacity, competence, potential, power, talent

inaccessible impassable, out of reach, out of the way, remote, unapproachable, unattainable, un-get-at-able (*informal*), unreachable
Antonyms accessible, approachable, attainable, reachable

inaccuracy 1. erroneousness, imprecision, incorrectness, inexactness, unfaithfulness, unreliability 2. blunder, boob (*Brit. slang*), corrigendum, defect, erratum, error, fault, howler (*informal*), lapse, literal (*Printing*), miscalculation, mistake, slip, typo (*informal, Printing*)

inaccurate careless, defective, discrepant, erroneous, faulty, imprecise, incorrect, in error, inexact, mistaken, off base (*U.S. & Canad. informal*), off beam (*informal*), out, unfaithful, unreliable, unsound, way off beam (*informal*), wide of the mark, wild, wrong
Antonyms accurate, correct, exact, precise, reliable, sound

inaccurately carelessly, clumsily, imprecisely, inexactly, unfaithfully, unreliably

inaction dormancy, idleness, immobility, inactivity, inertia, rest, torpidity, torpor

The only thing necessary for the triumph of evil is for good men to do nothing

Edmund Burke

inactive 1. abeyant, dormant, idle, immobile, inert, inoperative, jobless, kicking one's heels, latent, mothballed, out of service, out of work, unemployed, unoccupied, unused 2. dull, indolent, lazy, lethargic, low-key (*informal*), passive, quiet, sedentary, slothful, slow, sluggish, somnolent, torpid
Antonyms (*sense 1*) employed, mobile, occupied, operative, running, used, working (*sense 2*) active, busy, diligent, energetic, industrious, vibrant

inactivity 1. dormancy, hibernation, immobility, inaction, passivity, unemployment 2. dilatoriness, *dolce far niente*, dullness, heaviness, indolence, inertia, inertness, lassitude, laziness, lethargy, quiescence, sloth, sluggishness, stagnation, torpor, vegetation
Antonyms action, activeness, bustle, employment, exertion, mobility, movement

inadequacy 1. dearth, deficiency, inadequateness, incompleteness, insufficiency, meagreness, paucity, poverty, scantiness, shortage, skimpiness 2. defectiveness, faultiness, inability, inaptness, incapacity, incompetence, incompetency, ineffectiveness, inefficacy, unfitness, unsuitableness 3. defect, failing, imperfection, lack, shortage, shortcoming, weakness

inadequate 1. defective, deficient, faulty, imperfect, incommensurate, incomplete, insubstantial, insufficient, meagre, niggardly, pathetic, scant, scanty, short, sketchy, skimpy, sparse 2. found wanting, inapt, incapable, incompetent, not up to scratch (*informal*), unequal, unfitted, unqualified
Antonyms (*sense 1*) adequate, ample, complete, perfect, satisfactory, substantial, sufficient (*sense 2*) apt, capable, competent, equal, fit, qualified

inadequately imperfectly, insufficiently, meagrely, poorly, scantily, sketchily, skimpily, sparsely, thinly

inadmissible immaterial, improper, inappropriate, incompetent, irrelevant, unacceptable, unallowable, unqualified, unreasonable

inadvertence, inadvertency blunder, carelessness, error, heedlessness, inattention, inconsideration, inobservance, mistake, neglect, negligence, oversight, remissness, thoughtlessness

inadvertent accidental, careless, chance, heedless, negligent, thoughtless, unheeding, unintended, unintentional, unplanned, unpremeditated, unthinking, unwitting

inadvertently 1. carelessly, heedlessly, in an unguarded moment, negligently, thoughtlessly, unguardedly, unthinkingly 2. accidentally, by accident, by mistake, involuntarily, mistakenly, unintentionally, unwittingly
Antonyms carefully, consciously, deliberately, heedfully, intentionally

inadvisable ill-advised, impolitic, imprudent, inexpedient, injudicious, unwise

inalienable absolute, entailed (*Law*), inherent, inviolable, non-negotiable, nontransferable, sacrosanct, unassailable, untransferable

inane asinine, daft (*informal*), devoid of intelligence, empty, fatuous, frivolous, futile, goofy (*informal*), idiotic, imbecilic, mindless, puerile, senseless, silly, stupid, trifling, unintelligent, vacuous, vain, vapid, worthless
Antonyms meaningful, profound, sensible, serious, significant, weighty, worthwhile

inanimate cold, dead, defunct, extinct, inactive, inert, insensate, insentient, lifeless, quiescent, soulless, spiritless
Antonyms active, alive, alive and kicking, animate, full of beans (*informal*), lively, living, moving

inanity asininity, bêtise (*rare*), daftness (*informal*), emptiness, fatuity, folly, frivolity, imbecility, puerility, senselessness, silliness, vacuity, vapidity, worthlessness

inapplicable inapposite, inappropriate, inapt, irrelevant, unsuitable, unsuited
Antonyms applicable, apposite, appropriate, apt, fitting, pertinent, relevant, suitable

inapposite impertinent, inapplicable, inappropriate, infelicitous, irrelevant, out of place, unfit, unsuitable

inappreciable imperceptible, infinitesimal, insignificant, minuscule, negligible

inappropriate disproportionate, ill-fitted, ill-suited, ill-timed, improper, incongruous, malapropos, out of place, tasteless, unbecoming, unbefitting, unfit, unfitting, unseemly, unsuitable, untimely
Antonyms appropriate, becoming, congruous, fitting, proper, seemly, suitable, timely

inapt 1. ill-fitted, ill-suited, inapposite, inappropriate, infelicitous, unsuitable, unsuited 2. awkward, clumsy, dull, gauche, incompetent, inept, inexpert, maladroit, slow, stupid
Antonyms (*sense 1*) apposite, appropriate, apt, felicitous, fitting, suitable, suited

inaptitude awkwardness, clumsiness, incompetence, maladroitness, unfitness, unreadiness, unsuitableness

inarticulate 1. blurred, incoherent, incomprehensible, indistinct, muffled, mumbled, unclear, unintelligible 2. dumb, mute, silent, speechless, tongue-tied, unspoken, unuttered, unvoiced, voiceless, wordless 3. faltering, halting, hesitant, poorly spoken
Antonyms (*senses 1 & 3*) articulate, clear, coherent, comprehensible, intelligible, well-spoken

inattention absent-mindedness, carelessness, daydreaming, disregard, forgetfulness, heedlessness, inadvertence, inattentiveness, indifference, neglect, preoccupation, thoughtlessness, woolgathering

inattentive absent-minded, careless, distracted, distrait, dreamy, heedless, inadvertent, neglectful, negligent, preoccupied, regardless, remiss, slapdash, slipshod, thoughtless, unheeding, unmindful, unobservant, vague
Antonyms attentive, aware, careful, considerate, heeding, mindful, observant, thoughtful

inaudible indistinct, low, mumbling, out of earshot, stifled, unheard
Antonyms audible, clear, discernible, distinct, perceptible

inaugural dedicatory, first, initial, introductory, maiden, opening

inaugurate 1. begin, commence, get under way, initiate, institute, introduce, kick off (*informal*), launch, originate, set in motion, set up, usher in 2. induct, install, instate, invest 3. commission, dedicate, open, ordain

inauguration 1. initiation, institution, launch, launching, opening, setting up 2. induction, installation, investiture

inauspicious bad, black, bodeful, discouraging, ill-omened, ominous, unfavourable, unfortunate, unlucky, unpromising, unpropitious, untoward
Antonyms auspicious, encouraging, favourable, fortunate, good, lucky, promising, propitious

inborn congenital, connate, hereditary, immanent, inbred, ingrained, inherent, inherited, innate, in one's blood, instinctive, intuitive, native, natural

inbred constitutional, deep-seated, immanent, ingrained, inherent, innate, native, natural

in-built built-in, component, incorporated, integral

incalculable boundless, countless, enormous, immense, incomputable, inestimable, infinite, innumerable, limitless, measureless, numberless, uncountable, untold, vast, without number

incandescent brilliant, Day-Glo, glowing, luminous, phosphorescent, radiant, red-hot, shining, white-hot

incantation abracadabra, chant, charm, conjuration, formula, hex (*U.S. & Canad. informal*), invocation, spell

incapable 1. feeble, inadequate, incompetent, ineffective, inept, inexpert, insufficient, not equal to, not up to, unfit, unfitted, unqualified, weak 2. helpless, impotent, powerless, unable, unfit 3. *with* **of** impervious, not admitting of, not susceptible to, resistant
Antonyms (*sense 1*) adequate, capable, competent, efficient, expert, fit, qualified, sufficient

incapacitate cripple, disable, disqualify, immobilize, lay up (*informal*), paralyse, prostrate, put out of action (*informal*), scupper (*Brit. slang*), unfit (*rare*)

incapacitated disqualified, *hors de combat*, immobilized, indisposed, laid up (*informal*), out of action (*informal*), unfit

incapacity disqualification, feebleness, impotence, inability, inadequacy, incapability, incompetency, ineffectiveness, powerlessness, unfitness, weakness

incapsulate *see* ENCAPSULATE

incarcerate commit, confine, coop up, detain, gaol, immure, impound, imprison, intern, jail, lock up, put under lock and key, restrain, restrict, send down (*Brit.*), throw in jail

incarceration bondage, captivity, confinement, detention, imprisonment, internment, porridge (*slang*), restraint

incarnate 1. in bodily form, in human form, in the flesh, made flesh 2. embodied, personified, typified

incarnation avatar, bodily form, embodiment, epitome, exemplification, impersonation, manifestation, personification, type

incautious careless, hasty, heedless, ill-advised, ill-judged, improvident, imprudent, impulsive, inconsiderate, indiscreet, injudicious, negligent, precipitate, rash, reckless, thoughtless, unguarded, unthinking, unwary
Antonyms careful, cautious, considerate, discreet, guarded, heedful, judicious, prudent, thoughtful, wary

incautiously imprudently, impulsively, indiscreetly, precipitately, rashly, recklessly, thoughtlessly, unthinkingly

incendiary *adjective* 1. dissentious, inflammatory, provocative, rabble-rousing, seditious, subversive *~noun* 2. arsonist, firebug (*informal*), fire raiser, pyromaniac 3. agitator, demagogue, firebrand, insurgent, rabble-rouser, revolutionary

incense[1] *verb* anger, enrage, exasperate, excite, gall, get one's hackles up, inflame, infuriate, irritate, madden, make one's blood boil (*informal*), make one see red (*informal*), make one's hackles rise, nark (*Brit., Austral. & N.Z. slang*), provoke, raise one's hackles, rile (*informal*), rub one up the wrong way

incense[2] *noun* aroma, balm, bouquet, fragrance, perfume, redolence, scent

incensed angry, choked, cross, enraged, exasperated, fit to be tied (*slang*), fuming, furious, hot under the collar (*informal*), indignant, infuriated, irate, ireful (*literary*), mad (*informal*), maddened, on the warpath (*informal*), steamed up (*slang*), up in arms, wrathful

incentive bait, carrot (*informal*), carrot and stick, encouragement, enticement, goad, impetus, impulse, inducement, lure, motivation, motive, spur, stimulant, stimulus
Antonyms deterrent, discouragement, disincentive, dissuasion, warning

inception beginning, birth, commencement, dawn, inauguration, initiation, kickoff (*informal*), origin, outset, rise, start
Antonyms completion, conclusion, end, ending, finish, termination

incessant ceaseless, constant, continual, continuous, endless, eternal, everlasting, interminable, never-ending, nonstop, perpetual, persistent, relentless, unbroken, unceasing, unending, unrelenting, unremitting
Antonyms infrequent, intermittent, occasional, periodic, rare, sporadic

incessantly all the time, ceaselessly, constantly, continually, endlessly, eternally, everlastingly, interminably, nonstop, perpetually, persistently, without a break

incest

You should make a point of trying everything once, excepting incest and folk-dancing
Arnold Bax *Farewell My Youth*

inchoate 1. beginning, inceptive, incipient, nascent 2. elementary, embryonic, formless, immature, imperfect, rudimentary, undeveloped, unformed

incidence amount, degree, extent, frequency, occurrence, prevalence, rate

incident 1. adventure, circumstance, episode, event, fact, happening, matter, occasion, occurrence 2. brush, clash, commotion, confrontation, contretemps, disturbance, mishap, scene, skirmish

incidental 1. accidental, casual, chance, fortuitous, odd, random 2. *with* **to** accompanying, attendant, by-the-way, concomitant, contingent, contributory, related 3. ancillary, minor, nonessential, occasional, secondary, subordinate, subsidiary
Antonyms (*sense 3*) crucial, essential, important, necessary, vital

incidentally 1. accidentally, by chance, casually, fortuitously 2. by the bye, by the way, in passing, parenthetically

incidentals contingencies, extras, minutiae, odds and ends

incinerate burn up, carbonize, char, consume by fire, cremate, reduce to ashes

incipient beginning, commencing, developing, embryonic, inceptive, inchoate, nascent, originating, starting

incise carve, chisel, cut (into), engrave, etch, inscribe

incision cut, gash, notch, opening, slash, slit

incisive **1.** acute, keen, penetrating, perspicacious, piercing, trenchant **2.** acid, biting, caustic, cutting, mordacious, mordant, sarcastic, sardonic, satirical, severe, sharp, vitriolic
Antonyms (*sense 1*) dense, dull, superficial, vague, woolly

incisiveness **1.** keenness, penetration, perspicacity, sharpness, trenchancy **2.** acidity, pungency, sarcasm

incite agitate for *or* against, animate, drive, egg on, encourage, excite, foment, goad, impel, inflame, instigate, prod, prompt, provoke, put up to, rouse, set on, spur, stimulate, stir up, urge, whip up
Antonyms dampen, deter, discourage, dishearten, dissuade, restrain

incitement agitation, clarion call, encouragement, goad, impetus, impulse, inducement, instigation, motivation, motive, prompting, provocation, spur, stimulus

incivility bad manners, boorishness, discourteousness, discourtesy, disrespect, ill-breeding, impoliteness, rudeness, unmannerliness
Antonyms civility, courteousness, courtesy, good manners, mannerliness, politeness, respect

inclemency **1.** bitterness, boisterousness, rawness, rigour, roughness, severity, storminess **2.** callousness, cruelty, harshness, mercilessness, severity, tyranny, unfeelingness

inclement **1.** bitter, boisterous, foul, harsh, intemperate, rigorous, rough, severe, stormy, tempestuous **2.** callous, cruel, draconian, harsh, intemperate, merciless, pitiless, rigorous, severe, tyrannical, unfeeling, unmerciful
Antonyms (*sense 1*) balmy, calm, clement, fine, mild, pleasant, temperate (*sense 2*) compassionate, gentle, humane, kind, merciful, tender

inclination **1.** affection, aptitude, bent, bias, desire, disposition, fancy, fondness, leaning, liking, partiality, penchant, predilection, predisposition, prejudice, proclivity, proneness, propensity, stomach, taste, tendency, thirst, turn, turn of mind, wish **2.** bending, bow, bowing, nod **3.** angle, bend, bending, deviation, gradient, incline, leaning, pitch, slant, slope, tilt
Antonyms (*sense 1*) antipathy, aversion, disinclination, dislike, revulsion

incline *verb* **1.** be disposed *or* predisposed, bias, influence, persuade, predispose, prejudice, sway, tend, turn **2.** bend, bow, lower, nod, nutate (*rare*), stoop **3.** bend, bevel, cant, deviate, diverge, heel, lean, slant, slope, tend, tilt, tip, veer *~noun* **4.** acclivity, ascent, declivity, descent, dip, grade, gradient, ramp, rise, slope

inclined apt, disposed, given, liable, likely, minded, of a mind (*informal*), predisposed, prone, willing

inclose *see* ENCLOSE

include **1.** comprehend, comprise, contain, cover, embody, embrace, encompass, incorporate, involve, subsume, take in, take into account **2.** add, allow for, build in, count, enter, insert, introduce, number among
Antonyms eliminate, exclude, leave out, omit, rule out

including as well as, containing, counting, inclusive of, plus, together with, with

inclusion addition, incorporation, insertion
Antonyms exception, exclusion, omission, rejection

inclusive across-the-board, all-embracing, all in, all together, blanket, catch-all (*chiefly U.S.*), comprehensive, full, general, global, *in toto*, overall, sweeping, umbrella, without exception
Antonyms confined, exclusive, limited, narrow, restricted, unique

incognito disguised, in disguise, under an assumed name, unknown, unrecognized

incoherence disconnectedness, disjointedness, inarticulateness, unintelligibility

incoherent confused, disconnected, disjointed, disordered, inarticulate, inconsistent, jumbled, loose, muddled, rambling, stammering, stuttering, unconnected, uncoordinated, unintelligible, wandering, wild
Antonyms coherent, connected, intelligible, logical, rational

incombustible fireproof, flameproof, noncombustible, nonflammable, noninflammable

income earnings, gains, interest, means, pay, proceeds, profits, receipts, revenue, salary, takings, wages

There are few sorrows, however poignant, in which a good income is of no avail
Logan Pearsall Smith

incomer immigrant

incoming approaching, arriving, entering, homeward, landing, new, returning, succeeding
Antonyms departing, exiting, leaving, outgoing

incommensurate disproportionate, inadequate, inequitable, insufficient, unequal

incommode annoy, be a trouble to, bother, disturb, embarrass, get in one's hair (*informal*), give (someone) bother *or* trouble, hassle (*informal*), hinder, impede, inconvenience, irk, put out, put (someone) to trouble, trouble, upset, vex

incommodious awkward, confined, cramped, inconvenient, narrow, restricted, small, uncomfortable

incommunicable indescribable, ineffable, inexpressible, unspeakable, unutterable

incommunicado in purdah, under house arrest

incomparable beyond compare, inimitable, matchless, paramount, peerless, superlative, supreme, transcendent, unequalled, unmatched, unparalleled, unrivalled

incomparably beyond compare, by far, easily, eminently, far and away, immeasurably

incompatibility antagonism, conflict, discrepancy, disparateness, incongruity, inconsistency, irreconcilability, uncongeniality

incompatible antagonistic, antipathetic, conflicting, contradictory, discordant, discrepant, disparate, ill-assorted, incongruous, inconsistent, inconsonant, irreconcilable, mismatched, uncongenial, unsuitable, unsuited
Antonyms alike, appropriate, compatible, congenial, consistent, harmonious, reconcilable, suitable, suited

incompetence inability, inadequacy, incapability, incapacity, incompetency, ineffectiveness, ineptitude, ineptness, insufficiency, skill-lessness, unfitness, uselessness

incompetent bungling, cowboy (*informal*), floundering, incapable, incapacitated, ineffectual, inept, inexpert, insufficient, skill-less, unable, unfit, unfitted, unskilful, useless
Antonyms able, capable, competent, expert, fit, proficient, skilful

incomplete broken, defective, deficient, fragmentary, imperfect, insufficient, lacking, partial, short, unaccomplished, undeveloped, undone, unexecuted, unfinished, wanting
Antonyms accomplished, complete, developed, finished, perfect, unified, whole

incomprehensible above one's head, all Greek to one (*informal*), baffling, beyond comprehension, beyond one's grasp, enigmatic, impenetrable, inconceivable, inscrutable, mysterious, obscure, opaque, perplexing, puzzling, unfathomable, unimaginable, unintelligible, unthinkable
Antonyms apparent, clear, comprehensible, conceivable, evident, intelligible, manifest, obvious, understandable

inconceivable beyond belief, impossible, incomprehensible, incredible, mind-boggling (*informal*), not to be thought of, out of the question, staggering (*informal*), unbelievable, unheard-of, unimaginable, unknowable, unthinkable
Antonyms believable, comprehensible, conceivable, credible, imaginable, likely, plausible, possible, reasonable

inconclusive ambiguous, indecisive, indeterminate, open, uncertain, unconvincing, undecided, unsettled, up in the air (*informal*), vague

incongruity conflict, discrepancy, disparity, inappropriateness, inaptness, incompatibility, inconsistency, inharmoniousness, unsuitability

incongruous absurd, conflicting, contradictory, contrary, disconsonant, discordant, extraneous, improper, inappropriate, inapt, incoherent, incompatible, inconsistent, out of keeping, out of place, unbecoming, unsuitable, unsuited
Antonyms appropriate, becoming, compatible, consistent, harmonious, suitable, suited

inconsequential immaterial, inconsiderable, insignificant, measly, minor, negligible, nickel-and-dime (*U.S. slang*), of no significance, paltry, petty, trifling, trivial, unimportant, wanky (*taboo slang*)

inconsiderable exiguous, inconsequential, insignificant, light, minor, negligible, petty, slight, small, small-time (*informal*), trifling, trivial, unimportant

inconsiderate careless, indelicate, insensitive, intolerant, rude, self-centred, selfish, tactless, thoughtless, uncharitable, ungracious, unkind, unthinking
Antonyms attentive, careful, considerate, gracious, kind, sensitive, tactful, thoughtful, tolerant

inconsistency **1.** contrariety, disagreement, discrepancy, disparity, divergence, incompatibility, incongruity, inconsonance, paradox, variance **2.** fickleness, instability, unpredictability, unreliability, unsteadiness

inconsistent **1.** at odds, at variance, conflicting, contradictory, contrary, discordant, discrepant, incoherent, incompatible, in conflict, incongruous, inconstant, irreconcilable, out of step **2.** capricious, changeable, erratic, fickle, inconstant, irregular, uneven, unpredictable, unstable, unsteady, vagarious (*rare*), variable
Antonyms (*sense 1*) coherent, compatible, homogenous, orderly, reconcilable, uniform (*sense 2*) consistent, constant, predictable, reliable, stable, steady, unchanging

inconsistently contradictorily, differently, eccentrically, erratically, inequably, randomly, unequally, unfairly, unpredictably, variably

inconsolable brokenhearted, desolate, despairing, heartbroken, heartsick, prostrate with grief, sick at heart

inconspicuous camouflaged, hidden, insignificant, modest, muted, ordinary, plain, quiet, retiring, unassuming, unnoticeable, unobtrusive, unostentatious
Antonyms bold, conspicuous, noticeable, obtrusive, obvious, salient, significant, visible

inconstant blowing hot and cold (*informal*), capricious, changeable, changeful, erratic, fickle, fluctuating, inconsistent, irresolute, mercurial, mutable, temperamental, uncertain, undependable, uneven, unreliable, unsettled, unstable, unsteady, vacillating, vagarious (*rare*), variable, volatile, wavering, wayward

incontestable beyond doubt, beyond question, certain, incontrovertible, indisputable, indubitable, irrefutable, self-evident, sure, undeniable, unquestionable

incontinent 1. unbridled, unchecked, uncontrollable, uncontrolled, ungovernable, ungoverned, unrestrained 2. debauched, lascivious, lecherous, lewd, loose, lustful, profligate, promiscuous, unchaste, wanton

incontrovertible beyond dispute, certain, established, incontestable, indisputable, indubitable, irrefutable, positive, sure, undeniable, unquestionable, unshakable

inconvenience *noun* 1. annoyance, awkwardness, bother, difficulty, disadvantage, disruption, disturbance, downside, drawback, fuss, hassle (*informal*), hindrance, nuisance, trouble, uneasiness, upset, vexation 2. awkwardness, cumbersomeness, unfitness, unhandiness, unsuitableness, untimeliness, unwieldiness *~verb* 3. bother, discommode, disrupt, disturb, give (someone) bother *or* trouble, hassle (*informal*), irk, make (someone) go out of his way, put out, put to trouble, trouble, upset

An adventure is only an inconvenience rightly considered. An inconvenience is only an adventure wrongly considered
G.K. Chesterton *All Things Considered*

inconvenient 1. annoying, awkward, bothersome, disadvantageous, disturbing, embarrassing, inopportune, tiresome, troublesome, unseasonable, unsuitable, untimely, vexatious 2. awkward, cumbersome, difficult, unhandy, unmanageable, unwieldy
Antonyms (*sense 1*) convenient, handy, opportune, seasonable, suitable, timely

incorporate absorb, amalgamate, assimilate, blend, coalesce, combine, consolidate, embody, fuse, include, integrate, meld, merge, mix, subsume, unite

incorporation absorption, amalgamation, assimilation, blend, coalescence, federation, fusion, inclusion, integration, merger, unifying

incorrect erroneous, false, faulty, flawed, improper, inaccurate, inappropriate, inexact, mistaken, off base (*U.S. & Canad. informal*), off beam (*informal*), out, specious, unfitting, unsuitable, untrue, way off beam (*informal*), wide of the mark (*informal*), wrong
Antonyms accurate, correct, exact, faultless, fitting, flawless, right, suitable, true

incorrectness erroneousness, error, fallacy, faultiness, impreciseness, imprecision, impropriety, inaccuracy, inexactness, speciousness, unsoundness, unsuitability, wrongness

incorrigible hardened, hopeless, incurable, intractable, inveterate, irredeemable, unreformed

incorruptibility honesty, honour, integrity, justness, uprightness

incorruptible 1. above suspicion, honest, honourable, just, straight, trustworthy, unbribable, upright 2. everlasting, imperishable, undecaying

increase *verb* 1. add to, advance, aggrandize, amplify, augment, boost, build up, develop, dilate, enhance, enlarge, escalate, expand, extend, grow, heighten, inflate, intensify, magnify, mount, multiply, proliferate, prolong, raise, snowball, spread, step up (*informal*), strengthen, swell, wax *~noun* 2. addition, augmentation, boost, development, enlargement, escalation, expansion, extension, gain, growth, increment, intensification, rise, upsurge, upturn 3. **on the increase** developing, escalating, expanding, growing, increasing, multiplying, on the rise, proliferating, spreading
Antonyms *verb* abate, abbreviate, abridge, condense, curtail, decline, decrease, deflate, diminish, dwindle, lessen, reduce, shorten, shrink

increasingly more and more, progressively, to an increasing extent

incredible 1. absurd, beyond belief, cock-and-bull (*informal*), far-fetched, implausible, impossible, improbable, inconceivable, not hold water, preposterous, unbelievable, unimaginable, unthinkable 2. *informal* ace (*informal*), amazing, astonishing, astounding, awe-inspiring, brilliant, def (*slang*), extraordinary, far-out (*slang*), great, marvellous, mega (*slang*), prodigious, rad (*informal*), sensational (*informal*), superhuman, wonderful

incredulity disbelief, distrust, doubt, scepticism, unbelief

incredulous disbelieving, distrustful, doubtful, doubting, dubious, mistrustful, sceptical, suspicious, unbelieving, unconvinced, wet behind

the ears (*informal*)
Antonyms believing, credulous, gullible, na~ive, trusting, unsuspecting

increment accretion, accrual, accruement, ad~dition, advancement, augmentation, enlarge~ment, gain, increase, step (up), supplement

incriminate accuse, arraign, blacken the name of, blame, charge, impeach, implicate, incul~pate, indict, involve, point the finger at (*in~formal*), stigmatize

inculcate drill, drum into, hammer into (*infor~mal*), implant, impress, indoctrinate, infuse, instil

inculpate accuse, blame, censure, charge, drag into (*informal*), impeach, implicate, incrimi~nate, involve

incumbent binding, compulsory, mandatory, necessary, obligatory

incur arouse, bring (upon oneself), contract, draw, earn, expose oneself to, gain, induce, lay oneself open to, meet with, provoke

incurable *adjective* **1.** dyed-in-the-wool, hope~less, incorrigible, inveterate **2.** fatal, inoper~able, irrecoverable, irremediable, remediless, terminal

incurious apathetic, indifferent, pococurante, unconcerned, uninquiring, uninterested

incursion foray, infiltration, inroad, invasion, irruption, penetration, raid

indebted beholden, grateful, in debt, obligated, obliged, under an obligation

indecency bawdiness, coarseness, crudity, foulness, grossness, immodesty, impropriety, impurity, indecorum, indelicacy, lewdness, li~centiousness, obscenity, outrageousness, por~nography, smut, smuttiness, unseemliness, vileness, vulgarity
Antonyms decency, decorum, delicacy, modes~ty, propriety, purity, seemliness

indecent **1.** blue, coarse, crude, dirty, filthy, foul, gross, immodest, improper, impure, in~delicate, lewd, licentious, pornographic, sala~cious, scatological, smutty, vile **2.** ill-bred, im~proper, in bad taste, indecorous, offensive, outrageous, tasteless, unbecoming, unseemly, vulgar
Antonyms decent, decorous, delicate, modest, proper, pure, respectable, seemly, tasteful

indecipherable crabbed, illegible, indistin~guishable, unintelligible, unreadable

indecision ambivalence, dithering (*chiefly Brit.*), doubt, hesitancy, hesitation, indecisive~ness, irresolution, shilly-shallying (*informal*), uncertainty, vacillation, wavering

There is no more miserable human being than one in whom nothing is habitual but indecision
William James *Varieties of Religious Experience*

The cat would eat fish, but would not wet her feet

indecisive **1.** dithering (*chiefly Brit.*), doubtful, faltering, hesitating, in two minds (*informal*), irresolute, pussyfooting (*informal*), tentative, uncertain, undecided, undetermined, vacillat~ing, wavering **2.** inconclusive, indefinite, inde~terminate, unclear, undecided
Antonyms (*sense 1*) certain, decided, deter~mined, positive, resolute, unhesitating (*sense 2*) clear, conclusive, decisive, definite, deter~minate, final

indecorous boorish, churlish, coarse, ill-bred, immodest, impolite, improper, indecent, rude, tasteless, uncivil, uncouth, undignified, un~mannerly, unseemly, untoward

indeed actually, certainly, doubtlessly, in point of fact, in truth, positively, really, strictly, to be sure, truly, undeniably, undoubtedly, verily (*archaic*), veritably

indefatigable assiduous, diligent, dogged, in~exhaustible, patient, persevering, pertinacious, relentless, sedulous, tireless, unflagging, un~remitting, untiring, unwearied, unwearying

indefensible faulty, inexcusable, insupportable, unforgivable, unjustifiable, unpardonable, un~tenable, unwarrantable, wrong
Antonyms defensible, excusable, forgivable, justifiable, legitimate, pardonable, support~able, tenable, warrantable

indefinable dim, hazy, impalpable, indescrib~able, indistinct, inexpressible, nameless, ob~scure, unrealized, vague

indefinite ambiguous, confused, doubtful, equivocal, evasive, general, ill-defined, impre~cise, indeterminate, indistinct, inexact, loose, obscure, oracular, uncertain, unclear, unde~fined, undetermined, unfixed, unknown, un~limited, unsettled, vague
Antonyms certain, clear, definite, determi~nate, distinct, exact, fixed, settled, specific

indefinitely ad infinitum, continually, endless~ly, for ever, *sine die*, till the cows come home (*informal*)

indelible enduring, indestructible, ineffaceable, ineradicable, inexpungible, inextirpable, in~grained, lasting, permanent
Antonyms eradicable, erasable, impermanent, removable, short-lived, temporary, washable

indelicacy bad taste, coarseness, crudity, grossness, immodesty, impropriety, indecency, obscenity, offensiveness, rudeness, smuttiness, suggestiveness, tastelessness, vulgarity

indelicate blue, coarse, crude, embarrassing, gross, immodest, improper, indecent, indeco~rous, low, near the knuckle (*informal*), ob~scene, off-colour, offensive, risqué, rude, sug~gestive, tasteless, unbecoming, unseemly, un~toward, vulgar, X-rated (*informal*)

Antonyms becoming, decent, decorous, delicate, modest, proper, refined, seemly

indemnify 1. endorse, guarantee, insure, protect, secure, underwrite 2. compensate, pay, reimburse, remunerate, repair, repay, requite, satisfy

indemnity 1. guarantee, insurance, protection, security 2. compensation, redress, reimbursement, remuneration, reparation, requital, restitution, satisfaction 3. *Law* exemption, immunity, impunity, privilege

indent *verb* 1. ask for, order, request, requisition 2. cut, dint, mark, nick, notch, pink, scallop, score, serrate

indentation bash (*informal*), cut, dent, depression, dimple, dip, hollow, jag, nick, notch, pit

independence autarchy, autonomy, freedom, home rule, liberty, self-determination, self-government, self-reliance, self-rule, self-sufficiency, separation, sovereignty

Antonyms bondage, dependence, subjection, subjugation, subordination, subservience

A woman without a man is like a fish without a bicycle

Gloria Steinem

He travels the fastest who travels alone

Rudyard Kipling *The Story of the Gadsbys*

If we had independence tomorrow, life would change very little. But for nationalists, that is not a reason not to want it

Inaki Perez Beotegi

independent 1. absolute, free, liberated, separate, unconnected, unconstrained, uncontrolled, unrelated 2. autarchic, autarchical, autonomous, decontrolled, nonaligned, self-determining, self-governing, separated, sovereign 3. bold, individualistic, liberated, self-contained, self-reliant, self-sufficient, self-supporting, unaided, unconventional

Antonyms (*sense 2*) aligned, controlled, dependent, restrained, subject, submissive, subordinate, subservient, subsidiary

independently alone, autonomously, by oneself, individually, on one's own, separately, solo, unaided, under one's own steam

indescribable beggaring description, beyond description, beyond words, incommunicable, indefinable, ineffable, inexpressible, unutterable

indestructible abiding, durable, enduring, everlasting, immortal, imperishable, incorruptible, indelible, indissoluble, lasting, nonperishable, permanent, unbreakable, unfading

Antonyms breakable, corruptible, destructible, fading, impermanent, mortal, perishable

indeterminate imprecise, inconclusive, indefinite, inexact, uncertain, undefined, undetermined, unfixed, unspecified, unstipulated, vague

Antonyms certain, clear, conclusive, definite, determinate, exact, fixed, precise, specified, stipulated

index 1. clue, guide, indication, mark, sign, symptom, token 2. director, forefinger, hand, indicator, needle, pointer

indicate 1. add up to (*informal*), bespeak, be symptomatic of, betoken, denote, evince, imply, manifest, point to, reveal, show, signify, suggest 2. designate, point out, point to, specify 3. display, express, mark, read, record, register, show

indicated advisable, called-for, desirable, necessary, needed, recommended, suggested

indication clue, evidence, explanation, forewarning, hint, index, inkling, intimation, manifestation, mark, note, omen, portent, sign, signal, suggestion, symptom, warning

indicative exhibitive, indicatory, indicial, pointing to, significant, suggestive, symptomatic

indicator display, gauge, guide, index, mark, marker, meter, pointer, sign, signal, signpost, symbol

indict accuse, arraign, charge, impeach, prosecute, serve with a summons, summon, summons, tax

indictment accusation, allegation, charge, impeachment, prosecution, summons

indifference 1. absence of feeling, aloofness, apathy, callousness, carelessness, coldness, coolness, detachment, disregard, heedlessness, inattention, lack of interest, negligence, nonchalance, stoicalness, unconcern 2. disinterestedness, dispassion, equity, impartiality, neutrality, objectivity 3. insignificance, irrelevance, triviality, unimportance

Antonyms (*sense 1*) attention, care, commitment, concern, enthusiasm, heed, regard

I regard you with an indifference closely bordering on aversion

Robert Louis Stevenson *The New Arabian Nights*

indifferent 1. aloof, apathetic, callous, careless, cold, cool, detached, distant, heedless, impervious, inattentive, not give a monkey's (*slang*), regardless, uncaring, unconcerned, unimpressed, uninterested, unmoved, unresponsive, unsympathetic 2. immaterial, insignificant, of no consequence, unimportant 3. average, fair, mediocre, middling, moderate, no great shakes (*informal*), ordinary, passable, perfunctory, so-so (*informal*), undistinguished, uninspired 4. disinterested, dispassionate, equitable, impartial, neutral, nonaligned, nonpartisan, objective, unbiased, uninvolved, unprejudiced

Antonyms (*sense 1*) avid, compassionate, concerned, eager, enthusiastic, interested, keen, responsive, sensitive, susceptible, sympathetic (*sense 3*) excellent, exceptional, fine, first-class, notable, remarkable

indigence destitution, distress, necessity, need, penury, poverty, privation, want

indigenous 1. aboriginal, autochthonous, home-grown, native, original 2. congenital, connate, immanent, inborn, inbred, inherent, innate

indigent destitute, dirt-poor, down and out, down at heel (*informal*), flat broke (*informal*), impecunious, impoverished, in want, necessitous, needy, on one's uppers (*informal*), on the breadline, penniless, penurious, poor, poverty-stricken, short, straitened, without two pennies to rub together (*informal*)
Antonyms affluent, prosperous, rich, wealthy, well-off, well-to-do

indigestion dyspepsia, dyspepsy, heartburn, upset stomach

indignant angry, annoyed, choked, disgruntled, exasperated, fuming (*informal*), furious, hacked (off) (*U.S. slang*), heated, hot under the collar (*informal*), huffy (*informal*), in a huff, incensed, in high dudgeon, irate, livid (*informal*), mad (*informal*), miffed (*informal*), narked (*Brit., Austral., & N.Z. slang*), peeved (*informal*), pissed off (*taboo slang*), provoked, resentful, riled, scornful, seeing red (*informal*), sore (*informal*), up in arms (*informal*), wrathful

indignation anger, exasperation, fury, ire (*literary*), pique, rage, resentment, righteous anger, scorn, umbrage, wrath

indignity abuse, affront, contumely, dishonour, disrespect, humiliation, injury, insult, obloquy, opprobrium, outrage, reproach, slap in the face (*informal*), slight, snub

indirect 1. backhanded, circuitous, circumlocutory, crooked, devious, long-drawn-out, meandering, oblique, periphrastic, rambling, roundabout, tortuous, wandering, winding, zigzag 2. ancillary, collateral, contingent, incidental, secondary, subsidiary, unintended
Antonyms (*sense 1*) clear-cut, direct, straight, straightforward, undeviating, uninterrupted (*sense 2*) direct, explicit, express, intended

indirectly by implication, circumlocutorily, in a roundabout way, obliquely, periphrastically, second-hand

indiscernible hidden, impalpable, imperceptible, indistinct, indistinguishable, invisible, unapparent, undiscernible
Antonyms apparent, clear, discernible, distinct, distinguishable, perceptible, visible

indiscreet foolish, hasty, heedless, ill-advised, ill-considered, ill-judged, impolitic, imprudent, incautious, injudicious, naive, rash, reckless, tactless, undiplomatic, unthinking, unwise
Antonyms cautious, diplomatic, discreet, judicious, politic, prudent, tactful, wise

indiscretion bloomer (*Brit. informal*), boob (*Brit. slang*), error, faux pas, folly, foolishness, gaffe, gaucherie, imprudence, lapse, mistake, rashness, recklessness, slip, slip of the tongue, tactlessness

Careless talk costs lives
Second World War security slogan

indiscriminate 1. aimless, careless, desultory, general, hit or miss (*informal*), random, sweeping, uncritical, undiscriminating, unmethodical, unselective, unsystematic, wholesale 2. chaotic, confused, haphazard, higgledy-piggledy (*informal*), jumbled, mingled, miscellaneous, mixed, mongrel, motley, promiscuous, undistinguishable
Antonyms (*sense 1*) deliberate, discriminating, exclusive, methodical, selective, systematic

indispensable crucial, essential, imperative, key, necessary, needed, needful, requisite, vital
Antonyms dispensable, disposable, nonessential, superfluous, unimportant, unnecessary

indisposed 1. ailing, confined to bed, ill, laid up (*informal*), on the sick list (*informal*), poorly (*informal*), sick, under the weather, unwell 2. averse, disinclined, loath, reluctant, unwilling
Antonyms (*sense 1*) fine, fit, hardy, healthy, sound, well

indisposition 1. ailment, ill health, illness, sickness 2. aversion, disinclination, dislike, distaste, hesitancy, reluctance, unwillingness

indisputable absolute, beyond doubt, certain, evident, incontestable, incontrovertible, indubitable, irrefutable, positive, sure, unassailable, undeniable, unquestionable
Antonyms assailable, disputable, doubtful, indefinite, questionable, refutable, uncertain, vague

indissoluble abiding, binding, enduring, eternal, fixed, imperishable, incorruptible, indestructible, inseparable, lasting, permanent, solid, unbreakable

indistinct ambiguous, bleary, blurred, confused, dim, doubtful, faint, fuzzy, hazy, ill-defined, indefinite, indeterminate, indiscernible, indistinguishable, misty, muffled, obscure, out of focus, shadowy, unclear, undefined, unintelligible, vague, weak
Antonyms clear, defined, determinate, discernible, distinct, distinguishable, evident, intelligible

indistinguishable 1. alike, cut from the same cloth, identical, like as two peas in a pod (*informal*), (the) same, twin 2. imperceptible, indiscernible, invisible, obscure

individual 1. *adjective* characteristic, discrete, distinct, distinctive, exclusive, identical, idiosyncratic, own, particular, peculiar, personal, personalized, proper, respective, separate, several, single, singular, special, specific, unique 2. *noun* being, body (*informal*), character, creature, mortal, party, person, personage, soul, type, unit
Antonyms *adjective* collective, common, conventional, general, indistinct, ordinary, universal

individualism egocentricity, egoism, freethinking, independence, originality, self-direction, self-interest, self-reliance

individualist freethinker, independent, loner, lone wolf, maverick, nonconformist, original

individualistic 1. characteristic, distinctive, idiosyncratic, individual, original, particular, special, typical, unique 2. egocentric, egoistic, independent, self-reliant

individuality character, discreteness, distinction, distinctiveness, originality, peculiarity, personality, separateness, singularity, uniqueness

individually apart, independently, one at a time, one by one, personally, separately, severally, singly

indoctrinate brainwash, drill, ground, imbue, initiate, instruct, school, teach, train

indoctrination brainwashing, drilling, grounding, inculcation, instruction, schooling, training

indolence faineance, faineancy, heaviness, idleness, inactivity, inertia, inertness, languidness, languor, laziness, lethargy, shirking, skiving (*Brit. slang*), slacking, sloth, sluggishness, torpidity, torpor

I look upon indolence as a sort of suicide
Lord Chesterfield

indolent fainéant, good-for-nothing, idle, inactive, inert, lackadaisical, languid, lazy, lethargic, listless, lumpish, slack, slothful, slow, sluggish, torpid, workshy
Antonyms active, assiduous, busy, conscientious, diligent, energetic, industrious, vigorous

indomitable bold, invincible, resolute, staunch, steadfast, unbeatable, unconquerable, unflinching, untameable, unyielding
Antonyms cowardly, faltering, feeble, shrinking, wavering, weak, yielding

indorse *see* ENDORSE

indorsement *see* ENDORSEMENT

indubitable certain, evident, incontestable, incontrovertible, indisputable, irrefutable, obvious, open-and-shut, sure, unarguable, undeniable, undoubted, unquestionable, veritable

induce 1. actuate, convince, draw, encourage, get, impel, incite, influence, instigate, move, persuade, press, prevail upon, prompt, talk into 2. bring about, cause, effect, engender, generate, give rise to, lead to, occasion, produce, set in motion, set off
Antonyms curb, deter, discourage, dissuade, hinder, prevent, restrain, stop, suppress

inducement attraction, bait, carrot (*informal*), cause, clarion call, come-on (*informal*), consideration, encouragement, impulse, incentive, incitement, influence, lure, motive, reward, spur, stimulus, urge

induct inaugurate, initiate, install, introduce, invest, swear in

induction 1. inauguration, initiation, installation, institution, introduction, investiture 2. conclusion, generalization, inference

indulge 1. cater to, feed, give way to, gratify, pander to, regale, satiate, satisfy, treat oneself to, yield to 2. *with* **in** bask in, give free rein to, give oneself up to, luxuriate in, revel in, wallow in 3. baby, coddle, cosset, favour, fawn on, foster, give in to, go along with, humour, mollycoddle, pamper, pet, spoil

indulgence 1. excess, fondness, immoderation, intemperance, intemperateness, kindness, leniency, pampering, partiality, permissiveness, profligacy, profligateness, spoiling 2. appeasement, fulfilment, gratification, satiation, satisfaction 3. extravagance, favour, luxury, privilege, treat 4. courtesy, forbearance, goodwill, patience, tolerance, understanding
Antonyms (*sense 1*) moderation, strictness, temperance, temperateness

indulgent compliant, easy-going, favourable, fond, forbearing, gentle, gratifying, kind, kindly, lenient, liberal, mild, permissive, tender, tolerant, understanding
Antonyms austere, demanding, harsh, intolerant, rigorous, stern, strict, stringent, unmerciful

industrialist baron, big businessman, boss, capitalist, captain of industry, financier, magnate, manufacturer, producer, tycoon

industrious active, assiduous, busy, conscientious, diligent, energetic, hard-working, laborious, persevering, persistent, productive, purposeful, sedulous, steady, tireless, zealous
Antonyms good-for-nothing, idle, indolent, lackadaisical, lazy, shiftless, slothful

industriously assiduously, conscientiously, diligently, doggedly, hard, like a Trojan, nose to the grindstone (*informal*), perseveringly, sedulously, steadily, without slacking

industry 1. business, commerce, commercial enterprise, manufacturing, production, trade 2. activity, application, assiduity, determination, diligence, effort, labour, perseverance, persistence, tirelessness, toil, vigour, zeal

Go to the ant, thou sluggard; consider her ways, and be wise

Bible: Proverbs

If you have great talents, industry will improve them; if you have but moderate abilities, industry will supply their deficiency

Joshua Reynolds *Discourses on Art*

inebriate *verb* **1.** intoxicate, make drunk, stupefy **2.** animate, arouse, carry away, excite, exhilarate, fire, stimulate ~*noun* **3.** alcoholic, boozer (*informal*), dipsomaniac, drunk, drunkard, heavy drinker, lush (*slang*), soak (*slang*), sot, toper

inebriated befuddled, bevvied (*dialect*), blind drunk, blitzed (*slang*), blotto (*slang*), bombed (*slang*), Brahms and Liszt (*slang*), drunk, drunk as a skunk, flying (*slang*), fou *or* fu' (*Scot.*), half-cut (*informal*), half seas over (*informal*), high (*informal*), high as a kite (*informal*), inebriate, in one's cups, intoxicated, legless (*informal*), lit up (*slang*), merry (*Brit. informal*), out of it (*slang*), out to it (*Austral. & N.Z. slang*), paralytic (*informal*), pie-eyed (*slang*), pissed (*taboo slang*), plastered (*slang*), rat-arsed (*taboo slang*), smashed (*slang*), sozzled (*informal*), steamboats (*Scot. slang*), steaming (*slang*), stoned (*slang*), the worse for drink, three sheets in the wind (*informal*), tight (*informal*), tipsy, under the influence (*informal*), under the weather (*informal*), wasted (*slang*), wrecked (*slang*), zonked (*slang*)

inebriation crapulence, drunkenness, inebriety, insobriety, intemperance, intoxication, sottishness

ineffable beyond words, incommunicable, indefinable, indescribable, inexpressible, unspeakable, unutterable

ineffective barren, basket case, bootless, feeble, fruitless, futile, idle, impotent, inadequate, ineffectual, inefficacious, inefficient, pathetic, unavailing, unproductive, useless, vain, weak, worthless

Antonyms effective, efficacious, efficient, fruitful, potent, productive, useful, worthwhile

ineffectual abortive, basket case, bootless, emasculate, feeble, fruitless, futile, idle, impotent, inadequate, incompetent, ineffective, inefficacious, inefficient, inept, lame, pathetic, powerless, unavailing, useless, vain, weak

inefficacious abortive, futile, ineffective, ineffectual, unavailing, unproductive, unsuccessful

inefficacy futility, inadequacy, ineffectiveness, ineffectuality, nonsuccess, unproductiveness, uselessness

inefficiency carelessness, disorganization, incompetence, muddle, slackness, sloppiness

inefficient cowboy (*informal*), disorganized, feeble, incapable, incompetent, ineffectual, inefficacious, inept, inexpert, slipshod, sloppy, wasteful, weak

Antonyms able, capable, competent, effective, efficient, expert, organized, skilled

inelegant awkward, clumsy, coarse, crass, crude, gauche, graceless, indelicate, laboured, rough, uncouth, uncultivated, ungainly, ungraceful, unpolished, unrefined

ineligible disqualified, incompetent (*Law*), objectionable, ruled out, unacceptable, undesirable, unequipped, unfit, unfitted, unqualified, unsuitable

inept **1.** awkward, bumbling, bungling, cack-handed (*informal*), clumsy, cowboy (*informal*), gauche, incompetent, inexpert, maladroit, unhandy, unskilful, unworkmanlike **2.** absurd, improper, inappropriate, inapt, infelicitous, malapropos, meaningless, out of place, pointless, ridiculous, unfit, unsuitable

Antonyms able, adroit, appropriate, apt, competent, dexterous, effectual, efficient, germane, qualified, sensible, skilful, suitable, talented

ineptitude **1.** clumsiness, gaucheness, incapacity, incompetence, inexpertness, unfitness, unhandiness **2.** absurdity, inappropriateness, pointlessness, uselessness

inequality bias, difference, disparity, disproportion, diversity, imparity, irregularity, lack of balance, preferentiality, prejudice, unevenness

The worker is the slave of capitalist society, the female worker the slave of that slave

James Connolly *The Re-conquest of Ireland*

inequitable biased, discriminatory, one-sided, partial, partisan, preferential, prejudiced, unfair, unjust

Antonyms even-handed, fair, impartial, just, unbiased, unprejudiced

inequity bias, discrimination, injustice, one-sidedness, prejudice, unfairness, unjustness

inert dead, dormant, dull, idle, immobile, inactive, inanimate, indolent, lazy, leaden, lifeless, motionless, passive, quiescent, slack, slothful, sluggish, slumberous (*chiefly poetic*), static, still, torpid, unmoving, unreactive, unresponsive

Antonyms active, alive, alive and kicking, animated, energetic, full of beans (*informal*), living, mobile, moving, reactive, responsive, vital

inertia apathy, deadness, disinclination to move, drowsiness, dullness, idleness, immobility, inactivity, indolence, languor, lassitude, laziness, lethargy, listlessness, passivity, sloth, sluggishness, stillness, stupor, torpor, unresponsiveness

Antonyms action, activity, animation, brio, energy, liveliness, vigour, vitality

inescapable certain, destined, fated, ineluctable, ineludible (*rare*), inevitable, inexorable, sure, unavoidable

inessential 1. *adjective* dispensable, extraneous, extrinsic, needless, optional, redundant, spare, superfluous, surplus, uncalled-for, unnecessary 2. *noun* accessory, extra, extravagance, luxury, makeweight, superfluity, trimming

inestimable beyond price, immeasurable, incalculable, invaluable, precious, priceless, prodigious

inevitability certainty, fate, ineluctability, inexorability *or* inexorableness, sureness, unavoidability *or* unavoidableness

The glass is falling hour by hour, the glass will fall for ever
But if you break the bloody glass you won't hold up the weather
Louis MacNeice *Bagpipe Music*

One does not argue against the sun

inevitable assured, certain, decreed, destined, fixed, ineluctable, inescapable, inexorable, necessary, ordained, settled, sure, unavoidable, unpreventable
Antonyms avoidable, escapable, evadable, preventable, uncertain

inevitably as a necessary consequence, as a result, automatically, certainly, necessarily, of necessity, perforce, surely, unavoidably, willy-nilly

inexact imprecise, inaccurate, incorrect, indefinite, indeterminate, off

It is the nature of all greatness not to be exact
Edmund Burke

inexcusable indefensible, inexpiable, outrageous, unforgivable, unjustifiable, unpardonable, unwarrantable
Antonyms defensible, excusable, forgivable, justifiable, pardonable

inexhaustible 1. bottomless, boundless, endless, illimitable, infinite, limitless, measureless, never-ending, unbounded 2. indefatigable, tireless, undaunted, unfailing, unflagging, untiring, unwearied, unwearying
Antonyms (*sense 1*) bounded, exhaustible, finite, limitable, limited, measurable (*sense 2*) daunted, enervated, failing, flagging, tiring, wearied

inexorable adamant, cruel, hard, harsh, immovable, implacable, ineluctable, inescapable, inflexible, merciless, obdurate, pitiless, relentless, remorseless, severe, unappeasable, unbending, unrelenting, unyielding
Antonyms bending, flexible, lenient, movable, relenting, yielding

inexorably implacably, inevitably, irresistibly, relentlessly, remorselessly, unrelentingly

inexpedient disadvantageous, ill-advised, ill-considered, ill-judged, impolitic, impractical, improper, imprudent, inadvisable, inappropriate, indiscreet, injudicious, misguided, unadvisable, undesirable, undiplomatic, unsuitable, unwise

inexpensive bargain, budget, cheap, economical, low-cost, low-priced, modest, reasonable
Antonyms costly, dear, exorbitant, expensive, high-priced, pricey, uneconomical

inexperience callowness, greenness, ignorance, newness, rawness, unexpertness, unfamiliarity

You cannot put an old head on young shoulders

inexperienced amateur, callow, fresh, green, immature, new, raw, unaccustomed, unacquainted, unfamiliar, unfledged, unpractised, unschooled, unseasoned, unskilled, untrained, untried, unused, unversed, wet behind the ears (*informal*)
Antonyms experienced, familiar, knowledgeable, practised, seasoned, skilled, trained, versed

inexpert amateurish, awkward, bungling, cack-handed (*informal*), clumsy, inept, maladroit, skill-less, unhandy, unpractised, unprofessional, unskilful, unskilled, unworkmanlike

inexplicable baffling, beyond comprehension, enigmatic, incomprehensible, inscrutable, insoluble, mysterious, mystifying, strange, unaccountable, unfathomable, unintelligible
Antonyms comprehensible, explainable, explicable, fathomable, intelligible, soluble, understandable

inexpressible incommunicable, indefinable, indescribable, ineffable, unspeakable, unutterable

inexpressive bland, blank, cold, dead, deadpan, emotionless, empty, expressionless, impassive, inanimate, inscrutable, lifeless, stony, vacant

inextinguishable enduring, eternal, immortal, imperishable, indestructible, irrepressible, undying, unquenchable, unsuppressible

inextricably indissolubly, indistinguishably, inseparably, intricately, irretrievably, totally

infallibility 1. faultlessness, impeccability, irrefutability, omniscience, perfection, supremacy, unerringness 2. dependability, reliability, safety, sureness, trustworthiness

infallible 1. faultless, impeccable, omniscient, perfect, unerring, unimpeachable 2. certain, dependable, foolproof, reliable, sure, sure-fire (*informal*), trustworthy, unbeatable, unfailing
Antonyms (*sense 1*) errant, fallible, human, imperfect, mortal (*sense 2*) doubtful, dubious, uncertain, undependable, unreliable, unsure

infamous abominable, atrocious, base, detestable, disgraceful, dishonourable, disreputable

egregious, flagitious, hateful, heinous, ignominious, ill-famed, iniquitous, loathsome, monstrous, nefarious, notorious, odious, opprobrious, outrageous, scandalous, scurvy, shameful, shocking, vile, villainous, wicked
Antonyms esteemed, glorious, honourable, noble, reputable, virtuous

infamy abomination, atrocity, discredit, disgrace, dishonour, disrepute, ignominy, notoriety, obloquy, odium, opprobrium, outrageousness, scandal, shame, stigma, villainy

infancy 1. babyhood, early childhood 2. beginnings, cradle, dawn, early stages, emergence, inception, origins, outset, start
Antonyms (*sense 2*) close, conclusion, death, end, expiration, finish, termination

Heaven lies about us in our infancy
William Wordsworth *Intimations of Immortality*

infant 1. *noun* ankle-biter (*Austral. slang*), babe, babe in arms, baby, bairn (*Scot.*), child, little one, neonate, newborn child, rug rat (*slang*), sprog (*slang*), suckling, toddler, tot, wean (*Scot.*) 2. *adjective* baby, dawning, developing, early, emergent, growing, immature, initial, nascent, newborn, unfledged, young

At first the infant,
Mewling and puking in the nurse's arms
William Shakespeare *As You Like It*

infantile babyish, childish, immature, puerile, tender, weak, young
Antonyms adult, developed, mature

infatuate befool, beguile, besot, bewitch, captivate, delude, enchant, enrapture, enravish, fascinate, make a fool of, mislead, obsess, stupefy, sweep one off one's feet, turn (someone's) head

infatuated beguiled, besotted, bewitched, captivated, carried away, crazy about (*informal*), enamoured, enraptured, fascinated, head over heels in love with, inflamed, intoxicated, obsessed, possessed, smitten (*informal*), spellbound, swept off one's feet, under the spell of

infatuation crush (*informal*), fixation, folly, foolishness, madness, obsession, passion, thing (*informal*)

infect affect, blight, contaminate, corrupt, defile, influence, poison, pollute, spread to *or* among, taint, touch, vitiate

infection contagion, contamination, corruption, defilement, poison, pollution, septicity, virus

infectious catching, communicable, contagious, contaminating, corrupting, defiling, infective, pestilential, poisoning, polluting, spreading, transmittable, virulent, vitiating

infelicity 1. inappropriateness, inaptness, incongruity, unsuitability, wrongness 2. bad luck, misery, misfortune, sadness, unhappiness, woe, wretchedness

infer conclude, conjecture, deduce, derive, gather, presume, put two and two together, read between the lines, surmise, understand

inference assumption, conclusion, conjecture, consequence, corollary, deduction, illation (*rare*), presumption, reading, surmise

inferior *adjective* 1. junior, lesser, lower, menial, minor, secondary, subordinate, subsidiary, under, underneath 2. bad, bush-league (*Austral. & N.Z. informal*), chickenshit (*U.S. slang*), crappy (*slang*), dime-a-dozen (*informal*), duff (*Brit. informal*), for the birds (*informal*), imperfect, indifferent, low-grade, low-rent (*informal, chiefly U.S.*), mean, mediocre, no great shakes (*informal*), not a patch on, not much cop (*Brit. slang*), of a sort *or* of sorts, piss-poor (*taboo slang*), poor, poorer, poxy (*slang*), second-class, second-rate, shoddy, strictly for the birds (*informal*), substandard, tinhorn (*U.S. slang*), two-bit (*U.S. & Canad. slang*), worse ~*noun* 3. junior, menial, subordinate, underling
Antonyms (*sense 1*) greater, higher, senior, superior, top (*sense 2*) excellent, fine, first-class

No-one can make you feel inferior without your consent
Eleanor Roosevelt

inferiority 1. badness, deficiency, imperfection, inadequacy, insignificance, meanness, mediocrity, shoddiness, unimportance, worthlessness 2. abasement, inferior status *or* standing, lowliness, subordination, subservience
Antonyms advantage, ascendancy, dominance, eminence, excellence, superiority

infernal 1. chthonian, Hadean, hellish, lower, nether, Plutonian, Stygian, Tartarean (*literary*), underworld 2. accursed, damnable, damned, demonic, devilish, diabolical, fiendish, hellish, malevolent, malicious, satanic
Antonyms angelic, celestial, glorious, godlike, heavenly, seraphic

infertile barren, infecund, nonproductive, sterile, unfruitful, unproductive
Antonyms fecund, fertile, fruitful, generative, productive

infertility barrenness, infecundity, sterility, unfruitfulness, unproductiveness

infest beset, flood, invade, overrun, penetrate, permeate, ravage, swarm, throng

infested alive, beset, crawling, lousy (*slang*), overrun, pervaded, plagued, ravaged, ridden, swarming, teeming

infidel atheist, freethinker, Gentile, giaour (*Turkish*), heathen, heretic, pagan, sceptic, unbeliever

infidelity 1. adultery, bad faith, betrayal, cheating (*informal*), disloyalty, duplicity, faithlessness, false-heartedness, falseness, perfidy, unfaithfulness **2.** apostasy, disbelief, irreligion, scepticism, treachery, unbelief

infiltrate creep in, filter through, insinuate oneself, make inroads (into), penetrate, percolate, permeate, pervade, sneak in (*informal*), work *or* worm one's way into

infinite absolute, all-embracing, bottomless, boundless, enormous, eternal, everlasting, illimitable, immeasurable, immense, inestimable, inexhaustible, interminable, limitless, measureless, never-ending, numberless, perpetual, stupendous, total, unbounded, uncounted, untold, vast, wide, without end, without number
Antonyms bounded, circumscribed, finite, limited, measurable, restricted

infinitesimal atomic, inappreciable, insignificant, microscopic, minuscule, minute, negligible, teensy-weensy, teeny, teeny-weeny, tiny, unnoticeable, wee
Antonyms enormous, great, huge, infinite, large, vast

infinity boundlessness, endlessness, eternity, immensity, infinitude, perpetuity, vastness

I can't help it:- in spite of myself, infinity torments me
Alfred de Musset *L'Espoir en Dieu*

infirm 1. ailing, debilitated, decrepit, doddering, doddery, enfeebled, failing, feeble, frail, lame, weak **2.** faltering, indecisive, insecure, irresolute, shaky, unsound, unstable, vacillating, wavering, weak, wobbly
Antonyms (*sense 1*) healthy, hearty, robust, sound, strong, sturdy, vigorous

infirmity 1. debility, decrepitude, deficiency, feebleness, frailty, ill health, imperfection, sickliness, vulnerability **2.** ailment, defect, disorder, failing, fault, malady, sickness, weakness
Antonyms health, soundness, stability, strength, vigour

infix 1. engraft, fasten, implant, insert, inset, introduce, place, set **2.** drum into, entrench, impress, inculcate, ingrain, instil

inflame 1. agitate, anger, arouse, embitter, enrage, exasperate, excite, fire, foment, heat, ignite, impassion, incense, infuriate, intoxicate, kindle, madden, make one's blood boil, provoke, rile, rouse, stimulate **2.** aggravate, exacerbate, exasperate, fan, increase, intensify, worsen
Antonyms allay, calm, cool, discourage, extinguish, pacify, quench, quiet, soothe, suppress

inflamed angry, chafing, festering, fevered, heated, hot, infected, red, septic, sore, swollen

inflammable combustible, flammable, incendiary

inflammation burning, heat, painfulness, rash, redness, sore, soreness, tenderness

inflammatory anarchic, demagogic, explosive, fiery, incendiary, inflaming, instigative, insurgent, intemperate, provocative, rabble-rousing, rabid, red rag to a bull, riotous, seditious

inflate aerate, aggrandize, amplify, balloon, bloat, blow up, boost, dilate, distend, enlarge, escalate, exaggerate, expand, increase, puff up *or* out, pump up, swell
Antonyms collapse, compress, contract, deflate, diminish, lessen, shrink

inflated bombastic, exaggerated, grandiloquent, ostentatious, overblown, swollen

inflation aggrandizement, blowing up, distension, enhancement, enlargement, escalation, expansion, extension, increase, intensification, puffiness, rise, spread, swelling, tumefaction

inflect 1. intonate, modulate **2.** *Grammar* conjugate, decline **3.** arch, bend, bow, crook, curve, flex, round

inflection 1. accentuation, bend, bow, crook, curvature, intonation, modulation **2.** *Grammar* conjugation, declension **3.** angle, arc, arch

inflexibility 1. hardness, immovability, inelasticity, rigidity, stiffness, stringency **2.** fixity, intransigence, obduracy, obstinacy, steeliness

inflexible 1. adamant, brassbound, dyed-in-the-wool, firm, fixed, hard and fast, immovable, immutable, implacable, inexorable, intractable, iron, obdurate, obstinate, relentless, resolute, rigorous, set, set in one's ways, steadfast, steely, stiff-necked, strict, stringent, stubborn, unadaptable, unbending, unchangeable, uncompromising, unyielding **2.** hard, hardened, inelastic, nonflexible, rigid, stiff, taut
Antonyms elastic, flexible, irresolute, lissom(e), movable, pliable, pliant, supple, variable, yielding

inflict administer, apply, deliver, exact, impose, levy, mete *or* deal out, visit, wreak

infliction 1. administration, exaction, imposition, perpetration, wreaking **2.** affliction, penalty, punishment, trouble, visitation, worry

influence *noun* **1.** agency, ascendancy, authority, control, credit, direction, domination, effect, guidance, magnetism, mastery, power, pressure, rule, spell, sway, weight **2.** bottom, clout (*informal*), connections, good offices, hold, importance, leverage, power, prestige, pull (*informal*), weight *~verb* **3.** act *or* work upon, affect, arouse, bias, control, count, direct, dispose, guide, impact, impel, impress, incite, incline, induce, instigate, lead to believe, manipulate, modify, move, persuade, predispose, prompt, rouse, sway **4.** bring pressure to bear upon, carry weight with, make oneself felt, pull strings (*informal*)

influential authoritative, controlling, effective, efficacious, forcible, guiding, important, in~ strumental, leading, meaningful, momentous, moving, persuasive, potent, powerful, signifi~ cant, telling, weighty
Antonyms impotent, ineffective, ineffectual, powerless, unimportant, uninfluential, unper~ suasive, weak

influx arrival, convergence, flow, incursion, in~ flow, inrush, inundation, invasion, rush

infold *see* ENFOLD

inform 1. acquaint, advise, apprise, clue in (*in~ formal*), communicate, enlighten, give (some~ one) to understand, instruct, keep (someone) posted, leak to, let know, make conversant (with), notify, put (someone) in the picture (*informal*), send word to, teach, tell, tip off 2. *often with* **against** *or* **on** betray, blab, blow the gaff (*Brit. slang*), blow the whistle on (*in~ formal*), clype (*Scot.*), denounce, grass (*Brit. slang*), incriminate, inculpate, let the cat out of the bag, nark (*Brit., Austral., & N.Z. slang*), peach (*slang*), put the finger on (*infor~ mal*), rat (*informal*), shop (*slang, chiefly Brit.*), sing (*slang, chiefly U.S.*), snitch (*slang*), spill one's guts (*slang*), spill the beans (*informal*), squeal (*slang*), tell all, tell on (*informal*) 3. animate, characterize, illuminate, imbue, in~ spire, permeate, suffuse, typify

Never tell tales out of school

informal casual, colloquial, cosy, easy, familiar, natural, relaxed, simple, unceremonious, un~ constrained, unofficial
Antonyms ceremonious, constrained, conven~ tional, formal, official, stiff

informality casualness, ease, familiarity, lack of ceremony, naturalness, relaxation, simplic~ ity

information advice, blurb, counsel, data, dope (*informal*), facts, gen (*Brit. informal*), info (*informal*), inside story, instruction, intelli~ gence, knowledge, latest (*informal*), lowdown (*informal*), material, message, news, notice, report, tidings, word

informative chatty, communicative, edifying, educational, enlightening, forthcoming, gos~ sipy, illuminating, instructive, newsy, reveal~ ing

informed abreast, acquainted, *au courant*, *au fait*, briefed, conversant, enlightened, erudite, expert, familiar, genned up (*Brit. informal*), in the know (*informal*), in the picture, keeping one's finger on the pulse, knowledgeable, learned, posted, primed, reliable, up, up to date, versed, well-read

informer accuser, betrayer, grass (*Brit. slang*), Judas, nark (*Brit., Austral., & N.Z. slang*), sneak, squealer (*slang*), stool pigeon

infraction breach, breaking, contravention, in~ fringement, nonfulfilment, transgression, tres~ pass, violation

infrequent few and far between, occasional, once in a blue moon, rare, sporadic, uncom~ mon, unusual
Antonyms common, customary, frequent, ha~ bitual, often, regular, usual

infringe 1. break, contravene, disobey, trans~ gress, violate 2. *with* **on** *or* **upon** encroach, intrude, trespass

infringement breach, contravention, infraction, noncompliance, nonobservance, transgression, trespass, violation

infuriate anger, be like a red rag to a bull, en~ rage, exasperate, gall, get one's back up, get one's goat (*slang*), incense, irritate, madden, make one's blood boil, make one see red (*in~ formal*), make one's hackles rise, nark (*Brit., Austral., & N.Z. slang*), provoke, put one's back up, raise one's hackles, rile
Antonyms appease, calm, mollify, pacify, pla~ cate, propitiate, soothe

infuriating aggravating (*informal*), annoying, exasperating, galling, irritating, maddening, mortifying, pestilential, provoking, vexatious

infuse 1. breathe into, engraft, impart to, im~ plant, inculcate, inspire, instil, introduce 2. brew, macerate, soak, steep

ingenious adroit, bright, brilliant, clever, crafty, creative, dexterous, fertile, inventive, masterly, original, ready, resourceful, shrewd, skilful, subtle
Antonyms artless, clumsy, unimaginative, uninventive, unoriginal, unresourceful, un~ skilful

ingenuity adroitness, cleverness, faculty, flair, genius, gift, ingeniousness, inventiveness, knack, originality, resourcefulness, sharpness, shrewdness, skill, turn
Antonyms clumsiness, dullness, incompe~ tence, ineptitude, ineptness

ingenuous artless, candid, childlike, frank, guileless, honest, innocent, naive, open, plain, simple, sincere, trustful, trusting, unreserved, unsophisticated, unstudied
Antonyms artful, crafty, devious, insincere, reserved, sly, sophisticated, subtle, wily

ingenuousness artlessness, candour, frank~ ness, guilelessness, innocence, naivety, open~ ness, trustingness, unsuspiciousness
Antonyms artfulness, craftiness, insincerity, slyness, sophistication, subterfuge, subtlety

inglorious discreditable, disgraceful, dishon~ ourable, disreputable, failed, humiliating, ig~ noble, ignominious, infamous, obscure, shameful, unheroic, unknown, unsuccessful, unsung

ingraft *see* ENGRAFT

ingrain embed, entrench, fix, imbue, implant, impress, imprint, instil, root, sow the seeds

ingrained brassbound, constitutional, deep-rooted, deep-seated, fixed, fundamental, hereditary, inborn, inbred, inbuilt, indelible, ineradicable, inherent, in the blood, intrinsic, inveterate, rooted

ingratiate be a yes man, blandish, brown-nose (*taboo slang*), crawl, curry favour, fawn, flatter, get in with, get on the right side of, grovel, insinuate oneself, keep (someone) sweet, kiss (someone's) ass (*U.S. & Canad. taboo slang*), lick someone's arse (*taboo slang*), lick (someone's) boots, pander to, play up to, rub (someone) up the right way (*informal*), seek the favour (of someone), suck up to (*informal*), toady, worm oneself into (someone's) favour

ingratiating bootlicking (*informal*), crawling, fawning, flattering, humble, obsequious, servile, sycophantic, timeserving, toadying, unctuous

ingratitude thanklessness, unappreciativeness, ungratefulness
Antonyms appreciation, gratefulness, gratitude, thankfulness, thanks, thanksgiving

How sharper than a serpent's tooth it is
To have a thankless child!
William Shakespeare *King Lear*

Neither cast ye your pearls before swine
Bible: St. Matthew

ingredient component, constituent, element, part

ingress access, admission, admittance, door, entrance, entrée, entry, right of entry, way in

ingulf *see* ENGULF

inhabit abide, dwell, live, lodge, make one's home, occupy, people, populate, possess, reside, take up residence in, tenant

inhabitant aborigine, citizen, denizen, dweller, indigene, indweller, inmate, native, occupant, occupier, resident, tenant

inhabited colonized, developed, held, occupied, peopled, populated, settled, tenanted

inhalation breath, breathing, inhaling, inspiration

inhale breathe in, draw in, gasp, respire, suck in
Antonyms blow, breathe out, exhale, expire

inharmonious antipathetic, cacophonous, clashing, discordant, dissonant, grating, harsh, incompatible, inconsonant, jangling, jarring, strident, tuneless, unharmonious, unmelodious, unmusical

inherent basic, congenital, connate, essential, hereditary, immanent, inborn, inbred, inbuilt, ingrained, inherited, innate, in one's blood, instinctive, intrinsic, native, natural
Antonyms alien, extraneous, extrinsic, imposed, superficial, supplementary

inherit accede to, be bequeathed, be left, come into, fall heir to, succeed to

inheritance bequest, birthright, heritage, legacy, patrimony

inheritor beneficiary, heir, legatee, recipient, successor

inhibit arrest, bar, bridle, check, constrain, cramp (someone's) style (*informal*), curb, debar, discourage, forbid, frustrate, hinder, hold back *or* in, impede, obstruct, prevent, prohibit, restrain, stem the flow, stop, throw a spanner in the works
Antonyms abet, allow, enable, encourage, further, let, permit, support

inhibited constrained, frustrated, guarded, repressed, reserved, reticent, self-conscious, shy, subdued, uptight (*informal*), withdrawn
Antonyms free, natural, outgoing, relaxed, spontaneous, uninhibited, unreserved

inhibition bar, block, check, embargo, hang-up (*informal*), hindrance, interdict, mental blockage, obstacle, prohibition, reserve, restraint, restriction, reticence, self-consciousness, shyness

inhospitable **1.** cool, uncongenial, unfriendly, ungenerous, unkind, unreceptive, unsociable, unwelcoming, xenophobic **2.** bare, barren, bleak, desolate, empty, forbidding, godforsaken, hostile, lonely, sterile, unfavourable, uninhabitable
Antonyms (*sense 1*) amicable, friendly, generous, genial, gracious, hospitable, sociable, welcoming

inhuman animal, barbaric, barbarous, bestial, brutal, cold-blooded, cruel, diabolical, fiendish, heartless, merciless, pitiless, remorseless, ruthless, savage, unfeeling, vicious
Antonyms charitable, compassionate, feeling, humane, merciful, sensitive, tender, warmhearted

inhumane brutal, cruel, heartless, pitiless, uncompassionate, unfeeling, unkind, unsympathetic

inhumanity atrocity, barbarism, brutality, brutishness, cold-bloodedness, cold-heartedness, cruelty, hardheartedness, heartlessness, pitilessness, ruthlessness, unkindness, viciousness

Man's inhumanity to man
Makes countless thousands mourn
Robert Burns *Man was Made to Mourn*

inhumation burial, entombment, interment, sepulture

inhume bury, entomb, inter, lay to rest, sepulchre

inimical adverse, antagonistic, antipathetic, contrary, destructive, disaffected, harmful

hostile, hurtful, ill-disposed, injurious, noxious, opposed, oppugnant (*rare*), pernicious, repugnant, unfavourable, unfriendly, unwelcoming
Antonyms affable, amicable, congenial, favourable, friendly, good, helpful, kindly, sympathetic, welcoming

inimitable consummate, incomparable, matchless, nonpareil, peerless, supreme, unequalled, unexampled, unique, unmatched, unparalleled, unrivalled, unsurpassable

iniquitous abominable, accursed, atrocious, base, criminal, evil, heinous, immoral, infamous, nefarious, reprehensible, reprobate, sinful, unjust, unrighteous, vicious, wicked

iniquity abomination, baseness, crime, evil, evildoing, heinousness, infamy, injustice, misdeed, offence, sin, sinfulness, unrighteousness, wickedness, wrong, wrongdoing
Antonyms fairness, goodness, honesty, integrity, justice, morality, righteousness, uprightness, virtue

initial *adjective* beginning, commencing, early, first, inaugural, inceptive, inchoate, incipient, introductory, opening, primary
Antonyms closing, concluding, ending, final, last, terminal, ultimate

initially at first, at *or* in the beginning, at the outset, at the start, first, firstly, in the early stages, originally, primarily, to begin with

initiate *verb* **1.** begin, break the ice, commence, get under way, inaugurate, institute, kick off (*informal*), kick-start, launch, lay the foundations of, open, originate, pioneer, set going, set in motion, set the ball rolling, start **2.** acquaint with, coach, familiarize with, indoctrinate, induct, instate, instruct, introduce, invest, teach, train *~noun* **3.** beginner, convert, entrant, learner, member, novice, probationer, proselyte, tyro

initiation admission, baptism of fire, commencement, debut, enrolment, entrance, inauguration, inception, induction, installation, instatement, introduction, investiture

initiative **1.** advantage, beginning, commencement, first move, first step, lead **2.** ambition, drive, dynamism, enterprise, get-up-and-go (*informal*), inventiveness, leadership, originality, push (*informal*), resource, resourcefulness

inject **1.** inoculate, jab (*informal*), shoot (*informal*), vaccinate **2.** bring in, infuse, insert, instil, interject, introduce

injection **1.** inoculation, jab (*informal*), shot (*informal*), vaccination, vaccine **2.** dose, infusion, insertion, interjection, introduction

injudicious foolish, hasty, ill-advised, ill-judged, ill-timed, impolitic, imprudent, incautious, inconsiderate, indiscreet, inexpedient, rash, unthinking, unwise
Antonyms cautious, considerate, discreet, expedient, judicious, polite, prudent, well-timed, wise

injunction admonition, command, dictate, exhortation, instruction, mandate, order, precept, ruling

injure abuse, blemish, blight, break, damage, deface, disable, harm, hurt, impair, maltreat, mar, ruin, spoil, tarnish, undermine, vitiate, weaken, wound, wrong

injured **1.** broken, disabled, hurt, lamed, undermined, weakened, wounded **2.** cut to the quick, disgruntled, displeased, hurt, long-suffering, put out, reproachful, stung, unhappy, upset, wounded **3.** abused, blackened, blemished, defamed, ill-treated, maligned, maltreated, offended, tarnished, vilified, wronged

injurious adverse, bad, baneful (*archaic*), corrupting, damaging, deleterious, destructive, detrimental, disadvantageous, harmful, hurtful, iniquitous, maleficent, mischievous, noxious, pernicious, ruinous, slanderous, unconducive, unhealthy, unjust, wrongful

injury abuse, damage, detriment, disservice, evil, grievance, harm, hurt, ill, injustice, mischief, ruin, trauma (*Pathology*), wound, wrong

injustice bias, discrimination, favouritism, inequality, inequity, iniquity, one-sidedness, oppression, partiality, partisanship, prejudice, unfairness, unjustness, unlawfulness, wrong
Antonyms equality, equity, fairness, impartiality, justice, lawfulness, rectitude, right

inkling clue, conception, faintest *or* foggiest idea, glimmering, hint, idea, indication, intimation, notion, suggestion, suspicion, whisper

inland *adjective* domestic, interior, internal, upcountry

inlet arm (of the sea), bay, bight, cove, creek, entrance, firth *or* frith (*Scot.*), ingress, passage, sea loch (*Scot.*)

inmost *or* **innermost** basic, buried, central, deep, deepest, essential, intimate, personal, private, secret

innards **1.** entrails, guts, insides (*informal*), intestines, inwards, viscera, vitals **2.** guts (*informal*), mechanism, works

innate congenital, connate, constitutional, essential, immanent, inborn, inbred, indigenous, ingrained, inherent, inherited, in one's blood, instinctive, intrinsic, intuitive, native, natural
Antonyms accidental, acquired, affected, assumed, cultivated, fostered, incidental, learned, nurtured, unnatural

inner **1.** central, essential, inside, interior, internal, intestinal, inward, middle **2.** esoteric, hidden, intimate, personal, private, repressed, secret, unrevealed **3.** emotional, mental, psychological, spiritual

Antonyms (*sense 1*) exterior, external, outer, outside, outward (*sense 2*) exposed, obvious, overt, revealed, surface, unconcealed, unrepressed, visible

innkeeper host, hostess, hotelier, landlady, landlord, mine host, publican

innocence 1. blamelessness, chastity, clean hands, guiltlessness, incorruptibility, probity, purity, righteousness, sinlessness, stainlessness, uprightness, virginity, virtue 2. harmlessness, innocuousness, innoxiousness, inoffensiveness 3. artlessness, credulousness, freshness, guilelessness, gullibility, inexperience, ingenuousness, naïveté, simplicity, unsophistication, unworldliness 4. ignorance, lack of knowledge, nescience (*literary*), unawareness, unfamiliarity
Antonyms (*sense 1*) corruption, guilt, impurity, offensiveness, sinfulness, wrongness (*sense 3*) artfulness, cunning, disingenuousness, guile, wiliness, worldliness

He's armed without that's innocent within
Alexander Pope *Epilogue to the Satires*

If you would live innocently, seek solitude
Publilius Syrus *Sententiae*

Whoever blushes is already guilty; true innocence is ashamed of nothing
Jean Jacques Rousseau *Émile*

innocent *adjective* 1. blameless, clear, faultless, guiltless, honest, in the clear, not guilty, uninvolved, unoffending 2. chaste, immaculate, impeccable, incorrupt, pristine, pure, righteous, sinless, spotless, stainless, unblemished, unsullied, upright, virgin, virginal 3. *with* **of** clear of, empty of, free from, ignorant, lacking, nescient, unacquainted with, unaware, unfamiliar with, untouched by 4. harmless, innocuous, inoffensive, unmalicious, unobjectionable, well-intentioned, well-meant 5. artless, childlike, credulous, frank, guileless, gullible, ingenuous, naive, open, simple, unsuspicious, unworldly, wet behind the ears (*informal*) ~*noun* 6. babe (in arms) (*informal*), child, greenhorn (*informal*), ingénue *or* *(masc.)* ingénu
Antonyms (*sense 1*) blameworthy, culpable, dishonest, guilty, responsible (*sense 2*) corrupt, immoral, impure, sinful, wrong (*sense 4*) evil, harmful, iniquitous, malicious, offensive, wicked (*sense 5*) artful, disingenuous, sophisticated, worldly

innocuous harmless, innocent, innoxious, inoffensive, safe, unobjectionable

innovation alteration, change, departure, introduction, modernism, modernization, newness, novelty, variation

innovative alterative, inventive, new, novel, transformational, variational

innovator changer, introducer, inventor, modernizer, transformer

innuendo aspersion, hint, implication, imputation, insinuation, intimation, overtone, suggestion, whisper

innumerable beyond number, countless, incalculable, infinite, many, multitudinous, myriad, numberless, numerous, unnumbered, untold
Antonyms calculable, computable, finite, limited, measurable, numbered

inoffensive harmless, humble, innocent, innocuous, innoxious, mild, neutral, nonprovocative, peaceable, quiet, retiring, unobjectionable, unobtrusive, unoffending
Antonyms abrasive, harmful, irksome, irritating, malicious, objectionable, offensive, provocative

inoperable impracticable, impractical, nonviable, unrealistic, unworkable

inoperative broken, broken-down, buggered (*slang, chiefly Brit.*), defective, *hors de combat*, ineffective, ineffectual, inefficacious, invalid, nonactive, null and void, on the fritz (*U.S. slang*), out of action, out of commission, out of order, out of service, unserviceable, unworkable, useless

inopportune ill-chosen, ill-timed, inappropriate, inauspicious, inconvenient, malapropos, mistimed, unfavourable, unfortunate, unpropitious, unseasonable, unsuitable, untimely
Antonyms appropriate, auspicious, convenient, favourable, fortunate, opportune, seasonable, suitable, timely, well-timed

inordinate disproportionate, excessive, exorbitant, extravagant, immoderate, intemperate, preposterous, unconscionable, undue, unreasonable, unrestrained, unwarranted
Antonyms inhibited, moderate, reasonable, restrained, rightful, sensible, temperate

inorganic artificial, chemical, man-made, mineral

inquest inquiry, inquisition, investigation, probe

inquietude anxiety, apprehension, disquiet, disquietude, jumpiness, nervousness, restlessness, the jitters (*informal*), trepidation, unease, uneasiness, worry

inquire 1. examine, explore, inspect, investigate, look into, make inquiries, probe, research, scrutinize, search 2. *Also* **enquire** ask, query, question, request information, seek information

inquiring analytical, curious, doubtful, inquisitive, interested, investigative, nosy (*informal*), outward-looking, probing, questioning, searching, wondering

inquiry 1. examination, exploration, inquest, interrogation, investigation, probe, research scrutiny, search, study, survey **2.** *Also* **enquiry** query, question

inquisition cross-examination, examination, grilling (*informal*), inquest, inquiry, investigation, question, quizzing, third degree (*informal*)

inquisitive curious, inquiring, intrusive, nosy (*informal*), nosy-parkering (*informal*), peering, probing, prying, questioning, scrutinizing, snooping (*informal*), snoopy (*informal*)
Antonyms apathetic, incurious, indifferent, unconcerned, uninterested, unquestioning

inroad 1. advance, encroachment, foray, incursion, intrusion, invasion, irruption, onslaught, raid **2. make inroads upon** consume, eat away, eat up *or* into, encroach upon, use up

insalubrious injurious, insanitary, noxious, unhealthful, unhealthy, unwholesome

insane 1. as daft as a brush (*informal, chiefly Brit.*), barking (*slang*), barking mad (*slang*), crackpot (*informal*), crazed, crazy, demented, deranged, doolally (*slang*), gonzo (*slang*), loopy (*informal*), mad, mentally disordered, mentally ill, *non compos mentis*, not the full shilling (*informal*), off one's trolley (*slang*), of unsound mind, out of one's mind, out to lunch (*informal*), unhinged, up the pole (*informal*), wacko *or* whacko (*informal*) **2.** barking (*slang*), barking mad (*slang*), barmy (*slang*), batty (*slang*), bonkers (*slang, chiefly Brit.*), cracked (*slang*), crackers (*Brit. slang*), cuckoo (*informal*), having a screw loose (*informal*), loony (*slang*), loopy (*informal*), mental (*slang*), not right in the head, nuts (*slang*), nutty (*slang*), off one's chump (*slang*), off one's head (*slang*), off one's nut (*slang*), off one's rocker (*slang*), off one's trolley (*slang*), round the bend (*informal*), round the twist (*informal*), screwy (*informal*) **3.** bizarre, daft (*informal*), fatuous, foolish, idiotic, impractical, inane, irrational, irresponsible, lunatic, preposterous, senseless, stupid
Antonyms logical, lucid, normal, practical, rational, reasonable, reasoned, sane, sensible, sound

insanitary contaminated, dirtied, dirty, disease-ridden, feculent, filthy, impure, infected, infested, insalubrious, noxious, polluted, unclean, unhealthy, unhygienic
Antonyms clean, healthy, hygienic, pure, salubrious, unpolluted

insanity 1. aberration, craziness, delirium, dementia, frenzy, madness, mental derangement, mental disorder, mental illness **2.** folly, irresponsibility, lunacy, preposterousness, senselessness, stupidity
Antonyms logic, lucidity, normality, rationality, reason, sanity, sense, soundness, wisdom

insatiable edacious, gluttonous, greedy, insatiate, intemperate, quenchless, rapacious, ravenous, unappeasable, unquenchable, voracious
Antonyms appeasable, limited, quenchable, satiable, temperate

inscribe 1. carve, cut, engrave, etch, impress, imprint **2.** engross, enlist, enrol, enter, record, register, write **3.** address, dedicate

inscription dedication, engraving, label, legend, lettering, saying, words

inscrutable 1. blank, deadpan, enigmatic, impenetrable, poker-faced (*informal*), sphinxlike, unreadable **2.** hidden, incomprehensible, inexplicable, mysterious, undiscoverable, unexplainable, unfathomable, unintelligible
Antonyms clear, comprehensible, evident, explainable, explicable, intelligible, lucid, manifest, obvious, open, palpable, patent, penetrable, plain, readable, revealing, transparent, understandable

insect

Insects

Amazon ant
ant *or (archaic or dialect)* emmet
antlion *or* antlion fly
aphid *or* plant louse
aphis
apollo
apple blight *or* American blight
apple maggot
argus
army ant *or* legionary ant
bacon beetle
bag moth (*N.Z.*)
bagworm moth
bark beetle
bedbug *or (Southern U.S.)* chinch
bee
bee fly
beetfly *or* mangold fly
beetle
bell moth
blackfly *or* bean aphid
blister beetle
bloody-nosed beetle
blowfly *or* bluebottle
body louse, cootie *(U.S. & N.Z.) or (N.Z. slang)* kutu
bogong *or* bugong
boll weevil
bollworm
booklouse
bookworm
botfly
bristletail
brown-tail moth
buffalo gnat *or* black fly
buff-tip moth
bulb fly
bulldog ant *or* bull ant
bumblebee *or* humblebee
burying beetle *or* sexton
bushfly
butterfly
cabbageworm
cabinet beetle
cadelle
caddis worm *or* caseworm
Camberwell beauty *or (U.S.)* mourning cloak
cankerworm
cardinal beetle
carpenter bee
carpenter moth
carpet beetle *or (U.S.)* carpet bug
carpet moth
carrion beetle
carrot fly
cecropia moth
chafer
chalcid *or* chalcid fly
Christmas beetle
cicada *or* cicala
cinnabar
clearwing *or* clearwing moth
cleopatra
click beetle, snapping beetle *or* skipjack
Clifden nonpareil

cluster fly
cochineal *or* cochineal insect
cockchafer, May beetle *or* May bug
cockroach
codlin(g) moth
Colorado beetle *or* potato beetle
comma butterfly
copper
corkwing
cotton stainer
crab (louse)
crane fly *or (Brit.)* daddy-longlegs
cricket
cuckoo bee
curculio
damsel bug
damselfly
death's-head moth
deathwatch beetle
debris bug
devil's coach-horse
digger wasp
diving beetle
dobsonfly
dor
dragonfly *or (colloquial)* devil's darning-needle
drinker moth *or* drinker
driver ant
drosophila, fruit fly *or* vinegar fly
dung beetle *or* chafer
earwig *or (Scots dialect)* clipshears *or* clipshear
egger *or* eggar
ermine moth *or* ermine
firefly
flea
fly
frit fly
froghopper, spittle insect *or* spittle bug
fruit fly
furniture beetle
gadfly
gallfly
gall wasp
German cockroach *or (U.S.)* Croton bug
ghost moth
gipsy moth
glow-worm
gnat
gold beetle *or* goldbug
goldsmith beetle
goldtail moth *or* yellowtail (moth)
grannom
grasshopper
grass moth
greenbottle
greenfly
grey sedge
ground beetle
hairstreak
harlequin bug
hawk moth, sphinx moth *or* hummingbird moth
herald moth
Hercules beetle
Hessian fly
honeybee *or* hive bee
hornet
horntail *or* wood wasp
horsefly *or* cleg
housefly
house moth
hover fly
huhu
ichneumon fly *or* ichneumon wasp
Io moth
Japanese beetle
June bug, June beetle, May bug *or* May beetle
katydid
Kentish glory
killer bee
kissing bug
kitten moth
lace bug
lacewing
lac insect
lackey moth
ladybird *or (US & Canad.)* ladybug
lantern fly
lappet moth
large white *or* cabbage white
leaf beetle
leafcutter ant
leafcutter bee
leaf-hopper
leopard moth
lobster moth
locust
longicorn (beetle) *or* long-horned beetle
louse
luna moth
magpie moth
mantis *or* praying mantis
Maori bug
marbled white
mason bee
mason wasp
mayfly *or* dayfly
mealy bug
measuring worm, looper *or* inchworm
Mediterranean fruit fly *or* Medfly
midge
mining bee
mole cricket
monarch
mosquito
moth
mother-of-pearl moth
Mother Shipton
mud dauber
needle fly
nit
oil beetle
old lady
onion fly
orange-tip
painted lady
peacock butterfly
peppered moth
Pharaoh ant
phylloxera
pill beetle
pond-skater, water strider *or* water skater
privet hawk
processionary moth
purple emperor
puss moth
red admiral
red underwing
rhinoceros beetle
ringlet
robber fly, bee killer *or* assassin fly
rose chafer *or* rose beetle
rove beetle
ruby-tail wasp
sandfly
sand wasp
sawfly
scale insect
scarab
scavenger beetle
scorpion fly
screwworm fly
seventeen-year locust *or* periodical cicada
sheep ked *or* sheep tick
shield bug *or* stink bug
silkworm
silverfish
silverhorn
silver-Y (moth)
skipper
slave ant
small white
snake fly
snout (moth)
soldier beetle
Spanish fly
speckled wood
spider-hunting wasp
stable fly
stag beetle
stick insect *or (U.S. & Canad.)* walking stick
stonefly
sucking louse
swallowtail
swift (moth)
tachina fly
tapestry moth
tent caterpillar
termite *or* white ant
thorn (moth)
thrips
tiger (moth)
tortoise beetle
treehopper
tsetse fly *or* tzetze fly
tussock moth
two-tailed pasha
umber (moth)
vapourer moth
vedalia
velvet ant
vinegar fly
wall brown
warble fly
wasp
water beetle
water boatman
water bug
water scorpion
wave (moth)
wax insect
wax moth, honeycomb moth *or* bee moth
web spinner
weevil *or* snout beetle
weevil, pea weevil *or* bean weevil
weta
wheel bug
whirligig beetle
white

white admiral
whitefly
willow fly
winter moth
wireworm
wood ant
woodworm
yellow
yellow jacket (*U.S. & Canad.*)
yellow underwing

insecure 1. afraid, anxious, uncertain, unconfident, unsure 2. dangerous, defenceless, exposed, hazardous, ill-protected, open to attack, perilous, unguarded, unprotected, unsafe, unshielded, vulnerable, wide-open 3. built upon sand, flimsy, frail, insubstantial, loose, on thin ice, precarious, rickety, rocky, shaky, unreliable, unsound, unstable, unsteady, weak, wobbly
Antonyms (*sense 1*) assured, certain, confident, decisive, secure (*senses 2 & 3*) firm, protected, reliable, safe, secure, sound, stable, steady, substantial, sure

insecurity 1. anxiety, fear, uncertainty, unsureness, worry 2. danger, defencelessness, hazard, peril, risk, uncertainty, vulnerability, weakness 3. dubiety, frailness, instability, precariousness, shakiness, uncertainty, unreliability, unsteadiness, weakness
Antonyms (*sense 1*) assurance, certainty, confidence, security (*senses 2 & 3*) dependability, firmness, reliability, safety, security, stability, steadiness

insensate 1. anaesthetized, dead, inanimate, inert, insensible, insentient, lifeless, numbed, out (*informal*), unconscious 2. hardened, imperceptive, impercipient, indifferent, insensitive, inured, obtuse, stolid, thick-skinned, thoughtless, unfeeling, unperceiving 3. brainless, fatuous, foolish, mindless, senseless, stupid, thoughtless, unreasonable, witless

insensibility 1. apathy, callousness, dullness, indifference, inertia, insensitivity, lethargy, thoughtlessness, torpor 2. inertness, numbness, unconsciousness

insensible 1. anaesthetized, benumbed, dull, inert, insensate, numbed, senseless, stupid, torpid 2. apathetic, callous, cold, deaf, hard-hearted, impassive, impervious, indifferent, oblivious, unaffected, unaware, unconscious, unfeeling, unmindful, unmoved, unresponsive, unsusceptible, untouched 3. imperceivable, imperceptible, minuscule, negligible, unnoticeable
Antonyms (*sense 2*) affected, aware, conscious, feeling, mindful, responsive, sensible

insensibly by degrees, gradually, imperceptibly, invisibly, little by little, slightly, unnoticeably

insensitive 1. callous, crass, hardened, imperceptive, indifferent, obtuse, tactless, thick-skinned, tough, uncaring, unconcerned, unfeeling, unresponsive, unsusceptible 2. *with* **to** dead to, immune to, impervious to, nonreactive, proof against, unaffected by, unmoved by
Antonyms (*sense 1*) caring, concerned, perceptive, responsive, sensitive, sentient, susceptible, tactful, tender

inseparable 1. conjoined, inalienable, indissoluble, indivisible, inseverable 2. bosom, close, devoted, intimate

insert embed, enter, implant, infix, interject, interpolate, interpose, introduce, place, pop in (*informal*), put, set, stick in, tuck in, work in
Antonyms delete, extract, pull out, remove, take out, withdraw

insertion addition, implant, inclusion, insert, inset, interpolation, introduction, supplement

inside *noun* 1. contents, inner part, interior 2. *often plural informal* belly, bowels, entrails, gut, guts, innards (*informal*), internal organs, stomach, viscera, vitals *~adverb* 3. indoors, under cover, within *~adjective* 4. inner, innermost, interior, internal, intramural, inward 5. classified, confidential, esoteric, exclusive, internal, limited, private, restricted, secret
Antonyms (*sense 4*) exterior, external, extramural, outer, outermost, outside, outward

insidious artful, crafty, crooked, cunning, deceitful, deceptive, designing, disingenuous, duplicitous, guileful, intriguing, Machiavellian, slick, sly, smooth, sneaking, stealthy, subtle, surreptitious, treacherous, tricky, wily
Antonyms artless, conspicuous, forthright, harmless, honest, ingenuous, obvious, open, sincere, straightforward, upright

insight acumen, awareness, comprehension, discernment, intuition, intuitiveness, judgment, observation, penetration, perception, perspicacity, understanding, vision

insightful astute, discerning, knowledgeable, observant, penetrating, perceptive, perspicacious, sagacious, shrewd, understanding, wise

insignia badge, crest, decoration, distinguishing mark, earmark, emblem, ensign, symbol

insignificance immateriality, inconsequence, irrelevance, meaninglessness, negligibility, paltriness, pettiness, triviality, unimportance, worthlessness
Antonyms consequence, importance, matter, meaningfulness, relevance, significance, weight, worth

insignificant flimsy, immaterial, inconsequential, inconsiderable, irrelevant, meagre, meaningless, measly, minor, negligible, nickel-and-dime (*U.S. slang*), nondescript, nonessential, not worth mentioning, nugatory, of no account (consequence, moment), paltry, petty, scanty, small potatoes, trifling, trivial, unimportant, unsubstantial, wanky (*taboo slang*)
Antonyms consequential, considerable, essen~

tial, important, meaningful, momentous, rel~ evant, significant, substantial, vital, weighty

insincere deceitful, deceptive, devious, dishon~ est, disingenuous, dissembling, dissimulating, double-dealing, duplicitous, evasive, faithless, false, hollow, hypocritical, Janus-faced, lying, mendacious, perfidious, pretended, two-faced, unfaithful, untrue, untruthful, with tongue in cheek

Antonyms direct, earnest, faithful, genuine, honest, sincere, straightforward, true, truthful

insincerity deceitfulness, deviousness, dishon~ esty, disingenuousness, dissimulation, duplic~ ity, faithlessness, hypocrisy, lip service, men~ dacity, perfidy, pretence, untruthfulness

Antonyms directness, faithfulness, honesty, sincerity, truthfulness

The great enemy of clear language is insincerity. When there is a gap between one's real and one's declared aims, one turns as it were in~ stinctively to long words and exhausted idioms, like a cuttlefish squirting out ink

George Orwell *Politics and the English Language*

insinuate **1.** allude, hint, imply, indicate, inti~ mate, suggest **2.** infiltrate, infuse, inject, in~ stil, introduce **3.** curry favour, get in with, in~ gratiate, worm *or* work one's way in

insinuation **1.** allusion, aspersion, hint, impli~ cation, innuendo, slur, suggestion **2.** infiltra~ tion, infusion, ingratiating, injection, instilla~ tion, introduction

insipid **1.** anaemic, banal, bland, characterless, colourless, drab, dry, dull, flat, ho-hum (*infor~ mal*), jejune, lifeless, limp, pointless, prosaic, prosy, spiritless, stale, stupid, tame, tedious, tiresome, trite, unimaginative, uninteresting, vapid, weak, wearisome, wishy-washy (*infor~ mal*) **2.** bland, flavourless, savourless, taste~ less, unappetizing, watered down, watery, wishy-washy (*informal*)

Antonyms (*sense 1*) colourful, engaging, excit~ ing, interesting, lively, provocative, spirited, stimulating (*sense 2*) appetizing, fiery, palat~ able, piquant, pungent, savoury, tasteful

insipidity, insipidness **1.** banality, colourless~ ness, dullness, flatness, lack of imagination, pointlessness, staleness, tameness, tedious~ ness, triteness, uninterestingness, vapidity **2.** blandness, flavourlessness, lack of flavour, tastelessness

Antonyms (*sense 1*) animation, character, dy~ namism, gaiety, liveliness, spirit, vitality, vi~ vacity

insist **1.** be firm, brook no refusal, demand, lay down the law, not take no for an answer, persist, press (someone), put one's foot down (*informal*), require, stand firm, stand one's ground, take *or* make a stand, urge **2.** assert, asseverate, aver, claim, contend, hold, main~ tain, reiterate, repeat, swear, urge, vow

insistence assertion, contention, demands, em~ phasis, importunity, insistency, persistence, pressing, reiteration, stress, urging

insistent demanding, dogged, emphatic, exi~ gent, forceful, importunate, incessant, per~ emptory, persevering, persistent, pressing, unrelenting, urgent

insobriety crapulence, drunkenness, inebriety, intemperance, intoxication

insolence abuse, audacity, backchat (*informal*), boldness, cheek (*informal*), chutzpah (*U.S. & Canad. informal*), contemptuousness, contu~ mely, disrespect, effrontery, front, gall (*infor~ mal*), impertinence, impudence, incivility, in~ subordination, offensiveness, pertness, rude~ ness, sassiness (*U.S. informal*), sauce (*infor~ mal*), uncivility

Antonyms civility, courtesy, deference, es~ teem, mannerliness, politeness, respect, sub~ mission

insolent abusive, bold, brazen-faced, contemp~ tuous, fresh (*informal*), impertinent, impu~ dent, insubordinate, insulting, pert, rude, saucy, uncivil

Antonyms civil, courteous, deferential, man~ nerly, polite, respectful, submissive

insoluble baffling, impenetrable, indecipher~ able, inexplicable, mysterious, mystifying, ob~ scure, unaccountable, unfathomable, unsolv~ able

Antonyms accountable, comprehensible, ex~ plicable, fathomable, penetrable, soluble, solv~ able

insolvency bankruptcy, failure, liquidation, ruin

insolvent bankrupt, broke (*informal*), failed, gone bust (*informal*), gone to the wall, in queer street (*informal*), in receivership, in the hands of the receivers, on the rocks (*infor~ mal*), ruined

insomnia sleeplessness, wakefulness

insouciance airiness, breeziness, carefreeness, jauntiness, light-heartedness, nonchalance

insouciant airy, breezy, buoyant, carefree, cas~ ual, free and easy, gay, happy-go-lucky, jaun~ ty, light-hearted, nonchalant, sunny, uncon~ cerned, untroubled, unworried

inspect audit, check, check out (*informal*), ex~ amine, eyeball (*U.S. slang*), give (something *or* someone) the once-over (*informal*), go over *or* through, investigate, look over, oversee, recce (*slang*), research, scan, scrutinize, search, superintend, supervise, survey, take a dekko at (*Brit. slang*), vet, work over

inspection check, checkup, examination, in~ vestigation, look-over, once-over (*informal*), recce (*slang*), review, scan, scrutiny, search, superintendence, supervision, surveillance survey

inspector censor, checker, critic, examiner, investigator, overseer, scrutineer, scrutinizer, superintendent, supervisor

inspiration **1.** arousal, awakening, encouragement, influence, muse, spur, stimulus **2.** afflatus, creativity, elevation, enthusiasm, exaltation, genius, illumination, insight, revelation, stimulation
Antonyms depressant, deterrent, discouragement, disenchantment

inspire **1.** animate, be responsible for, encourage, enliven, fire *or* touch the imagination of, galvanize, hearten, imbue, influence, infuse, inspirit, instil, rouse, spark off, spur, stimulate **2.** arouse, enkindle, excite, give rise to, produce, quicken, rouse, stir
Antonyms daunt, deflate, depress, discourage, disenchant, dishearten, dispirit

inspired **1.** brilliant, dazzling, enthralling, exciting, impressive, memorable, of genius, outstanding, superlative, thrilling, wonderful **2.** *of a guess* instinctive, instinctual, intuitive **3.** aroused, elated, enthused, exalted, exhilarated, galvanized, possessed, stimulated, stirred up, uplifted

inspiring affecting, encouraging, exciting, exhilarating, heartening, moving, rousing, stimulating, stirring, uplifting
Antonyms boring, depressing, discouraging, disheartening, dispiriting, dull, uninspiring

inspirit animate, cheer, embolden, encourage, enliven, exhilarate, fire, galvanize, give hope to, hearten, incite, inspire, invigorate, move, nerve, put (new) heart into, rouse, stimulate

instability capriciousness, changeableness, disequilibrium, fickleness, fitfulness, fluctuation, fluidity, frailty, imbalance, impermanence, inconstancy, insecurity, irresolution, mutability, oscillation, precariousness, restlessness, shakiness, transience, unpredictability, unsteadiness, vacillation, variability, volatility, wavering, weakness
Antonyms balance, constancy, equilibrium, permanence, predictability, resolution, security, stability, steadiness, strength

install, instal **1.** fix, lay, lodge, place, position, put in, set up, station **2.** establish, inaugurate, induct, instate, institute, introduce, invest, set up **3.** ensconce, position, settle

installation **1.** establishment, fitting, instalment, placing, positioning, setting up **2.** inauguration, induction, instatement, investiture **3.** equipment, machinery, plant, system **4.** *Military* base, establishment, post, station

instalment chapter, division, episode, part, portion, repayment, section

instance *noun* **1.** case, case in point, example, illustration, occasion, occurrence, precedent, situation, time **2.** application, behest, demand, entreaty, importunity, impulse, incitement, insistence, instigation, pressure, prompting, request, solicitation, urging *~verb* **3.** adduce, cite, mention, name, quote, specify

instant *noun* **1.** bat of an eye (*informal*), flash, jiffy (*informal*), moment, second, shake (*informal*), split second, tick (*Brit. informal*), trice, twinkling, twinkling of an eye (*informal*), two shakes of a lamb's tail (*informal*) **2. on the instant** forthwith, immediately, instantly, now, right away, without delay **3.** juncture, moment, occasion, point, time *~adjective* **4.** direct, immediate, instantaneous, on-the-spot, prompt, quick, quickie (*informal*), split-second, urgent **5.** convenience, fast, precooked, ready-mixed **6.** burning, exigent, imperative, importunate, pressing, urgent

instantaneous direct, immediate, instant, on-the-spot

instantaneously at once, forthwith, immediately, in a fraction of a second, instantly, in the bat of an eye (*informal*), in the same breath, in the twinkling of an eye (*informal*), like a bat out of hell (*slang*), like greased lightning (*informal*), on the instant, on the spot, posthaste, promptly, pronto (*informal*), quick as lightning, straight away, then and there

instantly at once, directly, forthwith, immediately, instantaneously, instanter (*Law*), now, on the spot, posthaste, pronto (*informal*), right away, right now, straight away, there and then, this minute, *tout de suite*, without delay

instate establish, inaugurate, induct, install, invest, put in office

instead **1.** alternatively, in lieu, in preference, on second thoughts, preferably, rather **2.** *with* **of** as an alternative *or* equivalent to, in lieu of, in place of, rather than

instigate actuate, bring about, encourage, foment, get going, impel, incite, influence, initiate, kick-start, kindle, move, persuade, prod, prompt, provoke, rouse, set off, set on, spur, start, stimulate, stir up, trigger, urge, whip up
Antonyms discourage, repress, restrain, stop, suppress

instigation behest, bidding, encouragement, incentive, incitement, prompting, urging

instigator agitator, firebrand, fomenter, goad, incendiary, inciter, leader, mischief-maker, motivator, prime mover, ringleader, spur, stirrer (*informal*), troublemaker

instil, instill engender, engraft, imbue, implant, impress, inculcate, infix, infuse, insinuate, introduce, sow the seeds

instinct aptitude, faculty, feeling, gift, gut feeling (*informal*), gut reaction (*informal*), im~

pulse, intuition, knack, natural inclination, predisposition, proclivity, sixth sense, talent, tendency, urge

instinctive automatic, inborn, inherent, innate, instinctual, intuitional, intuitive, involuntary, mechanical, native, natural, reflex, spontaneous, unlearned, unpremeditated, unthinking, visceral
Antonyms acquired, calculated, considered, learned, mindful, premeditated, thinking, voluntary, willed

instinctively automatically, by instinct, in one's bones, intuitively, involuntarily, naturally, without thinking

institute[1] *verb* appoint, begin, bring into being, commence, constitute, enact, establish, fix, found, induct, initiate, install, introduce, invest, launch, ordain, organize, originate, pioneer, put into operation, set in motion, settle, set up, start
Antonyms abandon, abolish, cancel, cease, discontinue, end, stop, suspend, terminate

institute[2] *noun* **1.** academy, association, college, conservatory, foundation, guild, institution, school, seat of learning, seminary, society **2.** custom, decree, doctrine, dogma, edict, law, maxim, precedent, precept, principle, regulation, rule, tenet

institution **1.** constitution, creation, enactment, establishment, formation, foundation, initiation, introduction, investiture, investment, organization **2.** academy, college, establishment, foundation, hospital, institute, school, seminary, society, university **3.** convention, custom, fixture, law, practice, ritual, rule, tradition

institutional **1.** accepted, bureaucratic, conventional, established, establishment (*informal*), formal, organized, orthodox, societal **2.** cheerless, clinical, cold, drab, dreary, dull, forbidding, formal, impersonal, monotonous, regimented, routine, uniform, unwelcoming

instruct **1.** bid, canon, charge, command, direct, enjoin, order, tell **2.** coach, discipline, drill, educate, enlighten, ground, guide, inform, school, teach, train, tutor **3.** acquaint, advise, apprise, brief, counsel, inform, notify, tell

instruction **1.** apprenticeship, coaching, discipline, drilling, education, enlightenment, grounding, guidance, information, lesson(s), preparation, schooling, teaching, training, tuition, tutelage **2.** briefing, command, demand, direction, directive, injunction, mandate, order, ruling

instructions advice, directions, guidance, information, key, orders, recommendations, rules

instructive cautionary, didactic, edifying, educational, enlightening, helpful, illuminating, informative, instructional, revealing, useful

instructor adviser, coach, demonstrator, exponent, guide, handler, master, mentor, mistress, pedagogue, preceptor (*rare*), schoolmaster, schoolmistress, teacher, trainer, tutor

instrument **1.** apparatus, appliance, contraption (*informal*), contrivance, device, gadget, implement, mechanism, tool, utensil, waldo **2.** agency, agent, channel, factor, force, means, mechanism, medium, organ, vehicle **3.** *informal* cat's-paw, dupe, pawn, puppet, tool

instrumental active, assisting, auxiliary, conducive, contributory, helpful, helping, influential, involved, of help *or* service, subsidiary, useful

instrumentality agency, assistance, good offices, intercession, intervention, mediation, medium, vehicle

insubordinate contumacious, defiant, disobedient, disorderly, fractious, insurgent, mutinous, rebellious, recalcitrant, refractory, riotous, seditious, turbulent, undisciplined, ungovernable, unruly
Antonyms compliant, deferential, disciplined, docile, obedient, orderly, submissive, subservient

insubordination defiance, disobedience, indiscipline, insurrection, mutinousness, mutiny, rebellion, recalcitrance, revolt, riotousness, sedition, ungovernability
Antonyms acquiescence, compliance, deference, discipline, docility, obedience, submission, subordination

insubstantial **1.** feeble, flimsy, frail, poor, slight, tenuous, thin, weak **2.** chimerical, ephemeral, false, fanciful, idle, illusory, imaginary, immaterial, incorporeal, unreal
Antonyms (*sense 1*) firm, solid, strong, substantial, weighty

insufferable detestable, dreadful, enough to test the patience of a saint, enough to try the patience of Job, impossible, insupportable, intolerable, more than flesh and blood can stand, outrageous, past bearing, too much, unbearable, unendurable, unspeakable
Antonyms appealing, attractive, bearable, charming, disarming, pleasant

insufficiency dearth, deficiency, inadequacy, inadequateness, lack, paucity, poverty, scantiness, scarcity, shortage, short supply, want

insufficient deficient, inadequate, incapable, incommensurate, incompetent, lacking, scant, short, unfitted, unqualified
Antonyms adequate, ample, commensurate, competent, enough, plentiful, qualified, sufficient

insular *figurative* blinkered, circumscribed, closed, contracted, cut off, illiberal, inward-looking, isolated, limited, narrow, narrow-minded, parish-pump, parochial, petty, preju-

diced, provincial
Antonyms broad-minded, cosmopolitan, experienced, liberal, open-minded, tolerant, worldly

insulate *figurative* close off, cocoon, cushion, cut off, isolate, protect, sequester, shield, wrap up in cotton wool

insult **1.** *noun* abuse, affront, aspersion, contumely, indignity, insolence, offence, outrage, put-down, rudeness, slap in the face (*informal*), slight, snub **2.** *verb* abuse, affront, call names, give offence to, injure, miscall (*dialect*), offend, outrage, put down, revile, slag (off) (*slang*), slander, slight, snub
Antonyms *noun* compliment, flattery, honour ~*verb* flatter, please, praise

This is adding insult to injuries
Edward Moore *The Foundling*

insulting abusive, affronting, contemptuous, degrading, disparaging, insolent, offensive, rude, scurrilous, slighting
Antonyms complimentary, deferential, flattering, laudatory, respectful

insuperable impassable, insurmountable, invincible, unconquerable
Antonyms conquerable, possible, surmountable

insupportable **1.** insufferable, intolerable, past bearing, unbearable, unendurable **2.** indefensible, unjustifiable, untenable

insurance assurance, cover, coverage, guarantee, indemnification, indemnity, protection, provision, safeguard, security, something to fall back on (*informal*), warranty

insure assure, cover, guarantee, indemnify, underwrite, warrant

insurgent **1.** *noun* insurrectionist, mutineer, rebel, resister, revolter, revolutionary, revolutionist, rioter **2.** *adjective* disobedient, insubordinate, insurrectionary, mutinous, rebellious, revolting, revolutionary, riotous, seditious

insurmountable hopeless, impassable, impossible, insuperable, invincible, overwhelming, unconquerable

insurrection coup, insurgency, mutiny, putsch, rebellion, revolt, revolution, riot, rising, sedition, uprising

insusceptible immovable, immune, indifferent, insensible, insensitive, proof against, unimpressible, unmoved, unresponsive

intact all in one piece, complete, entire, perfect, scatheless, sound, together, unbroken, undamaged, undefiled, unharmed, unhurt, unimpaired, uninjured, unscathed, untouched, unviolated, virgin, whole
Antonyms broken, damaged, harmed, impaired, injured

intangible airy, dim, elusive, ethereal, evanescent, impalpable, imperceptible, incorporeal, indefinite, invisible, shadowy, unreal, unsubstantial, vague

integral **1.** basic, component, constituent, elemental, essential, fundamental, indispensable, intrinsic, necessary, requisite **2.** complete, entire, full, intact, undivided, whole
Antonyms fractional, inessential, unimportant, unnecessary

integrate accommodate, amalgamate, assimilate, blend, coalesce, combine, fuse, harmonize, incorporate, intermix, join, knit, meld, merge, mesh, unite
Antonyms disperse, divide, segregate, separate

integration amalgamation, assimilation, blending, combining, commingling, fusing, harmony, incorporation, mixing, unification

integrity **1.** candour, goodness, honesty, honour, incorruptibility, principle, probity, purity, rectitude, righteousness, uprightness, virtue **2.** coherence, cohesion, completeness, soundness, unity, wholeness
Antonyms (*sense 1*) corruption, deceit, dishonesty, disrepute, duplicity, faultiness, flimsiness, fragility, immorality, uncertainty, unsoundness

This above all: to thine own self be true
William Shakespeare *Hamlet*

intellect **1.** brains (*informal*), intelligence, judgment, mind, reason, sense, understanding **2.** *informal* brain (*informal*), egghead (*informal*), genius, intellectual, intelligence, mind, thinker

I care not whether a man is good or evil; all that I care
Is whether he is a wise man or a fool. Go! put off holiness
And put on intellect
William Blake *Jerusalem*

intellectual **1.** *adjective* bookish, cerebral, highbrow, intelligent, mental, rational, scholarly, studious, thoughtful **2.** *noun* academic, bluestocking (*usually disparaging*), egghead (*informal*), highbrow, thinker
Antonyms *adjective* ignorant, illiterate, material, physical, stupid, unintellectual, unlearned ~*noun* idiot, moron

An intellectual is someone whose mind watches itself
Albert Camus *Notebooks 1935 - 42*

To the man in-the-street, who, I'm sorry to say
Is a keen observer of life
The word "Intellectual" suggests straight away
A man who's untrue to his wife
W.H. Auden *New Year Letter*

intelligence **1.** acumen, alertness, aptitude, brain power, brains (*informal*), brightness,

capacity, cleverness, comprehension, discernment, grey matter (*informal*), intellect, mind, nous (*Brit. slang*), penetration, perception, quickness, reason, smarts (*slang, chiefly U.S.*), understanding **2.** advice, data, disclosure, facts, findings, gen (*Brit. informal*), information, knowledge, low-down (*informal*), news, notice, notification, report, rumour, tidings, tip-off, word
Antonyms (*sense 1*) dullness, ignorance, stupidity (*sense 2*) concealment, misinformation

Intelligence is characterised by a natural incomprehension of life
Henri Bergson *L'Évolution Créatrice*

Intelligence in chains loses in lucidity what it gains in intensity
Albert Camus *The Rebel*

The test of a first-rate intelligence is the ability to hold two opposed ideas in the mind at the same time, and still retain the ability to function
F. Scott Fitzgerald *The Crack-Up*

Intelligence is quickness in seeing things as they are
George Santayana *The Life of Reason: Reason in Common Sense*

intelligent acute, alert, apt, brainy (*informal*), bright, clever, discerning, enlightened, instructed, knowing, penetrating, perspicacious, quick, quick-witted, rational, sharp, smart, thinking, well-informed
Antonyms dim-witted, dull, foolish, ignorant, obtuse, stupid, unintelligent

intelligentsia eggheads (*informal*), highbrows, illuminati, intellectuals, literati, masterminds, the learned

intelligibility clarity, clearness, comprehensibility, distinctness, explicitness, lucidity, plainness, precision, simplicity

intelligible clear, comprehensible, distinct, lucid, open, plain, understandable
Antonyms confused, garbled, incomprehensible, puzzling, unclear, unintelligible

intemperance crapulence, excess, extravagance, immoderation, inebriation, insobriety, intoxication, overindulgence, unrestraint

intemperate excessive, extravagant, extreme, immoderate, incontinent, inordinate, intoxicated, O.T.T. (*slang*), over the top (*slang*), passionate, prodigal, profligate, self-indulgent, severe, tempestuous, unbridled, uncontrollable, ungovernable, unrestrained, violent, wild
Antonyms continent, disciplined, moderate, restrained, self-controlled, temperate

intend **1.** aim, be resolved *or* determined, contemplate, determine, have in mind *or* view, mean, meditate, plan, propose, purpose, scheme **2.** *often with* **for** aim, consign, design, destine, earmark, mark out, mean, set apart

intended **1.** *adjective* betrothed, destined, future, planned, proposed **2.** *noun, informal* betrothed, fiancé, fiancée, future wife *or* husband, husband- *or* wife-to-be

intense **1.** acute, agonizing, close, concentrated, deep, drastic, excessive, exquisite, extreme, fierce, forceful, great, harsh, intensive, powerful, profound, protracted, serious (*informal*), severe, strained, unqualified **2.** ardent, burning, consuming, eager, earnest, energetic, fanatical, fervent, fervid, fierce, flaming, forcible, heightened, impassioned, keen, passionate, speaking, vehement
Antonyms (*sense 1*) easy, gentle, mild, moderate, relaxed, slight (*sense 2*) casual, cool, indifferent, subdued, weak

intensely deeply, extremely, fiercely, passionately, profoundly, seriously (*informal*), strongly

intensify add fuel to the flames (*informal*), add to, aggravate, augment, boost, concentrate, deepen, emphasize, enhance, escalate, exacerbate, fan the flames of, heighten, increase, magnify, quicken, redouble, reinforce, set off, sharpen, step up (*informal*), strengthen, whet
Antonyms damp down, decrease, dilute, diminish, dull, lessen, minimize, weaken

intensity ardour, concentration, depth, earnestness, emotion, energy, excess, extremity, fanaticism, fervency, fervour, fierceness, fire, force, intenseness, keenness, passion, potency, power, severity, strain, strength, tension, vehemence, vigour

intensive all-out, comprehensive, concentrated, demanding, exhaustive, in-depth, thorough, thoroughgoing
Antonyms apathetic, careless, feeble, hit-or-miss, superficial, weakened

intent *adjective* **1.** absorbed, alert, attentive, committed, concentrated, determined, eager, earnest, engrossed, fixed, industrious, intense, occupied, piercing, preoccupied, rapt, resolute, resolved, steadfast, steady, watchful, wrapped up **2.** bent, hellbent (*informal*), set *~noun* **3.** aim, design, end, goal, intention, meaning, object, objective, plan, purpose **4.** **to all intents and purposes** as good as, practically, virtually
Antonyms *adjective* (*sense 1*) casual, indifferent, irresolute, unsteady, wavering *~noun* chance, fortune

intention aim, design, end, end in view, goal, idea, intent, meaning, object, objective, point, purpose, scope, target, view

The road to hell is paved with good intentions

intentional calculated, deliberate, designed, done on purpose, intended, meant, planned, prearranged, preconcerted, premeditated, purposed, studied, wilful

Antonyms accidental, inadvertent, unintentional, unplanned

intentionally by design, deliberately, designedly, on purpose, wilfully

intently attentively, closely, fixedly, hard, keenly, searchingly, steadily, watchfully

inter bury, entomb, inhume, inurn, lay to rest, sepulchre

intercede advocate, arbitrate, interpose, intervene, mediate, plead, speak

intercept arrest, block, catch, check, cut off, deflect, head off, interrupt, obstruct, seize, stop, take

intercession advocacy, entreaty, good offices, intervention, mediation, plea, pleading, prayer, solicitation, supplication

intercessor advocate, arbitrator, go-between, interceder, intermediary, mediator, middleman, negotiator, pleader

interchange **1.** *verb* alternate, bandy, barter, exchange, reciprocate, swap (*informal*), switch, trade **2.** *noun* alternation, crossfire, exchange, give and take, intersection, junction, reciprocation

interchangeable commutable, equivalent, exchangeable, identical, reciprocal, synonymous, the same, transposable

intercourse **1.** association, commerce, communication, communion, connection, contact, converse, correspondence, dealings, intercommunication, trade, traffic, truck **2.** carnal knowledge, coition, coitus, congress, copulation, intimacy, legover (*slang*), nookie (*slang*), rumpy-pumpy (*slang*), sex (*informal*), sexual act, sexual intercourse, sexual relations, the other (*informal*)

interdict **1.** *verb* ban, bar, debar, disallow, forbid, outlaw, prevent, prohibit, proscribe, veto **2.** *noun* ban, disallowance, disqualification, interdiction, prohibition, taboo, veto

interest *noun* **1.** affection, attention, attentiveness, attraction, concern, curiosity, notice, regard, suspicion, sympathy **2.** concern, consequence, importance, moment, note, relevance, significance, weight **3.** activity, diversion, hobby, leisure activity, pastime, preoccupation, pursuit, relaxation **4.** advantage, benefit, boot (*dialect*), gain, good, profit **5.** **in the interest of** for the sake of, on behalf of, on the part of, profitable to, to the advantage of **6.** authority, claim, commitment, influence, investment, involvement, participation, portion, right, share, stake **7.** *often plural* affair, business, care, concern, matter *~verb* **8.** amuse, arouse one's curiosity, attract, catch one's eye, divert, engross, fascinate, hold the attention of, intrigue, move, touch **9.** affect, concern, engage, involve
Antonyms *noun* (*sense 1*) boredom, coolness, disinterest, dispassion, disregard, unconcern (*sense 2*) inconsequence, insignificance, irrelevance, worthlessness *~verb* bore, burden, irk, repel, tire, weary

interested **1.** affected, attentive, attracted, curious, drawn, excited, fascinated, intent, into (*informal*), keen, moved, responsive, stimulated **2.** biased, concerned, implicated, involved, partial, partisan, predisposed, prejudiced
Antonyms (*sense 1*) apathetic, bored, detached, inattentive, indifferent, unconcerned, uninterested, wearied

interesting absorbing, amusing, appealing, attractive, compelling, curious, engaging, engrossing, entertaining, gripping, intriguing, pleasing, provocative, stimulating, suspicious, thought-provoking, unusual
Antonyms boring, dull, mind-numbing, tedious, tiresome, uninteresting

interfere **1.** butt in, get involved, intermeddle, intervene, intrude, meddle, poke one's nose in (*informal*), put one's two cents in (*U.S. slang*), stick one's oar in (*informal*), tamper **2.** *often with* **with** be a drag upon (*informal*), block, clash, collide, conflict, cramp, frustrate, get in the way of, hamper, handicap, hinder, impede, inhibit, obstruct, trammel

interference **1.** intermeddling, intervention, intrusion, meddlesomeness, meddling, prying **2.** clashing, collision, conflict, impedance, obstruction, opposition

interfering interruptive, intrusive, meddlesome, meddling, obtrusive, prying

interim **1.** *adjective* acting, caretaker, improvised, intervening, makeshift, pro tem, provisional, stopgap, temporary **2.** *noun* entr'acte, interregnum, interval, meantime, meanwhile, respite

interior *adjective* **1.** inner, inside, internal, inward **2.** *Geography* central, inland, remote, upcountry **3.** *Politics* domestic, home **4.** hidden, inner, intimate, mental, personal, private, secret, spiritual *~noun* **5.** bosom, centre, contents, core, heart, innards (*informal*), inside **6.** *Geography* centre, heartland, upcountry
Antonyms (*sense 1*) exposed, exterior, external, outer, outside, outward

interject interpolate, interpose, interrupt with, introduce, put in, throw in

interjection cry, ejaculation, exclamation, interpolation, interposition

interlace braid, cross, entwine, interlock, intersperse, intertwine, interweave, interwreathe, knit, plait, reticulate, twine

interlink interconnect, interlock, intertwine, interweave, knit, link, mesh

interloper gate-crasher (*informal*), inter~

meddler, intruder, meddler, trespasser, uninvited guest, unwanted visitor

interlude break, breathing space, delay, entr'acte, episode, halt, hiatus, intermission, interval, pause, respite, rest, spell, stop, stoppage, wait

intermediary *noun* agent, broker, entrepreneur, go-between, mediator, middleman

intermediate halfway, in-between (*informal*), intermediary, interposed, intervening, mean, mid, middle, midway, transitional

interment burial, burying, funeral, inhumation, sepulture

interminable boundless, ceaseless, dragging, endless, everlasting, immeasurable, infinite, limitless, long, long-drawn-out, long-winded, never-ending, perpetual, protracted, unbounded, unlimited, wearisome

Antonyms bounded, finite, limited, measurable, restricted, temporary

intermingle amalgamate, blend, combine, commingle, commix, fuse, interlace, intermix, interweave, meld, merge, mix

intermission break, breathing space, cessation, entr'acte, interlude, interruption, interval, let-up (*informal*), lull, pause, recess, respite, rest, stop, stoppage, suspense, suspension

intermittent broken, discontinuous, fitful, irregular, occasional, periodic, punctuated, recurrent, recurring, spasmodic, sporadic, stop-go (*informal*)

Antonyms continuous, steady, unceasing

intern confine, detain, hold, hold in custody

internal **1.** inner, inside, interior, intimate, private, subjective **2.** civic, domestic, home, in-house, intramural

Antonyms (*sense 1*) exposed, exterior, external, outer, outermost, outside, revealed, unconcealed

international cosmopolitan, ecumenical (*rare*), global, intercontinental, universal, worldwide

internecine bloody, deadly, destructive, exterminating, exterminatory, fatal, mortal, ruinous

interplay give-and-take, interaction, meshing, reciprocation, reciprocity

interpolate add, insert, intercalate, introduce

interpolation addition, aside, insert, insertion, intercalation, interjection, introduction

interpose **1.** come *or* place between, intercede, interfere, intermediate, intervene, intrude, mediate, step in **2.** insert, interject, interrupt (with), introduce, put forth, put one's oar in

interpret adapt, clarify, construe, decipher, decode, define, elucidate, explain, explicate, expound, make sense of, paraphrase, read, render, solve, spell out, take, throw light on, translate, understand

interpretation analysis, clarification, construction, diagnosis, elucidation, exegesis, explanation, explication, exposition, meaning, performance, portrayal, reading, rendering, rendition, sense, signification, translation, understanding, version

interpreter annotator, commentator, exponent, scholiast, translator

interrogate ask, catechize, cross-examine, cross-question, enquire, examine, give (someone) the third degree (*informal*), grill (*informal*), inquire, investigate, pump, put the screws on (*informal*), question, quiz

interrogation cross-examination, cross-questioning, enquiry, examination, grilling (*informal*), inquiry, inquisition, probing, questioning, third degree (*informal*)

interrogative curious, inquiring, inquisitive, inquisitorial, questioning, quizzical

interrupt barge in (*informal*), break, break in, break off, break (someone's) train of thought, butt in, check, cut, cut off, cut short, delay, disconnect, discontinue, disjoin, disturb, disunite, divide, heckle, hinder, hold up, interfere (with), intrude, lay aside, obstruct, punctuate, separate, sever, stay, stop, suspend

interrupted broken, cut off, disconnected, discontinuous, disturbed, incomplete, intermittent, uneven

interruption break, cessation, disconnection, discontinuance, disruption, dissolution, disturbance, disuniting, division, halt, hiatus, hindrance, hitch, impediment, intrusion, obstacle, obstruction, pause, separation, severance, stop, stoppage, suspension

intersect bisect, crisscross, cross, cut, cut across, divide, meet

intersection crossing, crossroads, interchange, junction

intersperse bestrew, interlard, intermix, pepper, scatter, sprinkle

interstice aperture, chink, cleft, crack, cranny, crevice, fissure, gap, interval, opening, rift, slit, space, vent

intertwine braid, convolute, cross, entwine, interlace, interweave, interwreathe, inweave, link, reticulate, twist

interval break, delay, distance, entr'acte, gap, hiatus, interim, interlude, intermission, meantime, meanwhile, opening, pause, period, playtime, respite, rest, season, space, spell, term, time, wait

intervene **1.** arbitrate, intercede, interfere, interpose oneself, intrude, involve oneself, mediate, put one's oar in, put one's two cents in (*U.S. slang*), step in (*informal*), take a hand (*informal*) **2.** befall, come to pass, ensue, happen, occur, succeed, supervene, take place

intervention agency, intercession, interference, interposition, intrusion, mediation

interview 1. *noun* audience, conference, consultation, dialogue, evaluation, meeting, oral (examination), press conference, talk 2. *verb* examine, interrogate, question, sound out, talk to

interviewer examiner, interlocutor, interrogator, investigator, questioner, reporter

interweave blend, braid, crisscross, cross, interlace, intertwine, interwreathe, inweave, reticulate, splice

interwoven blended, connected, entwined, inmixed, interconnected, interlaced, interlocked, intermingled, knit

intestinal abdominal, coeliac, duodenal, gut (*informal*), inner, stomachic, visceral

intestines bowels, entrails, guts, innards (*informal*), insides (*informal*), internal organs, viscera, vitals

intimacy closeness, confidence, confidentiality, familiarity, fraternization, understanding
Antonyms alienation, aloofness, coldness, detachment, distance, estrangement, remoteness, separation

intimate[1] *adjective* 1. bosom, cherished, close, confidential, dear, friendly, near, nearest and dearest, thick (*informal*), warm 2. confidential, personal, private, privy, secret 3. deep, detailed, exhaustive, experienced, first-hand, immediate, in-depth, penetrating, personal, profound, thorough 4. comfy (*informal*), cosy, friendly, informal, snug, tête-à-tête, warm ~*noun* 5. bosom friend, buddy (*informal*), china (*Brit. slang*), chum (*informal*), close friend, cock (*Brit. informal*), comrade, confidant, confidante, (constant) companion, crony, familiar, friend, gossip (*archaic*), homeboy (*slang, chiefly U.S.*), mate (*informal*), mucker (*Brit. slang*), pal
Antonyms *noun* (*sense 1*) distant, remote, superficial (*sense 2*) known, open, public ~*noun* enemy, foe, stranger

intimate[2] *verb* allude, announce, communicate, declare, drop a hint, give (someone) to understand, hint, impart, imply, indicate, insinuate, let it be known, make known, remind, state, suggest, tip (someone) the wink (*Brit. informal*), warn

intimately 1. affectionately, closely, confidentially, confidingly, familiarly, personally, tenderly, very well, warmly 2. fully, in detail, inside out, thoroughly, through and through, to the core, very well

intimation 1. allusion, hint, indication, inkling, insinuation, reminder, suggestion, warning 2. announcement, communication, declaration, notice

intimidate affright (*archaic*), alarm, appal, browbeat, bully, coerce, cow, daunt, dishearten, dismay, dispirit, frighten, lean on (*informal*), overawe, scare, scare off (*informal*), subdue, terrify, terrorize, threaten, twist someone's arm (*informal*)

intimidation arm-twisting (*informal*), browbeating, bullying, coercion, fear, menaces, pressure, terror, terrorization, threat(s)

intolerable beyond bearing, excruciating, impossible, insufferable, insupportable, more than flesh and blood can stand, not to be borne, painful, unbearable, unendurable
Antonyms bearable, endurable, painless, possible, sufferable, supportable, tolerable

intolerance bigotry, chauvinism, discrimination, dogmatism, fanaticism, illiberality, impatience, jingoism, narrow-mindedness, narrowness, prejudice, racialism, racism, xenophobia
Antonyms broad-mindedness, liberality, open-mindedness, patience, tolerance, understanding

intolerant bigoted, chauvinistic, dictatorial, dogmatic, fanatical, illiberal, impatient, narrow, narrow-minded, one-sided, prejudiced, racialist, racist, small-minded, uncharitable, xenophobic
Antonyms broad-minded, charitable, lenient, liberal, open-minded, patient, tolerant, understanding

intonation 1. accentuation, cadence, inflection, modulation, tone 2. chant, incantation

intone chant, croon, intonate, recite, sing

in toto as a whole, completely, entirely, in its entirety, totally, unabridged, uncut, wholly

intoxicate 1. addle, befuddle, fuddle, go to one's head, inebriate, put (someone) under the table (*informal*), stupefy 2. *figurative* elate, excite, exhilarate, go to one's head, inflame, make one's head spin, stimulate

intoxicated 1. bevvied (*dialect*), blitzed (*slang*), blotto (*slang*), bombed (*slang*), Brahms and Liszt (*slang*), canned (*slang*), cut (*Brit. slang*), drunk, drunk as a skunk, drunken, flying (*slang*), fuddled, half seas over (*Brit. informal*), high (*informal*), inebriated, in one's cups (*informal*), legless (*informal*), lit up (*slang*), out of it (*slang*), out to it (*Austral. & N.Z. slang*), paralytic (*informal*), pissed (*taboo slang*), plastered (*slang*), rat-arsed (*taboo slang*), smashed (*slang*), sozzled (*informal*), steamboats (*Scot. slang*), steaming (*slang*), stewed (*slang*), stiff (*slang*), stoned (*slang*), the worse for drink, three sheets in the wind (*informal*), tight (*informal*), tipsy, under the influence, wasted (*slang*), wrecked (*slang*), zonked (*slang*) 2. *figurative* dizzy, elated, en~

raptured, euphoric, excited, exhilarated, high (*informal*), infatuated, sent (*slang*), stimulated

intoxicating 1. alcoholic, inebriant, intoxicant, spirituous, strong 2. *figurative* exciting, exhilarating, heady, sexy (*informal*), stimulating, thrilling

intoxication 1. drunkenness, inebriation, inebriety, insobriety, tipsiness 2. *figurative* delirium, elation, euphoria, exaltation, excitement, exhilaration, infatuation

intractability awkwardness, cantankerousness, contrariness, incorrigibility, indiscipline, indocility, mulishness, obduracy, obstinacy, perverseness, perversity, pig-headedness, stubbornness, uncooperativeness, ungovernability, waywardness

intractable awkward, bull-headed, cantankerous, contrary, difficult, fractious, headstrong, incurable, insoluble, intransigent, obdurate, obstinate, perverse, pig-headed, refractory, self-willed, stiff-necked, stubborn, unbending, uncooperative, undisciplined, ungovernable, unmanageable, unruly, unyielding, wayward, wild, wilful

intransigent hardline, immovable, intractable, obdurate, obstinate, stiff-necked, stubborn, tenacious, tough, unbending, unbudgeable, uncompromising, unyielding
Antonyms acquiescent, compliant, compromising, flexible, open-minded

intrenched *see* ENTRENCHED

intrepid audacious, bold, brave, courageous, daring, dauntless, doughty, fearless, gallant, game (*informal*), have-a-go (*informal*), heroic, lion-hearted, nerveless, plucky, resolute, stalwart, stouthearted, unafraid, undaunted, unflinching, valiant, valorous
Antonyms afraid, cautious, cowardly, craven, daunted, faint-hearted, fearful, flinching, irresolute, timid

intrepidity audacity, boldness, bravery, courage, daring, dauntlessness, doughtiness, fearlessness, fortitude, gallantry, guts (*informal*), heroism, lion-heartedness, nerve, pluck, prowess, spirit, stoutheartedness, valour

intricacy complexity, complication, convolutions, elaborateness, entanglement, intricateness, involution, involvement, knottiness, obscurity

intricate baroque, Byzantine, complex, complicated, convoluted, daedal (*literary*), difficult, elaborate, fancy, involved, knotty, labyrinthine, obscure, perplexing, rococo, sophisticated, tangled, tortuous
Antonyms clear, easy, obvious, plain, simple, straightforward

intrigue *verb* 1. arouse the curiosity of, attract, charm, fascinate, interest, pique, rivet, tickle one's fancy, titillate 2. connive, conspire, machinate, manoeuvre, plot, scheme *~noun* 3. cabal, chicanery, collusion, conspiracy, double-dealing, knavery, machination, manipulation, manoeuvre, plot, ruse, scheme, sharp practice, stratagem, trickery, wile 4. affair, amour, intimacy, liaison, romance

intriguing beguiling, compelling, diverting, exciting, fascinating, interesting, tantalizing, titillating

intrinsic basic, built-in, central, congenital, constitutional, elemental, essential, fundamental, genuine, inborn, inbred, inherent, native, natural, radical, real, true, underlying
Antonyms acquired, added, appended, artificial, extraneous, extrinsic, incidental

intrinsically as such, at heart, basically, by definition, constitutionally, essentially, fundamentally, in itself, per se

introduce 1. acquaint, do the honours, familiarize, make known, make the introduction, present 2. begin, bring in, commence, establish, found, inaugurate, initiate, institute, launch, organize, pioneer, set up, start, usher in 3. advance, air, bring up, broach, moot, offer, propose, put forward, recommend, set forth, submit, suggest, ventilate 4. announce, lead into, lead off, open, preface 5. add, inject, insert, interpolate, interpose, put in, throw in (*informal*)

introduction 1. baptism, debut, establishment, first acquaintance, inauguration, induction, initiation, institution, launch, pioneering, presentation 2. commencement, exordium, foreword, intro (*informal*), lead-in, opening, opening passage, opening remarks, overture, preamble, preface, preliminaries, prelude, proem, prolegomena, prolegomenon, prologue 3. addition, insertion, interpolation
Antonyms (*sense 1*) completion, elimination, termination (*sense 2*) afterward, conclusion, end, epilogue (*sense 3*) extraction, removal, withdrawal

introductory early, elementary, first, inaugural, initial, initiatory, opening, precursory, prefatory, preliminary, preparatory, starting
Antonyms closing, concluding, final, last, terminating

introspection brooding, heart-searching, introversion, navel-gazing (*slang*), self-analysis, self-examination

introspective brooding, contemplative, inner-directed, introverted, inward-looking, meditative, pensive, subjective

introverted indrawn, inner-directed, introspective, inward-looking, self-centred, self-contained, withdrawn

intrude butt in, encroach, infringe, interfere, interrupt, meddle, obtrude, push in, put one's two cents in (*U.S. slang*), thrust oneself in *or* forward, trespass, violate

intruder burglar, gate-crasher (*informal*), infiltrator, interloper, invader, prowler, raider, snooper (*informal*), squatter, thief, trespasser

intrusion encroachment, infringement, interference, interruption, invasion, trespass, violation

intrusive disturbing, forward, impertinent, importunate, interfering, invasive, meddlesome, nosy (*informal*), officious, presumptuous, pushy (*informal*), uncalled-for, unwanted

intrust *see* ENTRUST

intuition discernment, hunch, insight, instinct, perception, presentiment, sixth sense

intuitive innate, instinctive, instinctual, involuntary, spontaneous, unreflecting, untaught

intuitively automatically, innately, instinctively, instinctually, involuntarily, spontaneously

intwine *see* ENTWINE

inundate deluge, drown, engulf, flood, glut, immerse, overflow, overrun, overwhelm, submerge, swamp

inundation deluge, flood, overflow, tidal wave, torrent

inure accustom, anneal, case-harden, desensitize, familiarize, habituate, harden, strengthen, temper, toughen, train

invade **1.** assail, assault, attack, burst in, descend upon, encroach, infringe, make inroads, occupy, raid, violate **2.** infect, infest, overrun, overspread, penetrate, permeate, pervade, swarm over

invader aggressor, alien, attacker, looter, plunderer, raider, trespasser

invalid[1] **1.** *adjective* ailing, bedridden, disabled, feeble, frail, ill, infirm, poorly (*informal*), sick, sickly, valetudinarian, weak **2.** *noun* convalescent, patient, valetudinarian

invalid[2] *adjective* baseless, fallacious, false, ill-founded, illogical, inoperative, irrational, not binding, nugatory, null, null and void, unfounded, unscientific, unsound, untrue, void, worthless
Antonyms logical, operative, rational, solid, sound, true, valid, viable

invalidate abrogate, annul, cancel, nullify, overrule, overthrow, quash, render null and void, rescind, undermine, undo, weaken
Antonyms authorize, empower, ratify, sanction, strengthen, validate

invalidism chronic illness, valetudinarianism

invalidity fallaciousness, fallacy, falsity, illogicality, inconsistency, irrationality, sophism, speciousness, unsoundness

invaluable beyond price, costly, inestimable, precious, priceless, valuable, worth one's *or* its weight in gold
Antonyms cheap, rubbishy, valueless, worthless

invariable changeless, consistent, constant, fixed, immutable, inflexible, regular, rigid, set, unalterable, unchangeable, unchanging, unfailing, uniform, unvarying, unwavering
Antonyms alterable, changeable, changing, differing, flexible, inconsistent, irregular, uneven, variable, varying

invariably always, consistently, customarily, day in, day out, ever, every time, habitually, inevitably, on every occasion, perpetually, regularly, unfailingly, without exception

invasion **1.** aggression, assault, attack, campaign, foray, incursion, inroad, irruption, offensive, onslaught, raid **2.** breach, encroachment, infiltration, infraction, infringement, intrusion, overstepping, usurpation, violation

invective abuse, berating, billingsgate, castigation, censure, contumely, denunciation, diatribe, obloquy, philippic(s), reproach, revilement, sarcasm, tirade, tongue-lashing, vilification, vituperation

inveigh berate, blame, castigate, censure, condemn, denounce, excoriate, expostulate, lambast(e), rail, recriminate, reproach, sound off, tongue-lash, upbraid, vituperate

inveigle allure, bamboozle (*informal*), beguile, cajole, coax, con (*slang*), decoy, ensnare, entice, entrap, lead on, lure, manipulate, manoeuvre, persuade, seduce, sweet-talk (*informal*), wheedle

invent **1.** coin, come up with (*informal*), conceive, contrive, create, design, devise, discover, dream up (*informal*), formulate, imagine, improvise, originate, think up **2.** concoct, cook up (*informal*), fabricate, feign, forge, make up, manufacture, trump up

invention **1.** brainchild (*informal*), contraption, contrivance, creation, design, development, device, discovery, gadget, instrument, waldo **2.** coinage, creativeness, creativity, genius, imagination, ingenuity, inspiration, inventiveness, originality, resourcefulness **3.** deceit, fabrication, fake, falsehood, fantasy, fib (*informal*), fiction, figment *or* product of (someone's) imagination, forgery, lie, prevarication, sham, story, tall story (*informal*), untruth, yarn

inventive creative, fertile, gifted, ground-breaking, imaginative, ingenious, innovative, inspired, original, resourceful
Antonyms imitative, pedestrian, trite, unimaginative, uninspired, uninventive

inventor architect, author, coiner, creator, designer, father, framer, maker, originator

inventory *noun* account, catalogue, file, list, record, register, roll, roster, schedule, stock book

inverse *adjective* contrary, converse, inverted, opposite, reverse, reversed, transposed

inversion antipode, antithesis, contraposition, contrariety, contrary, opposite, reversal, transposal, transposition

invert capsize, introvert, intussuscept (*Pathology*), invaginate (*Pathology*), overset, overturn, reverse, transpose, turn inside out, turn turtle, turn upside down, upset, upturn

invertebrate

Invertebrates

abalone *or* ear shell
amoeba *or (U.S.)* ameba
animalcule *or* animalculum
arrowworm
arthropod
barnacle
bird spider
bivalve
black widow
bladder worm
book scorpion
box jellyfish *or (Austral.)* sea wasp
brachiopod *or* lamp shell
brandling
bryozoan *or (colloquial)* sea mat
cardinal spider
catworm, white worm *or* white cat
centipede
cheese mite
chicken louse
chigger, chigoe *or (U.S. & Canad.)* redbug
chigoe, chigger, jigger *or* sand flea
chiton *or* coat-of-mail shell
clam
clappy-doo *or* clabby-doo (*Scot.*)
cockle
conch
cone (shell)
coral
cowrie *or* cowry
crab
crayfish, crawfish *(U.S.) or (Austral. & N.Z. informal)* craw
crown-of-thorns
ctenophore *or* comb jelly
cuttlefish *or* cuttle
daphnia
Dublin Bay prawn
earthworm
eelworm
false scorpion
freshwater shrimp
funnel-web
gaper
gapeworm
gastropod
goose barnacle
gribble
Guinea worm
harvestman *or (U.S. & Canad.)* daddy-longlegs
hermit crab
horseleech
horseshoe crab *or* king crab
house spider
itch mite
jellyfish
jumping spider
katipo
king prawn
krill
lancelet *or* amphioxus
land crab
langoustine
leech
limpet
liver fluke
lobster
lugworm, lug *or* lobworm
lungworm
millipede, millepede *or* milleped
mite
mollusc
money spider
murex
mussel
Norway lobster
nudibranch *or* sea slug
octopus *or* devilfish
opossum shrimp
ormer *or* sea-ear
otter shell
oyster
oyster crab
paddle worm
paper nautilus, nautilus *or* argonaut
pearly nautilus, nautilus *or* chambered nautilus
periwinkle *or* winkle
piddock
pinworm *or* threadworm
Portuguese man-of-war
prawn
quahog, hard-shell clam, hard-shell *or* round clam
ragworm *or (U.S.)* clamworm
ramshorn snail
razor-shell *or (U.S.)* razor clam
redback spider
red coral *or* precious coral
robber crab
Roman snail
roundworm
sand hopper, beach flea *or* sand flea
sand shrimp
sandworm
scallop
scorpion
sea anemone
sea cucumber
sea hare
sea lily
sea mouse
sea pen
sea slater
sea spider
sea squirt
sea urchin
seed oyster
shrimp
slug
snail
soft-shell (clam)
soft-shell crab
spider
spider crab
spider mite
spiny lobster, rock lobster, crawfish *or* langouste
sponge
squid
starfish
stomach worm
stony coral
sunstar
tapeworm
tarantula
tardigrade *or* water bear
tellin
teredo *or* shipworm
tick
top-shell
trap-door spider
trepang *or* bêche-de-mer
triton
tube worm
tubifex
tusk shell *or* tooth shell
Venus's flower basket
Venus's-girdle
Venus shell
vinegar eel, vinegar worm *or* eelworm
vinegarroon
water flea
water louse *or* water slater
water measurer
water spider
water stick insect
wentletrap
wheatworm
whelk
whip scorpion
whipworm
wolf spider *or* hunting spider
woodborer
worm

Extinct invertebrates

ammonite
belemnite
eurypterid
graptolite
trilobite

invest 1. advance, devote, lay out, put in, sink, spend 2. endow, endue, provide, supply 3 authorize, charge, empower, license, sanction vest 4. adopt, consecrate, enthrone, establish inaugurate, induct, install, ordain **5.** *Military* beleaguer, beset, besiege, enclose, lay siege to, surround **6.** *archaic* array, bedeck, bedizen (*archaic*), clothe, deck, drape, dress, robe

investigate consider, enquire into, examine, explore, go into, inquire into, inspect, look into, make enquiries, probe, put to the test, recce (*slang*), research, scrutinize, search, sift, study, work over

investigation analysis, enquiry, examination, exploration, fact finding, hearing, inquest, in~quiry, inspection, probe, recce (*slang*), re~search, review, scrutiny, search, study, survey

investigative fact-finding, inspecting, investi~gating, research, researching

investigator dick (*slang, chiefly U.S.*), examin~er, gumshoe (*U.S. slang*), inquirer, (private) detective, private eye (*informal*), researcher, reviewer, sleuth *or* sleuthhound (*informal*)

investiture admission, enthronement, inaugu~ration, induction, installation, instatement, investing, investment, ordination

investment **1.** asset, investing, speculation, transaction, venture **2.** ante (*informal*), contri~bution, stake **3.** *Military* beleaguering, besieg~ing, blockading, siege, surrounding

inveterate chronic, confirmed, deep-dyed (*usually derogatory*), deep-rooted, deep-seated, dyed-in-the-wool, entrenched, established, ha~bitual, hard-core, hardened, incorrigible, in~curable, ineradicable, ingrained, long-standing, obstinate

invidious discriminatory, envious (*obsolete*), hateful, obnoxious, odious, offensive, repug~nant, slighting, undesirable
Antonyms benevolent, desirable, generous, gratifying, kind, pleasant, pleasing

invigorate animate, brace, buck up (*informal*), energize, enliven, exhilarate, fortify, freshen (up), galvanize, harden, liven up, nerve, pep up, perk up, put new heart into, quicken, re~fresh, rejuvenate, revitalize, stimulate, strengthen

invigorating bracing, energizing, exhilarating, fresh, healthful, refreshing, rejuvenating, rejuvenative, restorative, salubrious, stimu~lating, tonic, uplifting

invincible impregnable, indestructible, indomi~table, inseparable, insuperable, invulnerable, unassailable, unbeatable, unconquerable, un~surmountable, unyielding
Antonyms assailable, beatable, conquerable, defenceless, fallible, powerless, unprotected, vulnerable, weak, yielding

inviolability holiness, inalienability, inviolacy, invulnerability, sacredness, sanctity

inviolable hallowed, holy, inalienable, sacred, sacrosanct, unalterable

inviolate entire, intact, pure, sacred, stainless, unbroken, undefiled, undisturbed, unhurt, unpolluted, unstained, unsullied, untouched, virgin, whole
Antonyms abused, broken, defiled, polluted, stained, sullied, touched, violated

invisible **1.** imperceptible, indiscernible, out of sight, unperceivable, unseen **2.** concealed, dis~guised, hidden, inappreciable, inconspicuous, infinitesimal, microscopic
Antonyms (*sense 1*) discernible, distinct, obvi~ous, perceptible, seen, visible

invitation **1.** asking, begging, bidding, call, in~vite (*informal*), request, solicitation, summons, supplication **2.** allurement, challenge, come-on (*informal*), coquetry, enticement, glad eye (*in~formal*), incitement, inducement, open door, overture, provocation, temptation

invite **1.** ask, beg, bid, call, request, request the pleasure of (someone's) company, solicit, sum~mon **2.** allure, ask for (*informal*), attract, bring on, court, draw, encourage, entice, lead, leave the door open to, provoke, solicit, tempt, welcome

inviting alluring, appealing, attractive, beguil~ing, captivating, delightful, engaging, enticing, fascinating, intriguing, magnetic, mouth~watering, pleasing, seductive, tempting, warm, welcoming, winning
Antonyms disagreeable, offensive, off-putting (*Brit. informal*), repellent, unappealing, unat~tractive, undesirable, uninviting, unpleasant

invocation appeal, beseeching, entreaty, peti~tion, prayer, supplication

invoke **1.** adjure, appeal to, beg, beseech, call upon, conjure, entreat, implore, petition, pray, solicit, supplicate **2.** apply, call in, have re~course to, implement, initiate, put into effect, resort to, use

involuntary **1.** compulsory, forced, obligatory, reluctant, unwilling **2.** automatic, blind, con~ditioned, instinctive, instinctual, reflex, spon~taneous, unconscious, uncontrolled, uninten~tional, unthinking
Antonyms (*sense 1*) optional, unconstrained, volitional, voluntary, willing (*sense 2*) calcu~lated, deliberate, intentional, planned, pur~posed, wilful

involve **1.** entail, imply, mean, necessitate, presuppose, require **2.** affect, associate, com~promise, concern, connect, draw in, implicate, incriminate, inculpate, mix up (*informal*), stitch up (*slang*), touch **3.** comprehend, com~prise, contain, cover, embrace, include, incor~porate, number among, take in **4.** absorb, bind, commit, engage, engross, grip, hold, preoccupy, rivet, wrap up **5.** complicate, em~broil, enmesh, entangle, link, mire, mix up, snarl up, tangle

involved 1. Byzantine, complex, complicated, confusing, convoluted, difficult, elaborate, intricate, knotty, labyrinthine, sophisticated, tangled, tortuous 2. caught (up), concerned, implicated, in on (*informal*), mixed up in *or* with, occupied, participating, taking part, up to one's ears in
Antonyms (*sense 1*) easy, easy-peasy (*slang*), elementary, simple, simplified, straightforward, uncomplicated, unsophisticated

involvement 1. association, commitment, concern, connection, dedication, interest, participation, responsibility 2. complexity, complication, difficulty, embarrassment, entanglement, imbroglio, intricacy, problem, ramification

invulnerability impenetrability, inviolability, safety, security, strength, unassailability, untouchability

invulnerable impenetrable, indestructible, insusceptible, invincible, proof against, safe, secure, unassailable
Antonyms assailable, defenceless, insecure, susceptible, unprotected, vulnerable, weak

inward *adjective* 1. entering, inbound, incoming, inflowing, ingoing, inpouring, penetrating 2. confidential, hidden, inmost, inner, innermost, inside, interior, internal, personal, private, privy, secret
Antonyms (*sense 2*) exterior, external, open, outer, outermost, outside, outward, public

inwardly at heart, deep down, in one's head, in one's inmost heart, inside, privately, secretly, to oneself, within

iota atom, bit, grain, hint, jot, mite, particle, scintilla (*rare*), scrap, speck, tittle, trace, whit

irascibility asperity, bad temper, cantankerousness, choler, crossness, edginess, fieriness, ill temper, impatience, irritability, irritation, petulance, shortness, snappishness, testiness, touchiness, uncertain temper

irascible cantankerous, choleric, crabbed, cross, hasty, hot-tempered, irritable, narky (*Brit. slang*), peppery, petulant, quick-tempered, ratty (*Brit. & N.Z. informal*), short-tempered, testy, tetchy, touchy

irate angered, angry, annoyed, as black as thunder, choked, cross, enraged, exasperated, fit to be tied (*slang*), fuming (*informal*), furious, hacked (off) (*U.S. slang*), hot under the collar (*informal*), incensed, indignant, infuriated, irritated, livid, mad (*informal*), piqued, pissed off (*taboo slang*), provoked, riled, up in arms, worked up, wrathful, wroth (*archaic*)

ire anger, annoyance, choler, displeasure, exasperation, fury, indignation, passion, rage, wrath

iridescent nacreous, opalescent, opaline, pearly, polychromatic, prismatic, rainbow-coloured, shimmering, shot

Irish green, Hibernian

irk aggravate (*informal*), annoy, be on one's back (*slang*), bug (*informal*), gall, get in one's hair (*informal*), get one's back up, get on one's nerves (*informal*), irritate, miff (*informal*), nark (*Brit., Austral., & N.Z. slang*), nettle, peeve (*informal*), piss one off (*taboo slang*), provoke, put one's back up, put one's nose out of joint (*informal*), put out (*informal*), rile, rub one up the wrong way (*informal*), ruffle, vex

irksome aggravating, annoying, boring, bothersome, burdensome, disagreeable, exasperating, irritating, tedious, tiresome, troublesome, uninteresting, unwelcome, vexatious, vexing, wearisome
Antonyms agreeable, enjoyable, gratifying, interesting, pleasant, pleasing, welcome

iron *adjective* 1. chalybeate, ferric, ferrous, irony 2. *figurative* adamant, cruel, hard, heavy, immovable, implacable, indomitable, inflexible, obdurate, rigid, robust, steel, steely, strong, tough, unbending, unyielding
Antonyms (*sense 2*) bending, easy, flexible, light, malleable, pliable, soft, weak, yielding

ironic, ironical 1. double-edged, mocking, mordacious, sarcastic, sardonic, satirical, scoffing, sneering, with tongue in cheek, wry 2. incongruous, paradoxical

iron out clear up, eliminate, eradicate, erase, expedite, get rid of, harmonize, put right, reconcile, resolve, settle, simplify, smooth over, sort out, straighten out, unravel

irons bonds, chains, fetters, gyves (*archaic*), manacles, shackles

irony 1. mockery, sarcasm, satire 2. contrariness, incongruity, paradox

irradiate brighten, cast light upon, enlighten, illume (*poetic*), illuminate, illumine, lighten, light up, shine upon

irrational 1. absurd, crackpot (*informal*), crazy, foolish, illogical, injudicious, loopy (*informal*), nonsensical, preposterous, silly, unreasonable, unreasoning, unsound, unthinking, unwise 2. aberrant, brainless, crazy, demented, insane, mindless, muddle-headed, raving, senseless, unstable, wild
Antonyms (*sense 1*) circumspect, judicious, logical, rational, reasonable, sensible, sound, wise

irrationality absurdity, brainlessness, illogicality, insanity, lack of judgment, lunacy, madness, preposterousness, senselessness, unreasonableness, unsoundness

irreconcilable 1. hardline, implacable, inexorable, inflexible, intransigent, unappeasable, uncompromising 2. clashing, conflicting, diametrically opposed, incompatible, incongruous, inconsistent, opposed

irrecoverable gone for ever, irreclaimable, irredeemable, irremediable, irreparable, irretrievable, lost, unregainable, unsalvageable, unsavable

irrefutable apodeictic, apodictic, beyond question, certain, incontestable, incontrovertible, indisputable, indubitable, invincible, irrefragable, irresistible, sure, unanswerable, unassailable, undeniable, unquestionable

irregular *adjective* **1.** desultory, disconnected, eccentric, erratic, fitful, fluctuating, fragmentary, haphazard, inconstant, intermittent, nonuniform, occasional, out of order, patchy, random, shifting, spasmodic, sporadic, uncertain, uneven, unmethodical, unpunctual, unsteady, unsystematic, variable, wavering **2.** abnormal, anomalous, capricious, disorderly, eccentric, exceptional, extraordinary, immoderate, improper, inappropriate, inordinate, odd, peculiar, queer, quirky, rum (*Brit. slang*), unconventional, unofficial, unorthodox, unsuitable, unusual **3.** asymmetrical, broken, bumpy, craggy, crooked, elliptic, elliptical, holey, jagged, lopsided, lumpy, pitted, ragged, rough, serrated, unequal, uneven, unsymmetrical *~noun* **4.** guerrilla, partisan, volunteer
Antonyms (*sense 1*) certain, invariable, methodical, punctual, reliable, steady, systematic (*sense 2*) appropriate, conventional, normal, orthodox, proper, regular, usual (*sense 3*) balanced, equal, even, regular, smooth, symmetrical

irregularity **1.** asymmetry, bumpiness, crookedness, jaggedness, lack of symmetry, lopsidedness, lumpiness, patchiness, raggedness, roughness, spottiness, unevenness **2.** aberration, abnormality, anomaly, breach, deviation, eccentricity, freak, malfunction, malpractice, oddity, peculiarity, singularity, unconventionality, unorthodoxy **3.** confusion, desultoriness, disorderliness, disorganization, haphazardness, lack of method, randomness, uncertainty, unpunctuality, unsteadiness

irregularly anyhow, by fits and starts, disconnectedly, eccentrically, erratically, fitfully, haphazardly, in snatches, intermittently, jerkily, now and again, occasionally, off and on, out of sequence, spasmodically, unevenly, unmethodically, unpunctually

irrelevance, irrelevancy inappositeness, inappropriateness, inaptness, inconsequence, non sequitur
Antonyms appositeness, appropriateness, aptness, consequence, pertinence, point, relevance, suitability

irrelevant beside the point, extraneous, immaterial, impertinent, inapplicable, inapposite, inappropriate, inapt, inconsequent, neither here nor there, unconnected, unrelated
Antonyms applicable, apposite, appropriate, apt, connected, fitting, pertinent, related, relevant, suitable

irreligious **1.** agnostic, atheistic, freethinking, godless, pagan, sceptical, unbelieving **2.** blasphemous, iconoclastic, impious, irreverent, profane, sacrilegious, sinful, undevout, ungodly, unholy, unrighteous, wicked

irremediable beyond redress, deadly, fatal, final, hopeless, incurable, irrecoverable, irredeemable, irreparable, irreversible, mortal, remediless, terminal

irreparable beyond repair, incurable, irrecoverable, irremediable, irreplaceable, irretrievable, irreversible

irreplaceable indispensable, invaluable, priceless, unique, vital

irrepressible boisterous, bubbling over, buoyant, ebullient, effervescent, insuppressible, uncontainable, uncontrollable, unmanageable, unquenchable, unrestrainable, unstoppable

irreproachable beyond reproach, blameless, faultless, guiltless, impeccable, inculpable, innocent, irreprehensible, irreprovable, perfect, pure, unblemished, unimpeachable

irresistible **1.** compelling, compulsive, imperative, overmastering, overpowering, overwhelming, potent, urgent **2.** ineluctable, inescapable, inevitable, inexorable, unavoidable **3.** alluring, beckoning, enchanting, fascinating, ravishing, seductive, tempting

irresolute doubtful, fickle, half-arsed (*Brit. slang*), half-assed (*U.S. & Canad. slang*), half-hearted, hesitant, hesitating, indecisive, infirm, in two minds, tentative, undecided, undetermined, unsettled, unstable, unsteady, vacillating, wavering, weak
Antonyms decisive, determined, firm, fixed, resolute, resolved, settled, stable, stalwart, steadfast, steady, strong

irresolution dithering (*chiefly Brit.*), faint-heartedness, half-heartedness, hesitancy, hesitation, indecisiveness, infirmity (of purpose), shillyshallying (*informal*), uncertainty, vacillation, wavering

irrespective of apart from, despite, discounting, in spite of, notwithstanding, regardless of, without reference to, without regard to

irresponsible careless, featherbrained, flighty, giddy, good-for-nothing, harebrained, harum-scarum, ill-considered, immature, reckless, scatter-brained, shiftless, thoughtless, undependable, unreliable, untrustworthy, wild
Antonyms careful, dependable, level-headed, mature, reliable, responsible, sensible, trustworthy

irreverence cheek (*informal*), cheekiness (*informal*), chutzpah (*U.S. & Canad. informal*), derision, disrespect, flippancy, impertinence, impudence, lack of respect, mockery, sauce (*informal*)

irreverent cheeky (*informal*), contemptuous, derisive, disrespectful, flip (*informal*), flippant, fresh (*informal*), iconoclastic, impertinent, im~pious, impudent, mocking, sassy (*U.S. informal*), saucy, tongue-in-cheek
Antonyms awed, deferential, meek, pious, re~spectful, reverent, submissive

irreversible final, incurable, irreparable, ir~revocable, unalterable

irrevocable changeless, fated, fixed, immu~table, invariable, irremediable, irretrievable, irreversible, predestined, predetermined, set~tled, unalterable, unchangeable, unreversible

The moving finger writes; and having writ,
Moves on; nor all thy piety nor wit
Shall lure it back to cancel half a line,
Nor all thy tears wash out a word of it.
Edward Fitzgerald *Rubaiyat of Omar Khayyam*

One cannot step twice into the same river
Heraclitus

irrigate flood, inundate, moisten, water, wet

irritability bad temper, ill humour, impatience, irascibility, peevishness, petulance, prickli~ness, testiness, tetchiness, touchiness
Antonyms bonhomie, cheerfulness, compla~cence, good humour, patience

irritable bad-tempered, cantankerous, choleric, crabbed, crabby, cross, crotchety (*informal*), dyspeptic, edgy, exasperated, fiery, fretful, hasty, hot, ill-humoured, ill-tempered, iras~cible, narky (*Brit. slang*), out of humour, oversensitive, peevish, petulant, prickly, ratty (*Brit. & N.Z. informal*), snappish, snappy, snarling, tense, testy, tetchy, touchy
Antonyms agreeable, calm, cheerful, compla~cent, composed, even-tempered, good-natured, imperturbable, patient, unexcitable

irritate 1. aggravate (*informal*), anger, annoy, bother, drive one up the wall (*slang*), enrage, exasperate, fret, gall, get in one's hair (*informal*), get one's back up, get one's dander up (*informal*), get one's goat (*slang*), get one's hackles up, get on one's nerves (*informal*), get on one's wick (*informal*), get under one's skin (*informal*), harass, incense, inflame, infuriate, nark (*Brit., Austral., & N.Z. slang*), needle (*informal*), nettle, offend, pester, piss one off (*taboo slang*), provoke, put one's back up, raise one's hackles, rankle with, rub up the wrong way (*informal*), ruffle, try one's pa~tience, vex 2. aggravate, chafe, fret, inflame, intensify, pain, rub
Antonyms (*sense 1*) calm, comfort, gratify, mollify, placate, please, soothe

irritated angry, annoyed, bothered, cross, dis~pleased, exasperated, flustered, hacked (off) (*U.S. slang*), harassed, impatient, irritable, nettled, out of humour, peeved (*informal*), piqued, pissed off (*taboo slang*), put out, ruf~fled, vexed

irritating aggravating (*informal*), annoying, displeasing, disquieting, disturbing, galling, infuriating, irksome, maddening, nagging, pestilential, provoking, thorny, troublesome, trying, upsetting, vexatious, worrisome
Antonyms agreeable, assuaging, calming, comforting, mollifying, pleasant, pleasing, quieting, soothing

irritation 1. anger, annoyance, crossness, dis~pleasure, exasperation, ill humour, ill temper, impatience, indignation, irritability, resent~ment, shortness, snappiness, testiness, vexa~tion, wrath 2. aggravation (*informal*), annoy~ance, drag (*informal*), gall, goad, irritant, nuisance, pain (*informal*), pain in the arse (*taboo informal*), pain in the neck (*informal*), pest, provocation, tease, thorn in one's flesh
Antonyms (*sense 1*) calm, composure, ease, pleasure, quietude, satisfaction, serenity, tranquillity

irrupt break in, burst in, crash in (*informal*), invade, rush in, storm in

irruption breaking in, foray, forcible entry, in~cursion, inroad, intrusion, invasion, raid

island ait *or* eyot (*dialect*), atoll, cay *or* key, holm (*dialect*), inch (*Scot. & Irish*), isle, islet
Related adjective: insular

Islands and island groups

Achill	Balearic
Admiralty	Bali
Aegean	Banaba
Aegina	Bangka
Alcatraz	Banks
Aldabra	Baranof
Alderney	Barbados
Aleutian	Barbuda
Alexander	Bardsey
Amboina	Barra
Andaman	Basilan
Andaman and Nicobar	Basse-Terre
Andreanof	Batan
Andros	Belau
Anglesey	Belle
Anguilla	Benbecula
Anticosti	Bermuda
Antigua	Biak
Antilles	Billiton
Antipodes	Bioko
Aran	Bohol
Arran	Bonaire
Aru *or* Arru	Bonin
Aruba	Bora Bora
Ascension	Borneo
Auckland	Bornholm
Azores	Bougainville
Baffin	British
Bahamas	Bute

Butung
Caicos
Caldy
Calf of Man
Campobello
Canary
Canna
Canvey
Cape Breton
Capri
Caroline
Cayman
Cebú
Ceylon
Channel
Chatham
Cheju
Chichagof
Chiloé
Chios
Choiseul
Christmas
Cocos
Coll
Colonsay
Coney
Cook
Corfu
Corregidor
Corsica
Crete
Cuba
Curaçao
Cyclades
Cyprus
Cythera
Delos
D'Entrecasteaux
Diomede
Disko
Diu
Djerba *or* Jerba
Dodecanese
Dominica
Dry Tortugas
Easter
Eigg
Elba
Ellesmere
Espíritu Santo
Euboea
Faeroes
Faial *or* Fayal
Fair
Falkland
Falster
Farquhar
Fernando de Noronha
Fiji
Flannan
Flinders
Flores
Florida Keys
Foula
Foulness
Franz Josef Land
French West Indies
Frisian
Fyn
Galapagos
Gambier
Gigha
Gilbert
Gotland, Gothland *or* Gottland
Grand Bahama
Grand Canary
Grande-Terre
Grand Manan
Greater Antilles
Greater Sunda
Greenland
Grenada
Grenadines
Guadalcanal
Guam
Guernsey
Hainan *or* Hainan Tao
Handa
Hawaii
Hayling
Heard and McDonald
Hebrides
Heimaey
Heligoland
Herm
Hispaniola
Hokkaido
Holy
Hong Kong
Honshu
Hormuz *or* Ormuz
Howland
Ibiza
Icaria
Iceland
Imbros
Iona
Ionian
Ireland
Ischia
Islay
Isle Royale
Ithaca
Iwo Jima
Jamaica
Jan Mayen
Java
Jersey
Jolo
Juan Fernández
Jura
Kangaroo
Kauai
Keos
Kerrera
Kiritimati
Kodiak
Kos *or* Cos
Kosrae
Krakatoa *or* Krakatau
Kuril *or* Kurile
Kyushu *or* Kiushu
La Palma
Labuan
Lakshadweep
Lampedusa
Lanai
Lavongai
Leeward
Lemnos
Lesbos
Lesser Antilles
Levkás, Leukas *or* Leucas
Lewis with Harris *or* Lewis and Harris
Leyte
Liberty
Lindisfarne
Line
Lipari
Lismore
Lolland *or* Laaland
Lombok
Long
Longa
Lord Howe
Luing
Lundy
Luzon
Mackinac
Macquarie
Madagascar
Madeira
Madura
Maewo
Mahé
Mainland
Majorca
Maldives
Malé
Malta
Man
Manhattan
Manitoulin
Marajó
Margarita
Marie Galante
Marinduque
Marquesas
Marshall
Martinique
Masbate
Mascarene
Matsu *or* Mazu
Maui
Mauritius
May
Mayotte
Melanesia
Melos
Melville
Mersea
Micronesia
Mindanao
Mindoro
Minorca
Miquelon
Molokai
Moluccas
Montserrat
Mount Desert
Muck
Mull
Mykonos
Nantucket
Nauru
Naxos
Negros
Netherlands Antilles
Nevis
New Britain
New Caledonia
Newfoundland
New Georgia
New Guinea
New Ireland
New Providence
New Siberian
Nicobar
Niue
Norfolk
North
North Uist
Nusa Tenggara
Oahu
Oceania
Okinawa
Orkneys *or* Orkney
Palawan
Palmyra
Panay
Pantelleria
Páros
Patmos
Pelagian
Pemba
Penang
Pescadores
Philae
Philippines
Phoenix

Pitcairn
Polynesia
Ponape
Pribilof
Prince Edward
Prince of Wales
Principe
Qeshm *or* Qishm
Queen Charlotte
Queen Elizabeth
Quemoy
Raasey
Ramsey
Rarotonga
Rathlin
Réunion
Rhodes
Rhum
Rialto
Roanoke
Robben
Rockall
Rona
Ross
Ryukyu
Saba
Safety
Saipan
Sakhalin
Salamis
Saltee
Samar
Samoa
Samos
Samothrace
San Cristóbal
San Juan
San Salvador
Santa Catalina
Sao Miguel
Sao Tomé
Sardinia
Sark
Savaii
Scalpay
Schouten
Scilly
Sea
Seil
Seram *or* Ceram
Seychelles
Sheppey
Shetland
Sicily
Singapore
Sjælland
Skikoku
Skokholm
Skomer
Skye
Skyros *or* Scyros
Society
Socotra
South
Southampton
South Georgia
South Orkney
South Shetland
South Uist
Spitsbergen
Sporades
Sri Lanka
St. Croix
St. Helena
St. John
St. Kilda
St. Kitts *or* St. Christopher
St. Lucia
St. Martin
St. Tudwal's
St. Vincent
Staffa
Staten
Stewart
Stroma
Stromboli
Sulawesi
Sumatra
Sumba *or* Soemba
Sumbawa *or* Soembawa
Summer
Sunda *or* Soenda
Tahiti
Taiwan
Tasmania
Tenedos
Tenerife
Terceira
Thanet
Thásos
Thera
Thousand
Thursday
Timor
Tiree
Tobago
Tokelau
Tombo
Tonga
Tortola
Tortuga
Trinidad
Tristan da Cunha
Trobriand
Truk
Tsushima
Tuamotu
Tubuai
Turks
Tutuila
Tuvalu
Ulva
Unimak
Upolu
Ushant
Vancouver
Vanua Levu
Vanuatu
Vestmannaeyjar
Victoria
Virgin
Visayan
Viti Levu
Volcano
Walcheren
Walney
West Indies
Western
Wight
Windward
Wrangel
Yap
Youth
Zante
Zanzibar

isolate cut off, detach, disconnect, divorce, insulate, quarantine, segregate, separate, sequester, set apart

isolated 1. backwoods, hidden, incommunicado, in the middle of nowhere, lonely, off the beaten track, outlying, out-of-the-way, remote, retired, secluded, unfrequented **2.** abnormal, anomalous, exceptional, freak, out on a limb, random, single, solitary, special, unique, unrelated, untypical, unusual

isolation aloofness, detachment, disconnection, exile, insularity, insulation, ivory tower, loneliness, quarantine, remoteness, retirement, seclusion, segregation, self-sufficiency, separation, solitude, withdrawal

No man is an Island, entire of it self
John Donne *Meditation XVII*

issue *noun* **1.** affair, argument, bone of contention, can of worms (*informal*), concern, controversy, matter, matter of contention, point, point in question, problem, question, subject, topic **2. at issue** at variance, controversial, in disagreement, in dispute, to be decided, under discussion, unsettled **3. take issue** challenge, disagree, dispute, object, oppose, raise an objection, take exception **4.** conclusion, consequence, culmination, effect, end, end result, finale, outcome, pay-off (*informal*), result, termination, upshot **5.** copy, edition, impression, instalment, number, printing **6.** circulation, delivery, dispersion, dissemination, distribution, granting, issuance, issuing, publication, sending out, supply, supplying **7.** children, descendants, heirs, offspring, progeny, scions, seed (*chiefly biblical*) *~verb* **8.** announce, broadcast, circulate, deliver, distribute, emit, give out, promulgate, publish, put in circulation, put out, release **9.** arise, be a consequence of, come forth, emanate, emerge, flow, originate, proceed, rise, spring, stem
Antonyms *noun* (*sense 4*) beginning, cause, inception, start (*sense 6*) cancellation, recall (*sense 7*) parent, sire *~verb* cause, revoke, withdraw

itch *verb* **1.** crawl, irritate, prickle, tickle, tingle **2.** ache, burn, crave, hanker, hunger, long, lust, pant, pine, yearn *~noun* **3.** irritation, itchiness, prickling, tingling **4.** craving, desire, hankering, hunger, longing, lust, passion, restlessness, yearning, yen (*informal*)

itching agog, aquiver, atremble, avid, burning, consumed with curiosity, eager, impatient, inquisitive, longing, mad keen (*informal*), raring, spoiling for

itchy eager, edgy, fidgety, impatient, restive, restless, unsettled

item **1.** article, aspect, component, consideration, detail, entry, matter, particular, point, thing **2.** account, article, bulletin, dispatch, feature, note, notice, paragraph, piece, report

itemize count, detail, document, enumerate, instance, inventory, list, number, particularize, record, set out, specify

iterate go over, recap (*informal*), recapitulate, reiterate, repeat, restate

itinerant *adjective* ambulatory, Gypsy, journeying, migratory, nomadic, peripatetic, roaming, roving, travelling, unsettled, vagabond, vagrant, wandering, wayfaring
Antonyms established, fixed, resident, rooted, settled, stable

itinerary **1.** circuit, journey, line, programme, route, schedule, timetable, tour **2.** Baedeker, guide, guidebook

ivory tower cloister, refuge, remoteness, retreat, sanctum, seclusion, splendid isolation, unreality, world of one's own

ivory-towered **1.** cloistered, far from the madding crowd, remote, retired, sequestered, sheltered, withdrawn **2.** academic, airy-fairy (*informal*), idealistic, quixotic, unrealizable, visionary

J

jab *verb/noun* dig, lunge, nudge, poke, prod, punch, stab, tap, thrust

jabber babble, blather, blether, chatter, drivel, gabble, mumble, prate, rabbit (on) (*Brit. informal*), ramble, run off at the mouth (*slang*), tattle, waffle (*informal, chiefly Brit.*), yap (*informal*)

jackass berk (*Brit. slang*), blockhead, charlie (*Brit. informal*), coot, dickhead (*slang*), dickwit (*slang*), dimwit (*informal*), dipstick (*Brit. slang*), divvy (*Brit. slang*), dolt, dork (*slang*), dweeb (*U.S. slang*), fool, fuckwit (*taboo slang*), geek (*slang*), gobshite (*Irish taboo slang*), gonzo (*slang*), idiot, imbecile, jerk (*slang, chiefly U.S. & Canad.*), lamebrain (*informal*), nerd *or* nurd (*slang*), nincompoop, ninny, nitwit (*informal*), numpty (*Scot. informal*), numskull *or* numbskull, oaf, pillock (*Brit. slang*), plank (*Brit. slang*), plonker (*slang*), prat (*slang*), prick (*slang*), schmuck (*U.S. slang*), simpleton, twit (*informal, chiefly Brit.*), wally (*slang*)

jacket case, casing, coat, covering, envelope, folder, sheath, skin, wrapper, wrapping

Jackets
see CLOTHES

jackpot award, bonanza, kitty, pool, pot, pot of gold at the end of the rainbow, prize, reward, winnings

jack up **1.** elevate, heave, hoist, lift, lift up, raise, rear **2.** accelerate, augment, boost, escalate, increase, inflate, put up, raise

jade harridan, hussy, nag, shrew, slattern, slut, trollop, vixen, wench

jaded **1.** clapped out (*Austral. & N.Z. informal*), exhausted, fagged (out) (*informal*), fatigued, spent, tired, tired-out, weary, zonked (*slang*) **2.** bored, cloyed, dulled, glutted, gorged, sated, satiated, surfeited, tired
Antonyms bright-eyed and bushy-tailed (*informal*), eager, enthusiastic, fresh, keen, life-loving, naive, refreshed

jag[1] *noun* notch, point, projection, protuberance, snag, spur, tooth

jag[2] *noun* binge (*informal*), bout, carousal, carouse, fit, orgy, period, spell, spree

jagged barbed, broken, cleft, craggy, denticulate, indented, notched, pointed, ragged, ridged, rough, serrated, snaggy, spiked, toothed, uneven
Antonyms glassy, level, regular, rounded, smooth

jail, gaol **1.** *noun* borstal, brig (*chiefly U.S.*), calaboose (*U.S. informal*), can (*slang*), clink (*slang*), cooler (*slang*), inside (*slang*), jailhouse (*Southern U.S.*), jug (*slang*), lockup, nick (*Brit. slang*), penitentiary (*U.S.*), poky *or* pokey (*U.S. & Canad. slang*), prison, quod (*slang*), reformatory, slammer (*slang*), stir (*slang*) **2.** *verb* confine, detain, immure, impound, imprison, incarcerate, lock up, send down

jailbird *or* **gaolbird** con (*slang*), convict, felon, lag (*slang*), malefactor, prisoner, ticket-of-leave man (*Historical*), trusty

jailer, gaoler captor, guard, keeper, screw (*slang*), turnkey (*archaic*), warden, warder

jam *verb* **1.** cram, crowd, crush, force, pack, press, ram, squeeze, stuff, throng, wedge **2.** block, cease, clog, congest, halt, obstruct, stall, stick ~*noun* **3.** crowd, crush, horde, mass, mob, multitude, pack, press, swarm, throng **4.** bind, deep water, dilemma, fix (*informal*), hole (*slang*), hot water, pickle (*informal*), plight, predicament, quandary, scrape (*informal*), spot (*informal*), strait, tight spot, trouble

> *The rule is, jam tomorrow and jam yesterday - but never jam today*
> Lewis Carroll *Alice Through the Looking Glass*

jamboree beano (*Brit. slang*), blast (*U.S. slang*), carnival, carousal, carouse, celebration, festival, festivity, fête, frolic, hooley *or* hoolie (*chiefly Irish & N.Z.*), jubilee, merriment, party, rave (*Brit. slang*), rave-up (*Brit. slang*), revelry, spree

jammy **1.** comfortable, cushy (*Informal*), easy, enviable, pleasant, plum (*Informal*), snug, soft, undemanding **2.** favoured, fortunate, lucky

jangle **1.** *verb* chime, clank, clash, clatter, jingle, rattle, vibrate **2.** *noun* cacophony, clang, clangour, clash, din, dissonance, jar, racket, rattle, reverberation
Antonyms (*sense 2*) harmoniousness, mellifluousness, quiet, silence

janitor caretaker, concierge, custodian, doorkeeper, porter

jar[1] *noun* amphora, carafe, container, crock, flagon, jug, pitcher, pot, receptacle, urn, vase, vessel

jar[2] *verb* **1.** bicker, clash, contend, disagree, interfere, oppose, quarrel, wrangle **2.** agitate, convulse, disturb, grate, irritate, jolt, offend, rasp, rattle (*informal*), rock, shake, vibrate **3.** annoy, clash, discompose, gall, get on one's nerves (*informal*), grate, grind, irk, irritate, nark (*Brit., Austral., & N.Z. slang*), nettle, piss one off (*taboo slang*) ~*noun* **4.** agitation, altercation, bickering, disagreement, discord, grating, irritation, jolt, quarrel, rasping, wrangling

jargon **1.** argot, cant, dialect, idiom, lingo (*informal*), parlance, patois, patter, slang, tongue, usage **2.** balderdash, bunkum *or* buncombe (*chiefly U.S.*), drivel, gabble, gibberish, gobbledegook, Greek (*informal*), mumbo jumbo, nonsense, palaver, rigmarole, twaddle

jaundiced **1.** cynical, preconceived, sceptical **2.** biased, bigoted, bitter, distorted, envious, hostile, jealous, partial, prejudiced, resentful, spiteful, suspicious
Antonyms credulous, ingenuous, naive, open-minded, optimistic, trusting, unbiased

jaunt airing, excursion, expedition, outing, promenade, ramble, stroll, tour, trip

jaunty airy, breezy, buoyant, carefree, dapper, gay, high-spirited, lively, perky, self-confident, showy, smart, sparky, sprightly, spruce, trim
Antonyms dignified, dull, lifeless, sedate, serious, staid

jaw *verb* **1.** babble, chat, chatter, chew the fat *or* rag (*slang*), gossip, lecture, run off at the mouth (*slang*), spout, talk **2.** abuse, censure, criticize, revile, scold ~*noun* **3.** chat, chinwag (*Brit. informal*), conversation, gabfest (*informal, chiefly U.S. & Canad.*), gossip, natter, talk

jaws abyss, aperture, entrance, gates, ingress, maw, mouth, opening, orifice

jazz up animate, enhance, enliven, heighten, improve

jazzy animated, fancy, flashy, gaudy, lively, smart, snazzy (*informal*), spirited, vivacious, wild, zestful

jealous **1.** covetous, desirous, emulous, envious, green, green-eyed, grudging, intolerant, invidious, resentful, rival **2.** anxious, apprehensive, attentive, guarded, mistrustful, protective, solicitous, suspicious, vigilant, wary, watchful, zealous
Antonyms carefree, indifferent, satisfied, trusting

jealousy covetousness, distrust, envy, heart-burning, ill-will, mistrust, possessiveness, resentment, spite, suspicion

Love is strong as death; jealousy is cruel as the grave
Bible: Song of Solomon

It is not love that is blind, but jealousy
Lawrence Durrell *Justine*

Jealousy is no more than feeling alone against smiling enemies
Elizabeth Bowen *The House in Paris*

Jealousy is always born with love, but does not always die with it
Duc de la Rochefoucauld *Maxims*

Jealousy is the greatest of all evils, and the one which arouses the least pity in the person who causes it
Duc de la Rochefoucauld *Maxims*

Love that is fed by jealousy dies hard
Ovid *Remedia Amoris*

To jealousy, nothing is more frightful than laughter
Françoise Sagan *La Chamade*

O! beware, my lord, of jealousy;
It is the green-eyed monster which doth mock
The meat it feeds on
William Shakespeare *Othello*

Anger and jealousy can no more bear to lose sight of their objects than love
George Eliot *The Mill on the Floss*

the injured lover's hell
John Milton *Paradise Lost*

jeer **1.** *verb* banter, barrack, cock a snook at (*Brit.*), contemn (*formal*), deride, flout, gibe, heckle, hector, knock (*informal*), mock, ridicule, scoff, sneer, taunt **2.** *noun* abuse, aspersion, boo, catcall, derision, gibe, hiss, hoot, obloquy, ridicule, scoff, sneer, taunt
Antonyms (*sense 1*) acclaim, applaud, cheer, clap, praise (*sense 2*) adulation, applause, cheers, encouragement, praise

jejune **1.** childish, immature, juvenile, naive, pointless, puerile, senseless, silly, simple, unsophisticated **2.** banal, colourless, dry, dull, inane, insipid, prosaic, uninteresting, vapid, wishy-washy (*informal*)

jell **1.** congeal, harden, set, solidify, thicken **2.** come together, crystallize, finalize, form, materialize, take shape

jeopardize chance, endanger, expose, gamble, hazard, imperil, risk, stake, venture

jeopardy danger, endangerment, exposure, hazard, insecurity, liability, peril, pitfall, precariousness, risk, venture, vulnerability

jeremiad complaint, groan, keen, lament, lamentation, moan, plaint, wail

jerk *verb/noun* jolt, lurch, pull, throw, thrust, tug, tweak, twitch, wrench, yank

jerky bouncy, bumpy, convulsive, fitful, jolting, jumpy, rough, shaky, spasmodic, tremulous, twitchy, uncontrolled

Antonyms flowing, frictionless, gliding, smooth

jerry-built cheap, defective, faulty, flimsy, ramshackle, rickety, shabby, slipshod, thrown together, unsubstantial
Antonyms sturdy, substantial, well-built, well-constructed

jest 1. *noun* banter, bon mot, crack (*slang*), fun, gag (*informal*), hoax, jape, joke, josh (*slang, chiefly U.S. & Canad.*), play, pleasantry, prank, quip, sally, sport, wisecrack (*informal*), witticism 2. *verb* banter, chaff, deride, gibe, jeer, joke, josh (*slang, chiefly U.S. & Canad.*), kid (*informal*), mock, quip, scoff, sneer, tease

a fellow of infinite jest
William Shakespeare *Hamlet*

The jests of the rich are ever successful
Oliver Goldsmith

jester 1. comedian, comic, humorist, joculator *or (fem.)* joculatrix, joker, quipster, wag, wit 2. buffoon, clown, fool, harlequin, madcap, mummer, pantaloon, prankster, zany

jet[1] *adjective* black, coal-black, ebony, inky, pitch-black, raven, sable

jet[2] *noun* 1. flow, fountain, gush, spout, spray, spring, stream 2. atomizer, nose, nozzle, rose, spout, sprayer, sprinkler ~*verb* 3. flow, gush, issue, rush, shoot, spew, spout, squirt, stream, surge 4. fly, soar, zoom

jetsetting cosmopolitan, fashionable, high-society, rich, ritzy (*slang*), sophisticated, tony (*U.S. & Canad. slang*), trendsetting, trendy (*Brit informal*), well-off

jettison abandon, discard, dump, eject, expel, heave, scrap, throw overboard, unload

jetty breakwater, dock, groyne, mole, pier, quay, wharf

jewel 1. brilliant, gemstone, ornament, precious stone, rock (*slang*), sparkler (*informal*), trinket 2. charm, collector's item, find, gem, humdinger (*slang*), masterpiece, paragon, pearl, prize, rarity, treasure, wonder

jewellery finery, gems, jewels, ornaments, precious stones, regalia, treasure, trinkets

I never hated a man enough to give him his diamonds back
Zsa Zsa Gabor

Jezebel harlot, harridan, hussy, jade, virago, wanton, witch

jib balk, recoil, refuse, retreat, shrink, stop short

jibe *see* GIBE

jiffy bat of an eye (*informal*), flash, instant, moment, second, split second, trice, twinkling

jig *verb* bob, bounce, caper, jiggle, jounce, prance, shake, skip, twitch, wiggle, wobble

jiggle agitate, bounce, fidget, jerk, jig, jog, joggle, shake, shimmy, twitch, wiggle

jilt *verb* abandon, betray, break with, coquette, deceive, desert, disappoint, discard, ditch (*slang*), drop, forsake, leave (someone) in the lurch, reject, throw over

Say what you will, 'tis better to be left than never to have been loved
William Congreve *The Way of the World*

jingle *verb* 1. chime, clatter, clink, jangle, rattle, ring, tinkle, tintinnabulate ~*noun* 2. clang, clangour, clink, rattle, reverberation, ringing, tinkle 3. chorus, ditty, doggerel, limerick, melody, song, tune

jingoism belligerence, bigotry, chauvinism, flag-waving (*informal*), hawkishness, insularity, xenophobia

jinx 1. *noun* black magic, curse, evil eye, hex (*U.S. & Canad. informal*), hoodoo (*informal*), nemesis, plague, voodoo 2. *verb* bewitch, curse, hex (*U.S. & Canad. informal*)

jitters anxiety, butterflies (in one's stomach) (*informal*), cold feet (*informal*), fidgets, heebie-jeebies (*slang*), nerves, nervousness, tenseness, the shakes (*informal*), the willies (*informal*)

jittery agitated, anxious, fidgety, hyper (*informal*), jumpy, nervous, neurotic, quivering, shaky, trembling, twitchy (*informal*), wired (*slang*)
Antonyms calm, composed, laid-back (*informal*), relaxed, together (*slang*), unfazed (*informal*), unflustered

job 1. affair, assignment, charge, chore, concern, contribution, duty, enterprise, errand, function, pursuit, responsibility, role, stint, task, undertaking, venture, work 2. activity, bread and butter (*informal*), business, calling, capacity, career, craft, employment, function, livelihood, métier, occupation, office, position, post, profession, situation, trade, vocation 3. allotment, assignment, batch, commission, consignment, contract, lot, output, piece, portion, product, share

If you have a job without aggravations, you don't have a job
Malcolm S. Forbes

jobless idle, inactive, out of work, unemployed, unoccupied

jockey *verb* 1. bamboozle, cheat, con (*informal*), deceive, dupe, fool, hoax, hoodwink, trick 2. cajole, engineer, finagle (*informal*), ingratiate, insinuate, manage, manipulate, manoeuvre, negotiate, trim, wheedle

jocose blithe, comical, droll, facetious, funny, humorous, jesting, jocular, jovial, joyous, merry, mischievous, playful, pleasant, sportive, teasing, waggish, witty

jocular amusing, comical, droll, facetious, frolicsome, funny, humorous, jesting, jocose, jocund, joking, jolly, jovial, ludic (*literary*), playful, roguish, sportive, teasing, waggish, whimsical, witty
Antonyms earnest, humourless, serious, solemn

jog 1. activate, arouse, nudge, prod, prompt, push, remind, shake, stimulate, stir, suggest 2. bounce, jar, jerk, jiggle, joggle, jolt, jostle, jounce, rock, shake 3. canter, dogtrot, lope, run, trot 4. lumber, plod, traipse (*informal*), tramp, trudge

joie de vivre ebullience, enjoyment, enthusiasm, gaiety, gusto, joy, joyfulness, pleasure, relish, zest
Antonyms apathy, depression, distaste

join 1. accompany, add, adhere, annex, append, attach, cement, combine, connect, couple, fasten, knit, link, marry, splice, tie, unite, yoke 2. affiliate with, associate with, enlist, enrol, enter, sign up 3. adjoin, border, border on, butt, conjoin, extend, meet, reach, touch, verge on
Antonyms detach, disconnect, disengage, disentangle, divide, leave, part, quit, resign, separate, sever, unfasten

If you can't beat them, join them

joint *noun* 1. articulation, connection, hinge, intersection, junction, juncture, knot, nexus, node, seam, union *~adjective* 2. collective, combined, communal, concerted, consolidated, cooperative, joined, mutual, shared, united *~verb* 3. connect, couple, fasten, fit, join, unite 4. carve, cut up, dismember, dissect, divide, segment, sever, sunder

jointly as one, collectively, in common, in conjunction, in league, in partnership, mutually, together, unitedly
Antonyms individually, separately, singly

joke *noun* 1. frolic, fun, gag (*informal*), jape, jest, josh (*slang, chiefly U.S. & Canad.*), lark, play, prank, pun, quip, quirk, sally, sport, whimsy, wisecrack (*informal*), witticism, yarn 2. buffoon, butt, clown, laughing stock, simpleton, target *~verb* 3. banter, chaff, deride, frolic, gambol, jest, josh (*slang, chiefly U.S. & Canad.*), kid (*informal*), mock, play the fool, quip, ridicule, taunt, tease, wind up (*Brit. slang*)

Many a true word is spoken in jest

joker buffoon, clown, comedian, comic, humorist, jester, kidder (*informal*), prankster, trickster, wag, wit

jokey amusing, droll, facetious, funny, humorous, jesting, mischievous, nonserious, playful, prankish, teasing, waggish, wisecracking
Antonyms dry, grave, humourless, solemn, straight-faced, unsmiling

jollification beano (*Brit slang*), carousal, celebration, festivity, jolly (*informal, chiefly Brit*), knees-up (*Brit informal*), merrymaking, party, rave (*Brit slang*), rave-up (*Brit slang*), reception, shindig (*informal*)

jollity conviviality, fun, gaiety, liveliness, merriment, merrymaking, mirth, revelry

jolly blithesome, carefree, cheerful, chirpy (*informal*), convivial, festive, frolicsome, funny, gay, genial, gladsome (*archaic*), hilarious, jocund, jovial, joyful, joyous, jubilant, ludic (*literary*), merry, mirthful, playful, sportive, sprightly, upbeat (*informal*)
Antonyms doleful, down in the dumps (*informal*), gaunt, grave, lugubrious, miserable, morose, saturnine, serious, solemn

jolt *verb* 1. jar, jerk, jog, jostle, knock, push, shake, shove 2. astonish, discompose, disturb, perturb, stagger, startle, stun, surprise, upset *~noun* 3. bump, jar, jerk, jog, jump, lurch, quiver, shake, start 4. blow, bolt from the blue, bombshell, reversal, setback, shock, surprise, thunderbolt, whammy (*informal, chiefly U.S.*)

jostle bump, butt, crowd, elbow, hustle, jog, joggle, jolt, press, push, scramble, shake, shove, squeeze, throng, thrust

jot 1. *noun* ace, atom, bit, detail, fraction, grain, iota, mite, morsel, particle, scintilla, scrap, smidgen *or* smidgin (*informal, chiefly U.S. & Canad.*), speck, tittle, trifle, whit 2. *verb* list, note, note down, record, register, scribble, tad (*informal, chiefly U.S.*), tally

jotter Filofax (*Trademark*), notebook, notepad, pad

journal 1. chronicle, daily, gazette, magazine, monthly, newspaper, paper, periodical, record, register, review, tabloid, weekly 2. chronicle, commonplace book, daybook, diary, log, record

journalism

Most rock journalism is people who can't write interviewing people who can't talk for people who can't read

Frank Zappa

I hope we never see the day when a thing is as bad as some of our newspapers make it

Will Rogers

Four hostile newspapers are to be feared more than a thousand bayonets

Napoleon Bonaparte

Modern journalism....justifies its own existence by the great Darwinian principle of the survival of the vulgarest

Oscar Wilde

I'm with you on the free press. It's the newspapers I can't stand

Tom Stoppard *Night and Day*

Freedom of the press in Britain means freedom to

print such of the proprietor's prejudices as the advertisers don't object to

Hannen Swaffer

Editor: a person employed by a newspaper, whose business it is to separate the wheat from the chaff, and to see that the chaff is printed

Elbert Hubbard *The Roycroft Dictionary*

I read the newspapers avidly. It is my one form of continuous fiction

Aneurin Bevan

The art of newspaper paragraphing is to stroke a platitude until it purrs like an epigram

Don Marquis

A good newspaper, I suppose, is a nation talking to itself

Arthur Miller

The power of the press is very great, but not so great as the power of suppress

Lord Northcliff

journalist broadcaster, columnist, commentator, contributor, correspondent, hack, journo (*slang*), newsman, newspaperman, pressman, reporter, scribe (*informal*), stringer

Journalists say a thing that they know isn't true, in the hope that if they keep on saying it long enough it will be true

Arnold Bennett *The Title*

journey **1.** *noun* excursion, expedition, jaunt, odyssey, outing, passage, peregrination, pilgrimage, progress, ramble, tour, travel, trek, trip, voyage **2.** *verb* fare, fly, go, peregrinate, proceed, ramble, range, roam, rove, tour, travel, traverse, trek, voyage, wander, wend

A journey of a thousand miles must begin with a single step

Lao-tze *Tao Te Ching*

Whenever I prepare for a journey I prepare as though for death. Should I never return, all is in order

Katherine Mansfield

joust **1.** *noun* combat, duel, encounter, engagement, lists, match, passage of arms, set-to, tilt, tournament, tourney **2.** *verb* break a lance, cross swords, engage, enter the lists, fight, tilt, trade blows

jovial airy, animated, blithe, buoyant, cheery, convivial, cordial, gay, glad, happy, hilarious, jocose, jocund, jolly, jubilant, merry, mirthful
Antonyms antisocial, doleful, grumpy, morose, solemn, unfriendly

joviality fun, gaiety, glee, hilarity, jollity, merriment, mirth

joy **1.** bliss, delight, ecstasy, elation, exaltation, exultation, felicity, festivity, gaiety, gladness, glee, hilarity, pleasure, rapture, ravishment, satisfaction, transport **2.** charm, delight, gem, jewel, pride, prize, treasure, treat, wonder
Antonyms bane, despair, grief, misery, sorrow, tribulation, unhappiness

Joy cometh in the morning

Bible: Psalm 30

joyful blithesome, cock-a-hoop, delighted, elated, enraptured, floating on air, glad, gladsome (*archaic*), gratified, happy, jocund, jolly, jovial, jubilant, light-hearted, merry, on cloud nine (*informal*), over the moon (*informal*), pleased, rapt, satisfied

joyless cheerless, dejected, depressed, dismal, dispirited, downcast, down in the dumps (*informal*), dreary, gloomy, miserable, sad, unhappy

joyous cheerful, festive, heartening, joyful, merry, rapturous

jubilant cock-a-hoop, elated, enraptured, euphoric, excited, exuberant, exultant, glad, joyous, overjoyed, over the moon (*informal*), rejoicing, rhapsodic, thrilled, triumphal, triumphant
Antonyms despondent, doleful, downcast, melancholy, sad, sorrowful

jubilation celebration, ecstasy, elation, excitement, exultation, festivity, jamboree, joy, jubilee, triumph

jubilee carnival, celebration, festival, festivity, fête, gala, holiday

Judas betrayer, deceiver, renegade, traitor, turncoat

judge *noun* **1.** adjudicator, arbiter, arbitrator, moderator, referee, umpire **2.** appraiser, arbiter, assessor, authority, connoisseur, critic, evaluator, expert **3.** beak (*Brit. slang*), justice, magistrate *~verb* **4.** adjudge, adjudicate, arbitrate, ascertain, conclude, decide, determine, discern, distinguish, mediate, referee, umpire **5.** appraise, appreciate, assess, consider, criticize, esteem, estimate, evaluate, examine, rate, review, value **6.** adjudge, condemn, decree, doom, find, pass sentence, pronounce sentence, rule, sentence, sit, try

He who has the judge for his father goes into court with an easy mind

Miguel de Cervantes *Don Quixote*

Forbear to judge, for we are sinners all

William Shakespeare *Henry VI, part II*

No one should be judge in his own cause

judgment **1.** acumen, common sense, discernment, discrimination, intelligence, penetration, percipience, perspicacity, prudence, sagacity, sense, shrewdness, smarts (*slang, chiefly U.S.*), taste, understanding, wisdom **2.** arbitration, award, conclusion, decision, decree, determination, finding, order, result, ruling, sentence, verdict **3.** appraisal, assessment, belief, conviction, deduction, diagnosis, estimate, finding, opinion, valuation, view **4.** damnation, doom, fate, misfortune, punishment, retribution

Judge not, that ye be not judged
Bible: St. Matthew

'Tis with our judgments as our watches: none
Go just alike, yet each believes his own
Alexander Pope *Essay on Criticism*

judgmental censorious, condemnatory, pharisaic, self-righteous

judicial **1.** judiciary, juridical, legal, official **2.** discriminating, distinguished, impartial, judgelike, magisterial, magistral

judicious acute, astute, careful, cautious, circumspect, considered, diplomatic, discerning, discreet, discriminating, enlightened, expedient, informed, politic, prudent, rational, reasonable, sagacious, sage, sane, sapient, sensible, shrewd, skilful, sober, sound, thoughtful, well-advised, well-judged, wise
Antonyms imprudent, indiscreet, injudicious, tactless, thoughtless

jug carafe, container, crock, ewer, jar, pitcher, urn, vessel

juggle alter, change, disguise, doctor (*informal*), falsify, fix (*informal*), manipulate, manoeuvre, misrepresent, modify, tamper with

juice extract, fluid, liquid, liquor, nectar, sap, secretion, serum

juicy **1.** lush, moist, sappy, succulent, watery **2.** colourful, interesting, provocative, racy, risqué, sensational, spicy (*informal*), suggestive, vivid

jumble **1.** *verb* confound, confuse, disarrange, dishevel, disorder, disorganize, entangle, mistake, mix, muddle, ravel, shuffle, tangle **2.** *noun* chaos, clutter, confusion, disarrangement, disarray, disorder, farrago, gallimaufry, hodgepodge, hotchpotch (*U.S.*), litter, medley, *mélange*, mess, miscellany, mishmash, mixture, muddle, pig's breakfast (*informal*)

jumbo elephantine, giant, gigantic, ginormous (*informal*), huge, humongous *or* humungous (*U.S. slang*), immense, large, mega (*informal*), oversized
Antonyms baby, dwarf, micro, mini, pocket, tiny, wee

jump *verb* **1.** bounce, bound, caper, clear, gambol, hop, hurdle, leap, skip, spring, vault **2.** flinch, jerk, recoil, start, wince **3.** avoid, digress, evade, miss, omit, overshoot, skip, switch **4.** advance, ascend, boost, escalate, gain, hike, increase, mount, rise, surge *~noun* **5.** bound, buck, caper, hop, leap, skip, spring, vault **6.** barricade, barrier, fence, hurdle, impediment, obstacle, rail **7.** breach, break, gap, hiatus, interruption, lacuna, space **8.** advance, augmentation, boost, increase, increment, rise, upsurge, upturn **9.** jar, jerk, jolt, lurch, shock, start, swerve, twitch, wrench

jumper jersey, pullover, sweater, woolly
Sweaters
see CLOTHES

jumpy agitated, anxious, apprehensive, fidgety, hyper (*informal*), jittery (*informal*), nervous, neurotic, on edge, restless, shaky, tense, timorous, twitchy (*informal*), wired (*slang*)
Antonyms calm, composed, laid-back (*informal*), nerveless, together (*slang*), unfazed (*informal*), unflustered

junction alliance, combination, connection, coupling, joint, juncture, linking, seam, union

juncture **1.** conjuncture, contingency, crisis, crux, emergency, exigency, moment, occasion, point, predicament, strait, time **2.** bond, connection, convergence, edge, intersection, junction, link, seam, weld

junior inferior, lesser, lower, minor, secondary, subordinate, younger
Antonyms elder, higher-ranking, older, senior, superior

junk clutter, debris, dreck (*slang, chiefly U.S.*), leavings, litter, oddments, odds and ends, refuse, rubbish, rummage, scrap, trash, waste

junkie, junky acidhead (*slang*), addict, cokehead (*slang*), drug addict, druggie (*informal*), freak (*informal*), hashhead (*slang*), head (*slang*), mainliner (*slang*), pill-popper (*slang*), pothead (*slang*), smackhead (*slang*), user, weedhead (*slang*)

junta assembly, cabal, camp, clique, combination, confederacy, convocation, coterie, council, crew, faction, gang, league, party, ring, schism, set

jurisdiction **1.** authority, command, control, dominion, influence, power, prerogative, rule, say, sway **2.** area, bounds, circuit, compass, district, dominion, field, orbit, province, range, scope, sphere, zone

just *adjective* **1.** blameless, conscientious, decent, equitable, fair, fairminded, good, honest, honourable, impartial, lawful, pure, right, righteous, unbiased, upright, virtuous **2.** accurate, correct, exact, faithful, normal, precise, proper, regular, sound, true **3.** appropriate, apt, condign, deserved, due, fitting, justified, legitimate, merited, proper, reasonable, rightful, sensible, suitable, well-deserved *~adverb* **4.** absolutely, completely, entirely, exactly, perfectly, precisely **5.** hardly, lately, only now, recently, scarcely **6.** at a push, at most, but, by the skin of one's teeth, merely, no more than, nothing but, only, simply, solely
Antonyms *adjective* corrupt, devious, dishonest, inappropriate, inequitable, prejudiced, undeserved, unfair, unfit, unjust, unlawful, unreasonable, untrue

Thrice is he arm'd that hath his quarrel just
William Shakespeare *Henry VI, part II*

just about all but, almost, around, close to, nearly, not quite, practically, well-nigh

justice 1. equity, fairness, honesty, impartiality, integrity, justness, law, legality, legitimacy, reasonableness, rectitude, right 2. amends, compensation, correction, penalty, recompense, redress, reparation 3. judge, magistrate
Antonyms dishonesty, favouritism, inequity, injustice, partiality, unfairness, unlawfulness, unreasonableness, untruth, wrong

It is better that ten guilty persons escape than one innocent suffer
William Blackstone *Commentaries*

Things go wrong in life. Justice is not done, and people sort of get used to it
Patricia Highsmith

In England, justice is open to all - like the Ritz Hotel
James Mathew

Justice should not only be done, but should manifestly and undoubtedly be seen to be done
Lord Hewart

justifiable acceptable, defensible, excusable, fit, lawful, legitimate, proper, reasonable, right, sensible, sound, tenable, understandable, valid, vindicable, warrantable, well-founded
Antonyms arbitrary, capricious, indefensible, inexcusable, unreasonable, unwarranted

justification 1. absolution, apology, approval, defence, exculpation, excuse, exoneration, explanation, extenuation, plea, rationalization, vindication 2. basis, defence, grounds, plea, reason, warrant

justify absolve, acquit, approve, confirm, defend, establish, exculpate, excuse, exonerate, explain, legalize, legitimize, maintain, substantiate, support, sustain, uphold, validate, vindicate, warrant

justly accurately, correctly, equally, equitably, fairly, honestly, impartially, lawfully, properly

jut bulge, extend, impend, overhang, poke, project, protrude, stick out

juvenile 1. *noun* adolescent, boy, child, girl, infant, minor, youth 2. *adjective* babyish, boyish, callow, childish, girlish, immature, inexperienced, infantile, jejune, puerile, undeveloped, unsophisticated, young, youthful
Antonyms *noun* adult, grown-up *~adjective* adult, grown-up, mature, responsible

juxtaposition adjacency, closeness, contact, contiguity, nearness, propinquity, proximity, vicinity

K

kaleidoscopic 1. changeable, fluctuating, fluid, many-coloured, mobile, motley, mutable, unstable, variegated 2. complex, complicated, confused, convoluted, disordered, intricate, jumbled, varied

kamikaze *adjective* foolhardy, self-destructive, suicidal

kaput broken, dead, defunct, destroyed, extinct, finished, ruined, undone, wrecked

keel over black out (*informal*), capsize, collapse, faint, founder, overturn, pass out, swoon (*literary*), topple over, upset

keen[1] *adjective* 1. ardent, avid, bright-eyed and bushy-tailed (*informal*), devoted to, eager, earnest, ebullient, enthusiastic, fervid, fierce, fond of, impassioned, intense, into (*informal*), zealous 2. acid, acute, biting, caustic, cutting, edged, finely honed, incisive, penetrating, piercing, pointed, razorlike, sardonic, satirical, sharp, tart, trenchant, vitriolic 3. astute, brilliant, canny, clever, discerning, discriminating, perceptive, perspicacious, quick, sagacious, sapient, sensitive, shrewd, wise

Antonyms (*sense 1*) apathetic, half-hearted, indifferent, laodicean, lukewarm, unenthusiastic, uninterested (*sense 2*) blunt, dull (*sense 3*) dull, obtuse, unperceptive

keen[2] 1. *verb* bewail, grieve, lament, mourn, wail, weep 2. *noun* coronach (*Scot. & Irish*), dirge, lament, lamentation, mourning, wailing, weeping

keenness 1. ardour, avidity, avidness, diligence, eagerness, earnestness, ebullience, enthusiasm, fervour, impatience, intensity, passion, zeal, zest 2. acerbity, harshness, incisiveness, mordancy, penetration, pungency, rigour, severity, sharpness, sternness, trenchancy, unkindness, virulence 3. astuteness, canniness, cleverness, discernment, insight, sagacity, sapience, sensitivity, shrewdness, wisdom

keep *verb* 1. conserve, control, hold, maintain, possess, preserve, retain 2. accumulate, amass, carry, deal in, deposit, furnish, garner, heap, hold, pile, place, stack, stock, store, trade in 3. care for, defend, guard, look after, maintain, manage, mind, operate, protect, safeguard, shelter, shield, tend, watch over 4. board, feed, foster, maintain, nourish, nurture, provide for, provision, subsidize, support, sustain, victual 5. accompany, associate with, consort with, fraternize with 6. arrest, block, check, constrain, control, curb, delay, detain, deter, hamper, hamstring, hinder, hold, hold back, impede, inhibit, keep back, limit, obstruct, prevent, restrain, retard, shackle, stall, withhold 7. adhere to, celebrate, commemorate, comply with, fulfil, hold, honour, obey, observe, perform, respect, ritualize, solemnize ~*noun* 8. board, food, livelihood, living, maintenance, means, nourishment, subsistence, support 9. castle, citadel, donjon, dungeon, fastness, stronghold, tower

Antonyms abandon, discard, disregard, expedite, free, give up, ignore, liberate, lose, release, speed

keep at be steadfast, carry on, complete, continue, drudge, endure, finish, grind, labour, last, maintain, persevere, persist, remain, slave, stay, stick, toil

keep back 1. check, constrain, control, curb, delay, hold back, keep a tight rein on, limit, prohibit, restrain, restrict, retard, withhold 2. censor, conceal, hide, keep dark, keep under one's hat, reserve, suppress, withhold

keeper attendant, caretaker, curator, custodian, defender, gaoler, governor, guard, guardian, jailer, overseer, preserver, steward, superintendent, warden, warder

keeping 1. aegis, auspices, care, charge, custody, guardianship, keep, maintenance, patronage, possession, protection, safekeeping, trust 2. accord, agreement, balance, compliance, conformity, congruity, consistency, correspondence, harmony, observance, proportion

keep on carry on, continue, endure, last, persevere, persist, prolong, remain

keepsake emblem, favour, memento, relic, remembrance, reminder, souvenir, symbol, token

keep up balance, compete, contend, continue, emulate, keep pace, maintain, match, persevere, preserve, rival, sustain, vie

keg barrel, cask, drum, firkin, hogshead, tun, vat

ken 1. compass, field, range, scope, sight, view, vision 2. acquaintance, awareness, cognizance, comprehension, knowledge, notice, understanding

kerchief babushka, headscarf, headsquare, scarf, square

kernel core, essence, germ, gist, grain, marrow, nub, pith, seed, substance

key *noun* 1. latchkey, opener 2. *figurative* answer, clue, cue, explanation, guide, indicator, interpretation, lead, means, pointer, sign, solution, translation *~adjective* 3. basic, chief, crucial, decisive, essential, fundamental, important, leading, main, major, pivotal, principal

Antonyms (*sense 3*) minor, secondary, subsidiary, superficial

key in enter, input, keyboard, type

keynote centre, core, essence, gist, heart, kernel, marrow, pith, substance, theme

keystone basis, core, cornerstone, crux, fundament, ground, linchpin, mainspring, motive, principle, quoin, root, source, spring

kick *verb* 1. boot, punt, put the boot in(to) (*slang*) 2. *figurative* complain, gripe (*informal*), grumble, object, oppose, protest, rebel, resist, spurn 3. *informal* abandon, desist from, give up, leave off, quit, stop *~noun* 4. force, intensity, pep, power, punch, pungency, snap (*informal*), sparkle, strength, tang, verve, vitality, zest 5. buzz (*slang*), enjoyment, excitement, fun, gratification, jollies (*slang*), pleasure, stimulation, thrill

kickback bribe, cut (*informal*), gift, graft (*informal*), payment, payoff, recompense, reward, share, sop, sweetener (*slang*)

kickoff *noun* beginning, commencement, opening, outset, start

kick off *verb* begin, commence, get the show on the road, get under way, initiate, kick-start, open, start

kick out discharge, dismiss, eject, evict, expel, get rid of, give (someone) their marching orders, give the boot (*slang*), give the bum's rush (*slang*), give the push, kiss off (*slang, chiefly U.S. & Canad.*), oust, reject, remove, sack (*informal*), show one the door, throw out on one's ear (*informal*), toss out

kid 1. *noun* ankle-biter (*Austral. slang*), baby, bairn, boy, child, girl, infant, lad, lass, little one, rug rat (*U.S. & Canad. informal*), sprog (*slang*), stripling, teenager, tot, youngster, youth 2. *verb* bamboozle, beguile, cozen, delude, fool, gull (*archaic*), hoax, hoodwink, jest, joke, mock, plague, pretend, rag (*Brit.*), ridicule, tease, trick, wind up (*Brit. slang*)

kidnap abduct, capture, hijack, hold to ransom, remove, seize, steal

kill 1. annihilate, assassinate, blow away (*slang, chiefly U.S.*), bump off (*slang*), butcher, destroy, dispatch, do away with, do in (*slang*), eradicate, execute, exterminate, extirpate, knock off (*slang*), liquidate, massacre, murder, neutralize, obliterate, slaughter, slay, take out (*slang*), take (someone's) life, waste (*informal*), wipe from the face of the earth (*informal*) 2. *figurative* cancel, cease, deaden, defeat, extinguish, halt, quash, quell, ruin, scotch, smother, stifle, still, stop, suppress, veto

Kill one man and you are a murderer. Kill millions and you are a conqueror. Kill all and you are a God

Jean Rostand

Thou shalt not kill; but needst not strive
Officiously, to keep alive

Arthur Hugh Clough *The Latest Decalogue*

killer assassin, butcher, cutthroat, destroyer, executioner, exterminator, gunman, hit man (*slang*), liquidator, murderer, slaughterer, slayer

killing *noun* 1. bloodshed, carnage, execution, extermination, fatality, homicide, manslaughter, massacre, murder, necktie party (*informal*), slaughter, slaying 2. *informal* bomb (*slang*), bonanza, cleanup (*informal*), coup, gain, profit, success, windfall *~adjective* 3. deadly, death-dealing, deathly, fatal, lethal, mortal, murderous 4. *informal* debilitating, enervating, exhausting, fatiguing, punishing, tiring 5. *informal* absurd, amusing, comical, hilarious, ludicrous, uproarious

kill-joy dampener, damper, spoilsport, wet blanket (*informal*)

kin *noun* 1. affinity, blood, connection, consanguinity, extraction, kinship, lineage, relationship, stock 2. connections, family, kindred, kinsfolk, kinsmen, kith, people, relations, relatives *~adjective* 3. akin, allied, close, cognate, consanguine, consanguineous, kindred, near, related

kind[1] *noun* 1. brand, breed, class, family, genus, ilk, race, set, sort, species, stamp, variety 2. character, description, essence, habit, manner, mould, nature, persuasion, sort, style, temperament, type

kind[2] *adjective* affectionate, amiable, amicable, beneficent, benevolent, benign, bounteous, charitable, clement, compassionate, congenial, considerate, cordial, courteous, friendly, generous, gentle, good, gracious, humane, indulgent, kind-hearted, kindly, lenient, loving, mild, neighbourly, obliging, philanthropic, propitious, sympathetic, tender-hearted, thoughtful, understanding

Antonyms cruel, hard-hearted, harsh, heartless, merciless, severe, unkind, unsympathetic, vicious

kind-hearted altruistic, amicable, compassionate, considerate, generous, good-natured, gracious, helpful, humane, kind, sympathetic, tender-hearted

Antonyms cold, cold-hearted, cruel, hard-hearted, harsh, heartless, selfish, severe, unkind, unsympathetic

kindle 1. fire, ignite, inflame, light, set fire to 2. *figurative* agitate, animate, arouse, awaken, bestir, enkindle, exasperate, excite, foment, incite, induce, inflame, inspire, provoke, rouse, sharpen, stimulate, stir, thrill
Antonyms douse, extinguish, quell, quench

kindliness amiability, beneficence, benevolence, benignity, charity, compassion, friendliness, gentleness, humanity, kind-heartedness, kindness, sympathy

kindly 1. *adjective* affable, beneficial, benevolent, benign, compassionate, cordial, favourable, genial, gentle, good-natured, hearty, helpful, kind, mild, pleasant, polite, sympathetic, warm 2. *adverb* agreeably, cordially, graciously, politely, tenderly, thoughtfully
Antonyms *adjective* cruel, harsh, malevolent, malicious, mean, severe, spiteful, unkindly, unsympathetic ~*adverb* cruelly, harshly, malevolently, maliciously, meanly, spitefully, unkindly, unsympathetically

kindness 1. affection, amiability, beneficence, benevolence, charity, clemency, compassion, decency, fellow-feeling, generosity, gentleness, goodness, goodwill, grace, hospitality, humanity, indulgence, kindliness, magnanimity, patience, philanthropy, tenderness, tolerance, understanding 2. aid, assistance, benefaction, bounty, favour, generosity, good deed, help, service
Antonyms (*sense 1*) animosity, callousness, cold-heartedness, cruelty, hard-heartedness, heartlessness, ill will, inhumanity, malevolence, malice, misanthropy, viciousness

Kindness acts
Not always as you think; a hated hand
Renders it odious
Corneille *Cinna*

You can accomplish by kindness what you cannot do by force
Publilius Syrus *Sententiae*

True kindness presupposes the faculty of imagining as one's own the suffering and joys of others
André Gide *Portraits and Aphorisms*

That best portion of a good man's life,
His little, nameless, unremembered acts
Of kindness and of love
William Wordsworth *Lines Composed a Few Miles Above Tintern Abbey*

the milk of human kindness
William Shakespeare *Macbeth*

kindred *noun* 1. affinity, consanguinity, relationship 2. connections, family, flesh, kin, kinsfolk, kinsmen, lineage, relations, relatives ~*adjective* 3. affiliated, akin, allied, cognate, congenial, corresponding, kin, like, matching, related, similar

king crowned head, emperor, majesty, monarch, overlord, prince, ruler, sovereign

I know I have the body of a weak and feeble woman, but I have the heart and stomach of a king, and of a king of England too
Queen Elizabeth I

kingdom 1. dominion, dynasty, empire, monarchy, realm, reign, sovereignty 2. commonwealth, county, division, nation, province, state, territory, tract 3. area, domain, field, province, sphere, territory

kingly 1. imperial, monarchical, regal, royal, sovereign 2. august, glorious, grand, grandiose, imposing, majestic, noble, splendid, stately

kink 1. bend, coil, corkscrew, crimp, entanglement, frizz, knot, tangle, twist, wrinkle 2. cramp, crick, pang, pinch, spasm, stab, tweak, twinge 3. complication, defect, difficulty, flaw, hitch, imperfection, knot, tangle 4. crotchet, eccentricity, fetish, foible, idiosyncrasy, quirk, singularity, vagary, whim

kinky 1. bizarre, eccentric, odd, oddball (*informal*), off-the-wall (*slang*), outlandish, outré, peculiar, queer, quirky, strange, unconventional, wacko (*slang*), weird 2. degenerated, depraved, deviant, licentious, perverted, pervy (*slang*), unnatural, warped 3. coiled, crimped, curled, curly, frizzled, frizzy, tangled, twisted

kinsfolk connections, family, kin, kindred, kinsmen, relations, relatives

kinship 1. blood relationship, consanguinity, kin, relation, ties of blood 2. affinity, alliance, association, bearing, connection, correspondence, relationship, similarity

kinsman blood relative, fellow clansman, fellow tribesman, relation, relative

kiosk bookstall, booth, counter, newsstand, stall, stand

kismet destiny, fate, fortune, karma, lot, portion, preordination, Providence

kiss *verb* 1. buss (*archaic*), canoodle (*slang*), greet, neck (*informal*), osculate, peck (*informal*), salute, smooch (*informal*) 2. brush, caress, glance, graze, scrape, touch ~*noun* 3. buss (*archaic*), osculation, peck (*informal*), smacker (*slang*)

You must not kiss and tell
William Congreve *Love for Love*

I wasn't kissing her, I was just whispering in her mouth
attributed to Groucho Marx

kit accoutrements, apparatus, effects, equipment, gear, impedimenta, implements, instruments, outfit, paraphernalia, provisions, rig, supplies, tackle, tools, trappings, utensils

kitchen cookhouse, galley, kitchenette

kit out *or* **up** accoutre, arm, deck out, equip, fit out, fix up, furnish, outfit, provide with, supply

kittenish coquettish, coy, flirtatious, frisky, frolicsome, funloving, ludic (*literary*), playful, sportive

knack ability, adroitness, aptitude, bent, ca~ pacity, dexterity, expertise, expertness, facil~ ity, flair, forte, genius, gift, handiness, in~ genuity, propensity, quickness, skilfulness, skill, talent, trick
Antonyms awkwardness, clumsiness, disabil~ ity, ineptitude

knackered all in (*slang*), beat (*slang*), bug~ gered (*Brit. slang*), dead beat (*slang*), dead tired, debilitated, dog-tired (*informal*), done in (*informal*), drained, enervated, exhausted, prostrated, ready to drop, tired out, worn out, zonked (*slang*)

knave blackguard, bounder (*old-fashioned Brit. slang*), cheat, cocksucker (*taboo slang*), rap~ scallion, rascal, reprobate, rogue, rotter (*slang, chiefly Brit.*), scally (*Northwest English dialect*), scallywag (*informal*), scamp, scape~ grace, scoundrel, scumbag (*slang*), swindler, varlet (*archaic*), villain

knavery chicanery, corruption, deceit, decep~ tion, dishonesty, double-dealing, duplicity, fraud, imposture, rascality, roguery, trickery, villainy

knavish deceitful, deceptive, dishonest, dishon~ ourable, fraudulent, lying, rascally, roguish, scoundrelly, tricky, unprincipled, unscrupu~ lous, villainous
Antonyms honest, honourable, noble, princi~ pled, trustworthy

knead blend, form, manipulate, massage, mould, press, rub, shape, squeeze, stroke, work

kneel bow, bow down, curtsey, curtsy, genu~ flect, get down on one's knees, kowtow, make obeisance, stoop

knell **1.** *verb* announce, chime, herald, peal, re~ sound, ring, sound, toll **2.** *noun* chime, peal, ringing, sound, toll

knickers bloomers, briefs, drawers, panties, smalls, underwear

knick-knack bagatelle, bauble, bibelot, bric-a-brac, gewgaw, gimcrack, kickshaw, plaything, trifle, trinket

knife **1.** *noun* blade, cutter, cutting tool **2.** *verb* cut, impale, lacerate, pierce, slash, stab, wound

knightly chivalrous, courageous, courtly, gal~ lant, gracious, heroic, noble, valiant

knit **1.** affix, ally, bind, connect, contract, fas~ ten, heal, interlace, intertwine, join, link, loop, mend, secure, tie, unite, weave **2.** crease, furrow, knot, pucker, wrinkle

knob boss, bulk, bump, bunch, hump, knot, knurl, lump, nub, projection, protrusion, pro~ tuberance, snag, stud, swell, swelling, tumour

knock *verb* **1.** belt (*informal*), buffet, chin (*slang*), clap, cuff, deck (*slang*), hit, lay one on (*slang*), punch, rap, slap, smack, smite (*ar~ chaic*), strike, thump, thwack *~noun* **2.** belt (*informal*), blow, box, clip, clout (*informal*), cuff, hammering, rap, slap, smack, thump *~verb* **3.** *informal* abuse, asperse, belittle, carp, cavil, censure, condemn, criticize, deni~ grate, deprecate, disparage, find fault, have a go (at) (*informal*), lambast(e), run down, slag (off) (*slang*), slam (*slang*) *~noun* **4.** blame, censure, condemnation, criticism, defeat, fail~ ure, heat (*slang, chiefly U.S. & Canad.*), re~ buff, rejection, reversal, setback, slagging (off) (*slang*), stick (*slang*), stricture

knock about *or* **around** **1.** ramble, range, roam, rove, traipse, travel, wander **2.** abuse, batter, beat up (*informal*), bruise, buffet, clobber (*slang*), damage, hit, hurt, lambast(e), maltreat, manhandle, maul, mistreat, strike, work over (*slang*), wound

knock down batter, clout (*informal*), deck (*slang*), demolish, destroy, fell, floor, level, pound, raze, smash, wallop (*informal*), wreck

knock off **1.** clock off, clock out, complete, con~ clude, finish, stop work, terminate **2.** blag (*slang*), cabbage (*Brit. slang*), filch, nick (*slang, chiefly Brit.*), pilfer, pinch, purloin, rob, steal, thieve **3.** assassinate, blow away (*slang, chiefly U.S.*), bump off (*slang*), do away with, do in (*slang*), kill, liquidate, mur~ der, slay, take out (*slang*), waste (*informal*)

knockout **1.** *coup de grâce*, kayo (*slang*), KO *or* K.O. (*slang*) **2.** hit, sensation, smash, smasheroo (*informal*), smash-hit, stunner (*in~ formal*), success, triumph, winner
Antonyms (*sense 2*) failure, flop (*informal*), turkey (*informal*)

knoll barrow, hill, hillock, hummock, mound, swell

knot *verb* **1.** bind, complicate, entangle, knit, loop, secure, tether, tie, weave *~noun* **2.** bond, bow, braid, connection, joint, ligature, loop, rosette, tie **3.** aggregation, bunch, clump, clus~ ter, collection, heap, mass, pile, tuft **4.** assem~ blage, band, circle, clique, company, crew (*in~ formal*), crowd, gang, group, mob, pack, set, squad

knotty **1.** bumpy, gnarled, knobby, knotted, nodular, rough, rugged **2.** baffling, complex, complicated, difficult, hard, intricate, mystify~ ing, perplexing, problematical, puzzling, thorny, tricky, troublesome

know **1.** apprehend, comprehend, experience, fathom, feel certain, ken (*Scot.*), learn, notice, perceive, realize, recognize, see, undergo,

understand **2.** associate with, be acquainted with, be familiar with, fraternize with, have dealings with, have knowledge of, recognize **3.** differentiate, discern, distinguish, identify, make out, perceive, recognize, see, tell
Antonyms be ignorant, be unfamiliar with, misunderstand

To really know someone is to have loved and hated him in turn
Marcel Jouhandeau

What you don't know can't hurt you

Know thyself

know-all clever-clogs (*informal*), clever Dick (*informal*), smart aleck (*informal*), smartarse (*slang*), smarty (*informal*), smarty-boots (*informal*), smarty-pants (*informal*), wiseacre, wise guy (*informal*)

know-how ability, adroitness, aptitude, capability, craft, dexterity, experience, expertise, faculty, flair, ingenuity, knack, knowledge, proficiency, savoir-faire, skill, talent

knowing 1. astute, clever, clued-up (*informal*), competent, discerning, experienced, expert, intelligent, qualified, skilful, well-informed **2.** acute, cunning, eloquent, expressive, meaningful, perceptive, sagacious, shrewd, significant **3.** aware, conscious, deliberate, intended, intentional
Antonyms accidental, ignorant, ingenuous, naive, obtuse, unintentional, wet behind the ears (*informal*)

knowingly consciously, deliberately, intentionally, on purpose, purposely, wilfully, wittingly

knowledge 1. education, enlightenment, erudition, instruction, intelligence, learning, scholarship, schooling, science, tuition, wisdom **2.** ability, apprehension, cognition, comprehension, consciousness, discernment, grasp, judgment, recognition, understanding **3.** acquaintance, cognizance, familiarity, information, intimacy, notice
Antonyms ignorance, illiteracy, misunderstanding, unawareness, unfamiliarity

Knowledge is power
Francis Bacon *Meditationes Sacrae*

Knowledge is power. Unfortunate dupes of this saying will keep on reading, ambitiously, till they have stunned their native initiative, and made their thoughts weak
Clarence Day *This Simian World*

That knowledge which stops at what it does not know, is the highest knowledge
Chang Tzu *The Music of Heaven and Earth*

No man's knowledge here can go beyond his experience
John Locke *Essay concerning Human Understanding*

Nothing that is worth knowing can be taught
Oscar Wilde *The Critic as Artist*

Knowledge is power, if you know it about the right person
Ethel Watts Mumford

All I know is that I know nothing
ascribed to Socrates

Knowledge is not knowledge until someone else knows that one knows
Lucilius *fragment*

He that increaseth knowledge increaseth sorrow
Bible: Ecclesiastes

Knowledge is of two kinds. We know a subject ourselves, or we know where we can find information upon it
Dr. Johnson

Knowledge puffeth up, but charity edifieth
Bible: I Corinthians

It is the province of knowledge to speak and it is the privilege of wisdom to listen
Oliver Wendell Holmes *The Poet at the Breakfast-Table*

If a little knowledge is dangerous, where is the man who has so much as to be out of danger?
T.H. Huxley *Collected Essays*

Owl hasn't exactly got Brain, but he Knows Things
A.A. Milne *Winnie-the-Pooh*

A little knowledge is a dangerous thing

An old poacher makes the best gamekeeper

knowledgeable 1. acquainted, *au courant*, *au fait*, aware, clued-up (*informal*), cognizant, conscious, conversant, experienced, familiar, in the know (*informal*), understanding, well-informed **2.** educated, erudite, intelligent, learned, lettered, scholarly

known acknowledged, admitted, avowed, celebrated, common, confessed, familiar, famous, manifest, noted, obvious, patent, plain, popular, published, recognized, well-known
Antonyms closet (*informal*), concealed, hidden, secret, unfamiliar, unknown, unrecognized, unrevealed

knuckle under *verb* accede, acquiesce, capitulate, give in, give way, submit, succumb, surrender, yield
Antonyms be defiant, dig one's heels in (*informal*), hold out (against), kick up (a fuss *or* stink), rebel, resist

knurl bulb, bulge, burl, gnarl, knot, lump, node, protuberance, ridge

kowtow 1. bow, genuflect, kneel **2.** brown-nose (*taboo slang*), court, cringe, fawn, flatter, grovel, kiss (someone's) ass (*U.S. & Canad. taboo slang*), lick someone's arse (*taboo slang*), lick someone's boots, pander to, suck up to (*slang*), toady, truckle

kudos acclaim, applause, distinction, esteem, fame, glory, honour, laudation, notability, plaudits, praise, prestige, regard, renown, repute

L

label *noun* **1.** docket (*chiefly Brit.*), flag, marker, sticker, tag, tally, ticket **2.** characterization, classification, description, epithet **3.** brand, company, mark, trademark *~verb* **4.** docket (*chiefly Brit.*), flag, mark, stamp, sticker, tag, tally **5.** brand, call, characterize, class, classify, define, describe, designate, identify, name

laborious **1.** arduous, backbreaking, burdensome, difficult, exhausting, fatiguing, hard, herculean, onerous, strenuous, tiresome, tiring, toilsome, tough, uphill, wearing, wearisome **2.** assiduous, diligent, hard-working, indefatigable, industrious, painstaking, persevering, sedulous, tireless, unflagging **3.** *of literary style, etc.* forced, laboured, not fluent, ponderous, strained
Antonyms easy, easy-peasy (*slang*), effortless, light, natural, simple

labour *noun* **1.** industry, toil, work **2.** employees, hands, labourers, workers, workforce, workmen **3.** donkey-work, drudgery, effort, exertion, grind (*informal*), industry, pains, painstaking, sweat (*informal*), toil, travail **4.** chore, job, task, undertaking **5.** childbirth, contractions, delivery, labour pains, pains, parturition, throes, travail *~verb* **6.** drudge, endeavour, grind (*informal*), peg along *or* away (*chiefly Brit.*), plod, plug along *or* away (*informal*), slave, strive, struggle, sweat (*informal*), toil, travail, work **7.** *usually with* **under** be a victim of, be burdened by, be disadvantaged, suffer **8.** dwell on, elaborate, make a federal case of (*U.S. informal*), make a production (out) of (*informal*), overdo, overemphasize, strain **9.** *of a ship* heave, pitch, roll, toss
Antonyms *noun* ease, idleness, leisure, relaxation, repose, respite, rest *~verb* relax, rest

laboured **1.** awkward, difficult, forced, heavy, stiff, strained **2.** affected, contrived, overdone, overwrought, ponderous, studied, unnatural

labourer blue-collar worker, drudge, hand, labouring man, manual worker, navvy (*Brit. informal*), unskilled worker, worker, working man, workman

The labourer is worthy of his hire

labyrinth coil, complexity, complication, convolution, entanglement, intricacy, jungle, knotty problem, maze, perplexity, puzzle, riddle, snarl, tangle, windings

labyrinthine Byzantine, complex, confused, convoluted, Daedalian, Gordian, intricate, involved, knotty, mazelike, mazy, perplexing, puzzling, tangled, tortuous, winding

lace *noun* **1.** filigree, netting, openwork, tatting **2.** bootlace, cord, shoelace, string, thong, tie *~verb* **3.** attach, bind, close, do up, fasten, intertwine, interweave, thread, tie, twine **4.** add to, fortify, mix in, spike

Lacedaemonian Spartan

lace into assail, attack, belabour, berate, castigate, flay, lay into (*informal*), light into (*informal*), set about, vituperate

lacerate **1.** claw, cut, gash, jag, maim, mangle, rend, rip, slash, tear, wound **2.** *figurative* afflict, distress, harrow, rend, torment, torture, wound

laceration cut, gash, injury, mutilation, rent, rip, slash, tear, trauma (*Pathology*), wound

lachrymose crying, dolorous, lugubrious, mournful, sad, tearful, weeping, weepy (*informal*), woeful

lack **1.** *noun* absence, dearth, deficiency, deprivation, destitution, insufficiency, need, privation, scantiness, scarcity, shortage, shortcoming, shortness, want **2.** *verb* be deficient in, be short of, be without, miss, need, require, want
Antonyms *noun* abundance, adequacy, excess, plentifulness, sufficiency, surplus *~verb* enjoy, have, own, possess

lackadaisical **1.** apathetic, dull, enervated, half-arsed (*Brit. slang*), half-assed (*U.S. & Canad. slang*), half-hearted, indifferent, languid, languorous, lethargic, limp, listless, spiritless **2.** abstracted, dreamy, idle, indolent, inert, lazy
Antonyms ambitious, diligent, excited, inspired, spirited

lackey **1.** ass-kisser (*U.S. & Canad. taboo slang*), brown-noser (*taboo slang*), creature, fawner, flatterer, flunky, hanger-on, instrument, menial, minion, parasite, pawn, sycophant, toady, tool, yes man **2.** attendant, cohort (*chiefly U.S.*), flunky, footman, manservant, valet, varlet (*archaic*)

lacking defective, deficient, flawed, impaired, inadequate, minus (*informal*), missing, needing, sans (*archaic*), wanting, without

lacklustre boring, dim, drab, dry, dull, flat, leaden, lifeless, lustreless, muted, prosaic, sombre, unimaginative, uninspired, vapid

laconic brief, clipped, compact, concise, crisp, curt, monosyllabic, pithy, sententious, short, succinct, terse, to the point
Antonyms long-winded, loquacious, rambling, verbose, voluble, wordy

lacuna blank, break, gap, hiatus, omission, space, void

lacy delicate, filigree, fine, frilly, gauzy, gossamer, lacelike, meshy, netlike, open, sheer

lad boy, chap (*informal*), fellow, guy (*informal*), juvenile, kid (*informal*), laddie (*Scot.*), schoolboy, shaver (*informal*), stripling, youngster, youth

laden burdened, charged, encumbered, fraught, full, hampered, loaded, oppressed, taxed, weighed down, weighted

la-di-da affected, conceited, highfalutin (*informal*), mannered, mincing, overrefined, posh (*informal, chiefly Brit.*), precious, pretentious, snobbish, snooty (*informal*), stuck-up (*informal*), toffee-nosed (*slang, chiefly Brit.*), too-too

lady **1.** dame, gentlewoman **2.** female, woman

lady-killer Casanova, Don Juan, heartbreaker, ladies' man, libertine, Lothario, philanderer, rake, roué, wolf (*informal*), womanizer

ladylike courtly, cultured, decorous, elegant, genteel, modest, polite, proper, refined, respectable, sophisticated, well-bred
Antonyms discourteous, ill-bred, ill-mannered, impolite, rude, uncultured, unladylike, unmannerly, unrefined

lag **1.** be behind, dawdle, delay, drag (behind), drag one's feet (*informal*), hang back, idle, linger, loiter, saunter, straggle, tarry, trail **2.** decrease, diminish, ebb, fail, fall off, flag, lose strength, slacken, wane

laggard dawdler, idler, lingerer, loafer, loiterer, lounger, saunterer, skiver (*Brit. slang*), slowcoach (*Brit. informal*), slowpoke (*U.S. & Canad. informal*), sluggard, snail, straggler

laid-back at ease, casual, easy-going, easy-oasy (*slang*), free and easy, relaxed, together (*slang*), unflappable (*informal*), unhurried
Antonyms edgy, jittery (*informal*), jumpy, keyed-up, nervous, on edge, tense, twitchy (*informal*), uptight (*informal*), wound-up (*informal*)

laid up bedridden, disabled, housebound, ill, immobilized, incapacitated, injured, on the sick list, out of action (*informal*), sick

lair **1.** burrow, den, earth, form, hole, nest, resting place **2.** *informal* den, hide-out, refuge, retreat, sanctuary

laissez faire *or* **laisser faire** *noun* free enterprise, free trade, individualism, live and let live, nonintervention

lake lagoon, loch (*Scot.*), lough (*Irish*), mere, reservoir, tarn
Related adjective: lacustrine

Lakes, lochs, and loughs

Allen
Annecy
Aral Sea *or* Lake Aral
Ard
Athabaska
Averno
Awe
Baikal
Bala
Balaton
Balkhash
Bangweulu
Bassenthwaite
Belfast
Biel
Bodensee
Buttermere
Caspian Sea
Chad
Champlain
Como
Coniston Water
Constance
Crummock Water
Dead Sea
Derwentwater
Dongting
Earn
Edward
Ennerdale Water
Erie
Erne
Eyre
Frome
Fyne
Garda
Gatún
Geneva
Grasmere
Great Bear
Great Bitter
Great Lakes
Great Salt
Great Slave
Hawes Water
Huron
Ijsselmeer *or* Ysselmeer
Iliamna
Ilmen
Issyk-Kul
Kariba
Katrine
Kivu
Koko Nor *or* Kuku Nor
Kootenay
Ladoga
Laggan
Lake of the Woods
Leven
Linnhe
Little Bitter
Lochy
Lomond
Lucerne
Lugano
Léman
Maggiore
Malawi
Managua
Manitoba
Maracaibo
Mead
Meech
Memphremagog
Menteith
Michigan
Miraflores
Mistassini
Mobutu
Morar
Mweru
Nam Co *or* Nam Tso
Nasser
Neagh
Ness
Neuchâtel
Nicaragua
Nipigon
Nipissing
No
Nyasa
Okanagan
Okeechobee
Onega
Oneida
Onondaga
Ontario
Patos
Peipus
Pontchartrain
Poopó
Poyang *pr* P'o-yang
Pskov
Rannoch

Reindeer
Rudolf
Saint Clair
Saint John
Sea of Galilee
Sevan
Stanley Pool
Superior
Sween
Taal
Tahoe
Tana
Tanganyika
Taupo
Tay
Thirlmere
Thun
Tien
Titicaca
Tonle Sap
Torrens
Torridon
Trasimene
Tummel
Turkana
Ullswater
Urmia
Van
Victoria
Volta
Waikaremoana
Washington
Wast Water
Windermere
Winnebago
Winnipeg
Zug
Zürich

lam batter, beat, hit, knock, lambast(e), pelt, pound, strike, thrash

lambast(e) **1.** beat, bludgeon, cosh (*Brit.*), cudgel, drub, flog, strike, thrash, whip **2.** bawl out (*informal*), berate, carpet (*informal*), castigate, censure, chew out (*U.S. & Canad. informal*), excoriate, flay, give a rocket (*Brit. & N.Z. informal*), rap over the knuckles, read the riot act, rebuke, reprimand, scold, slap on the wrist, tear into (*informal*), tear (someone) off a strip (*Brit. informal*), upbraid

lambent **1.** dancing, flickering, fluttering, licking, touching, twinkling **2.** gleaming, glistening, glowing, luminous, lustrous, radiant, refulgent, shimmering **3.** *of wit or humour* brilliant, light, sparkling

lamblike **1.** gentle, meek, mild, passive, peaceable, submissive **2.** artless, childlike, guileless, innocent, naive, simple, trusting

lame **1.** crippled, defective, disabled, game, halt (*archaic*), handicapped, hobbling, limping **2.** *figurative* feeble, flimsy, inadequate, insufficient, pathetic, poor, thin, unconvincing, unsatisfactory, weak

lament *verb* **1.** bemoan, bewail, complain, deplore, grieve, mourn, regret, sorrow, wail, weep *~noun* **2.** complaint, keening, lamentation, moan, moaning, plaint, ululation, wail, wailing **3.** coronach (*Scot. & Irish*), dirge, elegy, monody, requiem, threnody

lamentable **1.** deplorable, distressing, grievous, harrowing, mournful, regrettable, sorrowful, tragic, unfortunate, woeful **2.** low, meagre, mean, miserable, not much cop (*Brit. slang*), pitiful, poor, unsatisfactory, wretched

lamentation dirge, grief, grieving, keening, lament, moan, mourning, plaint, sobbing, sorrow, ululation, wailing, weeping

laminate **1.** coat, cover, face, foliate, layer, stratify, veneer **2.** exfoliate, flake, separate, split

lamp

> *The lamps are going out all over Europe; we shall not see them lit again in our lifetime*
>
> Lord Grey *25 Years*

lampoon **1.** *noun* burlesque, caricature, parody, pasquinade, satire, send-up (*Brit. informal*), skit, squib, takeoff (*informal*) **2.** *verb* burlesque, caricature, make fun of, mock, parody, pasquinade, ridicule, satirize, send up (*Brit. informal*), squib, take off (*informal*)

land *noun* **1.** dry land, earth, ground, terra firma **2.** dirt, ground, loam, soil **3.** countryside, farming, farmland, rural districts **4.** acres, estate, grounds, property, real property, realty **5.** country, district, fatherland, motherland, nation, province, region, territory, tract *~verb* **6.** alight, arrive, berth, come to rest, debark, disembark, dock, touch down **7.** *sometimes with* **up** arrive, bring, carry, cause, end up, lead, turn up, wind up **8.** *informal* acquire, gain, get, obtain, score (*slang*), secure, win
Related adjective: terrestrial

landing **1.** arrival, coming in, disembarkation, disembarkment, touchdown **2.** jetty, landing stage, platform, quayside

landlord **1.** host, hotelier, hotel-keeper, innkeeper **2.** freeholder, lessor, owner, proprietor

landmark **1.** feature, monument **2.** crisis, milestone, turning point, watershed **3.** benchmark, boundary, cairn, milepost, signpost

landscape countryside, outlook, panorama, prospect, scene, scenery, view, vista

landslide **1.** *noun* avalanche, landslip, rockfall **2.** *adjective* decisive, overwhelming, runaway

lane aisle, alley, corridor, footpath, passageway, path, pathway, road, street, strip, way

language **1.** communication, conversation, discourse, expression, interchange, parlance, speech, talk, utterance, verbalization, vocalization **2.** argot, cant, dialect, idiom, jargon, lingo (*informal*), lingua franca, patois, patter, speech, terminology, tongue, vernacular, vocabulary **3.** diction, expression, phraseology, phrasing, style, wording

European Languages

Albanian
Alemannic
Basque
Bohemian
Bokmål
Breton
Bulgarian
Byelorussian
Castilian
Catalan
Cheremiss *or* Cheremis
Cornish
Croatian
Cymric *or* Kymric
Czech
Danish
Dutch
English
Erse
Estonian
Faeroese
Finnish
Flemish

French
Frisian
Friulian
Gaelic
Gagauzi
Galician
Georgian
German
Greek
Hungarian
Icelandic
Italian
Karelian
Komi
Ladin
Ladino
Lallans *or* Lallan
Lapp
Latvian *or* Lettish
Lithuanian
Lusatian
Macedonian
Magyar
Maltese
Manx
Mingrelian *or* Mingrel
Mordvin
Norwegian
Nynorsk *or* Landsmål
Polish
Portuguese
Provençal
Romanian
Romansch *or* Ro~mansh
Romany *or* Romanes
Russian
Samoyed
Sardinian
Serbo-Croat *or* Serbo-Croatian
Shelta
Slovak
Slovene
Sorbian
Spanish
Swedish
Turkish
Udmurt
Ukrainian
Vogul
Votyak
Welsh
Yiddish
Zyrian

African Languages

Adamawa
Afrikaans
Akan
Amharic
Bambara
Barotse
Bashkir
Bemba
Berber
Chewa
Chichewa
Coptic
Damara
Duala
Dyula
Edo, Bini *or* Beni
Ewe
Fanagalo *or* Fanakalo
Fang
Fanti
Fula, Fulah *or* Fulani
Ga *or* Gã
Galla
Ganda
Griqua *or* Grikwa
Hausa
Herero
Hottentot
Hutu
Ibibio *or* Efik
Ibo *or* Igbo
Kabyle
Kikuyu
Kingwana
Kirundi
Kongo
Krio
Lozi
Luba *or* Tshiluba
Luganda
Luo
Malagasy
Malinke *or* Maninke
Masai
Matabele
Mossi *or* Moore
Nama *or* Namaqua
Ndebele
Nuba
Nupe
Nyanja
Nyoro
Ovambo
Pedi *or* Northern So~tho
Pondo
Rwanda
Sango
Sesotho
Shona
Somali
Songhai
Sotho
Susu
Swahili
Swazi
Temne
Tigré
Tigrinya
Tiv
Tonga
Tsonga
Tswana
Tuareg
Twi *or (formerly)* Ashanti
Venda
Wolof
Xhosa
Yoruba
Zulu

Asian Languages

Abkhaz, Abkhazi *or* Abkhazian
Adygei *or* Adyghe
Afghan
Ainu
Arabic
Aramaic
Armenian
Assamese
Azerbaijani
Bahasa Indonesia
Balinese
Baluchi *or* Balochi
Bengali
Bihari
Brahui
Burmese
Buryat *or* Buriat
Cantonese
Chukchee *or* Chukchi
Chuvash
Chinese
Cham
Circassian
Dinka
Divehi
Dzongka
Evenki
Farsi
Filipino
Gondi
Gujarati *or* Gujerati
Gurkhali
Hebrew
Hindi
Hindustani, Hindoo~stani *or* Hindostani
Iranian
Japanese
Javanese
Kabardian
Kafiri
Kalmuck *or* Kalmyk
Kannada, Kanarese *or* Canarese
Kara-Kalpak
Karen
Kashmiri
Kazakh *or* Kazak
Kazan Tatar
Khalkha
Khmer
Kirghiz
Korean
Kurdish
Lahnda
Lao
Lepcha
Malay
Malayalam *or* Mala~yalaam
Manchu
Mandarin
Marathi *or* Mahratti
Mishmi
Mon
Mongol
Mongolian
Moro
Naga
Nepali
Nuri
Oriya
Ossetian *or* Ossetic
Ostyak
Pashto, Pushto *or* Pushtu
Punjabi
Shan
Sindhi
Sinhalese
Sogdian
Tadzhiki *or* Tadzhik
Tagalog
Tamil
Tatar
Telugu *or* Telegu
Thai
Tibetan
Tungus
Turkmen
Turkoman *or* Turk~man
Uigur *or* Uighur
Urdu
Uzbek
Vietnamese
Yakut

South American Languages

Araucanian
Aymara
Chibchan
Galibi
Guarani
Nahuatl
Quechua, Kechua *or* Quichua
Tupi
Zapotec

North American Languages

Abnaki
Aleut *or* Aleutian
Algonquin *or* Algonkin
Apache
Arapaho
Assiniboine
Blackfoot
Caddoan
Catawba
Cayuga
Cherokee
Cheyenne
Chickasaw
Chinook
Choctaw
Comanche
Creek
Crow
Delaware
Erie
Eskimo
Fox
Haida
Hopi
Huron
Inuktitut
Iroquois
Kwakiutl
Mahican *or* Mohican
Massachuset *or* Massachusetts
Menomini
Micmac
Mixtec
Mohave *or* Mojave
Mohawk
Narraganset *or* Narragansett
Navaho *or* Navajo
Nez Percé
Nootka
Ojibwa
Okanagan, Okanogan *or* Okinagan
Oneida
Onondaga
Osage
Paiute *or* Piute
Pawnee
Pequot
Sahaptin, Sahaptan *or* Sahaptian
Seminole
Seneca
Shawnee
Shoshone *or* Shoshoni
Sioux
Tahltan
Taino
Tlingit
Tuscarora
Ute
Winnebago
Zuñi

Australasian Languages

Aranda
Beach-la-Mar
Dinka
Fijian
Gurindji
Hawaiian
Hiri Motu
kamilaroi
Krio
Maori
Moriori
Motu
Nauruan
Neo-Melanesian
Papuan
Pintubi
Police Motu
Samoan
Solomon Islands Pidgin
Tongan
Tuvaluan
Warlpiri

Ancient Languages

Akkadian
Ancient Greek
Anglo-Saxon
Assyrian
Avar
Avestan *or* Avestic
Aztec
Babylonian
Canaanite
Celtiberian
Chaldee
Edomite
Egyptian
Elamite
Ethiopic
Etruscan
Faliscan
Frankish
Gallo-Romance *or* Gallo-Roman
Ge'ez
Gothic
Hebrew
Himyaritic
Hittite
Illyrian
Inca
Ionic
Koine
Langobardic
langue d'oc
langue d'oïl
Latin
Libyan
Lycian
Lydian
Maya *or* Mayan
Messapian *or* Messapìc
Norn
Old Church Slavonic
Old High German
Old Norse
Old Prussian
Oscan
Osco-Umbrian
Pahlavi *or* Pehlevi
Pali
Phoenician
Phrygian
Pictish
Punic
Sabaean *or* Sabean
Sabellian
Sanskrit
Scythian
Sumerian
Syriac
Thracian
Thraco-Phrygian
Tocharian *or* Tokharian
Ugaritic
Umbrian
Vedic
Venetic
Volscian
Wendish

Artificial Languages

Esperanto
Ido
interlingua
Volapuk *or* Volapük

Language Groups

Afro-Asiatic
Albanian
Algonquian *or* Algonkian
Altaic
Anatolian
Athapascan, Athapaskan, Athabascan *or* Athabaskan
Arawakan
Armenian
Australian
Austro-Asiatic
Austronesian
Baltic
Bantu
Benue-Congo
Brythonic
Caddoan
Canaanitic
Carib
Caucasian
Celtic
Chadic
Chari-Nile
Cushitic
Cymric
Dardic
Dravidian
East Germanic
East Iranian
Eskimo
Finnic
Germanic
Gur
Hamitic
Hamito-Semitic
Hellenic
Hindustani
Indic
Indo-Aryan
Indo-European
Indo-Iranian
Indo-Pacific
Iranian
Iroquoian
Italic
Khoisan
Kordofanian
Kwa
Malayo-Polynesian
Mande
Mayan
Melanesian
Micronesian
Mongolic

Mon-Khmer
Munda
Muskogean *or* Muskhogean
Na-Dene *or* Na-Déné
Nguni
Niger-Congo
Nilo-Saharan
Nilotic
Norse
North Germanic
Oceanic
Pahari
Pama-Nyungan
Penutian
Polynesian
Rhaetian
Romance
Saharan
Salish *or* Salishan
San
Sanskritic
Semi-Bantu
Semitic
Semito-Hamitic
Shoshonean
Siouan
Sinitic
Sino-Tibetan
Slavonic
Sudanic
Tibeto-Burman
Trans-New Guinea phylum
Tungusic
Tupi-Guarani
Turkic
Ugric
Uralic
Uto-Aztecan
Voltaic
Wakashan
West Atlantic
West Germanic
West Iranian
West Slavonic
Yuman

Language is the dress of thought
Dr. Johnson *Lives of the English Poets: Cowley*

Languages are the pedigrees of nations
Dr. Johnson

We've come intil a gey queer time
Whan scrievin Scots is near a crime
"There's no-one speaks like that", they fleer
But wha the deil spoke like King Lear?
Sydney Goodsir Smith *Epistle to John Guthrie*

A language is a dialect with an army and a navy
Max Weinrich

To God I speak Spanish, to women Italian, to men French, and to my horse - German
attributed to Emperor Charles V

In language, the ignorant have prescribed laws to the learned
Richard Duppa *Maxims*

Language is fossil poetry
Ralph Waldo Emerson *Essays: Nominalist and Realist*

Political language... is designed to make lies sound truthful and murder respectable, and to give an appearance of solidity to pure wind
George Orwell *Shooting an Elephant*

languid 1. drooping, faint, feeble, languorous, limp, pining, sickly, weak, weary **2.** indifferent, lackadaisical, languorous, lazy, listless, spiritless, unenthusiastic, uninterested **3.** dull, heavy, inactive, inert, lethargic, sluggish, torpid
Antonyms active, alive and kicking, energetic, strong, tireless, vigorous

languish 1. decline, droop, fade, fail, faint, flag, sicken, waste, weaken, wilt, wither **2.** *often with* **for** desire, eat one's heart out over, hanker, hunger, long, pine, sigh, suspire, want, yearn **3.** be abandoned, be disregarded, be neglected, rot, suffer, waste away **4.** brood, despond, grieve, repine, sorrow
Antonyms bloom, flourish, prosper, thrive

languishing 1. declining, deteriorating, drooping, droopy, fading, failing, flagging, sickening, sinking, wasting away, weak, weakening, wilting, withering **2.** dreamy, longing, lovelorn, lovesick, melancholic, nostalgic, pensive, pining, soulful, tender, wistful, woebegone, yearning

languor 1. apathy, debility, enervation, ennui, faintness, fatigue, feebleness, frailty, heaviness, inertia, lassitude, lethargy, listlessness, torpor, weakness, weariness **2.** dreaminess, drowsiness, indolence, laziness, lotus-eating, relaxation, sleepiness, sloth **3.** calm, hush, lull, oppressiveness, silence, stillness

lank 1. dull, lifeless, limp, long, lustreless, straggling **2.** attenuated, emaciated, gaunt, lanky, lean, rawboned, scraggy, scrawny, skinny, slender, slim, spare, thin

lanky angular, bony, gangling, gaunt, loose-jointed, rangy, rawboned, scraggy, scrawny, spare, tall, thin, weedy (*informal*)
Antonyms brawny, burly, chubby, fat, muscular, plump, portly, rotund, rounded, short, sinewy, stocky, stout

lap[1] 1. *noun* circle, circuit, course, distance, loop, orbit, round, tour **2.** *verb* cover, enfold, envelop, fold, swaddle, swathe, turn, twist, wrap

lap[2] *verb* **1.** gurgle, plash, purl, ripple, slap, splash, swish, wash **2.** drink, lick, sip, sup

lapse *noun* **1.** error, failing, fault, indiscretion, mistake, negligence, omission, oversight, slip **2.** break, breathing space, gap, intermission, interruption, interval, lull, passage, pause **3.** backsliding, decline, descent, deterioration, drop, fall, relapse *~verb* **4.** decline, degenerate, deteriorate, drop, fail, fall, sink, slide, slip **5.** become obsolete, become void, end, expire, run out, stop, terminate

lapsed 1. discontinued, ended, expired, finished, invalid, out of date, run out, unrenewed **2.** backsliding, lacking faith, nonpractising

larceny burglary, misappropriation, pilfering, purloining, robbery, stealing, theft

large 1. big, bulky, colossal, considerable, elephantine, enormous, giant, gigantic, ginormous (*informal*), goodly, great, huge, humongous *or* humungous (*U.S. slang*), immense, jumbo (*informal*), king-size, man-size, massive, mega (*slang*), monumental, sizable *or* sizeable, stellar (*informal*), substantial, tidy (*informal*), vast **2.** abundant, ample, broad, capacious, comprehensive, copious, extensive,

full, generous, grand, grandiose, liberal, plentiful, roomy, spacious, sweeping, wide **3. at large a.** at liberty, free, on the loose, on the run, roaming, unconfined **b.** as a whole, chiefly, generally, in general, in the main, mainly **c.** at length, considerably, exhaustively, greatly, in full detail
Antonyms brief, inconsiderable, infinitesimal, little, minute, narrow, petty, scanty, scarce, short, slender, slight, slim, small, sparse, thin, tiny, trivial

large-hearted big-hearted, compassionate, good, good-hearted, kind, kind-hearted, large-souled, magnanimous, sympathetic, understanding

largely as a rule, by and large, chiefly, considerably, extensively, generally, mainly, mostly, predominantly, primarily, principally, to a great extent, widely

large-scale broad, extensive, far-reaching, global, sweeping, vast, wholesale, wide, wide-ranging

largess, largesse 1. alms-giving, benefaction, bounty, charity, generosity, liberality, munificence, open-handedness, philanthropy **2.** bequest, bounty, donation, endowment, gift, grant, present

lark 1. *noun* antic, caper, escapade, fling, frolic, fun, gambol, game, jape, mischief, prank, revel, rollick, romp, skylark, spree **2.** *verb* caper, cavort, cut capers, frolic, gambol, have fun, make mischief, play, rollick, romp, sport

lascivious 1. horny (*slang*), lecherous, lewd, libidinous, licentious, lustful, prurient, randy (*informal, chiefly Brit.*), salacious, sensual, unchaste, voluptuous, wanton **2.** bawdy, blue, coarse, crude, dirty, indecent, obscene, offensive, pornographic, ribald, scurrilous, smutty, suggestive, vulgar, X-rated (*informal*)

lash[1] *noun* **1.** blow, hit, stripe, stroke, swipe (*informal*) *~verb* **2.** beat, birch, chastise, flagellate, flog, horsewhip, lam (*slang*), lambast(e), scourge, thrash, whip **3.** beat, buffet, dash, drum, hammer, hit, knock, lambast(e), larrup (*dialect*), pound, punch, smack, strike **4.** attack, belabour, berate, blast, castigate, censure, criticize, flay, lambast(e), lampoon, put down, ridicule, satirize, scold, slate (*informal, chiefly Brit.*), tear into (*informal*), upbraid

lash[2] *verb* bind, fasten, join, make fast, rope, secure, strap, tie

lass bird (*slang*), chick (*slang*), colleen (*Irish*), damsel, girl, lassie (*informal*), maid, maiden, miss, schoolgirl, wench (*facetious*), young woman

lassitude apathy, drowsiness, dullness, enervation, ennui, exhaustion, fatigue, heaviness, inertia, languor, lethargy, listlessness, prostration, sluggardliness, sluggishness, tiredness, torpor, weariness

last[1] *adjective* **1.** aftermost, at the end, hindmost, rearmost **2.** latest, most recent **3.** closing, concluding, extreme, final, furthest, remotest, terminal, ultimate, utmost *~adverb* **4.** after, behind, bringing up the rear, in *or* at the end, in the rear *~noun* **5.** close, completion, conclusion, end, ending, finale, finish, termination **6. at last** at length, at the end of the day, eventually, finally, in conclusion, in the end, in the fullness of time, ultimately
Antonyms (*sense 1*) first, foremost, leading (*sense 3*) earliest, first, initial, introductory, opening

Many that are first shall be last; and the last shall be first

Bible: St. Mark

last[2] *verb* abide, carry on, continue, endure, hold on, hold out, keep, keep on, persist, remain, stand up, survive, wear
Antonyms cease, depart, die, end, expire, fade, fail, stop, terminate

last-ditch all-out (*informal*), desperate, final, frantic, heroic, straining, struggling

lasting abiding, continuing, deep-rooted, durable, enduring, eternal, indelible, lifelong, long-standing, long-term, perennial, permanent, perpetual, unceasing, undying, unending
Antonyms ephemeral, fleeting, momentary, passing, short-lived, transient, transitory

lastly after all, all in all, at last, finally, in conclusion, in the end, to conclude, to sum up, ultimately

last-minute deathbed, eleventh hour, last-ditch, last-gasp, late

last word, the 1. final say, finis, mother (of all), summation, ultimatum **2.** best, cream, *crème de la crème*, crown, epitome, *ne plus ultra*, perfection, quintessence, ultimate **3.** *dernier cri*, fashion, latest, newest, rage, vogue

latch 1. *noun* bar, bolt, catch, clamp, fastening, hasp, hook, lock, sneck (*dialect*) **2.** *verb* bar, bolt, fasten, lock, make fast, secure, sneck (*dialect*)

late *adjective* **1.** behind, behindhand, belated, delayed, last-minute, overdue, slow, tardy, unpunctual **2.** advanced, fresh, modern, new, recent **3.** dead, deceased, defunct, departed, ex-, former, old, past, preceding, previous *~adverb* **4.** at the last minute, behindhand, behind time, belatedly, dilatorily, slowly, tardily, unpunctually
Antonyms *adjective* (*sense 1*) beforehand, early, prompt, punctual, seasoned, timely (*sense 2*) old (*sense 3*) alive, existing *~adverb* beforehand, early, in advance

Better late than never

It is never too late

lately in recent times, just now, latterly, not long ago, of late, recently

lateness advanced hour, belatedness, delay, late date, retardation, tardiness, unpunctuality

latent concealed, dormant, hidden, immanent, inherent, invisible, lurking, potential, quiescent, secret, undeveloped, unexpressed, unrealized, unseen, veiled
Antonyms apparent, conspicuous, developed, evident, expressed, manifest, obvious, realized

later *adverb* after, afterwards, by and by, in a while, in time, later on, next, subsequently, thereafter

lateral edgeways, flanking, side, sideward, sideways

latest *adjective* current, fashionable, happening (*informal*), in, modern, most recent, newest, now, up-to-date, up-to-the-minute, with it (*informal*)

lather *noun* **1.** bubbles, foam, froth, soap, soapsuds, suds **2.** *informal* dither (*chiefly Brit.*), fever, flap (*informal*), fluster, fuss, pother, state (*informal*), stew (*informal*), sweat, tizzy (*informal*), twitter (*informal*) *~verb* **3.** foam, froth, soap **4.** *informal* beat, cane, drub, flog, lambast(e), strike, thrash, whip

lathery bubbly, foamy, frothy, soapy, sudsy

Latin

If the Romans had been obliged to learn Latin they would never have found time to conquer the world
Heinrich Heine

latitude **1.** breadth, compass, extent, range, reach, room, scope, space, span, spread, sweep, width **2.** a free hand, elbowroom, freedom, indulgence, laxity, leeway, liberty, licence, play, unrestrictedness

latter closing, concluding, last, last-mentioned, later, latest, modern, recent, second
Antonyms antecedent, earlier, foregoing, former, preceding, previous, prior

latterly hitherto, lately, of late, recently

lattice fretwork, grating, grid, grille, latticework, mesh, network, openwork, reticulation, tracery, trellis, web

laud acclaim, approve, celebrate, crack up (*informal*), extol, glorify, honour, magnify (*archaic*), praise, sing *or* sound the praises of

laudable admirable, commendable, creditable, estimable, excellent, meritorious, of note, praiseworthy, worthy
Antonyms base, blameworthy, contemptible, ignoble, lowly, unworthy

laudatory acclamatory, adulatory, approbatory, approving, commendatory, complimentary, eulogistic, panegyrical

laugh *verb* **1.** be convulsed (*informal*), be in stitches, be rolling in the aisles (*informal*), bust a gut (*informal*), chortle, chuckle, crack up (*informal*), crease up (*informal*), giggle, guffaw, roar with laughter, snigger, split one's sides, titter **2. laugh at** belittle, deride, jeer, lampoon, make a mock of, make fun of, mock, ridicule, scoff at, take the mickey (out of) (*informal*), taunt *~noun* **3.** belly laugh (*informal*), chortle, chuckle, giggle, guffaw, roar *or* shriek of laughter, snigger, titter **4.** *informal* card (*informal*), caution (*informal*), clown, comedian, comic, entertainer, hoot (*informal*), humorist, joke, lark, scream (*informal*), wag, wit

the loud laugh that spoke the vacant mind
Oliver Goldsmith *The Deserted Village*

Laugh and the world laughs with you;
Weep, and you weep alone;
For the sad old earth must borrow its mirth,
But has enough trouble of its own
Ella Wheeler Wilcox *Solitude*

He who laughs last, laughs longest

laughable **1.** absurd, derisive, derisory, ludicrous, nonsensical, preposterous, ridiculous, worthy of scorn **2.** amusing, comical, diverting, droll, farcical, funny, hilarious, humorous, mirthful, risible

laughing stock Aunt Sally (*Brit.*), butt, everybody's fool, fair game, figure of fun, target, victim

laugh off brush aside, dismiss, disregard, ignore, minimize, pooh-pooh, shrug off

laughter **1.** cachinnation, chortling, chuckling, giggling, guffawing, laughing, tittering **2.** amusement, glee, hilarity, merriment, mirth

Laughter is pleasant, but the exertion is too much for me
Thomas Love Peacock *Nightmare Abbey*

Delight hath a joy in it either permanent or pleasant. Laughter hath only a scornful tickling
Sir Philip Sidney *The Defence of Poetry*

If we may believe our logicians, man is distinguished from all other creatures by the faculty of laughter
Joseph Addison

As the crackling of thorns under a pot, so is the laughter of a fool
Bible: Ecclesiastes

launch **1.** cast, discharge, dispatch, fire, project, propel, send off, set afloat, set in motion, throw **2.** begin, commence, embark upon, inaugurate, initiate, instigate, introduce, open, start

launching **1.** projection, propelling, sendoff **2.** beginning, commencement, inauguration, initiation, instigation, introduction, opening, start

launder 1. clean, tub, wash 2. cook (*slang*), doctor, manipulate, process

laurels acclaim, awards, bays, Brownie points, commendation, credit, distinction, fame, glory, honour, kudos, praise, prestige, recognition, renown, reward

lavatory bathroom, bog (*slang*), can (*U.S. & Canad. slang*), cloakroom (*Brit.*), crapper (*taboo slang*), Gents, head(s) (*Nautical slang*), john (*slang, chiefly U.S. & Canad.*), khazi (*slang*), Ladies, latrine, little boy's room (*informal*), little girl's room (*informal*), loo (*Brit. informal*), *pissoir*, powder room, (public) convenience, toilet, washroom, water closet, W.C.

lavish *adjective* 1. abundant, copious, exuberant, lush, luxuriant, opulent, plentiful, profuse, prolific, sumptuous 2. bountiful, effusive, free, generous, liberal, munificent, openhanded, unstinting 3. exaggerated, excessive, extravagant, immoderate, improvident, intemperate, prodigal, thriftless, unreasonable, unrestrained, wasteful, wild *~verb* 4. deluge, dissipate, expend, heap, pour, shower, spend, squander, waste

Antonyms *adjective* cheap, frugal, meagre, miserly, parsimonious, scanty, sparing, stingy, thrifty, tight-fisted *~verb* begrudge, economize, stint, withhold

law 1. charter, code, constitution, jurisprudence 2. act, canon, code, command, commandment, covenant, decree, demand, edict, enactment, order, ordinance, rule, statute 3. axiom, canon, criterion, formula, precept, principle, regulation, standard 4. **lay down the law** dictate, dogmatize, emphasize, pontificate

Related adjectives: legal, judicial, juridicial

Law terms

abandonee
abate
abator
abet
abeyance
able
absente reo
absolute
acceptance (*Contract law*)
accessory *or* accessary
accretion
accrue
accusation
accusatorial
accuse
accused, the
acquit
action
actionable
act of God
adjective
ad litem
adminicle
administration order
admissible
adopt
adult
advocate
advocation
affiant
affidavit
affiliate *or* filiate
affiliation *or* filiation
affiliation order
affiliation proceedings *or (U.S.)* paternity suit
affirm
affirmation
affray
agist
alibi
alienable
alienate
alienation
alienee
alienor
alimony
allege
alluvion
ambulatory
a mensa et thoro
amerce (*obsolete*)
amicus curiae
amnesty
ancient
annulment
answer
Anton Piller order
appeal
appearance
appellant
appellate
appellee
appendant
approve
arbitrary
arbitration
arraign
array
arrest judgment
arrest of judgement
articled clerk
assault
assessor
assets
assign
assignee
assignment
assignor
assumpsit
attach
attachment
attainder
attaint (*archaic*)
attorn
attorney
attorney-at-law
attorney general
authentic
authority
automatism
aver
avoid
avoidance
avow (*rare*)
avulsion
award
bail
bailable
bailee (*Contract law*)
bailiff
bailiwick
bailment (*Contract law*)
bailor (*Contract law*)
bailsman (*rare*)
ban
bankrupt
bar
baron (*English law*)
barratry *or* barretry
barrister *or* barrister-at-law
bench, the
bencher
beneficial
beneficiary
bequeath
bequest
bigamy
bill of attainder
bill of indictment
bill of sale
blasphemy *or* blasphemous libel
body corporate
bona fides
bona vacantia
bond
bondsman
breach of promise
breach of the peace
breach of trust
brief
briefless
bring
burden of proof
capias
capital
caption
carnal knowledge
cartulary *or* chartulary
case
case law
case stated *or* stated case
cassation
cause
caution
CAV, Cur. adv. vult *or* Curia advisari vult
caveat
caveator
certificate of incorporation (*Company law*)
chamber counsel *or* counsellor
chambers
certification certiorari
cessor
cessionary
challenge
challenge to the array

challenge to the polls
champerty
chance-medley
chancery
change of venue
charge
chargeable
cheat
chief justice
chose
circuit (*English law*)
citation
cite
civil death
civil marriage
clerk to the justices
close
codicil
codification
coexecutor
cognizable *or* cognisable
cognizance *or* cognisance
collusion
come on
commitment, committal *or (especially formerly)* mittimus
common
commonage
common law
commutable
commutation
commute
competence
competency
competent
complainant
complaint (*English law*)
complete (*Land law*)
compound
compliance officer
composition
compurgation
conclusion
condemn
condition
condone
confiscate
connivance
connive
conscience clause
consensual
consideration
consolidation
consortium
constituent
constitute
constructive
contempt
contentious
continuance (*U.S.*)
contraband
contract
contractor
contributory (*Company law*)
contributory negligence
contumacy
convene
conventional
conversion
convert
conveyance
convincing
coparcenary *or* coparceny
coparcener *or* parcener
copyhold
copyholder
co-respondent
coroner
coroner's inquest
coroner's jury
corpus delicti
corpus juris
Corpus Juris Civilis
costs
counsel
counselor *or* counselor-at-law (*U.S.*)
count
countercharge
counterclaim
counterpart
countersign
county court
court
court of first instance
covenant
coverture
covin
criminal conversation
criminate (*rare*)
cross-examine
crown court (*English law*)
cruelty
culpa
Civil law
culprit
cumulative evidence
custodian
custody
custom
customary
cy pres
damages
damnify
dead letter
debatable
decedent (*chiefly U.S.*)
declarant
declaration
declaratory
decree
decree absolute
decree nisi
deed
deed poll
defalcate
defamation
default
defeasible
defeat
defence
defendant
deferred sentence
de jure
delict (*Roman law*)
demand
demandant
demisit sine prole
demur
demurrer
denunciation (*obsolete*)
deodand (*English law*)
deponent
depose
deposition
deraign *or* darraign (*obsolete*)
dereliction
descendible *or* descendable
desertion
detainer
determinable
determination
determine
detinue
devil
devisable
devise
devolve
dies non *or* dies non juridicus
digest
diligence
diminished responsibility
direct evidence
disaffirm
disafforest *or* disforest (*English law*)
disannul
disbar
discharge
disclaim
discommon
discontinue
discovert
discovery
disinherit
dismiss
disorderly
disorderly conduct
disorderly house
dissent
distrain *or* distress
distrainee
distraint
distributee (*chiefly U.S.*)
distribution
distringas
disturbance
dividend
divorce from bed and board (*U.S.*)
docket
documentation
Doe
domain
donee
donor
dot (*Civil law*)
dotation
dowable
dower
droit
due process of law
duress
earnest *or* earnest money (*Contract law*)
effectual
emblements
eminent domain
empanel *or* impanel
encumbrance
encumbrancer
enfranchise (*English law*)
engross
engrossment
enjoin
enter
equitable
equity
escheat
escrow
estop
estoppel
estovers
estray

estreat
evict
evidence
evocation (*French law*)
examination
examine
examine-in-chief
exception
execute
execution
executor *or (fem.)* executrix
executory
exemplary damages
exemplify
exhibit
ex parte
expectancy
expropriate
extend
extent (*U.S.*)
extinguish
extraditable
extradite
extrajudicial
eyre (*English legal history*)
fact
factor (*Commercial law*)
false imprisonment
Family Division
felo de se
feme
feme covert
feme sole
fiction
fideicommissary (*Civil law*)
fideicommissum (*Civil law*)
fiduciary *or* fiducial
fieri facias
file
filiate
filiation
find
finding
first offender
fiscal
flaw
folio
forbearance
force majeure
foreclose
foreign
foreman
forensic
forensic medicine, legal medicine *or* medical jurisprudence
forest
forfeit
forjudge *or* forejudge
fornication
free
fungible
garnish
garnishee
garnishment
gavelkind (*English law*)
gist
goods and chattels
grand jury (*chiefly U.S.*)
grand larceny
grantee
grant
grantor
gratuitous
gravamen
grith (*English legal history*)
ground rent
guarantee
guardian
guilty
habeas corpus
hand down (*U.S. & Canad.*)
handling
hear
hearing
hearsay
heir *or (fem.)* heiress (*Civil law*)
heirship
hereditary
heres *or* haeres (*Civil law*)
heritable
heritage
heritor
holder
homologate
hung jury
hypothec (*Roman law*)
hypothecate
immovable
impartible
impediment
imperfect
implead (*rare*)
imprescriptable
in articles
in banc
in camera
incapacitate
incapacity
in chancery
incompetent
incorporeal
incriminate
indefeasible
indemnity
indenture
indeterminate sentence
inducement
in escrow
infant
in fee
inferior court
infirm
in flagrante delicto *or* flagrante delicto
ingoing
inheritance
injunction
injury
innuendo
in personam
in posse
inquest
inquisition
inquisitorial
in rem
insanity
in specie
instanter
institutes
instruct
instructions
instrument
insurable interest
intendment
intent
intention
interdict (*Civil law*)
interlocutory
interplead
interpleader
interrogatories
intervene
inter vivos
intestate
invalidate
in venter
ipso jure
irrepleviable *or* irreplevisable
issuable
issue
jail delivery (*English law*)
jeopardy
joinder
joint
jointress
jointure
judge
judge-made
judges' rules
judgment *or* judgement
judgment by default
judicable
judicative
judicatory
judicature
judicial
judicial separation (*Family law*)
judiciary
junior
jural
jurat
juratory
juridical
jurisconsult
jurisprudence
jurisprudent
jurist
juristic
juror
jury
juryman *or (fem.)* jurywoman
jury process
jus
jus gentium (*Roman law*)
jus naturale (*Roman law*)
jus sanguinis
jus soli
justice
justice court
justice of the peace
justiciable
justices in eyre (*English legal history*)
justify
juvenile court
laches
land
lapse
larceny
Law French
Law Lords
law merchant (*Mercantile law*)
lawsuit
law term
lawyer
leasehold
leaseholder
legist
letters of administration

lex loci
lex non scripta
lex scripta
lex talionis
libel
lien
limit
limitation
lis pendens
litigable
litigant
litigation
locus standi
magistrate
magistrates' court *or* petty sessions
maintenance
malfeasance
malice
manager
mandamus
mandate (*Roman or Contract law*)
manslaughter
manus
mare clausum
mare liberum
material
matter
mayhem *or* maihem
memorandum
mens rea
mental disorder
mental impairment
merger
merits
mesne
ministerial
misadventure
mise
misfeasance
misjoinder
mispleading
mistrial
misuser
mittimus
monopoly
moral
moratorium
morganatic *or* left-handed
mortgagee
mortmain *or (less commonly)* dead hand
motion
moveable *or* movable
muniments
mute
naked
Napoleonic Code
necessaries
negligence
next friend
nisi
nisi prius (*history or* U.S.)
nolle prosequi, nol. pros. *or* nolle pros.
nolo contendere (*chiefly U.S.*)
nonage
non compos mentis
nonfeasance
nonjoinder
non liquet
non prosequitur *or* non pros.
nonsuit
notary public
not guilty
novation
novel (*Roman law*)
nude
nudum pactum
nuisance
oath
obiter dictum
obligation
oblivion
obreption
obscene
obtaining by deception
occupancy
occupant
offer (*Contract law*)
Official Referee
onerous
onomastic
on, upon *or* under oath
onus probandi
open
opening
ordinary
overt
owelty
oyer (*English legal history*)
oyer and terminer
panel
paraphernalia
pardon
parol
Particulars of Claim
party
paterfamilias (*Roman law*)
peculium (*Roman law*)
pecuniary
pecuniary advantage
pendente lite
perception
peremptory
persistent cruelty
personal
personal property *or* personalty
petit
petition
petitioner
petit jury *or* petty jury
petit larceny *or* petty larceny
petty
place of safety order
plaint
plaintiff
plea
plea bargaining
plead
pleading
pleadings
portion
port of entry
posse
posse comitatus
possessory
post-obit
prayer
precedent
precept
predispose
pre-emption
prefer
preference
premeditation
premises
prescribe
prescription
presentment (*chiefly U.S.*)
presents
presume
presumption
preterition (*Roman law*)
prima facie
primogeniture
principal
private law
private nuisance
privilege
privileged
privity
privy
prize court
probable cause
probate
proceed
proceeding
process
process-server
procuration
procuratory
prohibition
promisee (*Contract law*)
promisor (*Contract law*)
proof
property centre
proponent
propositus
propound (*English law*)
prosecute
prosecuting attorney (*U.S.*)
prosecution
prosecutor
prothonotary *or* protonotary
prove
provocation (*English criminal law*)
psychopathic disorder
public defender (*U.S.*)
public law
public nuisance
public prosecutor
pupil (*Civil law*)
pupillage
pursuant
purview
quarter sessions
queen's *or* king's evidence
question
question of fact (*English law*)
question of law (*English law*)
quitclaim
quo warranto
real
real property
rebutter
recaption
receivership
recital
recognizance *or* recognisance
recognizee *or* recognisee
recognizor *or* recognisor
recorder
recoup
recover
recovery
recrimination

re-examine
reference
refresher (*English law*)
rejoin
rejoinder
relation
relator (*English or U.S. law*)
release
relief
remand
remise
remission
remit
repetition (*Civil law*)
replevin
replevy
replication
reply
report
reporter
representation (*Contract law*)
reprieve
rescue
reservation
res gestae
residuary
residue
res ipsa loquitur
res judicata *or* res adjudicata
resolutive
respondent
rest
restitution
restrictive covenant
retain
retry
return
returnable
reverse
review
right of common
riot
rout
rule
ruling
run
salvo
saving
scandal
schedule
scienter
scire facias (*rare*)
script
secularize *or* secularise
self-defence
self-executing
sentence
separation (*Family law*)
sequester *or* sequestrate
sequestration
serjeant at law, serjeant, sergeant at law *or* sergeant
servitude
session
settlement
settlor
severable
several
severance
sign
signatory
sine
sine prole
slander
smart money (*U.S.*)
socage (*English law*)
soke (*English legal history*)
solatium (*chiefly U.S.*)
sole
solemnity
solicitor
solution
sound
sound in
special case
special pleading
specialty
specific performance
spinster
spoliation
squat
stale
stand by (*English law*)
stand down
statement
statement of claim
state's evidence (*U.S.*)
statute law
statutory declaration
stillicide
stipulate (*Roman law*)
stranger
stultify
submission
subpoena
subreption (*rare*)
subrogate
subrogation
substantive
succeed
sue
sui juris
suit
suitor
summary
summary jurisdiction
summary offence
summation (*U.S. law*)
summing-up
summons
suo jure
suo loco
surcharge
surety
surplusage
surrebuttal
surrebutter
surrejoinder
surrender
suspension
swear
swear in
swear out (*U.S.*)
tales
tenancy
tenantry
tender
tenor
term
termor *or* termer
territorial court (*U.S.*)
testament
testamentary
testate
testify
testimony
thing
third party
time immemorial
tipstaff
title
tort
tort-feasor
tortious
traffic court
transfer
transitory action
traverse
treasure-trove
trespass
triable
trial
trial court
tribunal
trover
try
udal
ultimogeniture
ultra vires
unalienable
unappealable
unavoidable
uncovenanted
unilateral
unincorporated
unlawful assembly
unreasonable behaviour
unwritten law
use
user
utter barrister
vacant
vacate
variance
vendee
vendor
venire facias
venireman (*U.S.*)
venue
verdict
verification
verify
versus
vesture
vexatious
view
viewer
vindicate (*Roman law*)
vindictive (*English law*)
vitiate
voidable
voir dire
voluntary
voluntary arrangement
volunteer
voucher (*English law, obsolete*)
wager of law (*English legal history*)
waif (*obsolete*)
waive
waiver
ward
ward of court
warrant
warranty (*Contract or Insurance law*)
waste
will
witness
without prejudice
writ
writ of execution
wrong
year and a day (*English law*)

Criminal law terms

acquittal
actual bodily harm
arson
bailment
battery
burglary (*English law*)
deception *or (formerly)* false pretences
embrace
embraceor *or* embracer
embracery
entry
felon
felonious
felony
force
forgery
grievous bodily harm
hard labour
housebreaking
impeach
indictable
indictment
infamous
malice aforethought
misdemeanant
misdemeanour
penal servitude (*English law*)
perjure
perjury
personate
Riot Act
robbery
suborn
theft
thief
true bill (*U.S. law*)
utter

Property law terms

abatement
abstract of title
abuttals
abutter
accession
ademption
administration
administrator
advancement
adverse
amortize *or* amortise
appoint
appointee
appointment
appointor
appurtenance
betterment
chattel
chattel personal
chattel real
convey *or* assure
deforce
demesne
demise
descent
devisee
devisor
dilapidation
disentail
disseise
divest
dominant tenement
dominium *or (rare)* dominion
easement
ejectment
enfeoff
entail
entry
equity of redemption
estate
fee
fee simple
fee tail
fixture
freehold
freeholder
heir apparent
heir-at-law
heirdom
heirloom
heriditament
hotchpot
intrusion
messuage
mortgagor *or* mortgager
oust
ouster
particular
partition
party wall
perpetuity
power of appointment
reconvert
remainder
remainderman
remitter
result
reversion
reversioner
revert
riparian
seisin *or (U.S.)* seizin
servient tenement
severalty
survivor
tail
tenure
transferee
transferor *or* transferrer
unity of interest
vested
vested interest
warranty

Scots law terms

advocate
Advocate Depute
agent
aliment
alimentary
approbate
approbate and reprobate
arrestment
assignation
assize
avizandum
condescendence
continue
crown agent
culpable homicide
curator
decern
declarator
decreet
defender
delict
depone
desert
district court *or (formerly)* justice of the peace court
feu
feu duty
fire raising
hypothec
interdict
interlocutor
law agent
location
lockfast
mandate
multiplepoinding
notour
notour bankrupt
not proven
poind
poinding
precognition
procurator fiscal *or* fiscal
pupil
repetition
repone
sasine
sequestrate
sheriff officer
thirlage
tradition
tutor
wadset
warrant sale

No brilliance is needed in the law. Nothing but common sense, and relatively clean finger nails
John Mortimer *A Voyage Round My Father*

A jury consists of twelve persons chosen to decide who has the better lawyer
Robert Frost

Laws were made to be broken
John Wilson *Noctes Ambrosianae*

The Common Law of England has been laboriously built about a mythical figure - the figure of "The Reasonable Man"
A.P. Herbert *Uncommon Law*

We do not get good laws to restrain bad people. We get good people to restrain bad laws
G.K. Chesterton *All Things Considered*

The law is a ass - a idiot
Charles Dickens *Oliver Twist*

Ignorance of the law excuses no man; not that all men know the law, but because 'tis an excuse every man will plead, and no man can tell how to confute him
John Selden *Table Talk*

Written laws are like spider's webs; they will catch, it is true, the weak and poor, but would be torn in pieces by the rich and powerful
Anacharsis

Law is a bottomless pit
Dr. Arbuthnot *The History of John Bull*

It is better that ten guilty persons escape than one innocent suffer
William Blackstone *Commentaries on the Laws of England*

The one great principle of the English law is to make business for itself
Charles Dickens *Bleak House*

No poet ever interpreted nature as freely as a lawyer interprets the truth
Jean Giraudoux *La Guerre de Troie n'aura pas lieu*

The end of law is, not to abolish or restrain, but to preserve and enlarge freedom
John Locke *Second Treatise of Civil Government*

The laws of most countries are far worse than the people who execute them, and many of them are only able to remain laws by being seldom or never carried into effect
John Stuart Mill *The Subjection of Women*

Hard cases make bad laws

One law for the rich, and another for the poor

law-abiding compliant, dutiful, good, honest, honourable, lawful, obedient, orderly, peaceable, peaceful

lawbreaker convict, criminal, crook (*informal*), culprit, delinquent, felon (*formerly criminal law*), miscreant, offender, sinner, transgressor, trespasser, villain, violater, wrongdoer

lawful allowable, authorized, constitutional, just, legal, legalized, legitimate, licit, permissible, proper, rightful, valid, warranted
Antonyms banned, forbidden, illegal, illegitimate, illicit, prohibited, unauthorized, unlawful

lawless anarchic, chaotic, disorderly, insubordinate, insurgent, mutinous, rebellious, reckless, riotous, seditious, ungoverned, unrestrained, unruly, wild
Antonyms civilized, compliant, disciplined, law-abiding, lawful, legitimate, licit, obedient, orderly, regimented, restrained, well-governed

lawlessness anarchy, chaos, disorder, mobocracy, mob rule, ochlocracy, reign of terror

lawsuit action, argument, case, cause, contest, dispute, industrial tribunal, litigation, proceedings, prosecution, suit, trial

lawyer advocate, attorney, barrister, counsel, counsellor, legal adviser, solicitor

The laws I love; the lawyers I suspect
Charles Churchill *The Farewell*

I don't want a lawyer to tell me what I cannot do; I hire him to tell me how to do what I want to do
J. Pierpoint Morgan

Woe unto you, lawyers! For ye have taken away the key of knowledge
Bible: St. Luke

lawyer: one skilled in circumvention of the law
Ambrose Bierce *The Devil's Dictionary*

A lawyer with his briefcase can steal more than a hundred men with guns
Mario Puzo *The Godfather*

A man who is his own lawyer has a fool for a client

lax **1.** careless, casual, easy-going, easy-oasy (*slang*), lenient, neglectful, negligent, overindulgent, remiss, slack, slapdash, slipshod **2.** broad, general, imprecise, inaccurate, indefinite, inexact, nonspecific, shapeless, vague **3.** flabby, flaccid, loose, slack, soft, yielding
Antonyms (*sense 1*) conscientious, disciplined, firm, heedful, moral, rigid, scrupulous, severe, stern, strict, stringent (*sense 3*) firm, rigid

laxative aperient, cathartic, physic (*rare*), purgative, purge, salts

lay[1] *verb* **1.** deposit, establish, leave, place, plant, posit, put, set, set down, settle, spread **2.** arrange, dispose, locate, organize, position, set out **3.** bear, deposit, produce **4.** advance, bring forward, lodge, offer, present, put forward, submit **5.** allocate, allot, ascribe, assign, attribute, charge, impute **6.** concoct, contrive, design, devise, hatch, plan, plot, prepare, work out **7.** apply, assess, burden, charge, encumber, impose, saddle, tax **8.** bet, gamble, give odds, hazard, risk, stake, wager **9.** allay, alleviate, appease, assuage, calm, quiet, relieve, soothe, still, suppress **10. lay bare** disclose, divulge, explain, expose, reveal, show, unveil **11. lay hands on a.** acquire, get, get hold of, grab, grasp, seize **b.** assault, attack, beat up, lay into (*informal*), set on, work over (*slang*), **c.** discover, find, unearth **d.** *Christianity* bless, confirm, consecrate, ordain **12. lay hold of** get, get hold of, grab, grasp, grip, seize, snatch

lay[2] *adjective* **1.** laic, laical, nonclerical, secular **2.** amateur, inexpert, nonprofessional, nonspecialist

lay[3] *noun* ballad, lyric, ode, poem, song

layabout beachcomber, couch potato (*slang*), good-for-nothing, idler, laggard, loafer, lounger, ne'er-do-well, shirker, skiver (*Brit. slang*), slubberdegullion (*archaic*), vagrant, wastrel

lay aside abandon, cast aside, dismiss, postpone, put aside, put off, reject, shelve

lay away accumulate, collect, hoard, keep, lay aside, lay in, salt away, save, stash (*informal*), stockpile, store

lay down **1.** discard, drop, give, give up, relinquish, surrender, yield **2.** affirm, assume, es~

tablish, formulate, ordain, postulate, prescribe, stipulate

layer 1. bed, ply, row, seam, stratum, thickness, tier 2. blanket, coat, coating, cover, covering, film, mantle, sheet

lay in accumulate, amass, build up, collect, hoard, stockpile, stock up, store (up)

lay into assail, attack, belabour, go for the jugular, hit out at, lambast(e), let fly at, pitch into (*informal*), set about

layman amateur, lay person, nonprofessional, outsider

lay-off discharge, dismissal, unemployment

lay off 1. discharge, dismiss, drop, give the boot to (*slang*), let go, make redundant, oust, pay off 2. *informal* belay (*Nautical*), cease, desist, get off someone's back (*informal*), give it a rest (*informal*), give over (*informal*), give up, leave alone, leave off, let up, quit, stop

lay on 1. cater (for), furnish, give, provide, purvey, supply 2. **lay it on** *slang* butter up, exaggerate, flatter, overdo it, overpraise, soft-soap (*informal*)

layout arrangement, design, draft, formation, geography, outline, plan

lay out 1. arrange, design, display, exhibit, plan, spread out 2. *informal* disburse, expend, fork out (*slang*), invest, pay, shell out (*informal*), spend 3. *informal* kayo (*slang*), knock for six (*informal*), knock out, knock unconscious, KO *or* K.O. (*slang*)

lay up 1. accumulate, amass, garner, hoard, keep, preserve, put away, save, store up, treasure 2. *informal* confine (to bed), hospitalize, incapacitate

laze 1. hang around, idle, loaf, loll, lounge, stand around 2. *often with* **away** fool away, fritter away, kill time, pass time, veg out (*slang, chiefly U.S.*), waste time, while away the hours

laziness dilatoriness, do-nothingness, faineance, faineancy, idleness, inactivity, indolence, lackadaisicalness, slackness, sloth, slothfulness, slowness, sluggishness, tardiness

lazy 1. good-for-nothing, idle, inactive, indolent, inert, remiss, shiftless, slack, slothful, slow, workshy 2. drowsy, languid, languorous, lethargic, sleepy, slow-moving, sluggish, somnolent, torpid
Antonyms active, assiduous, diligent, energetic, industrious, quick, stimulated

lazybones couch potato (*slang*), loafer, lounger, shirker, skiver (*Brit. slang*), sleepyhead, slugabed, sluggard

leach drain, extract, filter, filtrate, lixiviate (*Chemistry*), percolate, seep, strain

lead *verb* 1. conduct, escort, guide, pilot, precede, show the way, steer, usher 2. cause, dispose, draw, incline, induce, influence, persuade, prevail, prompt 3. command, direct, govern, head, manage, preside over, supervise 4. be ahead (of), blaze a trail, come first, exceed, excel, outdo, outstrip, surpass, transcend 5. experience, have, live, pass, spend, undergo 6. bring on, cause, conduce, contribute, produce, result in, serve, tend *~noun* 7. advance, advantage, cutting edge, edge, first place, margin, precedence, primacy, priority, start, supremacy, van, vanguard 8. direction, example, guidance, leadership, model 9. clue, guide, hint, indication, suggestion, tip, trace 10. leading role, principal, protagonist, star part, title role *~adjective* 11. chief, first, foremost, head, leading, main, most important, premier, primary, prime, principal

leaden 1. burdensome, crushing, cumbersome, heavy, inert, lead, onerous, oppressive 2. humdrum, laboured, plodding, sluggish, stiff, stilted, wooden 3. dismal, dreary, dull, gloomy, languid, lifeless, listless, spiritless 4. dingy, grey, greyish, lacklustre, louring *or* lowering, lustreless, overcast, sombre

leader bellwether, boss (*informal*), captain, chief, chieftain, commander, conductor, counsellor, director, guide, head, number one, principal, ringleader, ruler, superior, torchbearer
Antonyms adherent, disciple, follower, hanger-on, henchman, sidekick (*slang*), supporter

leadership 1. administration, direction, directorship, domination, guidance, management, running, superintendency 2. authority, command, control, influence, initiative, pre-eminence, supremacy, sway

leading chief, dominant, first, foremost, governing, greatest, highest, main, number one, outstanding, pre-eminent, primary, principal, ruling, superior
Antonyms following, hindmost, incidental, inferior, lesser, minor, secondary, subordinate, superficial

lead off begin, commence, get going, get under way, inaugurate, initiate, kick off (*informal*), open, set out, start, start the ball rolling (*informal*)

lead on beguile, deceive, draw on, entice, inveigle, lure, seduce, string along (*informal*), tempt

lead up to approach, intimate, introduce, make advances, make overtures, pave the way, prepare for, prepare the way, work round to

leaf *noun* 1. blade, bract, flag, foliole, frond, needle, pad 2. folio, page, sheet 3. **turn over a new leaf** amend, begin anew, change, change one's ways, improve, reform *~verb* 4.

bud, green, put out leaves, turn green **5.** browse, flip, glance, riffle, skim, thumb (through)

leaflet advert (*Brit. informal*), bill, booklet, brochure, circular, handbill, mailshot, pamphlet

leafy bosky (*literary*), green, in foliage, leafed, leaved, shaded, shady, springlike, summery, verdant, wooded

league *noun* **1.** alliance, association, band, coalition, combination, combine, compact, confederacy, confederation, consortium, federation, fellowship, fraternity, group, guild, order, partnership, union **2.** ability group, category, class, level **3. in league (with)** allied, collaborating, hand in glove, in cahoots (*informal*), leagued *~verb* **4.** ally, amalgamate, associate, band, collaborate, combine, confederate, join forces, unite

leak *noun* **1.** aperture, chink, crack, crevice, fissure, hole, opening, puncture **2.** drip, leakage, leaking, oozing, percolation, seepage **3.** disclosure, divulgence *~verb* **4.** discharge, drip, escape, exude, ooze, pass, percolate, seep, spill, trickle **5.** blow wide open (*slang*), disclose, divulge, give away, let slip, let the cat out of the bag, make known, make public, pass on, reveal, spill the beans (*informal*), tell

leaky cracked, holey, leaking, not watertight, perforated, porous, punctured, split, waterlogged

lean[1] *verb* **1.** be supported, prop, recline, repose, rest **2.** bend, heel, incline, slant, slope, tilt, tip **3.** be disposed to, be prone to, favour, gravitate towards, have a propensity, prefer, tend **4.** confide, count on, depend, have faith in, rely, trust

lean[2] *adjective* **1.** angular, bony, emaciated, gaunt, lank, macilent (*rare*), rangy, scraggy, scrawny, skinny, slender, slim, spare, thin, unfatty, wiry **2.** bare, barren, inadequate, infertile, meagre, pathetic, pitiful, poor, scanty, sparse, unfruitful, unproductive

Antonyms abundant, ample, brawny, burly, fat, fertile, full, obese, plentiful, plump, portly, profuse, rich

leaning aptitude, bent, bias, disposition, inclination, liking, partiality, penchant, predilection, proclivity, proneness, propensity, taste, tendency

leap *verb* **1.** bounce, bound, caper, cavort, frisk, gambol, hop, jump, skip, spring **2.** *figurative* arrive at, come to, form hastily, hasten, hurry, jump, reach, rush **3.** clear, jump (over), vault **4.** advance, become prominent, escalate, gain attention, increase, rocket, soar, surge *~noun* **5.** bound, caper, frisk, hop, jump, skip, spring, vault **6.** escalation, increase, rise, surge, upsurge, upswing

learn **1.** acquire, attain, become able, grasp, imbibe, master, pick up **2.** commit to memory, con (*archaic*), get off pat, get (something) word-perfect, learn by heart, memorize **3.** ascertain, detect, determine, discern, discover, find out, gain, gather, hear, suss (out) (*slang*), understand

learned academic, cultured, erudite, experienced, expert, highbrow, intellectual, lettered, literate, scholarly, skilled, versed, well-informed, well-read

Antonyms ignorant, illiterate, uneducated, unlearned

learner **1.** apprentice, beginner, neophyte, novice, tyro **2.** disciple, pupil, scholar, student, trainee

Antonyms (*sense 1*) adept, expert, grandmaster, master, maven, pastmaster, virtuoso, wizard (*sense 2*) coach, instructor, mentor, teacher, tutor

learning acquirements, attainments, culture, education, erudition, information, knowledge, letters, literature, lore, research, scholarship, schooling, study, tuition, wisdom

Much learning doth make thee mad
Bible: Acts

The further one goes, the less one knows
Lao-tze *Tao Te Ching*

Try to learn something about everything and everything about something
Thomas Henry Huxley *memorial stone*

Learning without thought is labour lost; thought without learning is perilous
Confucius *Analects*

A little learning is a dangerous thing;
Drink deep, or taste not the Pierian spring:
There shallow draughts intoxicate the brain,
And drinking largely sobers us again
Alexander Pope *An Essay on Criticism*

The bookful blockhead, ignorantly read,
With loads of learned lumber in his head
Alexander Pope *An Essay on Criticism*

lease *verb* charter, hire, let, loan, rent

leash *noun* **1.** lead, rein, tether **2.** check, control, curb, hold, restraint *~verb* **3.** fasten, secure, tether, tie up **4.** check, control, curb, hold back, restrain, suppress

least feeblest, fewest, last, lowest, meanest, minimum, minutest, poorest, slightest, smallest, tiniest

leathery coriaceous, durable, hard, hardened, leatherlike, leathern (*archaic*), rough, rugged, tough, wrinkled

leave[1] *verb* **1.** abandon, abscond, decamp, depart, desert, disappear, do a bunk (*Brit. slang*), exit, flit (*informal*), forsake, go, go away, hook it (*slang*), make tracks, move, pack one's bags (*informal*), pull out, quit, relinquish, retire, set out, sling one's hook (*Brit.*

slang), slope off, take off (*informal*), withdraw **2.** forget, lay down, leave behind, mislay **3.** cause, deposit, generate, produce, result in **4.** abandon, cease, desert, desist, drop, evacuate, forbear, give up, refrain, relinquish, renounce, stop, surrender **5.** allot, assign, cede, commit, consign, entrust, give over, refer **6.** bequeath, demise, devise (*Law*), hand down, transmit, will

Antonyms appear, arrive, assume, come, continue, emerge, hold, persist, remove, retain, stay

Let sleeping dogs lie

leave² *noun* **1.** allowance, authorization, concession, consent, dispensation, freedom, liberty, permission, sanction **2.** furlough, holiday, leave of absence, sabbatical, time off, vacation **3.** adieu, departure, farewell, goodbye, leave-taking, parting, retirement, withdrawal

Antonyms (*sense 1*) denial, prohibition, refusal, rejection (*sense 2*) duty (*sense 3*) arrival, stay

leaven *noun* **1.** barm, ferment, leavening, yeast **2.** *figurative* catalyst, influence, inspiration *~verb* **3.** ferment, lighten, raise, work **4.** *figurative* elevate, imbue, inspire, permeate, pervade, quicken, stimulate, suffuse

leave off abstain, belay (*Nautical*), break off, cease, desist, discontinue, end, give over (*informal*), give up, halt, kick (*informal*), knock off (*informal*), refrain, stop

leave out bar, cast aside, count out, disregard, except, exclude, ignore, neglect, omit, overlook, reject

leave-taking departure, farewell, going, goodbye, leaving, parting, sendoff (*informal*), valediction

leavings bits, dregs, fragments, leftovers, orts (*archaic or dialect*), pieces, refuse, remains, remnants, residue, scraps, spoil, sweepings, waste

lecher adulterer, Casanova, debauchee, dirty old man (*slang*), Don Juan, fornicator, goat (*informal*), lech *or* letch (*informal*), libertine, profligate, rake, roué, satyr, seducer, sensualist, wanton, wolf (*informal*), womanizer

lecherous carnal, concupiscent, goatish (*archaic or literary*), lascivious, lewd, libidinous, licentious, lubricious (*U.S. slang*), lubricous, lustful, prurient, randy (*informal, chiefly Brit.*), raunchy (*slang*), ruttish, salacious, unchaste, wanton

Antonyms prim, proper, prudish, puritanical, strait-laced, virginal, virtuous

lechery carnality, concupiscence, debauchery, lasciviousness, lecherousness, leching (*informal*), lewdness, libertinism, libidinousness, licentiousness, lubricity, lust, lustfulness, profligacy, prurience, rakishness, randiness (*informal, chiefly Brit.*), salaciousness, sensuality, wantonness, womanizing

lecture *noun* **1.** address, discourse, disquisition, harangue, instruction, lesson, speech, talk *~verb* **2.** address, discourse, expound, give a talk, harangue, hold forth, speak, spout, talk, teach *~noun* **3.** castigation, censure, chiding, dressing-down (*informal*), going-over (*informal*), heat (*slang, chiefly U.S. & Canad.*), rebuke, reprimand, reproof, scolding, talking-to (*informal*), telling off (*informal*), wigging (*Brit. slang*) *~verb* **4.** admonish, bawl out (*informal*), berate, carpet (*informal*), castigate, censure, chew out (*U.S. & Canad. informal*), chide, give a rocket (*Brit. & N.Z. informal*), rate, read the riot act, reprimand, reprove, scold, tear into (*informal*), tear (someone) off a strip (*Brit. informal*), tell off (*informal*)

ledge mantle, projection, ridge, shelf, sill, step

lee cover, protection, refuge, screen, shade, shadow, shelter, shield

leech *figurative* bloodsucker (*informal*), freeloader (*slang*), hanger-on, ligger (*slang*), parasite, sponger (*informal*), sycophant

leer *noun/verb* drool, eye, gloat, goggle, grin, ogle, smirk, squint, stare, wink

leery careful, cautious, chary, distrustful, doubting, dubious, on one's guard, sceptical, shy, suspicious, uncertain, unsure, wary

lees deposit, dregs, grounds, precipitate, refuse, sediment, settlings

leeway elbowroom, latitude, margin, play, room, scope, space

left *adjective* **1.** larboard (*Nautical*), left-hand, port, sinistral **2.** *of politics* leftist, left-wing, liberal, progressive, radical, socialist

left-handed **1.** *archaic* awkward, cack-handed (*informal*), careless, clumsy, fumbling, gauche, maladroit **2.** ambiguous, backhanded, double-edged, enigmatic, equivocal, indirect, ironic, sardonic

leftover *noun* **1.** legacy, remainder, residue, surplus, survivor **2.** *plural* leavings, oddments, odds and ends, remains, remnants, scraps *~adjective* **3.** excess, extra, remaining, surplus, uneaten, unused, unwanted

leg *noun* **1.** limb, lower limb, member, pin (*informal*), stump (*informal*) **2.** brace, prop, support, upright **3.** lap, part, portion, section, segment, stage, stretch **4. a leg up** assistance, boost, help, helping hand, push, support **5. not have a leg to stand on** *informal* be defenceless, be full of holes, be illogical, be invalid, be undermined, be vulnerable, lack support **6. on one's (its) last legs** about to break down, about to collapse, at death's door, dying, exhausted, failing, giving up the ghost, worn out **7. pull someone's leg** *informal* chaff, deceive, fool, kid (*informal*), make fun of, tease, trick, wind up (*Brit. slang*) 8. **shake a leg** *slang* **a.** get a move on (*informal*), get cracking (*informal*), hasten, hurry, look lively (*informal*), rush, stir one's stumps **b.** boogie (*slang*), dance, get down (*informal, chiefly U.S.*), hoof it (*slang*), trip the light fantastic 9. **stretch one's legs** exercise, go for a walk, move about, promenade, stroll, take a walk, take the air ~*verb* 10. **leg it** *informal* go on foot, hotfoot, hurry, run, skedaddle (*informal*), walk

legacy 1. bequest, devise (*Law*), estate, gift, heirloom, inheritance 2. birthright, endow~ment, heritage, inheritance, patrimony, throwback, tradition

legal 1. allowable, allowed, authorized, consti~tutional, lawful, legalized, legitimate, licit, permissible, proper, rightful, sanctioned, valid 2. forensic, judicial, juridical

legalistic contentious, disputatious, hair~splitting, literal, litigious, narrow, narrow-minded, polemical, strict

legality accordance with the law, admissible~ness, lawfulness, legitimacy, permissibility, rightfulness, validity

legalize allow, approve, authorize, decriminal~ize, legitimate, legitimatize, license, permit, sanction, validate

legate ambassador, delegate, depute (*Scot.*), deputy, emissary, envoy, messenger, nuncio

legatee beneficiary, heir, inheritor, recipient

legation consulate, delegation, diplomatic mis~sion, embassy, envoys, ministry, representa~tion

legend 1. fable, fiction, folk tale, myth, narra~tive, saga, story, tale, urban legend 2. big name, celeb (*informal*), celebrity, luminary, marvel, megastar (*informal*), phenomenon, prodigy, spectacle, wonder 3. caption, device, inscription, motto 4. cipher, code, key, table of symbols

legendary 1. apocryphal, fabled, fabulous, fan~ciful, fictitious, mythical, romantic, storied, traditional 2. celebrated, famed, famous, illus~trious, immortal, renowned, well-known
Antonyms (*sense 1*) factual, genuine, histori~cal (*sense 2*) unknown

legerdemain 1. prestidigitation, sleight of hand 2. artfulness, artifice, chicanery, contrivance, craftiness, cunning, deception, feint, hocus-pocus, manipulation, manoeuvring, subter~fuge, trickery

legibility clarity, decipherability, ease of read~ing, legibleness, neatness, plainness, read~ability, readableness

legible bold, clear, decipherable, distinct, easily read, easy to read, neat, plain, readable

legion *noun* 1. army, brigade, company, divi~sion, force, troop 2. drove, horde, host, mass, multitude, myriad, number, throng ~*adjective* 3. countless, multitudinous, myriad, number~less, numerous, very many

legislate codify, constitute, enact, establish, make laws, ordain, pass laws, prescribe, put in force

legislation 1. codification, enactment, law~making, prescription, regulation 2. act, bill, charter, law, measure, regulation, ruling, statute

legislative *adjective* congressional, judicial, ju~ridical, jurisdictive, lawgiving, lawmaking, or~daining, parliamentary

legislator lawgiver, lawmaker, parliamentarian

legislature assembly, chamber, congress, diet, house, lawmaking body, parliament, senate

legitimate *adjective* 1. acknowledged, authen~tic, authorized, genuine, kosher (*informal*), lawful, legal, legit (*slang*), licit, proper, real, rightful, sanctioned, statutory, true 2. admis~sible, correct, just, justifiable, logical, reason~able, sensible, valid, warranted, well-founded ~*verb* 3. authorize, give the green light for, legalize, legitimatize, legitimize, permit, pro~nounce lawful, sanction
Antonyms *adjective* false, fraudulent, illegal, illegitimate, unfair, unfounded, unjustified, unlawful, unreasonable, unsound

legitimatize, legitimize authorize, give the green light for, legalize, legitimate, permit, pronounce lawful, sanction

leisure 1. breathing space, ease, freedom, free time, holiday, liberty, opportunity, pause, quiet, recreation, relaxation, respite, rest, re~tirement, spare moments, spare time, time off, vacation 2. **at leisure a.** available, free, not booked up, on holiday, unengaged, unoc~cupied **b.** *Also* **at one's leisure** at an unhur~ried pace, at one's convenience, deliberately, in one's own (good) time, unhurriedly, when it suits one, when one gets round to it (*infor~mal*), without hurry
Antonyms business, duty, employment, la~bour, obligation, occupation, work

All intellectual improvement arises from leisure
Dr. Johnson

leisurely 1. *adjective* comfortable, easy, gentle, laid-back (*informal*), lazy, relaxed, restful, slow, unhurried 2. *adverb* at one's conveni~ence, at one's leisure, comfortably, deliberate~ly, easily, indolently, lazily, lingeringly, slow~ly, unhurriedly, without haste
Antonyms *adjective* brisk, fast, hasty, hectic, hurried, quick, rapid, rushed ~*adverb* briskly, hastily, hurriedly, quickly, rapidly

leitmotif *all with* **recurrent** *or* **recurring** air, convention, device, idea, melody, motif, phrase, strain, theme

lend 1. accommodate one with, advance, loan 2. add, afford, bestow, confer, contribute, furnish, give, grant, hand out, impart, present, provide, supply 3. **lend an ear** give ear, hearken (*archaic*), heed, listen, take notice 4. **lend a hand** aid, assist, give a (helping) hand, help, help out 5. **lend itself to** be adaptable, be appropriate, be serviceable, fit, present opportunities of, suit 6. **lend oneself to** agree, consent, cooperate, countenance, espouse, support

Neither a borrower nor a lender be
William Shakespeare *Hamlet*

length 1. *of linear extent* distance, extent, longitude, measure, reach, span 2. *of time* duration, period, space, span, stretch, term 3. measure, piece, portion, section, segment 4. elongation, extensiveness, lengthiness, protractedness 5. **at length a.** completely, fully, in depth, in detail, thoroughly, to the full **b.** for ages, for a long time, for hours, interminably **c.** at last, at long last, eventually, finally, in the end

lengthen continue, draw out, elongate, expand, extend, increase, make longer, prolong, protract, spin out, stretch
Antonyms abbreviate, abridge, curtail, cut, cut down, diminish, shorten, trim

lengthy diffuse, drawn-out, extended, interminable, lengthened, long, long-drawn-out, long-winded, overlong, prolix, prolonged, protracted, tedious, verbose, very long
Antonyms brief, concise, condensed, limited, short, succinct, terse, to the point

leniency, lenience clemency, compassion, forbearance, gentleness, indulgence, lenity, mercy, mildness, moderation, pity, quarter, tenderness, tolerance

lenient clement, compassionate, forbearing, forgiving, gentle, indulgent, kind, merciful, mild, sparing, tender, tolerant
Antonyms harsh, merciless, rigid, rigorous, severe, stern, strict, stringent

lenitive alleviative, assuaging, calming, easing, mitigative, mollifying, palliative, relieving, soothing

leper lazar (*archaic*), outcast, pariah, untouchable

lepidopterist butterfly collector

lesbian 1. *noun* butch (*slang*), dyke (*slang*), sapphist, tribade 2. *adjective* butch (*slang*), gay, homosexual, sapphic, tribadic

lesion abrasion, bruise, contusion, hurt, impairment, injury, sore, trauma (*Pathology*), wound

less *adjective* 1. shorter, slighter, smaller 2. inferior, minor, secondary, subordinate *~adverb* 3. barely, little, meagrely, to a smaller extent *~preposition* 4. excepting, lacking, minus, subtracting, without

lessen abate, abridge, contract, curtail, decrease, de-escalate, degrade, die down, diminish, downsize, dwindle, ease, erode, grow less, impair, lighten, lower, minimize, moderate, narrow, reduce, relax, shrink, slacken, slow down, weaken, wind down
Antonyms add to, augment, boost, enhance, enlarge, expand, increase, magnify, multiply, raise

lessening abatement, contraction, curtailment, decline, decrease, de-escalation, diminution, dwindling, ebbing, erosion, let-up (*informal*), meltdown (*informal*), minimization, moderation, petering out, reduction, shrinkage, slackening, slowing down, waning, weakening

lesser inferior, less important, lower, minor, secondary, slighter, subordinate, under-
Antonyms greater, higher, major, primary, superior

lesson 1. class, coaching, instruction, period, schooling, teaching, tutoring 2. assignment, drill, exercise, homework, lecture, practice, reading, recitation, task 3. deterrent, example, exemplar, message, model, moral, precept 4. admonition, censure, chiding, punishment, rebuke, reprimand, reproof, scolding, warning

let[1] *verb* 1. allow, authorize, entitle, give leave, give permission, give the go-ahead (green light, O.K. *or* okay (*informal*)) (*informal*), grant, permit, sanction, suffer (*archaic*), tolerate, warrant 2. hire, lease, rent 3. allow, cause, enable, grant, make, permit

let[2] *noun* constraint, hindrance, impediment, interference, obstacle, obstruction, prohibition, restriction

letdown anticlimax, bitter pill, blow, comedown (*informal*), disappointment, disgruntlement, disillusionment, frustration, setback, washout (*informal*), whammy (*informal, chiefly U.S.*)

let down disappoint, disenchant, disillusion, dissatisfy, fail, fall short, leave in the lurch, leave stranded

lethal baneful, dangerous, deadly, deathly, destructive, devastating, fatal, mortal, murderous, noxious, pernicious, poisonous, virulent
Antonyms harmless, healthy, innocuous, safe, wholesome

lethargic apathetic, comatose, debilitated, drowsy, dull, enervated, heavy, inactive, indifferent, inert, languid, lazy, listless, sleepy, slothful, slow, sluggish, somnolent, stupefied, torpid
Antonyms active, alert, animated, energetic, responsive, spirited, stimulated, vigorous

lethargy apathy, drowsiness, dullness, hebetude (*rare*), inaction, indifference, inertia,

languor, lassitude, listlessness, sleepiness, sloth, slowness, sluggishness, stupor, torpidity, torpor
Antonyms animation, brio, energy, life, liveliness, spirit, verve, vigour, vim, vitality, vivacity, zeal, zest

let in admit, allow to enter, give access to, greet, include, incorporate, receive, take in, welcome

let off 1. detonate, discharge, emit, explode, exude, fire, give off, leak, release 2. absolve, discharge, dispense, excuse, exempt, exonerate, forgive, pardon, release, spare

let on 1. admit, disclose, divulge, give away, let the cat out of the bag (*informal*), make known, reveal, say 2. act, counterfeit, dissemble, dissimulate, feign, make believe, make out, pretend, profess, simulate

let out 1. emit, give vent to, produce 2. discharge, free, let go, liberate, release 3. betray, blow wide open (*slang*), disclose, leak, let fall, let slip, make known, reveal, take the wraps off

letter 1. character, sign, symbol 2. acknowledgment, answer, billet (*archaic*), communication, dispatch, epistle, line, message, missive, note, reply 3. **to the letter** accurately, exactly, literally, precisely, strictly, word for word

Sir, more than kisses, letters mingle souls
John Donne *To Sir Henry Wotton*

All letters, methinks, should be free and easy as one's discourse, not studied as an oration, not made up of hard words like a charm
Dorothy Osborne

I have made this [letter] longer than usual, only because I have not had the time to make it shorter
Blaise Pascal *Lettres Provinciales*

lettered accomplished, cultivated, cultured, educated, erudite, informed, knowledgeable, learned, literate, scholarly, versed, well-educated, well-read

letters belles-lettres, culture, erudition, humanities, learning, literature, scholarship

let-up abatement, break, breathing space, cessation, interval, lessening, lull, pause, recess, remission, respite, slackening

let up abate, decrease, diminish, ease (up), moderate, relax, slacken, stop, subside

levee ceremony, entertainment, gathering, party, reception

level *adjective* 1. as flat as a pancake, consistent, even, flat, horizontal, plain, plane, smooth, uniform 2. aligned, balanced, commensurate, comparable, equal, equivalent, even, flush, in line, neck and neck, on a line, on a par, proportionate 3. calm, equable, even, even-tempered, stable, steady ~*verb* 4. even off *or* out, flatten, make flat, plane, smooth 5. bulldoze, demolish, destroy, devastate, equalize, flatten, knock down, lay low, pull down, raze, smooth, tear down, wreck 6. aim, beam, direct, focus, point, train 7. *informal* be above board, be frank, be honest, be open, be straightforward, be up front (*slang*), come clean (*informal*), keep nothing back ~*noun* 8. altitude, elevation, height, vertical position 9. achievement, degree, grade, position, rank, stage, standard, standing, status 10. bed, floor, layer, storey, stratum, zone 11. flat surface, horizontal, plain, plane 12. **on the level** *informal* above board, fair, genuine, honest, open, sincere, square, straight, straightforward, up front (*slang*)
Antonyms *adjective* (*sense 1*) bumpy, hilly, slanted, tilted, uneven, vertical, warped (*sense 2*) above, below ~*verb* (*sense 5*) build, erect, raise, roughen

level-headed balanced, calm, collected, composed, cool, dependable, even-tempered, reasonable, sane, self-possessed, sensible, steady, together (*slang*), unflappable (*informal*)

lever 1. *noun* bar, crowbar, handle, handspike, jemmy 2. *verb* force, jemmy, move, prise, pry (*U.S.*), purchase, raise

leverage ascendancy, authority, clout (*informal*), influence, pull (*informal*), purchasing power, rank, weight

leviathan behemoth, colossus, hulk, mammoth, monster, Titan, whale

levity buoyancy, facetiousness, fickleness, flightiness, flippancy, frivolity, giddiness, light-heartedness, light-mindedness, silliness, skittishness, triviality
Antonyms earnestness, gravity, seriousness, solemnity

levy *verb* 1. charge, collect, demand, exact, gather, impose, tax 2. call, call up, conscript, mobilize, muster, press, raise, summon ~*noun* 3. assessment, collection, exaction, gathering, imposition 4. assessment, duty, excise, fee, imposition, impost, tariff, tax, toll

lewd bawdy, blue, dirty, impure, indecent, lascivious, libidinous, licentious, loose, lustful, obscene, pornographic, profligate, salacious, smutty, unchaste, vile, vulgar, wanton, wicked, X-rated (*informal*)

lewdness bawdiness, carnality, crudity, debauchery, depravity, impurity, indecency, lasciviousness, lechery, licentiousness, lubricity, obscenity, pornography, profligacy, salaciousness, smut, smuttiness, unchastity, vulgarity, wantonness

lexicon dictionary, glossary, vocabulary, wordbook, word list

liabilities accounts payable, debts, expenditure, obligations

liability 1. accountability, answerability, culpability, duty, obligation, onus, responsibility 2. arrear, debit, debt, indebtedness, obligation 3. albatross, burden, disadvantage, drag, drawback, encumbrance, handicap, hindrance, impediment, inconvenience, millstone, minus (*informal*), nuisance 4. likelihood, probability, proneness, susceptibility, tendency

liable 1. accountable, amenable, answerable, bound, chargeable, obligated, responsible 2. exposed, open, subject, susceptible, vulnerable 3. apt, disposed, inclined, likely, prone, tending 4. **render oneself liable to** expose oneself to, incur, lay oneself open to, run the risk of

liaise communicate, connect, hook up, interchange, intermediate, keep contact, link, mediate

liaison 1. communication, connection, contact, go-between, hook-up, interchange, intermediary 2. affair, amour, entanglement, illicit romance, intrigue, love affair, romance

liar fabricator, falsifier, fibber, perjurer, prevaricator, storyteller (*informal*)

A liar should have a good memory
Quintilian *Institutio Oratoria*

libel 1. *noun* aspersion, calumny, defamation, denigration, obloquy, slander, smear, vituperation 2. *verb* blacken, calumniate, defame, derogate, drag (someone's) name through the mud, malign, revile, slander, slur, smear, traduce, vilify

libellous aspersive, calumniatory, calumnious, defamatory, derogatory, false, injurious, malicious, maligning, scurrilous, slanderous, traducing, untrue, vilifying, vituperative

liberal 1. advanced, humanistic, latitudinarian, libertarian, politically correct *or* PC, progressive, radical, reformist, right-on (*informal*) 2. altruistic, beneficent, bounteous, bountiful, charitable, free-handed, generous, kind, open-handed, open-hearted, prodigal, unstinting 3. advanced, broad-minded, catholic, enlightened, high-minded, humanitarian, indulgent, magnanimous, permissive, politically correct *or* PC, right-on (*informal*), tolerant, unbiased, unbigoted, unprejudiced 4. abundant, ample, bountiful, copious, handsome, lavish, munificent, plentiful, profuse, rich 5. broad, flexible, free, general, inexact, lenient, loose, not close, not literal, not strict
Antonyms biased, bigoted, cheap, conservative, fixed, inadequate, inflexible, intolerant, left-wing, limited, literal, prejudiced, reactionary, right-wing, skimpy, small, stingy, strict

conservative: a statesman who is enamoured of existing evils, as distinguished from the Liberal, who wishes to replace them with others
Ambrose Bierce *The Devil's Dictionary*

liberalism freethinking, humanitarianism, latitudinarianism, libertarianism, progressivism, radicalism

liberality 1. altruism, beneficence, benevolence, bounty, charity, free-handedness, generosity, kindness, largess *or* largesse, munificence, open-handedness, philanthropy 2. breadth, broad-mindedness, candour, catholicity, impartiality, latitude, liberalism, libertarianism, magnanimity, permissiveness, progressivism, toleration

liberalize ameliorate, broaden, ease, expand, extend, loosen, mitigate, moderate, modify, relax, slacken, soften, stretch

liberate deliver, discharge, disenthral, emancipate, free, let loose, let out, manumit, redeem, release, rescue, set free
Antonyms confine, detain, immure, imprison, incarcerate, intern, jail, lock up, put away

liberation deliverance, emancipation, enfranchisement, freedom, freeing, liberating, liberty, manumission, redemption, release, unfettering, unshackling

liberator deliverer, emancipator, freer, manumitter, redeemer, rescuer, saviour

libertine 1. *noun* debauchee, lech *or* letch (*informal*), lecher, loose liver, profligate, rake, reprobate, roué, seducer, sensualist, voluptuary, womanizer 2. *adjective* abandoned, corrupt, debauched, decadent, degenerate, depraved, dissolute, immoral, licentious, profligate, rakish, reprobate, voluptuous, wanton

liberty 1. autonomy, emancipation, freedom, immunity, independence, liberation, release, self-determination, sovereignty 2. authorization, blank cheque, carte blanche, dispensation, exemption, franchise, freedom, leave, licence, permission, prerogative, privilege, right, sanction 3. *often plural* disrespect, familiarity, forwardness, impertinence, impropriety, impudence, insolence, overfamiliarity, presumption, presumptuousness 4. **at liberty** free, not confined, on the loose, unlimited, unoccupied, unrestricted
Antonyms captivity, compulsion, constraint, duress, enslavement, imprisonment, restraint, restriction, slavery, tyranny

I know not what course others may take; but as for me, give me liberty, or give me death!
Patrick Henry

Liberty is liberty, not equality or fairness or justice or human happiness or a quiet conscience
Isaiah Berlin *Two Concepts of Liberty*

The tree of liberty must be refreshed from time to time with the blood of patriots and tyrants. It is its natural manure
Thomas Jefferson

Liberty is precious - so precious that it must be rationed

Lenin

Liberty means responsibility. That is why most men dread it

George Bernard Shaw *Man and Superman*

Liberty too must be limited in order to be possessed

Edmund Burke *Letter to the Sheriffs of Bristol*

The liberty of the individual must be thus far limited; he must not make himself a nuisance to other people

John Stuart Mill *On Liberty*

libidinous carnal, concupiscent, debauched, impure, incontinent, lascivious, lecherous, lickerish (*archaic*), loose, lustful, prurient, randy (*informal, chiefly Brit.*), ruttish, salacious, sensual, unchaste, wanton, wicked

libretto book, lines, lyrics, script, words

licence *noun* **1.** authority, authorization, blank cheque, carte blanche, certificate, charter, dispensation, entitlement, exemption, immunity, leave, liberty, permission, permit, privilege, right, warrant **2.** a free hand, freedom, independence, latitude, liberty, self-determination **3.** abandon, anarchy, disorder, excess, immoderation, impropriety, indulgence, irresponsibility, lawlessness, laxity, profligacy, unruliness

Antonyms constraint, denial, moderation, prohibition, restraint, restriction, strictness

license *verb* accredit, allow, authorize, certify, commission, empower, enable, entitle, give a blank cheque to, permit, sanction, warrant

Antonyms ban, debar, disallow, forbid, outlaw, prohibit, proscribe, rule out, veto

licentious abandoned, debauched, disorderly, dissolute, immoral, impure, lascivious, lax, lewd, libertine, libidinous, lubricious, lubricous, lustful, profligate, promiscuous, sensual, uncontrollable, uncontrolled, uncurbed, unruly, wanton

Antonyms chaste, law-abiding, lawful, moral, principled, proper, scrupulous, virtuous

licentiousness abandon, debauchery, dissipation, dissoluteness, lechery, lewdness, libertinism, libidinousness, lubricity, lust, lustfulness, profligacy, promiscuity, prurience, salaciousness, salacity, wantonness

lick *verb* **1.** brush, lap, taste, tongue, touch, wash **2.** *of flames* dart, flick, flicker, ignite, kindle, play over, ripple, touch **3.** *informal* **a.** blow out of the water (*slang*), clobber (*slang*), defeat, master, overcome, rout, run rings around (*informal*), stuff (*slang*), tank (*slang*), trounce, undo, vanquish, wipe the floor with (*informal*), **b.** beat, clobber (*slang*), flog, lambast(e), slap, spank, strike, thrash, wallop (*informal*), **c.** beat, best, blow out of the water (*slang*), clobber (*slang*), excel, outdo, outstrip, run rings around (*informal*), surpass, tank (*slang*), top, wipe the floor with (*informal*) ~*noun* **4.** bit, brush, dab, little, sample, speck, stroke, taste, touch **5.** *informal* clip (*informal*), pace, rate, speed

licking 1. beating, drubbing, flogging, hiding (*informal*), spanking, tanning (*slang*), thrashing, whipping **2.** beating, defeat, drubbing, pasting (*slang*), trouncing

lie[1] **1.** *verb* dissimulate, equivocate, fabricate, falsify, fib, forswear oneself, invent, misrepresent, perjure, prevaricate, tell a lie, tell untruths **2.** *noun* deceit, fabrication, falsehood, falsification, falsity, fib, fiction, invention, mendacity, pork pie (*Brit. slang*), porky (*Brit. slang*), prevarication, untruth, white lie

There is no worse lie than a truth misunderstood by those who hear it

William James *Varieties of Religious Experience*

Whoever would lie usefully should lie seldom

Lord Hervey *Memoirs of the Reign of George II*

The lie in the soul is a true lie

Benjamin Jowett *Introduction to his translation of Plato's Republic*

I cannot tell a lie

George Washington

The broad mass of a nation.... will more easily fall victim to a big lie than to a small one

Adolf Hitler *Mein Kampf*

Every word she writes is a lie, including "and" and "the"

Mary McCarthy (on Lillian Hellman)

It contains a misleading impression, not a lie. It was being economical with the truth

Sir Robert Armstrong (during the "Spycatcher" trial)

lie[2] *verb* **1.** be prone, be prostrate, be recumbent, be supine, couch, loll, lounge, recline, repose, rest, sprawl, stretch out **2.** be, be buried, be found, be interred, be located, belong, be placed, be situated, exist, extend, remain **3.** *usually with* **on** *or* **upon** burden, oppress, press, rest, weigh **4.** *usually with* **in** be present, consist, dwell, exist, inhere, pertain **5. lie low** conceal oneself, go to earth, go underground, hide, hide away, hide out, hole up, keep a low profile, keep out of sight, lurk, skulk, take cover

liege chieftain, feudal lord, master, overlord, seigneur, sovereign, superior, suzerain

lieu place, room, stead

life 1. animation, being, breath, entity, growth, sentience, viability, vitality **2.** being, career, continuance, course, duration, existence, lifetime, span, time **3.** human, human being, individual, mortal, person, soul **4.** autobiography, biography, career, confessions, history, life story, memoirs, story **5.** behaviour, conduct, life style, way of life **6.** the human con~

dition, the school of hard knocks, the times, the world, this mortal coil, trials and tribulations, vicissitudes **7**. activity, animation, brio, energy, get-up-and-go (*informal*), go (*informal*), high spirits, liveliness, oomph (*informal*), pep, sparkle, spirit, verve, vigour, vitality, vivacity, zest **8**. animating spirit, *élan vital*, essence, heart, lifeblood, soul, spirit, vital spark **9**. creatures, living beings, living things, organisms, wildlife **10**. **come to life** awaken, become animate, revive, rouse, show signs of life **11**. **for dear life** *informal* desperately, for all one is worth, intensely, quickly, urgently, vigorously

Oh, what a day-to-day business life is
Jules Laforgue *Complainte sur certains ennuis*

Believe me! The secret of reaping the greatest fruitfulness and the greatest enjoyment from life is to live dangerously!
Friedrich Nietzsche *Die fröhliche Wissenschaft*

Life is just one damned thing after another
Frank Ward O'Malley

Lift not the painted veil which those who live
Call Life
Percy Bysshe Shelley *Sonnet*

The unexamined life is not worth living
Socrates

It's a great life if you don't weaken
John Buchan *Mr. Standfast*

Life is one long process of getting tired
Samuel Butler *Notebooks*

Life well spent is long
Leonardo da Vinci

Anything for a quiet life
Thomas Middleton

Life is a foreign language: all men mispronounce it
Christopher Morley *Thunder on the Left*

Man is born to live, not to prepare for life
Boris Pasternak *Doctor Zhivago*

There is no wealth but life
John Ruskin *Unto this Last*

Human life begins on the far side of despair
Jean-Paul Sartre *Les Mouches*

Life would be very pleasant if it were not for its enjoyments
R.S. Surtees *Mr. Facey Romford's Hounds*

Every man regards his own life as the New Year's Eve of time
Jean Paul Richter *Levana*

Life is a theatre in which the worst people often have the best seats
attributed to Aristonymus

Life is long to the miserable, but short to the happy
Publilius Syrus *Sententiae*

Life's but a walking shadow, a poor player
That struts and frets his hour upon the stage,
And then is heard no more
William Shakespeare *Macbeth*

Life isn't all beer and skittles
Thomas Hughes *Tom Brown's Schooldays*

Life is far too important a thing ever to talk seriously about
Oscar Wilde *Lady Windermere's Fan*

Life can only be understood backwards; but it must be lived forwards
Søren Kierkegaard

The meaning of life is that it stops
Franz Kafka

We are born crying, live complaining, and die disappointed
Thomas Fuller *Gnomologia*

It is the essence of life that it exists for its own sake
A.N. Whitehead *Nature and Life*

This world is a comedy to those that think, and a tragedy to those that feel
Horace Walpole

Every man desires to live long; but no man would be old
Jonathan Swift

Old and young, we are all on our last cruise
Robert Louis Stevenson *Virginibus Puerisque*

Life exists in the universe only because the carbon atom possesses certain exceptional qualities
James Jeans *The Mysterious Universe*

Human life is everywhere a state in which much is to be endured, and little to be enjoyed
Dr. Johnson *Rasselas*

Life is a sexually transmitted disease
Anon.

life: a spiritual pickle preserving the body from decay
Ambrose Bierce *The Devil's Dictionary*

'Tis all a chequer-board of nights and days
Where Destiny with men for pieces plays;
Hither and thither moves, and mates, and slays,
And one by one back in the closet lays
Edward Fitzgerald *The Rubáiyát of Omar Khayyám*

Life is real! Life is earnest!
And the grave is not its goal;
Dust thou art, to dust returnest,
Was not spoken of the soul
Henry Wadsworth Longfellow *A Psalm of Life*

One crowded hour of glorious life
Is worth an age without a name
Thomas Osbert Mordaunt

Some people say that life is the thing, but I prefer reading
Logan Pearsall Smith *Afterthoughts*

Life begins at forty

lifeblood animating force, driving force, essence, guts (*informal*), heart, inspiration, life, stimulus, vital spark

lifeless 1. cold, dead, deceased, defunct, extinct, inanimate, inert 2. bare, barren, desert, empty, sterile, uninhabited, unproductive, waste 3. cold, colourless, dull, flat, heavy, hollow, lacklustre, lethargic, listless, passive, pointless, slow, sluggish, spent, spiritless, static, stiff, torpid, wooden 4. comatose, dead to the world (*informal*), in a faint, inert, insensate, insensible, out cold, out for six, unconscious
Antonyms active, alive, alive and kicking, animate, animated, live, lively, living, spirited, vital

lifelike authentic, exact, faithful, graphic, natural, photographic, real, realistic, true-to-life, undistorted, vivid

lifelong constant, deep-rooted, enduring, for all one's life, for life, lasting, lifetime, long-lasting, long-standing, perennial, permanent, persistent

lifetime all one's born days, career, course, day(s), existence, life span, one's natural life, period, span, time

life work business, calling, career, interest, mission, occupation, profession, purpose, pursuit, vocation, work

lift *verb* 1. bear aloft, buoy up, draw up, elevate, heft (*informal*), hoist, pick up, raise, raise high, rear, upheave, uplift, upraise 2. advance, ameliorate, boost, dignify, elevate, enhance, exalt, improve, promote, raise, upgrade 3. annul, cancel, countermand, end, relax, remove, rescind, revoke, stop, terminate 4. ascend, be dispelled, climb, disappear, disperse, dissipate, mount, rise, vanish 5. *informal* appropriate, blag (*slang*), cabbage (*Brit. slang*), copy, crib (*informal*), half-inch (*old-fashioned slang*), nick (*slang, chiefly Brit.*), pilfer, pinch (*informal*), pirate, plagiarize, pocket, purloin, steal, take, thieve *~noun* 6. car ride, drive, ride, run, transport 7. boost, encouragement, fillip, pick-me-up, reassurance, shot in the arm (*informal*), uplift 8. elevator (*chiefly U.S.*)
Antonyms *verb* (*sense 1*) dash, depress, drop, hang, lower (*sense 3*) establish, impose (*sense 4*) descend, drop, fall, lower *~noun* (*sense 7*) blow, letdown

ligature band, bandage, binding, bond, connection, ligament, link, tie

light[1] *noun* 1. blaze, brightness, brilliance, effulgence, flash, glare, gleam, glint, glow, illumination, incandescence, lambency, luminescence, luminosity, lustre, phosphorescence, radiance, ray, refulgence, scintillation, shine, sparkle 2. beacon, bulb, candle, flare, lamp, lantern, lighthouse, star, taper, torch, windowpane 3. broad day, cockcrow, dawn, daybreak, daylight, daytime, morn (*poetic*), morning, sun, sunbeam, sunrise, sunshine 4. *figurative* angle, approach, aspect, attitude, context, interpretation, point of view, slant, vantage point, viewpoint 5. awareness, comprehension, elucidation, explanation, illustration, information, insight, knowledge, understanding 6. example, exemplar, guiding light, model, paragon, shining example 7. flame, lighter, match 8. **bring to light** disclose, discover, expose, reveal, show, uncover, unearth, unveil 9. **come to light** appear, be disclosed, be discovered, be revealed, come out, transpire, turn up 10. **in (the) light of** bearing in mind, because of, considering, in view of, taking into account, with knowledge of 11. **shed** *or* **throw light on** clarify, clear up, elucidate, explain, simplify *~adjective* 12. aglow, bright, brilliant, glowing, illuminated, luminous, lustrous, shining, sunny, well-lighted, well-lit 13. bleached, blond, faded, fair, light-hued, light-toned, pale, pastel *~verb* 14. fire, ignite, inflame, kindle, set a match to, torch 15. brighten, clarify, floodlight, flood with light, illuminate, illumine, irradiate, lighten, light up, put on, switch on, turn on 16. animate, brighten, cheer, irradiate, lighten
Antonyms *noun* cloud, dark, darkness, dusk, mystery, obscurity, shade, shadow *~adjective* dark, deep, dim, dusky, gloomy *~verb* cloud, darken, douse, dull, extinguish, put out, quench

> *And God said, Let there be light; and there was light*
>
> Bible: Genesis

light[2] *adjective* 1. airy, buoyant, delicate, easy, flimsy, imponderous, insubstantial, lightsome, lightweight, portable, slight, underweight 2. faint, gentle, indistinct, mild, moderate, slight, soft, weak 3. inconsequential, inconsiderable, insignificant, minute, scanty, slight, small, thin, tiny, trifling, trivial, unsubstantial, wee 4. cushy (*informal*), easy, effortless, manageable, moderate, simple, undemanding, unexacting, untaxing 5. agile, airy, graceful, light-footed, lithe, nimble, sprightly, sylphlike 6. amusing, diverting, entertaining, frivolous, funny, gay, humorous, light-hearted, pleasing, superficial, trifling, trivial, witty 7. airy, animated, blithe, carefree, cheerful, cheery, fickle, frivolous, gay, lively, merry, sunny 8. dizzy, giddy, light-headed, reeling, unsteady, volatile 9. digestible, frugal, modest, not heavy, not rich, restricted, small 10. crumbly, friable, loose, porous, sandy, spongy *~verb* 11. alight, land, perch, settle 12. *with* **on** *or* **upon** chance, come across, discover, encounter, find, happen upon, hit upon, stumble on
Antonyms *adjective* burdensome, clumsy, deep, forceful, hard, heavy, intense, profound, rich, serious, sombre, strenuous, strong, substantial, weighty

lighten[1] *verb* become light, brighten, flash, gleam, illuminate, irradiate, light up, make bright, shine

lighten[2] *verb* **1.** disburden, ease, make lighter, reduce in weight, unload **2.** allay, alleviate, ameliorate, assuage, ease, facilitate, lessen, mitigate, reduce, relieve **3.** brighten, buoy up, cheer, elate, encourage, gladden, hearten, inspire, lift, perk up, revive
Antonyms (*sense 1*) burden, encumber, handicap (*sense 2*) aggravate, heighten, increase, intensify, make worse, worsen (*sense 3*) depress, oppress, sadden, weigh down

light-fingered crafty, crooked (*informal*), dishonest, furtive, pilfering, pinching (*informal*), shifty, sly, stealing, thieving, underhand

light-footed agile, buoyant, graceful, lithe, nimble, sprightly, spry, swift, tripping, winged

light-headed **1.** bird-brained (*informal*), featherbrained, fickle, flighty, flippant, foolish, frivolous, giddy, inane, rattlebrained (*slang*), shallow, silly, superficial, trifling **2.** delirious, dizzy, faint, giddy, hazy, vertiginous, woozy (*informal*)

light-hearted blithe, blithesome (*literary*), bright, carefree, cheerful, chirpy (*informal*), effervescent, frolicsome, gay, genial, glad, gleeful, happy-go-lucky, insouciant, jocund, jolly, jovial, joyful, joyous, ludic (*literary*), merry, playful, sunny, untroubled, upbeat (*informal*)
Antonyms cheerless, dejected, depressed, despondent, gloomy, heavy-hearted, low, melancholy, morose, sad

light into assail, attack, belabour, clobber (*slang*), flail, flay, go at hammer and tongs, lambast(e), lay into (*informal*), let fly at, pitch into (*informal*), sail into (*informal*), set about, tear into (*informal*)

lightless caliginous (*archaic*), dark, dim, dusky, gloomy, inky, jet black, murky, pitch-black, pitch-dark, pitchy, Stygian, sunless, tenebrous, unilluminated, unlighted, unlit

lightly **1.** airily, delicately, faintly, gently, gingerly, slightly, softly, timidly **2.** moderately, sparingly, sparsely, thinly **3.** easily, effortlessly, readily, simply **4.** breezily, carelessly, flippantly, frivolously, heedlessly, indifferently, slightingly, thoughtlessly
Antonyms abundantly, arduously, awkwardly, carefully, earnestly, firmly, forcefully, heavily, ponderously, seriously, slowly, thickly, with difficulty

light out abscond, depart, do a bunk (*Brit. slang*), do a runner (*slang*), escape, fly the coop (*U.S. & Canad. informal*), make off, quit, run away, scarper (*Brit. slang*), skedaddle (*informal*), take a powder (*U.S. & Canad. slang*), take it on the lam (*U.S. & Canad. slang*)

lightweight *adjective* inconsequential, insignificant, nickel-and-dime (*U.S. slang*), of no account, paltry, petty, slight, trifling, trivial, unimportant, wanky (*taboo slang*), worthless
Antonyms important, momentous, serious, significant, substantial, weighty

likable, likeable agreeable, amiable, appealing, attractive, charming, engaging, friendly, genial, nice, pleasant, pleasing, sympathetic, winning, winsome

like[1] **1.** *adjective* akin, alike, allied, analogous, approximating, cognate, corresponding, equivalent, identical, parallel, relating, resembling, same, similar **2.** *noun* counterpart, equal, fellow, match, parallel, twin
Antonyms *adjective* contrasted, different, dissimilar, divergent, diverse, opposite, unlike ~*noun* opposite
Like breeds like

like[2] *verb* **1.** adore (*informal*), be fond of, be keen on, be partial to, delight in, dig (*slang*), enjoy, go for, love, relish, revel in **2.** admire, appreciate, approve, cherish, esteem, hold dear, prize, take a shine to (*informal*), take to **3.** care to, choose, choose to, desire, fancy, feel inclined, prefer, select, want, wish ~*noun* **4.** *usually plural* cup of tea (*informal*), favourite, liking, partiality, predilection, preference
Antonyms *verb* abominate, despise, detest, dislike, hate, loathe

likelihood chance, good chance, liability, likeliness, possibility, probability, prospect, reasonableness, strong possibility

likely *adjective* **1.** anticipated, apt, disposed, expected, in a fair way, inclined, liable, on the cards, possible, probable, prone, tending, to be expected **2. be** *or* **seem likely** be in the running for, bid fair, incline towards, promise, stand a good chance, suggest, tend **3.** believable, credible, feasible, plausible, reasonable, verisimilar **4.** acceptable, agreeable, appropriate, befitting, fit, pleasing, proper, qualified, suitable **5.** fair, favourite, hopeful, odds-on, promising, up-and-coming ~*adverb* **6.** doubtlessly, in all probability, like as not (*informal*), like enough (*informal*), no doubt, presumably, probably

like-minded agreeing, compatible, *en rapport*, harmonious, in accord, in harmony, of one mind, of the same mind, unanimous

liken compare, equate, juxtapose, match, mention in the same breath, parallel, relate, set beside

likeness **1.** affinity, correspondence, resemblance, similarity, similitude **2.** copy, counterpart, delineation, depiction, effigy, facsimile, image, model, photograph, picture, portrait, replica, representation, reproduction, study **3.** appearance, form, guise, semblance

likewise **1.** also, besides, further, furthermore, in addition, moreover, too **2.** in like manner, in the same way, similarly

liking affection, affinity, appreciation, attraction, bent, bias, desire, fondness, inclination, love, partiality, penchant, predilection, preference, proneness, propensity, soft spot, stomach, taste, tendency, thirst, weakness
Antonyms abhorrence, aversion, dislike, hatred, loathing, repugnance

Lilliputian **1.** *noun* dwarf, homunculus, hop-o'-my-thumb, manikin, midget, munchkin (*informal, chiefly U.S.*), pygmy *or* pigmy, Tom Thumb **2.** *adjective* baby, bantam, diminutive, dwarf, little, mini, miniature, minuscule, petite, pocket-sized, pygmy *or* pigmy, small, teensy-weensy, teeny, teeny-weeny, tiny, wee

lilt beat, cadence, rhythm, sway, swing

lily-livered abject, boneless, chicken (*slang*), chicken-hearted, chickenshit (*U.S. slang*), cowardly, craven, faint-hearted, fearful, gutless (*informal*), pusillanimous, scared, spineless, timid, timorous, yellow (*informal*), yellow-bellied (*slang*)

lily-white **1.** milk-white, pure white, white, white as snow, white-skinned **2.** *informal* chaste, impeccable, innocent, irreproachable, pure, spotless, unsullied, untainted, untarnished, virgin, virtuous

limb **1.** appendage, arm, extension, extremity, leg, member, part, wing **2.** bough, branch, offshoot, projection, spur

limber *adjective* **1.** elastic, flexible, plastic, pliable, pliant, supple **2.** agile, graceful, lissom(e), lithe, loose-jointed, loose-limbed, supple ~*verb* **3.** *with* **up** exercise, get ready, loosen up, prepare, warm up

limelight attention, celebrity, fame, glare of publicity, prominence, public eye, publicity, public notice, recognition, stardom, the spotlight

limit *noun* **1.** bound, breaking point, cutoff point, deadline, end, end point, furthest bound, greatest extent, termination, the bitter end, ultimate, utmost **2.** *often plural* border, boundary, confines, edge, end, extent, frontier, pale, perimeter, periphery, precinct **3.** ceiling, check, curb, limitation, maximum, obstruction, restraint, restriction **4.** **the limit** *informal* enough, it (*informal*), the end, the last straw ~*verb* **5.** bound, check, circumscribe, confine, curb, delimit, demarcate, fix, hem in, hinder, ration, restrain, restrict, specify, straiten

limitation block, check, condition, constraint, control, curb, disadvantage, drawback, impediment, obstruction, qualification, reservation, restraint, restriction, snag

limited **1.** bounded, checked, circumscribed, confined, constrained, controlled, curbed, defined, finite, fixed, hampered, hemmed in, restricted **2.** cramped, diminished, inadequate, insufficient, minimal, narrow, reduced, restricted, scant, short, unsatisfactory
Antonyms boundless, limitless, unlimited, unrestricted

limitless boundless, countless, endless, illimitable, immeasurable, immense, inexhaustible, infinite, measureless, never-ending, numberless, unbounded, uncalculable, undefined, unending, unlimited, untold, vast

limp[1] **1.** *verb* falter, halt (*archaic*), hobble, hop, shamble, shuffle **2.** *noun* hobble, lameness

limp[2] *adjective* **1.** drooping, flabby, flaccid, flexible, floppy, lax, limber, loose, pliable, relaxed, slack, soft **2.** debilitated, enervated, exhausted, lethargic, spent, tired, weak, worn out
Antonyms (*sense 1*) firm, hard, rigid, solid, stiff, taut, tense, unyielding (*sense 2*) hardy, powerful, robust, strong, sturdy, tough

limpid **1.** bright, clear, crystal-clear, crystalline, pellucid, pure, translucent, transparent **2.** clear, comprehensible, intelligible, lucid, perspicuous, unambiguous **3.** calm, peaceful, placid, quiet, serene, still, tranquil, unruffled, untroubled

limp-wristed effete, feeble, impotent, inadequate, ineffective, ineffectual, inept, useless, weak

linchpin chief, co-ordinator, cornerstone, director, driving force, principal

line[1] *noun* **1.** band, bar, channel, dash, groove, mark, rule, score, scratch, streak, stripe, stroke, underline **2.** crease, crow's foot, furrow, mark, wrinkle **3.** border, borderline, boundary, demarcation, edge, frontier, limit, mark **4.** configuration, contour, features, figure, outline, profile, silhouette **5.** cable, cord, filament, rope, strand, string, thread, wire, wisp **6.** axis, course, direction, path, route, track, trajectory **7.** approach, avenue, belief, course, course of action, ideology, method, policy, position, practice, procedure, scheme, system **8.** activity, area, bag (*slang*), business, calling, department, employment, field, forte, interest, job, occupation, profession, province, pursuit, specialization, trade, vocation **9.** column, crocodile (*Brit.*), file, procession, queue, rank, row, sequence, series **10.** ancestry, breed, family, lineage, race, stock, strain, succession **11.** card, letter, message, note, postcard, report, word **12.** clue, hint, indication, information, lead **13.** *Military* disposition, firing line, formation, front, front line, position, trenches **14.** **draw the line** lay down the law, object, prohibit, put one's foot down, restrict, set a limit **15.** **in line** **a.** in alignment, in a row, plumb, straight, true **b.** in accord, in agree~

ment, in conformity, in harmony, in step **16. in line for** a candidate for, being considered for, due for, in the running for, next in succession to, on the short list for *~verb* **17.** crease, cut, draw; furrow, inscribe, mark, rule, score, trace, underline **18.** border, bound, edge, fringe, rank, rim, skirt, verge

line² *verb* ceil, cover, face, fill, interline

lineage ancestry, birth, breed, descendants, descent, extraction, family, forebears, forefathers, genealogy, heredity, house, line, offspring, pedigree, progeny, stirps, stock, succession

lineaments configuration, countenance, face, features, line, outline, phiz *or* phizog (*slang, chiefly Brit.*), physiognomy, trait, visage

lined 1. feint, ruled **2.** furrowed, wizened, worn, wrinkled

lines 1. appearance, configuration, contour, cut, outline, shape, style **2.** convention, example, model, pattern, plan, principle, procedure **3.** part, script, words

line-up arrangement, array, row, selection, team

line up 1. fall in, form ranks, queue up **2.** assemble, come up with, lay on, obtain, organize, prepare, procure, produce, secure **3.** align, arrange, array, marshal, order, range, regiment, sequence, straighten

linger 1. hang around, hang in the air, loiter, remain, stay, stop, tarry, wait **2.** dally, dawdle, delay, drag one's feet *or* heels, idle, lag, procrastinate, take one's time **3.** cling to life, die slowly, hang on, last, survive **4.** abide, continue, endure, persist, remain, stay

lingering dragging, long-drawn-out, persistent, protracted, remaining, slow

lingo argot, cant, dialect, idiom, jargon, language, patois, patter, speech, talk, tongue, vernacular

liniment balm, balsam, cream, embrocation, emollient, lotion, ointment, salve, unguent

link *noun* **1.** component, constituent, division, element, member, part, piece **2.** affiliation, affinity, association, attachment, bond, connection, joint, knot, liaison, relationship, tie, tie-up, vinculum *~verb* **3.** attach, bind, connect, couple, fasten, join, tie, unite, yoke **4.** associate, bracket, connect, identify, relate
Antonyms *verb* detach, disconnect, divide, separate, sever, split, sunder

lion *figurative* **1.** brave man, champion, conqueror, fighter, hero, warrior **2.** big name, celeb (*informal*), celebrity, idol, luminary, megastar (*informal*), notable, prodigy, star, superstar, V.I.P., wonder **3. beard the lion in his den** brave, confront, court destruction, defy danger, face, stand up to, tempt providence

lion-hearted bold, brave, courageous, daring, dauntless, heroic, intrepid, resolute, stalwart, valiant, valorous
Antonyms chicken-hearted, chickenshit (*U.S. slang*), cowardly, craven, faint-hearted, gutless (*informal*), lily-livered, pusillanimous, spineless, timorous, wimpish *or* wimpy (*informal*), yellow (*informal*)

lionize acclaim, adulate, aggrandize, celebrate, crack up (*informal*), eulogize, exalt, fête, glorify, hero-worship, honour, idolize, make much of, mob, sing *or* sound the praises of

lip 1. brim, brink, edge, flange, margin, rim **2.** *slang* backchat (*informal*), cheek (*informal*), effrontery, impertinence, insolence, rudeness, sauce (*informal*) **3.** *Music* control, embouchure **4. smack *or* lick one's lips** anticipate, delight in, drool over, enjoy, gloat over, relish, savour, slaver over

liquefaction deliquescence, dissolution, dissolving, fusion, melting, thawing

liquefy deliquesce, dissolve, flux, fuse, liquesce, liquidize, melt, run, thaw

liquid *noun* **1.** fluid, juice, liquor, solution *~adjective* **2.** aqueous, flowing, fluid, liquefied, melted, molten, running, runny, thawed, wet **3.** bright, brilliant, clear, limpid, shining, translucent, transparent **4.** dulcet, fluent, mellifluent, mellifluous, melting, smooth, soft, sweet **5.** *of assets* convertible, negotiable

liquidate 1. clear, discharge, honour, pay, pay off, settle, square **2.** abolish, annul, cancel, dissolve, terminate **3.** cash, convert to cash, realize, sell off, sell up **4.** annihilate, blow away (*slang, chiefly U.S.*), bump off (*slang*), destroy, dispatch, do away with, do in (*slang*), eliminate, exterminate, finish off, get rid of, kill, murder, remove, rub out (*U.S. slang*), silence, take out (*slang*), wipe out (*informal*)

liquor 1. alcohol, booze (*informal*), drink, Dutch courage (*informal*), grog, hard stuff (*informal*), hooch *or* hootch (*informal, chiefly U.S. & Canad.*), intoxicant, juice (*informal*), spirits, strong drink **2.** broth, extract, gravy, infusion, juice, liquid, stock

lissom(e) agile, flexible, graceful, light, limber, lithe, loose-jointed, loose-limbed, nimble, pliable, pliant, supple, willowy

list¹ 1. *noun* catalogue, directory, file, index, inventory, invoice, leet (*Scot.*), listing, record, register, roll, schedule, series, syllabus, tabulation, tally **2.** *verb* bill, book, catalogue, enrol, enter, enumerate, file, index, itemize, note, record, register, schedule, set down, tabulate, write down

list² 1. *verb* cant, careen, heel, heel over, incline, lean, tilt, tip **2.** *noun* cant, leaning, slant, tilt

listen 1. attend, be all ears, be attentive, give ear, hang on (someone's) words, hark, hear, hearken (*archaic*), keep one's ears open, lend an ear, pin back one's ears (*informal*), prick up one's ears 2. concentrate, do as one is told, give heed to, heed, mind, obey, observe, pay attention, take notice

Friends, Romans, countrymen, lend me your ears
William Shakespeare *Julius Caesar*

We have two ears and only one tongue in order that we may hear more and speak less
Diogenes Laertius *Lives of the Philosophers*

listless apathetic, enervated, heavy, impassive, inattentive, indifferent, indolent, inert, languid, languishing, lethargic, lifeless, limp, lymphatic, mopish, sluggish, spiritless, supine, torpid, vacant

Antonyms active, alert, alive and kicking, attentive, energetic, full of beans (*informal*), lively, sparky, spirited, wide-awake

listlessness apathy, enervation, ennui, inattention, indifference, indolence, inertia, languidness, languor, lethargy, lifelessness, sluggishness, spiritlessness, supineness, torpidity

litany 1. invocation, petition, prayer, supplication 2. account, catalogue, enumeration, list, recital, recitation, refrain, repetition, tale

literacy ability, articulacy, articulateness, cultivation, education, knowledge, learning, proficiency, scholarship

literal 1. accurate, close, exact, faithful, strict, verbatim, word for word 2. boring, colourless, down-to-earth, dull, factual, matter-of-fact, prosaic, prosy, unimaginative, uninspired 3. actual, bona fide, genuine, gospel, plain, real, simple, true, unexaggerated, unvarnished

literally actually, exactly, faithfully, plainly, precisely, really, simply, strictly, to the letter, truly, verbatim, word for word

literary bookish, erudite, formal, learned, lettered, literate, scholarly, well-read

literate cultivated, cultured, educated, erudite, informed, knowledgeable, learned, lettered, scholarly, well-informed, well-read

literature 1. belles-lettres, letters, lore, writings, written works 2. brochure, information, leaflet, mailshot, pamphlet

Literature terms

allegory
alliteration
allusion
amphigory *or* amphigouri
Angry Young Men
anti-hero
antinovel
anti-roman
aphorism
archaism
Augustan
bathos
Beat Generation *or* Beats
belles-lettres
belletrist
Bildungsroman
black comedy
Bloomsbury group
bodice-ripper
bombast
bowdlerization
Brechtian
bricolage
Byronic
campus novel
causerie
Celtic Revival
cento
chiller
Ciceronian
classicism
coda
colloquialism
comedy
comedy of manners
commedia dell'arte
conceit
courtly love
cut-up technique
cyberpunk
decadence
deconstruction
dénouement
dialogue
Dickensian
discourse
double entendre
drama
epilogue
epistle
epistolary novel
epitaph
erasure
essay
exegesis
expressionism
fable
faction
fantasy
festschrift
figure of speech
fin de siècle
foreward
Futurism
gloss
Gongorism
Gothic
hagiography
Hellenism
hermeneutics
historical novel
Homeric
Horatian
hudibrastic verse
imagery
interior monologue
intertextuality
invective
Jacobean
Janeite
Johnsonian
journalese
Joycean
Juvenalian
Kafkaesque
kenning
lampoon
Laurentian *or* Lawrentian
legend
literary criticism
littérateur
locus classicus
Lost Generation
magic realism *or* magical realism
maxim
melodrama
metafiction
metalanguage
metaphor
mock-heroic
modernism
motif
myth
mythopoeia
narrative
narrator
naturalism
nom de plume
nouveau roman
novel
novelette
novella
onomatopoeia
oxymoron
palindrome
paraphrase
parody
pastiche
pastoral
pathos
picaresque
plagarism
plot
polemic
pornography
postmodernism
post-structuralism
pot-boiler
realism
Restoration comedy
roman
roman à clef
Romanticism
saga
samizdat
satire
science fiction
sentimental novel

shopping-and-fucking *or* S & F novel
short story
simile
sketch
socialist realism
Spoonerism
story
stream of consciousness
structuralism
Sturm und Drang
subplot
subtext
Surrealism
Swiftian
theme
thesis
tragedy
tragicomedy
trope
verse
vignette

Characters in literature	**Book**	**Author**
Captain Ahab	Moby Dick	Herman Melville
Aladdin	The Arabian Nights' Entertainments	Traditional
Alice	Alice's Adventures in Wonderland, Through the Looking-Glass	Lewis Carroll
Bridget Allworthy	Tom Jones	Henry Fielding
Squire Allworthy	Tom Jones	Henry Fielding
Blanch Amory	Pendennis	William Makepeace Thackeray
Harry Angstrom	Rabbit, Run et al.	John Updike
Artful Dodger	Oliver Twist	Charles Dickens
Jack Aubrey	Master and Commander et al.	Patrick O'Brian
Aunt Polly	Tom Sawyer	Mark Twain
Joe Bagstock	Dombey and Son	Charles Dickens
David Balfour	Kidnapped, Catriona	Robert Louis Stevenson
Mrs. Bardell	The Pickwick Papers	Charles Dickens
Barkis	David Copperfield	Charles Dickens
Jake Barnes	The Sun Also Rises	Ernest Hemingway
Adam Bede	Adam Bede	George Eliot
Seth Bede	Adam Bede	George Eliot
Laura Bell	Pendennis	William Makepeace Thackeray
Elizabeth Bennet	Pride and Prejudice	Jane Austen
Jane Bennet	Pride and Prejudice	Jane Austen
Kitty Bennet	Pride and Prejudice	Jane Austen
Lydia Bennet	Pride and Prejudice	Jane Austen
Mary Bennet	Pride and Prejudice	Jane Austen
Mr. Bennet	Pride and Prejudice	Jane Austen
Mrs. Bennet	Pride and Prejudice	Jane Austen
Edmund Bertram	Mansfield Park	Jane Austen
Julia Bertram	Mansfield Park	Jane Austen
Lady Bertram	Mansfield Park	Jane Austen
Maria Bertram	Mansfield Park	Jane Austen
Sir Thomas Bertram	Mansfield Park	Jane Austen
Tom Bertram	Mansfield Park	Jane Austen
Biddy	Great Expectations	Charles Dickens
Charles Bingley	Pride and Prejudice	Jane Austen
Stephen Blackpool	Hard Times	Charles Dickens
Anthony Blanche	Brideshead Revisited	Evelyn Waugh
Leopold Bloom	Ulysses	James Joyce
Molly Bloom	Ulysses	James Joyce
Mr. Boffin	Our Mutual Friend	Charles Dickens
Mrs. Boffin	Our Mutual Friend	Charles Dickens
Farmer Boldwood	Far from the Madding Crowd	Thomas Hardy
Josiah Bounderby	Hard Times	Charles Dickens
Madeline Bray	Nicholas Nickleby	Charles Dickens
Alan Breck	Kidnapped, Catriona	Robert Louis Stevenson
Sue Bridehead	Jude the Obscure	Thomas Hardy
Miss Briggs	Vanity Fair	William Makepeace Thackeray
Dorothea Brooke	Middlemarch	George Eliot
Mr. Brooke	Middlemarch	George Eliot
Mr. Brownlow	Oliver Twist	Charles Dickens

Daisy Buchanan	The Great Gatsby	F. Scott Fitzgerald
Rosa Bud	Edwin Drood	Charles Dickens
Billy Budd	Billy Budd, Foretopman	Herman Melville
Mr. Bulstrode	Middlemarch	George Eliot
Bumble	Oliver Twist	Charles Dickens
Mrs. Cadwallader	Middlemarch	George Eliot
Carker	Dombey and Son	Charles Dickens
Richard Carstone	Bleak House	Charles Dickens
Sydney Carton	A Tale of Two Cities	Charles Dickens
Mr. Casaubon	Middlemarch	George Eliot
Casby	Little Dorrit	Charles Dickens
Flora Casby	Little Dorrit	Charles Dickens
Dunstan Cass	Silas Marner	George Eliot
Godfrey Cass	Silas Marner	George Eliot
Lady Castlewood	Henry Esmond	William Makepeace Thackeray
Lord Castlewood	Henry Esmond	William Makepeace Thackeray
Holden Caulfield	The Catcher in the Rye	J. D. Salinger
Chadband	Bleak House	Charles Dickens
Constance Chatterley	Lady Chatterley's Lover	D. H. Lawrence
The Cheeryble Brothers	Nicholas Nickleby	Charles Dickens
Edward Chester	Barnaby Rudge	Charles Dickens
Sir James Chettam	Middlemarch	George Eliot
Chuffey	Martin Chuzzlewit	Charles Dickens
Frank Churchill	Emma	Jane Austen
Jonas Chuzzlewit	Martin Chuzzlewit	Charles Dickens
Martin Chuzzlewit	Martin Chuzzlewit	Charles Dickens
Ada Clare	Bleak House	Charles Dickens
Angel Clare	Tess of the D'Urbervilles	Thomas Hardy
Arthur Clennam	Little Dorrit	Charles Dickens
Humphry Clinker	Humphry Clinker	Tobias Smollett
William Collins	Pride and Prejudice	Jane Austen
Benjy Compson	The Sound and the Fury	William Faulkner
David Copperfield	David Copperfield	Charles Dickens
Emily Costigan	Pendennis	William Makepeace Thackeray
Bob Cratchit	A Christmas Carol	Charles Dickens
Henry Crawford	Mansfield Park	Jane Austen
Mary Crawford	Mansfield Park	Jane Austen
Bute Crawley	Vanity Fair	William Makepeace Thackeray
Miss Crawley	Vanity Fair	William Makepeace Thackeray
Mrs. Bute Crawley	Vanity Fair	William Makepeace Thackeray
Pitt Crawley	Vanity Fair	William Makepeace Thackeray
Rawdon Crawley	Vanity Fair	William Makepeace Thackeray
Sir Pitt Crawley	Vanity Fair	William Makepeace Thackeray
Septimus Crisparkle	Edwin Drood	Charles Dickens
Vincent Crummles	Nicholas Nickleby	Charles Dickens
Jerry Cruncher	A Tale of Two Cities	Charles Dickens
Robinson Crusoe	Robinson Crusoe	Daniel Defoe
Captain Cuttle	Dombey and Son	Charles Dickens
Sebastian Dangerfield	The Ginger Man	J. P. Donleavy
Fitzwilliam Darcy	Pride and Prejudice	Jane Austen
Charles Darnay	A Tale of Two Cities	Charles Dickens
Elinor Dashwood	Sense and Sensibility	Jane Austen
John Dashwood	Sense and Sensibility	Jane Austen
Margaret Dashwood	Sense and Sensibility	Jane Austen

Marianne Dashwood	Sense and Sensibility	Jane Austen
Mrs. Henry Dashwood	Sense and Sensibility	Jane Austen
Dick Datchery	Edwin Drood	Charles Dickens
Fancy Day	Under The Greenwood Tree	Thomas Hardy
Lady Catherine de Bourgh	Pride and Prejudice	Jane Austen
Stephen Dedalus	A Portrait of the Artist as a Young Man, Ulysses	James Joyce
Sir Leicester Dedlock	Bleak House	Charles Dickens
Lady Dedlock	Bleak House	Charles Dickens
Madame Defarge	A Tale of Two Cities	Charles Dickens
Dick Dewy	Under The Greenwood Tree	Thomas Hardy
Mr. Dick	David Copperfield	Charles Dickens
Jim Dixon	Lucky Jim	Kingsley Amis
William Dobbin	Vanity Fair	William Makepeace Thackeray
Mr. Dombey	Dombey and Son	Charles Dickens
Florence Dombey	Dombey and Son	Charles Dickens
Don Quixote	Don Quixote de la Mancha	Miguel de Cervantes
Arabella Donn	Jude the Obscure	Thomas Hardy
Lorna Doone	Lorna Doone	R. D. Blackmore
Amy Dorrit *or* Little Dorrit	Little Dorrit	Charles Dickens
Fanny Dorrit	Little Dorrit	Charles Dickens
Tip Dorrit	Little Dorrit	Charles Dickens
William Dorrit	Little Dorrit	Charles Dickens
Edwin Drood	Edwin Drood	Charles Dickens
Bentley Drummle	Great Expectations	Charles Dickens
Catriona Drummond	Catriona	Robert Louis Stevenson
Alec D'Urberville	Tess of the D'Urbervilles	Thomas Hardy
Tess Durbeyfield	Tess of the D'Urbervilles	Thomas Hardy
Catherine Earnshaw	Wuthering Heights	Emily Brontë
Hareton Earnshaw	Wuthering Heights	Emily Brontë
Hindley Earnshaw	Wuthering Heights	Emily Brontë
Anne Elliot	Persuasion	Jane Austen
Elizabeth Elliot	Persuasion	Jane Austen
Sir Walter Elliot	Persuasion	Jane Austen
Em'ly	David Copperfield	Charles Dickens
Eppie	Silas Marner	George Eliot
Esmeralda	Notre Dame de Paris	Victor Hugo
Beatrix Esmond	Henry Esmond	William Makepeace Thackeray
Henry Esmond	Henry Esmond	William Makepeace Thackeray
Estella	Great Expectations	Charles Dickens
Bathsheba Everdene	Far from the Madding Crowd	Thomas Hardy
Jane Eyre	Jane Eyre	Charlotte Brontë
Fagin	Oliver Twist	Charles Dickens
Andrew Fairservice	Rob Roy	Sir Walter Scott
Donald Farfrae	The Mayor of Casterbridge	Thomas Hardy
Jude Fawley	Jude the Obscure	Thomas Hardy
Edward Ferrars	Sense and Sensibility	Jane Austen
Huck *or* Huckleberry Finn	Tom Sawyer, Huckleberry Finn	Mark Twain
Miss Flite	Bleak House	Charles Dickens
Julia Flyte	Brideshead Revisited	Evelyn Waugh
Sebastian Flyte	Brideshead Revisited	Evelyn Waugh
Phileas Fogg	Around the World in Eighty Days	Jules Verne

Man Friday	Robinson Crusoe	Daniel Defoe
Sarah Gamp	Martin Chuzzlewit	Charles Dickens
Joe Gargery	Great Expectations	Charles Dickens
Jay Gatsby	The Great Gatsby	F. Scott Fitzgerald
Walter Gay	Dombey and Son	Charles Dickens
Solomon Gills	Dombey and Son	Charles Dickens
Louisa Gradgrind	Hard Times	Charles Dickens
Thomas Gradgrind	Hard Times	Charles Dickens
Tom Gradgrind	Hard Times	Charles Dickens
Mary Graham	Martin Chuzzlewit	Charles Dickens
Edith Granger	Dombey and Son	Charles Dickens
Dorian Gray	The Picture of Dorian Gray	Oscar Wilde
Mr. Grewgious	Edwin Drood	Charles Dickens
Mrs. Grundy	Speed the Plough	T. Morton
Ben Gunn	Treasure Island	Robert Louis Stevenson
Chris Guthrie	Sunset Song et al.	Lewis Grassic Gibbon
Ham	David Copperfield	Charles Dickens
Richard Hannay	The Thirty-nine Steps et al.	John Buchan
Emma Haredale	Barnaby Rudge	Charles Dickens
John Harmon	Our Mutual Friend	Charles Dickens
James Harthouse	Hard Times	Charles Dickens
Miss Havisham	Great Expectations	Charles Dickens
Sir Mulberry Hawk	Nicholas Nickleby	Charles Dickens
Jim Hawkins	Treasure Island	Robert Louis Stevenson
Bradley Headstone	Our Mutual Friend	Charles Dickens
Heathcliff	Wuthering Heights	Emily Brontë
Uriah Heep	David Copperfield	Charles Dickens
Michael Henchard	The Mayor of Casterbridge	Thomas Hardy
Lizzy Hexam	Our Mutual Friend	Charles Dickens
Betty Higden	Our Mutual Friend	Charles Dickens
Sherlock Holmes	The Adventures of Sherlock Holmes et al.	Sir Arthur Conan Doyle
Humbert Humbert	Lolita	Vladimir Nabokov
Mr. Hyde	The Strange Case of Dr. Jekyll and Mr. Hyde	Robert Louis Stevenson
Injun Joe	Tom Sawyer	Mark Twain
Ishmael	Moby Dick	Herman Melville
Jaggers	Great Expectations	Charles Dickens
John Jarndyce	Bleak House	Charles Dickens
Bailie Nicol Jarvie	Rob Roy	Sir Walter Scott
John Jasper	Edwin Drood	Charles Dickens
Jeeves	My Man Jeeves et al.	P. G. Wodehouse
Dr. Jekyll	The Strange Case of Dr. Jekyll and Mr. Hyde	Robert Louis Stevenson
Mrs. Jellyby	Bleak House	Charles Dickens
Mrs. Jennings	Sense and Sensibility	Jane Austen
Jim	Huckleberry Finn	Mark Twain
Lord Jim	Lord Jim	Joseph Conrad
Jingle	The Pickwick Papers	Charles Dickens
Jo	Bleak House	Charles Dickens
Cissy Jupe	Hard Times	Charles Dickens
Joseph K.	The Trial	Franz Kafka
George Knightley	Emma	Jane Austen
Krook	Bleak House	Charles Dickens
Kurtz	Heart of Darkness	Joseph Conrad
Will Ladislaw	Middlemarch	George Eliot

Helena Landless	Edwin Drood	Charles Dickens
Neville Landless	Edwin Drood	Charles Dickens
Edgar Linton	Wuthering Heights	Emily Brontë
Isabella Linton	Wuthering Heights	Emily Brontë
Dr. Livesey	Treasure Island	Robert Louis Stevenson
Tertius Lydgate	Middlemarch	George Eliot
Rob Roy Macgregor	Rob Roy	Sir Walter Scott
Randle P. McMurphy	One Flew Over the Cuckoo's Nest	Ken Kesey
Abel Magwitch	Great Expectations	Charles Dickens
Dr. Manette	A Tale of Two Cities	Charles Dickens
Lucie Manette	A Tale of Two Cities	Charles Dickens
Madame Mantalini	Nicholas Nickleby	Charles Dickens
The Marchioness	The Old Curiosity Shop	Charles Dickens
Jacob Marley	A Christmas Carol	Charles Dickens
Philip Marlowe	The Big Sleep et al.	Raymond Chandler
Silas Marner	Silas Marner	George Eliot
Stephen Maturin	Master and Commander et al.	Patrick O'Brian
Oliver Mellors	Lady Chatterley's Lover	D. H. Lawrence
Merdle	Little Dorrit	Charles Dickens
Mrs. Merdle	Little Dorrit	Charles Dickens
Wilkins Micawber	David Copperfield	Charles Dickens
Walter Mitty	The Secret Life of Walter Mitty	James Thurber
Lord Mohun	Henry Esmond	William Makepeace Thackeray
Monks	Oliver Twist	Charles Dickens
Dean Moriarty	On the Road	Jack Kerouac
Professor Moriarty	The Adventures of Sherlock Holmes et al.	Sir Arthur Conan Doyle
Dinah Morris	Adam Bede	George Eliot
Murdstone	David Copperfield	Charles Dickens
Baron Münchhausen	Münchhausen, Baron, Narrative of His Marvellous Travels	R. E. Raspe
Nancy	Oliver Twist	Charles Dickens
Little Nell	The Old Curiosity Shop	Charles Dickens
Captain Nemo	Twenty Thousand Leagues under the Sea	Jules Verne
Kate Nickleby	Nicholas Nickleby	Charles Dickens
Nicholas Nickleby	Nicholas Nickleby	Charles Dickens
Ralph Nickleby	Nicholas Nickleby	Charles Dickens
Newman Noggs	Nicholas Nickleby	Charles Dickens
Susan Nipper	Dombey and Son	Charles Dickens
Kit Nubbles	The Old Curiosity Shop	Charles Dickens
Gabriel Oak	Far from the Madding Crowd	Thomas Hardy
Glorvina O'Dowd	Vanity Fair	William Makepeace Thackeray
Major O'Dowd	Vanity Fair	William Makepeace Thackeray
Mrs. O'Dowd	Vanity Fair	William Makepeace Thackeray
Francis Osbaldistone	Rob Roy	Sir Walter Scott
Rashleigh Osbaldistone	Rob Roy	Sir Walter Scott
George Osborne	Vanity Fair	William Makepeace Thackeray
Pancks	Little Dorrit	Charles Dickens

Sancho Panza	Don Quixote de la Mancha	Miguel de Cervantes
Sal Paradise	On the Road	Jack Kerouac
Passepartout	Around the World in Eighty Days	Jules Verne
Pecksniff	Martin Chuzzlewit	Charles Dickens
Charity Pecksniff	Martin Chuzzlewit	Charles Dickens
Mercy Pecksniff	Martin Chuzzlewit	Charles Dickens
Peggoty	David Copperfield	Charles Dickens
Arthur Pendennis	Pendennis	William Makepeace Thackeray
Helen Pendennis	Pendennis	William Makepeace Thackeray
Pew	Treasure Island	Robert Louis Stevenson
Samuel Pickwick	The Pickwick Papers	Charles Dickens
Ruth Pinch	Martin Chuzzlewit	Charles Dickens
Tom Pinch	Martin Chuzzlewit	Charles Dickens
Pip *or* Philip Pirrip	Great Expectations	Charles Dickens
Herbert Pocket	Great Expectations	Charles Dickens
Charles Pooter	The Diary of a Nobody	G. and W. Grossmith
Martin Poyser	Adam Bede	George Eliot
Mrs. Poyser	Adam Bede	George Eliot
Fanny Price	Mansfield Park	Jane Austen
J. Alfred Prufrock	Prufrock and Other Observations	T. S. Eliot
Pumblechook	Great Expectations	Charles Dickens
Quasimodo	Notre Dame de Paris	Victor Hugo
Queequeg	Moby Dick	Herman Melville
Daniel Quilp	The Old Curiosity Shop	Charles Dickens
Roderick Random	Roderick Random	Tobias Smollett
Riah	Our Mutual Friend	Charles Dickens
Rogue Riderhood	Our Mutual Friend	Charles Dickens
Fanny Robin	Far from the Madding Crowd	Thomas Hardy
Mr. Rochester	Jane Eyre	Charlotte Brontë
Barnaby Rudge	Barnaby Rudge	Charles Dickens
Lady Russell	Persuasion	Jane Austen
Charles Ryder	Brideshead Revisited	Evelyn Waugh
Tom Sawyer	Tom Sawyer	Mark Twain
Scrooge	A Christmas Carol	Charles Dickens
Amelia Sedley	Vanity Fair	William Makepeace Thackeray
Jos Sedley	Vanity Fair	William Makepeace Thackeray
Tristram Shandy	The Life and Opinions of Tristram Shandy	Laurence Sterne
Becky *or* Rebecca Sharp	Vanity Fair	William Makepeace Thackeray
Bill Sikes	Oliver Twist	Charles Dickens
Long John Silver	Treasure Island	Robert Louis Stevenson
Harold Skimpole	Bleak House	Charles Dickens
Sleary	Hard Times	Charles Dickens
Smike	Nicholas Nickleby	Charles Dickens
Harriet Smith	Emma	Jane Austen
Winston Smith	Nineteen Eighty-four	George Orwell
Augustus Snodgrass	The Pickwick Papers	Charles Dickens
Hetty Sorrel	Adam Bede	George Eliot
Lady Southdown	Vanity Fair	William Makepeace Thackeray
Mrs. Sparsit	Hard Times	Charles Dickens
Dora Spenlow	David Copperfield	Charles Dickens
Wackford Squeers	Nicholas Nickleby	Charles Dickens

Starbuck	Moby Dick	Herman Melville
Lucy Steele	Sense and Sensibility	Jane Austen
James Steerforth	David Copperfield	Charles Dickens
Lord Steyne	Vanity Fair	William Makepeace Thackeray
Esther Summerson	Bleak House	Charles Dickens
Dick Swiveller	The Old Curiosity Shop	Charles Dickens
Mark Tapley	Martin Chuzzlewit	Charles Dickens
Tartuffe	Tartuffe	Molière
Mr. Tartar	Edwin Drood	Charles Dickens
Tarzan	Tarzan of the Apes	Edgar Rice Burroughs
Becky Thatcher	Tom Sawyer	Mark Twain
Montague Tigg	Martin Chuzzlewit	Charles Dickens
Tiny Tim	A Christmas Carol	Charles Dickens
Mrs. Todgers	Martin Chuzzlewit	Charles Dickens
Toots	Dombey and Son	Charles Dickens
Traddles	David Copperfield	Charles Dickens
Squire Trelawney	Treasure Island	Robert Louis Stevenson
Fred Trent	The Old Curiosity Shop	Charles Dickens
Job Trotter	The Pickwick Papers	Charles Dickens
Betsey Trotwood	David Copperfield	Charles Dickens
Sergeant Troy	Far from the Madding Crowd	Thomas Hardy
Tulkinghorn	Bleak House	Charles Dickens
Tracy Tupman	The Pickwick Papers	Charles Dickens
Thomas Tusher	Henry Esmond	William Makepeace Thackeray
Oliver Twist	Oliver Twist	Charles Dickens
Gabriel Varden	Barnaby Rudge	Charles Dickens
Dolly Varden	Barnaby Rudge	Charles Dickens

Mr. Veneering	Our Mutual Friend	Charles Dickens
Mrs. Veneering	Our Mutual Friend	Charles Dickens
Diggory Venn	Return of the Native	Thomas Hardy
Diana Vernon	Rob Roy	Sir Walter Scott
Rosamond Vincy	Middlemarch	George Eliot
Johann Voss	Voss	Patrick White
Eustacia Vye	Return of the Native	Thomas Hardy
George Warrington	Pendennis	William Makepeace Thackeray
Dr. Watson	The Adventures of Sherlock Holmes et al.	Sir Arthur Conan Doyle
Silas Wegg	Our Mutual Friend	Charles Dickens
Sam Weller	The Pickwick Papers	Charles Dickens
Wemmick	Great Expectations	Charles Dickens
Frank Wentworth	Persuasion	Jane Austen
Agnes Wickfield	David Copperfield	Charles Dickens
George Wickham	Pride and Prejudice	Jane Austen
Damon Wildeve	Return of the Native	Thomas Hardy
Bella Wilfer	Our Mutual Friend	Charles Dickens
John Willoughby	Sense and Sensibility	Jane Austen
Nathaniel Winkle	The Pickwick Papers	Charles Dickens
Dolly Winthrop	Silas Marner	George Eliot
Allan Woodcourt	Bleak House	Charles Dickens
Emma Woodhouse	Emma	Jane Austen
Mr. Woodhouse	Emma	Jane Austen
Bertie Wooster	My Man Jeeves et al.	P. G. Wodehouse
Eugene Wrayburn	Our Mutual Friend	Charles Dickens
Jenny Wren	Our Mutual Friend	Charles Dickens
Clym Yeobright	Return of the Native	Thomas Hardy

Thomasin Yeobright	Return of the Native	Thomas Hardy
Yossarian	Catch-22	Joseph Heller
Yuri Zhivago	Doctor Zhivago	Boris Pasternak
Zorba *or* Alexis Zorbas	Zorba the Greek	Nikos Kazantzakis

Characters in Shakespeare	**Play**
Sir Andrew Aguecheek	Twelfth Night
Antonio	The Merchant of Venice
Antony	Antony and Cleopatra, Julius Caesar
Ariel	The Tempest
Aufidius	Coriolanus
Autolycus	The Winter's Tale
Banquo	Macbeth
Bassanio	The Merchant of Venice
Beatrice	Much Ado About Nothing
Sir Toby Belch	Twelfth Night
Benedick	Much Ado About Nothing
Bolingbroke	Richard II
Bottom	A Midsummer Night's Dream
Brutus	Julius Caesar
Caliban	The Tempest
Casca	Julius Caesar
Cassio	Othello
Cassius	Julius Caesar
Claudio	Much Ado About Nothing, Measure for Measure
Claudius	Hamlet
Cleopatra	Antony and Cleopatra
Cordelia	King Lear
Coriolanus	Coriolanus
Cressida	Troilus and Cressida
Demetrius	A Midsummer Night's Dream
Desdemona	Othello
Dogberry	Much Ado About Nothing
Edmund	King Lear
Enobarbus	Antony and Cleopatra
Falstaff	Henry IV Parts I and II, The Merry Wives of Windsor
Ferdinand	The Tempest
Feste	Twelfth Night
Fluellen	Henry V
Fool	King Lear
Gertrude	Hamlet
Gloucester	King Lear
Goneril	King Lear
Guildenstern	Hamlet
Hamlet	Hamlet
Helena	All's Well that Ends Well, A Midsummer Night's Dream
Hermia	A Midsummer Night's Dream
Hero	Much Ado About Nothing
Hotspur	Henry IV Part I
Iago	Othello
Jaques	As You Like It
John of Gaunt	Richard II
Juliet	Romeo and Juliet
Julius Caesar	Julius Caesar
Katharina *or* Kate	The Taming of the Shrew
Kent	King Lear
Laertes	Hamlet
Lear	King Lear
Lysander	A Midsummer Night's Dream
Macbeth	Macbeth
Lady Macbeth	Macbeth
Macduff	Macbeth
Malcolm	Macbeth
Malvolio	Twelfth Night
Mercutio	Romeo and Juliet
Miranda	The Tempest
Oberon	A Midsummer Night's Dream
Octavius	Antony and Cleopatra
Olivia	Twelfth Night
Ophelia	Hamlet
Orlando	As You Like It
Orsino	Twelfth Night
Othello	Othello
Pandarus	Troilus and Cressida
Perdita	The Winter's Tale
Petruchio	The Taming of the Shrew
Pistol	Henry IV Part II, Henry V, The Merry Wives of Windsor
Polonius	Hamlet
Portia	The Merchant of Venice
Prospero	The Tempest
Puck	A Midsummer Night's Dream
Mistress Quickly	The Merry Wives of Windsor
Regan	King Lear
Romeo	Romeo and Juliet
Rosalind	As You Like It
Rosencrantz	Hamlet

Sebastian	The Tempest, Twelfth Night
Shylock	The Merchant of Venice
Thersites	Troilus and Cressida
Timon	Timon of Athens
Titania	A Midsummer Night's Dream
Touchstone	As You Like It
Troilus	Troilus and Cressida
Tybalt	Romeo and Juliet
Viola	Twelfth Night

Plays of Shakespeare

All's Well that Ends Well	The Merry Wives of Windsor
Antony and Cleopatra	A Midsummer Night's Dream
As You Like It	Much Ado About Nothing
The Comedy of Errors	Othello
Coriolanus	Pericles, Prince of Tyre
Cymbeline	Richard II
Hamlet	Richard III
Henry IV Part I	Romeo and Juliet
Henry IV Part II	The Taming of the Shrew
Henry V	The Tempest
Henry VI Part I	Timon of Athens
Henry VI Part II	Titus Andronicus
Henry VI Part III	Troilus and Cressida
Henry VIII	Twelfth Night
Julius Caesar	The Two Gentlemen of Verona
King John	The Winter's Tale
King Lear	
Love's Labour's Lost	
Macbeth	
Measure for Measure	
The Merchant of Venice	

Poems of Shakespeare

The Passionate Pilgrim	The Rape of Lucrece
The Phoenix and the Turtle	Sonnets
	Venus and Adonis

It takes a great deal of history to produce a little literature
Henry James *Hawthorne*

Remarks are not literature
Gloria Steinem *Autobiography of Alice B. Toklas*

Literature is mostly about having sex and not much about children; life is the other way around
David Lodge *The British Museum is Falling Down*

Literature is news that STAYS news
Ezra Pound *ABC of Reading*

Literature is a luxury. Fiction is a necessity
G.K. Chesterton *The Defendant*

Our American professors like their literature clear and cold and pure and very dead
Sinclair Lewis *The American Fear of Literature*

When once the itch of literature comes over a man, nothing can cure it but the scratching of a pen
Samuel Lover *Handy Andy*

lithe flexible, limber, lissom(e), loose-jointed, loose-limbed, pliable, pliant, supple

litigant claimant, contestant, disputant, litigator, party, plaintiff

litigate contest at law, file a suit, go to court, go to law, institute legal proceedings, press charges, prosecute, sue

litigation action, case, contending, disputing, lawsuit, process, prosecution

litigious argumentative, belligerent, contentious, disputatious, quarrelsome

litter *noun* **1.** debris, detritus, fragments, garbage (*chiefly U.S.*), grot (*slang*), muck, refuse, rubbish, shreds, trash **2.** clutter, confusion, disarray, disorder, jumble, mess, scatter, untidiness **3.** brood, family, offspring, progeny, young **4.** bedding, couch, floor cover, mulch, straw-bed **5.** palanquin, stretcher *~verb* **6.** clutter, derange, disarrange, disorder, mess up, scatter, strew

little *adjective* **1.** diminutive, dwarf, elfin, infinitesimal, Lilliputian, mini, miniature, minute, munchkin (*informal, chiefly U.S.*), petite, pygmy *or* pigmy, short, slender, small, teensy-weensy, teeny-weeny, tiny, wee **2.** babyish, immature, infant, junior, undeveloped, young **3.** hardly any, insufficient, meagre, measly, scant, skimpy, small, sparse **4.** brief, fleeting, hasty, passing, short, short-lived **5.** inconsiderable, insignificant, minor, negligible, paltry, trifling, trivial, unimportant **6.** base, cheap, illiberal, mean, narrow-minded, petty, small-minded *~adverb* **7.** barely, hardly, not much, not quite, only just **8.** hardly ever, not often, rarely, scarcely, seldom **9. little by little** bit by bit, by degrees, gradually, imperceptibly, piecemeal, progressively, slowly, step by step *~noun* **10.** bit, dab, dash, fragment, hint, modicum, particle, pinch, small amount, snippet, speck, spot, tad (*informal, chiefly U.S.*), taste, touch, trace, trifle

Antonyms *adjective* abundant, ample, big, colossal, considerable, enormous, giant, ginormous (*informal*), grave, great, huge, immense, important, large, long, major, mega (*slang*), momentous, much, plentiful, serious, significant *~adverb* always, certainly, much, surely *~noun* lot, many, much

Little things affect little minds
Benjamin Disraeli *Sybil*

liturgical ceremonial, eucharistic, formal, ritual, sacramental, solemn

liturgy celebration, ceremony, form of worship, formula, rite, ritual, sacrament, service, services, worship

livable **1.** adequate, comfortable, fit (for human habitation), habitable, inhabitable, satisfac~

tory **2.** acceptable, bearable, endurable, passable, sufferable, supportable, tolerable, worth living, worthwhile **3.** *with* **with** companionable, compatible, congenial, easy, easy to live with, harmonious, sociable

live[1] *verb* **1.** be, be alive, breathe, draw breath, exist, have life **2.** be permanent, be remembered, last, persist, prevail, remain alive **3.** *sometimes with* **in** abide, dwell, hang out (*informal*), inhabit, lodge, occupy, reside, settle, stay (*chiefly Scot.*) **4.** abide, continue, earn a living, endure, fare, feed, get along, lead, make ends meet, pass, remain, subsist, support oneself, survive **5.** be happy, enjoy life, flourish, luxuriate, make the most of life, prosper, thrive **6.** **live it up** *informal* celebrate, enjoy oneself, have a ball (*informal*), have fun, make whoopee (*informal*), paint the town red, push the boat out (*Brit. informal*), revel

Live and learn

Live and let live

They that live longest see most

He lives long who lives well

live[2] *adjective* **1.** alive, animate, breathing, existent, living, quick (*archaic*), vital **2.** active, burning, controversial, current, hot, pertinent, pressing, prevalent, topical, unsettled, vital **3.** *informal* active, alert, brisk, dynamic, earnest, energetic, lively, sparky, vigorous, vivid, wide-awake **4.** active, alight, blazing, burning, connected, glowing, hot, ignited, smouldering, switched on

livelihood bread and butter (*informal*), employment, job, living, maintenance, means, (means of) support, occupation, (source of) income, subsistence, sustenance, work

liveliness activity, animation, boisterousness, brio, briskness, dynamism, energy, gaiety, quickness, smartness, spirit, sprightliness, vitality, vivacity

livelong complete, dragged out, entire, everlasting, full, long-drawn-out, unbroken, whole

lively **1.** active, agile, alert, alive and kicking, bright-eyed and bushy-tailed, brisk, chipper (*informal*), chirpy (*informal*), energetic, full of beans (*informal*), full of pep (*informal*), keen, nimble, perky, quick, sprightly, spry, vigorous **2.** animated, blithe, blithesome, cheerful, chirpy (*informal*), frisky, frolicsome, gay, merry, sparkling, sparky, spirited, upbeat (*informal*), vivacious **3.** astir, bustling, busy, buzzing, crowded, eventful, moving, stirring **4.** bright, colourful, exciting, forceful, invigorating, racy, refreshing, stimulating, vivid
Antonyms apathetic, debilitated, disabled, dull, inactive, lifeless, listless, slow, sluggish, torpid

liven (up) animate, brighten, buck up (*informal*), enliven, hot up (*informal*), pep up, perk up, put life into, rouse, stir, vitalize, vivify

liverish **1.** bilious, queasy, sick **2.** crotchety (*informal*), crusty, disagreeable, fratchy (*informal*), grumpy, ill-humoured, irascible, irritable, like a bear with a sore head, peevish, ratty (*Brit. & N.Z. informal*), snappy, splenetic, tetchy

livery attire, clothing, costume, dress, garb, raiment (*archaic or poetic*), regalia, suit, uniform, vestments

live wire ball of fire (*informal*), dynamo, go-getter (*informal*), hustler (*U.S. & Canad. slang*), life and soul of the party, self-starter

livid **1.** angry, black-and-blue, bruised, contused, discoloured, purple **2.** ashen, blanched, bloodless, doughy, greyish, leaden, pale, pallid, pasty, wan, waxen **3.** *informal* angry, as black as thunder, beside oneself, boiling, choked, cross, enraged, exasperated, fit to be tied (*slang*), fuming, furious, hot under the collar (*informal*), incensed, indignant, infuriated, mad (*informal*), outraged
Antonyms (*sense 3*) assuaged, blissful, content, delighted, enchanted, forgiving, happy, mollified, overjoyed, pleased

living *adjective* **1.** active, alive, alive and kicking, animated, breathing, existing, in the land of the living (*informal*), lively, quick (*archaic*), strong, vigorous, vital **2.** active, contemporary, continuing, current, developing, extant, in use, ongoing, operative, persisting *~noun* **3.** animation, being, existence, existing, life, subsistence **4.** life style, mode of living, way of life **5.** bread and butter (*informal*), job, livelihood, maintenance, (means of) support, occupation, (source of) income, subsistence, sustenance, work **6.** *Church of England* benefice, incumbency, stipend **7.** **the living** flesh and blood, the quick (*archaic*)
Antonyms *adjective* (*sense 1*) dead, deceased, defunct, departed, expired, late, lifeless, perished (*sense 2*) obsolescent, obsolete, out-of-date, vanishing

The living are the dead on holiday
Maurice Maeterlinck

load *noun* **1.** bale, cargo, consignment, freight, lading, shipment **2.** affliction, albatross, burden, encumbrance, incubus, millstone, onus, oppression, pressure, trouble, weight, worry *~verb* **3.** cram, fill, freight, heap, lade, pack, pile, stack, stuff **4.** burden, encumber, hamper, oppress, saddle with, trouble, weigh down, worry **5.** *of firearms* charge, make ready, prepare to fire, prime **6.** **load the dice** fix, rig, set up

loaded **1.** burdened, charged, freighted, full, laden, weighted **2.** biased, distorted, weighted

3. artful, insidious, manipulative, prejudicial, tricky 4. at the ready, charged, primed, ready to shoot *or* fire 5. *slang* affluent, flush (*informal*), moneyed, rich, rolling (*slang*), wealthy, well-heeled (*informal*), well off, well-to-do

loaf[1] *noun* 1. block, cake, cube, lump, slab 2. *slang* block (*informal*), chump (*Brit. slang*), gumption (*Brit. informal*), head, noddle (*informal, chiefly Brit.*), nous (*Brit. slang*), sense

loaf[2] *verb* 1. be indolent, idle, laze, lie around, loiter, loll, lounge around, take it easy 2. *with* **away** fritter away, kill time, pass time, veg out (*slang, chiefly U.S.*), waste time, while away the hours

loafer bum (*informal*), couch potato (*slang*), drone (*Brit.*), idler, layabout, lazybones (*informal*), lounger, ne'er-do-well, shirker, skiver (*Brit. slang*), time-waster, wastrel

loan 1. *noun* accommodation, advance, allowance, credit, mortgage, touch (*slang*) 2. *verb* accommodate, advance, allow, credit, lend, let out

loath, loth against, averse, backward, counter, disinclined, indisposed, opposed, reluctant, resisting, unwilling
Antonyms anxious, avid, desirous, eager, enthusiastic, keen, willing

loathe abhor, abominate, despise, detest, dislike, execrate, feel repugnance towards, find disgusting, hate, have a strong aversion to, not be able to bear *or* abide

loathing abhorrence, abomination, antipathy, aversion, detestation, disgust, execration, hatred, horror, odium, repugnance, repulsion, revulsion

loathsome abhorrent, abominable, detestable, disgusting, execrable, hateful, horrible, nasty, nauseating, obnoxious, obscene, odious, offensive, repugnant, repulsive, revolting, vile, yucky *or* yukky (*slang*)
Antonyms adorable, attractive, charming, delightful, enchanting, engaging, fetching, likable *or* likeable, lovable, lovely

lob *verb* fling, launch, lift, loft, pitch, shy (*informal*), throw, toss

lobby *noun* 1. corridor, entrance hall, foyer, hall, hallway, passage, passageway, porch, vestibule 2. pressure group *~verb* 3. bring pressure to bear, campaign for, exert influence, influence, persuade, press for, pressure, promote, pull strings (*Brit. informal*), push for, solicit votes, urge

local *adjective* 1. community, district, neighbourhood, parish, provincial, regional 2. confined, limited, narrow, parish pump, parochial, provincial, restricted, small-town *~noun* 3. character (*informal*), inhabitant, local yokel (*disparaging*), native, resident

locale locality, location, locus, place, position, scene, setting, site, spot, venue

locality 1. area, district, neck of the woods (*informal*), neighbourhood, region, vicinity 2. locale, location, place, position, scene, setting, site, spot

localize 1. circumscribe, concentrate, confine, contain, delimit, delimitate, limit, restrain, restrict 2. ascribe, assign, narrow down, pinpoint, specify

locate 1. come across, detect, discover, find, lay one's hands on, pin down, pinpoint, run to earth *or* ground, track down, unearth 2. establish, fix, place, put, seat, set, settle, situate

location bearings, locale, locus, place, point, position, site, situation, spot, venue, whereabouts

lock[1] *noun* 1. bolt, clasp, fastening, padlock *~verb* 2. bolt, close, fasten, latch, seal, secure, shut, sneck (*dialect*) 3. clench, engage, entangle, entwine, join, link, mesh, unite 4. clasp, clutch, embrace, encircle, enclose, grapple, grasp, hug, press

lock[2] *noun* curl, ringlet, strand, tress, tuft

lock out ban, bar, debar, exclude, keep out, refuse admittance to, shut out

lockup can (*slang*), cell, cooler (*slang*), gaol, jail, jug (*slang*), police cell

lock up cage, confine, detain, imprison, incarcerate, jail, put behind bars, shut up

locomotion action, headway, motion, movement, moving, progress, progression, travel, travelling

locution 1. collocation, expression, idiom, phrase, term, turn of speech, wording 2. accent, articulation, diction, inflection, intonation, manner of speech, phrasing, style

lodestar beacon, guide, model, par, pattern, signal, standard

lodestone beacon, focal point, focus, lodestar, magnet

lodge *noun* 1. cabin, chalet, cottage, gatehouse, house, hunting lodge, hut, shelter 2. assemblage, association, branch, chapter, club, group, society 3. den, haunt, lair, retreat *~verb* 4. accommodate, billet, board, entertain, harbour, put up, quarter, room, shelter, sojourn, stay, stop 5. become fixed, catch, come to rest, imbed, implant, stick 6. deposit, file, lay, place, put, put on record, register, set, submit

lodger boarder, guest, paying guest, P.G., resident, roomer, tenant

lodging *often plural* abode, accommodation, apartments, boarding, digs (*Brit. informal*), dwelling, habitation, quarters, residence, rooms, shelter

lofty **1.** elevated, high, raised, sky-high, soaring, tall, towering **2.** dignified, distinguished, elevated, exalted, grand, illustrious, imposing, majestic, noble, renowned, stately, sublime, superior **3.** arrogant, condescending, disdainful, haughty, high and mighty (*informal*), lordly, patronizing, proud, snooty (*informal*), supercilious, toffee-nosed (*slang, chiefly Brit.*)
Antonyms debased, degraded, dwarfed, friendly, humble, low, lowly, mean, modest, short, stunted, unassuming, warm

log *noun* **1.** block, bole, chunk, piece of timber, stump, trunk *~verb* **2.** chop, cut, fell, hew *~noun* **3.** account, chart, daybook, journal, listing, logbook, record, tally *~verb* **4.** book, chart, make a note of, note, record, register, report, set down, tally

loggerhead at loggerheads at daggers drawn, at each other's throats, at enmity, at odds, estranged, feuding, in dispute, opposed, quarrelling

logic **1.** argumentation, deduction, dialectics, ratiocination, science of reasoning, syllogistic reasoning **2.** good reason, good sense, reason, sense, sound judgment **3.** chain of thought, coherence, connection, link, rationale, relationship

logical **1.** clear, cogent, coherent, consistent, deducible, pertinent, rational, reasonable, relevant, sound, valid, well-organized **2.** judicious, most likely, necessary, obvious, plausible, reasonable, sensible, wise
Antonyms illogical, implausible, instinctive, irrational, unlikely, unorganized, unreasonable

logistics coordination, engineering, management, masterminding, orchestration, organization, plans, strategy

loiter dally, dawdle, delay, dilly-dally (*informal*), hang about *or* around, idle, lag, linger, loaf, loll, saunter, skulk, stroll

loll **1.** flop, lean, loaf, lounge, recline, relax, slouch, slump, sprawl **2.** dangle, droop, drop, flap, flop, hang, hang loosely, sag

London

When a man is tired of London, he is tired of life; for there is in London all that life can afford
Dr. Johnson

London: a nation, not a city
Benjamin Disraeli

London, that great cesspool into which all the loungers and idlers of the Empire are irresistibly drained
Sir Arthur Conan Doyle *A Study in Scarlet*

city of refuge, the mansion-house of liberty
John Milton *Areopagitica*

lone by oneself, deserted, isolated, lonesome, one, only, separate, separated, single, sole, solitary, unaccompanied

loneliness aloneness, desertedness, desolation, dreariness, forlornness, isolation, lonesomeness, seclusion, solitariness, solitude

Alone, alone, all, all alone,
Alone on a wide wide sea!
And never a saint took pity on
My soul in agony.
Samuel Taylor Coleridge *The Ancient Mariner*

lonely **1.** abandoned, destitute, estranged, forlorn, forsaken, friendless, lonesome, outcast **2.** alone, apart, by oneself, companionless, isolated, lone, single, solitary, withdrawn **3.** deserted, desolate, godforsaken, isolated, off the beaten track (*informal*), out-of-the-way, remote, secluded, sequestered, solitary, unfrequented, uninhabited
Antonyms (*sense 1*) accompanied, befriended, popular, together (*sense 2*) bustling, crowded, frequented, populous, teeming

loner hermit, individualist, lone wolf, maverick, misanthrope, outsider, recluse, solitary

lonesome cheerless, companionless, deserted, desolate, dreary, forlorn, friendless, gloomy, isolated, lone, lonely

long[1] *adjective* **1.** elongated, expanded, extended, extensive, far-reaching, lengthy, spread out, stretched **2.** dragging, interminable, late, lengthy, lingering, long-drawn-out, prolonged, protracted, slow, sustained, tardy
Antonyms abbreviated, abridged, brief, compressed, contracted, little, momentary, quick, short, short-lived, small

long[2] *verb* ache, covet, crave, desire, dream of, eat one's heart out over, hanker, hunger, itch, lust, pine, set one's heart on, want, wish, would give one's eyeteeth for, yearn

long-drawn-out dragged out, interminable, lengthy, marathon, overextended, overlong, prolonged, protracted, spun out

long-headed acute, astute, discerning, far-sighted, penetrating, perceptive, sagacious, shrewd, wise

longing **1.** *noun* ache, ambition, aspiration, coveting, craving, desire, hankering, hope, hungering, itch, thirst, urge, wish, yearning, yen (*informal*) **2.** *adjective* anxious, ardent, avid, craving, desirous, eager, hungry, languishing, pining, wishful, wistful, yearning
Antonyms *noun* abhorrence, antipathy, apathy, disgust, indifference, loathing, revulsion, unconcern *~adjective* apathetic, cold, disgusted, hateful, indifferent, loathing, unconcerned, uninterested

long-lived enduring, full of years, longevous, long-lasting, old as Methuselah

long-standing abiding, enduring, established,

fixed, hallowed by time, long-established, long-lasting, long-lived, time-honoured

long-suffering easygoing, forbearing, forgiving, patient, resigned, stoical, tolerant, uncom~plaining

long-winded diffuse, discursive, garrulous, lengthy, long-drawn-out, overlong, prolix, pro~longed, rambling, repetitious, tedious, tire~some, verbose, wordy
Antonyms brief, concise, crisp, curt, laconic, pithy, sententious, short, succinct, terse, to the point

look *verb* **1.** behold (*archaic*), check, check out (*informal*), clock (*Brit. slang*), consider, con~template, examine, eye, eyeball (*U.S. slang*), feast one's eyes upon, gaze, get a load of (*in~formal*), glance, inspect, observe, peep, recce (*slang*), regard, scan, scrutinize, see, study, survey, take a dekko at (*Brit. slang*), take a gander at (*informal*), view, watch **2.** appear, display, evidence, exhibit, look like, make clear, manifest, present, seem, seem to be, show, strike one as **3.** face, front, front on, give onto, overlook **4.** anticipate, await, expect, hope, reckon on **5.** forage, hunt, search, seek **6.** gape, gawk, gawp (*Brit. slang*), glower, goggle, ogle, rubberneck (*slang*), stare **7. look like** be the image of, favour, make one think of, put one in mind of, remind one of, resem~ble, take after *~noun* **8.** butcher's (*Brit. slang*), examination, eyeful (*informal*), gander (*informal*), gaze, glance, glimpse, inspection, look-see (*slang*), observation, once-over (*infor~mal*), peek, recce (*slang*), review, shufti (*Brit. slang*), sight, squint (*informal*), survey, view **9.** air, appearance, aspect, bearing, cast, com~plexion, countenance, demeanour, effect, ex~pression, face, fashion, guise, manner, mien (*literary*), semblance

Look before you leap

look after attend to, care for, guard, keep an eye on, mind, nurse, protect, sit with, super~vise, take care of, take charge of, tend, watch

lookalike clone, dead ringer (*slang*), double, exact match, living image, replica, ringer (*slang*), spit (*informal, chiefly Brit.*), spit and image (*informal*), spitting image (*informal*), twin

look down on *or* **upon** contemn, despise, dis~dain, hold in contempt, look down one's nose at (*informal*), misprize, scorn, sneer, spurn, treat with contempt, turn one's nose up (at) (*informal*)

look forward to anticipate, await, count on, count the days until, expect, hope for, long for, look for, set one's heart on, wait for

look into check out, delve into, examine, ex~plore, follow up, go into, inquire about, in~spect, investigate, look over, make enquiries, make inquiries, probe, research, scrutinize, study

lookout **1.** guard, qui vive, readiness, vigil, watch **2.** guard, sentinel, sentry, vedette (*Military*), watchman **3.** beacon, citadel, obser~vation post, observatory, post, tower, watch~tower **4.** *informal* business, concern, funeral (*informal*), pigeon (*Brit. informal*), worry **5.** chances, future, likelihood, outlook, prospect, view

look out be alert, be careful, be on guard, be on the qui vive, be vigilant, beware, keep an eye out, keep one's eyes open (peeled, skinned), pay attention, watch out

look over cast an eye over, check, check out (*informal*), examine, eyeball (*U.S. slang*), flick through, inspect, look through, monitor, pe~ruse, scan, take a dekko at (*Brit. slang*), view, work over

look up **1.** find, hunt for, research, search for, seek out, track down **2.** ameliorate, come along, get better, improve, perk up, pick up, progress, shape up (*informal*), show improve~ment **3.** *with* **to** admire, defer to, esteem, have a high opinion of, honour, regard highly, re~spect, revere **4.** call (on), drop in on (*infor~mal*), go to see, look in on, pay a visit to, visit

loom **1.** appear, become visible, be imminent, bulk, emerge, hover, impend, menace, take shape, threaten **2.** dominate, hang over, mount, overhang, overshadow, overtop, rise, soar, tower

loop **1.** *noun* bend, circle, coil, convolution, curl, curve, eyelet, hoop, kink, loophole, noose, ring, spiral, twirl, twist, whorl **2.** *verb* bend, braid, circle, coil, connect, curl, curve round, encircle, fold, join, knot, roll, spiral, turn, twist, wind round

loophole **1.** aperture, knothole, opening, slot **2.** *figurative* avoidance, escape, evasion, excuse, let-out, means of escape, plea, pretence, pre~text, subterfuge

loose *adjective* **1.** floating, free, insecure, movable, released, unattached, unbound, unconfined, un~fastened, unfettered, unrestricted, unsecured, untied, wobbly **2.** baggy, easy, hanging, loosened, not fitting, not tight, relaxed, slack, slackened, sloppy **3.** diffuse, disconnected, disordered, ill-defined, imprecise, inaccurate, indefinite, indis~tinct, inexact, rambling, random, vague **4.** aban~doned, debauched, disreputable, dissipated, dis~solute, fast, immoral, lewd, libertine, licentious, profligate, promiscuous, unchaste, wanton **5.** careless, heedless, imprudent, lax, negligent, rash, thoughtless, unmindful *~verb* **6.** detach, disconnect, disengage, ease, free, let go, liberate, loosen, release, set free, slacken, unbind, unbri~dle, undo, unfasten, unleash, unloose, untie

Antonyms *adjective* (*sense 1*) bound, curbed, fastened, fettered, restrained, secured, tethered, tied (*sense 2*) tight (*sense 3*) accurate, clear, concise, exact, precise (*sense 4*) chaste, disciplined, moral, virtuous *~verb* bind, cage, capture, fasten, fetter, imprison, tether

loose-jointed *or* **loose-limbed** agile, elastic, flexible, limber, lissom(e), lithe, pliable, pliant, supple

loosen **1.** detach, let out, separate, slacken, unbind, undo, unloose, unstick, untie, work free, work loose **2.** deliver, free, let go, liberate, release, set free **3.** *often with* **up** ease up *or* off, go easy (*informal*), lessen, let up, lighten up (*slang*), mitigate, moderate, relax, soften, weaken

loot **1.** *noun* booty, goods, haul, plunder, prize, spoils, swag (*slang*) **2.** *verb* despoil, pillage, plunder, raid, ransack, ravage, rifle, rob, sack

lop chop, clip, crop, curtail, cut, detach, dock, hack, prune, sever, shorten, trim, truncate

lope bound, canter, gallop, lollop, spring, stride

lopsided askew, asymmetrical, awry, cockeyed, crooked, disproportionate, off balance, one-sided, out of shape, out of true, skewwhiff (*Brit. informal*), squint, tilting, unbalanced, unequal, uneven, warped

loquacious babbling, blathering, chattering, chatty, gabby (*informal*), garrulous, gassy (*informal*), gossipy, talkative, voluble, wordy

loquacity babbling, chattering, chattiness, effusiveness, gabbling, garrulity, gassiness (*informal*), talkativeness, volubility

lord **1.** commander, governor, king, leader, liege, master, monarch, overlord, potentate, prince, ruler, seigneur, sovereign, superior **2.** childe (*archaic*), earl, noble, nobleman, peer, viscount **3.** **lord it over** act big (*slang*), be overbearing, boss around (*informal*), domineer, order around, play the lord, pull rank, put on airs, swagger

Lord, Our *or* **The** the Almighty, Christ, the Galilean, God, the Good Shepherd, Jehovah, Jesus Christ, the Nazarene

lordly **1.** arrogant, condescending, despotic, dictatorial, disdainful, domineering, haughty, high and mighty (*informal*), high-handed, hoity-toity (*informal*), imperious, lofty, overbearing, patronizing, proud, stuck-up (*informal*), supercilious, toffee-nosed (*slang, chiefly Brit.*), tyrannical **2.** aristocratic, dignified, exalted, gracious, grand, imperial, lofty, majestic, noble, princely, regal, stately

lore **1.** beliefs, doctrine, experience, folk-wisdom, mythos, saws, sayings, teaching, traditional wisdom, traditions, wisdom **2.** erudition, knowhow (*informal*), knowledge, learning, letters, scholarship

lose **1.** be deprived of, displace, drop, fail to keep, forget, mislay, misplace, miss, suffer loss **2.** capitulate, default, fail, fall short, forfeit, lose out on (*informal*), miss, pass up (*informal*), yield **3.** be defeated, be the loser, be worsted, come a cropper (*informal*), come to grief, get the worst of, lose out, suffer defeat, take a licking (*informal*) **4.** consume, deplete, dissipate, drain, exhaust, expend, lavish, misspend, squander, use up, waste **5.** confuse, miss, stray from, wander from **6.** lap, leave behind, outdistance, outrun, outstrip, overtake, pass **7.** dodge, duck, elude, escape, evade, give someone the slip, shake off, slip away, throw off

You cannot lose what you never had

loser also-ran, clinker (*slang, chiefly U.S.*), dud (*informal*), failure, flop (*informal*), lemon (*slang*), no-hoper (*Austral. slang*), underdog, washout (*informal*)

> *Show me a good loser and I will show you a loser*
>
> Paul Newman

loss **1.** bereavement, deprivation, disappearance, drain, failure, forfeiture, losing, misfortune, mislaying, privation, squandering, waste **2.** cost, damage, defeat, destruction, detriment, disadvantage, harm, hurt, impairment, injury, ruin **3.** *plural* casualties, dead, death toll, fatalities, number killed (captured, injured, missing, wounded) **4.** *sometimes plural* debit, debt, deficiency, deficit, depletion, losings, shrinkage **5.** **at a loss** at one's wits' end, baffled, bewildered, confused, helpless, nonplussed, perplexed, puzzled, stuck (*informal*), stumped
Antonyms acquisition, advantage, finding, gain, preservation, recovery, reimbursement, restoration, saving, winning

One man's loss is another man's gain

lossmaking unfruitful, unprofitable
Antonyms money spinning, profitable

lost **1.** disappeared, forfeited, mislaid, misplaced, missed, missing, strayed, vanished, wayward **2.** adrift, astray, at sea, disoriented, off-course, off-track **3.** baffled, bewildered, clueless (*slang*), confused, helpless, ignorant, mystified, perplexed, puzzled **4.** abolished, annihilated, demolished, destroyed, devastated, eradicated, exterminated, obliterated, perished, ruined, wasted, wiped out, wrecked **5.** absent, absorbed, abstracted, distracted, dreamy, engrossed, entranced, preoccupied, rapt, spellbound, taken up **6.** consumed, dissipated, frittered away, misapplied, misdirected, misspent, misused, squandered, wasted **7.** bygone, dead, extinct, forgotten, gone, lapsed, obsolete, out-of-date, past, unremembered **8.** abandoned, corrupt, damned, depraved, disso~

lute, fallen, irreclaimable, licentious, profligate, unchaste, wanton

lot 1. assortment, batch, bunch (*informal*), collection, consignment, crowd, group, quantity, set 2. accident, chance, destiny, doom, fate, fortune, hazard, plight, portion 3. allowance, cut (*informal*), parcel, part, percentage, piece, portion, quota, ration, share 4. **a lot** *or* **lots** abundance, a great deal, an arm and a leg (*informal*), heap(s), large amount, load(s) (*informal*), masses (*informal*), numbers, ocean(s), oodles (*informal*), piles (*informal*), plenty, quantities, reams (*informal*), scores, stack(s) 5. **draw lots** choose, cut for aces, cut straws (*informal*), decide, pick, select, spin a coin, toss up 6. **throw in one's lot with** ally *or* align oneself with, join, join forces with, join fortunes with, make common cause with, support

loth *see* LOATH

lotion balm, cream, embrocation, liniment, salve, solution

lottery 1. draw, raffle, sweepstake 2. chance, gamble, hazard, risk, toss-up (*informal*), venture

loud 1. blaring, blatant, boisterous, booming, clamorous, deafening, ear-piercing, ear-splitting, forte (*Music*), high-sounding, noisy, obstreperous, piercing, resounding, rowdy, sonorous, stentorian, strident, strong, thundering, tumultuous, turbulent, vehement, vociferous 2. *figurative* brash, brassy, flamboyant, flashy, garish, gaudy, glaring, lurid, naff (*Brit. slang*), ostentatious, showy, tacky (*informal*), tasteless, tawdry, vulgar 3. brash, brazen, coarse, crass, crude, loud-mouthed (*informal*), offensive, raucous, vulgar

Antonyms (*sense 1*) gentle, inaudible, low, low-pitched, quiet, silent, soft, soundless, subdued (*sense 2*) conservative, dull, sober, sombre (*sense 3*) quiet, reserved, retiring, shy, unassuming

loudly at full volume, at the top of one's voice, clamorously, deafeningly, fortissimo (*Music*), lustily, noisily, shrilly, uproariously, vehemently, vigorously, vociferously

loudmouth bigmouth (*slang*), blowhard (*informal*), blusterer, brag, braggadocio, braggart, bullshit artist (*taboo slang*), bullshitter (*taboo slang*), gasbag (*informal*), swaggerer, windbag (*slang*)

lounge *verb* 1. laze, lie about, loaf, loiter, loll, make oneself at home, recline, relax, saunter, sprawl, take it easy 2. dawdle, fritter time away, hang out (*informal*), idle, kill time, pass time idly, potter, veg out (*slang, chiefly U.S.*), waste time

lour, lower 1. be brewing, blacken, cloud up *or* over, darken, loom, menace, threaten 2. frown, give a dirty look, glare, glower, look daggers, look sullen, scowl

louring, lowering 1. black, clouded, cloudy, dark, darkening, forbidding, foreboding, gloomy, grey, heavy, menacing, ominous, overcast, threatening 2. brooding, forbidding, frowning, glowering, grim, scowling, sullen, surly

lousy 1. *slang* base, contemptible, despicable, dirty, hateful, low, mean, rotten (*informal*), shitty (*taboo slang*), vicious, vile 2. *slang* awful, bad, bush-league (*Austral. & N.Z. informal*), chickenshit (*U.S. slang*), dime-a-dozen (*informal*), duff, for the birds (*informal*), inferior, low-rent (*informal, chiefly U.S.*), miserable, no good, not much cop (*Brit. slang*), of a sort *or* of sorts, piss-poor (*taboo slang*), poor, poxy (*slang*), rotten (*informal*), second-rate, shitty (*taboo slang*), shoddy, slovenly, strictly for the birds (*informal*), terrible, tinhorn (*U.S. slang*), two-bit (*U.S. & Canad. slang*) 3. lice-infected, lice-infested, lice-ridden, pedicular, pediculous 4. **lousy with** *slang* **a.** amply supplied with, not short of, rolling in (*slang*), well-supplied with **b.** alive with, overrun by, swarming with, teeming with

lout bear, boor, bumpkin, churl, clod, clumsy idiot, dolt, gawk, lubber, lummox (*informal*), ned (*slang*), oaf, yahoo, yob *or* yobbo (*Brit. slang*)

loutish boorish, bungling, churlish, clodhopping (*informal*), coarse, doltish, gawky, gross, ill-bred, ill-mannered, lubberly, lumpen (*informal*), lumpish, oafish, rough, stolid, swinish, uncouth, unmannerly

lovable adorable, amiable, attractive, captivating, charming, cuddly, cute, delightful, enchanting, endearing, engaging, fetching (*informal*), likable *or* likeable, lovely, pleasing, sweet, winning, winsome

Antonyms abhorrent, abominable, detestable, hateful, loathsome, obnoxious, odious, offensive, revolting

love *verb* 1. adore, adulate, be attached to, be in love with, cherish, dote on, have affection for, hold dear, idolize, prize, think the world of, treasure, worship 2. appreciate, delight in, desire, enjoy, fancy, have a weakness for, like, relish, savour, take pleasure in 3. canoodle (*slang*), caress, cuddle, embrace, fondle, kiss, neck (*informal*), pet ~*noun* 4. adoration, adulation, affection, amity, ardour, attachment, devotion, fondness, friendship, infatuation, liking, passion, rapture, regard, tenderness, warmth 5. delight, devotion, enjoyment, fondness, inclination, liking, partiality, relish, soft spot, taste, weakness 6. angel, beloved, darling, dear, dearest, dear one, inamorata, inamorato, leman (*archaic*), loved one, lover, sweet, sweetheart, truelove 7. **for love** for nothing, freely, free of charge, gratis, pleasurably, without payment **8. for love or money** by any means, ever, under any conditions **9. in love** besotted, charmed, enamoured, enraptured, infatuated, smitten **10. fall in love (with)** bestow one's affections on, be taken with, fall for, lose one's heart (to), take a shine to (*informal*)

Antonyms *verb* (*senses 1 & 2*) abhor, abominate, detest, dislike, hate, scorn *~noun* (*senses 4 & 5*) abhorrence, abomination, animosity, antagonism, antipathy, aversion, bad blood, bitterness, detestation, disgust, dislike, hate, hatred, hostility, ill will, incompatibility, loathing, malice, repugnance, resentment, scorn (*sense 6*) enemy, foe

How do I love thee? Let me count the ways
Elizabeth Barrett Browning *Sonnets from the Portuguese*

All that matters is love and work
attributed to Sigmund Freud

Money was scarce but new love has no need of money. Somewhere to go, to be together is all and we were lucky. We had that. Hell is love with no place to go
Dilys Rose *All the Little Loved Ones*

To be overtopped in anything else I can bear: but in the tests of generous love I defy all mankind
Robert Burns *letter to Clarinda*

Love's pleasure lasts but a moment; love's sorrow lasts all through life
Jean-Pierre Claris de Florian *Celestine*

What love is, if thou wouldst be taught,
Thy heart must teach alone -
Two souls with but a single thought,
Two hearts that beat as one
Friedrich Halm *Der Sohn der Wildnis*

Love is like the measles; we all have to go through it
Jerome K. Jerome *The Idle Thoughts of an Idle Fellow*

Love's like the measles - all the worse when it comes late in life
Douglas Jerrold *Wit and Opinions of Douglas Jerrold*

No, there's nothing half so sweet in life
As love's young dream
Thomas Moore *Love's Young Dream*

And all for love, and nothing for reward
Edmund Spenser *The Faerie Queene*

'Tis better to have loved and lost
Than never to have loved at all
Alfred, Lord Tennyson *In Memoriam A.H.H.*

In the Spring a livelier iris changes on the burnish'd dove;
In the Spring a young man's fancy lightly turns to thoughts of love
Alfred, Lord Tennyson *Locksley Hall*

Love is like any other luxury. You have no right to it unless you can afford it
Anthony Trollope *The Way we Live Now*

Love conquers all things; let us too give in to love
Virgil *Eclogue*

Love and do what you will
Saint Augustine of Hippo *In Epistolam Joannis ad Parthos*

Those have most power to hurt us that we love
Francis Beaumont and John Fletcher *The Maid's Tragedy*

My love's a noble madness
John Dryden *All for Love*

And love's the noblest frailty of the mind
John Dryden *The Indian Emperor*

Love's tongue is in the eyes
Phineas Fletcher *Piscatory Eclogues*

Love is only one of many passions
Dr. Johnson *Plays of William Shakespeare, preface*

Where both deliberate, the love is slight;
Whoever loved that loved not at first sight?
Christopher Marlowe *Hero and Leander*

Men love in haste, but they detest at leisure
Lord Byron *Don Juan*

Men have died from time to time and worms have eaten them, but not for love
William Shakespeare *As You Like It*

The course of true love never did run smooth
William Shakespeare *A Midsummer Night's Dream*

Love is not love
Which alters when it alteration finds
William Shakespeare *Sonnets*

Love is like linen - often changed, the sweeter
Phineas Fletcher *Sicelides*

O my love's like a red, red rose
Robert Burns *A Red, Red Rose*

Two things a man cannot hide: that he is drunk, and that he is in love
Antiphanes

Every man is a poet when he is in love
Plato *Symposium*

one that lov'd not wisely but too well
William Shakespeare *Othello*

Love is like quicksilver in the hand. Leave the fingers open and it stays. Clutch it, and it darts away
Dorothy Parker

Love does not consist in gazing at each other, but in looking outward in the same direction
Antoine de Saint-Exupéry

Love ceases to be a pleasure, when it ceases to be a secret
Aphra Behn *The Lover's Watch, Four O'Clock*

Women who love the same man have a kind of bitter freemasonry
Max Beerbohm *Zuleika Dobson*

Many waters cannot quench love, neither can the floods drown it
Bible: Song of Solomon

Greater love hath no man than this, that a man lay down his life for his friends
Bible: St. John

O lyric Love, half-angel and half-bird
And all a wonder and a wild desire
Robert Browning *The Ring and the Book*

Man's love is of man's life a thing apart,
'Tis woman's whole existence
Lord Byron *Don Juan*

Whoever loves, if he do not propose
The right true end of love, he's one that goes
To sea for nothing but to make him sick
John Donne *Love's Progress*

I am two fools, I know,
For loving, and for saying so
In whining poetry
John Donne *The Triple Fool*

How alike are the groans of love to those of the dying
Malcolm Lowry *Under the Volcano*

Love is the delusion that one woman differs from another
H.L. Mencken *Chrestomathy*

After all, my erstwhile dear,
My no longer cherished,
Need we say it was not love,
Now that love has perished?
Edna St. Vincent Millay *Passer Mortuus Est*

If I am pressed to say why I loved him, I feel it can only be explained by replying: "Because it was he; because it was me."
Montaigne *Essais*

Love built on beauty, soon as beauty, dies
John Donne *The Anagram*

Love thy neighbour as thyself
Bible: Leviticus

All's fair in love and war

Love is blind

One cannot love and be wise

Love makes the world go round

Love will find a way

love affair 1. affair, *affaire de coeur*, amour, intrigue, liaison, relationship, romance 2. appreciation, devotion, enthusiasm, love, mania, passion

loveless 1. disliked, forsaken, friendless, lovelorn, unappreciated, uncherished, unloved, unvalued 2. cold, cold-hearted, frigid, hard, heartless, icy, insensitive, unfeeling, unfriendly, unloving, unresponsive

lovelorn crossed in love, jilted, languishing, lovesick, mooning, moping, pining, slighted, spurned, unrequited, yearning

lovely 1. admirable, adorable, amiable, attractive, beautiful, charming, comely, exquisite, graceful, handsome, pretty, sweet, winning 2. agreeable, captivating, delightful, enchanting, engaging, enjoyable, gratifying, nice, pleasant, pleasing

Antonyms abhorrent, detestable, hateful, hideous, loathsome, odious, repellent, repugnant, revolting, ugly, unattractive

lovemaking act of love, carnal knowledge, coition, coitus, copulation, intercourse, intimacy, mating, nookie (*slang*), rumpy-pumpy (*slang*), sexual intercourse, sexual relations, sexual union *or* congress, the other (*informal*)

lover admirer, beau, beloved, boyfriend, fancy bit (*slang*), fancy man (*slang*), fancy woman (*slang*), fiancé, fiancée, flame (*informal*), girlfriend, inamorata, inamorato, leman (*archaic*), mistress, paramour, suitor, swain (*archaic*), sweetheart, toy boy

All mankind love a lover
Ralph Waldo Emerson *Spiritual Laws*

lovesick desiring, languishing, longing, lovelorn, pining, yearning

loving affectionate, amorous, ardent, cordial, dear, demonstrative, devoted, doting, fond, friendly, kind, solicitous, tender, warm, warm-hearted

Antonyms aloof, cold, contemptuous, cruel, detached, distasteful, hateful, hostile, indifferent, mean, scornful, unconcerned, unloving

low[1] *adjective* 1. fubsy (*archaic or dialect*), little, short, small, squat, stunted 2. deep, depressed, ground-level, low-lying, shallow, subsided, sunken 3. depleted, insignificant, little, meagre, measly, paltry, reduced, scant, small, sparse, trifling 4. deficient, inadequate, inferior, low-grade, low-rent (*informal, chiefly U.S.*), mediocre, pathetic, poor, puny, second-rate, shoddy, substandard, worthless 5. coarse, common, crude, disgraceful, dishonourable, disreputable, gross, ill-bred, obscene, rough, rude, unbecoming, undignified, unrefined, vulgar 6. humble, lowborn, lowly, meek, obscure, plain, plebeian, poor, simple, unpretentious 7. blue, brassed off (*Brit. slang*), dejected, depressed, despondent, disheartened, dismal, down, downcast, down in the dumps (*informal*), fed up, forlorn, gloomy, glum, miserable, morose, sad, sick as a parrot (*informal*), unhappy 8. debilitated, dying, exhausted, feeble, frail, ill, prostrate, reduced, sinking, stricken, weak 9. gentle, hushed, muffled, muted, quiet, soft, subdued, whispered 10. cheap, economical, inexpensive, moderate, modest, reasonable 11. abject, base, contemptible, dastardly, degraded, depraved, despicable, ignoble, mean, menial, nasty, scurvy, servile, sordid, unworthy, vile, vulgar

Antonyms admirable, alert, brave, cheerful, elated, elevated, eminent, energetic, enthusiastic, exalted, fine, grand, happy, high, high-ranking, honourable, important, laudable, lofty, loud, noisy, praiseworthy, significant, strong, superior, tall, towering, worthy

low[2] 1. *verb* bellow, moo 2. *noun* bellow, bel~ lowing, lowing, moo, mooing

lowdown *informal* dope (*informal*), gen (*Brit. informal*), info (*informal*), information, inside story, intelligence

low-down base, cheap (*informal*), contempt~ ible, despicable, low, mean, nasty, reprehen~ sible, scurvy, ugly, underhand

lower[1] *adjective* 1. inferior, junior, lesser, low-level, minor, secondary, second-class, smaller, subordinate, under 2. curtailed, decreased, di~ minished, lessened, pared down, reduced ~*verb* 3. depress, drop, fall, let down, make lower, sink, submerge, take down 4. abase, belittle, condescend, debase, degrade, deign, demean, devalue, disgrace, downgrade, hum~ ble, humiliate, stoop 5. abate, curtail, cut, de~ crease, diminish, lessen, minimize, moderate, prune, reduce, slash 6. soften, tone down
Antonyms *adjective* enlarged, higher, in~ creased ~*verb* amplify, augment, boost, el~ evate, enlarge, extend, hoist, increase, inflate, lift, magnify, raise

lower[2] *see* LOUR

lowering *see* LOURING

low-grade bad, bush-league (*Austral. & N.Z. informal*), chickenshit (*U.S. slang*), dime-a-dozen (*informal*), duff (*informal*), inferior, low-rent (*informal, chiefly U.S.*), not good enough, not up to snuff (*informal*), of a sort *or* of sorts, piss-poor (*taboo slang*), poor, poxy (*slang*), second-rate, substandard, tinhorn (*U.S. slang*), two-bit (*U.S. & Canad. slang*)

low-key keeping a low profile, low-pitched, muffled, muted, played down, quiet, re~ strained, subdued, toned down, understated

lowly 1. ignoble, inferior, lowborn, mean, ob~ scure, plebeian, proletarian, subordinate 2. docile, dutiful, gentle, humble, meek, mild, modest, submissive, unassuming 3. average, common, homespun, modest, ordinary, plain, poor, simple, unpretentious

low-minded coarse, crude, dirty, disgusting, filthy, foul, gross, indecent, obscene, rude, smutty, uncouth, vulgar

low-spirited apathetic, blue, brassed off (*Brit. slang*), dejected, depressed, despondent, dis~ mal, down, down-hearted, down in the dumps (*informal*), down in the mouth, fed up, gloomy, heavy-hearted, low, miserable, moody, sad, unhappy

low-tech basic, simple, unsophisticated
Antonyms high-tech *or* hi-tech, scientific, technical, technological

loyal attached, constant, dependable, devoted, dutiful, faithful, immovable, patriotic, staunch, steadfast, tried and true, true, true-blue, true-hearted, trustworthy, trusty, un~ swerving, unwavering
Antonyms disloyal, false, perfidious, traitor~ ous, treacherous, unfaithful, untrustworthy

loyalty allegiance, constancy, dependability, devotion, faithfulness, fealty, fidelity, patriot~ ism, reliability, staunchness, steadfastness, troth (*archaic*), true-heartedness, trueness, trustiness, trustworthiness

No man can serve two masters

Bible: St. Matthew

lozenge cough drop, jujube, pastille, tablet, troche

lubberly *adjective* awkward, blundering, bun~ gling, churlish, clodhopping (*informal*), clown~ ish, clumsy, coarse, crude, doltish, gawky, heavy-handed, loutish, lumbering, lumpen (*informal*), lumpish, oafish, uncouth, ungainly

lubricate grease, make slippery, make smooth, oil, oil the wheels, smear, smooth the way

lucid 1. clear, clear-cut, comprehensible, crystal clear, distinct, evident, explicit, intelligible, limpid, obvious, pellucid, plain, transparent 2. beaming, bright, brilliant, effulgent, gleaming, luminous, radiant, resplendent, shining 3. clear, crystalline, diaphanous, glassy, limpid, pellucid, pure, translucent, transparent 4. all there, clear-headed, *compos mentis*, in one's right mind, rational, reasonable, sane, sen~ sible, sober, sound
Antonyms (*sense 1*) ambiguous, clear as mud (*informal*), confused, equivocal, incomprehen~ sible, indistinct, muddled, unclear, unintelli~ gible, vague (*sense 2*) dull (*sense 3*) unclear (*sense 4*) confused, irrational, muddled, un~ clear, unperceptive, vague

luck 1. accident, chance, destiny, fate, fortuity, fortune, hap (*archaic*), hazard 2. advantage, blessing, break (*informal*), fluke, godsend, good fortune, good luck, prosperity, serendip~ ity, stroke, success, windfall

The more I practise the luckier I get

Gary Player

You win some, you lose some

luckily 1. favourably, fortunately, happily, op~ portunely, propitiously, providentially 2. as it chanced, as luck would have it, by chance, fortuitously

luckless calamitous, cursed, disastrous, doomed, hapless, hopeless, ill-fated, ill-starred, jinxed, star-crossed, unfortunate, un~ happy, unlucky, unpropitious, unsuccessful

lucky 1. advantageous, blessed, charmed, fa~ voured, fortunate, jammy (*Brit. slang*), on a roll (*informal*), prosperous, serendipitous, suc~ cessful 2. adventitious, auspicious, fortuitous, opportune, propitious, providential, timely
Antonyms bad, detrimental, ominous, unfa~

vourable, unfortunate, unhappy, unlucky, un~promising, untimely
Lucky at cards, unlucky in love
Third time lucky

lucrative advantageous, fat, fruitful, gainful, high-income, money-making, paying, produc~tive, profitable, remunerative, well-paid

lucre gain, mammon, money, pelf, profit, riches, spoils, wealth

lucubration 1. brainwork, grind (*informal*), meditation, study 2. dissertation, opus, pro~duction, treatise

ludicrous absurd, burlesque, comic, comical, crazy, droll, farcical, funny, incongruous, laughable, nonsensical, odd, outlandish, pre~posterous, ridiculous, silly, zany
Antonyms grave, logical, sad, sensible, seri~ous, solemn

lug carry, drag, haul, heave, hump (*Brit. slang*), pull, tow, yank

luggage baggage, bags, cases, gear, impedi~menta, paraphernalia, suitcases, things, trunks

lugubrious dirgelike, dismal, doleful, dreary, funereal, gloomy, melancholy, morose, mourn~ful, sad, serious, sombre, sorrowful, woebe~gone, woeful

lukewarm 1. blood-warm, tepid, warm 2. *fig~urative* apathetic, cold, cool, half-arsed (*Brit. slang*), half-assed (*U.S. & Canad. slang*), half-hearted, indifferent, laodicean, phlegmat~ic, unconcerned, unenthusiastic, uninterested, unresponsive

lull *verb* 1. allay, calm, compose, hush, lullaby, pacify, quell, quiet, rock to sleep, soothe, still, subdue, tranquillize 2. abate, cease, decrease, diminish, dwindle, ease off, let up, moderate, quieten down, slacken, subside, wane *~noun* 3. calm, calmness, hush, let-up (*informal*), pause, quiet, respite, silence, stillness, tran~quillity

lullaby berceuse, cradlesong

lumber¹ 1. *noun* castoffs, clutter, discards, jumble, junk, refuse, rubbish, trash, trump~ery, white elephants 2. *verb, Brit. slang* bur~den, encumber, impose upon, land, load, sad~dle

lumber² *verb* clump, lump along, plod, sham~ble, shuffle, stump, trudge, trundle, waddle

lumbering awkward, blundering, bovine, bum~bling, clumsy, elephantine, heavy, heavy-footed, hulking, lubberly, overgrown, ponder~ous, ungainly, unwieldy

luminary big name, celeb (*informal*), celebrity, dignitary, leading light, lion, megastar (*infor~mal*), notable, personage, somebody, star, V.I.P., worthy

luminescent Day-Glo, effulgent, fluorescent, glowing, luminous, phosphorescent, radiant, shining

luminous 1. bright, brilliant, glowing, illumi~nated, lighted, lit, luminescent, lustrous, ra~diant, resplendent, shining, vivid 2. clear, evi~dent, intelligible, lucid, obvious, perspicuous, plain, transparent

lump¹ *noun* 1. ball, bunch, cake, chunk, clod, cluster, dab, gob, gobbet, group, hunk, mass, nugget, piece, spot, wedge 2. bulge, bump, growth, hump, protrusion, protuberance, swelling, tumescence, tumour *~verb* 3. agglu~tinate, aggregate, batch, bunch, coalesce, col~lect, combine, conglomerate, consolidate, group, mass, pool, unite

lump² *verb* bear, brook, endure, hack (*slang*), put up with, stand, suffer, take, thole (*North~ern English dialect*), tolerate

lumpish awkward, bungling, clumsy, doltish, elephantine, gawky, heavy, lethargic, lumber~ing, oafish, obtuse, puddingy, stolid, stupid, ungainly

lumpy bumpy, clotted, curdled, full of lumps, grainy, granular, knobbly, uneven

lunacy 1. dementia, derangement, idiocy, in~sanity, madness, mania, psychosis 2. aberra~tion, absurdity, craziness, folly, foolhardiness, foolishness, idiocy, imbecility, madness, senselessness, stupidity, tomfoolery
Antonyms prudence, reason, sanity, sense

lunatic 1. *adjective* as daft as a brush (*infor~mal, chiefly Brit.*), barking (*slang*), barking mad (*slang*), barmy (*slang*), bonkers (*slang, chiefly Brit.*), crackbrained, crackpot (*infor~mal*), crazy, daft, demented, deranged, gonzo (*slang*), insane, irrational, loopy (*informal*), mad, maniacal, not the full shilling (*infor~mal*), nuts (*slang*), off one's trolley (*slang*), out to lunch (*informal*), psychotic, unhinged, up the pole (*informal*), wacko *or* whacko (*infor~mal*) 2. *noun* headbanger (*informal*), headcase (*informal*), loony (*slang*), madman, maniac, nut (*slang*), nutcase (*slang*), nutter (*Brit. slang*), psychopath

lunge 1. *noun* charge, cut, jab, pass, pounce, spring, stab, swing, swipe (*informal*), thrust 2. *verb* bound, charge, cut, dash, dive, fall upon, hit at, jab, leap, pitch into (*informal*), plunge, poke, pounce, set upon, stab, strike at, thrust

lurch 1. heave, heel, lean, list, pitch, rock, roll, tilt, wallow 2. reel, stagger, stumble, sway, totter, weave

lure 1. *verb* allure, attract, beckon, decoy, draw, ensnare, entice, inveigle, invite, lead on, se~duce, tempt 2. *noun* allurement, attraction, bait, carrot (*informal*), come-on (*informal*), decoy, enticement, incentive, inducement, magnet, siren song, temptation

lurid 1. exaggerated, graphic, melodramatic, sensational, shock-horror (*facetious*), shocking, startling, unrestrained, vivid, yellow (*of journalism*) 2. disgusting, ghastly, gory, grim, grisly, gruesome, macabre, revolting, savage, violent 3. ashen, ghastly, pale, pallid, sallow, wan 4. bloody, fiery, flaming, glaring, glowering, intense, livid, overbright, sanguine
Antonyms (*senses 1 & 2*) breezy, bright, carefree, controlled, factual, jaunty, light-hearted, mild (*sense 4*) pale, pastel, watery

lurk conceal oneself, crouch, go furtively, hide, lie in wait, move with stealth, prowl, skulk, slink, sneak, snoop

luscious appetizing, delectable, delicious, honeyed, juicy, mouth-watering, palatable, rich, savoury, scrumptious (*informal*), succulent, sweet, toothsome, yummy (*slang*)

lush 1. abundant, dense, flourishing, green, lavish, overgrown, prolific, rank, teeming, verdant 2. fresh, juicy, ripe, succulent, tender 3. elaborate, extravagant, grand, lavish, luxurious, opulent, ornate, palatial, plush (*informal*), ritzy (*slang*), sumptuous

lust *noun* 1. carnality, concupiscence, lasciviousness, lechery, lewdness, libido, licentiousness, pruriency, randiness (*informal, chiefly Brit.*), salaciousness, sensuality, the hots (*slang*), wantonness 2. appetence, appetite, avidity, covetousness, craving, cupidity, desire, greed, longing, passion, thirst ~*verb* 3. be consumed with desire for, covet, crave, desire, hunger for *or* after, lech after (*informal*), need, slaver over, want, yearn

Natural freedoms are but just;
There's something generous in mere lust
John Wilmot, Earl of Rochester *A Ramble in St. James' Park*

lustful carnal, concupiscent, craving, hankering, horny (*slang*), hot-blooded, lascivious, lecherous, lewd, libidinous, licentious, passionate, prurient, randy (*informal, chiefly Brit.*), raunchy (*slang*), sensual, sexy (*informal*), unchaste, wanton

lustily forcefully, hard, loudly, powerfully, strongly, vigorously, with all one's might, with might and main

lustre 1. burnish, gleam, glint, glitter, gloss, glow, sheen, shimmer, shine, sparkle 2. brightness, brilliance, dazzle, lambency, luminousness, radiance, resplendence 3. distinction, fame, glory, honour, illustriousness, prestige, renown

lustreless colourless, dingy, drab, dull, faded, flat, lacklustre, lifeless, matt, pale, tarnished, unpolished, washed out

lustrous bright, burnished, dazzling, gleaming, glistening, glossy, glowing, luminous, radiant, shimmering, shining, shiny, sparkling

lusty brawny, energetic, hale, healthy, hearty, in fine fettle, powerful, red-blooded (*informal*), robust, rugged, stalwart, stout, strapping, strong, sturdy, vigorous, virile

luxuriant 1. abundant, ample, copious, excessive, lavish, plenteous, plentiful, prodigal, profuse, superabundant 2. baroque, corinthian, decorated, elaborate, extravagant, fancy, festooned, flamboyant, florid, flowery, ornate, rococo, sumptuous 3. dense, exuberant, fecund, fertile, flourishing, fruitful, lush, overflowing, productive, prolific, rank, rich, riotous, teeming, thriving
Antonyms barren, meagre, plain, scanty, simple, sparse, thin, unadorned

luxuriate 1. bask, delight, enjoy, flourish, indulge, relish, revel, wallow 2. abound, bloom, burgeon, flourish, grow, prosper, thrive 3. be in clover, have the time of one's life, live in luxury, live the life of Riley, take it easy, wanton

luxurious 1. comfortable, costly, de luxe, expensive, lavish, magnificent, opulent, plush (*informal*), rich, ritzy (*slang*), splendid, sumptuous, well-appointed 2. epicurean, pampered, pleasure-loving, self-indulgent, sensual, sybaritic, voluptuous
Antonyms ascetic, austere, deprived, economical, plain, poor, sparing, Spartan, squalid, thrifty

luxury 1. affluence, hedonism, opulence, richness, splendour, sumptuousness, voluptuousness 2. bliss, comfort, delight, enjoyment, gratification, indulgence, pleasure, satisfaction, wellbeing 3. extra, extravagance, frill, indulgence, nonessential, treat
Antonyms austerity, burden, deprivation, destitution, difficulty, discomfort, hardship, infliction, misery, necessity, need, poverty, privation, want

Give us the luxuries of life, and we will dispense with its necessities
John Lothrop Motley

lying 1. *noun* deceit, dishonesty, dissimulation, double-dealing, duplicity, fabrication, falsity, fibbing, guile, mendacity, perjury, prevarication, untruthfulness 2. *adjective* deceitful, dishonest, dissembling, double-dealing, false, guileful, mendacious, perfidious, treacherous, two-faced, untruthful
Antonyms *adjective* candid, forthright, frank, honest, reliable, sincere, straight, straightforward, truthful, veracious

lyric *adjective* 1. *of poetry* expressive, lyrical, melodic, musical, songlike 2. *of a voice* clear, dulcet, flowing, graceful, light, silvery *~noun* **3.** *plural* book, libretto, text, the words, words of a song

lyrical carried away, ecstatic, effusive, emotional, enthusiastic, expressive, impassioned, inspired, poetic, rapturous, rhapsodic

M

macabre cadaverous, deathlike, deathly, dreadful, eerie, frightening, frightful, ghastly, ghostly, ghoulish, grim, grisly, gruesome, hideous, horrid, morbid, unearthly, weird
Antonyms appealing, beautiful, charming, delightful, lovely, pleasant

macerate mash, pulp, soak, soften, steep

machiavellian amoral, artful, astute, crafty, cunning, cynical, deceitful, designing, double-dealing, foxy, intriguing, opportunist, perfidious, scheming, shrewd, sly, underhand, unscrupulous, wily

machinate conspire, contrive, design, devise, engineer, hatch, intrigue, invent, manoeuvre, plan, plot, scheme

machination artifice, cabal, conspiracy, design, device, dodge, intrigue, manoeuvre, plot, ploy, ruse, scheme, stratagem, trick

machine **1.** apparatus, appliance, contraption, contrivance, device, engine, instrument, mechanism, tool **2.** agency, machinery, organization, party, setup (*informal*), structure, system **3.** *figurative* agent, automaton, mechanical man, puppet, robot, zombie

machinery **1.** apparatus, equipment, gear, instruments, mechanism, tackle, tools, works **2.** agency, channels, machine, organization, procedure, structure, system

The world is dying of machinery
George Moore *Confessions of a Young Man*

macho butch (*slang*), chauvinist, he-man, manly, masculine, virile

mad **1.** aberrant, as daft as a brush (*informal, chiefly Brit.*), bananas (*slang*), barking (*slang*), barking mad (*slang*), barmy (*slang*), batty (*slang*), bonkers (*slang, chiefly Brit.*), crackers (*Brit. slang*), crackpot (*informal*), crazed, crazy (*informal*), cuckoo (*informal*), delirious, demented, deranged, distracted, doolally (*slang*), flaky (*U.S. slang*), frantic, frenzied, gonzo (*slang*), insane, loony (*slang*), loopy (*informal*), lost one's marbles (*informal*), lunatic, mental (*slang*), *non compos mentis*, not right in the head, not the full shilling (*informal*), nuts (*slang*), nutty (*slang*), off one's chump (*slang*), off one's head (*slang*), off one's nut (*slang*), off one's rocker (*slang*), off one's trolley (*slang*), of unsound mind, out of one's mind, out to lunch (*informal*), psychotic, rabid, raving, round the bend (*Brit. slang*), round the twist (*Brit. slang*), screwy (*informal*), unbalanced, unhinged, unstable, up the pole (*informal*), wacko *or* whacko (*informal*) **2.** absurd, as daft as a brush (*informal, chiefly Brit.*), asinine, daft (*informal*), foolhardy, foolish, imprudent, inane, irrational, ludicrous, nonsensical, preposterous, senseless, unreasonable, unsafe, unsound, wild **3.** *informal* angry, ape (*slang*), apeshit (*slang*), berserk, choked, cross, enraged, exasperated, fit to be tied (*slang*), fuming, furious, in a wax (*informal, chiefly Brit.*), incensed, infuriated, irate, irritated, livid (*informal*), raging, resentful, seeing red (*informal*), wild, wrathful **4.** ardent, avid, crazy, daft (*informal*), devoted, dotty (*slang, chiefly Brit.*), enamoured, enthusiastic, fanatical, fond, hooked, impassioned, infatuated, in love with, keen, nuts (*slang*), wild, zealous **5.** abandoned, agitated, boisterous, ebullient, energetic, excited, frenetic, frenzied, full-on (*informal*), gay, riotous, uncontrolled, unrestrained, wild **6. like mad** *informal* energetically, enthusiastically, excitedly, furiously, hell for leather, like greased lightning (*informal*), like lightning, like nobody's business (*informal*), like the clappers (*Brit. informal*), madly, quickly, rapidly, speedily, unrestrainedly, violently, wildly, with might and main
Antonyms appeased, calm, composed, cool, mollified, nonchalant, rational, sane, sensible, sound, uncaring

The mad are all in God's keeping
Rudyard Kipling *Kim*

I'm mad as hell and I'm not going to take it any more!
Paddy Chayefsky *Network*

Whom God would destroy he first sends mad
James Duport *Homeri Gnomologia*

madcap **1.** *adjective* crackpot (*informal*), crazy, foolhardy, hare-brained, heedless, hot-headed, ill-advised, imprudent, impulsive, lively, rash, reckless, thoughtless, wild **2.** *noun* daredevil, hothead, tearaway, wild man

madden aggravate (*informal*), annoy, craze, derange, drive one crazy (off one's head (*slang*), out of one's mind, round the bend (*Brit. slang*), round the twist (*Brit. slang*), to distraction) (*informal*), enrage, exasperate, gall, get one's back up, get one's dander up

(*informal*), get one's goat (*slang*), get one's hackles up, incense, inflame, infuriate, irritate, make one's blood boil, make one see red (*informal*), make one's hackles rise, nark (*Brit., Austral., & N.Z. slang*), piss one off (*taboo slang*), provoke, put one's back up, raise one's hackles, unhinge, upset, vex
Antonyms appease, calm, mollify, pacify, soothe

made-up fabricated, false, fictional, imaginary, invented, make-believe, mythical, specious, trumped-up, unreal, untrue

madhouse 1. funny farm (*facetious*), insane asylum, laughing academy (*U.S. slang*), loony bin (*slang*), lunatic asylum, mental hospital, mental institution, nuthouse (*slang*), psychiatric hospital, rubber room (*U.S. slang*) 2. Babel, bedlam, chaos, pandemonium, turmoil, uproar

madly 1. crazily, deliriously, dementedly, distractedly, frantically, frenziedly, hysterically, insanely, rabidly 2. absurdly, foolishly, irrationally, ludicrously, nonsensically, senselessly, unreasonably, wildly 3. energetically, excitedly, furiously, hastily, hell for leather, hotfoot, hurriedly, like greased lightning (*informal*), like lightning, like mad (*informal*), like nobody's business (*informal*), like the clappers (*Brit. informal*), quickly, rapidly, recklessly, speedily, violently, wildly 4. *informal* desperately, devotedly, exceedingly, excessively, extremely, intensely, passionately, to distraction

madman *or* **madwoman** headbanger (*informal*), headcase (*informal*), loony (*slang*), lunatic, maniac, mental case (*slang*), nut (*slang*), nutcase (*slang*), nutter (*Brit. slang*), psycho (*slang*), psychopath, psychotic

madness 1. aberration, craziness, delusion, dementia, derangement, distraction, insanity, lunacy, mania, mental illness, psychopathy, psychosis 2. absurdity, daftness (*informal*), folly, foolhardiness, foolishness, idiocy, nonsense, preposterousness, wildness 3. anger, exasperation, frenzy, fury, ire, rage, raving, wildness, wrath 4. ardour, craze, enthusiasm, fanaticism, fondness, infatuation, keenness, passion, rage, zeal 5. abandon, agitation, excitement, frenzy, furore, intoxication, riot, unrestraint, uproar

We are all born mad. Some remain so
Samuel Beckett *Waiting for Godot*

Though this be madness, yet there's method in't
William Shakespeare *Hamlet*

That way madness lies
William Shakespeare *King Lear*

maelstrom 1. vortex, whirlpool 2. bedlam, chaos, confusion, disorder, pandemonium, tumult, turmoil, upheaval, uproar

maestro expert, genius, master, virtuoso

magazine 1. journal, pamphlet, paper, periodical 2. ammunition dump, arsenal, depot, powder room (*obsolete*), store, storehouse, warehouse

magic *noun* 1. black art, enchantment, necromancy, occultism, sorcery, sortilege, spell, theurgy, witchcraft, wizardry 2. conjuring, hocus-pocus, illusion, jiggery-pokery (*informal, chiefly Brit.*), jugglery, legerdemain, prestidigitation, sleight of hand, trickery 3. allurement, charm, enchantment, fascination, glamour, magnetism, power *~adjective* 4. *Also* **magical** bewitching, charismatic, charming, enchanting, entrancing, fascinating, magnetic, marvellous, miraculous, sorcerous, spellbinding

magician 1. archimage (*rare*), conjurer, conjuror, enchanter, enchantress, illusionist, necromancer, sorcerer, thaumaturge (*rare*), theurgist, warlock, witch, wizard 2. genius, marvel, miracle-worker, spellbinder, virtuoso, wizard, wonder-worker

magisterial arrogant, assertive, authoritative, bossy (*informal*), commanding, dictatorial, domineering, high-handed, imperious, lordly, masterful, overbearing, peremptory
Antonyms deferential, diffident, humble, servile, shy, submissive, subservient, wimpish *or* wimpy (*informal*)

magistrate bailie (*Scot.*), J.P., judge, justice, justice of the peace, provost (*Scot.*)

magnanimity beneficence, big-heartedness, bountifulness, charitableness, generosity, high-mindedness, largess *or* largesse, munificence, nobility, open-handedness, selflessness, unselfishness

magnanimous beneficent, big, big-hearted, bountiful, charitable, free, generous, great-hearted, handsome, high-minded, kind, kindly, munificent, noble, open-handed, selfless, ungrudging, unselfish, unstinting
Antonyms miserly, petty, resentful, selfish, small, unforgiving, vindictive

magnate 1. baron, big cheese (*slang, old-fashioned*), big noise (*informal*), big shot (*informal*), big wheel (*slang*), bigwig (*informal*), captain of industry, chief, fat cat (*slang, chiefly U.S.*), leader, Mister Big (*slang, chiefly U.S.*), mogul, nabob (*informal*), notable, plutocrat, tycoon, V.I.P. 2. aristo (*informal*), aristocrat, baron, bashaw, grandee, magnifico, merchant, nob (*slang, chiefly Brit.*), noble, notable, personage, prince

magnetic alluring, attractive, captivating, charismatic, charming, enchanting, entrancing, fascinating, hypnotic, irresistible, mesmerizing, seductive
Antonyms disagreeable, offensive, repellent,

repulsive, unappealing, unattractive, unlikable *or* unlikeable, unpleasant

magnetism allure, appeal, attraction, attractiveness, captivatingness, charisma, charm, draw, drawing power, enchantment, fascination, hypnotism, magic, mesmerism, power, pull, seductiveness, spell

magnification aggrandizement, amplification, augmentation, blow-up (*informal*), boost, build-up, deepening, dilation, enhancement, enlargement, exaggeration, expansion, heightening, increase, inflation, intensification

magnificence brilliance, éclat, glory, gorgeousness, grandeur, luxuriousness, luxury, majesty, nobility, opulence, pomp, resplendence, splendour, stateliness, sublimity, sumptuousness

magnificent august, brilliant, divine (*informal*), elegant, elevated, exalted, excellent, fine, glorious, gorgeous, grand, grandiose, imposing, impressive, lavish, luxurious, majestic, noble, opulent, outstanding, princely, regal, resplendent, rich, splendid, splendiferous (*facetious*), stately, striking, sublime, sumptuous, superb, superior, transcendent
Antonyms bad, humble, ignoble, lowly, mean, modest, ordinary, petty, poor, trivial, undistinguished, unimposing

magnifico 1. aristo (*informal*), aristocrat, grandee, lord, magnate, nob (*slang, chiefly Brit.*), noble, patrician, seigneur 2. bashaw, big cheese (*slang, old-fashioned*), big noise (*informal*), big shot (*informal*), big wheel (*slang*), bigwig (*informal*), mogul, nabob (*informal*), notable, personage, V.I.P.

magnify 1. aggrandize, amplify, augment, blow up (*informal*), boost, build up, deepen, dilate, enlarge, expand, heighten, increase, intensify 2. aggravate, blow up, blow up out of all proportion, dramatize, enhance, exaggerate, inflate, make a federal case of (*U.S. informal*), make a mountain out of a molehill, make a production (out) of (*informal*), overdo, overemphasize, overestimate, overplay, overrate, overstate
Antonyms belittle, decrease, deflate, denigrate, deprecate, diminish, disparage, lessen, lower, minimize, reduce, shrink, understate

magniloquence bombast, fustian, grandiloquence, loftiness, pomposity, pretentiousness, turgidity

magniloquent bombastic, declamatory, elevated, exalted, grandiloquent, high-flown, high-sounding, lofty, orotund, overblown, pompous, pretentious, rhetorical, sonorous, stilted, turgid

magnitude 1. consequence, eminence, grandeur, greatness, importance, mark, moment, note, significance, weight 2. amount, amplitude, bigness, bulk, capacity, dimensions, enormity, expanse, extent, hugeness, immensity, intensity, largeness, mass, measure, proportions, quantity, size, space, strength, vastness, volume
Antonyms insignificance, meanness, smallness, triviality, unimportance

maid 1. damsel, girl, lass, lassie (*informal*), maiden, miss, nymph (*poetic*), wench 2. abigail (*archaic*), handmaiden (*archaic*), housemaid, maidservant, servant, serving-maid

maiden *noun* 1. damsel, girl, lass, lassie (*informal*), maid, miss, nymph (*poetic*), virgin, wench *~adjective* 2. chaste, intact, pure, undefiled, unmarried, unwed, virgin, virginal 3. first, inaugural, initial, initiatory, introductory 4. fresh, new, unbroached, untapped, untried, unused

maidenly chaste, decent, decorous, demure, gentle, girlish, modest, pure, reserved, undefiled, unsullied, vestal, virginal, virtuous
Antonyms brazen, corrupt, defiled, depraved, dirty, immodest, immoral, impure, indecent, loose, promiscuous, shameless, sinful, unchaste, wanton, wicked

mail *noun* 1. correspondence, letters, packages, parcels, post 2. post, postal service, postal system *~verb* 3. dispatch, forward, post, send, send by mail *or* post

maim cripple, disable, hamstring, hurt, impair, incapacitate, injure, lame, mangle, mar, mutilate, put out of action, wound

main *adjective* 1. capital, cardinal, central, chief, critical, crucial, essential, foremost, head, leading, necessary, outstanding, paramount, particular, predominant, pre-eminent, premier, primary, prime, principal, special, supreme, vital 2. absolute, brute, direct, downright, entire, mere, pure, sheer, undisguised, utmost, utter *~noun* 3. cable, channel, conduit, duct, line, pipe 4. effort, force, might, potency, power, puissance, strength 5. **in** *or* **for the main** for the most part, generally, in general, mainly, mostly, on the whole
Antonyms *adjective* auxiliary, dependent, insignificant, least, lesser, minor, secondary, subordinate, trivial, unimportant

mainly above all, chiefly, first and foremost, for the most part, generally, in general, in the main, largely, mostly, most of all, on the whole, overall, predominantly, primarily, principally, substantially, to the greatest extent, usually

mainspring cause, driving force, generator, impulse, incentive, inspiration, motivation, motive, origin, prime mover, source

mainstay anchor, backbone, bulwark, buttress, chief support, linchpin, pillar, prop

mainstream *adjective* accepted, central, conventional, core, current, established, general, orthodox, prevailing, received
Antonyms fringe, marginal, peripheral, unconventional, unorthodox

maintain 1. care for, carry on, conserve, continue, finance, keep, keep up, look after, nurture, perpetuate, preserve, prolong, provide, retain, supply, support, sustain, take care of, uphold 2. affirm, allege, assert, asseverate, aver, avow, claim, contend, declare, hold, insist, profess, state 3. advocate, argue for, back, champion, defend, fight for, justify, plead for, stand by, take up the cudgels for, uphold, vindicate
Antonyms (*sense 1*) abolish, break off, conclude, discontinue, drop, end, finish, give up, relinquish, suspend, terminate (*sense 2*) disavow (*sense 3*) abandon, desert

maintenance 1. care, carrying-on, conservation, continuance, continuation, keeping, nurture, perpetuation, preservation, prolongation, provision, repairs, retainment, supply, support, sustainment, sustention, upkeep 2. aliment, alimony, allowance, food, keep, livelihood, living, subsistence, support, sustenance, upkeep

majestic august, awesome, dignified, elevated, exalted, grand, grandiose, imperial, imposing, impressive, kingly, lofty, magnificent, monumental, noble, pompous, princely, regal, royal, splendid, splendiferous (*facetious*), stately, sublime, superb
Antonyms humble, ignoble, lowly, mean, modest, ordinary, unassuming, undistinguished, unimposing

majesty augustness, awesomeness, dignity, exaltedness, glory, grandeur, imposingness, impressiveness, kingliness, loftiness, magnificence, nobility, pomp, queenliness, royalty, splendour, state, stateliness, sublimity
Antonyms disgrace, meanness, shame, triviality

major 1. better, bigger, chief, elder, greater, head, higher, larger, lead, leading, main, most, senior, superior, supreme, uppermost 2. critical, crucial, grave, great, important, mega (*slang*), notable, outstanding, pre-eminent, radical, serious, significant, vital, weighty
Antonyms auxiliary, inconsequential, insignificant, lesser, minor, secondary, smaller, subordinate, trivial, unimportant

majority 1. best part, bulk, greater number, mass, more, most, plurality, preponderance, superiority 2. adulthood, manhood, maturity, seniority, womanhood

One, on God's side, is a majority
Wendell Phillips

make *verb* 1. assemble, build, compose, constitute, construct, create, fabricate, fashion, forge, form, frame, manufacture, mould, originate, produce, put together, shape, synthesize 2. accomplish, beget, bring about, cause, create, effect, engender, generate, give rise to, lead to, occasion, produce 3. cause, coerce, compel, constrain, dragoon, drive, force, impel, induce, oblige, press, pressurize, prevail upon, railroad (*informal*), require 4. appoint, assign, create, designate, elect, install, invest, nominate, ordain 5. draw up, enact, establish, fix, form, frame, pass 6. add up to, amount to, compose, constitute, embody, form, represent 7. act, carry out, do, effect, engage in, execute, perform, practise, prosecute 8. calculate, estimate, gauge, judge, reckon, suppose, think 9. acquire, clear, earn, gain, get, net, obtain, realize, secure, take in, win 10. arrive at, arrive in time for, attain, catch, get to, meet, reach 11. **make it** *informal* arrive (*informal*), be successful, come through, crack it (*informal*), cut it (*informal*), get on, get somewhere, prosper, pull through, succeed, survive *~noun* 12. brand, build, character, composition, constitution, construction, cut, designation, form, kind, make-up, mark, model, shape, sort, structure, style, type, variety 13. cast of mind, character, disposition, frame of mind, humour, kidney, make-up, nature, stamp, temper, temperament

make as if *or* **though** act as if *or* though, affect, feign, feint, give the impression that, make a show of, pretend

make away 1. abscond, beat a hasty retreat, clear out (*informal*), cut and run (*informal*), decamp, depart, do a runner (*slang*), flee, fly, fly the coop (*U.S. & Canad. informal*), hook it (*slang*), make off, run away *or* off, run for it (*informal*), scoot, skedaddle (*informal*), slope off, take a powder (*U.S. & Canad. slang*), take it on the lam (*U.S. & Canad. slang*), take to one's heels 2. *with* **with** abduct, cabbage (*Brit. slang*), carry off, cart off (*slang*), filch, kidnap, knock off (*slang*), make off with, nab (*informal*), nick (*slang, chiefly Brit.*), pilfer, pinch (*informal*), purloin, steal, swipe (*slang*) 3. *with* **with** blow away (*slang, chiefly U.S.*), bump off (*slang*), destroy, dispose of, do away with, do in (*slang*), eliminate, get rid of, kill, murder, rub out (*U.S. slang*)

make-believe 1. *noun* charade, dream, fantasy, imagination, play-acting, pretence, unreality 2. *adjective* dream, fantasized, fantasy, imaginary, imagined, made-up, mock, pretend, pretended, sham, unreal
Antonyms *noun* actuality, fact, reality, truthfulness *~adjective* authentic, genuine, real, unfeigned

make believe act as if *or* though, dream, enact, fantasize, imagine, play, play-act, pretend

make do cope, get along *or* by, improvise, manage, muddle through, scrape along *or* by

make for 1. aim for, be bound for, head for *or* towards, proceed towards, steer (a course) for 2. assail, assault, attack, fall on, fly at, go for, have a go at (*informal*), lunge at, set upon 3. be conducive to, conduce to, contribute to, facilitate, favour, promote

make off 1. abscond, beat a hasty retreat, bolt, clear out (*informal*), cut and run (*informal*), decamp, do a runner (*slang*), flee, fly, fly the coop (*U.S. & Canad. informal*), hook it (*slang*), make away, run away *or* off, run for it (*informal*), skedaddle (*informal*), slope off, take a powder (*U.S. & Canad. slang*), take it on the lam (*U.S. & Canad. slang*), take to one's heels 2. *with* **with** abduct, cabbage (*Brit. slang*), carry off, cart off (*slang*), filch, kidnap, knock off (*slang*), make away with, nab (*informal*), nick (*slang, chiefly Brit.*), pilfer, pinch (*informal*), purloin, run away *or* off with, steal, swipe (*slang*)

make out 1. descry, detect, discern, discover, distinguish, espy, perceive, recognize, see 2. comprehend, decipher, fathom, follow, grasp, perceive, realize, see, suss (out) (*slang*), understand, work out 3. complete, draw up, fill in *or* out, inscribe, write (out) 4. demonstrate, describe, prove, represent, show 5. assert, claim, let on, make as if *or* though, pretend 6. fare, get on, manage, prosper, succeed, thrive

maker author, builder, constructor, director, fabricator, framer, manufacturer, producer

Maker Creator, God

makeshift 1. *adjective* expedient, jury (*chiefly nautical*), make-do, provisional, rough and ready, stopgap, substitute, temporary 2. *noun* expedient, shift, stopgap, substitute

make-up 1. cosmetics, face (*informal*), greasepaint (*Theatre*), *maquillage*, paint (*informal*), powder, war paint (*informal, humorous*) 2. arrangement, assembly, composition, configuration, constitution, construction, form, format, formation, organization, structure 3. build, cast of mind, character, constitution, disposition, figure, frame of mind, make, nature, stamp, temper, temperament

God has given you one face, and you make yourselves another
William Shakespeare *Hamlet*

Most women are not so young as they are painted
Max Beerbohm

make up 1. compose, comprise, constitute, form 2. coin, compose, concoct, construct, cook up (*informal*), create, devise, dream up, fabricate, formulate, frame, hatch, invent, manufacture, originate, trump up, write 3. complete, fill, meet, supply 4. *with* **for** atone, balance, compensate, make amends, offset, recompense, redeem, redress, requite 5. bury the hatchet, call it quits, come to terms, compose, forgive and forget, make peace, mend, reconcile, settle, shake hands 6. **make up one's mind** choose, come to a decision, decide, determine, make a decision, reach a decision, resolve, settle 7. **make up to** *informal* chat up (*informal*), court, curry favour with, flirt with, make overtures to, woo

making 1. assembly, building, composition, construction, creation, fabrication, forging, manufacture, production 2. **in the making** budding, coming, emergent, growing, nascent, potential

makings 1. beginnings, capability, capacity, ingredients, materials, potentiality, potential(s), qualities 2. earnings, income, proceeds, profits, returns, revenue, takings

maladjusted alienated, disturbed, estranged, hung-up (*slang*), neurotic, unstable

maladministration blundering, bungling, corruption, dishonesty, incompetence, inefficiency, malfeasance (*Law*), malpractice, misgovernment, mismanagement, misrule

maladroit 1. awkward, bungling, cack-handed (*informal*), clumsy, hamfisted *or* -handed (*informal*), inept, inexpert, unhandy, unskilful 2. gauche, inconsiderate, inelegant, insensitive, tactless, thoughtless, undiplomatic, untoward

malady affliction, ailment, complaint, disease, disorder, ill, illness, indisposition, infirmity, lurgi (*informal*), sickness

malaise angst, anxiety, depression, discomfort, disquiet, doldrums, enervation, illness, lassitude, melancholy, sickness, unease, weakness

malapropos 1. *adjective* ill-timed, impertinent, inapposite, inappropriate, inapt, inopportune, misapplied, out of place, unseemly, unsuitable 2. *adverb* impertinently, inappositely, inappropriately, inaptly, inopportunely, out of turn, unseasonably, unsuitably, untimely 3. *noun* blunder, faux pas, gaffe, malapropism, solecism

malcontent 1. *adjective* disaffected, discontented, disgruntled, disgusted, dissatisfied, dissentious, factious, ill-disposed, rebellious, resentful, restive, unhappy, unsatisfied 2. *noun* agitator, complainer, fault-finder, grouch (*informal*), grouser, grumbler, mischief-maker, rebel, stirrer (*informal*), troublemaker

male manful, manlike, manly, masculine, virile
Antonyms camp (*informal*), effeminate, female, feminine, unmanly, wimpish *or* wimpy (*informal*), womanish, womanly

malediction anathema, curse, damnation, damning, denunciation, execration, imprecation, malison (*archaic*)

malefactor convict, criminal, crook (*informal*), culprit, delinquent, evildoer, felon, lawbreaker, miscreant, offender, outlaw, transgressor, villain, wrongdoer

maleficent baleful, deleterious, destructive, detrimental, evil, harmful, hurtful, injurious, malign, malignant, noxious, pernicious

malevolence hate, hatred, ill will, malice, maliciousness, malignity, rancour, spite, spitefulness, vengefulness, vindictiveness

malevolent baleful, evil-minded, hateful (*archaic*), hostile, ill-natured, maleficent, malicious, malign, malignant, pernicious, rancorous, spiteful, vengeful, vicious, vindictive
Antonyms amiable, benevolent, benign, friendly, gracious, kind, warm-hearted

malformation crookedness, deformity, distortion, misshape, misshapenness

malformed abnormal, contorted, crooked, deformed, distorted, irregular, misshapen, twisted

malfunction 1. *verb* break down, develop a fault, fail, go wrong 2. *noun* breakdown, defect, failure, fault, flaw, glitch, impairment

malice animosity, animus, bad blood, bitterness, enmity, evil intent, hate, hatred, ill will, malevolence, maliciousness, malignity, rancour, spite, spitefulness, spleen, vengefulness, venom, vindictiveness

> *Malice is of a low stature, but it hath very long arms*
>
> George Savile, Marquess of Halifax *Political, Moral, and Miscellaneous Thoughts*

malicious baleful, bitchy (*informal*), bitter, catty (*informal*), evil-minded, hateful, ill-disposed, ill-natured, injurious, malevolent, malignant, mischievous, pernicious, rancorous, resentful, shrewish, spiteful, vengeful, vicious
Antonyms amiable, benevolent, friendly, kind, warm-hearted

malign 1. *adjective* bad, baleful, baneful, deleterious, destructive, evil, harmful, hostile, hurtful, injurious, maleficent, malevolent, malignant, pernicious, vicious, wicked 2. *verb* abuse, asperse, bad-mouth (*slang, chiefly U.S. & Canad.*), blacken (someone's name), calumniate, defame, denigrate, derogate, disparage, do a hatchet job on (*informal*), harm, injure, knock (*informal*), libel, revile, rubbish (*informal*), run down, slag (off) (*slang*), slander, smear, speak ill of, traduce, vilify
Antonyms *adjective* agreeable, amiable, beneficial, benevolent, benign, friendly, good, harmless, honourable, innocuous, kind, moral, virtuous, warm-hearted, wholesome ~*verb* commend, compliment, extol, praise

malignant 1. baleful, bitter, destructive, harmful, hostile, hurtful, inimical, injurious, maleficent, malevolent, malicious, malign, of evil intent, pernicious, spiteful, vicious 2. *Medical* cancerous, dangerous, deadly, evil, fatal, irremediable, metastatic, uncontrollable, virulent
Antonyms (*sense 1*) amicable, benign, friendly, kind, warm-hearted (*sense 2*) benign

malignity 1. animosity, animus, bad blood, bitterness, evil, hate, hatred, hostility, ill will, malevolence, malice, maliciousness, rancour, spite, vengefulness, venom, viciousness, vindictiveness, wickedness 2. balefulness, deadliness, destructiveness, harmfulness, hurtfulness, perniciousness, virulence

malleable 1. ductile, plastic, soft, tensile, workable 2. adaptable, biddable, compliant, governable, impressionable, like putty in one's hands, manageable, pliable, tractable

malodorous evil-smelling, fetid, foul-smelling, mephitic, nauseating, niffy (*Brit. slang*), noisome, offensive, olid, putrid, rank, reeking, smelly, stinking

malpractice 1. abuse, dereliction, misbehaviour, misconduct, mismanagement, negligence 2. abuse, misdeed, offence, transgression

maltreat abuse, bully, damage, handle roughly, harm, hurt, ill-treat, injure, mistreat

maltreatment abuse, bullying, harm, ill-treatment, ill-usage, injury, mistreatment, rough handling

mammal

Mammals

aardvark
aardwolf
acouchi *or* acouchy
addax
agouti
alpaca *or* alpacca
angwantibo *or* golden potto
anteater
antelope
aoudad
arctic fox
argali *or* argal
ariel
armadillo
ass
axis (*plural* axises) *or* chital
aye-aye
babirusa
baboon
Bactrian camel
badger
baleen whale
bandicoot
Barbary ape
barbastelle
bat *or* chiropter
bharal
bear
beaver
Belgian hare
bilby, rabbit bandicoot *or* dalgyte
binturong
bison
black bear
black rat
blacktail
black whale
blaubok
blesbok
blue whale
boar
bobcat
boer goat
bongo
bonnet monkey
bontebok
boongary
bottlenose dolphin
bowhead
brocket
brown bear
brown rat *or* Norway rat
bubal *or* bubalis
buffalo

bull *see* CATTLE
burramys
bushbaby *or* galago
bushbuck *or* boschbok
bushpig
cacomistle *or* cacomixle
camel *or (Anglo-Indian)* oont
cane rat
Cape buffalo
capuchin
capybara
caracal *or* desert lynx
caribou
cat *see* CAT
catamount, catamountain *or* cat-o'-mountain
cavy
chacma
chamois *or* izard
cheetah *or* chetah
chevrotain *or* mouse deer
chigetai *or* dziggetai
chimpanzee *or* chimp
chinchilla
Chinese water deer
chipmunk
cinnamon bear
civet
colobus
coney *or* cony
corsac
cow *see* CATTLE
coyote *or* prairie wolf
coypu *or* nutria
cuscus
dasyure
deer
deer mouse
desert rat
desman
dhole
dik-dik
dingo *or (Austral.)* native dog
dog *see* DOG
dolphin
donkey
dormouse
douc
douroucouli
drill
dromedary
duck-billed platypus *or (technical)* ornithorhynchus
dugong
duiker *or* duyker
eared seal
earless seal
echidna *or* spiny anteater
eland
elephant
elephant seal
elephant shrew
elk
ermine
fennec
ferret
fieldmouse
flying fox
flying phalanger
flying squirrel
fox
fox squirrel
flying lemur *or* colugo
flying phalanger *or* glider
flying squirrel
fruit bat
gaur
gayal
gazelle
gelada
gemsbok
genet *or* genette
gerbil, gerbille *or* jerbil
gerenuk
giant panda
gibbon
giraffe *or (obsolete)* camelopard
gnu
goa
goat
gopher *or* pocket gopher
gopher *or* ground squirrel
goral
gorilla
Greenland whale
green monkey
grey fox *(U.S.)*
grey squirrel
grey whale
grey wolf *or* timber wolf
grison
grivet
grizzly bear *or* grizzly
groundhog *or* woodchuck
ground squirrel *or* gopher
grysbok
guanaco
guenon
guereza
guinea pig *or* cavy
hamster
hare
harnessed antelope
harp seal
hartebeest *or* hartbeest
harvest mouse
hedgehog
hippopotamus
hog badger
hognosed skunk
honey mouse *or* phalanger
hooded seal
horse *see* HORSE
horseshoe bat
house mouse
howler monkey
humpback *or* humpback whale
hyena *or* hyaena
hyrax *or* dassie
ibex
ichneumon
impala
indris *or* indri
insectivorous bat
jackal
jack rabbit
Jacob *or* Jacob sheep
jaguar
jaguarondi *or* jaguarundi
jerboa
jumping mouse
kalong
kangaroo
kangaroo rat
karakul *or* caracul
Kashmir goat
keitloa
kiang
killer whale, grampus *or* orc
kinkajou, honey bear *or* potto
klipspringer
koala (bear) *or (Austral.)* native bear
kob
Kodiak bear
kolinsky
kongoni
kouprey
kudu *or* koodoo
kulan
langur
laughing hyena *or* spotted hyena
lemming
lemur
leopard *or* panther
linsang
lion
llama
loris
lynx
macaco
macaque
manatee
mandrill
mangabey
Maori rat
mara
margay
markhor *or* markhoor
marmoset
marmot
marshbuck
marsupial mole
marsupial mouse
marten
meerkat
mink
minke whale
mole
mole rat
mona
mongoose
monkey *or (archaic)* jackanapes
moon rat
moose
mouflon *or* moufflon
mountain goat
mountain lion
mouse
mule
mule deer
muntjac, muntjak *or* barking deer
musk deer
muskrat
musquash
narwhal *or* narwhale
nilgai, nilghau *or* nylghau
noctule
numbat *or* banded anteater
nyala
ocelot
okapi
onager
opossum *or* possum
orang-outang, orang-utan *or* orang
oribi
oryx

otter
otter shrew
ox *see* CATTLE
paca
pack rat
pademelon *or* paddy~melon
palm civet
panda
pangolin *or* scaly ant~eater
panther
peccary
Père David's deer
phalanger
pig *see* PIG
pika *or* cony
pilot whale *or* black~fish
pine marten *or* sweet marten
pipistrelle
pocket mouse
polar bear *or* *(N. Canad.)* nanook
polecat
porcupine
porpoise
prairie dog
proboscis monkey
pronghorn
pudu
puma *or* cougar
quokka
rabbit *or* cottontail
raccoon, racoon *or* coon
raccoon dog
rasse
rat
ratel
rat kangaroo
razorback
red deer
red fox
red squirrel *or* chickaree
reedbuck *or* nagor
reindeer
rhebok *or* reebok
rhesus monkey
rhinoceros
right whale
Rocky Mountain goat
roe deer
rooikat
rorqual
sable
sable antelope
saiga
saki
sambar *or* sambur
sassaby
sea cow
seal
sea lion
sea otter
sei whale
serotine
serow
serval
sheep *or* *(Austral. slang)* jumbuck *see* SHEEP
shrew *or* shrewmouse
shrew mole
siamang
sifaka
sika
silver fox
skunk
sloth *or* ai
sloth bear
snow leopard *or* ounce
snowshoe hare *or* snowshoe rabbit
solenodon
sperm whale *or* cachalot
spider monkey
springbok
springhaas
squirrel
squirrel monkey
stag
star-nosed mole
steenbok
stoat
stone marten
strandwolf
sugar glider
sun bear
suslik *or* souslik
swift fox *or* kit fox
taguan
tahr *or* thar
takin
talapoin
tamandu, tamandua *or* lesser anteater
tamarin
tammar
tana
tapir
tarsier
Tasmanian devil
tayra
teledu
tenrec
thylacine, Tasmanian wolf *or* Tasmanian tiger
tiger
tiger cat
timber wolf
titi
toothed whale
tree kangaroo
tree shrew
tuan
tucotuco
vampire bat
vervet
vicuña *or* vicuna
viscacha *or* vizcacha
vole
wallaby
wallaroo
walrus *or* *(archaic)* sea horse
wanderoo
wapiti
wart hog
waterbuck
water buffalo, water ox *or* carabao
water rat
water shrew
water vole *or* water rat
weasel
whale
white elephant
white-footed mouse
white rat
white-tailed deer
white whale *or* beluga
wild boar
wildebeest
wolf
wolverine, glutton *or* carcajou
wombat
woodchuck
yak
yapok
zebra
zebu
zibeline
zibet
zo *or* zho *or* dzo
zorilla *or* zorille

Extinct mammals

apeman
aurochs
australopithecine
baluchitherium
chalicothere
creodont
dinoceras *or* uinta~there
dinothere
dryopithecine
eohippus
glyptodont
Irish elk
labyrinthodont
mammoth
mastodon
megathere
nototherium
quagga
sabre-toothed tiger *or* cat
tarpan
titanothere

Tiger! Tiger! burning bright
In the forests of the night;
What immortal hand or eye,
Could frame thy fearful symmetry?

William Blake *The Tiger*

gnu: an animal of South Africa, which in its domesticated state resembles a horse, a buffalo, and a stag. In its wild condition it is something like a thunderbolt, an earthquake and a cyclone

Ambrose Bierce *The Devil's Dictionary*

nature's great masterpiece, an elephant
The only harmless great thing

John Donne *The Progress of the Soul*

mouse: an animal which strews its path with fainting women

Ambrose Bierce *The Devil's Dictionary*

The leopard does not change his spots

mammoth Brobdingnagian, colossal, elephan~tine, enormous, gargantuan, giant, gigantic, ginormous (*informal*), huge, humongous *or* humungous (*U.S. slang*), immense, jumbo (*in~formal*), massive, mega (*slang*), mighty,

monumental, mountainous, prodigious, stellar (*informal*), stupendous, titanic, vast
Antonyms diminutive, insignificant, little, miniature, minute, puny, small, tiny, trivial

man *noun* **1**. bloke (*Brit. informal*), chap (*informal*), gentleman, guy (*informal*), male **2**. adult, being, body, human, human being, individual, one, person, personage, somebody, soul **3**. Homo sapiens, humanity, humankind, human race, mankind, mortals, people **4**. attendant, employee, follower, hand, hireling, liegeman, manservant, retainer, servant, soldier, subject, subordinate, valet, vassal, worker, workman **5**. beau, boyfriend, husband, lover, partner, significant other (*U.S. informal*), spouse **6**. **to a man** bar none, every one, one and all, unanimously, without exception *~verb* **7**. crew, fill, furnish with men, garrison, occupy, people, staff
Related adjectives: anthropic, anthropoid, anthropoidal

Man is only a reed, the weakest thing in nature; but he is a thinking reed
Blaise Pascal *Pensées*

Man is the measure of all things
Protagoras

Man is heaven's masterpiece
Francis Quarles *Emblems*

The more I see of men, the better I like dogs
Mme Roland

There are many wonderful things, and nothing is more wonderful than man
Sophocles *Antigone*

Man is a noble animal, splendid in ashes, and pompous in the grave
Thomas Browne *Hydriotaphia*

Man is an embodied paradox, a bundle of contradictions
Charles Colton *Lacon*

Man has but three events in his life: to be born, to live, and to die. He is not conscious of his birth, he suffers at his death and he forgets to live
Jean de la Bruyère *The Characters, or the Manners of the Age*

The four stages of man are infancy, childhood, adolescence and obsolescence
Art Linkletter *A Child's Garden of Misinformation*

Man is a useless passion
Jean-Paul Sartre *L'Être et le néant*

Glory to Man in the highest! for Man is the master of things
Algernon Charles Swinburne *Atalanta in Calydon: Hymn of Man*

I sometimes think that God in creating man somewhat overestimated his ability
Oscar Wilde

What a piece of work is man!
William Shakespeare *Hamlet*

Man is nature's sole mistake
W.S. Gilbert *Princess Ida*

Man is something to be surpassed
Friedrich Nietzche *Thus Spake Zarathustra*

The human race, to which so many of my readers belong
G.K. Chesterton *The Napoleon of Notting Hill*

Man was formed for society
William Blackstone *Commentaries on the Laws of England*

The male is a domestic animal which, if treated with firmness and kindness, can be trained to do most things
Jilly Cooper

man: an animal so lost in rapturous contemplation of what he thinks he is as to overlook what he indubitably ought to be
Ambrose Bierce *The Devil's Dictionary*

Men are but children of a larger growth
John Dryden *All for Love*

A man is as old as he's feeling,
A woman as old as she looks
Mortimer Collins *The Unknown Quantity*

Men play the game, women know the score
Roger Woddis

The best of men are but men at best

manacle **1**. *noun* bond, chain, fetter, gyve (*archaic*), handcuff, iron, shackle, tie **2**. *verb* bind, chain, check, clap *or* put in irons, confine, constrain, curb, fetter, hamper, handcuff, inhibit, put in chains, restrain, shackle, tie one's hands

manage **1**. administer, be in charge (of), call the shots, call the tune, command, concert, conduct, direct, govern, handle, manipulate, oversee, preside over, rule, run, superintend, supervise **2**. accomplish, arrange, bring about *or* off, contrive, cope with, crack it (*informal*), cut it (*informal*), deal with, effect, engineer, succeed **3**. control, dominate, govern, guide, handle, influence, manipulate, operate, pilot, ply, steer, train, use, wield **4**. carry on, cope, fare, get along, get by (*informal*), get on, make do, make out, muddle through, shift, survive
Antonyms bodge (*informal*), botch, fail, follow, make a mess of, make a nonsense of, mismanage, muff, spoil, starve

manageable amenable, compliant, controllable, convenient, docile, easy, governable, handy, submissive, tamable, tractable, user-friendly, wieldy
Antonyms demanding, difficult, disobedient, hard, headstrong, obstinate, refractory, stubborn, ungovernable, unruly, unyielding, wild

management **1**. administration, board, bosses (*informal*), directorate, directors, employers, executive(s) **2**. administration, care, charge, command, conduct, control, direction, govern~

ance, government, guidance, handling, manipulation, operation, rule, running, superintendence, supervision

manager administrator, boss (*informal*), comptroller, conductor, controller, director, executive, gaffer (*informal, chiefly Brit.*), governor, head, organizer, overseer, proprietor, superintendent, supervisor

mandate authority, authorization, bidding, canon, charge, command, commission, decree, directive, edict, fiat, injunction, instruction, order, precept, sanction, warrant

mandatory binding, compulsory, obligatory, required, requisite
Antonyms discretionary, nonbinding, noncompulsory, nonobligatory, optional, unnecessary, voluntary

manful bold, brave, courageous, daring, determined, gallant, hardy, heroic, indomitable, intrepid, manly, noble, powerful, resolute, stalwart, stout, stout-hearted, strong, valiant, vigorous

manfully boldly, bravely, courageously, desperately, determinedly, gallantly, hard, heroically, intrepidly, like a Trojan, like one possessed, like the devil, nobly, powerfully, resolutely, stalwartly, stoutly, strongly, to the best of one's ability, valiantly, vigorously, with might and main

mangle butcher, cripple, crush, cut, deform, destroy, disfigure, distort, hack, lacerate, maim, mar, maul, mutilate, rend, ruin, spoil, tear, total (*slang*), trash (*slang*), wreck

mangy dirty, grungy (*slang, chiefly U.S.*), mean, moth-eaten, scabby (*informal*), scruffy, scuzzy (*slang, chiefly U.S.*), seedy, shabby, shoddy, squalid
Antonyms attractive, choice, clean, de luxe, fine, splendid, spotless, superb, tidy, well-dressed, well-kempt, well-kept

manhandle **1.** handle roughly, knock about *or* around, maul, paw (*informal*), pull, push, rough up **2.** carry, haul, heave, hump (*Brit. slang*), lift, manoeuvre, pull, push, shove, tug

manhood bravery, courage, determination, firmness, fortitude, hardihood, manfulness, manliness, masculinity, maturity, mettle, resolution, spirit, strength, valour, virility

mania **1.** aberration, craziness, delirium, dementia, derangement, disorder, frenzy, insanity, lunacy, madness **2.** cacoethes, craving, craze, desire, enthusiasm, fad (*informal*), fetish, fixation, obsession, partiality, passion, preoccupation, rage, thing (*informal*)

Types of mania

ablutomania	washing
agoramania	open spaces
ailuromania	cats
andromania	men
Anglomania	England
anthomania	flowers
apimania	bees
arithmomania	counting
automania	solitude
autophonomania	suicide
balletomania	ballet
ballistomania	bullets
bibliomania	books
chionomania	snow
choreomania	dancing
chrematomania	money
cremnomania	cliffs
cynomania	dogs
dipsomania	alcohol
doramania	fur
dromomania	travelling
egomania	one's self
eleuthromania	freedom
entheomania	religion
entomomania	insects
ergasiomania	work
eroticomania	erotica
erotomania	sex
florimania	plants
gamomania	marriage
graphomania	writing
gymnomania	nakedness
gynomania	women
hamartomania	sin
hedonomania	pleasure
heliomania	sun
hippomania	horses
homicidomania	murder
hydromania	water
hylomania	woods
hypnomania	sleep
ichthyomania	fish
iconomania	icons
kinesomania	movement
kleptomania	stealing
logomania	talking
macromania	becoming larger
megalomania	one's own importance
melomania	music
mentulomania	penises
micromania	becoming smaller
monomania	one thing
musicomania	music
musomania	mice
mythomania	lies
necromania	death
noctimania	night
nudomania	nudity
nymphomania	sex
ochlomania	crowds
oikomania	home
oinomania	wine
ophidiomania	reptiles
orchidomania	testicles

ornithomania	birds
phagomania	eating
pharmacomania	medicines
phonomania	noise
photomania	light
plutomania	great wealth
potomania	drinking
pyromania	fire
scribomania	writing
siderodromomania	railway travel
sitomania	food
sophomania	one's own wisdom
thalassomania	the sea
thanatomania	death
theatromania	theatre
timbromania	stamps
trichomania	hair
verbomania	words
xenomania	foreigners
zoomania	animals

maniac 1. headbanger (*informal*), headcase (*informal*), loony (*slang*), lunatic, madman, madwoman, nutcase (*slang*), nutter (*Brit. slang*), psycho (*slang*), psychopath 2. energumen, enthusiast, fan, fanatic, fiend (*informal*), freak (*informal*)

maniacal *or* **manic** berserk, crazed, crazy, demented, deranged, frenzied, gonzo (*slang*), insane, lunatic, mad, neurotic, nutty (*slang*), psychotic, raving, unbalanced, wild

manifest 1. *adjective* apparent, blatant, bold, clear, conspicuous, distinct, evident, glaring, noticeable, obvious, open, palpable, patent, plain, salient, unmistakable, visible 2. *verb* declare, demonstrate, display, establish, evince, exhibit, expose, express, make plain, prove, reveal, set forth, show
Antonyms *adjective* concealed, disguised, hidden, inconspicuous, indistinct, masked, suppressed, unapparent, vague, veiled *~verb* conceal, cover, cover up, deny, hide, mask, obscure, refute

manifestation appearance, demonstration, disclosure, display, exhibition, exposure, expression, indication, instance, mark, materialization, revelation, show, sign, symptom, token

manifold abundant, assorted, copious, diverse, diversified, many, multifarious, multifold, multiple, multiplied, multitudinous, numerous, varied, various

manipulate 1. employ, handle, operate, ply, use, wield, work 2. conduct, control, direct, do a number on (*chiefly U.S.*), engineer, guide, influence, manoeuvre, negotiate, steer, twist around one's little finger

mankind Homo sapiens, humanity, humankind, human race, man, people

I hate mankind, for I think myself one of the best of them, and I know how bad I am
Dr. Johnson

Mankind have been created for the sake of one another. Either instruct them, therefore, or endure them
Marcus Aurelius *Meditations*

manliness boldness, bravery, courage, fearlessness, firmness, hardihood, heroism, independence, intrepidity, machismo, manfulness, manhood, masculinity, mettle, resolution, stoutheartedness, valour, vigour, virility

manly bold, brave, butch (*slang*), courageous, daring, dauntless, fearless, gallant, hardy, heroic, macho, male, manful, masculine, muscular, noble, powerful, red-blooded (*informal*), resolute, robust, stout-hearted, strapping, strong, valiant, valorous, vigorous, virile, well-built
Antonyms camp (*informal*), cowardly, craven, delicate, effeminate, faint-hearted, feeble, feminine, frail, ignoble, irresolute, sickly, soft, timid, unmanly, weak, wimpish *or* wimpy (*informal*), womanish

man-made artificial, ersatz, manufactured, mock, plastic (*slang*), synthetic

manner 1. air, appearance, aspect, bearing, behaviour, comportment, conduct, demeanour, deportment, look, mien (*literary*), presence, tone 2. approach, custom, fashion, form, genre, habit, line, means, method, mode, practice, procedure, process, routine, style, tack, tenor, usage, way, wont 3. brand, breed, category, form, kind, nature, sort, type, variety

mannered affected, artificial, posed, pretentious, pseudo (*informal*), put-on, stilted
Antonyms genuine, honest, natural, real, sincere, unaffected, unpretentious

mannerism characteristic, foible, habit, idiosyncrasy, peculiarity, quirk, trait, trick

mannerly civil, civilized, courteous, decorous, genteel, gentlemanly, gracious, ladylike, polished, polite, refined, respectful, well-behaved, well-bred, well-mannered
Antonyms boorish, discourteous, disrespectful, ill-mannered, impertinent, impolite, impudent, insolent, rude, unmannerly

manners 1. bearing, behaviour, breeding, carriage, comportment, conduct, demeanour, deportment 2. ceremony, courtesy, decorum, etiquette, formalities, good form, polish, politeness, politesse, proprieties, protocol, p's and q's, refinement, social graces, the done thing

To Americans, English manners are far more frightening than none at all
Randall Jarrell *Pictures from an Institution*

Manners maketh man

manoeuvrable fast-moving, handleable, manipulatable, mobile, responsive, versatile

manoeuvre *noun* **1.** action, artifice, dodge, intrigue, machination, move, movement, plan, plot, ploy, ruse, scheme, stratagem, subterfuge, tactic, trick **2.** deployment, evolution, exercise, movement, operation *~verb* **3.** contrive, devise, engineer, intrigue, machinate, manage, manipulate, plan, plot, pull strings, scheme, wangle (*informal*) **4.** deploy, exercise, move **5.** direct, drive, guide, handle, navigate, negotiate, pilot, steer

mansion abode, dwelling, habitation, hall, manor, residence, seat, villa

mantle *noun* **1.** *archaic* cape, cloak, hood, shawl, wrap **2.** blanket, canopy, cloud, cover, covering, curtain, envelope, pall, screen, shroud, veil *~verb* **3.** blanket, cloak, cloud, cover, disguise, envelop, hide, mask, overspread, screen, shroud, veil, wrap

manual 1. *adjective* done by hand, hand-operated, human, physical **2.** *noun* bible, enchiridion (*rare*), guide, guidebook, handbook, instructions, workbook

manufacture *verb* **1.** assemble, build, compose, construct, create, fabricate, forge, form, make, mass-produce, mould, process, produce, put together, shape, turn out **2.** concoct, cook up (*informal*), devise, fabricate, hatch, invent, make up, think up, trump up *~noun* **3.** assembly, construction, creation, fabrication, making, mass-production, produce, production

manufacturer builder, constructor, creator, fabricator, factory-owner, industrialist, maker, producer

manumission deliverance, emancipation, enfranchisement, freeing, liberation, release, unchaining

manumit deliver, emancipate, enfranchise, free, liberate, release, set free, unchain

manure compost, droppings, dung, excrement, fertilizer, muck, ordure

many *adjective* **1.** abundant, copious, countless, divers (*archaic*), frequent, innumerable, manifold, multifarious, multifold, multitudinous, myriad, numerous, profuse, sundry, umpteen (*informal*), varied, various *~noun* **2.** a horde, a lot, a mass, a multitude, a thousand and one, heaps (*informal*), large numbers, lots (*informal*), piles (*informal*), plenty, scores, tons (*informal*), umpteen (*informal*) **3. the many** crowd, hoi polloi, majority, masses, multitude, people, rank and file

mar blemish, blight, blot, damage, deface, detract from, disfigure, harm, hurt, impair, injure, maim, mangle, mutilate, put a damper on, ruin, scar, spoil, stain, sully, taint, tarnish, vitiate

Antonyms adorn, ameliorate, better, embellish, improve, ornament

maraud despoil, forage, foray, harry, loot, pillage, plunder, raid, ransack, ravage, reive (*dialect*), sack

marauder bandit, brigand, buccaneer, cateran (*Scot.*), corsair, freebooter, mosstrooper, outlaw, pillager, pirate, plunderer, raider, ravager, reiver (*dialect*), robber

march *verb* **1.** file, footslog, pace, parade, stalk, stride, strut, tramp, tread, walk *~noun* **2.** hike, routemarch, tramp, trek, walk **3.** demo (*informal*), demonstration, parade, procession **4.** gait, pace, step, stride **5.** advance, development, evolution, progress, progression **6. on the march** advancing, afoot, astir, en route, marching, on one's way, on the way, proceeding, progressing, under way

marches borderland, borders, boundaries, confines, frontiers, limits, marchlands

margin 1. border, bound, boundary, brim, brink, confine, edge, limit, perimeter, periphery, rim, side, verge **2.** allowance, compass, elbowroom, extra, latitude, leeway, play, room, scope, space, surplus

marginal 1. bordering, borderline, on the edge, peripheral **2.** insignificant, low, minimal, minor, negligible, slight, small

marijuana bhang, blow (*slang*), cannabis, charas, dope (*slang*), gage (*U.S. old-fashioned slang*), ganja, grass (*slang*), hash (*slang*), hashish, hemp, kif, leaf (*slang*), mary jane (*U.S. slang*), pot (*slang*), sinsemilla, smoke (*informal*), stuff (*slang*), tea (*U.S. slang*), wacky baccy (*slang*), weed (*slang*)

I experimented with marijuana a time or two.
And I didn't like it, and I didn't inhale
Bill Clinton

marine maritime, nautical, naval, ocean-going, oceanic, pelagic, saltwater, sea, seafaring, seagoing, thalassic

mariner bluejacket, gob (*U.S. slang*), hand, Jack Tar, matelot (*slang, chiefly Brit.*), navigator, sailor, salt, sea dog, seafarer, seafaring man, seaman, tar

marital conjugal, connubial, married, matrimonial, nuptial, spousal, wedded

maritime 1. marine, nautical, naval, oceanic, sea, seafaring **2.** coastal, littoral, seaside

mark *noun* **1.** blemish, blot, blotch, bruise, dent, impression, line, nick, pock, scar, scratch, smirch, smudge, splotch, spot, stain, streak **2.** badge, blaze, brand, characteristic, device, earmark, emblem, evidence, feature, flag, hallmark, impression, incision, index, indication, label, note, print, proof, seal, sign, signet, stamp, symbol, symptom, token **3.** criterion, level, measure, norm, par, standard, yardstick **4.** aim, end, goal, object, objective, purpose, target **5.** consequence, dignity, distinction, eminence, fame, importance, influence, notability, note, notice, prestige, quality, regard, standing **6**. footmark, footprint, sign, trace, track, trail, vestige **7**. **make one's mark** achieve recognition, be a success, find a place in the sun, get on in the world, make a success of oneself, make good, make it (*informal*), make something of oneself, prosper, succeed *~verb* **8**. blemish, blot, blotch, brand, bruise, dent, impress, imprint, nick, scar, scratch, smirch, smudge, splotch, stain, streak **9**. brand, characterize, flag, identify, label, stamp **10**. betoken, denote, distinguish, evince, exemplify, illustrate, show **11**. attend, hearken (*archaic*), mind, note, notice, observe, pay attention, pay heed, regard, remark, watch **12**. appraise, assess, correct, evaluate, grade

marked apparent, blatant, clear, considerable, conspicuous, decided, distinct, dramatic, evident, manifest, notable, noted, noticeable, obvious, outstanding, patent, prominent, pronounced, remarkable, salient, signal, striking
Antonyms concealed, doubtful, dubious, hidden, imperceptible, inconspicuous, indistinct, insignificant, obscure, unclear, unnoticeable, vague

markedly clearly, considerably, conspicuously, decidedly, distinctly, evidently, greatly, manifestly, notably, noticeably, obviously, outstandingly, patently, remarkably, seriously (*informal*), signally, strikingly, to a great extent

market **1**. *noun* bazaar, fair, mart **2**. *verb* offer for sale, retail, sell, vend

marketable in demand, merchantable, saleable, sought after, vendible, wanted

marksman, -woman crack shot (*informal*), deadeye (*informal, chiefly U.S.*), dead shot (*informal*), good shot, sharpshooter

maroon abandon, cast ashore, cast away, desert, leave, leave high and dry (*informal*), strand

marriage **1**. espousal, match, matrimony, nuptial rites, nuptials, wedding, wedding ceremony, wedlock **2**. alliance, amalgamation, association, confederation, coupling, link, merger, union
Related adjectives: connubial, hymeneal, nuptial

Happiness in marriage is entirely a matter of chance
Jane Austen *Pride and Prejudice*

If there is one notion I hate more than another, it is that of marriage - I mean marriage in the vulgar, weak sense, as a mere matter of sentiment
Charlotte Bronte *Shirley*

Every woman should marry - and no man
Benjamin Disraeli *Lothair*

There are good marriages, but no delightful ones
Duc de la Rochefoucauld *Réflexions ou Sentences et Maximes Morales*

It doesn't much signify whom one marries, for one is sure to find next morning that it was someone else
Samuel Rogers *Table Talk*

It is a woman's business to get married as soon as possible, and a man's to keep unmarried as long as he can
George Bernard Shaw *Man and Superman*

Marriage is like life in this - that it is a field of battle, and not a bed of roses
Robert Louis Stevenson *Virginibus Puerisque*

If all men are born free, how is it that all women are born slaves?
Mary Astell *Some Reflections upon Marriage*

I married beneath me, all women do
Nancy Astor

Single women have a dreadful propensity for being poor - which is one very strong argument in favour of matrimony
Jane Austen *letter*

Marriage always demands the finest arts of insincerity possible between two human beings
Vicki Baum *Zwischenfall in Lohwinckel*

Marriage is the grave or tomb of wit
Margaret Cavendish, Duchess of Newcastle *Nature's Three Daughters*

Courtship to marriage, as a very witty prologue to a very dull play
William Congreve *The Old Bachelor*

I am to be married within these three days; married past redemption
John Dryden *Marriage à la Mode*

When I said I would die a bachelor I did not think I should live till I were married
William Shakespeare *Much Ado About Nothing*

Men are April when they woo, December when they wed
William Shakespeare *As You Like It*

One should always be in love. That is the reason one should never marry
Oscar Wilde *A Woman of No Importance*

Marriage is a great institution, but I'm not ready for an institution yet
Mae West

Marriage has many pains, but celibacy has no pleasures
Dr. Johnson

Marriages are made in Heaven
John Lyly *Euphues and his England*

Men marry because they are tired, women because they are curious; both are disappointed
Oscar Wilde *A Woman of No Importance*

A man in love is incomplete until he has married. Then he's finished
Zsa Zsa Gabor

A happy marriage is a long conversation which always seems too short
André Maurois *Memories*

Marriage is three parts love and seven parts forgiveness
Langdon Mitchell

Marriage is a great institution - no family should be without it
Bob Hope

Marriage is popular because it combines the maximum of temptation with the maximum of opportunity
George Bernard Shaw *Maxims for Revolutionists*

Strange to say what delight we married people have to see these poor fools decoyed into our condition
Samuel Pepys

Bigamy is having one husband too many. Monogamy is the same thing
Erica Jong

No man is genuinely happy, married, who has to drink worse whisky than he used to drink when he was single
H.L. Mencken *Selected Prejudices*

Kissing don't last: cookery do!
George Meredith *The Ordeal of Richard Feverel*

There is not one in a hundred of either sex who is not taken in when they marry... it is, of all transactions, the one in which people expect most from others, and are least honest themselves
Jane Austen *Mansfield Park*

Therefore shall a man leave his father and his mother, and shall cleave unto his wife: and they shall be one flesh
Bible: Genesis

It was very good of God to let Carlyle and Mrs. Carlyle marry one another and so make only two people miserable instead of four
Samuel Butler

one fool at least in every married couple
Henry Fielding *Amelia*

Hogamus, higamous
Man is polygamous
Higamus, hogamous
Woman monogamous
William James

There once was an old man of Lyme
Who married three wives at a time,
When asked "Why a third?"
He replied, "One's absurd!
And bigamy, Sir, is a crime!"
William Cosmo Monkhouse

Marriage may often be a stormy lake, but celibacy is almost always a muddy horsepond
Thomas Love Peacock *Melincourt*

married **1.** hitched (*slang*), joined, one, spliced (*informal*), united, wed, wedded **2.** conjugal, connubial, husbandly, marital, matrimonial, nuptial, spousal, wifely

marrow core, cream, essence, gist, heart, kernel, pith, quick, quintessence, soul, spirit, substance

marry **1.** become man and wife, espouse, get hitched (*slang*), get spliced (*informal*), plight one's troth (*old-fashioned*), take the plunge (*informal*), take to wife, tie the knot (*informal*), walk down the aisle (*informal*), wed, wive (*archaic*) **2.** ally, bond, join, knit, link, match, merge, splice, tie, unify, unite, yoke

Thus grief still treads upon the heels of pleasure:
Marry'd in haste, we may repent at leisure
William Congreve *The Old Bachelor*

It is better to marry than to burn
Bible: I Corinthians

Advice for persons about to marry. -'Don't.'
Punch

Never marry for money, but marry where money is

marsh bog, fen, morass, moss (*Scot. & northern English dialect*), quagmire, slough, swamp
Related adjective: paludal

marshal **1.** align, arrange, array, assemble, collect, deploy, dispose, draw up, gather, group, line up, muster, order, organize, rank, sequence **2.** conduct, escort, guide, lead, shepherd, usher

marshy boggy, fenny, miry, quaggy, spongy, swampy, waterlogged, wet

martial bellicose, belligerent, brave, heroic, military, soldierly, warlike

martinet disciplinarian, drillmaster, stickler

martyrdom agony, anguish, ordeal, persecution, suffering, torment, torture
Antonyms bliss, ecstasy, happiness, joy

marvel **1.** *verb* be amazed, be awed, be filled with surprise, gape, gaze, goggle, wonder **2.** *noun* genius, miracle, phenomenon, portent, prodigy, whiz (*informal*), wonder

marvellous **1.** amazing, astonishing, astounding, breathtaking, brilliant, extraordinary, miraculous, phenomenal, prodigious, remarkable, sensational (*informal*), singular, spectacular, stupendous, wondrous (*archaic or literary*) **2.** difficult *or* hard to believe, fabulous, fantastic, implausible, improbable, incredible, surprising, unbelievable, unlikely **3.** *informal* awesome (*slang*), bad (*slang*), bodacious (*slang, chiefly U.S.*), boffo (*slang*), brill (*informal*), chillin' (*U.S. slang*), colossal, cracking (*Brit. informal*), crucial (*slang*), def (*slang*), divine (*informal*), excellent, fabulous (*informal*), fantastic (*informal*), glorious, great (*informal*), jim-dandy (*slang*), magnificent, mean (*slang*), mega (*slang*), sensational (*informal*), smashing (*informal*), sovereign, splendid, stupendous, super (*informal*), superb, terrific (*informal*), topping (*Brit. slang*), wicked (*informal*), wonderful

Antonyms awful, bad, believable, commonplace, credible, everyday, ordinary, terrible

Marxism

I am a Groucho Marxist
French student graffitti, 1968

masculine 1. male, manful, manlike, manly, mannish, virile 2. bold, brave, butch (*slang*), gallant, hardy, macho, muscular, powerful, red-blooded (*informal*), resolute, robust, stout-hearted, strapping, strong, vigorous, well-built

mask *noun* 1. domino, false face, visor, vizard (*archaic*) 2. blind, camouflage, cloak, concealment, cover, cover-up, disguise, façade, front, guise, screen, semblance, show, veil, veneer *~verb* 3. camouflage, cloak, conceal, cover, disguise, hide, obscure, screen, veil

masquerade *noun* 1. costume ball, fancy dress party, mask, masked ball, masked party, mummery, revel 2. costume, disguise, domino 3. cloak, cover, cover-up, deception, disguise, dissimulation, front (*informal*), guise, imposture, mask, pose, pretence, put-on (*slang*), screen, subterfuge *~verb* 4. disguise, dissemble, dissimulate, impersonate, mask, pass oneself off, pose, pretend (to be)

mass *noun* 1. block, chunk, concretion, hunk, lump, piece 2. aggregate, body, collection, entirety, sum, sum total, totality, whole 3. accumulation, aggregation, assemblage, batch, bunch, collection, combination, conglomeration, heap, load, lot, pile, quantity, rick, stack 4. assemblage, band, body, bunch (*informal*), crowd, group, horde, host, lot, mob, number, throng, troop 5. body, bulk, greater part, lion's share, majority, preponderance 6. bulk, dimension, greatness, magnitude, size 7. **the masses** commonalty, common people, crowd, hoi polloi, multitude *~adjective* 8. extensive, general, indiscriminate, large-scale, pandemic, popular, wholesale, widespread *~verb* 9. accumulate, amass, assemble, collect, congregate, forgather, gather, mob, muster, rally, swarm, throng

massacre 1. *noun* annihilation, blood bath, butchery, carnage, extermination, holocaust, killing, mass slaughter, murder, slaughter 2. *verb* annihilate, blow away (*slang, chiefly U.S.*), butcher, cut to pieces, exterminate, kill, mow down, murder, slaughter, slay, take out (*slang*), wipe out

massage 1. *noun* acupressure, kneading, manipulation, reflexology, rubbing, rub-down, shiatsu 2. *verb* knead, manipulate, rub, rub down

massive big, bulky, colossal, elephantine, enormous, extensive, gargantuan, gigantic, ginormous (*informal*), great, heavy, hefty, huge, hulking, humongous *or* humungous (*U.S. slang*), immense, imposing, impressive, mammoth, mega (*slang*), monster, monumental, ponderous, solid, stellar (*informal*), substantial, titanic, vast, weighty, whacking (*informal*), whopping (*informal*)
Antonyms frail, light, little, minute, petty, slight, small, thin, tiny, trivial

master *noun* 1. boss (*informal*), captain, chief, commander, controller, director, employer, governor, head, lord, manager, overlord, overseer, owner, principal, ruler, skipper (*informal*), superintendent 2. ace (*informal*), adept, dab hand (*Brit. informal*), doyen, expert, genius, grandmaster, maestro, maven (*U.S.*), past master, pro (*informal*), virtuoso, wizard 3. guide, guru, instructor, pedagogue, preceptor, schoolmaster, spiritual leader, swami, teacher, torchbearer, tutor *~adjective* 4. adept, crack (*informal*), expert, masterly, proficient, skilful, skilled 5. chief, controlling, foremost, grand, great, leading, main, predominant, prime, principal *~verb* 6. acquire, become proficient in, get the hang of (*informal*), grasp, learn 7. bridle, check, conquer, curb, defeat, lick (*informal*), overcome, overpower, quash, quell, subdue, subjugate, suppress, tame, triumph over, vanquish 8. command, control, direct, dominate, govern, manage, regulate, rule
Antonyms *noun* (*sense 1*) crew, servant, slave, subject (*sense 2*) amateur, novice (*sense 3*) student *~adjective* (*sense 4*) amateurish, clumsy, incompetent, inept, novice, unaccomplished, unskilled, untalented (*sense 5*) lesser, minor *~verb* (*sense 7*) give in, surrender, yield
Related adjective: magistral

masterful 1. adept, adroit, clever, consummate, crack (*informal*), deft, dexterous, excellent, expert, exquisite, fine, finished, first-rate, masterly, skilful, skilled, superior, superlative, supreme, world-class 2. arrogant, authoritative, bossy (*informal*), despotic, dictatorial, domineering, high-handed, imperious, magisterial, overbearing, overweening, peremptory, self-willed, tyrannical
Antonyms (*sense 1*) amateurish, clumsy, incompetent, inept, unaccomplished, unskilled, untalented (*sense 2*) irresolute, meek, spineless, weak, wimpish *or* wimpy (*informal*)

masterly adept, adroit, clever, consummate, crack (*informal*), dexterous, excellent, expert, exquisite, fine, finished, first-rate, masterful, skilful, skilled, superior, superlative, supreme, world-class

mastermind 1. *verb* be the brains behind (*informal*), conceive, devise, direct, manage, organize, plan 2. *noun* architect, authority, brain(s) (*informal*), brainbox, director, engineer, genius, intellect, manager, organizer, planner, virtuoso

masterpiece *chef d'oeuvre*, classic, jewel, magnum opus, master work, *pièce de résistance*, *tour de force*

mastery **1.** command, comprehension, familiarity, grasp, grip, knowledge, understanding **2.** ability, acquirement, attainment, cleverness, deftness, dexterity, expertise, finesse, know-how (*informal*), proficiency, prowess, skill, virtuosity **3.** ascendancy, authority, command, conquest, control, domination, dominion, pre-eminence, rule, superiority, supremacy, sway, triumph, upper hand, victory, whip hand

masticate champ, chew, crunch, eat, munch

masturbation autoeroticism, onanism, playing with oneself (*slang*), self-abuse

> *Don't knock masturbation. It's sex with someone I love*
>
> Woody Allen *Annie Hall*

match *noun* **1.** bout, competition, contest, game, head-to-head, test, trial **2.** competitor, counterpart, equal, equivalent, peer, rival **3.** companion, complement, counterpart, equal, equivalent, fellow, mate, tally **4.** copy, dead ringer (*slang*), double, duplicate, equal, look-alike, replica, ringer (*slang*), spit (*informal, chiefly Brit.*), spit and image (*informal*), spitting image (*informal*), twin **5.** affiliation, alliance, combination, couple, duet, item (*informal*), marriage, pair, pairing, partnership, union *~verb* **6.** ally, combine, couple, join, link, marry, mate, pair, unite, yoke **7.** accompany, accord, adapt, agree, blend, coordinate, correspond, fit, go with, harmonize, suit, tally, tone with **8.** compare, compete, contend, emulate, equal, measure up to, oppose, pit against, rival, vie

matching analogous, comparable, coordinating, corresponding, double, duplicate, equal, equivalent, identical, like, paired, parallel, same, toning, twin

Antonyms different, disparate, dissimilar, distinct, divergent, diverse, nonparallel, other, unequal, unlike

matchless consummate, exquisite, incomparable, inimitable, peerless, perfect, superlative, supreme, unequalled, unique, unmatched, unparalleled, unrivalled, unsurpassed

Antonyms average, cheaper, common, commonplace, comparable, equalled, everyday, excelled, inferior, lesser, mediocre, no great shakes (*informal*), ordinary, second-class, surpassed

mate *noun* **1.** better half (*humorous*), husband, partner, significant other (*U.S. informal*), spouse, wife **2.** *informal* buddy (*informal*), china (*Brit. slang*), chum (*informal*), cock (*Brit. informal*), comrade, crony, friend, homeboy (*slang, chiefly U.S.*), pal (*informal*) **3.** associate, colleague, companion, compeer, co-worker, fellow-worker **4.** assistant, helper, subordinate **5.** companion, double, fellow, match, twin *~verb* **6.** breed, copulate, couple, pair **7.** marry, match, wed **8.** couple, join, match, pair, yoke

material *noun* **1.** body, constituents, element, matter, stuff, substance **2.** data, evidence, facts, information, notes, work **3.** cloth, fabric, stuff *~adjective* **4.** bodily, concrete, corporeal, fleshly, nonspiritual, palpable, physical, substantial, tangible, worldly **5.** consequential, essential, grave, important, indispensable, key, meaningful, momentous, serious, significant, vital, weighty **6.** applicable, apposite, apropos, germane, pertinent, relevant

materialize appear, come about, come into being, come to pass, happen, occur, take place, take shape, turn up

materially considerably, essentially, gravely, greatly, much, seriously, significantly, substantially

Antonyms barely, hardly, insignificantly, little, scarcely, superficially, unsubstantially

materiel accoutrements, apparatus, equipment, gear, hardware, machinery, materials, stores, supplies, tackle, tools

maternal motherly

maternity motherhood, motherliness

mathematics

Branches of mathematics

algebra
analysis
analytical geometry *or* coordinate geometry
applied mathematics
arithmetic
Boolean algebra
calculus
chaos geometry
conics
differential calculus
Euclidean geometry
game theory
geometry
group theory
integral calculus
nomography
non-Euclidean geometry
number theory
numerical analysis
probability theory
pure mathematics
set theory
statistics
topology
trigonometry

Mathematics terms

acute angle
addition
algorithm *or* algorism
angle
arc
area
average
axis
base
binary
binomial
cardinal number
Cartesian coordinates
chord
circle
circumference
closed set
coefficient
common denominator
common factor
complex number
concentric
cone
constant
coordinate *or* co-ordinate
cosecant
cosine

cotangent
cube
cube root
cuboid
curve
cusp
cylinder
decagon
decimal
denary
denominator
diagonal
diameter
digit
division
dodecahedron
ellipse
equals
equation
equilateral
even
exponential
factor
factorial
formula
fraction
frequency
function
graph
helix
hemisphere
heptagon
hexagon
hyperbola
hypotenuse
icosahedron
imaginary number
improper fraction
index
infinity
integer
integral
intersection
irrational number
isosceles
locus
logarithm *or* log
lowest common denominator
lowest common multiple
Mandelbrot set
matrix
mean
median
minus
mode
multiplication
natural logarithm
natural number
node
nonagon
number
numerator
oblong
obtuse angle
octagon
octahedron
odd
open set
operation
operator
ordinal number
origin
parabola
parallel
parallelogram
pentagon
percentage
perfect number
pi
plus
polygon
polyhedron
polynomial
power
prime number
prism
probability
product
proof
proper fraction
Pythagoras' theorem
quadrant
quadratic equation
quadrilateral
quotient
radian
radius
ratio
rational number
real number
reciprocal
rectangle
recurring decimal
reflex angle
remainder
rhombus
right angle
right-angled triangle
root
scalar
scalene
secant
sector
semicircle
set
significant figures
simultaneous equations
sine
slide rule
solid
sphere
square
square root
strange attractor
subset
subtraction
sum
surd
tangent
tetrahedron
torus
trapezium
triangle
union
universal set
value
variable
vector
Venn diagram
volume
vulgar fraction
x-axis
y-axis
z-axis
zero

Famous mathematicians

Archimedes [Greek]
George Boole [English]
René Descartes [French]
Eratosthenes [Greek]
Euclid [Greek]
Leonhard Euler [Swiss]
Pierre de Fermat [French]
Leonardo Fibonacci [Italian]
Karl Friedrich Gauss [German]
Pierre Simon Laplace [French]
John Napier [Scottish]
Blaise Pascal [French]
Siméon Denis Poisson [French]
Pythagoras [Greek]
Georg Friedrich Bernhard Riemann [German]

I don't believe in mathematics
Albert Einstein

I have often admired the mystical way of Pythagoras, and the secret magic of numbers
Thomas Browne *Religio Medici*

Beauty is the first test; there is no permanent place in the world for ugly mathematics
Godfrey Harold Hardy *A Mathematician's Apology*

matrimonial conjugal, connubial, hymeneal, marital, married, nuptial, spousal, wedded, wedding

matrimony marital rites, marriage, nuptials, wedding ceremony, wedlock

matrix forge, mould, origin, source, womb

matted knotted, tangled, tousled, uncombed

matter *noun* **1.** body, material, stuff, substance **2.** affair, business, concern, episode, event, incident, issue, occurrence, proceeding, question, situation, subject, thing, topic, transaction **3.** amount, quantity, sum **4.** argument, context, purport, sense, subject, substance, text, thesis **5.** consequence, import, importance, moment, note, significance, weight **6.** complication, difficulty, distress, problem, trouble, upset, worry **7.** *Medical* discharge, purulence, pus, secretion *~verb* **8.** be important, be of consequence, carry weight, count, have influence, make a difference, mean something, signify

What is matter? - Never mind.
What is mind? - No matter

Punch

matter-of-fact deadpan, down-to-earth, dry, dull, emotionless, flat, lifeless, mundane, plain, prosaic, sober, unembellished, unimaginative, unsentimental, unvarnished

mature 1. *adjective* adult, complete, fit, full-blown, full-grown, fully fledged, grown, grown-up, matured, mellow, of age, perfect, prepared, ready, ripe, ripened, seasoned 2. *verb* age, become adult, bloom, blossom, come of age, develop, grow up, maturate, mellow, perfect, reach adulthood, ripen, season
Antonyms adolescent, childish, green, immature, incomplete, juvenile, puerile, undeveloped, unfinished, unperfected, unripe, young, youthful

maturity adulthood, completion, experience, full bloom, full growth, fullness, majority, manhood, maturation, matureness, perfection, ripeness, wisdom, womanhood
Antonyms childishness, excitability, immaturity, imperfection, incompletion, irresponsibility, juvenility, puerility, youthfulness

maudlin lachrymose, mawkish, mushy (*informal*), overemotional, sentimental, slushy (*informal*), soppy (*Brit. informal*), tearful, weepy (*informal*)

maul 1. abuse, handle roughly, ill-treat, manhandle, molest, paw 2. batter, beat, beat up (*informal*), claw, knock about *or* around, lacerate, lambast(e), mangle, pummel, rough up, thrash, work over (*slang*)

maunder 1. dawdle, dilly-dally (*informal*), drift, idle, loaf, meander, mooch (*slang*), potter, ramble, straggle, stray, traipse (*informal*) 2. babble, blather, blether, chatter, gabble, prattle, rabbit (on) (*Brit. informal*), ramble, rattle on, waffle (*informal, chiefly Brit.*), witter (*informal*)

maw craw, crop, gullet, jaws, mouth, stomach, throat

mawkish 1. emotional, feeble, gushy (*informal*), maudlin, mushy (*informal*), schmaltzy (*slang*), sentimental, slushy (*informal*), soppy (*Brit. informal*), three-hankie (*informal*) 2. disgusting, flat, foul, insipid, jejune, loathsome, nauseous, offensive, stale, vapid

maxim adage, aphorism, apophthegm, axiom, byword, dictum, gnome, motto, proverb, rule, saw, saying

maximum 1. *noun* apogee, ceiling, crest, extremity, height, most, peak, pinnacle, summit, top, upper limit, utmost, uttermost, zenith 2. *adjective* greatest, highest, maximal, most, paramount, supreme, topmost, utmost
Antonyms bottom, least, lowest, minimum

maybe it could be, mayhap (*archaic*), peradventure (*archaic*), perchance (*archaic*), perhaps, possibly

mayhem chaos, commotion, confusion, destruction, disorder, fracas, havoc, trouble, violence

maze 1. convolutions, intricacy, labyrinth, meander 2. *figurative* bewilderment, confusion, imbroglio, mesh, perplexity, puzzle, snarl, tangle, uncertainty, web

mazy baffling, bewildering, confused, confusing, intricate, labyrinthine, perplexing, puzzling, serpentine, twisting, twisting and turning, winding

meadow field, grassland, lea (*poetic*), ley, pasture

meagre 1. deficient, exiguous, inadequate, insubstantial, little, measly, paltry, pathetic, poor, puny, scanty, scrimpy, short, skimpy, slender, slight, small, spare, sparse 2. bony, emaciated, gaunt, hungry, lank, lean, scraggy, scrawny, skinny, starved, thin, underfed 3. barren, infertile, poor, unfruitful, unproductive, weak

meal board, repast, spread (*informal*)
Related adjective: prandial

Types of meal

afternoon tea	feast
banquet	fish fry (*U.S.*)
barbecue *or (Austral.)* barbie	high tea *or* tea
beanfeast	lunch *or* luncheon
breakfast	picnic
brunch	smorgasbord
buffet	snack
cream tea	supper
dinner	tapas
elevenses	tiffin

mealy-mouthed afraid, equivocal, euphemistic, hesitant, indirect, mincing, overdelicate, prim, reticent

mean[1] *verb* 1. betoken, connote, convey, denote, drive at, express, hint at, imply, indicate, purport, represent, say, signify, spell, stand for, suggest, symbolize 2. aim, aspire, contemplate, design, desire, have in mind, intend, plan, propose, purpose, set out, want, wish 3. design, destine, fate, fit, make, match, predestine, preordain, suit 4. bring about, cause, engender, entail, give rise to, involve, lead to, necessitate, produce, result in 5. adumbrate, augur, betoken, foreshadow, foretell, herald, portend, presage, promise

mean[2] *adjective* 1. beggarly, close, mercenary, mingy (*Brit. informal*), miserly, near (*informal*), niggardly, parsimonious, penny-pinching, penurious, selfish, skimpy, stingy, tight, tight-arsed (*taboo slang*), tight as a duck's arse (*taboo slang*), tight-assed (*U.S. taboo slang*), tight-fisted, ungenerous 2. bad-tempered, cantankerous, churlish, disagreeable, hostile, ill-tempered, malicious, nasty, rude, sour, unfriendly, unpleasant **3**. abject, base, callous, contemptible, degenerate, de~ graded, despicable, disgraceful, dishonourable, hard-hearted, ignoble, low-minded, narrow-minded, petty, scurvy, shabby, shameful, sor~ did, vile, wretched **4**. beggarly, contemptible, down-at-heel, grungy (*slang, chiefly U.S.*), in~ significant, low-rent (*informal, chiefly U.S.*), miserable, paltry, petty, poor, run-down, scruffy, scuzzy (*slang, chiefly U.S.*), seedy, shabby, sordid, squalid, tawdry, wretched **5**. base, baseborn (*archaic*), common, humble, ignoble, inferior, low, lowborn, lowly, menial, modest, obscure, ordinary, plebeian, proletar~ ian, servile, undistinguished, vulgar

Antonyms agreeable, altruistic, attractive, big, bountiful, choice, compassionate, conse~ quential, de luxe, excellent, first-rate, gener~ ous, gentle, good, high, honourable, humane, important, kind, liberal, munificent, noble, pleasing, praiseworthy, princely, prodigal, significant, superb, superior, sympathetic, unselfish, warm-hearted

mean³ **1**. *noun* average, balance, compromise, happy medium, median, middle, middle course *or* way, mid-point, norm **2**. *adjective* average, intermediate, medial, median, me~ dium, middle, middling, normal, standard

meander **1**. *verb* ramble, snake, stravaig (*Scot. & northern English dialect*), stray, stroll, turn, wander, wind, zigzag **2**. *noun* bend, coil, curve, loop, turn, twist, zigzag

meandering anfractuous, circuitous, convolut~ ed, indirect, roundabout, serpentine, snaking, tortuous, wandering, winding

Antonyms direct, straight, straightforward, undeviating

meaning *noun* **1**. connotation, denotation, drift, explanation, gist, implication, import, inter~ pretation, message, purport, sense, signifi~ cance, signification, substance, upshot, value **2**. aim, design, end, goal, idea, intention, ob~ ject, plan, point, purpose, trend **3**. effect, effi~ cacy, force, point, thrust, use, usefulness, va~ lidity, value, worth *~adjective* **4**. eloquent, ex~ pressive, meaningful, pointed, pregnant, speaking, suggestive

meaningful **1**. important, material, purposeful, relevant, serious, significant, useful, valid, worthwhile **2**. eloquent, expressive, meaning, pointed, pregnant, speaking, suggestive

Antonyms inconsequential, insignificant, meaningless, senseless, superficial, trivial, unimportant, useless, worthless

meaningless aimless, empty, futile, hollow, inane, inconsequential, insignificant, insub~ stantial, nonsensical, nugatory, pointless, purposeless, senseless, trifling, trivial, useless, vain, valueless, wanky (*taboo slang*), worth~ less

Antonyms clear, coherent, comprehensible, consequential, decipherable, deep, evident, important, intelligible, legible, meaningful, obvious, purposeful, sensible, significant, understandable, useful, valuable, worthwhile

meanness **1**. minginess (*Brit. informal*), mi~ serliness, niggardliness, parsimony, penuri~ ousness, selfishness, stinginess, tight-fistedness **2**. bad temper, cantankerousness, churlishness, disagreeableness, hostility, ill temper, malice, maliciousness, nastiness, rudeness, sourness, unfriendliness, unpleas~ antness **3**. abjectness, baseness, degeneracy, degradation, despicableness, disgracefulness, dishonourableness, low-mindedness, narrow-mindedness, pettiness, scurviness, shabbiness, shamefulness, sordidness, vileness, wretched~ ness **4**. beggarliness, contemptibleness, insig~ nificance, paltriness, pettiness, poorness, scruffiness, seediness, shabbiness, sordidness, squalor, tawdriness, wretchedness **5**. baseness, humbleness, lowliness, obscurity, servility

Do not spoil the ship for a ha'porth of tar

means **1**. agency, avenue, channel, course, ex~ pedient, instrument, measure, medium, meth~ od, mode, process, way **2**. affluence, capital, estate, fortune, funds, income, money, proper~ ty, resources, riches, substance, wealth, wherewithal **3**. **by all means** absolutely, cer~ tainly, definitely, doubtlessly, of course, posi~ tively, surely **4**. **by means of** by dint of, by way of, through, using, utilizing, via, with the aid of **5**. **by no means** absolutely not, defi~ nitely not, in no way, not at all, not in the least, not in the slightest, not the least bit, no way, on no account

meantime, meanwhile at the same time, con~ currently, for now, for the duration, for the moment, for then, in the interim, in the in~ terval, in the intervening time, in the mean~ time, in the meanwhile, simultaneously

measly beggarly, contemptible, meagre, mean, mingy (*Brit. informal*), miserable, miserly, niggardly, paltry, pathetic, petty, pitiful, poor, puny, scanty, skimpy, stingy, ungenerous

measurable assessable, computable, determi~ nable, gaugeable, material, mensurable, per~ ceptible, quantifiable, quantitative, significant

measure *noun* **1**. allotment, allowance, amount, amplitude, capacity, degree, extent, magnitude, portion, proportion, quantity, quo~ ta, range, ration, reach, scope, share, size **2**. gauge, metre, rule, scale, yardstick **3**. method, standard, system **4**. criterion, example, model, norm, par, standard, test, touchstone, yard~ stick **5**. bounds, control, limit, limitation, moderation, restraint **6**. act, action, course, deed, expedient, manoeuvre, means, pro~ cedure, proceeding, step **7**. act, bill, enact~ ment, law, resolution, statute **8**. beat, cadence, foot, metre, rhythm, verse **9. for good measure** as a bonus, besides, in addition, into the bargain, to boot *~verb* **10.** appraise, assess, calculate, calibrate, compute, determine, estimate, evaluate, gauge, judge, mark out, quantify, rate, size, sound, survey, value, weigh **11.** adapt, adjust, calculate, choose, fit, judge, tailor

measured 1. exact, gauged, modulated, precise, predetermined, quantified, regulated, standard, verified **2.** dignified, even, leisurely, regular, sedate, slow, solemn, stately, steady, unhurried **3.** calculated, considered, deliberate, grave, planned, premeditated, reasoned, sober, studied, well-thought-out

measureless beyond measure, boundless, endless, immeasurable, immense, incalculable, inestimable, infinite, limitless, unbounded, vast

measurement 1. appraisal, assessment, calculation, calibration, computation, estimation, evaluation, judgment, mensuration, metage, survey, valuation **2.** amount, amplitude, area, capacity, depth, dimension, extent, height, length, magnitude, size, volume, weight, width

measure off circumscribe, delimit, demarcate, determine, fix, lay down, limit, mark out, pace out

measure out allot, apportion, assign, deal out, dispense, distribute, divide, dole out, issue, mete out, parcel out, pour out, share out

measure up (to) be adequate, be capable, be equal to, be fit, be suitable, be suited, come up to scratch (*informal*), come up to standard, compare, cut the mustard (*U.S. slang*), equal, fit *or* fill the bill, fulfil the expectations, make the grade (*informal*), match, meet, rival

meat 1. aliment, cheer, chow (*informal*), comestibles, eats (*slang*), fare, flesh, food, grub (*slang*), nosh (*slang*), nourishment, nutriment, provender, provisions, rations, subsistence, sustenance, viands, victuals **2.** core, essence, gist, heart, kernel, marrow, nub, nucleus, pith, point, substance

Types and cuts of meat

see FOOD

The nearer the bone, the sweeter the meat

meaty 1. hearty, nourishing, rich, substantial **2.** beefy (*informal*), brawny, burly, fleshy, heavily built, heavy, husky (*informal*), muscular, solid, strapping, sturdy **3.** interesting, meaningful, pithy, profound, rich, significant, substantial

mechanical 1. automated, automatic, machine-driven **2.** automatic, cold, cursory, dead, emotionless, habitual, impersonal, instinctive, involuntary, lacklustre, lifeless, machine-like, matter-of-fact, perfunctory, routine, spiritless, unconscious, unfeeling, unthinking

Antonyms (*sense 1*) manual (*sense 2*) conscious, genuine, sincere, thinking, voluntary, warm, wholehearted

mechanism 1. apparatus, appliance, contrivance, device, instrument, machine, structure, system, tool **2.** action, components, gears, innards (*informal*), machinery, motor, workings, works **3.** agency, execution, functioning, means, medium, method, operation, performance, procedure, process, system, technique, workings

meddle butt in, interfere, intermeddle, interpose, intervene, intrude, pry, put one's oar in, put one's two cents in (*U.S. slang*), stick one's nose in (*informal*), tamper

meddlesome interfering, intermeddling, intruding, intrusive, meddling, mischievous, officious, prying

mediate act as middleman, arbitrate, bring to an agreement, bring to terms, conciliate, intercede, interpose, intervene, make peace between, moderate, reconcile, referee, resolve, restore harmony, settle, step in (*informal*), umpire

mediation arbitration, conciliation, good offices, intercession, interposition, intervention, reconciliation

mediator advocate, arbiter, arbitrator, go-between, honest broker, interceder, intermediary, judge, middleman, moderator, negotiator, peacemaker, referee, umpire

medicable curable, healable, remediable, treatable

medicinal analeptic, curative, healing, medical, remedial, restorative, roborant, sanatory, therapeutic

medicine cure, drug, medicament, medication, nostrum, physic, remedy

Branches of medicine

aetiology *or* etiology	dermatology
anaesthetics	diagnostics
anaplasty	eccrinology
anatomy	electrophysiology
andrology	electrotherapeutics
angiology	embryology
audiology	encephalography
aviation medicine	endocrinology
bacteriology	endodontics
balneology	epidemiology
bioastronautics	exodontics
biomedicine	forensic *or* legal medicine
cardiology	gastroenterology
chiropody	genitourinary medicine
dental hygiene *or* oral hygiene	geratology
dental surgery	geriatrics
dentistry	

gerontology
gynaecology *or (U.S.)* gynecology
haematology *or (U.S.)* hematology
hydrotherapeutics
immunochemistry
immunology
industrial medicine
internal medicine
laryngology
materia medica
midwifery
morbid anatomy
myology
neonatology
nephrology
neuroanatomy
neuroendocrinology
neurology
neuropathology
neurophysiology
neuropsychiatry
neurosurgery
nosology
nostology
nuclear medicine
nutrition
obstetrics
odontology
oncology
ophthalmology
optometry
orthodontics *or* orthodontia
orthopaedics *or (U.S.)* orthopedics
orthoptics
orthotics
osteology
osteoplasty
otolaryngology
otology
paediatrics *or (U.S.)* pediatrics
pathology
periodontics
pharyngology
physical medicine
physiotherapy *or (U.S.)* physiatrics
plastic surgery
posology
preventive medicine
proctology
psychiatry
psychoanalysis
psychology
radiology
rheumatology
rhinology
serology
space medicine
spare-part surgery
speech therapy
sports medicine
stomatology
surgery
symptomatology
syphilology
therapeutics
tocology *or* tokology
toxicology
trichology
urology
venereology
veterinary science *or* medicine
virology

Medical practitioners and specialists

aetiologist *or* etiologist
anaesthetist
anatomist
andrologist
audiologist
bacteriologist
balneologist
barefoot doctor
cardiologist
chiropodist
consultant
dental hygienist *or* oral hygienist
dentist *or* dental surgeon
dermatologist
diagnostician
dietitian
district nurse
doctor
electrophysiologist
embryologist
endocrinologist
endodontist
epidemiologist
exodontist
extern *or* externe (*U.S. & Canad.*)
forensic scientist
gastroenterologist
general practitioner *or* GP
geriatrician *or* geriatrist
gerontologist
gynaecologist *or (U.S.)* gynecologist
haematologist *or (U.S.)* hematologist
health visitor
house physician
houseman
hydrotherapist
immunologist
intern *or* interne (*U.S. & Canad.*)
internist
junior doctor
laboratory technician
laryngologist
matron
midwife
myologist
neonatologist
nephrologist
neuroanatomist
neurologist
neuropathologist
neurophysiologist
neuropsychiatrist
neurosurgeon
nosologist
nurse
nursing officer
nutritionist
obstetrician
occupational therapist
odontologist
oncologist
ophthalmologist
optician
optometrist
orderly
orthodontist
orthopaedist *or (U.S.)* orthopedist
orthoptist
orthotist
osteologist
otolaryngologist
otologist
paediatrician *or (U.S.)* pediatrician
paramedic
pathologist
pharyngologist
physiotherapist *or* physio
plastic surgeon
proctologist
psychiatrist
psychoanalyst
psychologist
radiographer
radiologist
registrar
resident (*U.S. & Canad.*)
rheumatologist
rhinologist
serologist
speech therapist
surgeon
syphilologist
therapist
toxicologist
trichologist
urologist
venereologist
veterinary surgeon, vet *or (U.S.)* veterinarian
virologist

Medical and surgical instruments and equipment

arthroscope
artificial heart
artificial kidney
aspirator
bandage
bedpan
bistoury
bronchoscope
cannula *or* canula
cardiograph
catheter
catling
clamp
clinical thermometer
colonoscope
colposcope
compressor
CT scanner *or* CAT scanner
curet *or* curette
cystoscope
defibrillator
depressor
dialysis machine
drain
electrocardiograph
electroencephalograph
electromyograph
encephalogram
endoscope
fetoscope
fibrescope *or (U.S.)* fiberscope
fluoroscope
forceps
gamma camera
gastroscope
gonioscope
haemostat *or (U.S.)* hemostat

heart-lung machine
heat lamp
hypodermic *or* hypodermic needle
hypodermic *or* hypodermic syringe
inhalator
inspirator
iron lung
kidney machine
kymograph *or* cymograph
lancet *or* lance
laparoscope
laryngoscope
life-support machine
microscope
nebulizer
needle
nephroscope
oesophagoscope *or* *(U.S.)* esophagoscope
ophthalmoscope
orthoscope
otoscope
oxygen mask
oxygen tent
pacemaker
packing
perimeter
pharyngoscope
plaster cast
pneumatometer
pneumograph
probe
proctoscope
Pulmotor (*Trademark*)
raspatory
respirator
resuscitator
retinoscope
retractor
rheometer
rhinoscope
roentgenoscope *or* röntgenoscope
scalpel
scanner
skiascope
sling
sound
specimen bottle
speculum
sphygmograph
sphygmomanometer
spirograph
spirometer
splint
stethoscope
stomach pump
stretcher
stupe
stylet
styptic pencil
suture
swab
syringe
thoracoscope
tourniquet
trepan
trephine
trocar
ultrasound scanner
urethroscope
urinometer
ventilator
wet pack
X-ray machine

Branches of alternative medicine

acupressure
acupuncture
Alexander technique
aromatherapy
autogenic training
Bach flower remedy
biofeedback
chiropractic
herbalism
homeopathy *or* homoeopathy
hydrotherapy
hypnosis
hypnotherapy
iridology
kinesiology
massage
moxibustion
naturopathy
osteopathy
radionics
reflexology
shiatsu

Nearly all men die of their medicines, not of their diseases

Molière *Le Malade Imaginaire*

medieval 1. Gothic 2. *informal* antediluvian, antiquated, antique, archaic, old-fashioned, primitive, unenlightened

mediocre average, banal, bog-standard (*Brit. & Irish slang*), commonplace, fair to middling (*informal*), indifferent, inferior, insignificant, mean, medium, middling, no great shakes (*informal*), ordinary, passable, pedestrian, run-of-the-mill, second-rate, so-so (*informal*), tolerable, undistinguished, uninspired, vanilla (*slang*)
Antonyms distinctive, distinguished, excellent, extraordinary, fine, incomparable, superb, superior, unexcelled, unique, unrivalled, unsurpassed

Some men are born mediocre, some men achieve mediocrity, and some men have mediocrity thrust upon them. With Major it had been all three

Joseph Heller *Catch-22*

mediocrity 1. commonplaceness, indifference, inferiority, insignificance, ordinariness, poorness, unimportance 2. cipher, lightweight (*informal*), nobody, nonentity, second-rater

Mediocrity knows nothing higher than itself, but talent instantly recognizes genius

Sir Arthur Conan Doyle *The Valley of Fear*

meditate 1. be in a brown study, cogitate, consider, contemplate, deliberate, muse, ponder, reflect, ruminate, study, think 2. consider, contemplate, design, devise, have in mind, intend, mull over, plan, purpose, scheme, think over

meditation brown study, cerebration, cogitation, concentration, contemplation, musing, pondering, reflection, reverie, ruminating, rumination, study, thought

meditative cogitative, contemplative, deliberative, pensive, reflective, ruminative, studious, thoughtful

medium *adjective* 1. average, fair, intermediate, mean, medial, median, mediocre, middle, middling, midway *~noun* 2. average, centre, compromise, mean, middle, middle course (ground, path, way), midpoint 3. agency, avenue, channel, form, instrument, instrumentality, means, mode, organ, vehicle, way 4. atmosphere, conditions, element, environment, habitat, influences, milieu, setting, surroundings 5. channeller, spiritist, spiritualist
Antonyms *adjective* distinctive, extraordinary, extreme, uncommon, unique, unusual, utmost

The medium is the message

Marshall McLuhan *Understanding Media*

medley assortment, confusion, farrago, gallimaufry, hodgepodge, hotchpotch, jumble, *mélange*, miscellany, mishmash, mixed bag (*informal*), mixture, olio, omnium-gatherum, pastiche, patchwork, potpourri, salmagundi

meek 1. deferential, docile, forbearing, gentle, humble, long-suffering, mild, modest, patient, peaceful, soft, submissive, unassuming, un-

pretentious, yielding **2.** acquiescent, boneless, compliant, resigned, spineless, spiritless, tame, timid, unresisting, weak, weak-kneed (*informal*), wimpish *or* wimpy (*informal*)
Antonyms arrogant, bold, bossy, domineering, feisty (*informal, chiefly U.S. & Canad.*), for~ward, immodest, overbearing, presumptuous, pretentious, proud, self-assertive, spirited, wilful

The meek shall inherit the earth
Bible: Psalm 37

It's going to be fun to watch and see how long the meek can keep the earth after they inherit it
Kin Hubbard

meekness 1. deference, docility, forbearance, gentleness, humbleness, humility, long-suffering, lowliness, mildness, modesty, pa~tience, peacefulness, resignation, softness, submission, submissiveness **2.** acquiescence, compliance, resignation, spinelessness, spirit~lessness, tameness, timidity, weakness

meet 1. bump into, chance on, come across, confront, contact, encounter, find, happen on, run across, run into **2.** abut, adjoin, come to~gether, connect, converge, cross, intersect, join, link up, touch, unite **3.** answer, carry out, come up to, comply, cope with, discharge, equal, fulfil, gratify, handle, match, measure up, perform, satisfy **4.** assemble, collect, come together, congregate, convene, forgather, gather, muster, rally **5.** bear, encounter, en~dure, experience, face, go through, suffer, undergo
Antonyms (*sense 1*) avoid, elude, escape, miss (*sense 2*) diverge (*sense 3*) fail, fall short, re~nege (*sense 4*) adjourn, disperse, scatter

meeting 1. assignation, confrontation, encoun~ter, engagement, introduction, rendezvous, tryst (*archaic*) **2.** assembly, audience, compa~ny, conclave, conference, congregation, con~gress, convention, convocation, gathering, get-together (*informal*), meet, powwow, rally, reunion, session **3.** concourse, confluence, con~junction, convergence, crossing, intersection, junction, union

melancholy 1. *noun* blues, dejection, depres~sion, despondency, gloom, gloominess, low spirits, misery, pensiveness, sadness, sorrow, the hump (*Brit. informal*), unhappiness, woe **2.** *adjective* blue, dejected, depressed, de~spondent, disconsolate, dismal, dispirited, doleful, down, downcast, downhearted, down in the dumps (*informal*), down in the mouth, gloomy, glum, heavy-hearted, joyless, low, low-spirited, lugubrious, melancholic, miser~able, moody, mournful, pensive, sad, sombre, sorrowful, unhappy, woebegone, woeful
Antonyms *noun* delight, gladness, happiness, joy, pleasure *~adjective* blithe, bright, cheer~ful, gay, glad, happy, jolly, joyful, joyous, light-hearted, lively, merry, sunny

mélange assortment, confusion, farrago, galli~maufry, hodge-podge, hotch-potch, jumble, medley, miscellany, mishmash, mix, mixed bag (*informal*), mixture, olio, omnium-gatherum, pastiche, potpourri, salmagundi

melee, mêlée affray (*Law*), *bagarre*, battle royal, brawl, broil, donnybrook, fight, fracas, fray, free-for-all (*informal*), ruckus (*informal*), ruction (*informal*), rumpus, scrimmage, scuf~fle, set-to (*informal*), shindig (*informal*), shin~dy (*informal*), skirmish, stramash (*Scot.*), tus~sle

mellifluous, mellifluent dulcet, euphonious, honeyed, mellow, silvery, smooth, soft, sooth~ing, sweet, sweet-sounding

mellow *adjective* **1.** delicate, full-flavoured, juicy, mature, perfect, rich, ripe, soft, sweet, well-matured **2.** dulcet, euphonic, full, mellifluous, melodious, rich, rounded, smooth, sweet, tuneful, well-tuned **3.** cheerful, cordial, elevated, expansive, genial, half-tipsy, happy, jolly, jovial, merry (*Brit. informal*), relaxed *~verb* **4.** develop, improve, mature, perfect, ripen, season, soften, sweeten
Antonyms *adjective* green, harsh, immature, raw, sour, unripe *~verb* brutalize, harden

melodious concordant, dulcet, euphonic, euphonious, harmonious, melodic, musical, silvery, sweet-sounding, sweet-toned, tuneful
Antonyms cacophonous, discordant, grating, harsh, unharmonious, unmelodic, unmelodi~ous, unmusical, untuneful

melodramatic actressy, blood-and-thunder, ex~travagant, hammy (*informal*), histrionic, over~dramatic, overemotional, sensational, stagy, theatrical

melody 1. air, descant, music, refrain, song, strain, theme, tune **2.** euphony, harmony, me~lodiousness, music, musicality, tunefulness

melt 1. deliquesce, diffuse, dissolve, flux, fuse, liquefy, soften, thaw **2.** *often with* **away** dis~appear, disperse, dissolve, evanesce, evapo~rate, fade, vanish **3.** disarm, mollify, relax, soften, touch

member 1. associate, fellow, representative **2.** appendage, arm, component, constituent, el~ement, extremity, leg, limb, organ, part, por~tion

membership 1. associates, body, fellows, mem~bers **2.** belonging, enrolment, fellowship, par~ticipation

memento keepsake, memorial, relic, remem~brance, reminder, souvenir, token, trophy

memoir account, biography, essay, journal, life, monograph, narrative, record, register

memoirs 1. autobiography, diary, experiences, journals, life, life story, memories, recollec~

tions, reminiscences **2.** annals, chronicles, records, transactions

To write one's memoirs is to speak ill of everybody except oneself
Marshal Pétain

memorable catchy, celebrated, distinguished, extraordinary, famous, historic, illustrious, important, impressive, momentous, notable, noteworthy, remarkable, signal, significant, striking, unforgettable
Antonyms commonplace, forgettable, insignificant, ordinary, trivial, undistinguished, unimportant, unimpressive, unmemorable

memorial *adjective* **1.** commemorative, monumental *~noun* **2.** cairn, memento, monument, plaque, record, remembrance, souvenir **3.** address, memorandum, petition, statement

memorize commit to memory, con (*archaic*), get by heart, learn, learn by heart, learn by rote, remember

memory **1.** recall, recollection, remembrance, reminiscence, retention **2.** commemoration, honour, remembrance **3.** celebrity, fame, glory, name, renown, reputation, repute

Our memories are card-indexes consulted, and then put back in disorder by authorities whom we do not control
Cyril Connolly *The Unquiet Grave*

menace *verb* **1.** alarm, bode ill, browbeat, bully, frighten, impend, intimidate, loom, lour *or* lower, terrorize, threaten, utter threats to *~noun* **2.** commination, intimidation, scare, threat, warning **3.** danger, hazard, jeopardy, peril **4.** *informal* annoyance, nuisance, pest, plague, troublemaker

menacing alarming, baleful, bodeful, dangerous, forbidding, frightening, intimidating, intimidatory, looming, louring *or* lowering, minacious, minatory, ominous, threatening
Antonyms auspicious, encouraging, favourable, promising

mend *verb* **1.** cure, darn, fix, heal, patch, rectify, refit, reform, remedy, renew, renovate, repair, restore, retouch **2.** ameliorate, amend, better, correct, emend, improve, rectify, reform, revise **3.** convalesce, get better, heal, recover, recuperate *~noun* **4.** darn, patch, repair, stitch **5. on the mend** convalescent, convalescing, getting better, improving, recovering, recuperating

mendacious deceitful, deceptive, dishonest, duplicitous, fallacious, false, fraudulent, insincere, lying, perfidious, perjured, untrue, untruthful
Antonyms genuine, honest, true, truthful

mendacity deceit, deceitfulness, dishonesty, distortion, duplicity, falsehood, falsification, fraudulence, insincerity, inveracity, lie, lying, mendaciousness, misrepresentation, perfidy, perjury, untruth, untruthfulness

mendicant **1.** *adjective* begging **2.** *noun* beggar, pauper

menial *adjective* **1.** boring, dull, humdrum, low-status, routine, unskilled **2.** abject, base, degrading, demeaning, fawning, grovelling, humble, ignoble, ignominious, low, lowly, mean, obsequious, servile, slavish, sorry, subservient, sycophantic, vile *~noun* **3.** attendant, dogsbody (*informal*), domestic, drudge, flunky, labourer, lackey, serf, servant, skivvy (*chiefly Brit.*), slave, underling, varlet (*archaic*), vassal
Antonyms *adjective* aristocratic, autocratic, bossy, dignified, domineering, elevated, haughty, high, noble, overbearing, proud *~noun* boss, chief, commander, lord, master, superior

menstruation catamenia (*Physiology*), courses (*Physiology*), flow (*informal*), menses, menstrual cycle, monthly (*informal*), period, the curse (*informal*)

mensuration assessment, calculation, calibration, computation, estimation, measurement, measuring, metage, survey, surveying

mental **1.** cerebral, intellectual **2.** as daft as a brush (*informal, chiefly Brit.*), deranged, disturbed, insane, lunatic, mad, mentally ill, not right in the head, psychiatric, psychotic, round the bend (*Brit. slang*), unbalanced, unstable

mentality **1.** brainpower, brains, comprehension, grey matter (*informal*), intellect, intelligence quotient, I.Q., mental age, mind, rationality, understanding, wit **2.** attitude, cast of mind, character, disposition, frame of mind, make-up, outlook, personality, psychology, turn of mind, way of thinking

mentally in one's head, intellectually, in the mind, inwardly, psychologically, rationally, subjectively

mention *verb* **1.** acknowledge, adduce, allude to, bring up, broach, call attention to, cite, communicate, declare, disclose, divulge, hint at, impart, intimate, make known, name, point out, recount, refer to, report, reveal, speak about *or* of, state, tell, touch upon **2. not to mention** as well as, besides, not counting, to say nothing of *~noun* **3.** acknowledgment, citation, recognition, tribute **4.** allusion, announcement, indication, notification, observation, reference, remark

mentor adviser, coach, counsellor, guide, guru, instructor, teacher, tutor

menu bill of fare, carte du jour, tariff (*chiefly Brit.*)

mephitic baleful, baneful, evil- *or* ill-smelling, fetid, foul, foul-smelling, malodorous, miasmal, miasmatic, miasmic, noisome, noxious, olid, pestilential, poisonous, putrid, stinking

mercantile commercial, marketable, trade, trading

mercenary *adjective* 1. acquisitive, avaricious, bribable, covetous, grasping, greedy, money-grubbing (*informal*), sordid, venal 2. bought, hired, paid, venal *~noun* 3. condottiere (*History*), free companion (*History*), freelance (*History*), hireling, soldier of fortune
Antonyms altruistic, benevolent, generous, idealistic, liberal, munificent, philanthropic, unselfish

merchandise 1. *noun* commodities, goods, produce, products, staples, stock, stock in trade, truck, vendibles, wares 2. *verb* buy and sell, deal in, distribute, do business in, market, retail, sell, trade, traffic in, vend

merchant broker, dealer, purveyor, retailer, salesman, seller, shopkeeper, supplier, trader, tradesman, trafficker, vendor, wholesaler

> *A merchant shall hardly keep himself from doing wrong*
>
> Bible: Ecclesiasticus

merchantable marketable, saleable, tradable, vendible

merciful beneficent, benignant, clement, compassionate, forbearing, forgiving, generous, gracious, humane, kind, lenient, liberal, mild, pitying, soft, sparing, sympathetic, tender-hearted
Antonyms cruel, hard-hearted, inhumane, merciless, pitiless, uncompassionate, unfeeling

merciless barbarous, callous, cruel, fell (*archaic*), hard, hard-hearted, harsh, heartless, implacable, inexorable, inhumane, pitiless, relentless, ruthless, severe, unappeasable, unfeeling, unforgiving, unmerciful, unpitying, unsparing, unsympathetic

mercurial active, capricious, changeable, erratic, fickle, flighty, gay, impulsive, inconstant, irrepressible, light-hearted, lively, mobile, quicksilver, spirited, sprightly, temperamental, unpredictable, unstable, variable, volatile
Antonyms consistent, constant, dependable, reliable, stable, steady, unchanging

mercy 1. benevolence, charity, clemency, compassion, favour, forbearance, forgiveness, grace, kindness, leniency, pity, quarter 2. benison (*archaic*), blessing, boon, godsend, piece of luck, relief 3. **at the mercy of** defenceless against, exposed to, in the clutches of, in the power of, naked before, open to, prey to, subject to, threatened by, unprotected against, vulnerable to
Antonyms brutality, cruelty, harshness, inhumanity, pitilessness, severity

> *Yet I shall temper so*
> *Justice with mercy*
>
> John Milton *Paradise Lost*

mere *adjective* absolute, bare, common, complete, entire, nothing more than, plain, pure, pure and simple, sheer, simple, stark, unadulterated, unmitigated, unmixed, utter

meretricious 1. flashy, garish, gaudy, gimcrack, plastic (*slang*), showy, tawdry, tinsel, trashy 2. bogus, counterfeit, deceitful, false, hollow, insincere, mock, phoney *or* phony (*informal*), pseudo (*informal*), put-on, sham, specious, spurious

merge amalgamate, become lost in, be swallowed up by, blend, coalesce, combine, consolidate, converge, fuse, incorporate, intermix, join, meet, meld, melt into, mingle, mix, tone with, unite
Antonyms detach, diverge, divide, part, separate, sever

merger amalgamation, coalition, combination, consolidation, fusion, incorporation, union

meridian acme, apex, apogee, climax, crest, culmination, high noon, high-water mark, peak, pinnacle, summit, zenith

merit *noun* 1. advantage, asset, excellence, good, goodness, integrity, quality, strong point, talent, value, virtue, worth, worthiness 2. claim, credit, desert, due, right *~verb* 3. be entitled to, be worthy of, deserve, earn, have a claim to, have a right to, have coming to one, incur, rate, warrant

> *What is merit? The opinion one man entertains of another*
>
> Lord Palmerston

merited appropriate, condign, deserved, earned, entitled, just, justified, rightful, rightly due, warranted

meritorious admirable, commendable, creditable, deserving, excellent, exemplary, good, honourable, laudable, praiseworthy, right, righteous, virtuous, worthy
Antonyms discreditable, dishonourable, ignoble, unchivalrous, undeserving, unexceptional, ungenerous, unpraiseworthy

merriment amusement, conviviality, festivity, frolic, fun, gaiety, glee, hilarity, jocularity, jollity, joviality, laughter, levity, liveliness, merrymaking, mirth, revelry, sport

merry 1. blithe, blithesome, carefree, cheerful, chirpy (*informal*), convivial, festive, frolicsome, fun-loving, gay, genial, glad, gleeful, happy, jocund, jolly, joyful, joyous, light-hearted, mirthful, rollicking, sportive, upbeat (*informal*), vivacious 2. amusing, comic, comical, facetious, funny, hilarious, humorous, jocular, mirthful 3. *Brit. informal* elevated (*informal*), happy, mellow, squiffy (*Brit. informal*), tiddly (*slang, chiefly Brit.*), tipsy 4. **make merry** carouse, celebrate, enjoy one~

self, feast, frolic, have a good time, have fun, make whoopee (*informal*), revel
Antonyms dejected, dismal, down in the dumps (*informal*), gloomy, miserable, sad, unhappy

A merry heart maketh a cheerful countenance
Bible: Proverbs

merrymaking beano (*Brit. slang*), carousal, carouse, celebration, conviviality, festivity, fun, gaiety, hooley *or* hoolie (*chiefly Irish & N.Z.*), jollification, merriment, party, rave (*Brit. slang*), rave-up (*Brit. slang*), revelry

mesh *noun* **1.** net, netting, network, plexus, reticulation, tracery, web **2.** entanglement, snare, tangle, toils, trap, web *~verb* **3.** catch, enmesh, ensnare, entangle, net, snare, tangle, trap **4.** combine, come together, connect, coordinate, dovetail, engage, fit together, harmonize, interlock, knit

mesmerize absorb, captivate, enthral, entrance, fascinate, grip, hold spellbound, hypnotize, magnetize, spellbind

mess *noun* **1.** balls-up (*taboo slang*), bodge (*informal*), botch, chaos, clutter, cock-up (*Brit. slang*), confusion, dirtiness, disarray, disorder, disorganization, fuck-up (*offensive taboo slang*), grot (*slang*), hash, hodgepodge (*U.S.*), hotchpotch, jumble, litter, mishmash, pig's breakfast (*informal*), shambles, state, turmoil, untidiness **2.** deep water, difficulty, dilemma, fine kettle of fish (*informal*), fix (*informal*), hot water (*informal*), imbroglio, jam (*informal*), mix-up, muddle, perplexity, pickle (*informal*), plight, predicament, spot (*informal*), stew (*informal*), tight spot *~verb* **3.** *often with* **up** befoul, besmirch, botch, bungle, clutter, cock up (*Brit. slang*), dirty, disarrange, dishevel, foul, fuck up (*offensive taboo slang*), litter, make a hash of (*informal*), make a nonsense of, make a pig's ear of (*informal*), muck up (*Brit. slang*), muddle, pollute, scramble **4.** *often with* **with** fiddle (*informal*), interfere, meddle, play, tamper, tinker

mess about *or* **around** **1.** amuse oneself, dabble, fool (about *or* around), footle (*informal*), muck about (*informal*), piss about *or* around (*taboo slang*), play about *or* around, potter, trifle **2.** fiddle (*informal*), fool (about *or* around), interfere, meddle, piss about *or* around (*taboo slang*), play, tamper, tinker, toy

message **1.** bulletin, communication, communiqué, dispatch, intimation, letter, memorandum, missive, note, notice, tidings, word **2.** idea, import, meaning, moral, point, purport, theme **3.** commission, errand, job, mission, task **4.** **get the message** catch on (*informal*), comprehend, get it, get the point, see, take the hint, twig (*Brit. informal*), understand

messenger agent, bearer, carrier, courier, delivery boy, emissary, envoy, errand-boy, go-between, harbinger, herald, runner

messy chaotic, cluttered, confused, dirty, dishevelled, disordered, disorganized, grubby, littered, muddled, scuzzy (*slang, chiefly U.S.*), shambolic (*informal*), sloppy (*informal*), slovenly, unkempt, untidy
Antonyms clean, meticulous, neat, ordered, orderly, shipshape, smart, squeaky-clean, tidy

metal

Metal	Symbol
actinium	Ac
aluminium	Al
americium	Am
antimony	Sb
barium	Ba
berkelium	Bk
beryllium	Be
bismuth	Bi
cadmium	Cd
caesium *or (U.S.)* cesium	Cs
calcium	Ca
californium	Cf
cerium	Ce
chromium	Cr
cobalt	Co
copper	Cu
curium	Cm
dysprosium	Dy
einsteinium	Es
erbium	Er
europium	Eu
fermium	Fm
francium	Fr
gadolinium	Gd
gallium	Ga
germanium	Ge
gold	Au
hafnium	Hf
holmium	Ho
indium	In
iridium	Ir
iron	Fe
lanthanum	La
lawrencium	Lr
lead	Pb
lithium	Li
lutetium	Lu
magnesium	Mg
manganese	Mn
mendelevium	Md
mercury	Hg
molybdenum	Mo
neodymium	Nd
neptunium	Np
nickel	Ni
niobium	Nb
nobelium	No

osmium	Os
palladium	Pd
platinum	Pt
plutonium	Pu
polonium	Po
potassium	K
praseodymium	Pr
promethium	Pm
protactinium	Pa
radium	Ra
rhenium	Re
rhodium	Rh
rubidium	Rb
ruthenium	Ru
samarium	Sm
scandium	Sc
silver	Ag
sodium	Na
strontium	Sr
tantalum	Ta
technetium	Tc
terbium	Tb
thallium	Tl
thorium	Th
thulium	Tm
tin	Sn
titanium	Ti
tungsten *or* wolfram	W
uranium	U
vanadium	V
ytterbium	Yb
yttrium	Y
zinc	Zn
zirconium	Zr

metamorphose alter, be reborn, change, convert, mutate, remake, remodel, reshape, transfigure, transform, translate, transmogrify (*jocular*), transmute, transubstantiate

metamorphosis alteration, change, changeover, conversion, mutation, rebirth, transfiguration, transformation, translation, transmogrification (*jocular*), transmutation, transubstantiation

metaphor allegory, analogy, emblem, figure of speech, image, symbol, trope

metaphorical allegorical, emblematic, emblematical, figurative, symbolic, tropical (*rhetoric*)

metaphysical **1.** basic, esoteric, essential, eternal, fundamental, general, ideal, intellectual, philosophical, profound, speculative, spiritual, subjective, universal **2.** abstract, abstruse, deep, high-flown, oversubtle, recondite, theoretical, transcendental **3.** immaterial, impalpable, incorporeal, intangible, spiritual, supernatural, unreal, unsubstantial

mete *verb* administer, allot, apportion, assign, deal, dispense, distribute, divide, dole, measure, parcel, portion, ration, share

meteoric brief, brilliant, dazzling, ephemeral, fast, flashing, fleeting, momentary, overnight, rapid, spectacular, speedy, sudden, swift, transient

Antonyms gradual, lengthy, long, prolonged, slow, steady, unhurried

method **1.** approach, arrangement, course, fashion, form, manner, mode, modus operandi, plan, practice, procedure, process, programme, routine, rule, scheme, style, system, technique, way **2.** design, form, order, orderliness, organization, pattern, planning, purpose, regularity, structure, system

methodical businesslike, deliberate, disciplined, efficient, meticulous, neat, ordered, orderly, organized, painstaking, planned, precise, regular, structured, systematic, tidy, well-regulated

Antonyms casual, chaotic, confused, disordered, disorderly, haphazard, irregular, random, unmethodical

meticulous detailed, exact, fastidious, fussy, microscopic, painstaking, particular, perfectionist, precise, punctilious, scrupulous, strict, thorough

Antonyms careless, haphazard, imprecise, inexact, loose, negligent, slapdash, sloppy

métier **1.** calling, craft, line, occupation, profession, pursuit, trade, vocation **2.** forte, long suit (*informal*), speciality, specialty, strong point, strong suit

metropolis capital, city

mettle **1.** ardour, balls (*taboo slang*), boldness, bottle (*Brit. slang*), bravery, courage, daring, fire, fortitude, gallantry, gameness, grit, guts (*informal*), hardihood, heart, indomitability, life, nerve, pluck, resolution, resolve, spirit, spunk (*informal*), valour, vigour **2.** calibre, character, disposition, kidney, make-up, nature, quality, stamp, temper, temperament

mettlesome ardent, bold, brisk, courageous, daring, dashing, feisty (*informal, chiefly U.S. & Canad.*), fiery, frisky, game (*informal*), have-a-go (*informal*), high-spirited, lively, mettled, plucky, sprightly, valiant, vigorous

mewl blubber, cry, grizzle (*informal, chiefly Brit.*), pule, snivel, whimper, whine, whinge (*informal*)

miasma effluvium, fetor, mephitis, niff (*Brit. slang*), odour, pollution, reek, smell, stench

miasmal fetid, foul, insalubrious, malodorous, mephitic, niffy (*Brit. slang*), noisome, noxious, olid, polluted, putrid, reeking, smelly, stinking, unwholesome

microbe bacillus, bacterium, bug (*informal*), germ, microorganism, virus

microscopic imperceptible, infinitesimal, invisible, minuscule, minute, negligible, teensy-weensy, teeny-weeny, tiny

Antonyms enormous, gigantic, ginormous (*informal*), great, huge, immense, large, vast

midday noon, noonday, noontide, noontime, twelve noon, twelve o'clock

middle *adjective* **1.** central, halfway, inner, inside, intermediate, intervening, mean, medial, median, medium, mid *~noun* **2.** centre, focus, halfway point, heart, inside, mean, midpoint, midsection, midst, thick **3.** midriff, midsection, waist

middleman broker, distributor, entrepreneur, go-between, intermediary

middling adequate, all right, average, bog-standard (*Brit. & Irish slang*), fair, indifferent, mediocre, medium, moderate, modest, O.K. *or* okay (*informal*), ordinary, passable, run-of-the-mill, so-so (*informal*), tolerable, unexceptional, unremarkable

midget 1. *noun* dwarf, gnome, homuncule, homunculus, manikin, munchkin (*informal, chiefly U.S.*), pygmy *or* pigmy, shrimp (*informal*), Tom Thumb **2.** *adjective* baby, dwarf, Lilliputian, little, miniature, pocket, pygmy *or* pigmy, small, teensy-weensy, teeny-weeny, tiny

midnight dead of night, middle of the night, the witching hour, twelve o'clock (at night)

midst 1. bosom, centre, core, depths, heart, hub, interior, middle, thick **2. in the midst of** amidst, among, during, enveloped by, in the middle of, in the thick of, surrounded by

midway betwixt and between, halfway, in the middle

mien air, appearance, aspect, aura, bearing, carriage, countenance, demeanour, deportment, look, manner, presence

miffed aggrieved, annoyed, displeased, hacked (off) (*U.S. slang*), hurt, in a huff, irked, irritated, narked (*Brit., Austral., & N.Z. slang*), nettled, offended, piqued, pissed off (*taboo slang*), put out, resentful, upset, vexed

might 1. ability, capability, capacity, clout (*informal*), efficacy, efficiency, energy, force, potency, power, prowess, puissance, strength, sway, valour, vigour **2. (with) might and main** as hard as one can, as hard as possible, forcefully, full blast, full force, lustily, manfully, mightily, vigorously, with all one's might *or* strength

Might is right

mightily 1. decidedly, exceedingly, extremely, greatly, highly, hugely, intensely, much, seriously (*informal*), very, very much **2.** energetically, forcefully, lustily, manfully, powerfully, strongly, vigorously, with all one's might and main, with all one's strength

mighty 1. doughty, forceful, hardy, indomitable, lusty, manful, potent, powerful, puissant, robust, stalwart, stout, strapping, strong, sturdy, vigorous **2.** bulky, colossal, elephantine, enormous, gigantic, ginormous (*informal*), grand, great, huge, humongous *or* humungous (*U.S. slang*), immense, large, massive, mega (*slang*), monumental, prodigious, stellar (*informal*), stupendous, titanic, towering, tremendous, vast

Antonyms feeble, impotent, small, tiny, unimposing, unimpressive, weak, weedy (*informal*), wimpish *or* wimpy (*informal*)

How are the mighty fallen, and the weapons of war perished

Bible: II Samuel

migrant 1. *noun* drifter, emigrant, gypsy, immigrant, itinerant, nomad, rover, tinker, transient, traveller, vagrant, wanderer **2.** *adjective* drifting, gypsy, immigrant, itinerant, migratory, nomadic, roving, shifting, transient, travelling, vagrant, wandering

migrate drift, emigrate, journey, move, roam, rove, shift, travel, trek, voyage, wander

migration emigration, journey, movement, roving, shift, travel, trek, voyage, wandering

migratory gypsy, itinerant, migrant, nomadic, peripatetic, roving, shifting, transient, travelling, unsettled, vagrant, wandering

mild 1. amiable, balmy, bland, calm, clement, compassionate, docile, easy, easy-going, easy-oasy (*slang*), equable, forbearing, forgiving, gentle, indulgent, kind, meek, mellow, merciful, moderate, pacific, peaceable, placid, pleasant, serene, smooth, soft, temperate, tender, tranquil, warm **2.** demulcent, emollient, lenitive, mollifying, soothing

Antonyms (*sense 1*) bitter, cold, fierce, harsh, rough, stormy, unkind, unpleasant, violent, wild (*sense 2*) harsh, powerful, severe, sharp, strong

mildness blandness, calmness, clemency, docility, forbearance, gentleness, indulgence, kindness, leniency, lenity, meekness, mellowness, moderation, placidity, smoothness, softness, temperateness, tenderness, tranquillity, warmth

milieu background, element, environment, locale, location, *mise en scène*, scene, setting, sphere, surroundings

militant *adjective* **1.** active, aggressive, assertive, combative, vigorous **2.** belligerent, combating, contending, embattled, fighting, in arms, warring *~noun* **3.** activist, partisan **4.** belligerent, combatant, fighter, gladiator, warrior

Antonyms concessive, pacific, pacifist, peaceful

military 1. *adjective* armed, martial, soldierlike, soldierly, warlike **2.** *noun* armed forces, army, forces, services

Military ranks

able rating
able seaman *or* able-bodied seaman (AB)
acting sublieutenant
admiral (Adm)
admiral of the fleet
air chief marshal (ACM)
air commodore (AC)
aircraftmen (AC)
air marshal (AM)
air officer
air vice-marshal (AVM)
branch officer (BO)
brigadier (Brig)
captain (Capt)
chief of staff (COS)
chief petty officer (CPO)
chief technician
colonel (Col)
colour sergeant (Col Sgt)
commander (Cdr)
commander in chief (C-in-C)
commanding officer (CO)
commissioned officer
commodore (Cdre)
company sergeant major (CSM)
corporal (Corp, Cpl)
drum major
field marshal (FM)
field officer (FO)
fleet admiral
fleet chief petty officer
flight engineer
flight lieutenant (Flt Lt)
flight mechanic (FM)
flight sergeant (Flt Sgt)
flying officer (FO)
general (Gen, Genl)
group captain (G Capt)
junior technician
lance corporal (L-Cpl)
leading aircraftman (LAC)
leading rating
lieutenant (Lt)
lieutenant colonel (Lt-Col)
lieutenant commander (Lt-Comm)
lieutenant general (Lt-Gen)
major (Maj)
major general (Maj-Gen)
marine
marshal
marshal of the Royal Air Force (MRAF)
master aircrew
medical officer (MO)
midshipman
noncommissioned officer (NCO)
ordinary rating
ordinary seaman (OS)
petty officer (PO)
pilot officer (PO)
private (Pte)
quartermaster (QM)
rear admiral (RA)
regimental sergeant major (RSM)
second lieutenant
senior aircraftman
senior medical officer (SMO)
sergeant (Sgt, Sergt)
sergeant major (SM)
squadron leader (Sqn-Ldr)
staff sergeant
subaltern
sublieutenant (Sub L)
vice admiral (VA)
warrant officer (WO)
wing commander

militate 1. *with* **against** be detrimental to, conflict with, contend, count, counter, counteract, oppose, resist, tell, weigh 2. *with* **for** advance, aid, further, help, promote

militia fencibles (*History*), National Guard (*U.S.*), reserve(s), Territorial Army (*Brit.*), trainband (*History*), yeomanry (*History*)

milk *verb* 1. drain, draw off, express, extract, let out, press, siphon, tap 2. bleed, drain, exploit, extract, impose on, pump, take advantage of, use, wring

milk-and-water feeble, innocuous, insipid, jejune, nerdy *or* nurdy (*slang*), vapid, weak, weedy (*informal*), wimpish *or* wimpy (*informal*), wishy-washy (*informal*)

Antonyms effective, energetic, forceful, healthy, strong

milksop chinless wonder (*Brit. informal*), coward, dastard (*archaic*), jessie (*Scot. slang*), namby-pamby, sissy, weakling, wimp (*informal*), wuss (*U.S. slang*)

milky alabaster, clouded, cloudy, milk-white, opaque, white, whitish

mill *noun* 1. factory, foundry, plant, shop, works 2. crusher, grinder 3. **run of the mill** average, bog-standard (*Brit. & Irish slang*), commonplace, everyday, fair, middling, ordinary, routine, unexceptional, unremarkable ~*verb* 4. comminute, crush, granulate, grate, grind, pound, powder, press, pulverize 5. crowd, seethe, swarm, throng

millstone 1. grindstone, quernstone 2. affliction, albatross, burden, dead weight, drag, encumbrance, load, weight

mime 1. *noun* dumb show, gesture, mummery, pantomime 2. *verb* act out, gesture, pantomime, represent, simulate

mimic *verb* 1. ape, caricature, do (*informal*), imitate, impersonate, parody, take off (*informal*) 2. echo, look like, mirror, resemble, simulate, take on the appearance of ~*noun* 3. caricaturist, copycat (*informal*), imitator, impersonator, impressionist, parodist, parrot ~*adjective* 4. echoic, imitation, imitative, make-believe, mimetic, mock, sham, simulated

mimicry apery, burlesque, caricature, copying, imitating, imitation, impersonation, impression, mimicking, mockery, parody, take-off (*informal*)

minatory baleful, dangerous, menacing, minacious, minatorial, threatening

mince 1. chop, crumble, cut, grind, hash 2. diminish, euphemize, extenuate, hold back, moderate, palliate, soften, spare, tone down, weaken 3. attitudinize, give oneself airs, ponce (*slang*), pose, posture

mincing affected, camp (*informal*), dainty, effeminate, foppish, lah-di-dah (*informal*), nice, niminy-piminy, poncy (*slang*), precious, pretentious, sissy

mind *noun* 1. brain(s) (*informal*), grey matter (*informal*), intellect, intelligence, mentality, ratiocination, reason, sense, spirit, understanding, wits 2. memory, recollection, remembrance 3. brain, head, imagination, psyche 4. brain (*informal*), brainbox, genius, intellect, intellectual, thinker 5. attitude, belief, feeling, judgment, opinion, outlook, point of view, sentiment, thoughts, view, way of thinking 6. bent, desire, disposition, fancy, inclination, intention, leaning, notion, purpose, tendency, urge, will, wish 7. attention, concentration, thinking, thoughts 8. judgment, marbles (*informal*), mental balance, rational~

ity, reason, sanity, senses, wits **9. in** *or* **of two minds** dithering (*chiefly Brit.*), hesitant, shillyshallying (*informal*), swithering (*Scot.*), uncertain, undecided, unsure, vacillating, wa~vering **10. make up one's mind** choose, come to a decision, decide, determine, reach a deci~sion, resolve **11. bear** *or* **keep in mind** be cognizant of, be mindful of, remember, take note of *~verb* **12.** be affronted, be bothered, care, disapprove, dislike, look askance at, ob~ject, resent, take offence **13.** adhere to, attend, comply with, follow, heed, listen to, mark, note, notice, obey, observe, pay attention, pay heed to, regard, respect, take heed, watch **14.** be sure, ensure, make certain **15.** attend to, guard, have charge of, keep an eye on, look after, take care of, tend, watch **16.** be careful, be cautious, be on (one's) guard, be wary, take care, watch **17. never mind** disregard, do not concern yourself, don't bother, don't give (it) a second thought, forget (it), it does not matter, it's none of your business, it's nothing to do with you, pay no attention
Related adjectives: noetic, mental

> *The mind is at its best about the age of forty-nine*
>
> Aristotle *Rhetoric*

> *The mind is its own place, and in itself*
> *Can make a heaven of hell, a hell of heaven*
>
> John Milton *Paradise Lost*

> *What is matter? - Never mind.*
> *What is mind? - No matter*
>
> Punch

> *Great minds think alike, fools seldom differ*

mindful alert, alive to, attentive, aware, care~ful, chary, cognizant, conscious, heedful, re~gardful, respectful, sensible, thoughtful, wary, watchful
Antonyms heedless, inattentive, incautious, mindless, oblivious, thoughtless, unaware

mindless 1. asinine, braindead (*informal*), brutish, careless, dead from the neck up (*in~formal*), foolish, forgetful, gratuitous, heedless, idiotic, imbecilic, inane, inattentive, moronic, neglectful, negligent, oblivious, obtuse, stupid, thoughtless, unintelligent, unmindful, un~thinking, witless **2.** automatic, brainless, me~chanical
Antonyms attentive, aware, considerate, in~telligent, mindful, reasonable, reasoning, sane, sensitive, thinking

mind out be careful, be on one's guard, be~ware, keep one's eyes open, look out, pay at~tention, take care, watch

mind's eye head, imagination, memory, mind, recollection, remembrance

mine *noun* **1.** coalfield, colliery, deposit, exca~vation, lode, pit, shaft, vein **2.** abundance, fund, hoard, reserve, source, stock, store, sup~ply, treasury, wealth **3.** sap, trench, tunnel *~verb* **4.** delve, dig for, dig up, excavate, ex~tract, hew, quarry, unearth **5.** lay mines in *or* under, sow with mines **6.** sap, subvert, tunnel, undermine, weaken

miner coalminer, collier (*Brit.*), pitman (*Brit.*)

mineral

Minerals

actinolite
agate
albite
allanite
allophane
alunite
amalgam
amblygonite
analcite *or* analcime
anatase
andalusite
andesine
anglesite
anhydrite
ankerite
annabergite
anorthite
apatite
apophyllite
aragonite
argentite
arsenopyrite
augite
autunite
axinite
azurite
baddeleyite
barytes
bastnaesite *or* bast~nasite
bauxite
beryl
biotite
bismuthinite *or* bis~muth glance
Boehmite
boracite
borax
bornite
braunite
brookite
calaverite
calcite
carnallite
carnotite
cassiterite
celestite *or* celestine
cerargyrite
chabazite
chalcanthite
chalcocite
chalcopyrite
chlorite
chromite
chrysoberyl
chrysotile
cinnabar
clay mineral
cleveite
clinopyroxene
cobaltite *or* cobaltine
colemanite
columbite
cordierite
corundum
cristobalite
crocidolite
crocoite *or* crocoisite
cryolite
cuprite
cyanite
datolite
diallage
diamond
diaspore
diopside
dioptase
dolomite
dumortierite
emery
enstatite
epidote
erythrite
euxenite
fayalite
feldspar *or* felspar
feldspathoid
fluorapatite
fluorspar, fluor *or* *(U.S. & Canad.)* fluorite
forsterite
franklinite
gahnite
galena *or* galenite
garnet
garnierite
gehlenite
germanite
geyserite
gibbsite
glauconite
goethite *or* göthite
graphite

greenockite
gummite
gypsum
halitc
harmotome
hematite *or* haematite
hemimorphite
hessite
heulandite
hiddenite
hornblende
hyacinth
hypersthene
illite
ilmenite
jadeite
jarosite
jasper
kainite
kaolinite
kernite
kieserite
kunzite
labradorite
lapis lazuli
lazulite
lazurite
leucite
limonite
magnesite
magnetite
malachite
manganite
marcasite
margarite
massicot
meerschaum
metamict
mica
microcline
millerite
mimetite
molybdenite
monazite
montmorillonite
monzonite
mullite
muscovite
natrolite
nepheline *or* nephelite
nephrite
niccolite
norite
oligoclase
olivenite
olivine
opal
orpiment
orthoclase
ozocerite *or* ozokerite
pentlandite
periclase
perovskite
petuntse *or* petuntze
phenacite *or* phena~kite
phosgenite
phosphorite
piedmontite
pinite
pitchblende
pollucite
polybasite
proustite
psilomelane
pyrargyrite
pyrite
pyrolusite
pyromorphite
pyrophyllite
pyroxene
pyroxenite
pyrrhotite *or* pyrrho~tine
quartz
realgar
rhodochrosite
rhodonite
rutile
samarskite
saponite
sapphirine
scapolite
scheelite
scolecite
senarmontite
serpentine
siderite
sillimanite
smaltite
smaragdite
smectite
smithsonite
sodalite
sperrylite
sphalerite
sphene
spinel
spodumene
stannite
staurolite
stibnite
stilbite
strontianite
sylvanite
sylvite *or* sylvine
talc
tantalite
tenorite
tetradymite
tetrahedrite
thenardite
thorianite
thorite
tiemannite
topaz
torbernite
tourmaline
tremolite
triphylite
trona
troostite
tungstite
turgite
turquoise
uralite
uraninite
uranite
vanadinite
variscite
vermiculite
vesuvianite
wavellite
willemite
witherite
wolframite
wollastonite
wulfenite
zaratite
zeolite
zincite
zinkenite *or* zincken~ite
zircon
zoisite

mingle 1. alloy, blend, coalesce, combine, com~mingle, compound, intermingle, intermix, interweave, join, marry, meld, merge, mix, unite 2. associate, circulate, consort, frater~nize, hang about *or* around, hang out (*infor~mal*), hobnob, rub shoulders (*informal*), so~cialize
Antonyms avoid, detach, dissociate, dissolve, divide, estrange, part, separate

miniature *adjective* baby, diminutive, dwarf, Lilliputian, little, midget, mini, minuscule, minute, pocket, pygmy *or* pigmy, reduced, scaled-down, small, teensy-weensy, teeny-weeny, tiny, toy, wee
Antonyms big, enlarged, enormous, giant, gi~gantic, ginormous (*informal*), great, huge, im~mense, large, mega (*slang*), oversize

minimal least, least possible, littlest, mini~mum, nominal, slightest, smallest, token

minimize 1. abbreviate, attenuate, curtail, de~crease, diminish, downsize, miniaturize, prune, reduce, shrink 2. belittle, decry, depre~cate, depreciate, discount, disparage, make light *or* little of, play down, underestimate, underrate
Antonyms augment, boast about, elevate, en~hance, enlarge, exalt, expand, extend, height~en, increase, magnify, praise, vaunt

minimum 1. *noun* bottom, depth, least, lowest, nadir, slightest 2. *adjective* least, least pos~sible, littlest, lowest, minimal, slightest, smallest
Antonyms greatest, highest, largest, maxi~mum, most

minion bootlicker (*informal*), cohort (*chiefly U.S.*), creature, darling, dependant, favourite, flatterer, flunky, follower, hanger-on, hench~man, hireling, lackey, lickspittle, myrmidon, parasite, pet, sycophant, toady, underling, yes man

minister *noun* 1. chaplain, churchman, clergy~man, cleric, divine, ecclesiastic, padre (*infor~mal*), parson, pastor, preacher, priest, rector, vicar **2.** administrator, ambassador, cabinet member, delegate, diplomat, envoy, executive, office-holder, official, plenipotentiary **3.** agent, aide, assistant, lieutenant, servant, subordinate, underling *~verb* **4.** accommodate, administer, answer, attend, be solicitous of, cater to, pander to, serve, take care of, tend

ministration aid, assistance, favour, help, patronage, relief, service, succour, support

ministry **1.** administration, bureau, cabinet, council, department, government, office, quango **2.** holy orders, the church, the priesthood, the pulpit

minor inconsequential, inconsiderable, inferior, insignificant, junior, lesser, light, negligible, nickel-and-dime (*U.S. slang*), paltry, petty, secondary, slight, small, smaller, subordinate, trifling, trivial, unimportant, younger

Antonyms appreciable, consequential, considerable, essential, grand, great, heavy, important, major, profound, serious, significant, substantial, superior, vital, weighty

minstrel bard, harper, jongleur, musician, singer, songstress, troubadour

mint *noun* **1.** bomb (*Brit. slang*), bundle (*slang*), fortune, heap (*informal*), King's ransom, million, packet (*slang*), pile (*informal*) *~adjective* **2.** brand-new, excellent, first-class, fresh, perfect, unblemished, undamaged, untarnished *~verb* **3.** cast, coin, make, produce, punch, stamp, strike **4.** coin, construct, devise, fabricate, fashion, forge, invent, make up, produce, think up

minuscule diminutive, fine, infinitesimal, Lilliputian, little, microscopic, miniature, minute, teensy-weensy, teeny-weeny, tiny, very small

minute[1] *noun* **1.** sixtieth of an hour, sixty seconds **2.** flash, instant, jiffy (*informal*), moment, second, shake (*informal*), tick (*Brit. informal*), trice **3. any minute** any moment, any second, any time, at any time, before long, very soon **4. up to the minute** all the rage, in, latest, modish, (most) fashionable, newest, now (*informal*), smart, stylish, trendiest, trendy (*Brit. informal*), up to date, vogue, with it (*informal*)

minute[2] *adjective* **1.** diminutive, fine, infinitesimal, Lilliputian, little, microscopic, miniature, minuscule, slender, small, teensy-weensy, teeny-weeny, tiny **2.** inconsiderable, negligible, paltry, petty, picayune (*U.S.*), piddling (*informal*), puny, slight, trifling, trivial, unimportant **3.** close, critical, detailed, exact, exhaustive, meticulous, painstaking, precise, punctilious

Antonyms (*senses 1 & 2*) enormous, generous, gigantic, ginormous (*informal*), grand, great, huge, immense, important, major, mega (*slang*), monstrous, significant, vital (*sense 3*) careless, haphazard, imprecise, inexact, loose, quick, rough, superficial

minutely closely, critically, exactly, exhaustively, in detail, meticulously, painstakingly, precisely, with a fine-tooth comb

minutes memorandum, notes, proceedings, record(s), transactions, transcript

minutiae details, finer points, ins and outs, niceties, particulars, subtleties, trifles, trivia

minx baggage (*informal, old-fashioned*), coquette, flirt, hoyden, hussy, jade, tomboy, wanton

miracle marvel, phenomenon, prodigy, thaumaturgy, wonder

Except ye see signs and wonders, ye will not believe

Bible: St. John

The age of miracles is past

miraculous amazing, astonishing, astounding, extraordinary, incredible, inexplicable, magical, marvellous, phenomenal, preternatural, prodigious, superhuman, supernatural, thaumaturgic, unaccountable, unbelievable, wonderful, wondrous (*archaic or literary*)

Antonyms awful, bad, banal, common, commonplace, everyday, normal, ordinary, run-of-the-mill, terrible, unexceptional, unremarkable, usual

mirage hallucination, illusion, optical illusion, phantasm

mire *noun* **1.** bog, marsh, morass, quagmire, swamp **2.** dirt, gloop (*informal*), grot (*slang*), muck, mud, ooze, slime, slob (*Irish*) **3. in the mire** encumbered, entangled, in difficulties, in trouble *~verb* **4.** bog down, flounder, sink, stick in the mud **5.** begrime, besmirch, bespatter, cake, dirty, muddy, soil **6.** catch up, enmesh, entangle, involve

mirror *noun* **1.** glass, looking-glass, reflector, speculum **2.** copy, double, image, likeness, reflection, replica, representation, twin *~verb* **3.** copy, depict, echo, emulate, follow, reflect, represent, show

mirth amusement, cheerfulness, festivity, frolic, fun, gaiety, gladness, glee, hilarity, jocularity, jollity, joviality, joyousness, laughter, levity, merriment, merrymaking, pleasure, rejoicing, revelry, sport

mirthful amused, amusing, blithe, cheerful, cheery, festive, frolicsome, funny, gay, glad, gladsome (*archaic*), happy, hilarious, jocund, jolly, jovial, laughable, light-hearted, ludic (*literary*), merry, playful, sportive, uproarious, vivacious

Antonyms dejected, depressed, despondent, dismal, down in the dumps (*informal*), gloomy, grave, lugubrious, melancholy, miserable, morose, sad, saturnine, sedate, serious, solemn, sombre, sorrowful, unhappy

misadventure accident, bad break (*informal*), bad luck, bummer (*slang*), calamity, catastrophe, debacle, disaster, failure, ill fortune, ill luck, mischance, misfortune, mishap, reverse, setback

misanthrope cynic, egoist, egotist, mankind-hater, misanthropist

misanthropic antisocial, cynical, egoistic, inhumane, malevolent, unfriendly, unsociable

misanthropy cynicism, egoism, hatred of mankind, inhumanity, malevolence

I wish I loved the human race;
I wish I loved its silly face;
I wish I liked the way it walks;
I wish I liked the way it talks;
And when I'm introduced to one
I wish I thought What Jolly Fun!
Walter Raleigh *Wishes of an Elderly Man*

misapply abuse, misappropriate, misemploy, misuse, pervert

misapprehend get hold of the wrong end of the stick, get one's lines crossed, get the wrong idea *or* impression, misconceive, misconstrue, misinterpret, misread, mistake, misunderstand

misapprehension delusion, error, fallacy, false belief, false impression, misconception, misconstruction, misinterpretation, misreading, mistake, misunderstanding, wrong idea *or* impression

misappropriate cabbage (*Brit. slang*), defalcate (*Law*), embezzle, misapply, misspend, misuse, peculate, pocket, steal, swindle

misbegotten **1.** dishonest, disreputable, ill-gotten, illicit, purloined, shady (*informal*), stolen, unlawful, unrespectable **2.** abortive, hare-brained, ill-advised, ill-conceived, poorly thought-out **3.** *literary* bastard, born out of wedlock, illegitimate, natural, spurious (*rare*)

misbehave act up (*informal*), be bad, be insubordinate, be naughty, carry on (*informal*), get up to mischief (*informal*), muck about (*Brit. slang*)
Antonyms act correctly, be good, behave, conduct oneself properly, mind one's manners, mind one's p's and q's, toe the line

misbehaviour acting up (*informal*), bad behaviour, impropriety, incivility, indiscipline, insubordination, mischief, misconduct, misdeeds, misdemeanour, monkey business (*informal*), naughtiness, rudeness, shenanigans (*informal*)

misbelief delusion, error, fallacy, false belief, heresy, unorthodoxy

miscalculate blunder, calculate wrongly, err, get (it) wrong, go wrong, make a mistake, misjudge, overestimate, overrate, slip up, underestimate, underrate

miscarriage **1.** miss (*informal*), spontaneous abortion **2.** botch (*informal*), breakdown, error, failure, misadventure, mischance, misfire, mishap, mismanagement, nonsuccess, perversion, thwarting, undoing

miscarry **1.** abort **2.** come to grief, come to nothing, fail, fall through, gang agley (*Scot.*), go amiss, go astray, go awry, go wrong, misfire

miscellaneous assorted, confused, diverse, diversified, farraginous, heterogeneous, indiscriminate, jumbled, manifold, many, mingled, mixed, motley, multifarious, multiform, promiscuous, sundry, varied, various

miscellany anthology, assortment, collection, diversity, farrago, gallimaufry, hotchpotch, jumble, medley, *mélange*, mixed bag, mixture, omnium-gatherum, potpourri, salmagundi, variety

mischance accident, bad break (*informal*), bad luck, bummer (*slang*), calamity, contretemps, disaster, ill chance, ill fortune, ill luck, infelicity, misadventure, misfortune, mishap

mischief **1.** devilment, impishness, misbehaviour, monkey business (*informal*), naughtiness, pranks, roguery, roguishness, shenanigans (*informal*), trouble, waywardness **2.** damage, detriment, disadvantage, disruption, evil, harm, hurt, injury, misfortune, trouble **3.** devil, imp, monkey, nuisance, pest, rascal, rogue, scallywag (*informal*), scamp, tyke (*informal*), villain

mischievous **1.** arch, bad, badly behaved, exasperating, frolicsome, impish, ludic (*literary*), naughty, playful, puckish, rascally, roguish, sportive, teasing, troublesome, vexatious, wayward **2.** bad, damaging, deleterious, destructive, detrimental, evil, harmful, hurtful, injurious, malicious, malignant, pernicious, sinful, spiteful, troublesome, vicious, wicked

misconceive fail to understand, get one's lines crossed, get the wrong idea (about), misapprehend, misconstrue, misjudge, mistake, misunderstand

misconception delusion, error, fallacy, misapprehension, misconstruction, mistaken belief, misunderstanding, wrong end of the stick, wrong idea

misconduct **1.** *noun* delinquency, dereliction, immorality, impropriety, malfeasance (*Law*), malpractice, malversation (*rare*), misbehaviour, misdemeanour, mismanagement, naughtiness, rudeness, transgression, unethical behaviour, wrongdoing **2.** *verb* behave badly, botch (up), bungle, err, make a mess of, misdirect, mismanage, sin

misconstruction false interpretation, misapprehension, misinterpretation, misreading, mistake, mistaken *or* false impression, misunderstanding, wrong idea

misconstrue get a false impression, get one's lines crossed, make a wrong interpretation, misapprehend, misconceive, misinterpret, misjudge, misread, mistake, mistranslate, misunderstand, take the wrong way (*informal*)

miscreant 1. *noun* blackguard, caitiff (*archaic*), criminal, evildoer, knave (*archaic*), malefactor, rascal, reprobate, rogue, scally (*Northwest English dialect*), scoundrel, sinner, vagabond, villain, wrongdoer 2. *adjective* corrupt, criminal, depraved, evil, iniquitous, nefarious, rascally, reprehensible, reprobate, scoundrelly, unprincipled, vicious, villainous, wicked

misdeed crime, fault, misconduct, misdemeanour, offence, sin, transgression, trespass, villainy, wrong

misdemeanour fault, infringement, misbehaviour, misconduct, misdeed, offence, peccadillo, transgression, trespass

miser cheapskate (*informal*), churl (*archaic*), curmudgeon, hunks (*rare*), niggard, penny-pincher (*informal*), screw (*slang*), Scrooge, skinflint, tight-arse (*taboo slang*), tight-ass (*U.S. taboo slang*), tightwad (*U.S. & Canad. slang*)

miserable 1. afflicted, broken-hearted, crestfallen, dejected, depressed, desolate, despondent, disconsolate, dismal, distressed, doleful, down, downcast, down in the dumps (*informal*), down in the mouth (*informal*), forlorn, gloomy, heartbroken, low, melancholy, mournful, sorrowful, unhappy, woebegone, wretched 2. destitute, dirt-poor (*informal*), down and out, flat broke (*informal*), impoverished, indigent, meagre, needy, penniless, poor, poverty-stricken, scanty, short, without two pennies to rub together (*informal*) 3. abject, bad, contemptible, deplorable, despicable, detestable, disgraceful, lamentable, low, mean, pathetic, piteous, pitiable, scurvy, shabby, shameful, sordid, sorry, squalid, vile, worthless, wretched

Antonyms admirable, cheerful, comfortable, good, happy, respectable, rich

miserliness avarice, cheeseparing, churlishness, close- *or* tightfistedness, covetousness, graspingness, meanness, minginess (*Brit. informal*), nearness, niggardliness, parsimony, penny-pinching (*informal*), penuriousness, stinginess

How easy it is for a man to die rich, if he will be contented to live miserable
Henry Fielding

miserly avaricious, beggarly, close, close-fisted, covetous, grasping, illiberal, mean, mingy (*Brit. informal*), near, niggardly, parsimonious, penny-pinching (*informal*), penurious, sordid, stingy, tight-arsed (*taboo slang*), tight as a duck's arse (*taboo slang*), tight-assed (*U.S. taboo slang*), tightfisted, ungenerous

Antonyms charitable, extravagant, generous, prodigal, unselfish

misery 1. agony, anguish, depression, desolation, despair, discomfort, distress, gloom, grief, hardship, melancholy, sadness, sorrow, suffering, torment, torture, unhappiness, woe, wretchedness 2. affliction, bitter pill (*informal*), burden, calamity, catastrophe, curse, disaster, hardship, load, misfortune, ordeal, sorrow, trial, tribulation, trouble, woe 3. destitution, indigence, need, penury, poverty, privation, sordidness, squalor, want, wretchedness 4. *Brit. informal* grouch (*informal*), killjoy, moaner, pessimist, prophet of doom, sourpuss (*informal*), spoilsport, wet blanket (*informal*), wowser (*Austral. & N.Z. slang*)

Antonyms comfort, contentment, ease, enjoyment, happiness, joy, luxury, pleasure

misfire fail, fail to go off, fall through, go phut (*informal*), go wrong, miscarry

misfit eccentric, fish out of water (*informal*), nonconformist, oddball (*informal*), square peg (in a round hole) (*informal*)

misfortune 1. bad luck, evil fortune, hard luck, ill luck, infelicity 2. accident, adversity, affliction, blow, bummer (*slang*), calamity, disaster, evil chance, failure, hardship, harm, loss, misadventure, mischance, misery, mishap, reverse, setback, stroke of bad luck, tragedy, trial, tribulation, trouble, whammy (*informal, chiefly U.S.*)

Antonyms fortune, good luck, relief

In the misfortune of our best friends, we always find something which is not displeasing to us
Duc de la Rochefoucauld *Réflexions ou Maximes Morales*

misfortune: the kind of fortune which never misses
Ambrose Bierce *The Devil's Dictionary*

Misfortunes never come singly

misgiving anxiety, apprehension, distrust, doubt, dubiety, hesitation, qualm, reservation, scruple, suspicion, trepidation, uncertainty, unease, worry

misguided deluded, erroneous, foolish, ill-advised, imprudent, injudicious, labouring under a delusion *or* misapprehension, misled, misplaced, mistaken, uncalled-for, unreasonable, unwarranted, unwise

mishandle bodge (*informal*), botch, bungle, flub (*U.S. slang*), make a hash of (*informal*), make a mess of, make a nonsense of, mess up (*informal*), mismanage, muff, screw (up) (*informal*)

mishap accident, adversity, bad luck, calamity, contretemps, disaster, evil chance, evil for~

tune, hard luck, ill fortune, ill luck, infelicity, misadventure, mischance, misfortune

mishmash farrago, gallimaufry, hash, hotchpotch, jumble, medley, potpourri, salmagundi

misinform deceive, give (someone) a bum steer (*informal, chiefly U.S.*), give (someone) duff gen (*Brit. informal*), misdirect, misguide, mislead

misinterpret distort, falsify, get wrong, misapprehend, misconceive, misconstrue, misjudge, misread, misrepresent, mistake, misunderstand, pervert

misjudge be wrong about, get the wrong idea about, miscalculate, overestimate, overrate, underestimate, underrate

mislay be unable to find, be unable to put *or* lay one's hand on, forget the whereabouts of, lose, lose track of, misplace, miss

mislead beguile, bluff, deceive, delude, fool, give (someone) a bum steer (*informal, chiefly U.S.*), hoodwink, lead astray, misdirect, misguide, misinform, pull the wool over (someone's) eyes (*informal*), take for a ride (*informal*), take in (*informal*)

misleading ambiguous, casuistical, confusing, deceitful, deceptive, delusive, delusory, disingenuous, evasive, false, sophistical, specious, spurious, tricky (*informal*), unstraightforward
Antonyms candid, clear, correct, direct, explicit, frank, genuine, honest, obvious, open, plain, simple, sincere, straightforward, true, truthful

mismanage be incompetent, be inefficient, bodge (*informal*), botch, bungle, make a hash of (*informal*), make a mess of, make a nonsense of, maladminister, mess up, misconduct, misdirect, misgovern, mishandle

mismatched clashing, discordant, disparate, ill-assorted, incompatible, incongruous, irregular, misallied, unreconcilable, unsuited

misogyny

Nothing makes a man hate a woman more than her constant conversation
William Wycherley *The Country Wife*

Sir, a woman preaching is like a dog's walking on his hind legs. It is not done well; but you are surprised to find it done at all
Dr. Johnson

misplace **1.** be unable to find, be unable to put *or* lay one's hand on, forget the whereabouts of, lose, lose track of, misfile, mislay, miss, put in the wrong place **2.** place unwisely, place wrongly

misprint corrigendum, erratum, literal, mistake, printing error, typo (*informal*), typographical error

misprize disparage, fail to appreciate, hold cheap, look down on, set no store by, slight, underestimate, underrate, undervalue

misquote distort, falsify, garble, mangle, misreport, misrepresent, misstate, muddle, pervert, quote *or* take out of context, twist

misrepresent belie, disguise, distort, falsify, garble, misinterpret, misstate, pervert, twist

misrule **1.** bad government, maladministration, misgovernment, mismanagement **2.** anarchy, chaos, confusion, disorder, lawlessness, tumult, turmoil

miss[1] *verb* **1.** avoid, be late for, blunder, err, escape, evade, fail, fail to grasp, fail to notice, forego, lack, leave out, let go, let slip, lose, miscarry, mistake, omit, overlook, pass over, pass up, skip, slip, trip **2.** feel the loss of, hunger for, long for, need, pine for, want, wish, yearn for ~*noun* **3.** blunder, error, failure, fault, loss, mistake, omission, oversight, want

A miss is as good as a mile
Walter Scott *Journal*

What you've never had you never miss

miss[2] *noun* damsel, girl, lass, lassie (*informal*), maid, maiden, schoolgirl, spinster, young lady

misshapen contorted, crippled, crooked, deformed, distorted, grotesque, ill-made, ill-proportioned, malformed, twisted, ugly, ungainly, unshapely, unsightly, warped, wry

missile projectile, rocket, weapon

Missiles
see WEAPON

missing absent, astray, gone, lacking, left behind, left out, lost, mislaid, misplaced, not present, nowhere to be found, unaccounted-for, wanting
Antonyms accounted for, at hand, available, here, in attendance, on hand, present, there, to hand

mission **1.** aim, assignment, business, calling, charge, commission, duty, errand, goal, job, office, operation, purpose, pursuit, quest, task, trust, undertaking, vocation, work **2.** commission, delegation, deputation, embassy, legation, ministry, task force

missionary apostle, converter, evangelist, preacher, propagandist, proselytizer

missive communication, dispatch, epistle, letter, memorandum, message, note, report

misspent dissipated, idle, imprudent, misapplied, prodigal, profitless, squandered, thrown away, wasted
Antonyms active, fruitful, industrious, meaningful, profitable, unwasted, useful, worthwhile

misstate distort, falsify, garble, give a false impression, misquote, misreport, misrepresent, pervert, twist

misstep bad move, blunder, error, false step, faux pas, gaffe, indiscretion, lapse, mistake, slip, slip-up (*informal*), stumble, trip, wrong move

mist 1. *noun* cloud, condensation, dew, drizzle, film, fog, haar (*Eastern Brit.*), haze, smog, smur *or* smir (*Scot.*), spray, steam, vapour 2. *verb* becloud, befog, blear, blur, cloud, film, fog, obscure, steam (up)

mistake *noun* 1. bloomer (*Brit. informal*), blunder, boob (*Brit. slang*), boo-boo (*informal*), clanger (*informal*), erratum, error, error of judgment, false move, fault, faux pas, gaffe, goof (*informal*), howler (*informal*), inaccuracy, miscalculation, misconception, misstep, misunderstanding, oversight, slip, slip-up (*informal*), solecism ~*verb* 2. get wrong, misapprehend, misconceive, misconstrue, misinterpret, misjudge, misread, misunderstand 3. accept as, confound, confuse with, misinterpret as, mix up with, take for 4. be wide of *or* be off the mark, be wrong, blunder, boob (*Brit. slang*), drop a clanger (*informal*), err, goof (*informal*), miscalculate, misjudge, put one's foot in it (*informal*), slip up (*informal*)

The man who makes no mistakes does not usually make anything

Edward John Phelps

mistaken barking up the wrong tree (*informal*), erroneous, fallacious, false, faulty, getting the wrong end of the stick (*informal*), inaccurate, inappropriate, incorrect, in the wrong, labouring under a misapprehension, misguided, misinformed, misled, off base (*U.S. & Canad. informal*), off beam (*informal*), off target, off the mark, unfounded, unsound, way off beam (*informal*), wide of the mark, wrong

Antonyms accurate, correct, logical, right, sound, true

mistakenly by mistake, erroneously, fallaciously, falsely, inaccurately, inappropriately, incorrectly, in error, misguidedly, wrongly

mistimed badly timed, ill-timed, inconvenient, inopportune, unseasonable, unsynchronized, untimely

mistreat abuse, brutalize, handle roughly, harm, ill-treat, ill-use, injure, knock about *or* around, maltreat, manhandle, maul, misuse, molest, rough up, wrong

mistreatment abuse, brutalization, harm, ill-treatment, ill-usage, injury, maltreatment, manhandling, mauling, misuse, molestation, rough handling, roughing up, unkindness

mistress concubine, doxy (*archaic*), fancy bit (*slang*), fancy woman (*slang*), floozy (*slang*), girlfriend, inamorata, kept woman, ladylove (*rare*), lover, paramour

mistrust 1. *verb* apprehend, beware, be wary of, distrust, doubt, fear, have doubts about, suspect 2. *noun* apprehension, distrust, doubt, dubiety, fear, misgiving, scepticism, suspicion, uncertainty, wariness

mistrustful apprehensive, cautious, chary, cynical, distrustful, doubtful, dubious, fearful, hesitant, leery (*slang*), nervous, sceptical, suspicious, uncertain, wary

Antonyms certain, definite, positive, sure, unafraid

misty bleary, blurred, cloudy, dark, dim, foggy, fuzzy, hazy, indistinct, murky, nebulous, obscure, opaque, overcast, unclear, vague

Antonyms bright, clear, distinct, lucid, obvious, plain, sunny, well-defined

misunderstand be at cross-purposes, get (it) wrong, get one's lines crossed, get one's wires crossed, get the wrong end of the stick, get the wrong idea (about), misapprehend, misconceive, misconstrue, mishear, misinterpret, misjudge, misread, miss the point (of), mistake

misunderstanding 1. error, false impression, misapprehension, misconception, misconstruction, misinterpretation, misjudgment, misreading, mistake, mix-up, wrong idea 2. argument, breach, conflict, difference, difficulty, disagreement, discord, dissension, falling-out (*informal*), quarrel, rift, rupture, squabble, variance

misunderstood misconstrued, misheard, misinterpreted, misjudged, misread, unappreciated, unrecognized

misuse *noun* 1. abuse, barbarism, catachresis, corruption, desecration, dissipation, malapropism, misapplication, misemployment, misusage, perversion, profanation, solecism, squandering, waste 2. abuse, cruel treatment, exploitation, harm, ill-treatment, ill-usage, inhumane treatment, injury, maltreatment, manhandling, mistreatment, rough handling ~*verb* 3. abuse, corrupt, desecrate, dissipate, misapply, misemploy, pervert, profane, prostitute, squander, waste 4. abuse, brutalize, exploit, handle roughly, harm, ill-treat, ill-use, injure, maltreat, manhandle, maul, mistreat, molest, wrong

Antonyms *verb* appreciate, cherish, honour, prize, respect, treasure, use

mitigate abate, allay, appease, assuage, blunt, calm, check, diminish, dull, ease, extenuate, lessen, lighten, moderate, modify, mollify, pacify, palliate, placate, quiet, reduce the force of, remit, soften, soothe, subdue, take the edge off, temper, tone down, tranquillize, weaken

Antonyms aggravate, augment, enhance, heighten, increase, intensify, strengthen

mitigation abatement, allaying, alleviation, assuagement, diminution, easement, extenu~

ation, moderation, mollification, palliation, relief, remission

mix *verb* **1.** alloy, amalgamate, associate, blend, coalesce, combine, commingle, commix, compound, cross, fuse, incorporate, intermingle, interweave, join, jumble, meld, merge, mingle, put together, unite **2.** associate, come together, consort, fraternize, hang out (*informal*), hobnob, join, mingle, socialize *~noun* **3.** alloy, amalgam, assortment, blend, combination, compound, fusion, medley, meld, mixed bag (*informal*), mixture

mixed 1. alloyed, amalgamated, blended, combined, composite, compound, fused, incorporated, joint, mingled, united **2.** assorted, cosmopolitan, diverse, diversified, heterogeneous, manifold, miscellaneous, motley, varied **3.** crossbred, hybrid, interbred, interdenominational, mongrel **4.** ambivalent, equivocal, indecisive, uncertain
Antonyms homogeneous, isolated, pure, straight, unmixed

mixed-up at sea, bewildered, confused, distraught, disturbed, maladjusted, muddled, perplexed, puzzled, upset

mixture admixture, alloy, amalgam, amalgamation, association, assortment, blend, brew, combine, composite, compound, concoction, conglomeration, cross, fusion, hotchpotch, jumble, medley, *mélange*, meld, miscellany, mix, mixed bag (*informal*), potpourri, salmagundi, union, variety

mix-up confusion, disorder, fankle (*Scot.*), jumble, mess, mistake, misunderstanding, muddle, snarl-up (*informal, chiefly Brit.*), tangle

mix up 1. blend, combine, commix, mix **2.** confound, confuse, muddle **3.** bewilder, confuse, disturb, fluster, muddle, perplex, puzzle, throw into confusion, unnerve, upset **4.** embroil, entangle, implicate, involve, rope in

moan *noun* **1.** groan, lament, lamentation, sigh, sob, sough, wail, whine **2.** *informal* beef (*slang*), bitch (*slang*), complaint, gripe (*informal*), grouch (*informal*), grouse, grumble, kvetch (*U.S. slang*), protest, whine *~verb* **3.** bemoan, bewail, deplore, grieve, groan, keen, lament, mourn, sigh, sob, sough, whine **4.** *informal* beef (*slang*), bitch (*slang*), bleat, carp, complain, gripe (*informal*), groan, grouch (*informal*), grouse, grumble, moan and groan, whine, whinge (*informal*)

mob *noun* **1.** assemblage, body, collection, crowd, drove, flock, gang, gathering, herd, horde, host, mass, multitude, pack, press, swarm, throng **2.** class, company, crew (*informal*), gang, group, lot, set, troop **3.** *canaille*, commonalty, great unwashed (*informal & derogatory*), hoi polloi, masses, rabble, riffraff, scum *~verb* **4.** crowd around, jostle, overrun, set upon, surround, swarm around **5.** cram into, crowd, crowd into, fill, fill to overflowing, jam, pack

mobile 1. ambulatory, itinerant, locomotive, migrant, motile, movable, moving, peripatetic, portable, travelling, wandering **2.** animated, changeable, ever-changing, expressive

mobilize activate, animate, call to arms, call up, get *or* make ready, marshal, muster, organize, prepare, put in motion, rally, ready

mock *verb* **1.** chaff, deride, flout, insult, jeer, laugh at, laugh to scorn, make a monkey out of, make fun of, poke fun at, ridicule, scoff, scorn, show contempt for, sneer, take the mickey (out of) (*informal*), take the piss (out of) (*taboo slang*), taunt, tease, wind up (*Brit. slang*) **2.** ape, burlesque, caricature, counterfeit, do (*informal*), imitate, lampoon, mimic, parody, satirize, send up (*Brit. informal*), take off (*informal*), travesty **3.** belie, cheat, deceive, delude, disappoint, dupe, elude, fool, let down, mislead **4.** defeat, defy, disappoint, foil, frustrate, thwart *~noun* **5.** banter, derision, gibe, jeering, mockery, ridicule, scorn, sneer, sneering **6.** Aunt Sally (*Brit.*), butt, dupe, fool, jest, laughing stock, sport, travesty **7.** counterfeit, fake, forgery, fraud, imitation, phoney *or* phony (*informal*), sham *~adjective* **8.** artificial, bogus, counterfeit, dummy, ersatz, fake, faked, false, feigned, forged, fraudulent, imitation, phoney *or* phony (*informal*), pretended, pseudo (*informal*), sham, spurious
Antonyms *verb* encourage, praise, respect, revere *~adjective* authentic, genuine, natural, real, sincere, true, unfeigned

mockery 1. contempt, contumely, derision, disdain, disrespect, gibes, insults, jeering, ridicule, scoffing, scorn **2.** burlesque, caricature, deception, farce, imitation, lampoon, laughing stock, mimicry, parody, pretence, send-up (*Brit. informal*), sham, spoof (*informal*), take-off (*informal*), travesty **3.** apology, disappointment, farce, joke, letdown

mocking contemptuous, contumelious, derisive, derisory, disdainful, disrespectful, insulting, irreverent, sarcastic, sardonic, satiric, satirical, scoffing, scornful, taunting

mode 1. approach, condition, course, custom, fashion, form, manner, method, plan, practice, procedure, process, quality, rule, state, style, system, technique, vein, way **2.** craze, fashion, look, rage, style, trend, vogue

model *noun* **1.** copy, dummy, facsimile, image, imitation, miniature, mock-up, replica, representation **2.** archetype, design, epitome, example, exemplar, gauge, ideal, lodestar, mould, norm, original, par, paradigm, paragon, pattern, prototype, standard, type **3.** poser, sitter, subject **4.** mannequin **5.** configuration, design, form, kind, mark, mode, stamp, style, type, variety, version *~verb* **6.** base,

carve, cast, design, fashion, form, mould, pattern, plan, sculpt, shape, stamp **7.** display, show off, sport (*informal*), wear ~*adjective* **8.** copy, dummy, facsimile, imitation, miniature **9.** archetypal, exemplary, ideal, illustrative, paradigmatic, perfect, standard, typical
Antonyms *adjective* (*sense 9*) deficient, flawed, impaired, imperfect

Rules and models destroy genius and art
William Hazlitt *Sketches and Essays*

moderate *adjective* **1.** calm, controlled, cool, deliberate, equable, gentle, judicious, limited, middle-of-the-road, mild, modest, peaceable, reasonable, restrained, sober, steady, temperate **2.** average, fair, fairish, fair to middling (*informal*), indifferent, mediocre, medium, middling, ordinary, passable, so-so (*informal*), unexceptional ~*verb* **3.** abate, allay, appease, assuage, calm, clear the air, control, curb, decrease, diminish, ease, lessen, mitigate, modulate, pacify, play down, quiet, regulate, relax, repress, restrain, soften, soft-pedal (*informal*), subdue, tame, temper, tone down **4.** arbitrate, chair, judge, mediate, preside, referee, take the chair
Antonyms *adjective* (*sense 1*) extreme, intemperate, ruffled, unreasonable, wild (*sense 2*) excessive, expensive, extreme, immoderate, inordinate, unusual ~*verb* heighten, increase, intensify

moderately fairly, gently, in moderation, passably, quite, rather, reasonably, slightly, somewhat, to a degree, tolerably, to some extent, within limits, within reason

moderation **1.** calmness, composure, coolness, equanimity, fairness, judiciousness, justice, justness, mildness, moderateness, reasonableness, restraint, sedateness, temperance **2. in moderation** moderately, within limits, within reason

We know what happens to people who stay in the middle of the road. They get run down
Aneurin Bevan

Moderation in all things

modern contemporary, current, fresh, late, latest, neoteric (*rare*), new, newfangled, novel, present, present-day, recent, twentieth-century, up-to-date, up-to-the-minute, with it (*informal*)
Antonyms ancient, antiquated, archaic, former, obsolete, old, old-fashioned, old hat, outmoded, passé, past, square (*informal*), uncool (*slang*)

modernity contemporaneity, currency, freshness, innovation, newness, novelty, recentness

modernize bring into the twentieth century, bring up to date, face-lift, make over, rejuvenate, remake, remodel, renew, renovate, revamp, update

modest **1.** bashful, blushing, coy, demure, diffident, discreet, humble, meek, quiet, reserved, reticent, retiring, self-conscious, self-effacing, shy, simple, unassuming, unpretentious **2.** fair, limited, middling, moderate, ordinary, small, unexceptional

modesty bashfulness, coyness, decency, demureness, diffidence, discreetness, humbleness, humility, lack of pretension, meekness, propriety, quietness, reserve, reticence, self-effacement, shyness, simplicity, timidity, unobtrusiveness, unpretentiousness
Antonyms arrogance, assurance, boastfulness, boldness, conceit, confidence, egotism, extravagance, forwardness, haughtiness, immodesty, indecency, ostentation, presumption, pretentiousness, pride, showiness, vanity

Small is the worth
Of beauty from the light retir'd;
Bid her come forth,
Suffer herself to be desir'd,
And not blush so to be admir'd
Edmund Waller *Go Lovely Rose!*

modicum atom, bit, crumb, dash, drop, fragment, grain, inch, iota, little, mite, ounce, particle, pinch, scrap, shred, small amount, speck, tad (*informal, chiefly U.S.*), tinge, touch

modification adjustment, alteration, change, modulation, mutation, qualification, refinement, reformation, restriction, revision, variation

modify **1.** adapt, adjust, alter, change, convert, recast, redo, refashion, reform, remodel, reorganize, reshape, revise, rework, transform, tweak (*informal*), vary **2.** abate, ease, lessen, limit, lower, moderate, qualify, reduce, relax, restrain, restrict, soften, temper, tone down

modish à la mode, all the rage, chic, contemporary, current, fashionable, hip (*slang*), in, now (*informal*), smart, stylish, trendy (*Brit. informal*), up-to-the-minute, vogue, voguish, with it (*informal*)

modulate adjust, attune, balance, harmonize, inflect, regulate, tone, tune, vary

modus operandi method, operation, practice, praxis, procedure, process, system, technique, way

mogul baron, bashaw, big cheese (*slang, old-fashioned*), big gun (*informal*), big noise (*informal*), big shot (*informal*), big wheel (*slang*), lord, magnate, nabob (*informal*), nob (*slang, chiefly Brit.*), notable, personage, potentate, tycoon, V.I.P.

moiety fifty percent, half, part, piece, portion, share

moist clammy, damp, dampish, dank, dewy, dripping, drizzly, humid, not dry, rainy, soggy, wet, wettish

moisten bedew, damp, dampen, humidify, lick, moisturize, soak, water, wet

moisture damp, dampness, dankness, dew, humidity, liquid, perspiration, sweat, water, wateriness, wetness

mole breakwater, dike, dyke, embankment, groyne, jetty, pier, sea wall

molecule atom, iota, jot, mite, mote, particle, speck

molest **1.** abuse, afflict, annoy, badger, beset, bother, bug (*informal*), disturb, harass, harry, hector, irritate, persecute, pester, plague, tease, torment, upset, vex, worry **2.** abuse, accost, assail, attack, harm, hurt, ill-treat, injure, interfere with, maltreat, manhandle

mollify **1.** appease, calm, compose, conciliate, pacify, placate, pour oil on troubled waters, propitiate, quell, quiet, soothe, sweeten **2.** abate, allay, assuage, blunt, curb, cushion, ease, lessen, lull, mitigate, moderate, modify, relieve, soften, temper, tone down, tranquillize

mollycoddle **1.** *verb* baby, coddle, cosset, indulge, pamper, pet, ruin, spoil **2.** *noun* baby, chinless wonder (*Brit. informal*), crybaby, milksop, milquetoast (*U.S.*), namby-pamby, sissy, weakling

moment **1.** bat of an eye (*informal*), flash, instant, jiffy (*informal*), minute, no time, second, shake (*informal*), split second, tick (*Brit. informal*), trice, twinkling, two shakes (*informal*), two shakes of a lamb's tail (*informal*) **2.** hour, instant, juncture, point, point in time, stage, time **3.** concern, consequence, gravity, import, importance, seriousness, significance, substance, value, weight, weightiness, worth

in the twinkling of an eye
Bible: I Corinthians

momentarily briefly, for a moment (little while, minute, second, short time, short while), for an instant, for the nonce, temporarily

momentary brief, ephemeral, evanescent, fleeting, flying, fugitive, hasty, passing, quick, short, short-lived, temporary, transitory
Antonyms lasting, lengthy, long-lived, permanent

momentous consequential, critical, crucial, decisive, earth-shaking (*informal*), fateful, grave, historic, important, of moment, pivotal, serious, significant, vital, weighty
Antonyms inconsequential, insignificant, trifling, trivial, unimportant

momentum drive, energy, force, impetus, power, propulsion, push, strength, thrust

monarch crowned head, emperor, empress, king, potentate, prince, princess, queen, ruler, sovereign

monarchy **1.** absolutism, autocracy, despotism, kingship, monocracy, royalism, sovereignty **2.** empire, kingdom, principality, realm

monastery abbey, cloister, convent, friary, house, nunnery, priory, religious community

monastic ascetic, austere, celibate, cenobitic, cloistered, cloistral, coenobitic, contemplative, conventual, eremitic, hermit-like, monachal, monkish, recluse, reclusive, secluded, sequestered, withdrawn

monetary budgetary, capital, cash, financial, fiscal, pecuniary

money **1.** ackers (*slang*), banknotes, brass (*Northern English dialect*), bread (*slang*), capital, cash, coin, currency, dibs (*slang*), dosh (*Brit. & Austral. slang*), dough (*slang*), filthy lucre (*facetious*), funds, gelt (*slang, chiefly U.S.*), green (*slang*), hard cash, legal tender, lolly (*Brit. slang*), loot (*informal*), mazuma (*slang, chiefly U.S.*), megabucks (*U.S. & Canad. slang*), moolah (*slang*), necessary (*informal*), needful (*informal*), pelf (*contemptuous*), readies (*informal*), rhino (*Brit. slang*), riches, shekels (*informal*), silver, specie, spondulicks (*slang*), the ready (*informal*), the wherewithal, tin (*slang*), wealth **2. in the money** affluent, flush (*informal*), in clover (*informal*), loaded (*slang*), on Easy Street (*informal*), prosperous, rich, rolling (*slang*), wealthy, well-heeled (*informal*), well-off, well-to-do
Related adjective: pecuniary

Currencies
see CURRENCY

Money couldn't buy friends but you got a better class of enemy
Spike Milligan *Puckoon*

Money is our madness, our vast collective madness
D.H. Lawrence

The almighty dollar is the only object of worship
Philadelphia Public Ledger

Money speaks sense in a language all nations understand
Aphra Behn *The Lucky Chance*

Wine maketh merry, but money answereth all things
Bible: Ecclesiastes

Money is coined liberty
Fyodor Dostoevsky *House of the Dead*

Money is the sinews of love, as of war
George Farquhar

Better authentic mammon than a bogus god
Louis MacNiece

Money is like a sixth sense without which you cannot make a complete use of the other five
W. Somerset Maugham *Of Human Bondage*

but it is pretty to see what money will do
Samuel Pepys *Diary*

Money doesn't talk, it swears
Bob Dylan *It's Alright, Ma (I'm Only Bleeding)*
Money is like muck, not good except it be spread
Francis Bacon *Of Seditions and Troubles*
Money ... is none of the wheels of trade: it is the oil which renders the motion of the wheels more smooth and easy
David Hume *Essays: Moral and Political*
Bad money drives out good
Money isn't everything
Money talks
Money is power
Money makes money
Shrouds have no pockets
You can't take it with you when you go

moneyed, monied affluent, flush (*informal*), loaded (*slang*), prosperous, rich, wealthy, well-heeled (*informal*), well-off, well-to-do

moneymaking *adjective* gainful, going, lucrative, paying, profitable, remunerative, successful, thriving

mongrel 1. *noun* bigener (*Biology*), cross, crossbreed, half-breed, hybrid, mixed breed **2.** *adjective* bastard, crossbred, half-breed, hybrid, of mixed breed

monitor 1. *noun* guide, invigilator, overseer, prefect (*Brit.*), supervisor, watchdog **2.** *verb* check, follow, keep an eye on, keep tabs on, keep track of, observe, oversee, record, scan, supervise, survey, watch

monitory admonishing, admonitory, cautionary, cautioning, reproving, warning

monk brother, friar (*loosely*), monastic, religious
Related adjective: monastic

monkey *noun* **1.** jackanapes (*archaic*), primate, simian **2.** devil, imp, mischief maker, pickle (*Brit. informal*), rascal, rogue, scamp **3.** *slang* ass, butt, dupe, fool, laughing stock **4. make a monkey of** make a fool of, make (someone) a laughing stock, make fun of, make (someone) look foolish (ridiculous, silly), play a trick on, ridicule ~*verb* **5.** fiddle (*informal*), fool, interfere, meddle, mess, play, tamper, tinker, trifle

monkey: an arboreal animal which makes itself at home in genealogical trees
Ambrose Bierce *The Devil's Dictionary*

monkey business 1. carry-on (*informal, chiefly Brit.*), clowning, horseplay, mischief, monkey tricks, pranks, shenanigans (*informal*), skylarking (*informal*), tomfoolery **2.** chicanery, dishonesty, funny business, hanky-panky (*informal*), skulduggery (*informal*), trickery

monolithic colossal, giant, gigantic, huge, immovable, impenetrable, imposing, intractable, massive, monumental, solid, substantial, undifferentiated, undivided, unitary

monologue harangue, lecture, sermon, soliloquy, speech

monomania bee in one's bonnet (*informal*), fanaticism, fixation, hobbyhorse, *idée fixe*, obsession, one-track mind (*informal*)

monopolize control, corner, corner the market in, dominate, engross, exercise *or* have a monopoly of, hog (*slang*), keep to oneself, take over, take up

monotonous all the same, boring, colourless, droning, dull, flat, ho-hum (*informal*), humdrum, mind-numbing, plodding, repetitious, repetitive, samey (*informal*), soporific, tedious, tiresome, toneless, unchanging, uniform, uninflected, unvaried, wearisome
Antonyms animated, enjoyable, entertaining, enthralling, exciting, exhilarating, interesting, lively, sexy (*informal*), stimulating

monotony boredom, colourlessness, dullness, flatness, humdrumness, monotonousness, repetitiousness, repetitiveness, routine, sameness, tediousness, tedium, tiresomeness, uniformity, wearisomeness

monster *noun* **1.** barbarian, beast, bogeyman, brute, demon, devil, fiend, ghoul, ogre, savage, villain **2.** abortion, freak, lusus naturae, miscreation, monstrosity, mutant, teratism **3.** behemoth, Brobdingnagian, colossus, giant, leviathan, mammoth, titan ~*adjective* **4.** Brobdingnagian, colossal, elephantine, enormous, gargantuan, giant, gigantic, ginormous (*informal*), huge, humongous *or* humungous (*U.S. slang*), immense, jumbo (*informal*), mammoth, massive, mega (*slang*), monstrous, stellar (*informal*), stupendous, titanic, tremendous

monstrosity 1. abortion, eyesore, freak, horror, lusus naturae, miscreation, monster, mutant, ogre, teratism **2.** abnormality, atrocity, dreadfulness, evil, frightfulness, heinousness, hellishness, hideousness, horror, loathsomeness, obscenity

monstrous 1. abnormal, dreadful, enormous, fiendish, freakish, frightful, grotesque, gruesome, hellish, hideous, horrendous, horrible, miscreated, obscene, teratoid, terrible, unnatural **2.** atrocious, cruel, devilish, diabolical, disgraceful, egregious, evil, fiendish, foul, heinous, horrifying, infamous, inhuman, intolerable, loathsome, odious, outrageous, satanic, scandalous, shocking, vicious, villainous **3.** colossal, elephantine, enormous, gargantuan, giant, gigantic, ginormous (*informal*), great, huge, humongous *or* humungous (*U.S. slang*), immense, mammoth, massive, mega (*slang*), prodigious, stellar (*informal*), stupendous, titanic, towering, tremendous, vast
Antonyms (*sense 1*) appealing, attractive, beautiful, delightful, lovely, natural, normal, ordinary, pleasant (*sense 2*) admirable, decent, fine, good, honourable, humane, kind,

merciful, mild (*sense 3*) diminutive, insignificant, little, meagre, miniature, minute, puny, slight, small, tiny

month four weeks, moon, thirty days

monument **1.** cairn, cenotaph, commemoration, gravestone, headstone, marker, mausoleum, memorial, obelisk, pillar, shrine, statue, tombstone **2.** memento, record, remembrance, reminder, testament, token, witness

If you seek a monument, look around (Si monumentum requiris, circumspice)
son of Sir Christopher Wren *Inscription in St. Paul's Cathedral*

monumental **1.** awe-inspiring, awesome, classic, enduring, enormous, epoch-making, historic, immortal, important, lasting, majestic, memorable, outstanding, prodigious, significant, stupendous, unforgettable **2.** commemorative, cyclopean, funerary, memorial, monolithic, statuary **3.** *informal* catastrophic, colossal, egregious, gigantic, great, horrible, immense, indefensible, massive, staggering, terrible, tremendous, unforgivable, whopping (*informal*)
Antonyms (*sense 1*) ephemeral, inconsequential, insignificant, modest, negligible, ordinary, trivial, undistinguished, unimportant, unimpressive, unremarkable (*sense 3*) average, insignificant, mild, petty, slight, small, tiny, trivial

mood **1.** disposition, frame of mind, humour, spirit, state of mind, temper, tenor, vein **2.** bad temper, bate (*Brit. slang*), blues, depression, doldrums, dumps (*informal*), fit of pique, grumps (*informal*), low spirits, melancholy, sulk, the hump (*Brit. informal*), the sulks, wax (*informal, chiefly Brit.*) **3.** **in the mood** disposed (towards), eager, favourable, inclined, interested, in the (right) frame of mind, keen, minded, willing

moody **1.** angry, broody, cantankerous, crabbed, crabby, crestfallen, cross, crotchety (*informal*), crusty, curt, dismal, doleful, dour, downcast, down in the dumps (*informal*), down in the mouth (*informal*), frowning, gloomy, glum, huffish, huffy, ill-humoured, ill-tempered, in a huff, in the doldrums, introspective, irascible, irritable, lugubrious, melancholy, miserable, mopish, mopy, morose, offended, out of sorts (*informal*), pensive, petulant, piqued, sad, saturnine, short-tempered, splenetic, sulky, sullen, temperamental, testy, tetchy, touchy, waspish, wounded **2.** capricious, changeable, erratic, faddish, fickle, fitful, flighty, impulsive, inconstant, mercurial, temperamental, unpredictable, unstable, unsteady, volatile
Antonyms (*sense 1*) amiable, cheerful, compatible, gay, happy, optimistic (*sense 2*) constant, stable, steady

moon *noun* **1.** satellite **2.** **once in a blue moon** almost never, hardly ever, rarely, very seldom *~verb* **3.** daydream, idle, languish, mooch (*slang*), mope, waste time
Related adjective: lunar

Swear not by the moon, the inconstant moon
William Shakespeare *Romeo and Juliet*

moonshine **1.** moonbeams, moonlight **2.** *U.S.* bootleg, hooch *or* hootch (*informal, chiefly U.S. & Canad.*), poteen **3.** blather, blether, bosh (*informal*), bunk (*informal*), bunkum *or* buncombe (*chiefly U.S.*), claptrap (*informal*), foolish talk, gas (*informal*), guff (*slang*), havers (*Scot.*), hogwash, hot air (*informal*), nonsense, piffle (*informal*), rubbish, stuff and nonsense, tarradiddle, tosh (*slang, chiefly Brit.*), trash, tripe (*informal*), twaddle

moor[1] *noun* fell (*Brit.*), heath, moorland, muir (*Scot.*)

moor[2] *verb* anchor, berth, dock, fasten, fix, lash, make fast, secure, tie up

moot **1.** *adjective* arguable, at issue, contestable, controversial, debatable, disputable, doubtful, open, open to debate, undecided, unresolved, unsettled **2.** *verb* bring up, broach, introduce, propose, put forward, suggest, ventilate

mop *noun* **1.** sponge, squeegee, swab **2.** mane, shock, tangle, thatch *~verb* **3.** clean, soak up, sponge, swab, wash, wipe

mope be apathetic, be dejected, be down in the mouth (*informal*), be gloomy, brood, eat one's heart out, fret, go about like a half-shut knife (*informal*), hang around, have a long face, idle, languish, moon, pine, pout, sulk, waste time, wear a long face

mop up **1.** clean up, mop, soak up, sponge, swab, wash, wipe **2.** *Military* account for, clean out, clear, eliminate, finish off, neutralize, pacify, round up, secure

moral *adjective* **1.** ethical **2.** blameless, chaste, decent, ethical, good, high-minded, honest, honourable, incorruptible, innocent, just, meritorious, noble, principled, proper, pure, right, righteous, upright, upstanding, virtuous *~noun* **3.** lesson, meaning, message, point, significance **4.** adage, aphorism, apophthegm, epigram, gnome, maxim, motto, proverb, saw, saying
Antonyms amoral, dishonest, dishonourable, immoral, improper, sinful, unethical, unfair, unjust, wrong

An Englishman thinks he is moral when he is only uncomfortable
George Bernard Shaw *Man and Superman*

morale confidence, esprit de corps, heart, mettle, self-esteem, spirit, temper

morality **1.** chastity, decency, ethicality, ethicalness, goodness, honesty, integrity, justice, principle, rectitude, righteousness, rightness, uprightness, virtue **2.** conduct, ethics, habits, ideals, manners, moral code, morals, mores, philosophy, principles, standards

Morality is the herd-instinct in the individual
Friedrich Nietzsche *Die fröhliche Wissenschaft*

Morality is a private and costly luxury
Henry Brooks Adams *The Education of Henry Adams*

We know no spectacle so ridiculous as the British public in one of its periodical fits of morality
Lord Macaulay *Essays*

One becomes moral as soon as one is unhappy
Marcel Proust *Within a Budding Grove*

morals behaviour, conduct, ethics, habits, integrity, manners, morality, mores, principles, scruples, standards

Food first, then morals
Bertolt Brecht *The Threepenny Opera*

morass **1.** bog, fen, marsh, marshland, moss (*Scot. & northern English dialect*), quagmire, slough, swamp **2.** chaos, confusion, jam (*informal*), mess, mix-up, muddle, quagmire, tangle

moratorium freeze, halt, postponement, respite, standstill, stay, suspension

morbid **1.** brooding, funereal, ghoulish, gloomy, grim, melancholy, pessimistic, sick, sombre, unhealthy, unwholesome **2.** dreadful, ghastly, grisly, gruesome, hideous, horrid, macabre **3.** ailing, deadly, diseased, infected, malignant, pathological, sick, sickly, unhealthy, unsound
Antonyms bright, cheerful, happy, healthy, salubrious, wholesome

mordant **1.** acerbic, acid, acrimonious, astringent, biting, caustic, cutting, edged, harsh, incisive, mordacious, pungent, sarcastic, scathing, sharp, stinging, trenchant, venomous, vitriolic, waspish **2.** acid, acidic, caustic, corrosive, pungent, vitriolic

more **1.** *adjective* added, additional, extra, fresh, further, new, other, spare, supplementary **2.** *adverb* better, further, longer, to a greater extent

Please, sir, I want some more
Charles Dickens *Oliver Twist*

The more, the merrier

moreover additionally, also, as well, besides, further, furthermore, in addition, into the bargain, likewise, to boot, too, what is more, withal (*literary*)

morgue mortuary

moribund **1.** at death's door, breathing one's last, doomed, dying, fading fast, failing, (having) one foot in the grave, *in extremis*, near death, near the end, on one's deathbed, on one's last legs **2.** at a standstill, declining, forceless, obsolescent, on its last legs, on the way out, stagnant, stagnating, standing still, waning, weak

morning a.m., break of day, dawn, daybreak, forenoon, morn (*poetic*), morrow (*archaic*), sunrise
Related adjective: matutinal

Awake! For morning in the bowl of night
Has flung the stone that puts the stars to flight
And lo! the Hunter of the East has caught
The Sultan's turret in a noose of light
Edward Fitzgerald *The Rubáiyát of Omar Khayyám*

moron airhead (*slang*), ass, berk (*Brit. slang*), blockhead, bonehead (*slang*), charlie (*Brit. informal*), coot, cretin, dickhead (*slang*), dickwit (*slang*), dimwit (*informal*), dipstick (*Brit. slang*), divvy (*Brit. slang*), dolt, dope (*informal*), dork (*slang*), dummy (*slang*), dunce, dunderhead, dweeb (*U.S. slang*), fathead (*informal*), fool, fuckwit (*taboo slang*), geek (*slang*), gobshite (*Irish taboo slang*), gonzo (*slang*), halfwit, idiot, imbecile, jerk (*slang, chiefly U.S. & Canad.*), lamebrain (*informal*), mental defective, muttonhead (*slang*), nerd *or* nurd (*slang*), nitwit (*informal*), numpty (*Scot. informal*), numskull *or* numbskull, oaf, pillock (*Brit. slang*), plank (*Brit. slang*), plonker (*slang*), prat (*slang*), prick (*slang*), schmuck (*U.S. slang*), simpleton, thickhead, tosser (*Brit. slang*), twit (*informal, chiefly Brit.*), wally (*slang*), weenie (*U.S. informal*)

moronic asinine, Boeotian, braindead (*informal*), brainless, cretinous, daft (*informal*), dead from the neck up (*informal*), dimwitted (*informal*), doltish, foolish, gormless (*Brit. informal*), halfwitted, idiotic, imbecilic, mentally defective, mindless, muttonheaded (*slang*), retarded, simple, stupid, thick, unintelligent

morose blue, churlish, crabbed, crabby, cross, crusty, depressed, dour, down, down in the dumps (*informal*), gloomy, glum, grouchy (*informal*), gruff, ill-humoured, ill-natured, ill-tempered, in a bad mood, low, melancholy, miserable, moody, mournful, perverse, pessimistic, saturnine, sour, sulky, sullen, surly, taciturn
Antonyms amiable, blithe, cheerful, chirpy (*informal*), friendly, gay, genial, good-humoured, good-natured, happy, pleasant, sweet

morsel bit, bite, crumb, fraction, fragment, grain, mouthful, nibble, part, piece, scrap, segment, slice, snack, soupçon, tad (*informal, chiefly U.S.*), taste, titbit

mortal *adjective* **1.** corporeal, earthly, ephemeral, human, impermanent, passing, sublunary, temporal, transient, worldly **2.** deadly, death-dealing, destructive, fatal, killing, lethal, murderous, terminal **3.** bitter, deadly, implacable, irreconcilable, out-and-out, re~ morseless, sworn, to the death, unrelenting **4.** agonizing, awful, dire, enormous, extreme, grave, great, intense, serious, severe, terrible *~noun* **5.** being, body, earthling, human, hu~ man being, individual, man, person, woman

What fools these mortals be!
William Shakespeare *A Midsummer Night's Dream*

mortality **1.** ephemerality, humanity, imper~ manence, temporality, transience **2.** bloodshed, carnage, death, destruction, fatality, killing, loss of life

Old mortality, the ruins of forgotten times
Thomas Browne *Hydriotaphia*

Dust thou art, and unto dust thou shalt return
Bible: Genesis

Earth to earth, ashes to ashes, dust to dust
Book of Common Prayer

All men think all men mortal but themselves
Edward Young *Night Thoughts*

Man that is born of a woman is of few days, and full of trouble. He cometh forth like a flower, and is cut down; he fleeth also as a shadow, and continueth not
Bible: Job

All flesh is grass, and all the goodliness therefore is as the flower of the field
Bible: Isaiah

Here today and gone tomorrow

mortification **1.** abasement, annoyance, cha~ grin, discomfiture, dissatisfaction, embarrass~ ment, humiliation, loss of face, shame, vexa~ tion **2.** abasement, chastening, control, denial, discipline, subjugation **3.** *Medical* corruption, festering, gangrene, necrosis, putrescence

mortified **1.** abashed, affronted, annoyed, ashamed, chagrined, chastened, confounded, crushed, deflated, discomfited, displeased, em~ barrassed, given a showing-up (*informal*), humbled, humiliated, made to eat humble pie (*informal*), put down, put out (*informal*), put to shame, rendered speechless, shamed, vexed **2.** abased, chastened, conquered, controlled, crushed, disciplined, subdued **3.** *of flesh* de~ cayed, gangrenous, necrotic, rotted

mortify **1.** abase, abash, affront, annoy, cha~ grin, chasten, confound, crush, deflate, disap~ point, discomfit, displease, embarrass, hum~ ble, humiliate, make (someone) eat humble pie (*informal*), put down, put to shame, shame, take (someone) down a peg (*informal*), vex **2.** abase, chasten, control, deny, discipline, subdue **3.** *of flesh* become gangrenous, corrupt, deaden, die, fester, gangrene, necrose, putrefy

mortuary funeral home (*U.S.*), funeral parlour, morgue

mostly above all, almost entirely, as a rule, chiefly, customarily, for the most part, gener~ ally, largely, mainly, most often, on the whole, particularly, predominantly, primarily, principally, usually

mote atom, grain, mite, particle, speck, spot

moth-eaten antiquated, decayed, decrepit, di~ lapidated, grungy (*slang, chiefly U.S.*), obso~ lete, outdated, outworn, ragged, scuzzy (*slang, chiefly U.S.*), seedy, shabby, stale, tattered, threadbare, worn-out

mother *noun* **1.** dam, ma (*informal*), mater, mom (*U.S. informal*), mum (*Brit. informal*), mummy (*Brit. informal*), old lady (*informal*), old woman (*informal*) *~adjective* **2.** connate, inborn, innate, native, natural *~verb* **3.** bear, bring forth, drop, give birth to, produce **4.** care for, cherish, nurse, nurture, protect, raise, rear, tend **5.** baby, fuss over, indulge, pamper, spoil

All women become like their mothers. That is their tragedy. No man does. That is his
Oscar Wilde *The Importance of Being Earnest*

Few misfortunes can befall a boy which bring worse consequences than to have a really affection~ ate mother
W. Somerset Maugham *A Writer's Notebook*

motherhood

The hand that rocks the cradle
Is the hand that rules the world
William Ross Wallace *John O'London's Treasure Trove*

motherly affectionate, caring, comforting, fond, gentle, kind, loving, maternal, protective, sheltering, tender, warm

mother wit brains, common sense, gumption (*Brit. informal*), horse sense, judgment, native intelligence, nous (*Brit. slang*), savvy (*slang*), smarts (*slang, chiefly U.S.*)

motif **1.** concept, idea, leitmotiv, subject, theme **2.** decoration, design, form, ornament, shape

motion *noun* **1.** action, change, flow, kinesics, locomotion, mobility, motility, move, move~ ment, passage, passing, progress, travel **2.** gesticulation, gesture, sign, signal, wave **3.** proposal, proposition, recommendation, sub~ mission, suggestion **4. in motion** afoot, func~ tioning, going, in progress, moving, on the go (*informal*), on the move (*informal*), operation~ al, travelling, under way, working *~verb* **5.** beckon, direct, gesticulate, gesture, nod, sig~ nal, wave

Related adjective: kinetic

motionless at a standstill, at rest, calm, fixed, frozen, halted, immobile, inanimate, inert, lifeless, paralysed, standing, static, stationary, still, stock-still, transfixed, unmoved, unmov~ ing

Antonyms active, agitated, animated, frantic, lively, mobile, moving, restless, travelling

motivate actuate, arouse, bring, cause, draw, drive, get going, give incentive to, impel, in~

duce, inspire, inspirit, instigate, lead, move, persuade, prod, prompt, provoke, set off, set on, stimulate, stir, trigger

motivation 1. ambition, desire, drive, hunger, inspiration, interest, wish 2. carrot and stick, impulse, incentive, incitement, inducement, inspiration, instigation, motive, persuasion, reason, spur, stimulus

motive 1. *noun* cause, design, ground(s), incentive, incitement, inducement, influence, inspiration, intention, mainspring, motivation, object, occasion, purpose, rationale, reason, spur, stimulus, the why and wherefore, thinking 2. *adjective* activating, driving, impelling, motivating, moving, operative, prompting

motley 1. assorted, disparate, dissimilar, diversified, heterogeneous, mingled, miscellaneous, mixed, unlike, varied 2. chequered, multicoloured, particoloured, polychromatic, polychrome, polychromous, rainbow, variegated

Antonyms (*sense 1*) homogeneous, similar, uniform (*sense 2*) monochromatic, plain, self-coloured, solid

mottled blotchy, brindled, chequered, dappled, flecked, freckled, marbled, piebald, pied, speckled, spotted, stippled, streaked, tabby, variegated

motto adage, byword, cry, dictum, formula, gnome, maxim, precept, proverb, rule, saw, saying, slogan, watchword

mould[1] *noun* 1. cast, die, form, matrix, pattern, shape, stamp 2. brand, build, configuration, construction, cut, design, fashion, form, format, frame, kind, line, make, pattern, shape, stamp, structure, style 3. calibre, character, ilk, kidney, kind, nature, quality, sort, stamp, type ~*verb* 4. carve, cast, construct, create, fashion, forge, form, make, model, sculpt, shape, stamp, work 5. affect, control, direct, form, influence, make, shape

mould[2] *noun* blight, fungus, mildew, mouldiness, mustiness

mould[3] *noun* dirt, earth, humus, loam, soil

moulder break down, crumble, decay, decompose, disintegrate, perish, rot, waste

mouldy bad, blighted, decaying, fusty, mildewed, musty, rotten, rotting, spoiled, stale

mound 1. bing (*Scot.*), drift, heap, pile, rick, stack 2. bank, dune, embankment, hill, hillock, knoll, rise 3. *Archaeology* barrow, tumulus 4. bulwark, earthwork, motte (*History*), rampart

mount *verb* 1. ascend, clamber up, climb, escalade, go up, make one's way up, scale 2. bestride, climb onto, climb up on, get astride, get (up) on, jump on 3. arise, ascend, rise, soar, tower 4. accumulate, build, escalate, grow, increase, intensify, multiply, pile up, swell 5. display, frame, set, set off 6. exhibit, get up (*informal*), prepare, produce, put on, stage 7. *Military* deliver, launch, prepare, ready, set in motion, stage 8. emplace, fit, install, place, position, put in place, set up ~*noun* 9. backing, base, fixture, foil, frame, mounting, setting, stand, support 10. horse, steed (*literary*)

Antonyms (*sense 1*) descend, drop, go down, make one's way down (*sense 2*) climb down from, climb off, dismount, get down from, get off, jump off (*sense 4*) contract, decline, decrease, diminish, dwindle, fall, lessen, lower, reduce, shrink, wane

mountain 1. alp, ben (*Scot.*), elevation, eminence, fell (*Brit.*), height, mount, Munro, peak 2. abundance, heap, mass, mound, pile, stack, ton

Mountains

Aconcagua
Adams
Albert Edward
Anai Mudi
Aneto
Annapurna
Apo
Aragats
Aran Fawddwy
Ararat
Arber
Argentera
Belukha
Ben Lomond
Ben Macdhui
Ben Nevis
Blackburn
Blanca Peak
Blue Mountain Peak
Bona
Brocken
Carmarthen Van
Carmel
Cerro de Mulhacén
Citlaltépetl
Clingman's Dome
Cook
Corcovado
Corno
Croagh Patrick
Demavend
Dhaulagiri
Eiger
Elbert
Elbrus
El Capitan
Emi Koussi
Estrella
Everest
Finsteraarhorn
Fuji
Gannet Peak
Gerlachovka
Grand Teton
Gran Paradiso
Harney Peak
Helicon
Helvellyn
Hermon
Humphreys Peak
Hymettus
Ida
Illimani
Isto
Jebel Musa
Jungfrau
K2 *or* Godwin Austen
Kamet
Kangchenjunga
Kenya
Kilimanjaro
Kinabalu
Kings Peak
Klínovec
Kommunizma Peak
Kongur Shan
Kosciusko
Lenin Peak
Leone
Logan
Longs Peak
Mansfield
Marcy
Markham
Marmolada
Masharbrum
Matterhorn
McKinley
Mitchell
Mont Blanc

Mount of Olives
Mulhacén
Munku-Sardyk
Musala
Nanda Devi
Nanga Parbat
Narodnaya
Nebo
Negoiu
Olympus
Ossa
Palomar
Parnassus
Pelion
Pentelikon
Perdido
Petermann Peak
Pikes Peak
Pilatus
Piz Bernina
Pobeda Peak
Puy de Dôme
Rainier
Rigi
Robson
Rock Creek
Rosa
Rushmore
Scafell Pike
Schneekoppe
Scopus
Sinai
Siple
Sir Sandford
Sir Wilfrid Laurier
Skalitsy
Slide Mountain
Smólikas
Snowdon
Sorata
Stanley
Sugar Loaf Mountain
Table Mountain
Tabor
Teide
Tengri Khan
Thabana Ntlenyana
Timpanogos
Tirich Mir
Toubkal
Troglav
Ulugh Muztagh
Uncompahgre Peak
Venusberg
Victoria
Viso
Waddington
Washington
Waun Fach
Weisshorn
White Mountain
Whitney
Wrangell
Zard Kuh
Zugspitze

If the mountain will not come to Mahomet,
Mahomet must go to the mountain

mountainous 1. alpine, high, highland, rocky, soaring, steep, towering, upland 2. daunting, enormous, gigantic, great, huge, hulking, immense, mammoth, mighty, monumental, ponderous, prodigious
Antonyms (*sense 2*) diminutive, insignificant, little, minute, petty, puny, small, tiny, trivial, weak

mountebank charlatan, cheat, chiseller (*informal*), confidence trickster, con man (*informal*), fake, fraud, fraudster, grifter (*slang, chiefly U.S. & Canad.*), impostor, phoney *or* phony (*informal*), pretender, quack, rogue, swindler

mourn bemoan, bewail, deplore, grieve, keen, lament, miss, rue, sorrow, wail, wear black, weep

mournful 1. afflicting, calamitous, deplorable, distressing, grievous, harrowing, lamentable, melancholy, painful, piteous, plaintive, sad, sorrowful, tragic, unhappy, woeful 2. brokenhearted, cheerless, desolate, disconsolate, dismal, downcast, down in the dumps (*informal*), funereal, gloomy, grief-stricken, grieving, heartbroken, heavy, heavy-hearted, joyless, lugubrious, melancholy, miserable, rueful, sad, sombre, unhappy, woeful
Antonyms (*sense 1*) agreeable, cheerful, fortunate, happy, lucky, pleasant, satisfying (*sense 2*) bright, cheerful, chirpy (*informal*), genial, happy, jolly, joyful, light-hearted, sunny, upbeat (*informal*)

mourning 1. bereavement, grief, grieving, keening, lamentation, weeping, woe 2. black, sackcloth and ashes, weeds, widow's weeds

mousy, mousey 1. brownish, colourless, drab, dull, indeterminate, plain 2. diffident, ineffectual, quiet, self-effacing, shy, timid, timorous, unassertive

mouth *noun* 1. chops (*slang*), gob (*slang, especially Brit.*), jaws, lips, maw, trap (*slang*), yap (*slang*) 2. *informal* boasting, braggadocio, bragging, empty talk, gas (*informal*), hot air (*slang*), idle talk 3. *informal* backchat (*informal*), cheek (*informal*), impudence, insolence, lip (*slang*), rudeness, sauce (*informal*) 4. aperture, cavity, crevice, door, entrance, gateway, inlet, lips, opening, orifice, rim 5. face, grimace, *moue*, pout, wry face 6. **down in** *or* **at the mouth** blue, crestfallen, dejected, depressed, disheartened, dispirited, down, downcast, down in the dumps (*informal*), in low spirits, melancholy, miserable, sad, sick as a parrot (*informal*), unhappy

A shut mouth catches no flies

mouthful bit, bite, drop, forkful, little, morsel, sample, sip, spoonful, sup, swallow, taste

mouthpiece 1. agent, delegate, representative, spokesman, spokeswoman 2. journal, organ, periodical, publication

movable detachable, mobile, not fixed, portable, portative, transferable, transportable

movables belongings, chattels, effects, furniture, gear, goods, possessions, property, stuff (*informal*), things (*informal*)

move *verb* 1. advance, budge, change position, drift, go, march, proceed, progress, shift, stir, walk 2. carry, change, shift, switch, transfer, transport, transpose 3. change residence, flit (*Scot. & northern English dialect*), go away, leave, migrate, move house, pack one's bags (*informal*), quit, relocate, remove 4. activate, drive, impel, motivate, operate, prod, propel, push, set going, shift, shove, start, turn 5. actuate, affect, agitate, cause, excite, give rise to, impel, impress, incite, induce, influence, inspire, instigate, lead, make an impression on, motivate, persuade, prompt, rouse, stimulate, touch, tug at (someone's) heartstrings (*Often facetious*), urge 6. advocate, propose, put forward, recommend, suggest, urge ~*noun* 7. act, action, deed, manoeuvre, measure, motion, movement, ploy, shift, step, stratagem, stroke, turn 8. change of address, flit (*Scot. & northern English dialect*), flitting (*Scot. &*

northern English dialect), migration, relocation, removal, shift, transfer **9. get a move on** get cracking (*informal*), get going, hurry (up), make haste, shake a leg (*informal*), speed up, step on it (*informal*), stir oneself **10. on the move** *informal* **a.** in transit, journeying, moving, on the road (*informal*), on the run, on the wing, travelling, under way, voyaging **b.** active, advancing, astir, going forward, moving, progressing, stirring, succeeding

Antonyms (*sense 5*) deter, discourage, dissuade, prevent, stop

movement 1. act, action, activity, advance, agitation, change, development, displacement, exercise, flow, gesture, manoeuvre, motion, move, moving, operation, progress, progression, shift, steps, stir, stirring, transfer **2.** camp, campaign, crusade, drive, faction, front, group, grouping, organization, party **3.** current, drift, flow, swing, tendency, trend **4.** action, innards (*informal*), machinery, mechanism, workings, works **5.** *Music* division, part, passage, section **6.** beat, cadence, measure (*Prosody*), metre, pace, rhythm, swing, tempo

movie 1. feature, film, flick (*slang*), motion picture, moving picture (*U.S.*), picture **2.** *plural* cinema, film, films, flicks (*slang*), pictures (*informal*), silver screen (*informal*)

moving 1. affecting, arousing, emotional, emotive, exciting, impelling, impressive, inspiring, pathetic, persuasive, poignant, stirring, touching **2.** mobile, motile, movable, portable, running, unfixed **3.** dynamic, impelling, inspirational, motivating, propelling, stimulating, stimulative

Antonyms (*sense 1*) unemotional, unexciting, unimpressive, uninspiring (*sense 2*) fixed, immobile, immovable, stationary, still, unmoving

mow crop, cut, scythe, shear, trim

mow down blow away (*slang, chiefly U.S.*), butcher, cut down, cut to pieces, massacre, shoot down, slaughter

much 1. *adjective* abundant, a lot of, ample, considerable, copious, great, plenteous, plenty of, sizeable, substantial **2.** *adverb* a great deal, a lot, considerably, decidedly, exceedingly, frequently, greatly, indeed, often, regularly **3.** *noun* a good deal, a great deal, a lot, an appreciable amount, heaps (*informal*), loads (*informal*), lots (*informal*), plenty

Antonyms *adjective* inadequate, insufficient, little, scant *~adverb* barely, hardly, infrequently, irregularly, not a lot, not much, occasionally, only just, rarely, scarcely, seldom, slightly *~noun* hardly anything, little, next to nothing, not a lot, not much, practically nothing, very little

much of a muchness

John Vanburgh & Colley Cibber *The Provok'd Husband*

muck 1. crap (*taboo slang*), dung, manure, ordure, shit (*taboo slang*) **2.** crap (*slang*), crud (*slang*), dirt, filth, grot (*slang*), gunge (*informal*), gunk (*informal*), mire, mud, ooze, scum, sewage, shit (*taboo slang*), slime, slob (*Irish*), sludge **3. make a muck of** *slang* blow (*slang*), botch, bungle, cock up (*Brit. slang*), flub (*U.S. slang*), fuck up (*offensive taboo slang*), make a mess of, make a nonsense of, make a pig's ear of (*informal*), mar, mess up, muff, ruin, screw up (*informal*), spoil

Where there's muck, there's brass

muck up blow (*slang*), bodge (*informal*), botch, bungle, cock up (*Brit. slang*), flub (*U.S. slang*), fuck up (*offensive taboo slang*), make a mess of, make a muck of (*slang*), make a nonsense of, make a pig's ear of (*informal*), mar, mess up, muff, ruin, screw up (*informal*), spoil

mucky begrimed, bespattered, dirty, filthy, grimy, messy, mud-caked, muddy, soiled, sticky

mucous glutinous, gummy, mucilaginous, slimy, viscid, viscous

mud clay, dirt, gloop (*informal*), mire, ooze, silt, slime, slob (*Irish*), sludge

muddle *verb* **1.** confuse, disarrange, disorder, disorganize, jumble, make a mess of, mess, muddle, ravel, scramble, spoil, tangle **2.** befuddle, bewilder, confound, confuse, daze, disorient, perplex, stupefy *~noun* **3.** chaos, clutter, confusion, daze, disarray, disorder, disorganization, fankle (*Scot.*), hodgepodge (*U.S.*), hotchpotch, jumble, mess, mix-up, perplexity, pig's breakfast (*informal*), plight, predicament, ravel, tangle

muddle along *or* **through** cope, get along, get by (*informal*), make it, manage, manage somehow, scrape by

muddled 1. chaotic, confused, disarrayed, disordered, disorganized, higgledy-piggledy (*informal*), jumbled, messy, mixed-up, scrambled, tangled **2.** at sea, befuddled, bewildered, confused, dazed, disoriented, perplexed, stupefied, vague **3.** confused, incoherent, loose, muddleheaded, unclear, woolly

Antonyms clear, cut-and-dried (*informal*), exact, orderly, organized, precise

muddy *adjective* **1.** bespattered, boggy, clarty (*Scot., & northern English dialect*), dirty, grimy, marshy, miry, mucky, mud-caked, quaggy, soiled, swampy **2.** blurred, dingy, dull, flat, lustreless, smoky, unclear, washed-out **3.** cloudy, dirty, foul, impure, opaque, turbid **4.** confused, fuzzy, hazy, indistinct, muddled, unclear, vague, woolly *~verb* **5.** begrime, bespatter, cloud, dirty, smear, smirch, soil

muff *verb* bodge (*informal*), botch, bungle, cock up (*Brit. slang*), flub (*U.S. slang*), fluff (*informal*), fuck up (*offensive taboo slang*), make a mess of, make a muck of (*informal*), make a nonsense of, make a pig's ear of (*informal*), mess up, mismanage, screw up (*informal*), spoil

muffle 1. cloak, conceal, cover, disguise, envelop, hood, mask, shroud, swaddle, swathe, wrap up 2. deaden, dull, gag, hush, muzzle, quieten, silence, soften, stifle, suppress

muffled dim, dull, faint, indistinct, muted, stifled, strangled, subdued, suppressed

mug[1] *noun* beaker, cup, flagon, jug, pot, tankard, toby jug

mug[2] *noun* clock (*Brit. slang*), countenance, dial (*slang*), face, features, kisser (*slang*), mush (*Brit. slang*), phiz *or* phizog (*Brit. slang*), puss (*slang*), visage

mug[3] 1. *noun* charlie (*Brit. informal*), chump (*informal*), easy *or* soft touch (*slang*), fool, gull (*archaic*), innocent, mark (*slang*), muggins (*Brit. slang*), simpleton, sucker (*slang*), weenie (*U.S. informal*) 2. *verb* assail, assault, attack, beat up, do over (*Brit., Austral., & N.Z. slang*), duff up (*Brit. slang*), hold up, lay into (*informal*), put the boot in (*slang*), rob, set about *or* upon, steam (*informal*), work over (*slang*)

muggy clammy, close, damp, humid, moist, oppressive, sticky, stuffy, sultry

mug up bone up on (*informal*), burn the midnight oil (*informal*), cram (*informal*), get up (*informal*), study, swot (*Brit. informal*)

mulish bull-headed, cross-grained, difficult, headstrong, inflexible, intractable, intransigent, obstinate, perverse, pig-headed, recalcitrant, refractory, rigid, self-willed, stiff-necked, stubborn, unreasonable, wilful

mull consider, contemplate, deliberate, examine, meditate, muse on, ponder, reflect on, review, ruminate, study, think about, think over, turn over in one's mind, weigh

multifarious different, diverse, diversified, legion, manifold, many, miscellaneous, multiform, multiple, multitudinous, numerous, sundry, varied, variegated

multiple collective, manifold, many, multitudinous, numerous, several, sundry, various

multiplicity abundance, array, diversity, heaps (*informal*), host, loads (*informal*), lot, lots (*informal*), mass, myriad, number, oodles (*informal*), piles (*informal*), profusion, scores, stacks, tons, variety

multiply accumulate, augment, breed, build up, expand, extend, increase, proliferate, propagate, reproduce, spread

Antonyms abate, decline, decrease, diminish, lessen, reduce

multitude 1. army, assemblage, assembly, collection, concourse, congregation, crowd, great number, horde, host, legion, lot, lots (*informal*), mass, mob, myriad, sea, swarm, throng 2. commonalty, common people, herd, hoi polloi, mob, populace, proletariat, public, rabble

multitudinous abounding, abundant, considerable, copious, countless, great, infinite, innumerable, legion, manifold, many, myriad, numerous, profuse, teeming, very numerous

mum 1. closemouthed, dumb, mute, quiet, secretive, silent, tight-lipped, uncommunicative, unforthcoming 2. **mum's the word** don't let on, don't tell a soul, keep quiet, keep silent, keep (something) secret, keep (something) to oneself, keep (something) under one's hat, play dumb, say nothing, tell no-one

mumbo jumbo 1. abracadabra, chant, charm, conjuration, hocus-pocus, incantation, magic, rite, ritual, spell, superstition 2. cant, claptrap (*informal*), double talk, gibberish, gobbledegook (*informal*), Greek (*informal*), humbug, jargon, nonsense, rigmarole

mumsy dowdy, drab, fogyish, frumpish *or* frumpy, homely, old-fashioned, plain, square (*informal*), unfashionable, unglamorous, unsophisticated

Antonyms attractive, beautiful, chic, elegant, fashionable, glamorous, modern, modish, smart, sophisticated, well-dressed

munch champ, chew, chomp, crunch, masticate, scrunch

mundane 1. banal, commonplace, day-to-day, everyday, humdrum, ordinary, prosaic, routine, vanilla (*slang*), workaday 2. earthly, fleshly, human, material, mortal, secular, sublunary, temporal, terrestrial, worldly

Antonyms (*sense 1*) dramatic, exciting, extraordinary, ground-breaking, imaginative, interesting, left-field (*informal*), novel, original, special, uncommon, unusual (*sense 2*) ethereal, heavenly, spiritual, unworldly

municipal borough, city, civic, community, public, town, urban

municipality borough, burgh (*Scot.*), city, district, town, township, urban community

munificence beneficence, benevolence, big-heartedness, bounteousness, bounty, generosity, generousness, largess *or* largesse, liberality, magnanimousness, open-handedness, philanthropy

munificent beneficent, benevolent, big-hearted, bounteous, bountiful, free-handed, generous, lavish, liberal, magnanimous, open-handed, philanthropical, princely, rich, unstinting

Antonyms cheap, mean, miserly, parsimonious, small, stingy

murder *noun* 1. assassination, bloodshed, butchery, carnage, homicide, killing, man~

slaughter, massacre, slaying **2.** *informal* agony, an ordeal, a trial, danger, difficulty, hell (*informal*), misery, trouble ~*verb* **3.** assassinate, blow away (*slang, chiefly U.S.*), bump off (*slang*), butcher, destroy, dispatch, do in (*informal*), do to death, eliminate (*slang*), hit (*slang*), kill, massacre, rub out (*U.S. slang*), slaughter, slay, take out (*slang*), take the life of, waste (*informal*) **4.** abuse, butcher, destroy, mangle, mar, misuse, ruin, spoil **5.** *informal* beat decisively, blow out of the water (*slang*), cream (*slang, chiefly U.S.*), defeat utterly, drub, hammer (*informal*), lick (*informal*), make mincemeat of (*informal*), slaughter, stuff (*slang*), tank (*slang*), thrash, wipe the floor with (*informal*)

Thou shalt not kill

Bible: Exodus

Murder will out

Geoffrey Chaucer *The Nun's Priest's Tale*

murder most foul

William Shakespeare *Hamlet*

murderer assassin, butcher, cutthroat, hit man (*slang*), homicide, killer, slaughterer, slayer

Every murderer is probably somebody's old friend

Agatha Christie

murderous 1. barbarous, bloodthirsty, bloody, brutal, cruel, cutthroat, deadly, death-dealing, destructive, devastating, fatal, fell (*archaic*), ferocious, internecine, lethal, sanguinary, savage, slaughterous, withering **2.** *informal* arduous, dangerous, difficult, exhausting, harrowing, hellish (*informal*), killing (*informal*), sapping, strenuous, unpleasant

murky cheerless, cloudy, dark, dim, dismal, dreary, dull, dusky, foggy, gloomy, grey, impenetrable, misty, nebulous, obscure, overcast **Antonyms** bright, cheerful, clear, distinct, sunny

murmur 1. *noun* babble, buzzing, drone, humming, mumble, muttering, purr, rumble, susurrus (*literary*), undertone, whisper, whispering **2.** *verb* babble, buzz, drone, hum, mumble, mutter, purr, rumble, speak in an undertone, whisper **3.** *noun* beef (*slang*), complaint, gripe (*informal*), grouse, grumble, moan (*informal*), word **4.** *verb* beef (*slang*), carp, cavil, complain, gripe (*informal*), grouse, grumble, moan (*informal*)

muscle *noun* **1.** muscle tissue, sinew, tendon, thew **2.** brawn, clout (*informal*), force, forcefulness, might, potency, power, stamina, strength, sturdiness, weight ~*verb* **3. muscle in** *informal* butt in, elbow one's way in, force one's way in, impose oneself

Muscles

see BODY

muscular athletic, beefy (*informal*), brawny, husky (*informal*), lusty, powerful, powerfully built, robust, sinewy, stalwart, strapping, strong, sturdy, thickset, vigorous, well-knit

muse be in a brown study, be lost in thought, brood, cogitate, consider, contemplate, deliberate, dream, meditate, mull over, ponder, reflect, ruminate, speculate, think, think over, weigh

Muses, the *Greek myth* Camenae (*Roman myth*), Pierides

Muses

Calliope	epic poetry
Clio	history
Erato	love poetry
Euterpe	lyric poetry and music
Melpomene	tragedy
Polyhymnia	singing, mime, and sacred dance
Terpsichore	dance and choral song
Thalia	comedy and pastoral poetry
Urania	astronomy

mush 1. dough, mash, pap, paste, pulp **2.** *informal* corn (*informal*), mawkishness, schmaltz (*slang*), sentimentality, slush (*informal*)

mushroom *verb* boom, burgeon, expand, flourish, grow rapidly, increase, luxuriate, proliferate, shoot up, spread, spring up, sprout

Mushrooms and other edible fungi

see FOOD

mushy 1. doughy, pappy, paste-like, pulpy, semi-liquid, semi-solid, slushy, soft, squashy, squelchy, squidgy (*informal*) **2.** *informal* corny (*slang*), maudlin, mawkish, saccharine, schmaltzy (*slang*), sentimental, sloppy (*informal*), slushy (*informal*), sugary, syrupy, three-hankie (*informal*), weepy, wet (*Brit. informal*)

music

Classical music genres

ars antiqua	nationalist
ars nova	neoclassical
baroque	post-romantic
classical	Renaissance
early music	rococo
expressionist	romantic
galant	salon music
Gothic	serial music
impressionist	twelve-tone *or* dodecaphonic
minimalist	
music concrète	

Types of composition

air	anthem
albumblatt	aria
allemande	bagatelle

ballade
ballet
barcarole
bolero
bourrée
canon
cantata
canticle
canzona
canzone
canzonetta
capriccio
cavatina
chaconne
chorale
chorus
concertante
concertino
concerto
concerto grosso
concertstück
contredanse *or* contradance
czardas
dirge
divertimento
divertissement
duet
dumka
duo
ecossaise
elegy
étude
fantasy *or* fantasia
farandole
fugue
galliard
galop
gavotte
gigue
grand opera
hornpipe
humoresque
impromptu
interlude
lament
ländler
lied
madrigal
march
mass
mazurka
medley
minuet
motet
nocturne
nonet
notturno
octet
opera
opera buffa
opera seria
operetta
oratorio
overture
partita
part song
passacaglia
passepied
Passion
pastiche
pastorale
pavane
phantasy
pibroch
polka
polonaise
prelude
psalm
quadrille
quartet
quintet
raga
reel
Requiem
rhapsody
ricercar *or* ricercare
rigadoon *or* rigadoun
romance
scherzo
schottische
septet
serenade
sextet
sinfonia concertante
sinfonietta
Singspiel
sonata
sonatina
song
song cycle
strathspey
suite
symphonic poem
symphony
toccata
tone poem
trio
trio sonata
waltz

Popular Music Types

acid house
acid jazz
acid rock
ambient
bebop
bhangra
bluebeat
bluegrass
blues
boogie-woogie
bop
bubblegum
Cajun
calypso
cool jazz
country and western
country blues
country rock
Cu-bop
death metal
disco
Dixieland
doo-wop
dub
folk music
folk rock
free jazz
funk
fusion
gangsta rap
glam rock
gospel
Goth
grunge
hardbop
hardcore
harmolodics
heavy metal
hip-hop
House
Indie
industrial
jazz
jazz-funk
jazz-rock
jungle
mainstream jazz
Merseybeat
modern jazz
Motown (*Trademark*)
Muzak (*Trademark*)
New Age
New Country
New Orleans jazz
new romantic
New Wave
P-funk
pop
progressive rock
psychobilly
punk
ragga
rap
rave
reggae
rhythm and blues
rock
rockabilly
rock and roll
salsa
ska
skiffle
soul
surf music
swing
swingbeat
techno
thrash metal
trad jazz
world music
zydeco

Musical instruments

accordion
aeolian harp
alphorn *or* alpenhorn
althorn
Autoharp
baby grand
Bach trumpet
bagpipes
balalaika
bandore
banjo
barrel organ
baryton
bass drum
basset horn
bass guitar
bassoon
bass viol
bell
bodhrán
Böhm flute
bombardon
bongo
boudoir grand
bouzouki
bugle
calliope
carillon
castanets
celesta *or* celeste
cello *or* violoncello
cembalo
chamber organ
chime
Chinese block
chitarrone
cimbalon *or* cymbalon
cithara *or* kithara
cittern, cither *or* cithern
clarinet
clarion
clarsach
clave

clavicembalo
clavichord
clavier
concert grand
concertina
conga
contrabass
contrabassoon
cor anglais
cornet
cornett
cottage piano
cowbell
crumhorn *or* krummhorn
crwth
cymbal
cymbalo
didgeridoo
Dobro
double bass
double bassoon
drum
drum machine
dulcimer
electric guitar
electronic organ
English horn
euphonium
fiddle
fife
flageolet
flugelhorn
flute
French horn
gittarone
gittern
glass harmonica
glockenspiel
gong
gran cassa
grand piano
guitar
Hammond organ
handbell
harmonica
harmonium
harp
harpsichord
Hawaiian guitar
helicon
horn
hornpipe
hunting horn
hurdy-gurdy
idiophone
jew's-harp
kazoo
kettledrum
keyboard
kit
kora
koto
lur *or* lure
lute
lyra viol
lyre
mandola
mandolin *or* mandoline
maraca
marimba
mbira
mellophone
melodeon *or* melodion
metallophone
Moog
mouth organ
musette
naker
ngoma
nickelodeon
nose flute
oboe
oboe da caccia
oboe d'amore
ocarina
octachord
ondes Martenot
ophicleide
orchestrina *or* orchestrion
organ
orpharion
oud
panpipes
pedal steel guitar
penny whistle
piano
Pianola
piccolo
pipe
player piano
portative organ
racket
rebec *or* rebeck
recorder
reco-reco
reed organ
reed pipe
regal
rote
sackbut
samisen
sarangi
sarod
sarrusophone
saxhorn
saxophone
shawm
side drum
sistrum
sitar
slide guitar
snare drum
sousaphone
Spanish guitar
spinet
square piano
steam organ
steel guitar
stylophone
synthesizer
syrinx
tabla
tabor *or* tabour
tambour
tamboura
tambourine
tam-tam
theorbo
timbal *or* tymbal
timpani *or* tympani
tom-tom
triangle
trigon
trombone
trumpet
tuba
tubular bells
uillean pipes
ukulele *or* ukelele
upright piano
vibraphone
vihuela
vina
viol
viola
viola da braccio
viola da gamba
viola d'amore
violin
violone
virginal
vocoder
washboard
Welsh harp
whip
whistle
wood block
Wurlitzer
xylophone
xylorimba
zither

Classical composers

Adolphe Adam [French]
John Adams [U.S.]
Isaac Albéniz [Spanish]
Tomaso Albinoni [Italian]
Gregorio Allegri [Italian]
William Alwyn [British]
George Antheil [U.S.]
Thomas Arne [English]
Malcolm Arnold [British]
Daniel François Espirit Auber [French]
Georges Auric [French]
Carl Philipp Emanuel Bach [German]
Johann Christian Bach [German]
Johann Christoph Friedrich Bach [German]
Johann Sebastian Bach [German]
Wilhelm Friedemann Bach [German]
Mily Alexeyevich Balakirev [Russian]
Granville Bantock [British]
Samuel Barber [U.S.]
Béla Bartók [Hungarian]
Arnold Bax [British]
Ludwig van Beethoven [German]
Vincenzo Bellini [Italian]
Arthur Benjamin [Australian]
Richard Rodney Bennett [British]
Alban Berg [Austrian]
Luciano Berio [Italian]
Lennox Berkeley [British]
Hector Berlioz [French]
Heinrich Biber [German]
Harrison Birtwhistle [British]
Georges Bizet [French]
Arthur Bliss [British]
Ernest Bloch [U.S.]
Luigi Bocherini [Italian]
Arrigo Boito [Italian]

Francesco Antonio Bonporti [Italian]
Aleksandr Porfirevich Borodin [Russian]
Pierre Boulez [French]
William Boyce [English]
Johannes Brahms [German]
Havergal Brian [British]
Frank Bridge [British]
Benjamin Britten [British]
Max Bruch [German]
Anton Bruckner [Austrian]
John Bull [English]
George Butterworth [British]
Dietrich Buxtehude [Danish]
William Byrd [English]
John Cage [U.S.]
Joseph Canteloube [French]
John Alden Carpenter [U.S.]
Eliot Carter [U.S.]
Robert Carver [Scottish]
Pablo Casals [Spanish]
Emmanuel Chabrier [French]
Gustave Charpentier [French]
Marc-Antoine Charpentier [French]
Luigi Cherubini [Italian]
Frédéric Chopin [Polish-French]
Domenico Cimarosa [Italian]
Jeremiah Clarke [English]
Samuel Coleridge-Taylor [British]
Aaron Copland [U.S.]
Arcangelo Corelli [Italian]
François Couperin [French]
Karl Czerny [Austrian]
Luigi Dallapiccola [Italian]
Peter Maxwell Davies [British]
Claude Debussy [French]
Léo Delibes [French]
Frederick Delius [British]
Josquin des Prés [Flemish]
Vincent d'Indy [French]
Ernst von Dohnányi [Hungarian]
Gaetano Donizetti [Italian]
Antal Doráti [U.S.]
John Dowland [English]
Paul Dukas [French]
John Dunstable [English]
Henri Duparc [French]
Marcel Dupré [French]
Maurice Duruflé [French]
Antonín Dvořák [Czech]
Edward Elgar [British]
Georges Enesco [Romanian]
Manuel de Falla [Spanish]
John Farmer [English]
Gabriel Fauré [French]
John Field [Irish]
Gerald Finzi [British]
Friedrich von Flotow [German]
César Franck [Belgian-French]
Girolamo Frescobaldi [Italian]
Wilhelm Fürtwangler [German]
Andrea Gabrieli [Italian]
Giovanni Gabrieli [Italian]
George Gershwin [U.S.]
Carlo Gesualdo [Italian]
Orlando Gibbons [English]
Philip Glass [U.S.]
Aleksandr Konstantinovich Glazunov [Russian]
Mikhail Ivanovich Glinka [Russian]
Christoph Willibald Gluck [German]
Eugene Goossens [Belgian-British]
Henryk Górecki [Polish]
Charles François Gounod [French]
Percy Grainger [Australian]
Enrique Granados [Spanish]
Edvard Grieg [Norwegian]
Ivor Gurney [British]
Fromental Halévy [French]
George Frederick Handel [German]
Roy Harris [U.S.]
Franz Joseph Haydn [Austrian]
Michael Haydn [Austrian]
Hans Werner Henze [German]
Hildegard of Bingen [German]
Paul Hindemith [German]
Heinz Holliger [Swiss]
Gustav Holst [British]
Arthur Honegger [French]
Johann Nepomuk Hummel [German]
Englebert Humperdinck [German]
Jacques Ibert [French]
John Ireland [British]
Charles Ives [U.S.]
Leoš Janáček [Czech]
Émile Jaques-Dalcroze [Swiss]
Joseph Joachim [Hungarian]
Daniel Jones [British]
Aram Ilich Khachaturian [Armenian]
Otto Klemperer [German]
Oliver Knussen [British]
Zoltán Kodály [Hungarian]
Erich Korngold [Austrian]
Franz Krommer [Moravian]
Raphael Kubelik [Czech]
Édouard Lalo [French]
Constant Lambert [British]
Roland de Lassus [Flemish]
Henry Lawes [English]
William Lawes [English]
Franz Lehár [Hungarian]
Ruggiero Leoncavallo [Italian]
György Ligeti [Hungarian]
Franz Liszt [Hungarian]
George Lloyd [British]
Matthew Locke [English]
Karl Loewe [German]
Jean Baptiste Lully [Italian-French]
Witold Lutosławski [Polish]
Elisabeth Lutyens [British]
Guillaume de Machaut [French]
James MacMillan [British]
Elizabeth Maconchy [British]
Gustav Mahler [Austrian]
Luca Marenzio [Italian]
Frank Martin [Swiss]
Bohuslav Martinů [Czech]
Steve Martland [British]
Pietro Mascagni [Italian]
Jules Émile Frédéric Massenet [French]
Fanny Mendelssohn [German]
Felix Mendelssohn [German]
Gian Carlo Menotti [Italian]
André Messager [French]

Olivier Messiaen [French]
Giacomo Meyerbeer [German]
Darius Milhaud [French]
Claudio Monteverdi [Italian]
Thomas Morley [English]
Leopold Mozart [Austrian]
Wolfgang Amadeus Mozart [Austrian]
Thea Musgrave [British]
Modest Petrovich Mussorgsky [Russian]
Carl Otto Ehrenfried Nicolai [German]
Carl Nielsen [Danish]
Luigi Nono [Italian]
Michael Nyman [British]
Johannes Ockeghem [Flemish]
Jacques Offenbach [German-French]
John Ogdon [British]
Carl Orff [German]
Johann Pachelbel [German]
Ignace Jan Paderewski [Polish]
Niccolò Paganini [Italian]
Giovanni Pierluigi da Palestrina [Italian]
Andrzej Panufnik [Polish-British]
Hubert Parry [British]
Arvo Pärt [Estonian]
Krzystof Penderecki [Polish]
Giovanni Battista Pergolesi [Italian]
Francis Poulenc [French]
Michael Praetorius [German]
Sergei Sergeyevich Prokofiev [Russian]
Giacomo Puccini [Italian]
Henry Purcell [English]
Sergei Vassilievich Rachmaninov [Russian]
Jean Philippe Rameau [French]
Maurice Ravel [French]
Alan Rawsthorne [British]
Max Reger [German]
Steve Reich [U.S.]
Ottorino Respighi [Italian]
Nikolai Andreyevich Rimsky-Korsakov [Russian]
Joaquín Rodrigo [Spanish]
Sigmund Romberg [U.S.]
Gioacchino Antonio Rossini [Italian]
Mstislav Leopoldovich Rostropovich [Russian]
Claude Joseph Rouget de Lisle [French]
Edmund Rubbra [British]
Anton Grigorevich Rubinstein [Russian]
Camille Saint-Saëns [French]
Antonio Salieri [Italian]
Erik Satie [French]
Alessandro Scarlatti [Italian]
Domenico Scarlatti [Italian]
Artur Schnabel [Austrian-U.S.]
Alfred Schnittke [Russian]
Arnold Schoenberg [Austrian]
Franz Schubert [Austrian]
William Schuman [U.S.]
Clara Schumann [German]
Robert Schumann [German]
Heinrich Schütz [German]
Aleksandr Nikolayvich Scriabin [Russian]
Peter Sculthorpe [Australian]
Roger Sessions [U.S.]
Dmitri Dmitriyevich Shostakovich [Russian]
Jean Sibelius [Finnish]
Bedřich Smetana [Czech]
Ethel Smyth [British]
John Philip Sousa [U.S.]
John Stainer [British]
Charles Stanford [Irish]
Karlheinz Stockhausen [German]
Oscar Straus [French]
Johann Strauss, the elder [Austrian]
Johann Struass, the younger [Austrian]
Richard Strauss [German]
Igor Fyodorovich Stravinsky [Russian-U.S.]
Jan Pieterszoon Sweelinck [Dutch]
Karol Szymanowski [Polish]
Toru Takemitsu [Japanese]
Thomas Tallis [English]
John Tavener [British]
John Taverner [English]
Pyotr Ilyich Tchaikovsky [Russian]
Georg Philipp Telemann [German]
Mikis Theodorakis [Greek]
Ambroise Thomas [French]
Virgil Thomson [U.S.]
Michael Tippett [British]
Paul Tortelier [French]
Edgar Varèse [French-U.S.]
Ralph Vaughan Williams [British]
Giuseppi Verdi [Italian]
Tomás Luis de Victoria [Spanish]
Heitor Villa-Lobos [Brazilian]
Antonio Vivaldi [Italian]
Richard Wagner [German]
William Walton [British]
Peter Warlock [British]
Carl Maria von Weber [German]
Anton Webern [Austrian]
Thomas Weelkes [English]
Judith Weir [British]
Egon Wellesz [Austrian-British]
Malcolm Williamson [Australian]
Hugo Wolf [Austrian]
Ermanno Wolf-Ferrari [Italian]
Yannis Xenakis [Romanian-Greek]
Alexander Zemlinsky [Austrian]

Popular composers, songwriters, and lyricists

Harold Arlen [U.S.]
Burt Bacharach [U.S.]
Lionel Bart [British]
Irving Berlin [Russian-U.S.]
Leonard Bernstein [U.S.]
Jacques Brel [Belgian]
Sammy Cahn [U.S.]
Hoagy Carmichael [U.S.]
Leonard Cohen [Canadian]
Willie Dixon [U.S.]
Lamont Dozier [U.S.]
Vernon Duke [Russian-U.S.]
Bob Dylan [U.S.]
Duke Ellington [U.S.]
Stephen Foster [U.S.]
George Gershwin [U.S.]
W(illiam) S(chwenck) Gilbert [British]
Gerry Goffin [U.S.]
W(illiam) C(hristopher) Handy [U.S.]
Marvin Hamlisch [U.S.]

Oscar Hammerstein [U.S.]
Lorenz Hart [U.S.]
Brian Holland [U.S.]
Eddie Holland [U.S.]
Maurice Jarre [French]
Jerome (David) Kern [U.S.]
Huddie "Leadbelly" Ledbetter [U.S.]
Andrew Lloyd-Webber [British]
Antonio Carlos Jobim [Brazilian]
Robert Johnson [U.S.]
Carole King [U.S.]
Kris Kristofferson [U.S.]
John Lennon [British]
Alan Jay Lerner [U.S.]
Jerry Lieber [U.S.]
Frank Loesser [U.S.]
Frederick Loewe [Austrian-U.S.]
Paul McCartney [British]
Ewan McColl [British]
Henry Mancini [U.S.]
Barry Mann [U.S.]
Thelonious (Sphere) Monk [U.S.]
Willie Nelson [U.S.]
Ivor Novello [British]
Doc Pomus [U.S.]
William "Smokey" Robinson [U.S.]
Cole Porter [U.S.]
Tim Rice [British]
Richard Rodgers [U.S.]
Sigmund Romberg [Hungarian-U.S.]
Paul Simon [U.S.]
Stephen Sondheim [U.S.]
Mike Stoller [U.S.]
Billy Strayhorn [U.S.]
Barrett Strong [U.S.]
Jule Styne [U.S.]
Arthur Sullivan [British]
Allen Toussaint [U.S.]
Johnny Van Heusen [U.S.]
Jimmy Webb [U.S.]
Cynthia Weil [U.S.]
Kurt Weill [German-U.S.]
Norman Whitfield [U.S.]
Hank Williams [U.S.]
Brian Wilson [U.S.]
Vincent Youmans [U.S.]

Musical notes and rests: British name	**American name**
breve	double-whole note
semibreve	whole note
minim	half note
crotchet	quarter note
quaver	eighth note
semiquaver	sixteenth note
demisemiquaver	thirty-second note
hemidemisemiquaver	sixty-fourth note

Expression and tempo instructions	**Meanings**
accelerando	with increasing speed
adagio	slowly
agitato	in an agitated manner
allegretto	fairly quickly or briskly
allegro	quickly, in a brisk, lively manner
amoroso	lovingly
andante	at a moderately slow tempo
andantino	slightly faster than andante
animato	in a lively manner
appassionato	impassioned
assai	(in combination) very
calando	with gradually decreasing tone and speed
cantabile	in a singing style
con	(in combination) with
con affeto	with tender emotion
con amore	lovingly
con anima	with spirit
con brio	vigorously
con fuoco	with fire
con moto	quickly
crescendo	gradual increase in loudness
diminuendo	gradual decrease in loudness
dolce	gently and sweetly
doloroso	in a sorrowful manner
energico	energetically
espressivo	expressively
forte	loud or loudly
fortissimo	very loud
furioso	in a frantically rushing manner
giocoso	merry
grave	solemn and slow
grazioso	graceful
lacrimoso	sad and mournful
largo	slowly and broadly
larghetto	slowly and broadly, but less so than largo
legato	smoothly and connectedly
leggiero	light
lento	slowly
maestoso	majestically
marziale	martial
mezzo	(in combination) moderately
moderato	at a moderate tempo
molto	(in combination) very
non troppo *or* non tanto	not too much
pianissimo	very quietly
piano	softly
più	(in combination) more
pizzicato	(in music for stringed instruments) to be plucked with the finger
poco *or* un poco	(in combination) a little

pomposo	in a pompous manner
presto	very fast
prestissimo	faster than presto
quasi	(in combination) almost, as if
rallentando	becoming slower
rubato	with a flexible tempo
scherzando	in jocular style
sciolto	free and easy
semplice	simple and unforced
sforzando	with strong initial attack
smorzando	dying away
sospirando	'sighing', plaintive
sostenuto	in a smooth and sustained manner
sotto voce	extremely quiet
staccato	(of notes) short, clipped, and separate
strascinando	stretched out
strepitoso	noisy
stringendo	with increasing speed
tanto	too much
tardo	slow
troppo	too much
vivace	in a brisk lively manner
volante	'flying', fast and light

Musical modes	**Final notes**
I Dorian	D
II Hypodorian	D
III Phrygian	E
IV Hypophrygian	E
V Lydian	F
VI Hypolydian	F
VII Mixolydian	G
VIII Hypomixolydian	G
IX Aeolian	A
X Hypoaeolian	A
XI Ionian	C
XII Hypoionian	C

Music has charms to soothe a savage breast
William Congreve *The Mourning Bride*

There's no passion in the human soul,
But finds its food in music
George Lillo *The Fatal Curiosity*

The opera ain't over till the fat lady sings
Dan Cook

Opera is where a guy gets stabbed in the back and, instead of bleeding, he sings
Ed Gardner *Duffy's Tavern*

Such sweet compulsion doth in music lie
John Milton *Arcades*

Hell is full of musical amateurs; music is the brandy of the damned
George Bernard Shaw *Man and Superman*

Music is feeling, then, not sound
Wallace Stevens *Peter Quince at the Clavier*

If music be the food of love, play on;
Give me excess of it
William Shakespeare *Twelfth Night*

Without music life would be a mistake
Friedrich Nietzsche *The Twilight of the Idols*

I have been told that Wagner's music is better than it sounds
Mark Twain

A musicologist is a man who can read music but can't hear it
Thomas Beecham

He has Van Gogh's ear for music
Orson Welles

Music is essentially useless, as life is
George Santayana *Little Essays*

Music is the healing force of the universe
Albert Ayler

All music is folk music, I ain't never heard no horse sing a song
Louis Armstrong *New York Times*

The only sensual pleasure without vice
Dr. Johnson *attributed to him in "European Magazine"*

The English may not like music but they absolutely love the noise it makes
Thomas Beecham

Classic music is th'kind that we keep thinkin'll turn into a tune
Kin Hubbard *Comments of Abe Martin and His Neighbours*

There are two golden rules for an orchestra: start together and finish together. The public doesn't give a damn what goes on in between
Thomas Beecham

two skeletons copulating on a corrugated tin roof
Thomas Beecham (describing the harpsichord)

too much counterpoint; what is worse, Protestant counterpoint
Thomas Beecham (describing Bach's music)

fiddle: an instrument to tickle human ears by friction of a horse's tail on the entrails of a cat
Ambrose Bierce *The Devil's Dictionary*

Some say, that Signor Bononcini,
Compared to Handel's a mere ninny;
Others aver, that to him Handel
Is scarcely fit to hold a candle.
Strange! that such high dispute should be
'Twixt Tweedledum and Tweedledee
John Byrom *On the Feuds between Handel and Bononcini*

Extraordinary how potent cheap music is
Noël Coward *Private Lives*

opera: a play representing life in another world, whose inhabitants have no speech but song, no motions but gestures and no postures but attitudes
Ambrose Bierce *The Devil's Dictionary*

What passion cannot music raise and quell?
John Dryden *A Song for St. Cecilia's Day*

piano: a parlor utensil for subduing the impenitent visitor. It is operated by depressing the keys of the machine and the spirits of the audience
Ambrose Bierce *The Devil's Dictionary*

an exotic and irrational entertainment
Dr. Johnson (of Italian opera)

Sing 'em muck! It's all they can understand!
Dame Nellie Melba (of Australians)

Music and women I cannot but give way to, whatever my business is
Samuel Pepys *Diary*

Music begins to atrophy when it departs too far from the dance... poetry begins to atrophy when it gets too far from music
Ezra Pound *The ABC of Reading*

[Rock music] is still only certain elements in the blues isolated, coarsened and amplified. It may affect audiences more strongly but this is only to say that home-distilled hooch is more affecting than château-bottled claret, or a punch on the nose than a reasoned refutation under nineteen headings
Philip Larkin

musical dulcet, euphonic, euphonious, harmonious, lilting, lyrical, melodic, melodious, sweet-sounding, tuneful
Antonyms discordant, grating, harsh, unmelodious, unmusical

musician
I'm a concert pianist - that's a pretentious way of saying I'm unemployed
Alan Jay Lerner *An American in Paris*

musing *noun* absent-mindedness, abstraction, brown study, cerebration, cogitation, contemplation, day-dreaming, dreaming, introspection, meditation, navel gazing (*slang*), reflection, reverie, rumination, thinking, woolgathering

must[1] *noun* duty, essential, fundamental, imperative, necessary thing, necessity, obligation, prerequisite, requirement, requisite, *sine qua non*

must[2] *noun* decay, fetor, fustiness, mildew, mould, mouldiness, mustiness, rot

muster *verb* **1.** assemble, call together, call up, collect, come together, congregate, convene, convoke, enrol, gather, group, marshal, meet, mobilize, rally, round up, summon ~*noun* **2.** assemblage, assembly, collection, concourse, congregation, convention, convocation, gathering, meeting, mobilization, rally, roundup **3. pass muster** be acceptable, be *or* come up to scratch, fill the bill (*informal*), make the grade, measure up, qualify

musty **1.** airless, dank, decayed, frowsty, fusty, mildewed, mildewy, mouldy, old, smelly, stale, stuffy **2.** ancient, antediluvian, antiquated, banal, clichéd, dull, hackneyed, hoary, moth-eaten, obsolete, old-fashioned, stale, threadbare, trite, worn-out
Antonyms (*sense 2*) current, exciting, fashionable, fresh, imaginative, interesting, lively, modern, modish, new, novel, original, unusual, up-to-date, with it (*informal*)

mutability alteration, change, evolution, metamorphosis, transition, variation, vicissitude

mutable adaptable, alterable, changeable, changing, fickle, flexible, immutable, inconsistent, inconstant, irresolute, uncertain, undependable, unreliable, unsettled, unstable, unsteady, vacillating, variable, volatile, wavering

mutation **1.** alteration, change, deviation, evolution, metamorphosis, modification, transfiguration, transformation, variation **2.** anomaly, deviant, mutant

mute **1.** *adjective* aphasiac, aphasic, aphonic, dumb, mum, silent, speechless, unexpressed, unspeaking, unspoken, voiceless, wordless **2.** *verb* dampen, deaden, lower, moderate, muffle, soften, soft-pedal, subdue, tone down, turn down

mutilate **1.** amputate, butcher, cripple, cut to pieces, cut up, damage, disable, disfigure, dismember, hack, injure, lacerate, lame, maim, mangle **2.** adulterate, bowdlerize, butcher, censor, cut, damage, distort, expurgate, hack, mar, spoil

mutinous bolshie (*Brit. informal*), contumacious, disobedient, insubordinate, insurgent, rebellious, refractory, revolutionary, riotous, seditious, subversive, turbulent, ungovernable, unmanageable, unruly

mutiny **1.** *noun* defiance, disobedience, insubordination, insurrection, rebellion, refusal to obey orders, resistance, revolt, revolution, riot, rising, strike, uprising **2.** *verb* be insubordinate, defy authority, disobey, rebel, refuse to obey orders, resist, revolt, rise up, strike

mutt **1.** berk (*Brit. slang*), charlie (*Brit. informal*), coot, dickhead (*slang*), dickwit (*slang*), dipstick (*Brit. slang*), divvy (*Brit. slang*), dolt, dork (*slang*), dunderhead, dweeb (*U.S. slang*), fool, fuckwit (*taboo slang*), geek (*slang*), gobshite (*Irish taboo slang*), gonzo (*slang*), idiot, ignoramus, imbecile (*informal*), jerk (*slang, chiefly U.S. & Canad.*), moron, nerd *or* nurd (*slang*), numpty (*Scot. informal*), numskull *or* numbskull, pillock (*Brit. slang*), plank (*Brit. slang*), plonker (*slang*), prat (*slang*), prick (*slang*), schmuck (*U.S. slang*), thickhead, twit (*informal, chiefly Brit.*), wally (*slang*), weenie (*U.S. informal*) **2.** cur, dog, mongrel

mutter complain, grouch (*informal*), grouse, grumble, mumble, murmur, rumble

mutual common, communal, correlative, interactive, interchangeable, interchanged, joint, reciprocal, reciprocated, requited, returned, shared

muzzle *noun* **1.** jaws, mouth, nose, snout **2.** gag, guard *~verb* **3.** censor, choke, curb, gag, restrain, silence, stifle, suppress

myopic near-sighted, short-sighted

myriad **1.** *adjective* a thousand and one, countless, immeasurable, incalculable, innumerable, multitudinous, untold **2.** *noun* a million, army, a thousand, flood, horde, host, millions, mountain, multitude, scores, sea, swarm, thousands

mysterious abstruse, arcane, baffling, cloak-and-dagger, concealed, covert, cryptic, curious, dark, Delphic, enigmatic, furtive, hidden, impenetrable, incomprehensible, inexplicable, inscrutable, insoluble, mystical, mystifying, obscure, perplexing, puzzling, recondite, secret, secretive, sphinxlike, strange, uncanny, unfathomable, unknown, veiled, weird

Antonyms apparent, clear, intelligible, manifest, open, plain

God moves in a mysterious way
His wonders to perform;
He plants his footsteps in the sea,
And rides upon the storm

William Cowper *Olney Hymns*

mystery cloak and dagger, closed book, conundrum, enigma, problem, puzzle, question, riddle, secrecy, secret, teaser

mystic, mystical abstruse, arcane, cabalistic, cryptic, enigmatical, esoteric, hidden, inscrutable, metaphysical, mysterious, nonrational, occult, otherworldly, paranormal, preternatural, supernatural, transcendental

mystify baffle, bamboozle (*informal*), be all Greek to (*informal*), beat (*slang*), befog, bewilder, confound, confuse, elude, escape, flummox, nonplus, perplex, puzzle, stump

mystique awe, charisma, charm, fascination, glamour, magic, spell

myth **1.** allegory, fable, fairy story, fiction, folk tale, legend, parable, saga, story, tradition, urban legend **2.** delusion, fancy, fantasy, figment, illusion, imagination, superstition, tall story

mythical **1.** allegorical, chimerical, fabled, fabulous, fairy-tale, legendary, mythological, storied **2.** fabricated, fanciful, fantasy, fictitious, imaginary, invented, made-up, make-believe, nonexistent, pretended, unreal, untrue

mythological fabulous, folkloric, heroic, legendary, mythic, mythical, traditional

mythology folklore, folk tales, legend, lore, mythos, myths, stories, tradition

Characters in classical mythology

Achilles
Actaeon
Adonis
Aeneas
Agamemnon
Ajax
Amazons
Andromache
Andromeda
Antigone
Arachne
Argonauts
Ariadne
Atalanta
Atlas
Callisto
Calypso
Cassandra
Cassiopeia
Castor
Charon
Circe
Clytemnestra
Daedalus
Dido
Echo
Electra
Europa
Eurydice
Galatea
Ganymede
Hector
Hecuba
Helen
Heracles
Hercules
Hermaphroditus
Hippolytus
Hyacinthus
Icarus
Io
Ixion
Jason
Jocasta
Leda
Medea
Medusa
Menelaus
Midas
Minos
Muses
Narcissus
Niobe
Odysseus
Oedipus
Orestes
Orion
Orpheus
Pandora
Paris
Penelope
Persephone
Perseus
Pleiades
Pollux
Polydeuces
Polyphemus
Priam
Prometheus
Proserpina
Psyche
Pygmalion
Pyramus
Remus
Romulus
Semele
sibyl
Silenus
Sisyphus
Tantalus
Theseus
Thisbe
Tiresias
Ulysses

Creatures in mythology

afreet *or* afrit
androsphinx
banshee
basilisk
behemoth
bunyip
centaur
Cerberus
Charybdis
chimera *or* chimaera
cockatrice
Cyclops
dragon
dryad
dwarf
Echidna
elf
erlking
fairy
faun
fay
Fury
genie
Geryon
giant
goblin
Gorgon
gremlin
Grendel
griffin, griffon *or* gryphon
hamadryad
Harpy
hippocampus
hippogriff *or* hippogryph
hobbit

hobgoblin
Hydra
impundulu
jinni, jinnee, djinni *or* djinny
kelpie
kraken
kylin
lamia
leprechaun
leviathan
mermaid
merman
Minotaur
naiad
Nereid
nix *or* nixie
nymph
Oceanid
orc
oread
peri
phoenix
pixie
roc
salamander
satyr
Scylla
Siren
Sphinx
sylph
tokoloshe
tricorn
troll
unicorn
water nymph
wood nymph

Places in Classical Mythology

Acheron
Colchis
Elysium
Erebus
Hades
Helicon
Islands of the Blessed
Lethe
Olympus
Parnassus
Phlegethon
Styx
Tartarus
Thebes
Troy

Places in Norse Mythology

Asgard *or* Asgarth
Bifrost
Hel *or* Hela
Jotunheim *or* Jotunnheim
Midgard *or* Midgarth
Niflheim
Utgard
Valhalla

Places in Arthurian Legend

Astolat
Avalon
Camelot
Glastonbury
Lyonnesse
Tintagel

N

nab apprehend, arrest, capture, catch, catch in the act, collar (*informal*), feel one's collar (*slang*), grab, lift (*slang*), nail (*informal*), nick (*slang, chiefly Brit.*), seize, snatch

nabob billionaire, Croesus, millionaire, multimillionaire

nadir bottom, depths, lowest point, minimum, rock bottom, zero
Antonyms acme, apex, climax, crest, height, high point, peak, pinnacle, summit, top, vertex, zenith

naff bad, chickenshit (*U.S. slang*), crappy (*slang*), duff (*Brit. informal*), for the birds (*informal*), inferior, low-grade, low-quality, piss-poor (*taboo slang*), poor, poxy (*slang*), rubbishy, second-rate, shabby, shoddy, strictly for the birds (*informal*), substandard, trashy, twopenny-halfpenny, valueless, worthless
Antonyms excellent, exceptional, fine, first-class, first-rate, high-quality, superior

nag[1] **1.** *verb* annoy, badger, bend someone's ear (*informal*), be on one's back (*slang*), berate, breathe down someone's neck, chivvy, goad, harass, harry, hassle (*informal*), henpeck, irritate, nark (*Brit., Austral., & N.Z. slang*), pester, plague, provoke, scold, torment, upbraid, vex, worry **2.** *noun* harpy, scold, shrew, tartar, termagant, virago

nag[2] *noun* hack, horse, jade, plug (*U.S.*)

nagging continuous, critical, distressing, irritating, on someone's back (*informal*), painful, persistent, scolding, shrewish, worrying

Nagging is the repetition of unpalatable truths
Edith Summerskill

naiad nymph, Oceanid (*Greek myth*), sprite, undine, water nymph

nail *verb* attach, beat, fasten, fix, hammer, join, pin, secure, tack

naive **1.** artless, candid, childlike, confiding, frank, guileless, ingenuous, innocent, jejune, natural, open, simple, trusting, unaffected, unpretentious, unsophisticated, unworldly **2.** as green as grass, callow, credulous, green, gullible, unsuspicious, wet behind the ears (*informal*)
Antonyms artful, disingenuous, experienced, sly, sophisticated, urbane, worldly, worldly-wise

naïveté, naivety **1.** artlessness, candour, frankness, guilelessness, inexperience, ingenuousness, innocence, naturalness, openness, simplicity **2.** callowness, credulity, gullibility

naked **1.** bare, buck naked (*slang*), denuded, disrobed, divested, exposed, in one's birthday suit (*informal*), in the altogether (*informal*), in the bare scud (*slang*), in the buff (*informal*), in the raw (*informal*), naked as the day one was born (*informal*), nude, scuddy (*slang*), starkers (*informal*), stripped, unclothed, unconcealed, uncovered, undraped, undressed, without a stitch on (*informal*) **2.** blatant, evident, manifest, open, overt, patent, plain, simple, stark, unadorned, undisguised, unexaggerated, unmistakable, unqualified, unvarnished **3.** defenceless, helpless, insecure, unarmed, unguarded, unprotected, vulnerable, wide open
Antonyms clothed, concealed, covered, dressed, wrapped up

nakedness **1.** baldness, bareness, nudity, undress **2.** openness, plainness, simplicity, starkness

namby-pamby anaemic, boneless, colourless, feeble, insipid, mawkish, niminy-piminy, prim, prissy (*informal*), sentimental, spineless, vapid, weak, weedy (*informal*), wimpish *or* wimpy (*informal*), wishy-washy (*informal*)

name *noun* **1.** appellation, cognomen, denomination, designation, epithet, handle (*slang*), moniker *or* monicker (*slang*), nickname, sobriquet, term, title **2.** distinction, eminence, esteem, fame, honour, note, praise, renown, repute **3.** character, credit, reputation *~verb* **4.** baptize, call, christen, denominate, dub, entitle, label, style, term **5.** appoint, choose, cite, classify, commission, designate, flag, identify, mention, nominate, select, specify
Related adjective: nominal

What's in a name? That which we call a rose
By any other name would smell as sweet
William Shakespeare *Romeo and Juliet*

named **1.** baptized, called, christened, denominated, dubbed, entitled, known as, labelled, styled, termed **2.** appointed, chosen, cited, classified, commissioned, designated, identified, mentioned, nominated, picked, selected, singled out, specified

nameless 1. anonymous, innominate, undesignated, unnamed, untitled 2. incognito, obscure, undistinguished, unheard-of, unknown, unsung 3. abominable, horrible, indescribable, ineffable, inexpressible, unmentionable, unspeakable, unutterable

namely i.e., specifically, that is to say, to wit, viz.

nap[1] 1. *verb* catnap, doze, drop off (*informal*), drowse, kip (*Brit. slang*), nod, nod off (*informal*), rest, sleep, snooze (*informal*), zizz (*Brit. informal*) 2. *noun* catnap, forty winks (*informal*), kip (*Brit. slang*), rest, shuteye (*slang*), siesta, sleep, zizz (*Brit. informal*)

nap[2] *noun* down, fibre, grain, pile, shag, weave

narcissism egotism, self-admiration, self-love, vanity

narcotic 1. *noun* anaesthetic, analgesic, anodyne, drug, opiate, painkiller, sedative, tranquillizer 2. *adjective* analgesic, calming, dulling, hypnotic, Lethean, numbing, painkilling, sedative, somnolent, soporific, stupefacient, stupefactive, stupefying

nark aggravate (*informal*), annoy, bother, bug, exasperate, gall, get on one's nerves (*informal*), irk, irritate, miff (*informal*), nettle, peeve, pique, piss one off (*taboo slang*), provoke, rile

narrate chronicle, describe, detail, recite, recount, rehearse, relate, repeat, report, set forth, tell, unfold

narration description, explanation, reading, recital, rehearsal, relation, storytelling, telling, voice-over (*in film*)

narrative account, chronicle, detail, history, report, statement, story, tale

narrator annalist, author, bard, chronicler, commentator, raconteur, reciter, relater, reporter, storyteller, writer

narrow *adjective* 1. circumscribed, close, confined, constricted, contracted, cramped, incapacious, limited, meagre, near, pinched, restricted, scanty, straitened, tight 2. biased, bigoted, dogmatic, illiberal, intolerant, narrow-minded, partial, prejudiced, puritan, reactionary, small-minded 3. attenuated, fine, slender, slim, spare, tapering, thin 4. exclusive, select 5. *informal* avaricious, close (*informal*), mean, mercenary, niggardly, ungenerous *~verb* 6. circumscribe, constrict, diminish, limit, reduce, simplify, straiten, tighten

Antonyms ample, big, broad, broad-minded, generous, liberal, open, receptive, spacious, tolerant, wide

narrowly 1. barely, by a whisker *or* hair's-breadth, by the skin of one's teeth, just, only just, scarcely 2. carefully, closely, painstakingly, scrutinizingly

narrow-minded biased, bigoted, conservative, hidebound, illiberal, insular, intolerant, opinionated, parochial, petty, prejudiced, provincial, reactionary, short-sighted, small-minded, strait-laced

Antonyms broad-minded, catholic, cosmopolitan, freethinking, indulgent, open-minded, permissive, tolerant, unprejudiced

narrows channel, gulf, passage, sound, straits

nascent beginning, budding, dawning, developing, evolving, incipient

nastiness 1. defilement, dirtiness, filth, filthiness, foulness, impurity, pollution, squalor, uncleanliness 2. indecency, licentiousness, obscenity, pollution, porn (*informal*), pornography, ribaldry, smuttiness 3. disagreeableness, malice, meanness, offensiveness, spitefulness, unpleasantness

nasty 1. dirty, disagreeable, disgusting, filthy, foul, grotty (*slang*), horrible, loathsome, malodorous, mephitic, nauseating, noisome, objectionable, obnoxious, odious, offensive, polluted, repellent, repugnant, sickening, unappetizing, unpleasant, vile, yucky *or* yukky (*slang*) 2. blue, foul, gross, impure, indecent, lascivious, lewd, licentious, obscene, pornographic, ribald, smutty 3. abusive, annoying, bad-tempered, despicable, disagreeable, distasteful, malicious, mean, spiteful, unpleasant, vicious, vile 4. bad, critical, dangerous, painful, serious, severe

Antonyms admirable, agreeable, clean, decent, enjoyable, kind, nice, pleasant, sweet

nation commonwealth, community, country, people, population, race, realm, society, state, tribe

Nations, like men, have their infancy

Viscount Henry St. John Bolingbroke *On the Study of History*

The great nations have always acted like gangsters, and the small nations like prostitutes

Stanley Kubrick

national *adjective* 1. civil, countrywide, governmental, nationwide, public, state, widespread 2. domestic, internal, social *~noun* 3. citizen, inhabitant, native, resident, subject

nationalism allegiance, chauvinism, fealty, jingoism, loyalty, nationality, patriotism

I question the right of that great Moloch, national sovereignty, to burn its children to save its pride

Anthony Meyer

Patriotism is a lively sense of collective responsibility. Nationalism is a silly cock crowing on its own dunghill

Richard Aldington *The Colonel's Daughter*

nationalistic chauvinistic, jingoistic, loyal, patriotic, xenophobic

nationality birth, ethnic group, nation, race

nationwide countrywide, general, national, overall, widespread

native *adjective* **1.** built-in, congenital, endemic, hereditary, immanent, inborn, inbred, indigenous, ingrained, inherent, inherited, innate, instinctive, intrinsic, inveterate, natal, natural **2.** genuine, original, real **3.** domestic, home, home-grown, home-made, indigenous, local, mother, vernacular **4.** aboriginal, autochthonous *~noun* **5.** aborigine, autochthon, citizen, countryman, dweller, inhabitant, national, resident

Place	**Native or inhabitant**
Aberdeen	Aberdonian
Afghanistan	Afghan
Alabama	Alabaman *or* Alabamian
Alaska	Alaskan
Albania	Albanian
Alberta	Albertan
Algeria	Algerian
Alsace	Alsatian
American continent	American
American Samoa	American Samoan
Amsterdam	Amsterdammer
Anatolia	Anatolian
Andorra	Andorran
Angola	Angolan
Anjou	Angevin
Antigua	Antiguan
Argentinia	Argentine *or* Argentinian
Arizona	Arizonan
Arkansas	Arkansan *or (informal)* Arkie
Armenia	Armenian
Asia	Asian
Assam	Assamese
Assyria	Assyrian
Australia	Australian *or (informal)* Aussie
Austria	Austrian
Azerbaijan	Azerbaijani *or* Azeri
Babylon	Babylonian
Bahamas	Bahamian
Bahrain	Bahraini
Bangladesh	Bangladeshi
Bali	Balinese
Barbados	Barbadian, Bajan *(informal) or* Bim *(informal)*
Barbuda	Barbudan *or* Barbudian
Bavaria	Bavarian
Belarus *or* Byelorussia	Belarussian *or* Byelorussian
Belau	Belauan
Belgium	Belgian
Benin	Beninese *or* Beninois
Berlin	Berliner
Bhutan	Bhutanese
Birmingham	Brummie
Bohemia	Bohemian
Bolivia	Bolivian
Bordeaux	Bordelais
the Borders	Borderer
Bosnia	Bosnian
Boston	Bostonian *or (U.S. slang)* Bean-eater
Botswana	Botswanan
Brazil	Brazilian
Bristol	Bristolian
Brittany	Breton
British Columbia	British Columbian
Bulgaria	Bulgarian
Burgundy	Burgundian
Burkina-Faso	Burkinabe
Burma	Burmese
Burundi	Burundian
Byzantium	Byzantine
California	Californian
Cambridge	Cantabrigian
Cambodia	Cambodian
Cameroon	Cameroonian
Canada	Canadian *or (informal)* Canuck
Canada, Maritime Provinces	Downeaster
Cape Verde	Cape Verdean
Castile	Castilian
Catalonia	Catalan
the Caucusus	Caucasian
Cayman Islands	Cayman Islander
Chad	Chadian *or* Chadean
Chicago	Chicagoan
Chile	Chilean
China	Chinese
Circassia	Circassian
Colombia	Colombian
Colorado	Coloradan
Connecticut	Nutmegger
Cork	Corkonian
Comoros Islands	Comorian
Congo Republic	Congolese
Cornwall	Cornishman, Cornishwoman
Corsica	Corsican
Costa Rica	Costa Rican
Côte d'Ivoire	Ivorian *or* Ivorean
Croatia	Croat *or* Croatian
Cuba	Cuban
Cumbria	Cumbrian
Cyprus	Cypriot
Czech Republic	Czech
Czechoslovakia	Czechoslovak *or* Czechoslovakian
Delaware	Delawarean
Denmark	Dane
Delphi	Pythian
Devon	Devonian

Djibouti	Djiboutian *or* Djiboutien
Dominica	Dominican
Dominican Republic	Dominican
Dublin	Dubliner
Dundee	Dundonian
East Timor	East Timorese
Ecuador	Ecuadorean *or* Ecuadoran
Edinburgh	Edinburgher
Egypt	Egyptian
El Salvador	Salvadoran, Salvadorean *or* Salvadorian
England	Englishman, Englishwoman
Ephesus	Ephesian
Estonia	Estonian
Eritrea	Eritrean
Ethiopia	Ethiopian
Equatorial Guinea	Equatorian
Eritrea	Eritrean
Estonia	Estonian
Ethiopia	Ethiopian
Europe	European
Euzkadi	Basque
Faeroe Islands	Faeroese
Falkland Islands	Falkland Islanders *or* Falklander
Fife	Fifer
Fiji	Fijian
Finland	Finn
Flanders	Fleming
Florence	Florentine
Florida	Floridian
France	Frenchman, Frenchwoman
French Guiana	Guianese
Friesland	Frisian
Friuili	Friulian
Gabon	Gabonese
Galicia	Galician
Galilee	Galilean
Galloway	Gallovidian
Galway	Galwegian
Gambia	Gambian
Gascony	Gascon
Genoa	Genoese
Georgia (country)	Georgian
Georgia (U.S. state)	Georgian
Germany	German
Ghana	Ghanaian *or* Ghanian
Glasgow	Glaswegian
Greece	Greek
Greenland	Greenlander
Grenada	Grenadian
Guam	Guamanian
Guatemala	Guatemalan
Guinea	Guinean

Guyana	Guyanese *or* Guyanan
Haiti	Haitian
Hawaii	Hawaiian
Havana	Habanero
Hesse	Hessian
Hungary	Hungarian *or* Magyar
Honduras	Honduran
Hyderabad state	Mulki
Ibiza	Ibizan
Iceland	Icelander
Idaho	Idahoan
Illinois	Illinoian *or* Illinoisian
India	Indian
Indiana	Indianan, Indianian *or (informal)* Hoosier
Indonesia	Indonesian
Iowa	Iowan
Iran	Iranian
Iraq	Iraqi
Ireland	Irishman, Irishwoman
Israel	Israeli
Italy	Italian
Jamaica	Jamaican
Japan	Japanese
Java	Javanese
Jordan	Jordanian
Kansas	Kansan
Karelia	Karelian
Kazakhstan	Kazakh
Kent (East)	Man, Woman of Kent
Kent (West)	Kentish man, Woman
Kentucky	Kentuckian
Kenya	Kenyan
Kirghizia	Kirghiz
Korea	Korean
Kuwait	Kuwaiti
Lancashire	Lancastrian
Lancaster	Lancastrian
Laos	Laotian
Latvia	Latvian *or* Lett
Lebanon	Lebanese
Liberia	Liberian
Libya	Libyan
Liechtenstein	Liechtensteiner
Lincolnshire	yellow belly *(dialect)*
Lithuania	Lithuanian
Liverpool	Liverpudlian *or (informal)* Scouse *or* Scouser
Lombardy	Lombard
London	Londoner *or* Cockney
Los Angeles	Angeleno
Louisiana	Louisianan *or* Louisianian
Luxembourg	Luxembourger
Lyon	Lyonnais

Macao	Macaonese
Macedonia	Macedonian
Madagascar	Madagascan *or* Malagasy
Madrid	Madrileño, Madrileña
Maine	Mainer *or* Downeaster
Majorca	Majorcan
Malawi	Malawian
Malaya	Malayan
Malaysia	Malaysian
Maldive Islands	Maldivian
Malta	Maltese
Man, Isle of	Manxman, Manxwoman
Manchester	Mancunian
Manitoba	Manitoban
Marquesas Islands	Marquesan
Mars	Martian
Marseilles	Marsellais
Marshall Islands	Marshall Islander
Martinique	Martiniquean
Maryland	Marylander
Massachusetts	Bay Stater
Mauritania	Mauritanian
Mauritius	Mauritian
Melanesia	Melanesian
Melbourne	Melburnian
Mexico	Mexican
Michigan	Michigander, Michiganite *or* Michiganian
Micronesia	Micronesian
Milan	Milanese
Minnesota	Minnesotan
Mississippi	Mississippian
Missouri	Missourian
Moldavia	Moldavian
Monaco	Monegasque
Mongolia	Mongolian
Montana	Montanan
Montenegro	Montenegrin
Montserrat	Montserratian
Moravia	Moravian
Morroco	Morrocan
Moscow	Muscovite
Mozambique	Mozambican
Namibia	Namibian
Nauru	Nauruan
Naples	Neapolitan
Nebraska	Nebraskan
the Netherlands	Dutchman, Dutchwoman
New Brunswick	New Brunswicker
Newcastle upon Tyne	Geordie
New England	New Englander *or (informal)* Yankee *or* Downeaster
Newfoundland	Newfoundlander *or (informal)* Newfie
Newfoundland fishing village	Outporter
New Hampshire	New Hampshirite
New Jersey	New Jerseyan *or* New Jerseyite
New Mexico	New Mexican
New South Wales	New South Welshman, New South Welshwoman
New York	New Yorker *or* Knickerbocker
New Zealand	New Zealander *or (informal)* Kiwi *or* Enzedder
Nicaragua	Nicaraguan
Niger	Nigerien
Nigeria	Nigerian
Normandy	Norman
North Carolina	North Carolinian *or* Tarheel
North Dakota	North Dakotan
Northern Ireland	Northern Irishman, Northern Irishwoman
Northern Territory	Territorian
Northern Territory, northern part of	Top Ender
North Korea	North Korean
Northumbria	Northumbrian
Norway	Norwegian
Nova Scotia	Nova Scotian *or (informal)* Bluenose
Ohio	Ohioan
Okinawa	Okinawan
Oklahoma	Oklahoman *or (slang)* Okie
Oman	Omani
Ontario	Ontarian *or* Ontarioan
Oregon	Oregonian
Orkney	Orcadian
Oxford	Oxonian
Pakistan	Pakistani
Palestine	Palestinian
Panama	Panamanian
Papua New Guinea	Papua
Paraguay	Paraguayan
Paris	Parisian
Pennsylvania	Pennsylvanian
Persia	Persian
Perth	Perthite
Peru	Peruvian
the Philippines	Filipino
Poland	Pole
Pomerania	Pomeranian
Portugal	Portuguese
Prince Edward Island	Prince Edward Islander
Provence	Provençal

Prussia	Prussian
Puerto Rico	Puerto Rican
Qatar	Qatari
Quebec	Quebecer, Quebecker *or* Quebecois
Queensland	Queenslander
Rhode Island	Rhode Islander
Rhodes	Rhodian
Rhodesia	Rhodesian
Rio de Janeiro	Cariocan
Romania	Romanian
Rome	Roman
Russian Federation	Russian
Ruthenia	Ruthenian
Rwanda	Rwandan
Samaria	Samaritan
San Marino	San Marinese *or* Sammarinese
Sardinia	Sardinian
Saskatchewan	Saskatchewanian
Saxony	Saxon
Saudi Arabia	Saudi *or* Saudi Arabian
Savoy	Savoyard
Scandinavia	Scandinavian
Scotland	Scot, Scotsman, Scotswoman *or* Caledonian
Scottish Highlands	Highlander *or (old-fashioned)* Hielanman
Senegale	Senegalese
Serbia	Serb *or* Serbian
Seychelles	Seychellois
Shetland	Shetlander
Sierra Leone	Sierra Leonean
Sind	Sindhi
Singapore	Singaporean
Slovakia	Slovak
Slovenia	Slovene *or* Slovenian
Solomon Islands	Solomon Islander
South Africa	South African
South Australia	South Australian *or (informal)* Croweater
South Carolina	South Carolinian
South Dakota	South Dakota
South Korea	South Korean
Spain	Spaniard
Sri Lanka	Sri Lankan
Sudan	Sudanese
Suriname	Surinamese
Swaziland	Swazi
Switzerland	Swiss
Sweden	Swede
Sydney	Sydneysider
Sydney, Western suburbs of	Westie *(informal)*
Syria	Syrian
Taiwan	Taiwanese
Tajikstan	Tajik
Tanzania	Tanzanian
Tasmania	Tasmanian *or (informal)* Tassie *or* Apple Islander
Tennessee	Tennessean
Texas	Texan
Thailand	Thai
Thessalonika	Thessalonian
Tibet	Tibetan
Togo	Togolese
Tonga	Tongan
Trinidad	Trinidadian
Tobago	Tobagan *or* Tobagonian
Troy	Trojan
Tuscany	Tuscan
Tunisia	Tunisian
Turkey	Turk
Turkmenistan	Turkmen
Tuvalu	Tuvaluan
Tyneside	Geordie
Tyre	Tyrian
Uganda	Ugandan
Ukraine	Ukrainian
Ulster	Ulsterman, Ulsterwoman
Umbria	Umbrian
United Kingdom	Briton, Brit *(informal) or* Britisher
United States of America	American *or (informal)* Yank *or* Yankee
Uruguay	Uruguayan
Utah	Utahan *or* Utahn
Uzbekistan	Uzbek
Venezuela	Venezuelan
Venice	Venetian
Vermont	Vermonter
Victoria	Victorian
Vienna	Viennese
Vietnam	Vietnamese
Virginia	Virginian
Wales	Welshman, Welshwoman
Washington	Washingtonian
Wearside	Mackem
Wessex	West Saxon
Western Australia	Western Australian, Westralian *or (informal)* Sandgroper
Western Sahara	Sahwari
West Virginia	West Virginian
Winnipeg	Winnipegger
Wisconsin	Wisconsinite
Wyoming	Wyomingite
Yemen	Yemeni
Yorkshire	Yorkshireman, Yorkshirewoman
the Yukon	Yukoner
Zaire	Zairean
Zambia	Zambian

Zanzibar Zanzibari
Zimbabwe Zimbabwean

nativity 1. birth, delivery, parturition 2. crèche, manger scene
Antonyms (*sense 1*) death, demise, dying, ex~piration

natter 1. *verb* blather, blether, chatter, chew the fat *or* rag (*slang*), gabble, gossip, jabber, jaw (*slang*), palaver, prate, prattle, rabbit (on) (*Brit. informal*), run off at the mouth (*slang*), shoot the breeze (*informal*), talk, talk idly, witter (*informal*) 2. *noun* blather, blether, chat, chinwag (*Brit. informal*), chitchat, con~fabulation, conversation, gab (*informal*), gab~ble, gabfest (*informal, chiefly U.S. & Canad.*), gossip, jabber, jaw (*slang*), palaver, prattle, talk

natty chic, crucial (*slang*), dapper, elegant, fashionable, neat, smart, snazzy (*informal*), spruce, stylish, trendy (*Brit. informal*), trim, well-dressed, well-turned-out

natural 1. common, everyday, legitimate, logi~cal, normal, ordinary, regular, typical, usual 2. characteristic, congenital, essential, imma~nent, inborn, indigenous, inherent, innate, in one's blood, instinctive, intuitive, natal, native 3. artless, candid, frank, genuine, ingenuous, open, real, simple, spontaneous, unaffected, unpretentious, unsophisticated, unstudied 4. organic, plain, pure, unbleached, unmixed, unpolished, unrefined, whole
Antonyms (*sense 1*) abnormal, irregular, out of the ordinary, strange, untypical (*sense 3*) affected, artificial, assumed, counterfeit, feigned, phoney *or* phony (*informal*), unnatu~ral (*sense 4*) manufactured, processed, syn~thetic, unnatural

naturalism factualism, realism, verisimilitude

naturalist 1. biologist, botanist, ecologist, zo~ologist 2. factualist, realist

naturalistic factualistic, kitchen sink, lifelike, photographic, realistic, real-life, representa~tional, true-to-life, vérité, warts and all (*in~formal*)

naturalize acclimate, acclimatize, acculturate, accustom, adapt, adopt, domesticate, enfran~chise, familiarize, grant citizenship, habituate

naturally 1. *adverb* as anticipated, customarily, genuinely, informally, normally, simply, spon~taneously, typically, unaffectedly, unpre~tentiously 2. *interjection* absolutely, as a mat~ter of course, certainly, of course

naturalness 1. artlessness, candidness, frank~ness, genuineness, ingenuousness, openness, realism, simpleness, simplicity, spontaneous~ness, unaffectedness, unpretentiousness, un~sophisticatedness, unstudiedness 2. plainness, pureness, purity, wholeness

nature 1. attributes, character, complexion, constitution, essence, features, make-up, quality, traits 2. category, description, kind, sort, species, style, type, variety 3. cosmos, creation, earth, environment, universe, world 4. disposition, humour, mood, outlook, temper, temperament 5. country, countryside, land~scape, natural history, scenery

nature red in tooth and claw
Alfred, Lord Tennyson *In Memoriam*

Nature does nothing without purpose or uselessly
Aristotle *Politics*

You may drive out nature with a pitchfork, yet she'll be constantly running back
Horace *Epistles*

In nature there are neither rewards nor punish~ments - there are consequences
Robert G. Ingersoll *Some Reasons Why*

In her [Nature's] inventions nothing is lacking, and nothing is superfluous
Leonardo da Vinci

"I play for seasons; not eternities!"
Says Nature
George Meredith *Modern Love*

naturist nudist

naught nil, nothing, nothingness, nought, zero

naughty 1. annoying, bad, disobedient, exas~perating, fractious, impish, misbehaved, mis~chievous, perverse, playful, refractory, ro~guish, sinful, teasing, wayward, wicked, worthless 2. bawdy, blue, improper, lewd, ob~scene, off-colour, ribald, risqué, smutty, vul~gar, X-rated (*informal*)
Antonyms good, obedient, polite, proper, seemly, well-behaved, well-mannered

nausea 1. biliousness, qualm(s), queasiness, retching, sickness, squeamishness, vomiting 2. abhorrence, aversion, disgust, loathing, odium, repugnance, revulsion

nauseate disgust, gross out (*U.S. slang*), hor~rify, offend, repel, repulse, revolt, sicken, turn one's stomach

nauseous abhorrent, detestable, disgusting, distasteful, loathsome, nauseating, offensive, repugnant, repulsive, revolting, sickening, yucky *or* yukky (*slang*)

nautical marine, maritime, naval, oceanic, sea~faring, seagoing, yachting

naval marine, maritime, nautical, oceanic

navel 1. bellybutton (*informal*), omphalos (*lit~erary*), umbilicus 2. central point, centre, hub, middle

navigable 1. clear, negotiable, passable, tra~versable, unobstructed 2. controllable, dirig~ible, sailable, steerable

navigate con (*Nautical*), cross, cruise, direct, drive, guide, handle, journey, manoeuvre, pi~lot, plan, plot, sail, skipper, steer, voyage

navigation cruising, helmsmanship, pilotage, sailing, seamanship, steering, voyaging

navigator mariner, pilot, seaman

navvy ganger, labourer, worker, workman

navy argosy (*archaic*), armada, fleet, flotilla, warships

Don't talk to me about naval tradition. It's nothing but rum, sodomy, and the lash
Winston Churchill

near *adjective* **1.** adjacent, adjoining, a hop, skip and a jump away (*informal*), alongside, at close quarters, beside, bordering, close, close by, contiguous, just round the corner, nearby, neighbouring, nigh, proximate, touching, within sniffing distance (*informal*) **2.** approaching, forthcoming, imminent, impending, in the offing, looming, near-at-hand, next, on the cards (*informal*), upcoming **3.** akin, allied, attached, connected, dear, familiar, intimate, related **4.** *informal* close-fisted, mean, miserly, niggardly, parsimonious, stingy, tightfisted, ungenerous

Antonyms (*senses 1, 2 & 3*) distant, far, faraway, far-flung, far-off, far-removed, long, outlying, out-of-the-way, remote, removed

nearby **1.** *adjective* adjacent, adjoining, convenient, handy, neighbouring **2.** *adverb* at close quarters, close at hand, just round the corner, not far away, proximate, within reach, within sniffing distance (*informal*)

nearing advancing, approaching, approximating, coming, imminent, impending, upcoming

nearly *adverb* about, all but, almost, approaching, approximately, as good as, closely, just about, not quite, practically, roughly, virtually, well-nigh

nearness **1.** accessibility, availability, closeness, contiguity, handiness, juxtaposition, propinquity, proximity, vicinity **2.** immediacy, imminence **3.** dearness, familiarity, intimacy **4.** *informal* meanness, niggardliness, parsimony, stinginess

near-sighted myopic, short-sighted

near thing close shave (*informal*), narrow escape, near miss

neat **1.** accurate, dainty, fastidious, methodical, nice, orderly, shipshape, smart, spick-and-span, spruce, straight, systematic, tidy, trim, uncluttered **2.** adept, adroit, agile, apt, clever, deft, dexterous, efficient, effortless, elegant, expert, graceful, handy, nimble, practised, precise, skilful, stylish, well-judged **3.** *of alcoholic drinks* pure, straight, undiluted, unmixed

Antonyms (*senses 1 & 2*) awful, bad, clumsy, cluttered, disarrayed, disorderly, disorganized, incompetent, inefficient, inelegant, messy, slobby (*informal*), sloppy (*informal*), terrible, untidy

neaten arrange, clean up, groom, put to rights, straighten out *or* up, tidy, tidy up, trig (*archaic or dialect*), trim

neatly **1.** accurately, daintily, fastidiously, methodically, nicely, smartly, sprucely, systematically, tidily **2.** adeptly, adroitly, agilely, aptly, cleverly, deftly, dexterously, efficiently, effortlessly, elegantly, expertly, gracefully, handily, nimbly, precisely, skilfully, stylishly

neatness **1.** accuracy, daintiness, fastidiousness, methodicalness, niceness, nicety, orderliness, smartness, spruceness, straightness, tidiness, trimness **2.** adeptness, adroitness, agility, aptness, cleverness, deftness, dexterity, efficiency, effortlessness, elegance, expertness, grace, gracefulness, handiness, nimbleness, preciseness, precision, skilfulness, skill, style, stylishness

nebulous ambiguous, amorphous, cloudy, confused, dim, hazy, imprecise, indefinite, indeterminate, indistinct, misty, murky, obscure, shadowy, shapeless, uncertain, unclear, unformed, vague

necessarily accordingly, automatically, axiomatically, by definition, certainly, compulsorily, consequently, incontrovertibly, ineluctably, inevitably, inexorably, irresistibly, naturally, *nolens volens*, of course, of necessity, perforce, undoubtedly, willy-nilly

necessary **1.** compulsory, *de rigueur*, essential, imperative, indispensable, mandatory, needed, needful, obligatory, required, requisite, vital **2.** certain, fated, inescapable, inevitable, inexorable, unavoidable

Antonyms dispensable, expendable, inessential, nonessential, superfluous, unnecessary

necessitate call for, coerce, compel, constrain, demand, entail, force, impel, make necessary, oblige, require

necessities essentials, exigencies, fundamentals, indispensables, needs, requirements

necessitous destitute, distressed, impecunious, impoverished, indigent, needy, penniless, penurious, poor, poverty-stricken

necessity **1.** demand, exigency, indispensability, need, needfulness, requirement **2.** desideratum, essential, fundamental, necessary, need, prerequisite, requirement, requisite, *sine qua non*, want **3.** destitution, extremity, indigence, need, penury, poverty, privation **4.** compulsion, destiny, fate, inevitability, inexorableness, obligation

Necessity never made a good bargain
Benjamin Franklin *Poor Richard's Almanac*

Necessity is the plea for every infringement of human freedom; it is the argument of tyrants; it is the creed of slaves
William Pitt

You make a virtue of necessity
Saint Jerome *Apologeticum adversus Rufinum*
Necessity is the mother of invention
Jonathan Swift *Gulliver's Travels*
Give us the luxuries of life, and we will dispense with its necessities
John Lothrop Motley
Necessity knows no law
Needs must when the devil drives

neckcloth cravat, kerchief, neckerchief, scarf

necromancer black magician, diviner, en~ chanter, enchantress, magician, sorcerer, sor~ ceress, warlock, witch, wizard

necromancy black art, black magic, demonol~ ogy, divination, enchantment, magic, sorcery, thaumaturgy (*rare*), voodoo, witchcraft, witch~ ery, wizardry

necropolis burial ground, cemetery, church~ yard, God's acre, graveyard

need *verb* **1.** call for, demand, entail, have oc~ casion to *or* for, lack, miss, necessitate, re~ quire, want *~noun* **2.** longing, requisite, want, wish **3.** deprivation, destitution, distress, ex~ tremity, impecuniousness, inadequacy, indi~ gence, insufficiency, lack, neediness, paucity, penury, poverty, privation, shortage **4.** emer~ gency, exigency, necessity, obligation, urgency, want **5.** demand, desideratum, essential, re~ quirement, requisite

From each according to his abilities, to each ac~ cording to his needs
Karl Marx *Critique of the Gotha Programme*

needed called for, desired, lacked, necessary, required, wanted

needful essential, indispensable, necessary, needed, required, requisite, stipulated, vital

needle *verb* aggravate (*informal*), annoy, bait, be on one's back (*slang*), gall, get in one's hair (*informal*), get on one's nerves (*informal*), get under one's skin (*informal*), goad, harass, hassle (*informal*), irk, irritate, nag, nark (*Brit., Austral., & N.Z. slang*), nettle, pester, piss one off (*taboo slang*), prick, prod, pro~ voke, rile, ruffle, spur, sting, taunt

needless causeless, dispensable, excessive, ex~ pendable, gratuitous, groundless, nonessen~ tial, pointless, redundant, superfluous, uncalled-for, undesired, unnecessary, unwant~ ed, useless
Antonyms beneficial, essential, obligatory, re~ quired, useful

needlework embroidery, fancywork, needle~ craft, sewing, stitching, tailoring

needy deprived, destitute, dirt-poor, disadvan~ taged, down at heel (*informal*), impecunious, impoverished, indigent, on the breadline (*in~ formal*), penniless, poor, poverty-stricken, underprivileged
Antonyms affluent, comfortable, moneyed, prosperous, rich, wealthy, well-off, well-to-do

ne'er-do-well black sheep, good-for-nothing, idler, layabout, loafer, loser, skiver (*Brit. slang*), wastrel

nefarious abominable, atrocious, base, crimi~ nal, depraved, detestable, dreadful, evil, ex~ ecrable, foul, heinous, horrible, infamous, in~ fernal, iniquitous, monstrous, odious, oppro~ brious, shameful, sinful, vicious, vile, villain~ ous, wicked
Antonyms admirable, good, honest, honour~ able, just, noble, praiseworthy, upright, virtu~ ous

negate **1.** abrogate, annul, cancel, counter~ mand, invalidate, neutralize, nullify, obviate, repeal, rescind, retract, reverse, revoke, void, wipe out **2.** contradict, deny, disallow, dis~ prove, gainsay (*archaic or literary*), oppose, rebut, refute
Antonyms affirm, assert, attest, avouch, avow, certify, confirm, declare, maintain, pro~ nounce, ratify, state, swear, testify

negation **1.** antithesis, antonym, contradiction, contrary, converse, counterpart, denial, dis~ avowal, disclaimer, inverse, opposite, rejec~ tion, renunciation, reverse **2.** opposition, pro~ scription, refusal, repudiation, veto **3.** cancel~ lation, neutralization, nullification **4.** blank, nonexistence, nothingness, nullity, vacuity, void

negative *adjective* **1.** contradictory, contrary, denying, dissenting, opposing, recusant, re~ fusing, rejecting, resisting **2.** annulling, counteractive, invalidating, neutralizing, nul~ lifying **3.** antagonistic, colourless, contrary, cynical, gloomy, jaundiced, neutral, pessimis~ tic, uncooperative, unenthusiastic, uninterest~ ed, unwilling, weak *~noun* **4.** contradiction, denial, refusal
Antonyms *adjective* affirmative, approving, assenting, cheerful, concurring, enthusiastic, optimistic, positive

negativeness, negativity **1.** contradiction, contradictoriness, contrariness, denial, dis~ sent, opposition, recusancy, refusal, rejection, resistance **2.** antagonism, colourlessness, con~ trariness, cynicism, gloom, neutrality, pessi~ mism, uncooperativeness, uninterestedness, unwillingness, weakness

neglect *verb* **1.** contemn, discount, disdain, disregard, ignore, leave alone, overlook, pass by, rebuff, scorn, slight, spurn, turn one's back on **2.** be remiss, evade, forget, let slide, omit, pass over, procrastinate, shirk, skimp *~noun* **3.** disdain, disregard, disrespect, heed~ lessness, inattention, indifference, slight, un~ concern **4.** carelessness, default, dereliction, failure, forgetfulness, laxity, laxness, neglect~

fulness, negligence, oversight, remissness, slackness, slovenliness
Antonyms *verb* appreciate, attend to, notice, observe, regard, remember, value *~noun* attention, care, consideration, notice, regard, respect

neglected 1. abandoned, derelict, overgrown 2. disregarded, unappreciated, underestimated, undervalued

neglectful careless, disregardful, heedless, inattentive, indifferent, lax, negligent, remiss, thoughtless, uncaring, unmindful

negligence carelessness, default, dereliction, disregard, failure, forgetfulness, heedlessness, inadvertence, inattention, inattentiveness, indifference, laxity, laxness, neglect, omission, oversight, remissness, shortcoming, slackness, thoughtlessness

negligent careless, cursory, disregardful, forgetful, heedless, inadvertent, inattentive, indifferent, neglectful, nonchalant, offhand, regardless, remiss, slack, slapdash, slipshod, thoughtless, unmindful, unthinking
Antonyms attentive, careful, considerate, mindful, painstaking, rigorous, thorough, thoughtful

negligible imperceptible, inconsequential, insignificant, minor, minute, nickel-and-dime (*U.S. slang*), petty, small, trifling, trivial, unimportant
Antonyms important, noteworthy, significant, vital

negotiable debatable, discussable *or* discussible, transactional, transferable, variable

negotiate 1. adjudicate, arbitrate, arrange, bargain, conciliate, confer, consult, contract, deal, debate, discuss, handle, manage, mediate, parley, settle, transact, work out 2. clear, cross, get over, get past, get round, pass, pass through, surmount

negotiation arbitration, bargaining, debate, diplomacy, discussion, mediation, transaction, wheeling and dealing (*informal*)

negotiator adjudicator, ambassador, arbitrator, delegate, diplomat, honest broker, intermediary, mediator, moderator

neighbourhood community, confines, district, environs, locale, locality, precincts, proximity, purlieus, quarter, region, surroundings, vicinity

neighbouring abutting, adjacent, adjoining, bordering, connecting, contiguous, near, nearby, nearest, next, surrounding
Antonyms distant, far, far-off, remote

neighbourly amiable, civil, companionable, considerate, friendly, genial, harmonious, helpful, hospitable, kind, obliging, sociable, social, well-disposed

nemesis destiny, destruction, fate, retribution, vengeance

neologism buzz word (*informal*), coinage, new phrase, new word, nonce word, vogue word

neophyte amateur, apprentice, beginner, catechumen, disciple, learner, novice, novitiate, probationer, proselyte, pupil, recruit, student, trainee, tyro

ne plus ultra acme, culmination, extreme, perfection, the last word, ultimate, uttermost point

nerve *noun* 1. balls (*taboo slang*), ballsiness (*taboo slang*), bottle (*Brit. slang*), bravery, coolness, courage, daring, determination, endurance, energy, face (*informal*), fearlessness, firmness, force, fortitude, gameness, grit, guts (*informal*), hardihood, intrepidity, mettle, might, pluck, resolution, spirit, spunk (*informal*), steadfastness, vigour, will 2. *informal* audacity, boldness, brass (*informal*), brass neck (*Brit. informal*), brazenness, cheek (*informal*), chutzpah (*U.S. & Canad. informal*), effrontery, front, gall, impertinence, impudence, insolence, neck (*informal*), sassiness (*U.S. slang*), sauce (*informal*), temerity *~verb* 3. brace, embolden, encourage, fortify, hearten, invigorate, steel, strengthen

nerveless 1. calm, collected, composed, controlled, cool, impassive, imperturbable, self-possessed, unemotional 2. afraid, cowardly, debilitated, enervated, feeble, nervous, spineless, timid, weak

nerve-racking annoying, difficult, distressing, frightening, harassing, harrowing, maddening, stressful, tense, trying, worrying

nerves anxiety, butterflies (in one's stomach) (*informal*), cold feet (*informal*), fretfulness, heebie-jeebies (*slang*), imbalance, nervousness, strain, stress, tension, worry

nervous agitated, anxious, apprehensive, edgy, excitable, fearful, fidgety, flustered, hesitant, highly strung, hyper (*informal*), hysterical, jittery (*informal*), jumpy, nervy (*Brit. informal*), neurotic, on edge, ruffled, shaky, tense, timid, timorous, twitchy (*informal*), uneasy, uptight (*informal*), weak, wired (*slang*), worried
Antonyms bold, calm, confident, constant, cool, equable, even, laid-back (*informal*), peaceful, relaxed, steady, together (*slang*), unfazed (*informal*)

nervous breakdown breakdown, collapse, crack-up (*informal*), nervous disorder, neurasthenia (*obsolete*)

nervousness agitation, anxiety, disquiet, excitability, fluster, perturbation, tension, timidity, touchiness, tremulousness, worry

nervy agitated, anxious, excitable, fidgety, jittery (*informal*), jumpy, nervous, on edge, restless, tense, twitchy (*informal*), wired (*slang*)

nescience **1.** ignorance, lack of knowledge, obliviousness, unawareness, unconsciousness, unenlightenment **2.** agnosticism, doubt, irreligion, unbelief

nescient **1.** ignorant, oblivious, unaware, unconscious, unenlightened, unknowing, unknowledgeable **2.** agnostic, doubting, irreligious, unbelieving

nest **1.** den, haunt, hideaway, refuge, resort, retreat, snuggery **2.** breeding-ground, den, hotbed

nest egg cache, deposit, fall-back, fund(s), reserve, savings, store

nestle cuddle, curl up, huddle, nuzzle, snuggle

nestling **1.** chick, fledgling **2.** babe, babe in arms, baby, infant, suckling

net[1] **1.** *noun* lacework, lattice, mesh, netting, network, openwork, reticulum, tracery, web **2.** *verb* bag, capture, catch, enmesh, ensnare, entangle, nab (*informal*), trap

net[2], nett *adjective* **1.** after taxes, clear, final, take-home **2.** closing, conclusive, final *~verb* **3.** accumulate, bring in, clear, earn, gain, make, realize, reap

nether basal, below, beneath, bottom, inferior, lower, Stygian, under, underground

nether world Avernus, Hades, hell, infernal regions, nether regions, underworld

nettle aggravate (*informal*), annoy, chafe, exasperate, fret, gall, get on one's nerves (*informal*), goad, harass, hassle (*informal*), incense, irritate, nark (*Brit., Austral., & N.Z. slang*), pique, piss one off (*taboo slang*), provoke, ruffle, sting, tease, vex

nettled aggrieved, angry, annoyed, chafed, choked, cross, exasperated, galled, goaded, hacked (off) (*U.S. slang*), harassed, huffy, incensed, irritable, irritated, peeved, peevish, piqued, pissed off (*taboo slang*), provoked, put out, ratty (*Brit. & N.Z. informal*), riled, ruffled, stung, teased, tetchy, touchy, vexed

network arrangement, channels, circuitry, complex, convolution, grid, grill, interconnections, labyrinth, maze, mesh, net, nexus, organization, plexus, structure, system, tracks, web

neurosis abnormality, affliction, derangement, deviation, instability, maladjustment, mental disturbance, mental illness, obsession, phobia, psychological *or* emotional disorder

neurotic abnormal, anxious, compulsive, deviant, disordered, distraught, disturbed, hyper (*informal*), maladjusted, manic, nervous, obsessive, overwrought, twitchy (*informal*), unhealthy, unstable
Antonyms calm, laid-back (*informal*), level-headed, normal, rational, sane, stable, together (*slang*), well-adjusted, well-balanced

neuter *verb* castrate, doctor (*informal*), dress, emasculate, fix (*informal*), geld, spay

neutral **1.** disinterested, dispassionate, even-handed, impartial, indifferent, nonaligned, nonbelligerent, noncombatant, noncommittal, nonpartisan, sitting on the fence, unaligned, unbiased, uncommitted, undecided, uninvolved, unprejudiced **2.** achromatic, colourless, dull, expressionless, indeterminate, indistinct, indistinguishable, intermediate, toneless, undefined
Antonyms active, belligerent, biased, decided, interested, interfering, partial, participating, positive, prejudiced

neutrality detachment, disinterestedness, impartiality, nonalignment, noninterference, noninterventionism, noninvolvement, nonpartisanship

neutralize cancel, compensate for, counteract, counterbalance, frustrate, invalidate, negate, nullify, offset, undo

never at no time, not at all, not for love nor money (*informal*), not on your life (*informal*), not on your nelly (*Brit. slang*), no way, on no account, under no circumstances
Antonyms always, aye (*Scot.*), constantly, continually, every time, forever, perpetually, without exception

never-ending boundless, ceaseless, constant, continual, continuous, eternal, everlasting, incessant, interminable, nonstop, perpetual, persistent, relentless, unbroken, unceasing, unchanging, uninterrupted, unremitting

never-never hire-purchase (*Brit.*), H.P. (*Brit.*)

nevertheless but, even so, (even) though, however, nonetheless, notwithstanding, regardless, still, yet

new **1.** advanced, all-singing, all-dancing, contemporary, current, different, fresh, ground-breaking, happening (*informal*), latest, modern, modernistic, modish, newfangled, novel, original, recent, state-of-the-art, topical, ultramodern, unfamiliar, unknown, unused, unusual, up-to-date, virgin **2.** added, extra, more, supplementary **3.** altered, changed, improved, modernized, redesigned, renewed, restored
Antonyms aged, ancient, antiquated, antique, experienced, hackneyed, old, old-fashioned, outmoded, passé, stale, trite

There is no new thing under the sun
Bible: Ecclesiastes

newcomer alien, arrival, beginner, foreigner, immigrant, incomer, Johnny-come-lately (*informal*), novice, outsider, parvenu, settler, stranger

newfangled all-singing, all-dancing, contemporary, fashionable, gimmicky, modern, new, new-fashioned, novel, recent, state-of-the-art
Antonyms antiquated, dated, obsolete, old-fashioned, outmoded, out-of-date, passé

newly anew, freshly, just, lately, latterly, recently

newness freshness, innovation, novelty, oddity, originality, strangeness, unfamiliarity, uniqueness

news account, advice, bulletin, buzz, communiqué, dirt (*U.S. slang*), disclosure, dispatch, exposé, gen (*Brit. informal*), gossip, hearsay, information, intelligence, latest (*informal*), leak, news flash, release, report, revelation, rumour, scandal, scuttlebutt (*U.S. slang*), statement, story, tidings, word

As cold waters to a thirsty soul, so is good news from another country
Bible: Proverbs

When a dog bites a man, that is not news, because it happens so often. But if a man bites a dog, that is news
John B. Bogart

all the news that's fit to print
Adolph S. Ochs *motto of the New York Times*

No news is good news

newsworthy arresting, important, interesting, notable, noteworthy, remarkable, significant, stimulating

next *adjective* **1.** consequent, ensuing, following, later, subsequent, succeeding **2.** adjacent, adjoining, closest, nearest, neighbouring *~adverb* **3.** afterwards, closely, following, later, subsequently, thereafter

next world afterlife, afterworld, heaven, hereafter, nirvana, paradise

nexus bond, connection, joining, junction, link, tie

nibble **1.** *noun* bite, crumb, morsel, peck, snack, *soupçon*, taste, titbit **2.** *verb* bite, eat, gnaw, munch, nip, peck, pick at

nice **1.** agreeable, amiable, attractive, charming, commendable, courteous, delightful, friendly, good, kind, likable *or* likeable, pleasant, pleasurable, polite, prepossessing, refined, well-mannered **2.** dainty, fine, neat, tidy, trim **3.** accurate, careful, critical, delicate, discriminating, exact, exacting, fastidious, fine, meticulous, precise, rigorous, scrupulous, strict, subtle **4.** cultured, genteel, refined, respectable, virtuous, well-bred
Antonyms awful, careless, coarse, crude, disagreeable, dreadful, ill-bred, mean, miserable, rough, shabby, sloppy (*informal*), unfriendly, unkind, unpleasant, vague, vulgar

nicely **1.** acceptably, agreeably, amiably, attractively, charmingly, commendably, courteously, delightfully, kindly, likably, pleasantly, pleasingly, pleasurably, politely, prepossessingly, well **2.** daintily, finely, neatly, tidily, trimly **3.** accurately, carefully, critically, delicately, exactingly, exactly, fastidiously, finely, meticulously, precisely, rigorously, scrupulously, strictly, subtly **4.** genteelly, respectably, virtuously
Antonyms carelessly, sloppily (*informal*), unattractively, unfortunately, unpleasantly

niceness **1.** agreeableness, amiability, attractiveness, charm, courtesy, delightfulness, friendliness, good manners, goodness, kindness, likableness *or* likeableness, pleasantness, pleasurableness, politeness, refinement **2.** daintiness, fineness, neatness, tidiness, trimness **3.** accuracy, care, carefulness, criticalness, delicacy, discrimination, exactingness, exactitude, exactness, fastidiousness, fineness, meticulosity, meticulousness, preciseness, precision, rigorousness, rigour, scrupulosity, scrupulousness, strictness, subtleness, subtlety **4.** gentility, good breeding, refinement, respectability, virtue

nicety **1.** accuracy, exactness, fastidiousness, finesse, meticulousness, minuteness, precision **2.** daintiness, delicacy, discrimination, distinction, nuance, refinement, subtlety

niche **1.** alcove, corner, hollow, nook, opening, recess **2.** calling, pigeonhole (*informal*), place, position, slot (*informal*), vocation

nick[1] *noun/verb* chip, cut, damage, dent, mark, notch, scar, score, scratch, snick

nick[2] *verb* finger (*slang*), knock off (*slang*), pilfer, pinch (*informal*), snitch (*slang*), steal, swipe (*slang*)

nickname diminutive, epithet, familiar name, handle (*slang*), label, moniker *or* monicker (*slang*), pet name, sobriquet

nifty agile, apt, attractive, chic, clever, deft, enjoyable, excellent, neat, pleasing, quick, sharp, smart, spruce, stylish

niggard cheapskate (*informal*), cheeseparer, churl (*archaic*), meanie *or* meany (*informal, chiefly Brit.*), miser, penny-pincher (*informal*), screw (*slang*), Scrooge, skinflint, tight-arse (*taboo slang*), tight-ass (*U.S. taboo slang*)

niggardliness **1.** avarice, avariciousness, closeness, covetousness, frugality, grudgingness, meanness, mercenariness, miserliness, nearness (*informal*), parsimony, penuriousness, sordidness, sparingness, stinginess, thrift, tightfistedness, ungenerousness **2.** beggarliness, inadequacy, insufficiency, meagreness, meanness, miserableness, paltriness, scantiness, skimpiness, smallness, wretchedness

niggardly **1.** avaricious, close, covetous, frugal, grudging, mean, mercenary, miserly, near (*informal*), parsimonious, penurious, Scroogelike, sordid, sparing, stinging, stingy, tight-arse (*taboo slang*), tight-arsed (*taboo slang*), tight as a duck's arse (*taboo slang*), tight-ass (*U.S. taboo slang*), tight-assed (*U.S. taboo slang*), tightfisted, ungenerous **2.** beggarly, inadequate, insufficient, meagre, mean, measly, miserable, paltry, pathetic, scant, scanty, skimpy, small, wretched

Antonyms abundant, ample, bountiful, copious, generous, handsome, lavish, liberal, munificent, plentiful, prodigal, profuse

niggle **1.** carp, cavil, criticize, find fault, fuss **2.** annoy, irritate, rankle, worry

niggler carper, caviller, fault-finder, fusspot (*Brit. informal*), nag, nit-picker (*informal*), pettifogger, quibbler

niggling **1.** cavilling, finicky, fussy, insignificant, minor, nit-picking (*informal*), pettifogging, petty, picky (*informal*), piddling (*informal*), quibbling, trifling, unimportant **2.** gnawing, irritating, persistent, troubling, worrying

nigh **1.** *adjective* adjacent, adjoining, approximate, at hand, bordering, close, contiguous, imminent, impending, near, next, upcoming **2.** *adverb* about, almost, approximately, close, near, practically

night dark, darkness, dead of night, hours of darkness, night-time, night watches

Related adjective: nocturnal

Night hath a thousand eyes
John Lyly *Maides Metamorphose*

The night has a thousand eyes,
And the day but one
F.W. Bourdillon *Light*

Night is the half of life, and the better half
Johann Wolfgang von Goethe *Wilhelm Meisters Lehrjahre*

the huge and thoughtful night
Walt Whitman *When Lilacs Last in the Dooryard Bloom'd*

sable-vested night, eldest of things
John Milton *Paradise Lost*

night and day all the time, ceaselessly, constantly, continually, continuously, day in, day out, endlessly, incessantly, interminably, unremittingly

nightfall crepuscule, dusk, eve (*archaic*), evening, eventide, gloaming (*Scot. or poetic*), sundown, sunset, twilight, vespers

Antonyms aurora (*poetic*), cockcrow, dawn, dawning, daybreak, daylight, morning, sunrise

nightly **1.** *adverb / adjective* each night, every night, night after night, nights (*informal*) **2.** *adverb* after dark, at night, by night, in the night, nights (*informal*), nocturnally **3.** *adjective* night-time, nocturnal

nightmare **1.** bad dream, hallucination, incubus, night terror, succubus **2.** hell on earth, horror, ordeal, torment, trial, tribulation

nightmarish agonizing, alarming, creepy (*informal*), disturbing, frightening, harrowing, horrible, Kafkaesque, scaring, terrifying, unreal

nihilism **1.** abnegation, agnosticism, atheism, denial, disbelief, nonbelief, rejection, renunciation, repudiation, scepticism **2.** blank, emptiness, negation, nonexistence, nothingness, nullity, oblivion **3.** anarchy, disorder, lawlessness, terrorism

nihilist **1.** agnostic, atheist, cynic, disbeliever, nonbeliever, pessimist, sceptic **2.** agitator, anarchist, extremist, revolutionary, terrorist

nil duck, love, naught, *nihil*, none, nothing, zero, zilch (*slang*)

nimble active, agile, alert, bright (*informal*), brisk, deft, dexterous, lively, nippy (*Brit. informal*), pdq (*slang*), proficient, prompt, quick, quick-witted, ready, smart, sprightly, spry, swift

Antonyms awkward, clumsy, dull, heavy, inactive, indolent, lethargic, slow

nimbleness adroitness, agility, alacrity, alertness, dexterity, finesse, grace, lightness, nippiness (*Brit. informal*), skill, smartness, sprightliness, spryness

nimbly actively, acutely, agilely, alertly, briskly, deftly, dexterously, easily, fast, fleetly, hotfoot, pdq (*slang*), posthaste, proficiently, promptly, pronto (*informal*), quickly, quick-wittedly, readily, sharply, smartly, speedily, spryly, swiftly

nimbus ambience, atmosphere, aura, aureole, cloud, corona, glow, halo, irradiation

nincompoop berk (*Brit. slang*), blockhead, charlie (*Brit. informal*), coot, dickhead (*slang*), dickwit (*slang*), dimwit (*informal*), dipstick (*Brit. slang*), divvy (*slang*), dolt, dork (*slang*), dunce, dweeb (*U.S. slang*), fathead (*informal*), fool, fuckwit (*taboo slang*), geek (*slang*), gobshite (*Irish taboo slang*), gonzo (*slang*), idiot, jerk (*slang, chiefly U.S. & Canad.*), lamebrain (*informal*), nerd *or* nurd (*slang*), ninny, nitwit (*informal*), noodle, numpty (*Scot. informal*), numskull *or* numbskull, oaf, pillock (*Brit. slang*), plank (*Brit. slang*), plonker (*slang*), prat (*slang*), prick (*slang*), schmuck (*U.S. slang*), simpleton, twit (*informal, chiefly Brit.*), wally (*slang*)

nip¹ *verb* **1.** bite, catch, clip, compress, grip, nibble, pinch, snag, snap, snip, squeeze, tweak, twitch **2.** check, frustrate, thwart

nip² *noun* dram, draught, drop, finger, mouthful, peg (*Brit.*), portion, shot (*informal*), sip, snifter (*informal*), *soupçon*, sup, swallow, taste

nipper **1.** claw, pincer **2.** *informal* ankle-biter (*Austral. slang*), baby, boy, child, girl, infant, kid (*informal*), little one, rug rat (*slang*), sprog (*slang*), tot

nipple boob (*slang*), breast, dug, mamilla, pap, papilla, teat, tit, udder

nippy **1.** biting, chilly, nipping, sharp, stinging **2.** *Brit. informal* active, agile, fast, nimble, pdq (*slang*), quick, spry

nirvana bliss, joy, paradise, peace, serenity, tranquillity

nit-picking captious, carping, cavilling, finicky, fussy, hairsplitting, pedantic, pettifogging, quibbling

nitty-gritty basics, bottom line, brass tacks (*informal*), core, crux, essence, essentials, facts, fundamentals, gist, heart of the matter, ins and outs, nuts and bolts, reality, sub~ stance

nitwit *informal* dickhead (*slang*), dickwit (*slang*), dimwit (*informal*), dipstick (*Brit. slang*), divvy (*slang*), dork (*slang*), dummy (*slang*), fool, fuckwit (*taboo slang*), geek (*slang*), gobshite (*Irish taboo slang*), halfwit, lamebrain (*informal*), nincompoop, ninny, numpty (*Scot. informal*), oaf, plank (*Brit. slang*), simpleton

nob aristo (*informal*), aristocrat, big shot (*in~ formal*), bigwig (*informal*), celeb (*informal*), fat cat (*slang, chiefly U.S.*), nabob (*informal*), toff (*Brit. slang*), V.I.P.

nobble **1.** disable, handicap, incapacitate, weaken **2.** bribe, get at, influence, intimidate, outwit, win over **3.** filch, knock off (*slang*), nick (*slang, chiefly Brit.*), pilfer, pinch (*infor~ mal*), purloin, snitch (*slang*), steal, swipe (*slang*) **4.** get hold of, grab, take

nobbly nubby, projecting, protruding, protu~ berant, ridged, rough

nobility **1.** aristocracy, elite, high society, lords, nobles, patricians, peerage, ruling class, upper class **2.** dignity, eminence, excellence, gran~ deur, greatness, illustriousness, loftiness, magnificence, majesty, nobleness, stateliness, sublimity, superiority, worthiness **3.** honour, incorruptibility, integrity, uprightness, virtue *Related adjective:* nobiliary

Ranks of the British nobility (in order of precedence)

royal duke *or (fem.)* royal duchess	earl
duke *or (fem.)* duch~ ess	viscount *or (fem.)* viscountess
marquess *or* marquis *or (fem.)* marchion~ ess	baron *or (fem.)* bar~ oness
	baronet

Ranks of foreign nobility

archduke *or (fem.)* archduchess	count *or (fem.)* coun~ tess
boyar	grand duke *or (fem.)* grand duchess
burgrave	grandee
landgrave *or (fem.)* landgravine	margravine
marchese *or (fem.)* marchesa	marquis *or* marquise
margrave *or (fem.)*	prince
	vicomte *or (fem.)* vi~ comtesse

New nobility is but the act of power, but ancient nobility is the act of time

Francis Bacon *Essays*

noble *noun* **1.** aristo (*informal*), aristocrat, childe (*archaic*), lord, nobleman, peer *~adjec~ tive* **2.** aristocratic, blue-blooded, gentle (*ar~ chaic*), highborn, lordly, patrician, titled **3.** august, dignified, distinguished, elevated, eminent, excellent, grand, great, imposing, impressive, lofty, splendid, stately, superb **4.** generous, honourable, magnanimous, upright, virtuous, worthy

Antonyms *noun* commoner, peasant, serf *~adjective* base, contemptible, despicable, dis~ honest, humble, ignoble, insignificant, low~ born, lowly, mean, modest, peasant, plain, plebeian, selfish, vulgar

nobody **1.** no-one **2.** cipher, lightweight (*infor~ mal*), menial, nonentity, nothing (*informal*)

Antonyms big name, big noise (*informal*), big shot (*slang*), celeb (*informal*), celebrity, mega~ star (*informal*), personage, star, superstar, V.I.P.

nocturnal night, nightly, night-time, of the night

nod *verb* **1.** acknowledge, bob, bow, dip, duck, gesture, indicate, nutate (*rare*), salute, signal **2.** agree, assent, concur, show agreement **3.** be sleepy, doze, droop, drowse, kip (*Brit. slang*), nap, sleep, slump, zizz (*Brit. informal*) *~noun* **4.** acknowledgment, beck, gesture, greeting, indication, salute, sign, signal

node bud, bump, burl, growth, knob, knot, lump, nodule, protuberance, swelling

noggin **1.** gill, quarter-pint **2.** cup, dram, mug, nip, tot **3.** *informal* bean (*U.S. & Canad. slang*), block (*informal*), bonce (*Brit. slang*), conk (*slang*), dome (*slang*), head, napper (*slang*), noddle (*informal, chiefly Brit.*), nut (*slang*)

no go futile, hopeless, impossible, not on (*in~ formal*), vain

noise **1.** *noun* babble, blare, clamour, clatter, commotion, cry, din, fracas, hubbub, outcry, pandemonium, racket, row, sound, talk, tu~ mult, uproar **2.** *verb* advertise, bruit, circulate, gossip, publicize, repeat, report, rumour

noiseless hushed, inaudible, mute, muted, quiet, silent, soundless, still

noisome **1.** bad, baneful (*archaic*), deleterious, harmful, hurtful, injurious, mischievous, per~ nicious, pestiferous, pestilential, poisonous, unhealthy, unwholesome **2.** disgusting, fetid, foul, malodorous, mephitic, niffy (*Brit. slang*), noxious, offensive, olid, putrid, reeking, smelly, stinking

noisy boisterous, cacophonous, chattering, clamorous, deafening, ear-splitting, loud, ob~ streperous, piercing, riotous, strident, tumul~ tuous, turbulent, uproarious, vociferous
Antonyms hushed, quiet, silent, still, sub~ dued, tranquil, tuneful

nomad drifter, itinerant, migrant, rambler, rover, vagabond, wanderer

nomadic itinerant, migrant, migratory, pasto~ ral, peripatetic, roaming, roving, travelling, vagrant, wandering

nom de plume alias, assumed name, nom de guerre, pen name, pseudonym

nomenclature classification, codification, locu~ tion, phraseology, taxonomy, terminology, vo~ cabulary

nominal **1.** formal, ostensible, pretended, pro~ fessed, puppet, purported, self-styled, so-called, *soi-disant*, supposed, theorctical, titu~ lar **2.** inconsiderable, insignificant, minimal, small, symbolic, token, trifling, trivial

nominate appoint, assign, choose, commission, designate, elect, elevate, empower, name, pre~ sent, propose, recommend, select, submit, suggest, term

nomination appointment, choice, designation, election, proposal, recommendation, selection, suggestion

nominee aspirant, candidate, contestant, en~ trant, favourite, protégé, runner

> *nominee: a modest gentleman shrinking from the distinction of private life and diligently seeking the honorable obscurity of public office*
> Ambrose Bierce *The Devil's Dictionary*

nonaligned impartial, neutral, uncommitted, undecided

nonchalance calm, composure, cool (*slang*), equanimity, imperturbability, indifference, sang-froid, self-possession, unconcern

nonchalant airy, apathetic, blasé, calm, care~ less, casual, collected, cool, detached, dispas~ sionate, indifferent, insouciant, laid-back (*in~ formal*), offhand, unconcerned, unemotional, unfazed (*informal*), unperturbed
Antonyms anxious, caring, concerned, in~ volved, worried

noncombatant civilian, neutral, nonbelligerent

noncommittal ambiguous, careful, cautious, circumspect, discreet, equivocal, evasive, guarded, indefinite, neutral, politic, reserved, tactful, temporizing, tentative, unrevealing, vague, wary

non compos mentis crazy, deranged, insane, mentally ill, of unsound mind, unbalanced, unhinged
Antonyms all there (*informal*), *compos men~ tis*, in one's right mind, lucid, mentally sound, rational, sane

nonconformist dissenter, dissentient, eccen~ tric, heretic, iconoclast, individualist, maver~ ick, protester, radical, rebel
Antonyms Babbitt (*U.S.*), conventionalist, stick-in-the-mud (*informal*), traditionalist, yes man

nonconformity dissent, eccentricity, heresy, heterodoxy, unconventionality

nondescript bog-standard (*Brit. & Irish slang*), characterless, common or garden (*informal*), commonplace, dull, featureless, indeterminate, mousy, nothing to write home about, ordi~ nary, run-of-the-mill, unclassifiable, unclassi~ fied, undistinguished, unexceptional, unin~ spiring, uninteresting, unmemorable, unre~ markable, vague, vanilla (*informal*)
Antonyms distinctive, extraordinary, memo~ rable, remarkable, unique, unusual

none bugger all (*slang*), diddly (*U.S. slang*), f.a. (*Brit. slang*), fuck all (*Brit. taboo slang*), nil, nobody, no-one, no part, not a bit, not any, nothing, not one, sweet F.A. (*Brit. slang*), sweet Fanny Adams (*Brit. slang*), zero, zilch (*slang, chiefly U.S. & Canad.*)

nonentity cipher, lightweight (*informal*), medi~ ocrity, nobody, small fry, unimportant person

nonessential dispensable, excessive, expend~ able, extraneous, inessential, peripheral, superfluous, unimportant, unnecessary
Antonyms appropriate, essential, important, indispensable, significant, vital

nonetheless despite that, even so, however, in spite of that, nevertheless, yet

nonexistent chimerical, fancied, fictional, hal~ lucinatory, hypothetical, illusory, imaginary, imagined, insubstantial, legendary, missing, mythical, unreal
Antonyms actual, existent, existing, genuine, real, true, veritable

nonpareil **1.** *noun* ideal, nonesuch (*archaic*), paragon, perfection **2.** *adjective* incomparable, matchless, peerless, supreme, unequalled, unique, unmatched, unparalleled, unrivalled, unsurpassed

nonpartisan detached, impartial, independent, neutral, nonpolitical, objective, unaffiliated, unbiased, unprejudiced

nonplus astonish, astound, baffle, be all Greek to (*informal*), bewilder, confound, confuse, discomfit, disconcert, discountenance, dismay, dumbfound, embarrass, faze, flummox, mysti~ fy, perplex, puzzle, stump, stun, take aback

nonsense absurdity, balderdash, balls (*taboo slang*), bilge (*informal*), blather, bombast, bosh (*informal*), bull (*slang*), bullshit (*taboo slang*), bunk (*informal*), bunkum *or* buncombe

(*chiefly U.S.*), claptrap (*informal*), cobblers (*Brit. taboo slang*), crap (*slang*), double Dutch (*Brit. informal*), drivel, eyewash (*informal*), fatuity, folly, foolishness, garbage (*informal*), gibberish, guff (*slang*), hogwash, hokum (*slang, chiefly U.S. & Canad.*), horsefeathers (*U.S. slang*), hot air (*informal*), idiocy, inan~ity, jest, ludicrousness, moonshine, pap, piffle (*informal*), poppycock (*informal*), ridiculous~ness, rot, rubbish, senselessness, shit (*taboo slang*), silliness, stuff, stupidity, tommyrot, tosh (*slang, chiefly Brit.*), trash, tripe (*infor~mal*), twaddle, waffle (*informal, chiefly Brit.*)
Antonyms fact, reality, reason, sense, seri~ousness, truth, wisdom

nonsensical absurd, asinine, crazy, foolish, in~ane, incomprehensible, irrational, ludicrous, meaningless, ridiculous, senseless, silly

nonstarter dead loss, dud (*informal*), lemon (*informal*), loser, no-hoper (*informal*), turkey (*informal*), washout (*informal*), waste of space *or* time

nonstop **1.** *adjective* ceaseless, constant, con~tinuous, direct, endless, incessant, intermi~nable, relentless, steady, unbroken, unending, unfaltering, uninterrupted, unremitting **2.** *ad~verb* ceaselessly, constantly, continuously, di~rectly, endlessly, incessantly, interminably, relentlessly, steadily, unbrokenly, unendingly, unfalteringly, uninterruptedly, unremittingly, without stopping
Antonyms *adjective* broken, discontinuous, fitful, intermittent, irregular, occasional, peri~odic, punctuated, recurrent, spasmodic, spo~radic, stop-go (*informal*)

nonviolent nonbelligerent, pacifist, peaceable, peaceful

nook alcove, cavity, corner, cranny, crevice, cubbyhole, hide-out, inglenook (*Brit.*), niche, opening, recess, retreat

noon high noon, midday, noonday, noontide, noontime, twelve noon

norm average, benchmark, criterion, mean, measure, model, par, pattern, rule, standard, type, yardstick

normal **1.** accustomed, acknowledged, average, bog-standard (*Brit. & Irish slang*), common, conventional, habitual, natural, ordinary, popular, regular, routine, run-of-the-mill, standard, typical, usual **2.** rational, reason~able, sane, well-adjusted
Antonyms abnormal, exceptional, irregular, peculiar, rare, remarkable, singular, uncom~mon, unnatural, unusual

normality **1.** accustomedness, averageness, commonness, commonplaceness, conventional~ity, habitualness, naturalness, ordinariness, popularity, regularity, routineness, typicality, usualness **2.** adjustment, balance, rationality, reason, sanity

normally as a rule, commonly, habitually, or~dinarily, regularly, typically, usually

normative controlling, normalizing, prescrip~tive, regularizing, regulating, standardizing

north **1.** *adjective* Arctic, boreal, northerly, northern, polar **2.** *adverb* northerly, north~ward(s)

North Star lodestar, Polaris, Pole Star

nose *noun* **1.** beak, bill, conk (*slang*), hooter (*slang*), neb (*archaic or dialect*), proboscis, schnozzle (*slang, chiefly U.S.*), snitch (*slang*), snout (*slang*) ~*verb* **2.** detect, scent, search (for), smell, sniff **3.** ease forward, nudge, nuz~zle, push, shove **4.** meddle, pry, snoop (*infor~mal*)

Give me a man with a good allowance of nose
Napoleon Bonaparte

nose dive dive, drop, plummet, plunge

nosegay bouquet, posy

nosh **1.** *noun* aliment, chow (*informal*), comes~tibles, eats (*slang*), fare, feed, food, grub (*slang*), meal, nosebag (*slang*), repast, scoff (*slang*), sustenance, tack (*informal*), viands, victuals, vittles (*obsolete or dialect*) **2.** *verb* consume, eat, scoff (*slang*)

nostalgia homesickness, longing, pining, re~gret, regretfulness, remembrance, reminis~cence, wistfulness, yearning

Nostalgia isn't what it used to be
Anon.

nostalgic emotional, homesick, longing, maud~lin, regretful, sentimental, wistful

nostrum cure, cure-all, drug, elixir, medicine, panacea, patent medicine, potion, quack medicine, remedy, sovereign cure, specific, treatment

nosy, nosey curious, eavesdropping, inquisi~tive, interfering, intrusive, meddlesome, pry~ing, snooping (*informal*)

notability **1.** celebrity, distinction, eminence, esteem, fame, renown **2.** big name, celeb (*in~formal*), celebrity, dignitary, megastar (*infor~mal*), notable, personage, V.I.P., worthy

notable **1.** *adjective* celebrated, conspicuous, distinguished, eminent, evident, extraordi~nary, famous, manifest, marked, memorable, noteworthy, noticeable, notorious, outstanding, pre-eminent, pronounced, rare, remarkable, renowned, salient, striking, uncommon, un~usual, well-known **2.** *noun* big name, celeb (*informal*), celebrity, dignitary, megastar (*in~formal*), notability, personage, V.I.P., worthy
Antonyms anonymous, concealed, hidden, im~perceptible, obscure, unknown, vague

notably conspicuously, distinctly, especially, markedly, noticeably, outstandingly, particu~

larly, remarkably, seriously (*informal*), sig~ nally, strikingly, uncommonly

notation **1.** characters, code, script, signs, symbols, system **2.** jotting, notating, note, noting, record

notch *noun* **1.** cleft, cut, incision, indentation, mark, nick, score **2.** *informal* cut (*informal*), degree, grade, level, step *~verb* **3.** cut, indent, mark, nick, score, scratch

notch up achieve, gain, make, register, score

note *noun* **1.** annotation, comment, communi~ cation, epistle, gloss, jotting, letter, memo, memorandum, message, minute, record, re~ mark, reminder **2.** indication, mark, sign, symbol, token **3.** heed, notice, observation, re~ gard **4.** celebrity, character, consequence, dis~ tinction, eminence, fame, prestige, renown, reputation *~verb* **5.** denote, designate, indi~ cate, mark, mention, notice, observe, perceive, record, register, remark, see

notebook commonplace book, diary, exercise book, Filofax (*Trademark*), jotter, journal, memorandum book, notepad, record book

noted acclaimed, celebrated, conspicuous, dis~ tinguished, eminent, famous, illustrious, no~ table, notorious, prominent, recognized, re~ nowned, well-known

Antonyms infamous, obscure, undistin~ guished, unknown

notes impressions, jottings, outline, record, re~ port, sketch

noteworthy exceptional, extraordinary, impor~ tant, notable, outstanding, remarkable, sig~ nificant, unusual

Antonyms commonplace, insignificant, nor~ mal, ordinary, pedestrian, run-of-the-mill, un~ exceptional, unremarkable

nothing bagatelle, cipher, emptiness, naught, nobody, nonentity, nonexistence, nothingness, nought, nullity, trifle, void, zero

Nothing, like something, happens anywhere
Philip Larkin *I Remember, I Remember*

Nothing can be created out of nothing
Lucretius *De Rerum Natura*

Nothing will come of nothing
William Shakespeare *King Lear*

nothingness **1.** nihility, nonbeing, nonexist~ ence, nullity, oblivion **2.** insignificance, unimportance, worthlessness

notice *verb* **1.** behold (*archaic or literary*), de~ tect, discern, distinguish, heed, mark, mind, note, observe, perceive, remark, see, spot *~noun* **2.** cognizance, consideration, heed, in~ terest, note, observation, regard **3.** advice, an~ nouncement, communication, instruction, in~ telligence, intimation, news, notification, or~ der, warning **4.** advertisement, comment, criticism, poster, review, sign **5.** attention, ci~ vility, respect

Antonyms *verb* disregard, ignore, neglect, over-look *~noun* disregard, ignorance, neglect, omission, oversight

noticeable appreciable, blatant, bold, clear, conspicuous, distinct, evident, manifest, ob~ servable, obvious, perceptible, plain, salient, striking, unmistakable

notification advice, alert, announcement, dec~ laration, information, intelligence, message, notice, notifying, publication, statement, tell~ ing, warning

notify acquaint, advise, alert, announce, ap~ prise, declare, inform, publish, tell, warn

notion **1.** apprehension, belief, concept, concep~ tion, idea, impression, inkling, judgment, knowledge, opinion, sentiment, understanding, view **2.** caprice, desire, fancy, impulse, incli~ nation, whim, wish

notional abstract, conceptual, fanciful, hypo~ thetical, ideal, imagal (*Psychoanalysis*), im~ aginary, speculative, theoretical, unreal, vi~ sionary

Antonyms actual, factual, genuine, real

notoriety dishonour, disrepute, infamy, oblo~ quy, opprobrium, scandal

notorious **1.** dishonourable, disreputable, infa~ mous, opprobrious, scandalous **2.** blatant, fla~ grant, glaring, obvious, open, overt, patent, undisputed

notoriously **1.** dishonourably, disreputably, in~ famously, opprobriously, scandalously **2.** bla~ tantly, flagrantly, glaringly, notably, obvious~ ly, openly, overtly, particularly, patently, spectacularly, undisputedly

notwithstanding although, despite, (even) though, however, nevertheless, nonetheless, though, yet

nought naught, nil, nothing, nothingness, zero

nourish **1.** attend, feed, furnish, nurse, nur~ ture, supply, sustain, tend **2.** comfort, culti~ vate, encourage, foster, maintain, promote, support

nourishing alimentative, beneficial, healthful, health-giving, nutritious, nutritive, wholesome

nourishment aliment, diet, food, nutriment, nutrition, sustenance, tack (*informal*), viands, victuals, vittles (*obsolete or dialect*)

nouveau riche arriviste, new-rich, parvenu, upstart

novel **1.** *adjective* different, fresh, ground-breaking, innovative, left-field (*informal*), new, original, rare, singular, strange, uncommon, unfamiliar, unusual **2.** *noun* fiction, narrative, romance, story, tale

Antonyms *adjective* ancient, common, cus~ tomary, familiar, habitual, old-fashioned, or~ dinary, run-of-the-mill, traditional, usual

Yes - oh dear yes - the novel tells a story
E.M. Forster *Aspects of the Novel*
There are three rules for writing the novel. Unfortunately, no one knows what they are
W. Somerset Maugham
novel: a short story padded
Ambrose Bierce *The Devil's Dictionary*
If you try to nail anything down in the novel, either it kills the novel, or the novel gets up and walks away with the nail
D.H. Lawrence *Phoenix*

novelty 1. freshness, innovation, newness, oddity, originality, strangeness, surprise, unfamiliarity, uniqueness 2. bagatelle, bauble, curiosity, gadget, gewgaw, gimcrack, gimmick, knick-knack, memento, souvenir, trifle, trinket
A "new thinker", when studied closely, is merely a man who does not know what other people have thought
F.M. Colby

novice amateur, apprentice, beginner, convert, learner, neophyte, newcomer, novitiate, probationer, proselyte, pupil, trainee, tyro
Antonyms ace, doyen, expert, grandmaster, master, maven, old hand, professional, teacher

novitiate 1. apprenticeship, probation, training 2. novice

now 1. at once, immediately, instanter (*Law*), instantly, presently (*Scot. & U.S.*), promptly, straightaway 2. any more, at the moment, nowadays, these days 3. **now and then** *or* **again** at times, from time to time, infrequently, intermittently, occasionally, on and off, once in a while, on occasion, sometimes, sporadically

nowadays any more, at the moment, in this day and age, now, these days, today

noxious baneful (*archaic*), corrupting, deadly, deleterious, destructive, detrimental, foul, harmful, hurtful, injurious, insalubrious, noisome, pernicious, pestilential, poisonous, unhealthy, unwholesome
Antonyms innocuous, innoxious, inoffensive, nontoxic, not dangerous, safe, unobjectionable

nuance degree, distinction, gradation, graduation, hint, nicety, refinement, shade, shadow, subtlety, suggestion, suspicion, tinge, touch, trace

nub 1. core, crux, essence, gist, heart, kernel, nucleus, pith, point 2. bulge, bump, knob, knot, lump, node, protuberance, swelling

nubile marriageable, ripe (*informal*)

nucleus basis, centre, core, focus, heart, kernel, nub, pivot

nude *au naturel*, bare, buck naked (*slang*), disrobed, exposed, in one's birthday suit (*informal*), in the altogether (*informal*), in the bare scud (*slang*), in the buff (*informal*), in the raw (*informal*), naked, naked as the day one was born (*informal*), scuddy (*slang*), starkers (*informal*), stark-naked, stripped, unclad, unclothed, uncovered, undraped, undressed, without a stitch on (*informal*)
Antonyms attired, clothed, covered, dressed

nudge *verb* bump, dig, elbow, jog, poke, prod, push, shove, touch

nudity bareness, dishabille, nakedness, nudism, undress

nugatory 1. insignificant, trifling, trivial, valueless, worthless 2. bootless, futile, ineffectual, inoperative, invalid, null and void, unavailing, useless, vain

nugget chunk, clump, hunk, lump, mass, piece

nuisance annoyance, bore, bother, drag (*informal*), gall, hassle (*informal*), inconvenience, infliction, irritation, offence, pain in the arse (backside, butt, neck) (*taboo informal*), pest, plague, problem, trouble, vexation
Antonyms benefit, blessing, delight, happiness, joy, pleasure, satisfaction

null characterless, ineffectual, inoperative, invalid, nonexistent, null and void, powerless, useless, vain, valueless, void, worthless

nullify abolish, abrogate, annul, bring to naught, cancel, counteract, countervail, invalidate, negate, neutralize, obviate, quash, rebut, render null and void, repeal, rescind, revoke, veto, void
Antonyms authorize, confirm, endorse, ratify, validate

nullity characterlessness, ineffectualness, invalidity, nonexistence, powerlessness, uselessness, valuelessness, voidness, worthlessness

numb 1. *adjective* benumbed, dead, deadened, frozen, immobilized, insensible, insensitive, paralysed, stupefied, torpid, unfeeling 2. *verb* benumb, deaden, dull, freeze, immobilize, paralyse, stun, stupefy
Antonyms *adjective* feeling, responsive, sensitive, sentient

number *noun* 1. character, count, digit, figure, integer, numeral, sum, total, unit 2. aggregate, amount, collection, company, crowd, horde, many, multitude, quantity, throng 3. copy, edition, imprint, issue, printing *~verb* 4. account, add, calculate, compute, count, enumerate, include, reckon, tell, total
Antonyms *noun* insufficiency, lack, scantiness, scarcity, shortage, want *~verb* conjecture, guess, theorize

numbered categorized, contained, counted, designated, fixed, included, limited, limited in number, specified, totalled

numberless countless, endless, infinite, innumerable, multitudinous, myriad, unnumbered, untold

numbness deadness, dullness, insensibility, insensitivity, paralysis, stupefaction, torpor, unfeelingness

numeral character, cipher, digit, figure, integer, number, symbol

numerous abundant, copious, many, plentiful, profuse, several, thick on the ground
Antonyms few, not many, scarcely any

numinous awe-inspiring, divine, heavenly, holy, mysterious, religious, spiritual, supernatural

numskull, numbskull berk (*Brit. slang*), blockhead, bonehead (*slang*), buffoon, charlie (*Brit. informal*), clot (*Brit. informal*), coot, dickhead (*slang*), dickwit (*slang*), dimwit (*informal*), dipstick (*Brit. slang*), divvy (*slang*), dolt, dope (*informal*), dork (*slang*), dullard, dummy (*slang*), dunce, dunderhead, dweeb (*U.S. slang*), fathead (*informal*), fool, fuckwit (*taboo slang*), geek (*slang*), gobshite (*Irish taboo slang*), gonzo (*slang*), jerk (*slang, chiefly U.S. & Canad.*), lamebrain (*informal*), nerd *or* nurd (*slang*), nitwit (*informal*), numpty (*Scot. informal*), oaf, pillock (*Brit. slang*), plank (*Brit. slang*), plonker (*slang*), prat (*slang*), prick (*slang*), schmuck (*U.S. slang*), simpleton, thickhead, twit (*informal*), wally (*slang*)

nuncio ambassador, envoy, legate, messenger

nunnery abbey, cloister, convent, house, monastery

Get thee to a nunnery
William Shakespeare *Hamlet*

nuptial *adjective* bridal, conjugal, connubial, epithalamial (*poetic*), hymeneal (*poetic*), marital, matrimonial, wedded, wedding

nuptials espousal (*archaic*), marriage, matrimony, wedding

nurse *verb* **1.** care for, look after, minister to, tend, treat **2.** breast-feed, feed, nourish, nurture, suckle, wet-nurse **3.** *figurative* cherish, cultivate, encourage, foster, harbour, keep alive, preserve, promote, succour, support

nurture *noun* **1.** diet, food, nourishment **2.** development, discipline, education, instruction, rearing, training, upbringing *~verb* **3.** feed, nourish, nurse, support, sustain, tend **4.** bring up, cultivate, develop, discipline, educate, instruct, rear, school, train
Antonyms *verb* deprive, disregard, ignore, neglect, overlook

nut **1.** kernel, pip, seed, stone **2.** *slang* brain, head, mind, reason, senses **3.** *slang* crackpot (*informal*), crank (*informal*), eccentric, headbanger (*informal*), headcase (*informal*), loony (*slang*), lunatic, madman, maniac, nutcase (*slang*), nutter (*Brit. slang*), oddball (*informal*), psycho (*slang*), wacko (*slang*)

nutriment aliment, diet, food, foodstuff, nourishment, nutrition, subsistence, support, sustenance

nutrition food, nourishment, nutriment, sustenance

nutritious alimental, alimentative, beneficial, healthful, health-giving, invigorating, nourishing, nutritive, strengthening, wholesome

nuts as daft as a brush (*informal, chiefly Brit.*), bananas (*slang*), barking (*slang*), barking mad (*slang*), batty (*slang*), crazy (*informal*), demented, deranged, doolally (*slang*), eccentric, gonzo (*slang*), insane, irrational, loony (*slang*), loopy (*informal*), mad, not the full shilling (*informal*), nutty (*slang*), off one's trolley (*slang*), out to lunch (*informal*), psycho (*slang*), psychopathic, up the pole (*informal*), wacko *or* whacko (*informal*)

nuts and bolts basics, details, essentials, fundamentals, ins and outs, nitty-gritty (*informal*), practicalities

nuzzle burrow, cuddle, fondle, nestle, nudge, pet, snuggle

nymph damsel, dryad, girl, hamadryad, lass, maid, maiden, naiad, Oceanid (*Greek myth*), oread, sylph

O

oaf airhead (*slang*), berk (*Brit. slang*), blockhead, bonehead (*slang*), booby, brute, charlie (*Brit. informal*), clod, coot, dickhead (*slang*), dickwit (*slang*), dipstick (*Brit. slang*), divvy (*Brit. slang*), dolt, dork (*slang*), dullard, dummy (*slang*), dunce, dweeb (*U.S. slang*), fathead (*informal*), fool, fuckwit (*taboo slang*), galoot (*slang, chiefly U.S.*), gawk, geek (*slang*), gobshite (*Irish taboo slang*), gonzo (*slang*), goon, gorilla (*informal*), halfwit, idiot, imbecile, jerk (*slang, chiefly U.S. & Canad.*), lout, lummox (*informal*), moron, nerd *or* nurd (*slang*), nincompoop, nitwit (*informal*), numpty (*Scot. informal*), numskull *or* numbskull, pillock (*Brit. slang*), plank (*Brit. slang*), plonker (*slang*), prat (*slang*), sap (*slang*), schmuck (*U.S. slang*), simpleton, twit (*informal, chiefly Brit.*), wally (*slang*)
Antonyms brain (*informal*), egghead (*informal*), genius, intellect, smart aleck (*informal*), wiseacre

oafish blockish, Boeotian, boneheaded (*slang*), bovine, brutish, dense, dim, dim-witted (*informal*), doltish, dozy (*Brit. informal*), dull, dumb (*informal*), heavy, loutish, lubberly, lumbering, moronic, obtuse, slow on the uptake (*informal*), stupid, thick
Antonyms acute, brainy (*informal*), bright, clever, intelligent, quick-witted, sharp, smart

oasis *figurative* haven, island, refuge, resting place, retreat, sanctuary, sanctum

oath 1. affirmation, avowal, bond, pledge, promise, sworn statement, vow, word 2. blasphemy, curse, cuss (*informal*), expletive, imprecation, malediction, profanity, strong language, swearword

He who cheats with an oath acknowledges that he is afraid of his enemy, but that he thinks little of God
Plutarch *Lives: Lysander*

Oaths are but words, and words but wind
Samuel Butler *Hudibras*

Let your yea be yea; and your nay, nay
Bible: James

obdurate adamant, callous, dogged, firm, fixed, hard, hard-hearted, harsh, immovable, implacable, indurate (*rare*), inexorable, inflexible, iron, mulish, obstinate, perverse, pig-headed, proof against persuasion, relentless, stiff-necked, stubborn, unbending, unfeeling, unimpressible, unrelenting, unshakable, unyielding
Antonyms amenable, biddable, compliant, flexible, malleable, pliant, soft-hearted, submissive, tender, tractable, yielding

obedience accordance, acquiescence, agreement, assent, compliance, conformability, deference, docility, dutifulness, duty, observance, respect, reverence, submission, submissiveness, subservience, tractability
Antonyms defiance, disobedience, insubordination, obstinacy, recalcitrance, stubbornness, wilfulness

They who know the least obey the best
George Farquhar

obedient acquiescent, amenable, biddable, compliant, deferential, docile, duteous, dutiful, law-abiding, observant, regardful, respectful, submissive, subservient, tractable, under control, well-trained, yielding
Antonyms arrogant, contrary, disobedient, disrespectful, intractable, obdurate, obstinate, rebellious, stubborn, undutiful, ungovernable, unmanageable, unruly, wayward

obeisance bending of the knee, bow, curtsy *or* curtsey, deference, genuflection, homage, kowtow, respect, reverence, salaam, salutation

obelisk column, monolith, monument, needle, pillar, shaft

obese corpulent, Falstaffian, fat, fleshy, gross, heavy, outsize, overweight, paunchy, plump, podgy, portly, roly-poly, rotund, stout, tubby, well-upholstered (*informal*)
Antonyms emaciated, gaunt, lean, scraggy, skeletal, skinny, slender, thin

obesity beef (*informal*), bulk, corpulence, *embonpoint*, fatness, fleshiness, grossness, overweight, portliness, stoutness, tubbiness, weight problem
Antonyms emaciation, gauntness, leanness, skinniness, slenderness, thinness

obey 1. abide by, act upon, adhere to, be ruled by, carry out, comply, conform, discharge, do what is expected, embrace, execute, follow, fulfil, heed, keep, mind, observe, perform, respond, serve 2. bow to, come to heel, do what one is told, get into line, give in, give way, knuckle under (*informal*), submit, succumb,

surrender (to), take orders from, toe the line, yield
Antonyms contravene, defy, disobey, disregard, ignore, rebel, transgress, violate

obfuscate befog, bewilder, cloud, confuse, darken, muddy the waters, obscure, perplex

object[1] *noun* **1.** article, body, entity, fact, item, phenomenon, reality, thing **2.** aim, butt, focus, recipient, target, victim **3.** design, end, end in view, end purpose, goal, idea, intent, intention, motive, objective, point, purpose, reason, the why and wherefore

object[2] *verb* argue against, demur, draw the line (at something), expostulate, oppose, protest, raise objections, take exception
Antonyms accept, acquiesce, admire, agree, approve, assent, compliment, comply, concur, consent, like, relish, take on board, welcome

objection cavil, censure, counter-argument, demur, doubt, exception, niggle (*informal*), opposition, protest, remonstrance, scruple
Antonyms acceptance, affirmation, agreement, approbation, assent, concession, endorsement, support

objectionable abhorrent, beyond the pale, deplorable, disagreeable, dislikable *or* dislikeable, displeasing, distasteful, exceptionable, indecorous, insufferable, intolerable, noxious, obnoxious, offensive, regrettable, repugnant, unacceptable, undesirable, unpleasant, unseemly, unsociable
Antonyms acceptable, agreeable, desirable, likable *or* likeable, pleasant, pleasing, welcome

objective **1.** *adjective* detached, disinterested, dispassionate, equitable, even-handed, fair, impartial, impersonal, judicial, just, open-minded, unbiased, uncoloured, unemotional, uninvolved, unprejudiced **2.** *noun* aim, ambition, aspiration, design, end, end in view, goal, Holy Grail (*informal*), intention, mark, object, purpose, target
Antonyms (*sense 1*) abstract, biased, personal, prejudiced, subjective, theoretical, unfair, unjust

objectively disinterestedly, dispassionately, even-handedly, impartially, with an open mind, with objectivity *or* impartiality, without fear or favour

objectivity detachment, disinterest, disinterestedness, dispassion, equitableness, impartiality, impersonality
Antonyms bent, bias, partiality, predisposition, prejudice, subjectivity

obligation **1.** accountability, accountableness, burden, charge, compulsion, duty, liability, must, onus, pigeon (*informal*), requirement, responsibility, trust **2.** agreement, bond, commitment, contract, debt, engagement, promise, understanding **3.** **under an obligation** beholden, duty-bound, grateful, honour-bound, indebted, in (someone's) debt, obligated, obliged, owing a favour, thankful

obligatory binding, coercive, compulsory, *de rigueur*, enforced, essential, imperative, mandatory, necessary, required, requisite, unavoidable
Antonyms discretionary, elective, noncompulsory, optional, voluntary

oblige **1.** bind, coerce, compel, constrain, dragoon, force, impel, make, necessitate, obligate, railroad (*informal*), require **2.** accommodate, benefit, do (someone) a favour *or* a kindness, favour, gratify, indulge, please, put oneself out for, serve
Antonyms (*sense 2*) bother, discommode, disoblige, disrupt, inconvenience, put out, trouble

obliged **1.** appreciative, beholden, grateful, gratified, indebted, in (someone's) debt, thankful **2.** bound, compelled, forced, required, under an obligation, under compulsion, without any option

obliging accommodating, agreeable, amiable, civil, complaisant, considerate, cooperative, courteous, eager to please, friendly, good-natured, helpful, kind, polite, willing
Antonyms discourteous, disobliging, inconsiderate, rude, sullen, surly, unaccommodating, uncooperative, unhelpful, unobliging

oblique **1.** angled, aslant, at an angle, atilt, inclined, slanted, slanting, sloped, sloping, tilted **2.** backhanded, circuitous, circumlocutory, evasive, implied, indirect, roundabout, sidelong
Antonyms (*sense 2*) blunt, candid, direct, downright, forthright, frank, open, straightforward

obliquely **1.** aslant, aslope, at an angle, diagonally, slantwise **2.** circuitously, evasively, in a roundabout manner *or* way, indirectly, not in so many words

obliterate annihilate, blot out, blow sky-high, cancel, delete, destroy, destroy root and branch, efface, eradicate, erase, expunge, extirpate, root out, wipe from the face of the earth, wipe off the face of the earth, wipe out
Antonyms build, construct, create, establish, form, formulate, generate, make

obliteration annihilation, deletion, effacement, elimination, eradication, erasure, expunction, extirpation, wiping (blotting, rooting, sponging) out
Antonyms building, construction, creation, establishment, formation, generation, making

oblivion **1.** abeyance, disregard, forgetfulness, insensibility, neglect, obliviousness, unawareness, unconsciousness, (waters of) Lethe **2.** blackness, darkness, eclipse, extinction, limbo,

nothingness, obscurity, void
Antonyms (*sense 1*) awareness, consciousness, perception, realization, recognition, sensibility

oblivious blind, careless, deaf, disregardful, forgetful, heedless, ignorant, inattentive, insensible, neglectful, negligent, regardless, unaware, unconcerned, unconscious, unmindful, unobservant
Antonyms alert, attentive, aware, conscious, heedful, mindful, observant, watchful

obloquy 1. abuse, animadversion, aspersion, attack, bad press, blame, calumny, censure, character assassination, contumely, criticism, defamation, detraction, invective, opprobrium, reproach, slander, stick (*slang*), vilification 2. discredit, disfavour, disgrace, dishonour, humiliation, ignominy, ill fame, ill repute, infamy, odium, shame, stigma

obnoxious abhorrent, abominable, detestable, disagreeable, disgusting, dislikable *or* dislikeable, foul, hateable, hateful, horrid, insufferable, loathsome, nasty, nauseating, objectionable, obscene, odious, offensive, repellent, reprehensible, repugnant, repulsive, revolting, sickening, unpleasant
Antonyms agreeable, amiable, charming, congenial, delightful, likable *or* likeable, pleasant, pleasing

obscene 1. bawdy, blue, coarse, dirty, disgusting, Fescennine (*rare*), filthy, foul, gross, immodest, immoral, improper, impure, indecent, lewd, licentious, loose, offensive, pornographic, prurient, ribald, salacious, scabrous, shameless, smutty, suggestive, unchaste, unwholesome, X-rated (*informal*) 2. *figurative* atrocious, evil, heinous, loathsome, outrageous, shocking, sickening, vile, wicked
Antonyms (*sense 1*) chaste, decent, decorous, inoffensive, modest, proper, pure, refined, respectable, seemly

obscenity 1. bawdiness, blueness, coarseness, dirtiness, filthiness, foulness, grossness, immodesty, impurity, lewdness, licentiousness, pornography, prurience, salacity, smuttiness, suggestiveness, vileness 2. four-letter word, impropriety, indecency, indelicacy, profanity, smut, swearword, vulgarism 3. abomination, affront, atrocity, blight, evil, offence, outrage, vileness, wrong
Antonyms (*sense 1*) chastity, decency, decorum, delicacy, innocence, modesty, propriety, purity

obscure *adjective* 1. abstruse, ambiguous, arcane, clear as mud (*informal*), concealed, confusing, cryptic, deep, Delphic, doubtful, enigmatic, esoteric, hazy, hidden, incomprehensible, indefinite, intricate, involved, mysterious, occult, opaque, recondite, unclear, vague 2. blurred, clouded, cloudy, dim, dusky, faint, gloomy, indistinct, murky, obfuscated, shadowy, shady, sombre, tenebrous, unlit, veiled 3. humble, inconspicuous, inglorious, little-known, lowly, minor, nameless, out-of-the-way, remote, undistinguished, unheard-of, unhonoured, unimportant, unknown, unnoted, unseen, unsung *~verb* 4. conceal, cover, disguise, hide, muddy, obfuscate, screen, throw a veil over, veil 5. adumbrate, bedim, befog, block, block out, blur, cloak, cloud, darken, dim, dull, eclipse, mask, overshadow, shade, shroud
Antonyms *adjective* (*senses 1 & 2*) apparent, bright, clear, conspicuous, definite, distinct, evident, explicit, intelligible, lucid, manifest, obvious, plain, prominent, sharp, significant, straightforward, transparent, unmistakable, well-defined (*sense 3*) celebrated, distinguished, eminent, familiar, famous, illustrious, important, major, prominent, renowned, well-known, widely-known *~verb* brighten, clarify, disclose, explain, explicate, expose, interpret, reveal, show, uncover, unmask, unveil

obscurity 1. abstruseness, ambiguity, complexity, impenetrableness, incomprehensibility, intricacy, reconditeness, vagueness 2. darkness, dimness, dusk, duskiness, gloom, haze, haziness, indistinctness, murkiness, shadowiness, shadows 3. inconspicuousness, ingloriousness, insignificance, lowliness, namelessness, nonrecognition, unimportance
Antonyms (*sense 1*) clarity, clearness, comprehensibility, explicitness, lucidity, obviousness, transparency

obsequies burial, burial service, exequies, funeral, funeral rites, last offices

obsequious abject, cringing, deferential, fawning, flattering, grovelling, ingratiating, mealy-mouthed, menial, servile, slavish, smarmy (*Brit. informal*), submissive, sycophantic, toadying, unctuous

obsequiously abjectly, cringingly, deferentially, fawningly, ingratiatingly, on one's knees, servilely, slavishly, smarmily (*Brit. informal*), sycophantically, unctuously

observable apparent, appreciable, blatant, clear, detectable, discernible, evident, noticeable, obvious, open, patent, perceivable, perceptible, recognizable, visible

observance 1. adherence to, attention, carrying out, celebration, compliance, discharge, fulfilment, heeding, honouring, notice, observation, performance 2. ceremonial, ceremony, custom, fashion, form, formality, practice, rite, ritual, service, tradition
Antonyms (*sense 1*) disdain, disregard, evasion, heedlessness, inattention, neglect, nonobservance, omission, oversight

observant alert, attentive, eagle-eyed, heedful, mindful, obedient, perceptive, quick, sharp-

eyed, submissive, vigilant, watchful, wide-awake
Antonyms distracted, dreamy, heedless, inattentive, indifferent, negligent, preoccupied, unobservant, vague

observation **1.** attention, cognition, consideration, examination, experience, information, inspection, knowledge, monitoring, notice, review, scrutiny, study, surveillance, watching **2.** annotation, comment, finding, note, obiter dictum, opinion, pronouncement, reflection, remark, thought, utterance

observe **1.** detect, discern, discover, espy, note, notice, perceive, see, spot, witness **2.** behold (*archaic or literary*), check, check out (*informal*), clock (*Brit. slang*), contemplate, eyeball (*U.S. slang*), get a load of (*informal*), keep an eye on (*informal*), keep tabs on (*informal*), keep track of, keep under observation, look at, monitor, pay attention to, recce (*slang*), regard, scrutinize, study, survey, take a dekko at (*Brit. slang*), view, watch, watch like a hawk **3.** animadvert, comment, declare, mention, note, opine, remark, say, state **4.** abide by, adhere to, comply, conform to, follow, fulfil, heed, honour, keep, mind, obey, perform, respect **5.** celebrate, commemorate, keep, remember, solemnize
Antonyms (*sense 4*) disregard, ignore, miss, neglect, omit, overlook, violate

observer beholder, bystander, commentator, eyewitness, fly on the wall, looker-on, onlooker, spectator, spotter, viewer, watcher, witness

I am a camera with its shutter open, quite passive, recording, not thinking
Christopher Isherwood *Goodbye to Berlin*

obsess bedevil, be on one's mind, be uppermost in one's thoughts, consume, dominate, engross, grip, haunt, monopolize, plague, possess, preoccupy, prey on one's mind, rule, torment

obsessed beset, dominated, gripped, hag-ridden, haunted, having a one-track mind, hung up on (*slang*), immersed in, infatuated, in the grip of, preoccupied, troubled
Antonyms aloof, apathetic, detached, disinterested, impassive, indifferent, uncaring, unconcerned

obsession addiction, bee in one's bonnet (*informal*), complex, enthusiasm, fetish, fixation, hang-up (*informal*), *idée fixe*, infatuation, mania, phobia, preoccupation, ruling passion, thing (*informal*)

obsessive besetting, compulsive, consuming, fixed, gripping, haunting, tormenting, unforgettable

obsolescent ageing, declining, dying out, not with it (*informal*), on the decline, on the wane, on the way out, past its prime, waning

obsolete anachronistic, ancient, antediluvian, antiquated, antique, archaic, bygone, dated, *démodé*, discarded, disused, extinct, musty, old, old-fashioned, old hat, out, outmoded, out of date, out of fashion, out of the ark (*informal*), outworn, passé, past it, superannuated, *vieux jeu*
Antonyms à la mode, contemporary, current, fashionable, in, in vogue, modern, new, present day, trendy (*Brit. informal*), up-to-date

obstacle bar, barrier, block, check, difficulty, hindrance, hitch, hurdle, impediment, interference, interruption, obstruction, snag, stumbling block
Antonyms advantage, aid, asset, assistance, benefit, crutch, help, support

obstinacy doggedness, firmness, inflexibility, intransigence, mulishness, obduracy, perseverance, persistence, pertinacity, pig-headedness, resoluteness, stubbornness, tenacity, wilfulness
Antonyms compliance, cooperativeness, docility, flexibility, meekness, submissiveness, tractability

Obstinacy in a bad cause, is but constancy in a good
Thomas Browne *Religio Medici*

obstinate contumacious, determined, dogged, firm, headstrong, immovable, inflexible, intractable, intransigent, mulish, opinionated, persistent, pertinacious, perverse, pig-headed, recalcitrant, refractory, self-willed, steadfast, stiff-necked, strong-minded, stubborn, tenacious, unyielding, wilful
Antonyms amenable, biddable, complaisant, compliant, docile, flexible, irresolute, manageable, obedient, submissive, tractable, undecided, wavering

obstreperous boisterous, clamorous, disorderly, loud, noisy, out of control, out of hand, rackety, rambunctious (*informal*), rampaging, raucous, restive, riotous, rip-roaring (*informal*), roistering, roisterous, rough, rowdy, stroppy (*Brit. slang*), tempestuous, tumultuous, turbulent, uncontrolled, undisciplined, unmanageable, unruly, uproarious, vociferous, wild
Antonyms calm, controlled, disciplined, docile, gentle, orderly, peaceful, placid, quiet

obstruct arrest, bar, barricade, block, bring to a standstill, bung, check, choke, clog, cumber, curb, cut off, frustrate, get in the way of, hamper, hamstring, hide, hinder, hold up, impede, inhibit, interfere with, interrupt, mask, obscure, prevent, restrict, retard, shield, shut off, slow down, stop, thwart, trammel

Antonyms abet, advance, aid, assist, encourage, favour, further, help, promote, support

obstruction bar, barricade, barrier, block, blockage, check, difficulty, hazard, hindrance, impediment, obstacle, occlusion, snag, stop, stoppage, trammel
Antonyms aid, assistance, cooperation, encouragement, favour, furtherance, help, support

obstructive awkward, blocking, delaying, hindering, inhibiting, preventative, restrictive, stalling, uncooperative, unhelpful
Antonyms cooperative, encouraging, favourable, helpful, obliging, supportive

obtain **1.** achieve, acquire, attain, come by, earn, gain, get, get hold of, get one's hands on, land, procure, score (*slang*), secure **2.** be in force, be prevalent, be the case, exist, hold, prevail, stand
Antonyms (*sense 1*) forfeit, forgo, give up, hand over, lose, relinquish, renounce, surrender

obtainable achievable, at hand, attainable, available, on tap (*informal*), procurable, ready, realizable, to be had

obtrusive **1.** forward, importunate, interfering, intrusive, meddling, nosy, officious, prying, pushy (*informal*) **2.** blatant, noticeable, obvious, prominent, protruding, protuberant, sticking out
Antonyms (*sense 1*) bashful, decorous, diffident, modest, reserved, reticent, retiring, shy, unassuming (*sense 2*) concealed, covert, hidden, inconspicuous, low-key, muted, unnoticeable, unobtrusive

obtrusively blatantly, bluntly, boldly, crassly, importunately, obviously, officiously, pushily

obtuse **1.** boneheaded (*slang*), dead from the neck up (*informal*), dense, dopey (*informal*), dull, dull-witted, dumb (*informal*), heavy, imperceptive, insensitive, muttonheaded (*slang*), retarded, slow, slow on the uptake (*informal*), stolid, stupid, thick, thick-skinned, uncomprehending, unintelligent **2.** blunt, rounded
Antonyms (*sense 1*) astute, bright, clever, keen, quick, sensitive, sharp, shrewd, smart

obviate anticipate, avert, counter, counteract, do away with, preclude, prevent, remove, render unnecessary

obvious apparent, blatant, bold, clear, clear as a bell, conspicuous, cut-and-dried (*informal*), distinct, evident, indisputable, manifest, much in evidence, noticeable, open, open-and-shut, overt, palpable, patent, perceptible, plain, plain as the nose on your face (*informal*), pronounced, recognizable, right under one's nose (*informal*), salient, self-evident, self-explanatory, staring one in the face (*informal*), sticking out a mile (*informal*), straightforward, transparent, unconcealed, undeniable, undisguised, unmistakable, unsubtle, visible
Antonyms ambiguous, clear as mud (*informal*), concealed, dark, hidden, imperceptible, inconspicuous, indistinct, invisible, obscure, unapparent, unclear, vague

obviously certainly, clearly, distinctly, manifestly, needless to say, of course, palpably, patently, plainly, undeniably, unmistakably, unquestionably, without doubt

occasion *noun* **1.** chance, convenience, incident, moment, occurrence, opening, opportunity, time, window **2.** affair, celebration, event, experience, happening, occurrence **3.** call, cause, excuse, ground(s), inducement, influence, justification, motive, prompting, provocation, reason *~verb* **4.** bring about, cause, create, effect, elicit, engender, evoke, generate, give rise to, induce, influence, inspire, lead to, move, originate, persuade, produce, prompt, provoke

occasional casual, desultory, incidental, infrequent, intermittent, irregular, odd, rare, sporadic, uncommon
Antonyms constant, continual, customary, frequent, habitual, incessant, regular, routine, usual

occasionally at intervals, at times, (every) now and then, every so often, from time to time, irregularly, now and again, off and on, on and off, once in a while, on occasion, periodically, sometimes
Antonyms constantly, continually, continuously, frequently, habitually, often, regularly, routinely

occlude block, bung, choke, clog, close, fill, hinder, obstruct, plug, seal, shut, stop up

occult abstruse, arcane, cabbalistic, concealed, esoteric, hidden, invisible, magical, mysterious, mystic, mystical, obscure, preternatural, recondite, secret, supernatural, unknown, unrevealed, veiled
Antonyms apparent, blatant, evident, exposed, manifest, obvious, open, overt, plain, revealed, visible

occultism black magic, diabolism, magic, sorcery, supernaturalism, the black arts, witchcraft

occupancy habitation, holding, inhabitancy, occupation, possession, residence, tenancy, tenure, term, use

occupant addressee, denizen, holder, incumbent, indweller, inhabitant, inmate, lessee, occupier, resident, tenant, user

occupation **1.** activity, business, calling, craft, employment, job, line (of work), post, profession, pursuit, trade, vocation, walk of life, work **2.** control, holding, occupancy, posses~

sion, residence, tenancy, tenure, use **3.** conquest, foreign rule, invasion, seizure, subjugation

occupied **1.** busy, employed, engaged, hard at it (*informal*), tied up (*informal*), working **2.** engaged, full, in use, taken, unavailable **3.** full, inhabited, lived-in, peopled, settled, tenanted

Antonyms (*sense 3*) deserted, empty, tenantless, uninhabited, unoccupied, untenanted, vacant, void

occupy **1.** *often passive* absorb, amuse, busy, divert, employ, engage, engross, entertain, hold the attention of, immerse, interest, involve, keep busy *or* occupied, monopolize, preoccupy, take up, tie up **2.** be established in, be in residence in, dwell in, ensconce oneself in, establish oneself in, inhabit, live in, own, possess, reside in, stay in (*Scot.*), tenant **3.** cover, fill, hold, permeate, pervade, take up, use, utilize **4.** capture, garrison, hold, invade, keep, overrun, seize, take over, take possession of

Antonyms abandon, depart, desert, evacuate, quit, retreat, vacate, withdraw

occur **1.** arise, befall, betide, chance, come about, come off (*informal*), come to pass (*archaic*), crop up (*informal*), eventuate, happen, materialize, result, take place, turn up (*informal*) **2.** appear, be found, be met with, be present, develop, exist, manifest itself, obtain, show itself **3.** *with* **to** come to mind, come to one, cross one's mind, dawn on, enter one's head, spring to mind, strike one, suggest (offer, present) itself

occurrence **1.** adventure, affair, circumstance, episode, event, happening, incident, instance, proceeding, transaction **2.** appearance, development, existence, manifestation, materialization

odd **1.** abnormal, atypical, bizarre, curious, deviant, different, eccentric, exceptional, extraordinary, fantastic, freak, freakish, freaky (*slang*), funny, irregular, kinky (*informal*), left-field (*informal*), oddball (*informal*), off-the-wall (*slang*), outlandish, out of the ordinary, outré, peculiar, quaint, queer, rare, remarkable, rum (*Brit. slang*), singular, strange, uncanny, uncommon, unconventional, unusual, wacko (*slang*), weird, whimsical **2.** casual, fragmentary, incidental, irregular, miscellaneous, occasional, periodic, random, seasonal, sundry, varied, various **3.** leftover, lone, remaining, single, solitary, spare, surplus, unconsumed, uneven, unmatched, unpaired

Antonyms common, customary, even, familiar, habitual, matched, natural, normal, ordinary, paired, permanent, regular, steady, typical, unexceptional, unremarkable, usual

oddity **1.** abnormality, anomaly, eccentricity, freak, idiosyncrasy, irregularity, kink, peculiarity, phenomenon, quirk, rarity **2.** card (*informal*), crank (*informal*), fish out of water, maverick, misfit, nut (*slang*), oddball (*informal*), odd bird (*informal*), odd fish (*Brit. informal*), rara avis, screwball (*slang, chiefly U.S. & Canad.*), wacko (*slang*), weirdo *or* weirdie (*informal*) **3.** abnormality, bizarreness, eccentricity, extraordinariness, freakishness, incongruity, oddness, outlandishness, peculiarity, queerness, singularity, strangeness, unconventionality, unnaturalness

odd man out exception, freak, maverick, misfit, nonconformist, outsider, square peg in a round hole (*informal*)

oddment bit, butt, end, end of a line, fag end, fragment, leftover, off cut, remnant, scrap, shred, sliver, snippet, stub, tail end

odds **1.** advantage, allowance, edge, lead, superiority **2.** balance, chances, likelihood, probability **3.** *Brit.* difference, disparity, dissimilarity, distinction **4.** **at odds** at daggers drawn, at loggerheads, at sixes and sevens, at variance, in conflict, in disagreement, in opposition to, not in keeping, on bad terms, out of line

odds and ends bits, bits and pieces, debris, leavings, litter, oddments, remnants, rubbish, scraps, sundry *or* miscellaneous items

odious abhorrent, abominable, detestable, disgusting, execrable, foul, hateful, horrible, horrid, loathsome, obnoxious, obscene, offensive, repellent, repugnant, repulsive, revolting, unpleasant, vile, yucky *or* yukky (*slang*)

Antonyms agreeable, charming, congenial, delightful, enchanting, enjoyable, pleasant, pleasing, winsome

odium abhorrence, antipathy, censure, condemnation, detestation, disapprobation, disapproval, discredit, disfavour, disgrace, dishonour, dislike, disrepute, execration, hatred, infamy, obloquy, opprobrium, reprobation, shame

odorous aromatic, balmy, fragrant, odoriferous, perfumed, redolent, scented, sweet-smelling

odour **1.** aroma, bouquet, essence, fragrance, niff (*Brit. slang*), perfume, redolence, scent, smell, stench, stink **2.** air, atmosphere, aura, emanation, flavour, quality, spirit

odyssey crusade, journey, peregrination, pilgrimage, quest, trek, voyage

off *adjective* **1.** absent, cancelled, finished, gone, inoperative, postponed, unavailable **2.** bad, below par, disappointing, disheartening, displeasing, low-quality, mortifying, poor, quiet, slack, substandard, unrewarding, unsatisfactory **3.** bad, decomposed, high, mouldy, rancid, rotten, sour, turned *~adverb* **4.** apart, aside, away, elsewhere, out

off and on (every) now and again, every once in a while, from time to time, intermittently, now and then, occasionally, on and off, sometimes, sporadically

offbeat bizarre, Bohemian, eccentric, far-out (*slang*), freaky (*slang*), idiosyncratic, kinky (*informal*), left-field (*informal*), novel, oddball (*informal*), off-the-wall (*slang*), *outré*, rum (*Brit. slang*), strange, uncommon, unconventional, unorthodox, unusual, wacko (*slang*), way-out (*informal*), weird

Antonyms common, conventional, normal, ordinary, orthodox, run-of-the-mill, stereotyped, traditional, unoriginal, usual

off colour green about the gills, ill, not up to par, off form, out of sorts, peaky, peely-wally (*Scot.*), poorly (*informal*), queasy, run down, sick, under par, under the weather (*informal*), unwell, washed out

offence 1. breach of conduct, crime, delinquency, fault, lapse, misdeed, misdemeanour, peccadillo, sin, transgression, trespass, wrong, wrongdoing **2.** affront, displeasure, harm, hurt, indignity, injury, injustice, insult, outrage, put-down (*slang*), slight, snub **3.** anger, annoyance, displeasure, hard feelings, huff, indignation, ire (*literary*), needle (*informal*), pique, resentment, umbrage, wounded feelings, wrath **4. take offence** be disgruntled, be offended, get riled, go into a huff, resent, take the huff, take the needle (*informal*), take umbrage

offend 1. affront, aggravate (*informal*), annoy, cut to the quick, disgruntle, displease, fret, gall, get (someone's) goat (*slang*), give offence, hurt (someone's) feelings, insult, irritate, miff (*informal*), nark (*Brit., Austral., & N.Z. slang*), outrage, pain, pique, piss one off (*taboo slang*), provoke, put down, put (someone's) back up, put (someone's) nose out of joint, rile, slight, snub, tread on (someone's) toes (*informal*), upset, vex, wound **2.** be disagreeable to, disgust, gross out (*U.S. slang*), make (someone) sick, nauseate, repel, repulse, sicken, turn (someone) off (*informal*)

Antonyms (*sense 1*) appease, assuage, conciliate, delight, mollify, placate, please, soothe

offended affronted, disgruntled, displeased, huffy, in a huff, miffed (*informal*), outraged, pained, piqued, put out (*informal*), resentful, smarting, stung, upset

offender criminal, crook, culprit, delinquent, lawbreaker, malefactor, miscreant, sinner, transgressor, villain, wrongdoer

offensive *adjective* **1.** abusive, annoying, detestable, discourteous, displeasing, disrespectful, embarrassing, impertinent, insolent, insulting, irritating, objectionable, rude, uncivil, unmannerly **2.** abominable, detestable, disagreeable, disgusting, grisly, loathsome, nasty, nauseating, noisome, obnoxious, odious, repellent, revolting, sickening, unpalatable, unpleasant, unsavoury, vile, yucky *or* yukky (*slang*) **3.** aggressive, attacking, invading *~noun* **4.** attack, campaign, drive, onslaught, push (*informal*) **5. on the offensive** advancing, aggressive, attacking, invading, invasive, on the warpath (*informal*)

Antonyms *adjective* agreeable, attractive, captivating, charming, civil, conciliatory, courteous, defensive, deferential, delightful, pleasant, polite, respectful *~noun* defensive

offer *verb* **1.** bid, extend, give, hold out, proffer, put on the market, put under the hammer, put up for sale, tender **2.** afford, furnish, make available, place at (someone's) disposal, present, provide, purvey, show **3.** advance, extend, move, propose, put forth, put forward, submit, suggest **4.** be at (someone's) service, come forward, offer one's services, volunteer *~noun* **5.** attempt, bid, endeavour, essay, overture, proposal, proposition, submission, suggestion, tender

Antonyms (*sense 1*) recant, refuse, retract, revoke, take back, withdraw, withhold

offering contribution, donation, gift, hand-out, oblation (*in religious contexts*), present, sacrifice, subscription, widow's mite

off form below par, having lost one's touch, not at one's best, not up to scratch (*informal*), on a bad day, out of practice, out of training, unpractised

offhand 1. *adjective* abrupt, aloof, brusque, careless, casual, cavalier, couldn't-care-less, curt, glib, informal, offhanded, perfunctory, take-it-or-leave-it (*informal*), unceremonious, unconcerned, uninterested **2.** *adverb* ad lib, extempore, impromptu, just like that (*informal*), off the cuff (*informal*), off the top of one's head (*informal*), without preparation

Antonyms attentive, careful, grave, intent, planned, premeditated, prepared, responsible, serious, thoughtful

office 1. appointment, business, capacity, charge, commission, duty, employment, function, obligation, occupation, place, post, responsibility, role, service, situation, station, trust, work **2.** *plural* advocacy, aegis, aid, auspices, backing, favour, help, intercession, intervention, mediation, patronage, recommendation, referral, support, word

officer agent, appointee, bureaucrat, dignitary, executive, functionary, office-holder, official, public servant, representative

official 1. *adjective* accredited, authentic, authoritative, authorized, bona fide, certified, endorsed, ex cathedra, ex officio, formal, legitimate, licensed, proper, sanctioned, signed

and sealed, straight from the horse's mouth (*informal*) **2.** *noun* agent, bureaucrat, executive, functionary, office bearer, officer, representative
Antonyms (*sense 1*) casual, doubtful, dubious, informal, unauthorized, unofficial, unreliable

officiate chair, conduct, emcee (*informal*), manage, oversee, preside, serve, superintend

officious bustling, dictatorial, forward, impertinent, inquisitive, interfering, intrusive, meddlesome, meddling, mischievous, obtrusive, opinionated, overbusy, overzealous, pragmatical (*rare*), pushy (*informal*), self-important
Antonyms aloof, detached, indifferent, reserved, reticent, retiring, shy, taciturn, unforthcoming, withdrawn

offing in the offing close at hand, coming up, hovering, imminent, in prospect, in the immediate future, in the wings, on the horizon, on the way, upcoming

off key discordant, dissonant, inharmonious, jarring, out of keeping, out of tune

off-load disburden, discharge, dump, get rid of, jettison, lighten, shift, take off, transfer, unburden, unload, unship

off-putting daunting, discomfiting, disconcerting, discouraging, dismaying, dispiriting, disturbing, formidable, frustrating, intimidating, unnerving, unsettling, upsetting

offset 1. *verb* balance out, cancel out, compensate for, counteract, counterbalance, counterpoise, countervail, make up for, neutralize **2.** *noun* balance, compensation, counterbalance, counterweight, equipoise

offshoot adjunct, appendage, branch, by-product, development, limb, outgrowth, spin-off, sprout

offspring brood, child, children, descendant, descendants, family, fry, heir, heirs, issue, kids (*informal*), progeny, scion, seed (*chiefly biblical*), spawn, successor, successors, young
Antonyms ancestor, begetter, forebear, forefather, forerunner, parent, predecessor, procreator, progenitor

often again and again, frequently, generally, many a time, much, oft (*archaic or poetic*), oftentimes (*archaic*), ofttimes (*archaic*), over and over again, repeatedly, time after time, time and again
Antonyms hardly ever, infrequently, irregularly, never, now and then, occasionally, rarely, scarcely, seldom

ogle eye up (*informal*), gawp at (*Brit. slang*), give the glad eye (*informal*), give the once-over (*informal*), lech *or* letch after (*informal*), leer, make sheep's eyes at (*informal*)

ogre bogey, bogeyman, bugbear, demon, devil, giant, monster, spectre

oil *verb* grease, lubricate

oily 1. fatty, greasy, oiled, oleaginous, smeary, swimming **2.** flattering, fulsome, glib, hypocritical, obsequious, plausible, servile, smarmy (*Brit. informal*), smooth, unctuous

ointment balm, cerate, cream, embrocation, emollient, liniment, lotion, salve, unguent

O.K., okay 1. *adjective* acceptable, accurate, adequate, all right, approved, convenient, correct, fair, fine, good, in order, middling, not bad (*informal*), passable, permitted, satisfactory, so-so (*informal*), tolerable, up to scratch (*informal*) **2.** *noun* agreement, approbation, approval, assent, authorization, consent, endorsement, go-ahead (*informal*), green light, permission, sanction, say-so (*informal*), seal of approval **3.** *verb* agree to, approve, authorize, consent to, endorse, entitle, give one's consent to, give the go-ahead (green light, thumbs up) to (*informal*), pass, rubber-stamp (*informal*), sanction, say yes to **4.** *interjection* agreed, all right, right, roger, very good, very well, yes
Antonyms (*sense 1*) displeasing, inaccurate, inadequate, incorrect, not up to scratch (*informal*), poor, unacceptable, unsatisfactory, unsuitable

old 1. advanced in years, aged, ancient, decrepit, elderly, full of years, getting on, grey, grey-haired, grizzled, hoary, mature, over the hill (*informal*), past it, past one's prime, patriarchal, senescent, senile, venerable **2.** antediluvian, antiquated, antique, cast-off, cobwebby, crumbling, dated, decayed, done, hackneyed, obsolete, old-fashioned, outdated, outmoded, out of date, out of the ark (*informal*), passé, stale, superannuated, timeworn, unfashionable, unoriginal, worn-out **3.** aboriginal, antique, archaic, bygone, early, immemorial, of old, of yore, olden (*archaic*), original, primeval, primitive, primordial, pristine, remote **4.** age-old, experienced, familiar, hardened, long-established, of long standing, practised, skilled, time-honoured, traditional, versed, veteran, vintage **5.** earlier, erstwhile, ex-, former, one-time, previous, quondam
Antonyms current, fashionable, immature, juvenile, modern, modish, new, novel, recent, up-to-date, young, youthful

No man is ever so old but he thinks he can live another year
Cicero *De Senectute*

There's many a good tune played on an old fiddle

You can't teach an old dog new tricks

old age advancing years, age, agedness, Anno Domini (*informal*), autumn *or* evening of one's life, declining years, dotage, eld (*archaic*), senescence, senility, Third Age

Antonyms adolescence, childhood, early life, immaturity, juvenescence, young days, youth

I am grown peaceful as old age tonight.
I regret a little, would change still less
Robert Browning *Andrea del Sarto*

Do not go gentle into that good night,
Old age should burn and rave at close of day;
Rage, rage against the dying of the light
Dylan Thomas *Do not go gentle into that good night*

Old age is the most unexpected of all the things that happen to a man
Leon Trotsky *Diary in Exile*

sans teeth, sans eyes, sans taste, sans everything
William Shakespeare *As You Like It*

If I'd known I was gonna live this long, I'd have taken better care of myself
Eubie Blake

old-fashioned ancient, antiquated, archaic, behind the times, cobwebby, corny (*slang*), dated, dead, *démodé*, fusty, musty, not with it (*informal*), obsolescent, obsolete, oldfangled, (old-)fogyish, old hat, old-time, outdated, outmoded, out of date, out of style, out of the ark (*informal*), passé, past, square (*informal*), superannuated, unfashionable
Antonyms chic, contemporary, current, fashionable, happening (*informal*), modern, modish, trendy (*Brit. informal*), up-to-date, voguish, with it (*informal*)

old hand expert, old soldier, old-timer, one of the old school, past master, veteran

old man elder, elder statesman, father, gaffer, grandfather, greybeard, O.A.P. (*Brit.*), old codger (*informal*), old stager, oldster (*informal*), old-timer (*U.S.*), papa (*old-fashioned informal*), patriarch, senior citizen

old-time ancient, antique, bygone, former, old-fashioned, past, vintage

old womanish finicky, fussy, niggly, niminy-piminy, old-maidish (*informal*), overcautious, overparticular, pernickety (*informal*), prim, prudish, strait-laced, timid, timorous

old-world archaic, ceremonious, chivalrous, courtly, gallant, old-fashioned, picturesque, quaint, traditional

oleaginous adipose, fat, fatty, greasy, oily, sebaceous, unguinous (*obsolete*)

Olympian elevated, exalted, glorious, godlike, lofty, majestic, rarefied, splendid, sublime

omen augury, foreboding, foretoken, indication, portent, premonition, presage, prognostic, prognostication, sign, straw in the wind, warning, writing on the wall

omen: a sign that something will happen if nothing happens
Ambrose Bierce *The Devil's Dictionary*

ominous baleful, bodeful, dark, fateful, forbidding, foreboding, inauspicious, menacing, minatory, portentous, premonitory, sinister, threatening, unpromising, unpropitious
Antonyms auspicious, encouraging, favourable, promising, propitious

omission default, exclusion, failure, forgetfulness, gap, lack, leaving out, neglect, noninclusion, oversight
Antonyms addition, inclusion, incorporation, insertion

omit disregard, drop, eliminate, exclude, fail, forget, give (something) a miss (*informal*), leave out, leave (something) undone, let (something) slide, miss (out), neglect, overlook, pass over, skip
Antonyms add, enter, include, incorporate, insert, put in

omnipotence divine right, invincibility, mastery, sovereignty, supremacy, supreme power, undisputed sway
Antonyms frailty, impotence, inability, inferiority, powerlessness, vulnerability, weakness

omnipotent all-powerful, almighty, supreme
Antonyms feeble, frail, impotent, incapable, inferior, powerless, vulnerable, weak

omniscient all-knowing, all-seeing, all-wise

on and off by fits and starts, discontinuously, (every) now and again, fitfully, from time to time, intermittently, now and then, off and on, on occasion, sometimes, spasmodically

once 1. at one time, formerly, in the old days, in the past, in times gone by, in times past, long ago, once upon a time, previously 2. **at once a.** directly, forthwith, immediately, instantly, now, right away, straight away, straightway (*archaic*), this (very) minute, without delay, without hesitation **b.** at *or* in one go (*informal*), at the same time, simultaneously, together 3. **once and for all** conclusively, decisively, finally, for all time, for good, for the last time, permanently, positively, with finality 4. **once in a while** at intervals, at times, every now and then, from time to time, now and again, occasionally, once in a blue moon (*informal*), on occasion, sometimes

oncoming advancing, approaching, forthcoming, imminent, impending, looming, onrushing, upcoming

one-horse backwoods, inferior, minor, obscure, petty, quiet, sleepy, slow, small, small-time (*informal*), tinpot (*Brit. informal*), unimportant

onerous backbreaking, burdensome, crushing, demanding, difficult, exacting, exhausting, exigent, formidable, grave, hard, heavy, laborious, oppressive, responsible, taxing, weighty
Antonyms cushy (*informal*), easy, effortless,

facile, light, painless, simple, trifling, undemanding, unexacting, untaxing

one-sided biased, coloured, discriminatory, inequitable, lopsided, partial, partisan, prejudiced, unequal, unfair, unjust
Antonyms equal, equitable, fair, impartial, just, unbiased, uncoloured, unprejudiced

one-time erstwhile, ex-, former, late, previous, quondam, sometime

one-track fanatical, fixated, monomaniacal, obsessed, single-track

ongoing advancing, continuous, current, developing, evolving, extant, growing, in progress, progressing, successful, unfinished, unfolding

onlooker bystander, eyewitness, looker-on, observer, spectator, viewer, watcher, witness

only 1. *adverb* at most, barely, exclusively, just, merely, purely, simply 2. *adjective* exclusive, individual, lone, one and only, single, sole, solitary, unique

onomatopoeic echoic, imitative, onomatopoetic

onrush charge, flood, flow, onset, onslaught, push, rush, stampede, stream, surge

onset 1. assault, attack, charge, onrush, onslaught 2. beginning, inception, kick-off (*informal*), outbreak, start
Antonyms (*sense 2*) conclusion, culmination, end, ending, finish, outcome, termination, wind-up

onslaught assault, attack, blitz, charge, offensive, onrush, onset
Antonyms defensive, escape, flight, recession, retreat, rout, stampede, withdrawal

onus burden, liability, load, obligation, responsibility, task
Antonyms easement, exemption, exoneration, liberation, pardon, release, relief, remission

onward, onwards *adverb* ahead, beyond, forth, forward, in front, on

ooze 1. *verb* bleed, discharge, drain, dribble, drip, drop, emit, escape, exude, filter, leach, leak, overflow with, percolate, seep, strain, sweat, weep 2. *noun* alluvium, gloop (*informal*), mire, muck, mud, silt, slime, slob (*Irish*), sludge

oozy dewy, dripping, miry, moist, mucky, slimy, sloppy, sludgy, sweaty, weeping

opacity cloudiness, density, dullness, filminess, impermeability, milkiness, murkiness, obscurity, opaqueness

opalescent iridescent, lustrous, nacreous, opaline, pearly, prismatic, rainbow-hued, shot

opaque 1. clouded, cloudy, dim, dull, filmy, hazy, impenetrable, lustreless, muddied, muddy, murky, obfuscated, turbid 2. abstruse, baffling, cryptic, difficult, enigmatic, incomprehensible, obscure, unclear, unfathomable, unintelligible
Antonyms bright, clear, crystal clear, limpid, lucid, pellucid, transparent, transpicuous

open *adjective* 1. agape, ajar, expanded, extended, gaping, revealed, spread out, unbarred, unclosed, uncovered, unfastened, unfolded, unfurled, unlocked, unobstructed, unsealed, yawning 2. airy, bare, clear, exposed, extensive, free, navigable, not built-up, passable, rolling, spacious, sweeping, uncluttered, uncrowded, unenclosed, unfenced, unsheltered, wide, wide-open 3. accessible, available, free, general, nondiscriminatory, public, unconditional, unengaged, unoccupied, unqualified, unrestricted, up for grabs (*informal*), vacant 4. apparent, avowed, barefaced, blatant, bold, clear, conspicuous, downright, evident, flagrant, frank, manifest, noticeable, obvious, overt, plain, unconcealed, undisguised, visible 5. arguable, debatable, moot, undecided, unresolved, unsettled, up in the air, yet to be decided 6. disinterested, free, impartial, objective, receptive, unbiased, uncommitted, unprejudiced 7. *with* **to** an easy target for, at the mercy of, defenceless against, disposed, exposed, liable, susceptible, vulnerable 8. above board, artless, candid, fair, frank, guileless, honest, ingenuous, innocent, natural, sincere, transparent, unreserved 9. filigree, fretted, holey, honeycombed, lacy, loose, openwork, porous, spongy 10. bounteous, bountiful, generous, liberal, munificent, prodigal 11. exposed, undefended, unfortified, unprotected *~verb* 12. begin, begin business, commence, get *or* start the ball rolling, inaugurate, initiate, kick off (*informal*), launch, put up one's plate, set in motion, set up shop, start 13. clear, crack, throw wide, unbar, unblock, unclose, uncork, uncover, undo, unfasten, unlock, unseal, untie, unwrap 14. expand, spread (out), unfold, unfurl, unroll 15. come apart, crack, rupture, separate, split 16. disclose, divulge, exhibit, explain, lay bare, pour out, show, uncover
Antonyms *adjective* (*senses 1 & 2*) bounded, closed, concealed, confined, covered, crowded, enclosed, fastened, limited, locked, obstructed, restricted, sealed, shut (*senses 3 & 4*) covert, disguised, hidden, inaccessible, private, protected, restricted, secret, veiled (*sense 6*) biased, partial, prejudiced (*senses 7 & 11*) defended, protected (*sense 8*) artful, cunning, introverted, reserved, secretive, sly, withdrawn *~verb* (*sense 12*) close, conclude, end, finish, terminate (*sense 13*) block, close, fasten, lock, obstruct, seal, shut (*sense 14*) fold

open-air alfresco, outdoor

open-and-shut foregone, noncontroversial, obvious, simple, straightforward

open-handed bountiful, free, generous, lavish, liberal, munificent, prodigal, unstinting
Antonyms avaricious, close-fisted, grasping, grudging, mean, miserly, parsimonious, penny-pinching (*informal*), stingy, tight-fisted

opening *noun* **1.** aperture, breach, break, chink, cleft, crack, fissure, gap, hole, interstice, orifice, perforation, rent, rupture, slot, space, split, vent **2.** break (*informal*), chance, look-in (*informal*), occasion, opportunity, place, vacancy, window **3.** beginning, birth, commencement, dawn, inauguration, inception, initiation, kickoff (*informal*), launch, launching, onset, opening move, outset, overture, start *~adjective* **4.** beginning, commencing, early, first, inaugural, initial, initiatory, introductory, maiden, primary
Antonyms (*sense 1*) blockage, cessation, closing, closure, obstruction, occlusion, plug, seal, stoppage (*sense 3*) close, completion, conclusion, culmination, ending, finale, finish, termination, winding up (*informal*)

openly **1.** candidly, face to face, forthrightly, frankly, overtly, plainly, straight from the shoulder (*informal*), unhesitatingly, unreservedly **2.** blatantly, brazenly, flagrantly, in full view, in public, publicly, shamelessly, unabashedly, unashamedly, wantonly, without pretence
Antonyms covertly, furtively, in camera, privately, quietly, secretly, slyly, surreptitiously

open-minded broad, broad-minded, catholic, dispassionate, enlightened, free, impartial, liberal, reasonable, receptive, tolerant, unbiased, undogmatic, unprejudiced
Antonyms assertive, biased, bigoted, dogmatic, intolerant, narrow-minded, opinionated, pig-headed, prejudiced, uncompromising

openness artlessness, candidness, candour *or* (*U.S.*) candor, frankness, freedom, freeness, guilelessness, honesty, ingenuousness, naturalness, open-heartedness, sincerity *or* sincereness, transparency, unreservedness

I will wear my heart upon my sleeve
William Shakespeare *Othello*

operate **1.** act, be in action, be in business, function, go, perform, run, work **2.** be in charge of, handle, manage, manoeuvre, use, work **3.** perform surgery
Antonyms (*sense 1*) break down, conk out (*informal*), cut out (*informal*), fail, falter, halt, seize up, stall, stop

operation **1.** action, affair, course, exercise, motion, movement, performance, procedure, process, use, working **2. in operation** effective, functioning, going, in action, in business, in force, operative **3.** activity, agency, effect, effort, force, influence, instrumentality, manipulation **4.** affair, business, deal, enterprise, proceeding, transaction, undertaking **5.** assault, campaign, exercise, manoeuvre **6.** surgery

operational functional, going, in working order, operative, prepared, ready, up and running, usable, viable, workable, working
Antonyms broken, ineffective, inoperative, kaput (*informal*), nonfunctional, on the blink (*slang*), out of order

operative *adjective* **1.** active, current, effective, efficient, functional, functioning, in business, in force, in operation, operational, serviceable, standing, workable **2.** crucial, important, indicative, influential, key, relevant, significant *~noun* **3.** artisan, employee, hand, labourer, machinist, mechanic, worker
Antonyms (*sense 1*) ineffective, inefficient, inoperative, nonfunctional, powerless, unusable, unworkable

operator **1.** conductor, driver, handler, mechanic, operative, practitioner, skilled employee, technician, worker **2.** administrator, contractor, dealer, director, manager, speculator, trader **3.** *informal* Machiavellian, machinator, manipulator, mover, shyster (*slang, chiefly U.S.*), smart aleck (*informal*), wheeler-dealer (*informal*), wirepuller, worker

opiate anodyne, bromide, downer (*slang*), drug, narcotic, nepenthe, pacifier, sedative, soporific, tranquillizer

opine believe, conceive, conclude, conjecture, declare, give as one's opinion, judge, presume, say, suggest, suppose, surmise, think, venture, volunteer, ween (*poetic*)

opinion **1.** assessment, belief, conception, conjecture, estimation, feeling, idea, impression, judgment, mind, notion, persuasion, point of view, sentiment, theory, view **2. be of the opinion** be convinced, believe, be under the impression, conclude, consider, hold, judge, reckon, suppose, surmise, think **3. matter of opinion** debatable point, matter of judgment, moot point, open question, open to debate, up to the individual

We can never be sure that the opinion we are endeavouring to stifle is a false opinion; and if we were sure, stifling it would be an evil still
John Stuart Mill *On Liberty*

There are as many opinions as there are people; each has his own correct way
Terence *Phormio*

New opinions are always suspected, and usually opposed, without any other reason but because they are not already common
John Locke *Essay concerning Human Understanding*

A man can brave opinion, a woman must submit to it
Mme de Staël *Delphine*

Where an opinion is general, it is usually correct
Jane Austen *Mansfield Park*

When a man gives his opinion, he's a man. When a woman gives her opinion, she's a bitch
Bette Davis

They that approve a private opinion, call it opinion; but they that mislike it, heresy; and yet heresy signifies no more than private opinion
Thomas Hobbes *Leviathan*

Opinion in good men is but knowledge in the making
John Milton *Areopagitica*

opinionated adamant, biased, bigoted, bull-headed, cocksure, dictatorial, doctrinaire, dog~matic, inflexible, obdurate, obstinate, over~bearing, pig-headed, prejudiced, self-assertive, single-minded, stubborn, uncompromising
Antonyms broad-minded, compliant, compro~mising, dispassionate, flexible, open-minded, receptive, tolerant, unbiased, unbigoted, un~prejudiced

opponent adversary, antagonist, challenger, competitor, contestant, disputant, dissentient, enemy, foe, opposer, rival, the opposition
Antonyms accomplice, ally, associate, col~league, friend, helper, mate, supporter

opportune advantageous, appropriate, apt, auspicious, convenient, falling into one's lap, favourable, felicitous, fit, fitting, fortunate, happy, lucky, proper, propitious, seasonable, suitable, timely, well-timed
Antonyms inappropriate, inconvenient, inop~portune, unfavourable, unfortunate, unsuit~able, untimely

opportunism expediency, exploitation, Machiavellianism, making hay while the sun shines (*informal*), pragmatism, realism, *Real~politik*, striking while the iron is hot (*infor~mal*), trimming, unscrupulousness

There is a tide in the affairs of men,
Which, taken at the flood, leads on to fortune
William Shakespeare *Julius Caesar*

opportunity break (*informal*), chance, conveni~ence, hour, look-in (*informal*), moment, occa~sion, opening, scope, time, window

When the cat's away, the mice will play

Never look a gift horse in the mouth

When one door shuts, another door opens

Strike while the iron is hot

There is no time like the present

oppose 1. bar, block, check, combat, confront, contradict, counter, counterattack, defy, face, fight, fly in the face of, hinder, obstruct, pre~vent, resist, set one's face against, speak against, stand up to, take a stand against, take issue with, take on, thwart, withstand 2. compare, contrast, counterbalance, match, pit *or* set against, play off
Antonyms advance, advocate, aid, back, de~fend, espouse, help, promote, support

opposed against, antagonistic, anti (*informal*), antipathetic, antithetical, at daggers drawn, averse, clashing, conflicting, contra (*informal*), contrary, dissentient, hostile, incompatible, inimical, in opposition, opposing, opposite

opposing antagonistic, antipathetic, clashing, combatant, conflicting, contrary, enemy, hos~tile, incompatible, irreconcilable, opposed, op~posite, rival, warring

opposite *adjective* 1. corresponding, facing, fronting 2. adverse, antagonistic, antithetical, conflicting, contradictory, contrary, contrasted, diametrically opposed, different, differing, di~verse, hostile, inconsistent, inimical, irrecon~cilable, opposed, poles apart, reverse, unlike *~noun* 3. antithesis, contradiction, contrary, converse, inverse, reverse, the other extreme, the other side of the coin (*informal*)
Antonyms (*sense 2*) alike, consistent, corre~sponding, identical, like, matching, same, similar, uniform

Opposites attract

opposition 1. antagonism, competition, contra~riety, counteraction, disapproval, hostility, ob~struction, obstructiveness, prevention, resist~ance, unfriendliness 2. antagonist, competi~tion, foe, opponent, other side, rival
Antonyms (*sense 1*) agreement, approval, as~sent, collaboration, concurrence, cooperation, correspondence, friendliness, responsiveness

oppress 1. afflict, burden, depress, dispirit, harass, lie *or* weigh heavy upon, sadden, take the heart out of, torment, vex 2. abuse, crush, harry, maltreat, overpower, overwhelm, per~secute, rule with an iron hand, subdue, sub~jugate, suppress, trample underfoot, tyrannize over, wrong
Antonyms deliver, emancipate, free, liberate, loose, release, set free, unburden

oppressed abused, browbeaten, burdened, dis~advantaged, downtrodden, enslaved, harassed, henpecked, maltreated, misused, prostrate, slave, subject, troubled, tyrannized, under~privileged
Antonyms advantaged, exalted, favoured, honoured, liberated, privileged

oppression abuse, brutality, calamity, cruelty, hardship, harshness, injury, injustice, iron hand, maltreatment, misery, persecution, se~verity, subjection, suffering, tyranny
Antonyms benevolence, clemency, compassion, goodness, humaneness, justice, kindness, mercy, sympathy, tenderness

Oppression makes the wise man mad
Robert Browning *Luria*

oppressive 1. brutal, burdensome, cruel, des~potic, grinding, harsh, heavy, inhuman, oner~

ous, overbearing, overwhelming, repressive, severe, tyrannical, unjust **2.** airless, close, heavy, muggy, overpowering, stifling, stuffy, suffocating, sultry, torrid
Antonyms (*sense 1*) encouraging, gentle, humane, just, lenient, merciful, propitious, soft

oppressor autocrat, bully, despot, harrier, intimidator, iron hand, persecutor, scourge, slave-driver, taskmaster, tormentor, tyrant

opprobrious **1.** abusive, calumniatory, contemptuous, contumelious, damaging, defamatory, hateful, insolent, insulting, invective, offensive, scandalous, scurrilous, vitriolic, vituperative **2.** abominable, contemptible, despicable, dishonourable, disreputable, hateful, ignominious, infamous, notorious, reprehensible, shameful

opprobrium calumny, censure, contumely, discredit, disfavour, disgrace, dishonour, disrepute, ignominy, ill repute, infamy, obloquy, odium, reproach, scurrility, shame, slur, stigma

oppugn argue, assail, attack, call into question, cast doubt on, combat, dispute, oppose, resist, withstand

opt (for) choose, decide (on), elect, exercise one's discretion (in favour of), go for, make a selection, plump for, prefer
Antonyms decide against, dismiss, eliminate, exclude, preclude, reject, rule out, turn down

optimism

To travel hopefully is a better thing than to arrive, and the true success is to labour
Robert Louis Stevenson *Virginibus Puerisque*

an optimist is a guy
that has never had
much experience
Don Marquis *archy and mehitabel*

Every cloud has a silver lining

optimistic **1.** disposed to take a favourable view, idealistic, seen through rose-coloured spectacles, Utopian **2.** assured, bright, buoyant, buoyed up, can-do (*informal*), cheerful, confident, encouraged, expectant, hopeful, looking on the bright side, positive, sanguine
Antonyms bleak, cynical, despairing, despondent, downhearted, fatalistic, gloomy, glum, hopeless, pessimistic, resigned

optimum *adjective* A1 *or* A-one (*informal*), best, choicest, flawless, highest, ideal, most favourable *or* advantageous, optimal, peak, perfect, superlative
Antonyms inferior, least, lowest, minimal, poorest, worst

option alternative, choice, election, preference, selection

optional discretionary, elective, extra, noncompulsory, open, possible, up to the individual, voluntary
Antonyms compulsory, de rigeur, mandatory, obligatory, required

opulence **1.** affluence, big bucks (*informal, chiefly U.S.*), big money, easy circumstances, Easy Street (*informal*), fortune, lavishness, luxuriance, luxury, megabucks (*U.S. & Canad. slang*), plenty, pretty penny (*informal*), prosperity, riches, richness, sumptuousness, tidy sum (*informal*), wad (*U.S. & Canad. slang*), wealth **2.** abundance, copiousness, cornucopia, fullness, profusion, richness, superabundance
Antonyms dearth, impecuniousness, indigence, lack, paucity, penury, poverty, privation, scantiness, scarcity, want

opulent **1.** affluent, lavish, luxurious, moneyed, prosperous, rich, sumptuous, wealthy, well-heeled (*informal*), well-off, well-to-do **2.** abundant, copious, lavish, luxuriant, plentiful, profuse, prolific
Antonyms (*sense 1*) broke (*informal*), destitute, down and out, indigent, moneyless, needy, on the rocks, penurious, poor, poverty-stricken

opus brainchild, composition, creation, *oeuvre*, piece, production, work

oracle **1.** augur, Cassandra, prophet, seer, sibyl, soothsayer **2.** answer, augury, divination, divine utterance, prediction, prognostication, prophecy, revelation, vision **3.** adviser, authority, guru, high priest, horse's mouth, mastermind, mentor, pundit, source, wizard

oracular **1.** auspicious, bodeful, foreboding, haruspical, mantic, ominous, portentous, prescient, prophetic, pythonic, sibylline, vatic (*rare*) **2.** authoritative, dictatorial, dogmatic, grave, positive, sage, significant, venerable, wise **3.** ambiguous, arcane, cryptic, Delphic, equivocal, mysterious, obscure, two-edged

oral spoken, verbal, viva voce, vocal

orate declaim, discourse, hold forth, make a speech, pontificate, speak, speechify, talk

oration address, declamation, discourse, harangue, homily, lecture, speech, spiel (*informal*)

orator Cicero, declaimer, lecturer, public speaker, rhetorician, speaker, spellbinder, spieler (*informal*)

oratorical bombastic, Ciceronian, declamatory, eloquent, grandiloquent, high-flown, magniloquent, rhetorical, silver-tongued, sonorous

oratory declamation, elocution, eloquence, grandiloquence, public speaking, rhetoric, speechifying, speech-making, spieling (*informal*)

orb ball, circle, globe, ring, round, sphere

orbit *noun* **1.** circle, circumgyration, course, cycle, ellipse, path, revolution, rotation, track, trajectory **2.** *figurative* ambit, compass, course, domain, influence, range, reach, scope, sphere, sphere of influence, sweep *~verb* **3.** circle, circumnavigate, encircle, revolve around

orchestrate 1. arrange, score **2.** arrange, concert, coordinate, integrate, organize, present, put together, set up, stage-manage

ordain 1. anoint, appoint, call, consecrate, destine, elect, frock, invest, nominate **2.** fate, foreordain, intend, predestine, predetermine **3.** decree, demand, dictate, enact, enjoin, establish, fix, lay down, legislate, order, prescribe, pronounce, rule, set, will

ordeal affliction, agony, anguish, baptism of fire, hardship, nightmare, suffering, test, torture, trial, tribulation(s), trouble(s)
Antonyms bliss, delight, elation, enjoyment, gladness, happiness, joy, pleasure

order *noun* **1.** arrangement, harmony, method, neatness, orderliness, organization, pattern, plan, propriety, regularity, symmetry, system, tidiness **2.** arrangement, array, categorization, classification, codification, disposal, disposition, grouping, layout, line, line-up, ordering, placement, progression, sequence, series, setup (*informal*), structure, succession **3. in order a.** arranged, in sequence, neat, orderly, shipshape, tidy **b.** acceptable, appropriate, called for, correct, fitting, O.K. *or* okay (*informal*), right, suitable **4. out of order a.** broken, broken-down, buggered (*slang, chiefly Brit.*), bust (*informal*), gone haywire (*informal*), gone phut (*informal*), in disrepair, inoperative, kaput (*informal*), nonfunctional, not working, on the blink (*slang*), on the fritz (*U.S. slang*), out of commission, U.S. (*informal*), wonky (*Brit. slang*) **b.** improper, indecorous, not cricket (*informal*), not done, not on (*informal*), out of place, out of turn, uncalled-for, wrong **5.** calm, control, discipline, law, law and order, peace, quiet, tranquillity **6.** caste, class, degree, grade, hierarchy, pecking order (*informal*), position, rank, status **7.** breed, cast, class, family, genre, genus, ilk, kind, sort, species, subclass, taxonomic group, tribe, type **8.** behest, canon, command, decree, dictate, direction, directive, injunction, instruction, law, mandate, ordinance, precept, regulation, rule, say-so (*informal*), stipulation **9.** application, booking, commission, request, requisition, reservation **10.** association, brotherhood, community, company, fraternity, guild, league, lodge, organization, sect, sisterhood, society, sodality, union *~verb* **11.** adjure, bid, charge, command, decree, demand, direct, enact, enjoin, instruct, ordain, prescribe, require **12.** apply for, authorize, book, call for, contract for, demand, engage, prescribe, request, reserve, send away for **13.** adjust, align, arrange, catalogue, class, classify, conduct, control, dispose, group, lay out, manage, marshal, neaten, organize, put to rights, regulate, sequence, set in order, sort out, systematize, tabulate, tidy
Antonyms *noun (senses 1 & 2)* chaos, clutter, confusion, disarray, disorder, jumble, mess, muddle, pandemonium, shambles *~verb (sense 13)* clutter, confuse, disarrange, disorder, disturb, jumble up, mess up, mix up, muddle, scramble
A place for everything, and everything in its place
There's a time and a place for everything

orderly *adjective* **1.** businesslike, in apple-pie order (*informal*), in order, methodical, neat, regular, scientific, shipshape, systematic, systematized, tidy, trim, well-organized, well-regulated **2.** controlled, decorous, disciplined, law-abiding, nonviolent, peaceable, quiet, restrained, well-behaved
Antonyms chaotic, disorderly, disorganized, higgledy-piggledy (*informal*), messy, riotous, sloppy, uncontrolled, undisciplined, unsystematic

ordinance 1. canon, command, decree, dictum, edict, enactment, fiat, law, order, precept, regulation, rule, ruling, statute **2.** ceremony, institution, observance, practice, rite, ritual, sacrament, usage

ordinarily as a rule, commonly, customarily, generally, habitually, in general, in the general run (of things), in the usual way, normally, usually
Antonyms hardly ever, infrequently, occasionally, rarely, scarcely, seldom, uncommonly

ordinary 1. accustomed, banal, common, customary, established, everyday, habitual, humdrum, mundane, normal, prevailing, quotidian, regular, routine, settled, standard, stock, typical, usual, wonted **2.** common or garden (*informal*), conventional, down-to-earth, familiar, homespun, household, humble, modest, plain, prosaic, run-of-the-mill, simple, unmemorable, unpretentious, unremarkable, workaday **3.** average, commonplace, dime-a-dozen (*informal*), fair, indifferent, inferior, mean, mediocre, no great shakes (*informal*), pedestrian, second-rate, stereotyped, undistinguished, unexceptional, uninspired, unremarkable **4. out of the ordinary** atypical, distinguished, exceptional, exciting, extraordinary, high-calibre, imaginative, important, impressive, inspired, noteworthy, outstanding, rare, remarkable, significant, special, striking, superior, uncommon, unusual
Antonyms consequential, distinguished, exceptional, extraordinary, important, impressive, inspired, notable, novel, outstanding, rare, significant, superior, uncommon, unconventional, unique, unusual

ordnance arms, artillery, big guns, cannon, guns, materiel, munitions, weapons

organ 1. device, implement, instrument, tool 2. element, member, part, process, structure, unit 3. agency, channel, forum, journal, means, medium, mouthpiece, newspaper, paper, periodical, publication, vehicle, voice

organic 1. animate, biological, biotic, live, living, natural 2. integrated, methodical, ordered, organized, structured, systematic 3. anatomical, constitutional, fundamental, immanent, inherent, innate, integral, structural

organism animal, being, body, creature, entity, living thing, structure

organization 1. assembling, assembly, construction, coordination, direction, disposal, formation, forming, formulation, making, management, methodology, organizing, planning, regulation, running, standardization, structuring 2. arrangement, chemistry, composition, configuration, conformation, constitution, design, format, framework, grouping, make-up, method, organism, pattern, plan, structure, system, unity, whole 3. association, body, combine, company, concern, confederation, consortium, corporation, federation, group, institution, league, outfit (*informal*), syndicate

organize arrange, be responsible for, catalogue, classify, codify, constitute, construct, coordinate, dispose, establish, form, frame, get going, get together, group, lay the foundations of, lick into shape, look after, marshal, pigeonhole, put in order, put together, run, see to (*informal*), set up, shape, straighten out, systematize, tabulate, take care of
Antonyms confuse, derange, disorganize, disrupt, jumble, mix up, muddle, scramble, upset

orgasm climax, coming (*taboo slang*), pleasure, the big O (*informal*)

orgiastic abandoned, bacchanalian, bacchic, debauched, depraved, Dionysian, dissolute, frenetic, riotous, Saturnalian, wanton, wild

orgy 1. bacchanal, bacchanalia, carousal, carouse, debauch, revel, revelry, Saturnalia 2. binge (*informal*), bout, excess, indulgence, overindulgence, splurge, spree, surfeit

orient *verb* acclimatize, adapt, adjust, align, familiarize, find one's feet (*informal*), get one's bearings, get the lie of the land, orientate

orientation 1. bearings, coordination, direction, location, position, sense of direction 2. acclimatization, adaptation, adjustment, assimilation, breaking in, familiarization, introduction, settling in

orifice aperture, cleft, hole, mouth, opening, perforation, pore, rent, vent

origin 1. base, basis, cause, derivation, *fons et origo*, font (*poetic*), fount, fountain, fountainhead, occasion, provenance, root, roots, source, spring, wellspring 2. beginning, birth, commencement, creation, dawning, early stages, emergence, foundation, genesis, inauguration, inception, launch, origination, outset, start 3. ancestry, beginnings, birth, descent, extraction, family, heritage, lineage, parentage, pedigree, stirps, stock
Antonyms conclusion, culmination, death, end, expiry, finale, finish, outcome, termination

original *adjective* 1. aboriginal, autochthonous, commencing, earliest, early, embryonic, first, infant, initial, introductory, opening, primary, primitive, primordial, pristine, rudimentary, starting 2. creative, fertile, fresh, ground-breaking, imaginative, ingenious, innovative, innovatory, inventive, new, novel, resourceful, seminal, unconventional, unprecedented, untried, unusual 3. archetypal, authentic, first, first-hand, genuine, master, primary, prototypical *~noun* 4. archetype, master, model, paradigm, pattern, precedent, prototype, standard, type 5. anomaly, card (*informal*), case (*informal*), character, eccentric, nonconformist, nut (*slang*), oddball (*informal*), oddity, queer fish (*Brit. informal*), wacko (*slang*), weirdo *or* weirdie (*informal*)
Antonyms *adjective* antiquated, banal, borrowed, commonplace, conventional, copied, familiar, final, last, latest, normal, old, old-fashioned, ordinary, secondary, stale, standard, stock, traditional, typical, unimaginative, unoriginal, usual *~noun* copy, imitation, replica, reproduction

originality boldness, break with tradition, cleverness, creativeness, creative spirit, creativity, daring, freshness, imagination, imaginativeness, individuality, ingenuity, innovation, innovativeness, inventiveness, new ideas, newness, novelty, resourcefulness, unconventionality, unorthodoxy
Antonyms conformity, conventionality, imitativeness, normality, orthodoxy, regularity, staleness, traditionalism

He was dull in a new way, and that made many people think him great

Dr. Johnson

originally at first, at the outset, at the start, by origin (birth, derivation), first, initially, in the beginning, in the first place, to begin with

originate 1. arise, be born, begin, come, derive, emanate, emerge, flow, issue, proceed, result, rise, spring, start, stem 2. bring about, conceive, create, develop, discover, evolve, form, formulate, generate, give birth to, inaugurate, initiate, institute, introduce, invent, launch, pioneer, produce, set in motion, set up
Antonyms cease, conclude, culminate, end, expire, finish, terminate, wind up

originator architect, author, creator, father,

founder, generator, innovator, inventor, maker, mother, pioneer, prime mover

ornament *noun* **1.** accessory, adornment, bauble, decoration, embellishment, festoon, frill, furbelow, garnish, gewgaw, knick-knack, trimming, trinket **2.** flower, honour, jewel, leading light, pride, treasure *~verb* **3.** adorn, beautify, bedizen (*archaic*), brighten, deck, decorate, dress up, embellish, festoon, garnish, gild, grace, prettify, prink, trim

ornamental attractive, beautifying, decorative, embellishing, for show, showy

ornamentation adornment, decoration, elaboration, embellishment, embroidery, frills, ornateness

ornate aureate, baroque, beautiful, bedecked, busy, convoluted, decorated, elaborate, elegant, fancy, florid, flowery, fussy, high-wrought, ornamented, overelaborate, rococo
Antonyms austere, bare, basic, ordinary, plain, severe, simple, spartan, stark, subdued, unadorned, unfussy

orthodox accepted, approved, conformist, conventional, correct, customary, doctrinal, established, kosher (*informal*), official, received, sound, traditional, true, well-established
Antonyms eccentric, heretical, left-field (*informal*), liberal, nonconformist, novel, off-the-wall (*slang*), original, radical, unconventional, unorthodox, unusual

orthodox: an ox wearing the popular religious yoke

Ambrose Bierce *The Devil's Dictionary*

orthodoxy authenticity, authoritativeness, authority, conformism, conformity, conventionality, devotion, devoutness, faithfulness, inflexibility, received wisdom, soundness, traditionalism
Antonyms flexibility, heresy, heterodoxy, impiety, nonconformism, nonconformity, unconventionality

oscillate fluctuate, seesaw, sway, swing, vacillate, vary, vibrate, waver
Antonyms commit oneself, decide, determine, purpose, resolve, settle

oscillation fluctuation, instability, seesawing, swing, vacillation, variation, wavering

ossified bony, fixed, fossilized, frozen, hardened, indurated (*rare*), inflexible, petrified, rigid, rigidified, solid

ossify fossilize, freeze, harden, indurate (*rare*), petrify, solidify, stiffen

ostensible alleged, apparent, avowed, exhibited, manifest, outward, plausible, pretended, professed, purported, seeming, so-called, specious, superficial, supposed

ostensibly apparently, for the ostensible purpose of, on the face of it, on the surface, professedly, seemingly, supposedly, to all intents and purposes

ostentation affectation, boasting, display, exhibitionism, flamboyance, flashiness, flaunting, flourish, pageantry, parade, pomp, pretension, pretentiousness, show, showiness, showing off (*informal*), swank (*informal*), vaunting, window-dressing
Antonyms humility, inconspicuousness, modesty, plainness, reserve, simplicity, unpretentiousness

ostentatious boastful, brash, conspicuous, crass, dashing, extravagant, flamboyant, flash (*informal*), flashy, flaunted, gaudy, loud, obtrusive, pompous, pretentious, showy, swanky (*informal*), vain, vulgar
Antonyms conservative, inconspicuous, low-key, modest, plain, reserved, simple, sombre

ostracism avoidance, banishment, boycott, cold-shouldering, exclusion, exile, expulsion, isolation, rejection
Antonyms acceptance, admission, approval, inclusion, invitation, reception, welcome

ostracize avoid, banish, blackball, blacklist, boycott, cast out, cold-shoulder, exclude, excommunicate, exile, expatriate, expel, give (someone) the cold shoulder, reject, send to Coventry, shun, snub
Antonyms accept, admit, approve, embrace, greet, include, invite, receive, welcome

other *adjective* **1.** added, additional, alternative, auxiliary, extra, further, more, spare, supplementary **2.** contrasting, different, dissimilar, distinct, diverse, remaining, separate, unrelated, variant

otherwise *adverb* **1.** if not, or else, or then **2.** any other way, contrarily, differently

ounce atom, crumb, drop, grain, iota, particle, scrap, shred, speck, trace, whit

oust depose, disinherit, dislodge, displace, dispossess, eject, evict, expel, relegate, throw out, topple, turn out, unseat

out *adjective* **1.** impossible, not allowed, not on (*informal*), ruled out, unacceptable **2.** abroad, absent, away, elsewhere, gone, not at home, outside **3.** antiquated, behind the times, dated, dead, *démodé*, old-fashioned, old hat, passé, square (*informal*), unfashionable **4.** at an end, cold, dead, doused, ended, exhausted, expired, extinguished, finished, used up
Antonyms (*sense 3*) à la mode, fashionable, in, in fashion, latest, modern, trendy (*Brit. informal*), up-to-date, with it (*informal*)

out-and-out absolute, arrant, complete, consummate, deep-dyed (*usually derogatory*), downright, dyed-in-the-wool, outright, perfect, thoroughgoing, total, unmitigated, unqualified, utter

outbreak burst, epidemic, eruption, explosion, flare-up, flash, outburst, rash, spasm, upsurge

outburst access, attack, discharge, eruption, explosion, fit of temper, flare-up, gush, outbreak, outpouring, paroxysm, spasm, storm, surge

outcast *noun* castaway, derelict, displaced person, exile, leper, pariah, *persona non grata*, refugee, reprobate, untouchable, vagabond, wretch

outclass be a cut above (*informal*), beat, eclipse, exceed, excel, leave *or* put in the shade, leave standing (*informal*), outdistance, outdo, outrank, outshine, outstrip, overshadow, run rings around (*informal*), surpass

outcome aftereffect, aftermath, conclusion, consequence, end, end result, issue, payoff (*informal*), result, sequel, upshot

outcry clamour, commotion, complaint, cry, exclamation, howl, hue and cry, hullaballoo, noise, outburst, protest, scream, screech, uproar, yell

outdated antiquated, antique, archaic, behind the times, *démodé*, obsolete, old-fashioned, outmoded, out of date, out of style, out of the ark (*informal*), passé, unfashionable

Antonyms à la mode, all the rage, contemporary, current, fashionable, in vogue, modern, modish, stylish, trendy (*Brit. informal*), up-to-date, with it (*informal*)

outdistance leave behind, leave standing (*informal*), lose, outrun, outstrip, shake off

outdo beat, be one up on, best, eclipse, exceed, excel, get the better of, go one better than (*informal*), outclass, outdistance, outfox, outjockey, outmanoeuvre, outshine, outsmart (*informal*), overcome, run rings around (*informal*), score points off, surpass, top, transcend

outdoor alfresco, open-air, out-of-door(s), outside

Antonyms indoor, inside, interior, within

outer exposed, exterior, external, outlying, outside, outward, peripheral, remote, superficial, surface

Antonyms central, closer, inner, inside, interior, internal, inward, nearer

outface beard, brave, confront, defy, look straight in the eye, outstare, square up to, stare down, stare out (of countenance)

outfit *noun* **1.** accoutrements, clothes, costume, ensemble, garb, gear (*informal*), get-up (*informal*), kit, rigout (*informal*), schmutter (*slang*), suit, threads (*slang*), togs (*informal*), trappings **2.** *informal* clique, company, corps, coterie, crew, firm, *galère*, group, organization, set, setup (*informal*), squad, team, unit *~verb* **3.** accoutre, appoint, equip, fit out, furnish, kit out, provision, stock, supply, turn out

outfitter clothier, costumier, couturier, dressmaker, haberdasher (*U.S.*), modiste, tailor

outflow discharge, drainage, ebb, effluence, efflux, effusion, emanation, emergence, gush, issue, jet, outfall, outpouring, rush, spout

outgoing **1.** departing, ex-, former, last, leaving, past, retiring, withdrawing **2.** approachable, communicative, cordial, demonstrative, easy, expansive, extrovert, friendly, genial, gregarious, informal, open, sociable, sympathetic, unreserved, warm

Antonyms (*sense 1*) arriving, entering, incoming (*sense 2*) austere, cold, indifferent, reserved, retiring, withdrawn

outgoings costs, expenditure, expenses, outlay, overheads

outgrowth **1.** bulge, excrescence, node, offshoot, outcrop, process, projection, protuberance, shoot, sprout **2.** by-product, consequence, derivative, development, emergence, issue, product, result, spin-off, yield

outing excursion, expedition, jaunt, pleasure trip, spin (*informal*), trip

outlandish alien, barbarous, bizarre, eccentric, exotic, fantastic, far-out (*slang*), foreign, freakish, grotesque, left-field (*informal*), *outré*, preposterous, queer, strange, unheard-of, weird

Antonyms banal, commonplace, everyday, familiar, humdrum, mundane, normal, ordinary, usual, well-known

outlast endure beyond, outlive, outstay, outwear, survive

outlaw **1.** *noun* bandit, brigand, desperado, fugitive, highwayman, marauder, outcast, pariah, robber **2.** *verb* ban, banish, bar, condemn, disallow, embargo, exclude, forbid, interdict, make illegal, prohibit, proscribe, put a price on (someone's) head

Antonyms (*sense 2*) allow, approve, authorize, consent, endorse, legalise, permit, sanction, support

outlay *noun* cost, disbursement, expenditure, expenses, investment, outgoings, spending

outlet **1.** avenue, channel, duct, egress, exit, means of expression, opening, orifice, release, safety valve, vent, way out **2.** market, shop, store

outline *noun* **1.** draft, drawing, frame, framework, layout, lineament(s), plan, rough, skeleton, sketch, tracing **2.** bare facts, main features, recapitulation, résumé, rough idea, rundown, summary, synopsis, thumbnail sketch **3.** configuration, contour, delineation, figure, form, profile, shape, silhouette *~verb* **4.** adumbrate, delineate, draft, plan, rough out, sketch (in), summarize, trace

outlive come through, endure beyond, live through, outlast, survive

outlook 1. angle, attitude, frame of mind, per~ spective, point of view, slant, standpoint, viewpoint, views 2. expectations, forecast, fu~ ture, prospect 3. aspect, panorama, prospect, scene, view, vista

outlying backwoods, distant, far-flung, in the middle of nowhere, outer, out-of-the-way, pe~ ripheral, provincial, remote

outmanoeuvre circumvent, get the better of, outdo, outflank, outfox, outgeneral, outjockey, outsmart (*informal*), outwit, run rings round (*informal*), steal a march on (*informal*)

outmoded anachronistic, antediluvian, anti~ quated, antique, archaic, behind the times, bygone, dated, *démodé*, fossilized, obsolescent, obsolete, olden (*archaic*), oldfangled, old-fashioned, old-time, out, out of date, out of style, out of the ark (*informal*), outworn, pas~ sé, square (*informal*), superannuated, super~ seded, unfashionable, unusable
Antonyms all the rage, fashionable, fresh, in vogue, latest, modern, modish, new, recent, usable

out of date antiquated, archaic, dated, dis~ carded, elapsed, expired, extinct, invalid, lapsed, obsolete, old-fashioned, outmoded, out of the ark (*informal*), outworn, passé, stale, superannuated, superseded, unfashionable
Antonyms contemporary, current, fashionable, in, new, now (*informal*), trendy (*Brit. infor~ mal*), up to date, valid

out-of-the-way 1. distant, far-flung, inacces~ sible, isolated, lonely, obscure, off the beaten track, outlying, remote, secluded, unfrequent~ ed 2. abnormal, curious, exceptional, extraor~ dinary, odd, outlandish, out of the ordinary, peculiar, strange, uncommon, unusual
Antonyms (*sense 1*) accessible, close, conveni~ ent, frequented, handy, near, nearby, proxi~ mate, reachable, within sniffing distance (*in~ formal*)

out of work idle, jobless, laid off, on the dole (*Brit.*), out of a job, redundant, unemployed

outpouring cascade, debouchment, deluge, ef~ fluence, efflux, effusion, emanation, flow, flux, issue, outflow, spate, spurt, stream, torrent

output achievement, manufacture, outturn (*rare*), product, production, productivity, yield

outrage *noun* 1. atrocity, barbarism, enormity, evil, inhumanity 2. abuse, affront, desecration, indignity, injury, insult, offence, profanation, rape, ravishing, sacrilege, shock, violation, violence 3. anger, fury, hurt, indignation, re~ sentment, shock, wrath *~verb* 4. affront, in~ cense, infuriate, madden, make one's blood boil, offend, scandalize, shock 5. abuse, defile, desecrate, injure, insult, maltreat, rape, rav~ age, ravish, violate

outrageous 1. abominable, atrocious, barbaric, beastly, egregious, flagrant, heinous, horrible, infamous, inhuman, iniquitous, nefarious, scandalous, shocking, unspeakable, villainous, violent, wicked 2. disgraceful, excessive, exor~ bitant, extravagant, immoderate, offensive, O.T.T. (*slang*), over the top (*slang*), preposter~ ous, scandalous, shocking, steep (*informal*), unreasonable
Antonyms equitable, fair, just, mild, minor, moderate, reasonable, tolerable, trivial

outré bizarre, eccentric, extravagant, fantastic, freakish, freaky (*slang*), grotesque, indecorous, kinky (*informal*), left-field (*informal*), odd, off-the-wall (*slang*), outlandish, rum (*Brit. slang*), unconventional, way-out (*informal*), weird

outrider advance guard, advance man, attend~ ant, bodyguard, escort, guard, harbinger, her~ ald, precursor, scout, squire

outright *adjective* 1. absolute, arrant, complete, consummate, deep-dyed (*usually derogatory*), downright, out-and-out, perfect, pure, thor~ ough, thoroughgoing, total, unconditional, un~ deniable, unmitigated, unqualified, utter, wholesale 2. definite, direct, flat, straight~ forward, unequivocal, unqualified *~adverb* 3. absolutely, completely, explicitly, openly, overtly, straightforwardly, thoroughly, to the full, without hesitation, without restraint 4. at once, cleanly, immediately, instantaneously, instantly, on the spot, straight away, there and then, without more ado

outrun beat, escape, exceed, excel, get away from, leave behind, lose, outdistance, outdo, outpace, outstrip, shake off, surpass

outset beginning, commencement, early days, inauguration, inception, kickoff (*informal*), onset, opening, start, starting point
Antonyms closing, completion, conclusion, consummation, end, finale, finish, termination

outshine be head and shoulders above, be su~ perior to, eclipse, leave *or* put in the shade, outclass, outdo, outstrip, overshadow, surpass, top, transcend, upstage

outside *adjective* 1. exterior, external, extra~ mural, extraneous, extreme, out, outdoor, outer, outermost, outward, surface 2. distant, faint, marginal, negligible, remote, slight, slim, small, unlikely *~noun* 3. exterior, façade, face, front, skin, surface, topside
Antonyms (*sense 1*) in, indoor, inner, inner~ most, inside, interior, internal, intramural, inward

outsider alien, foreigner, incomer, interloper, intruder, newcomer, nonmember, odd man out, outlander, stranger

outsize enormous, extra-large, gargantuan, gi~ ant, gigantic, huge, humongous *or* humungous

(*U.S. slang*), immense, jumbo (*informal*), large, mammoth, monster, oversized
Antonyms baby, dwarf, micro, mini, pocket, tiny, undersized

outskirts borders, boundary, edge, environs, faubourgs, periphery, purlieus, suburbia, sub~urbs, vicinity

outsmart deceive, dupe, get the better of, go one better than (*informal*), make a fool of (*in~formal*), outfox, outjockey, outmanoeuvre, out~perform, outthink, outwit, pull a fast one on (*informal*), put one over on (*informal*), run rings round (*informal*), trick

outspoken abrupt, blunt, candid, direct, downright, explicit, forthright, frank, free, free-spoken, open, plain-spoken, round, uncer~emonious, undissembling, unequivocal, unre~served
Antonyms diplomatic, gracious, judicious, re~served, reticent, tactful

outspread **1.** *adjective* expanded, extended, fanlike, fanned out, flared, open, opened up, outstretched, unfolded, unfurled, wide-open **2.** *verb* expand, extend, fan out, open, open wide, outstretch, spread out, unfold, unfurl

outstanding **1.** celebrated, distinguished, emi~nent, excellent, exceptional, great, important, impressive, meritorious, pre-eminent, special, stellar (*informal*), superior, superlative, well-known **2.** arresting, conspicuous, eye-catching, marked, memorable, notable, noteworthy, prominent, salient, signal, striking **3.** due, on~going, open, owing, payable, pending, remain~ing, uncollected, unpaid, unresolved, unsettled
Antonyms (*senses 1 & 2*) dull, inferior, insig~nificant, mediocre, no great shakes (*informal*), ordinary, pedestrian, run-of-the-mill, unexcep~tional, unimpressive

outstrip beat, better, eclipse, exceed, excel, get ahead of, knock spots off (*informal*), leave be~hind, leave standing (*informal*), lose, outclass, outdistance, outdo, outpace, outperform, out~run, outshine, overtake, run rings around (*in~formal*), shake off, surpass, top, transcend

outward *adjective* apparent, evident, exterior, external, noticeable, observable, obvious, os~tensible, outer, outside, perceptible, superfi~cial, surface, visible
Antonyms inner, inside, interior, internal, in~visible, inward, obscure, unnoticeable

outwardly apparently, as far as one can see, externally, officially, on the face of it, on the surface, ostensibly, professedly, seemingly, superficially, to all appearances, to all intents and purposes, to the eye

outweigh cancel (out), compensate for, eclipse, make up for, outbalance, overcome, override, predominate, preponderate, prevail over, take precedence over, tip the scales

outwit cheat, circumvent, deceive, defraud, dupe, get the better of, gull (*archaic*), make a fool *or* monkey of, outfox, outjockey, outma~noeuvre, outsmart (*informal*), outthink, put one over on (*informal*), run rings round (*in~formal*), swindle, take in (*informal*)

outworn abandoned, antiquated, behind the times, defunct, discredited, disused, exhaust~ed, hackneyed, obsolete, outdated, outmoded, out of date, overused, rejected, stale, super~annuated, threadbare, tired, worn-out
Antonyms credited, fresh, modish, new, re~cent, up to date, used

oval *adjective* egg-shaped, ellipsoidal, elliptical, ovate, oviform, ovoid

ovation acclaim, acclamation, applause, big hand, cheering, cheers, clapping, laudation, plaudits, tribute
Antonyms abuse, booing, catcalls, derision, heckling, jeers, jibes, mockery, ridicule

over *adjective* **1.** accomplished, ancient history (*informal*), at an end, by, bygone, closed, completed, concluded, done (with), ended, fin~ished, gone, past, settled, up (*informal*) *adjective/adverb* **2.** beyond, extra, in addition, in excess, left over, remaining, superfluous, surplus, unused *~preposition* **3.** above, on, on top of, superior to, upon **4.** above, exceeding, in excess of, more than *~adverb* **5.** above, aloft, on high, overhead **6.** **over and above** added to, as well as, besides, in addition to, let alone, not to mention, on top of, plus **7.** **over and over (again)** ad nauseam, again and again, frequently, often, repeatedly, time and again

It isn't over till it's over

overabundance embarrassment of riches, ex~cess, glut, oversupply, plethora, profusion, superabundance, superfluity, surfeit, surplus, too much of a good thing

overact exaggerate, ham *or* ham up (*informal*), overdo, overplay

overall **1.** *adjective* all-embracing, blanket, complete, comprehensive, general, global, in~clusive, long-range, long-term, total, umbrella **2.** *adverb* generally speaking, in general, in (the) large, in the long term, on the whole

overawe abash, alarm, browbeat, cow, daunt, frighten, intimidate, scare, terrify
Antonyms bolster, buoy up, cheer up, com~fort, console, hearten, reassure

overbalance capsize, keel over, lose one's bal~ance, lose one's footing, overset, overturn, slip, take a tumble, tip over, topple over, tumble, turn turtle, upset

overbearing arrogant, autocratic, bossy (*infor~mal*), cavalier, despotic, dictatorial, dogmatic, domineering, haughty, high-handed, imperi~ous, lordly, magisterial, officious, oppressive,

overweening, peremptory, supercilious, superior, tyrannical
Antonyms deferential, humble, modest, self-effacing, submissive, unassertive, unassuming

overblown 1. disproportionate, excessive, fulsome, immoderate, inflated, overdone, over the top, undue 2. aureate, bombastic, euphuistic, florid, flowery, fustian, grandiloquent, magniloquent, pompous, turgid, windy

overcast clouded, clouded over, cloudy, darkened, dismal, dreary, dull, grey, hazy, leaden, louring *or* lowering, murky, sombre, sunless, threatening
Antonyms bright, brilliant, clear, cloudless, fine, sunny, unclouded

overcharge 1. cheat, clip (*slang*), diddle (*informal*), do (*slang*), fleece, rip off (*slang*), rook (*slang*), short-change, skin (*slang*), sting (*informal*), surcharge 2. burden, oppress, overburden, overload, overtask, overtax, strain, surfeit 3. *literary* embellish, embroider, exaggerate, hyperbolize, lay it on thick (*informal*), overstate

overcome 1. *verb* beat, best, be victorious, blow out of the water (*slang*), bring (someone) to their knees (*informal*), clobber (*slang*), come out on top (*informal*), conquer, crush, defeat, get the better of, lick (*informal*), make mincemeat of (*informal*), master, overpower, overthrow, overwhelm, prevail, render incapable (helpless, powerless), rise above, stuff (*slang*), subdue, subjugate, surmount, survive, tank (*slang*), triumph over, undo, vanquish, weather, wipe the floor with (*informal*), worst 2. *adjective* affected, at a loss for words, bowled over (*informal*), overwhelmed, speechless, swept off one's feet, unable to continue, visibly moved

overconfident brash, cocksure, foolhardy, hubristic, overweening, presumptuous, riding for a fall (*informal*), uppish (*Brit. informal*)
Antonyms cautious, diffident, doubtful, hesitant, insecure, timid, timorous, uncertain, unsure

overcritical captious, carping, cavilling, fault-finding, hairsplitting, hard to please, hypercritical, nit-picking (*informal*), overparticular, pedantic, pernickety (*informal*), picky (*informal*)
Antonyms easily pleased, easy-going, laid-back (*informal*), lenient, tolerant, uncritical, undemanding, unfussy

overcrowded bursting at the seams, choked, congested, crammed full, hoatching (*Scot.*), jam-packed, like the Black Hole of Calcutta, overloaded, overpopulated, packed (out), swarming
Antonyms abandoned, deserted, desolate, empty, forsaken, unoccupied, vacant

overdo 1. be intemperate, belabour, carry too far, do to death (*informal*), exaggerate, gild the lily, go overboard (*informal*), go to extremes, lay it on thick (*informal*), not know when to stop, overindulge, overplay, overreach, overstate, overuse, overwork, run riot 2. **overdo it** bite off more than one can chew, burn the candle at both ends (*informal*), drive oneself, fatigue, go too far, have too many irons in the fire, overburden, overload, overtax one's strength, overtire, overwork, strain *or* overstrain oneself, wear oneself out
Antonyms (*sense 1*) belittle, disparage, minimize, play down, underplay, underrate, understate, underuse, undervalue

overdone 1. beyond all bounds, exaggerated, excessive, fulsome, hyped, immoderate, inordinate, overelaborate, preposterous, too much, undue, unnecessary 2. burnt, burnt to a cinder, charred, dried up, overcooked, spoiled
Antonyms (*sense 1*) belittled, minimized, moderated, played down, underdone, underplayed, understated

overdue behindhand, behind schedule, behind time, belated, late, late in the day, long delayed, not before time (*informal*), owing, tardy, unpunctual
Antonyms ahead of time, beforehand, early, in advance, in good time, punctual

overeat binge (*informal*), eat like a horse (*informal*), gorge, gormandize, guzzle, make a pig of oneself (*informal*), overindulge, pack away (*slang*), pig away (*slang*), pig out (*slang*), stuff, stuff oneself

overemphasize belabour, blow up out of all proportion, lay too much stress on, make a big thing of (*informal*), make a federal case of (*U.S. informal*), make a mountain out of a molehill (*informal*), make a production (out) of (*informal*), make something out of nothing, make too much of, overdramatize, overstress
Antonyms belittle, downplay, make light of, minimize, play down, underplay, underrate, understate

overexert burn the candle at both ends (*informal*), do too much, drive (oneself), fatigue, knock (oneself) out, overstrain, overtax, overtire, overwork, push (oneself) too hard, strain, wear out, work to death

overflow *verb* 1. bubble (brim, fall, pour, run, slop, well) over, discharge, pour out, run with, shower, spill, spray, surge, teem 2. cover, deluge, drown, flood, inundate, soak, submerge, swamp ~*noun* 3. discharge, flash flood, flood, flooding, inundation, overabundance, spill, spilling over, surplus

overflowing abounding, bountiful, brimful, copious, plentiful, profuse, rife, superabundant, swarming, teeming, thronged

Antonyms deficient, inadequate, insufficient, lacking, missing, scarce, wanting

overhang *verb* beetle, bulge, cast a shadow, extend, impend, jut, loom, project, protrude, stick out, threaten

overhaul **1.** *verb* check, do up (*informal*), examine, inspect, recondition, re-examine, repair, restore, service, survey **2.** *noun* check, checkup, examination, going-over (*informal*), inspection, reconditioning, service **3.** *verb* catch up with, draw level with, get ahead of, overtake, pass

overhead **1.** *adverb* above, aloft, atop, in the sky, on high, skyward, up above, upward **2.** *adjective* aerial, overhanging, roof, upper

Antonyms (*sense 1*) below, beneath, downward, underfoot, underneath

overheads burden, oncosts, operating cost(s), running cost(s)

overheated agitated, fiery, flaming, impassioned, inflamed, overexcited, roused

Antonyms calm, collected, composed, cool, dispassionate, unemotional, unexcited, unfazed (*informal*), unruffled

overindulge be immoderate *or* intemperate, drink *or* eat too much, have a binge (*informal*), live it up (*informal*), make a pig of oneself (*informal*), overdo it, pig out (*slang*)

overindulgence excess, immoderation, intemperance, overeating, surfeit

overjoyed cock-a-hoop, delighted, deliriously happy, elated, euphoric, floating on air, happy as a lark, in raptures, joyful, jubilant, on cloud nine (*informal*), only too happy, over the moon (*informal*), rapt, rapturous, thrilled, tickled pink (*informal*), transported

Antonyms crestfallen, dejected, disappointed, downcast, down in the dumps (*informal*), heartbroken, miserable, sad, unhappy, woebegone

overlay **1.** *verb* adorn, blanket, cover, inlay, laminate, ornament, overspread, superimpose, veneer **2.** *noun* adornment, appliqué, covering, decoration, ornamentation, veneer

overload burden, encumber, oppress, overburden, overcharge, overtax, saddle (with), strain, weigh down

It is the last straw that breaks the camel's back

overlook **1.** disregard, fail to notice, forget, ignore, leave out of consideration, leave undone, miss, neglect, omit, pass, slight, slip up on **2.** blink at, condone, disregard, excuse, forgive, let bygones be bygones, let one off with, let pass, let ride, make allowances for, pardon, turn a blind eye to, wink at **3.** afford a view of, command a view of, front on to, give upon, have a view of, look over *or* out on

Antonyms (*sense 1*) discern, heed, mark, note, notice, observe, perceive, regard, spot

overly exceedingly, excessively, immoderately, inordinately, over, too, unduly, very much

overpower beat, clobber (*slang*), conquer, crush, defeat, get the upper hand over, immobilize, knock out, lick (*informal*), make mincemeat of (*informal*), master, overcome, overthrow, overwhelm, quell, subdue, subjugate, vanquish

overpowering compelling, compulsive, extreme, forceful, invincible, irrefutable, irresistible, nauseating, overwhelming, powerful, sickening, strong, suffocating, telling, unbearable, uncontrollable

overrate assess too highly, exaggerate, make too much of, overestimate, overpraise, overprize, oversell, overvalue, rate too highly, think *or* expect too much of, think too highly of

overreach **1. overreach oneself** be hoist with one's own petard, bite off more than one can chew, defeat one's own ends, go too far, have one's schemes rebound (backfire, boomerang) on one, try to be too clever **2.** cheat, circumvent, deceive, defraud, dupe, gull (*archaic*), outsmart (*informal*), outwit, swindle, trick, victimize

override annul, cancel, countermand, discount, disregard, ignore, nullify, outweigh, overrule, quash, reverse, ride roughshod over, set aside, supersede, take no account of, trample underfoot, upset, vanquish

overriding cardinal, compelling, determining, dominant, final, major, mother (of all) (*informal*), number one, overruling, paramount, pivotal, predominant, prevailing, primary, prime, ruling, supreme, ultimate

Antonyms immaterial, inconsequential, insignificant, irrelevant, minor, negligible, paltry, petty, trifling, trivial, unimportant

overrule **1.** alter, annul, cancel, countermand, disallow, invalidate, make null and void, outvote, override, overturn, recall, repeal, rescind, reverse, revoke, rule against, set aside, veto **2.** bend to one's will, control, direct, dominate, govern, influence, prevail over, sway

Antonyms (*sense 1*) allow, approve, consent to, endorse, pass, permit, sanction

overrun **1.** cut to pieces, invade, massacre, occupy, overwhelm, put to flight, rout, swamp **2.** choke, infest, inundate, overflow, overgrow, permeate, ravage, spread like wildfire, spread over, surge over, swarm over **3.** exceed, go beyond, overshoot, run over *or* on

overseer boss (*informal*), chief, foreman, gaffer (*informal, chiefly Brit.*), manager, master, super (*informal*), superintendent, superior, supervisor

overshadow **1.** dominate, dwarf, eclipse, excel, leave *or* put in the shade, outshine, outweigh, render insignificant by comparison, rise above, steal the limelight from, surpass, take precedence over, throw into the shade, tower above **2.** adumbrate, becloud, bedim, cloud, darken, dim, obfuscate, obscure, veil **3.** blight, cast a gloom upon, mar, put a damper on, ruin, spoil, take the edge off, take the pleasure *or* enjoyment out of, temper

oversight **1.** blunder, carelessness, delinquency, error, fault, inattention, lapse, laxity, mistake, neglect, omission, slip **2.** administration, care, charge, control, custody, direction, handling, inspection, keeping, management, superintendence, supervision, surveillance

overt apparent, blatant, bold, manifest, observable, obvious, open, patent, plain, public, unconcealed, undisguised, visible
Antonyms concealed, covert, disguised, hidden, hush-hush (*informal*), invisible, secret, surreptitious, underhand

overtake **1.** catch up with, do better than, draw level with, get past, leave behind, outdistance, outdo, outstrip, overhaul, pass **2.** befall, catch unprepared, come upon, engulf, happen, hit, overwhelm, strike, take by surprise

overthrow *verb* **1.** abolish, beat, bring down, conquer, crush, defeat, depose, dethrone, do away with, master, oust, overcome, overpower, overwhelm, subdue, subjugate, topple, unseat, vanquish **2.** bring to ruin, demolish, destroy, knock down, level, overturn, put an end to, put paid to, raze, ruin, subvert, upend, upset *~noun* **3.** defeat, deposition, destruction, dethronement, discomfiture, disestablishment, displacement, dispossession, downfall, end, fall, ousting, prostration, rout, ruin, subjugation, subversion, suppression, undoing, unseating
Antonyms *verb* defend, guard, keep, maintain, preserve, protect, restore, support, uphold *~noun* defence, preservation, protection

overtone association, connotation, flavour, hint, implication, innuendo, intimation, nuance, sense, suggestion, undercurrent

overture **1.** *often plural* advance, approach, conciliatory move, invitation, offer, opening move, proposal, proposition, signal, tender **2.** *Music* introduction, opening, prelude
Antonyms afterword, close, coda, epilogue, finale, rebuke, rejection, withdrawal

overturn **1.** capsize, keel over, knock over *or* down, overbalance, reverse, spill, tip over, topple, tumble, upend, upset, upturn **2.** abolish, annul, bring down, countermand, depose, destroy, invalidate, obviate, overthrow, repeal, rescind, reverse, set aside, unseat

overused cliché'd, hackneyed, platitudinous, played out, stale, stereotyped, threadbare, tired, unoriginal, worn (out)

overweening **1.** arrogant, cavalier, cocksure, cocky, conceited, egotistical, haughty, high and mighty (*informal*), high-handed, insolent, lordly, opinionated, pompous, presumptuous, proud, self-confident, supercilious, uppish (*Brit. informal*), vain, vainglorious **2.** blown up out of all proportion, excessive, extravagant, immoderate
Antonyms (*sense 1*) deferential, diffident, hesitant, modest, self-conscious, self-effacing, timid, unassuming, unobtrusive

overweight *adjective* ample, bulky, buxom, chubby, chunky, corpulent, fat, fleshy, gross, heavy, hefty, huge, massive, obese, on the plump side, outsize, plump, podgy, portly, stout, tubby (*informal*), well-padded (*informal*), well-upholstered (*informal*)
Antonyms emaciated, gaunt, lean, pinched, scraggy, scrawny, skinny, thin, underweight

overwhelm **1.** bury, crush, deluge, engulf, flood, inundate, snow under, submerge, swamp **2.** bowl over (*informal*), confuse, devastate, knock (someone) for six (*informal*), make mincemeat of (*informal*), overcome, overpower, prostrate, render speechless, stagger, sweep (someone) off his *or* her feet, take (someone's) breath away **3.** crush, cut to pieces, destroy, massacre, overpower, overrun, rout

overwhelming breathtaking, crushing, devastating, invincible, irresistible, overpowering, shattering, stunning, towering, uncontrollable, vast, vastly superior
Antonyms commonplace, incidental, insignificant, negligible, paltry, resistible, trivial, unimportant

overwork be a slave-driver *or* hard taskmaster to, burden, burn the candle at both ends, burn the midnight oil, drive into the ground, exhaust, exploit, fatigue, oppress, overstrain, overtax, overuse, prostrate, strain, sweat (*informal*), wear out, weary, work one's fingers to the bone

> *overwork: a dangerous disorder affecting high public functionaries who want to go fishing*
> Ambrose Bierce *The Devil's Dictionary*

overwrought **1.** agitated, beside oneself, distracted, excited, frantic, in a state (tizzy (*informal*), twitter (*informal*)) (*informal*), keyed up, on edge, overexcited, overworked, stirred, strung up (*informal*), tense, uptight (*informal*), wired (*slang*), worked up (*informal*), wound up (*informal*) **2.** baroque, busy, contrived, florid, flowery, fussy, overdone, overelaborate, overembellished, overornate, rococo
Antonyms (*sense 1*) calm, collected, controlled,

cool, dispassionate, emotionless, impassive, self-contained, unfazed (*informal*), unmoved

owe be beholden to, be in arrears, be in debt, be obligated *or* indebted, be under an obligation to

owing *adjective* due, outstanding, overdue, owed, payable, unpaid, unsettled

owing to *preposition* as a result of, because of, on account of

own *adjective* **1.** individual, particular, personal, private *~pronoun* **2. on one's own** alone, by oneself, by one's own efforts, independently, isolated, left to one's own devices, off one's own bat, on one's tod (*Brit. slang*), singly, (standing) on one's own two feet, unaided, unassisted, under one's own steam **3. hold one's own** compete, keep going, keep one's end up, keep one's head above water, maintain one's position *~verb* **4.** be in possession of, be responsible for, enjoy, have, hold, keep, possess, retain **5. own up (to)** admit, come clean (about), come out of the closet (*informal*), confess, cough (*slang*), 'fess up (*U.S.*), make a clean breast of, tell the truth (about) **6.** acknowledge, admit, allow, allow to be valid, avow, concede, confess, disclose, go along with, grant, recognize

owner holder, landlord, lord, master, mistress, possessor, proprietor, proprietress, proprietrix

ownership dominion, possession, proprietary rights, proprietorship, right of possession, title

P

pace *noun* **1.** gait, measure, step, stride, tread, walk **2.** clip (*informal*), lick (*informal*), mo~ mentum, motion, movement, progress, rate, speed, tempo, time, velocity *~verb* **3.** march, patrol, pound, stride, walk back and forth, walk up and down **4.** count, determine, mark out, measure, step

pacific **1.** appeasing, conciliatory, diplomatic, irenic, pacificatory, peacemaking, placatory, propitiatory **2.** dovelike, dovish, friendly, gen~ tle, mild, nonbelligerent, nonviolent, pacifist, peaceable, peace-loving **3.** at peace, calm, hal~ cyon, peaceful, placid, quiet, serene, smooth, still, tranquil, unruffled
Antonyms aggressive, antagonistic, belliger~ ent, hostile, nonconciliatory, pugnacious, un~ forgiving, unfriendly, violent, warlike

pacifist conchie (*informal*), conscientious objector, dove, passive resister, peace lover, peacemonger, peacenik (*informal*), satyagrahi

pacify **1.** allay, ameliorate, appease, assuage, calm, clear the air, compose, conciliate, make peace, moderate, mollify, placate, pour oil on troubled waters, propitiate, quiet, restore harmony, smooth down *or* over, smooth one's ruffled feathers, soften, soothe, still, tranquil~ lize **2.** chasten, crush, impose peace, put down, quell, repress, silence, subdue, tame

pack *noun* **1.** back pack, bale, bundle, burden, fardel (*archaic*), kit, kitbag, knapsack, load, package, packet, parcel, rucksack, truss **2.** as~ semblage, band, bunch, collection, company, crew, crowd, deck, drove, flock, gang, group, herd, lot, mob, set, troop *~verb* **3.** batch, bun~ dle, burden, load, package, packet, store, stow **4.** charge, compact, compress, cram, crowd, fill, jam, mob, press, ram, stuff, tamp, throng, wedge **5.** *with* **off** bundle out, dismiss, hustle out, send away, send packing (*informal*), send someone about his business

package *noun* **1.** box, carton, container, packet, parcel **2.** amalgamation, combination, entity, unit, whole *~verb* **3.** batch, box, pack, packet, parcel (up), wrap, wrap up

packaging **1.** box, casing, packing, wrapping **2.** appearance, exterior, facade, image, outward *or* external appearance, PR (*informal*), pres~ entation, surface show, window dressing

packed brimful, bursting at the seams, chock-a-block, chock-full, congested, cram-full, crammed, crowded, filled, full, hoatching (*Scot.*), jammed, jam-packed, loaded *or* full to the gunwales, overflowing, overloaded, packed like sardines, seething, swarming
Antonyms deserted, empty, uncongested, un~ crowded

packet **1.** bag, carton, container, package, par~ cel, poke (*dialect*), wrapper, wrapping **2.** *slang* a bob or two (*Brit. informal*), an arm and a leg (*informal*), big bucks (*informal, chiefly U.S.*), big money, bomb (*Brit. slang*), bundle (*slang*), fortune, king's ransom (*informal*), lot(s), megabucks (*U.S. & Canad. slang*), mint, pile (*informal*), pot(s) (*informal*), pretty penny (*informal*), tidy sum (*informal*), wad (*U.S. & Canad. slang*)

pack in **1.** attract, cram, draw, fill to capacity, squeeze in **2.** *Brit. informal* cease, chuck (*in~ formal*), desist, give up *or* over, jack in, kick (*informal*), leave off, stop

pack up **1.** put away, store, tidy up **2.** *informal* call it a day (*informal*), call it a night (*infor~ mal*), finish, give up, pack in (*Brit. informal*) **3.** break down, conk out (*informal*), fail, give out, stall, stop

pact agreement, alliance, arrangement, bar~ gain, bond, compact, concord, concordat, con~ tract, convention, covenant, deal, league, protocol, treaty, understanding

pad[1] *noun* **1.** buffer, cushion, protection, stiff~ ening, stuffing, wad **2.** block, jotter, notepad, tablet, writing pad **3.** foot, paw, sole **4.** *slang* apartment, flat, hang-out (*informal*), home, place, quarters, room *~verb* **5.** cushion, fill, line, pack, protect, shape, stuff **6.** *often with* **out** amplify, augment, eke, elaborate, fill out, flesh out, inflate, lengthen, protract, spin out, stretch

pad[2] *verb* **1.** creep, go barefoot, pussyfoot (*in~ formal*), sneak, steal **2.** hike, march, plod, traipse (*informal*), tramp, trek, trudge, walk

padding **1.** filling, packing, stuffing, wadding **2.** hot air (*informal*), prolixity, verbiage, verbos~ ity, waffle (*informal, chiefly Brit.*), wordiness

paddle[1] **1.** *noun* oar, scull, sweep **2.** *verb* oar, propel, pull, row, scull

paddle[2] *verb* dabble, plash, slop, splash (about), stir, wade

paddy bate (*Brit. slang*), fit of temper, paddy~ whack (*Brit. informal*), passion, rage, tan~ trum, temper, tiff, wax (*informal, chiefly Brit.*)

paean **1.** anthem, hymn, psalm, thanksgiving **2.** encomium, eulogy, hymn of praise, ovation, panegyric, rave review (*informal*)

pagan **1.** *noun* Gentile, heathen, idolater, infi~ del, polytheist, unbeliever **2.** *adjective* Gentile, heathen, heathenish, idolatrous, infidel, irre~ ligious, polytheistic

page¹ *noun* **1.** folio, leaf, sheet, side **2.** chapter, episode, epoch, era, event, incident, period, phase, point, stage, time *~verb* **3.** foliate, number, paginate

page² **1.** *noun* attendant, bellboy (*U.S.*), foot~ boy, pageboy, servant, squire **2.** *verb* an~ nounce, call, call out, preconize, seek, send for, summon

pageant display, extravaganza, parade, pro~ cession, ritual, show, spectacle, tableau

pageantry display, drama, extravagance, glamour, glitter, grandeur, magnificence, pa~ rade, pomp, show, showiness, spectacle, splash (*informal*), splendour, state, theatrical~ ity

pain *noun* **1.** ache, cramp, discomfort, hurt, ir~ ritation, pang, smarting, soreness, spasm, suffering, tenderness, throb, throe (*rare*), trouble, twinge **2.** affliction, agony, anguish, bitterness, distress, grief, hardship, heartache, misery, suffering, torment, torture, tribula~ tion, woe, wretchedness **3.** *informal* aggrava~ tion, annoyance, bore, bother, drag (*informal*), gall, headache (*informal*), irritation, nuisance, pain in the arse (*taboo informal*), pain in the neck (*informal*), pest, vexation *~verb* **4.** ail, chafe, discomfort, harm, hurt, inflame, injure, smart, sting, throb **5.** afflict, aggrieve, agonize, cut to the quick, disquiet, distress, grieve, hurt, sadden, torment, torture, vex, worry, wound **6.** *informal* annoy, exasperate, gall, harass, irritate, nark (*Brit., Austral., & N.Z. slang*), rile, vex

pained aggrieved, anguished, distressed, hurt, injured, miffed (*informal*), offended, reproach~ ful, stung, unhappy, upset, worried, wounded

painful **1.** afflictive, disagreeable, distasteful, distressing, grievous, saddening, unpleasant **2.** aching, agonizing, excruciating, harrowing, hurting, inflamed, raw, smarting, sore, tender, throbbing **3.** arduous, difficult, hard, laborious, severe, tedious, troublesome, trying, vexatious **4.** *informal* abysmal, awful, dire, dreadful, ex~ cruciating, extremely bad, godawful, terrible
Antonyms (*sense 1*) agreeable, enjoyable, pleasant, satisfying (*sense 2*) comforting, painless, relieving, soothing (*sense 3*) a piece of cake (*informal*), easy, effortless, interesting, short, simple, straightforward, undemanding

painfully alarmingly, clearly, deplorably, dis~ tressingly, dreadfully, excessively, markedly, sadly, unfortunately, woefully

painkiller anaesthetic, analgesic, anodyne, drug, palliative, remedy, sedative

painless easy, effortless, fast, no trouble, pain-free, quick, simple, trouble-free

pains **1.** assiduousness, bother, care, diligence, effort, industry, labour, special attention, trouble **2.** birth-pangs, childbirth, contractions, labour

painstaking assiduous, careful, conscientious, diligent, earnest, exacting, hard-working, in~ dustrious, meticulous, persevering, punctili~ ous, scrupulous, sedulous, strenuous, thor~ ough, thoroughgoing
Antonyms careless, half-hearted, haphazard, heedless, lazy, negligent, slapdash, slipshod, thoughtless

paint *noun* **1.** colour, colouring, dye, emulsion, pigment, stain, tint **2.** *informal* cosmetics, face (*informal*), greasepaint, make-up, *maquillage*, war paint (*informal*) *~verb* **3.** catch a likeness, delineate, depict, draw, figure, picture, por~ tray, represent, sketch **4.** apply, coat, colour, cover, daub, decorate, slap on (*informal*) **5.** bring to life, capture, conjure up a vision, de~ pict, describe, evoke, make one see, portray, put graphically, recount, tell vividly **6. paint the town red** *informal* carouse, celebrate, go on a binge (*informal*), go on a spree, go on the town, live it up (*informal*), make merry, make whoopee (*informal*), revel

Every time I paint a portrait I lose a friend
John Singer Sargent

painter

Good painters imitate nature, bad ones vomit it
Miguel de Cervantes *El Licenciado Vidriera*

pair **1.** *noun* brace, combination, couple, dou~ blet, duo, match, matched set, span, twins, two of a kind, twosome, yoke **2.** *verb* bracket, couple, join, marry, match, match up, mate, pair off, put together, team, twin, wed, yoke

pal boon companion, buddy (*informal*), chum (*informal*), cock (*Brit. informal*), companion, comrade, crony, friend, homeboy (*slang, chiefly U.S.*), mate (*informal*)

palatable **1.** appetizing, delectable, delicious, luscious, mouthwatering, savoury, tasty, toothsome **2.** acceptable, agreeable, attractive, enjoyable, fair, pleasant, satisfactory
Antonyms (*sense 1*) bland, flat, insipid, stale, tasteless, unappetizing, unpalatable

palate **1.** appetite, heart, stomach, taste **2.** ap~ preciation, enjoyment, gusto, liking, relish, zest

palatial de luxe, gorgeous, grand, grandiose, il~ lustrious, imposing, luxurious, magnificent, majestic, opulent, plush (*informal*), regal, spacious, splendid, splendiferous (*facetious*), stately, sumptuous

palaver *noun* 1. business (*informal*), carry-on (*informal, chiefly Brit.*), pantomime (*informal, chiefly Brit.*), performance (*informal*), procedure, rigmarole, song and dance (*Brit. informal*), to-do 2. babble, blather, blether, chatter, hubbub, natter (*Brit.*), prattle, tongue-wagging, yak (*slang*) 3. colloquy, confab (*informal*), conference, discussion, get-together (*informal*), parley, powwow, session ~*verb* 4. confab (*informal*), confer, discuss, go into a huddle (*informal*), parley, powwow, put heads together 5. blather, blether, chatter, gabble, jabber, jaw (*slang*), natter (*Brit.*), prattle, yak (*slang*)

pale¹ *adjective* 1. anaemic, ashen, ashy, bleached, bloodless, colourless, faded, light, like death warmed up (*informal*), pallid, pasty, sallow, wan, washed-out, white, whitish 2. dim, faint, feeble, inadequate, pathetic, poor, thin, weak ~*verb* 3. become pale, blanch, go white, lose colour, whiten 4. decrease, dim, diminish, dull, fade, grow dull, lessen, lose lustre

Antonyms (*sense 1*) blooming, florid, flushed, glowing, rosy-cheeked, rubicund, ruddy, sanguine

pale² *noun* 1. paling, palisade, picket, post, slat, stake, upright 2. barricade, barrier, fence, palisade, railing 3. border, boundary, bounds, confines, district, limits, region, territory 4. **beyond the pale** barbaric, forbidden, improper, inadmissible, indecent, irregular, not done, out of line, unacceptable, unseemly, unspeakable, unsuitable

palisade bulwark, defence, enclosure, fence, paling, stockade

pall¹ *noun* 1. cloud, mantle, shadow, shroud, veil 2. check, damp, damper, dismay, gloom, melancholy

pall² *verb* become dull *or* tedious, bore, cloy, glut, jade, satiate, sicken, surfeit, tire, weary

palliate 1. abate, allay, alleviate, assuage, diminish, ease, mitigate, moderate, mollify, relax, relieve, soften, soothe, temper 2. cloak, conceal, cover, excuse, extenuate, gloss over, hide, lessen, minimize, paper over the cracks (*informal*), varnish, whitewash (*informal*)

palliative 1. *adjective* alleviative, anodyne, assuasive, calmative, calming, demulcent, lenitive, mitigative, mitigatory, mollifying, soothing 2. *noun* analgesic, anodyne, calmative, demulcent, drug, lenitive, painkiller, sedative, tranquillizer

pallid 1. anaemic, ashen, ashy, cadaverous, colourless, like death warmed up (*informal*), pale, pasty, sallow, wan, waxen, wheyfaced, whitish 2. anaemic, bloodless, colourless, insipid, lifeless, spiritless, sterile, tame, tired, uninspired, vapid

pallor ashen hue, bloodlessness, lack of colour, paleness, pallidness, wanness, whiteness

pally affectionate, buddy-buddy (*slang, chiefly U.S. & Canad.*), chummy (*informal*), close, familiar, friendly, intimate, palsy-walsy (*informal*), thick as thieves (*informal*)

palm¹ *noun* 1. hand, hook, meathook (*slang*), mitt (*slang*), paw (*informal*) 2. **in the palm of one's hand** at one's mercy, in one's clutches (control, power) 3. **grease someone's palm** *slang* bribe, buy, corrupt, fix (*informal*), give a backhander (*slang*), induce, influence, pay off (*informal*), square, suborn

palm² *noun, figurative* bays, crown, fame, glory, honour, laurels, merit, prize, success, triumph, trophy, victory

palm off 1. *with* **on** *or* **with** fob off, foist off, pass off 2. *with* **on** foist on, force upon, impose upon, take advantage of, thrust upon, unload upon

palmy flourishing, fortunate, glorious, golden, halcyon, happy, joyous, luxurious, prosperous, thriving, triumphant

palpable 1. apparent, blatant, clear, conspicuous, evident, manifest, obvious, open, patent, plain, salient, unmistakable, visible 2. concrete, material, real, solid, substantial, tangible, touchable

palpitate beat, flutter, pitapat, pitter-patter, pound, pulsate, pulse, quiver, shiver, throb, tremble, vibrate

palsied arthritic, atonic (*Pathology*), crippled, debilitated, disabled, helpless, paralysed, paralytic, rheumatic, sclerotic, shaking, shaky, spastic, trembling

palter 1. be evasive, deceive, double-talk, equivocate, flannel (*Brit. informal*), fudge, hedge, mislead, prevaricate, shuffle, tergiversate, trifle 2. bargain, barter, chaffer, dicker (*chiefly U.S.*), haggle, higgle

paltry base, beggarly, chickenshit (*U.S. slang*), contemptible, crappy (*slang*), derisory, despicable, inconsiderable, insignificant, low, meagre, mean, measly, Mickey Mouse (*slang*), minor, miserable, nickel-and-dime (*U.S. slang*), petty, picayune (*U.S.*), piddling (*informal*), pitiful, poor, poxy (*slang*), puny, slight, small, sorry, trifling, trivial, twopenny-halfpenny (*Brit. informal*), unimportant, worthless, wretched

Antonyms consequential, considerable, essential, grand, important, major, mega (*slang*), significant, valuable

pamper baby, cater to one's every whim, coddle, cosset, fondle, gratify, humour, indulge, mollycoddle, pander to, pet, spoil, wait on (someone) hand and foot

pamphlet booklet, brochure, circular, folder, leaflet, tract

pan[1] *noun* **1.** container, pot, saucepan, vessel ~*verb* **2.** look for, search for, separate, sift out, wash **3.** *informal* blast, censure, criticize, flay, hammer (*Brit. informal*), knock (*informal*), lambast(e), put down, roast (*informal*), rubbish (*informal*), slag (off) (*slang*), slam (*slang*), slate (*informal*), tear into (*informal*), throw brickbats at (*informal*)

pan[2] *verb* follow, move, scan, sweep, swing, track, traverse

panacea catholicon, cure-all, elixir, nostrum, sovereign remedy, universal cure

panache a flourish, brio, dash, élan, flair, flamboyance, spirit, style, swagger, verve

pandemonium babel, bedlam, chaos, clamour, commotion, confusion, din, hubbub, hue and cry, hullabaloo, racket, ruckus (*informal*), ruction (*informal*), rumpus, tumult, turmoil, uproar
Antonyms arrangement, calm, hush, order, peace, peacefulness, quietude, repose, stillness, tranquillity

pander **1.** *verb with* **to** cater to, fawn on, gratify, indulge, play up to (*informal*), please, satisfy **2.** *noun* go-between, mack (*slang*), pimp, ponce (*slang*), procurer, white-slaver, whoremaster (*archaic*)

panegyric accolade, commendation, encomium, eulogy, homage, paean, praise, tribute

panegyrical commendatory, complimentary, encomiastic, eulogistic, favourable, flattering, glowing, laudatory

pang ache, agony, anguish, discomfort, distress, gripe, pain, prick, spasm, stab, sting, stitch, throe (*rare*), twinge, wrench

panic *noun* **1.** agitation, alarm, consternation, dismay, fear, fright, horror, hysteria, scare, terror ~*verb* **2.** become hysterical, be terror-stricken, go to pieces, have kittens (*informal*), lose one's bottle (*Brit. slang*), lose one's nerve, overreact **3.** alarm, put the wind up (someone) (*informal*), scare, startle, terrify, unnerve

panicky afraid, agitated, distressed, fearful, frantic, frenzied, frightened, hysterical, in a flap (*informal*), in a tizzy (*informal*), jittery (*informal*), nervous, windy (*slang*), worked up, worried
Antonyms calm, collected, composed, confident, cool, imperturbable, self-controlled, together (*slang*), unexcitable, unfazed (*informal*), unflappable, unruffled

panic-stricken *or* **panic-struck** aghast, agitated, alarmed, appalled, fearful, frenzied, frightened, frightened out of one's wits, frightened to death, horrified, horror-stricken, hysterical, in a cold sweat (*informal*), panicky, petrified, scared, scared shitless (*taboo slang*), scared stiff, shit-scared (*taboo slang*), startled, terrified, terror-stricken, unnerved

panoply array, attire, dress, garb, get-up (*informal*), insignia, raiment (*archaic or poetic*), regalia, show, trappings, turnout

panorama **1.** bird's-eye view, prospect, scenery, scenic view, view, vista **2.** overall picture, overview, perspective, survey

panoramic all-embracing, bird's-eye, comprehensive, extensive, far-reaching, general, inclusive, overall, scenic, sweeping, wide

pan out come out, come to pass (*archaic*), culminate, eventuate, happen, result, turn out, work out

pant *verb* **1.** blow, breathe, gasp, heave, huff, palpitate, puff, throb, wheeze **2.** *figurative* ache, covet, crave, desire, eat one's heart out over, hanker after, hunger, long, pine, set one's heart on, sigh, suspire (*archaic or poetic*), thirst, want, yearn ~*noun* **3.** gasp, huff, puff, wheeze

panting *adjective* **1.** breathless, gasping, out of breath, out of puff, out of whack (*informal*), puffed, puffed out, puffing, short of breath, winded **2.** agog, all agog, anxious, champing at the bit (*informal*), eager, impatient, raring to go

pants **1.** *Brit.* boxer shorts, briefs, drawers, knickers, panties, underpants, Y-fronts (*Trademark*) **2.** *U.S.* slacks, trousers

pap **1.** baby food, mash, mush, pulp **2.** drivel, rubbish, trash, trivia

paper *noun* **1.** *often plural* certificate, deed, documents, instrument, record **2.** *plural* archive, diaries, documents, dossier, file, letters, records **3.** blat, daily, gazette, journal, news, newspaper, organ, rag (*informal*) **4.** analysis, article, assignment, composition, critique, dissertation, essay, examination, monograph, report, script, study, thesis, treatise **5.** **on paper** ideally, in the abstract, in theory, theoretically ~*adjective* **6.** cardboard, disposable, flimsy, insubstantial, paper-thin, papery, thin ~*verb* **7.** cover with paper, hang, line, paste up, wallpaper
Related adjective: papyraceous

papery flimsy, fragile, frail, insubstantial, light, lightweight, paperlike, paper-thin, thin

par *noun* **1.** average, level, mean, median, norm, standard, usual **2.** balance, equal footing, equality, equilibrium, equivalence, parity **3.** **above par** excellent, exceptional, first-rate (*informal*), outstanding, superior **4.** **below par** **a.** below average, bush-league (*Austral. & N.Z. informal*), dime-a-dozen (*informal*), inferior, lacking, not up to scratch (*informal*), poor, second-rate, substandard, tinhorn (*U.S.

slang), two-bit (*U.S. & Canad. slang*), wanting **b.** not oneself, off colour (*chiefly Brit.*), off form, poorly (*informal*), sick, under the weather (*informal*), unfit, unhealthy **5. par for the course** average, expected, ordinary, predictable, standard, typical, usual **6. on a par** equal, much the same, the same, well-matched **7. up to par** acceptable, adequate, good enough, passable, satisfactory, up to scratch (*informal*), up to the mark

parable allegory, exemplum, fable, lesson, moral tale, story

parabolic allegorical, figurative, metaphoric, symbolic

parade *noun* **1.** array, cavalcade, ceremony, column, march, pageant, procession, review, spectacle, train **2.** array, display, exhibition, flaunting, ostentation, pomp, show, spectacle, vaunting *~verb* **3.** defile, march, process **4.** air, brandish, display, exhibit, flaunt, make a show of, show, show off (*informal*), strut, swagger, vaunt

paradigm archetype, example, exemplar, ideal, model, norm, original, pattern, prototype

paradise **1.** City of God, divine abode, Elysian fields, garden of delights, Happy Valley (*Islam*), heaven, heavenly kingdom, Olympus (*poetic*), Promised Land, Zion (*Christianity*) **2.** Eden, Garden of Eden **3.** bliss, delight, felicity, heaven, seventh heaven, utopia

Two paradises 'twere in one
To live in paradise alone

Andrew Marvell *The Garden*

paradisiacal blessed, blissful, celestial, divine, Elysian, glorious, golden, heavenly, out of this world (*informal*), utopian

paradox absurdity, ambiguity, anomaly, contradiction, enigma, inconsistency, mystery, oddity, puzzle

paradoxical absurd, ambiguous, baffling, confounding, contradictory, enigmatic, equivocal, illogical, impossible, improbable, inconsistent, oracular, puzzling, riddling

paragon apotheosis, archetype, best thing since sliced bread (*informal*), criterion, cynosure, epitome, exemplar, greatest thing since sliced bread (*informal*), ideal, jewel, masterpiece, model, nonesuch (*archaic*), nonpareil, norm, paradigm, pattern, prototype, quintessence, standard

paragraph clause, item, notice, part, passage, portion, section, subdivision

parallel *adjective* **1.** aligned, alongside, coextensive, equidistant, side by side **2.** akin, analogous, complementary, correspondent, corresponding, like, matching, resembling, similar, uniform *~noun* **3.** analogue, complement, corollary, counterpart, duplicate, equal, equivalent, likeness, match, twin **4.** analogy, comparison, correlation, correspondence, likeness, parallelism, resemblance, similarity *~verb* **5.** agree, be alike, chime with, compare, complement, conform, correlate, correspond, equal, keep pace (with), match

Antonyms *adjective* different, dissimilar, divergent, non-parallel, unlike *~noun* difference, dissimilarity, divergence, opposite, reverse *~verb* be unlike, differ, diverge

paralyse **1.** cripple, debilitate, disable, incapacitate, lame **2.** anaesthetize, arrest, benumb, freeze, halt, immobilize, numb, petrify, stop dead, stun, stupefy, transfix

paralysis **1.** immobility, palsy, paresis (*Pathology*) **2.** arrest, breakdown, halt, shutdown, stagnation, standstill, stoppage

paralytic *adjective* **1.** crippled, disabled, immobile, immobilized, incapacitated, lame, numb, palsied, paralysed **2.** *informal* bevvied (*dialect*), blitzed (*slang*), blotto (*slang*), bombed (*slang*), Brahms and Liszt (*slang*), canned (*slang*), drunk, flying (*slang*), inebriated, intoxicated, legless (*informal*), lit up (*slang*), out of it (*slang*), out to it (*Austral. & N.Z. slang*), pie-eyed (*slang*), pissed (*taboo slang*), plastered (*slang*), rat-arsed (*taboo slang*), sloshed (*slang*), smashed (*slang*), steamboats (*Scot. slang*), steaming (*slang*), stewed (*slang*), stoned (*slang*), tired and emotional (*euphemistic*), wasted (*slang*), wrecked (*slang*), zonked (*slang*)

parameter constant, criterion, framework, guideline, limit, limitation, restriction, specification

paramount capital, cardinal, chief, dominant, eminent, first, foremost, main, outstanding, predominant, pre-eminent, primary, prime, principal, superior, supreme

Antonyms inferior, insignificant, least, minor, negligible, secondary, slight, subordinate, trifling, unimportant

paramour beau, concubine, courtesan, fancy bit (*slang*), fancy man (*slang*), fancy woman (*slang*), inamorata, inamorato, kept woman, lover, mistress

paraphernalia accoutrements, apparatus, appurtenances, baggage, belongings, clobber (*Brit. slang*), effects, equipage, equipment, gear, impedimenta, material, stuff, tackle, things, trappings

paraphrase **1.** *noun* interpretation, rehash, rendering, rendition, rephrasing, restatement, rewording, translation, version **2.** *verb* express in other words *or* one's own words, interpret, rehash, render, rephrase, restate, reword

parasite bloodsucker (*informal*), cadger, drone (*Brit.*), hanger-on, leech, scrounger (*informal*), sponge (*informal*), sponger (*informal*)

parasitic, parasitical bloodsucking (*informal*), cadging, leechlike, scrounging (*informal*), sponging (*informal*)

parcel *noun* **1.** bundle, carton, pack, package, packet **2.** band, batch, bunch, collection, company, crew, crowd, gang, group, lot, pack **3.** piece of land, plot, property, tract *~verb* **4.** *often with* **up** do up, pack, package, tie up, wrap **5.** *often with* **out** allocate, allot, apportion, carve up, deal out, dispense, distribute, divide, dole out, mete out, portion, share out, split up

parch blister, burn, dehydrate, desiccate, dry up, evaporate, make thirsty, scorch, sear, shrivel, wither

parched arid, dehydrated, dried out *or* up, drouthy (*Scot.*), dry, scorched, shrivelled, thirsty, torrid, waterless, withered

parching *adjective* baking, blistering, burning, dry, drying, hot, roasting (*informal*), scorching, searing, sweltering, withering

pardon 1. *verb* absolve, acquit, amnesty, condone, exculpate, excuse, exonerate, forgive, free, let off (*informal*), liberate, overlook, release, remit, reprieve **2.** *noun* absolution, acquittal, allowance, amnesty, condonation, discharge, excuse, exoneration, forgiveness, grace, indulgence, mercy, release, remission, reprieve
Antonyms *verb* admonish, blame, castigate, censure, chasten, chastise, condemn, discipline, excoriate, fine, penalize, punish, rebuke *~noun* condemnation, guilt, penalty, punishment, redress, retaliation, retribution, revenge, vengeance

God will pardon me. It is His trade
Heinrich Heine

pardonable allowable, condonable, excusable, forgivable, minor, not serious, permissible, understandable, venial

pare 1. clip, cut, peel, shave, skin, trim **2.** crop, cut, cut back, decrease, dock, lop, prune, reduce, retrench, shear

parent 1. begetter, father, guardian, mother, procreator, progenitor, sire **2.** architect, author, cause, creator, forerunner, origin, originator, prototype, root, source, wellspring

They fuck you up, your Mum and Dad.
They may not mean to, but they do.
They fill you with the faults they had
And add some extra, just for you
Philip Larkin *This Be the Verse*

To lose one parent, Mr. Worthing, may be regarded as a misfortune; to lose both looks like carelessness
Oscar Wilde *The Importance of Being Earnest*

Parents are the very last people who ought to be allowed to have children
H.E. Bell

The first half of our life is ruined by our parents and the second half by our children
Clarence Darrow

Honour thy father and thy mother
Bible: Exodus

parentage ancestry, birth, derivation, descent, extraction, family, line, lineage, origin, paternity, pedigree, race, stirps, stock

Men are generally more careful of the breed of their horses and dogs than of their children
William Penn *Some Fruits of Solitude*

parenthetic, parenthetical bracketed, by-the-way, explanatory, extraneous, extrinsic, incidental, in parenthesis, inserted, interposed, qualifying

parenthetically by the bye, by the way, by way of explanation, incidentally, in parenthesis, in passing

parenthood baby *or* child care, bringing up, child rearing, fatherhood *or* motherhood, fathering *or* mothering, nurturing, parenting, rearing, upbringing

Before I got married I had six theories about bringing up children; now I have six children, and no theories
John Wilmot, Earl of Rochester

pariah exile, leper, outcast, outlaw, undesirable, unperson, untouchable

paring *noun* clipping, flake, fragment, peel, peeling, rind, shaving, shred, skin, slice, sliver, snippet

parish church, churchgoers, community, congregation, flock, fold, parishioners
Related adjective: parochial

parity 1. consistency, equality, equal terms, equivalence, par, parallelism, quits (*informal*), uniformity, unity **2.** affinity, agreement, analogy, conformity, congruity, correspondence, likeness, resemblance, sameness, similarity, similitude

park 1. *noun* estate, garden, grounds, parkland, pleasure garden, recreation ground, woodland **2.** *verb* leave, manoeuvre, position, station

The parks are the lungs of London
William Pitt, Earl of Chapman

parlance idiom, jargon, language, lingo (*informal*), manner of speaking, phraseology, -speak, speech, talk, tongue

parley 1. *noun* colloquy, confab (*informal*), conference, congress, council, dialogue, discussion, meeting, palaver, powwow, seminar, talk(s) **2.** *verb* confabulate, confer, deliberate, discuss, negotiate, palaver, powwow, speak, talk

parliament 1. assembly, congress, convention, convocation, council, diet, legislature, senate, talking shop (*informal*) **2. Parliament** Houses of Parliament, Mother of Parliaments, the

House, the House of Commons and the House of Lords, Westminster

A parliament can do any thing but make a man a woman, and a woman a man

2nd Earl of Pembroke

A Parliament is nothing less than a big meeting of more or less idle people

Walter Bagehot *The English Constitution*

England is the mother of Parliaments

John Bright

parliamentary congressional, deliberative, governmental, lawgiving, lawmaking, legislative

parlour best room, drawing room, front room, lounge, reception room, sitting room

parlous chancy (*informal*), dangerous, desperate, difficult, dire, hairy (*slang*), hazardous, perilous, risky

parochial insular, inward-looking, limited, narrow, narrow-minded, parish-pump, petty, provincial, restricted, small-minded
Antonyms all-embracing, broad, broad-minded, cosmopolitan, international, liberal, national, universal, world-wide

parochialism insularity, limitedness, localism, narrow-mindedness, narrowness, provincialism, restrictedness, small-mindedness

a quarrel in a far away country between people of whom we know nothing

Neville Chamberlain

parodist burlesquer, caricaturist, humorist, impressionist, ironist, lampooner, mimic, mocker, pasquinader, satirist

parody *noun* **1.** burlesque, caricature, imitation, lampoon, satire, send-up (*Brit. informal*), skit, spoof (*informal*), takeoff (*informal*) **2.** apology, caricature, farce, mockery, travesty *~verb* **3.** burlesque, caricature, do a takeoff of (*informal*), lampoon, mimic, poke fun at, satirize, send up (*Brit. informal*), spoof (*informal*), take off (*informal*), take the piss out of (*taboo slang*), travesty

paroxysm attack, convulsion, eruption, fit, flare-up (*informal*), outburst, seizure, spasm

parrot 1. *noun, figurative* copycat (*informal*), imitator, (little) echo, mimic **2.** *adverb* **parrot-fashion** *informal* by rote, mechanically, mindlessly **3.** *verb* copy, echo, imitate, mimic, reiterate, repeat

parry 1. block, deflect, fend off, hold at bay, rebuff, repel, repulse, stave off, ward off **2.** avoid, circumvent, dodge, duck (*informal*), evade, fence, fight shy of, shun, sidestep

parsimonious cheeseparing, close, close-fisted, frugal, grasping, mean, mingy (*Brit. informal*), miserable, miserly, near (*informal*), niggardly, penny-pinching (*informal*), penurious, saving, scrimpy, skinflinty, sparing, stingy, stinting, tight-arse (*taboo slang*), tight-arsed (*taboo slang*), tight as a duck's arse (*taboo slang*), tight-ass (*U.S. taboo slang*), tight-assed (*U.S. taboo slang*), tightfisted
Antonyms extravagant, generous, lavish, munificent, open-handed, spendthrift, wasteful

parsimony frugality, meanness, minginess (*Brit. informal*), miserliness, nearness (*informal*), niggardliness, penny-pinching (*informal*), stinginess, tightness

parson churchman, clergyman, cleric, divine, ecclesiastic, incumbent, man of God, man of the cloth, minister, pastor, preacher, priest, rector, reverend (*informal*), vicar

part *noun* **1.** bit, fraction, fragment, lot, particle, piece, portion, scrap, section, sector, segment, share, slice **2.** branch, component, constituent, department, division, element, ingredient, limb, member, module, organ, piece, unit **3.** behalf, cause, concern, faction, interest, party, side **4.** bit, business, capacity, charge, duty, function, involvement, office, place, responsibility, role, say, share, task, work **5.** *Theatre* character, lines, role **6.** *often plural* airt (*Scot.*), area, district, neck of the woods (*informal*), neighbourhood, quarter, region, territory, vicinity **7. for the most part** chiefly, generally, in the main, largely, mainly, mostly, on the whole, principally **8. in good part** cheerfully, cordially, good-naturedly, well, without offence **9. in part** a little, in some measure, partially, partly, slightly, somewhat, to a certain extent, to some degree **10. on the part of** for the sake of, in support of, in the name of, on behalf of **11. take part in** associate oneself with, be instrumental in, be involved in, have a hand in, join in, partake in, participate in, play a part in, put one's twopence-worth in, take a hand in *~verb* **12.** break, cleave, come apart, detach, disconnect, disjoin, dismantle, disunite, divide, rend, separate, sever, split, tear **13.** break up, depart, go, go away, go (their) separate ways, leave, part company, quit, say goodbye, separate, split up, take one's leave, withdraw **14. part with** abandon, discard, forgo, give up, let go of, relinquish, renounce, sacrifice, surrender, yield
Antonyms *noun* (*senses 1 & 2*) bulk, entirety, mass, totality, whole *~verb* (*sense 12*) adhere, close, combine, hold, join, stick, unite (*sense 13*) appear, arrive, come, gather, remain, show up (*informal*), stay, turn up

partake 1. *with* **in** engage, enter into, participate, share, take part **2.** *with* **of** consume, eat, receive, share, take **3.** *with* **of** evince, evoke, have the quality of, show, suggest

partial 1. fragmentary, imperfect, incomplete, limited, uncompleted, unfinished **2.** biased, discriminatory, influenced, interested, one-sided, partisan, predisposed, prejudiced, tendentious, unfair, unjust **3. be partial to** be

fond of, be keen on, be taken with, care for, have a liking (soft spot, weakness) for
Antonyms (*sense 1*) complete, entire, finished, full, total, whole (*sense 2*) impartial, objective, unbiased, unprejudiced

partiality **1.** bias, favouritism, partisanship, predisposition, preference, prejudice **2.** affinity, bag (*slang*), cup of tea (*informal*), fondness, inclination, liking, love, penchant, predilec~ tion, predisposition, preference, proclivity, taste, weakness
Antonyms (*sense 1*) disinterest, equity, fair~ ness, impartiality, objectivity (*sense 2*) abhor~ rence, antipathy, aversion, disgust, disinclina~ tion, dislike, distaste, loathing, revulsion

partially fractionally, halfway, incompletely, in part, moderately, not wholly, partly, piece~ meal, somewhat, to a certain extent *or* degree

participant associate, contributor, member, partaker, participator, party, player, share~ holder

participate be a participant, be a party to, en~ gage in, enter into, get in on the act, have a hand in, join in, partake, perform, share, take part
Antonyms abstain, boycott, forgo, forsake, forswear, opt out, pass up, refrain from, take no part of

participation assistance, contribution, involve~ ment, joining in, partaking, partnership, sharing in, taking part

particle atom, bit, crumb, grain, iota, jot, mite, molecule, mote, piece, scrap, shred, speck, tit~ tle, whit

particular *adjective* **1.** distinct, exact, express, peculiar, precise, special, specific **2.** especial, exceptional, marked, notable, noteworthy, re~ markable, singular, uncommon, unusual **3.** blow-by-blow, circumstantial, detailed, item~ ized, minute, painstaking, precise, selective, thorough **4.** choosy (*informal*), critical, dainty, demanding, discriminating, exacting, fastidi~ ous, finicky, fussy, meticulous, nice (*rare*), overnice, pernickety (*informal*), picky (*infor~ mal*) *~noun* **5.** *usually plural* circumstance, detail, fact, feature, item, specification **6. in particular** distinctly, especially, exactly, ex~ pressly, particularly, specifically
Antonyms (*sense 1*) general, imprecise, in~ definite, indistinct, inexact, unspecified, vague (*sense 4*) casual, easy, easy to please, indis~ criminate, negligent, slack, sloppy, uncritical

particularity **1.** *often plural* circumstance, de~ tail, fact, instance, item, point **2.** carefulness, choosiness (*informal*), fastidiousness, fussi~ ness, meticulousness **3.** accuracy, detail, pre~ cision, thoroughness **4.** characteristic, distinc~ tiveness, feature, idiosyncrasy, individuality, peculiarity, property, singularity, trait

particularize detail, enumerate, itemize, speci~ fy, spell out, stipulate

particularly **1.** decidedly, especially, exception~ ally, markedly, notably, outstandingly, pecu~ liarly, singularly, surprisingly, uncommonly, unusually **2.** distinctly, especially, explicitly, expressly, in particular, specifically

parting *noun* **1.** adieu, departure, farewell, go~ ing, goodbye, leave-taking, valediction **2.** breaking, detachment, divergence, division, partition, rift, rupture, separation, split *~ad~ jective* **3.** departing, farewell, final, last, val~ edictory

Parting is all we know of heaven,
And all we need of hell
Emily Dickinson *"My life closed twice before its close"*

Parting is such sweet sorrow
William Shakespeare *Romeo and Juliet*

the parting of the way
Bible: Ezekiel

Since there's no help, come let us kiss and part,
Nay, I have done: you get no more of me,
And I am glad, yea glad with all my heart,
That thus so cleanly, I myself can free,
Shake hands forever, cancel all our vows,
And when we meet at any time again,
Be it not seen in either of our brows,
That we one jot of former love retain.
Michael Drayton *Idea: Sonnet 61*

In every parting there is an image of death
George Eliot *Scenes of Clerical Life*

partisan *noun* **1.** adherent, backer, champion, devotee, disciple, follower, stalwart, supporter, upholder, votary *~adjective* **2.** biased, faction~ al, interested, one-sided, partial, prejudiced, sectarian, tendentious *~noun* **3.** guerrilla, ir~ regular, resistance fighter, underground fight~ er *~adjective* **4.** guerrilla, irregular, resistance, underground
Antonyms *noun* adversary, contender, critic, detractor, foe, knocker (*informal*), leader, op~ ponent, rival *~adjective* bipartisan, broad-minded, disinterested, impartial, non-partisan, unbiased, unprejudiced

partition *noun* **1.** dividing, division, segrega~ tion, separation, severance, splitting **2.** barri~ er, divider, room divider, screen, wall **3.** allot~ ment, apportionment, distribution, portion, rationing out, share *~verb* **4.** apportion, cut up, divide, parcel out, portion, section, seg~ ment, separate, share, split up, subdivide **5.** divide, fence off, screen, separate, wall off

partly halfway, incompletely, in part, in some measure, not fully, partially, relatively, slightly, somewhat, to a certain degree *or* ex~ tent, up to a certain point
Antonyms completely, entirely, fully, in full, totally, wholly

partner 1. accomplice, ally, associate, bedfellow, collaborator, colleague, companion, comrade, confederate, copartner, helper, mate, participant, team-mate 2. bedfellow, consort, helpmate, her indoors (*Brit. slang*), husband, mate, significant other (*U.S. informal*), spouse, wife

partnership 1. companionship, connection, co-operation, copartnership, fellowship, interest, participation, sharing 2. alliance, association, combine, company, conglomerate, cooperative, corporation, firm, house, society, union

parts 1. ability, accomplishments, attributes, calibre, capabilities, endowments, faculties, genius, gifts, intellect, intelligence, talents 2. bits and pieces, components, spare parts, spares

party 1. at-home, bash (*informal*), beano (*Brit. slang*), celebration, do (*informal*), festivity, function, gathering, get-together (*informal*), hooley *or* hoolie (*chiefly Irish & N.Z.*), knees-up (*Brit. informal*), rave (*Brit. slang*), rave-up (*Brit. slang*), reception, shindig (*informal*), social, social gathering, soirée 2. band, body, bunch (*informal*), company, crew, detachment (*Military*), gang, gathering, group, squad, team, unit 3. alliance, association, cabal, camp, clique, coalition, combination, confederacy, coterie, faction, grouping, league, schism, set, side 4. individual, person, somebody, someone 5. *Law* contractor (*Law*), defendant, litigant, participant, plaintiff

Under democracy, one party always devotes its chief energies to trying to prove that the other party is unfit to rule: and both commonly succeed, and are right

H.L. Mencken

parvenu 1. *noun* arriviste, *nouveau riche*, social climber, upstart 2. *adjective nouveau riche*, upstart

pass[1] *verb* 1. depart, elapse, flow, go, go by *or* past, lapse, leave, move, move onwards, proceed, roll, run 2. beat, exceed, excel, go beyond, outdistance, outdo, outstrip, surmount, surpass, transcend 3. answer, come up to scratch (*informal*), do, get through, graduate, pass muster, qualify, succeed, suffice, suit 4. beguile, devote, employ, experience, fill, occupy, spend, suffer, undergo, while away 5. befall, come up, develop, fall out, happen, occur, take place 6. convey, deliver, exchange, give, hand, kick, let have, reach, send, throw, transfer, transmit 7. accept, adopt, approve, authorize, decree, enact, establish, legislate, ordain, ratify, sanction, validate 8. declare, deliver, express, pronounce, utter 9. disregard, ignore, miss, neglect, not heed, omit, overlook, skip (*informal*) 10. crap (*taboo slang*), defecate, discharge, eliminate, empty, evacuate, excrete, expel, shit (*taboo slang*), void 11. blow over, cease, die, disappear, dissolve, dwindle, ebb, end, evaporate, expire, fade, go, melt away, terminate, vanish, wane 12. *with* **for** *or* **as** be accepted as, be mistaken for, be regarded as, be taken for, impersonate, serve as

Antonyms (*sense 1*) bring *or* come to a standstill, cease, halt, pause, stop (*senses 2 & 3*) be inadequate, be inferior to, be unsuccessful, come a cropper (*informal*), fail, lose, suffer defeat (*sense 7*) ban, disallow, invalidate, overrule, prohibit, refuse, reject, veto (*sense 9*) acknowledge, heed, note, notice, observe, pay attention to

pass[2] *noun* 1. canyon, col, defile, gap, gorge, ravine 2. authorization, identification, identity card, licence, passport, permission, permit, safe-conduct, ticket, warrant 3. *informal* advances, approach, overture, play (*informal*), proposition, suggestion 4. condition, juncture, pinch, plight, predicament, situation, stage, state, state of affairs, straits 5. feint, jab, lunge, push, swing, thrust

passable 1. acceptable, adequate, admissible, allowable, all right, average, fair, fair enough, mediocre, middling, moderate, not too bad, ordinary, presentable, so-so (*informal*), tolerable, unexceptional 2. clear, crossable, navigable, open, traversable, unobstructed

Antonyms (*sense 1*) A1 *or* A-one (*informal*), exceptional, extraordinary, first-class, inadequate, inadmissible, marvellous, outstanding, superb, tops (*slang*), unacceptable, unsatisfactory (*sense 2*) blocked, closed, impassable, obstructed, sealed off, unnavigable

passably after a fashion, fairly, moderately, pretty much, rather, relatively, somewhat, tolerably, well enough

passage 1. alley, avenue, channel, course, lane, opening, path, road, route, thoroughfare, way 2. corridor, doorway, entrance, entrance hall, exit, hall, hallway, lobby, passageway, vestibule 3. clause, excerpt, extract, paragraph, piece, quotation, reading, section, sentence, text, verse 4. crossing, journey, tour, trek, trip, voyage 5. advance, change, conversion, flow, motion, movement, passing, progress, progression, transit, transition 6. allowance, authorization, freedom, permission, right, safe-conduct, visa, warrant 7. acceptance, enactment, establishment, legalization, legislation, passing, ratification

passageway aisle, alley, corridor, cut, entrance, exit, hall, hallway, lane, lobby, passage, wynd (*Scot.*)

pass away buy it (*U.S. slang*), buy the farm (*U.S. slang*), check out (*U.S. slang*), croak (*slang*), decease, depart (this life), die, expire, go belly-up (*slang*), kick it (*slang*), kick the bucket (*slang*), pass on, pass over, peg it (*informal*), peg out (*informal*), pop one's clogs (*informal*), shuffle off this mortal coil, snuff it (*informal*)

pass by **1.** go past, leave, move past, pass **2.** disregard, miss, neglect, not choose, overlook, pass over

passé antiquated, dated, *démodé*, obsolete, old-fashioned, old hat, outdated, outmoded, out-of-date, outworn, unfashionable

passenger fare, hitchhiker, pillion rider, rider, traveller

passer-by bystander, onlooker, witness

passing *adjective* **1.** brief, ephemeral, fleeting, momentary, short, short-lived, temporary, transient, transitory **2.** casual, cursory, glancing, hasty, quick, shallow, short, slight, superficial *~noun* **3.** death, decease, demise, end, finish, loss, termination **4. in passing** accidentally, by the bye, by the way, en passant, incidentally, on the way

passion **1.** animation, ardour, eagerness, emotion, excitement, feeling, fervour, fire, heat, intensity, joy, rapture, spirit, transport, warmth, zeal, zest **2.** adoration, affection, ardour, attachment, concupiscence, desire, fondness, infatuation, itch, keenness, love, lust, the hots (*slang*) **3.** bug (*informal*), craving, craze, enthusiasm, fancy, fascination, idol, infatuation, mania, obsession **4.** anger, fit, flare-up (*informal*), frenzy, fury, indignation, ire, outburst, paroxysm, rage, resentment, storm, vehemence, wrath
Antonyms apathy, calmness, coldness, coolness, frigidity, hate, indifference, unconcern

> *A man who has not passed through the inferno of his passions has never overcome them*
> Carl Gustav Jung *Memories, Dreams, and Reflections*

passionate **1.** amorous, ardent, aroused, desirous, erotic, hot, loving, lustful, sensual, sexy (*informal*), steamy (*informal*), wanton **2.** ablaze, animated, ardent, eager, emotional, enthusiastic, excited, fervent, fervid, fierce, flaming, frenzied, heartfelt, impassioned, impetuous, impulsive, intense, strong, vehement, warm, wild, zealous **3.** choleric, excitable, fiery, hot-headed, hot-tempered, irascible, irritable, peppery, quick-tempered, stormy, tempestuous, violent
Antonyms (*sense 1*) cold, frigid, passionless, unloving, unresponsive (*sense 2*) apathetic, calm, cold, half-hearted, indifferent, languorous, nonchalant, subdued, unemotional, unenthusiastic (*sense 3*) agreeable, calm, easy-going, even-tempered, nonviolent, placid, unexcitable

passionately **1.** amorously, ardently, desirously, erotically, hot-bloodedly, libidinously, lovingly, lustfully, sensually, sexily (*informal*), steamily (*informal*), with passion **2.** animatedly, ardently, eagerly, emotionally, enthusiastically, excitedly, fervently, fervidly, fiercely, frenziedly, impetuously, impulsively, intensely, strongly, vehemently, warmly, wildly, with all one's heart, zealously **3.** excitably, fierily, hot-headedly, irascibly, stormily, tempestuously, violently
Antonyms (*sense 1*) coldly, frigidly, unlovingly, unresponsively (*sense 2*) apathetically, calmly, coldly, half-heartedly, indifferently, nonchalantly, unemotionally, unenthusiastically (*sense 3*) calmly, placidly, unexcitably

passionless **1.** apathetic, cold, cold-blooded, cold-hearted, emotionless, frigid, icy, indifferent, uncaring, unfeeling, unloving, unresponsive **2.** calm, detached, dispassionate, impartial, impassive, neutral, restrained, unemotional, uninvolved

passive acquiescent, compliant, docile, enduring, inactive, inert, lifeless, long-suffering, nonviolent, patient, quiescent, receptive, resigned, submissive, unassertive, uninvolved, unresisting
Antonyms active, alive, assertive, bossy (*informal*), defiant, domineering, energetic, feisty (*informal, chiefly U.S. & Canad.*), impatient, involved, lively, rebellious, spirited, violent, zippy (*informal*)

pass off **1.** counterfeit, fake, feign, make a pretence of, palm off **2.** come to an end, die away, disappear, fade out, vanish **3.** emit, evaporate, give off, send forth, vaporize **4.** be completed, go off, happen, occur, take place, turn out **5.** dismiss, disregard, ignore, pass by, wink at

pass out **1.** *informal* become unconscious, black out (*informal*), drop, faint, flake out (*informal*), keel over (*informal*), lose consciousness, swoon (*literary*) **2.** deal out, distribute, dole out, hand out

pass over discount, disregard, forget, ignore, not dwell on, omit, overlook, pass by, take no notice of

pass up abstain, decline, forgo, give (something) a miss (*informal*), ignore, let go, let slip, miss, neglect, refuse, reject

password countersign, key word, open sesame, signal, watchword

past *adjective* **1.** accomplished, completed, done, elapsed, ended, extinct, finished, forgotten, gone, over, over and done with, spent **2.** ancient, bygone, early, erstwhile, foregoing, former, late, long-ago, olden, preceding, previous, prior, quondam, recent *~noun* **3. the past** antiquity, days gone by, days of yore, former times, good old days, history, long ago, olden days, old times, times past, yesteryear (*literary*) **4.** background, experience, history,

life, past life *~adverb* **5.** across, beyond, by, on, over *~preposition* **6.** after, beyond, farther than, later than, outside, over, subsequent to
Antonyms *adjective* arrived, begun, coming, future, now, present *~noun* future, now, present, time to come, today, tomorrow

The past is a foreign country; they do things differently there
L.P. Hartley *The Go-Between*

The past is the only dead thing that smells sweet
Edward Thomas *Early One Morning*

Those who cannot remember the past are condemned to repeat it
George Santayana *The Life of Reason*

paste **1.** *noun* adhesive, cement, glue, gum, mucilage **2.** *verb* cement, fasten, fix, glue, gum, stick

pastel *adjective* delicate, light, muted, pale, soft, soft-hued
Antonyms bright, deep, rich, strong, vibrant, vivid

pastiche blend, farrago, gallimaufry, hotchpotch, medley, *mélange*, miscellany, mixture, motley

pastille cough drop, jujube, lozenge, tablet, troche (*Medical*)

pastime activity, amusement, distraction, diversion, entertainment, game, hobby, leisure, play, recreation, relaxation, sport

past master ace (*informal*), artist, dab hand (*Brit. informal*), expert, old hand, virtuoso, wizard

pastor churchman, clergyman, divine, ecclesiastic, minister, parson, priest, rector, vicar

pastoral *adjective* **1.** agrestic, Arcadian, bucolic, country, georgic (*literary*), idyllic, rural, rustic, simple **2.** clerical, ecclesiastical, ministerial, priestly

pasture grass, grassland, grazing, grazing land, lea (*poetic*), meadow, pasturage, shieling (*Scot.*)

pasty *adjective* **1.** doughy, glutinous, mucilaginous, starchy, sticky **2.** anaemic, like death warmed up (*informal*), pale, pallid, sallow, sickly, unhealthy, wan, wheyfaced

pat[1] *verb* **1.** caress, dab, fondle, pet, slap, stroke, tap, touch *~noun* **2.** clap, dab, light blow, slap, stroke, tap **3.** cake, dab, lump, portion, small piece

pat[2] *adverb* **1.** exactly, faultlessly, flawlessly, off pat, perfectly, precisely **2.** aptly, bang, dead on, fittingly, just right, opportunely, plumb (*informal*), relevantly, seasonably *~adjective* **3.** apposite, apropos, apt, felicitous, fitting, happy, neat, pertinent, relevant, spot-on (*Brit. informal*), suitable, to the point **4.** automatic, easy, facile, glib, ready, simplistic, slick, smooth

patch *noun* **1.** piece of material, reinforcement **2.** bit, scrap, shred, small piece, spot, stretch **3.** area, ground, land, plot, tract *~verb* **4.** cover, fix, mend, reinforce, repair, sew up **5.** *with* **up** bury the hatchet, conciliate, make friends, placate, restore, settle, settle differences, smooth

patchwork confusion, hash, hotchpotch, jumble, medley, mishmash, mixture, pastiche

patchy bitty, erratic, fitful, inconstant, irregular, random, sketchy, spotty, uneven, variable, varying
Antonyms constant, even, regular, unbroken, unvarying

patent **1.** *adjective* apparent, blatant, clear, conspicuous, downright, evident, flagrant, glaring, indisputable, manifest, obvious, open, palpable, transparent, unconcealed, unequivocal, unmistakable **2.** *noun* copyright, invention, licence

paternal **1.** benevolent, concerned, fatherlike, fatherly, protective, solicitous, vigilant **2.** patrilineal, patrimonial

paternity **1.** fatherhood, fathership **2.** descent, extraction, family, lineage, parentage **3.** authorship, derivation, origin, source

path **1.** footpath, footway, pathway, towpath, track, trail, walkway (*chiefly U.S.*) **2.** avenue, course, direction, passage, procedure, road, route, track, walk, way

pathetic **1.** affecting, distressing, harrowing, heartbreaking, heart-rending, melting, moving, pitiable, plaintive, poignant, sad, tender, touching **2.** deplorable, feeble, inadequate, lamentable, meagre, measly, miserable, not much cop (*Brit. slang*), paltry, petty, pitiful, poor, puny, sorry, wet (*Brit. informal*), woeful **3.** *slang* chickenshit (*U.S. slang*), crappy (*slang*), crummy (*slang*), poxy (*slang*), rubbishy, trashy, uninteresting, useless, wanky (*taboo slang*), worthless
Antonyms (*sense 1*) amusing, comical, droll, entertaining, funny, laughable, ludicrous, ridiculous

pathfinder discoverer, explorer, guide, pioneer, scout, trailblazer

pathless impassable, impenetrable, trackless, uncharted, unexplored, untrodden, waste, wild

pathos pitiableness, pitifulness, plaintiveness, poignancy, sadness

patience **1.** calmness, composure, cool (*slang*), equanimity, even temper, forbearance, imperturbability, restraint, serenity, sufferance, tolerance, toleration **2.** constancy, diligence, endurance, fortitude, long-suffering, perseverance, persistence, resignation, stoicism, submission
Antonyms (*sense 1*) agitation, exasperation, excitement, impatience, irritation, nervous~

ness, passion, restlessness (*sense 2*) irresolution, vacillation

Patience is the virtue of an ass
Lord Lansdowne

They also serve who only stand and wait
John Milton *Sonnet on his Blindness*

All things come to those who wait

Rome was not built in a day

Patience is a virtue

patient *adjective* **1.** calm, composed, enduring, long-suffering, persevering, persistent, philosophical, quiet, resigned, self-possessed, serene, stoical, submissive, uncomplaining, untiring **2.** accommodating, even-tempered, forbearing, forgiving, indulgent, lenient, mild, tolerant, understanding *~noun* **3.** case, invalid, sick person, sufferer

That patient is not like to recover who makes the doctor his heir.
Thomas Fuller *Gnomologia*

patois 1. dialect **2.** argot, cant, jargon, lingo (*informal*), patter, slang, vernacular

patriarch 1. father, paterfamilias, sire **2.** elder, grandfather, greybeard, old man

patrician 1. *noun* aristo (*informal*), aristocrat, childe (*archaic*), noble, nobleman, peer **2.** *adjective* aristocratic, blue-blooded, gentle (*archaic*), highborn, high-class, lordly, noble

patrimony bequest, birthright, heritage, inheritance, legacy, portion, share

patriot chauvinist, flag-waver (*informal*), jingo, lover of one's country, loyalist, nationalist

No man can be a patriot on an empty stomach
W.C. Brann *Old Glory*

patriotic chauvinistic, flag-waving (*informal*), jingoistic, loyal, nationalistic

patriotism flag-waving (*informal*), jingoism, love of one's country, loyalty, nationalism

I only regret that I have but one life to lose for my country
Nathan Hale

It is a sweet and honourable thing to die for one's country (dulce et decorum est pro patria mori)
Horace *Odes*

Patriotism is the last refuge of a scoundrel
Dr. Johnson

And so, my fellow Americans; ask not what your country can do for you - ask what you can do for your country. My fellow citizens of the world; ask not what America will do for you, but what together we can do for the freedom of man
John F. Kennedy

England expects that every man will do his duty
Horatio Nelson

Never was patriot yet, but was a fool
John Dryden *Absalom and Achitophel*

That kind of patriotism which consists in hating all other nations
Elizabeth Gaskell *Sylvia's Lovers*

You'll never have a quiet world until you knock the patriotism out of the human race
George Bernard Shaw *O'Flaherty V.C.*

our country, right or wrong!
Stephen Decatur

If I should die, think only this of me,
That there's some corner of a foreign field
That is for ever England
Rupert Brooke *The Soldier*

What pity is it
That we can die but once to serve our country!
Joseph Addison *Cato*

Patriotism is a lively sense of collective responsibility. Nationalism is a silly cock crowing on its own dunghill
Richard Aldington *The Colonel's Daughter*

patriotism: combustible rubbish ready to the torch of any one ambitious to illuminate his name
Ambrose Bierce *The Devil's Dictionary*

patrol *noun* **1.** guarding, policing, protecting, rounds, safeguarding, vigilance, watching **2.** garrison, guard, patrolman, sentinel, watch, watchman *~verb* **3.** cruise, guard, inspect, keep guard, keep watch, make the rounds, police, pound, range, safeguard, walk the beat

patron 1. advocate, angel (*informal*), backer, benefactor, champion, defender, friend, guardian, helper, philanthropist, protagonist, protector, sponsor, supporter **2.** buyer, client, customer, frequenter, habitué, shopper

patronage 1. aid, assistance, backing, benefaction, championship, encouragement, espousal, help, promotion, sponsorship, support **2.** business, clientele, commerce, custom, trade, trading, traffic **3.** condescension, deigning, disdain, patronizing, stooping

patronize 1. be lofty with, look down on, talk down to, treat as inferior, treat condescendingly, treat like a child **2.** assist, back, befriend, foster, fund, help, maintain, promote, sponsor, subscribe to, support **3.** be a customer *or* client of, buy from, deal with, do business with, frequent, shop at, trade with

patronizing condescending, contemptuous, disdainful, gracious, haughty, lofty, snobbish, stooping, supercilious, superior, toffee-nosed (*slang, chiefly Brit.*)

Antonyms deferential, humble, obsequious, respectful, servile

patter[1] *verb* **1.** scurry, scuttle, skip, tiptoe, trip, walk lightly **2.** beat, pat, pelt, pitapat, pitter-patter, rat-a-tat, spatter, tap *~noun* **3.** pattering, pitapat, pitter-patter, tapping

patter[2] *noun* **1.** line, monologue, pitch, spiel (*informal*) **2.** chatter, gabble, jabber, nattering, prattle, yak (*slang*) **3.** argot, cant, jargon, lin~

go (*informal*), patois, slang, vernacular *~verb* 4. babble, blab, chatter, hold forth, jabber, prate, rattle off, rattle on, spiel (*informal*), spout (*informal*), tattle

pattern *noun* 1. arrangement, decoration, decorative design, design, device, figure, motif, ornament 2. arrangement, method, order, orderliness, plan, sequence, system 3. kind, shape, sort, style, type, variety 4. design, diagram, guide, instructions, original, plan, stencil, template 5. archetype, criterion, cynosure, example, exemplar, guide, model, norm, original, par, paradigm, paragon, prototype, sample, specimen, standard *~verb* 6. copy, emulate, follow, form, imitate, model, mould, order, shape, style 7. decorate, design, trim

paucity dearth, deficiency, fewness, insufficiency, lack, meagreness, paltriness, poverty, rarity, scantiness, scarcity, shortage, slenderness, slightness, smallness, sparseness, sparsity

paunch abdomen, beer-belly (*informal*), belly, corporation (*informal*), middle-age spread (*informal*), pot, potbelly, spare tyre (*Brit. slang*), spread (*informal*)

pauper bankrupt, beggar, down-and-out, have-not, indigent, insolvent, mendicant, poor person

pauperism beggary, destitution, impecuniousness, indigence, mendicancy, need, neediness, pennilessness, penury, poverty, privation, want

pauperize bankrupt, beggar, break, bust (*informal*), cripple financially, impoverish, reduce to beggary, ruin

pause 1. *verb* break, cease, delay, deliberate, desist, discontinue, halt, have a breather (*informal*), hesitate, interrupt, rest, stop briefly, take a break, wait, waver 2. *noun* break, breather (*informal*), breathing space, caesura, cessation, delay, discontinuance, entr'acte, gap, halt, hesitation, interlude, intermission, interruption, interval, let-up (*informal*), lull, respite, rest, stay, stoppage, wait

Antonyms *verb* advance, continue, proceed, progress *~noun* advancement, continuance, progression

pave asphalt, concrete, cover, flag, floor, macadamize, surface, tar, tile

paw *verb* grab, handle roughly, manhandle, maul, molest

pawn[1] 1. *verb* deposit, gage (*archaic*), hazard, hock (*informal, chiefly U.S.*), mortgage, pledge, pop (*informal*), stake, wager 2. *noun* assurance, bond, collateral, gage, guarantee, guaranty, pledge, security

pawn[2] *noun* cat's-paw, creature, dupe, instrument, plaything, puppet, stooge (*slang*), tool, toy

pay *verb* 1. clear, compensate, cough up (*informal*), discharge, foot, give, honour, liquidate, meet, offer, recompense, reimburse, remit, remunerate, render, requite, reward, settle, square up 2. be advantageous, benefit, be worthwhile, repay, serve 3. bestow, extend, give, grant, hand out, present, proffer, render 4. *often with* **for** answer for, atone, be punished, compensate, get one's deserts, make amends, suffer, suffer the consequences 5. bring in, produce, profit, return, yield 6. be profitable, be remunerative, make a return, make money, provide a living 7. avenge oneself for, get even with (*informal*), get revenge on, pay back, punish, reciprocate, repay, requite, settle a score *~noun* 8. allowance, compensation, earnings, emoluments, fee, hand-out, hire, income, meed (*archaic*), payment, recompense, reimbursement, remuneration, reward, salary, stipend, takings, wages

He who pays the piper calls the tune

You pays your money and you takes your choice

payable due, mature, obligatory, outstanding, owed, owing, receivable, to be paid

pay back 1. get even with (*informal*), get one's own back, hit back, reciprocate, recompense, retaliate, settle a score 2. refund, reimburse, repay, return, settle up, square

payment 1. defrayal, discharge, outlay, paying, remittance, settlement 2. advance, deposit, instalment, portion, premium, remittance 3. fee, hire, remuneration, reward, wage

payoff *noun* 1. conclusion, day of reckoning, final reckoning, judgment, retribution, reward, settlement 2. *informal* climax, clincher (*informal*), consequence, culmination, finale, moment of truth, outcome, punch line, result, the crunch (*informal*), upshot

pay off 1. discharge, dismiss, fire, lay off, let go, sack (*informal*) 2. clear, discharge, liquidate, pay in full, settle, square 3. be effective (profitable, successful), succeed, work 4. get even with (*informal*), pay back, retaliate, settle a score 5. *informal* bribe, buy off, corrupt, get at, grease the palm of (*slang*), oil (*informal*), suborn

pay out 1. cough up (*informal*), disburse, expend, fork out *or* over *or* up (*slang*), lay out (*informal*), shell out (*informal*), spend 2. get even with (*informal*), pay back, retaliate, settle a score

peace 1. accord, agreement, amity, concord, harmony 2. armistice, cessation of hostilities, conciliation, pacification, treaty, truce 3. calm, composure, contentment, placidity, relaxation, repose, serenity 4. calm, calmness, hush, peacefulness, quiet, quietude, repose, rest, silence, stillness, tranquillity

Related adjective: irenic *or* eirenic

Peace hath her victories
No less renowned than war
John Milton *Sonnet, To the Lord General Cromwell, May 1652*

Let him who desires peace, prepare for war
Vegetius *De Re Militari*

If peace cannot be maintained with honour, it is no longer peace
Lord John Russell

In the arts of peace Man is a bungler
George Bernard Shaw *Man and Superman*

the peace of God, which passeth all understanding
Bible: Philippians

They shall beat their swords into ploughshares, and their spears into pruning-hooks
Bible: Isaiah

War makes rattling good history; but Peace is poor reading
Thomas Hardy *The Dynasts*

He that makes a good war makes a good peace
George Herbert *Outlandish Proverbs*

peace: in international affairs, a period of cheating between two periods of fighting
Ambrose Bierce *The Devil's Dictionary*

peaceable 1. amiable, amicable, conciliatory, dovish, friendly, gentle, inoffensive, mild, nonbelligerent, pacific, peaceful, peace-loving, placid, unwarlike 2. balmy, calm, peaceful, quiet, restful, serene, still, tranquil, undisturbed

peaceful 1. amicable, at peace, free from strife, friendly, harmonious, nonviolent, on friendly *or* good terms, without hostility 2. calm, gentle, placid, quiet, restful, serene, still, tranquil, undisturbed, unruffled, untroubled 3. conciliatory, irenic, pacific, peaceable, peace-loving, placatory, unwarlike
Antonyms agitated, antagonistic, belligerent, bitter, disquieted, disturbed, hostile, loud, nervous, noisy, raucous, restless, unfriendly, upset, violent, warlike, warring, wartime

peacemaker appeaser, arbitrator, conciliator, mediator, pacifier, peacemonger

Blessed are the peacemakers; for they shall be called the children of God
Bible: St. Matthew

peak *noun* 1. aiguille, apex, brow, crest, pinnacle, point, summit, tip, top 2. acme, apogee, climax, crown, culmination, high point, maximum point, *ne plus ultra*, zenith ~*verb* 3. be at its height, climax, come to a head, culminate, reach its highest point, reach the zenith

peaky emaciated, green about the gills, ill, in poor shape, like death warmed up (*informal*), off colour, pale, peelie-wally (*Scot.*), pinched, poorly (*informal*), sick, sickly, under the weather (*informal*), unwell, wan

peal 1. *noun* blast, carillon, chime, clamour, clang, clap, crash, resounding, reverberation, ring, ringing, roar, rumble, sound, tintinnabulation 2. *verb* chime, crack, crash, resonate, resound, reverberate, ring, roar, roll, rumble, sound, tintinnabulate, toll

pearly 1. iridescent, margaric, margaritic, mother-of-pearl, nacreous, opalescent 2. cream, ivory, milky, silvery

peasant 1. churl (*archaic*), countryman, hind (*obsolete*), rustic, son of the soil, swain (*archaic*) 2. *informal* boor, churl, country bumpkin, hayseed (*U.S. & Canad. informal*), hick (*informal, chiefly U.S. & Canad.*), lout, provincial, yokel

peccadillo error, indiscretion, infraction, lapse, misdeed, misdemeanour, petty offence, slip, trifling fault

peck *verb/noun* bite, dig, hit, jab, kiss, nibble, pick, poke, prick, strike, tap

peculate appropriate, defalcate (*Law*), defraud, embezzle, misapply, misappropriate, pilfer, purloin, rob, steal

peculiar 1. abnormal, bizarre, curious, eccentric, exceptional, extraordinary, far-out (*slang*), freakish, funny, odd, offbeat, off-the-wall (*slang*), outlandish, out-of-the-way, outré, quaint, queer, singular, strange, uncommon, unconventional, unusual, wacko (*slang*), weird 2. appropriate, characteristic, distinct, distinctive, distinguishing, endemic, idiosyncratic, individual, local, particular, personal, private, restricted, special, specific, unique
Antonyms (*sense 1*) commonplace, conventional, expected, familiar, ordinary, usual (*sense 2*) common, general, indistinctive, unspecific

peculiarity 1. abnormality, bizarreness, eccentricity, foible, freakishness, idiosyncrasy, mannerism, oddity, odd trait, queerness, quirk 2. attribute, characteristic, distinctiveness, feature, mark, particularity, property, quality, singularity, speciality, trait

pecuniary commercial, financial, fiscal, monetary

pedagogue dogmatist, dominie (*Scot.*), educator, instructor, master, mistress, pedant, schoolmaster, schoolmistress, teacher

pedant casuist, doctrinaire, dogmatist, hairsplitter, literalist, nit-picker (*informal*), pedagogue, pettifogger, precisian, quibbler, scholastic, sophist

pedantic abstruse, academic, bookish, didactic, donnish, erudite, formal, fussy, hairsplitting, nit-picking (*informal*), overnice, particular, pedagogic, picky (*informal*), pompous, precise, priggish, punctilious, scholastic, schoolmasterly, sententious, stilted

pedantry bookishness, finicality, hairsplitting, overnicety, pedagogism, pettifoggery, pompos~ity, punctiliousness, quibbling, sophistry, stuffiness

Pedantry is the dotage of knowledge
Holbrook Jackson *Anatomy of Bibliomania*

peddle flog (*slang*), hawk, huckster, market, push (*informal*), sell, sell door to door, trade, vend

pedestal 1. base, dado (*Architecture*), foot, foundation, mounting, pier, plinth, socle, stand, support 2. **put on a pedestal** apoth~eosize, deify, dignify, ennoble, exalt, glorify, idealize, worship

pedestrian 1. *noun* footslogger, foot-traveller, walker 2. *adjective* banal, boring, common~place, dull, flat, ho-hum (*informal*), humdrum, mediocre, mundane, no great shakes (*infor~mal*), ordinary, plodding, prosaic, run-of-the-mill, unimaginative, uninspired, uninteresting
Antonyms *noun* driver *~adjective* exciting, fascinating, imaginative, important, interest~ing, noteworthy, outstanding, remarkable, significant

pedigree 1. *noun* ancestry, blood, breed, deri~vation, descent, extraction, family, family tree, genealogy, heritage, line, lineage, race, stemma, stirps, stock 2. *adjective* full-blooded, purebred, thoroughbred

pedlar cheap-jack (*informal*), colporteur, door-to-door salesman, duffer (*dialect*), hawker, huckster, seller, vendor

peek 1. *verb* glance, keek (*Scot.*), look, peep, peer, snatch a glimpse, sneak a look, spy, squinny, take *or* have a gander (*informal*), take a look 2. *noun* blink, butcher's (*Brit. slang*), gander (*informal*), glance, glim (*Scot.*), glimpse, keek (*Scot.*), look, look-see (*slang*), peep, shufti (*Brit. slang*)

peel 1. *verb* decorticate, desquamate, flake off, pare, scale, skin, strip off 2. *noun* epicarp, exocarp, peeling, rind, skin

peep[1] *verb* 1. keek (*Scot.*), look from hiding, look surreptitiously, peek, peer, sneak a look, spy, steal a look 2. appear briefly, emerge, peer out, show partially *~noun* 3. butcher's (*Brit. slang*), gander (*informal*), glim (*Scot.*), glimpse, keek (*Scot.*), look, look-see (*slang*), peek, shufti (*Brit. slang*)

peep[2] *verb/noun* cheep, chirp, chirrup, pipe, squeak, tweet, twitter

peephole aperture, chink, crack, crevice, fis~sure, hole, keyhole, opening, pinhole, slit, spyhole

peer[1] *noun* 1. aristo (*informal*), aristocrat, bar~on, count, duke, earl, lord, marquess, mar~quis, noble, nobleman, viscount 2. coequal, compeer, equal, fellow, like, match

peer[2] *verb* 1. gaze, inspect, peep, scan, scruti~nize, snoop, spy, squinny, squint 2. appear, become visible, emerge, peep out

peerage aristocracy, lords and ladies, nobility, peers, titled classes

When I want a peerage, I shall buy it like an honest man
Lord Northcliff

peerless beyond compare, excellent, incompa~rable, matchless, nonpareil, outstanding, sec~ond to none, superlative, unequalled, unique, unmatched, unparalleled, unrivalled, unsur~passed
Antonyms commonplace, inferior, mediocre, no great shakes (*informal*), ordinary, poor, second-rate

peeve 1. *verb* annoy, bother, bug (*informal*), exasperate, gall, get (*informal*), get one's goat (*slang*), get on one's nerves (*informal*), irk, ir~ritate, nark (*Brit., Austral., & N.Z. slang*), nettle, pique, piss one off (*taboo slang*), pro~voke, rile, rub (up) the wrong way, vex 2. *noun* annoyance, bother, gripe (*informal*), nuisance, pest, sore point, vexation

peeved annoyed, exasperated, galled, hacked (off) (*U.S. slang*), irked, irritated, nettled, piqued, pissed off (*taboo slang*), put out, riled, sore, upset, vexed

peevish acrimonious, cantankerous, captious, childish, churlish, crabbed, cross, crotchety (*informal*), crusty, fractious, fretful, grumpy, huffy, ill-natured, ill-tempered, irritable, liv~erish, pettish, petulant, querulous, ratty (*Brit. & N.Z. informal*), short-tempered, shrewish, snappy, splenetic, sulky, sullen, surly, testy, tetchy, touchy, waspish, whingeing (*informal*)
Antonyms affable, agreeable, cheerful, cheery, easy-going, even-tempered, genial, good-natured, happy, merry, pleasant, sweet

peg *verb* 1. attach, fasten, fix, join, make fast, secure 2. *with* **along** *or* **away** apply oneself to, beaver away (*Brit. informal*), keep at it, keep going, keep on, persist, plod along, plug away at (*informal*), stick to it, work at, work away 3. *of prices, etc.* control, fix, freeze, limit, set

pejorative belittling, debasing, deprecatory, depreciatory, derogatory, detractive, detrac~tory, disparaging, negative, slighting, uncom~plimentary, unpleasant

pell-mell 1. *adverb* full tilt, hastily, heedlessly, helter-skelter, hurriedly, impetuously, post~haste, precipitously, rashly, recklessly 2. *ad~jective* chaotic, confused, disordered, disorgan~ized, haphazard, tumultuous 3. *noun* anarchy, chaos, confusion, disarray, disorder, ferment, helter-skelter, pandemonium, tumult, turmoil, upheaval

pellucid 1. bright, clear, crystalline, glassy, limpid, translucent, transparent 2. clear, com~

prehensible, limpid, lucid, perspicuous, plain, straightforward, unambiguous

pelt[1] *verb* **1.** assail, batter, beat, belabour, bombard, cast, hurl, pepper, pummel, shower, sling, strike, thrash, throw, wallop (*informal*) **2.** barrel (along) (*informal, chiefly U.S. & Canad.*), belt (*slang*), burn rubber (*informal*), career, charge, dash, hurry, run fast, rush, shoot, speed, stampede, tear, whiz (*informal*) **3.** bucket down (*informal*), pour, rain cats and dogs (*informal*), rain hard, teem

pelt[2] *noun* coat, fell, hide, skin

pen[1] *verb* commit to paper, compose, draft, draw up, jot down, write

Beneath the rule of men entirely great
The pen is mightier than the sword
Edward Bulwer-Lytton *Richelieu*

pen[2] **1.** *noun* cage, coop, corral (*chiefly U.S. & Canad.*), enclosure, fold, hutch, pound, sty **2.** *verb* cage, confine, coop up, enclose, fence in, hedge, hem in, hurdle, impound, mew (up), pound, shut up *or* in

penal corrective, disciplinary, penalizing, punitive, retributive

penalize award a penalty against (*Sport*), correct, discipline, handicap, impose a penalty on, inflict a handicap on, punish, put at a disadvantage

penalty disadvantage, fine, forfeit, forfeiture, handicap, mulct, price, punishment, retribution

penance **1.** atonement, mortification, penalty, punishment, reparation, sackcloth and ashes **2.** **do penance** accept punishment, atone, make amends, make reparation, mortify oneself, show contrition, suffer

penchant affinity, bent, bias, disposition, fondness, inclination, leaning, liking, partiality, predilection, predisposition, proclivity, proneness, propensity, taste, tendency, turn

pendent *adjective* dangling, drooping, hanging, pendulous, suspended, swinging

pending awaiting, forthcoming, hanging fire, imminent, impending, in the balance, in the offing, undecided, undetermined, unsettled, up in the air

pendulous dangling, drooping, hanging, pendent, sagging, swaying, swinging

penetrable accessible, clear, comprehensible, fathomable, intelligible, open, passable, permeable, pervious, porous

penetrate **1.** bore, enter, go through, impale, perforate, pierce, prick, probe, stab **2.** diffuse, enter, get in, infiltrate, make inroads (into), permeate, pervade, seep, suffuse **3.** *figurative* affect, become clear, be understood, come across, get through to, impress, touch **4.** *figurative* comprehend, decipher, discern, fathom, figure out (*informal*), get to the bottom of, grasp, suss (out) (*slang*), understand, unravel, work out

penetrating **1.** biting, carrying, harsh, intrusive, pervasive, piercing, pungent, sharp, shrill, stinging, strong **2.** *figurative* acute, astute, critical, discerning, discriminating, incisive, intelligent, keen, perceptive, perspicacious, profound, quick, sagacious, searching, sharp, sharp-witted, shrewd

Antonyms (*sense 1*) blunt, dull, mild, sweet (*sense 2*) apathetic, dull, indifferent, obtuse, shallow, stupid, uncomprehending, unperceptive

penetration **1.** entrance, entry, incision, inroad, invasion, perforation, piercing, puncturing **2.** acuteness, astuteness, discernment, insight, keenness, perception, perspicacity, sharpness, shrewdness, wit

penis chopper (*Brit. slang*), cock (*taboo slang*), dick (*taboo slang*), dong (*slang*), John Thomas (*taboo slang*), joystick (*slang*), knob (*Brit. taboo slang*), member, organ, pecker (*U.S. & Canad. taboo slang*), phallus, pizzle (*archaic & dialect*), plonker (*slang*), prick (*taboo slang*), schlong (*U.S. slang*), tadger (*Brit. slang*), tool (*taboo slang*), wang (*U.S. slang*), weenie (*U.S. slang*), whang (*U.S. slang*), willie *or* willy (*Brit. informal*), winkle (*Brit. slang*)

penitence compunction, contrition, regret, remorse, repentance, ruefulness, self-reproach, shame, sorrow

penitent *adjective* abject, apologetic, atoning, conscience-stricken, contrite, regretful, remorseful, repentant, rueful, sorrowful, sorry

Antonyms callous, impenitent, remorseless, unrepentant

penmanship calligraphy, chirography, fist (*informal*), hand, handwriting, longhand, script, writing

pen name allonym, nom de plume, pseudonym

pennant banderole, banner, burgee (*Nautical*), ensign, flag, jack, pennon, streamer

penniless bankrupt, broke (*informal*), cleaned out (*slang*), destitute, dirt-poor (*informal*), down and out, down at heel, flat broke (*informal*), impecunious, impoverished, indigent, in queer street, moneyless, necessitous, needy, on one's uppers, on the breadline, penurious, poor, poverty-stricken, ruined, short, skint (*Brit. slang*), stony-broke (*Brit. slang*), strapped (*slang*), without a penny to one's name, without two pennies to rub together (*informal*)

Antonyms affluent, filthy rich, loaded (*slang*), rich, rolling (*slang*), wealthy, well-heeled (*informal*)

penny-pincher meany (*informal*), miser, niggard, pinchpenny, screw (*slang*), Scrooge, skinflint, tight-arse (*taboo slang*), tight-ass (*U.S. taboo slang*)

penny-pinching *adjective* cheeseparing, close, frugal, mean, mingy (*Brit. informal*), miserly, near (*informal*), niggardly, scrimping, Scroogelike, stingy, tight-arse (*taboo slang*), tight-arsed (*taboo slang*), tight as a duck's arse (*taboo slang*), tight-ass (*U.S. taboo slang*), tight-assed (*U.S. taboo slang*), tight~fisted

Antonyms generous, kind, liberal, munificent, prodigal, unstinting

pennyworth bit, crumb, jot, little, mite, modi~cum, particle, scrap, small amount, tittle

pension allowance, annuity, benefit, superan~nuation

pensioner O.A.P., retired person, senior citizen

pensive blue (*informal*), cogitative, contempla~tive, dreamy, grave, in a brown study (*infor~mal*), meditative, melancholy, mournful, mus~ing, preoccupied, reflective, ruminative, sad, serious, sober, solemn, sorrowful, thoughtful, wistful

Antonyms active, carefree, cheerful, frivolous, gay, happy, joyous, light-hearted

pent-up bottled up, bridled, checked, con~strained, curbed, held back, inhibited, re~pressed, smothered, stifled, suppressed

penurious 1. cheeseparing, close, close-fisted, frugal, grudging, mean, miserly, near (*infor~mal*), niggardly, parsimonious, skimping, stingy, tight-arse (*taboo slang*), tight-arsed (*taboo slang*), tight as a duck's arse (*taboo slang*), tight-ass (*U.S. taboo slang*), tight-assed (*U.S. taboo slang*), tightfisted, ungener~ous 2. destitute, down and out, down at heel, impecunious, impoverished, indigent, needy, on the breadline, penniless, poor, poverty-stricken 3. beggarly, deficient, inadequate, meagre, miserable, miserly, paltry, pathetic, poor, scanty

penury 1. beggary, destitution, indigence, need, pauperism, poverty, privation, straitened cir~cumstances, want 2. dearth, deficiency, lack, paucity, scantiness, scarcity, shortage, sparse~ness

people *noun* 1. human beings, humanity, hu~mans, mankind, men and women, mortals, persons 2. citizens, clan, community, family, folk, inhabitants, nation, population, public, race, tribe 3. commonalty, crowd, general public, grass roots, hoi polloi, masses, mob, multitude, plebs, populace, rabble, rank and file, the herd ~*verb* 4. colonize, inhabit, occu~py, populate, settle

African peoples

Bantu
Barotse
Basotho
Berber
Bushman
Chewa
Damara
Dinka
Duala
Edo
Eritrean
Ethiopian
Ewe
Gabonese
Galla
Gambian
Ghanaian *or* Ghanian
Griqua *or* Grikwa
Gujarati *or* Gujerati
Hausa
Herero
Hottentot
Hutu
Ibibio
Ibo *or* Igbo
Kabyle
Kikuyu
Kongo
Luba
Luo
Malinke *or* Maninke
Masai
Matabele
Moor
Mosotho
Mossi
Nama *or* Namaqua
Ndebele
Negrillo
Negro
Nguni
Nuba
Nupe
Nyanja
Nyoro
Ovambo
Pondo
Pygmy *or* Pigmy
Rif *or* Riff *or* Rifi
Shangaan
Shluh
Shona
Somali
Songhai
Sotho
Strandloper
Susu
Swahili
Swazi
Temne
Tiv
Tsonga
Tswana
Tuareg
Tunisian
Tutsi
Venda
Watusi *or* Watutsi
Wolof
Xhosa
Yoruba
Zulu

Asian peoples

Adivasi
Ainu
Akkadian *or* Accadian
Amalekite
Amorite
Andamanese
Arab
Babylonian
Bakhtyari
Baluchi *or* Balochi
Bashkir
Bedouin *or* Beduin
Bengali
Bihari
Burmese
Buryat
Chaldean *or* Chal~daean
Cham
Chinese
Chukchee *or* Chukchi
Chuvash
Cossack
Cumans
Dani
Dard
Dyak *or* Dayak
Elamite
Ephesian
Ephraimite
Essene
Evenki
Fulani
Gond
Gurkha
Hittite
Hui
Hun
Hurrian
Igorot *or* Igorrote
Israeli
Jat
Jewish
Kabardian
Kalmuck *or* Kalmyk
Kanarese *or* Canarese
Kara-Kalpak
Karen
Kashmiri
Kassite
Kazakh *or* Kazak
Khmer

Kurd
Lao
Lepcha
Lycian
Lydian
Malay
Maratha *or* Mahratta
Mede
Mishmi
Mon
Mongol
Montagnard
Moro
Motu
Munda
Naga
Negrito
Nogay
Nuri *or* Kafir
Palestinian
Pathan, Pashto, Pushto *or* Pushtu
Phoenician
Punjabi *or* Panjabi
Sabaean *or* Sabean
Samoyed
Saracen
Semite
Shan
Sherpa
Sindhi
Sinhalese
Sogdian
Sumerian
Tadzhik, Tadjik *or* Tajik
Tagalog
Talaing
Tamil
Tatar *or* Tartar
Thai
Tocharian *or* Tokharian
Tongan
Tungus
Turanian
Turk
Turkmen
Uigur *or* Uighur
Uzbek
Vedda *or* Veddah
Visayan *or* Bisayan
Yakut

European peoples

Achaean *or* Achaian
Aeolian *or* Eolian
Albanian
Alemanni
Andalusian
Angle
Anglo-Norman
Anglo-Saxon
Aragonese
Armenian
Aryan
Ashkenazi
Austrian
Azerbaijani *or* Azeri
Azorean
Basque
Bavarian
Belgae
Belorussian
Bosnian Muslim
Breton
Briton
Brython
Bulgar
Bulgarian
Burgundian
Carinthian
Castilian
Catalan
Celt
Celtiberi
Chechen
Cheremis *or* Cheremiss
Cimbri
Cornish
Corsican
Croatian *or* Croat
Cymry *or* Kymry
Czech
Dane
Dorian
Dutch
English
Faeroese
Finn
Ephesian
Estonian *or* Esthonian
Etruscan *or* Etrurian
Fleming
Frank
French
Frisian
Gaelic
Galician
Gascon
Gaul
Georgian
German
Goidel
Goth
Greek
Gypsy *or* Gipsy
Hellenic
Iberian *or* Celtiberian
Icelandic
Iceni
Illyrian
Indo-European
Ingush
Ionian
Irish
Jute
Karelian
Komi
Latin
Lapp
Latvian
Lithuanian
Lombard *or* Langobard
Lusatian
Luxembourger
Macedonian
Magyar
Maltese
Manx
Montenegrin
Mordvin
Norman
Norse
Norwegian
Ostrogoth
Ostyak
Pict
Pole
Portuguese
Provençal
Prussian
Romanian
Russian
Sabellian
Sabine
Salain
Samnite
Samoyed
Sardinian
Saxon
Scot
Scythian
Sephardi
Serbian
Sicilian
Silures
Slav
Slovak
Slovene
Sorb
Swabian
Swede
Swiss
Teuton
Thracian
Turk
Tyrolese
Ugrian
Ukrainian
Vandal
Viking
Visigoth
Vlach *or* Walach
Volsci
Votyak
Walloon
Welsh
Wend

Eskimo peoples

Aleut *or* Aleutian
Caribou Eskimo
Inuit *or* Innuit
Yupik

Australasian peoples

Aborigine
Aranda
Dayak
Gurindji
Maori
Melanesian
Polynesian
Tagalog

Central and South American Indian peoples

Araucanian
Arawakan
Aymara
Aztec
Carib
Cashinahua
Chibca
Chimú
Ge
Guarani
Inca
Makuna
Maya
Mixtec
Nahuatl
Quechua, Kechua *or* Quichua
Toltec
Tupi
Zapotec

Native American tribes

Abnaki
Aguaruna
Algonquian *or* Algonkian

Algonquin *or* Algonkin
Apache
Apalachee
Arapaho
Araucan
Arikara
Ashochimi
Assiniboine
Athabascan
Aymara
Aztec
Bella Coola
Biloxi
Blackfoot
Blood
Caddo
Campa
Carib
Catawba
Cayuga
Cherokee
Cheyenne
Chickasaw
Chilcal
Chinook
Chippewa *or* Chippeway
Choctaw
Cocopa
Comanche
Cree
Creek
Crow
Dakota
Delaware
Dene
Dogrib
Flathead
Fox
Haida
Hidatsa
Hopi
Hupa
Huron
Illinois
Inca
Iowa
Iroquois
Kansa
Karankawa
Kichai
Kickapoo
Kiowa
Kootenay
Kwakiutl
Leni-Lenapé
Lipan
Mandan
Mapuche
Maya
Menomini *or* Menominee
Miami
Micmac
Minnetaree
Mixtec
Mohave *or* Mojave
Mohawk
Mohegan
Mohican *or* Mahican
Moki *or* Moqui
Montagnard
Muskogean *or* Muskhogean
Nahuatl
Narraganset
Natchez
Navaho *or* Navajo
Nez Percé
Nootka
Ojibwa *or* Ojibway
Omaha
Oneida
Onondaga
Orejone
Osage
Ostiak
Ottawa
Paiute
Pasamaquoddy
Pawnee
Penobscot
Pequot
Pericu
Piegan
Pima
Powhatan
Pueblo
Quakaw
Quechua, Quichua *or* Kechua
Root-digger
Salish
Santee
Sarcee
Sauk
Seminole
Seneca
Shawnee
Shoshoni
Shushwap
Sioux
Stonies
Susquehanna
Teton
Tlingit
Toltec
Tonkawa
Tuscarora
Ute
Wappo
Warrau
Wichita
Winnebago
Wyandot
Yaqui
Yuchi
Yuma
Yunca
Zuni

The voice of the people is the voice of God
Alcuin *Epistles*

pep 1. *noun* animation, brio, energy, get-up-and-go (*informal*), gusto, high spirits, life, liveliness, spirit, verve, vigour, vim (*slang*), vitality, vivacity, zip (*informal*) 2. *verb with* **up** animate, enliven, exhilarate, inspire, invigorate, jazz up (*informal*), quicken, stimulate, vitalize, vivify

pepper *verb* 1. flavour, season, spice 2. bespeckle, dot, fleck, spatter, speck, sprinkle, stipple, stud 3. bombard, pelt, riddle, scatter, shower

peppery 1. fiery, highly seasoned, hot, piquant, pungent, spicy 2. choleric, hot-tempered, irascible, irritable, quick-tempered, snappish, testy, touchy, vitriolic, waspish 3. astringent, biting, caustic, incisive, sarcastic, sharp, stinging, trenchant, vitriolic
Antonyms (*sense 1*) bland, insipid, mild, tasteless, vapid

perceive 1. be aware of, behold, descry, discern, discover, distinguish, espy, make out, note, notice, observe, recognize, remark, see, spot 2. appreciate, apprehend, comprehend, conclude, deduce, feel, gather, get (*informal*), get the message, get the picture, grasp, know, learn, realize, see, sense, suss (out) (*slang*), understand

perceptible apparent, appreciable, blatant, clear, conspicuous, detectable, discernible, distinct, evident, noticeable, observable, obvious, palpable, perceivable, recognizable, tangible, visible
Antonyms concealed, hidden, imperceptible, inconspicuous, indiscernible, invisible, unapparent, undetectable, unnoticeable

perception apprehension, awareness, conception, consciousness, discernment, feeling, grasp, idea, impression, insight, notion, observation, recognition, sensation, sense, taste, understanding

perceptive acute, alert, astute, aware, discerning, insightful, intuitive, observant, penetrating, percipient, perspicacious, quick, responsive, sensitive, sharp
Antonyms dull, indifferent, insensitive, obtuse, slow-witted, stupid, thick

perch 1. *noun* branch, pole, post, resting place, roost 2. *verb* alight, balance, land, rest, roost, settle, sit on

perchance by chance, for all one knows, haply (*archaic*), maybe, mayhap (*archaic*), peradventure (*archaic*), perhaps, possibly, probably

percipience acuity, alertness, astuteness, awareness, discernment, insight, intuition, penetration, perception, perspicacity, sagacity, sensitivity, understanding

percipient alert, alive, astute, aware, bright (*informal*), discerning, discriminating, intelligent, penetrating, perceptive, perspicacious, quick-witted, sharp, wide-awake

percolate drain, drip, exude, filter, filtrate, leach, ooze, penetrate, perk (*of coffee, informal*), permeate, pervade, seep, strain, transfuse

percussion blow, brunt, bump, clash, collision, concussion, crash, impact, jolt, knock, shock, smash, thump

perdition condemnation, damnation, destruction, doom, downfall, everlasting punishment, hell, hellfire, ruin

peregrination **1.** expedition, exploration, journey, odyssey, tour, trek, trip, voyage **2.** globetrotting, roaming, roving, travelling, trekking, wandering, wayfaring

peremptory **1.** absolute, binding, categorical, commanding, compelling, decisive, final, imperative, incontrovertible, irrefutable, obligatory, undeniable **2.** arbitrary, assertive, authoritative, autocratic, bossy (*informal*), dictatorial, dogmatic, domineering, high-handed, imperious, intolerant, overbearing

perennial **1.** abiding, chronic, constant, continual, continuing, enduring, incessant, inveterate, lasting, lifelong, persistent, recurrent, unchanging **2.** ceaseless, deathless, eternal, everlasting, immortal, imperishable, never-ending, permanent, perpetual, unceasing, undying, unfailing, uninterrupted

perfect *adjective* **1.** absolute, complete, completed, consummate, entire, finished, full, out-and-out, sheer, unadulterated, unalloyed, unmitigated, utter, whole **2.** blameless, clean, excellent, faultless, flawless, ideal, immaculate, impeccable, pure, splendid, spotless, sublime, superb, superlative, supreme, unblemished, unmarred, untarnished **3.** accurate, close, correct, exact, faithful, on the money (*U.S.*), precise, right, spot-on (*Brit. informal*), strict, true, unerring **4.** accomplished, adept, experienced, expert, finished, masterly, polished, practised, skilful, skilled *~verb* **5.** accomplish, achieve, carry out, complete, consummate, effect, finish, fulfil, perform, realize **6.** ameliorate, cultivate, develop, elaborate, hone, improve, polish, refine
Antonyms *adjective* bad, damaged, defective, deficient, faulty, flawed, impaired, imperfect, impure, incomplete, inferior, partial, poor, ruined, spoiled, unfinished, unskilled, worthless *~verb* mar

perfection **1.** accomplishment, achievement, achieving, completion, consummation, evolution, fulfilment, realization **2.** completeness, exactness, excellence, exquisiteness, faultlessness, integrity, maturity, perfectness, precision, purity, sublimity, superiority, wholeness **3.** acme, crown, ideal, paragon

Perfection is the child of Time
Bishop Joseph Hall *Works*

perfectionist formalist, precisian, precisionist, purist, stickler

perfectly **1.** absolutely, altogether, completely, consummately, entirely, every inch, fully, quite, thoroughly, totally, utterly, wholly **2.** admirably, exquisitely, faultlessly, flawlessly, ideally, impeccably, like a dream, superbly, superlatively, supremely, to perfection, wonderfully
Antonyms (*sense 1*) inaccurately, incompletely, mistakenly, partially (*sense 2*) badly, defectively, faultily, imperfectly, poorly

perfidious corrupt, deceitful, dishonest, disloyal, double-dealing, double-faced, faithless, false, recreant (*archaic*), traitorous, treacherous, treasonous, two-faced, unfaithful, untrustworthy

perfidy betrayal, deceit, disloyalty, double-dealing, duplicity, faithlessness, falsity, infidelity, perfidiousness, treachery, treason

perforate bore, drill, hole, honeycomb, penetrate, pierce, punch, puncture

perforce by force of circumstances, by necessity, inevitably, necessarily, needs must, of necessity, unavoidably, willy-nilly, without choice

perform **1.** accomplish, achieve, act, bring about, carry out, complete, comply with, discharge, do, effect, execute, fulfil, function, observe, pull off, satisfy, transact, work **2.** act, appear as, depict, enact, play, present, produce, put on, render, represent, stage

performance **1.** accomplishment, achievement, act, carrying out, completion, conduct, consummation, discharge, execution, exploit, feat, fulfilment, work **2.** acting, appearance, exhibition, gig (*informal*), interpretation, play, portrayal, presentation, production, representation, show **3.** action, conduct, efficiency, functioning, operation, practice, running, working **4.** *informal* act, behaviour, bother, business, carry-on (*informal, chiefly Brit.*), fuss, pantomime (*informal, chiefly Brit.*), pother, rigmarole, to-do

performer actor, actress, artiste, play-actor, player, Thespian, trouper

perfume aroma, attar, balminess, bouquet, cologne, essence, fragrance, incense, niff (*Brit. slang*), odour, redolence, scent, smell, sweetness

perfunctory automatic, careless, cursory, heedless, inattentive, indifferent, mechanical, negligent, offhand, routine, sketchy, slipshod, slovenly, stereotyped, superficial, unconcerned, unthinking, wooden
Antonyms ardent, assiduous, attentive, careful, diligent, keen, spirited, thorough, thoughtful, zealous

perhaps as the case may be, conceivably, feasibly, for all one knows, it may be, maybe, perchance (*archaic*), possibly

peril danger, exposure, hazard, insecurity, jeopardy, menace, pitfall, risk, uncertainty, vulnerability
Antonyms certainty, impregnability, invulnerability, safety, security, surety

perilous chancy (*informal*), dangerous, exposed, fraught with danger, hairy (*slang*), hazardous, parlous (*archaic*), precarious, risky, threatening, unsafe, unsure, vulnerable

perimeter ambit, border, borderline, boundary, bounds, circumference, confines, edge, limit, margin, periphery
Antonyms central part, centre, core, heart, hub, middle, nucleus

period **1.** interval, season, space, span, spell, stretch, term, time, while **2.** aeon, age, course, cycle, date, days, epoch, era, generation, season, stage, term, time, years

periodic at fixed intervals, cyclic, cyclical, every once in a while, every so often, infrequent, intermittent, occasional, periodical, recurrent, regular, repeated, seasonal, spasmodic, sporadic

periodical *noun* journal, magazine, monthly, organ, paper, publication, quarterly, review, serial, weekly

peripatetic ambulant, itinerant, migrant, mobile, nomadic, roaming, roving, travelling, vagabond, vagrant, wandering

peripheral **1.** beside the point, borderline, incidental, inessential, irrelevant, marginal, minor, secondary, superficial, tangential, unimportant **2.** exterior, external, outer, outermost, outside, perimetric, surface

periphery ambit, border, boundary, brim, brink, circumference, edge, fringe, hem, outer edge, outskirts, perimeter, rim, skirt, verge

periphrastic circuitous, circumlocutory, pleonastic, prolix, roundabout, tautological, verbose, wordy

perish **1.** be killed, be lost, decease, die, expire, lose one's life, pass away **2.** be destroyed, collapse, decline, disappear, fall, go under, vanish **3.** break down, decay, decompose, disintegrate, moulder, rot, waste, wither

perishable decaying, decomposable, destructible, easily spoilt, liable to rot, short-lived, unstable
Antonyms durable, lasting, long-life, long-lived, non-perishable

perjure (oneself) bear false witness, commit perjury, forswear, give false testimony, lie under oath, swear falsely

perjured deceitful, false, forsworn, lying, mendacious, perfidious, traitorous, treacherous, untrue, untruthful

perjury bearing false witness, false oath, false statement, false swearing, forswearing, giving false testimony, lying under oath, oath breaking, violation of an oath, wilful falsehood

perk benefit, bonus, dividend, extra, fringe benefit, icing on the cake, perquisite, plus

perk up brighten, buck up (*informal*), cheer up, liven up, look up, pep up, rally, recover, recuperate, revive, take heart

perky animated, bouncy, bright, bright-eyed and bushy-tailed (*informal*), bubbly, buoyant, cheerful, cheery, chirpy (*informal*), full of beans (*informal*), gay, genial, in fine fettle, jaunty, lively, spirited, sprightly, sunny, upbeat (*informal*), vivacious

permanence constancy, continuance, continuity, dependability, durability, duration, endurance, finality, fixedness, fixity, immortality, indestructibility, lastingness, perdurability (*rare*), permanency, perpetuity, stability, survival

permanent abiding, constant, durable, enduring, eternal, everlasting, fixed, immovable, immutable, imperishable, indestructible, invariable, lasting, long-lasting, perennial, perpetual, persistent, stable, steadfast, unchanging, unfading
Antonyms brief, changing, ephemeral, finite, fleeting, impermanent, inconstant, momentary, mortal, passing, short-lived, temporary, transitory, variable

permanently abidingly, always, constantly, continually, enduringly, eternally, for ever, immovably, immutably, indelibly, in perpetuity, invariably, lastingly, perennially, perpetually, persistently, steadfastly, unchangingly, unfadingly, unwaveringly
Antonyms briefly, ephemerally, fleetingly, impermanently, inconstantly, momentarily, temporarily, transitorily

permeable absorbent, absorptive, penetrable, pervious, porous, spongy

permeate charge, diffuse throughout, fill, filter through, imbue, impregnate, infiltrate, pass through, penetrate, percolate, pervade, saturate, seep through, soak through, spread throughout

permissible acceptable, admissible, allowable, all right, authorized, kosher (*informal*), lawful, legal, legit (*slang*), legitimate, licit, O.K.

or okay (*informal*), permitted, proper, sanctioned

Antonyms banned, forbidden, illegal, illicit, prohibited, unauthorized, unlawful

permission allowance, approval, assent, authorization, blank cheque, consent, dispensation, freedom, go-ahead (*informal*), green light, leave, liberty, licence, permit, sanction, sufferance, tolerance

permissive acquiescent, easy-going, easy-oasy (*slang*), forbearing, free, indulgent, latitudinarian, lax, lenient, liberal, open-minded, tolerant

Antonyms authoritarian, denying, domineering, forbidding, grudging, rigid, strict

permit **1.** *verb* admit, agree, allow, authorize, consent, empower, enable, endorse, endure, entitle, give leave *or* permission, give the green light to, grant, let, license, own, sanction, suffer, tolerate, warrant **2.** *noun* authorization, liberty, licence, pass, passport, permission, sanction, warrant

permutation alteration, change, shift, transformation, transmutation, transposition

pernicious bad, baleful, baneful (*archaic*), damaging, dangerous, deadly, deleterious, destructive, detrimental, evil, fatal, harmful, hurtful, injurious, maleficent, malevolent, malicious, malign, malignant, noisome, noxious, offensive, pestilent, poisonous, ruinous, venomous, wicked

pernickety **1.** careful, carping, difficult to please, exacting, fastidious, finicky, fussy, hairsplitting, nice, nit-picking (*informal*), overprecise, painstaking, particular, picky (*informal*), punctilious **2.** detailed, exacting, fiddly, fine, tricky

Antonyms (*sense 1*) careless, easy to please, haphazard, heedless, inattentive, lax, slack, slapdash, slipshod, sloppy, uncritical (*sense 2*) easy, simple

peroration closing remarks, conclusion, recapitulation, recapping (*informal*), reiteration, summing-up

perpendicular at right angles to, on end, plumb, straight, upright, vertical

perpetrate be responsible for, bring about, carry out, commit, do, effect, enact, execute, inflict, perform, wreak

perpetual **1.** abiding, endless, enduring, eternal, everlasting, immortal, infinite, lasting, never-ending, perennial, permanent, sempiternal (*literary*), unchanging, undying, unending **2.** ceaseless, constant, continual, continuous, endless, incessant, interminable, never-ending, perennial, persistent, recurrent, repeated, unceasing, unfailing, uninterrupted, unremitting

Antonyms brief, ephemeral, fleeting, impermanent, momentary, passing, short-lived, temporary, transitory

perpetuate continue, eternalize, immortalize, keep alive, keep going, keep up, maintain, preserve, sustain

Antonyms abolish, destroy, end, forget, ignore, put an end to, stamp out, suppress

perplex **1.** baffle, befuddle, beset, bewilder, confound, confuse, dumbfound, flummox, mix up, muddle, mystify, nonplus, puzzle, stump **2.** complicate, encumber, entangle, involve, jumble, mix up, snarl up, tangle, thicken

perplexing baffling, bewildering, complex, complicated, confusing, difficult, enigmatic, hard, inexplicable, intricate, involved, knotty, labyrinthine, mysterious, mystifying, paradoxical, puzzling, strange, taxing, thorny, unaccountable, weird

perplexity **1.** bafflement, bewilderment, confusion, incomprehension, mystification, puzzlement, stupefaction **2.** complexity, difficulty, inextricability, intricacy, involvement, obscurity **3.** can of worms (*informal*), difficulty, dilemma, enigma, fix (*informal*), how-do-you-do (*informal*), knotty problem, mystery, paradox, puzzle, snarl

perquisite benefit, bonus, dividend, extra, fringe benefit, icing on the cake, perk (*Brit. informal*), plus

per se as such, by definition, by itself, by its very nature, essentially, in essence, in itself, intrinsically, of itself

persecute **1.** afflict, be on one's back (*slang*), distress, dragoon, harass, hassle (*informal*), hound, hunt, ill-treat, injure, maltreat, martyr, molest, oppress, pursue, torment, torture, victimize **2.** annoy, badger, bait, bother, pester, tease, vex, worry

Antonyms accommodate, back, calm, coddle, comfort, console, cosset, humour, indulge, leave alone, let alone, mollycoddle, pamper, pet, spoil, support

perseverance constancy, dedication, determination, diligence, doggedness, endurance, indefatigability, persistence, pertinacity, purposefulness, resolution, sedulity, stamina, steadfastness, tenacity

If at first you don't succeed,
Try, try, try again
William E. Hickson *Try and Try Again*

The best way out is always through
Robert Frost *A Servant to Servants*

persevere be determined *or* resolved, carry on, continue, endure, go on, hang on, hold fast, hold on (*informal*), keep going, keep on *or* at, keep one's hand in, maintain, persist, plug away (*informal*), pursue, remain, stand firm, stay the course, stick at *or* to

Antonyms be irresolute, dither (*chiefly Brit.*),

end, falter, give in, give up, hesitate, quit, shillyshally (*informal*), swither (*Scot.*), throw in the towel, vacillate, waver

persiflage badinage, banter, chaff, frivolity, pleasantry, raillery, repartee, teasing, wit, wittiness, wordplay

persist 1. be resolute, continue, hold on (*informal*), insist, persevere, stand firm, stay the course 2. abide, carry on, continue, endure, hang in the air, keep up, last, linger, remain

persistence constancy, determination, diligence, doggedness, endurance, grit, indefatigability, perseverance, pertinacity, pluck, resolution, stamina, steadfastness, tenacity, tirelessness

persistent 1. assiduous, determined, dogged, enduring, fixed, immovable, indefatigable, obdurate, obstinate, persevering, pertinacious, resolute, steadfast, steady, stiff-necked, stubborn, tenacious, tireless, unflagging 2. constant, continual, continuous, endless, incessant, interminable, never-ending, perpetual, relentless, repeated, unrelenting, unremitting
Antonyms (*sense 1*) changeable, flexible, irresolute, tractable, yielding (*sense 2*) inconstant, intermittent, irregular, occasional, off-and-on, periodic

person 1. being, body, human, human being, individual, living soul, soul 2. **in person** bodily, in the flesh, oneself, personally

persona assumed role, character, façade, face, front, mask, part, personality, public face, role

personable affable, agreeable, amiable, attractive, charming, good-looking, handsome, likable *or* likeable, nice, pleasant, pleasing, presentable, winning
Antonyms disagreeable, sullen, surly, ugly, unattractive, unpleasant, unsightly

personage big name, big noise (*informal*), big shot (*informal*), celeb (*informal*), celebrity, dignitary, luminary, megastar (*informal*), notable, personality, public figure, somebody, V.I.P., well-known person, worthy

personal 1. exclusive, individual, intimate, own, particular, peculiar, private, privy, special 2. bodily, corporal, corporeal, exterior, material, physical 3. derogatory, disparaging, insulting, nasty, offensive, pejorative, slighting

personality 1. character, disposition, identity, individuality, make-up, nature, psyche, temper, temperament, traits 2. attraction, attractiveness, character, charisma, charm, dynamism, likableness *or* likeableness, magnetism, pleasantness 3. big name, celeb (*informal*), celebrity, famous name, household name, megastar (*informal*), notable, personage, star, well-known face, well-known person

personalized customized, distinctive, individual, individualized, monogrammed, private, special, tailor-made

personally 1. alone, by oneself, independently, in person, in the flesh, on one's own, solely 2. for oneself, for one's part, from one's own viewpoint, in one's books, in one's own view 3. individualistically, individually, privately, specially, subjectively

personate act, depict, do (*informal*), enact, feign, imitate, impersonate, play-act, portray, represent

personification embodiment, epitome, image, incarnation, likeness, portrayal, recreation, representation, semblance

personify body forth, embody, epitomize, exemplify, express, image (*rare*), incarnate, mirror, represent, symbolize, typify

personnel employees, helpers, human resources, liveware, members, men and women, people, staff, workers, workforce

perspective 1. angle, attitude, broad view, context, frame of reference, objectivity, outlook, overview, proportion, relation, relative importance, relativity, way of looking 2. outlook, panorama, prospect, scene, view, vista

perspicacious acute, alert, astute, aware, clear-sighted, clever, discerning, keen, observant, penetrating, perceptive, percipient, sagacious, sharp, sharp-witted, shrewd

perspicacity acumen, acuteness, discernment, discrimination, insight, keenness, penetration, perceptiveness, percipience, perspicaciousness, perspicuity, sagaciousness, sagacity, sharpness, shrewdness, smarts (*slang, chiefly U.S.*), suss (*slang*), wit

perspicuity clarity, clearness, comprehensibility, distinctness, explicitness, intelligibility, limpidity, limpidness, lucidity, plainness, precision, straightforwardness, transparency

perspicuous clear, comprehensible, crystal-clear, distinct, easily understood, explicit, intelligible, limpid, lucid, obvious, plain, self-evident, straightforward, transparent, unambiguous, understandable

perspiration exudation, moisture, sweat, wetness

perspire be damp, be wet, drip, exude, glow, pour with sweat, secrete, sweat, swelter

persuade 1. actuate, advise, allure, bring round (*informal*), coax, counsel, entice, impel, incite, induce, influence, inveigle, prevail upon, prompt, sway, talk into, twist (someone's) arm, urge, win over 2. cause to believe, convert, convince, satisfy
Antonyms deter, discourage, dissuade, forbid, prohibit

persuasion 1. blandishment, cajolery, conversion, enticement, exhortation, inducement, in~

fluencing, inveiglement, wheedling **2.** cogency, force, persuasiveness, potency, power, pull (*informal*) **3.** belief, certitude, conviction, credo, creed, faith, firm belief, fixed opinion, opinion, tenet, views **4.** camp, cult, denomination, faction, party, school, school of thought, sect, side

I stuffed their mouths with gold
Aneurin Bevan

persuasive cogent, compelling, convincing, credible, effective, eloquent, forceful, impelling, impressive, inducing, influential, logical, moving, plausible, sound, telling, touching, valid, weighty, winning
Antonyms feeble, flimsy, illogical, implausible, incredible, ineffective, invalid, unconvincing, unimpressive, weak

pert 1. bold, brash, cheeky, flip (*informal*), flippant, forward, fresh (*informal*), impertinent, impudent, insolent, lippy (*U.S. & Canad. slang*), presumptuous, pushy (*informal*), sassy (*U.S. informal*), saucy, smart **2.** brisk, dapper, daring, dashing, gay, jaunty, lively, nimble, perky, smart, spirited, sprightly

pertain appertain, apply, be appropriate, bear on, befit, belong, be part of, be relevant, concern, refer, regard, relate

pertinacious bull-headed, determined, dogged, headstrong, inflexible, intractable, mulish, obdurate, obstinate, persevering, persistent, perverse, pig-headed, relentless, resolute, self-willed, stiff-necked, strong-willed, stubborn, tenacious, unyielding, wilful

pertinent admissible, *ad rem*, applicable, apposite, appropriate, apropos, apt, fit, fitting, germane, material, pat, proper, relevant, suitable, to the point, to the purpose
Antonyms discordant, foreign, immaterial, inappropriate, incongruous, irrelevant, unfitting, unrelated, unsuitable

pertness audacity, brashness, brass (*informal*), bumptiousness, cheek (*informal*), cheekiness, chutzpah (*U.S. & Canad. informal*), cockiness, effrontery, forwardness, front, impertinence, impudence, insolence, presumption, rudeness, sauciness

perturb 1. agitate, alarm, bother, discompose, disconcert, discountenance, disquiet, disturb, faze, fluster, ruffle, trouble, unnerve, unsettle, upset, vex, worry **2.** confuse, disarrange, disorder, muddle, unsettle

perturbed agitated, alarmed, anxious, disconcerted, disquieted, disturbed, fearful, flurried, flustered, ill at ease, nervous, restless, shaken, troubled, uncomfortable, uneasy, upset, worried
Antonyms assured, at ease, comfortable, composed, cool, impassive, relaxed, unperturbed, unruffled

perusal browse, check, examination, inspection, look through, read, scrutiny, study

peruse browse, check, examine, inspect, look through, read, run one's eye over, scan, scrutinize, study, work over

pervade affect, charge, diffuse, extend, fill, imbue, infuse, overspread, penetrate, percolate, permeate, spread through, suffuse

pervasive common, extensive, general, inescapable, omnipresent, permeating, pervading, prevalent, rife, ubiquitous, universal, widespread

perverse 1. abnormal, contradictory, contrary, delinquent, depraved, deviant, disobedient, improper, incorrect, miscreant, rebellious, refractory, troublesome, unhealthy, unmanageable, unreasonable **2.** contrary, contumacious, cross-grained, dogged, headstrong, intractable, intransigent, obdurate, wilful, wrong-headed **3.** contrary, mulish, obstinate, pig-headed, stiff-necked, stubborn, unyielding, wayward **4.** cantankerous, churlish, crabbed, cross, fractious, ill-natured, ill-tempered, peevish, petulant, shrewish, spiteful, stroppy (*Brit. slang*), surly
Antonyms accommodating, agreeable, amiable, complaisant, cooperative, flexible, good-natured, malleable, obedient, obliging

perversion 1. aberration, abnormality, debauchery, depravity, deviation, immorality, kink (*Brit. informal*), kinkiness (*slang*), unnaturalness, vice, vitiation, wickedness **2.** corruption, distortion, falsification, misinterpretation, misrepresentation, misuse, twisting

perversity contradictiveness, contradictoriness, contrariness, contumacy, frowardness (*archaic*), intransigence, obduracy, refractoriness, waywardness, wrong-headedness

pervert *verb* **1.** abuse, distort, falsify, garble, misconstrue, misinterpret, misrepresent, misuse, twist, warp **2.** corrupt, debase, debauch, degrade, deprave, desecrate, initiate, lead astray, subvert *~noun* **3.** debauchee, degenerate, deviant, sicko (*informal*), sleazeball (*slang*), weirdo *or* weirdie (*informal*)

perverted aberrant, abnormal, corrupt, debased, debauched, depraved, deviant, distorted, evil, immoral, impaired, kinky (*slang*), misguided, pervy (*slang*), sick, sicko (*slang*), twisted, unhealthy, unnatural, vicious, vitiated, warped, wicked

pessimism cynicism, dejection, depression, despair, despondency, distrust, gloom, gloominess, gloomy outlook, glumness, hopelessness, melancholy, the hump (*Brit. informal*)

pessimist cynic, defeatist, doomster, gloom merchant (*informal*), kill-joy, melancholic, misanthrope, prophet of doom, wet blanket (*informal*), worrier

pessimistic bleak, cynical, dark, dejected, de~ pressed, despairing, despondent, distrustful, downhearted, fatalistic, foreboding, gloomy, glum, hopeless, melancholy, misanthropic, morose, resigned, sad
Antonyms assured, bright, buoyant, cheerful, cheery, encouraged, exhilarated, hopeful, in good heart, optimistic, sanguine

pest 1. annoyance, bane, bore, bother, drag (*informal*), gall, irritation, nuisance, pain (*in~ formal*), pain in the arse (*taboo informal*), pain in the neck (*informal*), thorn in one's flesh, trial, vexation 2. bane, blight, bug, curse, epidemic, infection, pestilence, plague, scourge

pester aggravate (*informal*), annoy, badger, bedevil, bend someone's ear (*informal*), be on one's back (*slang*), bother, bug (*informal*), chivvy, disturb, drive one up the wall (*slang*), fret, get at, get in one's hair (*informal*), get on one's nerves (*informal*), harass, harry, hassle (*informal*), irk, nag, pick on, plague, ride (*informal*), torment, worry

pestilence 1. Black Death, epidemic, pandemic, plague, visitation 2. affliction, bane, blight, cancer, canker, curse, scourge

pestilent 1. annoying, bothersome, galling, irk~ some, irritating, plaguy (*informal*), tiresome, vexing 2. corrupting, deleterious, destructive, detrimental, evil, harmful, injurious, perni~ cious, ruinous, vicious 3. catching, contagious, contaminated, diseased, disease-ridden, in~ fected, infectious, plague-ridden, tainted

pestilential 1. annoying, dangerous, deleteri~ ous, destructive, detrimental, evil, foul, harm~ ful, hazardous, injurious, pernicious, ruinous, troublesome 2. catching, contagious, contami~ nated, deadly, disease-ridden, infectious, ma~ lignant, noxious, pestiferous, poisonous, ven~ omous

pet[1] *noun* 1. apple of one's eye, blue-eyed boy (*informal*), darling, favourite, idol, jewel, treasure *~adjective* 2. cherished, dearest, dear to one's heart, favoured, favourite, particular, preferred, special 3. domesticated, house, house-broken, house-trained (*Brit.*), tame, trained *~verb* 4. baby, coddle, cosset, molly~ coddle, pamper, spoil 5. caress, fondle, pat, stroke 6. *informal* canoodle (*slang*), cuddle, kiss, neck (*informal*), smooch (*informal*), snog (*Brit. slang*)

pet[2] *noun* bad mood, bate (*Brit. slang*), huff, ill temper, miff (*informal*), paddy (*Brit. infor~ mal*), paddywhack (*Brit. informal*), pique, pout, sulk, sulks, tantrum, temper

peter out come to nothing, die out, dwindle, ebb, evaporate, fade, fail, give out, run dry, run out, stop, taper off, wane

petite dainty, delicate, dinky (*Brit. informal*), elfin, little, slight, small

petition 1. *noun* address, appeal, application, entreaty, invocation, memorial, plea, prayer, request, round robin, solicitation, suit, suppli~ cation 2. *verb* adjure, appeal, ask, beg, be~ seech, call upon, crave, entreat, plead, pray, press, solicit, sue, supplicate, urge

petrified 1. fossilized, ossified, rocklike 2. aghast, appalled, dazed, dumbfounded, frozen, horrified, numb, scared shitless (*taboo slang*), scared stiff, shit-scared (*taboo slang*), shocked, speechless, stunned, stupefied, terrified, terror-stricken

petrify 1. calcify, fossilize, harden, set, solidify, turn to stone 2. amaze, appal, astonish, astound, confound, dumbfound, horrify, im~ mobilize, paralyse, stun, stupefy, terrify, transfix

pettifoggery cheating, corruption, deceit, de~ ception, dishonesty, double-dealing, duplicity, fraud, gerrymandering, jobbery, swindling

pettifogging captious, casuistic, cavilling, equivocating, hairsplitting, insignificant, mean, niggling, nit-picking (*informal*), paltry, petty, piddling (*informal*), quibbling, sophisti~ cal, sophisticated, subtle

pettish cross, fractious, fretful, grumpy, huffy, ill-humoured, irritable, liverish, peevish, petulant, querulous, ratty (*Brit. & N.Z. infor~ mal*), sulky, tetchy, thin-skinned, touchy, waspish

petty 1. contemptible, inconsiderable, inessen~ tial, inferior, insignificant, little, measly (*in~ formal*), negligible, nickel-and-dime (*U.S. slang*), paltry, piddling (*informal*), slight, small, trifling, trivial, unimportant 2. cheap, grudging, mean, mean-minded, shabby, small-minded, spiteful, stingy, ungenerous 3. inferior, junior, lesser, lower, minor, second~ ary, subordinate
Antonyms (*sense 1*) consequential, consider~ able, essential, important, major, momentous, significant (*sense 2*) broad-minded, generous, liberal, magnanimous, open-minded, tolerant

petulance bad temper, crabbiness, ill humour, irritability, peevishness, pettishness, pique, pouts, querulousness, spleen, sulkiness, sul~ lenness, waspishness

petulant bad-tempered, captious, cavilling, crabbed, cross, crusty, fault-finding, fretful, huffy, ill-humoured, impatient, irritable, moody, peevish, perverse, pouting, querulous, ratty (*Brit. & N.Z. informal*), snappish, sour, sulky, sullen, ungracious, waspish
Antonyms affable, cheerful, congenial, easy-going, even-tempered, good-humoured, good-natured, happy, patient, smiling

phantasm 1. apparition, eidolon, ghost, phantom, revenant, shade (*literary*), spectre, spirit, spook (*informal*), wraith 2. chimera, figment, figment of the imagination, hallucination, illusion, vision

phantasmagoric, phantasmagorical chimerical, dreamlike, hallucinatory, illusory, Kafkaesque, kaleidoscopic, nightmarish, phantasmal, psychedelic, surreal, unreal

phantasmal chimerical, delusory, fancied, fanciful, ghostlike, ghostly, illusory, imaginary, imagined, phantasmagoric, phantasmagorical, phantomlike, shadowy, spectral, unreal, wraithlike

phantasy *see* FANTASY

phantom 1. apparition, eidolon, ghost, phantasm, revenant, shade (*literary*), spectre, spirit, spook (*informal*), wraith 2. chimera, figment, figment of the imagination, hallucination, illusion, vision

pharisaic, pharisaical canting, formal, goody-goody, holier-than-thou, hypocritical, insincere, Pecksniffian, pietistic, sanctimonious, self-righteous

pharisaism cant, false piety, hypocrisy, insincerity, lip service, pietism, religiosity, sanctimoniousness, self-righteousness

pharisee canter, dissembler, dissimulator, fraud, humbug, hypocrite, phoney *or* phony (*informal*), pietist, whited sepulchre

phase aspect, chapter, condition, development, juncture, period, point, position, stage, state, step, time

phase out axe (*informal*), close, deactivate, dispose of gradually, ease off, eliminate, pull, pull out, remove, replace, run down, taper off, terminate, wind down, wind up, withdraw
Antonyms activate, begin, create, establish, form, initiate, open, set up, start

phenomenal exceptional, extraordinary, fantastic, marvellous, miraculous, notable, outstanding, prodigious, remarkable, sensational, singular, stellar (*informal*), uncommon, unique, unparalleled, unusual, wondrous (*archaic or literary*)
Antonyms average, common, mediocre, no great shakes (*informal*), ordinary, poor, run-of-the-mill, second-rate, unexceptional, unremarkable, usual

phenomenon 1. circumstance, episode, event, fact, happening, incident, occurrence 2. exception, marvel, miracle, nonpareil, prodigy, rarity, sensation, sight, spectacle, wonder

philander coquet, court, dally, flirt, fool around (*informal*), toy, trifle, womanize (*informal*)

philanderer Casanova, dallier, Don Juan, flirt, gallant, gay dog, ladies' man, lady-killer (*informal*), Lothario, playboy, stud (*slang*), trifler, wolf (*informal*), womanizer (*informal*)

philanthropic alms-giving, altruistic, beneficent, benevolent, benignant, charitable, eleemosynary, gracious, humane, humanitarian, kind, kind-hearted, munificent, public-spirited
Antonyms egoistic, mean, miserly, niggardly, penurious, selfish, self-seeking, stingy

philanthropist alms-giver, altruist, benefactor, contributor, donor, giver, humanitarian, patron

philanthropy alms-giving, altruism, beneficence, benevolence, benignity, bounty, brotherly love, charitableness, charity, generosity, humanitarianism, kind-heartedness, largess *or* largesse, liberality, munificence, open-handedness, patronage, public-spiritedness

philippic condemnation, denunciation, diatribe, fulmination, harangue, invective, obloquy, stream of abuse, tirade, vituperation

philistine 1. *noun* barbarian, boor, bourgeois, Goth, ignoramus, lout, lowbrow, vulgarian, yahoo 2. *adjective* anti-intellectual, boorish, bourgeois, crass, ignorant, inartistic, lowbrow, tasteless, uncultivated, uncultured, uneducated, unrefined

philosopher dialectician, logician, mahatma, metaphysician, sage, seeker after truth, theorist, thinker, wise man

Philosophers

Peter Abelard [French]
Theodor Wiesengrund Adorno [German]
Maria Gaetana Agnesi [Italian]
Albertus Magnus [German]
Jean Le Rond d'Alembert [French]
Mohammed ibn Tarkhan al-Farabi [Arabian]
Louis Althusser [French]
Anaxagoras [Greek]
Anaximander [Greek]
Anaximenes [Greek]
Antisthenes [Greek]
Thomas Aquinas [Italian]
Hannah Arendt [U.S.]
Aristippus [Greek]
Aristotle [Greek]
J(ohn) L(angshaw) Austin [British]
Averroës [Arabian]
Avicenna [Arabian]
A(lfred) J(ules) Ayer [British]
Francis Bacon [English]
Alexander Gottlieb Baumgarten [German]
Pierre Bayle [French]
Julien Benda [French]
Jeremy Bentham [British]
Nikolai Aleksandrovich Berdyayev [Russian]
Henri Louis Bergson [French]
George Berkeley [Irish]
Isaiah Berlin [British]
Anicius Manlius Severinus Boethius [Roman]
Bonaventura [Italian]
F(rancis) H(erbert) Bradley [British]
Giordano Bruno [Italian]
Martin Buber [Austrian-Israeli]
Jean Buridan [French]
Tommaso Campanella [Italian]
Rudolf Carnap [German-U.S.]
Ernst Cassirer [Ger~

man]
Marcus Porcius Cato [Roman]
Chu Xi [Chinese]
Cleanthes [Greek]
Auguste Comte [French]
Étienne Bonnot de Condillac [French]
Marie Jean Antoine Nicholas de Caritat Condorcet [French]
Confucius [Chinese]
Victor Cousin [French]
Benedetto Croce [Italian]
Ralph Cudworth [English]
Richard Cumberland [English]
Democritus [Greek]
Jacques Derrida [French]
René Descartes [French]
John Dewey [U.S.]
Denis Diderot [French]
Dio Chrysostom [Greek]
Diogenes [Greek]
Johann August Eberhard [German]
Empedocles [Greek]
Friedrich Engels [German]
Epictetus [Greek]
Epicurus [Greek]
John Scotus Erigena [Irish]
Rudolph Christoph Eucken [German]
Gustav Theodor Fechner [German]
Ludwig Andreas Feuerbach [German]
Johann Gottlieb Fichte [German]
Marsilio Ficino [Ital~ ian]
Bernard le Bovier de Fontenelle [French]
Michel Foucault [French]
Gottlob Frege [Ger~ man]
Erich Fromm [German-U.S.]
Pierre Gassendi [French]
Giovanni Gentile [Italian]
T(homas) H(ill) Green [British]
Ernst Heinrich Haeckel [German]
Han Fei Zu [Chinese]
David Hartley [Eng~ lish]
Friedrich August von Hayek [Austrian-British]
Georg Wilhelm Friedrich Hegel [German]
Martin Heidegger [German]
Claude Adrien Helvétius [French]
Heracleides [Greek]
Heraclitus [Greek]
Edward Herbert [English]
Johann Gottfried von Herder [German]
Aleksandr Ivanovich Herzen [Russian]
Thomas Hobbes [English]
David Hume [British]
Edmund Husserl [German]
Francis Hutcheson [Scottish]
Hypatia [Alexandrian]
Solomon ibn-Gabirol [Spanish]
ibn-Khaldun [Ara~ bian]
Muhammad Iqbal [Indian]
William James [U.S.]
Karl Jaspers [Ger~ man]
Judah hah-Levi [Spanish]
Immanuel Kant [Ger~ man]
Søren Aabye Kierkegaard [Danish]
Lao Zi [Chinese]
Gottfried Wilhelm von Leibnitz [German]
Giacomo Leopardi [Italian]
Leucippus [Greek]
Lucien Lévy-Bruhl [French]
John Locke [English]
Lucretius [Roman]
Georg Lukács [Hun~ garian]
Ramón Lully [Span~ ish]
Ernst Mach [Aus~ trian]
Niccolò Machiavelli [Italian]
Maimonides [Spanish]
Nicolas Malebranche [French]
Gabriel Marcel [French]
Herbert Marcuse [German-U.S]
Jacques Maritain [French]
Marsilius of Padua [Italian]
Tomáš Garrigue Masaryk [Czech]
Mencius [Chinese]
Maurice Merleau-Ponty [French]
James Mill [British]
John Stuart Mill [British]
Baron de la Brède et de Montesquieu [French]
G(eorge) E(dward) Moore [British]
Mo-Zi [Chinese]
(Jean) Iris Murdoch [British]
Isaac Newton [Eng~ lish]
Nicholas of Cusa [German]
Friedrich Wilhelm Nietzsche [German]
William of Ockham [English]
José Ortega y Gasset [Spanish]
William Paley [Brit~ ish]
Parmenides [Greek]
Blaise Pascal [French]
Charles Sanders Peirce [U.S.]
Philo Judaeus [Alex~ andrian]
Giovanni Pico della Mirandola [Italian]
Plato [Greek]
Plotinus [Roman]
Plutarch [Greek]
Jules Henri Poincaré [French]
Karl Popper [Austrian-British]
Porphyry [Greek]
Proclus [Greek]
Protagoras [Greek]
Samuel von Pufendorf [German]
Pyrrho [Greek]
Pythagoras [Greek]
Willard van Orman Quine [U.S]
Ramanuja [Indian]
Thomas Reid [British]
(Joseph) Ernest Renan [French]
Paul Ricoeur [French]
Jean Jacques Rousseau [French]
Josiah Royce [U.S]
Bertrand Russell [British]
Gilbert Ryle [British]
Comte de Saint-Simon [French]
Sankara [Indian]
George Santayana [U.S.]
Jean-Paul Sartre [French]
Friedrich Wilhelm Joseph von Schelling [German]
Friedrich von Schlegel [German]
Friedrich Ernst Daniel Schleiermacher [German]
Moritz Schlick [Ger~ man]
Arthur Schopenhauer [German]
Albert Schweitzer [Franco-German]
Lucius Annaeus Sen~ eca [Roman]
Shankaracharya *or* Shankara [Indian]
Adam Smith [British]
Socrates [Greek]
Georges Sorel [French]
Herbert Spencer [British]
Oswald Spengler [German]
Baruch Spinoza [Dutch]
Rudolf Steiner [Aus~ trian]
Peter Strawson [Brit~ ish]

Francisco de Suárez [Spanish]
Rabindranath Tagore [Indian]
Pierre Teilhard de Chardin [French]
Thales [Greek]
Theophrastus [Greek]
Paul Johannes Tillich [German-U.S.]
Leo Tolstoy [Russian]
Miguel de Unamuno [Spanish]
Giovanni Battista Vico [Italian]
Voltaire [French]
Simone Weil [French]
A(lfred) N(orth) Whitehead [British]
Ludwig Josef Johann Wittgenstein [Austrian-British]
Xenocrates [Greek]
Xun Zi [Chinese]
Zeno of Citium [Greek]
Zeno of Elea [Greek]
Zhuangzi *or* Chuang-tzu [Chinese]

It is not the beard that makes the philosopher
Thomas Fuller *Gnomologia*

There is no statement so absurd that no philosopher will make it
Cicero *De Divinatione*

There was never yet philosopher
That could endure the toothache patiently
William Shakespeare *Much Ado About Nothing*

The philosophers have only interpreted the world in various ways; the point, however, is to change it
Karl Marx *Theses on Feuerbach*

I have tried too in my time to be a philosopher; but, I don't know how, cheerfulness was always breaking in
Oliver Edwards

what I understand by 'philosopher': a terrible explosive in the presence of which everything is in danger
Friedrich Nietzsche *Ecce Homo*

philosophical, philosophic **1.** abstract, erudite, learned, logical, rational, sagacious, theoretical, thoughtful, wise **2.** calm, collected, composed, cool, impassive, imperturbable, patient, resigned, sedate, serene, stoical, tranquil, unruffled
Antonyms (*sense 1*) factual, illogical, irrational, practical, pragmatic, scientific (*sense 2*) emotional, hot-headed, impulsive, perturbed, rash, restless, upset

What, knocked a tooth out? Never mind, dear, laugh it off, laugh it off; it's all part of life's rich pageant
Arthur Marshall *The Games Mistress*

philosophy **1.** aesthetics, knowledge, logic, metaphysics, rationalism, reason, reasoning, thinking, thought, wisdom **2.** attitude to life, basic idea, beliefs, convictions, doctrine, ideology, principle, tenets, thinking, values, viewpoint, *Weltanschauung*, world-view **3.** composure, coolness, dispassion, equanimity, resignation, restraint, self-possession, serenity, stoicism

Philosophical Schools and Doctrines

animism
Aristotelianism
atomism
behaviourism
Cartesianism
conceptualism
Confucianism
consequentialism
conventionalism
critical realism
cynicism
deism
determinism
dualism
Eleaticism
empiricism
epicureanism
essentialism
existentialism
fatalism
fideism
hedonism
Hegelianism
humanism
idealism
immaterialism
Kantianism
logical atomism
logical positivism
Marxism
materialism
monism
neo-Platonism
nihilism
nominalism
phenomenalism
Platonism
pluralism
positivism
pragmatism
Pyrrhonism
Pythagoreanism
rationalism
realism
scepticism
scholasticism
sensationalism
Stoicism
structuralism
Taoism
theism
Thomism
utilitarianism
utopianism

Philosophy! the lumber of the schools
Jonathan Swift *Ode to Sir W. Temple*

Philosophy may teach us to bear with equanimity the misfortunes of our neighbours
Oscar Wilde *The English Renaissance of Art*

Philosophy is a good horse in the stable, but an arrant jade on a journey
Oliver Goldsmith *The Good-Natur'd Man*

All good moral philosophy is but an handmaid to religion
Francis Bacon *The Advancement of Learning*

A little philosophy inclineth man's mind to atheism, but depth in philosophy bringeth men's minds about to religion
Francis Bacon *Essays*

philosophy: a route of many roads leading from nowhere to nothing
Ambrose Bierce *The Devil's Dictionary*

Philosophy will clip an Angel's wings
John Keats *Lamia*

How charming is divine philosophy!
Not harsh and crabbèd, as dull fools suppose,
But musical as Apollo's lute
John Milton *Comus*

phlegmatic apathetic, bovine, cold, dull, frigid, heavy, impassive, indifferent, lethargic, listless, lymphatic, matter-of-fact, placid, sluggish, stoical, stolid, undemonstrative, unemotional, unfeeling
Antonyms active, alert, animated, emotional, energetic, excited, hyper (*informal*), lively, passionate

phobia aversion, detestation, dislike, distaste, dread, fear, hatred, horror, irrational fear, loathing, obsession, overwhelming anxiety, répulsion, revulsion, terror, thing (*informal*)
Antonyms bent, fancy, fondness, inclination, liking, love, partiality, passion, penchant, soft spot

Phobias

acerophobia	sourness
achluophobia	darkness
acrophobia	heights
aerophobia	air
agoraphobia	open spaces
aichurophobia	points
ailurophobia	cats
akousticophobia	sound
algophobia	pain
amakaphobia	carriages
amathophobia	dust
androphobia	men
anemophobia	wind
anginophobia	narrowness
antlophobia	flood
anthropophobia	man
apeirophobia	infinity
aquaphobia	water
arachnophobia	spiders
asthenophobia	weakness
astraphobia	lightning
atephobia	ruin
aulophobia	flute
bacilliphobia	microbes
barophobia	gravity
basophobia	walking
batrachophobia	reptiles
belonephobia	needles
bibliophobia	books
brontophobia	thunder
cancerophobia	cancer
cheimaphobia	cold
chionophobia	snow
chromatophobia	money
chronophobia	duration
chrystallophobia	crystals
claustrophobia	closed spaces
cnidophobia	stings
cometophobia	comets
cromophobia	colour
cyberphobia	computers
cynophobia	dogs
demophobia	crowds
demonophobia	demons
dermatophobia	skin
dikephobia	justice
doraphobia	fur
eisoptrophobia	mirrors
electrophobia	electricity
entomophobia	insects
eosophobia	dawn
eremophobia	solitude
enetephobia	pins
ereuthophobia	blushing
ergasiophobia	work
genophobia	sex
geumaphobia	taste
graphophobia	writing
gymnophobia	nudity
gynophobia	women
hadephobia	hell
haematophobia	blood
hamartiophobia	sin
haptophobia	touch
harpaxophobia	robbers
hedonophobia	pleasure
helminthophobia	worms
hodophobia	travel
homichlophobia	fog
homophobia	homosexuals
hormephobia	shock
hydrophobia	water
hypegiaphobia	responsibility
hypnophobia	sleep
ideophobia	ideas
kakorraphiaphobia	failure
katagelophobia	ridicule
kenophobia	void
kinesophobia	motion
kleptophobia	stealing
kopophobia	fatigue
kristallophobia	ice
laliophobia	stuttering
linonophobia	string
logophobia	words
lyssophobia	insanity
maniaphobia	insanity
mastigophobia	flogging
mechanophobia	machinery
metallophobia	metals
meteorophobia	meteors
misophobia	contamination
monophobia	one thing
musicophobia	music
musophobia	mice
necrophobia	corpses
nelophobia	glass
neophobia	newness
nephophobia	clouds
nosophobia	disease
nyctophobia	night
ochlophobia	crowds
ochophobia	vehicles
odontophobia	teeth
oikophobia	home
olfactophobia	smell
ommatophobia	eyes
oneirophobia	dreams
ophidiophobia	snakes
ornithophobia	birds
ouranophobia	heaven
panphobia	everything
pantophobia	everything

parthenophobia	girls
pathophobia	disease
peniaphobia	poverty
phasmophobia	ghosts
phobophobia	fears
photophobia	light
pnigerophobia	smothering
poinephobia	punishment
polyphobia	many things
potophobia	drink
pteronophobia	feathers
pyrophobia	fire
Russophobia	Russia
rypophobia	soiling
Satanophobia	Satan
selaphobia	flesh
siderophobia	stars
sitophobia	food
spermaphobia	germs
spermatophobia	germs
stasiphobia	standing
stygiophobia	hell
taphephobia	being buried alive
technophobia	technology
teratophobia	giving birth to a monster
thaasophobia	sitting
thalassophobia	sea
thanatophobia	death
theophobia	God
thermophobia	heat
tonitrophobia	thunder
toxiphobia	poison
tremophobia	trembling
triskaidekaphobia	thirteen
xenophobia	strangers or foreign~ers
zelophobia	jealousy
zoophobia	animals

phone *noun* **1.** blower (*informal*), telephone **2.** bell (*Brit. slang*), buzz (*informal*), call, ring (*informal, chiefly Brit.*), tinkle (*Brit. informal*) ~*verb* **3.** buzz (*informal*), call, get on the blower (*informal*), give someone a bell (*Brit. slang*), give someone a buzz (*informal*), give someone a call, give someone a ring (*informal, chiefly Brit.*), give someone a tinkle (*Brit. in~formal*), make a call, ring (up) (*informal, chiefly Brit.*), telephone

phoney **1.** *adjective* affected, assumed, bogus, counterfeit, ersatz, fake, false, forged, imita~tion, pseudo (*informal*), put-on, sham, spuri~ous, trick **2.** *noun* counterfeit, fake, faker, for~gery, fraud, humbug, impostor, pretender, pseud (*informal*), sham
Antonyms authentic, bona fide, genuine, original, real, sincere, unaffected, unassumed, unfeigned

photograph **1.** *noun* image, likeness, photo (*informal*), picture, print, shot, slide, snap (*informal*), snapshot, transparency **2.** *verb* capture on film, film, get a shot of, record, shoot, snap (*informal*), take, take a picture of, take (someone's) picture

photographic accurate, cinematic, detailed, exact, faithful, filmic, graphic, lifelike, minute, natural, pictorial, precise, realistic, retentive, visual, vivid

phrase **1.** *noun* expression, group of words, idi~om, locution, motto, remark, saying, tag, utterance, way of speaking **2.** *verb* couch, ex~press, formulate, frame, present, put, put into words, say, term, utter, voice, word

phraseology choice of words, diction, expres~sion, idiom, language, parlance, phrase, phrasing, speech, style, syntax, wording

physical **1.** bodily, carnal, corporal, corporeal, earthly, fleshly, incarnate, mortal, somatic, unspiritual **2.** material, natural, palpable, real, sensible, solid, substantial, tangible, vis~ible

physician doc (*informal*), doctor, doctor of medicine, general practitioner, G.P., healer, M.D., medic (*informal*), medical practitioner, medico (*informal*), sawbones (*slang*), specialist

Physician, heal thyself

Bible: St. Luke

Cured yesterday of my disease,
I died last night of my physician

Matthew Prior *The Remedy Worse than the Dis~ease*

physics

Branches of physics

acoustics	magnetics *or* magnetism
aerodynamics	magnetostatics
aerostatics	mechanics
applied physics	mesoscopics
astrophysics	microphysics
atomic physics	nuclear physics
biophysics	nucleonics
condensed-matter physics *or* solid-state physics	optics
cosmology	photometry
cryogenics *or* low-temperature physics	pneumatics
dynamics	quantum mechanics
electromagnetism	quantum physics
electronics	rheology
electrostatics	solar physics
geophysics	sonics
harmonics	spectroscopy
high-energy physics *or* particle physics	statics
kinetics	statistical mechanics
macrophysics	superaerodynamics
	theoretical physics
	thermodynamics
	thermometry
	thermostatics
	ultrasonics

Physics terms

acceleration
alternating current
ampere
amplifier
angstrom
anion
antimatter
atom
baryon
becquerel
Boyle's law
Brownian motion
cacion
calorie
capacitance
cathode ray
centre of gravity
centrifugal force
centripetal force
charge
Charles' law
conductor
convection
cosmic ray
coulomb
current
cyclotron
decibel
density
diffraction
diffusion
diode
direct current
Doppler effect
earth
electricity
electromotive force
electron
energy
farad
field
fission
fluorescence
force
frequency
friction
fuse
fusion
gamma ray
generator
gravity
half-life
hertz
hyperon
impetus
inductance
inertia
infrared
joule
kelvin
kinetic energy
laser
lens
lepton
luminescence
mass
matter
meson
microwave
moment
momentum
muon
neutrino
neutron
newton
nucleon
nucleus
ohm
Ohm's law
particle
pascal
Planck constant *or* Planck's constant
potential difference
potential energy
proton
quantum
radiation
radioactivity
radio wave
red shift
reflection
refraction
relativity
resistance
rutherford
semiconductor
simple harmonic motion
spectrum
static electricity
subatomic particle
superconductivity
superfluidity
surface tension
tau particle
tension
terminal velocity
thermostat
transformer
transistor
ultraviolet
vacuum
velocity
viscosity
volt
watt
wave
wavelength
x-ray

Famous physicists

André Marie Ampère [French]
Anders Jonas Ångström [Swedish]
Amedeo Avogadro [Italian]
Antoine Henri Becquerel [French]
Daniel Bernoulli [Swiss]
Niels (Henrik David) Bohr [Danish]
Robert Boyle [Irish]
Charles Augustin de Coulomb [French]
Marie Curie [French]
Pierre Curie [French]
Paul Adrien Maurice Dirac [British]
Albert Einstein [German-U.S.]
Michael Faraday [British]
Enrico Fermi [Italian]
Richard Feynman [U.S.]
Jean Bernard Léon Foucault [French]
James Franck [U.S.]
Galileo (Galilei) [Italian]
Stephen William Hawking [British]
Werner Karl Heisenburg [German]
Gustav Hertz [German]
Heinrich Rudolph Hertz [German]
James Prescott Joule [British]
William Thomson Kelvin [British]
Guglielmo Marconi [Italian]
Isaac Newton [English]
Georg Simon Ohm [German]
J(ulius) Robert Oppenheimer [U.S.]
Max (Karl Ernst Ludwig) Planck [German]
Ernest Rutherford [British]
Alessandro Volta [Italian]

physiognomy clock (*Brit. slang*), countenance, dial (*Brit. slang*), face, features, look, phiz (*slang*), phizog (*slang*), visage

physique body, build, constitution, figure, form, frame, make-up, shape, structure

pick *verb* **1.** choose, decide upon, elect, fix upon, hand-pick, mark out, opt for, select, settle upon, sift out, single out, sort out **2.** collect, cull, cut, gather, harvest, pluck, pull **3.** have no appetite, nibble, peck at, play *or* toy with, push the food round the plate **4.** foment, incite, instigate, provoke, start **5.** break into, break open, crack, force, jemmy, open, prise open **6. pick one's way** be tentative, find *or* make one's way, move cautiously, tread carefully, work through *~noun* **7.** choice, choosing, decision, option, preference, selection **8.** choicest, *crème de la crème*, elect, elite, flower, pride, prize, the best, the cream, the tops (*slang*)
Antonyms (*sense 1*) cast aside, decline, discard, dismiss, reject, spurn, turn down

pick at carp, cavil, criticize, find fault, get at, nag, pick holes, pick to pieces, quibble

picket *noun* **1.** pale, paling, palisade, peg, post, stake, stanchion, upright **2.** demonstrator, flying picket, picketer, protester **3.** guard, lookout, patrol, scout, sentinel, sentry, spotter, vedette (*Military*), watch *~verb* **4.** blockade, boycott, demonstrate **5.** corral (*U.S.*), enclose, fence, hedge in, palisade, pen in, rail in, shut in, wall in

pickings booty, earnings, gravy (*slang*), ill-gotten gains, loot, plunder, proceeds, profits, returns, rewards, spoils, yield

pickle *noun* **1.** *informal* bind (*informal*), difficulty, dilemma, fix (*informal*), hot water (*informal*), jam (*informal*), predicament, quandary, scrape (*informal*), spot (*informal*), tight spot **2.** *Brit. informal* little horror, mischief, mischief maker, monkey, naughty child, rascal *~verb* **3.** cure, keep, marinade, preserve, steep

pick-me-up bracer (*informal*), drink, pick-up (*slang*), refreshment, restorative, roborant, shot in the arm (*informal*), stimulant, tonic

pick on badger, bait, blame, bully, goad, hector, tease, torment

pick out **1.** choose, cull, hand-pick, select, separate the sheep from the goats, single out, sort out **2.** discriminate, distinguish, make distinct, make out, notice, perceive, recognize, tell apart

pick-up *noun* **1.** acceleration, response, revving (*informal*), speed-up **2.** change for the better, gain, improvement, rally, recovery, revival, rise, strengthening, upswing, upturn

pick up *verb* **1.** gather, grasp, hoist, lift, raise, take up, uplift **2.** buy, come across, find, garner, happen upon, obtain, purchase, score (*slang*) **3.** be on the mend, gain, gain ground, get better, improve, make a comeback (*informal*), mend, perk up, rally, recover, take a turn for the better, turn the corner **4.** call for, collect, get, give someone a lift, go to get, uplift (*Scot.*) **5.** acquire, get the hang of (*informal*), learn, master **6.** *slang* apprehend, arrest, bust (*informal*), collar (*informal*), do (*slang*), feel one's collar (*slang*), lift (*slang*), nab (*informal*), nail (*informal*), nick (*slang, chiefly Brit.*), pinch (*informal*), pull in (*Brit. slang*), run in (*slang*), take into custody

picky captious, carping, cavilling, choosy, critical, dainty, fastidious, fault-finding, finicky, fussy, nice, particular, pernickety (*informal*)

picnic **1.** excursion, *fête champêtre*, outdoor meal, outing **2.** *informal* breeze (*U.S. & Canad. informal*), cakewalk (*informal*), child's play (*informal*), cinch (*slang*), duck soup (*U.S. slang*), piece of cake (*Brit. informal*), pushover (*slang*), snap (*informal*), walkover (*informal*)

pictorial expressive, graphic, illustrated, picturesque, representational, scenic, striking, vivid

picture *noun* **1.** delineation, drawing, effigy, engraving, illustration, image, likeness, painting, photograph, portrait, portrayal, print, representation, similitude, sketch **2.** account, depiction, description, image, impression, re-creation, report **3.** carbon copy, copy, dead ringer (*slang*), double, duplicate, image, likeness, living image, lookalike, replica, ringer (*slang*), spit (*informal, chiefly Brit.*), spit and image (*informal*), spitting image (*informal*), twin **4.** archetype, embodiment, epitome, essence, living example, perfect example, personification **5.** film, flick (*slang*), motion picture, movie (*U.S. informal*) *~verb* **6.** conceive of, envision, image, see, see in the mind's eye, visualize **7.** delineate, depict, describe, draw, illustrate, paint, photograph, portray, render, represent, show, sketch

One picture is worth ten thousand words
Frederick R. Barnard *Printers' Ink*

Every picture tells a story

picturesque attractive, beautiful, charming, colourful, graphic, pretty, quaint, scenic, striking, vivid
Antonyms commonplace, drab, dull, everyday, inartistic, unattractive, uninteresting

piddling chickenshit (*U.S. slang*), crappy (*slang*), derisory, fiddling, insignificant, little, measly (*informal*), Mickey Mouse (*slang*), nickel-and-dime (*U.S. slang*), paltry, petty, piffling, poxy (*slang*), puny, trifling, trivial, unimportant, useless, wanky (*taboo slang*), worthless
Antonyms considerable, important, major, significant, sizable *or* sizeable, substantial, tidy (*informal*), useful, valuable

piebald black and white, brindled, dappled, flecked, mottled, pied, speckled, spotted

piece *noun* **1.** allotment, bit, chunk, division, fraction, fragment, length, morsel, mouthful, part, portion, quantity, scrap, section, segment, share, shred, slice **2.** case, example, instance, occurrence, sample, specimen, stroke **3.** article, bit (*informal*), composition, creation, item, production, study, work, work of art **4.** **go to pieces** break down, crack up (*informal*), crumple, disintegrate, fall apart, lose control, lose one's head **5.** **in pieces** broken, bust (*informal*), damaged, disintegrated, in bits, in smithereens, ruined, shattered, smashed **6.** **of a piece** alike, analogous, consistent, identical, of the same kind, similar, the same, uniform *~verb* **7.** *often with* **together** assemble, compose, fix, join, mend, patch, repair, restore, unite

pièce de résistance *chef-d'oeuvre*, jewel, masterpiece, masterwork, showpiece

piecemeal **1.** *adverb* at intervals, bit by bit, by degrees, by fits and starts, fitfully, intermittently, little by little, partially, slowly **2.** *adjective* fragmentary, intermittent, interrupted, partial, patchy, spotty, unsystematic

pied dappled, flecked, irregular, motley, mott~

led, multicoloured, parti-coloured, piebald, spotted, streaked, varicoloured, variegated

pier *noun* **1.** jetty, landing place, promenade, quay, wharf **2.** buttress, column, pile, piling, pillar, post, support, upright

pierce **1.** bore, drill, enter, impale, penetrate, perforate, prick, probe, puncture, run through, spike, stab, stick into, transfix **2.** comprehend, discern, discover, fathom, grasp, realize, see, understand **3.** *figurative* affect, cut, cut to the quick, excite, hurt, move, pain, rouse, sting, stir, strike, thrill, touch, wound

piercing **1.** *usually of sound* ear-splitting, high-pitched, loud, penetrating, sharp, shattering, shrill **2.** alert, aware, bright (*informal*), keen, penetrating, perceptive, perspicacious, probing, quick-witted, searching, sharp, shrewd **3.** *usually of weather* arctic, biting, bitter, cold, freezing, frosty, keen, nipping, nippy, numbing, raw, wintry **4.** acute, agonizing, excruciating, exquisite, fierce, intense, painful, powerful, racking, severe, sharp, shooting, stabbing
Antonyms (*sense 1*) inaudible, low, low-pitched, mellifluous, quiet, soundless (*sense 2*) obtuse, slow, slow-witted, thick, unperceptive

piety devotion, devoutness, dutifulness, duty, faith, godliness, grace, holiness, piousness, religion, reverence, sanctity, veneration

piffle balderdash, balls (*taboo slang*), bilge (*informal*), bosh (*informal*), bull (*slang*), bullshit (*taboo slang*), bunk (*informal*), bunkum *or* buncombe (*chiefly U.S.*), cobblers (*Brit. taboo slang*), codswallop (*Brit. slang*), crap (*slang*), drivel, eyewash (*informal*), garbage (*informal*), guff (*slang*), hogwash, hokum (*slang, chiefly U.S. & Canad.*), hooey (*slang*), horsefeathers (*U.S. slang*), hot air (*informal*), moonshine, nonsense, pap, poppycock (*informal*), rot, rubbish, shit (*taboo slang*), tarradiddle, tommyrot, tosh (*slang, chiefly Brit.*), trash, tripe (*informal*), twaddle

piffling chickenshit (*U.S. slang*), crappy (*slang*), derisory, fiddling, insignificant, little, measly (*informal*), Mickey Mouse (*slang*), nickel-and-dime (*U.S. slang*), paltry, petty, piddling (*informal*), poxy (*slang*), puny, trifling, trivial, unimportant, useless, wanky (*taboo slang*), worthless

pig **1.** boar, grunter, hog, piggy, piglet, porker, shoat, sow, swine **2.** *informal* animal, beast, boor, brute, glutton, greedy guts (*slang*), guzzler, hog (*informal*), slob (*slang*), sloven, swine
Related adjective: porcine

Breeds of pig

Berkshire
Cheshire
Chester White
Duroc
Gloucester Old Spot
Hampshire
Landrace
Large Black
Large White
Middle White
Pietrain
Saddleback
Small White
Tamworth
Welsh
Vietnamese pot-bellied

pigeon **1.** bird, culver (*archaic*), cushat, dove, squab **2.** *slang* dupe, fall guy (*informal*), gull (*archaic*), mug (*Brit. slang*), sitting duck, sitting target, sucker (*slang*), victim **3.** *Brit. informal* baby (*slang*), business, concern, lookout (*informal*), responsibility, worry

pigeonhole *noun* **1.** compartment, cubbyhole, cubicle, locker, niche, place, section **2.** *informal* category, class, classification, slot (*informal*) *~verb* **3.** defer, file, postpone, put off, shelve **4.** catalogue, characterize, classify, codify, compartmentalize, ghettoize, label, slot (*informal*), sort

piggish **1.** boorish, crude, gluttonous, greedy, hoggish, piggy, rude, swinish, voracious **2.** *informal* hoggish, mean, obstinate, pig-headed, possessive, selfish, stubborn

pig-headed bull-headed, contrary, cross-grained, dense, froward (*archaic*), inflexible, mulish, obstinate, perverse, self-willed, stiff-necked, stubborn, stupid, unyielding, wilful, wrong-headed
Antonyms agreeable, amiable, complaisant, cooperative, flexible, obliging, open-minded, tractable

pigment colorant, colour, colouring, colouring matter, dye, dyestuff, paint, stain, tincture, tint

pile[1] *noun* **1.** accumulation, assemblage, assortment, collection, heap, hoard, mass, mound, mountain, rick, stack, stockpile **2.** *informal* big bucks (*informal, chiefly U.S.*), big money, bomb (*Brit. slang*), fortune, megabucks (*U.S. & Canad. slang*), mint, money, packet (*slang*), pot, pretty penny (*informal*), tidy sum (*informal*), wad (*U.S. & Canad. slang*), wealth **3.** *often plural informal* a lot, great deal, ocean, oodles (*informal*), quantity, stacks **4.** building, edifice, erection, structure *~verb* **5.** accumulate, amass, assemble, collect, gather, heap, hoard, load up, mass, stack, store **6.** charge, crowd, crush, flock, flood, jam, pack, rush, stream

pile[2] *noun* beam, column, foundation, pier, piling, pillar, post, support, upright

pile[3] *noun* down, fibre, filament, fur, hair, nap, plush, shag, surface

piles haemorrhoids

pile-up accident, collision, crash, multiple collision, smash, smash-up (*informal*)

pilfer appropriate, blag (*slang*), cabbage (*Brit. slang*), embezzle, filch, knock off (*slang*), lift (*informal*), nick (*slang, chiefly Brit.*), pinch (*informal*), purloin, rifle, rob, snaffle (*Brit. in~

formal), snitch (*slang*), steal, swipe (*slang*), take, thieve, walk off with

pilgrim crusader, hajji, palmer, traveller, wan~derer, wayfarer

pilgrim: a traveler that is taken seriously
Ambrose Bierce *The Devil's Dictionary*

pilgrimage crusade, excursion, expedition, hajj, journey, mission, tour, trip

pill 1. bolus, capsule, pellet, pilule, tablet **2. the pill** oral contraceptive **3.** *slang* bore, drag (*in~formal*), nuisance, pain (*informal*), pain in the neck (*informal*), pest, trial

pillage *verb* **1.** depredate (*rare*), despoil, free~boot, loot, maraud, plunder, raid, ransack, ravage, reive (*dialect*), rifle, rob, sack, spoil (*archaic*), spoliate, strip *~noun* **2.** depredation, devastation, marauding, plunder, rapine, rob~bery, sack, spoliation **3.** booty, loot, plunder, spoils

pillar 1. column, pier, pilaster, piling, post, prop, shaft, stanchion, support, upright **2.** leader, leading light (*informal*), mainstay, rock, supporter, torchbearer, tower of strength, upholder, worthy

pillory *verb* brand, cast a slur on, denounce, expose to ridicule, heap *or* pour scorn on, hold up to shame, lash, show up, stigmatize

pilot 1. *noun* airman, aviator, captain, conduc~tor, coxswain, director, flier, guide, helmsman, leader, navigator, steersman **2.** *verb* conduct, control, direct, drive, fly, guide, handle, lead, manage, navigate, operate, shepherd, steer **3.** *adjective* experimental, model, test, trial

pimp 1. *noun* bawd (*archaic*), go-between, pan~der, panderer, procurer, white-slaver, whore~master (*archaic*) **2.** *verb* live off immoral earnings, procure, sell, solicit, tout

pimple boil, papule (*Pathology*), plook (*Scot.*), pustule, spot, swelling, zit (*slang*)

pin *verb* **1.** affix, attach, fasten, fix, join, secure **2.** fix, hold down, hold fast, immobilize, pin~ion, press, restrain

pinch *verb* **1.** compress, grasp, nip, press, squeeze, tweak **2.** chafe, confine, cramp, crush, hurt, pain **3.** afflict, be stingy, distress, econo~mize, oppress, pinch pennies, press, scrimp, skimp, spare, stint, tighten one's belt **4.** *infor~mal* blag (*slang*), cabbage (*Brit. slang*), filch, knock off (*slang*), lift (*informal*), nick (*slang, chiefly Brit.*), pilfer, purloin, rob, snaffle (*Brit. informal*), snatch, snitch (*slang*), steal, swipe (*slang*) **5.** *informal* apprehend, arrest, bust (*informal*), collar (*informal*), do (*slang*), feel one's collar (*slang*), lift (*slang*), nab (*informal*), nail (*informal*), nick (*slang, chiefly Brit.*), pick up (*slang*), pull in (*Brit. slang*), run in (*slang*), take into custody *~noun* **6.** nip, squeeze, tweak **7.** bit, dash, jot, mite, small quantity, *soupçon*, speck, taste **8.** crisis, difficulty, emergency, exigency, hardship, necessity, op~pression, pass, plight, predicament, pressure, strait, stress

Antonyms (*sense 3*) be extravagant, blow (*slang*), fritter away, spend like water, squan~der, waste (*sense 5*) free, let go, let out, re~lease, set free

pinchbeck 1. *noun* counterfeit, fake, imitation, paste, phoney *or* phony (*informal*), sham **2.** *adjective* artificial, bogus, counterfeit, ersatz, fake, imitation, pseudo (*informal*), spurious

pinched careworn, drawn, gaunt, haggard, peaky, starved, thin, worn

Antonyms blooming, chubby, fat, glowing, hale and hearty, healthy, plump, radiant, ruddy, well-fed

pin down 1. compel, constrain, force, make, press, pressurize **2.** designate, determine, home in on, identify, locate, name, pinpoint, specify **3.** bind, confine, constrain, fix, hold, hold down, immobilize, nail down, tie down

pine 1. *often with* **for** ache, carry a torch for, covet, crave, desire, eat one's heart out over, hanker, hunger for, long, lust after, sigh, sus~pire (*archaic or poetic*), thirst for, wish, yearn **2.** decay, decline, droop, dwindle, fade, flag, languish, peak, sicken, sink, waste, weaken, wilt, wither

pinion *verb* bind, chain, confine, fasten, fetter, immobilize, manacle, pin down, shackle, tie

pink[1] 1. *noun* acme, best, height, peak, perfec~tion, summit **2.** *adjective* flesh, flushed, red~dish, rose, roseate, rosy, salmon

pink[2] *verb* incise, notch, perforate, prick, punch, scallop, score

pinnacle 1. acme, apex, apogee, crest, crown, eminence, height, meridian, peak, summit, top, vertex, zenith **2.** belfry, cone, needle, ob~elisk, pyramid, spire, steeple

pinpoint define, distinguish, get a fix on, home in on, identify, locate, spot

pint ale, beer, jar (*Brit. informal*), jug (*Brit. informal*)

pint-size diminutive, little, midget, miniature, pocket, pygmy *or* pigmy, small, teensy-weensy, teeny-weeny, tiny, wee

pioneer *noun* **1.** colonist, colonizer, explorer, frontiersman, settler **2.** developer, founder, founding father, innovator, leader, trailblazer *~verb* **3.** create, develop, discover, establish, initiate, instigate, institute, invent, launch, lay the groundwork, map out, open up, origi~nate, prepare, show the way, start, take the lead

pious 1. dedicated, devoted, devout, God-fearing, godly, holy, religious, reverent, right~eous, saintly, spiritual **2.** goody-goody, holier-than-thou, hypocritical, pietistic, religiose, sanctimonious, self-righteous, unctuous

Antonyms (*sense 1*) impious, irreligious, irreverent, ungodly, unholy (*sense 2*) humble, meek, sincere

pipe *noun* **1.** conduit, conveyor, duct, hose, line, main, passage, pipeline, tube **2.** briar, clay, meerschaum **3.** fife, horn, tooter, whistle, wind instrument *~verb* **4.** cheep, peep, play, sing, sound, tootle, trill, tweet, twitter, warble, whistle **5.** bring in, channel, conduct, convey, siphon, supply, transmit

Pipes
see TOBACCO

pipe down belt up (*slang*), be quiet, button it (*slang*), button one's lip (*slang*), hold one's tongue, hush, put a sock in it (*Brit. slang*), quieten down, shush, shut one's mouth, shut up (*informal*), silence

pipe dream castle in the air, chimera, daydream, delusion, dream, fantasy, notion, reverie, vagary

pipeline **1.** conduit, conveyor, duct, line, passage, pipe, tube **2. in the pipeline** brewing, coming, getting ready, in process, in production, on the way, under way

pipe up have one's say, make oneself heard, put one's oar in, raise one's voice, speak, speak up, volunteer

pipsqueak creep (*slang*), nobody, nonentity, nothing (*informal*), squirt (*informal*), upstart, whippersnapper

piquancy **1.** bite (*informal*), edge, flavour, kick (*informal*), pungency, relish, sharpness, spice, spiciness, tang, zest **2.** colour, excitement, interest, pep, pizzazz *or* pizazz (*informal*), raciness, spirit, vigour, vitality, zing (*informal*), zip (*informal*)

piquant **1.** acerb, biting, highly-seasoned, peppery, pungent, savoury, sharp, spicy, stinging, tangy, tart, with a kick (*informal*), zesty **2.** interesting, lively, provocative, racy, salty, scintillating, sparkling, spirited, stimulating
Antonyms banal, bland, boring, dull, insipid, mild, tame, uninteresting

pique *noun* **1.** annoyance, displeasure, huff, hurt feelings, irritation, miff (*informal*), offence, resentment, umbrage, vexation, wounded pride *~verb* **2.** affront, annoy, displease, gall, get (*informal*), incense, irk, irritate, miff (*informal*), mortify, nark (*Brit., Austral., & N.Z. slang*), nettle, offend, peeve (*informal*), provoke, put out, put someone's nose out of joint (*informal*), rile, sting, vex, wound **3.** arouse, excite, galvanize, goad, kindle, provoke, rouse, spur, stimulate, stir, whet **4.** *with* **on** *or* **upon** *of oneself* congratulate, flatter, plume, preen, pride

piracy buccaneering, freebooting, hijacking, infringement, plagiarism, rapine, robbery at sea, stealing, theft

pirate *noun* **1.** buccaneer, corsair, filibuster, freebooter, marauder, raider, rover, sea robber, sea rover, sea wolf **2.** cribber (*informal*), infringer, plagiarist, plagiarizer *~verb* **3.** appropriate, borrow, copy, crib (*informal*), lift (*informal*), plagiarize, poach, reproduce, steal

piratical buccaneering, criminal, dishonest, felonious, fraudulent, lawless, pillaging, plundering, rapacious, thieving, unprincipled, wolfish

pirouette *noun/verb* pivot, spin, turn, twirl, whirl

pit *noun* **1.** abyss, cavity, chasm, coal mine, crater, dent, depression, dimple, excavation, gulf, hole, hollow, indentation, mine, pockmark, pothole, trench *~verb* **2.** *often with* **against** match, oppose, put in opposition, set against **3.** dent, dint, gouge, hole, indent, mark, nick, notch, pockmark, scar

pitch *verb* **1.** bung (*Brit. slang*), cast, chuck (*informal*), fling, heave, hurl, launch, lob (*informal*), sling, throw, toss **2.** erect, fix, locate, place, plant, put up, raise, settle, set up, station **3.** flounder, lurch, make heavy weather, plunge, roll, toss, wallow, welter **4.** dive, drop, fall headlong, stagger, topple, tumble *~noun* **5.** angle, cant, dip, gradient, incline, slope, steepness, tilt **6.** degree, height, highest point, level, point, summit **7.** harmonic, modulation, sound, timbre, tone **8.** line, patter, sales talk, spiel (*informal*) **9.** field of play, ground, park (*U.S. & Canad.*), sports field

pitch-black dark, ebony, inky, jet, jet-black, pitch-dark, raven, sable, unlit

pitch-dark black, dark, pitch-black, pitchy, Stygian, unilluminated, unlit

pitch in **1.** chip in (*informal*), contribute, cooperate, do one's bit, help, join in, lend a hand, lend a helping hand, participate **2.** begin, fall to, get busy, get cracking (*informal*), plunge into, set about, set to, tackle

pitch into assail, assault, attack, get stuck into (*informal*), lace into, light into (*informal*), sail into (*informal*), tear into (*informal*)

pitch on *or* **upon** choose, decide on, determine, elect, light on, opt for, pick, plump for, select, single out

pitchy black, coal-black, dark, ebony, inky, jet, jetty, moonless, pitch-black, raven, sable, unilluminated, unlighted

piteous affecting, deplorable, dismal, distressing, doleful, grievous, harrowing, heartbreaking, heart-rending, lamentable, miserable, mournful, moving, pathetic, pitiable, pitiful, plaintive, poignant, sad, sorrowful, woeful, wretched

pitfall **1.** banana skin (*informal*), catch, danger, difficulty, drawback, hazard, peril, snag, trap **2.** deadfall, downfall, pit, snare, trap

pith 1. core, crux, essence, gist, heart, heart of the matter, kernel, marrow, meat, nub, point, quintessence, salient point, the long and the short of it 2. consequence, depth, force, import, importance, matter, moment, power, significance, strength, substance, value, weight

pithy brief, cogent, compact, concise, epigrammatic, expressive, finely honed, forceful, laconic, meaningful, pointed, short, succinct, terse, to the point, trenchant
Antonyms diffuse, garrulous, long, long-winded, loquacious, prolix, verbose, wordy

pitiable deplorable, dismal, distressing, doleful, grievous, harrowing, lamentable, miserable, mournful, pathetic, piteous, poor, sad, sorry, woeful, wretched

pitiful 1. deplorable, distressing, grievous, harrowing, heartbreaking, heart-rending, lamentable, miserable, pathetic, piteous, pitiable, sad, woeful, wretched 2. abject, base, beggarly, contemptible, despicable, dismal, inadequate, insignificant, low, mean, measly, miserable, paltry, scurvy, shabby, sorry, vile, worthless
Antonyms (*sense 1*) amusing, cheerful, cheering, comical, funny, happy, heartening, laughable, merry (*sense 2*) adequate, admirable, honourable, laudable, praiseworthy, significant, valuable

pitiless brutal, callous, cold-blooded, cold-hearted, cruel, hardhearted, harsh, heartless, implacable, inexorable, inhuman, merciless, relentless, ruthless, uncaring, unfeeling, unmerciful, unsympathetic
Antonyms caring, compassionate, kind, merciful, relenting, responsive, soft-hearted, sparing

pittance allowance, chicken feed (*slang*), drop, mite, modicum, peanuts (*slang*), portion, ration, slave wages, trifle

pitted blemished, dented, eaten away, holey, indented, marked, pockmarked, pocky, potholed, riddled, rough, rutty, scarred, scratched

pity *noun* 1. charity, clemency, commiseration, compassion, condolence, fellow feeling, forbearance, kindness, mercy, quarter, sympathy, tenderness, understanding 2. bummer (*slang*), crime (*informal*), crying shame, misfortune, regret, sad thing, shame, sin 3. **take pity on** feel compassion for, forgive, have mercy on, melt, pardon, put out of one's misery, relent, reprieve, show mercy, spare *~verb* 4. bleed for, commiserate with, condole with, feel for, feel sorry for, grieve for, have compassion for, sympathize with, weep for
Antonyms (*sense 1*) anger, apathy, brutality, cruelty, disdain, fury, hard-heartedness, indifference, inhumanity, mercilessness, pitilessness, ruthlessness, scorn, severity, unconcern, wrath

pivot *noun* 1. axis, axle, fulcrum, spindle, swivel 2. centre, focal point, heart, hinge, hub, kingpin *~verb* 3. revolve, rotate, spin, swivel, turn, twirl 4. be contingent, depend, hang, hinge, rely, revolve round, turn

pivotal central, climactic, critical, crucial, decisive, determining, focal, vital

pixie brownie, elf, fairy, peri, sprite

placard advertisement, *affiche*, bill, poster, public notice, sticker

placate appease, assuage, calm, conciliate, humour, mollify, pacify, propitiate, satisfy, soothe, win over

placatory appeasing, conciliatory, designed to please, pacificatory, peacemaking, propitiative

place *noun* 1. area, location, locus, point, position, site, situation, spot, station, venue, whereabouts 2. city, district, hamlet, locale, locality, neighbourhood, quarter, region, town, vicinity, village 3. grade, position, rank, station, status 4. appointment, berth (*informal*), billet (*informal*), employment, job, position, post 5. abode, apartment, domicile, dwelling, flat, home, house, manor, mansion, pad (*slang*), property, residence, seat 6. accommodation, room, space, stead 7. affair, charge, concern, duty, function, prerogative, responsibility, right, role 8. **in place of** as an alternative to, as a substitute for, in exchange for, in lieu of, instead of, taking the place of 9. **put (someone) in his place** bring down, cut down to size, humble, humiliate, make (someone) eat humble pie, make (someone) swallow his pride, mortify, take down a peg (*informal*) 10. **take place** befall, betide, come about, come to pass (*archaic*), go on, happen, occur, transpire (*informal*) *~verb* 11. bung (*Brit. slang*), deposit, dispose, establish, fix, install, lay, locate, plant, position, put, rest, set, settle, situate, stand, station, stick (*informal*) 12. arrange, class, classify, grade, group, order, rank, sort 13. associate, identify, know, put one's finger on, recognize, remember, set in context 14. allocate, appoint, assign, charge, commission, entrust, give

Place	Nickname
Aberdeen	the Granite City
Adelaide	the City of Churches
Amsterdam	the Venice of the North
Birmingham	Brum *or* the Venice of the North
Boston	Bean Town
Bruges	the Venice of the North
California	the Golden State
Chicago	the Windy City

Dallas	the Big D
Detroit	the Motor City
Dresden	Florence on the Elbe
Dublin	the Fair City
Dumfries	Queen of the South
Edinburgh	Auld Reekie *or* the Athens of the North
Florida	the Sunshine State
Fraserburgh	the Broch
Fremantle	Freo
Glasgow	the Dear Green Place
Hamburg	the Venice of the North
Indiana	the Hoosier State
Iowa	the Hawkeye State
Ireland	the Emerald Isle
Jamaica	J.A. *or* the Yard
Jerusalem	the Holy City
Kentucky	the Bluegrass State
Kuala Lumpur	K.L.
London	the Big Smoke *or* the Great Wen
Los Angeles	L.A.
New Jersey	the Garden State
New Orleans	the Crescent City *or* the Big Easy
New South Wales	Ma State
New York (City)	the Big Apple
New York (State)	the Empire State
New Zealand	Pig Island
North Carolina	the Tarheel State
Nottingham	Queen of the Midlands
Oklahoma	the Sooner State
Pennsylvania	the Keystone State
Philadelphia	Philly
Portsmouth	Pompey
Prince Edward Island	Spud Island
Queensland	Bananaland *or* the Deep North *(both derogatory)*
Rome	the Eternal City
San Francisco	Frisco
Southeastern U.S.A.	Dixie, Dixieland *or* the Deep South
Tasmania	Tassie *or* the Apple Isle
Texas	the Lone Star State
Utah	the Beehive State
Venice	La Serenissima

placement **1.** arrangement, deployment, disposition, distribution, emplacement, installation, locating, location, ordering, positioning, stationing **2.** appointment, assignment, employment, engagement

placid calm, collected, composed, cool, equable, even, even-tempered, gentle, halcyon, imperturbable, mild, peaceful, quiet, self-possessed, serene, still, tranquil, undisturbed, unexcitable, unfazed (*informal*), unmoved, unruffled, untroubled
Antonyms agitated, disturbed, emotional, excitable, impulsive, passionate, rough, temperamental, tempestuous

plagiarism appropriation, borrowing, copying, cribbing (*informal*), infringement, lifting (*informal*), piracy, theft

If you steal from one author, it's plagiarism; if you steal from many, it's research
Wilson Mizner

plagiarize appropriate, borrow, crib (*informal*), infringe, lift (*informal*), pirate, steal, thieve

Plagiarize! Let no one else's work evade your eyes,
Remember why the good Lord made your eyes
Ernest Lehman *Lobachevski*

plague *noun* **1.** contagion, disease, epidemic, infection, lurgi (*informal*), pandemic, pestilence **2.** *figurative* affliction, bane, blight, calamity, cancer, curse, evil, scourge, torment, trial **3.** *informal* aggravation (*informal*), annoyance, bother, hassle (*informal*), irritant, nuisance, pain (*informal*), pest, problem, thorn in one's flesh, vexation *~verb* **4.** afflict, annoy, badger, bedevil, be on one's back (*slang*), bother, disturb, fret, get in one's hair (*informal*), get on one's nerves (*informal*), harass, harry, hassle (*informal*), haunt, molest, pain, persecute, pester, tease, torment, torture, trouble, vex

plaguy annoying, disagreeable, harassing, impossible, irksome, irritating, provoking, troublesome, trying, vexing, wretched

plain *adjective* **1.** apparent, bold, clear, comprehensible, distinct, evident, legible, lucid, manifest, obvious, patent, transparent, unambiguous, understandable, unmistakable, visible **2.** artless, blunt, candid, direct, downright, forthright, frank, guileless, honest, ingenuous, open, outspoken, round, sincere, straightforward, upfront (*informal*) **3.** common, commonplace, everyday, frugal, homely, lowly, modest, ordinary, simple, unaffected, unpretentious, workaday **4.** austere, bare, basic, discreet, modest, muted, pure, restrained, severe, simple, Spartan, stark, unadorned, unembellished, unfussy, unornamented, unpatterned, unvarnished **5.** ill-favoured, no oil painting (*informal*), not beautiful, not striking, ordinary, ugly, unalluring, unattractive, unlovely, unprepossessing **6.** even, flat, level, plane, smooth *~noun* **7.** flatland, grassland, llano, lowland, mesa, open country, plateau, prairie, steppe, tableland
Antonyms (*sense 1*) ambiguous, complex, concealed, deceptive, difficult, disguised, hidden, illegible, incomprehensible, inconspicuous, indiscernible, indistinct, obscure, vague, veiled

(*sense 2*) circuitous, indirect, meandering, rambling, roundabout (*sense 3*) affected, distinguished, egotistic, ostentatious, pretentious, sophisticated, worldly (*sense 4*) adorned, decorated, fancy, ornate (*sense 5*) attractive, beautiful, comely, good-looking, gorgeous, handsome (*sense 6*) bumpy, not level, uneven

plain-spoken blunt, candid, direct, downright, explicit, forthright, frank, open, outright, outspoken, straightforward, unequivocal, upfront (*informal*)
Antonyms diplomatic, discreet, evasive, guarded, indirect, reticent, subtle, tactful, thoughtful

plaintive disconsolate, doleful, grief-stricken, grievous, heart-rending, melancholy, mournful, pathetic, piteous, pitiful, rueful, sad, sorrowful, wistful, woebegone, woeful

plan *noun* **1.** contrivance, design, device, idea, method, plot, procedure, programme, project, proposal, proposition, scenario, scheme, strategy, suggestion, system **2.** blueprint, chart, delineation, diagram, drawing, illustration, layout, map, representation, scale drawing, sketch *~verb* **3.** arrange, concoct, contrive, design, devise, draft, formulate, frame, invent, organize, outline, plot, prepare, represent, scheme, think out **4.** aim, contemplate, envisage, foresee, intend, mean, propose, purpose

plane *noun* **1.** flat surface, level surface **2.** condition, degree, footing, level, position, stratum **3.** aeroplane, aircraft, jet *~adjective* **4.** even, flat, flush, horizontal, level, plain, regular, smooth, uniform *~verb* **5.** glide, sail, skate, skim, volplane

planet

Planets

Earth
Jupiter
Mars
Mercury
Neptune
Pluto
Saturn
Uranus
Venus

planetary **1.** earthly, mundane, sublunary, tellurian, terrene, terrestrial **2.** aberrant, erratic, journeying, moving, travelling, vacillating, variable, wandering

plangent clangorous, deep-toned, loud, mournful, plaintive, resonant, resounding, reverberating, ringing, sonorous

plant *noun* **1.** bush, flower, herb, shrub, vegetable, weed **2.** factory, foundry, mill, shop, works, yard **3.** apparatus, equipment, gear, machinery *~verb* **4.** implant, put in the ground, scatter, seed, set out, sow, transplant **5.** establish, fix, found, imbed, insert, institute, lodge, root, set, settle, sow the seeds

Algae

bladderwrack
brown algae
carrageen, carragheen *or* carageen
diatom
dinoflagellate
dulse
euglena
fucoid *or* fucus
green algae
gulfweed
Iceland moss
Irish moss
kelp
laver
lichen
oarweed
phytoplankton *or* plankton
red algae
reindeer moss
rockweed
sargasso *or* sargassum
sea lettuce
sea tangle
seaweed
sea wrack
spirogyra
stonewort
wrack

Ferns

adder's-tongue
bladder fern
beech fern
bracken
buckler fern
hard fern
hart's-tongue
lady fern
maidenhair
male fern
marsh fern
moonwort
oak fern
parsley fern
pillwort
rock brake
royal fern
shield fern
sword fern
tree fern
Venus's-hair
walking fern
wall rue
woodsia

Fungi

agaric
bird's-nest fungus
boletus
bracket fungus
cramp ball
death cap
dry rot
earthstar
elf-cup
ergot
funnel cap
ink-cap
jelly fungus
horn of plenty
liberty cap
mildew
milk cap
miller
mould
mushroom
puffball
rust *or* rust fungus
shaggy cap
sickener
smut
stinkhorn
sulphur tuft
toadstool
truffle
velvet shank
wax cap
wet rot
wood hedgehog
wood woollyfoot
yeast

Grasses

barley
Bermuda grass
bluegrass
buffalo grass
cane
citronella
cotton grass
couch grass
crab grass
darnel
elephant grass
esparto
fescue
maize
marram grass
millet
oat
pampas grass
reed
rice
rye
rye-grass
sorghum
sugar cane

wheat	wild rye
wild oat	

Shrubs

acacia	heather
acanthus	honeysuckle
arbutus	hydrangea
bilberry	jasmine
blackcurrant	juniper
blackthorn	laburnum
blueberry	laurel
bramble	lilac
briar *or* brier	liquorice
broom	magnolia
buckthorn	mistletoe
buddleia	mock orange
camellia	myrtle
caper	oleander
clematis	poinsettia
coca	poison ivy
cotton	poison oak
cranberry	potentilla
crown-of-thorns	privet
daphne	pyracantha
dogwood	raspberry
forsythia	redcurrant
frangipani	rhododendron
fuchsia	rose
gardenia	rosemary
gooseberry	rue
gorse	strawberry
hawthorn	tea
heath	thyme

Flowers

see FLOWER

Trees

see TREE

What is a weed? A plant whose virtues have not been discovered

Ralph Waldo Emerson *Fortune of the Republic*

Just now the lilac is in bloom,
All before my little room

Rupert Brooke *Grantchester*

plaque badge, brooch, cartouch(e), medal, medallion, panel, plate, slab, tablet

plaster *noun* **1.** gypsum, mortar, plaster of Paris, stucco **2.** adhesive plaster, bandage, dressing, Elastoplast (*Trademark*), sticking plaster *~verb* **3.** bedaub, besmear, coat, cover, daub, overlay, smear, spread

plastic *adjective* **1.** compliant, docile, easily influenced, impressionable, malleable, manageable, pliable, receptive, responsive, tractable **2.** ductile, fictile, flexible, mouldable, pliable, pliant, soft, supple, tensile **3.** *slang* artificial, false, meretricious, mock, phoney *or* phony (*informal*), pseudo (*informal*), sham, specious, spurious, superficial, synthetic
Antonyms (*sense 1*) intractable, rebellious, recalcitrant, refractory, unmanageable, unreceptive (*sense 2*) brittle, hard, inflexible, rigid, stiff, unbending, unyielding (*sense 3*) authentic, genuine, natural, real, sincere, true

plasticity flexibility, malleability, pliability, pliableness, suppleness, tractability

plate *noun* **1.** dish, platter, trencher (*archaic*) **2.** course, dish, helping, portion, serving **3.** layer, panel, sheet, slab **4.** illustration, lithograph, print *~verb* **5.** anodize, coat, cover, electroplate, face, gild, laminate, nickel, overlay, platinize, silver

plateau **1.** highland, mesa, table, tableland, upland **2.** level, levelling off, stability, stage

platform **1.** dais, podium, rostrum, stage, stand **2.** manifesto, objective(s), party line, policy, principle, programme, tenet(s)

platitude **1.** banality, bromide, cliché, commonplace, hackneyed saying, inanity, stereotype, trite remark, truism **2.** banality, dullness, inanity, insipidity, triteness, triviality, vapidity, verbiage

platitudinous banal, clichéd, commonplace, corny (*slang*), hack, hackneyed, overworked, set, stale, stereotyped, stock, tired, trite, truistic, vapid, well-worn

platonic *all of love* ideal, idealistic, intellectual, nonphysical, spiritual, transcendent

platoon company, group, outfit (*informal*), patrol, squad, squadron, team

platter charger, dish, plate, salver, tray, trencher (*archaic*)

plaudit *usually plural* acclaim, acclamation, applause, approbation, approval, clapping, commendation, congratulation, hand, kudos, ovation, praise, round of applause

plausible believable, colourable, conceivable, credible, fair-spoken, glib, likely, persuasive, possible, probable, reasonable, smooth, smooth-talking, smooth-tongued, specious, tenable, verisimilar
Antonyms genuine, illogical, implausible, impossible, improbable, inconceivable, incredible, real, unbelievable, unlikely

play *verb* **1.** amuse oneself, caper, engage in games, entertain oneself, fool, frisk, frolic, gambol, have fun, revel, romp, sport, trifle **2.** be in a team, challenge, compete, contend against, participate, rival, take on, take part, vie with **3.** act, act the part of, execute, impersonate, perform, personate, portray, represent, take the part of **4.** bet, chance, gamble, hazard, punt (*chiefly Brit.*), risk, speculate, take, wager **5.** **play ball** *informal* collaborate, cooperate, go along, play along, reciprocate, respond, show willing **6.** **play by ear** ad lib, extemporize, improvise, rise to the occasion, take it as it comes **7.** **play for time** delay, drag one's feet (*informal*), filibuster, hang fire, procrastinate, stall, temporize **8.** **play the**

fool act the goat (*informal*), clown, clown around, horse around (*informal*), lark (about) (*informal*), mess about, monkey around, sky~lark (*informal*) **9. play the game** *informal* conform, follow the rules, go along with, keep in step, play by the rules, play fair, toe the line *~noun* **10.** comedy, drama, dramatic piece, entertainment, farce, masque, pantomime, performance, piece, radio play, show, soap op~era, stage show, television drama, tragedy **11.** amusement, caper, diversion, entertainment, frolic, fun, gambol, game, jest, pastime, prank, recreation, romp, sport **12.** gambling, gaming **13.** action, activity, elbowroom, exer~cise, give (*informal*), latitude, leeway, margin, motion, movement, operation, range, room, scope, space, sweep, swing **14.** action, activity, employment, function, operation, transaction, working **15.** foolery, fun, humour, jest, joking, lark (*informal*), prank, sport, teasing

The play's the thing

William Shakespeare *Hamlet*

play around dally, fool around, mess around, philander, take lightly, trifle, womanize

playboy gay dog, ladies' man, lady-killer (*in~formal*), lover boy (*slang*), man about town, philanderer, pleasure seeker, rake, roué, so~cialite, womanizer

play down gloss over, make light of, make lit~tle of, minimize, set no store by, soft-pedal (*informal*), underplay, underrate

player 1. competitor, contestant, participant, sportsman, sportswoman, team member **2.** ac~tor, actress, entertainer, performer, Thespian, trouper **3.** artist, instrumentalist, musician, music maker, performer, virtuoso

playful 1. cheerful, coltish, frisky, frolicsome, gay, impish, joyous, kittenish, larkish (*infor~mal*), lively, ludic (*literary*), merry, mischie~vous, puckish, rollicking, spirited, sportive, sprightly, vivacious **2.** arch, coy, flirtatious, good-natured, humorous, jesting, jokey, joking, roguish, teasing, tongue-in-cheek, waggish
Antonyms despondent, gloomy, grave, morose, sedate, serious

playmate chum (*informal*), companion, com~rade, friend, neighbour, pal (*informal*), play~fellow

play on *or* **upon** abuse, capitalize on, exploit, impose on, milk, profit by, take advantage of, trade on, turn to account, utilize

plaything amusement, bauble, game, gewgaw, gimcrack, pastime, toy, trifle, trinket

play up 1. accentuate, bring to the fore, call attention to, emphasize, highlight, magnify, point up, stress, turn the spotlight on, under~line **2.** *Brit. informal* be painful, be sore, bother, give one gyp (*Brit. & N.Z. slang*), give one trouble, hurt, pain, trouble **3.** *Brit. infor~mal* be awkward, be bolshie (*Brit. informal*), be cussed (*informal*), be disobedient, be strop~py (*Brit. slang*), give trouble, misbehave **4.** *Brit. informal* be on the blink (*slang*), be wonky (*Brit. slang*), malfunction, not work properly **5. play up to** *informal* bootlick (*in~formal*), brown-nose (*taboo slang*), butter up, curry favour, fawn, flatter, get in with, ingra~tiate oneself, keep (someone) sweet, kiss (someone's) ass (*U.S. & Canad. taboo slang*), pander to, suck up to (*informal*), toady

play with 1. amuse oneself with, flirt with, string along, toy with, trifle with **2.** fiddle with (*informal*), fidget with, fool around, interfere with, jiggle, mess about, waggle, wiggle

playwright dramatist, dramaturge, dramatur~gist

plea 1. appeal, begging, entreaty, intercession, overture, petition, prayer, request, suit, sup~plication **2.** *Law* action, allegation, cause, suit **3.** apology, claim, defence, excuse, explanation, extenuation, justification, pretext, vindication

plead 1. appeal (to), ask, beg, beseech, crave, entreat, implore, importune, petition, request, solicit, supplicate **2.** adduce, allege, argue, as~sert, maintain, put forward, use as an excuse

pleasant 1. acceptable, agreeable, amusing, de~lectable, delightful, enjoyable, fine, gratifying, lovely, nice, pleasing, pleasurable, refreshing, satisfying, welcome **2.** affable, agreeable, ami~able, charming, cheerful, cheery, congenial, engaging, friendly, genial, good-humoured, likable *or* likeable, nice
Antonyms awful, cold, disagreeable, distaste~ful, horrible, horrid, impolite, miserable, of~fensive, repulsive, rude, unfriendly, unlikable *or* unlikeable, unpleasant

pleasantry badinage, banter, bon mot, good-natured remark, jest, joke, josh (*slang, chiefly U.S. & Canad.*), quip, sally, witticism

please 1. amuse, charm, cheer, content, de~light, entertain, give pleasure to, gladden, gratify, humour, indulge, rejoice, satisfy, suit, tickle, tickle pink (*informal*) **2.** be inclined, choose, desire, like, opt, prefer, see fit, want, will, wish
Antonyms anger, annoy, depress, disgust, displease, dissatisfy, grieve, incense, offend, provoke, sadden, vex

pleased chuffed (*Brit. slang*), contented, de~lighted, euphoric, glad, gratified, happy, in high spirits, over the moon (*informal*), pleased as punch (*informal*), rapt, satisfied, thrilled, tickled, tickled pink (*informal*)

pleasing agreeable, amiable, amusing, attrac~tive, charming, delightful, engaging, enjoy~able, entertaining, gratifying, likable *or* like~able, pleasurable, polite, satisfying, winning

Antonyms boring, disagreeable, dull, monotonous, rude, unattractive, unlikable *or* unlikeable, unpleasant

pleasurable agreeable, congenial, delightful, diverting, enjoyable, entertaining, fun, good, gratifying, lovely, nice, pleasant, welcome

pleasure 1. amusement, beer and skittles (*informal*), bliss, comfort, contentment, delectation, delight, diversion, ease, enjoyment, gladness, gratification, happiness, jollies (*slang*), joy, recreation, satisfaction, solace **2.** choice, command, desire, inclination, mind, option, preference, purpose, will, wish
Antonyms abstinence, anger, disinclination, displeasure, duty, labour, misery, necessity, obligation, pain, sadness, sorrow, suffering, unhappiness

Everyone is dragged on by their favourite pleasure
Virgil *Eclogue*

Pleasure's a sin, and sometimes sin's a pleasure
Lord Byron *Don Juan*

Sweet is pleasure after pain
John Dryden *Alexander's Feast*

The rapturous, wild, and ineffable pleasure
Of drinking at somebody else's expense
Henry Sambrooke Leigh *Carols of Cockayne*

Pleasure is nothing else but the intermission of pain
John Selden *Table Talk*

One half of the world cannot understand the pleasures of the other
Jane Austen *Emma*

plebeian 1. *adjective* base, coarse, common, ignoble, low, lowborn, lower-class, mean, non-U (*Brit. informal*), proletarian, uncultivated, unrefined, vulgar, working-class **2.** *noun* commoner, common man, man in the street, peasant, pleb, prole (*derogatory slang, chiefly Brit.*), proletarian
Antonyms aristocratic, cultivated, highborn, high-class, patrician, polished, refined, upper-class, well-bred

plebiscite ballot, poll, referendum, vote

pledge *noun* **1.** assurance, covenant, oath, promise, undertaking, vow, warrant, word, word of honour **2.** bail, bond, collateral, deposit, earnest, gage, guarantee, pawn, security, surety **3.** health, toast *~verb* **4.** contract, engage, give one's oath (word, word of honour), promise, swear, undertake, vouch, vow **5.** bind, engage, gage (*archaic*), guarantee, mortgage, plight **6.** drink the health of, drink to, toast

plenary 1. absolute, complete, full, sweeping, thorough, unconditional, unlimited, unqualified, unrestricted **2.** *of assemblies, councils, etc.* complete, entire, full, general, open, whole

plenipotentiary ambassador, emissary, envoy, legate, minister

plenitude 1. abundance, bounty, copiousness, cornucopia, excess, plenteousness, plenty, plethora, profusion, wealth **2.** amplitude, completeness, fullness, repletion

plenteous 1. abundant, ample, bounteous (*literary*), bountiful, copious, generous, inexhaustible, infinite, lavish, liberal, overflowing, plentiful, profuse, thick on the ground **2.** bumper, fertile, fruitful, luxuriant, plentiful, productive, prolific

plentiful 1. abundant, ample, bounteous (*literary*), bountiful, complete, copious, generous, inexhaustible, infinite, lavish, liberal, overflowing, plenteous, profuse, thick on the ground **2.** bumper, fertile, fruitful, luxuriant, plenteous, productive, prolific
Antonyms deficient, inadequate, insufficient, scant, scarce, skimpy, small, sparing, sparse, thin on the ground

plenty 1. abundance, enough, fund, good deal, great deal, heap(s) (*informal*), lots (*informal*), mass, masses, mine, mountain(s), oodles (*informal*), pile(s) (*informal*), plethora, quantities, quantity, stack(s), store, sufficiency, volume **2.** abundance, affluence, copiousness, fertility, fruitfulness, luxury, opulence, plenitude, plenteousness, plentifulness, profusion, prosperity, wealth

Plenty has made me poor
Ovid *Metamorphoses*

pleonasm circuitousness, circumlocution, convolution, periphrasis, redundancy, repetition, tautology, verbiage, verbosity, wordiness

pleonastic circuitous, circumlocutory, convoluted, iterative, periphrastic, prolix, redundant, repetitious, superfluous, tautological, verbose, wordy

plethora excess, glut, overabundance, profusion, superabundance, superfluity, surfeit, surplus
Antonyms dearth, deficiency, lack, scarcity, shortage, want

pliability 1. bendability, ductility, elasticity, flexibility, malleability, mobility, plasticity, pliancy **2.** adaptability, amenability, compliance, docility, impressionableness, susceptibility, tractableness

pliable 1. bendable, bendy, ductile, flexible, limber, lithe, malleable, plastic, pliant, supple, tensile **2.** adaptable, compliant, docile, easily led, impressionable, influenceable, like putty in one's hands, manageable, persuadable, pliant, receptive, responsive, susceptible, tractable, yielding
Antonyms headstrong, inflexible, intractable, obdurate, obstinate, rigid, stiff, stubborn, unadaptable, unbending, unyielding, wilful

pliant **1.** bendable, bendy, ductile, flexible, lithe, plastic, pliable, supple, tensile **2.** adaptable, biddable, compliant, easily led, impressionable, influenceable, manageable, persuadable, pliable, susceptible, tractable, yielding

plight[1] *noun* case, circumstances, condition, difficulty, dilemma, extremity, hole (*slang*), hot water (*informal*), jam (*informal*), perplexity, pickle (*informal*), predicament, scrape (*informal*), situation, spot (*informal*), state, straits, tight spot, trouble

plight[2] *verb* contract, covenant, engage, guarantee, pledge, promise, propose, swear, vouch, vow

plod **1.** clump, drag, lumber, slog, stomp (*informal*), tramp, tread, trudge **2.** drudge, grind (*informal*), grub, labour, peg away, persevere, plough through, plug away (*informal*), slog, soldier on, toil

plodder **1.** dawdler, laggard, slowcoach (*Brit. informal*), slowpoke (*U.S. & Canad. informal*), tortoise **2.** drudge, hack, slogger, toiler, workhorse

plot[1] *noun* **1.** cabal, conspiracy, covin (*Law*), intrigue, machination, plan, scheme, stratagem **2.** action, narrative, outline, scenario, story, story line, subject, theme, thread *~verb* **3.** cabal, collude, conspire, contrive, hatch, intrigue, machinate, manoeuvre, plan, scheme **4.** calculate, chart, compute, draft, draw, locate, map, mark, outline **5.** brew, conceive, concoct, contrive, cook up (*informal*), design, devise, frame, hatch, imagine, lay, project

Ay, now the plot thickens very much upon us
George Villiers Buckingham *The Rehearsal*

plot[2] *noun* allotment, area, ground, lot, parcel, patch, tract

plotter architect, cabalist, conniver, conspirator, conspirer, intriguer, Machiavellian, planner, schemer, strategist

plough *verb* **1.** break ground, cultivate, dig, furrow, ridge, till, turn over **2.** *usually with* **through** cut, drive, flounder, forge, plod, plunge, press, push, stagger, surge, wade **3.** *with* **into** bulldoze, career, crash, hurtle, plunge, shove, smash

ploy contrivance, device, dodge, gambit, game, manoeuvre, move, ruse, scheme, stratagem, subterfuge, tactic, trick, wile

pluck[1] *noun* backbone, balls (*taboo slang*), ballsiness (*taboo slang*), boldness, bottle (*Brit. slang*), bravery, courage, determination, grit, guts (*informal*), hardihood, heart, intrepidity, mettle, nerve, resolution, spirit, spunk (*informal*)

pluck[2] *verb* **1.** collect, draw, gather, harvest, pick, pull out *or* off **2.** catch, clutch, jerk, pull at, snatch, tug, tweak, yank **3.** finger, pick, plunk, strum, thrum, twang

plucky ballsy (*taboo slang*), bold, brave, courageous, daring, doughty, feisty (*informal, chiefly U.S. & Canad.*), game, gritty, gutsy (*slang*), hardy, have-a-go (*informal*), heroic, intrepid, mettlesome, spirited, spunky (*informal*), undaunted, unflinching, valiant
Antonyms afraid, chicken (*slang*), cowardly, dastardly, dispirited, lifeless, scared, spineless, spiritless, timid, weary, yellow (*informal*)

plug *noun* **1.** bung, cork, spigot, stopper, stopple **2.** cake, chew, pigtail, quid, twist, wad **3.** *informal* advert (*Brit. informal*), advertisement, good word, hype, mention, publicity, puff, push *~verb* **4.** block, bung, choke, close, cork, cover, fill, pack, seal, stop, stopper, stopple, stop up, stuff **5.** *informal* advertise, build up, hype, mention, promote, publicize, puff, push, write up **6.** *slang* blow away (*slang, chiefly U.S.*), gun down, pick off, pop, pot, put a bullet in, shoot **7.** *with* **along** *or* **away** *informal* drudge, grind (*informal*), labour, peg away, plod, slog, toil

plum *figurative* **1.** *noun* bonus, cream, find, pick, prize, treasure **2.** *adjective* best, choice, first-class, prize

plumb *noun* **1.** lead, plumb bob, plummet, weight *~adverb* **2.** perpendicularly, up and down, vertically **3.** bang, exactly, precisely, slap, spot-on (*Brit. informal*) *~verb* **4.** delve, explore, fathom, gauge, go into, measure, penetrate, probe, search, sound, unravel

plume **1.** *noun* aigrette, crest, feather, pinion, quill **2.** *verb with* **on** *or* **upon** congratulate oneself, pat oneself on the back, pique oneself, preen oneself, pride oneself

plummet crash, descend, dive, drop down, fall, nose-dive, plunge, stoop, swoop, tumble

plummy *applied to speech* deep, fruity, posh (*informal, chiefly Brit.*), refined, resonant, upper-class

plump[1] *adjective* beefy (*informal*), burly, buxom, chubby, corpulent, dumpy, fat, fleshy, full, obese, podgy, portly, roly-poly, rotund, round, stout, tubby, well-covered, well-upholstered (*informal*)
Antonyms anorexic, bony, emaciated, lanky, lean, scrawny, skinny, slender, slim, sylphlike, thin

plump[2] *verb* **1.** drop, dump, fall, flop, sink, slump **2.** *with* **for** back, choose, come down in favour of, favour, opt for, side with, support *~adjective* **3.** abrupt, direct, downright, forthright, plain, unqualified, unreserved

plunder **1.** *verb* despoil, devastate, loot, pillage, raid, ransack, ravage, rifle, rob, sack, spoil, steal, strip **2.** *noun* booty, ill-gotten gains, loot, pillage, prey, prize, rapine, spoils, swag (*slang*)

plunge *verb* 1. cast, descend, dip, dive, douse, drop, fall, go down, immerse, jump, nose-dive, pitch, plummet, sink, submerge, swoop, throw, tumble 2. career, charge, dash, hurtle, lurch, rush, tear ~*noun* 3. descent, dive, drop, fall, immersion, jump, submersion, swoop

plurality 1. diversity, multiplicity, numerousness, profusion, variety 2. bulk, majority, mass, most, nearly all, overwhelming number, preponderance

plus 1. *preposition* added to, and, coupled with, with, with the addition of 2. *adjective* added, additional, add-on, extra, positive, supplementary 3. *noun, informal* advantage, asset, benefit, bonus, extra, gain, good point, icing on the cake, perk (*Brit. informal*), surplus

plush costly, de luxe, lavish, luxurious, luxury, opulent, palatial, rich, ritzy (*slang*), sumptuous

Antonyms cheap, cheap and nasty, inexpensive, ordinary, plain, spartan

plutocrat capitalist, Croesus, Dives, fat cat (*slang, chiefly U.S.*), magnate, millionaire, moneybags (*slang*), rich man, tycoon

ply[1] *verb* 1. carry on, exercise, follow, practise, pursue, work at 2. employ, handle, manipulate, swing, utilize, wield 3. assail, beset, besiege, bombard, harass, importune, press, urge

ply[2] *noun* fold, layer, leaf, sheet, strand, thickness

poach appropriate, encroach, hunt *or* fish illegally, infringe, intrude, plunder, rob, steal, steal game, trespass

pock blemish, flaw, mark, pimple, pockmark, pustule, scar, spot

pocket *noun* 1. bag, compartment, hollow, pouch, receptacle, sack ~*adjective* 2. abridged, compact, concise, little, miniature, pint-size(d) (*informal*), portable, potted (*informal*), small ~*verb* 3. appropriate, cabbage (*Brit. slang*), filch, help oneself to, lift (*informal*), pilfer, purloin, snaffle (*Brit. informal*), steal, take 4. accept, bear, brook, endure, put up with (*informal*), stomach, swallow, take, tolerate

pockmark blemish, pit, pock, scar

pod *noun/verb* hull, husk, shell, shuck

podgy chubby, chunky, dumpy, fat, fleshy, fubsy (*archaic or dialect*), plump, roly-poly, rotund, short and fat, squat, stout, stubby, stumpy, tubby

podium dais, platform, rostrum, stage

poem lyric, ode, rhyme, song, sonnet, verse

A poem should not mean
but be
Archibald McLeish *Ars Poetica*

poet bard, lyricist, maker (*archaic*), rhymer, versifier

Poets
see WRITER

The poet is the priest of the invisible
Wallace Stevens *Adagia*

A poet's hope: to be,
like some valley cheese,
local, but prized elsewhere
W.H. Auden *Shorts II*

For that fine madness still he did retain
Which rightly should possess a poet's brain
Michael Drayton *To Henry Reynolds, of Poets and Poesy*

Immature poets imitate; mature poets steal
T.S. Eliot *The Sacred Wood*

The poet is always indebted to the universe, paying interest and fines on sorrow
Vladimir Mayakovsky *Conversation with an Inspector of Taxes about Poetry*

All a poet can do today is warn
Wilfred Owen *Poems (preface)*

Sir, I admit your general rule
That every poet is a fool;
But you yourself may serve to show it,
That every fool is not a poet
Alexander Pope *Epigram from the French*

poetic elegiac, lyric, lyrical, metrical, rhythmical, songlike

poetry metrical composition, poems, poesy (*archaic*), rhyme, rhyming, verse

Poetry/ prosody terms

accentual metre
accentual-syllabic metre *or* stress-syllabic metre
Adonic
Alcaic
Alexandrine
alliteration
amoebaean *or* amoebean
amphibrach
amphimacer
anacrusis
arsis
anapaest *or* anapest
anapaestic *or* anapestic
antistrophe
assonance
bacchius
ballad stanza
blank verse
bob
cadence *or* cadency
caesura *or* cesura
canto
catalectic
choriamb *or* choriambus
closed couplet
common measure
common metre
consonance *or* consonancy
couplet
cretic *or* amphimacer
dactyl
dactylic
diaeresis *or* dieresis
dipody
distich
elision
end-stopped
enjambement
envoy *or* envoi
epode
eye rhyme
feminine ending
feminine rhyme
foot
free verse *or* vers libre
half-rhyme
hemistich
heptameter
heptastich
heroic couplet
hexameter

hypermeter
iamb *or* iambus
iambic
ictus
internal rhyme
ionic
jabberwocky
leonine rhyme
long metre
macaronic
masculine ending
masculine rhyme
metre
octameter
octave *or* octet
onomatopoeia
ottava rima
paeon
paeonic
pararhyme
pentameter
pentastich
perfect rhyme *or* full rhyme
Pindaric
pyhrric
quantitative metre
quatrain
quintain *or* quintet
refrain
rhyme
rhyme royal
rhyme scheme
rhythm
rime riche
Sapphic
scansion
septet
sestet
sestina *or* sextain
short metre
Spenserian stanza
spondee
spondaic
sprung rhythm
stanza
stichic
strophe
syllabic metre
tercet
terza rima
tetrabrach
tetrameter
tetrapody
tetrastich
triplet
trochaic
trochee
unstopped
verse paragraph
wheel

Poetry movements/ groupings

Alexandrians
Decadents
Georgian Poets
imagists
Lake Poets
Liverpool Poets
Metaphysical Poets
the Movement
Petrarchans
Romantics
Scottish Chaucerians
symbolists

Poetry is a kind of ingenious nonsense
Isaac Barrow

Poetry is what gets lost in translation
Robert Frost

Poetry is the spontaneous overflow of powerful feelings; it takes its origin from emotion recollected in tranquility
William Wordsworth *Lyrical Ballads (preface)*

Poetry is at bottom a criticism of life
Matthew Arnold *Essays in Criticism*

Poetry is a subject as precise as geometry
Gustave Flaubert *letter*

Poetry is a way of taking life by the throat
Robert Frost

As civilization advances, poetry almost necessarily declines
Lord Macaulay *Essays*

Poetry (is) a speaking picture, with this end; to teach and delight
Sir Philip Sidney *The Defence of Poetry*

Poetry is truth in its Sunday clothes
Joseph Roux *Meditations of a Parish Priest*

Prose = words in their best order; poetry = the best words in their best order
Samuel Taylor Coleridge *Table Talk*

Imaginary gardens with real toads in them
Marianne Moore *Poetry*

Poetry is something more philosophical and more worthy of serious attention than history
Aristotle *Poetics*

Prose is when all the lines except the last go on to the end. Poetry is when some of them fall short of it
Jeremy Bentham

I am two fools, I know,
For loving, and for saying so
In whining poetry
John Donne *The Triple Fool*

Poetry's a mere drug, Sir
George Farquhar *Love and a Battle*

I'd as soon write free verse as play tennis with the net down
Robert Frost

If poetry comes not as naturally as the leaves to a tree it had better not come at all
John Keats

Writing a book of poetry is like dropping a rose petal down the Grand Canyon and waiting for the echo
Don Marquis

rhyme being... but the invention of a barbarous age, to set off wretched matter and lame metre
John Milton *Paradise Lost (preface)*

Most people ignore most poetry
because
most poetry ignores most people
Adrian Mitchell *Poems*

All that is not prose is verse; and all that is not verse is prose
Molière *Le Bourgeois Gentilhomme*

My subject is War, and the pity of War. The Poetry is in the pity
Wilfred Owen *Poems (preface)*

it is not poetry, but prose run mad
Alexander Pope *An Epistle to Dr. Arbuthnot*

Music begins to atrophy when it departs too far from the dance... poetry begins to atrophy when it gets too far from music
Ezra Pound *The ABC of Reading*

po-faced disapproving, humourless, narrow-minded, prim, prudish, puritanical, solemn, stolid, strait-laced

poignancy **1.** emotion, emotionalism, evocativeness, feeling, pathos, piteousness, plaintiveness, sadness, sentiment, tenderness **2.** bitterness, intensity, keenness, piquancy, pungency, sharpness

poignant 1. affecting, agonizing, bitter, distressing, harrowing, heartbreaking, heart-rending, intense, moving, painful, pathetic, sad, touching, upsetting 2. acute, biting, caustic, keen, penetrating, piercing, pointed, sarcastic, severe 3. acrid, piquant, pungent, sharp, stinging, tangy

point *noun* 1. dot, full stop, mark, period, speck, stop 2. location, place, position, site, spot, stage, station 3. apex, end, nib, prong, sharp end, spike, spur, summit, tine, tip, top 4. bill, cape, foreland, head, headland, ness (*archaic*), promontory 5. circumstance, condition, degree, extent, position, stage 6. instant, juncture, moment, time, very minute 7. aim, design, end, goal, intent, intention, motive, object, objective, purpose, reason, use, usefulness, utility 8. burden, core, crux, drift, essence, gist, heart, import, main idea, marrow, matter, meaning, nub, pith, proposition, question, subject, text, theme, thrust 9. aspect, detail, facet, feature, instance, item, nicety, particular 10. aspect, attribute, characteristic, peculiarity, property, quality, respect, side, trait 11. score, tally, unit 12. **beside the point** immaterial, incidental, inconsequential, irrelevant, not to the purpose, off the subject, out of the way, pointless, unimportant, without connection 13. **to the point** applicable, apposite, appropriate, apropos, apt, brief, fitting, germane, pertinent, pithy, pointed, relevant, short, suitable, terse ~*verb* 14. bespeak, call attention to, denote, designate, direct, indicate, show, signify 15. aim, bring to bear, direct, level, train 16. barb, edge, sharpen, taper, whet

point-blank 1. *adjective* abrupt, blunt, categorical, direct, downright, explicit, express, plain, straight-from-the-shoulder, unreserved 2. *adverb* bluntly, brusquely, candidly, directly, explicitly, forthrightly, frankly, openly, overtly, plainly, straight, straightforwardly

pointed 1. acicular, acuminate, acute, barbed, cuspidate, edged, mucronate, sharp 2. accurate, acute, biting, cutting, incisive, keen, penetrating, pertinent, sharp, telling, trenchant

pointer 1. guide, hand, indicator, needle 2. advice, caution, hint, information, recommendation, suggestion, tip, warning

pointless absurd, aimless, fruitless, futile, inane, ineffectual, irrelevant, meaningless, nonsensical, senseless, silly, stupid, unavailing, unproductive, unprofitable, useless, vague, vain, without rhyme nor reason, worthless
Antonyms appropriate, beneficial, desirable, fitting, fruitful, logical, meaningful, productive, profitable, proper, sensible, to the point, useful, worthwhile

point of view 1. angle, orientation, outlook, perspective, position, standpoint 2. approach, attitude, belief, judgment, opinion, slant, view, viewpoint, way of looking at it

point out allude to, bring up, call attention to, identify, indicate, mention, remind, reveal, show, specify

point up accent, accentuate, emphasize, make clear, stress, underline

poise 1. *noun* aplomb, assurance, calmness, composure, cool (*slang*), coolness, dignity, elegance, equanimity, equilibrium, grace, presence, presence of mind, sang-froid, savoir-faire, self-possession, serenity 2. *verb* balance, float, hang, hang in midair, hang suspended, hold, hover, position, support, suspend

poised 1. calm, collected, composed, debonair, dignified, graceful, nonchalant, self-confident, self-possessed, serene, suave, together (*informal*), unfazed (*informal*), unruffled, urbane 2. all set, in the wings, on the brink, prepared, ready, standing by, waiting
Antonyms (*sense 1*) agitated, annoyed, discomposed, disturbed, excited, irritated, ruffled, worked up

poison *noun* 1. bane, toxin, venom 2. bane, blight, cancer, canker, contagion, contamination, corruption, malignancy, miasma, virus ~*verb* 3. adulterate, contaminate, envenom, give (someone) poison, infect, kill, murder, pollute 4. corrupt, defile, deprave, pervert, subvert, taint, undermine, vitiate, warp ~*adjective* 5. deadly, lethal, poisonous, toxic, venomous

Poisonous substances and gases

aconite
acrolein
adamsite
afterdamp
Agent Orange
aldrin
allyl alcohol
aniline
antimony potassium tartrate
arsenic *or* arsenic trioxide
arsine
atropine *or* atropin
barium hydroxide
benzene
benzidine
brucine
cacodyl
carbon disulphide
carbon monoxide
coniine, conin *or* conine
curare
cyanic acid
cyanide
cyanogen
digitalin
emetine
formaldehyde
hemlock
hydrastine
hydrogen cyanide
hydrogen fluoride
hydrogen iodide
hydrogen sulphide
hyoscyamine
lead monoxide
lewisite
lindane
mercuric chloride
mercuric oxide
methanol
methyl bromide
muscarine
mustard gas
nerve gas
nitrogen dioxide
osmium tetroxide
ouabain

oxalic acid
Paraquat
Paris green
phenol
phosgene
picrotoxin
poison gas
potassium cyanide
potassium permanganate
prussic acid
ratsbane
red lead
sarin
silver nitrate
sodium cyanide
sodium fluoroacetate
stibine
strychnine
tetramethyldiarsine
thallium
thebaine
tropine
urushiol
veratrine
whitedamp
zinc chloride

Types of poisoning

botulism
bromism
digitalism
ergotism
fluorosis
hydrargyria
iodism
lead poisoning
listeriosis
mercurialism
phosphorism
plumbism
ptomaine poisoning
salmonella
saturnism
strychninism

Poisonous plants

aconite
amanita
baneberry
belladonna
black bryony
black nightshade
castor-oil plant
cowbane
coyotillo
deadly nightshade
death camass
death cap *or* angel
destroying angel
dieffenbachia
dog's mercury
ergot
fly agaric
foxglove
hemlock
henbane
Indian liquorice
laburnum
liberty cap
locoweed
manchineel
monkshood
mountain laurel
Noogoora burr
nux vomica
oleander
poison dogwood *or* elder
poison ivy
poison oak
poison sumach
pokeweed, pokeberry *or* pokeroot
sassy, sasswood *or* sassy wood
staggerbush
stavesacre
thorn apple
tutu
upas
water hemlock
wolfsbane *or* wolf's-bane
woody nightshade

poisonous 1. baneful (*archaic*), deadly, fatal, lethal, mephitic, mortal, noxious, toxic, venomous, virulent 2. baleful, baneful (*archaic*), corruptive, evil, malicious, noxious, pernicious, pestiferous, pestilential, vicious

poke *verb* 1. butt, dig, elbow, hit, jab, nudge, prod, punch, push, shove, stab, stick, thrust 2. butt in, interfere, intrude, meddle, nose, peek, poke one's nose into (*informal*), pry, put one's two cents in (*U.S. slang*), snoop (*informal*), tamper 3. **poke fun at** chaff, jeer, make a mock of, make fun of, mock, rib (*informal*), ridicule, send up (*Brit. informal*), take the mickey (*informal*), take the piss (out of) (*taboo slang*), tease ~*noun* 4. butt, dig, hit, jab, nudge, prod, punch, thrust

poky confined, cramped, incommodious, narrow, small, tiny

Antonyms capacious, commodious, large, open, roomy, spacious, wide

polar 1. Antarctic, Arctic, cold, extreme, freezing, frozen, furthest, glacial, icy, terminal 2. beacon-like, cardinal, guiding, leading, pivotal 3. antagonistic, antipodal, antithetical, contradictory, contrary, diametric, opposed, opposite

polarity ambivalence, contradiction, contrariety, dichotomy, duality, opposition, paradox

pole[1] *noun* bar, mast, post, rod, shaft, spar, staff, standard, stick

pole[2] *noun* 1. antipode, extremity, limit, terminus 2. **poles apart** at opposite ends of the earth, at opposite extremes, incompatible, irreconcilable, miles apart, widely separated, worlds apart

polemic 1. *noun* argument, controversy, debate, dispute 2. *adjective* argumentative, contentious, controversial, disputatious, polemical

polemics argument, argumentation, contention, controversy, debate, disputation, dispute

police *noun* 1. boys in blue (*informal*), constabulary, fuzz (*slang*), law enforcement agency, police force, the law (*informal*), the Old Bill (*slang*) ~*verb* 2. control, guard, keep in order, keep the peace, patrol, protect, regulate, watch 3. *figurative* check, monitor, observe, oversee, supervise

policeman bobby (*informal*), bogey (*slang*), constable, cop (*slang*), copper (*slang*), flatfoot (*slang*), fuzz (*slang*), gendarme (*slang*), officer, peeler (*obsolete Brit. slang*), pig (*slang*), rozzer (*slang*), woodentop (*slang*)

> *A policeman's lot is not a happy one*
> W.S. Gilbert *The Pirates of Penzance*

policy 1. action, approach, code, course, custom, guideline, line, plan, practice, procedure, programme, protocol, rule, scheme, stratagem, theory 2. discretion, good sense, prudence, sagacity, shrewdness, wisdom

polish *verb* 1. brighten, buff, burnish, clean, furbish, rub, shine, smooth, wax 2. brush up, correct, cultivate, emend, enhance, finish, improve, perfect, refine, touch up ~*noun* 3. brightness, brilliance, finish, glaze, gloss, lustre, sheen, smoothness, sparkle, veneer 4. varnish, wax 5. *figurative* breeding, class (*informal*), elegance, finesse, finish, grace, politesse, refinement, style, suavity, urbanity

polished 1. bright, burnished, furbished, glassy, gleaming, glossy, shining, slippery, smooth 2. *figurative* civilized, courtly, cultivated, elegant, finished, genteel, polite, re~

fined, sophisticated, urbane, well-bred **3.** accomplished, adept, expert, faultless, fine, flawless, impeccable, masterly, outstanding, professional, skilful, superlative
Antonyms (*sense 1*) dark, dull, matt, rough (*sense 2*) inelegant, uncivilized, uncultivated, unrefined, unsophisticated (*sense 3*) amateurish, inept, inexpert, unaccomplished, unskilled

polish off **1.** consume, down, eat up, finish, put away, shift (*informal*), swill, wolf **2.** blow away (*slang, chiefly U.S.*), bump off (*informal*), dispose of, do away with, do in (*slang*), eliminate, get rid of, kill, liquidate, murder, take out (*slang*)

polite **1.** affable, civil, complaisant, courteous, deferential, gracious, mannerly, obliging, respectful, well-behaved, well-mannered **2.** civilized, courtly, cultured, elegant, genteel, polished, refined, sophisticated, urbane, well-bred
Antonyms crude, discourteous, ill-mannered, impertinent, impolite, impudent, insulting, rude, uncultured, unrefined

politeness civility, common courtesy, complaisance, correctness, courteousness, courtesy, decency, deference, etiquette, grace, graciousness, mannerliness, obligingness, respectfulness

Politeness is organized indifference
Paul Valéry *Tel Quel*

politic **1.** artful, astute, canny, crafty, cunning, designing, ingenious, intriguing, Machiavellian, scheming, shrewd, sly, subtle, unscrupulous **2.** advisable, diplomatic, discreet, expedient, in one's best interests, judicious, prudent, sagacious, sensible, tactful, wise

political **1.** civic, governmental, parliamentary, policy-making **2.** factional, partisan, party

Man is by nature a political animal
Aristotle *Politics*

politician legislator, Member of Parliament, M.P., office bearer, politico (*informal, chiefly U.S.*), public servant, statesman

British Prime Ministers	Party	Term of office
Robert Walpole	Whig	1721-42
Earl of Wilmington	Whig	1742-43
Henry Pelham	Whig	1743-54
Duke of Newcastle	Whig	1754-56
Duke of Devonshire	Whig	1756-57
Duke of Newcastle	Whig	1757-62
Earl of Bute	Tory	1762-63
George Grenville	Whig	1763-65
Marquess of Rockingham	Whig	1765-66
Duke of Grafton	Whig	1766-70
Lord North	Tory	1770-82
Marquess of Rockingham	Whig	1782
Earl of Sherbourne	Whig	1782-83
Duke of Portland	Coalition	1783
William Pitt	Tory	1783-1801
Henry Addington	Tory	1801-04
William Pitt	Tory	1804-06
Lord Grenville	Whig	1806-1807
Duke of Portland	Tory	1807-09
Spencer Perceval	Tory	1809-12
Earl of Liverpool	Tory	1812-27
George Canning	Tory	1827
Viscount Goderich	Tory	1827-28
Duke of Wellington	Tory	1828-30
Earl Grey	Whig	1830-34
Viscount Melbourne	Whig	1834
Robert Peel	Conservative	1834-35
Viscount Melbourne	Whig	1835-41
Robert Peel	Conservative	1841-46
Lord John Russell	Liberal	1846-52
Earl of Derby	Conservative	1852
Lord Aberdeen	Peelite	1852-55
Viscount Palmerston	Liberal	1855-58
Earl of Derby	Conservative	1858-59
Viscount Palmerston	Liberal	1859-65
Lord John Russell	Liberal	1865-66
Earl of Derby	Conservative	1866-68
Benjamin Disraeli	Conservative	1868
William Gladstone	Liberal	1868-74

Benjamin Disraeli	Conservative	1874-80
William Gladstone	Liberal	1880-85
Marquess of Salisbury	Conservative	1885-86
William Gladstone	Liberal	1886
Marquess of Salisbury	Conservative	1886-92
William Gladstone	Liberal	1892-94
Earl of Roseberry	Liberal	1894-95
Marquess of Salisbury	Conservative	1895-1902
Arthur James Balfour	Conservative	1902-95
Henry Campbell-Bannerman	Liberal	1905-08
Herbert Henry Asquith	Liberal	1908-15
Herbert Henry Asquith	Coalition	1915-16
David Lloyd George	Coalition	1916-22
Andrew Bonar Law	Conservative	1922-23
Stanley Baldwin	Conservative	1923-24
James Ramsay McDonald	Labour	1924
Stanley Baldwin	Conservative	1924-29
James Ramsay McDonald	Labour	1929-31
James Ramsay McDonald	Nationalist	1931-35
Stanley Baldwin	Nationalist	1935-37
Arthur Neville Chamberlain	Nationalist	1937-40
Winston Churchill	Coalition	1940-45
Clement Atlee	Labour	1945-51
Winston Churchill	Conservative	1951-55
Anthony Eden	Conservative	1955-57
Harold Macmillan	Conservative	1957-63
Alec Douglas-Home	Conservative	1963-64
Harold Wilson	Labour	1964-70
Edward Heath	Conservative	1970-74
Harold Wilson	Labour	1974-76
James Callaghan	Labour	1976-79
Margaret Thatcher	Conservative	1979-90
John Major	Conservative	1990-

U.S. Presidents	**Party**	**Term of office**
1. George Washington	Federalist	1789-97
2. John Adams	Federalist	1797-1801
3. Thomas Jefferson	Democratic Republican	1801-1809
4. James Madison	Democratic Republican	1809-1817
5. James Monroe	Democratic Republican	1817-25
6. John Quincy Adams	Democratic Republican	1825-29
7. Andrew Jackson	Democrat	1829-37
8. Martin Van Buren	Democrat	1837-41
9. William Henry Harrison	Whig	1841
10. John Tyler	Whig	1841-45
11. James K. Polk	Democrat	1845-49
12. Zachary Taylor	Whig	1849-50
13. Millard Fillmore	Whig	1850-53
14. Franklin Pierce	Democrat	1853-57
15. James Buchanan	Democrat	1857-61
16. Abraham Lincoln	Republican	1861-65
17. Andrew Johnson	Republican	1865-69
18. Ulysses S. Grant	Republican	1869-77
19. Rutherford B. Hayes	Republican	1877-81

20. James A. Garfield	Republican	1881
21. Chester A. Arthur	Republican	1881-85
22. Grover Cleveland	Democrat	1885-89
23. Benjamin Harrison	Republican	1889-93
24. Grover Cleveland	Democrat	1893-97
25. William McKinley	Republican	1897-1901
26. Theodore Roosevelt	Republican	1901-1909
27. William Howard Taft	Republican	1909-13
28. Woodrow Wilson	Democrat	1913-21
29. Warren G. Harding	Republican	1921-23
30. Calvin Coolidge	Republican	1923-29
31. Herbert C. Hoover	Republican	1929-33
32. Franklin D. Roosevelt	Democrat	1933-45
33. Harry S. Truman	Democrat	1945-53
34. Dwight D. Eisenhower	Republican	1953-61
35. John F. Kennedy	Democrat	1961-63
36. Lyndon B. Johnson	Democrat	1963-69
37. Richard M. Nixon	Republican	1969-74
38. Gerald R. Ford	Republican	1974-77
39. James E. Carter, Jr	Democrat	1977-81
40. Ronald W. Reagan	Republican	1981-89
41. George H. W. Bush	Republican	1989-93
42. William J. Clinton	Democrat	1993-

Australian Prime Ministers	**Party**	**Term of office**
Edmund Barton	Protectionist	1901-03
Alfred Deakin	Protectionist	1903-04
John Christian Watson	Labor	1904
George Houston Reid	Free Trade	1904-05
Alfred Deakin	Protectionist	1905-08
Andrew Fisher	Labor	1908-09
Alfred Deakin	Fusion	1909-10
Andrew Fisher	Labor	1910-13
Joseph Cook	Liberal	1913-14
Andrew Fisher	Labor	1914-15
William Morris Hughes	National Labor	1915-17
William Morris Hughes	Nationalist	1917-23
Stanley Melbourne Bruce	Nationalist	1923-29
James Henry Scullin	Labor	1929-32
Joseph Aloysius Lyons	United	1932-39
Earle Christmas Page	Country	1939
Robert Gordon Menzies	United	1939-41
Arthur William Fadden	Country	1941
John Joseph Curtin	Labor	1941-45
Joseph Benedict Chifley	Labor	1945-49
Robert Gordon Menzies	Liberal	1949-66
Harold Edward Holt	Liberal	1966-67
John McEwen	Country	1967-68
John Grey Gorton	Liberal	1968-71
William McMahon	Liberal	1972-72
Edward Gough Whitlam	Labor	1972-75

John Malcolm Fraser	Liberal	1975-83
Robert James Lee Hawke	Labor	1983-91
Paul Keating	Labor	1991-

Canadian Prime Ministers	**Party**	**Term of office**
John A. MacDonald	Conserva~tive	1867-73
Alexander Mackenzie	Liberal	1873-78
John A. MacDonald	Conserva~tive	1878-91
John J.C. Abbot	Conserva~tive	1891-92
John S.D. Thompson	Conserva~tive	1892-94
Mackenzie Bowell	Conserva~tive	1894-96
Charles Tupper	Conserva~tive	1896
Wilfred Laurier	Liberal	1896-1911
Robert Borden	Conserva~tive	1911-20
Arthur Meighen	Conserva~tive	1920-21
William Lyon McKenzie King	Liberal	1921-1926
Arthur Meighen	Conserva~tive	1926
William Lyon McKenzie King	Liberal	1926-30
Richard Bedford Bennet	Conserva~tive	1930-35
William Lyon McKenzie King	Liberal	1935-48
Louis St. Laurent	Liberal	1948-57
John George Diefenbaker	Conserva~tive	1957-63
Lester Bowles Pearson	Liberal	1963-68
Pierre Elliott Trudeau	Liberal	1968-79
Joseph Clark	Conserva~tive	1979-80
Pierre Elliott Trudeau	Liberal	1968-79
Joseph Clark	Conserva~tive	1979-80
Pierre Elliott Trudeau	Liberal	1980-84
John Turner	Liberal	1984
Brian Mulroney	Conserva~tive	1984-93
Kim Campbell	Conserva~tive	1993
Joseph Jacques Jean Chrétien	Liberal	1993-

Prime Ministers of New Zealand	**Party**	**Term of office**
Henry Sewell	-	1856
Henry Fox	-	1856
Edward William Stafford	-	1856-61
William Fox	-	1861-62
Alfred Domett	-	1862-63
Frederick Whitaker	-	1863-64
Frederick Aloysius Weld	-	1864-65
Edward William Stafford	-	1865-69
William Fox	-	1869-72
Edward William Stafford	-	1872
William Fox	-	1873
Julius Vogel	-	1873-75
Daniel Pol~len	-	1875-76
Julius Vogel	-	1876
Harry Al~bert Atkinson	-	1876-77
George Grey	-	1877-79
John Hall	-	1879-82
Frederic Whitaker	-	1882-83
Harry Al~bert Atkinson	-	1883-84
Robert Stout	-	1884

Harry Albert Atkinson	-	1884
Robert Stout	-	1884-87
Harry Albert Atkinson	-	1887-91
John Ballance	-	1891-93
Richard John Sneddon	Liberal	1893-1906
William Hall-Jones	Liberal	1906
Joseph George Ward	Liberal/ National	1906-12
Thomas Mackenzie	National	1912
William Ferguson Massey	Reform	1912-25
Francis Henry Dillon Bell	Reform	1925
Joseph Gordon Coates	Reform	1925-28
Joseph George Ward	Liberal/ National	1928-30
George William Forbes	United	1930-35
Michael Joseph Savage	Labour	1935-40
Peter Fraser	Labour	1935-49
Sidney George Holland	National	1949-47
Keith Jacka Holyoake	National	1957
Walter Nash	Labour	1957-60
Keith Jacka Holyoake	National	1960-72
John Ross Marshall	National	1972
Norman Eric Kirk	Labour	1972-74
Wallace Edward Rowling	Labour	1974-75
Robert David Muldoon	National	1975-84
David Russell Lange	Labour	1984-89
Geoffrey Palmer	Labour	1989-90
Mike Moore	Labour	1990-

An honest politician is one who when bought stays bought
Simon Cameron

A statesman is a politician who has been dead ten or fifteen years
Harry S. Truman

A politician is an animal that can sit on a fence and keep both ears to the ground
H.L. Mencken

Since a politician never believes what he says, he is always astonished when others do
Charles de Gaulle

Well, in politics, I'm a complete neutral; I think they're all scoundrels without exception
H.L. Mencken

a politician is an arse upon which everyone has sat except a man
e e cummings *1 X 1 (no. 10)*

There are no good and bad politicians, only bad ones and worse
Spanish anarchist slogan

"Do you pray for the senators, Dr. Hale?"
"No, I look at the senators and I pray for the country."
Edward Everett Hale

A statesman is a politician who places himself at the service of the nation. A politician is a statesman who places the nation at his service
Georges Pompidou

politics **1**. affairs of state, civics, government, government policy, political science, polity, statecraft, statesmanship **2**. Machiavellianism, machination, power struggle, *Realpolitik*

Major political parties in the United Kingdom (Mainland)

Conservative and Unionist Party
Labour Party
Liberal Democrats
Plaid Cymru
Scottish National Party

Northern Ireland

Democratic Unionist Party
Official Ulster Unionist Party
Sinn Féin
Social Democratic and Labour Party (SDLP)

Irish Republic

Democratic Left
Fianna Fáil
Fine Gael
Labour Party
Progressive Democrats

Australia

Australian Labor Party
Liberal Party of Australia
National Party of Australia

Austria

Freedom Party (FPÖ)
People's Party (ÖVP)
Socialist Party (SPÖ)

Belgium
Flemish Bloc (VB)
Flemish Green Party (Agalev)
French Green Party (Ecolo)
Flemish Liberal Party (PVV)
French Liberal Reform Party (PRL)
Flemish Social Christian Party (CVP)
French Social Christian Party (PSC)
Flemish Socialist Party (SP)
French Socialist Party (PS)

Canada
Bloc Quebecois
Liberal Party
New Democratic Party
Progressive Conservative
Reform Party
Social Credit Party

Denmark
Centre Democrats (CD)
Christian People's Party (KrF)
Conservative People's Party (KF)
Left Socialists
Liberals (V)
Progress Party (FP)
Radical Liberals (RV)
Social Democrats (SD)
Socialist People's Party (SF)

Finland
Centre Party (KP)
Democratic Alternative
Finnish People's Democratic League (SKDL)
Finnish Rural Party (SMP)
Green Party
National Coalition Party (KOK)
Social Democratic Party (SD)
Swedish People's Party (SFP)

France
Communist Party (PC)
National Front
Rally for the Republic (RDR)
Republican Party (PR)
Socialist Party (PS)
Union for French Democracy (UDF)

Germany
Christian-Democratic Union (CDU)
Christian-Social Union (CSU)
Free Democratic Party (FDP)
Green Party
Party of Democratic Socialism (PDS)
Social Democratic Party (SPD)

Greece
Greek Communist Party
New Democracy (ND)
Pan-Hellenic Socialist Movement (PASOK)
Political Spring (Politiki Aniksi)

India
Congress (I)
Janata Dal
Bharitiya Janata Party (BJP)

Israel
Labour Party
Likud

Italy
Centre Union
Christian Democrat Party
Democratic Party of the Left (PDS)
Forza Italia
National Alliance
Northern League

Japan
Democratic Socialist Party
Liberal Democratic Party
Komeito
Social Democratic Party

Luxembourg
Communist Party
Democratic Party (PD)
Luxembourg Socialist Workers' Party (POSL)
Christian Social Party (PCS)

Malta
Malta Labour Party
Nationalist Party

Mexico
Institutional Revolutionary Party (PRI)
National Action Party (PAN)
Party of the Democratic Revolution (PRD)
Revolutionary Workers' Party

The Netherlands
Christian Democratic Appeal (CDA)
Labour Party (PvdA)
People's Party for Freedom and Democracy (VVD)

New Zealand
Labour Party
National Party

Portugal
Democratic Renewal Party (PRD)
Democratic Social Centre Party (CDS)
Social Democratic Party (PSD)
Socialist Party (PS)

South Africa
African National Congress (ANC)
Conservative Party
Inkatha Freedom Party
National Party
Pan-Africanist Congress (PAC)

Spain
Basque Nationalist Party (PNV)
Convergencia i Uni (CiU)
Herri Batasuna (HB)
People's Party (PP)
Socialist Workers' Party (PSOE)
United Left (IU)

Sweden
Centre Party
Christian Democratic Party
Green Party
Left Party
Liberal Party
Moderate Party
Social Democratic Labour Party (SAP)

Turkey
Motherland Party (ANAP)
Social Democratic Populist Party
True Path Party

United States of America
Democratic Party
Republican Party

Politics is the art of the possible
Prince Otto von Bismarck

A week is a long time in politics
Harold Wilson

Politics...has always been the systematic organisation of hatreds
Henry Brooks Adams *The Education of Henry Adams*

Practical politics consists in ignoring facts
Henry Brooks Adams *The Education of Henry Adams*

In politics the middle way is none at all
John Adams

In politics, what begins in fear usually ends in folly
Samuel Taylor Coleridge *Table Talk*

There is a holy mistaken zeal in politics as well as in religion. By persuading others, we convince ourselves
Junius *Public Advertiser*

Politics is war without bloodshed while war is politics with bloodshed
Mao Tse-tung

The argument of the broken window pane is the most valuable argument in modern politics
Emmeline Pankhurst

Politics is perhaps the only profession for which no preparation is thought necessary
Robert Louis Stevenson *Familiar Studies of Men and Books*

Most schemes of political improvement are very laughable things
Dr. Johnson

politics: a strife of interests masquerading as a contest of principles. The conduct of public affairs for private advantage
Ambrose Bierce *The Devil's Dictionary*

Politics makes strange bedfellows

poll *noun* **1.** figures, returns, tally, vote, voting **2.** ballot, canvass, census, count, Gallup Poll, (public) opinion poll, sampling, survey *~verb* **3.** register, tally **4.** ballot, canvass, fly a kite, interview, question, sample, survey

pollute **1.** adulterate, befoul, contaminate, dirty, foul, infect, make filthy, mar, poison, smirch, soil, spoil, stain, taint **2.** besmirch, corrupt, debase, debauch, defile, deprave, desecrate, dishonour, profane, sully, violate
Antonyms (*sense 1*) clean, cleanse, decontaminate, disinfect, purge, sanitize, sterilize (*sense 2*) esteem, honour

pollution adulteration, contamination, corruption, defilement, dirtying, foulness, impurity, taint, uncleanness, vitiation

poltroon caitiff (*archaic*), chicken (*slang*), coward, craven, cur, dastard (*archaic*), recreant (*archaic*), skunk (*informal*), yellow-belly (*slang*)

polychromatic many-coloured, many-hued, multicoloured, of all the colours of the rainbow, polychrome, rainbow, varicoloured, variegated

pomp **1.** ceremony, éclat, flourish, grandeur, magnificence, pageant, pageantry, parade, solemnity, splendour, state **2.** display, grandiosity, ostentation, pomposity, show, vainglory

pomposity **1.** affectation, airs, arrogance, flaunting, grandiosity, haughtiness, pompousness, portentousness, presumption, pretension, pretentiousness, self-importance, vainglory, vanity **2.** bombast, fustian, grandiloquence, hot air (*informal*), loftiness, magniloquence, rant, turgidity

pompous **1.** affected, arrogant, bloated, grandiose, imperious, magisterial, ostentatious, overbearing, pontifical, portentous, pretentious, puffed up, self-important, showy, supercilious, vainglorious **2.** boastful, bombastic, flatulent, fustian, grandiloquent, high-flown, inflated, magniloquent, orotund, overblown, turgid, windy
Antonyms direct, humble, modest, natural, plain-spoken, self-effacing, simple, succinct, unaffected, unpretentious

ponce *derogatory slang, chiefly Brit.* **1.** beau, coxcomb (*archaic*), dandy, fop, popinjay, swell **2.** bawd (*archaic*), pander, pimp, procurer

pond dew pond, duck pond, fish pond, lochan (*Scot.*), millpond, pool, small lake, tarn

ponder brood, cerebrate, cogitate, consider, contemplate, deliberate, examine, excogitate, give thought to, meditate, mull over, muse, puzzle over, rack one's brains, reflect, ruminate, study, think, weigh

ponderous **1.** bulky, clunky (*informal*), cumbersome, cumbrous, heavy, hefty, huge, massive, unwieldy, weighty **2.** awkward, clumsy, elephantine, graceless, heavy-footed, laborious, lumbering **3.** dreary, dull, heavy, laboured, lifeless, long-winded, pedantic, pedestrian, plodding, prolix, stilted, stodgy, tedious, tiresome, verbose
Antonyms (*senses 1 & 2*) graceful, handy, light, light-footed, little, small, tiny, weightless

poniard bodkin (*archaic*), dagger, dirk, misericord (*archaic*), stiletto

pontifical **1.** apostolic, ecclesiastical, papal, prelatic **2.** bloated, condescending, dogmatic, imperious, magisterial, overbearing, pompous, portentous, pretentious, self-important

pontificate declaim, dogmatize, expound, hold forth, lay down the law, pontify, preach, pronounce, sound off

pooh-pooh belittle, brush aside, deride, disdain, dismiss, disregard, make little of, play down, scoff, scorn, slight, sneer, sniff at, spurn, turn up one's nose at (*informal*)
Antonyms exalt, extol, glorify, praise

pool[1] *noun* **1.** lake, mere, pond, puddle, splash, tarn **2.** swimming bath, swimming pool

pool[2] *noun* **1.** collective, combine, consortium, group, syndicate, team, trust **2.** bank, funds, jackpot, kitty, pot, stakes *~verb* **3.** amalgamate, combine, join forces, league, merge, put together, share

poor **1.** badly off, broke (*informal*), destitute, dirt-poor (*informal*), down and out, down at heel, flat broke (*informal*), hard up (*informal*), impecunious, impoverished, indigent, in need, in queer street, in want, necessitous, needy, not have two beans to rub together, on one's beam-ends, on one's uppers, on the breadline, on the rocks, penniless, penurious, poverty-stricken, short, skint (*Brit. slang*), stony-broke (*Brit. slang*), without two pennies to rub together (*informal*) **2.** deficient, exiguous, inadequate, incomplete, insufficient, lacking, meagre, measly, miserable, niggardly, pathetic, pitiable, reduced, scant, scanty, skimpy, slight, sparse, straitened **3.** below par, chickenshit (*U.S. slang*), crappy (*slang*), faulty, feeble, for the birds (*informal*), inferior, low-grade, low-rent (*informal chiefly U.S.*), mediocre, no great shakes (*informal*), not much cop (*Brit. slang*), piss-poor (*taboo slang*), poxy (*slang*), rotten (*informal*), rubbishy, second-rate, shabby, shoddy, sorry, strictly for the birds (*informal*), substandard, unsatisfactory, valueless, weak, worthless **4.** bad, bare, barren, depleted, exhausted, fruitless, impoverished, infertile, sterile, unfruitful, unproductive **5.** hapless, ill-fated, luckless, miserable, pathetic, pitiable, unfortunate, unhappy, unlucky, wretched **6.** humble, insignificant, lowly, mean, modest, paltry, plain, trivial

Antonyms (*sense 1*) affluent, comfortable (*informal*), prosperous, rich, wealthy, well-heeled (*informal*), well-off (*sense 2*) abundant, adequate, ample, complete, dense, plentiful, satisfactory, sufficient, thick (*sense 3*) excellent, exceptional, first-class, first-rate, satisfactory, superior, valuable (*sense 4*) fertile, fruitful, productive, teeming, yielding (*sense 5*) fortunate, happy, lucky, successful

The poor man is happy; he expects no change for the worse
Demetrius

The poor always ye have with you
Bible: St. John

Poor and content is rich and rich enough
William Shakespeare *Othello*

poorly **1.** *adverb* badly, crudely, inadequately, incompetently, inexpertly, inferiorly, insufficiently, meanly, shabbily, unsatisfactorily, unsuccessfully **2.** *adjective, informal* ailing, below par, ill, indisposed, off colour, out of sorts, rotten (*informal*), seedy (*informal*), sick, under the weather (*informal*), unwell

Antonyms (*sense 1*) acceptably, adequately, competently, expertly, satisfactorily, sufficiently, well (*sense 2*) fit, hale and hearty, healthy, in good health, in the pink, well

pop *verb* **1.** bang, burst, crack, explode, go off, report, snap **2.** *often with* **in, out,** *etc. informal* appear, call, come *or* go suddenly, drop in (*informal*), leave quickly, nip in (*Brit. informal*), nip out (*Brit. informal*), visit **3.** *especially of eyes* bulge, protrude, stick out **4.** insert, push, put, shove, slip, stick, thrust, tuck *~noun* **5.** bang, burst, crack, explosion, noise, report **6.** *informal* fizzy drink, ginger (*Scot.*), lemonade, soda water, soft drink

pope Bishop of Rome, Holy Father, pontiff, Vicar of Christ

Pope	Pontificate
Peter	until c.64
Linus	c.64-c.76
Anacletus	c.76-c.90
Clement I	c.90-c.99
Evaristus	c.99-c.105
Alexander I	c.105-c.117
Sixtus I	c.117-c.127
Telesphorus	c.127-c.137
Hyginus	c.137-c.140
Pius I	c.140-c.154
Anicetus	c.154-c.166
Soter	c.166-c.175
Eleutherius	175-89
Victor I	189-98
Zephyrinus	198-217
Callistus I	217-22
Urban I	222-30
Pontian	230-35
Anterus	235-36
Fabian	236-50
Cornelius	251-53
Lucius I	253-54
Stephen I	254-57
Sixtus II	257-58
Dionysius	259-68
Felix I	269-74
Eutychianus	275-83
Caius	283-96
Marcellinus	296-304
Marcellus I	308-09
Eusebius	310
Miltiades	311-14
Sylvester I	314-35
Mark	336
Julius I	337-52
Liberius	352-66
Damasus I	366-84
Siricius	384-99
Anastasius I	399-401
Innocent I	402-17
Zosimus	417-18
Boniface I	418-22
Celestine I	422-32

Sixtus III	432-40	Sergius II	844-47
Leo I	440-61	Leo IV	847-55
Hilarus	461-68	Benedict III	855-58
Simplicius	468-83	Nicholas I	858-67
Felix III (II)	483-92	Hadrian II	867-72
Gelasius I	492-96	John VIII	872-82
Anastasius II	496-98	Marinus I	882-84
Symmachus	498-514	Hadrian III	884-85
Hormisdas	514-23	Stephen V (VI)	885-91
John I	523-26	Formosus	891-96
Felix IV (III)	526-30	Boniface VI	896
Boniface II	530-32	Stephen VI (VII)	896-97
John II	533-35	Romanus	897
Agapetus I	535-36	Theodore II	897
Silverius	536-37	John IX	898-900
Vigilius	537-55	Benedict IV	900-03
Pelagius I	556-61	Leo V	903
John III	561-74	Sergius III	904-11
Benedict I	575-79	Anastasius III	911-13
Pelagius II	579-90	Lando	913-14
Gregory I	590-604	John X	914-28
Sabinianus	604-06	Leo VI	928
Boniface III	607	Stephen VII (VIII)	928-31
Boniface IV	608-15	John XI	931-35
Deusdedit *or* Adeodatus I	615-18	Leo VII	936-39
		Stephen IX	939-42
Boniface V	619-25	Marinus II	942-46
Honorious I	625-38	Agapetus II	946-55
Severinus	640	John XII	955-64
John IV	640-42	Leo VIII	963-65
Theodore I	642-49	Benedict V	964-66
Martin I	649-54	John XIII	965-72
Eugenius I	654-57	Benedict VI	973-74
Vitalian	657-72	Benedict VII	974-83
Adeotatus II	672-6	John XIV	983-84
Donus	676-78	John XV	985-96
Agatho	678-81	Gregory V	996-99
Leo II	682-83	Sylvester II	999-1003
Benedict II	684-85	John XVII	1003
John V	685-86	John XVIII	1004-09
Cono	686-87	Sergius IV	1009-12
Sergius I	687-701	Benedict VIII	1012-24
John VI	701-05	John XIX	1024-32
John VII	705-07	Benedict IX	1032-44
Sisinnius	708	Sylvester III	1045
Constantine	708-15	Benedict IX (second reign)	1045
Gregory II	715-31		
Gregory III	731-41	Gregory VI	1045-46
Zacharias	741-52	Clement II	1046-47
Stephen II (not consecrated)	752	Benedict IX (third reign)	1047-48
Stephen II (III)	752-7	Damasus II	1048
Paul I	757-67	Leo IX	1048-54
Stephen III (IV)	768-72	Victor II	1055-57
Hadrian I	772-95	Stephen IX (X)	1057-58
Leo III	795-816	Nicholas II	1059-61
Stephen IV (V)	816-17	Alexander II	1061-73
Paschal I	817-24	Gregory VII	1073-85
Eugenius II	824-27	Victor III	1086-87
Valentine	827	Urban II	1088-99
Gregory IV	827-44	Paschal II	1099-1118

Gelasius II	1118-19
Callistus II	1119-24
Honorious II	1124-30
Innocent II	1130-43
Celestine II	1143-44
Lucius II	1144-45
Eugenius III	1145-53
Anastasius IV	1153-54
Hadrian IV	1154-59
Alexander III	1159-81
Lucius III	1181-85
Urban III	1185-87
Gregory VIII	1187
Clement III	1187-91
Celestine III	1191-98
Innocent III	1198-1216
Honorious III	1216-27
Gregory IX	1227-41
Celestine IV	1241
Innocent IV	1243-54
Alexander IV	1254-61
Urban IV	1261-64
Clement IV	1265-68
Gregory X	1271-76
Innocent V	1276
Hadrian V	1276
John XXI	1276-77
Nicholas III	1277-80
Martin IV	1281-85
Honorious IV	1285-87
Nicholas IV	1288-92
Celestine V	1294
Boniface VIII	1294-1303
Benedict XI	1303-04
Clement V	1305-14
John XXII	1316-34
Benedict XII	1334-42
Clement VI	1342-52
Innocent VI	1352-62
Urban V	1362-70
Gregory XI	1370-78
Urban VI	1378-89
Boniface IX	1389-1404
Innocent VII	1404-06
Gregory XII	1406-15
Martin V	1417-41
Eugenius IV	1431-47
Nicholas V	1447-55
Callistus III	1455-58
Pius II	1458-64
Paul II	1464-71
Sixtus IV	1471-84
Innocent VIII	1484-92
Alexander VI	1492-1503
Pius III	1503
Julius II	1503-13
Leo X	1513-21
Hadrian VI	1522-23
Clement VII	1523-34
Paul III	1534-49
Julius III	1550-55
Marcellus II	1555
Paul IV	1555-59
Pius IV	1559-65
Pius V	1566-72
Gregory XIII	1572-85
Sixtus V	1585-90
Urban VII	1590
Gregory XIV	1590-91
Innocent IX	1591
Clement VIII	1592-1605
Leo XI	1605
Paul V	1605-21
Gregory XV	1621-23
Urban VIII	1623-44
Innocent X	1644-55
Alexander VII	1655-67
Clement IX	1667-69
Clement X	1670-76
Innocent XI	1676-89
Alexander VIII	1689-91
Innocent XII	1691-1700
Clement XI	1700-21
Innocent XIII	1721-24
Benedict XIII	1724-30
Clement XII	1730-40
Benedict XIV	1740-58
Clement XIII	1758-69
Clement XIV	1769-74
Pius VI	1775-99
Pius VII	1800-23
Leo XII	1823-29
Pius VIII	1829-30
Gregory XVI	1831-46
Pius IX	1846-78
Leo XIII	1878-1903
Pius X	1903-14
Benedict XV	1914-22
Pius XI	1922-39
Pius XII	1939-58
John XXIII	1958-63
Paul VI	1963-78
John Paul I	1978
John Paul II	1978-

popinjay buck (*archaic*), coxcomb (*archaic*), dandy, fop, jackanapes, peacock, swell (*informal*)

poppycock babble, balderdash, balls (*taboo slang*), baloney (*informal*), bilge (*informal*), bosh (*informal*), bull (*slang*), bullshit (*taboo slang*), bunk (*informal*), bunkum *or* buncombe (*chiefly U.S.*), cobblers (*Brit. taboo slang*), crap (*slang*), drivel, eyewash (*informal*), garbage (*informal*), gibberish, gobbledegook (*informal*), guff (*slang*), hogwash, hokum (*slang, chiefly U.S. & Canad.*), hooey (*slang*), horsefeathers (*U.S. slang*), hot air (*informal*), moonshine, nonsense, pap, piffle (*informal*), rot, rubbish, shit (*taboo slang*), tommyrot, tosh (*slang, chiefly Brit.*), trash, tripe (*informal*), twaddle

populace commonalty, crowd, general public, hoi polloi, inhabitants, Joe (and Eileen) Public (*slang*), Joe Six-Pack (*U.S. slang*), masses, mob, multitude, people, rabble, throng

popular 1. accepted, approved, celebrated, famous, fashionable, favoured, favourite, in, in demand, in favour, liked, sought-after, well-liked 2. common, conventional, current, general, prevailing, prevalent, public, standard, stock, ubiquitous, universal, widespread
Antonyms (*sense 1*) despised, detested, disliked, hated, loathed, unaccepted, unpopular (*sense 2*) infrequent, rare, uncommon, unusual

popularity acceptance, acclaim, adoration, approval, celebrity, currency, esteem, fame, favour, idolization, lionization, recognition, regard, renown, reputation, repute, vogue

popularize disseminate, familiarize, give currency to, give mass appeal, make available to all, simplify, spread, universalize

popularly commonly, conventionally, customarily, generally, ordinarily, regularly, traditionally, universally, usually, widely

populate colonize, inhabit, live in, occupy, people, settle

population citizenry, community, denizens, folk, inhabitants, natives, people, populace, residents, society

Population, when unchecked, increases in a geometrical ratio. Subsistence only increases in an arithmetical ratio
Thomas Malthus *The Principle of Population*

populous crowded, heavily populated, overpopulated, packed, populated, swarming, teeming, thronged

pore[1] *verb* brood, contemplate, dwell on, examine, go over, peruse, ponder, read, scrutinize, study, work over

pore[2] *noun* hole, opening, orifice, outlet, stoma

pornographic blue, dirty, filthy, indecent, lewd, obscene, offensive, prurient, salacious, smutty, X-rated (*informal*)

pornography dirt, erotica, filth, indecency, obscenity, porn (*informal*), porno (*informal*), smut

Pornography is the attempt to insult sex, to do dirt on it
D.H. Lawrence *Phoenix*

porous absorbent, absorptive, penetrable, permeable, pervious, spongy
Antonyms impenetrable, impermeable, impervious, nonporous

port *Nautical* anchorage, harbour, haven, roads, roadstead, seaport

Major ports of the world

Abidjan
Accra
Aden
Alexandria
Algiers
Alicante
Amsterdam
Anchorage
Antwerp
Apia
Aqaba
Archangel
Ashdod
Auckland
Baku
Baltimore
Bangkok
Barcelona
Basra
Bathurst
Batum
Beira
Beirut
Belize
Benghazi
Bergen
Bilbao
Bissau
Bombay
Bordeaux
Boston
Boulogne
Bridgetown
Brindisi
Brisbane
Bristol
Buenaventura
Buenos Aires
Cádiz
Cagliari
Calais
Calcutta
Callao
Cannes
Canton
Cape Town
Cap-Haitien
Casablanca
Catania
Cebu
Charleston
Cherbourg
Chicago
Chittagong
Colombo
Colón
Conakry
Copenhagen
Corinth
Dakar
Dar es Salaam
Darwin
Dieppe
Djibouti
Dubrovnik
Duluth
Dunedin
Dunkerque
Durban
East London
Eilat *or* Elat
Esbjerg
Europoort
Fray Bentos
Freetown
Fremantle
Gdańsk
Genoa
Georgetown
Gijón
Göteborg *or* Gothenburg
Guayaquil
Haifa
Halifax
Hamburg
Hamilton
Havana
Helsinki
Hobart
Ho Chi Minh City
Honolulu
Hook of Holland
Inchon
Istanbul
Izmir
Jacksonville
Jaffa
Jidda *or* Jedda
Juneau
Kaohsiung *or* Kaohsiung
Karachi
Kawasaki
Keflavik
Kiel
Kingston
Kobe
Kowloon
Kuwait
La Coruña
Lagos
La Guaira
Las Palmas
Launceston
Le Havre
Limassol
Lisbon
Liverpool
Livorno
Lomé
London
Los Angeles
Luanda
Lübeck
Macao
Madras
Malmo

Manama
Manaus
Manila
Maputo
Mar del Plata
Marseille
Melbourne
Mobile
Mogadiscio *or* Mogadishu
Mombasa
Monrovia
Montego Bay
Montevideo
Montreal
Murmansk
Muscat
Nagasaki
Naples
Nassau
New Orleans
New York
Oakland
Odense
Odessa
Oporto
Osaka
Oslo
Ostend
Phnom Penh
Piraeus
Port Adelaide
Port au Prince
Port Elizabeth
Portland
Port Louis
Port Moresby
Port Said
Portsmouth
Port Sudan
Punta Arenas
Pusan
Recife
Reykjavik
Riga
Rimini
Rio de Janeiro
Rostock
Rotterdam
Saint Petersburg
Salvador
San Diego
San Francisco
San Juan
San Sebastian
Santander
Santo Domingo
Santos
Savannah
Seattle
Sevastopol
Seville
Shanghai
Singapore
Southampton
Split
Stavanger
Stockholm
Suez
Suva
Sydney
Szczecin
Takoradi
Tallinn *or* Tallin
Tampa
Tandjungpriok
Tangier
Tokyo
Townsville
Trieste
Tripoli
Trondheim
Tunis
Turku
Tyre
Valencia
Valparaíso
Vancouver
Venice
Veracruz
Vigo
Vishakhapatnam
Vladivostok
Volgograd
Walvis Bay
Wellington
Yangon
Yokohama
Zeebrugge

Main British and Irish ports

Aberdeen
Arbroath
Ayr
Barry
Belfast
Birkenhead
Bristol
Caernarfon
Cardiff
Cóbh
Cork
Dover
Dundee
Dún Laoghaire
Ellesmere Port
Fishguard
Fleetwood
Folkestone
Galway
Glasgow
Grangemouth
Gravesend
Great Yarmouth
Greenock
Grimsby
Harwich
Holyhead
Hull
Immingham
Kirkcaldy
Larne
Leith
Lerwick
Limerick
Liverpool
London
Londonderry *or* Derry
Lowestoft
Milford Haven
Morecambe
Newcastle upon Tyne
Newhaven
Newport
Newry
Oban
Penzance
Plymouth
Poole
Portsmouth
Port Talbot
Ramsgate
Rosslare
Scarborough
Sheerness
Sligo
Southampton
South Shields
Stornoway
Stranraer
Sunderland
Swansea
Tynemouth
Waterford
Wexford
Weymouth
Whitby
Wicklow

Any port in a storm

portable compact, convenient, easily carried, handy, light, lightweight, manageable, movable, portative

portal door, doorway, entrance, entrance way, entry, gateway, way in

portend adumbrate, augur, bespeak, betoken, bode, foreshadow, foretell, foretoken, forewarn, harbinger, herald, indicate, omen, point to, predict, presage, prognosticate, promise, threaten, vaticinate (*rare*), warn of

portent augury, foreboding, foreshadowing, forewarning, harbinger, indication, omen, premonition, presage, presentiment, prognostic, prognostication, sign, threat, warning

portentous **1.** alarming, bodeful, crucial, fateful, forbidding, important, menacing, minatory, momentous, ominous, significant, sinister, threatening **2.** amazing, astounding, awe-inspiring, extraordinary, miraculous, phenomenal, prodigious, remarkable, wondrous (*archaic or literary*) **3.** bloated, elephantine, heavy, pompous, ponderous, pontifical, self-important, solemn

porter[1] *noun* baggage attendant, bearer, carrier

porter[2] *noun* caretaker, concierge, doorman, gatekeeper, janitor

portion *noun* **1.** bit, fraction, fragment, morsel, part, piece, scrap, section, segment **2.** allocation, allotment, allowance, division, lot, measure, parcel, quantity, quota, ration, share **3.** helping, piece, serving **4.** cup, destiny, fate, fortune, lot, luck *~verb* **5.** allocate, allot, ap~

portion, assign, deal, distribute, divide, divvy up (*informal*), dole out, parcel out, partition, share out

portly ample, beefy (*informal*), bulky, burly, corpulent, fat, fleshy, heavy, large, obese, overweight, plump, rotund, stout, tubby (*informal*)

portrait **1.** image, likeness, painting, photograph, picture, portraiture, representation, sketch **2.** account, characterization, depiction, description, portrayal, profile, thumbnail sketch, vignette

portray **1.** delineate, depict, draw, figure, illustrate, limn, paint, picture, render, represent, sketch **2.** characterize, depict, describe, paint a mental picture of, put in words **3.** act the part of, play, represent

portrayal characterization, delineation, depiction, description, impersonation, interpretation, performance, picture, rendering, representation, take (*informal, chiefly U.S.*)

pose *verb* **1.** arrange, model, position, sit, sit for **2.** *often with* **as** feign, impersonate, masquerade as, pass oneself off as, pretend to be, profess to be, sham **3.** affect, attitudinize, posture, put on airs, show off (*informal*), strike an attitude **4.** advance, posit, present, propound, put, put forward, set, state, submit ~*noun* **5.** attitude, bearing, mien (*literary*), position, posture, stance **6.** act, affectation, air, attitudinizing, façade, front, mannerism, masquerade, posturing, pretence, role

poser brain-teaser (*informal*), conundrum, enigma, knotty point, problem, puzzle, question, riddle, teaser, tough one, vexed question

poseur attitudinizer, exhibitionist, hot dog (*chiefly U.S.*), impostor, mannerist, masquerader, poser, posturer, self-publicist, show-off (*informal*)

posh classy (*slang*), elegant, exclusive, fashionable, grand, high-class, high-toned, la-di-da (*informal*), luxurious, luxury, ritzy (*slang*), smart, stylish, swanky (*informal*), swish (*informal, chiefly Brit.*), top-drawer, up-market, upper-class

posit advance, assert, assume, postulate, predicate, presume, propound, put forward, state, submit

position *noun* **1.** area, bearings, locale, locality, location, place, point, post, reference, site, situation, spot, station, whereabouts **2.** arrangement, attitude, disposition, pose, posture, stance **3.** angle, attitude, belief, opinion, outlook, point of view, slant, stance, stand, standpoint, view, viewpoint **4.** circumstances, condition, lie of the land, pass, plight, predicament, situation, state, strait(s) **5.** caste, class, consequence, eminence, importance, place, prestige, rank, reputation, standing, station, stature, status **6.** berth (*informal*), billet (*informal*), capacity, duty, employment, function, job, occupation, office, place, post, role, situation ~*verb* **7.** arrange, array, dispose, fix, lay out, locate, place, put, sequence, set, settle, stand, stick (*informal*)

positive **1.** absolute, actual, affirmative, categorical, certain, clear, clear-cut, conclusive, concrete, decisive, definite, direct, explicit, express, firm, incontrovertible, indisputable, real, unequivocal, unmistakable **2.** assured, certain, confident, convinced, sure **3.** assertive, cocksure, decided, dogmatic, emphatic, firm, forceful, opinionated, peremptory, resolute, stubborn **4.** beneficial, constructive, effective, efficacious, forward-looking, helpful, practical, productive, progressive, useful **5.** *informal* absolute, complete, consummate, out-and-out, perfect, rank, thorough, thoroughgoing, unmitigated, utter

Antonyms (*sense 1*) contestable, disputable, doubtful, inconclusive, indecisive, indefinite, uncertain (*sense 2*) not confident, unassured, uncertain, unconvinced, unsure (*sense 3*) diffident, open-minded, receptive, retiring, timid, unassertive, unobtrusive (*sense 4*) conservative, detrimental, harmful, impractical, reactionary, unhelpful, useless

positive: mistaken at the top of one's voice
Ambrose Bierce *The Devil's Dictionary*

You've got to ac-cent-tchu-ate the positive
Elim-my-nate the negative
Latch on to the affirmative
Don't mess with Mister In-Between
Johnny Mercer *Ac-cent-tchu-ate the Positive*

positively absolutely, assuredly, categorically, certainly, definitely, emphatically, firmly, surely, undeniably, unequivocally, unmistakably, unquestionably, with certainty, without qualification

possess **1.** be blessed with, be born with, be endowed with, enjoy, have, have to one's name, hold, own **2.** acquire, control, dominate, hold, occupy, seize, take over, take possession of **3.** bewitch, consume, control, dominate, enchant, fixate, influence, mesmerize, obsess, put under a spell

possessed bedevilled, berserk, bewitched, consumed, crazed, cursed, demented, enchanted, frenetic, frenzied, hag-ridden, haunted, maddened, obsessed, raving, under a spell

possession **1.** control, custody, hold, occupancy, occupation, ownership, proprietorship, tenure, title **2.** *plural* assets, belongings, chattels, effects, estate, goods and chattels, property, things, wealth **3.** colony, dominion, protectorate, province, territory

Lay not up for yourselves treasures upon earth,
where moth and rust doth corrupt, and where

thieves break through and steal
Bible: St. Matthew
A bird in the hand is worth two in the bush
Possession is nine points of the law

possessive acquisitive, controlling, covetous, dominating, domineering, grasping, jealous, overprotective, selfish

possibility 1. feasibility, likelihood, plausibility, potentiality, practicability, workableness 2. chance, hazard, hope, liability, likelihood, odds, probability, prospect, risk 3. *often plural* capabilities, potential, potentiality, promise, prospects, talent

Everything is possible, including the impossible
Benito Mussolini

Probable impossibilities are to be preferred to improbable possibilities
Aristotle *Poetics*

possible 1. conceivable, credible, hypothetical, imaginable, likely, potential 2. attainable, do~ able, feasible, on (*informal*), practicable, real~ izable, viable, within reach, workable 3. hope~ ful, likely, potential, probable, promising
Antonyms impossible, impracticable, improb~ able, inconceivable, incredible, unfeasible, un~ imaginable, unlikely, unobtainable, unreason~ able, unthinkable

With God all things are possible
Bible: St. Matthew

possibly 1. God willing, haply (*archaic*), may~ be, mayhap (*archaic*), peradventure (*archaic*), perchance (*archaic*), perhaps 2. at all, by any chance, by any means, in any way

post¹ 1. *noun* column, newel, pale, palisade, picket, pillar, pole, shaft, stake, standard, stock, support, upright 2. *verb* advertise, affix, announce, display, make known, pin up, pro~ claim, promulgate, publicize, publish, put up, stick up

post² *noun* 1. appointment, assignment, berth (*informal*), billet (*informal*), employment, job, office, place, position, situation 2. beat, place, position, station *~verb* 3. assign, establish, lo~ cate, place, position, put, situate, station

post³ *noun* 1. collection, delivery, mail, postal service *~verb* 2. dispatch, mail, send, transmit 3. advise, brief, fill in on (*informal*), inform, notify, report to

poster advertisement, *affiche*, announcement, bill, notice, placard, public notice, sticker

posterior *adjective* 1. after, back, behind, hind, hinder, rear 2. ensuing, following, later, latter, subsequent

posterity 1. children, descendants, family, heirs, issue, offspring, progeny, scions, seed (*chiefly biblical*) 2. future, future generations, succeeding generations

"We are always doing," says he, "something for Posterity, but I would fain see Posterity doing something for us."
Joseph Addison

posthaste at once, before one can say Jack Robinson, directly, double-quick, full tilt, hastily, hotfoot, pdq (*slang*), promptly, pronto (*informal*), quickly, speedily, straightaway, swiftly

postmortem *noun* analysis, autopsy, dissec~ tion, examination, necropsy

postpone adjourn, defer, delay, hold over, put back, put off, put on ice (*informal*), put on the back burner (*informal*), shelve, suspend, table, take a rain check on (*U.S. & Canad. infor~ mal*)
Antonyms advance, bring forward, call to or~ der, carry out, go ahead with

postponement adjournment, deferment, de~ ferral, delay, moratorium, respite, stay, sus~ pension

postscript addition, afterthought, afterword, appendix, P.S., supplement

postulate advance, assume, hypothesize, posit, predicate, presuppose, propose, put forward, suppose, take for granted, theorize

posture *noun* 1. attitude, bearing, carriage, disposition, mien (*literary*), pose, position, set, stance 2. circumstance, condition, mode, phase, position, situation, state 3. attitude, disposition, feeling, frame of mind, inclination, mood, outlook, point of view, stance, stand~ point *~verb* 4. affect, attitudinize, do for ef~ fect, hot-dog (*chiefly U.S.*), make a show, pose, put on airs, show off (*informal*), try to attract attention

posy bouquet, boutonniere, buttonhole, cor~ sage, nosegay, spray

pot¹ *noun* 1. bowl, container, crock, jug, pan, urn, utensil, vase, vessel 2. *informal* cup, tro~ phy 3. bank, jackpot, kitty, pool, stakes 4. beer belly *or* gut (*informal*), bulge, corporation (*in~ formal*), gut, paunch, potbelly, spare tyre (*Brit. slang*), spread (*informal*) 5. **go to pot** decline, deteriorate, go downhill (*informal*), go to rack and ruin, go to the dogs (*informal*), run to seed, slump, worsen *~verb* 6. hit, plug (*informal*), shoot, strike

potbellied bloated, corpulent, distended, fat, obese, overweight, paunchy

potbelly beer belly (*informal*), corporation (*in~ formal*), gut, middle-age spread (*informal*), paunch, pot, spare tyre (*Brit. slang*), spread (*informal*)

potency authority, capacity, control, effective~ ness, efficacy, energy, force, influence, might, muscle, potential, power, puissance, strength, sway, vigour

potent **1.** efficacious, forceful, mighty, powerful, puissant, strong, vigorous **2.** cogent, compelling, convincing, effective, forceful, impressive, persuasive, telling **3.** authoritative, commanding, dominant, dynamic, influential, powerful
Antonyms impotent, ineffective, unconvincing, weak

potentate emperor, king, mogul, monarch, overlord, prince, ruler, sovereign

potential **1.** *adjective* budding, dormant, embryonic, future, hidden, inherent, latent, likely, possible, promising, undeveloped, unrealized **2.** *noun* ability, aptitude, capability, capacity, possibility, potentiality, power, the makings, what it takes (*informal*), wherewithal

potentiality ability, aptitude, capability, capacity, likelihood, potential, promise, prospect, the makings

pother bother, carry-on (*informal, chiefly Brit.*), commotion, disturbance, flap (*informal*), fuss, hoo-ha, lather (*informal*), ruction (*informal*), stew (*informal*), tizzy (*informal*), to-do

potion brew, concoction, cup, dose, draught, elixir, mixture, philtre, tonic

potpourri collection, combination, gallimaufry, hotchpotch, medley, *mélange*, miscellany, mixed bag (*informal*), mixture, motley, pastiche, patchwork, salmagundi

potter dabble, fiddle (*informal*), footle (*informal*), fribble, fritter, mess about, poke along, tinker

pottery ceramics, earthenware, stoneware, terracotta

potty **1.** barmy (*slang*), crackers (*Brit. slang*), crackpot (*informal*), crazy, daft (*informal*), dippy (*slang*), doolally (*slang*), dotty (*slang, chiefly Brit.*), eccentric, foolish, gonzo (*slang*), loopy (*informal*), oddball (*informal*), off one's chump (*slang*), off one's trolley (*slang*), off the rails, off-the-wall (*slang*), out to lunch (*informal*), silly, soft (*informal*), touched, up the pole (*informal*), wacko *or* whacko (*informal*) **2.** footling (*informal*), insignificant, petty, piddling (*informal*), trifling, trivial

pouch bag, container, pocket, poke (*dialect*), purse, sack

pounce **1.** *verb* ambush, attack, bound onto, dash at, drop, fall upon, jump, leap at, snatch, spring, strike, swoop, take by surprise, take unawares **2.** *noun* assault, attack, bound, jump, leap, spring, swoop

pound[1] *verb* **1.** batter, beat, beat the living daylights out of, belabour, clobber (*slang*), hammer, pelt, pummel, strike, thrash, thump **2.** bray (*dialect*), bruise, comminute, crush, powder, pulverize, triturate **3.** din into, drub into, drum into, hammer into **4.** *with* **out** bang, beat, hammer, thump **5.** clomp, march, stomp (*informal*), thunder, tramp **6.** beat, palpitate, pitapat, pulsate, pulse, throb

pound[2] *noun* compound, corral (*chiefly U.S. & Canad.*), enclosure, pen, yard

pour **1.** decant, let flow, spill, splash **2.** course, emit, flow, gush, run, rush, spew, spout, stream **3.** bucket down (*informal*), come down in torrents, pelt (down), rain, rain cats and dogs (*informal*), rain hard *or* heavily, sheet, teem **4.** crowd, stream, swarm, teem, throng

pout **1.** *verb* glower, look petulant, look sullen, lour *or* lower, make a *moue*, mope, pull a long face, purse one's lips, sulk, turn down the corners of one's mouth **2.** *noun* glower, long face, *moue*, sullen look

pouting bad-tempered, cross, huffy, ill-humoured, long-faced, moody, moping, morose, peevish, petulant, sulky, sullen

poverty **1.** beggary, destitution, distress, hand-to-mouth existence, hardship, indigence, insolvency, necessitousness, necessity, need, pauperism, pennilessness, penury, privation, want **2.** dearth, deficiency, insufficiency, lack, paucity, scarcity, shortage **3.** aridity, bareness, barrenness, deficiency, infertility, meagreness, poorness, sterility, unfruitfulness
Antonyms (*sense 1*) affluence, comfort, luxury, opulence, richness, wealth (*sense 2*) abundance, plethora, sufficiency (*sense 3*) fecundity, fertility, fruitfulness, productiveness

The greatest of evils and the worst of crimes is poverty
George Bernard Shaw *Major Barbara*

Anyone who has ever struggled with poverty knows how extremely expensive it is to be poor
James Baldwin *Nobody Knows My Name*

Give me not poverty lest I steal
Daniel Defoe *Review (later incorporated into Moll Flanders)*

The want of money is the root of all evil
Samuel Butler *Erewhon*

No man should commend poverty unless he is poor
Saint Bernard

People don't resent having nothing nearly as much as too little
Ivy Compton-Burnett *A Family and a Fortune*

Poverty is not a crime

poverty-stricken bankrupt, beggared, broke (*informal*), destitute, dirt-poor (*informal*), distressed, down and out, down at heel, flat broke (*informal*), impecunious, impoverished, indigent, in queer street, needy, on one's beam-ends, on one's uppers, on the breadline, penniless, penurious, poor, short, skint (*Brit. slang*), stony-broke (*Brit. slang*), without two pennies to rub together (*informal*)

powder *noun* **1.** dust, fine grains, loose particles, pounce, talc ~*verb* **2.** crush, granulate, grind, pestle, pound, pulverize **3.** cover, dredge, dust, scatter, sprinkle, strew

powdery chalky, crumbling, crumbly, dry, dusty, fine, friable, grainy, granular, loose, pulverized, sandy

power **1.** ability, capability, capacity, competence, competency, faculty, potential **2.** brawn, energy, force, forcefulness, intensity, might, muscle, potency, strength, vigour, weight **3.** ascendancy, authority, bottom, command, control, dominance, domination, dominion, influence, mastery, rule, sovereignty, supremacy, sway **4.** authority, authorization, licence, prerogative, privilege, right, warrant

Antonyms (*sense 1*) inability, incapability, incapacity, incompetence (*sense 2*) enervation, feebleness, impotence, listlessness, weakness

Power tends to corrupt and absolute power corrupts absolutely

First Baron Acton *letter*

Unlimited power is apt to corrupt the minds of those who possess it

William Pitt, Earl of Chatham

Power is the great aphrodisiac

Henry Kissinger

Here we may reign secure, and in my choice
To reign is worth ambition though in hell;
Better to reign in hell, than serve in heav'n

John Milton *Paradise Lost*

there is no such thing as revolutionary power, for all power is reactionary by nature

Spanish anarchist slogan

Power without responsibility; the prerogative of the harlot throughout the ages

Rudyard Kipling *Kipling Journal*

Political power grows out of the barrel of a gun

Mao Tse-tung

A friend in power is a friend lost

Henry Brooks Adams *The Education of Henry Adams*

The only purpose for which power can be rightfully exercised over any member of a civilized community, against his will, is to prevent harm to others. His own good, either physical or moral, is not a sufficient warrant

John Stuart Mill *On Liberty*

powerful **1.** energetic, mighty, potent, robust, stalwart, strapping, strong, sturdy, vigorous **2.** authoritative, commanding, controlling, dominant, influential, prevailing, puissant, sovereign, supreme **3.** cogent, compelling, convincing, effective, effectual, forceful, forcible, impressive, persuasive, striking, telling, weighty

powerfully forcefully, forcibly, hard, mightily, strongly, vigorously, with might and main

powerless **1.** debilitated, disabled, etiolated, feeble, frail, helpless, impotent, incapable, incapacitated, ineffectual, infirm, paralysed, prostrate, weak **2.** defenceless, dependent, disenfranchised, disfranchised, ineffective, over a barrel (*informal*), subject, tied, unarmed, vulnerable

Antonyms (*sense 1*) able-bodied, fit, healthy, lusty, powerful, robust, strong, sturdy

powwow **1.** *noun* chinwag (*Brit. informal*), confab (*informal*), confabulation, conference, congress, consultation, council, discussion, get-together (*informal*), huddle (*informal*), meeting, palaver, parley, seminar, talk **2.** *verb* confab (*informal*), confer, discuss, get together, go into a huddle (*informal*), meet, palaver, parley, talk

practicability advantage, feasibility, operability, possibility, practicality, use, usefulness, value, viability, workability

practicable achievable, attainable, doable, feasible, performable, possible, viable, within the realm of possibility, workable

Antonyms beyond the bounds of possibility, impossible, out of the question, unachievable, unattainable, unfeasible, unworkable

practical **1.** applied, efficient, empirical, experimental, factual, functional, pragmatic, realistic, utilitarian **2.** businesslike, down-to-earth, everyday, hard-headed, matter-of-fact, mundane, ordinary, realistic, sensible, workaday **3.** doable, feasible, practicable, serviceable, sound, useful, workable **4.** accomplished, efficient, experienced, proficient, qualified, seasoned, skilled, trained, veteran, working

Antonyms (*senses 1, 2, & 3*) impossible, impracticable, impractical, inefficient, speculative, theoretical, unpractical, unrealistic, unsound, unworkable, useless (*sense 4*) inefficient, inexperienced, unaccomplished, unqualified, unskilled, untrained

practically **1.** all but, almost, basically, close to, essentially, fundamentally, in effect, just about, nearly, to all intents and purposes, very nearly, virtually, well-nigh **2.** clearly, matter-of-factly, rationally, realistically, reasonably, sensibly, unsentimentally, with common sense

practice **1.** custom, habit, method, mode, praxis, routine, rule, system, tradition, usage, use, usual procedure, way, wont **2.** discipline, drill, exercise, preparation, rehearsal, repetition, study, training, work-out **3.** action, application, effect, exercise, experience, operation, use **4.** business, career, profession, vocation, work

Practice makes perfect

practise **1.** discipline, drill, exercise, go over, go through, keep one's hand in, polish, prepare, rehearse, repeat, study, train, warm up, work out **2.** apply, carry out, do, follow, live up to, observe, perform, put into practice **3.** carry on, engage in, ply, pursue, specialize in, undertake, work at

practised able, accomplished, experienced, expert, proficient, qualified, seasoned, skilled, trained, versed
Antonyms amateurish, bungling, incompetent, inexperienced, inexpert, unqualified, unskilled, untrained

pragmatic businesslike, down-to-earth, efficient, hard-headed, matter-of-fact, practical, realistic, sensible, utilitarian
Antonyms airy-fairy, idealistic, impractical, inefficient, starry-eyed, stupid, theoretical, unprofessional, unrealistic

praise *noun* **1.** acclaim, acclamation, accolade, applause, approbation, approval, cheering, commendation, compliment, congratulation, encomium, eulogy, good word, kudos, laudation, ovation, panegyric, plaudit, tribute **2.** adoration, devotion, glory, homage, thanks, worship *~verb* **3.** acclaim, admire, applaud, approve, cheer, compliment, congratulate, crack up (*informal*), cry up, eulogize, extol, honour, laud, pat on the back, pay tribute to, sing the praises of, take one's hat off to **4.** adore, bless, exalt, give thanks to, glorify, magnify (*archaic*), pay homage to, worship

Self-praise is no recommendation

praiseworthy admirable, commendable, creditable, estimable, excellent, exemplary, fine, honourable, laudable, meritorious, worthy
Antonyms condemnable, deplorable, despicable, discreditable, disgraceful, dishonourable, ignoble, reprehensible

prance 1. bound, caper, cavort, cut a rug (*informal*), dance, frisk, gambol, jump, leap, romp, skip, spring, trip **2.** parade, show off (*informal*), stalk, strut, swagger, swank (*informal*)

prank antic, caper, escapade, frolic, jape, lark (*informal*), practical joke, skylarking (*informal*), trick

prate babble, blather, boast, brag, chatter, drivel, gab (*informal*), gas (*informal*), go on and on, jaw (*slang*), rabbit (on) (*Brit. informal*), shoot off one's mouth (*slang*), waffle (*informal, chiefly Brit.*), witter on (*informal*), yak (*slang*)

prattle babble, blather, blether, chatter, clack, drivel, gabble, jabber, patter, rabbit (on) (*Brit. informal*), rattle on, run off at the mouth (*slang*), run on, twitter, waffle (*informal, chiefly Brit.*), witter (*informal*)

pray 1. offer a prayer, recite the rosary, say one's prayers **2.** adjure, ask, beg, beseech, call upon, crave, cry for, entreat, implore, importune, invoke, petition, plead, request, solicit, sue, supplicate, urge

pray: to ask that the laws of the universe be annulled in behalf of a single petitioner confessedly unworthy
Ambrose Bierce *The Devil's Dictionary*

prayer 1. communion, devotion, invocation, litany, orison, supplication **2.** appeal, entreaty, petition, plea, request, suit, supplication

More things are wrought by prayer
Than this world dreams of
Alfred, Lord Tennyson *Morte d'Arthur*

When the gods wish to punish us they answer our prayers
Oscar Wilde *An Ideal Husband*

The wish for prayer is a prayer in itself
Georges Bernanos *Journal d'un cure de campagne*

In prayer the lips ne'er act the winning part,
Without the sweet concurrence of the heart
Robert Herrick *The Heart*

One single grateful thought raised to heaven is the most perfect prayer
G.E. Lessing *Minna von Barnhelm*

preach 1. address, deliver a sermon, evangelize, exhort, orate **2.** admonish, advocate, exhort, harangue, lecture, moralize, sermonize, urge

preacher clergyman, evangelist, minister, missionary, parson, revivalist

preachify drone on, go on and on, harangue, hold forth, lecture, moralize, prose, sermonize

preachy canting, didactic, edifying, holier-than-thou, homiletic, moralizing, pharisaic, pietistic, pontifical, religiose, sanctimonious, self-righteous

preamble exordium, foreword, introduction, opening move, opening statement *or* remarks, overture, preface, prelude, proem, prolegomenon

precarious built on sand, chancy (*informal*), dangerous, dicey (*informal, chiefly Brit.*), dodgy (*Brit., Austral., & N.Z. informal*), doubtful, dubious, hairy (*slang*), hazardous, insecure, perilous, risky, shaky, slippery, touch and go, tricky, uncertain, unreliable, unsafe, unsettled, unstable, unsteady, unsure
Antonyms certain, dependable, reliable, safe, secure, stable, steady

precaution 1. belt and braces (*informal*), insurance, preventative measure, protection, provision, safeguard, safety measure **2.** anticipation, care, caution, circumspection, foresight, forethought, providence, prudence, wariness

precede antecede, antedate, come first, forerun, go ahead of, go before, head, herald, introduce, lead, pave the way, preface, take precedence, usher

precedence antecedence, lead, pre-eminence,

preference, primacy, priority, rank, seniority, superiority, supremacy

precedent *noun* antecedent, authority, criterion, example, exemplar, instance, model, paradigm, pattern, previous example, prototype, standard

preceding above, aforementioned, aforesaid, anterior, earlier, foregoing, former, past, previous, prior

precept 1. behest, canon, command, commandment, decree, dictum, direction, instruction, law, mandate, order, ordinance, principle, regulation, rule, statute 2. axiom, byword, dictum, guideline, maxim, motto, principle, rule, saying

precinct 1. bound, boundary, confine, enclosure, limit 2. area, district, quarter, section, sector, zone

precincts borders, bounds, confines, district, environs, limits, milieu, neighbourhood, purlieus, region, surrounding area

precious 1. adored, beloved, cherished, darling, dear, dearest, favourite, idolized, loved, prized, treasured, valued, worth one's *or* its weight in gold 2. choice, costly, dear, expensive, exquisite, fine, high-priced, inestimable, invaluable, priceless, prized, rare, recherché, valuable 3. affected, alembicated, artificial, chichi, fastidious, overnice, overrefined, twee (*Brit. informal*)

precipice bluff, brink, cliff, cliff face, crag, height, rock face, sheer drop, steep

precipitate *verb* 1. accelerate, advance, bring on, dispatch, expedite, further, hasten, hurry, press, push forward, quicken, speed up, trigger 2. cast, discharge, fling, hurl, launch, let fly, send forth, throw ~*adjective* 3. breakneck, headlong, plunging, rapid, rushing, swift, violent 4. frantic, harum-scarum, hasty, heedless, hurried, ill-advised, impetuous, impulsive, indiscreet, madcap, precipitous, rash, reckless 5. abrupt, brief, quick, sudden, unexpected, without warning

precipitous 1. abrupt, dizzy, falling sharply, high, perpendicular, sheer, steep 2. abrupt, careless, harum-scarum, hasty, heedless, hurried, ill-advised, precipitate, rash, reckless, sudden

précis 1. *noun* abridgment, abstract, *aperçu*, compendium, condensation, digest, outline, résumé, rundown, sketch, summary, synopsis 2. *verb* abridge, abstract, compress, condense, outline, shorten, summarize, sum up

precise 1. absolute, accurate, actual, clear-cut, correct, definite, exact, explicit, express, fixed, literal, particular, specific, strict, unequivocal 2. careful, ceremonious, exact, fastidious, finicky, formal, inflexible, meticulous, nice, particular, prim, punctilious, puritanical, rigid, scrupulous, stiff, strict
Antonyms (*sense 1*) ambiguous, careless, equivocal, incorrect, indefinite, indistinct, inexact, loose, vague (*sense 2*) flexible, haphazard, inexact, informal, relaxed, unceremonious

precisely absolutely, accurately, bang, correctly, exactly, just, just so, literally, neither more nor less, on the button (*informal*), plumb (*informal*), slap (*informal*), smack (*informal*), square, squarely, strictly, to the letter

precision accuracy, care, correctness, definiteness, dotting the i's and crossing the t's, exactitude, exactness, fidelity, meticulousness, nicety, particularity, preciseness, rigour

preclude check, debar, exclude, forestall, hinder, inhibit, make impossible, make impracticable, obviate, prevent, prohibit, put a stop to, restrain, rule out, stop

precocious advanced, ahead, bright, developed, forward, quick, smart
Antonyms backward, dense, dull, retarded, slow, underdeveloped, unresponsive

preconceived forejudged, predetermined, prejudged, premature, presumed, presupposed

preconception bias, notion, preconceived idea *or* notion, predisposition, prejudice, prepossession, presumption, presupposition

precondition essential, must, necessity, prerequisite, requirement, *sine qua non*

precursor 1. forerunner, harbinger, herald, messenger, usher, vanguard 2. antecedent, forebear, forerunner, originator, pioneer, predecessor

precursory antecedent, introductory, preceding, prefatory, preliminary, preparatory, previous, prior

predatory 1. carnivorous, hunting, predacious, rapacious, raptorial, ravening 2. despoiling, greedy, marauding, pillaging, plundering, rapacious, ravaging, thieving, voracious, vulturine, vulturous

predecessor 1. antecedent, forerunner, precursor, previous (former, prior) job holder 2. ancestor, antecedent, forebear, forefather

predestination destiny, doom, election (*Theology*), fate, foreordainment, foreordination, lot, necessity, predetermination

predestine doom, fate, foreordain, mean, predestinate, predetermine, pre-elect, preordain

predetermined agreed, arranged in advance, cut and dried (*informal*), decided beforehand, fixed, prearranged, preplanned, set, settled, set up

predicament corner, dilemma, emergency, fix (*informal*), hole (*slang*), hot water (*informal*), how-do-you-do (*informal*), jam (*informal*), mess, pickle (*informal*), pinch, plight, quandary, scrape (*informal*), situation, spot (*informal*), state, tight spot

predicate 1. affirm, assert, aver, avouch, avow, contend, declare, maintain, proclaim, state 2. connote, imply, indicate, intimate, signify, suggest 3. *with* **on** *or* **upon** base, build, establish, found, ground, postulate, rest

predict augur, divine, forebode, forecast, foresee, foretell, portend, presage, prognosticate, prophesy, soothsay, vaticinate (*rare*)

predictable anticipated, calculable, certain, expected, foreseeable, foreseen, likely, on the cards, reliable, sure, sure-fire (*informal*)
Antonyms out of the blue, surprising, unexpected, unforeseen, unlikely, unpredictable

prediction augury, divination, forecast, prognosis, prognostication, prophecy, soothsaying, sortilege
Methods of divination
see DIVINATION

predilection bag (*slang*), bias, cup of tea (*informal*), fancy, fondness, inclination, leaning, liking, love, partiality, penchant, predisposition, preference, proclivity, proneness, propensity, taste, tendency, weakness

predispose affect, bias, dispose, incline, induce, influence, lead, make (one) of a mind to, prejudice, prepare, prime, prompt, sway

predisposed agreeable, amenable, given to, inclined, liable, minded, prone, ready, subject, susceptible, willing

predisposition bent, bias, disposition, inclination, likelihood, penchant, potentiality, predilection, proclivity, proneness, propensity, susceptibility, tendency, willingness

predominance ascendancy, control, dominance, dominion, edge, greater number, hold, leadership, mastery, paramountcy, preponderance, supremacy, sway, upper hand, weight

predominant ascendant, capital, chief, controlling, dominant, important, leading, main, notable, paramount, preponderant, prevailing, prevalent, primary, prime, principal, prominent, ruling, sovereign, superior, supreme, top-priority
Antonyms inferior, minor, secondary, subordinate, unimportant, uninfluential

predominantly chiefly, for the most part, generally, in the main, largely, mainly, mostly, on the whole, preponderantly, primarily, principally, to a great extent

predominate be most noticeable, carry weight, get the upper hand, hold sway, outweigh, overrule, overshadow, preponderate, prevail, reign, rule, tell

pre-eminence distinction, excellence, paramountcy, predominance, prestige, prominence, renown, superiority, supremacy, transcendence

pre-eminent chief, consummate, distinguished, excellent, foremost, incomparable, matchless, outstanding, paramount, peerless, predominant, renowned, superior, supreme, transcendent, unequalled, unrivalled, unsurpassed

pre-eminently above all, by far, conspicuously, eminently, emphatically, exceptionally, far and away, incomparably, inimitably, matchlessly, notably, *par excellence*, particularly, second to none, signally, singularly, strikingly, superlatively, supremely

pre-empt acquire, anticipate, appropriate, arrogate, assume, seize, take over, usurp

preen 1. *of birds* clean, plume 2. array, deck out, doll up (*slang*), dress up, prettify, primp, prink, spruce up, titivate, trig (*archaic or dialect*), trim 3. **preen oneself (on)** congratulate oneself, pique oneself, plume oneself, pride oneself

preface 1. *noun* exordium, foreword, introduction, preamble, preliminary, prelude, proem, prolegomenon, prologue 2. *verb* begin, introduce, launch, lead up to, open, precede, prefix

prefatory antecedent, introductory, opening, precursory, prefatorial, preliminary, prelusive, prelusory, preparatory, proemial, prolegomenal

prefer 1. adopt, be partial to, choose, desire, elect, fancy, favour, go for, incline towards, like better, opt for, pick, plump for, select, single out, wish, would rather, would sooner 2. file, lodge, place, present, press, put forward 3. advance, aggrandize, elevate, move up, promote, raise, upgrade

preferable best, better, choice, chosen, favoured, more desirable, more eligible, superior, worthier
Antonyms average, fair, ineligible, inferior, mediocre, poor, second-rate, undesirable

preferably as a matter of choice, by choice, first, in *or* for preference, much rather, much sooner, rather, sooner, willingly

preference 1. bag (*slang*), choice, cup of tea (*informal*), desire, election, favourite, first choice, option, partiality, pick, predilection, selection, top of the list 2. advantage, favoured treatment, favouritism, first place, precedence, pride of place, priority

preferential advantageous, better, favoured, partial, partisan, privileged, special, superior

preferment advancement, dignity, elevation, exaltation, promotion, rise, upgrading

prefigure 1. adumbrate, foreshadow, foretoken, indicate, intimate, portend, presage, shadow forth, suggest 2. consider, fancy, imagine, picture, presuppose

pregnancy gestation, gravidity

pregnant 1. big *or* heavy with child, enceinte, expectant, expecting (*informal*), gravid, in the club (*Brit. slang*), in the family way (*informal*), in the pudding club (*slang*), preggers (*Brit. informal*), with child **2.** charged, eloquent, expressive, loaded, meaningful, pointed, significant, suggestive, telling, weighty **3.** creative, imaginative, inventive, original, seminal **4.** abounding in, abundant, fecund, fertile, fraught, fruitful, full, productive, prolific, replete, rich in, teeming

prehistoric **1.** earliest, early, primeval, primitive, primordial **2.** ancient, antediluvian, antiquated, archaic, out of date, out of the ark (*informal*)

prejudge anticipate, forejudge, jump to conclusions, make a hasty assessment, presume, presuppose

prejudice *noun* **1.** bias, jaundiced eye, partiality, preconceived notion, preconception, prejudgment, warp **2.** bigotry, chauvinism, discrimination, injustice, intolerance, narrow-mindedness, racism, sexism, unfairness **3.** damage, detriment, disadvantage, harm, hurt, impairment, loss, mischief *~verb* **4.** bias, colour, distort, influence, jaundice, poison, predispose, prepossess, slant, sway, warp **5.** damage, harm, hinder, hurt, impair, injure, mar, spoil, undermine

> *Drive out prejudices through the door, and they will return through the window*
> Frederick the Great *letter to Voltaire*

> *prejudice: a vagrant opinion without visible means of support*
> Ambrose Bierce *The Devil's Dictionary*

> *Who's 'im, Bill?*
> *A stranger!*
> *'Eave 'arf a brick at 'im*
> Punch

prejudiced biased, bigoted, conditioned, discriminatory, influenced, intolerant, jaundiced, narrow-minded, one-sided, opinionated, partial, partisan, prepossessed, unfair
Antonyms fair, impartial, just, neutral, not bigoted, not prejudiced, open-minded, unbiased

prejudicial counterproductive, damaging, deleterious, detrimental, disadvantageous, harmful, hurtful, inimical, injurious, undermining, unfavourable

preliminary **1.** *adjective* exploratory, first, initial, initiatory, introductory, opening, pilot, precursory, prefatory, preparatory, prior, qualifying, test, trial **2.** *noun* beginning, first round, foundation, groundwork, initiation, introduction, opening, overture, preamble, preface, prelims, prelude, preparation, start

prelude beginning, commencement, curtain-raiser, exordium, foreword, intro (*informal*), introduction, overture, preamble, preface, preliminary, preparation, proem, prolegomenon, prologue, start

premature **1.** abortive, early, embryonic, forward, green, immature, incomplete, predeveloped, raw, undeveloped, unfledged, unripe, unseasonable, untimely **2.** *figurative* hasty, ill-considered, ill-timed, impulsive, inopportune, jumping the gun, overhasty, precipitate, previous (*informal*), rash, too soon, untimely

prematurely **1.** before one's time, too early, too soon, untimely **2.** at half-cock, half-cocked, overhastily, precipitately, rashly, too hastily, too soon

premeditated aforethought, calculated, conscious, considered, contrived, deliberate, intended, intentional, planned, prepense, studied, wilful
Antonyms accidental, inadvertent, unintentional, unplanned, unpremeditated, unwitting

premeditation deliberation, design, determination, forethought, intention, malice aforethought, planning, plotting, prearrangement, predetermination, purpose

premier *noun* **1.** chancellor, head of government, P.M., prime minister *~adjective* **2.** arch, chief, first, foremost, head, highest, leading, main, primary, prime, principal, top **3.** earliest, first, inaugural, initial, original

premiere debut, first night, first performance, first showing, opening

premise *verb* assume, hypothesize, posit, postulate, predicate, presuppose, state

premises building, establishment, place, property, site

premiss, premise argument, assertion, assumption, ground, hypothesis, postulate, postulation, presupposition, proposition, supposition, thesis

premium **1.** bonus, boon, bounty, fee, percentage (*informal*), perk (*Brit. informal*), perquisite, prize, recompense, remuneration, reward **2.** appreciation, regard, stock, store, value **3.** **at a premium** beyond one's means, costly, expensive, hard to come by, in great demand, in short supply, like gold dust, not to be had for love or money, rare, scarce, valuable

premonition apprehension, feeling, feeling in one's bones, foreboding, forewarning, funny feeling (*informal*), hunch, idea, intuition, misgiving, omen, portent, presage, presentiment, sign, suspicion, warning

preoccupation **1.** absence of mind, absent-mindedness, absorption, abstraction, brown study, daydreaming, engrossment, immersion, inattentiveness, musing, oblivion, pensiveness, prepossession, reverie, woolgathering **2.** bee in one's bonnet, concern, fixation, hang-up (*in~*

formal), hobbyhorse, *idée fixe*, obsession, pet subject

preoccupied absent-minded, absorbed, abstracted, caught up in, distracted, distrait, engrossed, faraway, heedless, immersed, in a brown study, intent, lost in, lost in thought, oblivious, rapt, taken up, unaware, wrapped up

preordain destine, doom, fate, map out in advance, predestine, predetermine

preparation 1. development, getting ready, groundwork, preparing, putting in order 2. alertness, anticipation, expectation, foresight, precaution, preparedness, provision, readiness, safeguard 3. *often plural* arrangement, measure, plan, provision 4. composition, compound, concoction, medicine, mixture, tincture 5. homework, prep (*informal*), revision, schoolwork, study, swotting (*Brit. informal*)

preparatory 1. basic, elementary, introductory, opening, prefatory, preliminary, preparative, primary 2. **preparatory to** before, in advance of, in anticipation of, in preparation for, prior to

prepare 1. adapt, adjust, anticipate, arrange, coach, dispose, form, groom, make provision, make ready, plan, practise, prime, put in order, train, warm up 2. brace, fortify, gird, ready, steel, strengthen 3. assemble, concoct, construct, contrive, draw up, fashion, fix up, get up (*informal*), make, produce, put together, turn out 4. accoutre, equip, fit, fit out, furnish, outfit, provide, supply

prepared 1. all set, all systems go (*informal*), arranged, fit, in order, in readiness, planned, primed, ready, set 2. able, disposed, inclined, minded, of a mind, predisposed, willing

preparedness alertness, fitness, order, preparation, readiness

preponderance ascendancy, bulk, dominance, domination, dominion, extensiveness, greater numbers, greater part, lion's share, mass, power, predominance, prevalence, superiority, supremacy, sway, weight

preponderant ascendant, dominant, extensive, foremost, greater, important, larger, paramount, predominant, prevailing, prevalent, significant

preponderate dominate, hold sway, outnumber, predominate, prevail, reign supreme, rule

prepossessed biased, inclined, partial, partisan, predisposed, prejudiced

prepossessing alluring, amiable, appealing, attractive, beautiful, bewitching, captivating, charming, engaging, fair, fascinating, fetching, glamorous, good-looking, handsome, inviting, likable *or* likeable, lovable, magnetic, pleasing, striking, taking, winning

Antonyms disagreeable, displeasing, objectionable, offensive, repulsive, ugly, unattractive, uninviting, unlikable *or* unlikeable

prepossession 1. absorption, engrossment, preoccupation 2. bias, inclination, liking, partiality, predilection, predisposition, prejudice

preposterous absurd, asinine, bizarre, crazy, excessive, exorbitant, extravagant, extreme, foolish, impossible, incredible, insane, irrational, laughable, ludicrous, monstrous, nonsensical, out of the question, outrageous, ridiculous, senseless, shocking, unreasonable, unthinkable

prerequisite 1. *adjective* called for, essential, imperative, indispensable, mandatory, necessary, needful, obligatory, of the essence, required, requisite, vital 2. *noun* condition, essential, imperative, must, necessity, precondition, qualification, requirement, requisite, *sine qua non*

prerogative advantage, authority, birthright, choice, claim, droit, due, exemption, immunity, liberty, perquisite, privilege, right, sanction, title

presage *noun* 1. augury, auspice, forecast, forewarning, harbinger, intimation, omen, portent, prediction, prognostic, prognostication, prophecy, sign, warning 2. apprehension, boding, feeling, foreboding, intuition, misgiving, premonition, presentiment ~*verb* 3. divine, feel, foresee, have a feeling, intuit, sense 4. adumbrate, augur, betoken, bode, forebode, foreshadow, foretoken, omen, point to, portend, signify, warn 5. forecast, foretell, forewarn, predict, prognosticate, prophesy, soothsay, vaticinate (*rare*)

prescience clairvoyance, foreknowledge, foresight, precognition, prevision (*rare*), second sight

prescient clairvoyant, discerning, divinatory, divining, far-sighted, foresighted, mantic, perceptive, prophetic, psychic

prescribe appoint, assign, command, decree, define, dictate, direct, enjoin, establish, fix, impose, lay down, ordain, order, require, rule, set, specify, stipulate

prescript canon, command, dictate, dictum, direction, directive, edict, instruction, law, mandate, order, ordinance, precept, regulation, requirement, rule

prescription 1. direction, formula, instruction, recipe 2. drug, medicine, mixture, preparation, remedy

prescriptive authoritarian, dictatorial, didactic, dogmatic, legislating, preceptive, rigid

presence 1. attendance, being, companionship, company, existence, habitation, inhabitance, occupancy, residence 2. closeness, immediate circle, nearness, neighbourhood, propinquity, proximity, vicinity 3. air, appearance, aspect, aura, bearing, carriage, comportment, de~meanour, ease, mien (*literary*), personality, poise, self-assurance **4.** apparition, eidolon, ghost, manifestation, revenant, shade (*liter~ary*), spectre, spirit, supernatural being, wraith

presence of mind alertness, aplomb, calm~ness, composure, cool (*slang*), coolness, imper~turbability, level-headedness, phlegm, quick~ness, sang-froid, self-assurance, self-command, self-possession, wits

present[1] *adjective* **1.** contemporary, current, existent, existing, extant, immediate, instant, present-day **2.** accounted for, at hand, avail~able, here, in attendance, near, nearby, ready, there, to hand *~noun* **3.** here and now, now, present moment, the time being, this day and age, today **4. at present** at the moment, just now, now, nowadays, right now **5. for the present** for a while, for the moment, for the nonce, for the time being, in the meantime, not for long, provisionally, temporarily

For present joys are more to flesh and blood
Than a dull prospect of a distant good
John Dryden *The Hindu and the Panther*

Ah, fill the cup: - what boots it to repeat
How time is slipping underneath our feet;
Unborn tomorrow, and dead yesterday,
Why fret about them if today be sweet!
Edward Fitzgerald *The Rubáiyát of Omar Khayyám*

Presents, I often say, endear Absents
Charles Lamb *Essays of Elia*

There is no time like the present

present[2] *verb* **1.** acquaint with, introduce, make known **2.** demonstrate, display, exhibit, give, mount, put before the public, put on, show, stage **3.** adduce, advance, declare, ex~pound, extend, hold out, introduce, offer, pose, produce, proffer, put forward, raise, recount, relate, state, submit, suggest, tender **4.** award, bestow, confer, donate, entrust, furnish, give, grant, hand out, hand over, offer, proffer, put at (someone's) disposal *~noun* **5.** benefaction, boon, bounty, donation, endowment, favour, gift, grant, gratuity, hand-out, largess *or* lar~gesse, offering, prezzie (*informal*)

presentable acceptable, becoming, decent, fit to be seen, good enough, not bad (*informal*), O.K. *or* okay (*informal*), passable, proper, re~spectable, satisfactory, suitable, tolerable
Antonyms below par, not good enough, not up to scratch, poor, rubbishy, unacceptable, un~presentable, unsatisfactory

presentation 1. award, bestowal, conferral, do~nation, giving, investiture, offering **2.** appear~ance, arrangement, delivery, exposition, pro~duction, rendition, staging, submission **3.** demonstration, display, exhibition, perfor~mance, production, representation, show **4.** coming out, debut, introduction, launch, launching, reception

present-day contemporary, current, latter-day, modern, newfangled, present, recent, up-to-date

presentiment anticipation, apprehension, ex~pectation, fear, feeling, foreboding, forecast, forethought, hunch, intuition, misgiving, premonition, presage

presently anon (*archaic*), before long, by and by, erelong (*archaic or poetic*), in a minute, in a moment, in a short while, pretty soon (*in~formal*), shortly, soon

preservation conservation, defence, keeping, maintenance, perpetuation, protection, safe~guarding, safekeeping, safety, salvation, secu~rity, storage, support, upholding

Self-preservation is the first law of nature

preserve *verb* **1.** care for, conserve, defend, guard, keep, protect, safeguard, save, secure, shelter, shield **2.** continue, keep, keep up, maintain, perpetuate, retain, sustain, uphold **3.** conserve, keep, put up, save, store *~noun* **4.** area, domain, field, realm, specialism, sphere **5.** *often plural* confection, confiture, conserve, jam, jelly, marmalade, sweetmeat **6.** game re~serve, reservation, reserve, sanctuary
Antonyms (*sense 1*) assail, assault, attack, leave unprotected, turn out (*sense 2*) abandon, discontinue, drop, end, give up (*sense 3*) blow (*slang*), consume, fritter away, spend, squan~der, waste

preside administer, be at the head of, be in authority, chair, conduct, control, direct, gov~ern, head, lead, manage, officiate, run, super~vise

press *verb* **1.** bear down on, compress, con~dense, crush, depress, force down, jam, mash, push, reduce, squeeze, stuff **2.** calender, finish, flatten, iron, mangle, put the creases in, smooth, steam **3.** clasp, crush, embrace, encir~cle, enfold, fold in one's arms, hold close, hug, squeeze **4.** compel, constrain, demand, enforce, enjoin, force, insist on **5.** beg, entreat, exhort, implore, importune, petition, plead, pressur~ize, sue, supplicate, urge **6.** afflict, assail, be~set, besiege, disquiet, harass, plague, torment, trouble, vex, worry **7. be pressed** be hard put, be pushed (hurried, rushed) (*informal*), be short of **8.** cluster, crowd, flock, gather, hasten, herd, hurry, mill, push, rush, seethe, surge, swarm, throng *~noun* **9. the press a.** Fleet Street, fourth estate, journalism, news media, newspapers, the papers **b.** columnists, correspondents, gentlemen of the press, jour~nalists, journos (*slang*), newsmen, photogra~phers, pressmen, reporters **10.** bunch, crowd, crush, flock, herd, horde, host, mob, multi~

tude, pack, push (*informal*), swarm, throng **11.** bustle, demand, hassle (*informal*), hurry, pressure, strain, stress, urgency

Thou god of our idolatry, the press...
Thou fountain, at which drink the good and wise;
Thou ever-bubbling spring of endless lies;
Like Eden's dread probationary tree,
Knowledge of good and evil is from thee
William Cowper *The Progress of Error*

pressing burning, constraining, crucial, exigent, high-priority, imperative, important, importunate, now or never, serious, urgent, vital
Antonyms dispensable, regular, routine, unimportant, unnecessary

pressure 1. compressing, compression, crushing, force, heaviness, squeezing, weight **2.** coercion, compulsion, constraint, force, influence, obligation, power, sway **3.** adversity, affliction, burden, demands, difficulty, distress, exigency, hassle (*informal*), heat, hurry, load, press, strain, stress, urgency

If you can't stand the heat, get out of the kitchen
Harry S. Truman

pressurize 1. compress, condense, constrict, press, squash, squeeze **2.** breathe down someone's neck, browbeat, coerce, compel, dragoon, drive, force, intimidate, press-gang, put the screws on (*slang*), turn on the heat (*informal*), twist one's arm (*informal*)

prestige authority, bottom, Brownie points, cachet, celebrity, credit, distinction, eminence, esteem, fame, honour, importance, influence, kudos, regard, renown, reputation, standing, stature, status, weight

prestigious celebrated, eminent, esteemed, exalted, great, illustrious, important, imposing, impressive, influential, notable, prominent, renowned, reputable, respected
Antonyms humble, lowly, minor, obscure, unimportant, unimpressive, unknown

presumably apparently, doubtless, doubtlessly, in all likelihood, in all probability, it would seem, likely, most likely, on the face of it, probably, seemingly

presume 1. assume, believe, conjecture, guess (*informal, chiefly U.S. & Canad.*), infer, posit, postulate, presuppose, suppose, surmise, take for granted, take it, think **2.** dare, go so far, have the audacity, make bold, make so bold, take the liberty, undertake, venture **3.** bank on, count on, depend, rely, trust

Dr. Livingstone, I presume
Henry Morton Stanley

presumption 1. assurance, audacity, boldness, brass (*informal*), brass neck (*Brit. informal*), cheek (*informal*), chutzpah (*U.S. & Canad. informal*), effrontery, forwardness, front, gall (*informal*), impudence, insolence, neck (*informal*), nerve (*informal*), presumptuousness, sassiness (*U.S. informal*), temerity **2.** anticipation, assumption, belief, conjecture, guess, hypothesis, opinion, premiss, presupposition, supposition, surmise **3.** basis, chance, grounds, likelihood, plausibility, probability, reason

presumptive 1. assumed, believed, expected, hypothetical, inferred, supposed, understood **2.** believable, conceivable, credible, likely, plausible, possible, probable, reasonable, verisimilar

presumptuous arrogant, audacious, bigheaded (*informal*), bold, conceited, foolhardy, forward, insolent, overconfident, overfamiliar, overweening, presuming, pushy (*informal*), rash, too big for one's boots, uppish (*Brit. informal*)
Antonyms bashful, humble, modest, retiring, shy, timid, unassuming

presuppose accept, assume, consider, imply, posit, postulate, presume, suppose, take as read, take for granted, take it

presupposition assumption, belief, hypothesis, preconceived idea, preconception, premiss, presumption, supposition, theory

pretence 1. acting, charade, deceit, deception, fabrication, fakery, faking, falsehood, feigning, invention, make-believe, sham, simulation, subterfuge, trickery **2.** affectation, appearance, artifice, display, façade, hokum (*slang, chiefly U.S. & Canad.*), posing, posturing, pretentiousness, show, veneer **3.** claim, cloak, colour, cover, excuse, façade, garb, guise, mask, masquerade, pretext, ruse, semblance, show, veil, wile
Antonyms (*sense 1*) actuality, fact, reality (*sense 2*) candour, frankness, honesty, ingenuousness, openness

pretend 1. affect, allege, assume, counterfeit, dissemble, dissimulate, fake, falsify, feign, impersonate, make out, pass oneself off as, profess, put on, sham, simulate **2.** act, imagine, make believe, make up, play, play the part of, suppose **3.** allege, aspire, claim, lay claim, profess, purport

pretended alleged, avowed, bogus, counterfeit, fake, false, feigned, fictitious, imaginary, ostensible, phoney *or* phony (*informal*), pretend (*informal*), professed, pseudo (*informal*), purported, sham, so-called, spurious

pretender aspirant, claimant, claimer

pretension 1. aspiration, assertion, assumption, claim, demand, pretence, profession **2.** affectation, airs, conceit, hypocrisy, ostentation, pomposity, pretentiousness, self-importance, show, showiness, snobbery, snobbishness, vainglory, vanity

pretentious affected, assuming, bombastic, conceited, exaggerated, extravagant, flaunting, grandiloquent, grandiose, highfalutin (*informal*), high-flown, high-sounding, hollow, inflated, magniloquent, mannered, ostentatious, overambitious, pompous, puffed up, showy, snobbish, specious, vainglorious
Antonyms modest, natural, plain, simple, unaffected, unassuming, unpretentious

preternatural abnormal, anomalous, extraordinary, inexplicable, irregular, marvellous, miraculous, mysterious, odd, peculiar, strange, supernatural, unaccountable, unearthly, unnatural, unusual

pretext affectation, alleged reason, appearance, cloak, cover, device, excuse, guise, mask, ploy, pretence, red herring, ruse, semblance, show, simulation, veil

prettify adorn, deck out, decorate, doll up (*slang*), do up, embellish, garnish, gild, ornament, pretty up, tart up (*Brit. slang*), titivate, trick out, trim

pretty *adjective* **1.** appealing, attractive, beautiful, bonny, charming, comely, cute, fair, good-looking, graceful, lovely, personable **2.** bijou, dainty, delicate, elegant, fine, neat, nice, pleasing, tasteful, trim *~adverb* **3.** *informal* fairly, kind of (*informal*), moderately, quite, rather, reasonably, somewhat
Antonyms plain, ugly, unattractive, unshapely, unsightly

prevail **1.** be victorious, carry the day, gain mastery, overcome, overrule, prove superior, succeed, triumph, win **2.** abound, be current (prevalent, widespread), exist generally, obtain, predominate, preponderate **3.** *often with* **on** *or* **upon** bring round, convince, dispose, incline, induce, influence, persuade, prompt, sway, talk into, win over

prevailing **1.** common, current, customary, established, fashionable, general, in style, in vogue, ordinary, popular, prevalent, set, usual, widespread **2.** dominant, influential, main, operative, predominating, preponderating, principal, ruling

prevalence **1.** acceptance, commonness, common occurrence, currency, frequency, pervasiveness, popularity, profusion, regularity, ubiquity, universality **2.** ascendancy, hold, mastery, predominance, preponderance, primacy, rule, sway

prevalent **1.** accepted, common, commonplace, current, customary, established, everyday, extensive, frequent, general, habitual, popular, rampant, rife, ubiquitous, universal, usual, widespread **2.** ascendant, compelling, dominant, governing, powerful, predominant, prevailing, successful, superior
Antonyms (*sense 1*) confined, infrequent, limited, localized, rare, restricted, uncommon, unusual

prevaricate beat about the bush, beg the question, cavil, deceive, dodge, equivocate, evade, flannel (*Brit. informal*), give a false colour to, hedge, lie, palter, quibble, shift, shuffle, stretch the truth, tergiversate
Antonyms be blunt, be direct, be frank, be straightforward, come straight to the point, not beat about the bush

prevarication cavilling, deceit, deception, equivocation, evasion, falsehood, falsification, lie, misrepresentation, pretence, quibbling, tergiversation, untruth

prevaricator Ananias, deceiver, dissembler, dodger, equivocator, evader, fibber, hypocrite, liar, pettifogger, quibbler, sophist

prevent anticipate, avert, avoid, balk, bar, block, check, counteract, defend against, foil, forestall, frustrate, hamper, head off, hinder, impede, inhibit, intercept, nip in the bud, obstruct, obviate, preclude, restrain, stave off, stop, thwart, ward off
Antonyms allow, encourage, help, incite, permit, support, urge

prevention **1.** anticipation, avoidance, deterrence, elimination, forestalling, obviation, precaution, preclusion, prophylaxis, safeguard, thwarting **2.** bar, check, deterrence, frustration, hindrance, impediment, interruption, obstacle, obstruction, stoppage

Prevention is better than cure
Desiderius Erasmus *Adagia*

preventive, preventative *adjective* **1.** hampering, hindering, impeding, obstructive **2.** counteractive, deterrent, inhibitory, precautionary, prophylactic, protective, shielding *~noun* **3.** block, hindrance, impediment, obstacle, obstruction **4.** deterrent, neutralizer, prevention, prophylactic, protection, protective, remedy, safeguard, shield

preview **1.** *noun* advance showing, foretaste, sample, sampler, sneak preview, taster, trailer **2.** *verb* foretaste, sample, taste

previous **1.** antecedent, anterior, earlier, erstwhile, ex-, foregoing, former, one-time, past, preceding, prior, quondam, sometime **2.** *informal* ahead of oneself, precipitate, premature, too early, too soon, untimely
Antonyms (*sense 1*) consequent, following, later, subsequent, succeeding

previously at one time, a while ago, before, beforehand, earlier, formerly, heretofore, hitherto, in advance, in anticipation, in days *or* years gone by, in the past, once, then, until now

prey *noun* **1.** game, kill, quarry **2.** dupe, fall guy (*informal*), mark, mug (*Brit. slang*), target, victim *~verb* **3.** devour, eat, feed upon, hunt, live off, seize **4.** blackmail, bleed (*informal*), bully, exploit, intimidate, take advantage of, terrorize, victimize **5.** burden, distress, hang over, haunt, oppress, trouble, weigh down, weigh heavily, worry

price *noun* **1.** amount, asking price, assessment, bill, charge, cost, damage (*informal*), estimate, expenditure, expense, face value, fee, figure, outlay, payment, rate, valuation, value, worth **2.** consequences, cost, penalty, sacrifice, toll **3.** bounty, compensation, premium, recompense, reward **4. at any price** anyhow, cost what it may, expense no object, no matter what the cost, regardless, whatever the cost **5. beyond price** inestimable, invaluable, of incalculable value, precious, priceless, treasured, without price *~verb* **6.** assess, cost, estimate, evaluate, put a price on, rate, value

There's no such thing as a free lunch
Milton Friedman

You don't get something for nothing

priceless **1.** beyond price, cherished, costly, dear, expensive, incalculable, incomparable, inestimable, invaluable, irreplaceable, precious, prized, rare, rich, treasured, worth a king's ransom, worth one's *or* its weight in gold **2.** *informal* absurd, amusing, comic, droll, funny, hilarious, killing (*informal*), rib-tickling, ridiculous, riotous, side-splitting
Antonyms cheap, cheapo (*informal*), common, inexpensive, worthless

pricey, pricy costly, dear, exorbitant, expensive, extortionate, high-priced, over the odds (*Brit. informal*), steep (*informal*)

prick *verb* **1.** bore, impale, jab, lance, perforate, pierce, pink, punch, puncture, stab **2.** bite, itch, prickle, smart, sting, tingle **3.** cut, distress, grieve, move, pain, stab, touch, trouble, wound **4.** *usually with* **up** point, raise, rise, stand erect *~noun* **5.** cut, gash, hole, perforation, pinhole, puncture, wound **6.** gnawing, pang, prickle, smart, spasm, sting, twinge

prickle *noun* **1.** barb, needle, point, spike, spine, spur, thorn **2.** chill, formication, goose flesh, paraesthesia (*Medical*), pins and needles (*informal*), smart, tickle, tingle, tingling *~verb* **3.** itch, smart, sting, tingle, twitch **4.** jab, nick, prick, stick

prickly **1.** barbed, brambly, briery, bristly, spiny, thorny **2.** crawling, itchy, pricking, prickling, scratchy, sharp, smarting, stinging, tingling **3.** bad-tempered, cantankerous, edgy, fractious, grumpy, irritable, liverish, peevish, pettish, petulant, ratty (*Brit. & N.Z. informal*), shirty (*slang, chiefly Brit.*), snappish, stroppy (*Brit. slang*), tetchy, touchy, waspish **4.** complicated, difficult, intricate, involved, knotty, thorny, ticklish, tricky, troublesome, trying

pride *noun* **1.** *amour-propre*, dignity, honour, self-esteem, self-respect, self-worth **2.** arrogance, bigheadedness (*informal*), conceit, egotism, haughtiness, hauteur, hubris, loftiness, *morgue*, presumption, pretension, pretentiousness, self-importance, self-love, smugness, snobbery, superciliousness, vainglory, vanity **3.** boast, gem, jewel, pride and joy, prize, treasure **4.** delight, gratification, joy, pleasure, satisfaction **5.** best, choice, cream, elite, flower, glory, pick *~verb* **6.** be proud of, boast, brag, congratulate oneself, crow, exult, flatter oneself, glory in, pique, plume, preen, revel in, take pride, vaunt
Antonyms (*sense 1*) humility, meekness, modesty

Pride goeth before destruction, and a haughty spirit before a fall
Bible: Proverbs

And the Devil did grin, for his darling sin
Is pride that apes humility
Samuel Taylor Coleridge *The Devil's Thoughts*

priest churchman, clergyman, cleric, curate, divine, ecclesiastic, father, father confessor, holy man, man of God, man of the cloth, minister, padre (*informal*), pastor, vicar
Related adjective: hieratic

Once we had wooden chalices and golden priests, now we have golden chalices and wooden priests
Ralph Waldo Emerson *The Preacher*

In all the ages of the world, priests have been the enemy of liberty
David Hume *Essays Moral, Political, and Literary*

A priest,
A piece of mere church furniture at best
William Cowper *Tirocinium*

priestly canonical, clerical, ecclesiastic, hieratic, pastoral, priestlike, sacerdotal

prig goody-goody (*informal*), Holy Joe (*informal*), Holy Willie (*informal*), Mrs. Grundy, old maid (*informal*), pedant, prude, puritan, stuffed shirt (*informal*)

priggish goody-goody (*informal*), holier-than-thou, narrow-minded, pedantic, prim, prudish, puritanical, self-righteous, self-satisfied, smug, starchy (*informal*), stiff, stuffy

prim demure, fastidious, formal, fussy, niminy-piminy, old-maidish (*informal*), particular, precise, priggish, prissy (*informal*), proper, prudish, puritanical, schoolmarmish (*Brit. informal*), starchy (*informal*), stiff, strait-laced
Antonyms carefree, casual, easy-going, informal, laid-back, relaxed

primacy ascendancy, command, dominance, dominion, leadership, pre-eminence, superiority, supremacy

prima donna diva, leading lady, star

primal 1. earliest, first, initial, original, primary, prime, primitive, primordial, pristine 2. central, chief, first, greatest, highest, main, major, most important, paramount, prime, principal

primarily 1. above all, basically, chiefly, especially, essentially, for the most part, fundamentally, generally, largely, mainly, mostly, on the whole, principally 2. at first, at *or* from the start, first and foremost, initially, in the beginning, in the first place, originally

primary 1. best, capital, cardinal, chief, dominant, first, greatest, highest, leading, main, paramount, prime, principal, top 2. aboriginal, earliest, initial, original, primal, primeval, primitive, primordial, pristine 3. basic, beginning, bog-standard (*informal*), elemental, essential, fundamental, radical, ultimate, underlying 4. elementary, introductory, rudimentary, simple
Antonyms (*sense 1*) inferior, lesser, lowest, subordinate, supplementary, unimportant (*sense 4*) ensuing, following, later, secondary, subsequent, succeeding

prime *adjective* 1. best, capital, choice, excellent, first-class, first-rate, grade A, highest, quality, select, selected, superior, top 2. basic, bog-standard (*informal*), earliest, fundamental, original, primary, underlying 3. chief, leading, main, predominant, pre-eminent, primary, principal, ruling, senior ~*noun* 4. best days, bloom, flower, full flowering, height, heyday, maturity, peak, perfection, zenith 5. beginning, morning, opening, spring, start ~*verb* 6. break in, coach, fit, get ready, groom, make ready, prepare, train 7. brief, clue in (*informal*), clue up (*informal*), fill in (*informal*), gen up (*Brit. informal*), give someone the lowdown (*informal*), inform, notify, tell

primeval, primaeval ancient, earliest, early, first, old, original, prehistoric, primal, primitive, primordial, pristine

primitive 1. earliest, early, elementary, first, original, primary, primeval, primordial, pristine 2. barbarian, barbaric, crude, rough, rude, rudimentary, savage, simple, uncivilized, uncultivated, undeveloped, unrefined 3. childlike, naive, simple, undeveloped, unsophisticated, untrained, untutored
Antonyms (*sense 1*) advanced, later, modern (*sense 2*) civilized, comfortable, developed, elaborate, refined (*sense 3*) adult, developed, mature, sophisticated, trained, tutored

primordial 1. earliest, first, prehistoric, primal, primeval, primitive, pristine 2. basic, elemental, fundamental, original, radical

primp be in full fig (*slang*), deck out, doll up (*slang*), dress up, fig up (*slang*), gussy up (*slang*), prank, preen, prink, put on one's best bib and tucker (*informal*), put on one's gladrags (*slang*)

prince lord, monarch, potentate, ruler, sovereign

princely 1. bounteous, bountiful, generous, gracious, lavish, liberal, magnanimous, munificent, open-handed, rich 2. august, dignified, grand, high-born, imperial, imposing, lofty, magnificent, majestic, noble, regal, royal, sovereign, stately

principal *adjective* 1. capital, cardinal, chief, controlling, dominant, essential, first, foremost, highest, key, leading, main, most important, paramount, pre-eminent, primary, prime, strongest ~*noun* 2. boss (*informal*), chief, director, head, leader, master, ruler, superintendent 3. dean, director, head (*informal*), headmaster, headmistress, head teacher, master, rector 4. assets, capital, capital funds, money 5. first violin, lead, leader, star
Antonyms auxiliary, inferior, minor, subordinate, subsidiary, supplementary, weakest

principally above all, chiefly, especially, first and foremost, for the most part, in the main, largely, mainly, mostly, particularly, predominantly, primarily

principle 1. assumption, axiom, canon, criterion, dictum, doctrine, dogma, ethic, formula, fundamental, golden rule, law, maxim, moral law, precept, proposition, rule, standard, truth, verity 2. attitude, belief, code, credo, ethic, morality, opinion, tenet 3. conscience, integrity, morals, probity, rectitude, scruples, sense of duty, sense of honour, uprightness 4. **in principle** ideally, in essence, in theory, theoretically

> *The most useful thing about a principle is that it can always be sacrificed to expediency*
> W. Somerset Maugham *The Circle*

principled conscientious, correct, decent, ethical, high-minded, honourable, just, moral, righteous, right-minded, scrupulous, upright, virtuous

prink adorn, deck, doll up (*slang*), dress to kill (*informal*), dress up, dress (up) to the nines (*informal*), fig up (*slang*), groom, gussy up (*slang*), prank, preen, primp, titivate, trick out

print *verb* 1. engrave, go to press, impress, imprint, issue, mark, publish, put to bed (*informal*), run off, stamp ~*noun* 2. book, magazine, newspaper, newsprint, periodical, printed matter, publication, typescript 3. **in print a.** in black and white, on paper, on the streets, out, printed, published **b.** available, current, in the shops, obtainable, on the market, on the shelves 4. **out of print** no longer published, o.p., unavailable, unobtainable 5. copy, engraving, photo (*informal*), photograph, pic~

ture, reproduction **6.** characters, face, font (*chiefly U.S.*), fount, lettering, letters, type, typeface

prior **1.** aforementioned, antecedent, anterior, earlier, foregoing, former, preceding, pre-existent, pre-existing, previous **2.** **prior to** before, earlier than, preceding, previous to

priority first concern, greater importance, precedence, pre-eminence, preference, prerogative, rank, right of way, seniority, superiority, supremacy, the lead

priory abbey, cloister, convent, monastery, nunnery, religious house

prison calaboose (*U.S. informal*), can (*slang*), choky (*slang*), clink (*slang*), confinement, cooler (*slang*), dungeon, gaol, glasshouse (*Military informal*), jail, jug (*slang*), lockup, nick (*Brit. slang*), penal institution, penitentiary (*U.S.*), poky *or* pokey (*U.S. & Canad. slang*), pound, quod (*slang*), slammer (*slang*), stir (*slang*)

Stone walls do not a prison make,
Nor iron bars a cage
Richard Lovelace *To Althea, from Prison*

Prisons are built with stones of Law, brothels with bricks of Religion
William Blake *The Marriage of Heaven and Hell*

prisoner **1.** con (*slang*), convict, jailbird, lag (*slang*) **2.** captive, detainee, hostage, internee

prissy fastidious, finicky, fussy, niminy-piminy, old-maidish (*informal*), overnice, precious, prim, prim and proper, prudish, schoolmarmish (*Brit. informal*), squeamish, strait-laced

pristine **1.** earliest, first, former, initial, original, primal, primary, primeval, primitive, primordial **2.** immaculate, new, pure, uncorrupted, undefiled, unspoiled, unsullied, untouched, virgin, virginal

privacy **1.** isolation, privateness, retirement, retreat, seclusion, separateness, sequestration, solitude **2.** clandestineness, concealment, confidentiality, secrecy

One does not wash one's dirty linen in public

private *adjective* **1.** clandestine, closet, confidential, covert, hush-hush (*informal*), in camera, inside, off the record, privy (*archaic*), secret, unofficial **2.** exclusive, individual, intimate, own, particular, personal, reserved, special **3.** independent, nonpublic **4.** concealed, isolated, not overlooked, retired, secluded, secret, separate, sequestered, solitary, withdrawn **5.** **in private** behind closed doors, confidentially, in camera, in secret, personally, privately *~noun* **6.** enlisted man (*U.S.*), private soldier, squaddie *or* squaddy (*Brit. slang*), tommy (*Brit. informal*), Tommy Atkins (*Brit. informal*)

Antonyms (*sense 1*) disclosed, known, official, open, public, revealed (*sense 2*) common, general, open, public, unlimited, unrestricted (*sense 3*) bustling, busy, frequented, outgoing, sociable, unsecluded

privation destitution, distress, hardship, indigence, lack, loss, misery, necessity, need, neediness, penury, poverty, suffering, want

privilege advantage, benefit, birthright, claim, concession, due, entitlement, franchise, freedom, immunity, liberty, prerogative, right, sanction

privileged **1.** advantaged, elite, entitled, favoured, honoured, indulged, powerful, ruling, special **2.** allowed, empowered, exempt, free, granted, licensed, sanctioned, vested **3.** *of information* confidential, exceptional, inside, not for publication, off the record, privy, special

privy *adjective* **1.** *with* **to** apprised of, aware of, cognizant of, hip to (*slang*), informed, in on, in the know (*informal*), wise to (*slang*) **2.** *archaic* confidential, hidden, hush-hush (*informal*), off the record, personal, private, secret *~noun* **3.** bog (*slang*), closet, earth closet, latrine, lavatory, outside toilet, *pissoir*

prize[1] *noun* **1.** accolade, award, honour, premium, reward, trophy **2.** haul, jackpot, purse, stakes, windfall, winnings **3.** aim, ambition, conquest, desire, gain, goal, Holy Grail (*informal*), hope **4.** booty, capture, loot, pickings, pillage, plunder, spoil(s), trophy *~adjective* **5.** award-winning, best, champion, first-rate, outstanding, top, topnotch (*informal*), winning

prize[2] *verb* appreciate, cherish, esteem, hold dear, regard highly, set store by, treasure, value

prizefighter boxer, bruiser (*informal*), fighter, pug (*slang*), pugilist

prizefighting boxing, fighting, pugilism, the noble art *or* science, the prize ring, the ring

probability chance(s), expectation, liability, likelihood, likeliness, odds, presumption, prospect

probable apparent, credible, feasible, likely, most likely, odds-on, on the cards, ostensible, plausible, possible, presumable, presumed, reasonable, seeming, verisimilar

Antonyms doubtful, improbable, not likely, unlikely

probably as likely as not, doubtless, in all likelihood, in all probability, likely, maybe, most likely, perchance (*archaic*), perhaps, possibly, presumably

probation apprenticeship, examination, initiation, novitiate, test, trial, trial period

probe *verb* **1.** examine, explore, go into, investigate, look into, query, research, scrutinize, search, sift, sound, test, verify, work over **2.** explore, feel around, poke, prod *~noun* **3.** detection, examination, exploration, inquest, inquiry, investigation, research, scrutiny, study

probity equity, fairness, fidelity, goodness, honesty, honour, integrity, justice, morality, rectitude, righteousness, sincerity, trustworthiness, truthfulness, uprightness, virtue, worth

problem *noun* **1.** can of worms (*informal*), complication, difficulty, dilemma, disagreement, dispute, disputed point, doubt, Gordian knot, hard nut to crack (*informal*), how-do-you-do (*informal*), point at issue, predicament, quandary, trouble **2.** brain-teaser (*informal*), conundrum, enigma, poser, puzzle, question, riddle, teaser *~adjective* **3.** delinquent, difficult, intractable, uncontrollable, unmanageable, unruly

A problem shared is a problem halved

problematic chancy (*informal*), debatable, doubtful, dubious, enigmatic, moot, open to doubt, problematical, puzzling, questionable, tricky, uncertain, unsettled
Antonyms beyond question, certain, clear, definite, indisputable, settled, undebatable, unquestionable

procedure action, conduct, course, custom, form, formula, method, modus operandi, operation, performance, plan of action, policy, practice, process, routine, scheme, step, strategy, system, transaction

proceed **1.** advance, carry on, continue, get going, get on with, get under way with, go ahead, go on, make a start, move on, press on, progress, set in motion **2.** arise, come, derive, emanate, ensue, flow, follow, issue, originate, result, spring, stem
Antonyms (*sense 1*) break off, cease, discontinue, end, get behind, halt, leave off, pack in (*Brit. informal*), retreat, stop

proceeding **1.** act, action, course of action, deed, measure, move, occurrence, procedure, process, step, undertaking, venture **2.** *plural* account, affairs, annals, archives, business, dealings, doings, matters, minutes, records, report, transactions

proceeds earnings, gain, income, produce, products, profit, receipts, returns, revenue, takings, yield

process *noun* **1.** action, course, course of action, manner, means, measure, method, mode, operation, performance, practice, procedure, proceeding, system, transaction **2.** advance, course, development, evolution, formation, growth, movement, progress, progression, stage, step, unfolding **3.** *Law* action, case, suit, trial *~verb* **4.** deal with, dispose of, fulfil, handle, take care of **5.** alter, convert, prepare, refine, transform, treat

procession **1.** cavalcade, column, cortege, file, march, motorcade, parade, train **2.** course, cycle, run, sequence, series, string, succession, train

proclaim advertise, affirm, announce, blaze (abroad), blazon (abroad), circulate, declare, enunciate, give out, herald, indicate, make known, profess, promulgate, publish, shout from the housetops (*informal*), show, trumpet
Antonyms conceal, hush up, keep back, keep secret, suppress, withhold

proclamation announcement, declaration, decree, edict, manifesto, notice, notification, promulgation, pronouncement, pronunciamento, publication

proclivity bent, bias, disposition, facility, inclination, leaning, liableness, penchant, predilection, predisposition, proneness, propensity, tendency, weakness

procrastinate adjourn, be dilatory, dally, defer, delay, drag one's feet (*informal*), gain time, play a waiting game, play for time, postpone, prolong, protract, put off, retard, stall, temporize
Antonyms advance, expedite, get on with, hasten, hurry (up), proceed, speed up

procrastination delay, dilatoriness, hesitation, slackness, slowness, temporization *or* temporisation

Procrastination is the thief of time
Edward Young *The Complaint: Night Thoughts*

Never put off till tomorrow what you can do today
Lord Chesterfield *letter to his son*

procrastination is the
art of keeping
up with yesterday
Don Marquis *archy and mehitabel*

procreate beget, breed, bring into being, engender, father, generate, mother, produce, propagate, reproduce, sire

procure acquire, appropriate, buy, come by, earn, effect, find, gain, get, get hold of, land, lay hands on, manage to get, obtain, pick up, purchase, score (*slang*), secure, win

procurer bawd (*archaic*), madam, pander, panderer, pimp, procuress, white-slaver, whoremaster (*archaic*)

prod *verb* **1.** dig, drive, elbow, jab, nudge, poke, prick, propel, push, shove **2.** egg on, goad, impel, incite, motivate, move, prompt, put a bomb under (*informal*), rouse, spur, stimulate, stir up, urge *~noun* **3.** boost, dig, elbow, jab, nudge, poke, push, shove **4.** goad, poker, spur, stick **5.** boost, cue, prompt, reminder, signal, stimulus

prodigal *adjective* **1.** excessive, extravagant, immoderate, improvident, intemperate, profligate, reckless, spendthrift, squandering, wanton, wasteful **2.** bounteous, bountiful, copious, exuberant, lavish, luxuriant, profuse, sumptuous, superabundant, teeming *~noun* **3.**

big spender, profligate, spendthrift, squanderer, wastrel
Antonyms (*sense 1*) economical, frugal, miserly, parsimonious, sparing, stingy, thrifty, tight (*sense 2*) deficient, lacking, meagre, scanty, scarce, short, sparse

prodigality 1. abandon, dissipation, excess, extravagance, immoderation, intemperance, profligacy, recklessness, squandering, wantonness, waste, wastefulness 2. abundance, amplitude, bounteousness, bounty, copiousness, cornucopia, exuberance, horn of plenty, lavishness, luxuriance, plenteousness, plenty, profusion, richness, sumptuousness

prodigious 1. colossal, enormous, giant, gigantic, huge, immeasurable, immense, inordinate, mammoth, massive, monstrous, monumental, stellar (*informal*), stupendous, tremendous, vast 2. abnormal, amazing, astounding, dramatic, exceptional, extraordinary, fabulous, fantastic (*informal*), flabbergasting (*informal*), impressive, marvellous, miraculous, phenomenal, remarkable, staggering, startling, striking, stupendous, unusual, wonderful
Antonyms negligible, normal, ordinary, small, tiny, unexceptional, unimpressive, unremarkable, usual

prodigy 1. brainbox, child genius, genius, mastermind, talent, whiz (*informal*), whiz kid (*informal*), wizard, wonder child, wunderkind 2. marvel, miracle, one in a million, phenomenon, rare bird (*informal*), sensation, wonder 3. abnormality, curiosity, freak, grotesque, monster, monstrosity, mutation, spectacle

produce *verb* 1. compose, construct, create, develop, fabricate, invent, make, manufacture, originate, put together, turn out 2. afford, bear, beget, breed, bring forth, deliver, engender, furnish, give, render, supply, yield 3. bring about, cause, effect, generate, give rise to, make for, occasion, provoke, set off 4. advance, bring forward, bring to light, demonstrate, exhibit, offer, present, put forward, set forth, show 5. direct, do, exhibit, mount, present, put before the public, put on, show, stage 6. *Geometry* extend, lengthen, prolong, protract *~noun* 7. crop, fruit and vegetables, greengrocery, harvest, product, yield

producer 1. director, impresario, *régisseur* 2. farmer, grower, maker, manufacturer

> *There'd be a great improvement if they shot less film and more producers*
>
> Samuel Goldwyn

product 1. artefact, commodity, concoction, creation, goods, invention, merchandise, produce, production, work 2. consequence, effect, end result, fruit, issue, legacy, offshoot, outcome, result, returns, spin-off, upshot, yield

production 1. assembly, construction, creation, fabrication, formation, making, manufacture, manufacturing, origination, preparation, producing 2. direction, management, presentation, staging

productive 1. creative, dynamic, energetic, fecund, fertile, fruitful, generative, inventive, plentiful, producing, prolific, rich, teeming, vigorous 2. advantageous, beneficial, constructive, effective, fruitful, gainful, gratifying, profitable, rewarding, useful, valuable, worthwhile
Antonyms barren, poor, sterile, unfertile, unfruitful, unproductive, unprofitable, useless

productivity abundance, mass production, output, production, productive capacity, productiveness, work rate, yield

profane *adjective* 1. disrespectful, godless, heathen, idolatrous, impious, impure, irreligious, irreverent, pagan, sacrilegious, sinful, ungodly, wicked 2. lay, secular, temporal, unconsecrated, unhallowed, unholy, unsanctified, worldly 3. abusive, blasphemous, coarse, crude, filthy, foul, obscene, vulgar *~verb* 4. abuse, commit sacrilege, contaminate, debase, defile, desecrate, misuse, pervert, pollute, prostitute, violate, vitiate
Antonyms clean, decorous, holy, proper, religious, respectful, reverent, sacred, spiritual

profanity abuse, blasphemy, curse, cursing, execration, foul language, four-letter word, impiety, imprecation, irreverence, malediction, obscenity, profaneness, sacrilege, swearing, swearword

profess 1. acknowledge, admit, affirm, announce, assert, asseverate, aver, avow, certify, confess, confirm, declare, maintain, own, proclaim, state, vouch 2. act as if, allege, call oneself, claim, dissemble, fake, feign, let on, make out, pretend, purport, sham

professed 1. avowed, certified, confirmed, declared, proclaimed, self-acknowledged, self-confessed 2. alleged, apparent, ostensible, pretended, purported, self-styled, so-called, *soi-disant*, supposed, would-be

professedly 1. allegedly, apparently, by one's own account, falsely, ostensibly, purportedly, supposedly, under the pretext of 2. admittedly, avowedly, by open declaration, confessedly

profession 1. business, calling, career, employment, line, line of work, métier, occupation, office, position, sphere, vocation, walk of life 2. acknowledgment, affirmation, assertion, attestation, avowal, claim, confession, declaration, statement, testimony, vow

professional 1. *adjective* ace (*informal*), adept, competent, crack (*slang*), efficient, experienced, expert, finished, masterly, polished, practised, proficient, qualified, skilled, slick,

trained **2.** *noun* adept, authority, buff (*informal*), dab hand (*Brit. informal*), expert, hotshot (*informal*), maestro, master, maven (*U.S.*), past master, pro (*informal*), specialist, virtuoso, whiz (*informal*), wizard
Antonyms amateurish, incapable, incompetent, inefficient, inept, inexperienced, unpolished, unqualified, unskilled, untrained

professor don (*Brit.*), fellow (*Brit.*), head of faculty, prof (*informal*)

> *A professor is one who talks in someone else's sleep*
>
> W.H. Auden

proffer extend, hand, hold out, offer, present, propose, propound, submit, suggest, tender, volunteer

proficiency ability, accomplishment, aptitude, competence, craft, dexterity, expertise, expertness, facility, knack, know-how (*informal*), mastery, skilfulness, skill, talent

proficient able, accomplished, adept, apt, capable, clever, competent, conversant, efficient, experienced, expert, gifted, masterly, qualified, skilful, skilled, talented, trained, versed
Antonyms bad, incapable, incompetent, inept, unaccomplished, unskilled

profile *noun* **1.** contour, drawing, figure, form, outline, portrait, shape, side view, silhouette, sketch **2.** biography, characterization, character sketch, sketch, thumbnail sketch, vignette **3.** analysis, chart, diagram, examination, graph, review, study, survey, table

profit *noun* **1.** *often plural* boot (*dialect*), bottom line, earnings, emoluments, gain, percentage (*informal*), proceeds, receipts, return, revenue, surplus, takings, winnings, yield **2.** advancement, advantage, avail, benefit, gain, good, interest, mileage (*informal*), use, value ~*verb* **3.** aid, avail, benefit, be of advantage to, better, contribute, gain, help, improve, promote, serve, stand in good stead **4.** capitalize on, cash in on (*informal*), exploit, learn from, make capital of, make good use of, make the most of, put to good use, rake in (*informal*), reap the benefit of, take advantage of, turn to advantage *or* account, use, utilize **5.** clean up (*informal*), clear, earn, gain, make a good thing of (*informal*), make a killing (*informal*), make money

profitable **1.** commercial, cost-effective, fruitful, gainful, lucrative, money-making, paying, remunerative, rewarding, worthwhile **2.** advantageous, beneficial, economic, expedient, fruitful, productive, rewarding, serviceable, useful, valuable, worthwhile
Antonyms disadvantageous, fruitless, unremunerative, unrewarding, useless, vain, worthless

profiteer **1.** *noun* exploiter, racketeer **2.** *verb* exploit, fleece, make a quick buck (*slang*), make someone pay through the nose, overcharge, racketeer, skin (*slang*), sting (*informal*)

profitless basket case, bootless, fruitless, futile, idle, ineffective, ineffectual, pointless, thankless, to no purpose, unavailing, unproductive, unprofitable, unremunerative, useless, vain, worthless

profligacy **1.** abandon, corruption, debauchery, degeneracy, depravity, dissipation, dissoluteness, dolce vita, immorality, laxity, libertinism, licentiousness, promiscuity, unrestraint, wantonness **2.** excess, extravagance, improvidence, lavishness, prodigality, recklessness, squandering, waste, wastefulness

profligate *adjective* **1.** abandoned, corrupt, debauched, degenerate, depraved, dissipated, dissolute, immoral, iniquitous, libertine, licentious, loose, promiscuous, shameless, sink, unprincipled, vicious, vitiated, wanton, wicked, wild **2.** extravagant, immoderate, improvident, prodigal, reckless, spendthrift, squandering, wasteful ~*noun* **3.** debauchee, degenerate, dissipater, libertine, rake, reprobate, roué **4.** prodigal, spendthrift, squanderer, waster, wastrel
Antonyms (*sense 1*) chaste, decent, moral, principled, pure, upright, virginal, virtuous

profound **1.** abstruse, deep, discerning, erudite, learned, penetrating, philosophical, recondite, sagacious, sage, serious, skilled, subtle, thoughtful, weighty, wise **2.** abysmal, bottomless, cavernous, deep, fathomless, yawning **3.** abject, acute, deeply felt, extreme, great, heartfelt, heartrending, hearty, intense, keen, sincere **4.** absolute, complete, consummate, exhaustive, extensive, extreme, far-reaching, intense, out-and-out, pronounced, serious (*informal*), thoroughgoing, total, unqualified, utter
Antonyms imprudent, insincere, shallow, slight, stupid, superficial, thoughtless, uneducated, uninformed, unknowledgeable, unwise

profoundly abjectly, acutely, deeply, extremely, from the bottom of one's heart, greatly, heartily, intensely, keenly, seriously, sincerely, thoroughly, to the core, to the nth degree, very

profundity **1.** acuity, acumen, depth, erudition, insight, intelligence, learning, penetration, perceptiveness, perspicacity, perspicuity, sagacity, wisdom **2.** depth, extremity, intensity, seriousness, severity, strength

profuse **1.** abundant, ample, bountiful, copious, luxuriant, overflowing, plentiful, prolific, teeming **2.** excessive, extravagant, exuberant, fulsome, generous, immoderate, lavish, liberal, open-handed, prodigal, unstinting

Antonyms (*sense 1*) deficient, inadequate, meagre, scanty, scarce, skimpy, sparse (*sense 2*) frugal, illiberal, moderate, provident, thrifty

profusion abundance, bounty, copiousness, cornucopia, excess, extravagance, exuberance, glut, lavishness, luxuriance, multitude, over~supply, plenitude, plethora, prodigality, quan~tity, riot, superabundance, superfluity, sur~plus, wealth

progenitor 1. ancestor, begetter, forebear, forefather, parent, primogenitor, procreator **2.** antecedent, forerunner, instigator, originator, precursor, predecessor, source

progeny breed, children, descendants, family, issue, lineage, offspring, posterity, race, sci~ons, seed (*chiefly biblical*), stock, young

prognosis diagnosis, expectation, forecast, prediction, prognostication, projection, specu~lation, surmise

prognostic 1. *adjective* diagnostic, foretelling, indicating, predicting, predictive, prophetic **2.** *noun* forecast, indication, omen, portent, preindication, sign, symptom, warning

prognosticate 1. divine, forecast, foretell, pre~dict, presage, prophesy, soothsay, vaticinate (*rare*) **2.** augur, betoken, forebode, foreshadow, harbinger, herald, point to, portend, presage

prognostication expectation, forecast, predic~tion, prognosis, projection, prophecy, specula~tion, surmise

programme *noun* **1.** agenda, curriculum, line-up, list, listing, list of players, order of events, order of the day, plan, schedule, syllabus, timetable **2.** broadcast, performance, presen~tation, production, show **3.** design, order of the day, plan, plan of action, procedure, proj~ect, scheme *~verb* **4.** arrange, bill, book, de~sign, engage, formulate, itemize, lay on, line up, list, map out, plan, prearrange, schedule, work out

progress *noun* **1.** advance, course, movement, onward course, passage, progression, way **2.** advance, advancement, amelioration, better~ment, breakthrough, development, gain, gain~ing ground, growth, headway, improvement, increase, progression, promotion, step forward **3. in progress** being done, going on, happen~ing, occurring, proceeding, taking place, under way *~verb* **4.** advance, come on, continue, cov~er ground, forge ahead, gain ground, gather way, get on, go forward, make headway, make inroads (into), make one's way, make strides, move on, proceed, travel **5.** advance, amelio~rate, better, blossom, develop, gain, grow, im~prove, increase, mature
Antonyms *noun* decline, failure, recession, regression, relapse, retrogression *~verb* de~crease, get behind, lose, lose ground, recede, regress, retrogress

Printing, gunpowder, and the magnet... these three have changed the whole face and state of things throughout the world
Francis Bacon *Essays*

What we call 'progress' is the exchange of one nuisance for another nuisance
Havelock Ellis *Impressions and Comments*

Is it progress if a cannibal uses a knife and fork?
Stanislaw Lec *Unkempt Thoughts*

You can't say civilization don't advance, however, for in every war they kill you in a new way
Will Rogers

That's one small step for a man, one giant leap for mankind
Neil Armstrong

one step at a time

progression 1. advance, advancement, further~ance, gain, headway, movement forward, pro~gress **2.** chain, course, cycle, order, sequence, series, string, succession

progressive 1. accelerating, advancing, con~tinuing, continuous, developing, escalating, growing, increasing, intensifying, ongoing **2.** advanced, avant-garde, dynamic, enlightened, enterprising, forward-looking, go-ahead, liber~al, modern, radical, reformist, revolutionary, up-and-coming

prohibit 1. ban, debar, disallow, forbid, inter~dict, outlaw, proscribe, veto **2.** constrain, hamper, hinder, impede, make impossible, obstruct, preclude, prevent, restrict, rule out, stop
Antonyms allow, authorize, command, con~sent to, endure, further, give leave, let, li~cense, order, permit, suffer, tolerate

prohibited banned, barred, forbidden, not al~lowed, off limits, proscribed, taboo, *verboten*, vetoed

prohibition 1. constraint, disqualification, ex~clusion, forbiddance, interdiction, negation, obstruction, prevention, restriction **2.** ban, bar, boycott, disallowance, embargo, injunction, interdict, proscription, veto

prohibitive 1. forbidding, prohibiting, proscrip~tive, repressive, restraining, restrictive, sup~pressive **2.** *especially of prices* beyond one's means, excessive, exorbitant, extortionate, high-priced, preposterous, sky-high, steep (*in~formal*)

project *noun* **1.** activity, assignment, design, enterprise, job, occupation, plan, programme, proposal, scheme, task, undertaking, venture, work *~verb* **2.** contemplate, contrive, design, devise, draft, frame, map out, outline, plan, propose, purpose, scheme **3.** cast, discharge, fling, hurl, launch, make carry, propel, shoot, throw, transmit **4.** beetle, bulge, extend, jut, overhang, protrude, stand out, stick out **5.** calculate, estimate, extrapolate, forecast, gauge, predetermine, predict, reckon

projectile bullet, missile, rocket, shell

projection **1.** bulge, eaves, jut, ledge, overhang, protrusion, protuberance, ridge, shelf, sill **2.** blueprint, diagram, map, outline, plan, representation **3.** calculation, computation, estimate, estimation, extrapolation, forecast, prediction, reckoning

proletarian **1.** *adjective* cloth-cap (*informal*), common, plebeian, working-class **2.** *noun* commoner, Joe Bloggs (*Brit. informal*), man of the people, pleb, plebeian, prole (*derogatory slang, chiefly Brit.*), worker

proletariat commonalty, commoners, hoi polloi, labouring classes, lower classes, lower orders, plebs, proles (*derogatory slang chiefly Brit.*), the common people, the great unwashed (*informal & derogatory*), the herd, the masses, the rabble, wage-earners, working class
Antonyms aristo (*informal*), aristocracy, gentry, nobility, peerage, ruling class, upper class, upper crust (*informal*)

proliferate breed, burgeon, escalate, expand, grow rapidly, increase, multiply, mushroom, run riot, snowball

proliferation build-up, concentration, escalation, expansion, extension, increase, intensification, multiplication, spread, step-up (*informal*)

prolific abundant, bountiful, copious, fecund, fertile, fruitful, generative, luxuriant, productive, profuse, rank, rich, teeming
Antonyms barren, fruitless, infertile, sterile, unfruitful, unproductive, unprolific

prolix boring, diffuse, digressive, discursive, dragged out, full of verbiage, lengthy, long, long-drawn-out, long-winded, prolonged, protracted, rambling, spun out, tedious, tiresome, verbose, wordy

prolixity boringness, circuity, diffuseness, discursiveness, long-windedness, maundering, pleonasm, rambling, redundancy, tautology, tediousness, verbiage, verboseness, verbosity, wandering, wordiness

prologue exordium, foreword, introduction, preamble, preface, preliminary, prelude, proem

prolong carry on, continue, delay, drag out, draw out, extend, lengthen, make longer, perpetuate, protract, spin out, stretch
Antonyms abbreviate, abridge, curtail, cut, cut down, shorten, summarize

promenade *noun* **1.** boulevard, esplanade, parade, prom, public walk, walkway **2.** airing, constitutional, saunter, stroll, turn, walk ~*verb* **3.** perambulate, saunter, stretch one's legs, stroll, take a walk, walk **4.** flaunt, parade, strut, swagger

prominence **1.** cliff, crag, crest, elevation, headland, height, high point, hummock, mound, pinnacle, projection, promontory, rise, rising ground, spur **2.** bulge, jutting, projection, protrusion, protuberance, swelling **3.** conspicuousness, markedness, outstandingness, precedence, salience, specialness, top billing, weight **4.** celebrity, distinction, eminence, fame, greatness, importance, name, notability, pre-eminence, prestige, rank, reputation, standing

prominent **1.** bulging, hanging over, jutting, projecting, protruding, protrusive, protuberant, standing out **2.** blatant, conspicuous, easily seen, eye-catching, in the foreground, noticeable, obtrusive, obvious, outstanding, pronounced, remarkable, salient, striking, to the fore, unmistakable **3.** big-time (*informal*), celebrated, chief, distinguished, eminent, famous, foremost, important, leading, main, major league (*informal*), notable, noted, outstanding, popular, pre-eminent, renowned, respected, top, well-known, well-thought-of
Antonyms (*sense 1*) concave, indented, receding (*sense 2*) inconspicuous, indistinct, insignificant, unnoticeable (*sense 3*) insignificant, minor, secondary, undistinguished, unimportant, unknown, unnotable

promiscuity abandon, amorality, debauchery, depravity, dissipation, immorality, incontinence, laxity, laxness, lechery, libertinism, licentiousness, looseness, permissiveness, profligacy, promiscuousness, sleeping around (*informal*), wantonness

> *She speaks eighteen languages. And she can't say no in any of them*
>
> Dorothy Parker

> *You were born with your legs apart. They'll send you to the grave in a Y-shaped coffin*
>
> Joe Orton *What the Butler Saw*

promiscuous **1.** abandoned, debauched, dissipated, dissolute, fast, immoral, lax, libertine, licentious, loose, of easy virtue, profligate, unbridled, unchaste, wanton, wild **2.** chaotic, confused, disordered, diverse, heterogeneous, ill-assorted, indiscriminate, intermingled, intermixed, jumbled, mingled, miscellaneous, mixed, motley **3.** careless, casual, haphazard, heedless, indifferent, indiscriminate, irregular, irresponsible, random, slovenly, uncontrolled, uncritical, undiscriminating, unfastidious, unselective
Antonyms (*sense 1*) chaste, decent, innocent, modest, moral, pure, undefiled, unsullied, vestal, virginal, virtuous (*sense 2*) homogeneous, identical, neat, ordered, orderly, organized, shipshape, uniform, unmixed (*sense*

3) careful, critical, discriminating, fastidious, responsible, selective

promise *verb* **1.** assure, contract, cross one's heart, engage, give an undertaking, give one's word, guarantee, pledge, plight, stipulate, swear, take an oath, undertake, vouch, vow, warrant **2.** augur, bespeak, betoken, bid fair, denote, give hope of, hint at, hold a probability, hold out hopes of, indicate, lead one to expect, look like, seem likely to, show signs of, suggest *~noun* **3.** assurance, bond, commitment, compact, covenant, engagement, guarantee, oath, pledge, undertaking, vow, word, word of honour **4.** ability, aptitude, capability, capacity, flair, potential, talent

Whom the gods wish to destroy they first call promising
Cyril Connolly *Enemies of Promise*

Promises and pie-crust are made to be broken
Jonathan Swift *Polite Conversation*

promising **1.** auspicious, bright, encouraging, favourable, full of promise, hopeful, likely, propitious, reassuring, rosy **2.** able, gifted, likely, rising, talented, up-and-coming
Antonyms *(sense 1)* discouraging, unauspicious, unfavourable, unpromising

promontory cape, foreland, head, headland, ness *(archaic)*, point, spur

promote **1.** advance, aid, assist, back, boost, contribute to, develop, encourage, forward, foster, further, help, nurture, stimulate, support **2.** aggrandize, dignify, elevate, exalt, honour, kick upstairs *(informal)*, prefer, raise, upgrade **3.** advocate, call attention to, champion, endorse, espouse, popularize, prescribe, push for, recommend, speak for, sponsor, support, urge, work for **4.** advertise, beat the drum for *(informal)*, hype, plug *(informal)*, publicize, puff, push, sell
Antonyms *(sense 1)* discourage, hinder, hold back, impede, obstruct, oppose, prevent *(sense 2)* demote, downgrade, lower *or* reduce in rank

promoter **1.** advocate, campaigner, champion, helper, mainstay, proponent, stalwart, supporter, upholder **2.** arranger, entrepreneur, impresario, matchmaker, organizer

promotion **1.** advancement, aggrandizement, elevation, ennoblement, exaltation, honour, move up, preferment, rise, upgrading **2.** advancement, advocacy, backing, boosting, cultivation, development, encouragement, espousal, furtherance, progress, support **3.** advertising, advertising campaign, ballyhoo *(informal)*, hard sell, hype, media hype, plugging *(informal)*, propaganda, publicity, puffery *(informal)*, pushing

prompt *adjective* **1.** early, immediate, instant, instantaneous, on time, pdq *(slang)*, punctual, quick, rapid, speedy, swift, timely, unhesitating **2.** alert, brisk, eager, efficient, expeditious, quick, ready, responsive, smart, willing *~adverb* **3.** *informal* exactly, on the dot, promptly, punctually, sharp *~verb* **4.** cause, impel, incite, induce, inspire, instigate, motivate, move, provoke, spur, stimulate, urge **5.** assist, cue, help out, jog the memory, prod, refresh the memory, remind **6.** call forth, cause, elicit, evoke, give rise to, occasion, provoke *~noun* **7.** cue, help, hint, jog, jolt, prod, reminder, spur, stimulus
Antonyms *adjective* hesitating, inactive, inattentive, inefficient, late, remiss, slack, slow, tardy, unresponsive *~verb* deter, discourage, prevent, restrain, talk out of

prompter **1.** autocue, idiot board *(slang)*, Teleprompter *(Trademark)* **2.** agitator, catalyst, gadfly, inspirer, instigator, moving spirit, prime mover

prompting assistance, clarion call, encouragement, hint, incitement, influence, jogging, persuasion, pressing, pressure, prodding, pushing, reminder, reminding, suggestion, urging

promptly at once, by return, directly, hotfoot, immediately, instantly, on the dot, on time, pdq *(slang)*, posthaste, pronto *(informal)*, punctually, quickly, speedily, swiftly, unhesitatingly

promptness alacrity, alertness, briskness, dispatch, eagerness, haste, promptitude, punctuality, quickness, readiness, speed, swiftness, willingness

promulgate advertise, announce, broadcast, circulate, communicate, declare, decree, disseminate, issue, make known, make public, notify, proclaim, promote, publish, spread

prone **1.** face down, flat, horizontal, lying down, procumbent, prostrate, recumbent, supine **2.** apt, bent, disposed, given, inclined, liable, likely, predisposed, subject, susceptible, tending
Antonyms *(sense 1)* erect, face up, perpendicular, supine, upright, vertical *(sense 2)* averse, disinclined, indisposed, not likely, unlikely

proneness bent, bias, disposition, inclination, leaning, liability, partiality, proclivity, propensity, susceptibility, tendency, weakness

prong point, projection, spike, tine, tip

pronounce **1.** accent, articulate, enunciate, say, sound, speak, stress, utter, vocalize, voice **2.** affirm, announce, assert, declare, decree, deliver, judge, proclaim

pronounced broad, clear, conspicuous, decided, definite, distinct, evident, marked, noticeable, obvious, salient, striking, strong, unmistakable

Antonyms concealed, hidden, imperceptible, inconspicuous, unapparent, unnoticeable, vague

pronouncement announcement, declaration, decree, dictum, edict, judgment, manifesto, notification, proclamation, promulgation, pronunciamento, statement

pronunciation accent, accentuation, articulation, diction, elocution, enunciation, inflection, intonation, speech, stress

proof *noun* **1.** attestation, authentication, certification, confirmation, corroboration, demonstration, evidence, substantiation, testimony, verification **2.** *As in* **put to the proof** assay, examination, experiment, ordeal, scrutiny, test, trial **3.** *Printing* galley, galley proof, page proof, pull, slip, trial impression, trial print *~adjective* **4.** impenetrable, impervious, repellent, resistant, strong, tight, treated **5. be proof against** hold out against, resist, stand firm against, stand up to, withstand

The proof of the pudding is in the eating

prop *verb* **1.** bolster, brace, buttress, hold up, maintain, shore, stay, support, sustain, truss, uphold **2.** lean, rest, set, stand *~noun* **3.** brace, buttress, mainstay, stanchion, stay, support, truss

propaganda advertising, agitprop, ballyhoo (*informal*), brainwashing, disinformation, hype, information, newspeak, promotion, publicity

propagandist advocate, evangelist, indoctrinator, pamphleteer, promoter, proponent, proselytizer, publicist

propagandize brainwash, convince, indoctrinate, instil, persuade, proselytize

propagate **1.** beget, breed, engender, generate, increase, multiply, procreate, produce, proliferate, reproduce **2.** broadcast, circulate, diffuse, disseminate, make known, proclaim, promote, promulgate, publicize, publish, spread, transmit

Antonyms (*sense 2*) cover up, hide, hush up, keep under wraps, stifle, suppress, withhold

propagation **1.** breeding, generation, increase, multiplication, procreation, proliferation, reproduction **2.** circulation, communication, diffusion, dissemination, distribution, promotion, promulgation, spread, spreading, transmission

propel drive, force, impel, launch, push, send, set in motion, shoot, shove, start, thrust

Antonyms check, delay, hold back, pull, slow, stop

propensity aptness, bent, bias, disposition, inclination, leaning, liability, penchant, predisposition, proclivity, proneness, susceptibility, tendency, weakness

proper **1.** appropriate, apt, becoming, befitting, fit, fitting, legitimate, meet (*archaic*), right, suitable, suited **2.** *comme il faut*, decent, decorous, *de rigueur*, genteel, gentlemanly, ladylike, mannerly, polite, punctilious, refined, respectable, seemly **3.** accepted, accurate, conventional, correct, established, exact, formal, kosher (*informal*), orthodox, precise, right **4.** characteristic, individual, own, particular, peculiar, personal, respective, special, specific

Antonyms (*senses 1, 2, & 3*) coarse, common, crude, discourteous, impolite, improper, inappropriate, indecent, rude, unbecoming, unconventional, ungentlemanly, unladylike, unorthodox, unrefined, unseemly, unsuitable, wrong

properly **1.** appropriately, aptly, deservedly, fittingly, legitimately, rightly, suitably **2.** decently, decorously, ethically, politely, punctiliously, respectably, respectfully **3.** accurately, as intended, correctly, in the accepted *or* approved manner, in the true sense

Antonyms (*sense 1*) improperly, inappropriately, inaptly, unfittingly, unsuitably, wrongly (*sense 2*) badly, disrespectfully, impolitely, improperly, indecently, indecorously, unethically (*sense 3*) improperly, inaccurately, incorrectly, wrongly

property **1.** assets, belongings, building(s), capital, chattels, effects, estate, goods, holdings, house(s), means, possessions, resources, riches, wealth **2.** acres, estate, freehold, holding, land, real estate, real property, realty, title **3.** ability, attribute, characteristic, feature, hallmark, idiosyncrasy, mark, peculiarity, quality, trait, virtue

Property is theft

Pierre-Joseph Proudhon *Qu'est-ce que la Propriété?*

prophecy augury, divination, forecast, foretelling, prediction, prognosis, prognostication, revelation, second sight, soothsaying, sortilege, vaticination (*rare*)

prophesy augur, divine, forecast, foresee, foretell, forewarn, predict, presage, prognosticate, soothsay, vaticinate (*rare*)

prophet augur, Cassandra, clairvoyant, diviner, forecaster, oracle, prognosticator, prophesier, seer, sibyl, soothsayer

A prophet is not without honour, but in his own country

Bible: St. Mark

prophetic augural, divinatory, fatidic (*rare*), foreshadowing, mantic, oracular, predictive, presaging, prescient, prognostic, sibylline, vatic (*rare*)

propinquity **1.** adjacency, closeness, contiguity, nearness, neighbourhood, proximity, vicinity **2.** affiliation, affinity, blood, connection, consanguinity, kindred, kinship, relation, relationship, tie, ties of blood

propitiate appease, conciliate, make peace, mollify, pacify, placate, reconcile, satisfy

propitiation appeasement, conciliation, mollification, peacemaking, placation, reconciliation

propitiatory appeasing, assuaging, conciliatory, pacificatory, pacifying, peacemaking, placative, placatory, propitiative, reconciliatory

propitious **1.** advantageous, auspicious, bright, encouraging, favourable, fortunate, full of promise, happy, lucky, opportune, promising, prosperous, rosy, timely **2.** benevolent, benign, favourably inclined, friendly, gracious, kind, well-disposed

proponent advocate, apologist, backer, champion, defender, enthusiast, exponent, friend, partisan, patron, spokesman, spokeswoman, subscriber, supporter, upholder, vindicator

proportion **1.** distribution, ratio, relationship, relative amount **2.** agreement, balance, congruity, correspondence, harmony, symmetry **3.** amount, cut (*informal*), division, fraction, measure, part, percentage, quota, segment, share **4.** *plural* amplitude, breadth, bulk, capacity, dimensions, expanse, extent, magnitude, measurements, range, scope, size, volume

proportional, proportionate balanced, commensurate, comparable, compatible, consistent, correspondent, corresponding, equitable, equivalent, even, in proportion, just

Antonyms different, discordant, disproportionate, dissimilar, incommensurable, incompatible, inconsistent, unequal

proposal bid, design, motion, offer, overture, plan, presentation, proffer, programme, project, proposition, recommendation, scheme, suggestion, tender, terms

Barkis is willin'

Charles Dickens *David Copperfield*

propose **1.** advance, come up with, present, proffer, propound, put forward, submit, suggest, tender **2.** introduce, invite, name, nominate, present, put up, recommend **3.** aim, design, have every intention, have in mind, intend, mean, plan, purpose, scheme **4.** ask for someone's hand (in marriage), offer marriage, pay suit, pop the question (*informal*)

proposition **1.** *noun* motion, plan, programme, project, proposal, recommendation, scheme, suggestion **2.** *verb* accost, make an improper suggestion, make an indecent proposal, make a pass at, solicit

It is more important that a proposition be interesting than that it be true

A.N. Whitehead *Adventures of Ideas*

propound advance, advocate, contend, lay down, postulate, present, propose, put forward, set forth, submit, suggest

proprietor, proprietress deed holder, freeholder, landlady, landlord, landowner, owner, possessor, titleholder

propriety **1.** appropriateness, aptness, becomingness, correctness, fitness, rightness, seemliness, suitableness **2.** breeding, courtesy, decency, decorum, delicacy, etiquette, good form, good manners, manners, modesty, politeness, protocol, punctilio, rectitude, refinement, respectability, seemliness **3.** **the proprieties** accepted conduct, amenities, civilities, etiquette, niceties, rules of conduct, social code, social conventions, social graces, the done thing

Antonyms (*sense 2*) bad form, bad manners, immodesty, impoliteness, indecency, indecorum, indelicacy, vulgarity

propulsion drive, impetus, impulse, impulsion, momentum, motive power, power, pressure, propelling force, push, thrust

prosaic banal, boring, commonplace, dry, dull, everyday, flat, hackneyed, humdrum, matter-of-fact, mundane, ordinary, pedestrian, routine, stale, tame, trite, unimaginative, uninspiring, vapid, workaday

Antonyms entertaining, exciting, extraordinary, fascinating, imaginative, interesting, poetical, unusual

proscribe **1.** ban, boycott, censure, condemn, damn, denounce, doom, embargo, forbid, interdict, prohibit, reject **2.** attaint (*archaic*), banish, blackball, deport, exclude, excommunicate, exile, expatriate, expel, ostracize, outlaw

Antonyms (*sense 1*) allow, authorize, endorse, give leave, give permission, license, permit, sanction, warrant

proscription **1.** ban, boycott, censure, condemnation, damning, denunciation, dooming, embargo, interdict, prohibition, rejection **2.** attainder (*archaic*), banishment, deportation, ejection, eviction, exclusion, excommunication, exile, expatriation, expulsion, ostracism, outlawry

prose

Prose = words in their best order; poetry = the best words in their best order

Samuel Taylor Coleridge *Table Talk*

Prose is when all the lines except the last go on to the end. Poetry is when some of them fall short of it

Jeremy Bentham

All that is not prose is verse; and all that is not verse is prose

Molière *Le Bourgeois Gentilhomme*

prosecute **1.** *Law* arraign, bring action against, bring suit against, bring to trial, do (*slang*), indict, litigate, prefer charges, put in the dock, put on trial, seek redress, sue, sum~

mon, take to court, try **2.** carry on, conduct, direct, discharge, engage in, manage, perform, practise, work at **3.** carry through, continue, follow through, persevere, persist, pursue, see through

proselyte catechumen, convert, initiate, neophyte, new believer, novice, tyro

proselytize bring into the fold, bring to God, convert, evangelize, make converts, propagandize, spread the gospel, win over

prospect *noun* **1.** anticipation, calculation, contemplation, expectation, future, hope, odds, opening, outlook, plan, presumption, probability, promise, proposal, thought **2.** landscape, outlook, panorama, perspective, scene, sight, spectacle, view, vision, vista **3. in prospect** in sight, in store, in the offing, in the wind, in view, on the cards, on the horizon, planned, projected **4.** *sometimes plural* chance, likelihood, possibility *~verb* **5.** explore, go after, look for, search, seek, survey

prospective about to be, anticipated, approaching, awaited, coming, destined, eventual, expected, forthcoming, future, hoped-for, imminent, intended, likely, looked-for, on the cards, possible, potential, soon-to-be, -to-be, to come, upcoming

prospectus announcement, catalogue, conspectus, list, outline, plan, programme, scheme, syllabus, synopsis

prosper advance, be fortunate, bloom, do well, fare well, flourish, flower, get on, grow rich, make good, make it (*informal*), progress, succeed, thrive

prosperity affluence, boom, ease, fortune, good fortune, good times, life of luxury, life of Riley (*informal*), luxury, plenty, prosperousness, riches, success, the good life, wealth, well-being

Antonyms adversity, depression, destitution, failure, indigence, misfortune, poverty, shortage, want

prosperous **1.** blooming, booming, doing well, flourishing, fortunate, lucky, on a roll, on the up and up (*Brit.*), palmy, prospering, successful, thriving **2.** affluent, in clover (*informal*), in the money (*informal*), moneyed, opulent, rich, wealthy, well-heeled (*informal*), well-off, well-to-do **3.** advantageous, auspicious, bright, favourable, good, profitable, promising, propitious, timely

Antonyms defeated, failing, impoverished, inauspicious, poor, unfavourable, unfortunate, unlucky, unpromising, unsuccessful, untimely

prostitute **1.** *noun* bawd (*archaic*), brass (*slang*), call girl, camp follower, cocotte, courtesan, fallen woman, *fille de joie*, harlot, hooker (*U.S. slang*), hustler (*U.S. & Canad. slang*), loose woman, moll (*slang*), pro (*slang*), scrubber (*Brit. & Austral. slang*), streetwalker, strumpet, tart (*informal*), trollop, white slave, whore, working girl (*facetious slang*) **2.** *verb* cheapen, debase, degrade, demean, devalue, misapply, pervert, profane

prostitution harlotry, harlot's trade, Mrs. Warren's profession, streetwalking, the game (*slang*), the oldest profession, vice, whoredom

prostrate *adjective* **1.** abject, bowed low, flat, horizontal, kowtowing, procumbent, prone **2.** at a low ebb, dejected, depressed, desolate, drained, exhausted, fagged out (*informal*), fallen, inconsolable, overcome, spent, worn out **3.** brought to one's knees, defenceless, disarmed, helpless, impotent, overwhelmed, paralysed, powerless, reduced *~verb* **4.** *of oneself* abase, bend the knee to, bow before, bow down to, cast oneself before, cringe, fall at (someone's) feet, fall on one's knees before, grovel, kneel, kowtow, submit **5.** bring low, crush, depress, disarm, lay low, overcome, overthrow, overturn, overwhelm, paralyse, reduce, ruin **6.** drain, exhaust, fag out (*informal*), fatigue, sap, tire, wear out, weary

prostration **1.** abasement, bow, genuflection, kneeling, kowtow, obeisance, submission **2.** collapse, dejection, depression, depth of misery, desolation, despair, despondency, exhaustion, grief, helplessness, paralysis, weakness, weariness

prosy boring, commonplace, dull, flat, humdrum, long, long-drawn-out, long-winded, monotonous, overlong, pedestrian, prosaic, prosing, stale, tedious, tiresome, unimaginative, uninteresting, wordy

protagonist **1.** central character, hero, heroine, lead, leading character, principal **2.** advocate, champion, exponent, leader, mainstay, moving spirit, prime mover, standard-bearer, supporter, torchbearer

protean changeable, ever-changing, many-sided, mercurial, multiform, mutable, polymorphous, temperamental, variable, versatile, volatile

protect care for, chaperon, cover, cover up for, defend, foster, give sanctuary, guard, harbour, keep, keep safe, look after, mount *or* stand guard over, preserve, safeguard, save, screen, secure, shelter, shield, stick up for (*informal*), support, take under one's wing, watch over

Antonyms assail, assault, attack, betray, endanger, expose, expose to danger, threaten

protection **1.** aegis, care, charge, custody, defence, guardianship, guarding, preservation, protecting, safeguard, safekeeping, safety, security **2.** armour, barrier, buffer, bulwark, cover, guard, refuge, safeguard, screen, shelter, shield

protective careful, covering, defensive, fatherly, insulating, jealous, maternal, motherly, paternal, possessive, protecting, safeguarding, sheltering, shielding, vigilant, warm, watchful

protector advocate, benefactor, bodyguard, champion, counsel, defender, guard, guardian, guardian angel, knight in shining armour, patron, safeguard, tower of strength

protégé, protégée charge, dependant, discovery, pupil, student, ward

protest *noun* **1.** complaint, declaration, demur, demurral, disapproval, dissent, formal complaint, objection, outcry, protestation, remonstrance *~verb* **2.** complain, cry out, demonstrate, demur, disagree, disapprove, expostulate, express disapproval, kick (against) (*informal*), object, oppose, remonstrate, say no to, take exception, take up the cudgels **3.** affirm, argue, assert, asseverate, attest, avow, contend, declare, insist, maintain, profess, testify, vow

The lady doth protest too much methinks
William Shakespeare *Hamlet*

protestation **1.** complaint, disagreement, dissent, expostulation, objection, outcry, protest, remonstrance, remonstration **2.** affirmation, asseveration, avowal, declaration, oath, pledge, profession, vow

protester agitator, demonstrator, dissenter, dissident, protest marcher, rebel

protocol **1.** code of behaviour, conventions, courtesies, customs, decorum, etiquette, formalities, good form, manners, politesse, propriety, p's and q's, rules of conduct **2.** agreement, compact, concordat, contract, convention, covenant, pact, treaty

prototype archetype, example, first, mock-up, model, norm, original, paradigm, pattern, precedent, standard, type

protract continue, drag on *or* out, draw out, extend, keep going, lengthen, prolong, spin out, stretch out
Antonyms abbreviate, abridge, compress, curtail, reduce, shorten, summarize

protracted dragged out, drawn-out, extended, interminable, lengthy, long, long-drawn-out, never-ending, overlong, prolonged, spun out, time-consuming

protrude bulge, come through, extend, jut, obtrude, point, pop (*of eyes*), project, shoot out, stand out, start (from), stick out, stick out like a sore thumb

protrusion bulge, bump, hump, jut, lump, outgrowth, projection, protuberance, swelling

protuberance bulge, bump, excrescence, hump, knob, lump, outgrowth, process, projection, prominence, protrusion, swelling, tumour

protuberant beetling, bulbous, bulging, gibbous, hanging over, jutting, popping (*of eyes*), prominent, protruding, protrusive, proud (*dialect*), swelling, swollen
Antonyms concave, flat, indented, receding, sunken

proud **1.** appreciative, content, contented, glad, gratified, honoured, pleased, satisfied, self-respecting, well-pleased **2.** arrogant, boastful, conceited, disdainful, egotistical, haughty, high and mighty (*informal*), imperious, lordly, narcissistic, orgulous (*archaic*), overbearing, presumptuous, self-important, self-satisfied, snobbish, snooty (*informal*), stuck-up (*informal*), supercilious, toffee-nosed (*slang, chiefly Brit.*), too big for one's boots *or* breeches, vain **3.** exalted, glorious, gratifying, illustrious, memorable, pleasing, red-letter, rewarding, satisfying **4.** august, distinguished, eminent, grand, great, illustrious, imposing, magnificent, majestic, noble, splendid, stately
Antonyms abject, ashamed, base, deferential, discontented, displeased, dissatisfied, humble, ignoble, ignominious, lowly, meek, modest, submissive, unassuming, undignified, unobtrusive

provable attestable, demonstrable, evincible, testable, verifiable

prove **1.** ascertain, attest, authenticate, bear out, confirm, corroborate, demonstrate, determine, establish, evidence, evince, justify, show, show clearly, substantiate, verify **2.** analyse, assay, check, examine, experiment, put to the test, put to trial, test, try **3.** be found to be, come out, end up, result, turn out
Antonyms (*sense 1*) discredit, disprove, give the lie to, refute, rule out

proven *adjective* accepted, attested, authentic, certified, checked, confirmed, definite, dependable, established, proved, reliable, tested, tried, trustworthy, undoubted, valid, verified

provenance birthplace, derivation, origin, source

provender **1.** feed, fodder, forage **2.** comestibles, eatables, eats (*slang*), edibles, fare, feed, food, foodstuffs, groceries, grub (*slang*), nosebag (*slang*), nosh (*slang*), provisions, rations, supplies, sustenance, tack (*informal*), victuals, vittles (*obsolete or dialect*)

proverb adage, aphorism, apophthegm, byword, dictum, gnome, maxim, saw, saying

proverbial accepted, acknowledged, archetypal, axiomatic, conventional, current, customary, famed, famous, legendary, notorious, self-evident, time-honoured, traditional, typical, unquestioned, well-known

provide **1.** accommodate, cater, contribute, equip, furnish, outfit, provision, purvey, stock up, supply **2.** add, afford, bring, give, impart, lend, present, produce, render, serve, yield **3.**

with **for** *or* **against** anticipate, arrange for, forearm, get ready, make arrangements, make plans, plan ahead, plan for, prepare for, take measures, take precautions **4.** *with* **for** care for, keep, look after, maintain, support, sus~tain, take care of **5.** determine, lay down, re~quire, specify, state, stipulate
Antonyms (*sense 1*) deprive, keep back, ref~use, withhold (*sense 3*) disregard, fail to no~tice, miss, neglect, overlook (*sense 4*) neglect

providence 1. destiny, divine intervention, fate, fortune, God's will, predestination **2.** care, caution, discretion, far-sightedness, fore~sight, forethought, perspicacity, presence of mind, prudence

provident canny, careful, cautious, discreet, economical, equipped, far-seeing, far-sighted, forearmed, foresighted, frugal, prudent, saga~cious, shrewd, thrifty, vigilant, well-prepared, wise
Antonyms careless, heedless, improvident, imprudent, negligent, prodigal, profligate, reckless, short-sighted, spendthrift, thought~less, thriftless, uneconomical, unthrifty, wasteful

providential fortuitous, fortunate, happy, heaven-sent, lucky, opportune, timely, wel~come

provider 1. benefactor, donor, giver, source, supplier **2.** breadwinner, earner, mainstay, supporter, wage earner

providing, provided *conjunction* as long as, contingent upon, given, if and only if, in case, in the event, on condition, on the assumption, subject to, upon these terms, with the proviso, with the understanding

province 1. colony, county, department, de~pendency, district, division, domain, patch, region, section, territory, tract, turf (*U.S. slang*), zone **2.** *figurative* area, business, ca~pacity, charge, concern, duty, employment, field, function, line, orbit, part, pigeon (*Brit. informal*), post, responsibility, role, sphere, turf (*U.S. slang*)

Canadian province	Abbreviation
Alberta	AB
British Columbia	BC
Manitoba	MB
New Brunswick	NB
Newfoundland	NF
Northwest Terri~tories	NWT
Nova Scotia	NS
Ontario	ON
Prince Edward Is~land	PE
Quebec	PQ
Saskatchewan	SK
Yukon Territory	YT

provincial *adjective* **1.** country, hick (*informal, chiefly U.S. & Canad.*), home-grown, home~spun, local, rural, rustic **2.** insular, inward-looking, limited, narrow, narrow-minded, parish-pump, parochial, small-minded, small-town (*U.S.*), uninformed, unsophisticated, up~country *~noun* **3.** country cousin, hayseed (*U.S. & Canad. informal*), hick (*informal, chiefly U.S. & Canad.*), rustic, yokel
Antonyms cosmopolitan, fashionable, pol~ished, refined, sophisticated, urban, urbane

provincialism 1. insularity, lack of sophistica~tion, narrow-mindedness, parochialism, sec~tionalism **2.** dialect, idiom, localism, patois, regionalism, vernacularism

There are few who would not rather be taken in adultery than in provincialism
Aldous Huxley *Antic Hay*

provision 1. accoutrement, catering, equipping, fitting out, furnishing, providing, supplying, victualling **2.** arrangement, plan, prearrange~ment, precaution, preparation **3.** *figurative* agreement, clause, condition, demand, proviso, requirement, rider, specification, stipulation, term

provisional conditional, contingent, interim, limited, pro tem, provisory, qualified, stopgap, temporary, tentative, transitional
Antonyms definite, fixed, permanent

provisions comestibles, eatables, eats (*slang*), edibles, fare, feed, food, foodstuff, groceries, grub (*slang*), nosebag (*slang*), provender, ra~tions, stores, supplies, sustenance, tack (*in~formal*), viands, victuals, vittles (*obsolete or dialect*)

proviso clause, condition, limitation, provision, qualification, requirement, reservation, re~striction, rider, stipulation, strings

provocation 1. *casus belli*, cause, grounds, in~citement, inducement, instigation, justifica~tion, motivation, reason, stimulus **2.** affront, annoyance, challenge, dare, grievance, indig~nity, injury, insult, offence, red rag, taunt, vexation

provocative 1. aggravating (*informal*), annoy~ing, challenging, disturbing, galling, goading, incensing, insulting, offensive, outrageous, provoking, stimulating **2.** alluring, arousing, erotic, exciting, inviting, seductive, sexy (*in~formal*), stimulating, suggestive, tantalizing, tempting

provoke 1. affront, aggravate (*informal*), anger, annoy, chafe, enrage, exasperate, gall, get in one's hair (*informal*), get one's back up, get on one's nerves (*informal*), hassle (*informal*), incense, infuriate, insult, irk, irritate, mad~den, make one's blood boil, nark (*Brit., Aus~tral., & N.Z. slang*), offend, pique, piss one off (*taboo slang*), put one's back up, put out, rile, rub (someone) up the wrong way (*informal*), take a rise out of, try one's patience, vex **2.** bring about, bring on *or* down, call forth, cause, draw forth, elicit, evoke, excite, fire, generate, give rise to, incite, induce, inflame, inspire, instigate, kindle, lead to, motivate, move, occasion, precipitate, produce, promote, prompt, rouse, stimulate, stir

Antonyms (*sense 1*) appease, calm, conciliate, mollify, pacify, placate, propitiate, quiet, soothe, sweeten (*sense 2*) abate, allay, as~suage, blunt, curb, ease, lessen, lull, mitigate, moderate, modify, relieve, temper

No-one provokes me with impunity (Nemo me impune lacessit)

Motto of the Crown of Scotland and of all Scottish regiments

provoking aggravating (*informal*), annoying, exasperating, galling, irking, irksome, irritat~ing, maddening, obstructive, offensive, tire~some, vexatious, vexing

prow bow(s), fore, forepart, front, head, nose, sharp end (*jocular*), stem

prowess 1. ability, accomplishment, adeptness, adroitness, aptitude, attainment, command, dexterity, excellence, expertise, expertness, facility, genius, mastery, skill, talent **2.** bold~ness, bravery, courage, daring, dauntlessness, doughtiness, fearlessness, gallantry, hardi~hood, heroism, intrepidity, mettle, valiance, valour

Antonyms (*sense 1*) clumsiness, inability, in~capability, incompetence, ineptitude, inept~ness, inexpertise (*sense 2*) cowardice, faint-heartedness, fear, gutlessness, timidity

prowl cruise, hunt, lurk, move stealthily, nose around, patrol, range, roam, rove, scavenge, skulk, slink, sneak, stalk, steal

proximity adjacency, closeness, contiguity, jux~taposition, nearness, neighbourhood, propin~quity, vicinity

proxy agent, attorney, delegate, deputy, factor, representative, substitute, surrogate

prude Grundy, old maid (*informal*), prig, puri~tan, schoolmarm (*Brit. informal*)

prudence 1. canniness, care, caution, circum~spection, common sense, discretion, good sense, heedfulness, judgment, judiciousness, sagacity, vigilance, wariness, wisdom **2.** care~ful budgeting, economizing, economy, far-sightedness, foresight, forethought, frugality, good management, husbandry, planning, pre~caution, preparedness, providence, saving, thrift

Prudence is a rich, ugly, old maid courted by incapacity

William Blake *Proverbs of Hell*

Take care of the pennies and the pounds will look after themselves

A stitch in time saves nine

Waste not, want not

prudent 1. canny, careful, cautious, circum~spect, discerning, discreet, judicious, politic, sagacious, sage, sensible, shrewd, vigilant, wary, wise **2.** canny, careful, economical, far-sighted, frugal, provident, sparing, thrifty

Antonyms careless, extravagant, heedless, improvident, imprudent, inconsiderate, indis~creet, irrational, rash, thoughtless, unwise, wasteful

prudery Grundyism, old-maidishness (*infor~mal*), overmodesty, priggishness, primness, prudishness, puritanicalness, squeamishness, starchiness (*informal*), strictness, stuffiness

prudish demure, narrow-minded, niminy-piminy, old-maidish (*informal*), overmodest, overnice, priggish, prim, prissy (*informal*), proper, puritanical, schoolmarmish (*Brit. in~formal*), squeamish, starchy (*informal*), strait-laced, stuffy, Victorian

Antonyms broad-minded, liberal, open-minded, permissive

prune clip, cut, cut back, dock, lop, pare down, reduce, shape, shorten, snip, trim

prurient 1. concupiscent, desirous, hankering, itching, lascivious, lecherous, libidinous, long~ing, lustful, salacious **2.** dirty, erotic, indecent, lewd, obscene, pornographic, salacious, smut~ty, steamy (*informal*), voyeuristic, X-rated (*informal*)

pry be a busybody, be inquisitive, be nosy (*in~formal*), ferret about, interfere, intrude, med~dle, nose into, peep, peer, poke, poke one's nose in *or* into (*informal*), snoop (*informal*)

prying curious, eavesdropping, impertinent, inquisitive, interfering, intrusive, meddlesome, meddling, nosy (*informal*), snooping (*infor~mal*), snoopy (*informal*), spying

psalm carol, chant, hymn, paean, song of praise

pseud *noun* fraud, humbug, phoney *or* phony (*informal*), poser (*informal*), trendy (*Brit. in~formal*)

pseudo *adjective* artificial, bogus, counterfeit, ersatz, fake, false, imitation, mock, not genu~ine, phoney *or* phony (*informal*), pretended, quasi-, sham, spurious

Antonyms actual, authentic, bona fide, genu~ine, heartfelt, honest, real, sincere, true, un~feigned

pseudonym alias, assumed name, false name, incognito, nom de guerre, nom de plume, pen name, professional name, stage name

psyche anima, essential nature, individuality, inner man, innermost self, mind, personality, pneuma (*Philosophy*), self, soul, spirit, sub~conscious, true being

psychedelic 1. consciousness-expanding, hallucinatory, hallucinogenic, mind-bending (*informal*), mind-blowing (*informal*), mind-expanding, psychoactive, psychotomimetic, psychotropic 2. *informal* crazy, freaky (*slang*), kaleidoscopic, multicoloured, wild

psychiatrist analyst, headshrinker (*slang*), psychoanalyser, psychoanalyst, psychologist, psychotherapist, shrink (*slang*), therapist

Anyone who goes to see a psychiatrist needs his head examined
Samuel Goldwyn

To us he is no more a person now but a whole climate of opinion
W.H. Auden (of Sigmund Freud) *In Memory of Sigmund Freud*

psychic 1. clairvoyant, extrasensory, mystic, occult, preternatural, supernatural, telekinetic, telepathic 2. mental, psychogenic, psychological, spiritual

psychological 1. cerebral, cognitive, intellectual, mental 2. all in the mind, emotional, imaginary, irrational, psychosomatic, subconscious, subjective, unconscious, unreal

psychology 1. behaviourism, science of mind, study of personality 2. *informal* attitude, mental make-up, mental processes, thought processes, way of thinking, what makes one tick

Branches of psychology
analytic psychology
child psychology
clinical psychology
comparative psychology
developmental psychology
educational psychology
experimental psychology
hedonics
industrial psychology
neuropsychology
organizational psychology
parapsychology
psychiatry
psycholinguistics
psychometrics
psychophysics
psychophysiology
social psychology

Psychology terms
alter ego
anal
analysis
angst
anxiety
complex
compulsion
conditioning
consciousness
death wish
delusion
dementia
depression
Electra complex
ego
extrovert
fixation
Freudian slip
Gestalt therapy
group therapy
hypnosis
hypochondria
hysteria
id
inferiority complex
introvert
mania
mind
neurosis
obsession
Oedipus complex
paranoia
persecution complex
persona
personality
personality disorder
phobia
primal therapy *or* primal scream therapy
psyche
psychoanalysis
psychosis
psychosomatic
regression
repression
Rorschach test *or* inkblot test
schizophrenia
self
stress
subconscious
sublimation
superego
syndrome
trauma
unconscious

Famous psychologists
Alfred Adler [Austrian]
Hans Jürgen Eysenck [German-British]
Sigmund Freud [Austrian]
Karen Horney [German-U.S.]
Carl Gustav Jung [Swiss]
Wolfgang Köhler [German]
Alexander Romanovich Luria [Russian]
Ivan Petrovich Pavlov [Russian]
Wilhelm Reich [Austrian]
B(urrhus) F(rederic) Skinner [U.S.]

The trouble with Freud is that he never had to play the old Glasgow Empire on a Saturday night after Rangers and Celtic had both lost
Ken Dodd

psychopath headbanger (*informal*), headcase (*informal*), insane person, lunatic, madman, maniac, mental case (*slang*), nutcase (*slang*), nutter (*Brit. slang*), psychotic, sociopath

psychotic *adjective* certifiable, demented, deranged, insane, lunatic, mad, mental (*slang*), *non compos mentis*, not right in the head, off one's chump (head (*slang*), rocker (*slang*), trolley (*slang*)) (*slang*), psychopathic, round the bend (*Brit. slang*), unbalanced

pub *or* **public house** alehouse (*archaic*), bar, boozer (*Brit., Austral., & N.Z. informal*), hostelry (*archaic or facetious*), inn, local (*Brit. informal*), roadhouse, taproom, tavern, watering hole (*facetious slang*)

There is nothing which has yet been contrived by man, by which so much happiness is produced, as by a good tavern or inn
Dr. Johnson

puberty adolescence, awkward age, juvenescence, pubescence, teenage, teens, young adulthood

public *adjective* 1. civic, civil, common, general, national, popular, social, state, universal, widespread 2. accessible, communal, community, free to all, not private, open, open to the public, unrestricted 3. acknowledged, exposed, in circulation, known, notorious, obvious, open, overt, patent, plain, published, recognized 4. important, prominent, respected,

well-known *~noun* **5**. citizens, commonalty, community, country, electorate, everyone, hoi polloi, Joe (and Eileen) Public (*slang*), Joe Six-Pack (*U.S. slang*), masses, multitude, nation, people, populace, population, society, voters **6**. audience, buyers, clientele, followers, following, patrons, supporters, those interested, trade **7**. **in public** *coram populo*, for all to see, in full view, openly, overtly, publicly
Antonyms (*sense 2*) barred, closed, exclusive, inaccessible, personal, private, restricted, unavailable (*sense 3*) hidden, secluded, secret, unknown, unrevealed

We know no spectacle so ridiculous as the British public in one of its periodical outbursts of morality
Lord Macaulay *Essays*

publication **1**. advertisement, airing, announcement, appearance, broadcasting, declaration, disclosure, dissemination, notification, proclamation, promulgation, publishing, reporting **2**. book, booklet, brochure, handbill, hardback, issue, leaflet, magazine, newspaper, pamphlet, paperback, periodical, title

publicity advertising, attention, ballyhoo (*informal*), boost, build-up, hype, plug (*informal*), press, promotion, public notice, puff, puffery (*informal*)

All publicity is good, except an obituary notice
Brendan Behan

publicize advertise, beat the drum for (*informal*), bring to public notice, broadcast, give publicity to, hype, make known, play up, plug (*informal*), promote, puff, push, spotlight, spread about, write up
Antonyms conceal, contain, cover up, keep dark, keep secret, smother, stifle, suppress, withhold

public-spirited altruistic, charitable, community-minded, generous, humanitarian, philanthropic, unselfish

publish **1**. bring out, issue, print, produce, put out **2**. advertise, announce, blow wide open (*slang*), broadcast, circulate, communicate, declare, disclose, distribute, divulge, impart, leak, proclaim, promulgate, publicize, reveal, shout from the rooftops (*informal*), spread

Publish and be damned
Duke of Wellington

pucker **1**. *verb* compress, contract, crease, crinkle, crumple, draw together, furrow, gather, knit, pout, purse, ruckle, ruck up, ruffle, screw up, tighten, wrinkle **2**. *noun* crease, crinkle, crumple, fold, ruck, ruckle, wrinkle

puckish frolicsome, impish, ludic (*literary*), mischievous, naughty, playful, roguish, sly, sportive, teasing, waggish, whimsical

pudding afters (*Brit. informal*), dessert, last course, pud (*informal*), second course, sweet

puerile babyish, childish, foolish, immature, inane, infantile, irresponsible, jejune, juvenile, naive, petty, ridiculous, silly, trivial, weak
Antonyms adult, grown-up, mature, responsible, sensible

puff *noun* **1**. blast, breath, draught, emanation, flurry, gust, whiff **2**. drag (*slang*), pull, smoke **3**. bulge, bunching, swelling **4**. advertisement, commendation, favourable mention, good word, plug (*informal*), sales talk *~verb* **5**. blow, breathe, exhale, gasp, gulp, pant, wheeze **6**. drag (*slang*), draw, inhale, pull at *or* on, smoke, suck **7**. *usually with* **up** bloat, dilate, distend, expand, inflate, swell **8**. crack up (*informal*), hype, overpraise, plug (*informal*), praise, promote, publicize, push

puffed **1**. breathless, done in (*informal*), exhausted, gasping, out of breath, out of whack (*informal*), panting, shagged out (*Brit. slang*), short of breath, spent, winded, wiped out (*informal*) **2**. **puffed up** bigheaded (*informal*), full of oneself, high and mighty (*informal*), proud, swollen-headed, too big for one's boots
Antonyms (*sense 2*) humble, modest, self-effacing

puffy bloated, distended, enlarged, inflamed, inflated, puffed up, swollen

pugilism boxing, fighting, prizefighting, the noble art *or* science, the prize ring, the ring

pugilist boxer, bruiser (*informal*), fighter, prizefighter, pug (*slang*)

pugnacious aggressive, antagonistic, argumentative, bellicose, belligerent, choleric, combative, contentious, disputatious, hot-tempered, irascible, irritable, petulant, quarrelsome
Antonyms calm, conciliatory, gentle, irenic, pacific, peaceable, peaceful, peace-loving, placatory, placid, quiet

puke barf (*U.S. slang*), be nauseated, be sick, chuck (up) (*slang, chiefly U.S.*), chunder (*slang, chiefly Austral.*), disgorge, do a technicolour yawn (*slang*), heave, regurgitate, retch, spew, throw up (*informal*), toss one's cookies (*U.S. slang*), upchuck (*U.S. slang*), vomit

pukka authentic, bona fide, genuine, official, on the level (*informal*), proper, real, the real McCoy

pull *verb* **1**. drag, draw, haul, jerk, tow, trail, tug, yank **2**. cull, draw out, extract, gather, pick, pluck, remove, take out, uproot, weed **3**. dislocate, rend, rip, sprain, strain, stretch, tear, wrench **4**. *informal* attract, draw, entice, lure, magnetize **5**. **pull apart** *or* **to pieces** attack, blast, criticize, find fault, flay, lambast(e), lay into (*informal*), pan (*informal*), pick holes in, put down, run down, slam (*slang*), slate (*informal*), tear into (*informal*) **6**. **pull oneself together** *informal* buck up (*in-*

formal), get a grip on oneself, get over it, regain composure, snap out of it (*informal*) 7. **pull strings** *Brit. informal* influence, pull wires (*U.S.*), use one's influence 8. **pull someone's leg** *informal* chaff, have (someone) on, joke, make fun of, poke fun at, rag, rib (*informal*), tease, twit, wind up (*Brit. slang*) ~*noun* 9. jerk, tug, twitch, yank 10. attraction, drawing power, effort, exertion, force, forcefulness, influence, lure, magnetism, power 11. *informal* advantage, bottom, clout (*informal*), influence, leverage, muscle, weight 12. drag (*slang*), inhalation, puff

Antonyms *verb* (*sense 1*) drive, nudge, push, ram, shove, thrust (*sense 2*) implant, insert, plant (*sense 4*) deter, discourage, put one off, repel ~*noun* (*sense 9*) nudge, push, shove, thrust

pull down bulldoze, demolish, destroy, raze, remove

Antonyms build, construct, erect, put up, raise, set up

pull in 1. arrive, come in, draw in, draw up, reach, stop 2. attract, bring in, draw 3. *Brit. slang* arrest, bust (*informal*), collar (*informal*), feel one's collar (*slang*), lift (*slang*), nab (*informal*), nail (*informal*), pinch (*informal*), run in (*slang*), take into custody 4. clear, earn, gain, gross, make, net, pocket, take home

pull off 1. detach, doff, remove, rip off, tear off, wrench off 2. accomplish, bring off, carry out, crack it (*informal*), cut it (*informal*), do the trick, manage, score a success, secure one's object, succeed

pull out abandon, back off, depart, evacuate, leave, quit, rat on, retreat, stop participating, withdraw

pull through come through, get better, get over, pull round, rally, recover, survive, turn the corner, weather

pull up 1. dig out, lift, raise, uproot 2. brake, come to a halt, halt, reach a standstill, stop 3. admonish, bawl out (*informal*), carpet (*informal*), castigate, chew out (*U.S. & Canad. informal*), dress down (*informal*), give a rocket (*Brit. & N.Z. informal*), rap over the knuckles, read the riot act, rebuke, reprimand, reprove, slap on the wrist, take to task, tear into (*informal*), tear (someone) off a strip (*Brit. informal*), tell off (*informal*), tick off (*informal*)

pulp *noun* 1. flesh, marrow, soft part 2. mash, mush, pap, paste, pomace, semiliquid, semisolid, triturate ~*verb* 3. crush, mash, pulverize, squash, triturate ~*adjective* 4. cheap, lurid, mushy (*informal*), rubbishy, sensational, trashy

pulpy fleshy, mushy, pappy, soft, squashy, succulent

pulsate beat, hammer, oscillate, palpitate, pound, pulse, quiver, throb, thud, thump, tick, vibrate

pulse 1. *noun* beat, beating, oscillation, pulsation, rhythm, stroke, throb, throbbing, vibration 2. *verb* beat, pulsate, throb, tick, vibrate

pulverize 1. bray, comminute, crush, granulate, grind, levigate (*Chemistry*), mill, pestle, pound, triturate 2. *figurative* annihilate, blow out of the water (*slang*), crush, defeat, demolish, destroy, flatten, lick (*informal*), smash, stuff (*slang*), tank (*slang*), vanquish, wipe the floor with (*informal*), wreck

pummel bang, batter, beat, beat the living daylights out of, belt (*informal*), clobber (*slang*), hammer, knock, lambast(e), pound, punch, rain blows upon, strike, thump

pump *verb* 1. *with* **out** bail out, drain, draw off, drive out, empty, force out, siphon 2. *with* **up** blow up, dilate, inflate 3. drive, force, inject, pour, push, send, supply 4. cross-examine, give (someone) the third degree, grill (*informal*), interrogate, probe, question closely, quiz, worm out of

pun double entendre, equivoque, paronomasia (*Rhetoric*), play on words, quip, witticism

A man who could make so vile a pun would not scruple to pick a pocket

John Dennis

punch[1] *verb* 1. bash (*informal*), belt (*informal*), biff (*slang*), bop (*informal*), box, clout (*informal*), hit, plug (*slang*), pummel, slam, slug, smash, sock (*slang*), strike, wallop (*informal*) ~*noun* 2. bash (*informal*), biff (*slang*), blow, bop (*informal*), clout (*informal*), hit, jab, knock, plug (*slang*), sock (*slang*), thump, wallop (*informal*) 3. *informal* bite, drive, effectiveness, force, forcefulness, impact, point, verve, vigour

punch[2] *verb* bore, cut, drill, perforate, pierce, pink, prick, puncture, stamp

punch-drunk befuddled, confused, dazed, groggy (*informal*), in a daze, knocked silly, punchy (*informal*), reeling, slaphappy (*informal*), staggering, stupefied, unsteady, woozy (*informal*)

punch-up argument, *bagarre*, battle royal, brawl, dingdong, dust-up (*informal*), fight, free-for-all (*informal*), row, scrap (*informal*), set-to (*informal*), shindig (*informal*), shindy (*informal*), stand-up fight (*informal*)

punchy aggressive, dynamic, effective, forceful, incisive, in-your-face (*slang*), lively, spirited, vigorous

punctilio 1. exactitude, finickiness, meticulousness, particularity, precision, punctiliousness, scrupulousness, strictness 2. convention, delicacy, distinction, fine point, formality, nicety, particular, refinement

punctilious careful, ceremonious, conscientious, exact, finicky, formal, fussy, meticulous, nice, particular, precise, proper, scrupulous, strict

punctual early, exact, in good time, on the dot, on time, precise, prompt, punctilious, seasonable, strict, timely
Antonyms behind, behindhand, belated, delayed, late, overdue, tardy, unpunctual

punctuality promptitude, promptness, readiness, regularity

Punctuality is the politeness of kings
Louis XVIII

Punctuality is the thief of time
Oscar Wilde

Punctuality is the virtue of the bored
Evelyn Waugh

punctuate **1.** break, interject, interrupt, intersperse, pepper, sprinkle **2.** accentuate, emphasize, lay stress on, mark, point up, stress, underline

puncture *noun* **1.** break, cut, damage, hole, leak, nick, opening, perforation, rupture, slit **2.** flat, flat tyre *~verb* **3.** bore, cut, impale, nick, penetrate, perforate, pierce, prick, rupture **4.** deflate, go down, go flat **5.** deflate, discourage, disillusion, flatten, humble, take down a peg (*informal*)

pundit buff (*informal*), maestro, one of the cognoscenti, (self-appointed) authority *or* expert

pungent **1.** acerb, acid, acrid, aromatic, bitter, highly flavoured, hot, peppery, piquant, seasoned, sharp, sour, spicy, stinging, strong, tangy, tart **2.** acrimonious, acute, barbed, biting, caustic, cutting, incisive, keen, mordacious, mordant, penetrating, piercing, poignant, pointed, sarcastic, scathing, sharp, stinging, stringent, telling, trenchant, vitriolic
Antonyms bland, dull, inane, mild, moderate, tasteless, unsavoury, unstimulating, weak

punish **1.** beat, bring to book, castigate, chasten, chastise, correct, discipline, flog, give a lesson to, give (someone) the works (*slang*), lash, penalize, rap someone's knuckles, scourge, sentence, slap someone's wrist, throw the book at, whip **2.** abuse, batter, give (someone) a going-over (*informal*), harm, hurt, injure, knock about, maltreat, manhandle, misuse, oppress, rough up

punishable blameworthy, chargeable, convictable, criminal, culpable, indictable

punishing arduous, backbreaking, burdensome, demanding, exhausting, grinding, gruelling, hard, strenuous, taxing, tiring, uphill, wearing
Antonyms cushy (*informal*), easy, effortless, light, simple, undemanding, unexacting, untaxing

punishment **1.** chastening, chastisement, comeuppance (*slang*), correction, discipline, just deserts, penalty, penance, punitive measures, retribution, sanction, what for (*informal*) **2.** *informal* abuse, beating, hard work, maltreatment, manhandling, pain, rough treatment, slave labour, torture, victimization

Let the punishment fit the crime
W.S. Gilbert *The Mikado*

Whoso sheddeth man's blood, by man shall his blood be shed
Bible: Genesis

They have sown the wind, and they shall reap the whirlwind
Bible: Hosea

Be not deceived; God is not mocked; for whatsoever a man soweth, that shall he also reap
Bible: Galatians

Men are not hanged for stealing horses, but that horses may not be stolen
George Savile, Marquess of Halifax *Political, Moral, and Miscellaneous Thoughts*

punitive in reprisal, in retaliation, punitory, retaliative, retaliatory, revengeful, vindictive

punk delinquent, juvenile delinquent, punk rocker, rebel

punt *verb* **1.** back, bet, gamble, lay, stake, wager *~noun* **2.** bet, gamble, stake, wager **3.** backer, better, gambler, punter

punter *noun* **1.** backer, better, gambler, punt (*chiefly Brit.*) **2.** *informal* bloke (*Brit. informal*), fellow, guy (*informal*), man in the street, person **3.** *informal* client, customer

puny **1.** diminutive, dwarfish, feeble, frail, little, pint-sized (*informal*), pygmy *or* pigmy, sickly, stunted, tiny, underfed, undersized, undeveloped, weak, weakly **2.** inconsequential, inferior, insignificant, minor, paltry, petty, piddling (*informal*), trifling, trivial, worthless
Antonyms (*sense 1*) brawny, burly, healthy, hefty (*informal*), husky (*informal*), powerful, robust, strong, sturdy, well-built, well-developed

pup *or* **puppy** *figurative* braggart, cub, jackanapes, popinjay, whelp, whippersnapper, young dog

pupil beginner, catechumen, disciple, learner, neophyte, novice, scholar, schoolboy, schoolgirl, student, trainee, tyro
Antonyms coach, instructor, master, mistress, schoolmaster, schoolmistress, schoolteacher, teacher, trainer, tutor

puppet **1.** doll, marionette **2.** *figurative* cat's-paw, creature, dupe, figurehead, gull (*archaic*), instrument, mouthpiece, pawn, stooge, tool

purchasable **1.** bribable, corrupt, corruptible, dishonest, having one's price, unscrupulous, venal **2.** available, for sale, in stock, obtainable, on sale, on the market, to be had

purchase *verb* **1.** acquire, buy, come by, gain, get, get hold of, invest in, make a purchase, obtain, pay for, pick up, procure, score (*slang*), secure, shop for **2.** achieve, attain, earn, gain, realize, win *~noun* **3.** acquisition, asset, buy, gain, investment, possession, property **4.** advantage, edge, foothold, footing, grasp, grip, hold, influence, lever, leverage, support, toehold

Antonyms *verb* (*sense 1*) hawk, market, mer~ chandise, peddle, retail, sell, trade in, vend *~noun* (*sense 3*) marketing, sale, selling, vending

purchaser buyer, consumer, customer, vendee (*Law*)

Antonyms dealer, merchant, retailer, sales~ man, salesperson, saleswoman, seller, shop~ keeper, tradesman, vendor

pure 1. authentic, clear, flawless, genuine, natural, neat, perfect, real, simple, straight, true, unalloyed, unmixed **2.** clean, disinfected, germ-free, immaculate, pasteurized, sanitary, spotless, squeaky-clean, sterile, sterilized, un~ adulterated, unblemished, uncontaminated, unpolluted, untainted, wholesome **3.** blame~ less, chaste, guileless, honest, immaculate, impeccable, innocent, maidenly, modest, true, uncorrupted, undefiled, unspotted, unstained, unsullied, upright, virgin, virginal, virtuous **4.** absolute, complete, mere, outright, sheer, thorough, unmitigated, unqualified, utter **5.** abstract, academic, philosophical, speculative, theoretical

Antonyms (*senses 1 & 2*) adulterated, con~ taminated, dirty, filthy, flawed, imperfect, im~ pure, infected, insincere, mixed, polluted, tainted (*sense 3*) contaminated, corrupt, de~ filed, guilty, immodest, immoral, impure, in~ decent, obscene, sinful, spoiled, unchaste, un~ clean, untrue (*sense 4*) qualified (*sense 5*) ap~ plied, practical

Blessed are the pure in heart; for they shall see God

Bible: St. Matthew

Unto the pure all things are pure

Bible: II Timothy

purebred blood, full-blooded, pedigree, thoroughbred

purely absolutely, completely, entirely, exclu~ sively, just, merely, only, plainly, simply, solely, totally, wholly

purgative 1. *noun* aperient (*Medical*), cathartic, depurative, emetic, enema, evacuant, laxative, physic (*rare*), purge **2.** *adjective* aperient (*Medical*), cleansing, depurative, evacuant, laxative, purging

purgatory *as used informally* agony, hell (*in~ formal*), hell on earth, misery, murder (*infor~ mal*), the rack, torment, torture

purge *verb* **1.** axe (*informal*), clean out, dis~ miss, do away with, eject, eradicate, expel, exterminate, get rid of, kill, liquidate, oust, remove, rid of, rout out, sweep out, wipe from the face of the earth, wipe out **2.** absolve, cleanse, clear, exonerate, expiate, forgive, pardon, purify, wash *~noun* **3.** cleanup, crushing, ejection, elimination, eradication, expulsion, liquidation, reign of terror, remov~ al, suppression, witch hunt **4.** aperient (*Medi~ cal*), cathartic, dose of salts, emetic, enema, laxative, physic (*rare*), purgative (*Medical*)

purify 1. clarify, clean, cleanse, decontaminate, disinfect, filter, fumigate, refine, sanitize, wash **2.** absolve, cleanse, exculpate, exonerate, lustrate, redeem, sanctify, shrive

Antonyms adulterate, befoul, contaminate, corrupt, defile, foul, infect, pollute, soil, stain, sully, taint, tarnish, vitiate

purist classicist, formalist, pedant, precisian, stickler

puritan 1. *noun* fanatic, moralist, pietist, prude, rigorist, zealot **2.** *adjective* ascetic, aus~ tere, hidebound, intolerant, moralistic, nar~ row, narrow-minded, prudish, puritanical, se~ vere, strait-laced, strict

The Puritan hated bear-baiting, not because it gave pain to the bear, but because it gave pleas~ ure to the spectators

Lord Macaulay *History of England*

puritanical ascetic, austere, bigoted, disap~ proving, fanatical, forbidding, narrow, narrow-minded, prim, proper, prudish, puri~ tan, rigid, severe, stiff, strait-laced, strict, stuffy

Antonyms broad-minded, hedonistic, indul~ gent, latitudinarian, liberal, permissive, toler~ ant

puritanism asceticism, austerity, fanaticism, moralism, narrowness, piety, piousness, prud~ ishness, rigidity, rigorism, severity, strictness, zeal

Puritanism: The haunting fear that someone, somewhere may be happy

H.L. Mencken *Chrestomathy*

purity 1. brilliance, clarity, cleanliness, clean~ ness, clearness, faultlessness, fineness, genu~ ineness, immaculateness, pureness, un~ taintedness, wholesomeness **2.** blameless~ ness, chasteness, chastity, decency, guileless~ ness, honesty, innocence, integrity, piety, rec~ titude, sincerity, virginity, virtue, virtuous~ ness

Antonyms cloudiness, contamination, immod~ esty, immorality, impurity, unchasteness, vice, wickedness

purlieus 1. borders, confines, environs, fringes, limits, neighbourhood, outskirts, periphery, precincts, suburbs, vicinity **2.** *sometimes sin~*

gular hang-out (*informal*), haunt, patch, resort, stamping ground, territory

purloin appropriate, blag (*slang*), cabbage (*Brit. slang*), filch, knock off (*slang*), lift (*informal*), nick (*slang, chiefly Brit.*), nobble (*Brit. slang*), pilfer, pinch (*informal*), prig (*Brit. slang*), rob, snaffle (*Brit. informal*), snitch (*slang*), steal, swipe (*slang*), thieve, walk off with

purport *verb* **1.** allege, assert, claim, declare, maintain, pose as, pretend, proclaim, profess **2.** betoken, convey, denote, express, imply, import, indicate, intend, mean, point to, signify, suggest *~noun* **3.** bearing, drift, gist, idea, implication, import, meaning, sense, significance, spirit, tendency, tenor **4.** aim, design, intent, intention, object, objective, plan, purpose

purpose *noun* **1.** aim, design, function, idea, intention, object, point, principle, reason, the why and wherefore **2.** aim, ambition, aspiration, design, desire, end, goal, Holy Grail (*informal*), hope, intention, object, objective, plan, project, scheme, target, view, wish **3.** constancy, determination, firmness, persistence, resolution, resolve, single-mindedness, steadfastness, tenacity, will **4.** advantage, avail, benefit, effect, gain, good, mileage (*informal*), outcome, profit, result, return, use, utility **5. on purpose** by design, deliberately, designedly, intentionally, knowingly, purposely, wilfully, wittingly *~verb* **6.** aim, aspire, commit oneself, contemplate, decide, design, determine, have a mind to, intend, make up one's mind, mean, meditate, plan, propose, resolve, set one's sights on, think to, work towards

purposeful decided, deliberate, determined, firm, fixed, immovable, positive, resolute, resolved, settled, single-minded, steadfast, strong-willed, tenacious, unfaltering
Antonyms aimless, faltering, irresolute, purposeless, undecided, undetermined, vacillating, wavering

purposeless aimless, empty, goalless, motiveless, needless, pointless, senseless, uncalled-for, unnecessary, useless, vacuous, wanky (*taboo slang*), wanton, without rhyme or reason

purposely by design, calculatedly, consciously, deliberately, designedly, expressly, intentionally, knowingly, on purpose, wilfully, with intent
Antonyms accidentally, by accident, by chance, by mistake, inadvertently, unconsciously, unintentionally, unknowingly, unwittingly

purse *noun* **1.** money-bag, pouch, wallet **2.** coffers, exchequer, funds, means, money, resources, treasury, wealth, wherewithal **3.** award, gift, present, prize, reward *~verb* **4.** close, contract, knit, pout, press together, pucker, tighten, wrinkle

pursuance bringing about, carrying out, discharge, doing, effecting, execution, following, performance, prosecution, pursuing

pursue **1.** accompany, attend, chase, dog, follow, give chase to, go after, harass, harry, haunt, hound, hunt, hunt down, plague, run after, shadow, stalk, tail (*informal*), track **2.** aim for, aspire to, desire, have as one's goal, purpose, seek, strive for, try for, work towards **3.** adhere to, carry on, continue, cultivate, hold to, keep on, maintain, persevere in, persist in, proceed, see through **4.** apply oneself, carry on, conduct, engage in, perform, ply, practise, prosecute, tackle, wage, work at **5.** chase after, court, make up to (*informal*), pay attention to, pay court to, set one's cap at, woo
Antonyms avoid, eschew, fight shy of, flee, give (someone *or* something) a wide berth, keep away from, run away from, shun, steer clear of

pursuit **1.** chase, hunt, hunting, inquiry, quest, search, seeking, tracking, trail, trailing **2.** activity, hobby, interest, line, occupation, pastime, pleasure, vocation

purvey **1.** cater, deal in, furnish, provide, provision, retail, sell, supply, trade in, victual **2.** communicate, make available, pass on, publish, retail, spread, transmit

purview **1.** ambit, compass, confine(s), extent, field, limit, orbit, province, range, reach, scope, sphere **2.** comprehension, ken, overview, perspective, range of view, understanding

push *verb* **1.** depress, drive, poke, press, propel, ram, shove, thrust **2.** elbow, jostle, make *or* force one's way, move, shoulder, shove, squeeze, thrust **3.** egg on, encourage, expedite, hurry, impel, incite, persuade, press, prod, speed (up), spur, urge **4.** advertise, boost, cry up, hype, make known, plug (*informal*), promote, propagandize, publicize, puff **5.** browbeat, coerce, constrain, dragoon, encourage, exert influence on, influence, oblige *~noun* **6.** butt, jolt, nudge, poke, prod, shove, thrust **7.** *informal* ambition, determination, drive, dynamism, energy, enterprise, get-up-and-go (*informal*), go (*informal*), gumption (*informal*), initiative, pep, vigour, vitality **8.** *informal* advance, assault, attack, campaign, charge, effort, offensive, onset, thrust **9. the push** *slang* discharge, dismissal, kiss-off (*slang, chiefly U.S. & Canad.*), marching orders (*informal*), one's books (*informal*), one's cards, the boot (*slang*), the (old) heave-ho (*informal*), the order of the boot (*slang*), the sack (*informal*)
Antonyms *verb* (*sense 1*) drag, draw, haul, jerk, pull, tow, trail, tug, yank (*sense 3*) deter,

discourage, dissuade, put off *~noun* (*sense 6*) jerk, pull, tug, yank

pushed *often with* **for** hurried, in difficulty, pressed, rushed, short of, tight, under pressure, up against it (*informal*)

pushing 1. ambitious, determined, driving, dynamic, enterprising, go-ahead, on the go, purposeful, resourceful 2. assertive, bold, brash, bumptious, forward, impertinent, intrusive, presumptuous, pushy (*informal*), self-assertive

push off beat it (*slang*), depart, get lost (*informal*), go away, hit the road (*slang*), hook it (*slang*), launch, leave, light out (*informal*), make oneself scarce (*informal*), make tracks, pack one's bags (*informal*), shove off (*informal*), slope off, take off (*informal*)

pushover 1. breeze (*U.S. & Canad. informal*), cakewalk (*informal*), child's play (*informal*), cinch (*slang*), doddle (*Brit. slang*), duck soup (*U.S. slang*), picnic (*informal*), piece of cake (*Brit. informal*), piece of piss (*taboo slang*), plain sailing, walkover (*informal*) 2. chump (*informal*), easy game (*informal*), easy *or* soft mark (*informal*), mug (*Brit. slang*), soft touch (*slang*), stooge (*slang*), sucker (*slang*), walkover (*informal*)
Antonyms (*sense 1*) challenge, hassle (*informal*), ordeal, test, trial, undertaking

pushy aggressive, ambitious, bold, brash, bumptious, forceful, loud, obnoxious, obtrusive, offensive, officious, presumptuous, pushing, self-assertive
Antonyms diffident, inoffensive, meek, mousy, quiet, reserved, retiring, self-effacing, shy, timid, unassertive, unassuming, unobtrusive

pusillanimous abject, chicken-hearted, cowardly, craven, faint-hearted, fearful, feeble, gutless (*informal*), lily-livered, recreant (*archaic*), spineless, timid, timorous, weak, yellow (*informal*)
Antonyms bold, brave, courageous, daring, dauntless, fearless, gallant, heroic, intrepid, plucky, valiant, valorous

pussyfoot 1. creep, prowl, slink, steal, tiptoe, tread warily 2. beat about the bush, be noncommittal, equivocate, flannel (*Brit. informal*), hedge, hum and haw, prevaricate, sit on the fence, tergiversate

pustule abscess, blister, boil, fester, gathering, pimple, ulcer, zit (*slang*)

put 1. bring, deposit, establish, fix, lay, place, position, rest, set, settle, situate 2. commit, condemn, consign, doom, enjoin, impose, inflict, levy, subject 3. assign, constrain, employ, force, induce, make, oblige, require, set, subject to 4. express, phrase, pose, set, state, utter, word 5. advance, bring forward, forward, offer, posit, present, propose, set before, submit, tender 6. cast, fling, heave, hurl, lob, pitch, throw, toss

put across *or* **over** communicate, convey, explain, get across, get through, make clear, make oneself understood, spell out

put aside *or* **by** 1. cache, deposit, keep in reserve, lay by, salt away, save, squirrel away, stockpile, store, stow away 2. bury, discount, disregard, forget, ignore

putative alleged, assumed, commonly believed, imputed, presumed, presumptive, reported, reputed, supposed

put away 1. put back, replace, return to (its) place, tidy away 2. deposit, keep, lay in, put by, save, set aside, store away 3. certify, commit, confine, institutionalize, lock up 4. consume, devour, eat up, gobble, gulp down, wolf down 5. destroy, do away with, put down, put out of its misery, put to sleep

put-down barb, dig, disparagement, gibe, humiliation, kick in the teeth (*slang*), knock (*informal*), one in the eye (*informal*), rebuff, sarcasm, slight, sneer, snub

put down 1. enter, inscribe, log, record, set down, take down, transcribe, write down 2. crush, quash, quell, repress, silence, stamp out, suppress 3. *with* **to** ascribe, attribute, impute, set down 4. destroy, do away with, put away, put out of its misery, put to sleep 5. *slang* condemn, crush, deflate, dismiss, disparage, humiliate, mortify, reject, shame, slight, snub

put forward advance, introduce, move, nominate, prescribe, present, press, proffer, propose, recommend, submit, suggest, tender

put off 1. defer, delay, hold over, postpone, put back, put on ice, put on the back burner (*informal*), reschedule, take a rain check on (*U.S. & Canad. informal*) 2. abash, confuse, discomfit, disconcert, dismay, distress, faze, nonplus, perturb, rattle (*informal*), take the wind out of someone's sails, throw (*informal*), unsettle 3. discourage, dishearten, dissuade
Antonyms (*sense 3*) egg on, encourage, incite, persuade, prompt, push, spur, urge

put on 1. change into, don, dress, get dressed in, slip into 2. affect, assume, fake, feign, make believe, play-act, pretend, sham, simulate 3. do, mount, present, produce, show, stage 4. add, gain, increase by 5. back, bet, lay, place, wager
Antonyms (*sense 1*) cast off, doff, remove, shed, slip off, slip out of, take off, throw off, undress

put out 1. anger, annoy, confound, disturb, exasperate, harass, irk, irritate, nettle, perturb, provoke, vex 2. blow out, douse, extinguish, quench, smother, snuff out, stamp out 3. bother, discomfit, discommode, discompose, disconcert, discountenance, disturb, embarrass, impose upon, incommode, inconvenience, put on the spot, take the wind out of someone's sails, trouble, upset **4.** bring out, broadcast, circulate, issue, make known, make public, publish, release

putrefy break down, corrupt, decay, decompose, deteriorate, go bad, rot, spoil, stink, taint

putrescent decaying, decomposing, going bad, rotting, stinking

putrid bad, contaminated, corrupt, decayed, decomposed, fetid, foul, off, olid, putrefied, rancid, rank, reeking, rotten, rotting, spoiled, stinking, tainted
Antonyms clean, fresh, pure, sweet, uncontaminated, untainted, wholesome

put through accomplish, achieve, bring off, carry through, conclude, do, effect, execute, manage, pull off, realize

put up **1.** build, construct, erect, fabricate, raise **2.** accommodate, board, entertain, give one lodging, house, lodge, take in **3.** float, nominate, offer, present, propose, put forward, recommend, submit **4.** advance, give, invest, pay, pledge, provide, supply **5. put up to** egg on, encourage, goad, incite, instigate, prompt, put the idea into one's head, urge **6. put up with** *informal* abide, bear, brook, endure, hack (*slang*), lump (*informal*), pocket, stand, stand for, stomach, suffer, swallow, take, tolerate
Antonyms (*sense 1*) demolish, destroy, flatten, knock down, level, pull down, raze, tear down (*sense 6*) not stand for, object to, oppose, protest against, reject, take exception to

put-upon abused, beset, exploited, harried, imposed upon, inconvenienced, overworked, put-out, saddled, taken advantage of, taken for a fool, taken for granted, troubled

puzzle *verb* **1.** baffle, beat (*slang*), bewilder, confound, confuse, flummox, mystify, nonplus, perplex, stump **2.** ask oneself, brood, cudgel *or* rack one's brains, mull over, muse, ponder, study, think about, think hard, wonder **3.** *usually with* **out** clear up, crack, crack the code, decipher, figure out, find the key, get it, get the answer, resolve, see, solve, sort out, suss (out) (*slang*), think through, unravel, work out *~noun* **4.** brain-teaser (*informal*), conundrum, enigma, labyrinth, maze, mystery, paradox, poser, problem, question, question mark, riddle, teaser **5.** bafflement, bewilderment, confusion, difficulty, dilemma, perplexity, quandary, uncertainty

puzzled at a loss, at sea, baffled, beaten, bewildered, clueless, confused, doubtful, flummoxed, in a fog, lost, mixed up, mystified, nonplussed, perplexed, stuck, stumped, without a clue

puzzlement bafflement, bewilderment, confusion, disorientation, doubt, doubtfulness, mystification, perplexity, questioning, surprise, uncertainty, wonder

puzzling abstruse, ambiguous, baffling, bewildering, beyond one, enigmatic, full of surprises, hard, incomprehensible, inexplicable, involved, knotty, labyrinthine, misleading, mystifying, oracular, perplexing, unaccountable, unclear, unfathomable
Antonyms clear, comprehensible, easy, evident, intelligible, lucid, manifest, obvious, patent, plain, simple, unambiguous, unequivocal, unmistakable

pygmy, pigmy *noun* **1.** dwarf, homunculus, Lilliputian, manikin, midget, munchkin (*informal, chiefly U.S.*), shrimp (*informal*), Tom Thumb **2.** cipher, lightweight (*informal*), mediocrity, nobody, nonentity, pipsqueak (*informal*), small fry *~adjective* **3.** baby, diminutive, dwarf, dwarfish, elfin, Lilliputian, midget, miniature, minuscule, pocket, pygmean, small, stunted, teensy-weensy, teeny-weeny, tiny, undersized, wee

pyromaniac arsonist, firebug (*informal*), fire raiser, incendiary

Q

quack 1. *noun* charlatan, fake, fraud, humbug, impostor, mountebank, phoney *or* phony (*informal*), pretender, quacksalver (*archaic*) 2. *adjective* counterfeit, fake, fraudulent, phoney *or* phony (*informal*), pretended, sham

quaff bend the elbow (*informal*), bevvy (*dialect*), carouse, down, drink, gulp, guzzle, imbibe, swallow, swig (*informal*), tope

quaggy boggy, fenny, marshy, miry, muddy, mushy, paludal, soft, soggy, squelchy, swampy, yielding

quagmire 1. bog, fen, marsh, mire, morass, quicksand, slough, swamp 2. difficulty, dilemma, entanglement, fix (*informal*), imbroglio, impasse, jam (*informal*), muddle, pass, pickle (*informal*), pinch, plight, predicament, quandary, scrape (*informal*)

quail blanch, blench, cower, cringe, droop, faint, falter, flinch, have cold feet (*informal*), quake, recoil, shake, shrink, shudder, tremble

quaint 1. bizarre, curious, droll, eccentric, fanciful, fantastic, odd, old-fashioned, original, peculiar, queer, rum (*Brit. slang*), singular, strange, unusual, whimsical 2. antiquated, antique, artful, charming, gothic, ingenious, old-fashioned, old-world, picturesque
Antonyms fashionable, modern, new, normal, ordinary, up-to-date

quake convulse, move, pulsate, quail, quiver, rock, shake, shiver, shudder, throb, totter, tremble, vibrate, waver, wobble

qualification 1. ability, accomplishment, aptitude, attribute, capability, capacity, eligibility, endowment(s), fitness, quality, skill, suitability, suitableness 2. allowance, caveat, condition, criterion, exception, exemption, limitation, modification, objection, prerequisite, proviso, requirement, reservation, restriction, rider, stipulation

qualified 1. able, accomplished, adept, capable, certificated, competent, efficient, eligible, equipped, experienced, expert, fit, knowledgeable, licensed, practised, proficient, skilful, talented, trained 2. bounded, circumscribed, conditional, confined, contingent, equivocal, guarded, limited, modified, provisional, reserved, restricted
Antonyms (*sense 1*) amateur, apprentice, self-styled, self-taught, trainee, uncertificated, unqualified, untrained (*sense 2*) categorical, outright, unconditional, unequivocal, wholehearted

qualify 1. capacitate, certify, commission, condition, empower, endow, equip, fit, ground, permit, prepare, ready, sanction, train 2. abate, adapt, assuage, circumscribe, diminish, ease, lessen, limit, mitigate, moderate, modify, modulate, reduce, regulate, restrain, restrict, soften, temper, vary 3. characterize, describe, designate, distinguish, modify, name
Antonyms (*sense 1*) ban, debar, disqualify, forbid, preclude, prevent

quality 1. aspect, attribute, characteristic, condition, feature, mark, peculiarity, property, trait 2. character, constitution, description, essence, kind, make, nature, sort 3. calibre, distinction, excellence, grade, merit, position, pre-eminence, rank, standing, status, superiority, value, worth 4. *obsolete* aristocracy, gentry, nobility, ruling class, upper class

qualm 1. anxiety, apprehension, compunction, disquiet, doubt, hesitation, misgiving, regret, reluctance, remorse, scruple, twinge *or* pang of conscience, uncertainty, uneasiness 2. agony, attack, nausea, pang, queasiness, sickness, spasm, throe (*rare*), twinge

quandary bewilderment, cleft stick, delicate situation, difficulty, dilemma, doubt, embarrassment, impasse, perplexity, plight, predicament, puzzle, strait, uncertainty

quantity 1. aggregate, allotment, amount, lot, number, part, portion, quota, sum, total 2. bulk, capacity, expanse, extent, greatness, length, magnitude, mass, measure, size, volume

quarrel *noun* 1. affray, altercation, argument, *bagarre*, brawl, breach, broil, commotion, contention, controversy, difference (of opinion), disagreement, discord, disputation, dispute, dissension, dissidence, disturbance, feud, fight, fracas, fray, misunderstanding, row, scrap (*informal*), shindig (*informal*), shindy (*informal*), skirmish, spat, squabble, strife, tiff, tumult, vendetta, wrangle ~*verb* 2. altercate, argue, bicker, brawl, clash, differ, disagree, dispute, fall out (*informal*), fight, fight like cat and dog, go at it hammer and tongs, row, spar, squabble, wrangle 3. carp, cavil,

complain, decry, disapprove, find fault, object to, take exception to
Antonyms *(sense 1)* accord, agreement, con~cord *(sense 2)* agree, get on *or* along (with)

Love-quarrels oft in pleasing concord end
John Milton *Samson Agonistes*

quarrelsome argumentative, belligerent, can~tankerous, cat-and-dog *(informal)*, choleric, combative, contentious, cross, disputatious, fractious, ill-tempered, irascible, irritable, liti~gious, peevish, petulant, pugnacious, queru~lous
Antonyms easy-going, equable, even-tempered, placid

quarry aim, game, goal, objective, prey, prize, victim

quarter *noun* **1.** area, direction, district, local~ity, location, neighbourhood, part, place, point, position, province, region, side, spot, station, territory, zone **2.** clemency, compassion, fa~vour, forgiveness, leniency, mercy, pity *~verb* **3.** accommodate, billet, board, house, install, lodge, place, post, put up, station

quarters abode, accommodation, barracks, bil~let, cantonment *(Military)*, chambers, digs *(Brit. informal)*, domicile, dwelling, habitation, lodging, lodgings, post, residence, rooms, shelter, station

quash 1. beat, crush, destroy, extinguish, ex~tirpate, overthrow, put down, quell, quench, repress, squash, subdue, suppress **2.** annul, cancel, declare null and void, invalidate, nul~lify, overrule, overthrow, rescind, reverse, re~voke, set aside, void

quasi- 1. almost, apparently, partly, seemingly, supposedly **2.** apparent, fake, mock, near, nominal, pretended, pseudo-, seeming, semi-, sham, so-called, synthetic, virtual, would-be

quaver 1. *verb* flicker, flutter, oscillate, pulsate, quake, quiver, shake, shudder, thrill, tremble, trill, twitter, vibrate, waver **2.** *noun* break, quiver, shake, sob, throb, tremble, trembling, tremor, trill, vibration, warble

queasy 1. bilious, giddy, green around the gills *(informal)*, groggy *(informal)*, ill, indisposed, nauseated, off colour, queer, sick, sickish, squeamish, uncomfortable, unwell, upset **2.** anxious, concerned, fidgety, ill at ease, rest~less, troubled, uncertain, uneasy, worried

queen 1. consort, monarch, ruler, sovereign **2.** diva, doyenne, ideal, idol, mistress, model, perfection, prima donna, star

queen: a woman by whom the realm is ruled when there is a king, and through whom it is ruled when there is not
Ambrose Bierce *The Devil's Dictionary*

queenly grand, imperial, majestic, noble, regal, royal, stately

queer *adjective* **1.** abnormal, anomalous, atypi~cal, curious, disquieting, droll, eerie, erratic, extraordinary, funny, left-field *(informal)*, odd, outlandish, *outré*, peculiar, remarkable, rum *(Brit. slang)*, singular, strange, uncanny, un~common, unconventional, unnatural, unortho~dox, unusual, weird **2.** doubtful, dubious, fishy *(informal)*, irregular, mysterious, puzzling, questionable, shady *(informal)*, suspicious **3.** dizzy, faint, giddy, light-headed, queasy, reel~ing, uneasy **4.** crazy, demented, eccentric, idiosyncratic, irrational, mad, odd, touched, unbalanced, unhinged *~verb* **5.** bodge *(infor~mal)*, botch, endanger, harm, impair, imperil, injure, jeopardize, mar, ruin, spoil, thwart, wreck
Antonyms *adjective* believable, common, con~ventional, customary, natural, normal, ordi~nary, orthodox, rational, regular, straight, unexceptional, unoriginal *~verb* aid, boost, enhance, help

quell 1. conquer, crush, defeat, extinguish, overcome, overpower, put down, quash, squelch, stamp out, stifle, subdue, suppress, vanquish **2.** allay, alleviate, appease, assuage, calm, compose, deaden, dull, mitigate, moder~ate, mollify, pacify, quiet, silence, soothe

quench 1. check, crush, destroy, douse, end, extinguish, put out, smother, snuff out, squelch, stifle, suppress **2.** allay, appease, cool, sate, satiate, satisfy, slake

querulous cantankerous, captious, carping, censorious, complaining, critical, cross, dis~contented, dissatisfied, fault-finding, fretful, grouchy *(informal)*, grumbling, hard to please, irascible, irritable, murmuring, peevish, petu~lant, plaintive, ratty *(Brit. & N.Z. informal)*, sour, testy, tetchy, touchy, waspish, whining
Antonyms contented, easy to please, equable, placid, uncomplaining, uncritical, undemand~ing

query *verb* **1.** ask, enquire, question **2.** chal~lenge, disbelieve, dispute, distrust, doubt, mistrust, suspect *~noun* **3.** demand, doubt, hesitation, inquiry, objection, problem, ques~tion, reservation, scepticism, suspicion

quest *noun* adventure, crusade, enterprise, ex~pedition, exploration, hunt, journey, mission, pilgrimage, pursuit, search, voyage

question *verb* **1.** ask, catechize, cross-examine, enquire, examine, grill *(informal)*, interrogate, interview, investigate, probe, pump *(informal)*, quiz, sound out **2.** call into question, cast doubt upon, challenge, controvert, disbelieve, dispute, distrust, doubt, impugn, mistrust, oppose, query, suspect *~noun* **3.** examination, inquiry, interrogation, investigation **4.** argu~ment, can of worms *(informal)*, confusion, contention, controversy, debate, difficulty, dis~pute, doubt, dubiety, misgiving, problem, que~

ry, uncertainty **5.** bone of contention, issue, motion, point, point at issue, proposal, proposition, subject, theme, topic **6. in question** at issue, in doubt, open to debate, under discussion **7. out of the question** impossible, inconceivable, not to be thought of, unthinkable
Antonyms (*senses 1 & 3*) answer, reply (*sense 2*) accept, believe, buy (*slang*), swallow (*informal*), take on board, take on trust

Ask a silly question and you get a silly answer

Ask no questions and hear no lies

questionable arguable, controversial, controvertible, debatable, disputable, dodgy (*Brit., Austral., & N.Z. informal*), doubtful, dubious, dubitable, equivocal, fishy (*informal*), iffy (*informal*), moot, paradoxical, problematical, shady (*informal*), suspect, suspicious, uncertain, unproven, unreliable
Antonyms authoritative, certain, incontrovertible, indisputable, straightforward, unequivocal

queue chain, concatenation, file, line, order, progression, sequence, series, string, succession, train

quibble 1. *verb* carp, cavil, equivocate, evade, pretend, prevaricate, shift, split hairs **2.** *noun* artifice, cavil, complaint, criticism, duplicity, equivocation, evasion, nicety, niggle, objection, pretence, prevarication, protest, quiddity, quirk, shift, sophism, subterfuge, subtlety

quibbling ambiguous, carping, caviling, critical, equivocal, evasive, hair-splitting, jesuitical, niggling, nit-picking (*informal*), overnice, sophistical

quick 1. active, brief, brisk, cursory, expeditious, express, fast, fleet, hasty, headlong, hurried, pdq (*slang*), perfunctory, prompt, quickie (*informal*), rapid, speedy, sudden, swift **2.** agile, alert, animated, energetic, flying, keen, lively, nimble, spirited, sprightly, spry, vivacious, winged **3.** able, acute, adept, adroit, all there (*informal*), apt, astute, bright (*informal*), clever, deft, dexterous, discerning, intelligent, nimble-witted, perceptive, quick on the uptake (*informal*), quick-witted, receptive, sharp, shrewd, skilful, smart **4.** abrupt, curt, excitable, hasty, impatient, irascible, irritable, passionate, petulant, testy, touchy **5.** *archaic* alive, animate, existing, live, living, viable
Antonyms calm, deliberate, dull, gradual, heavy, inactive, inexpert, lazy, lethargic, long, maladroit, patient, restrained, slow, sluggish, stupid, unintelligent, unresponsive, unskilful

quicken 1. accelerate, dispatch, expedite, hasten, hurry, impel, precipitate, speed **2.** activate, animate, arouse, energize, excite, galvanize, incite, inspire, invigorate, kindle, refresh, reinvigorate, resuscitate, revitalize, revive, rouse, stimulate, strengthen, vitalize, vivify

quickly abruptly, apace, at a rate of knots (*informal*), at *or* on the double, at speed, briskly, expeditiously, fast, hastily, hell for leather (*informal*), hotfoot, hurriedly, immediately, instantly, like greased lightning (*informal*), like lightning, like nobody's business (*informal*), like the clappers (*Brit. informal*), pdq (*slang*), posthaste, promptly, pronto (*informal*), quick, rapidly, soon, speedily, swiftly, with all speed
Antonyms carefully, eventually, slowly, sluggishly, unhurriedly

quick-tempered cantankerous, choleric, excitable, fiery, hot-tempered, impatient, impulsive, irascible, irritable, petulant, quarrelsome, ratty (*Brit. & N.Z. informal*), shrewish, splenetic, testy, tetchy, waspish
Antonyms cool, dispassionate, phlegmatic, placid, slow to anger, tolerant

quick-witted alert, astute, bright (*informal*), clever, keen, perceptive, sharp, shrewd, smart
Antonyms dull, obtuse, slow, slow-witted, stupid, thick (*informal*), unperceptive

quid pro quo compensation, equivalent, exchange, interchange, reprisal, retaliation, substitution, tit for tat

quiescent calm, dormant, in abeyance, inactive, latent, motionless, peaceful, placid, quiet, resting, serene, silent, smooth, still, tranquil, unagitated, undisturbed, unmoving, unruffled

quiet *adjective* **1.** dumb, hushed, inaudible, low, low-pitched, noiseless, peaceful, silent, soft, soundless **2.** calm, contented, gentle, mild, motionless, pacific, peaceful, placid, restful, serene, smooth, tranquil, untroubled **3.** isolated, private, retired, secluded, secret, sequestered, undisturbed, unfrequented **4.** conservative, modest, plain, restrained, simple, sober, subdued, unassuming, unobtrusive, unpretentious **5.** collected, docile, even-tempered, gentle, imperturbable, meek, mild, phlegmatic, reserved, retiring, sedate, shy, unexcitable *~noun* **6.** calmness, ease, peace, quietness, repose, rest, serenity, silence, stillness, tranquillity
Antonyms *adjective* (*sense 1*) deafening, ear-splitting, high-decibel, high-volume, loud, noisy, stentorian (*sense 2*) agitated, alert, excitable, exciting, frenetic, troubled, turbulent, violent (*sense 3*) bustling, busy, crowded, exciting, fashionable, lively, popular, vibrant (*sense 4*) blatant, brash, bright, conspicuous, glaring, loud, obtrusive, ostentatious, pretentious, showy (*sense 5*) excitable, excited, high-spirited, impatient, loquacious, passionate, restless, talkative, verbose, violent *~noun* (*sense 6*) activity, bustle, commotion, din, disturbance, noise, racket

quieten *verb* allay, alleviate, appease, assuage, blunt, calm, compose, deaden, dull, hush, lull, mitigate, mollify, muffle, mute, palliate, quell, quiet, shush (*informal*), silence, soothe, stifle, still, stop, subdue, tranquillize

Antonyms aggravate, exacerbate, intensify, provoke, upset, worsen

quietly 1. confidentially, dumbly, in a low voice *or* whisper, in an undertone, inaudibly, in hushed tones, in silence, mutely, noiselessly, privately, secretly, silently, softly, without talking 2. calmly, contentedly, dispassionately, meekly, mildly, patiently, placidly, serenely, undemonstratively 3. coyly, demurely, diffidently, humbly, modestly, unassumingly, unobtrusively, unostentatiously, unpretentiously

quietness calm, calmness, hush, peace, placidity, quiescence, quiet, quietude, repose, rest, serenity, silence, still, stillness, tranquillity

quietus clincher (*informal*), *coup de grâce*, death, deathblow, demise, end, final blow, finish

quilt bedspread, comforter (*U.S.*), continental quilt, counterpane, coverlet, doona (*Austral.*), downie (*informal*), duvet, eiderdown

quintessence core, distillation, essence, extract, gist, heart, kernel, lifeblood, marrow, pith, soul, spirit

quintessential archetypal, definitive, essential, fundamental, prototypical, typical, ultimate

quip *noun* badinage, *bon mot*, counterattack, gibe, jest, joke, pleasantry, repartee, retort, riposte, sally, wisecrack (*informal*), witticism

quirk aberration, bee in one's bonnet, caprice, characteristic, eccentricity, fancy, fetish, foible, habit, *idée fixe*, idiosyncrasy, kink, mannerism, oddity, peculiarity, singularity, trait, vagary, whim

quirky capricious, curious, eccentric, fanciful, idiosyncratic, odd, offbeat, peculiar, rum (*Brit. slang*), singular, unpredictable, unusual, whimsical

quisling betrayer, collaborator, fifth columnist, Judas, renegade, traitor, turncoat

quit *verb* 1. abandon, abdicate, decamp, depart, desert, exit, forsake, go, leave, pack one's bags (*informal*), pull out, relinquish, renounce, resign, retire, step down (*informal*), surrender, take off (*informal*), withdraw 2. abandon, belay (*Nautical*), cease, conclude, discontinue, drop, end, give up, halt, stop, suspend, throw in the towel *~adjective* 3. absolved, acquitted, clear, discharged, exculpated, exempt, exonerated, free, released, rid of

Antonyms (*sense 2*) complete, continue, finish, go on with, see through

quite 1. absolutely, completely, considerably, entirely, fully, in all respects, largely, perfectly, precisely, totally, wholly, without reservation 2. fairly, moderately, rather, reasonably, relatively, somewhat, to a certain extent, to some degree 3. in fact, in reality, in truth, really, truly

quiver 1. *verb* agitate, convulse, oscillate, palpitate, pulsate, quake, quaver, shake, shiver, shudder, tremble, vibrate 2. *noun* convulsion, oscillation, palpitation, pulsation, shake, shiver, shudder, spasm, throb, tic, tremble, tremor, vibration

quixotic absurd, chimerical, chivalrous, dreamy, fanciful, fantastical, idealistic, imaginary, impracticable, impractical, impulsive, mad, romantic, unrealistic, unworldly, Utopian, visionary, wild

quiz 1. *noun* examination, investigation, questioning, test 2. *verb* ask, catechize, examine, grill (*informal*), interrogate, investigate, pump (*informal*), question

quizzical arch, bantering, curious, derisive, inquiring, mocking, questioning, sardonic, supercilious, teasing

quondam bygone, earlier, ex-, foregoing, former, late, one-time, past, previous, retired, sometime

quota allocation, allowance, assignment, cut (*informal*), part, portion, proportion, ration, share, slice, whack (*informal*)

quotation 1. citation, cutting, excerpt, extract, passage, quote (*informal*), reference, selection 2. *Commerce* bid price, charge, cost, estimate, figure, price, quote (*informal*), rate, tender

> *Every quotation contributes something to the stability or enlargement of the language*
> Dr. Johnson *Dictionary of the English Language (preface)*

quote adduce, attest, cite, detail, extract, instance, name, paraphrase, proclaim, recall, recite, recollect, refer to, repeat, retell

quotidian 1. daily, diurnal 2. common, commonplace, customary, everyday, habitual, ordinary, regular, routine

R

rabble **1.** canaille, crowd, herd, horde, mob, swarm, throng **2.** *derogatory* canaille, commonalty, commoners, common people, crowd, dregs, hoi polloi, lower classes, lumpenproletariat, masses, peasantry, populace, proletariat, riffraff, scum, the great unwashed (*informal & derogatory*), trash (*chiefly U.S. & Canad.*)
Antonyms (*sense 2*) aristocracy, bourgeoisie, elite, gentry, high society, nobility, upper classes

rabble-rouser agitator, demagogue, firebrand, incendiary, stirrer (*informal*), troublemaker

Rabelaisian bawdy, broad, coarse, earthy, extravagant, exuberant, gross, lusty, raunchy (*slang*), robust, satirical, uninhibited, unrestrained

rabid **1.** hydrophobic, mad **2.** berserk, crazed, frantic, frenzied, furious, infuriated, mad, maniacal, raging, violent, wild **3.** bigoted, extreme, fanatical, fervent, intemperate, intolerant, irrational, narrow-minded, zealous
Antonyms (*sense 3*) half-hearted, moderate, wishy-washy (*informal*)

race[1] **1.** *noun* chase, competition, contention, contest, dash, pursuit, rivalry **2.** *verb* barrel (along) (*informal, chiefly U.S. & Canad.*), burn rubber (*informal*), career, compete, contest, dart, dash, fly, gallop, go like a bomb (*Brit. & N.Z. informal*), hare (*Brit. informal*), hasten, hurry, run, run like mad (*informal*), speed, tear, zoom

race[2] *noun* blood, breed, clan, ethnic group, family, folk, house, issue, kin, kindred, line, lineage, nation, offspring, people, progeny, seed (*chiefly biblical*), stock, tribe, type

Say it loud: I'm Black and I'm proud!
James Brown

racial ethnic, ethnological, folk, genealogical, genetic, national, tribal

rack *noun* **1.** frame, framework, stand, structure **2.** affliction, agony, anguish, misery, pain, pang, persecution, suffering, torment, torture *~verb* **3.** afflict, agonize, crucify, distress, excruciate, harass, harrow, oppress, pain, torment, torture **4.** force, pull, shake, strain, stress, stretch, tear, wrench

racket **1.** babel, ballyhoo (*informal*), clamour, commotion, din, disturbance, fuss, hubbub, hullabaloo, noise, outcry, pandemonium, row, shouting, tumult, uproar **2.** criminal activity, fraud, illegal enterprise, scheme **3.** *slang* business, game (*informal*), line, occupation

rackety blaring, boisterous, clamorous, disorderly, noisy, rowdy, uproarious

racy **1.** animated, buoyant, dramatic, energetic, entertaining, exciting, exhilarating, heady, lively, sexy (*informal*), sparkling, spirited, stimulating, vigorous, zestful **2.** distinctive, piquant, pungent, rich, sharp, spicy, strong, tangy, tart, tasty **3.** bawdy, blue, broad, immodest, indecent, indelicate, naughty, near the knuckle (*informal*), off colour, risqué, smutty, spicy (*informal*), suggestive

raddled broken-down, coarsened, dilapidated, dishevelled, haggard, run-down, tattered, the worse for wear, unkempt

radiance **1.** brightness, brilliance, effulgence, glare, gleam, glitter, glow, incandescence, light, luminosity, lustre, resplendence, shine **2.** delight, gaiety, happiness, joy, pleasure, rapture, warmth

radiant **1.** beaming, bright, brilliant, effulgent, gleaming, glittering, glorious, glowing, incandescent, luminous, lustrous, resplendent, shining, sparkling, sunny **2.** beaming, beatific, blissed out, blissful, delighted, ecstatic, floating on air, gay, glowing, happy, joyful, joyous, on cloud nine (*informal*), rapt, rapturous, sent
Antonyms (*sense 1*) black, dark, dull, gloomy, sombre (*sense 2*) disconsolate, down in the dumps (*informal*), gloomy, joyless, low, miserable, sad, sombre, sorrowful

radiate **1.** diffuse, disseminate, emanate, emit, give off *or* out, gleam, glitter, pour, scatter, send out, shed, shine, spread **2.** branch out, diverge, issue, spread out

radiation emanation, emission, rays

radical *adjective* **1.** basic, constitutional, deep-seated, essential, fundamental, innate, native, natural, organic, profound, thoroughgoing **2.** complete, drastic, entire, excessive, extreme, extremist, fanatical, revolutionary, severe, sweeping, thorough, violent *~noun* **3.** extremist, fanatic, militant, revolutionary
Antonyms *adjective* insignificant, minor, superficial, token, trivial *~noun* conservative, moderate, reactionary

A radical is a man with both feet firmly planted in the air
Franklin D. Roosevelt

raffish 1. bohemian, careless, casual, dashing, devil-may-care, disreputable, jaunty, rakish, sporty, unconventional 2. coarse, flash (*informal*), garish, gaudy, gross, loud, meretricious, showy, tasteless, tawdry, trashy, uncouth, vulgar

raffle draw, lottery, sweep, sweepstake

ragamuffin gamin, guttersnipe, scarecrow (*informal*), street arab, tatterdemalion (*rare*), urchin

ragbag 1. confusion, hotchpotch, jumble, medley, miscellany, mixed bag (*informal*), mixture, omnium-gatherum, potpourri 2. *informal* frump, scarecrow (*informal*), scruff (*informal*), slattern, sloven, slut, trollop

rage *noun* 1. agitation, anger, frenzy, fury, high dudgeon, ire, madness, mania, obsession, passion, rampage, raving, vehemence, violence, wrath 2. craze, enthusiasm, fad (*informal*), fashion, latest thing, mode, style, vogue ~*verb* 3. be beside oneself, be furious, blow a fuse (*slang, chiefly U.S.*), blow one's top, blow up (*informal*), chafe, crack up (*informal*), flip one's lid (*slang*), fly off the handle (*informal*), foam at the mouth, fret, fume, go ballistic (*slang, chiefly U.S.*), go off the deep end (*informal*), go up the wall (*slang*), rant and rave, rave, see red (*informal*), seethe, storm, throw a fit (*informal*), wig out (*slang*) 4. be at its height, be uncontrollable, rampage, storm, surge
Antonyms *noun* (*sense 1*) acceptance, calmness, equanimity, gladness, good humour, joy, pleasure, resignation ~*verb* (*sense 3*) accept, keep one's cool, remain unruffled, resign oneself to, stay calm

ragged 1. contemptible, down at heel, frayed, in holes, in rags, in tatters, mean, poor, rent, scraggy, shabby, shaggy, tattered, tatty, threadbare, torn, unkempt, worn-out 2. crude, jagged, notched, poor, rough, rugged, serrated, uneven, unfinished 3. broken, desultory, disorganized, fragmented, irregular, uneven
Antonyms (*sense 1*) fashionable, smart, well-dressed

raging beside oneself, boiling mad (*informal*), doing one's nut (*Brit. slang*), enraged, fit to be tied (*slang*), fizzing (*Scot.*), foaming at the mouth, frenzied, fuming, furious, incensed, infuriated, mad, raving, seething

rags 1. castoffs, old clothes, tattered clothing, tatters 2. **in rags** down at heel, out at elbow, ragged, seedy, shabby, tattered
Antonyms finery, gladrags, Sunday best

raid 1. *noun* attack, break-in, descent, foray, hit-and-run attack, incursion, inroad, invasion, irruption, onset, sally, seizure, sortie, surprise attack 2. *verb* assault, attack, break into, descend on, fall upon, forage (*Military*), foray, invade, pillage, plunder, reive (*dialect*), rifle, sack, sally forth, swoop down upon

raider attacker, forager (*Military*), invader, marauder, plunderer, reiver (*dialect*), robber, thief

rail *verb* abuse, attack, blast, castigate, censure, complain, criticize, fulminate, inveigh, lambast(e), put down, revile, scold, tear into (*informal*), upbraid, vituperate, vociferate

railing balustrade, barrier, fence, paling, rails

raillery badinage, banter, chaff, irony, jesting, joke, joking, josh (*slang, chiefly U.S. & Canad.*), kidding (*informal*), mockery, persiflage, pleasantry, repartee, ridicule, satire, sport, teasing

rain *noun* 1. cloudburst, deluge, downpour, drizzle, fall, precipitation, raindrops, rainfall, showers 2. deluge, flood, hail, shower, spate, stream, torrent, volley ~*verb* 3. bucket down (*informal*), come down in buckets (*informal*), drizzle, fall, pelt (down), pour, rain cats and dogs (*informal*), shower, teem 4. deposit, drop, fall, shower, sprinkle 5. bestow, lavish, pour, shower
Related adjectives: hyetal, pluvial

The rain it raineth every day
William Shakespeare *Twelfth Night*

It never rains but it pours

rainy damp, drizzly, showery, wet
Antonyms arid, dry, fine, sunny

raise 1. build, construct, elevate, erect, exalt, heave, hoist, lift, move up, promote, put up, rear, set upright, uplift 2. advance, aggravate, amplify, augment, boost, enhance, enlarge, escalate, exaggerate, heighten, hike (up) (*informal*), increase, inflate, intensify, jack up, magnify, put up, reinforce, strengthen 3. advance, aggrandize, elevate, exalt, prefer, promote, upgrade 4. activate, arouse, awaken, cause, evoke, excite, foment, foster, incite, instigate, kindle, motivate, provoke, rouse, set on foot, stir up, summon up, whip up 5. bring about, cause, create, engender, give rise to, occasion, originate, produce, provoke, start 6. advance, bring up, broach, introduce, moot, put forward, suggest 7. assemble, collect, form, gather, get, levy, mass, mobilize, muster, obtain, rally, recruit 8. breed, bring up, cultivate, develop, grow, nurture, produce, propagate, rear 9. abandon, end, give up, lift, relieve, relinquish, remove, terminate
Antonyms begin, calm, cut, decrease, demolish, depress, destroy, diminish, drop, establish, lessen, let down, level, lower, quash, quell, reduce, ruin, sink, soothe, start, suppress, wreck

rake[1] *verb* 1. collect, gather, remove, scrape up 2. break up, harrow, hoe, scour, scrape, scratch 3. *with* **up** *or* **together** assemble, collect, dig up, dredge up, gather, scrape together 4. comb, examine, forage, hunt, ransack, scan, scour, scrutinize, search 5. graze, scrape, scratch 6. enfilade, pepper, sweep

rake[2] *noun* debauchee, dissolute man, lech *or* letch (*informal*), lecher, libertine, playboy, profligate, rakehell (*archaic*), roué, sensualist, voluptuary
Antonyms ascetic, celibate, monk, puritan

rakish[1] *adjective* abandoned, debauched, depraved, dissipated, dissolute, immoral, lecherous, licentious, loose, prodigal, profligate, sinful, wanton

rakish[2] *adjective* breezy, dapper, dashing, debonair, devil-may-care, flashy, jaunty, natty (*informal*), raffish, smart, snazzy (*informal*), sporty

rally[1] 1. *verb* bring *or* come to order, reassemble, re-form, regroup, reorganize, unite 2. *noun* regrouping, reorganization, reunion, stand 3. *verb* assemble, bond together, bring *or* come together, collect, convene, gather, get together, marshal, mobilize, muster, organize, round up, summon, unite 4. *noun* assembly, conference, congregation, congress, convention, convocation, gathering, mass meeting, meeting, muster 5. *verb* be on the mend, come round, get better, get one's second wind, improve, perk up, pick up, pull through, recover, recuperate, regain one's strength, revive, take a turn for the better, turn the corner 6. *noun* comeback (*informal*), improvement, recovery, recuperation, renewal, resurgence, revival, turn for the better
Antonyms *verb* (*sense 3*) disband, disperse, separate, split up (*sense 5*) deteriorate, fail, get worse, relapse, take a turn for the worse, worsen ~*noun* (*sense 6*) collapse, deterioration, relapse, turn for the worse

rally[2] *verb* chaff, make fun of, mock, poke fun at, ridicule, send up (*Brit. informal*), take the mickey out of (*informal*), taunt, tease, twit

ram *verb* 1. butt, collide with, crash, dash, drive, force, hit, impact, run into, slam, smash, strike 2. beat, cram, crowd, drum, force, hammer, jam, pack, pound, stuff, tamp, thrust

ramble *verb* 1. amble, drift, perambulate, peregrinate, range, roam, rove, saunter, straggle, stravaig (*Scot. & northern English dialect*), stray, stroll, traipse (*informal*), walk, wander 2. meander, snake, twist and turn, wind, zigzag 3. babble, chatter, digress, expatiate, maunder, rabbit (on) (*Brit. informal*), rattle on, run off at the mouth (*slang*), waffle (*informal, chiefly Brit.*), wander, witter on (*informal*) ~*noun* 4. excursion, hike, perambulation, peregrination, roaming, roving, saunter, stroll, tour, traipse (*informal*), trip, walk

rambler drifter, hiker, roamer, rover, stroller, walker, wanderer, wayfarer

rambling 1. circuitous, desultory, diffuse, digressive, disconnected, discursive, disjointed, incoherent, irregular, long-winded, periphrastic, prolix, wordy 2. irregular, sprawling, spreading, straggling, trailing
Antonyms (*sense 1*) coherent, concise, direct, to the point

ramification 1. branch, development, divarication, division, excrescence, extension, forking, offshoot, outgrowth, subdivision 2. complication, consequence, development, result, sequel, upshot

ramify 1. branch, divaricate, divide, fork, separate, split up 2. become complicated, multiply, thicken

ramp grade, gradient, incline, inclined plane, rise, slope

rampage *verb* 1. go ape (*slang*), go apeshit (*slang*), go ballistic (*slang, chiefly U.S.*), go berserk, rage, run amuck, run riot, run wild, storm, tear ~*noun* 2. destruction, frenzy, fury, rage, storm, tempest, tumult, uproar, violence 3. **on the rampage** amuck, berserk, destructive, out of control, raging, rampant, riotous, violent, wild

rampant 1. aggressive, dominant, excessive, flagrant, on the rampage, out of control, out of hand, outrageous, raging, rampaging, riotous, unbridled, uncontrollable, ungovernable, unrestrained, vehement, violent, wanton, wild 2. epidemic, exuberant, luxuriant, prevalent, profuse, rank, rife, spreading like wildfire, unchecked, uncontrolled, unrestrained, widespread 3. *Heraldry* erect, rearing, standing, upright

rampart barricade, bastion, breastwork, bulwark, defence, earthwork, embankment, fence, fort, fortification, guard, parapet, security, stronghold, wall

ramshackle broken-down, crumbling, decrepit, derelict, dilapidated, flimsy, jerry-built, rickety, shaky, tottering, tumbledown, unsafe, unsteady
Antonyms solid, stable, steady, well-built

rancid bad, fetid, foul, frowsty, fusty, musty, off, putrid, rank, rotten, sour, stale, strong-smelling, tainted
Antonyms fresh, pure, undecayed

rancorous acrimonious, bitter, hostile, implacable, malevolent, malicious, malign, malignant, resentful, spiteful, splenetic, venomous, vindictive, virulent

rancour animosity, animus, antipathy, bad blood, bitterness, chip on one's shoulder (*informal*), enmity, grudge, hate, hatred, hostility, ill feeling, ill will, malevolence, malice, malignity, resentfulness, resentment, spite, spleen, venom

random 1. accidental, adventitious, aimless, arbitrary, casual, chance, desultory, fortuitous, haphazard, hit or miss, incidental, indiscriminate, purposeless, spot, stray, unplanned, unpremeditated 2. **at random** accidentally, adventitiously, aimlessly, arbitrarily, by chance, casually, haphazardly, indiscriminately, irregularly, purposelessly, randomly, unsystematically, willy-nilly

Antonyms definite, deliberate, intended, planned, premeditated, specific

randy amorous, aroused, concupiscent, horny (*slang*), hot, lascivious, lecherous, lustful, raunchy (*slang*), satyric, sexually excited, sexy (*informal*), turned-on (*slang*)

range *noun* 1. ambit, amplitude, area, bounds, compass, confines, distance, domain, extent, field, latitude, limits, orbit, pale, parameters (*informal*), province, purview, radius, reach, scope, span, sphere, sweep 2. chain, file, line, rank, row, sequence, series, string, tier 3. assortment, class, collection, gamut, kind, lot, order, selection, series, sort, variety *~verb* 4. align, arrange, array, dispose, draw up, line up, order, sequence 5. arrange, bracket, catalogue, categorize, class, classify, file, grade, group, pigeonhole, rank 6. aim, align, direct, level, point, train 7. cruise, explore, ramble, roam, rove, straggle, stray, stroll, sweep, traverse, wander 8. extend, fluctuate, go, reach, run, stretch, vary between

rangy gangling, lanky, leggy, long-legged, long-limbed

rank[1] *noun* 1. caste, class, classification, degree, dignity, division, echelon, grade, level, nobility, order, position, quality, sort, standing, station, status, stratum, type 2. column, file, formation, group, line, range, row, series, tier *~verb* 3. align, arrange, array, class, classify, dispose, grade, line up, locate, marshal, order, position, range, sequence, sort

rank[2] *adjective* 1. abundant, dense, exuberant, flourishing, lush, luxuriant, productive, profuse, strong-growing, vigorous 2. bad, disagreeable, disgusting, fetid, foul, fusty, gamy, mephitic, musty, noisome, noxious, off, offensive, olid, pungent, putrid, rancid, revolting, stale, stinking, strong-smelling, yucky *or* yukky (*slang*) 3. absolute, arrant, blatant, complete, downright, egregious, excessive, extravagant, flagrant, glaring, gross, rampant, sheer, thorough, total, undisguised, unmitigated, utter 4. abusive, atrocious, coarse, crass, filthy, foul, gross, indecent, nasty, obscene, outrageous, scurrilous, shocking, vulgar

rank and file 1. lower ranks, men, other ranks, private soldiers, soldiers, troops 2. body, general public, Joe (and Eileen) Public (*slang*), Joe Six-Pack (*U.S. slang*), majority, mass, masses

rankle anger, annoy, chafe, embitter, fester, gall, get one's goat (*slang*), get on one's nerves (*informal*), irk, irritate, piss one off (*taboo slang*), rile

ransack 1. comb, explore, forage, go through, rake, rummage, scour, search, turn inside out 2. despoil, gut, loot, pillage, plunder, raid, ravage, rifle, sack, strip

ransom *noun* 1. deliverance, liberation, redemption, release, rescue 2. money, payment, payoff, price *~verb* 3. buy (someone) out (*informal*), buy the freedom of, deliver, liberate, obtain *or* pay for the release of, redeem, release, rescue, set free

rant 1. *verb* bellow, bluster, cry, declaim, rave, roar, shout, spout (*informal*), vociferate, yell 2. *noun* bluster, bombast, diatribe, fanfaronade (*rare*), harangue, philippic, rhetoric, tirade, vociferation

rap *verb* 1. crack, hit, knock, strike, tap 2. bark, speak abruptly, spit 3. *slang, chiefly U.S.* chat, confabulate, converse, discourse, shoot the breeze (*slang, chiefly U.S.*), talk 4. blast, carpet (*informal*), castigate, censure, chew out (*U.S. & Canad. informal*), criticize, give a rocket (*Brit. & N.Z. informal*), knock (*informal*), lambast(e), pan (*informal*), read the riot act, reprimand, scold, tick off (*informal*) *~noun* 5. blow, clout (*informal*), crack, knock, tap 6. *slang, chiefly U.S.* chat, colloquy, confabulation, conversation, dialogue, discourse, discussion, talk 7. *slang* blame, censure, chiding, punishment, rebuke, responsibility, sentence

rapacious avaricious, extortionate, grasping, greedy, insatiable, marauding, plundering, predatory, preying, ravenous, usurious, voracious, wolfish

rapacity avarice, avidity, cupidity, graspingness, greed, greediness, insatiableness, predatoriness, rapaciousness, ravenousness, usury, voraciousness, voracity, wolfishness

rape *noun* 1. outrage, ravishment, sexual assault, violation 2. depredation, despoilment, despoliation, pillage, plundering, rapine, sack, spoliation 3. abuse, defilement, desecration, maltreatment, perversion, violation *~verb* 4. abuse, force, outrage, ravish, sexually assault, violate 5. despoil, loot, pillage, plunder, ransack, sack, spoliate

rapid brisk, expeditious, express, fast, fleet, flying, hasty, hurried, pdq (*slang*), precipitate, prompt, quick, quickie (*informal*), speedy, swift

Antonyms deliberate, gradual, leisurely, slow, tardy, unhurried

rapidity alacrity, briskness, celerity, dispatch, expedition, fleetness, haste, hurry, precipitateness, promptitude, promptness, quickness, rush, speed, speediness, swiftness, velocity

rapidly apace, at speed, briskly, expeditiously, fast, hastily, hell for leather, hotfoot, hurriedly, in a hurry, in a rush, in haste, like a shot, like greased lightning (*informal*), like lightning, like nobody's business (*informal*), like the clappers (*Brit. informal*), pdq (*slang*), posthaste, precipitately, promptly, pronto (*informal*), quickly, speedily, swiftly, with dispatch

rapine depredation, despoilment, despoliation, looting, marauding, pillage, plunder, ransacking, rape, robbery, sack, seizure, spoliation, theft

rapport affinity, bond, empathy, harmony, interrelationship, link, relationship, sympathy, tie, understanding

rapprochement détente, reconcilement, reconciliation, restoration of harmony, reunion, softening
Antonyms antagonism, dissension, exacerbation, falling-out, quarrel, resumption of hostilities, schism

rapscallion bad egg (*old-fashioned informal*), blackguard, black sheep, cad, disgrace, good-for-nothing, knave (*archaic*), ne'er-do-well, rascal, rogue, scally (*Northwest English dialect*), scallywag (*informal*), scamp, scoundrel, scrote (*slang*), wastrel

rapt **1.** absorbed, carried away, engrossed, enthralled, entranced, fascinated, gripped, held, intent, preoccupied, spellbound **2.** bewitched, blissed out, blissful, captivated, charmed, delighted, ecstatic, enchanted, enraptured, rapturous, ravished, sent, transported
Antonyms bored, detached, left cold, unaffected, uninterested, uninvolved, unmoved

rapture beatitude, bliss, cloud nine (*informal*), delectation, delight, ecstasy, enthusiasm, euphoria, exaltation, felicity, happiness, joy, ravishment, rhapsody, seventh heaven, spell, transport

rapturous blissed out, blissful, delighted, ecstatic, enthusiastic, euphoric, exalted, floating on air, happy, in seventh heaven, joyful, joyous, on cloud nine (*informal*), overjoyed, over the moon (*informal*), rapt, ravished, rhapsodic, sent, transported

rare[1] *adjective* **1.** exceptional, few, infrequent, out of the ordinary, recherché, scarce, singular, sparse, sporadic, strange, thin on the ground, uncommon, unusual **2.** admirable, choice, excellent, exquisite, extreme, fine, great, incomparable, peerless, superb, superlative **3.** invaluable, precious, priceless, rich
Antonyms abundant, bountiful, common, frequent, habitual, manifold, many, plentiful, profuse, regular

rare[2] *adjective* bloody, half-cooked, half-raw, undercooked, underdone

rarefied **1.** elevated, exalted, high, lofty, noble, spiritual, sublime **2.** clannish, cliquish, esoteric, exclusive, occult, private, select

rarefy attenuate, clarify, purify, refine, sublimate, subtilize, thin out

rarely **1.** almost never, hardly, hardly ever, infrequently, little, once in a blue moon, once in a while, only now and then, on rare occasions, scarcely ever, seldom **2.** exceptionally, extraordinarily, finely, notably, remarkably, singularly, uncommonly, unusually
Antonyms commonly, frequently, often, regularly, usually

raring athirst, avid, champing at the bit (*informal*), desperate, eager, enthusiastic, impatient, keen, keen as mustard, longing, ready, willing, yearning

rarity **1.** collector's item, curio, curiosity, find, gem, one-off, pearl, treasure **2.** infrequency, scarcity, shortage, singularity, sparseness, strangeness, uncommonness, unusualness **3.** choiceness, excellence, exquisiteness, fineness, incomparability, incomparableness, peerlessness, quality, superbness **4.** invaluableness, preciousness, pricelessness, richness, value, worth

rascal bad egg (*old-fashioned informal*), blackguard, caitiff (*archaic*), devil, disgrace, good-for-nothing, imp, knave (*archaic*), miscreant, ne'er-do-well, pickle (*Brit. informal*), rake, rapscallion, reprobate, rogue, scally (*Northwest English dialect*), scallywag (*informal*), scamp, scoundrel, varmint (*informal*), villain, wastrel, wretch

rascally bad, base, crooked, dishonest, disreputable, evil, good-for-nothing, low, mean, reprobate, scoundrelly, unscrupulous, vicious, villainous, wicked

rash[1] *adjective* adventurous, audacious, brash, careless, foolhardy, harebrained, harum-scarum, hasty, headlong, headstrong, heedless, helter-skelter, hot-headed, ill-advised, ill-considered, impetuous, imprudent, impulsive, incautious, indiscreet, injudicious, madcap, precipitate, premature, reckless, thoughtless, unguarded, unthinking, unwary, venturesome
Antonyms canny, careful, cautious, considered, premeditated, prudent, well-thought-out

rash[2] *noun* **1.** eruption, outbreak **2.** epidemic, flood, outbreak, plague, series, spate, succession, wave

rashness adventurousness, audacity, brashness, carelessness, foolhardiness, hastiness, heedlessness, indiscretion, precipitation, recklessness, temerity, thoughtlessness

rasp *noun* 1. grating, grinding, scrape, scratch *~verb* 2. abrade, excoriate, file, grind, rub, sand, scour, scrape 3. grate (upon), irk, irritate, jar (upon), rub (someone) up the wrong way, set one's teeth on edge, wear upon

rasping *or* **raspy** creaking, croaking, croaky, grating, gravelly, gruff, harsh, hoarse, husky, jarring, rough, scratchy

rat *informal noun* 1. bad lot, bastard (*offensive*), bounder (*old-fashioned Brit. slang*), cad (*old-fashioned Brit. informal*), heel (*slang*), ratfink (*slang, chiefly U.S. and Canad.*), rogue, rotter (*slang, chiefly Brit.*), scoundrel, shit (*taboo slang*), shyster (*informal, chiefly U.S.*) 2. betrayer, deceiver, defector, deserter, double-crosser, grass (*Brit. informal*), informer, nark (*slang*), quisling, snake in the grass, stool pigeon, traitor, two-timer (*informal*) *~verb* 3. *with* **on** abandon, betray, defect, desert, do the dirty on (*Brit. informal*), leave high and dry, leave (someone) in the lurch, run out on (*informal*), sell down the river (*informal*)

rate[1] *noun* 1. degree, percentage, proportion, ratio, relation, scale, standard 2. charge, cost, dues, duty, fee, figure, hire, price, tariff, tax, toll 3. gait, measure, pace, speed, tempo, time, velocity 4. class, classification, degree, grade, position, quality, rank, rating, status, value, worth 5. **at any rate** anyhow, anyway, at all events, in any case, nevertheless *~verb* 6. adjudge, appraise, assess, class, classify, consider, count, esteem, estimate, evaluate, grade, measure, rank, reckon, regard, value, weigh 7. be entitled to, be worthy of, deserve, merit 8. *slang* admire, esteem, respect, think highly of, value

rate[2] *verb* bawl out (*informal*), berate, blame, carpet (*informal*), castigate, censure, chew out (*U.S. & Canad. informal*), chide, criticize severely, give a rocket (*Brit. & N.Z. informal*), haul over the coals (*informal*), read the riot act, rebuke, reprimand, reprove, roast (*informal*), scold, take to task, tear into (*informal*), tear (someone) off a strip (*informal*), tell off (*informal*), tongue-lash, upbraid

rather 1. a bit, a little, fairly, kind of (*informal*), moderately, pretty (*informal*), quite, relatively, slightly, somewhat, sort of (*informal*), to some degree, to some extent 2. a good bit, noticeably, significantly, very 3. instead, more readily, more willingly, preferably, sooner

ratify affirm, approve, authenticate, authorize, bear out, bind, certify, confirm, consent to, corroborate, endorse, establish, sanction, sign, uphold, validate

Antonyms abrogate, annul, cancel, reject, repeal, repudiate, revoke

rating[1] *noun* class, classification, degree, designation, estimate, evaluation, grade, order, placing, position, rank, rate, standing, status

rating[2] *noun* chiding, dressing down (*informal*), lecture, piece of one's mind, rebuke, reprimand, reproof, roasting (*informal*), row (*informal*), scolding, telling-off (*informal*), ticking-off (*informal*), tongue-lashing, wigging (*Brit. slang*)

ratio arrangement, correlation, correspondence, equation, fraction, percentage, proportion, rate, relation, relationship

ration *noun* 1. allotment, allowance, dole, helping, measure, part, portion, provision, quota, share 2. *plural* commons (*Brit.*), food, provender, provisions, stores, supplies *~verb* 3. *with* **out** allocate, allot, apportion, deal, distribute, dole, give out, issue, measure out, mete, parcel out 4. budget, conserve, control, limit, restrict, save

rational 1. enlightened, intelligent, judicious, logical, lucid, realistic, reasonable, sagacious, sane, sensible, sound, wise 2. cerebral, cognitive, ratiocinative, reasoning, thinking 3. all there (*informal*), balanced, *compos mentis*, in one's right mind, lucid, normal, of sound mind, sane

Antonyms insane, irrational, unreasonable, unsound

rationale exposition, grounds, logic, motivation, philosophy, principle, *raison d'être*, reasons, theory

rationalize 1. account for, excuse, explain away, extenuate, justify, make allowance for, make excuses for, vindicate 2. apply logic to, elucidate, reason out, resolve, think through 3. make cuts, make more efficient, streamline, trim

rattle *verb* 1. bang, clatter, jangle 2. bounce, jar, jiggle, jolt, jounce, shake, vibrate 3. *with* **on** blether, cackle, chatter, gabble, gibber, jabber, prate, prattle, rabbit (on) (*Brit. informal*), run on, witter (*informal*), yak (away) (*slang*) 4. *informal* discomfit, discompose, disconcert, discountenance, disturb, faze, frighten, perturb, put (someone) off his stride, put (someone) out of countenance, scare, shake, upset 5. *with* **off** list, recite, reel off, rehearse, run through, spiel off (*informal*)

ratty angry, annoyed, crabbed, cross, impatient, irritable, short-tempered, snappy, testy, tetchy, touchy

raucous grating, harsh, hoarse, husky, loud, noisy, rasping, rough, strident

Antonyms dulcet, mellifluous, quiet, smooth, sweet

raunchy bawdy, coarse, earthy, lecherous, lewd, lustful, lusty, ribald, salacious, sexual, sexy, smutty, steamy (*informal*), suggestive

ravage 1. *verb* demolish, desolate, despoil, destroy, devastate, gut, lay waste, leave in ruins, loot, pillage, plunder, ransack, raze, ruin, sack, shatter, spoil, wreak havoc on, wreck 2. *noun often plural* damage, demolition, depredation, desolation, destruction, devastation, havoc, pillage, plunder, rapine, ruin, ruination, spoliation, waste

rave *verb* 1. babble, be delirious, fume, go mad (*informal*), rage, rant, roar, run amuck, splutter, storm, talk wildly, thunder 2. *with* **about** *informal* be delighted by, be mad about (*informal*), be wild about (*informal*), cry up, enthuse, gush, praise, rhapsodize *~noun* 3. *informal* acclaim, applause, encomium, praise 4. *Also* **rave-up** *Brit. slang* affair, bash (*informal*), beano (*Brit. slang*), blow-out (*slang*), celebration, do (*informal*), hooley *or* hoolie (*chiefly Irish & N.Z.*), party 5. *Brit. slang* craze, fad, fashion, vogue *~adjective* 6. *informal* ecstatic, enthusiastic, excellent, favourable, laudatory

ravenous 1. esurient, famished, starved, starving, very hungry 2. avaricious, covetous, devouring, edacious, ferocious, gluttonous, grasping, greedy, insatiable, insatiate, predatory, rapacious, ravening, voracious, wolfish
Antonyms full, glutted, sated, satiated

ravine canyon, clough (*dialect*), defile, flume, gap (*U.S.*), gorge, gulch (*U.S.*), gully, linn (*Scot.*), pass

raving berserk, crazed, crazy, delirious, frantic, frenzied, furious, gonzo (*slang*), hysterical, insane, irrational, mad, out of one's mind, rabid, raging, wild

ravish 1. captivate, charm, delight, enchant, enrapture, entrance, fascinate, overjoy, spellbind, transport 2. abuse, force, outrage, rape, sexually assault, violate

> *He in a few minutes ravished this fair creature, or at least would have ravished her, if she had not, by a timely compliance, prevented him*
> Henry Fielding *Jonathan Wild*

ravishing beautiful, bewitching, charming, dazzling, delightful, drop-dead (*slang*), enchanting, entrancing, gorgeous, lovely, radiant, stunning (*informal*)

raw 1. bloody (*of meat*), fresh, natural, uncooked, undressed, unprepared 2. basic, coarse, crude, green, natural, organic, rough, unfinished, unprocessed, unrefined, unripe, untreated 3. abraded, chafed, grazed, open, scratched, sensitive, skinned, sore, tender 4. callow, green, ignorant, immature, inexperienced, new, undisciplined, unpractised, unseasoned, unskilled, untrained, untried 5. bare, blunt, brutal, candid, frank, naked, plain, realistic, unembellished, unvarnished 6. biting, bitter, bleak, chill, chilly, cold, damp, freezing, harsh, parky (*Brit. informal*), piercing, unpleasant, wet
Antonyms (*sense 1*) baked, cooked, done (*sense 2*) finished, prepared, refined (*sense 4*) experienced, practised, professional, skilled, trained (*sense 5*) embellished, gilded

ray 1. bar, beam, flash, gleam, shaft 2. flicker, glimmer, hint, indication, scintilla, spark, trace

raze 1. bulldoze, demolish, destroy, flatten, knock down, level, pull down, remove, ruin, tear down, throw down 2. delete, efface, erase, excise, expunge, extinguish, extirpate, obliterate, rub out, scratch out, strike out, wipe from the face of the earth, wipe out

razzmatazz carry-on (*informal, chiefly Brit.*), commotion, fuss, hullabaloo, performance (*informal*), rigmarole, song and dance (*informal*), to-do

re about, anent (*Scot.*), apropos, concerning, in respect of, on the subject of, regarding, respecting, with reference to, with regard to

reach *verb* 1. arrive at, attain, get as far as, get to, land at, make 2. contact, extend to, get (a) hold of, go as far as, grasp, stretch to, touch 3. amount to, arrive at, attain, climb to, come to, drop, fall, move, rise, sink 4. *informal* hand, hold out, pass, stretch 5. communicate with, contact, establish contact with, find, get, get hold of, get in touch with, get through to, make contact with *~noun* 6. ambit, capacity, command, compass, distance, extension, extent, grasp, influence, jurisdiction, mastery, power, range, scope, spread, stretch, sweep

react 1. acknowledge, answer, reply, respond, rise to the bait, take the bait 2. act, behave, conduct oneself, function, operate, proceed, work

reaction 1. acknowledgment, answer, feedback, reply, response 2. compensation, counteraction, counterbalance, counterpoise, recoil 3. conservatism, counter-revolution, obscurantism, the right

reactionary 1. *adjective* blimpish, conservative, counter-revolutionary, obscurantist, rightist 2. *noun* Colonel Blimp, conservative, counter-revolutionary, die-hard, obscurantist, rightist, right-winger
Antonyms (*senses 1 & 2*) leftist, progressive, radical, reformist, revolutionary, socialist

read 1. glance at, look at, peruse, pore over, refer to, run one's eye over, scan, study 2. announce, declaim, deliver, recite, speak, utter 3. comprehend, construe, decipher, discover, interpret, perceive the meaning of, see, under~

stand 4. display, indicate, record, register, show

Read, mark, learn, and inwardly digest
Book of Common Prayer

readable 1. clear, comprehensible, decipher~able, intelligible, legible, plain, understand~able 2. easy to read, enjoyable, entertaining, enthralling, gripping, interesting, pleasant, worth reading
Antonyms (*sense 1*) illegible, incomprehen~sible, indecipherable, unintelligible, unread~able (*sense 2*) as dry as dust, badly-written, boring, dull, heavy, heavy going, pretentious, turgid, unreadable

readily 1. cheerfully, eagerly, freely, gladly, lief (*rare*), promptly, quickly, voluntarily, willing~ly, with good grace, with pleasure 2. at once, easily, effortlessly, hotfoot, in no time, pdq (*slang*), quickly, right away, smoothly, speedi~ly, straight away, unhesitatingly, without de~lay, without demur, without difficulty, without hesitation
Antonyms hesitatingly, reluctantly, slowly, unwillingly, with difficulty

readiness 1. fitness, maturity, preparation, preparedness, ripeness 2. aptness, eagerness, gameness (*informal*), inclination, keenness, willingness 3. adroitness, dexterity, ease, fa~cility, handiness, promptitude, promptness, quickness, rapidity, skill 4. **in readiness** all set, at *or* on hand, at the ready, fit, prepared, primed, ready, set, waiting, waiting in the wings

reading 1. examination, inspection, perusal, review, scrutiny, study 2. homily, lecture, les~son, performance, recital, rendering, rendition, sermon 3. conception, construction, grasp, impression, interpretation, take (*informal, chiefly U.S.*), treatment, understanding, ver~sion 4. book-learning, edification, education, erudition, knowledge, learning, scholarship

Reading is to the mind what exercise is to the body
Richard Steele *The Tatler*

Some people say that life is the thing, but I prefer reading
Logan Pearsall Smith *Afterthoughts*

ready *adjective* 1. all set, arranged, completed, fit, in readiness, organized, prepared, primed, ripe, set 2. agreeable, apt, disposed, eager, game (*informal*), glad, happy, have-a-go (*in~formal*), inclined, keen, minded, predisposed, prone, willing 3. acute, adroit, alert, apt, as~tute, bright, clever, deft, dexterous, expert, handy, intelligent, keen, perceptive, prompt, quick, quick-witted, rapid, resourceful, sharp, skilful, smart 4. about, close, in danger of, liable, likely, on the brink of, on the point of, on the verge of 5. accessible, at *or* on hand, at one's fingertips, at the ready, available, close to hand, convenient, handy, near, on call, on tap (*informal*), present *~noun* 6. **at the ready** all systems go, in readiness, poised, prepared, ready for action, waiting *~verb* 7. arrange, equip, fit out, get ready, make ready, order, organize, prepare, set
Antonyms *adjective* disinclined, distant, hesi~tant, immature, inaccessible, inexpert, late, loath, reluctant, slow, unavailable, un~equipped, unfit, unhandy, unprepared, un~willing

real absolute, actual, authentic, bona fide, cer~tain, essential, existent, factual, genuine, heartfelt, honest, intrinsic, legitimate, posi~tive, right, rightful, sincere, true, unaffected, unfeigned, valid, veritable
Antonyms affected, counterfeit, fake, faked, false, feigned, imaginary, imitation, insincere

realistic 1. businesslike, common-sense, down-to-earth, hard-headed, level-headed, matter-of-fact, practical, pragmatic, rational, real, sensible, sober, unromantic, unsentimental 2. authentic, faithful, genuine, graphic, lifelike, natural, naturalistic, representational, true, true to life, truthful, vérité
Antonyms fanciful, idealistic, impractical, un~realistic

reality 1. actuality, authenticity, certainty, cor~poreality, fact, genuineness, materiality, real~ism, truth, validity, verisimilitude, verity 2. **in reality** actually, as a matter of fact, in actu~ality, in fact, in point of fact, in truth, really

Human kind
Cannot bear very much reality
T.S. Eliot *East Coker*

realization 1. appreciation, apprehension, awareness, cognizance, comprehension, con~ception, consciousness, grasp, imagination, perception, recognition, the penny drops (*in~formal*), understanding 2. accomplishment, achievement, carrying-out, completion, con~summation, effectuation, fulfilment

realize 1. appreciate, apprehend, be cognizant of, become aware of, become conscious of, catch on (*informal*), comprehend, conceive, get the message, grasp, imagine, recognize, take in, twig (*Brit. informal*), understand 2. accom~plish, actualize, bring about, bring off, bring to fruition, carry out *or* through, complete, consummate, do, effect, effectuate, fulfil, in~carnate, make concrete, make happen, per~form, reify 3. acquire, bring *or* take in, clear, earn, gain, get, go for, make, net, obtain, pro~duce, sell for

really absolutely, actually, assuredly, categori~cally, certainly, genuinely, in actuality, in~deed, in fact, in reality, positively, surely, truly, undoubtedly, verily, without a doubt

realm 1. country, domain, dominion, empire, kingdom, land, monarchy, principality, province, state 2. area, branch, department, field, orbit, patch, province, region, sphere, territory, turf (*U.S. slang*), world, zone

reap acquire, bring in, collect, cut, derive, gain, garner, gather, get, harvest, obtain, win

rear[1] 1. *noun* back, back end, end, rearguard, stern, tail, tail end 2. *adjective* aft, after (*Nautical*), back, following, hind, hindmost, last, trailing
Antonyms *noun* bow, forward end, front, nose, stem, vanguard ~*adjective* foremost, forward, front, leading

rear[2] *verb* 1. breed, bring up, care for, cultivate, educate, foster, grow, nurse, nurture, raise, train 2. elevate, hoist, hold up, lift, raise, set upright 3. build, construct, erect, fabricate, put up 4. loom, rise, soar, tower

reason *noun* 1. apprehension, brains, comprehension, intellect, judgment, logic, mentality, mind, ratiocination, rationality, reasoning, sanity, sense(s), sound mind, soundness, understanding 2. aim, basis, cause, design, end, goal, grounds, impetus, incentive, inducement, intention, motive, object, occasion, purpose, target, warrant, why and wherefore (*informal*) 3. apologia, apology, argument, case, defence, excuse, explanation, exposition, ground, justification, rationale, vindication 4. bounds, limits, moderation, propriety, reasonableness, sense, sensibleness, wisdom 5. **in** *or* **within reason** in moderation, proper, reasonable, sensible, warrantable, within bounds, within limits ~*verb* 6. conclude, deduce, draw conclusions, infer, make out, ratiocinate, resolve, solve, syllogize, think, work out 7. *with* **with** argue, bring round (*informal*), debate, dispute, dissuade, expostulate, move, persuade, prevail upon, remonstrate, show (someone) the error of his ways, talk into *or* out of, urge, win over
Antonyms (*sense 1*) emotion, feeling, instinct, sentiment

The heart has reasons that reason knows not of
Blaise Pascal *Pensées*

The reason of the strongest is always the best
Jean de la Fontaine *Fables*

There is nothing without a reason
Gottfried Wilhelm Leibniz *Studies in Physics and the Nature of Body*

Reason is natural revelation
John Locke *Essay concerning Human Understanding*

Reason, an ignis fatuus of the mind,
Which leaves the light of nature, sense, behind
John Wilmot, Earl of Rochester *A Satire against Mankind*

reasonable 1. advisable, arguable, believable, credible, intelligent, judicious, justifiable, logical, plausible, practical, rational, reasoned, sane, sensible, sober, sound, tenable, well-advised, well-thought-out, wise 2. acceptable, average, equitable, fair, fit, honest, inexpensive, just, moderate, modest, O.K. *or* okay (*informal*), proper, right, tolerable, within reason
Antonyms impossible, irrational, unfair, unintelligent, unreasonable, unsound

reasoned clear, judicious, logical, sensible, systematic, well expressed, well presented, well-thought-out

reasoning 1. analysis, cogitation, deduction, logic, ratiocination, reason, thinking, thought 2. argument, case, exposition, hypothesis, interpretation, proof, train of thought

reassure bolster, buoy up, cheer up, comfort, encourage, hearten, inspirit, put *or* set one's mind at rest, relieve (someone) of anxiety, restore confidence to

rebate allowance, bonus, deduction, discount, reduction, refund

rebel *verb* 1. man the barricades, mutiny, resist, revolt, rise up, take to the streets, take up arms 2. come out against, defy, dig one's heels in (*informal*), disobey, dissent, refuse to obey 3. flinch, recoil, show repugnance, shrink, shy away ~*noun* 4. insurgent, insurrectionary, mutineer, resistance fighter, revolutionary, revolutionist, secessionist 5. apostate, dissenter, heretic, nonconformist, schismatic ~*adjective* 6. insubordinate, insurgent, insurrectionary, mutinous, rebellious, revolutionary

What is a rebel? A man who says no
Albert Camus *The Rebel*

rebellion 1. insurgence, insurgency, insurrection, mutiny, resistance, revolt, revolution, rising, uprising 2. apostasy, defiance, disobedience, dissent, heresy, insubordination, nonconformity, schism

A little rebellion now and then is a good thing
Thomas Jefferson *letter to James Madison*

Rebellion to tyrants is obedience to God
John Bradshaw

rebellious 1. contumacious, defiant, disaffected, disloyal, disobedient, disorderly, insubordinate, insurgent, insurrectionary, intractable, mutinous, rebel, recalcitrant, revolutionary, seditious, turbulent, ungovernable, unruly 2. difficult, incorrigible, obstinate, recalcitrant, refractory, resistant, unmanageable
Antonyms dutiful, loyal, obedient, patriotic, subordinate, subservient

rebirth new beginning, regeneration, reincarnation, renaissance, renascence, renewal, res~

toration, resurgence, resurrection, revitalization, revival

rebound *verb* 1. bounce, recoil, resound, return, ricochet, spring back 2. backfire, boomerang, misfire, recoil *~noun* 3. bounce, comeback, kickback, repercussion, return, ricochet

rebuff 1. *verb* brush off (*slang*), check, cold-shoulder, cut, decline, deny, discourage, put off, refuse, reject, repulse, resist, slight, snub, spurn, turn down 2. *noun* brush-off (*slang*), bum's rush (*slang*), check, cold shoulder, defeat, denial, discouragement, kick in the teeth (*slang*), knock-back (*slang*), opposition, refusal, rejection, repulse, slap in the face (*informal*), slight, snub, the (old) heave-ho (*informal*), thumbs down
Antonyms *verb* encourage, lead on (*informal*), submit to, welcome *~noun* come-on (*informal*), encouragement, thumbs up, welcome

rebuke 1. *verb* admonish, bawl out (*informal*), berate, blame, carpet (*informal*), castigate, censure, chew out (*U.S. & Canad. informal*), chew (someone's) ass (*U.S. & Canad. taboo slang*), chide, dress down (*informal*), give a rocket (*Brit. & N.Z. informal*), haul (someone) over the coals (*informal*), lecture, read the riot act, reprehend, reprimand, reproach, reprove, scold, take to task, tear into (*informal*), tear (someone) off a strip (*informal*), tell off (*informal*), tick off (*informal*), upbraid 2. *noun* admonition, blame, castigation, censure, dressing down (*informal*), lecture, reprimand, reproach, reproof, reproval, row, telling-off (*informal*), ticking-off (*informal*), tongue-lashing, wigging (*Brit. slang*)
Antonyms *verb* applaud, approve, commend, compliment, congratulate, laud, praise *~noun* commendation, compliment, laudation, praise

rebut confute, defeat, disprove, invalidate, negate, overturn, prove wrong, quash, refute

rebuttal confutation, defeat, disproof, invalidation, negation, refutation

recalcitrant contrary, contumacious, defiant, disobedient, insubordinate, intractable, obstinate, refractory, stubborn, uncontrollable, ungovernable, unmanageable, unruly, unwilling, wayward, wilful
Antonyms amenable, compliant, docile, obedient, submissive

recall *verb* 1. bring *or* call to mind, call *or* summon up, evoke, look *or* think back to, mind (*dialect*), recollect, remember, reminisce about 2. abjure, annul, call back, call in, cancel, countermand, nullify, repeal, rescind, retract, revoke, take back, withdraw *~noun* 3. annulment, cancellation, nullification, recision, repeal, rescindment, rescission, retraction, revocation, withdrawal 4. memory, recollection, remembrance

recant abjure, apostatize, deny, disavow, disclaim, disown, forswear, recall, renege, renounce, repudiate, retract, revoke, take back, unsay, withdraw
Antonyms insist, maintain, profess, reaffirm, reiterate, repeat, restate, uphold

recapitulate epitomize, go over again, outline, recap (*informal*), recount, reiterate, repeat, restate, review, run over, run through again, summarize, sum up

recede 1. abate, back off, draw back, ebb, fall back, go back, regress, retire, retreat, retrocede, retrogress, return, subside, withdraw 2. decline, diminish, dwindle, fade, lessen, shrink, sink, wane

receipt 1. acknowledgment, counterfoil, proof of purchase, sales slip, stub, voucher 2. acceptance, delivery, receiving, reception, recipience 3. *plural* gains, gate, income, proceeds, profits, return, takings

receive 1. accept, accept delivery of, acquire, be given, be in receipt of, collect, derive, get, obtain, pick up, take 2. apprehend, be informed of, be told, gather, hear, perceive 3. bear, be subjected to, encounter, experience, go through, meet with, suffer, sustain, undergo 4. accommodate, admit, be at home to, entertain, greet, meet, take in, welcome

recent contemporary, current, fresh, happening (*informal*), late, latter, latter-day, modern, new, novel, present-day, up-to-date, young
Antonyms ancient, antique, earlier, early, former, historical, old

recently currently, freshly, lately, latterly, newly, not long ago, of late

receptacle container, holder, repository

reception 1. acceptance, admission, receipt, receiving, recipience 2. acknowledgment, greeting, reaction, recognition, response, treatment, welcome 3. do (*informal*), entertainment, function, levee, party, soirée

receptive 1. alert, bright, perceptive, quick on the uptake (*informal*), responsive, sensitive 2. accessible, amenable, approachable, favourable, friendly, hospitable, interested, open, open-minded, open to suggestions, susceptible, sympathetic, welcoming
Antonyms biased, narrow-minded, prejudiced, unreceptive, unresponsive

recess 1. alcove, bay, cavity, corner, depression, hollow, indentation, niche, nook, oriel 2. *plural* bowels, depths, heart, innards (*informal*), innermost parts, penetralia, reaches, retreats, secret places 3. break, cessation of business, closure, holiday, intermission, interval, respite, rest, vacation

recession decline, depression, downturn, drop, slump
Antonyms boom, upturn

It's a recession when your neighbour loses his job; it's a depression when you lose yours
Harry S. Truman

recherché arcane, choice, esoteric, exotic, far-fetched, rare, refined

recipe 1. directions, ingredients, instructions, receipt (*obsolete*) 2. formula, method, modus operandi, prescription, procedure, process, programme, technique

reciprocal alternate, complementary, correlative, corresponding, equivalent, exchanged, give-and-take, interchangeable, interdependent, mutual, reciprocative, reciprocatory
Antonyms one-way, unilateral, unreciprocated

reciprocate 1. barter, exchange, feel in return, interchange, reply, requite, respond, return, return the compliment, swap, trade 2. be equivalent, correspond, equal, match

recital account, description, detailing, enumeration, narration, narrative, performance, reading, recapitulation, recitation, rehearsal, relation, rendering, repetition, statement, story, tale, telling

recitation lecture, narration, passage, performance, piece, reading, recital, rendering, telling

recite declaim, deliver, describe, detail, do one's party piece (*informal*), enumerate, itemize, narrate, perform, recapitulate, recount, rehearse, relate, repeat, speak, tell

reckless careless, daredevil, devil-may-care, foolhardy, harebrained, harum-scarum, hasty, headlong, heedless, ill-advised, imprudent, inattentive, incautious, indiscreet, irresponsible, madcap, mindless, negligent, overventuresome, precipitate, rash, regardless, thoughtless, wild
Antonyms careful, cautious, heedful, mindful, observant, responsible, thoughtful, wary

reckon 1. add up, calculate, compute, count, enumerate, figure, number, tally, total 2. account, appraise, consider, count, deem, esteem, estimate, evaluate, gauge, hold, judge, look upon, rate, regard, think of 3. assume, believe, be of the opinion, conjecture, expect, fancy, guess (*informal, chiefly U.S. & Canad.*), imagine, suppose, surmise, think 4. *with* **with** cope, deal, face, handle, settle accounts, treat 5. *with* **with** anticipate, bargain for, bear in mind, be prepared for, expect, foresee, plan for, take cognizance of, take into account 6. *with* **on** *or* **upon** bank, calculate, count, depend, hope for, rely, take for granted, trust in 7. **to be reckoned with** consequential, considerable, important, influential, powerful, significant, strong, weighty

reckoning 1. adding, addition, calculation, computation, count, counting, estimate, summation, working 2. account, bill, charge, due, score, settlement 3. doom, judgment, last judgment, retribution

reclaim get *or* take back, recapture, recover, redeem, reform, regain, regenerate, reinstate, rescue, restore, retrieve, salvage

recline be recumbent, lay (something) down, lean, lie (down), loll, lounge, repose, rest, sprawl, stretch out
Antonyms get up, rise, sit up, stand, stand up, stand upright

recluse anchoress, anchorite, ascetic, eremite, hermit, monk, solitary

reclusive ascetic, cloistered, eremitic, hermitic, hermit-like, isolated, monastic, recluse, retiring, secluded, sequestered, solitary, withdrawn
Antonyms gregarious, sociable

recognition 1. detection, discovery, identification, recall, recollection, remembrance 2. acceptance, acknowledgment, admission, allowance, appreciation, avowal, awareness, cognizance, concession, confession, notice, perception, realization, respect, understanding 3. acknowledgment, appreciation, approval, gratitude, greeting, honour, salute

recognize 1. identify, know, know again, make out, notice, place, put one's finger on, recall, recollect, remember, spot 2. accept, acknowledge, admit, allow, appreciate, avow, be aware of, concede, confess, grant, own, perceive, realize, respect, see, take on board, understand 3. acknowledge, appreciate, approve, greet, honour, salute
Antonyms (*sense 2*) be unaware of, forget, ignore, overlook

recoil *verb* 1. jerk back, kick, react, rebound, resile, spring back 2. balk at, draw back, falter, flinch, quail, shrink, shy away 3. backfire, boomerang, go wrong, misfire, rebound *~noun* 4. backlash, kick, reaction, rebound, repercussion

recollect call to mind, mind (*dialect*), place, recall, remember, reminisce, summon up

recollection impression, memory, mental image, recall, remembrance, reminiscence

recommend 1. advance, advise, advocate, counsel, enjoin, exhort, prescribe, propose, put forward, suggest, urge 2. approve, commend, endorse, praise, put in a good word for, speak well of, vouch for 3. make attractive (acceptable, appealing, interesting)
Antonyms argue against, disapprove of, reject, veto

recommendation 1. advice, counsel, proposal, suggestion, urging 2. advocacy, approbation, approval, blessing, commendation, endorsement, favourable mention, good word, plug (*informal*), praise, reference, sanction, testimonial

recompense *verb* 1. pay, remunerate, reward 2. compensate, indemnify, make amends for, make good, make restitution for, make up for, pay for, redress, reimburse, repay, requite, satisfy ~*noun* 3. amends, compensation, damages, emolument, indemnification, indemnity, meed (*archaic*), pay, payment, remuneration, reparation, repayment, requital, restitution, return, reward, satisfaction, wages

reconcilable 1. compatible, congruous, consistent 2. appeasable, conciliatory, forgiving, peaceable, placable

reconcile 1. accept, accommodate, get used, make the best of, put up with (*informal*), resign, submit, yield 2. appease, bring to terms, conciliate, make peace between, pacify, placate, propitiate, re-establish friendly relations between, restore harmony between, reunite 3. adjust, compose, harmonize, patch up, put to rights, rectify, resolve, settle, square

reconciliation 1. appeasement, conciliation, détente, pacification, propitiation, *rapprochement*, reconcilement, reunion, understanding 2. accommodation, adjustment, compromise, harmony, rectification, settlement
Antonyms alienation, antagonism, break-up, estrangement, falling-out, separation

recondite abstruse, arcane, cabbalistic, concealed, dark, deep, difficult, esoteric, hidden, involved, mysterious, mystical, obscure, occult, profound, secret
Antonyms exoteric, simple, straightforward

recondition do up (*informal*), fix up (*informal, chiefly U.S. & Canad.*), overhaul, remodel, renew, renovate, repair, restore, revamp

reconnaissance exploration, inspection, investigation, observation, patrol, recce (*slang*), reconnoitring, scan, scouting, scrutiny, survey

reconnoitre case (*slang*), explore, get the lie of the land, inspect, investigate, make a reconnaissance (of), observe, patrol, recce (*slang*), scan, scout, scrutinize, see how the land lies, spy out, survey

reconsider change one's mind, have second thoughts, reassess, re-evaluate, re-examine, rethink, review, revise, take another look at, think again, think better of, think over, think twice

Second thoughts are the wisest
Euripides *Hippolytus*

reconstruct 1. reassemble, rebuild, recreate, re-establish, reform, regenerate, remake, remodel, renovate, reorganize, restore 2. build up, build up a picture of, deduce, piece together

record *noun* 1. account, annals, archives, chronicle, diary, document, entry, file, journal, log, memoir, memorandum, memorial, minute, register, report 2. documentation, evidence, memorial, remembrance, testimony, trace, witness 3. background, career, curriculum vitae, history, performance, track record (*informal*) 4. album, black disc, disc, EP, forty-five, gramophone record, LP, platter (*U.S. slang*), recording, release, seventy-eight, single, vinyl, waxing (*informal*) 5. **off the record** confidential, confidentially, in confidence, in private, not for publication, private, sub rosa, under the rose, unofficial, unofficially ~*verb* 6. chalk up (*informal*), chronicle, document, enrol, enter, inscribe, log, minute, note, preserve, put down, put on file, put on record, register, report, set down, take down, transcribe, write down 7. contain, give evidence of, indicate, read, register, say, show 8. cut, lay down (*slang*), make a recording of, put on wax (*informal*), tape, tape-record, video, video-tape, wax (*informal*)

recorder annalist, archivist, chronicler, clerk, diarist, historian, registrar, scorekeeper, scorer, scribe

recording cut (*informal*), disc, gramophone record, record, tape, video

recount delineate, depict, describe, detail, enumerate, give an account of, narrate, portray, recite, rehearse, relate, repeat, report, tell, tell the story of

recoup 1. make good, recover, redeem, regain, retrieve, win back 2. compensate, make redress for, make up for, refund, reimburse, remunerate, repay, requite, satisfy

recourse alternative, appeal, choice, expedient, option, refuge, remedy, resort, resource, way out

recover 1. find again, get back, make good, recapture, reclaim, recoup, redeem, regain, repair, repossess, restore, retake, retrieve, take back, win back 2. be on the mend, bounce back, come round, convalesce, feel oneself again, get back on one's feet, get better, get well, heal, improve, mend, pick up, pull through, rally, recuperate, regain one's health *or* strength, revive, take a turn for the better, turn the corner
Antonyms (*sense 1*) abandon, forfeit, lose (*sense 2*) deteriorate, go downhill, relapse, take a turn for the worse, weaken, worsen

recovery 1. convalescence, healing, improvement, mending, rally, recuperation, return to health, revival, turn for the better 2. amelioration, betterment, improvement, rally, rehabilitation, restoration, revival, upturn 3. recapture, reclamation, redemption, repair, repossession, restoration, retrieval

recreation amusement, beer and skittles (*informal*), distraction, diversion, enjoyment, entertainment, exercise, fun, hobby, leisure ac~

tivity, pastime, play, pleasure, refreshment, relaxation, relief, sport

recrimination bickering, counterattack, countercharge, mutual accusation, name-calling, quarrel, retaliation, retort, squabbling

recruit *verb* **1.** draft, enlist, enrol, impress, levy, mobilize, muster, raise, strengthen **2.** engage, enrol, gather, obtain, procure, proselytize, round up, take on, win (over) **3.** augment, build up, refresh, reinforce, renew, replenish, restore, strengthen, supply *~noun* **4.** apprentice, beginner, convert, greenhorn (*informal*), helper, initiate, learner, neophyte, novice, proselyte, rookie (*informal*), trainee, tyro

Antonyms (*sense 1*) dismiss, fire, lay off, make redundant, sack (*informal*)

rectify **1.** adjust, amend, correct, emend, fix, improve, make good, mend, put right, redress, reform, remedy, repair, right, set the record straight, square **2.** *Chemistry* distil, purify, refine, separate

rectitude **1.** correctness, decency, equity, goodness, honesty, honour, incorruptibility, integrity, justice, morality, principle, probity, righteousness, scrupulousness, uprightness, virtue **2.** accuracy, correctness, exactness, justice, precision, rightness, soundness, verity

Antonyms (*sense 1*) baseness, corruption, dishonesty, dishonour, immorality, scandalousness

recumbent flat, flat on one's back, horizontal, leaning, lying, lying down, prone, prostrate, reclining, resting, stretched out, supine

recuperate be on the mend, convalesce, get back on one's feet, get better, improve, mend, pick up, recover, regain one's health, turn the corner

recur **1.** come again, come and go, come back, happen again, persist, reappear, repeat, return, revert **2.** be remembered, come back, haunt one's thoughts, return to mind, run through one's mind

recurrent continued, cyclical, frequent, habitual, periodic, recurring, regular, repeated, repetitive

Antonyms isolated, one-off

recycle reclaim, reprocess, reuse, salvage, save

red *adjective* **1.** cardinal, carmine, cherry, coral, crimson, gules (*Heraldry*), maroon, pink, rose, ruby, scarlet, vermeil, vermilion, wine **2.** bay, carroty, chestnut, flame-coloured, flaming, foxy, reddish, sandy, titian **3.** blushing, embarrassed, florid, flushed, rubicund, shamefaced, suffused **4.** blooming, glowing, healthy, roseate, rosy, ruddy **5.** bloodshot, inflamed, red-rimmed **6.** bloodstained, bloody, ensanguined (*literary*), gory, sanguine *~noun* **7.** colour, redness **8.** **in the red** *informal* bankrupt, in arrears, in debit, in debt, in deficit, insolvent, on the rocks, overdrawn, owing money, showing a loss **9.** **see red** *informal* be beside oneself with rage (*informal*), become enraged, be *or* get very angry, blow a fuse (*slang, chiefly U.S.*), blow one's top, boil, crack up (*informal*), fly off the handle (*informal*), go ballistic (*slang, chiefly U.S.*), go mad (*informal*), go off one's head (*slang*), go off the deep end (*informal*), go up the wall (*slang*), lose one's rag (*slang*), lose one's temper, seethe, wig out (*slang*)

red-blooded hearty, lusty, manly, robust, strong, vigorous, virile, vital

redden blush, colour (up), crimson, flush, go red, suffuse

redeem **1.** buy back, reclaim, recover, recover possession of, regain, repossess, repurchase, retrieve, win back **2.** cash (in), change, exchange, trade in **3.** abide by, acquit, adhere to, be faithful to, carry out, discharge, fulfil, hold to, keep, keep faith with, make good, meet, perform, satisfy **4.** absolve, rehabilitate, reinstate, restore to favour **5.** atone for, compensate for, defray, make amends for, make good, make up for, offset, outweigh, redress, save **6.** buy the freedom of, deliver, emancipate, extricate, free, liberate, pay the ransom of, ransom, rescue, save, set free

redemption **1.** reclamation, recovery, repossession, repurchase, retrieval **2.** discharge, exchange, fulfilment, performance, quid pro quo, trade-in **3.** amends, atonement, compensation, expiation, reparation **4.** deliverance, emancipation, liberation, ransom, release, rescue, salvation

red-handed bang to rights (*slang*), (in) flagrante delicto, in the act, with one's fingers *or* hand in the till (*informal*), with one's pants down (*U.S. slang*)

redolent **1.** aromatic, fragrant, odorous, perfumed, scented, sweet-smelling **2.** evocative, remindful, reminiscent, suggestive

redoubtable awful, doughty, dreadful, fearful, fearsome, formidable, mighty, powerful, resolute, strong, terrible, valiant

redound **1.** conduce, contribute, effect, lead to, militate for, tend **2.** accrue, come back, ensue, rebound, recoil, reflect, result

redress *verb* **1.** compensate for, make amends (reparation, restitution) for, make up for, pay for, put right, recompense for **2.** adjust, amend, balance, correct, ease, even up, mend, put right, rectify, reform, regulate, relieve, remedy, repair, restore the balance, square *~noun* **3.** aid, assistance, correction, cure, ease, help, justice, rectification, relief, remedy, satisfaction **4.** amends, atonement, compensa~

tion, payment, quittance, recompense, repara~ tion, requital, restitution

reduce 1. abate, abridge, contract, curtail, cut down, debase, decrease, depress, dilute, di~ minish, downsize, impair, lessen, lower, mod~ erate, shorten, slow down, tone down, trun~ cate, turn down, weaken, wind down 2. bank~ rupt, break, impoverish, pauperize, ruin 3. bring, bring to the point of, conquer, drive, force, master, overpower, subdue, vanquish 4. be *or* go on a diet, diet, lose weight, shed weight, slenderize (*chiefly U.S.*), slim, trim 5. bring down the price of, cheapen, cut, dis~ count, lower, mark down, slash 6. break, bring low, degrade, demote, downgrade, humble, humiliate, lower in rank, lower the status of, take down a peg (*informal*)
Antonyms augment, defend, elevate, enhance, enlarge, exalt, extend, heighten, increase, promote

redundant 1. *de trop*, excessive, extra, ines~ sential, inordinate, supererogatory, superflu~ ous, supernumerary, surplus, unnecessary, unwanted 2. diffuse, iterative, padded, peri~ phrastic, pleonastic, prolix, repetitious, tauto~ logical, verbose, wordy
Antonyms essential, necessary, needed, vital

reek *verb* 1. hum (*slang*), pong (*Brit. informal*), smell, smell to high heaven, stink 2. be char~ acterized by, be permeated by, be redolent of 3. *dialect* fume, give off smoke *or* fumes, smoke, steam *~noun* 4. effluvium, fetor, malodour, mephitis, niff (*Brit. slang*), odour, pong (*Brit. informal*), smell, stench, stink 5. *dialect* exhalation, fumes, smoke, steam, va~ pour

reel 1. falter, lurch, pitch, rock, roll, stagger, stumble, sway, totter, waver, wobble 2. go round and round, revolve, spin, swim, swirl, twirl, whirl

refer 1. advert, allude, bring up, cite, hint, in~ voke, make mention of, make reference, men~ tion, speak of, touch on 2. direct, guide, point, recommend, send 3. apply, consult, go, have recourse to, look up, seek information from, turn to 4. apply, be directed to, belong, be relevant to, concern, pertain, relate 5. accred~ it, ascribe, assign, attribute, credit, impute, put down to 6. commit, consign, deliver, hand over, pass on, submit, transfer, turn over

referee 1. *noun* adjudicator, arbiter, arbitrator, judge, ref (*informal*), umpire 2. *verb* adjudi~ cate, arbitrate, judge, mediate, umpire

reference 1. allusion, citation, mention, note, quotation, remark 2. applicability, bearing, concern, connection, consideration, regard, re~ lation, respect 3. certification, character, cre~ dentials, endorsement, good word, recommen~ dation, testimonial

referendum plebiscite, popular vote, public vote

refine 1. clarify, cleanse, distil, filter, process, purify, rarefy 2. civilize, cultivate, elevate, hone, improve, perfect, polish, temper

refined 1. civil, civilized, courtly, cultivated, cultured, elegant, genteel, gentlemanly, gra~ cious, ladylike, polished, polite, sophisticated, urbane, well-bred, well-mannered 2. cultured, delicate, discerning, discriminating, exact, fastidious, fine, nice, precise, punctilious, sen~ sitive, sublime, subtle 3. clarified, clean, dis~ tilled, filtered, processed, pure, purified
Antonyms boorish, coarse, common, ill-bred, impure, inelegant, uncultured, ungentlemanly, unladylike, unmannerly, unrefined

refinement 1. clarification, cleansing, distilla~ tion, filtering, processing, purification, rar~ efaction, rectification 2. fine point, fine tuning, nicety, nuance, subtlety 3. breeding, civility, civilization, courtesy, courtliness, cultivation, culture, delicacy, discrimination, elegance, fastidiousness, fineness, finesse, finish, gentil~ ity, good breeding, good manners, grace, gra~ ciousness, polish, politeness, politesse, preci~ sion, sophistication, style, taste, urbanity

reflect 1. echo, give back, imitate, mirror, re~ produce, return, throw back 2. bear out, be~ speak, communicate, demonstrate, display, evince, exhibit, express, indicate, manifest, reveal, show 3. cogitate, consider, contemplate, deliberate, meditate, mull over, muse, ponder, ruminate, think, wonder

reflection 1. counterpart, echo, image, mirror image 2. cerebration, cogitation, consideration, contemplation, deliberation, idea, impression, meditation, musing, observation, opinion, pe~ rusal, pondering, rumination, study, thinking, thought, view 3. aspersion, censure, criticism, derogation, imputation, reproach, slur

reflective cogitating, contemplative, delibera~ tive, meditative, pensive, pondering, reason~ ing, ruminative, thoughtful

reform *verb* 1. ameliorate, amend, better, cor~ rect, emend, improve, mend, rebuild, reclaim, reconstitute, reconstruct, rectify, regenerate, rehabilitate, remodel, renovate, reorganize, repair, restore, revolutionize 2. clean up one's act (*informal*), get back on the straight and narrow (*informal*), get it together (*informal*), get one's act together (*informal*), go straight (*informal*), mend one's ways, pull one's socks up (*Brit. informal*), shape up (*informal*), turn over a new leaf *~noun* 3. amelioration, amendment, betterment, correction, improve~ ment, rectification, rehabilitation, renovation

refractory cantankerous, contentious, contu~ macious, difficult, disobedient, disputatious, headstrong, intractable, mulish, obstinate, perverse, recalcitrant, stiff-necked, stubborn, uncontrollable, uncooperative, unmanageable, unruly, wilful

refrain[1] *verb* abstain, avoid, cease, desist, do without, eschew, forbear, give up, kick (*informal*), leave off, renounce, stop

refrain[2] *noun* burden, chorus, melody, song, tune

refresh **1.** brace, breathe new life into, cheer, cool, enliven, freshen, inspirit, kick-start (*informal*), reanimate, reinvigorate, rejuvenate, revitalize, revive, revivify, stimulate **2.** brush up (*informal*), jog, prod, prompt, renew, stimulate **3.** renew, renovate, repair, replenish, restore, top up

refreshing bracing, cooling, different, fresh, inspiriting, invigorating, new, novel, original, revivifying, stimulating, thirst-quenching
Antonyms enervating, exhausting, soporific, tiring, wearisome

refreshment **1.** enlivenment, freshening, reanimation, renewal, renovation, repair, restoration, revival, stimulation **2.** *plural* drinks, food and drink, snacks, titbits

refrigerate chill, cool, freeze, keep cold

refuge asylum, bolt hole, harbour, haven, hide-out, protection, resort, retreat, sanctuary, security, shelter

refugee displaced person, émigré, escapee, exile, fugitive, runaway

refulgent bright, brilliant, gleaming, irradiant, lambent, lustrous, radiant, resplendent, shining

refund **1.** *verb* give back, make good, pay back, reimburse, repay, restore, return **2.** *noun* reimbursement, repayment, return

refurbish clean up, do up (*informal*), fix up (*informal, chiefly U.S. & Canad.*), mend, overhaul, re-equip, refit, remodel, renovate, repair, restore, revamp, set to rights, spruce up

refusal **1.** defiance, denial, kick in the teeth (*slang*), knockback (*slang*), negation, no, rebuff, rejection, repudiation, thumbs down **2.** choice, consideration, opportunity, option

refuse[1] *verb* abstain, decline, deny, reject, repel, repudiate, say no, spurn, turn down, withhold
Antonyms accept, agree, allow, approve, consent, give, permit

refuse[2] *noun* dreck (*slang, chiefly U.S.*), dregs, dross, garbage, junk (*informal*), leavings, lees, litter, offscourings, rubbish, scum, sediment, sweepings, trash, waste

refute blow out of the water (*slang*), confute, counter, discredit, disprove, give the lie to, negate, overthrow, prove false, rebut, silence
Antonyms confirm, prove, substantiate

regain **1.** get back, recapture, recoup, recover, redeem, repossess, retake, retrieve, take back, win back **2.** get back to, reach again, reattain, return to

regal fit for a king *or* queen, kingly, magnificent, majestic, noble, princely, proud, queenly, royal, sovereign

regale amuse, delight, divert, entertain, feast, gratify, ply, refresh, serve

regalia accoutrements, apparatus, decorations, emblems, finery, garb, gear, paraphernalia, rigout (*informal*), trappings

regard *verb* **1.** behold, check, check out (*informal*), clock (*Brit. slang*), eye, eyeball (*U.S. slang*), gaze at, get a load of (*informal*), look closely at, mark, notice, observe, remark, scrutinize, take a dekko at (*Brit. slang*), view, watch **2.** account, adjudge, believe, consider, deem, esteem, estimate, hold, imagine, judge, look upon, rate, see, suppose, think, treat, value, view **3.** apply to, be relevant to, concern, have a bearing on, have to do with, interest, pertain to, relate to **4.** attend, heed, listen to, mind, note, pay attention to, respect, take into consideration, take notice of ~*noun* **5.** attention, heed, interest, mind, notice **6.** account, affection, attachment, care, concern, consideration, deference, esteem, honour, love, note, reputation, repute, respect, store, sympathy, thought **7.** aspect, detail, feature, item, matter, particular, point, respect **8.** gaze, glance, look, scrutiny, stare **9.** bearing, concern, connection, reference, relation, relevance **10.** *plural* best wishes, compliments, devoirs, good wishes, greetings, respects, salutations

regardful attentive, aware, careful, considerate, dutiful, heedful, mindful, observant, respectful, thoughtful, watchful

regarding about, apropos, as regards, as to, concerning, in *or* with regard to, in re, in respect of, in the matter of, on the subject of, re, respecting, with reference to

regardless **1.** *adjective* disregarding, heedless, inattentive, inconsiderate, indifferent, neglectful, negligent, rash, reckless, remiss, unconcerned, unmindful **2.** *adverb* anyway, come what may, despite everything, for all that, in any case, in spite of everything, nevertheless, no matter what, nonetheless, rain or shine
Antonyms *adjective* heedful, mindful, regardful

regenerate breathe new life into, change, give a shot in the arm, inspirit, invigorate, kick-start (*informal*), reawaken, reconstruct, re-establish, reinvigorate, rejuvenate, renew, renovate, reproduce, restore, revive, revivify, uplift
Antonyms become moribund, decline, degenerate, stagnate, stultify

regime administration, establishment, government, leadership, management, reign, rule, system

regiment *verb* bully, control, discipline, order, organize, regulate, systematize

region 1. area, country, district, division, expanse, land, locality, part, patch, place, province, quarter, section, sector, territory, tract, turf (*U.S. slang*), zone 2. domain, field, province, realm, sphere, world 3. area, locality, neighbourhood, range, scope, vicinity

regional district, local, parochial, provincial, sectional, zonal

register *noun* 1. annals, archives, catalogue, chronicle, diary, file, ledger, list, log, memorandum, record, roll, roster, schedule ~*verb* 2. catalogue, check in, chronicle, enlist, enrol, enter, inscribe, list, note, record, set down, sign on *or* up, take down 3. be shown, bespeak, betray, display, exhibit, express, indicate, manifest, mark, read, record, reflect, reveal, say, show 4. *informal* come home, dawn on, get through, have an effect, impress, make an impression, sink in, tell

regress backslide, degenerate, deteriorate, ebb, fall away *or* off, fall back, go back, lapse, lose ground, recede, relapse, retreat, retrocede, retrogress, return, revert, turn the clock back, wane
Antonyms advance, improve, progress, wax

regret 1. *verb* bemoan, be upset, bewail, cry over spilt milk, deplore, feel remorse for, feel sorry for, grieve, lament, miss, mourn, repent, rue, weep over 2. *noun* bitterness, compunction, contrition, disappointment, grief, lamentation, pang of conscience, penitence, remorse, repentance, ruefulness, self-reproach, sorrow
Antonyms *verb* be happy, be satisfied, feel satisfaction, have not looked back, rejoice ~*noun* callousness, contentment, impenitence, lack of compassion, pleasure, satisfaction

regretful apologetic, ashamed, contrite, disappointed, mournful, penitent, remorseful, repentant, rueful, sad, sorrowful, sorry

regrettable deplorable, disappointing, distressing, ill-advised, lamentable, pitiable, sad, shameful, unfortunate, unhappy, woeful, wrong

regular 1. common, commonplace, customary, daily, everyday, habitual, normal, ordinary, routine, typical, unvarying, usual 2. consistent, constant, established, even, fixed, ordered, periodic, rhythmic, set, stated, steady, systematic, uniform 3. dependable, efficient, formal, methodical, orderly, standardized, steady, systematic 4. balanced, even, flat, level, smooth, straight, symmetrical, uniform 5. approved, bona fide, classic, correct, established, formal, official, orthodox, prevailing, proper, sanctioned, standard, time-honoured, traditional
Antonyms abnormal, disorderly, erratic, exceptional, inconsistent, inconstant, infrequent, irregular, occasional, rare, uncommon, unconventional, uneven, unmethodical, unusual, varied

regulate adjust, administer, arrange, balance, conduct, control, direct, fit, govern, guide, handle, manage, moderate, modulate, monitor, order, organize, oversee, rule, run, settle, superintend, supervise, systematize, tune

regulation *noun* 1. adjustment, administration, arrangement, control, direction, governance, government, management, modulation, supervision, tuning 2. canon, commandment, decree, dictate, direction, edict, law, order, ordinance, precept, procedure, requirement, rule, standing order, statute ~*adjective* 3. customary, mandatory, normal, official, prescribed, required, standard, usual

regurgitate barf (*U.S. slang*), chuck (up) (*slang, chiefly U.S.*), chunder (*slang, chiefly Austral.*), disgorge, puke (*slang*), sick up (*informal*), spew (out *or* up), throw up (*informal*), vomit

rehabilitate 1. adjust, redeem, reform, reintegrate, save 2. clear, convert, fix up (*informal, chiefly U.S. & Canad.*), make good, mend, rebuild, recondition, reconstitute, reconstruct, re-establish, reinstate, reinvigorate, renew, renovate, restore

rehash 1. *verb* alter, change, make over, rearrange, refashion, rejig (*informal*), reshuffle, reuse, rework, rewrite 2. *noun* new version, rearrangement, reworking, rewrite

rehearsal 1. drill, going-over (*informal*), practice, practice session, preparation, reading, rehearsing, run-through 2. account, catalogue, description, enumeration, list, narration, recital, recounting, relation, telling

rehearse 1. act, drill, go over, practise, prepare, ready, recite, repeat, run through, study, train, try out 2. delineate, depict, describe, detail, enumerate, go over, list, narrate, recite, recount, relate, review, run through, spell out, tell, trot out (*informal*)

reign *noun* 1. ascendancy, command, control, dominion, empire, hegemony, influence, monarchy, power, rule, sovereignty, supremacy, sway ~*verb* 2. administer, be in power, command, govern, hold sway, influence, occupy *or* sit on the throne, rule, wear the crown, wield the sceptre 3. be rampant, be rife, be supreme, hold sway, obtain, predominate, prevail

Here we may reign secure, and in my choice
To reign is worth ambition though in hell;

Better to reign in hell, than serve in heav'n
John Milton *Paradise Lost*

reimburse compensate, indemnify, pay back, recompense, refund, remunerate, repay, restore, return, square up

rein *noun* **1.** brake, bridle, check, control, curb, harness, hold, restraint, restriction **2. give (a) free rein (to)** free, give a blank cheque (to), give a free hand, give carte blanche, give (someone) his *or* her head, give way to, indulge, let go, remove restraints *~verb* **3.** bridle, check, control, curb, halt, hold, hold back, limit, restrain, restrict, slow down

reincarnation metempsychosis, rebirth, transmigration of souls

reinforce augment, bolster, buttress, emphasize, fortify, harden, increase, prop, shore up, stiffen, strengthen, stress, supplement, support, toughen, underline
Antonyms contradict, undermine, weaken

reinforcement **1.** addition, amplification, augmentation, enlargement, fortification, increase, strengthening, supplement **2.** brace, buttress, prop, shore, stay, support **3.** *plural* additional *or* fresh troops, auxiliaries, reserves, support

reinstate bring back, recall, re-establish, rehabilitate, replace, restore, return

reiterate do again, iterate, recapitulate, repeat, restate, retell, say again

reject **1.** *verb* bin, cast aside, decline, deny, despise, disallow, discard, eliminate, exclude, jettison, jilt, rebuff, refuse, renounce, repel, repudiate, repulse, say no to, scrap, spurn, throw away *or* out, turn down, veto **2.** *noun* castoff, discard, failure, flotsam, second
Antonyms *verb* accept, agree, allow, approve, permit, receive, select *~noun* prize, treasure

rejection brushoff (*slang*), bum's rush (*slang*), denial, dismissal, elimination, exclusion, kick in the teeth (*slang*), knock-back (*slang*), rebuff, refusal, renunciation, repudiation, the (old) heave-ho (*informal*), thumbs down, veto
Antonyms acceptance, affirmation, approval, selection

rejig alter, juggle, manipulate, massage, rearrange, reorganize, reshuffle, tweak

rejoice be glad (happy, overjoyed), celebrate, delight, exult, glory, joy, jump for joy, make merry, revel, triumph
Antonyms be sad (unhappy,upset), grieve, lament, mourn

rejoicing celebration, cheer, delight, elation, exultation, festivity, gaiety, gladness, happiness, joy, jubilation, merrymaking, revelry, triumph

rejoin answer, come back with, reply, respond, retort, return, riposte

rejoinder answer, comeback (*informal*), counter, counterattack, reply, response, retort, riposte

rejuvenate breathe new life into, give new life to, make young again, reanimate, refresh, regenerate, reinvigorate, renew, restore, restore vitality to, revitalize, revivify

relapse *verb* **1.** backslide, degenerate, fail, fall back, lapse, regress, retrogress, revert, slip back, weaken **2.** deteriorate, fade, fail, sicken, sink, weaken, worsen *~noun* **3.** backsliding, fall from grace, lapse, recidivism, regression, retrogression, reversion **4.** deterioration, recurrence, setback, turn for the worse, weakening, worsening
Antonyms *verb* (*sense 2*) get better, improve, rally, recover *~noun* (*sense 4*) improvement, rally, recovery, turn for the better

relate **1.** chronicle, describe, detail, give an account of, impart, narrate, present, recite, recount, rehearse, report, set forth, tell **2.** ally, associate, connect, coordinate, correlate, couple, join, link **3.** appertain, apply, bear upon, be relevant to, concern, have reference to, have to do with, pertain, refer
Antonyms (*sense 2*) detach, disconnect, dissociate, divorce (*sense 3*) be irrelevant to, be unconnected, have nothing to do with

related **1.** accompanying, affiliated, agnate, akin, allied, associated, cognate, concomitant, connected, correlated, interconnected, joint, linked **2.** agnate, akin, cognate, consanguineous, kin, kindred
Antonyms separate, unconnected, unrelated

relation **1.** affiliation, affinity, consanguinity, kindred, kinship, propinquity, relationship **2.** kin, kinsman, kinswoman, relative **3.** application, bearing, bond, comparison, connection, correlation, interdependence, link, pertinence, reference, regard, similarity, tie-in **4.** account, description, narration, narrative, recital, recountal, report, story, tale

relations **1.** affairs, associations, communications, connections, contact, dealings, interaction, intercourse, liaison, meetings, rapport, relationship, terms **2.** clan, family, kin, kindred, kinsfolk, kinsmen, relatives, tribe

Relations are simply a tedious pack of people who haven't got the remotest knowledge of how to live nor the smallest instinct about when to die
Oscar Wilde

relationship affair, affinity, association, bond, communications, conjunction, connection, correlation, exchange, kinship, liaison, link, parallel, proportion, rapport, ratio, similarity, tie-up

relative *adjective* **1.** allied, associated, comparative, connected, contingent, correspond~

ing, dependent, proportionate, reciprocal, related, respective **2.** applicable, apposite, appropriate, appurtenant, apropos, germane, pertinent, relevant **3.** *with* **to** corresponding to, in proportion to, proportional to *~noun* **4.** connection, kinsman, kinswoman, member of one's *or* the family, relation

relatively comparatively, in *or* by comparison, rather, somewhat, to some extent

relax 1. abate, diminish, ease, ebb, lessen, let up, loosen, lower, mitigate, moderate, reduce, relieve, slacken, weaken **2.** be *or* feel at ease, calm, chill out (*slang, chiefly U.S.*), hang loose (*slang*), laze, let oneself go (*informal*), let one's hair down (*informal*), lighten up (*slang*), loosen up, make oneself at home, mellow out (*informal*), put one's feet up, rest, soften, take it easy, take one's ease, tranquillize, unbend, unwind
Antonyms alarm, alert, heighten, increase, intensify, tense, tighten, work

relaxation 1. amusement, beer and skittles (*informal*), enjoyment, entertainment, fun, leisure, pleasure, recreation, refreshment, rest **2.** abatement, diminution, easing, lessening, let-up (*informal*), moderation, reduction, slackening, weakening

relaxed casual, comfortable, downbeat (*informal*), easy, easy-going, free and easy, informal, insouciant, laid-back (*informal*), leisurely, mellow, mild, nonchalant, unhurried, untaxing

relay *noun* **1.** relief, shift, turn **2.** communication, dispatch, message, transmission *~verb* **3.** broadcast, carry, communicate, hand on, pass on, send, spread, transmit

release *verb* **1.** deliver, discharge, disengage, drop, emancipate, extricate, free, let go, let out, liberate, loose, manumit, set free, turn loose, unbridle, unchain, undo, unfasten, unfetter, unloose, unshackle, untie **2.** absolve, acquit, dispense, excuse, exempt, exonerate, let go, let off **3.** break, circulate, disseminate, distribute, issue, launch, make known, make public, present, publish, put out, unveil *~noun* **4.** acquittal, deliverance, delivery, discharge, emancipation, freedom, liberation, liberty, manumission, relief **5.** absolution, acquittance, dispensation, exemption, exoneration, let-off (*informal*) **6.** announcement, issue, offering, proclamation, publication
Antonyms *verb* detain, engage, fasten, hold, imprison, incarcerate, keep, suppress, withhold *~noun* detention, imprisonment, incarceration, internment

relegate 1. demote, downgrade **2.** assign, consign, delegate, entrust, pass on, refer, transfer **3.** banish, deport, eject, exile, expatriate, expel, oust, throw out

relent 1. acquiesce, be merciful, capitulate, change one's mind, come round, forbear, give in, give quarter, give way, have pity, melt, show mercy, soften, unbend, yield **2.** die down, drop, ease, fall, let up, relax, slacken, slow, weaken
Antonyms (*sense 1*) be unyielding, give no quarter, remain firm, show no mercy (*sense 2*) increase, intensify, strengthen

relentless 1. cruel, fierce, grim, hard, harsh, implacable, inexorable, inflexible, merciless, pitiless, remorseless, ruthless, uncompromising, undeviating, unforgiving, unrelenting, unstoppable, unyielding **2.** incessant, nonstop, persistent, punishing, sustained, unabated, unbroken, unfaltering, unflagging, unrelenting, unrelieved, unremitting, unstoppable
Antonyms (*sense 1*) compassionate, forgiving, merciful, submissive, yielding

relevant admissible, *ad rem*, applicable, apposite, appropriate, appurtenant, apt, fitting, germane, material, pertinent, proper, related, relative, significant, suited, to the point, to the purpose
Antonyms beside the point, extraneous, extrinsic, immaterial, inapplicable, inappropriate, irrelevant, unconnected, unrelated

reliable certain, dependable, faithful, honest, predictable, regular, reputable, responsible, safe, sound, stable, staunch, sure, tried and true, true, trustworthy, trusty, unfailing, upright
Antonyms irresponsible, undependable, unreliable, untrustworthy

reliance assurance, belief, confidence, credence, credit, dependence, faith, trust

relic fragment, keepsake, memento, remembrance, remnant, scrap, souvenir, survival, token, trace, vestige

relief 1. abatement, alleviation, assuagement, balm, comfort, cure, deliverance, ease, easement, mitigation, palliation, release, remedy, solace **2.** aid, assistance, help, succour, support, sustenance **3.** break, breather (*informal*), diversion, let-up (*informal*), refreshment, relaxation, remission, respite, rest

For this relief much thanks
William Shakespeare *Hamlet*

relieve 1. abate, allay, alleviate, appease, assuage, calm, comfort, console, cure, diminish, dull, ease, mitigate, mollify, palliate, relax, salve, soften, solace, soothe **2.** aid, assist, bring aid to, help, succour, support, sustain **3.** give (someone) a break *or* rest, stand in for, substitute for, take over from, take the place of **4.** deliver, discharge, disembarrass, disencumber, exempt, free, release, unburden **5.** break, brighten, interrupt, let up on (*informal*), lighten, slacken, vary

Antonyms (*sense 1*) aggravate, exacerbate, heighten, intensify, worsen

religion

Religions

animism
Babi *or* Babism
Baha'ism
Buddhism
Christianity
Confucianism
druidism
heliolatry
Hinduism *or* Hindooism
Islam
Jainism
Judaism
Macumba
Manichaeism *or* Manicheism
Mithraism *or* Mithraicism
Orphism
Rastafarianism
Ryobu Shinto
Santeria
Satanism
shamanism
Shango
Shembe
Shinto
Sikhism
Taoism
voodoo *or* voodooism
Yezidis
Zoroastrianism *or* Zoroastrism

Christian denominations and sects

Adventists
Amish
Anabaptism
Anglicanism
Baptist Church
Byzantine Church
Calvinism
Catholicism
Christadelphianism
Christian Science
Congregationalism
Coptic Church
Dutch Reformed Church
Eastern Orthodox Church
Episcopal Church
evangelicalism
Greek Orthodox Church
Jehovah's Witnesses
Lutheranism
Maronite Church
Methodism
Moravian Church
Mormons *or* Latter-day Saints
New Jerusalem Church
Orthodox Church
Pentecostalism
Plymouth Brethren
Presbyterianism
Protestantism
Quakerism
Roman Catholicism
Russian Orthodox Church
Salvation Army
Seventh-Day Adventists
Shakers
Society of Friends
Unification Church
Unitarianism

Moslem denominations and sects

Alaouites *or* Alawites
Druse *or* Druze
Imami
Ismaili *or* Isma'ili
Nizari
Shiah, Shia *or* Shiite
Sufism
Sunni
Wahhabism *or* Wahabism
Zaidi

Buddhist schools

Foism
Geluk
Hinayana
Jodo
Kagyü
Lamaism
Mahayana
Nichiren
Nyingma
Pure Land Buddhism
Rinjai
Sakya
Soka Gakkai
Soto
Tendai
Theravada
Vajrayana
Zen

Jewish denominations and sects

Chassidism, Chasidism, Hassidism *or* Hasidism
Conservative Judaism
Liberal Judaism
Orthodox Judaism
Reform Judaism
Zionism

Hindu denominations and sects

Hare Krishna
Saivaism
Saktas
Vaishnavism

Religious books

Adi Granth
Apocrypha
Atharveda
Bible
Book of Mormon
Granth *or* Guru Granth Sahib
I Ching
Koran *or* Quran
Li Chi
Lu
Mahabharata
New Testament
Old Testament
Ramayana
Rigveda
Samaveda
Shi Ching
Siddhanta
Su Ching
Talmud
Tipitaka
Torah
Tripitaka
Veda
Yajurveda

Religious festivals

Advent
Al Hijrah
Ascension Day
Ash Wednesday
Baisakhi
Bodhi Day
Candlemas
Chanukah *or* Hanukkah
Ching Ming
Christmas
Corpus Christi
Day of Atonement
Dhammacakka
Diwali
Dragon Boat Festival
Dussehra
Easter
Eid ul-Adha *or* Id-ul-Adha
Eid ul-Fitr *or* Id-ul-Fitr
Epiphany
Feast of Tabernacles
Good Friday
Guru Nanak's Birthday
Hirja
Hola Mohalla
Holi
Janamashtami
Lailat ul-Barah
Lailat ul-Isra Wal Mi'raj
Lailat ul-Qadr
Lent
Mahashivaratri
Maundy Thursday
Michaelmas
Moon Festival
Palm Sunday
Passion Sunday
Passover
Pentecost
Pesach
Purim
Quadragesima
Quinquagesima
Raksha Bandhan
Ramadan
Rama Naumi
Rogation
Rosh Hashanah
Septuagesima
Sexagesima
Shavuot
Shrove Tuesday
Sukkoth *or* Succoth
Trinity
Wesak
Whitsun
Winter Festival
Yom Kippur
Yuan Tan

Religious clothing

see CLOTHES

Religion is by no means a proper subject of con~ versation in a mixed company
Earl of Chesterfield

I count religion but a childish toy,
And hold there is no sin but ignorance
Christopher Marlowe *The Jew of Malta*

Religion...is the opium of the people
Karl Marx *Critique of Hegel's Philosophy of Right*

Things have come to a pretty pass when religion is allowed to invade the sphere of private life
Lord Melbourne

The true meaning of religion is thus not moral~ ity, but morality touched by emotion
Matthew Arnold *Literature and Dogma*

Any system of religion that has any thing in it that shocks the mind of a child cannot be a true system
Thomas Paine *The Age of Reason*

I am a Millionaire. That is my religion
George Bernard Shaw *Major Barbara*

I can't talk religion to a man with bodily hunger in his eyes
George Bernard Shaw *Major Barbara*

There is only one religion, though there are a hun~ dred versions of it
George Bernard Shaw *Plays Unpleasant (preface)*

The one certain way for a woman to hold a man is to leave him for religion
Muriel Spark *The Comforters*

We have just enough religion to make us hate, but not enough to make us love one another
Jonathan Swift *Thoughts on Various Subjects*

I am for religion against religions
Victor Hugo *Les Miserables*

Time consecrates;
And what is grey with age becomes religion
Friedrich von Schiller *Die Piccolomini*

If you talk to God you are praying; if God talks to you, you have schizophrenia
Thomas Szasz *The Second Sin*

One religion is as true as another
Robert Burton *Anatomy of Melancholy*

Christians have burnt each other, quite persuaded
That all the apostles would have done as they did
Lord Byron *Don Juan*

The nearer the Church the further from God
Bishop Lancelot Andrews *Of the Nativity*

Science without religion is lame, religion without science is blind
Albert Einstein *Science, Philosophy and Religion*

To become a popular religion, it is only necessary for a superstition to enslave a philosophy
Dean Inge *Idea of Progress*

Religion's in the heart, not in the knees
Douglas Jerrold *The Devil's Ducat*

Religion is the frozen thought of men out of which they build temples
Jiddu Krishnamurti

religious **1.** churchgoing, devotional, devout, divine, doctrinal, faithful, god-fearing, godly, holy, pious, pure, reverent, righteous, sacred, scriptural, sectarian, spiritual, theological **2.** conscientious, exact, faithful, fastidious, me~ ticulous, punctilious, rigid, rigorous, scrupu~ lous, unerring, unswerving
Antonyms (*sense 1*) godless, infidel, irreli~ gious, rational, secular, unbelieving

relinquish abandon, abdicate, cast off, cede, desert, drop, forgo, forsake, give up, hand over, kiss (something) goodbye, lay aside, leave, let go, quit, release, renounce, repudi~ ate, resign, retire from, say goodbye to, sur~ render, vacate, waive, withdraw from, yield

relish *verb* **1.** appreciate, delight in, enjoy, fan~ cy, lick one's lips, like, look forward to, luxu~ riate in, prefer, revel in, savour, taste *~noun* **2.** appetite, appreciation, enjoyment, fancy, fondness, gusto, liking, love, partiality, pen~ chant, predilection, stomach, taste, zest, zing (*informal*) **3.** appetizer, condiment, sauce, sea~ soning **4.** flavour, piquancy, savour, smack, spice, tang, taste, trace
Antonyms *verb* be unenthusiastic about, dis~ like, loathe *~noun* (*sense 2*) dislike, distaste, loathing

reluctance aversion, backwardness, disinclina~ tion, dislike, disrelish, distaste, hesitancy, in~ disposition, loathing, repugnance, unwilling~ ness

reluctant averse, backward, disinclined, grudging, hesitant, indisposed, loath, recalci~ trant, slow, unenthusiastic, unwilling
Antonyms eager, enthusiastic, inclined, keen, willing

rely bank, be confident of, be sure of, bet, count, depend, have confidence in, lean, reck~ on, repose trust in, swear by, trust

remain abide, be left, cling, continue, delay, dwell, endure, go on, hang in the air, last, linger, persist, prevail, rest, stand, stay, stay behind, stay put (*informal*), survive, tarry, wait
Antonyms depart, go, leave

remainder balance, butt, dregs, excess, leav~ ings, oddment, relic, remains, remnant, resi~ due, residuum, rest, stub, surplus, tail end, trace, vestige(s)

remaining abiding, extant, lasting, left, linger~ ing, outstanding, persisting, residual, surviv~ ing, unfinished

remains **1.** balance, crumbs, debris, detritus, dregs, fragments, leavings, leftovers, odd~ ments, odds and ends, pieces, relics, remain~ der, remnants, residue, rest, scraps, traces, vestiges **2.** body, cadaver, carcass, corpse

remark *verb* **1.** animadvert, comment, declare, mention, observe, pass comment, reflect, say, state 2. espy, heed, make out, mark, note, notice, observe, perceive, regard, see, take note *or* notice of *~noun* 3. assertion, comment, declaration, observation, opinion, reflection, statement, thought, utterance, word 4. acknowledgment, attention, comment, consideration, heed, mention, notice, observation, recognition, regard, thought

remarkable conspicuous, distinguished, extraordinary, famous, impressive, miraculous, notable, noteworthy, odd, outstanding, phenomenal, pre-eminent, prominent, rare, signal, singular, strange, striking, surprising, uncommon, unusual, wonderful
Antonyms banal, common, commonplace, everyday, insignificant, mundane, ordinary, unexceptional, unimpressive, unsurprising, usual

remediable corrigible, curable, medicable, repairable, soluble, solvable, treatable

remedy *noun* 1. antidote, counteractive, cure, medicament, medicine, nostrum, panacea, physic (*rare*), relief, restorative, specific, therapy, treatment 2. antidote, corrective, countermeasure, panacea, redress, relief, solution *~verb* 3. alleviate, assuage, control, cure, ease, heal, help, mitigate, palliate, relieve, restore, soothe, treat 4. ameliorate, correct, fix, put right, rectify, redress, reform, relieve, repair, set to rights, solve

remember bear in mind, call to mind, call up, commemorate, keep in mind, look back (on), put one's finger on, recall, recognize, recollect, reminisce, retain, summon up, think back
Antonyms disregard, forget, ignore, neglect, overlook

remembrance 1. anamnesis, memory, mind, recall, recognition, recollection, regard, reminiscence, retrospect, thought 2. commemoration, keepsake, memento, memorial, monument, relic, remembrancer (*archaic*), reminder, souvenir, testimonial, token

There's rosemary, that's for remembrance
William Shakespeare *Hamlet*

remind awaken memories of, bring back to, bring to mind, call to mind, call up, jog one's memory, make (someone) remember, prompt, put in mind, refresh one's memory

reminisce go over in the memory, hark back, live in the past, look back, recall, recollect, remember, review, think back

reminiscence anecdote, memoir, memory, recall, recollection, reflection, remembrance, retrospection, review

reminiscent evocative, redolent, remindful, similar, suggestive

remiss careless, culpable, delinquent, derelict, dilatory, forgetful, heedless, inattentive, indifferent, lackadaisical, lax, neglectful, negligent, regardless, slack, slapdash, slipshod, sloppy (*informal*), slothful, slow, tardy, thoughtless, unmindful
Antonyms attentive, careful, diligent, painstaking, scrupulous

remission 1. absolution, acquittal, amnesty, discharge, excuse, exemption, exoneration, forgiveness, indulgence, pardon, release, reprieve 2. abatement, abeyance, alleviation, amelioration, decrease, diminution, ebb, lessening, let-up (*informal*), lull, moderation, reduction, relaxation, respite, suspension

remit *verb* 1. dispatch, forward, mail, post, send, transmit 2. cancel, desist, forbear, halt, repeal, rescind, stop 3. abate, alleviate, decrease, diminish, dwindle, ease up, fall away, mitigate, moderate, reduce, relax, sink, slacken, soften, wane, weaken 4. defer, delay, postpone, put off, put on the back burner (*informal*), shelve, suspend, take a rain check on (*U.S. & Canad. informal*) *~noun* 5. authorization, brief, guidelines, instructions, orders, terms of reference

remittance allowance, consideration, fee, payment

remnant balance, bit, butt, end, fragment, hangover, leftovers, oddment, piece, remainder, remains, residue, residuum, rest, rump, scrap, shred, stub, survival, tail end, trace, vestige

remonstrance complaint, expostulation, grievance, objection, petition, protest, protestation, reprimand, reproof

remonstrate argue, challenge, complain, dispute, dissent, expostulate, object, protest, take exception, take issue

remorse anguish, bad *or* guilty conscience, compassion, compunction, contrition, grief, guilt, pangs of conscience, penitence, pity, regret, repentance, ruefulness, self-reproach, shame, sorrow

remorse, the fatal egg by pleasure laid
William Cowper *The Progress of Error*

remorseful apologetic, ashamed, chastened, conscience-stricken, contrite, guilt-ridden, guilty, penitent, regretful, repentant, rueful, sad, self-reproachful, sorrowful, sorry

remorseless 1. inexorable, relentless, unrelenting, unremitting, unstoppable 2. callous, cruel, hard, hardhearted, harsh, implacable, inhumane, merciless, pitiless, ruthless, savage, uncompassionate, unforgiving, unmerciful

remote 1. backwoods, distant, far, faraway, far-off, godforsaken, inaccessible, in the middle of nowhere, isolated, lonely, off the beaten track, outlying, out-of-the-way, secluded 2. alien, extraneous, extrinsic, foreign, immaterial, irrelevant, outside, removed, unconnected, unrelated 3. doubtful, dubious, faint, implau~

sible, inconsiderable, meagre, negligible, outside, poor, slender, slight, slim, small, unlikely **4.** abstracted, aloof, cold, detached, distant, faraway, indifferent, introspective, introverted, removed, reserved, standoffish, unapproachable, uncommunicative, uninterested, uninvolved, withdrawn

Antonyms (*sense 1*) adjacent, central, close, just round the corner, near, nearby, neighbouring (*sense 2*) intrinsic, related, relevant (*sense 3*) considerable, good, likely, strong (*sense 4*) alert, attentive, aware, gregarious, interested, involved, outgoing, sociable

removal **1.** abstraction, dislodgment, dismissal, displacement, dispossession, ejection, elimination, eradication, erasure, expulsion, expunction, extraction, purging, stripping, subtraction, taking off, uprooting, withdrawal **2.** departure, flitting (*Scot. & northern English dialect*), move, relocation, transfer

remove **1.** abolish, abstract, amputate, carry off *or* away, cart off (*slang*), delete, depose, detach, dethrone, discharge, dislodge, dismiss, displace, do away with, doff, efface, eject, eliminate, erase, excise, expel, expunge, extract, get rid of, give the bum's rush (*slang*), move, oust, pull, purge, relegate, see the back of, shed, show one the door, strike out, take away, take off, take out, throw out, throw out on one's ear (*informal*), transfer, transport, unseat, wipe from the face of the earth, wipe out, withdraw **2.** depart, flit (*Scot. & northern English dialect*), move, move away, quit, relocate, shift, transfer, transport, vacate **3.** *figurative* assassinate, bump off (*slang*), dispose of, do away with, do in (*slang*), eliminate, execute, get rid of, kill, liquidate, murder, take out (*slang*), wipe from the face of the earth

Antonyms (*sense 1*) appoint, don, insert, install, join, link, place, put, put back, put in, put on, replace, set

remunerate compensate, indemnify, pay, recompense, redress, reimburse, repay, requite, reward

remuneration compensation, earnings, emolument, fee, income, indemnity, meed (*archaic*), pay, payment, profit, recompense, reimbursement, reparation, repayment, retainer, return, reward, salary, stipend, wages

remunerative economic, gainful, lucrative, moneymaking, paying, profitable, recompensing, rewarding, rich, worthwhile

renaissance, renascence awakening, new birth, new dawn, reappearance, reawakening, rebirth, re-emergence, regeneration, renewal, restoration, resurgence, resurrection, revival

renascent reanimated, reawakening, reborn, redivivus (*rare*), re-emerging, renewed, resurgent, resurrected, reviving

rend **1.** break, burst, cleave, crack, dissever, disturb, divide, fracture, lacerate, pierce, pull, rip, rive, rupture, separate, sever, shatter, smash, splinter, split, sunder (*literary*), tear, tear to pieces, wrench **2.** afflict, anguish, break, distress, hurt, lacerate, pain, pierce, stab, torment, wound, wring

render **1.** contribute, deliver, furnish, give, hand out, make available, pay, present, provide, show, submit, supply, tender, turn over, yield **2.** display, evince, exhibit, manifest, show **3.** exchange, give, return, swap, trade **4.** cause to become, leave, make **5.** act, depict, do, give, interpret, perform, play, portray, present, represent **6.** construe, explain, interpret, put, reproduce, restate, transcribe, translate **7.** cede, deliver, give, give up, hand over, relinquish, surrender, turn over, yield **8.** give back, make restitution, pay back, repay, restore, return

rendezvous *noun* **1.** appointment, assignation, date, engagement, meeting, tryst (*archaic*) **2.** gathering point, meeting place, place of assignation, trysting-place (*archaic*), venue ~*verb* **3.** assemble, be reunited, collect, come together, converge, gather, get together, join up, meet, muster, rally

rendition **1.** arrangement, delivery, depiction, execution, interpretation, performance, portrayal, presentation, reading, rendering, take (*informal, chiefly U.S.*), version **2.** construction, explanation, interpretation, reading, transcription, translation, version

renegade **1.** *noun* apostate, backslider, betrayer, defector, deserter, dissident, mutineer, outlaw, rebel, recreant (*archaic*), runaway, traitor, turncoat **2.** *adjective* apostate, backsliding, disloyal, dissident, mutinous, outlaw, rebel, rebellious, recreant (*archaic*), runaway, traitorous, unfaithful

renege, renegue back out, break a promise, break one's word, default, go back, repudiate, welsh (*slang*)

renew begin again, breathe new life into, bring up to date, continue, extend, fix up (*informal, chiefly U.S. & Canad.*), mend, modernize, overhaul, prolong, reaffirm, recommence, recreate, re-establish, refit, refresh, refurbish, regenerate, rejuvenate, renovate, reopen, repair, repeat, replace, replenish, restate, restock, restore, resume, revitalize, transform

renounce abandon, abdicate, abjure, abnegate, abstain from, cast off, decline, deny, discard, disclaim, disown, eschew, forgo, forsake, forswear, give up, leave off, quit, recant, reject, relinquish, renege, repudiate, resign, retract, spurn, swear off, throw off, waive, wash one's hands of

Antonyms assert, avow, claim, maintain, reassert

renovate do up (*informal*), fix up (*informal, chiefly U.S. & Canad.*), modernize, overhaul, recondition, reconstitute, recreate, refit, re~form, refurbish, rehabilitate, remodel, renew, repair, restore, revamp

renown acclaim, celebrity, distinction, emi~nence, fame, glory, honour, illustriousness, lustre, mark, note, reputation, repute, star~dom

renowned acclaimed, celebrated, distin~guished, eminent, esteemed, famed, famous, illustrious, notable, noted, well-known
Antonyms forgotten, little-known, neglected, obscure, unknown

rent[1] 1. *noun* fee, hire, lease, payment, rental, tariff 2. *verb* charter, hire, lease, let

rent[2] *noun* 1. breach, break, chink, crack, flaw, gash, hole, opening, perforation, rip, slash, slit, split, tear 2. breach, break, cleavage, dis~cord, dissension, disunity, division, faction, rift, rupture, schism, split

renunciation abandonment, abdication, abju~ration, abnegation, abstention, denial, dis~avowal, disclaimer, eschewal, forswearing, giving up, rejection, relinquishment, repudia~tion, resignation, spurning, surrender, waiver

reorganize make a clean sweep, rationalize, rearrange, reshuffle, restructure, shake up, spring-clean

repair[1] *verb* 1. compensate for, fix, heal, make good, make up for, mend, patch, patch up, put back together, put right, recover, rectify, re~dress, renew, renovate, restore, restore to working order, retrieve, square ~*noun* 2. ad~justment, darn, mend, overhaul, patch, resto~ration 3. condition, fettle, form, nick (*infor~mal*), shape (*informal*), state
Antonyms *verb* damage, destroy, harm, ruin, wreck

repair[2] *verb* 1. betake oneself, go, head for, leave for, move, remove, retire, set off for, withdraw 2. have recourse, resort, turn

reparable corrigible, curable, recoverable, rec~tifiable, remediable, restorable, retrievable, salvageable

reparation amends, atonement, compensation, damages, indemnity, propitiation, recompense, redress, renewal, repair, requital, restitution, satisfaction

repartee badinage, banter, bon mot, persiflage, pleasantry, raillery, riposte, sally, wit, witti~cism, wittiness, wordplay

repast collation, food, meal, nourishment, re~fection, spread (*informal*), victuals

repay 1. compensate, make restitution, pay back, recompense, refund, reimburse, remu~nerate, requite, restore, return, reward, settle up with, square 2. avenge, even *or* settle the score with, get back at, get even with (*infor~mal*), get one's own back on (*informal*), hit back, make reprisal, pay (someone) back in his *or* her own coin, reciprocate, retaliate, re~turn the compliment, revenge

repeal 1. *verb* abolish, abrogate, annul, cancel, countermand, declare null and void, invali~date, nullify, obviate, recall, rescind, reverse, revoke, set aside, withdraw 2. *noun* abolition, abrogation, annulment, cancellation, invalida~tion, nullification, rescinding, rescindment, rescission, revocation, withdrawal
Antonyms *verb* confirm, enact, introduce, pass, ratify, reaffirm, validate ~*noun* confir~mation, enactment, introduction, passing, ratification, reaffirmation, validation

repeat 1. *verb* duplicate, echo, iterate, quote, recapitulate, recite, redo, rehearse, reiterate, relate, renew, replay, reproduce, rerun, reshow, restate, retell 2. *noun* duplicate, echo, recapitulation, reiteration, repetition, replay, reproduction, rerun, reshowing

repeatedly again and again, frequently, many a time and oft (*archaic or poetic*), many times, often, over and over, time after time, time and (time) again

repel 1. beat off, check, confront, decline, drive off, fight, hold off, keep at arm's length, op~pose, parry, put to flight, rebuff, refuse, reject, repulse, resist, ward off 2. disgust, give one the creeps (*informal*), gross out (*U.S. slang*), make one shudder, make one sick, nauseate, offend, put one off, revolt, sicken, turn one off (*informal*), turn one's stomach
Antonyms attract, delight, draw, entrance, fascinate, invite, please, submit

repellent 1. abhorrent, abominable, cringe-making (*Brit. informal*), discouraging, dis~gusting, distasteful, hateful, horrid, loath~some, nauseating, noxious, obnoxious, ob~scene, odious, offensive, off-putting (*Brit. in~formal*), repugnant, repulsive, revolting, sick~ening, yucky *or* yukky (*slang*) 2. impermeable, proof, repelling, resistant

repent atone, be ashamed, be contrite, be sor~ry, deplore, feel remorse, lament, regret, re~lent, reproach oneself, rue, see the error of one's ways, show penitence, sorrow

When I consider how my life is spent,
I hardly ever repent
Ogden Nash *Reminiscent Reflection*

repentance compunction, contrition, grief, guilt, penitence, regret, remorse, sackcloth and ashes, self-reproach, sorriness, sorrow

Repentance is the virtue of weak minds
John Dryden *The Indian Emperor*

Joy shall be in heaven over one sinner that repenteth, more than over ninety and nine just persons, which need no repentance
Bible: St. Luke

Repentance is but want of power to sin
John Dryden *Palamon and Arcite*

repentant apologetic, ashamed, chastened, contrite, penitent, regretful, remorseful, rue~ful, self-reproachful, sorry

repercussion backlash, consequence, echo, re~bound, recoil, result, reverberation, sequel, side effect

repertory collection, list, range, repertoire, re~pository, stock, store, supply

repetition duplication, echo, iteration, re~appearance, recapitulation, recital, recurrence, redundancy, rehearsal, reiteration, relation, renewal, repeat, repetitiousness, replication, restatement, return, tautology

repetitious iterative, long-winded, pleonastic, prolix, redundant, tautological, tedious, ver~bose, windy, wordy

repetitive boring, dull, mechanical, monoto~nous, recurrent, samey (*informal*), tedious, unchanging, unvaried

rephrase paraphrase, put differently, recast, reword, say in other words

repine brood, complain, eat one's heart out, fret, grieve, grumble, lament, languish, moan, mope, murmur, sulk

replace fill (someone's) shoes *or* boots, follow, oust, put back, re-establish, reinstate, restore, stand in lieu of, step into (someone's) shoes *or* boots, substitute, succeed, supersede, sup~plant, supply, take over from, take the place of

replacement double, fill-in, proxy, stand-in, substitute, successor, surrogate, understudy

replenish fill, furnish, make up, provide, refill, reload, renew, replace, restock, restore, stock, supply, top up
Antonyms consume, drain, empty, exhaust, use up

replete abounding, brimful, brimming, charged, chock-full, crammed, filled, full, full to bursting, full up, glutted, gorged, jammed, jam-packed, sated, satiated, stuffed, teeming, well-provided, well-stocked
Antonyms bare, barren, empty, esurient, famished, hungry, lacking, starving, wanting

repletion completeness, fullness, glut, overfullness, plethora, satiation, satiety, superfluity, surfeit

replica carbon copy (*informal*), copy, duplicate, facsimile, imitation, model, reproduction
Antonyms original

replicate ape, copy, duplicate, follow, mimic, recreate, reduplicate, repeat, reproduce

reply **1.** *verb* acknowledge, answer, come back, counter, echo, make answer, react, recipro~cate, rejoin, respond, retaliate, retort, return, riposte, write back **2.** *noun* acknowledgment, answer, comeback (*informal*), counter, counterattack, echo, reaction, reciprocation, rejoinder, response, retaliation, retort, return, riposte

report *noun* **1.** account, announcement, article, communication, communiqué, declaration, de~scription, detail, dispatch, information, mes~sage, narrative, news, note, paper, piece, re~cital, record, relation, statement, story, sum~mary, tale, tidings, version, word, write-up **2.** buzz, gossip, hearsay, rumour, scuttlebutt (*U.S. slang*), talk **3.** character, eminence, es~teem, fame, regard, reputation, repute **4.** bang, blast, boom, crack, crash, detonation, discharge, explosion, noise, reverberation, sound *~verb* **5.** air, announce, bring word, broadcast, circulate, communicate, cover, de~clare, describe, detail, document, give an ac~count of, inform of, mention, narrate, note, notify, pass on, proclaim, publish, recite, rec~ord, recount, relate, relay, state, tell, write up **6.** appear, arrive, be present, clock in *or* on, come, present oneself, show up (*informal*), turn up

reporter announcer, correspondent, hack (*de~rogatory*), journalist, journo (*slang*), news~caster, newshound (*informal*), newspaperman, newspaperwoman, pressman, writer

repose[1] *noun* **1.** ease, inactivity, peace, quiet, quietness, quietude, relaxation, respite, rest, restfulness, sleep, slumber, stillness, tranquil~lity **2.** aplomb, calmness, composure, dignity, equanimity, peace of mind, poise, self-possession, serenity, tranquillity *~verb* **3.** drowse, lay down, lie, lie down, lie upon, re~cline, relax, rest, rest upon, sleep, slumber, take it easy, take one's ease

repose[2] *verb* confide, deposit, entrust, invest, lodge, place, put, store

repository archive, charnel house, depository, depot, emporium, magazine, receptacle, store, storehouse, treasury, vault, warehouse

reprehensible bad, blameworthy, censurable, condemnable, culpable, delinquent, discredit~able, disgraceful, errant, erring, ignoble, ob~jectionable, opprobrious, remiss, shameful, unworthy
Antonyms acceptable, admirable, forgivable, laudable, pardonable, praiseworthy, unobjec~tionable

represent **1.** act for, be, betoken, correspond to, equal, equate with, express, mean, serve as, speak for, stand for, substitute for, symbolize **2.** embody, epitomize, exemplify, personify, symbolize, typify **3.** delineate, denote, depict, describe, designate, evoke, express, illustrate, outline, picture, portray, render, reproduce, show, sketch **4.** describe as, make out to be, pass off as, pose as, pretend to be **5.** act, ap~pear as, assume the role of, enact, exhibit, perform, play the part of, produce, put on, show, stage

representation 1. account, delineation, depiction, description, illustration, image, likeness, model, narration, narrative, picture, portrait, portrayal, relation, resemblance, sketch 2. body of representatives, committee, delegates, delegation, embassy 3. exhibition, performance, play, production, show, sight, spectacle 4. *often plural* account, argument, explanation, exposition, expostulation, remonstrance, statement

representative *noun* 1. agent, commercial traveller, rep, salesman, traveller 2. archetype, embodiment, epitome, exemplar, personification, type, typical example 3. agent, commissioner, councillor, delegate, depute (*Scot.*), deputy, member, member of parliament, M.P., proxy, spokesman, spokeswoman ~*adjective* 4. archetypal, characteristic, emblematic, evocative, exemplary, illustrative, symbolic, typical 5. chosen, delegated, elected, elective
Antonyms (*sense 4*) atypical, extraordinary, uncharacteristic

repress bottle up, chasten, check, control, crush, curb, hold back, hold in, inhibit, keep in check, master, muffle, overcome, overpower, quash, quell, restrain, silence, smother, stifle, subdue, subjugate, suppress, swallow
Antonyms encourage, express, free, give free rein to, let out, liberate, release, support

repression authoritarianism, censorship, coercion, constraint, control, despotism, domination, inhibition, restraint, subjugation, suppression, tyranny

repressive absolute, authoritarian, coercive, despotic, dictatorial, harsh, oppressive, severe, tough, tyrannical
Antonyms democratic, liberal, libertarian

reprieve *verb* 1. grant a stay of execution to, let off the hook (*slang*), pardon, postpone *or* remit the punishment of 2. abate, allay, alleviate, mitigate, palliate, relieve, respite ~*noun* 3. abeyance, amnesty, deferment, pardon, postponement, remission, stay of execution, suspension 4. abatement, alleviation, let-up (*informal*), mitigation, palliation, relief, respite

reprimand 1. *noun* admonition, blame, castigation, censure, dressing-down (*informal*), flea in one's ear (*informal*), lecture, rebuke, reprehension, reproach, reproof, row, talking-to (*informal*), telling-off (*informal*), ticking-off (*informal*), tongue-lashing, wigging (*Brit. slang*) 2. *verb* admonish, bawl out (*informal*), blame, carpet (*informal*), castigate, censure, check, chew out (*U.S. & Canad. informal*), chew someone's ass (*U.S. & Canad. taboo slang*), chide, dress down (*informal*), give a rocket (*Brit. & N.Z. informal*), give (someone) a row (*informal*), haul over the coals (*informal*), lecture, rap over the knuckles, read the riot act, rebuke, reprehend, reproach, reprove, scold, send one away with a flea in one's ear (*informal*), slap on the wrist (*informal*), take to task, tear into (*informal*), tear (someone) off a strip (*Brit. informal*), tell off (*informal*), tick off (*informal*), tongue-lash, upbraid
Antonyms *noun* commendation, compliment, congratulations, praise ~*verb* applaud, commend, compliment, congratulate, praise

reprisal an eye for an eye, counterstroke, requital, retaliation, retribution, revenge, vengeance

reproach 1. *verb* abuse, bawl out (*informal*), blame, blast, carpet (*informal*), censure, chew out (*U.S. & Canad. informal*), chide, condemn, criticize, defame, discredit, disparage, find fault with, give a rocket (*Brit. & N.Z. informal*), have a go at (*informal*), lambast(e), read the riot act, rebuke, reprehend, reprimand, reprove, scold, take to task, tear into (*informal*), tear (someone) off a strip (*Brit. informal*), upbraid 2. *noun* abuse, blame, blemish, censure, condemnation, contempt, disapproval, discredit, disgrace, dishonour, disrepute, ignominy, indignity, obloquy, odium, opprobrium, scorn, shame, slight, slur, stain, stigma

reproachful abusive, admonitory, castigatory, censorious, condemnatory, contemptuous, critical, disappointed, disapproving, fault-finding, reproving, scolding, upbraiding

reprobate 1. *adjective* abandoned, bad, base, corrupt, damned, degenerate, depraved, dissolute, hardened, immoral, incorrigible, profligate, shameless, sinful, sink, unprincipled, vile, wicked 2. *noun* asshole (*U.S. & Canad. taboo slang*), asswipe (*U.S. & Canad. taboo slang*), bad egg (*old-fashioned informal*), bastard (*offensive*), blackguard, bugger (*taboo slang*), cocksucker (*taboo slang*), degenerate, evildoer, miscreant, mother (*taboo slang, chiefly U.S.*), motherfucker (*taboo slang, chiefly U.S.*), ne'er-do-well, outcast, pariah, profligate, rake, rakehell (*archaic*), rascal, roué, scoundrel, scumbag (*slang*), shit (*taboo slang*), sinner, son-of-a-bitch (*slang, chiefly U.S. & Canad.*), turd (*taboo slang*), villain, wastrel, wretch, wrongdoer 3. *verb* condemn, damn, denounce, disapprove of, frown upon, reprehend, vilify

reproduce 1. copy, duplicate, echo, emulate, imitate, match, mirror, parallel, print, recreate, repeat, replicate, represent, transcribe 2. breed, generate, multiply, procreate, produce young, proliferate, propagate, spawn

reproduction 1. breeding, generation, increase, multiplication, procreation, proliferation,

propagation **2.** copy, duplicate, facsimile, imitation, picture, print, replica
Antonyms (*sense 2*) original

reproof admonition, blame, castigation, censure, chiding, condemnation, criticism, dressing-down (*informal*), rebuke, reprehension, reprimand, reproach, reproval, scolding, ticking-off (*informal*), tongue-lashing, upbraiding
Antonyms commendation, compliment, encouragement, praise

reprove abuse, admonish, bawl out (*informal*), berate, blame, carpet (*informal*), censure, check, chew out (*U.S. & Canad. informal*), chide, condemn, give a rocket (*Brit. & N.Z. informal*), read the riot act, rebuke, reprehend, reprimand, scold, take to task, tear into (*informal*), tear (someone) off a strip (*Brit. informal*), tell off (*informal*), tick off (*informal*), upbraid
Antonyms applaud, commend, compliment, encourage, praise

reptile

Reptiles

adder
agama
agamid
alligator
amphisbaena
anaconda *or (Caribbean)* camoodi
anole
asp
bandy-bandy
blacksnake
blind snake
blue racer
bluetongue
boa
boa constrictor
boomslang
box turtle
brown snake
bull snake *or* gopher snake
bushmaster
carpet snake *or* python
cayman *or* caiman
cerastes
chameleon
chuckwalla
cobra
cobra de capello
constrictor
copperhead
coral snake
crocodile
death adder
diamondback, diamondback terrapin *or* diamondback turtle
diamond snake
dugite
elapid
fer-de-lance
flying lizard *or* flying dragon
frilled lizard
gaboon viper
galliwasp
garter snake
gavial, gharial *or* garial
gecko
giant tortoise
Gila monster
glass snake
goanna
grass snake
green turtle
habu
harlequin snake
hawksbill *or* hawksbill turtle
hognose snake *or* puff adder
hoop snake
horned toad *or* lizard
horned viper
iguana
indigo snake
jew lizard, bearded lizard *or* bearded dragon
kabaragoya *or* Malayan monitor
king cobra *or* hamadryad
king snake
Komodo dragon *or* Komodo lizard
krait
leatherback *or (Brit.)* leathery turtle
leguan
lizard
loggerhead *or* loggerhead turtle
mamba
massasauga
milk snake
moloch
monitor
mud turtle
perentie *or* perenty
pit viper
puff adder
python
racer
rat snake
rattlesnake *or (U.S. & Canad. informal)* rattler
ringhals
rock snake *or* rock python
sand lizard
sand viper
sea snake
sidewinder
skink
slowworm *or* blindworm
smooth snake
snake
snapping turtle
soft-shelled turtle
swift
taipan
terrapin
tiger snake
tokay
tortoise
tree snake
tuatara *or (technical)* sphenodon
turtle
viper
wall lizard
water moccasin, moccasin *or* cottonmouth
water snake
whip snake
worm lizard

Be ye therefore wise as serpents, and harmless as doves
Bible: St. Matthew

The turtle lives 'twixt plated decks
Which practically conceal its sex.
I think it clever of the turtle
In such a fix to be so fertile
Ogden Nash *Autres Bêtes, Autres Moeurs*

repudiate abandon, abjure, cast off, cut off, deny, desert, disavow, discard, disclaim, disown, forsake, reject, renounce, rescind, retract, reverse, revoke, turn one's back on, wash one's hands of
Antonyms accept, acknowledge, admit, assert, avow, defend, own, proclaim, ratify

repugnance abhorrence, antipathy, aversion, disgust, dislike, disrelish, distaste, hatred, loathing, odium, reluctance, repulsion, revulsion

repugnant **1.** abhorrent, abominable, disgusting, distasteful, foul, hateful, horrid, loathsome, nauseating, objectionable, obnoxious, odious, offensive, repellent, revolting, sickening, vile, yucky *or* yukky (*slang*) **2.** adverse, antagonistic, antipathetic, averse, contradictory, hostile, incompatible, inconsistent, inimical, opposed
Antonyms agreeable, attractive, compatible, pleasant, unobjectionable

repulse *verb* **1.** beat off, check, defeat, drive back, fight off, rebuff, repel, throw back, ward off **2.** disdain, disregard, give the cold shoulder to, rebuff, refuse, reject, snub, spurn, turn down *~noun* **3.** check, defeat, disappointment, failure, reverse **4.** cold shoulder, kick in the teeth (*slang*), knock-back (*slang*), rebuff, refusal, rejection, snub, spurning, the (old) heave-ho (*informal*)

repulsion abhorrence, aversion, detestation, disgust, disrelish, distaste, hatred, loathing, odium, repugnance, revulsion

repulsive abhorrent, abominable, disagreeable, disgusting, distasteful, forbidding, foul, hateful, hideous, horrid, loathsome, nauseating, objectionable, obnoxious, obscene, odious, offensive, repellent, revolting, sickening, ugly, unpleasant, vile
Antonyms appealing, attractive, delightful, enticing, lovely, pleasant

reputable creditable, estimable, excellent, good, honourable, honoured, legitimate, of good repute, reliable, respectable, trustworthy, upright, well-thought-of, worthy
Antonyms cowboy (*informal*), disreputable, fly-by-night, shady (*informal*), unreliable, untrustworthy

reputation character, credit, distinction, eminence, esteem, estimation, fame, honour, name, opinion, renown, repute, standing, stature

repute celebrity, distinction, eminence, esteem, estimation, fame, name, renown, reputation, standing, stature

reputed accounted, alleged, believed, considered, deemed, estimated, held, ostensible, putative, reckoned, regarded, rumoured, said, seeming, supposed, thought

reputedly allegedly, apparently, ostensibly, seemingly, supposedly

request **1.** *verb* appeal for, apply for, ask (for), beg, beseech, call for, demand, desire, entreat, petition, pray, put in for, requisition, seek, solicit, sue for, supplicate **2.** *noun* appeal, application, asking, begging, call, demand, desire, entreaty, petition, prayer, requisition, solicitation, suit, supplication
Antonyms command, order

require **1.** crave, depend upon, desire, have need of, lack, miss, need, stand in need of, want, wish **2.** ask, beg, beseech, bid, call upon, command, compel, constrain, demand, direct, enjoin, exact, insist upon, instruct, oblige, order, request **3.** call for, demand, entail, involve, necessitate, take

required called for, compulsory, demanded, essential, mandatory, necessary, needed, obligatory, prescribed, recommended, requisite, set, unavoidable, vital
Antonyms elective, noncompulsory, not necessary, not vital, optional, unimportant, voluntary

requirement demand, desideratum, essential, lack, must, necessity, need, precondition, prerequisite, qualification, requisite, *sine qua non*, specification, stipulation, want

requisite **1.** *adjective* called for, essential, indispensable, mandatory, necessary, needed, needful, obligatory, prerequisite, required, vital **2.** *noun* condition, desideratum, essential, must, necessity, need, precondition, prerequisite, requirement, *sine qua non*

requisition *noun* **1.** application, call, demand, request, summons **2.** appropriation, commandeering, occupation, seizure, takeover *~verb* **3.** apply for, call for, demand, put in for, request **4.** appropriate, commandeer, occupy, seize, take over, take possession of

requital amends, compensation, payment, recompense, redress, reimbursement, remuneration, repayment, restitution, return, reward

requite compensate, get even, give in return, give tit for tat, make amends, make good, make restitution, pay, pay (someone) back in his *or* her own coin, reciprocate, recompense, redress, reimburse, remunerate, repay, respond, retaliate, return, return like for like, reward, satisfy

rescind abrogate, annul, cancel, countermand, declare null and void, invalidate, obviate, overturn, quash, recall, repeal, retract, reverse, revoke, set aside, void
Antonyms confirm, enact, implement, reaffirm, support, uphold, validate

rescission abrogation, annulment, cancellation, invalidation, recall, repeal, rescindment, retraction, reversal, revocation, setting aside, voidance

rescue **1.** *verb* deliver, extricate, free, get out, liberate, recover, redeem, release, salvage, save, save (someone's) bacon (*Brit. informal*), save the life of, set free **2.** *noun* deliverance, extrication, liberation, recovery, redemption, release, relief, salvage, salvation, saving
Antonyms (*sense 1*) abandon, desert, leave, leave behind, lose, strand

research **1.** *noun* analysis, delving, examination, experimentation, exploration, fact-finding, groundwork, inquiry, investigation, probe, scrutiny, study **2.** *verb* analyse, consult the archives, do tests, examine, experiment, explore, investigate, look into, make inquiries, probe, scrutinize, study, work over

resemblance affinity, analogy, closeness, comparability, comparison, conformity, correspondence, counterpart, facsimile, image, kinship, likeness, parallel, parity, sameness, semblance, similarity, similitude

Antonyms difference, disparity, dissimilarity, heterogeneity, unlikeness, variation

resemble bear a resemblance to, be like, be similar to, duplicate, echo, favour (*informal*), look like, mirror, parallel, put one in mind of, remind one of, take after

resent be angry about, bear a grudge about, begrudge, be in a huff about, be offended by, dislike, feel bitter about, grudge, harbour a grudge against, have hard feelings about, ob~ ject to, take amiss, take as an insult, take exception to, take offence at, take umbrage at
Antonyms accept, approve, be content with, be pleased by, feel flattered by, like, welcome

resentful aggrieved, angry, bitter, choked, em~ bittered, exasperated, grudging, huffish, huffy, hurt, in a huff, incensed, indignant, in high dudgeon, irate, jealous, miffed (*informal*), of~ fended, peeved (*informal*), piqued, put out, revengeful, unforgiving, wounded
Antonyms content, flattered, gratified, pleased, satisfied

resentment anger, animosity, bad blood, bit~ terness, chip on one's shoulder (*informal*), displeasure, fury, grudge, huff, hurt, ill feel~ ing, ill will, indignation, ire, irritation, malice, pique, rage, rancour, umbrage, vexation, wrath

> *It is very difficult to get up resentment towards persons whom one has never seen*
> Cardinal Newman *Apologia pro Vita Sua*

reservation 1. condition, demur, doubt, hesi~ tancy, proviso, qualification, rider, scepticism, scruple, stipulation 2. enclave, homeland, pre~ serve, reserve, sanctuary, territory, tract

reserve *verb* 1. conserve, hang on to, hoard, hold, husband, keep, keep back, lay up, pre~ serve, put by, retain, save, set aside, stock~ pile, store, withhold 2. bespeak, book, engage, prearrange, pre-engage, retain, secure 3. def~ er, delay, keep back, postpone, put off, with~ hold *~noun* 4. backlog, cache, capital, fall-back, fund, hoard, reservoir, savings, stock, stockpile, store, supply 5. park, preserve, res~ ervation, sanctuary, tract 6. aloofness, con~ straint, coolness, formality, modesty, reluc~ tance, reservation, restraint, reticence, secre~ tiveness, shyness, silence, taciturnity *~adjec~ tive* 7. alternate, auxiliary, extra, fall-back, secondary, spare, substitute

reserved 1. booked, engaged, held, kept, re~ stricted, retained, set aside, spoken for, taken 2. aloof, cautious, close-mouthed, cold, cool, demure, formal, modest, prim, restrained, reticent, retiring, secretive, shy, silent, stand~ offish, taciturn, unapproachable, uncommuni~ cative, undemonstrative, unforthcoming, un~ responsive, unsociable 3. bound, destined, fat~ ed, intended, meant, predestined
Antonyms (*senses 1 & 2*) ardent, demonstra~ tive, forward, open, sociable, uninhibited, un~ reserved, warm

reservoir 1. basin, lake, pond, tank 2. contain~ er, holder, receptacle, repository, store, tank 3. accumulation, fund, pool, reserves, source, stock, stockpile, store, supply

reshuffle 1. *noun* change, interchange, realign~ ment, rearrangement, redistribution, regroup~ ing, reorganization, restructuring, revision, shake-up (*informal*) 2. *verb* change around, change the line-up of, interchange, realign, rearrange, redistribute, regroup, reorganize, restructure, revise, shake up (*informal*)

reside 1. abide, dwell, hang out (*informal*), have one's home, inhabit, live, lodge, remain, settle, sojourn, stay 2. abide, be intrinsic to, be vested, consist, dwell, exist, inhere, lie, rest with
Antonyms (*sense 1*) holiday in, visit

residence 1. abode, domicile, dwelling, flat, habitation, home, house, household, lodging, pad (*slang*), place, quarters 2. hall, manor, mansion, palace, seat, villa 3. occupancy, oc~ cupation, sojourn, stay, tenancy

resident 1. *noun* citizen, denizen, indweller, inhabitant, local, lodger, occupant, tenant 2. *adjective* dwelling, inhabiting, living, local, neighbourhood, settled
Antonyms *noun* nonresident, visitor *~adjec~ tive* nonresident, visiting

residual leftover, net, nett, remaining, unconsumed, unused, vestigial

residue balance, dregs, excess, extra, leftovers, remainder, remains, remnant, residuum, rest, surplus

resign 1. abandon, abdicate, call it a day *or* night, cede, forgo, forsake, give in one's no~ tice, give up, hand over, leave, quit, relin~ quish, renounce, step down (*informal*), sur~ render, turn over, vacate, yield 2. **resign oneself** accept, acquiesce, bow, give in, give up, reconcile, submit, succumb, yield

resignation 1. abandonment, abdication, de~ parture, leaving, notice, relinquishment, re~ nunciation, retirement, surrender 2. accept~ ance, acquiescence, compliance, endurance, forbearing, fortitude, nonresistance, passivity, patience, submission, sufferance
Antonyms (*sense 2*) defiance, dissent, kicking up a fuss, protest, resistance

resigned acquiescent, compliant, long-suffering, patient, stoical, subdued, submis~ sive, unprotesting, unresisting

resilient 1. bouncy, elastic, flexible, plastic, pli~ able, rubbery, springy, supple, whippy 2. bouncy, buoyant, feisty (*informal, chiefly U.S. & Canad.*), hardy, irrepressible, quick to re~ cover, strong, tough
Antonyms (*sense 1*) flaccid, inflexible, limp,

rigid, stiff (*sense 2*) delicate, effete, sensitive, sickly, weak

resist 1. battle, be proof against, check, combat, confront, contend with, counteract, countervail, curb, defy, dispute, fight back, hinder, hold out against, oppose, put up a fight (against), refuse, repel, stand up to, struggle against, thwart, weather, withstand 2. abstain from, avoid, forbear, forgo, keep from, leave alone, prevent oneself from, refrain from, refuse, turn down
Antonyms (*sense 1*) accept, acquiesce, give in, submit, succumb, surrender, welcome, yield (*sense 2*) enjoy, give in to, indulge in, surrender to

resistance battle, combat, contention, counteraction, defiance, fight, fighting, hindrance, impediment, intransigence, obstruction, opposition, refusal, struggle

Resistance freedom fighters, guerrillas, irregulars, maquis, partisans, underground

resistant 1. hard, impervious, insusceptible, proof against, strong, tough, unaffected by, unyielding 2. antagonistic, combative, defiant, dissident, hostile, intractable, intransigent, opposed, recalcitrant, unwilling

resolute bold, constant, determined, dogged, firm, fixed, immovable, inflexible, obstinate, persevering, purposeful, relentless, set, stalwart, staunch, steadfast, strong-willed, stubborn, tenacious, unbending, undaunted, unflinching, unshakable, unshaken, unwavering
Antonyms doubtful, irresolute, undecided, undetermined, unresolved, unsteady, weak

resolution 1. boldness, constancy, courage, dedication, determination, doggedness, earnestness, energy, firmness, fortitude, obstinacy, perseverance, purpose, relentlessness, resoluteness, resolve, sincerity, staunchness, staying power, steadfastness, stubbornness, tenacity, willpower 2. aim, decision, declaration, determination, intent, intention, judgment, motion, purpose, resolve, verdict 3. answer, end, finding, outcome, settlement, solution, solving, sorting out, unravelling, upshot, working out

resolve *verb* 1. agree, conclude, decide, design, determine, fix, intend, make up one's mind, purpose, settle, undertake 2. answer, clear up, crack, elucidate, fathom, find the solution to, suss (out) (*slang*), work out 3. banish, clear up, dispel, explain, remove 4. analyse, anatomize, break down, clear, disentangle, disintegrate, dissect, dissolve, liquefy, melt, reduce, separate, solve, split up, unravel 5. alter, change, convert, metamorphose, transform, transmute ~*noun* 6. conclusion, decision, design, intention, objective, project, purpose, resolution, undertaking 7. boldness, courage, determination, earnestness, firmness, resoluteness, resolution, steadfastness, willpower
Antonyms (*sense 7*) cowardice, half-heartedness, indecision, vacillation, wavering

resonant booming, echoing, full, resounding, reverberant, reverberating, rich, ringing, sonorous, vibrant

resort *verb* 1. avail oneself of, bring into play, employ, exercise, fall back on, have recourse to, look to, make use of, turn to, use, utilize 2. frequent, go, haunt, head for, repair, visit ~*noun* 3. haunt, holiday centre, refuge, retreat, spot, tourist centre, watering place (*Brit.*) 4. alternative, chance, course, expedient, hope, possibility, recourse, reference

resound echo, fill the air, re-echo, resonate, reverberate, ring

resounding booming, echoing, full, powerful, resonant, reverberating, rich, ringing, sonorous, sounding, vibrant

resource 1. ability, capability, cleverness, ingenuity, initiative, inventiveness, quick-wittedness, resourcefulness, talent 2. hoard, reserve, source, stockpile, supply 3. appliance, contrivance, course, device, expedient, means, resort

resourceful able, bright, capable, clever, creative, imaginative, ingenious, inventive, quick-witted, sharp, talented
Antonyms fushionless (*Scot.*), gormless (*Brit. informal*), unimaginative, uninventive

resources assets, capital, funds, holdings, materials, means, money, property, reserves, riches, supplies, wealth, wherewithal

respect *noun* 1. admiration, appreciation, approbation, consideration, deference, esteem, estimation, honour, recognition, regard, reverence, veneration 2. aspect, characteristic, detail, facet, feature, matter, particular, point, sense, way 3. bearing, connection, reference, regard, relation 4. *plural* compliments, devoirs, good wishes, greetings, regards, salutations ~*verb* 5. admire, adore, appreciate, defer to, esteem, have a good *or* high opinion of, honour, look up to, recognize, regard, revere, reverence, set store by, show consideration for, think highly of, value, venerate 6. abide by, adhere to, attend, comply with, follow, heed, honour, notice, obey, observe, pay attention to, regard, show consideration for
Antonyms *noun* (*sense 1*) contempt, disdain, disregard, disrespect, irreverence, scorn ~*verb* abuse, disregard, disrespect, ignore, neglect, scorn

respectable 1. admirable, decent, decorous, dignified, estimable, good, honest, honourable, proper, reputable, respected, upright, venerable, worthy 2. ample, appreciable, considerable, decent, fair, fairly good, goodly, present~

able, reasonable, sizable *or* sizeable, substan~ tial, tidy (*informal*), tolerable
Antonyms (*sense 1*) dishonourable, disrepu~ table, ignoble, impolite, improper, indecent, unrefined, unworthy (*sense 2*) paltry, poor, small

respectful civil, courteous, courtly, deferential, dutiful, gracious, humble, mannerly, obedient, polite, regardful, reverent, reverential, self-effacing, solicitous, submissive, well-mannered

respective corresponding, individual, own, particular, personal, relevant, separate, sev~ eral, specific, various

respite **1.** break, breather (*informal*), breathing space, cessation, halt, hiatus, intermission, interruption, interval, let-up (*informal*), lull, pause, recess, relaxation, relief, rest **2.** ad~ journment, delay, moratorium, postponement, reprieve, stay, suspension

resplendent beaming, bright, brilliant, daz~ zling, effulgent, gleaming, glittering, glorious, irradiant, luminous, lustrous, radiant, reful~ gent (*literary*), shining, splendid

respond acknowledge, act in response, answer, come back, counter, react, reciprocate, rejoin, reply, retort, return, rise to the bait, take the bait
Antonyms ignore, remain silent, turn a blind eye

response acknowledgment, answer, comeback (*informal*), counterattack, counterblast, feed~ back, reaction, rejoinder, reply, retort, return, riposte

responsibility **1.** accountability, amenability, answerability, care, charge, duty, liability, ob~ ligation, onus, pigeon (*informal*), trust **2.** authority, importance, power **3.** blame, bur~ den, culpability, fault, guilt **4.** conscientious~ ness, dependability, level-headedness, matur~ ity, rationality, reliability, sensibleness, so~ berness, stability, trustworthiness

Uneasy lies the head that wears a crown
William Shakespeare *Henry IV, part 2*

The buck stops here
Harry S. Truman

responsible **1.** at the helm, carrying the can (*informal*), in authority, in charge, in control **2.** accountable, amenable, answerable, bound, chargeable, duty-bound, liable, subject, under obligation **3.** authoritative, decision-making, executive, high, important **4.** at fault, cul~ pable, guilty, to blame **5.** adult, conscientious, dependable, level-headed, mature, rational, reliable, sensible, sober, sound, stable, trust~ worthy
Antonyms irresponsible, unaccountable, un~ conscientious, undependable, unreliable, un~ trustworthy

responsive alive, awake, aware, forthcoming, impressionable, open, perceptive, quick to re~ act, reactive, receptive, sensitive, sharp, sus~ ceptible, sympathetic
Antonyms apathetic, impassive, insensitive, silent, unresponsive, unsympathetic

rest¹ *noun* **1.** calm, doze, forty winks (*infor~ mal*), idleness, inactivity, kip (*Brit. slang*), leisure, lie-down, motionlessness, nap, re~ freshment, relaxation, relief, repose, siesta, sleep, slumber, snooze (*informal*), somnolence, standstill, stillness, tranquillity, zizz (*Brit. in~ formal*) **2. at rest** asleep, at a standstill, at peace, calm, dead, motionless, peaceful, rest~ ing, sleeping, still, stopped, tranquil, unmov~ ing **3.** break, breather (*informal*), breathing space, cessation, halt, holiday, interlude, intermission, interval, lull, pause, respite, stop, time off, vacation **4.** haven, lodging, ref~ uge, retreat, shelter **5.** base, holder, prop, shelf, stand, support, trestle *~verb* **6.** be at ease, be calm, doze, drowse, have a snooze (*informal*), have forty winks (*informal*), idle, kip (*Brit. slang*), laze, lie down, lie still, mel~ low out (*informal*), nap, put one's feet up, re~ fresh oneself, relax, sit down, sleep, slumber, snooze (*informal*), take a nap, take it easy, take one's ease, zizz (*Brit. informal*) **7.** be supported, lay, lean, lie, prop, recline, repose, sit, stand, stretch out **8.** break off, cease, come to a standstill, desist, discontinue, halt, have a break, knock off (*informal*), stay, stop, take a breather (*informal*) **9.** base, be based, be founded, depend, found, hang, hinge, lie, rely, reside, turn
Antonyms *verb* keep going, slog away (*infor~ mal*), work *~noun* activity, bustle, work

rest² **1.** *noun* balance, excess, leftovers, others, remainder, remains, remnants, residue, resid~ uum, rump, surplus **2.** *verb* be left, continue being, go on being, keep, remain, stay

restful calm, calming, comfortable, languid, pacific, peaceful, placid, quiet, relaxed, relax~ ing, serene, sleepy, soothing, tranquil, tran~ quillizing, undisturbed, unhurried
Antonyms agitated, busy, disturbing, restless, uncomfortable, unrelaxed

restitution amends, compensation, indemnifi~ cation, indemnity, recompense, redress, re~ fund, reimbursement, remuneration, repara~ tion, repayment, requital, restoration, return, satisfaction

restive agitated, edgy, fidgety, fractious, fret~ ful, ill at ease, impatient, jittery (*informal*), jumpy, nervous, on edge, recalcitrant, refrac~ tory, restless, uneasy, unquiet, unruly
Antonyms at ease, calm, content, peaceful, relaxed, satisfied, serene, tranquil

restless **1.** active, bustling, changeable, foot~ loose, hurried, inconstant, irresolute, moving,

nomadic, roving, transient, turbulent, unsettled, unstable, unsteady, wandering **2.** agitated, anxious, disturbed, edgy, fidgeting, fidgety, fitful, fretful, having itchy feet, ill at ease, jumpy, nervous, on edge, restive, sleepless, tossing and turning, troubled, uneasy, unquiet, unruly, unsettled, worried
Antonyms comfortable, composed, easy, quiet, relaxed, restful, steady, undisturbed

restlessness **1.** activity, bustle, hurry, hurry-scurry, inconstancy, instability, movement, transience, turbulence, turmoil, unrest, unsettledness **2.** agitation, ants in one's pants (*slang*), anxiety, disquiet, disturbance, edginess, fitfulness, fretfulness, heebie-jeebies (*slang*), inquietude, insomnia, jitters (*informal*), jumpiness, nervousness, restiveness, uneasiness, worriedness

restoration **1.** reconstruction, recovery, refreshment, refurbishing, rehabilitation, rejuvenation, renewal, renovation, repair, revitalization, revival **2.** recovery, re-establishment, reinstallation, reinstatement, replacement, restitution, return
Antonyms (*sense 1*) demolition, scrapping, wrecking (*sense 2*) abolition, overthrow

restore **1.** fix, mend, rebuild, recondition, reconstruct, recover, refurbish, rehabilitate, renew, renovate, repair, retouch, set to rights, touch up **2.** bring back to health, build up, reanimate, refresh, rejuvenate, revitalize, revive, revivify, strengthen **3.** bring back, give back, hand back, recover, re-establish, reinstate, replace, retrocede, return, send back **4.** reconstitute, re-enforce, reimpose, reinstate, reintroduce
Antonyms (*sense 1*) demolish, scrap, wreck (*sense 2*) make worse, sicken, weaken (*sense 4*) abolish, abrogate, repeal, rescind

restrain **1.** bridle, check, confine, constrain, contain, control, curb, curtail, debar, govern, hamper, handicap, harness, have on a tight leash, hinder, hold, hold back, inhibit, keep, keep under control, limit, muzzle, prevent, rein, repress, restrict, straiten, subdue, suppress **2.** arrest, bind, chain, confine, detain, fetter, hold, imprison, jail, lock up, manacle, pinion, tie up
Antonyms (*sense 1*) assist, encourage, help, incite, urge on (*sense 2*) free, liberate, release

restrained **1.** calm, controlled, mild, moderate, muted, reasonable, reticent, self-controlled, soft, steady, temperate, undemonstrative **2.** discreet, quiet, subdued, tasteful, unobtrusive
Antonyms (*sense 1*) fiery, hot-headed, intemperate, unrestrained, wild (*sense 2*) garish, loud, over-the-top, self-indulgent, tasteless

restraint **1.** coercion, command, compulsion, confines, constraint, control, curtailment, grip, hindrance, hold, inhibition, limitation, moderation, prevention, pulling one's punches, restriction, self-control, self-discipline, self-possession, self-restraint, suppression **2.** arrest, bondage, bonds, captivity, chains, confinement, detention, fetters, imprisonment, manacles, pinions, straitjacket **3.** ban, boycott, bridle, check, curb, disqualification, embargo, interdict, limit, limitation, rein, taboo
Antonyms (*sense 1*) excess, immoderation, intemperance, licence, self-indulgence (*sense 2*) freedom, liberty

restrict bound, circumscribe, clip someone's wings, confine, contain, cramp, demarcate, hamper, handicap, hem in, impede, inhibit, keep within bounds *or* limits, limit, regulate, restrain, straiten
Antonyms broaden, encourage, foster, free, promote, widen

restriction check, condition, confinement, constraint, containment, control, curb, demarcation, handicap, inhibition, limitation, regulation, restraint, rule, stipulation

result *noun* **1.** conclusion, consequence, decision, development, effect, end, end result, event, fruit, issue, outcome, product, reaction, sequel, termination, upshot *~verb* **2.** appear, arise, derive, develop, emanate, ensue, eventuate, flow, follow, happen, issue, spring, stem, turn out **3.** *with* **in** culminate, end, finish, pan out (*informal*), terminate, wind up
Antonyms (*sense 1*) beginning, cause, germ, origin, outset, root, source

resume **1.** begin again, carry on, continue, go on, proceed, recommence, reinstitute, reopen, restart, take up *or* pick up where one left off **2.** assume again, occupy again, reoccupy, take back, take up again
Antonyms (*sense 1*) cease, discontinue, stop

résumé abstract, digest, epitome, précis, recapitulation, review, rundown, summary, synopsis

resumption carrying on, continuation, fresh outbreak, new beginning, re-establishment, renewal, reopening, restart, resurgence

resurgence rebirth, recrudescence, re-emergence, renaissance, renascence, resumption, resurrection, return, revival

resurrect breathe new life into, bring back, kick-start (*informal*), raise from the dead, reintroduce, renew, restore to life, revive

resurrection comeback (*informal*), raising *or* rising from the dead, reappearance, rebirth, renaissance, renascence, renewal, restoration, resurgence, resuscitation, return, return from the dead, revival
Antonyms burial, demise, killing off

I am the resurrection, and the life
Bible: St. John

resuscitate breathe new life into, bring round, bring to life, give artificial respiration to, give the kiss of life, quicken, reanimate, renew, rescue, restore, resurrect, revitalize, revive, revivify, save

retain **1.** absorb, contain, detain, grasp, grip, hang *or* hold onto, hold, hold back, hold fast, keep, keep possession of, maintain, preserve, reserve, restrain, save **2.** bear in mind, im~ press on the memory, keep in mind, memo~ rize, recall, recollect, remember **3.** commission, employ, engage, hire, pay, reserve
Antonyms (*sense 1*) let go, lose, release, use up (*sense 2*) forget

retainer **1.** attendant, dependant, domestic, flunky, footman, henchman, lackey, servant, supporter, valet, vassal **2.** advance, deposit, fee

retaliate even the score, exact retribution, get back at, get even with (*informal*), get one's own back (*informal*), give as good as one gets (*informal*), give (someone) a taste of his *or* her own medicine, give tit for tat, hit back, make reprisal, pay (someone) back in his *or* her own coin, reciprocate, return like for like, strike back, take an eye for an eye, take re~ venge, wreak vengeance
Antonyms accept, submit, turn the other cheek

retaliation an eye for an eye, a taste of one's own medicine, counterblow, counterstroke, re~ ciprocation, repayment, reprisal, requital, ret~ ribution, revenge, tit for tat, vengeance

The smallest worm will turn, being trodden on
William Shakespeare *Henry VI, part 3*

retard arrest, brake, check, clog, decelerate, defer, delay, detain, encumber, handicap, hin~ der, hold back *or* up, impede, obstruct, set back, slow down, stall
Antonyms accelerate, advance, expedite, has~ ten, speed, speed up, stimulate

retch barf (*U.S. slang*), be sick, chuck (up) (*slang, chiefly U.S.*), chunder (*slang, chiefly Austral.*), disgorge, do a technicolour yawn (*slang*), gag, heave, puke (*slang*), regurgitate, spew, throw up (*informal*), toss one's cookies (*U.S. slang*), upchuck (*U.S. slang*), vomit

reticence quietness, reserve, restraint, secre~ tiveness, silence, taciturnity, uncommunica~ tiveness, unforthcomingness

reticent close-mouthed, mum, quiet, reserved, restrained, secretive, silent, taciturn, tight-lipped, uncommunicative, unforthcoming, un~ speaking
Antonyms candid, communicative, expansive, frank, open, talkative, voluble

retinue aides, attendants, cortege, entourage, escort, followers, following, servants, suite, train

retire **1.** be pensioned off, (be) put out to grass (*informal*), give up work, stop working **2.** ab~ sent oneself, betake oneself, depart, exit, go away, leave, remove, withdraw **3.** go to bed, go to one's room, go to sleep, hit the hay (*slang*), hit the sack (*slang*), kip down (*Brit. slang*), turn in (*informal*) **4.** back off, decamp, ebb, fall back, give ground, give way, pull back, pull out, recede, retreat, withdraw

retirement loneliness, obscurity, privacy, re~ treat, seclusion, solitude, withdrawal

retiring bashful, coy, demure, diffident, hum~ ble, meek, modest, quiet, reclusive, reserved, reticent, self-effacing, shrinking, shy, timid, timorous, unassertive, unassuming
Antonyms audacious, bold, brassy, forward, gregarious, outgoing, sociable

retort **1.** *verb* answer, answer back, come back with, counter, rejoin, reply, respond, retaliate, return, riposte **2.** *noun* answer, comeback (*in~ formal*), rejoinder, reply, response, riposte

retouch brush up, correct, finish, improve, re~ condition, renovate, restore, touch up

retract **1.** draw in, pull back, pull in, reel in, sheathe **2.** abjure, cancel, deny, disavow, dis~ claim, disown, eat one's words, recall, recant, renege, renounce, repeal, repudiate, rescind, reverse, revoke, take back, unsay, withdraw **3.** back out of, go back on, renege on

retreat *verb* **1.** back away, back off, depart, draw back, ebb, fall back, give ground, go back, leave, pull back, recede, recoil, retire, shrink, turn tail, withdraw *~noun* **2.** depar~ ture, ebb, evacuation, flight, retirement, with~ drawal **3.** asylum, den, haunt, haven, hide~ away, privacy, refuge, resort, retirement, sanctuary, seclusion, shelter
Antonyms *verb* advance, engage, move for~ ward *~noun* (*sense 2*) advance, charge, en~ trance

retrench curtail, cut, cut back, decrease, di~ minish, economize, husband, lessen, limit, make economies, pare, prune, reduce, save, tighten one's belt, trim

retrenchment contraction, cost-cutting, cur~ tailment, cut, cutback, economy, pruning, re~ duction, rundown, tightening one's belt
Antonyms expansion, investment

retribution an eye for an eye, compensation, justice, Nemesis, punishment, reckoning, rec~ ompense, redress, repayment, reprisal, re~ quital, retaliation, revenge, reward, satisfac~ tion, vengeance

Though the mills of God grind slowly, yet they grind exceeding small;
Though with patience He stands waiting, with exactness grinds He all
Henry Wadsworth Longfellow *Retribution*

retrieve fetch back, get back, recall, recapture, recoup, recover, redeem, regain, repair, repossess, rescue, restore, salvage, save, win back

retro antique, bygone, former, nostalgia, of yesteryear, old, old-fashioned, old-time, old-world, past, period

retrograde **1.** *adjective* backward, declining, degenerative, deteriorating, downward, inverse, negative, regressive, relapsing, retreating, retrogressive, reverse, waning, worsening **2.** *verb* backslide, decline, degenerate, deteriorate, go downhill (*informal*), regress, relapse, retreat, retrogress, revert, wane, worsen

retrogress **1.** backslide, decline, deteriorate, go back, go downhill (*informal*), regress, relapse, retrocede, retrograde, return, revert, worsen **2.** drop, ebb, fall, go back, lose ground, recede, retire, retreat, sink, wane, withdraw

retrospect afterthought, hindsight, recollection, re-examination, remembrance, reminiscence, review, survey
Antonyms anticipation, foresight

return *verb* **1.** come back, come round again, go back, reappear, rebound, recoil, recur, repair, retreat, revert, turn back **2.** carry back, convey, give back, put back, re-establish, reinstate, remit, render, replace, restore, retrocede, send, send back, take back, transmit **3.** give back, pay back, reciprocate, recompense, refund, reimburse, repay, requite **4.** bring in, earn, make, net, repay, yield **5.** answer, come back (with), communicate, rejoin, reply, respond, retort **6.** choose, elect, pick, vote in **7.** announce, arrive at, bring in, come to, deliver, render, report, submit *~noun* **8.** homecoming, reappearance, rebound, recoil, recrudescence, recurrence, retreat, reversion **9.** re-establishment, reinstatement, replacement, restoration **10.** advantage, benefit, boot (*dialect*), gain, income, interest, proceeds, profit, revenue, takings, yield **11.** compensation, meed (*archaic*), reciprocation, recompense, reimbursement, reparation, repayment, requital, retaliation, reward **12.** account, form, list, report, statement, summary **13.** answer, comeback (*informal*), rejoinder, reply, response, retort, riposte
Antonyms *verb* (*sense 1*) depart, disappear, go away, leave (*senses 2 & 3*) hold, keep, leave, remove, retain (*sense 4*) lose *~noun* (*sense 8*) departure, leaving (*sense 9*) removal

revamp do up (*informal*), fix up (*informal, chiefly U.S. & Canad.*), give a face-lift to, overhaul, patch up, recondition, refit, refurbish, rehabilitate, renovate, repair, restore

reveal **1.** announce, betray, blow wide open (*slang*), broadcast, communicate, disclose, divulge, get off one's chest (*informal*), give away, give out, impart, leak, let on, let out, let slip, make known, make public, proclaim, publish, take the wraps off (*informal*), tell **2.** bare, bring to light, display, exhibit, expose to view, lay bare, manifest, open, show, uncover, unearth, unmask, unveil
Antonyms conceal, cover up, hide, keep quiet about, sweep under the carpet (*informal*)

revel *verb* **1.** *with* **in** bask, crow, delight, drool, gloat, indulge, joy, lap up, luxuriate, rejoice, relish, rub one's hands, savour, take pleasure, thrive on, wallow **2.** carouse, celebrate, go on a spree, live it up (*informal*), make merry, paint the town red (*informal*), push the boat out (*Brit. informal*), rave (*Brit. slang*), roister, whoop it up (*informal*) *~noun* **3.** *often plural* bacchanal, beano (*Brit. slang*), carousal, carouse, celebration, debauch, festivity, gala, hooley *or* hoolie (*chiefly Irish & N.Z.*), jollification, merrymaking, party, rave (*Brit. slang*), rave-up (*Brit. slang*), saturnalia, spree
Antonyms (*sense 1*) abhor, be uninterested in, dislike, hate, have no taste for

revelation announcement, betrayal, broadcasting, communication, disclosure, discovery, display, exhibition, exposé, exposition, exposure, giveaway, leak, manifestation, news, proclamation, publication, telling, uncovering, unearthing, unveiling

reveller carouser, celebrator, merrymaker, partygoer, pleasure-seeker, roisterer

revelry beano (*Brit. slang*), carousal, carouse, celebration, debauch, debauchery, festivity, fun, hooley *or* hoolie (*chiefly Irish & N.Z.*), jollification, jollity, merrymaking, party, rave (*Brit. slang*), rave-up (*Brit. slang*), roistering, saturnalia, spree

revenge **1.** *noun* an eye for an eye, reprisal, requital, retaliation, retribution, satisfaction, vengeance, vindictiveness **2.** *verb* avenge, even the score for, get even, get one's own back for (*informal*), hit back, make reprisal for, pay (someone) back in his *or* her own coin, repay, requite, retaliate, take an eye for an eye for, take revenge for, vindicate

> *Revenge is a kind of wild justice, which the more man's nature runs to, the more ought law to weed it out*
> Francis Bacon *Essays*

> *Sweet is revenge - especially to women*
> Lord Byron *Don Juan*

> *An eye for an eye, a tooth for a tooth*
> Bible: Exodus

> *Revenge is a dish best served cold*

> *Don't get mad, get even*

> *Revenge is sweet*

revengeful bitter, implacable, malevolent, malicious, malignant, merciless, pitiless, resentful, spiteful, unforgiving, unmerciful, vengeful, vindictive

revenue gain, income, interest, proceeds, profits, receipts, returns, rewards, takings, yield
Antonyms expenditure, expenses, outgoings

reverberate echo, rebound, recoil, re-echo, resound, ring, vibrate

reverberation 1. echo, rebound, recoil, re-echoing, reflection, resonance, resounding, ringing, vibration **2.** *figurative usually plural* consequences, effects, repercussions, results

revere adore, be in awe of, defer to, exalt, have a high opinion of, honour, look up to, put on a pedestal, respect, reverence, think highly of, venerate, worship
Antonyms deride, despise, hold in contempt, scorn, sneer at

reverence 1. *noun* admiration, adoration, awe, deference, devotion, high esteem, homage, honour, respect, veneration, worship **2.** *verb* admire, adore, be in awe of, hold in awe, honour, pay homage to, respect, revere, venerate, worship
Antonyms (*sense 1*) contempt, contumely, derision, disdain, scorn

reverent adoring, awed, decorous, deferential, devout, humble, loving, meek, pious, respectful, reverential, solemn, submissive
Antonyms cheeky, disrespectful, flippant, impious, irreverent, mocking, sacrilegious

reverie absent-mindedness, abstraction, brown study, castles in the air *or* Spain, daydream, daydreaming, inattention, musing, preoccupation, trance, woolgathering

reverse *verb* **1.** invert, transpose, turn back, turn over, turn round, turn upside down, upend **2.** alter, annul, cancel, change, countermand, declare null and void, invalidate, negate, obviate, overrule, overset, overthrow, overturn, quash, repeal, rescind, retract, revoke, set aside, undo, upset **3.** back, backtrack, back up, go backwards, move backwards, retreat *~noun* **4.** antithesis, contradiction, contrary, converse, inverse, opposite **5.** back, flip side, other side, rear, underside, verso, wrong side **6.** adversity, affliction, blow, check, defeat, disappointment, failure, hardship, misadventure, misfortune, mishap, repulse, reversal, setback, trial, vicissitude *~adjective* **7.** back to front, backward, contrary, converse, inverse, inverted, opposite
Antonyms *verb* (*sense 2*) carry out, enforce, implement, validate (*sense 3*) advance, go forward, move forward *~noun* (*sense 5*) forward side, front, obverse, recto, right side

revert backslide, come back, go back, hark back, lapse, recur, regress, relapse, resume, return, take up where one left off

review *verb* **1.** go over again, look at again, reassess, recapitulate, reconsider, re-evaluate, re-examine, rethink, revise, run over, take another look at, think over **2.** call to mind, look back on, recall, recollect, reflect on, remember, summon up **3.** assess, criticize, discuss, evaluate, examine, give one's opinion of, inspect, judge, read through, scrutinize, study, weigh, write a critique of *~noun* **4.** analysis, examination, perusal, report, scrutiny, study, survey **5.** commentary, critical assessment, criticism, critique, evaluation, judgment, notice, study **6.** journal, magazine, periodical **7.** another look, fresh look, reassessment, recapitulation, reconsideration, re-evaluation, re-examination, rethink, retrospect, revision, second look **8.** *Military* display, inspection, march past, parade, procession

reviewer arbiter, commentator, connoisseur, critic, essayist, judge

revile abuse, asperse, bad-mouth (*slang, chiefly U.S. & Canad.*), calumniate, defame, denigrate, knock (*informal*), libel, malign, reproach, rubbish (*informal*), run down, scorn, slag (off) (*slang*), slander, smear, traduce, vilify, vituperate

revise 1. alter, amend, change, correct, edit, emend, modify, reconsider, redo, re-examine, revamp, review, rework, rewrite, update **2.** go over, memorize, reread, run through, study, swot up (*Brit. informal*)

revision 1. alteration, amendment, change, correction, editing, emendation, modification, re-examination, review, rewriting, updating **2.** homework, memorizing, rereading, studying, swotting (*Brit. informal*)

revitalize breathe new life into, bring back to life, reanimate, refresh, rejuvenate, renew, restore, resurrect, revivify

revival awakening, quickening, reanimation, reawakening, rebirth, recrudescence, refreshment, renaissance, renascence, renewal, restoration, resurgence, resurrection, resuscitation, revitalization, revivification
Antonyms disappearance, extinction, falling off, suppression

revive animate, awaken, breathe new life into, bring back to life, bring round, cheer, come round, comfort, invigorate, kick-start (*informal*), quicken, rally, reanimate, recover, refresh, rekindle, renew, renovate, restore, resuscitate, revitalize, rouse, spring up again
Antonyms die out, disappear, enervate, exhaust, tire out, weary

revivify breathe new life into, give new life to, inspirit, invigorate, kick-start (*informal*), reanimate, refresh, renew, restore, resuscitate, revive

revoke abolish, abrogate, annul, call back, cancel, countermand, declare null and void, disclaim, invalidate, negate, nullify, obviate,

quash, recall, recant, renege, renounce, repeal, repudiate, rescind, retract, reverse, set aside, take back, withdraw
Antonyms confirm, endorse, implement, maintain, put into effect, uphold

revolt *noun* **1.** defection, insurgency, insurrection, mutiny, putsch, rebellion, revolution, rising, sedition, uprising *~verb* **2.** defect, mutiny, rebel, resist, rise, take to the streets, take up arms (against) **3.** disgust, give one the creeps (*informal*), gross out (*U.S. slang*), make one's flesh creep, nauseate, offend, repel, repulse, shock, sicken, turn off (*informal*), turn one's stomach

revolting abhorrent, abominable, appalling, cringe-making (*Brit. informal*), disgusting, distasteful, foul, horrible, horrid, loathsome, nasty, nauseating, nauseous, noisome, obnoxious, obscene, offensive, repellent, repugnant, repulsive, shocking, sickening, yucky *or* yukky (*slang*)
Antonyms agreeable, attractive, delightful, fragrant, palatable, pleasant

revolution *noun* **1.** coup, coup d'état, insurgency, mutiny, putsch, rebellion, revolt, rising, uprising **2.** drastic *or* radical change, innovation, metamorphosis, reformation, sea change, shift, transformation, upheaval **3.** circle, circuit, cycle, gyration, lap, orbit, rotation, round, spin, turn, wheel, whirl

revolutionary *noun* **1.** insurgent, insurrectionary, insurrectionist, mutineer, rebel, revolutionist *~adjective* **2.** extremist, insurgent, insurrectionary, mutinous, radical, rebel, seditious, subversive **3.** avant-garde, different, drastic, experimental, fundamental, groundbreaking, innovative, new, novel, progressive, radical, thoroughgoing
Antonyms (*senses 1 & 2*) counter-revolutionary, loyalist, reactionary (*sense 3*) conservative, conventional, mainstream, minor, traditional, trivial

The most radical revolutionary will become a conservative on the day after the revolution
Hannah Arendt

revolutionize break with the past, metamorphose, modernize, reform, revamp, transform

revolve 1. circle, go round, gyrate, orbit, rotate, spin, turn, twist, wheel, whirl **2.** consider, deliberate, meditate, mull over, ponder, reflect, ruminate, study, think about, think over, turn over (in one's mind)

revulsion abhorrence, abomination, aversion, detestation, disgust, distaste, loathing, odium, recoil, repugnance, repulsion
Antonyms attraction, desire, fascination, liking, pleasure

reward *noun* **1.** benefit, bonus, bounty, compensation, gain, honour, meed (*archaic*), merit, payment, premium, prize, profit, recompense, remuneration, repayment, requital, return, wages **2.** comeuppance (*slang*), desert, just deserts, punishment, requital, retribution *~verb* **3.** compensate, honour, make it worth one's while, pay, recompense, remunerate, repay, requite
Antonyms *noun* (*sense 1*) fine, penalty, punishment *~verb* (*sense 3*) fine, penalize, punish

rewarding advantageous, beneficial, economic, edifying, enriching, fruitful, fulfilling, gainful, gratifying, pleasing, productive, profitable, remunerative, satisfying, valuable, worthwhile
Antonyms barren, boring, fruitless, unproductive, unprofitable, unrewarding, vain

reword express differently, paraphrase, put another way, put in other words, recast, rephrase

rewrite correct, edit, emend, recast, redraft, revise, touch up

rhapsodize drool, enthuse, go into ecstasies, gush, rave (*informal*), wax lyrical

rhetoric 1. eloquence, oratory **2.** bombast, fustian, grandiloquence, hot air (*informal*), hyperbole, magniloquence, pomposity, rant, verbosity, wordiness

rhetorical 1. bombastic, declamatory, flamboyant, flashy, florid, flowery, grandiloquent, high-flown, high-sounding, hyperbolic, magniloquent, oratorical, pompous, pretentious, showy, silver-tongued, verbose, windy **2.** linguistic, oratorical, stylistic, verbal

rhyme *noun* **1.** ode, poem, poetry, song, verse **2. rhyme or reason** logic, meaning, method, plan, sense *~verb* **3.** chime, harmonize, sound like

rhythm accent, beat, cadence, flow, lilt, measure (*Prosody*), metre, movement, pattern, periodicity, pulse, swing, tempo, time

It don't mean a thing if it ain't got that swing
Duke Ellington

rhythmic, rhythmical cadenced, flowing, harmonious, lilting, melodious, metrical, musical, periodic, pulsating, throbbing

ribald bawdy, blue, broad, coarse, earthy, filthy, gross, indecent, licentious, naughty, near the knuckle (*informal*), obscene, off colour, Rabelaisian, racy, raunchy (*slang*), risqué, rude, scurrilous, smutty, vulgar, X-rated (*informal*)
Antonyms chaste, decent, decorous, genteel, inoffensive, polite, proper, refined, tasteful

ribaldry bawdiness, billingsgate, coarseness, earthiness, filth, grossness, indecency, licentiousness, naughtiness, obscenity, raciness, rudeness, scurrility, smut, smuttiness, vulgarity

rich 1. affluent, filthy rich, flush (*informal*), loaded (*slang*), made of money (*informal*), moneyed, opulent, propertied, prosperous, rolling (*slang*), stinking rich (*informal*), wealthy, well-heeled (*informal*), well-off, well-to-do **2**. abounding, full, productive, well-endowed, well-provided, well-stocked, well-supplied **3**. abounding, abundant, ample, copious, exuberant, fecund, fertile, fruitful, full, lush, luxurious, plenteous, plentiful, pro~ductive, prolific **4**. beyond price, costly, elabo~rate, elegant, expensive, exquisite, fine, gor~geous, lavish, palatial, precious, priceless, splendid, sumptuous, superb, valuable **5**. creamy, delicious, fatty, flavoursome, full-bodied, heavy, highly-flavoured, juicy, lus~cious, savoury, spicy, succulent, sweet, tasty **6**. bright, deep, gay, intense, strong, vibrant, vivid, warm **7**. deep, dulcet, full, mellifluous, mellow, resonant **8**. amusing, comical, funny, hilarious, humorous, laughable, ludicrous, ri~diculous, risible, side-splitting

Antonyms (*sense 1*) destitute, impoverished, needy, penniless, poor (*sense 2*) lacking, poor, scarce, wanting (*sense 3*) barren, poor, unfertile, unfruitful, unproductive (*sense 4*) cheap, cheapo (*informal*), inexpensive, value~less, worthless (*sense 5*) bland, dull (*sense 6*) dull, insipid, weak (*sense 7*) high-pitched

Let me tell you about the very rich. They are different from you and me

F. Scott Fitzgerald *The Rich Boy*

I am rich beyond the dreams of avarice

Edward Moore *The Gamester*

It is easier for a camel to go through the eye of a needle, than for a rich man to enter into the king~dom of God

Bible: St. Matthew

riches abundance, affluence, assets, fortune, gold, money, opulence, plenty, property, re~sources, richness, substance, treasure, wealth

Antonyms dearth, indigence, lack, need, pau~city, poverty, scantiness, scarcity, want

The chief enjoyment of riches consists in the pa~rade of riches

Adam Smith *Wealth of Nations*

Riches are a good handmaid, but the worst mistress

Francis Bacon *De Dignitate et Augmentis Scientiarum*

richly **1**. elaborately, elegantly, expensively, ex~quisitely, gorgeously, lavishly, luxuriously, opulently, palatially, splendidly, sumptuously **2**. amply, appropriately, fully, in full measure, properly, suitably, thoroughly, well

rickety broken, broken-down, decrepit, derelict, dilapidated, feeble, flimsy, frail, imperfect, in~firm, insecure, jerry-built, precarious, ram~shackle, shaky, tottering, unsound, unsteady, weak, wobbly

rid **1**. clear, deliver, disabuse, disburden, dis~embarrass, disencumber, free, lighten, make free, purge, relieve, unburden **2**. **get rid of** dispense with, dispose of, do away with, dump, eject, eliminate, expel, give the bum's rush (*slang*), jettison, remove, see the back of, shake off, throw away *or* out, unload, weed out, wipe from the face of the earth

riddance clearance, clearing out, deliverance, disposal, ejection, elimination, expulsion, free~dom, release, relief, removal

riddle[1] *noun* brain-teaser (*informal*), Chinese puzzle, conundrum, enigma, mystery, poser, problem, puzzle, rebus, teaser

riddle[2] *verb* **1**. honeycomb, pepper, perforate, pierce, puncture **2**. corrupt, damage, fill, im~pair, infest, mar, permeate, pervade, spoil **3**. bolt, filter, screen, sieve, sift, strain, winnow ~*noun* **4**. filter, screen, sieve, strainer

ride *verb* **1**. control, handle, manage, sit on **2**. be borne (carried, supported), float, go, jour~ney, move, progress, sit, travel **3**. dominate, enslave, grip, haunt, oppress, tyrannize over ~*noun* **4**. drive, jaunt, journey, lift, outing, spin (*informal*), trip, whirl (*informal*)

ridicule **1**. *noun* banter, chaff, derision, gibe, irony, jeer, laughter, make a monkey out of, mockery, raillery, sarcasm, satire, scorn, sneer, taunting **2**. *verb* banter, caricature, chaff, deride, humiliate, jeer, lampoon, laugh at, laugh out of court, laugh to scorn, make a fool of, make fun of, make one a laughing stock, mock, parody, poke fun at, pooh-pooh, satirize, scoff, send up (*Brit. informal*), sneer, take the mickey out of (*informal*), take the piss (out of) (*taboo slang*), taunt

ridiculous absurd, comical, contemptible, deri~sory, farcical, foolish, funny, hilarious, inane, incredible, laughable, ludicrous, nonsensical, outrageous, preposterous, risible, silly, stupid, unbelievable, zany

Antonyms bright, clever, intelligent, logical, prudent, rational, reasonable, sagacious, sane, sensible, serious, smart, solemn, well-thought-out, wise

It is only one step from the sublime to the ri~diculous

Napoleon Bonaparte

The sublime and the ridiculous are often so nearly related, that it is difficult to class them separately. One step above the sublime, makes the ridiculous; and one step above the ridiculous, makes the sublime again

Thomas Paine *The Age of Reason*

rife abundant, common, current, epidemic, fre~quent, general, plentiful, prevailing, preva~lent, raging, rampant, teeming, ubiquitous, universal, widespread

riffraff *canaille*, dregs of society, hoi polloi, rabble, ragtag and bobtail, scum, undesirables

rifle *verb* burgle, despoil, go through, gut, loot, pillage, plunder, ransack, rob, rummage, sack, strip

rift 1. breach, break, chink, cleavage, cleft, crack, cranny, crevice, fault, fissure, flaw, fracture, gap, opening, space, split 2. alienation, breach, difference, disagreement, division, estrangement, falling out (*informal*), quarrel, schism, separation, split

rig *verb* 1. accoutre, equip, fit out, furnish, kit out, outfit, provision, supply, turn out 2. arrange, doctor, engineer, fake, falsify, fiddle with (*informal*), fix (*informal*), gerrymander, juggle, manipulate, tamper with, trump up ~*noun* 3. accoutrements, apparatus, equipage, equipment, fitments, fittings, fixtures, gear, machinery, outfit, tackle

right *adjective* 1. equitable, ethical, fair, good, honest, honourable, just, lawful, moral, proper, righteous, true, upright, virtuous 2. accurate, admissible, authentic, correct, exact, factual, genuine, on the money (*U.S.*), precise, satisfactory, sound, spot-on (*Brit. informal*), true, unerring, valid, veracious 3. advantageous, appropriate, becoming, *comme il faut*, convenient, deserved, desirable, done, due, favourable, fit, fitting, ideal, opportune, proper, propitious, rightful, seemly, suitable 4. all there (*informal*), balanced, *compos mentis*, fine, fit, healthy, in good health, in the pink, lucid, normal, rational, reasonable, sane, sound, unimpaired, up to par, well 5. conservative, reactionary, Tory 6. absolute, complete, out-and-out, outright, pure, real, thorough, thoroughgoing, utter ~*adverb* 7. accurately, aright, correctly, exactly, factually, genuinely, precisely, truly 8. appropriately, aptly, befittingly, fittingly, properly, satisfactorily, suitably 9. directly, immediately, instantly, promptly, quickly, straight, straightaway, without delay 10. bang, exactly, precisely, slap-bang (*informal*), squarely 11. absolutely, all the way, altogether, completely, entirely, perfectly, quite, thoroughly, totally, utterly, wholly 12. ethically, fairly, honestly, honourably, justly, morally, properly, righteously, virtuously 13. advantageously, beneficially, favourably, for the better, fortunately, to advantage, well ~*noun* 14. authority, business, claim, due, freedom, interest, liberty, licence, permission, power, prerogative, privilege, title 15. equity, good, goodness, honour, integrity, justice, lawfulness, legality, morality, propriety, reason, rectitude, righteousness, truth, uprightness, virtue 16. **by rights** equitably, in fairness, justly, properly 17. **to rights** arranged, in order, straight, tidy ~*verb* 18. compensate for, correct, fix, put right, rectify, redress, repair, settle, set upright, sort out, straighten, vindicate

Antonyms *adjective* (*sense 1*) bad, dishonest, immoral, improper, indecent, unethical, unfair, unjust, wrong (*sense 2*) counterfeit, erroneous, fake, false, fraudulent, illegal, illicit, inaccurate, incorrect, inexact, invalid, mistaken, questionable, uncertain, unlawful, untruthful, wrong (*sense 3*) disadvantageous, inappropriate, inconvenient, undesirable, unfitting, unseemly, unsuitable, wrong (*sense 4*) abnormal, unsound (*sense 5*) left, leftist, left-wing, liberal, radical, right-on (*informal*), socialist ~*adverb* (*sense 7*) inaccurately, incorrectly (*sense 8*) improperly (*sense 9*) incompletely, indirectly, slowly (*sense 13*) badly, poorly, unfavourably ~*noun* (*sense 15*) badness, dishonour, evil, immorality, impropriety ~*verb* (*sense 18*) make crooked, topple

> *We hold these truths to be self-evident: that all men are created equal; that they are endowed by their Creator with inalienable rights; that among these are life, liberty, and the pursuit of happiness*
>
> Thomas Jefferson *The Declaration of Independence*

> *Natural rights is simple nonsense; natural and imprescriptible rights, rhetorical nonsense - nonsense upon stilts*
>
> Jeremy Bentham *Anarchical Fallacies*

right away at once, directly, forthwith, immediately, instantly, now, posthaste, promptly, pronto (*informal*), right off, straightaway, straight off (*informal*), this instant, without delay, without hesitation

righteous blameless, equitable, ethical, fair, good, honest, honourable, just, law-abiding, moral, pure, squeaky-clean, upright, virtuous
Antonyms bad, corrupt, dishonest, dishonourable, evil, false, guilty, immoral, improper, indecent, insincere, sinful, unethical, unfair, unjust, unprincipled, unrighteous, unscrupulous, unseemly, wicked

righteousness blamelessness, equity, ethicalness, faithfulness, goodness, honesty, honour, integrity, justice, morality, probity, purity, rectitude, uprightness, virtue

rightful authorized, bona fide, de jure, due, just, lawful, legal, legitimate, proper, real, suitable, true, valid

rigid adamant, austere, exact, fixed, harsh, inflexible, intransigent, invariable, rigorous, set, severe, stern, stiff, strict, stringent, unalterable, unbending, uncompromising, undeviating, unrelenting, unyielding
Antonyms bending, elastic, flexible, indulgent, lax, lenient, limber, lissom(e), merciful, mobile, pliable, pliant, soft, supple, tolerant, yielding

rigmarole balderdash, bother, carry-on (*informal, chiefly Brit.*), gibberish, hassle (*infor~*

mal), jargon, nonsense, palaver, pantomime (*informal*), performance (*informal*), red tape, to-do, trash, twaddle

rigorous 1. austere, challenging, demanding, exacting, firm, hard, harsh, inflexible, rigid, severe, stern, strict, stringent, tough 2. accurate, conscientious, exact, meticulous, nice, painstaking, precise, punctilious, scrupulous, thorough 3. bad, bleak, extreme, harsh, inclement, inhospitable, severe
Antonyms (*sense 1*) easy, flexible, friendly, genial, gentle, humane, indulgent, kind, lax, lenient, loose, merciful, mild, permissive, relaxed, soft, sympathetic, tolerant, weak (*sense 2*) careless, half-hearted, haphazard, imperfect, inaccurate, incorrect, inexact, loose, negligent, slapdash, sloppy, slovenly, unscrupulous (*sense 3*) agreeable, mild, pleasant

rigour 1. asperity, austerity, firmness, hardness, hardship, harshness, inflexibility, ordeal, privation, rigidity, sternness, strictness, stringency, suffering, trial 2. accuracy, conscientiousness, exactitude, exactness, meticulousness, preciseness, precision, punctiliousness, thoroughness

rig-out apparel, clobber (*Brit. slang*), clothing, costume, dress, garb, gear (*informal*), get-up (*informal*), habit, outfit, raiment (*archaic or poetic*), togs

rig out 1. accoutre, equip, fit, furnish, kit out, outfit, set up 2. array, attire, clothe, costume, dress, kit out

rig up arrange, assemble, build, cobble together, construct, erect, fix up, improvise, put together, put up, set up, throw together

rile aggravate (*informal*), anger, annoy, bug (*informal*), gall, get one's back up, get one's goat (*slang*), get on one's nerves (*informal*), get under one's skin (*informal*), irk, irritate, nark (*Brit., Austral., & N.Z. slang*), nettle, peeve (*informal*), pique, piss one off (*taboo slang*), provoke, put one's back up, rub one up the wrong way, try one's patience, upset, vex

rim border, brim, brink, circumference, edge, flange, lip, margin, verge

rind crust, epicarp, husk, integument, outer layer, peel, skin

ring[1] *noun* 1. band, circle, circuit, halo, hoop, loop, round 2. arena, circus, enclosure, rink 3. association, band, cabal, cartel, cell, circle, clique, combine, coterie, crew (*informal*), gang, group, junta, knot, mob, organization, syndicate ~*verb* 4. circumscribe, encircle, enclose, encompass, gird, girdle, hem in, seal off, surround

ring[2] *verb* 1. chime, clang, peal, resonate, resound, reverberate, sound, toll 2. buzz (*informal*), call, phone, telephone ~*noun* 3. chime, knell, peal 4. buzz (*informal*), call, phone call

rinse 1. *verb* bathe, clean, cleanse, dip, splash, wash, wash out, wet 2. *noun* bath, dip, splash, wash, wetting

riot *noun* 1. anarchy, commotion, confusion, disorder, disturbance, donnybrook, fray, lawlessness, mob violence, quarrel, row, street fighting, strife, tumult, turbulence, turmoil, upheaval, uproar 2. blast (*U.S. slang*), boisterousness, carousal, excess, festivity, frolic, high jinks, jollification, merrymaking, revelry, romp 3. display, extravaganza, flourish, show, splash 4. **run riot a.** be out of control, break *or* cut loose, go wild, let oneself go, raise hell, rampage, throw off all restraint **b.** grow like weeds, grow profusely, luxuriate, spread like wildfire ~*verb* 5. fight in the streets, go on the rampage, raise an uproar, rampage, run riot, take to the streets 6. carouse, cut loose, frolic, go on a binge (*informal*), go on a spree, make merry, paint the town red (*informal*), revel, roister, romp

Riots are the language of the unheard
Martin Luther King

riot: a popular entertainment given to the military by innocent bystanders
Ambrose Bierce *The Devil's Dictionary*

riotous 1. anarchic, disorderly, insubordinate, lawless, mutinous, rampageous, rebellious, refractory, rowdy, tumultuous, ungovernable, unruly, uproarious, violent 2. boisterous, loud, luxurious, noisy, orgiastic, rambunctious (*informal*), roisterous, rollicking, saturnalian, side-splitting, unrestrained, uproarious, wanton, wild
Antonyms calm, civilized, disciplined, gentle, lawful, mild, obedient, orderly, peaceful, quiet, restrained, well-behaved

rip 1. *verb* be rent, burst, claw, cut, gash, hack, lacerate, rend, score, slash, slit, split, tear 2. *noun* cleavage, cut, gash, hole, laceration, rent, slash, slit, split, tear

ripe 1. fully developed, fully grown, mature, mellow, ready, ripened, seasoned 2. accomplished, complete, finished, in readiness, perfect, prepared, ready 3. auspicious, favourable, ideal, opportune, right, suitable, timely
Antonyms (*sense 1*) green, immature, undeveloped, unripe (*sense 2*) imperfect, incomplete, unaccomplished, unfinished, unfit, unprepared (*sense 3*) disadvantageous, inappropriate, inconvenient, inopportune, unfavourable, unfitting, unseemly, unsuitable, untimely

ripen burgeon, come of age, come to fruition, develop, get ready, grow ripe, make ripe, mature, prepare, season

rip-off cheat, con (*informal*), con trick (*informal*), daylight robbery (*informal*), exploitation, fraud, robbery, scam (*slang*), sting (*informal*), swindle, theft

rip off cabbage (*Brit. slang*), cheat, con (*informal*), cozen, defraud, diddle (*informal*), do the dirty on (*Brit. informal*), dupe, filch, fleece, gyp (*slang*), knock off (*slang*), lift (*informal*), pilfer, pinch (*informal*), rob, skin (*slang*), steal from, stiff (*slang*), swindle, swipe (*slang*), thieve, trick

riposte **1.** *noun* answer, comeback (*informal*), counterattack, rejoinder, repartee, reply, response, retort, return, sally **2.** *verb* answer, come back, reciprocate, rejoin, reply, respond, retort, return

ripple *noun* **1.** undulation, wavelet **2.** flutter, frisson, oscillation, repercussion, reverberation, thrill, tingle, tremor

rise *verb* **1.** arise, get out of bed, get to one's feet, get up, rise and shine, stand up, surface **2.** arise, ascend, climb, enlarge, go up, grow, improve, increase, intensify, levitate, lift, mount, move up, soar, swell, wax **3.** advance, be promoted, climb the ladder, get on, get somewhere, go places (*informal*), progress, prosper, work one's way up **4.** appear, become apparent, crop up, emanate, emerge, eventuate, flow, happen, issue, occur, originate, spring, turn up **5.** mount the barricades, mutiny, rebel, resist, revolt, take up arms **6.** ascend, climb, get steeper, go uphill, mount, slope upwards *~noun* **7.** advance, ascent, climb, improvement, increase, upsurge, upswing, upturn, upward turn **8.** advancement, aggrandizement, climb, progress, promotion **9.** acclivity, ascent, elevation, hillock, incline, rising ground, upward slope **10.** increment, pay increase, raise (*U.S.*) **11. give rise to** bring about, bring on, cause, effect, produce, provoke, result in

Antonyms *verb* abate, abbreviate, abridge, condense, curtail, decline, decrease, descend, diminish, drop, dwindle, fall, lessen, plunge, reduce, shrink, sink, wane *~noun* blip, decline, decrease, downswing, downturn, drop, fall

risible absurd, amusing, comical, droll, farcical, funny, hilarious, humorous, laughable, ludicrous, rib-tickling (*informal*), ridiculous, side-splitting

risk **1.** *noun* chance, danger, gamble, hazard, jeopardy, peril, pitfall, possibility, speculation, uncertainty, venture **2.** *verb* chance, dare, endanger, expose to danger, gamble, hazard, imperil, jeopardize, put in jeopardy, skate on thin ice, take a chance on, take the plunge, venture

risky chancy (*informal*), dangerous, dicey (*informal, chiefly Brit.*), dodgy (*Brit., Austral., & N.Z. informal*), fraught with danger, hazardous, perilous, precarious, touch-and-go, tricky, uncertain, unsafe

Antonyms certain, reliable, safe, secure, stable, sure

risqué bawdy, blue, daring, immodest, improper, indelicate, naughty, near the knuckle (*informal*), off colour, Rabelaisian, racy, ribald, suggestive

rite act, ceremonial, ceremony, communion, custom, form, formality, liturgy, mystery, observance, ordinance, practice, procedure, ritual, sacrament, service, solemnity, usage

ritual *noun* **1.** ceremonial, ceremony, communion, liturgy, mystery, observance, rite, sacrament, service, solemnity **2.** convention, custom, form, formality, habit, ordinance, practice, prescription, procedure, protocol, red tape, routine, stereotype, tradition, usage *~adjective* **3.** ceremonial, ceremonious, conventional, customary, formal, habitual, prescribed, procedural, routine, stereotyped

ritzy de luxe, elegant, glamorous, glittering, grand, high-class, luxurious, luxury, opulent, plush (*informal*), posh (*informal, chiefly Brit.*), stylish, sumptuous, swanky (*informal*)

rival *noun* **1.** adversary, antagonist, challenger, competitor, contender, contestant, emulator, opponent **2.** compeer, equal, equivalent, fellow, match, peer *~adjective* **3.** competing, competitive, conflicting, emulating, opposed, opposing *~verb* **4.** be a match for, bear comparison with, come up to, compare with, compete, contend, emulate, equal, match, measure up to, oppose, seek to displace, vie with

Antonyms *noun* (*sense 1*) ally, friend, helper, supporter *~verb* (*sense 4*) aid, back, help, support

rivalry antagonism, competition, competitiveness, conflict, contention, contest, duel, emulation, opposition, struggle, vying

river **1.** beck, brook, burn (*Scot.*), creek, rivulet, stream, tributary, watercourse, waterway **2.** flood, flow, rush, spate, torrent

Related adjectives: fluvial, potamic

Rivers

Adige	Apurimac
Ain	Araguaia
Aire	Aras
Aisne	Arkansas
Alabama	Arno
Albany	Aruwimi
Aldan	Assiniboine
Allier	Atbara
Amazon	Athabaska
Amu Darya	Aube
Amur	Avon
Anadyr	Back
Anderson	Barrow
Angara	Beni
Apure	Benue

Berezina
Bermejo
Bío-Bío
Black Volta
Blue Nile
Bomu
Boyne
Brahmaputra
Bug
Cam
Canadian
Caquetá
Cauca
Cauvery *or* Kaveri
Chagres
Chao Phraya
Charente
Chari *or* Shari
Chenab
Cher
Chindwin
Churchill
Clutha
Clyde
Colorado
Columbia
Congo
Connecticut
Cooper's Creek
Courantyne
Cuiaba
Damodar
Danube
Darling
Dee
Delaware
Demerara
Derwent
Des Moines
Detroit
Dnieper
Dniester
Don
Donets
Dordogne
Doubs
Douro
Drava *or* Drave
Drin
Durance
Dvina
Ebro
Elbe
Ems
Erne
Essequibo
Euphrates
Fly
Forth
Fraser
Ganges
Garonne
Glomma
Godavari
Gogra
Göta
Granta
Green
Guadalquivir
Guadiana
Guaporé
Han
Havel
Helmand
Hooghly
Hudson
Iguaçú *or* Iguassú
IJssel *or* Yssel
Illinois
Indus
Inn
Irrawaddy
Irtysh *or* Irtish
Isar
Isère
Isis
Japurá
Javari
Jhelum
Jordan
Juba
Jumna
Juruá
Kabul
Kagera
Kama
Kasai
Kentucky
Kizil Irmak
Klondike
Kolyma
Komati
Kootenay *or* Kootenai
Krishna
Kuban
Kura
Kuskokwim
Lachlan
Lech
Lee
Lena
Liao
Liard
Liffey
Limpopo
Lippe
Little Bighorn
Loire
Lot
Lualaba
Mackenzie
Macquarie
Madeira
Madre de Dios
Magdalena
Mahanadi
Main
Mamoré
Marañón
Maritsa
Marne
Medway
Mekong
Menderes
Mersey
Meta
Meuse
Minnesota
Miño
Mississippi
Missouri
Mohawk
Molopo
Monongahela
Morava
Moselle
Moskva
Murray
Murrumbidgee
Narmada
Neckar
Negro
Neisse
Nelson
Neman *or* Nyeman
Neva
Niagara
Niger
Nile
Ob
Oder
Ogooué *or* Ogowe
Ohio
Oise
Okanagan
Okavango
Orange
Ord
Orinoco
Orontes
Ottawa
Ouachita *or* Washita
Ouse
Paraguay
Paraíba
Paraná
Parnaíba *or* Parnahi-ba
Peace
Pearl
Pechora
Pecos
Piave
Pilcomayo
Plate
Po
Potomac
Pripet
Prut
Purús
Putamayo
Red
Rhine *or* Rhein
Rhône
Ribble
Richelieu
Rio Branco
Rio Grande
Rubicon
Saar
Sacramento
Safid Rud
Saguenay
Saint Croix
Saint John
Saint Lawrence
Salado
Salambria
Salween
Sambre
San
Santee
Saône
Saskatchewan
Sava *or* Save
Savannah
Scheldt
Seine
Severn
Shannon
Shatt-al-Arab
Shiré
Siret
Skien
Slave
Snake
Snowy
Somme
Songhua
Spey
Struma
Susquehanna
Sutlej
Suwannee *or* Swanee
Swan
Swat
Syr Darya
Tagus
Tana
Tanana
Tapajós
Tarim
Tarn
Tarsus

Tay	Volta
Tees	Volturno
Tennessee	Waal
Thames	Wabash
Tiber	Waikato
Ticino	Warta
Tigris	Wear
Tisza	Weser
Tobol	White Volta
Tocantins	Wisconsin
Trent	Xi, Hsi *or* Si
Tugela	Xiang, Hsiang *or* Siang
Tunguska	Xingú
Tweed	Wye
Tyne	Yalu
Ubangi	Yangtze
Ucayali	Yaqui
Uele	Yarra
Ural	Yellow
Usk	Yellowstone
Ussuri	Yenisei
Vaal	Yonne
Var	Yser
Vardar	Yüan *or* Yüen
Vienne	Yukon
Vistula	Zambezi *or* Zambese
Vltava	Zhu Jiang
Volga	

riveting absorbing, arresting, captivating, en~ grossing, enthralling, fascinating, gripping, hypnotic, spellbinding

road **1.** avenue, course, direction, highway, lane, motorway, path, pathway, roadway, route, street, thoroughfare, track, way **2.** *Nautical* anchorage, roadstead

roam drift, meander, peregrinate, prowl, ram~ ble, range, rove, stravaig (*Scot. & northern English dialect*), stray, stroll, travel, walk, wander

roar *verb* **1.** bawl, bay, bell, bellow, clamour, crash, cry, howl, rumble, shout, thunder, vo~ ciferate, yell **2.** bust a gut (*informal*), crack up (*informal*), guffaw, hoot, laugh heartily, split one's sides (*informal*) *~noun* **3.** bellow, clam~ our, crash, cry, howl, outcry, rumble, shout, thunder, yell **4.** belly laugh (*informal*), guffaw, hoot

rob bereave, burgle, cheat, con (*informal*), de~ fraud, deprive, despoil, dispossess, do out of (*informal*), gyp (*slang*), hold up, loot, mug (*informal*), pillage, plunder, raid, ransack, rifle, rip off (*slang*), sack, skin (*slang*), steam (*informal*), stiff (*slang*), strip, swindle

robber bandit, brigand, burglar, cheat, con man (*informal*), fraud, fraudster, grifter (*slang, chiefly U.S. & Canad.*), highwayman, looter, mugger (*informal*), pirate, plunderer, raider, stealer, swindler, thief

robbery burglary, depredation, embezzlement, filching, fraud, hold-up, larceny, mugging (*in~ formal*), pillage, plunder, raid, rapine, rip-off (*slang*), spoliation, stealing, steaming (*infor~ mal*), stick-up (*slang, chiefly U.S.*), swindle, theft, thievery

robe *noun* **1.** costume, gown, habit, vestment **2.** bathrobe, dressing gown, housecoat, negligee, peignoir, wrapper *~verb* **3.** apparel (*archaic*), attire, clothe, drape, dress, garb

robot android, automaton, machine, mechani~ cal man

> *The three fundamental Rules of Robotics... One, a robot may not injure a human being, or, through inaction, allow a human being to come to harm... Two... a robot must obey the orders given it by human beings except where such or~ ders would conflict with the First law... Three, a robot must protect its own existence as long as such protection does not conflict with the First or Second Laws*
>
> Isaac Asimov *I, Robot*

robust **1.** able-bodied, alive and kicking, ath~ letic, brawny, fighting fit, fit, fit as a fiddle (*informal*), hale, hardy, healthy, hearty, husky (*informal*), in fine fettle, in good health, lusty, muscular, powerful, rude, rugged, sinewy, sound, staunch, stout, strapping, strong, stur~ dy, thickset, tough, vigorous, well **2.** boister~ ous, coarse, earthy, indecorous, raunchy (*slang*), raw, roisterous, rollicking, rough, rude, unsubtle **3.** common-sensical, down-to-earth, hard-headed, practical, pragmatic, re~ alistic, sensible, straightforward

Antonyms delicate, feeble, frail, hothouse (*in~ formal, often disparaging*), infirm, refined, sickly, slender, unfit, unhealthy, unsound, weak, weedy (*informal*), wimpish *or* wimpy (*informal*)

rock[1] *noun* **1.** boulder, stone **2.** anchor, bul~ wark, cornerstone, foundation, mainstay, pro~ tection, support, tower of strength

Types of rock

andesite	gneiss
anorthosite	granite
anthracite	granodiorite
arkose	gravel
basalt	greywacke *or (U.S.)* graywacke
breccia	grit
chalk	hornblendite
chert	hornfels
clay	lamprophyre
coal	lava
conglomerate	lignite
diorite	limestone
dolerite	loess
dolomite	marble
dunite	monzonite
eclogite	mudstone
felsite *or* felstone	obsidian
flint	pegmatite
gabbro	

peridotite
perknite
phyllite
pitchstone
pumice
pyroxenite
quartzite
rhyolite
sandstone
schist
shale
skarn
slate
soapstone
syenite
trachyte

rock[2] *verb* **1.** lurch, pitch, reel, roll, sway, swing, toss, wobble **2.** astonish, astound, daze, dumbfound, jar, set one back on one's heels (*informal*), shake, shock, stagger, stun, surprise

rocky[1] *adjective* **1.** boulder-strewn, craggy, pebbly, rough, rugged, stony **2.** adamant, firm, flinty, hard, rocklike, rugged, solid, steady, tough, unyielding

rocky[2] *adjective* **1.** doubtful, rickety, shaky, uncertain, undependable, unreliable, unstable, unsteady, weak, wobbly **2.** *informal* dizzy, ill, sick, sickly, staggering, tottering, unsteady, unwell, weak, wobbly

rod bar, baton, birch, cane, crook, dowel, mace, pole, sceptre, shaft, staff, stick, switch, wand

rogue blackguard, charlatan, cheat, con man (*informal*), crook (*informal*), deceiver, devil, fraud, fraudster, grifter (*slang, chiefly U.S. & Canad.*), knave (*archaic*), mountebank, ne'er-do-well, rapscallion, rascal, reprobate, scally (*Northwest English dialect*), scamp, scoundrel, scumbag (*slang*), sharper, swindler, villain

roguish **1.** criminal, crooked, deceitful, deceiving, dishonest, fraudulent, knavish, raffish, rascally, shady (*informal*), swindling, unprincipled, unscrupulous, villainous **2.** arch, cheeky, coquettish, frolicsome, impish, ludic (*literary*), mischievous, playful, puckish, sportive, waggish

roister **1.** carouse, celebrate, frolic, go on a spree, live it up (*informal*), make merry, paint the town red (*informal*), push the boat out (*Brit. informal*), rave (*Brit. slang*), revel, rollick, romp, whoop it up (*informal*) **2.** bluster, boast, brag, show off (*informal*), strut, swagger

role **1.** character, impersonation, part, portrayal, representation **2.** capacity, duty, function, job, part, position, post, task

roll *verb* **1.** elapse, flow, go past, go round, gyrate, pass, pivot, reel, revolve, rock, rotate, run, spin, swivel, trundle, turn, twirl, undulate, wheel, whirl **2.** bind, coil, curl, enfold, entwine, envelop, furl, swathe, twist, wind, wrap **3.** even, flatten, level, press, smooth, spread **4.** boom, drum, echo, grumble, resound, reverberate, roar, rumble, thunder **5.** billow, lurch, reel, rock, sway, swing, toss, tumble, wallow, welter **6.** lumber, lurch, reel, stagger, swagger, sway, waddle *~noun* **7.** cycle, gyration, reel, revolution, rotation, run, spin, turn, twirl, undulation, wheel, whirl **8.** ball, bobbin, cylinder, reel, scroll, spool **9.** annals, catalogue, census, chronicle, directory, index, inventory, list, record, register, roster, schedule, scroll, table **10.** billowing, lurching, pitching, rocking, rolling, swell, tossing, undulation, wallowing, waves **11.** boom, drumming, growl, grumble, resonance, reverberation, roar, rumble, thunder

rollick caper, cavort, frisk, galumph (*informal*), gambol, make merry, revel, romp

rollicking[1] *adjective* boisterous, carefree, cavorting, devil-may-care, exuberant, frisky, frolicsome, full of beans (*informal*), hearty, jaunty, jovial, joyous, lively, merry, playful, rip-roaring (*informal*), romping, spirited, sportive, sprightly, swashbuckling
Antonyms cheerless, despondent, dull, gloomy, lifeless, melancholy, morose, sad, sedate, serious, unhappy

rollicking[2] *noun* dressing-down (*informal*), lecture, reprimand, roasting (*informal*), scolding, telling-off (*informal*), ticking off (*informal*), tongue-lashing, wigging (*Brit. slang*)

roly-poly buxom, chubby, fat, overweight, plump, podgy, pudgy, rotund, rounded, tubby

romance *noun* **1.** affair, *affaire (du coeur)*, affair of the heart, amour, attachment, intrigue, liaison, love affair, passion, relationship **2.** adventure, charm, colour, excitement, exoticness, fascination, glamour, mystery, nostalgia, sentiment **3.** fairy tale, fantasy, fiction, idyll, legend, love story, melodrama, novel, story, tale, tear-jerker (*informal*) **4.** absurdity, exaggeration, fabrication, fairy tale, falsehood, fiction, flight of fancy, invention, lie, tall story (*informal*), trumped-up story *~verb* **5.** be economical with the truth, exaggerate, fantasize, let one's imagination run away with one, lie, make up stories, stretch the truth, tell stories

It begins when you sink in his arms. It ends with your arms in his sink

feminist slogan

romantic *adjective* **1.** amorous, fond, lovey-dovey, loving, mushy (*informal*), passionate, sentimental, sloppy (*informal*), soppy (*Brit. informal*), tender **2.** charming, colourful, exciting, exotic, fascinating, glamorous, mysterious, nostalgic, picturesque **3.** dreamy, high-flown, idealistic, impractical, quixotic, starry-eyed, unrealistic, utopian, visionary, whimsical **4.** chimerical, exaggerated, extravagant, fabulous, fairy-tale, fanciful, fantastic, fictitious, idyllic, imaginary, imaginative, improbable, legendary, made-up, unrealistic, wild *~noun* **5.** Don Quixote, dreamer, idealist, romancer, sentimentalist, utopian, visionary
Antonyms *adjective* cold-hearted, insensitive, practical, realistic, unaffectionate, unimpas~

sioned, uninspiring, unloving, unromantic, unsentimental

romp *verb* 1. caper, cavort, cut capers, frisk, frolic, gambol, have fun, make merry, revel, roister, rollick, skip, sport 2. **romp home** *or* **in** run away with it, walk it (*informal*), win by a mile (*informal*), win easily, win hands down *~noun* 3. caper, frolic, lark (*informal*)

rook *verb* bilk, cheat, clip (*slang*), cozen, de~ fraud, diddle (*informal*), do (*slang*), fleece, gyp (*slang*), mulct, overcharge, rip off (*slang*), skin (*slang*), stiff (*slang*), sting (*informal*), swindle

room 1. allowance, area, capacity, compass, elbowroom, expanse, extent, latitude, leeway, margin, play, range, scope, space, territory, volume 2. apartment, chamber, office 3. chance, occasion, opportunity, scope

roomy ample, broad, capacious, commodious, extensive, generous, large, sizable *or* sizeable, spacious, wide

Antonyms bounded, confined, cramped, nar~ row, small, tiny, uncomfortable

root[1] *noun* 1. radicle, radix, rhizome, stem, tu~ ber 2. base, beginnings, bottom, cause, core, crux, derivation, essence, foundation, fountainhead, fundamental, germ, heart, mainspring, nub, nucleus, occasion, origin, seat, seed, source, starting point 3. *plural* birthplace, cradle, family, heritage, home, ori~ gins, sense of belonging 4. **root and branch** completely, entirely, finally, radically, thor~ oughly, totally, to the last man, utterly, whol~ ly, without exception *~verb* 5. anchor, become established, become settled, embed, entrench, establish, fasten, fix, ground, implant, moor, set, stick, take root

Related adjective: radical

root[2] *verb* burrow, delve, dig, ferret, forage, hunt, nose, poke, pry, rootle, rummage

rooted confirmed, deep, deeply felt, deep-seated, entrenched, established, firm, fixed, ingrained, radical, rigid

rootless footloose, homeless, itinerant, roving, transient, vagabond

root out 1. *Also* **root up** abolish, cut out, de~ stroy, dig up by the roots, do away with, ef~ face, eliminate, eradicate, erase, exterminate, extirpate, get rid of, remove, tear out by the roots, uproot, weed out, wipe from the face of the earth 2. bring to light, dig out, discover, dredge up, produce, turn up, unearth

rope *noun* 1. cable, cord, hawser, line, strand 2. **the rope** capital punishment, halter, hang~ ing, lynching, noose 3. **know the ropes** be an old hand, be experienced, be knowledgeable, know all the ins and outs, know one's way around, know the score (*informal*), know what's what, know where it's at (*slang*) *~verb* 4. bind, fasten, hitch, lash, lasso, moor, pin~ ion, tether, tie

Give a man enough rope and he will hang himself

rope in drag in, engage, enlist, inveigle, in~ volve, persuade, talk into

ropy, ropey 1. deficient, inadequate, indiffer~ ent, inferior, mediocre, no great shakes (*in~ formal*), of poor quality, poor, sketchy, sub~ standard 2. *informal* below par, off colour, poorly (*informal*), rough (*informal*), sickish, under the weather (*informal*), unwell

roseate 1. blooming, blushing, pink, pinkish, red, rose-coloured, rosy, rubicund, ruddy 2. idealistic, overoptimistic, rose-coloured, unre~ alistic, utopian

roster agenda, catalogue, inventory, list, list~ ing, register, roll, rota, schedule, scroll, table

rostrum dais, platform, podium, stage

rosy 1. pink, red, roseate, rose-coloured 2. blooming, blushing, flushed, fresh, glowing, healthy-looking, radiant, reddish, roseate, ru~ bicund, ruddy 3. auspicious, bright, cheerful, encouraging, favourable, hopeful, optimistic, promising, reassuring, roseate, rose-coloured, sunny

Antonyms (*sense 2*) ashen, colourless, grey, pale, pallid, sickly, wan, white (*sense 3*) cheerless, depressing, discouraging, dismal, down in the dumps (*informal*), dull, gloomy, hopeless, miserable, pessimistic, unhappy, unpromising

rot *verb* 1. break down, corrode, corrupt, crum~ ble, decay, decompose, degenerate, deteriorate, disintegrate, fester, go bad, moulder, perish, putrefy, spoil, taint 2. decline, degenerate, de~ teriorate, languish, waste away, wither away *~noun* 3. blight, canker, corrosion, corruption, decay, decomposition, deterioration, disinte~ gration, mould, putrefaction, putrescence 4. balderdash, balls (*taboo slang*), bilge (*infor~ mal*), bosh (*informal*), bull (*slang*), bullshit (*taboo slang*), bunk (*informal*), bunkum *or* buncombe (*chiefly U.S.*), claptrap (*informal*), cobblers (*Brit. taboo slang*), codswallop (*Brit. slang*), crap (*slang*), drivel, eyewash (*infor~ mal*), flapdoodle (*slang*), garbage (*chiefly U.S.*), guff (*slang*), hogwash, hokum (*slang, chiefly U.S. & Canad.*), horsefeathers (*U.S. slang*), hot air (*informal*), moonshine, nonsense, pap, piffle (*informal*), poppycock (*informal*), rub~ bish, shit (*taboo slang*), stuff and nonsense, tommyrot, tosh (*slang, chiefly Brit.*), trash, tripe (*informal*), twaddle

rotary gyratory, revolving, rotating, rotational, rotatory, spinning, turning

rotate 1. go round, gyrate, pirouette, pivot, reel, revolve, spin, swivel, turn, wheel 2. al~ ternate, follow in sequence, interchange, switch, take turns

rotation 1. gyration, orbit, pirouette, reel, revolution, spin, spinning, turn, turning, wheel 2. alternation, cycle, interchanging, sequence, succession, switching

rotten 1. bad, corroded, corrupt, crumbling, decayed, decaying, decomposed, decomposing, disintegrating, festering, fetid, foul, mouldering, mouldy, perished, putrescent, putrid, rank, sour, stinking, tainted, unsound 2. bent (*slang*), corrupt, crooked (*informal*), deceitful, degenerate, dishonest, dishonourable, disloyal, faithless, immoral, mercenary, perfidious, sink, treacherous, untrustworthy, venal, vicious 3. *informal* base, contemptible, despicable, dirty, disagreeable, filthy, mean, nasty, scurrilous, shitty (*taboo slang*), unpleasant, vile, wicked 4. *informal* bad, deplorable, disappointing, regrettable, unfortunate, unlucky 5. *informal* chickenshit (*U.S. slang*), crummy (*slang*), duff (*Brit. informal*), ill-considered, ill-thought-out, inadequate, inferior, lousy (*slang*), low-grade, of a sort *or* of sorts, poor, poxy (*slang*), punk, ropy *or* ropey (*Brit. informal*), sorry, substandard, unacceptable, unsatisfactory 6. *informal* bad, below par, ill, off colour, poorly (*informal*), ropy *or* ropey (*Brit. informal*), rough (*informal*), sick, under the weather (*informal*), unwell
Antonyms (*sense 1*) fresh, good, pure, wholesome (*sense 2*) decent, honest, honourable, moral, scrupulous, trustworthy (*sense 3*) sweet

rotter bad lot, blackguard, blighter (*Brit. informal*), bounder (*old-fashioned Brit. slang*), cad (*Brit. informal*), cocksucker (*taboo slang*), cur, louse (*slang*), rat (*informal*), scrote (*slang*), scumbag (*slang*), stinker (*slang*), swine

rotund 1. bulbous, globular, orbicular, round, rounded, spherical 2. chubby, corpulent, fat, fleshy, heavy, obese, plump, podgy, portly, roly-poly, rounded, stout, tubby 3. full, grandiloquent, magniloquent, orotund, resonant, rich, round, sonorous
Antonyms (*sense 2*) angular, gaunt, lank, lanky, lean, scrawny, skinny, slender, slight, slim, thin

roué debauchee, dirty old man (*slang*), lech *or* letch (*informal*), lecher, libertine, profligate, rake, sensualist, wanton

rough *adjective* 1. broken, bumpy, craggy, irregular, jagged, rocky, rugged, stony, uneven 2. bristly, bushy, coarse, dishevelled, disordered, fuzzy, hairy, shaggy, tangled, tousled, uncut, unshaven, unshorn 3. agitated, boisterous, choppy, inclement, squally, stormy, tempestuous, turbulent, wild 4. bearish, bluff, blunt, brusque, churlish, coarse, curt, discourteous, ill-bred, ill-mannered, impolite, inconsiderate, indelicate, loutish, rude, unceremonious, uncivil, uncouth, uncultured, ungracious, unmannerly, unpolished, unrefined, untutored 5. boisterous, cruel, curt, drastic, extreme, hard, harsh, nasty, rowdy, severe, sharp, tough, unfeeling, unjust, unpleasant, violent 6. *informal* below par, ill, not a hundred per cent (*informal*), off colour, poorly (*informal*), ropy *or* ropey (*Brit. informal*), rotten (*informal*), sick, under the weather (*informal*), unwell, upset 7. cacophonous, discordant, grating, gruff, harsh, husky, inharmonious, jarring, rasping, raucous, unmusical 8. arduous, austere, hard, rugged, spartan, tough, uncomfortable, unpleasant, unrefined 9. basic, crude, cursory, formless, hasty, imperfect, incomplete, quick, raw, rough-and-ready, rough-hewn, rudimentary, shapeless, sketchy, unfinished, unpolished, unrefined, untutored 10. crude, raw, rough-hewn, uncut, undressed, unhewn, unpolished, unprocessed, unwrought 11. amorphous, approximate, estimated, foggy, general, hazy, imprecise, inexact, sketchy, vague ~*noun* 12. draft, mock-up, outline, preliminary sketch, suggestion 13. *informal* bruiser, bully boy, casual, lager lout, ned (*slang*), roughneck (*slang*), rowdy, ruffian, thug, tough ~*verb* 14. **rough out** adumbrate, block out, delineate, draft, outline, plan, sketch, suggest 15. **rough up** bash up (*informal*), batter, beat the living daylights out of (*informal*), beat up, do over (*Brit., Austral., & N.Z. slang*), knock about *or* around, maltreat, manhandle, mistreat, thrash, work over (*slang*)
Antonyms (*sense 1*) even, level, regular, smooth, unbroken (*sense 2*) smooth, soft (*sense 3*) calm, gentle, quiet, smooth, tranquil (*sense 4*) civil, considerate, courteous, courtly, delicate, elegant, graceful, gracious, pleasant, polite, refined, smooth, sophisticated, urbane, well-bred, well-mannered (*sense 5*) gentle, just, kind, mild, pleasant, quiet, soft (*sense 7*) harmonious, smooth (*sense 8*) comfortable, cushy (*informal*), easy, pleasant, soft (*sense 9*) complete, detailed, finished, perfected, polished, refined, specific (*sense 10*) smooth (*sense 11*) exact, perfected, specific

rough-and-ready adequate, cobbled together, crude, improvised, makeshift, provisional, sketchy, stopgap, thrown together, unpolished, unrefined

rough-and-tumble 1. *noun* affray (*Law*), brawl, donnybrook, dust-up (*informal*), fight, fracas, melee *or* mêlée, punch-up (*Brit. informal*), roughhouse (*slang*), scrap (*informal*), scrimmage, scuffle, shindig (*informal*), shindy (*informal*), struggle 2. *adjective* boisterous, disorderly, haphazard, indisciplined, irregular, rough, rowdy, scrambled, scrambling

roughhouse 1. *noun* boisterousness, brawl, brawling, disorderliness, disturbance, horse~

play, rough behaviour, row, rowdiness, rowdyism, skylarking (*informal*) **2.** *verb* brawl, handle roughly, ill-treat, kick up a row (*informal*), knock about *or* around, maltreat, manhandle, mistreat, paw, skylark (*informal*)

roughneck bruiser (*informal*), bully boy, heavy (*slang*), rough (*informal*), rowdy, ruffian, thug, tough

round *adjective* **1.** annular, ball-shaped, bowed, bulbous, circular, curved, curvilinear, cylindrical, discoid, disc-shaped, globular, orbicular, ring-shaped, rotund, rounded, spherical **2.** complete, entire, full, solid, unbroken, undivided, whole **3.** ample, bounteous, bountiful, considerable, generous, great, large, liberal, substantial **4.** ample, fleshy, full, full-fleshed, plump, roly-poly, rotund, rounded **5.** full, mellifluous, orotund, resonant, rich, rotund, sonorous **6.** blunt, candid, direct, downright, frank, outspoken, plain, straightforward, unmodified *~noun* **7.** ball, band, circle, disc, globe, orb, ring, sphere **8.** bout, cycle, sequence, series, session, succession **9.** division, lap, level, period, session, stage, turn **10.** ambit, beat, circuit, compass, course, routine, schedule, series, tour, turn **11.** bullet, cartridge, discharge, shell, shot *~verb* **12.** bypass, circle, circumnavigate, encircle, flank, go round, skirt, turn

roundabout *adjective* circuitous, circumlocutory, devious, discursive, evasive, indirect, meandering, oblique, periphrastic, tortuous
Antonyms direct, straight, straightforward

roundly bitterly, bluntly, fiercely, frankly, intensely, outspokenly, rigorously, severely, sharply, thoroughly, vehemently, violently

round off bring to a close, cap, close, complete, conclude, crown, finish off, put the finishing touch to, settle
Antonyms begin, commence, initiate, open, start

round on abuse, attack, bite (someone's) head off (*informal*), have a go at (*Brit. slang*), lose one's temper with, retaliate, snap at, turn on, wade into

roundup 1. assembly, collection, gathering, herding, marshalling, muster, rally **2.** *informal* collation, summary, survey

round up assemble, bring together, collect, drive, gather, group, herd, marshal, muster, rally

rouse 1. arouse, awaken, call, get up, rise, wake, wake up **2.** agitate, anger, animate, arouse, bestir, disturb, excite, exhilarate, galvanize, get going, incite, inflame, instigate, move, prod, provoke, startle, stimulate, stir, whip up

rousing brisk, electrifying, exciting, exhilarating, inflammatory, inspiring, lively, moving, spirited, stimulating, stirring, vigorous
Antonyms boring, dreary, dull, lifeless, sluggish, spiritless, unenergetic, wearisome, wishy-washy (*informal*)

rout 1. *noun* beating, debacle, defeat, disorderly retreat, drubbing, headlong flight, hiding (*informal*), licking (*informal*), overthrow, overwhelming defeat, pasting (*slang*), ruin, shambles, thrashing **2.** *verb* beat, chase, clobber (*slang*), conquer, crush, cut to pieces, defeat, destroy, dispel, drive off, drub, lick (*informal*), overpower, overthrow, put to flight, put to rout, scatter, stuff (*slang*), tank (*slang*), thrash, throw back in confusion, wipe the floor with (*informal*), worst

route 1. *noun* avenue, beat, circuit, course, direction, itinerary, journey, passage, path, road, round, run, way **2.** *verb* convey, direct, dispatch, forward, send, steer

routine *noun* **1.** custom, formula, grind (*informal*), groove, method, order, pattern, practice, procedure, programme, usage, way, wont **2.** *informal* act, bit (*informal*), line, performance, piece, spiel (*informal*) *~adjective* **3.** conventional, customary, everyday, familiar, habitual, normal, ordinary, standard, typical, usual, wonted, workaday **4.** boring, clichéd, dull, hackneyed, humdrum, mind-numbing, predictable, run-of-the-mill, shtick (*slang*), tedious, tiresome, unimaginative, uninspired, unoriginal
Antonyms *adjective* abnormal, different, exceptional, irregular, special, unusual

rove cruise, drift, gad about, gallivant, meander, ramble, range, roam, stravaig (*Scot. & northern English dialect*), stray, stroll, traipse (*informal*), wander

rover bird of passage, drifter, gadabout (*informal*), gypsy, itinerant, nomad, rambler, ranger, rolling stone, stroller, transient, traveller, vagrant, wanderer

row[1] *noun* bank, column, file, line, queue, range, rank, sequence, series, string, tier

row[2] *noun* **1.** altercation, *bagarre*, brawl, commotion, controversy, dispute, disturbance, falling-out (*informal*), fracas, fray, fuss, noise, quarrel, racket, ruckus (*informal*), ruction (*informal*), rumpus, scrap (*informal*), shindig (*informal*), shindy (*informal*), shouting match (*informal*), slanging match (*Brit.*), squabble, tiff, trouble, tumult, uproar **2.** castigation, dressing-down (*informal*), flea in one's ear (*informal*), lecture, reprimand, reproof, rollicking (*Brit. informal*), talking-to (*informal*), telling-off (*informal*), ticking-off (*informal*), tongue-lashing *~verb* **3.** argue, brawl, dispute, fight, go at it hammer and tongs, scrap (*informal*), spar, squabble, wrangle

rowdy **1.** *adjective* boisterous, disorderly, loud, loutish, noisy, obstreperous, rough, unruly, uproarious, wild **2.** *noun* brawler, casual, hooligan, lager lout, lout, ned (*slang*), rough (*informal*), ruffian, tearaway (*Brit.*), tough, troublemaker, yahoo, yob *or* yobbo (*Brit. slang*)
Antonyms *adjective* decorous, gentle, law-abiding, mannerly, orderly, peaceful, refined

royal **1.** imperial, kinglike, kingly, monarchical, princely, queenly, regal, sovereign **2.** august, grand, impressive, magnificent, majestic, splendid, stately, superb, superior

Royalty is the gold filling in a mouthful of decay

John Osborne *They call it cricket*

rub *verb* **1.** abrade, caress, chafe, clean, fray, grate, knead, massage, polish, scour, scrape, shine, smooth, stroke, wipe **2.** apply, put, smear, spread **3. rub up the wrong way** aggravate (*informal*), anger, annoy, bug (*informal*), get in one's hair (*informal*), get one's goat (*slang*), get on one's nerves (*informal*), get under one's skin (*informal*), irk, irritate, nark (*Brit., Austral., & N.Z. slang*), peeve (*informal*), piss one off (*taboo slang*), vex ~*noun* **4.** caress, kneading, massage, polish, shine, stroke, wipe **5.** catch, difficulty, drawback, hazard, hindrance, hitch, impediment, obstacle, problem, snag, trouble

rubbish **1.** crap (*slang*), debris, dreck (*slang, chiefly U.S.*), dregs, dross, flotsam and jetsam, garbage (*chiefly U.S.*), grot (*slang*), junk (*informal*), litter, lumber, offal, offscourings, refuse, scrap, trash, waste **2.** balderdash, balls (*taboo slang*), bilge (*informal*), bosh (*informal*), bull (*slang*), bullshit (*taboo slang*), bunkum *or* buncombe (*chiefly U.S.*), claptrap (*informal*), cobblers (*Brit. taboo slang*), codswallop (*Brit. slang*), crap (*slang*), drivel, eyewash (*informal*), flapdoodle (*slang*), garbage (*chiefly U.S.*), gibberish, guff (*slang*), havers (*Scot.*), hogwash, hokum (*slang, chiefly U.S. & Canad.*), horsefeathers (*U.S. slang*), hot air (*informal*), moonshine, nonsense, pap, piffle (*informal*), poppycock (*informal*), rot, shit (*taboo slang*), stuff and nonsense, tommyrot, tosh (*slang, chiefly Brit.*), trash, tripe (*informal*), twaddle, wack (*U.S. slang*)

rubbishy brummagem, cheap, gimcrack, paltry, shoddy, tatty, tawdry, throwaway, trashy, twopenny, twopenny-halfpenny, valueless, worthless

rubicund blushing, florid, flushed, pink, reddish, roseate, rosy, ruddy

rub out **1.** cancel, delete, efface, erase, excise, expunge, obliterate, remove, wipe out **2.** *U.S. slang* assassinate, blow away (*slang, chiefly U.S.*), bump off (*slang*), butcher, dispatch, do in (*informal*), eliminate (*slang*), hit (*slang*), kill, knock off (*slang*), murder, slaughter, slay, take out (*slang*), waste (*informal*)

ruction altercation, brawl, commotion, dispute, disturbance, fracas, fuss, hue and cry, quarrel, racket, row, rumpus, scrap (*informal*), scrimmage, shindig (*informal*), shindy (*informal*), storm, to-do, trouble, uproar

ruddy **1.** blooming, blushing, florid, flushed, fresh, glowing, healthy, radiant, red, reddish, rosy, rosy-cheeked, rubicund, sanguine, sunburnt **2.** crimson, pink, red, reddish, roseate, ruby, scarlet
Antonyms (*sense 1*) anaemic, ashen, colourless, grey, pale, pallid, sickly, wan, white

rude **1.** abrupt, abusive, blunt, brusque, cheeky, churlish, curt, discourteous, disrespectful, ill-mannered, impertinent, impolite, impudent, inconsiderate, insolent, insulting, offhand, peremptory, short, uncivil, unmannerly **2.** barbarous, boorish, brutish, coarse, crude, graceless, gross, ignorant, illiterate, loutish, low, oafish, obscene, rough, savage, scurrilous, uncivilized, uncouth, uncultured, uneducated, ungracious, unpolished, unrefined, untutored, vulgar **3.** artless, crude, inartistic, inelegant, makeshift, primitive, raw, rough, rough-hewn, roughly-made, simple **4.** abrupt, harsh, sharp, startling, sudden, unpleasant, violent
Antonyms (*sense 1*) civil, considerate, cordial, courteous, courtly, decent, gentlemanly, gracious, ladylike, mannerly, polite, respectful, sociable, urbane, well-bred (*sense 2*) artful, civilized, cultured, educated, elegant, learned, polished, refined, sophisticated, urbane (*sense 3*) even, finished, shapely, smooth, well-made

rudimentary basic, early, elementary, embryonic, fundamental, immature, initial, introductory, primary, primitive, undeveloped, vestigial
Antonyms advanced, complete, developed, higher, later, mature, refined, secondary, sophisticated, supplementary

rudiments basics, beginnings, elements, essentials, first principles, foundation, fundamentals, nuts and bolts

rue bemoan, be sorry for, bewail, deplore, grieve, kick oneself for, lament, mourn, regret, repent, reproach oneself for, sorrow for, weep over

rueful conscience-stricken, contrite, dismal, doleful, grievous, lugubrious, melancholy, mournful, penitent, pitiable, pitiful, plaintive, regretful, remorseful, repentant, sad, self-reproachful, sorrowful, sorry, woebegone, woeful
Antonyms cheerful, delighted, glad, happy, joyful, pleased, unrepentant

ruffian bruiser (*informal*), brute, bully, bully boy, casual, heavy (*slang*), hoodlum, hooligan, lager lout, miscreant, ned (*slang*), rascal, rogue, rough (*informal*), roughneck (*slang*), rowdy, scoundrel, thug, tough, villain, wretch, yardie

ruffle **1.** derange, disarrange, discompose, dishevel, disorder, mess up, rumple, tousle, wrinkle **2.** agitate, annoy, confuse, disconcert, disquiet, disturb, faze, fluster, harass, hassle (*informal*), irritate, nettle, peeve (*informal*), perturb, put out, rattle (*informal*), shake up (*informal*), stir, torment, trouble, unnerve, unsettle, upset, vex, worry
Antonyms (*sense 2*) appease, calm, comfort, compose, console, ease, mollify, solace, soothe

rugged **1.** broken, bumpy, craggy, difficult, irregular, jagged, ragged, rocky, rough, stark, uneven **2.** furrowed, leathery, lined, rough-hewn, strong-featured, weather-beaten, weathered, worn, wrinkled **3.** austere, crabbed, dour, gruff, hard, harsh, rough, rude, severe, sour, stern, surly **4.** barbarous, blunt, churlish, crude, graceless, rude, uncouth, uncultured, unpolished, unrefined **5.** arduous, demanding, difficult, exacting, hard, harsh, laborious, rigorous, stern, strenuous, taxing, tough, trying, uncompromising **6.** beefy (*informal*), brawny, burly, hale, hardy, husky (*informal*), muscular, robust, strong, sturdy, tough, vigorous, well-built
Antonyms (*sense 1*) even, gentle, level, regular, smooth, unbroken (*sense 2*) delicate, pretty, refined, smooth, unmarked, youthful (*sense 4*) civil, courteous, cultivated, cultured, elegant, polished, polite, refined, sophisticated, subtle, urbane, well-bred (*sense 5*) agreeable, easy, gentle, mild, pleasant, simple, soft, tender, uncomplicated, unexacting (*sense 6*) delicate, feeble, fragile, frail, infirm, sickly, skinny, soft, weak

ruin *noun* **1.** bankruptcy, breakdown, collapse, crackup (*informal*), crash, damage, decay, defeat, destitution, destruction, devastation, disintegration, disrepair, dissolution, downfall, failure, fall, havoc, insolvency, nemesis, overthrow, ruination, subversion, the end, undoing, Waterloo, wreck, wreckage *~verb* **2.** bankrupt, break, bring down, bring to nothing, bring to ruin, crush, defeat, demolish, destroy, devastate, impoverish, lay in ruins, lay waste, overthrow, overturn, overwhelm, pauperize, raze, shatter, smash, total (*slang*), trash (*slang*), wreak havoc upon, wreck **3.** blow (*slang*), bodge (*informal*), botch, cock up (*Brit. slang*), damage, disfigure, fuck up (*offensive taboo slang*), injure, make a mess of, mangle, mar, mess up, screw up (*informal*), spoil, undo
Antonyms *noun* creation, preservation, success, triumph, victory *~verb* build, construct, create, enhance, enrich, improve, keep, mend, preserve, repair, restore, save, start, strengthen, submit to, succumb to, support, surrender to, yield to

ruinous **1.** baleful, baneful (*archaic*), calamitous, catastrophic, crippling, deadly, deleterious, destructive, devastating, dire, disastrous, extravagant, fatal, immoderate, injurious, murderous, noxious, pernicious, shattering, wasteful, withering **2.** broken-down, decrepit, derelict, dilapidated, in ruins, ramshackle, ruined

rule *noun* **1.** axiom, canon, criterion, decree, dictum, direction, guide, guideline, law, maxim, order, ordinance, precept, principle, regulation, ruling, standard, tenet **2.** administration, ascendancy, authority, command, control, direction, domination, dominion, empire, government, influence, jurisdiction, leadership, mastery, power, regime, reign, supremacy, sway **3.** condition, convention, custom, form, habit, order *or* way of things, practice, procedure, routine, tradition, wont **4.** course, formula, method, policy, procedure, way **5.** **as a rule** customarily, for the most part, generally, mainly, normally, on the whole, ordinarily, usually *~verb* **6.** administer, be in authority, be in power, be number one (*informal*), command, control, direct, dominate, govern, guide, hold sway, lead, manage, preside over, regulate, reign, wear the crown **7.** adjudge, adjudicate, decide, decree, determine, establish, find, judge, lay down, pronounce, resolve, settle **8.** be customary (pre-eminent, prevalent, superior), hold sway, obtain, predominate, preponderate, prevail

He shall rule them with a rod of iron
Bible: Revelation

My people and I have come to an agreement which satisfies us both. They are to say what they please, and I am to do what I please
Frederick the Great

The hand that rocks the cradle
Is the hand that rules the world
William Ross Wallace *John O'London's Treasure Trove*

Rules and models destroy genius and art
William Hazlitt *Sketches and Essays*

rule out ban, debar, dismiss, disqualify, eliminate, exclude, forbid, leave out, obviate, preclude, prevent, prohibit, proscribe, reject
Antonyms allow, approve, authorize, let, license, order, permit, sanction

ruler **1.** commander, controller, crowned head, emperor, empress, governor, head of state, king, leader, lord, monarch, potentate, prince, princess, queen, sovereign **2.** measure, rule, straight edge, yardstick

Titles of rulers

amir *or* ameer	maharani *or* maharanee
archduke	mikado
Caesar	nawab *or* nabob
caliph, calif, kalif *or* khalif	Negus
chief	Nizam
Chogyal	oba
Dalai Lama	pasha *or* pacha
doge	Pharaoh
duke	podesta
emir	pope
emperor *or* *(fem.)* empress	queen
Gaekwar *or* Gaikwar	rajah *or* raja
Great Mogul	rani *or* ranee
hospodar	satrap
imam *or* imaum	shah
Inca	sheik *or* sheikh
kabaka	sherif, shereef *or* sharif
Kaiser	shogun
khan	stadholder *or* stadtholder
khedive	sultan
king	tenno
maharajah *or* maharaja	tsar *or* czar
	viceroy *or* *(fem.)* vicereine

Famous rulers

Alexander the Great	Lenin
Alfred the Great	Louis XIV
Amin	Mao Ze Dong *or* Mao Tse-tung
Augustus	Montezuma
Bismarck	Mussolini
Boudicca	Napoleon Bonaparte
Caligula	Nasser
Castro	Nero
Catherine the Great	Nicholas II
Charlemagne	Pericles
Churchill	Peter the Great
Cleopatra	Richard the Lionheart
Cromwell	Saladin
de Gaulle	Stalin
Edward the Confessor	Suleiman the Magnificent
Elizabeth I	Tamerlane *or* Tamburlaine
Franco	Tutankhamen *or* Tutankhamun
Genghis Khan	Victoria
Haile Selassie	William the Conqueror
Herod	
Hirohito	
Hitler	
Ivan the Terrible	
Julius Caesar	
Kublai Khan	

ruling *noun* **1.** adjudication, decision, decree, finding, judgment, pronouncement, resolution, verdict *~adjective* **2.** commanding, controlling, dominant, governing, leading, regnant, reigning, upper **3.** chief, current, dominant, main, predominant, pre-eminent, preponderant, prevailing, prevalent, principal, regnant, supreme

Antonyms (*sense 3*) auxiliary, inferior, least, minor, secondary, subordinate, subsidiary, unimportant

rum curious, dodgy (*Brit., Austral., & N.Z. informal*), funny, odd, peculiar, queer, singular, strange, suspect, suspicious, unusual, weird

rumbustious boisterous, clamorous, disorderly, exuberant, loud, noisy, obstreperous, refractory, robust, rough, rowdy, unmanageable, unruly, uproarious, wayward, wild, wilful

ruminate brood, chew over, cogitate, consider, contemplate, deliberate, meditate, mull over, muse, ponder, rack one's brains, reflect, revolve, think, turn over in one's mind, weigh

rummage delve, examine, explore, forage, hunt, ransack, root, rootle, search

rumour 1. *noun* bruit (*archaic*), bush telegraph, buzz, canard, dirt (*U.S. slang*), gossip, hearsay, news, report, scuttlebutt (*U.S. slang*), story, talk, tidings, whisper, word **2.** *verb* bruit, circulate, gossip, noise abroad, pass around, publish, put about, report, say, tell, whisper

rump arse (*taboo slang*), ass (*U.S. & Canad. taboo slang*), backside (*informal*), bottom, bum (*Brit. slang*), buns (*U.S. slang*), butt (*U.S. & Canad. informal*), buttocks, croup, derrière (*euphemistic*), haunch, hindquarters, jacksy (*Brit. slang*), posterior, rear, rear end, seat, tail (*informal*)

rumple crease, crinkle, crumple, crush, derange, dishevel, disorder, mess up, pucker, ruffle, screw up, scrunch, tousle, wrinkle

rumpus brouhaha, commotion, confusion, disruption, disturbance, furore, fuss, hue and cry, kerfuffle (*informal*), noise, row, shindig (*informal*), shindy (*informal*), tumult, uproar

run *verb* **1.** barrel (along) (*informal, chiefly U.S. & Canad.*), bolt, career, dart, dash, gallop, hare (*Brit. informal*), hasten, hie, hotfoot, hurry, jog, leg it (*informal*), lope, race, rush, scamper, scramble, scud, scurry, speed, sprint, stampede **2.** abscond, beat a retreat, beat it (*slang*), bolt, clear out, cut and run (*informal*), decamp, depart, do a runner (*slang*), escape, flee, fly the coop (*U.S. & Canad. informal*), leg it (*informal*), make a run for it, make off, scarper (*Brit. slang*), show a clean pair of heels, skedaddle (*informal*), slope off, take a powder (*U.S. & Canad. slang*), take flight, take it on the lam (*U.S. & Canad. slang*), take off (*informal*), take to one's heels **3.** course, glide, go, move, pass, roll, skim, slide **4.** bear, carry, convey, drive, give a lift to, manoeuvre, operate, propel, transport **5.** go, operate, ply **6.** function, go, operate, perform, tick, work **7.** administer, be in charge of, boss (*informal*), carry on, conduct, control, coordinate, direct, handle, head, lead, look after, manage, mastermind, operate, oversee, own, regulate, superintend, supervise, take care of **8.** continue, extend, go, last, lie, proceed, range, reach, stretch **9.** cascade, discharge, flow, go, gush, issue, leak, move, pour, proceed, spill, spout, stream **10.** dissolve, fuse, go soft, liquefy, melt, turn to liquid **11.** be diffused, bleed, lose colour, mix, spread **12.** come apart, come undone, ladder, tear, unravel **13.** be current, circulate, climb, creep, go round, spread, trail **14.** display, feature, print, publish **15.** be a candidate, challenge, compete, contend, put oneself up for, stand, take part **16.** bootleg, deal in, ship, smuggle, sneak, traffic in **17. run for it** abscond, bolt, cut and run (*informal*), decamp, do a bunk (*Brit. slang*), do a runner (*slang*), escape, flee, fly, fly the coop (*U.S. & Canad. informal*), make a break for it, make off, scarper (*Brit. slang*), scram (*informal*), show a clean pair of heels, skedaddle (*informal*), take a powder (*U.S. & Canad. slang*), take flight, take it on the lam (*U.S. & Canad. slang*), take off *~noun* **18.** dash, gallop, jog, race, rush, sprint, spurt **19.** drive, excursion, jaunt, journey, joy ride (*informal*), lift, outing, ride, round, spin (*informal*), trip **20.** chain, course, cycle, passage, period, round, season, sequence, series, spell, streak, stretch, string **21.** category, class, kind, order, sort, type, variety **22.** application, demand, pressure, rush **23.** ladder, rip, snag, tear **24.** course, current, direction, drift, flow, motion, movement, passage, path, progress, stream, tendency, tenor, tide, trend, way **25.** coop, enclosure, pen **26. in the long run** at the end of the day, eventually, in the end, in the final analysis, in the fullness of time, in time, ultimately, when all is said and done **27. on the run a.** at liberty, escaping, fugitive, in flight, on the lam (*U.S. slang*), on the loose **b.** defeated, falling back, fleeing, in flight, in retreat, retreating, running away **c.** at speed, hastily, hurriedly, hurrying, in a hurry, in a rush, in haste

Antonyms (*sense 1*) crawl, creep, dawdle, walk (*sense 2*) remain, stay (*sense 8*) cease, stop

run across bump into, chance upon, come across, come upon, encounter, meet, meet with, run into

run after chase, follow, give chase, pursue

runaway *noun* **1.** absconder, deserter, escapee, escaper, fugitive, refugee, truant *~adjective* **2.** escaped, fleeing, fugitive, loose, out of control, uncontrolled, wild **3.** easily won, easy, effortless

run away 1. abscond, beat it (*slang*), bolt, clear out, cut and run (*informal*), decamp, do a bunk (*Brit. slang*), do a runner (*slang*), escape, flee, fly the coop (*U.S. & Canad. informal*), hook it (*slang*), make a run for it, run off, scarper (*Brit. slang*), scram (*informal*), show a clean pair of heels, skedaddle (*informal*), take a powder (*U.S. & Canad. slang*), take flight, take it on the lam (*U.S. & Canad. slang*), take off, take to one's heels, turn tail **2.** *with* **with a.** abduct, abscond, elope **b.** abscond, make off, pinch (*informal*), run off, snatch, steal **c.** romp home, walk it (*informal*), win by a mile (*informal*), win easily, win hands down

He who fights and runs away
May live to fight another day
Oliver Goldsmith *The Art of Poetry on a New Plan*

rundown briefing, outline, précis, recap (*informal*), résumé, review, run-through, sketch, summary, synopsis

run-down 1. below par, debilitated, drained, enervated, exhausted, fatigued, out of condition, peaky, tired, under the weather (*informal*), unhealthy, weak, weary, worn-out **2.** broken-down, decrepit, dilapidated, dingy, ramshackle, seedy, shabby, tumble-down, worn-out

Antonyms (*sense 1*) fighting fit, fine, fit, fit as a fiddle, full of beans (*informal*), healthy, well

run down 1. curtail, cut, cut back, decrease, downsize, drop, pare down, reduce, trim **2.** debilitate, exhaust, sap the strength of, tire, undermine the health of, weaken **3.** asperse, bad-mouth (*slang, chiefly U.S. & Canad.*), belittle, criticize adversely, decry, defame, denigrate, disparage, knock (*informal*), put down, revile, rubbish (*informal*), slag (off) (*slang*), speak ill of, vilify **4.** hit, knock down, knock over, run into, run over, strike

run-in altercation, argument, brush, confrontation, contretemps, dispute, dust-up (*informal*), encounter, face-off (*slang*), fight, quarrel, row, set-to (*informal*), skirmish, tussle

run in 1. break in gently, run gently **2.** *slang* apprehend, arrest, bust (*informal*), collar (*informal*), feel one's collar (*slang*), jail, lift (*slang*), nab (*informal*), nail (*informal*), pick up, pinch (*informal*), pull in (*Brit. slang*), take into custody, take to jail, throw in jail

run into 1. bump into, collide with, crash into, dash against, hit, ram, strike **2.** be beset by, be confronted by, bump into, chance upon, come across, come upon, encounter, meet, meet with, run across

runner 1. athlete, harrier, jogger, miler, sprinter **2.** courier, dispatch bearer, errand boy, messenger **3.** offshoot, shoot, sprig, sprout, stem, stolon (*Botany*), tendril

running *adjective* **1.** constant, continuous, incessant, in succession, on the trot (*informal*), perpetual, together, unbroken, unceasing, un~

interrupted **2.** flowing, moving, streaming *~noun* **3.** administration, charge, conduct, control, coordination, direction, leadership, management, organization, regulation, superintendency, supervision **4.** functioning, maintenance, operation, performance, working **5.** competition, contention, contest

runny diluted, flowing, fluid, liquefied, liquid, melted, streaming, watery

run off **1.** bolt, clear out, cut and run (*informal*), decamp, do a runner (*slang*), escape, flee, fly the coop (*U.S. & Canad. informal*), hook it (*slang*), make off, run away, scarper (*Brit. slang*), show a clean pair of heels, skedaddle (*informal*), take a powder (*U.S. & Canad. slang*), take flight, take it on the lam (*U.S. & Canad. slang*), take to one's heels, turn tail **2.** churn out (*informal*), duplicate, print, produce **3.** bleed, drain, flow away, siphon, tap **4.** *with* **with a.** lift (*informal*), make off, pinch (*informal*), purloin, run away, steal, swipe (*slang*) **b.** abscond, elope, run away

run-of-the-mill average, banal, bog-standard (*Brit. & Irish slang*), common, commonplace, dime-a-dozen (*informal*), fair, mediocre, middling, modest, no great shakes (*informal*), ordinary, passable, tolerable, undistinguished, unexceptional, unexciting, unimpressive, vanilla (*informal*)
Antonyms excellent, exceptional, extraordinary, marvellous, out of the ordinary, splendid, unusual

run out **1.** be exhausted, cease, close, come to a close, dry up, end, expire, fail, finish, give out, peter out, terminate **2.** *with* **of** be cleaned out, be out of, exhaust one's supply of, have no more of, have none left, have no remaining **3.** *with* **on** *informal* abandon, desert, forsake, leave high and dry, leave holding the baby, leave in the lurch, rat (*informal*), run away from, strand

run over **1.** hit, knock down, knock over, run down, strike **2.** brim over, overflow, spill, spill over **3.** check, examine, go over, go through, rehearse, reiterate, review, run through, survey

run through **1.** impale, pierce, spit, stab, stick, transfix **2.** blow (*slang*), dissipate, exhaust, fritter away, spend like water, squander, throw away, waste **3.** go over, practise, read, rehearse, run over **4.** check, examine, go through, look over, review, run over, survey

run-up approach, build-up, preliminaries

rupture *noun* **1.** breach, break, burst, cleavage, cleft, crack, fissure, fracture, rent, split, tear **2.** altercation, breach, break, bust-up (*informal*), contention, disagreement, disruption, dissolution, estrangement, falling-out (*informal*), feud, hostility, quarrel, rift, schism, split **3.** *Medical* hernia *~verb* **4.** break, burst, cleave, crack, fracture, puncture, rend, separate, sever, split, tear **5.** break off, cause a breach, come between, disrupt, dissever, divide, split

rural agrarian, agrestic, agricultural, Arcadian, bucolic, countrified, country, hick (*informal, chiefly U.S. & Canad.*), pastoral, rustic, sylvan, upcountry
Antonyms city, cosmopolitan, town, urban

ruse artifice, blind, deception, device, dodge, hoax, imposture, manoeuvre, ploy, sham, stratagem, subterfuge, trick, wile

rush *verb* **1.** accelerate, barrel (along) (*informal, chiefly U.S. & Canad.*), bolt, burn rubber (*informal*), career, dart, dash, dispatch, expedite, fly, hasten, hotfoot, hurry, hustle, lose no time, make haste, make short work of, press, push, quicken, race, run, scramble, scurry, shoot, speed, speed up, sprint, stampede, tear *~noun* **2.** charge, dash, dispatch, expedition, haste, hurry, race, scramble, speed, stampede, surge, swiftness, urgency *~verb* **3.** attack, capture, charge, overcome, storm, take by storm *~noun* **4.** assault, charge, onslaught, push, storm, surge *~adjective* **5.** brisk, cursory, emergency, expeditious, fast, hasty, hurried, prompt, quick, rapid, swift, urgent
Antonyms (*sense 1*) dally, dawdle, delay, procrastinate, slow down, tarry, wait (*sense 5*) careful, detailed, leisurely, not urgent, slow, thorough, unhurried

rust *noun* **1.** corrosion, oxidation *~verb* **2.** corrode, oxidize *~noun* **3.** blight, mildew, mould, must, rot *~verb* **4.** atrophy, decay, decline, deteriorate, go stale, stagnate, tarnish

rustic *adjective* **1.** agrestic, Arcadian, bucolic, countrified, country, pastoral, rural, sylvan, upcountry **2.** artless, homely, homespun, plain, simple, unaffected, unpolished, unrefined, unsophisticated **3.** awkward, boorish, churlish, cloddish, clodhopping (*informal*), clownish, coarse, crude, graceless, hick (*informal, chiefly U.S. & Canad.*), loutish, lumpish, maladroit, rough, uncouth, uncultured, unmannerly *~noun* **4.** boor, bumpkin, clod, clodhopper (*informal*), clown, country boy, country cousin, countryman, countrywoman, hayseed (*U.S. & Canad. informal*), hick (*informal, chiefly U.S. & Canad.*), hillbilly, Hodge, peasant, son of the soil, swain (*archaic*), yokel
Antonyms *adjective* cosmopolitan, courtly, elegant, grand, polished, refined, sophisticated, urban, urbane *~noun* city slicker, cosmopolitan, courtier, sophisticate, townee, townsman

rustle **1.** *verb* crackle, crepitate, crinkle, susurrate (*literary*), swish, whish, whisper, whoosh **2.** *noun* crackle, crepitation, crinkling, rustling, susurration *or* susurrus (*literary*), whisper

rusty **1**. corroded, oxidized, rust-covered, rusted **2**. chestnut, coppery, reddish, reddish-brown, russet, rust-coloured **3**. cracked, creaking, croaking, croaky, hoarse **4**. ancient, antiquated, antique, dated, old-fashioned, outmoded, out of date, passé **5**. deficient, impaired, not what it was, out of practice, sluggish, stale, unpractised, weak

rut *noun* **1**. furrow, gouge, groove, indentation, pothole, score, track, trough, wheelmark **2**. dead end, groove, habit, humdrum existence, pattern, routine, system *~verb* **3**. cut, furrow, gouge, groove, hole, indent, mark, score

ruthless adamant, barbarous, brutal, callous, cruel, ferocious, fierce, hard, hard-hearted, harsh, heartless, inexorable, inhuman, merciless, pitiless, relentless, remorseless, savage, severe, stern, unfeeling, unmerciful, unpitying, unrelenting, without pity
Antonyms compassionate, forgiving, gentle, humane, kind, lenient, merciful, pitying, sparing

ruttish **1**. in heat, in rut, in season, sexually excited **2**. aroused, horny (*slang*), lascivious, lecherous, lewd, libidinous, lustful, randy (*informal, chiefly Brit.*), salacious

S

sabbath

The sabbath was made for man, and not man for the sabbath

Bible: St. Mark

Remember the sabbath day, to keep it holy

Bible: Exodus

sable *adjective* black, dark, dusty, ebon (*poetic*), ebony, jet, jetty, raven, sombre

sabotage 1. *verb* cripple, damage, destroy, disable, disrupt, incapacitate, sap the foundations of, subvert, throw a spanner in the works (*Brit. informal*), undermine, vandalize, wreck 2. *noun* damage, destruction, disruption, subversion, treachery, treason, wrecking

sac bag, bladder, bursa, cyst, pocket, pod, pouch, vesicle

saccharine cloying, honeyed, icky (*informal*), maudlin, mawkish, nauseating, oversweet, sentimental, sickly, soppy (*Brit. informal*), sugary, syrupy (*informal*), treacly

sack[1] 1. *verb* axe (*informal*), discharge, dismiss, fire (*informal*), give (someone) his books (*informal*), give (someone) his cards, give (someone) his marching orders, give (someone) the boot (*slang*), give (someone) the bullet (*Brit. slang*), give (someone) the elbow, give (someone) the push (*informal*), kick out (*informal*), kiss off (*slang, chiefly U.S. & Canad.*) 2. *noun* **the sack** discharge, dismissal, termination of employment, the axe (*informal*), the boot (*slang*), the chop (*Brit. slang*), the (old) heave-ho (*informal*), the order of the boot (*slang*), the push (*slang*)

sack[2] 1. *verb* demolish, depredate (*rare*), despoil, destroy, devastate, lay waste, loot, maraud, pillage, plunder, raid, ravage, rifle, rob, ruin, spoil, strip 2. *noun* depredation, despoliation, destruction, devastation, looting, pillage, plunder, plundering, rape, rapine, ravage, ruin, waste

sack[3] *noun* **hit the sack** bed down, go to bed, hit the hay (*slang*), retire, turn in (*informal*)

sackcloth and ashes compunction, contrition, grief, hair shirt, mortification, mourning, penitence, remorse, repentance

sacred 1. blessed, consecrated, divine, hallowed, holy, revered, sanctified, venerable 2. inviolable, inviolate, invulnerable, protected, sacrosanct, secure 3. ecclesiastical, holy, religious, solemn
Antonyms lay, nonspiritual, profane, secular, temporal, unconsecrated, worldly

sacrifice 1. *verb* forego, forfeit, give up, immolate, let go, lose, offer, offer up, say goodbye to, surrender 2. *noun* burnt offering, destruction, hecatomb, holocaust (*rare*), immolation, loss, oblation, renunciation, surrender, votive offering

Never in the field of human conflict was so much owed by so many to so few

Winston Churchill

Too long a sacrifice
Can make a stone of the heart

W.B. Yeats *Easter 1916*

Greater love hath no man than this, that a man lay down his life for his friends

Bible: St. John

You cannot make an omelette without breaking eggs

sacrificial atoning, expiatory, oblatory, propitiatory, reparative

sacrilege blasphemy, desecration, heresy, impiety, irreverence, mockery, profanation, profaneness, profanity, violation
Antonyms piety, respect, reverence

sacrilegious blasphemous, desecrating, godless, impious, irreligious, irreverent, profane, ungodly, unholy

sacrosanct hallowed, inviolable, inviolate, sacred, sanctified, set apart, untouchable

sad 1. blue, cheerless, dejected, depressed, disconsolate, dismal, doleful, down, downcast, down in the dumps (*informal*), down in the mouth (*informal*), gloomy, glum, grief-stricken, grieved, heavy-hearted, low, low-spirited, lugubrious, melancholy, mournful, pensive, sick at heart, sombre, triste (*archaic*), unhappy, wistful, woebegone 2. calamitous, dark, depressing, disastrous, dismal, grievous, harrowing, heart-rending, lachrymose, moving, pathetic, pitiable, pitiful, poignant, sorry, tearful, tragic, upsetting 3. bad, deplorable, dismal, distressing, grave, lamentable, miserable, regrettable, serious, shabby, sorry, to be deplored, unfortunate, unhappy, unsatisfactory, wretched
Antonyms blithe, cheerful, cheery, chirpy (*informal*), fortunate, glad, good, happy, in good

spirits, jolly, joyful, joyous, light-hearted, merry, pleased

sadden aggrieve, bring tears to one's eyes, cast a gloom upon, cast down, dash, deject, de~ press, desolate, dispirit, distress, grieve, make blue, make one's heart bleed, upset

saddle *verb* burden, charge, encumber, load, lumber (*Brit. informal*), task, tax

sadistic barbarous, beastly, brutal, cruel, fiendish, inhuman, perverse, perverted, ruth~ less, savage, vicious

sadness bleakness, cheerlessness, dejection, depression, despondency, dolefulness, dolour (*poetic*), gloominess, grief, heavy heart, mel~ ancholy, misery, mournfulness, poignancy, sorrow, sorrowfulness, the blues, the dumps (*informal*), the hump (*Brit. informal*), tragedy, unhappiness, wretchedness

safe *adjective* **1.** all right, free from harm, im~ pregnable, in safe hands, in safety, intact, O.K. *or* okay (*informal*), out of danger, out of harm's way, out of the woods, protected, safe and sound, secure, undamaged, unharmed, unhurt, unscathed **2.** harmless, innocuous, nonpoisonous, nontoxic, pure, tame, unpollut~ ed, wholesome **3.** cautious, circumspect, con~ servative, dependable, discreet, on the safe side, prudent, realistic, reliable, sure, tried and true, trustworthy, unadventurous **4.** cer~ tain, impregnable, risk-free, riskless, secure, sound *~noun* **5.** coffer, deposit box, repository, safe-deposit box, strongbox, vault

Antonyms (*sense 1*) at risk, damaged, endan~ gered, imperilled, insecure, jeopardized, put at risk, put in danger, threatened (*sense 2*) baneful, dangerous, harmful, hazardous, hurtful, injurious, noxious, pernicious, unsafe (*sense 3*) imprudent, incautious, reckless, risky, unsafe

Better safe than sorry

safe-conduct authorization, licence, pass, passport, permit, safeguard, warrant

safeguard 1. *verb* defend, guard, look after, preserve, protect, screen, shield, watch over **2.** *noun* aegis, armour, bulwark, convoy, defence, escort, guard, protection, security, shield, surety

safekeeping care, charge, custody, guardian~ ship, keeping, protection, supervision, surveil~ lance, trust, tutelage, ward

safely in one piece, in safety, safe and sound, securely, with impunity, without risk, with safety

safety assurance, cover, immunity, impreg~ nability, protection, refuge, sanctuary, secu~ rity, shelter

There is safety in numbers

sag *verb* **1.** bag, bulge, cave in, dip, droop, drop, fall, fall unevenly, give way, hang loosely, seat (*of skirts, etc.*), settle, sink, slump, swag **2.** decline, droop, fall, flag, slide, slip, slump, wane, weaken, wilt *~noun* **3.** de~ cline, depression, dip, downturn, drop, fall, lapse, slip, slump

saga adventure, chronicle, epic, narrative, *roman-fleuve*, soap opera, story, tale, yarn

sagacious able, acute, apt, astute, canny, clear-sighted, discerning, downy (*Brit. slang*), far-sighted, fly (*slang*), insightful, intelligent, judicious, knowing, long-headed, perceptive, perspicacious, sage, sharp, sharp-witted, shrewd, smart, wise

sagacity acuteness, astuteness, canniness, dis~ cernment, foresight, insight, judiciousness, knowingness, penetration, perspicacity, pru~ dence, sapience, sense, sharpness, shrewd~ ness, understanding, wisdom

sage 1. *adjective* acute, canny, discerning, in~ telligent, judicious, learned, perspicacious, politic, prudent, sagacious, sapient, sensible, wise **2.** *noun* authority, elder, expert, guru, mahatma, man of learning, master, Nestor, philosopher, pundit, savant, Solomon, Solon, wise man

sail *verb* **1.** cast *or* weigh anchor, embark, get under way, hoist the blue peter, put to sea, set sail **2.** captain, cruise, go by water, navi~ gate, pilot, ride the waves, skipper, steer, vo~ yage **3.** drift, float, fly, glide, scud, shoot, skim, skirr, soar, sweep, wing **4.** *informal with* **in** *or* **into** assault, attack, begin, bela~ bour, fall upon, get going, get to work on, lambast(e), set about, tear into (*informal*)

sailor hearty (*informal*), Jack Tar, lascar, leatherneck (*slang*), marine, mariner, matelot (*slang, chiefly Brit.*), navigator, salt, sea dog, seafarer, seafaring man, seaman, tar (*infor~ mal*)

saint

Saint	Feast day
Agatha	5 February
Agnes	31 January
Aidan	31 August
Alban	June 22
Albertus Magnus	November 15
Aloysius (patron saint of youth)	21 June
Ambrose	7 December
Andrew (Scotland)	30 November
Anne	26 July
Anselm	21 April
Anthony *or* Antony	17 January
Anthony *or* Antony of Padua	13 June
Athanasius	2 May
Augustine of Hippo	28 August
Barnabas	11 June
Bartholomew	24 August

Basil	2 January
Bede	25 May
Benedict	11 July
Bernadette of Lourdes	16 April
Bernard of Clairvaux	20 August
Bernard of Menthon	28 May
Bonaventura *or* Bonaventure	15 July
Boniface	5 June
Brendan	16 May
Bridget, Bride *or* Brigid (Ireland)	1 February
Bridget *or* Birgitta (Sweden)	23 July
Catherine of Alexandria	25 November
Catherine of Siena (the Dominican Order)	29 April
Cecilia (music)	22 November
Charles Borromeo	4 November
Christopher (travellers)	25 July
Clare of Assisi	11 August
Clement I	23 November
Clement of Alexandria	5 December
Columba *or* Colmcille	9 June
Crispin (shoemakers)	25 October
Crispinian (shoemakers)	25 October
Cuthbert	20 March
Cyprian	16 September
Cyril	14 February
Cyril of Alexandria	27 June
David (Wales)	1 March
Denis (France)	9 October
Dominic	7 August
Dorothy	6 February
Dunstan	19 May
Edmund	20 November
Edward the Confessor	13 October
Edward the Martyr	18 March
Elizabeth	5 November
Elizabeth of Hungary	17 November
Elmo	2 June
Ethelbert *or* Æthelbert	25 February
Francis of Assisi	4 October
Francis of Sales	24 January
Francis Xavier	3 December
Geneviève (Paris)	3 January
George (England)	23 April
Gertrude	16 November
Gilbert of Sempringham	4 February
Giles (cripples, beggars, and lepers)	1 September
Gregory I (the Great)	3 September
Gregory VII *or* Hildebrand	25 May
Gregory of Nazianzus	2 January
Gregory of Nyssa	9 March
Gregory of Tours	17 November
Hilary of Poitiers	13 January
Hildegard of Bingen	17 September
Helen *or* Helena	18 August
Helier	16 July
Ignatius	17 October
Ignatius of Loyola	31 July
Isidore of Seville	4 April
James	23 October
James the Less	3 May
Jane Frances de Chantal	12 December
Jerome	30 September
Joachim	26 July
Joan of Arc	30 May
John	27 December
John Bosco	31 January
John Chrysostom	13 September
John Ogilvie	10 March
John of Damascus	4 December
John of the Cross	14 December
John the Baptist	24 June
Joseph	19 March
Joseph of Arimathaea	17 March
Joseph of Copertino	18 September
Jude	28 October
Justin	1 June
Kentigern *or* Mungo	14 January
Kevin	3 June
Lawrence	10 August
Lawrence O'Toole	14 November
Leger	2 October
Leo I (the Great)	10 November
Leo II	3 July
Leo III	12 June
Leo IV	17 July
Leonard	6 November
Lucy	13 December
Luke	18 October
Malachy	3 November
Margaret	20 July
Margaret of Scotland	10 June, 16 November (in Scotland)
Maria Goretti	6 July
Mark	25 April
Martha	29 July
Martin de Porres	3 November
Martin of Tours (France)	11 November
Mary	15 August
Mary Magdalene	22 July

Matthew *or* Levi	21 September
Matthias	14 May
Methodius	14 February
Michael	29 September
Neot	31 July
Nicholas (Russia, children, sailors, merchants, and pawnbrokers)	6 December
Nicholas I (the Great)	13 November
Ninian	16 September
Olaf *or* Olav (Norway)	29 July
Oliver Plunket *or* Plunkett	1 July
Oswald	28 February
Pachomius	14 May
Patrick (Ireland)	17 March
Paul	29 June
Paulinus	10 October
Paulinus of Nola	22 June
Peter *or* Simon Peter	29 June
Philip	3 May
Philip Neri	26 May
Pius V	30 April
Pius X	21 August
Polycarp	26 January *or* 23 February
Rose of Lima	23 August
Sebastian	20 January
Silas	13 July
Simon Zelotes	28 October
Stanislaw *or* Stanislaus (Poland)	11 April
Stanislaus Kostka	13 November
Stephen	26 *or* 27 December
Stephen of Hungary	16 *or* 20 August
Swithin *or* Swithun	15 July
Teresa *or* Theresa of Avila	15 October
Thérèse de Lisieux	1 October
Thomas	3 July
Thomas à Becket	29 December
Thomas Aquinas	28 January
Thomas More	22 June
Timothy	26 January
Titus	26 January
Ursula	21 October
Valentine	14 February
Veronica	12 July
Vincent de Paul	27 September
Vitus	15 June
Vladimir	15 July
Wenceslaus *or* Wenceslas	28 September
Wilfrid	12 October

saint: a dead sinner revised and edited
Ambrose Bierce *The Devil's Dictionary*

saintly angelic, beatific, blameless, blessed, devout, full of good works, god-fearing, godly, holy, pious, religious, righteous, sainted, saintlike, sinless, virtuous, worthy

sake **1.** account, advantage, behalf, benefit, consideration, gain, good, interest, profit, regard, respect, welfare, wellbeing **2.** aim, cause, end, motive, objective, principle, purpose, reason

salacious bawdy, blue, carnal, concupiscent, erotic, indecent, lascivious, lecherous, lewd, libidinous, lickerish (*archaic*), lustful, obscene, pornographic, prurient, ribald, ruttish, smutty, steamy (*informal*), wanton, X-rated (*informal*)

salary earnings, emolument, income, pay, remuneration, stipend, wage, wages

sale **1.** auction, deal, disposal, marketing, selling, transaction, vending **2.** buyers, consumers, customers, demand, market, outlet, purchasers **3. for sale** available, in stock, obtainable, on offer, on sale, on the market

salient arresting, conspicuous, important, jutting, marked, noticeable, outstanding, projecting, prominent, pronounced, protruding, remarkable, signal, striking

sallow anaemic, bilious, jaundiced-looking, pale, pallid, pasty, peely-wally (*Scot.*), sickly, unhealthy, wan, yellowish
Antonyms glowing, healthy-looking, radiant, rosy, ruddy

sally *verb* **1.** erupt, go forth, issue, rush, set out, surge *~noun* **2.** *Military* campaign, foray, incursion, offensive, raid, sortie, thrust **3.** *figurative* bon mot, crack (*informal*), jest, joke, quip, retort, riposte, smart remark, wisecrack (*informal*), witticism **4.** escapade, excursion, frolic, jaunt, trip

salt *noun* **1.** flavour, relish, savour, seasoning, taste **2. with a grain** *or* **pinch of salt** cynically, disbelievingly, doubtfully, sceptically, suspiciously, with reservations **3.** *figurative* Attic wit, bite, dry humour, liveliness, piquancy, punch, pungency, sarcasm, sharpness, wit, zest, zip (*informal*) **4.** mariner, sailor, sea dog, seaman, tar (*informal*) *~adjective* **5.** brackish, briny, saline, salted, salty

salt away accumulate, amass, bank, cache, hide, hoard up, lay by, lay in, lay up, put by, save, save for a rainy day, stash away (*informal*), stockpile

salty **1.** brackish, briny, over-salted, saline, salt, salted **2.** colourful, humorous, lively, piquant, pungent, racy, sharp, snappy (*informal*), spicy, tangy, tart, witty, zestful

salubrious beneficial, good for one, healthful, health-giving, healthy, invigorating, salutary, wholesome

salutary 1. advantageous, beneficial, good, good for one, helpful, practical, profitable, timely, useful, valuable 2. healthful, healthy, salubrious

salutation address, greeting, obeisance, salute, welcome

salute *verb* 1. accost, acknowledge, address, doff one's cap to, greet, hail, kiss, pay one's respects to, salaam, welcome 2. acknowledge, honour, pay tribute *or* homage to, present arms, recognize, take one's hat off to (*informal*) ~*noun* 3. address, greeting, kiss, obeisance, recognition, salaam, salutation, tribute

salvage *verb* glean, recover, redeem, rescue, restore, retrieve, save

salvation deliverance, escape, lifeline, preservation, redemption, rescue, restoration, saving
Antonyms condemnation, damnation, doom, downfall, hell, loss, perdition, ruin

> *Work out your own salvation with fear and trembling*
>
> Bible: Philippians

salve *noun* balm, cream, dressing, emollient, liniment, lotion, lubricant, medication, ointment, unguent

same *adjective* 1. aforementioned, aforesaid, selfsame, very 2. alike, corresponding, duplicate, equal, equivalent, identical, indistinguishable, interchangeable, synonymous, twin 3. changeless, consistent, constant, invariable, unaltered, unchanged, unfailing, uniform, unvarying 4. **all the same a.** after all, anyhow, be that as it may, in any event, just the same, nevertheless, nonetheless, still **b.** immaterial, not worth mentioning, of no consequence, unimportant
Antonyms altered, different, dissimilar, diverse, inconsistent, miscellaneous, other, variable

sameness consistency, identicalness, identity, indistinguishability, lack of variety, likeness, monotony, oneness, predictability, repetition, resemblance, similarity, standardization, tedium, uniformity

sample 1. *noun* cross section, example, exemplification, illustration, indication, instance, model, pattern, representative, sign, specimen 2. *verb* experience, inspect, partake of, taste, test, try 3. *adjective* illustrative, pilot, representative, specimen, test, trial

sanctify absolve, anoint, bless, cleanse, consecrate, hallow, purify, set apart

sanctimonious canting, false, goody-goody (*informal*), holier-than-thou, hypocritical, pharisaical, pi (*Brit. slang*), pietistic, pious, priggish, self-righteous, self-satisfied, smug, Tartuffian *or* Tartufian, too good to be true, unctuous

sanction *noun* 1. allowance, approbation, approval, authority, authorization, backing, confirmation, countenance, endorsement, O.K. *or* okay (*informal*), ratification, stamp *or* seal of approval, support 2. *often plural* ban, boycott, coercive measures, embargo, penalty ~*verb* 3. allow, approve, authorize, back, countenance, endorse, entitle, lend one's name to, permit, support, vouch for 4. confirm, ratify, warrant
Antonyms *noun* (*sense 1*) ban, disapproval, embargo, prohibition, proscription, refusal, veto (*sense 2*) approbation, approval, authority, authorization, dispensation, licence, permission ~*verb* ban, boycott, disallow, forbid, refuse, reject, veto

sanctity 1. devotion, godliness, goodness, grace, holiness, piety, purity, religiousness, righteousness, sanctitude, spirituality 2. inviolability, sacredness, solemnity

sanctuary 1. altar, church, Holy of Holies, sanctum, shrine, temple 2. asylum, haven, protection, refuge, retreat, shelter 3. conservation area, national park, nature reserve, reserve

sanctum 1. Holy of Holies, sanctuary, shrine 2. den, private room, refuge, retreat, study

sane 1. all there (*informal*), *compos mentis*, in one's right mind, in possession of all one's faculties, lucid, mentally sound, normal, of sound mind, rational 2. balanced, judicious, level-headed, moderate, reasonable, sensible, sober, sound
Antonyms bonkers (*slang, chiefly Brit.*), crackpot (*informal*), crazy, daft (*informal*), doolally (*slang*), foolish, insane, loony (*slang*), loopy (*informal*), mad, mentally ill, *non compos mentis*, nuts (*slang*), off one's head (*slang*), off one's trolley (*slang*), out to lunch (*informal*), round the bend *or* twist (*slang*), stupid, unreasonable, unsound, up the pole (*informal*), wacko *or* whacko (*informal*)

sang-froid aplomb, calmness, composure, cool (*slang*), cool-headedness, coolness, equanimity, imperturbability, indifference, nonchalance, phlegm, poise, self-possession, unflappability (*informal*)

sanguinary bloodied, bloodthirsty, bloody, cruel, fell (*archaic*), flowing with blood, gory, grim, merciless, murderous, pitiless, ruthless, savage

sanguine 1. animated, assured, buoyant, cheerful, confident, hopeful, in good heart, lively, optimistic, spirited 2. florid, red, rubicund, ruddy
Antonyms (*sense 1*) despondent, dispirited, down, gloomy, heavy-hearted, melancholy, pessimistic (*sense 2*) anaemic, ashen, pale, pallid, peely-wally (*Scot.*)

sanitary clean, germ-free, healthy, hygienic, salubrious, unpolluted, wholesome

sanitize cleanse, decontaminate, disinfect, fumigate, pasteurize, purge, purify, sterilize

sanity **1.** mental health, normality, rationality, reason, right mind (*informal*), saneness, stability **2.** common sense, good sense, judiciousness, level-headedness, rationality, sense, soundness of judgment
Antonyms craziness, dementia, folly, insanity, lunacy, madness, mental derangement, mental illness, senselessness, stupidity

sap[1] *noun* **1.** animating force, essence, lifeblood, vital fluid **2.** *informal* charlie (*Brit. informal*), chump (*informal*), drip (*informal*), dweeb (*U.S. slang*), fool, gobshite (*Irish taboo slang*), gull (*archaic*), idiot, jerk (*slang, chiefly U.S. & Canad.*), muggins (*Brit. slang*), nerd *or* nurd (*slang*), nincompoop, ninny, nitwit (*informal*), noddy, noodle, numpty (*Scot. informal*), numskull *or* numbskull, oaf, plonker (*slang*), prat (*slang*), Simple Simon, simpleton, twit (*informal*), wally (*slang*), weakling, weenie (*U.S. informal*), wet (*Brit. informal*)

sap[2] *verb* bleed, deplete, devitalize, drain, enervate, erode, exhaust, rob, undermine, weaken, wear down

sapience acuity, acuteness, discernment, insight, mother wit, nous (*Brit. slang*), perspicacity, sagacity, sense, shrewdness, suss (*slang*), understanding, wisdom

sapient acute, canny, discerning, discriminating, intelligent, judicious, knowing, long-headed, perspicacious, sagacious, sage, shrewd, wise, would-be-wise

sarcasm bitterness, causticness, contempt, cynicism, derision, irony, mockery, mordancy, satire, scorn, sneering, venom, vitriol

sarcastic acerb, acerbic, acid, acrimonious, backhanded, bitchy (*informal*), biting, caustic, contemptuous, cutting, cynical, derisive, disparaging, ironical, mocking, mordacious, mordant, sardonic, sarky (*Brit. informal*), satirical, sharp, sneering, taunting, vitriolic

sardonic bitter, cynical, derisive, dry, ironical, jeering, malevolent, malicious, malignant, mocking, mordacious, mordant, sarcastic, sneering, wry

Satan Apollyon, Beelzebub, Lord of the Flies, Lucifer, Mephistopheles, Old Nick (*informal*), Old Scratch (*informal*), Prince of Darkness, The Devil, The Evil One

satanic accursed, black, demoniac, demoniacal, demonic, devilish, diabolic, evil, fiendish, hellish, infernal, inhuman, iniquitous, malevolent, malignant, wicked
Antonyms benevolent, benign, divine, godly, holy

sate **1.** indulge to the full, satiate, satisfy, slake **2.** cloy, glut, gorge, overfill, saturate, sicken, surfeit, weary

satellite *noun* **1.** communications satellite, moon, sputnik **2.** *figurative* attendant, cohort (*chiefly U.S.*), dependant, follower, hanger-on, lackey, minion, parasite, retainer, sidekick (*slang*), sycophant, vassal *~adjective* **3.** *figurative* client, dependent, puppet, subordinate, tributary, vassal

satiate **1.** cloy, glut, gorge, jade, nauseate, overfill, stuff **2.** sate, satisfy, slake, surfeit

satiety **1.** overindulgence, saturation, surfeit **2.** fullness, gratification, repletion, satiation, satisfaction

satire burlesque, caricature, irony, lampoon, parody, pasquinade, raillery, ridicule, sarcasm, send-up (*Brit. informal*), skit, spoof (*informal*), takeoff (*informal*), travesty, wit

It's hard not to write satire
Juvenal *Satires*

Satire is a sort of glass, wherein beholders do generally discover everybody's face but their own
Jonathan Swift *The Battle of the Books*

satirical, satiric biting, bitter, burlesque, caustic, censorious, cutting, cynical, incisive, ironical, mocking, mordacious, mordant, pungent, Rabelaisian, sarcastic, sardonic, taunting, vitriolic

satirize abuse, burlesque, censure, criticize, deride, hold up to ridicule, lampoon, lash, parody, pillory, ridicule, send up (*Brit. informal*), take off (*informal*), travesty

satisfaction **1.** comfort, complacency, content, contentedness, contentment, ease, enjoyment, gratification, happiness, peace of mind, pleasure, pride, repletion, satiety, well-being **2.** achievement, appeasing, assuaging, fulfilment, gratification, resolution, settlement **3.** amends, atonement, compensation, damages, indemnification, justice, recompense, redress, reimbursement, remuneration, reparation, requital, restitution, settlement, vindication
Antonyms (*senses 1 & 2*) annoyance, discontent, displeasure, dissatisfaction, frustration, grief, injury, misgivings, pain, shame, unhappiness

satisfactory acceptable, adequate, all right, average, competent, fair, good enough, passable, sufficient, suitable, up to scratch, up to standard, up to the mark
Antonyms bad, below par, inadequate, insufficient, leaving a lot to be desired, mediocre, no great shakes (*informal*), not up to scratch (*informal*), poor, sub-standard, unacceptable, unsatisfactory, unsuitable

satisfied at ease, complacent, content, contented, convinced, easy in one's mind, happy, like the cat that swallowed the canary (*informal*), pacified, positive, smug, sure

satisfy **1**. appease, assuage, content, feed, fill, gratify, indulge, mollify, pacify, pander to, please, quench, sate, satiate, slake, surfeit **2**. answer, be enough (adequate, sufficient), come up to expectations, cut the mustard, do, fill the bill (*informal*), fulfil, meet, qualify, serve, serve the purpose, suffice **3**. assure, convince, dispel (someone's) doubts, persuade, put (someone's) mind at rest, quiet, reassure **4**. answer, comply with, discharge, fulfil, meet, pay (off), settle, square up **5**. atone, compen~sate, indemnify, make good, make reparation for, recompense, remunerate, requite, reward
Antonyms (*senses 1, 2, 3 & 4*) annoy, dis~please, dissatisfy, dissuade, exasperate, fail to meet, fail to persuade, frustrate, give cause for complaint

satisfying cheering, convincing, filling, gratify~ing, pleasing, pleasurable, satisfactory

saturate douse, drench, drouk (*Scot.*), imbue, impregnate, ret (*used of flax, etc.*), seep, soak, souse, steep, suffuse, waterlog, wet through

saturated drenched, dripping, droukit *or* drookit (*Scot.*), soaked, soaked to the skin, soaking (wet), sodden, sopping (wet), water~logged, wet through, wringing wet

saturnine dour, dull, gloomy, glum, grave, heavy, morose, phlegmatic, sedate, sluggish, sombre, taciturn, uncommunicative

sauce *noun* audacity, backchat (*informal*), brass (*informal*), brass neck (*Brit. informal*), cheek (*informal*), cheekiness, disrespectful~ness, face (*informal*), front, impertinence, im~pudence, insolence, lip (*slang*), neck (*infor~mal*), nerve (*informal*), rudeness

Sauces
see FOOD

sauciness backchat (*informal*), brass (*infor~mal*), brazenness, cheek (*informal*), flippancy, impertinence, impudence, insolence, lip (*slang*), pertness, rudeness, sauce (*informal*)

saucy **1**. cheeky (*informal*), disrespectful, flip (*informal*), flippant, forward, fresh (*informal*), impertinent, impudent, insolent, lippy (*U.S. & Canad. slang*), pert, presumptuous, rude, sas~sy (*U.S. informal*), smart-alecky (*informal*) **2**. dashing, gay, jaunty, natty (*informal*), perky, rakish, sporty

saunter **1**. *verb* amble, dally, linger, loiter, me~ander, mosey (*informal*), ramble, roam, rove, stravaig (*Scot. & northern English dialect*), stroll, take a stroll, tarry, wander **2**. *noun* airing, amble, breather, constitutional, per~ambulation, promenade, ramble, stroll, turn, walk

savage *adjective* **1**. feral, rough, rugged, un~civilized, uncultivated, undomesticated, un~tamed, wild **2**. barbarous, beastly, bestial, bloodthirsty, bloody, brutal, brutish, cruel, devilish, diabolical, ferocious, fierce, harsh, inhuman, merciless, murderous, pitiless, rav~ening, ruthless, sadistic, vicious **3**. in a state of nature, nonliterate, primitive, rude, un~spoilt *~noun* **4**. autochthon, barbarian, hea~then, indigene, native, primitive **5**. barbarian, bear, boor, lout, roughneck (*slang*), yahoo, yob (*Brit. slang*), yobbo (*Brit. slang*) **6**. beast, brute, fiend, monster *~verb* **7**. attack, lacerate, mangle, maul, tear into (*informal*)
Antonyms *adjective* balmy, civilized, cultivat~ed, domesticated, gentle, humane, kind, mer~ciful, mild, refined, restrained, tame *~verb* acclaim, celebrate, praise, rave about (*infor~mal*)

as savage as a bear with a sore head
Captain Marryat *The King's Own*

savagery barbarity, bestiality, bloodthirstiness, brutality, cruelty, ferocity, fierceness, inhu~manity, ruthlessness, sadism, viciousness

savant authority, intellectual, mahatma, mas~ter, mastermind, philosopher, sage, scholar

save **1**. bail (someone) out, come to (someone's) rescue, deliver, free, liberate, recover, redeem, rescue, salvage, save (someone's) bacon (*Brit~ish informal*), set free **2**. be frugal, be thrifty, collect, economize, gather, hide away, hoard, hold, husband, keep, keep up one's sleeve (*in~formal*), lay by, put aside for a rainy day, put by, reserve, retrench, salt away, set aside, store, tighten one's belt (*informal*), treasure up **3**. conserve, guard, keep safe, look after, preserve, protect, safeguard, screen, shield, take care of **4**. hinder, obviate, prevent, rule out, spare
Antonyms (*senses 1 & 3*) abandon, condemn, discard, endanger, expose, imperil, risk, threaten (*sense 2*) be extravagant, blow (*slang*), consume, fritter away, spend, splurge, squander, use, use up, waste

saving **1**. *adjective* compensatory, extenuating, qualifying, redeeming **2**. *noun* bargain, dis~count, economy, reduction

savings fall-back, fund, nest egg, provision for a rainy day, reserves, resources, store

saviour defender, deliverer, friend in need, Good Samaritan, guardian, knight in shining armour, liberator, preserver, protector, re~deemer, rescuer, salvation

Saviour, Our *or* **The** Christ, Jesus, Messiah, Redeemer

savoir-faire accomplishment, address, diplo~macy, discretion, finesse, poise, social graces, social know-how (*informal*), tact, urbanity

savour *noun* **1**. flavour, piquancy, relish, smack, smell, tang, taste, zest, zing (*informal*) **2**. distinctive quality, excitement, flavour, in~

terest, salt, spice, zest *~verb* **3.** *often with* **of** bear the hallmarks, be indicative, be suggestive, partake, show signs, smack, suggest, verge on **4.** appreciate, delight in, drool, enjoy, enjoy to the full, gloat over, like, luxuriate in, partake, relish, revel in, smack one's lips over

savoury 1. agreeable, appetizing, dainty, delectable, delicious, full-flavoured, good, luscious, mouthwatering, palatable, piquant, rich, scrumptious (*informal*), spicy, tangy, tasty, toothsome **2.** apple-pie (*informal*), decent, edifying, honest, reputable, respectable, wholesome

Antonyms disreputable, distasteful, insipid, nasty, tasteless, unappetizing, unpalatable, unpleasant, unsavoury, wersh (*Scots.*)

savvy *slang* **1.** *verb* apprehend, catch on, catch the drift, comprehend, get the gist, grasp, perceive, take in, understand **2.** *noun* apprehension, comprehension, grasp, ken, perception, understanding

saw adage, aphorism, apophthegm, axiom, byword, dictum, gnome, maxim, proverb, saying

saw-toothed crenate (*Botany, Zoology*), dentate, denticulate (*Biology*), notched, serrate, serrated

say *verb* **1.** add, affirm, announce, assert, asseverate, come out with (*informal*), declare, give voice *or* utterance to, maintain, mention, pronounce, put into words, remark, speak, state, utter, voice **2.** answer, disclose, divulge, give as one's opinion, make known, reply, respond, reveal, tell **3.** allege, bruit, claim, noise abroad, put about, report, rumour, suggest **4.** deliver, do, orate, perform, read, recite, rehearse, render, repeat **5.** assume, conjecture, dare say, estimate, guess, hazard a guess, imagine, judge, presume, suppose, surmise **6.** communicate, convey, express, give the impression that, imply **7. go without saying** be accepted, be a matter of course, be obvious, be self-evident, be taken as read, be taken for granted, be understood **8. to say the least** at the very least, to put it mildly, without any exaggeration *~noun* **9.** crack (*informal*), turn (chance, opportunity), to speak voice, vote **10.** authority, clout (*informal*), influence, power, sway, weight

saying adage, aphorism, apophthegm, axiom, byword, dictum, gnome, maxim, proverb, saw, slogan

say-so 1. assertion, asseveration, assurance, dictum, guarantee, word **2.** agreement, assent, authority, authorization, consent, O.K. *or* okay (*informal*), permission, sanction

scalding blistering, boiling, burning, piping hot, searing

scale[1] *noun* **1.** calibration, degrees, gamut, gradation, graduated system, graduation, hierarchy, ladder, pecking order (*informal*), progression, ranking, register, seniority system, sequence, series, spectrum, spread, steps **2.** proportion, ratio **3.** degree, extent, range, reach, scope, way *~verb* **4.** ascend, clamber, climb, escalade, mount, surmount **5.** adjust, proportion, prorate (*chiefly U.S.*), regulate

scale[2] *noun* flake, lamina, layer, plate, squama (*Biology*)

scaly flaky, furfuraceous (*Medical*), scabrous, scurfy, squamous *or* squamose (*Biology*), squamulose

scam diddle, fiddle, racket, stratagem, swindle

scamp devil, imp, knave (*archaic*), mischief-maker, monkey, pickle (*Brit. informal*), prankster, rascal, rogue, scallywag (*informal*), scapegrace, toe-rag (*slang*), tyke (*informal*), whippersnapper, wretch

scamper beetle, dart, dash, fly, hasten, hie (*archaic*), hurry, romp, run, scoot, scurry, scuttle, sprint

scan check, check out (*informal*), clock (*Brit. slang*), con (*archaic*), examine, eyeball (*U.S. slang*), get a load of (*informal*), glance over, investigate, look one up and down, look through, recce (*slang*), run one's eye over, run over, scour, scrutinize, search, size up (*informal*), skim, survey, sweep, take a dekko at (*Brit. slang*), take stock of

scandal 1. crime, crying shame (*informal*), disgrace, embarrassment, offence, sin, wrongdoing **2.** calumny, defamation, detraction, discredit, disgrace, dishonour, ignominy, infamy, obloquy, offence, opprobrium, reproach, shame, stigma **3.** abuse, aspersion, backbiting, dirt, dirty linen (*informal*), gossip, rumours, skeleton in the cupboard, slander, talk, tattle

It is public scandal that constitutes offence, and to sin in secret is not to sin at all

Molière *Le Tartuffe*

scandalize affront, appal, cause a few raised eyebrows (*informal*), disgust, horrify, offend, outrage, raise eyebrows, shock

scandalmonger calumniator, defamer, destroyer of reputations, gossip, muckraker, tattle, tattler, traducer

scandalous 1. atrocious, disgraceful, disreputable, highly improper, infamous, monstrous, odious, opprobrious, outrageous, shameful, shocking, unseemly **2.** defamatory, gossiping, libellous, scurrilous, slanderous, untrue

Antonyms decent, kind, laudatory, proper, reputable, respectable, seemly, unimpeachable, upright

scant bare, barely sufficient, deficient, inadequate, insufficient, limited, little, minimal, sparse

Antonyms abundant, adequate, ample, full, generous, plentiful, satisfactory, sufficient

scanty bare, deficient, exiguous, inadequate, insufficient, meagre, narrow, pathetic, poor, restricted, scant, short, skimpy, slender, sparing, sparse, thin

scapegoat fall guy (*informal*), whipping boy

scapegrace bad lot (*informal*), good-for-nothing, limb of Satan, ne'er-do-well, rascal, rogue, scallywag (*informal*), scamp, the despair of

scar **1.** *noun* blemish, cicatrix, injury, mark, trauma (*Pathology*), wound **2.** *verb* brand, damage, disfigure, mark, traumatize

scarce at a premium, deficient, few, few and far between, infrequent, in short supply, insufficient, rare, seldom met with, thin on the ground, uncommon, unusual, wanting
Antonyms abundant, ample, common, commonplace, frequent, numerous, plenteous, plentiful, sufficient

scarcely **1.** barely, hardly, only just, scarce (*archaic*) **2.** by no means, definitely not, hardly, not at all, on no account, under no circumstances

scarcity dearth, deficiency, infrequency, insufficiency, lack, paucity, poverty, rareness, shortage, undersupply, want
Antonyms abundance, excess, glut, superfluity, surfeit, surplus

scare **1.** *verb* affright (*archaic*), alarm, daunt, dismay, frighten, give (someone) a fright, give (someone) a turn (*informal*), intimidate, panic, put the wind up (someone) (*informal*), shock, startle, terrify, terrorize **2.** *noun* alarm, alert, fright, panic, shock, start, terror

scared fearful, frightened, panicky, panic-stricken, petrified, scared shitless (*taboo slang*), shaken, shit-scared (*taboo slang*), startled, terrified

scaremonger alarmist, Calamity Jane, doom merchant (*informal*), prophet of doom, spreader of despair and despondency

scarper abscond, beat a hasty retreat, beat it (*slang*), clear off (*informal*), cut and run (*informal*), decamp, depart, disappear, do a bunk (*Brit. slang*), flee, go, hook it (*slang*), make off, make oneself scarce (*informal*), run away, run for it, scram (*informal*), skedaddle (*informal*), slope off, take flight, take oneself off, take to one's heels, vamoose (*slang, chiefly U.S.*)

scary alarming, bloodcurdling, chilling, creepy (*informal*), frightening, hair-raising, hairy (*slang*), horrendous, horrifying, intimidating, shocking, spine-chilling, spooky (*informal*), terrifying, unnerving

scathing belittling, biting, brutal, caustic, critical, cutting, harsh, mordacious, mordant, sarcastic, savage, scornful, searing, trenchant, vitriolic, withering

scatter **1.** broadcast, diffuse, disseminate, fling, litter, shower, sow, spread, sprinkle, strew **2.** disband, dispel, disperse, dissipate, disunite, put to flight, separate
Antonyms assemble, cluster, collect, congregate, converge, rally, unite

scatterbrain bird-brain (*informal*), butterfly, featherbrain, flibbertigibbet, grasshopper mind, madcap

scatterbrained bird-brained (*informal*), careless, empty-headed, featherbrained, forgetful, frivolous, giddy, goofy (*informal*), inattentive, irresponsible, madcap, scatty (*Brit. informal*), silly, slaphappy (*informal*), thoughtless

scattering few, handful, scatter, smatter, smattering, sprinkling

scenario master plan, outline, résumé, rundown, scheme, sequence of events, sketch, story line, summary, synopsis

scene **1.** display, drama, exhibition, pageant, picture, representation, show, sight, spectacle, tableau **2.** area, locality, place, position, setting, site, situation, spot, whereabouts **3.** backdrop, background, location, *mise en scène*, set, setting **4.** act, division, episode, incident, part, stage **5.** carry-on (*informal, chiefly Brit.*), commotion, confrontation, display of emotion, drama, exhibition, fuss, hue and cry, performance, row, tantrum, to-do, upset **6.** landscape, panorama, prospect, view, vista **7.** *informal* arena, business, environment, field of interest, milieu, world

scenery **1.** landscape, surroundings, terrain, view, vista **2.** *Theatre* backdrop, décor, flats, *mise en scène*, set, setting, stage set

scenic beautiful, breathtaking, grand, impressive, panoramic, picturesque, spectacular, striking

scent *noun* **1.** aroma, bouquet, fragrance, niff (*Brit. slang*), odour, perfume, redolence, smell **2.** spoor, track, trail ~*verb* **3.** be on the track *or* trail of, detect, discern, get wind of (*informal*), nose out, recognize, sense, smell, sniff, sniff out

scented aromatic, fragrant, odoriferous, perfumed, redolent, sweet-smelling

sceptic agnostic, cynic, disbeliever, doubter, doubting Thomas, Pyrrhonist, scoffer, unbeliever

I am too much of a sceptic to deny the possibility of anything

T.H. Huxley

sceptical cynical, disbelieving, doubtful, doubting, dubious, hesitating, incredulous, mistrustful, questioning, quizzical, scoffing, take with a pinch of salt, unbelieving, unconvinced
Antonyms believing, certain, convinced, credulous, dogmatic, free from doubt, of fixed

mind, sure, trusting, undoubting, unquestioning

scepticism agnosticism, cynicism, disbelief, doubt, incredulity, Pyrrhonism, suspicion, unbelief

schedule 1. *noun* agenda, calendar, catalogue, inventory, itinerary, list, list of appointments, plan, programme, timetable 2. *verb* appoint, arrange, be due, book, organize, plan, programme, slot (*informal*), time

schematic diagrammatic, diagrammatical, graphic, illustrative, representational

schematize arrange, catalogue, categorize, classify, file, grade, methodize, order, pigeonhole, put into order, regulate, sort, standardize, systematize, systemize, tabulate

scheme *noun* 1. contrivance, course of action, design, device, plan, programme, project, proposal, strategy, system, tactics, theory 2. arrangement, blueprint, chart, codification, diagram, disposition, draft, layout, outline, pattern, schedule, schema, system 3. conspiracy, dodge, game (*informal*), intrigue, machinations, manoeuvre, plot, ploy, ruse, shift, stratagem, subterfuge *~verb* 4. contrive, design, devise, frame, imagine, lay plans, plan, project, work out 5. collude, conspire, intrigue, machinate, manoeuvre, plot, wheel and deal (*informal*)

The best laid schemes o' mice an' men
Gang aft a-gley

Robert Burns *To a Mouse*

schemer conniver, deceiver, intriguer, Machiavelli, plotter, slyboots (*informal*), wangler (*informal*), wheeler-dealer (*informal*)

scheming artful, calculating, conniving, cunning, deceitful, designing, duplicitous, foxy, Machiavellian, slippery, sly, tricky, underhand, wily

Antonyms above-board, artless, guileless, honest, ingenuous, naive, straightforward, trustworthy, undesigning

schism breach, break, discord, disunion, division, rift, rupture, separation, splintering, split

schismatic, schismatical *adjective* discordant, dissentient, dissenting, dissident, heretical, heterodox, seceding, separatist, splinter

schmaltzy bathetic, cloying, corny (*slang*), gooey (*informal*), maudlin, mawkish, mushy (*informal*), overemotional, sentimental, sloppy (*informal*), slushy (*informal*), soppy (*informal*), tear-jerking

scholar 1. academic, bluestocking (*usually disparaging*), bookworm, egghead (*informal*), intellectual, man of letters, savant 2. disciple, learner, pupil, schoolboy, schoolgirl, student

The ink of the scholar is more sacred than the blood of the martyr

Mohammed

scholarly academic, bookish, erudite, intellectual, learned, lettered, scholastic, studious, well-read

Antonyms lowbrow, middlebrow, philistine, unacademic, uneducated, unintellectual, unlettered

scholarship 1. accomplishments, attainments, book-learning, education, erudition, knowledge, learning, lore 2. bursary, exhibition, fellowship

scholastic 1. academic, bookish, learned, lettered, literary, scholarly 2. pedagogic, pedantic, precise

school *noun* 1. academy, alma mater, college, department, discipline, faculty, institute, institution, seminary 2. adherents, circle, class, clique, denomination, devotees, disciples, faction, followers, following, group, pupils, schism, sect, set 3. creed, faith, outlook, persuasion, school of thought, stamp, way of life *~verb* 4. coach, discipline, drill, educate, indoctrinate, instruct, prepare, prime, train, tutor, verse

School is where you go between when your parents can't take you and industry can't take you

John Updike

schooling 1. book-learning, education, formal education, teaching, tuition 2. coaching, drill, grounding, guidance, instruction, preparation, training

schoolteacher dominie (*Scot.*), instructor, pedagogue, schoolmarm (*informal*), schoolmaster, schoolmistress

science 1. body of knowledge, branch of knowledge, discipline 2. art, skill, technique

Art is meant to disturb. Science reassures

Georges Braque *Pensées sur l'art*

Science is the record of dead religions

Oscar Wilde *Phrases and Philosophies for the Use of the Young*

Science is a collection of successful remedies

Paul Valéry

Science is nothing but trained and organized common sense

T.H. Huxley

Our scientific power has outrun our spiritual power. We have guided missiles and misguided men

Martin Luther King

the great tragedy of Science - the slaying of a beautiful hypothesis by an ugly fact

T.H. Huxley *Biogenesis and Abiogenesis*

the essence of science: ask an impertinent question, and you are on the way to a pertinent answer

Jacob Bronowski *The Ascent of Man*

In science the credit goes to the man who convinces the world, not to the man to whom the idea first occurs
Francis Darwin

Science is an edged tool, with which men play like children, and cut their own fingers
Arthur Eddington

Science without religion is lame, religion without science is blind
Albert Einstein *Science, Philosophy and Religion*

There are no such things as applied sciences, only applications of science
Louis Pasteur

Science is built up of facts, as a house is built of stones; but an accumulation of facts is no more a science than a heap of stones is a house
Henri Poincaré *Science and Hypothesis*

Science must begin with myths, and the criticism of myths
Karl Popper *The Philosophy of Science*

scientific accurate, controlled, exact, mathematical, precise, systematic

scientist

When a distinguished but elderly scientist states that something is possible, he is almost certainly right. When he states that something is impossible, he is very probably wrong. (Clarke's First Law)
Arthur C. Clarke *Profile of the Future*

When I find myself in the company of scientists, I feel like a shabby curate who has strayed by mistake into a drawing room full of dukes
W.H. Auden *The Dyer's Hand*

I don't know what I may seem to the world, but as to myself, I seem to have been only like a boy playing on the sea-shore and diverting myself in now and then finding a smoother pebble or a prettier shell than ordinary, whilst the great ocean of truth lay all undiscovered before me
Isaac Newton

The physicists have known sin; and this is a knowledge which they cannot lose
J. Robert Oppenheimer *Open Mind*

Nature, and Nature's laws lay hid in night
God said, Let Newton be! and all was light
Alexander Pope *Epitaph: Intended for Sir Isaac Newton*

scintillate blaze, coruscate, flash, give off sparks, gleam, glint, glisten, glitter, sparkle, twinkle

scintillating animated, bright, brilliant, dazzling, ebullient, exciting, glittering, lively, sparkling, stimulating, witty

scion **1.** child, descendant, heir, offspring, successor **2.** branch, graft, offshoot, shoot, slip, sprout, twig

scoff[1] *verb* belittle, deride, despise, flout, gibe, jeer, knock (*informal*), laugh at, make light of, make sport of, mock, poke fun at, pooh-pooh, revile, ridicule, scorn, scout (*archaic*), slag (off) (*slang*), sneer, take the piss (out of) (*taboo slang*), taunt, twit

scoff[2] **1.** *verb* bolt, cram, devour, gobble (up), gollop, gorge (cram, stuff) oneself on, gulp down, guzzle, make a pig of oneself on (*informal*), put away, wolf **2.** *noun* chow (*informal*), eats (*slang*), fare, feed, food, grub (*slang*), meal, nosh (*slang*), nosh-up (*Brit. slang*), rations

scold **1.** *verb* bawl out (*informal*), berate, blame, bring (someone) to book, carpet (*informal*), castigate, censure, chew out (*U.S. & Canad. informal*), chide, find fault with, give a rocket (*Brit. & N.Z. informal*), give (someone) a dressing-down (row, talking-to) (*informal*), go on at, haul (someone) over the coals (*informal*), have (someone) on the carpet (*informal*), lecture, nag, rate, read the riot act, rebuke, remonstrate with, reprimand, reproach, reprove, slate (*informal, chiefly Brit.*), take (someone) to task, tear into (*informal*), tear (someone) off a strip (*Brit. informal*), tell off (*informal*), tick off (*informal*), upbraid, vituperate **2.** *noun* nag, shrew, termagant (*rare*), Xanthippe
Antonyms *verb* acclaim, applaud, approve, commend, compliment, extol, laud, praise

scolding dressing-down (*informal*), (good) talking-to (*informal*), lecture, piece of one's mind, rebuke, row, telling-off (*informal*), ticking-off (*informal*), tongue-lashing, wigging (*Brit. slang*)

scoop *noun* **1.** dipper, ladle, spoon **2.** coup, exclusive, exposé, inside story, revelation, sensation ~*verb* **3.** *often with* **up** clear away, gather up, lift, pick up, remove, sweep up *or* away, take up **4.** bail, dig, dip, empty, excavate, gouge, hollow, ladle, scrape, shovel

scoot bolt, dart, dash, run, scamper, scurry, scuttle, skedaddle (*informal*), skirr, skitter, sprint, zip

scope ambit, area, capacity, compass, confines, elbowroom, extent, field of reference, freedom, latitude, liberty, opportunity, orbit, outlook, purview, range, reach, room, space, span, sphere

scorch blacken, blister, burn, char, parch, roast, sear, shrivel, singe, wither

scorching baking, boiling, broiling, burning, fiery, flaming, red-hot, roasting, searing, sizzling, sweltering, torrid, tropical, unbearably hot

score *noun* **1.** grade, mark, outcome, points, record, result, total **2. the score** *informal* the facts, the lie of the land, the reality, the setup (*informal*), the situation, the truth **3.** *plural* a flock, a great number, an army, a throng, crowds, droves, hosts, hundreds, legions, lots, masses, millions, multitudes, myriads, swarms, very many **4.** account, basis, cause, ground, grounds, reason **5.** a bone to pick, grievance, grudge, injury, injustice, wrong **6. pay off old scores** avenge, get even with (*informal*), get one's own back (*informal*), give an eye for an eye, give like for like *or* tit for tat, give (someone) a taste of his own medicine, hit back, pay (someone) back (in his own coin), repay, requite, retaliate **7.** account, amount due, bill, charge, debt, obligation, reckoning, tab (*U.S. informal*), tally, total ~*verb* **8.** achieve, amass, chalk up (*informal*), gain, make, notch up (*informal*), win **9.** count, keep a tally of, keep count, record, register, tally **10.** crosshatch, cut, deface, gouge, graze, indent, mar, mark, nick, notch, scrape, scratch, slash **11.** *with* **out** *or* **through** cancel, cross out, delete, obliterate, put a line through, strike out **12.** *Music* adapt, arrange, orchestrate, set **13.** gain an advantage, go down well with (someone), impress, make a hit (*informal*), make an impact *or* impression, make a point, put oneself across, triumph

score off be one up on (*informal*), get the better of, have the laugh on, humiliate, make a fool of, make (someone) look silly, worst

scorn **1.** *noun* contempt, contemptuousness, contumely, derision, despite, disdain, disparagement, mockery, sarcasm, scornfulness, slight, sneer **2.** *verb* be above, consider beneath one, contemn, curl one's lip at, deride, disdain, flout, hold in contempt, look down on, make fun of, reject, scoff at, scout (*archaic*), slight, sneer at, spurn, turn up one's nose at (*informal*)

Antonyms *noun* acceptance, admiration, affection, esteem, high regard, respect, tolerance, toleration, veneration, worship ~*verb* accept, admire, esteem, look favourably on, respect, revere, tolerate, venerate, worship

Heav'n has no rage, like love to hatred turn'd,
Nor Hell a fury, like a woman scorn'd
William Congreve *The Mourning Bride*

scornful contemptuous, contumelious, defiant, derisive, disdainful, haughty, insolent, insulting, jeering, mocking, sarcastic, sardonic, scathing, scoffing, slighting, sneering, supercilious, withering

scornfully contemptuously, disdainfully, dismissively, scathingly, slightingly, with a sneer, with contempt, with disdain, witheringly, with lip curled

scot-free clear, safe, scatheless (*archaic*), undamaged, unharmed, unhurt, uninjured, unpunished, unscathed, without a scratch

Scots Caledonian, Scottish

There are few more impressive sights in the world than a Scotsman on the make
J.M. Barrie *What Every Woman Knows*

scoundrel asshole (*U.S. & Canad. taboo slang*), asswipe (*U.S. & Canad. taboo slang*), bad egg (*old-fashioned informal*), bastard (*offensive*), blackguard, bugger (*taboo slang*), caitiff (*archaic*), cheat, cocksucker (*taboo slang*), dastard (*archaic*), good-for-nothing, heel (*slang*), incorrigible, knave (*archaic*), miscreant, mother, motherfucker (*taboo slang chiefly U.S.*), ne'er-do-well, rascal, reprobate, rogue, rotter (*slang, chiefly Brit.*), scally (*Northwest English dialect*), scamp, scapegrace, scumbag (*slang*), shit (*taboo slang*), son-of-a-bitch (*slang, chiefly U.S. & Canad.*), swine, turd (*taboo slang*), vagabond, villain, wretch

scour[1] *verb* abrade, buff, burnish, clean, cleanse, flush, furbish, polish, purge, rub, scrub, wash, whiten

scour[2] *verb* beat, comb, forage, go over with a fine-tooth comb, hunt, look high and low, rake, ransack, search

scourge *noun* **1.** affliction, bane, curse, infliction, misfortune, penalty, pest, plague, punishment, terror, torment, visitation **2.** cat, cat-o'-nine-tails, lash, strap, switch, thong, whip ~*verb* **3.** beat, belt (*informal*), cane, castigate, chastise, discipline, flog, horsewhip, lash, lather (*informal*), leather, punish, take a strap to, tan (someone's) hide (*slang*), thrash, trounce, wallop (*informal*), whale, whip **4.** afflict, curse, excoriate, harass, plague, terrorize, torment

Antonyms *noun* (*sense 1*) benefit, blessing, boon, favour, gift, godsend

scout *verb* **1.** case (*slang*), check out, investigate, make a reconnaissance, nark (*Brit., Austral., & N.Z. slang*), observe, probe, recce (*slang*), reconnoitre, see how the land lies, spy, spy out, survey, watch **2.** *often with* **out, up,** *or* **around** cast around for, ferret out, hunt for, look for, rustle up, search for, search out, seek, track down ~*noun* **3.** advance guard, escort, lookout, outrider, precursor, reconnoitrer, vanguard **4.** recruiter, talent scout

scowl **1.** *verb* frown, glower, grimace, look daggers at, lour *or* lower **2.** *noun* black look, dirty look, frown, glower, grimace

scrabble clamber, claw, dig, grope, paw, scramble, scrape, scratch

scraggy **1.** angular, bony, emaciated, gangling, gaunt, lanky, lean, rawboned, scrawny, skinny, undernourished **2.** draggletailed (*archaic*), grotty (*slang*), lank, meagre, rough, scanty, scruffy, tousled, unkempt

scram abscond, beat it (*slang*), bugger off (*taboo slang*), clear off (*informal*), depart, disappear, fuck off (*offensive taboo slang*), get lost (*informal*), get on one's bike (*Brit. slang*), go away, go to hell (*informal*), hook it (*slang*), leave, make oneself scarce (*informal*), make tracks, pack one's bags (*informal*), quit, scarper (*Brit. slang*), scoot, skedaddle (*informal*), sling one's hook (*Brit. slang*), slope off, take oneself off, vamoose (*slang, chiefly U.S.*)

scramble *verb* **1.** clamber, climb, crawl, move with difficulty, push, scrabble, struggle, swarm **2.** contend, hasten, jockey for position, jostle, look lively *or* snappy (*informal*), make haste, push, run, rush, strive, vie *~noun* **3.** climb, trek **4.** commotion, competition, confusion, free-for-all (*informal*), hassle (*informal*), hustle, melee *or* mêlée, muddle, race, rat race, rush, struggle, tussle

scrap[1] *noun* **1.** atom, bit, bite, crumb, fragment, grain, iota, mite, modicum, morsel, mouthful, part, particle, piece, portion, remnant, sliver, snatch, snippet, trace **2.** junk, off cuts, waste **3. on the scrap heap** discarded, ditched (*slang*), jettisoned, put out to grass (*informal*), redundant, written off **4.** *plural* bits, leavings, leftovers, remains, scrapings *~verb* **5.** abandon, break up, chuck (*informal*), demolish, discard, dispense with, ditch (*slang*), drop, get rid of, jettison, junk (*informal*), shed, throw away *or* out, throw on the scrapheap, toss out, trash (*slang*), write off

Antonyms *verb* bring back, recall, re-establish, reinstall, reinstate, restore, return

scrap[2] **1.** *noun* argument, *bagarre*, battle, brawl, disagreement, dispute, dust-up (*informal*), fight, quarrel, row, scrimmage, scuffle, set-to (*informal*), shindig (*informal*), shindy (*informal*), squabble, tiff, wrangle **2.** *verb* argue, barney (*informal*), bicker, come to blows, fall out (*informal*), fight, have a shouting match (*informal*), have words, row, spar, squabble, wrangle

scrape *verb* **1.** abrade, bark, graze, rub, scratch, scuff, skin **2.** grate, grind, rasp, scratch, screech, set one's teeth on edge, squeak **3.** clean, erase, file, remove, rub, scour **4.** live from hand to mouth, pinch, save, scrimp, skimp, stint, tighten one's belt **5. scrape by, in,** *or* **through** barely make it, cut it fine (*informal*), get by (*informal*), have a close shave (*informal*), struggle *~noun* **6.** *informal* awkward *or* embarrassing situation, difficulty, dilemma, distress, fix (*informal*), mess, plight, predicament, pretty pickle (*informal*), spot (*informal*), tight spot, trouble

scrape together amass, dredge up, get hold of, glean, hoard, muster, rake up *or* together, save

scrappy bitty, disjointed, fragmentary, incomplete, perfunctory, piecemeal, sketchy, thrown together

scraps bits, leavings, leftovers, remains, scrapings

scratch *verb* **1.** claw, cut, damage, etch, grate, graze, incise, lacerate, make a mark on, mark, rub, score, scrape **2.** annul, cancel, delete, eliminate, erase, pull out, stand down, strike off, withdraw *~noun* **3.** blemish, claw mark, gash, graze, laceration, mark, scrape **4. up to scratch** acceptable, adequate, capable, competent, satisfactory, sufficient, up to snuff (*informal*), up to standard *~adjective* **5.** haphazard, hastily prepared, impromptu, improvised, rough, rough-and-ready

scrawl doodle, scrabble, scratch, scribble, squiggle, writing

scrawny angular, bony, gaunt, lanky, lean, macilent (*rare*), rawboned, scraggy, skeletal, skin-and-bones (*informal*), skinny, thin, undernourished

scream *verb* **1.** bawl, cry, holler (*informal*), screech, shriek, shrill, sing out, squeal, yell **2.** *figurative* be conspicuous, clash, jar, shriek *~noun* **3.** howl, outcry, screech, shriek, wail, yell, yelp **4.** *informal* card (*informal*), caution (*informal*), character (*informal*), comedian, comic, entertainer, hoot (*informal*), joker, laugh, riot (*slang*), sensation, wag, wit

screech cry, scream, shriek, squawk, squeal, yelp

screed passage, speech

screen *verb* **1.** cloak, conceal, cover, hide, mask, shade, shroud, shut out, veil **2.** defend, guard, protect, safeguard, shelter, shield **3.** cull, evaluate, examine, filter, gauge, grade, process, riddle, scan, sieve, sift, sort, vet **4.** broadcast, present, put on, show *~noun* **5.** awning, canopy, cloak, concealment, cover, guard, hedge, mantle, shade, shelter, shield, shroud **6.** mesh, net, partition, room divider

screw *verb* **1.** tighten, turn, twist, work in **2.** contort, contract, crumple, distort, pucker, wrinkle **3.** *informal* bring pressure to bear on, coerce, constrain, force, hold a knife to (someone's) throat, oppress, pressurize, put the screws on (*informal*), squeeze **4.** *informal, often with* **out of** bleed, extort, extract, wrest, wring

screwed up anxious, apprehensive, confused, edgy, in a mess, keyed up, mixed up, nervous, neurotic, on edge, strung up (*informal*), tense, uptight (*informal*), wired (*slang*), worked up, worried

screw up 1. contort, contract, crumple, distort, knit, knot, pucker, wrinkle **2.** *informal* bitch (up) (*slang*), bodge (*informal*), botch, bungle, cock up (*Brit. slang*), flub (*U.S. slang*), fuck up (*offensive taboo slang*), louse up (*slang*), make a hash of (*informal*), make a mess *or* muck-up of (*slang*), make a nonsense of, mess up, mishandle, mismanage, queer (*informal*), spoil

screwy batty (*slang*), cracked (*slang*), crackers (*Brit. slang*), crackpot (*informal*), crazy, doolally (*slang*), dotty (*slang, chiefly Brit.*), eccentric, gonzo (*slang*), loopy (*informal*), nutty (*slang*), odd, oddball (*informal*), off one's trolley (*slang*), off-the-wall (*slang*), outré, out to lunch (*informal*), queer (*informal*), round the bend (*Brit. slang*), rum (*Brit. slang*), up the pole (*informal*), wacko *or* whacko (*informal*), weird

scribble *verb* dash off, doodle, jot, pen, scratch, scrawl, write

scribe amanuensis, clerk, copyist, notary (*archaic*), penman (*rare*), scrivener (*archaic*), secretary, writer

scrimmage affray (*Law*), *bagarre*, bovver (*Brit. slang*), brawl, disturbance, dust-up (*informal*), fight, fray, free-for-all (*informal*), melee *or* mêlée, riot, row, scrap (*informal*), scuffle, set-to (*informal*), shindig (*informal*), shindy (*informal*), skirmish, squabble, struggle

scrimp be frugal, curtail, economize, limit, pinch, pinch pennies, reduce, save, scrape, shorten, skimp, stint, straiten, tighten one's belt

script 1. calligraphy, hand, handwriting, letters, longhand, penmanship, writing 2. book, copy, dialogue, libretto, lines, manuscript, text, words

Scripture Holy Bible, Holy Scripture, Holy Writ, The Bible, The Book of Books, The Good Book, The Gospels, The Scriptures, The Word, The Word of God

> *The devil can cite Scripture for his purpose*
> William Shakespeare *The Merchant of Venice*

scroll inventory, list, parchment, roll

Scrooge cheapskate (*informal*), meanie *or* meany (*informal, chiefly Brit.*), miser, money-grubber (*informal*), niggard, penny-pincher (*informal*), skinflint, tight-arse (*taboo slang*), tight-ass (*U.S. taboo slang*), tightwad (*U.S. & Canad. slang*)

scrounge beg, blag (*slang*), bum (*informal*), cadge, forage for, freeload (*slang*), hunt around (for), mooch (*slang*), sorn (*Scot.*), sponge (*informal*), touch (someone) for (*slang*), wheedle

scrounger bum (*informal*), cadger, freeloader (*slang*), parasite, sorner (*Scot.*), sponger (*informal*)

scrub *verb* 1. clean, cleanse, rub, scour 2. *informal* abandon, abolish, call off, cancel, delete, discontinue, do away with, drop, forget about, give up

scrubby insignificant, meagre, paltry, scrawny, spindly, stunted, underdeveloped, undersized

scruff 1. nape, scrag (*informal*) 2. *informal* ragamuffin, ragbag (*informal*), scarecrow, sloven, tatterdemalion (*rare*), tramp

scruffy disreputable, draggletailed (*archaic*), frowzy, grungy, ill-groomed, mangy, messy, ragged, run-down, scrubby (*Brit. informal*), seedy, shabby, slatternly, sloppy (*informal*), slovenly, sluttish, squalid, tattered, tatty, ungroomed, unkempt, untidy
Antonyms chic, dapper, natty, neat, soigné *or* soignée, spruce, tidy, well-dressed, well-groomed, well-turned-out

scrumptious appetizing, delectable, delicious, exquisite, inviting, luscious, magnificent, moreish (*informal*), mouthwatering, succulent, yummy (*slang*)

scrunch champ, chew, crumple, crunch, crush, mash, ruck up, squash

scruple 1. *verb* balk at, be loath, be reluctant, demur, doubt, falter, have misgivings about, have qualms about, hesitate, stick at, think twice about, vacillate, waver 2. *noun* caution, compunction, difficulty, doubt, hesitation, misgiving, perplexity, qualm, reluctance, second thoughts, squeamishness, twinge of conscience, uneasiness

scrupulous careful, conscientious, exact, fastidious, honourable, meticulous, minute, moral, nice, painstaking, precise, principled, punctilious, rigorous, strict, upright
Antonyms amoral, careless, dishonest, inexact, reckless, slapdash, superficial, uncaring, unconscientious, unprincipled, unscrupulous, without scruples

scrutinize analyse, dissect, examine, explore, go over with a fine-tooth comb, inquire into, inspect, investigate, peruse, pore over, probe, research, scan, search, sift, study, work over

scrutiny analysis, close study, examination, exploration, inquiry, inspection, investigation, once-over (*informal*), perusal, search, sifting, study

scud blow, fly, haste, hasten, race, sail, shoot, skim, speed

scuffle 1. *verb* clash, come to blows, contend, exchange blows, fight, grapple, jostle, struggle, tussle 2. *noun* affray (*Law*), *bagarre*, barney (*informal*), brawl, commotion, disturbance, fight, fray, ruck (*slang*), ruckus (*informal*), ruction (*informal*), rumpus, scrap (*informal*), scrimmage, set-to (*informal*), shindig (*informal*), shindy (*informal*), skirmish, tussle

sculpture *verb* carve, chisel, cut, fashion, form, hew, model, mould, sculp, sculpt, shape

scum 1. algae, crust, dross, film, froth, impurities, offscourings, scruff 2. *figurative canaille*, dregs of society, dross, lowest of the low, rabble, ragtag and bobtail, riffraff, rubbish, trash (*chiefly U.S. & Canad.*)

scupper defeat, demolish, destroy, disable, discomfit, overthrow, overwhelm, put paid to, ruin, torpedo, undo, wreck

scurrility abusiveness, billingsgate, coarseness, grossness, indecency, infamousness, invective, obloquy, obscenity, offensiveness, scurrilousness, vituperation

scurrilous abusive, coarse, defamatory, foul, foul-mouthed, gross, indecent, infamous, insulting, low, obscene, offensive, Rabelaisian, ribald, salacious, scabrous, scandalous, slanderous, vituperative, vulgar
Antonyms civilized, decent, polite, proper, refined, respectful

scurry 1. *verb* beetle, dart, dash, fly, hurry, race, scamper, scoot, scud, scuttle, skim, sprint, whisk 2. *noun* bustle, flurry, scampering, whirl
Antonyms *verb* amble, mooch (*slang*), mosey (*informal*), saunter, stroll, toddle, wander

scurvy *adjective* abject, bad, base, contemptible, despicable, dishonourable, ignoble, low, low-down (*informal*), mean, pitiful, rotten, scabby (*informal*), shabby, sorry, vile, worthless

scuttle beetle, bustle, hare (*Brit. informal*), hasten, hurry, run, rush, scamper, scoot, scramble, scud, scurry, scutter (*Brit. informal*)

sea *noun* 1. main, ocean, the briny (*informal*), the deep, the drink (*informal*), the waves 2. *figurative* abundance, expanse, mass, multitude, plethora, profusion, sheet, vast number 3. **at sea** adrift, astray, at a loss, at sixes and sevens, baffled, bewildered, confused, disoriented, lost, mystified, puzzled, upset ~*adjective* 4. aquatic, briny, marine, maritime, ocean, ocean-going, oceanic, pelagic, salt, saltwater, seagoing
Related adjective: thalassic

Seas

Adriatic
Aegean
Amundsen
Andaman
Arabian
Arafura
Aral
Azov
Baltic
Banda
Barents
Beaufort
Bellingshausen
Bering
Bismarck
Black *or* Euxine
Caribbean
Caspian
Celebes
Ceram
China
Chukchi
Coral
East China
East Siberian
Flores
Icarian
Inland
Ionian
Irish
Japan
Java
Kara
Laptev
Ligurian
Lincoln
Marmara *or* Marmora
Mediterranean
Nordenskjöld
North
Norwegian
Okhotsk
Philippine
Red
Ross
Sargasso
Scotia
Solomon
South China
Sulu
Tasman
Timor
Tyrrhenian
Weddell
White
Yellow *or* Hwang Hai

Oceans

Antarctic *or* Southern
Arctic
Atlantic
Indian
Pacific

the wine-dark sea
Homer *Iliad*

ocean: a body of water occupying about two-thirds of a world made for man - who has no gills
Ambrose Bierce *The Devil's Dictionary*

seafaring marine, maritime, nautical, naval, oceanic

seal *verb* 1. bung, close, cork, enclose, fasten, make airtight, plug, secure, shut, stop, stopper, stop up, waterproof 2. assure, attest, authenticate, confirm, establish, ratify, stamp, validate 3. clinch, conclude, consummate, finalize, settle, shake hands on (*informal*) 4. *with* **off** board up, fence off, isolate, put out of bounds, quarantine, segregate ~*noun* 5. assurance, attestation, authentication, confirmation, imprimatur, insignia, notification, ratification, stamp

seam *noun* 1. closure, joint, suture (*Surgery*) 2. layer, lode, stratum, vein 3. furrow, line, ridge, scar, wrinkle

seamy corrupt, dark, degraded, disagreeable, disreputable, low, nasty, rough, sordid, squalid, unpleasant, unwholesome

sear blight, brand, burn, cauterize, desiccate, dry up *or* out, scorch, seal, shrivel, sizzle, wilt, wither

search *verb* 1. cast around, check, comb, examine, explore, ferret, forage, frisk (*informal*), go over with a fine-tooth comb, inquire, inspect, investigate, leave no stone unturned, look, look high and low, probe, pry, ransack, rifle through, rummage through, scour, scrutinize, seek, sift, turn inside out, turn upside down ~*noun* 2. examination, exploration, going-over (*informal*), hunt, inquiry, inspection, investigation, pursuit, quest, researches, rummage, scrutiny 3. **in search of** hunting for, in need of, in pursuit of, looking for, making enquiries concerning, on the lookout for, on the track of, seeking

searching *adjective* close, intent, keen, minute, penetrating, piercing, probing, quizzical, severe, sharp, thorough
Antonyms cursory, perfunctory, peripheral, sketchy, superficial

seasickness *mal de mer*

season *noun* **1.** division, interval, juncture, occasion, opportunity, period, spell, term, time, time of year *~verb* **2.** colour, enliven, flavour, lace, leaven, pep up, salt, salt and pepper, spice **3.** acclimatize, accustom, anneal, discipline, habituate, harden, inure, mature, prepare, toughen, train **4.** mitigate, moderate, qualify, temper

Season	**Related adjective**
spring	vernal
summer	aestival *or* estival
autumn	autumnal
winter	hibernal *or* hiemal

To everything there is a season, and a time to every purpose under the heaven
Bible: Ecclesiastes

Summer has set in with its usual severity
Samuel Taylor Coleridge

summer afternoon - summer afternoon... the two most beautiful words in the English language
Henry James

Shall I compare thee to a Summer's day?
Thou art more lovely and more temperate
William Shakespeare *Sonnets*

season of mists and mellow fruitfulness
John Keats *To Autumn*

If Winter comes, can Spring be far behind?
Percy Bysshe Shelley *Ode to the West Wind*

in the bleak mid-winter
Christina Rosetti *Mid-Winter*

the English winter - ending in July to recommence in August
Lord Byron

In the Spring a young man's fancy lightly turns to thoughts of love
Alfred, Lord Tennyson *Locksley Hall*

One swallow does not make a summer

seasonable appropriate, convenient, fit, opportune, providential, suitable, timely, welcome, well-timed

seasoned battle-scarred, experienced, hardened, long-serving, mature, old, practised, time-served, veteran, weathered, well-versed **Antonyms** callow, green, inexperienced, new, novice, unpractised, unseasoned, unskilled

seasoning condiment, dressing, flavouring, relish, salt and pepper, sauce, spice

Herbs, spices and seasonings
see FOOD

seat *noun* **1.** bench, chair, pew, settle, stall, stool, throne **2.** axis, capital, centre, cradle, headquarters, heart, hub, location, place, site, situation, source, station **3.** base, bed, bottom, cause, footing, foundation, ground, groundwork **4.** abode, ancestral hall, house, mansion, residence **5.** chair, constituency, incumbency, membership, place *~verb* **6.** accommodate, cater for, contain, have room *or* capacity for, hold, sit, take **7.** deposit, fix, install, locate, place, set, settle, sit

seating accommodation, chairs, places, room, seats

secede apostatize, break with, disaffiliate, leave, pull out, quit, resign, retire, separate, split from, withdraw

secession apostasy, break, defection, disaffiliation, seceding, split, withdrawal

secluded cloistered, cut off, isolated, lonely, off the beaten track, out-of-the-way, private, reclusive, remote, retired, sequestered, sheltered, solitary, tucked away, unfrequented **Antonyms** accessible, busy, frequented, open, public, sociable

seclusion concealment, hiding, isolation, ivory tower, privacy, purdah, remoteness, retirement, retreat, shelter, solitude

second[1] *adjective* **1.** following, next, subsequent, succeeding **2.** additional, alternative, extra, further, other, repeated **3.** inferior, lesser, lower, secondary, subordinate, supporting **4.** double, duplicate, reproduction, twin *~noun* **5.** assistant, backer, helper, supporter *~verb* **6.** advance, aid, approve, assist, back, commend, encourage, endorse, forward, further, give moral support to, go along with, help, promote, support

second[2] *noun* bat of an eye (*informal*), flash, instant, jiffy (*informal*), minute, moment, sec (*informal*), split second, tick (*Brit. informal*), trice, twinkling, twinkling of an eye, two shakes of a lamb's tail (*informal*)

secondary 1. derivative, derived, indirect, resultant, resulting, second-hand **2.** consequential, contingent, inferior, lesser, lower, minor, second-rate, subordinate, unimportant **3.** alternate, auxiliary, backup, extra, fall-back, relief, reserve, second, subsidiary, supporting **Antonyms** cardinal, chief, head, larger, main, major, more important, only, original, preceding, primary, prime, principal, superior

second childhood Alzheimer's disease, caducity, dotage, senility

second class *adjective* déclassé, indifferent, inferior, mediocre, no great shakes (*informal*), outclassed, second-best, second-rate, undistinguished, uninspiring

second-hand 1. *adjective* handed down, hand-me-down (*informal*), nearly new, reach-me-down (*informal*), used **2.** *adverb* at second-hand, indirectly, on the grapevine (*informal*)

second in command depute (*Scot.*), deputy, number two, right-hand man, successor designate

secondly in the second place, next, second

second-rate bush-league (*Austral. & N.Z. informal*), cheap, cheap and nasty (*informal*), commonplace, dime-a-dozen (*informal*), for the

birds (*informal*), inferior, low-grade, low-quality, low-rent (*informal, chiefly U.S.*), mediocre, no great shakes (*informal*), not much cop (*Brit. slang*), piss-poor (*taboo slang*), poor, rubbishy, shoddy, strictly for the birds (*informal*), substandard, tacky (*informal*), tawdry, tinhorn (*U.S. slang*), two-bit (*U.S. & Canad. slang*)
Antonyms a cut above (*informal*), choice, de luxe, excellent, fine, first-class, first-rate, good quality, high-class, quality, superior

secrecy 1. cloak and dagger, concealment, confidentiality, huggermugger (*rare*), mystery, privacy, retirement, seclusion, silence, solitude, surreptitiousness 2. clandestineness, covertness, furtiveness, secretiveness, stealth

If you would wish another to keep your secret, first keep it yourself
Seneca *Hippolytus*

secret *adjective* 1. backstairs, behind someone's back, camouflaged, cloak-and-dagger, close, closet (*informal*), concealed, conspiratorial, covered, covert, disguised, furtive, hidden, hole-and-corner (*informal*), hush-hush (*informal*), reticent, shrouded, undercover, underground, under wraps, undisclosed, unknown, unpublished, unrevealed, unseen 2. abstruse, arcane, cabbalistic, clandestine, classified, cryptic, esoteric, mysterious, occult, recondite 3. hidden, out-of-the-way, private, retired, secluded, unfrequented, unknown 4. close, deep, discreet, reticent, secretive, sly, stealthy, underhand ~*noun* 5. code, confidence, enigma, formula, key, mystery, recipe, skeleton in the cupboard 6. **in secret** behind closed doors, by stealth, huggermugger (*archaic*), in camera, incognito, secretly, slyly, surreptitiously
Antonyms *adjective* apparent, candid, disclosed, exoteric, frank, manifest, obvious, open, overt, public, straightforward, unconcealed, visible, well-known

They have a skeleton in their closet
William Makepeace Thackeray *The Newcomes*

I know that's a secret, for it's whispered every where
William Congreve *Love for Love*

For secrets are edged tools,
And must be kept from children and from fools
John Dryden *Sir Martin Mar-All*

secret agent cloak-and-dagger man, nark (*Brit., Austral., & N.Z. slang*), spook (*U.S. & Canad. informal*), spy, undercover agent

secrete[1] *verb* bury, cache, conceal, cover, disguise, harbour, hide, screen, secure, shroud, stash (*informal*), stash away (*informal*), stow, veil
Antonyms bare, display, exhibit, expose to view, leave in the open, reveal, show, uncover, unmask, unveil

secrete[2] *verb* emanate, emit, extravasate (*Medical*), extrude, exude, give off

secretion discharge, emission, excretion, extravasation (*Medical*), exudation

secretive cagey (*informal*), clamlike, close, cryptic, deep, enigmatic, playing one's cards close to one's chest, reserved, reticent, tight-lipped, uncommunicative, unforthcoming, withdrawn
Antonyms candid, communicative, expansive, forthcoming, frank, open, unreserved

secretly behind closed doors, behind (someone's) back, clandestinely, confidentially, covertly, furtively, in camera, in confidence, in one's heart, in one's heart of hearts, in one's innermost thoughts, in secret, on the fly (*slang, chiefly Brit.*), on the q.t. (*informal*), on the sly, privately, quietly, stealthily, surreptitiously, under the counter, unobserved

sect camp, denomination, division, faction, group, party, schism, school, school of thought, splinter group, wing

sectarian 1. *adjective* bigoted, clannish, cliquish, doctrinaire, dogmatic, exclusive, factional, fanatic, fanatical, hidebound, insular, limited, narrow-minded, parochial, partisan, rigid 2. *noun* adherent, bigot, disciple, dogmatist, extremist, fanatic, partisan, true believer, zealot
Antonyms *adjective* broad-minded, catholic, free-thinking, liberal, non-sectarian, open-minded, tolerant, unbigoted, unprejudiced

section *noun* 1. component, cross section, division, fraction, fragment, instalment, part, passage, piece, portion, sample, segment, slice, subdivision 2. *chiefly U.S.* area, department, district, region, sector, zone

sectional divided, exclusive, factional, local, localized, partial, regional, separate, separatist

sector area, category, district, division, part, quarter, region, stratum, subdivision, zone

secular civil, earthly, laic, laical, lay, nonspiritual, profane, state, temporal, worldly
Antonyms divine, holy, religious, sacred, spiritual, theological

secure *adjective* 1. immune, impregnable, in safe hands, out of harm's way, protected, safe, sheltered, shielded, unassailable, undamaged, unharmed 2. dependable, fast, fastened, firm, fixed, fortified, immovable, stable, steady, tight 3. assured, certain, confident, easy, reassured, sure 4. absolute, conclusive, definite, in the bag (*informal*), reliable, solid, steadfast, tried and true, well-founded ~*verb* 5. acquire, come by, gain, get, get hold of, land (*informal*), make sure of, obtain, pick up, procure, score (*slang*), win possession of 6. attach, batten down, bolt, chain, fasten, fix, lash, lock,

lock up, make fast, moor, padlock, rivet, tie up **7.** assure, ensure, guarantee, insure
Antonyms *adjective* endangered, ill-at-ease, insecure, loose, not fastened, precarious, unassured, uncertain, uneasy, unfixed, unpro~ tected, unsafe, unsound, unsure *~verb* endan~ ger, give up, imperil, leave unguaranteed, let (something) slip through (one's) fingers, loose, lose, unloose, untie

security **1.** asylum, care, cover, custody, im~ munity, preservation, protection, refuge, re~ treat, safekeeping, safety, sanctuary **2.** de~ fence, guards, precautions, protection, safe~ guards, safety measures, surveillance **3.** as~ surance, certainty, confidence, conviction, ease of mind, freedom from doubt, positiveness, re~ liance, sureness **4.** collateral, gage, guarantee, hostage, insurance, pawn, pledge, surety
Antonyms (*senses 1, 2 & 3*) exposure, insecu~ rity, jeopardy, uncertainty, vulnerability

sedate calm, collected, composed, cool, deco~ rous, deliberate, demure, dignified, earnest, grave, imperturbable, middle-aged, placid, proper, quiet, seemly, serene, serious, slow-moving, sober, solemn, staid, tranquil, un~ flappable (*informal*), unruffled
Antonyms agitated, excitable, excited, flighty, impassioned, jumpy, nervous, undignified, un~ inhibited, unsteady, wild

sedative **1.** *adjective* allaying, anodyne, calma~ tive, calming, lenitive, relaxing, sleep-inducing, soothing, soporific, tranquillizing **2.** *noun* anodyne, calmative, downer *or* down (*slang*), narcotic, opiate, sleeping pill, tran~ quillizer

sedentary desk, desk-bound, inactive, motion~ less, seated, sitting, torpid
Antonyms active, mobile, motile, moving, on the go (*informal*)

sediment deposit, dregs, grounds, lees, pre~ cipitate, residuum, settlings

sedition agitation, disloyalty, incitement to riot, rabble-rousing, subversion, treason

seditious disloyal, dissident, insubordinate, mutinous, rebellious, refractory, revolutionary, subversive, treasonable

seduce **1.** betray, corrupt, debauch, deflower, deprave, dishonour, ruin (*archaic*) **2.** allure, attract, beguile, deceive, decoy, ensnare, en~ tice, inveigle, lead astray, lure, mislead, tempt

seduction **1.** corruption, defloration, ruin (*ar~ chaic*) **2.** allure, enticement, lure, snare, temptation

seductive alluring, attractive, beguiling, be~ witching, captivating, come-hither (*informal*), come-to-bed (*informal*), enticing, flirtatious, inviting, irresistible, provocative, ravishing, sexy (*informal*), siren, specious, tempting

seductress Circe, enchantress, *femme fatale*, Lorelei, siren, temptress, vamp (*informal*)

sedulous assiduous, busy, conscientious, con~ stant, diligent, industrious, laborious, pains~ taking, persevering, persistent, tireless, un~ flagging, unremitting

see[1] *verb* **1.** behold, catch a glimpse of, catch sight of, check, check out (*informal*), clock (*Brit. slang*), descry, discern, distinguish, espy, eyeball (*U.S. slang*), get a load of (*slang*), glimpse, heed, identify, lay *or* clap eyes on (*informal*), look, make out, mark, note, notice, observe, perceive, recognize, re~ gard, sight, spot, take a dekko at (*Brit. slang*), view, witness **2.** appreciate, catch on (*informal*), comprehend, fathom, feel, follow, get, get the drift of, get the hang of (*infor~ mal*), grasp, know, make out, realize, take in, understand **3.** ascertain, determine, discover, find out, investigate, learn, make enquiries, refer to **4.** ensure, guarantee, make certain, make sure, mind, see to it, take care **5.** con~ sider, decide, deliberate, give some thought to, judge, make up one's mind, mull over, reflect, think over **6.** confer with, consult, encounter, interview, meet, receive, run into, speak to, visit **7.** accompany, attend, escort, lead, show, usher, walk **8.** consort *or* associate with, court, date (*informal, chiefly U.S.*), go out with, go steady with (*informal*), keep company with, walk out with (*obsolete*) **9.** anticipate, divine, envisage, foresee, foretell, imagine, picture, visualize

What the eye doesn't see, the heart doesn't grieve over

What you see is what you get

Seeing is believing

see[2] *noun* bishopric, diocese

see about **1.** attend to, consider, deal with, give some thought to, look after, see to, take care of **2.** investigate, look into, make en~ quiries, research

seed **1.** egg, egg cell, embryo, germ, grain, ker~ nel, ovule, ovum, pip, spore **2.** beginning, germ, inkling, nucleus, source, start, suspicion **3.** *figurative* children, descendants, heirs, is~ sue, offspring, progeny, race, scions, spawn, successors **4. go** *or* **run to seed** decay, decline, degenerate, deteriorate, go downhill (*infor~ mal*), go to pieces, go to pot, go to rack and ruin, go to waste, let oneself go, retrogress
Related adjective: seminal

seedy **1.** crummy (*slang*), decaying, dilapidated, down at heel, faded, grotty (*slang*), grubby, mangy, manky (*Scot. dialect*), old, run-down, scruffy, shabby, sleazy, slovenly, squalid, tat~ ty, unkempt, worn **2.** *informal* ailing, ill, off colour, out of sorts, peely-wally (*Scot.*), poorly (*informal*), sickly, under the weather (*infor~*

mal), unwell
Antonyms (*sense 1*) classy, elegant, fashion~ able, high-toned, posh (*informal, chiefly Brit.*), ritzy (*slang*), smart, swanky (*informal*), swish (*informal, chiefly Brit.*), top-drawer, up-market

see eye to eye accord, agree, click, coincide, concur, correspond, fit, get along, get on like a house on fire (*informal*), get on (together), harmonize, speak the same language

seeing *conjunction* as, inasmuch as, in view of the fact that, since

seek **1.** be after, follow, go gunning for, go in pursuit (quest, search), of hunt, inquire, look for, pursue, search for **2.** aim, aspire to, at~ tempt, endeavour, essay, have a go (*informal*), strive, try **3.** ask, beg, entreat, inquire, invite, petition, request, solicit

Seek, and ye shall find
Bible: St. Matthew

seem appear, assume, give the impression, have the *or* every appearance of, look, look as if, look like, look to be, pretend, sound like, strike one as being

seeming *adjective* apparent, appearing, illuso~ ry, ostensible, outward, quasi-, specious, sur~ face

seemingly apparently, as far as anyone could tell, on the face of it, on the surface, osten~ sibly, outwardly, to all appearances, to all in~ tents and purposes

seemly appropriate, becoming, befitting, *comme il faut*, decent, decorous, fit, fitting, in good taste, meet (*archaic*), nice, proper, suit~ able, suited, the done thing
Antonyms improper, inappropriate, indeco~ rous, in poor taste, out of keeping, out of place, unbecoming, unbefitting, unseemly, un~ suitable

see over inspect, look round, see round, tour

seep bleed, exude, leach, leak, ooze, percolate, permeate, soak, trickle, weep, well

seepage exudation, leak, leakage, oozing, per~ colation

seer augur, predictor, prophet, sibyl, soothsay~ er

seesaw *verb* alternate, fluctuate, go from one extreme to the other, oscillate, pitch, swing, teeter

seethe **1.** boil, bubble, churn, ferment, fizz, foam, froth **2.** be in a state (*informal*), be livid (furious, incensed), breathe fire and slaughter, foam at the mouth, fume, get hot under the collar (*informal*), go ballistic (*slang, chiefly U.S.*), rage, see red (*informal*), simmer, storm, wig out (*slang*) **3.** be alive with, swarm, teem

see-through diaphanous, filmy, fine, flimsy, gauzy, gossamer, sheer, thin, translucent, transparent

see through *verb* **1.** be undeceived by, be wise to (*informal*), fathom, get to the bottom of, have (someone's) number (*informal*), not fall for, penetrate, read (someone) like a book **2.** **see (something** *or* **someone) through** help out, keep at, persevere (with), persist, see out, stay to the bitter end, stick by, stick out (*in~ formal*), support

see to arrange, attend to, be responsible for, do, look after, manage, organize, sort out, take care of, take charge of

segment bit, compartment, division, part, piece, portion, section, slice, wedge

segregate discriminate against, dissociate, iso~ late, separate, set apart, single out
Antonyms amalgamate, desegregate, join to~ gether, mix, unify, unite

segregation apartheid (*in South Africa*), dis~ crimination, isolation, separation

seize **1.** catch up, clutch, collar (*informal*), fas~ ten, grab, grasp, grip, lay hands on, snatch, take **2.** apprehend, catch, get, grasp, nab (*in~ formal*), nail (*informal*) **3.** abduct, annex, ap~ propriate, arrest, capture, commandeer, con~ fiscate, hijack, impound, take by storm, take captive, take possession of
Antonyms free, hand back, let go, let pass, loose, release, relinquish, set free, turn loose

seizure **1.** abduction, annexation, apprehension, arrest, capture, commandeering, confiscation, grabbing, taking **2.** attack, convulsion, fit, paroxysm, spasm

seldom hardly ever, infrequently, not often, occasionally, once in a blue moon (*informal*), rarely, scarcely ever
Antonyms again and again, frequently, many a time, much, often, over and over again, time after time, time and again

select *verb* **1.** choose, opt for, pick, prefer, sin~ gle out, sort out *~adjective* **2.** choice, excellent, first-class, first-rate, hand-picked, picked, posh (*informal, chiefly Brit.*), preferable, prime, rare, recherché, selected, special, superior, topnotch (*informal*) **3.** cliquish, elite, exclusive, limited, privileged
Antonyms *verb* eliminate, reject, turn down *~adjective* cheap, indifferent, indiscriminate, inferior, ordinary, random, run-of-the-mill, second-rate, shoddy, substandard, unremark~ able

selection **1.** choice, choosing, option, pick, pref~ erence **2.** anthology, assortment, choice, col~ lection, line-up, medley, miscellany, mixed bag (*informal*), pick 'n' mix, potpourri, range, va~ riety

selective careful, discerning, discriminating, discriminatory, eclectic, particular
Antonyms all-embracing, careless, desultory, indiscriminate, unselective

self-assurance assertiveness, confidence, positiveness, self-confidence, self-possession

self-centred egotistic, inward looking, narcissistic, self-absorbed, selfish, self-seeking, wrapped up in oneself

self-confidence aplomb, confidence, high morale, nerve, poise, self-assurance, self-reliance, self-respect

self-confident assured, confident, fearless, poised, secure, self-assured, self-reliant, sure of oneself

self-conscious affected, awkward, bashful, diffident, embarrassed, ill at ease, insecure, like a fish out of water, nervous, out of countenance, shamefaced, sheepish, uncomfortable

self-control calmness, cool, coolness, restraint, self-discipline, self-mastery, self-restraint, strength of mind *or* will, willpower

He that would govern others, first should be
The master of himself

Philip Massinger *The Bondman*

self-denial abstemiousness, asceticism, renunciation, self-abnegation, selflessness, self-sacrifice, unselfishness

Deny yourself! You must deny yourself! That is the song that never ends

Johann Wolfgang Von Goethe *Faust*

self-esteem *amour-propre*, confidence, faith in oneself, pride, self-assurance, self-regard, self-respect, vanity

self-evident axiomatic, clear, cut-and-dried (*informal*), incontrovertible, inescapable, manifestly *or* patently true, obvious, undeniable, written all over (something)

self-government autonomy, democracy, home rule, independence, self-determination, self-rule, sovereignty

self-important arrogant, big-headed, bumptious, cocky, conceited, full of oneself, overbearing, pompous, presumptuous, pushy (*informal*), strutting, swaggering, swollen-headed

self-indulgence dissipation, excess, extravagance, incontinence, intemperance, self-gratification, sensualism

selfish egoistic, egoistical, egotistic, egotistical, greedy, looking out for number one (*informal*), mean, mercenary, narrow, self-centred, self-interested, self-seeking, ungenerous

Antonyms altruistic, benevolent, considerate, generous, magnanimous, philanthropic, self-denying, selfless, self-sacrificing, ungrudging, unselfish

self-knowledge

Know then thyself, presume not God to scan,
The proper study of mankind is man

Alexander Pope *An Essay on Man*

All our knowledge is, our selves to know

Alexander Pope *An Essay on Man*

The greatest thing in the world is to know how to be oneself

Montaigne *Essais*

Man is man's ABC. There is none that can
Read God aright, unless he first spell Man

Francis Quarles *Hieroglyphics of the Life of Man*

selfless altruistic, generous, magnanimous, self-denying, self-sacrificing, ungrudging, unselfish

self-possessed collected, confident, cool, cool as a cucumber (*informal*), poised, self-assured, sure of oneself, together (*slang*), unruffled

self-possession aplomb, composure, confidence, cool (*slang*), poise, sang-froid, self-command, unflappability (*informal*)

self-reliant able to stand on one's own two feet (*informal*), capable, independent, self-sufficient, self-supporting

Antonyms dependent, helpless, reliant, relying on

self-respect *amour-propre*, dignity, faith in oneself, morale, one's own image, pride, self-esteem

self-restraint abstemiousness, forbearance, patience, self-command, self-control, self-discipline, willpower

self-righteous complacent, goody-goody (*informal*), holier-than-thou, hypocritical, pharisaic, pi (*Brit. slang*), pietistic, pious, priggish, sanctimonious, self-satisfied, smug, superior, too good to be true

self-sacrifice altruism, generosity, self-abnegation, self-denial, selflessness

self-satisfaction complacency, contentment, ease of mind, flush of success, glow of achievement, pride, self-approbation, self-approval, smugness

self-satisfied complacent, flushed with success, like a cat that has swallowed the cream *or* the canary, pleased with oneself, proud of oneself, puffed up, self-congratulatory, smug, too big for one's boots *or* breeches, well-pleased

self-seeking *adjective* acquisitive, calculating, careerist, fortune-hunting, gold-digging, looking out for number one (*informal*), mercenary, on the make (*slang*), opportunistic, out for what one can get, self-interested, selfish, self-serving

self-styled professed, quasi-, self-appointed, so-called, *soi-disant*, would-be

self-willed cussed (*informal*), headstrong, intractable, obstinate, opinionated, pig-headed, refractory, stiff-necked, stubborn, stubborn as a mule, ungovernable, wilful

sell **1.** barter, dispose of, exchange, put up for sale, trade **2.** be in the business of, deal in, handle, hawk, market, merchandise, peddle,

retail, stock, trade in, traffic in, vend **3.** gain acceptance for, promote, put across **4.** *informal with* **on** convert to, convince of, get (someone) hooked on, persuade of, talk (someone) into, win (someone) over to **5.** betray, deliver up, give up, sell down the river (*informal*), sell out (*informal*), surrender
Antonyms (*senses 1 & 2*) acquire, get, invest in, obtain, pay for, procure, purchase, shop for

seller agent, dealer, merchant, purveyor, rep, representative, retailer, salesman, saleswoman, shopkeeper, supplier, tradesman, traveller, vendor

selling 1. business, commercial transactions, dealing, trading, traffic **2.** marketing, merchandising, promotion, salesmanship

sell out 1. be out of stock of, dispose of, get rid of, run out of, sell up **2.** *informal* betray, break faith with, double-cross (*informal*), fail, give away, play false, rat on (*informal*), sell down the river (*informal*), stab in the back

semblance air, appearance, aspect, bearing, façade, figure, form, front, guise, image, likeness, mask, mien, pretence, resemblance, show, similarity, veneer

semen come *or* cum (*taboo*), jissom (*taboo*), scum (*U.S. slang*), seed (*archaic or dialect*), seminal fluid, sperm, spermatic fluid, spunk (*taboo*)

semidarkness dusk, gloaming (*Scot. or poetic*), gloom, half-light, murk, twilight, waning light

seminal *figurative* creative, formative, ground-breaking, imaginative, important, influential, innovative, original, productive

seminary academy, college, high school, institute, institution, school

send 1. communicate, consign, convey, direct, dispatch, forward, remit, transmit **2.** cast, deliver, fire, fling, hurl, let fly, propel, shoot **3.** *with* **off, out,** *etc.* broadcast, discharge, emit, exude, give off, radiate **4.** *slang* charm, delight, electrify, enrapture, enthrall, excite, intoxicate, move, please, ravish, stir, thrill, titillate, turn (someone) on (*slang*) **5. send (someone) packing** discharge, dismiss, give (someone) the bird (*informal*), give (someone) the brushoff (*slang*), send away, send (someone) about his *or* her business, send (someone) away with a flea in his *or* her ear (*informal*)

send for call for, demand, order, request, summon

sendoff departure, farewell, going-away party, leave-taking, start, valediction

send-up imitation, mickey-take (*informal*), mockery, parody, satire, skit, spoof (*informal*), take-off (*informal*)

send up burlesque, imitate, lampoon, make fun of, mimic, mock, parody, satirize, spoof (*informal*), take off (*informal*), take the mickey out of (*informal*), take the piss out of (*taboo slang*)

senile decrepit, doddering, doting, failing, imbecile, in one's dotage, in one's second childhood

senility Alzheimer's disease, caducity, decrepitude, dotage, infirmity, loss of one's faculties, second childhood, senescence, senile dementia

senior *adjective* elder, higher ranking, major (*Brit.*), older, superior
Antonyms inferior, junior, lesser, lower, minor, subordinate, younger

senior citizen elder, O.A.P., old age pensioner, old *or* elderly person, pensioner, retired person

seniority eldership, longer service, precedence, priority, rank, superiority

sensation 1. awareness, consciousness, feeling, impression, perception, sense, tingle **2.** agitation, commotion, crowd puller (*informal*), excitement, furore, hit (*informal*), scandal, stir, surprise, thrill, vibes (*slang*), wow (*slang, chiefly U.S.*)

sensational 1. amazing, astounding, breathtaking, dramatic, electrifying, exciting, hair-raising, horrifying, lurid, melodramatic, revealing, scandalous, sensationalistic, shock-horror (*facetious*), shocking, spectacular, staggering, startling, thrilling, yellow (*of the press*) **2.** *informal* awesome (*slang*), bodacious (*slang, chiefly U.S.*), boffo (*slang*), brill (*informal*), brilliant, chillin' (*U.S. slang*), cracking (*Brit. informal*), crucial (*slang*), def (*slang*), excellent, exceptional, fabulous (*informal*), first class, impressive, jim-dandy (*slang*), marvellous, mean (*slang*), mega (*slang*), mind-blowing (*informal*), out of this world (*informal*), smashing (*informal*), sovereign, superb, topping (*Brit. slang*)
Antonyms boring, commonplace, dull, humdrum, in good taste, mediocre, no great shakes (*informal*), ordinary, prosaic, run-of-the-mill, understated, undramatic, unexaggerated, unexciting, vanilla (*informal*)

sense *noun* **1.** faculty, feeling, sensation, sensibility **2.** appreciation, atmosphere, aura, awareness, consciousness, feel, impression, intuition, perception, premonition, presentiment, sentiment **3.** definition, denotation, drift, gist, implication, import, interpretation, meaning, message, nuance, purport, significance, signification, substance **4.** *sometimes plural* brains (*informal*), clear-headedness, cleverness, common sense, discernment, discrimination, gumption (*Brit. informal*), intelligence, judgment, mother wit, nous (*Brit. slang*), quickness, reason, sagacity, sanity, sharpness, smarts (*slang, chiefly U.S.*), tact,

understanding, wisdom, wit(s) **5.** advantage, good, logic, point, purpose, reason, use, value, worth *~verb* **6.** appreciate, apprehend, be aware of, discern, divine, feel, get the impression, grasp, have a feeling in one's bones (*informal*), have a funny feeling (*informal*), have a hunch, just know, notice, observe, perceive, pick up, realize, suspect, understand
Antonyms *noun* (*sense 4*) bêtise (*rare*), folly, foolishness, idiocy, nonsense, silliness, stupidity *~verb* be unaware of, fail to grasp *or* notice, miss, misunderstand, overlook

senseless **1.** absurd, asinine, crazy, daft (*informal*), fatuous, foolish, goofy (*informal*), half-witted, idiotic, illogical, imbecilic, inane, incongruous, inconsistent, irrational, ludicrous, mad, meaningless, mindless, moronic, nonsensical, pointless, ridiculous, silly, simple, stupid, unintelligent, unreasonable, unwise, without rhyme or reason **2.** anaesthetized, cold, deadened, insensate, insensible, numb, numbed, out, out cold, stunned, unconscious, unfeeling
Antonyms conscious, intelligent, meaningful, rational, reasonable, sensible, sensitive, useful, valid, wise, worthwhile

sensibility **1.** responsiveness, sensitiveness, sensitivity, susceptibility **2.** *often plural* emotions, feelings, moral sense, sentiments, susceptibilities **3.** appreciation, awareness, delicacy, discernment, insight, intuition, perceptiveness, taste
Antonyms deadness, insensibility, insensitivity, lack of awareness, numbness, unconsciousness, unperceptiveness, unresponsiveness

sensible **1.** canny, discreet, discriminating, down-to-earth, far-sighted, intelligent, judicious, matter-of-fact, practical, prudent, rational, realistic, reasonable, sagacious, sage, sane, shrewd, sober, sound, well-reasoned, well-thought-out, wise **2.** *usually with* **of** acquainted with, alive to, aware, conscious, convinced, mindful, observant, sensitive to, understanding **3.** appreciable, considerable, discernable, noticeable, palpable, perceptible, significant, tangible, visible
Antonyms (*senses 1 & 2*) blind, daft (*informal*), foolish, idiotic, ignorant, injudicious, insensible, insensitive, irrational, senseless, silly, stupid, unaware, unmindful, unreasonable, unwise

sensitive **1.** acute, delicate, easily affected, fine, impressionable, keen, perceptive, precise, reactive, responsive, sentient, susceptible, touchy-feely (*informal*) **2.** delicate, easily upset (hurt, offended), irritable, temperamental, tender, thin-skinned, touchy, umbrageous (*rare*)
Antonyms approximate, callous, hard, hardened, imprecise, inexact, insensitive, obtuse, thick-skinned, tough, uncaring, unfeeling, unperceptive

sensitivity delicacy, reactiveness, reactivity, receptiveness, responsiveness, sensitiveness, susceptibility

sensual **1.** animal, bodily, carnal, epicurean, fleshly, luxurious, physical, unspiritual, voluptuous **2.** erotic, lascivious, lecherous, lewd, libidinous, licentious, lustful, randy (*informal, chiefly Brit.*), raunchy (*slang*), sexual, sexy (*informal*), steamy (*informal*), unchaste

sensualist *bon vivant*, bon viveur, epicure, epicurean, hedonist, pleasure-lover, sybarite, voluptuary

sensuality animalism, carnality, eroticism, lasciviousness, lecherousness, lewdness, libidinousness, licentiousness, prurience, salaciousness, sexiness (*informal*), voluptuousness

sensuous bacchanalian, epicurean, gratifying, hedonistic, lush, pleasurable, rich, sensory, sumptuous, sybaritic
Antonyms abstemious, ascetic, celibate, plain, self-denying, Spartan

sentence **1.** *noun* condemnation, decision, decree, doom, judgment, order, pronouncement, ruling, verdict **2.** *verb* condemn, doom, mete out justice to, pass judgment on, penalize

sententious **1.** aphoristic, axiomatic, brief, compact, concise, epigrammatic, gnomic, laconic, pithy, pointed, short, succinct, terse **2.** canting, judgmental, moralistic, pompous, ponderous, preachifying (*informal*), sanctimonious

sentient conscious, feeling, live, living, reactive, sensitive

sentiment **1.** emotion, sensibility, soft-heartedness, tender feeling, tenderness **2.** *often plural* attitude, belief, feeling, idea, judgment, opinion, persuasion, saying, thought, view, way of thinking **3.** emotionalism, mawkishness, overemotionalism, romanticism, sentimentality, slush (*informal*)

sentimental corny (*slang*), dewy-eyed, drippy (*informal*), emotional, gushy (*informal*), impressionable, maudlin, mawkish, mushy (*informal*), nostalgic, overemotional, pathetic, romantic, schmaltzy (*slang*), simpering, sloppy (*informal*), slushy (*informal*), soft-hearted, tearful, tear-jerking (*informal*), tender, three-hankie (*informal*), touching, weepy (*informal*)
Antonyms commonsensical, dispassionate, down-to-earth, earthy, hard-headed, practical, realistic, undemonstrative, unemotional, unfeeling, unromantic, unsentimental

sentimentality bathos, corniness (*slang*), emotionalism, gush (*informal*), mawkishness, mush (*informal*), nostalgia, pathos, play on the emotions, romanticism, schmaltz (*slang*), sloppiness (*informal*), slush (*informal*), sob stuff (*informal*), tenderness

sentinel *or* **sentry** guard, lookout, picket, watch, watchman

separable detachable, distinguishable, divisible, scissile, severable

separate *verb* **1.** break off, cleave, come apart, come away, come between, detach, disconnect, disentangle, disjoin, divide, keep apart, remove, sever, split, sunder, uncouple **2.** discriminate between, isolate, put on one side, segregate, single out, sort out **3.** bifurcate, break up, disunite, diverge, divorce, estrange, go different ways, part, part company, set at variance *or* at odds, split up *~adjective* **4.** detached, disconnected, discrete, disjointed, divided, divorced, isolated, unattached, unconnected **5.** alone, apart, autonomous, distinct, independent, individual, particular, single, solitary
Antonyms *verb* amalgamate, combine, connect, join, link, merge, mix, unite *~adjective* affiliated, alike, connected, interdependent, joined, similar, unified, united

separated apart, broken up, disassociated, disconnected, disunited, divided, living apart, parted, put asunder, separate, split up, sundered

separately alone, apart, independently, individually, one at a time, one by one, personally, severally, singly
Antonyms as a group, as one, collectively, in a body, in concert, in unison, jointly, together

separation **1.** break, detachment, disconnection, disengagement, disjunction, dissociation, disunion, division, gap, segregation, severance **2.** break-up, divorce, estrangement, farewell, leave-taking, parting, rift, split, split-up

septic festering, infected, poisoned, pussy, putrefactive, putrefying, putrid, suppurating, toxic

sepulchral **1.** cheerless, dismal, funereal, gloomy, grave, lugubrious, melancholy, morbid, mournful, sad, sombre, Stygian, woeful **2.** deep, hollow, lugubrious, reverberating, sonorous

sepulchre burial place, grave, mausoleum, sarcophagus, tomb, vault

sequel conclusion, consequence, continuation, development, end, follow-up, issue, outcome, payoff (*informal*), result, upshot

sequence arrangement, chain, course, cycle, order, procession, progression, series, succession

sequestered cloistered, isolated, lonely, out-of-the-way, private, quiet, remote, retired, secluded, unfrequented

seraphic angelic, beatific, blissful, celestial, divine, heavenly, holy, pure, sublime

serene **1.** calm, composed, imperturbable, peaceful, placid, sedate, tranquil, undisturbed, unruffled, untroubled **2.** bright, clear, cloudless, fair, halcyon, unclouded
Antonyms (*sense 1*) agitated, anxious, disturbed, excitable, flustered, perturbed, troubled, uptight (*informal*)

serenity **1.** calm, calmness, composure, peace, peacefulness, peace of mind, placidity, quietness, quietude, stillness, tranquillity **2.** brightness, clearness, fairness

serf bondsman, helot, liegeman, servant, slave, thrall, varlet (*archaic*), vassal, villein

series arrangement, chain, course, line, order, progression, run, sequence, set, string, succession, train

serious **1.** grave, humourless, long-faced, pensive, sedate, sober, solemn, stern, thoughtful, unsmiling **2.** deliberate, determined, earnest, genuine, honest, in earnest, resolute, resolved, sincere **3.** crucial, deep, difficult, far-reaching, fateful, grim, important, momentous, no laughing matter, of moment *or* consequence, pressing, significant, urgent, weighty, worrying **4.** acute, alarming, critical, dangerous, grave, severe
Antonyms capricious, carefree, flighty, flippant, frivolous, insignificant, insincere, jolly, joyful, light-hearted, minor, slight, smiling, trivial, uncommitted, undecided, unimportant

seriously **1.** all joking aside, earnestly, gravely, in all conscience, in earnest, no joking (*informal*), sincerely, solemnly, thoughtfully, with a straight face **2.** acutely, badly, critically, dangerously, distressingly, gravely, grievously, severely, sorely

seriousness **1.** earnestness, gravitas, gravity, humourlessness, sedateness, sobriety, solemnity, staidness, sternness **2.** danger, gravity, importance, moment, significance, urgency, weight

sermon **1.** address, exhortation, homily **2.** dressing-down (*informal*), harangue, lecture, talking-to (*informal*)

serpentine coiling, crooked, meandering, sinuous, snaking, snaky, tortuous, twisting, twisty, winding

serrated notched, sawlike, sawtoothed, serrate, serriform (*Biology*), serrulate, toothed

serried assembled, close, compact, dense, massed, phalanxed

servant attendant, domestic, drudge, help, helper, lackey, liegeman, maid, menial, retainer, servitor (*archaic*), skivvy (*chiefly Brit.*), slave, varlet (*archaic*), vassal

serve **1.** aid, assist, attend to, be in the service of, be of assistance, be of use, help, minister to, oblige, succour, wait on, work for **2.** act, attend, complete, discharge, do, fulfil, go through, observe, officiate, pass, perform **3.** answer, answer the purpose, be acceptable, be adequate, be good enough, content, do, do duty as, do the work of, fill the bill (*informal*), function as, satisfy, suffice, suit **4.** arrange, deal, deliver, dish up, distribute, handle, present, provide, purvey, set out, supply

They also serve who only stand and wait
John Milton *Sonnet 16*

If you would be well served, serve yourself

service *noun* **1.** advantage, assistance, avail, benefit, help, ministrations, supply, use, usefulness, utility **2.** check, maintenance, overhaul, servicing **3.** business, duty, employ, employment, labour, office, work **4.** ceremony, function, observance, rite, worship *~verb* **5.** check, fine tune, go over, maintain, overhaul, recondition, repair, tune (up)

serviceable advantageous, beneficial, convenient, dependable, durable, efficient, functional, hard-wearing, helpful, operative, practical, profitable, usable, useful, utilitarian
Antonyms impractical, inefficient, unserviceable, unusable, useless, worn-out

servile abject, base, bootlicking (*informal*), craven, cringing, fawning, grovelling, humble, low, mean, menial, obsequious, slavish, submissive, subservient, sycophantic, toadying, toadyish, unctuous

servility abjection, baseness, bootlicking (*informal*), fawning, grovelling, meanness, obsequiousness, self-abasement, slavishness, submissiveness, subservience, sycophancy, toadyism, unctuousness

serving *noun* helping, plateful, portion

servitude bondage, bonds, chains, enslavement, obedience, serfdom, slavery, subjugation, thraldom, thrall, vassalage

session assembly, conference, congress, discussion, get-together (*informal*), hearing, meeting, period, seminar, sitting, term

set[1] *verb* **1.** aim, apply, deposit, direct, embed, fasten, fix, install, lay, locate, lodge, mount, park (*informal*), place, plant, plonk, plump, position, put, rest, seat, situate, station, stick, turn **2.** agree upon, allocate, appoint, arrange, assign, conclude, decide (upon), designate, determine, establish, fix, fix up, name, ordain, regulate, resolve, schedule, settle, specify **3.** arrange, lay, make ready, prepare, spread **4.** adjust, coordinate, rectify, regulate, synchronize **5.** cake, condense, congeal, crystallize, gelatinize, harden, jell, solidify, stiffen, thicken **6.** allot, decree, impose, lay down, ordain, prescribe, specify **7.** decline, dip, disappear, go down, sink, subside, vanish *~noun* **8.** attitude, bearing, carriage, fit, hang, position, posture, turn **9.** *mise-en-scène*, scene, scenery, setting, stage set, stage setting *~adjective* **10.** agreed, appointed, arranged, customary, decided, definite, established, firm, fixed, prearranged, predetermined, prescribed, regular, scheduled, settled, usual **11.** artificial, conventional, formal, hackneyed, rehearsed, routine, standard, stereotyped, stock, traditional, unspontaneous **12.** entrenched, firm, hard and fast, hardened, hidebound, immovable, inflexible, rigid, strict, stubborn **13.** *with* **on** *or* **upon** bent, determined, intent, resolute
Antonyms (*sense 12*) flexible, free, open, open-minded, undecided

set[2] *noun* **1.** band, circle, class, clique, company, coterie, crew (*informal*), crowd, faction, gang, group, outfit, posse (*informal*), schism, sect **2.** assemblage, assortment, batch, collection, compendium, coordinated group, kit, outfit, series

set about 1. address oneself to, attack, begin, get cracking (*informal*), get down to, get to work, get weaving (*informal*), make a start on, put one's shoulder to the wheel (*informal*), roll up one's sleeves, sail into (*informal*), set to, start, tackle, take the first step, wade into **2.** assail, assault, attack, belabour, lambast(e), mug (*informal*), sail into (*informal*)

set against 1. balance, compare, contrast, juxtapose, weigh **2.** alienate, disunite, divide, drive a wedge between, estrange, make bad blood, make mischief, oppose, set at cross purposes, set at odds, set by the ears (*informal*), sow dissension

set aside 1. keep, keep back, put on one side, reserve, save, select, separate, set apart, single out **2.** abrogate, annul, cancel, discard, dismiss, nullify, overrule, overturn, quash, reject, render null and void, repudiate, reverse

setback bit of trouble, blow, bummer (*slang*), check, defeat, disappointment, hitch, hold-up, misfortune, rebuff, reverse, upset, whammy (*informal, chiefly U.S.*)

set back delay, hinder, hold up, impede, retard, slow

set off 1. depart, embark, leave, sally forth, set out, start out **2.** detonate, explode, ignite, kick-start, light, set in motion, touch off, trigger (off) **3.** bring out the highlights in, enhance, show off, throw into relief

set on assail, assault, attack, fall upon, fly at, go for, incite, instigate, let fly at, pitch into (*informal*), pounce on, sail into (*informal*), set about, sic, spur on, urge

set out 1. arrange, array, describe, detail, display, dispose, elaborate, elucidate, exhibit, explain, expose to view, lay out, present, set forth **2.** begin, embark, get under way, hit the road (*slang*), sally forth, set off, start out, take to the road

setting backdrop, background, back story, context, frame, locale, location, *mise en scène*, mounting, perspective, scene, scenery, set, site, surround, surroundings

settle **1.** adjust, dispose, order, put into order, regulate, set to rights, straighten out, work out **2.** choose, clear up, complete, conclude, decide, dispose of, put an end to, reconcile, resolve **3.** *often with* **on** *or* **upon** agree, appoint, arrange, choose, come to an agreement, confirm, decide, determine, establish, fix **4.** allay, calm, compose, lull, pacify, quell, quiet, quieten, reassure, relax, relieve, sedate, soothe, tranquillize **5.** alight, bed down, come to rest, descend, land, light, make oneself comfortable **6.** dwell, inhabit, live, make one's home, move to, put down roots, reside, set up home, take up residence **7.** colonize, found, people, pioneer, plant, populate **8.** acquit oneself of, clear, discharge, liquidate, pay, quit, square (up) **9.** decline, fall, sink, subside

Antonyms (*sense 4*) agitate, bother, discompose, disquieten, disturb, rattle, trouble, unsettle, upset

settlement **1.** adjustment, agreement, arrangement, completion, conclusion, confirmation, disposition, establishment, resolution, termination, working out **2.** clearance, clearing, defrayal, discharge, liquidation, payment, satisfaction **3.** colonization, colony, community, encampment, hamlet, outpost, peopling

settler colonist, colonizer, frontiersman, immigrant, pioneer, planter

set-to argument, argy-bargy (*Brit. informal*), barney (*informal*), brush, disagreement, dust-up (*informal*), fight, fracas, quarrel, row, scrap (*informal*), slanging match (*Brit.*), spat, squabble, wrangle

setup arrangement, circumstances, conditions, organization, regime, structure, system

set up **1.** arrange, begin, compose, establish, found, initiate, install, institute, make provision for, organize, prearrange, prepare **2.** back, build up, establish, finance, promote, put some beef into (*informal*), strengthen, subsidize **3.** assemble, build, construct, elevate, erect, put together, put up, raise

set upon ambush, assail, assault, attack, beat up, fall upon, go for, lay into (*informal*), mug (*informal*), put the boot in (*slang*), set about, turn on, work over (*slang*)

sever **1.** bisect, cleave, cut, cut in two, detach, disconnect, disjoin, disunite, divide, part, rend, separate, split, sunder **2.** abandon, break off, dissociate, dissolve, put an end to, terminate

Antonyms attach, connect, continue, fix together, join, link, maintain, unite, uphold

several *adjective* assorted, different, disparate, distinct, divers (*archaic*), diverse, indefinite, individual, manifold, many, particular, respective, single, some, sundry, various

severe **1.** austere, cruel, Draconian, drastic, hard, harsh, inexorable, iron-handed, oppressive, pitiless, relentless, rigid, strict, unbending, unrelenting **2.** cold, disapproving, dour, flinty, forbidding, grave, grim, serious, sober, stern, strait-laced, tight-lipped, unsmiling **3.** acute, bitter, critical, dangerous, distressing, extreme, fierce, grinding, inclement, intense, violent **4.** ascetic, austere, chaste, classic, forbidding, functional, plain, restrained, severe, simple, Spartan, unadorned, unembellished, unfussy **5.** arduous, demanding, difficult, exacting, fierce, hard, punishing, rigorous, stringent, taxing, tough, unrelenting **6.** astringent, biting, caustic, cutting, harsh, mordacious, mordant, satirical, scathing, unsparing, vitriolic

Antonyms (*senses 1, 2, 3, 5 & 6*) affable, clement, compassionate, easy, genial, gentle, kind, lax, lenient, manageable, mild, minor, moderate, relaxed, temperate, tractable (*sense 4*) embellished, fancy, ornamental, ornate

severely **1.** harshly, like a ton of bricks (*informal*), rigorously, sharply, sternly, strictly, with an iron hand, with a rod of iron **2.** acutely, badly, critically, dangerously, extremely, gravely, hard, seriously, sorely

severity austerity, gravity, hardness, harshness, plainness, rigour, seriousness, severeness, sternness, strictness, stringency, toughness

sex **1.** gender **2.** *informal* coition, coitus, copulation, fornication, going to bed (with someone), intimacy, legover (*slang*), lovemaking, nookie (*slang*), rumpy-pumpy (*slang*), (sexual) intercourse, sexual relations, the other (*informal*) **3.** desire, facts of life, libido, reproduction, sexuality, the birds and the bees (*informal*)

Sexual practices and terms

adultery
afterplay
algolagnia
anal intercourse, sodomy *or* buggery
anilingus
autoeroticism
bagpiping
bestiality
bisexuality
bondage
coprophilia
cottaging
cunnilingus
felching
fellatio
fetishism
fisting *or* fist-fucking
flagellation
foreplay
fornication
frottage
heterosexuality
homosexuality
impotence
incest
lesbianism
masochism

masturbation
narcissism
necrophilia
nymphomania
oral sex
paedophilia
paraphilia
pederasty
premature ejaculation
rimming
rough trade
sadism
sadomasochism *or* S&M
safe sex
satyriasis
scopophilia
shrimping
soixante-neuf *or* sixty-nine
tribadism
troilism
voyeurism
water sports, urolagnia *or* golden shower
zoophilia

The pleasure is momentary, the position ridiculous, and the expense damnable
attributed to Lord Chesterfield

When I hear his steps outside my door I lie down on my bed, close my eyes, open my legs, and think of England
Lady Hillingdon

Sexual intercourse began
In nineteen sixty-three
(Which was rather late for me) -
Between the end of the "Chatterley" ban
And the Beatles' first LP
Philip Larkin *Annus Mirabilis*

Continental people have sex lives; the English have hot-water bottles
George Mikes *How to be an Alien*

Is sex dirty? Only if it's done right
Woody Allen *Everything You Always Wanted to Know About Sex*

[Sex] was the most fun I ever had without laughing
Woody Allen *Annie Hall*

My mother used to say, Delia, if S-E-X ever rears its ugly head, close your eyes before you see the rest of it
Alan Ayckbourn *Bedroom Farce*

It doesn't matter what you do in the bedroom as long as you don't do it in the street and frighten the horses
Mrs. Patrick Campbell

While we have sex in the mind, we truly have none in the body
D.H. Lawrence *Leave Sex Alone*

sex appeal allure, desirability, glamour, it (*informal*), magnetism, oomph (*informal*), seductiveness, sensuality, sexiness (*informal*), voluptuousness

sexless androgynous, asexual, epicene, hermaphrodite, neuter, nonsexual, parthenogenetic

sexual **1.** carnal, coital, erotic, intimate, of the flesh, sensual, sexy **2.** genital, procreative, reproductive, sex, venereal

sexual intercourse bonking (*informal*), carnal knowledge, coition, coitus, commerce (*archaic*), congress, consummation, copulation, coupling, fucking (*taboo*), intimacy, legover (*slang*), mating, nookie (*slang*), penetration, rumpy-pumpy (*slang*), screwing (*taboo*), shagging (*taboo*), the other (*informal*), union

sexuality bodily appetites, carnality, desire, eroticism, lust, sensuality, sexiness (*informal*), virility, voluptuousness

sexy arousing, beddable, bedroom, come-hither (*informal*), cuddly, erotic, flirtatious, inviting, kissable, naughty, provocative, provoking, seductive, sensual, sensuous, slinky, suggestive, titillating, voluptuous

shabby **1.** dilapidated, down at heel, faded, frayed, having seen better days, mean, neglected, poor, ragged, run-down, scruffy, seedy, tattered, tatty, the worse for wear, threadbare, worn, worn-out **2.** cheap, contemptible, despicable, dirty, dishonourable, ignoble, low, low-down (*informal*), mean, rotten (*informal*), scurvy, shameful, shoddy, ungentlemanly, unworthy
Antonyms fair, generous, handsome, honourable, in mint condition, neat, new, praiseworthy, smart, well-dressed, well-kempt, well-kept, well-to-do, worthy

shack cabin, dump (*informal*), hovel, hut, lean-to, shanty, shiel (*Scot.*), shieling (*Scot.*)

shackle *noun* **1.** *often plural* bond, chain, fetter, gyve (*archaic*), handcuff, hobble, iron, leg-iron, manacle, rope, tether *~verb* **2.** bind, chain, fetter, handcuff, hobble, manacle, pinion, put in irons, secure, tether, tie, trammel **3.** constrain, embarrass, encumber, hamper, hamstring, impede, inhibit, limit, obstruct, restrain, restrict, tie (someone's) hands

shade *noun* **1.** coolness, dimness, dusk, gloom, gloominess, obscurity, screen, semidarkness, shadiness, shadow, shadows **2.** **put into the shade** eclipse, make pale by comparison, outclass, outshine, overshadow **3.** blind, canopy, cover, covering, curtain, screen, shield, veil **4.** colour, hue, stain, tinge, tint, tone **5.** amount, dash, degree, difference, gradation, graduation, hint, nuance, semblance, suggestion, suspicion, trace, variety **6.** apparition, eidolon, ghost, manes, phantom, shadow, spectre, spirit *~verb* **7.** cast a shadow over, cloud, conceal, cover, darken, dim, hide, mute, obscure, protect, screen, shadow, shield, shut out the light, veil

shadow *noun* **1.** cover, darkness, dimness, dusk, gathering darkness, gloaming (*Scot. or poetic*), gloom, obscurity, protection, shade, shelter **2.** hint, suggestion, suspicion, trace **3.** eidolon, ghost, image, phantom, remnant, representation, spectre, vestige **4.** blight, cloud, gloom, sadness *~verb* **5.** cast a shadow over, darken, overhang, screen, shade, shield

6. dog, follow, spy on, stalk, tail (*informal*), trail

shadowy 1. crepuscular, dark, dim, dusky, funereal, gloomy, indistinct, murky, obscure, shaded, shady, tenebrious, tenebrous **2.** dim, dreamlike, faint, ghostly, illusory, imaginary, impalpable, intangible, nebulous, obscure, phantom, spectral, undefined, unreal, unsubstantial, vague, wraithlike

shady 1. bosky (*literary*), bowery, cool, dim, leafy, shaded, shadowy, umbrageous **2.** *informal* crooked, disreputable, dodgy (*Brit., Austral., & N.Z. informal*), dubious, fishy (*informal*), questionable, shifty, slippery, suspect, suspicious, unethical, unscrupulous, untrustworthy

Antonyms (*sense 1*) bright, exposed, open, out in the open, sunlit, sunny, unshaded (*sense 2*) above-board, ethical, honest, honourable, reputable, respectable, straight, trustworthy, upright

shaft 1. handle, pole, rod, shank, stem, upright **2.** beam, gleam, ray, streak **3.** barb, cut, dart, gibe, sting, thrust

shaggy hairy, hirsute, long-haired, rough, tousled, unkempt, unshorn

Antonyms close-cropped, crew-cut, cropped, flat-woven, neatly-trimmed, shorn, short-haired, short-piled, smooth

shake *verb* **1.** bump, fluctuate, jar, joggle, jolt, jounce, oscillate, quake, quiver, rock, shiver, shudder, sway, totter, tremble, vibrate, waver, wobble **2.** brandish, flourish, wave **3.** *often with* **up** agitate, churn, convulse, rouse, stir **4.** discompose, distress, disturb, frighten, intimidate, move, rattle (*informal*), shock, unnerve, upset **5.** impair, pull the rug out from under (*informal*), undermine, weaken *~noun* **6.** agitation, convulsion, disturbance, jar, jerk, jolt, jounce, pulsation, quaking, shiver, shock, shudder, trembling, tremor, vibration **7.** *informal* instant, jiffy (*informal*), moment, second, tick (*Brit. informal*), trice

shake off dislodge, elude, get away from, get rid of, get shot of (*slang*), give the slip, leave behind, lose, rid oneself of, throw off

shake up agitate, churn (up), disturb, mix, overturn, reorganize, shock, stir (up), turn upside down, unsettle, upset

shaky 1. all of a quiver (*informal*), faltering, insecure, precarious, quivery, rickety, tottering, trembling, tremulous, unstable, unsteady, weak, wobbly **2.** dubious, iffy (*informal*), questionable, suspect, uncertain, undependable, unreliable, unsound, unsupported

Antonyms dependable, firm, secure, stable, steady, strong

shallow 1. *adjective, figurative* empty, flimsy, foolish, frivolous, idle, ignorant, meaningless, puerile, simple, skin-deep, slight, superficial, surface, trivial, unintelligent **2.** *noun often plural* bank, flat, sandbank, sand bar, shelf, shoal

Antonyms *adjective* analytical, comprehensive, deep, in-depth, meaningful, penetrating, perceptive, profound, searching, serious, thoughtful, weighty *~noun* abyss, chasm, deep, depth, gorge, gulf, pit, void

sham 1. *noun* counterfeit, feint, forgery, fraud, hoax, humbug, imitation, impostor, imposture, phoney *or* phony (*informal*), pretence, pretender, pseud (*informal*), wolf in sheep's clothing **2.** *adjective* artificial, bogus, counterfeit, ersatz, false, feigned, imitation, mock, phoney *or* phony (*informal*), pretended, pseud (*informal*), pseudo (*informal*), simulated, spurious, synthetic **3.** *verb* affect, assume, counterfeit, fake, feign, imitate, play possum, pretend, put on, simulate

Antonyms *noun* master, original, the genuine article, the real McCoy (*or* McKay), the real thing *~adjective* authentic, bona fide, genuine, legitimate, natural, real, sound, true, unfeigned, veritable

shambles anarchy, chaos, confusion, disarray, disorder, disorganization, havoc, madhouse, mess, muddle

shambling awkward, clumsy, lumbering, lurching, shuffling, ungainly, unsteady

shambolic anarchic, at sixes and sevens, chaotic, confused, disordered, disorganized, inefficient, in total disarray, muddled, topsy-turvy, unsystematic

shame *noun* **1.** blot, contempt, degradation, derision, discredit, disgrace, dishonour, disrepute, ill repute, infamy, obloquy, odium, opprobrium, reproach, scandal, skeleton in the cupboard, smear **2.** abashment, chagrin, compunction, embarrassment, humiliation, ignominy, loss of face, mortification, shamefacedness **3. put to shame** disgrace, eclipse, outclass, outdo, outstrip, show up, surpass *~verb* **4.** abash, confound, disconcert, disgrace, embarrass, humble, humiliate, mortify, reproach, ridicule, take (someone) down a peg (*informal*) **5.** blot, debase, defile, degrade, discredit, dishonour, smear, stain

Antonyms *noun* (*sense 1*) credit, distinction, esteem, glory, honour, pride, renown, self-respect (*sense 2*) brass neck (*Brit. informal*), brazenness, cheek, shamelessness, unabashedness *~verb* acclaim, credit, do credit to, enhance the reputation of, honour, make proud

> *It is a most miserable thing to feel ashamed of home*
>
> Charles Dickens *Great Expectations*

shamefaced 1. bashful, blushing, diffident, hesitant, modest, shrinking, shy, timid **2.**

abashed, ashamed, chagrined, conscience-stricken, contrite, discomfited, embarrassed, humiliated, mortified, red-faced, remorseful, sheepish

shameful 1. atrocious, base, dastardly, degrading, disgraceful, dishonourable, ignominious, indecent, infamous, low, mean, outrageous, reprehensible, scandalous, unbecoming, unworthy, vile, wicked 2. blush-making (*informal*), cringe-making (*Brit. informal*), degrading, embarrassing, humiliating, mortifying, shaming
Antonyms admirable, creditable, estimable, exemplary, honourable, laudable, right, worthy

shameless abandoned, audacious, barefaced, brash, brazen, corrupt, depraved, dissolute, flagrant, hardened, immodest, improper, impudent, incorrigible, indecent, insolent, profligate, reprobate, unabashed, unashamed, unblushing, unprincipled, wanton

shanty bothy (*Scot.*), cabin, hovel, hut, lean-to, shack, shed, shiel (*Scot.*), shieling (*Scot.*)

shape *noun* 1. build, configuration, contours, cut, figure, form, lines, make, outline, profile, silhouette 2. frame, model, mould, pattern 3. appearance, aspect, form, guise, likeness, semblance 4. condition, fettle, health, kilter, state, trim *~verb* 5. create, fashion, form, make, model, mould, produce 6. accommodate, adapt, convert, define, develop, devise, frame, guide, modify, plan, prepare, regulate, remodel

shapeless amorphous, asymmetrical, battered, embryonic, formless, indeterminate, irregular, misshapen, nebulous, undeveloped, unstructured
Antonyms comely, curvaceous, elegant, graceful, neat, trim, well-formed, well-proportioned, well-turned

shapely comely, curvaceous, elegant, graceful, neat, sightly, trim, well-formed, well-proportioned, well-turned

shape up be promising, come on, develop, look good, proceed, progress, turn out

share 1. *verb* apportion, assign, distribute, divide, go Dutch (*informal*), go fifty-fifty (*informal*), go halves, parcel out, partake, participate, receive, split, use in common 2. *noun* allotment, allowance, contribution, cut (*informal*), division, due, lot, part, portion, proportion, quota, ration, whack (*informal*)

sharp *adjective* 1. acute, cutting, honed, jagged, keen, knife-edged, knifelike, pointed, razor-sharp, serrated, sharpened, spiky 2. abrupt, distinct, extreme, marked, sudden 3. alert, apt, astute, bright, clever, discerning, knowing, long-headed, observant, on the ball (*informal*), penetrating, perceptive, quick, quick-witted, ready, subtle 4. artful, crafty, cunning, dishonest, fly (*slang*), shrewd, sly, smart, unscrupulous, wily 5. acute, distressing, excruciating, fierce, intense, painful, piercing, severe, shooting, sore, stabbing, stinging, violent 6. clear, clear-cut, crisp, distinct, well-defined 7. *informal* chic, classy (*slang*), dressy, fashionable, natty (*informal*), smart, snappy, stylish, trendy (*informal*) 8. acerb, acrimonious, barbed, biting, bitter, caustic, cutting, harsh, hurtful, mordacious, mordant, sarcastic, sardonic, scathing, severe, trenchant, vitriolic 9. acerb, acerbic, acetic, acid, acrid, burning, hot, piquant, pungent, sour, tart, vinegary *~adverb* 10. exactly, on the dot, on time, precisely, promptly, punctually 11. abruptly, suddenly, unexpectedly, without warning
Antonyms *adjective* (*sense 1*) blunt, dull, edgeless, pointed, rounded, unsharpened (*sense 2*) even, gentle, gradual, moderate, progressive (*sense 3*) dim, dull-witted, dumb (*informal*), slow, slow-on-the-uptake, stupid (*sense 4*) artless, guileless, ingenuous, innocent, naive, simple, undesigning (*sense 6*) blurred, fuzzy, ill-defined, indistinct, unclear (*sense 8*) amicable, courteous, friendly, gentle, kindly, mild (*sense 9*) bland, mild, tasteless *~adverb* (*sense 10*) approximately, more or less, roughly, round about, vaguely (*sense 11*) bit by bit, gently, gradually, slowly

sharpen edge, grind, hone, put an edge on, strop, whet

sharp-eyed Argus-eyed, eagle-eyed, hawk-eyed, keen-sighted, lynx-eyed

shatter 1. break, burst, crack, crush, crush to smithereens, demolish, explode, implode, pulverize, shiver, smash, split 2. blast, blight, bring to nought, demolish, destroy, disable, exhaust, impair, overturn, ruin, torpedo, wreck 3. break (someone's) heart, crush, devastate, dumbfound, knock the stuffing out of (someone) (*informal*), upset

shattered all in (*slang*), clapped out (*Austral. & N.Z. informal*), crushed, dead beat (*informal*), dead tired (*informal*), devastated, dog-tired (*informal*), done in (*informal*), drained, exhausted, jiggered (*informal*), knackered (*slang*), ready to drop, shagged out (*Brit. slang*), spent, tired out, weary, wiped out (*informal*), worn out, zonked (*slang*)

shattering crushing, devastating, overwhelming, paralysing, severe, stunning

shave *verb* 1. crop, pare, plane, shear, trim 2. brush, graze, touch

shed[1] *verb* 1. afford, cast, diffuse, drop, emit, give, give forth, pour forth, radiate, scatter, shower, spill, throw 2. cast off, discard, exuviate, moult, slough

shed² *noun* bothy (*chiefly Scot.*), hut, lean-to, lockup, outhouse, shack

sheen brightness, burnish, gleam, gloss, lustre, patina, polish, shine, shininess

sheep
Related adjective: ovine

Breeds of sheep

- Beulah Speckled-face
- bighorn *or* mountain sheep
- Blackface
- Black Welsh Mountain
- Blue-faced *or* Hexham Leicester
- Border Leicester
- Boreray
- Brecknock Hill Cheviot
- British Bleu du Maine
- British Charollais
- British Friesland
- British Milksheep
- British Oldenburg
- British Texel
- British Vendéen
- Cambridge
- Cheviot
- Clun Forest
- Colbred
- Corriedale
- Cotswold
- Dalesbred
- Dartmoor
- Derbyshire Gritstone
- Devon and Cornwall Longwool
- Devon Closewool
- Dorset Down
- Dorset Horn
- East Friesland
- English Halfbred
- Exmoor Horn
- Hampshire Down
- Hebridian *or* St. Kilda
- Herdwick
- Hill Radnor
- Île de France
- Jacob
- karakul, caracul *or* broadtail
- Kerry Hill
- Leicester Longwool
- Lincoln Longwool
- Llanwenog
- Lleyn
- Lonk
- Manx Loghtan
- Masham
- Merino
- Mule
- Norfolk Horn
- North Country Cheviot
- Orkney *or* North Ronaldsay
- Oxford *or* Oxfordshire Down
- Polwarth
- Portland
- Rambouillet
- Romney Marsh
- Rouge de l'Ouest
- Rough Fell
- Ryeland
- Scottish Blackface
- Scottish Halfbred
- Shetland
- Shropshire
- Soay
- Southdown
- South Wales Mountain
- Suffolk
- Swaledale
- Teeswater
- Texel
- Welsh Halfbred
- Welsh Hill Speckled
- Welsh Mountain
- Welsh Mountain Badger Faced
- Welsh Mule
- Wensleydale Longwool
- White Face Dartmoor
- Whitefaced Woodland
- Wiltshire Horn

He is brought as a lamb to the slaughter
Bible: Isaiah

sheepish abashed, ashamed, chagrined, embarrassed, foolish, mortified, self-conscious, shamefaced, silly, uncomfortable
Antonyms assertive, audacious, bold, brash, brass-necked (*Brit. informal*), brazen, confident, intractable, obdurate, unabashed, unapologetic, unblushing, unembarrassed

sheer **1.** abrupt, headlong (*archaic*), perpendicular, precipitous, steep **2.** absolute, arrant, complete, downright, out-and-out, pure, rank, thoroughgoing, total, unadulterated, unalloyed, unmitigated, unqualified, utter **3.** *of fabrics* diaphanous, fine, gauzy, gossamer, see-through, thin, transparent
Antonyms (*sense 1*) gentle, gradual, horizontal, moderate, slanting, sloping (*sense 3*) coarse, heavy, impenetrable, opaque, thick

sheet **1.** coat, film, folio, lamina, layer, leaf, membrane, overlay, pane, panel, piece, plate, slab, stratum, surface, veneer **2.** area, blanket, covering, expanse, stretch, sweep

shell *noun* **1.** carapace, case, husk, pod *~verb* **2.** husk, shuck **3.** attack, barrage, blitz, bomb, bombard, strafe, strike *~noun* **4.** chassis, frame, framework, hull, skeleton, structure

shell out ante up (*informal, chiefly U.S.*), disburse, expend, fork out (*slang*), give, hand over, lay out (*informal*), pay out

shelter **1.** *verb* cover, defend, guard, harbour, hide, protect, safeguard, seek refuge, shield, take in, take shelter **2.** *noun* asylum, awning, cover, covert, defence, guard, haven, protection, refuge, retreat, roof over one's head, safety, sanctuary, screen, security, shiel (*Scot.*), umbrella
Antonyms *verb* endanger, expose, hazard, imperil, lay open, leave open, make vulnerable, risk, subject

sheltered cloistered, conventual, ensconced, hermitic, isolated, protected, quiet, reclusive, retired, screened, secluded, shaded, shielded, withdrawn
Antonyms exposed, laid bare, made public, open, public, unconcealed, unprotected, unsheltered

shelve defer, dismiss, freeze, hold in abeyance, hold over, lay aside, mothball, pigeonhole, postpone, put aside, put off, put on ice, put on the back burner (*informal*), suspend, table (*U.S.*), take a rain check on (*U.S. & Canad. informal*)

shepherd *verb* conduct, convoy, guide, herd, marshal, steer, usher

The Lord is my shepherd; I shall not want
Bible: Psalm 23

shield *noun* **1.** buckler, escutcheon (*Heraldry*), targe (*archaic*) **2.** aegis, bulwark, cover, defence, guard, protection, rampart, safeguard, screen, shelter, ward (*archaic*) *~verb* **3.** cover, defend, guard, protect, safeguard, screen, shelter, ward off

shift *verb* **1.** alter, budge, change, displace, fluctuate, move, move around, rearrange, relocate, remove, reposition, swerve, switch, transfer, transpose, vary, veer **2.** *As in* **shift for oneself** assume responsibility, contrive, devise, fend, get along, look after, make do, manage, plan, scheme, take care of *~noun* **3.** about-turn, alteration, change, displacement, fluctuation, modification, move, permutation, rearrangement, removal, shifting, switch, transfer, veering **4.** artifice, contrivance, craft, device, dodge, equivocation, evasion, expedi~ ent, move, resource, ruse, stratagem, subter~ fuge, trick, wile

shiftless aimless, good-for-nothing, idle, in~ competent, indolent, inefficient, inept, irre~ sponsible, lackadaisical, lazy, slothful, unam~ bitious, unenterprising

shifty contriving, crafty, deceitful, devious, du~ plicitous, evasive, fly-by-night (*informal*), fur~ tive, scheming, slippery, sly, tricky, under~ hand, unprincipled, untrustworthy, wily
Antonyms dependable, guileless, honest, hon~ ourable, open, reliable, trustworthy, upright

shillyshally *verb* be irresolute *or* indecisive, dilly-dally (*informal*), dither (*chiefly Brit.*), falter, fluctuate, haver (*Brit.*), hem and haw, hesitate, hum and haw, seesaw, swither (*Scot.*), vacillate, waver, yo-yo (*informal*)

shimmer **1.** *verb* dance, gleam, glisten, phos~ phoresce, scintillate, twinkle **2.** *noun* diffused light, gleam, glimmer, glow, incandescence, iridescence, lustre, phosphorescence, unsteady light

shin *verb* ascend, clamber, climb, scale, scram~ ble, swarm

shine *verb* **1.** beam, emit light, flash, give off light, glare, gleam, glimmer, glisten, glitter, glow, radiate, scintillate, shimmer, sparkle, twinkle **2.** be conspicuous (distinguished, out~ standing, pre-eminent), excel, stand out, stand out in a crowd, star, steal the show **3.** brush, buff, burnish, polish, rub up *~noun* **4.** bright~ ness, glare, gleam, lambency, light, luminos~ ity, radiance, shimmer, sparkle **5.** glaze, gloss, lustre, patina, polish, sheen

shining **1.** beaming, bright, brilliant, effulgent, gleaming, glistening, glittering, luminous, ra~ diant, resplendent, shimmering, sparkling **2.** *figurative* brilliant, celebrated, conspicuous, distinguished, eminent, glorious, illustrious, leading, outstanding, splendid

shiny agleam, bright, burnished, gleaming, glistening, glossy, lustrous, nitid (*poetic*), pol~ ished, satiny, sheeny

ship boat, craft, vessel

ships that pass in the night
Henry Wadsworth Longfellow *Tales of a Way~ side Inn*

shipshape Bristol fashion, businesslike, neat, orderly, spick-and-span, tidy, trig (*archaic or dialect*), trim, uncluttered, well-ordered, well-organized, well-regulated

shirk avoid, bob off (*Brit. slang*), body-swerve (*Scot.*), dodge, duck (out of) (*informal*), evade, get out of, scrimshank (*Brit. military slang*), shun, sidestep, skive (*Brit. slang*), slack

shirker clock-watcher, dodger, gold brick (*U.S. slang*), idler, malingerer, quitter, scrim~ shanker (*Brit. military slang*), shirk, skiver (*Brit. slang*), slacker

shiver[1] *verb* **1.** palpitate, quake, quiver, shake, shudder, tremble *~noun* **2.** flutter, *frisson*, quiver, shudder, thrill, tremble, trembling, tremor **3.** **the shivers** chattering teeth, chill, goose flesh, goose pimples, the shakes (*infor~ mal*)

shiver[2] *verb* break, crack, fragment, shatter, smash, smash to smithereens, splinter

shivery chilled, chilly, cold, quaking, quivery, shaking, shuddery, trembly

shoal sandbank, sand bar, shallow, shelf

shock *verb* **1.** agitate, appal, astound, disgust, disquiet, give (someone) a turn (*informal*), gross out (*U.S. slang*), horrify, jar, jolt, nau~ seate, numb, offend, outrage, paralyse, raise eyebrows, revolt, scandalize, shake, shake out of one's complacency, shake up (*informal*), sicken, stagger, stun, stupefy, traumatize, unsettle *~noun* **2.** blow, bolt from the blue, bombshell, breakdown, collapse, consternation, distress, disturbance, prostration, rude awak~ ening, state of shock, stupefaction, stupor, trauma, turn (*informal*), upset, whammy (*in~ formal, chiefly U.S.*) **3.** blow, clash, collision, encounter, impact, jarring, jolt

shocking abominable, appalling, atrocious, de~ testable, disgraceful, disgusting, disquieting, distressing, dreadful, foul, frightful, from hell (*informal*), ghastly, hellacious (*U.S. slang*), hideous, horrible, horrifying, loathsome, mon~ strous, nauseating, obscene, odious, offensive, outrageous, repulsive, revolting, scandalous, sickening, stupefying, unspeakable, X-rated (*informal*)
Antonyms admirable, decent, delightful, ex~ cellent, expected, fine, first-rate, gratifying, honourable, laudable, marvellous, pleasant, praiseworthy, satisfying, unsurprising, won~ derful

shoddy cheap-jack (*informal*), cheapo (*infor~ mal*), inferior, junky (*informal*), low-rent (*in~ formal, chiefly U.S.*), poor, rubbishy, second-rate, slipshod, tacky (*informal*), tatty, tawdry, trashy
Antonyms accurate, careful, considerate, craftsman-like, excellent, fastidious, fine, first-rate, meticulous, noble, quality, superla~ tive, well-made

shoemaker bootmaker, cobbler, souter (*Scot.*)

shoot[1] *verb* **1.** bag, blast (*slang*), blow away (*slang, chiefly U.S.*), bring down, hit, kill, open fire, pick off, plug (*slang*), pump full of lead (*slang*), zap (*slang*) **2.** discharge, emit, fire, fling, hurl, launch, let fly, project, propel **3.** barrel (along) (*informal, chiefly U.S. & Canad.*), bolt, burn rubber (*informal*), charge, dart, dash, flash, fly, hurtle, race, rush, scoot, speed, spring, streak, tear, whisk, whiz (*informal*)

shoot[2] **1.** *noun* branch, bud, offshoot, scion, slip, sprig, sprout, twig **2.** *verb* bud, burgeon, germinate, put forth new growth, sprout

shop boutique, emporium, hypermarket, market, mart, store, supermarket

shore *noun* beach, coast, foreshore, lakeside, sands, seaboard (*chiefly U.S.*), seashore, strand (*poetic*), waterside
Related adjective: littoral

shore (up) augment, brace, buttress, hold, prop, reinforce, strengthen, support, underpin

short *adjective* **1.** abridged, brief, clipped, compendious, compressed, concise, curtailed, laconic, pithy, sententious, succinct, summary, terse **2.** diminutive, dumpy, fubsy (*archaic or dialect*), knee high to a gnat (grasshopper), little, low, petite, small, squat, wee **3.** brief, fleeting, momentary, short-lived, short-term **4.** *often with* **of** deficient, inadequate, insufficient, lacking, limited, low (on), meagre, poor, scant, scanty, scarce, short-handed, slender, slim, sparse, strapped (for) (*slang*), tight, wanting **5.** abrupt, blunt, brusque, crusty, curt, discourteous, gruff, impolite, offhand, sharp, terse, testy, uncivil **6.** direct, straight **7.** *of pastry* brittle, crisp, crumbly, friable ~*adverb* **8.** abruptly, by surprise, suddenly, unaware, without warning **9. cut short** abbreviate, arrest, butt in, curtail, cut in on, dock, halt, interrupt, nip (something) in the bud, reduce, stop, terminate **10. fall short** be inadequate, disappoint, fail, fall down on (*informal*), not come up to expectations *or* scratch (*informal*) **11. in short** briefly, in a nutshell, in a word, in essence, to come to the point, to cut a long story short, to put it briefly **12. short of a.** apart from, except, other than, unless **b.** deficient in, in need of, lacking, low (on), missing, wanting
Antonyms *adjective* (*sense 1*) diffuse, lengthy, long, long-drawn-out, long-winded, prolonged, rambling, unabridged, verbose, wordy (*sense 2*) big, high, lanky, lofty, tall (*sense 3*) extended, long, long-term (*sense 4*) abundant, adequate, ample, bountiful, copious, inexhaustible, plentiful, sufficient, well-stocked (*sense 5*) civil, courteous, polite ~*adverb* (*sense 8*) bit by bit, gently, gradually, little by little, slowly

shortage dearth, deficiency, deficit, failure, inadequacy, insufficiency, lack, leanness, paucity, poverty, scarcity, shortfall, want
Antonyms abundance, adequate amount, excess, overabundance, plethora, profusion, sufficiency, surfeit, surplus

shortcoming defect, drawback, failing, fault, flaw, foible, frailty, imperfection, weakness, weak point

shorten abbreviate, abridge, curtail, cut, cut back, cut down, decrease, diminish, dock, downsize, lessen, prune, reduce, trim, truncate, turn up
Antonyms draw out, elongate, expand, extend, increase, lengthen, make longer, prolong, protract, spin out, stretch

short-lived brief, ephemeral, fleeting, impermanent, passing, short, temporary, transient, transitory

shortly 1. anon (*archaic*), any minute now, before long, erelong (*archaic or poetic*), in a little while, presently, soon **2.** abruptly, curtly, sharply, tartly, tersely **3.** briefly, concisely, in a few words, succinctly

short-sighted 1. blind as a bat, myopic, near-sighted **2.** careless, ill-advised, ill-considered, impolitic, impractical, improvident, imprudent, injudicious, seeing no further than (the end of) one's nose, unthinking

short-staffed below strength, short-handed, undermanned, understaffed

short-tempered choleric, fiery, hot-tempered, impatient, irascible, peppery, quick-tempered, ratty (*Brit. & N.Z. informal*), testy, touchy

shot[1] *noun* **1.** discharge, lob, pot shot, throw **2.** ball, bullet, lead, pellet, projectile, slug **3.** marksman, shooter **4.** *informal* attempt, chance, conjecture, crack (*informal*), effort, endeavour, essay, go (*informal*), guess, opportunity, stab (*informal*), surmise, try, turn **5. by a long shot a.** by far, easily, far and away, indubitably, undoubtedly, without doubt **b.** by any means, in any circumstances, on any account **6. have a shot** *informal* attempt, have a go (bash (*informal*), crack (*informal*), stab (*informal*)) (*informal*), tackle, try, try one's luck **7. like a shot** at once, eagerly, immediately, like a bat out of hell (*slang*), like a flash, quickly, unhesitatingly **8. shot in the arm** *informal* boost, encouragement, fillip, impetus, lift, stimulus

shot[2] *adjective* iridescent, moiré, opalescent, watered

shoulder *noun* **1. give (someone) the cold shoulder** cut (*informal*), ignore, kick in the teeth (*slang*), ostracize, put down, rebuff, send (someone) to Coventry, shun, snub **2. put one's shoulder to the wheel** *informal* apply oneself, buckle down to (*informal*), exert oneself, get down to, make every effort, set to work, strive **3.** **rub shoulders with** *informal* associate with, consort with, fraternize with, hobnob with, mix with, socialize with **4.** **shoulder to shoulder** as one, in cooperation, in partnership, in unity, jointly, side by side, together, united **5.** **straight from the shoulder** candidly, directly, frankly, man to man, outright, plainly, pulling no punches (*informal*), straight, unequivocally, with no holds barred *~verb* **6.** accept, assume, bear, be responsible for, carry, take on, take upon oneself **7.** elbow, jostle, press, push, shove, thrust

shoulder blade scapula

shout **1.** *noun* bellow, call, cry, roar, scream, yell **2.** *verb* bawl, bay, bellow, call (out), cry (out), holler (*informal*), hollo, raise one's voice, roar, scream, yell

shout down drown, drown out, overwhelm, silence

shove *verb* crowd, drive, elbow, impel, jostle, press, propel, push, shoulder, thrust

shovel *verb* convey, dredge, heap, ladle, load, move, scoop, shift, spoon, toss

shove off bugger off (*taboo slang*), clear off (*informal*), depart, fuck off (*offensive taboo slang*), get on one's bike (*Brit. slang*), go away, go to hell (*informal*), leave, pack one's bags (*informal*), push off (*informal*), scram (*informal*), sling one's hook (*Brit. slang*), slope off, take oneself off, vamoose (*slang, chiefly U.S.*)

show *verb* **1.** appear, be visible, blow wide open (*slang*), disclose, display, divulge, evidence, evince, exhibit, indicate, make known, manifest, present, register, reveal, testify to **2.** assert, clarify, demonstrate, elucidate, evince, explain, instruct, point out, present, prove, teach **3.** accompany, attend, conduct, escort, guide, lead **4.** accord, act with, bestow, confer, grant *~noun* **5.** array, demonstration, display, exhibition, expo (*informal*), exposition, fair, manifestation, pageant, pageantry, parade, representation, sight, spectacle, view **6.** affectation, air, appearance, display, illusion, likeness, ostentation, parade, pose, pretence, pretext, profession, semblance **7.** entertainment, presentation, production
Antonyms (*senses 1 & 2*) be invisible, conceal, deny, disprove, gainsay (*archaic or literary*), hide, keep secret, mask, obscure, refute, suppress, veil, withhold

showdown breaking point, clash, climax, confrontation, crisis, culmination, *dénouement*, exposé, face-off (*slang*), moment of truth

shower *noun* **1.** *figurative* barrage, deluge, downpour, fusillade, plethora, rain, stream, torrent, volley **2.** *Brit. slang* bunch of layabouts, crew, rabble *~verb* **3.** deluge, heap, inundate, lavish, load, pour, rain, spray, sprinkle

showing *noun* **1.** demonstration, display, exhibition, presentation, staging **2.** account of oneself, appearance, demonstration, impression, performance, show, track record **3.** evidence, representation, statement

showman entertainer, impresario, performer, publicist, stage manager

show-off boaster, braggadocio, braggart, egotist, exhibitionist, hot dog (*chiefly U.S.*), peacock, poseur, swaggerer

show off **1.** advertise, demonstrate, display, exhibit, flaunt, parade, spread out **2.** blow one's own trumpet, boast, brag, hot-dog (*chiefly U.S.*), make a spectacle of oneself, shoot a line (*informal*), strut one's stuff (*chiefly U.S.*), swagger

show up **1.** expose, highlight, lay bare, pinpoint, put the spotlight on, reveal, unmask **2.** appear, be conspicuous, be visible, catch the eye, leap to the eye, stand out **3.** *informal* embarrass, let down, mortify, put to shame, shame, show in a bad light **4.** *informal* appear, arrive, come, make an appearance, put in an appearance, show one's face, turn up

showy brash, flamboyant, flash (*informal*), flashy, garish, gaudy, loud, ostentatious, over the top (*informal*), pompous, pretentious, splashy (*informal*), tawdry, tinselly
Antonyms discreet, low-key, muted, quiet, restrained, subdued, tasteful, unobtrusive

shred *noun* **1.** bit, fragment, piece, rag, ribbon, scrap, sliver, snippet, tatter **2.** *figurative* atom, grain, iota, jot, particle, scrap, trace, whit

shrew ballbreaker (*slang*), dragon (*informal*), fury, harridan, nag, scold, spitfire, termagant (*rare*), virago, vixen, Xanthippe

It is better to dwell in a corner of the housetop, than with a brawling woman in a wide house
Bible: Proverbs

A continual dropping in a very rainy day and a contentious woman are alike
Bible: Proverbs

shrewd acute, artful, astute, calculated, calculating, canny, clever, crafty, cunning, discerning, discriminating, far-seeing, far-sighted, fly (*slang*), intelligent, keen, knowing, long-headed, perceptive, perspicacious, sagacious, sharp, sly, smart, wily
Antonyms artless, dull, gullible, imprudent, ingenuous, innocent, naive, obtuse, slow-witted, stupid, trusting, undiscerning, unsophisticated, unworldly

shrewdly artfully, astutely, cannily, cleverly, far-sightedly, knowingly, perceptively, perspicaciously, sagaciously, with all one's wits about one, with consummate skill

shrewdness acumen, acuteness, astuteness, canniness, discernment, grasp, judgment, penetration, perspicacity, quick wits, sagacity, sharpness, smartness, suss (*slang*)

shrewish bad-tempered, cantankerous, complaining, discontented, fault-finding, ill-humoured, ill-natured, ill-tempered, litigious, nagging, peevish, petulant, quarrelsome, scolding, sharp-tongued, vixenish

shriek *verb/noun* cry, holler, howl, scream, screech, squeal, wail, whoop, yell

shrill acute, ear-piercing, ear-splitting, high, high-pitched, penetrating, piercing, piping, screeching, sharp
Antonyms deep, dulcet, mellifluous, silver-toned, soft, soothing, sweet-sounding, velvety, well-modulated

shrink **1.** contract, decrease, deflate, diminish, downsize, drop off, dwindle, fall off, grow smaller, lessen, narrow, shorten, shrivel, wither, wrinkle **2.** cower, cringe, draw back, flinch, hang back, quail, recoil, retire, shy away, wince, withdraw
Antonyms (*sense 1*) balloon, dilate, distend, enlarge, expand, increase, inflate, mushroom, stretch, swell (*sense 2*) attack, challenge, confront, embrace, face, receive, welcome

shrivel **1.** burn, dry (up), parch, scorch, sear **2.** dehydrate, desiccate, dwindle, shrink, wilt, wither, wizen, wrinkle

shrivelled desiccated, dried up, dry, sere (*archaic*), shrunken, withered, wizened, wrinkled

shroud *verb* **1.** blanket, cloak, conceal, cover, envelop, hide, screen, swathe, veil *~noun* **2.** cerecloth, cerement, covering, grave clothes, winding sheet **3.** cloud, mantle, pall, screen, veil

shudder **1.** *verb* convulse, quake, quiver, shake, shiver, tremble **2.** *noun* convulsion, quiver, spasm, trembling, tremor

shuffle **1.** drag, scrape, scuff, scuffle, shamble **2.** confuse, disarrange, disorder, intermix, jumble, mix, rearrange, shift **3.** *usually with* **off** *or* **out** of beat about the bush, beg the question, cavil, dodge, equivocate, evade, flannel (*Brit. informal*), gloss over, hedge, prevaricate, pussyfoot (*informal*), quibble

shun avoid, body-swerve (*Scot.*), cold-shoulder, elude, eschew, evade, fight shy of, give (someone *or* something) a wide berth, have no part in, keep away from, shy away from, steer clear of

shut **1.** bar, close, draw to, fasten, push to, seal, secure, slam **2.** *with* **in, out,** *etc.* cage, confine, enclose, exclude, impound, imprison, pound, wall off *or* up
Antonyms open, throw wide, unbar, unclose, undo, unfasten, unlock

shut down cease, cease operating, close, discontinue, halt, shut up, stop, switch off

shut out **1.** bar, black, blackball, debar, exclude, keep out, lock out, ostracize **2.** block out, conceal, cover, hide, mask, screen, veil

shuttle *verb* alternate, commute, go back and forth, go to and fro, ply, seesaw, shunt

shut up **1.** bottle up, box in, cage, confine, coop up, immure, imprison, incarcerate, intern, keep in **2.** *informal* be quiet, button it (*slang*), button one's lip (*slang*), cut the cackle (*informal*), fall silent, gag, hold one's tongue, hush, keep one's trap shut (*slang*), muzzle, pipe down (*slang*), put a sock in it (*Brit. slang*), silence

shy[1] **1.** *adjective* backward, bashful, cautious, chary, coy, diffident, distrustful, hesitant, modest, mousy, nervous, reserved, reticent, retiring, self-conscious, self-effacing, shrinking, suspicious, timid, wary **2.** *verb sometimes with* **off** *or* **away** balk, buck, draw back, flinch, quail, rear, recoil, start, swerve, take fright, wince
Antonyms *adjective* assured, bold, brash, cheeky, confident, fearless, forward, pushy (*informal*), rash, reckless, self-assured, self-confident, unsuspecting, unwary

shy[2] *verb* cast, chuck (*informal*), fling, hurl, lob (*informal*), pitch, propel, send, sling, throw, toss

shyness bashfulness, diffidence, lack of confidence, modesty, mousiness, nervousness, reticence, self-consciousness, timidity, timidness, timorousness

sibyl Cassandra, oracle, prophetess, Pythia, pythoness, seer

sick **1.** green about the gills (*informal*), green around the gills (*informal*), ill, nauseated, nauseous, puking (*slang*), qualmish, queasy **2.** ailing, diseased, feeble, indisposed, laid up (*informal*), on the sick list (*informal*), poorly (*informal*), under par (*informal*), under the weather, unwell, weak **3.** *informal* black, ghoulish, macabre, morbid, sadistic **4.** *informal often with* **of** blasé, bored, disgusted, displeased, fed up, jaded, revolted, satiated, tired, weary
Antonyms (*senses 1 & 2*) able-bodied, fine, fit, fit and well, fit as a fiddle, hale and hearty, healthy, robust, tranquil, untroubled, unworried, up to par, well

sicken **1.** disgust, gross out (*U.S. slang*), make one's gorge rise, nauseate, repel, revolt, turn one's stomach **2.** ail, be stricken by, contract, fall ill, go down with, show symptoms of, take sick

sickening cringe-making (*Brit. informal*), disgusting, distasteful, foul, loathsome, nauseating, nauseous, noisome, offensive, putrid, re~

pulsive, revolting, stomach-turning (*informal*), vile, yucky *or* yukky (*slang*)
Antonyms curative, delightful, health-giving, heartening, inviting, marvellous, mouth-watering, pleasant, salutary, tempting, thera~peutic, wholesome, wonderful

sickly **1.** ailing, bilious, bloodless, delicate, faint, feeble, indisposed, infirm, in poor health, lacklustre, languid, pallid, peaky, pin~ing, unhealthy, wan, weak **2.** bilious (*infor~mal*), cloying, icky (*informal*), mawkish, nau~seating, revolting (*informal*), syrupy (*infor~mal*)

sickness **1.** barfing (*U.S. slang*), (the) colly~wobbles (*slang*), nausea, queasiness, puking (*slang*), vomiting **2.** affliction, ailment, bug (*informal*), complaint, disease, disorder, ill~ness, indisposition, infirmity, lurgi (*informal*), malady

side *noun* **1.** border, boundary, division, edge, limit, margin, part, perimeter, periphery, rim, sector, verge **2.** aspect, face, facet, flank, hand, part, surface, view **3.** angle, light, opinion, point of view, position, slant, stand, stand~point, viewpoint **4.** camp, cause, faction, party, sect, team **5.** *Brit. slang* airs, arrogance, inso~lence, pretentiousness *~adjective* **6.** flanking, lateral **7.** ancillary, incidental, indirect, lesser, marginal, minor, oblique, roundabout, second~ary, subordinate, subsidiary *~verb* **8.** *usually with* **with** ally with, associate oneself with, befriend, favour, go along with, join with, se~cond, support, take the part of, team up with (*informal*)
Antonyms *noun* (*sense 1*) centre, core, heart, middle *~adjective* central, essential, focal, fundamental, key, main, middle, primary, principal *~verb* counter, oppose, stand against, withstand
There are two sides to every question

sideline **1.** border, boundary, edge, fringe, margin, periphery **2.** subsidiary, supplement

sidelong *adjective* covert, indirect, oblique, sideways

side-splitting farcical, hilarious, hysterical, rollicking, uproarious

sidestep avoid, body-swerve (*Scot.*), bypass, circumvent, dodge, duck (*informal*), elude, evade, find a way round, skip, skirt

sidetrack deflect, distract, divert, lead off the subject

sideways **1.** *adverb* crabwise, edgeways, later~ally, obliquely, sidelong, sidewards, to the side **2.** *adjective* oblique, side, sidelong, slanted

sidle creep, edge, inch, slink, sneak, steal

siesta catnap, doze, forty winks (*informal*), kip (*Brit. slang*), nap, rest, sleep, snooze (*infor~mal*), zizz (*Brit. informal*)

sieve **1.** *noun* colander, riddle, screen, sifter, strainer, tammy cloth **2.** *verb* bolt, remove, riddle, separate, sift, strain

sift **1.** bolt, filter, pan, part, riddle, separate, sieve **2.** analyse, examine, fathom, go through, investigate, pore over, probe, research, screen, scrutinize, work over

sigh *verb* **1.** breathe, complain, grieve, lament, moan, sorrow, sough, suspire (*archaic*) **2.** *often with* **for** eat one's heart out over, languish, long, mourn, pine, yearn

sight *noun* **1.** eye, eyes, eyesight, seeing, vision **2.** appearance, apprehension, eyeshot, field of vision, ken, perception, range of vision, view, viewing, visibility **3.** display, exhibition, pag~eant, scene, show, spectacle, vista **4.** *informal* blot on the landscape (*informal*), eyesore, fright (*informal*), mess, monstrosity, spectacle **5.** **catch sight of** descry, espy, glimpse, rec~ognize, spot, view *~verb* **6.** behold, discern, distinguish, make out, observe, perceive, see, spot
Related adjective: visual
Out of sight, out of mind

sign *noun* **1.** clue, evidence, gesture, giveaway, hint, indication, manifestation, mark, note, proof, signal, spoor, suggestion, symptom, to~ken, trace, vestige **2.** board, notice, placard, warning **3.** badge, character, cipher, device, emblem, ensign, figure, logo, mark, represen~tation, symbol **4.** augury, auspice, foreboding, forewarning, omen, portent, presage, warning, writing on the wall *~verb* **5.** autograph, en~dorse, initial, inscribe, set one's hand to, sub~scribe **6.** beckon, gesticulate, gesture, indicate, signal, use sign language, wave

signal **1.** *noun* beacon, cue, flare, gesture, go-ahead (*informal*), green light, indication, indi~cator, mark, sign, token **2.** *adjective* conspicu~ous, distinguished, eminent, exceptional, extraordinary, famous, memorable, momen~tous, notable, noteworthy, outstanding, re~markable, serious (*informal*), significant, striking **3.** *verb* beckon, communicate, gesticu~late, gesture, give a sign to, indicate, motion, nod, sign, wave

sign away abandon, dispose of, forgo, give up all claim to, lose, relinquish, renounce, sur~render, transfer, waive

significance **1.** force, implication(s), import, meaning, message, point, purport, sense, sig~nification **2.** consequence, consideration, im~portance, impressiveness, matter, moment, relevance, weight

significant **1.** denoting, eloquent, expressing, expressive, indicative, knowing, meaning, meaningful, pregnant, suggestive **2.** critical, important, material, momentous, noteworthy, serious, vital, weighty

Antonyms immaterial, inconsequential, insignificant, irrelevant, meaningless, nit-picking, nugatory, of no consequence, paltry, petty, trivial, unimportant, worthless

signify 1. announce, be a sign of, betoken, communicate, connote, convey, denote, evidence, exhibit, express, imply, indicate, intimate, matter, mean, portend, proclaim, represent, show, stand for, suggest, symbolize 2. *informal* be of importance *or* significance, carry weight, count, matter

sign on *or* **up** 1. contract with, enlist, enrol, join, join up, register, volunteer 2. employ, engage, hire, put on the payroll, recruit, take into service, take on, take on board (*informal*)

silence *noun* 1. calm, hush, lull, noiselessness, peace, quiescence, quiet, stillness 2. dumbness, muteness, reticence, speechlessness, taciturnity, uncommunicativeness *~verb* 3. cut off, cut short, deaden, extinguish, gag, muffle, quell, quiet, quieten, stifle, still, strike dumb, subdue, suppress

Antonyms *noun* babble, bawling, cacophony, chatter, clamour, din, garrulousness, hubbub, loquaciousness, murmuring, noise, prattle, racket, shouting, sound, speech, talk, talking, tumult, uproar, verbosity, whispering, yelling *~verb* amplify, broadcast, champion, disseminate, encourage, foster, make louder, promote, promulgate, publicize, rouse, spread, support, ungag

Silence is the virtue of fools
Francis Bacon *Advancement of Learning*

Silence is more eloquent than words
Thomas Carlyle *Heroes and Hero-Worship*

Silence is golden

Silence means consent

silent 1. hushed, muted, noiseless, quiet, soundless, still, stilly (*poetic*) 2. dumb, mum, mute, nonvocal, not talkative, speechless, struck dumb, taciturn, tongue-tied, uncommunicative, unspeaking, voiceless, wordless 3. aphonic (*Phonetics*), implicit, implied, tacit, understood, unexpressed, unpronounced, unspoken

silently as quietly as a mouse (*informal*), dumbly, inaudibly, in silence, mutely, noiselessly, quietly, soundlessly, speechlessly, without a sound, wordlessly

silhouette 1. *noun* delineation, form, outline, profile, shape 2. *verb* delineate, etch, outline, stand out

silky silken, sleek, smooth, velvety

silly *adjective* 1. absurd, asinine, brainless, childish, dopy (*slang*), dozy (*Brit. informal*), fatuous, foolhardy, foolish, frivolous, giddy, goofy (*informal*), idiotic, immature, imprudent, inane, inappropriate, irresponsible, meaningless, pointless, preposterous, puerile, ridiculous, senseless, stupid, unwise, witless 2. *informal* benumbed, dazed, groggy (*informal*), in a daze, muzzy, stunned, stupefied *~noun* 3. *informal* clot (*Brit. informal*), duffer (*informal*), dweeb (*U.S. slang*), goose (*informal*), ignoramus, nerd *or* nurd (*slang*), ninny, nitwit (*informal*), plonker (*slang*), prat (*slang*), silly-billy (*informal*), simpleton, twit (*informal*), wally (*slang*)

Antonyms *adjective* acute, aware, bright, clever, intelligent, mature, perceptive, profound, prudent, reasonable, sane, sensible, serious, smart, thoughtful, well-thought-out, wise

silt 1. *noun* alluvium, deposit, ooze, residue, sediment, sludge 2. *verb usually with* **up** choke, clog, congest, dam

silver 1. *adjective* argent (*poetic*), pearly, silvered, silvery 2. *noun* silver plate, silverware

similar alike, analogous, close, comparable, congruous, corresponding, cut from the same cloth, homogeneous, homogenous, in agreement, much the same, of a piece, resembling, uniform

Antonyms antithetical, clashing, contradictory, contrary, different, disparate, dissimilar, diverse, heterogeneous, irreconcilable, opposite, unalike, unrelated, various, varying

similarity affinity, agreement, analogy, closeness, comparability, concordance, congruence, correspondence, likeness, point of comparison, relation, resemblance, sameness, similitude

Antonyms antithesis, contradictoriness, difference, disagreement, discordance, discrepancy, disparity, dissimilarity, diversity, heterogeneity, incomparability, irreconcilability, unalikeness, variation, variety

Birds of a feather flock together

similarly by the same token, correspondingly, in like manner, likewise

simmer *verb, figurative* be angry (agitated, tense, uptight (*informal*)) boil, burn, fume, rage, see red (*informal*), seethe, smart, smoulder

simmer down calm down, collect oneself, contain oneself, control oneself, cool off *or* down, get down off one's high horse (*informal*), grow quieter, unwind (*informal*)

simper grimace, smile affectedly (coyly, self-consciously), smirk, titter

simpering *adjective* affected, coy, self-conscious

simple 1. clear, easy, easy-peasy (*slang*), elementary, intelligible, lucid, manageable, plain, straightforward, uncomplicated, understandable, uninvolved 2. classic, clean, natural, plain, severe, Spartan, unadorned, uncluttered, unembellished, unfussy 3. elementary, pure, single, unalloyed, unblended, uncombined, undivided, unmixed 4. artless, childlike, frank, green, guileless, ingenuous, innocent, naive, natural, simplistic, sincere, unaffected, unpretentious, unsophisticated **5**. bald, basic, direct, frank, honest, naked, plain, sincere, stark, undeniable, unvarnished **6**. homely, humble, lowly, modest, rustic, unpretentious **7**. brainless, credulous, dense, dumb (*informal*), feeble, feeble-minded, foolish, half-witted, moronic, obtuse, shallow, silly, slow, stupid, thick

Antonyms (*senses 1 & 3*) advanced, complex, complicated, convoluted, difficult, elaborate, highly developed, intricate, involved, refined, sophisticated (*senses 2, 4 & 6*) artful, contrived, elaborate, extravagant, fancy, flashy, fussy, intricate, ornate, smart, sophisticated, worldly, worldly-wise (*sense 7*) astute, bright, clever, intelligent, knowing, on the ball, quick, quick on the uptake, quick-witted, sharp, smart, wise

simple-minded 1. a bit lacking (*informal*), addle-brained, backward, brainless, dead from the neck up (*informal*), dim-witted, feeble-minded, foolish, idiot, idiotic, moronic, retarded, simple, stupid **2**. artless, natural, unsophisticated

simpleton berk (*Brit. slang*), blockhead, booby, charlie (*Brit. informal*), coot, dickhead (*slang*), dickwit (*slang*), dipstick (*Brit. slang*), divvy (*Brit. slang*), dolt, dope (*informal*), dork (*slang*), dullard, dunce, dweeb (*U.S. slang*), fathead (*informal*), fool, fuckwit (*taboo slang*), geek (*slang*), gobshite (*Irish taboo slang*), gonzo (*slang*), goose (*informal*), greenhorn (*informal*), idiot, imbecile (*informal*), jackass, jerk (*slang, chiefly U.S. & Canad.*), moron, nerd *or* nurd (*slang*), nincompoop, ninny, nitwit (*informal*), numpty (*Scot. informal*), numskull *or* numbskull, oaf, plank (*Brit. slang*), schmuck (*U.S. slang*), Simple Simon, stupid (*informal*), twerp *or* twirp (*informal*), twit (*informal, chiefly Brit.*), wally (*slang*), weenie (*U.S. informal*)

simplicity 1. absence of complications, clarity, clearness, ease, easiness, elementariness, obviousness, straightforwardness **2**. clean lines, lack of adornment, modesty, naturalness, plainness, purity, restraint **3**. artlessness, candour, directness, guilelessness, innocence, lack of sophistication, naivety, openness

Antonyms (*sense 1*) complexity, complicatedness, difficulty, intricacy, lack of clarity (*sense 2*) decoration, elaborateness, embellishment, fanciness, fussiness, ornateness, ostentation (*sense 3*) brains, craftiness, cunning, deviousness, guile, insincerity, knowingness, sharpness, slyness, smartness, sophistication, wariness, wisdom, worldliness

simplify abridge, decipher, disentangle, facilitate, make intelligible, reduce to essentials, streamline

simplistic naive, oversimplified

simply 1. clearly, directly, easily, intelligibly, modestly, naturally, plainly, straightforwardly, unaffectedly, unpretentiously, without any elaboration **2**. just, merely, only, purely, solely **3**. absolutely, altogether, completely, really, totally, unreservedly, utterly, wholly

simulate act, affect, assume, counterfeit, fabricate, feign, imitate, make believe, pretend, put on, reproduce, sham

simulated 1. artificial, fake, imitation, man-made, mock, pseudo (*informal*), sham, substitute, synthetic **2**. artificial, assumed, feigned, insincere, make-believe, phoney *or* phony (*informal*), pretended, put-on

simultaneous at the same time, coincident, coinciding, concurrent, contemporaneous, synchronous

simultaneously all together, at the same time, concurrently, in chorus, in concert, in the same breath, in unison, together

sin 1. *noun* crime, damnation, error, evil, guilt, iniquity, misdeed, offence, sinfulness, transgression, trespass, ungodliness, unrighteousness, wickedness, wrong, wrongdoing **2**. *verb* err, fall, fall from grace, go astray, lapse, offend, transgress, trespass (*archaic*)

Seven deadly sins

anger	gluttony
covetousness *or* avarice	lust
envy	pride
	sloth

I count religion but a childish toy
And hold there is no sin but ignorance
Christopher Marlowe *The Jew of Malta*

Be sure your sin will find you out
Bible: Numbers

I used to be Snow White - but I drifted
Mae West

The wages of sin is death
Bible: Romans

more sinn'd against than sinning
William Shakespeare *King Lear*

There's no such thing as an original sin
Elvis Costello *I'm not Angry*

Though your sins be as scarlet, they shall be as white as snow
Bible: Isaiah

He that toucheth pitch shall be defiled therewith
Bible: Ecclesiasticus

If we say that we have no sin, we decieve ourselves, and the truth is not in us
Bible: I John

It is public scandal that constitutes offence, and to sin in secret is not to sin at all
Molière *Le Tartuffe*

Old sins cast long shadows

sincere artless, bona fide, candid, earnest, frank, genuine, guileless, heartfelt, honest, natural, no-nonsense, open, real, serious, straightforward, true, unaffected, unfeigned, upfront (*informal*), wholehearted
Antonyms affected, artful, artificial, deceitful, deceptive, dishonest, false, feigned, hollow, insincere, phoney *or* phony (*informal*), pretended, put on, synthetic, token, two-faced

sincerely earnestly, from the bottom of one's heart, genuinely, honestly, in all sincerity, in earnest, in good faith, really, seriously, truly, wholeheartedly

sincerity artlessness, bona fides, candour, frankness, genuineness, good faith, guilelessness, honesty, probity, seriousness, straightforwardness, truth, wholeheartedness

sinecure cushy number (*informal*), gravy train (*slang*), money for jam *or* old rope (*informal*), soft job (*informal*), soft option

sinewy athletic, brawny, lusty, muscular, powerful, robust, strong, sturdy, vigorous, wiry

sinful bad, corrupt, criminal, depraved, erring, guilty, immoral, iniquitous, irreligious, morally wrong, ungodly, unholy, unrighteous, wicked
Antonyms beatified, blessed, chaste, decent, free from sin, godly, holy, honest, honourable, immaculate, moral, pure, righteous, sinless, spotless, unblemished, upright, virtuous, without sin

sing 1. carol, chant, chirp, croon, make melody, pipe, trill, vocalize, warble, yodel 2. *slang, chiefly U.S.* betray, blow the whistle (on) (*informal*), fink (on) (*slang, chiefly U.S.*), grass (*Brit. slang*), inform (on), peach (*slang*), rat (on) (*informal*), shop (*slang, chiefly Brit.*), spill one's guts (*slang*), spill the beans (*informal*), squeal (*slang*), tell all, turn in (*informal*) 3. buzz, hum, purr, whine, whistle

singe burn, char, scorch, sear

singer balladeer, cantor, chanteuse (*fem.*), chorister, crooner, minstrel, soloist, songster, songstress, troubadour, vocalist

single *adjective* 1. distinct, individual, lone, one, only, particular, separate, singular, sole, solitary, unique 2. free, unattached, unmarried, unwed 3. exclusive, individual, separate, simple, unblended, uncompounded, undivided, unmixed, unshared *~verb* 4. *usually with* **out** choose, cull, distinguish, fix on, pick, pick on *or* out, put on one side, select, separate, set apart, winnow

single-handed alone, by oneself, independently, on one's own, solo, unaided, unassisted, under one's own steam, without help

single-minded dedicated, determined, dogged, fixed, hellbent (*informal*), monomaniacal, steadfast, stubborn, tireless, undeviating, unswerving, unwavering

singly individually, one at a time, one by one, separately

sing out call (out), cooee, cry (out), halloo, holler (*informal*), make oneself heard, shout, shout ahoy, yell

singsong *adjective* droning, monotone, monotonous, repetitious, toneless

singular 1. conspicuous, eminent, exceptional, notable, noteworthy, outstanding, prodigious, rare, remarkable, uncommon, unique, unparalleled 2. atypical, curious, eccentric, extraordinary, odd, oddball (*informal*), out-of-the-way, outré, peculiar, puzzling, queer, strange, unusual, wacko (*slang*) 3. individual, separate, single, sole
Antonyms common, common or garden, commonplace, conventional, everyday, familiar, normal, routine, run-of-the-mill, unexceptional, unremarkable, usual

singularity 1. abnormality, curiousness, extraordinariness, irregularity, oddness, peculiarity, queerness, strangeness 2. eccentricity, idiosyncrasy, oddity, particularity, peculiarity, quirk, twist

singularly conspicuously, especially, exceptionally, extraordinarily, notably, outstandingly, particularly, prodigiously, remarkably, seriously (*informal*), surprisingly, uncommonly, unusually

sinister baleful, bodeful, dire, disquieting, evil, forbidding, injurious, malevolent, malign, malignant, menacing, ominous, threatening
Antonyms auspicious, benevolent, benign, calming, encouraging, good, heartening, heroic, honourable, just, noble, promising, propitious, reassuring, righteous, upright, worthy

sink *verb* 1. cave in, decline, descend, dip, disappear, droop, drop, drown, ebb, engulf, fall, founder, go down, go under, lower, merge, plummet, plunge, sag, slope, submerge, subside 2. abate, collapse, drop, fall, lapse, relapse, retrogress, slip, slump, subside 3. decay, decline, decrease, degenerate, depreciate, deteriorate, die, diminish, dwindle, fade, fail, flag, go downhill (*informal*), lessen, weaken, worsen 4. bore, dig, drill, drive, excavate, lay, put down 5. be the ruin of, defeat, destroy, finish, overwhelm, ruin, scupper (*Brit. slang*), seal the doom of 6. be reduced to, debase oneself, lower oneself, stoop, succumb
Antonyms (*senses 1, 2 & 3*) arise, ascend, climb, enlarge, go up, grow, improve, increase, intensify, move up, rise, rise up, swell, wax

sink in be understood, get through to, make an impression, penetrate, register (*informal*), take hold of

sinless faultless, guiltless, immaculate, innocent, pure, unblemished, uncorrupted, undefiled, unsullied, virtuous, without fault, without sin

sinner evildoer, malefactor, miscreant, offender, reprobate, transgressor, trespasser (*archaic*), wrongdoer

sinuous coiling, crooked, curved, curvy, lithe, mazy, meandering, serpentine, supple, tortuous, twisty, undulating, winding

sip **1.** *verb* sample, sup, taste **2.** *noun* drop, swallow, taste, thimbleful

siren charmer, Circe, *femme fatale*, Lorelei, seductress, temptress, vamp (*informal*), witch

sissy **1.** *noun* baby, coward, jessie (*Scot. slang*), milksop, milquetoast (*U.S.*), mollycoddle, mummy's boy, namby-pamby, pansy, sisspot (*informal*), softy (*informal*), weakling, wet (*Brit. informal*), wimp (*informal*) **2.** *adjective* cowardly, effeminate, feeble, namby-pamby, sissified (*informal*), soft (*informal*), unmanly, weak, wet (*Brit. informal*), wimpish *or* wimpy (*informal*)

sit **1.** be seated, perch, rest, settle, take a seat, take the weight off one's feet **2.** assemble, be in session, convene, deliberate, meet, officiate, preside **3.** accommodate, contain, have space for, hold, seat

site **1.** *noun* ground, location, place, plot, position, setting, spot **2.** *verb* install, locate, place, position, set, situate

sitting *noun* congress, consultation, get-together (*informal*), hearing, meeting, period, session

situation **1.** locale, locality, location, place, position, seat, setting, site, spot **2.** ball game (*informal*), case, circumstances, condition, kettle of fish (*informal*), lie of the land, plight, scenario, state, state of affairs, status quo, the picture (*informal*) **3.** rank, sphere, station, status **4.** berth (*informal*), employment, job, office, place, position, post

sixth sense clairvoyance, feyness, intuition, second sight

sizable *or* **sizeable** considerable, decent, decent-sized, goodly, large, largish, respectable, substantial, tidy (*informal*)

size amount, bigness, bulk, dimensions, extent, greatness, hugeness, immensity, largeness, magnitude, mass, measurement(s), proportions, range, vastness, volume

size up appraise, assess, evaluate, eye up, get (something) taped (*Brit. informal*), get the measure of, take stock of

sizzle crackle, frizzle, fry, hiss, spit, sputter

skedaddle abscond, beat a hasty retreat, bolt, decamp, disappear, do a bunk (*Brit. slang*), flee, hook it (*slang*), hop it (*Brit. slang*), run away, scarper (*Brit. slang*), scoot, scram (*informal*), scurry away, scuttle away, vamoose (*slang, chiefly U.S.*)

skeletal cadaverous, emaciated, fleshless, gaunt, hollow-cheeked, lantern-jawed, skin-and-bone (*informal*), wasted, worn to a shadow

skeleton *figurative* bare bones, bones, draft, frame, framework, outline, sketch, structure

sketch **1.** *verb* block out, delineate, depict, draft, draw, outline, paint, plot, portray, represent, rough out **2.** *noun* delineation, design, draft, drawing, outline, plan, skeleton

sketchily cursorily, hastily, imperfectly, incompletely, patchily, perfunctorily, roughly

sketchy bitty, cobbled together, crude, cursory, inadequate, incomplete, outline, perfunctory, rough, scrappy, skimpy, slight, superficial, unfinished, vague
Antonyms complete, detailed, full, thorough

skewwhiff askew, aslant, cockeyed (*informal*), crooked, out of true, squint (*informal*), tilted

skilful able, accomplished, adept, adroit, apt, clever, competent, dexterous, experienced, expert, handy, masterly, practised, professional, proficient, quick, ready, skilled, trained
Antonyms amateurish, awkward, bungling, cack-handed, clumsy, cowboy (*informal*), ham-fisted, incompetent, inept, inexperienced, inexpert, maladroit, slapdash, unaccomplished, unqualified, unskilful, unskilled

skill ability, accomplishment, adroitness, aptitude, art, cleverness, competence, craft, dexterity, experience, expertise, expertness, facility, finesse, handiness, ingenuity, intelligence, knack, proficiency, quickness, readiness, skilfulness, talent, technique
Antonyms awkwardness, brute force, cack-handedness, clumsiness, gaucheness, ham-fistedness, inability, incompetence, ineptitude, inexperience, lack of finesse, maladroitness, unhandiness

skilled able, accomplished, a dab hand at (*Brit. informal*), experienced, expert, masterly, practised, professional, proficient, skilful, trained
Antonyms amateurish, cowboy (*informal*), inexperienced, inexpert, uneducated, unprofessional, unqualified, unskilled, untalented, untrained

skim **1.** cream, separate **2.** brush, coast, dart, float, fly, glide, sail, soar **3.** *usually with* **through** glance, run one's eye over, scan, skip (*informal*), thumb *or* leaf through

skimp be mean with, be niggardly, be sparing with, cut corners, pinch, scamp, scant, scrimp, stint, tighten one's belt, withhold
Antonyms act as if one had money to burn, be extravagant, be generous with, be prodigal, blow (*slang*), fritter away, lavish, overspend,

pour on, splurge, squander, throw money away

skimpy exiguous, inadequate, insufficient, meagre, miserly, niggardly, scant, scanty, short, sparse, thin, tight

skin *noun* **1.** fell, hide, integument, pelt, tegument **2.** casing, coating, crust, film, husk, membrane, outside, peel, rind **3. by the skin of one's teeth** by a hair's-breadth, by a narrow margin, by a whisker (*informal*), narrowly, only just **4. get under one's skin** aggravate (*informal*), annoy, get in one's hair (*informal*), get on one's nerves (*informal*), grate on, irk, irritate, needle (*informal*), nettle, piss one off (*taboo slang*), rub up the wrong way ~*verb* **5.** abrade, bark, excoriate, flay, graze, peel, scrape

skin-deep artificial, external, meaningless, on the surface, shallow, superficial, surface

skinflint meanie *or* meany (*informal, chiefly Brit.*), miser, niggard, penny-pincher (*informal*), Scrooge, tight-arse (*taboo slang*), tight-ass (*U.S. taboo slang*), tightwad (*U.S. & Canad. slang*)

skinny emaciated, lean, macilent (*rare*), scraggy, skeletal, skin-and-bone (*informal*), thin, twiggy, undernourished

Antonyms beefy (*informal*), broad in the beam (*informal*), fat, fleshy, heavy, obese, plump, podgy, portly, stout, tubby

skip *verb* **1.** bob, bounce, caper, cavort, dance, flit, frisk, gambol, hop, prance, trip **2.** eschew, give (something) a miss, leave out, miss out, omit, pass over, skim over **3.** *informal* bunk off (*slang*), cut (*informal*), dog it *or* dog off (*dialect*), miss, play truant from, wag (*dialect*)

skirmish **1.** *noun* affair, affray (*Law*), battle, brush, clash, combat, conflict, contest, dust-up (*informal*), encounter, engagement, fracas, incident, scrap (*informal*), scrimmage, set-to (*informal*), spat, tussle **2.** *verb* clash, collide, come to blows, scrap (*informal*), tussle

skirt *verb* **1.** border, edge, flank, lie alongside **2.** *often with* **around** *or* **round** avoid, body-swerve (*Scot.*), bypass, circumvent, detour, evade, steer clear of ~*noun* **3.** *often plural* border, edge, fringe, hem, margin, outskirts, periphery, purlieus, rim

skit burlesque, parody, sketch, spoof (*informal*), takeoff (*informal*), travesty, turn

skittish excitable, fickle, fidgety, frivolous, highly strung, jumpy, lively, nervous, playful, restive

Antonyms calm, composed, demure, laid-back, placid, relaxed, sober, staid, steady, unexcitable, unfazed (*informal*), unflappable, unruffled

skive *verb* bob off (*Brit. slang*), dodge, goldbrick (*U.S. slang*), idle, malinger, scrimshank (*Brit. military slang*), shirk, skulk, slack, swing the lead

skiver dodger, do-nothing, gold brick (*U.S. slang*), idler, loafer, scrimshanker (*Brit. military slang*), shirker, slacker

skulduggery double-dealing, duplicity, fraudulence, machinations, shenanigan(s) (*informal*), swindling, trickery, underhandedness, unscrupulousness

skulk creep, lie in wait, loiter, lurk, pad, prowl, slink, sneak

sky *noun* **1.** azure (*poetic*), empyrean (*poetic*), firmament, heavens, upper atmosphere, vault of heaven, welkin (*archaic*) **2. to the skies** excessively, extravagantly, fulsomely, highly, immoderately, inordinately, profusely

slab chunk, hunk, lump, nugget, piece, portion, slice, wedge, wodge (*Brit. informal*)

slack *adjective* **1.** baggy, easy, flaccid, flexible, lax, limp, loose, not taut, relaxed **2.** asleep on the job (*informal*), easy-going, idle, inactive, inattentive, lax, lazy, neglectful, negligent, permissive, remiss, slapdash, slipshod, tardy **3.** dull, inactive, quiet, slow, slow-moving, sluggish ~*noun* **4.** excess, give (*informal*), leeway, looseness, play, room ~*verb* **5.** bob off (*Brit. slang*), dodge, flag, idle, neglect, relax, shirk, skive (*Brit. slang*), slacken

Antonyms *adjective* (*sense 1*) inflexible, rigid, stiff, strained, stretched, taut, tight (*senses 2 & 3*) active, bustling, busy, concerned, diligent, exacting, fast-moving, hard, hard-working, hectic, meticulous, stern, strict

slacken (off) abate, decrease, diminish, drop off, ease (off), lessen, let up, loosen, moderate, reduce, relax, release, slack off, slow down, tire

slacker dodger, do-nothing, gold brick (*U.S. slang*), good-for-nothing, idler, layabout, loafer, passenger, scrimshanker (*Brit. military slang*), shirker, skiver (*Brit. slang*)

slag (off) *verb* abuse, berate, criticise, deride, insult, lambast(e), malign, mock, slam, slander, slang, slate

slake assuage, gratify, quench, sate, satiate, satisfy

slam **1.** bang, crash, dash, fling, hurl, smash, throw, thump **2.** *slang* attack, blast, castigate, criticize, damn, excoriate, lambast(e), pan (*informal*), pillory, shoot down (*informal*), slate (*informal*), tear into (*informal*), vilify

slander **1.** *noun* aspersion, backbiting, calumny, defamation, detraction, libel, misrepresentation, muckraking, obloquy, scandal, smear **2.** *verb* backbite, blacken (someone's) name, calumniate, decry, defame, detract, disparage, libel, malign, muckrake, slur, smear, traduce, vilify

Antonyms *noun* acclaim, acclamation, ap~

proval, laudation, praise, tribute *~verb* acclaim, applaud, approve, compliment, eulogize, laud, praise, sing the praises of

Throw enough dirt and some will stick

Give a dog a bad name and hang him

slanderous abusive, calumnious, damaging, defamatory, libellous, malicious

slang *verb* abuse, berate, call names, hurl insults at, insult, inveigh against, malign, rail against, revile, vilify, vituperate

slanging match altercation, argument, argy-bargy (*Brit. informal*), barney (*informal*), battle of words, ding-dong, quarrel, row, set-to (*informal*), spat

slant *verb* **1.** angle off, bend, bevel, cant, heel, incline, lean, list, shelve, skew, slope, tilt *~noun* **2.** camber, declination, diagonal, gradient, incline, pitch, rake, ramp, slope, tilt *~verb* **3.** angle, bias, colour, distort, twist, weight *~noun* **4.** angle, attitude, bias, emphasis, leaning, one-sidedness, point of view, prejudice, viewpoint

slanting angled, aslant, asymmetrical, at an angle, atilt, bent, canted, cater-cornered (*U.S. informal*), diagonal, inclined, oblique, on the bias, sideways, slanted, slantwise, sloping, tilted, tilting

slap *noun* **1.** bang, blow, chin (*slang*), clout (*informal*), cuff, deck (*slang*), lay one on (*slang*), smack, spank, wallop (*informal*), whack **2. a slap in the face** affront, blow, humiliation, insult, put-down, rebuff, rebuke, rejection, repulse, snub *~verb* **3.** bang, clap, clout (*informal*), cuff, hit, spank, strike, whack **4.** *informal* daub, plaster, plonk, spread *~adverb* **5.** *informal* bang, directly, exactly, plumb (*informal*), precisely, slap-bang (*informal*), smack (*informal*)

slapdash careless, clumsy, disorderly, haphazard, hasty, hurried, last-minute, messy, negligent, perfunctory, slipshod, sloppy (*informal*), slovenly, thoughtless, thrown-together, untidy
Antonyms careful, conscientious, fastidious, meticulous, ordered, orderly, painstaking, precise, punctilious, thoughtful, tidy

slap down bring to heel, put (someone) in his place, rebuke, reprimand, restrain, squash

slaphappy **1.** casual, haphazard, happy-go-lucky, hit-or-miss (*informal*), irresponsible, nonchalant **2.** dazed, giddy, punch-drunk, reeling, woozy (*informal*)

slapstick *noun* buffoonery, farce, horseplay, knockabout comedy

slap-up elaborate, excellent, first-rate, fit for a king, lavish, luxurious, magnificent, no-expense-spared, princely, splendid, sumptuous, superb

slash **1.** *verb* cut, gash, hack, lacerate, rend, rip, score, slit **2.** *noun* cut, gash, incision, laceration, rent, rip, slit **3.** *verb* cut, drop, lower, reduce

slashing aggressive, biting, brutal, ferocious, harsh, savage, searing, vicious

slate *verb* berate, blame, blast, castigate, censure, criticize, excoriate, haul over the coals (*informal*), lambas(t)e, lay into (*informal*), pan (*informal*), pitch into (*informal*), rail against, rap (someone's) knuckles, rebuke, roast (*informal*), scold, slam (*slang*), slang, take to task, tear into (*informal*), tear (someone) off a strip (*informal*)

slattern drab (*archaic*), sloven, slut, trollop

slatternly bedraggled, dirty, draggletailed (*archaic*), frowzy, slipshod, sloppy (*informal*), slovenly, sluttish, unclean, unkempt, untidy

slaughter *noun* **1.** blood bath, bloodshed, butchery, carnage, extermination, holocaust, killing, liquidation, massacre, murder, slaying *~verb* **2.** butcher, destroy, do to death, exterminate, kill, liquidate, massacre, murder, put to the sword, slay, take out (*slang*) **3.** *informal* blow out of the water (*slang*), crush, defeat, hammer (*informal*), lick (*informal*), overwhelm, rout, stuff (*slang*), tank (*slang*), thrash, trounce, undo, vanquish, wipe the floor with (*informal*)

slaughterhouse abattoir, butchery, shambles

slave **1.** *noun* bondservant, bondsman, drudge, scullion (*archaic*), serf, servant, skivvy (*chiefly Brit.*), slavey (*Brit. informal*), varlet (*archaic*), vassal, villein **2.** *verb* drudge, grind (*informal*), skivvy (*Brit.*), slog, sweat, toil, work one's fingers to the bone

slaver dribble, drool, salivate, slobber

slavery bondage, captivity, enslavement, serfdom, servitude, subjugation, thraldom, thrall, vassalage
Antonyms emancipation, freedom, liberty, manumission, release

Slavery they can have anywhere. It is a weed that grows on every soil
Edmund Burke *On Conciliation with America*

That state is a state of slavery in which a man does what he likes to do in his spare time and in his working time that which is required of him
Eric Gill *Art-nonsense and Other Essays*

slavish **1.** abject, base, cringing, despicable, fawning, grovelling, low, mean, menial, obsequious, servile, submissive, sycophantic **2.** conventional, imitative, second-hand, unimaginative, uninspired, unoriginal
Antonyms assertive, creative, domineering, imaginative, independent, inventive, masterful, original, radical, rebellious, revolutionary, self-willed, wilful

slay **1.** annihilate, assassinate, butcher, destroy, dispatch, do away with, do in (*slang*), eliminate, exterminate, kill, massacre, mow down, murder, rub out (*U.S. slang*), slaughter **2.** *informal* amuse, be the death of (*informal*), impress, make a hit with (*informal*), wow (*slang, chiefly U.S.*)

sleazy crummy, disreputable, low, run-down, seedy, sordid, squalid, tacky (*informal*)

sleek glossy, lustrous, shiny, smooth, well-fed, well-groomed
Antonyms badly groomed, bedraggled, dishevelled, frowzy, ill-nourished, in poor condition, ratty (*informal*), rough, shaggy, sloppy, slovenly, unkempt

sleep 1. *verb* be in the land of Nod, catnap, doze, drop off (*informal*), drowse, go out like a light, hibernate, kip (*Brit. slang*), nod off (*informal*), rest in the arms of Morpheus, slumber, snooze (*informal*), snore, take a nap, take forty winks (*informal*), zizz (*Brit. informal*) **2.** *noun* beauty sleep (*informal*), dormancy, doze, forty winks (*informal*), hibernation, kip (*Brit. slang*), nap, repose, rest, shuteye (*slang*), siesta, slumber(s), snooze (*informal*), zizz (*Brit. informal*)

Oh Sleep! it is a gentle thing,
Beloved from pole to pole,
To Mary Queen the praise be given!
She sent the gentle sleep from Heaven,
That slid into my soul.
Samuel Taylor Coleridge *The Ancient Mariner*

Come, sleep, O sleep, the certain knot of peace,
The baiting place of wit, the balm of woe
Philip Sidney *Astrophil and Stella*

to sleep: perchance to dream
William Shakespeare *Hamlet*

sleep the twin of death
Homer *Iliad*

The sleep of a labouring man is sweet
Bible: Ecclesiastes

Care-charmer Sleep, son of the sable Night,
Brother to Death, in silent darkness born
Samuel Daniel *Delia*

Care-charming Sleep, thou easer of all woes,
Brother to Death
John Fletcher *Wit Without Money*

I sleep like a baby. I wake up every 10 minutes screaming
Boris Jordan

One hour's sleep before midnight is worth two after

sleepiness doziness, drowsiness, heaviness, lethargy, somnolence, torpor

sleepless 1. disturbed, insomniac, restless, unsleeping, wakeful **2.** alert, unsleeping, vigilant, watchful, wide awake

sleeplessness insomnia, wakefulness

sleepwalker noctambulist, somnambulist

sleepwalking noctambulation, noctambulism, somnambulation, somnambulism

sleepy 1. drowsy, dull, heavy, inactive, lethargic, sluggish, slumbersome, somnolent, torpid **2.** dull, hypnotic, inactive, quiet, sleep-inducing, slow, slumberous, somnolent, soporific
Antonyms active, alert, alive and kicking, animated, attentive, awake, boisterous, bustling, busy, energetic, full of beans (*informal*), lively, restless, thriving, wakeful, wide-awake

sleight of hand adroitness, artifice, dexterity, legerdemain, manipulation, prestidigitation, skill

slender 1. lean, narrow, slight, slim, svelte, sylphlike, willowy **2.** inadequate, inconsiderable, insufficient, little, meagre, scant, scanty, small, spare **3.** faint, feeble, flimsy, fragile, poor, remote, slight, slim, tenuous, thin, weak
Antonyms ample, appreciable, bulky, chubby, considerable, fat, generous, good, heavy, large, podgy, solid, stout, strong, substantial, tubby, well-built

sleuth detective, dick (*slang, chiefly U.S.*), gumshoe (*U.S. slang*), private eye (*informal*), (private) investigator, sleuthhound (*informal*), tail (*informal*)

slice 1. *noun* cut, helping, piece, portion, segment, share, sliver, wedge **2.** *verb* carve, cut, divide, sever

slick *adjective* **1.** glib, meretricious, plausible, polished, smooth, sophistical, specious **2.** adroit, deft, dexterous, dextrous, polished, professional, sharp, skilful *~verb* **3.** make glossy, plaster down, sleek, smarm down (*Brit. informal*), smooth
Antonyms *adjective* amateur, amateurish, clumsy, crude, inexpert, unaccomplished, unpolished, unprofessional, unskilful

slide *verb* **1.** coast, glide, glissade, skim, slip, slither, toboggan, veer **2. let slide** forget, gloss over, ignore, let ride, neglect, pass over, push to the back of one's mind, turn a blind eye to

slight *adjective* **1.** feeble, inconsiderable, insignificant, insubstantial, meagre, measly, minor, modest, negligible, paltry, scanty, small, superficial, trifling, trivial, unimportant, weak **2.** delicate, feeble, fragile, lightly-built, slim, small, spare *~verb* **3.** affront, cold-shoulder, despise, disdain, disparage, give offence *or* umbrage to, ignore, insult, neglect, put down, scorn, show disrespect for, snub, treat with contempt *~noun* **4.** affront, contempt, discourtesy, disdain, disregard, disrespect, inattention, indifference, insult, neglect, rebuff, slap in the face (*informal*), snub, (the) cold shoulder
Antonyms *adjective* appreciable, considerable, great, heavy, important, large, muscular, noticeable, obvious, significant, solid, strong, sturdy, substantial, well-built *~verb* compli~

ment, flatter, praise, speak well of, treat considerately ~*noun* compliment, flattery, praise

slighting belittling, derogatory, disdainful, disparaging, disrespectful, insulting, offensive, scornful, supercilious, uncomplimentary

slightly a little, marginally, on a small scale, somewhat, to some extent *or* degree

slim *adjective* **1.** lean, narrow, slender, slight, svelte, sylphlike, thin, trim **2.** faint, poor, remote, slender, slight ~*verb* **3.** diet, lose weight, reduce, slenderize (*chiefly U.S.*)
Antonyms *adjective* broad, bulky, chubby, fat, good, heavy, muscular, obese, overweight, strong, sturdy, tubby, well-built, wide ~*verb* build oneself up, put on weight

slimy **1.** clammy, gloopy (*informal*), glutinous, miry, mucous, muddy, oozy, viscous **2.** creeping, grovelling, obsequious, oily, servile, smarmy (*Brit. informal*), soapy (*slang*), sycophantic, toadying, unctuous

sling *verb* **1.** cast, chuck (*informal*), fling, heave, hurl, lob (*informal*), shy, throw, toss **2.** dangle, hang, suspend, swing

slink creep, prowl, pussyfoot (*informal*), skulk, slip, sneak, steal

slinky clinging, close-fitting, feline, figure-hugging, sinuous, skintight, sleek

slip[1] *verb* **1.** glide, skate, slide, slither **2.** fall, lose one's balance, miss *or* lose one's footing, skid, trip (over) **3.** conceal, creep, hide, insinuate oneself, sneak, steal **4.** *sometimes with* **up** blunder, boob (*Brit. slang*), drop a brick *or* clanger (*informal*), err, go wrong, make a mistake, miscalculate, misjudge, mistake **5.** break away from, break free from, disappear, escape, get away, get clear of, take French leave **6. let slip** blurt out, come out with (*informal*), disclose, divulge, give away, leak, let out (*informal*), let the cat out of the bag, reveal ~*noun* **7.** bloomer (*Brit. informal*), blunder, boob (*Brit. slang*), error, failure, fault, faux pas, imprudence, indiscretion, lapse, mistake, omission, oversight, slip of the tongue, slip-up (*informal*) **8. give (someone) the slip** dodge, elude, escape from, evade, get away from, lose (someone), outwit, shake (someone) off

slip[2] *noun* **1.** piece, sliver, strip **2.** cutting, offshoot, runner, scion, shoot, sprig, sprout

slippery **1.** glassy, greasy, icy, lubricious (*rare*), perilous, skiddy (*informal*), slippy (*informal or dialect*), smooth, unsafe, unstable, unsteady **2.** crafty, cunning, devious, dishonest, duplicitous, evasive, false, foxy, shifty, sneaky, treacherous, tricky, two-faced, unpredictable, unreliable, untrustworthy

slipshod careless, casual, loose, slapdash, sloppy (*informal*), slovenly, unsystematic, untidy

slit **1.** *verb* cut (open), gash, impale, knife, lance, pierce, rip, slash, split open **2.** *noun* cut, fissure, gash, incision, opening, rent, split, tear

slither *verb* glide, skitter, slide, slink, slip, snake, undulate

sliver *noun* flake, fragment, paring, shaving, shred, slip, splinter

slob boor, churl, couch potato (*slang*), lout, oaf, yahoo, yob (*Brit. slang*)

slobber *verb* dribble, drivel, drool, salivate, slabber (*dialect*), slaver, water at the mouth

slobbish messy, slatternly, sloppy (*informal*), slovenly, unclean, unkempt, untidy

slog *verb* **1.** hit, hit for six, punch, slosh (*Brit. slang*), slug, sock (*slang*), strike, thump, wallop (*informal*) **2.** apply oneself to, keep one's nose to the grindstone, labour, peg away at, persevere, plod, plough through, slave, sweat blood (*informal*), toil, tramp, trek, trudge, work, work one's fingers to the bone ~*noun* **3.** blood, sweat, and tears (*informal*), effort, exertion, hike, labour, struggle, tramp, trek, trudge

slogan catch-phrase, catchword, jingle, motto, rallying cry

slop *verb* overflow, slosh (*informal*), spatter, spill, splash, splatter

slop around *or* **about** flop, loaf, lollop, lounge, shamble, shuffle, slouch, slump, sprawl, veg out (*slang, chiefly U.S.*)

slope *verb* **1.** drop away, fall, incline, lean, pitch, rise, slant, tilt ~*noun* **2.** brae (*Scot.*), declination, declivity, descent, downgrade (*chiefly U.S.*), gradient, inclination, incline, ramp, rise, scarp, slant, tilt ~*verb* **3.** *with* **off, away,** *etc.* creep, make oneself scarce, skulk, slink, slip, steal

sloping atilt, bevelled, cant, inclined, inclining, leaning, oblique, slanting

sloppy **1.** sludgy, slushy, splashy, watery, wet **2.** *informal* amateurish, careless, clumsy, hit-or-miss (*informal*), inattentive, messy, slipshod, slovenly, unkempt, untidy, weak **3.** banal, gushing, mawkish, mushy (*informal*), overemotional, sentimental, slushy (*informal*), soppy (*Brit. informal*), three-hankie (*informal*), trite, wet (*Brit. informal*)

slosh *verb* **1.** flounder, plash, pour, shower, slap, slop, splash, spray, swash, wade **2.** *Brit. slang* bash (*informal*), belt (*informal*), biff (*slang*), hit, punch, slog, slug, sock (*slang*), strike, swipe (*informal*), thwack, wallop (*informal*)

slot *noun* **1.** aperture, channel, groove, hole, slit, vent **2.** *informal* niche, opening, place, position, space, time, vacancy ~*verb* **3.** adjust, assign, fit, fit in, insert, pigeonhole

sloth faineance, idleness, inactivity, indolence, inertia, laziness, slackness, slothfulness, sluggishness, torpor

slothful do-nothing (*informal*), fainéant, good-for-nothing, idle, inactive, indolent, inert, lazy, skiving (*Brit. slang*), slack, sluggish, torpid, workshy

slouch *verb* droop, loll, slump, stoop

slouching awkward, loutish, lumbering, shambling, uncouth, ungainly

slovenly careless, disorderly, heedless, loose, negligent, slack, slapdash, slatternly, slipshod, sloppy (*informal*), unkempt, untidy
Antonyms careful, clean, conscientious, disciplined, methodical, meticulous, neat, orderly, shipshape, smart, soigné *or* soignée, tidy, trim, well-groomed, well-ordered

slow *adjective* **1.** creeping, dawdling, deliberate, easy, lackadaisical, laggard, lagging, lazy, leaden, leisurely, loitering, measured, plodding, ponderous, slow-moving, sluggardly, sluggish, tortoise-like, unhurried **2.** backward, behind, behindhand, delayed, dilatory, late, long-delayed, tardy, unpunctual **3.** gradual, lingering, long-drawn-out, prolonged, protracted, time-consuming **4.** behind the times, boring, conservative, dead, dead-and-alive (*Brit.*), dull, inactive, one-horse (*informal*), quiet, slack, sleepy, sluggish, stagnant, tame, tedious, uneventful, uninteresting, unproductive, unprogressive, wearisome **5.** blockish, bovine, braindead (*informal*), dense, dim, dozy (*Brit. informal*), dull, dull-witted, dumb (*informal*), obtuse, retarded, slow on the uptake (*informal*), slow-witted, stupid, thick, unresponsive **6.** *with* **to** averse, disinclined, hesitant, indisposed, loath, reluctant, unwilling ~*verb* **7.** *often with* **up** *or* **down** brake, check, curb, decelerate, delay, detain, handicap, hold up, lag, reduce speed, rein in, relax, restrict, retard, slacken (off), spin out
Antonyms *adjective* (*senses 1, 2, 3 & 4*) action-packed, animated, brisk, eager, exciting, fast, hectic, hurried, interesting, lively, precipitate, prompt, quick, quickie (*informal*), quick-moving, sharp, speedy, stimulating, swift (*sense 5*) bright, clever, intelligent, perceptive, quick, quick-witted, sharp, smart ~*verb* accelerate, advance, aid, boost, help, pick up speed, quicken, speed up

slowly at a snail's pace, at one's leisure, by degrees, gradually, inchmeal, in one's own (good) time, leisurely, ploddingly, steadily, taking one's time, unhurriedly, with leaden steps

sludge dregs, gloop (*informal*), mire, muck, mud, ooze, residue, sediment, silt, slime, slob (*Irish*), slop, slush

sluggish dull, heavy, inactive, indolent, inert, lethargic, lifeless, listless, phlegmatic, slothful, slow, slow-moving, torpid, unresponsive
Antonyms alive and kicking, animated, brisk, dynamic, energetic, enthusiastic, fast, free-flowing, full of beans (*informal*), full of life, industrious, lively, swift, vigorous

sluggishness apathy, drowsiness, dullness, heaviness, indolence, inertia, languor, lassitude, lethargy, listlessness, slothfulness, somnolence, stagnation, torpor

sluice *verb* cleanse, drain, drench, flush, irrigate, wash down, wash out

slum ghetto, hovel, rookery (*archaic*), warren

slumber *verb* be inactive, doze, drowse, kip (*Brit. slang*), lie dormant, nap, repose, sleep, snooze (*informal*), zizz (*Brit. informal*)

slummy decayed, overcrowded, run-down, seedy, sleazy, sordid, squalid, wretched

slump *verb* **1.** collapse, crash, decline, deteriorate, fall, fall off, go downhill (*informal*), plummet, plunge, reach a new low, sink, slip ~*noun* **2.** collapse, crash, decline, depreciation, depression, downturn, drop, failure, fall, falling-off, lapse, low, meltdown (*informal*), recession, reverse, stagnation, trough ~*verb* **3.** bend, droop, hunch, loll, sag, slouch
Antonyms *verb* advance, boom, develop, expand, flourish, grow, increase, prosper, thrive ~*noun* advance, boom, boost, development, expansion, gain, growth, improvement, increase, upsurge, upswing, upturn

slur *noun* affront, aspersion, blot, blot on one's escutcheon, brand, calumny, discredit, disgrace, innuendo, insinuation, insult, reproach, smear, stain, stigma

slut drab (*archaic*), scrubber (*Brit. & Austral. slang*), slattern, sloven, tart, trollop

sluttish **1.** dirty, slatternly, slovenly, trollopy **2.** coarse, dissipated, immoral, promiscuous, tarty (*informal*), whorish

sly *adjective* **1.** artful, astute, clever, conniving, covert, crafty, cunning, devious, foxy, furtive, guileful, insidious, scheming, secret, shifty, stealthy, subtle, underhand, wily **2.** arch, impish, knowing, mischievous, roguish ~*noun* **3.** **on the sly** behind (someone's) back, covertly, like a thief in the night, on the q.t. (*informal*), on the quiet, privately, secretly, surreptitiously, underhandedly, under the counter (*informal*)
Antonyms *adjective* above-board, artless, direct, frank, guileless, honest, ingenuous, open, straightforward, trustworthy ~*noun* above-board, candidly, forthrightly, on the level, openly, overtly, publicly

smack *verb* **1.** box, clap, cuff, hit, pat, slap, sock (*slang*), spank, strike, tap ~*noun* **2.** blow, crack, slap **3.** **smack in the eye** blow, rebuff, repulse, setback, slap in the face, snub ~*adverb* **4.** *informal* directly, exactly, plumb, point-blank, precisely, right, slap (*informal*), squarely, straight

smack of bear the stamp of, be redolent of, be suggestive *or* indicative of, betoken, have all the hallmarks of, reek of, smell of, suggest, testify to

small 1. diminutive, immature, Lilliputian, little, mini, miniature, minute, petite, pint-sized (*informal*), pocket-sized, puny, pygmy *or* pigmy, slight, teensy-weensy, teeny, teeny-weeny, tiny, undersized, wee, young 2. insignificant, lesser, minor, negligible, paltry, petty, trifling, trivial, unimportant 3. inadequate, inconsiderable, insufficient, limited, meagre, measly, scant, scanty 4. humble, modest, small-scale, unpretentious 5. base, grudging, illiberal, mean, narrow, petty, selfish 6. **make (someone) feel small** chagrin, disconcert, humble, humiliate, make (someone) look foolish, mortify, put down (*slang*), show up (*informal*), take down a peg or two (*informal*)
Antonyms (*sense 1*) ample, big, colossal, enormous, great, huge, immense, massive, mega (*slang*), sizable *or* sizeable, stellar (*informal*), vast (*senses 2, 3 & 4*) appreciable, considerable, generous, grand, important, large-scale, major, powerful, serious, significant, substantial, urgent, vital, weighty

Small is beautiful
Professor E.F. Schumacher *title of book*
The best things come in small packages

small-minded bigoted, envious, grudging, hidebound, intolerant, mean, narrow-minded, petty, rigid, ungenerous
Antonyms broad-minded, far-sighted, generous, liberal, open, open-minded, tolerant, unbigoted

small-time insignificant, minor, no-account (*U.S. informal*), of no account, of no consequence, petty, piddling (*informal*), unimportant

smarmy bootlicking (*informal*), bowing and scraping, crawling, fawning, fulsome, greasy, ingratiating, obsequious, oily, servile, slimy, smooth, soapy (*slang*), suave, sycophantic, toadying, unctuous

smart[1] *adjective* 1. acute, adept, agile, apt, astute, bright, brisk, canny, clever, ingenious, intelligent, keen, nimble, quick, quick-witted, ready, sharp, shrewd 2. as fresh as a daisy, chic, elegant, fashionable, fine, modish, natty (*informal*), neat, smart, snappy, spruce, stylish, trendy (*Brit. informal*), trim, well turned-out 3. effective, impertinent, nimble-witted, pointed, ready, saucy, smart-alecky (*informal*), witty 4. brisk, cracking (*informal*), jaunty, lively, quick, spanking, spirited, vigorous
Antonyms (*sense 1*) daft (*informal*), dense, dim-witted (*informal*), dull, dumb (*informal*), foolish, idiotic, moronic, slow, stupid, thick, unintelligent (*sense 2*) dowdy, dull, fogeyish, naff (*Brit. slang*), old-fashioned, outmoded, out-of-date, passé, scruffy, sloppy, uncool, unfashionable, untrendy (*Brit. informal*), (*sense 3*) modest, polite, respectful, restrained, unobtrusive

smart[2] 1. *verb* burn, hurt, pain, sting, throb, tingle 2. *adjective* hard, keen, painful, piercing, resounding, sharp, stinging 3. *noun* burning sensation, pain, pang, smarting, soreness, sting

smart aleck clever-clogs (*informal*), clever Dick (*informal*), know-all (*informal*), smartarse (*slang*), smarty boots (*informal*), smarty pants (*informal*), wise guy (*informal*)

smarten beautify, groom, gussy up (*slang, chiefly U.S.*), put in order, put to rights, spruce up, tidy

smash *verb* 1. break, collide, crash, crush, demolish, disintegrate, pulverize, shatter, shiver *~noun* 2. accident, collision, crash, pile-up (*informal*), smash-up (*informal*) *~verb* 3. defeat, destroy, lay waste, overthrow, ruin, total (*slang*), trash (*slang*), wreck *~noun* 4. collapse, defeat, destruction, disaster, downfall, failure, ruin, shattering

smashing awesome (*slang*), bodacious (*slang, chiefly U.S.*), boffo (*slang*), brill (*informal*), brilliant (*informal*), chillin' (*U.S. slang*), cracking (*Brit. informal*), crucial (*slang*), def (*slang*), excellent, exhilarating, fab (*informal, chiefly Brit.*), fabulous (*informal*), fantastic (*informal*), first-class, first-rate, great (*informal*), jim-dandy (*slang*), magnificent, marvellous, mean (*slang*), mega (*slang*), out of this world (*informal*), sensational (*informal*), sovereign, stupendous, super (*informal*), superb, superlative, terrific (*informal*), topping (*Brit. slang*), wonderful, world-class
Antonyms abysmal, appalling, average, awful, bad, boring, crap (*slang*), disappointing, disgraceful, disgusting, dreadful, dreary, dull, hideous, horrible, mediocre, no great shakes (*informal*), ordinary, rotten, run-of-the-mill, sickening, terrible, unexciting, uninspired, vile

smattering bit, dash, elements, modicum, nodding acquaintance, passing acquaintance, rudiments, smatter, sprinkling

smear *verb* 1. bedaub, bedim, besmirch, blur, coat, cover, daub, dirty, patch, plaster, rub on, smirch, smudge, soil, spread over, stain, sully *~noun* 2. blot, blotch, daub, smirch, smudge, splotch, streak *~verb* 3. asperse, besmirch, blacken, calumniate, drag (someone's) name through the mud, malign, sully, tarnish, traduce, vilify *~noun* 4. calumny, defamation, libel, mudslinging, slander, vilification, whispering campaign

smell *noun* **1.** aroma, bouquet, fragrance, niff (*Brit. slang*), odour, perfume, redolence, scent, whiff *~verb* **2.** get a whiff of, nose, scent, sniff *~noun* **3.** fetor, malodour, niff (*Brit. slang*), pong (*Brit. informal*), stench, stink *~verb* **4.** be malodorous, hum (*slang*), niff (*Brit. slang*), pong (*Brit. informal*), reek, stink, stink to high heaven (*informal*), whiff (*Brit. slang*) *Related adjective:* olfactory

smelly evil-smelling, fetid, foul, foul-smelling, high, malodorous, mephitic, niffy (*Brit. slang*), noisome, olid, pongy (*Brit. informal*), putrid, reeking, stinking, stinky (*informal*), strong, strong-smelling, whiffy (*Brit. slang*)

smile *verb* beam, grin

smirk *noun* grin, leer, simper, smug look, sneer

smitten **1.** afflicted, beset, laid low, plagued, struck **2.** beguiled, bewitched, bowled over (*informal*), captivated, charmed, enamoured, infatuated, swept off one's feet

smoky begrimed, black, caliginous (*archaic*), grey, grimy, hazy, murky, reeky, smoke-darkened, sooty, thick

smooth *adjective* **1.** even, flat, flush, horizontal, level, plain, plane, unwrinkled **2.** glossy, polished, shiny, silky, sleek, soft, velvety **3.** calm, equable, glassy, mirror-like, peaceful, serene, tranquil, undisturbed, unruffled **4.** agreeable, bland, mellow, mild, pleasant, soothing **5.** debonair, facile, glib, ingratiating, persuasive, silky, slick, smarmy (*Brit. informal*), suave, unctuous, urbane **6.** easy, effortless, flowing, fluent, frictionless, regular, rhythmic, steady, unbroken, uneventful, uniform, uninterrupted, untroubled, well-ordered *~verb* **7.** flatten, iron, level, plane, polish, press **8.** allay, alleviate, appease, assuage, calm, ease, extenuate, facilitate, iron out the difficulties of, mitigate, mollify, palliate, pave the way, soften
Antonyms *adjective* (*senses 1 & 2*) abrasive, bumpy, coarse, irregular, jagged, lumpy, rough, sharp, uneven (*sense 3*) agitated, disturbed, edgy, excitable, nervous, ruffled, troubled, troublesome, turbulent, uneasy *~verb* aggravate, exacerbate, hamper, hinder, intensify, make worse, roughen

smoothness **1.** evenness, flushness, levelness, regularity, unbrokenness **2.** silkiness, sleekness, smooth texture, softness, velvetiness **3.** calmness, glassiness, placidity, serenity, stillness, unruffled surface **4.** glibness, oiliness, smarminess (*Brit. informal*), suavity, urbanity **5.** ease, efficiency, effortlessness, felicity, finish, flow, fluency, polish, rhythm, slickness, smooth running

smother *verb* **1.** choke, extinguish, snuff, stifle, strangle, suffocate **2.** conceal, hide, keep back, muffle, repress, stifle, suppress **3.** be swimming in, cocoon, cover, envelop, heap, inundate, overwhelm, shower, shroud, surround *~noun* **4.** fug (*chiefly Brit.*), smog

smoulder *figurative* be resentful, boil, burn, fester, fume, rage, seethe, simmer, smart under

smudge **1.** *verb* blacken, blur, daub, dirty, mark, smear, smirch, soil **2.** *noun* blemish, blot, blur, smear, smut, smutch

smug complacent, conceited, holier-than-thou, priggish, self-opinionated, self-righteous, self-satisfied, superior

smuggler bootlegger, contrabandist, gentleman, moonshiner (*U.S.*), rum-runner, runner, trafficker, wrecker

smutty bawdy, blue, coarse, crude, dirty, filthy, improper, indecent, indelicate, lewd, obscene, off colour, pornographic, prurient, racy, raunchy (*U.S. slang*), risqué, salacious, suggestive, vulgar, X-rated (*informal*)

snack bite, bite to eat, break, elevenses (*Brit. informal*), light meal, nibble, refreshment(s), titbit

snag **1.** *noun* catch, complication, difficulty, disadvantage, downside, drawback, hazard, hitch, inconvenience, obstacle, problem, stumbling block, the rub **2.** *verb* catch, hole, rip, tear

snaky **1.** convoluted, serpentine, sinuous, tortuous, twisting, twisty, writhing **2.** crafty, insidious, perfidious, sly, treacherous, venomous

snap *verb* **1.** break, come apart, crack, give way, separate **2.** bite, bite at, catch, grip, nip, seize, snatch **3.** bark, flare out, flash, fly off the handle at (*informal*), growl, jump down (someone's) throat (*informal*), lash out at, retort, snarl, speak sharply **4.** click, crackle, pop **5.** **snap one's fingers at** cock a snook at (*Brit.*), defy, flout, pay no attention to, scorn, set at naught, wave two fingers at (*slang*) **6.** **snap out of it** cheer up, get a grip on oneself, get over, liven up, perk up, pull oneself together (*informal*), recover *~noun* **7.** crackle, fillip, flick, pop **8.** bite, grab, nip **9.** *informal* energy, get-up-and-go (*informal*), go (*informal*), liveliness, pep, pizzazz *or* pizazz (*informal*), vigour, zip (*informal*) *~adjective* **10.** abrupt, immediate, instant, on-the-spot, sudden, unpremeditated

snappy **1.** apt to fly off the handle (*informal*), cross, edgy, hasty, impatient, irritable, like a bear with a sore head (*informal*), quick-tempered, ratty (*Brit. & N.Z. informal*), snappish, tart, testy, tetchy, touchy, waspish **2.** chic, dapper, fashionable, modish, natty (*informal*), smart, stylish, trendy (*Brit. informal*), up-to-the-minute, voguish **3.** **look snappy** be quick, buck up (*informal*), get a move on (*informal*), get one's skates on, hurry (up), look lively, make haste

snap up avail oneself of, grab, grasp, nab (*informal*), pounce upon, seize, swoop down on, take advantage of

snare 1. *verb* catch, entrap, net, seize, springe, trap, trepan (*archaic*), wire 2. *noun* catch, gin, net, noose, pitfall, springe, trap, wire

snarl[1] *verb* complain, growl, grumble, mumble, murmur, show its teeth (*of an animal*)

snarl[2] *verb often with* **up** complicate, confuse, embroil, enmesh, entangle, entwine, muddle, ravel, tangle

snarl-up confusion, entanglement, muddle, tangle, (traffic) jam

snatch 1. *verb* catch up, clutch, gain, grab, grasp, grip, make off with, pluck, pull, rescue, seize, take, win, wrench, wrest 2. *noun* bit, fragment, part, piece, smattering, snippet, spell

snazzy attractive, dashing, flamboyant, flashy, jazzy (*informal*), raffish, ritzy (*slang*), showy, smart, sophisticated, sporty, stylish, swinging (*slang*), with it (*informal*)

sneak *verb* 1. cower, lurk, pad, sidle, skulk, slink, slip, smuggle, spirit, steal 2. *informal* grass on (*Brit. slang*), inform on, peach (*slang*), shop (*slang, chiefly Brit.*), sing (*slang, chiefly U.S.*), spill one's guts (*slang*), tell on (*informal*), tell tales ~*noun* 3. informer, snake in the grass, telltale ~*adjective* 4. clandestine, furtive, quick, secret, stealthy, surprise

sneaking 1. hidden, private, secret, suppressed, unavowed, unconfessed, undivulged, unexpressed, unvoiced 2. intuitive, nagging, niggling, persistent, uncomfortable, worrying 3. contemptible, furtive, mean, sly, sneaky, surreptitious, two-faced, underhand

sneaky base, contemptible, cowardly, deceitful, devious, dishonest, disingenuous, double-dealing, furtive, low, malicious, mean, nasty, shifty, slippery, sly, snide, unreliable, unscrupulous, untrustworthy

sneer 1. *verb* curl one's lip, deride, disdain, gibe, hold in contempt, hold up to ridicule, jeer, laugh, look down on, mock, ridicule, scoff, scorn, sniff at, snigger, turn up one's nose (*informal*) 2. *noun* derision, disdain, gibe, jeer, mockery, ridicule, scorn, snidery, snigger

> *Who can refute a sneer?*
>
> Revd. William Paley *Principles of Moral and Political Philosophy*

> *Damn with faint praise, assent with civil leer,*
> *And, without sneering, teach the rest to sneer*
>
> Alexander Pope *Epistle to Dr. Arbuthnot*

sneezing sternutation

snide cynical, disparaging, hurtful, ill-natured, insinuating, malicious, mean, nasty, sarcastic, scornful, shrewish, sneering, spiteful, unkind

sniff *verb* breathe, inhale, smell, snuff, snuffle

sniffy condescending, contemptuous, disdainful, haughty, supercilious, superior

snigger giggle, laugh, smirk, sneer, snicker, titter

snip *verb* 1. clip, crop, cut, dock, nick, nip off, notch, shave, trim ~*noun* 2. bit, clipping, fragment, piece, scrap, shred, snippet 3. *informal* bargain, giveaway, good buy, steal (*informal*)

snippet fragment, part, particle, piece, scrap, shred, snatch

snivel blubber, cry, girn (*Scot. & northern English dialect*), gripe (*informal*), grizzle (*informal, chiefly Brit.*), mewl, moan, sniffle, snuffle, weep, whimper, whine, whinge (*informal*)

snobbery airs, arrogance, condescension, pretension, pride, side (*Brit. slang*), snobbishness, snootiness (*informal*), uppishness (*Brit. informal*)

snobbish arrogant, condescending, high and mighty (*informal*), high-hat (*informal, chiefly U.S.*), hoity-toity (*informal*), patronizing, pretentious, snooty (*informal*), stuck-up (*informal*), superior, toffee-nosed (*slang, chiefly Brit.*), uppish (*Brit. informal*), uppity

Antonyms down to earth, humble, modest, natural, unassuming, unostentatious, unpretentious, without airs

snoop interfere, poke one's nose in (*informal*), pry, spy

snooper busybody, meddler, nosy parker (*informal*), Paul Pry, pry, snoop (*informal*), stickybeak (*Austral. informal*)

snooty aloof, condescending, disdainful, haughty, high and mighty (*informal*), high-hat (*informal, chiefly U.S.*), hoity-toity (*informal*), pretentious, proud, snobbish, snotty, stuck-up (*informal*), supercilious, superior, toffee-nosed (*slang, chiefly Brit*), toplofty (*informal*), uppish (*Brit. informal*), uppity

Antonyms down to earth, humble, modest, natural, unassuming, unpretentious, without airs

snooze 1. *verb* catnap, doze, drop off (*informal*), drowse, kip (*Brit. slang*), nap, nod off (*informal*), take forty winks (*informal*) 2. *noun* catnap, doze, forty winks (*informal*), kip (*Brit. slang*), nap, siesta

snub 1. *verb* cold-shoulder, cut (*informal*), cut dead (*informal*), give (someone) the brush-off (*slang*), give (someone) the cold shoulder, humble, humiliate, kick in the teeth (*slang*), mortify, put down, rebuff, shame, slight 2. *noun* affront, brush-off (*slang*), bum's rush (*slang*), humiliation, insult, put-down, slap in the face

snug **1.** comfortable, comfy (*informal*), cosy, homely, intimate, sheltered, warm **2.** close, compact, neat, trim

snuggle cuddle, nestle, nuzzle

soak *verb* **1.** bathe, damp, drench, immerse, infuse, marinate (*Cookery*), moisten, penetrate, permeate, saturate, seep, steep, wet **2.** *with* **up** absorb, assimilate, drink in, take up *or* in

soaking drenched, dripping, droukit *or* drookit (*Scot.*), like a drowned rat, saturated, soaked, soaked to the skin, sodden, sopping, streaming, waterlogged, wet through, wringing wet

soar **1.** ascend, fly, mount, rise, tower, wing **2.** climb, escalate, rise, rocket, shoot up
Antonyms descend, dive, drop down, fall, nose-dive, plummet, plunge, swoop

sob *verb* bawl, blubber, boohoo, cry, greet (*Scot. or archaic*), howl, shed tears, snivel, weep

sober *adjective* **1.** abstemious, abstinent, moderate, on the wagon (*informal*), temperate **2.** calm, clear-headed, cold, composed, cool, dispassionate, grave, level-headed, lucid, peaceful, practical, rational, realistic, reasonable, sedate, serene, serious, solemn, sound, staid, steady, unexcited, unruffled **3.** dark, drab, plain, quiet, severe, sombre, subdued *~verb* **4.** *usually with* **up** bring (someone) back to earth, calm down, clear one's head, come *or* bring to one's senses, give (someone) pause for thought, make (someone) stop and think
Antonyms *adjective* (*sense 1*) bevvied (*dialect*), blitzed (*slang*), blotto (*slang*), bombed (*slang*), Brahms and Liszt (*slang*), drunk, flying (*slang*), fu' (*Scot.*), guttered (*slang*), had one too many, inebriated, intoxicated, merry (*Brit. informal*), paralytic (*informal*), pie-eyed (*slang*), pissed (*taboo slang*), plastered, rat-arsed (*taboo slang*), sloshed (*slang*), smashed (*slang*), steamboats (*Scot. slang*), steaming (*slang*), tiddly (*slang, chiefly Brit.*), tight (*informal*), tipsy, tired and emotional (*euphemistic*), wasted (*slang*), wrecked (*slang*), zonked (*slang*) (*senses 2 & 3*) bright, excessive, flamboyant, flashy, frivolous, garish, gaudy, giddy, happy, immoderate, imprudent, injudicious, irrational, light, lighthearted, lively, sensational, unrealistic *~verb* become intoxicated, get drunk

sobersides prig, square (*informal*)

sobriety **1.** abstemiousness, abstinence, moderation, nonindulgence, self-restraint, soberness, temperance **2.** calmness, composure, coolness, gravity, level-headedness, reasonableness, restraint, sedateness, seriousness, solemnity, staidness, steadiness

so-called alleged, ostensible, pretended, professed, self-styled, *soi-disant*, supposed

sociability affability, companionability, congeniality, conviviality, cordiality, friendliness, gregariousness, neighbourliness

sociable accessible, affable, approachable, companionable, conversable, convivial, cordial, familiar, friendly, genial, gregarious, neighbourly, outgoing, social, warm
Antonyms antisocial, boorish, businesslike, cold, distant, formal, introverted, reclusive, standoffish, stiff, tense, uncommunicative, unfriendly, unsociable, withdrawn

social *adjective* **1.** collective, common, communal, community, general, group, organized, public, societal **2.** companionable, friendly, gregarious, neighbourly, sociable *~noun* **3.** do (*informal*), gathering, get-together (*informal*), party

socialism

The worst advertisement for Socialism is its adherents
George Orwell

The language of priorities is the religion of Socialism
Aneurin Bevan

To the ordinary working man, the sort you would meet in any pub on Saturday night, Socialism does not mean much more than better wages and shorter hours and nobody bossing you about
George Orwell *The Road to Wigan Pier*

socialize be a good mixer, break the ice, entertain, fraternize, get about *or* around, get together, go out, mix

society **1.** civilization, culture, humanity, mankind, people, population, social order, the community, the general public, the public, the world at large **2.** camaraderie, companionship, company, fellowship, friendship **3.** association, brotherhood, circle, club, corporation, fellowship, fraternity, group, guild, institute, league, order, organization, sisterhood, union **4.** beau monde, elite, gentry, *haut monde*, high society, polite society, the country set, the nobs (*slang*), the smart set, the swells (*informal*), the toffs (*Brit. slang*), the top drawer, upper classes, upper crust (*informal*)

There is no such thing as society
Margaret Thatcher

He who is unable to live in society, or who has no need because he is sufficient for himself, must be either a beast or a god
Aristotle *Politics*

sodden boggy, drenched, droukit *or* drookit (*Scot.*), marshy, miry, saturated, soaked, soggy, sopping, waterlogged

sodomy anal intercourse, anal sex, buggery

soft **1.** creamy, cushioned, cushiony, doughy, elastic, gelatinous, pulpy, quaggy, spongy, squashy, swampy, yielding **2.** bendable, ductile

(*of metals*), elastic, flexible, impressible, malleable, mouldable, plastic, pliable, supple, tensile **3.** downy, feathery, fleecy, flowing, fluid, furry, like a baby's bottom (*informal*), rounded, silky, smooth, velvety **4.** balmy, bland, caressing, delicate, diffuse, dim, dimmed, dulcet, faint, gentle, light, low, mellifluous, mellow, melodious, mild, murmured, muted, pale, pastel, pleasing, quiet, restful, shaded, soft-toned, soothing, subdued, sweet, temperate, twilight, understated, whispered **5.** compassionate, gentle, kind, pitying, sensitive, sentimental, sympathetic, tender, tenderhearted, touchy-feely (*informal*) **6.** boneless, easy-going, indulgent, lax, lenient, liberal, overindulgent, permissive, spineless, weak **7.** *informal* comfortable, cushy (*informal*), easy, easy-peasy (*slang*), undemanding **8.** effeminate, flabby, flaccid, limp, namby-pamby, out of condition, out of training, overindulged, pampered, podgy, weak **9.** *informal* a bit lacking (*informal*), daft (*informal*), feeble-minded, foolish, silly, simple, soft in the head (*informal*), soppy (*Brit. informal*)
Antonyms (*senses 1, 2 & 3*) abrasive, coarse, firm, grating, hard, inflexible, irritating, rigid, rough, solid, stiff, tough, unyielding (*sense 4*) bright, garish, gaudy, glaring, hard, harsh, loud, noisy, strident, unpleasant (*sense 6*) austere, harsh, no-nonsense, stern, strict

soften abate, allay, alleviate, appease, assuage, calm, cushion, diminish, ease, lessen, lighten, lower, melt, mitigate, moderate, modify, mollify, muffle, palliate, quell, relax, soothe, still, subdue, temper, tone down, turn down

soften up conciliate, disarm, melt, soft-soap (*informal*), weaken, win over, work on

softhearted charitable, compassionate, generous, indulgent, kind, sentimental, sympathetic, tender, tenderhearted, warm-hearted
Antonyms callous, cold, cruel, hard, hard-hearted, heartless, insensitive, uncaring, unkind, unsympathetic

softly-softly careful, cautious, circumspect, delicate, discreet, gradual, tactful, tentative

soft pedal de-emphasize, go easy (*informal*), moderate, play down, tone down

soft spot fondness, liking, partiality, weakness

soggy dripping, heavy, moist, mushy, pulpy, saturated, soaked, sodden, sopping, spongy, waterlogged

soil[1] *noun* **1.** clay, dirt, dust, earth, ground, loam **2.** country, land, region, terra firma

soil[2] *verb* bedraggle, befoul, begrime, besmirch, defile, dirty, foul, maculate (*literary*), muddy, pollute, smear, smirch, spatter, spot, stain, sully, tarnish

sojourn 1. *noun* rest, stay, stop, stopover, visit **2.** *verb* abide, dwell, lodge, reside, rest, stay, stop, tarry

solace 1. *noun* alleviation, assuagement, comfort, consolation, relief **2.** *verb* allay, alleviate, comfort, console, mitigate, soften, soothe

soldier enlisted man (*U.S.*), fighter, GI (*U.S. informal*), man-at-arms, military man, redcoat, serviceman, squaddie *or* squaddy (*Brit. slang*), Tommy (*Brit. informal*), trooper, warrior

Then it's Tommy this, an' Tommy that, an'
"Tommy, go away";
But it's "Thank you, Mister Atkins," when the band begins to play

Rudyard Kipling *Tommy*

sole alone, exclusive, individual, one, one and only, only, single, singular, solitary

solecism bloomer (*Brit. informal*), blunder, boo-boo (*informal*), breach of etiquette, cacology, faux pas, gaffe, gaucherie, impropriety, incongruity, indecorum, lapse, mistake

solely alone, completely, entirely, exclusively, merely, only, single-handedly, singly

solemn 1. earnest, glum, grave, portentous, sedate, serious, sober, staid, thoughtful **2.** august, awe-inspiring, ceremonial, ceremonious, dignified, formal, grand, grave, imposing, impressive, majestic, momentous, stately **3.** devotional, hallowed, holy, religious, reverential, ritual, sacred, sanctified, venerable
Antonyms (*senses 1 & 2*) bright, cheerful, chirpy (*informal*), comical, frivolous, genial, happy, informal, jovial, light-hearted, merry, relaxed, unceremonious (*sense 3*) irreligious, irreverent, unholy

solemnity 1. earnestness, grandeur, gravitas, gravity, impressiveness, momentousness, portentousness, sacredness, sanctity, seriousness **2.** *often plural* celebration, ceremonial, ceremony, formalities, observance, proceedings, rite, ritual

solemnize celebrate, commemorate, honour, keep, observe

solicit ask, beg, beseech, canvass, crave, entreat, implore, importune, petition, plead for, pray, seek, supplicate

solicitous anxious, apprehensive, attentive, careful, caring, concerned, eager, earnest, troubled, uneasy, worried, zealous

solicitude anxiety, attentiveness, care, concern, considerateness, consideration, regard, worry

solid *adjective* **1.** compact, concrete, dense, firm, hard, massed, stable, strong, sturdy, substantial, unshakable **2.** genuine, good, pure, real, reliable, sound **3.** agreed, complete, continuous, unalloyed, unanimous, unbroken, undivided, uninterrupted, united, unmixed **4.** constant, decent, dependable, estimable, law-abiding, level-headed, reliable, sensible, seri~

ous, sober, trusty, upright, upstanding, wor~thy
Antonyms (*sense 1*) broken, crumbling, de~caying, flimsy, gaseous, hollow, liquid, perme~able, precarious, shaky, unstable, unsteady, unsubstantial (*sense 2*) impure, unreliable, unsound (*sense 3*) at odds, divided, mixed, split, undecided (*sense 4*) flighty, irrespon~sible, unreliable, unsound, unstable, unsteady

solidarity accord, camaraderie, cohesion, com~munity of interest, concordance, esprit de corps, harmony, like-mindedness, singleness of purpose, soundness, stability, team spirit, unanimity, unification, unity

solidify cake, coagulate, cohere, congeal, hard~en, jell, set

solitary *adjective* **1.** desolate, hidden, isolated, lonely, out-of-the-way, remote, retired, seclud~ed, sequestered, unfrequented, unvisited **2.** alone, lone, single, sole **3.** cloistered, compan~ionless, friendless, hermitical, lonely, lone~some, reclusive, unsociable, unsocial *~noun* **4.** hermit, introvert, loner (*informal*), lone wolf, recluse
Antonyms *adjective* (*sense 1*) bustling, busy, frequented, public, well-frequented (*senses 2 & 3*) companionable, convivial, cordial, gre~garious, one of a group, outgoing, sociable, social *~noun* extrovert, mixer, socialite

If you are idle, be not solitary; if you are soli~tary, be not idle
Dr. Johnson

solitude **1.** isolation, ivory tower, loneliness, privacy, reclusiveness, retirement, seclusion **2.** *poetic* desert, emptiness, waste, wasteland, wilderness

far from the madding crowd's ignoble strife
Thomas Gray *Elegy Written in a Country Churchyard*

Solitude should teach us how to die
Lord Byron *Childe Harold*

That inward eye
Which is the bliss of solitude
William Wordsworth *I Wandered Lonely as a Cloud*

Two paradises 'twere in one
To live in paradise alone
Andrew Marvell *The Garden*

solution **1.** answer, clarification, elucidation, explanation, explication, key, resolution, re~sult, solving, unfolding, unravelling **2.** blend, compound, emulsion, mix, mixture, solvent, suspension (*Chemistry*) **3.** disconnection, dis~solution, liquefaction, melting

solve answer, clarify, clear up, crack, decipher, disentangle, elucidate, explain, expound, get to the bottom of, interpret, resolve, suss (out) (*slang*), unfold, unravel, work out

solvent **1.** solid, sound, unindebted **2.** dissol~vent (*rare*), resolvent

sombre dark, dim, dismal, doleful, drab, dull, dusky, funereal, gloomy, grave, joyless, lugu~brious, melancholy, mournful, obscure, sad, sepulchral, shadowy, shady, sober
Antonyms bright, cheerful, chirpy (*informal*), colourful, dazzling, effusive, full of beans, garish, gaudy, genial, happy, lively, sunny, upbeat (*informal*)

somebody *noun* big name, big noise (*infor~mal*), big shot (*informal*), big wheel (*slang*), bigwig (*informal*), celeb (*informal*), celebrity, dignitary, heavyweight (*informal*), household name, luminary, megastar (*informal*), name, notable, personage, person of note, public fig~ure, star, superstar, V.I.P.
Antonyms also-ran, cipher, lightweight (*in~formal*), menial, nobody, nonentity, nothing (*informal*)

someday eventually, in the fullness of time, one day, one of these (fine) days, sooner or later, ultimately

somehow by fair means or foul, by hook or (by) crook, by some means or other, come hell or high water (*informal*), come what may, one way or another

sometimes at times, every now and then, every so often, from time to time, now and again, now and then, occasionally, off and on, once in a while, on occasion
Antonyms always, consistently, constantly, continually, eternally, ever, everlastingly, evermore, forever, invariably, perpetually, unceasingly, without exception

somnolent comatose, dozy, drowsy, half-awake, heavy-eyed, nodding off (*informal*), sleepy, soporific, torpid

son
Related adjective: filial

A wise son maketh a glad father; but a foolish son is the heaviness of his mother
Bible: Proverbs

Like father like son

song air, anthem, ballad, canticle, canzonet, carol, chant, chorus, ditty, hymn, lay, lyric, melody, number, pop song, psalm, shanty, strain, tune

song and dance ado, commotion, flap (*infor~mal*), fuss, hoo-ha, kerfuffle (*informal*), panto~mime (*informal*), performance (*informal*), pother, shindig (*informal*), shindy (*informal*), stir, to-do

sonorous full, grandiloquent, high-flown, high-sounding, loud, orotund, plangent, reso~nant, resounding, rich, ringing, rounded, sounding

soon anon (*archaic*), any minute now, before long, betimes (*archaic*), erelong (*archaic or* *poetic*), in a couple of shakes, in a little while, in a minute, in a short time, in the near future, in two shakes of a lamb's tail, shortly

soothe allay, alleviate, appease, assuage, calm, calm down, compose, ease, hush, lull, mitigate, mollify, pacify, quiet, relieve, settle, smooth down, soften, still, tranquillize

Antonyms aggravate (*informal*), agitate, annoy, disquiet, disturb, exacerbate, excite, get on one's nerves (*informal*), hassle (*informal*), increase, inflame, irritate, rouse, stimulate, upset, vex, worry

soothing balsamic, calming, demulcent, easeful, emollient, lenitive, palliative, relaxing, restful

soothsayer augur, diviner, foreteller, prophet, seer, sibyl

sophisticated **1.** blasé, citified, cosmopolitan, cultivated, cultured, jet-set, refined, seasoned, urbane, worldly, worldly-wise, world-weary **2.** advanced, complex, complicated, delicate, elaborate, highly-developed, intricate, multifaceted, refined, subtle

Antonyms basic, naive, old-fashioned, plain, primitive, simple, uncomplicated, unrefined, unsophisticated, unsubtle, unworldly, wet behind the ears (*informal*)

sophistication finesse, poise, savoir-faire, *savoir-vivre*, urbanity, worldliness, worldly wisdom

sophistry casuistry, fallacy, quibble, sophism

soporific **1.** *adjective* hypnotic, sedative, sleep-inducing, sleepy, somniferous (*rare*), somnolent, tranquillizing **2.** *noun* anaesthetic, hypnotic, narcotic, opiate, sedative, tranquillizer

It is said that the effect of eating too much lettuce is 'soporific'
Beatrix Potter *The Tale of the Flopsy Bunnies*

soppy corny (*slang*), daft (*informal*), drippy (*informal*), gushy (*informal*), lovey-dovey, mawkish, overemotional, schmaltzy (*slang*), sentimental, silly, slushy (*informal*), soft (*informal*), three-hankie (*informal*), weepy (*informal*)

sorcerer enchanter, mage (*archaic*), magician, magus, necromancer, sorceress, warlock, witch, wizard

sorcery black art, black magic, charm, divination, enchantment, incantation, magic, necromancy, spell, witchcraft, witchery, wizardry

sordid **1.** dirty, filthy, foul, mean, seamy, seedy, sleazy, slovenly, slummy, squalid, unclean, wretched **2.** base, debauched, degenerate, degraded, despicable, disreputable, low, shabby, shameful, vicious, vile **3.** avaricious, corrupt, covetous, grasping, mercenary, miserly, niggardly, selfish, self-seeking, ungenerous, venal

Antonyms blameless, clean, decent, fresh, honourable, noble, pure, spotless, squeaky-clean, unblemished, undefiled, unsullied, upright

sore *adjective* **1.** angry, burning, chafed, choked, inflamed, irritated, painful, raw, reddened, sensitive, smarting, tender **2.** annoying, distressing, grievous, harrowing, severe, sharp, troublesome **3.** acute, critical, desperate, dire, extreme, pressing, urgent **4.** afflicted, aggrieved, angry, annoyed, cross, grieved, hurt, irked, irritated, pained, peeved (*informal*), resentful, stung, upset, vexed *~noun* **5.** abscess, boil, chafe, gathering, inflammation, ulcer

sorrow *noun* **1.** affliction, anguish, distress, grief, heartache, heartbreak, misery, mourning, regret, sadness, unhappiness, woe **2.** affliction, blow, bummer (*slang*), hardship, misfortune, trial, tribulation, trouble, woe, worry *~verb* **3.** agonize, bemoan, be sad, bewail, eat one's heart out, grieve, lament, moan, mourn, weep

Antonyms *noun* bliss, delight, elation, exaltation, exultation, gladness, good fortune, happiness, joy, lucky break, pleasure *~verb* celebrate, delight, exult, jump for joy, rejoice, revel

There is no greater sorrow than to recall a time of happiness in misery
Dante *Divine Comedy*

Into each life some rain must fall
Henry Wadsworth Longfellow

Sorrow makes us wise
Alfred Tennyson *In Memoriam*

Sorrow is tranquillity remembered in emotion
Dorothy Parker *Here Lies*

sorrowful affecting, afflicted, dejected, depressed, disconsolate, dismal, distressing, doleful, down in the dumps (*informal*), grievous, harrowing, heartbroken, heart-rending, heavy-hearted, lamentable, lugubrious, melancholy, miserable, mournful, painful, piteous, rueful, sad, sick at heart, sorry, tearful, unhappy, woebegone, woeful, wretched

sorry **1.** apologetic, conscience-stricken, contrite, guilt-ridden, in sackcloth and ashes, penitent, regretful, remorseful, repentant, self-reproachful, shamefaced **2.** disconsolate, distressed, grieved, melancholy, mournful, sad, sorrowful, unhappy **3.** commiserative, compassionate, full of pity, moved, pitying, sympathetic **4.** abject, base, deplorable, dismal, distressing, mean, miserable, paltry, pathetic, piteous, pitiable, pitiful, poor, sad, shabby, vile, wretched

Antonyms (*sense 1*) impenitent, not contrite, shameless, unapologetic, unashamed, unremorseful, unrepentant (*sense 2*) cheerful, delighted, elated, happy, joyful (*sense 3*)

compassionless (*rare*), heartless, indifferent, uncompassionate, unconcerned, unmoved, unpitying, unsympathetic

sort *noun* **1.** brand, breed, category, character, class, denomination, description, family, genus, group, ilk, kind, make, nature, order, quality, race, species, stamp, style, type, variety **2. out of sorts** crotchety, down in the dumps (*informal*), down in the mouth (*informal*), grouchy (*informal*), in low spirits, mopy, not up to par, not up to snuff (*informal*), off colour, poorly (*informal*), under the weather (*informal*) **3. sort of** as it were, in part, moderately, rather, reasonably, slightly, somewhat, to some extent *~verb* **4.** arrange, assort, catalogue, categorize, choose, class, classify, distribute, divide, file, grade, group, order, put in order, rank, select, separate, sequence, systematize, tabulate

sort out **1.** clarify, clear up, organize, put *or* get straight, resolve, tidy up **2.** pick out, put on one side, segregate, select, separate, sift

so-so *adjective* adequate, average, fair, fair to middling (*informal*), indifferent, middling, moderate, not bad (*informal*), O.K. *or* okay (*informal*), ordinary, passable, respectable, run-of-the-mill, tolerable, undistinguished

sought-after coveted, desirable, enviable, in demand, like gold dust, longed-for, wanted

soul **1.** animating principle, essence, intellect, life, mind, psyche, reason, spirit, vital force **2.** being, body, creature, individual, man, mortal, person, woman **3.** embodiment, epitome, essence, incarnation, personification, quintessence, type **4.** animation, ardour, courage, energy, feeling, fervour, force, inspiration, nobility, vitality, vivacity

soul-destroying dreary, dull, humdrum, mind-numbing, monotonous, tedious, tiresome, treadmill, unvarying, wearisome

soulful eloquent, expressive, heartfelt, meaningful, mournful, moving, profound, sensitive

soulless **1.** callous, cold, cruel, harsh, inhuman, unfeeling, unkind, unsympathetic **2.** dead, lifeless, mechanical, soul-destroying, spiritless, uninteresting

sound[1] *noun* **1.** din, noise, report, resonance, reverberation, tone, voice **2.** drift, idea, implication(s), impression, look, tenor **3.** earshot, hearing, range *~verb* **4.** echo, resonate, resound, reverberate **5.** appear, give the impression of, look, seem, strike one as being **6.** announce, articulate, declare, enunciate, express, pronounce, signal, utter

sound[2] *adjective* **1.** complete, entire, firm, fit, hale, hale and hearty, healthy, intact, perfect, robust, solid, sturdy, substantial, undamaged, unhurt, unimpaired, uninjured, vigorous, well-constructed, whole **2.** correct, fair, just, level-headed, logical, orthodox, proper, prudent, rational, reasonable, reliable, responsible, right, right-thinking, sensible, true, trustworthy, valid, well-founded, well-grounded, wise **3.** established, orthodox, proven, recognized, reliable, reputable, safe, secure, solid, solvent, stable, tried-and-true **4.** deep, peaceful, unbroken, undisturbed, untroubled

Antonyms (*sense 1*) ailing, damaged, flimsy, frail, light, shaky, sketchy, superficial, unbalanced, unstable, weak (*senses 2 & 3*) fallacious, faulty, flawed, incompetent, irrational, irresponsible, specious, unreliable, unsound, unstable (*sense 4*) broken, fitful, shallow, troubled

a sound mind in a sound body

Juvenal *Satires*

sound[3] *verb* **1.** fathom, plumb, probe **2.** examine, inspect, investigate, test

sound[4] *noun* **1.** channel, passage, strait **2.** arm of the sea, fjord, inlet, voe

sound out canvass, examine, probe, pump, put out feelers to, question, see how the land lies, test the water

sour *adjective* **1.** acerb, acetic, acid, acidulated, bitter, pungent, sharp, tart, unpleasant **2.** bad, curdled, fermented, gone off, rancid, turned, unsavoury, unwholesome **3.** acrid, acrimonious, churlish, crabbed, cynical, disagreeable, discontented, embittered, grouchy (*informal*), grudging, ill-natured, ill-tempered, jaundiced, peevish, tart, ungenerous, waspish *~verb* **4.** alienate, disenchant, embitter, envenom, exacerbate, exasperate, turn off (*informal*)

Antonyms *adjective* (*sense 1*) agreeable, bland, mild, pleasant, savoury, sugary, sweet (*sense 2*) fresh, unimpaired, unspoiled (*sense 3*) affable, amiable, congenial, friendly, genial, good-humoured, good-natured, good-tempered, pleasant, warm-hearted *~verb* enhance, improve, strengthen

source **1.** author, begetter, beginning, cause, commencement, derivation, fount, fountainhead, origin, originator, rise, spring, wellspring **2.** authority, informant

sourpuss crosspatch (*informal*), grouser, grump (*informal*), killjoy, misery (*Brit. informal*), prophet of doom, shrew, wowser (*Austral. & N.Z. slang*)

souse drench, dunk, immerse, marinate (*Cookery*), pickle, soak, steep

souvenir keepsake, memento, relic, remembrancer (*archaic*), reminder, token

sovereign *noun* **1.** chief, emperor, empress, king, monarch, potentate, prince, queen, ruler, shah, supreme ruler, tsar *~adjective* **2.** absolute, chief, dominant, imperial, kingly, mo~

narchal, paramount, predominant, principal, queenly, regal, royal, ruling, supreme, unlimited **3.** effectual, efficacious, efficient, excellent

sovereignty ascendancy, domination, kingship, primacy, supremacy, supreme power, suzerainty, sway

sow broadcast, disseminate, implant, inseminate, lodge, plant, scatter, seed

space 1. amplitude, capacity, elbowroom, expanse, extension, extent, leeway, margin, play, room, scope, spaciousness, volume **2.** blank, distance, gap, interval, lacuna, omission **3.** duration, interval, period, span, time, while **4.** accommodation, berth, place, seat

spaceman *or* **spacewoman** astronaut, cosmonaut

spacious ample, broad, capacious, comfortable, commodious, expansive, extensive, huge, large, roomy, sizable *or* sizeable, uncrowded, vast

Antonyms close, confined, cramped, crowded, limited, narrow, poky, restricted, small

spadework donkey-work, groundwork, labour, preparation

span *noun* **1.** amount, distance, extent, length, reach, spread, stretch **2.** duration, period, spell, term *~verb* **3.** arch across, bridge, cover, cross, extend across, link, range over, traverse, vault

spank *verb* belt (*informal*), cuff, give (someone) a hiding (*informal*), put (someone) over one's knee, slap, slipper (*informal*), smack, tan (*slang*), wallop (*informal*), whack

spanking *adjective* **1.** brisk, energetic, fast, invigorating, lively, quick, smart, snappy, vigorous **2.** *informal* brand-new, fine, gleaming, smart

spar *verb* argue, bicker, dispute, exchange blows, fall out (*informal*), have a tiff, lead a cat-and-dog life, row, scrap (*informal*), skirmish, spat (*U.S.*), squabble, wrangle, wrestle

spare *adjective* **1.** additional, emergency, extra, free, going begging, in excess, in reserve, leftover, odd, over, superfluous, supernumerary, surplus, unoccupied, unused, unwanted **2.** gaunt, lank, lean, macilent (*rare*), meagre, slender, slight, slim, wiry **3.** economical, frugal, meagre, modest, scanty, sparing **4. go spare** *Brit. slang* become angry (distracted, distraught, enraged, mad (*informal*), upset), blow one's top (*informal*), do one's nut (*Brit. slang*), go mental (*slang*), go up the wall (*slang*), have *or* throw a fit (*informal*) *~verb* **5.** afford, allow, bestow, dispense with, do without, give, grant, let (someone) have, manage without, part with, relinquish **6.** be merciful to, deal leniently with, go easy on (*informal*), have mercy on, leave, let off (*informal*), pardon, refrain from, release, relieve from, save from

Antonyms *adjective* (*sense 1*) allocated, designated, earmarked, in use, necessary, needed, set aside, spoken for (*sense 2*) corpulent, fat, flabby, fleshy, generous, heavy, large, plump *~verb* (*sense 6*) afflict, condemn, damn, destroy, hurt, punish, show no mercy to

spare time free time, leisure, odd moments, time on one's hands, time to kill

sparing careful, chary, cost-conscious, economical, frugal, money-conscious, prudent, saving, thrifty

Antonyms extravagant, lavish, liberal, open-handed, prodigal, spendthrift

spark *noun* **1.** flare, flash, flicker, gleam, glint, scintillation, spit **2.** atom, hint, jot, scintilla, scrap, trace, vestige *~verb* **3.** *often with* **off** animate, excite, inspire, kick-start, kindle, precipitate, prod, provoke, rouse, set in motion, set off, start, stimulate, stir, touch off, trigger (off)

sparkle *verb* **1.** beam, coruscate, dance, flash, gleam, glint, glisten, glister (*archaic*), glitter, glow, scintillate, shimmer, shine, spark, twinkle, wink **2.** bubble, effervesce, fizz, fizzle *~noun* **3.** brilliance, coruscation, dazzle, flash, flicker, gleam, glint, radiance, spark, twinkle **4.** animation, brio, dash, élan, gaiety, life, panache, spirit, vim (*slang*), vitality, vivacity, zip (*informal*)

sparse few and far between, meagre, scanty, scarce, scattered, sporadic

Antonyms crowded, dense, lavish, lush, luxuriant, numerous, plentiful, thick

spartan 1. abstemious, ascetic, austere, bleak, disciplined, extreme, frugal, plain, rigorous, self-denying, severe, stern, strict, stringent **2.** bold, brave, courageous, daring, dauntless, doughty, fearless, hardy, heroic, intrepid, resolute, unflinching, valorous

spasm 1. contraction, convulsion, paroxysm, throe (*rare*), twitch **2.** access, burst, eruption, fit, frenzy, outburst, seizure

spasmodic convulsive, erratic, fitful, intermittent, irregular, jerky, sporadic

spat altercation, bicker, contention, controversy, dispute, quarrel, squabble, tiff

spate deluge, flood, flow, outpouring, rush, torrent

spatter bespatter, bestrew, daub, dirty, scatter, soil, speckle, splash, splodge, spray, sprinkle

spawn *often derogatory* issue, offspring, product, progeny, seed (*chiefly biblical*), yield

speak 1. articulate, communicate, converse, discourse, enunciate, express, make known, pronounce, say, state, talk, tell, utter, voice **2.** address, argue, declaim, deliver an address, descant, discourse, harangue, hold forth, lecture, plead, speechify, spiel (*informal*), spout

3. *with* **of** advert to, allude to, comment on, deal with, discuss, make reference to, mention, refer to

speaker lecturer, mouthpiece, orator, public speaker, spieler (*informal*), spokesman, spokesperson, spokeswoman, word-spinner

speak for act for *or* on behalf of, appear for, hold a brief for, hold a mandate for, represent

speaking *adjective* eloquent, expressive, moving, noticeable, striking

speak out *or* **up** 1. make oneself heard, say it loud and clear, speak loudly 2. have one's say, make one's position plain, sound off, speak one's mind, stand up and be counted

speak to 1. accost, address, apostrophize, direct one's words at, talk to 2. admonish, bring to book, dress down (*informal*), lecture, rebuke, reprimand, scold, tell off (*informal*), tick off (*informal*), warn

spearhead *verb* be in the van, blaze the trail, head, initiate, launch, lay the first stone, lead, lead the way, pioneer, set in motion, set off

special 1. distinguished, especial, exceptional, extraordinary, festive, gala, important, memorable, momentous, one in a million, out of the ordinary, red-letter, significant, uncommon, unique, unusual 2. appropriate, certain, characteristic, distinctive, especial, individual, particular, peculiar, precise, specialized, specific 3. chief, main, major, particular, primary

Antonyms common, everyday, general, humdrum, mediocre, multi-purpose, no great shakes (*informal*), normal, ordinary, routine, run-of-the-mill, undistinctive, undistinguished, unexceptional, unspecialized, usual

specialist *noun* authority, buff (*informal*), connoisseur, consultant, expert, hotshot (*informal*), master, maven (*U.S.*), professional, whiz (*informal*)

speciality bag (*slang*), claim to fame, distinctive *or* distinguishing feature, forte, métier, *pièce de résistance*, special, specialty

species breed, category, class, collection, description, genus, group, kind, sort, type, variety

specific *adjective* 1. clear-cut, definite, exact, explicit, express, limited, particular, precise, unambiguous, unequivocal 2. characteristic, distinguishing, especial, peculiar, special

Antonyms approximate, common, general, hazy, imprecise, non-specific, uncertain, unclear, vague, woolly

specification condition, detail, item, particular, qualification, requirement, stipulation

specify be specific about, cite, define, designate, detail, enumerate, indicate, individualize, itemize, mention, name, particularize, spell out, stipulate

specimen copy, embodiment, example, exemplar, exemplification, exhibit, individual, instance, model, pattern, proof, representative, sample, type

specious casuistic, deceptive, fallacious, misleading, plausible, sophistic, sophistical, unsound

speck 1. blemish, blot, defect, dot, fault, flaw, fleck, mark, mote, speckle, spot, stain 2. atom, bit, dot, grain, iota, jot, mite, modicum, particle, shred, tittle, whit

speckled brindled, dappled, dotted, flecked, freckled, mottled, speckledy, spotted, spotty, sprinkled, stippled

spectacle 1. display, event, exhibition, extravaganza, pageant, parade, performance, show, sight 2. curiosity, laughing stock, marvel, phenomenon, scene, sight, wonder

spectacular 1. *adjective* breathtaking, daring, dazzling, dramatic, eye-catching, fantastic (*informal*), grand, impressive, magnificent, marked, remarkable, sensational, splendid, staggering, striking, stunning (*informal*) 2. *noun* display, extravaganza, show, spectacle

Antonyms *adjective* easy, everyday, modest, ordinary, plain, run-of-the-mill, simple, unimpressive, unostentatious, unspectacular

spectator beholder, bystander, eyewitness, looker-on, observer, onlooker, viewer, watcher, witness

Antonyms contestant, contributor, partaker, participant, participator, party, player

spectral eerie, ghostly, incorporeal, insubstantial, phantom, shadowy, spooky (*informal*), supernatural, uncanny, unearthly, weird, wraithlike

spectre apparition, eidolon, ghost, phantom, presence, shade (*literary*), shadow, spirit, vision, wraith

speculate 1. cogitate, conjecture, consider, contemplate, deliberate, hypothesize, meditate, muse, scheme, suppose, surmise, theorize, wonder 2. gamble, have a flutter (*informal*), hazard, play the market, risk, take a chance with, venture

speculation 1. conjecture, consideration, contemplation, deliberation, guess, guesswork, hypothesis, opinion, supposition, surmise, theory 2. gamble, gambling, hazard, risk

speculative 1. abstract, academic, conjectural, hypothetical, notional, suppositional, tentative, theoretical 2. chancy (*informal*), dicey (*informal, chiefly Brit.*), hazardous, risky, uncertain, unpredictable

speech 1. communication, conversation, dialogue, discussion, intercourse, talk 2. address, discourse, disquisition, harangue, homily, lecture, oration, spiel (*informal*) 3. articulation, dialect, diction, enunciation, idiom, jargon, language, lingo (*informal*), parlance, tongue, utterance, voice

An after-dinner speech should be like a lady's dress - long enough to cover the subject and short enough to be interesting
R.A. Butler

A speech is like a love-affair. Any fool can start it, but to end it requires considerable skill
Lord Mancroft

Speech is the small-change of silence
George Meredith

Let your speech be alway with grace, seasoned with salt
Bible: Colossians

Half the sorrows of women would be averted if they could repress the speech they know to be useless; nay, the speech they have resolved not to make
George Eliot *Felix Holt*

Human speech is like a cracked kettle on which we tap crude rhythms for bears to dance to, while we long to make music that will melt the stars
Gustave Flaubert *Madame Bovary*

speechless **1.** dumb, inarticulate, lost for words, mum, mute, silent, tongue-tied, unable to get a word out (*informal*), wordless **2.** *figurative* aghast, amazed, astounded, dazed, dumbfounded, dumbstruck, shocked, thunderstruck

speed *noun* **1.** acceleration, celerity, expedition, fleetness, haste, hurry, momentum, pace, precipitation, quickness, rapidity, rush, swiftness, velocity *~verb* **2.** barrel (along) (*informal, chiefly U.S. & Canad.*), belt (along) (*slang*), bomb (along), bowl along, burn rubber (*informal*), career, dispatch, exceed the speed limit, expedite, flash, gallop, get a move on (*informal*), go hell for leather (*informal*), go like a bat out of hell, go like a bomb (*Brit. & N.Z. informal*), go like the wind, hasten, hurry, lose no time, make haste, press on, put one's foot down (*informal*), quicken, race, rush, sprint, step on it (*informal*), tear, urge, zoom **3.** advance, aid, assist, boost, expedite, facilitate, further, help, impel, promote
Antonyms *noun* delay, slowness, sluggishness, tardiness *~verb* crawl, creep, dawdle, delay, hamper, hinder, hold up, retard, slow, take one's time, tarry

speed up accelerate, gather momentum, get moving, get under way, increase, increase the tempo, open up the throttle, put one's foot down (*informal*), put on speed
Antonyms brake, decelerate, reduce speed, rein in, slacken (off), slow down

speedy expeditious, express, fast, fleet, fleet of foot, hasty, headlong, hurried, immediate, nimble, pdq (*slang*), precipitate, prompt, quick, quickie (*informal*), rapid, summary, swift, winged
Antonyms dead slow and stop, delayed, dilatory, late, leisurely, lingering, long-drawn-out, plodding, slow, sluggish, tardy, unhurried, unrushed

spell[1] *noun* bout, course, interval, patch, period, season, stint, stretch, term, time, tour of duty, turn

spell[2] *noun* **1.** abracadabra, charm, conjuration, exorcism, incantation, sorcery, witchery **2.** allure, bewitchment, enchantment, fascination, glamour, magic, trance

spell[3] *verb* amount to, augur, herald, imply, indicate, mean, point to, portend, presage, promise, signify, suggest

spellbound bemused, bewitched, captivated, charmed, enthralled, entranced, fascinated, gripped, hooked, mesmerized, possessed, rapt, transfixed, transported, under a spell

spelling orthography

My spelling is Wobbly. It's good spelling but it Wobbles, and the letters get in the wrong place
A.A. Milne *Winnie the Pooh*

"Do you spell it with a 'V' or a 'W'?"... "That depends upon the taste and fancy of the speller, my Lord."
Charles Dickens *Pickwick Papers*

orthography: the science of spelling by the eye instead of the ear
Ambrose Bierce *The Devil's Dictionary*

spell out **1.** clarify, elucidate, explicate, make clear *or* plain, make explicit, specify **2.** discern, make out, puzzle out

spend **1.** disburse, expend, fork out (*slang*), lay out, pay out, shell out (*informal*), splash out (*Brit. informal*) **2.** blow (*slang*), consume, deplete, dispense, dissipate, drain, empty, exhaust, fritter away, run through, squander, use up, waste **3.** apply, bestow, concentrate, devote, employ, exert, invest, lavish, put in, use **4.** fill, occupy, pass, while away
Antonyms (*senses 1 & 2*) hoard, invest, keep, put aside, put by, save, store

spendthrift **1.** *noun* big spender, prodigal, profligate, spender, squanderer, waster, wastrel **2.** *adjective* extravagant, improvident, prodigal, profligate, wasteful
Antonyms *noun* meanie *or* meany (*informal, chiefly Brit.*), miser, penny-pincher (*informal*), Scrooge, skinflint, tight-arse (*taboo slang*), tight-ass (*U.S. taboo slang*), tightwad (*U.S. & Canad. slang*) *~adjective* careful, economical, frugal, parsimonious, provident, prudent, sparing, thrifty

spent *adjective* **1.** all in (*slang*), burnt out, bushed (*informal*), clapped out (*Austral. & N.Z. informal*), dead beat (*informal*), debilitated, dog-tired (*informal*), done in *or* up (*informal*), drained, effete, exhausted, fagged (out) (*informal*), knackered (*slang*), played out (*informal*), prostrate, ready to drop (*informal*), shagged out (*Brit. slang*), shattered (*informal*), tired out, weakened, wearied, weary, whacked (*Brit. informal*), wiped out (*informal*), worn out, zonked (*informal*) **2.** consumed, expended, finished, gone, used up

sperm **1.** come *or* cum (*taboo*), jissom (*taboo*), scum (*U.S. slang*), seed (*archaic or dialect*), semen, spermatozoa **2.** male gamete, reproductive cell, spermatozoon

spew barf (*U.S. slang*), belch forth, chuck (up) (*slang, chiefly U.S.*), chunder (*slang, chiefly Austral.*), disgorge, do a technicolour yawn (*slang*), puke (*slang*), regurgitate, spit out, throw up (*informal*), toss one's cookies (*U.S. slang*), upchuck (*U.S. slang*), vomit

sphere **1.** ball, circle, globe, globule, orb **2.** capacity, compass, department, domain, employment, field, function, pale, patch, province, range, rank, realm, scope, station, stratum, territory, turf (*U.S. slang*), walk of life

spherical globe-shaped, globular, orbicular, rotund, round

spice *noun* **1.** relish, savour, seasoning **2.** colour, excitement, gusto, kick (*informal*), pep, piquancy, tang, zap (*slang*), zest, zing (*informal*), zip (*informal*)

Herbs, spices and seasonings
see FOOD

spick-and-span clean, fresh as paint, immaculate, impeccable, in apple-pie order (*informal*), neat as a new pin, shipshape, spotless, spruce, tidy, trim

spicy **1.** aromatic, flavoursome, hot, piquant, pungent, savoury, seasoned, tangy **2.** *informal* broad, hot (*informal*), improper, indecorous, indelicate, off-colour, racy, ribald, risqué, scandalous, sensational, suggestive, titillating, unseemly

spiel **1.** *verb* expatiate on, hold forth, lecture, recite, speechify, spout (*informal*) **2.** *noun* harangue, patter, pitch, recital, sales patter, sales talk, speech

spike *noun* **1.** barb, point, prong, spine ~*verb* **2.** impale, spear, spit, stick **3.** block, foil, frustrate, render ineffective, thwart

spill *verb* **1.** discharge, disgorge, overflow, overturn, scatter, shed, slop over, spill *or* run over, teem, throw off, upset **2. spill the beans** *informal* betray a secret, blab, blow the gaff (*Brit. slang*), give the game away, grass (*Brit. slang*), inform, let the cat out of the bag, shop (*slang, chiefly Brit.*), sing (*slang, chiefly U.S.*), spill one's guts (*slang*), split (*slang*), squeal (*slang*), talk out of turn, tattle, tell all ~*noun* **3.** *informal* accident, cropper (*informal*), fall, tumble

spin *verb* **1.** birl (*Scot.*), gyrate, pirouette, reel, revolve, rotate, turn, twirl, twist, wheel, whirl **2.** concoct, develop, invent, narrate, recount, relate, tell, unfold **3.** be giddy, be in a whirl, grow dizzy, reel, swim, whirl ~*noun* **4.** gyration, revolution, roll, twist, whirl **5. (flat) spin** *informal* agitation, commotion, flap (*informal*), mind-fuck (*taboo slang*), panic, state (*informal*), tiz-woz (*informal*), tizzy (*informal*) **6.** *informal* drive, hurl (*Scot.*), joy ride (*informal*), ride, turn, whirl

spindly attenuated, gangling, gangly, lanky, leggy, spidery, spindle-shanked, twiggy

spine **1.** backbone, spinal column, vertebrae, vertebral column **2.** barb, needle, quill, rachis, ray, spike, spur

spine-chilling bloodcurdling, eerie, frightening, hair-raising, horrifying, scary (*informal*), spooky (*informal*), terrifying

spineless boneless, chickenshit (*U.S. slang*), cowardly, faint-hearted, feeble, gutless (*informal*), inadequate, ineffective, irresolute, lily-livered, pathetic, soft, spiritless, squeamish, submissive, vacillating, weak, weak-kneed (*informal*), weak-willed, without a will of one's own, yellow (*informal*)
Antonyms ballsy (*taboo slang*), bold, brave, courageous, gritty, strong, strong-willed

spin out amplify, delay, drag out, draw out, extend, lengthen, pad out, prolong, prolongate, protract

spiral **1.** *adjective* circular, cochlear, cochleate (*Biology*), coiled, corkscrew, helical, scrolled, voluted, whorled, winding **2.** *noun* coil, corkscrew, curlicue, gyre (*literary*), helix, screw, volute, whorl

spirit *noun* **1.** air, breath, life, life force, psyche, soul, vital spark **2.** attitude, character, complexion, disposition, essence, humour, outlook, quality, temper, temperament **3.** animation, ardour, backbone, balls (*taboo slang*), ballsiness (*taboo slang*), brio, courage, dauntlessness, earnestness, energy, enterprise, enthusiasm, fire, force, gameness, grit, guts (*informal*), life, liveliness, mettle, resolution, sparkle, spunk (*informal*), stoutheartedness, vigour, warmth, zest **4.** motivation, resolution, resolve, will, willpower **5.** atmosphere, feeling, gist, humour, tenor, tone **6.** essence, intent, intention, meaning, purport, purpose, sense, substance **7.** *plural* feelings, frame of mind, humour, mood, morale **8.** apparition, eidolon, ghost, phantom, shade (*literary*), shadow, spectre, spook (*informal*), sprite, vision ~*verb* **9.** *with* **away** *or* **off** abduct, abstract, carry, convey, make away with, purloin, remove, seize, snaffle (*Brit. informal*), steal, whisk

spirited active, animated, ardent, bold, courageous, energetic, feisty (*informal, chiefly U.S.*

& *Canad.*), game, have-a-go (*informal*), high-spirited, lively, mettlesome, plucky, sparkling, sprightly, spunky (*informal*), vigorous, vivacious
Antonyms apathetic, bland, calm, dispirited, dull, feeble, half-hearted, lacklustre, lifeless, low-key, spiritless, timid, token, unenthusiastic, weary

spiritless apathetic, dejected, depressed, despondent, dispirited, droopy, dull, lacklustre, languid, lifeless, listless, low (*informal*), melancholic, melancholy, mopy, torpid, unenthusiastic, unmoved

spirits alcohol, firewater, liquor, strong liquor, the hard stuff (*informal*)

Spirits
see DRINK

spiritual devotional, divine, ethereal, ghostly, holy, immaterial, incorporeal, nonmaterial, otherworldly, pure, religious, sacred
Antonyms concrete, corporeal, material, nonspiritual, palpable, physical, substantial, tangible

spit **1.** *verb* discharge, eject, expectorate, hiss, spew, splutter, sputter, throw out **2.** *noun* dribble, drool, saliva, slaver, spittle, sputum

spite *noun* **1.** animosity, bitchiness (*slang*), gall, grudge, hate, hatred, ill will, malevolence, malice, malignity, pique, rancour, spitefulness, spleen, venom **2. in spite of** despite, (even) though, in defiance of, notwithstanding, regardless of ~*verb* **3.** annoy, discomfit, gall, harm, hurt, injure, needle (*informal*), nettle, offend, pique, provoke, put out, put (someone's) nose out of joint (*informal*), vex
Antonyms *noun* benevolence, big-heartedness, charity, compassion, generosity of spirit, goodwill, kindliness, kindness, love, warm-heartedness ~*verb* aid, benefit, encourage, go along with, help, please, serve, support

Don't cut off your nose to spite your face

spiteful barbed, bitchy (*informal*), catty (*informal*), cruel, ill-disposed, ill-natured, malevolent, malicious, malignant, nasty, rancorous, shrewish, snide, splenetic, venomous, vindictive

spitting image clone, (dead) ringer (*slang*), double, likeness, living image, lookalike, picture, replica, spit (*informal, chiefly Brit.*), spit and image (*informal*)

splash *verb* **1.** bespatter, shower, slop, slosh (*informal*), spatter, splodge, spray, spread, sprinkle, squirt, strew, wet **2.** bathe, dabble, paddle, plunge, wade, wallow **3.** batter, break, buffet, dash, plash, plop, smack, strike, surge, wash **4.** blazon, broadcast, flaunt, headline, plaster, publicize, tout, trumpet ~*noun* **5.** burst, dash, patch, spattering, splodge, touch **6.** *informal* display, effect, impact, sensation, splurge, stir **7. make a splash** be ostentatious, cause a stir, cut a dash, go overboard (*informal*), go to town, splurge

splash out be extravagant, lash out (*informal*), push the boat out (*Brit. informal*), spare no expense, spend, splurge

spleen acrimony, anger, animosity, animus, bad temper, bile, bitterness, gall, hatred, hostility, ill humour, ill will, malevolence, malice, malignity, peevishness, pique, rancour, resentment, spite, spitefulness, venom, vindictiveness, wrath

splendid **1.** admirable, brilliant, exceptional, glorious, grand, heroic, illustrious, magnificent, outstanding, rare, remarkable, renowned, sterling, sublime, superb, supreme **2.** costly, dazzling, gorgeous, imposing, impressive, lavish, luxurious, magnificent, ornate, resplendent, rich, splendiferous (*facetious*), sumptuous, superb **3.** awesome (*slang*), bodacious (*slang, chiefly U.S.*), boffo (*slang*), brill (*informal*), chillin' (*U.S. slang*), cracking (*Brit. informal*), crucial (*slang*), def (*slang*), excellent, fantastic (*informal*), fine, first-class, glorious, great (*informal*), marvellous, mean (*slang*), mega (*slang*), sovereign, topping (*Brit. slang*), wonderful **4.** beaming, bright, brilliant, glittering, glowing, lustrous, radiant, refulgent
Antonyms beggarly, depressing, disgusting, distressed, drab, dull, ignoble, ignominious, lacklustre, low, mean, mediocre, miserable, no great shakes (*informal*), ordinary, pathetic, plain, poor, poverty-stricken, rotten, run-of-the-mill, sombre, sordid, squalid, tarnished, tawdry, undistinguished, unexceptional

splendour brightness, brilliance, ceremony, dazzle, display, éclat, effulgence, glory, gorgeousness, grandeur, lustre, magnificence, majesty, pomp, radiance, refulgence, renown, resplendence, richness, show, solemnity, spectacle, stateliness, sumptuousness
Antonyms dullness, ignominy, lacklustreness, meanness, ordinariness, plainness, poverty, simplicity, sobriety, squalor, tawdriness

splenetic acid, bitchy (*informal*), choleric, churlish, crabbed, crabby, cross, envenomed, fretful, irascible, irritable, morose, peevish, petulant, rancorous, ratty (*Brit. & N.Z. informal*), sour, spiteful, sullen, testy, tetchy, touchy

splice *verb* braid, entwine, graft, interlace, intertwine, intertwist, interweave, join, knit, marry, mesh, plait, unite, wed, yoke

splinter **1.** *noun* chip, flake, fragment, needle, paring, shaving, sliver **2.** *verb* break into smithereens, disintegrate, fracture, shatter, shiver, split

split *verb* **1.** bifurcate, branch, break, break up, burst, cleave, come apart, come undone, crack, disband, disunite, diverge, fork, gape, give way, go separate ways, open, part, pull apart, rend, rip, separate, slash, slit, snap, splinter **2.** allocate, allot, apportion, carve up, distribute, divide, divvy up (*informal*), dole out, halve, parcel out, partition, share out, slice up **3.** *with* **on** *slang* betray, give away, grass (*Brit. slang*), inform on, peach (*slang*), shop (*slang, chiefly Brit.*), sing (*slang, chiefly U.S.*), spill one's guts (*slang*), squeal (*slang*) *~noun* **4.** breach, crack, damage, division, fissure, gap, rent, rip, separation, slash, slit, tear **5.** breach, break, break-up, difference, discord, disruption, dissension, disunion, divergence, division, estrangement, partition, rift, rupture, schism *~adjective* **6.** ambivalent, bisected, broken, cleft, cracked, divided, dual, fractured, ruptured, twofold

split up break up, disband, divorce, go separate ways, part, part company, separate

spoil *verb* **1.** blemish, blow (*slang*), damage, debase, deface, destroy, disfigure, harm, impair, injure, mar, mess up, put a damper on, ruin, scar, total (*slang*), trash (*slang*), undo, upset, wreck **2.** baby, cocker (*rare*), coddle, cosset, indulge, kill with kindness, mollycoddle, overindulge, pamper, spoon-feed **3.** addle, become tainted, curdle, decay, decompose, go bad, go off (*Brit. informal*), mildew, putrefy, rot, turn **4. spoiling for** bent upon, desirous of, eager for, enthusiastic about, keen to, looking for, out to get (*informal*), raring to
Antonyms (*sense 1*) augment, conserve, enhance, improve, keep, preserve, save (*sense 2*) be strict with, deprive, ignore, pay no attention to, treat harshly

spoils boodle (*slang, chiefly U.S.*), booty, gain, loot, pickings, pillage, plunder, prey, prizes, rapine, swag (*slang*)

spoilsport damper, dog in the manger, kill-joy, misery (*Brit. informal*), party-pooper (*U.S. slang*), wet blanket (*informal*)

spoken by word of mouth, expressed, oral, phonetic, put into words, said, told, unwritten, uttered, verbal, viva voce, voiced

sponger bloodsucker (*informal*), cadge (*Brit.*), cadger, freeloader (*slang*), hanger-on, leech, parasite, scrounger (*informal*)

spongy absorbent, cushioned, cushiony, elastic, light, porous, springy

sponsor 1. *noun* angel (*informal*), backer, godparent, guarantor, patron, promoter **2.** *verb* back, finance, fund, guarantee, lend one's name to, patronize, promote, put up the money for, subsidize

spontaneous extempore, free, impromptu, impulsive, instinctive, natural, unbidden, uncompelled, unconstrained, unforced, unpremeditated, unprompted, voluntary, willing
Antonyms arranged, calculated, contrived, deliberate, forced, mannered, orchestrated, planned, prearranged, premeditated, preplanned, stage-managed, studied

spontaneously extempore, freely, impromptu, impulsively, instinctively, in the heat of the moment, off one's own bat, off the cuff (*informal*), of one's own accord, on impulse, quite unprompted, voluntarily

spoof *noun* **1.** burlesque, caricature, lampoon, mockery, parody, satire, send-up (*Brit. informal*), take-off (*informal*), travesty **2.** bluff, canard, deception, game, hoax, joke, leg-pull (*Brit. informal*), prank, trick

spooky chilling, creepy (*informal*), eerie, frightening, ghostly, mysterious, scary (*informal*), spine-chilling, supernatural, uncanny, unearthly, weird

spoon-feed baby, cosset, featherbed, mollycoddle, overindulge, overprotect, spoil, wrap up in cotton wool (*informal*)

sporadic infrequent, intermittent, irregular, isolated, occasional, on and off, random, scattered, spasmodic
Antonyms consistent, frequent, recurrent, regular, set, steady, systematic

sport *noun* **1.** amusement, diversion, entertainment, exercise, game, pastime, physical activity, play, recreation **2.** badinage, banter, frolic, fun, jest, joking, josh (*slang, chiefly U.S. & Canad.*), kidding (*informal*), merriment, mirth, raillery, teasing **3.** buffoon, butt, derision, fair game, game, laughing stock, mockery, plaything, ridicule *~verb* **4.** *with* **with** amuse oneself, dally, flirt, fool, play, take advantage of, toy, treat lightly *or* cavalierly, trifle **5.** *informal* display, exhibit, show off, wear **6.** caper, disport, frolic, gambol, play, romp

Team sports

American football
association football *or* soccer
Australian Rules *or* Australian Rules football
baseball
bandy
basketball
camogie
Canadian football
cricket
curling
five-a-side football
football
Gaelic football
goalball
handball
hockey
hurling *or* hurley
ice hockey
kabbadi
korfball
lacrosse
netball
polo
roller hockey
rounders
rugby *or* rugby football
rugby league
rugby union
shinty
softball

stool ball
tug-of-war

Motor sports

autocross
drag racing
karting
motocross
motor-cycle racing
motor racing
motor rallying *or* ral~ lying
rallycross
scrambling
speedway
stock car racing

Winter sports

Alpine skiing
biathlon
bobsleigh
curling
downhill racing
ice dancing
ice hockey
ice skating *or* figure skating
luge
Nordic skiing
skating
skibobbing
skiing
skijoring
ski jumping
slalom
snowboarding
speed skating
super-G
tobogganing

Water sports

aquabobbing
canoeing
canoe polo
diving
parasailing
powerboating *or* powerboat racing
rowing
sailing
skin diving
surfing
swimming
synchronized swim~ ming
water polo
water-skiing
windsurfing
yachting

Athletic events

100 metres
110 metres hurdles
200 metres
400 metres
400 metres hurdles
800 metres
1500 metres
3000 metres
5000 metres
10 000 metres
cross-country running
decathlon
discus
half marathon
hammer
heptathlon
high jump
javelin
long jump
marathon
orienteering
pole vault
relay
shot put
steeplechase
triple jump
walking

Other sports

angling *or* fishing
archery
badminton
ballooning
billiards
boules
bowls
bullfighting
candlepins
clay pigeon shooting
cockfighting
coursing
croquet
cycling
cyclo-cross
darts
falconry
fives
fly-fishing
fowling
fox-hunting
gliding
golf
greyhound racing
gymnastics
hang gliding
jai alai
lawn tennis
modern pentathlon
mountaineering
paddleball
parachuting
paragliding
parascending
paraskiing
pelota
pétanque
pigeon racing
pool
potholing
quoits
rackets
real tennis
rhythmic gymnastics
rock climbing
roller skating
shooting
skeet
skittles
skydiving
snooker
squash *or* squash rackets
table tennis
tennis
tenpin bowling
trampolining
trapshooting
triathlon
weightlifting

Terms used in (Association) Football

aggregate (score)
back
ballplayer
ballwinner
booking *or* caution
breakaway
cap
catenaccio
centre circle
centre forward
centre half
clearance
cross
crossbar *or* bar
corner (kick)
cut out
defender
derby
direct free kick
dribble
dummy
extra time
FA
FIFA
finishing
forward
foul
free kick
fullback
full time
goal
goal area *or* six-yard box
goalkeeper *or* goalie
goal kick *or* bye kick
goal net *or* net
goalpost *or* post
half
halfback
half time
half way line
handball
indirect free kick
inside left
inside right
inswinger
international
kick off
lay off
left back
linesman
long ball
mark
midfield
midfielder
nil
non-league
nutmeg
offside
offside trap
onside
one-two
outside left
outside right
own goal
pass
pass-back
penalty (kick) *or* spot kick
penalty area *or* pen~ alty box
penalty shoot-out
penalty spot
playoff
professional foul
promotion
red card
referee
relegation
reserves
right back
Route One
save
score draw

sending-off *or* ordering-off
SFA
shot
six-yard line
sliding tackle
stoppage time *or* injury time
striker
square
substitute
sweeper
tackle
target man
throw in
total football
touchline
transfer
trap
UEFA
wall
wall pass
wing
winger
yellow card

Terms used in Australian Rules Football

Australian Football League *or* AFL
back pocket
behind *or* point
behind line
behind post
boundary
eighteen, the
field umpire
flank
footy, Aussie Rules *or* *(jocular)* aerial ping-pong
follower
forward pocket
free kick
goal
goal umpire
guernsey
half-back
half-forward
handball
interchange
mark
nineteenth man
quarter
rove
rover
rub out
ruck
ruckrover
scrimmage
shepherd
shirt front
stab kick
stanza
throw in
twentieth man

American football terms

backfield
blitz
block
center
complete
cornerback
defense
defensive back
defensive end
down
end zone
field goal
football *or* pigskin
fullback
gridiron
guard
halfback
incomplete
interception
kicker
line *or* line of scrimmage
line backer
lineman
offense
overtime
pass
play
point after
punt
punter
quarterback
run *or* rush
running back
sack
safety
scrimmage
secondary
shotgun
snap
special team
Super Bowl
tackle
tight end
touchback
touchdown
turnover
wide receiver

Rugby terms

back
back row
ball
centre
conversion
crossbar
drop goal
lock forward
loose forward
loose head
five-eighth (*Austral. & N.Z.*)
flanker *or* wing forward (*rugby union*)
forward
front row
full back
garryowen (*rugby union*)
goalpost
half back
hooker
knock on
line-out (*rugby union*)
mark (*rugby union*)
maul (*rugby union*)
number eight forward (*rugby union*)
scrum *or* scrummage
stand-off half, fly half *or* outside half
pack
pass
penalty
prop forward
punt
referee
ruck (*rugby union*)
scrum half
second row
tackle
three-quarter
tight head
touch judge
try
up and under (*rugby league*)
winger

Tennis terms

ace
advantage
approach shot
backhand
ball
baseline
break of serve
break point
cannonball
centre line
centre mark
chip
clay court
court
deuce
double fault
doubles
drop shot
fault
foot fault
forecourt
forehand
game
grass court
ground stroke
half-volley
hard court
lawn tennis
let
line call
linesman
lob
love
love game
match
mixed doubles
net
net cord
passing shot
racket *or* racquet
rally
receiver
return
server
service
service line
set
set point
sideline
singles
slice
smash
tie-break *or* tie-breaker
topspin
tramline
umpire
undercut
volley

Cricket terms

appeal
Ashes
bail
ball
bat
batsman

bouncer *or* bumper
boundary
bowl
bowled
bowler
bye
catch
caught
century
chinaman
cover point
covers
crease
cut
declare
drive
duck
edge
extra
extra cover
fast bowler
fielder *or* fieldsman
fine leg
follow on
four
full toss
glance *or* glide
googly
gully
hit wicket
hook
in
innings
leg before wicket
leg break
leg bye
leg slip
long leg
long off
long on
maiden (over)
mid off
mid on
mid wicket
nightwatchman
no ball
off break
off side
on side *or* leg side
opener *or* opening batsman
out
over
pad
pitch
pull
run
run out
seam
short leg
silly mid on
silly mid off
single
six
slip
spin
square leg
stump
stumped
sweep
swing
test match
third man
twelfth man
umpire
wicket
wicketkeeper
wide
yorker

Golf terms

ace (*U.S.*)
air shot *or* fresh air shot
albatross
approach
apron
back nine (*chiefly U.S.*)
backswing
bag
ball
bandit
better-ball
birdie
blade
bogey
borrow
bunker, trap *or (esp. U.S. & Canad.)* sand trap
caddie
caddie car
carry
casual water
chip
club
clubhouse
course
cup
cut
divot
dormie
downswing
draw
drive
driver
driving range
duff
eagle
fade
fairway
fluff
foozle
fore
four-ball
foursome
front nine (*chiefly U.S.*)
gimme
green
green fee
green keeper
greensome
grip
half
half shot
handicap
hazard
heel
hole
hole in one
honour
hook
hosel
iron
ladies' tee
lag
lie
links
local rules
loft
long iron
marker
match play
medal play
medal tee
midiron
nine-hole course
nineteenth hole
par
pin
pitch and run
pitching wedge
pitch shot
play through
plus fours
plus twos
practice swing
pull
putt
putter
putting green
rabbit
recovery
rough
round
rub of the green
run
Royal and Ancient *or* R & A
sand wedge
sclaff
score
score card
scratch
shaft
shank
short iron
single
slice
slow play
spoon
Stableford system
stance
stroke
stroke play
stymie
sweetspot
swing
take-away
tee
thin
tiger
threesome
top
trolley
waggle
wedge
wood
yips

Snooker and billiards terms

baize
ball
baulk
baulkline
black
blue
boucleé
break
bricole
bridge
brown
cannon
carom (*chiefly U.S. & Canad*)
chalk
clearance
cue ball
cue extension
cue tip
cushion
d
double
draw
drop cannon
fluke
foul

frame
free ball
green
half-butt
hazard
headrail
in-off
jenny
kick
kiss
lag
long jenny
massé
maximum break *or* 147
miscue
nurse
nursery cannon
object ball
pink
plain ball
plant
pocket
pot
red
rest
safety
scratch
screw
short jenny
side *or (U.S. & Canad.)* English
snooker
spider
spot
spot ball
stun
top
triangle *or (U.S. & Canad.)* rack
white
Whitechapel
yellow

Equestrian events and sports

Ascot
Badminton
buckjumping (*Austral.*)
cavalcade
claiming race (*U.S. & Canad.*)
classic
Derby
dressage
eventing
Grand National
gymkhana
harness racing
horse racing
hunt
joust
jump-off
Kentucky Derby
meeting
nursery stakes
Oaks
One Thousand Guineas
picnic race (*Austral.*)
plate
point-to-point
polo
puissance
race meeting
races, the
Saint Leger
showjumping
steeplechase
sweepstake *or (esp. U.S.)* sweepstakes
three-day eventing
Two Thousand Guineas

Classic English horse races	**Course**	**Distance**
One Thousand Guineas (fillies)	Newmarket	one mile
Two Thousand Guineas (colts)	Newmarket	one mile
Derby (colts)	Epsom	one and a half miles
the Oaks (fillies)	Epsom	one and a half miles
St. Leger (colts and fillies)	Doncaster	one and three quarter miles

Horse racing terms

accumulator
allowance
also-ran
ante post betting
apprentice
auction plate
away
blanket finish
boring
break
break away
card *or* race card
chaser
claiming race (*U.S. & Canad.*)
classic
clerk of the course
clerk of the scales
colt
come in
course
daily double
dead heat
distance
dope sheet (*slang*)
draw
each way *or (U.S.)* across-the-board
faller
fence
filly
finish
flat
flat jockey
flat racing
flight
furlong
gate
going
green horse
handicap
handicapper
handy
harness race *or (N.Z)* trotting race
head
home straight *or (U.S.)* home stretch
hurdle
hurdling
impost
jockey
Jockey Club
jump jockey
length
maiden
meeting
milepost
nap
National Hunt
neck
novice
objection
pacemaker *or* pace~setter
pacer
paddock
photo finish
place
plater
point-to-point (*Brit.*)
pole (*chiefly U.S. & Canad.*)
post
roughie
scratch
scurry
selling race *or* plate
short head
silver ring
stakes
starter
starting post
starting price
starting stalls *or (U.S.)* starting gate
stayer
steeplechase *or* chase
steward
stewards' enquiry
straight *or (U.S.)* straightaway
stretch
sweat (*chiefly U.S.*)
sweat up
ticktack
track
trainer
turf
under starter's orders
unplaced
unseated rider
walkover
weigh in
winning post
wire (*U.S. & Canad.*)
yearling

Types of jump

brush and rails
double oxer
gate
hog's back
narrow stile
parallel poles
planks
post and rails
triple bars
wall
water jump

Combat sports

boxing
fencing
sambo *or* sambo wrestling
savate
wrestling

Boxing weights	Amateur	Professional
Light flyweight	48 kg	49 kg
Flyweight	51 kg	51 kg
Bantamweight	54 kg	53.5 kg
Featherweight	57 kg	57 kg
Junior lightweight	-	59 kg
Lightweight	60 kg	61 kg
Light welterweight	63.5 kg	63.5 kg
Welterweight	67 kg	66.6 kg
Light middleweight	71 kg	70 kg
Middleweight	75 kg	72.5 kg
Light heavyweight	81 kg	79 kg
Cruiserweight	-	88.5 kg
Heavyweight	91 kg	+88.5 kg
Superheavyweight	+91 kg	-

Martial arts

aikido
capoeira
Crane style kung fu
Goju Kai karate
Goju Ryu karate
hapkido
Hung Gar *or* Tiger style kung fu
iai-do
iai-jutsu
Ishin Ryu karate
Jeet Kune Do
judo
ju jitsu, jiu jitsu *or* ju-jutsu
karate *or* karate-do
kendo
kick boxing
kung fu
Kyokushinkai karate
kyudo
naginata-do
ninjitsu *or* ninjutsu
Praying Mantis style kung fu
Sankukai karate
Shito Ryu karate
Shotokai karate
Shotokan karate
Shukokai karate
sumo *or* sumo wrestling
tae kwon-do
tai chi chuan
tai chi qi gong
Ta Sheng Men *or* Monkey style kung fu
Thai boxing *or* Muay Thai
Tomiki aikido
Tukido (*Trademark*)
Wado Ryu karate
Wing Chun *or* Wing Tsun kung fu
yari-jutsu

Martial arts terms	Meaning
basho	sumo turnament
bo	staff
bogu	kendo armour
bokuto	kendo wooden sword
budo *or* bushido	warrior's way
dan	black belt grade
do	kendo breastplate
-do	the way
dohyo	sumo ring
dojo	practice room or mat
gi	suit
hachimaki *or* tenugui	kendo headcloth
hakama	divided skirt
ippon	one competition point
jiu-kumite	freestyle karate competition
-jutsu	fighting art
-ka	student
kama	hand sickle
kata	sequence of techniques
katana	kendo sword
katsu	resuscitation techniques
keikogi	kendo jacket
kesho-mawashi	embroidered sumo apron
ki, chi *or* qi	inner power
kiai	yell accompanying movement
kihon	repetition of techniques
kote	kendo gauntlets
kyu	student grade
makiwara	practice block
mawashi	sumo fighting belt
men	kendo mask
nage-waza *or* tachi-waza	ju jitsu competition
naginata	curved-blade spear
ne-waza	ju jitsu competition
ninin-dori	aikido competition
ninja	Japanese trained assassin
nunchaku	hinged flails
obi	coloured belt
ozeki	sumo champion
qi gong	breath control
randori kyoghi	aikido competition
rikishi	sumo wrestler
rokushakubo	six-foot staff
ryu	martial arts school

sai	short trident
samurai	Japanese warrior caste
sensei	teacher
shinai	kendo bamboo sword
sifu	teacher
suneate	naginata shin guards
tanto randori	aikido competition
tare	kendo apron
te	hand fighting
ton-fa *or* tui-fa	hardwood weapon
tsuna	sumo grand champion's belt
waza-ari	half competition point
yari	spear
yokozuna	sumo grand champion
zanshin	total awareness

When a man wants to murder a tiger he calls it sport; when the tiger wants to murder him he calls it ferocity
George Bernard Shaw *Maxims for Revolutionists*

The flannelled fools at the wicket or the muddied oafs at the goals
Rudyard Kipling *The Islanders*

It's more than a game. It's an institution
Thomas Hughes (of cricket) *Tom Brown's Schooldays*

cricket - a game which the English, not being a spiritual people, have invented in order to give themselves some conception of eternity
Lord Mancroft *Bees in Some Bonnets*

Golf is a good walk spoiled
Mark Twain

sporting fair, game (*informal*), gentlemanly, sportsman-like
Antonyms unfair, unsporting, unsportsman~like

sportive coltish, frisky, frolicsome, full of beans (*informal*), full of fun, gamesome, gay, joyous, kittenish, lively, ludic (*literary*), merry, playful, prankish, rollicking, skittish, spright~ly

sporty **1.** casual, flashy, gay, informal, jaunty, jazzy (*informal*), loud, raffish, rakish, showy, snazzy (*informal*), stylish, trendy (*Brit. infor~mal*) **2.** athletic, energetic, hearty, outdoor

spot *noun* **1.** blemish, blot, blotch, daub, dis~coloration, flaw, mark, pimple, plook (*Scot.*), pustule, scar, smudge, speck, speckle, stain, taint, zit (*slang*) **2.** locality, location, place, point, position, scene, site, situation **3.** *infor~mal* bit, little, morsel, splash **4.** *informal* diffi~culty, hot water (*informal*), mess, plight, pre~dicament, quandary, tight spot, trouble *~verb* **5.** behold (*archaic or literary*), catch sight of, descry, detect, discern, espy, identify, make out, observe, pick out, recognize, see, sight **6.** besmirch, blot, dirty, dot, fleck, mark, mottle, scar, smirch, soil, spatter, speckle, splodge, splotch, stain, sully, taint, tarnish

Out, damned spot!
William Shakespeare *Macbeth*

spotless above reproach, blameless, chaste, clean, faultless, flawless, gleaming, immacu~late, impeccable, innocent, irreproachable, pure, shining, snowy, unblemished, unim~peachable, unstained, unsullied, untarnished, virgin, virginal, white
Antonyms besmirched, bespattered, blem~ished, defiled, dirty, filthy, flawed, impure, messy, notorious, reprehensible, soiled, spot~ted, stained, sullied, tainted, tarnished, un~chaste, untidy

spotlight *figurative* **1.** *verb* accentuate, draw attention to, feature, focus attention on, give prominence to, highlight, illuminate, point up, throw into relief **2.** *noun* attention, fame, in~terest, limelight, notoriety, public attention, public eye

spot-on accurate, correct, exact, hitting the nail on the head (*informal*), on the bull's-eye (*informal*), on the money (*U.S.*), precise, punctual (to the minute), right, unerring

spotted dappled, dotted, flecked, mottled, pied, polka-dot, specked, speckled

spotty **1.** blotchy, pimpled, pimply, plooky-faced (*Scot.*), poor-complexioned **2.** erratic, fluctuating, irregular, patchy, sporadic, un~even

spouse better half (*humorous*), companion, consort, helpmate, her indoors (*Brit. slang*), husband, mate, partner, significant other (*U.S. informal*), wife

spout *verb* **1.** discharge, emit, erupt, gush, jet, shoot, spray, spurt, squirt, stream, surge **2.** *informal* declaim, expatiate, go on (*informal*), hold forth, orate, pontificate, rabbit (on) (*Brit. informal*), ramble (on), rant, speechify, spiel (*informal*), talk

sprawl *verb* flop, loll, lounge, ramble, slouch, slump, spread, straggle, trail

spray[1] *verb* **1.** atomize, diffuse, scatter, shower, sprinkle *~noun* **2.** drizzle, droplets, fine mist, moisture, spindrift, spoondrift **3.** aerosol, at~omizer, sprinkler

spray[2] *noun* bough, branch, corsage, floral ar~rangement, shoot, sprig

spread *verb* **1.** be displayed, bloat, broaden, di~late, expand, extend, fan out, open, open out, sprawl, stretch, swell, unfold, unfurl, unroll, widen **2.** escalate, multiply, mushroom, prolif~erate **3.** advertise, blazon, broadcast, bruit, cast, circulate, cover, diffuse, disseminate, distribute, make known, make public, pro~claim, promulgate, propagate, publicize, pub~lish, radiate, scatter, shed, strew, transmit **4.**

arrange, array, cover, furnish, lay, prepare, set *~noun* **5.** advance, advancement, development, diffusion, dispersion, dissemination, escalation, expansion, increase, proliferation, spreading, suffusion, transmission **6.** compass, extent, period, reach, span, stretch, sweep, term **7.** *informal* array, banquet, blowout (*slang*), feast, repast
Antonyms *verb* (*sense 3*) contain, control, curb, hold back, hold in, repress, restrain, stifle

spree bacchanalia, beano (*Brit. slang*), bender (*informal*), binge (*informal*), carousal, carouse, debauch, fling, jag (*slang*), junketing, orgy, revel, splurge

sprightly active, agile, airy, alert, animated, blithe, bright-eyed and bushy-tailed, brisk, cheerful, energetic, frolicsome, gay, jaunty, joyous, lively, ludic (*literary*), nimble, perky, playful, spirited, sportive, spry, vivacious
Antonyms dull, inactive, lethargic, sedentary, sluggish, torpid, unenergetic

spring *verb* **1.** bounce, bound, hop, jump, leap, rebound, recoil, vault **2.** *often with* **from** arise, be derived, be descended, come, derive, descend, emanate, emerge, grow, issue, originate, proceed, start, stem **3.** *with* **up** appear, burgeon, come into existence *or* being, develop, mushroom, shoot up *~noun* **4.** bound, buck, hop, jump, leap, saltation, vault **5.** bounce, bounciness, buoyancy, elasticity, flexibility, give (*informal*), recoil, resilience, springiness **6.** beginning, cause, fount, fountainhead, origin, root, source, well, wellspring *~adjective* **7.** *of the season* springlike, vernal

April is the cruellest month, breeding
Lilacs out of the dead land, mixing
Memory and desire, stirring
Dull roots with spring rain
T.S. Eliot *The Waste Land*

springy bouncy, buoyant, elastic, flexible, resilient, rubbery, spongy

sprinkle *verb* dredge, dust, pepper, powder, scatter, shower, spray, strew

sprinkling admixture, dash, dusting, few, handful, scatter, scattering, smattering, sprinkle

sprint *verb* barrel (along) (*informal, chiefly U.S. & Canad.*), dart, dash, go at top speed, go like a bomb (*Brit. & N.Z. informal*), hare (*Brit. informal*), hotfoot, put on a burst of speed, race, scamper, shoot, tear, whiz (*informal*)

sprite apparition, brownie, dryad, elf, fairy, goblin, imp, leprechaun, naiad, nymph, Oceanid (*Greek myth*), peri, pixie, spirit, sylph

sprout *verb* bud, develop, germinate, grow, push, shoot, spring, vegetate

spruce as if one had just stepped out of a bandbox, dainty, dapper, elegant, natty (*informal*), neat, smart, soigné *or* soignée, trig (*archaic or dialect*), trim, well-groomed, well turned out
Antonyms bedraggled, disarrayed, dishevelled, frowsy, messy, rumpled, uncombed, unkempt, untidy

spruce up groom, gussy up (*slang, chiefly U.S.*), have a wash and brush-up (*Brit.*), smarten up, tidy, titivate

spry active, agile, alert, brisk, nimble, nippy (*Brit. informal*), quick, ready, sprightly, supple
Antonyms awkward, decrepit, doddering, inactive, lethargic, slow, sluggish, stiff

spunk backbone, balls (*taboo slang*), ballsiness (*taboo slang*), bottle (*Brit. slang*), courage, gameness, grit, gumption (*informal*), guts (*informal*), mettle, nerve, pluck, resolution, spirit, toughness

spur *verb* **1.** animate, drive, goad, impel, incite, press, prick, prod, prompt, put a bomb under (*informal*), stimulate, urge *~noun* **2.** goad, prick, rowel **3.** impetus, impulse, incentive, incitement, inducement, kick up the backside (*informal*), motive, stimulus **4. on the spur of the moment** impetuously, impromptu, impulsively, on impulse, on the spot, unpremeditatedly, unthinkingly, without planning, without thinking

spurious artificial, bogus, contrived, counterfeit, deceitful, ersatz, fake, false, feigned, forged, imitation, mock, phoney *or* phony (*informal*), pretended, pseudo (*informal*), sham, simulated, specious, unauthentic
Antonyms authentic, bona fide, genuine, honest, kosher (*informal*), legitimate, real, sound, unfeigned, valid

spurn cold-shoulder, contemn, despise, disdain, disregard, kick in the teeth (*slang*), put down, rebuff, reject, repulse, scorn, slight, snub, turn one's nose up at (*informal*)
Antonyms embrace, grasp, seize, take up, welcome

spurt **1.** *verb* burst, erupt, gush, jet, shoot, spew, squirt, surge **2.** *noun* access, burst, fit, rush, spate, surge

spy *noun* **1.** double agent, fifth columnist, foreign agent, mole, nark (*Brit., Austral., & N.Z. slang*), secret agent, secret service agent, undercover agent *~verb* **2.** *usually with* **on** follow, keep under surveillance, keep watch on, shadow, tail (*informal*), trail, watch **3.** behold (*archaic or literary*), catch sight of, descry, espy, glimpse, notice, observe, set eyes on, spot

spying *noun* espionage, secret service

squabble 1. *verb* argue, bicker, brawl, clash, dispute, fall out (*informal*), fight, fight like cat and dog, go at it hammer and tongs, have words, quarrel, row, scrap (*informal*), spar, wrangle 2. *noun* argument, *bagarre*, barney (*informal*), difference of opinion, disagreement, dispute, fight, row, scrap (*informal*), set-to (*informal*), spat, tiff

squad band, company, crew, force, gang, group, team, troop

squalid broken-down, decayed, dirty, disgusting, fetid, filthy, foul, low, nasty, poverty-stricken, repulsive, run-down, seedy, sleazy, slovenly, slummy, sordid, unclean, yucky *or* yukky (*slang*)
Antonyms attractive, clean, genial, hygienic, in good condition, pleasant, salubrious, spick-and-span, spotless, tidy, well-kempt, well looked-after

squally blustery, gusty, inclement, rough, stormy, tempestuous, turbulent, wild, windy

squalor decay, filth, foulness, meanness, sleaziness, slumminess, squalidness, wretchedness
Antonyms beauty, cleanliness, fine condition, luxury, neatness, order, pleasantness, splendour

squander be prodigal with, blow (*slang*), consume, dissipate, expend, fritter away, frivol away, lavish, misspend, misuse, run through, scatter, spend, spend like water, throw away, waste
Antonyms be frugal, be thrifty, economize, keep, put aside for a rainy day, save, store

square *figurative verb* 1. *often with* **with** accord, agree, conform, correspond, fit, harmonize, match, reconcile, tally 2. *sometimes with* **up** balance, clear (up), discharge, liquidate, make even, pay off, quit, satisfy, settle 3. accommodate, adapt, adjust, align, even up, level, regulate, suit, tailor, true (up) 4. *slang* bribe, buy off, corrupt, fix (*informal*), rig, suborn *~adjective* 5. aboveboard, decent, equitable, ethical, fair, fair and square, genuine, honest, just, kosher (*informal*), on the level (*informal*), on the up and up, straight, straightforward, upfront (*informal*), upright 6. *informal* behind the times, bourgeois, conservative, conventional, old-fashioned, out of date, out of the ark (*informal*), Pooterish, straight (*slang*), strait-laced, stuffy *~noun* 7. *informal* antediluvian, back number (*informal*), conservative, die-hard, dinosaur, fuddy-duddy (*informal*), old buffer (*Brit. informal*), (old) fogy, stick-in-the-mud (*informal*), traditionalist
Antonyms *adjective* (*sense 6*) fashionable, in vogue, modern, modish, stylish, trendy (*Brit. informal*), voguish

squash *verb* 1. compress, crush, distort, flatten, mash, pound, press, pulp, smash, stamp on, trample down 2. annihilate, crush, humiliate, put down (*slang*), put (someone) in his (*or* her) place, quash, quell, silence, sit on (*informal*), suppress

squashy mushy, pappy, pulpy, soft, spongy, yielding

squawk *verb* 1. cackle, crow, cry, hoot, screech, yelp 2. *informal* complain, kick up a fuss (*informal*), protest, raise Cain (*slang*), squeal (*informal, chiefly Brit.*)

squeak *verb* peep, pipe, shrill, squeal, whine, yelp

squeal *noun* 1. scream, screech, shriek, wail, yell, yelp, yowl *~verb* 2. scream, screech, shout, shriek, shrill, wail, yelp 3. *slang* betray, blab, blow the gaff (*Brit. slang*), grass (*Brit. slang*), inform on, peach (*slang*), rat on (*informal*), sell (someone) down the river (*informal*), shop (*slang, chiefly Brit.*), sing (*slang, chiefly U.S.*), snitch (*slang*), spill one's guts (*slang*), spill the beans (*informal*), tell all 4. *informal* complain, kick up a fuss (*informal*), moan, protest, squawk (*informal*)

squeamish 1. delicate, fastidious, finicky, nice (*rare*), particular, prissy (*informal*), prudish, punctilious, scrupulous, strait-laced 2. nauseous, qualmish, queasy, queer, sick, sickish
Antonyms bold, brassy, brazen, coarse, earthy, immodest, indifferent, strong-stomached, tough, wanton

squeeze *verb* 1. clutch, compress, crush, grip, nip, pinch, press, squash, wring 2. cram, crowd, force, jam, jostle, pack, press, ram, stuff, thrust, wedge 3. clasp, cuddle, embrace, enfold, hold tight, hug 4. bleed (*informal*), bring pressure to bear on, extort, lean on (*informal*), milk, oppress, pressurize, put the screws on (*informal*), put the squeeze on (*informal*), wrest *~noun* 5. clasp, embrace, handclasp, hold, hug 6. congestion, crowd, crush, jam, press, squash

squint askew, aslant, awry, cockeyed, crooked, oblique, off-centre, skew-whiff (*informal*)
Antonyms aligned, even, horizontal, in line, level, perpendicular, plum, square, straight, true, vertical

squire *verb* accompany, attend, companion, escort

squirm agonize, fidget, flounder, shift, twist, wiggle, wriggle, writhe

stab *verb* 1. bayonet, cut, gore, impale, injure, jab, knife, pierce, puncture, run through, spear, spill blood, stick, thrust, transfix, wound 2. **stab in the back** betray, break faith with, deceive, do the dirty on (*Brit. slang*), double-cross (*informal*), give the Judas kiss to, inform on, let down, play false, sell, sell out (*informal*), slander *~noun* 3. gash, incision, jab, puncture, rent, thrust, wound 4.

ache, pang, prick, twinge **5. make a stab at** attempt, endeavour, essay, give it one's best shot (*informal*), have a go (crack (*informal*), shot (*informal*), stab (*informal*)) (*informal*), try, try one's hand at, venture

stability constancy, durability, firmness, permanence, solidity, soundness, steadfastness, steadiness, strength
Antonyms changeableness, fickleness, fragility, frailty, inconstancy, instability, unpredictability, unreliability, unsteadiness

stable abiding, constant, deep-rooted, durable, enduring, established, fast, firm, fixed, immovable, immutable, invariable, lasting, permanent, reliable, secure, sound, staunch, steadfast, steady, strong, sturdy, sure, unalterable, unchangeable, unwavering, well-founded
Antonyms changeable, deteriorating, erratic, excitable, fickle, frail, inconstant, insecure, irresolute, mercurial, mutable, over-emotional, shaky, shifting, temperamental, uncertain, unpredictable, unreliable, unstable, unsteady, variable, volatile, wavering

stack **1.** *noun* clamp (*Brit. agriculture*), cock, heap, hoard, load, mass, mound, mountain, pile, rick **2.** *verb* accumulate, amass, assemble, bank up, heap up, load, pile, stockpile

staff *noun* **1.** employees, lecturers, officers, organization, personnel, teachers, team, workers, workforce **2.** cane, crook, pole, prop, rod, sceptre, stave, wand

stage **1.** *noun* division, juncture, lap, leg, length, level, period, phase, point, step **2.** *verb* arrange, do, engineer, give, lay on, mount, orchestrate, organize, perform, play, present, produce, put on

stagger *verb* **1.** falter, hesitate, lurch, reel, sway, teeter, totter, vacillate, waver, wobble **2.** amaze, astonish, astound, bowl over (*informal*), confound, dumbfound, flabbergast, give (someone) a shock, nonplus, overwhelm, shake, shock, strike (someone) dumb, stun, stupefy, surprise, take (someone) aback, take (someone's) breath away, throw off balance **3.** alternate, overlap, step, zigzag

stagnant brackish, motionless, quiet, sluggish, stale, standing, still
Antonyms active, clear, flowing, fresh, lively, moving, pure, running, thriving, unpolluted

stagnate decay, decline, deteriorate, fester, go to seed, idle, languish, lie fallow, rot, rust, stand still, vegetate

staid calm, composed, decorous, demure, grave, quiet, sedate, self-restrained, serious, set in one's ways, sober, solemn, steady
Antonyms adventurous, capricious, demonstrative, exuberant, flighty, giddy, indecorous, lively, rowdy, sportive, wild

stain *verb* **1.** blemish, blot, colour, dirty, discolour, dye, mark, smirch, soil, spot, tarnish, tinge **2.** besmirch, blacken, contaminate, corrupt, defile, deprave, disgrace, drag through the mud, sully, taint *~noun* **3.** blemish, blot, discoloration, dye, smirch, spot, tint **4.** blemish, blot on the escutcheon, disgrace, dishonour, infamy, reproach, shame, slur, stigma

stake[1] *noun* **1.** pale, paling, palisade, picket, pole, post, spike, stave, stick *~verb* **2.** brace, prop, secure, support, tether, tie up **3.** *often with* **out** define, delimit, demarcate, lay claim to, mark out, outline, reserve

stake[2] *noun* **1.** ante, bet, chance, hazard, peril, pledge, risk, venture, wager **2.** claim, concern, interest, investment, involvement, share *~verb* **3.** bet, chance, gamble, hazard, imperil, jeopardize, pledge, put on, risk, venture, wager

stale **1.** decayed, dry, faded, fetid, flat, fusty, hard, insipid, musty, old, sour, stagnant, tasteless **2.** antiquated, banal, cliché-ridden, common, commonplace, drab, effete, flat, hackneyed, insipid, old hat, overused, platitudinous, repetitious, stereotyped, threadbare, trite, unoriginal, worn-out
Antonyms crisp, different, fresh, imaginative, innovative, lively, new, novel, original, refreshing

stalemate deadlock, draw, impasse, standstill, tie

stalk *verb* **1.** creep up on, follow, haunt, hunt, pursue, shadow, tail (*informal*), track **2.** flounce, march, pace, stride, strut

stall *verb* beat about the bush (*informal*), hedge, play for time, stonewall, temporize

stalwart athletic, beefy (*informal*), brawny, daring, dependable, hefty (*informal*), husky (*informal*), indomitable, intrepid, lusty, manly, muscular, redoubtable, robust, rugged, sinewy, staunch, stout, strapping, strong, sturdy, valiant, vigorous
Antonyms faint-hearted, feeble, frail, infirm, namby-pamby, puny, shilpit (*Scot.*), sickly, timid, weak

stamina endurance, energy, force, grit, indefatigability, lustiness, power, power of endurance, resilience, resistance, staying power, strength, tenacity, vigour

stammer *verb* falter, hem and haw, hesitate, pause, splutter, stumble, stutter

stamp *verb* **1.** beat, crush, trample **2.** engrave, fix, impress, imprint, inscribe, mark, mould, print **3.** betray, brand, categorize, exhibit, identify, label, mark, pronounce, reveal, show to be, typecast *~noun* **4.** brand, cast, earmark, hallmark, imprint, mark, mould, signature **5.** breed, cast, character, cut, description, fashion, form, kind, sort, type

stamp collecting philately

stampede *noun* charge, flight, rout, rush, scattering

stamp out crush, destroy, eliminate, eradicate, extinguish, extirpate, put down, put out, quell, quench, scotch, suppress

stance **1.** bearing, carriage, deportment, posture **2.** attitude, position, stand, standpoint, viewpoint

stanch, staunch arrest, check, dam, halt, plug, stay, stem, stop

stand *verb* **1.** be erect, be upright, be vertical, rise **2.** mount, place, position, put, rank, set **3.** be in force, belong, be situated *or* located, be valid, continue, exist, halt, hold, obtain, pause, prevail, remain, rest, stay, stop **4.** abide, allow, bear, brook, cope with, countenance, endure, experience, hack (*slang*), handle, put up with (*informal*), stomach, submit to, suffer, support, sustain, take, thole (*dialect*), tolerate, undergo, wear (*Brit. slang*), weather, withstand *~noun* **5.** halt, rest, standstill, stay, stop, stopover **6.** attitude, determination, firm stand, opinion, position, stance, standpoint **7.** base, booth, bracket, dais, frame, grandstand, place, platform, rack, rank, stage, staging, stall, stance (*chiefly Scot.*), support, table

standard[1] *noun* **1.** average, benchmark, canon, criterion, example, gauge, grade, guide, guideline, measure, model, norm, par, pattern, principle, requirement, rule, sample, specification, touchstone, type, yardstick **2.** *often plural* code of honour, ethics, ideals, moral principles, morals, principles *~adjective* **3.** accepted, average, basic, customary, normal, orthodox, popular, prevailing, regular, set, staple, stock, typical, usual **4.** approved, authoritative, classic, definitive, established, official, recognized

Antonyms *adjective* abnormal, atypical, exceptional, extraordinary, irregular, singular, strange, unauthorised, uncommon, unconventional, unofficial, unusual

> *Standards are always out of date. That's what makes them standards*
>
> Alan Bennett *Forty Years On*

standard[2] *noun* banner, colours, ensign, flag, pennant, pennon, streamer

standardize assimilate, bring into line, institutionalize, mass-produce, regiment, stereotype

stand by **1.** back, befriend, be loyal to, champion, defend, stick up for (*informal*), support, take (someone's) part, uphold **2.** be prepared, wait, wait in the wings

stand for **1.** betoken, denote, exemplify, indicate, mean, represent, signify, symbolize **2.** *informal* bear, brook, endure, lie down under (*informal*), put up with, suffer, tolerate, wear (*Brit. informal*)

stand in for cover for, deputize for, do duty for, hold the fort for, replace, represent, substitute for, take the place of, understudy

standing *noun* **1.** condition, credit, eminence, estimation, footing, position, rank, reputation, repute, station, status **2.** continuance, duration, existence, experience *~adjective* **3.** fixed, lasting, permanent, perpetual, regular, repeated **4.** erect, perpendicular, rampant (*Heraldry*), upended, upright, vertical

standoffish aloof, cold, distant, haughty, remote, reserved, unapproachable, unsociable

Antonyms affable, approachable, congenial, cordial, friendly, open, sociable, warm

stand out attract attention, be highlighted, be prominent (conspicuous, distinct, obvious, striking), be thrown into relief, bulk large, catch the eye, leap to the eye, project, stare one in the face (*informal*), stick out a mile (*informal*), stick out like a sore thumb (*informal*)

standpoint angle, point of view, position, post, stance, station, vantage point, viewpoint

stand up for champion, come to the defence of, defend, side with, stick up for (*informal*), support, uphold

stand up to brave, confront, defy, endure, oppose, resist, tackle, withstand

staple *adjective* basic, chief, essential, fundamental, key, main, predominant, primary, principal

star *noun* **1.** heavenly body **2.** big name, celeb (*informal*), celebrity, draw, idol, lead, leading man *or* lady, luminary, main attraction, megastar (*informal*), name *~adjective* **3.** brilliant, celebrated, illustrious, leading, major, paramount, principal, prominent, talented, well-known

Related adjectives: astral, sidereal, stellar

Stars

Aldebaran
Betelgeuse *or* Betelgeux
Polaris, the Pole Star *or* the North Star
Sirius, the Dog Star, Canicula *or* Sothis
the Sun

Constellations: Latin name	**English name**
Andromeda	Andromeda
Antila	Air Pump
Apus	Bird of Paradise
Aquarius	Water Bearer
Aquila	Eagle
Ara	Altar
Aries	Ram
Auriga	Charioteer
Boötes	Herdsman
Caelum	Chisel
Camelopardalis	Giraffe

Cancer	Crab
Canes Venatici	Hunting Dogs
Canis Major	Great Dog
Canis Minor	Little Dog
Capricornus	Sea Goat
Carina	Keel
Cassiopeia	Cassiopeia
Centaurus	Centaur
Cepheus	Cepheus
Cetus	Whale
Chamaeleon	Chameleon
Circinus	Compasses
Columba	Dove
Coma Bernices	Bernice's Hair
Corona Australis	Southern Crown
Corona Borealis	Northern Crown
Corvus	Crow
Crater	Cup
Crux	Southern Cross
Cygnus	Swan
Delphinus	Dolphin
Dorado	Swordfish
Draco	Dragon
Equuleus	Little Horse
Eridanus	River Eridanus
Fornax	Furnace
Gemini	Twins
Grus	Crane
Hercules	Hercules
Horologium	Clock
Hydra	Sea Serpent
Hydrus	Water Snake
Indus	Indian
Lacerta	Lizard
Leo	Lion
Leo Minor	Little Lion
Lepus	Hare
Libra	Scales
Lupus	Wolf
Lynx	Lynx
Lyra	Harp
Mensa	Table
Microscopium	Microscope
Monoceros	Unicorn
Musca	Fly
Norma	Level
Octans	Octant
Ophiuchus	Serpent Bearer
Orion	Orion
Pavo	Peacock
Pegasus	Winged Horse
Perseus	Perseus
Phoenix	Phoenix
Pictor	Easel
Pisces	Fishes
Piscis Austrinus	Southern Fish
Puppis	Ship's Stern
Pyxis	Mariner's Compass
Reticulum	Net
Sagitta	Arrow
Sagittarius	Archer
Scorpius	Scorpion
Sculptor	Sculptor
Scutum	Shield
Serpens	Serpent
Sextans	Sextant
Taurus	Bull
Telescopium	Telescope
Triangulum	Triangle
Triangulum Australe	Southern Triangle
Tucana	Toucan
Ursa Major	Great Bear (contains the Plough *or (U.S.)* Big Dipper)
Ursa Minor	Little Bear *or (U.S.)* Little Dipper
Vela	Sails
Virgo	Virgin
Volans	Flying Fish
Vulpecula	Fox

starchy ceremonious, conventional, formal, precise, prim, punctilious, stiff, stuffy

stare *verb* gape, gawk, gawp (*Brit. slang*), gaze, goggle, look, ogle, rubberneck (*slang*), watch

stark *adjective* **1.** absolute, arrant, bald, bare, blunt, consummate, downright, entire, flagrant, out-and-out, palpable, patent, pure, sheer, simple, unalloyed, unmitigated, utter **2.** austere, bare, barren, bleak, cold, depressing, desolate, drear (*literary*), dreary, forsaken, godforsaken, grim, hard, harsh, plain, severe, solitary, unadorned *~adverb* **3.** absolutely, altogether, clean, completely, entirely, quite, utterly, wholly

stark-naked buck naked (*slang*), in a state of nature, in one's birthday suit (*informal*), in the altogether (*informal*), in the bare scud (*slang*), in the buff (*informal*), in the raw (*informal*), naked, naked as the day one was born (*informal*), nude, scuddy (*slang*), stark, starkers (*informal*), stripped, unclad, undressed, without a stitch on (*informal*)

start *verb* **1.** appear, arise, begin, come into being, come into existence, commence, depart, first see the light of day, get on the road, get under way, go ahead, hit the road (*informal*), issue, leave, originate, pitch in (*informal*), sally forth, set off, set out **2.** activate, embark upon, engender, enter upon, get going, get (something) off the ground (*informal*), get the ball rolling, initiate, instigate, kick off (*informal*), kick-start, make a beginning, open, originate, put one's hand to the plough (*informal*), set about, set in motion, set the ball rolling, start the ball rolling, take the first step, take the plunge (*informal*), trigger, turn on **3.** begin, create, establish, father, found, inaugurate, initiate, institute, introduce, launch, lay the foundations of, pioneer, set up **4.** blench, flinch, jerk, jump, recoil, shy, twitch

~*noun* **5**. beginning, birth, commencement, dawn, first step(s), foundation, inauguration, inception, initiation, kickoff (*informal*), onset, opening, opening move, outset **6**. advantage, edge, head start, lead **7**. backing, break (*informal*), chance, helping hand, introduction, opening, opportunity, sponsorship **8**. convulsion, jar, jump, spasm, twitch

Antonyms *verb* (*senses 1, 2 & 3*) abandon, bring to an end, call it a day (*informal*), cease, conclude, delay, desist, end, finish, give up, put aside, put off, quit, stop, switch off, terminate, turn off, wind up ~*noun* (*sense 5*) cessation, conclusion, dénouement, end, finale, finish, outcome, result, stop, termination, turning off, wind-up

startle agitate, alarm, amaze, astonish, astound, frighten, give (someone) a turn (*informal*), make (someone) jump, scare, shock, surprise, take (someone) aback

startling alarming, astonishing, astounding, extraordinary, shocking, staggering, sudden, surprising, unexpected, unforeseen

starving esurient, faint from lack of food, famished, hungering, hungry, ravenous, ready to eat a horse (*informal*), sharp-set, starved

stash *verb* cache, hide, hoard, lay up, put aside for a rainy day, salt away, save up, secrete, stockpile, stow

state[1] *verb* **1**. affirm, articulate, assert, asseverate, aver, declare, enumerate, explain, expound, express, present, propound, put, report, say, specify, utter, voice ~*noun* **2**. case, category, circumstances, condition, mode, pass, plight, position, predicament, shape, situation, state of affairs **3**. attitude, frame of mind, humour, mood, spirits **4**. ceremony, dignity, display, glory, grandeur, majesty, pomp, splendour, style **5**. *informal* bother, flap (*informal*), mind-fuck (*taboo slang*), panic, pother, tiz-woz (*informal*), tizzy (*informal*) **6**. **in a state** *informal* agitated, all steamed up (*slang*), anxious, distressed, disturbed, flustered, het up, panic-stricken, ruffled, upset, uptight (*informal*)

state[2] *noun* body politic, commonwealth, country, federation, government, kingdom, land, nation, republic, territory

US states	Abbreviation	Zip code
Alabama	Ala.	AL
Alaska	Alas.	AK
Arizona	Ariz.	AZ
Arkansas	Ark.	AR
California	Cal.	CA
Colorado	Colo.	CO
Connecticut	Conn.	CT
Delaware	Del.	DE
District of Columbia	D.C.	DC
Florida	Fla.	FL
Georgia	Ga.	GA
Hawaii	Haw.	HI
Idaho	Id. *or* Ida.	ID
Illinois	Ill.	IL
Indiana	Ind.	IN
Iowa	Ia. *or* Io.	IA
Kansas	Kan. *or* Kans.	KS
Kentucky	Ken.	KY
Louisiana	La.	LA
Maine	Me.	ME
Maryland	Md.	MD
Massachusetts	Mass.	MA
Michigan	Mich.	MI
Minnesota	Minn.	MN
Mississippi	Miss.	MS
Missouri	Mo.	MO
Montana	Mont.	MT
Nebraska	Neb.	NE
Nevada	Nev.	NV
New Hampshire	N.H.	NH
New Jersey	N.J.	NJ
New Mexico	N.M. *or* N.Mex.	NM
New York	N.Y.	NY
North Carolina	N.C.	NC
North Dakota	N.D. *or* N.Dak.	ND
Ohio	O.	OH
Oklahoma	Okla.	OK
Oregon	Oreg.	OR
Pennsylvania	Pa. *or* Penn. *or* Penna.	PA
Rhode Island	R.I.	RI
South Carolina	S.C.	SC
South Dakota	S.Dak.	SD
Tennessee	Tenn.	TN
Texas	Tex.	TX
Utah	Ut.	UT
Vermont	Vt.	VT
Virginia	Va.	VA
Washington	Wash.	WA
West Virginia	W.Va.	WV
Wisconsin	Wis.	WI
Wyoming	Wyo.	WY

Australian states and territories

Australian Capital Territory
New South Wales
Northern Territory
Queensland
South Australia
Tasmania
Victoria
Western Australia

stately august, ceremonious, deliberate, dignified, elegant, grand, imperial, imposing, impressive, lofty, majestic, measured, noble, pompous, regal, royal, solemn
Antonyms common, humble, lowly, modest, simple, undignified, undistinguished, unimpressive

statement account, announcement, communication, communiqué, declaration, explanation, proclamation, recital, relation, report, testimony, utterance

state-of-the-art latest, newest, up-to-date, up-to-the-minute
Antonyms obsolescent, obsolete, old-fashioned, outdated, outmoded, out of date, out of the ark (*informal*)

static changeless, constant, fixed, immobile, inert, motionless, stagnant, stationary, still, unmoving, unvarying
Antonyms active, dynamic, kinetic, lively, mobile, moving, travelling, varied

station *noun* **1.** base, depot, headquarters, location, place, position, post, seat, situation **2.** appointment, business, calling, employment, grade, occupation, position, post, rank, situation, sphere, standing, status *~verb* **3.** assign, establish, fix, garrison, install, locate, post, set

stationary at a standstill, fixed, inert, moored, motionless, parked, standing, static, stock-still, unmoving
Antonyms changeable, changing, inconstant, mobile, moving, shifting, travelling, unstable, variable, varying, volatile

statistics

There are three kinds of lies: lies, damned lies, and statistics
Benjamin Disraeli

He uses statistics like a drunken man uses lamp-posts - for support rather than illumination
Andrew Lang

statuesque dignified, imposing, Junoesque, majestic, regal, stately

stature consequence, eminence, high station, importance, prestige, prominence, rank, size, standing

status condition, consequence, degree, distinction, eminence, grade, position, prestige, rank, standing

statute act, decree, edict, enactment, ordinance, regulation, rule

staunch constant, dependable, faithful, firm, immovable, loyal, reliable, resolute, sound, stalwart, steadfast, stout, strong, sure, tried and true, true, true-blue, trustworthy, trusty

stave off avert, evade, fend off, foil, hold off, keep at arm's length, keep at bay, parry, ward off

stay[1] *verb* **1.** abide, continue, delay, establish oneself, halt, hang around (*informal*), hang in the air, hover, linger, loiter, pause, put down roots, remain, reside, settle, sojourn, stand, stay put, stop, tarry, wait **2.** *often with* **at** be accommodated at, lodge, put up at, sojourn, visit **3.** adjourn, defer, discontinue, hold in abeyance, hold over, prorogue, put off, suspend **4.** *archaic* arrest, check, curb, delay, detain, hinder, hold, impede, obstruct, prevent *~noun* **5.** holiday, sojourn, stop, stopover, visit **6.** deferment, delay, halt, pause, postponement, remission, reprieve, stopping, suspension
Antonyms *verb* (*sense 1*) abandon, depart, exit, go, leave, move on, pack one's bags (*informal*), pass through, quit, withdraw

stay[2] *noun* brace, buttress, prop, reinforcement, shoring, stanchion, support

staying power endurance, stamina, strength, toughness

steadfast constant, dedicated, dependable, established, faithful, fast, firm, fixed, immovable, intent, loyal, persevering, reliable, resolute, single-minded, stable, stalwart, staunch, steady, unfaltering, unflinching, unswerving, unwavering
Antonyms capricious, faint-hearted, faltering, fickle, flagging, half-hearted, inconstant, irresolute, uncommitted, undependable, unreliable, unstable, vacillating, wavering

steady *adjective* **1.** firm, fixed, immovable, on an even keel, safe, stable, substantial, unchangeable, uniform **2.** balanced, calm, dependable, equable, having both feet on the ground, imperturbable, level-headed, reliable, sedate, sensible, serene, serious-minded, settled, sober, staid, staunch, steadfast **3.** ceaseless, confirmed, consistent, constant, continuous, even, faithful, habitual, incessant, nonstop, persistent, regular, rhythmic, unbroken, unfaltering, unfluctuating, uninterrupted, unremitting, unvarying, unwavering *~verb* **4.** balance, brace, secure, stabilize, support **5.** compose *or* calm oneself, cool down, get a grip on oneself, sober (up)
Antonyms *adjective* careless, changeable, faltering, fickle, fluctuating, half-hearted, inconsistent, infrequent, insecure, intermittent, in two minds, irregular, occasional, sporadic, uncommitted, unconscientious, undependable, unpredictable, unreliable, unsettled, unstable, unsteady, vacillating, wavering *~verb* agitate, shake, tilt, upset, worry

slow but sure

steal **1.** appropriate, be light-fingered, blag (*slang*), cabbage (*Brit. slang*), embezzle, filch, half-inch (*old-fashioned slang*), heist (*U.S. slang*), lift (*informal*), misappropriate, nick (*slang, chiefly Brit.*), peculate, pilfer, pinch (*informal*), pirate, plagiarize, poach, prig (*Brit. slang*), purloin, shoplift, snitch (*slang*), swipe (*slang*), take, thieve, walk *or* make off with **2.** creep, flit, insinuate oneself, slink, slip, sneak, tiptoe

stealing embezzlement, larceny, misappropriation, pilferage, pilfering, plagiarism, robbery, shoplifting, theft, thievery, thieving

stealth furtiveness, secrecy, slyness, sneakiness, stealthiness, surreptitiousness, unobtrusiveness

•stealthy clandestine, covert, furtive, secret, secretive, skulking, sly, sneaking, sneaky, surreptitious, underhand

steamy *informal* carnal, erotic, hot (*slang*), lascivious, lewd, lubricious (*formal or literary*), lustful, prurient, raunchy (*slang*), sensual, sexy (*informal*), titillating

steel *verb* brace, fortify, grit one's teeth, harden, make up one's mind

steep[1] *adjective* **1.** abrupt, headlong, precipitous, sheer **2.** *informal* excessive, exorbitant, extortionate, extreme, high, overpriced, stiff, uncalled-for, unreasonable
Antonyms (*sense 1*) easy, gentle, gradual, moderate, slight (*sense 2*) fair, moderate, reasonable

steep[2] *verb* **1.** damp, drench, imbrue (*rare*), immerse, macerate, marinate (*Cookery*), moisten, soak, souse, submerge **2.** fill, imbue, infuse, permeate, pervade, saturate, suffuse

steer 1. administer, be in the driver's seat, conduct, control, direct, govern, guide, handle, pilot **2. steer clear of** avoid, body-swerve (*Scot.*), circumvent, eschew, evade, give a wide berth to, sheer off, shun

steersman cox, coxswain, helmsman, pilot, wheelman (*U.S.*)

stem[1] **1.** *noun* axis, branch, peduncle, shoot, stalk, stock, trunk **2.** *verb usually with* **from** arise, be caused (bred, brought about, generated), by derive, develop, emanate, flow, issue, originate

stem[2] *verb* bring to a standstill, check, contain, curb, dam, hold back, oppose, resist, restrain, stanch, staunch, stay (*archaic*), stop, withstand

stench foul odour, malodour, mephitis, niff (*Brit. slang*), noisomeness, pong (*Brit. informal*), reek, stink, whiff (*Brit. slang*)

stentorian blaring, booming, carrying, full, loud, powerful, resonant, resounding, ringing, sonorous, strident, strong, thundering
Antonyms gentle, hushed, low, low-pitched, quiet, soft, subdued

step *noun* **1.** footfall, footprint, footstep, gait, impression, pace, print, stride, trace, track, walk **2.** act, action, deed, expedient, manoeuvre, means, measure, move, procedure, proceeding **3. take steps** act, intervene, move in, prepare, take action, take measures, take the initiative **4.** advance, advancement, move, phase, point, process, progression, stage **5.** degree, level, rank, remove **6.** doorstep, round, rung, stair, tread **7. in step** coinciding, conforming, in harmony (agreement, conformity, unison), in line **8. out of step** erratic, incongruous, in disagreement, out of harmony, out of line, out of phase, pulling different ways **9. watch one's step** be discreet (canny, careful, cautious), be on one's guard, have one's wits about one, look out, mind how one goes, mind one's p's and q's, take care, take heed, tread carefully *~verb* **10.** move, pace, tread, walk

one step at a time

step down abdicate, bow out, give up, hand over, leave, pull out, quit, resign, retire

step in become involved, chip in (*informal*), intercede, intervene, take action, take a hand

step up accelerate, augment, boost, escalate, increase, intensify, raise, speed up, up

stereotype 1. *noun* formula, mould, pattern, received idea **2.** *verb* categorize, conventionalize, dub, ghettoize, pigeonhole, standardize, take to be, typecast

stereotyped banal, cliché-ridden, conventional, corny (*slang*), hackneyed, mass-produced, overused, platitudinous, played out, stale, standard, standardized, stock, threadbare, tired, trite, unoriginal

sterile 1. abortive, bare, barren, dry, empty, fruitless, infecund, unfruitful, unproductive, unprofitable, unprolific **2.** antiseptic, aseptic, disinfected, germ-free, sterilized
Antonyms (*sense 1*) fecund, fertile, fruitful, productive, prolific (*sense 2*) contaminated, dirty, germ-ridden, infected, insanitary, unhygienic, unsterile

sterilize autoclave, disinfect, fumigate, purify

sterling authentic, excellent, fine, first-class, genuine, pure, real, sound, standard, substantial, superlative, true

stern austere, authoritarian, bitter, cruel, drastic, flinty, forbidding, frowning, grim, hard, harsh, inflexible, relentless, rigid, rigorous, serious, severe, steely, strict, unrelenting, unsparing, unyielding
Antonyms amused, approachable, compassionate, flexible, friendly, gentle, kind, lenient, liberal, permissive, soft, sympathetic, tolerant, warm

stew 1. goulash, hash, olio, olla, olla podrida, potpourri, ragout **2.** anxiety, concern, fret, lather (*informal*), panic, worry **3.** blend, hash, hodgepodge (*U.S. & Canad.*), hotchpotch, medley, miscellany, mix, mixture, olio, olla, potpourri

stick[1] *verb* **1.** adhere, affix, attach, bind, bond, cement, cleave, cling, fasten, fix, fuse, glue, hold, hold on, join, paste, weld **2.** dig, gore, insert, jab, penetrate, pierce, pin, poke, prod, puncture, spear, stab, thrust, transfix **3.** *with* **out, up,** *etc.* bulge, extend, jut, obtrude, poke, project, protrude, show **4.** *informal* deposit, drop, fix, install, lay, place, plant, plonk, position, put, set, store, stuff **5.** be bogged down, become immobilized, be embedded, catch, clog, come to a standstill, jam, lodge, snag, stop **6.** linger, persist, remain, stay **7.** *slang* abide, bear up under, endure, get on with, hack (*slang*), stand, stomach, take, tolerate **8. stick it out** *informal* bear, endure, grin and bear it (*informal*), last out, put up with (*informal*), see it through, see through to the bitter end, soldier on, take it (*informal*), weather **9. stick up for** *informal* champion, defend, stand up for, support, take the part *or* side of, uphold

stick[2] *noun* **1.** baton, birch, cane, crook, pole, rod, sceptre, staff, stake, switch, twig, wand **2.** *informal* dinosaur, fuddy-duddy (*informal*), (old) fogy, pain (*informal*), prig, stick-in-the-mud (*informal*) **3.** *Brit. slang* abuse, blame, criticism, flak (*informal*), hostility, punishment

stick at **1.** continue, keep at, persevere in, persist, plug away at (*informal*), see (something) through **2.** balk, be conscience-stricken, be deterred by, demur, doubt, hesitate, pause, recoil, scruple, shrink from, stop at

stick-in-the-mud Colonel Blimp, conservative, die-hard, dinosaur, fuddy-duddy (*informal*), (old) fogy, reactionary, sobersides, stick (*informal*)

stickler fanatic, fusspot (*Brit. informal*), hard taskmaster, maniac (*informal*), martinet, nut (*slang*), pedant, perfectionist, purist

stick to adhere to, cleave to, continue in, honour, keep, persevere in, remain loyal (faithful, true), stick at

sticky **1.** adhesive, claggy (*dialect*), clinging, gluey, glutinous, gooey (*informal*), gummy, syrupy, tacky, tenacious, viscid, viscous **2.** *informal* awkward, delicate, difficult, discomforting, embarrassing, hairy (*slang*), nasty, painful, thorny, tricky, unpleasant **3.** clammy, close, humid, muggy, oppressive, sultry, sweltering

stiff **1.** brittle, firm, hard, hardened, inelastic, inflexible, rigid, solid, solidified, taut, tense, tight, unbending, unyielding **2.** artificial, austere, ceremonious, chilly, cold, constrained, forced, formal, laboured, mannered, pompous, priggish, prim, punctilious, standoffish, starchy (*informal*), stilted, uneasy, unnatural, unrelaxed, wooden **3.** arthritic, awkward, clumsy, creaky (*informal*), crude, graceless, inelegant, jerky, rheumaticky (*informal*), ungainly, ungraceful, unsupple **4.** arduous, difficult, exacting, fatiguing, formidable, hard, laborious, tough, trying, uphill **5.** austere, cruel, drastic, extreme, great, hard, harsh, heavy, inexorable, oppressive, pitiless, rigorous, severe, sharp, strict, stringent **6.** brisk, fresh, powerful, strong, vigorous

Antonyms (*senses 1 & 3*) bendable, ductile, elastic, flexible, limber, lissom(e), lithe, pliable, pliant, supple, yielding (*sense 2*) casual, easy, informal, laid-back, natural, relaxed, spontaneous, unceremonious, unofficial

stiffen brace, coagulate, congeal, crystallize, harden, jell, reinforce, set, solidify, starch, tauten, tense, thicken

stiff-necked boneheaded (*slang*), contumacious, haughty, obstinate, opinionated, stubborn, uncompromising, unreceptive

stifle **1.** asphyxiate, choke, smother, strangle, suffocate **2.** check, choke back, cover up, curb, extinguish, hush, muffle, prevent, repress, restrain, silence, smother, stop, suppress

stigma blot, brand, disgrace, dishonour, imputation, mark, reproach, shame, slur, smirch, spot, stain

stigmatize brand, cast a slur upon, defame, denounce, discredit, label, mark, pillory

still **1.** *adjective* at rest, calm, hushed, inert, lifeless, motionless, noiseless, pacific, peaceful, placid, quiet, restful, serene, silent, smooth, stationary, stilly (*poetic*), tranquil, undisturbed, unruffled, unstirring **2.** *verb* allay, alleviate, appease, calm, hush, lull, pacify, quiet, quieten, settle, silence, smooth, smooth over, soothe, subdue, tranquillize **3.** *conjunction* but, for all that, however, nevertheless, notwithstanding, yet **4.** *noun, poetic* hush, peace, quiet, silence, stillness, tranquillity

Antonyms *adjective* active, agitated, astir, bustling, busy, humming, lively, moving, noisy, restless, turbulent *~verb* aggravate, agitate, exacerbate, increase, inflame, rouse, stir up *~noun* bustle, clamour, hubbub, noise, uproar

stilted artificial, bombastic, constrained, forced, grandiloquent, high-flown, high-sounding, inflated, laboured, pedantic, pompous, pretentious, stiff, unnatural, wooden

Antonyms flowing, fluid, free, natural, spontaneous, unaffected, unpretentious

stimulant analeptic, bracer (*informal*), energizer, excitant, pep pill (*informal*), pick-me-up (*informal*), restorative, reviver, tonic, upper (*slang*)

Antonyms calmant, depressant, downer (*slang*), sedative, tranquilliser

stimulate animate, arouse, encourage, fan, fire, foment, goad, impel, incite, inflame, instigate, prod, prompt, provoke, quicken, rouse, spur, turn on (*slang*), urge, whet

stimulating exciting, exhilarating, galvanic, inspiring, intriguing, provocative, provoking, rousing, stirring, thought-provoking
Antonyms as dry as dust, boring, dull, mind-numbing, unexciting, unimaginative, uninspiring, uninteresting, unstimulating

stimulus clarion call, encouragement, fillip, goad, incentive, incitement, inducement, provocation, shot in the arm (*informal*), spur

sting *verb* **1.** burn, hurt, pain, smart, tingle, wound **2.** anger, gall, incense, inflame, infuri~ ate, nettle, pique, provoke, rile **3.** *informal* cheat, defraud, do (*slang*), fleece, overcharge, rip off (*slang*), skin (*slang*), stiff (*slang*), swindle, take for a ride (*informal*)

stingy 1. avaricious, cheeseparing, close-fisted, covetous, illiberal, mean, mingy (*Brit. infor~ mal*), miserly, near, niggardly, parsimonious, penny-pinching (*informal*), penurious, scrimp~ ing, tight-arse (*taboo slang*), tight-arsed (*taboo slang*), tight as a duck's arse (*taboo slang*), tight-ass (*U.S. taboo slang*), tight-assed (*U.S. taboo slang*), tightfisted, ungenerous **2.** inad~ equate, insufficient, meagre, measly (*infor~ mal*), mouldy (*informal*), on the small side, pathetic, scant, scanty, skimpy, small

stink *verb* **1.** offend the nostrils, pong (*Brit. in~ formal*), reek, stink to high heaven (*informal*), whiff (*Brit. slang*) **2.** *slang* be held in disre~ pute, be no good, be offensive, be rotten (ab~ horrent, bad, detestable), have a bad name *~noun* **3.** fetor, foulness, foul odour, malodour, noisomeness, pong (*Brit. informal*), stench **4.** *slang* brouhaha, commotion, deal of trouble (*informal*), disturbance, fuss, hubbub, row, rumpus, scandal, stir, to-do, uproar, upset

stinker 1. bounder (*old-fashioned Brit. slang*), cad (*Brit. informal*), cocksucker (*taboo slang*), cur, dastard (*archaic*), heel, nasty piece of work (*informal*), rotter (*slang, chiefly Brit.*), scab, scoundrel, scrote (*slang*), sod (*slang*), swine **2.** affliction, beast, difficulty, fine how-do-you-do (*informal*), horror, impediment, plight, poser, predicament, problem, shocker

stinking 1. fetid, foul-smelling, ill-smelling, malodorous, mephitic, niffy (*Brit. slang*), noi~ some, olid, pongy (*Brit. informal*), reeking, smelly, whiffy (*Brit. slang*) **2.** *informal* con~ temptible, disgusting, low, low-down (*infor~ mal*), mean, rotten, shitty (*taboo slang*), un~ pleasant, vile, wretched **3.** *slang* bevvied (*dia~ lect*), blitzed (*slang*), blotto (*slang*), bombed (*slang*), boozed, Brahms and Liszt (*slang*), canned (*slang*), drunk, drunk as a lord, flying (*slang*), intoxicated, legless (*informal*), lit up (*slang*), out of it (*slang*), out to it (*Austral. & N.Z. slang*), paralytic (*informal*), pissed (*taboo slang*), plastered (*slang*), rat-arsed (*taboo slang*), smashed (*slang*), sozzled (*informal*), steamboats (*Scot. slang*), steaming (*slang*), stewed (*slang*), stoned (*slang*), wasted (*slang*), wrecked (*slang*), zonked (*slang*)

stint 1. *noun* assignment, bit, period, quota, share, shift, spell, stretch, term, time, tour, turn **2.** *verb* begrudge, be sparing (frugal, mean, mingy (*Brit. informal*), parsimonious), economize, hold back, save, scrimp, skimp on, spoil the ship for a ha'porth of tar, withhold

stipulate agree, contract, covenant, engage, guarantee, insist upon, lay down, lay down *or* impose conditions, make a point of, pledge, postulate, promise, require, settle, specify

stipulation agreement, clause, condition, con~ tract, engagement, precondition, prerequisite, provision, proviso, qualification, requirement, restriction, rider, settlement, *sine qua non*, specification, term

stir *verb* **1.** agitate, beat, disturb, flutter, mix, move, quiver, rustle, shake, tremble **2.** *often with* **up** animate, arouse, awaken, excite, in~ cite, inflame, instigate, kindle, prod, prompt, provoke, quicken, raise, rouse, spur, stimu~ late, urge **3.** affect, electrify, excite, fire, in~ spire, move, thrill, touch **4.** bestir, be up and about (*informal*), budge, exert oneself, get a move on (*informal*), get moving, hasten, look lively (*informal*), make an effort, mill about, move, shake a leg (*informal*) *~noun* **5.** activ~ ity, ado, agitation, bustle, commotion, disor~ der, disturbance, excitement, ferment, flurry, fuss, movement, to-do, tumult, uproar
Antonyms *verb* (*senses 2 & 3*) check, curb, dampen, inhibit, restrain, stifle, suppress, throw cold water on (*informal*)

stirring animating, dramatic, emotive, exciting, exhilarating, heady, impassioned, inspiring, intoxicating, lively, moving, rousing, spirited, stimulating, thrilling

stock *noun* **1.** array, assets, assortment, cache, choice, commodities, fund, goods, hoard, in~ ventory, merchandise, range, reserve, reser~ voir, selection, stockpile, store, supply, vari~ ety, wares **2.** *animals* beasts, cattle, domestic animals, flocks, herds, horses, livestock, sheep **3.** ancestry, background, breed, descent, ex~ traction, family, forebears, house, line, line~ age, line of descent, parentage, pedigree, race, strain, type, variety **4.** *Money* capital, funds, investment, property **5. take stock** appraise, estimate, review the situation, see how the land lies, size up (*informal*), weigh up *~ad~ jective* **6.** banal, basic, commonplace, conven~ tional, customary, formal, hackneyed, ordi~ nary, overused, regular, routine, run-of-the-mill, set, standard, staple, stereotyped, tradi~ tional, trite, usual, worn-out *~verb* **7.** deal in, handle, keep, sell, supply, trade in **8.** *with* **up** accumulate, amass, buy up, gather, hoard, lay in, put away, replenish, save, store (up), supply **9.** equip, fill, fit out, furnish, kit out, provide with, provision, supply

stocky chunky, dumpy, mesomorphic, solid, stubby, stumpy, sturdy, thickset

stodgy **1.** filling, heavy, leaden, starchy, substantial **2.** boring, dull, dull as ditchwater, formal, fuddy-duddy (*informal*), heavy going, ho-hum, laboured, staid, stuffy, tedious, tiresome, turgid, unexciting, unimaginative, uninspired
Antonyms (*sense 1*) appetizing, fluffy, insubstantial, light (*sense 2*) animated, exciting, fashionable, fresh, interesting, light, lively, readable, stimulating, trendy (*Brit. informal*), up-to-date

stoical calm, cool, dispassionate, impassive, imperturbable, indifferent, long-suffering, philosophic, phlegmatic, resigned, stoic, stolid

stoicism acceptance, calmness, dispassion, fatalism, forbearance, fortitude, impassivity, imperturbability, indifference, long-suffering, patience, resignation, stolidity

stolen bent (*slang*), hooky (*slang*), hot (*slang*)

stolid apathetic, bovine, doltish, dozy (*Brit. informal*), dull, heavy, lumpish, obtuse, slow, stupid, unemotional, wooden
Antonyms acute, animated, bright, emotional, energetic, excitable, intelligent, interested, lively, passionate, sharp, smart

stomach *noun* **1.** abdomen, belly, breadbasket (*slang*), gut (*informal*), inside(s) (*informal*), paunch, pot, potbelly, spare tyre (*informal*), tummy (*informal*) **2.** appetite, desire, inclination, mind, relish, taste *~verb* **3.** abide, bear, endure, hack (*slang*), put up with (*informal*), reconcile *or* resign oneself to, submit to, suffer, swallow, take, tolerate

An army marches on its stomach

The way to a man's heart is through his stomach

stony *figurative* adamant, blank, callous, chilly, cold as ice, expressionless, frigid, hard, harsh, heartless, hostile, icy, indifferent, inexorable, merciless, obdurate, pitiless, unfeeling, unforgiving, unresponsive

stooge **1.** *noun* butt, dupe, fall guy (*informal*), foil, henchman, lackey, patsy (*slang, chiefly U.S. & Canad.*), pawn, puppet **2.** *verb, informal* flit, fly, hang about (*informal*), meander, mooch (*slang*), mosey (*informal*), move, wander

stoop *verb* **1.** be bowed *or* round-shouldered, bend, bow, crouch, descend, duck, hunch, incline, kneel, lean, squat **2.** *often with* **to** condescend, deign, demean oneself, descend, lower oneself, resort, sink, vouchsafe *~noun* **3.** bad posture, droop, round-shoulderedness, sag, slouch, slump

stop *verb* **1.** axe (*informal*), belay (*Nautical*), be over, break off, bring *or* come to a halt, bring *or* come to a standstill, call it a day (*informal*), cease, come to an end, conclude, cut out (*informal*), cut short, desist, discontinue, draw up, end, finish, halt, leave off, pack in (*Brit. informal*), pause, peter out, pull up, put an end to, quit, refrain, run down, run its course, shut down, stall, terminate **2.** arrest, bar, block, break, bung, check, close, forestall, frustrate, hinder, hold back, impede, intercept, interrupt, nip (something) in the bud, obstruct, plug, prevent, rein in, repress, restrain, seal, silence, staunch, stem, suspend **3.** break one's journey, lodge, put up, rest, sojourn, stay, tarry *~noun* **4.** cessation, conclusion, discontinuation, end, finish, halt, standstill **5.** break, rest, sojourn, stay, stopover, visit **6.** bar, block, break, check, control, hindrance, impediment, plug, stoppage **7.** depot, destination, halt, stage, station, termination, terminus
Antonyms *verb* (*senses 1 & 3*) advance, begin, commence, continue, get going, get under way, give the go ahead, go, institute, keep going, keep on, kick off (*informal*), proceed, set in motion, set off, start (*sense 2*) assist, boost, encourage, expedite, facilitate, further, hasten, promote, push *~noun* (*sense 4*) beginning, commencement, kick-off (*informal*), start (*sense 6*) boost, encouragement, incitement

stopgap **1.** *noun* improvisation, makeshift, resort, shift, substitute, temporary expedient **2.** *adjective* emergency, impromptu, improvised, makeshift, provisional, rough-and-ready, temporary

stoppage **1.** abeyance, arrest, close, closure, cutoff, deduction, discontinuance, halt, hindrance, lay-off, shutdown, standstill, stopping **2.** blockage, check, curtailment, interruption, obstruction, occlusion, stopping up

store *verb* **1.** accumulate, deposit, garner, hoard, husband, keep, keep in reserve, lay by *or* in, lock away, put aside, put aside for a rainy day, put by, put in storage, reserve, salt away, save, stash (*informal*), stock, stockpile *~noun* **2.** abundance, accumulation, cache, fund, hoard, lot, mine, plenty, plethora, provision, quantity, reserve, reservoir, stock, stockpile, supply, wealth **3.** chain store, department store, emporium, market, mart, outlet, shop, supermarket **4.** depository, repository, storehouse, storeroom, warehouse **5.** **set store by** appreciate, esteem, hold in high regard, prize, think highly of, value

storm *noun* **1.** blast, blizzard, cyclone, gale, gust, hurricane, squall, tempest, tornado, whirlwind **2.** *figurative* agitation, anger, clamour, commotion, disturbance, furore, hubbub, outbreak, outburst, outcry, passion, roar, row, rumpus, stir, strife, tumult, turmoil, violence *~verb* **3.** assail, assault, beset, charge, rush, take by storm *~noun* **4.** assault, attack, blitz, blitzkrieg, offensive, onset, onslaught, rush *~verb* **5.** bluster, complain, fly off the handle (*informal*), fume, go ballistic (*slang, chiefly U.S.*), rage, rant, rave, scold, thunder, wig out (*slang*) **6.** flounce, fly, rush, stalk, stamp, stomp (*informal*)

stormy blustering, blustery, boisterous, dirty, foul, gusty, inclement, raging, rough, squally, tempestuous, turbulent, wild, windy

story **1.** account, anecdote, chronicle, fictional account, history, legend, narration, narrative, novel, recital, record, relation, romance, tale, urban legend, version, yarn **2.** *informal* false~hood, fib, fiction, lie, pork pie (*Brit. slang*), porky (*Brit. slang*), untruth, white lie **3.** arti~cle, feature, news, news item, report, scoop

storyteller anecdotist, author, bard, chronicler, fabulist, narrator, novelist, raconteur, roman~cer, spinner of yarns

stout **1.** big, bulky, burly, corpulent, fat, fleshy, heavy, obese, on the large *or* heavy side, overweight, plump, portly, rotund, substan~tial, tubby **2.** able-bodied, athletic, beefy (*in~formal*), brawny, hardy, hulking, husky (*in~formal*), lusty, muscular, robust, stalwart, strapping, strong, sturdy, substantial, thick~set, tough, vigorous **3.** bold, brave, courageous, dauntless, doughty, fearless, gallant, intrepid, lion-hearted, manly, plucky, resolute, valiant, valorous
Antonyms (*senses 1 & 2*) feeble, flimsy, frail, insubstantial, lanky, lean, puny, skin-and-bones (*informal*), skinny, slender, slight, slim (*sense 3*) cowardly, faint-hearted, fearful, ir~resolute, shrinking, soft, spineless, timid, weak

stouthearted ballsy (*taboo slang*), bold, brave, courageous, dauntless, doughty, fearless, great-hearted, gutsy (*slang*), heroic, indomi~table, intrepid, lion-hearted, plucky, spirited, stalwart, valiant, valorous

stow bundle, cram, deposit, jam, load, pack, put away, secrete, stash (*informal*), store, stuff, tuck

straggle drift, lag, loiter, ramble, range, roam, rove, spread, stray, string out, trail, wander

straggly aimless, disorganized, drifting, ir~regular, loose, rambling, random, spreading, spread out, straggling, straying, untidy

straight *adjective* **1.** direct, near, short, undeviating, unswerving **2.** aligned, erect, even, horizontal, in line, level, perpendicular, plumb, right, smooth, square, true, upright, vertical **3.** blunt, bold, candid, downright, forthright, frank, honest, outright, plain, point-blank, straightforward, unqualified, up~front (*informal*) **4.** above board, accurate, authentic, decent, equitable, fair, fair and square, honest, honourable, just, law-abiding, reliable, respectable, trustworthy, upright **5.** arranged, in order, neat, orderly, organized, put to rights, shipshape, sorted out, tidy **6.** consecutive, continuous, nonstop, running, solid, successive, sustained, through, uninter~rupted, unrelieved **7.** *slang* bourgeois, con~servative, conventional, orthodox, Pooterish, square (*informal*), traditional **8.** neat, pure, unadulterated, undiluted, unmixed *~adverb* **9.** as the crow flies, at once, directly, immedi~ately, instantly **10.** candidly, frankly, honestly, in plain English, point-blank, pulling no punches (*informal*), with no holds barred
Antonyms *adjective* (*sense 1*) circuitous, indi~rect, roundabout, winding, zigzag (*sense 2*) askew, bent, crooked, curved, skewwhiff (*Brit. informal*), twisted, uneven (*sense 3*) ambigu~ous, cryptic, equivocal, evasive, indirect, vague (*sense 4*) bent (*slang*), crooked (*infor~mal*), dishonest, dishonourable, shady (*infor~mal*), unlawful (*sense 5*) confused, disorderly, disorganized, in disarray, messy, untidy (*sense 6*) broken, discontinuous, interrupted, non-consecutive (*sense 7*) *slang* cool, fashionable, trendy (*Brit. informal*), voguish

straightaway at once, directly, immediately, instantly, now, on the spot, right away, straightway (*archaic*), there and then, this minute, without any delay, without more ado

straighten arrange, neaten, order, put in or~der, set *or* put to rights, smarten up, spruce up, tidy (up)

straighten out become clear, clear up, correct, disentangle, put right, rectify, regularize, re~solve, settle, sort out, unsnarl, work out

straightforward **1.** above board, candid, direct, forthright, genuine, guileless, honest, open, sincere, truthful, upfront (*informal*) **2.** clear-cut, easy, easy-peasy (*slang*), elementary, routine, simple, uncomplicated, undemanding
Antonyms complex, complicated, confused, convoluted, devious, disingenuous, round~about, shady, sharp, unclear, unscrupulous

strain[1] *verb* **1.** distend, draw tight, extend, stretch, tauten, tighten **2.** drive, exert, fatigue, injure, overexert, overtax, overwork, pull, push to the limit, sprain, tax, tear, test, tire, twist, weaken, wrench **3.** bend over backwards (*informal*), break one's back, break one's neck (*informal*), bust a gut (*informal*), do one's damnedest (*informal*), endeavour, give it one's all (*informal*), give it one's best shot (*infor~mal*), go all out for (*informal*), go for broke (*slang*), go for it (*informal*), knock oneself out (*informal*), labour, make an all-out effort (*in~formal*), make a supreme effort, rupture one~self (*informal*), strive, struggle **4.** filter, perco~

late, purify, riddle, screen, seep, separate, sieve, sift *~noun* **5**. effort, exertion, force, in~ jury, pull, sprain, struggle, tautness, tension, tensity (*rare*), wrench **6**. anxiety, burden, pressure, stress, tension **7**. *often plural* air, lay, measure (*poetic*), melody, song, theme, tune

Antonyms *verb* (*senses 2 & 3*) idle, loose, pamper, relax, rest, slacken, take it easy, yield *~noun* (*senses 5 & 6*) ease, effortless~ ness, lack of tension, relaxation

strain[2] *noun* **1**. ancestry, blood, descent, ex~ traction, family, lineage, pedigree, race, stock **2**. streak, suggestion, suspicion, tendency, trace, trait **3**. humour, manner, spirit, style, temper, tone, vein, way

strained artificial, awkward, constrained, diffi~ cult, embarrassed, false, forced, laboured, put on, self-conscious, stiff, tense, uncomfortable, uneasy, unnatural, unrelaxed

Antonyms comfortable, natural, relaxed

straitened difficult, distressed, embarrassed, limited, reduced, restricted

strait-laced moralistic, narrow, narrow-minded, niminy-piminy, of the old school, old-maidish (*informal*), overscrupulous, prim, proper, prudish, puritanical, strict, Victorian

Antonyms broad-minded, earthy, immoral, loose, relaxed, uninhibited, unreserved

straits *noun sometimes singular* **1**. crisis, diffi~ culty, dilemma, distress, embarrassment, emergency, extremity, hardship, hole (*slang*), mess, panic stations (*informal*), pass, perplex~ ity, plight, predicament, pretty *or* fine kettle of fish (*informal*) **2**. channel, narrows, sound

strand *noun* fibre, filament, length, lock, rope, string, thread, tress, twist, wisp

stranded **1**. aground, ashore, beached, cast away, grounded, marooned, wrecked **2**. *figura~ tive* abandoned, helpless, high and dry, home~ less, left in the lurch, penniless

strange **1**. abnormal, astonishing, bizarre, cu~ rious, curiouser and curiouser, eccentric, ex~ ceptional, extraordinary, fantastic, funny, ir~ regular, left-field (*informal*), marvellous, mys~ tifying, odd, oddball (*informal*), off-the-wall (*slang*), out-of-the-way, outré, peculiar, per~ plexing, queer, rare, remarkable, rum (*Brit. slang*), singular, unaccountable, uncanny, un~ common, unheard of, weird, wonderful **2**. al~ ien, exotic, foreign, new, novel, outside one's experience, remote, unexplored, unfamiliar, unknown, untried **3**. *often with* **to** a stranger to, ignorant of, inexperienced, new to, unac~ customed, unpractised, unseasoned, unused, unversed in **4**. awkward, bewildered, disori~ ented, ill at ease, like a fish out of water, lost, out of place, uncomfortable

Antonyms (*senses 1 & 2*) accustomed, bog-standard (*Brit. & Irish slang*), common, commonplace, conventional, familiar, habitual, ordinary, regular, routine, run-of-the-mill, standard, typical, unexceptional, usual, well-known (*sense 3*) accustomed, familiar, habitu~ al (*sense 4*) at ease, at home, comfortable, re~ laxed

stranger alien, foreigner, guest, incomer, new arrival, newcomer, outlander, unknown, visi~ tor

a stranger in a strange land

Bible: Exodus

strangle **1**. asphyxiate, choke, garrotte, smoth~ er, strangulate, suffocate, throttle **2**. gag, in~ hibit, repress, stifle, suppress

strap *noun* **1**. belt, leash, thong, tie *~verb* **2**. bind, buckle, fasten, lash, secure, tie, truss **3**. beat, belt (*informal*), flog, lash, scourge, whip

strapped distressed, embarrassed, financially embarrassed, in need, pinched, reduced, short, squeezed, straitened, stuck

strapping beefy (*informal*), big, brawny, burly, hefty (*informal*), hulking, husky (*informal*), powerful, robust, stalwart, sturdy, well-built, well set-up

stratagem artifice, device, dodge, feint, in~ trigue, manoeuvre, plan, plot, ploy, ruse, scheme, subterfuge, trick, wile

strategic **1**. cardinal, critical, crucial, decisive, important, key, vital **2**. calculated, deliberate, diplomatic, planned, politic, tactical

strategy approach, grand design, manoeuvring, plan, planning, policy, procedure, programme, scheme

stratum **1**. bed, layer, level, lode, seam, strati~ fication, table, tier, vein **2**. bracket, caste, cat~ egory, class, estate, grade, group, level, rank, station

stray *verb* **1**. deviate, digress, diverge, get off the point, get sidetracked, go off at a tangent, ramble **2**. be abandoned *or* lost, drift, err, go astray, lose one's way, meander, range, roam, rove, straggle, wander *~adjective* **3**. aban~ doned, homeless, lost, roaming, vagrant **4**. ac~ cidental, chance, erratic, freak, odd, random, scattered

streak *noun* **1**. band, layer, line, slash, smear, strip, stripe, stroke, vein **2**. dash, element, strain, touch, trace, vein *~verb* **3**. band, daub, fleck, slash, smear, striate, stripe **4**. barrel (along) (*informal, chiefly U.S. & Canad.*), burn rubber (*informal*), dart, flash, fly, hurtle, move like greased lightning (*informal*), speed, sprint, sweep, tear, whistle, whiz (*informal*), zoom

stream **1**. *noun* bayou, beck, brook, burn, course, creek (*U.S.*), current, drift, flow, freshet, outpouring, rill, river, rivulet, run, rush, surge, tide, tideway, torrent, tributary, undertow **2.** *verb* cascade, course, emit, flood, flow, glide, gush, issue, pour, run, shed, spill, spout

streamer banner, colours, ensign, flag, gonfalon, pennant, pennon, ribbon, standard

streamlined efficient, modernized, organized, rationalized, sleek, slick, smooth, smooth-running, time-saving, well-run

street **1.** avenue, boulevard, lane, road, roadway, row, terrace, thoroughfare **2. (right) up one's street** acceptable, compatible, congenial, familiar, one's cup of tea (*informal*), pleasing, suitable, to one's liking, to one's taste

strength **1.** backbone, brawn, brawniness, courage, firmness, fortitude, health, lustiness, might, muscle, robustness, sinew, stamina, stoutness, sturdiness, toughness **2.** cogency, concentration, effectiveness, efficacy, energy, force, intensity, potency, power, resolution, spirit, vehemence, vigour, virtue (*archaic*) **3.** advantage, anchor, asset, mainstay, security, strong point, succour, tower of strength
Antonyms (*senses 1 & 2*) debility, feebleness, frailty, impotence, infirmity, powerlessness, weakness (*sense 3*) Achilles heel, chink in one's armour, defect, failing, flaw, shortcoming, weakness

Out of the mouths of very babes and sucklings hast thou ordained strength
Bible: Psalm 8

strengthen **1.** animate, brace up, consolidate, encourage, fortify, give new energy to, harden, hearten, invigorate, nerve, nourish, rejuvenate, restore, stiffen, toughen **2.** augment, bolster, brace, build up, buttress, confirm, corroborate, enhance, establish, give a boost to, harden, heighten, increase, intensify, justify, reinforce, steel, substantiate, support
Antonyms crush, debilitate, destroy, dilute, enervate, render impotent, sap, subvert, undermine, weaken

strenuous **1.** arduous, demanding, exhausting, hard, Herculean, laborious, taxing, toilsome, tough, tough going, unrelaxing, uphill **2.** active, bold, determined, eager, earnest, energetic, persistent, resolute, spirited, strong, tireless, vigorous, zealous
Antonyms easy, effortless, relaxed, relaxing, undemanding, unenergetic, untaxing

stress *noun* **1.** emphasis, force, importance, significance, urgency, weight **2.** anxiety, burden, hassle (*informal*), nervous tension, oppression, pressure, strain, tautness, tension, trauma, worry **3.** accent, accentuation, beat, emphasis, ictus *~verb* **4.** accentuate, belabour, dwell on, emphasize, harp on, lay emphasis upon, point up, repeat, rub in, underline, underscore

I don't have ulcers, I give them
Harry Cohn

stressful agitating, anxious, tense, traumatic, worrying

stretch *verb* **1.** cover, extend, put forth, reach, spread, unfold, unroll **2.** distend, draw out, elongate, expand, inflate, lengthen, pull, pull out of shape, rack, strain, swell, tighten *~noun* **3.** area, distance, expanse, extent, spread, sweep, tract **4.** bit, period, run, space, spell, stint, term, time

strew bestrew, disperse, litter, scatter, spread, sprinkle, toss

stricken affected, afflicted, hit, injured, laid low, smitten, struck, struck down

strict **1.** austere, authoritarian, firm, harsh, no-nonsense, rigid, rigorous, severe, stern, stringent **2.** accurate, close, exact, faithful, meticulous, particular, precise, religious, scrupulous, true **3.** absolute, complete, perfect, total, utter
Antonyms (*sense 1*) easy-going, easy-oasy (*slang*), flexible, laid-back (*informal*), lax, mild, moderate, soft, tolerant

stricture animadversion, bad press, blame, censure, criticism, flak (*informal*), rebuke, stick (*slang*)

strident clamorous, clashing, discordant, grating, harsh, jangling, jarring, rasping, raucous, screeching, shrill, stridulant, stridulous, unmusical, vociferous
Antonyms calm, dulcet, gentle, harmonious, mellifluous, mellow, quiet, soft, soothing, sweet

strife animosity, battle, bickering, clash, clashes, combat, conflict, contention, contest, controversy, discord, dissension, friction, quarrel, rivalry, row, squabbling, struggle, warfare, wrangling

strike *verb* **1.** bang, beat, box, buffet, chastise, chin (*slang*), clobber (*slang*), clout (*informal*), clump (*slang*), cuff, deck (*slang*), hammer, hit, knock, lambast(e), lay a finger on (*informal*), lay one on (*slang*), pound, punch, punish, slap, smack, smite, sock (*slang*), thump, wallop (*informal*) **2.** be in collision with, bump into, clash, collide with, come into contact with, dash, hit, knock into, run into, smash into, touch **3.** drive, force, hit, impel, thrust **4.** affect, come to, come to the mind of, dawn on *or* upon, hit, impress, make an impact on, occur to, reach, register (*informal*), seem **5.** *sometimes with* **upon** come upon *or* across, discover, encounter, find, happen *or* chance upon, hit upon, light upon, reach, stumble upon *or* across, turn up, uncover, unearth **6.** affect, assail, assault, attack, deal a blow to, devastate, fall upon, hit, invade, set upon, smite **7.** achieve, arrange, arrive at, attain, effect, reach **8.** down tools, mutiny, revolt, walk out

strike down afflict, bring low, deal a death~blow to, destroy, kill, ruin, slay, smite

strike out **1.** *Also* **strike off, strike through** cancel, cross out, delete, efface, erase, excise, expunge, remove, score out **2.** begin, get under way, set out, start out

striking astonishing, conspicuous, dazzling, dramatic, drop-dead (*slang*), extraordinary, forcible, impressive, memorable, noticeable, out of the ordinary, outstanding, stunning (*informal*), wonderful
Antonyms average, dull, indifferent, undis~tinguished, unexceptional, unextraordinary, unimpressive, uninteresting, vanilla (*infor~mal*)

string *noun* **1.** cord, fibre, twine **2.** chain, file, line, procession, queue, row, sequence, series, strand, succession *~verb* **3.** festoon, hang, link, loop, sling, stretch, suspend, thread **4.** *with* **out** disperse, extend, fan out, lengthen, pro~tract, space out, spread out, straggle

string along **1.** *often with* **with** agree, assent, collaborate, go along with **2.** *Also* **string on** bluff, deceive, dupe, fool, hoax, kid (*informal*), play fast and loose with (someone) (*informal*), play (someone) false, put one over on (some~one) (*informal*), take (someone) for a ride (*in~formal*)

stringent binding, demanding, exacting, inflex~ible, rigid, rigorous, severe, strict, tight, tough
Antonyms equivocal, flexible, inconclusive, lax, loose, relaxed, slack, unrigorous, vague

strings *figurative* catches (*informal*), complica~tions, conditions, obligations, prerequisites, provisos, qualifications, requirements, riders, stipulations

stringy chewy, fibrous, gristly, sinewy, tough, wiry

strip[1] *verb* **1.** bare, denude, deprive, despoil, dismantle, divest, empty, gut, lay bare, loot, peel, pillage, plunder, ransack, rob, sack, skin, spoil **2.** disrobe, unclothe, uncover, undress

strip[2] *noun* band, belt, bit, fillet, piece, ribbon, shred, slip, swathe, tongue

striped banded, barred, striated, stripy

stripling adolescent, boy, fledgling, hobble~dehoy (*archaic*), lad, shaver (*informal*), young fellow, youngster, youth

strive attempt, bend over backwards (*infor~mal*), break one's neck (*informal*), bust a gut (*informal*), compete, contend, do all one can, do one's best, do one's damnedest (*informal*), do one's utmost, endeavour, exert oneself, fight, give it one's all (*informal*), give it one's best shot (*informal*), go all out (*informal*), go for broke (*slang*), go for it (*informal*), jump through hoops (*informal*), knock oneself out (*informal*), labour, leave no stone unturned, make an all-out effort (*informal*), make every effort, rupture oneself (*informal*), strain, struggle, toil, try, try hard

stroke *noun* **1.** accomplishment, achievement, blow, feat, flourish, hit, knock, move, move~ment, pat, rap, thump **2.** apoplexy, attack, collapse, fit, seizure, shock *~verb* **3.** caress, fondle, pat, pet, rub

stroll **1.** *verb* amble, make one's way, mooch (*slang*), mosey (*informal*), promenade, ramble, saunter, stooge (*slang*), stretch one's legs, take a turn, toddle, wander **2.** *noun* airing, breath of air, constitutional, excursion, prom~enade, ramble, turn, walk

strong **1.** athletic, beefy (*informal*), brawny, burly, capable, fighting fit, fit, fit as a fiddle, hale, hardy, healthy, Herculean, lusty, mus~cular, powerful, robust, sinewy, sound, stal~wart, stout, strapping, sturdy, tough, virile **2.** aggressive, brave, courageous, determined, feisty (*informal, chiefly U.S. & Canad.*), firm in spirit, forceful, hard as nails, hard-nosed (*informal*), high-powered, plucky, resilient, resolute, resourceful, self-assertive, steadfast, stouthearted, tenacious, tough, unyielding **3.** acute, dedicated, deep, deep-rooted, eager, fervent, fervid, fierce, firm, intense, keen, se~vere, staunch, vehement, violent, zealous **4.** clear, clear-cut, cogent, compelling, convinc~ing, distinct, effective, formidable, great, marked, overpowering, persuasive, potent, re~doubtable, sound, telling, trenchant, unmis~takable, urgent, weighty, well-established, well-founded **5.** Draconian, drastic, extreme, forceful, severe **6.** durable, hard-wearing, heavy-duty, on a firm foundation, reinforced, sturdy, substantial, well-armed, well-built, well-protected **7.** bold, bright, brilliant, daz~zling, glaring, loud, stark **8.** biting, concen~trated, heady, highly-flavoured, highly-seasoned, hot, intoxicating, piquant, pungent, pure, sharp, spicy, undiluted
Antonyms (*senses 1, 2, 3, 4, 5 & 6*) charac~terless, delicate, faint-hearted, feeble, frail, ineffectual, lacking drive, namby-pamby, puny, slight, spineless, timid, unassertive, uncommitted, unimpassioned, weak (*sense 7*) dull, insipid, pale, pastel, washed-out (*sense 8*) bland, mild, tasteless, vapid, weak

strong-arm *adjective* aggressive, bullying, co~ercive, forceful, high-pressure, terror, terror~izing, threatening, thuggish, violent

stronghold bastion, bulwark, castle, citadel, fastness, fort, fortress, keep, refuge

strong-minded determined, firm, independent, iron-willed, resolute, strong-willed, unbending, uncompromising

strong point advantage, asset, forte, long suit

(*informal*), métier, speciality, strength, strong suit

stroppy awkward, bloody-minded (*Brit. informal*), cantankerous, destructive, difficult, litigious, obstreperous, perverse, quarrelsome, uncooperative, unhelpful

structure *noun* **1.** arrangement, configuration, conformation, construction, design, fabric, form, formation, interrelation of parts, make, make-up, organization **2.** building, construction, edifice, erection, pile *~verb* **3.** arrange, assemble, build up, design, organize, put together, shape

struggle *verb* **1.** bend over backwards (*informal*), break one's neck (*informal*), bust a gut (*informal*), do one's damnedest (*informal*), exert oneself, give it one's all (*informal*), give it one's best shot (*informal*), go all out (*informal*), go for broke (*slang*), go for it (*informal*), knock oneself out (*informal*), labour, make an all-out effort (*informal*), make every effort, rupture oneself (*informal*), strain, strive, toil, work, work like a Trojan *~noun* **2.** effort, exertion, grind (*informal*), labour, long haul, pains, scramble, toil, work *~verb* **3.** battle, compete, contend, fight, grapple, lock horns, scuffle, wrestle *~noun* **4.** battle, brush, clash, combat, conflict, contest, encounter, hostilities, skirmish, strife, tussle

strung up a bundle of nerves (*informal*), edgy, jittery (*informal*), keyed up, nervous, on edge, on tenterhooks, tense, twitchy (*informal*), under a strain, uptight (*informal*), wired (*slang*)

strut *verb* parade, peacock, prance, stalk, swagger

stub *noun* butt, counterfoil, dog-end (*informal*), end, fag end (*informal*), remnant, stump, tail, tail end

stubborn bull-headed, contumacious, cross-grained, dogged, dour, fixed, headstrong, inflexible, intractable, mulish, obdurate, obstinate, opinionated, persistent, pig-headed, recalcitrant, refractory, self-willed, stiff-necked, tenacious, unbending, unmanageable, unshakable, unyielding, wilful

Antonyms biddable, compliant, docile, flexible, half-hearted, irresolute, malleable, manageable, pliable, pliant, tractable, vacillating, wavering, yielding

stubby **1.** chunky, dumpy, fubsy (*archaic or dialect*), short, squat, stocky, stumpy, thickset **2.** bristling, bristly, prickly, rough, stubbly

stuck **1.** cemented, fast, fastened, firm, fixed, glued, joined **2.** *informal* at a loss, at a standstill, at one's wits' end, baffled, beaten, bereft of ideas, nonplussed, stumped, up against a brick wall (*informal*) **3.** *slang with* **on** crazy about, for, *or* over (*informal*), enthusiastic about, hung up on (*slang*), infatuated, keen, mad, obsessed with, wild about (*informal*) **4.** **get stuck into** *informal* get down to, make a start on, set about, tackle, take the bit between one's teeth

stuck-up arrogant, big-headed (*informal*), conceited, condescending, haughty, high and mighty (*informal*), hoity-toity (*informal*), patronizing, proud, snobbish, snooty (*informal*), swollen-headed, toffee-nosed (*slang, chiefly Brit.*), uppish (*Brit. informal*), uppity (*informal*)

stud *verb* bejewel, bespangle, dot, fleck, ornament, spangle, speckle, spot, sprinkle

student apprentice, disciple, learner, observer, pupil, scholar, trainee, undergraduate

studied calculated, conscious, deliberate, intentional, planned, premeditated, purposeful, well-considered, wilful

Antonyms impulsive, natural, spontaneous, spur-of-the-moment, unplanned, unpremeditated

studio atelier, workshop

studious academic, assiduous, attentive, bookish, careful, diligent, eager, earnest, hard-working, intellectual, meditative, reflective, scholarly, sedulous, serious, thoughtful

Antonyms careless, frivolous, idle, inattentive, indifferent, lazy, loafing, negligent, unacademic, unintellectual, unscholarly

study *verb* **1.** apply oneself (to), bone up on (*informal*), burn the midnight oil, cogitate, con (*archaic*), consider, contemplate, cram (*informal*), examine, go into, hammer away at, learn, lucubrate (*rare*), meditate, mug up (*Brit. slang*), ponder, pore over, read, read up, swot (up) (*Brit. informal*) **2.** analyse, deliberate, examine, investigate, look into, peruse, research, scrutinize, survey, work over *~noun* **3.** academic work, application, book work, cramming (*informal*), learning, lessons, reading, research, school work, swotting (*Brit. informal*), thought **4.** analysis, attention, cogitation, consideration, contemplation, examination, inquiry, inspection, investigation, perusal, review, scrutiny, survey

Of making many books there is no end; and much study is a weariness of the flesh
Bible: Ecclesiastes

stuff *verb* **1.** compress, cram, crowd, fill, force, jam, load, pack, pad, push, ram, shove, squeeze, stow, wedge **2.** gobble, gorge, gormandize, guzzle, make a pig of oneself (*informal*), overindulge, pig out (*slang*), sate, satiate *~noun* **3.** belongings, bits and pieces, clobber (*Brit. slang*), effects, equipment, gear, goods and chattels, impedimenta, junk, kit, luggage, materials, objects, paraphernalia, possessions, tackle, things, trappings **4.** cloth, fabric, material, raw material, textile **5.** es~

sence, matter, pith, quintessence, staple, sub~ stance **6.** balderdash, baloney (*informal*), bosh (*informal*), bunk (*informal*), bunkum, claptrap (*informal*), foolishness, humbug, nonsense, poppycock (*informal*), rot, rubbish, stuff and nonsense, tommyrot, trash, tripe (*informal*), twaddle, verbiage

stuffing **1.** filler, kapok, packing, quilting, wadding **2.** farce, farcemeat, forcemeat

stuffy **1.** airless, close, fetid, frowsty, fuggy, heavy, muggy, oppressive, stale, stifling, suf~ focating, sultry, unventilated **2.** as dry as dust, conventional, deadly, dreary, dull, fusty, humourless, musty, niminy-piminy, old-fashioned, old-fogyish, pompous, priggish, prim, prim and proper, staid, stilted, stodgy, strait-laced, uninteresting

Antonyms (*sense 1*) airy, breezy, cool, draughty, fresh, gusty, pleasant, well-ventilated

stumble **1.** blunder about, come a cropper (*in~ formal*), fall, falter, flounder, hesitate, lose one's balance, lurch, reel, slip, stagger, trip **2.** *with* **on** *or* **upon** blunder upon, chance upon, come across, discover, encounter, find, happen upon, light upon, run across, turn up **3.** falter, fluff (*informal*), stammer, stutter

stumbling block bar, barrier, difficulty, haz~ ard, hindrance, hurdle, impediment, obstacle, obstruction, snag

stump *verb* **1.** baffle, bewilder, bring (someone) up short, confound, confuse, dumbfound, flummox, foil, mystify, nonplus, outwit, per~ plex, puzzle, stop, stymie **2.** clomp, clump, lumber, plod, stamp, stomp (*informal*), trudge

stumped at a loss, at one's wits' end, at sea, baffled, brought to a standstill, floored (*infor~ mal*), flummoxed, in despair, nonplussed, per~ plexed, stymied, uncertain which way to turn

stump up chip in (*informal*), come across with (*informal*), contribute, cough up (*informal*), donate, fork out (*slang*), hand over, pay, shell out (*informal*)

stumpy chunky, dumpy, fubsy (*archaic or dia~ lect*), heavy, short, squat, stocky, stubby, thick, thickset

stun *figurative* amaze, astonish, astound, be~ wilder, confound, confuse, daze, dumbfound, flabbergast (*informal*), hit (someone) like a ton of bricks (*informal*), knock out, knock (someone) for six (*informal*), overcome, over~ power, shock, stagger, strike (someone) dumb, stupefy, take (someone's) breath away

stung angered, exasperated, goaded, hurt, in~ censed, nettled, piqued, resentful, roused, wounded

stunned *figurative* astounded, at a loss for words, bowled over (*informal*), dazed, devas~ tated, dumbfounded, flabbergasted (*informal*), gobsmacked (*Brit. slang*), numb, shocked, staggered, struck dumb

stunner beauty, charmer, dazzler, dish (*infor~ mal*), dolly (*slang*), eyeful (*informal*), glamour puss, good-looker, heart-throb, honey (*infor~ mal*), humdinger (*slang*), knockout (*informal*), looker (*informal, chiefly U.S.*), lovely (*slang*), peach (*informal*), sensation, smasher (*infor~ mal*), wow (*slang, chiefly U.S.*)

stunning beautiful, brilliant, dazzling, devas~ tating (*informal*), dramatic, drop-dead (*slang*), gorgeous, great (*informal*), heavenly, impres~ sive, lovely, marvellous, out of this world (*in~ formal*), ravishing, remarkable, sensational (*informal*), smashing (*informal*), spectacular, striking, wonderful

Antonyms average, dreadful, horrible, medio~ cre, no great shakes (*informal*), ordinary, plain, poor, rotten, run-of-the-mill, ugly, un~ attractive, unimpressive, uninspiring, unre~ markable

stunt *noun* act, deed, exploit, feat, feature, gest (*archaic*), *tour de force*, trick

stunted diminutive, dwarfed, dwarfish, little, small, tiny, undersized

stupefaction amazement, astonishment, awe, wonder, wonderment

stupefy amaze, astound, bewilder, confound, daze, dumbfound, knock senseless, numb, shock, stagger, stun

stupendous amazing, astounding, breath~ taking, brilliant, colossal, enormous, fabulous (*informal*), fantastic (*informal*), gigantic, huge, marvellous, mega (*slang*), mind-blowing (*in~ formal*), mind-boggling (*informal*), out of this world (*informal*), overwhelming, phenomenal, prodigious, sensational (*informal*), staggering, stunning (*informal*), superb, surpassing belief, surprising, tremendous (*informal*), vast, won~ derful, wondrous (*archaic or literary*)

Antonyms average, diminutive, mediocre, modest, no great shakes (*informal*), ordinary, petty, puny, tiny, unexciting, unimpressive, unremarkable, unsurprising

stupid **1.** Boeotian, braindead (*informal*), brain~ less, cretinous, dead from the neck up, deficient, dense, dim, doltish, dopey (*informal*), dozy (*Brit. informal*), dull, dumb (*informal*), foolish, gul~ lible, half-witted, moronic, naive, obtuse, simple, simple-minded, slow, slow on the uptake (*infor~ mal*), slow-witted, sluggish, stolid, thick, thick as mince (*Scot. informal*), thickheaded, unintelli~ gent, witless, woodenheaded (*informal*) **2.** asi~ nine, crackbrained, daft (*informal*), futile, half-baked (*informal*), idiotic, ill-advised, imbecilic, inane, indiscreet, irrelevant, irresponsible, laughable, ludicrous, meaningless, mindless, nonsensical, pointless, puerile, rash, senseless, short-sighted, trivial, unintelligent, unthinking

3. dazed, groggy, in a daze, insensate, punch-drunk, semiconscious, senseless, stunned, stu~pefied
Antonyms astute, brainy, bright, brilliant, clear-headed, clever, intelligent, lucid, on the ball (*informal*), prudent, quick, quick on the uptake, quick-witted, realistic, reasonable, sensible, sharp, shrewd, smart, thoughtful, well-thought-out, wise

He's so dumb he can't fart and chew gum at the same time (often euphemistically "walk and chew gum")

Lyndon B Johnson (of Gerald Ford)

stupidity 1. asininity, brainlessness, denseness, dimness, dopiness (*slang*), doziness (*Brit. informal*), dullness, dumbness (*informal*), feeble-mindedness, imbecility, lack of brain, lack of intelligence, naivety, obtuseness, puer~ility, simplicity, slowness, thickheadedness, thickness 2. absurdity, bêtise (*rare*), fatuity, fatuousness, folly, foolhardiness, foolishness, futility, idiocy, impracticality, inanity, indis~cretion, ineptitude, irresponsibility, ludicrous~ness, lunacy, madness, pointlessness, rash~ness, senselessness, silliness

stupor coma, daze, inertia, insensibility, leth~argy, numbness, stupefaction, torpor, trance, unconsciousness

sturdy athletic, brawny, built to last, deter~mined, durable, firm, flourishing, hardy, hearty, lusty, muscular, powerful, resolute, robust, secure, solid, stalwart, staunch, stead~fast, stouthearted, substantial, thickset, vig~orous, well-built, well-made
Antonyms feeble, flimsy, frail, infirm, irreso~lute, puny, rickety, skinny, uncertain, unsub~stantial, weak, weakly

stutter *verb* falter, hesitate, speak haltingly, splutter, stammer, stumble

Stygian black, caliginous (*archaic*), dark, dreary, gloomy, Hadean, hellish, infernal, sombre, Tartarean, tenebrous

style *noun* 1. cut, design, form, hand, manner, technique 2. fashion, mode, rage, trend, vogue 3. approach, custom, manner, method, mode, way 4. *bon ton*, chic, cosmopolitanism, dash, dressiness (*informal*), élan, elegance, fashion~ableness, flair, grace, panache, polish, refine~ment, savoir-faire, smartness, sophistication, stylishness, taste, urbanity 5. affluence, com~fort, ease, elegance, gracious living, grandeur, luxury 6. appearance, category, characteristic, genre, kind, pattern, sort, spirit, strain, tenor, tone, type, variety 7. diction, expression, mode of expression, phraseology, phrasing, treat~ment, turn of phrase, vein, wording *~verb* 8. adapt, arrange, cut, design, dress, fashion, shape, tailor 9. address, call, christen, de~nominate, designate, dub, entitle, label, name, term

stylish à la mode, chic, classy (*slang*), dapper, dressy (*informal*), fashionable, in fashion, in vogue, modish, natty (*informal*), polished, smart, snappy, snazzy (*informal*), trendy (*Brit. informal*), urbane, voguish, well turned-out
Antonyms badly-tailored, naff (*Brit. slang*), old-fashioned, outmoded, out-of-date, passé, scruffy, shabby, slovenly, tacky, tawdry, un~fashionable, unstylish, untrendy (*Brit. infor~mal*)

stymie balk, confound, defeat, flummox, foil, frustrate, hinder, mystify, nonplus, puzzle, snooker, spike (someone's) guns, stump, throw a spanner in the works (*Brit. informal*), thwart

suave affable, agreeable, bland, charming, civilized, cool (*informal*), courteous, debonair, diplomatic, gracious, obliging, pleasing, polite, smooth, smooth-tongued, sophisticated, svelte, urbane, worldly

subconscious *adjective* hidden, inner, inner~most, intuitive, latent, repressed, subliminal, suppressed
Antonyms aware, conscious, knowing, sen~sible, sentient

subdue 1. beat down, break, conquer, control, crush, defeat, discipline, gain ascendancy over, get the better of, get the upper hand over, get under control, humble, master, over~come, overpower, overrun, put down, quell, tame, trample, triumph over, vanquish 2. check, control, mellow, moderate, quieten down, repress, soften, suppress, tone down
Antonyms (*sense 2*) agitate, arouse, awaken, incite, provoke, stir up, waken, whip up

subdued 1. chastened, crestfallen, dejected, downcast, down in the mouth, grave, out of spirits, quiet, repentant, repressed, restrained, sad, sadder and wiser, serious, sobered, sol~emn 2. dim, hushed, low-key, muted, quiet, shaded, sober, soft, subtle, toned down, unob~trusive
Antonyms bright, cheerful, enthusiastic, full of beans (*informal*), happy, lively, loud, stri~dent, vivacious

subject *noun* 1. affair, business, field of en~quiry *or* reference, issue, matter, object, point, question, subject matter, substance, theme, topic 2. case, client, guinea pig (*informal*), participant, patient, victim 3. citizen, depend~ant, liegeman, national, subordinate, vassal *~adjective* 4. at the mercy of, disposed, ex~posed, in danger of, liable, open, prone, sus~ceptible, vulnerable 5. conditional, contingent, dependent 6. answerable, bound by, captive, dependent, enslaved, inferior, obedient, satel~lite, subjugated, submissive, subordinate, subservient *~verb* 7. expose, lay open, make liable, put through, submit, treat

subjective biased, emotional, idiosyncratic, instinctive, intuitive, nonobjective, personal, prejudiced
Antonyms concrete, detached, disinterested, dispassionate, impartial, impersonal, objective, open-minded, unbiased

subjugate bring (someone) to his knees, bring to heel, bring under the yoke, conquer, crush, defeat, enslave, hold sway over, lick (*informal*), master, overcome, overpower, overthrow, put down, quell, reduce, rule over, subdue, suppress, tame, vanquish

sublimate **1.** channel, divert, redirect, transfer, turn **2.** elevate, exalt, heighten, refine

sublime elevated, eminent, exalted, glorious, grand, great, high, imposing, lofty, magnificent, majestic, noble, transcendent
Antonyms bad, commonplace, lowly, mundane, ordinary, poor, ridiculous, worldly

It is only one step from the sublime to the ridiculous
Napoleon Bonaparte

The sublime and the ridiculous are often so nearly related, that it is difficult to class them separately. One step above the sublime, makes the ridiculous; and one step above the ridiculous, makes the sublime again
Thomas Paine *The Age of Reason*

subliminal subconscious, unconscious

submerge deluge, dip, drown, duck, dunk, engulf, flood, immerse, inundate, overflow, overwhelm, plunge, sink, swamp

submerged drowned, immersed, subaquatic, subaqueous, submarine, submersed, sunk, sunken, undersea, underwater

submission **1.** acquiescence, assent, capitulation, giving in, surrender, yielding **2.** compliance, deference, docility, meekness, obedience, passivity, resignation, submissiveness, tractability, unassertiveness **3.** argument, contention, proposal **4.** entry, handing in, presentation, submitting, tendering

submissive abject, accommodating, acquiescent, amenable, biddable, bootlicking (*informal*), compliant, deferential, docile, dutiful, humble, ingratiating, lowly, malleable, meek, obedient, obeisant, obsequious, passive, patient, pliant, resigned, subdued, tractable, uncomplaining, unresisting, yielding
Antonyms awkward, difficult, disobedient, headstrong, intractable, obstinate, stubborn, uncooperative, unyielding

submit **1.** accede, acquiesce, agree, bend, bow, capitulate, comply, defer, endure, give in, hoist the white flag, knuckle under, lay down arms, put up with (*informal*), resign oneself, stoop, succumb, surrender, throw in the sponge, toe the line, tolerate, yield **2.** commit, hand in, present, proffer, put forward, refer, table, tender **3.** advance, argue, assert, claim, contend, move, propose, propound, put, state, suggest, volunteer

subnormal cretinous, E.S.N., feeble-minded, imbecilic, mentally defective, moronic, retarded, simple, slow

subordinate *adjective* **1.** dependent, inferior, junior, lesser, lower, minor, secondary, subject, subservient **2.** ancillary, auxiliary, subsidiary, supplementary *~noun* **3.** aide, assistant, attendant, dependant, inferior, junior, second, subaltern, underling
Antonyms *adjective* central, essential, greater, higher, key, main, necessary, predominant, senior, superior, vital *~noun* boss (*informal*), captain, chief, commander, head, leader, master, principal, senior, superior

subordination inferiority, inferior *or* secondary status, servitude, subjection, submission

sub rosa behind closed doors, in camera, in secret, in strict confidence, secretly

subscribe **1.** chip in (*informal*), contribute, donate, give, offer, pledge, promise **2.** acquiesce, advocate, agree, consent, countenance, endorse, support

subscription annual payment, contribution, donation, dues, gift, membership fee, offering

subsequent after, consequent, consequential, ensuing, following, later, succeeding, successive
Antonyms antecedent, earlier, erstwhile, former, on-time, past, preceding, previous, prior

subsequently afterwards, at a later date, consequently, in the aftermath (of), in the end, later

subservient **1.** abject, bootlicking (*informal*), deferential, inferior, obsequious, servile, slavish, subject, submissive, sycophantic, truckling **2.** accessory, ancillary, auxiliary, conducive, helpful, instrumental, serviceable, subordinate, subsidiary, useful
Antonyms (*sense 1*) bolshie, bossy, disobedient, domineering, overbearing, overriding, rebellious, superior, wilful

subside **1.** abate, decrease, de-escalate, diminish, dwindle, ease, ebb, lessen, let up, level off, melt away, moderate, peter out, quieten, recede, slacken, wane **2.** cave in, collapse, decline, descend, drop, ebb, lower, settle, sink
Antonyms escalate, grow, heighten, increase, inflate, intensify, mount, rise, soar, swell, tumefy, wax

subsidence **1.** decline, descent, ebb, settlement, settling, sinking **2.** abatement, decrease, de-escalation, diminution, easing off, lessening, slackening

subsidiary aiding, ancillary, assistant, auxiliary, contributory, cooperative, helpful, lesser, minor, secondary, serviceable, subordinate,

subservient, supplemental, supplementary, useful
Antonyms central, chief, head, key, leading, main, major, primary, principal, vital

subsidize finance, fund, promote, put up the money for, sponsor, support, underwrite

subsidy aid, allowance, assistance, contribu~ tion, financial aid, grant, help, stipend, sub~ vention, support

subsist be, continue, eke out an existence, en~ dure, exist, keep going, keep one's head above water, last, live, make ends meet, remain, stay alive, survive, sustain oneself

subsistence aliment, existence, food, keep, livelihood, living, maintenance, provision, ra~ tions, support, survival, sustenance, upkeep, victuals

substance **1.** body, element, fabric, material, stuff, texture **2.** burden, essence, gist, grava~ men (*Law*), import, main point, matter, meaning, pith, significance, subject, sum and substance, theme **3.** actuality, concreteness, entity, force, reality **4.** affluence, assets, es~ tate, means, property, resources, wealth

substandard damaged, imperfect, inadequate, inferior, second-rate, shoddy, unacceptable

substantial **1.** ample, big, considerable, gener~ ous, goodly, important, large, significant, siz~ able *or* sizeable, tidy (*informal*), worthwhile **2.** bulky, durable, firm, hefty, massive, solid, sound, stout, strong, sturdy, well-built **3.** ac~ tual, existent, material, positive, real, true, valid, weighty
Antonyms (*senses 1 & 2*) feeble, frail, inad~ equate, inconsiderable, infirm, insignificant, insubstantial, jerry-built, light-weight, mea~ gre, niggardly, pathetic, poor, rickety, skimpy, small, weak (*sense 3*) fictitious, imaginary, imagined, insubstantial, nonexistent, unreal

substantially essentially, in essence, in essen~ tials, in substance, in the main, largely, ma~ terially, to a large extent

substantiate affirm, attest to, authenticate, bear out, confirm, corroborate, establish, prove, support, validate, verify
Antonyms confute, contradict, controvert, dis~ prove, expose, invalidate, make a nonsense of, negate, prove false, rebut, refute

substitute *verb* **1.** change, commute, exchange, interchange, replace, swap (*informal*), switch **2.** *with* **for** act for, be in place of, cover for, deputize, double for, fill in for, hold the fort for, relieve, stand in for, take over *~noun* **3.** agent, depute (*Scot.*), deputy, equivalent, ex~ pedient, locum, locum tenens, makeshift, proxy, relief, replacement, representative, re~ serve, stand-by, stopgap, sub, supply, surro~ gate, temp (*informal*), temporary *~adjective* **4.** acting, additional, alternative, fall-back, proxy, replacement, reserve, second, surro~ gate, temporary

substitution change, exchange, interchange, replacement, swap (*informal*), switch

subterfuge artifice, deception, deviousness, dodge, duplicity, evasion, excuse, machination, manoeuvre, ploy, pretence, pretext, quibble, ruse, shift, stall, stratagem, trick

subtle **1.** deep, delicate, discriminating, ingen~ ious, nice, penetrating, profound, refined, so~ phisticated **2.** delicate, faint, implied, indirect, insinuated, slight, understated **3.** artful, as~ tute, crafty, cunning, designing, devious, in~ triguing, keen, Machiavellian, scheming, shrewd, sly, wily
Antonyms artless, blunt, crass, direct, down~ right, guileless, heavy-handed, lacking finesse, obvious, overwhelming, simple, straight~ forward, strong, tactless, unsophisticated, un~ subtle

subtlety **1.** acumen, acuteness, cleverness, delicacy, discernment, fine point, intricacy, nicety, refinement, sagacity, skill, sophistica~ tion **2.** discernment, discrimination, finesse, penetration **3.** artfulness, astuteness, crafti~ ness, cunning, deviousness, guile, slyness, wiliness

subtract deduct, detract, diminish, remove, take away, take from, take off, withdraw
Antonyms add, add to, append, increase by, supplement

suburbs dormitory area (*Brit.*), environs, fau~ bourgs, neighbourhood, outskirts, precincts, purlieus, residential areas, suburbia

subversive **1.** *adjective* destructive, incendiary, inflammatory, insurrectionary, overthrowing, perversive, riotous, seditious, treasonous, underground, undermining **2.** *noun* deviation~ ist, dissident, fifth columnist, insurrectionary, quisling, saboteur, seditionary, seditionist, terrorist, traitor

subvert **1.** demolish, destroy, invalidate, over~ turn, raze, ruin, sabotage, undermine, upset, wreck **2.** confound, contaminate, corrupt, de~ base, demoralize, deprave, pervert, poison, vi~ tiate

succeed **1.** arrive (*informal*), be successful, bring home the bacon (*informal*), carry all be~ fore one, come off (*informal*), crack it (*infor~ mal*), cut it (*informal*), do all right for oneself (*informal*), do the trick (*informal*), flourish, gain one's end, get to the top, go down a bomb (*informal, chiefly Brit.*), go like a bomb (*Brit. & N.Z. informal*), hit the jackpot (*infor~ mal*), make good, make it (*informal*), make one's mark (*informal*), make the grade (*infor~ mal*), prosper, thrive, triumph, turn out well, work **2.** be subsequent, come next, ensue, fol~ low, result, supervene **3.** *usually with* **to** ac~

cede, assume the office of, come into, come into possession of, enter upon, fill (someone's) boots, inherit, replace, step into (someone's) boots, take over
Antonyms (*sense 1*) be unsuccessful, collapse, come a cropper (*informal*), fail, fall by the wayside, fall flat, fall short, flop (*informal*), go belly up (*informal*), go by the board, not make the grade, not manage to (*sense 2*) be a precursor of, come before, go ahead of, go before, pave the way, precede

succeeding ensuing, following, next, subsequent, successive
Antonyms antecedent, earlier, former, preceding, previous, prior

success 1. ascendancy, eminence, fame, favourable outcome, fortune, happiness, hit (*informal*), luck, prosperity, triumph 2. best seller, big name, celebrity, hit (*informal*), market leader, megastar (*informal*), sensation, smasheroo (*slang*), smash hit (*informal*), somebody, star, V.I.P., winner
Antonyms collapse, dead duck (*slang*), disaster, downfall, failure, fiasco, flop (*informal*), loser, misfortune, nobody, no-hoper, washout

Getting on is the opium of the middle classes
Walter James

To succeed in the world we must look foolish but be wise
C.L. de Montesquieu *Pensées*

Success has ruin'd many a man
Benjamin Franklin *Poor Richard's Almanac*

The road to success is full of women pushing their husbands along
Lord Thomas Dewar

The moral flabbiness born of the exclusive worship of the bitch-goddess success
William James *Letter to H G Wells*

The secret of business success is honesty and sincerity. If you can fake those, you've got it made
attributed to Groucho Marx

If A is success in life, then A equals x plus y plus z. Work is x; y is play; and z is keeping your mouth shut
Albert Einstein

Success is relative;
It is what we can make of the mess we have made of things
T.S. Eliot *The Family Reunion*

success: the one unpardonable sin against one's fellows
Ambrose Bierce *The Devil's Dictionary*

Be nice to people on your way up because you'll meet 'em on your way down
Wilson Mizner

Nothing succeeds like success

There is always room at the top

successful acknowledged, at the top of the tree, best-selling, booming, efficacious, favourable, flourishing, fortunate, fruitful, going places, home and dry (*Brit. informal*), lucky, lucrative, moneymaking, on a roll, out in front (*informal*), paying, profitable, prosperous, rewarding, thriving, top, unbeaten, victorious, wealthy
Antonyms defeated, failed, ineffective, losing, luckless, uneconomic, unprofitable, unsuccessful, useless

A successful man is one who makes more money than his wife can spend
Lana Turner

successfully famously (*informal*), favourably, in triumph, swimmingly, victoriously, well, with flying colours

succession 1. chain, continuation, course, cycle, flow, order, procession, progression, run, sequence, series, train 2. **in succession** consecutively, one after the other, one behind the other, on the trot (*informal*), running, successively 3. accession, assumption, elevation, entering upon, inheritance, taking over 4. descendants, descent, line, lineage, race

successive consecutive, following, in a row, in succession, sequent, succeeding

succinct brief, compact, compendious, concise, condensed, gnomic, in a few well-chosen words, laconic, pithy, summary, terse, to the point
Antonyms circuitous, circumlocutory, diffuse, discursive, long-winded, prolix, rambling, verbose, wordy

succour 1. *verb* aid, assist, befriend, comfort, encourage, foster, give aid and encouragement to, help, minister to, nurse, relieve, render assistance to, support 2. *noun* aid, assistance, comfort, help, relief, support

succulent juicy, luscious, lush, mellow, moist, mouthwatering, rich

succumb capitulate, die, fall, fall victim to, give in, give way, go under, knuckle under, submit, surrender, yield
Antonyms beat, conquer, get the better of, master, overcome, rise above, surmount, triumph over

sucker butt, cat's paw, dupe, easy game *or* mark (*informal*), fool, mug (*Brit. slang*), nerd *or* nurd (*slang*), pushover (*slang*), sap (*slang*), sitting duck (*informal*), sitting target, victim

suck up to brown-nose (*taboo slang*), butter up, curry favour with, dance attendance on, fawn on, flatter, get on the right side of, ingratiate oneself with, keep in with (*informal*), kiss (someone's) ass (*U.S. & Canad. taboo slang*), lick (someone's) boots, pander to, play up to (*informal*), toady, truckle, worm oneself into (someone's) favour

sudden abrupt, hasty, hurried, impulsive, quick, rapid, rash, swift, unexpected, unforeseen, unusual
Antonyms anticipated, deliberate, expected, foreseen, gentle, gradual, slow, unhasty

suddenly abruptly, all at once, all of a sudden, on the spur of the moment, out of the blue (*informal*), unexpectedly, without warning

sue 1. *Law* bring an action against (someone), charge, have the law on (someone) (*informal*), indict, institute legal proceedings against (someone), prefer charges against (someone), prosecute, summon, take (someone) to court **2.** appeal for, beg, beseech, entreat, petition, plead, solicit, supplicate

suffer 1. ache, agonize, be affected, be in pain, be racked, feel wretched, go through a lot (*informal*), go through the mill (*informal*), grieve, have a thin *or* bad time, hurt **2.** bear, endure, experience, feel, go through, put up with (*informal*), support, sustain, tolerate, undergo **3.** appear in a poor light, be handicapped, be impaired, deteriorate, fall off, show to disadvantage **4.** *archaic* allow, let, permit

suffering *noun* affliction, agony, anguish, discomfort, distress, hardship, martyrdom, misery, ordeal, pain, torment, torture

suffice answer, be sufficient (adequate, enough), content, do, fill the bill (*informal*), meet requirements, satisfy, serve

sufficient adequate, competent, enough, enow (*archaic*), satisfactory
Antonyms deficient, inadequate, insufficient, meagre, not enough, poor, scant, short, sparse

suffocate asphyxiate, choke, smother, stifle, strangle

suffrage ballot, consent, franchise, right to vote, voice (*figurative*), vote

suffuse bathe, cover, flood, imbue, infuse, mantle, overspread, permeate, pervade, spread over, steep, transfuse

suggest 1. advise, advocate, move, offer a suggestion, prescribe, propose, put forward, recommend **2.** bring to mind, connote, evoke, put one in mind of **3.** hint, imply, indicate, insinuate, intimate, lead one to believe

suggestible accessible, amenable, impressionable, influencable, malleable, open, open-minded, persuadable, pervious, pliant, receptive, susceptible, tractable
Antonyms firm, headstrong, impervious, obdurate, single-minded, unwavering

suggestion 1. motion, plan, proposal, proposition, recommendation **2.** breath, hint, indication, insinuation, intimation, suspicion, trace, whisper

suggestive 1. *with* **of** evocative, expressive, indicative, redolent, reminiscent **2.** bawdy, blue, immodest, improper, indecent, indelicate, off colour, provocative, prurient, racy, ribald, risqué, rude, smutty, spicy (*informal*), titillating, unseemly

suicide

Suicide is confession

Daniel Webster

It is cowardice to commit suicide

Napoleon Bonaparte

A suicide kills two people, Maggie, that's what it's for!

Arthur Miller *After the Fall*

suit *verb* **1.** agree, agree with, answer, be acceptable to, become, befit, be seemly, conform to, correspond, do, go with, gratify, harmonize, match, please, satisfy, tally **2.** accommodate, adapt, adjust, customize, fashion, fit, modify, proportion, tailor ~*noun* **3.** addresses, appeal, attentions, courtship, entreaty, invocation, petition, prayer, request **4.** *Law* action, case, cause, industrial tribunal, lawsuit, proceeding, prosecution, trial **5.** clothing, costume, dress, ensemble, habit, outfit **6. follow suit** accord with, copy, emulate, run with the herd, take one's cue from

Suits
see CLOTHES

suitability appropriateness, aptness, fitness, opportuneness, rightness, timeliness

suitable acceptable, applicable, apposite, appropriate, apt, becoming, befitting, convenient, cut out for, due, fit, fitting, in character, in keeping, opportune, pertinent, proper, relevant, right, satisfactory, seemly, suited
Antonyms discordant, inapposite, inappropriate, incorrect, inopportune, jarring, out of character, out of keeping, unbecoming, unfitting, unseemly, unsuitable, unsuited

suite 1. apartment, collection, furniture, rooms, series, set **2.** attendants, entourage, escort, followers, retainers, retinue, train

suitor admirer, beau, follower (*obsolete*), swain (*archaic*), wooer, young man

sulk be in a huff, be put out, brood, have the hump (*Brit. informal*), look sullen, pout

sulky aloof, churlish, cross, disgruntled, huffy, ill-humoured, in the sulks, moody, morose, perverse, petulant, put out, querulous, resentful, sullen, vexed

sullen brooding, cheerless, cross, dismal, dull, gloomy, glowering, heavy, moody, morose, obstinate, out of humour, perverse, silent, sombre, sour, stubborn, surly, unsociable
Antonyms amiable, bright, cheerful, cheery, chirpy (*informal*), genial, good-humoured, good-natured, pleasant, sociable, sunny, warm, warm-hearted

sullenness glumness, heaviness, ill humour,

moodiness, moroseness, sourness, sulkiness, sulks

sully befoul, besmirch, blemish, contaminate, darken, defile, dirty, disgrace, dishonour, pollute, smirch, spoil, spot, stain, taint, tarnish

sultry **1.** close, hot, humid, muggy, oppressive, sticky, stifling, stuffy, sweltering **2.** amorous, come-hither (*informal*), erotic, passionate, provocative, seductive, sensual, sexy (*informal*), voluptuous
Antonyms (*sense 1*) cool, fresh, invigorating, refreshing

sum aggregate, amount, entirety, quantity, reckoning, score, sum total, tally, total, totality, whole

summarily arbitrarily, at short notice, expeditiously, forthwith, immediately, on the spot, peremptorily, promptly, speedily, swiftly, without delay, without wasting words

summarize abridge, condense, encapsulate, epitomize, give a rundown of, give the main points of, outline, précis, put in a nutshell, review, sum up

summary **1.** *noun* abridgment, abstract, compendium, digest, epitome, essence, extract, outline, précis, recapitulation, résumé, review, rundown, summing-up, synopsis **2.** *adjective* arbitrary, brief, compact, compendious, concise, condensed, cursory, hasty, laconic, perfunctory, pithy, succinct

summit acme, apex, crest, crown, crowning point, culmination, head, height, peak, pinnacle, top, zenith
Antonyms base, bottom, depths, foot, lowest point, nadir

summon **1.** arouse, assemble, bid, call, call together, cite, convene, convoke, invite, rally, rouse, send for **2.** *often with* **up** call into action, draw on, gather, invoke, mobilize, muster

sumptuous costly, dear, de luxe, expensive, extravagant, gorgeous, grand, lavish, luxurious, magnificent, opulent, plush (*informal*), posh (*informal, chiefly Brit.*), rich, ritzy (*slang*), splendid, splendiferous (*facetious*), superb
Antonyms austere, basic, cheap, frugal, inexpensive, meagre, mean, miserly, plain, shabby, wretched

sum up **1.** close, conclude, put in a nutshell, recapitulate, review, summarize **2.** estimate, form an opinion of, get the measure of, size up (*informal*)

sun **1.** *noun* daystar (*poetic*), eye of heaven, Helios (*Greek myth*), Phoebus (*Greek myth*), Phoebus Apollo (*Greek myth*), Sol (*Roman myth*) **2.** *verb* bake, bask, sunbathe, tan
Related adjective: solar

sunburnt bronzed, brown, brown as a berry, burnt, burnt to a crisp, like a lobster, peeling, red, ruddy, scarlet, tanned

sundry assorted, different, divers (*archaic*), miscellaneous, several, some, varied, various

sunk all washed up (*informal*), done for (*informal*), finished, lost, on the rocks, ruined, up the creek without a paddle (*informal*)

sunken **1.** concave, drawn, haggard, hollow, hollowed **2.** at a lower level, below ground, buried, depressed, immersed, lower, recessed, submerged

sunless bleak, cheerless, cloudy, dark, depressing, gloomy, grey, hazy, overcast, sombre

sunny **1.** bright, brilliant, clear, fine, luminous, radiant, summery, sunlit, sunshiny, unclouded, without a cloud in the sky **2.** *figurative* beaming, blithe, buoyant, cheerful, cheery, chirpy (*informal*), genial, happy, joyful, light-hearted, optimistic, pleasant, smiling
Antonyms cloudy, depressing, doleful, down in the dumps (*informal*), dreary, dreich (*Scot.*), dull, gloomy, miserable, morbid, murky, overcast, rainy, shaded, shadowy, sunless, unsmiling, wet, wintry

sunrise aurora (*poetic*), break of day, cockcrow, dawn, daybreak, daylight, dayspring (*poetic*), sunup

sunset close of (the) day, dusk, eventide, gloaming (*Scot. or poetic*), nightfall, sundown
Related adjective: acronychal, acronycal, *or (U.S.)* acronical

super awesome (*slang*), boffo (*slang*), brill (*informal*), chillin' (*U.S. slang*), cracking (*Brit. informal*), crucial (*slang*), def (*slang*), excellent, glorious, incomparable, jim-dandy (*slang*), magnificent, marvellous, matchless, mean (*slang*), mega (*slang*), out of this world (*informal*), outstanding, peerless, sensational (*informal*), smashing (*informal*), sovereign, superb, terrific (*informal*), topnotch (*informal*), topping (*Brit. slang*), wonderful

superannuated aged, antiquated, decrepit, discharged, obsolete, old, past it (*informal*), pensioned off, put out to grass (*informal*), retired, senile, unfit

superb admirable, awesome (*slang*), bodacious (*slang, chiefly U.S.*), boffo (*slang*), breathtaking, brill (*informal*), chillin' (*U.S. slang*), choice, divine, excellent, exquisite, fine, first-rate, gorgeous, grand, magnificent, marvellous, mega (*slang*), of the first water, splendid, splendiferous (*facetious*), superior, topping (*Brit. slang*), unrivalled, world-class
Antonyms abysmal, awful, bad, disappointing, dreadful, inferior, mediocre, no great shakes (*informal*), pathetic, poor quality, run-of-the-mill, terrible, third-rate, uninspired, woeful

supercilious arrogant, condescending, contemptuous, disdainful, haughty, high and mighty (*informal*), hoity-toity (*informal*), imperious, insolent, lofty, lordly, overbearing, patronizing, proud, scornful, snooty (*informal*), stuck-up (*informal*), toffee-nosed (*slang, chiefly Brit.*), uppish (*Brit. informal*), vainglorious
Antonyms deferential, generous, humble, meek, modest, obsequious, self-effacing, submissive, unassuming, unpretentious, warm-hearted

superficial 1. exterior, external, on the surface, peripheral, shallow, skin-deep, slight, surface 2. casual, cosmetic, cursory, desultory, hasty, hurried, inattentive, nodding, passing, perfunctory, sketchy, slapdash 3. empty, empty-headed, frivolous, lightweight, shallow, silly, trivial 4. apparent, evident, ostensible, outward, seeming
Antonyms complete, comprehensive, deep, detailed, earnest, exhaustive, in depth, major, penetrating, probing, profound, serious, substantial, thorough

superficiality emptiness, lack of depth, lack of substance, shallowness, triviality

superficially apparently, at face value, at first glance, externally, on the surface, ostensibly, to the casual eye

superfluity excess, exuberance, glut, plethora, redundancy, superabundance, surfeit, surplus

superfluous excess, excessive, extra, in excess, left over, needless, on one's hands, pleonastic (*Rhetoric*), redundant, remaining, residuary, spare, superabundant, supererogatory, supernumerary, surplus, surplus to requirements, uncalled-for, unnecessary, unneeded, unrequired
Antonyms called for, essential, imperative, indispensable, necessary, needed, requisite, vital, wanted

superhuman 1. herculean, heroic, phenomenal, prodigious, stupendous, valiant 2. divine, paranormal, preternatural, supernatural

superintend administer, control, direct, handle, inspect, look after, manage, overlook, oversee, run, supervise

superintendence care, charge, control, direction, government, guidance, inspection, management, supervision, surveillance

superintendent administrator, chief, conductor, controller, director, governor, inspector, manager, overseer, supervisor

superior *adjective* 1. better, grander, greater, higher, more advanced (expert, extensive, skilful), paramount, predominant, preferred, prevailing, surpassing, unrivalled 2. a cut above (*informal*), admirable, choice, de luxe, distinguished, excellent, exceptional, exclusive, fine, first-class, first-rate, good, good quality, high calibre, high-class, of the first order, running rings around (*informal*), streets ahead (*informal*), world-class 3. airy, condescending, disdainful, haughty, lofty, lordly, on one's high horse (*informal*), patronizing, pretentious, snobbish, stuck-up (*informal*), supercilious ~*noun* 4. boss (*informal*), chief, director, manager, principal, senior, supervisor
Antonyms *adjective* (*senses 1 & 2*) average, inferior, less, lesser, lower, mediocre, no great shakes (*informal*), not as good, ordinary, poorer, second-class, second-rate, substandard, unremarkable, worse ~*noun* assistant, cohort (*chiefly U.S.*), dogsbody, inferior, junior, lackey, minion, subordinate, underling

superiority advantage, ascendancy, excellence, lead, predominance, pre-eminence, preponderance, prevalence, supremacy

Superiority is always detested
Baltasar Gracián *The Art of Worldly Wisdom*

superlative *adjective* consummate, crack (*slang*), excellent, greatest, highest, magnificent, matchless, of the first water, of the highest order, outstanding, peerless, stellar (*informal*), supreme, surpassing, transcendent, unparalleled, unrivalled, unsurpassed
Antonyms abysmal, appalling, average, dreadful, easily outclassed, inferior, ordinary, poor, rotten, run-of-the-mill, undistinguished, unexceptional, uninspired, unspectacular

supernatural abnormal, dark, ghostly, hidden, miraculous, mysterious, mystic, occult, paranormal, phantom, preternatural, psychic, spectral, supranatural, uncanny, unearthly, unnatural

People with supernatural powers

archimage	rainmaker
channeller	seer
clairaudient	shaman
clairvoyant	siren
conjurer	sorcerer
diviner	sorceress
dowser	spaewife (*Scot.*)
enchanter	superhero
enchantress	thaumaturge
exorcist	warlock
fortune-teller	water diviner
hag	water witch
hex	white witch
mage	witch
magician	witch doctor
magus	witch master
medium	wizard
necromancer	

Supernatural creatures

angel	devil
banshee	dwarf
brownie	dybbuk
demon	elf

fairy
fairy godmother
familiar
fay
genie
ghost
ghoul
giant
gnome
goblin
god *or* goddess
golem
gremlin
guardian angel
hobgoblin
imp
incubus
jinni, jinnee, djinni *or* djinny
kachina
kelpie
lamia
leprechaun
little people *or* folk
monster
ogre
peri
phantom
pixie
poltergeist
sandman
selkie *or* silkie (*Scot.*)
spectre
sprite
succubus
sylph
troll
vampire
werewolf *or* lycan~thrope
wraith
zombie *or* zombi

Supernatural terms

abracadabra
amulet
apport
aura
black magic *or* the Black Art
charm
clairaudience
clairvoyance
cryptaesthesia
curse
divination
ectoplasm
evil eye
exorcism
extrasensory percep~tion *or* ESP
fate
fetish
grigri, gris-gris *or* greegree
grimoire
hex
hoodoo
incantation
invultuation
Indian sign
jinx
juju
kismet
levitation
magic circle
magic spell
magic wand
mojo
necromancy
obi *or* obeah
Ouija (*Trademark*)
parapsychology
pentagram
philtre
portent
possession
premonition
reincarnation
rune
seance *or* séance
second sight
sigil
sixth sense
spell
talisman
talking in tongues *or* xenoglossia *or* xeno~glossy
telaesthesia
telegnosis
telekinesis *or* psycho~kinesis
telepathy
voodoo
wand
white magic
witching hour

There are more things in Heaven and earth, Horatio,
Than are dreamt of in your philosophy
William Shakespeare *Hamlet*

supernumerary excess, excessive, extra, in ex~cess, odd, redundant, spare, superfluous, sur~plus, unrequired

supersede annul, displace, fill (someone's) boots, oust, overrule, remove, replace, set aside, step into (someone's) boots, supplant, supplement, suspend, take over, take the place of, usurp

superstition

Superstition is the religion of feeble minds
Edmund Burke *Reflections on the Revolution in France*

Superstition is the poetry of life
Johann Wolfgang von Goethe *Maximen und Reflexionen*

supervise administer, be on duty at, be re~sponsible for, conduct, control, direct, handle, have *or* be in charge of, inspect, keep an eye on, look after, manage, oversee, preside over, run, superintend

supervision administration, auspices, care, charge, control, direction, guidance, instruc~tion, management, oversight, stewardship, superintendence, surveillance

supervisor administrator, boss (*informal*), chief, foreman, gaffer (*informal, chiefly Brit.*), inspector, manager, overseer, steward, super~intendent

supervisory administrative, executive, mana~gerial, overseeing, superintendent

supine **1.** flat, flat on one's back, horizontal, recumbent **2.** apathetic, careless, heedless, idle, incurious, indifferent, indolent, inert, languid, lazy, lethargic, listless, lymphatic, negligent, passive, slothful, sluggish, spine~less, spiritless, torpid, uninterested
Antonyms (*sense 1*) prone, prostrate

supplant displace, oust, overthrow, remove, replace, supersede, take over, take the place of, undermine, unseat

supple bending, elastic, flexible, limber, lis~som(e), lithe, loose-limbed, plastic, pliable, pliant
Antonyms awkward, creaky (*informal*), firm, graceless, inflexible, rigid, stiff, taut, unbend~ing, unsupple, unyielding

supplement **1.** *noun* added feature, addendum, addition, add-on, appendix, codicil, comple~ment, extra, insert, postscript, pull-out, sequel **2.** *verb* add, augment, complement, extend, fill out, reinforce, supply, top up

supplementary accompanying, additional, add-on, ancillary, auxiliary, complementary, extra, secondary, supplemental

suppliant **1.** *adjective* begging, beseeching, craving, entreating, imploring, importunate, on bended knee **2.** *noun* applicant, petitioner, suitor, supplicant

supplication appeal, entreaty, invocation, petition, plea, pleading, prayer, request, solicitation, suit

supply *verb* 1. afford, cater to *or* for, come up with, contribute, endow, fill, furnish, give, grant, minister, outfit, produce, provide, purvey, replenish, satisfy, stock, store, victual, yield *~noun* 2. cache, fund, hoard, quantity, reserve, reservoir, source, stock, stockpile, store 3. *usually plural* equipment, food, foodstuff, items, materials, necessities, provender, provisions, rations, stores

support *verb* 1. bear, bolster, brace, buttress, carry, hold, hold up, prop, reinforce, shore up, sustain, underpin, uphold 2. be a source of strength to, buoy up, cherish, encourage, finance, foster, fund, hold (someone's) hand, keep, look after, maintain, nourish, provide for, strengthen, subsidize, succour, sustain, take care of, underwrite 3. advocate, aid, assist, back, boost (someone's) morale, champion, defend, espouse, forward, go along with, help, promote, second, side with, stand behind, stand up for, stick up for (*informal*), take (someone's) part, take up the cudgels for, uphold 4. attest to, authenticate, bear out, confirm, corroborate, document, endorse, lend credence to, substantiate, verify 5. bear, brook, countenance, endure, put up with (*informal*), stand (for), stomach, submit, suffer, thole (*dialect*), tolerate, undergo *~noun* 6. abutment, back, brace, foundation, lining, pillar, post, prop, shore, stanchion, stay, stiffener, underpinning 7. aid, approval, assistance, backing, blessing, championship, comfort, encouragement, espousal, friendship, furtherance, help, loyalty, moral support, patronage, promotion, protection, relief, succour, sustenance 8. keep, livelihood, maintenance, subsistence, sustenance, upkeep 9. backbone, backer, comforter, mainstay, prop, second, stay, supporter, tower of strength
Antonyms *verb* (*sense 2*) live off, sponge off (*senses 3, 4 & 5*) challenge, contradict, deny, go against, hinder, hold out against, oppose, refute, reject, stab in the back, turn one's back on, undermine, walk away from *~noun* (*senses 7 & 9*) antagonist, burden, denial, encumbrance, hindrance, impediment, opposition, refutation, rejection, undermining

supporter adherent, advocate, ally, apologist, champion, co-worker, defender, fan, follower, friend, helper, henchman, patron, protagonist, sponsor, upholder, well-wisher
Antonyms adversary, antagonist, challenger, competitor, foe, opponent, rival

supportive caring, encouraging, helpful, reassuring, sympathetic, understanding

suppose 1. assume, calculate (*U.S. dialect*), conjecture, dare say, expect, guess (*informal, chiefly U.S. & Canad.*), imagine, infer, judge, opine, presume, presuppose, surmise, take as read, take for granted, think 2. believe, conceive, conclude, conjecture, consider, fancy, hypothesize, imagine, postulate, pretend

supposed 1. accepted, alleged, assumed, hypothetical, presumed, presupposed, professed, putative, reputed, rumoured 2. *with* **to** expected, meant, obliged, ought, required

supposedly allegedly, at a guess, avowedly, by all accounts, hypothetically, ostensibly, presumably, professedly, purportedly, theoretically
Antonyms absolutely, actually, certainly, in actuality, in fact, really, surely, truly, undoubtedly, without a doubt

supposition conjecture, doubt, guess, guesswork, hypothesis, idea, notion, postulate, presumption, speculation, surmise, theory

suppress 1. beat down, check, clamp down on, conquer, crack down on, crush, drive underground, extinguish, overpower, overthrow, put an end to, quash, quell, quench, snuff out, stamp out, stop, subdue, trample on 2. censor, conceal, contain, cover up, curb, hold in *or* back, hold in check, keep secret, muffle, muzzle, repress, restrain, silence, smother, stifle, sweep under the carpet (*informal*), withhold
Antonyms encourage, foster, further, incite, inflame, promote, rouse, spread, stimulate, stir up, whip up

suppression check, clampdown, crackdown, crushing, dissolution, elimination, extinction, inhibition, prohibition, quashing, smothering, termination

suppurate discharge, fester, gather, maturate, ooze, weep

supremacy absolute rule, ascendancy, dominance, domination, dominion, lordship, mastery, paramountcy, predominance, pre-eminence, primacy, sovereignty, supreme authority, sway

supreme cardinal, chief, crowning, culminating, extreme, final, first, foremost, greatest, head, highest, incomparable, leading, matchless, mother (of all), paramount, peerless, predominant, pre-eminent, prevailing, prime, principal, sovereign, superlative, surpassing, top, ultimate, unsurpassed, utmost
Antonyms least, least successful, lowest, most inferior, most minor, most subordinate, most trivial, poorest, worst

sure 1. assured, certain, clear, confident, convinced, decided, definite, free from doubt, persuaded, positive, satisfied 2. accurate, dependable, effective, foolproof, honest, indisputable, infallible, never-failing, precise, reliable, sure-fire (*informal*), tried and true, trustworthy, trusty, undeniable, undoubted, unerr~

ing, unfailing, unmistakable, well-proven **3.** assured, bound, guaranteed, ineluctable, inescapable, inevitable, in the bag (*slang*), irrevocable **4.** fast, firm, fixed, safe, secure, solid, stable, staunch, steady
Antonyms distrustful, dodgy (*Brit., Austral., & N.Z. informal*), doubtful, dubious, fallible, iffy (*informal*), insecure, sceptical, touch-and-go, unassured, uncertain, unconvinced, undependable, uneasy, unreliable, unsure, untrustworthy, vague

surely assuredly, beyond the shadow of a doubt, certainly, come what may, definitely, doubtlessly, for certain, indubitably, inevitably, inexorably, undoubtedly, unquestionably, without doubt, without fail

surety **1.** bail, bond, deposit, guarantee, indemnity, insurance, pledge, safety, security, warranty **2.** bondsman, guarantor, hostage, mortgagor, sponsor

surface *noun* **1.** covering, exterior, façade, face, facet, outside, plane, side, skin, superficies (*rare*), top, veneer **2. on the surface** apparently, at first glance, ostensibly, outwardly, superficially, to all appearances, to the casual eye *~adjective* **3.** apparent, exterior, external, outward, superficial *~verb* **4.** appear, come to light, come up, crop up (*informal*), emerge, materialize, rise, transpire

surfeit **1.** *noun* excess, glut, overindulgence, plethora, satiety, superabundance, superfluity **2.** *verb* cram, fill, glut, gorge, overfeed, overfill, satiate, stuff
Antonyms *noun* dearth, deficiency, insufficiency, lack, scarcity, shortage, shortness, want

surge **1.** *verb* billow, eddy, gush, heave, rise, roll, rush, swell, swirl, tower, undulate, well forth **2.** *noun* billow, breaker, efflux, flood, flow, gush, intensification, outpouring, roller, rush, swell, uprush, upsurge, wave

surly bearish, brusque, churlish, crabbed, cross, crusty, curmudgeonly, grouchy (*informal*), gruff, ill-natured, morose, perverse, shrewish, sulky, sullen, testy, uncivil, ungracious
Antonyms agreeable, cheerful, cheery, genial, good-natured, happy, pleasant, sunny

surmise **1.** *verb* come to the conclusion, conclude, conjecture, consider, deduce, fancy, guess, hazard a guess, imagine, infer, opine, presume, speculate, suppose, suspect **2.** *noun* assumption, conclusion, conjecture, deduction, guess, hypothesis, idea, inference, notion, possibility, presumption, speculation, supposition, suspicion, thought

surmount conquer, exceed, master, overcome, overpower, overtop, pass, prevail over, surpass, triumph over, vanquish

surpass beat, best, eclipse, exceed, excel, go one better than (*informal*), outdo, outshine, outstrip, override, overshadow, put in the shade, top, tower above, transcend

surpassing exceptional, extraordinary, incomparable, matchless, outstanding, phenomenal, rare, stellar (*informal*), supreme, transcendent, unrivalled

surplus **1.** *noun* balance, excess, remainder, residue, superabundance, superfluity, surfeit **2.** *adjective* excess, extra, in excess, left over, odd, remaining, spare, superfluous, unused
Antonyms *noun* dearth, deficiency, deficit, insufficiency, lack, paucity, shortage, shortfall *~adjective* deficient, falling short, inadequate, insufficient, lacking, limited, scant, scanty, scarce

surprise *verb* **1.** amaze, astonish, astound, bewilder, bowl over (*informal*), confuse, disconcert, flabbergast (*informal*), leave open-mouthed, nonplus, stagger, stun, take aback, take (someone's) breath away **2.** burst in on, catch in the act *or* red-handed, catch napping, catch on the hop (*informal*), catch unawares *or* off-guard, come down on like a bolt from the blue, discover, spring upon, startle *~noun* **3.** amazement, astonishment, bewilderment, incredulity, stupefaction, wonder **4.** bolt from the blue, bombshell, eye-opener (*informal*), jolt, revelation, shock, start (*informal*), turn-up for the books (*informal*)

> *Surprises are foolish things. The pleasure is not enhanced, and the inconvenience is often considerable*
>
> Jane Austen *Emma*

surprised amazed, astonished, at a loss, caught on the hop (*Brit. informal*), caught on the wrong foot (*informal*), disconcerted, incredulous, nonplussed, open-mouthed, speechless, startled, taken aback, taken by surprise, thunderstruck, unable to believe one's eyes

surprising amazing, astonishing, astounding, extraordinary, incredible, marvellous, remarkable, staggering, startling, unexpected, unlooked-for, unusual, wonderful

surrender *verb* **1.** abandon, cede, concede, deliver up, forego, give up, part with, relinquish, renounce, resign, waive, yield **2.** capitulate, give in, give oneself up, give way, lay down arms, quit, show the white flag, submit, succumb, throw in the towel, yield *~noun* **3.** capitulation, delivery, relinquishment, renunciation, resignation, submission, yielding
Antonyms *verb* defy, fight (on), make a stand against, oppose, resist, stand up to, withstand

surreptitious clandestine, covert, fraudulent, furtive, secret, sly, sneaking, stealthy, unauthorized, underhand, veiled
Antonyms blatant, conspicuous, frank, hon~

est, manifest, obvious, open, overt, uncon~cealed, undisguised

surrogate *noun* deputy, proxy, representative, stand-in, substitute

surround 1. close in on, encircle, enclose, en~compass, envelop, environ, enwreath, fence in, girdle, hem in, ring 2. *Military* besiege, invest (*rare*), lay siege to

surrounding nearby, neighbouring

surroundings background, environment, envi~rons, location, milieu, neighbourhood, setting

surveillance care, control, direction, inspection, observation, scrutiny, superintendence, super~vision, vigilance, watch

Big Brother is watching you
George Orwell *1984*

survey *verb* 1. contemplate, examine, eye up, inspect, look over, observe, recce (*slang*), rec~onnoitre, research, review, scan, scrutinize, study, supervise, view 2. appraise, assess, es~timate, eye up, measure, plan, plot, prospect, size up, take stock of, triangulate *~noun* 3. examination, inquiry, inspection, once-over (*informal*), overview, perusal, random sample, review, scrutiny, study

survive be extant, endure, exist, fight for one's life, hold out, keep body and soul together (*informal*), keep one's head above water, last, live, live on, outlast, outlive, pull through, re~main alive, subsist

susceptibility liability, predisposition, prone~ness, propensity, responsiveness, sensitivity, suggestibility, vulnerability, weakness

susceptible 1. *usually with* **to** disposed, given, inclined, liable, open, predisposed, prone, sub~ject, vulnerable 2. alive to, easily moved, im~pressionable, receptive, responsive, sensitive, suggestible, tender
Antonyms immune, incapable, insensible, in~susceptible, invulnerable, resistant, unaffected by, unmoved by, unresponsive

suspect *verb* 1. distrust, doubt, harbour suspi~cions about, have one's doubts about, mis~trust, smell a rat (*informal*) 2. believe, con~clude, conjecture, consider, fancy, feel, guess, have a sneaking suspicion, hazard a guess, speculate, suppose, surmise, think probable *~adjective* 3. dodgy (*Brit., Austral., & N.Z. in~formal*), doubtful, dubious, fishy (*informal*), iffy (*informal*), open to suspicion, questionable
Antonyms *verb* accept, be certain, be confi~dent of, believe, buy (*slang*), have faith in, know, swallow (*informal*), think innocent, trust *~adjective* above suspicion, innocent, re~liable, straightforward, trustworthy, trusty

suspend 1. append, attach, dangle, hang, swing 2. adjourn, arrest, cease, cut short, de~bar, defer, delay, discontinue, hold off, inter~rupt, lay aside, pigeonhole, postpone, put in cold storage, put off, shelve, stay, withhold
Antonyms (*sense 2*) carry on, continue, reestablish, reinstate, restore, resume, re~turn

suspense 1. anticipation, anxiety, apprehen~sion, doubt, expectancy, expectation, indeci~sion, insecurity, irresolution, tension, uncer~tainty, wavering 2. **in suspense** anxious, in an agony of doubt, keyed up, on edge, on tenterhooks, with bated breath

suspenseful cliffhanging, exciting, gripping, hair-raising, spine-chilling, thrilling

suspension abeyance, adjournment, break, breaking off, deferment, delay, disbarment, discontinuation, interruption, moratorium, postponement, remission, respite, stay

suspicion 1. bad vibes (*slang*), chariness, dis~trust, doubt, dubiety, funny feeling (*informal*), jealousy, lack of confidence, misgiving, mis~trust, qualm, scepticism, wariness 2. **above suspicion** above reproach, blameless, hon~ourable, like Caesar's wife, pure, sinless, un~impeachable, virtuous 3. conjecture, guess, gut feeling (*informal*), hunch, idea, impression, notion, supposition, surmise 4. glimmer, hint, shade, shadow, *soupçon*, strain, streak, sug~gestion, tinge, touch, trace

Caesar's wife should be above suspicion
Julius Caesar

There is no smoke without fire
Plautus *Curculio*

suspicious 1. apprehensive, distrustful, doubt~ful, jealous, leery (*slang*), mistrustful, scepti~cal, suspecting, unbelieving, wary 2. dodgy (*Brit., Austral., & N.Z. informal*), doubtful, dubious, fishy (*informal*), funny, irregular, of doubtful honesty, open to doubt *or* miscon~struction, queer, questionable, shady (*infor~mal*), suspect
Antonyms (*sense 1*) believing, credulous, gul~lible, open, trustful, trusting, unsuspecting, unsuspicious (*sense 2*) above board, beyond suspicion, not open to question, open, straight, straightforward, unquestionable, upright

suss *slang* 1. *verb with* **out** calculate, clear up, figure out, find out, puzzle out, resolve, solve, work out 2. *noun* adroitness, astuteness, can~niness, guile, intelligence, intuition, keenness, perceptiveness, quickness, sharp-mindedness, sharpness, smartness

sustain 1. bear, carry, keep from falling, keep up, support, uphold 2. bear, bear up under, endure, experience, feel, suffer, undergo, withstand 3. aid, assist, comfort, foster, help, keep alive, nourish, nurture, provide for, re~lieve 4. approve, confirm, continue, keep alive, keep going, keep up, maintain, prolong, pro~tract, ratify 5. endorse, uphold, validate, veri~fy

sustained constant, continuous, nonstop, perpetual, prolonged, steady, unremitting
Antonyms broken, discontinuous, intermittent, irregular, periodic, spasmodic, sporadic

sustenance **1.** aliment, comestibles, daily bread, eatables, edibles, food, nourishment, provender, provisions, rations, refection, refreshments, victuals **2.** livelihood, maintenance, subsistence, support

svelte **1.** graceful, lissom(e), lithe, slender, slinky, sylphlike, willowy **2.** polished, smooth, sophisticated, urbane

swagger **1.** *verb* bluster, boast, brag, bully, gasconade (*rare*), hector, hot-dog (*chiefly U.S.*), parade, prance, show off (*informal*), strut, swank (*informal*) **2.** *noun* arrogance, bluster, braggadocio, display, gasconade (*rare*), ostentation, pomposity, show, showing off (*informal*), swank (*informal*), swashbuckling

swallow *verb* **1.** absorb, consume, devour, down (*informal*), drink, eat, gulp, ingest, swig (*informal*), swill, wash down **2.** *often with* **up** absorb, assimilate, consume, engulf, envelop, overrun, overwhelm, use up, waste **3.** choke back, hold in, repress **4.** *informal* accept, believe, buy (*slang*), fall for, take (something) as gospel

swamp *noun* **1.** bog, everglade(s) (*U.S.*), fen, marsh, mire, morass, moss (*Scot. & northern English dialect*), quagmire, slough *~verb* **2.** capsize, drench, engulf, flood, inundate, overwhelm, sink, submerge, swallow up, upset, wash over, waterlog **3.** beset, besiege, deluge, flood, inundate, overload, overwhelm, snow under

swampy boggy, fenny, marish (*obsolete*), marshy, miry, quaggy, waterlogged, wet

swank *verb* **1.** give oneself airs, hot-dog (*chiefly U.S.*), posture, put on side (*Brit. slang*), show off (*informal*), swagger *~noun* **2.** attitudinizer, braggadocio, hot dog (*chiefly U.S.*), poser, poseur, show-off (*informal*), swankpot (*informal*), swashbuckler **3.** boastfulness, display, ostentation, show, swagger, vainglory

swanky de luxe, exclusive, expensive, fancy, fashionable, flash, flashy, glamorous, glitzy (*slang*), gorgeous, grand, lavish, luxurious, ostentatious, plush (*informal*), plushy (*informal*), posh (*informal, chiefly Brit.*), rich, ritzy (*slang*), showy, smart, stylish, sumptuous, swank (*informal*), swish (*informal, chiefly Brit.*)
Antonyms discreet, humble, inconspicuous, low-key, low-profile, modest, subdued, unassuming, unostentatious, unpretentious

swap, swop *verb* bandy, barter, exchange, interchange, switch, trade, traffic

swarm *noun* **1.** army, bevy, concourse, crowd, drove, flock, herd, horde, host, mass, multitude, myriad, shoal, throng *~verb* **2.** congregate, crowd, flock, mass, stream, throng **3.** *with* **with** abound, be alive (infested, overrun), bristle, crawl, teem

swarthy black, brown, dark, dark-complexioned, dark-skinned, dusky, swart (*archaic*), tawny

swashbuckling bold, daredevil, dashing, flamboyant, gallant, mettlesome, roisterous, spirited, swaggering

swastika crooked cross, fylfot

swathe bandage, bind, bundle up, cloak, drape, envelop, enwrap, fold, furl, lap, muffle up, sheathe, shroud, swaddle, wrap

sway *verb* **1.** bend, fluctuate, incline, lean, lurch, oscillate, rock, roll, swing, wave **2.** affect, control, direct, dominate, govern, guide, induce, influence, persuade, prevail on, win over *~noun* **3.** ascendency, authority, clout (*informal*), command, control, dominion, government, influence, jurisdiction, power, predominance, rule, sovereignty **4.** **hold sway** predominate, prevail, reign, rule, run

swear **1.** affirm, assert, asseverate, attest, avow, declare, depose, give one's word, pledge oneself, promise, state under oath, swear blind, take an oath, testify, vow, warrant **2.** be foul-mouthed, blaspheme, curse, cuss (*informal*), imprecate, take the Lord's name in vain, turn the air blue (*informal*), utter profanities **3.** *with* **by** depend on, have confidence in, rely on, trust

Swear not by the moon, the inconstant moon
William Shakespeare *Romeo and Juliet*

As he knew not what to say, he swore
Lord Byron *The Island*

swearing bad language, blasphemy, cursing, cussing (*informal*), foul language, imprecations, malediction, profanity

Expletive deleted
editor of Nixon's Watergate tapes

swearword curse, cuss (*informal*), expletive, four-letter word, oath, obscenity, profanity

sweat *noun* **1.** diaphoresis (*Medical*), exudation, perspiration, sudor (*Medical*) **2.** *informal* agitation, anxiety, distress, flap (*informal*), panic, strain, worry **3.** *informal* backbreaking task, chore, drudgery, effort, labour, toil *~verb* **4.** break out in a sweat, exude moisture, glow, perspire **5.** *informal* agonize, be on pins and needles (*informal*), be on tenterhooks, chafe, fret, lose sleep over, suffer, torture oneself, worry **6.** **sweat it out** *informal* endure, see (something) through, stay the course, stick it out (*informal*)

sweaty clammy, drenched (bathed, soaked), in perspiration glowing, perspiring, sticky, sweating

sweep *verb* **1.** brush, clean, clear, remove **2.** career, flounce, fly, glance, glide, hurtle, pass, sail, scud, skim, tear, zoom *~noun* **3.** arc, bend, curve, gesture, move, movement, stroke, swing **4.** compass, extent, range, scope, span, stretch, vista **5.** draw, lottery, raffle, sweep~stake

sweeping **1.** all-embracing, all-inclusive, bird's-eye, broad, comprehensive, extensive, global, radical, thoroughgoing, wide, wide-ranging **2.** across-the-board, blanket, exagger~ated, indiscriminate, overdrawn, overstated, unqualified, wholesale
Antonyms constrained, limited, minor, mod~est, narrow, qualified, restricted, token, tri~fling, unimportant

sweet *adjective* **1.** cloying, honeyed, icky (*in~formal*), luscious, melting, saccharine, sugary, sweetened, syrupy, toothsome, treacly **2.** af~fectionate, agreeable, amiable, appealing, at~tractive, beautiful, charming, cute, delightful, engaging, fair, gentle, kind, likable *or* like~able, lovable, sweet-tempered, taking, tender, unselfish, winning, winsome **3.** beloved, cher~ished, darling, dear, dearest, pet, precious, treasured **4.** aromatic, balmy, clean, fragrant, fresh, new, perfumed, pure, redolent, sweet-smelling, wholesome **5.** dulcet, euphonic, euphonious, harmonious, mellow, melodious, musical, silver-toned, silvery, soft, sweet-sounding, tuneful **6. sweet on** enamoured of, gone on (*slang*), head over heels in love with, infatuated by, in love with, keen on, obsessed *or* bewitched by, taken with, wild *or* mad about (*informal*) *~noun* **7.** afters (*Brit. infor~mal*), dessert, pudding, sweet course **8.** *usually plural* bonbon, candy (*U.S.*), confec~tionery, sweetie, sweetmeats
Antonyms *adjective* (*sense 1*) acerbic, acetic, acid, bitter, savoury, sharp, sour, tart, vin~egary (*senses 2, 3 & 4*) bad-tempered, dis~agreeable, fetid, foul, grouchy (*informal*), grumpy, hated, ill-tempered, loathsome, nasty, noisome, objectionable, obnoxious, rank, stinking, unappealing, unattractive, unlovable, unpleasant, unwanted (*sense 5*) cacophonous, discordant, grating, harsh, shrill, strident, unharmonious, unmusical, unpleasant

Desserts and sweet dishes
see FOOD

sweeten **1.** honey, sugar, sugar-coat **2.** allevi~ate, appease, mollify, pacify, soften up, soothe, sugar the pill

sweetheart admirer, beau, beloved, boyfriend, darling, dear, flame (*informal*), follower (*obso~lete*), girlfriend, inamorata, inamorato, leman (*archaic*), love, lover, steady (*informal*), suitor, swain (*archaic*), sweetie (*informal*), truelove, valentine

sweet-scented ambrosial, aromatic, fragrant, perfumed, sweet-smelling
Antonyms fetid, foul-smelling, malodorous, niffy (*Brit. slang*), noisome, olid, pongy (*Brit. informal*), smelly, stinking, stinky (*informal*), whiffy (*Brit. slang*)

sweet-talk *informal* beguile, blandish, cajole, chat up, coax, dupe, entice, flatter, inveigle, manoeuvre, mislead, palaver, persuade, se~duce, soft-soap (*informal*), tempt, wheedle

swell *verb* **1.** balloon, become bloated *or* dis~tended, become larger, be inflated, belly, bil~low, bloat, bulge, dilate, distend, enlarge, ex~pand, extend, fatten, grow, increase, protrude, puff up, rise, round out, tumefy, well up **2.** add to, aggravate, augment, enhance, height~en, intensify, mount, surge *~noun* **3.** billow, rise, surge, undulation, wave **4.** *informal* beau, blade (*archaic*), cockscomb (*informal*), dandy, fashion plate, fop, nob (*slang*), toff (*Brit. slang*) *~adjective* **5.** *informal* de luxe, exclusive, fashionable, grand, plush *or* plushy (*informal*), posh (*informal, chiefly Brit.*), ritzy (*slang*), smart, stylish
Antonyms *verb* become smaller, contract, de~crease, deflate, diminish, ebb, fall, go down, lessen, reduce, shrink, wane *~adjective* com~mon, grotty (*slang*), ordinary, plebeian, poor, run down, seedy, shabby, sordid, tatty, unim~pressive, vulgar

swelling *noun* blister, bruise, bulge, bump, di~lation, distension, enlargement, inflammation, lump, protuberance, puffiness, tumescence

sweltering airless, baking, boiling, burning, hot, humid, oppressive, roasting, scorching, steaming, stifling, sultry, torrid

swerve *verb* bend, deflect, depart from, devi~ate, diverge, incline, sheer off, shift, skew, stray, swing, turn, turn aside, veer, wander, wind

swift abrupt, expeditious, express, fast, fleet, fleet-footed, flying, hurried, nimble, nippy (*Brit. informal*), pdq (*slang*), prompt, quick, quickie (*informal*), rapid, ready, short, short-lived, spanking, speedy, sudden, winged
Antonyms lead-footed, lingering, plodding, ponderous, slow, sluggish, tardy, tortoise-like, unhurried

swiftly apace, as fast as one's legs can carry one, (at) full tilt, double-quick, fast, hell for leather, hotfoot, hurriedly, in less than no time, like greased lightning (*informal*), like lightning, like the clappers (*Brit. informal*), nippily (*Brit. informal*), posthaste, promptly, pronto (*informal*), rapidly, speedily, without losing time

swiftness alacrity, celerity, dispatch, expedi~tion, fleetness, promptness, quickness, rapid~ity, speed, speediness, velocity

swill *verb* 1. bend the elbow (*informal*), bevvy (*dialect*), consume, drain, drink (down), gulp, guzzle, imbibe, pour down one's gullet, quaff, swallow, swig (*informal*), toss off 2. *often with* **out** drench, flush, rinse, sluice, wash down, wash out ~*noun* 3. hogwash, mash, mush, pigswill, scourings, slops, waste

swimmingly as planned, cosily, effortlessly, like a dream, like clockwork, smoothly, successfully, very well, with no trouble, without a hitch

swindle 1. *verb* bamboozle (*informal*), bilk (of), cheat, con, cozen, deceive, defraud, diddle (*informal*), do (*slang*), dupe, fleece, hornswoggle (*slang*), overcharge, pull a fast one (on someone) (*informal*), put one over on (someone) (*informal*), rip (someone) off (*slang*), rook (*slang*), sell a pup (to) (*slang*), skin (*slang*), stiff (*slang*), sting (*informal*), take (someone) for a ride (*informal*), take to the cleaners (*informal*), trick 2. *noun* con trick (*informal*), deceit, deception, double-dealing, fiddle (*Brit. informal*), fraud, imposition, knavery, racket, rip-off (*slang*), roguery, scam (*slang*), sharp practice, sting (*informal*), swizz (*Brit. informal*), swizzle (*Brit. informal*), trickery

swindler charlatan, cheat, chiseller (*informal*), confidence man, con man (*informal*), fraud, fraudster, grifter (*slang, chiefly U.S. & Canad.*), impostor, knave (*archaic*), mountebank, rascal, rogue, rook (*slang*), shark, sharper, trickster

swing *verb* 1. be pendent, be suspended, dangle, hang, move back and forth, suspend 2. fluctuate, oscillate, rock, sway, vary, veer, vibrate, wave 3. *usually with* **round** curve, pivot, rotate, swivel, turn, turn on one's heel, wheel ~*noun* 4. fluctuation, oscillation, stroke, sway, swaying, vibration 5. **in full swing** animated, at its height, lively, on the go (*informal*), under way

swingeing daunting, Draconian, drastic, excessive, exorbitant, harsh, heavy, huge, oppressive, punishing, severe, stringent

swinging dynamic, fashionable, full of go *or* pep (*informal*), groovy (*dated slang*), happening (*informal*), hip (*slang*), in the swim (*informal*), lively, trendy (*Brit. informal*), up-to-date, up to the minute, with it (*informal*)

swipe *verb* 1. chin (*slang*), clip (*informal*), deck (*slang*), fetch (someone) a blow, hit, lash out at, lay one on (*slang*), slap, slosh (*Brit. slang*), sock (*slang*), strike, wallop (*informal*) ~*noun* 2. blow, clip (*informal*), clout (*informal*), clump (*slang*), cuff, slap, smack, wallop (*informal*) ~*verb* 3. *slang* appropriate, cabbage (*Brit. slang*), filch, lift (*informal*), make off with, nick (*slang, chiefly Brit.*), pilfer, pinch (*informal*), purloin, snaffle (*Brit. informal*), steal

swirl *verb* agitate, boil, churn, eddy, spin, surge, twirl, twist, whirl

swish *adjective* de luxe, elegant, exclusive, fashionable, grand, plush *or* plushy (*informal*), posh (*informal, chiefly Brit.*), ritzy (*slang*), smart, sumptuous, swell (*informal*)

switch *verb* 1. change, change course, deflect, deviate, divert, exchange, interchange, rearrange, replace by, shift, substitute, swap (*informal*), trade, turn aside ~*noun* 2. about-turn, alteration, change, change of direction, exchange, reversal, shift, substitution, swap (*informal*) ~*verb* 3. lash, swish, twitch, wave, whip

swivel *verb* pirouette, pivot, revolve, rotate, spin, swing round, turn

swollen bloated, distended, dropsical, edematous, enlarged, inflamed, oedematous, puffed up, puffy, tumescent, tumid

swollen-headed bigheaded (*informal*), bumptious, cocky, full of oneself, proud, puffed up, self-important, too big for one's boots, too big for one's breeches, vain, vainglorious

swoop 1. *verb* descend, dive, pounce, rush, stoop, sweep 2. *noun* descent, drop, lunge, plunge, pounce, rush, stoop, sweep

swop *see* SWAP

sword 1. blade, brand (*archaic*), trusty steel 2. **cross swords** argue, come to blows, dispute, fight, spar, wrangle 3. **the sword** aggression, arms, butchery, death, massacre, military might, murder, slaying, violence, war

The pen is mightier than the sword
E.G. Bulwer-Lytton *Richelieu*

All they that take the sword shall perish with the sword
Bible: St. Matthew

swot *verb* apply oneself to, bone up on (*informal*), burn the midnight oil, cram (*informal*), get up (*informal*), lucubrate (*rare*), mug up (*Brit. slang*), pore over, revise, study, toil over, work

sybarite epicure, epicurean, hedonist, playboy, sensualist, voluptuary

sybaritic bacchanalian, epicurean, hedonistic, Lucullan, luxurious, luxury-loving, pleasure-loving, self-indulgent, sensual, voluptuous

sycophancy adulation, bootlicking (*informal*), cringing, fawning, flattery, grovelling, kowtowing, obsequiousness, servility, slavishness, toadyism, truckling

sycophant apple polisher (*U.S. slang*), ass-kisser (*U.S. & Canad. taboo slang*), bootlicker (*informal*), brown-noser (*taboo slang*), cringer, fawner, flatterer, hanger-on, lickspittle, parasite, slave, sponger, toadeater (*rare*), toady, truckler, yes man

sycophantic all over (someone) (*informal*), arse-licking (*taboo slang*), bootlicking (*informal*), cringing, fawning, flattering, grovelling, ingratiating, obsequious, parasitical, servile, slavish, slimy, smarmy (*Brit. informal*), time-serving, toadying, unctuous

syllabus course of study, curriculum

sylphlike graceful, lithe, slender, svelte, willowy

symbol badge, emblem, figure, image, logo, mark, representation, sign, token, type

symbolic, symbolical allegorical, emblematic, figurative, representative, significant, token, typical

symbolize betoken, body forth, connote, denote, exemplify, mean, personify, represent, signify, stand for, typify

symmetrical balanced, in proportion, proportional, regular, well-proportioned
Antonyms asymmetrical, disorderly, irregular, lopsided, unbalanced, unequal, unsymmetrical

symmetry agreement, balance, correspondence, evenness, form, harmony, order, proportion, regularity

sympathetic 1. affectionate, caring, commiserating, compassionate, concerned, condoling, feeling, interested, kind, kindly, pitying, responsive, supportive, tender, understanding, warm, warm-hearted 2. *often with* **to** agreeable, approving, encouraging, favourably disposed, friendly, in sympathy with, pro, well-disposed 3. agreeable, appreciative, companionable, compatible, congenial, friendly, like-minded, responsive, well-intentioned
Antonyms apathetic, callous, cold, cold-hearted, disdainful, disinterested, indifferent, inhumane, insensitive, scornful, steely, uncaring, uncompassionate, uncongenial, unfeeling, uninterested, unmoved, unresponsive, unsympathetic

sympathetically appreciatively, feelingly, kindly, perceptively, responsively, sensitively, understandingly, warm-heartedly, warmly, with compassion, with feeling, with interest

sympathize 1. bleed for, commiserate, condole, empathize, feel for, feel one's heart go out to, grieve with, have compassion, offer consolation, pity, share another's sorrow 2. agree, be in accord, be in sympathy, go along with, identify with, side with, understand
Antonyms disagree, disregard, fail to understand, have no feelings for, misunderstand, mock, oppose, reject, scorn

sympathizer condoler, fellow traveller, partisan, protagonist, supporter, well-wisher

sympathy 1. commiseration, compassion, condolence(s), empathy, pity, tenderness, thoughtfulness, understanding 2. affinity, agreement, congeniality, correspondence, fellow feeling, harmony, rapport, union, warmth
Antonyms (*sense 1*) callousness, coldness, disdain, hard-heartedness, indifference, insensitivity, lack of feeling *or* understanding *or* sympathy, pitilessness, scorn (*sense 2*) antagonism, disapproval, hostility, opposition, resistance, unfriendliness

> *A fellow-feeling makes one wond'rous kind*
> David Garrick *An Occasional Prologue on Quitting the Theatre*

symptom expression, indication, mark, note, sign, syndrome, token, warning

symptomatic characteristic, indicative, suggestive

synonymous equal, equivalent, identical, identified, interchangeable, one and the same, similar, tantamount, the same

synopsis abridgment, abstract, *aperçu*, compendium, condensation, conspectus, digest, epitome, outline, outline sketch, précis, résumé, review, rundown, summary

synthesis 1. amalgamation, coalescence, combination, integration, unification, welding 2. amalgam, blend, combination, composite, compound, fusion, meld, union

synthetic artificial, ersatz, fake, man-made, manufactured, mock, pseudo (*informal*), sham, simulated
Antonyms authentic, genuine, kosher (*informal*), natural, real

system 1. arrangement, classification, combination, coordination, organization, scheme, setup (*informal*), structure 2. fixed order, frame of reference, method, methodology, modus operandi, practice, procedure, routine, technique, theory, usage 3. definite plan, logical process, method, methodicalness, orderliness, regularity, systematization

systematic businesslike, efficient, methodical, orderly, organized, precise, standardized, systematized, well-ordered
Antonyms arbitrary, cursory, disorderly, disorganized, haphazard, indiscriminate, random, slapdash, unbusinesslike, unmethodical, unpremeditated, unsystematic

systematize arrange, classify, dispose, make uniform, methodize, organize, put in order, rationalize, regulate, schematize, sequence, standardize, tabulate

T

tab flag, flap, label, marker, sticker, tag, ticket

tabby banded, brindled, streaked, striped, stripy, wavy

table *noun* **1.** bench, board, counter, slab, stand **2.** board, diet, fare, food, spread (*informal*), victuals **3.** flat, flatland, mesa, plain, plateau, tableland **4.** agenda, catalogue, chart, diagram, digest, graph, index, inventory, list, plan, record, register, roll, schedule, synopsis, tabulation *~verb* **5.** enter, move, propose, put forward, submit, suggest

Tables and desks
see FURNITURE

tableau picture, representation, scene, spectacle

tableland flat, flatland, mesa, plain, plateau, table

taboo 1. *adjective* anathema, banned, beyond the pale, disapproved of, forbidden, frowned on, not allowed, not permitted, off limits, outlawed, prohibited, proscribed, ruled out, unacceptable, unmentionable, unthinkable **2.** *noun* anathema, ban, disapproval, interdict, prohibition, proscription, restriction
Antonyms *adjective* acceptable, allowed, permitted, sanctioned

tabulate arrange, catalogue, categorize, chart, classify, codify, index, list, order, range, systematize, tabularize

tacit implicit, implied, inferred, silent, taken for granted, undeclared, understood, unexpressed, unspoken, unstated, wordless
Antonyms explicit, express, spelled-out, spoken, stated

taciturn aloof, antisocial, close-lipped, cold, distant, dumb, mute, quiet, reserved, reticent, silent, tight-lipped, uncommunicative, unforthcoming, withdrawn
Antonyms blethering, chatty, communicative, forthcoming, garrulous, loquacious, open, outgoing, prattling, sociable, talkative, unreserved, verbose, voluble, wordy

tack *noun* **1.** drawing pin, nail, pin, staple, thumbtack (*U.S.*), tintack **2.** approach, bearing, course, direction, heading, line, method, path, plan, procedure, tactic, tenor, way *~verb* **3.** affix, attach, fasten, fix, nail, pin, staple **4.** baste, stitch **5.** add, annex, append, attach, tag

tackle *noun* **1.** accoutrements, apparatus, equipment, gear, implements, outfit, paraphernalia, rig, rigging, tools, trappings **2.** block, challenge, stop *~verb* **3.** apply oneself to, attempt, begin, come *or* get to grips with, deal with, embark upon, engage in, essay, get stuck into (*informal*), have a go at (*informal*), have a stab at (*informal*), set about, sink one's teeth into, take on, take the bit between one's teeth, try, turn one's hand to, undertake, wade into **4.** block, bring down, challenge, clutch, confront, grab, grasp, halt, intercept, seize, stop, take hold of, throw

tacky 1. adhesive, gluey, gummy, sticky, wet **2.** *informal* cheap, messy, naff (*Brit. slang*), nasty, seedy, shabby, shoddy, sleazy, tasteless, tatty, vulgar

tact address, adroitness, consideration, delicacy, diplomacy, discretion, finesse, judgment, perception, savoir-faire, sensitivity, skill, thoughtfulness, understanding
Antonyms awkwardness, clumsiness, gaucherie, heavy-handedness, indiscretion, insensitivity, lack of consideration, lack of discretion, tactlessness

Least said, soonest mended

tactful careful, considerate, delicate, diplomatic, discreet, judicious, perceptive, polished, polite, politic, prudent, sensitive, subtle, thoughtful, treating with kid gloves, understanding
Antonyms awkward, clumsy, gauche, inconsiderate, indiscreet, insensitive, tactless, tasteless, thoughtless, undiplomatic, unsubtle, untoward

tactic 1. approach, course, device, line, manoeuvre, means, method, move, ploy, policy, scheme, stratagem, tack, trick, way **2.** *plural* campaign, generalship, manoeuvres, plans, strategy

tactical adroit, artful, clever, cunning, diplomatic, foxy, politic, shrewd, skilful, smart, strategic
Antonyms blundering, clumsy, gauche, impolitic, inept

tactician brain (*informal*), campaigner, coordinator, director, general, mastermind, planner, strategist

tactless blundering, boorish, careless, clumsy, discourteous, gauche, harsh, impolite, impolitic, imprudent, inconsiderate, indelicate, indiscreet, inept, injudicious, insensitive, maladroit, rough, rude, sharp, thoughtless, uncivil, undiplomatic, unfeeling, unkind, unsubtle
Antonyms considerate, diplomatic, discreet, polite, subtle, tactful

tag *noun* **1.** docket, flag, flap, identification, label, mark, marker, note, slip, sticker, tab, ticket *~verb* **2.** earmark, flag, identify, label, mark, ticket **3.** add, adjoin, affix, annex, append, fasten, tack **4.** *with* **on** *or* **along** accompany, attend, dog, follow, shadow, tail (*informal*), trail **5.** call, christen, dub, label, name, nickname, style, term

tail *noun* **1.** appendage, conclusion, empennage, end, extremity, rear end, tailpiece, train **2.** file, line, queue, tailback, train **3.** *of hair* braid, pigtail, plait, ponytail, tress **4.** *informal* arse (*taboo slang*), ass (*U.S. & Canad. taboo slang*), backside (*informal*), behind (*informal*), bottom, bum (*Brit. slang*), buns (*U.S. slang*), butt (*U.S. & Canad. informal*), buttocks, croup, derrière (*euphemistic*), jacksy (*Brit. slang*), posterior, rear (*informal*), rear end, rump **5.** **turn tail** cut and run, escape, flee, hook it (*slang*), make off, retreat, run away, run for it (*informal*), run off, scarper (*Brit. slang*), show a clean pair of heels, skedaddle (*informal*), take off (*informal*), take to one's heels *~verb* **6.** *informal* dog the footsteps of, follow, keep an eye on, shadow, stalk, track, trail
Related adjective: caudal

tail off *or* **away** decrease, die out, drop, dwindle, fade, fall away, peter out, wane
Antonyms grow, increase, intensify, wax

tailor **1.** *noun* clothier, costumier, couturier, dressmaker, garment maker, outfitter, seamstress **2.** *verb* accommodate, adapt, adjust, alter, convert, customize, cut, fashion, fit, modify, mould, shape, style, suit
Related adjective: sartorial

tailor-made **1.** cut to fit, fitted, made-to-measure, made to order **2.** custom-made, ideal, just right, perfect, right, right up one's street (*informal*), suitable, up one's alley

taint *verb* **1.** adulterate, blight, contaminate, corrupt, dirty, foul, infect, poison, pollute, soil, spoil **2.** besmirch, blacken, blemish, blot, brand, damage, defile, disgrace, dishonour, muddy, ruin, shame, smear, smirch, stain, stigmatize, sully, tarnish, vitiate *~noun* **3.** black mark, blemish, blot, blot on one's escutcheon, defect, demerit, disgrace, dishonour, fault, flaw, shame, smear, smirch, spot, stain, stigma **4.** contagion, contamination, infection, pollution
Antonyms *verb* clean, cleanse, decontaminate, disinfect, purify

take *verb* **1.** abduct, acquire, arrest, capture, carry off, cart off (*slang*), catch, clutch, ensnare, entrap, gain possession of, get, get hold of, grasp, grip, have, help oneself to, lay hold of, obtain, receive, secure, seize, win **2.** abstract, appropriate, blag (*slang*), cabbage (*Brit. slang*), carry off, filch, misappropriate, nick (*slang, chiefly Brit.*), pinch (*informal*), pocket, purloin, run off with, steal, swipe (*slang*), walk off with **3.** book, buy, engage, hire, lease, pay for, pick, purchase, rent, reserve, select **4.** abide, bear, brave, brook, endure, go through, hack (*slang*), pocket, put up with (*informal*), stand, stomach, submit to, suffer, swallow, thole (*Scot.*), tolerate, undergo, weather, withstand **5.** consume, drink, eat, imbibe, ingest, inhale, swallow **6.** accept, adopt, assume, enter upon, undertake **7.** do, effect, execute, have, make, perform **8.** assume, believe, consider, deem, hold, interpret as, perceive, presume, receive, regard, see as, think of as, understand **9.** be efficacious, do the trick (*informal*), have effect, operate, succeed, work **10.** bear, bring, carry, cart, convey, ferry, fetch, haul, tote (*informal*), transport **11.** accompany, bring, conduct, convoy, escort, guide, hold (someone's) hand, lead, usher **12.** attract, become popular, captivate, charm, delight, enchant, fascinate, please, win favour **13.** call for, demand, necessitate, need, require **14.** deduct, eliminate, remove, subtract **15.** accept, accommodate, contain, have room for, hold **16.** *slang* bilk, cheat, con (*informal*), deceive, defraud, do (*slang*), dupe, fiddle (*informal*), gull (*archaic*), pull a fast one on (*informal*), stiff (*slang*), swindle *~noun* **17.** catch, gate, haul, proceeds, profits, receipts, return, revenue, takings, yield
Antonyms add, avoid, decline, dismiss, dodge, eschew, fail, flop (*informal*), free, give, give back, give in, give way, hand over, ignore, let go, put, refuse, reject, release, restore, return, scorn, send, spurn, surrender, yield

take aback astonish, astound, bewilder, disconcert, flabbergast (*informal*), floor (*informal*), nonplus, stagger, startle, stun, surprise

take back **1.** disavow, disclaim, recant, renege, renounce, retract, unsay, withdraw **2.** get back, recapture, reclaim, reconquer, regain, repossess, retake **3.** accept back, exchange, give one a refund for

take down **1.** make a note of, minute, note, put on record, record, set down, transcribe, write down **2.** depress, drop, haul down, let down, lower, pull down, remove, take off **3.** demolish, disassemble, dismantle, level, raze, take apart, take to pieces, tear down **4.** de~

flate, humble, humiliate, mortify, put down (*slang*)

take in 1. absorb, assimilate, comprehend, digest, get the hang of (*informal*), grasp, understand 2. comprise, contain, cover, embrace, encompass, include 3. accommodate, admit, let in, receive 4. *informal* bilk, cheat, con (*informal*), cozen, deceive, do (*slang*), dupe, fool, gull (*archaic*), hoodwink, mislead, pull the wool over (someone's) eyes (*informal*), stiff (*slang*), swindle, trick

takeoff 1. departure, launch, liftoff 2. *informal* caricature, imitation, lampoon, mocking, parody, satire, send-up (*Brit. informal*), spoof (*informal*), travesty

take off 1. discard, divest oneself of, doff, drop, peel off, remove, strip off 2. become airborne, leave the ground, lift off, take to the air 3. *informal* abscond, beat it (*slang*), decamp, depart, disappear, go, hit the road (*slang*), hook it (*slang*), leave, pack one's bags (*informal*), set out, slope off, split (*slang*), strike out 4. *informal* caricature, hit off, imitate, lampoon, mimic, mock, parody, satirize, send up (*Brit. informal*), spoof (*informal*), take the piss (out of) (*taboo slang*), travesty

take on 1. employ, engage, enlist, enrol, hire, retain 2. acquire, assume, come to have 3. accept, address oneself to, agree to do, have a go at (*informal*), tackle, undertake 4. compete against, contend with, enter the lists against, face, fight, match oneself against, oppose, pit oneself against, vie with 5. *informal* break down, get excited, get upset, give way, make a fuss

takeover change of leadership, coup, incorporation, merger

take over assume control of, become leader of, come to power, gain control of, succeed to, take command of

take to 1. flee to, head for, make for, man, run for 2. become friendly, be pleased by, be taken with, conceive an affection for, get on with, like, warm to 3. have recourse to, make a habit of, resort to

take up 1. adopt, assume, become involved in, engage in, start 2. begin again, carry on, continue, follow on, go on, pick up, proceed, recommence, restart, resume 3. absorb, consume, cover, extend over, fill, occupy, use up

taking *adjective* 1. attractive, beguiling, captivating, charming, compelling, cute, delightful, enchanting, engaging, fascinating, fetching (*informal*), intriguing, likable *or* likeable, pleasing, prepossessing, winning 2. *informal* catching, contagious, infectious *~noun* 3. *plural* earnings, gain, gate, income, pickings, proceeds, profits, receipts, returns, revenue, take, yield

Antonyms (*sense 1*) abhorrent, loathsome, offensive, repulsive, unattractive, unpleasant

tale 1. account, anecdote, *conte*, fable, fiction, legend, narration, narrative, novel, relation, report, romance, saga, short story, spiel (*informal*), story, urban legend, yarn (*informal*) 2. cock-and-bull story (*informal*), fabrication, falsehood, fib, lie, rigmarole, rumour, spiel (*informal*), tall story (*informal*), untruth

and thereby hangs a tale

William Shakespeare *As You Like It*

A tale never loses in the telling

talent ability, aptitude, bent, capacity, endowment, faculty, flair, forte, genius, gift, knack, parts, power

Genius does what it must, and talent does what it can

E.G. Bulwer-Lytton

Mediocrity knows nothing higher than itself, but talent instantly recognizes genius

Sir Arthur Conan Doyle *The Valley of Fear*

talented able, artistic, brilliant, gifted, well-endowed

talisman amulet, charm, fetish, juju, lucky charm, mascot, periapt (*rare*)

talk *verb* 1. articulate, chat, chatter, communicate, converse, crack (*Scot. & Irish*), express oneself, gab (*informal*), give voice to, gossip, natter, prate, prattle, rap (*slang*), run off at the mouth (*slang*), say, shoot the breeze (*U.S. slang*), speak, spout, utter, verbalize, witter (*informal*) 2. chew the rag *or* fat (*slang*), confabulate, confer, have a confab (*informal*), hold discussions, negotiate, palaver, parley 3. blab, crack, give the game away, grass (*Brit. slang*), inform, let the cat out of the bag, reveal information, shop (*slang, chiefly Brit.*), sing (*slang, chiefly U.S.*), spill one's guts (*slang*), spill the beans (*informal*), squeak (*informal*), squeal (*slang*), tell all *~noun* 4. address, discourse, disquisition, dissertation, harangue, lecture, oration, sermon, speech 5. blather, blether, chat, chatter, chitchat, conversation, crack (*Scot. & Irish*), gab (*informal*), gossip, hearsay, jaw (*slang*), natter, rap (*slang*), rumour, tittle-tattle 6. colloquy, conclave, confab (*informal*), confabulation, conference, congress, consultation, dialogue, discussion, meeting, negotiation, palaver, parley, seminar, symposium 7. argot, dialect, jargon, language, lingo (*informal*), patois, slang, speech, words

A fool may talk, but a wise man speaks

Ben Jonson *Discoveries*

Fine words butter no parsnips

Talk is cheap

talkative big-mouthed (*slang*), chatty, effusive, gabby (*informal*), garrulous, gossipy, long-

winded, loquacious, mouthy, prolix, verbose, voluble, wordy
Antonyms quiet, reserved, reticent, silent, taciturn, tight-lipped, uncommunicative, unforthcoming

talk big blow one's own trumpet, bluster, boast, brag, crow, exaggerate, vaunt

talker chatterbox, conversationalist, lecturer, orator, speaker, speechmaker

talking-to criticism, dressing-down (*informal*), lecture, rap on the knuckles, rebuke, reprimand, reproach, reproof, row, scolding, slating (*informal*), telling-off (*informal*), ticking-off (*informal*), wigging (*Brit. slang*)
Antonyms acclaim, approbation, commendation, encouragement, praise

talk into bring round (*informal*), convince, persuade, prevail on *or* upon, sway, win over

tall **1.** big, elevated, giant, high, lanky, lofty, soaring, towering **2.** *informal* absurd, cock-and-bull (*informal*), embellished, exaggerated, far-fetched, implausible, incredible, overblown, preposterous, steep (*Brit. informal*), unbelievable **3.** *informal* demanding, difficult, exorbitant, hard, unreasonable, well-nigh impossible
Antonyms (*sense 1*) fubsy (*archaic or dialect*), short, small, squat, stumpy, tiny, wee (*sense 2*) accurate, believable, easy, plausible, realistic, reasonable, true, unexaggerated

tally *verb* **1.** accord, agree, coincide, concur, conform, correspond, fit, harmonize, jibe (*informal*), match, parallel, square, suit **2.** compute, count up, keep score, mark, reckon, record, register, total *~noun* **3.** count, mark, reckoning, record, running total, score, total **4.** counterfoil, counterpart, duplicate, match, mate, stub
Antonyms (*sense 1*) clash, conflict, contradict, differ, disagree

tame *adjective* **1.** amenable, broken, cultivated, disciplined, docile, domesticated, gentle, obedient, tractable **2.** fearless, unafraid, used to human contact **3.** compliant, docile, manageable, meek, obedient, spiritless, subdued, submissive, unresisting **4.** bland, boring, dull, flat, humdrum, insipid, lifeless, prosaic, tedious, tiresome, unexciting, uninspiring, uninteresting, vapid, wearisome *~verb* **5.** break in, domesticate, gentle, house-train, make tame, pacify, train **6.** break the spirit of, bridle, bring to heel, conquer, curb, discipline, enslave, humble, master, repress, subdue, subjugate, suppress **7.** mitigate, mute, soften, soft-pedal (*informal*), subdue, temper, tone down, water down
Antonyms *adjective* aggressive, argumentative, exciting, feral, ferocious, frenzied, hot, interesting, lively, obdurate, savage, stimulating, strong-willed, stubborn, undomesticated, unmanageable, untamed, wild *~verb* arouse, incite, intensify, make fiercer

tamper **1.** alter, damage, fiddle (*informal*), fool about (*informal*), interfere, intrude, meddle, mess about, monkey around, muck about (*Brit. slang*), poke one's nose into (*informal*), tinker **2.** bribe, corrupt, fix (*informal*), get at, influence, manipulate, rig

tang **1.** aroma, bite, flavour, odour, piquancy, reek, savour, scent, smack, smell, taste **2.** hint, suggestion, tinge, touch, trace, whiff

tangible actual, concrete, corporeal, definite, discernible, evident, manifest, material, objective, palpable, perceptible, physical, positive, real, solid, substantial, tactile, touchable
Antonyms abstract, disembodied, ethereal, immaterial, impalpable, imperceptible, indiscernible, insubstantial, intangible, theoretical, unreal

tangle *noun* **1.** coil, confusion, entanglement, jam, jungle, knot, mass, mat, mesh, ravel, snarl, twist, web **2.** complication, entanglement, fix (*informal*), imbroglio, labyrinth, maze, mess, mix-up *~verb* **3.** coil, confuse, entangle, interlace, interlock, intertwist, interweave, jam, kink, knot, mat, mesh, ravel, snarl, twist **4.** *often with* **with** come into conflict, come up against, contend, contest, cross swords, dispute, lock horns **5.** catch, drag into, embroil, enmesh, ensnare, entangle, entrap, implicate, involve
Antonyms (*sense 3*) disentangle, extricate, free, straighten out, unravel, untangle

tangled **1.** entangled, jumbled, knotted, knotty, matted, messy, scrambled, snarled, tousled, twisted **2.** complex, complicated, confused, convoluted, involved, knotty, messy, mixed-up

tangy acerb, biting, briny, fresh, piquant, pungent, sharp, spicy, tart

tantalize baffle, balk, disappoint, entice, frustrate, keep (someone) hanging on, lead on, make (someone's) mouth water, provoke, taunt, tease, thwart, titillate, torment, torture

tantamount as good as, commensurate, equal, equivalent, synonymous, the same as

tantrum bate (*Brit. slang*), fit, flare-up, hysterics, ill humour, outburst, paddy (*Brit. informal*), paroxysm, storm, temper, wax (*informal, chiefly Brit.*)

tap[1] **1.** *verb* beat, drum, knock, pat, rap, strike, touch **2.** *noun* beat, knock, light blow, pat, rap, touch

tap[2] *noun* **1.** faucet (*U.S.*), spigot, spout, stopcock, valve **2.** bung, plug, spile, stopper **3.** bug (*informal*), listening device **4.** **on tap a.** *informal* at hand, available, in reserve, on hand, ready **b.** on draught *~verb* **5.** bleed, broach, drain, draw off, open, pierce, siphon off, unplug **6.** draw on, exploit, make use of, milk, mine, put to use, turn to account, use, utilize **7.** bug (*informal*), eavesdrop on, listen in on

tape *noun* **1.** band, ribbon, strip ~*verb* **2.** bind, seal, secure, stick, wrap **3.** record, tape-record, video

taper 1. come to a point, narrow, thin **2.** *with* **off** decrease, die away, die out, dwindle, fade, lessen, reduce, subside, thin out, wane, weaken, wind down

Antonyms (*sense 2*) grow, increase, intensify, step up, strengthen, swell, widen

tardiness belatedness, delay, dilatoriness, lateness, procrastination, slowness, unpunctuality

tardy backward, behindhand, belated, dawdling, dilatory, late, loitering, overdue, procrastinating, retarded, slack, slow, sluggish, unpunctual

target 1. aim, ambition, bull's-eye, end, goal, Holy Grail (*informal*), intention, mark, object, objective **2.** butt, quarry, scapegoat, victim

tariff 1. assessment, duty, excise, impost, levy, rate, tax, toll **2.** bill of fare, charges, menu, price list, schedule

tarnish 1. *verb* befoul, blacken, blemish, blot, darken, dim, discolour, drag through the mud, dull, lose lustre *or* shine, rust, smirch, soil, spot, stain, sully, taint **2.** *noun* blackening, black mark, blemish, blot, discoloration, rust, smirch, spot, stain, taint

Antonyms *verb* brighten, enhance, gleam, polish up, shine

tarry abide, bide, dally, dawdle, delay, drag one's feet *or* heels, dwell, hang around (*informal*), linger, lodge, loiter, lose time, pause, remain, rest, sojourn, stay, take one's time, wait

Antonyms hasten, hurry, move on, rush, scoot, step on it (*informal*)

tart[1] *noun* **1.** pastry, pie, tartlet **2.** call girl, fallen woman, *fille de joie*, floozy (*slang*), harlot, hooker (*U.S. slang*), loose woman, prostitute, scrubber (*Brit. & Austral. slang*), slag (*Brit. slang*), slut, streetwalker, strumpet, trollop, whore, woman of easy virtue, working girl (*facetious slang*)

tart[2] *adjective* **1.** acerb, acid, acidulous, astringent, bitter, piquant, pungent, sharp, sour, tangy, vinegary **2.** acrimonious, astringent, barbed, biting, caustic, crusty, cutting, harsh, mordacious, mordant, nasty, scathing, sharp, short, snappish, testy, trenchant, vitriolic, wounding

Antonyms (*sense 1*) honeyed, sugary, sweet, syrupy, toothsome (*sense 2*) agreeable, delightful, gentle, kind, pleasant

task *noun* **1.** assignment, business, charge, chore, duty, employment, enterprise, exercise, job, labour, mission, occupation, toil, undertaking, work **2. take to task** bawl out (*informal*), blame, blast, carpet (*informal*), censure, chew out (*U.S. & Canad. informal*), criticize, give a rocket (*Brit. & N.Z. informal*), lambast(e), lecture, read the riot act, reprimand, reproach, reprove, scold, tear into (*informal*), tear (someone) off a strip (*Brit. informal*), tell off (*informal*), upbraid ~*verb* **3.** assign to, charge, entrust **4.** burden, exhaust, load, lumber (*Brit. informal*), oppress, overload, push, saddle, strain, tax, test, weary

taste *noun* **1.** flavour, relish, savour, smack, tang **2.** bit, bite, dash, drop, morsel, mouthful, nip, sample, sip, *soupçon*, spoonful, swallow, titbit, touch **3.** appetite, bent, desire, fancy, fondness, inclination, leaning, liking, palate, partiality, penchant, predilection, preference, relish **4.** appreciation, cultivation, culture, discernment, discrimination, elegance, grace, judgment, perception, polish, refinement, sophistication, style **5.** correctness, decorum, delicacy, discretion, nicety, politeness, propriety, restraint, tact, tactfulness ~*verb* **6.** differentiate, discern, distinguish, perceive **7.** assay, nibble, relish, sample, savour, sip, test, try **8.** have a flavour of, savour of, smack **9.** come up against, encounter, experience, feel, have knowledge of, know, meet with, partake of, undergo

Antonyms *noun* bawdiness, blandness, blueness, coarseness, crudeness, disinclination, dislike, distaste, hatred, impropriety, indelicacy, insipidity, lack of discernment, lack of judgment, loathing, mawkishness, obscenity, tackiness (*informal*), tactlessness, tastelessness, unsubtlety ~*verb* fail to achieve, fail to discern, miss, remain ignorant of

Related noun: gustation

Taste is the feminine of genius
Edward Fitzgerald *Letters*

No one ever went broke underestimating the taste of the American public
H.L. Mencken

Taste is the enemy of creativeness
Pablo Picasso

There's no accounting for tastes

Beauty is in the eye of the beholder

One man's meat is another man's poison

tasteful aesthetically pleasing, artistic, beautiful, charming, cultivated, cultured, delicate, discriminating, elegant, exquisite, fastidious, graceful, handsome, harmonious, in good taste, polished, refined, restrained, smart, stylish, urbane

Antonyms brash, flashy, garish, gaudy, inelegant, loud, objectionable, offensive, showy, sick, tacky (*informal*), tasteless, tawdry, twee, uncultured, unrefined, vulgar

tasteless 1. bland, boring, dull, flat, flavourless, insipid, mild, stale, tame, thin, uninspired, uninteresting, vapid, watered-down, weak 2. cheap, coarse, crass, crude, flashy, garish, gaudy, graceless, gross, impolite, improper, indecorous, indelicate, indiscreet, inelegant, low, naff (*Brit. slang*), rude, tacky (*informal*), tactless, tawdry, uncouth, unseemly, vulgar
Antonyms (*sense 1*) appetizing, delectable, delicious, flavoursome, savoury, scrumptious (*informal*), tasty (*sense 2*) elegant, graceful, refined, tasteful

tasty appetizing, delectable, delicious, flavourful, flavoursome, full-flavoured, good-tasting, luscious, palatable, sapid, savoury, scrumptious (*informal*), toothsome, yummy (*slang*)
Antonyms bland, flavourless, insipid, tasteless, unappetizing, unsavoury

tatter 1. bit, piece, rag, scrap, shred 2. **in tatters** down at heel, in rags, in shreds, ragged, ripped, tattered, threadbare, torn

tattle 1. *verb* babble, blab, blather, blether, chat, chatter, gossip, jabber, natter, prate, prattle, run off at the mouth (*slang*), spread rumours, talk idly, tell tales, tittle-tattle, yak (*slang*) 2. *noun* babble, blather, blether, chat, chatter, chitchat, gossip, hearsay, idle talk, jabber, prattle, small talk, tittle-tattle, yak (*slang*), yap (*slang*)

tattler bigmouth (*slang*), gossip, quidnunc, rumourmonger, scandalmonger, talebearer, taleteller, telltale

tatty bedraggled, dilapidated, down at heel, frayed, having seen better days, neglected, poor, ragged, rumpled, run-down, scruffy, seedy, shabby, tattered, tawdry, the worse for wear, threadbare, unkempt, worn, worn out
Antonyms good, new, smart, well-preserved

taunt 1. *verb* deride, flout, gibe, guy (*informal*), insult, jeer, mock, provoke, reproach, revile, ridicule, sneer, take the piss (out of) (*taboo slang*), tease, torment, twit, upbraid 2. *noun* barb, censure, cut, derision, dig, gibe, insult, jeer, provocation, reproach, ridicule, sarcasm, teasing

taut 1. flexed, rigid, strained, stressed, stretched, tense, tight 2. *Nautical* in good order, neat, orderly, shipshape, spruce, tidy, tight, trim, well-ordered, well-regulated
Antonyms (*sense 1*) loose, relaxed, slack

tautological iterative, pleonastic, prolix, redundant, repetitious, repetitive, verbose

tautology iteration, pleonasm, prolixity, redundancy, repetition, repetitiousness, repetitiveness, verbiage, verbosity

tavern alehouse (*archaic*), bar, boozer (*Brit., Austral. & N.Z. informal*), hostelry, inn, pub (*informal, chiefly Brit.*), public house, taproom, watering hole (*facetious slang*)

There is nothing which has yet been contrived by man, by which so much happiness is produced as by a good tavern or inn
Dr. Johnson

tawdry brummagem, cheap, cheap-jack (*informal*), flashy, gaudy, gimcrack, glittering, meretricious, naff (*Brit. slang*), plastic (*slang*), raffish, showy, tacky (*informal*), tasteless, tatty, tinsel, tinselly, vulgar
Antonyms elegant, graceful, plain, refined, simple, stylish, tasteful, unflashy, unostentatious, well-tailored

tax *noun* 1. assessment, charge, contribution, customs, duty, excise, imposition, impost, levy, rate, tariff, tithe, toll, tribute 2. burden, demand, drain, load, pressure, strain, weight ~*verb* 3. assess, charge, demand, exact, extract, impose, levy a tax on, rate, tithe 4. burden, drain, enervate, exhaust, load, make heavy demands on, overburden, push, put pressure on, sap, strain, stretch, task, test, try, weaken, wear out, weary, weigh heavily on 5. accuse, arraign, blame, charge, impeach, impugn, incriminate, lay at one's door
Antonyms (*sense 5*) acquit, clear, exculpate, exonerate, vindicate

In this world nothing is certain but death and taxes
Benjamin Franklin

To tax and to please, no more than to love and to be wise, is not given to men
Edmund Burke *On American Taxation*

Only the little people pay taxes
Leona Helmsley

The Chancellor of the Exchequer is a man whose duties make him more or less of a taxing machine. He is intrusted with a certain amount of misery which it is his duty to distribute as fairly as he can
Robert Lowe, Viscount Sherbrooke

Death and taxes and childbirth! There's never any convenient time for any of them
Margaret Mitchell *Gone with the Wind*

Taxation without representation is tyranny
James Otis

Income Tax has made more Liars out of the American people than Golf
Will Rogers *The Illiterate Digest*

taxing burdensome, demanding, enervating, exacting, heavy, onerous, punishing, sapping, stressful, tiring, tough, trying, wearing, wearisome
Antonyms easy, easy-peasy (*slang*), effortless, light, unburdensome, undemanding

tea

Teas

Assam	Indian tea
bohea	jasmine tea
camomile tea	Lapsang Souchong
Ceylon	lemon tea
Chinese tea	mint tea
congou *or* congo	oolong
Darjeeling	orange pekoe
Earl Grey	post-and-rail tea (*archaic*)
green tea	Russian tea
gunpowder tea	
herb *or* herbal tea	

Look here, Steward, if this is coffee, I want tea; but if this is tea, then I wish for coffee

Punch

teach advise, coach, demonstrate, direct, discipline, drill, edify, educate, enlighten, give lessons in, guide, impart, implant, inculcate, inform, instil, instruct, school, show, train, tutor

He who can, does. He who cannot teaches

George Bernard Shaw *Maxims for Revolutionists*

teacher coach, dominie (*Scot.*), don, educator, guide, guru, handler, instructor, lecturer, master, mentor, mistress, pedagogue, professor, schoolmaster, schoolmistress, schoolteacher, trainer, tutor

I owe a lot to my teachers and mean to pay them back some day

Stephen Leacock

It is when the gods hate a man with uncommon abhorrence that they drive him into the profession of a schoolmaster

Seneca

A teacher affects eternity; he can never tell where his influence stops

Henry Brooks Adams *The Education of Henry Adams*

team *noun* **1.** band, body, bunch, company, crew, gang, group, line-up, posse (*informal*), set, side, squad, troupe **2.** pair, span, yoke *~verb* **3.** *often with* **up** band together, cooperate, couple, get together, join, link, unite, work together, yoke

teamwork collaboration, concert, cooperation, coordination, esprit de corps, fellowship, harmony, joint action, unity

tear *verb* **1.** claw, divide, lacerate, mangle, mutilate, pull apart, rend, rip, rive, run, rupture, scratch, sever, shred, split, sunder **2.** barrel (along) (*informal, chiefly U.S. & Canad.*), belt (*slang*), bolt, burn rubber (*informal*), career, charge, dart, dash, fly, gallop, hurry, race, run, rush, shoot, speed, sprint, zoom **3.** grab, pluck, pull, rip, seize, snatch, wrench, wrest, yank *~noun* **4.** hole, laceration, mutilation, rent, rip, run, rupture, scratch, split

tearaway daredevil, delinquent, good-for-nothing, hooligan, madcap, rough (*informal*), roughneck (*slang*), rowdy, ruffian, tough

tearful **1.** blubbering, crying, in tears, lachrymose, sobbing, weeping, weepy (*informal*), whimpering **2.** distressing, dolorous, harrowing, lamentable, mournful, pathetic, pitiable, pitiful, poignant, sad, sorrowful, upsetting, woeful

tears **1.** blubbering, crying, distress, lamentation, mourning, pain, regret, sadness, sobbing, sorrow, wailing, weeping, whimpering, woe **2.** **in tears** blubbering, crying, distressed, sobbing, visibly moved, weeping, whimpering
Related adjectives: lacrimal, lachrymal *or* lacrymal

tease aggravate (*informal*), annoy, badger, bait, bedevil, bother, chaff, gibe, goad, guy (*informal*), lead on, mock, needle (*informal*), pester, plague (*informal*), provoke, pull someone's leg (*informal*), rag, rib (*informal*), ridicule, take the mickey (*informal*), take the piss (out of) (*taboo slang*), tantalize, taunt, torment, twit, vex, wind up (*Brit. slang*), worry

technical hi-tech *or* high-tech, scientific, skilled, specialist, specialized, technological

technique **1.** approach, course, fashion, manner, means, method, mode, modus operandi, procedure, style, system, way **2.** address, adroitness, art, artistry, craft, craftsmanship, delivery, execution, facility, knack, know-how (*informal*), performance, proficiency, skill, touch

tedious annoying, banal, boring, deadly dull, drab, dreary, dreich (*Scot.*), dull, fatiguing, ho-hum (*informal*), humdrum, irksome, laborious, lifeless, long-drawn-out, mind-numbing, monotonous, prosaic, prosy, soporific, tiresome, tiring, unexciting, uninteresting, vapid, wearisome
Antonyms enjoyable, enthralling, exciting, exhilarating, imaginative, inspiring, interesting, quickly finished, short, stimulating

tedium banality, boredom, deadness, drabness, dreariness, dullness, ennui, lifelessness, monotony, routine, sameness, tediousness, the doldrums
Antonyms challenge, excitement, exhilaration, fascination, interest, liveliness, stimulation

teem[1] *verb* abound, be abundant, bear, be crawling with, be full of, be prolific, brim, bristle, burst at the seams, overflow, produce, pullulate, swarm

teem[2] *verb* belt (*slang*), bucket down (*informal*), lash, pelt (down), pour, rain cats and dogs (*informal*), sheet, stream

teeming[1] *adjective* abundant, alive, brimful, brimming, bristling, bursting, chock-a-block, chock-full, crawling, fruitful, full, numerous, overflowing, packed, replete, swarming, thick
Antonyms deficient, lacking, short, wanting

teeming[2] *adjective* belting (*slang*), bucketing down (*informal*), lashing, pelting, pouring, sheeting, streaming

teenage adolescent, immature, juvenile, youthful

teenager adolescent, boy, girl, juvenile, minor, youth

teeny diminutive, microscopic, miniature, minuscule, minute, teensy-weensy, teeny-weeny, tiny, wee

teeter balance, pivot, rock, seesaw, stagger, sway, totter, tremble, waver, wobble

teetotaller abstainer, nondrinker, Rechabite

teetotaller: one who abstains from strong drink, sometimes totally, sometimes tolerably totally
Ambrose Bierce *The Devil's Dictionary*

telegram cable, radiogram, telegraph, telex, wire (*informal*)

telegraph *noun* **1.** tape machine (*Stock Exchange*), teleprinter, telex **2.** cable, radiogram, telegram, telex, wire (*informal*) ~*verb* **3.** cable, send, telex, transmit, wire (*informal*)

telepathy mind-reading, sixth sense, thought transference

telephone **1.** *noun* blower (*informal*), handset, line, phone **2.** *verb* buzz (*informal*), call, call up, dial, get on the blower (*informal*), give (someone) a bell (*Brit. slang*), give (someone) a buzz (*informal*), give (someone) a call, give (someone) a ring (*informal, chiefly Brit.*), give someone a tinkle (*Brit. informal*), phone, put a call through to, ring (*informal, chiefly Brit.*)

telephone: an invention of the devil which abrogates some of the advantages of making a disagreeable person keep his distance
Ambrose Bierce *The Devil's Dictionary*

telescope *noun* **1.** glass, spyglass ~*verb* **2.** concertina, crush, squash **3.** abbreviate, abridge, capsulize, compress, condense, consolidate, contract, curtail, cut, shorten, shrink, tighten, trim, truncate

Antonyms (*sense 3*) amplify, draw out, elongate, extend, flesh out, lengthen, protract, spread out

television gogglebox (*Brit. slang*), idiot box (*slang*), receiver, small screen (*informal*), telly (*Brit. informal*), the box (*Brit. informal*), the tube (*slang*), TV, TV set

Television has brought back murder into the home - where it belongs
Alfred Hitchcock

tell *verb* **1.** acquaint, announce, apprise, communicate, confess, disclose, divulge, express, get off one's chest (*informal*), impart, inform, let know, make known, mention, notify, proclaim, reveal, say, speak, state, utter **2.** authorize, bid, call upon, command, direct, enjoin, instruct, order, require, summon **3.** chronicle, depict, describe, give an account of, narrate, portray, recount, rehearse, relate, report **4.** comprehend, discern, discover, make out, see, understand **5.** differentiate, discern, discriminate, distinguish, identify **6.** carry weight, count, have *or* take effect, have force, make its presence felt, register, take its toll, weigh **7.** calculate, compute, count, enumerate, number, reckon, tally

telling considerable, decisive, effective, effectual, forceful, forcible, impressive, influential, marked, potent, powerful, significant, solid, striking, trenchant, weighty

Antonyms easily ignored, inconsequential, indecisive, ineffectual, insignificant, lightweight, minor, negligible, slight, trivial, unimportant

tell off bawl out (*informal*), berate, carpet (*informal*), censure, chew out (*U.S. & Canad. informal*), chide, give (someone) a piece of one's mind, give (someone) a rocket (*Brit. & N.Z. informal*), haul over the coals (*informal*), lecture, read the riot act, rebuke, reprimand, reproach, reprove, scold, take to task, tear into (*informal*), tear (someone) off a strip (*Brit. informal*), tick off (*informal*), upbraid

temerity assurance, audacity, boldness, brass neck (*Brit. informal*), chutzpah (*U.S. & Canad. informal*), effrontery, foolhardiness, forwardness, front, gall (*informal*), heedlessness, impudence, impulsiveness, intrepidity, nerve (*informal*), pluck, rashness, recklessness, sassiness (*U.S. informal*)

temper *noun* **1.** attitude, character, constitution, disposition, frame of mind, humour, mind, mood, nature, temperament, tenor, vein **2.** bad mood, bate (*Brit. slang*), fit of pique, fury, gall, paddy (*Brit. informal*), passion, rage, tantrum, wax (*informal, chiefly Brit.*) **3.** anger, annoyance, heat, hot-headedness, ill humour, irascibility, irritability, irritation, passion, peevishness, petulance, resentment, surliness **4.** calm, calmness, composure, cool (*slang*), coolness, equanimity, good humour, moderation, self-control, tranquillity ~*verb* **5.** abate, admix, allay, assuage, calm, lessen, mitigate, moderate, mollify, palliate, restrain, soften, soft-pedal (*informal*), soothe, tone down **6.** anneal, harden, strengthen, toughen

Antonyms *noun* (*sense 3*) contentment, goodwill, pleasant mood (*sense 4*) agitation, anger, bad mood, excitability, foul humour, fury, grumpiness, indignation, irascibility, irritation, pique, vexation, wrath ~*verb* (*sense 5*) aggravate, arouse, excite, heighten, intensify, provoke, stir (*sense 6*) soften

temperament **1.** bent, cast of mind, character, complexion, constitution, disposition, frame of mind, humour, make-up, mettle, nature, outlook, personality, quality, soul, spirit, stamp, temper, tendencies, tendency **2.** anger, excit~

ability, explosiveness, hot-headedness, impatience, mercurialness, moodiness, moods, petulance, volatility

temperamental 1. capricious, easily upset, emotional, erratic, excitable, explosive, fiery, highly strung, hot-headed, hypersensitive, impatient, irritable, mercurial, moody, neurotic, passionate, petulant, sensitive, touchy, volatile 2. congenital, constitutional, inborn, ingrained, inherent, innate, natural 3. erratic, inconsistent, inconstant, undependable, unpredictable, unreliable
Antonyms calm, constant, cool-headed, dependable, easy-going, even-tempered, level-headed, phlegmatic, reliable, stable, steady, unexcitable, unflappable, unperturbable

temperance 1. continence, discretion, forbearance, moderation, restraint, self-control, self-discipline, self-restraint 2. abstemiousness, abstinence, prohibition, sobriety, teetotalism
Antonyms crapulence, excess, immoderation, intemperance, overindulgence, prodigality

Temperance is the greatest of all the virtues
Plutarch *Moralia*

temperate 1. agreeable, balmy, calm, clement, cool, fair, gentle, mild, moderate, pleasant, soft 2. calm, composed, dispassionate, equable, even-tempered, mild, moderate, reasonable, self-controlled, self-restrained, sensible, stable 3. abstemious, abstinent, continent, moderate, sober
Antonyms excessive, extreme, harsh, immoderate, inclement, inordinate, intemperate, prodigal, severe, torrid, uncontrolled, undisciplined, unreasonable, unrestrained, wild

tempest 1. cyclone, gale, hurricane, squall, storm, tornado, typhoon 2. commotion, disturbance, ferment, furore, storm, tumult, upheaval, uproar
Antonyms (*sense 2*) calm, peace, quiet, serenity, stillness, tranquillity

tempestuous 1. agitated, blustery, boisterous, breezy, gusty, inclement, raging, squally, stormy, turbulent, windy 2. ablaze, agitated, boisterous, emotional, excited, feverish, flaming, furious, heated, hysterical, impassioned, intense, passionate, stormy, turbulent, uncontrolled, violent, wild
Antonyms (*sense 2*) calm, peaceful, quiet, serene, still, tranquil, undisturbed, unruffled

temple church, holy place, place of worship, sanctuary, shrine

tempo beat, cadence, measure (*Prosody*), metre, pace, pulse, rate, rhythm, speed, time

temporal 1. carnal, civil, earthly, fleshly, lay, material, mortal, mundane, profane, secular, sublunary, terrestrial, worldly 2. evanescent, fleeting, fugacious, fugitive, impermanent, momentary, passing, short-lived, temporary, transient, transitory

temporarily briefly, fleetingly, for a little while, for a moment, for a short time, for a short while, for the moment, for the nonce, for the time being, momentarily, pro tem

temporary brief, ephemeral, evanescent, fleeting, fugacious, fugitive, here today and gone tomorrow, impermanent, interim, momentary, passing, pro tem, *pro tempore*, provisional, short-lived, transient, transitory
Antonyms durable, enduring, eternal, everlasting, long-lasting, long-term, permanent

temporize beat about the bush, be evasive, delay, equivocate, gain time, hum and haw, play a waiting game, play for time, procrastinate, stall, tergiversate

tempt 1. allure, appeal to, attract, coax, decoy, draw, entice, inveigle, invite, lead on, lure, make one's mouth water, seduce, tantalize, whet the appetite of, woo 2. bait, dare, fly in the face of, provoke, risk, test, try
Antonyms (*sense 1*) deter, discourage, dissuade, hinder, inhibit, put off

temptation allurement, appeal, attraction, attractiveness, bait, blandishments, coaxing, come-on (*informal*), decoy, draw, enticement, inducement, invitation, lure, pull, seduction, snare, tantalization

The best way to get the better of temptation is to yield to it
Clementina Stirling Graham *Mystifications*

Music and women I cannot but give way to, whatever my business is
Samuel Pepys *Diary*

I couldn't help it. I can resist everything except temptation
Oscar Wilde *Lady Windermere's Fan*

The serpent beguiled me, and I did eat
Bible: Genesis

Get thee behind me, Satan
Bible: St. Matthew

Watch and pray, that ye enter not into temptation; the spirit indeed is willing but the flesh is weak
Bible: St. Matthew

tempting alluring, appetizing, attractive, enticing, inviting, mouthwatering, seductive, tantalizing
Antonyms off-putting (*Brit. informal*), unappetizing, unattractive, undesirable, uninviting, untempting

tenable arguable, believable, defendable, defensible, justifiable, maintainable, plausible, rational, reasonable, sound, viable
Antonyms indefensible, insupportable, unjustifiable, untenable

tenacious 1. clinging, fast, firm, forceful, immovable, iron, strong, tight, unshakable 2. retentive, unforgetful 3. adamant, determined,

dogged, firm, immovable, inflexible, intransigent, obdurate, obstinate, persistent, pertinacious, resolute, staunch, steadfast, stiff-necked, strong-willed, stubborn, sure, unswerving, unyielding **4.** coherent, cohesive, solid, strong, tough **5.** adhesive, clinging, gluey, glutinous, mucilaginous, sticky
Antonyms (*sense 3*) changeable, flexible, irresolute, vacillating, wavering, yielding

tenacity **1.** fastness, firmness, force, forcefulness, power, strength **2.** firm grasp, retention, retentiveness **3.** application, determination, diligence, doggedness, firmness, inflexibility, intransigence, obduracy, obstinacy, perseverance, persistence, pertinacity, resoluteness, resolution, resolve, staunchness, steadfastness, strength of purpose, strength of will, stubbornness **4.** coherence, cohesiveness, solidity, solidness, strength, toughness **5.** adhesiveness, clingingness, stickiness
Antonyms (*sense 1*) looseness, powerlessness, slackness, weakness

tenancy **1.** holding, lease, occupancy, occupation, possession, renting, residence **2.** incumbency, period of office, tenure, time in office

tenant holder, inhabitant, leaseholder, lessee, occupant, occupier, renter, resident

tend¹ *verb* **1.** be apt, be biased, be disposed, be inclined, be liable, be likely, gravitate, have a leaning, have an inclination, have a tendency, incline, lean, trend **2.** aim, bear, be conducive, conduce, contribute, go, head, influence, lead, make for, move, point

tend² *verb* attend, care for, cater to, control, cultivate, feed, guard, handle, keep, keep an eye on, look after, maintain, manage, minister to, nurse, nurture, protect, see to, serve, take care of, wait on, watch, watch over
Antonyms disregard, ignore, neglect, overlook, shirk

tendency **1.** bent, disposition, inclination, leaning, liability, partiality, penchant, predilection, predisposition, proclivity, proneness, propensity, readiness, susceptibility **2.** bearing, bias, course, direction, drift, drive, heading, movement, purport, tenor, trend, turning

tender¹ *adjective* **1.** breakable, delicate, feeble, fragile, frail, soft, weak **2.** callow, green, immature, impressionable, inexperienced, new, raw, sensitive, unripe, vulnerable, wet behind the ears (*informal*), young, youthful **3.** affectionate, amorous, benevolent, caring, compassionate, considerate, fond, gentle, humane, kind, loving, merciful, pitiful, sentimental, softhearted, sympathetic, tenderhearted, touchy-feely (*informal*), warm, warm-hearted **4.** emotional, evocative, moving, poignant, romantic, touching **5.** complicated, dangerous, difficult, risky, sensitive, ticklish, touchy, tricky **6.** aching, acute, bruised, inflamed, irritated, painful, raw, sensitive, smarting, sore
Antonyms advanced, brutal, cold-hearted, cruel, elderly, experienced, grown-up, hard, hard-hearted, inhuman, insensitive, leathery, mature, pitiless, seasoned, sophisticated, strong, tough, uncaring, unkind, unsympathetic, worldly, worldly-wise

tender² *verb* **1.** extend, give, hand in, offer, present, proffer, propose, put forward, submit, suggest, volunteer *~noun* **2.** bid, estimate, offer, proffer, proposal, submission, suggestion **3.** currency, medium, money, payment, specie

tenderhearted affectionate, benevolent, benign, caring, compassionate, considerate, fond, gentle, humane, kind, kind-hearted, kindly, loving, merciful, mild, responsive, sensitive, sentimental, softhearted, sympathetic, touchy-feely (*informal*), warm, warm-hearted

tenderness **1.** delicateness, feebleness, fragility, frailness, sensitiveness, sensitivity, softness, vulnerability, weakness **2.** callowness, greenness, immaturity, impressionableness, inexperience, newness, rawness, sensitivity, vulnerability, youth, youthfulness **3.** affection, amorousness, attachment, benevolence, care, compassion, consideration, devotion, fondness, gentleness, humaneness, humanity, kindness, liking, love, mercy, pity, sentimentality, softheartedness, sympathy, tenderheartedness, warm-heartedness, warmth **4.** ache, aching, bruising, inflammation, irritation, pain, painfulness, rawness, sensitiveness, sensitivity, smart, soreness
Antonyms (*sense 3*) cruelty, hardness, harshness, indifference, insensitivity, unkindness

tenebrous dark, dim, dingy, dusky, gloomy, murky, obscure, shadowy, shady, sombre, Stygian, sunless, unlit

tenet article of faith, belief, canon, conviction, creed, doctrine, dogma, maxim, opinion, precept, principle, rule, teaching, thesis, view

tenor aim, burden, course, direction, drift, evolution, intent, meaning, path, purport, purpose, sense, substance, tendency, theme, trend, way

tense *adjective* **1.** rigid, strained, stretched, taut, tight **2.** anxious, apprehensive, edgy, fidgety, jittery (*informal*), jumpy, keyed up, nervous, on edge, on tenterhooks, overwrought, restless, strained, strung up (*informal*), twitchy (*informal*), under pressure, uptight (*informal*), wired (*slang*), wound up (*informal*), wrought up **3.** exciting, moving, nerve-racking, stressful, worrying *~verb* **4.** brace, flex, strain, stretch, tauten, tighten
Antonyms *adjective* boring, calm, collected, cool-headed, dull, easy-going, flaccid, flexible, limp, loose, pliant, relaxed, self-possessed, serene, unconcerned, uninteresting, unruffled, unworried *~verb* loosen, relax, slacken

tension 1. pressure, rigidity, stiffness, straining, stress, stretching, tautness, tightness 2. anxiety, apprehension, edginess, hostility, ill feeling, nervousness, pressure, restlessness, strain, stress, suspense, the jitters (*informal*), unease
Antonyms (*sense 2*) calmness, peacefulness, relaxation, restfulness, serenity, tranquillity

tentative 1. conjectural, experimental, indefinite, provisional, speculative, unconfirmed, unsettled 2. backward, cautious, diffident, doubtful, faltering, hesitant, timid, uncertain, undecided, unsure
Antonyms (*sense 1*) conclusive, decisive, definite, final, fixed, resolved, settled (*sense 2*) assured, bold, certain, confident, unhesitating

tenuous 1. doubtful, dubious, flimsy, insignificant, insubstantial, nebulous, questionable, shaky, sketchy, slight, weak 2. attenuated, delicate, fine, gossamer, slim
Antonyms (*sense 1*) significant, solid, sound, strong, substantial

tenure holding, incumbency, occupancy, occupation, possession, proprietorship, residence, tenancy, term, time

tepid 1. lukewarm, slightly warm, warmish 2. apathetic, cool, half-arsed (*Brit. slang*), half-assed (*U.S. & Canad. slang*), half-hearted, indifferent, lukewarm, unenthusiastic
Antonyms (*sense 2*) animated, eager, enthusiastic, excited, keen, passionate, vibrant, zealous

tergiversate 1. apostatize, change sides, defect, desert, go over to the other side, renege, turn traitor 2. beat about the bush, blow hot and cold (*informal*), dodge, equivocate, fence, hedge, prevaricate, pussyfoot (*informal*), vacillate

term *noun* 1. appellation, denomination, designation, expression, locution, name, phrase, title, word 2. duration, interval, period, season, space, span, spell, time, while 3. course, session 4. bound, boundary, close, conclusion, confine, culmination, end, finish, fruition, limit, terminus *~verb* 5. call, denominate, designate, dub, entitle, label, name, style

terminal *adjective* 1. bounding, concluding, extreme, final, last, limiting, ultimate, utmost 2. deadly, fatal, incurable, killing, lethal, mortal *~noun* 3. boundary, end, extremity, limit, termination, terminus 4. depot, end of the line, station, terminus
Antonyms (*sense 1*) beginning, commencing, first, initial, introductory, opening

terminate abort, axe (*informal*), belay (*Nautical*), bring *or* come to an end, cease, close, complete, conclude, cut off, discontinue, end, expire, finish, issue, lapse, pull the plug on (*informal*), put an end to, result, run out, stop, wind up
Antonyms begin, commence, inaugurate, initiate, instigate, introduce, open, start

termination abortion, cessation, close, completion, conclusion, consequence, cut-off point, discontinuation, effect, end, ending, expiry, finale, finis, finish, issue, result, wind-up
Antonyms beginning, commencement, inauguration, initiation, opening, start

terminology argot, cant, jargon, language, lingo (*informal*), nomenclature, patois, phraseology, terms, vocabulary

terminus 1. boundary, close, end, extremity, final point, goal, limit, target, termination 2. depot, end of the line, garage, last stop, station

terms 1. language, manner of speaking, phraseology, terminology 2. conditions, particulars, premises (*Law*), provisions, provisos, qualifications, specifications, stipulations 3. charges, fee, payment, price, rates 4. footing, position, relations, relationship, standing, status 5. **come to terms** be reconciled, come to an agreement, come to an understanding, conclude agreement, learn to live with, reach acceptance, reach agreement

terrain country, going, ground, land, landscape, topography

terrestrial 1. *adjective* earthly, global, mundane, sublunary, tellurian, terrene, worldly 2. *noun* earthling, earthman, earthwoman, human

terrible 1. bad, dangerous, desperate, extreme, serious, severe 2. *informal* abhorrent, abysmal, awful, bad, beastly (*informal*), dire, dreadful, duff (*Brit. informal*), foul, frightful, from hell (*informal*), godawful (*slang*), hateful, hideous, loathsome, obnoxious, obscene, odious, offensive, poor, repulsive, revolting, rotten (*informal*), shitty (*taboo slang*), unpleasant, vile 3. appalling, awful, dread, dreaded, dreadful, fearful, frightful, gruesome, harrowing, hellacious (*U.S. slang*), horrendous, horrible, horrid, horrifying, monstrous, shocking, terrifying, unspeakable
Antonyms (*sense 1*) harmless, insignificant, mild, moderate, paltry, small (*sense 2*) admirable, brilliant, delightful, excellent, fine, great, magic, noteworthy, pleasant, remarkable, super, superb, terrific, very good, wonderful (*sense 3*) calming, comforting, encouraging, reassuring, settling, soothing

terribly awfully (*informal*), decidedly, desperately, exceedingly, extremely, gravely, greatly, much, seriously, thoroughly, very

terrific 1. awesome, awful, dreadful, enormous, excessive, extreme, fearful, fierce, gigantic, great, harsh, horrific, huge, intense, monstrous, severe, terrible, tremendous 2. *infor~*

mal ace (*informal*), amazing, awesome (*slang*), bodacious (*slang, chiefly U.S.*), boffo (*slang*), breathtaking, brill (*informal*), brilliant, chillin' (*U.S. slang*), cracking (*Brit. informal*), excel~ lent, fabulous (*informal*), fantastic (*informal*), fine, great (*informal*), jim-dandy (*slang*), mag~ nificent, marvellous, mean (*slang*), outstand~ ing, sensational (*informal*), smashing (*infor~ mal*), sovereign, stupendous, super (*informal*), superb, topping (*Brit. slang*), very good, won~ derful
Antonyms appalling, awful, bad, calming, comforting, dreadful, encouraging, harmless, hideous, insignificant, lousy (*slang*), mediocre, mild, moderate, no great shakes (*informal*), paltry, reassuring, rotten, settling (*informal*), shocking, soothing, terrible, uninspired, un~ pleasant

terrified alarmed, appalled, awed, dismayed, frightened, frightened out of one's wits, horri~ fied, horror-struck, intimidated, panic-stricken, petrified, scared, scared shitless (*ta~ boo slang*), scared stiff, scared to death, shit-scared (*taboo slang*), shocked, terror-stricken

terrify alarm, appal, awe, dismay, fill with ter~ ror, frighten, frighten out of one's wits, horri~ fy, intimidate, make one's blood run cold, make one's flesh creep, make one's hair stand on end, petrify, put the fear of God into, scare, scare to death, shock, terrorize

territory area, bailiwick, country, district, do~ main, land, patch, province, region, sector, state, terrain, tract, turf (*U.S. slang*), zone

terror **1.** alarm, anxiety, awe, consternation, dismay, dread, fear, fear and trembling, fright, horror, intimidation, panic, shock **2.** bogeyman, bugbear, devil, fiend, monster, scourge

terrorize **1.** browbeat, bully, coerce, intimidate, menace, oppress, strong-arm (*informal*), threaten **2.** alarm, appal, awe, dismay, fill with terror, frighten, frighten out of one's wits, horrify, inspire panic in, intimidate, make one's blood run cold, make one's flesh creep, make one's hair stand on end, petrify, put the fear of God into, scare, scare to death, shock, strike terror into, terrify

terse **1.** aphoristic, brief, clipped, compact, con~ cise, condensed, crisp, elliptical, epigrammat~ ic, gnomic, incisive, laconic, monosyllabic, neat, pithy, sententious, short, succinct, sum~ mary, to the point **2.** abrupt, brusque, curt, short, snappy
Antonyms ambiguous, chatty, circumlocutory, confused, discursive, lengthy, long-winded, polite, rambling, roundabout, vague, verbose, wordy

test **1.** *verb* analyse, assay, assess, check, ex~ amine, experiment, investigate, prove, put through their paces, put to the proof, put to the test, research, try, try out, verify, work over **2.** *noun* acid test, analysis, assessment, attempt, catechism, check, evaluation, exami~ nation, investigation, ordeal, probation, proof, research, trial

testament **1.** last wishes, will **2.** attestation, demonstration, earnest, evidence, exemplifica~ tion, proof, testimony, tribute, witness

testicles balls (*taboo slang*), bollocks *or* bal~ locks (*taboo slang*), *cojones* (*U.S. taboo slang*), family jewels (*slang*), nuts (*taboo slang*), rocks (*U.S. taboo slang*)

testify affirm, assert, asseverate, attest, bear witness, certify, corroborate, declare, depone (*Scots Law*), depose (*Law*), evince, give testi~ mony, show, state, swear, vouch, witness
Antonyms belie, contradict, controvert, dis~ prove, dispute, gainsay (*archaic or literary*), oppose

testimonial certificate, character, commenda~ tion, credential, endorsement, recommenda~ tion, reference, tribute

testimony **1.** affidavit, affirmation, attestation, avowal, confirmation, corroboration, declara~ tion, deposition, evidence, information, profes~ sion, statement, submission, witness **2.** cor~ roboration, demonstration, evidence, indica~ tion, manifestation, proof, support, verification

testing arduous, challenging, demanding, diffi~ cult, exacting, formidable, rigorous, searching, strenuous, taxing, tough, trying
Antonyms easy, friendly, gentle, mild, simple, straightforward, undemanding

testy bad-tempered, cantankerous, captious, crabbed, cross, fretful, grumpy, impatient, irascible, irritable, liverish, peevish, peppery, petulant, quarrelsome, quick-tempered, ratty (*Brit. & N.Z. informal*), short-tempered, snap~ pish, snappy, splenetic, sullen, tetchy, touchy, waspish

tetchy bad-tempered, cantankerous, captious, crabbed, cross, fretful, grumpy, impatient, irascible, irritable, liverish, peevish, peppery, petulant, quarrelsome, quick-tempered, ratty (*Brit. & N.Z. informal*), short-tempered, snap~ pish, snappy, splenetic, sullen, testy, touchy, waspish

tête-à-tête **1.** *noun* chat, confab (*informal*), cosy chat, parley, private conversation, pri~ vate word, talk **2.** *adverb* in private, intimate~ ly, privately

tether *noun* **1.** bond, chain, fastening, fetter, halter, lead, leash, restraint, rope, shackle **2.** **at the end of one's tether** at one's wits' end, at the limit of one's endurance, exasper~ ated, exhausted, finished, out of patience ~*verb* **3.** bind, chain, fasten, fetter, leash, manacle, picket, restrain, rope, secure, shack~ le, tie

text 1. body, contents, main body, matter 2. wording, words 3. *Bible* paragraph, passage, sentence, verse 4. argument, matter, motif, subject, theme, topic 5. reader, reference book, source, textbook

texture character, composition, consistency, constitution, fabric, feel, grain, make, quality, structure, surface, tissue, weave

thank express gratitude, say thank you, show gratitude, show one's appreciation

thankful appreciative, beholden, grateful, indebted, obliged, pleased, relieved
Antonyms thankless, unappreciative, ungrateful

thankless 1. fruitless, unappreciated, unprofitable, unrequited, unrewarding, useless 2. inconsiderate, unappreciative, ungracious, ungrateful, unmindful, unthankful
Antonyms (*sense 1*) fruitful, productive, profitable, rewarding, useful, worthwhile (*sense 2*) appreciative, grateful, thankful

thanks 1. acknowledgment, appreciation, Brownie points, credit, gratefulness, gratitude, recognition, thanksgiving 2. **thanks to** as a result of, because of, by reason of, due to, owing to, through

thaw defrost, dissolve, liquefy, melt, soften, unfreeze, warm
Antonyms chill, congeal, freeze, harden, solidify, stiffen

theatrical 1. dramatic, dramaturgic, melodramatic, scenic, Thespian 2. actorly, actressy, affected, artificial, camp (*informal*), ceremonious, dramatic, exaggerated, hammy (*informal*), histrionic, mannered, ostentatious, overdone, pompous, showy, stagy, stilted, unreal
Antonyms (*sense 2*) natural, plain, simple, straightforward, unaffected, unassuming, unexaggerated, unpretentious, unsophisticated

theft embezzlement, fraud, larceny, pilfering, purloining, rip-off (*slang*), robbery, stealing, swindling, thievery, thieving

theme 1. argument, burden, idea, keynote, matter, subject, subject matter, text, thesis, topic 2. leitmotiv, motif, recurrent image, unifying idea 3. composition, dissertation, essay, exercise, paper

theological divine, doctrinal, ecclesiastical, religious

theorem deduction, dictum, formula, hypothesis, principle, proposition, rule, statement

theoretical abstract, academic, conjectural, hypothetical, ideal, impractical, notional, pure, speculative
Antonyms applied, experiential, factual, practical, realistic

theorize conjecture, formulate, guess, hypothesize, project, propound, speculate, suppose

theory 1. assumption, conjecture, guess, hypothesis, presumption, speculation, supposition, surmise, thesis 2. philosophy, plan, proposal, scheme, system
Antonyms certainty, experience, fact, practice, reality

therapeutic ameliorative, analeptic, beneficial, corrective, curative, good, healing, remedial, restorative, salubrious, salutary, sanative
Antonyms adverse, damaging, destructive, detrimental, harmful

therapy cure, healing, remedial treatment, remedy, treatment

therefore accordingly, as a result, consequently, ergo, for that reason, hence, so, then, thence, thus, whence

thesaurus dictionary, encyclopedia, repository, storehouse, treasury, wordbook

thesis 1. composition, disquisition, dissertation, essay, monograph, paper, treatise 2. contention, hypothesis, idea, line of argument, opinion, proposal, proposition, theory, view 3. area, subject, theme, topic 4. assumption, postulate, premise, proposition, statement, supposition, surmise

thick *adjective* 1. broad, bulky, deep, fat, solid, substantial, wide 2. close, clotted, coagulated, compact, concentrated, condensed, crowded, deep, dense, heavy, impenetrable, opaque 3. abundant, brimming, bristling, bursting, chock-a-block, chock-full, covered, crawling, frequent, full, numerous, packed, replete, swarming, teeming 4. blockheaded, braindead (*informal*), brainless, dense, dim-witted (*informal*), dopey (*informal*), dozy (*Brit. informal*), dull, insensitive, moronic, obtuse, slow, slow-witted, stupid, thickheaded 5. dense, heavy, impenetrable, soupy 6. distorted, guttural, hoarse, husky, inarticulate, indistinct, throaty 7. broad, decided, distinct, marked, pronounced, rich, strong 8. *informal* buddy-buddy (*slang, chiefly U.S. & Canad.*), chummy (*informal*), close, confidential, devoted, familiar, friendly, hand in glove, inseparable, intimate, matey *or* maty (*Brit. informal*), on good terms, pally (*informal*), palsy-walsy (*informal*), well in (*informal*) 9. **a bit thick** excessive, over the score (*informal*), too much, unfair, unjust, unreasonable ~*noun* 10. centre, heart, middle, midst
Antonyms (*sense 1*) narrow, slight, slim, thin (*sense 2*) clear, diluted, runny, thin, watery, weak (*sense 3*) bare, clear, devoid of, empty, free from, sparse, thin (*sense 4*) articulate, brainy, bright, clever, intellectual, intelligent, quick-witted, sharp, smart (*sense 5*) clear, thin (*sense 6*) articulate, clear, distinct, sharp, shrill, thin (*sense 7*) faint, slight, vague, weak (*sense 8*) antagonistic, distant, hostile, unfriendly

thicken cake, clot, coagulate, condense, con~geal, deepen, gel, inspissate (*archaic*), jell, set
Antonyms dilute, thin, water down, weaken

thicket brake, clump, coppice, copse, covert, grove, hurst (*archaic*), spinney (*Brit.*), wood, woodland

thickhead berk (*Brit. slang*), blockhead, bone~head (*slang*), charlie (*Brit. informal*), clot (*Brit. informal*), dickhead (*slang*), dickwit (*slang*), dimwit (*informal*), dipstick (*Brit. slang*), divvy (*Brit. slang*), dolt, dope (*infor~mal*), dork (*slang*), dummy (*slang*), dunce, dunderhead, dweeb (*U.S. slang*), fathead (*in~formal*), fool, fuckwit (*taboo slang*), geek (*slang*), gobshite (*Irish taboo slang*), gonzo (*slang*), idiot, imbecile, lamebrain (*informal*), moron, nerd *or* nurd (*slang*), numpty (*Scot. informal*), numskull *or* numbskull, pillock (*Brit. slang*), pinhead (*slang*), plank (*Brit. slang*), plonker (*slang*), prat (*slang*), prick (*slang*), twit (*informal, chiefly Brit.*), wally (*slang*)

thickheaded blockheaded, braindead (*infor~mal*), brainless, dense, dim-witted (*informal*), doltish, dopey (*informal*), dozy (*Brit. infor~mal*), idiotic, moronic, obtuse, slow, slow-witted, stupid, thick

thickset **1.** beefy (*informal*), brawny, bulky, burly, heavy, muscular, powerfully built, stocky, strong, stubby, sturdy, well-built **2.** closely packed, dense, densely planted, solid, thick
Antonyms angular, bony, gangling, gaunt, lanky, rawboned, scraggy, scrawny, weedy (*informal*)

thick-skinned callous, case-hardened, hard-boiled (*informal*), hardened, impervious, in~sensitive, stolid, tough, unfeeling, unsuscep~tible
Antonyms concerned, feeling, sensitive, ten~der, thin-skinned, touchy

thief bandit, burglar, cheat, cracksman (*slang*), crook (*informal*), embezzler, housebreaker, larcenist, mugger (*informal*), pickpocket, pil~ferer, plunderer, purloiner, robber, shoplifter, stealer, swindler

Thieves respect property. They merely wish the property to become their property that they may more perfectly respect it
G.K. Chesterton *The Man who was Thursday*

Set a thief to catch a thief

thieve blag (*slang*), cabbage (*Brit. slang*), cheat, embezzle, filch, half-inch (*old-fashioned slang*), have sticky fingers (*informal*), knock off (*slang*), lift (*informal*), misappropriate, nick (*slang, chiefly Brit.*), peculate, pilfer, pinch (*informal*), plunder, poach, purloin, rip off (*slang*), rob, run off with, snitch (*slang*), steal, swindle, swipe (*slang*)

thievery banditry, burglary, crookedness (*in~formal*), embezzlement, larceny, mugging (*in~formal*), pilfering, plundering, robbery, shop~lifting, stealing, theft, thieving

thievish crooked (*informal*), dishonest, fraudu~lent, larcenous, light-fingered, predatory, ra~pacious, sticky-fingered (*informal*), thieving

thimbleful capful, dab, dash, dram, drop, jot, modicum, nip, pinch, sip, *soupçon*, spoonful, spot, taste, toothful

thin *adjective* **1.** attenuate, attenuated, fine, narrow, threadlike **2.** delicate, diaphanous, filmy, fine, flimsy, gossamer, see-through, sheer, translucent, transparent, unsubstantial **3.** bony, emaciated, lank, lanky, lean, light, macilent (*rare*), meagre, scraggy, scrawny, skeletal, skin and bone, skinny, slender, slight, slim, spare, spindly, thin as a rake, undernourished, underweight **4.** deficient, meagre, scanty, scarce, scattered, skimpy, sparse, wispy **5.** dilute, diluted, rarefied, run~ny, watery, weak, wishy-washy (*informal*) **6.** feeble, flimsy, inadequate, insufficient, lame, poor, scant, scanty, shallow, slight, superficial, unconvincing, unsubstantial, weak *~verb* **7.** attenuate, cut back, dilute, diminish, emaci~ate, prune, rarefy, reduce, refine, trim, water down, weaken, weed out
Antonyms (*sense 1*) heavy, thick (*sense 2*) bulky, dense, heavy, strong, substantial, thick (*sense 3*) bulky, corpulent, fat, heavy, obese, stout (*sense 4*) abundant, adequate, plentiful, profuse (*sense 5*) concentrated, dense, strong, thick, viscous (*sense 6*) adequate, convincing, strong, substantial

thing **1.** affair, article, being, body, circum~stance, concept, entity, fact, matter, object, part, portion, something, substance **2.** act, deed, event, eventuality, feat, happening, in~cident, occurrence, phenomenon, proceeding **3.** apparatus, contrivance, device, gadget, imple~ment, instrument, machine, means, mecha~nism, tool **4.** aspect, detail, facet, factor, fea~ture, item, particular, point, statement, thought **5.** *plural* baggage, belongings, bits and pieces, clobber (*Brit. slang*), clothes, ef~fects, equipment, gear, goods, impedimenta, luggage, odds and ends, paraphernalia, pos~sessions, stuff **6.** *informal* attitude, bee in one's bonnet, fetish, fixation, hang-up (*infor~mal*), *idée fixe*, mania, obsession, phobia, pre~occupation, quirk

think *verb* **1.** believe, conceive, conclude, con~sider, deem, determine, esteem, estimate, guess (*informal, chiefly U.S. & Canad.*), hold, imagine, judge, reckon, regard, suppose, sur~mise **2.** brood, cerebrate, chew over (*informal*), cogitate, consider, contemplate, deliberate, have in mind, meditate, mull over, muse, ponder, rack one's brains, reason, reflect, re~

volve, ruminate, turn over in one's mind, weigh up **3.** call to mind, recall, recollect, remember **4.** anticipate, envisage, expect, foresee, imagine, plan for, presume, suppose **5.** **think better of** change one's mind about, decide against, go back on, have second thoughts about, reconsider, repent, think again, think twice about **6.** **think much of** admire, attach importance to, esteem, have a high opinion of, hold in high regard, rate (*slang*), respect, set store by, think highly of, value **7.** **think nothing of** consider unimportant, have no compunction about, have no hesitation about, regard as routine, set no store by, take in one's stride *~noun* **8.** assessment, consideration, contemplation, deliberation, look, reflection

I think, therefore I am

René Descartes *Le Discours de la Méthode*

thinkable conceivable, feasible, imaginable, likely, possible, reasonable, within the bounds of possibility
Antonyms absurd, impossible, inconceivable, not on (*informal*), out of the question, unlikely, unreasonable, unthinkable

thinker brain (*informal*), intellect (*informal*), mahatma, mastermind, philosopher, sage, theorist, wise man

thinking **1.** *noun* assessment, conclusions, conjecture, idea, judgment, opinion, outlook, philosophy, position, reasoning, theory, thoughts, view **2.** *adjective* contemplative, cultured, intelligent, meditative, philosophical, ratiocinative, rational, reasoning, reflective, sophisticated, thoughtful

think over chew over (*informal*), consider, consider the pros and cons of, contemplate, give thought to, mull over, ponder, rack one's brains, reflect upon, turn over in one's mind, weigh up

think up come up with, concoct, contrive, create, devise, dream up, imagine, improvise, invent, manufacture, trump up, visualize

thin-skinned easily hurt, hypersensitive, quick to take offence, sensitive, soft, susceptible, tender, touchy, vulnerable
Antonyms callous, hard, heartless, insensitive, obdurate, stolid, thick-skinned, tough, unfeeling

third-rate bad, cheap-jack, chickenshit (*U.S. slang*), duff (*Brit. informal*), indifferent, inferior, low-grade, mediocre, no great shakes (*informal*), not much cop (*informal*), of a sort *or* of sorts, poor, poor-quality, ropy *or* ropey (*Brit. informal*), shoddy

thirst *noun* **1.** craving to drink, drought, dryness, thirstiness **2.** ache, appetite, craving, desire, eagerness, hankering, hunger, keenness, longing, lust, passion, yearning, yen (*informal*)
Antonyms (*sense 2*) apathy, aversion, disinclination, dislike, distaste, loathing, revulsion

thirsty **1.** arid, dehydrated, dry, parched **2.** athirst, avid, burning, craving, desirous, dying, eager, greedy, hankering, hungry, itching, longing, lusting, thirsting, yearning

thorn **1.** barb, prickle, spike, spine **2.** affliction, annoyance, bane, bother, curse, hassle (*informal*), irritant, irritation, nuisance, pest, plague, scourge, torment, torture, trouble
Antonyms (*sense 2*) balm, benefaction, blessing, comfort, manna, solace, succour

thorny **1.** barbed, bristling with thorns, bristly, pointed, prickly, sharp, spiky, spinous, spiny **2.** awkward, difficult, harassing, hard, irksome, problematic(al), sticky (*informal*), ticklish, tough, troublesome, trying, unpleasant, upsetting, vexatious, worrying

thorough *or* **thoroughgoing** **1.** all-embracing, all-inclusive, assiduous, careful, complete, comprehensive, conscientious, efficient, exhaustive, full, in-depth, intensive, leaving no stone unturned, meticulous, painstaking, scrupulous, sweeping **2.** absolute, arrant, complete, deep-dyed (*usually derogatory*), downright, entire, out-and-out, outright, perfect, pure, sheer, total, unmitigated, unqualified, utter
Antonyms careless, cursory, half-hearted, haphazard, imperfect, incomplete, lackadaisical, partial, sloppy, superficial

thoroughbred *adjective* blood, full-blooded, of unmixed stock, pedigree, pure-blooded, purebred
Antonyms crossbred, crossed, half-breed, hybrid, mongrel, of mixed breed

thoroughfare access, avenue, highway, passage, passageway, road, roadway, street, way

thoroughly **1.** assiduously, carefully, completely, comprehensively, conscientiously, efficiently, exhaustively, from top to bottom, fully, inside out, intensively, leaving no stone unturned, meticulously, painstakingly, scrupulously, sweepingly, through and through, throughout **2.** absolutely, completely, downright, entirely, perfectly, quite, totally, to the full, to the hilt, utterly, without reservation
Antonyms carelessly, cursorily, half-heartedly, haphazardly, imperfectly, incompletely, in part, lackadaisically, partly, sloppily, somewhat, superficially

though **1.** *conjunction* albeit, allowing, although, despite the fact that, even if, even supposing, even though, granted, notwithstanding, tho' (*U.S. or poetic*), while **2.** *adverb* all the same, for all that, however, nevertheless, nonetheless, notwithstanding, still, yet

thought 1. brainwork, cerebration, cogitation, consideration, contemplation, deliberation, introspection, meditation, musing, navel-gazing (*slang*), reflection, regard, rumination, thinking 2. assessment, belief, concept, conception, conclusion, conjecture, conviction, estimation, idea, judgment, notion, opinion, thinking, view 3. attention, consideration, heed, regard, scrutiny, study 4. aim, design, idea, intention, notion, object, plan, purpose 5. anticipation, aspiration, dream, expectation, hope, prospect 6. dash, jot, little, small amount, *soupçon*, touch, trifle, whisker (*informal*) 7. anxiety, attentiveness, care, compassion, concern, kindness, regard, solicitude, sympathy, thoughtfulness

Thought flies and words go on foot
Julien Green *Journal*

Learning without thought is labour lost; thought without learning is perilous
Confucius *Analects*

thoughtful 1. attentive, caring, considerate, helpful, kind, kindly, solicitous, unselfish 2. astute, canny, careful, cautious, circumspect, deliberate, discreet, heedful, mindful, prudent, wary, well-thought-out 3. contemplative, deliberative, in a brown study, introspective, lost in thought, meditative, musing, pensive, rapt, reflective, ruminative, serious, studious, thinking, wistful
Antonyms cold-hearted, extrovert, flippant, heedless, impolite, inconsiderate, insensitive, irresponsible, neglectful, rash, selfish, shallow, superficial, thoughtless, uncaring, unthinking

thoughtless 1. impolite, inconsiderate, indiscreet, insensitive, rude, selfish, tactless, uncaring, undiplomatic, unkind 2. absent-minded, careless, foolish, heedless, ill-considered, imprudent, inadvertent, inattentive, injudicious, mindless, neglectful, negligent, rash, reckless, regardless, remiss, silly, slapdash, slipshod, stupid, unmindful, unobservant, unthinking
Antonyms attentive, considerate, considered, diplomatic, intelligent, prudent, smart, tactful, thoughtful, unselfish, well-advised, well-thought-out, wise

thraldom bondage, enslavement, serfdom, servitude, slavery, subjection, subjugation, thrall, vassalage

thrall 1. bondage, enslavement, serfdom, servitude, slavery, subjection, subjugation, thraldom, vassalage 2. bondservant, bondsman, serf, slave, subject, varlet (*archaic*), vassal

thrash 1. beat, belt (*informal*), birch, cane, chastise, clobber (*slang*), drub, flagellate, flog, give (someone) a (good) hiding (*informal*), hide (*informal*), horsewhip, lambast(e), leather, lick (*informal*), paste (*slang*), punish, scourge, spank, take a stick to, tan (*slang*), whip 2. beat, beat (someone) hollow (*Brit. informal*), blow out of the water (*slang*), clobber (*slang*), crush, defeat, drub, hammer (*informal*), lick (*informal*), make mincemeat of (*informal*), maul, overwhelm, paste (*slang*), rout, run rings around (*informal*), slaughter (*informal*), stuff (*slang*), tank (*slang*), trounce, wipe the floor with (*informal*) 3. flail, heave, jerk, plunge, squirm, thresh, toss, toss and turn, writhe

thrashing 1. beating, belting (*informal*), caning, chastisement, drubbing, flogging, hiding (*informal*), lashing, pasting (*slang*), punishment, tanning (*slang*), whipping 2. beating, defeat, drubbing, hammering (*informal*), hiding (*informal*), mauling, pasting (*slang*), rout, trouncing

thrash out argue out, debate, discuss, have out, resolve, settle, solve, talk over

thread *noun* 1. cotton, fibre, filament, line, strand, string, yarn 2. course, direction, drift, motif, plot, story line, strain, tenor, theme, train of thought *~verb* 3. ease, inch, loop, meander, pass, pick (one's way), squeeze through, string, wind

threadbare 1. down at heel, frayed, old, ragged, scruffy, shabby, tattered, tatty, used, worn, worn-out 2. clichéd, cliché-ridden, common, commonplace, conventional, corny (*slang*), familiar, hackneyed, overused, stale, stereotyped, stock, tired, trite, well-worn
Antonyms (*sense 1*) brand-new, good, new, smart, unused, well-preserved (*sense 2*) different, fresh, new, novel, original, unconventional, unfamiliar, unusual

threat 1. commination, intimidatory remark, menace, threatening remark, warning 2. foreboding, foreshadowing, omen, portent, presage, warning, writing on the wall 3. danger, hazard, menace, peril, risk

threaten 1. endanger, imperil, jeopardize, put at risk, put in jeopardy, put on the line 2. be imminent, be in the air, be in the offing, forebode, foreshadow, hang over, hang over (someone's) head, impend, loom over, portend, presage, warn 3. browbeat, bully, cow, intimidate, lean on (*slang*), make threats to, menace, pressurize, terrorize, warn
Antonyms defend, guard, protect, safeguard, shelter, shield

threatening 1. bullying, cautionary, comminatory, intimidatory, menacing, minatory, terrorizing, warning 2. baleful, bodeful, forbidding, grim, inauspicious, ominous, sinister
Antonyms (*sense 2*) auspicious, bright, comforting, encouraging, favourable, promising, propitious, reassuring

threesome triad, trilogy, trine, trinity, trio,

triple, triplet, triplex, triptych, triumvirate, triune, troika

threnody coronach (*Scot. & Irish*), dirge, elegy, funeral ode, keen, lament, monody, requiem

threshold 1. door, doorsill, doorstep, doorway, entrance, sill 2. beginning, brink, dawn, inception, opening, outset, start, starting point, verge 3. lower limit, minimum
Antonyms (*sense 2*) close, decline, end, finish, twilight
Related adjective: liminal

thrift carefulness, economy, frugality, good husbandry, parsimony, prudence, saving, thriftiness
Antonyms carelessness, extravagance, prodigality, profligacy, recklessness, squandering, waste

thriftless extravagant, improvident, imprudent, lavish, prodigal, profligate, spendthrift, unthrifty, wasteful
Antonyms careful, economical, frugal, provident, prudent, sparing, thrifty

thrifty careful, economical, frugal, parsimonious, provident, prudent, saving, sparing
Antonyms extravagant, free-spending, generous, improvident, prodigal, spendthrift, wasteful

thrill *noun* 1. adventure, buzz (*slang*), charge (*slang*), flush of excitement, glow, kick (*informal*), pleasure, sensation, stimulation, tingle, titillation 2. flutter, fluttering, quiver, shudder, throb, tremble, tremor, vibration *~verb* 3. arouse, electrify, excite, flush, get a charge (*slang*), get a kick (*informal*), glow, move, send (*slang*), stimulate, stir, tingle, titillate 4. flutter, quake, quiver, shake, shudder, throb, tremble, vibrate
Antonyms (*sense 1*) boredom, dreariness, dullness, ennui, monotony, tedium

thrilling 1. electrifying, exciting, gripping, hair-raising, rip-roaring (*informal*), riveting, rousing, sensational, sexy (*informal*), stimulating, stirring 2. quaking, shaking, shivering, shuddering, trembling, vibrating
Antonyms boring, dreary, dull, monotonous, quiet, staid, tedious, tiresome, uninteresting, unmoving

thrive advance, bloom, boom, burgeon, develop, do well, flourish, get on, grow, grow rich, increase, prosper, succeed, wax
Antonyms decline, droop, fail, languish, perish, shrivel, stagnate, wane, wilt, wither

thriving blooming, booming, burgeoning, developing, doing well, flourishing, going strong, growing, healthy, prosperous, successful, wealthy, well
Antonyms ailing, bankrupt, failing, impoverished, languishing, on the rocks, poverty-stricken, unsuccessful, withering

throaty deep, gruff, guttural, hoarse, husky, low, thick

throb 1. *verb* beat, palpitate, pound, pulsate, pulse, thump, vibrate 2. *noun* beat, palpitation, pounding, pulsating, pulse, thump, thumping, vibration

throe 1. convulsion, fit, pain, pang, paroxysm, spasm, stab 2. *plural* agony, anguish, pain, suffering, torture, travail 3. **in the throes of** agonized by, anguished by, in the midst of, in the pangs of, in the process of, struggling with, suffering from, toiling with, wrestling with

throng 1. *noun* assemblage, concourse, congregation, crowd, crush, horde, host, jam, mass, mob, multitude, pack, press, swarm 2. *verb* bunch, congregate, converge, cram, crowd, fill, flock, hem in, herd, jam, mill around, pack, press, swarm around, troop
Antonyms *verb* break up, disband, dispel, disperse, scatter, separate, spread out

throttle *verb* 1. choke, garrotte, strangle, strangulate 2. control, gag, inhibit, silence, stifle, suppress

through *preposition* 1. between, by, from end to end of, from one side to the other of, in and out of, past 2. as a consequence *or* result of, because of, by means of, by virtue of, by way of, using, via, with the help of 3. during, in, in the middle of, throughout 4. *with* **with** at the end of, done, finished, having completed, having had enough of *~adjective* 5. completed, done, ended, finished, terminated, washed up (*informal*) *~adverb* 6. **through and through** altogether, completely, entirely, fully, thoroughly, totally, to the core, unreservedly, utterly, wholly
Antonyms *adverb* moderately, more or less, partially, partly, somewhat, to some extent

throughout all over, all the time, all through, during the whole of, everywhere, for the duration of, from beginning to end, from end to end, from start to finish, from the start, in every nook and cranny, over the length and breadth of, right through, the whole time, through the whole of

throw *verb* 1. cast, chuck (*informal*), fling, heave, hurl, launch, lob (*informal*), pitch, project, propel, put, send, shy, sling, toss 2. *informal* astonish, baffle, confound, confuse, disconcert, dumbfound, faze, put one off one's stroke, throw off, throw one off one's stride, throw out 3. bring down, dislodge, fell, floor, hurl to the ground, overturn, unseat, upset *~noun* 4. cast, fling, heave, lob (*informal*), pitch, projection, put, shy, sling, toss 5. *informal* attempt, chance, essay, gamble, hazard, try, venture, wager

throwaway *adjective* careless, casual, offhand, passing, understated

throw away 1. axe (*informal*), bin (*informal*), cast off, chuck (*informal*), discard, dispense with, dispose of, ditch (*slang*), dump (*informal*), get rid of, jettison, junk (*informal*), reject, scrap, throw out 2. blow (*slang*), fail to exploit, fritter away, lose, make poor use of, squander, waste
Antonyms (*sense 1*) conserve, keep, preserve, rescue, retain, retrieve, salvage, save

throw off 1. abandon, cast off, discard, drop, free oneself of, rid oneself of, shake off 2. elude, escape from, evade, get away from, give (someone) the slip, leave behind, lose, outdistance, outrun, shake off, show a clean pair of heels to 3. confuse, disconcert, disturb, faze, put one off one's stroke, throw (*informal*), throw one off one's stride, unsettle, upset

throw out 1. bin (*informal*), cast off, chuck (*informal*), discard, dismiss, dispense with, ditch (*slang*), dump (*informal*), eject, evict, expel, get rid of, give the bum's rush (*slang*), jettison, junk (*informal*), kick out (*informal*), kiss off (*slang, chiefly U.S. & Canad.*), oust, reject, relegate, scrap, show one the door, throw away, turf out (*Brit. informal*), turn down 2. confuse, disconcert, disturb, put one off one's stroke, throw (*informal*), throw one off one's stride, unsettle, upset 3. diffuse, disseminate, emit, give off, put forth, radiate

throw over abandon, break with, chuck (*informal*), desert, discard, drop (*informal*), finish with, forsake, jilt, leave, quit, split up with, walk out on (*informal*)

throw up 1. abandon, chuck (*informal*), give up, jack in, leave, quit, relinquish, renounce, resign from, step down from (*informal*) 2. bring forward, bring to light, bring to notice, bring to the surface, produce, reveal 3. *informal* barf (*U.S. slang*), be sick, bring up, chuck (up) (*slang, chiefly U.S.*), chunder (*slang, chiefly Austral.*), disgorge, do a technicolour yawn (*slang*), heave, puke (*slang*), regurgitate, retch, spew, toss one's cookies (*U.S. slang*), upchuck (*U.S. slang*), vomit 4. jerry-build, run up, slap together, throw together

thrust *verb* 1. butt, drive, elbow *or* shoulder one's way, force, impel, jam, plunge, poke, press, prod, propel, push, ram, shove, urge 2. jab, lunge, pierce, stab, stick ~*noun* 3. drive, lunge, poke, prod, push, shove, stab 4. impetus, momentum, motive force, motive power, propulsive force

thud *noun/verb* clonk, clump, clunk, crash, knock, smack, thump, wallop (*informal*)

thug assassin, bandit, bruiser (*informal*), bully boy, cutthroat, gangster, heavy (*slang*), hooligan, killer, mugger (*informal*), murderer, robber, ruffian, tough

thumb *noun* 1. pollex 2. **all thumbs** butter-fingered (*informal*), cack-handed (*informal*), clumsy, ham-fisted (*informal*), inept, maladroit 3. **thumbs down** disapproval, negation, no, rebuff, refusal, rejection 4. **thumbs up** acceptance, affirmation, approval, encouragement, go-ahead (*informal*), green light, O.K. *or* okay (*informal*), yes ~*verb* 5. hitch (*informal*), hitchhike 6. *often with* **through** browse through, flick through, flip through, glance at, leaf through, riffle through, run one's eye over, scan the pages of, skim through, turn over 7. dog-ear, finger, handle, mark 8. **thumb one's nose at** be contemptuous of, cock a snook at, deride, flout, jeer at, laugh at, laugh in the face of, mock, ridicule, show contempt for, show disrespect to

thumbnail *adjective* brief, compact, concise, pithy, quick, short, succinct

thump 1. *noun* bang, blow, clout (*informal*), clunk, crash, knock, punch, rap, smack, thud, thwack, wallop (*informal*), whack 2. *verb* bang, batter, beat, belabour, chin (*slang*), clobber (*slang*), clout (*informal*), crash, deck (*slang*), hit, knock, lambast(e), lay one on (*slang*), pound, punch, rap, smack, strike, thrash, throb, thud, thwack, wallop (*informal*), whack

thumping colossal, elephantine, enormous, excessive, exorbitant, gargantuan, gigantic, great, huge, humongous *or* humungous (*U.S. slang*), impressive, mammoth, massive, monumental, stellar (*informal*), terrific, thundering (*slang*), titanic, tremendous, whopping (*informal*)
Antonyms inconsequential, insignificant, meagre, measly (*informal*), negligible, paltry, petty, piddling (*informal*), trifling, trivial

thunder *noun* 1. boom, booming, cracking, crash, crashing, detonation, explosion, pealing, rumble, rumbling ~*verb* 2. blast, boom, clap, crack, crash, detonate, explode, peal, resound, reverberate, roar, rumble 3. bark, bellow, declaim, roar, shout, yell 4. curse, denounce, fulminate, rail, threaten, utter threats

thundering decided, enormous, excessive, great, monumental, remarkable, unmitigated, utter

thunderous booming, deafening, ear-splitting, loud, noisy, resounding, roaring, tumultuous

thunderstruck aghast, amazed, astonished, astounded, bowled over (*informal*), dazed, dumbfounded, flabbergasted (*informal*), floored (*informal*), flummoxed, gobsmacked (*Brit. slang*), knocked for six (*informal*), left speechless, nonplussed, open-mouthed, paralysed, petrified, rooted to the spot, shocked, staggered, struck dumb, stunned, taken aback

thus **1.** as follows, in this fashion (manner, way), like so, like this, so, to such a degree **2.** accordingly, consequently, ergo, for this reason, hence, on that account, so, then, therefore

thwack **1.** *verb* bash (*informal*), beat, chin (*slang*), clout (*informal*), deck (*slang*), flog, hit, lambast(e), lay one on (*slang*), smack, thump, wallop (*informal*), whack **2.** *noun* bash (*informal*), blow, clout (*informal*), smack, thump, wallop (*informal*), whack

thwart baffle, balk, check, cook (someone's) goose (*informal*), defeat, foil, frustrate, hinder, impede, obstruct, oppose, outwit, prevent, put a spoke in someone's wheel (*informal*), stop, stymie
Antonyms aggravate, aid, assist, encourage, exacerbate, facilitate, hasten, help, intensify, support

tic jerk, spasm, twitch

tick[1] *noun* **1.** clack, click, clicking, tap, tapping, ticktock **2.** *Brit. informal* bat of an eye (*informal*), flash, half a mo (*Brit. informal*), instant, jiffy (*informal*), minute, moment, sec (*informal*), second, shake (*informal*), split second, trice, twinkling, two shakes of a lamb's tail (*informal*) **3.** dash, mark, stroke *~verb* **4.** clack, click, tap, ticktock **5.** check off, choose, indicate, mark, mark off, select **6.** **what makes someone tick** drive, motivation, motive, *raison d'être*

tick[2] *noun* account, credit, deferred payment, the slate (*Brit. informal*)

ticket **1.** card, certificate, coupon, pass, slip, token, voucher **2.** card, docket, label, marker, slip, sticker, tab, tag

tickle *figurative* amuse, delight, divert, entertain, excite, gratify, please, thrill, titillate
Antonyms annoy, bore, bother, irritate, pester, trouble, vex, weary

ticklish awkward, critical, delicate, difficult, nice, risky, sensitive, thorny, touchy, tricky, uncertain, unstable, unsteady

tick off **1.** check off, mark off, put a tick at **2.** *informal* bawl out (*informal*), berate, carpet (*informal*), censure, chew out (*U.S. & Canad. informal*), chide, give a rocket (*Brit. & N.Z. informal*), haul over the coals (*informal*), lecture, read the riot act, rebuke, reprimand, reproach, reprove, scold, take to task, tear into (*informal*), tear (someone) off a strip (*Brit. informal*), tell off (*informal*), upbraid

tide **1.** course, current, ebb, flow, stream, tideway, undertow **2.** course, current, direction, drift, movement, tendency, trend

tide over aid, assist, bridge the gap, help, keep one going, keep one's head above water, keep the wolf from the door, see one through

tidings advice, bulletin, communication, gen (*Brit. informal*), greetings, information, intelligence, latest (*informal*), message, news, report, word

tidy *adjective* **1.** businesslike, clean, cleanly, in apple-pie order (*informal*), methodical, neat, ordered, orderly, shipshape, spick-and-span, spruce, systematic, trig (*archaic or dialect*), trim, well-groomed, well-kept, well-ordered **2.** *informal* ample, considerable, fair, generous, good, goodly, handsome, healthy, large, largish, respectable, sizable *or* sizeable, substantial *~verb* **3.** clean, groom, neaten, order, put in order, put in trim, put to rights, spruce up, straighten
Antonyms (*sense 1*) careless, dirty, dishevelled, disordered, disorderly, filthy, in disarray, messy, scruffy, sloppy, slovenly, unbusinesslike, unkempt, unmethodical, unsystematic, untidy (*sense 2*) inconsiderable, insignificant, little, small, tiny (*sense 3*) dirty, dishevel, disorder, mess, mess up

tie *verb* **1.** attach, bind, connect, fasten, interlace, join, knot, lash, link, make fast, moor, rope, secure, tether, truss, unite **2.** bind, confine, hamper, hinder, hold, limit, restrain, restrict **3.** be even, be neck and neck, draw, equal, match *~noun* **4.** band, bond, connection, cord, fastening, fetter, joint, knot, ligature, link, rope, string **5.** affiliation, affinity, allegiance, bond, commitment, connection, duty, kinship, liaison, obligation, relationship **6.** encumbrance, hindrance, limitation, restraint, restriction **7.** dead heat, deadlock, draw, stalemate **8.** *Brit.* contest, fixture, game, match
Antonyms free, loose, release, separate, undo, unfasten, unhitch, unknot, untie

tie-in association, connection, coordination, hook-up, liaison, link, relation, relationship, tie-up

tie in be relevant, come in, connect, coordinate, fit in, have bearing, link, relate

tier bank, echelon, file, layer, level, line, order, rank, row, series, storey, stratum

tie-up association, connection, coordination, hook-up, liaison, link, linkup, relation, relationship, tie-in

tie up **1.** attach, bind, pinion, restrain, tether, truss **2.** lash, make fast, moor, rope, secure **3.** engage, engross, keep busy, occupy **4.** bring to a close, conclude, end, finish off, settle, terminate, wind up, wrap up (*informal*)

tiff **1.** difference, disagreement, dispute, falling-out (*informal*), petty quarrel, quarrel, row, scrap (*informal*), squabble, words **2.** bad mood, fit of ill humour, fit of pique, huff, ill humour, pet, sulk, tantrum, temper, wax (*informal, chiefly Brit.*)

tight 1. close, close-fitting, compact, constricted, cramped, fast, firm, fixed, narrow, rigid, secure, snug, stiff, stretched, taut, tense 2. hermetic, impervious, proof, sealed, sound, watertight 3. harsh, inflexible, rigid, rigorous, severe, stern, strict, stringent, tough, uncompromising, unyielding 4. close, grasping, mean, miserly, niggardly, parsimonious, penurious, sparing, stingy, tight-arse (*taboo slang*), tight-arsed (*taboo slang*), tight as a duck's arse (*taboo slang*), tight-ass (*U.S. taboo slang*), tight-assed (*U.S. taboo slang*), tightfisted 5. dangerous, difficult, hazardous, perilous, precarious, problematic, sticky (*informal*), ticklish, tough, tricky, troublesome, worrisome 6. close, even, evenly-balanced, near, well-matched 7. *informal* bevvied (*dialect*), blitzed (*slang*), blotto (*slang*), bombed (*slang*), Brahms and Liszt (*slang*), drunk, flying (*slang*), half cut (*Brit. slang*), half seas over (*Brit. informal*), inebriated, in one's cups, intoxicated, legless (*informal*), lit up (*slang*), out of it (*slang*), out to it (*Austral. & N.Z. slang*), paralytic (*informal*), pickled (*informal*), pie-eyed (*slang*), pissed (*taboo slang*), plastered (*slang*), rat-arsed (*taboo slang*), smashed (*slang*), sozzled (*informal*), steamboats (*Scot. slang*), steaming (*slang*), stewed (*slang*), stoned (*slang*), three sheets in the wind (*slang*), tiddly (*slang, chiefly Brit.*), tipsy, under the influence (*informal*), wasted (*slang*), wrecked (*slang*), zonked (*slang*)
Antonyms (*sense 1*) lax, loose, relaxed, slack, spacious (*sense 2*) loose, open, porous (*sense 3*) easy, easy-going, generous, lax, lenient, liberal, relaxed, soft, undemanding (*sense 4*) abundant, extravagant, generous, lavish, munificent, open, prodigal, profuse, spendthrift (*sense 5*) easy (*sense 6*) easy, landslide, overwhelming, runaway, uneven (*sense 7*) sober

tighten close, constrict, cramp, fasten, fix, narrow, rigidify, screw, secure, squeeze, stiffen, stretch, tauten, tense
Antonyms ease off, let out, loosen, relax, slacken, unbind, weaken

tightfisted close, close-fisted, grasping, mean, mingy (*Brit. informal*), miserly, niggardly, parsimonious, penurious, sparing, stingy, tight, tight-arse (*taboo slang*), tight-arsed (*taboo slang*), tight as a duck's arse (*taboo slang*), tight-ass (*U.S. taboo slang*), tight-assed (*U.S. taboo slang*)

tight-lipped close-lipped, close-mouthed, mum, mute, quiet, reserved, reticent, secretive, silent, taciturn, uncommunicative, unforthcoming

till[1] *verb* cultivate, dig, plough, turn over, work

till[2] *noun* cash box, cash drawer, cash register

tilt *verb* 1. cant, heel, incline, lean, list, slant, slope, tip 2. attack, break a lance, clash, contend, cross swords, duel, encounter, fight, joust, lock horns, overthrow, spar *~noun* 3. angle, cant, inclination, incline, list, pitch, slant, slope 4. *Medieval history* clash, combat, duel, encounter, fight, joust, lists, set-to (*informal*), tournament, tourney 5. **(at) full tilt** for dear life, full force, full speed, headlong, like a bat out of hell (*slang*), like the clappers (*Brit. informal*)

timber beams, boards, forest, logs, planks, trees, wood

timbre colour, quality of sound, resonance, ring, tonality, tone, tone colour

time *noun* 1. age, chronology, date, duration, epoch, era, generation, hour, interval, period, season, space, span, spell, stretch, term, while 2. instance, juncture, occasion, point, stage 3. allotted span, day, duration, life, life span, lifetime, season 4. heyday, hour, peak 5. *Music* beat, measure, metre, rhythm, tempo 6. **all the time** always, at all times, constantly, continually, continuously, ever, for the duration, perpetually, throughout 7. **at one time** **a.** for a while, formerly, hitherto, once, once upon a time, previously **b.** all at once, at the same time, simultaneously, together 8. **at times** every now and then, every so often, from time to time, now and then, occasionally, once in a while, on occasion, sometimes 9. **behind the times** antiquated, dated, obsolete, old-fashioned, old hat, outdated, outmoded, out of date, out of fashion, out of style, passé, square (*informal*) 10. **for the time being** for now, for the moment, for the nonce, for the present, in the meantime, meantime, meanwhile, pro tem, temporarily 11. **from time to time** at times, every now and then, every so often, now and then, occasionally, once in a while, on occasion, sometimes 12. **in good time** **a.** early, on time, with time to spare **b.** quickly, rapidly, speedily, swiftly, with dispatch 13. **in no time** apace, before one knows it, before you can say Jack Robinson, in an instant, in a trice (flash, jiffy (*informal*), moment), in two shakes of a lamb's tail (*informal*), quickly, rapidly, speedily, swiftly 14. **in time** **a.** at the appointed time, early, in good time, on schedule, on time, with time to spare **b.** by and by, eventually, in the fullness of time, one day, someday, sooner or later, ultimately 15. **on time** in good time, on the dot, punctually 16. **time and again** frequently, many times, often, on many occasions, over and over again, repeatedly, time after time *~verb* 17. clock, control, count, judge, measure, regulate, schedule, set
Related adjective: temporal

Related vocabulary

calends *or* kalends
civil day
civil year
day
Gregorian calendar
ides
intercalary
Julian calendar
leap year
lunar month
lunar year
month
nones
Roman calendar
synodic month
week
year

Gregorian Calendar

January
February
March
April
May
June
July
August
September
October
November
December

Jewish Calendar

Tishri
Cheshvan *or* Heshvan
Kislev
Tevet
Shevat *or* Shebat
Adar
Nisan
Iyar *or* Iyyar
Sivan
Tammuz
Av *or* Ab
Elul

Muslim Calendar

Muharram *or* Moharram
Safar *or* Saphar
Rabia I
Rabia II
Jumada I
Jumada II
Rajab
Shaban *or* Shaaban
Ramadan, Rhamadhan *or* Ramazan
Shawwal
Dhu'l-Qa'dah
Dhu'l-Hijjah

French Revolutionary Calendar

Vendémiaire
Brumaire
Frimaire
Nivôse
Pluviôse
Ventôse
Germinal
Floréal
Prairial
Messidor
Thermidor *or* Fervidor
Fructidor

Time zones

Atlantic Daylight Time
Atlantic Standard Time
British Summer Time
Central Daylight Time
Central European Time
Central Standard Time
Eastern Daylight Time
Eastern Standard Time
Greenwich Mean Time
Mountain Daylight Time
Mountain Standard Time
Newfoundland Daylight Time
Newfoundland Standard Time
Pacific Daylight Time
Pacific Standard Time
Yukon Daylight Time
Yukon Standard Time

Remember, that time is money
Benjamin Franklin *Advice to Young Tradesman*

But meanwhile it is flying, irretrievable time is flying
Virgil *Georgics*

The innocent and the beautiful
Have no enemy but time
W.B. Yeats *In memory of Eva Gore-Booth and Con Markiewicz*

Every instant of time is a pinprick of eternity
Marcus Aurelius *Meditations*

Tomorrow, and tomorrow, and tomorrow,
Creeps in this petty pace from day to day,
To the last syllable of recorded time;
And all our yesterdays have lighted fools
The way to dusty death
William Shakespeare *Macbeth*

Time is the best medicine
Ovid *Remedia Amoris*

Gather ye rose-buds while ye may,
Old time is still a flying
Robert Herrick *Hesperides*

The time is out of joint
William Shakespeare *Hamlet*

Men talk of killing time, while time quietly kills them
Dion Boucicault *London Assurance*

Thirty days hath September
April, June and November
All the rest have thirty-one
Excepting February alone
Which has but twenty-eight days clear
And twenty-nine in each leap year
Anon.

My days are swifter than a weaver's shuttle
Bible: Job

time the subtle thief of youth
John Milton *Sonnet 7*

time the devourer of everything
Ovid *Metamorphoses*

Time and tide wait for no man
Time flies (tempus fugit)
Time is a great healer
Time will tell

time-honoured age-old, ancient, conventional, customary, established, fixed, long-established, old, traditional, usual, venerable

timeless abiding, ageless, ceaseless, changeless, deathless, endless, enduring, eternal, everlasting, immortal, immutable, imperishable, indestructible, lasting, permanent, persistent, undying
Antonyms ephemeral, evanescent, momentary, mortal, passing, temporal, temporary, transitory

timely appropriate, at the right time, convenient, judicious, opportune, prompt, propitious, punctual, seasonable, suitable, well-timed
Antonyms ill-timed, inconvenient, inopportune, late, tardy, unseasonable, untimely

timeserver hypocrite, opportunist, self-seeker, trimmer, Vicar of Bray, weathercock

timeserving hypocritical, opportunist, self-seeking, temporizing, trimming

timetable agenda, calendar, curriculum, diary, list, order of the day, programme, schedule

timeworn 1. aged, ancient, broken-down, decrepit, dog-eared, lined, ragged, run-down, shabby, the worse for wear, weathered, worn, wrinkled 2. ancient, clichéd, dated, hackneyed, hoary, old hat, out of date, outworn, passé, stale, stock, threadbare, tired, trite, well-worn

timid afraid, apprehensive, bashful, cowardly, coy, diffident, faint-hearted, fearful, irresolute, modest, mousy, nervous, pusillanimous, retiring, shrinking, shy, timorous
Antonyms aggressive, arrogant, ballsy (*taboo slang*), bold, brave, confident, daring, fearless, fierce, forceful, forward, presumptuous, self-assured, self-confident, shameless, unabashed

timorous afraid, apprehensive, bashful, cowardly, coy, diffident, faint-hearted, fearful, frightened, irresolute, mousy, nervous, pusillanimous, retiring, shrinking, shy, timid, trembling
Antonyms assertive, assured, audacious, bold, confident, courageous, daring, fearless

tincture 1. *noun* aroma, colour, dash, flavour, hint, hue, seasoning, shade, smack, *soupçon*, stain, suggestion, tinge, tint, touch, trace 2. *verb* colour, dye, flavour, scent, season, stain, tinge, tint

tinge *noun* 1. cast, colour, dye, shade, stain, tincture, tint, wash 2. bit, dash, drop, pinch, smack, smattering, *soupçon*, sprinkling, suggestion, touch, trace ~*verb* 3. colour, dye, imbue, shade, stain, suffuse, tinge, tint

tingle 1. *verb* have goose pimples, itch, prickle, sting, tickle 2. *noun* goose pimples, itch, itching, pins and needles (*informal*), prickling, quiver, shiver, stinging, thrill, tickle, tickling

tinker *verb* dabble, fiddle (*informal*), meddle, mess about, monkey, muck about (*Brit. slang*), play, potter, toy

tinpot chickenshit (*U.S. slang*), inferior, measly (*informal*), Mickey Mouse (*slang*), miserable, paltry, pathetic, poxy (*slang*), second-class, second-rate, two-bit (*U.S. & Canad. slang*), twopenny-halfpenny, worthless, wretched

tinsel *adjective* brummagem, cheap, flashy, gaudy, gimcrack, meretricious, ostentatious, pinchbeck, plastic (*slang*), sham, showy, specious, superficial, tawdry, trashy

tint *noun* 1. cast, colour, hue, shade, tone 2. dye, rinse, stain, tincture, tinge, wash 3. hint, shade, suggestion, tinge, touch, trace ~*verb* 4. colour, dye, rinse, stain, tincture, tinge 5. affect, colour, influence, taint, tinge

tiny diminutive, dwarfish, infinitesimal, insignificant, Lilliputian, little, microscopic, mini, miniature, minute, negligible, petite, pint-sized (*informal*), puny, pygmy *or* pigmy, slight, small, teensy-weensy, teeny-weeny, trifling, wee
Antonyms colossal, enormous, extra-large, gargantuan, giant, gigantic, great, huge, immense, mammoth, massive, monstrous, titanic, vast

tip[1] 1. *noun* apex, cap, crown, end, extremity, head, peak, pinnacle, point, summit, top 2. *verb* cap, crown, finish, surmount, top

tip[2] *verb* 1. cant, capsize, incline, lean, list, overturn, slant, spill, tilt, topple over, upend, upset 2. *Brit.* ditch (*slang*), dump, empty, pour out, unload ~*noun* 3. *Brit.* dump, midden (*dialect*), refuse heap, rubbish heap

tip[3] *noun* 1. baksheesh, gift, gratuity, perquisite, *pourboire* 2. *Also* **tip-off** clue, forecast, gen (*Brit. informal*), hint, information, inside information, pointer, suggestion, warning, word, word of advice ~*verb* 3. remunerate, reward 4. *Also* **tip off** advise, caution, forewarn, give a clue, give a hint, suggest, tip (someone) the wink (*Brit. informal*), warn

tipple 1. *verb* bend the elbow (*informal*), bevvy (*dialect*), drink, imbibe, indulge (*informal*), quaff, swig, take a drink, tope 2. *noun* alcohol, booze (*informal*), drink, John Barleycorn, liquor, poison (*informal*)

tippler bibber, boozer (*informal*), drinker, drunk, drunkard, inebriate, soak (*slang*), sot, sponge (*informal*), toper

tipsy elevated (*informal*), fuddled, happy (*informal*), mellow, merry (*Brit. informal*), slightly drunk, tiddly (*slang, chiefly Brit.*), woozy (*informal*)

tirade abuse, denunciation, diatribe, fulmination, harangue, invective, lecture, outburst, philippic

tire 1. drain, droop, enervate, exhaust, fag (*informal*), fail, fatigue, flag, jade, knacker (*slang*), sink, take it out of (*informal*), wear down, wear out, weary, whack (*Brit. informal*) 2. aggravate (*informal*), annoy, bore, exasperate, get on one's nerves (*informal*), harass, hassle (*informal*), irk, irritate, piss one off (*taboo slang*), weary
Antonyms (*sense 1*) energize, enliven, exhilarate, invigorate, liven up, pep up, refresh, restore, revive

tired 1. all in (*slang*), asleep *or* dead on one's feet (*informal*), clapped out (*Austral. & N.Z. informal*), dead beat (*informal*), dog-tired (*informal*), done in (*informal*), drained, drooping, drowsy, enervated, exhausted, fagged (*informal*), fatigued, flagging, jaded, knackered (*slang*), ready to drop, sleepy, spent, weary, whacked (*Brit. informal*), worn out, zonked (*slang*) 2. *with* **of** annoyed with, bored with,

exasperated by, fed up with, irked by, irritated by, pissed off with (*taboo slang*), sick of, weary of **3.** clichéd, conventional, corny (*slang*), familiar, hackneyed, old, outworn, stale, stock, threadbare, trite, well-worn
Antonyms alive and kicking, energetic, enthusiastic about, fond of, fresh, full of beans (*informal*), innovative, keen on, lively, original, refreshed, rested, wide-awake

tireless determined, energetic, indefatigable, industrious, resolute, unflagging, untiring, unwearied, vigorous
Antonyms drained, exhausted, fatigued, flagging, tired, weak, weary, worn out

tiresome annoying, boring, dull, exasperating, flat, irksome, irritating, laborious, monotonous, tedious, trying, uninteresting, vexatious, wearing, wearisome
Antonyms exhilarating, inspiring, interesting, refreshing, rousing, stimulating

tiring arduous, demanding, enervative, exacting, exhausting, fatiguing, laborious, strenuous, tough, wearing, wearying

tiro *see* TYRO

tissue **1.** fabric, gauze, mesh, structure, stuff, texture, web **2.** paper, paper handkerchief, wrapping paper **3.** accumulation, chain, collection, combination, concatenation, conglomeration, fabrication, mass, network, pack, series, web

titan colossus, giant, leviathan, ogre, superman

titanic Brobdingnagian, colossal, elephantine, enormous, giant, gigantic, herculean, huge, humongous *or* humungous (*U.S. slang*), immense, jumbo (*informal*), mammoth, massive, mighty, monstrous, mountainous, prodigious, stellar (*informal*), stupendous, towering, vast

titbit *bonne bouche*, choice item, dainty, delicacy, goody, juicy bit, morsel, scrap, snack, treat

tit for tat an eye for an eye, as good as one gets, a tooth for a tooth, blow for blow, like for like, measure for measure, retaliation

tithe *noun* **1.** assessment, duty, impost, levy, tariff, tax, tenth, toll, tribute *~verb* **2.** assess, charge, levy, rate, tax **3.** give up, pay, pay a tithe on, render, surrender, turn over

titillate arouse, excite, interest, provoke, stimulate, tantalize, tease, thrill, tickle, turn on (*slang*)

titillating arousing, exciting, interesting, lewd, lurid, provocative, sensational, stimulating, suggestive, teasing, thrilling

titivate doll up (*slang*), do up (*informal*), gussy up (*slang, chiefly U.S.*), make up, prank, preen, primp, prink, refurbish, smarten up, tart up (*Brit. slang*), touch up

title *noun* **1.** caption, heading, inscription, label, legend, name, style **2.** appellation, denomination, designation, epithet, handle (*slang*), moniker *or* monicker (*slang*), name, nickname, nom de plume, pseudonym, sobriquet, term **3.** championship, crown, laurels **4.** claim, entitlement, ownership, prerogative, privilege, right *~verb* **5.** call, designate, label, name, style, term

titter chortle (*informal*), chuckle, giggle, laugh, snigger, tee-hee, te-hee

tittle atom, bit, dash, drop, grain, iota, jot, mite, particle, scrap, shred, speck, whit

tittle-tattle **1.** *noun* babble, blather, blether, cackle, chatter, chitchat, clishmaclaver (*Scot.*), dirt (*U.S. slang*), gossip, hearsay, idle chat, jaw (*slang*), natter, prattle, rumour, twaddle, yackety-yak (*slang*), yatter (*informal*) **2.** *verb* babble, blather, blether, cackle, chat, chatter, chitchat, gossip, jaw (*slang*), natter, prattle, run off at the mouth (*slang*), witter (*informal*), yak (*slang*), yatter (*informal*)

titular honorary, in name only, nominal, puppet, putative, so-called, theoretical, token
Antonyms actual, effective, functioning, real, true

toady **1.** *noun* apple polisher (*U.S. slang*), ass-kisser (*U.S. & Canad. taboo slang*), bootlicker (*informal*), brown-noser (*taboo slang*), crawler (*slang*), creep (*slang*), fawner, flatterer, flunkey, groveller, hanger-on, jackal, lackey, lickspittle, minion, parasite, spaniel, sycophant, truckler, yes man **2.** *verb* be obsequious to, bow and scrape, brown-nose (*taboo slang*), butter up, crawl, creep, cringe, curry favour with, fawn on, flatter, grovel, kiss (someone's) ass (*U.S. & Canad. taboo slang*), kiss the feet of, kowtow to, lick (someone's) arse (*taboo slang*), lick (someone's) boots, pander to, suck up to (*informal*)
Antonyms (*sense 2*) confront, defy, oppose, rebel, resist, stand against, withstand

toast¹ *verb* brown, grill, heat, roast, warm

toast² *noun* **1.** compliment, drink, health, pledge, salutation, salute, tribute **2.** darling, favourite, heroine *~verb* **3.** drink to, drink (to) the health of, pledge, salute

If I am obliged to bring religion into after-dinner toasts (which indeed does not seem quite the thing) I shall drink... to Conscience first, and to the Pope afterwards
Cardinal Newman *Letter Addressed to the Duke of Norfolk*

Here's tae us; wha's like us?
Gey few, and they're a' deid
Scottish toast

tobacco

Tobacco types

broadleaf	chewing tobacco
Burley	cigar binder
canaster	cigar filler
caporal	cigar wrapper

Cuban cigar leaf
dark air-cured
filler
fire-cured
flue-cured
makhorka
Maryland
perique
rappee
shag
snout (*Brit. slang*)
snuff
Sumatra
Turkish
Virginia

Types of cigar and cigarette

breva
cheroot
cigarillo
claro
concha
corona
Havana
imperiale
maduro
Manila
panatella
perfecto
puritano
roll-up
roll-your-own
stogy *or* stogey
tailor-made (*slang*)

Pipes

briar
clay pipe
corncob pipe
churchwarden
hookah *or* hubble-bubble
meerschaum
peace pipe

General smoking terms

ash
ashtray
bowl
butt
calabash
cigarette case
cigarette holder
cigarette paper
dottle
filter tip
flint
humidor
lighter
makings (*slang*)
matches
pigtail
pipe
pipe cleaner
pipe rack
plug
rollings (*slang*)
smoking jacket
smoker *or* smoking compartment
smoke room *or* smoking room
snuffbox
splint
stem
tobacconist
tobacco pouch

And a woman is only a woman, but a good cigar is a Smoke
Rudyard Kipling *The Betrothed*

A cigarette is the perfect type of a perfect pleasure. It is exquisite, and it leaves one unsatisfied. What more can one want?
Oscar Wilde *Picture of Dorian Gray*

Neither do thou lust after that tawney weed tobacco
Ben Jonson *Bartholomew Fair*

pernicious weed! whose scent the fair annoys,
Unfriendly to society's chief joys
William Cowper *Conversation*

A custom loathsome to the eye, hateful to the nose, harmful to the brain, dangerous to the lungs, and in the black, stinking fume thereof, nearest resembling the horrible Stygian smoke of the pit that is bottomless
James I *A Counterblast to Tobacco*

to-do agitation, bother, brouhaha, bustle, commotion, disturbance, excitement, flap (*informal*), furore, fuss, hoo-ha, hue and cry, performance (*informal*), quarrel, ruction (*informal*), rumpus, stir, tumult, turmoil, unrest, upheaval, uproar

together *adverb* **1.** as a group, as one, cheek by jowl, closely, collectively, hand in glove, hand in hand, in a body, in concert, in co-operation, in unison, jointly, mutually, shoulder to shoulder, side by side **2.** all at once, as one, at one fell swoop, at the same time, concurrently, contemporaneously, en masse, in unison, simultaneously, with one accord **3.** consecutively, continuously, in a row, in succession, one after the other, on end, successively, without a break, without interruption **4.** *informal* arranged, fixed, ordered, organized, settled, sorted out, straight, to rights ~*adjective* **5.** *slang* calm, composed, cool, stable, well-adjusted, well-balanced, well-organized

Antonyms (*sense 1*) alone, apart, independently, individually, one at a time, one by one, separately, singly

toil 1. *noun* application, blood, sweat, and tears (*informal*), donkey-work, drudgery, effort, elbow grease (*informal*), exertion, graft (*informal*), hard work, industry, labour, pains, slog, sweat, travail **2.** *verb* bend over backwards (*informal*), break one's neck (*informal*), bust a gut (*informal*), do one's damnedest (*informal*), drag oneself, drudge, give it one's all (*informal*), give it one's best shot (*informal*), go for broke (*slang*), go for it (*informal*), graft (*informal*), grind (*informal*), grub, knock oneself out (*informal*), labour, make an all-out effort (*informal*), push oneself, rupture oneself (*informal*), slave, slog, strive, struggle, sweat (*informal*), work, work like a dog, work like a Trojan, work one's fingers to the bone

Antonyms (*sense 1*) idleness, inactivity, indolence, inertia, laziness, sloth, torpor

toilet 1. ablutions (*Military informal*), bathroom, bog (*slang*), can (*U.S. & Canad. slang*), closet, convenience, crapper (*taboo slang*), gents (*Brit. informal*), john (*slang, chiefly U.S. & Canad.*), khazi (*slang*), ladies' room, latrine, lavatory, little boy's room (*informal*), little girl's room (*informal*), loo (*Brit. informal*), outhouse, *pissoir*, powder room, privy, urinal, washroom, water closet, W.C. **2.** ablutions, bathing, dressing, grooming, toilette

toilsome arduous, backbreaking, difficult, fatiguing, hard, herculean, laborious, painful, severe, strenuous, taxing, tedious, tiresome, tough, wearisome

token *noun* **1.** badge, clue, demonstration, earnest, evidence, expression, index, indication, manifestation, mark, note, proof, representation, sign, symbol, warning **2.** keepsake, memento, memorial, remembrance, reminder, souvenir *~adjective* **3.** hollow, minimal, nominal, perfunctory, superficial, symbolic

tolerable **1.** acceptable, allowable, bearable, endurable, sufferable, supportable **2.** acceptable, adequate, all right, average, fair, fairly good, fair to middling, good enough, indifferent, mediocre, middling, not bad (*informal*), O.K. *or* okay (*informal*), ordinary, passable, run-of-the-mill, so-so (*informal*), unexceptional
Antonyms (*sense 1*) insufferable, intolerable, unacceptable, unbearable, unendurable (*sense 2*) awful, bad, dreadful, rotten

tolerance **1.** broad-mindedness, charity, forbearance, indulgence, lenity, magnanimity, open-mindedness, patience, permissiveness, sufferance, sympathy **2.** endurance, fortitude, hardiness, hardness, resilience, resistance, stamina, staying power, toughness **3.** fluctuation, play, swing, variation
Antonyms (*sense 1*) bigotry, discrimination, intolerance, narrow-mindedness, prejudice, sectarianism

Live and let live
J.C.F. Schiller *Wallenstein's Camp*

tolerant **1.** broad-minded, catholic, charitable, fair, forbearing, latitudinarian, liberal, long-suffering, magnanimous, open-minded, patient, sympathetic, unbigoted, understanding, unprejudiced **2.** complaisant, easy-going, easy-oasy (*slang*), free and easy, indulgent, kind-hearted, lax, lenient, permissive, soft
Antonyms authoritarian, biased, bigoted, despotic, dictatorial, dogmatic, illiberal, intolerant, narrow-minded, prejudiced, repressive, rigid, sectarian, stern, strict, tyrannical, uncharitable

tolerate abide, accept, admit, allow, bear, brook, condone, countenance, endure, hack (*slang*), indulge, permit, pocket, put up with (*informal*), receive, sanction, stand, stomach, submit to, suffer, swallow, take, thole (*Scot.*), turn a blind eye to, undergo, wink at
Antonyms ban, disallow, disapprove, forbid, outlaw, preclude, prohibit, veto

toleration **1.** acceptance, allowance, condonation, endurance, indulgence, permissiveness, sanction, sufferance **2.** freedom of conscience, freedom of worship, religious freedom

toll[1] *verb* **1.** chime, clang, knell, peal, ring, sound, strike **2.** announce, call, signal, summon, warn *~noun* **3.** chime, clang, knell, peal, ring, ringing, tolling

toll[2] *noun* **1.** assessment, charge, customs, demand, duty, fee, impost, levy, payment, rate, tariff, tax, tribute **2.** cost, damage, inroad, loss, penalty

tomb burial chamber, catacomb, crypt, grave, mausoleum, sarcophagus, sepulchre, vault

tombstone gravestone, headstone, marker, memorial, monument

tome book, title, volume, work

tomfool **1.** *noun* ass, berk (*Brit. slang*), blockhead, charlie (*Brit. informal*), chump (*informal*), clown, dickhead (*slang*), dickwit (*slang*), dipstick (*Brit. slang*), divvy (*Brit. slang*), dolt, dork (*slang*), dweeb (*U.S. slang*), fool, fuckwit (*taboo slang*), geek (*slang*), gonzo (*slang*), idiot, nerd *or* nurd (*slang*), nincompoop, ninny, nitwit (*informal*), numskull *or* numbskull, oaf, pillock (*Brit. slang*), plank (*Brit. slang*), plonker (*slang*), prat (*slang*), prick (*slang*), simpleton, twit (*informal, chiefly Brit.*), wally (*slang*) **2.** *adjective* asinine, crackbrained, crazy, daft (*informal*), foolish, halfwitted, harebrained, idiotic, inane, rash, senseless, silly, stupid

tomfoolery **1.** buffoonery, childishness, clowning, fooling around (*informal*), foolishness, horseplay, idiocy, larks (*informal*), messing around (*informal*), shenanigans (*informal*), silliness, skylarking (*informal*), stupidity **2.** balderdash, baloney (*informal*), bilge (*informal*), bosh (*informal*), bunk (*informal*), bunkum *or* buncombe (*chiefly U.S.*), claptrap (*informal*), hogwash, hooey (*slang*), inanity, nonsense, poppycock (*informal*), rot, rubbish, stuff and nonsense, tommyrot, tosh (*slang, chiefly Brit.*), trash, twaddle
Antonyms demureness, gravity, heaviness, reserve, sedateness, seriousness, sobriety, solemnity, sternness

tomorrow

Take therefore no thought for the morrow; for the morrow shall take thought for the things of itself
Bible: St. Matthew

Tomorrow is another day

Tomorrow never comes

tone *noun* **1.** accent, emphasis, force, inflection, intonation, modulation, pitch, strength, stress, timbre, tonality, volume **2.** air, approach, aspect, attitude, character, drift, effect, feel, frame, grain, manner, mood, note, quality, spirit, style, temper, tenor, vein **3.** cast, colour, hue, shade, tinge, tint *~verb* **4.** blend, go well with, harmonize, match, suit

tone down dampen, dim, mitigate, moderate, modulate, play down, reduce, restrain, soften, soft-pedal (*informal*), subdue, temper

tone up freshen, get in shape, get into condition, invigorate, limber up, shape up, sharpen up, trim, tune up

tongue **1.** argot, dialect, idiom, language, lingo (*informal*), parlance, patois, speech, talk, vernacular 2. articulation, speech, utterance, verbal expression, voice

tongue-lashing dressing-down (*informal*), lecture, rebuke, reprimand, reproach, reproof, scolding, slating (*informal*), talking-to (*informal*), telling-off (*informal*), ticking-off (*informal*), wigging (*Brit. slang*)

tongue-tied at a loss for words, dumb, dumbstruck, inarticulate, mute, speechless, struck dumb
Antonyms articulate, chatty, effusive, garrulous, loquacious, talkative, verbose, voluble, wordy

tonic analeptic, boost, bracer (*informal*), cordial, fillip, livener, pick-me-up (*informal*), refresher, restorative, roborant, shot in the arm (*informal*), stimulant

too 1. also, as well, besides, further, in addition, into the bargain, likewise, moreover, to boot 2. excessively, exorbitantly, extremely, immoderately, inordinately, over-, overly, unduly, unreasonably, very

tool *noun* 1. apparatus, appliance, contraption, contrivance, device, gadget, implement, instrument, machine, utensil 2. agency, agent, intermediary, means, medium, vehicle, wherewithal 3. cat's-paw, creature, dupe, flunkey, hireling, jackal, lackey, minion, pawn, puppet, stooge (*slang*) ~*verb* 4. chase, cut, decorate, ornament, shape, work

Tools

Allen key
alligator
auger
awl
axe
ball-peen hammer
beetle
billhook
bit
bitstock
bodkin
bolster
borer
bosh
brace and bit
broach
broad
burin
bushhammer
centre punch
chaser
chisel
claw hammer
clink
clippers
cold chisel
comb
comber
countersink
cradle
croze
diamond point
dibble
drawknife *or* drawshave
dresser
drift *or* driftpin
drill
drill press
drove *or* drove chisel
edge tool
eyeleteer
facer
file
fillet
firmer chisel
flange
flatter
float
floatcut file
fork
former
fraise
froe *or* frow
fuller
gab
gad
gavel
gimlet
gouger
graver
gympie (*Austral.*)
hack
hack hammer
half-round chisel
hammer
hammer drill
hob
hoe
hone
icebreaker
ice pick
jackhammer
jointer
jumper
kevel
knapping hammer
mallet
mattock
maul
mitre square
monkey wrench
nibbler
nippers
padsaw
percussion tool
pestle
pick
piledriver
pitching tool
plane
pliers
ploughstaff
pneumatic hammer
power drill
pruning hook
punch
rabble *or* rabbler
rake
rawhide hammer
ripple
rocker
rounder
router
sander
saw
sax
scorper *or* scauper
screwdriver
screw tap
scriber
scutch *or* scutcher
scythe
shave
shears
sickle
slasher (*Austral. & N.Z.*)
sledgehammer
snake
slick
soldering iron
spade
spanner
spider
spitsticker
spud *or* spudder
stiletto
stylus
swage
tack hammer
tilt hammer
triphammer
trepan
trowel
wimble
wrench

tooth

Teeth

canine
incisor *or* foretooth
molar
premolar
wisdom tooth

toothsome agreeable, appetizing, dainty, delectable, delicious, luscious, mouthwatering, nice, palatable, savoury, scrumptious (*informal*), sweet, tasty, tempting, yummy (*slang*)

top *noun* 1. acme, apex, apogee, crest, crown, culmination, head, height, high point, meridian, peak, pinnacle, summit, vertex, zenith 2. cap, cork, cover, lid, stopper 3. first place, head, highest rank, lead 4. **blow one's top** *informal* blow up (*informal*), do one's nut (*Brit. slang*), explode, fly into a temper, fly off the handle (*informal*), go spare (*Brit. slang*), have a fit (*informal*), lose one's temper, see red (*informal*), throw a tantrum 5. **over the top** a bit much (*informal*), excessive, going too far, immoderate, inordinate, over the limit, too much, uncalled-for *~adjective* **6.** best, chief, crack (*informal*), crowning, culminating, dominant, elite, finest, first, foremost, greatest, head, highest, lead, leading, pre-eminent, prime, principal, ruling, sovereign, superior, topmost, upper, uppermost *~verb* **7.** cap, cover, crown, finish, garnish, roof, tip **8.** ascend, climb, crest, reach the top of, scale, surmount **9.** be first, be in charge of, command, head, lead, rule **10.** beat, best, better, eclipse, exceed, excel, go beyond, outdo, outshine, outstrip, surpass, transcend

Antonyms *noun* base, bottom, foot, nadir, underneath, underside *~adjective* amateurish, bottom, incompetent, inept, inferior, least, lower, lowest, second-rate, unknown, unranked, worst *~verb* be at the bottom of, fail to equal, fall short of, not be as good as

topic issue, matter, point, question, subject, subject matter, text, theme, thesis

topical 1. contemporary, current, newsworthy, popular, up-to-date, up-to-the-minute **2.** local, parochial, regional, restricted

topmost dominant, foremost, highest, leading, loftiest, paramount, principal, supreme, top, upper, uppermost

Antonyms base, basic, bottom, bottommost, last, lowest, undermost

topple 1. capsize, collapse, fall, fall headlong, fall over, keel over, knock down, knock over, overbalance, overturn, tip over, totter, tumble, upset **2.** bring down, bring low, oust, overthrow, overturn, unseat

Antonyms (*sense 1*) ascend, build, mount, rise, tower

topsy-turvy chaotic, confused, disarranged, disorderly, disorganized, inside-out, jumbled, messy, mixed-up, untidy, upside-down

Antonyms neat, ordered, orderly, organized, shipshape, systematic, tidy

top up add to, augment, boost, enhance, fill out *or* up, supplement

torment *verb* **1.** afflict, agonize, crucify, distress, excruciate, harrow, pain, rack, torture **2.** aggravate (*informal*), annoy, bedevil, bother, chivvy, devil (*informal*), harass, harry, hassle (*informal*), hound, irritate, lead (someone) a merry dance (*Brit. informal*), nag, persecute, pester, plague, provoke, tease, trouble, vex, worry *~noun* **3.** agony, anguish, distress, hell, misery, pain, suffering, torture **4.** affliction, annoyance, bane, bother, harassment, hassle (*informal*), irritation, nag, nagging, nuisance, pain in the neck (*informal*), persecution, pest, plague, provocation, scourge, thorn in one's flesh, trouble, vexation, worry

Antonyms *verb* comfort, delight, ease, encourage, make happy, put at ease, reassure, soothe *~noun* bliss, comfort, ease, ecstasy, encouragement, happiness, joy, reassurance, rest

torn *adjective* **1.** cut, lacerated, ragged, rent, ripped, slit, split **2.** divided, in two minds (*informal*), irresolute, split, uncertain, undecided, unsure, vacillating, wavering

tornado cyclone, gale, hurricane, squall, storm, tempest, twister (*U.S. informal*), typhoon, whirlwind, windstorm

torpid apathetic, benumbed, dormant, drowsy, dull, fainéant, inactive, indolent, inert, lackadaisical, languid, languorous, lazy, lethargic, listless, lymphatic, motionless, numb, passive, slothful, slow, slow-moving, sluggish, somnolent, stagnant

torpor accidie, acedia, apathy, dormancy, drowsiness, dullness, inactivity, inanition, indolence, inertia, inertness, languor, laziness, lethargy, listlessness, numbness, passivity, sloth, sluggishness, somnolence, stagnancy, stupor, torpidity

Antonyms animation, energy, get-up-and-go (*informal*), go, liveliness, pep, vigour

torrent cascade, deluge, downpour, effusion, flood, flow, gush, outburst, rush, spate, stream, tide

torrid 1. arid, blistering, boiling, broiling, burning, dried, dry, fiery, flaming, hot, parched, parching, scorched, scorching, sizzling, stifling, sultry, sweltering, tropical **2.** ardent, erotic, fervent, flaming, hot, intense, passionate, sexy (*informal*), steamy (*informal*)

tortuous 1. bent, circuitous, convoluted, crooked, curved, indirect, mazy, meandering, serpentine, sinuous, twisted, twisting, twisty, winding, zigzag **2.** ambiguous, complicated, convoluted, cunning, deceptive, devious, indirect, involved, mazy, misleading, roundabout, tricky

Antonyms (*sense 2*) candid, direct, honest, ingenuous, open, reliable, straightforward, upright

torture 1. *verb* afflict, agonize, crucify, distress, excruciate, harrow, lacerate, martyr, pain, persecute, put on the rack, rack, torment **2.** *noun* affliction, agony, anguish, distress, hell, laceration, martyrdom, misery, pain, pang(s), persecution, rack, suffering, torment

Antonyms (*sense 1*) alleviate, comfort, console, ease, mollify, relieve, salve, solace, soothe (*sense 2*) amusement, bliss, delight, enjoyment, happiness, joy, pleasure, well-being

Instruments of torture

boot	Procrustean bed
brake	rack
cat-o'-nine-tails	scourge
iron maiden	thumbscrew
pilliwinks	wheel

Types of torture

bastinado	strappado
Chinese water torture	water cure
gauntlet	water torture

toss *verb* **1.** cast, chuck (*informal*), fling, flip, hurl, launch, lob (*informal*), pitch, project, propel, shy, sling, throw **2.** agitate, disturb, jiggle, joggle, jolt, rock, roll, shake, thrash, tumble, wriggle, writhe **3.** heave, labour, lurch, pitch, roll, wallow *~noun* **4.** cast, fling, lob (*informal*), pitch, shy, throw

tot[1] *noun* **1.** ankle-biter (*Austral. slang*), baby, child, infant, little one, mite, rug rat (*slang*), sprog (*slang*), toddler, wean (*Scot.*) **2.** dram, finger, measure, nip, shot (*informal*), slug, snifter (*informal*), toothful

tot[2] *verb* add up, calculate, count up, reckon, sum (up), tally, total

total 1. *noun* aggregate, all, amount, entirety, full amount, mass, sum, totality, whole **2.** *adjective* absolute, all-out, arrant, complete, comprehensive, consummate, deep-dyed (*usually derogatory*), downright, entire, full, gross, integral, out-and-out, outright, perfect, sheer, sweeping, thorough, thoroughgoing, unconditional, undisputed, undivided, unmitigated, unqualified, utter, whole **3.** *verb* add up, amount to, come to, mount up to, reach, reckon, sum up, tot up

Antonyms *noun* individual amount, part, subtotal *~adjective* conditional, fragmentary, incomplete, limited, mixed, part, partial, qualified, restricted, uncombined *~verb* deduct, subtract

totalitarian authoritarian, despotic, dictatorial, monolithic, one-party, oppressive, tyrannous, undemocratic

Antonyms autonomous, democratic, egalitarian, popular, self-governing

totality 1. aggregate, all, entirety, everything, sum, total, whole **2.** completeness, entireness, fullness, wholeness

totally absolutely, completely, comprehensively, consummately, entirely, fully, one hundred per cent, perfectly, quite, thoroughly, to the hilt, unconditionally, unmitigatedly, utterly, wholeheartedly, wholly

Antonyms incompletely, in part, partially, partly, somewhat, to a certain extent

totter falter, lurch, quiver, reel, rock, shake, stagger, stumble, sway, teeter, tremble, walk unsteadily, waver

touch *noun* **1.** feel, feeling, handling, palpation, physical contact, tactility **2.** blow, brush, caress, contact, fondling, hit, pat, push, stroke, tap **3.** bit, dash, detail, drop, hint, intimation, jot, pinch, smack, small amount, smattering, *soupçon*, speck, spot, suggestion, suspicion, taste, tincture, tinge, trace, whiff **4.** direction, effect, hand, influence **5.** approach, characteristic, handiwork, manner, method, style, technique, trademark, way **6.** ability, adroitness, art, artistry, command, craft, deftness, facility, flair, knack, mastery, skill, virtuosity **7.** acquaintance, awareness, communication, contact, correspondence, familiarity, understanding *~verb* **8.** brush, caress, contact, feel, finger, fondle, graze, handle, hit, lay a finger on, palpate, pat, push, strike, stroke, tap **9.** abut, adjoin, be in contact, border, brush, come together, contact, converge, graze, impinge upon, meet **10.** affect, disturb, get through to, get to (*informal*), have an effect on, impress, influence, inspire, make an impression on, mark, melt, move, soften, stir, strike, tug at (someone's) heartstrings (*often facetious*), upset **11.** be a party to, concern oneself with, consume, deal with, drink, eat, get involved in, handle, have to do with, partake of, use, utilize **12.** *with* **on** allude to, bring in, cover, deal with, mention, refer to, speak of **13.** bear upon, concern, have to do with, interest, pertain to, regard **14.** be a match for, be in the same league as, be on a par with, come near, come up to, compare with, equal, hold a candle to (*informal*), match, parallel, rival **15.** arrive at, attain, come to, reach

Related adjectives: haptic, tactile

touch-and-go close, critical, dangerous, hairy (*slang*), hazardous, near, nerve-racking, parlous, perilous, precarious, risky, sticky (*informal*), tricky

touched 1. affected, disturbed, impressed, melted, moved, softened, stirred, swayed, upset **2.** barmy (*slang*), batty (*slang*), bonkers (*slang, chiefly Brit.*), crackpot (*informal*), crazy, cuckoo (*informal*), daft (*informal*), doolally (*slang*), gonzo (*slang*), loopy (*informal*), not all there, not right in the head, nuts (*slang*), nutty (*slang*), nutty as a fruitcake (*slang*), off one's rocker (*slang*), off one's trolley (*slang*), out to lunch (*informal*), soft in the head (*informal*), up the pole (*informal*), wacko *or* whacko (*informal*)

touchiness bad temper, crabbedness, fretfulness, grouchiness (*informal*), irascibility, irritability, peevishness, pettishness, petulance, surliness, testiness, tetchiness, ticklishness

touching affecting, emotive, heartbreaking, melting, moving, pathetic, piteous, pitiable, pitiful, poignant, sad, stirring, tender

touch off 1. fire, ignite, light, put a match to, set off **2.** arouse, begin, cause, foment, give rise to, initiate, provoke, set in motion, spark off, trigger (off)

touchstone criterion, gauge, measure, norm, par, standard, yardstick

touch up 1. finish off, perfect, put the finishing touches to, round off 2. brush up, enhance, fake (up), falsify, give a face-lift to, gloss over, improve, patch up, polish up, renovate, re~touch, revamp, titivate, whitewash (*informal*)

touchy bad-tempered, captious, crabbed, cross, easily offended, grouchy (*informal*), grumpy, irascible, irritable, oversensitive, peevish, pet~tish, petulant, querulous, quick-tempered, ratty (*Brit. & N.Z. informal*), splenetic, surly, testy, tetchy, thin-skinned, ticklish
Antonyms affable, cheerful, easy-going, gen~ial, good-humoured, imperious, indifferent, in~sensitive, light-hearted, pleasant, sunny, sweet, thick-skinned, unconcerned

tough *adjective* 1. cohesive, durable, firm, hard, inflexible, leathery, resilient, resistant, rigid, rugged, solid, stiff, strong, sturdy, tenacious 2. brawny, fit, hard as nails, hardened, hardy, resilient, seasoned, stalwart, stout, strapping, strong, sturdy, vigorous 3. hard-bitten, pugna~cious, rough, ruffianly, ruthless, vicious, vio~lent 4. adamant, callous, exacting, firm, hard, hard-boiled (*informal*), hard-nosed (*informal*), inflexible, intractable, merciless, obdurate, obstinate, refractory, resolute, severe, stern, strict, stubborn, unbending, unforgiving, un~yielding 5. arduous, baffling, difficult, exact~ing, exhausting, hard, intractable, irksome, knotty, laborious, perplexing, puzzling, strenuous, thorny, troublesome, uphill 6. *in~formal* bad, hard cheese (*Brit. slang*), hard lines (*Brit. informal*), hard luck, lamentable, regrettable, too bad (*informal*), unfortunate, unlucky ~*noun* 7. bravo, bruiser (*informal*), brute, bully, bully boy, heavy (*slang*), hooli~gan, rough (*informal*), roughneck (*slang*), rowdy, ruffian, thug
Antonyms accommodating, benign, civilized, compassionate, considerate, delicate, easy, easy-peasy (*slang*), flexible, flimsy, fragile, gentle, humane, indulgent, kind, lenient, merciful, mild, simple, soft, sympathetic, ten~der, unexacting, weak

tour *noun* 1. excursion, expedition, jaunt, jour~ney, outing, peregrination, progress, trip 2. circuit, course, round ~*verb* 3. explore, go on the road, go round, holiday in, journey, sight~see, travel round, travel through, visit

tourist excursionist, globetrotter, holiday-maker, journeyer, sightseer, traveller, tripper, voyager

tournament 1. competition, contest, event, match, meeting, series 2. *Medieval* joust, the lists, tourney

tousle disarrange, disarray, dishevel, disorder, mess up, ruffle, rumple, tangle

tout *verb* 1. bark (*U.S. informal*), canvass, drum up, solicit, spiel 2. *informal* approve, commend, endorse, praise, promote, recom~mend, speak well of, support, tip, urge ~*noun* 3. barker, canvasser, solicitor, spieler 4. tipster

tow *verb* drag, draw, haul, lug, pull, trail, trawl, tug

towards 1. en route for, for, in the direction of, in the vicinity of, on the road to, on the way to, to 2. about, concerning, for, regarding, with regard to, with respect to 3. almost, close to, coming up to, getting on for, just before, nearing, nearly, not quite, shortly before

tower *noun* 1. belfry, column, obelisk, pillar, skyscraper, steeple, turret 2. castle, citadel, fort, fortification, fortress, keep, refuge, stronghold ~*verb* 3. ascend, be head and shoulders above, dominate, exceed, loom, mount, overlook, overtop, rear, rise, soar, sur~pass, top, transcend

towering 1. colossal, elevated, extraordinary, gigantic, great, high, imposing, impressive, lofty, magnificent, outstanding, paramount, prodigious, soaring, stellar (*informal*), strik~ing, sublime, superior, supreme, surpassing, tall, transcendent 2. burning, excessive, ex~treme, fiery, immoderate, inordinate, intem~perate, intense, mighty, passionate, vehement, violent

town
Related adjectives: oppidan, urban

God made the country, and man made the town
William Cowper *The Task*

toxic baneful (*archaic*), deadly, harmful, lethal, noxious, pernicious, pestilential, poisonous, septic
Antonyms harmless, invigorating, non-poisonous, nontoxic, safe, salubrious

toy *noun* 1. doll, game, plaything 2. bauble, gewgaw, knick-knack, trifle, trinket ~*verb* 3. amuse oneself, dally, fiddle (*informal*), flirt, fool (about *or* around), play, play fast and loose (*informal*), sport, trifle, wanton

trace *noun* 1. evidence, indication, mark, rec~ord, relic, remains, remnant, sign, survival, token, vestige 2. bit, dash, drop, hint, iota, jot, shadow, *soupçon*, suggestion, suspicion, tinc~ture, tinge, touch, trifle, whiff 3. footmark, footprint, footstep, path, slot, spoor, track, trail ~*verb* 4. ascertain, detect, determine, discover, ferret out, find, follow, hunt down, pursue, search for, seek, shadow, stalk, track, trail, unearth 5. chart, copy, delineate, depict, draw, map, mark out, outline, record, show, sketch

track *noun* 1. footmark, footprint, footstep, mark, path, scent, slipstream, slot, spoor, trace, trail, wake 2. course, flight path, line, orbit, path, pathway, road, track, trajectory, way 3. line, permanent way, rail, rails 4. **keep track of** follow, keep an eye on, keep in sight, keep in touch with, keep up to date with, keep up with, monitor, oversee, watch 5. **lose track of** lose, lose sight of, misplace ~*verb* 6. chase, dog, follow, follow the trail of, hunt down, pursue, shadow, stalk, tail (*informal*), trace, trail

track down apprehend, bring to light, capture, catch, dig up, discover, expose, ferret out, find, hunt down, run to earth *or* ground, sniff out, trace, unearth

trackless empty, pathless, solitary, uncharted, unexplored, unfrequented, untrodden, unused, virgin

tracks 1. footprints, impressions, imprints, tyremarks, tyreprints, wheelmarks 2. **make tracks** beat it (*slang*), depart, disappear, get going, get moving, go, head off, hit the road (*slang*), leave, pack one's bags (*informal*), set out, split (*slang*), take off (*informal*) 3. **stop in one's tracks** bring to a standstill, freeze, immobilize, petrify, rivet to the spot, stop dead, transfix

tract[1] *noun* area, district, estate, expanse, extent, lot, plot, quarter, region, stretch, territory, zone

tract[2] *noun* booklet, brochure, disquisition, dissertation, essay, homily, leaflet, monograph, pamphlet, tractate, treatise

tractable 1. amenable, biddable, compliant, controllable, docile, governable, manageable, obedient, persuadable, submissive, tame, willing, yielding 2. ductile, fictile, malleable, plastic, pliable, pliant, tensile, tractile, workable
Antonyms defiant, headstrong, obstinate, refractory, stiff-necked, stubborn, unruly, wilful

traction adhesion, drag, draught, drawing, friction, grip, haulage, pull, pulling, purchase, resistance

trade *noun* 1. barter, business, buying and selling, commerce, dealing, exchange, traffic, transactions, truck 2. avocation, business, calling, craft, employment, job, line, line of work, métier, occupation, profession, pursuit, skill 3. deal, exchange, interchange, swap 4. clientele, custom, customers, market, patrons, public ~*verb* 5. bargain, barter, buy and sell, deal, do business, exchange, have dealings, peddle, traffic, transact, truck 6. barter, exchange, swap, switch

trader broker, buyer, dealer, marketer, merchandiser, merchant, purveyor, seller, supplier

tradesman 1. dealer, merchant, purveyor, retailer, seller, shopkeeper, supplier, vendor 2. artisan, craftsman, journeyman, skilled worker, workman

tradition convention, custom, customs, established practice, folklore, habit, institution, lore, praxis, ritual, unwritten law, usage

traditional accustomed, ancestral, conventional, customary, established, fixed, folk, historic, long-established, old, oral, time-honoured, transmitted, unwritten, usual
Antonyms avant-garde, contemporary, ground-breaking, innovative, modern, new, novel, off-the-wall (*slang*), original, revolutionary, unconventional, unusual

traduce abuse, asperse, bad-mouth (*slang, chiefly U.S. & Canad.*), blacken, calumniate, decry, defame, denigrate, deprecate, depreciate, detract, disparage, drag through the mud, dump on (*slang, chiefly U.S.*), knock (*informal*), malign, misrepresent, revile, rubbish (*informal*), run down, slag (off) (*slang*), slander, smear, speak ill of, vilify

traducer abuser, asperser, calumniator, defamer, denigrator, deprecator, detractor, disparager, slanderer, smearer, vilifier

traffic *noun* 1. coming and going, freight, movement, passengers, transport, transportation, vehicles 2. barter, business, buying and selling, commerce, communication, dealing, dealings, doings, exchange, intercourse, peddling, relations, trade, truck ~*verb* 3. bargain, barter, buy and sell, deal, do business, exchange, have dealings, have transactions, market, peddle, trade, truck

tragedy adversity, affliction, bummer (*slang*), calamity, catastrophe, disaster, grievous blow, misfortune, whammy (*informal, chiefly U.S.*)
Antonyms fortune, happiness, joy, prosperity, success

Tragedy is clean, it is restful, it is flawless
Jean Anouilh *Antigone*

Tragedy ought to be a great kick at misery
D.H. Lawrence *letter*

All tragedies are finish'd by a death,
All comedies are ended by a marriage
Lord Byron *Don Juan*

The world is a comedy to those that think, a tragedy to those that feel
Horace Walpole, Fourth Earl of Orford *Letters*

tragic anguished, appalling, awful, calamitous, catastrophic, deadly, dire, disastrous, dismal, doleful, dreadful, fatal, grievous, heartbreaking, heart-rending, ill-fated, ill-starred, lamentable, miserable, mournful, pathetic, pitiable, ruinous, sad, shocking, sorrowful, unfortunate, woeful, wretched
Antonyms agreeable, beneficial, cheerful, comic, fortunate, glorious, happy, joyful, lucky, satisfying, worthwhile

trail *verb* 1. dangle, drag, draw, hang down, haul, pull, stream, tow 2. chase, follow, hunt, pursue, shadow, stalk, tail (*informal*), trace, track 3. bring up the rear, dawdle, drag oneself, fall behind, follow, hang back, lag, linger, loiter, straggle, traipse (*informal*) 4. dangle, droop, extend, hang, straggle ~*noun* 5. footprints, footsteps, mark, marks, path, scent, slipstream, spoor, trace, track, wake **6.** beaten track, footpath, path, road, route, track, way **7.** appendage, stream, tail, train

trail away *or* **off** decrease, die away, diminish, dwindle, fade away *or* out, fall away, grow faint, grow weak, lessen, peter out, shrink, sink, subside, tail off, taper off, weaken

train *verb* **1.** coach, discipline, drill, educate, guide, improve, instruct, prepare, rear, rehearse, school, teach, tutor **2.** exercise, improve, prepare, work out **3.** aim, bring to bear, direct, focus, level, line up, point *~noun* **4.** chain, concatenation, course, order, progression, sequence, series, set, string, succession **5.** caravan, column, convoy, file, procession **6.** appendage, tail, trail **7.** attendants, cortege, court, entourage, followers, following, household, retinue, staff, suite

trainer coach, handler

training **1.** coaching, discipline, education, grounding, guidance, instruction, schooling, teaching, tuition, tutelage, upbringing **2.** body building, exercise, practice, preparation, working-out

traipse **1.** *verb* drag oneself, footslog, slouch, trail, tramp, trudge **2.** *noun* long walk, slog, tramp, trek, trudge

trait attribute, characteristic, feature, idiosyncrasy, lineament, mannerism, peculiarity, quality, quirk

traitor apostate, back-stabber, betrayer, deceiver, defector, deserter, double-crosser (*informal*), fifth columnist, informer, Judas, miscreant, quisling, rebel, renegade, snake in the grass (*informal*), turncoat
Antonyms defender, loyalist, patriot, supporter

traitorous apostate, disloyal, double-crossing (*informal*), double-dealing, faithless, false, perfidious, renegade, seditious, treacherous, treasonable, unfaithful, untrue
Antonyms constant, faithful, loyal, patriotic, staunch, steadfast, true, trusty

trajectory course, flight, flight path, line, path, route, track

trammel **1.** *noun* bar, block, bond, chain, check, clog, curb, fetter, handicap, hazard, hindrance, impediment, obstacle, rein, shackle, stumbling block **2.** *verb* bar, block, capture, catch, check, clog, curb, enmesh, ensnare, entrap, fetter, hamper, handicap, hinder, impede, net, restrain, restrict, snag, tie
Antonyms *verb* advance, assist, expedite, facilitate, foster, further, promote, support

tramp *verb* **1.** footslog, hike, march, ramble, range, roam, rove, slog, trek, walk, yomp **2.** march, plod, stamp, stump, toil, traipse (*informal*), trudge, walk heavily **3.** crush, stamp, stomp (*informal*), trample, tread, walk over *~noun* **4.** bag lady (*chiefly U.S.*), bum (*informal*), derelict, dosser (*Brit. slang*), down-and-out, drifter, hobo (*chiefly U.S.*), vagabond, vagrant **5.** hike, march, ramble, slog, trek **6.** footfall, footstep, stamp, tread

trample **1.** crush, flatten, run over, squash, stamp, tread, walk over **2.** do violence to, encroach upon, hurt, infringe, ride roughshod over, show no consideration for, violate

trance abstraction, daze, dream, ecstasy, hypnotic state, muse, rapture, reverie, spell, stupor, unconsciousness

tranquil at peace, calm, composed, cool, pacific, peaceful, placid, quiet, restful, sedate, serene, still, undisturbed, unexcited, unperturbed, unruffled, untroubled
Antonyms agitated, busy, confused, disturbed, excited, hectic, restless, troubled

tranquillity ataraxia, calm, calmness, composure, coolness, equanimity, hush, imperturbability, peace, peacefulness, placidity, quiet, quietness, quietude, repose, rest, restfulness, sedateness, serenity, stillness
Antonyms agitation, commotion, confusion, disturbance, excitement, noise, restlessness, turmoil, upset

tranquillize calm, compose, lull, pacify, quell, quiet, relax, sedate, settle one's nerves, soothe
Antonyms agitate, confuse, distress, disturb, harass, perturb, ruffle, trouble, upset

tranquillizer barbiturate, bromide, downer (*slang*), opiate, red (*slang*), sedative

transact accomplish, carry on, carry out, conclude, conduct, discharge, do, enact, execute, handle, manage, negotiate, perform, prosecute, see to, settle, take care of

transaction **1.** action, affair, bargain, business, coup, deal, deed, enterprise, event, matter, negotiation, occurrence, proceeding, undertaking **2.** *plural* affairs, annals, doings, goings-on (*informal*), minutes, proceedings, record

transcend eclipse, exceed, excel, go above, go beyond, leave behind, leave in the shade (*informal*), outdo, outrival, outshine, outstrip, outvie, overstep, rise above, surpass

transcendence, transcendency ascendancy, excellence, greatness, incomparability, matchlessness, paramountcy, pre-eminence, sublimity, superiority, supremacy

transcendent consummate, exceeding, extraordinary, incomparable, matchless, peerless, pre-eminent, second to none, sublime, superior, transcendental, unequalled, unique, unparalleled, unrivalled

transcribe **1.** copy out, engross, note, reproduce, rewrite, set out, take down, transfer, write out **2.** interpret, render, translate, transliterate **3.** record, tape, tape-record

transcript carbon, carbon copy, copy, duplicate, manuscript, note, notes, record, reproduction, transcription, translation, transliteration, version

transfer 1. *verb* carry, change, consign, convey, displace, hand over, make over, move, pass on, relocate, remove, shift, translate, transmit, transplant, transport, transpose, turn over 2. *noun* change, displacement, handover, move, relocation, removal, shift, transference, translation, transmission, transposition

transfigure alter, apotheosize, change, convert, exalt, glorify, idealize, metamorphose, transform, transmute

transfix 1. engross, fascinate, halt *or* stop in one's tracks, hold, hypnotize, mesmerize, paralyse, petrify, rivet the attention of, root to the spot, spellbind, stop dead, stun 2. fix, impale, pierce, puncture, run through, skewer, spear, spit, transpierce
Antonyms (*sense 1*) bore, fatigue, tire, weary

transform alter, change, convert, make over, metamorphose, reconstruct, remodel, renew, revolutionize, transfigure, translate, transmogrify (*jocular*), transmute

transformation alteration, change, conversion, metamorphosis, radical change, renewal, revolution, revolutionary change, sea change, transfiguration, transmogrification (*jocular*), transmutation

transfuse permeate, pervade, spread over, suffuse

transgress be out of order, break, break the law, contravene, defy, disobey, do *or* go wrong, encroach, err, exceed, fall from grace, go astray, go beyond, infringe, lapse, misbehave, offend, overstep, sin, trespass, violate

transgression breach, contravention, crime, encroachment, error, fault, infraction, infringement, iniquity, lapse, misbehaviour, misdeed, misdemeanour, offence, peccadillo, sin, trespass, violation, wrong, wrongdoing

transgressor criminal, culprit, delinquent, evildoer, felon, lawbreaker, malefactor, miscreant, offender, sinner, trespasser, villain, wrongdoer

transience brevity, briefness, ephemerality, evanescence, fleetingness, fugacity, fugitiveness, impermanence, momentariness, shortness, transitoriness

transient brief, ephemeral, evanescent, fleeting, flying, fugacious, fugitive, here today and gone tomorrow, impermanent, momentary, passing, short, short-lived, short-term, temporary, transitory
Antonyms abiding, constant, durable, enduring, eternal, imperishable, long-lasting, long-term, permanent, perpetual, persistent, undying

transit *noun* 1. carriage, conveyance, crossing, motion, movement, passage, portage, shipment, transfer, transport, transportation, travel, traverse 2. alteration, change, changeover, conversion, shift, transition 3. **in transit** during passage, en route, on the journey, on the move, on the road, on the way, while travelling *~verb* 4. cross, journey, move, pass, travel, traverse

transition alteration, change, changeover, conversion, development, evolution, flux, metamorphosis, metastasis, passage, passing, progression, shift, transit, transmutation, upheaval

transitional changing, developmental, fluid, intermediate, passing, provisional, temporary, transitionary, unsettled

transitory brief, ephemeral, evanescent, fleeting, flying, fugacious, here today and gone tomorrow, impermanent, momentary, passing, short, short-lived, short-term, temporary, transient
Antonyms abiding, enduring, eternal, everlasting, lasting, long-lived, long-term, permanent, perpetual, persistent, undying

translate 1. construe, convert, decipher, decode, interpret, paraphrase, render, transcribe, transliterate 2. elucidate, explain, make clear, paraphrase, put in plain English, simplify, spell out, state in layman's language 3. alter, change, convert, metamorphose, transfigure, transform, transmute, turn 4. carry, convey, move, remove, send, transfer, transplant, transport, transpose

translation 1. construction, decoding, gloss, interpretation, paraphrase, rendering, rendition, transcription, transliteration, version 2. elucidation, explanation, paraphrase, rephrasing, rewording, simplification 3. alteration, change, conversion, metamorphosis, transfiguration, transformation, transmutation 4. conveyance, move, removal, transference, transposition

Translations, like wives, are seldom faithful if they are in the least attractive
Roy Campbell *The Poetry Review*

Some hold translation not unlike to be
The wrong side of a Turkish tapestry
Julia Ward Howe *Familiar Letters*

translator interpreter, linguist, metaphrast, paraphrast

translucent clear, diaphanous, limpid, lucent, pellucid, semitransparent

transmigration journey, metempsychosis, migration, movement, passage, rebirth, reincarnation, travel

transmission 1. carriage, communication, conveyance, diffusion, dispatch, dissemination, remission, sending, shipment, spread, transfer, transference, transport 2. broadcasting, dissemination, putting out, relaying, sending, showing **3.** broadcast, programme, show

transmit 1. bear, carry, communicate, convey, diffuse, dispatch, disseminate, forward, hand down, hand on, impart, pass on, remit, send, spread, take, transfer, transport **2.** broadcast, disseminate, put on the air, radio, relay, send, send out

transmute alchemize, alter, change, convert, metamorphose, remake, transfigure, transform

transparency 1. clarity, clearness, diaphaneity, diaphanousness, filminess, gauziness, limpidity, limpidness, pellucidity, pellucidness, sheerness, translucence, translucency, transparence **2.** apparentness, distinctness, explicitness, obviousness, patentness, perspicuousness, plainness, unambiguousness, visibility **3.** candidness, directness, forthrightness, frankness, openness, straightforwardness **4.** photograph, slide

Antonyms (*sense 1*) ambiguity, cloudiness, murkiness, obscurity, opacity, unclearness, vagueness

transparent 1. clear, crystal clear, crystalline, diaphanous, filmy, gauzy, limpid, lucent, lucid, pellucid, see-through, sheer, translucent, transpicuous **2.** apparent, as plain as the nose on one's face (*informal*), bold, distinct, easy, evident, explicit, manifest, obvious, patent, perspicuous, plain, recognizable, unambiguous, understandable, undisguised, visible **3.** candid, direct, forthright, frank, open, plain-spoken, straight, straightforward, unambiguous, unequivocal

Antonyms ambiguous, cloudy, deceptive, disingenuous, hidden, muddy, mysterious, opaque, thick, turbid, uncertain, unclear, vague

transpire 1. *informal* arise, befall, chance, come about, come to pass (*archaic*), happen, occur, take place, turn up **2.** become known, be disclosed, be discovered, be made public, come out, come to light, emerge

transplant displace, relocate, remove, resettle, shift, transfer, uproot

transport *verb* **1.** bear, bring, carry, convey, fetch, haul, move, remove, run, ship, take, transfer **2.** banish, deport, exile, sentence to transportation **3.** captivate, carry away, delight, electrify, enchant, enrapture, entrance, move, ravish, spellbind ~*noun* **4.** conveyance, transportation, vehicle, wheels (*informal*) **5.** carriage, conveyance, removal, shipment, shipping, transference, transportation **6.** cloud nine (*informal*), enchantment, euphoria, heaven, rapture, seventh heaven **7.** bliss, delight, ecstasy, happiness, ravishment

Antonyms (*sense 6*) blues (*informal*), depression, despondency, doldrums, dumps (*informal*), melancholy

transpose alter, change, exchange, interchange, move, rearrange, relocate, reorder, shift, substitute, swap (*informal*), switch, transfer

transverse athwart, crossways, crosswise, diagonal, oblique

trap *noun* **1.** ambush, gin, net, noose, pitfall, snare, springe, toils **2.** ambush, artifice, deception, device, ruse, stratagem, subterfuge, trick, wile ~*verb* **3.** catch, corner, enmesh, ensnare, entrap, snare, take **4.** ambush, beguile, deceive, dupe, ensnare, inveigle, trick

trapped ambushed, at bay, beguiled, caught, cornered, cut off, deceived, duped, ensnared, in a tight corner, in a tight spot, inveigled, netted, snared, stuck (*informal*), surrounded, tricked, with one's back to the wall

trappings accoutrements, adornments, bells and whistles, decorations, dress, equipment, finery, fittings, fixtures, fripperies, furnishings, gear, livery, ornaments, panoply, paraphernalia, raiment (*archaic or poetic*), things, trimmings

trash 1. balderdash, balls (*taboo slang*), bilge (*informal*), bosh (*informal*), bull (*slang*), bullshit (*taboo slang*), bunkum *or* buncombe (*chiefly U.S.*), cobblers (*Brit. taboo slang*), crap (*slang*), drivel, eyewash (*informal*), foolish talk, garbage (*informal*), guff (*slang*), hogwash, hokum (*slang, chiefly U.S. & Canad.*), horsefeathers (*U.S. slang*), hot air (*informal*), inanity, moonshine, nonsense, pap, piffle (*informal*), poppycock (*informal*), rot, rubbish, shit (*taboo slang*), tommyrot, tosh (*slang, chiefly Brit.*), tripe (*informal*), trumpery, twaddle **2.** dreck (*slang, chiefly U.S.*), dregs, dross, garbage, junk (*informal*), litter, off-scourings, refuse, rubbish, sweepings, waste

Antonyms (*sense 1*) logic, reason, sense, significance

trashy brummagem, catchpenny, cheap, cheap-jack (*informal*), chickenshit (*U.S. slang*), crappy (*slang*), flimsy, inferior, meretricious, of a sort *or* of sorts, poxy (*slang*), rubbishy, shabby, shoddy, tawdry, thrown together, tinsel, worthless

Antonyms A1 *or* A-one (*informal*), excellent, exceptional, first-class, first-rate, outstanding, superlative

trauma agony, anguish, damage, disturbance, hurt, injury, jolt, ordeal, pain, shock, strain, suffering, torture, upheaval, upset, wound

traumatic agonizing, damaging, disturbing, hurtful, injurious, painful, scarring, shocking, upsetting, wounding

Antonyms calming, healing, helpful, relaxing, therapeutic, wholesome

travail *noun* **1.** distress, drudgery, effort, exertion, grind (*informal*), hardship, hard work, labour, pain, slavery, slog, strain, stress, suffering, sweat, tears, toil **2.** birth pangs, childbirth, labour, labour pains *~verb* **3.** drudge, grind (*informal*), labour, slave, slog, suffer, sweat, toil

travel *verb* **1.** cross, go, journey, make a journey, make one's way, move, proceed, progress, ramble, roam, rove, take a trip, tour, traverse, trek, voyage, walk, wander, wend **2.** be transmitted, carry, get through, move *~noun* **3.** *usually plural* excursion, expedition, globetrotting, journey, movement, passage, peregrination, ramble, tour, touring, trip, voyage, walk, wandering

I'll put a girdle round the earth
In forty minutes
William Shakespeare *A Midsummer Night's Dream*

I have recently been all round the world and have formed a very poor opinion of it
Sir Thomas Beecham

They change their clime, but not their minds, who rush across the sea
Horace *Epistles*

Whenever I prepare for a journey I prepare as though for death
Katherine Mansfield *Journal*

A man who has not seen Italy, is always conscious of an inferiority, from his not having seen what it is expected a man should see. The grand object of travelling is to see the shores of the Mediterranean
Dr. Johnson

For my part, I travel not to go anywhere, but to go. I travel for travel's sake. The great affair is to move
Robert Louis Stevenson *Travels with a Donkey*

Travel broadens the mind

traveller **1.** excursionist, explorer, globetrotter, gypsy, hiker, holiday-maker, journeyer, migrant, nomad, passenger, tourist, tripper, voyager, wanderer, wayfarer **2.** agent, commercial traveller, rep, representative, salesman, travelling salesman

travelling *adjective* itinerant, migrant, migratory, mobile, moving, nomadic, peripatetic, restless, roaming, roving, touring, unsettled, wandering, wayfaring

traverse **1.** bridge, cover, cross, cut across, go across, go over, make one's way across, negotiate, pass over, ply, range, roam, span, travel over, wander **2.** balk, contravene, counter, counteract, deny, frustrate, go against, hinder, impede, obstruct, oppose, thwart **3.** check, consider, examine, eye, inspect, investigate, look into, look over, pore over, range over, review, scan, scrutinize, study

travesty **1.** *noun* burlesque, caricature, distortion, lampoon, mockery, parody, perversion, send-up (*Brit. informal*), sham, spoof (*informal*), takeoff (*informal*) **2.** *verb* burlesque, caricature, deride, distort, lampoon, make a mockery of, make fun of, mock, parody, pervert, ridicule, send up (*Brit. informal*), sham, spoof (*informal*), take off (*informal*)

treacherous **1.** deceitful, disloyal, double-crossing (*informal*), double-dealing, duplicitous, faithless, false, perfidious, recreant (*archaic*), traitorous, treasonable, unfaithful, unreliable, untrue, untrustworthy **2.** dangerous, deceptive, hazardous, icy, perilous, precarious, risky, slippery, slippy (*informal or dialect*), tricky, unreliable, unsafe, unstable

Antonyms dependable, faithful, loyal, reliable, safe, true, trustworthy

treachery betrayal, disloyalty, double-cross (*informal*), double-dealing, duplicity, faithlessness, infidelity, perfidiousness, perfidy, stab in the back, treason

Antonyms allegiance, dependability, faithfulness, fealty, fidelity, loyalty, reliability

tread *verb* **1.** hike, march, pace, plod, stamp, step, stride, tramp, trudge, walk **2.** crush underfoot, squash, trample **3.** bear down, crush, oppress, quell, repress, ride roughshod over, subdue, subjugate, suppress **4. tread on someone's toes** affront, annoy, bruise, disgruntle, get someone's back up, hurt, hurt someone's feelings, infringe, injure, irk, offend, vex *~noun* **5.** footfall, footstep, gait, pace, step, stride, walk

treason disaffection, disloyalty, duplicity, lese-majesty, mutiny, perfidy, sedition, subversion, traitorousness, treachery

Antonyms allegiance, faithfulness, fealty, fidelity, loyalty, patriotism

Treason doth never prosper, what's the reason
For if it prosper, none dare call it treason
Sir John Harington *Epigrams*

treasonable disloyal, false, mutinous, perfidious, seditious, subversive, traitorous, treacherous, treasonous

Antonyms dependable, faithful, loyal, patriotic, reliable, trustworthy

treasure *noun* **1.** cash, fortune, funds, gold, jewels, money, riches, valuables, wealth **2.** apple of one's eye, best thing since sliced bread (*informal*), darling, gem, greatest thing since sliced bread (*informal*), jewel, nonpareil, paragon, pearl, precious, pride and joy, prize *~verb* **3.** adore, cherish, dote upon, esteem, hold dear, idolize, love, prize, revere, value, venerate, worship **4.** accumulate, cache, collect, garner, hoard, husband, lay up, salt away, save, stash (away) (*informal*), store up

treasury **1.** bank, cache, hoard, repository, store, storehouse, vault **2.** assets, capital, coffers, exchequer, finances, funds, money, resources, revenues

treat *noun* 1. banquet, celebration, entertainment, feast, gift, party, refreshment 2. delight, enjoyment, fun, gratification, joy, pleasure, satisfaction, surprise, thrill *~verb* 3. act towards, behave towards, consider, deal with, handle, look upon, manage, regard, use 4. apply treatment to, attend to, care for, doctor, medicate, nurse 5. buy for, entertain, feast, foot *or* pay the bill, give, lay on, pay for, provide, regale, stand (*informal*), take out, wine and dine 6. be concerned with, contain, deal with, discourse upon, discuss, go into, touch upon 7. bargain, come to terms, confer, have talks, make terms, negotiate, parley

treatise disquisition, dissertation, essay, exposition, monograph, pamphlet, paper, study, thesis, tract, work, writing

treatment 1. care, cure, healing, medication, medicine, remedy, surgery, therapy 2. action towards, behaviour towards, conduct, dealing, handling, management, manipulation, reception, usage

treaty agreement, alliance, bargain, bond, compact, concordat, contract, convention, covenant, entente, pact

tree

Related adjectives: arboreal, arboreous

Trees

acacia
akee
alder
almond
aloe
apple
apricot
ash
aspen
balsa
banana
banyan
baobab
bay
beech
birch
bonsai
box
brazil
bunya
butternut
cacao
carob
cashew
cassia
cedar
cedar of Lebanon
cherry
chestnut
cinnamon
citrus
coco
coconut
coolabah
cork oak
cypress
date palm
deal
dogwood
Douglas fir
ebony
elder
elm
eucalyptus *or* eucalypt
fig
fir
grapefruit
ground ash
ground oak
guava
gum
gympie
hawthorn
hazel
hemlock
hickory
holly
hornbeam
horse chestnut
ilex
ironwood
jacaranda
Judas tree
juniper
karri
kauri
laburnum
larch
laurel
lemon
lilac
lime
lind
linden
lotus
macrocarpa
magnolia
mahogany
mango
mangrove
maple
melaleuca
mimosa
monkey puzzle *or* Chile pine
mountain ash
mulberry
nutmeg
oak
olive
orange
osier
palm
papaya
paperbark
pawpaw *or* papaw
peach
pear
persimmon
pine
plane
plum
pomegranate
poplar
pussy willow
quince
raffia
redwood
rosewood
rowan
sandalwood
sassafras
Scots fir
Scots pine
sequoia
silver birch
spruce
stringy-bark
sycamore
tamarind
teak
walnut
weeping willow
white ash
whitebeam
willow
witch
witch elm
yew
ylang-ylang
yucca

The tree is known by its fruit
Bible: St. Matthew

I think that I shall never see
A poem lovely as a tree
Joyce Kilmer *Trees*

Of all the trees that grow so fair,
Old England to adorn,
Greater are none beneath the Sun,
Than Oak, and Ash, and Thorn
Rudyard Kipling *Puck of Pook's Hill*

trek 1. *noun* expedition, footslog, hike, journey, long haul, march, odyssey, safari, slog, tramp 2. *verb* footslog, hike, journey, march, plod, range, roam, rove, slog, traipse (*informal*), tramp, trudge, yomp

tremble 1. *verb* oscillate, quake, quake in one's boots, quiver, rock, shake, shake in one's boots, shake in one's shoes, shiver, shudder, teeter, totter, vibrate, wobble 2. *noun* oscillation, quake, quiver, shake, shiver, shudder, tremor, vibration, wobble

tremendous 1. appalling, awesome, awful, colossal, deafening, dreadful, enormous, fearful, formidable, frightful, gargantuan, gigantic, great, huge, immense, mammoth, monstrous, prodigious, stellar (*informal*), stupendous, ter~

rible, terrific, titanic, towering, vast, whopping (*informal*) **2.** *informal* ace (*informal*), amazing, awesome (*slang*), bodacious (*slang, chiefly U.S.*), boffo (*slang*), brill (*informal*), brilliant, chillin' (*U.S. slang*), cracking (*Brit. informal*), excellent, exceptional, extraordinary, fabulous (*informal*), fantastic (*informal*), great, incredible, jim-dandy (*slang*), marvellous, mean (*slang*), sensational (*informal*), sovereign, super (*informal*), terrific (*informal*), topping (*Brit. slang*), wonderful
Antonyms abysmal, appalling, average, awful, diminutive, dreadful, little, mediocre, minuscule, minute, no great shakes (*informal*), ordinary, rotten, run-of-the-mill, small, so-so, terrible, tiny

tremor **1.** agitation, quaking, quaver, quiver, quivering, shake, shaking, shiver, tremble, trembling, trepidation, vibration, wobble **2.** earthquake, quake (*informal*), shock

tremulous aflutter, afraid, agitated, agog, anxious, aquiver, excited, fearful, frightened, jittery (*informal*), jumpy, nervous, quavering, quivering, quivery, scared, shaking, shivering, timid, trembling, vibrating, wavering

trench channel, cut, ditch, drain, earthwork, entrenchment, excavation, fosse, furrow, gutter, pit, trough, waterway

trenchant **1.** acerbic, acid, acidulous, acute, astringent, biting, caustic, cutting, hurtful, incisive, keen, mordacious, mordant, penetrating, piquant, pointed, pungent, sarcastic, scathing, severe, sharp, tart, vitriolic **2.** driving, effective, effectual, emphatic, energetic, forceful, potent, powerful, strong, vigorous **3.** clear, clear-cut, crisp, distinct, distinctly defined, explicit, salient, unequivocal, well-defined
Antonyms (*sense 1*) appeasing, kind, mollifying, soothing (*sense 3*) ill-defined, indistinct, nebulous, obscure, unclear, vague, woolly

trend *noun* **1.** bias, course, current, direction, drift, flow, inclination, leaning, tendency **2.** craze, fad (*informal*), fashion, look, mode, rage, style, thing, vogue *~verb* **3.** bend, flow, head, incline, lean, run, stretch, swing, tend, turn, veer

trendsetter arbiter of taste, avant-gardist, leader of fashion, pacemaker, pacesetter

trendy **1.** *adjective* fashionable, flash (*informal*), in (*slang*), in fashion, in vogue, latest, modish, now (*informal*), stylish, up to the minute, voguish, with it (*informal*) **2.** *noun* poser (*informal*), pseud (*informal*)

trepidation agitation, alarm, anxiety, apprehension, blue funk (*informal*), butterflies (*informal*), cold feet (*informal*), cold sweat (*informal*), consternation, dismay, disquiet, disturbance, dread, emotion, excitement, fear, fright, jitters (*informal*), nervousness, palpitation, perturbation, quivering, shaking, the heebie-jeebies (*slang*), trembling, tremor, uneasiness, worry
Antonyms aplomb, calm, composure, confidence, coolness, equanimity, self-assurance

trespass *verb* **1.** encroach, infringe, intrude, invade, obtrude, poach **2.** *archaic* offend, sin, transgress, violate, wrong *~noun* **3.** encroachment, infringement, intrusion, invasion, poaching, unlawful entry, wrongful entry **4.** breach, crime, delinquency, error, evildoing, fault, infraction, iniquity, injury, misbehaviour, misconduct, misdeed, misdemeanour, offence, sin, transgression, wrongdoing

trespasser **1.** infringer, interloper, intruder, invader, poacher, unwelcome visitor **2.** *archaic* criminal, delinquent, evildoer, malefactor, offender, sinner, transgressor, wrongdoer

tress braid, curl, lock, pigtail, plait, ringlet

triad threesome, trilogy, trine, trinity, trio, triple, triplet, triptych, triumvirate, triune

trial *noun* **1.** assay, audition, check, dry run (*informal*), examination, experience, experiment, probation, proof, test, testing, test-run **2.** contest, hearing, industrial tribunal, judicial examination, litigation, tribunal **3.** attempt, crack (*informal*), effort, endeavour, go (*informal*), shot (*informal*), stab (*informal*), try, venture, whack (*informal*) **4.** adversity, affliction, burden, cross to bear, distress, grief, hardship, hard times, load, misery, ordeal, pain, suffering, tribulation, trouble, unhappiness, vexation, woe, wretchedness **5.** bane, bother, drag (*informal*), hassle (*informal*), irritation, nuisance, pain in the arse (*taboo informal*), pain in the neck (*informal*), pest, plague (*informal*), thorn in one's flesh, vexation *~adjective* **6.** experimental, exploratory, pilot, probationary, provisional, testing

tribe blood, caste, clan, class, division, dynasty, ethnic group, family, gens, house, people, race, seed (*chiefly biblical*), sept, stock

tribulation adversity, affliction, bad luck, blow, bummer (*slang*), burden, care, cross to bear, curse, distress, grief, hardship, hassle (*informal*), heartache, ill fortune, misery, misfortune, ordeal, pain, reverse, sorrow, suffering, trial, trouble, unhappiness, vexation, woe, worry, wretchedness
Antonyms blessing, bliss, ease, good fortune, happiness, joy, pleasure, rest

tribunal bar, bench, court, hearing, industrial tribunal, judgment seat, judicial examination, trial

tribute **1.** accolade, acknowledgment, applause, commendation, compliment, encomium, esteem, eulogy, gift, gratitude, honour, laudation, panegyric, praise, recognition, respect, testimonial **2.** charge, contribution, customs,

duty, excise, homage, impost, offering, payment, ransom, subsidy, tax, toll
Antonyms (*sense 1*) blame, complaint, condemnation, criticism, disapproval, reproach, reproof

trice bat of an eye (*informal*), flash, instant, jiffy (*informal*), minute, moment, second, shake (*informal*), split second, tick (*Brit. informal*), twinkling, twinkling of an eye, two shakes of a lamb's tail (*informal*)

trick *noun* **1.** artifice, canard, con (*slang*), deceit, deception, device, dodge, feint, fraud, gimmick, hoax, imposition, imposture, manoeuvre, ploy, ruse, scam (*slang*), sting (*informal*), stratagem, subterfuge, swindle, trap, wile **2.** antic, cantrip (*Scot.*), caper, device, feat, frolic, gag (*informal*), gambol, jape, joke, juggle, legerdemain, leg-pull (*Brit. informal*), practical joke, prank, put-on (*slang*), sleight of hand, stunt **3.** art, command, craft, device, expertise, gift, hang (*informal*), knack, know-how (*informal*), secret, skill, technique **4.** characteristic, crotchet, foible, habit, idiosyncrasy, mannerism, peculiarity, practice, quirk, trait **5. do the trick** *informal* be effective *or* effectual, have effect, produce the desired result, work *~verb* **6.** bamboozle (*informal*), cheat, con (*informal*), deceive, defraud, delude, dupe, fool, gull (*archaic*), have (someone) on, hoax, hoodwink, impose upon, kid (*informal*), mislead, pull a fast one on (*informal*), pull the wool over (someone's) eyes, put one over on (someone) (*informal*), stiff (*slang*), sting (*informal*), swindle, take in (*informal*), trap

I know a trick worth two of that
William Shakespeare *Henry IV, part I*

trickery cheating, chicanery, con (*informal*), deceit, deception, dishonesty, double-dealing, fraud, funny business, guile, hanky-panky (*informal*), hoax, hokum (*slang, chiefly U.S. & Canad.*), imposture, jiggery-pokery (*informal, chiefly Brit.*), monkey business (*informal*), pretence, skulduggery (*informal*), swindling
Antonyms artlessness, candour, directness, frankness, honesty, openness, straightforwardness, uprightness

trickle 1. *verb* crawl, creep, dribble, drip, drop, exude, ooze, percolate, run, seep, stream **2.** *noun* dribble, drip, seepage

trick out *or* **up** adorn, array, attire, bedeck, deck out, doll up (*slang*), do up (*informal*), dress up, get up (*informal*), ornament, prank, prink

trickster cheat, chiseller (*informal*), con man (*informal*), deceiver, fraud, fraudster, grifter (*slang, chiefly U.S. & Canad.*), hoaxer, impostor, joker, practical joker, pretender, swindler

tricky 1. complicated, delicate, difficult, knotty, problematic, risky, sticky (*informal*), thorny, ticklish, touch-and-go **2.** artful, crafty, cunning, deceitful, deceptive, devious, foxy, scheming, slippery, sly, subtle, wily
Antonyms (*sense 1*) clear, easy, obvious, simple, straightforward, uncomplicated (*sense 2*) above board, artless, direct, genuine, honest, ingenuous, open, sincere, truthful

trifle *noun* **1.** bagatelle, bauble, child's play (*informal*), gewgaw, knick-knack, nothing, plaything, toy, triviality **2.** bit, dash, drop, jot, little, pinch, spot, touch, trace *~verb* **3.** amuse oneself, coquet, dally, dawdle, flirt, fritter, idle, mess about, palter, play, play fast and loose (*informal*), toy, wanton, waste, waste time

a snapper-up of unconsidered trifles
William Shakespeare *The Winter's Tale*

trifler dilettante, good-for-nothing, idler, layabout, loafer, ne'er-do-well, skiver (*Brit. slang*), waster

trifling empty, footling (*informal*), frivolous, idle, inconsiderable, insignificant, measly, minuscule, negligible, nickel-and-dime (*U.S. slang*), paltry, petty, piddling (*informal*), puny, shallow, silly, slight, small, tiny, trivial, unimportant, valueless, worthless
Antonyms considerable, crucial, important, large, major, serious, significant, vital, weighty

trigger *verb* activate, bring about, cause, elicit, generate, give rise to, produce, prompt, provoke, set in motion, set off, spark off, start
Antonyms bar, block, hinder, impede, inhibit, obstruct, prevent, repress, stop

trim *adjective* **1.** compact, dapper, natty (*informal*), neat, nice, orderly, shipshape, smart, soigné *or* soignée, spick-and-span, spruce, tidy, trig (*archaic or dialect*), well-groomed, well-ordered, well turned-out **2.** fit, shapely, sleek, slender, slim, streamlined, svelte, willowy *~verb* **3.** barber, clip, crop, curtail, cut, cut back, dock, even up, lop, pare, prune, shave, shear, tidy **4.** adorn, array, beautify, bedeck, deck out, decorate, dress, embellish, embroider, garnish, ornament, trick out **5.** adjust, arrange, balance, distribute, order, prepare, settle *~noun* **6.** adornment, border, decoration, edging, embellishment, frill, fringe, garnish, ornamentation, piping, trimming **7.** condition, fettle, fitness, form, health, order, repair, shape (*informal*), situation, state **8.** clipping, crop, cut, pruning, shave, shearing, tidying up, trimming **9.** array, attire, dress, equipment, gear, trappings
Antonyms (*sense 1*) disarrayed, disorderly, messy, scruffy, shabby, sloppy, ungroomed, unkempt, untidy

trimming 1. adornment, border, braid, decoration, edging, embellishment, festoon, frill, fringe, garnish, ornamentation, piping **2.** *plu~*

ral accessories, accompaniments, appurtenances, extras, frills, garnish, ornaments, paraphernalia, trappings **3.** *plural* brash, clippings, cuttings, ends, parings, shavings

trinity threesome, triad, trilogy, trine, trio, triple, triplet, triptych, triumvirate, triune

trinket bagatelle, bauble, bibelot, gewgaw, gimcrack, kickshaw, knick-knack, nothing, ornament, piece of bric-a-brac, toy, trifle

trio threesome, triad, trilogy, trine, trinity, triple, triplet, triptych, triumvirate, triune

trip *noun* **1.** errand, excursion, expedition, foray, jaunt, journey, outing, ramble, run, tour, travel, voyage **2.** bloomer (*Brit. informal*), blunder, boob (*Brit. slang*), error, fall, false move, false step, faux pas, indiscretion, lapse, misstep, slip, stumble ~*verb* **3.** blunder, boob (*Brit. slang*), err, fall, go wrong, lapse, lose one's balance, lose one's footing, make a false move, make a faux pas, miscalculate, misstep, slip, slip up (*informal*), stumble, tumble **4.** catch out, confuse, disconcert, put off one's stride, throw off, trap, unsettle **5.** go, ramble, tour, travel, voyage **6.** caper, dance, flit, frisk, gambol, hop, skip, spring, tread lightly **7.** *informal* get high (*informal*), get stoned (*slang*), take drugs, turn on (*slang*) **8.** activate, engage, flip, pull, release, set off, switch on, throw, turn on

tripe balderdash, balls (*taboo slang*), bilge (*informal*), bosh (*informal*), bull (*slang*), bullshit (*taboo slang*), bunkum *or* buncombe (*chiefly U.S.*), claptrap (*informal*), cobblers (*Brit. taboo slang*), crap (*slang*), drivel, eyewash (*informal*), foolish talk, garbage (*informal*), guff (*slang*), hogwash, hokum (*slang, chiefly U.S. & Canad.*), horsefeathers (*U.S. slang*), hot air (*informal*), inanity, moonshine, nonsense, pap, piffle (*informal*), poppycock (*informal*), rot, rubbish, shit (*taboo slang*), tommyrot, tosh (*slang, chiefly Brit.*), trash, trumpery, twaddle

triple 1. *adjective* threefold, three times as much, three-way, tripartite **2.** *noun* threesome, triad, trilogy, trine, trinity, trio, triplet, triumvirate, triune **3.** *verb* increase threefold, treble, triplicate

triplet threesome, triad, trilogy, trine, trinity, trio, triple, triumvirate, triune

tripper excursionist, holiday-maker, journeyer, sightseer, tourist, voyager

trite banal, bromidic, clichéd, common, commonplace, corny (*slang*), dull, hack, hackneyed, ordinary, pedestrian, routine, run-of-the-mill, stale, stereotyped, stock, threadbare, tired, uninspired, unoriginal, worn
Antonyms exciting, fresh, interesting, new, novel, original, out-of-the-ordinary, uncommon, unexpected, unfamiliar

triturate beat, bray, bruise, comminute, crush, grind, masticate, pound, powder, pulverize

triumph *noun* **1.** elation, exultation, happiness, joy, jubilation, pride, rejoicing **2.** accomplishment, achievement, ascendancy, attainment, conquest, coup, feat, feather in one's cap, hit (*informal*), mastery, sensation, smash (*informal*), smasheroo (*slang*), smash-hit (*informal*), success, *tour de force*, victory, walkover (*informal*) ~*verb* **3.** *often with* **over** best, carry the day, come out on top (*informal*), dominate, flourish, get the better of, overcome, overwhelm, prevail, prosper, subdue, succeed, take the honours, thrive, vanquish, win **4.** celebrate, crow, drool, exult, gloat, glory, jubilate, rejoice, revel, swagger
Antonyms (*sense 2*) catastrophe, defeat, disaster, failure, fiasco, flop (*informal*), washout (*informal*) (*sense 3*) come a cropper (*informal*), fail, fall, flop (*informal*), lose

triumphant boastful, celebratory, cock-a-hoop, conquering, dominant, elated, exultant, glorious, jubilant, proud, rejoicing, successful, swaggering, triumphal, undefeated, victorious, winning
Antonyms beaten, defeated, embarrassed, humbled, humiliated, shamed, unsuccessful

trivia details, minutiae, petty details, trifles, trivialities
Antonyms basics, brass tacks (*informal*), core, essentials, fundamentals, nitty-gritty (*informal*), rudiments

trivial chickenshit (*U.S. slang*), commonplace, everyday, frivolous, incidental, inconsequential, inconsiderable, insignificant, little, meaningless, minor, negligible, nickel-and-dime (*U.S. slang*), paltry, petty, puny, slight, small, trifling, trite, unimportant, valueless, wanky (*taboo slang*), worthless
Antonyms considerable, crucial, essential, important, profound, serious, significant, uncommon, unusual, vital, weighty, worthwhile

What mighty contests rise from trivial things
Alexander Pope *The Rape of the Lock*

triviality 1. frivolity, inconsequentiality, insignificance, littleness, meaninglessness, much ado about nothing, negligibility, paltriness, pettiness, slightness, smallness, triteness, unimportance, valuelessness, worthlessness **2.** detail, no big thing, no great matter, nothing, petty detail, technicality, trifle
Antonyms (*sense 1*) consequence, essential, importance, rudiment, significance, value, worth

Little things please little minds

trivialize belittle, laugh off, make light of, minimize, play down, scoff at, underestimate, underplay, undervalue

trollop fallen woman, floozy (*slang*), harlot, hussy, loose woman, prostitute, scrubber (*Brit. & Austral. slang*), slag (*Brit. slang*), slattern, slut, streetwalker, strumpet, tart (*informal*), wanton, whore, working girl (*facetious slang*)

troop *noun* **1.** assemblage, band, bevy, body, bunch (*informal*), company, contingent, crew (*informal*), crowd, drove, flock, gang, gathering, group, herd, horde, multitude, pack, posse (*informal*), squad, swarm, team, throng, unit **2.** *plural* armed forces, army, fighting men, men, military, servicemen, soldiers, soldiery *~verb* **3.** crowd, flock, march, parade, stream, swarm, throng, traipse (*informal*)

trophy award, bays, booty, cup, laurels, memento, prize, souvenir, spoils

tropical hot, humid, lush, steamy, stifling, sultry, sweltering, torrid
Antonyms arctic, chilly, cold, cool, freezing, frosty, frozen, parky (*Brit. informal*)

trot *verb* **1.** canter, go briskly, jog, lope, run, scamper *~noun* **2.** brisk pace, canter, jog, lope, run **3. on the trot** *informal* consecutively, in a row, in succession, one after the other, without break, without interruption

trot out bring forward, bring up, come out with, drag up, exhibit, recite, rehearse, reiterate, relate, repeat

troubadour balladeer, jongleur, lyric poet, minstrel, poet, singer

trouble *noun* **1.** agitation, annoyance, anxiety, bummer (*slang*), disquiet, distress, grief, hardship, hassle (*informal*), heartache, irritation, misfortune, pain, sorrow, suffering, torment, tribulation, vexation, woe, worry **2.** agitation, bother (*informal*), commotion, discontent, discord, disorder, dissatisfaction, disturbance, hassle (*informal*), Pandora's box, row, strife, tumult, unrest **3.** ailment, complaint, defect, disability, disease, disorder, failure, illness, malfunction, upset **4.** bother, concern, danger, deep water (*informal*), difficulty, dilemma, dire straits, hassle (*informal*), hot water (*informal*), mess, nuisance, pest, pickle (*informal*), predicament, problem, scrape (*informal*), spot (*informal*), tight spot **5.** attention, bother, care, effort, exertion, inconvenience, labour, pains, struggle, thought, work *~verb* **6.** afflict, agitate, annoy, bother, discompose, disconcert, disquiet, distress, disturb, faze, fret, grieve, harass, hassle (*informal*), inconvenience, pain, perplex, perturb, pester, plague, put *or* get someone's back up, sadden, torment, upset, vex, worry **7.** be concerned, bother, burden, discomfort, discommode, disturb, impose upon, incommode, inconvenience, put out **8.** exert oneself, go to the effort of, make an effort, take pains, take the time
Antonyms *noun* agreement, comfort, contentment, convenience, ease, facility, good fortune, happiness, harmony, peace, pleasure, tranquillity, unity *~verb* appease, avoid, be unharassed, calm, dodge, ease, mollify, please, relieve, soothe

Man is born unto trouble
Bible: Job

double, double, toil and trouble
William Shakespeare *Macbeth*

Never trouble trouble till trouble troubles you

troublemaker *agent provocateur*, agitator, bad apple (*U.S. informal*), firebrand, incendiary, instigator, meddler, mischief-maker, rabble-rouser, rotten apple (*Brit. informal*), stirrer (*informal*), stormy petrel
Antonyms appeaser, arbitrator, conciliator, pacifier, peace-maker

Better to have him inside the tent pissing out, than outside pissing in
Lyndon B Johnson (of J Edgar Hoover)

troublesome **1.** annoying, arduous, bothersome, burdensome, demanding, difficult, harassing, hard, importunate, inconvenient, irksome, irritating, laborious, oppressive, pestilential, plaguy (*informal*), taxing, tiresome, tricky, trying, upsetting, vexatious, wearisome, worrisome, worrying **2.** disorderly, insubordinate, rebellious, recalcitrant, refractory, rowdy, turbulent, uncooperative, undisciplined, unruly, violent
Antonyms agreeable, calming, congenial, disciplined, eager-to-please, easy, obedient, pleasant, simple, soothing, undemanding, well-behaved

trough **1.** crib, manger, water trough **2.** canal, channel, depression, ditch, duct, flume, furrow, gully, gutter, trench, watercourse

trounce beat, beat (someone) hollow (*Brit. informal*), blow out of the water (*slang*), clobber (*slang*), crush, defeat heavily *or* utterly, drub, give a hiding (*informal*), give a pasting (*slang*), hammer (*informal*), lick (*informal*), make mincemeat of, overwhelm, paste (*slang*), rout, run rings around (*informal*), slaughter (*informal*), stuff (*slang*), tank (*slang*), thrash, walk over (*informal*), wipe the floor with (*informal*)

troupe band, cast, company

trouper actor, artiste, entertainer, performer, player, theatrical, thespian

truancy absence, absence without leave, malingering, shirking, skiving (*Brit. slang*)

truant *noun* **1.** absentee, delinquent, deserter, dodger, malingerer, runaway, shirker, skiver (*Brit. slang*), straggler **2.** *adjective* absent, absent without leave, A.W.O.L., missing, skiving (*Brit. slang*) *~verb* **3.** absent oneself, bob off (*Brit. slang*), bunk off (*slang*), desert, dodge, go missing, malinger, play truant, run away, shirk, skive (*Brit. slang*), wag (*dialect*)

truce armistice, break, ceasefire, cessation, cessation of hostilities, intermission, interval, let-up (*informal*), lull, moratorium, peace, respite, rest, stay, treaty

truck *noun* **1.** commercial goods, commodities, goods, merchandise, stock, stuff, wares **2.** bar~ter, business, buying and selling, commerce, communication, connection, contact, dealings, exchange, relations, trade, traffic *~verb* **3.** bargain, barter, buy and sell, deal, do busi~ness, exchange, have dealings, negotiate, swap, trade, traffic, transact business

truckle bend the knee, bow and scrape, con~cede, cringe, crouch, defer, fawn, give in, give way, knuckle under, kowtow, lick (someone's) boots, pander to, stoop, submit, toady, yield

truculent aggressive, antagonistic, bad-tempered, bellicose, belligerent, combative, contentious, cross, defiant, fierce, hostile, ill-tempered, itching *or* spoiling for a fight (*in~formal*), obstreperous, pugnacious, scrappy (*informal*), sullen, violent
Antonyms agreeable, amiable, civil, co-operative, gentle, good-natured, peaceable, placid

trudge **1.** *verb* clump, drag oneself, footslog, hike, lumber, march, plod, slog, stump, traipse (*informal*), tramp, trek, walk heavily, yomp **2.** *noun* footslog, haul, hike, march, slog, traipse (*informal*), tramp, trek, yomp

true *adjective* **1.** accurate, actual, authentic, bona fide, correct, exact, factual, genuine, le~gitimate, natural, precise, pure, real, right, truthful, valid, veracious, veritable **2.** con~firmed, constant, dedicated, devoted, dutiful, faithful, fast, firm, honest, honourable, loyal, pure, reliable, sincere, staunch, steady, true-blue, trustworthy, trusty, unswerving, upright **3.** accurate, correct, exact, on target, perfect, precise, proper, spot-on (*Brit. informal*), un~erring *~adverb* **4.** honestly, rightly, truthfully, veraciously, veritably **5.** accurately, correctly, on target, perfectly, precisely, properly, un~erringly **6.** **come true** become reality, be granted, be realized, come to pass, happen, occur
Antonyms (*sense 1*) abnormal, artificial, atypical, bogus, counterfeit, erroneous, fake, false, fictional, fictitious, illegitimate, imagi~nary, inaccurate, incorrect, made-up, make-believe, phoney *or* phony (*informal*), pretend~ed, self-styled, spurious, unofficial, untrue, untruthful (*sense 2*) deceitful, disloyal, faith~less, false, treacherous, unreliable, untrue, untrustworthy (*sense 3*) askew, awry, erro~neous, inaccurate, incorrect, untrue

Many a true word is spoken in jest

true-blue confirmed, constant, dedicated, de~voted, dyed-in-the-wool, faithful, loyal, ortho~dox, staunch, trusty, uncompromising, unwa~vering

truism axiom, bromide, cliché, commonplace, platitude, stock phrase, trite saying

truly **1.** accurately, authentically, beyond doubt, beyond question, correctly, exactly, factually, genuinely, in actuality, in fact, in reality, in truth, legitimately, precisely, really, rightly, truthfully, veraciously, veritably, without a doubt **2.** confirmedly, constantly, devotedly, dutifully, faithfully, firmly, honestly, honour~ably, loyally, sincerely, staunchly, steadily, with all one's heart, with dedication, with de~votion **3.** exceptionally, extremely, greatly, in~deed, of course, really, seriously (*informal*), to be sure, verily, very
Antonyms (*sense 1*) doubtfully, falsely, fraudulently, inaccurately, incorrectly, mis~takenly

trump **1.** *noun/verb* ruff **2.** *verb* cap, excel, out~do, score points off, surpass, top

trumped-up concocted, contrived, cooked-up (*informal*), fabricated, fake, false, falsified, in~vented, made-up, manufactured, phoney *or* phony (*informal*), untrue
Antonyms actual, authentic, bona fide, genu~ine, real, sound, true, veritable

trumpery *noun* **1.** balderdash, balls (*taboo slang*), bilge (*informal*), bosh (*informal*), bull (*slang*), bullshit (*taboo slang*), bunkum *or* buncombe (*chiefly U.S.*), claptrap (*informal*), cobblers (*Brit. taboo slang*), crap (*slang*), driv~el, eyewash (*informal*), foolishness, foolish talk, garbage (*informal*), guff (*slang*), hog~wash, hokum (*slang, chiefly U.S. & Canad.*), horsefeathers (*U.S. slang*), hot air (*informal*), idiocy, inanity, moonshine, nonsense, pap, piffle (*informal*), poppycock (*informal*), rot, rubbish, shit (*taboo slang*), stuff, tommyrot, tosh (*slang, chiefly Brit.*), trash, tripe (*infor~mal*), twaddle **2.** bagatelle, bauble, gewgaw, kickshaw, knick-knack, toy, trifle, trinket *~adjective* **3.** brummagem, cheap, flashy, mer~etricious, nasty, rubbishy, shabby, shoddy, tawdry, trashy, trifling, useless, valueless, worthless

trumpet *noun* **1.** bugle, clarion, horn **2.** bay, bellow, call, cry, roar **3.** **blow one's own trumpet** boast, brag, crow, sing one's own praises, vaunt *~verb* **4.** advertise, announce, broadcast, crack up (*informal*), extol, noise abroad, proclaim, publish, shout from the rooftops, sound loudly, tout (*informal*)
Antonyms *verb* conceal, hide, hush up, keep secret, make light of, play down, soft pedal (*informal*)

trump up concoct, contrive, cook up (*informal*),

create, fabricate, fake, invent, make up, manufacture

truncate abbreviate, clip, crop, curtail, cut, cut short, dock, lop, pare, prune, shorten, trim
Antonyms drag out, draw out, extend, lengthen, prolong, protract, spin out, stretch

truncheon baton, club, cudgel, staff

trunk **1**. bole, stalk, stem, stock **2**. body, torso **3**. proboscis, snout **4**. bin, box, case, casket, chest, coffer, crate, kist (*Scot. & northern English dialect*), locker, portmanteau

truss *verb* **1**. bind, bundle, fasten, make fast, pack, pinion, secure, strap, tether, tie *~noun* **2**. beam, brace, buttress, joist, prop, shore, stanchion, stay, strut, support **3**. *Medical* bandage, support **4**. bale, bundle, package, packet

trust *noun* **1**. assurance, belief, certainty, certitude, confidence, conviction, credence, credit, expectation, faith, hope, reliance **2**. duty, obligation, responsibility **3**. care, charge, custody, guard, guardianship, protection, safekeeping, trusteeship *~verb* **4**. assume, believe, expect, hope, presume, suppose, surmise, think likely **5**. bank on, believe, count on, depend on, have faith in, lean on, pin one's faith on, place confidence in, place one's trust in, place reliance on, rely upon, swear by, take as gospel, take at face value **6**. assign, command, commit, confide, consign, delegate, entrust, give, put into the hands of, sign over, turn over
Antonyms *noun* distrust, doubt, fear, incredulity, lack of faith, mistrust, scepticism, suspicion, uncertainty, wariness *~verb* be sceptical of, beware, disbelieve, discredit, distrust, doubt, lack confidence in, lack faith in, mistrust, suspect
Related adjective: fiducial

trustful, trusting confiding, credulous, gullible, innocent, naive, optimistic, simple, unguarded, unsuspecting, unsuspicious, unwary
Antonyms cagey (*informal*), cautious, chary, distrustful, guarded, on one's guard, suspicious, wary

trustworthy dependable, ethical, honest, honourable, level-headed, mature, principled, reliable, reputable, responsible, righteous, sensible, staunch, steadfast, to be trusted, true, trusty, truthful, upright
Antonyms deceitful, dishonest, disloyal, irresponsible, treacherous, undependable, unethical, unprincipled, unreliable, untrustworthy

trusty dependable, faithful, firm, honest, reliable, responsible, solid, staunch, steady, straightforward, strong, true, trustworthy, upright
Antonyms dishonest, irresolute, irresponsible, undependable, unfaithful, unreliable

truth **1**. accuracy, actuality, exactness, fact, factuality, factualness, genuineness, legitimacy, precision, reality, truthfulness, validity, veracity, verity **2**. candour, constancy, dedication, devotion, dutifulness, faith, faithfulness, fidelity, frankness, honesty, integrity, loyalty, naturalism, realism, uprightness **3**. axiom, certainty, fact, law, maxim, proven principle, reality, truism, verity
Antonyms deceit, deception, delusion, dishonesty, error, fabrication, falsehood, falsity, fiction, inaccuracy, invention, legend, lie, make-believe, myth, old wives' tale, untruth

Truth sits upon the lips of dying men
Matthew Arnold *Sohrab and Rustum*

Beauty and Truth, though never found, are worthy to be sought
Robert Williams Buchanan *To David in Heaven*

Beauty is truth, truth beauty
John Keats *Ode on a Grecian Urn*

What is truth? said jesting Pilate; and would not stay for an answer
Francis Bacon *Essays*

Truth can never be told so as to be understood, and not believed
William Blake *Proverbs of Hell*

Truth never hurts the teller
Robert Browning *Fifine at the Fair*

Truth is within ourselves
Robert Browning *Paracelsus*

'Tis strange - but true; for truth is always strange; Stranger than fiction
Lord Byron *Don Juan*

It is the customary fate of new truths to begin as heresies and to end as superstitions
T.H. Huxley *Science and Culture*

The first casualty when war comes is truth
Philander Chase Johnson *Shooting Stars*

There was things that he stretched, but mainly he told the truth
Mark Twain *The Adventures of Huckleberry Finn*

The truth is rarely pure, and never simple
Oscar Wilde *The Importance of Being Earnest*

The truth is a terrible weapon of aggression. It is possible to lie, and even to murder, for the truth
Alfred Adler *The Problem of Neurosis*

The truth which makes men free is for the most part the truth which men prefer not to hear
Herbert Agar *A Time for Greatness*

When you have eliminated the impossible, whatever remains, however improbable, must be the truth
Sir Arthur Conan Doyle *The Sign of Four*

Truth...may bear all lights
3rd Earl of Shaftesbury *Sensus Communis*

The truth shall make you free
Bible: St. John

When you want to fool the world, tell the truth
Otto von Bismarck

It is always the best policy to speak the truth, unless of course you are an exceptionally good liar
Jerome K. Jerome

Irrationally held truths may be more harmful than reasoned errors
T.H. Huxley *Science and Culture and Other Essays*

Truth is the cry of all, but the game of the few
Bishop George Berkeley *Siris*

A truth that's told with bad intent
Beats all the lies you can invent
William Blake *Auguries of Innocence*

Truth lies within a little and certain compass, but error is immense
Henry St. John, 1st Viscount Bolingbroke *Reflections upon Exile*

There is truth in wine (in vino veritas)

truthful accurate, candid, correct, exact, faithful, forthright, frank, honest, literal, naturalistic, plain-spoken, precise, realistic, reliable, sincere, straight, straightforward, true, trustworthy, upfront (*informal*), veracious, veritable
Antonyms deceptive, dishonest, fabricated, false, fictional, fictitious, inaccurate, incorrect, insincere, lying, made-up, untrue, untruthful

truthless deceitful, deceptive, dishonest, faithless, false, fraudulent, insincere, lying, mendacious, perjured, treacherous, untrue, untrustworthy

try *verb* **1.** aim, attempt, bend over backwards (*informal*), break one's neck (*informal*), bust a gut (*informal*), do one's best, do one's damnedest (*informal*), endeavour, essay, exert oneself, give it one's all (*informal*), give it one's best shot (*informal*), go for broke (*slang*), go for it (*informal*), have a go (crack (*informal*), shot (*informal*), stab (*informal*), whack (*informal*)) (*informal*), knock oneself out (*informal*), make an all-out effort (*informal*), make an attempt, make an effort, move heaven and earth, rupture oneself (*informal*), seek, strive, struggle, undertake **2.** appraise, check out, evaluate, examine, experiment, inspect, investigate, prove, put to the test, sample, taste, test **3.** afflict, annoy, inconvenience, irk, irritate, pain, plague, strain, stress, tax, tire, trouble, upset, vex, weary **4.** adjudge, adjudicate, examine, hear *~noun* **5.** attempt, crack (*informal*), effort, endeavour, essay, go (*informal*), shot (*informal*), stab (*informal*), whack (*informal*) **6.** appraisal, evaluation, experiment, inspection, sample, taste, test, trial

trying aggravating (*informal*), annoying, arduous, bothersome, difficult, exasperating, fatiguing, hard, irksome, irritating, stressful, taxing, tiresome, tough, troublesome, upsetting, vexing, wearisome
Antonyms calming, easy, no bother, no trouble, painless, simple, straightforward, undemanding

try out appraise, check out, evaluate, experiment with, inspect, put into practice, put to the test, sample, taste, test

tsar, czar autocrat, despot, emperor, head, leader, overlord, ruler, sovereign, tyrant

tubby chubby, corpulent, fat, obese, overweight, paunchy, plump, podgy, portly, roly-poly, stout

tuck *verb* **1.** fold, gather, insert, push *~noun* **2.** fold, gather, pinch, pleat **3.** *informal* comestibles, eats (*slang*), food, grub (*slang*), nosebag (*slang*), nosh (*slang*), scoff (*slang*), tack (*informal*), victuals, vittles (*obsolete or dialect*)

tuck in 1. bed down, enfold, fold under, make snug, put to bed, swaddle, wrap up **2.** chow down (*slang*), eat heartily, eat up, fall to, get stuck in (*informal*)

tuft bunch, clump, cluster, collection, knot, shock, topknot, tussock

tug 1. *verb* drag, draw, haul, heave, jerk, lug, pull, tow, wrench, yank **2.** *noun* drag, haul, heave, jerk, pull, tow, traction, wrench, yank

tuition education, instruction, lessons, schooling, teaching, training, tutelage, tutoring

tumble 1. *verb* drop, fall, fall end over end, fall headlong, fall head over heels, flop, lose one's footing, pitch, plummet, roll, stumble, topple, toss, trip up **2.** *noun* collapse, drop, fall, flop, headlong fall, plunge, roll, spill, stumble, toss, trip

tumble-down crumbling, decrepit, dilapidated, disintegrating, falling to pieces, ramshackle, rickety, ruined, shaky, tottering
Antonyms durable, firm, solid, sound, stable, sturdy, substantial, well-kept

tumid 1. bloated, bulging, distended, enlarged, inflated, protuberant, puffed up, puffy, swollen, tumescent **2.** bombastic, flowery, fulsome, fustian, grandiloquent, grandiose, high-flown, inflated, magniloquent, orotund, overblown, pompous, pretentious, sesquipedalian, stilted, turgid

tummy *informal* abdomen, belly, breadbasket (*slang*), corporation (*informal*), gut (*informal*), inside(s) (*informal*), paunch, pot, potbelly, spare tyre (*informal*), stomach, tum (*informal*)

tumour cancer, carcinoma (*Pathology*), growth, lump, neoplasm (*Medical*), sarcoma (*Medical*), swelling

tumult ado, affray (*Law*), agitation, altercation, bedlam, brawl, brouhaha, clamour, commotion, din, disorder, disturbance, excitement, fracas, hubbub, hullabaloo, outbreak, pandemonium, quarrel, racket, riot, row, ruction (*informal*), stir, stramash (*Scot.*), strife, turmoil, unrest, upheaval, uproar

Antonyms calm, hush, peace, quiet, repose, serenity, silence, stillness

tumultuous agitated, boisterous, clamorous, confused, disorderly, disturbed, excited, fierce, full-on (*informal*), hectic, irregular, lawless, noisy, obstreperous, passionate, raging, restless, riotous, rowdy, rumbustious, stormy, turbulent, unrestrained, unruly, uproarious, violent, vociferous, wild
Antonyms calm, hushed, peaceful, quiet, restful, serene, still, tranquil

tune *noun* **1.** air, melody, melody line, motif, song, strain, theme **2.** agreement, concert, concord, consonance, euphony, harmony, pitch, sympathy, unison **3.** attitude, demeanour, disposition, frame of mind, mood **4. call the tune** be in charge (command, control), call the shots (*slang*), command, dictate, govern, lead, rule, rule the roost **5. change one's tune** change one's mind, do an about-face, have a change of heart, reconsider, take a different tack, think again *~verb* **6.** adapt, adjust, attune, bring into harmony, harmonize, pitch, regulate
Antonyms (*sense 2*) clashing, conflict, contention, disagreement, discord, discordance, disharmony, disunity, friction

tuneful catchy, consonant (*Music*), easy on the ear (*informal*), euphonic, euphonious, harmonious, mellifluous, melodic, melodious, musical, pleasant, symphonic
Antonyms cacophonous, clashing, discordant, dissonant, harsh, jangly, tuneless, unmelodious

tuneless atonal, cacophonous, clashing, discordant, dissonant, harsh, unmelodic, unmelodious, unmusical
Antonyms harmonious, melodious, musical, pleasing, sonorous, symphonic, tuneful

tunnel 1. *noun* burrow, channel, hole, passage, passageway, shaft, subway, underpass **2.** *verb* burrow, dig, dig one's way, excavate, mine, penetrate, scoop out, undermine

turbid clouded, cloudy, confused, dense, dim, dreggy, foggy, foul, fuzzy, hazy, impure, incoherent, muddled, muddy, murky, opaque, roiled, thick, unclear, unsettled

turbulence agitation, boiling, commotion, confusion, disorder, instability, pandemonium, roughness, storm, tumult, turmoil, unrest, upheaval
Antonyms calm, peace, quiet, repose, rest, stillness

turbulent 1. agitated, blustery, boiling, choppy, confused, disordered, foaming, furious, raging, rough, tempestuous, tumultuous, unsettled, unstable **2.** agitated, anarchic, boisterous, disorderly, insubordinate, lawless, mutinous, obstreperous, rebellious, refractory, riotous, rowdy, seditious, tumultuous, unbridled, undisciplined, ungovernable, unruly, uproarious, violent, wild
Antonyms (*sense 1*) calm, glassy, peaceful, quiet, smooth, still, unruffled

turf 1. clod, divot, grass, green, sod, sward **2. the turf** horse-racing, racecourse, racetrack, racing, the flat

turf out banish, bounce (*slang*), cast out, chuck out (*informal*), discharge, dismiss, dispossess, eject, evict, expel, fire (*informal*), fling out, give one the bum's rush (*slang*), give one the sack (*informal*), kick out (*informal*), kiss off (*slang, chiefly U.S. & Canad.*), oust, relegate, sack (*informal*), show one the door, throw out

turgid 1. bloated, bulging, congested, distended, inflated, protuberant, puffed up, puffy, swollen, tumescent, tumid **2.** bombastic, flowery, fulsome, fustian, grandiloquent, grandiose, high-flown, inflated, magniloquent, orotund, ostentatious, overblown, pompous, pretentious, sesquipedalian, stilted, tumid, windy

turmoil agitation, bedlam, brouhaha, bustle, chaos, commotion, confusion, disarray, disorder, disturbance, ferment, flurry, hubbub, noise, pandemonium, row, stir, strife, trouble, tumult, turbulence, upheaval, uproar, violence
Antonyms calm, peace, quiet, repose, rest, serenity, stillness, tranquillity

turn *verb* **1.** circle, go round, gyrate, move in a circle, pivot, revolve, roll, rotate, spin, swivel, twirl, twist, wheel, whirl **2.** change course, change position, go back, move, return, reverse, shift, swerve, switch, veer, wheel **3.** arc, come round, corner, go round, negotiate, pass, pass around, take a bend **4.** adapt, alter, become, change, convert, divert, fashion, fit, form, metamorphose, mould, mutate, remodel, shape, transfigure, transform, transmute **5.** become rancid, curdle, go bad, go off (*Brit. informal*), go sour, make rancid, sour, spoil, taint **6.** appeal, apply, approach, go, have recourse, look, resort **7.** nauseate, sicken, upset **8.** apostatize, bring round (*informal*), change one's mind, change sides, defect, desert, go over, influence, persuade, prejudice, prevail upon, renege, retract, talk into **9.** construct, deliver, execute, fashion, frame, make, mould, perform, shape, write **10. turn tail** beat a hasty retreat, bolt, cut and run (*informal*), flee, hook it (*slang*), run away, run off, show a clean pair of heels, take off (*informal*), take to one's heels *~noun* **11.** bend, change, circle, curve, cycle, gyration, pivot, reversal, revolution, rotation, spin, swing, turning, twist, whirl **12.** bias, direction, drift, heading, tendency, trend **13.** bend, change of course, change of direction, curve, departure, deviation, shift **14.** chance, crack (*informal*), fling, go, opportunity, period, round, shift, shot (*informal*), spell, stint, succession, time, try, whack (*informal*) **15.** airing, circuit, constitutional, drive, excursion, jaunt, outing, promenade, ride, saunter, spin (*informal*), stroll, walk **16.** affinity, aptitude, bent, bias, flair, gift, inclination, knack, leaning, propensity, talent **17.** cast, fashion, form, format, guise, make-up, manner, mode, mould, shape, style, way **18.** act, action, deed, favour, gesture, service **19.** bend, distortion, twist, warp **20.** *informal* fright, scare, shock, start, surprise **21. by turns** alternately, in succession, one after another, reciprocally, turn and turn about **22. to a turn** correctly, exactly, just right, perfectly, precisely

One good turn deserves another

turncoat apostate, backslider, defector, deserter, rat (*informal*), recreant (*archaic*), renegade, seceder, tergiversator, traitor

turn down 1. diminish, lessen, lower, muffle, mute, quieten, reduce the volume of, soften **2.** abstain from, decline, rebuff, refuse, reject, repudiate, say no to, spurn, throw out

Antonyms (*sense 1*) amplify, augment, boost, increase, raise, strengthen, swell, turn up (*sense 2*) accede, accept, acquiesce, agree, receive, take

turn in 1. go to bed, go to sleep, hit the hay (*slang*), hit the sack (*slang*), retire for the night **2.** deliver, give back, give up, hand in, hand over, return, submit, surrender, tender

turning bend, crossroads, curve, junction, side road, turn, turn-off

turning point change, climacteric, crisis, critical moment, crossroads, crux, decisive moment, moment of decision, moment of truth

turn-off branch, exit, side road, turn, turning

turn off 1. branch off, change direction, depart from, deviate, leave, quit, take another road, take a side road **2.** cut out, kill, put out, shut down, stop, switch off, turn out, unplug **3.** *informal* alienate, bore, disenchant, disgust, displease, gross out (*U.S. slang*), irritate, lose one's interest, nauseate, offend, put off, repel, sicken

turn on 1. activate, energize, ignite, kick-start, put on, set in motion, start, start up, switch on **2.** balance, be contingent on, be decided by, depend, hang, hinge, pivot, rest **3.** assail, assault, attack, fall on, lose one's temper with, round on **4.** *slang* arouse, arouse one's desire, attract, excite, please, ring (someone's) bell (*U.S. slang*), stimulate, thrill, titillate, work up **5.** *slang* get high (*informal*), get stoned (*slang*), take drugs, trip (*informal*) **6.** *slang* expose, get one started with, inform, initiate, introduce, show

Antonyms (*sense 1*) cut out, put out, shut off, stop, switch off, turn off

turnout 1. assemblage, assembly, attendance, audience, congregation, crowd, gate, number, throng **2.** amount produced, output, outturn (*rare*), production, production quota, productivity, turnover, volume, yield **3.** array, attire, costume, dress, equipage, equipment, gear (*informal*), get-up (*informal*), outfit, rigout (*informal*)

turn out 1. put out, switch off, turn off, unplug **2.** bring out, fabricate, finish, make, manufacture, process, produce, put out **3.** axe (*informal*), banish, cashier, cast out, deport, discharge, dismiss, dispossess, drive out, drum out, evict, expel, fire (*informal*), give one the sack (*informal*), give the bum's rush (*slang*), kick out (*informal*), kiss off (*slang, chiefly U.S. & Canad.*), oust, put out, relegate, sack (*informal*), show one the door, throw out, turf out (*Brit. informal*), unseat **4.** clean out, clear, discharge, empty, take out the contents of **5.** become, come about, come to be, come to light, crop up (*informal*), develop, emerge, end up, eventuate, evolve, happen, prove to be, result, transpire (*informal*), work out **6.** accoutre, apparel (*archaic*), attire, clothe, dress, fit, outfit, rig out **7.** appear, assemble, attend, be present, come, gather, go, put in an appearance, show up (*informal*), turn up

turnover 1. business, flow, output, outturn (*rare*), production, productivity, volume, yield **2.** change, coming and going, movement, replacement

turn over 1. capsize, flip over, keel over, overturn, reverse, tip over, upend, upset **2.** activate, crank, press the starter button, set going, set in motion, start up, switch on, switch on the ignition, warm up **3.** assign, commend, commit, deliver, give over, give up, hand over, pass on, render, surrender, transfer, yield **4.** consider, contemplate, deliberate, give thought to, mull over, ponder, reflect on, revolve, ruminate about, think about, think over, wonder about **5.** break up, dig, plough

turn up 1. appear, arrive, attend, come, put in an appearance, show (*informal*), show one's face, show up (*informal*) **2.** appear, become known, be found, bring to light, come to light, come to pass, come up with, crop up (*informal*), dig up, disclose, discover, expose, find, pop up, reveal, transpire, unearth **3.** amplify, boost, enhance, increase, increase the volume of, intensify, make louder, raise

Antonyms (*sense 2*) disappear, evaporate, fade, hide, vanish (*sense 3*) diminish, lessen, lower, reduce, soften, turn down

A bad penny always turns up

turpitude badness, baseness, corruption, criminality, degeneracy, depravity, evil, foulness, immorality, iniquity, nefariousness, sin~

fulness, viciousness, vileness, villainy, wickedness

tussle 1. *verb* battle, brawl, contend, fight, grapple, scrap (*informal*), scuffle, struggle, vie, wrestle 2. *noun bagarre*, battle, bout, brawl, competition, conflict, contention, contest, fight, fracas, fray, punch-up (*Brit. informal*), scrap (*informal*), scrimmage, scuffle, set-to (*informal*), shindig (*informal*), shindy (*informal*), struggle

tutelage care, charge, custody, dependence, education, guardianship, guidance, instruction, patronage, preparation, protection, schooling, teaching, tuition, wardship

tutor 1. *noun* coach, educator, governor, guardian, guide, guru, instructor, lecturer, master, mentor, preceptor, schoolmaster, teacher 2. *verb* coach, direct, discipline, drill, edify, educate, guide, instruct, lecture, school, teach, train

tutorial 1. *noun* individual instruction, lesson, seminar 2. *adjective* coaching, guiding, instructional, teaching

TV gogglebox (*Brit. slang*), idiot box (*slang*), receiver, small screen (*informal*), television, television set, telly (*Brit. informal*), the box (*Brit. informal*), the tube (*slang*), TV set

twaddle 1. *noun* balderdash, balls (*taboo slang*), bilge (*informal*), blather, bosh (*informal*), bull (*slang*), bullshit (*taboo slang*), bunkum *or* buncombe (*chiefly U.S.*), chatter, claptrap (*informal*), cobblers (*Brit. taboo slang*), crap (*slang*), drivel, eyewash (*informal*), foolish talk, gabble, garbage (*informal*), gobbledegook (*informal*), gossip, guff (*slang*), hogwash, hokum (*slang, chiefly U.S. & Canad.*), horsefeathers (*U.S. slang*), hot air (*informal*), inanity, moonshine, nonsense, pap, piffle (*informal*), poppycock (*informal*), rigmarole, rot, rubbish, shit (*taboo slang*), tattle, tommyrot, tosh (*slang, chiefly Brit.*), trash, tripe (*informal*), trumpery, verbiage, waffle (*informal, chiefly Brit.*) 2. *verb* blather, chatter, gabble, gossip, prattle, rattle on, talk nonsense, talk through one's hat, tattle, waffle (*informal, chiefly Brit.*)

tweak *verb/noun* jerk, nip, pinch, pull, squeeze, twist, twitch

twee bijou, cute, dainty, precious, pretty, quaint, sentimental, sweet

twiddle 1. adjust, fiddle (*informal*), finger, jiggle, juggle, monkey with (*informal*), play with, twirl, wiggle 2. **twiddle one's thumbs** be idle, be unoccupied, do nothing, have nothing to do, malinger, mark time, sit around

twig[1] *noun* branch, offshoot, shoot, spray, sprig, stick, withe

twig[2] *verb* catch on (*informal*), comprehend, fathom, find out, get, grasp, make out, rumble (*Brit. informal*), see, tumble to (*informal*), understand

twilight *noun* 1. dimness, dusk, evening, gloaming (*Scot. or poetic*), half-light, sundown, sunset 2. decline, ebb, last phase *~adjective* 3. crepuscular, darkening, dim, evening 4. declining, dying, ebbing, final, last

Antonyms climax, crowning moment, dawn, daybreak, height, morning, peak, sunrise, sunup

twin 1. *noun* clone, corollary, counterpart, double, duplicate, fellow, likeness, lookalike, match, mate, ringer (*slang*) 2. *adjective* corresponding, double, dual, duplicate, geminate, identical, matched, matching, paired, parallel, twofold 3. *verb* couple, join, link, match, pair, yoke

twine *noun* 1. cord, string, yarn 2. coil, convolution, interlacing, twist, whorl 3. knot, snarl, tangle *~verb* 4. braid, entwine, interlace, interweave, knit, plait, splice, twist, twist together, weave 5. bend, coil, curl, encircle, loop, meander, spiral, surround, twist, wind, wrap, wreathe

twinge bite, gripe, pain, pang, pinch, prick, sharp pain, spasm, stab, stitch, throb, throe (*rare*), tic, tweak, twist, twitch

twinkle *verb* 1. blink, coruscate, flash, flicker, gleam, glint, glisten, glitter, scintillate, shimmer, shine, sparkle, wink *~noun* 2. blink, coruscation, flash, flicker, gleam, glimmer, glistening, glittering, light, scintillation, shimmer, shine, spark, sparkle, wink 3. flash, instant, jiffy (*informal*), moment, second, shake (*informal*), split second, tick (*Brit. informal*), trice, twinkling, two shakes of a lamb's tail (*informal*)

twinkling 1. blink, coruscation, flash, flashing, flicker, gleam, glimmer, glistening, glittering, scintillation, shimmer, shining, sparkle, twinkle, wink 2. bat of an eye (*informal*), flash, instant, jiffy (*informal*), moment, second, shake (*informal*), split second, tick (*Brit. informal*), trice, twinkle, two shakes of a lamb's tail (*informal*)

twirl *verb* 1. gyrate, pirouette, pivot, revolve, rotate, spin, turn, turn on one's heel, twiddle, twist, wheel, whirl, wind *~noun* 2. gyration, pirouette, revolution, rotation, spin, turn, twist, wheel, whirl 3. coil, spiral, twist

twist *verb* 1. coil, corkscrew, curl, encircle, entwine, intertwine, screw, spin, swivel, twine, weave, wind, wrap, wreathe, wring 2. contort, distort, screw up 3. rick, sprain, turn, wrench 4. alter, change, distort, falsify, garble, misquote, misrepresent, pervert, warp 5. squirm, wriggle, writhe 6. **twist someone's arm** bully, coerce, force, persuade, pressurize, talk into *~noun* 7. coil, curl, spin, swivel, twine,

wind **8.** braid, coil, curl, hank, plug, quid, roll **9.** change, development, revelation, slant, surprise, turn, variation **10.** arc, bend, convolution, curve, meander, turn, undulation, zigzag **11.** defect, deformation, distortion, flaw, imperfection, kink, warp **12.** jerk, pull, sprain, turn, wrench **13.** aberration, bent, characteristic, crotchet, eccentricity, fault, foible, idiosyncrasy, oddity, peculiarity, proclivity, quirk, trait **14.** confusion, entanglement, kink, knot, mess, mix-up, ravel, snarl, tangle **15. round the twist** *Brit. slang* barmy (*slang*), batty (*slang*), bonkers (*slang, chiefly Brit.*), crazy, cuckoo (*informal*), daft (*informal*), gonzo (*slang*), insane, loopy (*informal*), mad, not all there, not right in the head, nuts (*slang*), nutty (*slang*), nutty as a fruitcake (*slang*), off one's rocker (*slang*), off one's trolley (*slang*), out to lunch (*informal*), up the pole (*informal*), wacko *or* whacko (*informal*)
Antonyms hold stationary, hold steady, hold still, straighten, uncoil, unravel, unroll, untwist, unwind

twister cheat, chiseller (*informal*), con man (*informal*), crook (*informal*), deceiver, fraud, fraudster, grifter (*slang, chiefly U.S. & Canad.*), rogue, swindler, trickster

twit¹ *verb* banter, berate, blame, censure, deride, jeer, make fun of, scorn, taunt, tease, upbraid

twit² *noun* airhead (*slang*), ass, berk (*Brit. slang*), blockhead, charlie (*Brit. informal*), chump (*informal*), clown, dickhead (*slang*), dickwit (*slang*), dipstick (*Brit. slang*), divvy (*Brit. slang*), dope (*informal*), dork (*slang*), dweeb (*U.S. slang*), fool, fuckwit (*taboo slang*), geek (*slang*), gobshite (*Irish taboo slang*), gonzo (*slang*), halfwit, idiot, jerk (*slang, chiefly U.S. & Canad.*), juggins (*Brit. informal*), nerd *or* nurd (*slang*), nincompoop, ninny, nitwit (*informal*), numpty (*Scot. informal*), numskull *or* numbskull, oaf, pillock (*Brit. slang*), plank (*Brit. slang*), plonker (*slang*), prat (*slang*), prick (*slang*), schmuck (*U.S. slang*), silly-billy (*informal*), simpleton, twerp *or* twirp (*informal*), wally (*slang*), weenie (*U.S. informal*)

twitch 1. *verb* blink, flutter, jerk, jump, pluck, pull, snatch, squirm, tug, yank **2.** *noun* blink, flutter, jerk, jump, pull, spasm, tic, tremor, twinge

twitter *verb* **1.** chatter, cheep, chirp, chirrup, trill, tweet, warble, whistle **2.** chatter, giggle, prattle, simper, snigger, titter ~*noun* **3.** call, chatter, cheep, chirp, chirrup, cry, song, trill, tweet, warble, whistle **4.** agitation, anxiety, bustle, dither (*chiefly Brit.*), excitement, flurry, fluster, flutter, nervousness, tizzy (*informal*), whirl

two-edged ambiguous, ambivalent, backhanded, double-edged, equivocal

two-faced deceitful, deceiving, dissembling, double-dealing, duplicitous, false, hypocritical, insincere, Janus-faced, perfidious, treacherous, untrustworthy
Antonyms artless, candid, frank, genuine, honest, ingenuous, sincere, trustworthy

tycoon baron, big cheese (*slang, old-fashioned*), big noise (*informal*), capitalist, captain of industry, fat cat (*slang, chiefly U.S.*), financier, industrialist, magnate, merchant prince, mogul, plutocrat, potentate, wealthy businessman

type 1. breed, category, class, classification, form, genre, group, ilk, kidney, kind, order, sort, species, stamp, strain, subdivision, variety **2.** case, characters, face, fount, print, printing **3.** archetype, epitome, essence, example, exemplar, model, norm, original, paradigm, pattern, personification, prototype, quintessence, specimen, standard

typhoon cyclone, squall, storm, tempest, tornado, tropical storm

typical archetypal, average, bog-standard (*Brit. & Irish slang*), characteristic, classic, conventional, essential, illustrative, in character, indicative, in keeping, model, normal, orthodox, representative, standard, stock, true to type, usual
Antonyms atypical, exceptional, out of keeping, out of the ordinary, singular, uncharacteristic, unconventional, unexpected, unique, unrepresentative, unusual

typify characterize, embody, epitomize, exemplify, illustrate, incarnate, personify, represent, sum up, symbolize

tyrannical absolute, arbitrary, authoritarian, autocratic, coercive, cruel, despotic, dictatorial, domineering, high-handed, imperious, inhuman, magisterial, oppressive, overbearing, overweening, peremptory, severe, tyrannous, unjust, unreasonable
Antonyms democratic, easy-going, lax, lenient, liberal, reasonable, tolerant, understanding

tyrannize browbeat, bully, coerce, dictate, domineer, enslave, have (someone) under one's thumb, intimidate, oppress, ride roughshod over, rule with an iron hand, subjugate, terrorize

tyranny absolutism, authoritarianism, autocracy, coercion, cruelty, despotism, dictatorship, harsh discipline, high-handedness, imperiousness, oppression, peremptoriness, reign of terror, unreasonableness
Antonyms democracy, ease, laxity, leniency, liberality, mercy, relaxation, tolerance, understanding

Tyranny is always better organised than freedom
Charles Péguy *Basic Verities*

tyrant absolutist, authoritarian, autocrat, bully, despot, dictator, Hitler, martinet, oppressor, slave-driver

The hand of vengeance found the bed
To which the purple tyrant fled;
The iron hand crushed the tyrant's head,
And became a tyrant in his stead
William Blake *The Grey Monk*

Tyrants seldom want pretexts
Edmund Burke

Nature has left this tincture in the blood,
That all men would be tyrants if they could
Daniel Defoe *The History of the Kentish Petition*

When he laughed, respectable senators burst with laughter,
And when he cried the little children died in the streets
W.H. Auden *Epitaph on a Tyrant*

tyro apprentice, beginner, catechumen, greenhorn (*informal*), initiate, learner, neophyte, novice, novitiate, pupil, student, trainee

U

ubiquitous all-over, ever-present, everywhere, omnipresent, pervasive, universal

ugly **1.** hard-favoured, hard-featured, homely (*chiefly U.S.*), ill-favoured, misshapen, no oil painting (*informal*), not much to look at, plain, unattractive, unlovely, unprepossessing, unsightly **2.** disagreeable, disgusting, distasteful, frightful, hideous, horrid, monstrous, objectionable, obscene, offensive, repugnant, repulsive, revolting, shocking, terrible, unpleasant, vile **3.** baleful, bodeful, dangerous, forbidding, menacing, ominous, sinister, threatening **4.** angry, bad-tempered, dark, evil, malevolent, nasty, spiteful, sullen, surly
Antonyms agreeable, attractive, auspicious, beautiful, cute, friendly, good-humoured, good-looking, good-natured, gorgeous, handsome, likable *or* likeable, lovely, peaceful, pleasant, pretty, promising

ulcer abscess, boil, fester, gathering, gumboil, peptic ulcer, pustule, sore

ulcerous cankered, cankerous, festering, furunculous (*Pathology*), suppurative, ulcerative

ulterior concealed, covert, hidden, personal, secondary, secret, selfish, undisclosed, unexpressed
Antonyms apparent, declared, manifest, obvious, overt, plain

ultimate *adjective* **1.** conclusive, decisive, end, eventual, extreme, final, furthest, last, terminal **2.** extreme, greatest, highest, maximum, most significant, paramount, superlative, supreme, topmost, utmost **3.** basic, elemental, fundamental, primary, radical *~noun* **4.** culmination, epitome, extreme, greatest, height, mother (of all), peak, perfection, summit, the last word

ultimately after all, at last, at the end of the day, basically, eventually, finally, fundamentally, in due time, in the end, in the fullness of time, sooner or later

ultra *adjective* excessive, extreme, fanatical, immoderate, rabid, radical, revolutionary

ultramodern advanced, ahead of its time, avant-garde, futuristic, modernistic, neoteric (*rare*), progressive, way-out (*informal*)

ululate bawl, cry, howl, keen, lament, moan, mourn, sob, wail, weep

umbrage anger, chagrin, displeasure, grudge, high dudgeon, huff, indignation, offence, pique, resentment, sense of injury
Antonyms amity, cordiality, goodwill, harmony, pleasure, understanding

umbrella **1.** brolly (*Brit. informal*), gamp (*Brit. informal*) **2.** aegis, agency, cover, patronage, protection

umpire **1.** *noun* adjudicator, arbiter, arbitrator, judge, moderator, ref (*informal*), referee **2.** *verb* adjudicate, arbitrate, call (*Sport*), judge, mediate, moderate, referee

umpteen a good many, a thousand and one, considerable, countless, ever so many, millions, n, numerous, very many

unabashed blatant, bold, brazen, confident, unawed, unblushing, unconcerned, undaunted, undismayed, unembarrassed
Antonyms abashed, embarrassed, humbled, mortified, shame-faced, sheepish

unable impotent, inadequate, incapable, ineffectual, no good, not able, not equal to, not up to, powerless, unfit, unfitted, unqualified
Antonyms able, adept, adequate, capable, competent, effective, potent, powerful

unabridged complete, full-length, uncondensed, uncut, unexpurgated, unshortened, whole

unacceptable beyond the pale, disagreeable, displeasing, distasteful, improper, inadmissible, insupportable, objectionable, offensive, undesirable, unpleasant, unsatisfactory, unwelcome
Antonyms acceptable, agreeable, delightful, desirable, pleasant, pleasing, welcome

unaccompanied a cappella (*Music*), alone, by oneself, lone, on one's own, solo, unescorted

unaccomplished **1.** incomplete, unachieved, uncompleted, undone, unfinished, unperformed **2.** inexpert, lacking finesse, uncultivated, unskilful, unskilled

unaccountable **1.** baffling, incomprehensible, inexplicable, inscrutable, mysterious, odd, peculiar, puzzling, strange, unexplainable, unfathomable, unintelligible **2.** astonishing, extraordinary, uncommon, unheard-of, unusual, unwonted **3.** clear, exempt, free, not answerable, not responsible, unliable
Antonyms (*sense 1*) accountable, comprehensible, explicable, intelligible, understandable

unaccounted-for lost, missing, not explained, not taken into consideration, not understood, unexplained

unaccustomed 1. *with* **to** a newcomer to, a novice at, green, inexperienced, not given to, not used to, unfamiliar with, unpractised, unused to, unversed in 2. new, out of the ordinary, remarkable, special, strange, surprising, uncommon, unexpected, unfamiliar, unprecedented, unusual, unwonted
Antonyms (*sense 1*) experienced, given to, habituated, practised, seasoned, used to, well-versed (*sense 2*) accustomed, familiar, ordinary, regular, usual

unadorned plain, restrained, severe, simple, stark, straightforward, unembellished, unfussy, unornamented, unvarnished

unadulterated absolute, neat, pure, sheer, unmixed

Antonyms contaminated, corrupted, debased, impure, mixed, weakened

unadventurous cagey (*informal*), careful, cautious, chary, circumspect, hesitant, prudent, safe, stay-at-home, tentative, timid, timorous, unenterprising, wary
Antonyms adventurous, audacious, bold, daredevil, daring, enterprising, intrepid, venturesome

unadvised 1. careless, hasty, heedless, ill-advised, imprudent, inadvisable, indiscreet, injudicious, rash, reckless, unwary, unwise 2. ignorant, in the dark, unaware, uninformed, unknowing, unsuspecting, unwarned

unaffected[1] *adjective* artless, genuine, honest, ingenuous, naive, natural, plain, simple, sincere, straightforward, unassuming, unpretentious, unsophisticated, unspoilt, unstudied, without airs
Antonyms affected, assumed, designing, devious, insincere, mannered, pretentious, put-on, snobbish, sophisticated

unaffected[2] *adjective* aloof, impervious, not influenced, proof, unaltered, unchanged, unimpressed, unmoved, unresponsive, unstirred, untouched
Antonyms affected, changed, concerned, disrupted, hard-hit, influenced, interested, responsive, sympathetic, touched

unafraid confident, daring, dauntless, fearless, intrepid, unfearing, unshakable
Antonyms afraid, alarmed, anxious, fearful, frightened, scared

unalterable fixed, fixed as the laws of the Medes and the Persians, immovable, immutable, invariable, permanent, steadfast, unchangeable, unchanging
Antonyms alterable, changeable, changing, flexible, mutable, variable

unanimity accord, agreement, assent, chorus, concert, concord, concurrence, consensus, harmony, like-mindedness, one mind, unison, unity
Antonyms difference, disagreement, discord, disunity, division, variance

unanimous agreed, agreeing, at one, common, concerted, concordant, harmonious, in agreement, in complete accord, like-minded, of one mind, united
Antonyms differing, discordant, dissident, disunited, divided, schismatic, split

unanimously by common consent, nem. con., unitedly, unopposed, with one accord, without exception, without opposition

unanswerable 1. absolute, conclusive, incontestable, incontrovertible, indisputable, irrefutable, unarguable, undeniable 2. insoluble, insolvable, unascertainable, unexplainable, unresolvable

unanswered disputed, ignored, in doubt, open, undecided, undenied, unnoticed, unrefuted, unresolved, unsettled, up in the air, vexed

unappetizing disagreeable, disgusting, distasteful, flavourless, foul-tasting, insipid, nauseating, off-putting (*Brit. informal*), repellent, repulsive, tasteless, unappealing, unattractive, uninteresting, uninviting, unpalatable, unpleasant, unsavoury, untempting, vapid

Antonyms agreeable, appealing, appetizing, attractive, delicious, interesting, inviting, mouthwatering, palatable, savoury, scrumptious (*informal*), succulent, tasty, tempting, toothsome

unapproachable 1. aloof, chilly, cool, distant, frigid, offish (*informal*), remote, reserved, standoffish, unfriendly, unsociable, withdrawn 2. inaccessible, out of reach, out-of-the-way, remote, un-get-at-able (*informal*), unreachable
Antonyms (*sense 1*) affable, approachable, congenial, cordial, friendly, sociable

unapt 1. inapplicable, inapposite, inappropriate, inapt, out of character, out of keeping, out of place, unfit, unfitted, unsuitable 2. backward, dim, dim-witted (*informal*), dull, incompetent, slow, stupid, thick 3. averse, disinclined, loath, not prone, reluctant, undisposed, unlikely, unwilling

unarmed assailable, defenceless, exposed, helpless, open, open to attack, unarmoured, unprotected, weak, weaponless, without arms
Antonyms armed, equipped, fortified, protected, ready, strengthened

unasked 1. gratuitous, spontaneous, unbidden, undemanded, undesired, uninvited, unprompted, unrequested, unsought, unwanted 2. off one's own bat, of one's own accord, voluntarily, without prompting

unassailable **1.** impregnable, invincible, invul~ nerable, secure, well-defended **2.** absolute, conclusive, incontestable, incontrovertible, in~ disputable, irrefutable, positive, proven, sound, undeniable
Antonyms (*sense 2*) debatable, doubtful, dubi~ ous, inconclusive, uncertain, unfounded, un~ proven, unsound

unassertive backward, bashful, diffident, meek, mousy, retiring, self-effacing, timid, timorous, unassuming
Antonyms aggressive, assertive, confident, feisty (*informal, chiefly U.S. & Canad.*), forceful, overbearing, pushy (*informal*)

unassuming diffident, humble, meek, modest, quiet, reserved, retiring, self-effacing, simple, unassertive, unobtrusive, unostentatious, un~ pretentious
Antonyms assuming, audacious, conceited, ostentatious, overconfident, presumptuous, pretentious

unattached **1.** autonomous, free, independent, nonaligned, unaffiliated, uncommitted **2.** a free agent, available, by oneself, footloose and fancy-free, left on the shelf, not spoken for, on one's own, single, unengaged, unmarried
Antonyms (*sense 1*) affiliated, aligned, at~ tached, committed, dependent, implicated, in~ volved

unattended **1.** abandoned, disregarded, ig~ nored, left alone, not cared for, unguarded, unwatched **2.** alone, on one's own, unaccom~ panied, unescorted

unauthorized illegal, off the record, unap~ proved, unconstitutional, under-the-table, un~ lawful, unofficial, unsanctioned, unwarranted
Antonyms authorized, constitutional, lawful, legal, official, sanctioned, warranted

unavailing abortive, bootless, fruitless, futile, idle, ineffective, ineffectual, of no avail, point~ less, to no purpose, unproductive, unsuccess~ ful, useless, vain
Antonyms effective, fruitful, productive, re~ warding, successful, useful, worthwhile

unavoidable bound to happen, certain, com~ pulsory, fated, ineluctable, inescapable, inevi~ table, inexorable, necessary, obligatory, sure

unaware heedless, ignorant, incognizant, oblivious, unconscious, unenlightened, unin~ formed, unknowing, unmindful, unsuspecting
Antonyms attentive, aware, conscious, in~ formed, knowing, mindful

unawares **1.** aback, abruptly, by surprise, caught napping, off guard, on the hop (*Brit. informal*), suddenly, unexpectedly, unpre~ pared, without warning **2.** accidentally, by ac~ cident, by mistake, inadvertently, mistakenly, unconsciously, unintentionally, unknowingly, unwittingly
Antonyms deliberately, forewarned, knowing~ ly, on purpose, on the lookout, prepared, wit~ tingly

unbalanced **1.** asymmetrical, irregular, lop~ sided, not balanced, shaky, unequal, uneven, unstable, unsymmetrical, wobbly **2.** barking (*slang*), barking mad (*slang*), crazy, demented, deranged, disturbed, doolally (*slang*), eccen~ tric, erratic, gonzo (*slang*), insane, irrational, loopy (*informal*), lunatic, mad, *non compos mentis*, not all there, not the full shilling (*in~ formal*), off one's trolley (*slang*), out to lunch (*informal*), touched, unhinged, unsound, un~ stable, up the pole (*informal*), wacko *or* whacko (*informal*) **3.** biased, inequitable, one-sided, partial, partisan, prejudiced, unfair, unjust
Antonyms (*sense 1*) balanced, equal, even, stable, symmetrical

unbearable insufferable, insupportable, intol~ erable, oppressive, too much (*informal*), unac~ ceptable, unendurable
Antonyms acceptable, bearable, endurable, supportable, tolerable

unbeatable indomitable, invincible, more than a match for, unconquerable, unstoppable, un~ surpassable

unbeaten **1.** triumphant, unbowed, undefeated, unsubdued, unsurpassed, unvanquished, vic~ torious, winning **2.** new, untouched, untried, untrodden, virgin

unbecoming **1.** ill-suited, inappropriate, incon~ gruous, unattractive, unbefitting, unfit, un~ flattering, unsightly, unsuitable, unsuited **2.** discreditable, improper, indecorous, indelicate, offensive, tasteless, unseemly
Antonyms (*sense 2*) becoming, decent, deco~ rous, delicate, proper, seemly

unbelief atheism, disbelief, distrust, doubt, in~ credulity, scepticism
Antonyms belief, credence, credulity, faith, trust

unbelievable astonishing, beyond belief, cock-and-bull (*informal*), far-fetched, implausible, impossible, improbable, inconceivable, incred~ ible, outlandish, preposterous, questionable, staggering, unconvincing, unimaginable, un~ thinkable
Antonyms authentic, believable, credible, likely, plausible, possible, probable, trust~ worthy

unbeliever agnostic, atheist, disbeliever, doubting Thomas, infidel, sceptic

unbelieving disbelieving, distrustful, doubtful, doubting, dubious, incredulous, sceptical, sus~ picious, unconvinced
Antonyms believing, convinced, credulous, trustful, undoubting, unsuspicious

unbend **1.** be informal, calm down, chill out (*slang, chiefly U.S.*), cool it (*slang*), ease up, let it all hang out (*slang*), let oneself go, let up, lighten up (*slang*), loosen up, relax, slacken, slow down, take it easy, unbutton (*informal*), unwind **2.** put straight, straighten, uncoil, uncurl

unbending **1.** aloof, distant, formal, inflexible, reserved, rigid, stiff, uptight (*informal*) **2.** firm, hardline, intractable, resolute, severe, strict, stubborn, tough, uncompromising, unyielding
Antonyms (*sense 1*) approachable, at ease, flexible, friendly, outgoing, relaxed, sociable

unbiased disinterested, dispassionate, equitable, even-handed, fair, impartial, just, neutral, objective, open-minded, unprejudiced
Antonyms biased, bigoted, partial, prejudiced, slanted, swayed, unfair, unjust

unbidden **1.** free, spontaneous, unforced, unprompted, voluntary, willing **2.** unasked, uninvited, unwanted, unwelcome

unbind free, loosen, release, set free, unbridle, unchain, undo, unfasten, unfetter, unloose, unshackle, untie, unyoke
Antonyms bind, chain, fasten, fetter, restrain, shackle, tie, yoke

unblemished flawless, immaculate, impeccable, perfect, pure, spotless, unflawed, unspotted, unstained, unsullied, untarnished
Antonyms blemished, flawed, imperfect, impure, stained, sullied, tarnished

unblinking **1.** calm, cool, emotionless, impassive, unemotional, unfaltering, unwavering **2.** fearless, steady, unafraid, unflinching, unshrinking

unblushing amoral, bold, brazen, forward, immodest, shameless, unabashed, unashamed, unembarrassed

unborn **1.** awaited, embryonic, expected, *in utero* **2.** coming, future, hereafter, latter, subsequent, to come

unbosom admit, confess, confide, disburden, disclose, divulge, get (something) off one's chest (*informal*), get (something) out of one's system, lay bare, let out, reveal, spill one's guts about (*slang*), tell, unburden
Antonyms conceal, cover up, guard, hold back, suppress, withhold

unbounded absolute, boundless, endless, immeasurable, infinite, lavish, limitless, unbridled, unchecked, unconstrained, uncontrolled, unlimited, unrestrained, vast
Antonyms bounded, confined, constrained, curbed, limited, restricted

unbreakable armoured, durable, indestructible, infrangible, lasting, nonbreakable, resistant, rugged, shatterproof, solid, strong, toughened
Antonyms breakable, brittle, delicate, flimsy, fragile, frangible

unbridled excessive, full-on (*informal*), intemperate, licentious, rampant, riotous, unchecked, unconstrained, uncontrolled, uncurbed, ungovernable, ungoverned, unrestrained, unruly, violent, wanton

unbroken **1.** complete, entire, intact, solid, total, unimpaired, whole **2.** ceaseless, constant, continuous, endless, incessant, progressive, serried, successive, uninterrupted, unremitting **3.** deep, fast, profound, sound, undisturbed, unruffled, untroubled **4.** unbowed, unsubdued, untamed
Antonyms (*sense 1*) broken, cracked, damaged, fragmented, in pieces, shattered (*sense 2*) erratic, fitful, intermittent, interrupted, irregular, occasional, off-and-on, uneven

unburden **1.** disburden, discharge, disencumber, ease the load, empty, lighten, relieve, unload **2.** come clean (*informal*), confess, confide, disclose, get (something) off one's chest (*informal*), lay bare, make a clean breast of, reveal, spill one's guts about (*slang*), tell all, unbosom

uncalled-for gratuitous, inappropriate, needless, undeserved, unjust, unjustified, unnecessary, unprovoked, unwarranted, unwelcome
Antonyms appropriate, deserved, just, justified, necessary, needed, provoked, warranted

uncanny **1.** creepy (*informal*), eerie, eldritch (*poetic*), mysterious, preternatural, queer, spooky (*informal*), strange, supernatural, unearthly, unnatural, weird **2.** astonishing, astounding, exceptional, extraordinary, fantastic, incredible, inspired, miraculous, prodigious, remarkable, singular, unheard-of, unusual

uncaring indifferent, negligent, unconcerned, unfeeling, uninterested, unmoved, unresponsive, unsympathetic

unceasing ceaseless, constant, continual, continuing, continuous, endless, incessant, never-ending, nonstop, perpetual, persistent, unending, unfailing, unremitting
Antonyms fitful, intermittent, irregular, occasional, periodic, spasmodic, sporadic

uncertain **1.** ambiguous, chancy, conjectural, doubtful, iffy (*informal*), incalculable, indefinite, indeterminate, indistinct, questionable, risky, speculative, undetermined, unforeseeable, unpredictable **2.** ambivalent, at a loss, doubtful, dubious, hazy, in the balance, in two minds, irresolute, unclear, unconfirmed, undecided, undetermined, unfixed, unresolved, unsettled, unsure, up in the air, vacillating, vague **3.** changeable, erratic, fitful, hesitant, iffy (*informal*), inconstant, insecure, irregular, precarious, unpredictable, unreliable, vacillat~

ing, variable, wavering
Antonyms certain, clear, clear-cut, decided, definite, firm, fixed, known, positive, predictable, resolute, settled, sure, unambiguous, unhesitating, unvarying, unwavering

uncertainty ambiguity, bewilderment, confusion, dilemma, doubt, dubiety, hesitancy, hesitation, inconclusiveness, indecision, irresolution, lack of confidence, misgiving, mystification, perplexity, puzzlement, qualm, quandary, scepticism, state of suspense, unpredictability, vagueness
Antonyms assurance, certainty, confidence, decision, predictability, resolution, sureness, trust

unchangeable changeless, constant, fixed, immovable, immutable, inevitable, invariable, irreversible, permanent, stable, steadfast, strong, unalterable
Antonyms changeable, inconstant, irregular, mutable, shifting, unstable, variable, wavering

unchanging abiding, changeless, constant, continuing, enduring, eternal, immutable, imperishable, lasting, permanent, perpetual, unchanged, unfading, unvarying

uncharitable cruel, hardhearted, insensitive, mean, merciless, stingy, unchristian, unfeeling, unforgiving, unfriendly, ungenerous, unkind, unsympathetic
Antonyms charitable, feeling, friendly, generous, kind, merciful, sensitive, sympathetic

uncharted not mapped, strange, undiscovered, unexplored, unfamiliar, unknown, unplumbed, virgin

unchaste depraved, dissolute, fallen, immodest, immoral, impure, lewd, loose, promiscuous, unvirtuous, wanton
Antonyms chaste, decent, innocent, modest, moral, pure, virtuous

uncivil bad-mannered, bearish, boorish, brusque, churlish, discourteous, disrespectful, gruff, ill-bred, ill-mannered, impolite, rude, surly, uncouth, unmannerly
Antonyms civil, courteous, mannerly, polished, polite, refined, respectful, well-bred, well-mannered

uncivilized 1. barbarian, barbaric, barbarous, illiterate, primitive, savage, wild 2. beyond the pale, boorish, brutish, churlish, coarse, gross, philistine, uncouth, uncultivated, uncultured, uneducated, unmannered, unpolished, unsophisticated, vulgar

unclad bare, buck naked (*slang*), in one's birthday suit (*informal*), in the altogether (*informal*), in the bare scud (*slang*), in the buff (*informal*), in the raw (*informal*), naked, naked as the day one was born (*informal*), nude, scuddy (*slang*), starkers (*informal*), stripped, unclothed, undressed, with nothing on, without a stitch on (*informal*)

unclean contaminated, corrupt, defiled, dirty, evil, filthy, foul, impure, nasty, polluted, scuzzy (*slang, chiefly U.S.*), soiled, spotted, stained, sullied, tainted
Antonyms clean, faultless, flawless, pure, spotless, unblemished, unstained, unsullied

unclear ambiguous, bleary, blurred, confused, dim, doubtful, faint, fuzzy, hazy, ill-defined, indefinite, indeterminate, indiscernible, indistinct, indistinguishable, misty, muffled, obscure, out of focus, shadowy, undefined, unintelligible, vague, weak
Antonyms clear, defined, determinate, discernible, distinct, distinguishable, evident, intelligible

uncomfortable 1. awkward, causing discomfort, cramped, disagreeable, hard, ill-fitting, incommodious, irritating, painful, rough, troublesome 2. awkward, confused, discomfited, disquieted, distressed, disturbed, embarrassed, ill at ease, like a fish out of water, out of place, self-conscious, troubled, uneasy
Antonyms (*sense 2*) at ease, at home, comfortable, easy, relaxed, serene, untroubled

uncommitted floating, free, free-floating, neutral, nonaligned, nonpartisan, not involved, (sitting) on the fence, unattached, uninvolved

uncommon 1. bizarre, curious, few and far between, infrequent, novel, odd, out of the ordinary, peculiar, queer, rare, scarce, singular, strange, thin on the ground, unfamiliar, unusual 2. distinctive, exceptional, extraordinary, incomparable, inimitable, notable, noteworthy, outstanding, rare, remarkable, singular, special, superior, unparalleled, unprecedented
Antonyms (*sense 1*) common, familiar, frequent, regular, routine, usual (*sense 2*) average, banal, commonplace, everyday, humdrum, mundane, ordinary, run-of-the-mill

uncommonly 1. hardly ever, infrequently, not often, occasionally, only now and then, rarely, scarcely ever, seldom 2. exceptionally, extremely, particularly, peculiarly, remarkably, seriously (*informal*), strangely, to the nth degree, unusually, very

uncommunicative close, curt, guarded, reserved, reticent, retiring, secretive, short, shy, silent, taciturn, tight-lipped, unforthcoming, unresponsive, unsociable, withdrawn
Antonyms chatty, communicative, forthcoming, garrulous, loquacious, responsive, talkative, voluble

uncompromising decided, die-hard, firm, hardline, inexorable, inflexible, intransigent, obdurate, obstinate, rigid, steadfast, stiff-necked, strict, stubborn, tough, unbending, unyielding

unconcern aloofness, apathy, detachment, indifference, insouciance, lack of interest, nonchalance, remoteness, uninterestedness

unconcerned **1.** aloof, apathetic, cool, detached, dispassionate, distant, incurious, indifferent, oblivious, uninterested, uninvolved, unmoved, unsympathetic **2.** blithe, callous, carefree, careless, easy, insouciant, nonchalant, not bothered, not giving a toss (*informal*), relaxed, serene, unperturbed, unruffled, untroubled, unworried

Antonyms (*sense 1*) avid, curious, eager, interested, involved (*sense 2*) agitated, anxious, concerned, distressed, perturbed, uneasy, worried

unconditional absolute, arrant, categorical, complete, downright, entire, explicit, full, out-and-out, outright, plenary, positive, thoroughgoing, total, unlimited, unqualified, unreserved, unrestricted, utter

Antonyms conditional, limited, partial, qualified, reserved, restricted

uncongenial antagonistic, antipathetic, disagreeable, discordant, displeasing, distasteful, incompatible, not one's cup of tea (*informal*), unharmonious, uninviting, unpleasant, unsuited, unsympathetic

Antonyms affable, agreeable, compatible, congenial, genial, harmonious, pleasant, pleasing, sympathetic

unconnected **1.** detached, disconnected, divided, independent, separate **2.** disconnected, disjointed, illogical, incoherent, irrelevant, meaningless, nonsensical, not related, unrelated

Antonyms (*sense 2*) coherent, connected, intelligible, logical, meaningful, related, relevant

unconquerable **1.** indomitable, invincible, unbeatable, undefeatable, unyielding **2.** enduring, ingrained, innate, insurmountable, inveterate, irrepressible, irresistible, overpowering

unconscionable **1.** amoral, criminal, unethical, unfair, unjust, unprincipled, unscrupulous **2.** excessive, exorbitant, extravagant, extreme, immoderate, inordinate, outrageous, preposterous, unreasonable

unconscious **1.** blacked out (*informal*), comatose, dead to the world (*informal*), insensible, knocked out, numb, out, out cold, out for the count (*Boxing*), senseless, stunned **2.** blind to, deaf to, heedless, ignorant, in ignorance, lost to, oblivious, unaware, unknowing, unmindful, unsuspecting **3.** accidental, inadvertent, unintended, unintentional, unpremeditated, unwitting **4.** automatic, gut (*informal*), inherent, innate, instinctive, involuntary, latent, reflex, repressed, subconscious, subliminal, suppressed, unrealized

Antonyms (*sense 1*) alert, awake, aware, conscious, responsive, sensible (*sense 3*) calculated, conscious, deliberate, intentional, planned, studied, wilful

uncontrollable beside oneself, carried away, frantic, furious, irrepressible, irresistible, like one possessed, mad, strong, ungovernable, unmanageable, unruly, violent, wild

uncontrolled boisterous, full-on (*informal*), furious, lacking self-control, out of control, out of hand, rampant, riotous, running wild, unbridled, unchecked, uncurbed, undisciplined, ungoverned, unrestrained, unruly, unsubmissive, untrammelled, violent

Antonyms contained, controlled, disciplined, restrained, subdued, submissive

unconventional atypical, bizarre, bohemian, different, eccentric, far-out (*slang*), freakish, idiosyncratic, individual, individualistic, informal, irregular, left-field (*informal*), nonconformist, odd, oddball (*informal*), offbeat, off-the-wall (*slang*), original, out of the ordinary, outré, uncustomary, unorthodox, unusual, wacko (*slang*), way-out (*informal*)

Antonyms conventional, normal, ordinary, orthodox, proper, regular, typical, usual

unconvincing cock-and-bull (*informal*), dubious, feeble, fishy (*informal*), flimsy, hard to believe, implausible, improbable, inconclusive, lame, questionable, specious, suspect, thin, unlikely, unpersuasive, weak

Antonyms believable, conclusive, convincing, credible, likely, persuasive, plausible, probable

uncooperative awkward, bloody-minded (*Brit. informal*), cussed (*informal*), difficult, disobliging, inconsiderate, obstructive, unaccommodating, unhelpful, unneighbourly, unreasonable, unresponsive, unsupportive

Antonyms accommodating, considerate, cooperative, helpful, neighbourly, obliging, reasonable, responsive, supportive

uncoordinated all thumbs, awkward, bumbling, bungling, butterfingered (*informal*), clodhopping (*informal*), clumsy, graceless, heavy-footed, inept, lumbering, maladroit, ungainly, ungraceful

uncounted countless, infinite, innumerable, legion, multitudinous, myriad, numberless, unnumbered, untold

uncouth awkward, barbaric, boorish, clownish, clumsy, coarse, crude, gawky, graceless, gross, ill-mannered, loutish, lubberly, oafish, rough, rude, rustic, uncivilized, uncultivated, ungainly, unrefined, unseemly, vulgar

Antonyms civilized, courteous, cultivated, elegant, graceful, refined, seemly, well-mannered

uncover **1.** bare, lay open, lift the lid, open, show, strip, take the wraps off, unwrap **2.**

blow wide open (*slang*), bring to light, disclose, discover, divulge, expose, lay bare, make known, reveal, unearth, unmask
Antonyms clothe, conceal, cover, cover up, drape, dress, hide, keep under wraps, suppress

uncritical easily pleased, indiscriminate, undiscerning, undiscriminating, unexacting, unfussy, unperceptive, unselective, unthinking
Antonyms critical, discerning, discriminating, fastidious, fussy, perceptive, selective

unctuous **1.** fawning, glib, gushing, ingratiating, insincere, obsequious, oily, plausible, slick, smarmy (*Brit. informal*), smooth, suave, sycophantic **2.** greasy, oily, oleaginous, slippery, slithery

undaunted bold, brave, courageous, dauntless, fearless, gallant, gritty, indomitable, intrepid, not discouraged, nothing daunted, not put off, resolute, steadfast, undeterred, undiscouraged, undismayed, unfaltering, unflinching, unshrinking

undeceive be honest with, correct, disabuse, disillusion, enlighten, open (someone's) eyes (to), put (someone) right, set (someone) straight, shatter (someone's) illusions

undecided **1.** ambivalent, dithering (*chiefly Brit.*), doubtful, dubious, hesitant, in two minds, irresolute, swithering (*Scot.*), torn, uncertain, uncommitted, unsure, wavering **2.** debatable, iffy (*informal*), indefinite, in the balance, moot, open, pending, tentative, unconcluded, undetermined, unsettled, up in the air, vague
Antonyms certain, committed, decided, definite, determined, resolute, resolved, settled, sure

undecipherable crabbed, cryptic, hieroglyphic, illegible, impenetrable, incomprehensible, indecipherable, indistinct, undistinguishable, unreadable, unrecognizable

undefended defenceless, exposed, naked, open to attack, unarmed, unfortified, unguarded, unprotected, vulnerable, wide open
Antonyms armed, defended, fortified, guarded, protected

undefiled chaste, clean, clear, flawless, immaculate, impeccable, pure, sinless, spotless, squeaky-clean, unblemished, unsoiled, unspotted, unstained, unsullied, virginal
Antonyms blemished, defiled, flawed, impure, sinful, soiled, spotted, stained, sullied

undefined **1.** formless, hazy, indefinite, indistinct, shadowy, tenuous, vague **2.** imprecise, indeterminate, inexact, unclear, unexplained, unspecified
Antonyms (*sense 2*) clear, defined, definite, determinate, exact, explicit, precise, specified

undemonstrative aloof, cold, contained, distant, formal, impassive, reserved, restrained, reticent, stiff, stolid, unaffectionate, uncommunicative, unemotional, unresponsive, withdrawn
Antonyms affectionate, demonstrative, emotional, expressive, friendly, outgoing, overemotional, unreserved, warm

undeniable beyond (a) doubt, beyond question, certain, clear, evident, incontestable, incontrovertible, indisputable, indubitable, irrefutable, manifest, obvious, patent, proven, sound, sure, unassailable, undoubted, unquestionable
Antonyms debatable, deniable, doubtful, dubious, questionable, uncertain, unproven

undependable capricious, changeable, erratic, fickle, inconsistent, inconstant, irresponsible, treacherous, uncertain, unpredictable, unreliable, unstable, untrustworthy, variable

under *preposition* **1.** below, beneath, on the bottom of, underneath **2.** directed by, governed by, inferior to, junior to, reporting to, secondary to, subject to, subordinate to, subservient to **3.** belonging to, comprised in, included in, subsumed under *~adverb* **4.** below, beneath, down, downward, lower, to the bottom
Antonyms (*senses 1 & 4*) above, over, up, upper, upward

underclothes lingerie, smalls (*informal*), underclothing, undergarments, underlinen, underthings, underwear, undies (*informal*), unmentionables (*humorous*)

Underwear
see CLOTHES

undercover clandestine, concealed, confidential, covert, hidden, hush-hush (*informal*), intelligence, private, secret, spy, surreptitious, underground
Antonyms manifest, open, overt, plain, unconcealed, visible

undercurrent **1.** crosscurrent, rip, rip current, riptide, tideway, underflow, undertow **2.** atmosphere, aura, drift, feeling, flavour, hidden feeling, hint, murmur, overtone, sense, suggestion, tendency, tenor, tinge, trend, undertone, vibes (*slang*), vibrations

undercut **1.** sacrifice, sell at a loss, sell cheaply, undercharge, underprice, undersell **2.** cut away, cut out, excavate, gouge out, hollow out, mine, undermine

underdog fall guy (*informal*), little fellow (*informal*), loser, victim, weaker party

underestimate belittle, hold cheap, minimize, miscalculate, misprize, not do justice to, rate too low, sell short (*informal*), set no store by, think too little of, underrate, undervalue
Antonyms exaggerate, inflate, overdo, overestimate, overrate, overstate

undergo bear, be subjected to, endure, experience, go through, stand, submit to, suffer, sustain, weather, withstand

underground *adjective* **1.** below ground, below the surface, buried, covered, subterranean **2.** clandestine, concealed, covert, hidden, secret, surreptitious, undercover **3.** alternative, avant-garde, experimental, radical, revolutionary, subversive *~noun* **the underground 4.** the metro, the subway, the tube (*Brit.*) **5.** partisans, the Maquis, the Resistance

undergrowth bracken, brambles, briars, brush, brushwood, scrub, underbrush, underbush, underwood

underhand below the belt (*informal*), clandestine, crafty, crooked (*informal*), deceitful, deceptive, devious, dishonest, dishonourable, fraudulent, furtive, secret, secretive, sly, sneaky, stealthy, surreptitious, treacherous, underhanded, unethical, unscrupulous

Antonyms above board, frank, honest, honourable, legal, open, outright, principled, scrupulous

underline 1. italicize, mark, rule a line under, underscore **2.** accentuate, bring home, call *or* draw attention to, emphasize, give emphasis to, highlight, point up, stress

Antonyms (*sense 2*) gloss over, make light of, minimize, play down, soft-pedal (*informal*), underrate

underling cohort (*chiefly U.S.*), flunky, hireling, inferior, lackey, menial, minion, nonentity, retainer, servant, slave, subordinate, understrapper

underlying 1. concealed, hidden, latent, lurking, veiled **2.** basal, basic, elementary, essential, fundamental, intrinsic, primary, prime, radical, root

undermine 1. dig out, eat away at, erode, excavate, mine, tunnel, undercut, wear away **2.** debilitate, disable, impair, sabotage, sap, subvert, threaten, weaken

Antonyms (*sense 2*) buttress, fortify, promote, reinforce, strengthen, sustain

underpinning 1. base, footing, foundation, groundwork, substructure, support **2.** *plural* backbone, basis, foundation, ground, support

underprivileged badly off, deprived, destitute, disadvantaged, impoverished, in need, in want, needy, on the breadline, poor

underrate belittle, discount, disparage, fail to appreciate, misprize, not do justice to, set (too) little store by, underestimate, undervalue

Antonyms exaggerate, overestimate, overprize, overrate, overvalue

undersell 1. cut, mark down, reduce, slash, undercharge, undercut **2.** play down, understate

undersized atrophied, dwarfish, miniature, pygmy *or* pigmy, runtish, runty, small, squat, stunted, teensy-weensy, teeny-weeny, tiny, underdeveloped, underweight

Antonyms big, colossal, giant, huge, massive, oversized, overweight

understand 1. appreciate, apprehend, be aware, catch on (*informal*), comprehend, conceive, cotton on (*informal*), discern, fathom, follow, get, get one's head round, get the hang of (*informal*), get to the bottom of, grasp, know, make head or tail of (*informal*), make out, penetrate, perceive, realize, recognize, savvy (*slang*), see, see the light, take in, tumble to (*informal*), twig (*Brit. informal*) **2.** assume, be informed, believe, conclude, gather, hear, learn, presume, suppose, take it, think **3.** accept, appreciate, be able to see, commiserate, show compassion for, sympathize with, tolerate

understandable justifiable, legitimate, logical, natural, normal, reasonable, to be expected

understanding *noun* **1.** appreciation, awareness, comprehension, discernment, grasp, insight, intelligence, judgment, knowledge, penetration, perception, sense **2.** belief, conclusion, estimation, idea, interpretation, judgment, notion, opinion, perception, view, viewpoint **3.** accord, agreement, common view, gentlemen's agreement, meeting of minds, pact *~adjective* **4.** accepting, compassionate, considerate, discerning, forbearing, forgiving, kind, kindly, patient, perceptive, responsive, sensitive, sympathetic, tolerant

Antonyms *noun* (*sense 1*) ignorance, incomprehension, insensitivity, misapprehension, misunderstanding, obtuseness (*sense 3*) aloofness, coldness, disagreement, dispute *~adjective* inconsiderate, insensitive, intolerant, obtuse, rigid, strict, unfeeling, unsympathetic

The ill and unfit choice of words wonderfully obstructs the understanding

Francis Bacon *Novum Organum*

I shall light a candle of understanding in thine heart, which shall not be put out

Bible: II Esdras

understood 1. implicit, implied, inferred, tacit, unspoken, unstated **2.** accepted, assumed, axiomatic, presumed, taken for granted

understudy *noun* double, fill-in, replacement, reserve, stand-in, sub, substitute

undertake 1. agree, bargain, commit oneself, contract, covenant, engage, guarantee, pledge, promise, stipulate, take upon oneself **2.** attempt, begin, commence, embark on, endeavour, enter upon, set about, tackle, take on, try

undertaker funeral director, mortician (*U.S.*)

undertaking 1. affair, attempt, business, effort, endeavour, enterprise, game, operation, pro~

ject, task, venture 2. assurance, commitment, pledge, promise, solemn word, vow, word, word of honour

undertone 1. low tone, murmur, subdued voice, whisper 2. atmosphere, feeling, flavour, hint, suggestion, tinge, touch, trace, undercurrent, vibes (*slang*)

undervalue depreciate, hold cheap, look down on, make light of, minimize, misjudge, misprize, set no store by, underestimate, underrate
Antonyms exaggerate, overestimate, overrate, overvalue

underwater submarine, submerged, sunken, undersea

under way afoot, begun, going on, in business, in motion, in operation, in progress, started

underwear lingerie, smalls (*informal*), underclothes, underclothing, undergarments, underlinen, underthings, undies (*informal*), unmentionables (*humorous*)

Underwear
see CLOTHES

underweight emaciated, half-starved, puny, skin and bone (*informal*), skinny, undernourished, undersized

underworld 1. criminal element, criminals, gangland (*informal*), gangsters, organized crime 2. abode of the dead, Hades, hell, infernal region, nether regions, nether world, the inferno

underwrite 1. back, finance, fund, guarantee, insure, provide security, sponsor, subsidize 2. countersign, endorse, initial, sign, subscribe 3. agree to, approve, consent, O.K. *or* okay (*informal*), sanction

undesigned accidental, fortuitous, inadvertent, not meant, unintended, unintentional, unpremeditated

undesirable disagreeable, disliked, distasteful, dreaded, for the birds (*informal*), objectionable, obnoxious, offensive, out of place, repugnant, strictly for the birds (*informal*), (to be) avoided, unacceptable, unattractive, unpleasing, unpopular, unsavoury, unsuitable, unwanted, unwelcome, unwished-for
Antonyms acceptable, agreeable, appealing, attractive, desirable, inviting, pleasing, popular, welcome

undeveloped embryonic, immature, inchoate, in embryo, latent, potential, primordial (*Biology*)

undignified beneath one, beneath one's dignity, improper, inappropriate, indecorous, inelegant, infra dig (*informal*), lacking dignity, unbecoming, ungentlemanly, unladylike, unrefined, unseemly, unsuitable
Antonyms appropriate, becoming, decorous, dignified, elegant, proper, refined, seemly, suitable

undisciplined disobedient, erratic, fitful, obstreperous, uncontrolled, unpredictable, unreliable, unrestrained, unruly, unschooled, unsteady, unsystematic, untrained, wayward, wild, wilful
Antonyms controlled, disciplined, obedient, predictable, reliable, restrained, steady, trained

undisguised blatant, complete, evident, explicit, genuine, manifest, obvious, open, out-and-out, overt, patent, thoroughgoing, transparent, unconcealed, unfeigned, unmistakable, utter, wholehearted
Antonyms concealed, covert, disguised, feigned, hidden, secret

undisputed accepted, acknowledged, beyond question, certain, conclusive, freely admitted, incontestable, incontrovertible, indisputable, irrefutable, not disputed, recognized, sure, unchallenged, uncontested, undeniable, undoubted, unquestioned
Antonyms deniable, disputed, doubtful, dubious, inconclusive, questioned, uncertain

undistinguished commonplace, everyday, indifferent, mediocre, no great shakes (*informal*), nothing to write home about (*informal*), ordinary, pedestrian, prosaic, run-of-the-mill, so-so (*informal*), unexceptional, unexciting, unimpressive, unremarkable, vanilla (*informal*)
Antonyms distinguished, exceptional, exciting, extraordinary, impressive, notable, outstanding, remarkable, striking

undisturbed 1. not moved, quiet, uninterrupted, untouched, without interruption 2. calm, collected, composed, equable, even, motionless, placid, sedate, serene, tranquil, unagitated, unbothered, unfazed (*informal*), unperturbed, unruffled, untroubled
Antonyms (*sense 1*) confused, disordered, interfered with, interrupted, moved, muddled (*sense 2*) agitated, bothered, busy, disturbed, excited, flustered, nervous, perturbed, troubled, upset

undivided combined, complete, concentrated, concerted, entire, exclusive, full, solid, thorough, unanimous, undistracted, united, whole, wholehearted

undo 1. disengage, disentangle, loose, loosen, open, unbutton, unfasten, unlock, untie, unwrap 2. annul, cancel, invalidate, neutralize, nullify, offset, reverse, wipe out 3. bring to naught, defeat, destroy, impoverish, invalidate, mar, overturn, quash, ruin, shatter, subvert, undermine, upset, wreck

undoing 1. collapse, defeat, destruction, disgrace, downfall, humiliation, overthrow, over~

turn, reversal, ruin, ruination, shame **2.** affliction, blight, curse, fatal flaw, misfortune, the last straw, trial, trouble, weakness

undone[1] *adjective* incomplete, left, neglected, not completed, not done, omitted, outstanding, passed over, unattended to, unfinished, unfulfilled, unperformed
Antonyms accomplished, attended to, complete, done, finished, fulfilled, performed

undone[2] *adjective* betrayed, destroyed, forlorn, hapless, overcome, prostrate, ruined, wretched

undoubted acknowledged, certain, definite, evident, incontrovertible, indisputable, indubitable, obvious, sure, undisputed, unquestionable, unquestioned

undoubtedly assuredly, beyond a shadow of (a) doubt, beyond question, certainly, come hell or high water (*informal*), definitely, doubtless, of course, surely, undeniably, unmistakably, unquestionably, without doubt

undreamed of astonishing, inconceivable, incredible, miraculous, undreamt, unexpected, unforeseen, unheard-of, unimagined, unsuspected, unthought-of

undress 1. *verb* disrobe, divest oneself of, peel off (*slang*), shed, strip, take off one's clothes **2.** *noun* disarray, dishabille, nakedness, nudity

undue disproportionate, excessive, extravagant, extreme, immoderate, improper, inordinate, intemperate, needless, overmuch, too great, too much, uncalled-for, undeserved, unnecessary, unseemly, unwarranted
Antonyms appropriate, due, fitting, justified, necessary, proper, suitable, well-considered

undulate billow, heave, ripple, rise and fall, roll, surge, swell, wave

unduly disproportionately, excessively, extravagantly, immoderately, improperly, inordinately, out of all proportion, overly, overmuch, unjustifiably, unnecessarily, unreasonably
Antonyms duly, justifiably, moderately, ordinately, properly, proportionately, reasonably

undying constant, continuing, deathless, eternal, everlasting, immortal, imperishable, indestructible, inextinguishable, infinite, perennial, permanent, perpetual, sempiternal (*literary*), undiminished, unending, unfading
Antonyms ephemeral, finite, fleeting, impermanent, inconstant, momentary, mortal, perishable, short-lived

unearth 1. dig up, disinter, dredge up, excavate, exhume **2.** bring to light, discover, expose, ferret out, find, reveal, root up, turn up, uncover

unearthly 1. eerie, eldritch (*poetic*), ghostly, haunted, nightmarish, phantom, spectral, spooky (*informal*), strange, uncanny, weird **2.** ethereal, heavenly, not of this world, preternatural, sublime, supernatural **3.** abnormal, absurd, extraordinary, ridiculous, strange, ungodly (*informal*), unholy (*informal*), unreasonable

uneasiness agitation, alarm, anxiety, apprehension, apprehensiveness, disquiet, doubt, dubiety, misgiving, nervousness, perturbation, qualms, suspicion, trepidation, worry
Antonyms calm, composure, cool, ease, peace, quiet, serenity

uneasy 1. agitated, anxious, apprehensive, discomposed, disturbed, edgy, ill at ease, impatient, jittery (*informal*), like a fish out of water, nervous, on edge, perturbed, restive, restless, troubled, twitchy (*informal*), uncomfortable, unsettled, upset, wired (*slang*), worried **2.** awkward, constrained, insecure, precarious, shaky, strained, tense, uncomfortable, unstable **3.** bothering, dismaying, disquieting, disturbing, troubling, upsetting, worrying
Antonyms at ease, calm, comfortable, relaxed, tranquil, unfazed (*informal*), unflustered, unperturbed, unruffled

uneconomic loss-making, nonpaying, nonprofit-making, nonviable, unprofitable
Antonyms economic, money-making, productive, profitable, remunerative, viable

uneducated 1. ignorant, illiterate, unlettered, unread, unschooled, untaught **2.** benighted, lowbrow, uncultivated, uncultured
Antonyms (*sense 1*) educated, informed, instructed, literate, schooled, taught, tutored

unembellished austere, bald, bare, functional, modest, plain, severe, simple, spartan, stark, unadorned, unfussy, unornamented, unvarnished

unemotional apathetic, cold, cool, impassive, indifferent, listless, passionless, phlegmatic, reserved, undemonstrative, unexcitable, unfeeling, unimpressionable, unresponsive
Antonyms demonstrative, emotional, excitable, feeling, passionate, responsive, sensitive

unemployed idle, jobless, laid off, on the dole (*Brit. informal*), out of a job, out of work, redundant, resting (*of an actor*), workless

unending ceaseless, constant, continual, endless, eternal, everlasting, incessant, interminable, never-ending, perpetual, unceasing, unremitting

unendurable insufferable, insupportable, intolerable, more than flesh and blood can stand, unbearable
Antonyms bearable, endurable, sufferable, supportable, tolerable

unenthusiastic apathetic, blasé, bored, half-arsed (*Brit. slang*), half-assed (*U.S. & Canad. slang*), half-hearted, indifferent, lukewarm,

neutral, nonchalant, unimpressed, uninterested, unmoved, unresponsive
Antonyms ardent, eager, enthusiastic, excited, interested, keen, passionate

unenviable disagreeable, painful, thankless, uncomfortable, undesirable, unpleasant
Antonyms agreeable, attractive, desirable, enviable, pleasant

unequal 1. different, differing, disparate, dissimilar, not uniform, unlike, unmatched, variable, varying 2. *with* **to** found wanting, inadequate, insufficient, not up to 3. asymmetrical, disproportionate, ill-matched, irregular, unbalanced, uneven
Antonyms (*sense 1*) equal, equivalent, identical, like, matched, similar, uniform

unequalled beyond compare, incomparable, inimitable, matchless, nonpareil, paramount, peerless, pre-eminent, second to none, supreme, transcendent, unmatched, unparalleled, unrivalled, unsurpassed, without equal

unequivocal absolute, black-and-white, certain, clear, clear-cut, cut-and-dried (*informal*), decisive, definite, direct, evident, explicit, incontrovertible, indubitable, manifest, plain, positive, straight, unambiguous, uncontestable, unmistakable
Antonyms ambiguous, doubtful, equivocal, evasive, indecisive, noncommittal, vague

unerring accurate, certain, exact, faultless, impeccable, infallible, perfect, sure, unfailing

unethical dirty, dishonest, dishonourable, disreputable, illegal, immoral, improper, not cricket (*informal*), shady (*informal*), underhand, under-the-table, unfair, unprincipled, unprofessional, unscrupulous, wrong
Antonyms ethical, honest, honourable, legal, moral, proper, scrupulous, upright

uneven 1. bumpy, not flat, not level, not smooth, rough 2. broken, changeable, fitful, fluctuating, intermittent, irregular, jerky, patchy, spasmodic, unsteady, variable 3. asymmetrical, lopsided, not parallel, odd, out of true, unbalanced 4. disparate, ill-matched, one-sided, unequal, unfair
Antonyms (*sense 1*) even, flat, level, plane, smooth

uneventful boring, commonplace, dull, ho-hum (*informal*), humdrum, monotonous, ordinary, quiet, routine, tedious, unexceptional, unexciting, uninteresting, unmemorable, unremarkable, unvaried
Antonyms eventful, exceptional, exciting, interesting, memorable, momentous, remarkable

unexampled unequalled, unheard-of, unique, unmatched, unparalleled, unprecedented

unexceptional bog-standard (*Brit. & Irish slang*), common or garden (*informal*), commonplace, conventional, insignificant, mediocre, no great shakes (*informal*), normal, nothing to write home about (*informal*), ordinary, pedestrian, run-of-the-mill, undistinguished, unimpressive, unremarkable, usual
Antonyms distinguished, exceptional, impressive, notable, noteworthy, outstanding, remarkable, significant, unusual

unexpected abrupt, accidental, astonishing, chance, fortuitous, not bargained for, out of the blue, startling, sudden, surprising, unanticipated, unforeseen, unlooked-for, unpredictable
Antonyms anticipated, awaited, expected, foreseen, normal, planned, predictable

Expect the unexpected

unexpressive blank, emotionless, expressionless, impassive, inexpressive, inscrutable, vacant

unfailing 1. bottomless, boundless, ceaseless, continual, continuous, endless, inexhaustible, never-failing, persistent, unflagging, unlimited 2. certain, constant, dependable, faithful, infallible, loyal, reliable, staunch, steadfast, sure, tried and true, true
Antonyms (*sense 2*) disloyal, fallible, inconstant, uncertain, unfaithful, unreliable, unsure, untrustworthy

unfair 1. arbitrary, biased, bigoted, discriminatory, inequitable, one-sided, partial, partisan, prejudiced, unjust 2. crooked (*informal*), dishonest, dishonourable, uncalled-for, unethical, unprincipled, unscrupulous, unsporting, unwarranted, wrongful
Antonyms (*sense 2*) ethical, fair, honest, just, principled, scrupulous

unfaithful 1. deceitful, disloyal, faithless, false, false-hearted, perfidious, recreant (*archaic*), traitorous, treacherous, treasonable, unreliable, untrustworthy 2. adulterous, faithless, fickle, inconstant, two-timing (*informal*), unchaste, untrue 3. distorted, erroneous, imperfect, imprecise, inaccurate, inexact, unreliable, untrustworthy
Antonyms (*sense 1*) constant, faithful, loyal, steadfast, true, trustworthy (*sense 3*) accurate, exact, perfect, precise, reliable

unfaltering firm, indefatigable, persevering, resolute, steadfast, steady, tireless, unfailing, unflagging, unflinching, unswerving, untiring, unwavering

unfamiliar 1. alien, beyond one's ken, curious, different, little known, new, novel, out-of-the-way, strange, unaccustomed, uncommon, unknown, unusual 2. *with* **with** a stranger to, inexperienced in, unaccustomed to, unacquainted, unconversant, uninformed about, uninitiated in, unpractised in, unskilled at, unversed in
Antonyms accustomed, acquainted, average,

common, commonplace, conversant, everyday, experienced, familiar, knowledgeable, normal, unexceptional, well-known, well-versed

unfashionable antiquated, behind the times, dated, obsolete, old-fashioned, old hat, out, outmoded, out of date, out of fashion, out of the ark (*informal*), passé, square (*informal*), unpopular
Antonyms à la mode, fashionable, modern, popular, stylish, trendy (*Brit. informal*)

unfasten detach, disconnect, let go, loosen, open, separate, uncouple, undo, unlace, unlock, untie

unfathomable 1. bottomless, immeasurable, unmeasured, unplumbed, unsounded 2. abstruse, baffling, deep, esoteric, impenetrable, incomprehensible, indecipherable, inexplicable, profound, unknowable

unfavourable 1. adverse, bad, contrary, disadvantageous, hostile, ill-suited, infelicitous, inimical, low, negative, poor, unfortunate, unfriendly, unsuited 2. inauspicious, inopportune, ominous, threatening, unlucky, unpromising, unpropitious, unseasonable, untimely, untoward
Antonyms (*sense 1*) amicable, approving, favourable, friendly, positive, warm, well-disposed

unfeeling 1. apathetic, callous, cold, cruel, hardened, hardhearted, heartless, inhuman, insensitive, pitiless, stony, uncaring, unsympathetic 2. insensate, insensible, numb, sensationless
Antonyms (*sense 1*) benevolent, caring, concerned, feeling, gentle, humane, kind, sensitive, sympathetic

unfeigned genuine, heartfelt, natural, pure, real, sincere, unaffected, unforced, wholehearted

unfettered free, unbridled, unchecked, unconfined, unconstrained, unrestrained, unshackled, untrammelled

unfinished 1. deficient, half-done, imperfect, incomplete, in the making, lacking, unaccomplished, uncompleted, undone, unfulfilled, wanting 2. bare, crude, natural, raw, rough, sketchy, unpolished, unrefined, unvarnished
Antonyms (*sense 2*) finished, flawless, perfected, polished, refined, smooth, varnished

unfit 1. ill-equipped, inadequate, incapable, incompetent, ineligible, no good, not cut out for, not equal to, not up to, unprepared, unqualified, untrained, useless 2. ill-adapted, inadequate, inappropriate, ineffective, not designed, not fit, unsuitable, unsuited, useless 3. debilitated, decrepit, feeble, flabby, in poor condition, out of kelter, out of shape, out of trim, unhealthy
Antonyms (*senses 1 & 2*) able, acceptable, capable, competent, equipped, qualified, ready, suitable (*sense 3*) fit, healthy, in good condition, strong, sturdy, well

unflagging constant, fixed, indefatigable, persevering, persistent, staunch, steady, tireless, unceasing, undeviating, unfailing, unfaltering, unremitting, untiring, unwearied

unflappable calm, collected, composed, cool, impassive, imperturbable, level-headed, not given to worry, self-possessed, unfazed (*informal*), unruffled
Antonyms excitable, flappable, hot-headed, nervous, temperamental, twitchy (*informal*), volatile

unflattering 1. blunt, candid, critical, honest, uncomplimentary, warts and all 2. not shown in the best light, not shown to advantage, plain, unattractive, unbecoming, unprepossessing

unfledged callow, green, immature, inexperienced, raw, undeveloped, untried, young

unflinching bold, constant, determined, firm, immovable, resolute, stalwart, staunch, steadfast, steady, unfaltering, unshaken, unshrinking, unswerving, unwavering
Antonyms cowed, faltering, scared, shaken, shrinking, wavering

unfold 1. disentangle, expand, flatten, open, spread out, straighten, stretch out, undo, unfurl, unravel, unroll, unwrap 2. *figurative* clarify, describe, disclose, divulge, explain, illustrate, make known, present, reveal, show, uncover 3. bear fruit, blossom, develop, evolve, expand, grow, mature

unforeseen abrupt, accidental, out of the blue, startling, sudden, surprise, surprising, unanticipated, unexpected, unlooked-for, unpredicted
Antonyms anticipated, envisaged, expected, foreseen, intended, predicted

unforgettable exceptional, extraordinary, fixed in the mind, impressive, memorable, never to be forgotten, notable, striking

unforgivable deplorable, disgraceful, indefensible, inexcusable, shameful, unjustifiable, unpardonable, unwarrantable
Antonyms allowable, excusable, forgivable, justifiable, pardonable, venial

unfortunate 1. adverse, calamitous, disastrous, ill-fated, ill-starred, inopportune, ruinous, unfavourable, untoward 2. cursed, doomed, hapless, hopeless, luckless, out of luck, poor, star-crossed, unhappy, unlucky, unprosperous, unsuccessful, wretched 3. deplorable, ill-advised, inappropriate, infelicitous, lamentable, regrettable, unbecoming, unsuitable
Antonyms (*senses 1 & 3*) appropriate, opportune, suitable, tactful, timely (*sense 2*) auspi~

cious, felicitous, fortuitous, fortunate, happy, lucky, successful

unfounded baseless, fabricated, false, groundless, idle, spurious, trumped up, unjustified, unproven, unsubstantiated, vain, without basis, without foundation
Antonyms attested, confirmed, factual, justified, proven, substantiated, verified

unfrequented deserted, godforsaken, isolated, lone, lonely, off the beaten track, remote, sequestered, solitary, uninhabited, unvisited

unfriendly 1. aloof, antagonistic, chilly, cold, disagreeable, distant, hostile, ill-disposed, inhospitable, not on speaking terms, quarrelsome, sour, surly, uncongenial, unneighbourly, unsociable 2. alien, hostile, inauspicious, inhospitable, inimical, unfavourable, unpropitious
Antonyms affable, amiable, auspicious, congenial, convivial, friendly, hospitable, propitious, sociable, warm

unfruitful barren, fruitless, infecund, infertile, sterile, unproductive, unprofitable, unprolific, unrewarding
Antonyms abundant, fecund, fertile, fruitful, productive, profuse, prolific, rewarding

ungainly awkward, clumsy, gangling, gawky, inelegant, loutish, lubberly, lumbering, slouching, uncoordinated, uncouth, ungraceful
Antonyms attractive, comely, elegant, graceful, pleasing

ungodly 1. blasphemous, corrupt, depraved, godless, immoral, impious, irreligious, profane, sinful, vile, wicked 2. *informal* dreadful, horrendous, intolerable, outrageous, unearthly, unholy (*informal*), unreasonable, unseemly

ungovernable rebellious, refractory, uncontrollable, unmanageable, unrestrainable, unruly, wild

ungraceful all thumbs, awkward, clumsy, elephantine, gawky, heavy, inelegant, laboured, lumbering, ponderous, stiff, ugly, uncoordinated, ungainly, unnatural, unwieldy
Antonyms aesthetic, agile, coordinated, easy, elegant, flowing, graceful, natural, pleasing, smooth

ungracious bad-mannered, churlish, discourteous, ill-bred, impolite, offhand, rude, uncivil, unmannerly
Antonyms affable, civil, courteous, gracious, mannerly, polite, well-mannered

ungrateful heedless, ingrate (*archaic*), selfish, thankless, unappreciative, unmindful, unthankful
Antonyms appreciative, aware, grateful, mindful, thankful

unguarded 1. careless, foolhardy, heedless, ill-considered, impolitic, imprudent, incautious, indiscreet, rash, thoughtless, uncircumspect, undiplomatic, unthinking, unwary 2. defenceless, open to attack, undefended, unpatrolled, unprotected, vulnerable 3. artless, candid, direct, frank, guileless, open, straightforward
Antonyms (*sense 1*) cagey (*informal*), careful, cautious, diplomatic, discreet, guarded, prudent, wary

unhallowed 1. not sacred, unblessed, unconsecrated, unholy, unsanctified 2. damnable, evil, godless, irreverent, profane, sinful, wicked

unhandy 1. awkward, bumbling, bungling, clumsy, fumbling, heavy-handed, incompetent, inept, inexpert, maladroit, unskilful 2. awkward, cumbersome, hampering, ill-arranged, ill-contrived, inconvenient, unwieldy

unhappiness blues, dejection, depression, despondency, discontent, dissatisfaction, gloom, heartache, low spirits, melancholy, misery, sadness, sorrow, wretchedness

He felt the loyalty we all feel to unhappiness - the sense that that is where we really belong
Graham Greene *The Heart of the Matter*

Unhappiness is not knowing what we want and killing ourselves to get it
Don Herold

Unhappiness is best defined as the difference between our talents and our expectations
Edward de Bono

unhappy 1. blue, crestfallen, dejected, depressed, despondent, disconsolate, dispirited, down, downcast, down in the dumps (*informal*), gloomy, long-faced, low, melancholy, miserable, mournful, sad, sorrowful 2. cursed, hapless, ill-fated, ill-omened, luckless, unfortunate, unlucky, wretched 3. awkward, clumsy, gauche, ill-advised, ill-timed, inappropriate, inept, infelicitous, injudicious, malapropos, tactless, unsuitable, untactful
Antonyms (*sense 1*) cheerful, chirpy (*informal*), content, exuberant, genial, good-humoured, happy, joyful, light-hearted, overjoyed, over the moon (*informal*), satisfied (*senses 2 & 3*) apt, becoming, fortunate, lucky, prudent, suitable, tactful

unharmed in one piece (*informal*), intact, safe, safe and sound, sound, undamaged, unhurt, uninjured, unscarred, unscathed, untouched, whole, without a scratch
Antonyms damaged, harmed, hurt, impaired, injured, scarred, scathed

unhealthy 1. ailing, delicate, feeble, frail, infirm, in poor health, invalid, poorly (*informal*), sick, sickly, unsound, unwell, weak 2. deleterious, detrimental, harmful, insalubrious, insanitary, noisome, noxious, unwholesome 3. bad, baneful (*archaic*), corrupt, corrupting, degrading, demoralizing, morbid, negative, undesirable

Antonyms (*senses 1 & 2*) beneficial, fit, good, healthy, robust, salubrious, salutary, well, wholesome (*sense 3*) desirable, moral, positive

unheard-of 1. little known, obscure, undiscovered, unfamiliar, unknown, unregarded, unremarked, unsung 2. ground-breaking, inconceivable, never before encountered, new, novel, singular, unbelievable, undreamed of, unexampled, unique, unprecedented, unusual 3. disgraceful, extreme, offensive, outlandish, outrageous, preposterous, shocking, unacceptable, unthinkable

unheeded disobeyed, disregarded, forgotten, ignored, neglected, overlooked, unfollowed, unnoticed, unobserved, untaken
Antonyms heeded, noted, noticed, obeyed, observed, regarded, remembered

unheralded out of the blue, surprise, unacclaimed, unannounced, unexpected, unforeseen, unnoticed, unproclaimed, unpublicized, unrecognized, unsung

unhesitating 1. implicit, resolute, steadfast, unfaltering, unquestioning, unreserved, unswerving, unwavering, wholehearted 2. immediate, instant, instantaneous, prompt, ready, without delay
Antonyms (*sense 1*) diffident, hesitant, irresolute, questioning, tentative, uncertain, unsure, wavering

unhinge 1. confound, confuse, craze, derange, disorder, distemper (*archaic*), drive out of one's mind, madden, unbalance, unsettle 2. detach, disconnect, disjoint, dislodge, remove

unholy 1. base, corrupt, depraved, dishonest, evil, heinous, immoral, iniquitous, irreligious, profane, sinful, ungodly, vile, wicked 2. *informal* appalling, awful, dreadful, horrendous, outrageous, shocking, unearthly, ungodly (*informal*), unnatural, unreasonable
Antonyms (*sense 1*) devout, faithful, godly, holy, pious, religious, saintly, virtuous

unhoped-for beyond one's wildest dreams, incredible, like a dream come true, out of the blue, surprising, unanticipated, unbelievable, undreamed of, unexpected, unimaginable, unlooked-for

unhurried calm, deliberate, easy, easy-going, leisurely, sedate, slow, slow and steady, slow-paced
Antonyms brief, cursory, hasty, hectic, hurried, quick, rushed, speedy, swift

unidentified anonymous, mysterious, nameless, unclassified, unfamiliar, unknown, unmarked, unnamed, unrecognized, unrevealed
Antonyms classified, familiar, identified, known, marked, named, recognized

unification alliance, amalgamation, coalescence, coalition, combination, confederation, federation, fusion, merger, union, uniting

uniform *noun* 1. costume, dress, garb, habit, livery, outfit, regalia, regimentals, suit ~*adjective* 2. consistent, constant, equable, even, regular, smooth, unbroken, unchanging, undeviating, unvarying 3. alike, equal, identical, like, same, selfsame, similar
Antonyms *adjective* (*sense 2*) changeable, changing, deviating, inconsistent, irregular, uneven, variable

uniformity 1. constancy, evenness, homogeneity, invariability, regularity, sameness, similarity 2. drabness, dullness, flatness, lack of diversity, monotony, sameness, tedium

unify amalgamate, bind, bring together, combine, confederate, consolidate, federate, fuse, join, merge, unite
Antonyms alienate, disconnect, disjoin, disunite, divide, separate, sever, split

unimaginable beyond one's wildest dreams, fantastic, impossible, inconceivable, incredible, indescribable, ineffable, mind-boggling (*informal*), unbelievable, unheard-of, unthinkable

unimaginative banal, barren, commonplace, derivative, dry, dull, hackneyed, lifeless, matter-of-fact, ordinary, pedestrian, predictable, prosaic, routine, tame, uncreative, uninspired, unoriginal, unromantic, usual, vanilla (*informal*)
Antonyms creative, different, exciting, fresh, ground-breaking, imaginative, innovative, inventive, original, unhackneyed, unusual

unimpassioned calm, collected, composed, controlled, cool, dispassionate, impassive, moderate, rational, sedate, temperate, tranquil, undemonstrative, unemotional, unmoved

unimpeachable above reproach, beyond criticism, beyond question, blameless, faultless, impeccable, irreproachable, perfect, unassailable, unblemished, unchallengeable, unexceptionable, unquestionable
Antonyms blameworthy, faulty, imperfect, reprehensible, reproachable, shameful

unimpeded free, open, unblocked, unchecked, unconstrained, unhampered, unhindered, unrestrained, untrammelled
Antonyms blocked, checked, constrained, hampered, hindered, impeded, restrained

unimportant immaterial, inconsequential, insignificant, irrelevant, low-ranking, minor, nickel-and-dime (*U.S. slang*), not worth mentioning, nugatory, of no account, of no consequence, of no moment, paltry, petty, slight, trifling, trivial, worthless
Antonyms essential, grave, important, major, significant, urgent, vital, weighty

uninhabited abandoned, barren, desert, deserted, desolate, empty, unoccupied, unpopulated, unsettled, untenanted, vacant, waste

uninhibited 1. candid, frank, free, free and easy, informal, instinctive, liberated, natural, open, relaxed, spontaneous, unrepressed, unreserved, unselfconscious 2. free, unbridled, unchecked, unconstrained, uncontrolled, uncurbed, unrestrained, unrestricted
Antonyms bashful, careful, checked, constrained, controlled, curbed, demure, hampered, inhibited, modest, restrained, self-conscious, shy, uptight (*informal*)

uninspired banal, commonplace, dull, humdrum, indifferent, ordinary, prosaic, stale, stock, unexciting, unimaginative, uninspiring, uninteresting, unoriginal, vanilla (*informal*)
Antonyms brilliant, different, exciting, imaginative, inspired, interesting, original, outstanding

uninspiring as dry as dust, boring, drab, dreary, dry, dull, flat, humdrum, insipid, mundane, pedestrian, plain, prosaic, spiritless, unexciting, uninteresting
Antonyms affecting, encouraging, exciting, exhilarating, heartening, inspiring, moving, rousing, stimulating, stirring, uplifting

unintelligent braindead (*informal*), brainless, dense, dozy (*Brit. informal*), dull, empty-headed, foolish, gormless (*Brit. informal*), obtuse, slow, stupid, thick, unreasoning, unthinking
Antonyms bright, clever, intelligent, sharp, smart, thinking

unintelligible double Dutch (*Brit. informal*), Greek (*informal*), illegible, inarticulate, incoherent, incomprehensible, indecipherable, indistinct, jumbled, meaningless, muddled, unfathomable
Antonyms clear, coherent, comprehensible, intelligible, legible, lucid, understandable

unintentional accidental, casual, fortuitous, inadvertent, involuntary, unconscious, undesigned, unintended, unpremeditated, unthinking, unwitting
Antonyms conscious, deliberate, designed, intended, intentional, premeditated, voluntary, wilful

uninterested apathetic, blasé, bored, distant, impassive, incurious, indifferent, listless, unconcerned, uninvolved, unresponsive
Antonyms alert, concerned, curious, enthusiastic, interested, involved, keen, responsive

uninteresting as dry as dust, boring, commonplace, drab, dreary, dry, dull, flat, ho-hum (*informal*), humdrum, mind-numbing, monotonous, tedious, tiresome, unenjoyable, uneventful, unexciting, uninspiring, wearisome
Antonyms absorbing, compelling, enjoyable, exciting, gripping, inspiring, interesting, intriguing, stimulating

uninterrupted constant, continual, continuous, nonstop, peaceful, steady, sustained, unbroken, undisturbed, unending

uninvited not asked, not invited, unasked, unbidden, unwanted, unwelcome

uninviting disagreeable, offensive, off-putting (*Brit. informal*), repellent, repulsive, unappealing, unappetizing, unattractive, undesirable, unpleasant, untempting, unwelcoming
Antonyms agreeable, appealing, appetizing, attractive, desirable, inviting, pleasant, tempting, welcoming

union 1. amalgam, amalgamation, blend, combination, conjunction, fusion, junction, mixture, synthesis, uniting 2. alliance, association, Bund, coalition, confederacy, confederation, federation, league 3. accord, agreement, concord, concurrence, harmony, unanimity, unison, unity 4. coition, coitus, copulation, coupling, intercourse, marriage, matrimony, nookie (*slang*), rumpy-pumpy (*slang*), the other (*informal*), wedlock
Union is strength

unique 1. lone, one and only, only, single, solitary, sui generis 2. incomparable, inimitable, matchless, nonpareil, peerless, unequalled, unexampled, unmatched, unparalleled, unrivalled, without equal

unison accord, accordance, agreement, concert, concord, cooperation, harmony, unanimity, unity
Antonyms disagreement, discord, disharmony, dissension, dissidence, dissonance

unit 1. assembly, detachment, entity, group, section, system, whole 2. component, constituent, element, item, member, module, part, piece, portion, section, segment 3. measure, measurement, module, quantity

unite 1. amalgamate, blend, coalesce, combine, confederate, consolidate, couple, fuse, incorporate, join, link, marry, meld, merge, unify, wed 2. ally, associate, band, close ranks, club together, cooperate, join forces, join together, league, pool, pull together
Antonyms break, detach, disunite, divide, divorce, part, separate, sever, split

united 1. affiliated, allied, banded together, collective, combined, concerted, in partnership, leagued, pooled, unified 2. agreed, in accord, in agreement, like-minded, of like mind, of one mind, of the same opinion, one, unanimous

unity 1. entity, integrity, oneness, singleness, undividedness, unification, union, wholeness 2. accord, agreement, assent, concord, concurrence, consensus, harmony, peace, solidarity, unanimity, unison
Antonyms disagreement, discord, disunity, division, factionalism, heterogeneity, ill will,

independence, individuality, in-fighting, mul~tiplicity, separation, strife

We must indeed all hang together, or, most as~suredly, we shall all hang separately
Benjamin Franklin

All for one; one for all
Alexandre Dumas *The Three Musketeers*

By uniting we stand, by dividing we fall
John Dickinson *The Patriot's Appeal*

universal all-embracing, catholic, common, ecumenical, entire, general, omnipresent, to~tal, unlimited, whole, widespread, worldwide

universality all-inclusiveness, completeness, comprehensiveness, entirety, generality, gen~eralization, totality, ubiquity

universally across the board, always, every~where, in all cases, in every instance, invari~ably, uniformly, without exception

universe cosmos, creation, everything, macro~cosm, nature, the natural world

The universe is not hostile, nor yet is it friendly. It is simply indifferent
Revd. John H. Holmes *A Sensible Man's View of Religion*

Had I been present at the Creation, I would have given some useful hints for the better ordering of the universe
attributed to Alfonso "the Wise", King of Cas~tile

Now, my own suspicion is that the universe is not only queerer than we suppose, but queerer than we can suppose
J.B.S. Haldane *Possible Worlds*

university

Oxford gave the world marmalade and a manner, Cambridge science and a sausage
Anon.

The use of a university is to make young gentlemen as unlike their fathers as possible
Woodrow Wilson

unjust biased, inequitable, one-sided, partial, partisan, prejudiced, undeserved, unfair, un~justified, unmerited, wrong, wrongful
Antonyms equitable, ethical, fair, impartial, just, justified, right, unbiased

unjustifiable indefensible, inexcusable, outra~geous, unacceptable, unforgivable, unjust, un~pardonable, unwarrantable, wrong

unkempt bedraggled, blowzy, disarranged, dis~arrayed, dishevelled, disordered, frowzy, messy, rumpled, scruffy, shabby, shaggy, slat~ternly, sloppy (*informal*), slovenly, sluttish, tousled, uncombed, ungroomed, untidy
Antonyms neat, presentable, soigné *or* soi~gnée, spruce, tidy, trim, well-groomed

unkind cruel, hardhearted, harsh, inconsider~ate, inhuman, insensitive, malicious, mean, nasty, spiteful, thoughtless, uncaring, un~charitable, unchristian, unfeeling, unfriendly, unsympathetic
Antonyms benevolent, caring, charitable, con~siderate, generous, kind, soft-hearted, sympa~thetic, thoughtful

unkindness cruelty, hardheartedness, harsh~ness, ill will, inhumanity, insensitivity, ma~levolence, malice, maliciousness, meanness, spite, spitefulness, unfeeling
Antonyms benevolence, charity, friendliness, generosity, goodwill, kindness, sympathy, thoughtfulness

This was the most unkindest cut of all
William Shakespeare *Julius Caesar*

unknown **1.** alien, concealed, dark, hidden, mysterious, new, secret, strange, unrecog~nized, unrevealed, untold **2.** anonymous, be~yond one's ken, nameless, uncharted, undis~covered, unexplored, unidentified, unnamed **3.** humble, little known, obscure, undistin~guished, unfamiliar, unheard-of, unrenowned, unsung
Antonyms (*sense 3*) celebrated, distinguished, familiar, known, recognized, renowned, well-known

unladylike coarse, ill-bred, impolite, indelicate, rude, uncivil, ungracious, unmannerly, unre~fined
Antonyms civil, delicate, gracious, ladylike, mannerly, polite, refined, seemly

unlamented unbemoaned, unbewailed, unde~plored, unmissed, unmourned, unregret~ted, unwept

unlawful actionable, against the law, banned, criminal, forbidden, illegal, illegitimate, illicit, outlawed, prohibited, unauthorized, under-the-table, unlicensed

unleash free, let go, let loose, release, unbri~dle, unloose, untie

unlettered ignorant, illiterate, uneducated, unlearned, unschooled, untaught, untutored
Antonyms educated, learned, literate, schooled, taught, tutored

unlike as different as chalk and cheese (*infor~mal*), contrasted, different, dissimilar, distinct, divergent, diverse, ill-matched, incompatible, not alike, opposite, unequal, unrelated
Antonyms compatible, equal, like, matched, related, similar

unlikely **1.** doubtful, faint, improbable, not likely, remote, slight, unimaginable **2.** cock-and-bull (*informal*), implausible, incredible, questionable, unbelievable, unconvincing

unlimited **1.** boundless, countless, endless, ex~tensive, great, illimitable, immeasurable, im~mense, incalculable, infinite, limitless, stellar (*informal*), unbounded, vast **2.** absolute, all-encompassing, complete, full, total, uncondi~

tional, unconstrained, unfettered, unqualified, unrestricted
Antonyms (*sense 1*) bounded, circumscribed, confined, constrained, finite, limited, restricted

unload disburden, discharge, dump, empty, lighten, off-load, relieve, unburden, unlade, unpack

unlock free, let loose, open, release, unbar, unbolt, undo, unfasten, unlatch

unlooked-for chance, fortuitous, out of the blue, surprise, surprising, unanticipated, undreamed of, unexpected, unforeseen, unhoped-for, unpredicted, unthought-of

unlovable abhorrent, abominable, despicable, detestable, dislikable *or* dislikeable, hateful, loathsome, obnoxious, odious, offensive, repellent, repulsive, revolting, unadorable, unattractive, uncaptivating, undesirable, unlovely, unpleasant
Antonyms adorable, amiable, attractive, captivating, charming, cuddly, cute, desirable, enchanting, endearing, engaging, likable *or* likeable, lovable, lovely, winsome

unloved disliked, forsaken, loveless, neglected, rejected, spurned, uncared-for, uncherished, unpopular, unwanted
Antonyms adored, beloved, cherished, liked, loved, popular, precious, wanted

unlucky **1.** cursed, disastrous, hapless, luckless, miserable, unfortunate, unhappy, unsuccessful, wretched **2.** doomed, ill-fated, ill-omened, ill-starred, inauspicious, ominous, unfavourable, untimely
Antonyms (*sense 1*) blessed, favoured, fortunate, happy, lucky, prosperous

now and then
there is a person born
who is so unlucky
that he runs into accidents
which started to happen
to someone else

Don Marquis *archys life of mehitabel*

unman daunt, demoralize, discourage, dispirit, emasculate, enervate, enfeeble, intimidate, psych out (*informal*), unnerve, weaken

unmanageable **1.** awkward, bulky, clunky (*informal*), cumbersome, difficult to handle, inconvenient, unhandy, unwieldy **2.** difficult, fractious, intractable, obstreperous, out of hand, refractory, stroppy (*Brit. slang*), uncontrollable, unruly, wild
Antonyms (*sense 2*) amenable, compliant, docile, easy, manageable, submissive, tractable, wieldy

unmanly **1.** camp (*informal*), effeminate, feeble, sissy, soft (*informal*), weak, womanish **2.** abject, chicken-hearted, cowardly, craven, dishonourable, ignoble, weak-kneed (*informal*), yellow (*informal*)

unmannerly badly behaved, bad-mannered, discourteous, disrespectful, ill-bred, ill-mannered, impolite, misbehaved, rude, uncivil, uncouth
Antonyms civil, courteous, mannerly, polite, respectful, well-behaved, well-bred, well-mannered

unmarried bachelor, celibate, maiden, on the shelf, single, unattached, unwed, unwedded, virgin

unmask bare, bring to light, disclose, discover, expose, lay bare, reveal, show up, uncloak, uncover, unveil

unmatched beyond compare, consummate, incomparable, matchless, paramount, peerless, second to none, supreme, unequalled, unparalleled, unrivalled, unsurpassed

unmentionable disgraceful, disreputable, forbidden, frowned on, immodest, indecent, obscene, scandalous, shameful, shocking, taboo, unspeakable, unutterable, X-rated (*informal*)

unmerciful brutal, cruel, hard, heartless, implacable, merciless, pitiless, relentless, remorseless, ruthless, uncaring, unfeeling, unsparing
Antonyms beneficent, caring, feeling, humane, merciful, pitying, sparing, tender-hearted

unmethodical confused, desultory, disorderly, haphazard, irregular, muddled, orderless, random, systemless, unorganized, unsystematic

unmindful careless, forgetful, heedless, inattentive, indifferent, lax, neglectful, negligent, oblivious, remiss, slack, unheeding
Antonyms alert, attentive, aware, careful, heedful, mindful, regardful, watchful

unmistakable blatant, certain, clear, conspicuous, decided, distinct, evident, glaring, indisputable, manifest, obvious, palpable, patent, plain, positive, pronounced, sure, unambiguous, unequivocal
Antonyms ambiguous, dim, doubtful, equivocal, hidden, mistakable, obscure, uncertain, unclear, unsure

unmitigated **1.** grim, harsh, intense, oppressive, persistent, relentless, unabated, unalleviated, unbroken, undiminished, unmodified, unqualified, unredeemed, unrelieved **2.** absolute, arrant, complete, consummate, deep-dyed (*usually derogatory*), downright, out-and-out, outright, perfect, rank, sheer, thorough, thoroughgoing, utter

unmoved **1.** fast, firm, in place, in position, steady, unchanged, untouched **2.** cold, dry-eyed, impassive, indifferent, unaffected, unfeeling, unimpressed, unresponsive, unstirred, untouched **3.** determined, firm, inflexible,

resolute, resolved, steadfast, undeviating, unshaken, unwavering
Antonyms (*sense 1*) shifted, touched, transferred (*sense 2*) affected, concerned, impressed, moved, persuaded, stirred, swayed, touched (*sense 3*) adaptable, flexible, shaken, wavering

unnatural 1. aberrant, abnormal, anomalous, irregular, odd, perverse, perverted, unusual 2. bizarre, extraordinary, freakish, outlandish, queer, strange, supernatural, unaccountable, uncanny 3. affected, artificial, assumed, contrived, factitious, false, feigned, forced, insincere, laboured, mannered, phoney *or* phony (*informal*), self-conscious, stagy, stiff, stilted, strained, studied, theatrical 4. brutal, callous, cold-blooded, evil, fiendish, heartless, inhuman, monstrous, ruthless, savage, unfeeling, wicked
Antonyms (*senses 1 & 2*) normal, ordinary, typical (*sense 3*) genuine, honest, natural, sincere, unaffected, unfeigned, unpretentious (*sense 4*) caring, humane, loving, warm

unnecessary dispensable, expendable, inessential, needless, nonessential, redundant, supererogatory, superfluous, surplus to requirements, uncalled-for, unneeded, unrequired, useless
Antonyms essential, indispensable, necessary, needed, required, vital

unnerve confound, daunt, demoralize, disarm, disconcert, discourage, dishearten, dismay, dispirit, faze, fluster, frighten, intimidate, psych out (*informal*), rattle (*informal*), shake, throw off balance, unhinge, unman, upset
Antonyms arm, brace, encourage, hearten, nerve, steel, strengthen, support

unnoticed disregarded, ignored, neglected, overlooked, undiscovered, unheeded, unobserved, unperceived, unrecognized, unremarked, unseen
Antonyms discovered, heeded, noted, noticed, observed, perceived, recognized, remarked

unobtrusive humble, inconspicuous, keeping a low profile, low-key, meek, modest, quiet, restrained, retiring, self-effacing, subdued, unassuming, unnoticeable, unostentatious, unpretentious
Antonyms assertive, blatant, bold, conspicuous, eccentric, eye-catching, getting in the way, high-profile, noticeable, obtrusive, outgoing, prominent

unoccupied 1. empty, tenantless, uninhabited, untenanted, vacant 2. at a loose end, at leisure, disengaged, idle, inactive, unemployed

unofficial informal, off the record, personal, private, unauthorized, unconfirmed, wildcat

unorthodox abnormal, heterodox, irregular, off-the-wall (*slang*), unconventional, uncustomary, unusual, unwonted
Antonyms conventional, customary, established, orthodox, sound, traditional, usual

unpaid 1. due, not discharged, outstanding, overdue, owing, payable, unsettled 2. honorary, unsalaried, voluntary

unpalatable bitter, disagreeable, displeasing, distasteful, horrid, offensive, repugnant, unappetizing, unattractive, uneatable, unpleasant, unsavoury
Antonyms agreeable, appetizing, attractive, eatable, palatable, pleasant, pleasing, savoury, tasteful

unparalleled beyond compare, consummate, exceptional, incomparable, matchless, peerless, rare, singular, superlative, unequalled, unique, unmatched, unprecedented, unrivalled, unsurpassed, without equal

unpardonable deplorable, disgraceful, indefensible, inexcusable, outrageous, scandalous, shameful, unforgivable, unjustifiable

unperturbed as cool as a cucumber, calm, collected, composed, cool, placid, poised, self-possessed, tranquil, undismayed, unfazed (*informal*), unflustered, unruffled, untroubled, unworried
Antonyms anxious, dismayed, flustered, perturbed, ruffled, troubled, worried

unpleasant abhorrent, bad, disagreeable, displeasing, distasteful, horrid, ill-natured, irksome, nasty, objectionable, obnoxious, repulsive, troublesome, unattractive, unlikable *or* unlikeable, unlovely, unpalatable
Antonyms agreeable, congenial, delicious, good-natured, likable *or* likeable, lovely, nice, pleasant

unpleasantness 1. awfulness, disagreeableness, displeasure, dreadfulness, grimness, horridness, misery, trouble, ugliness, unacceptability, woe 2. abrasiveness, animosity, antagonism, argumentativeness, bad feeling, hostility, ill humour *or* will, malice, nastiness, offensiveness, quarrelsomeness, rudeness, unfriendliness
Antonyms acceptability, agreeableness, amusement, congeniality, delectation, delight, enjoyment, good humour *or* will, pleasantness, pleasure

unpolished 1. crude, rough, rough and ready, rude, sketchy, unfashioned, unfinished, unworked 2. uncivilized, uncouth, uncultivated, uncultured, unrefined, unsophisticated, vulgar

unpopular avoided, detested, disliked, not sought out, out in the cold, out of favour, rejected, shunned, unattractive, undesirable, unloved, unwanted, unwelcome
Antonyms desirable, favoured, liked, loved, popular, wanted, welcome

unprecedented abnormal, exceptional, extraordinary, freakish, ground-breaking, new, novel, original, remarkable, singular, unexampled, unheard-of, unparalleled, unrivalled, unusual

unpredictable chance, changeable, doubtful, erratic, fickle, fluky (*informal*), hit-and-miss (*informal*), hit-or-miss (*informal*), iffy (*informal*), inconstant, random, unforeseeable, unreliable, unstable, variable
Antonyms certain, constant, dependable, foreseeable, predictable, reliable, stable, steady, unchanging

unprejudiced balanced, even-handed, fair, fair-minded, impartial, just, nonpartisan, objective, open-minded, unbiased, uninfluenced
Antonyms biased, bigoted, influenced, narrow-minded, partial, prejudiced, unfair, unjust

unpremeditated extempore, impromptu, impulsive, offhand, off the cuff (*informal*), spontaneous, spur-of-the-moment, unplanned, unprepared

unprepared **1.** half-baked (*informal*), ill-considered, incomplete, not thought out, unfinished, unplanned **2.** caught napping, caught on the hop (*Brit. informal*), surprised, taken aback, taken off guard, unaware, unready, unsuspecting **3.** ad-lib, extemporaneous, improvised, off the cuff (*informal*), spontaneous

unpretentious homely, honest, humble, modest, plain, simple, straightforward, unaffected, unassuming, unimposing, unobtrusive, unostentatious, unspoiled
Antonyms affected, assuming, brash, conceited, flaunting, inflated, obtrusive, ostentatious, pretentious, showy

unprincipled amoral, corrupt, crooked, deceitful, devious, dishonest, immoral, sink, tricky, unconscionable, underhand, unethical, unprofessional, unscrupulous
Antonyms decent, ethical, honest, honourable, moral, righteous, scrupulous, upright, virtuous

unproductive **1.** basket case, bootless, fruitless, futile, idle, ineffective, inefficacious, otiose, unavailing, unprofitable, unremunerative, unrewarding, useless, vain, valueless, worthless **2.** barren, dry, fruitless, sterile, unprolific
Antonyms (*sense 1*) effective, fruitful, profitable, remunerative, rewarding, useful, worthwhile (*sense 2*) abundant, fertile, fruitful, productive, prolific

unprofessional **1.** improper, lax, negligent, unethical, unfitting, unprincipled, unseemly, unworthy **2.** amateur, amateurish, cowboy (*informal*), incompetent, inefficient, inexperienced, inexpert, slapdash, slipshod, untrained
Antonyms (*sense 2*) adept, competent, efficient, experienced, expert, professional, skilful

unpromising adverse, discouraging, doubtful, gloomy, inauspicious, infelicitous, ominous, unfavourable, unpropitious

unprotected defenceless, exposed, helpless, naked, open, open to attack, pregnable, unarmed, undefended, unguarded, unsheltered, unshielded, vulnerable
Antonyms defended, guarded, immune, protected, safe, secure, shielded

unqualified **1.** ill-equipped, incapable, incompetent, ineligible, not equal to, not up to, unfit, unprepared **2.** categorical, downright, outright, unconditional, unmitigated, unreserved, unrestricted, without reservation **3.** absolute, arrant, complete, consummate, deep-dyed (*usually derogatory*), downright, out-and-out, outright, thorough, thoroughgoing, total, utter

unquestionable absolute, beyond a shadow of doubt, certain, clear, conclusive, definite, faultless, flawless, incontestable, incontrovertible, indisputable, indubitable, irrefutable, manifest, patent, perfect, self-evident, sure, undeniable, unequivocal, unmistakable
Antonyms ambiguous, doubtful, dubious, inconclusive, questionable, uncertain, unclear

unravel **1.** disentangle, extricate, free, separate, straighten out, undo, unknot, untangle, unwind **2.** clear up, explain, figure out (*informal*), get straight, get to the bottom of, interpret, make out, puzzle out, resolve, solve, suss (out) (*slang*), work out

unreadable **1.** crabbed, illegible, undecipherable **2.** badly written, dry as dust, heavy going, turgid

unreal **1.** chimerical, dreamlike, fabulous, fanciful, fictitious, illusory, imaginary, make-believe, phantasmagoric, storybook, visionary **2.** hypothetical, immaterial, impalpable, insubstantial, intangible, mythical, nebulous **3.** artificial, fake, false, insincere, mock, ostensible, pretended, seeming, sham
Antonyms authentic, bona fide, genuine, real, realistic, sincere, true, veritable

unrealistic **1.** half-baked (*informal*), impracticable, impractical, improbable, quixotic, romantic, starry-eyed, theoretical, unworkable **2.** non-naturalistic, unauthentic, unlifelike, unreal
Antonyms (*sense 1*) practical, pragmatic, probable, realistic, sensible, unromantic, workable

unreasonable **1.** excessive, exorbitant, extortionate, extravagant, immoderate, steep (*informal*), too great, uncalled-for, undue, unfair, unjust, unwarranted **2.** arbitrary, biased, blinkered, capricious, erratic, headstrong, inconsistent, opinionated, quirky **3.** absurd, far-fetched, foolish, illogical, irrational, mad,

nonsensical, preposterous, senseless, silly, stupid
Antonyms (*sense 1*) fair, just, justified, moderate, reasonable, temperate, warranted (*sense 2*) fair-minded, flexible, open-minded (*sense 3*) logical, rational, sensible, wise

unrefined 1. crude, raw, unfinished, unpolished, unpurified, untreated 2. boorish, coarse, inelegant, rude, uncultured, unsophisticated, vulgar

unregenerate 1. godless, impious, profane, sinful, unconverted, unreformed, unrepentant, wicked 2. hardened, intractable, obdurate, obstinate, recalcitrant, refractory, self-willed, stubborn
Antonyms (*sense 1*) converted, godly, pious, reformed, regenerate, repentant, virtuous

unrelated 1. different, dissimilar, not kin, not kindred, not related, unconnected, unlike 2. beside the point, extraneous, inapplicable, inappropriate, irrelevant, not germane, unassociated, unconnected

unrelenting 1. cruel, implacable, inexorable, intransigent, merciless, pitiless, relentless, remorseless, ruthless, stern, tough, unsparing 2. ceaseless, constant, continual, continuous, endless, incessant, perpetual, steady, unabated, unbroken, unremitting, unwavering

unreliable 1. disreputable, irresponsible, not conscientious, treacherous, undependable, unstable, untrustworthy 2. deceptive, delusive, erroneous, fake, fallible, false, implausible, inaccurate, mistaken, specious, uncertain, unconvincing, unsound
Antonyms (*sense 1*) conscientious, dependable, regular, reliable, responsible, stable, trustworthy (*sense 2*) accurate, infallible

unremitting assiduous, constant, continual, continuous, diligent, incessant, indefatigable, perpetual, relentless, remorseless, sedulous, unabated, unbroken, unceasing, unwavering, unwearied

unrepentant abandoned, callous, hardened, impenitent, incorrigible, not contrite, obdurate, shameless, unregenerate, unremorseful, unrepenting
Antonyms ashamed, contrite, penitent, remorseful, repentant, rueful, sorry

Farewell, remorse! All good to me is lost;
Evil, be thou my good
John Milton *Paradise Lost*

unreserved 1. demonstrative, extrovert, forthright, frank, free, open, open-hearted, outgoing, outspoken, uninhibited, unrestrained, unreticent 2. absolute, complete, entire, full, total, unconditional, unlimited, unqualified, wholehearted, without reservation
Antonyms demure, inhibited, modest, reserved, restrained, reticent, shy, undemonstrative

unresolved doubtful, moot, open to question, pending, problematical, unanswered, undecided, undetermined, unsettled, unsolved, up in the air, vague, yet to be decided

unrest 1. agitation, disaffection, discontent, discord, dissatisfaction, dissension, protest, rebellion, sedition, strife, tumult, turmoil, upheaval 2. agitation, anxiety, disquiet, distress, perturbation, restlessness, trepidation, uneasiness, worry
Antonyms calm, contentment, peace, relaxation, repose, rest, stillness, tranquillity

unrestrained abandoned, boisterous, free, immoderate, inordinate, intemperate, natural, unbounded, unbridled, unchecked, unconstrained, uncontrolled, unhindered, uninhibited, unrepressed
Antonyms checked, constrained, frustrated, hindered, inhibited, repressed, restrained

unrestricted 1. absolute, free, free-for-all (*informal*), freewheeling (*informal*), open, unbounded, uncircumscribed, unhindered, unlimited, unregulated 2. clear, open, public, unobstructed, unopposed

unrivalled beyond compare, incomparable, matchless, nonpareil, peerless, supreme, unequalled, unexcelled, unmatched, unparalleled, unsurpassed, without equal

unruffled 1. calm, collected, composed, cool, peaceful, placid, sedate, serene, tranquil, undisturbed, unfazed (*informal*), unflustered, unmoved, unperturbed 2. even, flat, level, smooth, unbroken

unruly disobedient, disorderly, fractious, headstrong, insubordinate, intractable, lawless, mutinous, obstreperous, rebellious, refractory, riotous, rowdy, turbulent, uncontrollable, ungovernable, unmanageable, wayward, wild, wilful
Antonyms amenable, biddable, docile, governable, manageable, obedient, orderly, tractable

unsafe dangerous, hazardous, insecure, perilous, precarious, risky, threatening, treacherous, uncertain, unreliable, unsound, unstable
Antonyms certain, harmless, reliable, safe, secure, sound, stable, sure

unsaid left to the imagination, tacit, undeclared, unexpressed, unspoken, unstated, unuttered, unvoiced

unsanitary dirty, filthy, germ-ridden, infected, insalubrious, insanitary, sordid, squalid, unclean, unhealthy, unhygienic

unsatisfactory deficient, disappointing, displeasing, inadequate, insufficient, mediocre, no great shakes (*informal*), not good enough, not much cop (*Brit. slang*), not up to par, not

up to scratch (*informal*), pathetic, poor, unacceptable, unsuitable, unworthy, weak
Antonyms acceptable, adequate, passable, pleasing, satisfactory, sufficient, suitable

unsavoury **1.** distasteful, nasty, objectionable, obnoxious, offensive, repellent, repugnant, repulsive, revolting, unpleasant **2.** disagreeable, distasteful, nauseating, sickening, unappetizing, unpalatable
Antonyms appetizing, palatable, pleasant, savoury, tasteful, tasty, toothsome

unscathed in one piece, safe, sound, unharmed, unhurt, uninjured, unmarked, unscarred, unscratched, untouched, whole

unscrupulous conscienceless, corrupt, crooked (*informal*), dishonest, dishonourable, exploitative, immoral, improper, knavish, roguish, ruthless, sink, unconscientious, unconscionable, unethical, unprincipled
Antonyms ethical, honest, honourable, moral, principled, proper, scrupulous, upright

unseasonable ill-timed, inappropriate, inopportune, mistimed, out of keeping, unsuitable, untimely

unseat **1.** throw, unhorse, unsaddle **2.** depose, dethrone, discharge, dismiss, displace, oust, overthrow, remove

unseemly discreditable, disreputable, improper, inappropriate, indecorous, indelicate, in poor taste, out of keeping, out of place, unbecoming, unbefitting, undignified, unrefined, unsuitable
Antonyms acceptable, appropriate, becoming, decorous, fitting, proper, refined, seemly, suitable

unseen concealed, hidden, invisible, lurking, obscure, undetected, unnoticed, unobserved, unobtrusive, unperceived, veiled

unselfish altruistic, charitable, devoted, disinterested, generous, humanitarian, kind, liberal, magnanimous, noble, self-denying, selfless, self-sacrificing

unsettle agitate, bother, confuse, discompose, disconcert, disorder, disturb, faze, fluster, perturb, rattle (*informal*), ruffle, throw (*informal*), throw into confusion (disorder, uproar), throw off balance, trouble, unbalance, unnerve, upset

unsettled **1.** disorderly, insecure, shaky, unstable, unsteady **2.** changeable, changing, inconstant, uncertain, unpredictable, variable **3.** agitated, anxious, confused, disturbed, flustered, on edge, perturbed, restive, restless, shaken, tense, troubled, uneasy, unnerved, wired (*slang*) **4.** debatable, doubtful, moot, open, undecided, undetermined, unresolved, up in the air **5.** due, in arrears, outstanding, owing, payable, pending **6.** uninhabited, unoccupied, unpeopled, unpopulated

unshakable absolute, constant, firm, fixed, immovable, resolute, staunch, steadfast, sure, unassailable, unswerving, unwavering, well-founded
Antonyms insecure, shaky, uncertain, unsure, wavering, wobbly

unshaken calm, collected, composed, impassive, unaffected, unalarmed, undaunted, undismayed, undisturbed, unfazed (*informal*), unmoved, unperturbed, unruffled

unsheltered exposed, open, out in the open, unprotected, unscreened, unshielded

unsightly disagreeable, hideous, horrid, repulsive, revolting (*informal*), ugly, unattractive, unpleasant, unprepossessing
Antonyms agreeable, attractive, beautiful, comely, cute, handsome, pleasing, prepossessing, pretty

unskilful awkward, bungling, clumsy, cowboy (*informal*), fumbling, incompetent, inept, inexpert, maladroit, unhandy, unpractised, unworkmanlike

unskilled amateurish, cowboy (*informal*), inexperienced, uneducated, unprofessional, unqualified, untalented, untrained
Antonyms adept, expert, masterly, professional, qualified, skilled, talented

unsociable chilly, cold, distant, hostile, inhospitable, introverted, reclusive, retiring, standoffish, uncongenial, unforthcoming, unfriendly, unneighbourly, unsocial, withdrawn
Antonyms congenial, convivial, friendly, gregarious, hospitable, neighbourly, outgoing, sociable

unsolicited free-will, gratuitous, spontaneous, unasked for, uncalled-for, unforced, uninvited, unrequested, unsought, unwelcome, voluntary, volunteered

unsophisticated **1.** artless, childlike, guileless, inexperienced, ingenuous, innocent, naive, natural, unaffected, untutored, unworldly **2.** plain, simple, straightforward, uncomplex, uncomplicated, uninvolved, unrefined, unspecialized **3.** genuine, not artificial, pure, unadulterated
Antonyms (*sense 2*) advanced, complex, complicated, elegant, esoteric, intricate, sophisticated

unsound **1.** ailing, defective, delicate, deranged, diseased, frail, ill, in poor health, unbalanced, unhealthy, unhinged, unstable, unwell, weak **2.** defective, erroneous, fallacious, false, faulty, flawed, ill-founded, illogical, invalid, shaky, specious, unreliable, weak **3.** flimsy, insecure, not solid, rickety, shaky, tottering, unreliable, unsafe, unstable, unsteady, wobbly
Antonyms (*sense 3*) reliable, safe, solid,

sound, stable, steady, strong, sturdy, substantial

unsparing 1. abundant, bountiful, generous, lavish, liberal, munificent, open-handed, plenteous, prodigal, profuse, ungrudging, unstinting 2. cold-blooded, hard, harsh, implacable, inexorable, relentless, rigorous, ruthless, severe, stern, stringent, uncompromising, unforgiving, unmerciful

unspeakable 1. beyond description, beyond words, inconceivable, indescribable, ineffable, inexpressible, overwhelming, unbelievable, unimaginable, unutterable, wonderful 2. abominable, abysmal, appalling, awful, bad, dreadful, evil, execrable, frightful, from hell (*informal*), heinous, hellacious (*U.S. slang*), horrible, loathsome, monstrous, odious, repellent, shocking, too horrible for words

unspoiled, unspoilt 1. intact, perfect, preserved, unaffected, unblemished, unchanged, undamaged, unharmed, unimpaired, untouched 2. artless, innocent, natural, unaffected, unassuming, unstudied, wholesome
Antonyms (*sense 1*) affected, blemished, changed, damaged, harmed, impaired, imperfect, spoilt, touched

unspoken 1. assumed, implicit, implied, inferred, left to the imagination, not put into words, not spelt out, tacit, taken for granted, undeclared, understood, unexpressed, unstated 2. mute, silent, unsaid, unuttered, voiceless, wordless
Antonyms (*sense 1*) clear, declared, explicit, expressed, spoken, stated

unstable 1. insecure, not fixed, precarious, rickety, risky, shaky, tottering, unsettled, unsteady, wobbly 2. capricious, changeable, erratic, fitful, fluctuating, inconsistent, inconstant, irrational, temperamental, unpredictable, unsteady, untrustworthy, vacillating, variable, volatile
Antonyms (*sense 2*) consistent, constant, level-headed, predictable, rational, reliable, stable, steady, trustworthy

unsteady 1. infirm, insecure, precarious, reeling, rickety, shaky, tottering, treacherous, unsafe, unstable, wobbly 2. changeable, erratic, flickering, flighty, fluctuating, inconstant, irregular, temperamental, unreliable, unsettled, vacillating, variable, volatile, wavering

unstinted abundant, ample, bountiful, full, generous, large, lavish, liberal, plentiful, prodigal, profuse

unsubstantial 1. airy, flimsy, fragile, frail, inadequate, light, slight, thin 2. erroneous, full of holes, ill-founded, superficial, tenuous, unsound, unsupported, weak 3. dreamlike, fanciful, illusory, imaginary, immaterial, impalpable, visionary

unsubstantiated open to question, unattested, unconfirmed, uncorroborated, unestablished, unproven, unsupported
Antonyms attested, confirmed, corroborated, established, proven, substantiated, supported

unsuccessful 1. abortive, bootless, failed, fruitless, futile, ineffective, unavailing, unproductive, useless, vain 2. at a low ebb, balked, defeated, foiled, frustrated, hapless, ill-starred, losing, luckless, unfortunate, unlucky
Antonyms (*sense 1*) flourishing, fruitful, productive, prosperous, remunerative, successful, thriving, useful, worthwhile (*sense 2*) fortunate, lucky, triumphant, victorious, winning

unsuitable improper, inapposite, inappropriate, inapt, incompatible, incongruous, ineligible, infelicitous, out of character, out of keeping, out of place, unacceptable, unbecoming, unbefitting, unfitting, unseasonable, unseemly, unsuited
Antonyms acceptable, apposite, appropriate, apt, compatible, eligible, fitting, proper, suitable

unsullied clean, immaculate, impeccable, pristine, pure, spotless, squeaky-clean, stainless, unblackened, unblemished, uncorrupted, undefiled, unsoiled, untainted, untarnished, untouched

unsung anonymous, disregarded, neglected, unacclaimed, unacknowledged, uncelebrated, unhailed, unhonoured, unknown, unnamed, unrecognized

unsure 1. insecure, lacking in confidence, unassured, unconfident 2. distrustful, doubtful, dubious, hesitant, in a quandary, irresolute, mistrustful, sceptical, suspicious, unconvinced, undecided
Antonyms assured, certain, confident, convinced, decided, persuaded, resolute, sure

unsurpassed consummate, exceptional, incomparable, matchless, nonpareil, paramount, peerless, second to none, superlative, supreme, transcendent, unequalled, unexcelled, unparalleled, unrivalled, without an equal

unsuspecting confiding, credulous, gullible, inexperienced, ingenuous, innocent, naive, off guard, trustful, trusting, unconscious, unsuspicious, unwarned, unwary

unswerving constant, dedicated, devoted, direct, firm, resolute, single-minded, staunch, steadfast, steady, true, undeviating, unfaltering, unflagging, untiring, unwavering

unsympathetic apathetic, callous, cold, compassionless (*rare*), cruel, hard, harsh, heartless, indifferent, insensitive, soulless, stony-hearted, uncompassionate, unconcerned, unfeeling, unkind, unmoved, unpitying, unresponsive
Antonyms caring, compassionate, concerned,

kind, pitying, sensitive, supportive, sympathetic, understanding

unsystematic chaotic, confused, disorderly, disorganized, haphazard, irregular, jumbled, muddled, random, slapdash, unmethodical, unorganized, unplanned, unsystematized

untamed barbarous, feral, fierce, not broken in, savage, unbroken, uncontrollable, undomesticated, untameable, wild

untangle clear up, disentangle, explain, extricate, solve, straighten out, unravel, unsnarl
Antonyms complicate, confuse, enmesh, entangle, jumble, muddle, puzzle, snarl, tangle

untarnished bright, burnished, clean, glowing, immaculate, impeccable, polished, pure, shining, spotless, squeaky-clean, unblemished, unimpeachable, unsoiled, unspotted, unstained, unsullied

untenable fallacious, flawed, groundless, illogical, indefensible, insupportable, shaky, unreasonable, unsound, unsustainable, weak
Antonyms justified, logical, rational, reasonable, sensible, supported, unarguable, uncontestable, valid, verifiable, well-grounded

unthinkable 1. absurd, illogical, impossible, improbable, not on (*informal*), out of the question, preposterous, unlikely, unreasonable 2. beyond belief, beyond the bounds of possibility, implausible, inconceivable, incredible, insupportable, unbelievable, unimaginable

unthinking 1. blundering, inconsiderate, insensitive, rude, selfish, tactless, thoughtless, undiplomatic 2. careless, heedless, impulsive, inadvertent, instinctive, mechanical, negligent, oblivious, rash, senseless, unconscious, unmindful, vacant, witless
Antonyms (*sense 2*) careful, conscious, deliberate, heedful, mindful, sensible, witting

untidy bedraggled, chaotic, cluttered, disarrayed, disorderly, higgledy-piggledy (*informal*), jumbled, littered, messy, muddled, muddly, mussy (*U.S. informal*), rumpled, shambolic, slatternly, slipshod, sloppy (*informal*), slovenly, topsy-turvy, unkempt
Antonyms methodical, neat, orderly, presentable, ship-shape, spruce, systematic, tidy, well-kept

untie free, loosen, release, unbind, unbridle, undo, unfasten, unknot, unlace

untimely awkward, badly timed, early, ill-timed, inappropriate, inauspicious, inconvenient, inopportune, mistimed, premature, unfortunate, unseasonable, unsuitable
Antonyms appropriate, auspicious, convenient, fortunate, opportune, seasonable, suitable, timely, welcome, well-timed

untiring constant, dedicated, determined, devoted, dogged, incessant, indefatigable, patient, persevering, persistent, staunch, steady, tireless, unfaltering, unflagging, unremitting, unwearied

untold 1. indescribable, inexpressible, undreamed of, unimaginable, unspeakable, unthinkable, unutterable 2. countless, incalculable, innumerable, measureless, myriad, numberless, uncountable, uncounted, unnumbered 3. hidden, private, secret, undisclosed, unknown, unpublished, unrecounted, unrelated, unrevealed

untouched 1. intact, safe and sound, undamaged, unharmed, unhurt, uninjured, unscathed, without a scratch 2. dry-eyed, indifferent, unaffected, unconcerned, unimpressed, unmoved, unstirred
Antonyms (*sense 2*) affected, concerned, impressed, moved, softened, stirred, touched

untoward 1. annoying, awkward, disastrous, ill-timed, inconvenient, inimical, irritating, troublesome, unfortunate, vexatious 2. adverse, contrary, inauspicious, inopportune, unfavourable, unlucky, untimely 3. improper, inappropriate, indecorous, out of place, unbecoming, unfitting, unseemly, unsuitable

untrained amateur, green, inexperienced, raw, uneducated, unpractised, unqualified, unschooled, unskilled, untaught, untutored
Antonyms educated, experienced, expert, qualified, schooled, skilled, taught, trained

untried in the experimental stage, new, novel, unattempted, unessayed, unproved, untested

untroubled calm, composed, cool, peaceful, placid, sedate, serene, steady, tranquil, unagitated, unconcerned, undisturbed, unfazed (*informal*), unflappable (*informal*), unflustered, unperturbed, unruffled, unstirred, unworried
Antonyms agitated, anxious, concerned, disturbed, flustered, perturbed, ruffled, troubled, worried

untrue 1. deceptive, dishonest, erroneous, fallacious, false, inaccurate, incorrect, lying, misleading, mistaken, sham, spurious, untruthful, wrong 2. deceitful, disloyal, faithless, false, forsworn, inconstant, perfidious, traitorous, treacherous, two-faced, unfaithful, untrustworthy 3. deviant, distorted, inaccurate, off, out of line, out of true, wide
Antonyms (*sense 1*) accurate, correct, factual, right, true (*sense 2*) constant, dependable, faithful, honest, honourable, loyal, truthful, virtuous

untrustworthy capricious, deceitful, devious, dishonest, disloyal, fair-weather, faithless, false, fickle, fly-by-night (*informal*), not to be depended on, slippery, treacherous, tricky, two-faced, undependable, unfaithful, unreliable, untrue, untrusty
Antonyms dependable, faithful, honest, loyal,

reliable, reputable, steadfast, true, trust~worthy, trusty

untruth 1. deceitfulness, duplicity, falsity, in~veracity (*rare*), lying, mendacity, perjury, truthlessness, untruthfulness 2. deceit, fabri~cation, falsehood, falsification, fib, fiction, lie, pork pie (*Brit. slang*), porky (*Brit. slang*), prevarication, story, tale, trick, whopper (*in~formal*)

untruthful crooked (*informal*), deceitful, decep~tive, dishonest, dissembling, false, fibbing, hypocritical, lying, mendacious
Antonyms candid, honest, sincere, true, truthful, veracious

untutored 1. ignorant, illiterate, uneducated, unlearned, unschooled, untrained, unversed 2. artless, inexperienced, simple, unpractised, unrefined, unsophisticated

unused 1. fresh, intact, new, pristine, un~touched 2. *with* **to** a stranger to, inexperi~enced in, new to, not ready for, not up to, unaccustomed to, unfamiliar with, un~habituated to 3. available, extra, left, leftover, remaining, unconsumed, unexhausted, unutilized

unusual abnormal, atypical, bizarre, curious, different, exceptional, extraordinary, left-field (*informal*), notable, odd, out of the ordinary, phenomenal, queer, rare, remarkable, singu~lar, strange, surprising, uncommon, uncon~ventional, unexpected, unfamiliar, unwonted
Antonyms average, banal, commonplace, con~ventional, everyday, familiar, normal, routine, traditional, typical, unremarkable, usual

unutterable beyond words, extreme, indescrib~able, ineffable, overwhelming, unimaginable, unspeakable

unvarnished bare, candid, frank, honest, na~ked, plain, pure, pure and simple, simple, sincere, stark, straightforward, unadorned, unembellished

unveil bare, bring to light, disclose, divulge, expose, lay bare, lay open, make known, make public, reveal, uncover
Antonyms cloak, conceal, cover, disguise, hide, mask, obscure, veil

unwanted *de trop*, going begging, outcast, re~jected, superfluous, surplus to requirements, unasked, undesired, uninvited, unneeded, un~solicited, unwelcome, useless
Antonyms desired, necessary, needed, useful, wanted, welcome

unwarranted gratuitous, groundless, indefen~sible, inexcusable, uncalled-for, unjust, unjus~tified, unprovoked, unreasonable, wrong

unwary careless, hasty, heedless, imprudent, incautious, indiscreet, rash, reckless, thought~less, uncircumspect, unguarded, unwatchful
Antonyms cautious, chary, circumspect, dis~creet, guarded, prudent, wary, watchful

unwavering consistent, dedicated, determined, immovable, resolute, single-minded, staunch, steadfast, steady, undeviating, unfaltering, unflagging, unshakable, unshaken, unswerv~ing, untiring

unwelcome 1. excluded, rejected, unacceptable, undesirable, uninvited, unpopular, unwanted, unwished for 2. disagreeable, displeasing, dis~tasteful, thankless, undesirable, unpleasant
Antonyms acceptable, agreeable, desirable, pleasant, pleasing, popular, wanted, welcome

unwell ailing, at death's door, green about the gills, ill, indisposed, in poor health, off colour, out of sorts, poorly (*informal*), sick, sickly, under the weather (*informal*), unhealthy
Antonyms fine, healthy, robust, sound, well

unwholesome 1. deleterious, harmful, insalu~brious, junk (*informal*), noxious, poisonous, tainted, unhealthy, unnourishing 2. bad, cor~rupting, degrading, demoralizing, depraving, evil, immoral, maleficent, perverting, wicked 3. anaemic, pale, pallid, pasty, sickly, wan
Antonyms (*sense 1*) beneficial, germ-free, healthy, hygienic, salubrious, sanitary, whole~some (*sense 2*) edifying, moral

unwieldy 1. awkward, burdensome, cumber~some, inconvenient, unhandy, unmanageable 2. bulky, clumsy, clunky (*informal*), hefty, massive, ponderous, ungainly, weighty

unwilling averse, demurring, disinclined, grudging, indisposed, laggard (*rare*), loath, not in the mood, opposed, reluctant, resistant, unenthusiastic
Antonyms amenable, compliant, disposed, eager, enthusiastic, inclined, voluntary, will~ing

unwind 1. disentangle, slacken, uncoil, undo, unravel, unreel, unroll, untwine, untwist 2. calm down, let oneself go, loosen up, make oneself at home, mellow out (*informal*), quiet~en down, relax, sit back, slow down, take a break, take it easy, wind down

unwise asinine, foolhardy, foolish, ill-advised, ill-considered, ill-judged, impolitic, improvi~dent, imprudent, inadvisable, inane, indis~creet, injudicious, irresponsible, rash, reckless, senseless, short-sighted, silly, stupid
Antonyms discreet, judicious, politic, prudent, responsible, sensible, shrewd, wise

unwitting 1. ignorant, innocent, unaware, un~conscious, unknowing, unsuspecting 2. acci~dental, chance, inadvertent, involuntary, un~designed, unintended, unintentional, un~meant, unplanned
Antonyms (*sense 2*) conscious, deliberate, de~signed, intended, intentional, knowing, meant, planned, witting

unwonted atypical, extraordinary, infrequent, out of the ordinary, peculiar, rare, seldom seen, singular, unaccustomed, uncommon, uncustomary, unexpected, unfamiliar, unheard-of, unusual

unworldly 1. abstract, celestial, metaphysical, nonmaterialistic, religious, spiritual, transcendental 2. as green as grass, green, idealistic, inexperienced, innocent, naive, raw, trusting, unsophisticated, wet behind the ears (*informal*) 3. ethereal, extraterrestrial, otherworldly, unearthly

unworthy 1. *with* **of** beneath the dignity of, improper, inappropriate, out of character, out of place, unbecoming, unbefitting, unfitting, unseemly, unsuitable 2. base, contemptible, degrading, discreditable, disgraceful, dishonourable, disreputable, ignoble, shameful 3. ineligible, not deserving of, not fit for, not good enough, not worth, undeserving
Antonyms (*sense 3*) commendable, creditable, deserving, eligible, fit, honourable, meritorious, worthy

unwritten 1. oral, unrecorded, vocal, word-of-mouth 2. accepted, conventional, customary, tacit, traditional, understood, unformulated

unyielding adamant, determined, firm, hardline, immovable, inexorable, inflexible, intractable, obdurate, obstinate, relentless, resolute, rigid, staunch, steadfast, stiff-necked, stubborn, tough, unbending, uncompromising, unwavering
Antonyms adaptable, compliant, compromising, cooperative, flexible, movable, tractable, yielding

up-and-coming ambitious, eager, go-getting (*informal*), on the make (*slang*), promising, pushing

upbeat *adjective* buoyant, cheerful, cheery, encouraging, favourable, forward-looking, heartening, hopeful, looking up, optimistic, positive, promising, rosy

upbraid admonish, bawl out (*informal*), berate, blame, carpet (*informal*), castigate, censure, chew out (*U.S. & Canad. informal*), chide, condemn, dress down (*informal*), excoriate, give (someone) a rocket (*Brit. & N.Z. informal*), lecture, rap (someone) over the knuckles, read the riot act, rebuke, reprimand, reproach, reprove, scold, slap on the wrist, take to task, tear into (*informal*), tear (someone) off a strip (*Brit. informal*), tell off (*informal*), tick off (*informal*)

upbringing breeding, bringing-up, care, cultivation, education, nurture, raising, rearing, tending, training

update amend, bring up to date, modernize, renew, revise

upgrade advance, ameliorate, better, elevate, enhance, improve, promote, raise
Antonyms decry, degrade, demote, denigrate, downgrade, lower

upheaval cataclysm, disorder, disruption, disturbance, eruption, overthrow, revolution, turmoil, violent change

uphill *adjective* 1. ascending, climbing, mounting, rising 2. arduous, difficult, exhausting, gruelling, hard, laborious, punishing, Sisyphean, strenuous, taxing, tough, wearisome
Antonyms (*sense 1*) descending, downhill, lowering

uphold advocate, aid, back, champion, defend, encourage, endorse, hold to, justify, maintain, promote, stand by, stick up for (*informal*), support, sustain, vindicate

upkeep 1. conservation, keep, maintenance, preservation, repair, running, subsistence, support, sustenance 2. expenditure, expenses, oncosts (*Brit.*), operating costs, outlay, overheads, running costs

uplift *verb* 1. elevate, heave, hoist, lift up, raise 2. advance, ameliorate, better, civilize, cultivate, edify, improve, inspire, raise, refine, upgrade *~noun* 3. advancement, betterment, cultivation, edification, enhancement, enlightenment, enrichment, improvement, refinement

upper 1. high, higher, loftier, top, topmost 2. elevated, eminent, greater, important, superior
Antonyms bottom, inferior, junior, low, lower

upper-class aristocratic, blue-blooded, highborn, high-class, noble, patrician, top-drawer, well-bred

upper hand advantage, ascendancy, control, dominion, edge, mastery, superiority, supremacy, sway, whip hand

uppermost 1. highest, loftiest, most elevated, top, topmost, upmost 2. chief, dominant, foremost, greatest, leading, main, paramount, predominant, pre-eminent, primary, principal, supreme
Antonyms bottom, bottommost, humblest, least, lowermost, lowest, lowliest, slightest

uppish affected, arrogant, cocky, conceited, high and mighty (*informal*), hoity-toity (*informal*), overweening, presumptuous, putting on airs, self-important, snobbish, stuck-up (*informal*), supercilious, toffee-nosed (*slang, chiefly Brit.*), uppity (*informal*)
Antonyms diffident, humble, lowly, meek, obsequious, servile, unaffected, unassertive

uppity bigheaded (*informal*), bumptious, cocky, conceited, full of oneself, impertinent, on one's high horse (*informal*), overweening, self-important, swanky (*informal*), too big for one's boots *or* breeches (*informal*), uppish (*Brit. informal*)

upright 1. erect, on end, perpendicular, straight, vertical 2. *figurative* above board, conscientious, ethical, faithful, good, high-minded, honest, honourable, incorruptible, just, principled, righteous, straightforward, true, trustworthy, unimpeachable, virtuous
Antonyms (*sense 1*) flat, horizontal, lying, prone, prostrate, supine (*sense 2*) corrupt, de~vious, dishonest, dishonourable, unethical, unjust, untrustworthy, wicked

uprightness fairness, faithfulness, goodness, high-mindedness, honesty, incorruptibility, integrity, justice, probity, rectitude, right~eousness, straightforwardness, trustworthi~ness, virtue

uprising disturbance, insurgence, insurrection, mutiny, outbreak, putsch, rebellion, revolt, revolution, rising, upheaval

uproar *bagarre*, brawl, brouhaha, clamour, commotion, confusion, din, furore, hubbub, hullabaloo, hurly-burly, mayhem, noise, out~cry, pandemonium, racket, riot, ruckus (*infor~mal*), ruction (*informal*), rumpus, turbulence, turmoil

uproarious 1. clamorous, confused, disorderly, loud, noisy, riotous, rowdy, tempestuous, tu~multuous, turbulent, wild 2. convulsive (*infor~mal*), hilarious, hysterical, killing (*infor~mal*), rib-tickling, rip-roaring (*informal*), screamingly funny, side-splitting, very funny 3. boisterous, gleeful, loud, rollicking, unre~strained
Antonyms (*sense 1*) inaudible, low-key, order~ly, peaceful, quiet, still (*sense 2*) morose, mournful, sad, serious, sorrowful, tragic

uproot 1. deracinate, dig up, extirpate, grub up, pull out by the roots, pull up, rip up, root out, weed out 2. deracinate, disorient, dis~place, exile 3. destroy, do away with, elimi~nate, eradicate, extirpate, remove, wipe out

ups and downs changes, ebb and flow, fluc~tuations, moods, vicissitudes, wheel of fortune

upset *verb* 1. capsize, knock over, overturn, spill, tip over, topple over 2. change, disorder, disorganize, disturb, mess up, mix up, put out of order, spoil, turn topsy-turvy 3. agitate, bother, discompose, disconcert, dismay, dis~quiet, distress, disturb, faze, fluster, grieve, hassle (*informal*), perturb, ruffle, throw (someone) off balance, trouble, unnerve 4. be victorious over, conquer, defeat, get the better of, overcome, overthrow, triumph over, win against the odds *~noun* 5. defeat, reverse, shake-up (*informal*), sudden change, surprise 6. bug (*informal*), complaint, disorder, dis~turbance, illness, indisposition, malady, quea~siness, sickness 7. agitation, bother, discom~posure, disquiet, distress, disturbance, hassle (*informal*), shock, trouble, worry *~adjective* 8. capsized, overturned, spilled, tipped over, top~pled, tumbled, upside down 9. disordered, dis~turbed, gippy (*slang*), ill, poorly (*informal*), queasy, sick 10. agitated, bothered, confused, disconcerted, dismayed, disquieted, distressed, disturbed, frantic, grieved, hassled (*informal*), hurt, overwrought, put out, ruffled, troubled, worried 11. at sixes and sevens, chaotic, con~fused, disarrayed, disordered, in disarray *or* disorder, messed up, muddled, topsy-turvy 12. beaten, conquered, defeated, overcome, over~thrown, vanquished

upshot conclusion, consequence, culmination, end, end result, event, finale, issue, outcome, payoff (*informal*), result, sequel

upside down 1. bottom up, inverted, on its head, overturned, upturned, wrong side up 2. *informal* chaotic, confused, disordered, higgledy-piggledy (*informal*), in confusion (chaos, disarray, disorder), jumbled, muddled, topsy-turvy

upstanding 1. ethical, good, honest, honour~able, incorruptible, moral, principled, true, trustworthy, upright 2. firm, hale and hearty, hardy, healthy, robust, stalwart, strong, stur~dy, upright, vigorous
Antonyms (*sense 1*) bad, corrupt, dishonest, false, immoral, unethical, unprincipled, un~trustworthy (*sense 2*) delicate, feeble, frail, in~firm, puny, unhealthy, weak

upstart arriviste, nobody, *nouveau riche*, par~venu, social climber, status seeker

uptight anxious, edgy, nervy (*Brit. informal*), neurotic, on edge, on the defensive, prickly, tense, uneasy, wired (*slang*), withdrawn

up-to-date all the rage, current, fashionable, happening (*informal*), having one's finger on the pulse, in, in vogue, modern, newest, now (*informal*), stylish, trendy (*Brit. informal*), up-to-the-minute, with it (*informal*)
Antonyms antiquated, dated, *démodé*, obso~lete, old fashioned, outmoded, out of date, out of the ark (*informal*), passé

upturn *noun* advancement, boost, improve~ment, increase, recovery, revival, rise, upsurge, upswing

urban city, civic, inner-city, metropolitan, mu~nicipal, oppidan (*rare*), town

urbane civil, civilized, cosmopolitan, courteous, cultivated, cultured, debonair, elegant, man~nerly, polished, refined, smooth, sophisticated, suave, well-bred, well-mannered
Antonyms boorish, clownish, discourteous, gauche, impolite, rude, uncivilized, uncouth, uncultured

urbanity charm, civility, courtesy, culture, el~egance, grace, mannerliness, polish, refine~ment, sophistication, suavity, worldliness

urchin brat, gamin, guttersnipe, mudlark

(*slang*), ragamuffin, street Arab (*offensive*), waif, young rogue

urge *verb* **1.** appeal to, beg, beseech, entreat, exhort, implore, plead, press, solicit **2.** advise, advocate, champion, counsel, insist on, push for, recommend, support **3.** compel, constrain, drive, egg on, encourage, force, goad, hasten, impel, incite, induce, instigate, press, prompt, propel, push, spur, stimulate *~noun* **4.** compulsion, desire, drive, fancy, impulse, itch, longing, thirst, wish, yearning, yen (*informal*)
Antonyms *verb* (*senses 1 & 2*) caution, deter, discourage, dissuade, remonstrate, warn *~noun* aversion, disinclination, distaste, indisposition, reluctance, repugnance

urgency exigency, extremity, gravity, hurry, imperativeness, importance, importunity, necessity, need, pressure, seriousness, stress

urgent 1. compelling, critical, crucial, immediate, imperative, important, instant, not to be delayed, now or never, pressing, top-priority **2.** clamorous, earnest, importunate, insistent, intense, persistent, persuasive
Antonyms apathetic, casual, feeble, half-hearted, lackadaisical, low-priority, minor, perfunctory, trivial, unimportant, weak

urinate leak (*slang*), make water, micturate, pass water, pee (*slang*), piddle (*informal*), piss (*taboo slang*), spend a penny (*Brit. informal*), tinkle (*Brit. informal*), wee (*informal*), wee-wee (*informal*)

usable at one's disposal, available, current, fit for use, functional, in running order, practical, ready for use, serviceable, utilizable, valid, working

usage 1. control, employment, handling, management, operation, regulation, running, treatment, use **2.** convention, custom, form, habit, matter of course, method, mode, practice, procedure, regime, routine, rule, tradition, wont

use *verb* **1.** apply, avail oneself of, bring into play, employ, exercise, exert, find a use for, make use of, operate, ply, practise, profit by, put to use, turn to account, utilize, wield, work **2.** act towards, behave towards, deal with, exploit, handle, manipulate, misuse, take advantage of, treat **3.** consume, exhaust, expend, run through, spend, waste *~noun* **4.** application, employment, exercise, handling, operation, practice, service, treatment, usage, wear and tear **5.** advantage, application, avail, benefit, good, help, mileage (*informal*), point, profit, service, usefulness, utility, value, worth **6.** custom, habit, practice, usage, way, wont **7.** call, cause, end, necessity, need, object, occasion, point, purpose, reason

used cast-off, hand-me-down (*informal*), nearly new, not new, reach-me-down (*informal*), second-hand, shopsoiled, worn
Antonyms brand-new, fresh, intact, new, pristine, unused

used to accustomed to, at home in, attuned to, familiar with, given to, habituated to, hardened to, in the habit of, inured to, tolerant of, wont to

useful advantageous, all-purpose, beneficial, effective, fruitful, general-purpose, helpful, of help, of service, of use, practical, profitable, salutary, serviceable, valuable, worthwhile
Antonyms inadequate, ineffective, unbeneficial, unhelpful, unproductive, useless, vain, worthless

usefulness benefit, convenience, effectiveness, efficacy, help, helpfulness, practicality, profit, service, use, utility, value, worth

useless 1. basket case, bootless, disadvantageous, fruitless, futile, hopeless, idle, impractical, ineffective, ineffectual, of no use, pointless, profitless, unavailing, unproductive, unworkable, vain, valueless, wanky (*taboo slang*), worthless **2.** *informal* a dead loss, hopeless, incompetent, ineffectual, inept, no good, stupid, weak
Antonyms (*sense 1*) advantageous, effective, fruitful, practical, productive, profitable, useful, valuable, workable, worthwhile

use up absorb, burn up, consume, deplete, devour, drain, exhaust, finish, fritter away, run through, squander, swallow up, waste

usher *noun* **1.** attendant, doorkeeper, escort, guide, usherette *~verb* **2.** conduct, direct, escort, guide, lead, pilot, show in *or* out, steer **3.** *usually with* **in** bring in, herald, inaugurate, initiate, introduce, launch, open the door to, pave the way for, precede, ring in

usual accustomed, bog-standard (*Brit. & Irish slang*), common, constant, customary, everyday, expected, familiar, fixed, general, habitual, normal, ordinary, regular, routine, standard, stock, typical, wonted
Antonyms exceptional, extraordinary, new, novel, off-beat, out of the ordinary, peculiar, rare, singular, strange, uncommon, unexpected, unhackneyed, unique, unorthodox, unusual

usually as a rule, as is the custom, as is usual, by and large, commonly, for the most part, generally, habitually, in the main, mainly, mostly, most often, normally, on the whole, ordinarily, regularly, routinely

usurp appropriate, arrogate, assume, commandeer, infringe upon, lay hold of, seize, take, take over, wrest

utility advantageousness, avail, benefit, convenience, efficacy, fitness, mileage (*informal*), point, practicality, profit, service, serviceableness, use, usefulness

utilize appropriate, avail oneself of, employ, have recourse to, make the most of, make use of, profit by, put to use, resort to, take ad~ vantage of, turn to account, use

utmost *adjective* 1. chief, extreme, greatest, highest, maximum, paramount, pre-eminent, supreme 2. extreme, farthest, final, last, most distant, outermost, remotest, uttermost *~noun* 3. best, greatest, hardest, highest, most

Utopia bliss, Eden, Erewhon, Garden of Eden, Happy Valley, heaven, ideal life, paradise, perfect place, seventh heaven, Shangri-la

Utopian 1. *adjective* airy, chimerical, dream, fanciful, fantasy, ideal, idealistic, illusory, im~ aginary, impractical, perfect, romantic, vi~ sionary 2. *noun* Don Quixote, dreamer, ideal~ ist, romanticist, visionary

utter[1] *verb* 1. articulate, enunciate, express, pronounce, put into words, say, speak, ver~ balize, vocalize, voice 2. declare, divulge, give expression to, make known, proclaim, prom~ ulgate, publish, reveal, state

utter[2] *adjective* absolute, arrant, complete, consummate, deep-dyed (*usually derogatory*), downright, entire, out-and-out, outright, per~ fect, sheer, stark, thorough, thoroughgoing, total, unmitigated, unqualified

utterance 1. announcement, declaration, ex~ pression, opinion, remark, speech, statement, words 2. articulation, delivery, ejaculation, expression, verbalization, vocalization, vocif~ eration

utterly absolutely, completely, entirely, ex~ tremely, fully, one hundred per cent, perfect~ ly, thoroughly, totally, to the core, to the nth degree, wholly

uttermost extreme, farthest, final, last, outer~ most, remotest, utmost

V

vacancy 1. job, opening, opportunity, position, post, room, situation 2. absent-mindedness, abstraction, blankness, inanity, inattentiveness, incomprehension, incuriousness, lack of interest, vacuousness 3. emptiness, gap, space, vacuum, void

vacant 1. available, disengaged, empty, free, idle, not in use, to let, unemployed, unengaged, unfilled, unoccupied, untenanted, void 2. absent-minded, abstracted, blank, dreaming, dreamy, expressionless, idle, inane, incurious, thoughtless, unthinking, vacuous, vague
Antonyms (*sense 1*) busy, engaged, full, inhabited, in use, occupied, taken (*sense 2*) animated, engrossed, expressive, lively, reflective, thoughtful

vacate depart, evacuate, give up, go away, leave, leave empty, move out of, quit, relinquish possession of, withdraw

vacillate be irresolute *or* indecisive, blow hot and cold (*informal*), chop and change, dither (*chiefly Brit.*), fluctuate, haver, hesitate, keep changing one's mind, oscillate, reel, rock, shillyshally (*informal*), sway, swither (*Scot.*), waver

vacillating hesitant, in two minds (*informal*), irresolute, oscillating, shillyshallying (*informal*), uncertain, unresolved, wavering

vacillation dithering (*chiefly Brit.*), fluctuation, hesitation, inconstancy, indecisiveness, irresoluteness, irresolution, shillyshallying (*informal*), unsteadiness, wavering

My mind is not a bed to be made and re-made
James Agate *Ego*

Some praise at morning what they blame at night;
But always think the last opinion right
Alexander Pope *An Essay on Criticism*

Don't change horses in midstream

vacuity 1. blankness, emptiness, inanity, incognizance, incomprehension, vacuousness 2. emptiness, nothingness, space, vacuum, void

vacuous 1. blank, inane, stupid, uncomprehending, unintelligent, vacant 2. empty, unfilled, vacant, void

vacuum emptiness, free space, gap, nothingness, space, vacuity, void

Nature abhors a vacuum
François Rabelais *Gargantua*

vagabond 1. *noun* bag lady (*chiefly U.S.*), beggar, bum (*informal*), down-and-out, hobo (*U.S.*), itinerant, knight of the road, migrant, nomad, outcast, rascal, rover, tramp, vagrant, wanderer, wayfarer 2. *adjective* destitute, down and out, drifting, fly-by-night (*informal*), footloose, homeless, idle, itinerant, journeying, nomadic, rootless, roving, shiftless, vagrant, wandering

vagary caprice, crotchet, fancy, humour, megrim (*archaic*), notion, whim, whimsy

vagina beaver (*taboo slang*), box (*taboo slang*), crack (*taboo slang*), cunt (*taboo*), fanny (*Brit. taboo slang*), hole (*taboo slang*), muff (*taboo slang*), pussy (*taboo slang*), quim (*Brit. taboo*), snatch (*taboo slang*), twat (*taboo slang*), vulva, yoni

vagrant 1. *noun* bag lady (*chiefly U.S.*), beggar, bird of passage, bum (*informal*), drifter, hobo (*U.S.*), itinerant, person of no fixed address, rolling stone, tramp, wanderer 2. *adjective* itinerant, nomadic, roaming, rootless, roving, unsettled, vagabond
Antonyms *adjective* established, fixed, purposeful, rooted, settled

vague amorphous, blurred, dim, doubtful, fuzzy, generalized, hazy, ill-defined, imprecise, indefinite, indeterminate, indistinct, lax, loose, nebulous, obscure, shadowy, uncertain, unclear, unknown, unspecified, woolly
Antonyms clear, clear-cut, definite, distinct, exact, explicit, lucid, precise, specific, well-defined

vaguely absent-mindedly, dimly, evasively, imprecisely, in a general way, obscurely, slightly, through a glass darkly, vacantly

vagueness ambiguity, impreciseness, inexactitude, lack of preciseness, looseness, obscurity, undecidedness, woolliness
Antonyms clarity, clearness, definition, exactness, obviousness, preciseness, precision

vain 1. arrogant, bigheaded (*informal*), cocky, conceited, egotistical, inflated, narcissistic, ostentatious, overweening, peacockish, pleased with oneself, proud, self-important, stuck-up (*informal*), swaggering, swanky (*informal*), swollen-headed (*informal*), vainglorious 2. abortive, empty, fruitless, futile, hollow, idle, nugatory, pointless, senseless, time-wasting, trifling, trivial, unavailing, unimportant, un~

productive, unprofitable, useless, wanky (*taboo slang*), worthless **3. be vain** have a high opinion of oneself, have a swelled head (*informal*), have one's head turned, think a lot of oneself, think oneself it (*informal*), think oneself the cat's whiskers *or* pyjamas (*slang*) **4. in vain** bootless, fruitless(ly), ineffectual(ly), to no avail, to no purpose, unsuccessful(ly), useless(ly), vain(ly), wasted, without success
Antonyms (*sense 1*) bashful, humble, meek, modest, self-deprecating (*sense 2*) fruitful, profitable, serious, successful, useful, valid, worthwhile, worthy

valediction adieu, farewell, goodbye, leave-taking, sendoff (*informal*), *vale*

valedictory *adjective* farewell, final, parting

valetudinarian *adjective* delicate, feeble, frail, hypochondriac, infirm, in poor health, invalid, sickly, weakly

valiant bold, brave, courageous, dauntless, doughty, fearless, gallant, heroic, indomitable, intrepid, lion-hearted, plucky, redoubtable, stouthearted, valorous, worthy
Antonyms cowardly, craven, fearful, shrinking, spineless, timid, weak

valid 1. acceptable, binding, cogent, conclusive, convincing, efficacious, efficient, good, just, logical, powerful, sensible, sound, substantial, telling, weighty, well-founded, well-grounded **2.** authentic, bona fide, genuine, in force, lawful, legal, legally binding, legitimate, official, signed and sealed
Antonyms (*sense 1*) baseless, bogus, fallacious, false, illogical, sham, spurious, unacceptable, unfounded, unrealistic, unrecognized, untrue, weak (*sense 2*) illegal, inoperative, invalid, unlawful, unofficial

validate authenticate, authorize, certify, confirm, corroborate, endorse, legalize, make legally binding, ratify, set one's seal on *or* to, substantiate

validity 1. cogency, force, foundation, grounds, point, power, soundness, strength, substance, weight **2.** authority, lawfulness, legality, legitimacy, right

valley coomb, cwm (*Welsh*), dale, dell, depression, dingle, glen, hollow, strath (*Scot.*), vale

valorous bold, brave, courageous, dauntless, doughty, fearless, gallant, heroic, intrepid, lion-hearted, plucky, valiant

valour boldness, bravery, courage, derring-do (*archaic*), doughtiness, fearlessness, gallantry, heroism, intrepidity, lion-heartedness, spirit
Antonyms cowardice, dread, fear, timidity, trepidation, weakness

valuable *adjective* **1.** costly, dear, expensive, high-priced, precious **2.** beneficial, cherished, esteemed, estimable, held dear, helpful, important, prized, profitable, serviceable, treasured, useful, valued, worth one's *or* its weight in gold, worthwhile, worthy *~noun* **3.** *usually plural* heirloom, treasure(s)
Antonyms *adjective* (*sense 1*) cheap, cheapo (*informal*), chickenshit (*U.S. slang*), crappy (*slang*), inexpensive, worthless (*sense 2*) insignificant, pointless, silly, trifling, trivial, unimportant, useless, worthless

value *noun* **1.** cost, equivalent, market price, monetary worth, rate **2.** advantage, benefit, desirability, help, importance, merit, mileage (*informal*), profit, serviceableness, significance, use, usefulness, utility, worth **3.** *plural* code of behaviour, ethics, (moral) standards, principles *~verb* **4.** account, appraise, assess, compute, estimate, evaluate, price, put a price on, rate, set at, survey **5.** appreciate, cherish, esteem, hold dear, hold in high regard *or* esteem, prize, regard highly, respect, set store by, treasure
Antonyms *noun* (*sense 2*) insignificance, unimportance, uselessness, worthlessness *~verb* disregard, have no time for, hold a low opinion of, underestimate, undervalue

valued cherished, dear, esteemed, highly regarded, loved, prized, treasured

valueless miserable, no good, of no earthly use, of no value, unsaleable, useless, worthless

vamoose bugger off (*taboo slang*), clear off (*informal*), decamp, do a bunk (*Brit. slang*), fuck off (*offensive taboo slang*), get on one's bike (*Brit. slang*), go away, go to hell (*informal*), hook it (*slang*), make off, make oneself scarce (*informal*), run away, scarper (*Brit. slang*), scram (*informal*), skedaddle (*informal*), sling one's hook (*Brit. slang*), take flight, take oneself off

vandal delinquent, graffiti artist, hooligan, lager lout, ned (*slang*), rowdy, yob *or* yobbo (*Brit. slang*)

vanguard advance guard, cutting edge, forefront, forerunners, front, front line, front rank, leaders, spearhead, trailblazers, trendsetters, van
Antonyms back, rear, rearguard, stern, tail, tail end

vanish become invisible, be lost to sight, die out, disappear, disappear from sight *or* from the face of the earth, dissolve, evanesce, evaporate, exit, fade (away), melt (away), vanish off the face of the earth
Antonyms appear, arrive, become visible, come into view, materialize, pop up

vanity 1. affected ways, airs, arrogance, bigheadedness (*informal*), conceit, conceitedness, egotism, narcissism, ostentation, pretension, pride, self-admiration, self-love, showing off (*informal*), swollen-headedness (*informal*),

vainglory 2. emptiness, frivolity, fruitlessness, futility, hollowness, inanity, pointlessness, profitlessness, triviality, unproductiveness, unreality, unsubstantiality, uselessness, worthlessness
Antonyms (*sense 1*) humility, meekness, modesty, self-abasement, self-deprecation (*sense 2*) importance, value, worth

Vanity, like murder, will out
Hannah Cowley *The Belle's Stratagem*

Vanity of vanities, all is vanity
Bible: Ecclesiastes

We are so vain that we even care for the opinion of those we don't care for
Marie von Ebner-Eschenbach

vanquish beat, blow out of the water (*slang*), clobber (*slang*), conquer, crush, defeat, get the upper hand over, lick (*informal*), master, overcome, overpower, overwhelm, put down, put to flight, put to rout, quell, reduce, repress, rout, run rings around (*informal*), stuff (*slang*), subdue, subjugate, tank (*slang*), triumph over, undo, wipe the floor with (*informal*)

vapid 1. bland, dead, flat, flavourless, insipid, lifeless, milk-and-water, stale, tasteless, unpalatable, watery, weak, wishy-washy (*informal*) 2. boring, colourless, dull, flat, limp, tame, tedious, tiresome, uninspiring, uninteresting

vapour breath, dampness, exhalation, fog, fumes, haze, miasma, mist, smoke, steam

variable capricious, chameleonic, changeable, fickle, fitful, flexible, fluctuating, inconstant, mercurial, mutable, protean, shifting, temperamental, uneven, unstable, unsteady, vacillating, wavering
Antonyms constant, firm, fixed, settled, stable, steady, unalterable, unchanging

variance 1. difference, difference of opinion, disagreement, discord, discrepancy, dissension, dissent, divergence, inconsistency, lack of harmony, strife, variation 2. **at variance** at loggerheads, at odds, at sixes and sevens (*informal*), conflicting, in disagreement, in opposition, out of harmony, out of line
Antonyms (*sense 1*) accord, agreement, congruity, correspondence, harmony, similarity, unison

variant 1. *adjective* alternative, derived, different, divergent, exceptional, modified 2. *noun* alternative, derived form, development, modification, sport (*Biology*), variation

variation alteration, break in routine, change, departure, departure from the norm, deviation, difference, discrepancy, diversification, diversity, innovation, modification, novelty, variety
Antonyms dullness, monotony, sameness, tedium, uniformity

varied assorted, different, diverse, heterogeneous, manifold, miscellaneous, mixed, motley, sundry, various
Antonyms homogeneous, repetitive, similar, standardized, uniform, unvarying

variegated diversified, many-coloured, motley, mottled, parti-coloured, pied, streaked, varicoloured

variety 1. change, difference, discrepancy, diversification, diversity, many-sidedness, multifariousness, variation 2. array, assortment, collection, cross section, intermixture, medley, miscellany, mixed bag (*informal*), mixture, multiplicity, range 3. brand, breed, category, class, kind, make, order, sort, species, strain, type
Antonyms (*sense 1*) homogeneity, invariability, monotony, similarity, similitude, uniformity

Variety's the very spice of life,
That gives all its flavour
William Cowper *The Task*

You should make a point of trying everything once, excepting incest and folk-dancing
Sir Arnold Bax *Farewell My Youth*

Different strokes for different folks

various assorted, different, differing, disparate, distinct, divers (*archaic*), diverse, diversified, heterogeneous, manifold, many, many-sided, miscellaneous, several, sundry, varied, variegated
Antonyms alike, equivalent, matching, same, similar, uniform

varnish *verb* adorn, decorate, embellish, gild, glaze, gloss, japan, lacquer, polish, shellac

vary alter, alternate, be unlike, change, depart, differ, disagree, diverge, diversify, fluctuate, intermix, modify, permutate, reorder, transform

varying changing, different, distinct, distinguishable, diverse, fluctuating, inconsistent
Antonyms consistent, fixed, monotonous, regular, settled, unchanging, unvarying

vassal bondman, bondservant, bondsman, liegeman, retainer, serf, slave, subject, thrall, varlet (*archaic*)

vassalage bondage, dependence, serfdom, servitude, slavery, subjection, thraldom

vast astronomical, boundless, colossal, elephantine, enormous, extensive, gigantic, ginormous (*informal*), great, huge, humongous *or* humungous (*U.S. slang*), illimitable, immeasurable, immense, limitless, mammoth, massive, measureless, mega (*slang*), monstrous, monumental, never-ending, prodigious, sweeping, tremendous, unbounded, unlimited, vasty (*archaic*), voluminous, wide

Antonyms bounded, limited, microscopic, narrow, negligible, paltry, puny, small, tiny, trifling

vault[1] *verb* bound, clear, hurdle, jump, leap, spring

vault[2] *noun* **1.** arch, ceiling, roof, span **2.** catacomb, cellar, charnel house, crypt, mausoleum, tomb, undercroft **3.** depository, repository, strongroom *~verb* **4.** arch, bend, bow, curve, overarch, span

vaulted arched, cavernous, domed, hemispheric

vaunt boast about, brag about, crow about, exult in, flaunt, give oneself airs about, make a display of, make much of, parade, prate about, show off, talk big about (*informal*)

veer be deflected, change, change course, change direction, sheer, shift, swerve, tack, turn

vegetate **1.** be inert, deteriorate, exist, go to seed, idle, languish, loaf, moulder, stagnate, veg out (*slang, chiefly U.S.*) **2.** burgeon, germinate, grow, shoot, spring, sprout, swell
Antonyms (*sense 1*) accomplish, develop, grow, participate, perform, react, respond

vehemence ardour, eagerness, earnestness, emphasis, energy, enthusiasm, fervency, fervour, fire, force, forcefulness, heat, impetuosity, intensity, keenness, passion, verve, vigour, violence, warmth, zeal
Antonyms apathy, coolness, indifference, inertia, lethargy, listlessness, passivity, stoicism, torpor

vehement ablaze, ardent, eager, earnest, emphatic, enthusiastic, fervent, fervid, fierce, flaming, forceful, forcible, impassioned, impetuous, intense, passionate, powerful, strong, violent, zealous
Antonyms apathetic, calm, cool, dispassionate, half-hearted, impassive, lukewarm, moderate

vehicle[1] *noun* conveyance, means of transport, transport, transportation

Types of vehicle

aircraft *see* AIRCRAFT
ambulance
articulated lorry *or* (*informal*) artic
autocycle
autorickshaw
barrow
bicycle *or* (*informal*) bike
Black Maria
boat *see* VESSEL
bulldozer
bus
cab
cabriolet
camion
camper (*U.S. & Canad.*)
camper van
car
caravan
carriage
Caterpillar (*Trademark*)
chaise
charabanc (*Brit.*)
chariot
coach
combine harvester
Conestoga wagon (*U.S. & Canad.*)
coupé
cycle
delivery van *or* (*U.S. & Canad.*) panel truck
Dormobile (*Trademark*)
double-decker (*chiefly Brit.*)
dray
dump truck *or* dumper-truck
dustcart *or* (*U.S. & Canad.*) garbage truck
estate car
fire engine
fork-lift truck
gritter (*Brit.*)
hansom *or* hansom cab
hatchback *or* hatch
hog (*informal*)
jaunting car *or* jaunty car
JCB (*Trademark*)
Jeep (*Trademark*)
jet ski
jinricksha, jinrickshaw, jinrikisha *or* jinriksha
jitney (*U.S., rare*)
kart, go-cart *or* go-kart
kibitka
komatik
koneke (*N.Z.*)
landaulet *or* landaulette
light engine *or* (*U.S.*) wildcat
limousine
litter
locomotive
lorry
low-loader
luge
milk float
minibus
moped
motorbicycle
motorbike
motorbus
motorcar
motor caravan
motorcycle
motor scooter
motor vehicle
off-road vehicle
omnibus
panda car (*Brit.*)
pantechnicon (*Brit.*)
pick-up *or* (*Austral. & N.Z.*) utility truck *or* (*informal*) ute
police car
postbus
post chaise
pram
racing car
railcar
ratha
rickshaw
roadroller
road train (*Austral.*)
rocket
scooter
scout car
shandrydan
ship *see* VESSEL
single-decker (*Brit. informal*)
skibob
sledge *or* (*especially U.S. & Canad.*) sled
sleigh
Sno-Cat (*Trademark*)
snowmobile
snow plough
space capsule
spacecraft
space probe
spaceship
space shuttle
sports car
stagecoach
steamroller
sulky
tandem
tank
tank engine *or* locomotive
tanker
tarantass
taxi
telega
three-wheeler
tipper truck *or* lorry
toboggan
tonga
tourer *or* (*especially U.S.*) touring car
traction engine
tractor
trail bike
trailer
train
tram *or* tramcar *or* (*U.S. & Canad.*) streetcar *or* trolley car
travois
tricycle

troika	unicycle
trolley	van
trolleybus	wagon *or* waggon
troop carrier	wagonette *or* waggon~ette
truck	
tumbrel *or* tumbril	wheelbarrow

vehicle[2] *noun, figurative* apparatus, channel, means, means of expression, mechanism, medium, organ

veil 1. *verb* cloak, conceal, cover, dim, disguise, hide, mantle, mask, obscure, screen, shield **2.** *noun* blind, cloak, cover, curtain, disguise, film, mask, screen, shade, shroud
Antonyms *verb* disclose, display, divulge, expose, lay bare, reveal, uncover, unveil

veiled concealed, covert, disguised, hinted at, implied, masked, suppressed

vein 1. blood vessel, course, current, lode, seam, stratum, streak, stripe **2.** dash, hint, strain, streak, thread, trait **3.** attitude, bent, character, faculty, humour, mode, mood, note, style, temper, tenor, tone, turn

velocity celerity, fleetness, impetus, pace, quickness, rapidity, speed, swiftness

velvety delicate, downy, mossy, smooth, soft, velutinous, velvet-like

venal bent (*slang*), corrupt, corruptible, crooked (*informal*), dishonourable, grafting (*informal*), mercenary, prostituted, purchasable, rapacious, simoniacal, sordid, unprincipled
Antonyms honest, honourable, incorruptible, law-abiding, principled, upright

vendetta bad blood, blood feud, feud, quarrel

veneer *noun, figurative* appearance, façade, false front, finish, front, gloss, guise, mask, pretence, semblance, show

venerable august, esteemed, grave, honoured, respected, revered, reverenced, sage, sedate, wise, worshipped
Antonyms callow, discredited, disdained, disgraced, dishonourable, disreputable, green, ignominious, immature, inexperienced, inglorious, scorned, young, youthful

venerate adore, esteem, hold in awe, honour, look up to, respect, revere, reverence, worship
Antonyms deride, dishonour, disregard, execrate, mock, scorn, spurn

veneration adoration, awe, deference, esteem, respect, reverence, worship

vengeance 1. an eye for an eye, avenging, lex talionis, reprisal, requital, retaliation, retribution, revenge, settling of scores **2. with a vengeance a.** forcefully, furiously, vehemently, violently **b.** and no mistake, extremely, greatly, to the full, to the nth degree, to the utmost, with no holds barred
Antonyms (*sense 1*) absolution, acquittal, exoneration, forbearance, forgiveness, mercy, pardon, remission

Vengeance is mine; I will repay, saith the Lord
Bible: Romans

vengeful avenging, implacable, punitive, rancorous, relentless, retaliatory, revengeful, spiteful, thirsting for revenge, unforgiving, vindictive

venial allowable, excusable, forgivable, insignificant, minor, pardonable, slight, trivial

venom 1. bane, poison, toxin **2.** acidity, acrimony, bitterness, gall, grudge, hate, ill will, malevolence, malice, maliciousness, malignity, pungency, rancour, spite, spitefulness, spleen, virulence
Antonyms (*sense 2*) benevolence, charity, compassion, favour, goodwill, kindness, love, mercy

venomous 1. baneful (*archaic*), envenomed, mephitic, noxious, poison, poisonous, toxic, virulent **2.** baleful, hostile, malicious, malignant, rancorous, savage, spiteful, vicious, vindictive, virulent
Antonyms (*sense 1*) harmless, nonpoisonous, nontoxic, nonvenomous (*sense 2*) affectionate, benevolent, compassionate, forgiving, harmless, loving, magnanimous

vent 1. *noun* aperture, duct, hole, opening, orifice, outlet, split **2.** *verb* air, come out with, discharge, emit, empty, express, give expression to, give vent to, pour out, release, utter, voice
Antonyms *verb* bottle up, curb, hold back, inhibit, quash, quell, repress, stifle, subdue

ventilate *figurative* air, bring out into the open, broadcast, debate, discuss, examine, make known, scrutinize, sift, talk about

venture *verb* **1.** chance, endanger, hazard, imperil, jeopardize, put in jeopardy, risk, speculate, stake, wager **2.** advance, dare, dare say, hazard, make bold, presume, stick one's neck out (*informal*), take the liberty, volunteer **3.** *with* **out, forth,** *etc.* embark on, go, plunge into, set out ~*noun* **4.** adventure, chance, endeavour, enterprise, fling, gamble, hazard, jeopardy, project, risk, speculation, undertaking

Nothing ventured, nothing gained

venturesome adventurous, bold, courageous, daredevil, daring, doughty, enterprising, fearless, intrepid, plucky, spirited

veracious accurate, credible, dependable, ethical, factual, faithful, frank, genuine, high-principled, honest, reliable, straightforward, true, trustworthy, truthful, veridical

veracity accuracy, candour, credibility, exactitude, frankness, honesty, integrity, precision, probity, rectitude, trustworthiness, truth, truthfulness, uprightness

verbal literal, oral, spoken, unwritten, verbatim, word-of-mouth

verbally by word of mouth, orally

verbatim exactly, precisely, to the letter, word for word

verbiage circumlocution, periphrasis, pleonasm, prolixity, redundancy, repetition, tautology, verbosity

verbose circumlocutory, diffuse, garrulous, long-winded, periphrastic, pleonastic, prolix, tautological, windy, wordy
Antonyms brief, brusque, concise, curt, quiet, reticent, short, succinct, terse, untalkative

verbosely at great length, at undue length, long-windedly, wordily

verbosity garrulity, logorrhoea, long-windedness, loquaciousness, prolixity, rambling, verbiage, verboseness, windiness, wordiness

verdant flourishing, fresh, grassy, green, leafy, lush

verdict adjudication, conclusion, decision, finding, judgment, opinion, sentence

verge 1. *noun* border, boundary, brim, brink, edge, extreme, limit, lip, margin, roadside, threshold **2.** *verb* approach, border, come near

verification authentication, confirmation, corroboration, proof, substantiation, validation

verify attest, attest to, authenticate, bear out, check, confirm, corroborate, prove, substantiate, support, validate
Antonyms deny, discount, discredit, dispute, invalidate, nullify, undermine, weaken

verisimilitude authenticity, colour, credibility, likeliness, likeness, plausibility, realism, resemblance, semblance, show of

verminous alive, crawling, flea-ridden, lousy, rat-infested

vernacular 1. *adjective* colloquial, common, indigenous, informal, local, mother, native, popular, vulgar **2.** *noun* argot, cant, dialect, idiom, jargon, native language, parlance, patois, speech, vulgar tongue

versatile adaptable, adjustable, all-purpose, all-round, all-singing, all-dancing, flexible, functional, handy, many-sided, multifaceted, protean, resourceful, variable
Antonyms fixed, inflexible, invariable, limited, one-sided, unadaptable

versed accomplished, acquainted, competent, conversant, experienced, familiar, knowledgeable, practised, proficient, qualified, seasoned, skilled, well informed, well up in (*informal*)
Antonyms callow, green, ignorant, inexperienced, new, raw, unacquainted, unfledged, unpractised, unschooled, unskilled, unversed

version 1. account, adaptation, exercise, interpretation, portrayal, reading, rendering, side, take (*informal, chiefly U.S.*), translation **2.** design, form, kind, model, style, type, variant

vertex acme, apex, apogee, crest, crown, culmination, extremity, height, pinnacle, summit, top, zenith

vertical erect, on end, perpendicular, upright
Antonyms flat, horizontal, level, plane, prone

vertigo dizziness, giddiness, light-headedness, loss of equilibrium, swimming of the head

verve animation, brio, dash, élan, energy, enthusiasm, force, get-up-and-go (*informal*), gusto, life, liveliness, pep, punch (*informal*), sparkle, spirit, vigour, vim (*slang*), vitality, vivacity, zeal, zip (*informal*)
Antonyms apathy, disdain, half-heartedness, indifference, inertia, lack of enthusiasm, languor, lethargy, lifelessness, reluctance, torpor

very *adverb* **1.** absolutely, acutely, awfully (*informal*), decidedly, deeply, eminently, exceedingly, excessively, extremely, greatly, highly, jolly (*Brit.*), noticeably, particularly, profoundly, really, remarkably, seriously (*informal*), superlatively, surpassingly, terribly, truly, uncommonly, unusually, wonderfully ~*adjective* **2.** actual, appropriate, exact, express, identical, perfect, precise, real, same, selfsame, unqualified **3.** bare, mere, plain, pure, sheer, simple

vessel 1. barque (*poetic*), boat, craft, ship **2.** container, pot, receptacle, utensil

Vessels

airboat
aircraft carrier
auxiliary
barge
barque
barquentine *or* barquantine
bateau
bathyscaph, bathyscaphe, *or* bathyscape
battlecruiser
battleship
Bermuda rig
brigantine
bulk carrier
bumboat
cabin cruiser
canal boat
canoe
caravel *or* carvel
carrack
catamaran
catboat
caïque
clipper
coble
cockboat *or* cockleboat
cockleshell
coracle
corvette
cruiser
cutter
destroyer
destroyer escort
dhow
dinghy
dogger
dreadnought *or* dreadnaught
drifter
dromond *or* dromon
E-boat
factory ship
faltboat
felucca
ferry
fireboat
fishing boat
flatboat
flotel *or* floatel
flyboat
fore-and-after
freighter
frigate
galleass
galleon
galley
gig
gondola
gunboat
hooker

houseboat
hoy
hydrofoil
icebreaker
Indiaman
ironclad
jolly boat
junk
kayak
keelboat
ketch
laker
lapstrake *or* lapstreak
launch
lifeboat
lightship
liner
longboat
longship
lugger
man-of-war *or* man o' war
merchantman
minehunter
minelayer
minesweeper
monitor
monohull
motorboat
MTB (motor torpedo boat)
multihull
narrow boat
nuggar
outboard
outrigger
oysterman
packet boat
paddle steamer
pink
pocket battleship
polacre *or* polacca
powerboat
proa *or* prau
punt
púcán
quinquereme
raft
randan
revenue cutter
rowing boat
sailing boat *or (U.S. & Canad.)* sailboat
schooner
scull
sealer
shallop
shell
ship of the line
sidewheeler
skiff
sloop
square-rigger
steamboat
steamer
steamship
sternwheeler
submarine
supertanker
surfboat
swamp boat
tall ship
tanker
tartan
tender
threedecker
torpedo boat
torpedo-boat destroyer
trawler
trimaran
trireme
troopship
tub
tug *or* tugboat
U-boat
umiak *or* oomiak
vaporetto
vedette
warship
weather ship
whaler
wherry
windjammer
xebec, zebec *or* zebeck
yacht
yawl

vest *verb* **1.** *with* **in** *or* **with** authorize, be devolved upon, bestow, confer, consign, empower, endow, entrust, furnish, invest, lodge, place, put in the hands of, settle **2.** apparel, bedeck, clothe, cover, dress, envelop, garb, robe

vestibule anteroom, entrance hall, foyer, hall, lobby, porch, portico

vestige evidence, glimmer, hint, indication, relic, remainder, remains, remnant, residue, scrap, sign, suspicion, token, trace, track

vestigial imperfect, incomplete, nonfunctional, rudimentary, surviving, undeveloped
Antonyms complete, developed, functional, perfect, practical, useful

vet *verb* appraise, check, check out, examine, give (someone *or* something) the once-over (*informal*), investigate, look over, pass under review, review, scan, scrutinize, size up (*informal*)

veteran 1. *noun* master, old hand, old stager, old-timer, past master, past mistress, pro (*informal*), trouper, warhorse (*informal*) **2.** *adjective* adept, battle-scarred, expert, long-serving, old, proficient, seasoned
Antonyms *noun* apprentice, beginner, freshman, initiate, neophyte, novice, recruit, tyro

veto 1. *verb* ban, boycott, disallow, forbid, give the thumbs down to, interdict, kill (*informal*), negative, prohibit, put the kibosh on (*slang*), refuse permission, reject, rule out, turn down **2.** *noun* ban, boycott, embargo, interdict, nonconsent, prohibition
Antonyms *verb* approve, endorse, O.K. *or* okay (*informal*), pass, ratify *~noun* approval, endorsement, go-ahead (*informal*), ratification

vex afflict, aggravate (*informal*), agitate, annoy, bother, bug (*informal*), displease, distress, disturb, exasperate, fret, gall, get one's back up, get on one's nerves (*informal*), grate on, harass, hassle (*informal*), irritate, molest, nark (*Brit., Austral., & N.Z. slang*), needle (*informal*), nettle, offend, peeve (*informal*), perplex, pester, pique, plague, provoke, put one's back up, put out, rile, tease, torment, trouble, upset, worry
Antonyms allay, appease, comfort, console, gratify, hush, mollify, please, quiet, soothe

vexation 1. aggravation (*informal*), annoyance, displeasure, dissatisfaction, exasperation, frustration, irritation, pique **2.** bother, difficulty, hassle (*informal*), headache (*informal*), irritant, misfortune, nuisance, problem, thorn in one's flesh, trouble, upset, worry

vexatious afflicting, aggravating (*informal*), annoying, bothersome, burdensome, disagreeable, disappointing, distressing, exasperating, harassing, irksome, irritating, nagging, plaguy (*archaic*), provoking, teasing, tormenting, troublesome, trying, unpleasant, upsetting, worrisome, worrying
Antonyms agreeable, balmy, calming, comforting, pleasant, reassuring, relaxing, soothing

vexed 1. afflicted, aggravated (*informal*), agitated, annoyed, bothered, confused, displeased, distressed, disturbed, exasperated, fed up, hacked (off) (*U.S. slang*), harassed, irritated, miffed (*informal*), nettled, out of countenance, peeved (*informal*), perplexed, pissed off (*taboo slang*), provoked, put out, riled, ruffled, tormented, troubled, upset, worried **2.** contested, controversial, disputed, moot, much debated

viable applicable, feasible, operable, practicable, usable, within the bounds of possibility, workable
Antonyms hopeless, impossible, impracticable, inconceivable, out of the question, unthinkable, unworkable

vibes atmosphere, aura, emanation, emotions, feelings, reaction, response, vibrations

vibrant **1.** aquiver, oscillating, palpitating, pulsating, quivering, trembling **2.** alive, animated, colourful, dynamic, electrifying, full of pep (*informal*), responsive, sensitive, sparkling, spirited, vivacious, vivid

vibrate fluctuate, judder (*informal*), oscillate, pulsate, pulse, quiver, resonate, reverberate, shake, shiver, sway, swing, throb, tremble, undulate

vibration juddering (*informal*), oscillation, pulsation, pulse, quiver, resonance, reverberation, shaking, throb, throbbing, trembling, tremor

vicarious acting, at one remove, commissioned, delegated, deputed, empathetic, indirect, substituted, surrogate

vice **1.** corruption, degeneracy, depravity, evil, evildoing, immorality, iniquity, profligacy, sin, turpitude, venality, wickedness **2.** blemish, defect, failing, fault, imperfection, shortcoming, weakness
Antonyms (*sense 1*) honour, morality, virtue (*sense 2*) attainment, gift, good point, strong point, talent

vice versa contrariwise, conversely, in reverse, the other way round

vicinity area, district, environs, locality, neck of the woods (*informal*), neighbourhood, precincts, propinquity, proximity, purlieus

vicious **1.** abandoned, abhorrent, atrocious, bad, barbarous, corrupt, cruel, dangerous, debased, degenerate, degraded, depraved, diabolical, ferocious, fiendish, foul, heinous, immoral, infamous, monstrous, profligate, savage, sinful, unprincipled, vile, violent, wicked, worthless, wrong **2.** backbiting, bitchy (*informal*), cruel, defamatory, malicious, mean, rancorous, slanderous, spiteful, venomous, vindictive
Antonyms complimentary, docile, friendly, gentle, good, honourable, kind, playful, tame, upright, virtuous

You can't expect a boy to be vicious till he's been to a good school
Saki *Reginald in Russia*

viciousness **1.** badness, corruption, cruelty, depravity, ferocity, immorality, profligacy, savagery, wickedness **2.** bitchiness (*slang*), malice, rancour, spite, spitefulness, venom
Antonyms (*sense 2*) gentleness, goodness, goodwill, graciousness, kindness, mercy, virtue

vicissitude alteration, alternation, change, fluctuation of fortune, mutation, one of life's ups and downs (*informal*), revolution, shift, variation

victim **1.** casualty, fatality, injured party, martyr, sacrifice, scapegoat, sufferer **2.** dupe, easy prey, fall guy (*informal*), gull (*archaic*), innocent, patsy (*slang, chiefly U.S. & Canad.*), sitting duck (*informal*), sitting target, sucker (*slang*)
Antonyms (*sense 1*) survivor (*sense 2*) assailant, attacker, culprit, guilty party, offender

He is brought as a lamb to the slaughter
Bible: Isaiah

victimize **1.** demonize, discriminate against, have a down on (someone) (*informal*), have it in for (someone) (*informal*), have one's knife into (someone), persecute, pick on **2.** cheat, deceive, defraud, dupe, exploit, fool, gull (*archaic*), hoodwink, prey on, swindle, take advantage of, use

victor champ (*informal*), champion, conquering hero, conqueror, first, prizewinner, top dog (*informal*), vanquisher, winner
Antonyms also-ran, dud (*informal*), failure, flop (*informal*), loser, vanquished

victorious champion, conquering, first, prizewinning, successful, triumphant, vanquishing, winning
Antonyms beaten, conquered, defeated, failed, losing, overcome, unsuccessful, vanquished

victory conquest, laurels, mastery, success, superiority, the palm, the prize, triumph, win
Antonyms defeat, failure, loss

victuals bread, comestibles, eatables, eats (*slang*), edibles, food, grub (*slang*), meat, nosebag (*slang*), nosh (*slang*), provisions, rations, stores, supplies, tack (*informal*), viands, vittles (*obsolete*)

vie be rivals, compete, contend, contest, match oneself against, strive, struggle

view *noun* **1.** aspect, landscape, outlook, panorama, perspective, picture, prospect, scene, spectacle, vista **2.** range *or* field of vision, sight, vision **3.** *sometimes plural* attitude, belief, conviction, feeling, impression, judgment, notion, opinion, point of view, sentiment, thought, way of thinking **4.** contemplation, display, examination, inspection, look, recce (*slang*), scan, scrutiny, sight, survey, viewing **5. with a view to** in order to, in the hope of, so as to, with the aim *or* intention of ~*verb* **6.** behold, check, check out (*informal*), clock (*Brit. slang*), contemplate, examine, explore, eye, eyeball (*U.S. slang*), gaze at, get a load of (*informal*), inspect, look at, observe, recce (*slang*), regard, scan, spectate, stare at, survey, take a dekko at (*Brit. slang*), watch, witness **7.** consider, deem, judge, look on, regard, think about

viewer observer, one of an audience, onlooker, spectator, TV watcher, watcher

viewpoint angle, frame of reference, perspective, point of view, position, slant, stance, standpoint, vantage point, way of thinking

vigilance alertness, attentiveness, carefulness, caution, circumspection, observance, watchfulness

vigilant alert, Argus-eyed, attentive, careful, cautious, circumspect, keeping one's eyes peeled *or* skinned (*informal*), on one's guard, on one's toes, on the alert, on the lookout, on the qui vive, on the watch, sleepless, unsleeping, wakeful, watchful, wide awake
Antonyms careless, inattentive, lax, neglectful, negligent, remiss, slack

vigorous active, alive and kicking, brisk, dynamic, effective, efficient, energetic, enterprising, fighting fit, fit as a fiddle (*informal*), flourishing, forceful, forcible, full of beans (*informal*), full of energy, hale, hale and hearty, hardy, healthy, intense, lively, lusty, powerful, red-blooded, robust, sound, spanking, spirited, strenuous, strong, virile, vital, zippy (*informal*)
Antonyms apathetic, effete, enervated, feeble, frail, inactive, indolent, lethargic, lifeless, spiritless, torpid, weak, weedy (*informal*), wimpish *or* wimpy (*informal*), wishy-washy

vigorously all out, eagerly, energetically, forcefully, hammer and tongs, hard, like mad (*slang*), lustily, strenuously, strongly, with a vengeance, with might and main

vigour activity, animation, balls (*taboo slang*), brio, dash, dynamism, energy, force, forcefulness, gusto, health, liveliness, might, oomph (*informal*), pep, power, punch (*informal*), robustness, snap (*informal*), soundness, spirit, strength, verve, vim (*slang*), virility, vitality, zip (*informal*)
Antonyms apathy, feebleness, fragility, frailty, impotence, inactivity, inertia, infirmity, lethargy, sluggishness, weakness

vile 1. abandoned, abject, appalling, bad, base, coarse, contemptible, corrupt, debased, degenerate, degrading, depraved, despicable, disgraceful, evil, humiliating, ignoble, impure, loathsome, low, mean, miserable, nefarious, perverted, shocking, sinful, ugly, vicious, vulgar, wicked, worthless, wretched **2.** disgusting, foul, horrid, loathsome, nasty, nauseating, noxious, obscene, offensive, repellent, repugnant, repulsive, revolting, sickening, yucky *or* yukky (*slang*)
Antonyms agreeable, chaste, cultured, delicate, genteel, honourable, lovely, marvellous, noble, pleasant, polite, pure, refined, righteous, splendid, sublime, upright, worthy

vileness coarseness, corruption, degeneracy, depravity, dreadfulness, enormity, evil, foulness, heinousness, noxiousness, offensiveness, outrage, profanity, turpitude, ugliness, wickedness

vilification abuse, aspersion, calumniation, calumny, contumely, defamation, denigration, disparagement, invective, mudslinging, scurrility, vituperation

vilify abuse, asperse, bad-mouth (*slang, chiefly U.S. & Canad.*), berate, calumniate, debase, decry, defame, denigrate, disparage, dump on (*slang, chiefly U.S.*), knock (*informal*), malign, pull to pieces (*informal*), revile, rubbish (*informal*), run down, slag (off) (*slang*), slander, smear, speak ill of, traduce, vilipend (*rare*), vituperate
Antonyms adore, commend, esteem, exalt, glorify, honour, praise, revere, venerate

villain 1. blackguard, caitiff (*archaic*), criminal, evildoer, knave (*archaic*), libertine, malefactor, miscreant, profligate, rapscallion, reprobate, rogue, scoundrel, wretch **2.** antihero, baddy (*informal*) **3.** devil, monkey, rascal, rogue, scallywag (*informal*), scamp
Antonyms (*senses 2 & 3*) angel, goody, hero, heroine, idol

villainous atrocious, bad, base, blackguardly, criminal, cruel, debased, degenerate, depraved, detestable, diabolical, evil, fiendish, hateful, heinous, ignoble, infamous, inhuman, mean, nefarious, outrageous, ruffianly, scoundrelly, sinful, terrible, thievish, vicious, vile, wicked
Antonyms angelic, good, heroic, humane, moral, noble, righteous, saintly, virtuous

villainy atrocity, baseness, crime, criminality, delinquency, depravity, devilry, iniquity, knavery, rascality, sin, turpitude, vice, wickedness

vindicate 1. absolve, acquit, clear, defend, do justice to, exculpate, excuse, exonerate, free from blame, justify, rehabilitate **2.** advocate, assert, establish, maintain, support, uphold
Antonyms (*sense 1*) accuse, blame, condemn, convict, incriminate, punish, reproach

vindication apology, assertion, defence, exculpating, exculpation, excuse, exoneration, justification, maintenance, plea, rehabilitation, substantiation, support

vindictive full of spleen, implacable, malicious, malignant, rancorous, relentless, resentful, revengeful, spiteful, unforgiving, unrelenting, vengeful, venomous
Antonyms forgiving, generous, magnanimous, merciful, relenting, unvindictive

vintage 1. *noun* collection, crop, epoch, era, generation, harvest, origin, year 2. *adjective* best, choice, classic, mature, prime, rare, ripe, select, superior, venerable

violate 1. break, contravene, disobey, disregard, encroach upon, infract, infringe, transgress 2. abuse, assault, befoul, debauch, defile, desecrate, dishonour, invade, outrage, pollute, profane, rape, ravish
Antonyms (*sense 1*) honour, obey, respect, uphold (*sense 2*) defend, honour, protect, respect, revere, set on a pedestal

violation 1. abuse, breach, contravention, encroachment, infraction, infringement, transgression, trespass 2. defilement, desecration, profanation, sacrilege, spoliation

violence 1. bestiality, bloodshed, bloodthirstiness, brutality, brute force, cruelty, destructiveness, ferocity, fierceness, fighting, force, frenzy, fury, murderousness, passion, rough handling, savagery, strong-arm tactics (*informal*), terrorism, thuggery, vehemence, wildness 2. boisterousness, power, raging, roughness, storminess, tumult, turbulence, wildness 3. abandon, acuteness, fervour, force, harshness, intensity, severity, sharpness, vehemence

I say violence is necessary. It is as American as cherry pie
H. Rap Brown

All they that take the sword shall perish with the sword
Bible: St. Matthew

Keep violence in the mind
Where it belongs
Brian Aldiss *Barefoot in the Head*

violent 1. berserk, bloodthirsty, brutal, cruel, destructive, fiery, flaming, forcible, furious, headstrong, homicidal, hot-headed, impetuous, intemperate, maddened, maniacal, murderous, passionate, powerful, raging, riotous, rough, savage, strong, tempestuous, uncontrollable, ungovernable, unrestrained, vehement, vicious, wild 2. blustery, boisterous, devastating, full of force, gale force, powerful, raging, ruinous, strong, tempestuous, tumultuous, turbulent, wild 3. acute, agonizing, biting, excruciating, extreme, harsh, inordinate, intense, outrageous, painful, severe, sharp
Antonyms calm, composed, gentle, mild, peaceful, quiet, rational, sane, serene, unruffled, well-behaved

V.I.P. big name, big noise (*informal*), big shot (*informal*), bigwig (*informal*), celebrity, leading light (*informal*), lion, luminary, man *or* woman of the hour, notable, personage, public figure, somebody, star

virago ballbreaker (*slang*), battle-axe (*informal*), fury, harridan, scold, shrew, termagant (*rare*), vixen, Xanthippe

virgin 1. *noun* damsel (*archaic*), girl, maid (*archaic*), maiden (*archaic*), vestal, virgo intacta 2. *adjective* chaste, fresh, immaculate, maidenly, modest, new, pristine, pure, snowy, uncorrupted, undefiled, unsullied, untouched, unused, vestal, virginal
Antonyms *adjective* contaminated, corrupted, defiled, dirty, impure, polluted, spoiled, used

virginal celibate, chaste, fresh, immaculate, maidenly, pristine, pure, snowy, spotless, uncorrupted, undefiled, undisturbed, untouched, virgin, white

virginity chastity, maidenhead, maidenhood

virile forceful, lusty, macho, male, manlike, manly, masculine, potent, red-blooded, robust, strong, vigorous
Antonyms camp (*informal*), effeminate, emasculate, feminine, impotent, unmanly, weak, weedy (*informal*), wimpish *or* wimpy (*informal*)

virility machismo, manhood, masculinity, potency, vigour
Antonyms effeminacy, femininity, impotence, softness, unmanliness, weakness

virtual essential, implicit, implied, in all but name, indirect, potential, practical, tacit, unacknowledged

virtually as good as, effectually, for all practical purposes, in all but name, in effect, in essence, nearly, practically, to all intents and purposes

virtue 1. ethicalness, excellence, goodness, high-mindedness, incorruptibility, integrity, justice, morality, probity, quality, rectitude, righteousness, uprightness, worth, worthiness 2. advantage, asset, attribute, credit, good point, good quality, merit, plus (*informal*), strength 3. chastity, honour, innocence, morality, purity, virginity 4. **by virtue of** as a result of, by dint of, by reason of, in view of, on account of, owing to, thanks to
Antonyms (*sense 1*) corruption, debauchery, depravity, dishonesty, dishonour, evil, immorality, sin, sinfulness, turpitude, vice (*sense 2*) drawback, failing, frailty, shortcoming, weak point (*sense 3*) promiscuity, unchastity

Virtue is the fount whence honour springs
Christopher Marlowe *Tamburlaine the Great*

Virtue is its own reward
Cicero *De Finibus*

Virtue is like a rich stone, best plain set
Francis Bacon *Essays*

Who can find a virtuous woman? For her price is far above rubies
Bible: Proverbs

For 'tis some virtue, virtue to commend
William Congreve

Virtue could see to do what Virtue would
By her own radiant light, though sun and moon
Were in the flat sea sunk
John Milton *Comus*

Against the threats
Of malice or of sorcery, or that power
Which erring men call chance, this I hold firm,
Virtue may be assailed, but never hurt,
Surprised by unjust force, but not enthralled
John Milton *Comus*

I cannot praise a fugitive and cloistered virtue, unexercised and unbreathed, that never sallies out and sees her adversary, but slinks out of the race, where that immortal garland is to be run for, not without dust and heat... that which purifies us is trial, and trial is by what is contrary
John Milton *Areopagitica*

virtuosity brilliance, craft, éclat, expertise, fin~ish, flair, mastery, panache, polish, skill

virtuoso **1.** *noun* artist, genius, grandmaster, maestro, magician, master, master hand, ma~ven (*U.S.*) **2.** *adjective* bravura (*Music*), bril~liant, dazzling, masterly

virtuous **1.** blameless, ethical, excellent, exem~plary, good, high-principled, honest, honour~able, incorruptible, moral, praiseworthy, pure, righteous, squeaky-clean, upright, worthy **2.** celibate, chaste, clean-living, innocent, pure, spotless, virginal
Antonyms (*sense 1*) corrupt, debauched, de~praved, dishonest, evil, immoral, sinful, un~righteous, vicious, wicked (*sense 2*) impure, loose, promiscuous, unchaste

virulence **1.** deadliness, harmfulness, hurtful~ness, infectiousness, injuriousness, malignan~cy, noxiousness, poisonousness, toxicity, viru~lency **2.** acrimony, antagonism, bitterness, ha~tred, hostility, ill will, malevolence, malice, poison, pungency, rancour, resentment, spite, spleen, venom, viciousness, vindictiveness

virulent **1.** baneful (*archaic*), deadly, infective, injurious, lethal, malignant, pernicious, poi~sonous, septic, toxic, venomous **2.** acrimonious, bitter, envenomed, hostile, malevolent, mali~cious, rancorous, resentful, spiteful, splenetic, venomous, vicious, vindictive
Antonyms (*sense 1*) harmless, innocuous, nonpoisonous, nontoxic (*sense 2*) amiable, be~nign, compassionate, kind, magnanimous, sympathetic, warm

viscous adhesive, clammy, gelatinous, gluey, glutinous, gooey (*informal*), gummy, mucilagi~nous, sticky, syrupy, tenacious, thick, treacly, viscid

visible anywhere to be seen, apparent, bold, clear, conspicuous, detectable, discernible, discoverable, distinguishable, evident, in sight, in view, manifest, not hidden, notice~able, observable, obvious, palpable, patent, perceivable, perceptible, plain, salient, to be seen, unconcealed, unmistakable
Antonyms concealed, hidden, imperceptible, invisible, obscured, unnoticeable, unseen

vision **1.** eyes, eyesight, perception, seeing, sight, view **2.** breadth of view, discernment, farsightedness, foresight, imagination, insight, intuition, penetration, prescience **3.** castle in the air, concept, conception, daydream, dream, fantasy, idea, ideal, image, imago (*Psycho~anal.*), mental picture, pipe dream **4.** appari~tion, chimera, delusion, eidolon, ghost, hallu~cination, illusion, mirage, phantasm, phan~tom, revelation, spectre, wraith **5.** dream, feast for the eyes, perfect picture, picture, sight, sight for sore eyes, spectacle

Your old men shall dream dreams, your young men shall see visions
Bible: Joel

Where there is no vision, the people perish
Bible: Proverbs

visionary *adjective* **1.** dreaming, dreamy, ideal~istic, quixotic, romantic, starry-eyed, with one's head in the clouds **2.** chimerical, deluso~ry, fanciful, fantastic, ideal, idealized, illusory, imaginal (*Psychoanal.*), imaginary, impracti~cal, prophetic, speculative, unreal, unrealistic, unworkable, utopian *~noun* **3.** daydreamer, Don Quixote, dreamer, enthusiast (*archaic*), idealist, mystic, prophet, romantic, seer, theo~rist, utopian, zealot
Antonyms *adjective* actual, mundane, prag~matic, real, realistic, unimaginary *~noun* cynic, pessimist, pragmatist, realist

visit *verb* **1.** be the guest of, call in, call on, drop in on (*informal*), go to see, inspect, look (someone) up, pay a call on, pop in (*informal*), stay at, stay with, stop by, take in (*informal*) **2.** afflict, assail, attack, befall, descend upon, haunt, smite, trouble **3.** *with* **on** *or* **upon** bring down upon, execute, impose, inflict, wreak *~noun* **4.** call, sojourn, stay, stop

visitation **1.** examination, inspection, visit **2.** bane, blight, calamity, cataclysm, catastrophe, disaster, infliction, ordeal, punishment, scourge, trial

visitor caller, company, guest, visitant

vista panorama, perspective, prospect, view

visual **1.** ocular, optic, optical **2.** discernible, observable, perceptible, visible
Antonyms (*sense 2*) imperceptible, indiscern~ible, invisible, out of sight, unnoticeable, unperceivable

visualize conceive of, conjure up a mental pic~ture of, envisage, imagine, picture, see in the mind's eye

vital **1.** basic, cardinal, essential, fundamental, imperative, indispensable, necessary, radical, requisite **2.** critical, crucial, decisive, impor~

tant, key, life-or-death, significant, urgent **3.** animated, dynamic, energetic, forceful, full of beans (*informal*), full of the joy of living, lively, sparky, spirited, vibrant, vigorous, vivacious, zestful **4.** alive, alive and kicking, animate, generative, invigorative, life-giving, live, living, quickening
Antonyms (*sense 1*) dispensable, inessential, nonessential, unnecessary (*sense 2*) minor, trivial, unimportant (*sense 3*) apathetic, lethargic, listless, uninvolved (*sense 4*) dead, dying, inanimate, moribund

vitality animation, brio, energy, exuberance, go (*informal*), life, liveliness, lustiness, pep, robustness, sparkle, stamina, strength, vigour, vim (*slang*), vivaciousness, vivacity
Antonyms apathy, inertia, lethargy, listlessness, sluggishness, weakness

vitiate 1. blemish, devalue, harm, impair, injure, invalidate, mar, spoil, undermine, water down **2.** blight, contaminate, corrupt, debase, defile, deprave, deteriorate, pervert, pollute, sully, taint

vitiation 1. deterioration, devaluation, dilution, impairment, marring, reduction, spoiling, undermining **2.** adulteration, contamination, corruption, debasement, degradation, perversion, pollution, sullying

vitriolic *figurative* acerbic, acid, bitchy (*informal*), bitter, caustic, destructive, dripping with malice, envenomed, sardonic, scathing, venomous, virulent, withering

vituperate abuse, asperse, berate, blame, castigate, censure, cry down, denounce, excoriate, find fault with, rail against, rate, reproach, revile, run down, slang, slate (*informal*), tear into (*informal*), upbraid, vilify

vituperation abuse, billingsgate, blame, castigation, censure, fault-finding, flak (*informal*), invective, obloquy, rebuke, reprimand, reproach, scurrility, tongue-lashing, vilification
Antonyms acclaim, approval, commendation, eulogy, flattery, praise, tribute

vituperative abusive, belittling, calumniatory, censorious, defamatory, denunciatory, derogatory, harsh, insulting, malign, opprobrious, sardonic, scurrilous, withering

vivacious animated, bubbling, cheerful, chirpy (*informal*), ebullient, effervescent, frolicsome, full of beans (*informal*), full of life, gay, high-spirited, jolly, light-hearted, lively, merry, scintillating, sparkling, sparky, spirited, sportive, sprightly, upbeat (*informal*), vital
Antonyms boring, dull, languid, lifeless, listless, melancholy, spiritless, unenthusiastic

vivacity animation, brio, ebullience, effervescence, energy, gaiety, high spirits, life, liveliness, pep, quickness, sparkle, spirit, sprightliness
Antonyms apathy, ennui, fatigue, heaviness, inertia, languor, lethargy, listlessness, weariness

vivid 1. bright, brilliant, clear, colourful, glowing, intense, rich **2.** distinct, dramatic, graphic, highly-coloured, lifelike, memorable, powerful, realistic, sharp, sharply-etched, stirring, strong, telling, true to life **3.** active, animated, dynamic, energetic, expressive, flamboyant, lively, quick, spirited, striking, strong, vigorous
Antonyms colourless, cool, drab, dull, lifeless, nondescript, ordinary, pale, pastel, quiet, routine, run-of-the-mill, sombre, unclear, unmemorable, unremarkable, vague

vividness 1. brightness, brilliancy, glow, life, radiance, resplendence, sprightliness **2.** clarity, distinctness, graphicness, immediacy, intensity, realism, sharpness, strength

vixen *figurative* ballbreaker (*slang*), fury, harpy, harridan, hellcat, scold, shrew, spitfire, termagant (*rare*), virago, Xanthippe

viz. namely, that is to say, to wit, videlicet

vocabulary dictionary, glossary, language, lexicon, wordbook, word hoard, words, word stock

vocal *adjective* **1.** articulate, articulated, oral, put into words, said, spoken, uttered, voiced **2.** articulate, blunt, clamorous, eloquent, expressive, forthright, frank, free-spoken, noisy, outspoken, plain-spoken, strident, vociferous
Antonyms (*sense 2*) inarticulate, quiet, reserved, reticent, retiring, shy, silent, uncommunicative

vocation business, calling, career, employment, job, life's work, life work, métier, mission, office, post, profession, pursuit, role, trade

Many are called, but few are chosen
Bible: St. Matthew

vociferous clamant, clamorous, loud, loudmouthed (*informal*), noisy, obstreperous, outspoken, ranting, shouting, strident, uproarious, vehement, vocal
Antonyms hushed, muted, noiseless, quiet, silent, still

vogue *noun* **1.** craze, custom, *dernier cri*, fashion, last word, mode, style, the latest, the rage, the thing (*informal*), trend, way **2.** acceptance, currency, fashionableness, favour, popularity, prevalence, usage, use *~adjective* **3.** fashionable, in, modish, now (*informal*), popular, prevalent, trendy (*Brit. informal*), up-to-the-minute, voguish, with it (*informal*)

voice *noun* **1.** articulation, language, power of speech, sound, tone, utterance, words **2.** decision, expression, part, say, view, vote, will, wish **3.** agency, instrument, medium, mouthpiece, organ, spokesman, spokesperson, spokeswoman, vehicle *~verb* **4.** air, articulate, assert, come out with (*informal*), declare, divulge, enunciate, express, give expression *or* utterance to, put into words, say, utter, ventilate

void *adjective* **1.** bare, clear, drained, emptied, empty, free, tenantless, unfilled, unoccupied, vacant **2.** *with* **of** destitute, devoid, lacking, without **3.** dead, ineffective, ineffectual, inoperative, invalid, nonviable, nugatory, null and void, unenforceable, useless, vain, worthless ~*noun* **4.** blank, blankness, emptiness, gap, lack, opening, space, vacuity, vacuum, want ~*verb* **5.** discharge, drain, eject, eliminate (*Physiology*), emit, empty, evacuate **6.** abnegate, cancel, invalidate, nullify, rescind
Antonyms *adjective* (*sense 1*) abounding, complete, filled, full, occupied, replete, tenanted

volatile airy, changeable, erratic, explosive, fickle, flighty, gay, giddy, inconstant, lively, mercurial, sprightly, temperamental, unsettled, unstable, unsteady, up and down (*informal*), variable, whimsical
Antonyms calm, consistent, constant, cool-headed, dependable, inert, reliable, self-controlled, settled, sober, stable, steady

volcano

Volcanoes

Antisana	Kazbek
Apo	Kenya
Askja	Krakatoa *or* Krakatau
Cameroon	Lassen Peak
Chimborazo	Mauna Kea
Citlaltépetl	Mauna Loa
Corcovado	Mayon
Cotopaxi	Mount St. Helens
Egmont	Nevado de Colima
Elgon	Nevado de Toluca
El Misti	Paricutín
Erciyas Dagi	Pelée
Erebus	Popocatépetl
Etna	Santa Maria
Fuji	Semeru *or* Semeroe
Haleakala	Soufrière
Hekla	Stromboli
Helgafell	Suribachi
Huascarán *or* Huascán	Taal
Iliamna	Tambora
Ixtaccihuatl *or* Iztaccihuatl	Teide *or* Teyde
Katmai	Tolima
	Tristan da Cunha
	Vesuvius

volition choice, choosing, determination, discretion, election, free will, option, preference, purpose, resolution, will

volley *noun* barrage, blast, bombardment, burst, cannonade, discharge, explosion, fusillade, hail, salvo, shower

volubility fluency, garrulity, gift of the gab, glibness, loquaciousness, loquacity

voluble articulate, blessed with the gift of the gab, fluent, forthcoming, glib, loquacious, talkative
Antonyms hesitant, inarticulate, reticent, succinct, taciturn, terse, tongue-tied, unforthcoming

volume 1. aggregate, amount, body, bulk, capacity, compass, cubic content, dimensions, mass, quantity, total **2.** book, publication, title, tome, treatise

voluminous ample, big, billowing, bulky, capacious, cavernous, copious, full, large, massive, prolific, roomy, vast
Antonyms inadequate, insufficient, scanty, skimpy, slight, small, tiny

voluntarily by choice, freely, lief (*rare*), off one's own bat, of one's own accord, of one's own free will, on one's own initiative, willingly, without being asked, without prompting

voluntary discretional, discretionary, free, gratuitous, honorary, intended, intentional, optional, spontaneous, uncompelled, unconstrained, unforced, unpaid, volunteer, willing
Antonyms automatic, conscripted, forced, instinctive, involuntary, obligatory, unintentional

volunteer *verb* advance, let oneself in for (*informal*), need no invitation, offer, offer one's services, present, proffer, propose, put forward, put oneself at (someone's) disposal, step forward, suggest, tender
Antonyms begrudge, deny, keep, refuse, retain, withdraw, withhold

voluptuary *bon vivant*, epicurean, hedonist, luxury-lover, playboy, pleasure seeker, profligate, sensualist, sybarite

voluptuous 1. bacchanalian, epicurean, hedonistic, licentious, luxurious, pleasure-loving, self-indulgent, sensual, sybaritic **2.** ample, buxom, curvaceous (*informal*), enticing, erotic, full-bosomed, provocative, seductive, shapely, well-stacked (*Brit. slang*)
Antonyms (*sense 1*) abstemious, ascetic, celibate, rigorous, self-denying, Spartan

voluptuousness carnality, curvaceousness (*informal*), licentiousness, opulence, seductiveness, sensuality, shapeliness

vomit *verb* barf (*U.S. slang*), belch forth, be sick, bring up, chuck (up) (*slang, chiefly U.S.*), chunder (*slang, chiefly Austral.*), disgorge, do a technicolour yawn (*slang*), eject, emit, heave, puke (*slang*), regurgitate, retch, sick up (*informal*), spew out *or* up, throw up (*informal*), toss one's cookies (*U.S. slang*), upchuck (*U.S. slang*)

voracious avid, devouring, edacious, esurient, gluttonous, greedy, hungry, insatiable, omnivorous, prodigious, rapacious, ravening, ravenous, uncontrolled, unquenchable

Antonyms moderate, sated, satisfied, self-controlled, temperate

voracity avidity, eagerness, edacity, greed, hunger, rapacity, ravenousness

vortex eddy, maelstrom, whirlpool

votary adherent, aficionado, believer, devotee, disciple, follower

vote *noun* **1.** ballot, franchise, plebiscite, poll, referendum, right to vote, show of hands, suffrage *~verb* **2.** ballot, cast one's vote, elect, go to the polls, opt, return **3.** *informal* declare, judge, pronounce, propose, recommend, suggest

vouch *usually with* **for** affirm, answer for, assert, asseverate, attest to, back, certify, confirm, give assurance of, go bail for, guarantee, stand witness, support, swear to, uphold

voucher coupon, ticket, token

vouchsafe accord, cede, condescend to give, confer, deign, favour (someone) with, grant, yield

vow **1.** *verb* affirm, consecrate, dedicate, devote, pledge, promise, swear, undertake solemnly **2.** *noun* oath, pledge, promise, troth (*archaic*)

voyage *noun* crossing, cruise, journey, passage, travels, trip

vulgar **1.** blue, boorish, cheap and nasty, coarse, common, common as muck, crude, dirty, flashy, gaudy, gross, ill-bred, impolite, improper, indecent, indecorous, indelicate, low, nasty, naughty, off colour, ribald, risqué, rude, suggestive, tasteless, tawdry, uncouth, unmannerly, unrefined **2.** general, native, ordinary, unrefined, vernacular
Antonyms aristocratic, classical, decorous, elegant, genteel, high-brow, polite, refined, sophisticated, tasteful, upper-class, urbane, well-mannered

It's worse than wicked, my dear, it's vulgar
Punch

vulgarian arriviste, boor, churl, *nouveau riche*, parvenu, philistine, upstart

vulgarity bad taste, coarseness, crudeness, crudity, gaudiness, grossness, indecorum, indelicacy, lack of refinement, ribaldry, rudeness, suggestiveness, tastelessness, tawdriness
Antonyms decorum, gentility, good breeding, good manners, good taste, refinement, sensitivity, sophistication, tastefulness

vulnerable accessible, assailable, defenceless, exposed, open to attack, sensitive, susceptible, tender, thin-skinned, unprotected, weak, wide open
Antonyms guarded, immune, impervious, insensitive, invulnerable, thick-skinned, unassailable, well-protected

W

wacky crazy, daft (*informal*), eccentric, erratic, gonzo (*slang*), goofy (*informal*), irrational, loony (*slang*), nutty (*slang*), odd, oddball (*informal*), off-the-wall (*slang*), outré, screwy (*informal*), silly, unpredictable, wacko *or* whacko (*informal*), wild, zany

wad ball, block, bundle, chunk, hunk, lump, mass, plug, roll

wadding filler, lining, packing, padding, stuffing

waddle rock, shuffle, sway, toddle, totter, wobble

wade 1. ford, paddle, splash, walk through 2. *with* **through** drudge, labour, peg away, plough through, toil, work one's way 3. *with* **in** *or* **into** assail, attack, get stuck in (*informal*), go for, launch oneself at, light into (*informal*), set about, tackle, tear into (*informal*)

waffle 1. *verb* blather, jabber, prate, prattle, rabbit (on) (*Brit. informal*), verbalize, witter on (*informal*) 2. *noun* blather, jabber, padding, prating, prattle, prolixity, verbiage, verbosity, wordiness

waft 1. *verb* bear, be carried, carry, convey, drift, float, ride, transmit, transport 2. *noun* breath, breeze, current, draught, puff, whiff

wag¹ 1. *verb* bob, flutter, nod, oscillate, quiver, rock, shake, stir, vibrate, waggle, wave, wiggle 2. *noun* bob, flutter, nod, oscillation, quiver, shake, toss, vibration, waggle, wave, wiggle

wag² *noun* card (*informal*), clown, comedian, comic, humorist, jester, joculator *or* (*fem.*) joculatrix, joker, wit

wage 1. *noun Also* **wages** allowance, compensation, earnings, emolument, fee, hire, pay, payment, recompense, remuneration, reward, stipend 2. *verb* carry on, conduct, engage in, practise, proceed with, prosecute, pursue, undertake

For the labourer is worthy of his hire
Bible: St. Luke

wager 1. *noun* bet, flutter (*Brit. informal*), gamble, pledge, punt (*chiefly Brit.*), stake, venture 2. *verb* bet, chance, gamble, hazard, lay, pledge, punt (*chiefly Brit.*), put on, risk, speculate, stake, venture

waggish amusing, comical, droll, facetious, funny, humorous, impish, jesting, jocose, jocular, ludic (*literary*), merry, mischievous, playful, puckish, risible, sportive, witty

waggle 1. *verb* flutter, oscillate, shake, wag, wave, wiggle, wobble 2. *noun* flutter, oscillation, shake, wag, wave, wiggle, wobble

waif foundling, orphan, stray

wail 1. *verb* bawl, bemoan, bewail, cry, deplore, grieve, howl, keen, lament, ululate, weep, yowl 2. *noun* complaint, cry, grief, howl, keen, lament, lamentation, moan, ululation, weeping, yowl

wait 1. *verb* abide, bide one's time, cool one's heels, dally, delay, hang fire, hold back, hold on (*informal*), kick one's heels, linger, mark time, pause, remain, rest, stand by, stay, tarry 2. *noun* delay, entr'acte, halt, hold-up, interval, pause, rest, stay
Antonyms (*sense 1*) depart, go, go away, leave, move off, quit, set off, take off (*informal*)
Don't count your chickens before they are hatched
Don't cross the bridge till you come to it

waiter, waitress attendant, server, steward, stewardess

wait on *or* **upon** attend, minister to, serve, tend

waive abandon, defer, dispense with, forgo, give up, postpone, put off, refrain from, relinquish, remit, renounce, resign, set aside, surrender
Antonyms claim, demand, insist, maintain, press, profess, pursue, uphold

waiver abandonment, abdication, disclaimer, giving up, relinquishment, remission, renunciation, resignation, setting aside, surrender

wake¹ *verb* 1. arise, awake, awaken, bestir, come to, get up, rouse, rouse from sleep, stir 2. activate, animate, arouse, awaken, enliven, excite, fire, galvanize, kindle, provoke, quicken, rouse, stimulate, stir up ~*noun* 3. deathwatch, funeral, vigil, watch
Antonyms (*sense 1*) catnap, doze, drop off (*informal*), hibernate, nod off (*informal*), sleep, snooze (*informal*), take a nap

wake² *noun* aftermath, backwash, path, slipstream, track, trail, train, wash, waves

wakeful 1. insomniac, restless, sleepless, unsleeping 2. alert, alive, attentive, heedful, observant, on guard, on the alert, on the

lookout, on the qui vive, unsleeping, vigilant, wary, watchful
Antonyms (*sense 2*) asleep, dormant, dozing, dreamy, drowsy, heedless, inattentive, off guard, sleepy

waken activate, animate, arouse, awake, awaken, be roused, come awake, come to, en~liven, fire, galvanize, get up, kindle, quicken, rouse, stimulate, stir
Antonyms be inactive, doze, lie dormant, nap, repose, sleep, slumber, snooze (*informal*)

wale contusion, mark, scar, streak, stripe, weal, welt, wheal

walk *verb* **1.** advance, amble, foot it, go, go by shanks's pony (*informal*), go on foot, hike, hoof it (*slang*), march, move, pace, perambu~late, promenade, saunter, step, stride, stroll, traipse (*informal*), tramp, travel on foot, trek, trudge **2.** accompany, convoy, escort, take ~*noun* **3.** constitutional, hike, march, peram~bulation, promenade, ramble, saunter, stroll, traipse (*informal*), tramp, trek, trudge, turn **4.** carriage, gait, manner of walking, pace, step, stride **5.** aisle, alley, avenue, esplanade, foot~path, lane, path, pathway, pavement, prom~enade, sidewalk, trail **6.** area, arena, calling, career, course, field, line, métier, profession, sphere, trade, vocation
We must learn to walk before we can run

walker footslogger, hiker, pedestrian, rambler, wayfarer

walkout industrial action, protest, stoppage, strike

walk out 1. flounce out, get up and go, leave suddenly, storm out, take off (*informal*), vote with one's feet **2.** down tools, go on strike, stop work, strike, take industrial action, withdraw one's labour **3.** *with* **on** abandon, chuck (*informal*), desert, forsake, jilt, leave, leave in the lurch, pack in (*informal*), run away from, strand, throw over
Antonyms (*sense 3*) be loyal to, defend, re~main, stand by, stay, stick with, support, uphold

walkover breeze (*U.S. & Canad. informal*), cakewalk (*informal*), child's play (*informal*), cinch (*slang*), doddle (*Brit. slang*), duck soup (*U.S. slang*), easy victory, picnic (*informal*), piece of cake (*informal*), pushover (*slang*), snap (*informal*)
Antonyms drudgery, effort, grind (*informal*), labour, ordeal, strain, struggle, trial

wall 1. divider, enclosure, panel, partition, screen **2.** barricade, breastwork, bulwark, em~bankment, fortification, palisade, parapet, rampart, stockade **3.** barrier, block, fence, hedge, impediment, obstacle, obstruction **4. go to the wall** *informal* be ruined, collapse, fail, fall, go bust (*informal*), go under **5. drive up the wall** *slang* aggravate (*informal*), annoy, dement, derange, drive crazy (*informal*), drive insane, exasperate, get on one's nerves (*infor~mal*), infuriate, irritate, madden, piss one off (*taboo slang*), send off one's head (*slang*), try
Related adjective: mural

wallet case, holder, notecase, pocketbook, pouch, purse

wallop *verb* **1.** batter, beat, belt (*informal*), buffet, chin (*slang*), clobber (*slang*), deck (*slang*), hit, lambast(e), lay one on (*slang*), paste (*slang*), pound, pummel, punch, slug, smack, strike, thrash, thump, whack **2.** beat, best, blow out of the water (*slang*), clobber (*slang*), crush, defeat, drub, hammer (*infor~mal*), lick (*informal*), rout, run rings around (*informal*), stuff (*slang*), thrash, trounce, van~quish, wipe the floor with (*informal*), worst ~*noun* **3.** bash, belt (*informal*), blow, hay~maker (*slang*), kick, punch, slug, smack, thump, thwack, whack

wallow 1. lie, roll about, splash around, tum~ble, welter **2.** flounder, lurch, stagger, stum~ble, wade **3.** bask, delight, glory, indulge one~self, luxuriate, relish, revel, take pleasure
Antonyms (*sense 3*) abstain, avoid, do with~out, eschew, forgo, give up, refrain

wan 1. anaemic, ashen, bloodless, cadaverous, colourless, discoloured, ghastly, like death warmed up (*informal*), livid, pale, pallid, pasty, sickly, washed out, waxen, wheyfaced, white **2.** dim, faint, feeble, pale, weak
Antonyms (*sense 1*) blooming, bright, flour~ishing, glowing, healthy, roseate, rosy, rubi~cund, ruddy, vibrant

wand baton, rod, sprig, stick, twig, withe, withy

wander *verb* **1.** cruise, drift, knock about *or* around, meander, mooch around (*slang*), per~egrinate, ramble, range, roam, rove, straggle, stravaig (*Scot. & northern English dialect*), stray, stroll, traipse (*informal*) **2.** depart, de~viate, digress, divagate (*rare*), diverge, err, get lost, go astray, go off at a tangent, go off course, lapse, lose concentration, lose one's train of thought, lose one's way, swerve, veer **3.** babble, be delirious, be incoherent, ramble, rave, speak incoherently, talk nonsense ~*noun* **4.** cruise, excursion, meander, peregri~nation, ramble, traipse (*informal*)
Antonyms (*sense 2*) comply, conform, fall in with, follow, run with the pack, toe the line

wanderer bird of passage, drifter, gypsy, itin~erant, nomad, rambler, ranger, rolling stone, rover, stroller, traveller, vagabond, vagrant, voyager

wandering drifting, homeless, itinerant, mi~gratory, nomadic, peripatetic, rambling, root~

less, roving, strolling, travelling, vagabond, vagrant, voyaging, wayfaring

wanderlust itchy feet (*informal*), restlessness, urge to travel

wane *verb* **1.** abate, atrophy, decline, decrease, die out, dim, diminish, draw to a close, drop, dwindle, ebb, fade, fade away, fail, lessen, sink, subside, taper off, weaken, wind down, wither *~noun* **2.** abatement, atrophy, decay, declension, decrease, diminution, drop, dwin~dling, ebb, fading, failure, fall, falling off, lessening, sinking, subsidence, tapering off, withering **3. on the wane** at its lowest ebb, declining, dropping, dwindling, dying out, ebbing, fading, lessening, obsolescent, on its last legs, on the decline, on the way out, sub~siding, tapering off, weakening, withering

Antonyms *verb* blossom, brighten, develop, expand, grow, improve, increase, rise, strengthen, wax *~noun* advancement, devel~opment, expansion, growth, increase, rise, strengthening, waxing

wangle arrange, bring off, contrive, engineer, fiddle (*informal*), finagle (*informal*), fix (*infor~mal*), manipulate, manoeuvre, pull off, scheme, work (*informal*)

want *verb* **1.** covet, crave, desire, eat one's heart out over, feel a need for, hanker after, have a fancy for, have a yen for (*informal*), hope for, hunger for, long for, need, pine for, require, set one's heart on, thirst for, wish, would give one's eyeteeth for, yearn for **2.** be able to do with, be deficient in, be short of, be without, call for, demand, fall short in, have need of, lack, miss, need, require, stand in need of *~noun* **3.** appetite, craving, demand, desire, fancy, hankering, hunger, longing, ne~cessity, need, requirement, thirst, wish, yearning, yen (*informal*) **4.** absence, dearth, default, deficiency, famine, insufficiency, lack, paucity, scantiness, scarcity, shortage **5.** des~titution, indigence, need, neediness, pauper~ism, penury, poverty, privation

Antonyms *verb* be sated, detest, dislike, en~joy, hate, have, loathe, own, possess, reject, spurn, surfeit *~noun* abundance, adequacy, comfort, ease, excess, luxury, plenty, suffi~ciency, surplus, wealth

wanting **1.** absent, incomplete, lacking, less, missing, short, shy **2.** defective, deficient, dis~appointing, faulty, imperfect, inadequate, in~ferior, leaving much to be desired, not good enough, not much cop (*Brit. slang*), not up to expectations, not up to par, patchy, pathetic, poor, sketchy, substandard, unsound

Antonyms adequate, complete, enough, full, replete, satisfactory, saturated, sufficient

wanton *adjective* **1.** abandoned, dissipated, dissolute, fast, immoral, lecherous, lewd, lib~ertine, libidinous, licentious, loose, lustful, of easy virtue, promiscuous, rakish, shameless, unchaste **2.** arbitrary, cruel, evil, gratuitous, groundless, malevolent, malicious, motiveless, needless, senseless, spiteful, uncalled-for, un~justifiable, unjustified, unprovoked, vicious, wicked, wilful **3.** careless, devil-may-care, ex~travagant, heedless, immoderate, intemperate, lavish, outrageous, rash, reckless, unre~strained, wild *~noun* **4.** Casanova, debauchee, Don Juan, gigolo, harlot, lech *or* letch (*infor~mal*), lecher, libertine, loose woman, profligate, prostitute, rake, roué, scrubber (*Brit. & Austral. slang*), slag (*Brit. slang*), slut, strumpet, tart (*informal*), trollop, volup~tuary, whore, woman of easy virtue *~verb* **5.** debauch, dissipate, revel, riot, sleep around (*informal*), wench (*archaic*), whore **6.** fritter away, misspend, squander, throw away, waste

Antonyms (*sense 1*) overmodest, priggish, prim, prudish, puritanical, rigid, strait-laced, stuffy, Victorian (*sense 2*) called-for, excus~able, justified, legitimate, motivated, pro~voked, warranted (*sense 3*) cautious, circum~spect, guarded, inhibited, moderate, prudent, reserved, restrained, temperate

war **1.** *noun* armed conflict, battle, bloodshed, combat, conflict, contention, contest, enmity, fighting, hostilities, hostility, strife, struggle, warfare **2.** *verb* battle, campaign against, car~ry on hostilities, clash, combat, conduct a war, contend, contest, fight, make war, strive, struggle, take up arms, wage war

Antonyms *noun* accord, armistice, cease-fire, co-existence, compliance, co-operation, harmo~ny, peace, peace-time, treaty, truce *~verb* call a ceasefire, co-exist, co-operate, make peace

There was never a good war, or a bad peace
Benjamin Franklin

War makes rattling good history; but Peace is poor reading
Thomas Hardy *The Dynasts*

He that makes a good war makes a good peace
George Herbert *Outlandish Proverbs*

For what can war but endless war still breed?
John Milton *Sonnet, On the Lord General Fairfax*

Above all, this book is not concerned with Poetry,
The subject of it is War, and the Pity of War.
The Poetry is in the Pity.
Wilfred Owen *Poems, Preface*

As long as war is regarded as wicked, it will al~ways have its fascination. When it is looked upon as vulgar, it will cease to be popular
Oscar Wilde *The Critic as Artist*

In war, whichever side may call itself the victor, there are no winners, but all are losers
Neville Chamberlain

War is too serious a matter to entrust to military men
Georges Clemenceau

It is easier to make war than to make peace
Georges Clemenceau

During the time men live without a common power to keep them all in awe, they are in that condition which is called war; and such a war as is of every man against every man
Thomas Hobbes *Leviathan*

History is littered with the wars which everybody knew would never happen
Enoch Powell

War is capitalism with the gloves off
Tom Stoppard *Travesties*

Let slip the dogs of war
William Shakespeare *Julius Caesar*

War is the trade of kings
John Dryden *King Arthur*

The quickest way of ending a war is to lose it
George Orwell *Shooting an Elephant*

Sometime they'll give a war and nobody will come
Carl Sandburg *"The People, Yes"*

War is nothing but the continuation of politics by other means
Karl von Clausewitz *On War*

Since war begins in the minds of men, it is in the minds of men that the defences of peace must be constructed
Constitution of UNESCO

The next war will be fought with atom bombs and the one after that with spears
Harold Urey

A bayonet is a weapon with a worker at each end
pacifist slogan

Fighting for peace is like fucking for virginity
anti-war graffitti

War will cease when men refuse to fight
pacifist slogan

After each war there is a little less democracy to save
Brooks Atkinson *Once Around the Sun*

The Falklands thing was a fight between two bald men over a comb
Jorge Luis Borges

All's fair in love and war

warble 1. *verb* chirp, chirrup, quaver, sing, trill, twitter 2. *noun* call, chirp, chirrup, cry, quaver, song, trill, twitter

war cry battle cry, rallying cry, slogan, war whoop

ward 1. area, district, division, precinct, quarter, zone 2. apartment, cubicle, room 3. charge, dependant, minor, protégé, pupil 4. care, charge, custody, guardianship, keeping, protection, safekeeping

warden administrator, caretaker, curator, custodian, guardian, janitor, keeper, ranger, steward, superintendent, warder, watchman

warder, wardress custodian, gaoler, guard, jailer, keeper, prison officer, screw (*slang*), turnkey (*archaic*)

ward off avert, avoid, beat off, block, deflect, fend off, forestall, keep at arm's length, keep at bay, parry, repel, stave off, thwart, turn aside, turn away
Antonyms accept, admit, allow, embrace, permit, receive, take in, welcome

wardrobe 1. closet, clothes cupboard, clothes-press 2. apparel, attire, clothes, collection of clothes, outfit

warehouse depository, depot, stockroom, store, storehouse

wares commodities, goods, lines, manufactures, merchandise, produce, products, stock, stuff

warfare armed conflict, armed struggle, arms, battle, blows, campaigning, clash of arms, combat, conflict, contest, discord, fighting, hostilities, passage of arms, strategy, strife, struggle, war
Antonyms accord, amity, armistice, ceasefire, cessation of hostilities, conciliation, harmony, peace, treaty, truce

warily cagily (*informal*), carefully, cautiously, charily, circumspectly, distrustfully, gingerly, guardedly, suspiciously, vigilantly, watchfully, with care
Antonyms carelessly, hastily, heedlessly, irresponsibly, rashly, recklessly, thoughtlessly, unwarily

wariness alertness, attention, caginess (*informal*), care, carefulness, caution, circumspection, discretion, distrust, foresight, heedfulness, mindfulness, prudence, suspicion, vigilance, watchfulness
Antonyms carelessness, heedlessness, inattention, mindlessness, negligence, oblivion, recklessness, thoughtlessness

Call no man foe, but never love a stranger
Stella Benson *This is the End*

warlike aggressive, bellicose, belligerent, bloodthirsty, combative, hawkish, hostile, inimical, jingoistic, martial, militaristic, military, pugnacious, sabre-rattling, unfriendly, warmongering
Antonyms amicable, conciliatory, friendly, nonbelligerent, pacific, peaceable, peaceful, placid, unwarlike

warlock conjurer, enchanter, magician, necromancer, sorcerer, witch, wizard

warm *adjective* 1. balmy, heated, lukewarm, moderately hot, pleasant, sunny, tepid, thermal 2. affable, affectionate, amiable, amorous, cheerful, congenial, cordial, friendly, genial, happy, hearty, hospitable, kindly, likable *or* likeable, loving, pleasant, tender 3. ablaze,

animated, ardent, cordial, earnest, effusive, emotional, enthusiastic, excited, fervent, glowing, heated, intense, keen, lively, passionate, spirited, stormy, vehement, vigorous, violent, zealous **4**. irascible, irritable, passionate, quick, sensitive, short, touchy **5**. *informal* dangerous, disagreeable, hazardous, perilous, tricky, uncomfortable, unpleasant *~verb* **6**. heat, heat up, melt, thaw, warm up **7**. animate, awaken, excite, get going, interest, make enthusiastic, put some life into, rouse, stimulate, stir, turn on (*slang*)
Antonyms *adjective* aloof, apathetic, chilly, cold, cool, distant, freezing, half-hearted, hostile, icy, phlegmatic, remote, stand-offish, uncaring, unenthusiastic, unfriendly, unwelcoming *~verb* alienate, chill, cool, cool down, depress, freeze, sadden

warm-blooded ardent, earnest, emotional, enthusiastic, excitable, fervent, impetuous, lively, passionate, rash, spirited, vivacious

warm-hearted affectionate, compassionate, cordial, generous, kind-hearted, kindly, loving, sympathetic, tender, tender-hearted
Antonyms callous, cold, cold-hearted, hard, hard-hearted, harsh, heartless, insensitive, mean, merciless, unfeeling, unsympathetic

warmonger belligerent, hawk, jingo, militarist, sabre-rattler

warmth **1**. heat, hotness, warmness **2**. animation, ardour, eagerness, earnestness, effusiveness, enthusiasm, excitement, fervency, fervour, fire, heat, intensity, passion, spirit, transport, vehemence, vigour, violence, zeal, zest **3**. affability, affection, amorousness, cheerfulness, cordiality, happiness, heartiness, hospitableness, kindliness, love, tenderness
Antonyms aloofness, apathy, austerity, chill, chilliness, cold, cold-heartedness, coldness, coolness, hard-heartedness, hostility, iciness, indifference, insincerity, lack of enthusiasm, remoteness, sternness

warn admonish, advise, alert, apprise, caution, forewarn, give fair warning, give notice, inform, make (someone) aware, notify, put one on one's guard, summon, tip off

warning **1**. *noun* admonition, advice, alarm, alert, augury, caution, caveat, foretoken, hint, notice, notification, omen, premonition, presage, sign, signal, threat, tip, tip-off, token, word, word to the wise **2**. *adjective* admonitory, bodeful, cautionary, monitory, ominous, premonitory, threatening

warp **1**. *verb* bend, contort, deform, deviate, distort, misshape, pervert, swerve, turn, twist **2**. *noun* bend, bent, bias, contortion, deformation, deviation, distortion, kink, perversion, quirk, turn, twist

warrant *noun* **1**. assurance, authority, authorization, carte blanche, commission, guarantee, licence, permission, permit, pledge, sanction, security, warranty *~verb* **2**. affirm, answer for, assure, attest, avouch, certify, declare, guarantee, pledge, secure, stand behind, underwrite, uphold, vouch for **3**. approve, authorize, call for, commission, demand, deserve, empower, entail, entitle, excuse, give ground for, justify, license, necessitate, permit, require, sanction

warrantable accountable, allowable, defensible, justifiable, lawful, necessary, permissible, proper, reasonable, right
Antonyms indefensible, reasonable, uncalled-for, undue, unjustifiable, unnecessary, unwarrantable, wrong

warranty assurance, bond, certificate, contract, covenant, guarantee, pledge

warring at daggers drawn, at war, belligerent, combatant, conflicting, contending, embattled, fighting, hostile, opposed

warrior champion, combatant, fighter, fighting man, gladiator, man-at-arms, soldier

wary alert, attentive, cagey (*informal*), careful, cautious, chary, circumspect, distrustful, guarded, heedful, leery (*slang*), on one's guard, on the lookout, on the qui vive, prudent, suspicious, vigilant, watchful, wide-awake
Antonyms careless, foolhardy, imprudent, negligent, rash, reckless, remiss, unguarded, unsuspecting, unwary

wash *verb* **1**. bath, bathe, clean, cleanse, launder, moisten, rinse, scrub, shampoo, shower, wet **2**. *with* **away** bear away, carry off, erode, move, sweep away, wash off **3**. *informal* bear scrutiny, be convincing, be plausible, carry weight, hold up, hold water, stand up, stick **4**. **wash one's hands of** abandon, accept no responsibility for, give up on, have nothing to do with, leave to one's own devices *~noun* **5**. ablution, bath, bathe, cleaning, cleansing, laundering, rinse, scrub, shampoo, shower, washing **6**. ebb and flow, flow, roll, surge, sweep, swell, wave **7**. coat, coating, film, layer, overlay, screen, stain, suffusion

washed out **1**. blanched, bleached, colourless, etiolated, faded, flat, lacklustre, mat, pale **2**. all in (*slang*), clapped out (*Austral. & N.Z. informal*), dead on one's feet (*informal*), dog-tired (*informal*), done in (*informal*), drained, drawn, exhausted, fatigued, haggard, knackered (*slang*), pale, spent, tired-out, wan, weary, wiped out (*informal*), worn-out, zonked (*slang*)
Antonyms (*sense 2*) alert, chirpy, energetic, full of beans (*informal*), full of pep (*informal*), lively, perky, refreshed, sprightly, zippy (*informal*)

washout 1. clinker (*slang, chiefly U.S.*), disappointment, disaster, dud (*informal*), failure, fiasco, flop (*informal*), mess 2. failure, incompetent, loser
Antonyms (*sense 1*) conquest, feat, success, triumph, victory, winner

washy attenuated, diluted, feeble, insipid, overdiluted, thin, watered-down, watery, weak, wishy-washy (*informal*)

waspish bad-tempered, cantankerous, captious, crabbed, crabby, cross, crotchety (*informal*), fretful, grumpy, ill-tempered, irascible, irritable, liverish, peevish, peppery, pettish, petulant, ratty (*Brit. & N.Z. informal*), snappish, splenetic, testy, tetchy, touchy, waxy (*informal, chiefly Brit.*)
Antonyms affable, agreeable, cheerful, easy-going, genial, good-humoured, good-natured, jovial, pleasant

waste *verb* 1. blow (*slang*), dissipate, fritter away, frivol away (*informal*), lavish, misuse, run through, squander, throw away 2. atrophy, consume, corrode, crumble, debilitate, decay, decline, deplete, disable, drain, dwindle, eat away, ebb, emaciate, enfeeble, exhaust, fade, gnaw, perish, sap the strength of, sink, undermine, wane, wear out, wither 3. despoil, destroy, devastate, lay waste, pillage, rape, ravage, raze, ruin, sack, spoil, total (*slang*), trash (*slang*), undo, wreak havoc upon *~noun* 4. dissipation, expenditure, extravagance, frittering away, loss, lost opportunity, misapplication, misuse, prodigality, squandering, unthriftiness, wastefulness 5. desolation, destruction, devastation, havoc, ravage, ruin 6. debris, dregs, dross, garbage, leavings, leftovers, litter, offal, offscourings, refuse, rubbish, scrap, sweepings, trash 7. desert, solitude, void, wasteland, wild, wilderness *~adjective* 8. leftover, superfluous, supernumerary, unused, unwanted, useless, worthless 9. bare, barren, desolate, devastated, dismal, dreary, empty, uncultivated, uninhabited, unproductive, wild 10. **lay waste** depredate (*rare*), despoil, destroy, devastate, pillage, rape, ravage, raze, ruin, sack, spoil, wreak havoc upon
Antonyms *verb* build, conserve, defend, develop, economize, husband, increase, preserve, protect, rally, restore, save, strengthen *~noun* economy, frugality, good housekeeping, saving, thrift *~adjective* arable, developed, fruitful, habitable, in use, necessary, needed, productive, utilized, verdant

It's no use making shoes for geese

wasteful extravagant, improvident, lavish, prodigal, profligate, ruinous, spendthrift, thriftless, uneconomical, unthrifty
Antonyms economical, frugal, money-saving, parsimonious, penny-wise, provident, sparing, thrifty

wasteland desert, void, waste, wild, wilderness

waster drone, good-for-nothing, idler, layabout, loafer, loser, malingerer, ne'er-do-well, shirker, skiver (*Brit. slang*), wastrel

wastrel 1. prodigal, profligate, spendthrift, squanderer 2. drone, good-for-nothing, idler, layabout, loafer, loser, malingerer, ne'er-do-well, shirker, skiver (*Brit. slang*), waster

watch *verb* 1. check, check out (*informal*), clock (*Brit. slang*), contemplate, eye, eyeball (*U.S. slang*), feast one's eyes on, gaze at, get a load of (*informal*), look, look at, look on, mark, note, observe, pay attention, peer at, regard, see, stare at, take a dekko at (*Brit. slang*), view 2. attend, be on the alert, be on the lookout, be vigilant, be wary, be watchful, keep an eye open (*informal*), look out, take heed, wait 3. guard, keep, look after, mind, protect, superintend, take care of, tend *~noun* 4. chronometer, clock, pocket watch, timepiece, wristwatch 5. alertness, attention, eye, heed, inspection, lookout, notice, observation, supervision, surveillance, vigil, vigilance, watchfulness

A watched kettle never boils

watchdog 1. guard dog 2. custodian, guardian, inspector, monitor, protector, scrutineer

watcher fly on the wall, looker-on, lookout, observer, onlooker, spectator, spy, viewer, witness

watchful alert, attentive, circumspect, guarded, heedful, observant, on one's guard, on the lookout, on the qui vive, on the watch, suspicious, vigilant, wary, wide awake
Antonyms careless, inattentive, reckless, thoughtless, unaware, unguarded, unmindful, unobservant, unwary

watchfulness alertness, attention, attentiveness, caution, cautiousness, circumspection, heedfulness, vigilance, wariness
Antonyms carelessness, heedlessness, inattention, indiscretion, irresponsibility, neglect, recklessness, thoughtlessness

watchman caretaker, custodian, guard, security guard, security man

watch out be alert, be careful, be on one's guard, be on the alert, be on (the) watch, be vigilant, be watchful, have a care, keep a sharp lookout, keep a weather eye open, keep one's eyes open, keep one's eyes peeled *or* skinned (*informal*), look out, mind out, watch oneself

watch over defend, guard, keep safe, look after, preserve, protect, shelter, shield, stand guard over

watchword 1. countersign, magic word, password, shibboleth 2. battle cry, byword, catch phrase, catchword, maxim, motto, rallying cry, slogan

water *noun* **1.** Adam's ale *or* wine, aqua, H_2O **2. hold water** bear examination *or* scrutiny, be credible (logical, sound), make sense, pass the test, ring true, work **3. of the first water** excellent, of the best, of the best quality, of the finest quality, of the highest degree, of the highest grade *~verb* **4.** damp, dampen, douse, drench, flood, hose, irrigate, moisten, soak, souse, spray, sprinkle **5.** add water to, adulterate, dilute, put water in, thin, water down, weaken
Related adjectives: aquatic, aqueous

Water, water, every where,
And all the boards did shrink;
Water, water, every where.
Nor any drop to drink.
Samuel Taylor Coleridge *The Ancient Mariner*

Water taken in moderation cannot hurt anybody
Mark Twain *Notebook*

water down 1. add water to, adulterate, dilute, put water in, thin, water, weaken **2.** adulterate, mitigate, qualify, soften, tone down, weaken
Antonyms (*sense 1*) fortify, purify, strengthen, thicken

waterfall cascade, cataract, chute, fall, force (*Northern English dialect*), linn (*Scot.*)

Waterfalls

Angel Falls	Pilao
Churchill Falls	Ribbon
Cleve-Garth	Roraima
Cuquenan	Sutherland Falls
Iguaçú Falls	Tysse
Itatinga	Vestre Mardola
Kaieteur Falls	Victoria Falls
Niagara Falls	Yellowstone Falls
Ormeli	Yosemite Falls

watertight 1. sound, waterproof **2.** airtight, firm, flawless, foolproof, impregnable, incontrovertible, sound, unassailable
Antonyms defective, flawed, leaky, questionable, shaky, tenuous, uncertain, unsound, weak

watery 1. aqueous, damp, fluid, humid, liquid, marshy, moist, soggy, squelchy, wet **2.** rheumy, tear-filled, tearful, weepy **3.** adulterated, dilute, diluted, flavourless, insipid, runny, tasteless, thin, washy, watered-down, waterish, weak, wishy-washy (*informal*)
Antonyms concentrated, condensed, dense, fortified, solid, strong, thick

wave *verb* **1.** brandish, flap, flourish, flutter, move to and fro, oscillate, quiver, ripple, shake, stir, sway, swing, undulate, wag, waver, wield **2.** beckon, direct, gesticulate, gesture, indicate, sign, signal *~noun* **3.** billow, breaker, comber, ridge, ripple, roller, sea surf, swell, undulation, unevenness **4.** current, drift, flood, ground swell, movement, outbreak, rash, rush, stream, surge, sweep, tendency, trend, upsurge

waver 1. be indecisive, be irresolute, be unable to decide, be unable to make up one's mind, blow hot and cold (*informal*), dither (*chiefly Brit.*), falter, fluctuate, hesitate, hum and haw, seesaw, shillyshally (*informal*), swither (*Scot.*), vacillate **2.** flicker, fluctuate, quiver, reel, shake, sway, totter, tremble, undulate, vary, wave, weave, wobble
Antonyms be decisive, be determined, be of fixed opinion, be resolute, determine, resolve, stand firm

wax *verb* become fuller, become larger, develop, dilate, enlarge, expand, fill out, get bigger, grow, increase, magnify, mount, rise, swell
Antonyms contract, decline, decrease, diminish, dwindle, fade, lessen, narrow, shrink, wane

waxen anaemic, ashen, bloodless, colourless, ghastly, pale, pallid, wan, white, whitish

way 1. approach, course of action, fashion, manner, means, method, mode, plan, practice, procedure, process, scheme, system, technique **2.** access, avenue, channel, course, direction, highway, lane, path, pathway, road, route, street, thoroughfare, track, trail **3.** elbowroom, opening, room, space **4.** distance, journey, length, stretch, trail **5.** advance, approach, journey, march, passage, progress **6.** characteristic, conduct, custom, habit, idiosyncrasy, manner, nature, personality, practice, style, trait, usage, wont **7.** aspect, detail, feature, particular, point, respect, sense **8.** aim, ambition, choice, demand, desire, goal, pleasure, will, wish **9.** *informal* circumstance, condition, fettle, shape (*informal*), situation, state, status **10.** forward motion, headway, movement, passage, progress **11. by the way** by the bye, en passant, incidentally, in parenthesis, in passing **12. give way a.** break down, cave in, collapse, crack, crumple, fall, fall to pieces, give, go to pieces, subside **b.** accede, acknowledge defeat, acquiesce, back down, concede, make concessions, withdraw, yield **13. under way** afoot, begun, going, in motion, in progress, moving, on the go (*informal*), on the move, started

The longest way round is the shortest way home

wayfarer bird of passage, globetrotter, Gypsy, itinerant, journeyer, nomad, rover, traveller, trekker, voyager, walker, wanderer

wayfaring *adjective* drifting, itinerant, journeying, nomadic, peripatetic, rambling, roving, travelling, voyaging, walking, wandering

waylay accost, ambush, attack, catch, hold up, intercept, lie in wait for, pounce on, set upon, surprise, swoop down on

way-out **1**. advanced, avant-garde, bizarre, crazy, eccentric, experimental, far-out (*slang*), freaky (*slang*), oddball (*informal*), offbeat, off-the-wall (*slang*), outlandish, outré, progressive, unconventional, unorthodox, wacko *or* whacko (*informal*), weird, wild **2**. amazing, awesome (*informal*), brilliant, excellent, fantastic (*informal*), great (*informal*), marvellous, sensational (*informal*), tremendous (*informal*), wonderful

ways and means ability, capability, capacity, course, funds, methods, procedure, reserves, resources, tools, way, wherewithal

wayward capricious, changeable, contrary, contumacious, cross-grained, disobedient, erratic, fickle, flighty, froward (*archaic*), headstrong, inconstant, incorrigible, insubordinate, intractable, mulish, obdurate, obstinate, perverse, rebellious, refractory, self-willed, stubborn, undependable, ungovernable, unmanageable, unpredictable, unruly, wilful
Antonyms complaisant, compliant, dependable, good-natured, malleable, manageable, obedient, obliging, predictable, reliable, submissive, tractable

weak **1**. anaemic, debilitated, decrepit, delicate, effete, enervated, exhausted, faint, feeble, fragile, frail, infirm, languid, puny, shaky, sickly, spent, tender, unsound, unsteady, wasted, weakly **2**. boneless, cowardly, impotent, indecisive, ineffectual, infirm, irresolute, namby-pamby, pathetic, powerless, soft, spineless, timorous, weak-kneed (*informal*) **3**. distant, dull, faint, imperceptible, low, muffled, poor, quiet, slight, small, soft **4**. deficient, faulty, inadequate, lacking, pathetic, poor, substandard, under-strength, wanting **5**. feeble, flimsy, hollow, inconclusive, invalid, lame, pathetic, shallow, slight, unconvincing, unsatisfactory **6**. defenceless, exposed, helpless, unguarded, unprotected, unsafe, untenable, vulnerable, wide open **7**. diluted, insipid, milk-and-water, runny, tasteless, thin, under-strength, waterish, watery, wishy-washy (*informal*)
Antonyms able, capable, conclusive, convincing, effective, energetic, firm, flavoursome, forceful, hardy, healthy, hefty, intoxicating, invulnerable, mighty, obvious, potent, powerful, safe, secure, solid, strong, substantial, tasty, tough, trustworthy, uncontrovertible, valid, well-defended

The weakest goes to the wall
William Shakespeare *Romeo and Juliet*

weaken **1**. abate, debilitate, depress, diminish, droop, dwindle, ease up, enervate, fade, fail, flag, give way, impair, invalidate, lessen, lower, mitigate, moderate, reduce, sap, sap the strength of, soften up, take the edge off, temper, tire, undermine, wane **2**. adulterate, cut, debase, dilute, thin, thin out, water down
Antonyms boost, enhance, grow, improve, increase, invigorate, revitalize, strengthen

weakling coward, doormat (*slang*), drip (*informal*), jellyfish (*informal*), jessie (*Scot. slang*), milksop, mouse, sissy, wet (*Brit. informal*), wimp (*informal*), wuss (*U.S. slang*)

weakness **1**. debility, decrepitude, enervation, faintness, feebleness, fragility, frailty, impotence, infirmity, irresolution, powerlessness, vulnerability **2**. Achilles heel, blemish, chink in one's armour, defect, deficiency, failing, fault, flaw, imperfection, lack, shortcoming **3**. fondness, inclination, liking, partiality, passion, penchant, predilection, proclivity, proneness, soft spot
Antonyms advantage, aversion, dislike, forte, hardiness, hatred, health, impregnability, loathing, potency, power, stamina, strength, strong point, sturdiness, validity, vigour, virtue, vitality

Frailty, thy name is woman!
William Shakespeare *Hamlet*

A chain is no stronger than its weakest link

weak-willed feeble, feeble-minded, indecisive, infirm, irresolute, namby-pamby, soft, spineless, weak-kneed (*informal*), weak-minded, wimpish (*informal*)

weal contusion, mark, ridge, scar, streak, stripe, wale, welt, wheal

wealth **1**. affluence, assets, big bucks (*informal, chiefly U.S.*), big money, capital, cash, estate, fortune, funds, goods, lucre, means, megabucks (*U.S. & Canad. slang*), money, opulence, pelf, possessions, pretty penny (*informal*), property, prosperity, resources, riches, substance, tidy sum (*informal*), wad (*U.S. & Canad. slang*) **2**. abundance, bounty, copiousness, cornucopia, fullness, plenitude, plenty, profusion, richness, store
Antonyms dearth, deprivation, destitution, indigence, lack, need, paucity, penury, poverty, scarcity, shortage, want, wretchedness

In every well-governed state, wealth is a sacred thing; in democracies it is the only sacred thing
Anatole France *L'Île des pingouins*

It is easier for a camel to go through the eye of a needle, than for a rich man to enter the kingdom of God
Bible: St. Mark

I am rich beyond the dreams of avarice
Edward Moore *The Gamester*

wealthy affluent, comfortable, filthy rich, flush (*informal*), in the money (*informal*), loaded (*slang*), made of money (*informal*), moneyed, on Easy Street (*informal*), opulent, prosperous, quids in (*slang*), rich, rolling in it (*slang*), stinking rich (*slang*), well-heeled (*informal*), well-off, well-to-do

Antonyms broke (*informal*), deprived, destitute, dirt-poor (*informal*), down and out, down at heel, flat broke (*informal*), impoverished, indigent, needy, on the breadline, penniless, poor, poverty-stricken, short, skint (*Brit. slang*), without two pennies to rub together (*informal*)

weapon

Weapons with blades

assegai *or* assagai	pike
backsword	poleaxe
battle-axe	poniard
bayonet	rapier
bill	sabre *or* saber
bowie knife	scimitar
broadsword	sgian-dhu
claymore	sheath knife
cutlass	skean
dagger	smallsword
dirk	snickersnee
falchion	spear
foil	spontoon
halberd	stiletto
hatchet	stone axe
jackknife	sword *or (archaic)* glaive
jerid, jereed *or* jerreed	sword bayonet
knife *or (slang)* chiv	swordstick
kris	tomahawk
kukri	trench knife
machete	yataghan *or* ataghan
parang	
partisan	

Missiles

cruise missile	Scud
Exocet	SLBM *or* submarine-launched ballistic missile
guided missile	SLCM *or* sea-launched cruise missile
ICBM *or* intercontinental ballistic missile	SS-18
Minuteman	SS-20
MIRV *or* multiple independently targeted re-entry vehicle	standoff missile
Patriot	Trident
Pershing	V-1, doodlebug, buzz bomb, *or* flying bomb
Polaris	V-2
rocket	

Projectile weapons

ballista	gun *see* GUN
bazooka	longbow
blowpipe	onager
catapult	quarrel
crossbow	rifle grenade
fléchette	torpedo
grapeshot	trebuchet *or* trebucket

Miscellaneous weapons

biological warfare	death ray
bomb *see* BOMB	flame-thrower
chemical warfare	germ warfare *or* bacteriological warfare
club *see* CLUB	mustard gas
Greek fire	napalm
knuckle-duster	poison gas
mace	

The only arms I allow myself to use, silence, exile, and cunning
James Joyce *A Portrait of the Artist as a Young Man*

Our swords shall play the orators for us
Christopher Marlowe *Tamburlaine the Great*

wear *verb* **1.** bear, be clothed in, be dressed in, carry, clothe oneself, don, dress in, have on, put on, sport (*informal*) **2.** display, exhibit, fly, show **3.** abrade, consume, corrode, deteriorate, erode, fray, grind, impair, rub, use, wash away, waste **4.** bear up, be durable, endure, hold up, last, stand up **5.** annoy, drain, enervate, exasperate, fatigue, get on one's nerves (*informal*), harass, irk, pester, tax, undermine, vex, weaken, weary **6.** *Brit. slang* accept, allow, brook, countenance, fall for, permit, put up with (*informal*), stand for, stomach, swallow (*informal*), take ~*noun* **7.** employment, mileage (*informal*), service, use, usefulness, utility **8.** apparel, attire, clothes, costume, dress, garb, garments, gear (*informal*), habit, outfit, things, threads (*slang*) **9.** abrasion, attrition, corrosion, damage, depreciation, deterioration, erosion, friction, use, wear and tear

Antonyms (*sense 9*) conservation, maintenance, preservation, repair, upkeep

wear down 1. abrade, be consumed, consume, corrode, erode, grind down, rub away **2.** chip away at (*informal*), fight a war of attrition against, overcome gradually, reduce, undermine

weariness drowsiness, enervation, exhaustion, fatigue, languor, lassitude, lethargy, listlessness, prostration, tiredness

Antonyms drive, energy, freshness, get-up-and-go (*informal*), liveliness, stamina, vigour, vitality, zeal, zest

wearing exasperating, exhausting, fatiguing, irksome, oppressive, taxing, tiresome, tiring, trying, wearisome

Antonyms easy, effortless, light, no bother, painless, refreshing, stimulating, undemanding

wearisome annoying, boring, bothersome, burdensome, dull, exasperating, exhausting, fatiguing, humdrum, irksome, mind-numbing, monotonous, oppressive, pestilential, prosaic, tedious, tiresome, troublesome, trying, uninteresting, vexatious, wearing

Antonyms agreeable, delightful, enjoyable, exhilarating, interesting, invigorating, pleasurable, refreshing, stimulating

wear off 1. abate, decrease, diminish, disappear, dwindle, ebb, fade, lose effect, lose

strength, peter out, subside, wane, weaken **2**. abrade, disappear, efface, fade, rub away
Antonyms grow, increase, intensify, magnify, persist, reinforce, step up, strengthen, wax

wear out **1**. become useless, become worn, consume, deteriorate, erode, fray, impair, use up, wear through **2**. enervate, exhaust, fag out (*informal*), fatigue, frazzle (*informal*), knacker (*slang*), prostrate, sap, tire, weary
Antonyms (*sense 2*) buck up (*informal*), energize, invigorate, pep up, perk up, refresh, revitalize, stimulate, strengthen

weary *adjective* **1**. all in (*slang*), asleep *or* dead on one's feet (*informal*), clapped out (*Austral. & N.Z. informal*), dead beat (*informal*), dog-tired (*informal*), done in (*informal*), drained, drooping, drowsy, enervated, exhausted, fagged (*informal*), fatigued, flagging, jaded, knackered (*slang*), ready to drop, sleepy, spent, tired, wearied, whacked (*Brit. informal*), worn out, zonked (*slang*) **2**. arduous, enervative, irksome, laborious, taxing, tiresome, tiring, wearing, wearisome **3**. bored, browned-off (*informal*), discontented, fed up, impatient, indifferent, jaded, sick (*informal*), sick and tired (*informal*) *~verb* **4**. burden, debilitate, drain, droop, enervate, fade, fag (*informal*), fail, fatigue, grow tired, sap, take it out of (*informal*), tax, tire, tire out, wear out **5**. annoy, become bored, bore, exasperate, have had enough, irk, jade, make discontented, plague, sicken, try the patience of, vex
Antonyms *adjective* amused, energetic, excited, exciting, forebearing, fresh, full of beans (*informal*), full of get-up-and-go (*informal*), invigorated, invigorating, lively, original, patient, refreshed, refreshing, stimulated *~verb* amuse, enliven, excite, interest, invigorate, refresh, revive, stimulate

weather *noun* **1**. climate, conditions **2**. **under the weather a.** ailing, below par, ill, indisposed, nauseous, not well, off-colour, out of sorts, poorly (*informal*), seedy (*informal*), sick **b.** crapulent, crapulous, drunk, flying (*slang*), groggy (*informal*), hung over (*informal*), inebriated, intoxicated, one over the eight (*slang*), the worse for drink, three sheets in the wind (*informal*), under the influence (*informal*) *~verb* **3**. expose, harden, season, toughen **4**. bear up against, brave, come through, endure, get through, live through, make it (*informal*), overcome, pull through, resist, ride out, rise above, stand, stick it out (*informal*), suffer, surmount, survive, withstand
Antonyms (*sense 4*) cave in, collapse, fail, fall, give in, go under, succumb, surrender, yield

Weather descriptions

arctic	balmy
baking	bland
blistering	icy
blustery	inclement
breezy	mild
clammy	misty
clear	muggy
clement	nippy
close	overcast
cloudy	parky (*informal*)
cold	perishing (*informal*)
dirty	rainy
dreich (*Scot.*)	raw
drizzly	scorching (*informal*)
dry	showery
dull	snowy
filthy	sticky
fine	stormy
foggy	sultry
foul	sunny
freezing (*informal*)	thundery
fresh	tropical
hazy	wet
hot	windy
humid	wintry

Weather phenomena

acid rain	pressure
ball lightning	rain
breeze	sandstorm
cloud	sheet lightning
cold snap	shower
cyclone	sleet
drizzle	smirr (*Scot.*)
dust devil	snow
dust storm	squall
fog	storm
freeze	sunshine
gale	tempest (*literary*)
gust	thaw
haar (*Scot.*)	thunder
hail	tidal wave
heatwave	tornado
hurricane	tsunami
ice	typhoon
lightning	waterspout
mist	whirlwind
peasouper (*chiefly Brit.*)	wind
	willy-willy (*Austral.*)
precipitation	zephyr

Cloud types

altocumulus	false cirrus
altostratus	fractocumulus
cirrocumulus	fractostratus
cirrostratus	nimbostratus
cirrus	nimbus
cumulonimbus	stratocumulus
cumulus	stratus

Meteorological terms

anticyclone	front
cold front	heat-island
cyclone	isallobar
depression	isobar

lee wave	thermal
occluded front	trough
ridge	virga
scud	warm front
synoptic chart	

Gatherers of weather data

dropsonde	radiosonde
meteorograph	weather ship
Meteorological Office *or* Met. Office	weather station
	weatherman
pilot balloon	weatherwoman

Measuring instrument	**Phenomena measured**
anemometer	wind velocity
anemoscope	wind direction
atmometer	rate of water evaporation into atmosphere
barograph	atmospheric pressure
barometer	atmospheric pressure
baroscope	atmospheric pressure
hygrometer	humidity
maximum-minimum thermometer	temperature variation
nephoscope	cloud velocity, altitude, and direction of movement
psychrometer	humidity
rain gauge	rainfall and snowfall
rawinsonde	atmospheric wind velocity
Stevenson's screen	temperature
sunshine recorder	hours of sunshine
thermometer	temperature
weathercock	wind direction
weather vane	wind direction
wet-and-dry-bulb thermometer	humidity
wind gauge	wind velocity
wind tee	wind direction

Layers of the atmosphere

see ATMOSPHERE

Summer has set in with its usual severity
Samuel Taylor Coleridge

'Tis the hard grey weather
Breeds hard English men
Charles Kingsley *The Three Fishers*

weather: the climate of an hour
Ambrose Bierce *The Devil's Dictionary*

Red sky at night, shepherd's delight; red sky in the morning, shepherd's warning

weave 1. blend, braid, entwine, fuse, incorporate, interlace, intermingle, intertwine, introduce, knit, mat, merge, plait, twist, unite 2. build, construct, contrive, create, fabricate, make, make up, put together, spin 3. crisscross, move in and out, weave one's way, wind, zigzag 4. **get weaving** *informal* get a move on, get going, get one's finger out (*Brit. informal*), get under way, hurry, make a start, shake a leg (*slang*), start

web 1. cobweb, spider's web 2. interlacing, lattice, mesh, net, netting, network, screen, tangle, toils, weave, webbing

wed 1. become man and wife, be married to, espouse, get hitched (*slang*), get married, join, make one, marry, plight one's troth (*old-fashioned*), splice (*informal*), take as one's husband, take as one's wife, take the plunge (*informal*), take to wife, tie the knot (*informal*), unite 2. ally, blend, coalesce, combine, commingle, dedicate, fuse, interweave, join, link, marry, merge, unify, unite, yoke
Antonyms (*sense 2*) break up, disunite, divide, divorce, part, separate, sever, split

wedding espousals, marriage, marriage ceremony, nuptial rite, nuptials, wedlock

wedge 1. *noun* block, chock, chunk, lump, wodge (*Brit. informal*) 2. *verb* block, cram, crowd, force, jam, lodge, pack, ram, split, squeeze, stuff, thrust

wedlock marriage, matrimony

wee diminutive, insignificant, itsy-bitsy (*informal*), Lilliputian, little, microscopic, miniature, minuscule, minute, negligible, pygmy *or* pigmy, small, teensy-weensy, teeny, teeny-weeny, tiny

weed out dispense with, eliminate, eradicate, extirpate, get rid of, remove, root out, separate out, shed, uproot

weedy feeble, frail, ineffectual, namby-pamby, nerdy *or* nurdy (*slang*), puny, skinny, thin, undersized, weak, weak-kneed (*informal*)

weekly by the week, every week, hebdomadal, hebdomadally, hebdomadary, once a week

weep bemoan, bewail, blub (*slang*), blubber, boohoo, complain, cry, greet (*Scot. or archaic*), keen, lament, moan, mourn, shed tears, snivel, sob, ululate, whimper, whinge (*informal*)
Antonyms be glad, celebrate, delight, exult, joy, rejoice, revel, triumph

weepy 1. *adjective* blubbering, close to tears, crying, lachrymose, on the verge of tears, sobbing, tearful, weeping, whimpering 2. *noun* tear-jerker (*informal*)

weigh 1. have a weight of, measure the weight of, put on the scales, tip the scales at (*informal*) 2. apportion, deal out, dole out, measure 3. consider, contemplate, deliberate upon, evaluate, examine, eye up, give thought to, meditate upon, mull over, ponder, reflect upon, study, think over 4. be influential, carry weight, count, cut any ice (*informal*), have influence, impress, matter, tell 5. bear down, burden, oppress, prey

weigh down bear down, burden, depress, get down, oppress, overburden, overload, press down, trouble, weigh upon, worry

Antonyms alleviate, ease, hearten, help, lift, lighten, refresh, relieve, unburden

weight *noun* **1.** avoirdupois, burden, gravity, heaviness, heft (*informal*), load, mass, poundage, pressure, tonnage **2.** ballast, heavy object, load, mass **3.** albatross, burden, load, millstone, oppression, pressure, strain **4.** greatest force, main force, onus, preponderance **5.** authority, bottom, clout (*informal*), consequence, consideration, efficacy, emphasis, impact, import, importance, influence, moment, persuasiveness, power, significance, substance, value *~verb* **6.** add weight to, ballast, charge, freight, increase the load on, increase the weight of, load, make heavier **7.** burden, encumber, handicap, impede, oppress, overburden, weigh down **8.** bias, load, unbalance

weighty **1.** burdensome, cumbersome, dense, heavy, hefty (*informal*), massive, ponderous **2.** consequential, considerable, critical, crucial, forcible, grave, important, momentous, portentous, serious, significant, solemn, substantial **3.** backbreaking, burdensome, crushing, demanding, difficult, exacting, onerous, oppressive, taxing, worrisome, worrying

Antonyms (*sense 2*) frivolous, immaterial, incidental, inconsequential, insignificant, minor, petty, trivial, unimportant

weird bizarre, creepy (*informal*), eerie, eldritch (*poetic*), far-out (*slang*), freakish, ghostly, grotesque, mysterious, odd, outlandish, queer, spooky (*informal*), strange, supernatural, uncanny, unearthly, unnatural

Antonyms common, mundane, natural, normal, ordinary, regular, typical, usual

weirdo, weirdie crackpot (*informal*), crank (*informal*), eccentric, freak (*informal*), headbanger (*informal*), headcase (*informal*), loony (*slang*), nut (*slang*), nutcase (*slang*), nutter (*Brit. slang*), oddball (*informal*), queer fish (*Brit. informal*)

welcome *adjective* **1.** acceptable, accepted, agreeable, appreciated, delightful, desirable, gladly received, gratifying, pleasant, pleasing, pleasurable, refreshing, wanted **2.** at home, free, invited, under no obligation *~noun* **3.** acceptance, entertainment, greeting, hospitality, reception, salutation *~verb* **4.** accept gladly, bid welcome, embrace, greet, hail, meet, offer hospitality to, receive, receive with open arms, roll out the red carpet for, usher in

Antonyms (*sense 1*) disagreeable, excluded, rebuffed, rejected, unacceptable, undesirable, unpleasant, unwanted, unwelcome (*sense 3*) cold shoulder, exclusion, ostracism, rebuff, rejection, slight, snub (*sense 4*) exclude, rebuff, refuse, reject, slight, snub, spurn, turn away

weld **1.** *verb* bind, bond, braze, cement, connect, fuse, join, link, solder, unite **2.** *noun* bond, joint, juncture, seam

welfare advantage, benefit, good, happiness, health, interest, profit, prosperity, success, wellbeing

well[1] *adverb* **1.** agreeably, capitally, famously (*informal*), happily, in a satisfactory manner, like nobody's business (*informal*), nicely, pleasantly, satisfactorily, smoothly, splendidly, successfully **2.** ably, adeptly, adequately, admirably, conscientiously, correctly, effectively, efficiently, expertly, proficiently, properly, skilfully, with skill **3.** accurately, attentively, carefully, closely **4.** comfortably, flourishingly, prosperously **5.** correctly, easily, fairly, fittingly, in all fairness, justly, properly, readily, rightly, suitably **6.** closely, completely, deeply, fully, intimately, personally, profoundly, thoroughly **7.** approvingly, favourably, glowingly, graciously, highly, kindly, warmly **8.** abundantly, amply, completely, considerably, fully, greatly, heartily, highly, substantially, sufficiently, thoroughly, very much **9.** **as well** also, besides, in addition, into the bargain, to boot, too **10.** **as well as** along with, at the same time as, in addition to, including, over and above *~adjective* **11.** able-bodied, alive and kicking, fighting fit (*informal*), fit, fit as a fiddle, hale, healthy, hearty, in fine fettle, in good health, robust, sound, strong, up to par **12.** advisable, agreeable, bright, fine, fitting, flourishing, fortunate, good, happy, lucky, pleasing, profitable, proper, prudent, right, satisfactory, thriving, useful

Antonyms *adverb* badly, coldly, disapprovingly, gracelessly, ham-fistedly, inadequately, incompetently, incorrectly, ineptly, inexpertly, poorly, slightly, sloppily, somewhat, unfairly, unjustly, unkindly, unskilfully, unsympathetically, vaguely, wrongly *~adjective* ailing, at death's door, below par, feeble, frail, going badly, green about the gills, ill, improper, infirm, poorly, run-down, sick, sickly, under-the-weather, unfitting, unsatisfactory, unsuccessful, unwell, weak, wrong

well[2] *noun* **1.** fount, fountain, pool, source, spring, waterhole **2.** bore, hole, pit, shaft **3.** fount, mine, repository, source, wellspring *~verb* **4.** exude, flow, gush, jet, ooze, pour, rise, run, seep, spout, spring, spurt, stream, surge, trickle

well-balanced **1.** graceful, harmonious, proportional, symmetrical, well-proportioned **2.** judicious, level-headed, rational, reasonable, sane, sensible, sober, sound, together (*slang*), well-adjusted

Antonyms (*sense 2*) erratic, insane, irrational, neurotic, unbalanced, unreasonable, unsound, unstable, volatile

well-behaved disciplined, docile, good, obedient, orderly, restrained

Antonyms bad, devilish, disorderly, disrup~

tive, misbehaving, mischievous, naughty, roguish

well-bred 1. aristocratic, blue-blooded, gentle, highborn, noble, patrician, well-born 2. civil, courteous, courtly, cultivated, cultured, gallant, genteel, gentlemanly, ladylike, mannerly, polished, polite, refined, sophisticated, urbane, well-brought-up, well-mannered
Antonyms (*sense 2*) bad-mannered, base, coarse, discourteous, ill-bred, rude, uncivilized, uncouth, uncultured, vulgar

well-dressed chic, dapper, dressed to kill, dressed up to the nines, elegant, smart, soigné *or* soignée, spruce, stylish, well turned out

The sense of being well-dressed gives a feeling of inward tranquillity which religion is powerless to bestow

Miss C. F. Forbes

well-favoured attractive, beautiful, bonny, comely, fair, good-looking, handsome, lovely, nice-looking, pretty

well-fed 1. healthy, in good condition, well-nourished 2. chubby, fat, fleshy, plump, podgy, portly, rotund, rounded, stout

well-groomed dapper, neat, smart, soigné *or* soignée, spruce, tidy, trim, well-dressed, well turned out

well-heeled *informal* affluent, comfortable, flush (*informal*), in clover (*informal*), in the money (*informal*), loaded (*slang*), moneyed, opulent, prosperous, rich, wealthy, well-off, well-situated, well-to-do

well-informed acquainted, *au courant*, *au fait*, aware, clued-up (*informal*), cognizant *or* cognisant, conversant, educated, informed, in the know (*informal*), knowledgeable *or* knowledgable, understanding, well-educated, well-grounded, well-read, well-versed

well-known celebrated, familiar, famous, illustrious, notable, noted, on the map, popular, renowned, widely known

well-mannered civil, courteous, genteel, gentlemanly, gracious, ladylike, mannerly, polite, respectful, well-bred

well-nigh all but, almost, just about, more or less, nearly, next to, practically, virtually

well-off 1. comfortable, flourishing, fortunate, lucky, successful, thriving 2. affluent, comfortable, flush (*informal*), loaded (*slang*), moneyed, prosperous, rich, wealthy, well-heeled (*informal*), well-to-do
Antonyms (*sense 2*) badly off, broke (*informal*), destitute, dirt-poor (*informal*), down and out, down at heel, flat broke (*informal*), hard up (*informal*), impoverished, indigent, needy, on the breadline, on the rocks (*informal*), penniless, poor, poverty-stricken, short, without two pennies to rub together (*informal*)

wellspring 1. fount, fountainhead, origin, source, wellhead 2. fount, fund, mine, repository, reserve, reservoir, source, supply, well

well-thought-of admired, esteemed, highly regarded, of good repute, reputable, respected, revered, venerated
Antonyms abhorred, derided, despised, disdained, reviled, scorned, spurned

well-to-do affluent, comfortable, flush (*informal*), loaded (*slang*), moneyed, prosperous, rich, wealthy, well-heeled (*informal*), well-off
Antonyms bankrupt, broke (*informal*), destitute, down at heel, hard up (*informal*), indigent, insolvent, needy, on the breadline, poor, ruined

well-worn banal, commonplace, hackneyed, overused, stale, stereotyped, threadbare, timeworn, tired, trite

welt contusion, mark, ridge, scar, streak, stripe, wale, weal, wheal

welter *verb* 1. flounder, lie, roll, splash, tumble, wade, wallow, writhe 2. billow, heave, pitch, roll, surge, swell, toss *~noun* 3. confusion, hotchpotch, jumble, mess, muddle, tangle, web

wend direct one's course, go, make for, move, proceed, progress, travel

wet *adjective* 1. aqueous, damp, dank, drenched, dripping, humid, moist, moistened, saturated, soaked, soaking, sodden, soggy, sopping, waterlogged, watery, wringing wet 2. clammy, dank, drizzling, humid, misty, pouring, raining, rainy, showery, teeming 3. *Brit. informal* boneless, effete, feeble, foolish, ineffectual, irresolute, namby-pamby, nerdy *or* nurdy (*slang*), silly, soft, spineless, timorous, weak, weedy (*informal*) 4. **wet behind the ears** *informal* as green as grass, born yesterday, callow, green, immature, inexperienced, innocent, naive, new, raw *~noun* 5. clamminess, condensation, damp, dampness, humidity, liquid, moisture, water, wetness 6. damp weather, drizzle, rain, rains, rainy season, rainy weather 7. *Brit. informal* drip (*informal*), milksop, weakling, weed (*informal*), wimp (*informal*), wuss (*U.S. slang*) *~verb* 8. damp, dampen, dip, douse, drench, humidify, irrigate, moisten, saturate, soak, splash, spray, sprinkle, steep, water
Antonyms *adjective* arid, bone-dry, dried, dry, fine, hardened, parched, set, sunny *~noun* dryness, dry weather, fine weather *~verb* dehydrate, desiccate, dry, parch

wetness clamminess, condensation, damp, dampness, humidity, liquid, moisture, sogginess, water, wet

whack *verb* 1. bang, bash (*informal*), beat, belabour, belt (*informal*), box, buffet, chin (*slang*), clobber (*slang*), clout (*informal*), cuff, deck (*slang*), hit, lambast(e), lay one on (*slang*), rap, slap, slug, smack, sock (*slang*), strike, thrash, thump, thwack, wallop (*informal*) ~*noun* **2**. bang, bash (*informal*), belt (*informal*), blow, box, buffet, clout (*informal*), cuff, hit, rap, slap, slug, smack, sock (*slang*), stroke, thump, thwack, wallop (*informal*), wham **3**. *informal* allotment, bit, cut (*informal*), part, portion, quota, share **4**. *informal* attempt, bash (*informal*), crack (*informal*), go (*informal*), shot (*informal*), stab (*informal*), try, turn

whacking big, elephantine, enormous, extraordinary, giant, gigantic, great, huge, humongous *or* humungous (*U.S. slang*), large, mammoth, monstrous, prodigious, tremendous, whopping (*informal*)

wham bang, bash (*informal*), blow, concussion, impact, slam, smack, thump, thwack, wallop (*informal*), whack, whang

wharf dock, jetty, landing stage, pier, quay

wheal contusion, mark, ridge, scar, streak, stripe, wale, weal

wheedle butter up, cajole, charm, coax, court, draw, entice, flatter, inveigle, persuade, talk into, worm

wheel *noun* **1**. circle, gyration, pivot, revolution, roll, rotation, spin, turn, twirl, whirl **2**. **at the wheel** at the helm, driving, in charge, in command, in control, in the driving seat, steering ~*verb* **3**. circle, gyrate, orbit, pirouette, revolve, roll, rotate, spin, swing, swivel, turn, twirl, whirl

wheeze *verb* **1**. breathe roughly, catch one's breath, cough, gasp, hiss, rasp, whistle ~*noun* **2**. cough, gasp, hiss, rasp, whistle **3**. *Brit. slang* expedient, idea, plan, ploy, ruse, scheme, stunt, trick, wrinkle (*informal*) **4**. *informal* anecdote, chestnut (*informal*), crack (*slang*), gag (*informal*), joke, old joke, one-liner (*slang*), story

whereabouts location, position, site, situation

wherewithal capital, equipment, essentials, funds, means, money, ready (*informal*), ready money, resources, supplies

whet **1**. edge, file, grind, hone, sharpen, strop **2**. animate, arouse, awaken, enhance, excite, incite, increase, kindle, pique, provoke, quicken, rouse, stimulate, stir

Antonyms (*sense 2*) blunt, dampen, deaden, depress, dull, numb, smother, stifle, subdue, suppress

whiff *noun* **1**. aroma, blast, breath, draught, gust, hint, niff (*Brit. slang*), odour, puff, scent, smell, sniff ~*verb* **2**. breathe, inhale, puff, smell, smoke, sniff, waft **3**. *Brit. slang* hum (*slang*), malodour, niff (*Brit. slang*), pong (*Brit. informal*), reek, stink

whim caprice, conceit, craze, crotchet, fad (*informal*), fancy, freak, humour, impulse, notion, passing thought, quirk, sport, sudden notion, urge, vagary, whimsy

whimper **1**. *verb* blub (*slang*), blubber, cry, grizzle (*informal, chiefly Brit.*), mewl, moan, pule, snivel, sob, weep, whine, whinge (*informal*) **2**. *noun* moan, snivel, sob, whine

whimsical capricious, chimerical, crotchety, curious, droll, eccentric, fanciful, fantastic, fantastical, freakish, funny, mischievous, odd, peculiar, playful, quaint, queer, singular, unusual, waggish, weird

whine *noun* **1**. cry, moan, plaintive cry, sob, wail, whimper **2**. beef (*slang*), complaint, gripe (*informal*), grouch (*informal*), grouse, grumble, moan ~*verb* **3**. beef (*slang*), bellyache (*slang*), bleat, carp, complain, cry, gripe (*informal*), grizzle (*informal, chiefly Brit.*), grouch (*informal*), grouse, grumble, kvetch (*U.S. slang*), moan, sob, wail, whimper, whinge (*informal*)

whiner complainer, fault-finder, grouch (*informal*), grouser, grumbler, malcontent, moaner, whinger (*informal*)

whinge *informal verb* **1**. cry, fret, grizzle (*informal, chiefly Brit.*), moan, wail, whimper, whine **2**. beef (*slang*), bellyache (*slang*), bleat, carp, complain, gripe (*informal*), grizzle (*informal, chiefly Brit.*), grouch (*informal*), grouse, grumble, kvetch (*U.S. slang*), moan ~*noun* **3**. beef (*slang*), complaint, gripe (*informal*), grouch, grouse, grumble, moan, whine

whip *verb* **1**. beat, birch, cane, castigate, flagellate, flog, give a hiding (*informal*), lambast(e), lash, leather, lick (*informal*), punish, scourge, spank, strap, switch, tan (*slang*), thrash **2**. exhibit, flash, jerk, produce, pull, remove, seize, show, snatch, whisk **3**. *informal* dart, dash, dive, flit, flounce, fly, rush, shoot, tear, whisk **4**. *informal* beat, best, blow out of the water (*slang*), clobber (*slang*), conquer, defeat, drub, hammer (*informal*), lick (*informal*), make mincemeat out of (*informal*), outdo, overcome, overpower, overwhelm, rout, run rings around (*informal*), stuff (*slang*), take apart (*slang*), thrash, trounce, wipe the floor with (*informal*), worst **5**. agitate, compel, drive, foment, goad, hound, incite, instigate, prick, prod, provoke, push, spur, stir, urge, work up **6**. beat, whisk ~*noun* **7**. birch, bullwhip, cane, cat-o'-nine-tails, crop, horsewhip, knout, lash, rawhide, riding crop, scourge, switch, thong

whipping beating, birching, caning, castigation, flagellation, flogging, hiding (*informal*), lashing, leathering, punishment, spanking, tanning (*slang*), the strap, thrashing

whip up agitate, arouse, excite, foment, incite,

inflame, instigate, kindle, provoke, rouse, stir up, work up

whirl *verb* 1. circle, gyrate, pirouette, pivot, reel, revolve, roll, rotate, spin, swirl, turn, twirl, twist, wheel 2. feel dizzy, reel, spin *~noun* 3. birl (*Scot.*), circle, gyration, pirou~ette, reel, revolution, roll, rotation, spin, swirl, turn, twirl, twist, wheel 4. confusion, daze, dither (*chiefly Brit.*), flurry, giddiness, spin 5. flurry, merry-go-round, round, series, succes~sion 6. agitation, bustle, commotion, confusion, flurry, hurly-burly, stir, tumult, uproar 7. **give (something) a whirl** *informal* attempt, have a bash (crack (*informal*), go (*informal*), shot (*informal*), stab (*informal*), whack (*infor~mal*)) (*informal*), try

whirlwind 1. *noun* dust devil, tornado, water~spout 2. *adjective* hasty, headlong, impetuous, impulsive, lightning, quick, quickie (*informal*), rapid, rash, short, speedy, swift
Antonyms (*sense 2*) calculated, cautious, con~sidered, deliberate, measured, prudent, slow, unhurried

whisk *verb* 1. brush, flick, sweep, whip, wipe 2. barrel (along) (*informal, chiefly U.S. & Canad.*), burn rubber (*informal*), dart, dash, fly, hasten, hurry, race, rush, shoot, speed, sweep, tear 3. beat, fluff up, whip *~noun* 4. brush, flick, sweep, whip, wipe 5. beater

whisky barley-bree (*Scot.*), bourbon, John Barleycorn, malt, rye, Scotch, usquebaugh

Whiskies

blend	redeye (*U.S. slang*)
blended whisky	rye
bourbon	Scotch
corn whisky	shebeen *or* shebean (*Irish*)
grain whisky	single malt
hokonui (*N.Z.*)	sour mash
Irish whiskey	vatted malt
malt *or* malt whisky	
poteen *or* poitín	

Freedom and Whisky gang thegither!
Robert Burns *The Author's Earnest Cry and Prayer*

a torchlight procession marching down your throat
John L. O'Sullivan (of whisky)

whisper *verb* 1. breathe, murmur, say softly, speak in hushed tones, utter under the breath 2. gossip, hint, insinuate, intimate, murmur, spread rumours 3. hiss, murmur, rustle, sigh, sough, susurrate (*literary*), swish *~noun* 4. hushed tone, low voice, murmur, soft voice, undertone 5. hiss, murmur, rustle, sigh, sigh~ing, soughing, susurration *or* susurrus (*liter~ary*), swish 6. breath, fraction, hint, shadow, suggestion, suspicion, tinge, trace, whiff 7. *in~formal* buzz, dirt (*U.S. slang*), gossip, innuen~do, insinuation, report, rumour, scuttlebutt (*U.S. slang*), word
Antonyms (*sense 1*) bawl, bellow, clamour, roar, shout, thunder, yell

whit atom, bit, crumb, dash, drop, fragment, grain, iota, jot, least bit, little, mite, modicum, particle, piece, pinch, scrap, shred, speck, trace

white 1. ashen, bloodless, ghastly, grey, like death warmed up (*informal*), pale, pallid, pasty, wan, waxen, wheyfaced 2. grey, griz~zled, hoary, silver, snowy 3. clean, immacu~late, impeccable, innocent, pure, spotless, squeaky-clean, stainless, unblemished, unsul~lied
Antonyms (*senses 2 & 3*) black, blackish, blemished, dark, dirty, impure, soiled, stained, tarnished

white-collar clerical, executive, nonmanual, of~fice, professional, salaried

whiten blanch, bleach, blench, etiolate, fade, go white, pale, turn pale
Antonyms blacken, colour, darken

whitewash 1. *noun* camouflage, concealment, cover-up, deception, extenuation 2. *verb* camouflage, conceal, cover up, extenuate, gloss over, make light of, suppress
Antonyms *verb* disclose, expose, lay bare, re~veal, uncover, unmask, unveil

whittle 1. carve, cut, hew, pare, shape, shave, trim 2. consume, destroy, eat away, erode, re~duce, undermine, wear away

whizz kid *informal* child genius, genius, mastermind, phenom (*U.S. informal*), prodigy, talent, whiz (*informal*), wonder kid, wunder~kind

whole *adjective* 1. complete, entire, full, in one piece, integral, total, unabridged, uncut, un~divided 2. faultless, flawless, good, in one piece, intact, inviolate, mint, perfect, sound, unbroken, undamaged, unharmed, unhurt, unimpaired, uninjured, unmutilated, un~scathed, untouched 3. able-bodied, better, cured, fit, hale, healed, healthy, in fine fettle, in good health, recovered, robust, sound, strong, well *~adverb* 4. in one, in one piece *~noun* 5. aggregate, all, everything, lot, sum total, the entire amount, total 6. ensemble, entirety, entity, fullness, piece, totality, unit, unity 7. **on the whole a.** all in all, all things considered, by and large, taking everything into consideration **b.** as a rule, for the most part, generally, in general, in the main, mostly, predominantly
Antonyms *adjective* ailing, broken, cut, dam~aged, diseased, divided, fragmented, ill, in~complete, in pieces, partial, sick, sickly, under-the-weather, unwell *~noun* bit, compo~nent, constituent, division, element, fragment, part, piece, portion

wholehearted committed, complete, dedicated, determined, devoted, earnest, emphatic, enthusiastic, genuine, heartfelt, hearty, real, sincere, true, unfeigned, unqualified, unreserved, unstinting, warm, zealous

Antonyms cool, grudging, half-hearted, insincere, qualified, reserved, unreal

wholesale **1.** *adjective* all-inclusive, broad, comprehensive, extensive, far-reaching, indiscriminate, mass, sweeping, wide-ranging **2.** *adverb* all at once, comprehensively, extensively, indiscriminately, on a large scale, without exception

Antonyms *adjective* confined, discriminate, limited, partial, restricted, selective

wholesome **1.** beneficial, good, healthful, health-giving, healthy, helpful, hygienic, invigorating, nourishing, nutritious, salubrious, salutary, sanitary, strengthening **2.** apple-pie (*informal*), clean, decent, edifying, ethical, exemplary, honourable, improving, innocent, moral, nice, pure, respectable, righteous, squeaky-clean, uplifting, virtuous, worthy

Antonyms blue, corrupt, degrading, dirty, dishonest, evil, filthy, immoral, lewd, obscene, pernicious, pornographic, putrid, rotten, tasteless, trashy, unhealthy, unhygienic, unprincipled, unwholesome, X-rated (*informal*)

wholly **1.** all, altogether, completely, comprehensively, entirely, fully, heart and soul, in every respect, one hundred per cent (*informal*), perfectly, thoroughly, totally, utterly **2.** exclusively, only, solely, without exception

Antonyms (*sense 1*) incompletely, in part, moderately, partially, partly, relatively, slightly, somewhat

whoop cheer, cry, halloo, holler (*informal*), hoot, hurrah, scream, shout, shriek, yell

whopper **1.** colossus, crackerjack (*informal*), giant, jumbo (*informal*), leviathan, mammoth, monster **2.** big lie, fable, fabrication, falsehood, tall story (*informal*), untruth

whopping big, elephantine, enormous, extraordinary, giant, gigantic, great, huge, humongous *or* humungous (*U.S. slang*), large, mammoth, massive, monstrous, prodigious, tremendous, whacking (*informal*)

whore *noun* **1.** brass (*slang*), call girl, cocotte, courtesan, demimondaine, demirep (*rare*), fallen woman, *fille de joie*, harlot, hooker (*U.S. slang*), hustler (*U.S. & Canad. slang*), lady of the night, loose woman, prostitute, scrubber (*Brit. & Austral. slang*), slag (*Brit. slang*), streetwalker, strumpet, tart (*informal*), trollop, woman of easy virtue, woman of ill repute, working girl (*facetious slang*) ~*verb* **2.** be on the game (*slang*), hustle (*U.S. & Canad. slang*), prostitute oneself, sell one's body, sell oneself, solicit, walk the streets **3.** fornicate, lech *or* letch (*informal*), sleep around (*informal*), wanton, wench (*archaic*), womanize

whorehouse bagnio, bordello, brothel, cathouse (*U.S. slang*), disorderly house, house of ill fame *or* repute, house of prostitution, knocking-shop (*Brit. slang*)

whorl coil, corkscrew, helix, spiral, swirl, twist, vortex

wicked **1.** abandoned, abominable, amoral, atrocious, bad, black-hearted, corrupt, debased, depraved, devilish, dissolute, egregious, evil, fiendish, flagitious, foul, guilty, heinous, immoral, impious, iniquitous, irreligious, maleficent, nefarious, scandalous, shameful, sinful, sink, unprincipled, unrighteous, vicious, vile, villainous, worthless **2.** arch, impish, incorrigible, mischievous, naughty, rascally, roguish **3.** acute, agonizing, awful, crashing, destructive, dreadful, fearful, fierce, harmful, injurious, intense, mighty, painful, severe, terrible **4.** bothersome, difficult, distressing, galling, offensive, troublesome, trying, unpleasant **5.** *slang* adept, adroit, deft, expert, masterly, mighty, outstanding, powerful, skilful, strong

Antonyms benevolent, ethical, good, harmless, honourable, innocuous, mannerly, mild, moral, noble, obedient, pleasant, principled, virtuous, well-behaved, wholesome

There is no peace unto the wicked

Bible: Isaiah

wide *adjective* **1.** ample, broad, catholic, comprehensive, distended, encyclopedic, expanded, expansive, extensive, far-reaching, general, immense, inclusive, large, sweeping, vast **2.** away, distant, off, off course, off target, remote **3.** dilated, distended, expanded, fully open, outspread, outstretched **4.** ample, baggy, capacious, commodious, full, loose, roomy, spacious ~*adverb* **5.** as far as possible, completely, fully, right out, to the furthest extent **6.** astray, nowhere near, off course, off target, off the mark, out

Antonyms *adjective* closed, confined, constricted, cramped, limited, narrow, restricted, shut, strict, tight ~*adverb* barely, narrowly, partially, partly

wide-awake **1.** conscious, fully awake, roused, wakened **2.** alert, aware, heedful, keen, observant, on one's toes, on the alert, on the ball (*informal*), on the qui vive, vigilant, wary, watchful

Antonyms (*sense 2*) distracted, dreamy, heedless, inattentive, negligent, oblivious, preoccupied, unaware, unobservant

wide-eyed as green as grass, credulous, green, impressionable, ingenuous, innocent, naive, simple, trusting, unsophisticated, unsuspicious, wet behind the ears (*informal*)

widen broaden, dilate, enlarge, expand, extend, open out *or* up, open wide, spread, stretch
Antonyms compress, constrict, contract, cramp, diminish, narrow, reduce, shrink, tighten

wide-open 1. fully extended, fully open, gaping, outspread, outstretched, splayed, spread 2. at risk, defenceless, exposed, in danger, in peril, open, susceptible, unprotected, vulnerable 3. anybody's guess (*informal*), indeterminate, uncertain, unpredictable, unsettled, up for grabs (*informal*)

widespread broad, common, epidemic, extensive, far-flung, far-reaching, general, pervasive, popular, prevalent, rife, sweeping, universal, wholesale
Antonyms confined, exclusive, limited, local, narrow, rare, sporadic, uncommon

width breadth, compass, diameter, extent, girth, measure, range, reach, scope, span, thickness, wideness

wield 1. brandish, employ, flourish, handle, manage, manipulate, ply, swing, use 2. apply, be possessed of, command, control, exercise, exert, have, have at one's disposal, hold, maintain, make use of, manage, possess, put to use, utilize

wife better half (*humorous*), bride, helpmate, helpmeet, her indoors (*Brit. slang*), little woman (*informal*), mate, old lady (*informal*), old woman (*informal*), partner, significant other (*U.S. informal*), spouse, (the) missis *or* missus (*informal*), woman (*informal*)
Related adjective: uxorial

If you get a good wife you'll become happy; if you get a bad one, you'll become a philosopher
Socrates

Wives are young men's mistresses, companions for middle age, and old men's nurses
Francis Bacon

An ideal wife is any woman who has an ideal husband
Booth Tarkington

I... chose my wife, as she did her wedding gown, not for a fine glossy surface, but such qualities as would wear well
Oliver Goldsmith *The Vicar of Wakefield*

My fairest, my espoused, my latest found,
Heaven's last best gift, my ever new delight
John Milton *Paradise Lost*

best image of myself and dearer half
John Milton *Paradise Lost*

A good husband should be deaf and a good wife blind
French proverb

wiggle *verb/noun* jerk, jiggle, shake, shimmy, squirm, twitch, wag, waggle, writhe

wild *adjective* 1. feral, ferocious, fierce, savage, unbroken, undomesticated, untamed 2. free, indigenous, native, natural, uncultivated 3. desert, deserted, desolate, empty, godforsaken, trackless, uncivilized, uncultivated, uninhabited, unpopulated, virgin 4. barbaric, barbarous, brutish, ferocious, fierce, primitive, rude, savage, uncivilized 5. boisterous, chaotic, disorderly, impetuous, lawless, noisy, riotous, rough, rowdy, self-willed, turbulent, unbridled, uncontrolled, undisciplined, unfettered, ungovernable, unmanageable, unrestrained, unruly, uproarious, violent, wayward 6. blustery, choppy, furious, howling, intense, raging, rough, tempestuous, violent 7. dishevelled, disordered, straggly, tousled, unkempt, untidy, windblown 8. at one's wits' end, berserk, beside oneself, crazed, crazy, delirious, demented, excited, frantic, frenzied, hysterical, irrational, mad, maniacal, rabid, raving 9. extravagant, fantastic, flighty, foolhardy, foolish, giddy, ill-considered, impracticable, imprudent, madcap, outrageous, preposterous, rash, reckless 10. *informal* agog, avid, crazy (*informal*), daft (*informal*), eager, enthusiastic, excited, gonzo (*slang*), mad (*informal*), nuts (*slang*), potty (*Brit. informal*) ~*adverb* 11. **run wild a.** grow unchecked, ramble, spread, straggle **b.** abandon all restraint, cut loose, go on the rampage, kick over the traces, rampage, run free, run riot, stray ~*noun* 12. *often plural* back of beyond (*informal*), desert, middle of nowhere (*informal*), uninhabited area, wasteland, wilderness
Antonyms *adjective* advanced, broken, calm, careful, controlled, disciplined, domesticated, friendly, genteel, gentle, lawful, logical, mild, ordered, orderly, peaceful, polite, practical, quiet, realistic, restrained, self-controlled, tame, thoughtful, unenthusiastic, uninterested, well-behaved, well-thought-out (*senses 2 & 3*) civilized, cultivated, farmed, inhabited, planted, populated, urban

wilderness 1. desert, jungle, waste, wasteland, wild 2. clutter, confused mass, confusion, congeries, jumble, maze, muddle, tangle, welter

wildlife flora and fauna

wile 1. artfulness, artifice, cheating, chicanery, craft, craftiness, cunning, fraud, guile, slyness, trickery 2. *usually plural* artifice, contrivance, device, dodge, imposition, lure, manoeuvre, ploy, ruse, stratagem, subterfuge, trick

wilful 1. adamant, bull-headed, determined, dogged, froward (*archaic*), headstrong, inflexible, intractable, intransigent, mulish, obdurate, obstinate, persistent, perverse, pig-headed, refractory, self-willed, stiff-necked, stubborn, uncompromising, unyielding 2. conscious, deliberate, intended, intentional, pur~

poseful, volitional, voluntary, willed
Antonyms (*sense 1*) biddable, complaisant, compromising, docile, flexible, good-natured, obedient, pliant, tractable, yielding (*sense 2*) accidental, involuntary, uncalculated, unconscious, unintentional, unplanned, unwitting

will *noun* **1.** choice, decision, determination, discretion, option, prerogative, volition **2.** declaration, last wishes, testament **3.** choice, decision, decree, desire, fancy, inclination, mind, pleasure, preference, wish **4.** aim, determination, intention, purpose, resolution, resolve, willpower **5.** attitude, disposition, feeling **6. at will** as one pleases, as one thinks fit, as one wishes, at one's desire (discretion, inclination, pleasure, whim, wish) *~verb* **7.** bid, bring about, cause, command, decree, determine, direct, effect, ordain, order, resolve **8.** choose, desire, elect, opt, prefer, see fit, want, wish **9.** bequeath, confer, give, leave, pass on, transfer

Where there's a will there's a way

willing agreeable, amenable, compliant, consenting, content, desirous, disposed, eager, enthusiastic, favourable, game (*informal*), happy, inclined, in favour, in the mood, nothing loath, pleased, prepared, ready, so-minded
Antonyms averse, disinclined, grudging, indisposed, loath, not keen, reluctant, unenthusiastic, unwilling

willingly by choice, cheerfully, eagerly, freely, gladly, happily, of one's own accord, of one's own free will, readily, voluntarily, with all one's heart, without hesitation, with pleasure
Antonyms grudgingly, hesitantly, involuntarily, reluctantly, unwillingly

willingness agreeableness, agreement, consent, desire, disposition, enthusiasm, favour, goodwill, inclination, volition, will, wish
Antonyms aversion, disagreement, disinclination, hesitation, loathing, reluctance, unwillingness

willowy graceful, limber, lissom(e), lithe, slender, slim, supple, svelte, sylphlike

willpower determination, drive, firmness of purpose *or* will, fixity of purpose, force *or* strength of will, grit, resolution, resolve, self-control, self-discipline, single-mindedness
Antonyms apathy, hesitancy, indecision, irresolution, languor, lethargy, shilly-shallying (*informal*), torpor, uncertainty, weakness

willy-nilly **1.** *adverb* necessarily, *nolens volens*, of necessity, perforce, whether desired or not, whether one likes it or not, whether or no **2.** *adjective* inevitable, irrespective of one's wishes, necessary, unavoidable

wilt **1.** become limp *or* flaccid, droop, sag, shrivel, wither **2.** diminish, dwindle, ebb, fade, fail, flag, languish, lose courage, melt away, sag, sink, wane, weaken, wither

wily arch, artful, astute, cagey (*informal*), crafty, crooked, cunning, deceitful, deceptive, designing, fly (*slang*), foxy, guileful, intriguing, scheming, sharp, shifty, shrewd, sly, tricky, underhand
Antonyms above-board, artless, candid, dull, guileless, honest, ingenuous, naive, simple, straightforward

wimp coward, doormat (*slang*), *informal* drip (*informal*), jellyfish (*informal*), jessie (*Scot. slang*), milksop, mouse, sissy, softy *or* softie, weakling, wet (*Brit. slang*)

win *verb* **1.** achieve first place, achieve mastery, be victorious, carry all before one, carry the day, come first, conquer, finish first, gain victory, overcome, prevail, succeed, sweep the board, take the prize, triumph **2.** accomplish, achieve, acquire, attain, bag (*informal*), catch, collect, come away with, earn, gain, get, land, net, obtain, pick up, procure, receive, secure **3.** *often with* **over** allure, attract, bring *or* talk round, carry, charm, convert, convince, disarm, induce, influence, persuade, prevail upon, sway *~noun* **4.** *informal* conquest, success, triumph, victory
Antonyms *verb* fail, fall, forfeit, lose, miss, suffer defeat, suffer loss *~noun* beating, defeat, downfall, failure, loss, washout (*informal*)

You can't win them all

wince **1.** *verb* blench, cower, cringe, draw back, flinch, quail, recoil, shrink, start **2.** *noun* cringe, flinch, start

wind[1] **1.** *noun* air, air-current, blast, breath, breeze, current of air, draught, gust, zephyr **2.** *informal* clue, hint, inkling, intimation, notice, report, rumour, suggestion, tidings, warning, whisper **3.** babble, blather, bluster, boasting, empty talk, gab (*informal*), hot air, humbug, idle talk, talk, verbalizing **4.** breath, puff, respiration **5.** *informal* flatulence, flatus, gas **6. get** *or* have the wind up *informal* be afraid (alarmed, frightened, scared), fear, take fright **7. in the wind** about to happen, approaching, close at hand, coming, imminent, impending, in the offing, near, on the cards (*informal*), on the way **8. put the wind up** *informal* alarm, discourage, frighten, frighten off, scare, scare off

Related adjective: aeolian

Wind force	Beaufort number	Speed (kph)
Calm	0	less than 1
Light air	1	1-5
Light breeze	2	6-11
Gentle breeze	3	12-19
Moderate breeze	4	20-28
Fresh	5	29-38

Strong	6		39-49
Near gale	7		50-61
Gale	8		62-74
Strong gale	9		75-88
Storm	10		89-102
Violent storm	11		103-117
Hurricane	12		over 118

Wind	**Location**
berg wind	South Africa
bise	Switzerland
bora	Adriatic Sea
buran *or* bura	central Asia
Cape doctor	Cape Town, South Africa
chinook	Washington & Oregon coasts
föhn *or* foehn	N slopes of the Alps
harmattan	W African coast
khamsin, kamseen *or* kamsin	Egypt
levanter	W Mediterranean
libeccio *or* libecchio	Corsica
meltemi *or* etesian wind	NE Mediterranean
mistral	S France to Mediterranean
monsoon	S Asia
nor'wester	Southern Alps, New Zealand
pampero	S America
simoom *or* simoon	Arabia & N Africa
sirocco	N Africa to S Europe
tramontane *or* tramontana	W coast of Italy

It's an ill wind that blows nobody any good

wind² *verb* **1**. coil, curl, encircle, furl, loop, reel, roll, spiral, turn around, twine, twist, wreathe **2**. bend, curve, deviate, meander, ramble, snake, turn, twist, zigzag *~noun* **3**. bend, curve, meander, turn, twist, zigzag

windbag bigmouth (*slang*), blether (*Scot.*), blowhard (*informal*), boaster, bore, braggart, bullshit artist (*taboo slang*), bullshitter (*taboo slang*), gasbag (*informal*), gossip, loudmouth (*informal*), prattler

wind down cool off, decline, diminish, dwindle, lessen, reduce, relax, slacken, subside, taper off, unwind
Antonyms accelerate, amplify, escalate, expand, heat up, increase, intensify, magnify, step up

winded breathless, gasping for breath, out of breath, out of puff, out of whack (*informal*), panting, puffed, puffed out

windfall bonanza, find, godsend, jackpot, manna from heaven, pot of gold at the end of the rainbow, stroke of luck
Antonyms bad luck, disaster, infelicity, misadventure, mischance, misfortune, mishap

winding 1. *noun* bend, convolution, curve, meander, turn, twist, undulation **2**. *adjective* anfractuous, bending, circuitous, convoluted, crooked, curving, flexuous, indirect, meandering, roundabout, serpentine, sinuous, spiral, tortuous, turning, twisting, twisty
Antonyms *adjective* direct, even, level, plumb, smooth, straight, undeviating, unswerving

wind-up close, conclusion, culmination, dénouement, end, finale, finish, termination

wind up 1. bring to a close, close, close down, conclude, end, finalize, finish, liquidate, settle, terminate, tie up the loose ends (*informal*), wrap up **2**. *informal* excite, make nervous, make tense, put on edge, work up **3**. *informal* be left, end one's days, end up, find oneself, finish up
Antonyms (*sense 1*) begin, commence, embark on, initiate, instigate, institute, open, start

windy 1. blowy, blustering, blustery, boisterous, breezy, gusty, inclement, squally, stormy, tempestuous, wild, windswept **2**. boastful, bombastic, diffuse, empty, garrulous, long-winded, loquacious, meandering, pompous, prolix, rambling, turgid, verbose, wordy **3**. *slang* afraid, chicken (*slang*), chickenshit (*U.S. slang*), cowardly, fearful, frightened, nervous, scared, timid
Antonyms (*sense 1*) becalmed, calm, motionless, smooth, still, windless (*sense 2*) modest, quiet, reserved, restrained, reticent, shy, taciturn, unforthcoming (*sense 3*) bold, brave, courageous, daring, fearless, gallant, unafraid, undaunted

wine

Wines

Amarone	Bikaver
Asti Spumante	Burgundy
Bairrada	Cahors
Bandol	canary
Banyuls	Carema
Barbaresco	Cava
Barbera d'Albi	Chablis
Barbera d'Asti	Chambertin
Barolo	Champagne
Barsac	chardonnay
beaujolais	chianti
beaujolais nouveau	Colheita Port
Bereich Bernkastel	claret
Bergerac	Condrieu
blanc de blancs	Constantia
Blanquette de Limoux	Corbières
Bordeaux	Coteaux du Tricastin
Bourgogne	Côte de Beaune-Villages
Bourgueil	Côte Rôtie
Brouilly	Côtes du Rhône
Brunello di Montalcino	Crémant d'Alsace
Bucelas	Crémant de Loire
Bull's Blood *or* Egri	Crozes-Hermitage

crusted Port
Dão
Entre-Deux-Mers
Faugères
Fitou
Fleurie
Frascati
Fumé Blanc
Gaillac
Gattinara
Gavi
Gevrey-Chambertin
Gigondas
Grange Hermitage
Graves
Hermitage
hock
jerepigo
Jurançon
lachryma Christi
Lambrusco
Liebfraumilch
Lirac
Liqueur Muscat
Liqueur Tokay
Mâcon
Mâcon-Villages
Madeira
Málaga
Margaux
Marsala
Médoc
Meursault
Minervois
Monbazillac
Montepulciano d'Abruzzo
montilla
Moscato d'Asti
Moselle
muscadet
Muscat de Beaumes-de-Venise
muscatel
Niersteiner
Nuits-Saint-Georges
Orvieto
Parrina
Pauillac
Pessac-Léognan
Piesporter
Pomerol
Pommard
port
Pouilly-Fuissé
Pouilly-Fumé
Quarts de Chaume
Quincy
retsina
Rhine wine
riesling
Rioja
Roero
Rosé d'Anjou
Rosso Cònero
Rüdesheimer
Rueda
Rully
sack
Saint-Émilion
Saint-Estèphe
Saint-Julien
Saint-Véran
Salice Salentino
Sancerre
Saumur
Sauternes
scuppernong
sherry
straw wine
Tavel
Teroldego Rotaliano
Tokaji
Tokay-Pinot Gris
Valdepeñas
Valpolicella
Verdicchio
Vinho Verde
vin ordinaire
Vino Nobile di Montepulciano
Vosne-Romanée
Vouvray

Grapes used in making white wine

aligoté
chardonnay
chenin blanc *or* steen
colombard
furmint
gewürztraminer
grüner veltliner
hárslevelü
malvasia
marsanne
müller-thurgau
muscadelle
muscat *or* moscatel
pinot blanc
pinot gris, pinot grigio, ruländer *or* Tokay-Pinot Gris
riesling *or* rhine riesling
sauvignon blanc
scheurebe
semillon *or* sémillon
seyval blanc
silvaner *or* sylvaner
trebbiano *or* ugni blanc
verdelho
verdicchio
viognier
viura
welschriesling, olasz rizling *or* laski rizling

Grapes used in making red wine

barbera
cabernet franc
cabernet sauvignon
cinsault
dolcetto
gamay
grenache *or* garnacha
kékfrankos
malbec
merlot
montepulciano
mourvèdre
nebbiolo *or* spanna
negroamoro
pinotage
pinot noir *or* spätburgunder
sangiovese
shiraz *or* syrah
tempranillo
zinfandel

Wine-producing areas	**Country**
Ahr	Germany
Alsace	France
Alto Adige *or* Südtirol	Italy
Anjou	France
Argentina	--
Austria	--
Barossa Valley	Australia
Baden	Germany
Bordeaux	France
Bulgaria	--
Burgundy	France
California	U.S.A.
Chablis	France
Champagne	France
Chianti	Italy
Chile	--
Clare Valley	Australia
Coonawarra	Australia
Côte d'Or	France
Finger Lakes	U.S.A.
Franken	Germany
Friuli	Italy
Gisborne	New Zealand
Goulburn Valley	Australia
Hawkes Bay	New Zealand
Hessiches Bergstrasse	Germany
Greece	--
Hungary	--
Hunter Valley	Australia
Languedoc	France
Loire	France
Marlborough	New Zealand
Margaret River	Australia
Martinborough	New Zealand
McLaren Vale	Australia
Mendocino	U.S.A.
Mittelrhein	Germany
Moldavia	--

Mornington Peninsula	Australia
Mosel-Saar-Ruwer	Germany
Nahe	Germany
Napa Valley	U.S.A.
Navarra	Spain
New York State	U.S.A.
Oregon	U.S.A.
Padthaway	Australia
Penedès	Spain
Piedmont	Italy
Portugal	--
Provence	France
Rheingau	Germany
Rheinhessen	Germany
Rheinpfalz	Germany
Rhône	France
Ribera del Duro	Spain
Rioja	Spain
Romania	--
Sicily	Italy
Sonoma	U.S.A.
South Africa	--
Switzerland	--
Touraine	France
Tuscany	Italy
Umbria	Italy
Valdepeñas	Spain
Veneto	Italy
Washington State	U.S.A.
Württemberg	Germany
Yarra Valley	Australia

Wine terms

abbocatto
AC *or* appellation contrôlée
amabile
amontillado
AOC *or* appellation d'origine contrôlée
aszú
Ausbruch
Auslese
Baumé
Beerenauslese
botrytis
botrytized
Brix
brut
cream
crianza
cru bourgeois
cru classé
cuvée
demi-sec
dessert wine
DO
DOC *or* denominazione di origine controllata
DOCG *or* denominazione di origine controllata e garantita
dolce
dry
Einzellage
Eiswein
erzeugerabfüllung
estate bottled
flor
fino
fortified wine
garrafeira
grand cru
gran reserva
Grosslage
halbtrocken
Kabinett
late harvest
LBV *or* Late-Bottled Vintage Port
malmsey
malolactic fermentation
manzanilla
medium
medium-dry
medium-sweet
méthode champenoise
moelleux
mousseux
noble rot
NV *or* non-vintage
Oechsle
oloroso
organic
pale cream
passito
pétillant
plonk
pourriture noble
prädikat
premier cru
puttonyos
QbA, Qualitätswein bestimmter Anbaugebiet *or* Qualitätswein
QmP *or* Qualitätswein mit Prädikat
recioto
récolte
reserva
rosé
riserva
Ruby Port
sec
secco
second wine
Sekt
sin crianza
Sigle Quinta Port
solera
sparkling wine
Spätlese
spumante
sur lie
sweet
table wine
Tafelwein
tannin
Tawny Port
terroir
tinto
trocken
Trockenbeerenauslese *or* TBA
varietal
VDQS *or* Vin Délimité de Qualité Supérieure
vendage tardive
vieilles vignes
vigneron
vignoble
vin de pays
vin de table
vin doux naturel
vin gris
vino da tavola
vintage
Weingut
Weissherbst
Winzergenossenschaft

A sight of the label is worth fifty years' experience
Michael Broadbent *Wine Tasting*

God made only water, but man made wine
Victor Hugo *Les Contemplations*

Wine is the drink of the gods, milk the drink of babies, tea the drink of women, and water the drink of beasts
John Stuart Blackie

When the wine is in, the wit is out
Thomas Becon *Catechism*

strong brother in God and last companion, Wine
Hilaire Belloc *Heroic Poem upon Wine*

It would be port if it could
Richard Bentley (describing claret)

Wine is a mocker, strong drink is raging
Bible: Proverbs

Look not thou upon the wine when it is red, when it giveth his colour in the cup... at the last it biteth like a serpent, and stingeth like an adder
Bible: Proverbs

Give strong drink unto him that is ready to perish, and wine unto those that be of heavy hearts
Bible: Proverbs

Wine, madame, is God's next best gift to man
Ambrose Bierce *The Devil's Dictionary*

There is truth in wine (in vino veritas)

wing *noun* **1.** organ of flight, pennon (*poetic*), pinion (*poetic*) **2.** arm, branch, cabal, circle, clique, coterie, faction, group, grouping, schism, section, segment, set, side **3.** adjunct, annexe, ell, extension *~verb* **4.** fly, glide, soar **5.** fleet, fly, hasten, hurry, race, speed, zoom **6.** clip, hit, nick, wound

wink *verb* **1.** bat, blink, flutter, nictate, nictitate **2.** flash, gleam, glimmer, sparkle, twinkle *~noun* **3.** blink, flutter, nictation **4.** flash, gleam, glimmering, sparkle, twinkle **5.** instant, jiffy (*informal*), moment, second, split second, twinkling

wink at allow, blink at, condone, connive at, disregard, ignore, overlook, pretend not to notice, put up with (*informal*), shut one's eyes to, tolerate, turn a blind eye to

winkle out dig out, dislodge, draw out, extract, extricate, force out, prise out, smoke out, worm out

winner champ (*informal*), champion, conquering hero, conqueror, first, master, vanquisher, victor

winning 1. alluring, amiable, attractive, bewitching, captivating, charming, cute, delectable, delightful, disarming, enchanting, endearing, engaging, fascinating, fetching, likable *or* likeable, lovely, pleasing, prepossessing, sweet, taking, winsome **2.** conquering, successful, triumphant, victorious
Antonyms (*sense 1*) disagreeable, irksome, offensive, repellent, tiresome, unappealing, unattractive, uninteresting, unpleasant

winnings booty, gains, prize(s), proceeds, profits, spoils, takings

winnow comb, cull, divide, fan, part, screen, select, separate, separate the wheat from the chaff, sift, sort out

winsome agreeable, alluring, amiable, attractive, bewitching, captivating, charming, comely, cute, delectable, disarming, enchanting, endearing, engaging, fair, fascinating, fetching, likable *or* likeable, pleasant, pleasing, pretty, sweet, taking, winning

wintry 1. brumal, chilly, cold, freezing, frosty, frozen, harsh, hibernal, hiemal, icy, snowy **2.** bleak, cheerless, cold, desolate, dismal
Antonyms balmy, bright, mild, pleasant, summery, sunny, tepid, warm

wipe *verb* **1.** brush, clean, dry, dust, mop, rub, sponge, swab **2.** clean off, erase, get rid of, remove, rub off, take away, take off *~noun* **3.** brush, lick, rub, swab

wipe out annihilate, blot out, blow away (*slang, chiefly U.S.*), destroy, efface, eradicate, erase, expunge, exterminate, extirpate, kill to the last man, massacre, obliterate, take out (*slang*), wipe from the face of the earth

wiry 1. lean, sinewy, strong, tough **2.** bristly, kinky, stiff
Antonyms (*sense 1*) fat, feeble, flabby, fleshy, frail, podgy, puny, spineless, weak

wisdom astuteness, circumspection, comprehension, discernment, enlightenment, erudition, foresight, insight, intelligence, judgment, judiciousness, knowledge, learning, penetration, prudence, reason, sagacity, sapience, sense, smarts (*slang, chiefly U.S.*), sound judgment, understanding
Antonyms absurdity, bêtise (*rare*), daftness (*informal*), folly, foolishness, idiocy, injudiciousness, nonsense, senselessness, silliness, stupidity

Knowledge comes, but wisdom lingers
Alfred, Lord Tennyson *Locksley Hall*

Wisdom denotes the pursuing of the best ends by the best means
Francis Hutcheson *Inquiry into the Original of our Ideas of Beauty and Virtue*

The art of being wise is the art of knowing what to overlook
William James *Principles of Psychology*

Be wiser than other people if you can, but do not tell them so
Lord Chesterfield

wise enough to play the fool
William Shakespeare *Twelfth Night*

The price of wisdom is above rubies
Bible: Job

Some folks are wise, and some are otherwise
Tobias Smollett *Roderick Random*

But where shall wisdom be found? And where is the place of understanding?
Bible: Job

Wisdom is the principal thing; therefore get wisdom; and with all thy getting get understanding
Bible: Proverbs

It is the province of knowledge to speak and it is the privilege of wisdom to listen
Oliver Wendell Holmes *The Poet at the Breakfast-Table*

Don't teach your grandmother to suck eggs

wise 1. aware, clever, clued-up (*informal*), discerning, enlightened, erudite, informed, intelligent, judicious, knowing, perceptive, politic, prudent, rational, reasonable, sagacious, sage, sapient, sensible, shrewd, sound, understanding, well-advised, well-informed **2. put wise** *slang* alert, apprise, clue in *or* up (*informal*), inform, let (someone) into the secret, notify, tell, tip off, warn
Antonyms daft (*informal*), foolish, injudicious, rash, silly, stupid, unintelligent, unwise

The stupid neither forgive nor forget; the naive forgive and forget; the wise forgive but do not forget

Thomas Szasz *The Second Sin*

It's a wise child that knows its own father

A word to the wise is enough

It is easy to be wise after the event

wisecrack 1. *noun* barb, funny (*informal*), gag (*informal*), jest, jibe, joke, pithy remark, quip, sardonic remark, smart remark, witticism 2. *verb* be facetious, jest, jibe, joke, quip, tell jokes

wish *verb* 1. aspire, covet, crave, desiderate, desire, hanker, hope, hunger, long, need, set one's heart on, sigh for, thirst, want, yearn 2. bid, greet with 3. ask, bid, command, desire, direct, instruct, order, require ~*noun* 4. aspiration, desire, hankering, hope, hunger, inclination, intention, liking, longing, thirst, urge, want, whim, will, yearning 5. bidding, command, desire, order, request, will

Antonyms (*sense 4*) aversion, disinclination, dislike, distaste, loathing, reluctance, repulsion, revulsion

The wish is father to the thought

If wishes were horses, beggars would ride

wishy-washy bland, feeble, flat, ineffective, ineffectual, insipid, jejune, tasteless, thin, vapid, watered-down, watery, weak

wisp piece, shred, snippet, strand, thread, twist

wispy attenuate, attenuated, delicate, diaphanous, ethereal, faint, fine, flimsy, fragile, frail, gossamer, insubstantial, light, thin, wisplike

wistful contemplative, disconsolate, dreaming, dreamy, forlorn, longing, meditative, melancholy, mournful, musing, pensive, reflective, sad, thoughtful, yearning

wit 1. badinage, banter, drollery, facetiousness, fun, humour, jocularity, levity, pleasantry, raillery, repartee, wordplay 2. card (*informal*), comedian, epigrammatist, *farceur*, humorist, joker, punster, wag 3. acumen, brains, cleverness, common sense, comprehension, discernment, ingenuity, insight, intellect, judgment, mind, nous (*Brit. slang*), perception, practical intelligence, reason, sense, smarts (*slang, chiefly U.S.*), understanding, wisdom

Antonyms dullness, folly, foolishness, gravity, humourlessness, ignorance, lack of perception, obtuseness, seriousness, silliness, sobriety, solemnity, stupidity

True wit is nature to advantage dress'd,
What oft was thought, but ne'er so well expressed

Alexander Pope *An Essay on Criticism*

Brevity is the soul of wit

William Shakespeare *Hamlet*

Next to being witty yourself, the best thing is being able to quote another's wit

Christian N. Bovee

Wit is the epitaph of an emotion

Friedrich Nietzsche *Menschliches, Allzumenschliches*

witch crone, enchantress, magician, necromancer, occultist, sorceress

witch: (1) An ugly and repulsive old woman, in a wicked league with the devil. (2) A beautiful and attractive young woman, in wickedness a league beyond the devil

Ambrose Bierce *The Devil's Dictionary*

witchcraft enchantment, incantation, magic, necromancy, occultism, sorcery, sortilege, spell, the black art, the occult, voodoo, witchery, witching, wizardry

withdraw 1. draw back, draw out, extract, pull, pull out, remove, take away, take off 2. abjure, disavow, disclaim, recall, recant, rescind, retract, revoke, take back, unsay 3. absent oneself, back off, back out, cop out (*slang*), depart, detach oneself, disengage, drop out, fall back, go, leave, make oneself scarce (*informal*), pull back, pull out, retire, retreat, secede

Antonyms (*senses 1 & 3*) advance, forge ahead, go on, move forward, persist, press on, proceed, progress

withdrawal 1. extraction, removal 2. abjuration, disavowal, disclaimer, recall, recantation, repudiation, rescission, retraction, revocation 3. departure, disengagement, exit, exodus, retirement, retreat, secession

withdrawn 1. aloof, detached, distant, introverted, quiet, reserved, retiring, shrinking, shy, silent, taciturn, timorous, uncommunicative, unforthcoming 2. hidden, isolated, out-of-the-way, private, remote, secluded, solitary

Antonyms boisterous, bustling, busy, easily accessible, extrovert, forward, friendly, gregarious, open, outgoing, sociable

wither 1. blast, blight, decay, decline, desiccate, disintegrate, droop, dry, fade, languish, perish, shrink, shrivel, wane, waste, wilt 2. abash, blast, humiliate, mortify, put down, shame, snub

Antonyms (*sense 1*) bloom, blossom, develop, flourish, increase, prosper, succeed, thrive, wax

withering 1. blasting, blighting, devastating, humiliating, hurtful, mortifying, scornful, snubbing 2. deadly, death-dealing, destructive, devastating, killing, murderous, slaughterous

withhold 1. check, conceal, deduct, hide, hold back, keep, keep back, keep secret, refuse, repress, reserve, resist, restrain, retain, sit on (*informal*), suppress 2. *with* **from** forbear, keep oneself, refrain, stop oneself

Antonyms (*sense 1*) accord, expose, get off one's chest (*informal*), give, grant, hand over, let go, release, relinquish, reveal

with it fashionable, happening (*informal*), in (*informal*), latest (*informal*), modern, modish, progressive, stylish, swinging (*slang*), trendy (*Brit. informal*), up-to-date, up-to-the-minute, vogue

withstand **1.** bear, brave, combat, confront, cope with, defy, endure, face, grapple with, hold off, hold out against, oppose, put up with (*informal*), resist, stand up to, suffer, take, take on, thwart, tolerate, weather **2.** endure, hold *or* stand one's ground, hold out, remain firm, stand, stand fast, stand firm
Antonyms capitulate, falter, give in, give way, relent, succumb, surrender, weaken, yield

witless asinine, braindead (*informal*), crackpot (*informal*), crazy, daft (*informal*), dozy (*Brit. informal*), dull, empty-headed, foolish, goofy (*informal*), halfwitted, idiotic, imbecilic, inane, loopy (*informal*), moronic, obtuse, rattlebrained (*slang*), senseless, silly, stupid, unintelligent

witness *noun* **1.** beholder, bystander, eyewitness, looker-on, observer, onlooker, spectator, viewer, watcher **2.** attestant, corroborator, deponent, testifier **3. bear witness a.** depone, depose, give evidence, give testimony, testify **b.** attest to, bear out, be evidence of, be proof of, betoken, confirm, constitute proof of, corroborate, demonstrate, evince, prove, show, testify to, vouch for ~*verb* **4.** attend, behold (*archaic or literary*), be present at, look on, mark, note, notice, observe, perceive, see, view, watch **5.** attest, authenticate, bear out, bear witness, confirm, corroborate, depone, depose, give evidence, give testimony, testify **6.** countersign, endorse, sign

wits **1.** acumen, astuteness, brains (*informal*), cleverness, comprehension, faculties, ingenuity, intelligence, judgment, nous (*Brit. slang*), reason, sense, smarts (*slang, chiefly U.S.*), understanding **2. at one's wits' end** at a loss, at the end of one's tether, baffled, bewildered, in despair, lost, stuck (*informal*), stumped

witter *verb* **1.** babble, blab, blather, blether, burble, cackle, chat, chatter, clack, gab (*informal*), gabble, jabber, prate, prattle, rabbit (on) (*Brit. informal*), tattle, twaddle, waffle (*informal, chiefly Brit.*) ~*noun* **2.** babble, blather, blether, burble, chat, chatter, clack, gab (*informal*), gabble, jabber, prate, prattle, tattle, twaddle, waffle (*informal, chiefly Brit.*)

witticism bon mot, clever remark, epigram, one-liner (*slang*), play on words, pleasantry, pun, quip, repartee, riposte, sally, witty remark

witty amusing, brilliant, clever, droll, epigrammatic, facetious, fanciful, funny, gay, humorous, ingenious, jocular, lively, original, piquant, sparkling, waggish, whimsical
Antonyms boring, dull, humourless, stupid, tedious, tiresome, unamusing, uninteresting, witless

> *A witty woman is a treasure; a witty beauty is a power*
>
> George Meredith *Diana of the Crossways*

wizard **1.** conjurer, enchanter, mage (*archaic*), magician, magus, necromancer, occultist, shaman, sorcerer, thaumaturge (*rare*), warlock, witch **2.** ace (*informal*), adept, buff (*informal*), expert, genius, hotshot (*informal*), maestro, master, maven (*U.S.*), prodigy, star, virtuoso, whiz (*informal*), whizz kid (*informal*), wiz (*informal*)

wizardry conjuration, enchantment, magic, necromancy, occultism, sorcery, sortilege, the black art, voodoo, witchcraft, witchery, witching

wizened dried up, gnarled, lined, sere (*archaic*), shrivelled, shrunken, withered, worn, wrinkled
Antonyms bloated, plump, rounded, smooth, swollen, turgid

wobble *verb* **1.** quake, rock, seesaw, shake, sway, teeter, totter, tremble, vibrate, waver **2.** be unable to make up one's mind, be undecided, dither (*chiefly Brit.*), fluctuate, hesitate, shillyshally (*informal*), swither (*Scot.*), vacillate, waver ~*noun* **3.** quaking, shake, tremble, tremor, unsteadiness, vibration

wobbly rickety, shaky, teetering, tottering, unbalanced, uneven, unsafe, unstable, unsteady, wonky (*Brit. slang*)

woe adversity, affliction, agony, anguish, burden, curse, dejection, depression, disaster, distress, gloom, grief, hardship, heartache, heartbreak, melancholy, misery, misfortune, pain, sadness, sorrow, suffering, trial, tribulation, trouble, unhappiness, wretchedness
Antonyms bliss, elation, felicity, fortune, happiness, joy, jubilation, pleasure, prosperity, rapture

woebegone blue, chapfallen, cheerless, crestfallen, dejected, disconsolate, doleful, downcast, downhearted, down in the dumps (*informal*), down in the mouth (*informal*), forlorn, funereal, gloomy, grief-stricken, hangdog, long-faced, low, lugubrious, miserable, mournful, sad, sorrowful, troubled, wretched

woeful **1.** afflicted, agonized, anguished, calamitous, catastrophic, cruel, deplorable, disastrous, disconsolate, dismal, distressing, doleful, dreadful, gloomy, grieving, grievous, harrowing, heartbreaking, heart-rending, lamentable, miserable, mournful, pathetic,

piteous, pitiable, pitiful, plaintive, sad, sorrowful, tragic, unhappy, wretched **2.** abysmal, appalling, awful, bad, deplorable, disappointing, disgraceful, dreadful, duff (*Brit. informal*), feeble, godawful (*slang*), hopeless, inadequate, lousy (*slang*), mean, miserable, not much cop (*Brit. slang*), paltry, pathetic, pitiable, pitiful, poor, rotten (*informal*), shitty (*taboo slang*), shocking, sorry, terrible, wretched
Antonyms (*sense 1*) carefree, cheerful, chirpy (*informal*), contented, delighted, glad, happy, jolly, joyful, jubilant, light-hearted (*sense 2*) abundant, ample, bountiful, enviable, extensive, generous, lavish, luxurious, profuse, prosperous

wolf *noun* **1.** *figurative* devil, fiend, killer, mercenary, pirate, predator, robber, savage, shark **2.** *informal* Casanova, Don Juan, lady-killer, lech *or* letch (*informal*), lecher, Lothario, philanderer, seducer, womanizer *~verb* **3.** *with* **down** bolt, cram, devour, eat like a horse, gobble, gollop, gorge, gulp, pack away (*informal*), pig out (*slang*), scoff (*slang*), stuff
Antonyms *verb* bite, nibble, nip, peck, pick at

wolfish avaricious, edacious, fierce, gluttonous, greedy, insatiable, predatory, rapacious, ravenous, savage, voracious

woman **1.** bird (*slang*), chick (*slang*), dame (*slang*), female, gal (*slang*), girl, ho (*U.S. derogatory slang*), lady, lass, lassie (*informal*), maid (*archaic*), maiden (*archaic*), miss, she, wench (*facetious*) **2.** chambermaid, char (*informal*), charwoman, domestic, female servant, handmaiden, housekeeper, lady-in-waiting, maid, maidservant **3.** *informal* bride, girl, girlfriend, ladylove, mate, mistress, old lady (*informal*), partner, significant other (*U.S. informal*), spouse, sweetheart, wife
Antonyms (*sense 1*) bloke (*Brit. informal*), boy, chap (*informal*), gentleman, guy (*informal*), lad, laddie, male, man

She floats, she hesitates; in a word, she's a woman
Jean Racine *Athalie*

Fickle and changeable always is woman
Virgil *Aeneid*

A man is as old as he's feeling,
A woman as old as she looks
Mortimer Collins *The Unknown Quantity*

Men play the game, women know the score
Roger Woddis

The prime truth of woman, the universal mother...that if a thing is worth doing, it is worth doing badly
G.K. Chesterton *What's Wrong with the World*

One is not born a woman; one becomes one
Simone de Beauvoir *The Second Sex*

Woman was God's second blunder
Friedrich Nietzsche *Der Antichrist*

The greatest glory of a woman is to be least talked about by men
Pericles

A woman seldom writes her mind but in her postscript
Sir Richard Steele *The Spectator*

A woman without a man is like a fish without a bicycle
attributed to Gloria Steinem

Frailty, thy name is woman!
William Shakespeare *Hamlet*

Men, at most, differ as Heaven and earth,
But women, worst and best, as Heaven and Hell
Alfred, Lord Tennyson *Merlin and Vivien*

A woman, especially, if she have the misfortune of knowing anything, should conceal it as well as she can
Jane Austen *Northanger Abbey*

A woman's place is in the wrong
James Thurber

I expect that woman will be the last thing civilized by man
George Meredith

A woman who thinks she is intelligent demands equal rights with men. A woman who is intelligent does not
Colette

Whatever women do they must do twice as well as men to be thought half as good. Luckily this is not difficult
Charlotte Whitton

I hate women because they always know where things are
James Thurber

Most women are not as young as they are painted
Sir Max Beerbohm

She's the sort of woman who lives for others - you can tell the others by their hunted expression
C.S. Lewis *The Screwtape Letters*

A woman knows enough if she knows enough to mend our shirts and cook us a steak
Pierre-Joseph Proudhon

Man has his will; but woman has her way
O.W. Holmes

All women become like their mothers. That is their tragedy. No man does. That's his
Oscar Wilde *The Importance of Being Ernest*

When women go wrong, men go right after them
Mae West

Women - one half of the human race at least - care fifty times more for a marriage than a ministry
Walter Bagehot *The English Constitution*

Women can't forgive failure
Anton Chekhov *The Seagull*
Women, then, are only children of a larger growth
Lord Chesterfield *Letters to his Son*
Can anything be more absurd than keeping women in a state of ignorance, and yet so vehemently to insist on their resisting temptation?
Vicesimus Knox
Women are really much nicer than men: no wonder we like them
Kingsley Amis *A Bookshop Idyll*
If all men are born free, how is it that all women are born slaves?
Mary Astell *Some Reflections upon Marriage*
Good women always think it is their fault when someone else is being offensive. Bad women never take the blame for anything
Anita Brookner *Hotel du Lac*
O fairest of creation, last and best
Of all God's works
John Milton *Paradise Lost*
Music and women I cannot but give way to, whatever my business is
Samuel Pepys *Diary*
A woman's place is in the home
Hell hath no fury like a woman scorned
A woman's work is never done

womanizer Casanova, Don Juan, lady-killer, lech *or* letch (*informal*), lecher, Lothario, phi~ landerer, seducer, wolf (*informal*)

womanly female, feminine, ladylike, matronly, motherly, tender, warm

womb uterus

wonder *noun* **1.** admiration, amazement, astonishment, awe, bewilderment, curiosity, fascination, stupefaction, surprise, wonder~ ment **2.** curiosity, marvel, miracle, nonpareil, phenomenon, portent, prodigy, rarity, sight, spectacle, wonderment *~verb* **3.** ask oneself, be curious, be inquisitive, conjecture, cudgel one's brains (*informal*), doubt, inquire, medi~ tate, ponder, puzzle, query, question, specu~ late, think **4.** be amazed (astonished, awed, dumbstruck), be flabbergasted (*informal*), boggle, gape, gawk, marvel, stand amazed, stare

Seven wonders of the ancient world
Colossus of Rhodes
Hanging Gardens of Babylon
mausoleum of Hali~ carnassus
Pharos of Alexandria
Phidias' statue of Zeus at Olympia
Pyramids of Egypt
temple of Artemis at Ephesus

wonderful **1.** amazing, astonishing, astounding, awe-inspiring, awesome, extraordinary, fan~ tastic, incredible, marvellous, miraculous, odd, peculiar, phenomenal, remarkable, staggering, startling, strange, surprising, unheard-of, wondrous (*archaic or literary*) **2.** ace (*infor~ mal*), admirable, awesome (*slang*), bodacious (*slang, chiefly U.S.*), boffo (*slang*), brill (*infor~ mal*), brilliant, chillin' (*U.S. slang*), cracking (*Brit. informal*), excellent, fabulous (*informal*), fantastic (*informal*), great (*informal*), jim-dandy (*slang*), like a dream come true, mag~ nificent, marvellous, mean (*slang*), out of this world (*informal*), outstanding, sensational (*in~ formal*), smashing (*informal*), sovereign, stu~ pendous, super (*informal*), superb, terrific, tiptop, topping (*Brit. slang*), tremendous
Antonyms abominable, abysmal, appalling, average, awful, bad, common, commonplace, depressing, dire, dreadful, frightful, grim, hellacious (*U.S. slang*), indifferent, lousy (*slang*), mediocre, miserable, modest, no great shakes (*informal*), ordinary, paltry, rotten, run-of-the-mill, terrible, uninteresting, un~ pleasant, unremarkable, usual, vile

wonky **1.** groggy (*informal*), infirm, shaky, un~ steady, weak, wobbly, woozy (*informal*) **2.** askew, awry, out of alignment, skewwhiff (*Brit. informal*), squint (*informal*)

wont **1.** *adjective* accustomed, given, in the habit of, used **2.** *noun* custom, habit, practice, rule, use, way

wonted **1.** accustomed, given, habituated, in the habit of, used **2.** accustomed, common, conventional, customary, familiar, frequent, habitual, normal, regular, usual

woo chase, court, cultivate, importune, pay court to, pay one's addresses to, pay suit to, press one's suit with, pursue, seek after, seek the hand of, seek to win, solicit the goodwill of, spark (*rare*)

wood **1.** *Also* **woods** coppice, copse, forest, grove, hurst (*archaic*), thicket, trees, wood~ land **2.** **out of the wood(s)** clear, home and dry (*Brit. slang*), in the clear, out of danger, safe, safe and sound, secure **3.** planks, timber
Related adjectives: ligneous, sylvan

Woods
African mahogany
afrormosia
alerce
amboyna *or* amboina
apple
ash
assegai *or* assagai
balsa
basswood
baywood
beech
beefwood
birch
black walnut
bog oak
boxwood
brazil, brasil, *or* bra~ zil wood
bulletwood
butternut
cade
calamander
camwood
candlewood
cedar
cherry
chestnut
citron wood
coachwood
corkwood
crabwood
cypress
durmast *or* durmast oak

eaglewood
ebony
elm
fiddlewood
fir
gaboon
gopher wood
greenheart
guaiacum *or* guaiocum
gumtree *or* gumwood
hackberry
hardwood
hazel
hemlock
hickory
hornbeam
iroko
ironwood
jacaranda
jelutong
kauri
kiaat
kingwood
koa
lancewood
larch
locust
mahogany
maple
marblewood
nutwood
oak
olive
orangewood
padauk *or* padouk
Paraná pine
partridge-wood
pear
persimmon
pine
pitch pine
poon
poplar
pulpwood
quassia
quebracho
red cedar
red fir
red gum
red oak
ribbonwood
rosewood
sandalwood
sandarac
sappanwood
sassy, sasswood *or* sassy wood
satinwood
Scots pine
shagbark *or* shellbark
sneezewood
softwood
spotted gum
spruce
stinkwood
sumach *or* sumac (*U.S.*)
sycamore
tamarack
tamarind
teak
thorn
toon
torchwood
tulipwood
tupelo
walnut
western red cedar
white cedar
white pine
whitewood
willow
yellowwood
yew
zebrawood

wooded forested, sylvan (*poetic*), timbered, tree-clad, tree-covered, woody

wooden 1. ligneous, made of wood, of wood, timber, woody 2. awkward, clumsy, gauche, gawky, graceless, inelegant, maladroit, rigid, stiff, ungainly 3. blank, colourless, deadpan, dull, emotionless, empty, expressionless, glassy, lifeless, spiritless, unemotional, unresponsive, vacant 4. inflexible, obstinate, rigid, stiff, unbending, unyielding 5. dense, dim, dim-witted (*informal*), dozy (*Brit. informal*), dull, dull-witted, obtuse, slow, stupid, thick, witless, woodenheaded (*informal*) 6. dull, muffled
Antonyms (*senses 2 & 4*) agile, comely, elegant, flexible, flowing, graceful, lissom(e), nimble, supple

wool 1. fleece, hair, yarn 2. **dyed in the wool** confirmed, diehard, fixed, hardened, inflexible, inveterate, settled, unchangeable, uncompromising, unshakable 3. **pull the wool over someone's eyes** bamboozle (*informal*), con (*slang*), deceive, delude, dupe, fool, hoodwink, kid (*informal*), lead (someone) up the garden path (*informal*), pull a fast one (on someone) (*informal*), put one over on (*slang*), take in (*informal*), trick

woolgathering absent-mindedness, abstraction, building castles in the air, daydreaming, dreaming, inattention, musing, preoccupation, reverie
Antonyms alertness, attention, awareness, concentration, heed, observation, thoughtfulness, vigilance, watchfulness

woolly *adjective* 1. fleecy, flocculent, hairy, made of wool, shaggy, woollen 2. blurred, clouded, confused, foggy, fuzzy, hazy, ill-defined, indefinite, indistinct, muddled, nebulous, unclear, vague
Antonyms (*sense 2*) clear, clear-cut, definite, distinct, exact, obvious, precise, sharp, well-defined

woozy befuddled, bemused, confused, dazed, dizzy, nauseated, rocky (*informal*), tipsy, unsteady, wobbly

word *noun* 1. brief conversation, chat, chitchat, colloquy, confab (*informal*), confabulation, consultation, discussion, talk, tête-à-tête 2. brief statement, comment, declaration, expression, remark, utterance 3. expression, locution, name, term, vocable 4. account, advice, bulletin, communication, communiqué, dispatch, gen (*Brit. informal*), information, intelligence, intimation, latest (*informal*), message, news, notice, report, tidings 5. command, go-ahead (*informal*), green light, order, signal 6. affirmation, assertion, assurance, guarantee, oath, parole, pledge, promise, solemn oath, solemn word, undertaking, vow, word of honour 7. bidding, command, commandment, decree, edict, mandate, order, ukase (*rare*), will 8. countersign, password, slogan, watchword 9. **in a word** briefly, concisely, in a nutshell, in short, succinctly, to put it briefly, to sum up ~*verb* 10. couch, express, phrase, put, say, state, utter
Related adjective: lexical

In the beginning was the Word
Bible: St. John

Words are, of course, the most powerful drug used by mankind
Rudyard Kipling

I am a bear of Very Little Brain, and long words Bother me
A.A. Milne *Winnie-the-Pooh*

"When I use a word," Humpty Dumpty said in a rather scornful tone, "it means just what I choose it to mean - neither more nor less."
Lewis Carroll *Through the Looking-Glass*

Words just say what you want them to say; they don't know any better
A.L. Kennedy *The Role of Notable Silences in Scottish History*

and once sent out, a word takes wing beyond recall
Horace *Epistles*

Words are the physicians of a mind diseased
Aeschylus *Prometheus Bound*

Thought flies and words go on foot
Julien Green *Journal*

How often misused words generate misleading thoughts
Herbert Spencer *Principles of Ethics*

Words are the tokens current and accepted for con~ceits, as moneys are for values
Francis Bacon *The Advancement of Learning*

Words are wise men's counters, they do but reckon by them
Thomas Hobbes *Leviathan*

Oaths are but words, and words but wind
Samuel Butler *Hudibras*

wording choice of words, language, mode of expression, phraseology, phrasing, terminol~ogy, words

wordplay punning, puns, repartee, wit, witti~cisms

words **1.** lyrics, text **2.** altercation, angry ex~change, angry speech, argument, barney (*in~formal*), bickering, disagreement, dispute, falling-out (*informal*), quarrel, row, run-in (*informal*), set-to (*informal*), squabble

wordy diffuse, discursive, garrulous, long-winded, loquacious, pleonastic, prolix, ram~bling, verbose, windy
Antonyms brief, concise, laconic, pithy, short, succinct, terse, to the point

work *noun* **1.** drudgery, effort, elbow grease (*facetious*), exertion, grind (*informal*), indus~try, labour, slog, sweat, toil, travail (*literary*) **2.** bread and butter (*informal*), business, call~ing, craft, duty, employment, job, line, liveli~hood, métier, occupation, office, profession, pursuit, trade **3.** assignment, chore, commis~sion, duty, job, stint, task, undertaking **4.** achievement, composition, creation, handi~work, *oeuvre*, opus, performance, piece, pro~duction **5.** art, craft, skill, workmanship **6. out of work** idle, jobless, on the dole (*Brit. infor~mal*), on the street, out of a job, unemployed *~verb* **7.** break one's back, drudge, exert one~self, labour, peg away, slave, slog (away), sweat, toil **8.** be employed, be in work, do business, earn a living, have a job **9.** act, con~trol, direct, drive, handle, manage, manipu~late, move, operate, ply, use, wield **10.** func~tion, go, operate, perform, run **11.** cultivate, dig, farm, till **12.** fashion, form, handle, knead, make, manipulate, mould, process, shape **13.** be agitated, convulse, move, twitch, writhe **14.** *often with* **up** arouse, excite, move, prompt, provoke, rouse, stir **15.** accomplish, achieve, bring about, carry out, cause, contrive, create, effect, encompass, execute, implement **16.** force, make one's way, manoeuvre, move, pro~gress **17.** *informal* arrange, bring off, contrive, exploit, fiddle (*informal*), fix (*informal*), han~dle, manipulate, pull off, swing (*informal*)
Antonyms *noun* (*sense 1*) ease, leisure, re~laxation, rest (*sense 2*) entertainment, hobby, holiday, play, recreation, retirement, spare time, unemployment (*sense 3*) child's play (*in~formal*) *~verb* (*sense 7*) have fun, mark time, play, relax, skive (*Brit. slang*), take it easy (*sense 10*) be broken, be out of order (*sense 15*) counteract, nullify, prevent, reverse (*sense 16*) remain

Work expands so as to fill the time available for its completion
N. Northcote Parkinson *Parkinson's Law*

Work is the curse of the drinking classes
Oscar Wilde

Work is the great cure of all maladies and mis~eries that ever beset mankind
Thomas Carlyle

If any would not work, neither should he eat
Bible: II Thessalonians

All that matters is love and work
attributed to Sigmund Freud

All work and no play makes Jack a dull boy

workable doable, feasible, possible, practicable, practical, viable
Antonyms hopeless, impossible, impractical, inconceivable, unattainable, unthinkable, un~workable, useless

workaday bog-standard (*Brit. & Irish slang*), common, commonplace, everyday, familiar, humdrum, mundane, ordinary, practical, pro~saic, routine, run-of-the-mill
Antonyms atypical, different, exciting, extraordinary, rare, special, uncommon, unfa~miliar, unusual

worker artisan, craftsman, employee, hand, labourer, proletarian, tradesman, wage earn~er, working man, working woman, workman

The proletarians have nothing to lose but their chains. They have a world to win. Workers of all countries unite!
Marx & Engels *The Communist Manifesto*

working *noun* **1.** action, functioning, manner, method, mode of operation, operation, running **2.** *plural* diggings, excavations, mine, pit, quarry, shaft *~adjective* **3.** active, employed, in a job, in work, labouring **4.** functioning, go~

ing, operative, running **5.** effective, practical, useful, viable

workman artificer, artisan, craftsman, employee, hand, journeyman, labourer, mechanic, operative, tradesman, worker

A bad workman always blames his tools

workmanlike, workmanly adept, careful, efficient, expert, masterly, painstaking, professional, proficient, satisfactory, skilful, skilled, thorough

Antonyms amateurish, botchy, careless, clumsy, cowboy (*informal*), incompetent, slap-dash, slipshod, unprofessional, unskilful

workmanship art, artistry, craft, craftsmanship, execution, expertise, handicraft, handiwork, manufacture, skill, technique, work

work-out drill, exercise, exercise session, practice session, training, training session, warm-up

work out **1.** accomplish, achieve, attain, win **2.** calculate, clear up, figure out, find out, puzzle out, resolve, solve, suss (out) (*slang*) **3.** arrange, construct, contrive, develop, devise, elaborate, evolve, form, formulate, plan, put together **4.** be effective, flourish, go as planned, go well, prosper, prove satisfactory, succeed **5.** come out, develop, evolve, go, happen, pan out (*informal*), result, turn out **6.** do exercises, drill, exercise, practise, train, warm up **7.** add up to, amount to, come to, reach, reach a total of

works **1.** factory, mill, plant, shop, workshop **2.** canon, *oeuvre*, output, productions, writings **3.** actions, acts, deeds, doings **4.** action, guts (*informal*), innards (*informal*), insides (*informal*), machinery, mechanism, movement, moving parts, parts, workings

workshop **1.** atelier, factory, mill, plant, shop, studio, workroom, works **2.** class, discussion group, seminar, study group

work up agitate, animate, arouse, enkindle, excite, foment, generate, get (someone) all steamed up (*slang*), incite, inflame, instigate, move, rouse, spur, stir up, wind up (*informal*)

world **1.** earth, earthly sphere, globe **2.** everybody, everyone, humanity, humankind, human race, man, mankind, men, the public, the race of man **3.** cosmos, creation, existence, life, nature, universe **4.** heavenly body, planet, star **5.** area, domain, environment, field, kingdom, province, realm, sphere, system **6.** age, days, epoch, era, period, times **7. for all the world** exactly, in every respect, in every way, just as if, just like, precisely, to all intents and purposes **8. on top of the world** *informal* beside oneself with joy, cock-a-hoop, ecstatic, elated, exultant, happy, in raptures, on cloud nine (*informal*), overjoyed, over the moon (*informal*) **9. out of this world** *informal* awesome (*slang*), bodacious (*slang, chiefly U.S.*), excellent, fabulous (*informal*), fantastic (*informal*), great (*informal*), incredible, indescribable, marvellous, superb, unbelievable, wonderful

All the world's a stage
William Shakespeare *As you Like It*

The world's mine oyster
William Shakespeare *The Merry Wives of Windsor*

The world is everything that is the case
Ludwig Wittgenstein *Tractatus Logico-philosophicus*

worldly **1.** carnal, earthly, fleshly, lay, mundane, physical, profane, secular, sublunary, temporal, terrestrial **2.** avaricious, covetous, grasping, greedy, materialistic, selfish, worldly-minded **3.** blasé, cosmopolitan, experienced, knowing, politic, sophisticated, urbane, well versed in the ways of the world, worldly-wise

Antonyms (*sense 1*) divine, ethereal, heavenly, immaterial, noncorporeal, spiritual, transcendental, unworldly (*sense 2*) moral, nonmaterialistic, unworldly (*sense 3*) ingenuous, innocent, naive, unsophisticated, unworldly

Be wisely worldly, be not worldly wise
Francis Quarles *Emblems*

worldly-wise experienced, knowing, sophisticated, worldly

Antonyms callow, inexperienced, ingenuous, innocent, jejune, naive, unsophisticated, unworldly

worldwide general, global, international, omnipresent, pandemic, ubiquitous, universal

Antonyms confined, insular, limited, local, narrow, national, parochial, provincial, restricted

worn **1.** frayed, ragged, shabby, shiny, tattered, tatty, the worse for wear, threadbare **2.** careworn, drawn, haggard, lined, pinched, wizened **3.** exhausted, fatigued, jaded, played-out (*informal*), spent, tired, tired out, wearied, weary, worn-out

worn-out **1.** broken-down, clapped out (*Brit., Austral., & N.Z. informal*), decrepit, done, frayed, moth-eaten, on its last legs, ragged, run-down, shabby, tattered, tatty, threadbare, used, used-up, useless, worn **2.** all in (*slang*), clapped out (*Austral. & N.Z. informal*), dead or out on one's feet (*informal*), dog-tired (*informal*), done in (*informal*), exhausted, fatigued, fit to drop, jiggered (*dialect*), knackered (*slang*), played-out, prostrate, shagged out (*Brit. slang*), spent, tired, tired out, weary, wiped out (*informal*), zonked (*slang*)

Antonyms (*sense 2*) fresh, refreshed, relaxed, renewed, rested, restored, revived, strengthened

worried afraid, anxious, apprehensive, both~ ered, concerned, distracted, distraught, dis~ tressed, disturbed, fearful, fretful, frightened, hot and bothered, ill at ease, nervous, on edge, overwrought, perturbed, tense, torment~ ed, troubled, uneasy, unquiet, upset, wired (*slang*)
Antonyms calm, fearless, peaceful, quiet, tranquil, unafraid, unconcerned, unfazed (*in~ formal*), unworried

worrisome 1. bothersome, disquieting, dis~ tressing, disturbing, irksome, perturbing, troublesome, upsetting, vexing, worrying 2. anxious, apprehensive, fretful, insecure, jit~ tery (*informal*), nervous, neurotic, uneasy

worry *verb* 1. agonize, annoy, badger, be anx~ ious, bother, brood, disquiet, distress, disturb, feel uneasy, fret, harass, harry, hassle (*infor~ mal*), hector, importune, irritate, make anx~ ious, perturb, pester, plague, tantalize, tease, torment, trouble, unsettle, upset, vex 2. at~ tack, bite, gnaw at, go for, harass, harry, kill, lacerate, savage, tear ~*noun* 3. annoyance, bother, care, hassle (*informal*), irritation, pest, plague, problem, torment, trial, trouble, vexa~ tion 4. annoyance, anxiety, apprehension, care, concern, disturbance, fear, irritation, misery, misgiving, perplexity, torment, trepi~ dation, trouble, unease, vexation, woe
Antonyms *verb* be apathetic, be unconcerned, be unperturbed, calm, comfort, console, solace, soothe ~*noun* calm, comfort, consolation, peace of mind, reassurance, serenity, solace, tranquillity

worsen aggravate, damage, decay, decline, de~ generate, deteriorate, exacerbate, get worse, go downhill (*informal*), go from bad to worse, retrogress, sink, take a turn for the worse
Antonyms ameliorate, be on the mend, better, enhance, improve, mend, recover, rectify, up~ grade

worship 1. *verb* adore, adulate, deify, exalt, glorify, honour, idolize, laud, love, praise, pray to, put on a pedestal, respect, revere, reverence, venerate 2. *noun* adoration, adula~ tion, deification, devotion, exaltation, glorifi~ cation, glory, homage, honour, laudation, love, praise, prayer(s), regard, respect, reverence
Antonyms *verb* blaspheme, deride, despise, disdain, dishonour, flout, mock, revile, ridi~ cule, scoff at, spurn

worst *verb* beat, best, blow out of the water (*slang*), clobber (*slang*), conquer, crush, defeat, gain the advantage over, get the better of, lick (*informal*), master, overcome, overpower, overthrow, run rings around (*informal*), sub~ due, subjugate, undo, vanquish, wipe the floor with (*informal*)

worth 1. aid, assistance, avail, benefit, credit, desert(s), estimation, excellence, goodness, help, importance, merit, quality, usefulness, utility, value, virtue, worthiness 2. cost, price, rate, valuation, value
Antonyms (*sense 1*) futility, insignificance, paltriness, triviality, unworthiness, use~ lessness, worthlessness, wretchedness

worthless 1. a dime a dozen, chickenshit (*U.S. slang*), futile, ineffectual, insignificant, inutile, meaningless, measly, miserable, nickel-and-dime (*U.S. slang*), not much cop (*Brit.slang*), not worth a hill of beans (*chiefly U.S.*), no use, nugatory, paltry, pointless, poor, poxy (*slang*), rubbishy, trashy, trifling, trivial, two a penny (*informal*), unavailing, unimportant, unusable, useless, valueless, wanky (*taboo slang*), wretched 2. abandoned, abject, base, contemptible, depraved, despicable, good-for-nothing, ignoble, useless, vile
Antonyms consequential, decent, effective, fruitful, honourable, important, noble, pre~ cious, productive, profitable, significant, upright, useful, valuable, worthwhile, worthy

worthwhile beneficial, constructive, expedient, gainful, good, helpful, justifiable, productive, profitable, useful, valuable, worthy
Antonyms inconsequential, pointless, trivial, unimportant, unworthy, useless, vain, value~ less, wasteful, worthless

worthy 1. *adjective* admirable, commendable, creditable, decent, dependable, deserving, es~ timable, excellent, good, honest, honourable, laudable, meritorious, praiseworthy, reliable, reputable, respectable, righteous, upright, valuable, virtuous, worthwhile 2. *noun* big shot (*informal*), bigwig (*informal*), dignitary, luminary, notable, personage
Antonyms *adjective* demeaning, disreputable, dubious, ignoble, undeserving, unproductive, untrustworthy, unworthy, useless ~*noun* member of the rank and file, nobody, pleb, punter (*informal*)

would-be budding, dormant, latent, manqué, potential, professed, quasi-, self-appointed, self-styled, so-called, *soi-disant*, undeveloped, unfulfilled, unrealized

wound *noun* 1. cut, damage, gash, harm, hurt, injury, laceration, lesion, slash, trauma (*Pa~ thology*) 2. anguish, distress, grief, heartbreak, injury, insult, offence, pain, pang, sense of loss, shock, slight, torment, torture, trauma ~*verb* 3. cut, damage, gash, harm, hit, hurt, injure, irritate, lacerate, pierce, slash, wing 4. annoy, cut (someone) to the quick, distress, grieve, hurt, hurt the feelings of, mortify, of~ fend, pain, shock, sting, traumatize

what wound did ever heal but by degrees?
William Shakespeare *Othello*

wounding acid, barbed, bitter, caustic, cruel, cutting, damaging, destructive, distressing, grievous, harmful, hurtful, injurious, insult~

ing, maleficent, malicious, mordacious, offensive, pernicious, pointed, savage, scathing, slighting, spiteful, stinging, trenchant, unkind, vitriolic

wraith apparition, eidolon, ghost, phantom, revenant, shade (*literary*), spectre, spirit, spook (*informal*)

wrangle **1.** *verb* altercate, argue, bicker, brawl, contend, disagree, dispute, fall out (*informal*), fight, have words, quarrel, row, scrap, spar, squabble **2.** *noun* altercation, angry exchange, argy-bargy (*Brit. informal*), *bagarre*, barney (*informal*), bickering, brawl, clash, contest, controversy, dispute, falling-out (*informal*), quarrel, row, set-to (*informal*), slanging match (*Brit.*), squabble, tiff

wrap **1.** *verb* absorb, bind, bundle up, cloak, cover, encase, enclose, enfold, envelop, fold, immerse, muffle, pack, package, roll up, sheathe, shroud, surround, swathe, wind **2.** *noun* cape, cloak, mantle, shawl, stole
Antonyms *verb* disclose, open, strip, uncover, unfold, unpack, unwind, unwrap

wrapper case, cover, envelope, jacket, packaging, paper, sheath, sleeve, wrapping

wrap up **1.** bundle up, enclose, enwrap, giftwrap, pack, package **2.** dress warmly, muffle up, put warm clothes on, wear something warm **3.** *slang* be quiet, be silent, button it (*slang*), button one's lip (*slang*), hold one's tongue, put a sock in it (*Brit. slang*), shut one's face (*Brit. slang*), shut one's mouth (*slang*), shut one's trap (*slang*), shut up **4.** *informal* bring to a close, conclude, end, finish off, polish off, round off, terminate, tidy up, wind up

wrath anger, choler, displeasure, exasperation, fury, indignation, ire, irritation, passion, rage, resentment, temper
Antonyms amusement, contentment, delight, enjoyment, gladness, gratification, happiness, joy, pleasure, satisfaction

The tigers of wrath are wiser than the horses of instruction
William Blake *Proverbs of Hell*

I was angry with my friend,
I told my wrath, my wrath did end.
I was angry with my foe,
I told it not, my wrath did grow
William Blake *A Poison Tree*

nursing her wrath to keep it warm
Robert Burns *Tam o'Shanter*

wrath: anger of a superior quality and degree, appropriate to exalted characters and momentous occasions
Ambrose Bierce *The Devil's Dictionary*

wrathful angry, beside oneself with rage, choked, displeased, enraged, furious, incensed, indignant, infuriated, irate, on the warpath (*informal*), raging, wroth (*archaic*)
Antonyms amused, calm, contented, delighted, glad, gratified, happy, joyful, pleased, satisfied

wreak **1.** bring about, carry out, cause, create, effect, execute, exercise, inflict, visit, work **2.** express, give free rein to, give vent to, gratify, indulge, unleash, vent

wreath band, chaplet, coronet, crown, festoon, garland, loop, ring

wreathe adorn, coil, crown, encircle, enfold, engarland, entwine, envelop, enwrap, festoon, intertwine, interweave, surround, twine, twist, wind, wrap, writhe

wreck *verb* **1.** blow (*slang*), break, cock up (*Brit. slang*), dash to pieces, demolish, destroy, devastate, fuck up (*offensive taboo slang*), mar, play havoc with, ravage, ruin, screw up (*informal*), shatter, smash, spoil, total (*slang*), trash (*slang*), undo **2.** founder, go *or* run aground, run onto the rocks, shipwreck, strand *~noun* **3.** derelict, hulk, shipwreck, sunken vessel **4.** desolation, destruction, devastation, disruption, mess, overthrow, ruin, undoing
Antonyms *verb* build, conserve, create, fulfil, make possible, preserve, reconstruct, salvage, save *~noun* conservation, creation, formation, fulfilment, preservation, restoration, salvage, saving

wreckage debris, fragments, hulk, pieces, remains, rubble, ruin, wrack

wrench *verb* **1.** force, jerk, pull, rip, tear, tug, twist, wrest, wring, yank **2.** distort, rick, sprain, strain *~noun* **3.** jerk, pull, rip, tug, twist, yank **4.** sprain, strain, twist **5.** ache, blow, pain, pang, shock, upheaval, uprooting **6.** adjustable spanner, shifting spanner, spanner

wrest extract, force, pull, seize, strain, take, twist, win, wrench, wring

wrestle battle, combat, contend, fight, grapple, scuffle, strive, struggle, tussle

wretch **1.** asshole (*U.S. & Canad. taboo slang*), asswipe (*U.S. & Canad. taboo slang*), bad egg (*old-fashioned informal*), bastard (*offensive*), blackguard, bugger (*taboo slang*), cocksucker (*taboo slang*), cur, good-for-nothing, miscreant, mother (*taboo slang chiefly U.S.*), motherfucker (*taboo slang chiefly U.S.*), outcast, profligate, rascal, rat (*informal*), rogue, rotter (*slang, chiefly Brit.*), ruffian, scoundrel, scumbag (*slang*), shit (*taboo slang*), son-of-a-bitch (*slang, chiefly U.S. & Canad.*), swine, turd (*taboo slang*), vagabond, villain, worm **2.** poor thing, unfortunate

wretched **1.** abject, brokenhearted, cheerless, comfortless, crestfallen, dejected, deplorable, depressed, disconsolate, dismal, distressed, doleful, downcast, down in the dumps (*informal*), forlorn, funereal, gloomy, hapless, hopeless, melancholy, miserable, pathetic, pitiable, pitiful, poor, sorry, unfortunate, unhappy, woebegone, woeful, worthless **2.** calamitous, deplorable, inferior, miserable, paltry, pathetic, poor, sorry, worthless **3.** base, contemptible, crappy (*slang*), despicable, low, low-down (*informal*), mean, paltry, poxy (*slang*), scurvy, shabby, shameful, vile

Antonyms admirable, carefree, cheerful, contented, decent, enviable, excellent, flourishing, fortunate, great, happy, jovial, light-hearted, noble, prosperous, splendid, successful, thriving, untroubled, wonderful, worthy

wriggle *verb* **1.** jerk, jiggle, squirm, turn, twist, wag, waggle, wiggle, writhe **2.** crawl, slink, snake, twist and turn, worm, zigzag **3.** crawl, dodge, extricate oneself, manoeuvre, sneak, talk one's way out, worm ~*noun* **4.** jerk, jiggle, squirm, turn, twist, wag, waggle, wiggle

wring **1.** coerce, extort, extract, force, screw, squeeze, twist, wrench, wrest **2.** distress, hurt, lacerate, pain, pierce, rack, rend, stab, tear at, wound

wrinkle[1] **1.** *noun* corrugation, crease, crinkle, crow's-foot, crumple, fold, furrow, gather, line, pucker, rumple **2.** *verb* corrugate, crease, crinkle, crumple, fold, furrow, gather, line, pucker, ruck, rumple

Antonyms *verb* even out, flatten, iron, level, press, smooth, straighten, unfold

wrinkle[2] *noun* device, dodge, gimmick, idea, plan, ploy, ruse, scheme, stunt, tip, trick, wheeze (*Brit. slang*)

writ court order, decree, document, summons

write author (*nonstandard*), commit to paper, compose, copy, correspond, create, draft, draw up, indite, inscribe, jot down, pen, put down in black and white, put in writing, record, scribble, set down, take down, tell, transcribe

No man but a blockhead ever wrote, except for money

Dr. Johnson

write off **1.** cancel, cross out, disregard, forget about, give up for lost, score out, shelve **2.** *informal* crash, damage beyond repair, destroy, smash up, total (*slang*), trash (*slang*), wreck

writer author, columnist, essayist, hack, littérateur, man of letters, novelist, penman, penny-a-liner (*rare*), penpusher, scribbler, scribe, wordsmith

Novelists

Alain-Fournier [French]
Kingsley Amis [English]
Jane Austen [English]
Honoré de Balzac [French]
Simone de Beauvoir [French]
(Enoch) Arnold Bennett [English]
R(ichard) D(oddridge) Blackmore [English]
Anne Brontë [English]
Charlotte Brontë [English]
Emily (Jane) Brontë [English]
Mikhail Afanaseyev Bulgakov [Russian]
Anthony Burgess [British]
Samuel Butler [English]
Albert Camus [French]
Miguel de Cervantes [Spanish]
Agatha (Mary Clarissa) Christie [English]
Colette [French]
(William) Wilkie Collins [English]
Joseph Conrad [Polish-British]
James Fenimore Cooper [U.S.]
Stephen Crane [U.S.]
Daniel Defoe [English]
Charles (John Huffam) Dickens [English]
Fyodor Mikhailovich Dostoevsky [Russian]
Alexandre Dumas [French]
Daphne Du Maurier [English]
George Eliot [English]
William Faulkner [U.S.]
Henry Fielding [English]
F(rancis) Scott (Key) Fitzgerald [U.S.]
Gustave Flaubert [French]
E(dward) M(organ) Forster [English]
John Galsworthy [English]
Gabriel García Márquez [Colombian]
Mrs. Gaskell [English]
André Gide [French]
Nikolai Vasilievich Gogol [Russian]
William (Gerald) Golding [English]
Ivan Aleksandrovich Goncharov [Russian]
Maxim Gorki *or* Gorky [Russian]
Günter (Wilhelm) Grass [German]
Graham Greene [English]
Thomas Hardy [English]
L(eslie) P(oles) Hartley [English]
Nathaniel Hawthorne [U.S.]
Joseph Heller [U.S.]
Ernest Hemingway [U.S.]
Hermann Hesse [German]
Anthony Hope [English]
Victor (Marie) Hugo [French]
Aldous (Leonard) Huxley [English]
Christopher Isherwood [English-U.S.]
Henry James [U.S.-British]
James (Augustine Aloysius) Joyce [Irish]
Franz Kafka [Czech]
Jack Kerouac [U.S.]
D(avid) H(erbert) Lawrence [English]
Mikhail Yurievich Lermontov [Russian]
Jack London [U.S.]
(Clarence) Malcolm Lowry [English]
Thomas Mann [German]
Frederick Marryat [English]
Herman Melville [U.S.]
Vladimir Vladimirovich Nabokov [Russian-U.S.]
Baroness Emmuska Orczy [Hungarian-British]
George Orwell [English]
Boris Leonidovich Pasternak [Russian]
Marcel Proust [French]
Samuel Richardson [English]

(Ahmed) Salman Rushdie [Indian-British]
Antoine de Saint-Exupéry [French]
George Sand [French]
Jean-Paul Sartre [French]
Walter Scott [Scottish]
Georges Simenon [Belgian]
Tobias George Smollett [Scottish]
Alexander Isayevich Solzhenitsyn [Russian]
John (Ernst) Steinbeck [U.S.]
Stendhal [French]
Laurence Sterne [Irish-British]
Robert Louis (Balfour) Stevenson [Scottish]
Bram Stoker [Irish]
Harriet Elizabeth Beecher Stowe [U.S.]
William Makepeace Thackeray [English]
J(ohn) R(onald) R(euel) Tolkien [English]
Leo Tolstoy [Russian]
Anthony Trollope [English]
Ivan Sergeyevich Turgenev [Russian]
Mark Twain [U.S.]
Jules Verne [French]
Evelyn (Arthur Saint John) Waugh [English]
H(erbert) G(eorge) Wells [English]
Thornton Wilder [U.S.]
P(elham) G(renville) Wodehouse [English-U.S.]
Virginia Woolf [English]
Emile Zola [French]

Poets

Ludovico Ariosto [Italian]
Matthew Arnold [English]
W(ystan) H(ugh) Auden [English-U.S.]
Charles Pierre Baudelaire [French]
John Betjeman [English]
William Blake [English]
Rupert (Chawner) Brooke [English]
Elizabeth Barrett Browning [English]
Robert Browning [English]
Robert Burns [Scottish]
George Gordon Byron [English]
Callimachus [Greek]
Luis Vaz de Camoëns [Portuguese]
Gaius Valerius Catullus [Roman]
Geoffrey Chaucer [English]
John Clare [English]
Samuel Taylor Coleridge [English]
William Cowper [English]
e(dward) e(stlin) cummings [U.S.]
Dante (Alighieri) [Italian]
Emily Dickinson [U.S.]
John Donne [English]
John Dryden [English]
T(homas) S(tearns) Eliot [U.S.-British]
Edward Fitzgerald [English]
Robert (Lee) Frost [U.S.]
Johann Wolfgang von Goethe [German]
Thomas Gray [English]
George Herbert [English]
Hesiod [Greek]
Homer [Greek]
Thomas Hood [English]
Gerard Manley Hopkins [English]
Horace [Roman]
A(lfred) E(dward) Housman [English]
Ted Hughes [English]
Juvenal [Roman]
John Keats [English]
(Joseph) Rudyard Kipling [English]
Alphonse Marie Louis de Prat de Lamartine [French]
Walter Savage Landor [English]
William Langland [English]
Philip Larkin [English]
Henry Wadsworth Longfellow [U.S.]
Richard Lovelace [English]
Lucretius [Roman]
Martial [Roman]
Andrew Marvell [English]
John Milton [English]
Pablo Neruda [Chilean]
Omar Khayyam [Persian]
Ovid [Roman]
Wilfred Owen [British]
Petrarch [Italian]
Pindar [Greek]
Sylvia Plath [U.S.]
Alexander Pope [English]
Ezra (Loomis) Pound [U.S.]
Sextus Propertius [Roman]
Aleksander Sergeyevich Pushkin [Russian]
Rainer Maria Rilke [Austro-German]
Arthur Rimbaud [French]
Christina Georgina Rossetti [English]
Dante Gabriel Rossetti [English]
Sappho [Greek]
Johann Christoph Friedrich von Schiller [German]
Sir Walter Scott [Scottish]
William Shakespeare [English]
Percy Bysshe Shelley [English]
Sir Philip Sidney [English]
Robert Southey [English]
Edmund Spenser [English]
Algernon Charles Swinburne [English]
Torquato Tasso [Italian]
Alfred, Lord Tennyson [English]
Dylan (Marlais) Thomas [Welsh]
Paul Verlaine [French]
Alfred Victor de Vigny [French]
François Villon [French]
Virgil [Roman]
Walt(er) Whitman [U.S.]
William Wordsworth [English]
W(illiam) B(utler) Yeats [Irish]

Dramatists

Jean Anouilh [French]
Aristophanes [Greek]
Pierre Augustin Caron de Beaumarchais [French]
Samuel (Barclay) Beckett [Irish]
Bertolt Brecht [German]
Pedro Calderón de la Barca [Spanish]
Anton Pavlovich Chekhov [Russian]
William Congreve [English]
Pierre Corneille [French]
Noël (Pierce) Coward [English]
Euripides [Greek]
John Fletcher [English]
John Ford [English]
W(illiam) S(chwenk) Gilbert [English]
Oliver Goldsmith [Irish]
Václav Havel [Czech]
Henrik Ibsen [Norwegian]
Eugène Ionesco

[Romanian-French]
Ben Jonson [English]
Thomas Kyd [English]
Lope de Vega [Spanish]
Federico Garcia Lorca [Spanish]
Christopher Marlowe [English]
Menander [Greek]
Arthur Miller [U.S.]
Molière [French]
Sean O'Casey [Irish]
Eugene (Gladstone) O'Neill [U.S.]
Joe (Kingsley) Orton [English]
John (James) Osborne [English]
Arthur Wing Pinero [English]
Harold Pinter [English]
Luigi Pirandello [Italian]
Titus Maccius Plautus [Roman]
Aleksander Sergeyevich Pushkin [Russian]
Jean Baptiste Racine [French]
Terence Mervyn Rattigan [English]
William Shakespeare [English]
George Bernard Shaw [Irish]
Richard Brinsley Sheridan [Irish]
Sophocles [Greek]
Tom Stoppard [Czech-British]
August Strindberg [Swedish]
John Millington Synge [Irish]
Terence [Roman]
John Webster [English]
Oscar (Fingal O'Flahertie Wills) Wilde [Irish]
Thornton Wilder [U.S.]
Tennessee Williams [U.S.]

Short story writers
Giovanni Boccaccio [Italian]
Jorge Luis Borges [Argentinian]
Arthur Conan Doyle [British]
Joel Chandler Harris [U.S.]
Washington Irving [U.S.]
Katherine Mansfield [N.Z.-British]
W(illiam) Somerset Maugham [English]
(Henri Rene Albert) Guy de Maupassant [French]
O. Henry [U.S.]
Edgar Allan Poe [U.S.]

Children's writers
Louisa May Alcott [U.S.]
Hans Christian Andersen [Danish]
J(ames) M(atthew) Barrie [Scottish]
Enid (Mary) Blyton [English]
Lewis Carroll [English]
Roald Dahl [British]
Kenneth Grahame [Scottish]
C(live) S(taples) Lewis [English]
A(lan) A(lexander) Milne [English]

Other writers
Aesop [Greek]
James Boswell [Scottish]
John Bunyan [English]
Thomas Carlyle [Scottish]
Marcus Tullius Cicero [Roman]
William Cobbett [English]
Desiderius Erasmus [Dutch]
Edward Gibbon [English]
William Hazlitt [English]
Jerome K(lapka) Jerome [English]
Samuel Johnson [English]
Thomas Malory [English]
Michel Eyquem de Montaigne [French]
Samuel Pepys [English]
François Rabelais [French]
John Ruskin [English]

Some editors are failed writers - but so are most writers
T.S. Eliot

Writers, like teeth, are divided into incisors and grinders
Walter Bagehot *Estimates of some Englishmen and Scotchmen*

writhe contort, distort, jerk, squirm, struggle, thrash, thresh, toss, twist, wiggle, wriggle

writing **1.** calligraphy, chirography, hand, handwriting, penmanship, print, scrawl, scribble, script **2.** book, composition, document, letter, opus, publication, title, work **3.** belles-lettres, letters, literature

What is written without effort is in general read without pleasure
Dr. Johnson *Johnsonian Miscellanies*

Many suffer from the incurable disease of writing, and it becomes chronic in their sick minds
Juvenal *Satires*

All writing is garbage
Antonin Artaud *Selected Writings*

wrong *adjective* **1.** erroneous, fallacious, false, faulty, inaccurate, incorrect, in error, mistaken, off base (*U.S. & Canad. informal*), off beam (*informal*), off target, out, unsound, untrue, way off beam (*informal*), wide of the mark **2.** bad, blameworthy, criminal, crooked, dishonest, dishonourable, evil, felonious, illegal, illicit, immoral, iniquitous, not cricket (*informal*), reprehensible, sinful, under-the-table, unethical, unfair, unjust, unlawful, wicked, wrongful **3.** funny, improper, inappropriate, inapt, incongruous, incorrect, indecorous, infelicitous, malapropos, not done, unacceptable, unbecoming, unconventional, undesirable, unfitting, unhappy, unseemly, unsuitable **4.** amiss, askew, awry, defective, faulty, not working, out of commission, out of order **5.** inside, inverse, opposite, reverse *~adverb* **6.** amiss, askew, astray, awry, badly, erroneously, inaccurately, incorrectly, mistakenly, wrongly **7.** **go wrong a.** come to grief (*informal*), come to nothing, fail, fall through, flop (*informal*), miscarry, misfire **b.** boob (*Brit. slang*), err, go astray, make a mistake, slip up (*informal*), **c.** break down, cease to function, conk out (*informal*), fail, go kaput (*informal*), go on the blink (*slang*), go phut (*informal*), malfunction, misfire **d.** err, fall from grace, go astray, go off the straight and narrow (*informal*), go to the bad, lapse, sin *~noun* **8.** abuse, bad *or* evil deed, crime, error, grievance, im~

morality, inequity, infraction, infringement, iniquity, injury, injustice, misdeed, offence, sin, sinfulness, transgression, trespass, unfairness, wickedness **9. in the wrong** at fault, blameworthy, guilty, in error, mistaken, off beam (*informal*), off course, off target, to be blamed *~verb* **10.** abuse, cheat, discredit, dishonour, dump on (*slang, chiefly U.S.*), harm, hurt, ill-treat, ill-use, impose upon, injure, malign, maltreat, misrepresent, mistreat, oppress, shit on (*taboo slang*), take advantage of **Antonyms** *adjective* accurate, appropriate, apt, becoming, commendable, correct, ethical, fair, fitting, godly, honest, honourable, just, laudable, lawful, legal, moral, praiseworthy, precise, proper, righteous, rightful, seemly, sensible, square, suitable, true, upright, virtuous *~adverb* accurately, correctly, exactly, precisely, properly, squarely, truly *~noun* decency, fairness, favour, good, good deed, goodness, good turn, high-mindedness, honesty, lawfulness, legality, morality, propriety, virtue *~verb* aid, do a favour, help, support, treat well

A man should never be ashamed to own he has been in the wrong, which is but saying, in other words, that he is wiser today than he was yesterday

Alexander Pope *Miscellanies*

Two wrongs don't make a right

wrongdoer criminal, culprit, delinquent, evildoer, lawbreaker, malefactor, miscreant, offender, sinner, transgressor, trespasser (*archaic*), villain

wrongful blameworthy, criminal, dishonest, dishonourable, evil, felonious, illegal, illegitimate, illicit, immoral, improper, reprehensible, under-the-table, unethical, unfair, unjust, unlawful, wicked
Antonyms ethical, fair, honest, honourable, just, lawful, legal, legitimate, moral, proper, rightful

wrong-headed **1.** bull-headed, contrary, cross-grained, dogged, froward (*archaic*), inflexible, intransigent, mulish, obdurate, obstinate, perverse, pig-headed, refractory, self-willed, stubborn, wilful **2.** erroneous, fallacious, false, faulty, incorrect, in error, misguided, mistaken, off target, unsound, wrong

wrought-up agitated, animated, aroused, at fever pitch, beside oneself, excited, inflamed, keyed up, moved, overwrought, roused, stirred, strung up (*informal*), worked-up, wound up (*informal*)

wry **1.** askew, aslant, awry, contorted, crooked, deformed, distorted, off the level, skewwhiff (*Brit. informal*), twisted, uneven, warped **2.** droll, dry, ironic, mocking, mordacious, pawky (*Scot.*), sarcastic, sardonic
Antonyms (*sense 1*) aligned, even, level, smooth, straight, unbent

X

Xmas Christmas, Christmastide, festive season, Noel, Yule (*archaic*), Yuletide (*archaic*)

'Twas the night before Christmas, when all
through the house
Not a creature was stirring, not even a mouse
Clement C. Moore *A Visit from St. Nichola*

X-rays Röntgen rays (*old name*)

Y

yahoo barbarian, beast, boor, brute, churl, lout, philistine, roughneck (*slang*), rowdy, savage, yob *or* yobbo (*Brit. slang*)

yak 1. *verb* blather, chatter, chew the fat *or* rag (*slang*), gab (*informal*), gossip, jabber, jaw (*slang*), rabbit (on) (*Brit. informal*), run off at the mouth (*sang*), run on, spout, tattle, waffle (*informal, chiefly Brit.*), witter on (*informal*), yap (*informal*) 2. *noun* blather, chat, chinwag (*Brit. informal*), confab (*informal*), gossip, hot air (*informal*), jaw (*slang*), waffle (*informal, chiefly Brit.*), yackety-yak (*slang*), yammer (*informal*)

yank *verb/noun* hitch, jerk, pull, snatch, tug, wrench

yap *verb* 1. yammer (*informal*), yelp, yip (*chiefly U.S.*) 2. *informal* babble, blather, chatter, chew the fat *or* rag, go on, gossip, jabber, jaw (*slang*), prattle, rabbit (on) (*Brit. informal*), run off at the mouth (*slang*), spout, talk, tattle, waffle (*informal, chiefly Brit.*)

yardstick benchmark, criterion, gauge, meas~ ure, par, standard, touchstone

yarn *noun* 1. fibre, thread 2. *informal* anecdote, cock-and-bull story (*informal*), fable, story, tale, tall story

yawning cavernous, chasmal, gaping, vast, wide, wide-open

yearly annual, annually, every year, once a year, per annum

yearn ache, covet, crave, desire, eat one's heart out over, hanker, have a yen for (*informal*), hunger, itch, languish, long, lust, pant, pine, set one's heart upon, suspire (*archaic or poet~ ic*), would give one's eyeteeth for

years 1. age, dotage, eld (*archaic*), old age, se~ cond childhood, senescence, senility 2. days, generation(s), lifetime, span, time

yell 1. *verb* bawl, holler (*informal*), howl, scream, screech, shout, shriek, squeal 2. *noun* cry, howl, scream, screech, shriek, whoop
Antonyms *verb* mumble, murmur, mutter, say softly, whisper

yelp cry, yammer (*informal*), yap, yip (*chiefly U.S.*), yowl

yen *noun* ache, craving, desire, hankering, hunger, itch, longing, passion, thirst, yearning

yes man ass-kisser (*U.S. & Canad. taboo slang*), bootlicker (*informal*), bosses' lackey, company man, crawler (*slang*), creature, min~ ion, sycophant, timeserver, toady

yet 1. as yet, so far, thus far, until now, up to now 2. however, nevertheless, notwithstand~ ing, still 3. additionally, as well, besides, fur~ ther, in addition, into the bargain, moreover, over and above, still, to boot 4. already, just now, now, right now, so soon

yield *verb* 1. afford, bear, bring forth, bring in, earn, furnish, generate, give, net, pay, prod~ uce, provide, return, supply *~noun* 2. crop, earnings, harvest, income, output, produce, profit, return, revenue, takings *~verb* 3. aban~ don, abdicate, admit defeat, bow, capitulate, cave in (*informal*), cede, cry quits, give in, give up the struggle, give way, knuckle under, lay down one's arms, part with, raise the white flag, relinquish, resign, resign oneself, submit, succumb, surrender, throw in the towel 4. accede, agree, allow, bow, comply, concede, consent, go along with, grant, permit
Antonyms *verb* appropriate, attack, combat, commandeer, consume, counterattack, defy, grab, hold on to, hold out, keep, lose, main~ tain, oppose, reserve, resist, retain, seize, struggle, use, use up *~noun* consumption, in~ put, loss

yielding 1. accommodating, acquiescent, bid~ dable, compliant, docile, easy, flexible, obedi~ ent, pliant, submissive, tractable 2. elastic, pliable, quaggy, resilient, soft, spongy, springy, supple, unresisting
Antonyms (*sense 1*) dogged, headstrong, mul~ ish, obstinate, opinionated, perverse, stiff-necked, stubborn, tenacious, wilful

yob, yobbo heavy (*slang*), hoodlum, hooligan, lout, rough (*informal*), roughneck (*slang*), rowdy, ruffian, thug, tough, yahoo

yoke *noun* 1. bond, chain, coupling, ligament, link, tie 2. bondage, burden, enslavement, helotry, oppression, serfdom, service, servility, servitude, slavery, thraldom, vassalage *~verb* 3. bracket, connect, couple, harness, hitch, join, link, tie, unite

yokel boor, bucolic, clodhopper (*informal*), (country) bumpkin, country cousin, country~ man, hayseed (*U.S. & Canad. informal*), hick (*informal, chiefly U.S. & Canad.*), hillbilly, hind (*obsolete*), peasant (*informal*), rustic

young *adjective* **1.** adolescent, callow, green, growing, immature, infant, in the springtime of life, junior, juvenile, little, unfledged, youthful **2.** at an early stage, early, fledgling, new, newish, not far advanced, recent, undeveloped *~noun* **3.** babies, brood, family, issue, litter, little ones, offspring, progeny
Antonyms *adjective* adult, advanced, aged, developed, elderly, experienced, full-grown, grown-up, mature, old, ripe, senior, venerable *~noun* adult, grown-up, parent

youngster boy, cub, girl, juvenile, kid (*informal*), lad, lass, pup (*informal, chiefly Brit.*), teenager, teenybopper (*slang*), urchin, young adult, young hopeful, young person, young shaver (*informal*), young 'un (*informal*), youth

youth 1. adolescence, boyhood, early life, girlhood, immaturity, juvenescence, salad days, young days **2.** adolescent, boy, kid (*informal*), lad, shaveling (*archaic*), stripling, teenager, young man, young shaver (*informal*), youngster **3.** teenagers, the rising generation, the young, younger generation, young people
Antonyms adult, adulthood, age, grown-up, later life, manhood, maturity, OAP, old age, pensioner, senior citizen, the aged, the elderly, the old, womanhood

Young men have more virtue than old men; they have more generous sentiments in every respect
Dr. Johnson

Youth, which is forgiven everything, forgives itself nothing: age, which forgives itself anything, is forgiven nothing
George Bernard Shaw *Maxims for Revolutionists*

Whom the gods love dies young
Menander *Mouostichoi*

The whining schoolboy, with his satchel
And shining morning face, creeping like snail
Unwillingly to school
William Shakespeare *As You Like It*

Bliss was it in that dawn to be alive,
But to be young was very heaven
William Wordsworth *The Prelude*

Youth is a disease that must be borne with patiently! Time, indeed, will cure it
R.H. Benson

Hope I die before I get old
Pete Townshend *My Generation*

The atrocious crime of being a young man... I shall neither attempt to palliate nor deny
William Pitt, Earl of Chapman

Youth must be served

youthful 1. boyish, childish, girlish, immature, inexperienced, juvenile, pubescent, puerile, young **2.** active, fresh, spry, vigorous, young at heart, young looking
Antonyms adult, aged, ageing, ancient, careworn, decaying, decrepit, elderly, grown-up, hoary, mature, old, over the hill, senile, senior, tired, waning, weary

yowl *verb* bawl, bay, caterwaul, cry, give tongue, howl, screech, squall, ululate, wail, yell

yucky, yukky beastly, dirty, disgusting, foul, grotty (*slang*), horrible, messy, mucky, revolting (*informal*), unpleasant

Z

zany 1. *adjective* clownish, comical, crazy, eccentric, funny, goofy (*informal*), kooky (*U.S. informal*), loony (*slang*), madcap, nutty (*slang*), oddball (*informal*), wacko *or* whacko (*informal*), wacky (*slang*) 2. *noun* buffoon, clown, comedian, jester, joculator *or* (*fem.*) joculatrix, joker, merry-andrew, nut (*slang*), screwball (*slang, chiefly U.S. & Canad.*), wag

zeal ardour, devotion, eagerness, earnestness, enthusiasm, fanaticism, fervency, fervour, fire, gusto, keenness, militancy, passion, spirit, verve, warmth, zest
Antonyms apathy, coolness, indifference, passivity, stoicism, torpor, unresponsiveness

zealot bigot, energumen, enthusiast, extremist, fanatic, fiend (*informal*), maniac, militant

zealous ablaze, afire, ardent, burning, devoted, eager, earnest, enthusiastic, fanatical, fervent, fervid, impassioned, keen, militant, passionate, rabid, spirited
Antonyms apathetic, cold, cool, half-hearted, indifferent, lackadaisical, lacklustre, languorous, listless, low-key, sceptical, torpid, unenthusiastic, unimpassioned

zenith acme, apex, apogee, climax, crest, height, high noon, high point, meridian, peak, pinnacle, summit, top, vertex
Antonyms base, bottom, depths, lowest point, nadir, rock bottom

zero 1. cipher, naught, nil, nothing, nought 2. bottom, lowest point *or* ebb, nadir, nothing, rock bottom

zero hour appointed hour, crisis, moment of decision, moment of truth, turning point, vital moment

zero in (on) aim, bring to bear, concentrate, converge, direct, focus, home in, level, pinpoint, train

zest 1. appetite, delectation, enjoyment, gusto, keenness, relish, zeal, zing (*informal*) 2. charm, flavour, interest, kick (*informal*), piquancy, pungency, relish, savour, smack, spice, tang, taste
Antonyms abhorrence, apathy, aversion, disinclination, distaste, indifference, lack of enthusiasm, loathing, repugnance, weariness

zing animation, brio, dash, energy, go (*informal*), life, liveliness, oomph (*informal*), pep, pizzazz *or* pizazz (*informal*), spirit, vigour, vitality, zest, zip (*informal*)

zip 1. *noun, figurative* brio, drive, energy, get-up-and-go (*informal*), go (*informal*), gusto, life, liveliness, oomph (*informal*), pep, pizzazz *or* pizazz (*informal*), punch (*informal*), sparkle, spirit, verve, vigour, vim (*slang*), vitality, zest, zing (*informal*) 2. *verb* barrel (along) (*informal, chiefly U.S. & Canad.*), burn rubber (*informal*), dash, flash, fly, hurry, rush, shoot, speed, tear, whiz (*informal*), zoom
Antonyms apathy, indifference, inertia, laziness, lethargy, listlessness, sloth, sluggishness

zone area, belt, district, region, section, sector, sphere

zoology

Branches of zoology

arachnology
archaeozoology
cetology
entomology
ethology
herpetology
ichthyology
malacology
mammalogy
myrmecology
ophiology
ornithology
palaeozoology
primatology
protozoology
zoogeography
zoography
zoometry
zootomy

Zoology terms

abdomen
aestivation
amphibian
antenna
anterior
appendage
arachnid
arthropod
biped
bivalve
carnivore
caudal
chordate
chrysalis
cocoon
coelenterate
coelem
colony
crustacean
decapod
dipteran
dorsal
echinoderm
edentate
fin
gastropod *or* gasteropod
gill
herbivore
hibernation
imago
insectivore
invertebrate
larva
lepidopteran
marsupial
metamorphosis
migration
omnivore
parenchyma
passerine
pectoral
placenta
posterior

predator
prey
primate
protozoan
pupa
quadruped
raptor
reptile
rodent
ruminant
segment
skeleton
spawn
spine
sucker
thorax
ventral
vertebrate

Famous zoologists

Charles (Robert) Darwin [English]
Richard Dawkins [British]
Gerald (Malcolm) Durrell [British]
Karl von Frisch [Austrian]
Paul Kammerer [Austrian]
Alfred Charles Kinsey [U.S.]
Jean Baptiste Pierre Antoine de Monet Lamarck [French]
Konrad Zacharias Lorenz [Austrian]
Thomas Hunt Morgan [U.S.]
Nikolaas Tinbergen [British]
Alfred Russel Wallace [British]
Solly Zuckerman [British]

zoom *verb* barrel (along) (*informal, chiefly U.S. & Canad.*), burn rubber (*informal*), buzz, dash, dive, flash, fly, hare (*Brit. informal*), hum (*slang*), hurtle, pelt, rip (*informal*), rush, shoot, speed, streak, tear, whirl, whiz (*informal*), zip (*informal*)

Supplements

Languages and Alphabets

A simplified tree of Indo-European languages

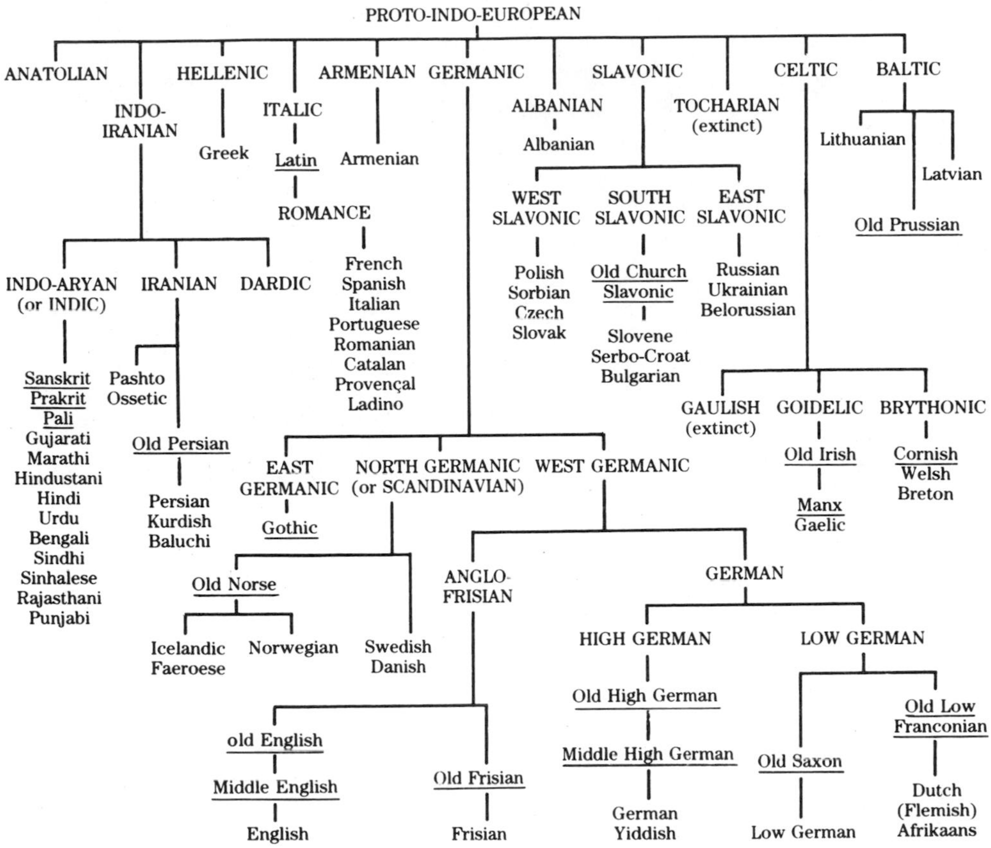

Note: underlined languages
are no longer spoken

The development of the modern Roman alphabet

Phoenician
Early Hebrew
Early Aramaic
Early Greek
Classical Greek
Etruscan
Early Latin
Classical Latin
Russian-Cyrillic
Modern Roman
A B C D E F G H I J K L M N O P Q R S T U V W X Y Z

The Plant Kingdom

A simplified classification

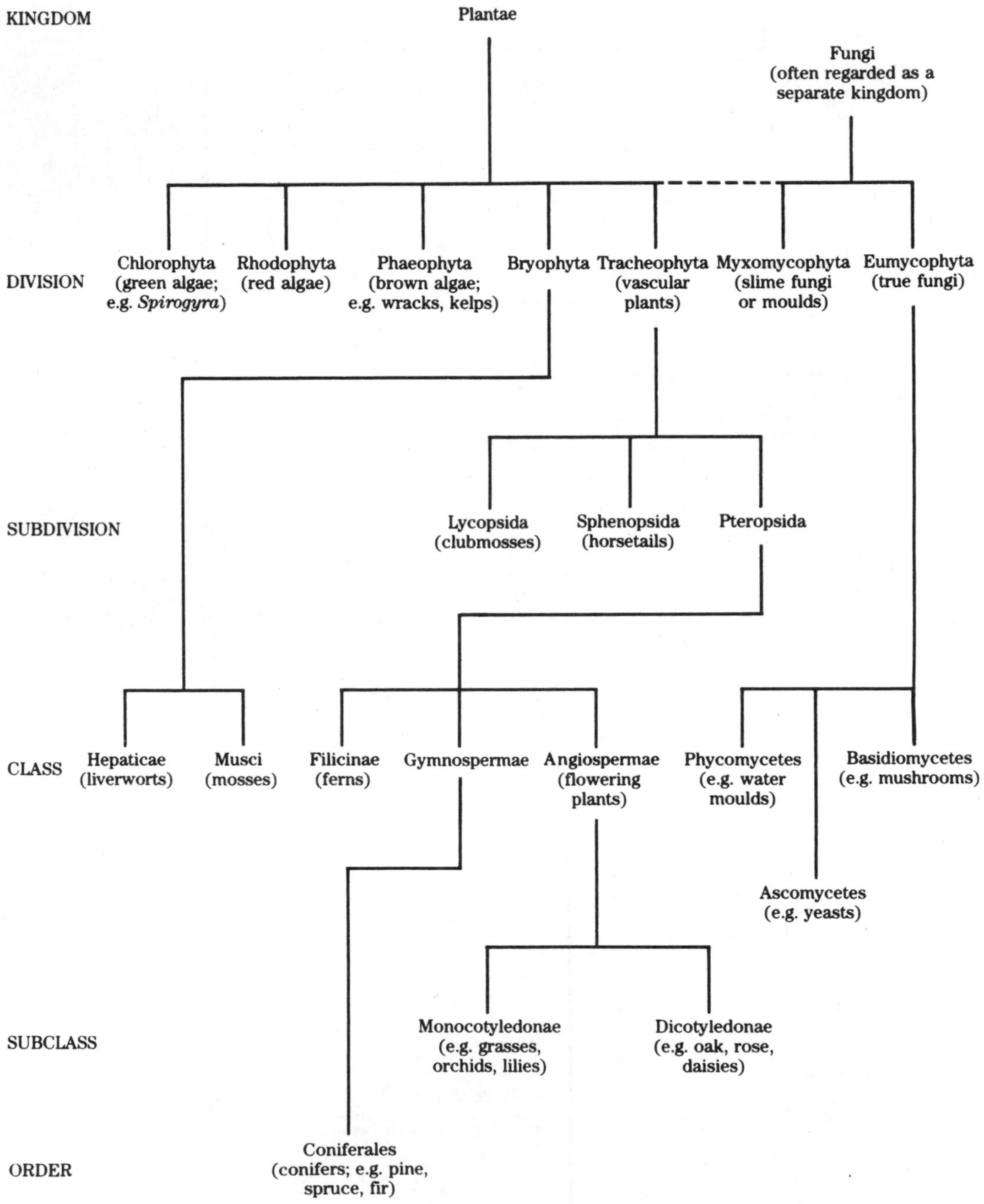

The Animal Kingdom

A simplified classification

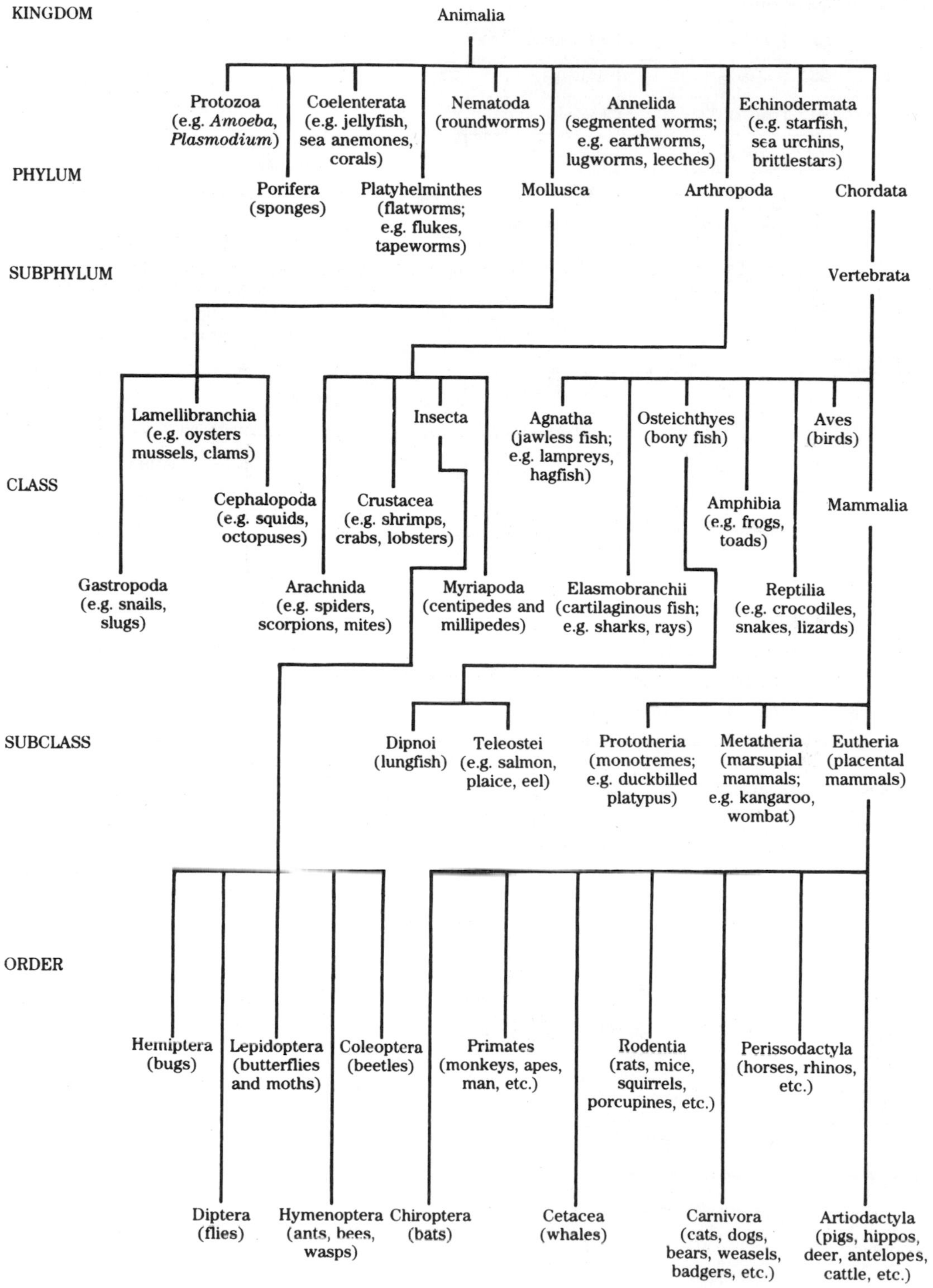

Music Symbols, etc.

Notes and rests

Note	*Rest*	*British*	*American*
𝅜	𝄺	breve	double-whole note
𝅝	𝄻	semibreve	whole note
𝅗𝅥	𝄼	minim	half note
𝅘𝅥	𝄽 *or* 𝄿	crotchet	quarter note
𝅘𝅥𝅮	𝄾	quaver	eighth note
𝅘𝅥𝅯	𝄿	semiquaver	sixteenth note
𝅘𝅥𝅰	𝅀	demisemiquaver	thirty-second note
𝅘𝅥𝅱	𝅁	hemidemisemiquaver	sixty-fourth note

Clefs

Fixed note	*Position of middle C*	*Clef*
		G *or* treble clef
		F *or* bass clef
		C (soprano) clef
		C (alto) clef
		C (tenor) clef

Accidentals

♯ sharp; raising note one semitone

𝄪 double sharp; raising note one tone

♭ flat; lowering note one semitone

𝄫 double flat; lowering note one tone

♮ natural; restoring note to normal pitch after sharp or flat

Ornaments and decorations

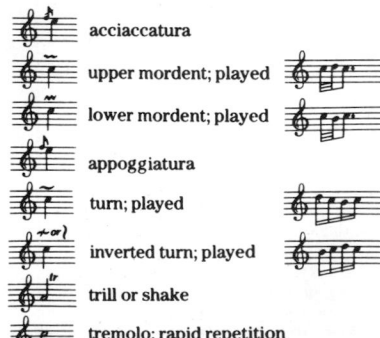

acciaccatura

upper mordent; played

lower mordent; played

appoggiatura

turn; played

inverted turn; played

trill or shake

tremolo; rapid repetition

Staccato marks and signs of accentuation

mezzo-staccato: shorten note by about ¼

staccato: shorten note by about ½

staccatissimo: shorten note by about ¾

detached: accented

attack

Time signatures

Simple duple:

- 2/2 *or* ¢ two minim beats
- 2/4 two crotchet beats
- 2/8 two quaver beats

Compound duple:

- 6/4 two dotted minim beats
- 6/8 two dotted crotchet beats
- 6/16 two dotted quaver beats

Simple triple:

- 3/2 three minim beats
- 3/4 three crotchet beats
- 3/8 three quaver beats

Compound triple:

- 9/4 three dotted minim beats
- 9/8 three dotted crotchet beats
- 9/16 three dotted quaver beats

Simple quadruple:

- 4/2 four minim beats
- 4/4 *or* C four crotchet beats
- 4/8 four quaver beats

Compound quadruple:

- 12/4 four dotted minim beats
- 12/8 four dotted crotchet beats
- 12/16 four dotted quaver beats

Irregular rhythms

2 duplet or couplet

3 triplet

4 quadruplet

5 quintruplet

Dynamics

crescendo

diminuendo

Curved lines

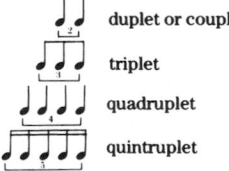

tie or bind; two notes played as one

slur or legato; play smoothly (in one bow on stringed instrument)

Other

repeat preceding section

end of section or piece

𝄐 pause

8^e play an octave above notes written

Music Symbols, etc.

Range of some musical instruments

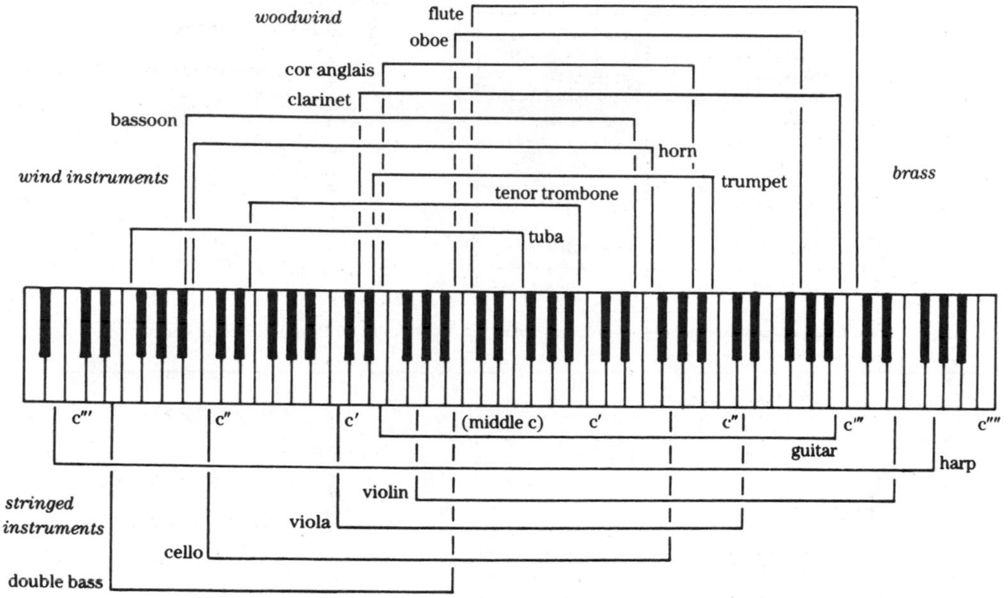

Keys and key signatures

Major key	*Relative minor key*	*Key signature (sharp keys)*	*Key signature (flat keys)*
C	A	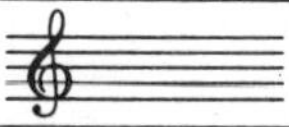	
G	E	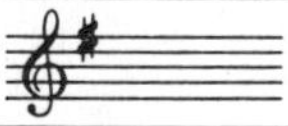	
D	B		
A	F♯		
E	C♯		
B = C♭	G♯		
F♯ = G♭	E♭		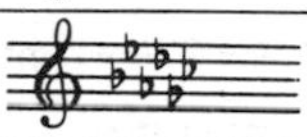
C♯ = D♭	B♭		
A♭	F		
E♭	C		
B♭	G		
F	D		

The Solar System

The Planets

Planet	*Equatorial diameter (kilometres)*	*Mass (earth masses* = 5.974 × 10^{24} kg)	*Mean distance from sun (millions of kilometres)*	*Sidereal period*
Mercury	4878	0.06	57.91	87.97 days
Venus	12 104	0.82	108.21	224.70 days
Earth	12 756	1.000	149.60	365.26 days
Mars	6787	0.11	227.94	686.980 days
Jupiter	142 800	317.83	778.34	11.86 years
Saturn	120 000	95.17	1427.01	29.46 years
Uranus	50 800	14.50	2869.6	84.01 years
Neptune	48 600	17.20	4496.7	164.79 years
Pluto	3000?	0.002	5907	247.70 years

Planetary Satellites

Planet & satellite	*Diameter (km)*	*Distance from primary (1000km)*	*Year of discovery*
EARTH			
Moon	3 476	384.40	–
MARS			
Phobos	22	9.38	1877
Deimos	13	23.46	1877
JUPITER			
Metis	40	128	1979
Adrastea	20	129	1979
Amalthea	190	181	1892
Thebe	100	222	1979
Io	3 630	422	1610
Europa	3 140	671	1610
Ganymede	5 260	1 070	1610
Callisto	4 800	1 883	1610
Leda	15	11 094	1974
Himalia	185	11 480	1904
Lysithea	35	11 720	1938
Elara	75	11 737	1905
Ananke	30	21 200	1951
Carme	40	22 600	1938
Pasiphae	50	23 500	1908
Sinope	35	23 700	1914
SATURN			
Atlas	30	138	1980
Prometheus	105	139	1980
Pandora	90	142	1980
Janus	90	151	1966
Epimetheus	120	151	1966
Mimas	390	186	1789
Enceladus	500	238	1789
Tethys	1 060	295	1684
Telesto	30	295	1980
Calypso	25	295	1980
Dione	1 120	377	1684
Helene	30	377	1980
Rhea	1 530	527	1672
Titan	5 150	1 222	1655
Hyperion	290	1 481	1848
Iapetus	1 460	3 561	1671
Phoebe	220	12 952	1898
URANUS			
Cordelia	40	50	1986
Ophelia	50	54	1986
Bianca	50	59	1986
Cressida	60	62	1986
Desdemona	60	63	1986
Juliet	80	64	1986
Portia	90	66	1986
Rosalind	60	70	1986
Belinda	50	75	1986
Puck	170	86	1985
Miranda	480	129	1948
Ariel	1 160	191	1851
Umbriel	1 190	266	1851
Titania	1 610	436	1787
Oberon	1 550	584	1787
NEPTUNE			
1989 N6	50	48	1989
1989 N5	90	50	1989
1989 N3	140	53	1989
1989 N4	160	62	1989
1989 N2	200	74	1989
1989 N1	420	118	1989
Triton	2 720	354	1846
Nereid	340	5 511	1949
PLUTO			
Charon	1 200	19	1978

Classical and Foreign Words and Phrases

Abbreviations - L. Latin; G. Greek; F. French; It. Italian; Ger. German.

à bas [F.] down with.
ab initio [L.] from the beginning.
ab ovo [L.] from the beginning.
absit omen [L.] may there be no ill omen.
accouchement [F.] childbirth, confinement.
à cheval [F.] on horseback, astride.
à deux [F.] of, for two persons.
ad hoc [L.] for this special object.
ad hominem [L.] to the man.
ad infinitum [L.] to infinity.
ad interim [L.] in the meanwhile.
ad majorem Dei gloriam [L.] for the greater glory of God.
ad nauseam [L.] to the point of disgust.
ad referendum [L.] for consideration.
ad rem [L.] to the point.
adsum [L.] I am here; present!
ad valorem [L.] according to value.
affaire d'amour [F.] a love affair.
affaire d'honneur [F.] an affair of honour, a duel.
affaire du coeur [F.] an affair of the heart.
a fortiori [L.] with stronger reason.
agent provocateur [F.] a police or secret service spy.
aide mémoire [F.] memorandum; summary.
à la carte [F.] picking from the bill of fare; *see* **table d'hote**.
à la française [F.] in the French style.
à la mode [F.] in the fashion.
al dente [It.] cooked so as to be firm when eaten.
al fresco [It.] in the open air.
alma mater [L.] benign mother; the term is used by former students in referring to their university.
alter ego [L.] another self, a close friend.
alto relievo [It.] high relief.
amende honorable [F.] apology.
amor patriae [L.] love of country.
amour propre [F.] self-esteem.
ancien régime [F.] the old order.
anglice [L.] in English.
anno Domini [L.] in the year of our Lord.
anno regni [L.] in the year of the reign.
anno urbis conditae [L.] (**A.U.C.**) in the year from the time of the building of the City (Rome).
annus mirabilis [L.] year of wonder.
ante meridiem [L.] before noon.
aperçu [F.] summary; insight.
à propos [F.] to the point.
arrière-pensée [F.] mental reservation.
arrivederci [It.] goodbye.
au contraire [F.] on the contrary.
au courant [F.] fully acquainted (with).
au fait [F.] fully informed; expert.
au fond [F.] fundamentally; essentially.
au naturel [F.] naked; uncooked or plainly cooked.
au revoir [F.] good-bye, till we meet again.
auf Wiedersehen [Ger.] good-bye, till we meet again.
auto da fé [Portuguese] act of faith, the public burning of heretics.

beau geste [F.] noble or gracious act.
beau idéal [F.] ideal excellence, imagined state of perfection.
beau monde [F.] fashionable world.
bel esprit [F.] a man of wit.
bête noire [F.] an object of special detestation, pet aversion.
billet doux [F.] a love-letter.
blitzkrieg [Ger.] lightning war.
bona fide [L.] in good faith.
bonhomie [F.] good nature.
bonjour [F.] good-morning, good-day.
bon marché [F.] cheaply.
bonne bouche [F.] titbit.
bonsoir [F.] good-evening, good-night.
bon ton [F.] good breeding.

carpe diem [L.] enjoy the present day.
carte blanche [F.] full powers.
casus belli [L.] something which involves war.
cause célèbre [F.] famous lawsuit or controversy.
ça va sans dire [F.] that is a matter of course.
caveat emptor [L.] let the buyer beware.
cave canem [L.] beware of the dog.
c'est la vie [F.] that's life.
chacun à son gout [F.] every one to his taste.
ceteris paribus [L.] other things being equal.
chef-d'oeuvre [F.] masterpiece.
cherchez la femme [F.] look for the woman; there is a woman at the bottom of the business.
che sarà, sarà [It.] what will be, will be.
ciao [It.] hello, goodbye.
ci-devant [F.] former.
cogito, ergo sum [L.] I think, therefore I am.
comme il faut [F.] as it should be.
compos mentis [L.] sane.
compte rendu [F.] a report.
con amore [It.] with love, earnestly.
concierge [F.] a porter or doorkeeper.
coram populo [L.] in the presence of the people, openly.
corpus delicti [L.] the substance of the offence; the body of the victim of murder.
corrigenda [L.] things to be corrected.
coup d'état [F.] a stroke of policy, a sudden decisive political move, an abuse of authority.

coup de foudre [F.] sudden amazing event.
coup de grâce [F.] a finishing blow.
coup de théâtre [F.] a theatrical effect, a sudden change in a situation.
cui bono? [L.] for whose benefit is it? (i.e. the crime - in a law-case).
cum grano salis [L.] with a grain of salt, with reservation.

de facto [L.] actually, in fact.
Dei gratia [L.] by the grace of God.
de jure [L.] in law, by right.
de mortuis nil nisi bonum [L.] say nothing but good about the dead.
de novo [L.] anew.
Deo gratias [L.] thanks to God.
Deo volente [L.] (**D.V.**) God willing.
de profundis [L.] out of the depths. (The first words of the Latin version of Psalm 130.)
de rigueur [F.] indispensable, obligatory.
dernier cri [F.] latest fashion.
de trop [F.] superfluous, intrusive.
deus ex machina [L.] literally, a god out of the (theatrical) machine, i.e. a too obvious device in the plot of a play or story.
dies non [L.] a day on which judges do not sit.
Dieu et mon droit [F.] God and my right; motto of the British crown.
disjecta membra [L.] the scattered remains.
distingué [F.] of distinguished appearance.
distrait [F.] absent-minded.
dolce far niente [It.] pleasant idleness.
double entendre [F.] double meaning.
douceur [F.] a tip, a bribe.
dramatis personae [L.] the characters in a drama.

ecce homo! [L.] behold the man! (Spoken by Pilate; St. John, c.19, v.5.)
embarras de richesses [F.] perplexing wealth.
emeritus [L.] retired from office.
éminence grise [F.] person who wields power unofficially or behind the scenes.
en famille [F.] with one's family; at home; informally.
enfant terrible [F.] literally, "a terrible child."
en fête [F.] on holiday, in a state of festivity.
en masse [F.] in a body.
en passant [F.] in passing, by the way.
en rapport [F.] in sympathy with.
en règle [F.] in due order.
en route [F.] on the way; march!
entente cordiale [F.] friendly understanding between two nations.
entre nous [F.] between ourselves.
e pluribus unum [L.] one out of many. (Motto of the U.S.A.)
erratum (*pl.* **errata**) [L.] error.
esprit de corps [F.] team-spirit.
eureka! (**heureka**) [G.] I have found it! (The exclamation of Archimedes.)
ex cathedra [L.] from the chair of office, hence, authoritatively.
exeat [L.] literally, "let him go out"; formal leave of absence.
exempli gratia [L.] (**e.g.**) for example.
exeunt omnes [L.] all go out.
exit [L.] goes out.
ex libris [L.] from the books ... (followed by the name of the owner).
ex officio [L.] by virtue of his office.
ex parte [L.] on one side, partisan.

facile princeps [L.] an easy first.
fait accompli [F.] a thing done.
faute de mieux [F.] for lack of anything better.
faux pas [F.] a false step, a mistake.
felo de se [L.] a suicide, literally, a "felon of himself."
femme fatale [F.] seductive woman.
festina lente [L.] hasten slowly.
fête champêtre [F.] a rural festival.
feu de joie [F.] a bonfire; gun salute.
fiat lux [L.] let there be light.
fidei defensor [L.] defender of the faith.
fille de joie [F.] prostitute.
fin de siècle [F.] end of the 19th century; decadent.
finis [L.] the end.
flagrante delicto [L.] in the very act, red-handed.
folie de grandeur [F.] delusions of grandeur.
fons et origo [L.] the source and origin.

gaudeamus igitur [L.] let us then rejoice.
gendarme [F.] one of the *gendarmerie*, a body of armed police in France.

haute couture [F.] high fashion.
haute cuisine [F.] high-class cooking.
hic jacet [L.] here lies.
honi soit qui mal y pense [Old F.] shame to him who thinks ill of it.
horribile dictu [L.] horrible to relate.
hors de combat [F.] out of condition to fight.

ibidem (abbreviated as **ib;** or **ibid;**) [L.] in the same place.
ich dien [Ger.] I serve.
idée fixe [F.] an obsession, monomania.
id est [L.] (usually **i.e.**) that is.
idem [L.] the same.
ignis fatuus [L.] a will-o'-the-wisp.
imprimatur [L.] literally, "let it be printed", a licence to print, sanction.

in camera [L.] in a (judge's private) room.
in extremis [L.] at the point of death.
infra dignitatem [L.] (**infra dig.**) below one's dignity.
in loco parentis [L.] in the place of a parent.
in medias res [L.] into the midst of things.
in memoriam [L.] to the memory of.
in perpetuum [L.] for ever.
in re [L.] in the matter of.
in situ [L.] in its original position.
in statu quo [L.] in the former state.
inter alia [L.] among other things.
in toto [L.] entirely.
in vino veritas [L.] in wine the truth (comes out).
ipse dixit [L.] "he himself said it"; his unsupported word.
ipsissima verba [L.] the very words.
ipso facto [L.] by the fact itself.

je ne sais quoi [F.] "I don't know what", a something or other.
jeu d'esprit [F.] a witticism.
joie de vivre [F.] joy of living; ebullience.

laissez faire [F.] policy of inaction.
lapsus linguae [L.] a slip of the tongue.
lares et penates [L.] household gods.
leitmotif [Ger.] a theme used to indicate a person, idea, etc. in opera, etc.
lèse-majesté [F.] high treason.
l'état, c'est moi [F.] I am the state. (Saying of Louis XIV).
lettre de cachet [F.] a sealed letter; a royal warrant for imprisonment.
locum tenens [L.] "one occupying the place", a deputy or substitute.

magnum opus [L.] a great work.
mal à propos [F.] ill-timed.
mal de mer [F.] sea-sickness.
malentendu [F.] a misunderstanding.
manqué [F.] potential; would-be.
mariage de convenance [F.] a marriage from motives of interest rather than love.
mauvaise honte [F.] false modesty, bashfulness.
mauvais quart d'heure [F.] a brief unpleasant experience.
mea culpa [L.] by my fault.
memento mori [L.] remember death.
ménage à trois [F.] sexual arrangement involving a married couple and the lover of one of them.
mens sana in corpore sano [L.] a sound mind in a sound body.
mésalliance [F.] marriage with someone of lower social status.
meum et tuum [L.] mine and thine.
mirabile dictu [L.] wonderful to relate.
mise en scène [F.] scenic setting.
modus operandi [L.] manner of working.
mot juste [F.] the exact right word.
moue [F.] a disdainful or pouting look.
multum in parvo [L.] much in little.
mutatis mutandis [L.] with the necessary changes.

née [F.] "born", her maiden name being; e.g. *Mrs. Brown née Smith.*
nemine contradicente [L.] (often as **nem.con.**) without opposition.
nemo me impune lacessit [L.] no one hurts me with impunity.
ne plus ultra [L.] nothing further; the uttermost point.
nihil obstat [L.] there is no obstacle.
nil desperandum [L.] despair of nothing.
noblesse oblige [F.] nobility imposes obligations.
nolens volens [L.] whether he will or not.
noli me tangere [L.] don't touch me.
nom de guerre [F.] an assumed name. (**nom de plume** is hardly used in French.)
non compos mentis [L.] insane.
non sequitur [L.] it does not follow.
nota bene [L.] (**N.B.**) note well.
nous avons changé tout cela [F.] we have changed all that.
nouveau riche [F.] one newly enriched, an upstart.
nulli secundus [L.] second to none.

obiit [L.] he (or she) died.
obiter dictum [L.] (*pl.* **obiter dicta**) something said by the way.
on dit [F.] they say; a rumour.
ora pro nobis [L.] pray for us.
O tempora! O mores! [L.] literally, "O the times! O the manners!"; what dreadful times and doings.

pace [L.] by leave of.
par avion [F.] by aeroplane (of mail sent by air).
par excellence [F.] pre-eminently.
pari passu [L.] with equal pace; together.
passim [L.] here and there, everywhere.
pax vobiscum [L.] peace be with you.
peccavi [L.] I have sinned.
per ardua ad astra [L.] through difficulties to the stars.
persona non grata [L.] unacceptable or unwelcome person.
post hoc, ergo propter hoc [L.] after this, therefore because of this (a fallacy in reasoning.)

pour encourager les autres [F.] in order to encourage the others.
prima facie [L.] at a first view.
primus inter pares [L.] first among equals.
pro patria [L.] for one's country.
pro tempore [L.] for the time being.

quis custodiet ipsos custodes? [L.] who will guard the guards?
qui vive? [F.] who goes there?
quod erat demonstrandum [L.] (**Q.E.D.**) which was to be proved.
quot homines, tot sententiae [L.] as many men as there are opinions.
quo vadis? [L.] whither goest thou?

rara avis [L.] a rare bird, something prodigious.
reductio ad absurdum [L.] a reducing to the absurd.
répondez s'il vous plait [F.] (**R.S.V.P.**) please reply.
requiescat in pace [L.] (**R.I.P.**) may he (or she) rest in peace.
rus in urbe [L.] the country in the town.

sans peur et sans reproche [F.] without fear and without reproach.
sans souci [F.] without care.
sauve qui peut [F.] save himself who can - the cry of disorderly retreat.
semper fidelis [L.] always faithful.
seriatim [L.] in order.
sic [L.] thus. Often used to call attention to some quoted mistake.
sic transit gloria mundi [L.] so passes the glory of the world.
sine die [L.] without date, indefinitely postponed.
si monumentum requiris, circumspice [L.] if you seek (his) monument, look around you. (The inscription on the architect Wren's tomb in St. Paul's.)
sine qua non [L.] an indispensable condition.
soi-disant [F.] so-called; self-styled.
status quo [L.] "the state in which", the pre-existing state of affairs.
stet [L.] let it stand.
Sturm und Drang [Ger.] storm and stress.
sub judice [L.] under consideration.
sub rosa [L.] "under the rose", secretly.
sub voce [L.] under that heading.
sursum corda [L.] lift up your hearts (to God).

table d'hôte [F.] general guest-table, meal at a fixed price.
tant mieux [F.] so much the better.
tant pis [F.] so much the worse.
tempore [L.] in the time of.
tempus fugit [L.] time flies.
terra firma [L.] solid earth.
terra incognita [L.] unexplored land or area of study.
tour de force [F.] a feat of strength or skill.
tout de suite [F.] at once.
tout ensemble [F.] the whole taken together, the general effect.
tout le monde [F.] all the world, everyone.

ubique [L.] everywhere.
ultima Thule [L.] the utmost boundary or limit.
ultra vires [L.] beyond one's powers.

vade in pace [L.] go in peace.
vade mecum [L.] go with me; a constant companion, work of reference.
vale [L.] farewell.
veni, vidi, vici [L.] I came, I saw, I conquered.
ventre à terre [F.] belly to the ground; at high speed.
verbum sapienti satis [L.] (**verb.sap.**) a word is enough for a wise man.
via media [L.] a middle course.
videlicet [L.] (**viz.**) namely, to wit.
volente Deo [L.] God willing.

Weltschmerz [Ger.] world-weariness; sentimental pessimism.

Zeitgeist [Ger.] the spirit of the times.